Happy Birthday, Dad!
4/27/03
Love, Bob + Shirley.

# ENCYCLOPEDIA OF AMERICAN CARS

A Comprehensive History of the Automakers and the Cars They Built.

BY THE AUTO EDITORS OF CONSUMER GUIDE®

pil Publications International, Ltd.

Copyright © 2002 Publications International, Ltd. All rights reserved. This book may not be reproduced or quoted in whole or in part by any means whatsoever without written permission from:

Louis Weber, CEO
Publications International, Ltd.
7373 North Cicero Avenue
Lincolnwood, Illinois 60712

Permission is never granted for commercial purposes.

Manufactured in China.

8 7 6 5 4 3 2 1

ISBN: 0-7853-6275-4

Library of Congress Control Number:   2002102208

**Photo Credits**

**Owners:**
Special thanks to the owners of the cars featured in this book for their enthusiastic cooperation. They are listed below along with the page number(s) on which their cars appear:

**Harrah's National Auto Museum** - 161; **Norman and Joyce Booth** - 161; **Jeff Tranberg** - 162; **James and Robert Lojewski** - 162; **Brad and Barb Hillick** - 163; **Jerry Richman** - 163; **R.C. "Buzz" Pitzen** - 164; **Mike Kaminsky** - 165; **Ray Somers** - 165; **Larry Hoeckelberg** 166; **Ted Onufryk** - 166; **Les Raye** - 167; **Sheryl Sommers** - 167; **Richard Stanley** - 168; **Harry Nicks** - 168; **R. Wayne Turner** - 169; **Gene and Magdalena Asbury** - 169; **Eugene Fattone, Jr.** - 170; **Ron Walker** - 170; **Steven D. Wilson** - 171; **Carmine A. Palazzo** - 172; **Chuck Misetich** - 172; **Steve Bergin** - 173; **Bill and Rita Malik** - 173; **Mike Kuhn** - 174; **Fairway Chevrolet** - 174; **Rod Ryan** - 175; **Jeanne C. Finster** - 176; **Dr. Dennis Pagliano** - 176; **Bill and Pat Locke** - 321; **Harry A. Demenge** - 322; **Lloyd and Martha Mayes** - 323; **James McLeod** - 323; **James Harland** - 324; **Stephan M. Thomas** - 325; **Esther Day Candies Corporation** - 325; **Walter G. Serviss** - 326; **Gary Loomer** - 326; **Robert R. Helfenstein** - 327; **Michael A. Porto** - 327, 647, 654; **S. Ray Miller, Jr.** - 328, 332, 811; **Art Astor** - 328; **Larry Martin** - 329; **Thomas J. Sory** - 329; **Scott Swaydrak** - 330; **Frank Goderre** - 330; **Joseph B. Folladori** - 331; **Alfred Ferrara** - 332; **Jerry Robbin** - 333; **Cliff Felpel** - 334; **Jim Perrault** - 334; **John Webber** - 336; **Dick Colarossi** - 336; **Sherm Smith** - 481; **Sandra Simpkin** - 481; **Robert M. Forker** - 482; **Anthony A. Lucarz** - 482; **Allan St. Jacques** - 483; **Luis A. Chanes** - 484; **Sigfried Grunze** - 484; **Judy Bruggenthies** - 485; **Neil Swartz** - 486; **Rob and Dottie Sharkey** - 486; **Bill Hubert** - 488, 491, 494; **Neil Greener** - 488; **James P. Manak** - 489; **Steve Carey** - 490; **Eldon and Esta Hostetler** - 490; **Steve Blake** - 491; **Billy F. Wilson** - 492; **Michael W. Riebe** - 492; **Henry Hopkins** - 493; **Allan S. Murray** - 493; **Rosemary and Duane Sell** - 494; **Jim Mueller** - 495; **Ed Johnson** - 495; **Larry Klein** - 496; **Warren and Sylvia Lauridsen** - 496; **Lee Gurvey** - 641; **Thomas F. Lerch** - 641; **Jerry Capizzi, The Cappy Collection** - 642; **Len Berman** - 642; **Richard Krist** - 643; **Nick Alexander** - 644; **Thomas Amendola, Sr.** - 644; **Linda Wade** - 645; **Judge Lewis Weinstein** - 645; **Melvin R. Hull** - 646; **Bob Clarke** - 647; **Clarence Becker** - 648; **Glen Patch** - 648; **Bud Dutton** - 649; **Glenn Eisenhamer** - 649; **John Strewe** - 650; **Ed Musial** - 650; **Mike and Charlene Izzo** 651; **Walt Cunny** - 652; **Bill Laur** - 652; **John Shanahan** 653; **Mark and Jan Hilbert** - 653; **Thomas Derro** - 654; **Harris Laskey** - 655; **John Thomas** - 655; **Carroll and Dawn Bramble** - 656; **Ralph Neubauer** - 656; **Carl Sable** 801; **Donald Phillips** - 801; **Phil Newcomb** - 802; **Jim McGrew** - 803; **Kyle J. Wood** - 803; **Gary J. Kistinger** - 804; **Robert J. and Charlene Matteoli** - 804; **Greg Minor** - 805; **Anthony Fusco** - 805; **Ted Hinkle** - 806; **Terry Magestro** - 807; **Frank McLiesh** - 807; **Joe Hayes** 809; **Darryl Schleger, MD** - 810; **Wilbert Endres** - 811; **Burt Van Flue** - 812; **Mr. and Mrs. Ken Mooney** - 812; **Robert Thorton** - 813; **Bruce McBroom** - 814; **Wayne R. Graefen** - 814; **Dave Cammack** - 815; **Jim Flicek** - 815; **David M. Kronk** - 816; **Roy Umberger** - 816.

**Photography:**
The editors gratefully acknowledge the cooperation of the following people who supplied photography to help make this book possible:

**Nicky Wright** - 161, 328, 332, 493, 648, 813; **Vince Manocchi** - 161, 164, 165, 166, 168, 172, 173, 176, 322, 323, 326, 327, 328, 336, 481, 486, 643, 644, 647, 649, 651, 652, 653, 654, 802, 805, 814; **Thomas Glatch** - 162, 175, 806, 807; **Sam Griffith** - 162, 170, 321, 325, 642; **Mark Garcia** 163; **Don Heiny** - 163, 330, 492, 644, 645, 654, 805; **Avanti** 164; **Mike Spenner** - 166; **Milton Kieft** - 167, 169, 325, 331, 332, 492, 494, 641, 642, 648, 816; **Les Bidrawn** - 167; **W.C. Waymack** - 170, 174, 329, 481, 482, 488, 490, 491, 494, 655, 656, 811; **GM Photographic** - 171, 321, 651, 806, 808, 809; **Joe Joliet** - 171; **Doug Mitchel** - 173, 175, 321, 324, 330, 333, 482, 485, 487, 489, 495, 496, 641, 645, 649, 650, 652, 656, 801, 807, 809, 810, 816; **Nina Padgett-Russin** - 174, 323, 812; **DaimlerChrysler Media Archives** - 324, 331, 333, 802, 810; **Jim Frenak** - 327; **Dan Lyons** - 334, 490, 804, 812; **Jeff Rose** - 334; **Excalibur** - 335; **Ford Photographic Services** - 483, 485, 487, 643, 646; **David Newhardt** - 483, 484; **Rick Lenz** - 488; **Paul Hostetler** - 489; **Phil Toy** - 493; **Gary Greene** - 495; **Bud Juneau** - 496, 647, 655, 804; **David Temple** - 801, 803; **Jay Peck** - 803; **David Gooley** - 813; **Jim Thompson** - 815; **Willoughby Photo** - 815.

Very special thanks to the following: American Automobile Manufacturers Association; Jon Bill, Auburn-Cord-Duesenberg Museum; Buick Public Relations; Cadillac Public Relations; Chevrolet Public Relations; Pamela Clark, Oldsmobile History Center; Kelley Enright, DaimlerChrysler Public Relations; Ford Division Public Affairs; Ford Photographic Services; GM Design Staff; Dean E. McCaig, General Motors; Pontiac Public Relations.

# Contents

| | |
|---|---|
| Introduction ...................... 6 | Chrysler ........................ 268 |
| Qualifications/Exceptions ... 10 | Continental .................... 317 |
| Allstate ........................... 13 | Cord .............................. 319 |
| American Austin .............. 14 | Crosley .......................... 339 |
| American Bantam ........... 16 | DeSoto .......................... 342 |
| AMC ............................... 18 | Dodge ........................... 357 |
| Auburn ........................... 42 | Duesenberg ................... 414 |
| Avanti/Avanti II ............... 47 | Eagle ............................. 417 |
| Buick .............................. 51 | Edsel ............................. 420 |
| Cadillac ......................... 104 | Essex ............................. 422 |
| Checker ........................ 157 | Excalibur ....................... 424 |
| Chevrolet ...................... 178 | Ford .............................. 430 |
| Chevrolet Corvair .......... 243 | Ford Mustang ................ 506 |
| Chevrolet Corvette ........ 247 | Ford Thunderbird .......... 524 |
| | Franklin ......................... 543 |

| | |
|---|---|
| Frazer | 546 |
| Graham | 549 |
| Henry J | 556 |
| Hudson | 558 |
| Hupmobile | 573 |
| Imperial | 578 |
| Kaiser | 587 |
| LaSalle | 592 |
| Lincoln | 596 |
| Marmon | 628 |
| Mercury | 631 |
| Muntz | 690 |
| Nash | 691 |
| Oldsmobile | 705 |
| Packard | 757 |
| Panoz | 774 |
| Pierce-Arrow | 775 |
| Plymouth | 780 |
| Pontiac | 842 |
| Rambler | 900 |
| Reo | 908 |
| Saturn | 912 |
| Shelby | 921 |
| Studebaker | 925 |
| Stutz | 942 |
| Terraplane | 945 |
| Tucker | 947 |
| Willys | 948 |
| Minor Makes | 954 |

# Introduction

In the dawn of its age, the automobile took many forms. Internal combustion engines vied with steam and electricity as a source of motive power, while chassis designs varied greatly as to engine placement, steering mechanisms, and the number of wheels.

By some counts, there were more than 2500 "manufacturers" in the early part of the 20th century, but a great many were backyard tinkerers who bought a proprietary engine and placed it in a chassis bearing their own name. Many went under when the first mass-produced car, the famous Ford Model T, was introduced at a starting price of $825—far less than it took for most people to build one themselves.

While the Model T wasn't the first horseless carriage manufactured by the Ford Motor Company, it certainly had the most impact. During its 19-year production run, it not only put America on wheels by selling over 15 million copies, it also established the four-wheeled, gasoline-powered, front engine/rear drive, left-hand steering layout as the national standard that would be featured on most American cars for the next 70-odd years.

Ironically, once this standard was accepted, cars began to look markedly alike. In the 1920s, even the most car-crazed youngster must have had difficulty distinguishing one make from another. Body designs seemed to follow the same pattern, exceptions existing mainly in high-priced cars like Cadillac and Lincoln—though that was due more to their sheer size and adornment than to any distinction of line. It wasn't until the early 1930s that styling became distinguishable between the popularly priced makes, a trend started largely by General Motors with its Art and Colour Section headed by Harley Earl. By 1933, even the "low-priced three"—Chevy, Ford, and Plymouth—sported distinct faces.

In looking back over the development of the automobile, one can't help noting how world events have had a hand in shaping its history. World War I prompted our engineers to accelerate mechanical technology, advancements that soon found their way into production cars. The Depression forced many companies out of business, narrowing our choices and muting the flamboyant attitude of the Roaring Twenties. World War II virtually halted development for half a decade—longer, really, since few cars changed much in the first four years after production resumed.

In more recent times, a nationwide recession during 1958 not only helped kill off venerable Packard and newcomer Edsel, it also prompted a resurgence of economical compacts, which had been tried before and were abandoned due to lack of buyer interest. Their popularity this time around started the turn to "niche" vehicles, from which came muscle cars, ponycars, and personal coupes, along with the first automobiles to find commercial success despite (or perhaps because of) the fact that they deviated from the basic design principles set down by the Model T over half-a-century before. The result was an automotive free-for-all in Detroit, an "anything goes" period where the horsepower race begun in the 1950s was run with reckless abandon towards a seemingly nonexistent finish line.

But the line was soon to be drawn. By the late-1960s, government safety and emission regulations were playing a growing part in automotive design, and together with the insurance lobby, conspired to dump a heavy rain on Detroit's parade. A final blow was dealt by the Arab oil embargo in the fall of 1973, when OPEC became a four-letter word. What had been a rosy picture five years earlier had now turned decidedly grey.

It is said, however, that necessity is the mother of invention, and the 1970s proved to be a decade of transformation if not excitement. Some of the greatest changes in the history of the automobile took place during this period, as manufacturers learned to cope with a much more-restrictive environment. While few automotive aficionados look back on the '70s with a great sense of longing, it did bring about some interesting experimentation with technologies that would be refined as time went on: turbocharging, alternate materials, electronics, and the science of aerodynamics. All these came at a price, however, and the decade would also bring extraordinary increases in the cost of buying, owning, and manufacturing cars.

If the Seventies go down in history as a decade of discouragement, then the Eighties and Nineties must be considered nothing less than the renaissance of the automobile. As manufacturers learned to cope with emission rules through fuel injection and electronic engine controls, power once again began to creep upward. Impact-absorbing bumpers became more subtle and integrated, styling dispatched with the gaudy tape stripes and opera windows, and silhouettes bore the smooth mark of aerodynamics. By century's end, it looked as though the American auto industry was once again producing the kind of cars that one day would be coveted classics.

The 70-plus years covered in this encyclopedia represent what many consider to be the golden age of the automobile. At least 85 percent of the people collecting and restoring old cars today are concerned with the post-1930 period, as the pre-1930 antiques that once dominated the hobby have, to a large extent, long since been relegated to museums. Meanwhile, collector focus has moved forward with time and the addition of younger enthusiasts. People generally tend to be interested in the cars they remember from their youth, which explains the current high popularity of late-'60s muscle cars.

In the first edition of this book we suggested that the "age of collectible cars" might actually end with 1970, but have since come to think otherwise. While it is still too early for collectors to have expressed much interest in the cars of the '70s and '80s, one day they undoubtedly will. The latest domestic models, many the product and expression of fascinating new technology, are arguably the best cars ever built in this country.

From the '30s on through to the '90s, America has produced some of the most unique and coveted automobiles manufactured anywhere in the world. All of these classics—and classics yet to be—are celebrated within the pages of this book. We hope you enjoy it.

## Genesis of an Era: The 1930s

Ironically, the automotive styling and engineering develop-

# Introduction

ments of 1940-75 were almost wholly the result of lessons learned during the greatest economic disaster in modern history. The Depression may have meant the end for many automobile producers, but it forced the survivors to think, plan, and invent. In so doing, they altered the shape of the American automobile almost completely.

During the 1930s, the industry parted company with unsynchronized manual transmissions, wood-framed bodies, mechanical brakes, and solid front axles. In their place came synchromesh gears, semiautomatic and fully automatic transmissions, all-steel bodies composed of fewer and larger panels welded together, hydraulic brakes, and independent front suspension. As roads improved, buyers demanded more speed, so higher-revving engines were needed. This led to new foundry and engine-building techniques that guaranteed high-rpm reliability. Cars could then be geared higher to travel faster. The advent of automatic shiftless transmissions made it less important to gear and "cam" a car so the lazy driver could pull away from a crawl without changing out of "High." As we learned how independent front suspensions and rubber engine mounts could help absorb road shocks, we were able to design stiffer chassis, which made overall construction tighter and more solid. Compared to its 1930 forebear—an upright box on artillery wheels wheezing along on four or six small cylinders—the automobile of 1940 was a sleek torpedo on slotted steel wheels, with more room inside, a longer wheelbase, and a vibration-free, rubber-mounted engine—and it was a good 20 mph faster.

In the process of thinning out industry ranks, the Depression years largely determined the nature of the major producers as we know them today—and selected those independents strong enough to survive. Ever since its founding by W. C. Durant in 1908, General Motors had been striving for managerial and creative decentralization through its division structure. While Henry Ford ruled his strongly centralized company almost single-handedly, the division concept put GM ahead in production during the early 1920s. Only after Henry Ford II took over his grandfather's troubled firm in 1945 did Ford begin to decentralize—and to rebuild.

Walter P. Chrysler was an old GM man, and saw the light very early on. Although Chrysler Corporation was founded in the '20s, it came of age during the '30s. Following a division structure not unlike GM's, Chrysler built the second-largest car company in the nation during the decade, and it remained so until the early 1950s.

By 1940, only a few independent manufacturers were left. After the war there were just four major ones remaining, all with high hopes: Nash, Hudson, Packard, and Studebaker. Together with newcomer Kaiser-Frazer and later joined by Crosley and Willys, the independents enjoyed as much as a 15-percent market share in the late '40s and early '50s. But it didn't last. Nash's president George Mason was the only high-ranking executive among the independents who could envision the benefits of merger. He had managed to add Hudson to his empire in 1954, thus forming American Motors, but died before he could meld in Packard and Studebaker. One by one, the other independents vanished, though Studebaker-Packard lasted longer than most. Only AMC hung on longer, though even it faded away when the struggling company was purchased by Chrysler Corporation in 1987.

## The 1940s

Although classic four-square styling was largely abandoned after World War II, some of its finest expressions appeared in 1940-42: the senior Packards, the Hupp Skylark and Graham Hollywood, and the last production LaSalle. Other cars, like the sleek Fords and Mercurys of 1940, offered near-perfection in line and form. Chrysler's 1949 products, boxy and upright, symbolized that corporation's concern for ample interior space within compact exterior dimensions.

The modern V-8 engine was perhaps the most significant engineering development of the decade. Of course, V-8s had been around for years—at Cadillac since 1915, and at Ford since 1932. But these were relatively heavy, long-stroke, low-compression engines, known for smoothness rather than performance. In 1949, Cadillac and Oldsmobile pioneered a new generation of V-8s, the forerunners of the powerplants found in most large U.S. cars today. America's light, efficient, and powerful V-8 soon became famous worldwide for its performance and reliability. The '40s also offered traditionally designed engines for those who preferred them. Packard's magnificent 356 cubic-inch straight eight and Cadillac's 346 V-8 were L-head units known for quietness and smooth operation. Both are highly prized by collectors.

Most engines of the 1940s, however, were work-a-day inline sixes and eights that may not have been revolutionary, but were dependable and economical. The 230- and 170-cid sixes sold by Plymouth and Studebaker, respectively, served their makers well right on through the '50s, and were well-known for thriftiness. Studebaker's powerplant was a traditional winner in the Mobilgas Economy Run.

Racing was not emphasized by the industry as a whole during the '40s, but many individuals recorded performances that indicated the competition potential of certain production models. The supercharged Graham of 1940-41 was among the fastest cars powered by a conventional sidevalve six. The Hudson Super Six, the Graham's postwar counterpart, could reach speeds that far exceeded what was normally expected from six cylinders. Oldsmobile and Cadillac achieved early competition success with their overhead-valve V-8s. Cadillac scored unbelievable 10th- and 11th-place finishes at the grueling 1950 24 hours of Le Mans. Oldsmobile's fast, lightweight 88 dominated stock-car racing from 1949 through 1951.

Another extremely important engineering highlight of the '40s was the increasing use of the modern automatic transmission. Before, there had been only semiautomatics. Oldsmobile offered one for 1938, then dropped it the next year for Hydra-Matic—the most-successful completely shift-free transmission of all time. Chrysler enthusiastically marketed its Fluid Drive (which eliminated most shift motions) well into the 1950s. Ford was conservative, and stayed with the manual gearshift (both with and without overdrive) for all 1940-49 Fords and Mercurys. It offered the GM-built Hydra-Matic for the 1949 Lincoln, but did not manufacture an automatic of its own until 1951. Nash and Kaiser-Frazer stayed with stickshifts until 1950, then gave in and also purchased Hydra-Matic.

Two independents that did strike out with automatics of their own were Packard and Studebaker. Packard's Ultramatic was the only such unit developed entirely by an independent without any help from a transmission firm. It was a smooth-shifting gearbox, but not amenable to the extra

# Introduction

power delivered by later Packard engines. Studebaker teamed up with Detroit Gear to create a fine three-speed automatic, but it didn't arrive until 1950.

GM really had the automatic market to itself in the 1940s. Cadillac began offering Hydra-Matic in 1948; Buick debuted its Dynaflow Drive the same year. Though smooth in operation, Dynaflow was not in the same performance league as Hydra-Matic. The '40s were years of attrition and false starts for the smaller automakers. American Bantam, Hupmobile, and Graham all ceased production well before World War II—and did not return afterward. Willys-Overland, which offered conventional passenger cars through the 1942 model year, came back after the war with an interesting line of Jeep-like vehicles. These included the unique Jeepster that appeared for 1948—the last true touring car in the American industry. The decade's best-known failure was the Tucker—a brilliant concept that nevertheless saw no more than 50 copies. For years, the assumption was that the Tucker had been killed—prematurely—by General Motors and its cohorts. Yet even though its admirable design caused the big manufacturers a bit of concern, it was not actually a serious threat to them. Whether the car could have been realistically produced at the price Preston Tucker claimed will probably never be known.

## The 1950s

A lot of people think the cars of the '50s are responsible for the sorry state of the automotive scene today. Critics tell us they were heavy, ungainly, dumb-looking beasts with no—or at best few—redeeming virtues. Yet, they were nowhere near as uniformly bad as skeptics like to insist. In fact, several important advances were made between 1950 and 1960.

Consider, for example, torsion bar suspension, short-stroke V-8s, efficient automatic transmissions, and unit construction—which we tried and liked—and air suspension, tailfins, and pushbutton transmissions—which we tried, disliked, and discarded. Notwithstanding the emphasis on chrome-laden gimmickry, the 1950s also brought some innovative new body styles such as the two- and four-door pillarless hardtop, and the all-steel station wagon that became (for the first time in its history) more like a car than a truck.

If these years are remembered for some of the industry's worst styling excesses, they were also marked by some of the finest automotive designs of all time: the Studebaker "Loewy coupes," the Continental Mark II, the Darrin-styled Kaisers, and the two-seat Thunderbirds. Finally—and this may come as a surprise—American cars of this decade are considered by many experts to have been safer than cars had ever been before. Maybe the seatbelts, padded dashes, and dished steering wheels weren't merely sales gimmicks after all.

There's something else about these automobiles that even their admirers often fail to mention, perhaps because it's so obvious. These cars have an intrinsic character—a special appeal—which the industry somehow lost in the late '60s. They were different—vastly different—from the cars of today. This was probably the last decade when a manufacturer dared sell something clearly unique, like the "Step-down" Hudson, the tiny Nash Metropolitan, or the fiberglass Woodill Wildfire. Cars of the '50s were also built differently: Interiors were trimmed in comfortable mohair or genuine leather; bodies were made of heavy-gauge steel. Their makers shunned things like plastic, cardboard, and decals. While the average family car of 1950-59 probably handled as sloppily as everyone said it did, it was also built with more pure integrity than its more-nimble successors. Every piece of trim met every other piece precisely where intended. Each door, trunklid, and hood closed with a resounding clunk, swinging shut on vaultlike hinges. Collectors still discover rust-free examples with six-figure mileage, and interiors, paint, and mechanical components in approximately the same shape as when the car left the factory. And this, despite the industry's reputation for haphazard assembly quality.

## The 1960s

That turbulent era produced memorable autos. It's not at all difficult to remember the cars: the 18-foot-long luxury hardtops, the bucket-seat sporty compacts, the personal cars, the ponycars, and the muscle cars. An incredibly diverse assortment of automobiles streamed out of the factory gates in those years, a car for every taste and budget; anything from the $1700 Metropolitan to the $18,500 Crown Imperial limousine.

Government demands that the industry clean up exhaust emissions and make cars safer were good ideas, even if the legislation that followed was often controversial. But the mandates that took effect in the late '60s also guaranteed an end to the uninhibited experimentation that characterized the early years of the decade.

In a way, the public had as much to do with the decline of innovation as the government. What incentive was there for automakers to develop something really new or different when buyers seemed interested mainly in performance, styling, and "pizzazz"? Consider the record. After generating high initial interest, the sophisticated Corvair was soon forgotten—long before Ralph Nader came along. Buyers yawned at the first Pontiac Tempest, not sure what to make of its all-independent suspension and rear-mounted transaxle. The Tempest sold well, but it might have done even better with a more-ordinary drivetrain. In 1966, Oldsmobile introduced its radical, superbly engineered front-wheel-drive Toronado—which was consistently outsold by the conventionally designed Buick Riviera. Pontiac's overhead-cam six of 1966, an engine that offered as good a balance between economy and performance as any engine on the market, was almost completely ignored as most customers insisted on V-8s. Sales records aside, there is something significant about the technological tour de force of the '60s: Nearly all of them came from General Motors. There are many reasons for this. The decline of the independents after World War II (the mergers and demise of Nash and Hudson, Packard and Studebaker, plus the disappearance of Kaiser and Willys) radically altered the nature of the industry. Soon, the high-volume manufacturers discovered there were not just one or two kinds of buyers, but six or eight. The result was a raft of new sizes and concepts designed for distinct segments of the market—and new categories like compact, sporty-compact, intermediate, standard, luxury, and personal-specialty. Yet ironically, all this variety gradually blurred the distinction in price or status between makes. What had happened was that the market began subdividing after about 1955, but wasn't really expanding. This can be seen in the production figures. Chevrolet, for example, wasn't actually turning out any more cars in 1970 than it did in 1960, but it was building a far greater variety of models.

General Motors was best able to adapt to this new situation. Although Ford had its successes—the Mustang and

# Introduction

Continental Mark III for instance—they were triumphs of packaging or marketing, not technology. But GM had grown so large by the mid-'60s that it could just as easily produce either unusual, technically interesting designs like the Corvair or Toronado or boringly ordinary cars like the Chevy II or Impala.

Despite the domination of the market by GM and Ford, a few specialty manufacturers operated profitably during the '60s by appealing to small but significant groups of buyers overlooked by the industry giants. The Avanti II continued to occupy its own market niche for years after its parent company fell apart. The original Shelby GT 350 was little more than a reengineered Mustang designed by a former racer who believed there was a tiny—but vocal—market for all-out performance. Checker still sold cars to practical folk looking for taxicab toughness and simplicity. Brooks Stevens found that others shared his dream of driving a "modern classic," and would buy an Excalibur.

Buyers did not always react enthusiastically to important engineering advances in the 1960s, but they did become more discriminating in their judgments of gimmicky or useless features. As the decade began, the public almost immediately started rejecting such things as tailfins, pushbutton transmissions, and chrome-encrusted super-cruisers. Rapidly, new models appeared from the likes of Pontiac, Lincoln, Dodge, and Chevrolet—cars that illustrated that good design meant more than a five-pound hood ornament. The early compacts proved that the industry could still build practical cars—and that they could be designed to sell—after a generation of offering impractical ones. The sporty compacts brought home a point the Europeans had long accepted: The best car is not necessarily the biggest. Heading into the 1970s, it was clear that America's automotive values were slowly beginning to change. As events were to prove, the changes couldn't have been more timely.

## The 1970s

In the early 1970s the industry was beset by a lengthening list of government regulations, complicated by a new set of equally stark realities resulting from the Arab oil embargo. With the sudden recognition of how interdependent the world had become, Detroit executives made key decisions that would change the nature of the American car more dramatically and more swiftly than ever before. General Motors would lead the way—and where GM went, the rest would follow. Reacting quickly to the change in consumer needs, GM embarked on a daring long-term program to downsize its entire fleet. The first results appeared on the 1977 B- and C-body full-size models. It represented a huge gamble even for the number one producer, for "standards" were still crucially important to profits. But it worked: The new cars were as large or larger than their predecessors on the inside yet astonishingly smaller on the outside—and up to 800 pounds lighter. More importantly, they sold quite well. GM went on to apply the same formula to its intermediates, specialty cars, and compacts in rapid succession, while other makers rushed to follow. Meanwhile, there were advances in allied areas. Ford designer Bill Boyer told us that 96 inches is about as short as a wheelbase should be. "When you can't downsize any more," he declares, "you improve efficiency by more complicated means: aerodynamics, front drive/transverse engines." And you provide performance through turbocharging a smaller engine for "power on demand," to quote an old Kaiser slogan, rather than relying on a big V-8 with a surfeit of power.

## The 1980s

It is often said that every cloud has a silver lining, and however black the cloud of government regulations appeared in the 1970s, the technology that it spawned in the '80s made the interim suffering seem ultimately worthwhile. One result of the drain on horsepower that accompanied tightening EPA and CAFE requirements was that the focus of performance switched from straight-line acceleration to more-adroit handling and braking. The resulting automobiles became more-capable all-around performers.

Yet around 1982, horsepower began making a comeback. One of the first signs that the slump was over appeared in that year's Mustang GT, which was fitted with a 157-bhp version of the venerable 302-cid small-block V-8—up from a 120-bhp 255 which was the '81 ponycar's most-potent V-8. This engine got stronger each year, and was joined by increasingly sophisticated turbocharged fours. GM's offerings likewise began building more muscle: The Z28 Camaro's top engine went from 165 bhp in 1982 to 215 by '85. And these were not exceptions to the rule.

Another indication that the sober '70s were at an end also occurred in 1982—the rebirth of the ragtop. Convertibles had been discontinued by 1976 due to waning popularity and anticipation of government rollover standards that never materialized. Chrysler Corporation usually takes the kudos for reviving "wind-in-your-hair" motoring, though Buick introduced a ragtop Riviera the same year. Other manufacturers soon followed suit, and by decade's end there were nine American droptops to choose from, with more on the way.

## The 1990s

The trials experienced by the American auto industry in the previous two decades proved to be character builders. During the '90s Detroit saw something of a renaissance. Staid General Motors—of all companies—shook up the way the industry did business with the 1991 introduction of the Saturn. Prior to its 1996 redesign, the Ford Taurus returned a domestic nameplate to the top of the U.S. sales rankings. Chrysler, meanwhile, came out with a slew of cutting-edge models built around "cab-forward" design and walked on the wild side with cars like the ferocious Dodge Viper and playful Plymouth Prowler. In 1998, Chrysler surprised everyone by merging with Daimler-Benz. Ford and General Motors acquired or formed alliances with foreign automakers. Foreign design and engineering would prove to have more influence on domestic products during this decade.

## The 2000s

The new century got off to a rocky start with a recession. Ford was hit hard by a scandal involving Firestone tire blow-outs on its best-selling Explorer line. The Daimler/Chrysler merger created losses instead of the "synergy" promised at its announcement. General Motors continued to lose market share. However, it was hoped that Robert Lutz, in charge of new product development, would do for GM what he had done for Chrysler in the '90s. Chrysler continued to create exciting concept cars that were likely to go into production. William Ford had taken control of the family firm and promised to bring stability as well as get Ford back on track.

# Qualifications and Exceptions

Even the best system of terminology and classification has its exceptions. For the Major Makes section, the intent was to include every volume manufacturer that did business in America between 1930 and 2002. Thus, makes like Essex, Franklin, and Marmon are listed even though all were active only briefly in the early '30s. Similarly, there is a listing for AMC, activated as a separate nameplate in 1966.

Several makes usually considered "minor" by the industry are the first exceptions. Avanti II, Checker, Duesenberg, Excalibur, Panoz, and Shelby are treated as majors even though their production was a mere fraction of total industry volume. The reasoning was subjective, though their volume was never substantial, we felt these cars warranted more than a mere notation among the "minors." Shelby as a marque saw only sporadic production since its formation in 1965, but in some years its volume was quite considerable for a tiny company—not to mention its impact. The last is reason enough to include Duesenberg.

Canadian models are not officially covered here, but again there is an exception: the 1965-66 Studebaker, which was nominally a Canadian product in those years. This decision was made on the grounds that Studebaker had been too much a part of the American scene in previous years to leave out its final offerings. The problem, of course, is that if these cars are listed, then Canadian Plymouths, for example, should be included, too. An argument, though perhaps tenuous, can be made for the 1965-66 Studebakers, because including them effectively caps a story; lumping in Canadian Plymouths would only have exceeded the basic scope of the book.

A different problem arose in deciding how to treat major models of certain makes, cars substantially different in technology or character from the marque's usual products. For improved clarity and coverage, the rear-engine Corvair and the singular Corvette have their own chapters apart from the main Chevrolet entry. Likewise, Mustang and Thunderbird are treated separately from Ford. But this led to more exceptions. The Kaiser-Darrin is not listed separately from Kaiser, for example. Another reason for treating the aforementioned models individually is that the main Chevrolet and Ford entries were already enormous. The Nash Metropolitan involved two more exceptions. Because of its individual character, it is considered distinct from other Nash models by many authorities. Yet it was labeled a Nash until 1958, when that nameplate disappeared and Metropolitan became a make in its own right. To avoid confusing the issue any further, we have included it in the Nash chapter—appropriate, we feel, considering its origins. We have treated similar cases in the same manner. Clipper was a Packard model before it became a distinct marque for 1956, but since it was little different than the Packard product and only lasted one year on its own, we included it with its parent company. Likewise the Valiant, officially a separate make upon its introduction in 1960, but a Plymouth model thereafter.

In other cases, we follow industry practice. For example, Continental was a distinct Ford Motor Company make in 1956-1958, and there was no problem separating the appropriate models from Lincoln in the period covered. The same principle applies to AMC (the make, not the corporation). The company used the Rambler nameplate exclusively from 1957 through 1965, and the '65 Ambassador and Marlin both bore the appropriate script and emblems. For 1966-67, however, these models had new "AMC" identification, and the AMX and Javelin appeared for 1968 as AMC products, not Ramblers. For 1970, the Rambler name disappeared entirely in favor of AMC. Thus, the reader will find the 1965 Marlin, for example, discussed under "Rambler," and the 1966-67 models under "AMC."

Willys posed some of the most serious problems encountered. Officially, the Willys passenger car ended after 1955 with the expiration of the domestic Aero-based models. But a steel-bodied station wagon continued to be offered through 1961—variously called a Willys, a Kaiser-Jeep, and a Jeep. From 1963 on, Jeep Corporation marketed the four-wheel-drive Wagoneer much like a passenger model and, in 1967, Kaiser-Jeep Corporation released the Jeepster 2, designed in the image of the 1948 original. Most industry sources and the collector hobby consider the 1948-51 Jeepster a passenger car, but none list the Jeep wagons, Wagoneer, or Jeepster 2, which are all defined as "trucks." Including the original Jeepster might seem to imply including these other products as well. The problem was that by leaving in those models, the book would be opened up to similar contemporary competitors like the Ford Bronco or International Scout, which were definitely beyond our scope. Ultimately, it was decided to make two more exceptions: The original Jeepster and Aero passenger cars are the only postwar Willys models discussed.

## Chapter Texts

The general text of each entry presents a detailed account of the make's history. There is, we think, sound reason for this even in a reference work. Too often, "encyclopedias" simply report statistics. But to understand what was done, it is essential to know how and why it was done and what the results were. Therefore, we have included information on the designers, engineers, and executives who shaped these cars; the reasons why they did what they did, the alternative plans they rejected, and the successes or failures that followed. Each chapter is intended to offer a concise, yet complete, description of each major manufacturer—a basic outline for the casual user, a quick education for the uninitiated, and a solid review for the expert. In the process of writing these entries, we have attempted to puncture many hoary automotive legends—that the Corvair was torpedoed by Ralph Nader, for example, or that Studebaker was a victim of a plot at Ford. You'll find the real stories no less interesting.

## Photographs

Selecting photographs for a work like this can be more difficult than editing text. Limited space and the great variety of cars offered by the larger companies dictates that

# Qualifications and Exceptions

it is not always possible to provide a truly representative sample for each model year over such a broad time span. While this book cannot contain the detailed photographic references of a single-make history, the most important and influential models are shown.

Unlike some other automotive encyclopedias, this one includes pictures of selected prototypes, experimentals, and showcars as well as production models—all clearly labeled as such. The reasons are the inordinate interest in such nonproduction designs among today's enthusiasts, and the importance of these proposals as benchmarks. While there are hundreds, even thousands, of styling studies for each model and model year among most of the major makes, there are those interesting or key design ideas that either evolved into production or were abruptly dismissed. The prototypes selected represent the industry at its best and its worst in line with the major goal of this book: to present a broad, clear, and factual account of the American automobile industry.

## Tables

At the end of each chapter is a series of tables listing every model and body style offered by that make in the 1930-2002 period. Again, however, there are exceptions. The Duesenberg and Tucker entries have no accompanying charts because the former built chassis that were then fitted with custom bodywork, and the latter produced only prototypes that are adequately described in the text.

Of all the elements in a book like this, charts are the most time consuming and pose the greatest problems of style and accuracy. Space naturally played a part in the choice of material shown here. The object was to provide, at a glance, the data most readers would be likely to require in a hurry: models, wheelbases, body styles, weights, prices, model-year production, and engine availability. In using the tables, the reader should keep the following in mind:

## Series or Model Entries

Each group of body styles is listed under a series or model heading. This indicates the factory model or series code number (where applicable), name, and wheelbase (in inches). Code numbers posed many problems. On several occasions, it was unclear whether a code applied to the series or model line as a whole, to specific body styles, or both. In instances where they were misleading or irrelevant, the code numbers were omitted. Where a code applies to both model/series and body style, the first part is shown with the model/series and the second with the body style. An example is found in the 1959 Dodge chart. Officially, that year's Coronet six-cylinder club sedan was designated by the factory as MD1-L21, but "MD1-L" applied to all Coronet sixes, and "21" only to the club sedan. The number is therefore divided accordingly.

In the '60s, some code systems became more complex, so numbers are listed as the situation required. In 1961, for example, codes for the Dodge Lancer followed '59 practice. But the 1961 Dart Six series consisted of Seneca, Pioneer, and Phoenix subseries. In this case, only the series number "RD3" is shown in the heading, the rest of the designation appearing alongside the corresponding body styles. In reality, a 1961 Dart Six Phoenix hardtop sedan went by the code RD3-H434; it is shown as model RD3, body style H434.

## Abbreviations

For best readability, it was important to limit each entry to one line. To do this, the following standard abbreviations were adopted for the body style listings:

| abbreviation | meaning |
| --- | --- |
| A/S | auxiliary seats |
| A/W | all-weather |
| brghm/b'ham | brougham (sedan, convertible, etc.) |
| bus | business, as in coupe |
| cab | cabriolet |
| comm/comcl | commercial |
| conv cpe | two-door convertible |
| conv sdn | four-door convertible |
| cpe | coupe |
| CQ | closed rear roof quarters |
| div | division window (limousine) |
| fstbk | fastback ("torpedo") |
| form | formal, as in sedan |
| FQ | formal rear roof quarters |
| htchbk | hatchback |
| htp cpe | two-door pillarless hardtop |
| htp sdn | four-door pillarless hardtop |
| htp wgn | pillarless station wagon |
| J/B | "jet back" (fastback) |
| lndu | landau |
| limo | limousine |
| phtn | phaeton |
| proto | prototype |
| rdstr | two-passenger roadster |
| R/S | rumble seat, as in roadster |
| sdn | sedan |
| SQ | solid rear roof quarters |
| spdstr | speedster |
| spt | sport, as in coupe |
| T/B | "trunkback" |
| tng | touring |
| util | utility, usually a two-door sedan |
| wgn | station wagon |

Generally, all body styles except sports cars and very small models like American Bantam have five- or six-passenger capacity; exceptions are specified. There are also cases where it is necessary to differentiate between otherwise similar types. These abbreviations are:

| P (7P, 8P, etc.) | passenger capacity |
| --- | --- |
| S (2S, 3S) | number of seats (wagons) |
| W (4W, 6W) | number of side windows |
| FW | fixed window |

Engine abbreviations also follow a consistent pattern: block configuration is followed by the number of cylinders and, where needed, a suffix letter. The letters are as follows:

| I (I-6, I-8, etc.) | inline or straight |
| --- | --- |
| V (V-6, V-8, etc.) | V-block |
| S | supercharged |
| T | turbocharged |
| D | diesel |

Manufacturers differ widely in treating engine options.

# Qualifications and Exceptions

Some group both standard and extra-cost engines under the same model code; others distinguish between them and even give them separate model numbers. The charts follow the practice each manufacturer used for a given model year. The Pontiac Six and Eight, for example, were distinct models and are shown as such. Plymouth engines were usually listed as options for a given model and are combined. This difference is emphasized by spelling out and capitalizing the words "Six" and "Eight" in cases like Pontiac and by using the abbreviations "I-6" and "V-8" in cases like Plymouth.

Where options are combined, prices shown are for base-engine models. Production figures shown are for the total number of that model built, regardless of engine.

## Weight

The column marked "wght" provides the initial advertised curb weight (not adjusted for passengers, fuel, or cargo) for each body style as listed in industry sources, usually National Automobile Dealers Association (NADA) guides. The reader may expect these to differ slightly from other published figures, because weights varied depending on equipment fitted or even the scales used.

It is important to note, however, that when more than one engine was standard for a given model, curb weights shown are averages, deemed necessary for maximum readability. For example, the 1955 Chevrolet Bel Air convertible weighed 3315 pounds with the six and 3285 pounds with the V-8. Our listed weight is the average: 3300 pounds. However, many manufacturers only quoted weight for cars with the standard engine. Usually, the choice of engine did not change curb weight by more than 100-150 pounds.

## Prices

Figures shown in the "price" column are based on initial advertised prices (as delivered) according to NADA and similar sources, and represent contemporary dollars ("as-new" price). Oftentimes, prices varied during the model year. When more than one standard engine was available, however, prices were not averaged, the figure for the least-expensive power unit being shown instead.

## Model-Year Production

The question most often asked about older cars—and one of the most important in a reference work about them—is "How many did they make?" The answer is not always clear-cut, and in some cases production has been a subject of research—and dispute—among automotive historians for decades. However, the figures listed are the most recent and accurate available and have been thoroughly researched and cross-checked. Note that mainly model year, not calendar year, figures are used in both the tables and the text. The reason for this is that calendar year totals always include some portion of at least two model years, which creates confusion when comparing one make with another. Model year figures normally represent production of cars marketed as the 1939, 1949, 1959, 1969, etc. models. For makes and/or years where precise model-year totals were not available, registrations or calendar-year figures are given and are always identified as such. These exceptions apply mainly to the early years of the '30s, before the model-year concept had been universally adopted by the industry, and to low-volume independents like Duesenberg, where the idea had relatively little meaning in the context of company operations. Starting in the '90's manufacturers were more likely to publish calendar-year totals and model-year figures were sometimes not available.

Production received long and painstaking analysis in preparing this book. Too often, published totals have been based on company handouts that are often misleading and sometimes inaccurate. The 1953 Buick Skylark, for example, is listed by the division (and at least one other source) as the "Roadmaster Anniversary Convertible." The contradictions and false trails of factory lists were fully explored and compared to other lists from a dozen different sources. Sometimes, it was discovered that there were cars built that weren't "officially" listed; in other cases, models were listed but not actually produced.

There were a few cases where it was possible to go beyond known information by estimating, such as when a company provided only a combined total for two or three model years. In those cases where we felt confident to do so, production was proportioned over individual model years. The usual standard for these breakdowns was calendar-year output in cases where it very nearly coincided with model-year output (usually when a model year began in January rather than September or October).

In some instances, available factory figures included non-production models, usually styles intended for production but not produced in volume. These are retained in the charts and are clearly labeled as nonproduction. While not all records documented nonproduction models, the ones available are shown for completeness.

There were a few cases where even estimating proved impossible, or where a large group of models or body styles were lumped together. Through research, we were able to add a number of previously missing figures to this latest edition; it is hoped that we will be able to add even more to the next edition.

## Engine

Under each model year roster is a list of standard (S) and optional (O) engines and their model or series availability. Other basic information provided includes block configuration, number of cylinders, displacement (to the nearest 0.1 cubic inch), bore and stroke (to the nearest .01 inch), and SAE gross horsepower (SAE net starting in 1972). In cases where there was more than one standard engine, all are shown as "S."

## Additions and Corrections

Much care has been taken in compiling this book to ensure a high degree of accuracy. Nevertheless, additional research may yield data or conclusions other than those presented here. The publishers welcome additions and suggestions. They may be addressed to Encyclopedia of American Cars, c/o Consumer Guide® Publications, 7373 North Cicero Avenue, Lincolnwood, Illinois 60712, e-mail: jstewart@pubint.com

—The Auto Editors of Consumer Guide®

# Allstate

Imagine Chrysler selling shirts, Ford merchandising mattresses, or GM pushing power tools. Sound strange? No more so than retailing giant Sears, Roebuck getting into the car business, which it did for a brief time in the '50s.

The story begins in the late '40s with Theodore V. Houser, then vice president of merchandising for Sears, but also on the board of Kaiser-Frazer, the upstart postwar automaker. In 1949, Houser broached the idea of marketing a K-F product under Sears' familiar Allstate name—a complete car to be sold along with parts and accessories for it at the new auto shops Sears was then opening up next to its retail stores. A hookup with K-F was a natural. At the time, Houser was buying Homart enamelware from Kaiser Metals Company in which Sears held a 45-percent interest.

The first thought was simply to put Allstate logos on Kaiser-Frazer's large 1949 models, but Sears was dubious. Then the compact Henry J came along for 1951 (see entry), exactly the car Houser had been looking for: simple, inexpensive, and easy to service.

Somehow, K-F president Edgar F. Kaiser managed to convince his dealers to accept a chain department store as a competitor, and the Allstate was announced that November. It was the only new American make for 1952, and the first car Sears had offered since its high-wheeler of 40 years earlier. In an apparent attempt to feel out the market, Sears initially concentrated promotion in the Southeast, though the Allstate was ostensibly available nationwide through the Sears catalog.

Though obviously a Henry J, the Allstate sported a distinctive front end designed by Alex Tremulis (lately involved with the Tucker fiasco), plus a major interior upgrade in line with Sears' policy of improving on proprietary products. K-F interior specialist Carleton Spencer used quilted saran plastic combined with a coated-paper fiber encapsulated in vinyl, a material he'd discovered in use on the transatlantic telegraph cable. Seemingly impervious to normal wear, it was superior to the upholstery of most Henry Js.

Not surprisingly, Sears specified its own Allstate batteries, spark plugs, and tube tires, each with the appropriate guarantee. The entire vehicle was covered for 90 days or 4000 miles, K-F's standard warranty. Allstate's Deluxe models had trunklids and dashboard gloveboxes, items found less often on Henry Js, though basic and standard Allstates lacked the opening trunk. The costlier Deluxe Six also had armrests and a horn ring that weren't available on lesser versions even at extra cost.

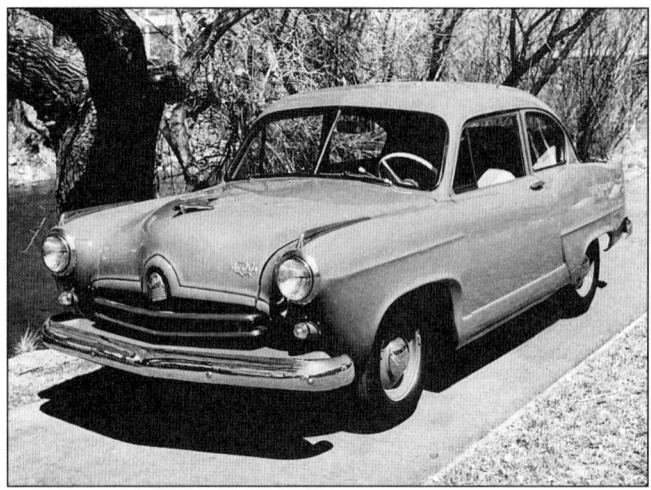

**1952 fastback two-door sedan**

Otherwise, everything else was the same. That meant K-F's pudgy-looking little two-door fastback sedan with a choice of two L-head Willys engines: a four and a six. Sears' marketing was more aggressive, though, with five Allstate models to four Henry Js. The cheapest '52 Allstate, the basic Four, was priced just below the standard Henry J.

There was little change for '53. A full-width rubber-covered pad was added to the dash, taillights were relocated to the rear fenders, and models reduced to two Fours and the Six.

But by then, it was clear the Allstate had failed. Whether it was because people didn't take to buying cars in department stores or because of the narrow marketing approach is difficult to determine. Both factors probably contributed. Only 1566 Allstates were built for 1952. The count was 797 when Sears canceled the project in early '53, leaving plans for future models stillborn. Among these was a pair of proposals for a two-door station wagon, one by industrial designer Brooks Stevens, the other by Gordon Tercey of K-F Styling.

Allstates are extremely rare today, and thus more desired by collectors than comparable Henry Js. In 1971, Allstate Insurance purchased an Allstate car for historical purposes. In the '60s it would have been hard to convince the folks at Sears' parts counters that the car had ever existed.

## Specifications

### 1952—1,566 built

| A2304 Four (wb 100.0) | | Wght | Price | Prod |
|---|---|---|---|---|
| 110 | basic sdn 2d | 2,300 | 1,395 | 200 |
| 111 | std sdn 2d | 2,300 | 1,486 | 500 |
| 113 | Deluxe sdn 2d | 2,300 | 1,539 | 200 |
| **A2404 Six (wb 100.0)** | | | | |
| — | basic sdn 2d | 2,325 | 1,594 | 200 |
| 115 | Deluxe sdn 2d | 2,325 | 1,693 | 466 |

| 1952 Engines | bore × stroke | bhp | availability |
|---|---|---|---|
| I-4, 134.2 | 3.11 × 4.38 | 68 | S-Allstate Four |
| I-6, 161.0 | 3.13 × 3.50 | 80 | S-Allstate Six |

### 1953—797 built

| A3304 Four (wb 100.0) | | Wght | Price | Prod |
|---|---|---|---|---|
| 210 | std sdn 2d | 2,405 | 1,528 | 200 |
| 213 | Deluxe sdn 2d | 2,405 | 1,589 | 225 |
| **A3404 Six (wb 100.0)** | | | | |
| 215 | Deluxe sdn 2d | 2,455 | 1,785 | 372 |

| 1953 Engines | bore × stroke | bhp | availability |
|---|---|---|---|
| I-4, 134.2 | 3.11 × 4.38 | 68 | S-Allstate Four |
| I-6, 161.0 | 3.13 × 3.50 | 80 | S-Allstate Six |

Note: Model-by-model production totals are estimated.

# American Austin

**1930 Model A 2-passenger coupe**

When Sir Herbert Austin came to America in 1929, the well-known English manufacturer had many people excited over his plan to build cars in the USA. After a tour of the country, he announced that the American Austin would be built in Butler, Pennsylvania. Detroit shook its collective head, but Butler wasn't such a strange choice. It had access to industrial services and an eager work force, and it was close enough to East Coast ports to make importing components from England quite feasible. The basic concept of the car itself seemed promising, too, and as production started in May 1930, the company claimed it had close to 200,000 orders for its new ultralight, ultra-economical car.

The American Austin was built through 1934, and the same engine was used throughout the production run. It was an L-head four that displaced 46 cubic inches, had only two main bearings, and developed 13-14 brake horsepower at 3200 rpm. A roadster and coupe were initially offered. In 1931, a business coupe, Deluxe coupe, and 2/4 passenger cabriolet were added. Once production fired up, some of the original prices were cut, and the figures were reduced again in 1933 in an effort to boost sales.

For a while, prospects for the American Austin looked good—but only for a while. The 1930 output of 8558 units would never be exceeded. Two factors were largely responsible for the lackluster reception. One was the general business decline brought on by the Depression. The other was the fact that, even in bad times, Americans didn't take to midget cars. To be sure, the American Austin was a midget. Its 75-inch wheelbase was fully 16 inches less than that of the future VW Beetle. Also, the Austin weighed only 1100-1200 pounds, and Americans were notoriously leery about light cars in those years, as many still are. It was an attractive little car, designed in part by Alexis de Sakhnoffsky, but that didn't seem to matter, and production ground to a halt in 1935.

Austins provided a welcome touch of amusement in a drab period for America. And, for a few people, they became a sort of reverse status symbol, much like the Beetle would be in the 1950s. Al Jolson, who loved cars and usually drove Packards or Lincolns, bought the first Austin coupe delivered to a private buyer. He was followed by numerous other Hollywood stars: Buster Keaton, Slim Summerville, and the "Our Gang" kiddies. Austins even starred in a movie. They were used as "steeds" for a knightly battle in Will Rogers' A Connecticut Yankee in King Arthur's Court. It made for a great movie scene, but it didn't help to sell Austins.

# American Austin

1930 Model A 2-passenger coupe

1930 Model A 2-passenger coupe

## Specifications

### 1930—8,558 built*

| Model A (wb 75.0) | Wght | Price | Prod |
|---|---|---|---|
| rdstr | 1,100 | 445 | — |
| cpe 2P | 1,130 | 465 | — |

| 1930 Engine | bore × stroke | bhp | availability |
|---|---|---|---|
| I-4, 46.0 | 2.20 × 3.00 | 14 | S-all |

*Calendar year

### 1931—1,279 built*

| Model A (wb 75.0) | Wght | Price | Prod |
|---|---|---|---|
| rdstr | 1,040 | 395 | — |
| bus cpe | 1,130 | 330 | — |
| cpe 2P | 1,130 | 395 | — |
| DeLuxe cpe 2P | 1,130 | 525 | — |
| cabriolet 2-4P | 1,175 | 550 | — |

| 1931 Engine | bore × stroke | bhp | availability |
|---|---|---|---|
| I-4, 46.0 | 2.20 × 3.00 | 14 | S-all |

*Calendar year

### 1932—3,846 built*

| Model A (wb 75.0) | Wght | Price | Prod |
|---|---|---|---|
| rdstr | 1,040 | 395 | — |
| bus cpe | 1,130 | 330 | — |
| cpe 2P | 1,130 | 395 | — |

| 1932 Engine | bore × stroke | bhp | availability |
|---|---|---|---|
| I-4, 46.0 | 2.20 × 3.00 | 14 | S-all |

*Calendar year

### 1933—4,726 built*

| Model 2-75 (wb 75.0) | Wght | Price | Prod |
|---|---|---|---|
| rdstr | 1,020 | 315 | — |
| bus cpe | 1,100 | 275 | — |
| Special bus cpe | 1,100 | 295 | — |
| cpe 2P | 1,130 | 315 | — |

| Model 3-75 (wb 75.0) | Wght | Price | Prod |
|---|---|---|---|
| rdstr | 1,929 | 365 | — |
| bus cpe | 1,100 | 295 | — |
| cpe 2P | 1,130 | 345 | — |
| DeLuxe cpe | 1,130 | 365 | — |

| 1933 Engine | bore × stroke | bhp | availability |
|---|---|---|---|
| I-4, 46.0 | 2.20 × 3.00 | 13 | S-all |

*Calendar year

### 1934—1,300 built (est.)*

| Model 375 (wb 75.0) | Wght | Price | Prod |
|---|---|---|---|
| rdstr | 1,020 | 365 | — |
| bus cpe | 1,130 | 295 | — |
| cpe 2P | 1,130 | 345 | — |
| DeLuxe cpe 2P | 1,130 | 365 | — |

| 1934 Engine | bore × stroke | bhp | availability |
|---|---|---|---|
| I-4, 46.0 | 2.20 × 3.00 | 13 | S-all |

*Calendar year

### 1935-36

Models listed in industry records, but no production.

# American Bantam

**1938 Model 60 Playboy roadster**

**1938 Model 60 Speedster 4-passenger**

Small cars never made it big in prewar America, but that didn't stop people from pushing them. Among the more energetic proponents was Roy S. Evans, who took over the moribund American Austin Car Company in 1935 with hopes of succeeding where Sir Herbert Austin had failed.

Evans' hopes were tempered by the Depression, which still seemed endless, and Austin's formidable debts: $75,000 in back taxes and interest, plus a $150,000 property mortgage to the Pullman Standard Company. But the federal court overseeing American Austin's bankruptcy felt Evans might salvage things, and gave him the place for only $5000 cash—a mere 1/2000th of its appraised value. Evans secured a $250,000 loan from the Reconstruction Finance Corporation, then hired the necessary talent to help him create a new car called American Bantam.

Like American Austin, the Bantam was styled by the artistic Alexis de Sakhnoffsky, who conjured a new front with a smooth hood and rounded grille, plus reworked fenders and rear deck. His bill was only $300, and Evans was able to retool the entire line for a mere $7000. Indy race-car builder Harry Miller was hired to improve mechanicals, but lack of funds confined him to a redesigned manifold. Butler's own engineers replaced the Austin's expensive roller bearings with cheap babbitt bearings, and added full-pressure lubrication, a new three-speed transmission, Hotchkiss final drive, and Ross cam-and-lever steering. They also devised a heavier frame. Engine size was unchanged, but three main bearings were used instead of two after 1939. Wheel diameter shrank from 18 to 16 inches for 1937 and to 15 inches for 1938.

The debut 1936 Bantam line comprised a roadster and five coupes in the $295-$385 range. Two roadsters and three

**1937 panel truck**

coupes were listed for '37 at somewhat higher prices ($385-$492). Several new models arrived for 1938, including a Speedster with pretty "Duesenberg sweep" side panels, and the novel Boulevard Delivery with a rear half-roof. For 1939 came a smart Riviera convertible, designed by the young Alex Tremulis, who later recalled that it could cruise at 75-80 mph and average 42.5 mpg—a rather questionable claim.

Bantam production continued into 1941, but not even the dynamic Evans could convince Americans of the value in his tiny package. Output was about 2000 units in 1938, just 1229 the following year, under 1000 in 1940-41, then none. The firm found temporary salvation by winning a contract to design what became the World War II Army Jeep. Bantam built the first prototype, but the army was concerned about its ability to produce Jeeps in the quantities needed. Ford and Willys were supplied with Bantam's blueprints and asked to submit their own versions. Bantam received contracts for only 2,643 units, while Ford and Willys built more than 600,000 during the war. Bantam did get a contract to build two-wheel Jeeptrailers. The company produced utility trailers until 1956.

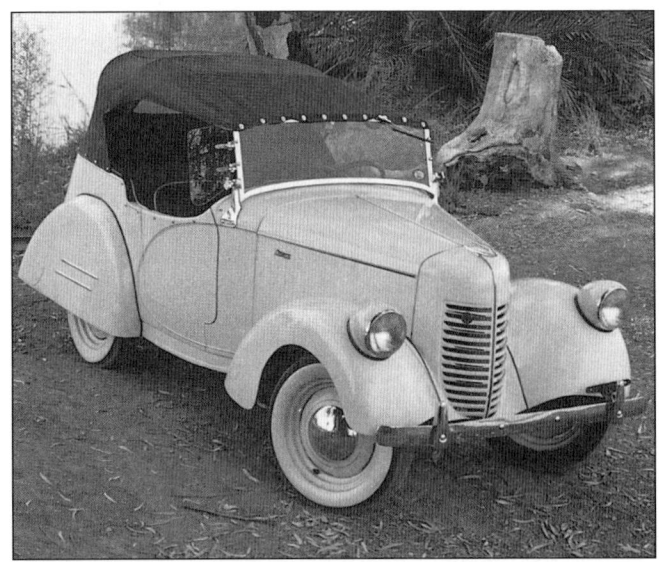

1940 Series 65 Speedster 4-passenger

## Specifications

### 1936

| Model 575 (wb 75.0) | Wght | Price | Prod* |
|---|---|---|---|
| rdstr 2P | 1,040 | 385 | — |
| bus cpe 1P | 1,130 | 295 | — |
| bus cpe 2P | 1,130 | 307 | — |
| Standard cpe | 1,130 | 355 | — |
| DeLuxe cpe | 1,130 | 385 | — |

| 1936 Engine | bore × stroke | bhp | availability |
|---|---|---|---|
| I-4, 46.0 | 2.20 × 3.00 | 13 | all |

*Under 500, all models

### 1937—3,500 built (est.)

| Model 575 (wb 75.0) | Wght | Price | Prod |
|---|---|---|---|
| rdstr | 1,100 | 431 | — |
| Custom rdstr | 1,100 | 492 | — |
| bus cpe | 1,100 | 385 | — |
| cpe 2P | 1,100 | 411 | — |
| DeLuxe cpe 2P | 1,100 | 431 | — |

| 1937 Engine | bore × stroke | bhp | availability |
|---|---|---|---|
| I-4, 46.0 | 2.20 × 3.00 | 20 | S-all |

### 1938—2,000 built (est.)

| Model 60 (wb 75.0) | Wght | Price | Prod |
|---|---|---|---|
| Special rdstr | 1,130 | 449 | — |
| rdstr | 1,140 | 479 | — |
| DeLuxe rdstr | 1,160 | 525 | — |
| bus cpe | 1,230 | 399 | — |
| cpe 2P | 1,230 | 399 | — |
| Master cpe 2P | 1,250 | 439 | — |
| DeLuxe cpe 2P | 1,250 | 465 | — |
| Foursome spdstr 4P | 1,265 | 497 | — |
| wgn 2d | 1,434 | 565 | — |

| 1938 Engine | bore × stroke | bhp | availability |
|---|---|---|---|
| I-4, 46.0 | 2.20 × 3.00 | 20 | S-all |

### 1939—1,229 built*

| Model 62 (wb 75.0) | Wght | Price | Prod |
|---|---|---|---|
| rdstr | 1,130 | 449 | — |
| Special rdstr | 1,140 | 479 | — |
| DeLuxe rdstr | 1,160 | 525 | — |
| cpe 2P | 1,230 | 399 | — |
| Special cpe 2P | 1,240 | 439 | — |
| DeLuxe cpe 2P | 1,250 | 469 | — |
| Sunair cpe 2P | 1,250 | 479 | — |
| Foursome spdstr 4P | 1,265 | 497 | — |
| DeLuxe Foursome spdstr 4P | 1,280 | 549 | — |
| wgn 2d | 1,434 | 565 | — |

| 1939 Engine | bore × stroke | bhp | availability |
|---|---|---|---|
| I-4, 46.0 | 2.20 × 3.00 | 20 | S-all |

### 1940—800 built

| Series 65 (wb 75.0) | | Wght | Price | Prod |
|---|---|---|---|---|
| 65 | cpe | 1,261 | 399 | — |
| 65 | Master cpe | 1,275 | 449 | — |
| 65 | conv cpe | 1,340 | 525 | — |
| 65 | Master rdstr | 1,211 | 449 | — |
| 65 | conv sdn | 1,296 | 549 | — |
| 65 | wgn 2d | 1,400 | 565 | — |

| 1940 Engine | bore × stroke | bhp | availability |
|---|---|---|---|
| I-4, 50.1 | 2.26 × 3.13 | 22 | S-all |

### 1941—138 built

| Series 65 (wb 75.0) | | Wght | Price | Prod |
|---|---|---|---|---|
| 65 | cpe | 1,261 | 399 | — |
| 65 | Master cpe | 1,275 | 449 | — |
| 65 | conv cpe | 1,340 | 525 | — |
| 65 | Master rdstr | 1,211 | 449 | — |
| 65 | conv sdn | 1,296 | 549 | — |
| 65 | wgn 2d | 1,400 | 565 | — |

| 1941 Engine | bore × stroke | bhp | availability |
|---|---|---|---|
| I-4, 50.1 | 2.26 × 3.13 | 22 | S-all |

*Calendar-year figures.

# AMC

AMC became a distinct make for 1966, as American Motors substituted this badge for Rambler nameplates on the full-size Ambassador and midsize fastback Marlin. The intermediate Rambler Rebel followed suit for '68, when the Javelin ponycar and two-seat AMX arrived as new AMC models. Rambler disappeared after the final, 1969 edition of the 1964-vintage American compact, which was replaced for 1970 by the AMC Hornet and Gremlin.

The 1966 Ambassador was a face-lifted version of the redesigned '65 Rambler model, one of the better efforts from the studios of AMC design vice president Richard A. Teague. Squarish but clean, it spanned a 116-inch wheelbase, four inches longer than the '64 Ambassador's. A new special edition for '66 was the DPL hardtop coupe, elegantly appointed with reclining bucket seats, fold-down center armrests, pile carpeting, and many other standards.

Ranked below were Ambassador sedans, wagons, and hardtops in 880 and 990 trim, plus a 990 convertible. All offered the long-running 232-cubic-inch Typhoon six or optional 287- and 327-cid V-8s. Only the 270-horsepower 327 required premium

**1966 Ambassador DPL hardtop coupe**

**1966 Ambassador 660 station wagon**

**1966 Ambassador DPL hardtop coupe**

**1966 Ambassador 880 two-door sedan**

**1966 Rambler Classic Rebel hardtop coupe**

**1967 Ambassador 990 four-door sedan**

**1967 Ambassador DPL hardtop coupe**

**1967 Ambassador DPL convertible coupe**

# AMC

**1967 Rambler Rebel SST hardtop coupe**

**1967 Rambler Rebel 770 Cross Country station wagon**

fuel. Most Ambassadors were ordered with automatic, but a few carried a three-speed manual transmission or AMC's "Twin-Stick" overdrive. A four-speed manual was also listed for 990s and the DPL.

The big Ambassador evolved nicely through the late '60s. Wheelbase was stretched two inches for '67, when semifastback styling with more-rounded contours was adopted. The '68s were little changed save a slightly altered hood and a revised model sequence: standard, DPL, and SST. New frontal styling with a more-sculpted hood, plastic grille, and horizontal quad headlights marked the '69s, riding a new 122-inch wheelbase and sporting standard air conditioning. A minor restyle for 1970 brought new rear fenders and taillamps to sedans and hardtops, and new roof panels and taillamps to wagons.

AMC made an unsuccessful first stab at the booming personal-car market with the radically styled 1965 Rambler Marlin, renamed AMC Marlin for 1966-67. This was a big fastback hardtop coupe, initially based on the midsize 1965-66 Rambler

**1967 Rambler Rebel SST convertible coupe**

**1967 Marlin fastback hardtop coupe**

**1967 Marlin fastback hardtop coupe**

**1968 Ambassador SST hardtop coupe**

**1968 Ambassador SST four-door sedan**

**1968 Rebel 770 four-door sedan**

19

# AMC

1968 Rebel SST convertible coupe

1968 Javelin SST fastback hardtop coupe

1968 Javelin SST fastback hardtop coupe

1968 AMX 2-passenger coupe

1968 Javelin SST hardtop coupe

1968 Javelin fastback hardtop coupe

1968 AMX 2-passenger coupe

1968 AMX 2-passenger coupe

Classic, with the same 112-inch wheelbase and similar front sheetmetal. Teague penned sweeping, elliptical rear side windows so the C-pillars wouldn't look heavy, but the overall styling was somewhat clumsy nonetheless. The '66 changed only in detail: revised grille, standard front antiroll bar on six-cylinder models, and newly optional vinyl roof treatment.

The '67 Marlin was switched to that year's new Ambassador platform and ended up much better proportioned on its longer wheelbase. Teague helped with handsome lower-body lines of the same hippy sort applied to that year's Ambassador and Rebel. Measuring 6.5-inches longer than previous Marlins, the '67 was perhaps the best of this school, but it arrived too late to save the day. Sales had been low from the start, and 1965-66 sales were less than 5000 and 3000, respectively. Marlin offered some sports-car features (optional four-speed gearbox, tachometer, bucket seats, and V-8s with up to 280 bhp) but lacked a sports car's taut, precise handling and manageable size.

Replacing Marlin for 1968 was the smaller and far more popular Javelin, a "ponycar" in the image of Ford's wildly successful Mustang. Beautifully shaped and exciting, the Javelin sold like hotcakes. Over 56,000 of the '68s were built, helping AMC out of a four-year sales slump. With standard 232 six, a Javelin cruised at 80 mph; the optional 290 V-8 boosted top speed to 100 mph. An optional "Go Package" offered a 343 V-8 with four-barrel carburetor and dual exhausts, plus power front-disc brakes, heavy-duty suspension, and wide tires—good for eight seconds in the 0-60-mph dash and a top speed approaching 120 mph. On its 109-inch wheelbase, Javelin was a bit roomier, larger, and longer than the rival Mustang, Chevy Camaro, and Plymouth Barracuda. Its styling was arguably the cleanest of the lot.

Javelin was face-lifted for 1969, mainly via an altered grille. A "twin-venturi" nose, revised wheel covers, and a new hood with simulated air scoops arrived for 1970. But sales failed to match the first-year total because of additional ponycar competition—notably a sleek new Camaro.

An exciting mid 1968 newcomer was the AMX, a two-seat coupe created by sectioning the Javelin bodyshell to a trim 97-inch wheelbase. This car introduced a new 390-cid V-8 with forged-steel crankshaft and connecting rods. Output was a healthy 315 bhp and 425 pound-feet of torque. AMX's standard engine was a 290 V-8; a 343 was optional. Tight suspension, bucket seats, and extra-cost four-speed gearbox made for a capable semisports car; the AMC also did well in competition. As with the Marlin, the handsomest AMX was the last, the 1970 edition looking more-integrated and "serious." But again, demand was always much lower than management hoped, with production for all three model years combined failing to top 20,000 units.

As mentioned, Rebel switched to an AMC nameplate for 1968, though the basic car had appeared the previous year as a Rambler, taking over from the old Classic. It remained AMC's midsize, however, riding a 114-inch wheelbase and offering a variety of sixes and V-8s. Prices were competitive, starting at around $2500. Sedans, hardtop coupes, and wagons were available in three series—550, 770, and SST. Rebel also offered AMC's sole 1968 convertibles, but few were built: just 377 in the 550 series and another 823 SSTs. They would be AMC's last factory droptops (not counting the later Renault-based Alliance models). The '69 Rebel line was trimmed to just basic and SST series. A wider track and a new grille, plus a restyled rear deck and taillights, were the only changes of note.

For 1970, Rebel sedans and hardtops were lengthened two inches to accommodate redesigned roof panels and rear fenders, and new taillights appeared. Series stayed the same, but AMC again went after the performance crowd with "The Machine." A Rebel with a cause, this hardtop coupe packed the company's most-potent V-8, plus four-speed manual gearbox with Hurst linkage and a 3.54:1 rear axle. Providing easy exterior identification were a bold, functional hood air scoop,

**1969 Ambassador SST four-door sedan**

**1969 Rebel SST four-door station wagon**

**1969 Rebel hardtop coupe**

**1969 Javelin SST fastback hardtop coupe**

**1969 Javelin SST fastback hardtop coupe**

**1969 AMX 2-passenger coupe**

# AMC

1970 AMX 2-passenger coupe

1970 Rebel SST hardtop coupe

1970 Rebel SST hardtop coupe

1970 Hornet SST two-door sedan

1970 Javelin SST fastback hardtop coupe

1970 Ambassador SST hardtop coupe

1970 Rebel hardtop coupe

1970 Rebel "The Machine" hardtop coupe

1970 Hornet two-door sedan

1970 Javelin SST hardtop coupe

# AMC

special red-white-and-blue paint, and 15-inch mag wheels with raised-white-letter tires. An 8000-rpm tachometer, dual exhausts with low-restriction mufflers, and a definite front-end rake completed this expensive package ($3475). The Machine certainly looked like a hot performer, but Javelin won the competition laurels, Mark Donohue piloting one to win the Sports Car Club of America's 1970 Trans-Am road-racing series.

AMC spent $40 million, a million man-hours and three years on its new 1970 Hornet compact, which revived a time-honored name not seen since the last Hudsons of 1957. It bowed as two- and four-door notchback sedans on a 108-inch wheelbase (two inches up on the predecessor American) with a choice of two sixes and base or SST trim. First-year sales were 92,458, a strong showing that helped AMC's sagging finances. Still, Kenosha lost money that year—$58.2 million on sales of over $1 billion.

April 1970 brought the clever Gremlin, America's first subcompact. With AMC's thriftiest six and base prices below $2000, this import-fighter initially sold well: over 26,000 for its abbreviated first model year. Gremlin related to Hornet as AMX did to Javelin. Sheetmetal was similar ahead of the B-posts, but Gremlin wheelbase was trimmed to 96 inches to match a

**1970 Gremlin hatchback coupe**

**1970 Gremlin hatchback coupe**

**1971 Matador four-door station wagon**

**1971 Hornet SC/360 two-door sedan**

**1971 Hornet SC/360 two-door sedan**

**1971 Javelin AMX fastback hardtop coupe**

**1971 Javelin SST fastback hardtop coupe**

**1971 Javelin AMX fastback hardtop coupe**

# AMC

1971 Javelin SST Mark Donohue Edition

1972 Ambassador Brougham station wagon

1972 Hornet SST two-door sedan

1971 Gremlin hatchback coupe

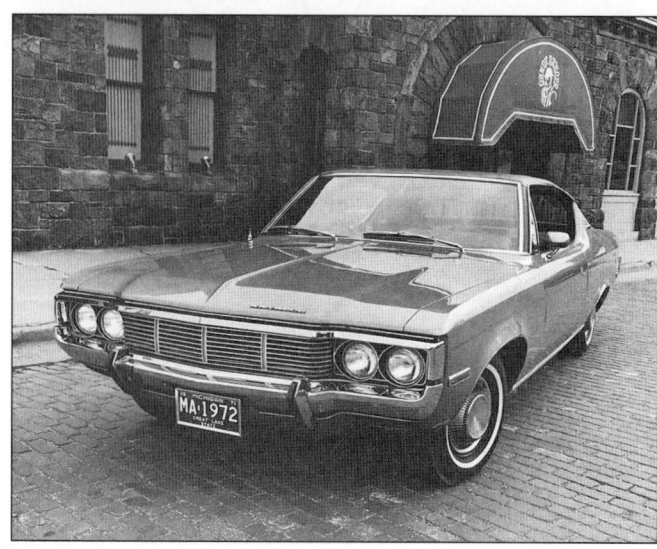

1972 Matador hardtop coupe

severely truncated rear body with lift-up wagon-style rear window. Though this styling proved controversial, designer Teague insisted it was the only way to go. "Nobody would have paid it any attention if it had looked like one of the Big Three," he said.

With Hornet and Gremlin, AMC gave up trying to be a "full-line" automaker slugging toe-to-toe with the Big Three, returning to its original role as a "niche" marketer specializing in small cars. But the transition took a long time, and it wasn't until model-year '79 that AMC fully returned to the formula it had found so profitable in the late '50s and early '60s. In a way,

it was strange that this tiny outfit would have ever tried to match the giants model-for-model, but president Roy Abernethy and even market-wise chairman Roy D. Chapin, Jr., were somehow persuaded to abandon the course pursued long before by George Romney.

An important development toward more specialized products was the February 1970 acquisition of Toledo-based Kaiser-Jeep Corporation, which instantly made AMC the nation's leading builder of four-wheel-drive vehicles. Though uncharted territory for AMC, Jeep's long experience in the field would prove

1972 Hornet Sportabout Gucci Edition sedan/wagon

1972 Javelin SST fastback hardtop coupe

valuable, eventually finding its way into the passenger-car line.

Though it took nearly a decade to complete, AMC's market reorientation was evident as early as 1971. The jazzy Rebel Machine and slow-selling AMX were dropped, though the latter's name was applied to a new top-line Javelin. The ponycar was given heavy—and not altogether successful—sheetmetal surgery on an inch-longer wheelbase, with crisper lines highlighted by pronounced bulges over the front wheel openings in the manner of the contemporary Chevrolet Corvette. Inside was a reworked dash curved inward at the center, as in Pontiac's then-current Grand Prix, so as to bring minor controls closer to the driver.

Javelin stumbled along in this form through 1974, a vestige of the past. Annual production never broke 30,000 in this period, reflecting the general fast decline in ponycar demand after 1970. AMC decided against a direct replacement—reasonable, considering the only such cars still selling in decent numbers by then were the Chevrolet Camaro/Pontiac Firebird. Still, Javelin remained faithful to the cause. For example, the big 401-cid V-8 introduced for '71 was optionally available through the end, though with diminished power both on paper (with the 1971 industry switch to more realistic SAE net power ratings) and in fact (due to detuning for lower exhaust emissions).

Another AMC nameplate, Ambassador, disappeared after 1974. Continued with only minor trim and equipment changes in its final years, the firm's full-size was ultimately done in by lack of interest. Sales had never been great, and though its aging 1967 design was more sensible in some ways than that of concurrent Big Three rivals, the lack of change increasingly weighed against it. The crowning blow was probably the Middle East oil embargo of 1973-74, which triggered America's first energy crisis and temporarily crippled sales of most all full-size cars.

Another holdover fared only slightly better. This was the mid-size Matador, a renamed, restyled Rebel appearing for 1971 as a continuation of that basic 1967 design. Offered in the same three body styles through 1973, it was pretty ordinary stuff and failed to generate much showroom traffic. In later years, AMC tacitly acknowledged the line's near invisibility with a series of humorous TV commercials that asked "What's a Matador?" Few

**1972 Javelin SST Pierre Cardin Edition**

**1972 Gremlin X hatchback coupe**

**1972 Gremlin X hatchback coupe**

**1973 Matador four-door station wagon**

**1973 Matador four-door sedan**

**1973 Hornet Sportabout D/L sedan/wagon**

# AMC

1973 Ambassador Brougham station wagon

1973 Ambassador Brougham hardtop coupe

1973 Hornet hatchback coupe

1973 Javelin SST fastback hardtop coupe

1973 Gremlin X "Levi's" hatchback coupe

1974 Ambassador Brougham station wagon

1974 Matador four-door sedan

1974 Matador X fastback coupe

1974 Hornet Sportabout D/L sedan/wagon

1974 Hornet two-door sedan

buyers apparently cared.

An attempt to perk up Matador's staid image arrived for 1974, when the notchback hardtop coupe gave way to a completely different pillared fastback that AMC boldly announced would race in NASCAR. Designer Teague gave it smooth, curvaceous contours and an unusual front with the hood shaped to form the upper portions of huge headlamp nacelles. Despite special "designer" interiors (then a favored AMC marketing ploy) and sporty options like the X package, the fastback provided only temporary relief and Matador sales remained underwhelming. Like Ambassador, the midsize suffered in the aftermath of the first energy crisis. By 1978 it was quite passé, even the coupes, which had been progressively hoked up in the interim. After that, it was adios, Matador.

Gremlin was one "sow's ear" that Teague made into the proverbial silk purse. In fact, it was generally AMC's number-two seller in the '70s, after Hornet. Special trim options appeared almost yearly to help keep interest alive. Among the most popular was the X package, which typically delivered tape stripes, black grille, slotted wheels, wider tires, custom bucket-seat interior, sports steering wheel, and similar dress-up items. Prices were reasonable, about $300 at first. The "LEVI's®" edition, new for '73, sported seats and door panels done up in blue spun nylon with copper rivets to look just like the cotton denim of Levi Strauss & Company, which happily collaborated on the package, even allowing use of its distinctive red jeans label. This was probably the most winsome Gremlin, and if anybody ever collects these cars, it may well be the most sought-after.

Gremlin vanished after 1978 but lived on in Spirit—the same thing with smoother, more-conventional styling. Joining the familiar chopped-tail two-door was a slick new hatchback coupe with a particularly graceful superstructure for such a short car. Both body styles offered three trim levels, and the AMX tag was revived for a special "paint-on performance" coupe in 1980. Spirits moved via a standard 2.5-liter (151-cid) four purchased from Pontiac or, at extra cost, the long-lived

**1974 Javelin fastback hardtop coupe**

**1974 Javelin fastback hardtop coupe**

**1975 Matador fastback coupe**

**1974 Javelin AMX fastback hardtop coupe**

**1974 Gremlin X "Levi's" hatchback coupe**

**1975 Hornet D/L four-door sedan**

# AMC

**1975 Hornet hatchback coupe**

**1975 Hornet Sportabout sedan/wagon**

AMC six. A heavy emphasis on quality made Spirits generally better-built than Gremlins, if not Big Three rivals. But there was no escaping the aged '60s-style design, and while the four was fairly thrifty, it had very little power; the six was quicker but thirstier.

In a similar transformation, the compact Hornet became the Concord for 1978. Reflecting AMC's limited new-model development funds, it wasn't all that different structurally or mechanically, but it looked more "important" and, like its linemates, benefited from an urgent stress on workmanship prompted by the growing success of Japanese imports. Concord was AMC's volume seller from the time it appeared. By 1980 it boasted a thriftier standard engine, cleaner looks, more comfort and convenience extras, and a broader antirust warranty.

Not to be overlooked are three early-'70s Hornet developments. One was the SC/360, a performance-oriented two-door offered only for 1971. As the name suggested, it packed AMC's 360-cid small-block V-8, rated at 245 bhp with standard two-barrel carb or 285 bhp with extra-cost four-pot induction. Acceleration was quite vivid, and a large functional hood scoop, heavy-duty suspension, styled wheels, fat tires, tape stripes, and Hurst four-speed were either standard or available.

**1975 Pacer D/L hatchback coupe**

**1975 Gremlin hatchback coupe**

**1976 Matador Brougham fastback coupe**

**1976 Matador Brougham fastback coupe**

**1976 Hornet Sportabout sedan/wagon**

**1976 Hornet D/L four-door sedan**

# AMC

1976 Gremlin hatchback coupe

1976 Gremlin X hatchback coupe

1977 Matador four-door sedan

1977 Matador fastback coupe

1977 Hornet hatchback coupe

1977 Hornet D/L two-door sedan

1977 Hornet D/L four-door sedan

1977 Hornet AMX hatchback coupe

But as had so often been the case, AMC was a day late and a dollar short: only 784 were built, making the SC/360 one of the '70s rarest production Detroiters and thus something of a collector's item.

A more sensible and successful innovation was the Hornet Sportabout, a graceful four-door wagon with a one-piece tailgate. Another '71 newcomer, it would prove uncommonly long-lived. Even lovelier was the new-for-'73 Hornet hatchback coupe. Offering vast load space, it could be quite sporty with an optional X package. Needless styling gimmicks made some versions quite tacky by the time the Concord came in, and the hatchback was discontinued after '79. There was also a special AMX model with this bodyshell, a limited 1977-78 offering.

Concord spawned a novel offshoot for 1980, the four-wheel-drive Eagle, reviving a name that AMC owned via the Jeep takeover and, with it, the dregs of Willys-Overland. A natural for a firm with AMC's particular, but limited, resources, Eagle was essentially the Concord platform equipped with a new full-time 4WD system called Quadra-Trac, whose transfer case apportioned driving torque between front and rear wheels via a center differential with clutches running in a slip-limiting silicone compound.

# AMC

Eagle arrived with Concord's three body styles and a nominal 1.3-inch-longer wheelbase. Its ride height was greater too, thanks to larger tires and the required extra ground clearance for the differentials. The drivetrain comprised the firm's well-known 258-cid six (a stroked 232, first offered for 1971) mated to three-speed Torque Command automatic transmission (actually Chrysler TorqueFlite). Power steering and brakes and all-season radial tires were standard. Eagles flew with prominent (and necessary) wheel-arch flares made of color-keyed Krayton plastic, and a Sport-package option offered black extensions and other trim, plus Goodyear Tiempo tires.

Predictably, the Eagle drove and felt much like any Concord. AMC didn't intend it for off-road use, stressing the safety advantages of 4WD traction for everyday driving, particularly in the snowbelt. A full range of luxury and convenience features was offered, but there was no V-8 option for the sake of fuel economy—and the government's corporate average fuel-economy (CAFE) mandates. The Spirit/Concord Pontiac-built four became available for '81.

AMC's biggest '70s disappointment was the Pacer, announced for 1975 as "the first wide small car." It was planned for a lightweight Wankel rotary engine that GM was developing in the early '70s but quickly shelved. Designer Teague penned distinctive lines with acres of glass, a short nose, and a hatchback body that looked

**1977 Pacer D/L two-door station wagon**

**1977 Pacer X hatchback coupe**

**1977 Pacer D/L two-door station wagon**

**1977 Gremlin X hatchback coupe**

**1978 Matador four-door station wagon**

**1978 Matador Barcelona four-door sedan**

**1978 Matador Barcelona fastback coupe**

**1978 Concord D/L two-door sedan**

# AMC

1978 AMX fastback coupe

1978 Concord D/L sedan/wagon

1978 Concord D/L sedan/wagon

1978 Concord D/L two-door sedan

1978 Pacer D/L wagon

1978 Pacer D/L hatchback coupe

1978 Gremlin hatchback coupe

1978 Gremlin hatchback coupe

nearly as wide as it was long.

Unhappily, cancellation of the GM Wankel forced AMC into patchwork engineering alterations that seriously compromised the original concept. While the rotary would have provided decent performance and fuel economy, AMC had to use its relatively big and weighty six, to the detriment of both as well as handling. With that and all its heavy glass, Pacer ended up quite portly for a subcompact, and its styling seemed frankly odd to many eyes (though doors wrapped into the roof were predictive of '80s design). By 1979, annual sales were down to only 10,000 or so despite the interim addition of wagons and an optional V-8, and Pacer was unceremoniously dumped after 1980.

An aging product line that didn't generate sufficient sales for funding more-modern replacements proved an increasingly vicious cycle for AMC as the '70s wore on. Eagle, for instance, owed much to Concord, which dated from the then decade-old Hornet. At decade's end, mounting losses were aggravated by a deep national recession that cut sales further, and AMC soon found itself the object of a takeover bid by Renault of France, which acquired a controlling interest by 1982.

Thus was born what some were quick to call "Franco-American Motors." Renault executives came in to run things

31

# AMC

alongside AMC officials, and the old Nash factory in Kenosha was retooled at great expense to produce an Americanized version of the European Renault 9 subcompact, which was aptly renamed Alliance.

Trouble was, acquiring AMC made Renault no wiser about the American market, and it had little more impact as a back-door "domestic" than it had as an independent import. Odd Renault products like the tinny-tiny Le Car and lumpy Fuego coupe didn't help AMC dealers very much. The Alliance did, but not for long. As a car, it was no more than adequate, and not really up to the huge task of improving Renault's second-rate image among U.S. buyers.

Still, Alliance seemed just what the doctor ordered: modern two- and four-door front-drive sedans with a 97.8-inch wheelbase and a thrifty, transverse 85-cid four-cylinder engine. And for a time it sold well: over 142,000 of the debut 1983 models. Bolstered by two- and four-door hatchback derivatives called Encore, sales zoomed to over 208,000 the following year.

**1978 Gremlin GT hatchback coupe**

**1979 Concord DL hatchback coupe**

**1979 Pacer DL two-door station wagon**

**1979 Spirit Liftback coupe**

**1979 Concord Limited two-door sedan**

**1979 Pacer DL two-door station wagon**

**1979 Spirit Limited hatchback coupe**

**1979 AMX hatchback coupe**

But mechanical problems and indifferent workmanship were as evident here as on French-built Renaults. Once word got around, sales tumbled: to 150,000 for '85, then to 65,000 and finally to only some 35,000. AMC tried to stop the slide for '85 with an optional 105-cid/78-bhp engine and a brace of new Alliance convertibles—Kenosha's first droptops since '68—but to no avail.

By 1987, with AMC's continued losses and several years of withering home-market sales, Renault was in financial trouble and ready to pull out. Fortunately, Lee Iacocca, the miracle worker who'd lately turned Chrysler Corporation from penniless to prosperous, was willing to take over, mainly to get his hands on AMC's lucrative Jeep business. Thus did America's last sizable independent automaker pass into history, transformed almost overnight into a new Chrysler division called Jeep-Eagle.

AMC's own products departed much earlier, dropped after 1983 in the rush to Renaults. The sole exceptions were the Eagle wagon and four-door sedan, which hung on until the Chrysler takeover, then disappeared with Alliance.

**1980 Concord DL two-door sedan**

**1980 Concord DL four-door sedan**

**1980 Concord Limited sedan/wagon**

**1980 AMX hatchback coupe**

**1980 Pacer DL two-door station wagon**

**1980 Pacer DL hatchback coupe**

**1981 Eagle Limited two-door sedan**

**1981 Eagle sedan/wagon**

# AMC

Before the end, AMC slipped the Eagle's full-time 4WD under the Spirit coupe and ex-Gremlin two-door bodies to create a pair of "Eaglets." The most interesting of these was the SX/4 Sport, Teague's pretty little fastback bedecked with foglights, distinctive striping, rear spoiler, and plush bucket-seat interior. Though pleasant and distinctive, it was no sprinter, and buyers continued to prefer "real" 4WDs—like Jeep CJs and Wagoneers—to these passenger-car pretenders.

Still, low production, a drivetrain unique among American cars, and status as AMC's last attempt at something different suggest the short-lived junior Eagles will be minor collector's items one day. Only about 37,500 Eagles of all kinds were sold for 1981 and less than half that number for '82 and '83; exact breakdowns aren't available, but the smaller ones probably accounted for no more than a third of each year's total. After 1983, the big Eagles carried on alone, virtually unchanged and garnering some 6000-7000 annual sales—too paltry for industry statisticians to even bother with.

For 1988, Chrysler began to re-establish Eagle as an "upscale" brand aimed at would-be import buyers—but with only inherited front-drive Renault's: the competent but dull midsize Premier (built in Canada) and the compact Medallion (imported from France). The latter didn't last past 1989, but the former carried on with minor success through 1991 (and as the 1990-91 Dodge

**1981 Eagle SX/4 Sport hatchback coupe**

**1982 Spirit GT Liftback coupe**

**1985 Renault Encore GS hatchback coupe**

**1985 Renault Alliance DL two-door sedan**

**1986 Renault Alliance DL convertible coupe**

**1986 Renault Alliance DL four-door sedan**

**1986 Renault Encore S hatchback sedan**

**1986 Renault Encore Electronic hatchback coupe**

# AMC

Monaco). Medallion gave way to rebadged designs by Mitsubishi of Japan, but Premier's successor would be an all-American Eagle, the exciting 1993 Vision, one of Chrysler's breakthrough "LH" sedans with "cab-forward" styling (see Eagle).

Chrysler's Eagle was no more successful as a niche make than AMC was in its later years and was dropped after 1998—proof that in the auto business at least, history can and often does repeat itself.

## Specifications
(also see Rambler) **Note:** Some production figures approximated.

### 1966

| Marlin (wb 112.0) | Wght | Price | Prod |
|---|---|---|---|
| 6659-7  fstbk cpe | 3,050 | 2,601 | 4,547 |
| **Ambassador 880 (wb 116.0)** | | | |
| 6685-2  sdn 4d | 3,006 | 2,455 | 13,974 |
| 6686-2  sdn 2d | 2,970 | 2,404 | 1,493 |
| 6688-2  wgn 4d | 3,160 | 2,759 | 4,791 |
| **Ambassador 990 (wb 116.0)** | | | |
| 6685-5  sdn 4d | 3,034 | 2,574 | 25,986 |
| 6687-5  conv cpe | 3,462 | 2,968 | 1,814 |
| 6688-5  wgn 4d | 3,180 | 2,880 | 8,852 |
| 6689-5  htp cpe | 3,056 | 2,600 | 4,324 |
| **Ambassador DPL (wb 116.0)** | | | |
| 6689-7  htp cpe | 3,090 | 2,756 | 10,458 |

| 1966 Engines | bore × stroke | bhp | availability |
|---|---|---|---|
| I-6, 232 | 3.75 × 3.50 | 145 | S-Marlin |
| I-6, 232 | 2.75 × 3.50 | 155 | S-Ambassador |
| V-8, 287 | 3.75 × 3.25 | 198 | O-all |
| V-8, 327 | 4.00 × 3.25 | 250/270 | O-all |

### 1967

| Marlin (wb 118.0) | Wght | Price | Prod |
|---|---|---|---|
| 6759-7  fstbk cpe | 3,342 | 2,963 | 2,545 |
| **Ambassador 880 (wb 118.0)** | | | |
| 6785-2  sdn 4d | 3,279 | 2,657 | 9,772 |
| 6786-2  sdn 2d | 3,310 | 2,519 | 3,623 |
| 6788-2  wgn 4d | 3,486 | 2,962 | 3,540 |
| **Ambassador 990 (wb 118.0)** | | | |
| 6785-5  sdn 4d | 3,324 | 2,776 | 18,033 |
| 6788-5  wgn 4d | 3,545 | 3,083 | 7,919 |
| 6789-5  htp cpe | 3,376 | 2,803 | 6,140 |
| **Ambassador DPL (wb 118.0)** | | | |
| 6787-7  conv cpe | 3,434 | 3,143 | 1,260 |
| 6789-7  htp cpe | 3,394 | 2,958 | 12,552 |

| 1967 Engines | bore × stroke | bhp | availability |
|---|---|---|---|
| I-6, 232 | 3.75 × 3.50 | 145 | S-Marlin |
| I-6, 232 | 3.75 × 3.50 | 155 | S-Ambassador; O-Marlin |
| V-8, 290 | 3.75 × 3.28 | 200 | S-Amb conv; O-others |
| V-8, 343 | 4.08 × 3.28 | 235 | O-all |
| V-8, 343 | 4.08 × 3.28 | 280 | O-all |

### 1968

| Rebel 550 (wb 114.0) | Wght | Price | Prod |
|---|---|---|---|
| 6815  sdn 4d | 3,062 | 2,443 | 11,329 |
| 6817  conv 2d | 3,195 | 2,736 | 377 |
| 6818  wgn 4d | 3,301 | 2,729 | 7,228 |
| 6819  htp cpe | 3,117 | 2,454 | 7,385 |

| Rebel 770 (wb 114.0) | Wght | Price | Prod |
|---|---|---|---|
| 6815-5  sdn 4d | 3,074 | 2,542 | 19,640 |
| 6818-5  wgn 4d | 3,306 | 2,854 | 11,169 |
| 6819-5  htp cpe | 3,116 | 2,556 | 4,428 |
| **Rebel SST (wb 114.0)** | | | |
| 6817-7  conv cpe | 3,427 | 2,999 | 823 |
| 6819-7  htp cpe | 3,348 | 2,775 | 11,516 |
| **AMX (wb 97.0)** | | | |
| 6839-7  fstbk cpe 2S | 3,097 | 3,245 | 6,725 |
| **Javelin (wb 109.0)—56, 462 built** | | | |
| 6879-5  fstbk cpe | 2,826 | 2,482 | 29,097 |
| 6879-7  SST fstbk cpe | 2,836 | 2,587 | 27,347 |
| **Ambassador (wb 118.0)** | | | |
| 6885-2  sdn 4d | 3,193 | 2,820 | 6,272 |
| 6889-2  htp cpe | 3,258 | 2,892 | 3,360 |
| **Ambassador DPL (wb 118.0)** | | | |
| 6885-5  sdn 4d | 3,265 | 2,920 | 9,362 |
| 6888-5  wgn 4d | 3,475 | 3,207 | 10,698 |
| 6889-5  htp cpe | 3,321 | 2,947 | 3,696 |
| **Ambassador SST (wb 118.0)** | | | |
| 6885-7  sdn 4d | 3,496 | 3,151 | 13,387 |
| 6889-7  htp cpe | 3,530 | 3,172 | 7,876 |

| 1968 Engines | bore × stroke | bhp | availability |
|---|---|---|---|
| I-6, 232 | 3.75 × 3.50 | 145 | S-Javelin, Rebel exc SST |
| I-6, 232 | 3.75 × 3.50 | 155 | S-Amb exc SST |
| V-8, 290 | 3.75 × 3.28 | 200 | S-Rebel SST, Amb SST; O-all |
| V-8, 290 | 3.75 × 3.28 | 225 | S-AMX; O-Javelin |
| V-8, 343 | 4.08 × 3.28 | 235 | O-Rebel, Ambassador |
| V-8, 343 | 4.08 × 3.28 | 280 | O-AMX Javelin, Rebel, Amb |
| V-8, 390 | 4.17 × 3.57 | 315 | O-all |

### 1969

| Rebel (wb 114.0) | Wght | Price | Prod |
|---|---|---|---|
| 6915  sdn 4d | 3,062 | 2,484 | 10,885 |
| 6918  wgn 4d | 3,301 | 2,817 | 8,569 |
| 6919  htp cpe | 3,117 | 2,496 | 5,396 |
| **Rebel SST (wb 114.0)** | | | |
| 6915-7  sdn 4d | 3,074 | 2,584 | 20,595 |
| 6918-7  wgn 4d | 3,306 | 2,947 | 9,256 |
| 6919-7  htp cpe | 3,140 | 2,598 | 5,405 |
| **AMX (wb 97.0)** | | | |
| 6939-7  fstbk cpe 2S | 3,097 | 3,297 | 8,293 |
| **Javelin (wb 109.0)** | | | |
| 6979-5  fstbk cpe | 2,826 | 2,512 | 17,389 |
| 6979-7  SST fstbk cpe | 2,836 | 2,633 | 23,286 |
| **Ambassador (wb 122.0)** | | | |
| 6985-2  sdn 4d | 3,276 | 2,914 | 14,617 |
| **Ambassador DPL (WB 122.0)** | | | |
| 6985-5  sdn 4d | 3,358 | 3,165 | 12,665 |

# AMC

| Ambassador DPL (WB 122.0) | Wght | Price | Prod |
|---|---|---|---|
| 6988-5 wgn 4d | 3,561 | 3,504 | 8,866 |
| 6989-5 htp cpe | 3,403 | 3,182 | 4,504 |
| **Ambassador SST (wb 122.0)** | | | |
| 6985-7 sdn 4d | 3,508 | 3,605 | 18,719 |
| 6988-7 wgn 4d | 3,732 | 3,998 | 7,825 |
| 6989-7 htp cpe | 3,566 | 3,622 | 8,998 |

| 1969 Engines | bore × stroke | bhp | availability |
|---|---|---|---|
| I-6,232 | 3.75 × 3.50 | 145 | S-Javelin, Rebel |
| I-6,232 | 3.75 × 3.50 | 155 | S-Amb, Amb DPL; O-Rebel |
| V-8,290 | 3.75 × 3.28 | 200 | S-Amb SST; O-Amb, Reb, Jav |
| V-8,290 | 3.75 × 3.28 | 225 | S-AMX; O-Javelin |
| V-8,343 | 4.08 × 3.28 | 235 | O-Rebel, Ambassador |
| V-8,343 | 4.08 × 3.28 | 280 | O-AMX, Jav, Rebel, Amb |
| V-8,390 | 4.17 × 3.57 | 315 | O-AMX, Jav SST, Amb SST |

## 1970*

| Hornet (wb 108.0) | Wght | Price | Prod |
|---|---|---|---|
| 7005-0 sdn 4d | 2,748 | 2,072 | — |
| 7006-0 sdn 2d | 2,677 | 1,994 | — |
| **Hornet SST (wb 108.0)** | | | |
| 7005-7 sdn 4d | 2,765 | 2,221 | — |
| 7006-7 sdn 2d | 2,705 | 2,144 | — |
| **Rebel (wb 114.0)** | | | |
| 7015-0 sdn 4d | 3,129 | 2,636 | — |
| 7018-0 wgn 4d | 3,356 | 2,766 | — |
| 7019-0 htp cpe | 3,148 | 2,660 | — |
| **Rebel SST (wb 114.0)** | | | |
| 7015-7 sdn 4d | 3,155 | 2,684 | — |
| 7018-0 wgn 4d | 3,375 | 3,072 | — |
| 7019-7 htp cpe | 3,206 | 2,718 | — |
| **Rebel Machine (wb 114.0)** | | | |
| 7019-0 htp cpe | 3,650 | 3,475 | 2,326 |
| **AMX (wb 97.0)—4,116 built** | | | |
| 7039-7 fstbk cpe 2S | 3,126 | 3,395 | — |
| **Gremlin (wb 96.0)** | | | |
| 7046-0 sdn 2d | 2,497 | 1,879 | — |
| 7046-5 sdn 2d | 2,557 | 1,959 | — |
| **Javelin (wb 109.0)—28,210 built** | | | |
| 7079-5 fstbk cpe | 2,845 | 2,720 | — |
| 7079-7 SST fstbk cpe | 2,863 | 2,848 | — |
| 7079-7 SST/Trans-Am fstbk cpe | 3,340 | 3,995 | — |
| **Ambassador (wb 122.0)** | | | |
| 7085-2 sdn 4d | 3,328 | 3,020 | — |
| **Ambassador DPL (wb 122.0)** | | | |
| 7085-5 sdn 4d | 3,523 | 3,588 | — |
| 7088-5 wgn 4d | 3,817 | 3,946 | — |
| 7089-5 htp cpe | 3,555 | 3,605 | — |
| **Ambassador SST (wb 122.0)** | | | |
| 7085-7 sdn 4d | 3,557 | 3,722 | — |
| 7088-5 wgn 4d | 3,852 | 4,122 | — |
| 7089-5 htp cpe | 3,606 | 3,739 | — |

*Total 1970 calendar year, 276,110

| 1970 Engines | bore × stroke | bhp | availability |
|---|---|---|---|
| I-6, 199 | 3.75 × 3.00 | 128 | S-Hornet, Gremlin |
| I-6, 232 | 3.75 × 3.50 | 145 | S-Hornet SST, Rebel, Javelin; O-Hornet, Gremlin |
| I-6, 232 | 3.75 × 3.50 | 155 | S-Amb; O-Hornet, Rebel |
| V-8, 304 | 3.75 × 3.44 | 210 | S-DPL, SST; O-all exc AMX |
| V-8, 360 | 4.08 × 3.44 | 245 | O-Rebel, Amb, Jav |
| V-8, 360 | 4.08 × 3.44 | 290 | S-AMX; O-Reb; Amb |
| V-8, 390 | 4.17 × 3.57 | 325 | O-AMX, Jav, Reb SST, Amb SST |
| V-8, 390 | 4.17 × 3.57 | 340 | S-Rebel Machine; O-all |

## 1971

| Gremlin (wb 96.0) | Wght | Price | Prod* |
|---|---|---|---|
| 7146-0 sdn 2d 2P | 2,503 | 1,899 | 53,480 |
| 7146-5 sdn 2d 4P | 2,552 | 1,999 | |
| **Hornet (wb 108.0)** | | | |
| 7105-0 sdn 4d I-6 | 2,731 | 2,234 | 23,500** |
| 7106-0 sdn 2d V-8 | 2,654 | 2,174 | |
| 7105-7 SST sdn 4d I-6 | 2,732 | 2,334 | |
| 7106-7 SST sdn 2d V-8 | 2,691 | 2,274 | 49,500*** |
| 7108-7 Sportabout wgn 4d | 2,827 | 2,594 | |
| 7106-1 SC/360 sdn 2d | 3,057 | 2,663 | 784 |
| **Javelin (wb 110.0)** | | | |
| 7179-5 htp cpe I-6 | 2,887 | 2,879 | 3,500 |
| 7179-7 SST htp cpe I-6 | 2,890 | 2,999 | 1,000 |
| 7179-5 htp cpe V-8 | 3,144 | 2,980 | 4,000 |
| 7179-7 SST htp cpe V-8 | 3,147 | 3,100 | 17,000 |
| 7979-8 AMX htp cpe V-8 | 3,244 | 3,432 | 2,054 |
| **Matador (wb 118.0)—45,789 built (approx. 30,000 I-6)** | | | |
| 7155-7 sdn 4d I-6 | 3,165 | 2,770 | — |
| 7119-7 htp cpe I-6 | 3,201 | 2,799 | — |
| 7118-7 wgn 4d I-6 | 3,437 | 3,163 | 6,800 |
| 7115-7 sdn 4d V-8 | 3,324 | 3,100 | — |
| 7119-7 htp cpe V-8 | 3,360 | 3,129 | — |
| 7118-7 wgn 4d V-8 | 3,596 | 3,493 | 4,200 |
| **Ambassador (wb 122.0)** | | | |
| 7185-2 DPL sdn 4d I-6 | 3,315 | 3,616 | 650 |
| 7185-2 DPL sdn 4d V-8 | 3,488 | 3,717 | 6,000 |
| 7185-5 SST sdn 4d V-8 | 3,520 | 3,852 | 7,500 |
| 7189-5 SST htp cpe V-8 | 3,561 | 3,870 | |
| 7188-5 SST wgn 4d V-8 | 3,815 | 4,253 | 8,000 |
| 7185-7 Brougham sdn 4d V-8 | 3,541 | 3,983 | 10,000 |
| 7189-7 Brougham htp cpe V-8 | 3,580 | 3,999 | |
| 7188-7 Brougham wgn 4d V-8 | 3,862 | 4,430 | 10,000 |

*Estimates  **Includes 500 V-8s  ***Includes 9,500 V-8s

| 1971 Engines | bore × stroke | bhp | availability |
|---|---|---|---|
| I-6, 232.0 | 3.75 × 3.50 | 135 | S-Grem, Hrnt, Jav, Mat |
| I-6, 258.0 | 3.75 × 3.90 | 150 | S-Amb; O-Grem, Hrnt, Jav, Mat |
| V-8, 304.0 | 3.75 × 3.44 | 210 | S-Jav, Mat, Amb; O-Hrnt |
| V-8, 360.0 | 4.08 × 3.44 | 245 | S-Hrnt SC; O-Jav, Mat, Amb |
| V-8, 360.0 | 4.08 × 3.44 | 285 | O-Hrnt SC, Jav, Mat, Amb |
| V-8, 401.0 | 4.17 × 3.68 | 330 | O-Amb |

## 1972

| Gremlin (wb 96.0)—61,717 built | Wght | Price | Prod* |
|---|---|---|---|
| 46-5  sdn 2d I-6 | 2,494 | 1,999 | 53,000 |
| 46-5  sdn 2d V-8 | 2,746 | 2,153 | 8,500 |

# AMC

| Hornet SST (wb 108.0)—71,056 built | | Wght | Price | Prod |
|---|---|---|---|---|
| 05-7 | sdn 4d I-6 | 2,691 | 2,265 | ⎤ 35,000 |
| 06-7 | sdn 2d I-6 | 2,627 | 2,199 | ⎦ |
| 08-7 | Sportabout wgn 4d I-6 | 2,769 | 2,587 | 30,000 |
| 05-7 | sdn 4d V-8 | 2,925 | 2,403 | ⎤ 2,000 |
| 06-7 | sdn 2d V-8 | 2,861 | 2,337 | ⎦ |
| 08-7 | Sportabout wgn 4d V-8 | 2,998 | 2,725 | 5,000 |
| **Javelin (wb 110.0)** | | | | |
| 79-7 | SST htp cpe I-6 | 2,876 | 2,807 | ⎤ 23,455 |
| 79-7 | SST htp cpe V-8 | 3,118 | 2,901 | ⎦ |
| 79-8 | AMX htp cpe V-8 | 3,149 | 3,109 | 2,729 |
| **Matador (wb 118.0)—54,813 built** | | | | |
| 15-7 | sdn 4d I-6 | 3,171 | 2,784 | ⎤ 11,000 |
| 19-7 | htp cpe I-6 | 3,210 | 2,818 | ⎦ |
| 18-7 | wgn 4d I-6 | 3,480 | 3,140 | 3,000 |
| 15-7 | sdn 4d V-8 | 3,355 | 2,883 | ⎤ 34,000 |
| 19-7 | htp cpe V-8 | 3,394 | 2,917 | ⎦ |
| 18-7 | wgn 4d V-8 | 3,653 | 3,239 | 7,500 |
| **Ambassador (wb 122.0)—44,364 built** | | | | |
| 85-5 | SST sdn 4d | 3,537 | 3,885 | ⎤ 18,000 |
| 89-5 | SST htp cpe | 3,579 | 3,902 | ⎦ |
| 88-5 | SST wgn 4d | 3,833 | 4,270 | 5,500 |
| 85-7 | Brougham sdn 4d | 3,551 | 4,002 | ⎤ 15,000 |
| 89-5 | Brougham htp cpe | 3,581 | 4,018 | ⎦ |
| 88-5 | Brougham wgn 4d | 3,857 | 4,437 | 5,500 |

*Estimates

| 1972 Engines | bore × stroke | bhp | availability |
|---|---|---|---|
| I-6, 232.0 | 3.75 × 3.50 | 100 | S-Grem, Hrnt, Jav, Mat exc wgn |
| I-6, 258.0 | 3.75 × 3.90 | 110 | S-Mat wgn, Grem, Hrnt; O-Jav, Mat |
| V-8, 304.0 | 3.75 × 3.44 | 150 | S-all base V-8 models |
| V-8, 360.0 | 4.08 × 3.44 | 175 | O-all exc Gremlin |
| V-8, 360.0 | 4.08 × 3.44 | 195 | O-Jav, Mat, Amb |
| V-8, 401.0 | 4.17 × 3.68 | 255 | O-Jav, Mat, Amb |

## 1973

| Gremlin (wb 96.0) | | Wght | Price | Prod |
|---|---|---|---|---|
| 46-5 | sdn 2d I-6 | 2,642 | 2,098 | — |
| 46-5 | sdn 2d V-8 | 2,867 | 2,252 | — |
| **Hornet (wb 108.0)** | | | | |
| 05-7 | sdn 4d I-6 | 2,854 | 2,343 | — |
| 06-7 | sdn 2d I-6 | 2,777 | 2,298 | — |
| 03-7 | htchbk cpe I-6 | 2,818 | 2,449 | — |
| 08-7 | Sportabout wgn 4d I-6 | 2,921 | 2,675 | — |
| 05-7 | sdn 4d V-8 | 3,067 | 2,481 | — |
| 06-7 | sdn 2d V-8 | 2,990 | 2,436 | — |
| 03-7 | htchbk cpe V-8 | 3,031 | 2,587 | — |
| 08-7 | Sportabout wgn 4d V-8 | 3,134 | 2,813 | — |
| **Javelin (wb 110.0)** | | | | |
| 79-7 | htp cpe I-6 | 2,868 | 2,889 | ⎤ 22,556 |
| 79-7 | htp cpe V-8 | 3,104 | 2,983 | ⎦ |
| 79-8 | AMX htp cpe V-8 | 3,170 | 3,191 | 4,980 |
| **Matador (wb 118.0)** | | | | |
| 15-7 | sdn 4d I-6 | 3,289 | 2,853 | — |
| 19-7 | htp cpe I-6 | 3,314 | 2,887 | — |
| 18-7 | wgn 4d I-6 | 3,627 | 3,179 | — |
| 15-7 | sdn 4d V-8 | 3,502 | 2,952 | — |
| 19-7 | htp cpe V-8 | 3,527 | 2,986 | — |
| 18-7 | wgn 4d V-8 | 3,815 | 3,278 | — |
| **Ambassador Brougham (wb 122.0)** | | | | |
| 85-7 | sdn 4d | 3,763 | 4,461 | — |
| 89-7 | htp cpe | 3,774 | 4,477 | — |
| 88-7 | wgn 4d | 4,054 | 4,861 | — |

| 1973 Engines | bore × stroke | bhp | availability |
|---|---|---|---|
| I-6, 232.0 | 3.75 × 3.50 | 100 | S-Grem, Hrnt, Jav, Mat exc wgn |
| I-6, 258.0 | 3.75 × 3.90 | 110 | S-Mat wgn; O-Grem, Hrnt, Jav, Mat |
| V-8, 304.0 | 3.75 × 3.44 | 150 | S-all base V-8 models |
| V-8, 360.0 | 4.08 × 3.44 | 175 | O-all exc Gremlin |
| V-8, 360.0 | 4.08 × 3.44 | 195 | O-Jav, Mat, Amb |
| V-8, 401.0 | 4.17 × 3.68 | 255 | O-Jav, Mat, Amb |

## 1974

| Gremlin (wb 96.0) | | Wght | Price | Prod |
|---|---|---|---|---|
| 46-5 | sdn 2d I-6 | 2,649 | 2,481 | 119,642 |
| 46-5 | sdn 2d V-8 | 2,888 | 2,635 | 12,263 |
| **Hornet (wb 108.0)** | | | | |
| 05-7 | sdn 4d I-6 | 2,833 | 2,824 | ⎤ |
| 06-7 | sdn 2d I-6 | 2,767 | 2,774 | ⎬ 70,052 |
| 03-7 | htchbk cpe I-6 | 2,791 | 2,849 | ⎦ |
| 08-7 | Sportabout wgn 4d I-6 | 2,900 | 3,049 | 57,414 |
| 05-7 | sdn 4d V-8 | 3,077 | 2,962 | ⎤ |
| 06-7 | sdn 2d V-8 | 3,011 | 2,912 | ⎬ 7,697 |
| 03-7 | htchbk cpe V-8 | 3,035 | 2,987 | ⎦ |
| 08-7 | Sportabout wgn 4d V-8 | 3,144 | 3,187 | 10,295 |
| **Javelin (wb 110.0)** | | | | |
| 79-7 | htp cpe I-6 | 2,869 | 2,999 | 5,036 |
| 79-7 | htp cpe V-8 | 3,116 | 3,093 | 19,520 |
| 79-8 | AMX htp cpe V-8 | 3,184 | 3,299 | 4,980 |
| **Matador (wb 118.0; cpe 114.0)—99,922 built** | | | | |
| 15-7 | sdn 4d I-6 | 3,425 | 3,052 | ⎤ 25,826 |
| 16-7 | cpe I-6 | 3,437 | 3,096 | ⎦ |
| 18-7 | wgn 4d I-6 | 3,739 | 3,378 | 2,975 |
| 15-7 | sdn 4d V-8 | 3,632 | 3,151 | ⎤ 35,000 |
| 16-7 | cpe V-8 | 3,634 | 3,195 | ⎦ |
| 18-7 | wgn 4d V-8 | 3,925 | 3,477 | 6,734 |
| 16-9 | Brougham cpe I-6 | 3,456 | 3,249 | ⎤ 28,000 |
| 16-9 | Brougham cpe V-8 | 3,663 | 3,348 | ⎦ |
| 16-8 | X htp cpe V-8 | 3,672 | 3,699 | 1,500 |
| **Ambassador Brougham (wb 122.0)** | | | | |
| 85-7 | sdn 4d | 3,851 | 4,559 | 17,901 |
| 88-7 | wgn 4d | 4,125 | 4,960 | 7,070 |

| 1974 Engines | bore × stroke | bhp | availability |
|---|---|---|---|
| I-6, 232.0 | 3.75 × 3.50 | 100 | S-Grem, Hrnt, Jav, Mat wgn |
| I-6, 258.0 | 3.75 × 3.90 | 110 | S-Mat wgn; O-Grem, Hrnt, Jav, Mat |
| V-8, 304.0 | 3.75 × 3.44 | 150 | S-all base V-8 models |
| V-8, 360.0 | 4.08 × 3.44 | 175 | O-all exc Gremlin |
| V-8, 360.0 | 4.08 × 3.44 | 195 | O-Jav, Mat, Amb |
| V-8, 401.0 | 4.17 × 3.68 | 235 | O-Jav, Mat, Amb |

## 1975

| Gremlin (wb 96.0) | | Wght | Price | Prod |
|---|---|---|---|---|
| 46-5 | sdn 2d I-6 | 2,694 | 2,798 | 42,630 |
| 46-5 | sdn 2d V-8 | 2,952 | 2,952 | 3,218 |
| **Hornet (wb 108.0)** | | | | |
| 05-7 | sdn 4d I-6 | 2,881 | 3,124 | |

# AMC

| Hornet (wb 108.0) | | Wght | Price | Prod |
|---|---|---|---|---|
| 06-7 | sdn 2d I-6 | 2,815 | 3,074 | ⎫ 36,305 |
| 03-7 | htchbk cpe I-6 | 2,839 | 3,174 | ⎭ |
| 08-7 | Sportabout wgn 4d I-6 | 2,948 | 3,374 | 3,016 |
| 05-7 | sdn 4d V-8 | 3,127 | 3,262 | ⎫ |
| 06-7 | sdn 2d V-8 | 3,061 | 3,212 | 20,369 |
| 03-7 | htchbk cpe V-8 | 3,085 | 3,312 | ⎭ |
| 08-7 | Sportabout wgn 4d V-8 | 3,194 | 3,512 | 4,223 |

| Pacer (wb 100.0) | | | | |
|---|---|---|---|---|
| 66-7 | htchbk sdn 2d | 2,995 | 3,299 | 72,158 |

| Matador (wb 118.0; cpe 114.0) | | | | |
|---|---|---|---|---|
| 85-7 | sdn 4d I-6 | 3,586 | 3,452 | ⎫ 9,390 |
| 16-7 | cpe I-6 | 3,562 | 3,446 | ⎭ |
| 88-7 | wgn 4d I-6 | 3,878 | 3,844 | 1,575 |
| 85-7 | sdn 4d V-8 | 3,746 | 3,551 | ⎫ 40,500 |
| 16-7 | cpe V-8 | 3,734 | 3,545 | ⎭ |
| 88-7 | wgn 4d V-8 | 4,038 | 3,943 | 8,117 |

| 1975 Engines | bore × stroke | bhp | availability |
|---|---|---|---|
| I-6, 232.0 | 3.75 × 3.50 | 100 | S-Grem, Hrnt, Pcr |
| I-6, 258.0 | 3.75 × 3.90 | 110 | S-Mat; O-Grem, Hrnt, Pcr |
| V-8, 304.0 | 3.75 × 3.44 | 150 | S-Grem, Hrnt, Mat |
| V-8, 360.0 | 4.08 × 3.44 | 175 | O-Matador |

## 1976

| Gremlin (wb 96.0) | | Wght | Price | Prod |
|---|---|---|---|---|
| 46-3 | sdn 2d I-6 | 2,771 | 2,889 | ⎫ 52,115 |
| 46-5 | Cus sdn 2d I-6 | 2,774 | 2,998 | ⎭ |
| 46-3 | sdn 2d V-8 | 3,020 | 3,051 | ⎫ 826 |
| 46-5 | Cus sdn 2d V-8 | 3,023 | 3,160 | ⎭ |

| Pacer (wb 100.0) | | | | |
|---|---|---|---|---|
| 66-7 | htchbk sdn 2d | 3,114 | 3,499 | 117,244 |

| Hornet (wb 108.0) | | | | |
|---|---|---|---|---|
| 05-7 | sdn 4d I-6 | 2,971 | 3,199 | ⎫ |
| 06-7 | sdn 2d I-6 | 2,909 | 3,199 | 41,025 |
| 03-7 | htchbk cpe I-6 | 2,920 | 3,199 | ⎭ |
| 08-7 | Sportabout wgn 4d I-6 | 3,040 | 3,549 | 26,787 |
| 05-7 | sdn 4d V-8 | 3,220 | 3,344 | ⎫ |
| 06-7 | sdn 2d V-8 | 3,158 | 3,344 | 789 |
| 03-7 | htchbk cpe V-8 | 3,169 | 3,344 | ⎭ |
| 08-7 | Sportabout wgn 4d V-8 | 3,289 | 3,694 | 2,976 |

| Matador (wb 118.0; cpe 114.0) | | | | |
|---|---|---|---|---|
| 85-7 | sdn 4d I-6 | 3,589 | 3,627 | ⎫ 4,993 |
| 16-7 | cpe I-6 | 3,562 | 3,621 | ⎭ |
| 85-7 | sdn 4d V-8 | 3,838 | 3,731 | ⎫ 25,471 |
| 16-7 | cpe V-8 | 3,811 | 3,725 | ⎭ |
| 88-7 | wgn 4d V-8 | 4,015 | 4,373 | 11,049 |

| 1976 Engines | bore × stroke | bhp | availability |
|---|---|---|---|
| I-6, 232.0 | 3.75 × 3.50 | 90 | S-all exc Mat |
| I-6, 258.0 | 3.75 × 3.90 | 95 | S-Mat; O-others |
| I-6, 258.0 | 3.75 × 3.90 | 120 | O-Pacer |
| V-8, 304.0 | 3.75 × 3.44 | 120 | S-all exc Pcr |
| V-8, 360.0 | 4.08 × 3.44 | 140/180 | O-Mat sdn/wgn |

## 1977

| Gremlin (wb 96.0) | | Wght | Price | Prod |
|---|---|---|---|---|
| 46-4 | sdn 2d I-4 | 2,654 | 3,248 | 7,558 |
| 46-5 | sdn 2d I-6 | 2,811 | 2,995 | ⎫ 8,613 |
| 36-7 | Custom sdn 2d I-6 | 2,824 | 3,248 | ⎭ |

| Pacer (wb 100.0) | | | | |
|---|---|---|---|---|
| 66-7 | htchbk sdn 2d | 3,156 | 3,649 | 20,265 |
| 68-7 | wgn 2d | 3,202 | 3,799 | 37,999 |

| Hornet (wb 108.0) | | | | |
|---|---|---|---|---|
| 05-7 | sdn 4d I-6 | 3,035 | 2,449 | ⎫ |
| 06-7 | sdn 2d I-6 | 2,971 | 3,399 | 73,752 |
| 03-7 | htchbk cpe I-6 | 3,012 | 3,419 | |
| 08-7 | wgn 4d I-6 | 3,100 | 3,699 | ⎭ |
| 05-7 | sdn 4d V-8 | 3,268 | 3,613 | ⎫ |
| 06-7 | sdn 2d V-8 | 3,204 | 3,563 | 4,091 |
| 03-7 | htchbk cpe V-8 | 3,245 | 3,662 | |
| 08-7 | wgn 4d V-8 | 3,333 | 3,863 | ⎭ |

| Matador (wb. 118.0; cpe 114.0) | | | | |
|---|---|---|---|---|
| 85-7 | sdn 4d I-6 | 3,713 | 4,549 | ⎫ 2,447 |
| 16-7 | cpe I-6 | 3,704 | 4,499 | ⎭ |
| 85-7 | sdn 4d V-8 | 3,876 | 4,669 | ⎫ 17,322 |
| 16-7 | cpe V-8 | 3,872 | 4,619 | ⎭ |
| 88-7 | wgn 4d V-8 | 4,104 | 4,899 | 11,078 |

| 1977 Engines | bore × stroke | bhp | availability |
|---|---|---|---|
| I-4, 121.0 | 3.41 × 3.32 | 80 | S-Gremlin |
| I-6, 232.0 | 3.75 × 3.50 | 88 | S-all exc Matador |
| I-6, 258.0 | 3.75 × 3.90 | 98 | S-Matador |
| I-6, 258.0 | 3.75 × 3.90 | 114 | O-all exc Matador |
| V-8, 304.0 | 3.75 × 3.44 | 121 | S-Hornet |
| V-8, 304.0 | 3.75 × 3.44 | 126 | S-Matador |
| V-8, 360.0 | 4.08 × 3.44 | 129 | O-Matador |

## 1978

| Gremlin (wb 96.0) | | Wght | Price | Prod |
|---|---|---|---|---|
| 46-4 | sdn 2d I-4 | 2,656 | 3,789 | 6,349 |
| 46-5 | sdn 2d I-6 | 2,834 | 3,539 | ⎫ 15,755 |
| 46-7 | Custom sdn 2d I-6 | 2,822 | 3,789 | ⎭ |

| Concord (wb 108.0) | | | | |
|---|---|---|---|---|
| 05-7 | sdn 4d I-6 | 3,099 | 3,849 | ⎫ |
| 06-7 | sdn 2d I-6 | 3,029 | 3,749 | 110,972 |
| 03-7 | htchbk cpe I-6 | 3,051 | 3,849 | |
| 08-7 | wgn 4d I-6 | 3,133 | 4,049 | ⎭ |
| 05-7 | sdn 4d V-8 | 3,332 | 4,099 | ⎫ |
| 06-7 | sdn 2d V-8 | 3,262 | 3,999 | 6,541 |
| 03-7 | htchbk cpe V-8 | 3,284 | 4,099 | |
| 08-7 | wgn 4d V-8 | 3,366 | 4,299 | ⎭ |

Note: A total of 3,780 4-cyl. Concords were produced.

| Pacer (wb 100.0) | | | | |
|---|---|---|---|---|
| 66-7 | htchbk sdn 2d I-6 | 3,197 | 4,048 | ⎫ 18,717 |
| 68-7 | wgn 2d I-6 | 3,245 | 4,193 | ⎭ |
| 66-7 | htchbk sdn 2d V-8 | 3,430 | 4,298 | ⎫ 2,514 |
| 68-7 | wgn 2d V-8 | 3,478 | 4,443 | ⎭ |

| AMX (wb 108.0) | | | | |
|---|---|---|---|---|
| 03-9 | htchbk cpe I-6 | 3,159 | 4,649 | ⎫ 2,540 |
| 03-9 | htchbk cpe V-8 | 3,381 | 4,899 | ⎭ |

| Matador (wb 118.0; cpe 114.0) | | | | |
|---|---|---|---|---|
| 85-7 | sdn 4d I-6 | 3,718 | 4,849 | ⎫ 23 |
| 16-7 | cpe I-6 | 3,709 | 4,799 | ⎭ |
| 85-7 | sdn 4d V-8 | 3,921 | 5,039 | ⎫ 6,807 |
| 16-7 | cpe V-8 | 3,916 | 4,989 | ⎭ |
| 88-7 | wgn 4d V-8 | 4,146 | 5,299 | 3,746 |

| 1978 Engines | bore × stroke | bhp | availability |
|---|---|---|---|
| I-4, 121.0 | 3.41 × 3.32 | 80 | S-Gremlin, Concord |
| I-6, 232.0 | 3.75 × 3.50 | 90 | S-all exc Matador, AMX |
| I-6, 258.0 | 3.75 × 3.90 | 120 | S-Mat, AMX; O-others |
| V-8, 304.0 | 3.75 × 3.44 | 130 | S-Con, Pacer, AMX |
| V-8, 360.0 | 4.08 × 3.44 | 140 | S-Mat wgn; O-Matador |

# AMC

## 1979

| Spirit (wb 96.0) | | Wght | Price | Prod |
|---|---|---|---|---|
| 43-7 | htchbk cpe I-4 | 2,545 | 3,953 | ⎤ |
| 46-7 | sdn 2d I-4 | 2,489 | 3,853 | |
| 43-7 | DL htchbk cpe I-4 | 2,635 | 4,190 | 16,237 |
| 46-7 | DL sdn 2d I-4 | 2,579 | 4,090 | |
| 43-7 | Limited htchbk cpe I-4 | 2,732 | 5,190 | |
| 46-7 | Limited sdn 2d I-4 | 2,676 | 5,090 | ⎦ |
| 43-7 | htchbk cpe I-6 | 2,762 | 4,133 | ⎤ |
| 46-7 | sdn 2d I-6 | 2,706 | 4,033 | |
| 43-7 | DL htchbk cpe I-6 | 2,852 | 4,370 | 36,241 |
| 46-7 | DL sdn 2d I-6 | 2,798 | 4,270 | |
| 43-7 | Limited htchbk cpe I-6 | 2,949 | 5,370 | |
| 46-7 | Limited sdn 2d I-6 | 2,893 | 5,270 | ⎦ |

| Concord (wb 108.0) | | Wght | Price | Prod |
|---|---|---|---|---|
| 05-7 | sdn 4d I-6 | 2,939 | 4,489 | ⎤ |
| 06-7 | sdn 2d I-6 | 2,873 | 4,389 | |
| 03-7 | htchbk cpe I-6 | 2,888 | 4,324 | |
| 08-7 | wgn 4d I-6 | 2,977 | 4,689 | |
| 05-7 | DL sdn 4d I-6 | 3,040 | 4,788 | |
| 06-7 | DL sdn 2d I-6 | 2,982 | 4,688 | 91,842 |
| 03-7 | DL htchbk cpe I-6 | 3,003 | 4,623 | |
| 08-7 | DL wgn 4d I-6 | 3,072 | 4,988 | |
| 05-7 | Limited sdn 4d I-6 | 3,146 | 5,788 | |
| 06-7 | Limited sdn 2d I-6 | 3,090 | 5,688 | |
| 08-7 | Limited wgn 4d I-6 | 3,177 | 5,988 | ⎦ |
| 05-7 | sdn 4d V-8 | 3,146 | 4,889 | ⎤ |
| 06-7 | sdn 2d V-8 | 3,080 | 4,789 | |
| 03-7 | htchbk cpe V-8 | 3,095 | 4,724 | |
| 08-7 | wgn 4d V-8 | 3,184 | 5,089 | |
| 05-7 | DL sdn 4d V-8 | 3,247 | 5,188 | |
| 06-7 | DL sdn 2d V-8 | 3,189 | 5,088 | 4,656 |
| 03-7 | DL htchbk cpe V-8 | 3,210 | 5,023 | |
| 08-7 | DL wgn 4d V-8 | 3,279 | 5,388 | |
| 05-7 | Limited sdn 4d V-8 | 3,353 | 6,188 | |
| 06-7 | Limited sdn 2d V-8 | 3,297 | 6,088 | |
| 08-7 | Limited wgn 4d V-8 | 3,384 | 6,888 | ⎦ |

Note: 6,355 4-cyl. Concords were produced.

| Pacer (wb 100.0) | | Wght | Price | Prod |
|---|---|---|---|---|
| 66-7 | DL htchbk sdn 2d I-6 | 3,133 | 5,039 | ⎤ |
| 68-7 | DL wgn 2d I-6 | 3,170 | 5,189 | 9,201 |
| 66-7 | Limited htchbk sdn 2d I-6 | 3,218 | 6,039 | |
| 68-7 | Limited wgn 2d I-6 | 3,255 | 6,189 | ⎦ |
| 66-7 | DL htchbk sdn 2d V-8 | 3,360 | 5,439 | ⎤ |
| 68-7 | DL wgn 2d V-8 | 3,397 | 5,589 | 1,014 |
| 66-7 | Limited htckbk sdn 2d V-8 | 3,445 | 6,439 | |
| 68-7 | Limited wgn 2d V-8 | 3,482 | 6,589 | ⎦ |

| AMX (wb 96.0) | | Wght | Price | Prod |
|---|---|---|---|---|
| 43-9 | htchbk cpe I-6 | 2,899 | 6,090 | ⎤ 3,657* |
| 43-9 | htchbk cpe V-8 | 3,092 | 6,465 | ⎦ |

*included in Spirit total.

| 1979 Engines | bore × stroke | bhp | availability |
|---|---|---|---|
| I-4, 121.0 | 3.41 × 3.32 | 80 | S-Spirit; O-Con exc wgn |
| I-6, 232.0 | 3.75 × 3.50 | 90 | S-Con; O-Spirit |
| I-6, 258.0 | 3.75 × 3.90 | 100 | S-Pacer |
| I-6, 258.0 | 3.75 × 3.90 | 110 | S-Sprt, AMX; O-Con |
| V-8, 304.0 | 3.75 × 3.44 | 125 | S-all V-8 models |

## 1980

| Spirit (wb 96.0) | | Wght | Price | Prod |
|---|---|---|---|---|
| 43-0 | htchbk cpe I-4 | 2,556 | 4,605 | ⎤ |
| 46-0 | sdn 2d I-4 | 2,512 | 4,505 | |
| 43-5 | DL htchbk cpe I-4 | 2,656 | 5,004 | |
| 46-5 | DL sdn 2d I-4 | 2,611 | 4,904 | 37,799 |
| 43-7 | Limited htckbk cpe I-4 | 2,675 | 5,451 | |
| 46-7 | Limited sdn 2d I-4 | 2,630 | 5,351 | ⎦ |
| 43-0 | htchbk cpe I-6 | 2,758 | 4,734 | ⎤ |
| 46-0 | sdn 2d I-6 | 2,714 | 4,634 | |
| 43-5 | DL htchbk cpe I-6 | 2,858 | 5,133 | 33,233 |
| 46-5 | DL sdn 2d I-6 | 2,813 | 5,033 | |
| 43-7 | Limited htckbk cpe I-6 | 2,877 | 5,580 | |
| 46-7 | Limited sdn 2d I-6 | 2,832 | 5,480 | ⎦ |

| Concord (wb 108.0) | | Wght | Price | Prod |
|---|---|---|---|---|
| 05-0 | sdn 4d I-4 | 2,712 | 5,219 | ⎤ |
| 06-0 | sdn 2d I-4 | 2,646 | 5,094 | |
| 08-0 | wgn 4d I-4 | 2,741 | 5,419 | |
| 05-5 | DL sdn 4d I-4 | 2,834 | 5,618 | 9,949 |
| 06-5 | DL sdn 2d I-4 | 2,764 | 5,493 | |
| 08-5 | DL wgn 4d I-4 | 2,855 | 5,818 | |
| 05-7 | Limited sdn 4d I-4 | 2,859 | 6,065 | |
| 06-7 | Limited sdn 2d I-4 | 2,789 | 5,940 | |
| 08-7 | Limited wgn 4d I-4 | 2,886 | 6,265 | ⎦ |
| 05-0 | sdn 4d I-6 | 2,910 | 5,348 | ⎤ |
| 06-0 | sdn 2d I-6 | 2,844 | 5,223 | |
| 08-0 | wgn 4d I-6 | 2,939 | 5,548 | |
| 05-5 | DL sdn 4d I-6 | 3,032 | 5,747 | |
| 06-5 | DL sdn 2d I-6 | 2,962 | 5,622 | 70,507 |
| 08-5 | DL wgn 4d I-6 | 3,053 | 5,947 | |
| 05-7 | Limited sdn 4d I-6 | 3,057 | 6,194 | |
| 06-7 | Limited sdn 2d I-6 | 2,987 | 6,069 | |
| 08-7 | Limited wgn 4d I-6 | 3,084 | 6,394 | ⎦ |

| Pacer (wb 100.0) | | Wght | Price | Prod |
|---|---|---|---|---|
| 66-5 | DL htckbk 2d I-6 | 3,147 | 5,407 | 405 |
| 68-5 | DL wgn 2d I-6 | 3,195 | 5,558 | 1,341 |
| 66-7 | Limited htchbk 2d I-6 | 3,172 | 6,031 | — |
| 68-7 | Limited wgn 2d I-6 | 3,220 | 6,182 | — |

| AMX (wb 96.0) | | Wght | Price | Prod |
|---|---|---|---|---|
| 43-9 | htchbk cpe I-4 | 2,901 | 5,653 | — |

| Eagle (wb 109.3) | | Wght | Price | Prod |
|---|---|---|---|---|
| 35-5 | sdn 4d I-6 | 3,450 | 7,418 | 9,956 |
| 36-5 | sdn 2d I-6 | 3,382 | 7,168 | 10,616 |
| 38-5 | wgn 4d I-6 | 3,470 | 7,718 | 25,807 |
| 35-7 | Limited sdn 4d I-6 | 3,465 | 7,815 | — |
| 36-7 | Limited sdn 2d I-6 | 3,397 | 7,565 | — |
| 38-7 | Limited wgn 4d I-6 | 3,491 | 8,115 | — |

| 1980 Engines | bore × stroke | bhp | availability |
|---|---|---|---|
| I-4, 151.0 | 4.00 × 3.00 | 90 | S-all 4-cyl models |
| I-6, 258.0 | 3.75 × 3.90 | 110 | S-all 6-cyl models |

## 1981

| Spirit (wb 96.0) | | Wght | Price | Prod |
|---|---|---|---|---|
| 43-0 | htckbk cpe I-4 | 2,587 | 5,190 | ⎤ |
| 43-0 | htchbk cpe I-6 | 2,716 | 5,326 | 42,252 |
| 43-5 | DL htckbk cpe I-4 | 2,673 | 5,589 | |
| 43-5 | DL htchbk cpe I-6 | 2,802 | 5,725 | ⎦ |
| 46-0 | sdn 2d I-4 | 2,543 | 5,090 | ⎤ |
| 46-0 | sdn 2d I-6 | 2,671 | 5,226 | 2,367 |
| 46-5 | DL sdn 2d I-4 | 2,627 | 5,489 | |
| 46-5 | DL sdn 2d I-6 | 2,756 | 5,625 | ⎦ |

| Concord (wb 108.0) | | Wght | Price | Prod |
|---|---|---|---|---|
| 05-0 | sdn 4d I-4 | 2,738 | 5,944 | ⎤ |
| 05-0 | sdn 4d I-6 | 2,864 | 6,080 | |
| 05-5 | DL sdn 4d I-4 | 2,837 | 6,343 | 24,403 |
| 05-5 | DL sdn 4d I-6 | 2,963 | 6,479 | |

39

# AMC

| Concord (wb 108.0) | | Wght | Price | Prod |
|---|---|---|---|---|
| 05-7 | Limited sdn 4d I-4 | 2,859 | 6,790 | |
| 05-7 | Limited sdn 4d I-6 | 2,985 | 6,926 | |
| 06-0 | sdn 2d I-4 | 2,672 | 5,819 | |
| 06-0 | sdn 2d I-6 | 2,798 | 5,955 | |
| 06-5 | DL sdn 2d I-4 | 2,767 | 6,218 | 15,496 |
| 06-5 | DL sdn 2d I-6 | 2,893 | 6,354 | |
| 06-7 | Limited sdn 2d I-4 | 2,789 | 6,665 | |
| 06-7 | Limited sdn 2d I-6 | 2,915 | 6,801 | |
| 08-0 | wgn 4d I-4 | 2,768 | 6,144 | |
| 08-0 | wgn 4d I-6 | 2,894 | 6,280 | |
| 08-5 | DL wgn 4d I-4 | 2,852 | 6,543 | 15,198 |
| 08-5 | DL wgn 4d I-6 | 2,978 | 6,679 | |
| 08-7 | Limited wgn 4d I-4 | 2,880 | 6,990 | |
| 08-7 | Limited wgn 4d I-6 | 3,006 | 7,126 | |

| Eagle 50 (wb 97.2) | | | | |
|---|---|---|---|---|
| 53-0 | SX/4 liftbk cpe 2d I-4 | 2,967 | 6,717 | |
| 53-0 | SX/4 liftbk cpe 2d I-6 | 3,123 | 6,853 | |
| 53-5 | DL SX/4 liftbk cpe 2d I-4 | 3,040 | 7,119 | 17,340 |
| 53-5 | DL SX/4 liftbk cpe 2d I-6 | 3,196 | 7,255 | |
| 56-0 | Kammback sdn 2d I-4 | 2,919 | 5,995 | |
| 56-0 | Kammback sdn 2d I-6 | 3,015 | 6,131 | |
| 56-5 | DL Kammback sdn 2d I-4 | 2,990 | 6,515 | 5,603 |
| 56-5 | DL Kammback sdn 2d I-6 | 3,146 | 6,651 | |

| Eagle 30 (wb 109.3) | | | | |
|---|---|---|---|---|
| 35-5 | sdn 4d I-4 | 3,172 | 8,097 | |
| 35-5 | sdn 4d I-6 | 3,328 | 8,233 | |
| 35-7 | Limited sdn 4d I-4 | 3,180 | 8,494 | 1,737 |
| 35-7 | Limited sdn 4d I-6 | 3,336 | 8,630 | |
| 36-5 | sdn 2d I-4 | 3,104 | 7,847 | |
| 36-5 | sdn 2d I-6 | 3,260 | 7,983 | |
| 36-7 | Limited sdn 2d I-4 | 3,114 | 8,244 | 2,378 |
| 36-7 | Limited sdn 2d I-6 | 3,270 | 8,380 | |
| 38-5 | wgn 4d I-4 | 3,184 | 8,397 | |
| 38-5 | wgn 4d I-6 | 3,340 | 8,533 | |
| 38-7 | Limited wgn 4d I-4 | 3,198 | 8,794 | 10,371 |
| 38-7 | Limited wgn 4d I-6 | 3,354 | 8,930 | |

| 1981 Engines | bore × stroke | bhp | availability |
|---|---|---|---|
| I-4, 151.0 | 4.00 × 3.00 | 82 | S-all 4-cyl models |
| I-6, 258.0 | 3.75 × 3.90 | 110 | S-all 6-cyl models |

## 1982

| Spirit (wb. 96.0) | | Wght | Price | Prod |
|---|---|---|---|---|
| 43-0 | htchbk cpe I-4 | 2,588 | 5,576 | |
| 43-0 | htchbk cpe I-6 | 2,687 | 5,726 | |
| 43-5 | DL htchbk cpe I-4 | 2,666 | 5,959 | 20,063 |
| 43-5 | DL htchbk cpe I-6 | 2,765 | 6,109 | |
| 46-0 | sdn 2d I-4 | 2,538 | 5,476 | |
| 46-0 | sdn 2d I-6 | 2,637 | 5,626 | |
| 46-5 | DL sdn 2d I-4 | 2,614 | 5,859 | 119 |
| 46-5 | DL sdn 2d I-6 | 2,713 | 6,009 | |

| Concord (wb 108.0) | | | | |
|---|---|---|---|---|
| 05-0 | sdn 4d I-4 | 2,752 | 6,254 | |
| 05-0 | sdn 4d I-6 | 2,842 | 6,404 | |
| 05-5 | DL sdn 4d I-4 | 2,841 | 6,761 | |
| 05-5 | DL sdn 4d I-6 | 2,931 | 6,911 | 25,572 |
| 05-7 | Limited sdn 4d I-4 | 2,862 | 7,258 | |
| 05-7 | Limited sdn 4d I-6 | 2,952 | 7,408 | |
| 06-0 | sdn 2d I-4 | 2,683 | 5,954 | |
| 06-0 | sdn 2d I-6 | 2,773 | 6,104 | |
| 06-5 | DL sdn 2d I-4 | 2,768 | 6,716 | |
| 06-5 | DL sdn 2d I-6 | 2,858 | 6,866 | 6,132 |
| 06-7 | Limited sdn 2d I-4 | 2,790 | 7,213 | |
| 06-7 | Limited sdn 2d I-6 | 2,880 | 7,363 | |

| Concord (wb 108.0) | | Wght | Price | Prod |
|---|---|---|---|---|
| 08-0 | wgn 4d I-4 | 2,786 | 7,013 | |
| 08-0 | wgn 4d I-6 | 2,876 | 7,163 | |
| 08-5 | DL wgn 4d I-4 | 2,940 | 7,462 | 12,106 |
| 08-5 | DL wgn 4d I-6 | 3,030 | 7,612 | |
| 08-7 | Limited wgn 4d I-4 | 2,892 | 7,959 | |
| 08-7 | Limited wgn 4d I-6 | 2,982 | 8,109 | |

| Eagle 50 (wb 97.2) | | | | |
|---|---|---|---|---|
| 53-0 | SX/4 liftbk cpe 2d I-4 | 2,972 | 7,451 | |
| 53-0 | SX/4 liftbk cpe 2d I-6 | 3,100 | 7,601 | 10,445 |
| 53-5 | DL SX/4 liftbk cpe 2d I-4 | 3,041 | 7,903 | |
| 53-5 | DL SX/4 liftbk cpe 2d I-6 | 3,169 | 8,053 | |
| 56-0 | Kammback sdn 2d I-4 | 2,933 | 6,799 | |
| 56-0 | Kammback sdn 2d I-6 | 3,061 | 6,949 | 520 |
| 56-5 | DL Kammback sdn 2d I-4 | 3,000 | 7,369 | |
| 56-5 | DL Kammback sdn 2d I-6 | 3,128 | 7,519 | |

| Eagle 30 (wb 109.3 in.) | | | | |
|---|---|---|---|---|
| 35-5 | sdn 4d I-4 | 3,172 | 8,869 | |
| 35-5 | sdn 4D I-6 | 3,310 | 9,019 | 4,091 |
| 35-7 | Limited sdn 4d I-4 | 3,180 | 9,316 | |
| 35-7 | Limited sdn 4d I-6 | 3,308 | 9,466 | |
| 36-5 | sdn 2d I-4 | 3,107 | 8,719 | |
| 36-5 | sdn 2d I-6 | 3,235 | 8,869 | 1,968 |
| 36-7 | Limited sdn 2d I-4 | 3,115 | 9,166 | |
| 36-7 | Limited sdn 2d I-6 | 3,243 | 9,316 | |
| 38-5 | wgn 4d I-4 | 3,299 | 9,566 | |
| 38-5 | wgn 4d I-6 | 3,327 | 9,716 | 20,899 |
| 38-7 | Limited wgn 4d I-4 | 3,213 | 10,013 | |
| 38-7 | Limited wgn 4d I-6 | 3,341 | 10,163 | |

| 1982 Engines | bore × stroke | bhp | availability |
|---|---|---|---|
| I-4, 151.0 | 4.00 × 3.00 | 82 | S-all 4-cyl models |
| I-6, 258.0 | 3.75 × 3.90 | 110 | S-all 6-cyl models |

## 1983

| Alliance (wb 97.8) | | Wght | Price | Prod |
|---|---|---|---|---|
| 96-0 | sdn 2d | 1,945 | 5,595 | |
| 96-3 | L sdn 2d | 1,945 | 6,020 | 55,556 |
| 96-6 | DL sdn 2d | 1,945 | 6,655 | |
| 96-6 | MT sdn 2d | — | 7,450 | |
| 95-3 | L sdn 4d | 1,980 | 6,270 | |
| 95-6 | DL sdn 4d | 1,980 | 6,905 | 86,649 |
| 95-8 | Limited sdn 4d | 1,980 | 7,470 | |
| 95-6 | MT sdn 4d | — | 7,700 | |

| Spirit (wb 96.0) | | | | |
|---|---|---|---|---|
| 43-5 | DL htchbk cpe I-6 | 2,810 | 5,995 | 3,491 |
| 43-9 | GT htchbk cpe I-6 | 2,817 | 6,495 | |

| Concord (wb 108.0) | | | | |
|---|---|---|---|---|
| 05-0 | sdn 4d I-6 | 2,904 | 6,724 | 4,433 |
| 05-5 | DL sdn 4d I-6 | 2,999 | 6,995 | |
| 08-0 | wgn 4d I-6 | 2,948 | 7,449 | |
| 08-5 | DL wgn 4d I-6 | 3,037 | 7,730 | 867 |
| 08-7 | Limited wgn 4d I-6 | 3,061 | 8,117 | |

| Eagle 50 (wb 97.2) | | Wght | Price | Prod |
|---|---|---|---|---|
| 53-0 | SX/4 liftbk cpe 2d I-4 | 3,034 | 7,697 | |
| 53-0 | SX/4 liftbk cpe 2d I-6 | 3,165 | 7,852 | 2,259 |
| 53-5 | DL SX/4 liftbk cpe 2d I-4 | 3,094 | 8,164 | |
| 53-5 | DL SX/4 liftbk cpe 2d I-6 | 3,225 | 8,319 | |

| Eagle 30 (wb 109.3) | | | | |
|---|---|---|---|---|
| 35-5 | sdn 4d I-4 | 3,265 | 9,162 | 3,093 |
| 35-5 | sdn 4d I-6 | 3,396 | 9,317 | |
| 38-5 | wgn 4d I-4 | 3,285 | 9,882 | 12,378 |
| 38-5 | wgn 4d I-6 | 3,416 | 10,037 | |

# AMC

| Eagle 30 (wb 109.3) | | Wght | Price | Prod |
|---|---|---|---|---|
| 38-7 | Limited wgn 4d I-4 | 3,301 | 10,343 | |
| 38-7 | Limited wgn 4d I-6 | 3,432 | 10,498 | |

| 1983 Engines | bore × stroke | bhp | availability |
|---|---|---|---|
| I-4, 85.2 | 2.99 × 3.03 | 56 | S-Alliance |
| I-4, 151.0 | 4.00 × 3.00 | 84 | S-early Eagle |
| I-4, 150.0 | 3.88 × 3.19 | — | S-late Eagle |
| I-6, 258.0 | 3.75 × 3.90 | 110 | S-Spirit, Conc; O-Eagle |

## 1984

| Encore (wb 97.8) | | Wght | Price | Prod |
|---|---|---|---|---|
| 93-0 | htchbk sdn 2d | 2,010 | 5,755 | |
| 93-3 | S htchbk sdn 2d | 2,021 | 6,365 | |
| 93-6 | LS htchbk sdn 2d | 2,069 | 6,995 | 55,343 |
| 93-9 | GS htchbk sdn 2d | 2,079 | 7,547 | |
| 93-6 | Diamond Ed htchbk sdn 2d | — | 7,570 | |
| 99-3 | S htchbk sdn 4d | 2,044 | 6,615 | |
| 99-6 | LS htchbk sdn 4d | 2,095 | 7,195 | 32,266 |
| 99-6 | Diamond Ed htchbk sdn 4d | — | 7,770 | |

| Alliance (wb 97.8) | | Wght | Price | Prod |
|---|---|---|---|---|
| 96-0 | sdn 2d | 1,970 | 5,959 | |
| 96-3 | L sdn 2d | 1,972 | 6,465 | |
| 96-6 | DL sdn 2d | 2,011 | 7,065 | 50,978 |
| 96-6 | Diamond Ed sdn 2d | — | 7,715 | |
| 95-3 | L sdn 4d | 2,000 | 6,715 | |
| 95-6 | DL sdn 4d | 2,038 | 7,365 | |
| 95-6 | Diamond Ed sdn 4d | — | 8,015 | 70,037 |
| 95-8 | Limited sdn 4d | 2,055 | 8,027 | |

| Eagle 30 (wb 109.3 in.) | | Wght | Price | Prod |
|---|---|---|---|---|
| 35-5 | sdn 4d I-4 | 3,273 | 9,495 | |
| 35-5 | sdn 4d I-6 | 3,391 | 9,666 | 4,241 |
| 38-5 | wgn 4d I-4 | 3,304 | 10,225 | |
| 38-5 | wgn 4d I-6 | 3,422 | 10,396 | |
| 38-7 | Limited wgn 4d I-4 | 3,320 | 10,695 | 21,294 |
| 38-7 | Limited wgn 4d I-6 | 3,438 | 10,866 | |

| 1984 Engines | bore × stroke | bhp | availability |
|---|---|---|---|
| I-4, 85.2 | 2.99 × 3.03 | 56 | S-Alliance, Encore |
| I-4, 150.0 | 3.88 × 3.19 | NA | S-Eagle |
| I-6, 258.0 | 3.75 × 3.90 | 110 | O-Eagle |

## 1985

| Encore (wb 97.8) | | Wght | Price | Prod |
|---|---|---|---|---|
| 93-0 | htchbk sdn 2d | 1,982 | 5,895 | |
| 93-3 | S htchbk sdn 2d | 2,021 | 6,360 | |
| 93-6 | LS htchbk sdn 2d | 2,069 | 7,060 | 38,623 |
| 93-9 | GS htchbk sdn 2d | 2,079 | 7,560 | |
| 99-3 | S htchbk sdn 4d | 2,044 | 6,610 | 19,902 |
| 99-6 | LS htchbk sdn 4d | 2,095 | 7,310 | |

| Alliance (wb 97.8) | | Wght | Price | Prod |
|---|---|---|---|---|
| 96-0 | sdn 2d | 1,958 | 5,995 | |
| 96-3 | L sdn 2d | 1,965 | 6,400 | 33,617 |
| 96-6 | DL sdn 2d | 1,998 | 7,000 | |
| 95-3 | L sdn 4d | 2,000 | 6,650 | |
| 95-6 | DL sdn 4d | 2,037 | 7,250 | 50,906 |
| 95-8 | Limited sdn 4d | 2,087 | 7,750 | |
| 97-3 | L conv cpe | 2,189 | 10,295 | 7,141 |
| 97-6 | DL conv cpe | 2,226 | 11,295 | |

| Eagle 30 (wb 109.3) | | Wght | Price | Prod |
|---|---|---|---|---|
| 35-5 | sdn 4d I-6 | 3,390 | 10,457 | 2,655 |
| 38-5 | wgn 4d I-6 | 3,421 | 11,217 | 13,535 |
| 38-7 | Limited wgn 4d I-6 | 3,452 | 11,893 | |

| 1985 Engines | bore × stroke | bhp | availability |
|---|---|---|---|
| I-4, 85.2 | 2.99 × 3.03 | 56 | S-Alliance, Encore |
| I-4, 105.0 | 3.19 × 3.29 | 77 | S-Alliance conv, Encore GS; O-Alliance, Encore |
| I-6, 258.0 | 3.75 × 3.90 | 110 | S-Eagle |

## 1986

| Encore (wb 97.8) | | Wght | Price | Prod |
|---|---|---|---|---|
| 93-3 | S htchbk sdn 2d | 2,006 | 6,710 | |
| 93-6 | LS htchbk sdn 2d | 2,010 | 7,310 | 12,239 |
| 93-9 | GS htchbk sdn 2d | 2,013 | 7,968 | |
| 93-4 | Electronic htchbk sdn 2d | 2,051 | 7,498 | |
| 99-3 | S htchbk sdn 4d | 2,039 | 6,960 | 6,870 |
| 99-6 | LS htchbk sdn 4d | 2,043 | 7,560 | |

| Alliance (wb 97.8) | | Wght | Price | Prod |
|---|---|---|---|---|
| 96-0 | sdn 2d | 1,959 | 5,999 | |
| 96-3 | L sdn 2d | 1,964 | 6,510 | 23,204 |
| 96-6 | DL sdn 2d | 1,971 | 7,110 | |
| 95-0 | sdn 4d | 1,993 | 6,199 | |
| 95-3 | L sdn 4d | 1,998 | 6,760 | 41,891 |
| 95-6 | DL sdn 4d | 2,005 | 7,360 | |
| 97-3 | L conv cpe | 2,222 | 10,557 | 2,015 |
| 97-6 | DL conv cpe | 2,228 | 11,557 | |

| Eagle 30 (wb 109.3) | | Wght | Price | Prod |
|---|---|---|---|---|
| 35-5 | sdn 4d I-6 | 3,391 | 10,719 | 1,274 |
| 38-5 | wgn 4d I-6 | 3,425 | 11,489 | 6,943 |
| 38-7 | Limited wgn 4d I-6 | 3,456 | 12,719 | |

| 1986 Engines | bore × stroke | bhp | availability |
|---|---|---|---|
| I-4, 85.2 | 2.99 × 3.03 | 56 | S-Alliance, Encore |
| I-4, 105.0 | 3.19 × 3.29 | 77 | S-Alliance conv, Encore Elect/GS; O-Alliance, Encore |
| I-6, 258.0 | 3.75 × 3.90 | 110 | S-Eagle |

## 1987

| Alliance (wb 97.8) | | Wght | Price | Prod |
|---|---|---|---|---|
| 96-0 | sdn 2d | 1,959 | 6,399 | |
| 96-3 | L sdn 2d | 1,965 | 6,925 | 13,132 |
| 96-6 | DL sdn 2d | 2,000 | 7,625 | |
| 96-7 | GTA sdn 2d | 2,104 | 8,999 | |
| 95-0 | sdn 4d | 1,997 | 6,599 | |
| 95-3 | L sdn 4d | 2,003 | 7,200 | 16,214 |
| 95-8 | DL sdn 4d | 2,038 | 7,900 | |
| 97-3 | L conv cpe | 2,206 | 11,099 | |
| 97-6 | DL conv cpe | 2,239 | 12,099 | 1,991 |
| 97-7 | GTA conv cpe | 2,298 | 12,899 | |
| 93-0 | htchbk sdn 2d | 1,985 | 6,599 | |
| 93-3 | L htchbk sdn 2d | 1,991 | 6,975 | 2,857 |
| 93-6 | DL htchbk sdn 2d | 2,028 | 7,675 | |
| 93-9 | GS htckbk sdn 2d | 2,057 | 8,499 | |
| 99-3 | L htchbk sdn 4d | 2,039 | 7,250 | 2,142 |
| 99-6 | DL htchbk sdn 4d | 2,081 | 7,950 | |

| Eagle (wb 109.3) | | Wght | Price | Prod |
|---|---|---|---|---|
| 35-5 | sdn 4d I-6 | 3,383 | 11,150 | 751 |
| 38-5 | wgn 4d I-6 | 3,417 | 11,943 | 4,452 |
| 38-7 | Limited wgn 4d I-6 | 3,431 | 12,653 | |

| 1987 Engines | bore × stroke | bhp | availability |
|---|---|---|---|
| I-4, 85.2 | 2.99 × 3.03 | 56 | S-Alliance |
| I-4, 105.0 | 3.19 × 3.29 | 77 | S-Alliance conv; O=Alliance |
| I-4, 120.0 | 3.23 × 3.66 | 95 | S-Alliance GTA |
| I-6, 258.0 | 3.75 × 3.90 | 112 | S-Eagle |

Note: Production totals that were unavailable from AMC have been compiled from industry sources.

# Auburn

Though the Auburns best remembered today were built in the '30s and late '20s, the marque was established way back in 1903. That's when brothers Frank and Morris Eckhart, buggy-builders in the northeast Indiana town of Auburn, began selling an $800 chain-drive runabout with a single-cylinder engine. Two-, four-, and six-cylinder models followed quickly in the years through 1912. Like other small, marginally capitalized automakers of the time, Auburn offered "assembled cars" built from a variety of proven, but brought-in, components.

As a result, Auburn was nearly stagnant by 1919, when the Eckharts sold out to a Chicago group headed by chewing-gum king William K. Wrigley, Jr. New capital and more-aggressive marketing were put behind a new model, the "Beauty Six," with streamlined body, disc wheels, step plates instead of running boards, and windshield vent wings—all very advanced for the day. But a deep post-World War I recession cut greatly into car sales. With annual output below 4000 units, Auburn was on the ropes again by 1924.

Then came a second savior, Errett Lobban Cord, a brash young entrepreneur described as both "boy wonder" and "profane, bespectacled capitalist." Salesmanship was his claim to fame. Responsible for the selling and distribution of the majority of Moon Motor Car Company's production in the Chicago market alone, Cord attracted the attention of Auburn's Chicago owners. Wanting to try the production end of the car business, Cord accepted the position of Auburn general manager. After promptly disposing of some 700 leftover 1924s, which netted enough cash to pay off Auburn's debts, he was made vice president. By 1926, he was both the firm's president and its chief stockholder.

Auburn prospered under Cord, gaining a modest competition image, greatly increasing exports, expanding its dealer body,

**1934 Eight Cabriolet 2/4 passenger**

**1932 12-160 Speedster**

**1930 Custom Eight Cabriolet 2/4 passenger**

# Auburn

**1935 851 Speedster**

**1932 Custom Eight Cabriolet 2/4 passenger**

and adding eight-cylinder models in 1925. With fast, handsome, and reliable cars priced incredibly low, Auburn passed the 20,000 mark in annual production by 1929. Though Eights naturally offered more vivid performance than Sixes, all Auburns were appreciated for their good looks and high value.

Deciding to concentrate on Eights and, ultimately, a Twelve, Cord dropped the Auburn Six after 1930. That year's final 6-85 series offered just a cabriolet, sedan, and sport sedan. Power was supplied by Lycoming, a Pennsylvania company Cord had purchased in 1929. The sturdy 185-cubic-inch engine produced 70 horsepower at 3400 rpm. Despite modest $1000-$1100 pricing, the 6-85 was by no means dull: smooth and clean on a 120-inch wheelbase. Even so, Auburn sales dropped almost 50 percent for calendar 1930, and model-year volume declined to 14,360. With the Depression hitting hard, management concluded that the Six was just not profitable enough to retain, though it would return.

There were two Auburn Eights for 1930. The lower-priced 125-inch-wheelbase 8-95 was an unquestioned bargain, offering four models (the six-cylinder trio plus a five-seat phaeton) in the $1200-$1400 range. Its 247-cid inline engine was basically the 6-85 unit with two more cylinders and 100 bhp. For $1500-$1700 you could have the same foursome as Custom Eight 125s, with that many horses from 298.6 cid. Mounting a 130-inch chassis, they weighed some 3900 pounds but could do almost 90 mph—astonishing for the day. In 1929, this engine had powered a 3000-pound speedster to 100 mph—a first for Auburn.

Auburn was one of the few automakers to see higher sales after the 1929 Wall Street Crash. Calendar-year 1931 production zoomed to a record of over 32,000 on the strength of more dealers and a line of fleet, luxurious, bargain-priced Eights. Reflecting Cord's cagey sales strategy, the bigger eight was dropped along with the six, the smaller eight bored to 268.6 cid and 98 bhp. Larger, more-rakish bodies were placed on longer 127-inch wheelbases for identical Eight and Custom Eight series. The latter featured standard freewheeling, but both lines offered speedster, coupe, cabriolet, brougham, phaeton-sedan, and closed-sedan bodies, plus seven-seat sedans on a special

**1932 Custom Eight four-door sedan**

# Auburn

136-inch chassis. All this moved Business Week to hail Auburn as "more car for the money than the public had ever seen."

If the 1931 Eight was a remarkable buy, the 1932 Twelve was even more so: the least-costly V-12 on the market at prices ranging from $975 for the Standard coupe to $1275 for the top-line Custom Speedster. The engine, a 391-cid Lycoming designed by Auburn chief engineer George Kublin, packed a healthy 160 bhp at 3500 rpm. It was mounted in an X-braced frame spanning a kingly 133-inch wheelbase. Custom Twelves featured the well-known Columbia dual-ratio rear axle with 4.55 and 3.04:1 gear sets that could be selected below 40 mph, which effectively provided six forward speeds. Eights continued as before, as did the usual body types, including eight-cylinder long sedans. The beautiful V-12 boattail speedsters, so rare today, were the best expressions of that year's Auburn styling.

Yet despite these peerless cars, sales plunged in 1932 to a calendar-year output of just over 11,000. Red ink continued gushing in 1933, as volume fell to under 5000. While all this mystified E. L. Cord, hindsight reveals that a V-12 at any price just couldn't interest many buyers in the depths of the Depression. Unsold '33 V-12s were retitled and sold as '34s. Auburn's Eight, which had exhausted what demand it had enjoyed in 1931, was little changed for '32 and '33.

Worse, Cord was now spread very thin building his far-flung business empire. He'd bought Duesenberg in 1926, launched the front-drive Cord L-29 three years later, then acquired Lycoming, the Ansted engine company, several midwestern corporations, and even Checker Cab—plus shipbuilding and aviation interests. Perhaps to avoid a brewing scandal over his management of these enterprises, Cord fled to England in 1934 and promptly dropped from sight. Eventually, his conglomerate's fortunes were handed over to Duesenberg president Harold T. Ames.

The 1934 line featured all-steel bodies with more-streamlined, but less-distinctive styling by Alan Leamy of L-29 renown. The Six was revived with a 210-cid Lycoming engine making 85 bhp at 3500 rpm. Eights used a revised, 280-inch version of the previous straight eight developing 100 bhp with a cast-iron head or 115 bhp with a high-compression aluminum head. Standard and Custom models on a 119-inch (Six) or 126-inch Eight chassis were offered for as little as $695 (Standard Six) in an effort to win Depression-depleted dollars. But these cars didn't sell. Poorly received styling (especially the "shovel front") often get the blame, but 1934 wasn't a good sales year for any make.

The '35 Auburns benefited from the talents of two automotive legends—designer Gordon Buehrig and engineer August Duesenberg. Buehrig was given a modest $50,000 and told to do what he could to improve Auburn styling. Adding a bold grille and massive hood to the existing body did the trick. Augie, meantime, was asked to adapt a Schwitzer-Cummins supercharger to the eight. Horsepower jumped to a hefty 150 horsepower. Supercharged cars were identified by external exhausts. The six and 115-bhp eight were carried over. The result was a line of very pretty cars that would include Auburn's final glory—the superb 851/852 speedster.

Buehrig didn't have enough money for a complete redesign

1936 Supercharged Eight Dual Ratio four-door sedan

# Auburn

so he worked with the midsection of leftover '33 Speedsters, giving the old bodies the new front-end treatment, beautifully curved pontoon fenders, and a new boattail. All Speedsters were supercharged and could hit 100 mph right out of the showroom, yet they sold for as little as $2245. Once again Auburn was offering truly unbelievable value.

But 1935 proved a confused and ultimately disappointing year, so the 1936 Auburns were predictably almost unchanged. The six-cylinder 653 became Series 654, still offered in standard form as well as Custom and Salon "Dual Ratio" models. The same arrangement, plus supercharged models, applied to the 1936 Series 852. Yet despite this still-brilliant fleet of cabriolets, broughams, phaetons, sedans, and the 852 Supercharged Speedster, sales refused to improve. Speedster production, for instance, came to less than 500 for both years.

Like a prodigal son, E.L. Cord returned from England in 1936 to salvage his crumbling empire, only to find the IRS and the Securities and Exchange Commission ready to launch major investigations of his doings. One result was the cancellation of planned 1937 Auburns. The make was dead.

Cord would manage to keep most of his fortune, and in later years got involved in western land speculation. Though he is not remembered fondly by Auburn fans, it's doubtful the make would have risen so high without him. It's a shame that its life at the pinnacle was so short.

## Specifications

### 1930

| 6-85 Six (wb 120.0) | | Wght | Price | Prod* |
|---|---|---|---|---|
| 685A | sdn 4d | 3,300 | 1,095 | — |
| 685B | spt sdn 2W | 3,300 | 995 | — |
| 685F | cab, 2-4P | 3,125 | 1,095 | — |
| **8-95 Eight (wb 125.0)** | | | | |
| 895A | sdn 4d | 3,590 | 1,295 | — |
| 895B | spt sdn 2W | 3,590 | 1,195 | — |
| 895F | cab 2-4P | 3,410 | 1,295 | — |
| 895H | phtn sdn 5P | 3,600 | 1,395 | — |
| **125 Custom Eight (wb 130.0)** | | | | |
| 125A | sdn 4d | 3,995 | 1,595 | — |
| 125B | spt sdn 2W | 3,995 | 1,495 | — |
| 125F | cab 2-4P | 3,800 | 1,595 | — |
| 125H | phtn sdn 5P | 3,990 | 1,695 | — |

| 1930 Engines | bore × stroke | bhp | availability |
|---|---|---|---|
| I-6, 185.0 | 2.88 × 4.75 | 70 | 6-85 |
| I-8, 247.0 | 2.88 × 4.75 | 100 | 8-95 |
| I-8, 298.6 | 3.25 × 4.50 | 125 | 125 |

* Calendar-year production: 11,357

### 1931

| 8-98 Eight (wb 127.0; 7P-136.0) | Wght | Price | Prod* |
|---|---|---|---|
| b'ham 2d 5P | 3,580 | 945 | — |
| spdstr 2P | 3,320 | 945 | — |
| sdn 4d | 3,700 | 995 | — |
| cpe 2P | 3,460 | 995 | — |
| cab 2-4P | 3,540 | 1,045 | — |
| phtn sdn 5P | 3,650 | 1,145 | — |
| sdn 7P | 3,990 | 1,195 | — |
| **8-98A Custom Eight (wb 127.0; 7P-136.0)** | | | |
| b'ham 2d 5P | 3,630 | 1,145 | — |
| sdn 4d | 3,750 | 1,195 | — |
| cpe 2P | 3,510 | 1,195 | — |
| cab 2-4P | 3,490 | 1,245 | — |
| phtn sdn 5P | 3,700 | 1,345 | — |
| spdstr 2P | 3,370 | 1,395 | — |
| sdn 7P | 4,040 | 1,395 | — |

| 1931 Engine | bore × stroke | bhp | availability |
|---|---|---|---|
| I-8, 268.6 | 3.00 × 4.75 | 98 | 8-98, 8-98A |

*Calendar-year production: 32,301

### 1932

| 8-100 Eight (wb 127.0; 7P-136.0) | Wght | Price | Prod* |
|---|---|---|---|
| cpe 2P | 3,485 | 675 | — |
| b'ham 2d 5P | 3,605 | 725 | — |
| sdn 4d | 3,725 | 775 | — |
| cab 2-4P | 3,495 | 795 | — |
| phtn sdn 5P | 3,675 | 845 | — |
| spdstr 2P | 3,345 | 845 | — |
| sdn 7P | 4,015 | 875 | — |
| **8-100A Custom Eight Dual Ratio (wb 127.0; 7P-136.0)** | | | |
| cpe 2P | 3,575 | 805 | — |
| b'ham 2d 5P | 3,695 | 855 | — |
| sdn 4d | 3,815 | 905 | — |
| cab 2-4P | 3,585 | 925 | — |
| phtn sdn 5P | 3,765 | 975 | — |
| spdstr 2P | 3,435 | 975 | — |
| sdn 7P | 4,105 | 1,005 | — |
| **12-160 Twelve (wb 133.0)** | | | |
| cpe 2P | 4,275 | 975 | — |
| b'ham 2d 5P | 4,395 | 1,025 | — |
| sdn 4d | 4,515 | 1,075 | — |
| cab 2-4P | 4,285 | 1,095 | — |
| phtn sdn 5P | 4,465 | 1,145 | — |
| spdstr 2P | 4,135 | 1,145 | — |
| **12-160A Custom Twelve Dual Ratio (wb 133.0)** | | | |
| cpe 2P | 4,375 | 1,105 | — |
| b'ham 2d 5P | 4,495 | 1,155 | — |
| sdn 4d | 4,615 | 1,205 | — |
| cab 2-4P | 4,385 | 1,225 | — |
| phtn sdn 5P | 4,565 | 1,275 | — |
| spdstr 2P | 4,235 | 1,275 | — |

| 1932 Engines | bore × stroke | bhp | availability |
|---|---|---|---|
| I-8, 268.6 | 3.00 × 4.75 | 100 | all Eights |
| V-12, 391.6 | 3.13 × 4.25 | 160 | all Twelves |

* Total 1932 registrations: 11,345

### 1933

| 8-101 Eight (wb 1276.0; 7P-136.0) | Wght | Price | Prod* |
|---|---|---|---|
| cpe 2P | 3,485 | 745 | — |
| b'ham 2d 5P | 3,605 | 795 | — |
| sdn 4d | 3,725 | 845 | — |
| cab 2-4P | 3,495 | 895 | — |
| phtn sdn 5P | 3,675 | 945 | — |
| spdstr 2P | 3,345 | 945 | — |
| sdn 7P | 4,015 | 945 | — |

# Auburn

| 8-101A Custom Eight Dual Ratio (wb 127.0; 7P-136.0) | Wght | Price | Prod* |
|---|---|---|---|
| cpe 2P | 3,575 | 895 | — |
| b'ham 2d 5P | 3,695 | 945 | — |
| sdn 4d | 3,815 | 995 | — |
| cab 2-4P | 3,585 | 1,045 | — |
| phtn sdn 5P | 3,765 | 1,095 | — |
| spdstr 2P | 3,435 | 1,095 | — |
| sdn 7P | 4,105 | 1,095 | — |
| **8-105 Salon Eight Dual Ratio (wb 127.0)** | | | |
| b'ham 2d 5P | 3,800 | 1,045 | — |
| sdn 4d | 3,920 | 1,095 | — |
| cab 2-4P | 3,640 | 1,145 | — |
| phtn sdn 5P | 3,835 | 1,195 | — |
| spdstr 2P | 3,510 | 1,195 | — |
| **12-161 Twelve (wb 133.0)** | | | |
| cpe 2P | 4,275 | 1,145 | — |
| b'ham 2d 5P | 4,395 | 1,195 | — |
| sdn 4d | 4,515 | 1,245 | — |
| cab 2-4P | 4,285 | 1,295 | — |
| phtn sdn 5P | 4,465 | 1,345 | — |
| spdstr 2P | 4,135 | 1,345 | — |
| **12-161A Custom Twelve Dual Ratio (wb 133.0)** | | | |
| cpe 2P | 4,355 | 1,295 | — |
| b'ham 2d 5P | 4,495 | 1,345 | — |
| sdn 4d | 4,615 | 1,395 | — |
| cab 2-4P | 4,385 | 1,445 | — |
| phtn sdn 5P | 4,565 | 1,495 | — |
| spdstr 2P | 4,235 | 1,495 | — |
| **12-165 Salon Twelve Dual Ratio (wb 133.0)** | | | |
| b'ham 2d 5P | 4,715 | 1,595 | — |
| sdn 4d | 4,870 | 1,645 | — |
| cab 2-4P | 4,570 | 1,695 | — |
| phtn sdn 5P | 4,710 | 1,745 | — |
| spdstr 2P | 4,440 | 1,745 | — |

| 1933 Engines | bore × stroke | bhp | availability |
|---|---|---|---|
| I-8, 268.6 | 3.00 × 4.75 | 100 | all Eights |
| V-12, 391.6 | 3.13 × 4.25 | 160 | all Twelves |

* Calendar-year production: 4,813

## 1934

| 652X Six (wb 119.0) | Wght | Price | Prod* |
|---|---|---|---|
| b'ham 2d 5P | 3,215 | 695 | — |
| sdn 4d | 3,263 | 745 | — |
| cab 2-4P | 3,105 | 795 | — |
| **652Y Custom Six Dual Ratio (wb 119.0)** | | | |
| b'ham 2d 5P | 3,305 | 795 | — |
| sdn 4d | 3,353 | 845 | — |
| cab 2-4P | 3,195 | 895 | — |
| phtn sdn 5P | 3,375 | 945 | — |
| **850X Eight (wb 126.0)** | | | |
| b'ham 2d 5P | 3,628 | 945 | — |
| sdn 4d | 3,668 | 995 | — |
| cab 2-4P | 3,603 | 1,045 | — |
| **850Y Custom Eight Dual Ratio (wb 126.0)** | | | |
| b'ham 2d 5P | 3,688 | 1,075 | — |
| sdn 4d | 3,755 | 1,125 | — |
| cab 2-4P | 3,653 | 1,175 | — |
| phtn sdn 5P | 3,773 | 1,225 | — |
| **1250 Salon Twelve Dual Ratio (wb 133.0)** | | | |
| b'ham 2d 5P | 4,715 | 1,395 | — |
| sdn 4d | 4,870 | 1,445 | — |
| cab 2-4P | 4,570 | 1,495 | — |
| phtn sdn 5P | 4,710 | 1,545 | — |

| 1934 Engines | bore × stroke | bhp | availability |
|---|---|---|---|
| I-6, 210.0 | 3.06 × 4.75 | 85 | all Sixes |
| I-8, 280.0 | 3.06 × 4.75 | 100 | 850X |
| I-8, 280.0 | 3.06 × 4.75 | 115 | 850Y |
| V-12, 391.6 | 3.13 × 4.25 | 160 | 1250 |

*Calendar-year production: 7,770

## 1935/36

| 653/654 Six (wb 120.0) | Wght | Price | Prod* |
|---|---|---|---|
| b'ham 2d 5P | 3,214 | 745 | — |
| sdn 4d | 3,279 | 795 | — |
| cpe 2P | 3,105 | 835 | — |
| cab 2-4P | 3,182 | 945 | — |
| phtn sdn 5P | 3,248 | 995 | — |
| **653 Custom Six Dual Ratio (from February 1935)(wb 120.0)** | | | |
| b'ham 2d 4P | 3,321 | 852 | — |
| cpe 2P | 3,201 | 942 | — |
| sdn 4d | 3,388 | 952 | — |
| cab 2-4P | 3,282 | 1,052 | — |
| phtn sdn 5P | 3,248 | 1,102 | — |
| **653 Salon Six Dual Ratio (wb 120.0)** | | | |
| b'ham 2d 4P | 3,471 | 932 | — |
| sdn 4d | 3,533 | 982 | — |
| cpe 2P | 3,371 | 990 | — |
| cab 2-4P | 3,432 | 1,100 | — |
| phtn sdn 5P | 3,498 | 1,182 | — |
| **851/852 Eight (wb 127.0)** | | | |
| b'ham 2d 5P | 3,475 | 995 | — |
| cpe 2P | 3,395 | 1,085 | — |
| sdn 4d | 3,580 | 1,095 | — |
| cab 2-4P | 3,415 | 1,225 | — |
| phtn sdn 5P | 3,565 | 1,275 | — |
| sdn 7P | 3,870 | 1,195 | — |
| **851/852 Custom Eight Dual Ratio (wb 127.0)** | | | |
| b'ham 2d 5P | 3,574 | 1,088 | — |
| cpe 2P | 3,493 | 1,173 | — |
| sdn 4d | 3,679 | 1,188 | — |
| cab 2-4P | 3,511 | 1,313 | — |
| phtn sdn 5P | 3,664 | 1,368 | — |
| sdn 7P | 3,969 | 1,288 | — |
| **851/852 Salon Eight Dual Ratio (wb 127.0)** | | | |
| b'ham 2d 5P | 3,724 | 1,168 | — |
| cpe 2P | 3,643 | 1,221 | — |
| sdn 4d | 3,835 | 1,268 | — |
| cab 2-4P | 3,641 | 1,361 | — |
| phtn sdn 5P | 3,814 | 1,448 | — |
| sdn 7P | 4,125 | 1,368 | — |
| **851/852 Supercharged Eight Dual Ratio (wb 127.0)** | | | |
| b'ham 2d 5P | 3,655 | 1,445 | — |
| sdn 4d | 3,729 | 1,545 | — |
| cpe 2P | 3,565 | 1,545 | — |
| cab 2-4P | 3,633 | 1,675 | — |
| phtn sdn 5P | 3,714 | 1,725 | — |
| spdstr 2P | 3,706 | 2,245 | — |

| 1935/36 Engines | bore × stroke | bhp | availability |
|---|---|---|---|
| I-6, 210.0 | 3.06 × 4.75 | 85 | all Sixes |
| I-8, 280.0 | 3.06 × 4.75 | 115 | Eights exc Suprchd |
| I-8S, 280.0 | 3.06 × 4.75 | 150 | Supercharged |

* 1935 calendar-year production: 6,316; 1936 calendar-year production: 1,263

# Avanti/Avanti II

Studebaker fled to Canada in late 1963 and left the auto business three years later. By that time, Leo Newman and Nathan Altman had resurrected the Avanti, Studebaker's most interesting car of the '60s.

Designed by a team under Raymond Loewy, the Avanti had failed Studebaker in the marketplace but succeeded greatly with enthusiasts—the only Studebaker in two generations to inspire such interest. Before its phaseout on Studebaker's departure from South Bend, the Avanti had broken virtually every major U.S. Auto Club speed record (see Studebaker).

Newman and Altman were partners in a South Bend Studebaker dealership, one of the oldest. Knowing the Avanti was too good to lose, they bought the name, production rights, tooling, and a portion of the century-old South Bend plant where the Avanti had been built. In 1965, they began turning out a revised version called Avanti II. They hoped to make 300 a year, which they'd never manage, but output was adequate and consistent.

Unlike the original, Avanti II was a commercial success. Its fiberglass body meant no expensive sheetmetal dies to maintain. And because Newman and Altman had conceived their Avanti as more exclusive than Studebaker's, they could build it carefully and largely by hand on a small assembly line. That meant they could tailor each car to the customer's wishes.

Well-heeled buyers could push the $6550 base price beyond $10,000. Options included Hurst four-speed manual transmission, power steering, air conditioning, electric window lifts, tinted glass, AM/FM radio, Eppe fog or driving lights, limited-slip differential, Magnum 500 chrome wheels, and Firestone bias-ply or Michelin radial tires. Early Avanti IIs had vinyl interiors, but textured "Raphael vinyl" could be ordered for $200. Genuine leather seat and door trim added $300, full leather $500. Paint colors were anything a buyer wanted, as were interior trims in later years. Though this led to some bizarre cars, it was part of the "custom-built" aura and it helped sales.

Early IIs retained the original Avanti's modified Lark convertible frame, but Studebaker V-8s were gone by the time Newman and Altman started, so they followed Studebaker's own lead by adopting the same 327-cubic-inch Chevrolet small-block in 300-horsepower Corvette tune. Chevy then introduced a 350-cid enlargement, and Avantis got it in 1969, though rated power was unchanged. Transmissions were either a fully synchronized Borg-Warner four-speed manual or a "Power-Shift" automatic that permitted manual hold of first and second gears.

These new mechanicals resided in a body almost identical to the original Avanti's. The main visual differences were a more level stance (Altman's customers disliked the Studebaker's marked front-end rake), Avanti logos with suffix Roman-numeral IIs, and reduced-radius wheel openings.

Corvette power made for fine performance in the sleek four-place Avanti. The typical automatic car could run 0-60 mph in under nine seconds and hit 125 mph with 3.54:1 rear axle. Better still, the Chevy engines were lighter than the old Studebaker V-8, so front/rear weight balance improved from 59/41 percent to 57/43. Power front-disc/rear-drum brakes resisted fade admirably, while providing quick deceleration of nearly 1g in 80-mph panic stops. Obviously, Newman and Altman cared about safety as much as straight-line performance.

Being custom-built, the Avanti II necessarily cost more than Studebaker's version, competing in Cadillac Eldorado territory instead of Chrysler country like the $4,445 original. Realizing this meant a change in market orientation, Newman and Altman pitched the II more on "personal-luxury" than performance.

And indeed, the car was in its element on the open road. Magazine testers gave it points for safety, quietness, structural rigidity, and a firm but comfortable ride. "In this day of great concern over automotive safety," wrote John R. Bond in 1966, "the Avanti II should make new friends, for obviously there was more thought given to safety in its conception than in most American cars . . . It's a better car than it was three years ago."

Avanti II saw few changes in the '70s save those needed to meet federal safety and emissions rules. Among the more obvious—and depressing—was the ugly, rubber-tipped "cow catcher" grafted on to meet 1973's new five-mph bumper standard, although Avanti Motor Corporation was small enough to win exemption from the required 2½-mph side-impact door beams. Also for '73, the engine was changed to Chevrolet's new detoxed 400 V-8. With net horsepower ratings in force for '74, the 400 came in at an anemic 180-bhp SAE net (245 gross). The 350 returned for '77 and would remain standard into the early '80s.

With Nate Altman's untimely death in 1976, Avanti seemed to lose direction, at times appearing half-hearted about its product and its future. Workmanship declined even as prices, spurred by inflation, galloped upward (breaking $12,000 in '76 and pushing $23,000 in '82). Federal dictates prompted detail interior changes (mainly to switchgear) wrought with an afterthought carelessness suggesting less-than-professional engineering and design work. On the plus side, the firm reduced its plethora of paint and trim choices in the interest of higher build quality and lower inventory costs. But little money and effort were going into updating the concept, as Altman had done. Both car and company were surviving, but hardly thriving.

That was about to change. After rebuffing several buyout offers over the years, the Altman family and other Avanti board members gave audience to Stephen Blake, a young Washington, D.C., construction tycoon. Alas, Altman's death came only days after the parties agreed to serious negotiations, and another seven years would pass before Blake became owner, president, and CEO of Avanti Motor Corporation in October 1982.

**1970s Avanti II sport coupe**

**1989 Avanti sport coupe**

# Avanti

**1989 Avanti sport convertible**

**1998 AVX coupe**

Blake blew into South Bend like a tornado, rearranging work flow in the crumbling remains of the old Studebaker plant for improved efficiency and quality. He also resisted the UAW and dismissed many dealers, inking more businesslike contracts with established Cadillac stores in major markets. Recruiting needed engineering talent soon resulted in several improvements: a switch to premium DuPont Imron paint (as on Indy race cars), greater use of GM components, optional body-color bumpers and black trim, square headlights, revamped interior, minor chassis tweaks, and an optional 190-bhp 305-cid V-8 (versus 155 bhp standard) from the Chevy Camaro Z28. The name lost it's Roman numeral "II" and returned to plain "Avanti." Most of these changes came together in a special 20th Anniversary 1983 coupe offered in solid black, white, red, or silver.

Bolder still were Blake's plans for the first Avanti convertible (unveiled as a prototype in late '83) and a new drop-floor chassis with independent rear suspension designed by Herb Adams. Blake even made a stab at racing, entering an Avanti "GT" in the 1983 Pepsi Challenge 24-hour enduro at Daytona. Though it finished only 27th out of 30 survivors from a starting field of 79, its merely showing up suggested Avanti was moving forward again.

Sadly, Blake tried to do too much too fast, and unexpected peeling problems with the new race-car paint cost a bundle to fix. By early 1985, Blake had spent himself into a credit crunch with his prime lender, a South Bend bank, and was forced to sell.

Avanti might have died right there had it not been for Michael Kelly, a 36-year-old Texas ethanol baron who acquired Blake's interests for just $725,000 in April 1985. Operating as New Avanti Motor Corporation, Kelly's regime began building Blake's convertible alongside the familiar coupe in 1987. Both models received new seats, a "cockpit" dash, altered bumpers, and improved cooling and climate systems. The coupe still listed for about $30,000; the convertible was some $10,000 more. With this changing of the guard, no 1986 Avantis were built.

Even more ambitious than Blake, Kelly moved production to a new plant in Youngstown, Ohio. This occurred in August 1987, thus closing the old Studebaker factory at last. Avantis would still be mostly hand-built, but the modern facilities promised great strides in quality. And volume, which Kelly predicted would eventually reach an unprecedented 1000 cars a year.

To achieve that, Kelly literally stretched the Avanti line by adding three new models: a 117-inch-wheelbase Luxury Sport Coupe, an even longer four-door Luxury Touring Sedan on a 123-inch chassis, and a jumbo limousine on a huge 174-inch span. Purists moaned, though designer Loewy (who died in late 1987) had mocked up a pair of "Avanti-styled" sedans as 1965-66 Studebakers. At least the LSC looked as good as the standard coupe, a tribute to the "rightness" of the original design.

Besides 40 LSCs, Kelly's company managed 50 Silver Anniversary coupes in 1988 to honor Avanti's 25th birthday. These carried Chevy 305 V-8s that were muscled up to 250 bhp (from 170 standard) via Paxton superchargers supplied by the Grantelli brothers, just as in Studebaker days. Appropriately, the anniversary models were painted pearl silver. Interiors featured black or red leather, an "entertainment center" with TV, power moonroof, compact-disc player, and cellular telephone. There was also a fortified suspension with fat tires on handsome alloy wheels, and bodies gained a front spoiler with fog lamps, rocker-panel skirts, and reshaped bumpers.

Exceeding projected first-year production by 50 percent, New Avanti built 300 cars in 1987, the level Blake had hoped to attain but didn't. But Kelly, too, soon overreached himself, and this (plus legal hassles from one-time backers) forced him to sell in August 1988. The buyer turned out to be his principal partner, shopping-mall developer J.J. Cafaro, who changed the company name once again, this time to Avanti Automotive Corporation.

Both LSC and the planned limo were forgotten, but Cafaro did introduce a four-door Touring Sedan for 1990, though on a trimmer 116-inch wheelbase. Improbably, he claimed its body was molded directly from one of the old Loewy sedan mockups that had sat for years in the South Bend attic gathering dust and pigeon droppings. Though distinctive, the four-door wasn't as handsome as the classic coupe, but was definitely built better. High-tech composites replaced steel for its roof and (belatedly adopted) door beams, and Kevlar was substituted for fiberglass in floorpan, bumpers, and seatbelt and body mounts.

Cafaro's operation managed 150 Avantis in 1988 and some 350 in '89. Most were the standard coupe. The 1990 target was 500 cars, but actual output was much lower. There were heady plans for '91, including a switch to the 245-bhp Corvette L98 engine, plus a new chassis (engineered by Callaway Technologies) with all-independent suspension and the four-wheel disc brakes from Ford's Thunderbird Super Coupe. But these plans were derailed by a sharp recession that hurt sales industrywide. Instead of building its planned 1000 cars in '91, Avanti Automotive Corporation filed for bankruptcy. The firm produced only 15 cars that year, mostly convertibles with a few cosmetic changes and body-material substitutions like those on the sedan.

A postscript to the Cafaro bankruptcy concerns one Robert Lucarell, who stayed as caretaker for the Youngstown plant. Lucarell sold handfuls of assorted leftover parts to diehard owners, all the while insisting that the car and the company he loved would rise yet again. "Avanti is still a going business," he told Automotive News in May 1994. "I am here selling parts and helping people fix their cars over the telephone every day."

Among those customers was Jim Bunting, a retired advertising executive in Lancaster, Pennsylvania, who'd bought his first Avanti in the mid-'80s and became a fan. Bunting was intrigued by a two-seat Avanti drawn by the late Bob Andrews, a member of the Loewy team, and decided to build a real one. But no crude hatchet job would do, so he contacted Tom Kellogg, the team member who had done considerable detail work and most of the renderings for the Avanti project. Kellogg obliged with drawings of how the two-seater should look, but sent along a sketch with a playful note reading, "Let's do this one next." It showed a modernized Avanti of the sort Kellogg had been doodling for years, with the basic look evolved just as Studebaker might have done had it not folded.

Bunting loved Kellogg's "Avanti for the '90s," and decided to make it real. To keep costs reasonable, he started with a '94 Pontiac Firebird—a good choice, as its outer body panels were easily swapped for a new Avanti-look fiberglass skin custom-tailored by Kellogg. The transformation took place at the Harrisburg, Pennsylvania, shop of renowned hot-rod builder Bill Lang and was finished in January 1996. By that point, other people had seen the car and wanted one, too. Bunting then showed it—still in primer and a bit rough—at a major swap meet, where more favorable inquiries convinced him to offer copies. After further tweaks by Kellogg, the finished car was unveiled in June 1997 at the combined meet of the Studebaker and Avanti clubs. Because rights to the Avanti name were in limbo, the car was christened AVX—"AVanti eXperimental."

Incorporating AVX Cars in Lancaster, Bunting contracted with Lang's Custom Auto to convert post-'92 Firebirds at the rate of two a month. Initial price was $33,900, plus the donor coupe or convertible. Echoing Newman & Altman, AVX owners could have their car most anyway they liked. "Nothing is too outrageous," Bunting told Collectible Automobile® magazine. Ready-made packages were available: two for brakes, three for suspension, and four engine upgrades, including a Paxton-supercharged Corvette LS1 V-8 with 455 bhp up to an incredible 650.

The AVX was well-timed for the late-'90s luxury-car sales boom, but Bunting soon found that running a car company, even a tiny one, was more than he bargained for, and he decided to sell after building only a handful of AVXs. But the buyer was none other than Michael Kelly. No less surprising, the new owners also acquired the assets of all preceding Avanti companies, plus artifacts from Studebaker days and rights to the Avanti name and logo. In December 1999, Kelly announced the formation of a new Avanti Motor Corporation in tiny Villa Rica, Georgia. There, in a 74,000-square-foot former hosiery mill, up to 100 workers would convert Firebirds to the AVX design. Both the T-top coupe and convertible had a 320-bhp V-8, four-speed automatic or six-speed manual transmission, antilock brakes, all the regular Firebird features and, again, custom-built cachet. About 100 cars were sold in 2001. By 2002, production was expected to reach Kelly's goal of 150 units per year. A supercharger was available, adding $10,000 to the base price of $79,000 for the coupe and $83,000 for the convertible. With Firebird production ending with the 2002 model year, Avanti was developing its own platform for the 2004 AVX.

At least the Avanti survived into the 21st century, thanks to the never-say-die spirit of Jim Bunting, Tom Kellogg, and now Mike Kelly again. But can the old magic still cheat death in the future? Given the record, we wouldn't be surprised if it does.

## Specifications

### 1965
| (wb 109.0) | | Wght | Price | Prod |
|---|---|---|---|---|
| spt cpe | | 3,217 | 6,550 | 21 |

| 1965 Engine | bore × stroke | bhp | availability |
|---|---|---|---|
| V-8, 327.0 | 4.00 × 3.25 | 300 | S-all |

### 1966
| (wb 109.0) | | Wght | Price | Prod |
|---|---|---|---|---|
| spt cpe | | 3,181 | 7,200 | 98 |

| 1966 Engine | bore × stroke | bhp | availability |
|---|---|---|---|
| V-8, 327.0 | 4.00 × 3.25 | 300 | S-all |

### 1967
| (wb 109.0) | | Wght | Price | Prod |
|---|---|---|---|---|
| spt cpe | | 3,217 | 7,200 | 60 |

| 1967 Engine | bore × stroke | bhp | availability |
|---|---|---|---|
| V-8, 327.0 | 4.00 × 3.25 | 300 | S-all |

### 1968
| (wb 109.0) | | Wght | Price | Prod |
|---|---|---|---|---|
| spt cpe | | 3,217 | 6,645 | 89 |

| 1968 Engine | bore × stroke | bhp | availability |
|---|---|---|---|
| V-8, 327.0 | 4.00 × 3.25 | 300 | S-all |

### 1969
| (wb 109.0) | | Wght | Price | Prod |
|---|---|---|---|---|
| spt cpe | | 3,217 | 7,145 | 103 |

| 1969 Engines | bore × stroke | bhp | availability |
|---|---|---|---|
| V-8, 327.0 | 4.00 × 3.25 | 300 | S-all |
| V-8, 350.0 | 4.00 × 3.48 | 300 | O-all |

### 1970
| (wb 109.0) | | Wght | Price | Prod |
|---|---|---|---|---|
| spt cpe | | 3,342 | 7,500 | 111 |

| 1970 Engine | bore × stroke | bhp | availability |
|---|---|---|---|
| V-8, 350.0 | 4.00 × 3.48 | 300 | S-all |

### 1971
| (wb 109.0) | | Wght | Price | Prod |
|---|---|---|---|---|
| spt cpe | | 3,217 | 7,645 | 107 |

| 1971 Engine | bore × stroke | bhp | availability |
|---|---|---|---|
| V-8, 350.0 | 4.00 × 3.48 | 270 | S-all |

### 1972
| (wb 109.0) | | Wght | Price | Prod |
|---|---|---|---|---|
| spt cpe | | 3,217 | 8,145 | 127 |

| 1972 Engine | bore × stroke | bhp | availability |
|---|---|---|---|
| V-8, 400.0 | 4.13 × 3.75 | 270 | S-all |

### 1973
| (wb 109.0) | | Wght | Price | Prod |
|---|---|---|---|---|
| spt cpe | | 3,250 | 8,145 | 106 |

| 1973 Engine | bore × stroke | bhp | availability |
|---|---|---|---|
| V-8, 400.0 | 4.13 × 3.75 | — | S-all |

### 1974
| (wb 109.0) | | Wght | Price | Prod |
|---|---|---|---|---|
| spt cpe | | 3,250 | 8,645 | 123 |

| 1974 Engine | bore × stroke | bhp | availability |
|---|---|---|---|
| V-8, 400.0 | 4.13 × 3.75 | 180 | S-all |

### 1975
| (wb 109.0) | | Wght | Price | Prod |
|---|---|---|---|---|
| spt cpe | | 3,250 | 9,945 | 125 |

| 1975 Engine | bore × stroke | bhp | availability |
|---|---|---|---|
| V-8, 400.00 | 4.13 × 3.75 | 175 | S-all |

### 1976
| (wb 109.0) | | Wght | Price | Prod |
|---|---|---|---|---|
| spt cpe | | 3,500 | 12,195 | 175 |

# Avanti

| 1976 Engine | bore × stroke | bhp | availability |
|---|---|---|---|
| V-8, 400.0 | 4.13 × 3.75 | 175 | S-all |

## 1977
(wb 109.0)

| | Wght | Price | Prod |
|---|---|---|---|
| spt cpe | 3,500 | 13,195 | 180 |

| 1977 Engine | bore × stroke | bhp | availability |
|---|---|---|---|
| V-8, 350.0 | 4.00 × 3.48 | 180 | S-all |

## 1978
(wb 109.0)

| | Wght | Price | Prod |
|---|---|---|---|
| spt cpe | 3,500 | 15,980 | 190 |

| 1978 Engine | bore × stroke | bhp | availability |
|---|---|---|---|
| V-8, 350.0 | 4.00 × 3.48 | 180 | S-all |

## 1979
(wb 109.0)

| | Wght | Price | Prod |
|---|---|---|---|
| spt cpe | 3,570 | 17,670 | 195 |

| 1979 Engine | bore × stroke | bhp | availability |
|---|---|---|---|
| V-8, 350.0 | 4.00 × 3.48 | 185 | S-all |

## 1980
(wb 109.0)

| | Wght | Price | Prod |
|---|---|---|---|
| spt cpe | 3,570 | 18,995 | 190 |

| 1980 Engine | bore × stroke | bhp | availability |
|---|---|---|---|
| V-8, 350.0 | 4.00 × 3.48 | 190 | S-all |

## 1981
(wb 109.0)

| | Wght | Price | Prod* |
|---|---|---|---|
| spt cpe | 3,570 | 20,495 | 200 |

| 1981 Engine | bore × stroke | bhp | availability |
|---|---|---|---|
| V-8, 305.0 | 3.74 × 3.48 | 155 | S-all |

## 1982
(wb 109.0)

| | Wght | Price | Prod* |
|---|---|---|---|
| spt cpe | 3,570 | 22,995 | 200 |

| 1982 Engine | bore × stroke | bhp | availability |
|---|---|---|---|
| V-8, 305.0 | 3.74 × 3.48 | 155 | S-all |

*Calendar year figures (estimated)

## 1983
(wb 109.0)

| | Wght | Price | Prod |
|---|---|---|---|
| spt cpe | 3,690 | 24,995 | — |

| 1983 Engine | bore × stroke | bhp | availability |
|---|---|---|---|
| V-8, 305.0 | 3.74 × 3.48 | 155 | S-all |

## 1984
(wb 109.0)

| | Wght | Price | Prod |
|---|---|---|---|
| spt cpe | 3,680 | 31,860 | 287 |

| 1984 Engines | bore × stroke | bhp | availability |
|---|---|---|---|
| V-8, 305.0 | 3.74 × 3.48 | 155 | S-all |
| V-8, 305.0 | 3.74 × 3.48 | 190 | O-all |

## 1985
(wb 109.0)

| | Wght | Price | Prod |
|---|---|---|---|
| spt cpe | 3,680 | 37,995 | — |
| GT cpe | 3,210 | 37,995 | — |

| 1985 Engines | bore × stroke | bhp | availability |
|---|---|---|---|
| V-8, 305.0 | 3.74 × 3.48 | 190 | S-cpe |
| V-8, 305.0 | 3.74 × 3.48 | 205 | S-GT |

## 1987
(wb 109.0; luxury spt cpe 117.0)

| | Wght | Price | Prod |
|---|---|---|---|
| spt cpe | — | 29,995 | 300 (est.) |
| conv cpe | — | 39,995 | |
| luxury spt cpe | — | 55,900 | |

| 1987 Engine | bore × stroke | bhp | availability |
|---|---|---|---|
| V-8, 305.0 | 3.74 × 3.48 | 155 | S-all |

## 1988
(wb 109.0; luxury spt cpe 117.0)

| | Wght | Price | Prod |
|---|---|---|---|
| spt cpe | 3,750 | 35,000 | 150 (est.) |
| conv cpe | — | 45,000 | |
| luxury cpe | — | 53,000 | |

| 1988 Engines | bore × stroke | bhp | availability |
|---|---|---|---|
| V-8, 305.0 | 3.74 × 3.48 | 170 | S-all |
| V-8S, 305.0 | 3.74 × 3.48 | 250 | S-Silver Anniv, suprchrgd |

## 1989
(wb 109.0; luxury cpe 117.0)

| | Wght | Price | Prod |
|---|---|---|---|
| spt cpe | — | — | 350 (est.) |
| conv cpe | — | — | |
| luxury cpe | — | — | |

| 1989 Engine | bore × stroke | bhp | availability |
|---|---|---|---|
| V-8, 305.0 | 3.74 × 3.48 | — | S-all |

## 1990
(wb 109.0; sdn 116.0)

| | Wght | Price | Prod |
|---|---|---|---|
| spt cpe | — | — | — |
| conv cpe | — | — | — |
| sdn 4d | — | — | — |

| 1990 Engine | bore × stroke | bhp | availability |
|---|---|---|---|
| V-8, 305.0 | 3.74 × 3.48 | — | S-all |

## 1991
(wb 109.0)

| | Wght | Price | Prod |
|---|---|---|---|
| spt cpe | — | — | 15 |
| conv cpe | — | — | |

| 1991 Engine | bore × stroke | bhp | availability |
|---|---|---|---|
| V-8, 305.0 | 3.74 × 3.48 | — | S-all |

## 1998-99 AVX
(wb 101.1)

| | Wght | Price | Prod |
|---|---|---|---|
| T-top cpe | — | 33,900* | — |
| conv cpe | — | 33,900* | — |

| 1998-99 Engine | bore × stroke | bhp | availability |
|---|---|---|---|
| V-8, 350.0 | 4.00 × 3.48 | — | S-all |

* Requires donor Pontiac Firebird.

## 2001
(wb 101.1)

| | Wght | Price | Prod |
|---|---|---|---|
| T-top cpe | — | 69,000 | 100 (est.) |
| conv cpe | — | 83,000 | |

## 2002
(wb 101.1)

| | Wght | Price | Prod |
|---|---|---|---|
| T-top cpe | 3,640 | 79,000 | — |
| conv cpe | — | 83,000 | — |

| 2001-02 Engines | bore × stroke | bhp | availability |
|---|---|---|---|
| V-8, 350.0 | 4.00 × 3.48 | — | S-all |
| V-8S, 350.0 | 4.00 × 3.48 | — | O-all |

# Buick

David Dunbar Buick was a canny Scottish industrialist but an unlikely auto builder. After making his mark with a process for annealing porcelain to steel for bathtubs, he turned to the profit opportunities of the horseless-carriage phenomenon. His first car, appearing in 1903, was a simple little chain-drive runabout with flat-twin power. One engine feature, overhead valves, was a rarity then, but has been a hallmark of almost all Buicks since.

Soon prosperous, Buick Motor Company was one of the firms William C. Durant brought together to forge General Motors in 1908. Six-cylinder engines arrived in 1914, and were the only type Buick offered from 1925 to '30. By that point, Buick buyers were mostly upper middle-class professional types who'd moved up from a Chevrolet, Oakland, or Oldsmobile—hence the "doctor's car" sobriquet of the make's early years. The Depression considerably reduced the size of this clientele—and Buick sales—but the division would bounce back strongly, reaching fourth in industry production for model-year 1938 (from a decade-low seventh in 1934-36).

The decision to offer costlier eight-cylinder cars came before the Wall Street crash, so Buick's sales problems in the early '30s, stemmed mainly from bad timing. The 1930 line, for example, continued the bulged "pregnant" beltline styling that had been decidedly unpopular in 1929. Otherwise, they were conventional, arrayed in three series: the low-priced "40" on a 118-inch wheelbase, mid-range "50" on a 124-inch span, and deluxe "60" on a 132-inch chassis. All carried "valve-in-head" sixes, the last six-cylinder engines at Buick until the 1960s. The 40 used a 257.5-cubic-incher with 81 horsepower, the 50 and 60 a 331.3-cid engine with 99 bhp. The 50 offered just four-door sedan and four-place sport coupe; 40 and 60 listed a full range of models, some quite scarce (only 836 seven-seat Series 60 limousines, for instance). Despite the deepening Depression, Buick finished third in industry production for the model year, mainly because competitors fared far worse.

For 1931 came an expanded lineup powered by the first Buick eights, among the most-advanced engines of their day: smooth and reliable five-main-bearing units designed by division chief engineer F.A. Bower. They included a 77-bhp 220.7 for the 50, now the least-costly Buick; a 272.6 with 90 bhp for the 60, the new midranger; and a 104-bhp 344.8-cid engine for new top-echelon Series 80 and 90. The lengthened model roster again included sedans, coupes, phaetons, convertibles, and roadsters, plus Series 90 seven-seat sedan and limousine. The 50, which included a "second-series" group announced in early '31, rode the 114-inch wheelbase applied to the 1930 Marquette, Buick's short-lived junior make; 60, 80, and 90 spanned 118, 124, and 132 inches, respectively.

Straight eights would be Buick's mainstay for the next 22 years. The new 1931 engine proved its mettle at that year's Indianapolis 500 by powering a racer that Phil Shafer qualified at 105.1 mph; for the race he averaged 86.4 mph. Any '31 Buick was quick in showroom tune; 10-60 mph took about 25 seconds, quite speedy for the day, and 90 mph was possible.

The big news for 1932 was "Silent Second SynchroMesh" transmission, plus more horsepower for all engines. Power and most wheelbases went up again for 1933, but sales did not. As a partial consequence, Harlow H. Curtice was appointed Buick president in October that year.

Curtice believed in "more speed for less money," and backed it up with an all-new 117-inch-wheelbase Series 40 for 1934. The result was a sales upturn aided by more modern, streamlined styling that broke sharply with "Roaring '20s" squarishness. Also featured linewide was GM's new "Knee-Action" (Dubonnet-type) independent front suspension, then a great step forward. Though the 40 omitted flashy soft tops to emphasize far more popular coupes and sedans, its masterful blend of an inexpensive, Chevrolet-size platform and "important" Buick

**1930 Series 60 7-passenger sedan**

**1932 Series 90 sport phaeton**

**1931 Series 50 business coupe**

**1932 Series 90 convertible phaeton**

# Buick

1932 Series 60 business coupe

1933 Series 60 Victoria coupe

styling helped boost the division's 1934 output from some 47,000 to over 71,000. Buick then jumped way over 100,000 for model-year '36, and would reach even greater heights a few years hence.

Also in 1934, Curtice launched a $64 million factory modernization program that wasn't completed until 1940. However, plowing receipts back into facilities left little money for product improvements, so the 1935 Buicks weren't changed much. Offerings again comprised 40, 50, 60, and 90 with straight eights of 233, 235, 278, and 344 cid, respectively. There was one belated addition, though: a Series 40 convertible coupe.

More extensive changes occurred for 1936, as Buick adopted GM's all-steel "Turret Top" construction that eliminated the traditional fabric roof insert, gaining sleek all-new styling with it. The division also boasted more-potent engines with aluminum pistons. Series numbers began giving way to names that would last all the way through 1958—from the bottom, Special (40), Century (60), Roadmaster (80), and Limited (90). Respective wheelbases were 118, 122, 131, and 138 inches.

Styling was a big factor in Buick's 1936 resurgence. It was, of course, the work of Harley J. Earl, founder and head of GM's Art & Colour Section, the first formal styling department at a major automaker. Earl liked streamlining, and Buick had it for '36. Lines were rounder than ever, set off by more swept-back windshields, fully integrated trunks (instead of separate, detachable fixtures), and massive vertical-bar grilles. The public responded to this package by buying over 168,000 Buicks for the model year. Calendar-1936 production reached near 180,000 as division volume returned to its pre-Depression level.

Engines choices were reduced for '36 from four to just two. Special retained its 93-bhp 233-cid eight. Other '36s carried a new 320-cid unit with 120 bhp. The latter would be a Buick mainstay through the '50s. Putting it in the lighter Special body made the new '36 Century a fast car, with genuine 100-mph top speed and 10-60 acceleration of 18-19 seconds. Besides good performance and sleek good looks, Century was attractively priced: as little as $1035 for the sport coupe and $1135 for the rakish convertible. It quickly became known as a "factory hot rod" (arguably Detroit's first)—about the fastest thing you could buy for $1000 or so.

Such triumphs didn't imply much change for 1937. But Harley Earl wasn't satisfied, so Flint's Turret-Tops gained longer fenders with blunt trailing edges, plus horizontal grille bars and complementing side hood vents. Buick was perhaps GM's best-looking '37 car, and still an industry style-setter.

Mechanically, the bigger eight returned unchanged, but a longer stroke boosted Special's engine to 248 cid, horsepower to an even 100. Factory figures suggested a '37 Special could

1934 Series 60 convertible coupe

1937 Series 60 Century two-door sedan

1936 Series 60 Roadmaster four-door sedan

1938 Series 90 Limited 8-passenger sedan

# Buick

1939 Series 40 Special convertible coupe

1940 Series 40 Special convertible coupe

1940 Series 60 Century sport coupe

1941 Series 40A Special sport coupe

1941 Series 90 Limited limousine

1941 Series 60 Century business coupe

scale 10-60 mph in 19.2 seconds—fine performance for the class and only a second behind the hot Century. New for all '37s were hypoid rear axle, improved generator, standard windshield defroster, front/rear antiroll bars, and a claimed industry first: a steering-wheel horn ring (Cord introduced it in '36).

The top-line Limited became almost Cadillac-exclusive in 1936-37, so it's puzzling they'd be long overlooked as collector's items. All late-'30s Limiteds were of "trunkback" configuration and carried dual spare tires in long "pontoon" front fenders. The elegant formal sedan of 1936-37 came with a glass division between front and rear compartments, plus the expected grand luxe trim. Through 1939, the series included six- and eight-passenger sedans and a limousine. Limited chassis were supplied in fair numbers to custom coachbuilders such as Eureka, Miller, Sayers & Scoville, and Flexible for hearse, ambulance, and flower-car applications.

A new grille with fewer but thicker horizontal bars was the chief styling cue for 1938, but more mechanical changes made a good car even better. All-coil suspension—another Buick first—delivered a much-improved ride, aided by shock absorbers four times the typical size. Domed, high-compression pistons boosted horsepower on both engines, now dubbed "Dynaflash." A new item for Special was a five-speed semi-automatic transmission, though it proved troublesome and was dropped after one year. Flint wouldn't attempt another clutchless drive until fully automatic Dynaflow about a decade later.

Buick by now had expanded to encompass a broad market. Prices ranged from $945 for the 1938 Special business coupe to near $2500 for the opulent eight-passenger Limited limo. For big spenders, Brunn still offered custom-bodied Limiteds, though far fewer than in the halcyon pre-Depression days.

Flint closed out the decade with lower-looking 1939 models mildly face-lifted with "waterfall" grilles, "streamboards" (optional concealed running boards), and a sunroof option on some models. Sidemount spares were still available, but not as frequently ordered. Special's 122-inch wheelbase (from 1937-38) shrank two inches. Other spans were unchanged from '38: 126-inch Century, 133-inch Roadmaster, 140-inch Limited. Body choices were as plentiful as ever, prices as moderate. The natty Century convertible sport phaeton sold for just $1713, the sport coupe for $1175. Buick abandoned the increasingly unpopular rumble-seat ragtop for '39, but scored a safety innovation with flashing turn signals, installed at the rear as part of the trunk emblem. Also new were column-mounted gearshift and refillable shock absorbers.

Buick's buyers were quite loyal, and in the '40s the division would be GM's number-two seller, after Chevrolet. Throughout the decade, Buick usually ran fourth behind the "Low-Price Three" (Chevy, Ford, Plymouth), building upwards of 300,000 cars a year. GM endured an extended strike after World War II and Flint took awhile to regain momentum, but was back to over 324,000 cars for 1949. Buicks of the '40s reflected the division's period slogan "Valve in Head—Ahead in Value": big but reasonably priced cars that were a bit ostentatious. For those who felt status was everything, there was always Cadillac.

The early-'40s lineup was one of the widest in Buick history and wouldn't be matched until the mid '50s. Model groups expanded from four to six for 1940 with the addition of the Series 50 Super (another enduring name). It bowed with fewer models than the Special priced just below it, but included a handsome wood-bodied Estate wagon. Super and Special both rode a 121-inch wheelbase and carried the respected 248-cid straight eight, still with 107 bhp (as since 1938). Priced above them—and still with the brawny 320.2-cid eight—were Century (60) and Roadmaster (now Series 70) on 126-inch chassis, plus

# Buick

**1942 Series 40B Special four-door sedan**

**1942 Series 40A Special convertible coupe**

**1942 Series 40 Special station wagon**

**1946 Series 40 Special sedanet**

**1946 Roadmaster four-door sedan**

**1947 Special Sedanet fastback**

**1947 Roadmaster convertible coupe**

**1948 Super four-door station wagon**

two Limited lines: 133-inch-wheelbase Series 80 and 140-inch Series 90 (the latter confined to long sedans and limousines).

Buick again cataloged several interesting wares for 1940, but some were in their last season. Low sales had been thinning the ranks of convertible sedans. This year saw the final Century model; Super and Roadmaster versions would run one year more. "Streamlined Sedans" with fastback styling reminiscent of the Lincoln-Zephyr saw just 14 copies in the Series 80. More popular was the $1952 Series 80 convertible sedan (phaeton) with conventional lines, though only 250 were called for. Custom styles were still around, but not as "factory" models. One rakish town car by Brewster on the Series 90 chassis would be the first Buick named a "Classic" by the Classic Car Club of America. Buffalo's Brunn was also still doing customs in 1940, including one fairly conventional town car on the Roadmaster platform.

Flint had a banner 1941, with model-year production soaring to 374,000. Leading that year's line were beautiful and opulent Brunn customs on the Limited chassis: phaeton, town car, landau brougham, and full landau. Most flamboyant was the convertible coupe, offered to dealers for $3500. At that price, only the prototype sold, but it was significant for a "sweep-spear" side motif that prefigured a postwar Buick hallmark.

Among production '41s, the two Limited lines were combined into a single Series 90 on a 139-inch wheelbase. Century was shorn of its convertible, convertible sedan, and club coupe. The Estate wagon shifted from Super to Special but cost some $200 more than in 1940. Reflecting its strong sales, Special split into two subseries: 121-inch-wheelbase 40 and 118-inch 40A. Styling was evolutionary, with a bolder, heavier grille and revised "ports" on the hood sides. A new idea was the fastback, offered in Century and 40 Special trim as a four-door touring

# Buick

1949 Roadmaster convertible coupe

1949 Super Sedanet fastback

1949 Roadmaster Riviera hardtop coupe

1949 Roadmaster four-door sedan

sedan and two-door business coupe and sedanet. A clean break with the "trunkback" era, it had great buyer appeal. The Special touring sedan alone sold over 100,000.

The 1941 Special/Super engine gained new-design high-compression pistons for more-efficient combustion that lifted horsepower to 115. Available for the 40 touring sedan and sedanet was "Compound Carburetion"—two carburetors with a progressive linkage that added 10 bhp. This was standard on other '41s, resulting in 165 bhp for the 320 engine. Chassis were carryovers for all but Limited, which used a new X-member design.

World War II came at precisely the wrong time for Buick, which completely restyled for 1942 a la Harley Earl's 1939 "Y-Job" show car. The result was Flint's sleekest cars ever, with a wide, low, vertical-bar grille theme that would continue postwar. Fastback "torpedo" styling was more popular than ever. Century, which would go into postwar limbo until 1954, was down to only two models, both fastbacks. Their Special counterparts continued to dominate sales of that two-series line (realigned into 40A and 40B on 118- and 121-inch wheelbases, respectively). Two-door sedanets were new for Super and Roadmaster. Most '42 Buicks wore Earl's new "Airfoil" front fenders swept back through almost the entire length of the car to meet the rear-fender leading edges. Limiteds and Specials lacked this, but had front fenders extended well into the doors.

As elsewhere in Detroit, Buicks built after January 1, 1942, used painted metal instead of chromed parts per government order. For the same reason, Specials and Supers exchanged aluminum pistons for cast-iron slugs. This, plus lowered compression, dropped horsepower to 110 (118 with Compound Carburetion). Production ground to a halt in early February after some 92,000 units, and wouldn't begin again until October 1945.

But thanks to its '42 redesign, Buick resumed civilian production in fine fettle. While nearly all makes were forced to issue warmed-over prewar models, Flint's styling was technically but a year old in 1945, and thus still fairly fresh. Packard, by contrast, returned with the two-year-old styling of its very handsome 1941-42 Clipper, then felt obliged to undertake a severe facelift for 1948. Buick stretched its '42 tooling through the 1949 Special, then came back with a brand-new Special for 1950. (One year can make a big difference in the car business.) Exotic customs did not return; they simply weren't needed. A mere 2482 Buicks were built in the closing months of 1945, but output surged to more than 153,000 for model-year '46.

While the first postwar Buicks were basically '42s, there were fewer of them: Special, Super, and Roadmaster sedans and sedanets; Super and Roadmaster convertibles; Super Estate wagon; no Centurys or Limiteds; only one Special series. Styling was cleaned up via single instead of double side moldings, simpler grille, and the first of Buick's distinctive "gunsight" hood ornaments. Wheelbases were 121 inches for Special (as for 1942's Series 40B), 124 for Super, 129 for Roadmaster. Compound Carburetion didn't return either, so Special/Super remained at 110 bhp. This array of models, wheelbases, and engines would endure through 1948 with only minor changes.

Appearance alterations were also minor through '48, as GM was planning its first all-postwar models for 1949. The '47s gained a "wing-top" grille conferring a lower look; a new, more-elaborate crest appeared above it. The only changes for '48 were full-length belt moldings on Specials and chrome fender nameplates on Super/Roadmaster.

But Flint made big news for '48 with Dynaflow, its excellent new fully automatic transmission, arriving as a $244 option for Roadmaster only. Demand for this torque-converter unit proved so strong that Buick had to double planned installations. By 1951, Dynaflow was ordered by 85 percent of Buick buyers.

The all-new '49 models swelled Buick volume to 324,276 units—again right behind Chevy-Ford-Plymouth. These were sleek and graceful cars next to the 1946-48s, and reviewers agreed they were worth the great attention they got. Harley Earl's team successfully translated aircraft themes to an automobile, and only a hint of the old separate rear fenders remained on Super and Roadmaster. Also new was the first of Buick's trademark "portholes" or "VentiPorts," an idea from designer Ned Nickles.

Buick's most eye-catching '49 was the Roadmaster Riviera, introduced at midyear along with Cadillac's Coupe de Ville and Oldsmobile's Holiday. As Detroit's first modern mass-produced "hardtop convertibles," they began a trend that would eventu-

55

# Buick

1950 Roadmaster Riviera four-door sedan

1950 Special Jetback fastback sedan

1950 Super Riviera hardtop coupe

1951 Super four-door sedan

ally render real convertibles obsolete. The '49 Riviera was a handsome, luxurious brute with a beautiful pillarless roofline. It was sold with either conventional straight side moldings or "sweep-spear" trim, soon to join VentiPorts as a make trademark.

With the main emphasis on styling, the '49 Buicks changed little mechanically, though Dynaflow-equipped Supers got higher, 6.9:1 compression that improved horsepower to 120. Roadmaster had been similarly raised to 150 in 1948, and continued that way with Dynaflow standard. Body styles stayed the same, save the new hardtop. The woody wagon was reworked to fit '49 styling, but sales remained modest. Roadmaster was put on a 126-inch wheelbase and Super reassigned to the 121-inch Special chassis.

Buick would maintain this basic lineup through 1953. All 1950 models, Special now included, wore a new look dominated by big, "toothy" vertical-bar grilles and fuller body contours. This, too, would persist through '53. Specials also received a half-inch longer wheelbase. Though still attractively priced, the 1950s were a bit utilitarian. Offerings comprised standard and DeLuxe fastback and "Touring" notchback four-doors, fastback sedanet coupe, and a revived business coupe. With fastbacks quickly falling from buyer favor, the Special sedanet was Buick's only "jetback" for '51, when the Special received a Riviera hardtop, as had the Super for 1950.

The Riviera name also graced well-proportioned 1950-51 Super and Roadmaster four-door sedans with special long wheelbases (130.3 and 125.5 inches, respectively). Both lines also included woody Estate wagons through '53, with structural body parts of mahogany and white ash. These were big and expensive. The '53 Roadmaster Estate cost a hefty $4031 and weighed 4315 pounds.

Super was Buick's volume seller in the early '50s, offering standard and Riviera sedans, a convertible, Riviera hardtop and the Estate, plus a 1950 sedanet and a handful of notchback '52 two-door sedans. Roadmaster styles essentially duplicated these.

All 1950-52 Buicks and the '53 Special continued to rely on aging but proven valve-in-head straight eights. Displacement, compression, and power varied with model and year. The 1950 Special engine delivered 115 bhp (120 bhp with Dynaflow) from its usual 248 cid. Supers and 1951-53 Specials offered up to 130 bhp from a bored-out 263.3-cid version. Roadmasters still used the 320, which was bumped up for '52 from 152 to 170 bhp.

Dynaflow (some called it "Dyna-slush") had been an increasingly popular Super/Special option since 1950 (it remained standard on Roadmaster). It multiplied torque via a drive turbine induced to rotate through an oil bath by a facing crankshaft-driven turbine. Dynaflow was smooth, but gave poor performance. The successor Twin-Turbine Dynaflow of 1953 was more positive and gave better oomph. By decade's end an even better Triple-Turbine transmission was offered across the board at $296 extra. But no Dynaflow could deliver acceleration like the Cadillac/Oldsmobile Hydra-Matic, and was thus

1951 Roadmaster Riviera four-door sedan

1951 Roadmaster four-door station wagon

# Buick

handicapped in the burgeoning '50s "horsepower race."

Golden Anniversary 1953 brought first-time availability of power steering and a 12-volt electrical system, but the highlight was a fine new overhead-valve V-8 for Super and Roadmaster. An oversquare design of 322 cid, this "Fireball" engine packed up to 188 bhp on industry-topping 8.5:1 compression. Roadmasters were demoted to a 121.5-inch wheelbase save the Riviera sedan, which shared the Super's 125.5-inch span.

Also highlighting Buick's 50th year was a flashy new limited-edition Roadmaster convertible. Called Skylark, it was perfect for Hollywood types and Texas oil barons. Only 1690 were sold that year, largely because of the extraordinary $5000 price.

Skylark was another of those long-famous Harley Earl styling projects, but was planned for the broadest possible appeal. Instead of being a two-seat sports car—which accounted for only 0.27 percent of the '53 market—it was a luxurious and sporty "personal" four-seater similar to Ford's post-1957 Thunderbirds. Like 1953's corresponding Olds Fiesta and Cadillac Eldorado, Skylark was basically a customized standard convertible, with four-inch lower windshield and top, plus fully radiused rear wheel cutouts. Though bereft of the trademark portholes, it sported Kelsey-Hayes chrome wire wheels, then becoming fashionable throughout Detroit.

Along with Olds and Cadillac, Buick switched to longer, more-massively square bodies for 1954, but also revived its prewar "hot rod" with a new Century line offering the bigger Buick engine in the smaller Buick body. All models wore inverted-U grilles with fine vertical bars set under oval nacelles cradling headlamps and parking lamps. Windshields were newly wrapped as on recent GM showmobiles, and rear fenders kicked up to carry vertical pairs of bullet taillamps high in the trailing edges. Offerings regrouped to include convertibles, hardtops, and sedans in each series. Century and Special also offered new all-steel four-door Estate wagons (remarkably with no ersatz wood). A two-door sedan was exclusive to Special, and was the price-leader at $2207.

Special belatedly received its own Fireball V-8 for '54, a 264-cid unit with 143/150 bhp. Other models carried the 322 with power ratings of 177 (manual-shift Super) to 200 (Roadmaster and Skylark). Wheelbases were realigned once more: 122 inches for Special/Century, 127 for Super/Roadmaster.

Skylark also returned for '54, but was much less "custom" than the '53, though that enabled Buick to trim price down to $4483. Now more Century than Roadmaster, the '54 stood apart with tacked-on tailfins and huge chrome-plated diecast taillight housings, plus the circular rear wheel openings. Overall, it somewhat resembled Buick's '54 Wildcat II show car, but was evidently less-impressive than the '53 Skylark, for only 836 were sold before the model was dropped.

Much of Buick's 1954 styling was previewed by the XP-300 and 1951 LeSabre show cars, rolling testbeds for numerous postwar GM ideas. Both used an experimental 215-cid aluminum V-8, a very special job unrelated to Buick's same-size early-'60s engine. With exactly square dimensions (3.25-inch bore and stroke), 10:1 compression, and a Roots-type supercharger, it produced over 300 bhp—phenomenal for the day. However, it ran on a methanol/gasoline blend, not exactly common at local filling stations. Both showpieces were futuristic. The 116-inch-wheelbase LeSabre sported a wrapped windshield and "Dagmar" bumpers. The XP-300, on an inch-shorter wheelbase, prefigured production '54 Buicks in its frontal treatment.

Speaking of production, Buick had been pushing relentlessly toward number-three, breaking its all-time record in calendar 1950 with more than 550,000 cars. The 1954 tally of 531,000 left Buick trailing only Chevrolet and Ford, a position it hadn't held since the '40s. The division's 1955 volume was another record:

1951 Super Jetback fastback coupe

1952 Special sport coupe

1952 Roadmaster convertible coupe

1953 Roadmaster four-door station wagon

781,000, nearly 50 percent higher than the previous best.

This success was owed largely to the Special, which had become one of America's most popular cars. Over 380,000 were built for 1955, Detroit's banner year of the decade, including 155,000 Riviera two-door hardtops, that season's single best-selling Buick. A deft '55 restyle kept sales booming, aided by even-more-potent V-8s delivering 188 bhp on Specials, 236 bhp elsewhere. For mid-'55 came four-door Riviera hardtop sedans in the Special and Century series; Super and Roadmaster versions followed for '56. These (along with the Oldsmobile Holiday) were the first four-door hardtops, GM once again forcing the rest of the industry to play catch-up.

The '56 Buicks didn't sell as well as the '55s—but then, '56 was a "breather" for most everyone. Another facelift introduced model-year designation to exterior nameplates, which

57

# Buick

1954 Wildcat II show car

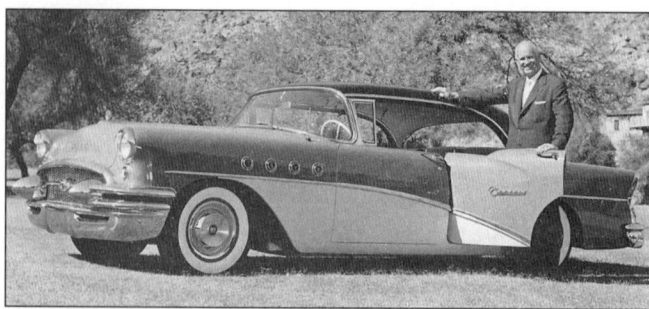
1955 Century Riviera hardtop sedan

1953 Roadmaster Riviera hardtop sedan

1956 Roadmaster Riviera hardtop sedan

1954 Roadmaster Riviera four-door sedan

1956 Roadmaster four-door sedan

1954 Century four-door sedan

1956 Special Riviera hardtop sedan

Buick would abandon after 1957 amid customer complaints that it made the cars obsolete that much sooner. The "horsepower race" was at full gallop, and the '56s were the most-powerful Buicks yet. The Special now offered 220 bhp, other models 255. A Century could leap from 0-60 mph in 10.5 seconds and top 110 mph, and every '56 Buick could do at least 100 mph.

Longer and lower new bodies arrived for '57 wearing slightly exaggerated '56 styling. Though division general manager Ed Ragsdale never said how much this makeover cost, it must have run several hundred million. Yet despite the most-sweeping alterations since '49, Buick's '57s didn't sell that well, mainly because rivals were pressing hard for industry design leadership. Chrysler, in fact, took over with its new fleet of longer, lower, glassier, and tailfinned cars created under Virgil Exner.

Still, Flint's '57s were dashing and fairly clean for the age. And horsepower was higher still: 250 for Special, an even 300 elsewhere, thanks to a bore/stroke job taking V-8 displacement to 364 cubes. Model changes were few but interesting: pillarless four-door wagons for Century and Special, plus a Series 75 Roadmaster Riviera hardtop coupe and sedan. The latter, just upmarket versions of the regular Series 70 models, had every possible standard luxury save air conditioning: Dynaflow, power steering and brakes, dual exhausts, automatic windshield washers, backup lights, clock, special interior with deep-pile carpeting, and more. But though 1957 was a decent year for Buick, it was even better for Plymouth, which pushed Flint from third to fourth in sales for the first time in three years.

Sales were far worse for 1958, notable for the gaudiest

# Buick

1957 Super Riviera hardtop sedan

1957 Century Caballero hardtop station wagon

1957 Century Riviera hardtop coupe

1957 Roadmaster convertible coupe

1958 Century convertible coupe

Buicks ever. From contrived chrome-draped fins to a monster grille holding 160 shiny little squares, Flint's "B-58" models looked overtly ornate—especially the heroically over-decorated Limited, newly revived: The '58s were also the fattest Buicks since the war—some 400 pounds heavier than the 1950s and three to four inches longer than the '57s—so performance suffered with unchanged horsepower.

No '58 Buick sold well, though the year's flash recession was as much to blame as the garish styling. Model-year production stopped at some 240,000, and Flint dropped behind Olds to fifth in sales. Air suspension was offered, but seldom ordered. In all, '58 was a very bad year for Buick.

So was 1959. But where the '58s were ostentatious, the '59s were tasteful. Though again dominated by omnipresent tailfins—bigger than ever now, and newly canted—the '59s were smooth, clean, and fairly dignified, with huge windshields, fewer chrome grille squares—and no sweep-spears. Buick now shared corporate A- and B-bodies with sister GM makes, but it wasn't obvious. Nor was the fact that '59 styling was a hasty reply to Chrysler's successful '57s. But thank goodness for it. Original '59 plans called for face-lifted '58s, which were gruesome.

For the first time in two decades, Buick retitled its series for '59. Special became LeSabre, Invicta replaced Century, and Super and Roadmaster were now Electra and Electra 225. The last two rode a 126.3-inch wheelbase, trimmed 1.2 inches from 1957-58. LeSabre/Invicta shared a 123-inch chassis and Special/Century body styles save hardtop wagons, which were dropped due to low sales. Electras were priced quite a bit lower than counterpart '58s, spanning a $3800-$4300 range. Buick was called 1959's most-changed car, and the changes were for the better.

On the mechanical side, 1959 brought a new 401-cid V-8 with 325 bhp for the upper three series; LeSabre stayed with the last Special's 364. Power brakes and steering were standard on Electras, a $150 option elsewhere. Air conditioning was $430 across the board. Air suspension (for the rear only) was still nominally available—and still almost never ordered due to unresolved reliability problems.

Significantly, Buick dealers sold more Opels than ever in '59. The "captive import" from GM's German subsidiary had been assigned to Buick in '58, and soon nabbed a fair number of customers weary of oversized, overweight cars. But Buick was already planning its own compact, and its star would rise again.

Indeed, Buick volume soared from about 250,000 cars and ninth place in 1960 to more than 665,000 and a tight hold on fifth by '69. This success was due partly to the advent of compacts and partly to increased demand for traditional Buicks. Electra sales, for instance, were only some 56,000 in 1960 but nearly 159,000 by '69. Corresponding LeSabre figures were about 152,000 and nearly 198,000. Wildcat, which replaced Invicta for '63, began at about 35,000 but was almost double that by decade's end.

The aforementioned compact appeared for 1961 as the smallest Buick in 50 years. Reviving the Special name, it was one of three "second-wave" GM compacts—the Buick-Olds-Pontiac models that followed Chevy's Corvair (and borrowed some of its body engineering). Riding a 112-inch wheelbase, Special offered base and DeLuxe coupe, sedan, and four-door wagon in the $2300-$2700 range. All carried a new 215-cid aluminum-block V-8 with 155 bhp—light, smooth, and efficient. (Amazingly, production lasted into the 21st century. GM sold manufacturing rights to Rover, which used it in Rover cars and Land Rover utility vehicles beginning in the late '60s.)

Responding quickly to the sporty-car craze begun by the 1960 Corvair Monza, Buick fielded a more special Special DeLuxe coupe for mid '61. This one resurrected another familiar name: Skylark. No-cost bucket seats, optional vinyl roof, and a 185-

# Buick

1958 Century Caballero hardtop station wagon

1960 Electra 225 hardtop sedan

1960 Electra 225 Riviera hardtop sedan

1960 Invicta hardtop coupe

bhp V-8 helped sell more than 12,000 in that short debut season. For 1962 came Skylark and Special DeLuxe convertibles, an optional Borg-Warner four-speed gearbox—and more than 42,000 Buick compact sales.

The big Buicks changed dramatically after the 1960 models, which were basically toned-down '59s. The '61s rode unchanged wheelbases but weighed 100-200 pounds less, looked much cleaner, and boasted fewer gimmicks. For 1962, Buick unleashed the Wildcat as a specialty Invicta: a two-ton, 123-inch-wheelbase luxury hardtop priced around $4000 and sporting bucket seats, vinyl roof, and unique exterior badging. First-

1961 Electra 225 convertible coupe

1961 Invicta hardtop coupe

year sales were so good that Wildcat replaced Invicta on all midrange senior Buicks for '63 save a single wagon (fewer than 3500 sold), after which the Invicta name disappeared.

As noted, the premium Electras attracted increased sales right away. Two series continued for 1960-61: standard Electra and the posher Electra 225, named for its overall length in inches and soon popularly known as the "Deuce-and-a-Quarter." This setup didn't last, however, as all Electras became 225s for '62. Buick then concentrated on fewer offerings. Electra's standard engine through 1966 was a 325-bhp 401 V-8. A bored-out 425 with 340/360 bhp became optionally available by 1964. Both then gave way to a standard 430 with 360 horses.

Buick styling wasn't exceptional in this decade, with one singular exception: the new-for-'63 Riviera (recycling yet another well-known Flint moniker). This svelte personal-luxury hardtop coupe changed Buicks' stodgy image almost overnight. Many people felt that GM styling chief William L. Mitchell (who'd succeeded Harley Earl on his retirement back in '58) had fathered one of the best automotive shapes of all time.

This new Riviera was first conceived as a LaSalle, reviving Cadillac's lower-priced nameplate of 1927-40. (It wasn't the first attempt. Buick head designer Ned Nickles had penned an experimental "LaSalle II" roadster and hardtop sedan for the 1955 Motorama, both with trademark vertical-themed grille.) The impetus was Ford's highly successful four-seat Thunderbird that bowed for 1958. At one time, a convertible, four-door hardtop, and even a convertible sedan were considered. Ultimately, the hardtop-coupe clay model approved in early 1961 was assigned to Buick to give it a shot in the sales arm. Not that there was much choice. Cadillac didn't have facilities to build the car (and didn't need it), Chevrolet was enjoying record sales, and Oldsmobile and Pontiac had other fish to fry.

Mitchell freely admitted to borrowing some of the '63 Riviera's design elements. Its razor-edge roof styling, for instance, was inspired by certain 1950s English custom bodywork. But the finished product was handsome and individual. As scheduled, model-year production was exactly 40,000.

Riding a 117-inch wheelbase, Riviera was about 14 inches

# Buick

1961 Special DeLuxe four-door sedan

1962 Invicta Estate wagon

1962 Special Skylark hardtop coupe

1962 Electra 225 hardtop coupe

1962 Invicta Wildcat hardtop sport coupe

1963 Electra 225 hardtop sedan

1963 Wildcat hardtop sedan

1963 Riviera hardtop coupe

shorter and 200-300 pounds lighter than other big '63 Buicks. At first, Electra's 325-bhp 401 V-8 was standard and the new 340-bhp 425 optional, but the latter became base power for '64, when optional horses increased to 360. Standard two-speed Turbine Drive was used for '63, three-speed Hydra-Matic thereafter. Handling was up to performance, which was strong. The typical 325-bhp Riv ran the quarter-mile in 16 seconds at 85 mph; a 360-bhp car managed 15.5 seconds and 90-plus mph.

For 1964, Buick joined Olds and Pontiac in offering larger, restyled compacts with GM's new midsize A-body platform, also used by Chevy's new Chevelle. Wheelbase stretched to 120 inches on wagons and 115 inches for other body styles. There were new engines, too: a 225-cid V-6 (a novelty for Detroit) with 155 bhp, and a cast-iron 300-cid V-8 with 210/250 bhp. With that, the plush Skylark rapidly became the most-popular smaller Buick. Skylark/Special production was about 9-to-10 for '64, but Skylark had reached a near 5-to-1 ratio by 1969.

Flint's 1964 standards were longer overall but unchanged in wheelbase. The compacts' new 300 V-8 became base LeSabre power. Like the Century of yore, Wildcat was the division's hot rod, carrying the Electra 401 in the lighter, shorter LeSabre chassis. Reflecting its popularity, a four-door sedan joined the convertible and two hardtops that year. All '64 seniors retained their '63 look, but with corners and edges rounded off. Riviera was little changed, but production dropped by about 2500 units.

The division's 1965 production was 50 percent above its 1960 total, putting Buick fifth in the annual industry race. An expanded lineup in general and the unique Riviera in particular were responsible, but so was a very strong overall market that bought Detroit cars in record numbers: over 9.3 million for the calendar year, the best since '55.

Like everyone else in 1965, Buick proliferated trim and model variations so buyers could virtually custom-build their cars. That year's junior line comprised V-6 and V-8 Skylarks and standard and DeLuxe Specials priced from about $2350 to $3000, plus V-8 Special "Sportwagons" in the $3000-$3200 range.

# Buick

**1963 LeSabre convertible coupe**

**1964 Wildcat hardtop sport coupe**

**1964 LeSabre hardtop sedan**

**1964 Riviera hardtop coupe**

**1964 Special Skylark convertible coupe**

**1965 Wildcat hardtop sport coupe**

**1965 LeSabre four-door sedan**

**1965 Electra 225 sport coupe hardtop**

Wildcat returned with three body types in standard, DeLuxe, and Custom trim, plus DeLuxe and Custom convertibles. LeSabre and Electra 225 offered the same in standard and Custom versions. At $4440 base, the Electra 225 Custom convertible was the priciest '65 Buick, with the elegant Riviera close behind at $4408. Engine assignments stood pat. Riviera gained added distinction via hidden headlights, the four beams moving from the main grille to stack vertically behind front-fender subgrilles reworked into "clamshells." Taillights moved down into the rear bumper.

A memorable new option arrived for '65: the Gran Sport package for Riviera and Skylark. It delivered some $250 worth of performance goodies, including oversize tires, Super-Turbine 300 automatic, and Wildcat 401 V-8. The Skylark Gran Sport was every inch a grand tourer, though it was really Buick's "muscle car" reply to Pontiac's hot-selling year-old GTO. The Riviera GS was even grander in its way, capable of 125 mph flat out. Motor Trend magazine said it "goes and handles better than before, and that's quite an improvement."

The big attraction for 1966 was a second-generation Riviera, a cousin to that year's new E-body front-drive Olds Toronado. The Riv retained rear drive and looked much more massive than the crisp 1963-65, yet wheelbase was only two inches longer. More-curvaceous contours, wide hidden-headlamp grille, and a sleek semifastback roof with vestiges of the previous razor edges made it impressive to the eye. Yet it sold for only about $4400, which today seems unbelievably low. Other '66 Buicks were mainly carryovers, but a stroked 340 version of the 300 V-8 was made standard for LeSabres and Skylark Sportwagons.

Modestly redone grilles, side trim, and taillights were again the principal alterations for '67 juniors, but that year's seniors got new GM B- and C-bodies with flowing semifastback profiles on hardtop coupes and more voluptuous lines everywhere else. Identifying the '67 Riviera was a horizontal-crossbar grille and revamped parking lights.

Specials and Skylarks continued with the 225 V-6 and 300/340

# Buick

1965 Electra 225 convertible coupe

1966 LeSabre four-door sedan

1966 Riviera hardtop coupe

1967 Skylark GS 400 hardtop sport coupe

1967 Electra 225 hardtop coupe

V-8s for '67, but a new 430 V-8—Buick's biggest engine—was now standard for Wildcat, Electra, and Riviera. Though no more potent than the 425, it was smoother and quieter. A new Special/Skylark option was a cast-iron 400, a bored-and-stroked 340. This formed the heart of a new Skylark subseries called GS 400 offering convertible, two-door hardtop, and pillared coupe with handling suspension, bucket seats, and other sporty touches. A similar hardtop with the 340 engine bowed as the GS 340. Model-year sales were excellent, exceeding 560,000.

Skylark sold in record numbers for 1968, partly because Specials were trimmed to just three DeLuxe models. Like other '68 GM intermediates, junior Buicks adopted a new "split-wheelbase" A-body making for 112-inch Special/Skylark two-doors, 116-inch Special four-doors and DeLuxe wagons, and 121-inch Sportwagons (versus 120 inches in 1964-67). The hot GS 400 returned minus coupe, while GS 340 gave way to a GS 350 with a bored 350-cid V-8 packing 280 bhp. A 230-bhp version was a new Special/Skylark option and standard for Sportwagon, Skylark Custom, and LeSabres; all these offered the tuned unit at extra cost. The 225 V-6 gave way to a Chevy-built 250 inline six with lower compression, reflecting 1968's new federal emissions rules.

Like the '67s, the big '68 Buicks had side sculpturing (traced with moldings on some models) recalling the '50s "sweepspear," plus divided grilles, big bumpers, and, new that season, hidden wipers. The rebodied midsizers wore similar down-sloped side "character" lines, plus new grilles, the hide-away wipers, pointy rear fenders, and taillamps in big back bumpers. Riviera got a heavy-handed divided grille that made it look more contrived than in 1966-67. Many Buicks returned to tradition with stylized front-fender "ventiports." Exceptions were Wildcats, GS 400s, and Skylark Customs, where rectangular trim was used to suggest air vents of various types.

No engine changes occurred for record-breaking 1969, when Buick built more than 665,000 cars, its decade high, though it still ran fifth in the industry. Seniors again received new bodies, this time with ventless side glass and a squarer, more-formal look. The year-old junior line displayed the expected minor trim shuffles; Gran Sports and Sportwagons remained separate series, as in '68. LeSabre still rode a 123-inch wheelbase, but so did Wildcat for the first time in four years.

This hot-selling line continued into 1970, but without Specials—the smaller workaday models were now Skylarks—and with Estate wagons in a separate series. The latter remained big upper-class two- and three-seat haulers battling the likes of Chrysler's Town & Country. All full-sizers acquired new grilles, bumpers, and taillights; intermediates received longer hoods, bulkier lower-body contours, and different grilles for each series. Riviera also gained a longer hood, reverted to exposed headlamps astride a thin-line vertical-bar grille, sported a wider rear window and altered bumpers, and offered rear fender skirts as a first-time option. The result was more dignified, if a tad stuffy.

Buick's main mechanical development was an enormous 455 V-8. An outgrowth of the 430 it supplanted, this monster gulped premium gas at the rate of 12 mpg on compression ratios of at least 10:1. The last mammoth V-8 Buick would build, the 455 bowed in '70 with 350, 360, or 370 bhp, and was standard for the GS and LeSabre 455s, Riviera, Electra 225, Wildcat, and Estates.

Flint would remain staunchly committed to big cars throughout the '70s, but energy economics and government mandates inevitably prompted smaller models as time passed. Nevertheless, full-size cars remained Buick's bread-and-butter through 1975, accounting for over 40 percent of total division sales.

GM completely redesigned its full-size models for 1971, and that year's big Buicks were the largest and heaviest yet—as big

63

# Buick

as American cars would ever get. Styling was more rounded, with smoothly curved "fuselage" bodysides, massive hoods, and broader expanses of glass. Wildcat was retitled Centurion (recalling a mid-'50s Buick show car), and shared its B-body platform with the popular LeSabre. The upmarket Electra remained a C-body cousin to Olds Ninety-Eight and Cadillac de Ville. Estate wagons moved up to its 127-inch wheelbase.

Big Buicks continued in this form through 1976, becoming busier and somewhat bulkier each year, but not significantly changed except where needed to satisfy blossoming safety and emissions rules. All were thirsty. The last 455-cid Electra, for example, was good for only 8.7 mpg in the Environmental Protection Agency's city-fuel-economy ratings.

Riviera also bulked up for '71, gaining three inches between wheel centers (to 122). It also gained about 120 needless pounds, though it looked like more. Dominating swoopy new Bill Mitchell styling was a dramatic "boattail" deck that proved controversial and was thus short-lived—gone after '73. The GS option, a last vestige of sport, vanished after 1975, but Buick tried to keep enthusiasts interested with a "Rallye" package offering reinforced front antiroll bar, a new rear bar, and heavy-duty springs and shocks. This was claimed to provide even better ride and handling than the GS, and probably should have been standard to handle the size and weight of these beasts. Oddball styling and outsize heft must have contributed to Riviera's sagging fortunes in this period; by 1975, sales were less than half of what they'd been five years before.

The last of the 1968-vintage Skylarks appeared for 1971-72. They remained solid, good-looking middleweights, though their engines were being emasculated by power-sapping emission-control devices, which meant Gran Sports weren't so hot anymore. Signaling the imminent demise of midsize Buick convertibles (ragtop sales were down to a trickle industrywide), Skylark hardtop coupes offered a fold-back cloth sunroof as a new '72 option. Trim packages created a bevy of models: base, 350 and Custom Skylarks, plus Sportwagons and Gran Sports.

Buick's last true muscle cars were also 1970-72 models. They've since become coveted collectibles for their performance and miniscule production. A prime example is the 1970 GSX, a bespoilered GS 455 hardtop with new "Stage I" engine

**1968 GS 400 hardtop sport coupe**

**1968 Wildcat Custom convertible coupe**

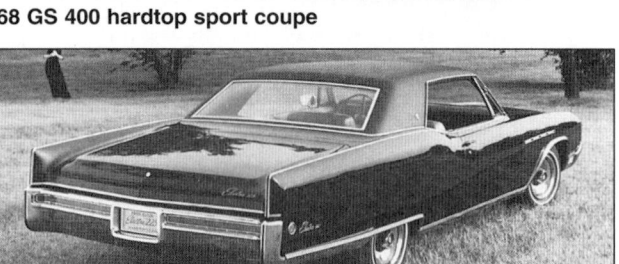
**1968 Electra 225 hardtop coupe**

**1969 Wildcat Custom hardtop sport coupe**

**1968 Sportwagon four-door**

**1969 Skylark Custom convertible coupe**

**1968 Electra 225 Custom hardtop sedan**

**1969 Special DeLuxe coupe**

# Buick

**1969 Riviera hardtop coupe**

**1970 Wildcat Custom hardtop sport coupe**

**1970 Riviera hardtop coupe**

**1970 GSX hardtop sport coupe**

**1971 GS 455 hardtop sport coupe**

**1971 Riviera GS hardtop sport coupe**

tuning; it saw only 678 copies; the GS 455 convertible was little higher at 1416. Both were back for '71 (GSX as an option package) with bold black body stripes and hood paint, special grille, chrome wheels, and fat tires. Figures aren't available for the '71 GSX, but only 902 GS ragtops were built and just 8268 hardtops, reflecting the big drop in performance-car demand after 1969.

For 1973, the respected Century name returned once more, this time on redesigned intermediate Buicks with unchanged wheelbases. All employed a new-generation A-body with so-called "Colonnade" styling that did away with pillarless coupes and sedans. Convertibles were no more, GM reacting to a proposed federal rule on rollover protection that would have outlawed ragtops but which ironically never materialized. Bolstered by spiffy Luxus and Regal submodels (the latter made a separate series after '74), the midsize Centurys sold well through 1977, providing an important "safety net" at times when inflation and rising fuel prices sent would-be big-car buyers scurrying for thriftier alternatives.

A compact also returned to Buick, its first in 10 years. Arriving for mid '73 as the Apollo, it was just a rebadged clone of the 111-inch-wheelbase X-body Chevrolet Nova from 1968, with the same three body styles (two- and four-door sedans and a hatchback two-door) plus, initially, the same 250-cid Chevy straight six as standard power. It was a definite asset during the big-car sales slump touched off by the Middle East oil embargo late that year, but intermediates would remain more important to Buick's overall health.

Confusing buyers for 1975 was the return of the Skylark name at the top of the compact line, where it would eventually supplant Apollo. In common with all X-body variants that year, Buick's version gained heavily revised outer panels that gave it something like European "sports sedan" flair.

A genuine surprise was the new-for-'75 Skyhawk, the smallest Buick in living memory. A near twin to the Vega-based Chevrolet Monza, this 97-inch-wheelbase subcompact "hatch-coupe" took a bit more than eight percent of total division sales in its first six months. Though not light for its size, Skyhawk offered a decent performance/economy blend thanks to a new 90-degree 231-cid V-6 engine, the only one available. Rated at 110 bhp, and also standard power for the '75 Skylark, Century, and Regal, this would be a significant engine in years to come.

Model-year 1977 brought the first of GM's downsized cars. Sometime before the first energy crisis, management had decided to move to smaller, lighter, more-economical designs in every size and price category. Its largest cars were the logical starting point, and they were rendered even more timely by the government corporate average fuel economy standards (CAFE) that took effect for '78.

The first fruits of this program were dramatically evident at Buick, where LeSabre and Electra shrank to almost Century size. Wheelbases contracted to 116 and 119 inches, respectively (Estate wagons rode the shorter one); curb weights dropped several hundred pounds. This made smaller engines feasible, yet interiors were within inches of the old behemoths' size. Riviera wasn't left out, becoming a high-spec version of the new B-body LeSabre (though it would soon return to the corporate E-body).

Electras through 1979 relied on a standard Chevy-built 350 V-8; a new 403 with 185 bhp was optional, courtesy of Olds. Convertibles were no more (killed after '75), but two- and four-door sedans were offered in LeSabre, LeSabre Custom, Electra 225, and 225 Limited series. The following year brought even

# Buick

**1971 Centurion hardtop coupe**

**1974 LeSabre Luxus coupe**

**1972 Riviera hardtop coupe**

**1974 Riviera GS two-door coupe**

**1973 Apollo hatchback coupe**

**1974 Electra 225 Limited hardtop sedan**

fancier Electra Park Avenue models. An interesting 1978 addition was the LeSabre sport coupe, powered by that year's new 165-bhp turbocharged version of the Buick V-6.

Big Buicks entered the '80s with subtly restyled sheetmetal said to reduce wind resistance as an aid to fuel economy. Toward the same end, more extensive use of lighter materials also netted an average 150-pound weight savings, about half that achieved with the '77s. It's odd how perspective changes. GM's first downsized big cars seemed quite small next to Big Three rivals of the day. Now they look just as large as their outsized predecessors.

Intermediates were next on the corporate slenderizing schedule, so a smaller Century bowed for 1978 along with a separate Regal series of personal-luxury coupes, all built on a new 108.1-inch-wheelbase A-body. Regal sold well from the start, but Century didn't. Sloped-roof "aeroback" styling on the two- and four-door sedans was out of phase with buyer tastes, though there was nothing wrong with the handsome wagon. Buick corrected this mistake for 1980 with a more-formal-looking notchback four-door bearing a faint resemblance to the first-generation Cadillac Seville, and sales took off. Buick had turbocharged its V-6 with the new midsize line in mind, offering it in sporty Century and Regal sport coupe models. But the sales pattern was the same, and the blown Century vanished with aerobacks.

Riviera was downsized a second time for '79. Styling was crisper and tighter, and front-wheel drive finally put the model in line with its Toronado and Cadillac Eldorado cousins. A turbo V-6 was available here, too. Though most buyers opted for standard powerplants, the blown Riv was a fine performer—able to leap from 0-60 mph in under 12 seconds while averaging close to 20 mpg in more-restrained driving, this despite a still-bulky 3800-pound curb weight. The 1980 Riviera was basically a reprise but introduced a long-time Cadillac feature: "Twilight Sentinel," the automatic on/off headlamp control with delay timer (for keeping the lights on for up to three minutes after switching off the ignition to illuminate your path).

Though it promised much, the little Skyhawk hatch-coupe was never a big seller and disappeared after 1980. One interesting 1979-80 variation was the Road Hawk, a package aimed at younger buyers more interested in sports-car looks than genuine ability. Fore and aft spoilers, special paint and tape stripes, identifying decals, mag-style wheels, and larger tires were included, but there was little action to back up the brag.

An important new Buick arrived in the spring of '79 as an early-1980 entry. This was a front-drive replacement for the long-running rear-drive Skylark, sharing GM's technically advanced new 104.9-inch-wheelbase X-body platform with siblings Chevrolet Citation, Pontiac Phoenix, and Oldsmobile Omega. Buick had learned its styling lesson, so this new, smaller

1974 Century Luxus Colonnade coupe

1975 Riviera coupe

1975 Electra 225 Limited hardtop sedan

1976 Skylark S/R Landau coupe

1976 Riviera S/R coupe

compact was offered only in traditional notchback form. Design highlights included rack-and-pinion steering, all-coil suspension, and transversely mounted engines—either 2.5-liter Pontiac-built inline-four or an optional 2.8-liter 60-degree V-6 from Chevrolet. Skylark performed well with the latter, and tastefully done sport coupe and sport sedan models offered firmer suspension and sportier appointments for more-serious drivers. Likely on the strength of the Buick name, Skylark became the second-best-selling X-car after the higher-volume, lower-priced Citation. Unfortunately, execution left much to be desired on all X-cars, which soon supplanted the Dodge Aspen/Plymouth Volare as the most-recalled cars from Detroit.

Yet despite the occasional flawed product and market miscalculation, Buick had moved with changing buyer demands in the '70s, reaping the benefit of good sales while some other makes faltered. Per tradition, Buick anticipated most market trends and responded with cars that, if not on the leading edge of design, were at least in tune with the times. Strong sales year after year were proof that Buick not only knew its market but how to satisfy it.

Flint continued doing that into the '80s. But though Buick suffered from rising sales of Japanese cars as much as any Detroit make, it could not escape the cumulative effects of misguided corporate policies that severely eroded GM's market share by 1990.

Buick began the '80s by again reaching out to the younger, more-affluent types who'd bought Gran Sports in the "flower power" era. This reflected the product policies of Lloyd Reuss, a former division chief engineer who became Buick general manager in 1980. A genuine "car guy," Reuss wanted some Buicks to be American-style BMWs, and he got his way. By 1983, there were sporty T type editions of every Buick save for the LeSabre and plush Electra, featuring black exterior trim, firmer chassis, more-potent engines, and "driver-oriented" interiors. Buick also mounted an Indy-car racing program for its V-6 and offered over-the-counter hop-up parts to cement its hoped-for image as a more youthful, performance-oriented outfit.

This strategy worked well for a time, but ultimately backfired. Buick jumped to third in industry production for 1982-83 and ran fourth in model years '81 and 1984-86. Even so, '86 volume was well down on '85's, and the slide continued into 1987, when Buick fell to fifth, behind Oldsmobile. A significant factor was strong new competition from Pontiac, which offered many of the same basic cars but had recently returned to its '60s-style performance theme and returned to third for the first time since 1970. Trying to be all things to all people, Reuss later conceded, only confused Buick's image—and its customers.

In the end, it didn't matter. Chairman Roger Smith's wholesale corporate reorganization, ordained in 1984 to reverse GM's withering market share and in evidence by '87, called for returning each GM make to its distinct rung on the price-and-prestige ladder fashioned back in the '30s by legendary president Alfred P. Sloan. At Flint, this meant a hasty retreat from T types and turbo V-6s, and by decade's end the division had mostly returned to its traditional brand of upper-middle-class luxury—a "doctor's car" once more.

Buick's generally strong sales in the '80s reflected a consistent model lineup, which evolved in step with those of other GM divisions but was, perhaps, more clear-cut to buyers from year to year. Some individual models certainly seemed ageless. The big 1977-vintage Electra and LeSabre, for example, hardly changed at all after their 1980 update, receiving only minor styling and equipment shuffles through mid-decade while accounting for about a quarter of division output each year.

The full-size Estate wagons continued in this vein through 1990, garnering fewer sales as time passed, but coupe and

# Buick

**1976 Regal Landau Colonnade coupe**

**1977 Riviera coupe**

**1977 Regal Landau coupe**

**1977 Electra four-door sedan**

**1977 Estate wagon Limited**

**1978 Century fastback sport coupe**

**1978 Riviera coupe**

**1979 Riviera S Type Turbo coupe**

**1979 LeSabre sport coupe**

**1980 Skyhawk Road Hawk fastback coupe**

sedan models gave way to more-efficient and popular front-drive successors, beginning with 1985's new C-body Electra. A similar H-body LeSabre arrived the following year.

Announcing a second wave of GM downsizing, these smaller big Buicks shared a 110.8-inch wheelbase and measured some two feet shorter and 400 pounds lighter than the 1977-84 models. Yet they hardly sacrificed any passenger room and were vastly more pleasurable to drive, thriftier with fuel, and adequately quick. Transverse-mounted V-6s mated to four-speed over-drive automatic transaxles across the board. Initially, 3.0-liter gasoline and 4.3-liter diesel engines were offered, but soon vanished in favor of the old reliable 3.8-liter gas unit, though updated with sequential multiport electronic fuel injection and, from '86, roller valve lifters. A modified "3800" engine with 165 bhp (versus 150) arrived on certain '88s. Electra coupes disappeared after 1987, when the top-line Park Avenue became a separate model and a laudable new antilock brake system (announced for '86) became more widely available for both series. Electra offered a subtly sporty T Type sedan, LeSabre a T Type coupe. But, as always, the traditional Custom and

# Buick

**1980 Skylark sport coupe**

**1980 Riviera S Type turbo coupe**

**1980 Century fastback sport coupe**

**1980 Regal sport coupe**

**1981 Century Limited four-door sedan**

**1981 Regal sport coupe**

**1981 Electra Estate wagon (diesel)**

**1981 Riviera coupe**

Limited lines sold better by far. And those sales were good: around 100,000-150,000 a year.

The same could not be said for the sixth-generation Riviera. New for '86, the third downsized personal-luxury Buick in 10 years laid a gigantic egg. Sales plunged to an 11-year Riviera low, the '86 tally off a whopping 70 percent from model-year '85. The 1987-88 results were even poorer.

In a way, this was curious. On a tighter 108-inch wheelbase, this new Riviera was far more nimble than the old, and its quiet, well-mannered drivetrain was basically the same as found in Electra/LeSabre. But it was evidently a bit too small for Riviera customers. An unfortunate styling resemblance to Buick's N-body Somerset/Skylark didn't help, and hardly anyone liked the gimmicky Graphic Control Center, a touch-sensitive TV-type screen that needlessly complicated even simple tasks like changing radio stations.

Hoping to turn things around, Buick made the '89 Riviera look more "important," adding 11 inches to overall length, ladling on chrome, and restyling the tail to resemble that of the 1979-85 models. Did it work? Yes and no. Production leaped from about 8600 for '88 to over 21,000 for '89, but the latter wasn't even half the total of a decade before. The 1990s sold only about 1300 units better. A more-conventional dash was a welcome change that season.

All this must have greatly disappointed Flint executives, who'd seen the 1981-84 Riviera average 50,000 model-year sales and the '85 over 65,000 (the increase no doubt due to buyers learning of the shrunken '86). Like the last rear-drive Buicks, these cars changed little after 1980. There was a mild facelift for '84, and an optional Olds-built 350 V-8 was offered through '82, but turbo and nonturbo V-6s were available all along (the latter a new 4.1-liter from '81), as was a 350 Olds diesel V-8 (a troublesome beast, and thus rarely ordered), and choice of standard and T Type coupes.

Riviera's most interesting '80s development was the advent of its first convertible, bowing at mid 1982. A coupe conversion performed by an outside contractor, it was a handsome rig, fairly solid for a droptop and as luxurious as any Riv. But it was heavier and slower with its standard 4.1 V-6 (fitted to most examples, though the turbo 3.8 was ostensibly available) and

# Buick

1981 Regal sport coupe

1982 Skylark Limited four-door sedan

1982 Century Custom coupe

1982 LeSabre F/E (Formal Edition) coupe

1982 Skylark sport coupe

1982 Riviera convertible coupe

1982 Regal Grand National coupe

1983 Skylark T Type coupe

found few takers at $25,000-plus. Production was predictably limited—just 1248, 1750, 500, and 400, respectively, for 1982-85—scarcity that guarantees this as a minor future collectible at least. Of course, the ragtop Riv died with the '86 E-body, which was deemed too small to be a practical four-seater in convertible form (though Buick later showed a prototype of just such a car).

Two more collectible '80s Buicks are found among the rear-drive Regal coupes, which were reskinned for '81 with crisper, more-aerodynamic lines that persisted through the end of series production in December 1987. These are the hot turbo-powered T Type and Grand National.

The new-for-'82 Regal T Type replaced the previous sport coupe as Flint's "factory hot rod," offering fat tires, beefier chassis, attention-getting exterior, and plush interior. Horsepower was rated at 175-180 bhp at first, then boosted to 200 bhp for 1984 via sequential-port fuel injection. The GN bowed at mid '82 as a low-volume commemorative car (named for the Chevy-powered Regals then starting to clean up on the NASCAR circuit), but in reality, it was just a fancy T Type.

After a one-year hiatus, though, Grand National returned with a mean all-black exterior and more unique touches. For 1986 came a turbo intercooler that swelled horses by 35 for both T Type and GN. Recalibrated engine electronics gave the '87s 10 bhp more—and truly phenomenal acceleration. In fact, these Buicks bid fair as the fastest cars in the land, able to bound from 0 to 60 in about six seconds.

Quicker still was the 1987 GNX, a $30,000 end-of-the-line limited edition (547 built, by contractor ASC) with higher turbo boost, "smarter" electronics, cleaner porting, bigger tires, meaner looks, a claimed 300 bhp (276 actual) and a mighty 355-420 pound-feet of torque. Magazine testers clocked 0-60 in the mid-fives and the quarter-mile in about 14.5 seconds at 95 mph.

For all this grandstanding, the Regal T Type was always a peripheral seller and the GN almost invisible (only 215 of the '82s, about 2000 for '84, even fewer for 1985-87). Still, they were great fun, even if Buick wasn't the place one expected to find a modern muscle car.

# Buick

1983 Riviera convertible

1983 Riviera T Type coupe

1983 Regal T Type turbo coupe

1983 Century Limited four-door sedan

1983 Skyhawk Limited station wagon

Smaller cars, particularly intermediates, were far more important to Buick's fortunes in the '80s. For 1981 these comprised the workaday Regal coupes and a mostly carryover group of Century sedans and wagons. All continued the 1978 A-body design that was renamed G-body for '82, when the Centurys became Regals and Buick's 4.1-liter V-6 replaced a 4.3 V-8 option. Model-year volume was some 384,500 for 1981 and over 328,000 for '82, not bad for two very difficult industry years. Production eased to some 226,000 for 1983-84, by which time four-speed automatic transmissions had been adopted as a much better bet for improved mileage.

Meantime, Buick had introduced the first front-drive Century, a notchback coupe and sedan built on the new 1982 A-body used by sister Chevy, Olds, and Pontiac models. Like them, this Century was just a "deluxe" X-car with more expansive sheet-metal and plusher interiors on the same 104.9-inch wheelbase. Initial engine choices were a 2.5-liter Pontiac four; a new 3.0-liter Buick V-6 (destroked from 3.8); and a 4.3-liter Olds diesel V-6. Euro-style T Types were added for '83. The following year brought a 3.8-liter option (standard for T Types) and new five-door Custom and Limited Estate wagons (replacing the old Regal models).

Though little changed for '85, Century displaced Regal (now down to coupes only) as Buick's best-seller, with annual production through 1987 of over a quarter-million units. The '86s were modestly restyled via a curiously unaerodynamic undercut nose. The T Type coupe vanished, Chevy's familiar 2.8 V-6 ousted Buick's 3.0 as the step-up engine, and the 3.8 gained 25 horses (for 150 total) via low-friction roller valve lifters, sequential-port injection, and distributorless triple-coil ignition. For 1987, the T Type became a package option, and both the four and 2.8 V-6 received "Generation II" improvements conferring slightly more power. More standard equipment eased the sticker shock of 1988 prices that were up to the $12,000-$15,000 range (versus $10,000-$12,000 five years before). The 1989s received a minor facelift and a new 160-bhp 3.3-liter V-6 derived from the veteran 3.8 (to replace the 2.8). Nevertheless, volume withered to some 150,000 for '88, then dropped below 90,000 for '89, thanks to a worsening national economy and other factors. Still, this was highly important business for Flint—and highly creditable for such an elderly basic design.

A notch below the front-drive Century was the compact Skylark, which was an X-body for 1981-85, an N-body thereafter. For all the recalls and attendant bad publicity that plagued GM's X-cars in these years, the Skylark continued to sell well. Buick built over a quarter-million of the '81s and more than 100,000 a year for 1982-84. The '85s ended the line at around 93,000. Changes in styling, engineering, and models were strictly evolutionary. There were always 2.5 four and 2.8 V-6 coupes and sedans (except '85, sedans only) in base/Custom and Limited trim. Sport versions through '82 and the two-door 1983-85 T Type could be had with a high-output V-6 (port-injected for '85) and came with distinctive exteriors and Buick's firmer "Gran Touring" suspension package. In all, this Skylark served Buick well.

Buick still peddled a subcompact Skyhawk in the '80s, though quite different from the same-named late-'70s hatch coupe. Bowing for '82, this was one of GM's five front-drive J-body models, riding a 101.2-inch-wheelbase chassis with all-coil suspension via front MacPherson struts and a rear beam axle on trailing arms. Buick wouldn't get a convertible version like Chevy and Pontiac, but did offer their two- and four-door notchback styles plus 5-door wagons from '83 and a "fasthatch" coupe from '86. Engines were the same four-cylinder fare used by sister Js: Chevy-built overhead-valve 2.0-liter (abandoned after '87) and a Brazilian-built overhead-cam unit. The latter,

# Buick

initially a 1.8, was also offered as a more-potent turbocharged version from 1984; both grew to 2.0 liters for '87, after which the blown engine was cancelled. Custom and plusher Limited trim was cataloged all along. The inevitable T Types arrived for '83—notchback two-doors first, then fasthatch coupes too. Styling changed little through the final '89 models save an optional hidden-headlamp nose from 1986. Coupes, turbos, and T Types were all dropped after '87 due to dwindling sales and the division's return to its more-traditional "Premium American Motorcars" thrust.

In sales, Skyhawk typically ran in the middle of the J-car pack—behind Chevy Cavalier and Pontiac's 2000/Sunbird but ahead of Olds Firenza and Cadillac Cimarron. While none of these cars matched certain Japanese rivals for refinement, workmanship, and economy, they were at least competent and sometimes pleasant. Skyhawk probably benefited as much from the Buick corporate badge as any design feature, but would surely have sold better without so much intramural competition. As it was, production peaked with the '84 models—over 145,000 built. After dropping for '85, volume recovered to some 91,500 for industry banner-year '86. But that spurt was a fluke. By '89, Skyhawk sales were down below 30,000.

Much of the J-car's basic engineering appeared in the 1985 Somerset Regal, a notchback two-door heralding the arrival of

**1983 Skyhawk T Type coupe**

**1984 Skylark T Type coupe**

**1983 Regal four-door sedan**

**1984 LeSabre Custom four-door sedan**

**1983 LeSabre Estate wagon (diesel)**

**1984 Regal Grand National coupe**

**1984 Century Estate wagon**

**1984 Regal T Type turbo coupe**

GM's new N-body. Buick wasn't able to trade on the popular Regal name the way Olds did with Cutlass, so this car soon became just Somerset. Companion N-body four-doors arrived for '86 under the Skylark, finishing off the last X-body models; Somersets became Skylarks two years later.

Through 1987, Somerset/Skylark engines comprised the familiar 2.5 four (updated to "Generation II" specs that season) and extra-cost Buick 3.0 V-6. An added option for '88 was Oldsmobile's new "Quad 4," a dual-overhead-cam 2.3-liter four with four valves per cylinder, an aluminum head, and a cast-iron block. With a healthy 150 bhp even in mild initial tune, the Quad-4 promised much. But it wasn't in the same league with similar Japanese engines for smoothness, quietness, and lugging power. Buick was thus wise to retain the V-6 (unlike Pontiac, which dropped it for the '88 Grand Am).

The N-body Buick got off to a good start. Some 86,000 were built for the abbreviated debut model year, followed by nearly 138,000 of the '86s. Like Skyhawk, this was not a state-of-the-art competitor, but it kept getting better. Among the more-notable improvements was the 1989 exchange of 3.0 V-6 for the torquier 160-bhp "3300" unit. The following year brought more logical ergonomics to all Skylarks, plus a new Luxury Edition four-door and a Gran Sport coupe.

Having learned with the J-cars that too many corporate

**1985 Electra Park Avenue coupe**

**1985 Skyhawk T Type coupe**

**1985 Riviera coupe**

**1985 Somerset Regal coupe**

**1985 LeSabre Limited four-door sedan**

**1986 LeSabre Limited coupe**

**1985 Regal Grand National coupe**

**1986 Skylark Limited four-door sedan**

clones spoil the sales broth, GM returned to more individual styling for a trio of 1988 midsize coupes. At Buick, this new front-drive GM10 or W-body design replaced the rear-drive Regal, but retained make appearance "cues" to stand apart more clearly from the related Pontiac Grand Prix and Olds Cutlass Supreme. Significantly, wheelbase was cut just 0.6-inch from the previous Regal's, to the benefit of passenger space; base curb weight slimmed some 250 pounds and overall length by 8.4 inches, to the benefit of economy and handling. The usual Custom and Limited versions were on hand, and a Gran Sport appearance/handling package offered front "bib" spoiler, rocker-panel skirts, black grille, aluminum road wheels, and other "Euro" touches.

All models initially carried a transverse, port-injected 2.8 Chevy V-6 of 125 bhp and four-speed overdrive automatic transaxle, plus all-disc brakes—uncommon in mass-market Detroiters. Equally laudable was the all-independent suspension with the expected front struts and coil springs, plus rear struts on single trailing links and dual lateral links connected by a single transverse plastic leaf spring, as on the big C/H-bodies.

Despite such technical finesse, Regal finished well-down on the midsize sales chart for 1988. The reason, said many pundits, was GM's delay in introducing planned four-door models, a style far preferred in this class. GM remedied its mistake for 1991, and Buick added Regal sedans with the same trim levels and wheelbase as its W-body coupes. By that point, the 2.8 V-6 had been enlarged to a 3.1 with 10 more bhp, and a praiseworthy antilock braking system (ABS) was offered optionally on Limited and GS models. Despite all this, Regal sales continued to disappoint.

Another '88 newcomer was a more telling sign of Buick's late-decade fortunes. It was Flint's first production two-seater, named Reatta (derived from an American Indian word for lariat). Though basically a Riviera cut down to a 98.5-inch wheelbase, Reatta was only 4.5 inches shorter overall and almost as heavy (at 3350 pounds). Powertrain and dashboard also came from the Riv, but styling was Reatta's own: smooth, rounded, "friendly."

Buick took pains to note that Reatta was not a sports car but a "mature" two-seater emphasizing luxury, comfort, even practicality. Extensive standard equipment limited options to just an electric sliding sunroof and a driver's seat with no fewer than 16 power adjustments. You had to contend with the dubious Graphic Control Center in 1988-89 models, but the roomy two-place cabin and a largish trunk with drop-down pass-through panel invited long-distance touring. Even better, Reatta was shrewdly priced: around $25,000 initially, about half as much as Cadillac's slow-selling Italian-bodied Allante convertible. An open-air Reatta bowed for 1990 as Buick's first "in-house" ragtop in 15 years. (It would have appeared in early '89 but for last-minute production troubles.) Both 1990 Reattas gained a standard driver-side airbag and conventional audio and climate controls. The '91s boasted a further-improved 3800 V-6, new electronic shift control for the four-speed automatic

**1986 Riviera T Type coupe**

**1987 Skylark Custom four-door sedan**

**1987 Regal Grand National coupe**

**1987 LeSabre T Type coupe**

**1987 Riviera T Type coupe**

**1988 Regal Custom two-door coupe**

# Buick

1988 Riviera coupe

1988 Reatta 2-passenger coupe

1988 LeSabre Limited coupe

1988 Electra T Type four-door sedan

1989 Skyhawk SE coupe

transmission, standard touring tires, and a shorter final drive for sprightlier pickup.

Yet for all its appealing qualities, the Reatta was a fish out of water: conceived in the heady days of Buick sportiness but born to a division fast returning to "The Great American Road." It did have the handcrafted aura of a genuine limited edition, built at a special new "Reatta Craft Centre" (though that was situated at Olds in Lansing, not at Flint). Yet Riviera offered the same basic car for less money—plus the bonus of a back seat. Worse, Reatta workmanship was erratic, especially on the convertible, which not only made do with a manual top but was downright pricey at an initial $34,995—$6700 above the coupe. With all this, Reatta failed to meet even its minimum yearly sales goal of 10,000 units and was thus dropped after 1991. Total production was precisely 21,850, including a mere 2437 ragtops (only 305 of which were built to '91 specs).

Reatta was a sad loss for those who appreciate interesting cars, but it died in a good cause. The aging of America's vast "baby-boom" generation implied growing demand for the sort of "modern conservatism" traditional from Flint.

Indeed, the division enjoyed something close to prosperity in the early '90s, running third in calendar-year sales among domestic makes before yielding to a resurgent Pontiac in 1993. Still, this success was only relative, as Buick volume was down to barely half its mid '80s level—about half-a-million cars per year. Worse, GM as a whole was losing money by the ton: $2 billion in 1990 alone, a massive $4.5 billion in '91.

Analysts found no mystery in that. Quite simply, they said, GM still had too many factories with too much capacity to build too many vehicles for too few customers. By contrast, Ford and Chrysler had become leaner and more efficient in the '80s. GM merely redrew its organizational chart to enter the '90s with the highest overhead and lowest per-unit profit of the Big Three (not to mention the Japanese "transplant" operations that now loomed large in the total U.S. picture). By 1993, GM's net losses over four years had reached a towering $18 billion.

By that point, GM had endured another painful reorganization and numerous plant closings, plus an unprecedented 1992 "palace coup" that summarily ousted chairman Robert Stempel and president Lloyd Reuss after just two years in office. GM was making money again just two years later, thanks to the efforts of new president John F. "Jack" Smith, who'd recently turned things around for GM Europe, and John Smale, the former CEO of Proctor & Gamble.

In a sense, Buick had long been showing the way to GM's future. As the purveyor of "Premium American Motorcars," it entered the '90s with one of Detroit's stronger "brand images," thanks to a well-established lineup of cars that made no apologies for being smooth, lush, and Detroit-traditional. Buick worked hard to strengthen its position even further in the '90s. Dropping Reatta had been but a first step.

A second one was the '91 debut of the first Roadmaster in 35 years. It was only that year's restyled Chevy Caprice in Buick dress, built on the same rear-drive B-body chassis from '77. But this new "Roadie" was big, spacious, and well-equipped in the best tradition of full-size Detroiters. In other words, it was a lot of car for the money, considering it was cheaper than the smaller, more efficient front-drive Park Avenue. An Estate wagon bowed first with fake-wood siding, eight-passenger seating, handy two-way tailgate with separate liftup window, and a $21,500 price tag. Six-passenger standard and Limited sedans followed for '92 in the $22,000-$24,000 range. That same year, the base 170-hp 5.0-liter V-8 was bolstered by a much torquier 5.7-liter option. The '94s could run close to $27,000, but they also ran with a standard 350 LT1 V-8 from Chevy's latest Corvette sports car, though in low-stress, 260-bhp tune. Car

# Buick

and Driver clocked one at 7.8 seconds 0-60, but pulling power, not sheer acceleration, was the name of this game—as in towing trailers and boats.

The reborn Roadmaster pulled a fair number of customers, all things considered: a best of 85,500 for '92, 30,000 to 40,000 for 1993-95. Though that wasn't much compared to the levels of 10 and 20 years before, each sale was almost pure gravy, as the elderly platform and other major components had been paid for long ago. But the Roadmaster would die after '96 to make room for more-profitable sport-utility vehicle production at the Arlington, Texas, factory that also built the Caprice. Like Reatta, the '90s Roadmaster served a purpose, but it was clearly a car of Buick's past, not its future.

How, then, to explain the aging front-drive Century as one of Flint's most profitable assets in this period? Again, there was no mystery. Buick increased quality and added features that customers wanted while keeping the lid on price. While holding on to an old design might seem questionable, Buick couldn't afford to let this one die, because the Century had come to have great appeal for rental-car companies and other fleet buyers; in fact, they now accounted for the majority of sales. The improved workmanship was just a timely bonus, the result of a gradual but wholesale reengineering effort for both Century and Oldsmobile's related Cutlass Ciera. And it paid off. In 1993, the influential J.D. Power organization ranked this elderly duo near the top of the industry for initial vehicle quality.

Sales, of course, were the most important payoff, and Century model-year production remained well above 100,000 for 1990-95. This was achieved with remarkably few changes: a more-orthodox face for '91, new downpriced Special models for '92 (recycling yet another familiar Buick name), a new 2.2-liter base four for '93 (ousting the old Iron Duke at last). A standard driver-side airbag and ABS arrived for '94, when offerings thinned to Custom and Special sedans and a Special wagon. By that point, Buick was into "value pricing" (like other GM divisions), which meant selling well-equipped cars for several hundred dollars less than if they were "optioned up" the usual way. Yet Century's price spread hadn't changed that much, with stickers still in the affordable $16,000-$18,000 range. Even more than Roadmaster, Buick's "old dog" A-body had learned some profitable new tricks—enough to earn a complete redesign for '97.

Century's one-time successor, the front-drive Regal, could be as quick and pleasant as any rival—and more so than some. Even so, production tumbled 27 percent from model-year '92 to just over 83,000 for '93, then to 78,600 before recovering to the 100,000 level for '95. Likely factors in this see-saw performance were styling that didn't age gracefully, a complete lack of airbags until '94 (the '95s got standard dual restraints), and the fact that the $15,000 Regals of 1990 cost well over $20,000 by '95. Happily, ABS was standard by then, even on base-trim

**1989 Century Custom four-door sedan**

**1990 Reatta 2-passenger convertible coupe**

**1989 Regal Gran Sport coupe**

**1992 Skylark coupe**

**1990 Skylark Luxury Edition four-door sedan**

**1993 Riviera coupe with Gran Touring Package**

# Buick

1993 Roadmaster Estate wagon

1994 Park Avenue Ultra four-door sedan

1996 Century Custom sedan

1996 Roadmaster Limited sedan

Customs, and the natty Gran Sport had been promoted from 1990-91 option package to separate coupe and sedan models.

Continuing as Buick's top-seller by far, the full-size H-body LeSabre drew well over 150,000 orders each model year in 1992-94. Its stellar second-place finish in J.D. Power's 1989 quality survey prompted Buick to bill itself as "the new symbol for quality in America." LeSabre also earned "best family car" honors from Family Circle magazine and a string of yearly Best Buy endorsements from Consumer Guide®. Helping the cause was a thorough 1992 redesign featuring a more rounded and contemporary look, a smoother 3800 V-6, standard driver-side airbag, and useful no-cost extras like power windows and GM's "PASS-Key" antitheft ignition. Coupes disappeared, but Custom and Limited sedans kept moving out the door on the strength of appealing high-teens starting prices and considered yearly feature upgrades like standard power door locks ('93), passenger airbag and heat-reflecting "solar control" glass ('94) and high-value "Select Series" models ('95). Though LeSabre had no more allure for enthusiasts than a Century or Regal, it offered solid family transport with a modicum of luxury at a fair price, a combination many folks found hard to resist.

Buick's flagship C-body line received a similar makeover for 1991, gaining more-fulsome lines inspired by the '89 Essence show car, plus plastic front fenders and eight inches in overall length (wheelbase was unchanged). Models thinned to a $24,385 Park Avenue sedan and a posh new $27,420 Park Avenue Ultra. Both carried 3800 V-6s with tuned-port injection and 170 bhp, plus four-speed automatic transaxles with electronic shift control newly integrated with the engine computer. Also on hand: standard driver-side airbag, ABS, solar-control windshield glass, and full power assists.

Befitting its name, the Ultra came with a leather-trimmed interior and a few unique styling touches. Come 1992, it added a supercharged V-6, the only such engine in U.S. production other than Ford's Thunderbird SC unit. Unlike Buick turbos of the '70s and '80s, Ultra's supercharged engine was tuned for low-speed torque, not high-end power. Still, its 205 bhp wasn't exactly puny, so neither was performance. Where the regular Park Avenue took 9.2 seconds 0-60, the Ultra needed about eight. Also new for '92 was optional traction control for both models (later extended to LeSabre as well). This praiseworthy feature was appreciated even more when the Ultra went to 225 bhp for 1994—good for seven seconds flat in the benchmark sprint to 60. The 1995 base model got a reengineered "Series II" 3800 with vibration-quelling "balance shafts." The blown V-6 followed suit for '96 and muscled up to 240 bhp—not bad for a lowly pushrod engine then over 20 years old.

Like their linemates, Park Avenue/Ultra added a few standard features each year. While that necessarily pushed up prices, customers seemed willing to go along. That was especially true for '91, when the series doubled its model-year production to over 100,000. Annual volume then settled to between 55,000 and 68,000 through mid-decade.

The compact N-body Skylark was much less important to Buick in the early '90s than it was in the '80s. Indeed, sales declined most every model year even as Pontiac's similar Grand Am steadily drew up to four times as many buyers. Skylark's 1992 redesign didn't help, with a flashy, sharp-lined exterior and an oddly drawn dash worthy of Salvador Dali.

Skylark offered coupes and sedans in base and Gran Sport trim for '92, then in Custom, Limited, and GS guise, through '95. GS models always had a standard V-6: a Buick 3.3 through '93, then a Chevy-built 3.1. Either was preferable to the otherwise-standard Quad-4, which remained a rough-and-rowdy runner despite GM's best efforts to civilize it (including the belated addition of twin balance shafts for '95, when it was prosaically retitled Twin Cam). A three-speed automatic was still the lone transmission and thus quite passé even for a compact. An optional four-speed unit arrived for '94, when all Skylarks gained a driver-side airbag as well as standard air conditioning, cruise control, tilt steering wheel, power windows, and automatic power door locks. By that point, Skylark had added special "value-priced" models in the hotly contested $14,000-$18,000 bracket. Yet despite such tactics and worthy interim changes, this was still one of those cars that seemed to aim more at Hertz and Avis than Joe and Jane America.

# Buick

Buick tried bolstering Skylark's showroom appeal with a 1996 facelift featuring a toned-down exterior and a more orthodox dashboard with standard passenger's airbag. At the same time, the base four was enlarged to 2.4 liters, mostly for better low-speed torque (horsepower was unchanged), and was teamed with the four-speed automatic like the V-6. And all models boasted standard traction control. But none of this helped sales, which actually declined to the 50,000-unit level. With that and a new cost-cutting push by GM managers, Buick exited the compact field after 1997.

A changing market and GM's steadily declining share of it—down to less than 30 percent by the mid '90s—would eventually claim another Buick, the once-proud Riviera. Its future certainly looked bleak as the decade opened, as the restyled '89 was left to soldier on for four model years without significant change. Though there were laudable technical advances like electronic transmission control and standard ABS, they only kept the car current without making it more compelling. Worse, the luxury-coupe market started to nosedive in an early-decade recession. As a result, Riv sales were flat for 1991-92 at some 12,000-13,000 per year, then plunged to a paltry 4555 for '93. And there were no '94s at all.

But that's only because Buick had prepared an all-new Riviera for a spring '94 debut. Artfully detailed and refreshingly different, the 1995 model marked a renaissance for the personal-luxury Buick—arguably the most-exciting Riviera in a quarter-century. Styling was a major attraction. Developed under studio chief Bill Porter, it had begun as a variation on the curvy Lucerne showmobile, but ended up like no Buick before. Some saw a hint of trendy "cab forward" proportioning, others a touch of Jaguar and even Ferrari Dino in the smoothly carved nose, tail, and profile. Even if you didn't like the new look—and not everyone did—you had to admire its audacity. Car and Driver, for one, praised "the boldness and coherence of the Riviera's design, [though] the shape somehow doesn't make our hearts flutter instantly. But neither did we tire of it quickly, for there's a wealth of visual detail that was gradually revealed to us as we spent time with the car."

The reborn Riviera was definitely larger and more "substantial" than the 1989-93 generation, growing nine inches longer, 1.9 inches wider, and 238 pounds heavier. The weight gain partly reflected the use of a new "G-car" platform, claimed to be the stiffest in GM history. It was the same structure used for Oldsmobile's new '95 Aurora sedan, but aside from sharing a few underskin components and a 113.8-inch wheelbase, the two cars were nothing alike.

The move from E-body to G-car gave Riviera a modern independent rear suspension with semitrailing arms, toe-control links, coil springs and antiroll bar. Together with a strut-type front end and Buick chassis tuning, the Riv handled with confi-

**1996 Regal Limited sedan**

**1997 LeSabre Limited sedan**

**1996 Skylark Gran Sport coupe**

**1998 Park Avenue Ultra sedan**

**1997 Century Custom sedan**

**1998 Regal GS sedan**

dence, if not Euro firmness, and delivered a great American-style ride. The interior enhanced comfort by offering space enough for six—five with available front buckets—plus the expected upscale decor and a handsome reverse-slant instrument panel that prompted faint memories of 1963.

Early '95 Rivieras carried the 225-bhp supercharged V-6 from that season's Park Avenue Ultra. Despite fair heft (nearly 3800 pounds) and mandatory four-speed autobox, the blown Riv clocked a brisk 7.9 seconds in 0-60 runs by Consumer Guide®. A less-expensive, standard model soon followed with the unblown 205-bhp Series II engine. Both versions packed standard four-wheel ABS, full power, dual-zone climate control, a remote-keyless-entry system and many other amenities now expected in the class. Even so, the base Riv stickered at just over $28,000, thousands less than pricey foreign luxury coupes, not to mention domestic rivals. The supercharged model was only some $1100 upstream, and even a full option load wouldn't push it much beyond $32 grand.

Enthusiasts must have been happy to see Riviera not only alive and well but more elegant and desirable than it had been in a long, long time. Buick was happy to see sales go through the roof, relatively speaking, turning out 41,442 for the extended 1995 run. But that would be the peak. With buyers fast deserting big coupes for upscale sport-utility vehicles (SUVs) and luxury import-brand sedans, Riviera sales dropped to just over 17,000 for '96, inched up to around 18,000 for '97, then plunged to 10,613 for '98. There were few changes along the way, though the supercharged engine was boosted to 240 bhp for '96 and was the only engine available for '98, when bucket seats were standardized too. But the market had spoken, and Riviera was consigned to history after a token 2000-unit run for 1999. Of those, about 200 were specially trimmed Silver Arrow models, a nostalgic nod to the Bill Mitchell show car previewing the classic '63 Riviera. Though the valedictory edition may emerge one day as a minor collector's item, it was a sad finale for what had been one of the most glamorous of all Buicks.

Losing Riviera and Skylark did not seriously affect Buick business in the late '90s, which stayed fairly steady with some 400,000 or more sales each calendar year through 2000. Timely redesigns were a big help, with 1997 a pivotal model year. Century and Regal were recast on a new corporate W-body platform shared with Pontiac Grand Prix and Oldsmobile's new midsize '98 Intrigue. Coupes were forgotten, but sedans got smooth, handsome lines on longer wheelbases that made for roomier interiors. Century targeted the family market with six-passenger Custom and Limited models using a 3.1-liter V-6. Regal catered to luxury seekers with LS and bucket-seat GS sedans using 3.8-liter V-6s—a 195-bhp version for LS, a hot 240-bhp supercharged version for GS, which also boasted leather upholstery, sporty styling accents, and handling-oriented Gran Touring suspension. Centurys base-priced some $2000-$3000 less than Regals and, perhaps as a result, were far more popular, drawing well over 100,000 calendar-year sales in 1998-2000 versus 65,000-75,000 for Regal. To its credit, Buick generally held the price line while adding features most every season. The '99 Centurys, for example, got standard traction control and a useful tire-pressure monitor, while GM's new OnStar communications system moved from optional to standard status for 2001 GS Regals and Limited Centurys.

The admirable G-platform was the basis for redesigned big Buicks, starting with 1997's Park Avenue and Park Avenue Ultra. Here, too, styling was more curvaceous, though still Buick-conservative, and interiors became more spacious thanks to a longer wheelbase (by three inches), though overall length was little changed. Predictably, Flint's flagships offered a pile of new features, including front shoulder belts conve-

1998 Skylark sedan

1999 Riviera coupe

2000 Century sedan

2001 Park Avenue Ultra sedan

2001 Regal Olympic Edition sedan

niently integrated with the seat, an aircraft-style head-up display projecting speed and other data onto the windshield at driver eye level, and "rain-sensing" wipers that varied intermittent sweeps according to moisture detected on the windshield. Arriving a bit later was Cadillac's praiseworthy "StabiliTrak" electronic antiskid system, which throttled back power and/or braked individual wheels to keep you on course. With all this, plus reasonable prices of $30,000-$35,000, Park Avenue calendar-year sales improved a healthy 44 percent in '97 and held in the 58,000-62,000 range before dipping below 48,000 in 2000—a fair success, all things considered.

LeSabre got a mild cosmetic freshening for '97 before it, too, became a G-car. Appropriately, the redesigned 2000 models bowed in early 1999, the 40th anniversary of the LeSabre nameplate—on production Buicks, that is. Interior room improved via a longer wheelbase, plus a little extra width and even height, yet overall length and weight were again little changed. Styling was more closely aligned with Park Avenue's, and many of the flagship's features were on hand. Even the sophisticated StabiliTrak system was available in a new "Driver Confidence" package that also included the head-up display and self-sealing tires, though it required the Gran Touring suspension option. Yet for all the changes—including more nimble handling, a benefit of the stout G-car structure—LeSabre remained a resolutely conservative, upper-middle-class Buick with a family-friendly character and value pricing in low-$20,000 territory. Trouble was, many families had long since preferred minivans and SUVs over full-size sedans, which partly explains why LeSabre calendar-year sales remained essentially flat at just under 150,000 per year through 2000.

Light-truck demand grew at a phenomenal pace throughout the 1990s, one of the most important market trends of the decade. Another was GM's steady loss of market share, which withered to only some 25 percent by the start of the new millennium. Attempting to turn things around, GM embraced "brand management," a philosophy that said good products were less important to sales than a good name with a good image. It was a new twist on the old "sell the sizzle, not the steak" idea, and it didn't work in the much more competitive late-'90s market. Worse for Buick, brand management was a distraction that left the division on the sidelines of the profitable light-truck action.

GM finally corrected the oversight with the 2002 Rendezvous, Buick's first truck in 70 years. Actually, this was one of a new breed of "crossover" vehicles that were raking in big money by combining truck-type styling and utility with carlike refinement and driving ease. Rendezvous was related to Pontiac's similarly conceived Aztek, which bowed about a year before it, but was far more attractive, as most critics said. Both amounted to clever reskins of GM's basic 1997 front-drive minivan design, with different outer sheetmetal giving a quasi-SUV appearance, plus four conventional side doors. As a Buick, Rendezvous one-upped Aztek with better standard trim and equipment, not to mention a 4-inch longer wheelbase that made room for included three-row seating for up to seven, a must feature for this new kind of vehicle. Each offered models with front-wheel drive or GM's new "VersaTrak" all-wheel drive, but the only engine was the corporation's hoary 3.4-liter pushrod V-6, which sent 185 bhp through a four-speed automatic transmission.

Despite the pedestrian underpinnings, Rendezvous emerged as a pleasant, well-equipped package that promised to expand Buick's market reach and perhaps rejuvenate a nameplate whose image has become rather stale. And even-more-exciting Buicks loom just over the horizon. On the eve of its 100th birthday, Buick seems to be redefining itself for a vastly changed market and a new generation of buyers. From where we sit, that's a good way to greet the future.

## Specifications

### 1930

| Series 40 (wb 118.0) | | Wght | Price | Prod |
|---|---|---|---|---|
| 30-40 | sdn 2d | 3,600 | 1,270 | 6,144 |
| 30-44 | spt rdstr 2P | 3,420 | 1,310 | 3,639 |
| 30-45 | phtn 4P | 3,410 | 1,310 | 1,100 |
| 30-46 | bus cpe | 3,540 | 1,260 | 5,716 |
| 30-46S | special cpe 4P | 3,600 | 1,300 | 10,748 |
| 30-47 | sdn 4d | 3,700 | 1,330 | 47,496 |
| — | chassis | — | — | 3,288 |
| **Series 50 (wb 124.0)** | | | | |
| 30-57 | sdn 4d | 4,235 | 1,540 | 23,139 |
| 30-58 | cpe 4P | 4,120 | 1,510 | 5,275 |
| **Series 60 (wb 132.0)** | | | | |
| 30-60 | sdn 7P | 4,415 | 1,910 | 6,650 |
| 30-60L | limo 7P | 4,475 | 2,070 | 836 |
| 30-61 | special sdn 4d | 4,330 | 1,760 | 12,557 |
| 30-64 | rdstr 2P | 4,015 | 1,585 | 2,009 |
| 30-64C | special cpe 4P | 4,225 | 1,695 | 5,381 |
| 30-68 | cpe 5P | 4,220 | 1,740 | 10,216 |
| 30-69 | phtn 7P | 4,110 | 1,595 | 1,618 |
| — | chassis | — | — | 924 |

| 1930 Engines | bore × stroke | bhp | availability |
|---|---|---|---|
| I-6, 257.5 | 3.44 × 4.63 | 81 | S-40 |
| I-6, 331.3 | 3.75 × 5.00 | 99 | S-50, 60 |

### 1931

| Series 50 (wb 114.0) | | Wght | Price | Prod |
|---|---|---|---|---|
| 8-50 | sdn 2d | 3,065 | 1,035 | combined |
| 8-54 | spt rdstr 2-4P | 2,840 | 1,055 | below |
| 8-55 | phtn 5p | 2,840 | 1,055 | |
| 8-56 | bus cpe | 2,980 | 1,025 | |
| 8-56S | spt cpe 2-4P | 3,060 | 1,055 | |
| 8-57 | sdn 4d | 3,170 | 1,095 | |
| **Series 50 (wb 114.0; intro. 1/31)** | | | | |
| 8-50 | sdn 2d | 3,145 | 1,035 | 3,677 |
| 8-54 | spt rdstr 2-4P | 2,935 | 1,055 | 977 |
| 8-55 | phtn 5P | 2,970 | 1,055 | 388 |
| 8-56 | bus cpe | 3,055 | 1,025 | 2,782 |
| 8-56C | conv cpe 4P | 3,095 | 1,095 | 1,540 |
| 8-56S | spt cpe 2-4P | 3,135 | 1,055 | 5,757 |
| 8-57 | sdn 4d | 3,265 | 1,095 | 33,358 |
| — | chassis | — | — | 2,008 |
| **Series 60 (wb 118.0)** | | | | |
| 8-64 | spt rdstr 2-4P | 3,465 | 1,335 | 1,078 |
| 8-65 | phtn 5P | 3,525 | 1,335 | 495 |
| 8-66 | bus cpe | 3,615 | 1,285 | 2,732 |
| 8-66S | spt cpe 2-4P | 3,695 | 1,325 | 30,775 |
| 8-67 | sdn 4d | 3,795 | 1,355 | 30,775 |
| — | chassis | — | — | 1,692 |
| **Series 80 (wb 124.0)** | | | | |
| 8-86 | cpe 4P | 4,120 | 1,535 | 3,579 |
| 8-87 | sdn 4d | 4,255 | 1,565 | 14,769 |
| **Series 90 (wb 132.0)** | | | | |
| 8-90 | sdn 7P | 4,435 | 1,935 | 4,202 |
| 8-90L | limo 7P | 4,505 | 2,035 | 620 |
| 8-91 | brgm 4d 5P | 4,340 | 1,785 | 7,858 |
| 8-94 | spt rdstr 4P | 4,010 | 1,610 | 843 |
| 8-95 | phtn 7P | 4,125 | 1,620 | 450 |
| 8-96 | cpe 5P | 4,260 | 1,765 | 7,715 |

# Buick

| Series 90 (wb 132.0) | | Wght | Price | Prod |
|---|---|---|---|---|
| 8-96C | conv cpe | 4,195 | 1,785 | 1,070 |
| 8-96S | spt cpe 2-4P | 4,250 | 1,720 | 2,993 |
| — | chassis | — | — | 290 |

| 1931 Engines | bore × stroke | bhp | availability |
|---|---|---|---|
| I-8, 220.7 | 2.88 × 4.25 | 77 | S-50 |
| I-8, 272.6 | 3.06 × 4.63 | 90 | S-60 |
| I-8, 344.8 | 3.13 × 5.00 | 104 | S-80, 90 |

## 1932

| Series 50 (wb 114.0) | | Wght | Price | Prod |
|---|---|---|---|---|
| 32-55 | spt phtn 5P | 3,270 | 1,155 | 116 |
| 32-56 | bus cpe | 3,275 | 935 | 1,726 |
| 32-56C | conv cpe-rdstr 4P | 3,335 | 1,080 | 643 |
| 32-56S | special cpe 4P | 3,395 | 1,040 | 1,914 |
| 32-57 | sdn 4d | 3,450 | 995 | 10,803 |
| 32-57S | special sdn 4d | 3,510 | 1,080 | 9,941 |
| 32-58 | victoria cpe 5P | 3,420 | 1,060 | 2,196 |
| 32-58C | conv phtn 5P | 3,425 | 1,080 | 400 |
| — | chassis | — | — | 664 |

| Series 60 (wb 118.0) | | Wght | Price | Prod |
|---|---|---|---|---|
| 32-65 | spt phtn 5P | 3,795 | 1,390 | 103 |
| 32-66 | bus cpe | 3,795 | 1,250 | 636 |
| 32-66C | cpe-rdstr 4P | 3,795 | 1,310 | 452 |
| 32-66S | special cpe 4P | 3,860 | 1,270 | 1,684 |
| 32-67 | sdn 4d | 3,980 | 1,310 | 9,060 |
| 32-68 | victoria cpe 5P | 3,875 | 1,290 | 1,514 |
| 32-68C | conv phtn 5P | 3,880 | 1,310 | 384 |
| — | chassis | — | — | 408 |

| Series 80 (wb 126.0) | | Wght | Price | Prod |
|---|---|---|---|---|
| 32-86 | victoria cpe 5P | 4,335 | 1,540 | 1,800 |
| 32-87 | sdn 4d | 4,450 | 1,570 | 4,092 |

| Series 90 (wb 134.0) | | Wght | Price | Prod |
|---|---|---|---|---|
| 32-90 | sdn 7P | 4,657 | 1,955 | 1,387 |
| 32-90L | limo 7P | 4,740 | 2,055 | 190 |
| 32-91 | club sdn 5P | 4,620 | 1,820 | 2,238 |
| 32-95 | spt phtn 7P | 4,400 | 1,675 | 146 |
| 32-96 | victoria cpe 5P | 4,460 | 1,785 | 1,460 |
| 32-96C | cpe rdstr 4P | 4,390 | 1,805 | 289 |
| 32-96S | Country Club cpe 4P | 4,470 | 1,740 | 586 |
| 32-97 | sdn 4d | 4,565 | 1,805 | 1,485 |
| 32-98 | conv phtn 5P | 4,480 | 1,830 | 269 |
| — | chassis | — | — | 216 |

| 1932 Engines | bore × stroke | bhp | availability |
|---|---|---|---|
| I-8, 230.4 | 2.94 × 4.25 | 82 | S-50 |
| I-8, 272.6 | 3.06 × 4.63 | 95 | S-60 |
| I-8, 344.8 | 3.13 × 5.00 | 113 | S-80, 90 |

## 1933

| Series 50 (wb 119.0) | | Wght | Price | Prod |
|---|---|---|---|---|
| 33-56 | bus cpe | 3,520 | 995 | 1,321 |
| 33-56C | conv cpe 4P | 3,525 | 1,115 | 350 |
| 33-56S | spt cpe 2-4P | 3,585 | 1,030 | 1,653 |
| 33-57 | sdn 4d | 3,705 | 1,045 | 19,259 |
| 33-58 | victoria cpe 5P | 3,605 | 1,065 | 4,123 |
| — | chassis | — | — | 870 |

| Series 60 (wb 127.0) | | Wght | Price | Prod |
|---|---|---|---|---|
| 33-66C | conv cpe 2-4P | 3,940 | 1,365 | 152 |
| 33-66S | spt cpe 2-4P | 3,975 | 1,270 | 1,000 |
| 33-67 | sdn 4d | 4,115 | 1,310 | 7,450 |
| 33-68 | victoria cpe 5P | 4,005 | 1,310 | 2,887 |
| 33-68C | conv phtn 5P | 4,110 | 1,585 | 183 |
| — | chassis | — | — | 399 |

| Series 80 (wb 130.0) | | Wght | Price | Prod |
|---|---|---|---|---|
| 33-86 | victoria cpe 5P | 4,420 | 1,540 | 758 |

| Series 80 (wb 130.0) | | Wght | Price | Prod |
|---|---|---|---|---|
| 33-86C | conv cpe 2-4P | 4,325 | 1,575 | 90 |
| 33-86S | spt cpe 2-4P | 4,355 | 1,495 | 401 |
| 33-87 | sdn 4d | 4,505 | 1,570 | 1,545 |
| 33-88C | conv phtn 5P | 4,525 | 1,845 | 124 |
| — | chassis | — | — | 90 |

| Series 90 (wb 138.0) | | Wght | Price | Prod |
|---|---|---|---|---|
| 33-90 | sdn 7P | 4,705 | 1,955 | 902 |
| 33-90L | limo 7P | 4,780 | 2,055 | 338 |
| 33-91 | club sdn 5P | 4,595 | 1,820 | 1,639 |
| 33-96 | victoria cpe 5P | 4,520 | 1,785 | 557 |
| 33-97 | sdn 4d | 4,595 | 1,805 | 641 |
| — | chassis | — | — | 192 |

| 1933 Engines | bore × stroke | bhp | availability |
|---|---|---|---|
| I-8, 230.4 | 2.94 × 4.25 | 86 | S-50 |
| I-8, 272.6 | 3.06 × 4.63 | 97 | S-60 |
| I-8, 344.8 | 3.13 × 5.00 | 113 | S-80, 90 |

## 1934

| Series 40 (wb 117.0) | | Wght | Price | Prod |
|---|---|---|---|---|
| 34-41 | club sdn T/B 5P | 3,175 | 925 | 11,495 |
| 34-46 | cpe 5P | 2,995 | 795 | 1,808 |
| 34-46S | spt cpe 2-4P | 3,085 | 855 | 1,279 |
| 34-47 | sdn 4d | 3,155 | 895 | 7,805 |
| 34-48 | tng sdn 2d T/B | 3,120 | 865 | 4,779 |
| — | chassis | — | — | 1,727 |

| Series 50 (wb 119.0) | | Wght | Price | Prod |
|---|---|---|---|---|
| 34-56 | bus cpe 2P | 3,682 | 1,110 | 1,082 |
| 34-56C | conv cpe 2-4P | 3,692 | 1,230 | 589 |
| 34-56S | spt cpe 2-4P | 3,712 | 1,145 | 1,192 |
| 34-57 | sdn 4d | 3,852 | 1,190 | 12,805 |
| 34-58 | victoria cpe 5P | 3,767 | 1,160 | 4,405 |
| — | chassis | — | — | 1,777 |

| Series 60 (wb 128.0) | | Wght | Price | Prod |
|---|---|---|---|---|
| 34-61 | club sdn 5P | 4,318 | 1,465 | 5,629 |
| 34-66C | conv cpe 2-4P | 4,133 | 1,495 | 263 |
| 34-66S | spt cpe 2-4P | 4,193 | 1,375 | 825 |
| 34-67 | sdn 4d | 4,303 | 1,425 | 5,365 |
| 34-68 | victoria T/B cpe 5P | 4,213 | 1,395 | 1,966 |
| 34-68C | conv phtn 5P | 4,353 | 1,675 | 587 |
| — | chassis | — | — | 717 |

| Series 90 (wb 136.0) | | Wght | Price | Prod |
|---|---|---|---|---|
| 34-90 | sdn 7P | 4,806 | 2,055 | 1,234 |
| 34-90L | limo 7P | 4,876 | 2,175 | 428 |
| 34-91 | club sdn 5P | 4,696 | 1,965 | 1,507 |
| 34-96C | conv cpe 4P | 4,511 | 1,945 | 83 |
| 34-96S | spt cpe 2-4P | 4,546 | 1,875 | 137 |
| 34-97 | sdn 4d | 4,691 | 1,945 | 654 |
| 34-98 | victoria cpe 5P | 4,571 | 1,895 | 348 |
| 34-98C | conv phtn 5P | 4,691 | 2,145 | 138 |
| — | chassis | — | — | 405 |

| 1934 Engines | bore × stroke | bhp | availability |
|---|---|---|---|
| I-8, 233.0 | 3.09 × 3.88 | 93 | S-40 |
| I-8, 235.3 | 2.97 × 4.25 | 88 | S-50 |
| I-8, 278.1 | 3.09 × 4.63 | 100 | S-60 |
| I-8, 344.8 | 3.13 × 5.00 | 116 | S-90 |

## 1935

| Series 40 (wb 117.0) | | Wght | Price | Prod |
|---|---|---|---|---|
| 35-41 | sdn T/B 4d | 3,210 | 925 | 19,173 |

# Buick

| Series 40 (wb 117.0) | | Wght | Price | Prod |
|---|---|---|---|---|
| 35-46 | bus cpe | 3,020 | 795 | 2,858 |
| **Series 40 (wb 117.0)** | | | | |
| 35-46C | conv cpe 2-4P | 3,140 | 925 | 1,000 |
| 35-46S | spt cpe 2-4P | 3,090 | 855 | 1,200 |
| 35-47 | sdn 4d | 3,180 | 895 | 6,641 |
| 35-48 | sdn 2d T/B | 3,160 | 865 | 5,027 |
| — | chassis | — | — | 2,621 |
| **Series 50 (wb 119.0)** | | | | |
| 35-56 | bus cpe | 3,652 | 1,110 | 257 |
| 35-56C | conv cpe 2-4P | 3,662 | 1,230 | 187 |
| 35-56S | spt cpe 2-4P | 3,682 | 1,145 | 279 |
| 35-57 | sdn 4d | 3,822 | 1,190 | 3,998 |
| 35-58 | victoria cpe 5P | 3,737 | 1,160 | 1,618 |
| — | chassis | — | — | 197 |
| **Series 60 (wb 128.0)** | | | | |
| 35-61 | club sdn 5P | 4,288 | 1,465 | 2,854 |
| 35-66C | conv cpe 2-4P | 4,103 | 1,495 | 111 |
| 35-66S | spt cpe 2-4P | 4,163 | 1,375 | 261 |
| 35-67 | sdn 4d | 4,273 | 1,425 | 1,792 |
| 35-68 | victoria cpe 5P | 4,183 | 1,395 | 603 |
| 35-68C | conv phtn 6W 5P | 4,323 | 1,675 | 308 |
| — | chassis | — | — | 309 |
| **Series 90 (wb 136.0)** | | | | |
| 35-90 | sdn 7P | 4,776 | 2,055 | 651 |
| 35-90L | limo 7P | 4,846 | 2,175 | 296 |
| 35-91 | club sdn 5P | 4,666 | 1,965 | 580 |
| 35-96C | conv cpe 2-4P | 4,481 | 1,945 | 11 |
| 35-96S | spt cpe 2-4P | 4,516 | 1,875 | 42 |
| 35-97 | sdn 4d | 4,661 | 1,945 | 119 |
| 35-98 | victoria cpe 5P | 4,541 | 1,895 | 32 |
| 35-98C | conv phtn 6W 5P | 4,661 | 2,145 | 43 |
| — | chassis | — | — | 181 |

| 1935 Engines | bore × stroke | bhp | availability |
|---|---|---|---|
| I-8, 233.0 | 3.09 × 3.88 | 93 | S-40 |
| I-8, 235.3 | 2.97 × 4.25 | 88 | S-50 |
| I-8, 278.1 | 3.09 × 4.63 | 100 | S-60 |
| I-8, 334.8 | 3.13 × 5.00 | 116 | S-90 |

## 1936

| Series 40 Special (wb 118.0) | | Wght | Price | Prod |
|---|---|---|---|---|
| 36-41 | sdn 4d T/B | 3,660 | 885 | 78,803 |
| 36-46 | bus cpe | 3,150 | 765 | 10,928 |
| 36-46C | conv cpe 2-4P | 3,590 | 905 | 1,650 |
| 36-46S | spt cpe 3P | 3,180 | 820 | 1,103 |
| 36-46S | spt cpe 2-4P R/S | 3,180 | 820 | 1,494 |
| 36-48 | victoria cpe T/B 5P | 3,305 | 835 | 22,323 |
| — | chassis | — | — | 5,413 |
| **Series 60 Century (wb 122.0)** | | | | |
| 36-61 | sdn 4d T/B | 3,780 | 1,090 | 18,203 |
| 36-66C | conv cpe 2-4P | 3,595 | 1,135 | 766 |
| 36-66S | spt cpe 3P T/B | 3,195 | 1,035 | 1,079 |
| 36-66S | spt cpe 2-4P R/S | 3,195 | 1,035 | 1,018 |
| 36-68 | victoria cpe T/B 5P | 3,730 | 1,055 | 3,799 |
| — | chassis | — | — | 1,115 |
| **Series 80 Roadmaster (wb 131.0)** | | | | |
| 36-80C | conv phtn T/B 6P | 4,100 | 1,565 | 1,230 |
| 36-81 | sdn 4d T/B 6P | 4,100 | 1,255 | 15,328 |
| — | chassis | — | — | 534 |
| **Series 90 Limited (wb 138.0)** | | | | |
| 36-90 | sdn T/B 8P | — | 1,845 | 1,709 |
| 36-90L | limo T/B 8P | — | 1,945 | 947 |

| Series 90 Limited (wb 138.0) | | Wght | Price | Prod |
|---|---|---|---|---|
| 36-91 | sdn T/B 6P | — | 1,695 | 1,726 |
| 36-91F | form sdn T/B 4d | 1,635 | 1,895 | 75 |
| — | chassis | — | — | 352 |

| 1936 Engines | bore × stroke | bhp | availability |
|---|---|---|---|
| I-8, 233.0 | 3.09 × 3.88 | 93 | S-40 |
| I-8, 320.2 | 3.44 × 4.31 | 120 | S-60, 80, 90 |

## 1937

| 40 Special (wb 122.0) | | Wght | Price | Prod |
|---|---|---|---|---|
| 37-40C | conv phtn 5P | 3,630 | 1,302 | 1,945 |
| 37-41 | sdn 4d T/B | 3,490 | 1,021 | 85,195 |
| 37-44 | sdn 2d | 3,490 | 959 | 9,342 |
| 37-46 | bus cpe | 3,380 | 913 | 13,773 |
| 37-46C | conv cpe 4P | 3,480 | 1,056 | 2,399 |
| 37-46S | spt cpe 4P | 3,445 | 975 | 5,284 |
| 37-47 | sdn 4d | 3,510 | 995 | 22,517 |
| 37-48 | tng sdn T/B 2d | 3,480 | 985 | 16,034 |
| — | chassis | — | — | 6,860 |
| **60 Century (wb 126.0)** | | | | |
| 37-60C | conv phtn 5P | 3,840 | 1,524 | 425 |
| 37-61 | tng sdn T/B 4d | 3,720 | 1,233 | 21,140 |
| 37-64 | sdn 2d | 3,720 | 1,172 | 1,118 |
| 37-66C | conv cpe 4P | 3,715 | 1,269 | 843 |
| 37-66S | spt cpe 4P | 3,660 | 1,187 | 2,873 |
| 37-67 | sdn 4d | 3,750 | 1,297 | 4,771 |
| 37-68 | tng sdn T/B 2d | 3,750 | 1,197 | 2,897 |
| — | chassis | — | — | 1,026 |
| **80 Roadmaster (wb 131.0)** | | | | |
| 37-80C | conv phtn T/B 6P | 4,214 | 1,856 | 1,155 |
| 37-81 | sdn T/B 4d | 4,159 | 1,518 | 14,981 |
| 37-81F | formal sdn 6P | 4,229 | 1,641 | 489 |
| — | chassis | — | — | 606 |
| **90 Limited (wb 138.0)** | | | | |
| 37-90 | sdn T/B 8P | 4,549 | 2,240 | 1,710 |
| 37-90L | limo T/B 8P | 4,599 | 2,342 | 965 |
| 37-91 | sdn T/B 4d | 4,469 | 2,066 | 1,242 |
| 37-91F | form sdn T/B 4d | 4,409 | 2,240 | 158 |
| — | chassis | — | — | 598 |

| 1937 Engines | bore × stroke | bhp | availability |
|---|---|---|---|
| I-8, 248.0 | 3.09 × 4.13 | 100 | S-40 |
| I-8, 320.2 | 3.44 × 4.31 | 130 | S-60, 80, 90 |

## 1938

| 40 Special (wb 122.0) | | Wght | Price | Prod |
|---|---|---|---|---|
| 38-40C | conv phtn 5P | 3,705 | 1,406 | 946 |
| 38-41 | tng sdn 4d T/B | 3,560 | 1,047 | 82,191 |
| 38-44 | spt sdn 2d 5P | 3,515 | 981 | 5,951 |
| 38-46 | bus cpe | 3,385 | 945 | 11,368 |
| 38-46C | conv cpe 4P | 3,575 | 1,103 | 2,625 |
| 38-46S | spt cpe T/B 4P | 3,425 | 1,001 | 5,574 |
| 38-47 | spt sdn 4d | 3,535 | 1,022 | 11,341 |
| 38-48 | tng sdn T/B 2d | 3,520 | 1,006 | 14,213 |
| — | chassis | — | — | 7,092 |
| **Series 60 Century (wb 126.0)** | | | | |
| 38-60C | conv phtn 5P | 3,950 | 1,713 | 219 |
| 38-61 | tng sdn T/B 4d | 3,780 | 1,297 | 12,673 |
| 38-66C | conv cpe 4P | 3,815 | 1,359 | 694 |
| 38-66S | spt cpe T/B 4P | 3,690 | 1,226 | 2,030 |
| 38-67 | spt sdn 4d | 3,785 | 1,272 | 1,516 |
| 38-68 | tng sdn T/B 2d | 3,760 | 1,256 | 1,393 |
| — | chassis | — | — | 762 |

# Buick

| Series 80 Roadmaster (wb 133.0) | | Wght | Price | Prod |
|---|---|---|---|---|
| 37-80C | conv phtn 6P | 4,235 | 1,983 | 411 |
| 37-81 | tng sdn T/B 4d | 4,245 | 1,645 | 4,704 |
| 37-81F | form sdn 6P | 4,305 | 1,758 | 296 |
| 37-87 | spt sdn 6P | 4,245 | 1,645 | 466 |
| — | chassis | — | — | 223 |
| **Series 90 Limited (wb 140.0)** | | | | |
| 37-90 | tng sdn T/B 8P | 4,585 | 2,350 | 706 |
| 37-90L | limo T/B 8P | 4,665 | 2,453 | 577 |
| 37-91 | tng sdn T/B 4d | 4,580 | 2,176 | 441 |
| — | chassis | — | — | 277 |

| 1938 Engines | bore × stroke | bhp | availability |
|---|---|---|---|
| I-8, 248.0 | 3.09 × 4.13 | 107 | S-40 |
| I-8, 320.2 | 3.44 × 4.31 | 141 | S-60, 80, 90 |

## 1939

| Series 40 Special (wb 120.0) | | Wght | Price | Prod |
|---|---|---|---|---|
| 41 | tng sdn T/B 4d | 3,482 | 966 | 111,473 |
| 41C | spt phtn T/B 5P | 3,642 | 1,406 | 830 |
| 46 | bus cpe | 3,322 | 894 | 14,609 |
| 46C | conv cpe T/B 4P | 3,452 | 1,077 | 4,809 |
| 46S | spt cpe T/B 4P | 3,372 | 950 | 10,276 |
| 48 | tng sdn T/B 2d | 3,417 | 955 | 27,290 |
| — | chassis | — | — | 6,281 |
| **Series 60 Century (wb 126.0)** | | | | |
| 61 | tng sdn T/B 4d | 3,782 | 1,246 | 18,783 |
| 61C | spt phtn T/B 5P | 3,917 | 1,713 | 269 |
| 66C | conv cpe T/B 4P | 3,712 | 1,343 | 850 |
| 66S | spt cpe T/B 4P | 3,637 | 1,175 | 3,470 |
| — | chassis | — | — | 518 |
| **Series 80 Roadmaster (wb 133.0)** | | | | |
| 80C | spt phtn 4d 6P | 4,237 | 1,983 | 3 |
| 81 | tng sdn T/B 4d | 4,247 | 1,543 | 5,619 |
| 81C | spt phtn T/B 4d | 4,392 | 1,983 | 364 |
| 81F | form sdn T/B 6P | 4,312 | 1,758 | 340 |
| 87 | spt sdn 6P | 4,262 | 1,543 | 20 |
| — | chassis | — | — | 143 |
| **Series 90 Limited (wb 140.0)** | | | | |
| 90 | tng sdn T/B 8P | 4,608 | 2,350 | 686 |
| 90L | limo T/B 8P | 4,653 | 2,453 | 543 |
| 91 | tng sdn T/B 4d | 4,568 | 2,074 | 382 |
| — | chassis | — | — | 176 |

| 1939 Engines | bore × stroke | bhp | availability |
|---|---|---|---|
| I-8, 248.0 | 3.09 × 4.13 | 107 | S-40 |
| I-8, 320.2 | 3.44 × 4.31 | 141 | S-60, 80, 90 |

## 1940

| Series 40 Special (wb 121.0) | | Wght | Price | Prod |
|---|---|---|---|---|
| 41 | sdn 4d | 3,660 | 996 | 68,816 |
| 41C | spt phtn | 3,755 | 1,355 | 597 |
| 41T | taxi | 3,700 | 1,000 | 48 |
| 46 | bus cpe | 3,505 | 895 | 12,382 |
| 46C | conv cpe | 3,665 | 1,077 | 3,763 |
| 46S | spt cpe | 3,540 | 950 | 8,401 |
| **Series 50 Super (wb 121.0)** | | **Wght** | **Price** | **Prod** |
| 48 | sdn 2d | 3,605 | 955 | 20,768 |
| 51 | sdn 4d | 3,790 | 1,109 | 97,226 |
| 51C | spt phtn | 3,895 | 1,549 | 534 |
| 56C | conv cpe | 3,785 | 1,211 | 4,804 |
| 56S | spt cpe | 3,735 | 1,058 | 26,462 |
| 59 | wgn 4d | 3,870 | 1,242 | 501 |

| Series 60 Century (wb 126.0) | | Wght | Price | Prod |
|---|---|---|---|---|
| 61 | sdn 4d | 3,935 | 1,210 | 8,708 |
| 61C | spt phtn | 4,050 | 1,620 | 203 |
| 66 | bus cpe | 3,800 | 1,128 | 44 |
| 66C | conv cpe | 3,915 | 1,343 | 550 |
| 66S | spt cpe | 3,765 | 1,175 | 96 |
| **Series 70 Roadmaster (wb 126.0)** | | | | |
| 71 | sdn 4d | 4,045 | 1,359 | 13,733 |
| 71C | spt phtn | 4,195 | 1,768 | 238 |
| 76C | conv cpe | 4,055 | 1,431 | 612 |
| 76S | spt cpe | 3,990 | 1,277 | 3,972 |
| **Series 80 Limited (wb 133.0)** | | | | |
| 80C | Streamlined spt phtn | 4,540 | 1,952 | 7 |
| 81 | sdn 4d | 4,440 | 1,553 | 3,898 |
| 81C | T/B spt phtn | 4,540 | 1,952 | 250 |
| 81F | T/B form sdn | 4,455 | 1,727 | 270 |
| 87 | Streamlined spt sdn 4d | 4,380 | 1,553 | 14 |
| 87F | Streamlined form sdn | 4,455 | 1,727 | 7 |
| **Series 90 Limited (wb 140.0)** | | | | |
| 90 | sdn 4d, 8P, A/S | 4,645 | 2,096 | 828 |
| 90L | limo 8P, A/S | 4,705 | 2,199 | 634 |
| 91 | sdn 4d | 4,590 | 1,942 | 418 |

| 1940 Engines | bore × stroke | bhp | availability |
|---|---|---|---|
| I-8, 248.0 | 3.09 × 4.13 | 107 | S-40, 50 |
| I-8, 320.2 | 3.44 × 4.31 | 141 | S-60, 70, 80, 90 |

## 1941

| Series 40 Special (wb 121.0) | | Wght | Price | Prod |
|---|---|---|---|---|
| 41 | sdn 4d | 3,730 | 1,052 | 92,528 |
| 41SE | sdn 4d | 3,790 | 1,134 | 13,402 |
| 46 | bus cpe | 3,630 | 935 | 9,201 |
| 46S | sedanet | 3,700 | 1,006 | 88,148 |
| 46SSE | sedanet | 3,690 | 1,063 | 9,614 |
| 49 | wgn 4d | 3,980 | 1,463 | 850 |
| **Series 40A Special (wb 118.0)** | | | | |
| 44 | bus cpe | 3,530 | 915 | 3,261 |
| 44C | conv cpe | 3,780 | 1,138 | 4,309 |
| 44S | spt cpe | 3,590 | 980 | 5,290 |
| 47 | sdn 4d | 3,670 | 1,021 | 14,139 |
| **Series 50 Super (wb 121.0)** | | | | |
| 51 | sdn 4d | 3,770 | 1,185 | 58,638 |
| 51C | conv phtn | 4,014 | 1,555 | 508 |
| 56 | bus cpe | 3,620 | 1,031 | 2,452 |
| 56C | conv cpe | 3,810 | 1,267 | 12,391 |
| 56S | spt cpe | 3,670 | 1,113 | 19,876 |
| **Series 60 Century (wb 126.0)** | | | | |
| 61 | sdn 4d | 4,025 | 1,288 | 15,136 |
| 66 | bus cpe | 3,870 | 1,195 | 222 |
| 66S | sedanet | 3,920 | 1,241 | 5,547 |
| **Series 70 Roadmaster (wb 126.0)** | | | | |
| 71 | sdn 4d | 4,010 | 1,364 | 10,553 |
| 71C | conv phtn | 4,469 | 1,775 | 326 |
| 76C | conv cpe | 4,045 | 1,457 | 1,869 |
| 76S | spt cpe | 3,920 | 1,282 | 2,834 |
| **Series 90 Limited (wb 139.0)** | | | | |
| 90 | sdn 4d, 8P, A/S | 4,680 | 2,360 | 906 |
| 90L | limo 8P, A/S | 4,760 | 2,465 | 669 |
| 91 | sdn 4d | 4,575 | 2,155 | 1,231 |
| 91F | form sdn, A/S | 4,665 | 2,310 | 296 |

| 1941 Engines | bore × stroke | bhp | availability |
|---|---|---|---|
| I-8, 248.0 | 3.09 × 4.13 | 115 | S-40A, 40 exc SE |

# Buick

| 1941 Engines | bore × stroke | bhp | availability |
|---|---|---|---|
| I-8, 248.0 | 3.09 × 4.13 | 125 | S-50, 41SE, 46SSE |
| I-8, 320.2 | 3.44 × 4.31 | 165 | S-60, 70, 90 |

## 1942

| Series 40A Special (wb 118.) | | Wght | Price | Prod |
|---|---|---|---|---|
| 44 | util cpe | 3,510 | 990 | 461 |
| 44C | conv cpe | 3,790 | 1,260 | 1,788 |
| 47 | sdn 4d | 3,650 | 1,080 | 1,652 |
| 48 | bus sedanet | 3,555 | 1,010 | 559 |
| 48S | fam sedanet | 3,610 | 1,045 | 5,990 |
| Series 40B Special (wb 121.0) | | | | |
| 41 | sdn 4d | 3,760 | 1,120 | 17,397 |
| 41SE | sdn 4d | 3,785 | 1,200 | 2,288 |
| 46 | bus sedanet | 3,650 | 1,020 | 1,408 |
| 46S | fam sedanet | 3,705 | 1,075 | 11,856 |
| 46SSE | fam sedanet | 3,725 | 1,130 | 1,809 |
| 49 | wgn 4d | 3,925 | 1,450 | 327 |
| Series 50 Super (wb 124.0) | | | | |
| 51 | sdn 4d | 3,890 | 1,280 | 16,265 |
| 56C | conv cpe | 4,025 | 1,450 | 2,489 |
| 56S | sedanet | 3,800 | 1,230 | 14,629 |
| Series 60 Century (wb 126.0) | | | | |
| 61 | sdn 4d | 4,065 | 1,350 | 3,319 |
| 66S | sedanet | 3,985 | 1,300 | 1,232 |
| Series 70 Roadmaster (wb 129.0) | | | | |
| 71 | sdn 4d | 4,150 | 1,465 | 5,418 |
| 76C | conv cpe | 4,300 | 1,675 | 511 |
| 76S | sedanet | 4,075 | 1,395 | 2,475 |
| Series 90 Limited (wb 139.0) | | | | |
| 90 | sdn 4d, 8P, A/S | 4,710 | 2,445 | 150 |
| 90L | limo 8P, A/S | 4,765 | 2,545 | 250 |
| 91 | sdn 4d | 4,665 | 2,245 | 215 |
| 91F | form sdn | 4,695 | 2,395 | 85 |

| 1942 Engines | bore × stroke | bhp | availability |
|---|---|---|---|
| I-8, 248.0 | 3.09 × 4.13 | 110 | S-40A, 40B exc SE |
| I-8, 248.0 | 3.09 × 4.13 | 118 | S-50, 46SSE, 41SE |
| I-8, 320.2 | 3.44 × 4.31 | 165 | S-60, 70, 90 |

## 1946

| Series 40 Special (wb 121.0) | | Wght | Price | Prod |
|---|---|---|---|---|
| 41 | sdn 4d | 3,720 | 1,580 | 1,650 |
| 46S | sedanet | 3,670 | 1,522 | 1,350 |
| Series 50 Super (wb 124.0) | | | | |
| 51 | sdn 4d | 3,935 | 1,822 | 77,724 |
| 56C | conv cpe | 4,050 | 2,046 | 5,987 |
| 56S | sedanet | 3,795 | 1,741 | 34,425 |
| 59 | wgn 4d | 4,170 | 2,594 | 748 |
| Series 70 Roadmaster (wb 129.0) | | | | |
| 71 | sdn 4d | 4,165 | 2,110 | 20,864 |
| 76C | conv cpe | 4,345 | 2,347 | 2,587 |
| 76S | sedanet | 4,095 | 2,014 | 8,292 |

| 1946 Engines | bore × stroke | bhp | availability |
|---|---|---|---|
| I-8, 248.0 | 3.09 × 4.13 | 110 | S-40, 50 |
| I-8, 320.2 | 3.44 × 4.31 | 144 | S-70 |

## 1947

| Series 40 Special (wb 121.0) | | Wght | Price | Prod |
|---|---|---|---|---|
| 41 | sdn 4d | 3,720 | 1,623 | 18,431 |
| 46S | sedanet | 3,760 | 1,611 | 14,603 |
| Series 50 Super (wb 124.0) | | | | |
| 51 | sdn 4d | 3,910 | 1,929 | 83,576 |
| 56C | conv cpe | 4,050 | 2,333 | 28,297 |
| 56S | sedanet | 3,795 | 1,843 | 46,917 |
| 59 | wgn 4d | 4,170 | 2,940 | 2,036 |
| Series 70 Roadmaster (wb 129.0) | | | | |
| 71 | sdn 4d | 4,190 | 2,232 | 47,152 |
| 76C | conv cpe | 4,345 | 2,651 | 12,074 |
| 76S | sedanet | 4,095 | 2,131 | 19,212 |
| 79 | wgn 4d | 4,445 | 3,249 | 300 |

| 1947 Engines | bore × stroke | bhp | availability |
|---|---|---|---|
| I-8, 248.0 | 3.09 × 4.13 | 110 | S-40, 50 |
| I-8, 320.2 | 3.44 × 4.31 | 144 | S-70 |

## 1948

| Series 40 Special (wb 121.0) | | Wght | Price | Prod |
|---|---|---|---|---|
| 41 | sdn 4d | 3,705 | 1,809 | 14,051 |
| 46S | sedanet | 3,635 | 1,735 | 11,176 |
| Series 50 Super (wb 124.0) | | | | |
| 51 | sdn 4d | 3,855 | 2,087 | 53,447 |
| 56C | conv cpe | 4,020 | 2,518 | 19,017 |
| 56S | sedanet | 3,770 | 1,987 | 33,819 |
| 59 | wgn 4d | 4,170 | 3,127 | 2,018 |
| Series 70 Roadmaster (wb 129.0) | | | | |
| 71 | sedan 4d | 4,160 | 2,418 | 47,569 |
| 76C | conv cpe | 4,315 | 2,837 | 11,503 |
| 76S | sedanet | 4,065 | 2,297 | 20,649 |
| 79 | wgn 4d | 4,460 | 3,433 | 350 |

| 1948 Engines | bore × stroke | bhp | availability |
|---|---|---|---|
| I-8, 248.0 | 3.09 × 4.13 | 110 | S-40 |
| I-8, 248.0 | 3.09 × 4.13 | 115 | S-50 |
| I-8, 320.2 | 3.44 × 4.31 | 144/150 | S-70 |

## 1949

| Series 40 Special (wb 121.0) | | Wght | Price | Prod |
|---|---|---|---|---|
| 41 | sdn 4d | 3,695 | 1,861 | 5,940 |
| 46S | sedanet | 3,625 | 1,787 | 4,687 |
| Series 50 Super (wb 121.0) | | | | |
| 51 | sedan 4d | 3,835 | 2,157 | 136,423 |
| 56C | conv cpe | 3,985 | 2,583 | 22,110 |
| 56S | sedanet | 3,735 | 2,059 | 66,250 |
| 59 | wgn 4d | 4,100 | 3,178 | 1,847 |
| Series 70 Roadmaster (wb 126.0) | | | | |
| 71 | sdn 4d | 4,205 | 2,735 | 55,242 |
| 76C | conv cpe | 4,370 | 3,150 | 8,244 |
| 76R | Riviera htp cpe | 4,420 | 3,203 | 4,343 |
| 76S | sedanet | 4,115 | 2,618 | 18,537 |
| 79 | wgn 4d | 4,490 | 3,734 | 653 |

| 1949 Engines | bore × stroke | bhp | availability |
|---|---|---|---|
| I-8, 248.0 | 3.09 × 4.13 | 110 | S-40 |
| I-8, 248.0 | 3.09 × 4.13 | 115/120 | S-50 |
| I-8, 320.2 | 3.44 × 4.31 | 150 | S-70 |

## 1950

| Series 40 Special (wb 121.5) | | Wght | Price | Prod |
|---|---|---|---|---|
| 41 | sdn 4d | 3,710 | 1,941 | 1,141 |
| 41D | DeLuxe sdn | 3,735 | 1,983 | 141,396 |
| 43 | J/B sdn 4d | 3,715 | 1,809 | 58,700 |
| 43D | DeLuxe J/B sdn, 4d | 3,720 | 1,952 | 14,335 |
| 46 | J/B cpe | 3,615 | 1,803 | 2,500 |
| 46D | DeLuxe J/B cpe | 3,665 | 1,899 | 76,902 |
| 46S | J/B sedanet | 3,655 | 1,856 | 42,935 |

# Buick

| Series 50 Super (wb 121.5) | | Wght | Price | Prod |
|---|---|---|---|---|
| 51 | sdn 4d | 3,745 | 2,139 | 55,672 |
| 56C | conv cpe | 3,965 | 2,476 | 12,259 |
| 56R | Riviera htp cpe | 3,790 | 2,139 | 56,030 |
| 56S | J/B sedanet | 3,645 | 2,041 | 10,697 |
| 59 | wgn 4d | 4,115 | 2,844 | 2,480 |
| **Series 50 Super (wb 125.5)** | | | | |
| 52 | sdn 4d | 3,870 | 2,212 | 114,745 |
| **Series 70 Roadmaster (wb 125.3; 72-130.3)** | | | | |
| 71 | sdn 4d | 4,135 | 2,633 | 6,738 |
| 72 | Riviera sdn 4d | 4,220 | 2,738 | 54,212 |
| 75R | Riviera htp cpe | 4,135 | 2,633 | 2,300 |
| 76R | Riv DeLuxe htp cpe | 4,245 | 2,854 | 8,432 |
| 76C | conv cpe | 4,345 | 2,981 | 2,964 |
| 76S | J/B sedanet | 4,025 | 2,528 | 2,968 |
| 79 | wgn 4d | 4,470 | 3,407 | 420 |

| 1950 Engines | bore × stroke | bhp | availability |
|---|---|---|---|
| I-8, 248.0 | 3.09 × 4.13 | 115/120 | S-40 |
| I-8, 263.3 | 3.19 × 4.13 | 124/128 | S-50 |
| I-8, 320.2 | 3.44 × 4.31 | 152 | S-70 |

## 1951

| Series 40 Special (wb 121.5) | | Wght | Price | Prod |
|---|---|---|---|---|
| 41 | sdn 4d | 3,605 | 2,139 | 999 |
| 41D | DeLuxe sdn 4d | 3,680 | 2,185 | 87,848 |
| 45R | Riviera sdn 2d | 3,645 | 2,225 | 16,491 |
| 46C | conv cpe | 3,830 | 2,561 | 2,099 |
| 46S | spt cpe | 3,600 | 2,046 | 2,700 |
| 48D | DeLuxe sdn 2d | 3,615 | 2,127 | 54,311 |
| **Series 50 Super (wb 121.5; 52-125.5)** | | | | |
| 51 | sdn 4d | 3,755 | 2,356 | 10,000 |
| 52 | Riviera sdn 4d | 3,845 | 2,437 | 92,886 |
| 56C | conv cpe | 3,965 | 2,728 | 8,116 |
| 56R | Riviera sdn 2d | 3,765 | 2,356 | 54,512 |
| 56S | DeLuxe sdn 2d | 3,685 | 2,248 | 1,500 |
| 59 | wgn 4d | 4,100 | 3,133 | 2,212 |
| **Series 70 Roadmaster (wb 126.3; 72R-130.3)** | | | | |
| 72R | Riviera sdn 4d | 4,240 | 3,044 | 48,758 |
| 76C | conv cpe | 4,355 | 3,283 | 2,911 |
| 76MR | Riviera htp cpe | 4,185 | 3,051 | 809 |
| 76R | Riv htp cpe, hydrlic cntrls | 4,235 | 3,143 | 12,901 |
| 79R | wgn 4d | 4,470 | 3,780 | 679 |

| 1951 Engines | bore × stroke | bhp | availability |
|---|---|---|---|
| I-8, 263.3 | 3.19 × 4.13 | 120/128 | S-40 |
| I-8, 263.3 | 3.19 × 4.13 | 124/128 | S-50 |
| I-8, 320.2 | 3.44 × 4.31 | 152 | S-70 |

## 1952

| Series 40 Special (wb 121.5) | | Wght | Price | Prod |
|---|---|---|---|---|
| 41 | sdn 4d | 3,650 | 2,209 | 137 |
| 41D | DeLuxe sdn 4d | 3,665 | 2,255 | 63,346 |
| 45R | Riviera htp cpe | 3,665 | 2,295 | 21,180 |
| 46C | conv cpe | 3,850 | 2,634 | 600 |
| 46S | spt cpe | 3,605 | 2,115 | 2,206 |
| 48D | sdn 2d | 3,620 | 2,197 | 32,684 |
| **Series 50 Super (wb 121.5; 52-125.5)** | | | | |
| 52 | sdn 4d | 3,825 | 2,563 | 71,387 |
| 56C | conv cpe | 3,970 | 2,869 | 6,904 |
| 56R | Riviera htp cpe | 3,775 | 2,478 | 55,400 |
| 59 | wgn 4d | 4,105 | 3,296 | 1,641 |
| **Series 70 Roadmaster (wb 126.3; 72R-130.3)** | | | | |
| 72R | sdn 4d | 4,285 | 3,200 | 32,069 |

| Series 70 Roadmaster (wb 126.3; 72R-130.3) | | Wght | Price | Prod |
|---|---|---|---|---|
| 76C | conv cpe | 4,395 | 3,453 | 2,402 |
| 76R | Riviera htp cpe | 4,235 | 3,306 | 11,387 |
| 79R | wgn 4d | 4,505 | 3,977 | 359 |

| 1952 Engines | bore × stroke | bhp | availability |
|---|---|---|---|
| I-8, 263.3 | 3.19 × 4.13 | 120/128 | S-40 |
| I-8, 263.3 | 3.19 × 4.13 | 124/128 | S-50 |
| I-8, 320.2 | 3.44 × 4.31 | 170 | S-70 |

## 1953

| Series 40 Special (wb 121.5) | | Wght | Price | Prod |
|---|---|---|---|---|
| 41D | DeLuxe sdn 4d | 3,710 | 2,255 | 100,312 |
| 45R | Riviera htp cpe | 3,705 | 2,295 | 58,780 |
| 46C | conv cpe | 3,815 | 2,553 | 4,282 |
| 48D | DeLuxe sdn 2d | 3,675 | 2,197 | 53,796 |
| **Series 50 Super (wb 121.5; 52-125.5)** | | | | |
| 52 | Riviera sdn 4d | 3,905 | 2,696 | 90,685 |
| 56C | conv cpe | 4,035 | 3,002 | 6,701 |
| 56R | Riviera htp cpe | 3,845 | 2,611 | 91,298 |
| 59 | wgn 4d | 4,150 | 3,430 | 1,830 |
| **Series 70 Roadmaster (wb 121.5; 72R-125.5)** | | | | |
| 72R | Riviera sdn 4d | 4,100 | 3,254 | 50,523 |
| 76C | conv cpe | 4,250 | 3,506 | 3,318 |
| 76R | Riviera htp cpe | 4,125 | 3,358 | 22,927 |
| 76X | Skylark conv cpe | 4,315 | 5,000 | 1,690 |
| 79R | wgn 4d | 4,315 | 4,031 | 670 |

| 1953 Engines | bore × stroke | bhp | availability |
|---|---|---|---|
| I-8, 263.3 | 3.19 × 4.13 | 125/130 | S-40 |
| V-8, 322.0 | 4.00 × 3.20 | 164/170 | S-50 |
| V-8, 322.0 | 4.00 × 3.20 | 188 | S-70 |

## 1954

| Series 40 Special (wb 122.0) | | Wght | Price | Prod |
|---|---|---|---|---|
| 41D | DeLuxe sdn 4d | 3,735 | 2,265 | 70,356 |
| 46C | conv cpe | 3,810 | 2,563 | 6,135 |
| 46R | Riviera htp cpe | 3,740 | 2,305 | 71,186 |
| 48D | DeLuxe sdn 2d | 3,690 | 2,207 | 41,557 |
| 49 | DeLuxe wgn 4d | 3,905 | 3,163 | 1,650 |
| **Series 50 Super (wb 127.0)** | | | | |
| 52 | Riviera sdn 4d | 4,105 | 2,711 | 41,756 |
| 56C | conv cpe | 4,145 | 2,964 | 3,343 |
| 56R | Riviera htp cpe | 4,035 | 2,626 | 73,531 |
| **Series 60 Century (wb 122.0)** | | | | |
| 61 | sdn 4d | 3,805 | 2,520 | 31,919 |
| 66C | conv cpe | 3,950 | 2,963 | 2,790 |
| 66R | Riviera htp cpe | 3,795 | 2,534 | 45,710 |
| 69 | wgn 4d | 3,975 | 3,470 | 1,563 |
| **Series 70 Roadmaster (wb 127.0)** | | | | |
| 72R | Riviera sdn 4d | 4,250 | 3,269 | 26,862 |
| 76C | conv cpe | 4,355 | 3,521 | 20,404 |
| 76R | Riviera htp cpe | 4,215 | 3,373 | 3,305 |
| **Series 100 Skylark (wb 122.0)** | | | | |
| 100M | conv cpe | 4,260 | 4,483 | 836 |

| 1954 Engines | bore × stroke | bhp | availability |
|---|---|---|---|
| V-8, 264.0 | 3.63 × 3.20 | 143/150 | S-40 |
| V-8, 322.0 | 4.00 × 3.20 | 177/182 | S-50 |
| V-8, 322.0 | 4.00 × 3.20 | 195/200 | S-60 |
| V-8, 322.0 | 4.00 × 3.20 | 200 | S-70, 100 |

## 1955

| Series 40 Special (wb 122.0) | | Wght | Price | Prod |
|---|---|---|---|---|
| 41 | sdn 4d | 3,745 | 2,291 | 84,182 |

| Series 40 Special (wb 122.0) | | Wght | Price | Prod |
|---|---|---|---|---|
| 43 | Riviera htp sdn | 3,820 | 2,409 | 66,409 |
| 46C | conv cpe | 3,825 | 2,590 | 10,009 |
| 46R | Riviera htp cpe | 3,720 | 2,332 | 155,818 |
| 48 | sdn 2d | 3,715 | 2,233 | 61,879 |
| 49 | wgn 4d | 3,940 | 2,974 | 2,952 |
| Series 50 Super (wb 127.0) | | | | |
| 52 | sdn 4d | 4,140 | 2,876 | 43,280 |
| 56C | conv cpe | 4,280 | 3,225 | 3,527 |
| 56R | Riviera htp cpe | 4,075 | 2,831 | 85,656 |
| Series 60 Century (wb 122.0) | | | | |
| 61 | sdn 4d | 3,825 | 2,548 | 13,269 |
| 63 | Riviera htp sdn | 3,900 | 2,733 | 55,088 |
| 66C | conv cpe | 3,950 | 2,991 | 5,588 |
| 66R | Riviera htp cpe | 3,805 | 2,601 | 80,338 |
| 68 | sdn 2d | 3,795 | 2,490 | 270 |
| 69 | wgn 4d | 3,995 | 3,175 | 4,243 |
| Series 70 Roadmaster (wb 127.0) | | | | |
| 72 | sdn 4d | 4,300 | 3,349 | 31,717 |
| 76C | conv cpe | 4,415 | 3,552 | 4,739 |
| 76R | Riviera htp cpe | 4,270 | 3,453 | 28,071 |

| 1955 Engines | bore × stroke | bhp | availability |
|---|---|---|---|
| V-8, 264.0 | 3.63 × 3.20 | 188 | S-40 |
| V-8, 322.0 | 4.00 × 3.20 | 236 | S-50, 60, 70 |

## 1956

| Series 40 Special (wb 122.0) | | Wght | Price | Prod |
|---|---|---|---|---|
| 41 | sdn 4d | 3,790 | 2,416 | 66,977 |
| 43 | Riviera htp sdn | 3,860 | 2,528 | 91,025 |
| 46C | Special conv cpe | 3,880 | 2,740 | 9,712 |
| 46R | Riviera htp cpe | 3,775 | 2,457 | 113,861 |
| 48 | sdn 2d | 3,750 | 2,357 | 38,672 |
| 49 | wgn 4d | 3,945 | 2,775 | 13,770 |
| Series 50 Super (wb 127.0) | | | | |
| 52 | sdn 4d | 4,200 | 3,250 | 14,940 |
| 53 | Riviera htp sdn | 4,265 | 3,340 | 34,029 |
| 56C | conv cpe | 4,340 | 3,544 | 2,889 |
| 56R | Riviera htp cpe | 4,140 | 3,204 | 29,540 |
| Series 60 Century (wb 122.0) | | | | |
| 61 | sdn 4d | 3,930 | exp | 1 |
| 63 | Riviera htp sdn | 4,000 | 3,025 | 20,891 |
| 63D | Riviera DeLuxe htp sdn | 4,000 | 3,041 | 35,082 |
| 66C | conv cpe | 4,045 | 3,306 | 4,721 |
| 66R | Riviera htp cpe | 3,890 | 2,963 | 33,334 |
| 69 | wgn 4d | 4,080 | 3,256 | 8,160 |
| Series 70 Roadmaster (wb 127.0) | | | | |
| 72 | sdn 4d | 4,280 | 3,503 | 11,804 |
| 73 | Riviera htp sdn | 4,355 | 3,692 | 24,779 |
| 76C | conv cpe | 4,395 | 3,704 | 4,354 |
| 76R | Riviera htp cpe | 4,235 | 3,591 | 12,490 |

| 1956 Engines | bore × stroke | bhp | availability |
|---|---|---|---|
| V-8, 322.0 | 4.00 × 3.20 | 220 | S-40 |
| V-8, 322.0 | 4.00 × 3.20 | 255 | S-50, 60, 70 |

## 1957

| Series 40 Special (wb 122.0) | | Wght | Price | Prod |
|---|---|---|---|---|
| 41 | sdn 4d | 4,012 | 2,660 | 59,739 |
| 43 | Riviera htp sdn | 4,041 | 2,780 | 50,563 |
| 46C | conv cpe | 4,082 | 2,987 | 8,505 |
| 46R | Riviera hpt cpe | 3,956 | 2,704 | 64,425 |
| 48 | sdn 2d | 3,955 | 2,596 | 23,180 |
| 49 | wgn 4d | 4,292 | 3,047 | 7,013 |
| 49D | Riviera Estate wgn 4d | 4,309 | 3,167 | 6,817 |
| Series 50 Super (wb 127.5) | | | | |
| 53 | Riviera htp sdn | 4,356 | 3,681 | 41,665 |
| 56C | conv cpe | 4,414 | 3,981 | 2,056 |
| 56R | Riviera htp cpe | 4,271 | 3,536 | 26,529 |
| Series 60 Century (wb 122.0) | | | | |
| 61 | sdn 4d | 4,137 | 3,234 | 8,075 |
| 63 | Riviera htp sdn | 4,163 | 3,354 | 26,589 |
| 66C | conv cpe | 4,234 | 3,598 | 4,085 |
| 66R | Riviera htp cpe | 4,081 | 3,270 | 17,029 |
| 68 | sdn 2d | 4,080 | exp | 2 |
| 69 | Caballero wgn 4d | 4,423 | 3,706 | 10,186 |
| Series 70 Roadmaster (wb 127.5) | | | | |
| 73 | Riviera htp sdn | 4,469 | 4,053 | 11,401 |
| 73A | Riviera htp sdn, 1-pc bcklt | 4,455 | 4,053 | 10,526 |
| 76C | conv cpe | 4,500 | 4,066 | 4,363 |
| 76R | Riviera htp cpe | 4,374 | 3,944 | 3,826 |
| 76A | Riviera htp cpe, 1-pc bcklt | 4,370 | 3,944 | 2,812 |
| Series 75 Roadmaster (wb 127.5) | | | | |
| 75 | Riviera htp sdn | 4,539 | 4,483 | 12,250 |
| 75R | Riviera htp cpe | 4,427 | 4,373 | 2,404 |

| 1957 Engines | bore × stroke | bhp | availability |
|---|---|---|---|
| V-8, 364.0 | 4.13 × 3.40 | 250 | S-40 |
| V-8, 364.0 | 4.13 × 3.40 | 300 | S-50, 60, 70, 75 |

## 1958

| Series 40 Special (wb 122.0) | | Wght | Price | Prod |
|---|---|---|---|---|
| 41 | sdn 4d | 4,115 | 2,700 | 48,238 |
| 43 | Riviera htp sdn | 4,180 | 2,820 | 31,921 |
| 46C | conv cpe | 4,165 | 3,041 | 5,502 |
| 46R | Riviera htp cpe | 4,058 | 2,744 | 34,903 |
| 48 | sdn 2d | 4,063 | 2,636 | 11,566 |
| 49 | wgn 4d | 4,396 | 3,154 | 3,663 |
| 49D | Riviera Estate htp wgn 4d | 4,408 | 3,261 | 3,420 |
| Series 50 Super (wb 127.5) | | | | |
| 53 | Riviera htp sdn | 4,500 | 3,789 | 28,460 |
| 56R | Riviera htp cpe | 4,392 | 3,644 | 13,928 |
| Series 60 Century (wb 122.0) | | | | |
| 61 | sdn 4d | 4,241 | 3,316 | 7,241 |
| 63 | Riviera htp sdn | 4,267 | 3,436 | 15,171 |
| 66C | conv cpe | 4,302 | 3,680 | 2,588 |
| 66R | Riviera htp cpe | 4,182 | 3,368 | 8,110 |
| 68 | sdn 2d | 4,189 | export | 2 |
| 69 | Caballero htp wgn 4d | 4,498 | 3,831 | 4,456 |
| Series 75 Roadmaster (wb 127.5) | | | | |
| 75 | Riviera htp sdn | 4,668 | 4,667 | 10,505 |
| 75C | conv cpe | 4,676 | 4,680 | 1,181 |
| 75R | Riviera htp cpe | 4,568 | 4,557 | 2,368 |
| Series 700 Limited (wb 127.5) | | | | |
| 750 | Riviera htp sdn | 4,710 | 5,112 | 5,571 |
| 755 | Riviera htp cpe | 4,691 | 5,002 | 1,026 |
| 756 | conv cpe | 4,603 | 5,125 | 839 |

| 1958 Engines | bore × stroke | bhp | availability |
|---|---|---|---|
| V-8, 364.0 | 4.13 × 3.40 | 250 | S-40 |
| V-8, 364.0 | 4.13 × 3.40 | 300 | S-50, 60, 75, 700 |

## 1959

| 4400 LeSabre (wb 123.0) | | Wght | Price | Prod |
|---|---|---|---|---|
| 4411 | sdn 2d | 4,159 | 2,740 | 13,492 |
| 4419 | sdn 4d | 4,229 | 2,804 | 51,379 |
| 4435 | wgn 4d | 4,565 | 3,320 | 8,286 |
| 4437 | htp cpe | 4,188 | 2,849 | 35,189 |
| 4439 | htp sdn | 4,266 | 2,925 | 46,069 |

# Buick

| 4400 LeSabre (wb 123.0) | | Wght | Price | Prod |
|---|---|---|---|---|
| 4467 | conv cpe | 4,216 | 3,129 | 10,489 |
| **4600 Invicta (wb 123.0)** | | | | |
| 4619 | sdn 4d | 4,331 | 3,357 | 10,566 |
| 4635 | wgn 4d | 4,660 | 3,841 | 5,231 |
| 4637 | htp cpe | 4,274 | 3,447 | 11,451 |
| 4639 | htp sdn | 4,373 | 3,515 | 20,156 |
| 4667 | conv cpe | 4,317 | 3,620 | 5,447 |
| **4700 Electra (wb 126.3)** | | | | |
| 4719 | sdn 4d | 4,557 | 3,856 | 12,357 |
| 4737 | htp cpe | 4,465 | 3,818 | 11,216 |
| 4739 | htp sdn | 4,573 | 3,963 | 20,612 |
| **4800 Electra 225 (wb 126.3)** | | | | |
| 4829 | Riviera htp sdn | 4,632 | 4,300 | 6,324 |
| 4839 | htp sdn | 4,641 | 4,300 | 10,491 |
| 4867 | conv cpe | 4,562 | 4,192 | 5,493 |

| 1959 Engines | bore × stroke | bhp | availability |
|---|---|---|---|
| V-8, 364.0 | 4.13 × 3.40 | 250 | S-LeSabre |
| V-8, 401.0 | 4.19 × 3.64 | 325 | S-others |

## 1960

| 4400 LeSabre (wb 123.0) | | Wght | Price | Prod |
|---|---|---|---|---|
| 4411 | sdn 2d | 4,139 | 2,756 | 14,388 |
| 4419 | sdn 4d | 4,219 | 2,870 | 54,033 |
| 4435 | wgn 4d, 2S | 4,568 | 3,386 | 5,331 |
| 4437 | htp cpe | 4,163 | 2,915 | 26,521 |
| 4439 | htp sdn | 4,269 | 2,991 | 35,999 |
| 4445 | wgn 4d, 3S | 4,574 | 3,493 | 2,222 |
| 4467 | conv cpe | 4,233 | 3,145 | 13,588 |
| **4600 Invicta (wb 123.0)** | | | | |
| 4619 | sdn 4d | 4,324 | 3,357 | 10,839 |
| 4635 | wgn 4d, 2S | 4,644 | 3,841 | 3,471 |
| 4637 | htp cpe | 4,255 | 3,447 | 8,960 |
| 4639 | htp sdn | 4,365 | 3,515 | 15,300 |
| 4645 | wgn 4d, 3S | 4,679 | 3,948 | 1,605 |
| 4667 | conv cpe | 4,347 | 3,620 | 5,236 |
| **4700 Electra (wb 126.3)** | | | | |
| 4719 | sdn 4d | 4,544 | 3,856 | 13,794 |
| 4737 | htp cpe | 4,453 | 3,818 | 7,416 |
| 4739 | htp sdn | 4,554 | 3,963 | 14,488 |
| **4800 Electra 225 (wb 126.3)** | | | | |
| 4829 | Riviera htp sdn | 4,653 | 4,300 | 8,029 |
| 4839 | htp sdn | 4,650 | 4,300 | 5,841 |
| 4867 | conv cpe | 4,571 | 4,192 | 6,746 |

| 1960 Engines | bore × stroke | bhp | availability |
|---|---|---|---|
| V-8, 364.0 | 4.13 × 3.40 | 235/250 | S-LeSabre |
| V-8, 364.0 | 4.13 × 3.40 | 300 | O-LeSabre |
| V-8, 401.0 | 4.19 × 3.40 | 325 | S-others |

## 1961

| 4000 Special (wb 112.0) | | Wght | Price | Prod |
|---|---|---|---|---|
| 4019 | sdn 4d | 2,610 | 2,384 | 18,339 |
| 4027 | spt cpe | 2,579 | 2,330 | 4,232 |
| 4035 | wgn 4d | 2,775 | 2,681 | 6,101 |
| 4045 | wgn 4d, 3S | 2,844 | 2,762 | 798 |
| 4119 | DeLuxe sdn 4d | 2,632 | 2,519 | 32,986 |
| 4135 | DeLuxe wgn 4d | 2,794 | 2,816 | 11,729 |
| 4317 | Skylark spt cpe | 2,687 | 2,621 | 12,683 |
| **4400 LeSabre (wb 123.0)** | | | | |
| 4411 | sdn 2d | 4,033 | 2,993 | 5,959 |
| 4435 | wgn 4d | 4,450 | 3,623 | 5,628 |
| 4437 | htp cpe | 4,054 | 3,152 | 14,474 |
| 4439 | htp sdn | 4,129 | 3,228 | 37,790 |
| 4445 | wgn 4d, 3S | 4,483 | 3,730 | 2,423 |
| 4467 | conv cpe | 4,186 | 3,382 | 11,951 |
| 4469 | sdn 4d | 4,102 | 3,107 | 35,005 |
| **4600 Invicta (wb 123.0)** | | | | |
| 4637 | htp cpe | 4,090 | 3,447 | 6,382 |
| 4639 | htp sdn | 4,179 | 3,515 | 18,398 |
| 4667 | conv cpe | 4,206 | 3,620 | 3,953 |
| **4700 Electra (wb 126.0)** | | | | |
| 4719 | sdn 4d | 4,298 | 3,825 | 13,818 |
| 4737 | htp cpe | 4,260 | 3,818 | 4,250 |
| 4739 | htp sdn | 4,333 | 3,932 | 8,978 |
| **4800 Electra 225 (wb 126.0)** | | | | |
| 4829 | Riviera htp sdn | 4,417 | 4,350 | 13,719 |
| 4867 | conv cpe | 4,441 | 4,192 | 7,158 |

| 1961 Engines | bore × stroke | bhp | availability |
|---|---|---|---|
| V-8, 215.0 | 3.50 × 2.80 | 155 | S-Special (Skylark 185 bhp) |
| V-8, 364.0 | 4.13 × 3.40 | 235/250 | S-LeSabre |
| V-8, 401.0 | 4.19 × 3.64 | 325 | S-others |

## 1962

| Special (wb 112.1) | | Wght | Price | Prod |
|---|---|---|---|---|
| 4019 | sdn 4d | 2,666 | 2,358 | 23,249 |
| 4027 | cpe | 2,638 | 2,304 | 19,135 |
| 4035 | wgn 4d | 2,876 | 2,655 | 7,382 |
| 4045 | wgn 4d, 3S | 2,896 | 2,736 | 2,814 |
| 4067 | conv cpe | 2,858 | 2,587 | 7,918 |
| 4119 | Del sdn 4d | 2,648 | 2,593 | 31,660 |
| 4135 | Del wgn 4d | 2,845 | 2,890 | 10,380 |
| 4167 | Del conv cpe | 2,820 | 2,879 | 8,332 |
| 4347 | Skylark htp cpe | 2,707 | 2,787 | 34,060 |
| 4367 | Skylark conv cpe | 2,871 | 3,012 | 8,913 |
| **LeSabre (wb 123.0)** | | | | |
| 4411 | sdn 2d | 4,041 | 3,091 | 7,418 |
| 4439 | spt sdn | 4,156 | 3,369 | 37,518 |
| 4447 | htp cpe | 4,054 | 3,293 | 25,479 |
| 4469 | sdn 4d | 4,104 | 3,227 | 56,783 |
| **Invicta (wb 123.0)** | | | | |
| 4435 | wgn 4d | 4,471 | 3,836 | 9,131 |
| 4639 | htp sdn | 4,159 | 3,667 | 16,443 |
| 4645 | wgn 4d, 3S | 4,505 | 3,917 | 4,617 |
| 4647 | Wildcat spt cpe | 4,150 | 3,927 | 2,000 est. |
| 4647 | spt cpe | 4,077 | 3,733 | 10,355 |
| 4667 | conv cpe | 4,217 | 3,617 | 13,471 |
| **Electra 225 (wb 126.0)** | | | | |
| 4819 | sdn 4d | 4,304 | 4,051 | 13,523 |
| 4829 | Riviera htp sdn 6W | 4,390 | 4,448 | 15,395 |
| 4839 | htp sdn | 4,309 | 4,186 | 16,734 |
| 4847 | htp cpe | 4,235 | 4,062 | 8,922 |
| 4867 | conv cpe | 4,396 | 4,366 | 7,894 |

| 1962 Engines | bore × stroke | bhp | availability |
|---|---|---|---|
| V-6, 198.0 | 3.63 × 3.20 | 135 | S-Special |
| V-8, 215.0 | 3.50 × 2.80 | 155 | S-Special DeLuxe |
| V-8, 215.0 | 3.50 × 2.80 | 190 | S-Skylark; O-Special |
| V-8, 401.0 | 4.19 × 3.64 | 265/280 | S-LeSabre |
| V-8, 401.0 | 4.19 × 3.64 | 325 | S-Invicta, Electra |

## 1963

| Special (wb 112.1) | | Wght | Price | Prod |
|---|---|---|---|---|
| 4019 | sdn 4d | 2,696 | 2,363 | 21,733 |

# Buick

| Special (wb 112.1) | | Wght | Price | Prod |
|---|---|---|---|---|
| 4027 | cpe | 2,661 | 2,309 | 21,886 |
| 4035 | wgn 4d | 2,866 | 2,659 | 5,867 |
| 4045 | wgn 4d, 3S | 2,903 | 2,740 | 2,415 |
| 4067 | conv cpe | 2,768 | 2,591 | 8,082 |
| 4119 | Del sdn 4d | 2,720 | 2,521 | 37,695 |
| 4135 | Del wgn 4d | 2,854 | 2,818 | 8,771 |
| 4347 | Skylark spt cpe | 2,757 | 2,857 | 32,109 |
| 4367 | Skylark conv cpe | 2,810 | 3,011 | 10,212 |
| **LeSabre (wb 123.0)** | | | | |
| 4411 | sdn 2d | 3,905 | 2,869 | 8,328 |
| 4435 | wgn 4d | 4,320 | 3,526 | 5,566 |
| 4439 | htp sdn | 4,007 | 3,146 | 50,420 |
| 4445 | wgn 4d, 3S | 4,340 | 3,606 | 3,922 |
| 4447 | htp cpe | 3,924 | 3,070 | 27,977 |
| 4467 | conv cpe | 4,052 | 3,339 | 9,975 |
| 4469 | sdn 4d | 3,970 | 3,004 | 64,995 |
| **Wildcat (wb 123.0)** | | | | |
| 4639 | htp sdn | 4,222 | 3,871 | 17,519 |
| 4647 | htp cpe | 4,123 | 3,849 | 12,185 |
| 4667 | conv cpe | 4,228 | 3,961 | 6,021 |
| **Invicta (wb 123.0)** | | | | |
| 4635 | wgn 4d | 4,397 | 3,969 | 3,495 |
| **Electra 225 (wb 126.0)** | | | | |
| 4819 | sdn 4d | 4,241 | 4,051 | 14,268 |
| 4829 | pillarless sdn | 4,284 | 4,254 | 11,468 |
| 4839 | htp sdn | 4,272 | 4,186 | 19,714 |
| 4847 | htp cpe | 4,153 | 4,062 | 6,848 |
| 4867 | conv cpe | 4,297 | 4,365 | 6,367 |
| **Riviera (wb 117.0)** | | | | |
| 4747 | htp cpe | 3,988 | 4,333 | 40,000 |

| 1963 Engines | bore × stroke | bhp | availability |
|---|---|---|---|
| V-6, 198.0 | 3.63 × 3.20 | 135 | S-Special, Special DeLuxe |
| V-8, 215.0 | 3.50 × 2.80 | 155 | O-Special DeLuxe, Skylark |
| V-8, 215.0 | 3.50 × 2.80 | 200 | S-Skylark; O-all Specials |
| V-8, 401.0 | 4.19 × 3.64 | 265/280 | S-LeSabre |
| V-8, 401.0 | 4.19 × 3.64 | 325 | S-Invicta, Wildcat, Electra, Riviera |
| V-8, 425.0 | 4.31 × 3.64 | 340 | O-Riviera |

## 1964

| Special (wb 115.0; wgns-120.0) | | Wght | Price | Prod |
|---|---|---|---|---|
| 4027 | cpe | 2,991 | 2,343 | 15,030 |
| 4035 | wgn | 3,266 | 2,689 | 6,270 |
| 4067 | conv cpe | 3,108 | 2,605 | 6,308 |
| 4069 | sdn 4d | 3,008 | 2,397 | 17,983 |
| 4127 | Del cpe | 3,006 | 2,457 | 11,962 |
| 4135 | Del wgn 4d | 3,285 | 2,787 | 9,467 |
| 4169 | Del sdn 4d | 3,026 | 2,490 | 31,742 |
| 4337 | Skylark spt cpe | 3,057 | 2,680 | 42,356 |
| 4367 | Skylark conv cpe | 3,175 | 2,834 | 10,225 |
| 4369 | Skylark sdn 4d | 3,070 | 2,669 | 19,635 |
| 4255 | Skylark Spt Wgn | 3,557 | 2,989 | 2,709 |
| 4355 | Skylark Custom Spt Wgn | 3,595 | 3,161 | 3,913 |
| 4265 | Skylark Spt Wgn 4d 3S | 3,689 | 3,124 | 2,586 |
| 4365 | Skylark Custom Spt Wgn | 3,727 | 3,286 | 4,446 |
| **LeSabre (wb 123.0)** | | | | |
| 4439 | htp sdn | 3,730 | 3,122 | 37,052 |
| 4447 | htp cpe | 3,629 | 3,061 | 24,177 |
| 4467 | conv cpe | 3,787 | 3,314 | 6,685 |

| LeSabre (wb 123.0) | | Wght | Price | Prod |
|---|---|---|---|---|
| 4469 | sdn 4d | 3,693 | 2,980 | 56,729 |
| 4635 | wgn 4d | 4,352 | 3,554 | 6,517 |
| 4645 | wgn 4d, 3S | 4,362 | 3,635 | 4,003 |
| **Wildcat (wb 123.0)** | | | | |
| 4639 | htp sdn | 4,058 | 3,327 | 33,358 |
| 4647 | htp cpe | 4,003 | 3,267 | 22,893 |
| 4667 | conv cpe | 4,076 | 3,455 | 7,850 |
| 4669 | sdn | 4,021 | 3,164 | 20,144 |
| **Electra 225 (wb 126.0)** | | | | |
| 4819 | sdn 4d | 4,212 | 4,059 | 15,968 |
| 4829 | pillarless sdn | 4,238 | 4,261 | 11,663 |
| 4839 | htp sdn | 4,229 | 4,194 | 24,935 |
| 4847 | htp cpe | 4,149 | 4,070 | 9,045 |
| 4867 | conv cpe | 4,280 | 4,374 | 7,181 |
| **Riviera (wb 117.0)** | | | | |
| 4747 | htp cpe | 3,951 | 4,385 | 37,658 |

| 1964 Engines | bore × stroke | bhp | availability |
|---|---|---|---|
| V-6, 225.0 | 3.75 × 3.40 | 155 | S-Special |
| V-8, 300.0 | 3.75 × 3.40 | 210/250 | S-LeSabre 4400; O-Special |
| V-8, 401.0 | 4.19 × 3.64 | 325 | S-LeS 4600, Wildcat, Elec |
| V-8, 425.0 | 4.31 × 3.64 | 340/360 | S-Riv; O-LeS 4600, Wldct, Elec |

## 1965

| Special (wb 115.0) | | Wght | Price | Prod |
|---|---|---|---|---|
| 43327 | cpe | 2,977 | 2,343 | 12,945 |
| 43335 | wgn 4d | 3,258 | 2,688 | 2,868 |
| 43367 | conv cpe | 3,087 | 2,605 | 3,357 |
| 43369 | sdn 4d | 3,010 | 2,397 | 13,828 |
| 43427 | cpe V-8 | 3,080 | 2,414 | 5,309 |
| 43435 | wgn 4d V-8 | 3,365 | 2,759 | 3,676 |
| 43467 | conv cpe V-8 | 3,197 | 2,676 | 3,365 |
| 43469 | sdn 4d V-8 | 3,117 | 2,468 | 8,121 |
| 43535 | Del wgn 4d | 3,242 | 2,787 | 1,677 |
| 43569 | Del sdn 4d | 3,016 | 2,669 | 11,033 |
| 43635 | Del wgn 4d | 3,369 | 2,858 | 9,123 |
| 43669 | Del sdn 4d | 3,143 | 2,561 | 26,299 |
| **Skylark (wb 115.0; wgns-120.0)** | | | | |
| 44255 | wgn 4d | 3,642 | 2,989 | 4,226 |
| 44265 | wgn 4d, 3S | 3,750 | 3,123 | 4,669 |
| 44327 | cpe | 3,035 | 2,537 | 4,195 |
| 44337 | htp cpe | 3,057 | 2,680 | 4,549 |
| 44367 | conv cpe | 3,149 | 2,834 | 1,181 |
| 44369 | sdn 4d | 3,086 | 2,669 | 3,385 |
| 44427 | GS cpe | 3,146 | 2,608 | 11,877 |
| 44437 | GS htp cpe | 3,198 | 2,751 | 47,034 |
| 44455 | Cus wgn 4d | 3,690 | 3,160 | 8,300 |
| 44465 | Cus wgn 3S | 3,802 | 3,285 | 11,166 |
| 44467 | GS conv cpe | 3,294 | 2,905 | 10,456 |
| 44469 | sdn 4d | 3,194 | 2,740 | 22,335 |
| **LeSabre (wb 123.0)** | | | | |
| 45237 | htp cpe | 3,753 | 3,030 | 15,786 |
| 45239 | htp sdn | 3,809 | 3,090 | 18,384 |
| 45269 | sdn 4d | 3,788 | 2,948 | 37,788 |
| 45437 | Cus htp cpe | 3,724 | 3,100 | 21,049 |
| 45439 | Cus htp sdn | 3,811 | 3,166 | 23,394 |
| 45467 | Cus conv cpe | 3,812 | 3,325 | 6,543 |
| 45469 | Cus sdn 4d | 3,777 | 3,024 | 22,052 |
| **Wildcat (wb 126.0)** | | | | |
| 46237 | htp cpe | 3,988 | 3,286 | 6,031 |

# Buick

| Wildcat (wb 126.0) | | Wght | Price | Prod |
|---|---|---|---|---|
| 46239 | htp sdn | 4,089 | 3,346 | 7,499 |
| 46269 | sdn 4d | 4,058 | 3,182 | 10,184 |
| 46437 | Del htp cpe | 4,014 | 3,340 | 11,617 |
| 46439 | Del htp sdn | 4,075 | 3,407 | 13,903 |
| 46467 | Del conv cpe | 4,069 | 3,502 | 4,616 |
| 46469 | Del sdn 4d | 4,046 | 3,285 | 9,765 |
| 46637 | Cus htp cpe | 4,047 | 3,566 | 15,896 |
| 46639 | Cus htp sdn | 4,160 | 3,626 | 14,878 |
| 46667 | Cus conv cpe | 4,087 | 3,727 | 4,398 |
| **Electra 225 (wb 126.0)** | | | | |
| 48237 | htp cpe | 4,208 | 4,082 | 6,302 |
| 48239 | htp sdn | 4,284 | 4,206 | 12,842 |
| 48269 | sdn 4d | 4,261 | 4,071 | 12,459 |
| 48437 | Cus htp cpe | 4,228 | 4,265 | 9,570 |
| 48439 | Cus htp sdn | 4,344 | 4,389 | 29,932 |
| 48467 | Cus conv cpe | 4,325 | 4,440 | 8,505 |
| 48469 | Cus sdn 4d | 4,272 | 4,254 | 7,197 |
| **Riviera (wb 117.0)** | | | | |
| 49447 | htp cpe | 4,036 | 4,408 | 34,586 |

| 1965 Engines | bore × stroke | bhp | availability |
|---|---|---|---|
| V-6, 225.0 | 3.75 × 3.40 | 155 | S-Special, Skylark |
| V-8, 300.0 | 3.75 × 3.40 | 210/250 | S-LeS; O-Special, Skylark |
| V-8, 401.0 | 4.19 × 3.64 | 325 | S-Wildcat, Electra, Riviera; O-LeS |
| V-8, 425.0 | 4.31 × 3.64 | 340/360 | O-Wildcat, Electra, Riviera |

## 1966

| Special (wb 115.0; wgns-120.0) | | Wght | Price | Prod |
|---|---|---|---|---|
| 43307 | cpe | 3,009 | 2,348 | 9,322 |
| 43335 | wgn 4d | 3,296 | 2,695 | 1,451 |
| 43367 | conv cpe | 3,092 | 2,604 | 1,357 |
| 43369 | sdn 4d | 3,046 | 2,401 | 8,797 |
| 43407 | cpe V-8 | 3,091 | 2,418 | 5,719 |
| 43435 | wgn 4d V-8 | 3,399 | 2,764 | 3,038 |
| 43467 | conv cpe V-8 | 3,223 | 2,671 | 2,036 |
| 43469 | sdn 4d V-8 | 3,148 | 2,471 | 9,355 |
| 43507 | Del cpe | 3,009 | 2,432 | 2,359 |
| 43517 | Del htp cpe | 3,038 | 2,504 | 2,507 |
| 43535 | Del wgn 4d | 3,290 | 2,783 | 824 |
| 43569 | Del sdn 4d | 3,045 | 2,485 | 5,573 |
| 43607 | Del cpe V-8 | 3,112 | 2,502 | 4,908 |
| 43617 | Del htp cpe V-8 | 3,130 | 2,574 | 10,350 |
| 43635 | Del wgn 4d V-8 | 3,427 | 2,853 | 7,592 |
| 43669 | Del sdn 4d V-8 | 3,156 | 2,555 | 27,909 |
| **Skylark (wb 115.0; wgns-120.0)** | | | | |
| 44255 | wgn 4d | 3,713 | 3,025 | 2,469 |
| 44265 | wgn 4d, 3S | 3,811 | 3,173 | 2,667 |
| 44307 | cpe V-6 | 3,034 | 2,624 | 1,454 |
| 44317 | htp cpe | 3,069 | 2,687 | 2,552 |
| 44339 | htp sdn | 3,172 | 2,846 | 1,422 |
| 44367 | conv cpe | 3,158 | 2,837 | 608 |
| 44407 | cpe V-8 | 3,145 | 2,694 | 6,427 |
| 44417 | htp cpe V-8 | 3,152 | 2,757 | 33,326 |
| 44439 | htp sdn V-8 | 3,285 | 2,916 | 18,873 |
| 44455 | Cus wgn 4d | 3,720 | 3,155 | 6,964 |
| 44465 | Cus wgn 4d, 3S | 3,844 | 3,293 | 9,510 |
| 44467 | conv cpe V-8 | 3,259 | 2,904 | 6,129 |
| 44607 | GS cpe | 3,479 | 2,956 | 1,835 |
| 44617 | GS htp cpe | 3,428 | 3,019 | 9,934 |
| 44667 | GS conv cpe | 3,532 | 3,167 | 2,047 |

| LeSabre (wb 123.0) | | Wght | Price | Prod |
|---|---|---|---|---|
| 45237 | htp cpe | 3,751 | 3,022 | 13,843 |
| 45239 | htp sdn | 3,828 | 3,081 | 17,740 |
| 45269 | sdn 4d | 3,796 | 2,942 | 39,146 |
| 45437 | Cus htp cpe | 3,746 | 3,109 | 18,830 |
| 45439 | Cus htp sdn | 3,824 | 3,174 | 21,914 |
| 45467 | Cus conv cpe | 3,833 | 3,326 | 4,994 |
| 45469 | Cus sdn 4d | 3,788 | 3,035 | 25,932 |
| **Wildcat (wb 126.0)** | | | | |
| 46437 | htp cpe | 4,003 | 3,326 | 9,774 |
| 46439 | htp sdn | 4,108 | 3,391 | 15,081 |
| 46467 | conv cpe | 4,065 | 3,480 | 2,690 |
| 46469 | sdn 4d | 4,070 | 3,233 | 14,389 |
| 46637 | Cus htp cpe | 4,018 | 3,547 | 10,800 |
| 46639 | Cus htp sdn | 4,176 | 3,606 | 13,060 |
| 46667 | Cus conv cpe | 4,079 | 3,701 | 2,790 |
| **Electra 225 (wb 126.0)** | | | | |
| 48237 | htp cpe | 4,176 | 4,032 | 4,882 |
| 48239 | htp sdn | 4,271 | 4,153 | 10,792 |
| 48269 | sdn 4d | 4,255 | 4,022 | 11,740 |
| 48437 | Cus htp cpe | 4,230 | 4,211 | 10,119 |
| 48439 | Cus htp sdn | 4,323 | 4,332 | 34,149 |
| 48467 | Cus conv cpe | 4,298 | 4,378 | 7,175 |
| 48469 | Cus sdn 4d | 4,292 | 4,201 | 9,368 |
| **Riviera (wb 119.0)** | | | | |
| 49487 | htp cpe | 4,180 | 4,424 | 45,348 |

| 1966 Engines | bore × stroke | bhp | availability |
|---|---|---|---|
| V-6, 225.0 | 3.75 × 3.40 | 160 | S-Special, Skylark |
| V-8, 300.0 | 3.75 × 3.40 | 210 | O-Special, Skylark |
| V-8, 340.0 | 3.75 × 3.85 | 220 | S-4440 wgn, LeSabre |
| V-8, 401.0 | 4.19 × 3.64 | 325 | S-Skylark GS, Wildcat, Electra |
| V-8, 425.0 | 4.31 × 3.64 | 340 | S-Riviera; O-Wildcat, Electra |

## 1967

| Special (wb 115.0; wgns-120.0) | | Wght | Price | Prod |
|---|---|---|---|---|
| 43307 | cpe | 3,071 | 2,411 | 6,989 |
| 43335 | wgn 4d | 3,343 | 2,742 | 908 |
| 43369 | sdn 4d | 3,077 | 2,462 | 4,711 |
| 43407 | cpe | 3,173 | 2,481 | 8,937 |
| 43435 | wgn 4d | 3,425 | 2,812 | 1,688 |
| 43469 | sdn 4d | 3,196 | 2,532 | 5,793 |
| 43517 | Del htp cpe | 3,127 | 2,566 | 2,357 |
| 43569 | Del sdn 4d | 3,142 | 2,545 | 3,650 |
| 43617 | Del htp cpe | 3,202 | 2,636 | 14,408 |
| 43635 | Del wgn 4d | 3,317 | 2,901 | 6,851 |
| 43669 | Del sdn 4d | 3,205 | 2,615 | 26,057 |
| **Skylark (wb 115.0; wgns-120.0)** | | | | |
| 34017 | GS 340 htp cpe | 3,283 | 2,845 | 3,692 |
| 44307 | cpe V-6 | 3,137 | 2,665 | 894 |
| 44407 | cpe V-8 | 3,229 | 2,735 | 3,165 |
| 44417 | htp cpe | 3,199 | 2,798 | 41,084 |
| 44439 | htp sdn | 3,373 | 2,950 | 13,721 |
| 44455 | wgn 4d | 3,713 | 3,025 | 5,440 |
| 44465 | wgn 4d, 3S | 3,811 | 3,173 | 5,970 |
| 44455 | Cust wgn 4d | 3,772 | 3,202 | 3,114 |
| 44465 | Cust wgn 4d, 3S | 3,876 | 3,340 | 4,559 |
| 44467 | conv cpe | 3,335 | 2,945 | 6,319 |
| 44469 | sdn 4d | 3,324 | 2,767 | 9,213 |
| 44607 | GS 400 cpe | 3,439 | 2,956 | 1,014 |
| 44617 | GS 400 htp cpe | 3,500 | 3,019 | 10,659 |
| 44667 | GS 400 conv cpe | 3,505 | 3,167 | 2,140 |

# Buick

| LeSabre (wb 123.0) | | Wght | Price | Prod |
|---|---|---|---|---|
| 45239 | htp sdn | 3,878 | 3,142 | 17,464 |
| 45269 | sdn 4d | 3,847 | 3,002 | 36,220 |
| 45287 | htp cpe | 3,819 | 3,084 | 13,760 |
| 45439 | Cus htp sdn | 3,873 | 3,236 | 32,526 |
| 45467 | Cus conv cpe | 3,890 | 3,388 | 4,624 |
| 45469 | Cus sdn 4d | 3,855 | 3,096 | 27,930 |
| 45487 | Cus htp cpe | 3,853 | 3,172 | 22,666 |
| **Wildcat (wb 126.0)** | | | | |
| 46439 | htp sdn | 4,069 | 3,437 | 15,110 |
| 46467 | conv cpe | 4,064 | 3,536 | 2,276 |
| 46469 | sdn 4d | 4,008 | 3,277 | 14,579 |
| 46487 | htp cpe | 4,021 | 3,382 | 10,585 |
| 46639 | Cus htp sdn | 4,119 | 3,652 | 13,547 |
| 46667 | Cus conv cpe | 4,046 | 3,757 | 2,913 |
| 46687 | Cus htp cpe | 4,055 | 3,603 | 11,871 |
| **Electra 225 (wb 126.0)** | | | | |
| 48239 | htp sdn | 4,293 | 4,184 | 12,491 |
| 48257 | htp cpe | 4,197 | 4,075 | 6,845 |
| 48269 | sdn 4d | 4,246 | 4,054 | 10,787 |
| 48439 | Cus htp sdn | 4,336 | 4,363 | 40,978 |
| 48457 | Cus htp cpe | 4,242 | 4,254 | 12,156 |
| 48467 | Cus conv cpe | 4,304 | 4,421 | 6,941 |
| 48469 | Cus sdn 4d | 4,312 | 4,270 | 10,106 |
| **Riviera (wb 119.0)** | | | | |
| 49487 | htp cpe | 4,189 | 4,469 | 42,799 |

| 1967 Engines | bore × stroke | bhp | availability |
|---|---|---|---|
| V-6, 225.0 | 3.75 × 3.40 | 160 | S-Special, Skylark |
| V-8, 300.0 | 3.75 × 3.40 | 210 | O-Special, Skylark |
| V-8, 340.0 | 3.75 × 3.85 | 220/260 | S-4400 wgn, LeS; O-Skylark |
| V-8, 400.0 | 4.04 × 3.90 | 340 | S-GS 400 |
| V-8, 430.0 | 4.19 × 3.90 | 360 | S-Wildcat, Electra, Riviera |

## 1968

| Special DeLuxe (wb 116; 2d-112) | | Wght | Price | Prod |
|---|---|---|---|---|
| 43327 | cpe | 3,185 | 2,513 | 21,988 |
| 43369 | sdn 4d | 3,277 | 2,564 | 16,571 |
| 43435 | wgn 4d | 3,670 | 3,001 | 10,916 |
| **Skylark (wb 116.0; 2d-112.0)** | | | | |
| 43537 | htp cpe | 3,240 | 2,688 | 32,795 |
| 43569 | sdn 4d | 3,278 | 2,666 | 27,387 |
| 44437 | Cus htp cpe | 3,344 | 2,956 | 44,143 |
| 44439 | Cus htp sdn | 3,481 | 3,108 | 12,984 |
| 44467 | Cus conv cpe | 3,394 | 3,098 | 8,188 |
| 44469 | Cus sdn 4d | 3,377 | 2,924 | 8,066 |
| **Sportwagon (wb 121.0)** | | | | |
| 44455 | wgn 4d | 3,975 | 3,341 | 10,530 |
| 44465 | wgn 4d, 3S | 4,118 | 3,499 | 12,378 |

Note: Sportwagon production includes 10,909 series 48000 woodgrain models.

| Gran Sport (wb 112.0) | | | | |
|---|---|---|---|---|
| 43437 | GS 350 htp cpe | 3,375 | 2,926 | 8,317 |
| 44637 | GS 400 htp cpe | 3,514 | 3,127 | 10,743 |
| 44667 | GS 400 conv cpe | 3,547 | 3,271 | 2,454 |
| **LeSabre (wb 123.0)** | | | | |
| 45239 | htp sdn | 3,980 | 3,281 | 18,058 |
| 45269 | sdn 4d | 3,946 | 3,141 | 37,433 |
| 45287 | htp cpe | 3,923 | 3,223 | 14,992 |
| 45439 | Cus htp sdn | 4,007 | 3,375 | 40,370 |
| 45467 | Cus conv cpe | 3,966 | 3,504 | 5,257 |

| LeSabre (wb 123.0) | | Wght | Price | Prod |
|---|---|---|---|---|
| 45469 | Cus sdn 4d | 3,950 | 3,235 | 34,112 |
| 45487 | Cus htp cpe | 3,932 | 3,311 | 29,596 |
| **Wildcat (wb 126.0)** | | | | |
| 46439 | htp sdn | 4,133 | 3,576 | 15,153 |
| 46469 | sdn 4d | 4,076 | 3,416 | 15,201 |
| 46487 | htp cpe | 4,065 | 3,521 | 10,708 |
| 46639 | Cus htp sdn | 4,162 | 3,791 | 14,059 |
| 46667 | Cus conv cpe | 4,118 | 3,873 | 3,572 |
| 46687 | Cus htp cpe | 4,082 | 3,742 | 11,276 |
| **Electra 225 (wb 126.0)** | | | | |
| 48239 | htp sdn | 4,270 | 4,330 | 15,376 |
| 48257 | htp cpe | 4,180 | 4,221 | 10,705 |
| 48269 | sdn 4d | 4,253 | 4,200 | 12,723 |
| 48439 | Cus htp sdn | 4,314 | 4,509 | 50,846 |
| 48457 | Cus htp cpe | 4,223 | 4,400 | 16,826 |
| 48467 | Cus conv cpe | 4,285 | 4,541 | 7,976 |
| 48469 | Cus sdn 4d | 4,304 | 4,415 | 10,910 |
| **Riviera (wb 119.0)** | | | | |
| 49487 | htp cpe | 4,222 | 4,615 | 49,284 |

| 1968 Engines | bore × stroke | bhp | availability |
|---|---|---|---|
| I-6, 250.0 | 3.88 × 3.53 | 155 | S-Special Del, Skylark |
| V-8, 350.0 | 3.80 × 3.85 | 230 | S-Swgn, Sky Cus, LeS; O-Spec, Sky |
| V-8, 350.0 | 3.80 × 3.85 | 280 | S-GS 350; O-Sp Del, Sky, LeS, Swgn |
| V-8, 400.0 | 4.04 × 3.90 | 340 | S-GS 400; Sportwagon 400 |
| V-8, 430.0 | 4.19 × 3.90 | 360 | S-Wildcat, Electra, Riviera |

## 1969

| Special DeLuxe (wb 116; 2d-112) | | Wght | Price | Prod |
|---|---|---|---|---|
| 43327 | cpe | 3,216 | 2,562 | 15,268 |
| 43369 | sdn 4d | 3,182 | 2,613 | 11,113 |
| 43435 | wgn 4d | 3,736 | 3,092 | 2,590 |
| 43436 | luxury wgn 4d | 3,783 | 3,124 | 6,677 |
| **Skylark (wb 116.0; 2d-112.0)** | | | | |
| 43537 | htp cpe | 3,240 | 2,736 | 38,658 |
| 43569 | sdn 4d | 3,270 | 2,715 | 22,349 |
| 44437 | Cus htp cpe | 3,341 | 3,009 | 35,639 |
| 44439 | Cus htp sdn | 3,477 | 3,151 | 9,609 |
| 44467 | Cus conv cpe | 3,398 | 3,152 | 6,552 |
| 44469 | Cus sdn 4d | 3,397 | 2,978 | 6,423 |
| **Sportwagon (wb 121.0)** | | | | |
| 44456 | wgn 4d | 4,106 | 3,465 | 9,157 |
| 44466 | wgn 4d,3S | 4,321 | 3,621 | 11,513 |
| **Gran Sport (wb 112.0)** | | | | |
| 43437 | GS 350 htp cpe | 3,406 | 2,980 | 4,933 |
| 44637 | GS 400 htp cpe | 3,549 | 3,181 | 6,356 |
| 44667 | GS 400 conv cpe | 3,594 | 3,325 | 1,776 |
| **LeSabre (wb 123.2)** | | | | |
| 45237 | htp cpe | 3,936 | 3,298 | 16,201 |
| 45239 | htp sdn | 3,983 | 3,356 | 17,235 |
| 45269 | sdn 4d | 3,966 | 3,216 | 36,664 |
| 45437 | Cus htp cpe | 4,018 | 3,386 | 38,887 |
| 45439 | Cus htp sdn | 4,073 | 3,450 | 48,123 |
| 45467 | Cus conv cpe | 3,958 | 3,579 | 3,620 |
| 45469 | Cus sdn 4d | 3,941 | 3,310 | 37,136 |
| **Wildcat (wb 123.2)** | | | | |
| 46437 | htp cpe | 3,926 | 3,596 | 12,416 |

# Buick

| Wildcat (wb 123.2) | | Wght | Price | Prod |
|---|---|---|---|---|
| 46439 | htp sdn | 4,304 | 3,651 | 13,805 |
| 46469 | sdn 4d | 4,102 | 3,491 | 13,126 |
| 46637 | Cus htp cpe | 4,134 | 3,817 | 12,136 |
| 46639 | Cus htp sdn | 4,220 | 3,866 | 13,596 |
| 46667 | Cus conv cpe | 4,152 | 3,948 | 2,374 |
| **Electra 225 (wb 126.2)** | | | | |
| 48239 | htp sdn | 4,294 | 4,432 | 15,983 |
| 48257 | htp cpe | 4,203 | 4,323 | 13,128 |
| 48269 | sdn 4d | 4,238 | 4,302 | 14,521 |
| 48439 | Cus htp sdn | 4,328 | 4,611 | 65,240 |
| 48457 | Cus htp cpe | 4,222 | 4,502 | 27,018 |
| 48467 | Cus conv cpe | 4,309 | 4,643 | 8,294 |
| 48469 | Cus sdn 4d | 4,281 | 4,517 | 14,434 |
| **Riviera (wb 119.0)** | | | | |
| 49487 | htp cpe | 4,199 | 4,701 | 52,872 |

| 1969 Engines | bore × stroke | bhp | availability |
|---|---|---|---|
| I-6, 250.0 | 3.88 × 3.53 | 155 | S-SD cpe & sdn, Sky |
| V-8, 350.0 | 3.80 × 3.85 | 230 | S-SD wgn, Sky Cus, Swgn, LeSabre |
| V-8, 350.0 | 3.80 × 3.85 | 280 | S-GS 350; O-LeS, SW, SD, Skylark |
| V-8, 400.0 | 4.04 × 3.90 | 340 | S-GS 400; O-LeS, Sportwagon |
| V-8, 430.0 | 4.19 × 3.90 | 360 | S-Riviera, Electra, Wildcat |

## 1970

| Skylark (wb 116.0; 2d-112.0) | | Wght | Price | Prod |
|---|---|---|---|---|
| 43327 | cpe | 3,250 | 2,685 | 18,620 |
| 43369 | sdn 4d | 3,311 | 2,736 | 13,420 |
| 43537 | 350 htp cpe | 3,277 | 2,859 | 70,918 |
| 43569 | 350 sdn 4d | 3,320 | 2,838 | 30,281 |
| 44437 | Cus htp cpe | 3,435 | 3,132 | 36,367 |
| 44439 | Cus htp sdn | 3,565 | 3,220 | 12,411 |
| 44467 | Cus conv cpe | 3,499 | 3,275 | 4,954 |
| 44469 | Cus sdn 4d | 3,499 | 3,101 | 7,113 |
| **Sportwagon (wb 116.0)** | | | | |
| 43435 | wgn 4d | 3,775 | 3,210 | 2,239 |
| 43436 | luxury wgn 4d | 3,898 | 3,242 | 10,002 |
| **Gran Sport (wb 112.0)** | | | | |
| 43437 | htp cpe | 3,434 | 3,098 | 9,948 |
| 44637 | 455 htp cpe | 3,562 | 3,283 | 8,732 |
| 44667 | 455 conv cpe | 3,619 | 3,469 | 1,416 |
| **LeSabre (wb 124.0)** | | | | |
| 45237 | htp cpe | 3,866 | 3,419 | 14,163 |
| 45239 | htp sdn | 4,018 | 3,477 | 14,817 |
| 45269 | sdn 4d | 3,970 | 3,337 | 35,404 |
| 45437 | Cus htp cpe | 3,921 | 3,507 | 35,641 |
| 45439 | Cus htp sdn | 3,988 | 3,571 | 43,863 |
| 45467 | Cus conv cpe | 3,947 | 3,700 | 2,487 |
| 45469 | Cus sdn 4d | 3,950 | 3,431 | 36,682 |
| 46437 | Cus 455 htp cpe | 4,066 | 3,675 | 5,469 |
| 46439 | Cus 455 htp sdn | 4,143 | 3,739 | 6,541 |
| 46469 | Cus 455 sdn 4d | 4,107 | 3,599 | 5,555 |
| **Estate wagon (wb 124.0)** | | | | |
| 46036 | wgn 4d | 4,691 | 3,923 | 11,427 |
| 46046 | wgn 4d, 3S | 4,779 | 4,068 | 16,879 |
| **Wildcat Custom (wb 124.0)** | | | | |
| 46637 | htp cpe | 4,099 | 3,949 | 9,447 |
| 46639 | htp sdn | 4,187 | 3,997 | 12,924 |
| 46667 | conv cpe | 4,214 | 4,079 | 1,244 |

| Electra 225 (wb 127.0) | | Wght | Price | Prod |
|---|---|---|---|---|
| 48239 | htp sdn | 4,296 | 4,592 | 14,338 |
| 48257 | htp cpe | 4,214 | 4,482 | 12,013 |
| 48269 | sdn 4d | 4,274 | 4,461 | 12,580 |
| 48439 | Cus htp sdn | 4,385 | 4,771 | 65,114 |
| 48457 | Cus stp cpe | 4,297 | 4,661 | 26,002 |
| 48467 | Cus conv cpe | 4,341 | 4,802 | 6,045 |
| 48469 | Cus sdn 4d | 4,283 | 4,677 | 14,109 |
| **Riviera (wb 119.0)** | | | | |
| 49487 | htp cpe | 4,216 | 4,854 | 37,336 |

| 1970 Engines | bore × stroke | bhp | availability |
|---|---|---|---|
| I-6, 250.0 | 3.88 × 3.53 | 155 | S-Skylark, Sky 350 |
| V-8, 350.0 | 3.80 × 3.85 | 260 | S-LeS, Sky Cus, SW; O-Skylark |
| V-8, 350.0 | 3.80 × 3.85 | 285 | O-LeS, Skylark, Sportwagon |
| V-8, 350.0 | 3.80 × 3.85 | 315 | S-GS; O-LeS, Sky, Sportwagon |
| V-8, 455.0 | 4.31 × 3.90 | 350/360 | S-GS 455 |
| V-8, 455.0 | 4.31 × 3.90 | 370 | S-Wildct, Est Wgn, LeS 455, Elec, Riv |

## 1971

| Skylark (wb 116.0; 2d 112.0) | | Wght | Price | Prod |
|---|---|---|---|---|
| 43327 | cpe | 3,254 | 2,847 | 14,500 |
| 43337 | htp cpe | 3,272 | 2,918 | 61,201 |
| 43369 | sdn 4d | 3,326 | 2,897 | 34,037 |
| 44437 | Custom htp cpe | 3,391 | 2,317 | 29,536 |
| 44439 | Custom htp sdn | 3,547 | 3,397 | 10,814 |
| 44467 | Custom conv cpe | 3,431 | 3,462 | 3,993 |
| 44469 | Custom sdn 4d | 3,455 | 3,288 | 8,299 |
| **Sportwagon (wb 116.0)** | | | | |
| 43436 | wgn 4d | 3,928 | 3,515 | 12,525 |
| **Gran Sport (wb 112.0)** | | | | |
| 43437 | htp cpe | 3,461 | 3,285 | 8,268 |
| 43467 | conv cpe | 3,497 | 3,476 | 902 |
| **LeSabre (wb 124.0)** | | | | |
| 45239 | htp sdn 4d | 4,109 | 4,119 | 14,234 |
| 45257 | htp cpe | 4,049 | 4,061 | 13,385 |
| 46269 | sdn 4d | 4,078 | 3,992 | 26,348 |
| 45439 | Custom htp sdn | 4,147 | 4,213 | 41,098 |
| 45457 | Custom htp cpe | 4,095 | 4,149 | 29,944 |
| 45467 | Custom conv cpe | 4,086 | 4,342 | 1,856 |
| 45469 | Custom sdn 4d | 4,107 | 4,085 | 26,970 |
| **Estate wagon (wb 127.0)** | | | | |
| 46035 | wgn 4d 2S | 4,906 | 4,640 | 8,699 |
| 46045 | wgn 4d 3S | 4,965 | 4,786 | 15,335 |
| **Centurion (wb 124.0)** | | | | |
| 46639 | htp sdn | 4,307 | 4,564 | 15,345 |
| 46647 | htp cpe | 4,195 | 4,678 | 11,892 |
| 46667 | conv cpe | 4,227 | 4,678 | 2,161 |
| **Electra 225 (wb 127.0)** | | | | |
| 48237 | htp cpe | 4,345 | 4,801 | 8,662 |
| 48239 | htp sdn | 4,381 | 4,915 | 17,589 |
| 48437 | Custom htp cpe | 4,359 | 4,980 | 26,831 |
| 48439 | Custom htp sdn | 4,421 | 5,093 | 72,954 |
| **Riviera (wb 122.0)** | | | | |
| 49487 | htp cpe | 4,325 | 5,253 | 33,810 |

| 1971 Engines | bore × stroke | bhp | availability |
|---|---|---|---|
| I-6, 250.0 | 3.88 × 3.53 | 145 | S-Skylark |
| V-8, 350.0 | 3.80 × 3.85 | 230 | S-SW, LeS, O-Sky |

# Buick

| 1971 Engines | bore × stroke | bhp | availability |
|---|---|---|---|
| V-8, 350.0 | 3.80 × 3.85 | 260 | S-Sky GS; O-Sky, LeS |
| V-8, 455.0 | 4.31 × 3.90 | 315 | S-Cent, Elec, EWgn; Riv, O-Sky, LeS, GS |
| V-8, 455.0 | 4.31 × 3.90 | 330 | O-Cent, Riv |
| V-8, 455.0 | 4.31 × 3.90 | 345 | O-Sky, LeS, GS |

## 1972

| Skylark (wb 116.0; 2d 112.0) | | Wght | Price | Prod |
|---|---|---|---|---|
| 4D69 | sed 4d | 3,475 | 2,973 | 42,206 |
| 4D69 | 350 sdn 4d | 3,600 | 3,104 | |
| 4D27 | cpe | 3,420 | 2,925 | 14,552 |
| 4D37 | htp cpe | 3,426 | 2,993 | 84,868 |
| 4D37 | 350 htp cpe | 3,600 | 3,124 | |
| 4G37 | GS htp cpe | 3,471 | 3,225 | 7,723 |
| 4G67 | GS conv cpe | 3,525 | 3,406 | 852 |
| 4H69 | Custom sdn 4d | 3,516 | 3,228 | 9,924 |
| 4H39 | Custom htp sdn | 3,609 | 3,331 | 12,925 |
| 4H37 | Custom htp cpe | 3,477 | 3,255 | 34,271 |
| 4H67 | Custom conv cpe | 3,534 | 3,393 | 3,608 |
| 4F36 | Sportwagon 4d 2S | 3,987 | 3,444 | 14,417 |
| **LeSabre (wb 124.0)** | | | | |
| 4L69 | sdn 4d | 4,201 | 3,958 | 29,505 |
| 4L39 | htp sdn | 4,211 | 4,079 | 15,160 |
| 4L57 | htp cpe | 4,166 | 4,024 | 14,011 |
| 4N69 | Custom sdn 4d | 4,221 | 4,047 | 35,295 |
| 4N39 | Custom htp sdn | 4,226 | 4,168 | 50,804 |
| 4N57 | Custom htp cpe | 4,181 | 4,107 | 36,510 |
| 4N67 | Custom conv cpe | 4,235 | 4,291 | 2,037 |
| **Estate wagon (wb 127.0)** | | | | |
| 4R45 | wgn 4d 3S | 5,060 | 4,728 | 18,793 |
| 4R35 | wgn 4d 2S | 4,975 | 4,589 | 10,175 |
| **Centurion (wb 124.0)** | | | | |
| 4P39 | htp sdn | 4,406 | 4,508 | 19,852 |
| 4P47 | htp cpe | 4,336 | 4,579 | 14,187 |
| 4P67 | conv cpe | 4,396 | 4,616 | 2,396 |
| **Electra 225 (wb 127.0)** | | | | |
| 4U39 | htp sdn | 4,515 | 4,890 | 19,433 |
| 4U37 | htp cpe | 4,445 | 4,782 | 9,961 |
| 4V39 | Custom sdn 4d | 4,530 | 5,060 | 104,754 |
| 4V37 | Custom htp cpe | 4,455 | 4,952 | 37,974 |
| **Riviera (wb 122.0)** | | | | |
| 4Y87 | htp cpe | 4,343 | 5,149 | 33,728 |

| 1972 Engines | bore × stroke | bhp | availability |
|---|---|---|---|
| V-8, 350.0 | 3.80 × 3.85 | 150 | S-Skylark, LeSabre |
| V-8, 350.0 | 3.80 × 3.85 | 190 | S-GS, O-Sky, LeS |
| V-8, 455.0 | 4.31 × 3.90 | 225 | S-Cent, Elec, EWgn; O-Sky GS, LeS |
| V-8, 455.0 | 4.31 × 3.90 | 250 | S-Riviera; O-Cent, LeS |
| V-8, 455.0 | 4.31 × 3.90 | 270 | O-GS |

## 1973

| Apollo (wb 111.0) | | Wght | Price | Prod |
|---|---|---|---|---|
| B69 | sdn 4d | 3,239 | 2,628 | 8,450 |
| B27 | sdn 2d | 3,195 | 2,605 | 14,475 |
| B17 | htchbk sdn 2d | 3,297 | 2,754 | 9,868 |
| **Century (wb 116.0; 2d 112.0)** | | | | |
| D29 | Colonnade sdn 4d | 3,780 | 3,057 | 38,202 |
| D37 | Colonnade cpe | 3,713 | 3,057 | 56,154 |
| F35/45 | wgn 4d 2S/3S | 4,156* | 3,486* | 7,760* |
| H29 | Luxus Colonnade sdn 4d | 3,797 | 3,326 | 22,438 |
| H57 | Luxus Colonnade cpe | 3,718 | 3,331 | 71,712 |
| K35/45 | Luxus wgn 4d 2S/3S | 4,190* | 3,652* | 10,645* |
| J57 | Regal Colonnade cpe | 3,743 | 3,470 | 91,557 |
| **LeSabre (wb 124.0)** | | | | |
| L69 | sdn 4d | 4,234 | 3,998 | 29,649 |
| L39 | htp sdn | 4,259 | 4,125 | 13,413 |
| L57 | htp cpe | 4,210 | 4,067 | 14,061 |
| N69 | Custom sdn 4d | 4,264 | 4,091 | 42,854 |
| N39 | Custom htp sdn | 4,284 | 4,217 | 55,879 |
| N57 | Custom htp cpe | 4,225 | 4,154 | 41,425 |
| **Centurion (wb 124.0)** | | | | |
| P39 | htp sdn | 4,329 | 4,390 | 22,354 |
| P57 | htp cpe | 4,260 | 3,336 | 16,883 |
| P67 | conv cpe | 4,316 | 4,534 | 5,739 |
| **Estate wagon (wb 127.0)** | | | | |
| R35 | wgn 4d 2S | 4,952 | 4,645 | 12,282 |
| R45 | wgn 4d 3S | 5,021 | 4,790 | 23,513 |
| **Electra 225 (wb 127.0)** | | | | |
| T39 | htp sdn | 4,581 | 4,928 | 17,189 |
| T37 | htp cpe | 4,488 | 4,815 | 9,224 |
| V39 | Custom htp sdn | 4,603 | 5,105 | 107,031 |
| V37 | Custom htp cpe | 4,505 | 4,993 | 44,328 |
| **Riviera (wb 122.0)** | | | | |
| Y87 | htp cpe | 4,486 | 5,221 | 34,080 |

| 1973 Engines | bore × stroke | bhp | availability |
|---|---|---|---|
| I-6, 250.0 | 3.87 × 3.50 | 100 | S-Apollo |
| V-8, 350.0 | 3.80 × 3.85 | 150 | S-Apollo, Cnty, LeS |
| V-8, 350.0 | 3.80 × 3.85 | 175 | S-Cnty; O-Ap, LeS |
| V-8, 455.0 | 4.31 × 3.90 | 225 | S-Ewgn, Elec; O-Cnty, LeS |
| V-8, 455.0 | 4.31 × 3.90 | 250 | S-Riv; O-LeS; Ewgn, Elec |
| V-8, 455.0 | 4.31 × 3.90 | 260/270 | O-Riviera |

*Figures for 2S (2 seat) wgns shown; for 3S wgns add approx. 40 lbs and $125. Production combined.

## 1974

| Apollo (wb 111.0) | | Wght | Price | Prod |
|---|---|---|---|---|
| B69 | sdn 4d | 3,362 | 3,060 | 16,779 |
| B27 | sdn 2d | 3,322 | 3,037 | 28,286 |
| B17 | htchbk sdn 2d | 3,428 | 3,160 | 11,644 |
| **Century (wb 116.0; 2d 112.0)** | | | | |
| D29 | 350 Colonnade sdn 4d | 3,890 | 3,836 | 22,856 |
| D37 | 350 Colonnade cpe | 3,845 | 3,790 | 33,166 |
| D37 | Grand Sport Colonnade cpe | 3,937 | 3,904 | |
| F35/45 | wgn 4d 2S/3S | 4,272* | 4,205* | 4,860* |
| H29 | Luxus Colonnade sdn 4d | 3,910 | 4,109 | 11,159 |
| H57 | Luxus Colonnade cpe | 3,835 | 4,089 | 44,930 |
| K35/45 | Luxus wgn 4d 2S/3S | 4,312* | 4,371* | 6,791* |
| J29 | Regal Colonnade htp sdn | 3,930 | 4,221 | 9,333 |
| J57 | Regal Colonnade htp cpe | 3,900 | 4,201 | 57,512 |
| **LeSabre (wb 124.0)** | | | | |
| N69 | sdn 4d | 4,337 | 4,355 | 18,572 |
| N39 | htp sdn | 4,387 | 4,482 | 11,879 |
| N57 | htp cpe | 4,297 | 4,424 | 12,522 |
| P69 | Luxus sdn 4d | 4,352 | 4,466 | 16,039 |
| P39 | Luxus htp sdn | 4,397 | 4,629 | 23,910 |
| P57 | Luxus htp cpe | 4,307 | 4,575 | 27,243 |
| P67 | Luxus conv cpe | 4,372 | 4,696 | 3,627 |

# Buick

| Estate wagon (wb 127.0) | | Wght | Price | Prod |
|---|---|---|---|---|
| R35 | wgn 4d 2S | 5,082 | 5,019 | 4,581 |
| R45 | wgn 4d 3S | 5,182 | 5,163 | 9,831 |
| **Electra 225 (wb 127.0)** | | | | |
| T39 | htp sdn | 4,682 | 5,373 | 5,750 |
| T37 | htp cpe | 4,607 | 5,260 | 3,339 |
| V39 | Custom htp sdn | 4,702 | 5,550 | 29,089 |
| V37 | Custom htp cpe | 4,627 | 5,438 | 15,099 |
| X39 | Limited htp sdn | 4,732 | 5,921 | 30,051 |
| X37 | Limited htp cpe | 4,682 | 5,886 | 16,086 |
| **Riviera (wb 122.0)** | | | | |
| Y87 | htp cpe | 4,572 | 5,678 | 20,129 |

| 1974 Engines | bore × stroke | bhp | availability |
|---|---|---|---|
| I-6, 250.0 | 3.87 × 3.50 | 100 | S-Apollo |
| V-8, 350.0 | 3.80 × 3.85 | 150 | S-Ap, Cnty, LeS |
| V-8, 350.0 | 3.80 × 3.85 | 175 | O-Ap, Cnty, LeS |
| V-8, 455.0 | 4.31 × 3.90 | 175 | O-Cnty, EWgn |
| V-8, 455.0 | 4.31 × 3.90 | 210 | S-EWgn, Elec, Riv; O-Cnty |
| V-8, 455.0 | 4.31 × 3.90 | 245 | O-Ewgn, Elec, Riv, Cnty |

*Figures for 2S wgns shown; for 3S wgs add approx. 30 lbs and $125. Production combined.

## 1975

| Skyhawk (wb 97.0) | | Wght | Price | Prod |
|---|---|---|---|---|
| S07 | htchbk cpe 2d | 2,891 | 4,173 | 29,448 |
| T07 | S htchbk cpe 2d | 2,851 | 3,860 | |
| **Apollo/Skylark (wb 111.0)*** | | | | |
| B69 | Apollo sdn 4d I-6 | 3,438 | 3,436 | 21,138 |
| W27 | Skylark "S" cpe V-6 | 3,405 | 3,234 | 27,689 |
| B27 | Skylark cpe V-6 | 3,438 | 3,463 | |
| B17 | Skylark htckbk sdn 2d V-6 | 3,512 | 3,586 | 6,814 |
| C69 | Apollo S/R sdn 4d I-6 | 3,478 | 4,092 | 2,241 |
| C27 | Skylark S/R cpe V-6 | 3,404 | 4,136 | 3,746 |
| C17 | Skylark S/R htckbk V-6 | 3,514 | 4,253 | 1,505 |
| **Century (wb 116.0; 2d 112.0)*** | | | | |
| D37 | Colonnade cpe | 3,762 | 3,894 | 39,556 |
| E37 | Special Colonnade cpe V-6 | 3,613 | 3,815 | |
| D29 | Colonnade sdn 4d | 3,818 | 3,944 | 22,075 |
| F35 | wgn 4d 2S V-8 | 4,320 | 4,636 | 4,416 |
| F45 | wgn 4d 3S V-8 | 4,370 | 4,751 | |
| H29 | Custom Colonnade sdn 4d | 3,851 | 4,211 | 9,995 |
| H57 | Custom Colonnade cpe | 3,759 | 4,154 | 32,966 |
| K35 | Custom wgn 4d 2S | 4,350 | 4,802 | 7,078 |
| K45 | Custom wgn 4d 3S | 4,400 | 4,917 | |
| **Regal (wb 116.0; 2d 112.0)*** | | | | |
| J29 | Colonnade sdn 4d V-6 | 3,888 | 4,311 | 10,726 |
| J57 | Colonnade cpe V-6 | 3,821 | 4,257 | 56,646 |
| **LeSabre (wb 123.5)** | | | | |
| N69 | sdn 4d | 4,355 | 4,771 | 14,088 |
| N39 | htp sdn | 4,411 | 4,898 | 9,119 |
| N57 | htp cpe | 4,294 | 4,840 | 8,647 |
| P69 | Custom sdn 4d | 4,388 | 4,934 | 17,026 |
| P39 | Custom htp sdn | 4,439 | 5,061 | 30,005 |
| P57 | Custom htp cpe | 4,316 | 5,007 | 25,016 |
| P67 | Custom conv cpe | 4,392 | 5,133 | 5,300 |
| **Estate wagon (wb 127.0)** | | | | |
| R35 | wgn 4d 2S | 5,055 | 5,447 | 4,128 |
| R45 | wgn 4d 3S | 5,135 | 5,591 | 9,612 |
| **Electra 225 (wb 127.0)** | | | | |
| V39 | Custom htp sdn | 4,706 | 6,201 | 27,357 |
| V37 | Custom htp cpe | 4,582 | 6,041 | 16,145 |

| Electra 225 (wb 127.0) | | Wght | Price | Prod |
|---|---|---|---|---|
| X39 | Limited htp sdn | 4,762 | 6,516 | 33,778 |
| X37 | Limited htp cpe | 4,633 | 6,352 | 17,750 |
| **Riviera (wb 122.0)** | | | | |
| Z87 | htp cpe | 4,539 | 6,420 | 17,306 |

| 1975 Engines | bore × stroke | bhp | availability |
|---|---|---|---|
| V-6, 231.0 | 3.80 × 3.40 | 110 | S-Skh, Skl, Cnty, Rgl |
| I-6, 250.0 | 3.87 × 3.50 | 105 | S-Apollo |
| V-8, 260.0 | 3.50 × 3.39 | 110 | S-Apollo, Skylark |
| V-8, 350.0 | 3.80 × 3.85 | 145 | S-Cnty exc wgns |
| V-8, 350.0 | 3.80 × 3.85 | 165 | S-Cnty wgns, Les; O-Cnty, Rgl |
| V-8, 400.0 | 4.12 × 3.75 | 185 | S-LeSabre (Cal.) |
| V-8, 455.0 | 4.31 × 3.90 | 205 | S-EWgn, Elec, Riv; O-LeS |

*Six & V-8 weights averaged. Prices for sixes shown; for V-8s add approx. $80 to I-6 or $20-30 to V-6 models.

## 1976

| Skyhawk (wb 97.0) | | Wght | Price | Prod |
|---|---|---|---|---|
| S07 | htchbk cpe 2d | 2,889 | 4,216 | 15,768 |
| T07 | S htchbk cpe 2d | 2,857 | 3,903 | |
| **Skylark (wb. 111.0)** | | | | |
| W27 | S cpe | 3,416 | 3,435 | 51,260 |
| B27 | cpe | 3,426 | 3,549 | |
| B69 | sdn 4d | 3,384 | 3,609 | 48,157 |
| B17 | htchbk cpe 2d | 3,494 | 3,687 | 6,703 |
| C69 | S/R sdn 4d | 3,406 | 4,324 | 3,243 |
| C27 | S/R cpe | 3,410 | 4,281 | 3,880 |
| C17 | S/R htchbk cpe 2d | 3,430 | 4,398 | 1,248 |
| **Century (wb 116.0; 2d 112.0)** | | | | |
| D37 | Colonnade cpe | 3,748 | 4,070 | 59,448 |
| E37 | Special Colonnade cpe V-6 | 3,508 | 3,935 | |
| D29 | Colonnade sdn 4d | 3,567 | 4,105 | 33,632 |
| H29 | Custom Colonnade sdn 4d | 3,817 | 4,424 | 19,728 |
| H57 | Custom Colonnade cpe | 3,705 | 4,346 | 34,036 |
| K35 | Custom wgn, 2S V-8 | 4,363 | 4,987 | 16,625 |
| K45 | Custom wgn, 4d 3S V-8 | 4,413 | 5,099 | |
| **Regal (wb 116.0; 2d 112.0)** | | | | |
| J29 | Colonnade sdn 4d V-8 | 4,104 | 4,825 | 17,118 |
| J57 | Colonnade cpe V-6 | 3,866 | 4,465 | 124,498 |
| **LeSabre (wb 124.0)** | | | | |
| N69 | sdn 4d V-6 | 4,170 | 4,747 | 4,315 |
| N39 | htp sdn V-6 | 4,059 | 4,871 | 2,312 |
| N57 | htp cpe V-6 | 4,129 | 4,815 | 3,861 |
| P69 | Custom sdn 4d V-8 | 4,328 | 5,046 | 34,841 |
| P39 | Custom htp sdn V-8 | 4,386 | 5,166 | 46,109 |
| P57 | Custom htp cpe V-8 | 4,275 | 5,144 | 45,669 |
| **Estate wagon (wb 127.0)** | | | | |
| R35 | wgn 4d 2S | 5,013 | 5,591 | 5,990 |
| R45 | wgn 4d 3S | 5,139 | 5,731 | 14,384 |
| **Electra 225 (wb 127.0)** | | | | |
| V39 | htp sdn | 4,641 | 6,527 | 26,655 |
| V37 | htp cpe | 4,502 | 6,367 | 18,442 |
| X39 | Limited htp sdn | 4,709 | 6,852 | 51,067 |
| X37 | Limited htp cpe | 4,521 | 6,689 | 28,395 |
| **Riviera (wb 122.0)** | | | | |
| Z87 | htp cpe | 4,531 | 6,798 | 20,082 |

# Buick

| 1976 Engines | bore × stroke | bhp | availability |
|---|---|---|---|
| V-6, 231.0 | 3.80 × 3.40 | 110 | S-Skh, Skl, Cnty, Rgl, LeS |
| V-8, 260.0 | 3.50 × 3.39 | 110 | S-Skylark |
| V-8, 350.0 | 3.80 × 3.85 | 145 | S-Rgl, Cnty exc wgn; O-Skl |
| V-8, 350.0 | 3.80 × 3.85 | 165 | S-Cnty wgn, LeS Cus; O-Skl, Cnty, Rgl |
| V-8, 455.0 | 4.31 × 3.90 | 205 | S-EWgn, Elec, Riv; O-LeS Cus |

## 1977

| Skyhawk (wb 97.0) | | Wght | Price | Prod |
|---|---|---|---|---|
| S07 | htchbk cpe 2d | 2,817 | 4,294 | 12,345 |
| T07 | S htchbk cpe 2d | 2,805 | 3,981 | |
| **Skylark (wb 111.0)*** | | | | |
| W27 | S cpe | 3,286 | 3,642 | 49,858 |
| B27 | cpe | 3,286 | 3,765 | |
| B69 | sdn 4d | 3,324 | 3,825 | 48,121 |
| B17 | htchbk cpe 2d | 3,408 | 3,942 | 5,316 |
| C69 | S/R sdn 4d | 3,324 | 4,587 | 4,000 |
| C27 | S/R cpe | 3,330 | 4,527 | 5,023 |
| C17 | S/R htchbk cpe | 3,358 | 4,695 | 1,154 |
| **Century (wb 116.0; 2d 112.0)*** | | | | |
| D37 | cpe | 3,582 | 4,304 | 52,864 |
| E37 | Special cpe | 3,590 | 4,170 | |
| D29 | sdn 4d | 3,754 | 4,364 | 29,065 |
| H29 | Custom sdn 4d | 3,750 | 4,688 | 13,645 |
| H57 | Custom htp cpe | 3,610 | 4,628 | 20,834 |
| K35 | Custom wgn 4d 2S V-8 | 4,260 | 5,219 | 19,282 |
| K45 | Custom wgn 4d 3S V-8 | 4,310 | 5,271 | |
| **Regal (wb 116.0; 2d 112.0)*** | | | | |
| J29 | sdn 4d V-8 | 3,928 | 5,244 | 17,946 |
| J57 | cpe V-6 | 3,612 | 4,713 | 174,560 |
| **LeSabre (wb 115.9)*** | | | | |
| N69 | sdn 4d | 3,560 | 5,093 | 19,827 |
| N37 | cpe | 3,522 | 5,033 | 8,455 |
| P69 | Custom sdn 4d | 3,572 | 5,382 | 103,855 |
| P37 | Custom cpe | 3,530 | 5,322 | 58,589 |
| F37 | Custom cpe V-8 | 3,634 | 5,819 | |
| **Estate wagon (115.9)** | | | | |
| R35 | wgn 4d 2S | 4,015 | 5,903 | 25,075 |
| R45 | wgn 4d 3S | 4,141 | 6,078 | |
| **Electra 225 (wb 119.0)** | | | | |
| V-69 | sdn | 3,814 | 6,866 | 25,633 |
| V37 | cpe | 3,761 | 6,673 | 15,762 |
| X69 | Limited sdn | 3,839 | 7,226 | 82,361 |
| X37 | Limited cpe | 3,785 | 7,033 | 37,871 |
| **Riviera (wb 116.0)** | | | | |
| Z37 | htp cpe | 3,784 | 7,385 | 26,138 |

| 1977 Engines | bore × stroke | bhp | availability |
|---|---|---|---|
| V-6, 231.0 | 3.80 × 3.40 | 105 | S-Skh, Skl, Cnty, Regl, LeS |
| V-8, 301.0 | 4.00 × 3.00 | 135 | S-Skl, LeS |
| V-8, 305.0 | 3.74 × 3.48 | 145 | O-Skl, Cnty wgn |
| V-8, 350.0 | 3.80 × 3.85 | 140 | S-Cnty exc wgn, Rgl; O-Skl |
| V-8, 350.0 | 3.80 × 3.85 | 155 | S-Cnty wgn, Elec, Riv; O-Skl, Cnty, Rgl |
| V-8, 350.0 | 4.06 × 3.39 | 170 | S-EWgn; O-LeS, Elec, Riv |
| V-8, 403.0 | 4.35 × 3.38 | 185 | O-Cnty, LeS, Elec, Riv |

*Six & V-8 weights averaged. Prices for sixes shown; for V-8s add $150

## 1978

| Skyhawk (wb 97.0) | | Wght | Price | Prod |
|---|---|---|---|---|
| S07 | htchbk cpe 2d | 2,707 | 4,414 | 24,589 |
| T07 | S htchbk cpe 2d | 2,678 | 4,146 | |
| **Skylark (wb 111.0)*** | | | | |
| W27 | S cpe | 3,285 | 3,911 | 42,087 |
| B27 | cpe | 3,287 | 4,035 | |
| B69 | sdn 4d | 3,318 | 4,120 | 40,951 |
| B17 | htchbk cpe 2d | 3,397 | 4,217 | 2,642 |
| C69 | Custom sdn 4d | 3,303 | 4,367 | 14,523 |
| C27 | Custom cpe | 3,270 | 4,282 | 12,740 |
| C17 | Custom htchbk cpe 2d | 3,369 | 4,464 | 1,277 |
| **Century (wb 108.1)*** | | | | |
| E09 | Special sdn 4d | 3,087 | 4,520 | 12,533 |
| E87 | Special sdn 2d | 3,096 | 4,413 | 10,818 |
| E37 | Special wgn 4d 2S | 3,231 | 5,021 | 9,586 |
| H09 | Custom sdn 4d | 3,111 | 4,768 | 18,361 |
| H87 | Custom sdn 2d | 3,084 | 4,658 | 12,434 |
| H35 | Custom wgn 4d 2S | 3,265 | 5,233 | 24,014 |
| G87 | sport coupe sdn 2d | 3,124 | 5,051 | — |
| L09 | Limited sdn 4d | 3,148 | 5,127 | — |
| L87 | Limited sdn 2d | 3,171 | 4,017 | — |
| **Regal (wb 108.1)*** | | | | |
| J47 | cpe | 3,065 | 4,885 | 236,652 |
| M47 | Limited cpe | 3,114 | 5,268 | — |
| K47 | sport coupe turbo V-6 | 3,153 | 5,958 | — |
| **LeSabre (wb 115.9)*** | | | | |
| N69 | sdn 4d | 3,522 | 5,536 | 23,354 |
| N37 | cpe | 3,531 | 5,451 | 8,265 |
| P69 | Custom sdn 4d | 3,534 | 6,045 | 86,638 |
| P37 | Custom cpe | 3,496 | 5,727 | 53,675 |
| F37 | sport coupe turbo V-6 | 3,559 | 6,346 | — |
| **Estate wagon (wb 115.9)** | | | | |
| R35 | wgn 4d 2S V-8 | 4,063 | 6,394 | 25,964 |
| **Electra 225 (wb 119.0)** | | | | |
| V-69 | sdn 4d | 3,730 | 7,431 | 14,590 |
| V37 | cpe | 3,682 | 7,252 | 8,259 |
| X69 | Limited sdn 4d | 3,757 | 7,817 | 65,335 |
| X37 | Limited cpe | 3,710 | 7,638 | 33,365 |
| U69 | Park Avenue sdn 4d | 3,777 | 8,208 | — |
| U37 | Park Avenue cpe | 3,730 | 7,952 | — |
| **Riviera (wb 116.0)** | | | | |
| Z37 | cpe | 3,701 | 9,224 | 20,535 |

| 1978 Engines | bore × stroke | bhp | availability |
|---|---|---|---|
| V-6, 196.0 | 3.50 × 3.40 | 90 | S-Cnty exc wgn, Rgl exc S/C |
| V-6, 231.0 | 3.80 × 3.40 | 105 | S-Skh, Skl, Cnty wgn, LeS; O-Rgl exc S/C, Century |
| V-6T, 231.0 | 3.80 × 3.40 | 150 | S-Rgl & LeS S/Cs; O-Rgl |
| V-6T, 231.0 | 3.80 × 3.40 | 165 | O-Rgl & LeS S/Cs |
| V-8, 301.0 | 4.00 × 3.00 | 140 | S-LeS exc wgn |
| V-8, 305.0 | 3.74 × 3.48 | 145 | S-Skl, Cnty wgn, Rgl exc S/C; O-Cnty |
| V-8, 305.0 | 3.74 × 3.48 | 160 | O-Cnty, Rgl exc S/C |
| V-8, 350.0 | 3.80 × 3.85 | 155 | S-EWgn, Elec, Riv O-LeS |
| V-8, 350.0 | 4.00 × 3.48 | 170 | O-Skl, Cnty |
| V-8, 403.0 | 4.35 × 3.38 | 185 | O-LeS, Elec, Riv |

*Six & V-8 weights averaged. Prices for sixes shown; for V-8s add $175.

# Buick

### 1979

| Skyhawk (wb 97.0) | | Wght | Price | Prod |
|---|---|---|---|---|
| S07 | htchbk cpe 2d | 2,740 | 4,778 | 23,139 |
| T07 | S htchbk cpe 2d | 2,724 | 4,560 | |

| Skylark (wb 111.0) | | | | |
|---|---|---|---|---|
| W27 | S cpe | 3,164 | 4,082 | 10,201 |
| B27 | cpe | 3,174 | 4,208 | |
| B69 | sdn 4d | 3,218 | 4,308 | 10,849 |
| B17 | htchbk cpe 2d | 3,254 | 4,357 | 608 |
| C69 | Custom sdn 4d | 3,226 | 4,562 | 3,822 |
| C27 | Custom cpe | 3,182 | 4,462 | 3,546 |

| Century (wb 108.1) | | | | |
|---|---|---|---|---|
| E09 | Special sdn 4d | 3,105 | 5,021 | 7,363 |
| E87 | Special sdn 2d | 3,090 | 4,921 | 4,805 |
| E35 | Special wgn 4d 2S | 3,222 | 5,492 | 10,413 |
| H09 | Custom sdn 4d | 3,123 | 5,290 | 9,681 |
| H87 | Custom sdn 2d | 3,103 | 5,165 | 2,474 |
| H37 | Custom wgn 4d 2S | 3,258 | 5,806 | 21,100 |
| G87 | sport coupe sdn 2d | 3,099 | 5,473 | 1,653 |
| L09 | Limited sdn 4d | 3,156 | 5,658 | 2,694 |

| Regal (wb 108.1) | | | | |
|---|---|---|---|---|
| J47 | cpe | 3,081 | 5,407 | 157,228 |
| M47 | Limited cpe | 3,123 | 5,814 | 94,748 |
| K47 | sport coupe turbo V-6 | 3,190 | 6,497 | 21,389 |

| LeSabre (wb 115.9) | | | | |
|---|---|---|---|---|
| N69 | sdn 4d | 3,523 | 6,110 | 25,431 |
| N37 | cpe | 3,492 | 6,010 | 7,542 |
| P69 | Limited sdn 4d | 3,567 | 6,620 | 75,939 |
| P37 | Limited cpe | 3,518 | 6,495 | 38,290 |
| F37 | sport coupe turbo V-6 | 3,545 | 6,953 | 3,582 |

| Estate wagon (wb 115.9) | | | | |
|---|---|---|---|---|
| R35 | wgn 4d 2S V-8 | 4,021 | 7,169 | 21,312 |

| Electra 225 (wb 119.0) | | | | |
|---|---|---|---|---|
| V-69 | sdn 4d | 3,831 | 8,878 | 11,055 |
| V37 | cpe | 3,767 | 8,703 | 5,358 |
| X69 | Limited sdn 4d | 3,853 | 9,278 | 76,340 |
| X37 | Limited cpe | 3,789 | 9,103 | 28,878 |
| U69 | Park Avenue sdn 4d | 3,860 | 9,959 | — |
| U37 | Park Avenue cpe | 3,794 | 9,784 | — |

| Riviera (wb 114.0) | | | | |
|---|---|---|---|---|
| Z57 | cpe V-8 | 3,759 | 10,684 | 52,181 |
| Y57 | S-Type cpe | 3,774 | 10,960 | |

| 1979 Engines | bore × stroke | bhp | availability |
|---|---|---|---|
| V-6, 196.0 | 3.50 × 3.40 | 105 | S-Cnty exc wgn, Rgl exc S/C |
| V-6, 231.0 | 3.80 × 3.40 | 115 | S-Skh, Skl, Cnty wgn, LeS; O-Cnty, Rgl |
| V-6T, 231.0 | 3.80 × 3.40 | 170-185 | S-Riv S; O-Cnty/Rgl/LeS Spt |
| V-8, 301.0 | 4.00 × 3.00 | 140 | S-Cnty, Rgl, LeS |
| V-8, 301.0 | 4.00 × 3.00 | 150 | O-Cnty, Rgl |
| V-8, 305.0 | 3.74 × 3.48 | 130 | S-Skl |
| V-8, 305.0 | 3.74 × 3.48 | 155 | O-Cnty, Rgl |
| V-8, 350.0 | 3.80 × 3.85 | 155 | S-EWgn, Elec; O-LeS |
| V-8, 350.0 | 4.00 × 3.48 | 165 | O-Sky, Cent wgn |
| V-8, 350.0 | 4.06 × 3.39 | 170 | S-Riv; O-Riv S |
| V-8, 403.0 | 4.35 × 3.38 | 185 | O-EWgn, Elec |

### 1980

| Skyhawk (wb 97.0) | | Wght | Price | Prod |
|---|---|---|---|---|
| S07 | htchbk cpe 2d | 2,754 | 5,211 | 8,322 |
| T07 | S htchbk cpe 2d | 2,754 | 4,993 | |

| Skylark (wb 104.9) | | | | |
|---|---|---|---|---|
| B69 | sdn 4d | 2,458 | 5,488 | 80,940 |
| B37 | sdn 2d | 2,430 | 5,342 | 55,114 |
| C69 | Limited sdn 4d | 2,498 | 5,912 | 86,948 |
| C37 | Limited sdn 2d | 2,458 | 5,765 | 42,652 |
| D69 | Sport Sedan 4d | 2,490 | 6,102 | — |
| D37 | sport coupe 2d I-4/V-6 | 2,450 | 5,955 | — |

| Century (wb 108.1)** | | | | |
|---|---|---|---|---|
| H69 | sdn 4d | 3,158 | 5,858 | 129,740 |
| L69 | Limited sdn 4d | 3,202 | 6,344 | — |
| H87 | sdn 2d | 3,138 | 5,758 | 1,074 |
| G87 | sport coupe sdn 2d | 3,202 | 6,275 | — |
| H35 | Estate wgn 4d 2S | 3,311 | 6,432 | 11,122 |
| E35 | wgn 4d 2S | 3,300 | 6,134 | 6,493 |

| Regal (wb 108.1)** | | | | |
|---|---|---|---|---|
| J47 | cpe 2d | 3,179 | 6,506 | 214,735 |
| M47 | Limited cpe 2d | 3,282 | 6,925 | |
| K47 | sport coupe turbo V-6 2d | 3,194 | 7,203 | |

| LeSabre (wb 115.9)** | | | | |
|---|---|---|---|---|
| N69 | sdn 4d | 3,433 | 6,940 | 23,873 |
| N37 | cpe 2d | 3,380 | 6,845 | 8,342 |
| P69 | Limited sdn 4d | 3,439 | 7,242 | 37,676 |
| P37 | Limited cpe 2d | 3,391 | 7,100 | 20,561 |
| F37 | sport coupe turbo V-6 | 3,430 | 8,003 | — |
| R35 | wgn 4d 2S V-8 | 3,898 | 7,844 | 9,318 |
| R35 | wgn 4d 3S V-8 | 3,982 | 8,037 | |

| Electra 225 (wb 119.0; wgns 115.9)** | | | | |
|---|---|---|---|---|
| X69 | Limited sdn 4d | 3,670 | 9,580 | 54,422 |
| W69 | Park Avenue sdn 4d | 3,670 | 10,676 | — |
| X37 | Limited cpe 2d | 3,664 | 9,425 | 14,058 |
| W37 | Park Avenue cpe 2d | 3,692 | 10,537 | — |
| V35 | Estate wgn 4d 2S V-8 | 4,105 | 10,806 | — |
| V35 | Estate wgn 4d 3S V-8 | 4,135 | 10,999 | — |

| Riviera (wb 114.0) | | | | |
|---|---|---|---|---|
| Z57 | cpe V-8 | 3,633 | 11,640 | 48,621 |
| Y57 | S-Type cpe | 3,734 | 12,151 | |

| 1980 Engines | bore × stroke | bhp | availability |
|---|---|---|---|
| I-4, 151.0 | 4.00 × 3.00 | 90 | S-Skylark |
| V-6, 173.0 | 3.50 × 3.00 | 115 | O-Skylark |
| V-6, 231.0 | 3.80 × 3.40 | 110 | S-Skyhawk, Cnty, Rgl, LeS |
| V-6T, 231.0 | 3.80 × 3.40 | 170 | S-Rgl S/C, LeS S/C; O-Cnty |
| V-6T, 231.0 | 3.80 × 3.40 | 175 | S-Cnty S/C |
| V-6T, 231.0 | 3.80 × 3.40 | 185 | S-Riv "S"; O-Riv |
| V-6, 252.0 | 3.97 × 3.40 | 125 | S-Elec; O-LeS |
| V-8, 265.0 | 3.75 × 3.00 | 120 | S-Cnty, Rgl |
| V-8, 301.0 | 4.00 × 3.00 | 140 | S-LeS, Elec, EWgn, O-Cnty, Rgl |
| V-8, 305.0 | 3.74 × 3.48 | 155 | O-Cnty, Rgl |
| V-8, 350.0 | 3.80 × 3.85 | 155 | O-LeS, Elec, EWgn |
| V-8, 350.0 | 4.06 × 3.39 | 160 | S-Elec, Riv; O-LeS, Riv S, EWgn |
| V-8D, 350.0 | 3.88 × 3.53 | 105 | O-EWgn, Elec |

* I-4 & V-6 weights averaged. Prices are for L4s; V-6s add $225
** V-6 & V-8 weights averaged. Prices are for V-6s; V-8s add $105

### 1981

| Skylark (wb 104.9) | | Wght | Price | Prod |
|---|---|---|---|---|
| B69 | sdn 4d | 2,479 | 6,551 | 104,091 |

# Buick

| Skylark (wb 104.9) | | Wght | Price | Prod |
|---|---|---|---|---|
| B37 | sdn 2d | 2,453 | 6,405 | 46,515 |
| C69 | Limited sdn 4d | 2,513 | 7,007 | 81,642 |
| C37 | Limited sdn 2d | 2,482 | 6,860 | 30,080 |
| D69 | Sport Sedan 4d | 2,512 | 7,186 | — |
| D37 | sport coupe 2d | 2,486 | 7,040 | — |
| **Century (wb 108.1)** | | | | |
| H69 | sdn 4d | 3,224 | 7,094 ⎤ | 127,119 |
| L69 | Limited sdn 4d | 3,249 | 7,999 ⎦ | |
| H35 | Estate wgn 4d 2S | 3,368 | 7,735 | 11,659 |
| E35 | wgn 4d 2S | 3,321 | 7,391 | 5,489 |
| **Regal (wb 108.1)** | | | | |
| J47 | cpe 2d | 3,245 | 7,555 ⎤ | 123,848 |
| K47 | sport coupe turbo V-6 2d | 3,261 | 8,528 ⎦ | |
| M47 | Limited cpe 2d | 3,382 | 8,024 | 116,352 |
| **LeSabre (wb 115.9)** | | | | |
| N69 | sdn 4d | 3,573 | 7,805 | 19,166 |
| N37 | cpe 2d | 3,544 | 7,715 | 4,909 |
| P69 | Limited sdn 4d | 3,595 | 8,101 | 39,006 |
| P37 | Limited cpe 2d | 3,562 | 7,966 | 14,862 |
| R35 | Estate wgn 4d 2S V-8 | 4,118 | 8,722 | 4,934 |
| **Electra (wb 118.9; wgn 115.9)** | | | | |
| X69 | Limited sdn 4d | 3,802 | 10,368 ⎤ | 58,832 |
| W69 | Park Avenue sdn 4d | 3,818 | 11,396 ⎦ | |
| X37 | Limited cpe 2d | 3,686 | 10,237 ⎤ | 10,151 |
| W37 | Park Avenue cpe 2d | 3,808 | 11,267 ⎦ | |
| V35 | Estate wgn 4d 2S V-8 | 4,290 | 11,291 | 6,334 |
| **Riviera (wb 114.0)** | | | | |
| Z57 | cpe 2d | 3,643 | 12,147 ⎤ | 52,007 |
| Y57 | T Type cpe turbo V-6 | 3,651 | 13,091 ⎦ | |

| 1981 Engines | bore × stroke | bhp | availability |
|---|---|---|---|
| I-4, 151.0 | 4.00 × 3.00 | 90 | S-Skylark |
| V-6, 173.0 | 3.50 × 3.00 | 115 | O-Skylark |
| V-6, 231.0 | 3.80 × 3.40 | 110 | S-Cnty, Rgl, LeS |
| V-6T, 231.0 | 3.80 × 3.40 | 170 | S-Rgl S/C |
| V-6T, 231.0 | 3.80 × 3.40 | 180 | S-Riv T; O-Riv |
| V-6, 252.0 | 3.97 × 3.40 | 125 | S-Elec, Riv; O-Les, Riv T |
| V-8, 265.0 | 3.75 × 3.00 | 119 | O-Cnty, Rgl |
| V-8, 307.0 | 3.80 × 3.39 | 140 | S-EWgn; O-LeS, Elec, Riv |
| V-8D, 350.0 | 4.06 × 3.39 | 105 | O-LeS, Elec, EWgn, Riv |

## 1982

| Skyhawk (wb 101.2) | | Wght | Price | Prod |
|---|---|---|---|---|
| S69 | Custom sdn 4d | 2,385 | 7,489 ⎤ | 22,540 |
| T69 | Limited sdn 4d | 2,411 | 7,931 ⎦ | |
| S27 | Custom cpe 2d | 2,327 | 7,297 ⎤ | 25,378 |
| T27 | Limited cpe 2d | 2,349 | 7,739 ⎦ | |
| **Skylark (wb 104.9)** | | | | |
| B69 | sdn 4d | 2,521 | 7,647 | 65,541 |
| B37 | cpe 2d | 2,490 | 7,477 | 21,017 |
| C69 | Limited sdn 4d | 2,547 | 8,079 | 44,290 |
| C37 | Limited cpe 2d | 2,517 | 7,917 | 13,712 |
| D69 | Sport Sedan 4d | 2,552 | 8,219 ⎤ | 1,295* |
| D37 | sport coupe 2d | 2,522 | 8,048 ⎦ | |
| **Century (wb 104.9)** | | | | |
| H19 | Custom sdn 4d | 2,671 | 9,141 ⎤ | 83,250 |
| L19 | Limited sdn 4d | 2,683 | 9,581 ⎦ | |
| H27 | Custom cpe 2d | 2,643 | 8,980 ⎤ | 19,715 |
| L27 | Limited cpe 2d | 2,654 | 9,417 ⎦ | |
| **Regal (wb 108.1)** | | | | |
| J47 | cpe 2d | 3,152 | 8,712 ⎤ | 134,237 |
| M47 | Limited cpe 2d | 3,192 | 9,266 ⎦ | |
| K47 | sport coupe turbo V-6 2d | 3,265 | 9,738 | 2,022 |
| J69 | sdn 4d | 3,167 | 8,862 ⎤ | 74,428 |
| M69 | Limited sdn 4d | 3,205 | 9,364 ⎦ | |
| J35 | wgn 4d | 3,410 | 9,058 | 14,732 |
| **LeSabre (wb 115.9)** | | | | |
| N69 | Custom sdn 4d | 3,594 | 8,876 | 23,220 |
| N37 | Custom cpe 2d | 3,565 | 8,774 | 5,165 |
| P69 | Limited sdn 4d | 3,666 | 9,331 | 47,224 |
| P37 | Limited cpe 2d | 3,583 | 9,177 | 16,062 |
| R35 | Estate wgn 4d 2s V-8 | 4,228 | 10,668 | 7,149 |
| **Electra (wb 118.9; wgn 115.9)** | | | | |
| X69 | Limited sdn 4d | 3,807 | 11,884 ⎤ | 59,601 |
| W69 | Park Avenue sdn 4d | 3,888 | 13,559 ⎦ | |
| X37 | Limited cpe 2d | 3,747 | 11,713 ⎤ | 8,449 |
| W37 | Park Avenue cpe 2d | 3,824 | 13,408 ⎦ | |
| V35 | Estate wgn 4d 2s V-8 | 4,229 | 12,911 | 8,182 |
| **Riviera (wb 114.0)** | | | | |
| Z57 | cpe 2d | 3,680 | 14,272 ⎤ | 42,823 |
| Y57 | T Type cpe turbo V-6 | — | 14,940 ⎦ | |
| Z67 | conv cpe | — | 23,994 | 1,248 |

| 1982 Engines | bore × stroke | bhp | availability |
|---|---|---|---|
| I-4, 112.0 | 3.50 × 2.91 | 88 | S-Skyhawk |
| I-4, 112.0 | 3.33 × 3.12 | 80 | O-Skyhawk |
| I-4, 121.0 | 3.50 × 3.15 | 90 | O-Skyhawk |
| I-4, 151.0 | 4.00 × 3.00 | 90 | O-Skylark, Century |
| V-6, 173.0 | 3.50 × 3.00 | 112 | O-Skylark |
| V-6, 173.0 | 3.50 × 3.00 | 135 | O-Skylark |
| V-6, 181.0 | 3.80 × 2.66 | 110 | O-Century |
| V-6, 231.0 | 3.80 × 3.40 | 110 | S-Rgl, LeS |
| V-6T, 231.0 | 3.80 × 3.40 | 175/180 | S-Rgl S/C, Riv T |
| V-6, 252.0 | 3.96 × 3.40 | 125 | S-Elec, Riv; O-Rgl, LeS |
| V-6D, 262.5 | 4.06 × 3.39 | 85 | O-Cnty, Rgl |
| V-8, 307.0 | 3.80 × 3.38 | 140 | S-EWgn; O-LeS, Elec, Riv |
| V-8D, 350.0 | 4.06 × 3.39 | 105 | O-Rgl, LeS, Elec, EWgn, Riv |

* Sport model production included in basic Skylark totals.

## 1983

| Skyhawk (wb 101.2) | | Wght | Price | Prod |
|---|---|---|---|---|
| S69 | Custom sdn 4d | 2,369 | 7,166 ⎤ | 19,847 |
| T69 | Limited sdn 4d | 2,411 | 7,649 ⎦ | |
| S27 | Custom cpe 2d | 2,316 | 6,958 ⎤ | 27,557 |
| T27 | Limited cpe 2d | 2,333 | 7,457 ⎦ | |
| S35 | Custom wgn 4d | 2,439 | 7,492 ⎤ | 10,653 |
| T35 | Limited wgn 4d | 2,462 | 7,934 ⎦ | |
| E27 | T Type cpe 2d | 2,336 | 7,961 | 5,095 |
| **Skylark (wb 104.9)** | | | | |
| B69 | Custom sdn 4d | 2,521 | 7,718 | 51,950 |
| B37 | Custom cpe 2d | 2,492 | 7,548 | 11,671 |
| C69 | Limited sdn 4d | 2,549 | 8,150 | 30,674 |
| C37 | Limited cpe 2d | 2,519 | 7,988 | 7,863 |
| D37 | T Type cpe 2d V-6 | 2,608 | 9,337 | 2,489 |
| **Century (wb 104.9)** | | | | |
| H19 | Custom sdn 4d | 2,692 | 9,002 ⎤ | 50,296 |
| H27 | Custom cpe 2d | 2,644 | 8,841 ⎦ | |
| L19 | Limited sdn 4d | 2,705 | 9,425 ⎤ | 73,030 |
| L27 | Limited cpe 2d | 2,662 | 9,261 ⎦ | |
| G27 | T Type cpe 2d V-6 | 2,749 | 10,017 | 4,600* |

# Buick

| Century (wb 104.9) | | Wght | Price | Prod |
|---|---|---|---|---|
| G19 | T Type sdn 4d V-6 | 2,801 | 10,178 | |
| **Regal (wb 108.1)** | | | | |
| J47 | cpe 2d | 3,123 | 9,100 | 147,935 |
| M47 | Limited cpe 2d | 3,164 | 9,722 | |
| K47 | T Type turbo V-6 cpe 2d | 3,194 | 10,366 | 3,732 |
| J69 | sdn 4d | 3,139 | 9,279 | 61,285 |
| M69 | Limited sdn 4d | 3,177 | 9,856 | |
| J35 | wgn 4d | 3,289 | 9,550 | 15,287 |
| **LeSabre (wb 115.9)** | | | | |
| N69 | Custom sdn 4d | 3,574 | 9,394 | 31,196 |
| N37 | Custom cpe 2d | 3,545 | 9,292 | 6,974 |
| P69 | Limited sdn 4d | 3,613 | 9,990 | 66,547 |
| P37 | Limited cpe 2d | 3,579 | 9,836 | 22,029 |
| R35 | Estate wgn 4d 2S V-8 | 4,105 | 11,187 | 9,306 |
| **Electra (wb 118.9; wgn 115.9)** | | | | |
| X69 | Limited sdn 4d | 3,794 | 12,586 | 79,700 |
| W69 | Park Avenue sdn 4d | 3,871 | 14,245 | |
| X37 | Limited cpe 2d | 3,734 | 12,415 | 8,885 |
| W37 | Park Avenue cpe 2d | 3,806 | 14,094 | |
| V35 | Estate wgn 4d 2S V-8 | 4,175 | 13,638 | 9,581 |
| **Riviera (wb 114.0)** | | | | |
| Z57 | cpe 2d | 3,689 | 15,238 | 47,153 |
| Y57 | T Type cpe turbo V-6 | 3,593 | 15,906 | 1,331 |
| Z67 | conv cpe | 3,875 | 24,960 | 1,750 |

| 1983 Engines | bore × stroke | bhp | availability |
|---|---|---|---|
| I-4, 112.0 | 3.34 × 3.13 | 84 | O-Skyhawk |
| I-4, 121.0 | 3.50 × 3.15 | 86 | S-Skyhawk |
| I-4, 151.0 | 4.00 × 3.00 | 90 | S-Skylark, Century |
| V-6, 173.0 | 3.50 × 2.99 | 112 | O-Skylark |
| V-6, 173.0 | 3.50 × 2.99 | 135 | S-Skylark T; O-Skylark |
| V-6, 181.0 | 3.80 × 2.66 | 110 | O-Century |
| V-6, 231.0 | 3.80 × 3.40 | 110 | S-Rgl, LeS |
| V-6T, 231.0 | 3.80 × 3.40 | 180 | S-Rgl T, Riv T |
| V-6, 252.0 | 3.97 × 3.40 | 125 | S-Elec, Riv; O-Rgl, LeS |
| V-6D, 262.5 | 4.06 × 3.39 | 85 | O-Cnty, Rgl |
| V-8, 307.0 | 3.80 × 3.39 | 140 | S-EWgn; O-LeS, Elec, Riv |
| V-8D, 350.0 | 4.06 × 3.39 | 105 | O-Rgl, LeS, Elec, EWgn, Riv |

*T Type production included in basic totals.

## 1984

| Skyhawk (wb 101.2) | | Wght | Price | Prod |
|---|---|---|---|---|
| S69 | Custom sdn 4d | 2,436 | 7,345 | 45,648 |
| T69 | Limited sdn 4d | 2,471 | 7,837 | |
| S27 | Custom cpe 2d | 2,383 | 7,133 | 74,760 |
| T27 | Limited cpe 2d | 2,424 | 7,641 | |
| S35 | Custom wgn 4d | 2,507 | 7,677 | 13,668 |
| T35 | Limited wgn 4d | 2,536 | 8,127 | |
| E27 | T Type cpe 2d | 2,399 | 8,152 | 11,317 |
| **Skylark (wb 104.9)** | | | | |
| B69 | Custom sdn 4d | 2,593 | 7,707 | 56,495 |
| B37 | Custom cpe 2d | 2,561 | 7,545 | 12,377 |
| C69 | Limited sdn 4d | 2,618 | 8,283 | 33,795 |
| C37 | Limited cpe 2d | 2,587 | 8,119 | 7,621 |
| D37 | T Type cpe 2d V-6 | 2,676 | 9,557 | 923 |
| **Century (wb 104.9)** | | | | |
| H19 | Custom sdn 4d | 2,790 | 9,274 | 178,454 |
| L19 | Limited sdn 4d | 2,811 | 9,729 | |
| H27 | Custom cpe 2d | 2,742 | 9,110 | 15,429 |
| L27 | Limited cpe 2d | 2,763 | 9,562 | |
| H35 | Custom wgn 4d | 2,958 | 9,660 | 25,975 |

| Century (wb 104.9) | | Wght | Price | Prod |
|---|---|---|---|---|
| L35 | Limited wgn 4d | 2,976 | 10,087 | |
| G27 | T Type cpe 2d V-6 | 2,855 | 10,510 | 3,477* |
| G19 | T Type sdn 4d V-6 | 2,903 | 10,674 | |
| **Regal (wb 108.1)** | | | | |
| J47 | cpe 2d | 3,172 | 9,487 | 160,638 |
| M47 | Limited cpe 2d | 3,210 | 10,125 | |
| K47 | T Type turbo V-6 cpe 2d | 3,254 | 12,118 | 5,401 |
| J69 | sdn 4d | 3,219 | 9,671 | 58,715 |
| M69 | Limited sdn 4d | 3,254 | 10,263 | |
| **LeSabre (wb 115.9)** | | | | |
| N69 | Custom sdn 4d | 3,717 | 10,129 | 36,072 |
| N37 | Custom cpe 2d | 3,684 | 9,984 | 3,890 |
| P69 | Limited sdn 4d | 3,763 | 10,940 | 86,418 |
| P37 | Limited cpe 2d | 3,730 | 10,780 | 28,332 |
| **Electra (wb 118.9; wgn 115.9)** | | | | |
| R69 | Limited sdn 4d | 3,944 | 13,332 | 52,551 |
| U69 | Park Avenue sdn 4d | 3,994 | 15,044 | |
| R37 | Limited cpe 2d | 3,884 | 13,155 | 4,075 |
| U37 | Park Avenue cpe 2d | 3,928 | 14,888 | |
| V35 | Estate wgn 4d 2s V-8 | 4,295 | 14,483 | 17,563 |
| **Riviera (wb 114.0)** | | | | |
| Z57 | cpe 2d | 3,766 | 15,967 | 56,210 |
| Y57 | T Type cpe turbo V-6 | 3,666 | 17,050 | 1,153 |
| Z67 | conv cpe | 3,873 | 25,832 | 500 |

| 1984 Engines | bore × stroke | bhp | availability |
|---|---|---|---|
| I-4, 112.0 | 3.34 × 3.13 | 84 | O-Skyhawk |
| I-4T, 112.0 | 3.34 × 3.13 | 150 | S-Skyhawk T; O-Skyh |
| I-4, 121.0 | 3.50 × 3.15 | 86 | S-Skyhawk |
| I-4, 151.0 | 4.00 × 3.00 | 92 | S-Skylark, Century |
| V-6, 173.0 | 3.50 × 2.99 | 112 | O-Skylark |
| V-6, 173.0 | 3.50 × 2.99 | 135 | S-Skylark T; O-Skyl |
| V-6, 181.0 | 3.80 × 2.66 | 110 | O-Century |
| V-6, 231.0 | 3.80 × 3.40 | 110 | S-Rgl, LeS |
| V-6, 231.0 | 3.80 × 3.40 | 125 | S-Century T; O-Cnty |
| V-6T, 231.0 | 3.80 × 3.40 | 200 | S-Rgl T |
| V-6T, 231.0 | 3.80 × 3.40 | 190 | S-Riv T |
| V-6, 252.0 | 3.97 × 3.40 | 125 | S-Elec, Riv; O-Rgl, LeS |
| V-6D, 262.5 | 4.06 × 3.39 | 85 | O-Cnty, Rgl |
| V-8, 307.0 | 3.80 × 3.39 | 140 | S-EWgn; O-LeS, Elec, Riv |
| V-8D, 350.0 | 4.06 × 3.39 | 105 | O-LeS, EWgn, Riv |

* T Type production included in basic totals.

## 1985

| Skyhawk (wb 101.2) | | Wght | Price | Prod |
|---|---|---|---|---|
| S69 | Custom sdn 4d | 2,392 | 7,581 | 27,906 |
| T69 | Limited sdn 4d | 2,424 | 8,083 | |
| S27 | Custom cpe 2d | 2,347 | 7,365 | 44,804 |
| T27 | Limited cpe 2d | 2,380 | 7,883 | |
| S35 | Custom wgn 4d | 2,469 | 7,919 | 5,285 |
| T35 | Limited wgn 4d | 2,496 | 8,379 | |
| E27 | T Type cpe 2d | 2,362 | 8,437 | 4,521 |
| **Skylark (wb 104.9)** | | | | |
| B69 | Custom sdn 4d | 2,618 | 7,707 | 65,667 |
| C69 | Limited sdn 4d | 2,655 | 8,283 | 27,490 |
| **Somerset Regal (wb 103.4)** | | | | |
| J27 | Custom cpe 2d | 2,567 | 8,857 | 48,470 |
| M27 | Limited cpe 2d | 2,571 | 9,466 | 37,601 |
| **Century (wb 104.9)** | | | | |
| H19 | Custom sdn 4d | 2,790 | 9,545 | 215,928 |
| L19 | Limited sdn 4d | 2,812 | 10,012 | |

# Buick

| Century (wb 104.9) | | Wght | Price | Prod |
|---|---|---|---|---|
| H27 | Custom cpe 2d | 2,742 | 9,377 | 13,043 |
| L27 | Limited cpe 2d | 2,764 | 9,841 | |
| H35 | Custom wgn 4d | 2,958 | 9,941 | 28,221 |
| L35 | Limited wgn 4d | 2,975 | 10,379 | |
| G27 | T Type cpe 2d V-6 | 2,881 | 11,249 | 4,043* |
| G19 | T Type sdn 4d V-6 | 2,930 | 11,418 | |
| **Regal (wb 108.1)** | | | | |
| J47 | cpe 2d | 3,172 | 9,928 | 60,597 |
| M47 | Limited cpe 2d | 3,199 | 10,585 | 59,780 |
| K47 | T Type turbo V-6 cpe 2d | 3,349 | 12,640 | 2,067 |
| K47 | Grand National V-6 cpe 2d | — | 13,315 | 2,102 |
| **LeSabre (wb 115.9)** | | | | |
| N69 | Custom sdn 4d | 3,683 | 10,603 | 32,091 |
| N37 | Custom cpe 2d | 3,672 | 10,455 | 5,156 |
| P69 | Limited sdn 4d | 3,729 | 11,916 | 84,432 |
| P37 | Limited cpe 2d | 3,696 | 11,751 | 22,211 |
| R35 | Estate wgn 4d | 4,153 | 12,704 | 5,597 |
| **Electra (wb 110.8; wgn 115.9)** | | | | |
| X69 | sdn 4d | 3,250 | 14,331 | 131,011 |
| W69 | Park Avenue sdn 4d | 3,269 | 16,240 | |
| X11 | cpe 2d | 3,205 | 14,149 | 5,852 |
| W11 | Park Avenue cpe 2d | 3,223 | 16,080 | |
| F69 | T Type sdn 4d V-6 | 3,261 | 15,568 | 4,644* |
| F11 | T Type cpe 2d V-6 | 3,216 | 15,386 | |
| V35 | Estate wgn 4d 2s V-8 | 4,231 | 15,323 | 7,769 |
| **Riviera (wb 114.0)** | | | | |
| Z57 | cpe 2d | 3,857 | 16,710 | 63,836 |
| Y57 | T Type cpe turbo V-6 | 3,668 | 17,654 | 1,069 |
| Z67 | conv cpe | 3,977 | 26,797 | 400 |

| 1985 Engines | bore × stroke | bhp | availability |
|---|---|---|---|
| I-4, 112.0 | 3.43 × 3.13 | 84 | S-Skyhawk T; O-Skyhawk |
| I-4T, 112.0 | 3.34 × 3.13 | 150 | O-Skyhawk T |
| I-4, 121.0 | 3.50 × 3.15 | 86 | S-Skyhawk |
| I-4, 151.0 | 4.00 × 3.00 | 92 | S-Skylark, Cnty, Somerset |
| V-6, 173.0 | 3.50 × 2.99 | 112 | O-Skylark, Century |
| V-6, 173.0 | 3.50 × 2.99 | 125 | O-Skylark |
| V-6, 181.0 | 3.80 × 2.66 | 110 | S-Electra; O-Century |
| V-6, 181.0 | 3.80 × 2.66 | 125 | O-Somerset |
| V-6, 231.0 | 3.80 × 3.40 | 110 | S-Rgl, LeS |
| V-6, 231.0 | 3.80 × 3.40 | 125 | S-Century T, Electra T/Park; O-Century, Electra |
| V-6T, 231.0 | 3.80 × 3.40 | 200 | S-Rgl T |
| V-6T, 231.0 | 3.80 × 3.40 | 190 | S-Riv T |
| V-6D, 262.5 | 4.06 × 3.39 | 85 | O-Cnty, Rgl, Elec |
| V-8, 307.0 | 3.80 × 3.39 | 140 | S-EWgn, Riv; O-LeS |
| V-8D, 350.0 | 4.06 × 3.39 | 105 | O-LeS, EWgn, Riv |

*T Type production included in basic totals.

## 1986

| Skyhawk (wb 101.2) | | Wght | Price | Prod |
|---|---|---|---|---|
| S69 | Custom sdn 4d | 2,392 | 8,073 | 29,959 |
| T69 | Limited sdn 4d | 2,425 | 8,598 | |
| S27 | Custom cpe 2d | 2,343 | 7,844 | 45,884 |
| T27 | Limited cpe 2d | 2,381 | 8,388 | |
| S35 | Custom wgn 4d | 2,469 | 8,426 | 6,079 |
| T35 | Limited wgn 4d | 2,498 | 8,910 | |
| E27 | T Type cpe 2d | 2,440 | 8,971 | 6,071 |
| E77 | T Type htchbk 2d | 2,526 | 9,414 | |
| S77 | Sport htchbk 2d | 2,433 | 8,184 | — |

| Skylark (wb 103.4) | | Wght | Price | Prod |
|---|---|---|---|---|
| J69 | Custom sdn | 2,601 | 9,620 | 62,235 |
| M69 | Limited sdn 4d | 2,608 | 10,290 | |
| **Somerset (wb 103.4)** | | | | |
| J27 | Custom cpe 2d | 2,557 | 9,425 | 72,062 |
| M27 | Limited cpe 2d | 2,577 | 10,095 | |
| K27 | T Type cpe 2d | 2,562 | 11,390 | 3,558 |
| **Century (wb 104.9)** | | | | |
| H19 | Custom sdn 4d | 2,773 | 10,228 | 229,066 |
| L19 | Limited sdn 4d | 2,795 | 10,729 | |
| H27 | Custom cpe 2d | 2,726 | 10,052 | 13,752 |
| L27 | Limited cpe 2d | 2,748 | 10,544 | |
| — | Gran Sport cpe 2d | — | — | 1,029 |
| H35 | Custom wgn 4d | 2,938 | 10,648 | 25,374 |
| L35 | Limited wgn 4d | 2,955 | 11,109 | |
| G19 | T Type sdn 4d V-6 | 2,941 | 12,223 | 5,286 |
| **Regal (wb 108.1)** | | | | |
| J47 | cpe 2d | 3,289 | 10,654 | 39,734 |
| M47 | Limited cpe 2d | 3,315 | 11,347 | 43,599 |
| K47 | T Type turbo V-6 cpe 2d | 3,380 | 13,714 | 7,896 |
| K47 | Grand National V-6 cpe 2d | — | 14,349 | 5,512* |
| **LeSabre (wb 110.8; wgn 115.9)** | | | | |
| P69 | Custom sdn 4d | 3,150 | 12,511 | 30,235 |
| P37 | Custom cpe 2d | 3,108 | 12,511 | 7,191 |
| R69 | Limited sdn 4d | 3,161 | 13,633 | 43,215 |
| R37 | Limited cpe 2d | 3,119 | 13,633 | 14,331 |
| R35 | Estate wgn 4d | 4,206 | 13,597 | 7,755 |
| **Electra (wb 110.8; wgn 115.9)** | | | | |
| X69 | sdn 4d | 3,256 | 15,588 | 109,042 |
| W69 | Park Avenue sdn 4d | 3,305 | 17,338 | |
| X11 | cpe 2d | 3,205 | 15,396 | 4,996 |
| W11 | Park Avenue cpe 2d | 3,250 | 17,158 | |
| F69 | T Type sdn 4d V-6 | 3,278 | 16,826 | 5,816 |
| V35 | Estate wgn 4d 2s V-8 | 4,242 | 16,402 | 10,371 |
| **Riviera (wb 108.0)** | | | | |
| Z57 | cpe 2d | 3,298 | 19,831 | 20,096 |
| Y57 | T Type cpe | 3,329 | 21,577 | 2,042 |

| 1986 Engines | bore × stroke | bhp | availability |
|---|---|---|---|
| I-4, 112.0 | 3.34 × 3.13 | 88 | S-Skyh T; O-Skyh |
| I-4T, 112.0 | 3.34 × 3.13 | 150 | O-Skyhawk T |
| I-4, 121.0 | 3.50 × 3.15 | 88 | S-Skyhawk |
| I-4, 151.0 | 4.00 × 3.00 | 92 | S-Skylark, Cnty, Somerset |
| V-6, 173.0 | 3.50 × 2.99 | 112 | O-Century |
| V-6, 181.0 | 3.80 × 2.66 | 125 | S-Smrst T, LeS; O-Somerset, Sky |
| V-6, 231.0 | 3.80 × 3.40 | 110 | S-Rgl |
| V-6, 231.0 | 3.80 × 3.40 | 140 | S-Elec, Riv |
| V-6, 231.0 | 3.80 × 3.40 | 150 | S-Century T; O-Century, LeS |
| V-6T 231.0 | 3.80 × 3.40 | 235 | S-Rgl T |
| V-8, 307.0 | 3.80 × 3.39 | 140 | S-EWgn; O-Regal |

*Production included in basic Regal total.

## 1987

| Skyhawk (wb 101.2) | | Wght | Price | Prod |
|---|---|---|---|---|
| S69 | Custom sdn 4d | 2,385 | 8,559 | 15,778 |
| T69 | Limited sdn 4d | 2,423 | 9,503 | 2,200 |
| S27 | Custom cpe 2d | 2,336 | 8,522 | 19,814 |
| T27 | Limited cpe 2d | 2,345 | 9,445 | 1,556 |
| S35 | Custom wgn 4d | 2,463 | 9,249 | 3,061 |
| T35 | Limited wgn 4d | 2,498 | 9,841 | 498 |

# Buick

| Skyhawk (wb 101.2) | | Wght | Price | Prod |
|---|---|---|---|---|
| S77 | Sport htchbk 2d | 2,396 | 8,965 | 3,757 |
| **Skylark (wb 103.4)** | | | | |
| J69 | Custom sdn 4d | 2,535 | 9,915 | 26,173 |
| M69 | Limited sdn 4d | 2,609 | 11,003 | 7,532 |
| **Somerset (wb 103.4)** | | | | |
| J27 | Custom cpe 2d | 2,489 | 9,957 | 34,916 |
| M27 | Limited cpe 2d | 2,574 | 11,003 | 11,585 |
| **Century (wb 104.9)** | | | | |
| H19 | Custom sdn 4d | 2,783 | 10,989 | 88,445 |
| L19 | Limited sdn 4d | 2,811 | 11,593 | 71,340 |
| H27 | Custom cpe 2d | 2,736 | 10,844 | 2,878 |
| L27 | Limited cpe 2d | 2,765 | 11,397 | 4,384 |
| H35 | Custom wgn 4d | 2,866 | 11,478 | 10,141 |
| L35 | Limited Estate wgn 4d | 2,866 | 11,998 | 6,990 |
| **Regal (wb 108.1)** | | | | |
| J47 | cpe 2d | 3,286 | 11,562 | 44,844 |
| M47 | Limited cpe 2d | 3,315 | 12,303 | 20,441 |
| J47/Y56 | T Type V-6 cpe 2d | — | 14,857 | 8,541* |
| J47/WE2 | Grand National V-6 cpe 2d | — | 15,136 | 20,193* |
| J47/T26 | GNX cpe | — | — | 547* |
| **LeSabre (wb 110.8)** | | | | |
| H69 | sdn 4d | 3,141 | 13,438 | 6,243 |
| P69 | Custom sdn 4d | 3,140 | 13,616 | 60,392 |
| R69 | Limited sdn 4d | 3,171 | 14,918 | 70,797 |
| P37 | Custom cpe 2d | 3,104 | 13,616 | 5,035 |
| R37 | Limited cpe 2d | 3,137 | 14,918 | 7,741 |
| L37 | T Type cpe 2d | — | 15,521 | 4,123 |
| **Electra (wb 110.8)** | | | | |
| X69 | sdn 4d | 3,269 | 16,902 | 7,787 |
| W69 | Park Avenue sdn 4d | 3,338 | 18,769 | 75,600 |
| W11 | Park Avenue cpe 2d | 3,236 | 18,577 | 4,084 |
| F69 | T Type sdn 4d | 3,278 | 18,224 | 2,570 |
| **Estate wagons (wb 115.9)** | | | | |
| R35 | LeSabre wgn 4d | 4,160 | 14,724 | 5,251 |
| V35 | Electra wgn 4d | 4,239 | 17,697 | 7,508 |
| **Riviera (wb 108.0)** | | | | |
| Z57 | cpe 2d | 3,320 | 20,337 | 12,636 |
| Z57/Y50 | T Type cpe | 3,360 | 22,181 | 2,587 |

| 1987 Engines | bore × stroke | bhp | availability |
|---|---|---|---|
| I-4, 121.0 | 3.50 × 3.15 | 90 | S-Skyhawk |
| I-4, 121.0 | 3.39 × 3.39 | 96 | O-Skyhawk |
| I-4T, 121.0 | 3.39 × 3.39 | 165 | O-Skyhawk |
| I-4, 151.0 | 4.00 × 3.00 | 98 | S-Skylark, Cnty, Somerset |
| V-6, 173.0 | 3.50 × 2.99 | 125 | O-Century |
| V-6, 181.0 | 3.80 × 2.66 | 125 | O-Somerset, Skyl |
| V-6, 231.0 | 3.80 × 3.40 | 110 | S-Regal |
| V-6, 231.0 | 3.80 × 3.40 | 150 | S-LeS, Elec, Riv; O-Cnty |
| V-6T, 231.0 | 3.80 × 3.40 | 245 | S-Rgl Grand Nat'l; O-Regal |
| V-6T, 231.0 | 3.80 × 3.40 | 276 | S-GNX |
| V-8, 307.0 | 3.80 × 3.39 | 140 | S-EWgn; O-Regal |

*Production included in basic Regal total.

## 1988

| Skyhawk (wb 101.2) | | Wght | Price | Prod |
|---|---|---|---|---|
| S69 | sdn 4d | 2,396 | 8,884 | 14,271 |
| S27 | cpe 2d | 2,336 | 8,884 | 9,857 |
| S35 | wgn 4d | 2,474 | 9,797 | 1,707 |
| S27/WN2 | S/E cpe 2d | — | 9,979 | 3,299 |
| **Skylark (wb 103.4)** | | | | |
| C69 | Custom sdn 4d | 2,601 | 10,399 | 24,940 |
| D69 | Limited sdn 4d | 2,622 | 11,721 | 5,316 |
| J27 | Custom cpe 2d | 2,555 | 10,684 | 19,590 |
| M27 | Limited cpe 2d | 2,576 | 11,791 | 4,946 |
| **Century (wb 104.9)** | | | | |
| H19 | Custom sdn 4d | 2,796 | 11,793 | 62,214 |
| L19 | Limited sdn 4d | 2,803 | 12,613 | 39,137 |
| H27 | Custom cpe 2d | 2,725 | 11,643 | 1,322 |
| L27 | Limited cpe 2d | 2,732 | 12,410 | 1,127 |
| H35 | Custom wgn 4d | 2,945 | 12,345 | 5,312 |
| L35 | Limited Estate wgn 4d | 2,949 | 13,077 | 4,146 |
| **Reatta (wb 98.5)** | | | | |
| C97 | cpe 2d | 3,350 | 25,000 | 4,708 |
| **Regal (wb 107.5)** | | | | |
| B57 | Custom cpe 2d | 2,953 | 12,449 | 64,773 |
| D57 | Limited cpe 2d | 2,972 | 12,782 | 65,224 |
| **LeSabre (wb 110.8)** | | | | |
| P37 | cpe 2d | 3,192 | 14,560 | 2,403 |
| P69 | Custom sdn 4d | 3,239 | 14,405 | 67,213 |
| R69 | Limited sdn 4d | 3,291 | 15,745 | 57,524 |
| R37 | Limited cpe 2d | 3,242 | 16,350 | 2,474 |
| P37/WE2 | T Type cpe 2d | — | 16,518 | 6,426 |
| **Electra (wb 110.8)** | | | | |
| X69 | Limited sdn 4d | 3,288 | 17,479 | 5,791 |
| W69 | Park Avenue sdn 4d | 3,326 | 19,464 | 84,853 |
| F69 | T Type sdn 4d | 3,333 | 20,229 | 1,869 |
| **Estate wagons (wb 115.9)** | | | | |
| R35 | LeSabre wgn 3S 4d | 4,156 | 16,040 | 3,723 |
| V35 | Electra wgn 3S 4d | 4,217 | 18,954 | 5,901 |
| **Riviera (wb 108.0)** | | | | |
| Z57 | cpe 2d | 3,364 | 21,615 | 6,560 |
| Z57/Y50 | T Type cpe | — | 23,380 | 2,065 |

| 1988 Engines | bore × stroke | bhp | availability |
|---|---|---|---|
| I-4, 121.0 | 3.39 × 3.39 | 96 | S-Skyhawk |
| I-4, 138.0 | 3.62 × 3.35 | 150 | O-Skylark (dohc) |
| I-4, 151.0 | 4.00 × 3.00 | 98 | S-Skylark, Century |
| V-6, 173.0 | 3.50 × 2.99 | 125 | O-Century, Regal |
| V-6, 181.0 | 3.80 × 2.66 | 125 | O-Skylark |
| V-6, 231.0 | 3.80 × 3.40 | 150 | S-LeS; O-Cnty |
| V-6, 231.0 | 3.80 × 3.40 | 165 | S-LeS T, Elec, Riv; O-LeS |
| V-6T, 231.0 | 3.80 × 3.40 | 245 | S-Regal Grand Nat'l |
| V-8, 307.0 | 3.80 × 3.39 | 140 | S-Estate Wgn |

## 1989

| Skyhawk (wb 101.2) | | Wght | Price | Prod |
|---|---|---|---|---|
| S69 | sdn 4d | 2,469 | 9,285 | 13,841 |
| S27 | cpe 2d | 2,420 | 9,285 | 7,837 |
| S35 | wgn 4d | 2,551 | 10,230 | 1,688 |
| **Skylark (wb 103.4)** | | | | |
| C69 | Custom sdn 4d | 2,640 | 11,115 | 42,636 |
| D69 | Limited sdn 4d | — | 12,345 | 4,774 |
| J27 | Custom cpe 2d | 2,583 | 11,115 | 12,714 |
| M27 | Limited cpe 2d | — | 12,345 | 1,416 |
| **Century (wb 104.9)** | | | | |
| H69 | Custom sdn 4d | 2,769 | 12,429 | 89,281 |
| L69 | Limited sdn 4d | — | 13,356 | 49,839 |
| H37 | Custom cpe 2d | 2,725 | 12,199 | 6,953 |
| H35 | Custom wgn 4d | 2,905 | 13,156 | 5,479 |
| L35 | Limited Estate wgn 4d | — | 13,956 | 3,980 |

# Buick

| Reatta (wb 98.5) | | Wght | Price | Prod |
|---|---|---|---|---|
| C97 | cpe 2d | 3,394 | 26,700 | 7,009 |
| **Regal (wb 107.5)** | | | | |
| B57 | Custom cpe 2d | 3,144 | 14,214 | 56,057 |
| D57 | Limited cpe 2d | — | 14,739 | 32,700 |
| **LeSabre (wb 110.8)** | | | | |
| P37 | cpe 2d | 3,227 | 15,425 | 7,219 |
| P69 | Custom sdn 4d | 3,267 | 15,330 | 78,738 |
| R69 | Limited sdn 4d | — | 16,730 | 61,328 |
| R37 | Limited cpe 2d | — | 16,630 | 2,287 |
| **Electra (wb 110.8)** | | | | |
| X69 | Limited sdn 4d | 3,289 | 18,525 | 5,814 |
| W69 | Park Avenue sdn 4d | — | 20,460 | 71,786 |
| U69 | Park Avenue Ultra sdn 4d | — | — | 4,815 |
| F69 | T Type sdn 4d | — | 21,325 | 1,151 |
| **Estate wagons (wb 115.9)** | | | | |
| R35 | LeSabre wgn 3S 4d | 4,209 | 16,770 | 2,971 |
| V35 | Electra wgn 3S 4d | 4,273 | 19,860 | 4,560 |
| **Riviera (wb 108.0)** | | | | |
| Z57 | cpe 2d | 3,436 | 22,540 | 21,189 |

| 1989 Engines | bore × stroke | bhp | availability |
|---|---|---|---|
| I-4, 121.0 | 3.50 × 3.15 | 90 | S-Skyhawk |
| I-4, 138.0 | 3.62 × 3.35 | 150 | O-Skylark (dohc) |
| I-4, 151.0 | 4.00 × 3.00 | 98 | S-Century |
| I-4, 151.0 | 4.00 × 3.00 | 110 | S-Skylark |
| V-6, 173.0 | 3.50 × 2.99 | 130 | S-Regal |
| V-6, 191.0 | 3.50 × 3.31 | 140 | S-late Regal |
| V-6, 204.0 | 3.70 × 3.16 | 160 | O-Skylark, Century |
| V-6, 231.0 | 3.80 × 3.40 | 165 | S-LeS, Elec, Reat, Riv |
| V-8, 307.0 | 3.80 × 3.39 | 140 | S-Estate Wgn |

## 1990

| Skylark (wb 103.4) | | Wght | Price | Prod |
|---|---|---|---|---|
| V-69 | sdn 4d | 2,636 | 10,465 | 46,705 |
| C69 | Custom sdn 4d | — | 11,460 | 24,469 |
| D69 | Luxury Edition sdn 4d | — | 13,145 | 3,019 |
| V27 | cpe 2d | 2,636 | 10,565 | 4,248 |
| J27 | Custom cpe 2d | 2,583 | 11,115 | 5,490 |
| M27 | Gran Sport cpe 2d | — | 12,935 | 1,637 |
| **Century (wb 104.9)** | | | | |
| H69 | Custom sdn 4d | 2,776 | 13,150 | 88,309 |
| L69 | Limited sdn 4d | — | 14,075 | 35,248 |
| H37 | Custom cpe 2d | 2,754 | 13,250 | 1,944 |
| H35 | Custom wgn 4d | 2,924 | 14,570 | 4,383 |
| L35 | Limited Estate wgn 4d | — | 15,455 | 2,837 |
| **Reatta (wb 98.5)** | | | | |
| C97 | cpe 2d | 3,379 | 28,335 | 6,383 |
| C67 | conv cpe 2d | 3,562 | 34,995 | 2,132 |
| **Regal (wb 107.5)** | | | | |
| B57 | Custom cpe 2d | 3,108 | 15,200 | 39,036 |
| D57 | Limited cpe 2d | — | 15,860 | 15,787 |
| **LeSabre (wb 110.8)** | | | | |
| P37 | cpe 2d | 3,242 | 16,145 | 2,406 |
| P69 | Custom sdn 4d | 3,269 | 16,050 | 96,616 |
| R69 | Limited sdn 4d | — | 17,400 | 62,504 |
| R37 | Limited cpe 2d | — | 16,300 | 1,855 |
| **Electra (wb 110.8)** | | | | |
| X69 | Limited sdn 4d | 3,288 | 20,225 | 2,621 |
| W69 | Park Avenue sdn 4d | — | 21,750 | 44,072 |
| U69 | Park Avenue Ultra sdn 4d | — | 27,825 | 1,967 |
| F69 | T Type sdn 4d | — | 23,025 | 478 |
| **Estate wagon (wb 115.9)** | | | | |
| R35 | wgn 3S 4d | 4,281 | 17,940 | 7,838 |
| **Riviera (wb 108.0)** | | | | |
| Z57 | cpe 2d | 3,464 | 23,040 | 22,526 |

| 1990 Engines | bore × stroke | bhp | availability |
|---|---|---|---|
| I-4, 138.0 | 3.62 × 3.35 | 160 | O-Skylark (dohc) |
| I-4, 151.0 | 4.00 × 3.00 | 110 | S-Century, Skylark |
| V-6, 191.0 | 3.50 × 3.31 | 135 | S-Regal |
| V-6, 204.0 | 3.70 × 3.16 | 160 | O-Skylark, Century |
| V-6, 231.0 | 3.80 × 3.40 | 165 | S-LeS, Elec, Reatta, Riv |
| V-6, 231.0 | 3.80 × 3.40 | 170 | O-Regal |
| V-8, 307.0 | 3.80 × 3.39 | 140 | S-Estate Wgn |

## 1991

| Skylark (wb 103.3) | | Wght | Price | Prod |
|---|---|---|---|---|
| V-69 | sdn 4d | 2,654 | $10,725 | 57,323 |
| C69 | Custom sdn 4d | 2,692 | 12,020 | 11,582 |
| D69 | Luxury Edition sdn 4d | 2,716 | 13,865 | 928 |
| V27 | cpe 2d | 2,593 | 10,825 | 5,108 |
| J27 | Custom cpe 2d | 2,628 | 12,020 | 1,706 |
| M27 | Gran Sport cpe 2d | 2,659 | 13,665 | 693 |
| **Century (wb 104.9)** | | | | |
| G69 | Special sdn 4d | 2,869 | 13,240 | 13,045 |
| H69 | Custom sdn 4d | 2,869 | 13,685 | 81,424 |
| L69 | Limited sdn 4d | 2,870 | 14,795 | 15,273 |
| H37 | Custom cpe 2d | 2,832 | 13,785 | 1,951 |
| H35 | Custom wgn 4d | 3,071 | 15,310 | 3,102 |
| L35 | Limited wgn 4d | 3,072 | 16,230 | 1,729 |
| **Reatta (wb 98.5)** | | | | |
| C97 | cpe 2d | 3,392 | 29,300 | 1,214 |
| C67 | conv cpe 2d | 3,593 | 35,965 | 305 |
| **Regal (wb 107.5)** | | | | |
| B19 | Custom sdn 4d | 3,321 | 15,910 | 59,496 |
| D19 | Limited sdn 4d | 3,324 | 16,735 | 60,155 |
| B19Z13 | Gran Sport sdn 4d | 3,385 | 18,458 | 12,965* |
| B57 | Custom cpe 2d | 3,247 | 15,960 | 17,428 |
| D57 | Limited cpe 2d | 3,251 | 16,455 | 6,901 |
| B57Z13 | Gran Sport cpe 2d | 3,315 | 18,647 | |
| **LeSabre (wb 110.8)** | | | | |
| P69 | Custom sdn 4d | 3,269 | 17,080 | 56,231 |
| R69 | Limited sdn 4d | 3,301 | 18,430 | 33,344 |
| P37 | cpe 2d | 3,231 | 17,180 | 695 |
| R37 | Limited cpe 2d | 3,264 | 18,330 | 486 |
| **Park Avenue (wb 110.8)** | | | | |
| W69 | sdn 4d | 3,580 | 24,385 | 87,461 |
| U69 | Ultra sdn 4d | 3,662 | 27,420 | 22,030 |
| **Roadmaster (wb 115.9)** | | | | |
| R35 | Estate wgn 4d | 4,415 | 21,445 | 7,291 |
| **Riviera (wb 108.0)** | | | | |
| Z57 | cpe 2d | 3,496 | 24,560 | 13,166 |

| 1991 Engines | bore × stroke | bhp | availability |
|---|---|---|---|
| I-4, 138.0 | 3.62 × 3.92 | 160 | O-Skylark (dohc) |
| I-4, 151.0 | 4.10 × 3.10 | 110 | S-Skylark, Century |
| V-6, 191.0 | 4.00 × 3.00 | 140 | S-Regal |
| V-6, 204.0 | 3.70 × 3.16 | 160 | O-Skylark, Century |
| V-6, 231.0 | 3.80 × 3.40 | 165 | S-LeSabre |
| V-6, 231.0 | 3.80 × 3.40 | 170 | S-Riviera, Reatta, Park Avenue, O-Regal |

# Buick

| 1991 Engines | bore × stroke | bhp | availability |
|---|---|---|---|
| V-8, 305.0 | 3.74 × 3.48 | 170 | S-Roadmaster |

*Combined Regal Gran Sport Sedan and Coupe production.

## 1992

| Skylark (wb 103.4) | | Wght | Price | Prod |
|---|---|---|---|---|
| J69 | sdn 4d | 2,846 | 13,560 | 43,630 |
| M69 | Gran Sport sdn 4d | 2,965 | 15,555 | 4,480 |
| J37 | cpe 2d | 2,782 | 13,560 | 7,788 |
| M37 | Gran Sport cpe 2d | 2,901 | 15,555 | 4,748 |
| **Century (wb 104.9)** | | | | |
| G69 | Special sdn 4d | 2,914 | 13,795 | 68,361 |
| H69 | Custom sdn 4d | 2,914 | 14,755 | 42,745 |
| L69 | Limited sdn 4d | 2,930 | 15,695 | 8,829 |
| H37 | Custom cpe 2d | 2,862 | 14,550 | 627 |
| H35 | Custom wgn 4d | 3,054 | 15,660 | 5,029 |
| L35 | Limited wgn 4d | 3,080 | 16,395 | 1,784 |
| **Regal (wb 107.5)** | | | | |
| B19 | Custom sdn 4d | 3,320 | 16,865 | 60,921 |
| D19 | Limited sdn 4d | 3,320 | 18,110 | 20,220 |
| F19 | Gran Sport sdn 4d | 3,380 | 19,300 | 10,754 |
| B57 | Custom cpe 2d | 3,236 | 16,610 | 12,152 |
| D57 | Limited cpe 2d | 3,236 | 17,790 | 4,921 |
| F57 | Gran Sport cpe 2d | 3,236 | 18,600 | 5,925 |
| **LeSabre (wb 110.8)** | | | | |
| H69 | Custom sdn 4d | 3,417 | 18,695 | 101,139 |
| R69 | Limited sdn 4d | 3,457 | 20,775 | 70,412 |
| **Park Avenue (wb 110.7)** | | | | |
| W69 | sdn 4d | 3,536 | 25,285 | 57,443 |
| U69 | Ultra sdn 4d | 3,640 | 28,780 | 11,499 |
| **Roadmaster (wb 115.9)** | | | | |
| N69 | sdn 4d | 4,073 | 21,865 | 30,415 |
| T69 | Limited sdn 4d | — | 24,195 | 43,402 |
| R35 | Estate wgn 4d | 4,468 | 23,040 | 11,491 |
| **Riviera (wb 108.0)** | | | | |
| Z57 | cpe 2d | 3,497 | 24,415 | 12,585 |

| 1992 Engines | bore × stroke | bhp | availability |
|---|---|---|---|
| I-4, 138.0 | 3.62 × 3.35 | 120 | S-Skylark (ohc) |
| I-4, 151.0 | 4.10 × 3.10 | 110 | S-Century |
| V-6, 191.0 | 3.51 × 3.31 | 140 | S-Regal |
| V-6, 204.0 | 3.70 × 3.16 | 160 | O-Skylark, Century |
| V-6, 231.0 | 3.80 × 3.40 | 170 | S-LeSabre, Riviera, Park Avenue, O-Regal, |
| V-6S, 231.0 | 3.80 × 3.40 | 205 | S-Park Avenue Ultra |
| V-8, 350.0 | 4.00 × 3.48 | 180 | S-Roadmaster |

## 1993

| Skylark (wb 103.4) | | Wght | Price | Prod |
|---|---|---|---|---|
| V-69 | Custom sdn 4d | 2,846 | 12,995 | 41,625 |
| J69 | Limited sdn 4d | 2,965 | 13,875 | 6,903 |
| M69 | Gran Sport sdn 4d | 2,965 | 15,760 | 1,627 |
| V37 | Custom cpe 2d | 2,782 | 12,995 | 5,691 |
| J37 | Limited cpe 2d | 2,965 | 13,875 | 894 |
| M37 | Gran Sport cpe 2d | 2,901 | 15,760 | 1,442 |
| **Century (wb 104.9)** | | | | |
| G69 | Special sdn 4d | 2,949 | 14,205 | 100,012 |
| H69 | Custom sdn 4d | 2,948 | 15,905 | 14,673 |
| L69 | Limited sdn 4d | 2,948 | 16,865 | 4,846 |
| H37 | Custom cpe 2d | 2,903 | 15,620 | 566 |

| Century (wb 104.9) | | Wght | Price | Prod |
|---|---|---|---|---|
| G35 | Special wgn 4d | 3,103 | 14,960 | 7,216 |
| H35 | Custom wgn 4d | 3,102 | 16,865 | 2,751 |
| **Regal (wb 107.5)** | | | | |
| B19 | Custom sdn 4d | 3,340 | 16,865 | 54,113 |
| D19 | Limited sdn 4d | 3,362 | 18,460 | 7,494 |
| F19 | Gran Sport sdn 4d | 3,472 | 19,310 | 7,625 |
| B57 | Custom cpe 2d | 3,250 | 16,610 | 7,443 |
| D57 | Limited cpe 2d | 3,258 | 18,260 | 2,523 |
| F57 | Gran Sport cpe 2d | 3,388 | 19,095 | 4,109 |
| **LeSabre (wb 110.8)** | | | | |
| P69 | Custom sdn 4d | 3,433 | 19,935 | 99,518 |
| R69 | Limited sdn 4d | 3,454 | 21,735 | 51,416 |
| **Park Avenue (wb 110.8)** | | | | |
| W69 | sdn 4d | 3,536 | 26,040 | 40,468 |
| U69 | Ultra sdn 4d | 3,639 | 29,395 | 14,738 |
| **Roadmaster (wb 115.9)** | | | | |
| N69 | sdn 4d | 3,973 | 22,555 | 13,233 |
| T69 | Limited sdn 4d | 3,988 | 24,920 | 17,725 |
| R35 | Estate wgn 4d | 4,508 | 23,850 | 9,541 |
| **Riviera (wb 108.0)** | | | | |
| Z57 | cpe 2d | 3,504 | 26,320 | 4,555 |

| 1993 Engines | bore × stroke | bhp | availability |
|---|---|---|---|
| I-4, 133.0 | 3.50 × 3.46 | 110 | S-Century |
| I-4, 138.0 | 3.62 × 3.92 | 115 | S-Skylark (ohc) |
| V-6, 191.0 | 3.51 × 3.31 | 140 | S-Regal |
| V-6, 204.0 | 3.70 × 3.16 | 160 | O-Skylark, Century |
| V-6, 231.0 | 3.80 × 3.40 | 170 | S-LeSabre, Riviera, Park Avenue, O-Regal |
| V-6S, 231.0 | 3.80 × 3.40 | 205 | S-Park Avenue Ultra |
| V-8, 350.0 | 4.00 × 3.48 | 180 | S-Roadmaster |

## 1994

| Skylark (wb 103.4) | | Wght | Price | Prod |
|---|---|---|---|---|
| V-69 | Custom sdn 4d | 2,855 | 13,599 | 46,548 |
| J69 | Limited sdn 4d | 2,939 | 16,199 | 2,010 |
| M69 | Gran Sport sdn 4d | 3,038 | 18,299 | 857 |
| V37 | Custom cpe 2d | 2,791 | 13,599 | 9,024 |
| M37 | Gran Sport cpe 2d | 2,985 | 18,299 | 626 |
| **Century (wb 104.9)** | | | | |
| G69 | Special sdn 4d | 2,974 | 15,495 | 122,916 |
| H69 | Custom sdn 4d | 2,976 | 16,695 | 5,853 |
| G35 | Special wgn 4d | 3,134 | 16,345 | 9,100 |
| **Regal (wb 107.5)** | | | | |
| B19 | Custom sdn 4d | 3,338 | 18,299 | 47,293 |
| D19 | Limited sdn 4d | 3,362 | 19,799 | 4,672 |
| F19 | Gran Sport sdn 4d | 3,429 | 20,299 | 8,528 |
| B57 | Custom cpe 2d | 3,240 | 17,999 | 10,828 |
| F57 | Gran Sport cpe 2d | 3,335 | 19,999 | 7,236 |
| **LeSabre (wb 110.8)** | | | | |
| P69 | Custom sdn 4d | 3,449 | 20,860 | 113,834 |
| R69 | Limited sdn 4d | 3,449 | 24,420 | 45,416 |
| **Park Avenue (wb 110.8)** | | | | |
| W69 | sdn 4d | 3,533 | 26,999 | 52,034 |
| U69 | Ultra sdn 4d | 3,637 | 31,699 | 12,630 |
| **Roadmaster (wb 115.9)** | | | | |
| N69 | sdn 4d | 4,191 | 23,999 | 15,311 |
| T69 | Limited sdn 4d | 4,279 | 26,399 | 14,831 |
| R35 | Estate wgn 4d | 4,572 | 25,599 | 8,767 |

| 1994 Engines | bore × stroke | bhp | availability |
|---|---|---|---|
| I-4, 133.0 | 3.50 × 3.46 | 120 | S-Century |

# Buick

| 1994 Engines | bore × stroke | bhp | availability |
|---|---|---|---|
| I-4, 138.0 | 3.62 × 3.35 | 115 | S-Skylark |
| V-6, 191.0 | 3.51 × 3.31 | 155 | O-Skylark |
| V-6, 191.0 | 3.51 × 3.31 | 160 | S-Regal, O-Century |
| V-6, 231.0 | 3.80 × 3.40 | 170 | S-LeSabre, Park Avenue, O-Regal |
| V-6S, 231.0 | 3.80 × 3.40 | 225 | S-Park Avenue Ultra |
| V-8, 350.0 | 4.00 × 3.48 | 260 | S-Roadmaster |

## 1995

### Skylark (wb 103.4)

| | | Wght | Price | Prod |
|---|---|---|---|---|
| V-69 | Custom sdn 4d | 2,941 | 14,320 | |
| V-69SK | Limited sdn 4d | 2,941 | 15,195 | |
| V-69SL | Gran Sport sdn 4d | 3,058 | 16,895 | 53,860 |
| V37 | Custom cpe 2d | 2,888 | 14,320 | |
| V37SK | Limited cpe 2d | 2,888 | 15,195 | |
| V37SL | Gran Sport cpe 2d | 3,005 | 16,895 | |

### Century (wb 104.9)

| | | Wght | Price | Prod |
|---|---|---|---|---|
| G69 | Special sdn 4d | 2,968 | 16,360 | |
| G69SL | Limited sdn 4d | 2,968 | 17,995 | 113,699 |
| H69 | Custom sdn 4d | 2,993 | 17,965 | |
| G35 | Special wgn 4d | 3,130 | 17,080 | |

### Regal (wb 107.5)

| | | Wght | Price | Prod |
|---|---|---|---|---|
| B19 | Custom sdn 4d | 3,335 | 19,920 | |
| D19 | Limited sdn 4d | 3,463 | 21,235 | |
| F19 | Gran Sport sdn 4d | 3,406 | 21,870 | 100,169 |
| B57 | Custom cpe 2d | 3,261 | 19,603 | |
| B57SE | Gran Sport cpe 2d | 3,328 | 19,995 | |

### LeSabre (wb 110.8)

| | | Wght | Price | Prod |
|---|---|---|---|---|
| P69 | Custom sdn 4d | 3,442 | 21,735 | 171,783 |
| R69 | Limited sdn 4d | 3,442 | 25,465 | |

### Park Avenue (wb 110.8)

| | | Wght | Price | Prod |
|---|---|---|---|---|
| W69 | sdn 4d | 3,532 | 28,244 | 62,994 |
| U69 | Ultra sdn 4d | 3,642 | 33,084 | |

### Roadmaster (wb 115.9)

| | | Wght | Price | Prod |
|---|---|---|---|---|
| N69 | sdn 4d | 4,211 | 25,265 | |
| R69 | Limited sdn 4d | 4,244 | 27,555 | 30,508 |
| R35 | Estate wgn 4d | 4,563 | 27,070 | |

### Riviera (wb 113.8)

| | | Wght | Price | Prod |
|---|---|---|---|---|
| D07 | cpe 2d | 3,748 | 27,632 | 41,442 |

| 1995 Engines | bore × stroke | bhp | availability |
|---|---|---|---|
| I-4, 133.0 | 3.50 × 3.46 | 120 | S-Century |
| I-4, 138.0 | 3.62 × 3.35 | 150 | S-Skylark (dohc) |
| V-6, 191.0 | 3.51 × 3.31 | 155 | O-Skylark |
| V-6, 191.0 | 3.51 × 3.31 | 160 | S-Regal, O-Century |
| V-6, 231.0 | 3.80 × 3.40 | 170 | S-LeSabre, O-Regal |
| V-6, 231.0 | 3.80 × 3.40 | 205 | S-Park Avenue, Riviera |
| V-6S, 231.0 | 3.80 × 3.40 | 225 | S-Park Avenue Ultra, O-Riviera |
| V-8, 350.0 | 4.00 × 3.48 | 260 | S-Roadmaster |

## 1996

### Skylark (wb 103.4)

| | | Wght | Price | Prod |
|---|---|---|---|---|
| J69 | Custom sdn 4d | 2,948 | 15,495 | |
| J69 | Limited sdn 4d | 2,948 | 16,518 | 35,089 |
| J69 | Gran Sport sdn 4d | — | 17,701 | |
| J37 | Custom cpe 2d | 2,917 | 15,495 | |
| J37 | Limited cpe 2d | 2,917 | 16,518 | 6,783 |
| J37 | Gran Sport cpe 2d | — | 17,701 | |

### Century (wb 104.9)

| | | Wght | Price | Prod |
|---|---|---|---|---|
| G69 | Special sdn 4d | 2,950 | 16,720 | |

### Century (wb 104.9)

| | | Wght | Price | Prod |
|---|---|---|---|---|
| G69 | Custom sdn 4d | — | 18,383 | 85,625 |
| G69 | Limited sdn 4d | — | 19,406 | |
| G35 | Special wgn 4d | 3,118 | 18,135 | 6,843 |

### Regal (wb 107.5)

| | | Wght | Price | Prod |
|---|---|---|---|---|
| B19 | Custom sdn 4d | 3,331 | 19,740 | |
| B19SE | Limited sdn 4d | — | 21,195 | 107,056 |
| F19SE | Gran Sport sdn 4d | — | 21,800 | |
| B57 | Custom cpe 2d | 3,232 | 19,445 | 5,991 |
| B57 | Gran Sport cpe 2d | — | 21,340 | |

### LeSabre (wb 110.8)—52,061 built

| | | Wght | Price | Prod |
|---|---|---|---|---|
| P69 | Custom sdn 4d | 3,430 | 21,380 | — |
| R69 | Limited sdn 4d | — | 25,385 | — |

### Park Avenue (wb 110.8)—46,953 built

| | | Wght | Price | Prod |
|---|---|---|---|---|
| W69 | sdn 4d | 3,536 | 28,205 | — |
| U69 | Ultra sdn 4d | 3,629 | 32,820 | — |

### Roadmaster (wb 115.9)

| | | Wght | Price | Prod |
|---|---|---|---|---|
| N69 | sdn 4d | 4,211 | 25,560 | 12,581 |
| T69 | Limited sdn 4d | 4,244 | 27,490 | |
| R35 | Estate wgn 4d | 4,563 | 27,575 | 8,962 |
| Z27 | Limited Estate wgn 4d | — | 29,445 | |

### Riviera (wb 113.8)

| | | Wght | Price | Prod |
|---|---|---|---|---|
| D07 | cpe 2d | 3,690 | 29,475 | 17,389 |

| 1996 Engines | bore × stroke | bhp | availability |
|---|---|---|---|
| I-4, 134.0 | 3.50 × 3.46 | 120 | S-Century |
| I-4, 146.0 | 3.54 × 3.70 | 150 | S-Skylark (dohc) |
| V-6, 191.0 | 3.51 × 3.31 | 155 | O-Skylark |
| V-6, 191.0 | 3.51 × 3.31 | 160 | S-Regal, O-Century |
| V-6, 231.0 | 3.80 × 3.40 | 205 | S-LeSabre, Park Avenue, Riviera, O-Regal |
| V-6S, 231.0 | 3.80 × 3.40 | 240 | S-Park Avenue Ultra, O-Riviera |
| V-8, 350.0 | 4.00 × 3.48 | 260 | S-Roadmaster |

## 1997

### Skylark (wb 103.4)

| | | Wght | Price | Prod |
|---|---|---|---|---|
| J69 | Custom sdn 4d | 2,985 | 15,970 | 53,863 |
| J37 | Custom cpe 2d | 2,945 | 15,970 | 4,041 |

### Century (wb 109.0)—53,486 built

| | | Wght | Price | Prod |
|---|---|---|---|---|
| G69 | Custom sdn 4d | 3,348 | 17,845 | — |
| G69 | Limited sdn 4d | 3,359 | 19,220 | — |

### Regal (wb 107.5)—50,691 built*

| | | Wght | Price | Prod |
|---|---|---|---|---|
| B19 | LS sdn 4d | 3,331 | 20,545 | — |
| F19 | GS sdn 4d | — | 22,945 | — |

### LeSabre (wb 110.8)—211,651 built

| | | Wght | Price | Prod |
|---|---|---|---|---|
| P69 | Custom sdn 4d | 3,441 | 22,015 | — |
| R69 | Limited sdn 4d | 3,462 | 25,565 | — |

### Park Avenue (wb 113.8)—59,637 built

| | | Wght | Price | Prod |
|---|---|---|---|---|
| W69 | sdn 4d | 3,788 | 29,995 | — |
| U69 | Ultra sdn 4d | 3,879 | 34,995 | — |

### Riviera (wb 113.8)

| | | Wght | Price | Prod |
|---|---|---|---|---|
| D07 | cpe 2d | 3,720 | 30,110 | 18,199 |

*Calendar year production.

| 1997 Engines | bore × stroke | bhp | availability |
|---|---|---|---|
| I-4, 146.0 | 3.54 × 3.70 | 150 | S-Skylark (dohc) |
| V-6, 191.0 | 3.51 × 3.31 | 155 | O-Skylark |
| V-6, 191.0 | 3.51 × 3.31 | 160 | S-Century |
| V-6, 231.0 | 3.80 × 3.40 | 195 | S-Regal |
| V-6, 231.0 | 3.80 × 3.40 | 205 | S-LeS, Pk Av, Riv |

# Buick

| 1997 Engines | bore × stroke | bhp | availability |
|---|---|---|---|
| V-6S, 231.0 | 3.80 × 3.40 | 240 | S-Pk Av Ult, O-Rgl, Riviera |

## 1998

### Century (wb 109.0)—128,587 built

| | | Wght | Price | Prod |
|---|---|---|---|---|
| G69 | Custom sdn 4d | 3,335 | 18,215 | — |
| G69 | Limited sdn 4d | 3,354 | 19,575 | — |

### Regal (wb 109.0)—70,257 built

| B19 | LS sdn 4d | 3,447 | 20,945 | — |
|---|---|---|---|---|
| F19 | GS sdn 4d | 3,562 | 23,690 | — |

### LeSabre (wb 110.8)—143,251 built

| P69 | Custom sdn 4d | 3,443 | 22,465 | — |
|---|---|---|---|---|
| R69 | Limited sdn 4d | 3,465 | 25,790 | — |

### Park Avenue (wb 113.8)—61,974 built

| W69 | sdn 4d | 3,740 | 30,675 | — |
|---|---|---|---|---|
| U69 | Ultra sdn 4d | 3,837 | 35,550 | — |

### Riviera (wb 113.8)

| D07 | cpe 2d | 3,699 | 32,500 | 10,613 |
|---|---|---|---|---|

*Calendar year production.

| 1998 Engines | bore × stroke | bhp | availability |
|---|---|---|---|
| V-6, 191.0 | 3.51 × 3.31 | 160 | S-Century |
| V-6, 231.0 | 3.80 × 3.40 | 195 | S-Regal |
| V-6, 231.0 | 3.80 × 3.40 | 205 | S-LeSabre, Park Avenue |
| V-6S, 231.0 | 3.80 × 3.40 | 240 | S-Park Avenue Ultra, Riviera, O-Regal |

## 1999

### Century (wb 109.0)—167,728

| | | Wght | Price | Prod* |
|---|---|---|---|---|
| G69 | Custom sdn 4d | 3,365 | 18,775 | — |
| G69 | Limited sdn 4d | 3,375 | 20,145 | — |

### Regal (wb 109.0)—79,733

| B19 | LS sdn 4d | 3,450 | 21,695 | — |
|---|---|---|---|---|
| F19 | GS sdn 4d | 3,545 | 24,395 | — |

### LeSabre (wb 110.8)—157,051

| P69 | Custom sdn 4d | 3,430 | 22,725 | — |
|---|---|---|---|---|
| R69 | Limited sdn 4d | — | 25,990 | — |

### Park Avenue (wb 113.8)—61,009

| W69 | sdn 4d | 3,790 | 31,130 | — |
|---|---|---|---|---|
| U69 | Ultra sdn 4d | 3,880 | 36,025 | — |

### Riviera (wb 113.8)

| D07 | cpe 2d | 3,720 | 33,820 | 10,613** |
|---|---|---|---|---|

*Calendar year production. **Model year production.

| 1999 Engines | bore × stroke | bhp | availability |
|---|---|---|---|
| V-6, 191.0 | 3.51 × 3.31 | 160 | S-Century |
| V-6, 231.0 | 3.80 × 3.40 | 200 | S-Regal |
| V-6, 231.0 | 3.80 × 3.40 | 205 | S-LeSabre, Park Avenue |
| V-6S, 231.0 | 3.80 × 3.40 | 240 | S-Park Avenue Ultra, Riviera, O-Regal |

## 2000

### Century (wb 109.0)—158,118

| | | Wght | Price | Prod* |
|---|---|---|---|---|
| G69 | Custom sdn 4d | 3,368 | 19,602 | — |
| G69 | Limited sdn 4d | 3,371 | 21,737 | — |

### Regal (wb 109.0)—77,879

| B19 | LS sdn 4d | 3,439 | 22,220 | — |
|---|---|---|---|---|

### Regal (wb 109.0)—77,879

| | | Wght | Price | Prod |
|---|---|---|---|---|
| F19 | GS sdn 4d | 3,543 | 25,065 | — |

### LeSabre (wb 112.2)—163,936

| P69 | Custom sdn 4d | 3,567 | 23,235 | — |
|---|---|---|---|---|
| R69 | Limited sdn 4d | 3,591 | 27,340 | — |

### Park Avenue (wb 113.8)—45,295

| W69 | sdn 4d | 3,778 | 31,725 | — |
|---|---|---|---|---|
| U69 | Ultra sdn 4d | 3,884 | 36,800 | — |

*Calendar year production.

| 2000 Engines | bore × stroke | bhp | availability |
|---|---|---|---|
| V-6, 191.0 | 3.51 × 3.31 | 175 | S-Century |
| V-6, 231.0 | 3.80 × 3.40 | 200 | S-Regal |
| V-6, 231.0 | 3.80 × 3.40 | 205 | S-LeSabre, Park Avenue |
| V-6S, 231.0 | 3.80 × 3.40 | 240 | S-Park Avenue Ultra, O-Regal |

## 2001

### Century (wb 109.0)—128,112 built

| | | Wght | Price | Prod* |
|---|---|---|---|---|
| G69 | Custom sdn 4d | 3,368 | 19,840 | — |
| G69 | Limited sdn 4d | 3,371 | 22,871 | — |

### Regal (wb 109.0)—63,100 built

| B19 | LS sdn 4d | 3,438 | 22,845 | — |
|---|---|---|---|---|
| F19 | GS sdn 4d | 3,543 | 26,095 | — |

### LeSabre (wb 112.2)—135,242 built

| P69 | Custom sdn 4d | 3,567 | 24,107 | — |
|---|---|---|---|---|
| R69 | Limited sdn 4d | 3,591 | 28,796 | — |

### Park Avenue (wb 113.8)—29,956 built

| W69 | sdn 4d | 3,778 | 32,980 | — |
|---|---|---|---|---|
| U69 | Ultra sdn 4d | 3,884 | 37,490 | — |

*Calendar year production.

| 2001 Engines | bore × stroke | bhp | availability |
|---|---|---|---|
| V-6, 191.0 | 3.51 × 3.31 | 175 | S-Century |
| V-6, 231.0 | 3.80 × 3.40 | 200 | S-Regal |
| V-6, 231.0 | 3.80 × 3.40 | 205 | S-LeSabre, Park Avenue |
| V-6S, 231.0 | 3.80 × 3.40 | 240 | S-Park Avenue Ultra, O-Regal |

## 2002

### Century (wb 109.0)

| | | Wght | Price | Prod* |
|---|---|---|---|---|
| G69 | Custom sdn 4d | 3,353 | 20,285 | — |
| G69 | Limited sdn 4d | 3,391 | 23,285 | — |

### Regal (wb 109.0)

| B19 | LS sdn 4d | 3,461 | 23,230 | — |
|---|---|---|---|---|
| F19 | GS sdn 4d | 3,536 | 27,285 | — |

### LeSabre (wb 112.2)

| P69 | Custom sdn 4d | 3,567 | 24,290 | — |
|---|---|---|---|---|
| R69 | Limited sdn 4d | 3,591 | 29,990 | — |

### Park Avenue (wb 113.8)

| W69 | sdn 4d | 3,778 | 33,420 | — |
|---|---|---|---|---|
| U69 | Ultra sdn 4d | 3,884 | 37,930 | — |

| 2002 Engines | bore × stroke | bhp | availability |
|---|---|---|---|
| V-6, 191.0 | 3.51 × 3.31 | 175 | S-Century |
| V-6, 231.0 | 3.80 × 3.40 | 200 | S-Regal |
| V-6, 231.0 | 3.80 × 3.40 | 205 | S-LeSabre, Park Avenue |
| V-6S, 231.0 | 3.80 × 3.40 | 240 | S-Park Avenue Ultra, O-Regal |

* Production figures not available at time of publication.

# Cadillac

Cadillac was founded in late 1902 by Henry Martyn Leland, a brilliant engineer who'd worked at Ford and Oldsmobile. His first cars were simple "one-lung" runabouts, but he soon developed a more civilized four-cylinder model, the successful Cadillac "30" of 1909-15. Leland's passion for precision craftsmanship and standardized parts, born of his experience as a gunmaker, was evident early on. In England in 1908, three Cadillacs were disassembled, their components mixed up, then reassembled into three cars that ran perfectly. This feat won Cadillac its first Dewar Trophy and inspired the make's now long-familiar slogan, "Standard of the World."

The following year, Cadillac became part of fledgling General Motors. As an upper-middle-priced car in those days, it didn't compete directly with Packard or Pierce-Arrow, but was always a high-quality item. Cadillac's pioneering 1915 V-8 set new standards for smoothness, power, and reliability, and sales increased steadily from the late Teens through the end of the '20s, when the make turned to luxury cars exclusively.

Had it not been part of GM, Cadillac might have perished in the Depression, a time when few people could afford—or wanted to be seen in—big, expensive automobiles no matter how superb. Unlike independent Packard, which was forced to survive with medium-priced products, Cadillac was protected by GM's vast size and enormous financial strength. Then, too, the division already had a medium-priced car, the LaSalle, introduced in 1927 (see entry). All this helped Cadillac endure "hard times" without squandering its blue-chip image even as it built ultra-luxury cars selling only in small numbers.

Foremost among them was that magnificent 1930 surprise, the Sixteen, carrying an overhead-valve, 452-cubic-inch engine producing 165 horsepower and 320 pound-feet of torque. An undoubted great in an era of greats, the Sixteen was ostensibly available in 33 different models, submodels or trim variations ranging from a $5350 two-passenger roadster to a $9700 town brougham. The typical example could return about eight miles to a 15-cent gallon of gas and 150 miles to a quart of oil, plus cruise at 70 and top 90 mph. But brute performance wasn't its forte. Rather, the Sixteen was intended to elevate Cadillac into the rarefied realm of Packard, Peerless, and Pierce-Arrow. That it did, offering superb luxury and smooth, effortless power with minimal shifting. Cadillac advertised its performance as "a continuous flow . . . constantly at full-volume efficiency . . . flexible . . . instantly responsive."

The Sixteen was only nine months old when Cadillac introduced another multicylinder engine, a 368-cid V-12. Essentially a V-16 with four fewer cylinders, it delivered 135 horsepower and 285 pound-feet of torque. The cars it powered also weren't quite as large the Sixteens, riding the Cadillac Eight's 140-inch wheelbase instead of an enormous 148-inch span. Predictably, the Twelve also wasn't as fast, but its free-revving engine was renowned for smooth, even power. And that power was quite ample. A roadster could do about 85 mph with standard rear-axle ratio, and most Twelves could cruise all day at 70. Of course, the Twelve was cheaper than the Sixteen—by far—offered with 11 body choices in the $3795-$4985 range.

But despite their refined performance and majestic proportions, the multicylinder Cadillacs were anachronisms in the devastated Depression market, and none sold in significant numbers. The peak was 1930-31 with exactly 3250 Sixteens and 5725 Twelves. Production was only fair for '32, then declined to about 700 and 400 units per year, respectively. Both models were dropped after 1937, but Cadillac made one more try starting the following year with an L-head V-16. At 431 cid and 185 bhp, this engine was smaller and lighter yet more potent than the earlier ohv design, but only 508 cars were so equipped through 1940, its final year.

There were two reasons why these grand Cadillacs fared so poorly. As noted, staggeringly expensive cars with more than eight cylinders seemed socially inappropriate to many people in the early '30s. After their initial sales spurt, these models were shunned by most customers for the cheaper, less-showy, but by no means inferior Cadillac Eights. Later, the big engines were simply outmoded by advancing technology. The introduction of precision-insert connecting-rod bearings helped eliminate knock and high-speed wear in engines with fewer than 12 cylinders, so there was little reason for Cadillac buyers to choose a Twelve or Sixteen over an Eight.

Fortunately for Cadillac, its V-8 line sold consistently and fairly well through the '30s. Model-year production hung around 10,000 units for 1930-31, plunged to 2000-3000 for 1932-33, then recovered rapidly. With the introduction of the low-priced Series 60 for 1936, V-8 volume passed 10,000, then reached over 13,000 by 1939. This highly creditable performance was owed to a reliable cast-iron L-head engine, competitive prices, and a wide range of body styles.

Cadillac's early-'30s V-8 was based on a 341-cid unit introduced in 1928. Sized at 353 cid for 1930-35, it delivered 95-130 bhp. A completely redesigned 346 with 135 bhp replaced it for 1936. That year's new Series 60 used a 322-cid version, then adopted the 346. This respected powerplant would remain in

**1930 Series 353 Eight 5-passenger sedan**

**1930 Series 353 Eight town sedan**

1931 Series 355 Eight 2-passenger coupe

1932 Series 355-B Eight 5-passenger coupe

1932 Series 355-B Eight four-door sedan

1933 Twelve Imperial 7-passenger sedan

production until Cadillac launched its new short-stroke ohv V-8 for 1949. Though the L-head had limits, it delivered excellent performance and reasonable economy. The lighter 1938-39 models could do nearly 100 mph and run 0-60 in 15-16 seconds—no mean feat for 4500-pound luxury liners before World War II.

Unlike luxury rivals, Cadillac designed and built most of its bodies in-house via Fisher and Fleetwood, two respected coach-makers that GM had acquired. (Cadillac also supplied chassis in fair numbers to independent body builders. This arrangement enabled designer Harley Earl to maintain a consistent look throughout the car instead of in just the radiator and hood. "Classic" Cadillac styling was undoubtedly epitomized by the 1930-31 models with their opulent, thick-collar vertical radiators; beautifully rounded hoods; and clean, flowing lines. Body styles were bewildering. The 1930 Fisher line spanned seven types in the $3300-$4000 range. Fleetwood Custom models numbered no fewer than 14, priced from $3450 to $5145. Most elegant of all were the several "Madame X"—after a stage play of the era—styles with their slender chrome door and windshield moldings.

Square-rigged styling began to dissolve with the more-rounded 1932 Cadillacs, but true streamlining wasn't evident until the 1933 models. While these retained the basic '32 bodies, Earl modernized appearance with items like skirted fenders, vee'd radiators, and more-swept-back windshields. A notable innovation was front-door ventwing windows, called "No-Draft Ventilation," a feature shared with sister GM divisions that year. All early-'30s Cadillacs have long been prized by enthusiasts as some of the best designs of the late Classic era.

Styling for 1934 was fully revised along the lines of the exotic, experimental "Aerodynamic" fastback coupe presented at the 1933 Chicago World's Fair. Earl now moved away completely from upright forms into the realm of pontoon fenders, sloped radiators, "bullet" headlights, and rakish rear decks. He also conjured novel two-piece front and rear bumpers likely inspired by the biplane configuration, but they proved fragile and unpopular, and were thus abandoned after one season. The 1935-36 models were relatively dumpy by comparison, with roundness prevailing over squareness throughout.

Everything changed again for 1938, when young William L. Mitchell, an Earl protégé, drew up the Sixty Special sedan as an addition to the 124-inch-wheelbase Series 60. Square yet crisply elegant and quite compact for a Cadillac, Mitchell's creation stood apart with chrome-edged side windows, square-back fenders, concealed running boards and a low profile on a wheelbase three inches longer than on other 60s—a coupe, a

1934 Eight Fleetwood Aero-Dynamic 5-passenger coupe

1934 Series 355-D Eight convertible sedan

# Cadillac

1934 Series 355-D Eight convertible coupe for two passengers

1935 Series 355-D Eight 5-passenger sedan

1936 Series Sixty convertible coupe 2/4 passenger

1936 Series Seventy-Five Fleetwood convertible sedan

1936 Eight Series Sixty 2-passenger coupe

1937 Series Sixty convertible sedan

1937 Series Seventy Fleetwood touring sedan

sedan, and two convertibles. It's long been judged one of the all-time design greats.

Cadillac's produced 10,000 units more for 1939 than for '38 (which had suffered in a national recession). Only mild facelifts occurred and engines were unchanged, but the division now blanketed the luxury field. A new 126-inch-wheelbase Series 61 offered four models priced from $1610 to $2170, while the Sixty Special returned as a series of its own priced from $2090 to $2315. The Series 75 listed the usual plethora of Fleetwood bodies on a 141-inch span, Cadillac's longest V-8 wheelbase yet.

The 1930s saw vast technical progress at Cadillac. Having introduced clashless "Syncro-Mesh" transmission in 1929, the division followed up for '32 with "Triple-Silent" Syncro-Mesh (helical-cut gears for all three forward speeds). "No-Draft" and vacuum-assisted brakes appeared for 1933, independent front suspension for '34. For 1935 came GM's all-steel "Turret Top" construction that eliminated fabric roof inserts. Hydraulic brakes arrived on all but Sixteens for 1936. Column-mounted gearshift arrived in '38 and optional turn signals one year later.

As mentioned, a "second-series" Sixteen arrived for 1938, and again led the Cadillac fleet for 1939-40. Its new short-stroke engine was smaller than the earlier V-16, but made the same 185 bhp. Like Cadillac's V-8, it featured rugged cast-iron construction and dual carburetors, as well as nine main bearings and separate manifolds, water pump, and distributor for each cylinder bank. Chassis was shared with the 75, as were body styles: two coupes, a convertible, touring sedans with and without division window, a "trunkback" convertible sedan, formal sedans seating five or seven, and several seven-passenger sedans. The big difference was price. The basic five-passenger sedan of 1940 sold for $1745 with V-8 but $5140 with V-16—a premium no longer really justified, as Cadillac's V-8 was one of

# Cadillac

1937 Series Seventy Fleetwood convertible coupe

1937 Series Seventy-Five Fleetwood convertible sedan

1938 Series Seventy-Five Fleetwood town sedan

1938 Series Seventy-Five Fleetwood convertible sedan

1938 Series Sixty-Five touring sedan

1938 Sixty Special touring sedan

1938 Series Seventy-Five Fleetwood convertible coupe

1939 Sixty Special touring sedan

the smoothest engines anywhere. With sales no better than in 1930-37, the opulent Sixteen was dropped for good after 1940—a relic of a grand age we would not see again.

Some of Cadillac's most important engineering developments—and some of its most beautiful cars—appeared in the '40s. Like Buick, the division face-lifted for 1940-41, then issued completely new styling for '42 that left it in a good market position when civilian car production resumed after World War II.

Most 1940 Cadillacs were relatively plain—in front, almost Chevrolet-like with their simple bar grilles. The exception was the splendid Sixteen, which wore the eggcrate radiator theme first seen for 1937, soon to be a Cadillac fixture. All models wore sealed-beam headlamps, as did most cars from Detroit that year.

Ranked below the 90 and 75 for 1940 was a new Series 72 with a 138-inch wheelbase and slightly fewer models, but also lower prices ($2670-$3695). Though impressive and well designed, it would be a one-year-only line, with sales limited by competition from the more luxurious 75. Yet, even counting 75s and Sixteens, Cadillac built only a little over 2500 long-wheelbase 1940 cars.

The crisp Sixty Special returned with minor styling tweaks in the same four models offered for '39. A predictive, if rarely ordered, new option (Cadillac sold only 1500 between 1938 and '41) was a sliding metal sunroof (called "Sunshine Turret Top Roof"). It was available on both the standard Sixty Special "town sedan" and division-window Imperial. There was also a "town car" offered with painted-metal or leather-covered roof. Just 15 were built; most 1940 Sixty Specials were the standard sedan (4472 units).

# Cadillac

**1940 Sixty Special Fleetwood touring sedan**

**1940 Series Seventy-Five Fleetwood coupe**

**1941 Series Sixty-Two convertible coupe**

**1941 Series Sixty-Two touring sedan**

**1942 Series Sixty-Three four-door sedan**

Displacing the 61 as 1940's most-affordable Cadillac was the Series 62, another future Cadillac fixture. Initial offerings comprised coupe, touring sedan, convertible coupe, and convertible sedan on a 129-inch wheelbase. Prices ranged from $1685 to $2195. As in later years, the 62 garnered the most sales by far of any 1940 Cadillac line.

The division's 1940 V-8 retained its familiar monoblock construction (unitized block and crankcase), three main bearings with counterweights, and dual downdraft carbs. Though heavy, it was reliable and exceptionally smooth. As in '39, it was tuned for 135 horsepower in the 62 and Sixty Special, 140 for the 72 and 75.

A significant and attractive design change occurred for 1941, when Cadillac revived the Series 61 to replace its junior LaSalle line. This was a marketing decision based on the success of Lincoln-Zephyr and Packard's One Ten/One Twenty, and it worked. While Packard continued to rely on medium-priced cars long after World War II, Cadillac (and Lincoln) returned to the luxury field exclusively, thus bolstering its "fine car" reputation—and sales—at Packard's expense.

The '41 Cadillacs wore a fresh face: a complex eggcrate grille with central bulge (carried down from the hood). Taillights were also more prominent, and one even concealed the gas filler, yet another feature destined for a long life. Departure of both the Sixteen and 72 reduced wheelbases to three: 136 inches for the 75, 139 on four new Series 67 sedans, and 126 for others.

Cadillac's big mechanical news for 1941 was a first in the luxury class: fully shiftless Hydra-Matic Drive. Developed by Oldsmobile, which had introduced it a year earlier, this excellent automatic transmission would remain an option for all models through 1949. Also, higher compression lifted the V-8 to 150 bhp. This combined with revised axle ratios to permit most '41 Caddys to reach a genuine 100 mph and scale 0-60 in about 14 seconds—impressive for the day.

Improved performance, the new Hydra-Matic, and a still-broad price span ($1345-$4045) pushed Cadillac production to a new high for the '41 model year: 66,130. That was only some 6700 short of Packard, which was selling a much higher proportion of less-costly cars. Most of the gain was owed to the revived 61, which was every inch a Cadillac despite its lower price. But the 62 was up dramatically, the Sixty Special scored a healthy 4100 sales, and a new Series 63 four-door attracted some 5000 customers all by itself.

The 1942 lineup was mostly the same but had a new look, dominated by big bullet-shape fenders front and rear, plus fastback rooflines (debuted on the '41 Series 61) for a Series 62 coupe named "sedanet." Unfortunately, this year's Sixty Special was more like other Cadillacs—far less "special." Cadillac built a total 16,511 of its '42s before war halted production in February 1942. The division then turned out tanks, aircraft engines, and munitions until V-J Day.

Resuming civilian operations took several months, so Cadillac managed only 1142 Series 62 sedans before the end of 1945 and 29,194 cars total for model-year '46. These were only slightly changed from '42, but the 63, 67, and division-window 60 Special were all dropped. What remained were fastback 61s, fastback and notchback 62s, a lone Sixty Special, and five 75s.

The '47s were little changed: round instead of rectangular parking lights (when large optional fog lamps weren't designated), script instead of block-letter fender nameplates, a five-bar grille theme in place of the six bars used the previous year, and the famed "sombrero" wheelcovers were first offered. Postwar inflation swelled prices by $150-$200, but production now regained its prewar stride, nearing 62,000 for the model year. As before, the 62 accounted for most of it with just under 40,000 units.

# Cadillac

1946 Series Sixty-One four-door sedan

1946 Sixty Special four-door sedan

1947 Series Sixty-Two sedanet (club coupe)

1947 Series Sixty-Two convertible coupe

1948 Series Sixty-One sedanet (club coupe)

1948 Series Sixty-Two four-door sedan

1948 Series Sixty-One four-door sedan

1949 Series Sixty-Two Coupe de Ville hardtop

Then came 1948, "The Year of the Tailfin." Before the war, designers Earl, Mitchell, Franklin Q. Hershey, and Art Ross had been shown the then-secret Lockheed P-38 "Lightning" pursuit fighter. During the war, a skeleton crew played with ideas for postwar styling inspired by some of the plane's design elements: pontoon front fenders, pointy front, cockpitlike curved windshields—and tailfins. This influence would be seen at other GM divisions. Olds, for example, adopted the P-38's engine air-scoop motif for the headlamp bezels on its 1949 "Futuramic" models. But the fin had the most lasting impact. As Mitchell later said: "From a design standpoint, the fins gave definition to the rear of the car for the first time. They made the back end as interesting as the front, and established a long-standing Cadillac-styling hallmark."

Tailfins were the crowning touch for Cadillac's masterful '48 design, which was executed by a small team working under Hershey at his farm in suburban Detroit. The make's traditional grille became more aggressive via larger eggcrates, complemented by a more-shapely hood. Roof and fenderlines were curvaceously beautiful from every angle. Inside was a new dashboard dominated by a huge "drum" housing gauges and controls. This lasted only a year, however, as it was complex and costly to produce. The '49s used a simpler instrument board that echoed the grille shape, a theme that would persist for the next eight years.

Models, body styles, and wheelbases stood pat for '48, but Series 75s wouldn't get the new look until 1950 (low production precluded early amortization of their prewar dies). The '49 line was a rerun too—except for two stunning developments. One was the Coupe de Ville, a $3497 entry in the Series 62 that

# Cadillac

**1949 Series Sixty-Two convertible coupe**

**1950 Sixty Special four-door sedan**

**1950 Series Sixty-One four-door sedan**

**1951 Series Sixty-Two Coupe de Ville hardtop**

**1951 Series Sixty-Two convertible coupe**

shares honors with that year's new Oldsmobile 98 Holiday and Buick Roadmaster Riviera as Detroit's first volume hardtop. Cadillac sold 2150 of the '49s, a higher percentage of its total production than either Buick or Olds. Of course, the idea behind all three was convertible airiness combined with closed-car comfort and solidness, and it proved enormously popular, starting a trend that would dominate Detroit by the mid-'50s. (Cadillac also built one 1949 Coupe de Ville on the 133-inch Sixty Special chassis, strictly an experiment.)

Equally revolutionary was Cadillac's exciting new 1949 overhead-valve V-8, the second blow of a potent one-two punch delivered directly to Packard, Lincoln, and Chrysler's Imperial. The product of 10 years' research and development, this engine was designed by Ed Cole, Jack Gordon, and Harry Barr, who aimed for less weight and higher compression (to take advantage of the higher-octane fuels promised after the war). This dictated valve rearrangement, a stroke shorter than bore, wedge-shape combustion chambers, and "slipper" pistons. The last, devised by Byron Ellis, traveled low between the crankshaft counterweights to allow for short connecting rods and, thus, low reciprocating mass.

Sized at 331 cid, the new V-8 arrived with 160 horsepower, 10 bhp more than the old 346 L-head despite less displacement, testifying to its efficiency. The ohv had other advantages. Though a cast-iron job like the L-head, it weighed nearly 200 pounds less. Compression was just 7.5:1, yet could be pushed up to 12:1; the L-head couldn't. The ohv also delivered more torque and 14-percent better mileage. It was no less durable nor reliable. And it had room enough to be greatly enlarged—as indeed it was. In a relatively light 1949-50 Series 62, it could produce 0-60 mph in around 13 seconds and an easy 100 mph.

Further proof of this V-8's prowess was provided by sportsman Briggs Cunningham, who entered a near-stock 1950 Cadillac in that year's Le Mans 24-Hour race in France. Driven by Sam and Miles Collier, it finished 10th overall, an achievement unmatched by any other luxury car. It tore down the Mulsanne Straight at around 120 mph and averaged 81.5 mph for the race. Cunningham himself drove a streamlined Cadillac-powered special that the French called Le Monstre. He went even faster than the Colliers, but lost top gear and finished right behind them.

This brilliant V-8 combined with best-in-class styling to put Cadillac firmly atop the luxury heap by 1950. Though the 331 would continue through '55, it would gain over 100 bhp in the interim.

Though Cadillac styling would deteriorate to chrome-laden glitter in the late '50s, its basic '48 design was good enough to remain popular—and thus largely intact—through 1953. As Mitchell once noted: "A traditional look is always preserved. If a grille is changed, the tail end is left alone; if a fin is changed, the grille is not monkeyed with."

And so it was: a new one-piece windshield and revamped grille for 1950, small auxiliary grilles under the headlamps for '51, a winged badge in that spot for '52, one-piece rear windows and suggestive "Dagmar" front bumper guards for '53. However, Cadillac gave up on fastbacks much earlier than sister GM makes, switching all of its 1950 coupes to notchback profiles with hardtop rooflines a la Coupe de Ville.

Models also didn't change much through '53. Still accounting for most sales, the 62 offered four-door sedan, hardtop coupe, Coupe de Ville, and convertible, all on the usual 126-inch wheelbase. Sixty Special remained a solitary super-luxury four-door on its own wheelbase, which was now 130 inches versus the 133 of 1942-48. The Series 75 again offered its customary array of limousines and long-wheelbase sedans on a 146.8-inch chassis. Cadillac also continued supplying chassis for various

# Cadillac

1952 Sixty Special four-door sedan

1953 Series Seventy-Five Fleetwood 8-passenger sedan

1953 Sixty Special four-door sedan

1953 Series Sixty-Two Coupe de Ville hardtop

1953 Series Sixty-Two convertible coupe

1954 Sixty Special Fleetwood four-door sedan

1954 Series Sixty-Two hardtop coupe

1954 Series Sixty-Two convertible coupe

1954 Series Seventy-Five Fleetwood 8-passenger sedan

# Cadillac

1958 Series Sixty-Two Coupe de Ville hardtop

1957 Series Sixty-Two hardtop coupe

1957 Eldorado Brougham hardtop sedan

1957 Eldorado Seville hardtop coupe

1957 Eldorado Biarritz convertible coupe

coach-builders, averaging about 2000 a year through 1959.

The "entry-level" Series 61 was still around in 1950, but its sedan and de Ville-inspired coupe were demoted to a 122-inch wheelbase (from 126 in the '40s). Manual shift was still standard here (and on 75s), but other Caddys now came with Hydra-Matic at no extra cost. The 61s still lacked chrome rocker moldings and had plainer interiors, but also lower prices (by about $575). But with record 1950 sales of 100,000-plus, Cadillac no longer needed a "price leader," so the 61 was cancelled after 1951, this time for good.

After observing its golden anniversary in 1952, Cadillac issued a flashy limited-edition convertible, the 1953 Series 62 Eldorado. Like that year's new Buick Skylark and Olds 98 Fiesta, it boasted features previewed on recent GM Motorama show cars: custom interior, special cut-down "Panoramic" wraparound windshield, a sporty "notched" beltline, and a metal lid instead of a canvas boot to cover the lowered top. A striking piece, the Eldorado was a preview of Cadillacs to come, but only 532 of the '53s were built, largely because price was a towering $7750.

Model-year '54 ushered in longer, lower, and wider Caddys with more power and an all-new GM C-body bearing the trendy wrapped windshield. Wheelbase lengthened to 129 inches on Series 62s and to 149.8 on 75s. The V-8 was boosted to 230 bhp, and power steering and windshield washers became standard linewide. Four-way power seat was a new option. Eldorado returned with standard gold-color trim and genuine wire wheels, but was much more like the standard 62 ragtop and thus far cheaper than the '53: $4738. Predictably, sales rose to 2150 for the model year. That improved to 3950 for '55, then rose 65 percent for '56, when Eldorados doubled to include a Seville hardtop coupe with the same $6556 base price as the ragtop, which was retitled Biarritz.

Eldorado became more-distinctive again after 1954, sprouting pointy "shark" fins above round taillights. Other models retained the small taillight-and-fin motif from prior years. Cadillac's basic '54 styling persisted through effective, if evolutionary, face-lifts for 1955 and '56. The latter year brought the division's first four-door hardtop, the Sedan de Ville, which immediately scored almost as many sales as the Coupe de Ville and standard 62 hardtop combined.

Division sales continued upward, reaching 140,777 for banner '55. But even that was a temporary plateau. Despite challenges from an all-new '56 Lincoln and revitalized '57 Imperial, Cadillac remained America's luxury sales leader by far. Combined Lincoln/Imperial volume never exceeded 40,000 cars a year in this era; at Cadillac, that was good quarterly output.

Horsepower seemed to climb right along with sales. For 1955 it reached 250 standard via higher compression and improved manifolding; Eldorado now boasted 270 bhp courtesy of dual four-barrel carburetors, optional for other models. For 1956, the milestone V-8 received the first of several enlargements, being bored to 365 cid. It now produced 285 bhp in standard models, 305 for Eldorado.

The ratings were 300/325 for 1957, when compression reached 10:1 and the line was again rebodied, emerging with blockier but still evolutionary styling inspired by the Orleans, Eldorado Brougham, and Park Avenue show cars of 1954-55. Reaching into the luxury stratosphere was a production Eldorado Brougham priced at a princely $13,074. One of the most-interesting '50s Cadillacs, this low-slung pillarless sedan on a "compact" 126-inch wheelbase featured center-opening doors and a brushed stainless-steel roof, the latter one of Harley Earl's favorite touches. Standard quad headlights were an industry first shared with that year's Nash.

The Brougham's most-intriguing mechanical feature was air suspension, the work of engineers Lester Milliken and Fred Cowin. Based on systems used for commercial vehicles since 1952, this employed an air "spring" at each wheel comprising a domed air chamber, rubber diaphragm, and pistons. Fed by a central air compressor, the domes continually adjusted for load and road conditions (via valves and solenoids) for a smooth, level ride. Cadillac's system differed from "air ride" options at other GM divisions in being "open" (taking in air from outside) rather than "closed." Unhappily, cost and complexity were high relative to benefits. The air domes leaked, and replacements were frequent, leading many owners to junk the system in favor of conventional coil springs. Following 1960, Cadillac and GM abandoned air suspension altogether.

After two years and 704 units, the Brougham was fully restyled, and assembly was farmed out to Pininfarina in Italy. Only 99 were built for '59, another 101 of the near-identical '60s. Though appearance was clean (and a preview of Cadillac's 1961 styling), these were larger (130-inch wheelbase) and heavier cars that weren't put together very well (bodies contained lots of lead filler). They're collector's items now, but restoring one is a chore.

Back to the volume Cadillacs, which were heavily face-lifted for 1958 in a manner typical of GM that year. The most-garish Caddys yet, they dripped with chrome and were far-less stylish than previous postwar models. Sales were poor, though a nationwide recession was probably more to blame than the styling, which was, after all, in vogue. At 121,778 units, model-year production was the lowest since 1954. Horsepower ratings, however, continued upward. The 365 V-8 was coaxed to 310 bhp on all but the Eldorado, where it was 335.

Forecasting the future, de Ville became a 62 subseries for '58, and pillared sedans were eliminated. The 62 line also gained a hardtop sedan with extended rear deck. All models were available with cruise control, high-pressure cooling system, two-speaker signal-seeking radio, and automatic parking-brake release. A special show Eldorado introduced a "thinking" convertible top that raised itself and the side windows when a sensor detected raindrops; this gimmick allegedly saw limited production, though probably less than air suspension.

Another new GM C-body arrived for 1959, bringing more curvaceous Cadillac styling devised as a hurried reply to Chrysler's resurgent '57 Imperial. Hallmarks included huge windshields,

1957 Fleetwood Sixty Special hardtop sedan

1957 Series Seventy-Five limousine

1958 Series Sixty-Two Coupe de Ville hardtop

thin-section rooflines, slim pillars—and soaring fins of ridiculous proportions, ending in bullet taillamps. Offsetting these excesses were some worthy suspension changes, improved power steering, and a V-8 stroked to 390 cid. Predictably, horsepower rose again, to 345 on Eldorados; other models were up to 325.

De Ville now became a distinct series, offering hardtop sedans with flat-top four-window styling and a curvier six-window roofline, plus a hardtop coupe. The Series 62 duplicated these, and added a convertible. Also still pillarless (as it had been since '57) was the lush Sixty Special, now on a 130-inch wheelbase shared with other standard models including the line-topping Eldorado Seville, Biarritz, and Brougham.

Prices were generally higher for '59, with 62s at around $5000 and Eldos going for $7400 and up. Still, Cadillac built over 142,000 cars, a fair gain on 1958. Though not appreciated then, these Caddys are sought-after today as the epitome of '50s styling with their massive size, sparkling trim, and especially those overblown fins.

Cadillac displayed several two-seat idea cars in the '50s. First came the 1953 Le Mans, which looked much like the '54 Eldorado but on a trim 115-inch wheelbase. That same dimension was used on the following year's El Camino coupe and La Espada convertible, which previewed '55 styling. A restyled Le Mans was also shown at the '55 Motorama. Wildest of all was the 1959 Cyclone, a rocketlike machine with 104-inch wheelbase,

# Cadillac

1959 Coupe de Ville hardtop

1959 Cyclone show car

1960 Fleetwood Sixty Special hardtop sedan

all-independent suspension, unit construction, and a clear-plastic "bubble" top. The canopy was coated inside with vaporized silver to resist the sun's rays, and slid away as the door was opened. And those doors were sliding types, as on the late Kaiser-Darrin, though they worked electrically. Cyclone was a parting gift from GM design chief Harley Earl, who retired in 1958. His successor was longtime understudy Bill Mitchell, who would return Cadillac to more-dignified styling in the '60s.

Indeed, Cadillac immediately backed away from wretched excess with a more-restrained 1960 line bearing cleaner grilles and lowered fins. Offerings stayed the same, as did prices, ranging from $4892 for the Series 62 hardtop coupe to $9748 for the big Series 75 limousine. Mechanical specifications also stood pat. Cadillac had run ninth in model-year production for 1956-57, then dropped to 10th, where it would remain through 1964. Still, that was impressive going for a luxury make.

Carrying another new GM C-body, the '61s were the cleanest Cadillacs in years. This reflected the influence of Bill Mitchell, who favored a more-chiseled look and less chrome than Harley Earl. The grille was reduced to a modest grid, and wrapped windshields were abandoned (except on 75s), though Mitchell contrived to improve visibility. The Eldorado Seville and Brougham disappeared, while the Biarritz convertible was downgraded to the 325-bhp engine.

1961 Coupe de Ville hardtop

GM settled into a styling groove under Mitchell, so Cadillac's '62s were basically toned-down '61s. Highlights included still-lower fins, front-fender cornering lights as a new option, and backup/turn/stop lights combined behind a single white lens. Four-window sedans received more-orthodox rooflines but still included a pair of short-deck variants, now called Series 62 town sedan and de Ville Park Avenue. A new braking system with dual master cylinder and separate front and rear hydraulic lines appeared. Model-year output rose to nearly 161,000, up some 23,000 over '61.

The long-running Cadillac V-8 got its first major revision in 14 years for 1963. Cylinder size was unchanged, as were valves, rocker arms, heads, compression (still 10.5:1), and connecting rods. But everything else was different: lighter, stronger crankshaft; a stiffer block weighing 50 pounds less; accessories relocated to improve service access. While all this did little for performance, the revised 390 was smoother and quieter by far. And performance was already good. The typical '63 Cadillac could reach 115-120 mph, do 0-60 mph in 10 seconds, return about 14 miles per gallon, and was near-silent at high speed. In fact, for refinement, many testers held Cadillac superior to Rolls-Royce. Styling departed from recent practice. Fins were lower than ever, the grille bulkier, new outer body panels and side moldings created a more slab-sided effect, and a more-massive rear end carried long vertical tail/backup lights.

Prices rose only slightly for '63, so Cadillac remained an excellent value for the money. No-cost features expanded to include self-adjusting power brakes and remote-control door mirror. A six-way power seat became standard on Eldorado, and power windows were standard for all except Series 62 sedans and coupes. Even power vent windows were offered. So were vinyl roof coverings, a new option. Remarkably, a 62 still cost as little as $5026; the Eldorado Biarritz was only $6608. With all this, Cadillac set another model-year production record, topping 163,000.

Revisions were minor for 1964. Even lower tailfins created an unbroken beltline, accentuating length; grilles got a body-color horizontal divider bar; and taillamp housings were reshaped. A newly optional automatic heating/air-conditioning

1962 Series Sixty-Two convertible coupe

1963 Sedan de Ville 4-window hardtop

1962 Sedan de Ville 6-window hardtop

1963 Coupe de Ville hardtop

system maintained a set temperature regardless of outside conditions. It's been a Cadillac staple ever since. Perhaps more significantly, the 390 was enlarged to 429 cid, good for 340 bhp. Unit volume improved once more, this time to near 166,000.

Cadillac had a resounding 1965, producing close to 200,000 cars. But it was a great year in general for Detroit, so that volume was only good for 11th place. The mainstay Series 62 was renamed Calais, while Eldorado and Sixty Special officially became Fleetwoods, like the Series 75, bearing the requisite nameplates, wreath-and-crest medallions, broad rocker panel and rear-quarter brightwork, and rectangular-pattern rear appliques. A new Fleetwood Brougham sedan (actually a Sixty Special trim option) offered a vinyl roof with "Brougham" script on the rear pillars.

Another body change gave '65 Caddys a longer, lower silhouette, with fins planed absolutely flat, though a hint of them remained in a recontoured rear deck. Also new were a straight back bumper and vertical lamp clusters. Up front, headlight pairs switched from horizontal to vertical, making for an even wider grille. Curved side windows appeared, six-window hardtop sedans disappeared, and pillared sedans returned in Calais, de Ville and Sixty Special guise. The Special also reverted to its exclusive 133-inch wheelbase (last used from 1954 to 1958).

Despite an unchanged V-8, the slightly lighter '65 Caddys boasted the luxury field's best power-to-weight ratio. "Dual driving range" Turbo Hydra-Matic and full-perimeter frames (replacing the X-type used since '57) arrived except on 75s, and all models came with a new "sonically balanced" exhaust system. Amazingly, prices weren't too far above what they'd been in 1961.

Cadillac enjoyed its first 200,000-car year for calendar '66, breaking the barrier by exactly 5001 units. A mild facelift brought a new front bumper and grille, plus more smoothly integrated taillights. Perimeter frames now supported Series 75s, which were also fully rebodied for the first time since 1959. Variable-ratio power steering, which "speeded up" the more the wheel was turned from straight-ahead, was a new option along with carbon-cloth seat heating pads. The Fleetwood Brougham became a separate model, more luxuriously trimmed than the plain-roof Sixty Special and priced about $320 higher.

Arriving for 1967 was the most-significant Cadillac of the decade: an all-new Eldorado with front-wheel drive. Based on Oldsmobile's new 1966 Toronado, it was a daring concept for the luxury field, though with six years of careful planning and research behind it. Front drive gave it outstanding roadability; Bill Mitchell gave it magnificent styling.

It had originated in 1959 with the XP-727 program, which underwent several rethinks through early 1962. Management

1964 Series Seventy-Five Fleetwood limousine

1964 Series Sixty-Two hardtop coupe

# Cadillac

**1964 Sedan de Ville 4-window hardtop**

**1965 Coupe de Ville hardtop**

**1965 Sixty-Special Fleetwood Brougham four-door sedan**

**1965 Calais hardtop coupe**

**1965 Series Seventy-Five Fleetwood Landau limousine**

**1965 Calais four-door sedan**

**1965 Fleetwood Eldorado convertible coupe**

**1966 Sixty Special Fleetwood Brougham four-door sedan**

then settled on front-wheel drive, and further prototypes evolved with that in mind. For awhile, Cadillac considered calling it LaSalle, but ultimately chose Eldorado as a name with higher recognition. A clay model called XP-825, with razor-edge lines and formal roof treatment, was essentially the final production design.

Unlike Toronado, the '67 Eldorado was a very low-key announcement. This was typical of Cadillac, which used the one-year delay to improve on Oldsmobile's package. The Eldo thus rode better, yet handled at least as well despite the same basic suspension (torsion bars, A-arms, and telescopic shocks up front; a beam axle on semi-elliptic leaf springs and four shock absorbers—two horizontal, two vertical—in back). Two unique additions were self-leveling control and optional radially vented caliper front-disc brakes.

On its own relatively compact 120-inch wheelbase, the '67 Eldorado was announced at $6277 and targeted for 10 percent of Cadillac's total 1967 model-year production—about 20,000 units. The final figure was 17,930. For 1968-70, sales ran 23,000-28,000. A technological tour de force, it quickly established itself as the ultimate Cadillac. And unlike the old Brougham, it made money from day one.

Cadillac didn't forget its bread-and-butter "standards" for '67, applying an extensive restyle marked by a front-end ensemble thrust forward at the top. New linewide features included printed mylar instrument-panel circuits, automatic level control (standard on all Fleetwoods), cruise control, and tilt steering wheel. Bolstered by the new Eldorado, also part of the Fleetwood series, Cadillac built precisely 200,000 cars for the model year.

The 1968 spotlight was on motive power: an all-new 472-cid V-8 with 375 bhp. Designed to meet the new government emission standards that took effect that year, it was extensively tested in the laboratory, running the equivalent of 500,000 miles. Though not as fuel-efficient as the 429, the 472 could launch a coupe de Ville from 0 to 100 mph in under half a minute.

Design-wise, the '68 Eldorado gained side-marker lights (also newly required) plus larger taillights, combined turn signal/parking lamps in front-fender caps, and a hood extended at the rear to conceal the windshield wipers. Standards also got the hidden wipers and side markers, plus a revised grille and a trunklid reshaped for increased cargo space. Calais lost its pil-

1966 Series Seventy-Five Fleetwood limousine

1966 Coupe de Ville hardtop

1967 Series Seventy-Five Fleetwood 9-passenger sedan

1967 Coupe de Ville hardtop

1967 Sixty Special Fleetwood Brougham four-door sedan

1967 Fleetwood Eldorado hardtop coupe

1968 Sixty Special Fleetwood Brougham four-door sedan

1968 Fleetwood Eldorado hardtop coupe

lared four-door sedan.

Cadillac built a record 266,798 cars for calendar '69, breezing past Chrysler and American Motors to grab ninth in the industry rankings. For the model year, though, it remained 11th at a little over 223,000, down almost 7000 units from '68.

The Eldorado was again little changed for 1969, save for exposed headlights. Standards, however, were fully restyled via squarer new bodyshells. Headlamps reverted to horizontal, while parking lights wrapped around to flank a higher grille, still prominently vee'd. A somewhat dubious change was the elimination of front vent windows. Per Washington edict, no-cost equipment again expanded to include front-seat headrests, energy-absorbing steering column, ignition-key warning buzzer, and antitheft steering-column/transmission lock. Prices ran from just above $5400 for a Calais to well over $10,000 for the 75 limousine.

Eldorado got a new engine for 1970, and a badge reading "8.2 litres" to prove it. At 500 cubic inches, this was the world's largest production-car engine, developing 400 bhp and a monumental 550 pound-feet of torque. Other models retained the 375 horsepower 472. All 1970 Cadillacs boasted new integral steering knuckles, fiberglass-belted tires, and a radio antenna imbedded in the windshield.

Senior styling was touched up for 1970: a new grille with bright vertical accents over a cross-hatch background, horizontal bright trim on parking lights, winged crests instead of V's on de Ville and Calais hoods, and new taillamps. Eldorado sported a narrowed grille separate from the headlamps, plus slimmer taillamps. Production results were mixed. Though model-year volume rose to near 239,000 units, Cadillac again finished 10th, but calendar output dropped by over 100,000 cars for 1970, and the division fell back to 11th behind Chrysler and AMC. Still, in a generally quiet year for the industry, Cadillac out-produced Lincoln 3-1 and Imperial by no less than 15-1. "The Standard of the World" still reigned supreme as America's luxury favorite.

Cadillac stayed with its successful late-'60s lineup through 1976, though styling didn't change much after '71 and Calais sales were 6000-8000 annually. Forecasting the '80s was the new compact Seville of 1975, the smallest Cadillac in 50 years, followed by a decisively downsized big-car range for 1977.

Along with its E-body Buick Riviera and Oldsmobile Toronado stablemates, the Eldorado became bulkier for 1971,

# Cadillac

**1968 Sedan de Ville hardtop**

**1968 de Ville convertible coupe**

**1968 Fleetwood Eldorado hardtop coupe**

**1969 Sedan de Ville hardtop**

**1969 Coupe de Ville hardtop**

**1969 Sixty Special Fleetwood Brougham four-door sedan**

**1969 Fleetwood Eldorado hardtop coupe**

**1970 Sedan de Ville hardtop**

**1970 Coupe de Ville hardtop**

**1970 de Ville convertible coupe**

though not drastically heavier. It would continue through 1978 with few changes apart from government-mandated safety and emissions equipment that, along with inflation, escalated prices each year. Though they accounted for upwards of 40,000 annual sales, these outsized cruisers were not svelte, good-handling cars like the 1967-70 models.

Arriving with the '71 redesign was the first front-drive Eldorado convertible, a body style not offered by its corporate cousins and the first open-air Eldo since 1966. By 1976, eroding ragtop sales and high attrition throughout Detroit rendered it the only factory-built convertible on the market. This prompted a special run of 2000 all-white "last convertibles" and a promise to build no more. Rabid opportunists bid prices to the skies in the hope of making a killing on the collector market with what looked like a gilt-edged investment. The division kept its word, but only for a while. As time would prove, the droptop's demise was only temporary, and the '76 Eldos were not Detroit's "last" convertibles—nor, by the mid-'80s, particularly worth keeping.

In what was a busy Cadillac year, 1971 also brought a smoother but larger new C-body for the standard line, with "fuselage" flanks and softer, more-massive contours. Calais remained the latter-day equivalent of the old Series 61, though it wasn't that much cheaper than the better-equipped de Ville. Perhaps because of this, sales declined to below 10,000 units by 1974, prompting Calais' cancellation for 1977. Only two- and four-door hardtops were listed in these years, with the two-door becoming a fixed-pillar style after '73.

The money-spinning de Ville was reduced to that same two-some after 1970. Its convertible was judged superfluous with the revived Eldorado ragtop; the pillared four-door was merely put on hold until 1977. Considering the history of the name, a pillared Coupe de Ville was a contradiction in terms and, possibly for that reason, proved less popular than the pillarless Sedan de Ville after 1973.

Though still low-volume specialty items, the premium Fleetwoods got a new GM D-body for '71, and thus fresh styling for the first time since 1966. The Sixty Special remained a four-door sedan on a unique 133-inch wheelbase, but there was only one version now. Called Fleetwood Sixty Special Brougham, it shared the Series 75's new roof styling with more distinctly separate side windows. It, too, would see little appearance change through 1976.

The main reason Cadillac styling evolved so slowly in this period is that engineering and design talent was engaged with the more-pressing concerns of the day: fuel economy, emissions, and occupant crash protection. As it was very difficult to reconcile those last two with the first, Cadillac's engineering emphasis fell on the emissions side with both of its V-8s. For example, exhaust-gas recirculation was added for 1973 to reduce oxides of nitrogen (NOx) emissions, while the air-injection pump and engine pulleys were altered to lessen noise.

Big-car sales slipped badly with the 1973-74 oil embargo. Cadillac was no exception, but it recovered smartly by 1975, when the Eldo's huge 500 V-8—by then down to a measly 190 bhp in SAE net measure—became standard for other Cadillacs save one.

And that one marked a big departure from tradition: a brand-new four-door sedan that was not only much smaller than anything else in the line, but also more expensive—outpriced only by the 75. It arrived in the spring of 1975 as the Seville, from Eldorado lineage. Cadillac had considered "Leland," to honor its founder, but decided most buyers were too young to make that connection. LaSalle (again!) was also in the running, but was ultimately rejected for the same reason—and because Cadillac's '30s companion make was still felt to have a "loser" image. But this Seville was no loser, being carefully planned for

1970 Fleetwood Eldorado hardtop coupe

1971 Fleetwood Sixty Special Brougham four-door sedan

1971 Fleetwood Eldorado convertible coupe

1971 Fleetwood Eldorado coupe

the one area of the luxury market that Cadillac had yet to exploit: the quality intermediate typified by Mercedes-Benz.

The Seville bowed to mixed reviews. Clean and trim on its 114.3-inch wheelbase, it compared favorably with German rivals for interior space. But styling struck some as unimaginative, and it was an open secret that this "baby Cadillac" was actually a heavily reengineered version of GM's workaday X-body compact, a serious deficit in the prestige class.

But the driving left little to criticize. Power came from a 350-cid V-8 built by Olds to Cadillac specifications, which included a new Bendix electronic-fuel-injection system exclusive to this model. The result was brisk, turbinelike performance, with

# Cadillac

**1972 Fleetwood Eldorado convertible coupe**

**1974 Fleetwood Eldorado convertible coupe**

**1973 Fleetwood Eldorado coupe**

**1975 Coupe de Ville**

**1973 Fleetwood Eldorado convertible coupe**

**1976 Seville four-door sedan**

**1973 Coupe de Ville hardtop**

**1976 Fleetwood Sixty Special Brougham four-door sedan**

**1974 Fleetwood Sixty Special Brougham four-door sedan**

**1977 Sedan de Ville**

# Cadillac

1977 Coupe de Ville

1977 Fleetwood Eldorado coupe

1977 Seville four-door sedan

1978 Coupe de Ville d'Elegance

1978 Seville Elegante four-door sedan

typical 0-60 acceleration of 10-11 seconds and a top speed of over 110 mph. Seville weighed 1000 pounds less and was 27 inches shorter than a '75 de Ville, yet its ride was as cloudlike as buyers expected. And it was the best-handling Cadillac since the '67 Eldorado—much closer to M-B and BMW than those makers might have admitted. To be sure, it wouldn't glide over washboard surfaces with the disdain of a big Mercedes, but it didn't cost nearly so much either. Buyers responded with enthusiasm. Seville sales totalled 43,000 in its first full model year, 1976, a healthy 15 percent of division output.

Other Cadillacs were mostly unchanged for '76, but improving energy supplies and a reviving economy spurred sales across the board, and the division broke 300,000 units for the first time since '73. Things were even better for 1977-78 despite cancellation of Calais and the Eldo convertible: about 350,000 per year. A second energy crisis depressed 1979-80 calendar-year volume, but Cadillac kept its usual two-three percent of the total industry, the share it had claimed for many years.

Perhaps only Cadillac could so drastically change its cars while setting new sales records. Its 1977 standards were fresh from the ground up—8½ inches shorter and nearly 1000 pounds lighter on average than the '76s. Wheelbases were now 121.5 inches for de Ville/Fleetwood Brougham, 144.5 for the Fleetwood limo. They also had a cleaner, more-efficient new engine: a fuel-injected 425 V-8 with 180 bhp; a 195-bhp version was optional except for limos. Upmarket "D'Elegance" trim options continued for de Villes, along with new pseudo-convertible "Cabriolet" roof coverings.

The story was much the same for 1979, when Eldorado was downsized to lose 1100 pounds, 20 inches in length, and 12.3 inches in wheelbase (to 114). An unusual touch for an upmarket domestic was independent rear suspension, more compact than the previous beam axle, which made it possible to reduce wheelbase with little loss of passenger room. Options for all '79 Cadillacs included dual electric remote-control door mirrors, integrated 40-channel CB radio, and "Tripmaster" on-board travel computer. First offered on the '78 de Ville, Tripmaster provided digital readouts for average mpg and speed, miles to destination and estimated arrival time, plus engine rpm, coolant temperature, and electrical system voltage.

Attention for 1980 focused on a completely overhauled second-generation Seville. Its most controversial aspect was a sloped "trunkback" rear, executed by designer Wayne Cady but also a parting shot for GM styling chief Bill Mitchell. Reminiscent of certain 1950s Rolls-Royce bodies, it made for the most-distinctive Cadillac since the tailfinned '48s, though not everyone liked it. For cost reasons, Seville now shared the latest Eldorado chassis, thus shifting from rear to front drive and gaining the same all-independent suspension with automatic self-leveling. As had been true since 1978, a spiffy Elegante version, usually two-toned, was a higher-cost alternative to the standard article.

A telling feature of the '80 Seville was its standard engine: a "dieselized" version of the existing Oldsmobile 350 gasoline V-8, built in Lansing for use by other GM divisions. Cadillac had first offered this as a 1978 option for the Seville; it was optional across-the-board for '79. Smooth and quiet for a diesel, it gave Cadillac a direct reply to compression-ignition Mercedes models. More importantly, it helped the division contribute to GM's compliance with the corporate average fuel economy (CAFE) mandates that took effect with model-year 1978.

As time went on, however, it became clear that most people bought diesel Mercedes not for their economy or longevity but the snob appeal of their three-pointed star. And unhappily for Cadillac's image, the Olds engine suffered early and persistent reliability problems that GM never could seem to fix. By the

# Cadillac

mid-'80s, a glut of cheap gasoline would wash away memories of the second "energy crisis" that played havoc with the market in 1979-82. Once buyers began rushing back to big cars and big engines, Cadillac had no trouble abandoning diesels. Neither did most anyone else who'd been peddling them in the U.S.

Before this came a further blow to Cadillac's reputation for quality: the problematic "V-8-6-4" variable-displacement gasoline engine, a costly stopgap also prompted by CAFE. Displacing 6.0 liters (368 cid) and tuned for a modest 140 bhp, it arrived as a 1981 option for Seville and was made standard elsewhere.

At its heart was an electromechanical system, developed by the Eaton Corporation, that opened and closed the valves on two or four cylinders (hence the name) when signaled by an electronic module controlling the engine's digital fuel injection. The aim, of course, was improved economy, the cylinders shutting down under part-throttle, low-load conditions when you didn't need all eight, such as in medium-speed highway cruising. It was a good idea, but too complex to be reliable, and Cadillac paid a big price in both image and dollars once angry consumers began suing for redress. Few mourned when the V-8-6-4 was terminated after just one year (though it persisted in limos through '82).

A better bet was Buick's 125-bhp 4.1-liter V-6, newly optional across the '81 board (except limousines) and the first six in Cadillac history. Another new extra was an electronic "memory"

**1978 Eldorado Custom Biarritz Classic Coupe**

**1980 Seville Elegante four-door sedan**

**1979 Seville Elegante four-door sedan**

**1981 Fleetwood Brougham coupe**

**1979 Eldorado coupe**

**1980 Eldorado Biarritz coupe**

**1979 Eldorado coupe**

**1981 Coupe de Ville**

power seat that assumed one of two preset positions at the touch of a button—shades of Mercury's mid-'50s "Seat-O-Matic."

There were a couple more surprises for '82. The biggest one was a Cadillac even smaller than the '75 Seville. Called Cimarron, it was just a high-zoot version of GM's new 101.2-inch wheelbase J-body subcompact, loaded to the gills but otherwise much like sister four-doors at every other GM division—except for price: initially $12,000. That looked very steep when a similar Chevy Cavalier or Pontiac J2000 could be had for half as much with comparable equipment. Cimarron did have a few J-car exclusives like leather upholstery and optional sliding-glass "Astroroof," but its humble origins were so obvious that nobody took it for a real Cadillac.

Cimarron was a frank embarrassment to Cadillac, caught in a flagrant act of "badge-engineering." Still, it was a logical development: needed to boost the division's fleet-average economy until its larger cars could be downsized again, and also to help stem a rising tide of upscale imports (typified by the BMW 3-Series) beginning to erode Cadillac sales. But the decision to field this gilded J came at the 11th hour, and it showed. The resulting criticism stung.

As a result, Cadillac immediately began distancing Cimarron from lesser Js, adding more standard features, ringing in a mild facelift and a lush "D'Oro" submodel for '83, making Chevy's 2.8 V-6 an option from mid-'85 and standard for '87 (replacing the original weak and noisy 2.0-liter four), tinkering with suspen-

1981 Seville four-door sedan (Diesel)

1982 Coupe de Ville

1981 Eldorado Biarritz coupe

1982 Fleetwood Brougham Coupe d'Elegance

1981 Eldorado coupe

1982 Eldorado Touring Coupe

1982 Cimarron four-door sedan

1982 Seville Elegante four-door sedan

# Cadillac

1983 Eldorado Biarritz coupe

1983 Fleetwood Brougham coupe

1983 Seville Elegante four-door sedan

1984 Coupe de Ville

1984 Fleetwood Brougham Sedan d'Elegance

sion to impart a more "European" feel. But buyers always stayed away in droves, and Cadillac struggled to move an average 20,000 Cimarrons per year through 1986. Demand then slid to less than 15,000, and the model was belatedly killed after the 1988 model year.

Not that Cadillac cried much on its way to the bank, because total output rose steadily from 1982 through '85—from about 235,500 to nearly 335,000. Though Cimarron and troublesome engines may have blotted its enviable engineering record, Cadillac still dominated the luxury market.

Which brings us back to 1982's other surprise, yet another new engine. This was a small 4.1-liter (249-cid) V-8 with a cast-iron head atop a lightweight aluminum block, plus digital fuel injection. Dubbed "HT4100," it was standard for all '82s (save Cimarron and limos). Initial rated output was 125 bhp, same as for the Buick 4.1 V-6, which remained as an option for that year, then disappeared entirely. However, the V-8 actually produced a bit less torque than the V-6. It was certainly far less torquey than the old 425 or even the V-8-6-4, so the big Cadillacs were far less rapid.

Happier '82 news involved a Touring Coupe package for Eldorado with blackout moldings, fatter tires on aluminum wheels, and standard buckets-and-console interior with unique trim. Traditionalists still had their usual choices of two- and four-door de Villes and Fleetwoods in plain and D'Elegance trim, plus standard and Biarritz Eldorados and base and Elegante Sevilles—all available with fake wire wheels and convertible-look tops.

The big Caddys changed little over the next two years. HT4100 horsepower and torque rose by 10 each for '83, when Eldo and Seville offered a new acoustically tailored sound system developed by GM's Delco Electronics Division in concert with the Bose speaker people.

All was again mostly quiet for '84 except for the return of an open-air Eldorado (though all the "last convertible" nonsense had already been silenced). Actually, Buick had issued a ragtop Riviera back in '82, which made Cadillac seem rather slow to follow suit with its related Eldo. The likely reason was not the no-more-convertibles promise but the Riviera's slow sales, which must have made Cadillac managers hesitate.

But they finally did it, and they did it big. Offered only in uplevel Biarritz trim (a staple option for coupes since the late '70s), the reborn ragtop Eldo base-priced at $31,286—in raw dollars the costliest U.S. production convertible ever offered. But like the open Riviera, it would die after 1985. Price didn't kill it as much as the advent of a smaller new E-body and the luxury market's continuing desertion to imports.

Model-year '85 was pivotal for Cadillac, as its best-selling de Ville was downsized again and given front-wheel drive for the first time. Its new GM C-body was shared with that year's similarly revised Buick Electra and Olds Ninety-Eight. So was the 110.8-inch-wheelbase chassis with all-independent coil-spring/strut suspension and power rack-and-pinion steering. Dimensionally, this trimmest de Ville ever was two feet shorter and some 600 pounds lighter than its rear-drive predecessor. There was also a new Seventy-Five limousine on a 134.4-inch platform. The 4.1 V-8 was turned sideways to provide comparable cabin space within the smaller new package, but necessary manifolding changes brought horsepower back to 125 and torque to 190 pound-feet. Still, Cadillac could claim the world's only transverse V-8.

Even better, the new Coupe and Sedan de Ville and their lush Fleetwood counterparts quickly outsold the popular rear-drive series. Cadillac built over 197,000 for the first full model year, versus an annual 137,000-175,000 of the 1981-84 C-bodies.

But before buyers had given this approval, Cadillac had

# Cadillac

1984 Seville four-door sedan (cabriolet roof)

1984 Eldorado Biarritz convertible coupe

1984 Eldorado Biarritz coupe

1984 Eldorado Touring Coupe

1984 Seville four-door sedan

1985 Seville Elegante four-door sedan

1985 Fleetwood Brougham four-door sedan

1985 Cimarron four-door sedan

decided to retain some rear-drive models as a hedge. This proved a shrewd move once the market began its strong recovery from the doldrums of '82. Badged Fleetwood Brougham through 1986, then just plain Brougham, these cars continued with few changes through the end of the decade, garnering about 50,000 orders a year, each one pure gravy. We should note the passing of the big Brougham coupe and the diesel V-8 option after 1985. The latter wouldn't be missed. Nor was it really needed for CAFE, since the government had relaxed those requirements somewhat. Indeed, Cadillac saw fit to switch these cars to a 5.0-liter (307-cid) Olds V-8 with 140 bhp in 1986.

As planned, the Cadillac line's second wholesale downsizing since '77 was completed when a new-generation Eldorado and Seville appeared for 1986. Remaining twins under the skin, they shared the new 108-inch-wheelbase E-body platform (technically, Seville was still GM's K-body) of that year's Riviera and Olds Toronado. The Cadillacs, of course, had a 4.1 V-8 (again situated transversely rather than longitudinally) instead of the others' Buick V-6. Designers again managed similar interior space within smaller envelopes, here trimmed 16 inches in length and 350-plus pounds in curb weight, and Seville shed its controversial "bustle" for a conventional notchback profile. Both had a raft of interesting new features: floor-mounted

# Cadillac

1985 Sedan de Ville

1985 Fleetwood four-door sedan

1985 Coupe de Ville

1985 Fleetwood Seventy-Five limousine

1985 Eldorado coupe (diesel)

1986 Eldorado Biarritz coupe

1986 Sedan de Ville

# Cadillac

shifters (for the mandatory four-speed overdrive automatic transaxle), flush-mount "composite" headlamps, and more electronic gadgets than ever.

Sadly, these cars proved even bigger sales disasters than Cimarron. Seville volume, a strong 40,000 a year for 1984-85, dropped by half; Eldorado, which garnered an annual 76,000-plus orders in the same period, plunged by more than two-thirds.

The reasons were obvious enough: bland styling that was too close to that of GM's much cheaper N-body compacts (which began arriving the previous year) and dimensions that just weren't impressive enough for the cars' regular clientele. A 1987 Newsweek article on GM's declining fortunes graphically highlighted the design problem by picturing a Seville tail-to-tail with an N-body Olds Calais; it was tough to tell them apart. Worse, workmanship slipped badly due to equipment problems at the highly automated new Detroit-Hamtramck plant dedicated solely to E/K production. Typical of the woes: robots painting each other instead of cars.

There was nothing to do but soldier on, so the '87s received only minor suspension tweaks. For 1988, Cadillac tried to rectify its styling mistake via time-honored methods. Seville thus gained a "power dome" hood and a more "important" grille. Eldorado was similarly treated but also received new squared-up lower-body sheetmetal that stretched overall length by three inches at the rear—shades of the '50s.

Happier developments included first-time availability of an antilock brake system (ABS) and a more-potent engine. The former was the same laudable option announced for the 1986 de Ville/Fleetwood—though not readily available until '87. The 4.1 V-8 was enlarged to 4.5 liters (273 cid), and this plus a new two-stage intake manifold, larger throttle bores, and other changes lifted horsepower by 25 (to 155 total) and torque by 40 pound-feet (to 240). The '88 Eldorado and Seville were thus usefully quicker off the line than the 1986-87s—quite punchy, in fact—and ABS made panic stops shorter and more controlled. A "touring" suspension package was still available for those seeking crisper handling with little sacrifice in ride comfort.

The bread-winning de Ville and Fleetwood were improving, too. Besides a slight power increase, the '86 line offered new Touring Coupe and Sedan de Villes with firm suspension, husky blackwall tires on aluminum wheels, a front airdam with built-in foglights, plus less chrome outside and special trim inside. The '87s were lengthened 1.5 inches via extended rear fender caps and got a new grille, while the Sixty Special designation returned on a stretched, 115.8-inch-wheelbase Fleetwood four-door—a nod to the "executive car" market. The front-drive Seventy-Five was in its last year. As Chrysler had lately realized, factory-built limousines were unprofitable and thus better left to aftermarket converters, of which there were plenty. The main changes for '88 involved the more-potent 4.5 V-8 and standardization of several former options including the timed Twilight Sentinel headlamp system, tilt/telescope steering wheel, illuminated entry system, and cruise control.

The de Ville and Fleetwood then finished out the '80s with a major revamping that produced a major sales gain. Again looking to the "longer-is-better" ploy, Cadillac stretched sedan models 8.8 inches in overall length, and increased wheelbase by three inches to 113.8. Coupes were 5.9 inches longer overall on an unchanged wheelbase. Styling on both body types was modified to suit the new dimensions, trunk space improved by some two cubic feet, and front fenders were rendered in a rust-free "nylon composite alloy" to save a little weight. Offerings also expanded with the return of a two-door Fleetwood after a two-year hiatus. Also returning (and again recalling the '50s) were rear fender skirts on the Fleetwoods, which again included a

1986 de Ville touring sedan

1986 de Ville touring coupe

1986 Eldorado coupe

1986 Seville Elegante four-door sedan

# Cadillac

1987 Cimarron four-door sedan

1987 Presidential Limousine

1987 Allanté 2-passenger convertible

1987 Seville four-door sedan

1987 Eldorado coupe

Sixty Special that actually lost two inches of wheelbase.

Several new linewide options also appeared for '89, including a supplemental air bag housed in the steering-wheel hub, "ElectriClear" heated windshield (to match the now-standard rear-window defroster), and GM's clever new "PASS-Key" theft-deterrent system. The powertrain was unchanged, but so was performance, as weight increases averaged only 100 pounds despite the added inches.

Those inches translated directly into higher sales, and total de Ville/Fleetwood production jumped by nearly 26,000 units—over 17 percent—to nearly 179,000 for the model year. The 1990s weren't greatly changed, but performance benefited by a switch from single-point to multipoint fuel injection that lifted the 4.5 V-8 from 155 to 180 bhp and improved torque by 5 pound-feet to 245 total. Safety-conscious customers applauded a newly standard driver-side air bag on all models, plus no-cost ABS on Fleetwoods. Series sales continued strong despite the start of a deep new recession, falling by only some 2300 units.

The 1990 Seville and Eldorado also carried the more-potent V-8, which was welcome, because both were becoming decidedly sporty. Still seeking to beat back imported sports sedans, Cadillac offered a limited-edition Seville Touring Sedan package in late '88, then made it a full-fledged option for 1989. Its chief attractions were a quieter monochrome exterior, beefy tires on handsome alloy rims, Touring Suspension, and a shorter final-drive for quicker acceleration.

The STS proved popular enough to rate separate-model status for 1990, when both Seville and Eldorado received a minor facelift, standard driver-side air bag and some miscellaneous no-cost extras. The STS also came with ABS now. Sales were better than they'd been a few years earlier, but still not what Cadillac wanted. Eldorado volume dropped from near 31,000 for '89 to about 22,000 for 1990. Seville, however, more than made up for this loss, soaring better than 40 percent from 23,000 to 33,000.

Cadillac's most ambitious car of the '80s—certainly its most publicized—was the Allanté, a sharp two-seat convertible aimed squarely at the big-bucks Mercedes 560SL. The first two-seat Caddy since 1941, it bowed with great fanfare for 1987 on a front-drive Eldorado chassis shortened to a 99.4-inch wheelbase. Power initially came from a tuned 4.1 V-8 with multi-point (instead of single- or dual-point) injection, roller valve lifters, high-flow cylinder heads, and tuned intake manifold, good for 170 bhp. Italy's renowned Pininfarina was contracted for the styling and to build the bodywork—more snob appeal that way. Modified Eldo understructures were flown in special 747 jets to a new PF plant set up in Turin especially for Allanté production; fully trimmed shells (galvanized unit hulls with aluminum hood and trunklid) were then air-shipped back to Detroit-Hamtramck for drivetrain installation and final assembly. Standard equipment included a lift-off hardtop to supplement the manual soft top. A cellular telephone was the lone option.

Though a pleasant, capable tourer and an entirely new breed of Cadillac, the Allanté failed to make the hoped-for impression. Cadillac predicted calendar-'87 sales of 4000 units, but moved only 1651 (of 3363 built); deliveries for the first full production year totaled just 3065 versus a planned 7000. Model-year production was just 2569. The results: an embarrassing pile-up of unsold cars, hefty rebates to clear it—and a further blow to Cadillac prestige. In fact, trade weekly Automotive News named Allanté its 1987 "Flop of the Year." Division chief John O. Grettenberger dismissed that dubious honor—and wide coverage of the car's slow start—as "just the latest round of GM bashing."

Still, for what it was, Allanté was judged too expensive: $54,000 at announcement, $56,500 for the little-changed '88.

# Cadillac

1988 Cimarron four-door sedan

1988 Fleetwood d'Elegance four-door sedan

1988 Allanté 2-passenger convertible

1988 Fleetwood Sixty Special four-door sedan

1988 Fleetwood Brougham four-door sedan

1989 Coupe de Ville

1988 Seville Touring Sedan (STS)

1989 Fleetwood four-door sedan

# Cadillac

**1989 Allanté 2-passenger convertible**

**1989 Seville Touring Sedan (STS)**

**1990 Eldorado Touring Coupe (ETC)**

**1989 Eldorado coupe**

**1990 Coupe de Ville**

And it depreciated by a third the minute it left a showroom, whereas a Mercedes SL actually went up in value. An assortment of niggling troubles—wind and water leaks, squeaks and rattles, horns that didn't work, and heaters that worked too well—hardly helped matters.

Cadillac scrambled, installing its bigger 4.5 V-8 for 1989, then tuning for a smashing 200 bhp and 270 pound-feet. Alas, that and a shorter final drive sufficiently lowered EPA mileage to incur a $650 Gas Guzzler penalty, which upped actual delivered price to $57,183. But 0-60 acceleration dropped from 10 seconds to 8.5 or less, and Cadillac kept things safe at every speed with new speed-sensitive power steering, bigger wheels and tires, and three-mode "speed-dependent damping" (auto-adjusting shock absorbers). Other improvements included comfier seats, a revised top mechanism (always manual), and PASS-Key anti-theft protection. Model-year production rose from 2569 to 3298, which was encouraging. But Allanté sales were now being propped up by a "guaranteed resale" scheme pegged to the SL's higher residual values; Cadillac promised to pay the difference if an Allanté owner traded for another new Cadillac.

Having fumbled its original mission as division flagship, Allanté got a new role for 1990: technology showcase. High-tech it had. The big news was a standard traction-control system—a first for a front-drive car—plus a revised "Speed Sensitive Suspension" (SSS) that stayed in "soft" mode up to 40 mph (instead of 25) for a smoother low-speed ride; as before, it then selected "normal," going into "firm" only above 60 mph. "Firm" also kicked in during hard acceleration, braking, or cornering. A no-cost driver-side airbag served safety, and a compact-disc player lengthened the standard-equipment list.

Straining to keep price attractive, Cadillac offered a 1990 Allanté sans hardtop for $51,500, a sizable $6313 below the "full" version, which was hiked to $57,813. Yet despite the arrival of new-design Mercedes SLs starting in the mid-$70,000s, Allanté sales only got worse, model-year output easing to 3101.

Allanté held on for three more seasons. Like some other GM cars that had been put to death too soon, the last one was the best. For one thing, the '93 packed Cadillac's new all-aluminum, dual-overhead-cam "Northstar" V-8 with 4.6 liters and a resounding 295 bhp. Also on hand were more-sophisticated traction control and a faster-acting "Road Sensing Suspension" (RSS). But by this point, a brilliant new Seville and Eldorado had done much to polish Cadillac's image, and Allanté was no longer needed to prove that "Standard of the World" still meant something. For the benefit of collectors—and make no mistake: Allantés will be collected—model-year volumes were 2500 for '91, just 1931 for '92, and 4670 for swan-song '93.

Meantime, other Cadillacs were doing quite nicely, both technically and commercially. Though the division lost about 45,000 calendar-year sales between 1990 and '91, demand then stabilized at around 214,000 through mid-decade (save for 1993's modest 10,000-unit dip). That was an admirable showing given GM's numerous troubles of the day, not to mention continued aggressive competition from Lincoln. On that score, Cadillac remained comfortably ahead of its perennial rival, though Lincoln narrowed Cadillac's lead down to 30,500 units in 1993 despite offering fewer models.

But Cadillac had more to worry about than just Lincoln. European luxury cars had not only multiplied, but were selling better than ever to the younger, affluent "baby boom" generation that still mostly ignored Cadillac. Then, too, the Japanese had lately weighed in with upscale coupes and sedans under the Acura, Infiniti, and Lexus banners. All these competitors were technically sophisticated, and most were outstanding to drive. To protect its position as the luxury leader, Cadillac had to respond—and fast.

Cadillac did, starting with an upsized iron-head V-8 for 1991. Now at 4.9 liters (300 cid), this engine was newly standard for all models except Allanté and the big old Brougham. Horsepower stood at 200, and newly integrated electronic transmission controls insured smooth, efficient delivery. That same year, ABS went from optional to standard status for de Ville, Eldorado, and the base Seville. The de Ville/Fleetwood line was also lightly face-lifted, mainly by a new grille and more-prominent hood bulge.

With one eye on the imports, Cadillac revived the de Ville Touring Sedan for 1991 after a three-year absence. Priced at around $35,200, it stood apart from sister de Villes with a subdued "monochromatic" exterior, stout 16-inch alloy wheels shod with blackwall performance tires, shorter final gearing for better pickup, thicker stabilizer bars for tighter handling, and posh wood-and-leather interior.

Taking even closer aim at the imports were the all-new 1992 Eldorado and Seville. Both were smooth and curvy, clean and elegant, a refreshing break with their recent boxy past. Styling, however, was no longer so similar between the two, and there were greater differences elsewhere as well. For example, Seville now strode its own 111-inch wheelbase, while the Eldo stuck to a 108-inch span. Both models grew some 12 inches

1991 Brougham four-door sedan

1991 Fleetwood Sixty Special four-door sedan

1991 Allanté 2-passenger convertible

1991 Seville Touring Sedan (STS)

1991 Eldorado coupe

# Cadillac

1992 Eldorado Touring Coupe (ETC)

1992 Sedan de Ville

1992 Fleetwood coupe

1992 Brougham four-door sedan

1993 Sedan de Ville

longer and 2.5 inches wider, but the new Seville was taut, purposeful, even bold for a Cadillac—enough to make the Eldo seem cautious to some eyes.

Prices opened some eyes. The Eldo now started at $32,000, while the Seville was up in $35,000-$38,000 territory. Then again, inflation had taken a toll, and both new models were really fine values against comparable imports. As before, the more-enthusiastic buyer opted for the Seville Touring Sedan or an Eldorado with extra-cost Touring Coupe package—which made an "ETC." Either choice meant firm suspension, wider tires on 16-inch wheels, less exterior chrome, and a more driver-oriented cabin with console, front buckets, and analog instead of electronic digi-graphic instruments.

The STS and ETC became more exciting for '93, as the pushrod 4.9 V-8 gave way to the sterling all-aluminum Northstar. As in the final Allantés, this 32-valver packed a 295-bhp punch that knocked 0-60 times down to 7.5 seconds or so in Consumer Guide® tests—more than a second quicker than before. Both models also gained speed-sensitive power steering and optional Road Sensing Suspension. Arriving for the base Eldo was a $3000 Sport Coupe package with a special 270-bhp Northstar tuned for 10 extra pound-feet (300 versus 290) at lower rpm—all the better for low-speed lugging power. An alternative new Sport Appearance option offered ETC-style looks and interior for just $875. All '93 Eldos and Sevilles benefited from standard passenger airbags, minor rear-suspension tweaks, and improved traction control that could throttle back on engine power as well as apply the brakes to keep you on the straight and narrow.

Eldorado's Sport Coupe package was dropped for '94, but the Touring Coupe became a separate model, the base Seville got the high-torque Northstar to become the SLS ("Seville Luxury Sedan"), and RSS was made standard for ETC and STS. For '95, both versions of the Northstar gained five horsepower, and there were subtle styling changes for all Eldos and Sevilles, including a body-color grille for ETC (thus matching the four-door STS). Typical of Cadillac was a new standard feature: headlamps that switched on automatically with the wipers.

In all, the new "personal" Cadillacs were everything expected of the marque—and more. Fittingly, they sold well. In fact, both almost doubled their model-year production from '91 to '92, the Eldorado exceeding 31,000, the Seville reaching almost 44,000. The '93s skidded to about 21,500 and 37,240, respectively, doubtless due to higher sticker prices reflecting the costlier Northstar engines. But 1994 brought a modest recovery, Seville climbing back to nearly 47,000 and Eldo to nearly 25,000. Though such numbers weren't great compared to early-'80s sales, they were a darn sight better than late-'80s volume. Just as important, these cars proved that at least some Cadillacs could set an American standard for an automotive world now vastly and forever changed.

The big rear-drive Brougham sedan hardly changed at all through 1992. As a late-'70s holdover it was now quite an anachronism, heroically overdecorated and obviously under-damped. But Cadillac was loath to let it go because some buyers wouldn't have a front-drive car—and because the Brougham made more money per sale than other Cadillacs. Besides, it was the longest car in American production, as the division was proud to advertise.

An old design long since paid for allowed Cadillac to keep updating the Brougham without eating into profits. Accordingly, the 1990 model gained standard antilock brakes while answering requests for more power with a newly optional 5.7-liter V-8, the biggest engine for this car in years. It came from Chevy and required an extra-cost trailering package, but its healthy 175 bhp was welcomed by "stretch limo" converters.

# Cadillac

1993 Allanté 2-passenger convertible

1994 Eldorado Touring Coupe (ETC)

1993 Fleetwood four-door sedan

1994 Fleetwood four-door sedan

1993 Eldorado Touring Coupe (ETC)

1995 Sedan de Ville

1994 Seville Touring Sedan (STS)

1995 Eldorado coupe

1994 de Ville Concours four-door sedan

1995 Seville Touring Sedan (STS)

133

# Cadillac

Base powerplants switched for '91, going from a 140-bhp Olds 307 (last descendant of the fabled '49 "Rocket") to Chevy's evergreen 305, now up to 170 horsepower. At the same time, the 5.7 was pushed to 185 bhp and made a freestanding option. No other major changes occurred—except for a worrisome 60-percent sales plunge from nearly 34,000 for 1990 to just under 14,000 for '92.

But Cadillac was still devoted to "traditional" cars, and proved it by launching a big new Fleetwood for '93. This was basically a rebodied Brougham *a la* '91 Chevy Caprice and Buick's reborn Roadmaster, though the Brougham name lived on for a spiffy interior-trim option. Styling remained "formal" but curvier and more contemporary, with plenty of applied trim and the usual expansive eggcrate face. Overall length stretched 4.1 inches to 225, but wheelbase was unchanged. Curb weight rose only 90 pounds despite the extra sheetmetal and added standards like the "Airbank"—dual airbags wide enough to protect all three occupants of the still-standard front bench seat. A plastic fuel tank helped minimize weight gain, while newly standard traction control helped drivers stay safely on course in foul weather.

The 5.7 was also standard for the '93 Fleetwood, but '94 brought even better performance with adoption of the new 260-bhp version of Chevrolet's LT1 5.7, with sequential multipoint fuel injection (instead of single-point). Electronic transmission control was also added. Only detail changes occurred for '95.

For so much massive opulence, the new-wave Fleetwood was reasonably priced in the mid-$30,000 area, and thus quite a bargain against comparably sized luxury imports. Buyers responded, and 1993 model-year production almost doubled to nearly 32,000 units. The '94s found fewer takers (just over 27,000), and calendar-year output was back to Brougham levels by 1995 at around 13,400 (off 7000 from calendar '94). But the sales issue was soon rendered moot, as GM decided to drop all its rear-drive cars after 1996 so its Texas factory could build more sport-utility trucks. That prompts one to wonder whether the final Fleetwoods will be scooped up by collectors someday as the last big Cadillacs of the grand old school. Stranger things have happened.

There was nothing strange about the mainstay front-drive Cadillacs of this period, which evolved through two distinct phases. The first ended the familiar square-rigged series after 1993 with no further changes of consequence. Among lesser but laudable improvements were standard traction control for '92 Fleetwoods and the de Ville Touring Sedan, followed by speed-sensitive steering and suspension for all '93s. When the Fleetwood name moved to the big rear-drive car, the front-drive Fleetwood coupe was dropped, leaving the Sixty Special sedan as the lone uplevel '93.

The Special disappeared the next year, as did the Coupe de

1995 Fleetwood four-door sedan

1996 Eldorado coupe

1996 Seville Touring Sedan (STS)

1996 Seville Luxury Sedan (SLS)

1996 de Ville four-door sedan

1996 Fleetwood four-door sedan

# Cadillac

1997 Eldorado Touring Coupe (ETC)

1998 Seville Touring Sedan (STS)

1999 Catera four-door sedan

1999 Catera four-door sedan

1999 Eldorado Touring Coupe (ETC)

Ville, thus ending those once-proud model names. But the Sedan de Ville returned with a thorough redesign, and there was a new Concours (borrowing an old Chevy name) to replace the de Ville Touring Sedan. Motive power was the main difference. Sedan de Ville used the 200-bhp pushrod 4.9 V-8, Concours the 270-bhp twincam Northstar. Both looked like slightly smaller versions of the '93 Fleetwood, so few would have guessed they were built on a new K-Special version of the Seville platform. Wheelbase grew 2.8 inches to 113.8 (to match the previous de Ville sedan stretch) and overall length extended 3.4 inches to 209.7, thus increasing passenger and parcel space. Styling had bit more "crease in the pants" than Fleetwood, but was conservatively handsome except for rather chubby rear flanks (slim vertical taillamps didn't help).

Predictably, the new de Ville/Concours were even more impressive than their predecessors: smooth, quiet performers with noticeably less engine and road noise. There was also new reassurance in a standard "Airbank" system, plus the usual arm-long list of comfort and convenience goodies. The Concours proved a virtual hot rod, Consumer Guide® clocking 0-60 at a very swift 6.8 seconds, and its standard traction control and Road Sensing Suspension struck a happy balance between Euro-style handling and American-style ride. As ever, Sedan de Ville aimed at older, less-energetic drivers, but was hardly the barge the Fleetwood was. Either model used fair amounts of premium gas, but that still didn't concern most Cadillac buyers. Amazingly, de Ville's base price was unchanged for '94 at $32,990; the Concours started little higher, a reasonable $36,950.

With all this, many felt Cadillac had worked minor miracles with the de Ville/Concours, so the division was doubtless dismayed to see sales go down instead of up. The '94 loss wasn't huge—about 10,000 units for the model year to just over 120,000—but calendar-year output dropped 20,000 units between '94 and '95 to around 111,000.

And to GM's undoubted frustration, the downward trend continued into the new millennium, with sales and production declining most every year through 2001. In a way, this was curious. The '92 Seville and Eldorado and '94 DeVille represented solid technical and design progress, and Cadillac was planning bold new initiatives intended to further defend against unprecedented competition, chiefly from foreign makes but also a suddenly and surprisingly resurgent Lincoln. Yet somehow, Cadillac couldn't put together a winning formula.

There were several problems, starting with a stale image. Journalists by now liked to quip that Cadillac buyers were typically "somewhere between 60 and death," meaning the make wasn't appealing to the younger upscale trend-setters who preferred BMWs, Mercedes, and Toyota's upstart Lexuses for their superior workmanship, cachet, and performance. And once customers are lost, they're awfully hard to win back. GM compounded this problem with "brand management," attempting to win sales more by clever marketing than imaginative design or superior quality. Though Cadillac did pioneer several praiseworthy innovations in the late '90s and began exploring new markets, the efforts were often too little, too late. As a result, the division's calendar-year sales plunged nearly 23 percent between 1995 and '99, and were down to around 130,500 by 2001. After decades as America's luxury leader, Cadillac was a mere also-ran.

A perfect symbol of Cadillac's plight was Eldorado, which languished with no further change of consequence before being summarily dropped after the 2002 model run. To be sure, demand for big luxury coupes had been withering since the early '90s—enough to claim Lincoln's Mark VIII after 1998—yet the Eldorado returned each year as one of the old-fogey cars

135

# Cadillac

that Cadillac said it wanted to get away from. What Cadillac really wanted was to attract younger buyers without turning off its older customers, but it ended up satisfying neither group entirely.

Still, Eldorado was hardly ignored in its later years. Model-year '96, for example, introduced optional "Rainsense" wipers that automatically activated when sensors detected moisture on the windshield (recalling a certain 1958 Eldo show car). For '97, the sporty ETC added a new Continuously Variable Road Sensing Suspension (CVRSS), which largely involved shock absorbers that automatically adjusted firmness according to input from sensors on road speed, wheel movement, steering angle and so forth. The '98 ETC introduced "Stabilitrak," Cadillac's new antiskid system. Also standard for that year's Seville STS and later standard or optional for other front-drive Cadillacs, Stabilitrak took the CVRSS idea a step further, using sensor input to brake either or both front wheels to keep the car on its intended path—a great boon for "dynamic" safety. Curiously, though, Eldorado would never get the "passive" safety benefit of front side airbags like other Caddys. However, the '99s did share an exclusive with Seville in optional "active" power front seats. These provided a gentle message via small powered rollers in the cushion and backrest, plus a series of air bladders that periodically inflated and deflated. The idea was to relieve pressure points that could induce body aches on long trips, and it worked tolerably well.

But creature comforts and moderate year-to-year price changes couldn't halt Eldorado's steady slide toward oblivion. By 2002, volume was only about a third of what it was a decade before—under 10,500 units. Approximately 1600 were Eldorado Collector Series (ECS) cars, which had the usual "Collector Edition" badges and extra trim, plus an exhaust system tuned to mimic the original 1953 Eldorado. With Eldorado's passing went a hallowed Cadillac name that's not likely to be revived, the division having decided that future models will have "letter" names like ETC or, as on post-1999 base Eldorados, ESC (Eldorado Sport Coupe).

Seville, the "international" Cadillac, retained its new-for-'92 design only through 1997, when the Continuously Variable Road Sensing Suspension became standard for the base SLS as well as the sporty STS. The latter was further upgraded for '97 with standard Stabilitrak, and both Sevilles offered GM's new OnStar communications system as a dealer-installed option. Using a cellular phone link to a satellite-based navigation system and a 24-hour staffed operations center, OnStar could provide "live" route and location assistance, track a stolen car, even remotely open the doors should you lock yourself out. The system would also automatically summon emergency help if the airbags deployed in an accident. Most people found OnStar much easier to use than the video-type in-car navigation systems then coming into vogue, and its emergency services were unique. OnStar eventually became a semi-independent company whose basic hardware and services, both steadily improved, would spread to other GM divisions and even a few other automakers. But Cadillac offered it first on '97 Sevilles, DeVilles, and Eldorados.

Seville base prices were trimmed $2500-$3000 for '97 in an effort to spark sales, but model-year production disappointed at just over 45,000. Even more disappointing, output fell nearly 11,000 units for '98 despite a full redesign. It should have gone up. Notwithstanding cautiously evolutionary styling and carry-over powertrains, the '98 was the best Seville yet. Built on a new G-car platform, the stiffest in GM history, it gained 1.2 inches in wheelbase, yet stood 3.1 inches shorter overall. The result was a roomier yet tighter-handling Seville that ceded little, if anything, to comparable import rivals in performance,

1997 Seville Touring Sedan (STS)

1997 de Ville four-door sedan

1999 Seville Touring Sedan (STS)

2000 de Ville DHS four-door sedan

2000 de Ville DHS four-door sedan

dynamic ability, ride, comfort, and luxury.

Audaciously, Cadillac earmarked 20 percent of Seville production for a special model to be sold in Europe, a bid to establish itself as a true "world-class" competitor; there was even a right-hand-drive STS for Britain. Yet despite being the most un-American Cadillac ever, the Seville bombed in Europe, judged unacceptably big and thirsty for local conditions and lacking the build quality of BMW and Mercedes. Said Britain's CAR magazine in November 2001: "The STS is massive, brash and worryingly vague to drive. [Its] V-8 engine nice, but the rest of the experience feels like a bad copy of a Lexus LS . . . Owning this car is a sign of terminally bad taste."

Back home, Seville volume recovered to near 42,500 for 1999, but shrank by nearly 8000 units in 2000 before thudding to just over 28,000 for '01. And more's the pity. Judged on its own merits, this Seville was a darn good car. It just wasn't quite as good as Cadillac needed it to be.

The same can be said for Catera, which also aimed at giving Cadillac international credibility, only in the even more-competitive "near luxury" class. The approach was the opposite of the G-based Seville's, Catera being basically a upscale "Cadillac-ized" version of the 1995-vintage Opel Omega from GM's German subsidiary. It was even built in Germany, allowing Cadillac to claim genuine European breeding. And indeed, Catera seemed to have all the right stuff for a modern sports sedan: trim size, an efficient 3.0-liter twincam V-6, all-independent suspension, tasteful design, and full-house equipment. It even dared depart from other contemporary Caddys in being rear-wheel drive. Trouble was, Catera was rather heavier than rivals BMW 3-Series and Mercedes C-Class, while being relatively short on power. To make matters worse, it didn't offer a manual transmission as a "proper" Eurosedan should. Initial advertising strained at youth appeal, using a cartoon duck and the tag line "Catera is the Cadillac that zigs," but critics dismissed the campaign as ineffective and rather juvenile, given Cadillac's aims. Later ads downplayed the duck, and a year-2000 update ushered in a more-serious Catera Sport with bigger wheels and tires, rear spoiler, firmer suspension and, belatedly, front side airbags. But despite this, plus a couple of interim price cuts and attractive lease deals, Catera never really caught on. Sales peaked in '98 at over 30,000, dropped below 15,000 the following model year, then limped along in the 12,000-16,000 area through 2001. Catera then vanished in favor of a new home-grown entry-level Cadillac, which will be covered in detail shortly.

The full-size DeVille was Cadillac's one real success in the late '90s, scoring over 100,000 sales each model year (except '95) through 1999. Thoughtful yearly improvements played their part. Optional OnStar arrived for 1997, when a discreet facelift omitted rear fender skirts, allowing a wider rear track for more-stable handling. Also new that year was a luxury D'Elegance model priced between the base sedan and the sporty Concours. For '98, the Concours' standard Stabilitrak was made optional for other DeVilles. A standard tip computer and optional massaging front seats were added for '99.

DeVille was then redesigned for 2000 on the Seville's capable G-car platform, yet sales dropped below 100,000 in another reversal that was hard to understand. The new DeVille not only looked trimmer, it was, giving up two inches in width and length but adding 1.5 inches in wheelbase, again for more interior space. Three models continued at surprisingly little-changed prices. D'Elegance was retitled DHS (for "DeVille High-luxury Sedan"), while Concours became the DTS ("DeVille Touring Sedan"). All boasted standard OnStar, front side airbags, newly available rear torso side airbags, plus ever-pleasing Northstar power. New LED taillamps were also added. These lit faster than traditional incandescent bulbs—a change that Cadillac said might preclude a rear-end crunch. The DHS was a near limousine. Rear passengers were coddled with heated seats, power lumbar adjustment, rear and side sunshades, and illuminated vanity mirrors. High-tech options abounded for DHS and DTS, including a touch-screen navigation system, an ultrasonic warning system to signal the presence of obstacles when backing up, and an industry first called Night Vision. The last, employing infrared technology proven in the Persian Gulf War, used a grille-mounted camera to detect the heat signatures

2000 Catera Sport four-door sedan

2001 de Ville DTS four-door sedan

2002 Escalade four-door wagon

2003 CTS four-door sedan

of objects beyond headlight range, which were projected as a "virtual" image onto the windshield near driver eye level. No other car offered anything like it, and though not a popular option at a hefty $2000, Night Vision represented the sort of technical innovation that had served Cadillac so well in the '50s and '60s.

But even without such gizmos, the 2000 DeVille was mighty impressive. Even the base model offered adroitly balanced ride and handling, and Motor Trend praised the DTS as "a technological tour de force, an efficient, elegant, and uniquely American approach to fine motoring and a true Cadillac." So why did sales drop? It certainly wasn't for lack of trying on the corporation's part.

By this point, though, Cadillac had charted a new course for a new century, yet another effort to regain former greatness. The master plan was slow to gel, but eventually came to include a new design signature called "Art & Science" for its hard, angular lines that were meant to look as if they'd come from a computer, not a stylist's hand. Cadillac also bowed to market trends by issuing its first truck, the 1999 Escalade, an upscale clone of the posh GMC Denali sport-utility wagon. Significantly, a redesigned 2001 Escalade brought the new design theme to Cadillac showrooms. Following for '02 was the similarly styled Escalade EXT, a luxury version of the multipurpose Chevrolet Avalanche four-door SUV/pickup. Most surprising of all, perhaps, was the new two-seat roadster Cadillac planned for 2003. Called XLR, it promised to be far more exciting than the old Allanté, being a sister to a new-generation Corvette and patterned on the striking (if controversial) 1999 Evoq showmobile. Other turn-of-millennium concepts like the Imaj sedan and Vizon "sport wagon" suggest Cadillac will continue to explore new ideas and new markets.

Meantime, the division takes another crack at the premium compact sedan with the 2003 CTS—"Cadillac Touring Sedan." Far more ambitious than the Catera it replaces, the U.S.-built CTS introduces the significant rear-drive Sigma platform destined for the next-generation Seville and several other future GM cars. Power comes from a larger, more-powerful version of Catera's V-6, but CTS offers manual transmission as well as automatic, and both are five-speed units, Cadillac's first. Engineers spent much time tuning the chassis on Germany's demanding Nürburgring circuit, and early reviews found little lacking in the handling department, especially with the firmer damping and 17-inch wheel/tire package available in the Luxury Sport option. The one debatable element is the bold "A&S" styling. Even so, Consumer Guide® initially judged CTS "an upper-echelon driving machine . . . a solid and sporty sedan [that] delivers good near-luxury value, listing for around $36,000 popularly equipped . . . There's more here than meets the eye."

That may also be true for Cadillac and all of GM. It's worth noting that the CTS debuted soon after Robert Lutz, the hard-charging "car guy" who masterminded Chrysler's early-'90s revival, was recruited as GM "product czar" and was then quickly named chairman of the company's North American unit. While one man cannot summon the future, the mere presence of an executive like Lutz implied GM was finally getting serious about building cars and trucks with real spirit, high style, and genuine quality, just like the glory days when GM so dominated the industry. While the task won't be easy in today's vastly different world, it is achievable. We sincerely hope they succeed.

## Specifications

### 1930

**353 Eight (wb 140.0)—11,005 built**

| | Wght | Price | Prod |
|---|---|---|---|
| *Fisher:* | | | |
| cpe 2P | 4,940 | 3,295 | — |
| conv cpe 2P | 4,845 | 3,595 | — |
| cpe 5P | 4,930 | 3,595 | — |
| town sdn 5P | 5,025 | 3,495 | — |
| sdn 5P | 5,055 | 3,695 | — |
| sdn 7P | 5,155 | 3,795 | — |
| Imperial sdn 7P | 5,195 | 3,995 | — |
| | | | |
| *Fleetwood:* | | | |
| rdstr 2P | 4,610 | 3,450 | — |
| sdn 5P | 5,135 | 4,195 | — |
| sdn cab 5P | 5,185 | 4,245 | — |
| Imperial sdn 5P | 5,205 | 4,395 | — |
| Imperial cab 5P | 5,225 | 4,445 | — |
| sdn 7P | 5,265 | 4,295 | — |
| Imperial sdn 7P | 5,305 | 4,595 | — |
| sdnt 5P | 5,055 | 4,500 | — |
| sdnt 4P | 5,055 | 4,595 | — |
| phtn A/W 4P | 4,975 | 4,700 | — |
| town cab | 5,215 | 4,995 | — |
| town cab "Fleetmont" | 5,135 | 5,145 | — |
| town cab "Fleetcrest" | 5,135 | 5,145 | — |
| Limo b'ham | 5,305 | 5,145 | — |

**370 Twelve (wb 140.0; 7P-143.0)—5,725 built (1930-31)**

| | Wght | Price | Prod |
|---|---|---|---|
| *Fisher:* | | | |
| rdstr 2P | 4,910 | 3,945 | — |
| phtn 5P | 4,950 | 4,055 | — |
| A/W phtn 5P | 5,290 | 4,895 | — |
| cpe 2P | 5,035 | 3,795 | — |
| conv cpe 2P | 5,005 | 4,045 | — |
| cpe 5P | 5,055 | 3,895 | — |
| sdn 5P | 5,215 | 3,895 | — |
| town sdn 5P | 5,230 | 3,945 | — |
| sdn 7P | 5,345 | 4,195 | — |
| Imperial sdn 7P | 5,420 | 4,345 | — |
| touring 7P | 5,005 | 4,295 | — |
| | | | |
| *Fleetwood:* | | | |
| sdn 5P | 5,350 | 4,995 | — |
| Imperial sdn 5P | 5,420 | 5,200 | — |
| sdn cab 5P | 5,400 | 5,095 | — |
| Imperial cab 5P | 5,440 | 5,300 | — |
| sdn 7P | 5,480 | 5,075 | — |
| Imperial sdn 7P | 5,520 | 5,275 | — |
| town cab 5P | 5,430 | 5,750 | — |
| town cab 5P CQ | 5,350 | 5,800 | — |
| limo b'ham 7P | 5,520 | 5,800 | — |

**Sixteen (wb 148.0)—3,250 built (1930-31)**

| | | Wght | Price | Prod |
|---|---|---|---|---|
| 4100 | *Madam X:* | | | |
| 4108C | Imperial landau cab 5P | 5,925 | — | 4 |

# Cadillac

| Sixteen (wb 148.0) | | Wght | Price | Prod |
|---|---|---|---|---|
| 4130 | Imperial sdn 5P | 5,905 | 7,300 | 17 |
| 4130S | sdn 5P | 5,835 | 6,950 | 49 |
| 4155 | Imperial cab 5P | 5,925 | 7,350 | 10 |
| 4155S | sdn cabriolet 5P | 5,885 | 7,125 | 7 |
| 4155C | Imperial landau cab 5P | 5,925 | — | 5 |
| 4155SC | landau sdn cab 5P | 5,885 | — | 2 |
| 4161 | Imperial club sdn 5P | 5,725 | — | 1 |
| 4161S | club sdn 5P | 5,655 | 6,950 | 43 |
| 4175 | Imperial sdn 7P | 6,005 | 7,525 | 110 |
| 4175S | sdn 7P | 5,965 | 7,225 | 47 |
| *4200 series:* | | | | |
| 4200 | stationary sdn cab 7P | — | — | 1 |
| 4206 | stationary cpe cab 2P | — | — | 1 |
| 4207 | stationary cpe cab 2P | — | — | 3 |
| 4208 | Imperial cab 5P | 5,885 | — | 7 |
| 4212 | transformable town cab 5P | 6,005 | 8,750 | 6 |
| 4212C | transformable town cab CQ 5P | 6,005 | — | 1 |
| 4220 | 4121C w/leather roof | 6,006 | 8,750 | 9 |
| 4220B | 4212C w/painted roof | 6,005 | — | 1 |
| 4225 | 4212C SQ | 6,005 | 8,750 | 6 |
| 4225C | 4212C CQ | 6,005 | — | 1 |
| 4235 | conv cpe 2P | 5,655 | 6,900 | 94 |
| 4257A | touring 5P | — | — | 1 |
| 4257H | touring 7P | — | — | 1 |
| 4260 | phtn 5P | — | 6,500 | 85 |
| 4260A | phtn 5p | — | — | 1 |
| 4262 | Imperial cab 7P | — | — | 1 |
| 4264 | transformable town b'ham 5P | 6,005 | 9,200 | 4 |
| 4264B | transformable town b'ham 5P | 6,005 | 9,700 | 6 |
| 4275 | Imperial sdn 7P | 6,005 | 6,525 | 1 |
| 4275C | Imperial Lnd sdn 7P | 6,005 | 7,525 | 2 |
| 4276 | cpe 2P | 5,750 | 6,850 | 70 |
| 4280 | A/W phtn 4P | 5,675 | 7,350 | 8 |
| 4285 | A/W spt cab 5P | — | — | 2 |
| 4291 | transformable limo b'ham 7P | 6,005 | 8,750 | 14 |
| *4300 series:* | | | | |
| 4302 | rdstr 2P | 5,310 | 5,350 | 105 |
| 4312 | transformable town cab 5P | — | 6,525 | 24 |
| 4320 | transformable town cab 7P Q/W | — | 7,150 | 25 |
| 4325 | transformable town cab 7P SQ | — | 7,150 | 35 |
| 4325C | transformable CQ | — | — | 3 |
| 4330 | Imperial sdn 5P | 5,905 | 6,300 | 50 |
| 4330S | sdn 5P | 5,835 | 5,950 | 394 |
| 4335 | conv cpe 2P | 5,655 | 5,900 | 100 |
| 4355 | Imperial cab 5P | 5,925 | 6,350 | 52 |
| 4355S | sdn cab 5P | 5,885 | 6,125 | 81 |
| 4355C | Imperial landau cab 5P | — | — | 1 |
| 4361 | Imperial club sdn 5P | — | — | 2 |
| 4361S | club sdn 5P | 5,725 | 5,950 | 258 |
| 4375 | Imperial sdn 7P | 6,005 | 6,525 | 438 |
| 4375S | sdn 7P | 5,965 | 6,225 | 501 |
| 4375C | Imperial landau sdn 7P | — | — | 2 |
| 4376 | cpe 2P | 5,750 | 5,800 | 98 |
| 4380 | A/W phtn 4P | — | 6,650 | 250 |
| 4381 | cpe 5P | 5,740 | 5,950 | 98 |
| 4391 | transformable limo b'ham 7P | 6,005 | 7,150 | 30 |
| *Misc. Fisher:* | | | | |
| 30-152 | town sdn 5P | — | — | 3 |
| 30-158 | cpe 2P | — | — | 3 |
| 30-158 | sdn 5P | — | — | 5 |
| 30-168 | conv cpe 2p | — | — | 17 |

| Sixteen (wb 148.0) | | Wght | Price | Prod |
|---|---|---|---|---|
| 30-172 | cpe 5P | — | — | 2 |
| 2901LX | sdn 7P | — | — | 1 |
| 2951LX | sdn 7P | — | — | 1 |
| 30-X | sdn test car 7P | — | — | 1 |
| LX 2905 | town sdn 5P | — | — | 1 |
| LX 2913 | cpe 5P | — | — | 1 |
| *Misc. Fleetwood:* | | | | |
| 3289B | transformable town cab 7P | — | — | 1 |
| 3981 | sdnt cab 4P | — | 6,450 | 1 |
| 3991 | transformable limo b'ham | — | — | 1 |
| 4412 | transformable town cab 5P | — | — | 1 |
| 4476 | cpe 2P | 5,750 | 5,800 | 11 |
| 2950X | special sdn 7P | — | — | 1 |
| | Misc. chassis and unknown | — | — | 37 |

| 1930 Engines | bore × stroke | bhp | availability |
|---|---|---|---|
| V-8, 353.0 | 3.63 × 4.94 | 95 | S-Eight |
| V-12, 368.0 | 3.13 × 4.00 | 135 | S-Twelve |
| V-16, 452.6 | 3.00 × 4.00 | 165 | S-Sixteen |

Editor's note: Cadillac Sixteens obviously appeared in a very broad number of body styles. This analysis, the clearest ever published, appears in *Sixteen Cylinder Motorcars* by Roy S. Schneider, Heritage House, 430 W. Longden Avenue, Arcadia, California 91006, with production figures researched from company records by Carl L. Steig.

## 1931

| 355 Eight (wb 134.0)—10,709 built | Wght | Price | Prod |
|---|---|---|---|
| rdstr 2P | 4,355 | 2,845 | — |
| phtn 5P | 4,395 | 2,945 | — |
| cpe 2P | 4,480 | 2,695 | — |
| conv cpe 2P | 4,450 | 2,945 | — |
| cpe 5P | 4,500 | 2,795 | — |
| sdn 4d 5P | 4,660 | 2,795 | — |
| town sdn 5P | 4,675 | 2,845 | — |
| A/W phtn 5P | 4,685 | 3,795 | — |
| sdn 4d 7P | 4,760 | 2,945 | — |
| Imperial sdn 7P | 4,835 | 3,095 | — |
| touring 7P | 4,450 | 3,195 | — |

**370A Twelve (wb 140.0; 7P-143.0)(see 1930)**

**Sixteen (wb 148.0)(see 1930)**

| 1931 Engines | bore × stroke | bhp | availability |
|---|---|---|---|
| V-8, 353.0 | 3.63 × 4.94 | 95 | S-Eight |
| V-12, 368.0 | 3.13 × 4.00 | 135 | S-Twelve |
| V-16, 452.6 | 3.00 × 4.00 | 165 | S-Sixteen |

## 1932

| 355B Eight (wb 134.0)—2,693 built* | Wght | Price | Prod |
|---|---|---|---|
| rdstr 2P | 4,635 | 2,895 | — |
| cpe 2P | 4,705 | 2,795 | — |
| conv cpe 2P | 4,675 | 2,945 | — |
| sdn 5P | 4,885 | 2,895 | — |

| 355B Eight (wb 140.0) | Wght | Price | Prod |
|---|---|---|---|
| *Fisher:* | | | |
| phtn 5P | 4,700 | 2,995 | |
| Special phtn 5P | 4,750 | 3,095 | |
| spt phtn 5P | 4,800 | 3,245 | |
| A/W phtn 5P | 5,070 | 3,495 | |
| cpe 5P | 4,715 | 2,995 | |
| special sdn 5P | 4,965 | 3,045 | |

# Cadillac

| 355B Eight (wb 140.0) | Wght | Price | Prod |
|---|---|---|---|
| town sdn 5P | 4,980 | 3,095 | — |
| sdn 7P | 5,110 | 3,145 | — |
| Imperial sdn 7P | 5,150 | 3,295 | — |
| *Fleetwood*: | | | |
| sdn 5P | 4,965 | 3,395 | — |
| town cpe 5P | 4,915 | 3,395 | — |
| sdn 7P | 5,110 | 3,545 | — |
| limo 7P | 5,150 | 3,745 | — |
| town cab 5P | 4,990 | 4,095 | — |
| town cab 7P | 5,100 | 4,245 | — |
| limo b'ham 7P | 5,100 | 4,245 | — |
| **370B Twelve (wb 134.0)—1,709 built*** | | | |
| rdstr 2P | 4,870 | 3,595 | — |
| cpe 2P | 5,085 | 3,495 | — |
| conv cpe 2P | 5,060 | 3,645 | — |
| sdn 5P | 5,175 | 3,595 | — |
| **370B Twelve (wb 140.0)** | | | |
| *Fisher*: | | | |
| phtn 5P | 5,240 | 3,695 | — |
| Special phtn 5P | 5,290 | 3,795 | — |
| spt phtn 5P | 5,340 | 3,945 | — |
| A/W phtn 5P | 5,385 | 4,195 | — |
| cpe 5P | 5,220 | 3,695 | — |
| Special sdn 5P | 5,345 | 3,745 | — |
| town sdn 5P | 5,370 | 3,795 | — |
| sdn 7P | 5,460 | 3,845 | — |
| Imperial sdn 7P | 5,500 | 3,995 | — |
| *Fleetwood*: | | | |
| town cpe 5P | 5,225 | 4,095 | — |
| sdn 5P | 5,345 | 4,095 | — |
| sdn 7P | 5,460 | 4,245 | — |
| limo 7P | 5,500 | 4,445 | — |
| town cab 5P | 5,380 | 4,795 | — |
| town cab 7P | 5,580 | 4,945 | — |
| limo b'ham 7P | 5,580 | 4,945 | — |
| **452B Sixteen (wb 143.0)—296 built**** | | | |
| rdstr 2P | 5,065 | 4,595 | 3 |
| cpe 2P | 5,530 | 4,495 | — |
| conv cpe 2P | 5,505 | 4,645 | — |
| sdn 5P | 5,625 | 4,595 | — |
| **452B Sixteen (wb 149.0)** | | | |
| *Fisher*: | | | |
| phtn 5P | 5,400 | 4,695 | 1 |
| Special phtn 5P | 5,450 | 4,795 | 3 |
| spt phtn 5P | 5,500 | 4,945 | 2 |
| A/W phtn 5P | 5,525 | 5,195 | 13 |
| *Fleetwood*: | | | |
| town cpe 5P | 5,605 | 5,095 | 24 |
| sdn 5P | 5,735 | 5,095 | — |
| conv cpe 5p | 5,505 | 4,645 | 1 |
| sdn 7P | 5,865 | 5,245 | 47 |
| limo 7P | 5,935 | 5,445 | — |
| Imperial cabriolet sedan | — | — | 4 |
| Imperial landaulette | — | — | 1 |
| town cab 5P | 5,775 | 5,795 | 4 |
| town cab 7P | 5,935 | 5,945 | 2 |
| limo b'ham 7P | 5,935 | 5,945 | 7 |

* incl. 140.0-in wb; ** incl. 149.0-in wb.

| 1932 Engines | bore × stroke | bhp | availability |
|---|---|---|---|
| V-8, 353.0 | 3.63 × 4.94 | 115 | S-Eights |
| V-12, 368.0 | 3.13 × 4.00 | 135 | S-Twelves |
| V-16, 452.6 | 3.00 × 4.00 | 165 | S-Sixteens |

Note: weights listed for five wire wheels, all models.

## 1933

| 355C Eight (wb 134.0)—2,906 built* | Wght | Price | Prod |
|---|---|---|---|
| rdstr 2P | 4,695 | 2,795 | — |
| cpe 2P | 4,855 | 2,695 | — |
| conv cpe 2P | 4,825 | 2,845 | — |
| **355 C Eight (wb 140.0)** | | | |
| *Fisher*: | | | |
| phtn 5P | 4,865 | 2,895 | — |
| A/W phtn 5P | 5,110 | 3,395 | — |
| cpe 5P | 4,850 | 2,895 | — |
| sdn 5P | 5,000 | 2,895 | — |
| town sdn 5P | 5,060 | 2,995 | — |
| sdn 7P | 5,105 | 3,045 | — |
| Imperial sdn 7P | 5,140 | 3,195 | — |
| *Fleetwood*: | | | |
| sdn 5P | 5,000 | 3,295 | — |
| sdn 7P | 5,105 | 3,445 | — |
| limo 7P | 5,140 | 3,645 | — |
| town cab 5P | 5,010 | 3,395 | — |
| town cab 7P | 5,200 | 4,145 | — |
| limo b'ham 7P | 5,225 | 4,145 | — |
| **370C Twelve (wb 134.0)—952 built*** | | | |
| rdstr 2P | 5,030 | 3,495 | — |
| cpe 2P | 5,165 | 3,395 | — |
| conv cpe 2P | 5,125 | 3,545 | — |
| **370C Twelve (wb 140.0)** | | | |
| *Fisher*: | | | |
| phtn 5P | 5,200 | 3,595 | — |
| A/W phtn 5P | 5,405 | 4,095 | — |
| cpe 5P | 5,200 | 3,595 | — |
| sdn 5P | 5,335 | 3,595 | — |
| town sdn 5P | 5,385 | 3,695 | — |
| sdn 7P | 5,440 | 3,745 | — |
| Imperial sdn 7P | 5,500 | 3,895 | — |
| *Fleetwood*: | | | |
| sdn 5P | 5,335 | 3,995 | — |
| sdn 7P | 5,440 | 4,145 | — |
| limo 7P | 5,500 | 4,345 | — |
| town cab 5P | 5,375 | 4,695 | — |
| town cab 7P | 5,575 | 4,845 | — |
| limo b'ham 7P | 5,575 | 4,845 | — |
| **452C Sixteen (wb 149.0)—125 built** | | | |
| *Fleetwood*: | | | |
| A/W phtn 5P | 6,110 | 8,000 | — |
| conv cpe 5P | 5,910 | 7,500 | 2 |
| town cpe 5P | 6,000 | 6,250 | 4 |
| Imperial cab 5P | 6,100 | 5,540 | 1 |
| sdn 5P | 6,070 | 6,250 | — |
| sdn 7P | 6,200 | 6,400 | — |
| limo 7P | 6,270 | 6,600 | — |
| town cab 5P | 6,110 | 6,850 | — |
| town cab 7P | 6,270 | 6,850 | — |
| limo b'ham 7P | 6,300 | 6,850 | — |
| Sport phaeton | — | — | 1 |
| Imperial town sdn | — | — | 1 |

* incl. 140-in. wb.

# Cadillac

| 1933 Engines | bore × stroke | bhp | availability |
|---|---|---|---|
| V-8, 353.0 | 3.38 × 4.94 | 115 | S-Eights |
| V-12, 368.0 | 3.13 × 4.00 | 135 | S-Twelves |
| V-16, 452.0 | 3.00 × 4.00 | 165 | S-Sixteens |

## 1934

### 355D Eight Series 10 (wb 128.0)—2,015 built

| | | Wght | Price | Prod |
|---|---|---|---|---|
| 702 | town sdn 5P | 4,735 | 2,695 | — |
| 709 | sdn 5P | 4,715 | 2,645 | — |
| 718 | conv cpe 2P | 4,515 | 2,645 | — |
| 721 | conv sdn 5P | 4,750 | 2,845 | — |
| 722 | town cpe 5P | 4,630 | 2,695 | — |
| 728 | cpe 2P | 4,550 | 2,545 | — |

### 355D Eight Series 20 (wb 136.0)—2,729 built

| 652 | town sdn 5P | 4,815 | 2,895 | — |
|---|---|---|---|---|
| 659 | sdn 5P | 4,825 | 2,845 | — |
| 662 | sdn 7P | 4,945 | 2,995 | — |
| 663 | Imperial sdn 7P | 4,970 | 3,145 | — |
| 668 | conv cpe 2P | 4,625 | 2,845 | — |
| 671 | conv sdn 5P | 4,860 | 3,045 | — |
| 678 | cpe 2P | 4,660 | 2,745 | — |

### 355D Eight Series 30 (wb 146.0)—336 built

*Fleetwood (straight windshield):*

| 6030FL | Imperial cab 5P | 5,500 | 3,895 | — |
|---|---|---|---|---|
| 6030S | sdn 5P | 5,465 | 3,495 | — |
| 6033S | town sdn 5P | 5,415 | 3,545 | — |
| 6075 | limo 7P | 5,580 | 3,845 | — |
| 6075FL | Imperial cab 7P | 5,580 | 4,045 | — |
| 6075S | sdn 7P | 5,545 | 3,645 | — |

*Fleetwood (mod. V windshield):*

| 5612 | town cab 5P | 5,540 | 5,695 | — |
|---|---|---|---|---|
| 5630FL | Special Imperial cab 5P | 5,500 | 4,345 | — |
| 5630S | Special sdn 5P | 5,465 | 3,945 | — |
| 5625 | town cab 7P | 5,650 | 5,795 | — |
| 5633S | Special town sdn 5P | 5,415 | 3,995 | — |
| 5635 | conv cpe 4P | 5,115 | 4,245 | — |
| 5675 | Special limo 7P | 5,580 | 4,295 | — |
| 5675FL | Imperial cab 7P | 5,580 | 4,495 | — |
| 5675S | Special sdn 7P | 5,545 | 4,095 | — |
| 5676 | cpe 4P | 5,150 | 4,095 | — |
| 5680 | Imperial conv sdn 5P | 5,465 | 4,495 | — |
| 5691 | limo b'ham 7P | 5,580 | 5,695 | — |

### 370D Twelve Series 40 (wb 146.0)—683 built

*Fleetwood (straight windshield):*

| 6130FL | Imperial cab 5P | 5,765 | 4,595 | — |
|---|---|---|---|---|
| 6130S | sdn 5P | 5,735 | 4,195 | — |
| 6133S | town sdn 5P | 5,700 | 4,245 | — |
| 6175 | limo 7P | 5,790 | 4,545 | — |
| 6175FL | Imperial cab 7P | 5,790 | 4,745 | — |
| 6175S | sdn 7P | 5,760 | 4,345 | — |

*Fleetwood (V windshield):*

| 5712 | town cab 5P | 5,990 | 6,395 | — |
|---|---|---|---|---|
| 5725 | town cab 7P | 6,040 | 6,495 | — |
| 5730FL | Special Imperial cab 5P | 5,765 | 5,045 | — |
| 5730S | Special sdn 5P | 5,735 | 4,645 | — |
| 5733S | Special town sdn 5P | 5,700 | 4,695 | — |
| 5735 | conv cpe 4P | 5,485 | 4,945 | — |
| 5775 | Special limo 7P | 5,790 | 4,995 | — |
| 5775FL | Special Imperial cab 7P | 5,790 | 5,195 | — |

### 370D Twelve Series 40

| | | Wght | Price | Prod |
|---|---|---|---|---|
| 5775S | Special sdn 7P | 5,760 | 4,795 | — |
| 5776 | cpe 4P | 5,520 | 4,795 | — |
| 5780 | Imperial conv sdn 5P | 5,800 | 5,195 | — |
| 5791 | limo b'ham 7P | 6,030 | 6,395 | — |

### 452D Sixteen Series 60 (wb 154.0)—56 built

*Fleetwood (straight windshield):*

| 6275 | limo 7P | 6,210 | 7,300 | 10 |
|---|---|---|---|---|
| 6275S | sdn 7P | 6,190 | 7,100 | 5 |

*Fleetwood (V windshield):*

| 5825 | town cab 7P | 6,390 | 9,250 | 4 |
|---|---|---|---|---|
| 5830 | Imperial sdn 5P | — | — | 1 |
| 5833 | Imperial town sdn 5P | — | — | 1 |
| 5833S | town sdn 5P | 6,085 | 7,350 | 2 |
| 5835 | conv cpe 2P | 5,900 | 7,900 | 2 |
| 5875 | limo 7P | 6,210 | 7,950 | 9 |
| 5875S | Special sdn 7P | 6,190 | 7,750 | 5 |
| 5875FL | Special Imperial sdn 7P | — | 8,150 | 1 |
| 5876 | stationary cpe 2P | 5,840 | 7,750 | 5 |
| 5880 | Imperial conv sdn 5P | 6,100 | 8,150 | 5 |
| 5880S | conv sdn 5P | — | 7,950 | 1 |
| 5885 | conv cpe 5P | — | 8,150 | 1 |
| 5899 | Aero cpe 5P | — | 8,150 | 3 |
| — | Chassis | — | — | 1 |

| 1934 Engines | bore × stroke | bhp | availability |
|---|---|---|---|
| V-8, 353.0 | 3.38 × 4.94 | 130 | S-Eights |
| V-12, 368.0 | 3.13 × 4.00 | 150 | S-Twelves |
| V-16, 452.0 | 3.00 × 4.00 | 185 | S-Sixteens |

## 1935

### 355D Eight Series 10 (wb 128.0)—1,130 built

| | | Wght | Price | Prod |
|---|---|---|---|---|
| 702 | town sdn 5P | 4,735 | 2,495 | — |
| 709 | sdn 5P | 4,715 | 2,445 | — |
| 718 | conv cpe 2-4P | 4,515 | 2,445 | — |
| 721 | conv sdn 5P | 4,750 | 2,755 | — |
| 722 | town cpe 5P | 4,630 | 2,495 | — |
| 728 | cpe 2-4P | 4,550 | 2,345 | — |

### 355D Eight Series 20 (wb 136.0)—1,859 built

| 652 | town sdn 5P | 4,815 | 2,695 | — |
|---|---|---|---|---|
| 659 | sdn 5P | 4,825 | 2,645 | — |
| 662 | sdn 7P | 4,945 | 2,995 | — |
| 663 | Imperial sdn 7P | 4,970 | 2,945 | — |
| 668 | conv cpe 2-4P | 3,625 | 2,645 | — |
| 671 | conv sdn 5P | 4,860 | 2,955 | — |
| 678 | cpe 2-4P | 4,660 | 2,545 | — |

### 355D Eight Series 30 (wb 146.0)—220 built

*Fleetwood (straight windshield):*

| 6030FL | Imperial cab | 5,500 | 3,695 | — |
|---|---|---|---|---|
| 6030S | sdn 5P | 5,465 | 2,295 | — |
| 6033S | town sdn 5P | 5,415 | 3,345 | — |
| 6075 | limo 7P | 5,580 | 3,645 | — |
| 6075 FL | Imperial cab 7P | 5,580 | 3,845 | — |
| 6075S | sdn 7P | 5,545 | 3,445 | — |

*Fleetwood (V windshield):*

| 5612 | town cab 5P | 5,540 | 5,495 | — |
|---|---|---|---|---|
| 5625 | town cab 7P | 5,650 | 5,595 | — |
| 5630FL | Special Imperial cab 5P | 5,500 | 4,145 | — |
| 5630S | Special sdn 5P | 5,465 | 3,745 | — |
| 5633S | Special cab sdn 5P | 5,415 | 3,795 | — |

# Cadillac

| 355D Eight Series 30 (wb 146.0) | | Wght | Price | Prod |
|---|---|---|---|---|
| 5635 | conv cpe 4P | 5,115 | 4,045 | — |
| 5675FL | Special Imperial cab 7P | 5,580 | 4,295 | — |
| 5675S | Special sdn 7P | 5,545 | 3,895 | — |
| 5675 | Special limo 7P | 5,580 | 4,095 | — |
| 5676 | cpe 4P | 5,150 | 3,895 | — |
| 5680 | Imperial conv sdn 5P | 5,465 | 4,295 | — |
| 5691 | limo b'ham 7P | 5,580 | 5,495 | — |

**370D Twelve Series 40 (wb 146.0)—377 built**

*Fleetwood (straight windshield):*

| | | Wght | Price | Prod |
|---|---|---|---|---|
| 6130FL | Imperial cab 5P | 5,765 | 4,395 | — |
| 6130S | sdn 5P | 5,735 | 3,995 | — |
| 6133S | town sdn 5P | 5,700 | 4,045 | — |
| 6175 | limo 7P | 5,790 | 4,345 | — |
| 6175FL | Imperial cab 7P | 5,790 | 4,545 | — |
| 6175S | sdn 7P | 5,760 | 4,145 | — |

*Fleetwood (V windshield):*

| | | Wght | Price | Prod |
|---|---|---|---|---|
| 5712 | town cab 5P | 5,990 | 6,195 | — |
| 5725 | town cab 7P | 6,040 | 6,295 | — |
| 5730FL | Special Imperial cab 5P | 5,765 | 4,845 | — |
| 5730S | Special sdn 5P | 5,735 | 4,445 | — |
| 5733S | Special town sdn 5P | 5,700 | 4,495 | — |
| 5735 | conv cpe 4P | 5,485 | 4,745 | — |
| 5775 | Special limo 7P | 5,790 | 4,795 | — |
| 5775FL | Special Imperial cab 7P | 5,790 | 4,995 | — |
| 5775S | Special sdn 7P | 5,760 | 4,595 | — |
| 5776 | cpe 4P | 5,520 | 4,595 | — |
| 5780 | Imperial conv sdn 5P | 5,800 | 4,995 | — |
| 5791 | limo b'ham 7P | 6,030 | 6,195 | — |

**452D Sixteen Series 60 (wb 154.0)—50 built**

*Fleetwood (straight windshield):*

| | | Wght | Price | Prod |
|---|---|---|---|---|
| 6233S | town sdn 5P | 6,085 | 6,800 | 2 |
| 6275 | limo 7P | 6,210 | 7,100 | 6 |
| 6275S | sdn 7P | 6,190 | 6,900 | 3 |
| 6275B | Imperial sdn 7P | — | — | 2 |
| 6275H3 | limo (extra headroom) 7P | — | — | 1 |

*Fleetwood (V windshield):*

| | | Wght | Price | Prod |
|---|---|---|---|---|
| 5825 | town cab 7P | 6,390 | 9,050 | 2 |
| 5830S | Special sdn 5P | 6,240 | 7,400 | 1 |
| 5833 | Imperial town sdn 5P | — | 8,000 | 2 |
| 5833S | town sdn 5P | 6,085 | 7,450 | 4 |
| 5875 | limo 7P | 6,210 | 7,750 | 15 |
| — | cpe 2p | 5,840 | 7,550 | 2 |
| 5875S | sdn 7P | 6,190 | 7,550 | 2 |
| 5875FL | Imperial cab 7P | 6,100 | 7,950 | 4 |
| 5876 | stationary cpe 2P | 5,840 | 7,550 | 2 |
| 5880 | conv sdn 5P | 6,100 | 7,950 | 4 |
| 5885 | conv cpe 5P | — | 8,150 | 2 |
| 5891B | limo b'ham 7P | — | 8,950 | 1 |
| Chassis | | — | — | 1 |

| 1935 Engines | bore × stroke | bhp | availability |
|---|---|---|---|
| V-8, 353.0 | 3.38 × 4.94 | 130 | S-Eights |
| V-12, 368.0 | 3.13 × 4.00 | 150 | S-Twelves |
| V-16, 452.0 | 3.00 × 4.00 | 185 | S-Sixteens |

## 1936

| Series 60 (wb 121.0)—6,700 built | | Wght | Price | Prod |
|---|---|---|---|---|
| 6019 | touring sdn 5P | 4,010 | 1,695 | — |
| 6067 | conv cpe 2-4P | 3,985 | 1,725 | — |
| 6077 | cpe 2P | 3,830 | 1,645 | — |

| Series 70 (wb 131.0)—2,000 built | | Wght | Price | Prod |
|---|---|---|---|---|
| 7019 | touring sdn 5P | 4,670 | 2,445 | — |
| 7029 | conv sdn 5P | 4,710 | 2,745 | — |
| 7057 | cpe 2P | 4,620 | 2,595 | — |
| 7067 | conv cpe 2-4P | 4,690 | 2,695 | — |

| Series 75 Fleetwood (wb 138.0)—3,227 built | | Wght | Price | Prod |
|---|---|---|---|---|
| 7503 | sdn 7P | 4,885 | 2,795 | — |
| 7509 | sdn 5P | 4,805 | 2,645 | — |
| 7513 | Imperial sdn 7P | 5,045 | 2,995 | — |
| 7519 | touring sdn 5P | 4,805 | 2,645 | — |
| 7523 | touring sdn 7P | 4,885 | 2,795 | — |
| 7529 | conv sdn 5P | 5,040 | 3,395 | — |
| 7519F | formal sdn 5P | 4,805 | 3,395 | — |
| 7533 | Imperial touring sdn 5P | 5,045 | 2,995 | — |
| 7539 | town sdn 5P | 4,840 | 3,145 | — |
| 7543 | town car 7P | 5,115 | 4,445 | — |

| Series 80 Fleetwood (wb 131.0)—250 built | | Wght | Price | Prod |
|---|---|---|---|---|
| 8019 | touring sdn 5P | 4,945 | 3,145 | — |
| 8029 | conv sdn 5P | 4,990 | 3,445 | — |
| 8057 | cpe 2P | 4,690 | 3,295 | — |
| 8067 | conv cpe 2-4P | 4,800 | 3,395 | — |

| Series 85 Fleetwood (wb 138.0)—651 built | | Wght | Price | Prod |
|---|---|---|---|---|
| 8503 | sdn 7P | 5,195 | 3,495 | — |
| 8509 | sdn 5P | 5,115 | 3,345 | — |
| 8513 | Imperial sdn 7P | 5,230 | 3,695 | — |
| 8519 | touring sdn 5P | 5,115 | 3,345 | — |
| 8519F | formal sdn 5P | 5,115 | 4,095 | — |
| 8523 | touring sdn 7P | 5,195 | 3,495 | — |
| 8529 | conv sdn 5P | 5,230 | 4,095 | — |
| 8533 | Imperial touring sdn 7P | 5,230 | 3,695 | — |
| 8539 | town sdn 5P | 5,065 | 3,845 | — |
| 8543 | town car 7P | 5,300 | 5,145 | — |

| Series 90 Fleetwood (wb 154.0)—52 built | | Wght | Price | Prod |
|---|---|---|---|---|
| 5825 | town cab | 6,390 | 8,850 | 1 |
| 5825C | town cab 7P CQ | 6,450 | — | 1 |
| 5830S | Special sdn 5P | — | 7,600 | 1 |
| 5830FL | Special Imperial cab | — | 8,000 | 3 |
| 5833S | town sdn 5P | 6,085 | 7,250 | 3 |
| 5835 | conv cpe 2P | — | 7,900 | 2 |
| 5875 | limo 7P | 6,190 | 7,750 | 24 |
| 5875S | sdn 7P | 6,190 | 7,550 | 2 |
| 5875FL | Imperial cab 7P | 6,210 | 7,850 | 1 |
| 5876 | stationary cpe 2P | — | 7,750 | 1 |
| 5880 | conv sdn 5P | 6,100 | 7,850 | 6 |
| 5899 | Aero cpe 5P | — | 8,150 | 4 |
| — | Chassis | — | 6,250 | 3 |

| 1936 Engines | bore × stroke | bhp | availability |
|---|---|---|---|
| V-8, 322.0 | 3.38 × 4.50 | 125 | S-60 |
| V-8, 346.0 | 3.50 × 4.50 | 135 | S-70, 75 |
| V-12, 368.0 | 3.13 × 2.00 | 150 | S-80, 85 |
| V-16, 452.0 | 3.00 × 4.00 | 185 | S-90 |

## 1937

| Series 60 (wb 124.0)—7,000 built* | | Wght | Price | Prod |
|---|---|---|---|---|
| — | club cpe 2P | — | 1,710 | — |
| 6019 | touring sdn 5P | 3,845 | 1,760 | — |
| 6027 | cpe 2P | 3,710 | 1,655 | — |
| 6049 | conv sdn 5P | 3,885 | 2,120 | — |
| 6067 | conv cpe 2P | 3,745 | 1,790 | — |

| Series 65 (wb 131.0) | | | | |
|---|---|---|---|---|
| 6519 | touring sdn 5P | 4,385 | 2,190 | 2,401 |

# Cadillac

| Series 70 Fleetwood (wb 131.0)—1,001 blt | | Wght | Price | Prod |
|---|---|---|---|---|
| 7019 | touring sdn 5P | 4,420 | 2,695 | — |
| 7029 | conv sdn 5P | 4,460 | 3,060 | — |
| 7057 | spt cpe 2P | 4,285 | 2,905 | — |
| 7067 | conv cpe 2P | 4,325 | 3,005 | — |
| **Series 75 Fleetwood (wb 138.0)—3,227 built*** | | | | |
| 7509F | formal sdn 5P | 4,745 | 3,785 | — |
| 7519 | touring sdn 5P | 4,745 | 2,915 | — |
| 7523 | touring sdn 7P | 4,825 | 3,070 | — |
| 7523S | touring spt sdn 7P | 4,825 | 2,710 | — |
| 7523SL | touring bus sdn 8P | 4,825 | 2,845 | — |
| 7529 | conv sdn 5P | 4,980 | 3,730 | — |
| 7533 | Imperial touring sdn 7P | 4,985 | 3,270 | — |
| 7533S | touring Spl Imperial sdn 7P | 4,985 | 2,910 | — |
| 7533SL | Imperial touring bus sdn 8P | 4,985 | 3,050 | — |
| 7539 | town sdn 5P | 4,780 | 3,425 | — |
| 7543 | town car 7P | 5,055 | 4,855 | — |
| **Series 85 Fleetwood (wb 138.0)—474 built** | | | | |
| 8509F | formal sdn 5P | 5,050 | 4,500 | — |
| 8519 | touring sdn 5P | 5,050 | 3,635 | — |
| 8523 | touring sdn 7P | 5,130 | 3,790 | — |
| 8529 | conv sdn 5P | 5,165 | 4,450 | — |
| 8533 | Imperial touring sdn 7P | 5,165 | 3,990 | — |
| 8539 | town sdn 5P | 5,000 | 4,145 | — |
| 8543 | town car 7P | 5,230 | 5,575 | — |
| **Series 90 (wb 154.0)—49 built** | | | | |
| 5825 | town cab | 6,390 | 9,230 | 2 |
| 5833S | town sdn 5P | 6,085 | 7,595 | 2 |
| 5875 | limo 7P | 6,190 | 7,900 | 24 |
| 5875S | sdn 7P | 6,190 | 7,645 | 2 |
| 5875SF | sdn 7P SQ | 6,200 | — | 1 |
| 5875FL | Imperial cab 7P | 6,210 | 8,155 | 3 |
| 5876 | stationary cpe 2P | 5,840 | 7,745 | 4 |
| 5880 | conv sdn 5P | 6,100 | 8,205 | 5 |
| 5885 | conv cpe 5P | — | 8,150 | 2 |
| 5891 | limo b'ham | — | 9,150 | 1 |
| 5899 | Aero cpe 5P | — | 8,150 | 1 |
| — | Chassis | — | — | 2 |

| 1937 Engines | bore × stroke | bhp | availability |
|---|---|---|---|
| V-8, 346.0 | 3.50 × 4.50 | 135 | S-60, 65, 70, 75 |
| V-12, 368.0 | 3.13 × 4.00 | 150 | S-85 |
| V-16, 452.0 | 3.00 × 4.00 | 185 | S-90 |

* Includes commercials on 160-in. wb; ** Includes commercials on 155-in. wb

## 1938

| Series 60 (wb 124.0) | | Wght | Price | Prod |
|---|---|---|---|---|
| 6119 | sdn 4d | 3,940 | 1,730 | 1,295 |
| 6119 | sdn 4d CKD | — | — | 12 |
| 6127 | cpe 2P | 3,855 | 1,695 | 438 |
| 6149 | conv sdn 5P | 3,980 | 2,215 | 60 |
| 6167 | conv cpe 2P | 3,845 | 1,815 | 145 |
| — | comm chassis (wb 159.0) | — | — | 101 |
| **Series 60 (wb 127.0)** | | | | |
| 6019S | sdn 4d | 4,170 | 2,090 | 3,587 |
| 6019S | sdn 4d CKD | — | — | 108 |
| — | chassis | — | — | 8 |
| **Series 65 (wb 132.0)** | | | | |
| 6519 | sdn 4d | 4,540 | 2,290 | 1,178 |
| 6519F | Imperial div sdn 5P | 4,580 | 2,360 | 110 |
| 6549 | conv sdn 5P | 4,5801 | 2,605 | 110 |

| Series 65 (wb 132.0) | | Wght | Price | Prod |
|---|---|---|---|---|
| — | chassis | — | — | 3 |
| **Series 75 (wb 141.3)** | | | | |
| 7519 | sdn 5P | 4,865 | 3,080 | 475 |
| 7519F | Imperial div sdn 5P | 4,925 | 3,155 | 34 |
| 7523 | sdn 7P | 4,945 | 3,210 | 380 |
| 7523L | bus sdn 7P | 4,945 | 3,105 | 25 |
| 7529 | conv sdn 5P | — | — | 58 |
| 7533 | Imperial sdn 7P | 5,105 | 3,360 | 479 |
| 7533 | Imperial sdn 7P CKD | — | — | 84 |
| 7533F | formal sdn 7P | 5,105 | 3,995 | 40 |
| 7533L | Imperial bus sdn 7P | 5,105 | 3,260 | 25 |
| 7539 | town sdn 5P | 4,900 | 3,635 | 56 |
| 7553 | town car 7P | 5,175 | 5,115 | 17 |
| 7557 | cpe 2P | 4,675 | 3,280 | 52 |
| 7557B | cpe 5P | 4,775 | 3,380 | 42 |
| — | chassis (inc. 8 CKD) | — | — | 24 |
| — | comm chassis (wb 161.0) | — | — | 11 |
| **Series 90 (wb 141.3)** | | | | |
| 9019 | sdn 5P | 5,105 | 5,140 | 43 |
| 9019F | Imperial sdn 5P | 5,165 | 5,215 | 5 |
| 9023 | sdn 7P | 5,185 | 5,270 | 65 |
| 9029 | conv sdn 5P | 5,350 | 6,000 | 13 |
| 9033 | Imperial sdn 7P | 5,345 | 5,420 | 95 |
| 9033F | formal sdn 7P | 5,345 | 6,055 | 17 |
| 9039 | town sdn 5P | 5,140 | 5,695 | 20 |
| 9053 | town car 7P | 5,415 | 7,175 | 11 |
| 9057 | cpe 2P | 4,915 | 5,340 | 11 |
| 9057B | cpe 5P | 5,015 | 5,440 | 8 |
| 9059 | formal sdn 5P | 5,105 | 6,055 | 8 |
| 9067 | conv cpe 2P | 4,905 | 5,440 | 10 |
| 9006 | Presidential limo (wb 161.0) | — | — | 2 |
| — | chassis | — | — | 3 |

| 1938 Engines | bore × stroke | bhp | availability |
|---|---|---|---|
| V-8, 346.0 | 3.50 × 4.50 | 135 | S-60, 65, 70 |
| V-8, 346.0 | 3.50 × 4.50 | 140 | S-75 |
| V-16, 431.0 | 3.25 × 3.25 | 185 | S-90 |

## 1939

| Series 61 (wb 126.0) | | Wght | Price | Prod |
|---|---|---|---|---|
| 6119 | sdn 4d | 3,770 | 1,680 | 3,955 |
| 6119 | sdn 4d CKD | — | — | 196 |
| 6119A | sunroof sdn 4d | — | — | 43 |
| 6119F | Imperial sdn 5P | — | — | 30 |
| 6127 | cpe 2-4P | 3,685 | 1,610 | 1,023 |
| 6129 | conv sdn 5P | 3,810 | 2,170 | 140 |
| 6167 | conv cpe 2-4P | 3,765 | 1,770 | 350 |
| — | comm chassis (wb 156.0) | — | — | 237 |
| **Series Sixty Special (wb 127.0)** | | | | |
| 6019S | sdn 4d | 4,110 | 2,090 | 5,135 |
| 6019S | sdn 4d CKD | — | — | 84 |
| 6019SA | sunroof sdn 4d | — | — | 225 |
| 6019SAF | Imperial sunroof sdn 4d | — | — | 55 |
| — | chassis | — | — | 7 |
| **Series 75 (wb 141.3)** | | | | |
| 7519 | sdn 5P | 4,785 | 2,995 | 543 |
| 7519F | Imperial div sdn 5P | 4,845 | 3,155 | 53 |
| 7523 | sdn 7P | 4,865 | 3,210 | 412 |
| 7523L | bus sdn 7P | 4,865 | 3,105 | 33 |
| 7529 | conv sdn 5P | 5,030 | 3,945 | 36 |
| 7533 | Imperial sdn 7P | 5,025 | 3,360 | 638 |

# Cadillac

| Series 75 (wb 141.3) | | Wght | Price | Prod |
|---|---|---|---|---|
| 7533 | Imperial sdn 7P CKD | — | — | 60 |
| 7533F | formal sdn 7P | 5,025 | 3,995 | 44 |
| 7533L | Imperial bus sdn 7P | 5,025 | 3,260 | 2 |
| 7539 | town sdn 5P | 4,820 | 3,635 | 51 |
| 7553 | town car 7P | 5,095 | 5,115 | 13 |
| 7557 | cpe 2P | 4,595 | 3,280 | 36 |
| 7557B | cpe 5P | 4,695 | 3,380 | 23 |
| 7559 | formal sdn 5P | 4,785 | 3,995 | 53 |
| 7567 | conv cpe 2P | 4,675 | 3,380 | 27 |
| — | chassis | — | — | 13 |
| — | comm chassis (wb 161.0) | — | — | 28 |
| **Series 90 (wb 141.3)** | | | | |
| 9019 | sdn 5P | 5,190 | 5,140 | 13 |
| 9019F | Imperial sdn 5P | 5,265 | 5,215 | 2 |
| 9023 | sdn 7P | 5,215 | 5,270 | 18 |
| 9029 | conv sdn 5P | 5,220 | 6,000 | 4 |
| 9033 | Imperial sdn 7P | 5,260 | 5,420 | 60 |
| 9033F | formal sdn 7P | 5,260 | 6,055 | 8 |
| 9039 | town sdn 5P | 5,230 | 5,695 | 2 |
| 9053 | town car 7P | 5,330 | 7,175 | 5 |
| 9057 | cpe 2P | 4,830 | 5,340 | 6 |
| 9057B | cpe 5P | 4,930 | 5,440 | 5 |
| 9059 | formal sdn 5P | 5,190 | 6,055 | 4 |
| 9067 | conv cpe 2P | 4,970 | 5,440 | 7 |
| — | chassis | — | — | 2 |

| 1939 Engines | bore × stroke | bhp | availability |
|---|---|---|---|
| V-8, 346.0 | 3.50 × 4.50 | 135 | S-60, 61 |
| V-8, 346.0 | 3.50 × 4.50 | 140 | S-75 |
| V-16, 431.0 | 3.25 × 3.25 | 185 | S-90 |

## 1940

| Series 62 (wb 129.0) | | Wght | Price | Prod |
|---|---|---|---|---|
| 6219 | sdn 4d | 4,065 | 1,745 | 4,302 |
| 6227 | cpe 2-4P | 3,975 | 1,685 | 1,322 |
| 6229 | conv sdn | 4,265 | 2,195 | 75 |
| 6267 | conv cpe | 4,080 | 1,795 | 200 |
| 62 | chassis | — | — | 1 |
| **Series Sixty Special (wb 127.0)** | | | | |
| 6019F | division sdn | 4,110 | 2,230 | 110 |
| 6019S | sdn 4d | 4,070 | 2,090 | 4,472 |
| 6053LB | town car-leather back | 4,365 | 3,820 | 6 |
| 6053MB | town car-metal back | 4,365 | 3,465 | 9 |
| **Series 72 (wb 138.0)** | | | | |
| 7219 | sdn 4d | 4,670 | 2,670 | 455 |
| 7219F | division sdn | 4,710 | 2,740 | 100 |
| 7223 | sdn 4d, 7P | 4,700 | 2,785 | 305 |
| 7223L | livery sdn 7P | 4,700 | 2,690 | 25 |
| 7233 | Imperial sdn 7P | 4,740 | 2,915 | 292 |
| 7233F | formal sdn 7P | 4,780 | 3,695 | 20 |
| 7233L | livery imp sdn 7P | 4,740 | 2,825 | 36 |
| 7259 | formal sdn | 4,670 | 3,695 | 18 |
| 72 | comm chassis (wb 165.0) | — | — | 275 |
| **Series 75 (wb 141.3)** | | | | |
| 7519 | sdn 4d | 4,900 | 2,995 | 155 |
| 7419F | division sdn | 4,940 | 3,155 | 25 |
| 7523 | sdn 4d, 7P | 4,930 | 3,210 | 166 |
| 7529 | conv sdn 7P, T/B | 5,110 | 3,945 | 45 |
| 7533 | Imperial sdn 7P | 4,970 | 3,360 | 338 |
| 7533F | formal sdn 7P | 4,970 | 3,995 | 42 |
| 7539 | town sdn | 4,935 | 3,635 | 14 |

| Series 75 (wb 141.3) | | Wght | Price | Prod |
|---|---|---|---|---|
| 7553 | town car 7P | 5,195 | 5,115 | 14 |
| 7557 | cpe 2-4P | 4,785 | 3,280 | 15 |
| 7557B | cpe | 4,810 | 3,380 | 12 |
| 7559 | formal sdn, T/B | 4,900 | 3,995 | 48 |
| 7567 | conv cpe | 4,915 | 3,380 | 30 |
| 75 | chassis | — | — | 3 |
| 75 | comm chassis (wb 161.0) | — | — | 52 |
| **Series 90 Sixteen (wb 141.3)** | | | | |
| 9019 | sdn 4d | 5,190 | 5,140 | 4 |
| 9023 | sdn 4d, 7P | 5,215 | 5,270 | 4 |
| 9029 | conv sdn, T/B | 5,265 | 5,795 | 2 |
| 9033 | Imperial sdn 7P | 5,260 | 5,225 | 20 |
| 9033F | formal sdn 7P, T/B | 5,260 | 5,845 | 20 |
| 9039 | town sdn, T/B | 5,220 | 5,495 | 1 |
| 9053 | town car 7P, T/B | 5,330 | 6,945 | 2 |
| 9057 | cpe 2-4P | 4,830 | 5,145 | 2 |
| 9057B | cpe | 4,930 | 5,245 | 1 |
| 9059 | formal sdn, T/B | 5,190 | 5,845 | 2 |
| 9067 | conv cpe 2-4P | 4,970 | 5,245 | 2 |
| 90 | chassis | — | 3,700 | 1 |

| 1940 Engines | bore × stroke | bhp | availability |
|---|---|---|---|
| V-8, 346.0 | 3.50 × 4.50 | 135 | S-62, 60S |
| V-8, 346.0 | 3.50 × 4.50 | 140 | S-72, 75 |
| V-16, 431.0 | 3.25 × 3.25 | 185 | S-Sixteen |

## 1941

| Series 61 (wb 126.0) | | Wght | Price | Prod |
|---|---|---|---|---|
| 6109 | sdn 4d | 4,065 | 1,445 | 10,925 |
| 6109D | del sdn 4d | 4,085 | 1,535 | 3,495 |
| 6127 | cpe | 3,985 | 1,345 | 11,812 |
| 6127D | del cpe | 4,005 | 1,435 | 3,015 |
| 61 | chassis | — | — | 3 |
| **Series 62 (wb 126.0)** | | | | |
| 6219 | sdn 4d | 4,030 | 1,495 | 8,012 |
| 6219D | del sdn 4d | 4,050 | 1,585 | 7,850 |
| 6227 | cpe 2-4P | 3,950 | 1,420 | 1,985 |
| 6227D | del cpe 2-4P | 3,970 | 1,510 | 1,900 |
| 6229D | conv sdn | 4,230 | 1,965 | 400 |
| 6267D | conv cpe | 4,055 | 1,645 | 3,100 |
| 62 | chassis | — | — | 4 |
| 62 | comm chassis (wb 163.0) | — | — | 1,475 |
| **Series 63 (wb 126.0)** | | | | |
| 6319 | sdn 4d | 4,140 | 1,695 | 5,050 |
| **Series Sixty Special (wb 126.0)** | | | | |
| 6019 | sdn 4d | 4,230 | 2,195 | 3,878 |
| 6019F | division sdn | 4,290 | 2,345 | 220 |
| 6053LB | town car | 4,485 | — | 1 |
| 60 | chassis | — | — | 1 |
| **Series 67 (wb 139.0)** | | | | |
| 6719 | sdn 4d | 4,555 | 2,595 | 315 |
| 6719F | division sdn | 4,615 | 2,745 | 95 |
| 6723 | sdn 4d, 7P | 4,630 | 2,735 | 280 |
| 6733 | Imperial sdn 7P | 4,705 | 2,890 | 210 |
| **Series 75 (wb 136.0)** | | | | |
| 7519 | sdn 4d | 4,750 | 2,995 | 422 |
| 7519F | division sdn | 4,810 | 3,150 | 132 |
| 7523 | sdn 4d, 7P | 4,800 | 3,140 | 405 |
| 7523L | business sdn 9P | 4,750 | 2,895 | 54 |
| 7533 | Imperial sdn 7P | 4,860 | 3,295 | 757 |

# Cadillac

| Series 75 (wb 136.0) | | Wght | Price | Prod |
|---|---|---|---|---|
| 7533F | formal sdn 7P | 4,915 | 4,045 | 98 |
| 7533L | business imperial sdn 7P | 4,810 | 3,050 | 6 |
| 7559 | formal sdn | 4,900 | 3,920 | 75 |
| 75 | chassis | — | — | 5 |
| 75 | comm chassis (wb 163.0) | — | — | 150 |

| 1941 Engine | bore × stroke | bhp | availability |
|---|---|---|---|
| V-8, 346.0 | 3.50 × 4.50 | 150 | S-all |

## 1942

| Series 61 (wb 126.0) | | Wght | Price | Prod |
|---|---|---|---|---|
| 6107 | club cpe | 4,035 | 1,450 | 2,482 |
| 6109 | sdn 4d | 4,115 | 1,530 | 3,218 |
| **Series 62 (wb 129.0)** | | | | |
| 6207 | club cpe | 4,105 | 1,545 | 515 |
| 6207D | club cpe | 4,125 | 1,630 | 530 |
| 6267D | conv cpe | 4,365 | 1,880 | 308 |
| 6269 | sdn 4d | 4,185 | 1,630 | 1,780 |
| 6269D | sdn 4d | 4,205 | 1,705 | 1,827 |
| **Series 63 (wb 126.0)** | | | | |
| 6319 | sdn 4d | 4,115 | 1,745 | 1,750 |
| **Series Sixty Special (wb 133.0)** | | | | |
| 6069 | sdn 4d | 4,310 | 2,265 | 1,684 |
| 6069F | division sdn | 4,365 | 2,415 | 190 |
| 60 | chassis | — | — | 1 |
| **Series 67 (wb 138.0)** | | | | |
| 6719 | sdn 4d | 4,605 | 2,700 | 200 |
| 6719F | division sdn | 4,665 | 2,845 | 50 |
| 6723 | sdn 7P | 4,680 | 2,845 | 260 |
| 6733 | Imperial sdn 7P | 4,755 | 2,995 | 190 |
| **Series 75 (wb 136.0)** | | | | |
| 7519 | sdn 4d | 4,750 | 3,080 | 205 |
| 7519F | division sdn | 4,810 | 3,230 | 65 |
| 7523 | sdn 4d, 7P | 4,800 | 3,230 | 225 |
| 7523L | business sdn 9P | 4,750 | 2,935 | 29 |
| 7533 | Imperial sdn 7P | 4,860 | 3,375 | 430 |
| 7533F | formal sdn 7P | 4,915 | 4,215 | 80 |
| 7533L | business imperial sdn 9P | 4,860 | 3,080 | 6 |
| 7559 | formal sdn | 4,900 | 4,060 | 60 |
| 75 | chassis | — | — | 1 |
| 75 | comm chassis (wb 163.0) | — | — | 425 |

| 1942 Engine | bore × stroke | bhp | availability |
|---|---|---|---|
| V-8, 346.0 | 3.50 × 4.50 | 150 | S-all |

## 1946

| Series 61 (wb 126.0) | | Wght | Price | Prod |
|---|---|---|---|---|
| 6107 | club cpe | 4,145 | 2,052 | 800 |
| 6109 | sdn 4d | 4,225 | 2,176 | 2,200 |
| 61 | chassis | — | — | 1 |
| **Series 62 (wb 129.0)** | | | | |
| 6207 | club cpe | 4,215 | 2,284 | 2,323 |
| 6267D | conv cpe | 4,475 | 2,556 | 1,342 |
| 6269 | sdn 4d | 4,295 | 2,359 | 14,900 |
| 62 | chassis | — | — | 1 |
| **Series Sixty Special (wb 133.0)** | | | | |
| 6069 | sdn 4d | 4,420 | 3,095 | 5,700 |

| Series 75 (wb 136.0) | | Wght | Price | Prod |
|---|---|---|---|---|
| 7519 | sdn 4d | 4,860 | 4,298 | 150 |
| 7523 | sdn 4d, 7P | 4,905 | 4,475 | 225 |
| 7523L | business sdn 9P | 4,920 | 4,153 | 22 |
| 7533 | Imperial sdn 7P | 4,925 | 4,669 | 221 |
| 7533L | business imperial sdn 9P | 4,925 | 4,346 | 17 |
| 75 | comm chassis (wb 163.0) | — | — | 1,292 |

| 1946 Engine | bore × stroke | bhp | availability |
|---|---|---|---|
| V-8, 346.0 | 3.50 × 4.50 | 150 | S-all |

## 1947

| Series 61 (wb 126.0) | | Wght | Price | Prod |
|---|---|---|---|---|
| 6107 | club cpe | 4,080 | 2,200 | 3,395 |
| 6109 | sdn 4d | 4,165 | 2,324 | 5,160 |
| **Series 62 (wb 129.0)** | | | | |
| 6207 | club cpe | 4,145 | 2,446 | 7,245 |
| 6267 | conv cpe | 4,455 | 2,902 | 6,755 |
| 6269 | sdn 4d | 4,235 | 2,523 | 25,834 |
| 62 | chassis | — | — | 1 |
| **Series Sixty Special (wb 133.0)** | | | | |
| 6069 | sdn 4d | 4,370 | 3,195 | 8,500 |
| **Series 75 (wb 136.0)** | | | | |
| 7519 | sdn 4d | 4,875 | 4,471 | 300 |
| 7523 | sdn 4d, 7P | 4,895 | 4,686 | 890 |
| 7523L | business sdn 9P | 4,790 | 4,368 | 135 |
| 7533 | Imperial sdn 7P | 4,930 | 4,887 | 1,005 |
| 7533L | business imperial sdn 9P | 4,800 | 4,560 | 80 |
| 75 | chassis | — | — | 3 |
| 75 | comm & bus chassis (wb 163.0) | — | — | 2,623 |

| 1947 Engine | bore × stroke | bhp | availability |
|---|---|---|---|
| V-8, 346.0 | 3.50 × 4.50 | 150 | S-all |

## 1948

| Series 61 (wb 126.0) | | Wght | Price | Prod |
|---|---|---|---|---|
| 6107 | club cpe | 4,068 | 2,728 | 3,521 |
| 6169 | sdn 4d | 4,150 | 2,833 | 5,081 |
| 61 | chassis | — | — | 1 |
| **Series 62 (wb 126.0)** | | | | |
| 6207 | club cpe | 4,125 | 2,912 | 4,764 |
| 6267 | conv cpe | 4,449 | 3,442 | 5,450 |
| 6259 | sdn 4d | 4,179 | 2,996 | 23,997 |
| 62 | chassis | — | — | 2 |
| **Series Sixty Special (wb 133.0)** | | | | |
| 6069 | sdn 4d | 4,356 | 3,820 | 6,561 |
| **Series 75 (wb 136.0)** | | | | |
| 7519 | sdn 4d | 4,875 | 4,779 | 225 |
| 7523 | sdn 4d, 7P | 4,878 | 4,999 | 499 |
| 7523L | business sdn 9P | 4,780 | 4,679 | 90 |
| 7533 | Imperial sdn 7P | 4,959 | 5,199 | 382 |
| 7533L | bus imperial sdn 9P | — | — | 64 |
| 75 | chassis | — | — | 2 |
| 75 | comm chassis (wb 163.0) | — | — | 2,067 |

| 1948 Engine | bore × stroke | bhp | availability |
|---|---|---|---|
| V-8, 346.0 | 3.50 × 4.50 | 150 | S-all |

# Cadillac

## 1949

| Series 61 (wb 126.0) | | Wght | Price | Prod |
|---|---|---|---|---|
| 6107 | club cpe | 3,838 | 2,788 | 6,409 |
| 6169 | sdn 4d | 3,915 | 2,893 | 15,738 |
| 61 | chassis | — | — | 1 |
| **Series 62 (wb 126.0)** | | | | |
| 6207 | club cpe | 3,862 | 2,966 | 7,515 |
| 6237 | Coupe de Ville htp cpe | 4,033 | 3,497 | 2,150 |
| 6267 | conv cpe | 4,218 | 3,523 | 8,000 |
| 6269 | sdn 4d | 3,956 | 3,050 | 37,977 |
| 62 | chassis | — | — | 1 |
| **Series Sixty Special (wb 133.0)** | | | | |
| 6037 | Coupe de Ville htp cpe | 4,200 | — | 1 |
| 6069 | sdn 4d | 4,129 | 3,828 | 11,399 |
| **Series 75 (wb 136.0)** | | | | |
| 7519 | sdn 4d | 4,579 | 4,750 | 220 |
| 7523 | sdn 4d, 7P | 4,626 | 4,970 | 595 |
| 7523L | business sdn 9P | 4,522 | 4,650 | 35 |
| 7533 | Imperial sdn 7P | 4,648 | 5,170 | 626 |
| 7533L | business imperial sdn 9P | 4,573 | 4,839 | 25 |
| 75 | chassis | — | — | 1 |
| 86 | comm chassis (wb 163.0) | — | — | 1,861 |

| 1949 Engine | bore × stroke | bhp | availability |
|---|---|---|---|
| V-8, 331.0 | 3.81 × 3.63 | 160 | S-all |

## 1950

| Series 61 (wb 122.0) | | Wght | Price | Prod |
|---|---|---|---|---|
| 6137 | htp cpe | 3,829 | 2,761 | 11,839 |
| 6169 | sdn 4d | 3,822 | 2,866 | 14,931 |
| 61 | chassis | — | — | 2 |
| **Series 62 (wb 126.0)** | | | | |
| 6219 | sdn 4d | 4,012 | 3,234 | 41,890 |
| 6237 | htp cpe | 3,933 | 3,150 | 6,434 |
| 6237D | Coupe de Ville htp cpe | 4,074 | 3,523 | 4,507 |
| 6267 | conv cpe | 4,316 | 3,654 | 6,986 |
| 62 | chassis | — | — | 1 |
| **Series Sixty Special (wb 130.0)** | | | | |
| 6019 | sdn 4d | 4,136 | 3,797 | 13,755 |
| **Series 75 (wb 146.8)** | | | | |
| 7523 | sdn 4d, 7P | 4,555 | 4,770 | 716 |
| 7523L | business sdn 9P | 4,235 | export | 1 |
| 7533 | Imperial sdn 7P | 4,586 | 4,959 | 743 |
| 86 | comm chassis (wb 157.0) | — | — | 2,052 |

| 1950 Engine | bore × stroke | bhp | availability |
|---|---|---|---|
| V-8, 331.0 | 3.81 × 3.63 | 160 | S-all |

## 1951

| Series 61 (wb 122.0) | | Wght | Price | Prod |
|---|---|---|---|---|
| 6137 | htp cpe | 3,829 | 2810 | 2,400 |
| 6189 | sdn 4d | 3,827 | 2,917 | 2,300 |
| **Series 62 (wb 126.0)** | | | | |
| 6219 | sdn 4d | 4,062 | 3,528 | 55,352 |
| 6237 | htp cpe | 4,081 | 3,436 | 10,132 |
| 6237D | Coupe de Ville htp cpe | 4,156 | 3,843 | 10,241 |
| 6267 | conv cpe | 4,377 | 3,987 | 6,117 |
| 62-126 | chassis | — | — | 2 |
| **Series Sixty Special (wb 130.0)** | | | | |
| 6019 | sdn 4d | 4,234 | 4,142 | 18,631 |
| **Series 75 (wb 146.8)** | | | | |
| 7523 | sdn 4d, 8P | 4,621 | 5,200 | 1,090 |
| 7523L | business sdn 9P | 4,300 | — | 30 |
| 7533 | Imperial sdn 8P | 4,652 | 5,405 | 1,085 |
| 86 | comm chassis (wb 157.0) | — | — | 2,960 |

| 1951 Engine | bore × stroke | bhp | availability |
|---|---|---|---|
| V-8, 331.0 | 3.81 × 3.63 | 160 | S-all |

## 1952

| Series 62 (wb 126.0) | | Wght | Price | Prod |
|---|---|---|---|---|
| 6219 | sdn 4d | 4,140 | 3,684 | 42,625 |
| 6237 | htp cpe | 4,173 | 3,587 | 10,065 |
| 6237D | Coupe de Ville htp cpe | 4,203 | 4,013 | 11,165 |
| 6267 | conv cpe | 4,416 | 4,163 | 6,400 |
| **Series Sixty Special (wb 130.0)** | | | | |
| 6019 | sdn 4d | 4,255 | 4,323 | 16,110 |
| **Series 75 (wb 146.8)** | | | | |
| 7523 | sdn 4d, 8P | 4,698 | 5,428 | 1,400 |
| 7533 | Imperial sdn 8P | 4,733 | 5,643 | 800 |
| 8680S | comm chassis (wb 157.0) | — | — | 1,694 |

| 1952 Engine | bore × stroke | bhp | availability |
|---|---|---|---|
| V-8, 331.0 | 3.81 × 3.63 | 190 | S-all |

## 1953

| Series 62 (wb 126.0) | | Wght | Price | Prod |
|---|---|---|---|---|
| 6219 | sdn 4d | 4,225 | 3,666 | 47,640 |
| 6237 | htp cpe | 4,230 | 3,571 | 14,353 |
| 6237D | Coupe de Ville htp cpe | 4,340 | 3,995 | 14,550 |
| 6267 | conv cpe | 4,500 | 4,144 | 8,367 |
| 6267S | Eldorado conv cpe | 4,800 | 7,750 | 532 |
| 62 | chassis | — | — | 4 |
| **Series Sixty Special (wb 130.0)** | | | | |
| 6019 | sdn 4d | 4,415 | 4,305 | 20,000 |
| **Series 75 (wb 146.8)** | | | | |
| 7523 | sdn 4d, 8P | 4,830 | 5,408 | 1,435 |
| 7533 | Imperial sdn 8P | 4,850 | 5,621 | 765 |
| 8680S | comm chassis (wb 157.0) | — | — | 2,005 |

| 1953 Engine | bore × stroke | bhp | availability |
|---|---|---|---|
| V-8, 331.0 | 3.81 × 3.63 | 210 | S-all |

## 1954

| Series 62 (wb 129.0) | | Wght | Price | Prod |
|---|---|---|---|---|
| 6219 | sdn 4d | 4,370 | 3,933 | 34,252 |
| 6219S | DeVille htp sdn | — | proto | 1 |
| 6237 | htp cpe | 4,365 | 3,838 | 17,460 |
| 6237D | Coupe de Ville htp cpe | 4,405 | 4,261 | 17,170 |
| 6267 | conv cpe | 4,610 | 4,404 | 6,310 |
| 6267S | Eldorado conv cpe | 4,815 | 5,738 | 2,150 |
| 62 | chassis | — | — | 1 |
| **Series Sixty Special (wb 133.0)** | | | | |
| 6019 | sdn 4d | 4,500 | 4,863 | 16,200 |
| **Series 75 (wb 149.8)** | | | | |
| 7523 | sdn 4d, 8P | 5,055 | 5,875 | 889 |
| 7533 | Imperial sdn 8P | 5,105 | 6,090 | 611 |
| 8680S | comm chassis (wb 158.0) | — | — | 1,635 |

# Cadillac

| 1954 Engine | bore × stroke | bhp | availability |
|---|---|---|---|
| V-8, 331.0 | 3.81 × 3.63 | 230 | S-all |

## 1955

### Series 62 (wb 129.0)
| | | Wght | Price | Prod |
|---|---|---|---|---|
| 6219 | sdn 4d | 4,370 | 3,977 | 45,300 |
| 6237 | htp cpe | 4,358 | 3,882 | 27,879 |
| 6237D | Coupe de Ville htp cpe | 4,424 | 4,305 | 33,300 |
| 6267 | conv cpe | 4,627 | 4,448 | 8,150 |
| 6267S | Eldorado conv cpe | 4,809 | 6,286 | 3,950 |
| 62 | chassis | — | — | 7 |

### Series Sixty Special (wb 133.0)
| | | Wght | Price | Prod |
|---|---|---|---|---|
| 6019 | sdn 4d | 4,540 | 4,728 | 18,300 |

### Series 75 (wb 149.8)
| | | Wght | Price | Prod |
|---|---|---|---|---|
| 7523 | sdn 4d, 8P | 5,020 | 6,187 | 1,075 |
| 7533 | limo 8P | 5,113 | 6,402 | 841 |
| 8680S | comm chassis (wb 158.0) | — | — | 1,975 |

| 1955 Engines | bore × stroke | bhp | availability |
|---|---|---|---|
| V-8, 331.0 | 3.81 × 3.63 | 250 | S-62, 60S, 75 |
| V-8, 331.0 | 3.81 × 3.63 | 270 | S-Eldorado |

## 1956

### Series 62 (wb 129.0)
| | | Wght | Price | Prod |
|---|---|---|---|---|
| 6219 | sdn 4d | 4,430 | 4,296 | 26,666 |
| 6237 | htp cpe | 4,420 | 4,201 | 26,649 |
| 6237D | Coupe de Ville htp cpe | 4,445 | 4,624 | 24,086 |
| 6237S | Eldorado Seville htp cpe | 4,665 | 6,556 | 3,900 |
| 6239D | Sedan de Ville htp sdn | 4,550 | 4,753 | 41,732 |
| 6267 | conv cpe | 4,645 | 4,766 | 8,300 |
| 6267S | Eldorado Biarritz conv cpe | 4,880 | 6,556 | 2,150 |
| 62 | chassis | — | — | 19 |

### Series Sixty Special (wb 133.0)
| | | Wght | Price | Prod |
|---|---|---|---|---|
| 6019 | sdn 4d | 4,610 | 5,047 | 17,000 |

### Series 75 (wb 149.8)
| | | Wght | Price | Prod |
|---|---|---|---|---|
| 7523 | sdn 4d, 8P | 5,050 | 6,613 | 1,095 |
| 7533 | limo 8P | 5,130 | 6,828 | 955 |
| 8680S | comm chassis (wb 158.0) | — | — | 2,025 |

| 1956 Engines | bore × stroke | bhp | availability |
|---|---|---|---|
| V-8, 365.0 | 4.00 × 3.63 | 285 | S-62, 60S, 75 |
| V-8, 365.0 | 4.00 × 3.63 | 305 | S-Eldorado |

## 1957

### Series 62 (wb 129.5)
| | | Wght | Price | Prod |
|---|---|---|---|---|
| 6237 | htp cpe | 4,565 | 4,677 | 25,120 |
| 6237D | Coupe de Ville htp cpe | 4,620 | 5,116 | 23,813 |
| 6237S | Eldorado Seville htp cpe | 4,810 | 7,286 | 2,100 |
| 6239 | htp sdn | 4,595 | 4,781 | 32,342 |
| 6239D | Sedan de Ville htp sdn | 4,655 | 5,256 | 23,808 |
| 6239S | Eldorado Seville htp sdn | 4,810 | 7,286 | 4 |
| 6267 | conv cpe | 4,730 | 5,293 | 9,000 |
| 6267S | Eldorado Biarritz conv cpe | 4,930 | 7,286 | 1,800 |
| 62 | chassis & export sdn | — | — | 385 |

### Series Sixty Special (wb 133.0)
| | | Wght | Price | Prod |
|---|---|---|---|---|
| 6039 | htp sdn | 4,735 | 5,614 | 24,000 |

### Series 70 Eldorado Brougham (wb 126.0)
| | | Wght | Price | Prod |
|---|---|---|---|---|
| 7059 | htp sdn | 5,315 | 13,074 | 400 |

### Series 75 (wb 149.8)
| | | Wght | Price | Prod |
|---|---|---|---|---|
| 7523 | sdn 4d, 8P | 5,340 | 7,440 | 1,010 |
| 7533 | limo 8P | 5,390 | 7,678 | 890 |
| 8680S | comm chassis (wb 156.0) | — | — | 2,169 |

| 1957 Engines | bore × stroke | bhp | availability |
|---|---|---|---|
| V-8, 365.0 | 4.00 × 3.63 | 300 | S-62, 60S |
| V-8, 365.0 | 4.00 × 3.63 | 325 | S-70, O-62, Eldorado |

## 1958

### Series 62 (wb 129.5)
| | | Wght | Price | Prod |
|---|---|---|---|---|
| 6237 | htp cpe | 4,630 | 4,784 | 18,736 |
| 6237D | Coupe de Ville htp cpe | 4,705 | 5,251 | 18,414 |
| 6237S | Eldorado Seville htp cpe | 4,910 | 7,500 | 855 |
| 6239 | htp sdn | 4,675 | 4,891 | 13,335 |
| 6239E | htp sdn (ext. deck) | 4,770 | 5,079 | 20,952 |
| 6239 | Sedan de Ville htp sdn | 4,855 | 5,497 | 23,989 |
| 6267 | conv cpe | 4,856 | 5,454 | 7,825 |
| 6267S | Eldorado Biarritz conv cpe | 5,070 | 7,500 | 815 |
| 62 | chassis & exp sdn | — | — | 206 |

### Series Sixty Special (wb 133.0)
| | | Wght | Price | Prod |
|---|---|---|---|---|
| 6039 | htp sdn | 4,930 | 6,232 | 12,900 |

### Series 70 Eldorado Brougham (wb 126.0)
| | | Wght | Price | Prod |
|---|---|---|---|---|
| 7059 | htp sdn | 5,315 | 13,074 | 304 |

### Series 75 (wb 149.8)
| | | Wght | Price | Prod |
|---|---|---|---|---|
| 7523 | sdn 4d, 9P | 5,360 | 8,460 | 802 |
| 7533 | limo 9P | 5,425 | 8,675 | 730 |
| 8680S | comm chassis (wb 156.0) | — | — | 1,915 |

| 1958 Engines | bore × stroke | bhp | availability |
|---|---|---|---|
| V-8, 365.0 | 4.00 × 3.63 | 310 | S-all exc Eldorado |
| V-8, 365.0 | 4.00 × 3.63 | 335 | S-Eldo; O-all |

## 1959

### Series 62 (wb 130.0)
| | | Wght | Price | Prod |
|---|---|---|---|---|
| 6229 | htp sdn 6W | 4,770 | 5,080 | 23,461 |
| 6237 | htp cpe | 4,690 | 4,892 | 21,947 |
| 6239 | htp sdn 9W | 4,835 | 5,080 | 14,138 |
| 6267 | conv cpe | 4,855 | 5,455 | 11,130 |
| 62 | export sdn | — | — | 60 |

### DeVille (wb 130.0)
| | | Wght | Price | Prod |
|---|---|---|---|---|
| 6329 | htp sdn 6W | 4,850 | 5,498 | 19,158 |
| 6337 | htp cpe | 4,720 | 5,252 | 21,924 |
| 6339 | htp sdn 4W | 4,825 | 5,498 | 12,308 |

### Eldorado (wb 130.0)
| | | Wght | Price | Prod |
|---|---|---|---|---|
| 6437 | Seville htp cpe | — | 7,401 | 975 |
| 6467 | Biarritz conv cpe | — | 7,401 | 1,320 |
| 6929 | Brougham htp sdn | — | 13,075 | 99 |

### Series Sixty Special (wb 130.0)
| | | Wght | Price | Prod |
|---|---|---|---|---|
| 6039 | htp sdn | 4,890 | 6,233 | 12,250 |

### Series 75 (wb 149.8)
| | | Wght | Price | Prod |
|---|---|---|---|---|
| 6723 | sdn 4d, 9P | 5,490 | 9,533 | 710 |
| 6733 | limo 9P | 5,570 | 9,748 | 690 |
| 6890 | comm chassis (wb 156.0) | — | — | 2,102 |

| 1959 Engines | bore × stroke | bhp | availability |
|---|---|---|---|
| V-8, 390.0 | 4.00 × 3.88 | 325 | S-62, DeVille, 60S, 75 |
| V-8, 390.0 | 4.00 × 3.88 | 345 | S-Eldorado |

# Cadillac

## 1960

### Series 62 (wb 130.0)
| | | Wght | Price | Prod |
|---|---|---|---|---|
| 6229 | htp sdn 6W | 4,805 | 5,080 | 26,824 |
| 6237 | htp cpe | 4,670 | 4,892 | 19,978 |
| 6239 | htp sdn 4W | 4,775 | 5,080 | 9,984 |
| 6267 | conv cpe | 4,850 | 5,455 | 14,000 |
| 62 | chassis & export sdn | — | — | 38 |

### DeVille (wb 130.0)
| | | Wght | Price | Prod |
|---|---|---|---|---|
| 6329 | htp sdn 6W | 4,835 | 5,498 | 22,579 |
| 6337 | htp cpe | 4,705 | 5,252 | 21,585 |
| 6339 | htp sdn 4W | 4,815 | 5,498 | 9,225 |

### Eldorado (wb 130.0)
| | | Wght | Price | Prod |
|---|---|---|---|---|
| 6437 | Seville htp cpe | — | 7,401 | 1,075 |
| 6467 | Biarritz conv cpe | — | 7,401 | 1,285 |
| 6929 | Brougham htp sdn | — | 13,075 | 101 |

### Series Sixty Special (wb 130.0)
| | | Wght | Price | Prod |
|---|---|---|---|---|
| 6039 | htp sdn | 4,880 | 6,233 | 11,800 |

### Series 75 (wb 149.8)
| | | Wght | Price | Prod |
|---|---|---|---|---|
| 6723 | sdn 4d, 9P | 5,475 | 9,533 | 718 |
| 6733 | limo 9P | 5,560 | 9,748 | 832 |
| 6890 | comm chassis (wb 156.0) | — | — | 2,160 |

### 1960 Engines
| | bore × stroke | bhp | availability |
|---|---|---|---|
| V-8, 390.0 | 4.00 × 3.88 | 325 | S-62, DeVille, 60S, 75 |
| V-8, 390.0 | 4.00 × 3.88 | 345 | S-Eldorado |

## 1961

### Series 62 (wb 129.5)
| | | Wght | Price | Prod |
|---|---|---|---|---|
| 6229 | htp sdn 6W | 4,680 | 5,080 | 26,216 |
| 6237 | htp cpe | 4,560 | 4,892 | 16,005 |
| 6239 | htp sdn 4W | 4,660 | 5,080 | 4,700 |
| 6267 | conv | 4,720 | 5,455 | 15,500 |
| 62 | chassis | — | — | 5 |
| 6399 | town sedan hpt 6W | — | — | 3,756 |

### DeVille (wb 129.5)
| | | Wght | Price | Prod |
|---|---|---|---|---|
| 6329 | hpt sdn 6W | 4,710 | 5,498 | 26,415 |
| 6337 | hpt cpe | 4,595 | 5,252 | 20,156 |
| 6339 | hpt sdn 4W | 4,715 | 5,498 | 4,847 |

### Eldorado (wb 129.5)
| | | Wght | Price | Prod |
|---|---|---|---|---|
| 6367 | Biarritz conv cpe | — | 6,477 | 1,450 |

### Series Sixty Special (wb 129.5)
| | | Wght | Price | Prod |
|---|---|---|---|---|
| 6039 | htp sdn | 4,770 | 6,233 | 15,500 |

### Series 75 (wb 149.8)
| | | Wght | Price | Prod |
|---|---|---|---|---|
| 6723 | sdn 4d, 9P | 5,390 | 9,533 | 699 |
| 6733 | limo 9P | 5,420 | 9,748 | 926 |
| 6890 | comm chassis (wb 156.0) | — | — | 2,204 |

### 1961 Engine
| | bore × stroke | bhp | availability |
|---|---|---|---|
| V-8, 390.0 | 4.00 × 3.88 | 325 | S-all |

## 1962

### Series 62 (wb 129.5)
| | | Wght | Price | Prod |
|---|---|---|---|---|
| 6229 | htp sdn 6W | 4,640 | 5,213 | 16,730 |
| 6239 | htp sdn 4W | 4,645 | 5,213 | 17,314 |
| 6247 | htp cpe | 4,530 | 5,025 | 16,833 |
| 6267 | conv cpe | 4,630 | 5,588 | 16,800 |
| 6289 | town sedan htp sdn | 4,590 | 5,213 | 2,600 |

### DeVille (wb 129.5)
| | | Wght | Price | Prod |
|---|---|---|---|---|
| 6329 | htp sdn 6W | 4,660 | 5,631 | 16,230 |
| 6339 | htp sdn 4W | 4,675 | 5,631 | 27,378 |
| 6347 | htp cpe | 4,595 | 5,385 | 25,675 |
| 6389 | Park Avenue htp sdn | 4,655 | 5,631 | 2,600 |

### Eldorado (wb 129.5)
| | | Wght | Price | Prod |
|---|---|---|---|---|
| 6367 | Biarritz conv cpe | 4,620 | 6,610 | 1,450 |

### Series Sixty Special (wb 129.5)
| | | Wght | Price | Prod |
|---|---|---|---|---|
| 6039 | htp sdn 6W | 4,710 | 6,366 | 13,350 |

### Series 75 (wb 149.8)
| | | Wght | Price | Prod |
|---|---|---|---|---|
| 6723 | sdn 4d, 9P | 5,325 | 9,722 | 696 |
| 6733 | limo 9P | 5,390 | 9,937 | 904 |
| 6890 | comm chassis (wb 156.0) | — | — | 2,280 |

### 1962 Engine
| | bore × stroke | bhp | availability |
|---|---|---|---|
| V-8, 390.0 | 4.00 × 3.88 | 325 | S-all |

## 1963

### Series 62 (wb 129.5)
| | | Wght | Price | Prod |
|---|---|---|---|---|
| 6229 | htp sdn 6W | 4,610 | 5,214 | 12,929 |
| 6239 | htp sdn 4W | 4,595 | 5,214 | 16,980 |
| 6257 | htp cpe | 4,505 | 5,026 | 17,786 |
| 6267 | conv cpe | 4,545 | 5,590 | 17,600 |
| 62 | chassis | — | — | 3 |

### DeVille (wb 129.5)
| | | Wght | Price | Prod |
|---|---|---|---|---|
| 6329 | htp sdn 6W | 4,650 | 5,633 | 15,146 |
| 6339 | htp sdn 4W | 4,605 | 5,633 | 30,579 |
| 6357 | htp cpe | 4,520 | 5,386 | 31,749 |
| 6389 | Park Avenue htp sdn | 4,590 | 5,633 | 1,575 |

### Eldorado (wb 129.5)
| | | Wght | Price | Prod |
|---|---|---|---|---|
| 6367 | Biarritz conv cpe | 4,640 | 6,608 | 1,825 |

### Series Sixty Special (wb 129.5)
| | | Wght | Price | Prod |
|---|---|---|---|---|
| 6039 | htp sdn | 4,690 | 6,366 | 14,000 |

### Series 75 (wb 149.8)
| | | Wght | Price | Prod |
|---|---|---|---|---|
| 6723 | sdn 4d, 9P | 5,240 | 9,724 | 680 |
| 6733 | limo 9P | 5,300 | 9,939 | 795 |
| 6890 | comm chassis (wb 156.0) | — | — | 2,527 |

### 1963 Engine
| | bore × stroke | bhp | availability |
|---|---|---|---|
| V-8, 390.0 | 4.00 × 3.88 | 325 | S-all |

## 1964

### Series 62 (wb 129.5)
| | | Wght | Price | Prod |
|---|---|---|---|---|
| 6229 | htp sdn 6W | 4,575 | 5,236 | 9,243 |
| 6239 | htp sdn 4W | 4,550 | 5,236 | 13,670 |
| 6257 | htp cpe | 4,475 | 5,048 | 12,166 |
| 6267 | conv cpe | 4,545 | 5,612 | 17,900 |

### DeVille (wb 129.5)
| | | Wght | Price | Prod |
|---|---|---|---|---|
| 6329 | htp sdn 6W | 4,600 | 5,655 | 14,627 |
| 6339 | htp cpe 4W | 4,575 | 5,655 | 39,674 |
| 6357 | htp cpe | 4,495 | 5,408 | 38,195 |

### Eldorado (wb 129.5)
| | | Wght | Price | Prod |
|---|---|---|---|---|
| 6367 | Biarritz conv cpe | 4,605 | 6,630 | 1,870 |

### Series Sixty Special (wb 129.5)
| | | Wght | Price | Prod |
|---|---|---|---|---|
| 6039 | htp sdn | 4,680 | 6,388 | 14,550 |

### Series 75 (wb 149.8)
| | | Wght | Price | Prod |
|---|---|---|---|---|
| 6723 | sdn 4d, 9P | 5,215 | 9,746 | 617 |
| 6733 | limo 9P | 5,300 | 9,960 | 808 |

# Cadillac

| Series 75 (wb 149.8) | Wght | Price | Prod |
|---|---|---|---|
| 6890 comm chassis (wb 156.0) | — | — | 2,639 |

| 1964 Engine | bore × stroke | bhp | availability |
|---|---|---|---|
| V-8, 429.0 | 4.13 × 4.00 | 340 | S-all |

## 1965

| Calais (wb 129.5) | Wght | Price | Prod |
|---|---|---|---|
| 68239 htp sdn | 4,500 | 5,247 | 13,975 |
| 68257 htp cpe | 4,435 | 5,059 | 12,515 |
| 68269 sdn 4d | 4,490 | 5,247 | 7,721 |
| **DeVille (wb 129.5)** | | | |
| 68339 htp sdn | 4,560 | 5,666 | 45,535 |
| 68357 htp cpe | 4,480 | 5,419 | 43,345 |
| 68367 conv cpe | 4,690 | 5,639 | 19,200 |
| 68369 sdn 4d | 4,555 | 5,666 | 15,000 |
| **Eldorado (wb 129.5)** | | | |
| 68467 conv cpe | 4,660 | 6,738 | 2,125 |
| **Sixty Special (wb 133.0)** | | | |
| 68069 sdn 4d | 4,670 | 6,479 | 18,100 |
| **Seventy-Five (wb 149.8)** | | | |
| 69723 sdn 4d, 9P | 5,190 | 9,746 | 455 |
| 69733 limo 9P | 5,260 | 9,960 | 795 |
| 69890 comm chassis (wb 156.0) | — | — | 2,669 |

| 1965 Engine | bore × stroke | bhp | availability |
|---|---|---|---|
| V-8, 429.0 | 4.13 × 4.00 | 340 | S-all |

## 1966

| Calais (wb 129.5) | Wght | Price | Prod |
|---|---|---|---|
| 68239 htp sdn | 4,465 | 5,171 | 13,025 |
| 68257 htp cpe | 4,390 | 4,986 | 11,080 |
| 68269 sdn 4d | 4,460 | 5,171 | 4,575 |
| **DeVille (wb 129.5)** | | | |
| 68339 htp sdn | 4,515 | 5,581 | 60,550 |
| 68357 htp cpe | 4,460 | 5,339 | 50,580 |
| 68367 conv cpe | 4,445 | 5,555 | 19,200 |
| 68369 sdn 4d | 4,535 | 5,581 | 11,860 |
| **Eldorado (wb 129.5)** | | | |
| 68467 conv cpe | 4,500 | 6,631 | 2,250 |
| **Sixty Special (wb 133.0)** | | | |
| 68069 sdn 4d | 4,615 | 6,378 | 5,455 |
| 68169 Fleetwood Brghm sdn 4d | 4,665 | 6,695 | 13,630 |
| **Seventy-Five (wb 149.8)** | | | |
| 69723 sdn 4d, 9P | 5,320 | 10,312 | 980 |
| 69733 limo 9P | 5,435 | 10,521 | 1,037 |
| 69890 comm chassis (wb 156.0) | — | — | 2,463 |

| 1966 Engine | bore × stroke | bhp | availability |
|---|---|---|---|
| V-8, 429.0 | 4.13 × 4.00 | 340 | S-all |

## 1967

| Calais (wb 129.5) | Wght | Price | Prod |
|---|---|---|---|
| 68247 htp cpe | 4,447 | 5,040 | 9,085 |
| 68249 htp sdn | 4,495 | 5,215 | 9,880 |
| 68269 sdn 4d | 4,499 | 5,215 | 2,865 |

| DeVille (wb 129.5) | Wght | Price | Prod |
|---|---|---|---|
| 68347 htp cpe | 4,486 | 5,392 | 52,905 |
| 68349 htp sdn | 4,532 | 5,625 | 59,902 |
| 68367 conv cpe | 4,479 | 5,608 | 18,202 |
| 68369 sdn 4d | 4,534 | 5,625 | 8,800 |
| **Eldorado (wb 120.0)** | | | |
| 69347 htp cpe | 4,500 | 6,277 | 17,930 |
| **Sixty Special (wb 133.0)** | | | |
| 68069 sdn 4d | 4,678 | 6,423 | 3,550 |
| 68169 Fleetwood Brghm sdn 4d | 4,715 | 6,739 | 12,750 |
| **Seventy-Five (wb 149.8.0)** | | | |
| 69723 sdn 4d, 9P | 5,344 | 10,360 | 835 |
| 69733 limo 9P | 5,436 | 10,571 | 965 |
| 68490 comm chassis (wb 156.0) | — | — | 2,333 |

| 1967 Engine | bore × stroke | bhp | availability |
|---|---|---|---|
| V-8, 429.0 | 4.13 × 4.00 | 340 | S-all |

## 1968

| Calais (wb 129.5) | Wght | Price | Prod |
|---|---|---|---|
| 68247 htp cpe | 4,570 | 5,315 | 8,165 |
| 68249 htp sdn | 4,640 | 5,491 | 10,025 |
| **DeVille (wb 129.5)** | | | |
| 68347 htp cpe | 4,595 | 5,552 | 63,935 |
| 68349 htp sdn | 4,675 | 5,785 | 72,662 |
| 68367 conv cpe | 4,600 | 5,736 | 18,025 |
| 68369 sdn 4d | 4,680 | 5,785 | 9,850 |
| **Eldorado (wb 120.0)** | | | |
| 69347 htp cpe | 4,580 | 6,605 | 24,528 |
| **Sixty Special (wb 133.0)** | | | |
| 68069 sdn 4d | 4,795 | 6,583 | 3,300 |
| 68169 Fleetwood Brghm sdn 4d | 4,805 | 6,899 | 15,300 |
| **Seventy-Five (wb 149.8)** | | | |
| 69723 sdn 4d, 9P | 5,300 | 10,629 | 805 |
| 69733 limo 9P | 5,385 | 10,768 | 995 |
| 69890 comm chassis (wb 156.0) | — | — | 2,413 |

| 1968 Engine | bore × stroke | bhp | availability |
|---|---|---|---|
| V-8, 472.0 | 4.30 × 4.06 | 375 | S-all |

## 1969

| Calais (wb 129.5) | Wght | Price | Prod |
|---|---|---|---|
| 68247 htp cpe | 4,555 | 5,484 | 5,600 |
| 68349 htp sdn | 4,630 | 5,660 | 6,825 |
| **DeVille (wb 129.5)** | | | |
| 68347 htp cpe | 4,595 | 5,721 | 65,755 |
| 68349 htp sdn | 4,660 | 5,954 | 72,958 |
| 68367 conv cpe | 4,590 | 5,905 | 16,445 |
| 68369 sdn 4d | 4,640 | 5,954 | 7,890 |
| **Eldorado (wb 120.0)** | | | |
| 69347 htp cpe | 4,550 | 6,711 | 23,333 |
| **Sixty Special (wb 133.0)** | | | |
| 68069 sdn 4d | 4,765 | 6,779 | 2,545 |
| 68169 Fleetwood Brghm sdn 4d | 4,770 | 7,110 | 17,300 |
| **Seventy-Five (wb 149.8)** | | | |
| 69723 sdn 4d, 9P | 5,430 | 10,841 | 880 |

## Cadillac

| Seventy-Five (wb 149.8) | | Wght | Price | Prod |
|---|---|---|---|---|
| 69733 | limo 9P | 5,555 | 10,979 | 1,156 |
| 69890 | comm chassis (wb 156.0) | — | — | 2,550 |
| **1969 Engine** | bore × stroke | bhp | availability | |
| V-8, 472.0 | 4.30 × 4.06 | 375 | S-all | |

### 1970

| Calais (wb 129.5) | | Wght | Price | Prod |
|---|---|---|---|---|
| 68247 | htp cpe | 4,620 | 5,637 | 4,724 |
| 68249 | htp sdn | 4,680 | 5,813 | 5,187 |
| **DeVille (wb 129.5)** | | | | |
| 68347 | htp cpe | 4,650 | 5,884 | 76,043 |
| 68349 | htp sdn | 4,725 | 6,118 | 83,274 |
| 68367 | conv cpe | 4,660 | 6,068 | 15,172 |
| 68369 | sdn 4d | 4,690 | 6,118 | 7,230 |
| **Eldorado (wb 120.0)** | | | | |
| 69347 | htp cpe | 4,630 | 6,903 | 23,842 |
| **Sixty Special (wb 133.0)** | | | | |
| 68089 | sdn 4d | 4,830 | 6,953 | 1,738 |
| 68189 | Fleetwood Brghm sdn 4d | 4,835 | 7,284 | 16,913 |
| **Seventy-Five (wb 149.8)** | | | | |
| 69723 | sdn 4d, 9P | 5,530 | 11,039 | 876 |
| 69733 | limo 9P | 5,630 | 11,178 | 1,240 |
| 69890 | comm chassis (wb 156.0) | — | — | 2,506 |
| **1970 Engines** | bore × stroke | bhp | availability | |
| V-8, 472.0 | 4.30 × 4.06 | 375 | S-all exc Eldorado | |
| V-8, 500.0 | 4.30 × 4.30 | 400 | S-Eldorado | |

### 1971

| Calais (wb 129.5) | | Wght | Price | Prod |
|---|---|---|---|---|
| 68247 | htp cpe | 4,635 | 5,899 | 3,360 |
| 68249 | htp sdn | 4,710 | 6,075 | 3,569 |
| **DeVille (wb 130.0)** | | | | |
| 68347 | htp cpe | 4,685 | 6,264 | 66,081 |
| 68349 | htp sdn | 4,730 | 6,498 | 69,345 |
| **Eldorado (wb 120.0)** | | | | |
| 69346 | htp cpe | 4,675 | 7,383 | 20,568 |
| 69367 | conv | 4,730 | 7,751 | 6,800 |
| **Sixty Special Brougham (wb 133.0)** | | | | |
| 68169 | Fleetwood sdn 4d | 4,815 | 7,763 | 15,200 |
| **Seventy-Five (wb 151.5)** | | | | |
| 69723 | sdn 4d | 5,510 | 11,869 | 752 |
| 69733 | limo 9P | 5,570 | 12,008 | 848 |
| 69890 | comm chassis (wb 157.5) | — | — | 2,014 |
| **1971 Engines** | bore × stroke | bhp | availability | |
| V-8, 472.0 | 4.30 × 4.06 | 345 | S-all exc Eldorado | |
| V-8, 500.0 | 4.30 × 4.30 | 365 | S-Eldorado | |

### 1972

| Calais (wb 130.0) | | Wght | Price | Prod |
|---|---|---|---|---|
| 68247 | htp cpe | 4,642 | 5,771 | 3,900 |
| 68249 | htp sdn | 4,698 | 5,938 | 3,875 |
| **DeVille (wb 130.0)** | | | | |
| 68347 | htp cpe | 4,682 | 6,168 | 95,280 |
| 68349 | htp sdn | 4,762 | 6,390 | 99,531 |
| **Eldorado (wb 126.3)** | | | | |
| 69347 | htp cpe | 4,682 | 7,230 | 32,099 |
| 69367 | conv | 4,772 | 7,546 | 7,975 |
| **Sixty Special Brougham (wb 133.0)** | | | | |
| 68169 | Fleetwood sdn 4d | 4,858 | 7,637 | 20,750 |
| **Seventy-Five (wb 151.5)** | | | | |
| 69723 | sdn 4d | 5,515 | 11,748 | 955 |
| 69733 | limo 9P | 5,637 | 11,880 | 960 |
| 69890 | comm chassis (wb 157.5) | — | — | 2,462 |
| **1972 Engines** | bore × stroke | bhp | availability | |
| V-8, 472.0 | 4.30 × 4.06 | 220 | S-all exc Eldorado | |
| V-8, 500.0 | 4.30 × 4.30 | 235 | S-Eldorado | |

### 1973

| Calais (wb 130.0) | | Wght | Price | Prod |
|---|---|---|---|---|
| 68247 | htp cpe | 4,900 | 5,866 | 4,275 |
| 68249 | htp sdn | 4,953 | 6,038 | 3,798 |
| **DeVille (wb 130.0)** | | | | |
| 68347 | htp cpe | 4,925 | 6,268 | 112,849 |
| 68349 | htp sdn | 4,985 | 6,500 | 103,394 |
| **Eldorado (wb 126.3)** | | | | |
| 69347 | hpt cpe | 4,880 | 7,360 | 42,136 |
| 69367 | conv | 4,966 | 7,681 | 9,315 |
| **Sixty Special Brougham (wb 133.0)** | | | | |
| 68169 | Fleetwood sdn 4d | 5,102 | 7,765 | 24,800 |
| **Seventy-Five (wb 151.5)** | | | | |
| 69723 | sdn 4d | 5,620 | 11,948 | 1,043 |
| 69733 | limo 9P | 5,742 | 12,080 | 1,017 |
| 69890 | comm chassis (wb 157.5) | — | — | 2,212 |
| **1973 Engines** | bore × stroke | bhp | availability | |
| V-8, 472.0 | 4.30 × 4.06 | 220 | S-all exc Eldorado | |
| V-8, 500.0 | 4.30 × 4.30 | 235 | S-Eldorado | |

### 1974

| Calais (wb 130.0) | | Wght | Price | Prod |
|---|---|---|---|---|
| 68247 | cpe | 4,900 | 7,371 | 4,559 |
| 68249 | htp sdn 4d | 4,979 | 7,545 | 2,324 |
| **DeVille (wb 130.0)** | | | | |
| 68347 | cpe | 4,924 | 7,867 | 112,201 |
| 68349 | htp sdn 4d | 5,032 | 8,100 | 60,419 |
| **Eldorado (wb 126.3)** | | | | |
| 69347 | htp cpe | 4,960 | 9,110 | 32,812 |
| 69367 | conv | 5,019 | 9,437 | 7,600 |
| **Sixty Special Brougham (wb 133.0)** | | | | |
| 68169 | Fleetwood sdn 4d | 5,143 | 9,537 | 18,250 |
| **Seventy-Five (wb 151.5)** | | | | |
| 69723 | sdn 4d | 5,719 | 13,120 | 895 |
| 69733 | limo 9P | 5,883 | 13,254 | 1,005 |
| 69890 | comm chassis (wb 157.5) | — | — | 2,265 |
| **1974 Engines** | bore × stroke | bhp | availability | |
| V-8, 472.0 | 4.30 × 4.06 | 205 | S-all exc Eldorado | |
| V-8, 500.0 | 4.30 × 4.30 | 210 | S-Eldorado | |

# Cadillac

## 1975

| Seville (wb 114.3) | | Wght | Price | Prod |
|---|---|---|---|---|
| S69 | sdn 4d | 4,232 | 12,479 | 16,355 |
| **Calais (wb 130.0)** | | | | |
| 68247 | cpe | 5,003 | 8,184 | 5,800 |
| 68249 | htp sdn 4d | 5,087 | 8,377 | 2,500 |
| **DeVille (wb 130.0)** | | | | |
| 68347 | cpe | 5,049 | 8,600 | 110,218 |
| 68349 | htp sdn 4d | 5,146 | 8,801 | 63,352 |
| **Eldorado (wb 126.3)** | | | | |
| 69347 | cpe | 5,108 | 9,935 | 35,802 |
| 69367 | conv | 5,167 | 10,354 | 8,950 |
| **Fleetwood Brougham (wb 133.0)** | | | | |
| 68169 | sdn 4d | 5,242 | 10,414 | 18,755 |
| **Seventy-Five (wb 151.5)** | | | | |
| 69723 | sdn 4d | 5,720 | 14,218 | 876 |
| 69733 | limo 9P | 5,862 | 14,557 | 795 |
| 69890 | comm chassis (wb 157.5) | — | — | 1,329 |

| 1975 Engines | bore × stroke | bhp | availability |
|---|---|---|---|
| V-8, 350.0 | 4.06 × 3.39 | 180 | S-Seville |
| V-8, 500.0 | 4.30 × 4.30 | 190 | S-all exc Seville |

## 1976

| Seville (wb 114.3) | | Wght | Price | Prod |
|---|---|---|---|---|
| S69 | sdn 4d | 4,232 | 12,479 | 43,772 |
| **Calais (wb 130.0)** | | | | |
| 68247 | cpe | 4,989 | 8,629 | 4,500 |
| 68249 | htp sdn 4d | 5,083 | 8,825 | 1,700 |
| **DeVille (wb 130.0)** | | | | |
| 68347 | cpe | 5,025 | 9,067 | 114,482 |
| 68349 | htp sdn 4d | 5,127 | 9,265 | 67,677 |
| **Eldorado (wb 126.3)** | | | | |
| 69347 | cpe | 5,085 | 10,586 | 35,184 |
| 69367 | conv | 5,153 | 11,049 | 14,000 |
| **Fleetwood Brougham (wb 133.0)** | | | | |
| 68169 | sdn 4d | 5,213 | 10,935 | 24,500 |
| **Seventy-Five (wb 151.5)** | | | | |
| 69723 | sdn 4d | 5,746 | 14,889 | 981 |
| 69733 | limo 9P | 5,889 | 15,239 | 834 |
| 69890 | comm chassis (wb 157.5) | — | — | 1,509 |

| 1976 Engines | bore × stroke | bhp | availability |
|---|---|---|---|
| V-8, 350.0 | 4.06 × 3.39 | 180 | S-Seville |
| V-8, 500.0 | 4.30 × 4.30 | 190 | S-all exc Seville |
| V-8, 500.0 | 4.30 × 4.30 | 215 | O-all exc Seville |

## 1977

| Seville (wb 114.3) | | Wght | Price | Prod |
|---|---|---|---|---|
| S69 | sdn 4d | 4,192 | 13,359 | 45,060 |
| **DeVille (wb 121.5)** | | | | |
| 68347 | cpe | 4,186 | 9,810 | 138,750 |
| 68349 | sdn 4d | 4,222 | 10,020 | 95,421 |
| **Eldorado (wb 126.3)** | | | | |
| 69347 | cpe | 4,955 | 11,187 | 47,344 |
| **Fleetwood Brougham (wb 121.5)** | | | | |
| 68169 | sdn 4d | 4,340 | 11,546 | 28,000 |
| **Fleetwood limousine (wb 144.5)** | | Wght | Price | Prod |
| 69723 | sdn 4d | 4,738 | 18,349 | 1,582 |
| 69773 | formal sdn 4d | 4,806 | 19,014 | 1,032 |
| 69890 | comm chassis (wb 157.5) | — | — | 1,299 |

| 1977 Engines | bore × stroke | bhp | availability |
|---|---|---|---|
| V-8, 350.0 | 4.06 × 3.39 | 180 | S-Seville |
| V-8, 425.0 | 4.08 × 4.06 | 180 | S-all exc Seville |
| V-8, 425.0 | 4.08 × 4.06 | 195 | O-Brgm, DeVille, Eldo |

## 1978

| Seville (wb 114.3) | | Wght | Price | Prod |
|---|---|---|---|---|
| S69 | sdn 4d | 4,179 | 14,161 | 56,985 |
| **DeVille (wb 121.5)** | | | | |
| 68347 | cpe | 4,163 | 10,584 | 117,750 |
| 68349 | sdn 4d | 4,236 | 10,924 | 88,951 |
| **Eldorado (wb 126.3)** | | | | |
| 69347 | cpe | 4,906 | 12,401 | 46,816 |
| **Fleetwood Brougham (wb 121.5)** | | | | |
| 68169 | sdn 4d | 4,314 | 12,842 | 36,800 |
| **Fleetwood limousine (wb 144.5)** | | | | |
| 69723 | sdn 4d | 4,772 | 20,007 | 848 |
| 69773 | formal sdn 4d | 4,858 | 10,742 | 682 |
| 69890 | comm chassis (wb 157.5) | — | — | 852 |

| 1978 Engines | bore × stroke | bhp | availability |
|---|---|---|---|
| V-8, 350.0 | 4.06 × 3.39 | 170 | S-Seville |
| V-8D, 350.0 | 4.06 × 3.39 | 120 | O-Seville |
| V-8, 425.0 | 4.08 × 4.06 | 180 | S-all exc Seville |
| V-8, 425.0 | 4.08 × 4.06 | 195 | S-Brgm, DeVille, Eldo |

## 1979

| Seville (wb 114.3) | | Wght | Price | Prod |
|---|---|---|---|---|
| S69 | sdn 4d | 4,179 | 16,224 | 53,487 |
| **Eldorado (wb 114.0)** | | | | |
| L57 | cpe | 3,792 | 14,668 | 67,436 |
| **DeVille (wb 121.5)** | | | | |
| D47 | cpe | 4,143 | 11,728 | 121,890 |
| D69 | sdn 4d | 4,212 | 12,093 | 93,211 |
| **Fleetwood Brougham (wb 121.5)** | | | | |
| B69 | sdn 4d | 4,240 | 14,102 | 42,200 |
| **Fleetwood limousine (wb 144.5)** | | | | |
| F23 | sdn 4d | 4,782 | 21,869 | 2,025 |
| F33 | formal sdn 4d | 4,866 | 22,640 | 2,025 |
| — | comm chassis (wb 157.5) | — | — | 864 |

| 1979 Engines | bore × stroke | bhp | availability |
|---|---|---|---|
| V-8, 350.0 | 4.06 × 3.39 | 170 | S-Seville, Eldo |
| V-8D, 350.0 | 4.06 × 3.39 | 125 | O-all, exc limo |
| V-8, 425.0 | 4.08 × 4.06 | 180 | S-all exc Seville |
| V-8, 425.0 | 4.08 × 4.06 | 195 | O-Brgm, DeVille |

## 1980

| Eldorado (wb 114.0) | | Wght | Price | Prod |
|---|---|---|---|---|
| L57 | cpe | 3,806 | 16,141 | 52,685 |

## Cadillac

| DeVille (wb 121.5) | | Wght | Price | Prod |
|---|---|---|---|---|
| D47 | cpe | 4,048 | 12,899 | 55,490 |
| D69 | sdn 4d | 4,084 | 13,282 | 49,188 |
| **Fleetwood Brougham (wb 121.5)** | | | | |
| B47 | cpe | 4,025 | 15,307 | 2,300 |
| B69 | sdn 4d | 4,092 | 15,564 | 29,659 |
| **Fleetwood limousine (wb 144.5)** | | | | |
| F23 | sdn 4d | 4,629 | 23,509 | 1,612 |
| F33 | formal sdn 4d | 4,718 | 24,343 | — |
| — | comm chassis (wb 157.5) | — | — | 750 |
| **Seville (wb 114.3)** | | | | |
| S69 | sdn 4d | 3,911 | 20,477 | 39,344 |

| 1980 Engines | bore × stroke | bhp | availability |
|---|---|---|---|
| V-8D, 350.0 | 4.06 × 3.39 | 105 | S-Seville; O-Flt/Brgm, Eldo |
| V-8, 350.0 | 4.06 × 3.39 | 160 | O-Seville, Eldo |
| V-8, 368.0 | 3.80 × 4.06 | 150 | S-DeV, Fltwd |
| V-8, 368.0 | 3.80 × 4.06 | 145 | S-Eldo; O-Seville |

### 1981

| Seville (wb 114.0) | | Wght | Price | Prod |
|---|---|---|---|---|
| S69 | sdn 4d | 4,167 | 21,088 | 28,631 |
| **Eldorado (wb 114.0)** | | | | |
| L57 | cpe | 3,930 | 16,492 | 60,643 |
| **DeVille (wb 121.4)** | | | | |
| D47 | cpe | 4,151 | 13,450 | 54,145 |
| D69 | sdn 4d | 4,202 | 13,847 | 55,100 |
| **Fleetwood Brougham (wb 121.4)** | | | | |
| B47 | cpe | 4,204 | 15,942 | 8,300 |
| B69 | sdn 4d | 4,250 | 16,365 | 31,500 |
| **Fleetwood limousine (wb 144.5)** | | | | |
| F23 | sdn 4d | 4,629 | 24,464 | 610 |
| F33 | formal sdn 4d | 4,717 | 25,323 | 590 |
| | commercial chassis | — | — | 670 |

| 1981 Engines | bore × stroke | bhp | availability |
|---|---|---|---|
| V-6, 252.0 | 3.97 × 3.40 | 125 | O-all except limos |
| V-8D, 350.0 | 4.06 × 3.39 | 105 | S-Seville; O-DeV, Brgm, Eldo |
| V-8-6-4, 368.0 | 3.80 × 4.06 | 140 | S-DeV, Brgm, Eldo; O-Seville |
| V-8, 368.0 | 3.80 × 4.06 | 150 | S-comm chassis |

### 1982

| Cimarron (wb 101.2) | | Wght | Price | Prod |
|---|---|---|---|---|
| G69 | sdn 4d | 2,594 | 12,131 | 25,968 |
| **Seville (wb 114.0)** | | | | |
| S69 | sdn 4d | 4,167 | 23,433 | 19,998 |
| **Eldorado (wb 114.0)** | | | | |
| L57 | cpe | 3,930 | 18,716 | 52,018 |
| **DeVille (wb 121.4)** | | | | |
| D47 | cpe | 3,923 | 15,249 | 44,950 |
| D69 | sdn 4d | 3,979 | 15,699 | 53,870 |
| **Fleetwood Brougham (wb 121.4)** | | | | |
| B47 | cpe | 3,965 | 18,096 | 5,180 |
| B69 | sdn 4d | 4,006 | 18,567 | 32,150 |

| Fleetwood limousine (wb 144.5) | | Wght | Price | Prod |
|---|---|---|---|---|
| F23 | sdn 4d | 4,628 | 27,961 | 514 |
| F33 | formal sdn 4d | 4,718 | 28,941 | 486 |
| | commercial chassis | — | — | 450 |

| 1982 Engines | bore × stroke | bhp | availability |
|---|---|---|---|
| I-4, 112.0 | 3.50 × 2.90 | 88 | S-Cimarron |
| V-8, 249.0 | 3.46 × 3.31 | 125 | S-Sev, Eldo, DeV, Fltwd |
| V-6, 252.0 | 3.97 × 3.40 | 125 | O-Sev, Eldo, DeV, Fltwd |
| V-8D, 350.0 | 4.06 × 3.39 | 105 | O-Seville, Eldo, DeV, Fltwd |
| V-8-6-4, 368.0 | 3.80 × 4.06 | 140 | S-limousines |
| V-8, 368.0 | 3.80 × 4.06 | 150 | S-comm chassis |

### 1983

| Cimarron (wb 101.2) | | Wght | Price | Prod |
|---|---|---|---|---|
| G69 | sdn 4d | 2,639 | 12,215 | 19,294 |
| **Seville (wb 114.0)** | | | | |
| S69 | sdn 4d | 3,844 | 21,440 | 30,430 |
| **Eldorado (wb 114.0)** | | | | |
| L57 | cpe | 3,748 | 19,334 | 67,416 |
| **DeVille (wb 121.5)** | | | | |
| D47 | cpe | 3,935 | 15,970 | 60,300 |
| D69 | sdn 4d | 3,993 | 16,441 | 70,423 |
| **Fleetwood Brougham (wb 121.5)** | | | | |
| B47 | cpe | 3,986 | 18,688 | 5,200 |
| B69 | sdn 4d | 4,029 | 19,182 | 38,300 |
| **Fleetwood limousine (wb 144.5)** | | | | |
| F23 | sdn 4d | 4,765 | 29,323 | 492 |
| F33 | formal sdn 4d | 4,852 | 30,349 | 508 |
| | commercial chassis | — | — | 451 |

| 1983 Engines | bore × stroke | bhp | availability |
|---|---|---|---|
| I-4, 121.0 | 3.50 × 3.15 | 88 | S-Cimarron |
| V-8, 249.0 | 3.46 × 3.30 | 135 | S-Sev, Eldo, DeV, Fltwd |
| V-8D, 350.0 | 4.06 × 3.39 | 105 | O-Seville, Eldo, DeV, Fltwd |
| V-8-6-4, 368.0 | 3.80 × 4.06 | 140 | S-limousines |
| V-8, 368.0 | 3.80 × 4.06 | 150 | S-comm chassis |

### 1984

| Cimarron (wb 101.2) | | Wght | Price | Prod |
|---|---|---|---|---|
| G69 | sdn 4d | 2,583 | 12,614 | 21,898 |
| **Seville (wb 114.0)** | | | | |
| S69 | sdn 4d | 3,804 | 22,468 | 39,997 |
| **Eldorado (wb 114.0)** | | | | |
| L57 | cpe | 3,734 | 20,342 | 74,506 |
| L67 | Biarritz conv cpe | 3,926 | 31,286 | 3,300 |
| **DeVille (wb 121.5)** | | | | |
| M47 | cpe | 3,940 | 17,140 | 46,340 |
| M69 | sdn 4d | 3,981 | 17,625 | 68,270 |
| **Fleetwood Brougham (wb 121.5)** | | | | |
| W47 | cpe | 3,990 | 19,942 | 4,500 |
| W69 | sdn 4d | 4,034 | 20,451 | 39,650 |

# Cadillac

| Fleetwood limousine (wb 144.5) | | Wght | Price | Prod |
|---|---|---|---|---|
| F23 | sdn 4d | 4,765 | 30,454 | 462 |
| F33 | formal sdn 4d | 4,855 | 31,512 | 631 |
| | commercial chassis | — | — | 746 |

| 1984 Engines | bore × stroke | bhp | availability |
|---|---|---|---|
| I-4, 121.0 | 3.50 × 3.15 | 88 | S-Cimarron |
| V-8, 249.0 | 3.46 × 3.30 | 135 | S-Sev, Eldo, DeV, Fltwd |
| V-8D, 350.0 | 4.06 × 3.39 | 105 | O-Seville, Eldo, DeV, Fltwd |
| V-8-6-4, 368.0 | 3.80 × 4.06 | 140 | S-limousines |

## 1985

| Cimarron (wb 101.2) | | Wght | Price | Prod |
|---|---|---|---|---|
| G69 | sdn 4d | 2,583 | 12,962 | 19,890 |

| Seville (wb 114.0) | | | | |
|---|---|---|---|---|
| S69 | sdn 4d | 3,803 | 23,259 | 39,755 |

| Eldorado (wb 114.0) | | | | |
|---|---|---|---|---|
| L57 | cpe | 3,724 | 20,931 | 74,101 |
| L67 | conv cpe | 3,915 | 22,105 | 2,300 |

Note: Production total includes 2,463 Commemorative Edition models.

| DeVille (wb 110.8) | | | | |
|---|---|---|---|---|
| D47 | cpe | 3,324 | 17,990 | 39,500* |
| D69 | sdn 4d | 3,396 | 18,571 | 101,366* |

| Fleetwood (wb 110.8) | | | | |
|---|---|---|---|---|
| B47 | cpe | 3,346 | 21,069 | * |
| B69 | sdn 4d | 3,422 | 21,040 | * |

* Fleetwood production included in DeVille coupe and sedan totals.

| Fleetwood Brougham RWD (wb 121.5) | | | | |
|---|---|---|---|---|
| W47 | cpe | 3,977 | 20,798 | 3,000 |
| W69 | sdn 4d | 4,020 | 21,402 | 52,450 |

| Fleetwood limousine (wb 134.4) | | | | |
|---|---|---|---|---|
| H23 | sdn 4d | 3,583 | 32,640 | 405 |
| H33 | formal sdn 4d | 3,642 | — | — |

| 1985 Engines | bore × stroke | bhp | availability |
|---|---|---|---|
| I-4, 121.0 | 3.50 × 3.15 | 88 | S-Cimarron |
| V-6, 173.0 | 3.50 × 2.99 | 125 | O-Cimarron |
| V-8, 249.0 | 3.46 × 3.30 | 125 | S-DeV, Fltwd, limo |
| V-8, 249.0 | 3.46 × 3.30 | 135 | S-Sev, Eldo, Brgm |
| V-6D, 262.0 | 4.06 × 3.39 | 85 | O-DeV, Fltwd |
| V-8D, 350.0 | 4.06 × 3.39 | 105 | O-Seville, Eldo, Brgm |

## 1986

| Cimarron (wb 101.2) | | Wght | Price | Prod |
|---|---|---|---|---|
| G69 | sdn 4d | 2,583 | 13,128 | 24,534 |

| Seville (wb 108.0) | | | | |
|---|---|---|---|---|
| S69 | sdn 4d | 3,428 | 26,756 | 19,098 |

| Eldorado (wb 108.0) | | | | |
|---|---|---|---|---|
| L57 | cpe | 3,365 | 24,251 | 21,342 |
| | American II cpe | — | — | 1,500 |

| DeVille (wb 110.8) | | | | |
|---|---|---|---|---|
| D47 | cpe | 3,319 | 19,669 | 36,350* |
| D69 | sdn 4d | 3,378 | 19,990 | 129,857* |

| Fleetwood (wb 110.8) | | | | |
|---|---|---|---|---|
| | cpe | — | 23,443 | * |

| Fleetwood (wb 110.8) | | Wght | Price | Prod |
|---|---|---|---|---|
| | sdn 4d | — | 23,764 | * |

* Fleetwood (option package) production included in DeVille coupe and sedan totals.

| Fleetwood Brougham RWD (wb 121.5) | | | | |
|---|---|---|---|---|
| W69 | sdn 4d | 4,020 | 21,265 | 49,137 |

| Fleetwood Seventy-Five limousine (wb 134.4) | | | | |
|---|---|---|---|---|
| H23 | sdn 4d | 3,637 | 33,895 | 650 |
| H33 | formal sdn 4d | 3,736 | 35,895 | 350 |
| | commercial chassis | — | — | 365 |

| 1986 Engines | bore × stroke | bhp | availability |
|---|---|---|---|
| L4, 121.0 | 3.50 × 3.15 | 85 | S-Cimarron |
| V-6, 173.0 | 3.50 × 2.99 | 120 | O-Cimarron |
| V-8, 249.0 | 3.46 × 3.30 | 130/135 | S-Sev, Eldo, DeV, Fltwd |
| V-8, 249.0 | 3.46 × 3.30 | 135 | S-limo |
| V-8, 307.0 | 3.80 × 3.39 | 140 | S-Brgm |

## 1987

| Cimarron (wb 101.2) | | Wght | Price | Prod |
|---|---|---|---|---|
| G69 | sdn 4d | 2,659 | 15,032 | 14,561 |

| Allanté (wb 99.4) | | | | |
|---|---|---|---|---|
| R67 | cpe | 3,494 | 54,700 | 3,363 |

| Seville (wb 108.0) | | | | |
|---|---|---|---|---|
| S69 | sdn 4d | 3,420 | 26,326 | 18,578 |

| Eldorado (wb 108.0) | | | | |
|---|---|---|---|---|
| L57 | cpe | 3,360 | 23,740 | 17,775 |

| DeVille (wb 110.8) | | | | |
|---|---|---|---|---|
| D47 | cpe | 3,312 | 21,316 | 32,700 |
| D69 | sdn 4d | 3,370 | 21,659 | 129,521 |

| Fleetwood d'Elegance (wb 110.8) | | | | |
|---|---|---|---|---|
| B69 | sdn 4d | 3,421 | 26,104 | — |

| Fleetwood Sixty Special (wb 115.8) | | | | |
|---|---|---|---|---|
| S19 | sdn 4d | 3,408 | 34,850 | — |

| Fleetwood Brougham RWD (wb 121.5) | | | | |
|---|---|---|---|---|
| W69 | sdn 4d | 4,046 | 22,637 | 65,504 |

| Fleetwood Seventy-Five limousine (wb 134.4) | | | | |
|---|---|---|---|---|
| H23 | sdn 4d | 3,678 | 36,510 | 302 |
| H33 | formal sdn 4d | 3,798 | 38,580 | — |
| | commercial chassis | — | — | 577 |

| 1987 Engines | bore × stroke | bhp | availability |
|---|---|---|---|
| V-6, 173.0 | 3.50 × 2.99 | 125 | S-Cimarron |
| V-8, 249.0 | 3.46 × 3.30 | 130 | S-Sev, Eldo, DeV, Fltwd, limo |
| V-8, 249.0 | 3.46 × 3.30 | 170 | S-Allanté |
| V-8, 307.0 | 3.80 × 3.39 | 140 | S-Brgm |

## 1988

| Cimarron (wb 101.2) | | Wght | Price | Prod |
|---|---|---|---|---|
| G69 | sdn 4d | 2,756 | 16,071 | 6,454 |

| Allanté (wb 99.4) | | | | |
|---|---|---|---|---|
| R67 | cpe | 3,489 | 56,533 | 2,569 |

| Seville (wb 108.0) | | | | |
|---|---|---|---|---|
| S69 | sdn 4d | 3,449 | 27,627 | 22,968 |

153

# Cadillac

| Eldorado (wb 108.0) | | Wght | Price | Prod |
|---|---|---|---|---|
| L57 | cpe | 3,399 | 24,891 | 33,210 |
| **DeVille (wb 110.8)** | | | | |
| D47 | cpe | 3,397 | 23,049 | 152,513* |
| D69 | sdn 4d | 3,437 | 23,404 | |
| **Fleetwood d'Elegance (wb 110.8)** | | | | |
| B69 | sdn 4d | 3,463 | 28,024 | * |
| **Fleetwood Sixty Special (wb 115.8)** | | | | |
| S19 | sdn 4d | 3,547 | 34,750 | * |
| *Fleetwood production included in DeVille. | | | | |
| **Fleetwood Brougham RWD (wb 121.5)** | | | | |
| W69 | sdn 4d | 4,156 | 23,846 | 53,130 |

| 1988 Engines | bore × stroke | bhp | availability |
|---|---|---|---|
| V-6, 173.0 | 3.50 × 2.99 | 125 | S-Cimarron |
| V-8, 249.0 | 3.46 × 3.30 | 170 | S-Allanté |
| V-8, 273.0 | 3.62 × 3.31 | 155 | S-Sev, Eldo, DeV, Fltwd |
| V-8, 307.0 | 3.80 × 3.39 | 140 | S-Brgm |

## 1989

| Allanté (wb 99.4) | | Wght | Price | Prod |
|---|---|---|---|---|
| R67 | conv cpe | 3,492 | 57,183 | 3,296 |
| **Seville (wb 108.0)** | | | | |
| S69 | sdn 4d | 3,422 | 29,750 | 22,909 |
| **Eldorado (wb 108.0)** | | | | |
| L57 | cpe | 3,422 | 26,738 | 30,925 |
| **DeVille (wb 110.8; sdn 113.8)** | | | | |
| D47 | cpe | 3,397 | 24,960 | 23,294 |
| D69 | sdn 4d | 3,470 | 25,435 | 122,693 |
| **Fleetwood (wb 110.8; sdn 113.8)** | | | | |
| 847 | cpe | 3,459 | 29,825 | 4,108 |
| 869 | sdn 4d | 3,545 | 30,300 | 26,641* |
| **Fleetwood Sixty Special (wb 113.8)** | | | | |
| S69 | sdn 4d | 3,598 | 34,230 | * |
| **Fleetwood Brougham RWD (wb 121.5)** | | | | |
| W69 | sdn 4d | 4,190 | 25,699 | 40,264 |

| 1989 Engines | bore × stroke | bhp | availability |
|---|---|---|---|
| V-8, 273.0 | 3.62 × 3.31 | 155 | S-Sev, Eldo, DeV, Fltwd |
| V-8, 273.0 | 3.62 × 3.31 | 200 | S-Allanté |
| V-8, 307.0 | 3.80 × 3.39 | 140 | S-Brgm |

* Sixty Special production included with Fleetwood sdn.

## 1990

| Allanté (wb 99.4) | | Wght | Price | Prod |
|---|---|---|---|---|
| R67 | conv cpe | 3,466 | 51,500 | 3,101 |
| **Seville (wb 108.0)** | | | | |
| S69 | sdn 4d | 3,480 | 31,830 | 33,128 |
| **Eldorado (wb 108.0)** | | | | |
| L57 | cpe | 3,426 | 28,885 | 22,291 |
| **DeVille (wb 110.8; sdn 113.8)** | | | | |
| D47 | cpe | 3,466 | 26,960 | 17,569 |
| D69 | sdn 4d | 3,546 | 27,540 | 131,717 |
| **Fleetwood (wb 110.8; sdn 113.8)** | | | | |
| 847 | cpe | — | 32,400 | 2,438 |
| 869 | sdn 4d | — | 32,980 | 22,889* |
| **Fleetwood Sixty Special (wb 113.8)** | | | | |
| S69 | sdn 4d | — | 36,980 | * |
| **Brougham RWD (wb 121.5)** | | | | |
| W69 | sdn 4d | 4,283 | 27,400 | 33,741 |

| 1990 Engines | bore × stroke | bhp | availability |
|---|---|---|---|
| V-8, 273.0 | 3.62 × 3.31 | 180 | S-Sev, Eldo, DeV, Fltwd |
| V-8, 273.0 | 3.62 × 3.31 | 200 | S-Allanté |
| V-8, 307.0 | 3.80 × 3.39 | 140 | S-Brgm |
| V-8, 350.0 | 4.00 × 3.48 | 175 | O-Brgm |

* Sixty Special production included with Fleetwood sdn.

## 1991

| Allanté (wb 99.4) | | Wght | Price | Prod |
|---|---|---|---|---|
| S67 | conv cpe | 3,479 | 57,260 | 2,500 |
| R67 | conv/htp cpe | 3,536 | 62,810 | |
| **Seville (wb 108.0)** | | | | |
| S69 | sdn 4d | 3,512 | 34,195 | 26,431 |
| Y69 | STS sdn 4d | 3,564 | 37,395 | |
| **Eldorado (wb 108.0)** | | | | |
| L57 | cpe 2d | 3,469 | 31,495 | 16,212 |
| **DeVille (wb 110.8; sdn 113.8)** | | | | |
| D69 | sdn 4d | 3,622 | 30,455 | 147,998 |
| D69TS | Touring Sedan 4d | — | 33,455 | |
| D47 | sdn 2d | 3,545 | 30,455 | |
| **Fleetwood (wb 110.8; sdn 113.8)** | | | | |
| B69 | sdn 4d | 3,675 | 35,195 | * |
| B47 | cpe 2d | 3,593 | 35,195 | * |
| **Fleetwood Sixty Special (wb 113.8)** | | | | |
| G69 | sdn 4d | 3,706 | 38,695 | * |
| **Brougham (wb 121.5)** | | | | |
| W69 | sdn 4d | 4,281 | 30,455 | 27,231 |

| 1991 Engines | bore × stroke | bhp | availability |
|---|---|---|---|
| V-8, 273.0 | 3.62 × 3.31 | 200 | S-Allanté |
| V-8, 300.0 | 3.62 × 3.62 | 200 | S-DeVille, Fleetwood, Sixty Special, Eldorado, Seville |
| V-8, 305.0 | 3.74 × 3.48 | 170 | S-Brougham |
| V-8, 350.0 | 4.00 × 3.48 | 185 | O-Brougham |

*Fleetwood production included with DeVille.

## 1992

| Allanté (wb 99.4) | | Wght | Price | Prod |
|---|---|---|---|---|
| S67 | conv cpe | 3,402 | 58,470 | 1,931 |
| R67 | conv/htp cpe | 3,462 | 64,090 | |
| **Seville (wb 111.0)** | | | | |
| S69 | sdn 4d | 3,648 | 34,975 | 43,954 |
| Y69 | STS sdn 4d | 3,721 | 37,975 | |
| **Eldorado (wb 108.0)** | | | | |
| L57 | cpe 2d | 3,604 | 32,470 | 31,151 |
| **DeVille (wb 110.8; sdn 113.8)** | | | | |
| D69 | sdn 4d | 3,591 | 31,740 | 142,328 |
| T69 | Touring Sedan 4d | 3,627 | 35,190 | |
| D47 | sdn 2d | 3,519 | 31,740 | |

# Cadillac

| Fleetwood (wb 110.8; sdn 113.8) | | Wght | Price | Prod |
|---|---|---|---|---|
| B69 | sdn 4d | 3,642 | 36,360 | * |
| B47 | cpe 2d | 3,566 | 36,360 | * |
| **Fleetwood Sixty Special (wb 113.8)** | | | | |
| G69 | sdn 4d | 3,653 | 39,860 | * |
| **Brougham (wb 121.5)** | | | | |
| W69 | sdn 4d | 4,277 | 31,740 | 13,761 |

| 1992 Engines | bore × stroke | bhp | availability |
|---|---|---|---|
| V-8, 273.0 | 3.62 × 3.31 | 200 | S-Allanté |
| V-8, 300.0 | 3.62 × 3.62 | 200 | S-DeVille, Fleetwood, Sixty Special, Eldorado, Seville |
| V-8, 305.0 | 3.74 × 3.48 | 170 | S-Brougham |
| V-8, 350.0 | 4.00 × 3.48 | 185 | O-Brougham |

*Fleetwood production included with DeVille.

## 1993

| Allanté (wb 99.4) | | Wght | Price | Prod |
|---|---|---|---|---|
| S67 | conv cpe | 3,776 | 61,675 | 4,670 |
| **Seville (wb 111.0)** | | | | |
| S69 | sdn 4d | 3,648 | 36,990 | 37,239 |
| Y69 | STS sdn 4d | 3,721 | 41,990 | |
| **Eldorado (wb 108.0)** | | | | |
| L57 | cpe 2d | 3,640 | 33,990 | 21,473 |
| **DeVille (wb 110.8; sdn 113.7)** | | | | |
| D69 | sdn 4d | 3,605 | 32,990 | 130,714 |
| T69 | Touring Sedan 4d | 3,651 | 36,310 | |
| D47 | sdn 2d | 3,519 | 33,915 | |
| **Sixty Special (wb 113.8)** | | | | |
| G69 | sdn 4d | 3,649 | 37,230 | * |

*Sixty Special production included with DeVille.

| Fleetwood (wb 121.5) | | | | |
|---|---|---|---|---|
| W69 | sdn 4d | 4,367 | 33,990 | 31,773 |

| 1993 Engines | bore × stroke | bhp | availability |
|---|---|---|---|
| V-8, 279.0 | 3.66 × 3.31 | 295 | S-Allanté |
| V-8, 279.0 | 3.66 × 3.31 | 270 | O-Eldorado |
| V-8, 279.0 | 3.66 × 3.31 | 295 | O-Eldorado, Seville |
| V-8, 299.0 | 3.62 × 3.62 | 200 | S-DeVille, Sixty Special, Eldorado, Seville |
| V-8, 350.0 | 4.00 × 3.48 | 185 | O-Fleetwood |

## 1994

| Seville (wb 111.0) | | Wght | Price | Prod |
|---|---|---|---|---|
| S69 | sdn 4d | 3,830 | 40,990 | 46,714 |
| Y69 | STS sdn 4d | 3,892 | 44,890 | |
| **Eldorado (wb 108.0)** | | | | |
| L57 | cpe 2d | 3,773 | 37,290 | 24,970 |
| T57 | TC cpe 2d | 3,818 | 40,590 | |
| **DeVille (sdn 113.7)** | | | | |
| D69 | sdn 4d | 3,757 | 32,990 | 120,352 |
| F69 | Concours sdn 4d | 3,984 | 36,950 | |
| **Fleetwood (wb 121.5)** | | | | |
| W69 | sdn 4d | 4,478 | 33,990 | 27,473 |

| 1994 Engines | bore × stroke | bhp | availability |
|---|---|---|---|
| V-8, 279.0 | 3.66 × 3.31 | 270 | S-Eldorado, Seville, Concours |
| V-8, 279.0 | 3.66 × 3.31 | 295 | O-Eldorado, Seville |
| V-8, 300.0 | 3.62 × 3.62 | 200 | S-DeVille |
| V-8, 350.0 | 4.00 × 3.48 | 260 | O-Fleetwood |

## 1995

| Seville (wb 111.0) | | Wght | Price | Prod |
|---|---|---|---|---|
| S69 | sdn 4d | 3,832 | 41,935 | 38,931 |
| Y69 | STS sdn 4d | 3,869 | 45,935 | |
| **Eldorado (wb 108.0)** | | | | |
| L57 | cpe 2d | 3,765 | 38,220 | 25,230 |
| T57 | TC cpe 2d | 3,801 | 41,535 | |
| **DeVille (wb 113.7)** | | | | |
| D69 | sdn 4d | 3,761 | 34,900 | 91,501 |
| F69 | Concours sdn 4d | 3,988 | 17,570 | |
| **Fleetwood (wb 121.5)** | | | | |
| W69 | sdn 4d | 4,351 | 35,595 | 16,180 |

| 1995 Engines | bore × stroke | bhp | availability |
|---|---|---|---|
| V-8, 279.0 | 3.66 × 3.31 | 275 | S-Eldorado, Seville, Concours |
| V-8, 279.0 | 3.66 × 3.31 | 300 | O-Eldorado, Seville |
| V-8, 299.0 | 3.62 × 3.62 | 200 | S-DeVille |
| V-8, 350.0 | 4.00 × 3.48 | 260 | O-Fleetwood |

## 1996

| Seville (wb 111.0) | | Wght | Price | Prod |
|---|---|---|---|---|
| S69 | sdn 4d | 3,832 | 42,995 | 38,241 |
| Y69 | STS sdn 4d | 3,869 | 47,495 | |
| **Eldorado (wb 108.0)** | | | | |
| L57 | cpe 2d | 3,765 | 39,595 | 20,816 |
| T57 | TC cpe 2d | 3,801 | 42,995 | |
| **DeVille (wb 113.7)** | | | | |
| D69 | sdn 4d | 3,981 | 35,995 | 111,279 |
| F69 | Concours sdn 4d | 3,959 | 40,495 | |
| **Fleetwood (wb 121.5)** | | | | |
| W69 | sdn 4d | 4,461 | 36,995 | 15,109 |

| 1996 Engines | bore × stroke | bhp | availability |
|---|---|---|---|
| V-8, 279.0 | 3.66 × 3.31 | 275 | S-Eldorado, Seville, DeVille |
| V-8, 279.0 | 3.66 × 3.31 | 300 | O-Eldorado, Seville, Concours |
| V-8, 350.0 | 4.00 × 3.48 | 260 | S-Fleetwood |

## 1997

| Catera (wb 107.4) | | Wght | Price | Prod |
|---|---|---|---|---|
| M69 | sdn 4d | 3,770 | 29,995 | 28,704 |
| **Seville (wb 111.0)** | | | | |
| S69 | SLS sdn 4d | 3,900 | 39,995 | 23,127 |
| Y69 | STS sdn 4d | 3,900 | 44,995 | 22,156 |
| **Eldorado (wb 108.0)** | | | | |
| L57 | cpe 2d | 3,821 | 37,995 | 11,521 |
| T57 | TC cpe 2d | 3,863 | 41,395 | 8,626 |
| **DeVille (wb 113.8)** | | | | |
| D69 | sdn 4d | 4,009 | 36,995 | 77,603 |
| E69 | d'Elegance sdn 4d | 4,009 | 39,995 | 14,095 |

# Cadillac

| DeVille (wb 113.8) | | Wght | Price | Prod |
|---|---|---|---|---|
| F69 | Concours sdn 4d | 4,052 | 41,995 | 9,665 |

| 1997 Engines | bore × stroke | bhp | availability |
|---|---|---|---|
| V-6, 181.0 | 3.40 × 3.40 | 200 | S-Catera |
| V-8, 279.0 | 3.66 × 3.31 | 275 | S-Eldorado, Seville, DeVille |
| V-8, 279.0 | 3.66 × 3.31 | 300 | O-Eldorado, Seville, Concours |

## 1998

| Catera (wb 107.4) | | Wght | Price | Prod |
|---|---|---|---|---|
| M69 | sdn 4d | 3,770 | 29,995 | 20,512 |
| R69 | leather int. sdn 4d | — | 33,610 | 9,635 |

| Seville (wb 112.2) | | | | |
|---|---|---|---|---|
| S69 | SLS sdn 4d | 3,972 | 42,495 | 16,460 |
| Y69 | STS sdn 4d | — | 46,995 | 18,061 |

| Eldorado (wb 108.0) | | | | |
|---|---|---|---|---|
| L57 | cpe 2d | 3,843 | 38,495 | 11,666 |
| T57 | TC cpe 2d | 3,876 | 42,695 | 6,749 |

| DeVille (wb 113.8) | | | | |
|---|---|---|---|---|
| D69 | sdn 4d | 4,012 | 37,695 | 83,798 |
| E69 | d'Elegance sdn 4d | 4,052 | 41,295 | 16,417 |
| F69 | Concours sdn 4d | 4,063 | 42,995 | 10,052 |

| 1998 Engines | bore × stroke | bhp | availability |
|---|---|---|---|
| V-6, 181.0 | 3.40 × 3.40 | 200 | S-Catera |
| V-8, 279.0 | 3.66 × 3.31 | 275 | S-Eldorado, Seville, DeVille |
| V-8, 279.0 | 3.66 × 3.31 | 300 | O-Eldorado, Seville, Concours |

## 1999

| Catera (wb 107.4) | | Wght | Price | Prod |
|---|---|---|---|---|
| R69 | sdn 4d | 3,770 | 34,180 | 14,495 |

| Seville (wb 112.2) | | | | |
|---|---|---|---|---|
| S69 | SLS sdn 4d | 3,970 | 43,355 | 20,891 |
| Y69 | STS sdn 4d | 4,001 | 47,850 | 21,561 |

| Eldorado (wb 108.0) | | | | |
|---|---|---|---|---|
| L57 | cpe 2d | 3,843 | 39,235 | 9,637 |
| T57 | TC cpe 2d | 3,876 | 43,495 | 6,535 |

| DeVille (wb 113.8) | | | | |
|---|---|---|---|---|
| D69 | sdn 4d | 4,012 | 38,630 | 85,561 |
| E69 | d'Elegance sdn 4d | 4,052 | 42,730 | 17,335 |
| F69 | Concours sdn 4d | 4,063 | 43,230 | 9,357 |

| 1999 Engines | bore × stroke | bhp | availability |
|---|---|---|---|
| V-6, 181.0 | 3.40 × 3.40 | 200 | S-Catera |
| V-8, 279.0 | 3.66 × 3.31 | 275 | S-Eldorado, Seville, DeVille |
| V-8, 279.0 | 3.66 × 3.31 | 300 | O-Eldorado, Seville, Concours |

## 2000

| Catera (wb 107.4) | | Wght | Price | Prod |
|---|---|---|---|---|
| R69 | sdn 4d | 3,770 | 31,010 | 16,072 |

| Seville (wb 112.2) | | | | |
|---|---|---|---|---|
| S69 | SLS sdn 4d | 3,970 | 43,880 | 16,904 |
| Y69 | STS sdn 4d | 4,001 | 48,480 | 17,688 |

| Eldorado (wb 108.0) | | | | |
|---|---|---|---|---|
| L57 | ESC cpe 2d | 3,843 | 39,120 | 8,396 |
| T57 | ETC cpe 2d | 3,876 | 42,695 | 5,597 |

| DeVille (wb 115.3) | | Wght | Price | Prod |
|---|---|---|---|---|
| D69 | sdn 4d | 3,978 | 39,500 | 69,085 |
| E69 | DHS sdn 4d | — | 44,700 | 12,365 |
| F69 | DTS sdn 4d | — | 44,700 | 17,006 |

| 2000 Engines | bore × stroke | bhp | availability |
|---|---|---|---|
| V-6, 181.0 | 3.40 × 3.40 | 200 | S-Catera |
| V-8, 279.0 | 3.66 × 3.31 | 275 | S-Eldorado, Seville, DeVille |
| V-8, 279.0 | 3.66 × 3.31 | 300 | O-Eldorado, Seville, DTS |

## 2001

| Catera (wb 107.5) | | Wght | Price | Prod |
|---|---|---|---|---|
| R69 | sdn 4d | 3,770 | 31,305 | 12,097 |

| Seville (wb 112.2) | | | | |
|---|---|---|---|---|
| S69 | SLS sdn 4d | 3,986 | 41,935 | 14,626 |
| Y69 | STS sdn 4d | 4,027 | 48,245 | 13,430 |

| Eldorado (wb 108.0) | | | | |
|---|---|---|---|---|
| L57 | ESC cpe 2d | 3,814 | 40,346 | 5,745 |
| T57 | ETC cpe 2d | 3,865 | 44,011 | 4,652 |

| DeVille (wb 115.3) | | | | |
|---|---|---|---|---|
| D69 | sdn 4d | 3,978 | 38,630 | 63,778 |
| E69 | DHS sdn 4d | 4,049 | 42,730 | 13,550 |
| F69 | DTS sdn 4d | 4,047 | 43,230 | 14,516 |

| 2001 Engines | bore × stroke | bhp | availability |
|---|---|---|---|
| V-6, 181.0 | 3.40 × 3.40 | 200 | S-Catera |
| V-8, 279.0 | 3.66 × 3.31 | 275 | S-Eldorado, Seville, DeVille |
| V-8, 279.0 | 3.66 × 3.31 | 300 | O-Eldorado, Seville, DTS |

## 2002

| Seville (wb 112.2) | | Wght | Price | Prod* |
|---|---|---|---|---|
| S69 | SLS sdn 4d | 3,992 | 43,524 | |
| Y69 | STS sdn 4d | 4,027 | 49,080 | |

| Eldorado (wb 108.0) | | | | |
|---|---|---|---|---|
| L57 | ESC cpe 2d | 3,814 | 41,865 | |
| T57 | ETC cpe 2d | 3,865 | 45,000 | |
| C5T | ECS cpe 2d | 3,865 | 47,660 | |

| DeVille (wb 115.3) | | | | |
|---|---|---|---|---|
| D69 | sdn 4d | 3,984 | 42,325 | |
| E69 | DHS sdn 4d | 4,048 | 47,255 | |
| F69 | DTS sdn 4d | 4,044 | 47,255 | |

| 2002 Engines | bore × stroke | bhp | availability |
|---|---|---|---|
| V-8, 279.0 | 3.66 × 3.31 | 275 | S-Eldorado, Seville, DeVille |
| V-8, 279.0 | 3.66 × 3.31 | 300 | O-Eldorado, Seville, DTS |

*Production numbers not available at time of publication.

## 2003*

| CTS (wb 113.4) | | Wght | Price | Prod* |
|---|---|---|---|---|
| M69 | sdn 4d | 3,509 | 29,350 | |

| 2003 Engines | bore × stroke | bhp | availability |
|---|---|---|---|
| V-6, 194.0 | 3.44 × 3.46 | 220 | S-CTS |

*Complete product line and production numbers not available at time of publication.

# Checker

Founded in 1922, Checker was long-famous for specially designed taxicabs and airport limousines when it began selling "civilian" models in 1959. Some sources say Checker offered "pleasure cars" as early as 1948, but the Kalamazoo factory always said 1959 was the first year for private sales.

Assuming one could find a Checker dealer (they were never very numerous), civilians bought what was initially called Superba, a four-door sedan or wagon in standard or Special trim. Specials were more deluxe inside, but not much. All were the same tanklike affairs familiar to anyone who ever hailed a cab from the mid-'50s to the mid-'80s. The A8 hit the streets in 1956 with a wheelbase of 120 inches—fairly compact for the time. Average curb weights were 3400 pounds for the sedans, and nearly 3800 for the boxy wagons.

Morris Markin, Checker's founder and president, was steadfast: There'd be no change to this dumpy but practical design so long as there were buyers for reliable, durable, "taxi-tough" cars. Not that there'd been many changes before. Aside from noncommercial paint jobs and leaving off the "hire light," the Superba differed from the A8 only in a front-end facelift with trendy quad headlamps.

Superba power came from Continental Motor Company, basically the same 226-cubic-inch L-head six once used by Kaiser (see entry). Here, though, it was available in side-valve and overhead-valve versions at no difference in price. The former had 7.3:1 compression and produced a mere 80 horsepower, so it must have been meant for areas where gas was of very poor quality. The ohv unit had a more-modern 8:1 squeeze and a more-respectable 122 bhp. Transmissions were the expected three-speed column-shift manual and Borg-Warner automatic.

True to its taxi traditions, the Superba sedan could be equipped with a pair of rear jump seats for carrying up to eight. The wagon, which came with a roll-down tailgate window, had the same roomy back seat, which folded down to make a truly voluminous cargo deck. Unusually, though, the seat-folding was accomplished by an electric servo. This gimmick and the different bodywork made the wagon some $350 more expensive than the sedan.

At a time when mainstream American cars rolled on 14-inch wheels, Checker stuck with 15s, which made for smoother taxi rides over the increasingly cratered streets of urban America. Also reflecting its taxi origins, the Superba boasted tall doors and ruler-flat floors for easy entry/exit and plenty of foot space. It did not, however, boast much in the way of luxury: rubber mats where carpeting might have been, pedestrian hardboard headliner, and a conspicuous absence of late-'50s safety features like padded dash and sun visors, dished steering wheel, and seatbelts. Plain round gauges nestled within a flat-faced dashboard that looked like something from a '51 Plymouth, a design that would be absolutely unchanged through the very last cars Checker built.

Seeking higher nonfleet sales, Checker applied the Marathon name to the Superba Special for 1961, substituted 14-inch wheels on both Superba and Marathon sedans, and standardized the ohv engine for wagons. Prices stood pat: $2542 for the base Superba sedan to $3004 for the Marathon wagon. Air conditioning cost $411 extra, power steering $64. The model quartet returned for 1962, the only change being a return to 15-inch wheels for sedans. But Checker now further plied the consumer market with a special new Town Custom limousine on a 129-inch wheelbase. Optimistically priced at $7500, it came with vinyl roof and a division window between front and rear compartments; there was also a full range of power options. But production was limited by low demand—understandable, as even the most-expensive nonlimousine Cadillac cost less. The only change for '63 was boosting the ohv engine to 141 bhp for all models.

In 1964, prices rose about $100 and Superba was dropped from the Checker line. The following year, Checker switched to more-modern Chevrolet engines: standard 140-bhp, 230-cid six and optional 283 and 327 V-8s with 195 and 250 bhp, respectively. The Town Custom limo was still around, but only by special order. The 283 cost $110 extra, automatic transmission $248, overdrive $108.

For 1966, Checker added a Marathon Deluxe sedan and a lower-priced limousine ($4541), thus re-establishing a four-model line. Both were dropped the following year, but the Deluxe sedan returned for '68, the limousine for 1969.

The Chevy V-8s naturally made post-1964 Checkers much faster than the earlier six-cylinder cars. And there was more power to come. The 283 was dropped for '67, and a 307-cid

**Circa 1961 Superba four-door sedan**

**1961 Superba four-door sedan**

**1963 Marathon four-door station wagon**

# Checker

1964 Marathon four-door sedan

1970 Marathon DeLuxe Limousine

1965 Marathon four-door sedan

1980 Marathon four-door sedan

1965-67 Marathon DeLuxe Limousine

replacement with 200 bhp was available for 1968 only. For 1969, the 327 was joined by a new 350 Chevy small-block with 300 bhp. Emissions tuning cut horses to 250 for 1970. Prices for the optional engines were usually low: in 1968, $108 for the 307 and $195 for the 327.

Checker sales were always moderate in the '60s, though adequate to sustain the firm's desired annual volume of 6000-7000 units. Checker's best year of the decade was 1962, when it built 8173 cars, though most were taxis.

Markin never wavered from his mission of building taxi-tough cars. It isn't widely known, but Nathan Altman once approached Checker about building his Avanti II (see entry). Markin replied that the Avanti was too ugly to bother with.

David Markin took over the helm in Kalamazoo on his father's death in 1970, but he didn't much change the company or its products until the mid-'70s. That's when Edward N. Cole, having retired as GM president in 1974, joined Checker to launch a new-model development program. Sadly, Cole was killed in a plane crash before his efforts reached fruition.

Checker began a long, steady decline in 1970. The main problem was increased competition for fleet sales from the major Detroit makers who needed this important outlet when passenger-car sales slowed in the mid-'70s (during the OPEC oil embargo) and again at decade's end. With its low fixed volume and relatively high overhead, tiny Checker just couldn't compete with the Big Three on price. As a result, its passenger-car volume was dramatically lower after 1969: fewer than 400 for 1970, a more encouraging 600-1000 units a year through 1974, less than 500 thereafter.

Relentless inflation-fueled price escalation didn't help. The standard sedan was up to almost $4000 by '73, to near $5400 by '75, over $6000 in '77, and close to $8000 by 1980. That was Chrysler or Buick money, and a lot to ask for such a dull car that wasn't put together all that well.

These difficulties were reflected in Checker's dwindling number of models and sales as the '70s wore on. The decade began with the usual Marathon sedan and wagon and long-wheelbase Deluxe sedan and limo. The latter proved unprofitable and was dropped after '71.

The wagon disappeared after 1974, but the sedan and long-wheelbase Deluxe sedan carried on to the end. The standard six after 1970 was the stroked 250 version of the Chevy 230, rated at 145 horsepower through '71, 100-115 thereafter. The 350 V-8 remained optional, down-rated to 145-170 bhp SAE net for 1972-79. A 145-bhp, 305-cid small-block became an additional option after 1976 and a 105 horsepower, 350-cid diesel was offered in 1980-82.

Through all of this, Checker clung to its extremely dated basic design, resisting all suggestions that it needed to be replaced. The addition of federal "crash" bumpers for 1974—big girderlike lumps of steel—rendered quite ugly a car that had once simply looked old. The famed Ghia coachworks in Italy devised a prototype for a handsome new-generation Checker in 1970, but it was refused. The same fate awaited "Galva II," a 1975 proposal by Autodynamics of Madison Heights, Michigan. This had extremely simple, rectilinear styling to keep tooling costs to an absolute minimum. It likely failed for lack of money, though managerial stubbornness was still a factor.

But that began to change once the dynamic Ed Cole started planning yet another new Checker soon after his arrival. Targeted for production sometime during 1983, this was a boxy, square-lined, four-door hatchback sedan with front-drive mechanicals borrowed from the GM X-car compacts, which Cole knew were in the works when he joined Checker. A sturdy new box-section chassis of undisclosed design was planned for three models: a 109-inch-wheelbase six-passenger version, a 122-inch eight-seater, and a 128-inch nine-seater. A variety of low-cost, easily replaced plastic body panels was contemplated, as was an interesting rear suspension with solid rubber springs. Design work progressed as far as a single full-scale mockup.

But it made no difference in the end. The project lost momentum with Cole's untimely death, and by that time even Checker's taxi business had become marginal. With that, Kalamazoo ceased all production in mid-1982.

Intriguingly, Checkers show signs of becoming minor collector's items, especially the low-volume Town Limousines and the huge multidoor "Aerobus" wagons built for airport shuttle service. Checkers, collectible? Morris Markin would be amazed.

## Specifications

### 1960—6,980 built, inc taxis

| Superba (wb 120.0) | Wght | Price | Prod |
|---|---|---|---|
| sdn 4d | 3,410 | 2,542 | — |
| Special sdn 4d | 3,410 | 2,650 | — |
| wgn 4d | 3,780 | 2,896 | — |
| Special wgn 4d | 3,780 | 3,004 | — |

| 1960 Engines | bore × stroke | bhp | availability |
|---|---|---|---|
| I-6, 226.0 | 3.31 × 4.38 | 80 | S-all |
| I-6, 226.0 | 3.31 × 4.38 | 122 | O-all |

### 1961—5,683 built, inc taxis

| Superba (wb 120.0) | Wght | Price | Prod |
|---|---|---|---|
| sdn 4d | 3,320 | 2,542 | — |
| wgn 4d | 3,570 | 2,896 | — |
| **Marathon (wb 120.0)** | | | |
| sdn 4d | 3,345 | 2,650 | — |
| wgn 4d | 3,615 | 3,004 | — |

| 1961 Engines | bore × stroke | bhp | availability |
|---|---|---|---|
| I-6, 226.0 | 3.31 × 4.38 | 80 | S-all |
| I-6, 226.0 | 3.31 × 4.38 | 122 | S-wgn; O-sdn |

### 1962—8,173 built, inc taxis

| Superba (wb 120.0) | Wght | Price | Prod |
|---|---|---|---|
| sdn 4d | 3,320 | 2,642 | — |
| wgn 4d | 3,570 | 2,991 | — |
| **Marathon (wb 120.0)** | | | |
| sdn 4d | 3,345 | 2,793 | — |
| wgn 4d | 3,615 | 3,140 | — |
| **Town Custom (wb 129.0)** | | | |
| limo 8P | 5,000 | 7,500 | — |

| 1962 Engines | bore × stroke | bhp | availability |
|---|---|---|---|
| I-6, 226.0 | 3.31 × 4.38 | 80 | S-all |
| I-6, 226.0 | 3.31 × 4.38 | 122 | O-all |

### 1963—7,050 built, inc taxis

| Superba (wb 120.0) | Wght | Price | Prod |
|---|---|---|---|
| sdn 4d | 3,485 | 2,642 | — |
| wgn 4d | 3,625 | 2,991 | — |

# Checker

| Marathon (wb 120.0) | | Wght | Price | Prod |
|---|---|---|---|---|
| sdn 4d | | 3,485 | 2,773 | — |
| wgn 4d | | 3,625 | 3,140 | — |
| **Town Custom (wb 129.0)** | | | | |
| limo 8P | | 5,000 | 7,500 | — |

| 1963 Engines | bore × stroke | bhp | availability |
|---|---|---|---|
| I-6, 226.0 | 3.31 × 4.38 | 80 | S-all |
| I-6, 226.0 | 3.31 × 4.38 | 141 | O-all |

### 1964—6,310 built, inc taxis

| Marathon (wb 120.0) | | Wght | Price | Prod |
|---|---|---|---|---|
| sdn 4d | | 3,625 | 2,814 | — |
| wgn 4d | | 3,720 | 3,160 | — |
| **Town Custom (wb 129.0)** | | | | |
| limo 8P | | 5,000 | 8,000 | — |

| 1964 Engines | bore × stroke | bhp | availability |
|---|---|---|---|
| I-6, 226.0 | 3.3 × 4.38 | 80 | S-all |
| I-6, 226.0 | 3.31 × 4.38 | 141 | O-all |

### 1965—6,136 built, inc taxis

| Marathon (wb 120.0) | | Wght | Price | Prod |
|---|---|---|---|---|
| A12 | sdn 4d | 3,360 | 2,793 | — |
| A12W | wgn 4d | 3,450 | 3,140 | — |
| **Town Custom (wb 129.0)** | | | | |
| A12E | limo 8P | 4,800 | 8,000 | — |

| 1965 Engines | bore × stroke | bhp | availability |
|---|---|---|---|
| I-6, 230.0 | 3.88 × 3.20 | 140 | S-all |
| V-8, 283.0 | 3.88 × 3.00 | 195 | O-all |
| V-8, 327.0 | 4.00 × 3.25 | 250 | O-all |

### 1966—1,056 built; 5,761 inc taxis

| Marathon (wb 120.0) | | Wght | Price | Prod |
|---|---|---|---|---|
| A12 | sdn 4d | 3,400 | 2,874 | — |
| A12E | Deluxe sdn 4d | 3,800 | 3,567 | — |
| A12E | limo 8P | 3,800 | 4,541 | — |
| A12W | wgn 4d | 3,500 | 3,500 | — |

| 1966 Engines | bore × stroke | bhp | availability |
|---|---|---|---|
| I-6, 230.0 | 3.88 × 3.25 | 140 | S-all |
| V-8, 283.0 | 3.88 × 3.00 | 195 | O-all |
| V-8, 327.0 | 4.00 × 3.25 | 250 | O-all |

### 1967—935 built; 5,822 inc taxis

| Marathon (wb 120.0) | | Wght | Price | Prod |
|---|---|---|---|---|
| A12 | sdn 4d | 3,400 | 2,874 | — |
| A12W | wgn 4d | 3,500 | 3,075 | — |

| 1967 Engines | bore × stroke | bhp | availability |
|---|---|---|---|
| I-6, 230.0 | 3.88 × 3.25 | 140 | S-all |
| V-8, 327.0 | 4.00 × 3.25 | 250 | O-all |

### 1968—992 built; 5,477 inc taxis

| Marathon (wb 120.0) | | Wght | Price | Prod |
|---|---|---|---|---|
| A12 | sdn 4d | 3,390 | 3,221 | — |
| A12E | Deluxe sdn 4d | 3,590 | 3,913 | — |
| A12W | wgn 4d | 3,480 | 3,491 | — |

| 1968 Engines | bore × stroke | bhp | availability |
|---|---|---|---|
| I-6, 230.0 | 3.88 × 3.25 | 140 | S-all |
| V-8, 307.0 | 3.88 × 3.25 | 200 | O-all |
| V-8, 327.0 | 4.00 × 3.25 | 275 | O-all |

### 1969—760 built; 5,417 inc taxis

| Marathon (wb 120.0) | | Wght | Price | Prod |
|---|---|---|---|---|
| A12 | sdn 4d | 3,390 | 3,290 | — |
| A12W | wgn 4d | 3,480 | 3,560 | — |
| **Deluxe (wb 129.0)** | | | | |
| A12E | sdn 4d | 3,590 | 3,984 | — |
| A12E | limo 8P | 3,802 | 4,969 | — |

| 1969 Engines | bore × stroke | bhp | availability |
|---|---|---|---|
| I-6, 230.0 | 3.88 × 3.25 | 155 | S-all |
| V-8, 327.0 | 4.00 × 3.25 | 235 | O-all |
| V-8, 350.0 | 4.00 × 3.48 | 300 | O-all |

### 1970—397 built

| Marathon (wb 120.0) | | Wght | Price | Prod |
|---|---|---|---|---|
| A12 | sdn 4d | 3,268 | 3,671 | — |
| A12W | wgn 4d | 3,470 | 3,941 | — |
| **Marathon Deluxe (wb 129.0)** | | | | |
| A12E | sdn 4d | 3,378 | 4,364 | — |
| A12E | limo 8P | 3,578 | 5,338 | — |

| 1970 Engines | bore × stroke | bhp | availability |
|---|---|---|---|
| I-6, 230.0 | 3.88 × 3.25 | 155 | S-all |
| V-8, 350.0 | 4.00 × 3.48 | 250 | O-all |

### 1971

| Marathon (wb 120.0) | | Wght* | Price* | Prod* |
|---|---|---|---|---|
| A12 | sdn 4d | 3,400 | 3,843 | 500 |
| A12W | wgn 4d | 3,600 | 4,113 | |
| **Marathon Deluxe (wb 129.0)** | | | | |
| A12E | sdn 4d | 3,700 | 4,536 | 100 |
| A12E | limo 8P | 3,975 | 5,510 | |

| 1971 Engines | bore × stroke | bhp | availability |
|---|---|---|---|
| I-6, 250.0 | 3.88 × 3.53 | 145 | S-all |
| V-8, 350.0 | 4.00 × 3.48 | 245 | O-all |

* I-6 weight/price given; V-8 adds 100 lbs & $110. Production estimated.

### 1972

| Marathon (wb 120.0) | | Wght* | Price* | Prod* |
|---|---|---|---|---|
| A12 | sdn 4d | 3,400 | 3,654 | 750 |
| A12W | wgn 4d | 3,600 | 3,910 | |
| **Marathon Deluxe (wb 129.0)** | | | | |
| A12E | sdn 4d | 3,700 | 4,312 | 100 |

| 1972 Engines | bore × stroke | bhp | availability |
|---|---|---|---|
| I-6, 250.0 | 3.88 × 3.53 | 110 | S-all |
| V-8, 350.0 | 4.00 × 3.48 | 165 | O-all |

*I-6 weight/price given; V-8 adds 100 lbs & $250. Production estimated.

### 1973

| Marathon (wb 120.0) | | Wght* | Price* | Prod* |
|---|---|---|---|---|
| A12 | sdn 4d | 3,622 | 3,955 | 800 |
| A12W | wgn 4d | 3,825 | 4,211 | |
| **Marathon Deluxe (wb 129.0)** | | | | |
| A12E | sdn 4d 8P I-6 | 3,822 | 4,612 | 100 |
| A12E | sdn 4d 8P V-8 | 3,923 | 4,727 | |

| 1973 Engines | bore × stroke | bhp | availability |
|---|---|---|---|
| I-6, 250.0 | 3.88 × 3.53 | 100 | S-all |
| V-8, 350.0 | 4.00 × 3.48 | 145 | O-Marathon |

*I-6 weight/price given; V-8 adds 100 lbs & $115. Production estimated.

▲ 1952 Allstate two-door sedan      ▼ 1939 American Bantam speedster

▲ 1966 AMC Ambassador 990 convertible    ▼ 1968 AMC AMX hardtop coupe

▲ 1970 AMC Javelin Trans Am hardtop coupe

▼ 1931 Auburn boattail speedster

▲ 1989 Avanti convertible and coupe ▼ 1931 Buick 95 phaeton

▲ 1941 Buick Super four-door convertible    ▼ 1953 Buick Skylark convertible

▲ 1958 Buick Century two-door hardtop coupe ▼ 1961 Buick LeSabre convertible

▲ 1963 Buick Riviera hardtop coupe    ▼ 1973 Buick Riviera hardtop coupe

▲ 1938 Cadillac Sixty Special sedan

▼ 1947 Cadillac Series Sixty-Two convertible

▲ 1955 Cadillac Fleetwood Sixty Special sedan ▼ 1959 Cadillac Series Sixty-Two hardtop coupe

▲ 1967 Cadillac Eldorado hardtop coupe

▼ 1971 Cadillac Coupe de Ville

▲ 1987 Cadillac Allanté convertible ▼ 1972 Checker station wagon

▲ 1931 Chevrolet station wagon ▼ 1947 Chevrolet Fleetline two-door Aerosedan

▲ 1951 Chevrolet Fleetline Deluxe four-door sedan ▼ 1957 Chevrolet Bel Air convertible

▲ 1965 Chevrolet Chevelle Super Sport hardtop coupe ▼ 1975 Chevrolet Caprice Classic convertible

▲ 2002 Chevrolet Impala four-door sedan police car ▼ 1960 Chevrolet Corvair 700 club coupe

175

▲ 1966 Chevrolet Corvair Monza convertible ▼ 1957 Chevrolet Corvette convertible

# Checker

### 1974

| Marathon (wb 120.0) | Wght* | Price* | Prod* |
|---|---|---|---|
| A12 sdn 4d | 3,720 | 4,453 | 900 |
| A12W wgn 4d | 3,925 | 4,710 | |

| Marathon Deluxe (wb 129.0) | | | |
|---|---|---|---|
| A12E sdn 4d 8P | 3,920 | 5,394 | 50 |

| 1974 Engines | bore × stroke | bhp | availability |
|---|---|---|---|
| I-6, 250.0 | 3.88 × 3.53 | 100 | S-all |
| V-8, 350.0 | 4.00 × 3.48 | 145 | O-all |

*I-6 weight/price given; V-8 adds 100 lbs & $150. Production estimated.

### 1975

| Marathon (wb 120.0; DeL 129.0) | Wght | Price | Prod* |
|---|---|---|---|
| A12 sdn 4d I-6 | 3,774 | 5,394 | 450 |
| A12 sdn 4d V-8 | 3,839 | 5,539 | |
| A12E Deluxe sdn 4d V-8 | 4,137 | 6,216 | |

| 1975 Engines | bore × stroke | bhp | availability |
|---|---|---|---|
| I-6, 250.0 | 3.88 × 3.53 | 105 | S-sixes |
| V-8, 350.0 | 4.00 × 3.48 | 145 | S-V-8s |

*Production estimated.

### 1976

| Marathon (wb 120.0) | Wght | Price | Prod* |
|---|---|---|---|
| A12 sdn 4d I-6 | 3,774 | 5,749 | 400 |
| A12 sdn 4d V-8 | 3,839 | 5,894 | |

| Marathon Deluxe (wb 129.0) | | | |
|---|---|---|---|
| A12E sdn 4d V-8 | 4,137 | 6,736 | — |

| 1976 Engines | bore × stroke | bhp | availability |
|---|---|---|---|
| I-6, 250.0 | 3.88 × 3.53 | 105 | S-sixes |
| V-8, 350.0 | 4.00 × 3.48 | 165 | S-V-8s |

*Production estimated.

### 1977

| Marathon (wb 120.0) | Wght | Price | Prod* |
|---|---|---|---|
| A12 sdn 4d I-6 | 3,765 | 6,156 | 300 |
| A12 sdn 4d V-8 | 3,830 | 6,301 | |

| Marathon Deluxe (wb 129.0) | | | |
|---|---|---|---|
| A12E sdn 4d V-8 | 4,137 | — | — |

| 1977 Engines | bore × stroke | bhp | availability |
|---|---|---|---|
| I-6, 250.0 | 3.88 × 3.53 | 110 | S-sixes |
| V-8, 305.0 | 3.74 × 3.48 | 145 | S-V-8s |
| V-8, 350.0 | 4.00 × 3.48 | 170 | O-V-8s |

*Production estimated.

### 1978

| Marathon (wb 120.0) | Wght | Price | Prod* |
|---|---|---|---|
| A12 sdn 4d I-6 | 3,765 | 6,814 | 300 |
| A12 sdn 4d V-8 | 3,830 | 6,959 | |

| Marathon Deluxe (wb 129.0) | | | |
|---|---|---|---|
| A12E sdn 4d V-8 | 4,062 | 7,867 | — |

| 1978 Engines | bore × stroke | bhp | availability |
|---|---|---|---|
| I-6, 250.0 | 3.88 × 3.53 | 110 | S-sixes |
| V-8, 305.0 | 3.74 × 3.53 | 145 | S-V-8s |
| V-8, 350.0 | 4.00 × 3.48 | 170 | O-V-8s |

*Production estimated.

### 1979

| Marathon (wb 120.0) | Wght | Price | Prod* |
|---|---|---|---|
| A12 sdn 4d I-6 | 3,765 | 7,314 | 200 |
| A12 sdn 4d V-8 | 3,830 | 7,515 | |

| Marathon Deluxe (wb 129.0) | | | |
|---|---|---|---|
| A12E sdn 4d V-8 | 3,999 | 8,389 | — |

| 1979 Engines | bore × stroke | bhp | availability |
|---|---|---|---|
| I-6, 250.0 | 3.88 × 3.53 | 115 | S-Sixes |
| V-8, 305.0 | 3.74 × 3.48 | 130 | S-V-8s |
| V-8, 350.0 | 4.00 × 3.48 | 170 | O-V-8s |

*Production estimated.

### 1980

| Marathon (wb 120.0) | Wght | Price | Prod* |
|---|---|---|---|
| A12 sdn 4d I-6 | 3,765 | 7,800 | 250 |
| A12 sdn 4d V-8 | 3,830 | 8,000 | |

| Marathon Deluxe (wb 129.0) | | | |
|---|---|---|---|
| A12E sdn 4d V-8 | 3,999 | 9,192 | — |

| 1980 Engines | bore × stroke | bhp | availability |
|---|---|---|---|
| V6, 229.0 | 3.74 × 3.48 | 115 | S-sixes |
| V-8, 267.0 | 3.50 × 3.48 | 120 | S-Del; O-all |
| V-8, 305.0 | 3.74 × 3.48 | 155 | O-V-8s |
| V-8D, 350.0 | 4.06 × 3.39 | 105 | O-V-8s |

*Production estimated.

### 1981—2,950 built, inc taxis

| Marathon (wb 120.0) | Wght | Price | Prod |
|---|---|---|---|
| A12 sdn 4d V6 | 3,680 | 9,632 | — |
| A12 sdn 4d V-8 | — | 9,869 | — |

| Marathon Deluxe (wb 129.0) | | | |
|---|---|---|---|
| A12E sdn 4d V-8 | 3,999 | 10,706 | — |

| 1981 Engines | bore × stroke | bhp | availability |
|---|---|---|---|
| V6, 229.0 | 3.73 × 3.48 | 110 | S-sixes |
| V-8, 267.0 | 3.50 × 3.48 | 115 | S-V-8s |
| V-8, 305.0 | 3.74 × 3.48 | 150 | O-V-8s |
| V-8D, 350.0 | 4.06 × 3.39 | 105 | O-V-8s |

### 1982—2,000 built, inc taxis

| Marathon (wb 120.0) | Wght | Price | Prod |
|---|---|---|---|
| A12 sdn 4d V6 | 3,680 | 10,950 | — |
| A12 sdn 4d V-8 | — | 11,187 | — |

| Marathon Deluxe (wb 129.0) | | | |
|---|---|---|---|
| A12E sdn 4d V-8 | 3,839 | 12,025 | — |

| 1982 Engines | bore X stroke | bhp | availability |
|---|---|---|---|
| V6, 229.0 | 3.73 × 3.48 | 110 | S-sixes |
| V-8, 267.0 | 3.50 × 3.48 | 115 | S-V-8s |
| V-8D, 350.0 | 4.06 × 3.39 | 105 | O-V-8s |

# Chevrolet

William C. Durant founded General Motors in 1908 but was ousted two years later, so he formed Chevrolet in 1911, intending to make it a powerful lever for regaining control. He did. By 1915, Chevrolet was a force to be reckoned with; by 1918 it was part of General Motors; by the mid-'20s, it was GM's largest volume division—and has been ever since.

Early Chevys were largish, medium-price cars with six-cylinder and even V-8 power. The make's historic turn to the low-price field came with the four-cylinder "490" of 1915, named for its advertised list price. It was a big success, outflanking Ford's Model T with more-attractive styling and more features. Its closely related successors were Chevy's mainstay products into the late '20s.

However, Chevy didn't pass Ford in production until 1927, the year Dearborn stopped building the aged T to retool for the Model A. Then, in 1929, Chevrolet introduced its new "Stovebolt Six," also known as the "Cast-Iron Wonder." The nicknames stemmed from the engine's cast-iron pistons and numerous ¼-inch slotted bolts—hardly esoteric, but wonderfully effective and reliable as Old Faithful.

The Stovebolt was engineered by Ormond E. Hunt from an earlier design by Henry M. Crane that had evolved into the 1926 Pontiac engine. By 1930, it produced an even 50 brake horsepower from 194 cubic inches. With various improvements, this solid, overhead-valve engine would remain Chevrolet's only powerplant for nearly three decades. For 1934, new combustion chambers prompted the name "Blue Flame," and two versions would be offered through 1935: 60-bhp, 181 cid and 80-bhp, 206.8 cid. The six was then redesigned for 1937 to be shorter and lighter. It also gained nearly "square" cylinder dimensions as well as four (versus three) main bearings. The result was 85 bhp from 216.5 cid. It was with this engine in 1940 that a young Juan Manuel Fangio won the car-breaking 5900-mile round-trip road race between Buenos Aires, Argentina, and Lima, Peru, at an average speed of 53.6 mph. Fangio continued to race Chevrolets after World War II, but eventually switched to Grand Prix cars and became a legend as the only five-time world champion driver.

Throughout its history, Chevrolet has usually made the right moves at the right time. To follow the Stovebolt, division general manager William "Big Bill" Knudsen and GM design director Harley Earl cooked up an elegant line of Cadillac-style cars for 1929-32. The 1930-31 line comprised a single series offering roadsters for two or four passengers, a phaeton, three coupes, and two sedans. Prices were attractively low: $495-$685.

The 1930-33 Chevys carried a different series name each year: in order, Universal, Independence, Confederate, then Eagle (deluxe) and Mercury (standard). This practice was ended for 1934, when models were grouped into Master and Standard lines. Master tacked on the "DeLuxe" handle for '35, and Standards became Masters for 1937-39.

Chevy styling in these years evolved along the lines of costlier GM cars. The '33s, with their skirted fenders and graceful lines, were perhaps the most-attractive Chevrolets of the decade. Body styles proliferated, and by 1932 included such exotics as a $625 landau phaeton. The 1933 Eagles offered many features designed to win buyers from Ford: a Fisher body with "No-Draft Ventilation" front-door ventwing windows, airplane-type instruments, Cadillac-style hood doors, a cowl vent, synchromesh transmission, selective free-wheeling, safety plate glass, adjustable driver's seat, even an octane selector. Many of these also appeared on the standard Mercury models. Wheelbases gradually lengthened, going from 1930's 107 inches to 109 for 1931-32, then to 107/110 for the '33 Mercury/Eagle; the '34 Master/Standard split 112/107.

Chevy fared well in this period despite the prevailing Depression. Production outpaced Ford's each year in 1931-33, bottoming to 313,000 units for '32, but recovering to 486,000 for '33. Volume then soared to nearly a million by 1936, though Ford was nearer.

Along with more-streamlined styling, 1934 brought new "Knee-Action" independent front suspension (IFS) to Master models, Bill Knudsen's last major decision before leaving Chevy in October 1933. According to writer Karl Ludvigsen, engineer Maurice Olley tried to discourage Knudsen from using it, saying there weren't enough centerless grinding machines in America to produce all the coil springs. Knudsen replied this was just what the machine-tool industry needed to get back on its feet. Still, he limited the new suspension to the one line.

**1930 AD Universal phaeton**

**1932 BA Confederate sports roadster 2/4 passenger**

**1933 CA Eagle sport coupe 2/4 passenger**

# Chevrolet

**1934 Master Six town sedan**

**1934 Master Six coach two-door**

**1935 Master DeLuxe coach two-door**

**1936 Master DeLuxe sport coupe 2/4 passenger**

**1937 Master DeLuxe sport sedan**

**1938 Master DeLuxe sedan four-door**

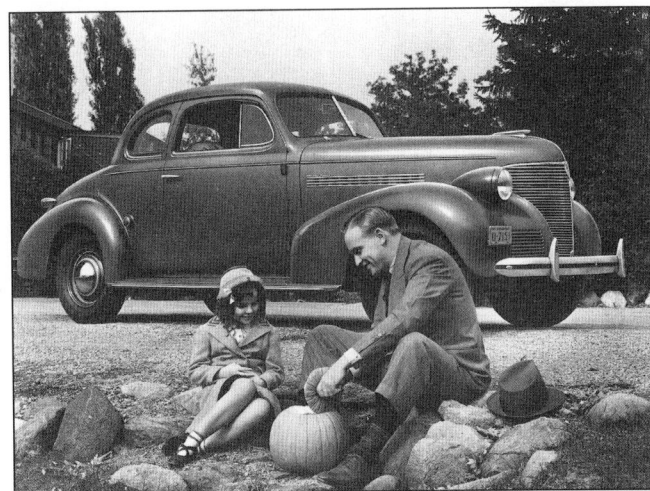
**1939 Master DeLuxe sport coupe 4-passenger**

Knee-Action wasn't universally liked, so Standard/Master retained solid front axles through 1940, after which all Chevys had IFS.

The 1935s were the last Chevys with any styling kinship to the "classic" era. Master DeLuxe added an inch of wheelbase to suit sleeker new bodies with vee'd windshield, streamlined fenders, and a raked-back radiator with cap concealed beneath the hood, then an innovation. Also new was the corporate all-steel "Turret Top" construction without the traditional fabric roof insert.

Modernization continued for 1936 as Chevrolet adopted still-rounder styling of the streamlined school, highlighted by die-cast "waterfall" grilles, steel-spoke wheels (wires remained optional), and sleeker fenders. As ever, Chevy relied on extra features to win sales from Ford. A big plus for '36 was hydraulic brakes, which Ford wouldn't offer until 1939 (thanks mainly to old Henry's stubbornness). Chevy was also quicker than Ford to drop body styles without roll-up windows, abandoning both roadsters and phaetons for 1936. The two series became more alike, as both used the 80-bhp 206.8-cid Stovebolt.

The redesigned 85-bhp engine of 1937 made Chevrolet particularly well equipped for the sales battle. However, styling became rather dull, as it did for other GM cars, with skinny, uninteresting grilles and high, bulky bodies that looked clumsy next to the increasingly streamlined Fords. Despite that, Chevy regained production supremacy for model-year '38, and until the '90s, at least, rarely surrendered it to Dearborn.

Renewed competitiveness was evident in an expanded 1940 line with what Chevy called "Royal Clipper" styling. Though not a drastic change from 1939, this facelift was sufficiently thorough to make the cars look much newer. Wheelbase was 113 inches, up from 1937-39's 112.3. Master 85 returned from '39 as the cheaper Chevy, with Master DeLuxe above it. Each offered business coupe, two-door town sedan, and four-door sport sedan; the 85 also listed a woody wagon, the DeLuxe line a sport coupe. A new top-line Special DeLuxe series had all these

# Chevrolet

**1940 Special DeLuxe town sedan two-door**

**1940 Special DeLuxe four-door station wagon**

**1941 Special DeLuxe Fleetline four-door sedan**

**1941 Special DeLuxe cabriolet coupe**

**1942 Fleetline Aerosedan fastback coupe**

**1942 Special DeLuxe sport sedan four-door**

**1946 Fleetline Aerosedan fastback coupe**

**1946 Fleetmaster cabriolet coupe**

**1947 Fleetline Sportmaster four-door sedan**

**1948 Fleetline Sportmaster four-door sedan**

plus Chevy's first true convertible coupe, which was quite successful (nearly 12,000 model-year sales). Specials and Master DeLuxes came with Knee-Action; Master 85s carried Chevy's last solid front axles. Model-year production soared from some 577,000 to nearly 765,000 as Chevrolet bested Ford by over 220,000 cars.

The gap widened to more than 300,000 for 1941 as Chevrolet scored its first million-car model year. Though no one knew it then, this year's substantial redesign would carry the make through 1948: 116-inch wheelbase, Knee-Action linewide, attractive new styling by Harley Earl's Art & Colour Section, and five extra horsepower achieved with higher compression (6.5:1); new pistons; and revised combustion chambers, valves, rocker arms, and water pump. Master 85s were dropped, but Special DeLuxe added a sleek Fleetline four-door sedan at midyear. Distinguished by a more-formal roofline with closed-in rear quarters *a la* the Cadillac Sixty Special, the newcomer managed a creditable 34,000 sales for its shortened debut model year.

Styling refinements marked the war-shortened '42s. Fenders were extended back into the front doors, as on costlier GM makes, and a smart, clean grille replaced the somewhat busy '41 face. Models stayed the same except for five-passenger coupes replacing business coupes, and series names continued as Master DeLuxe and Special DeLuxe. The latter now contained a Fleetline subseries with a new "torpedo-style" two-door Aerosedan that proved an instant hit and a conventional Sportmaster four-door, both bearing triple chrome bands on front and rear fenders.

By the time the government halted civilian car production in February 1942, Chevy's model-year total was over a quarter-million units, of which less than 50,000 were built in calendar '42. Convertibles and wagons numbered only about 1000 each. Like all 1942 Detroit cars, rarity has since rendered these Chevys coveted collector's items.

Strikes and material shortages hampered GM's postwar production startup, allowing Ford to outpace Chevy for '46. But Chevy was again "USA-1" for 1947-48 even though it followed most other makes (Ford included) by offering slightly modified '42s. The few differences involved grille treatments, medallions and other exterior trim. Models and specifications stood pat, but now Stylemaster and Fleetmaster names came in.

Meanwhile, Chevy contemplated a smaller companion model evolved under a program called "Cadet." Though different configurations were considered, the final prototype was an orthodox four-door sedan with smooth "bathtub" styling, 108-inch wheelbase, and a scaled-down Stovebolt Six. But after spending a few million dollars, management decided there was no need for a compact in the booming postwar seller's market, especially as the Cadet would have cost as much to build as a standard Chevy. Ford reached the same conclusions at about the same time. Still, the Cadet is significant as the first application of engineer Earle S. MacPherson's simple, effective strut-type front suspension, today almost universal among small cars. Ford would be the first to use it in production, however, as MacPherson went to Dearborn soon after the Cadet project was cancelled.

If production Chevys didn't change much in this period, management did, and new models were floated for the future: sports cars, hardtop-convertibles, all-steel station wagons. These and other ideas gained impetus with the June 1946 arrival of Cadillac chief Nicholas Dreystadt to replace M. E. Coyle as Chevrolet general manager. Dreystadt also encouraged a forceful engineering program that would ultimately breathe new life into a make that had acquired a respectable but stodgy image. Unfortunately, he died after just two years in office, and his successor, W. E. Armstrong, resigned early because of illness. Then came Thomas H. Keating, who continued Dreystadt's policies. Soon after he took charge, Edward N. Cole came over from Cadillac to be Chevy chief engineer.

**1949 Styleline DeLuxe sport sedan four-door**

**1949 Styleline DeLuxe station wagon**

Their first order of business was to make Chevys look more "with it." In a happy bit of timing, GM had scheduled most of its all-new postwar models for 1949, and Chevy's were among the best. Though wheelbase was actually cut an inch, to 115, the cleanly styled '49s contrived to look much longer than the 1946-48 models. They were definitely lower, accented by a newly curved two-piece windshield trimmed two inches in height, fenders swept back smoothly through the cowl and doors, and rear fenders rolled gracefully forward. Suspension revisions and a lower center of gravity made for the best-handling Chevys yet—and probably better than that year's Plymouth and Ford. The '49s were also beautifully put together, testifying that engineers and production people had taken great care to make them "right."

Matching all this newness was an equally new four-series model line. It began with an "entry-level" Special series of two- and four-door Fleetline fastback sedans and notchback Styleline town and sport sedans, sport coupe, and business coupe. All but the last were offered with more-luxurious DeLuxe trim, as was a Styleline convertible and eight-passenger station wagon. There were actually two wagons: an "early" '49 with vestigial wood in its body construction, and a midyear all-steel replacement. Fleetlines initially sold well, but the fastback fad soon faded, so offerings dwindled. The last was a lone 1952 DeLuxe two-door.

Having regained its production stride in 1947-48, Chevy rolled out a record 1,010,000 cars for 1949. Ford, however, managed about 108,000 more, thanks to a popular all-new design and an early introduction (in June '48).

No make better reflected the exuberant '50s than Chevrolet, which evolved from family freighter to hot hauler in just a few short years. Again, in this decade the division mostly made the right moves at the right times. By 1960, Chevrolet was no longer just one of the "low-priced three" but an alternative to Dodge, Mercury, and Pontiac.

# Chevrolet

1950 Styleline DeLuxe four-door sport sedan

1951 Special Styleline two-door sedan

1952 Styleline DeLuxe four-door sedan

1952 Styleline DeLuxe convertible coupe

1953 Two-Ten DeLuxe four-door sedan

1953 Bel Air convertible coupe

1954 Two-Ten DeLuxe two-door sedan

1955 Bel Air sport coupe hardtop

The 1950-52 models were the last of the traditional low-cost, low-suds Chevys, though DeLuxes accounted for 80-85 percent of production. The hoary old 216.5 Stovebolt was coaxed up to 92 bhp for 1950, when a new 105-bhp 235.5-cid version arrived for cars equipped with optional two-speed Powerglide. The last was Chevy's new fully automatic transmission, thus beating Ford, whose Ford-O-Matic was still a year off, and Plymouth, which wouldn't have a true self-shifter until '55. A torque-converter automatic similar to Buick's Dynaflow, Powerglide was a big reason why Chevy beat Ford in model-year car production by no less than 290,000, with a total of near 1.5 million.

Another factor was the new 1950 Bel Air, America's first low-priced hardtop coupe. Buyers couldn't get enough of it. Like the pioneering 1949 Buick, Cadillac, and Olds hardtops, this junior edition sported lush trim that included simulated convertible-top bows on the headliner. It debuted as a top-shelf Styleline DeLuxe priced at $1741, about $100 below the ragtop, but it outpaced the convertible by better than 2-to-1 with over 76,000 first-year sales.

Chevy took a breather the next two years, with no mechanical developments and only bulkier sheetmetal for '51, followed by detail trim revisions for '52. Yet Chevy remained "USA-1" for both years. The '51 total was 1.23 million to Ford's 1.01 million. Korean War restrictions forced industrywide cutbacks for '52,

# Chevrolet

**1955 Bel Air Beauville station wagon**

**1955 Two-Ten sport coupe hardtop**

**1956 Bel Air sport sedan hardtop**

**1956 Bel Air sport coupe hardtop**

**1956 Bel Air Nomad two-door station wagon**

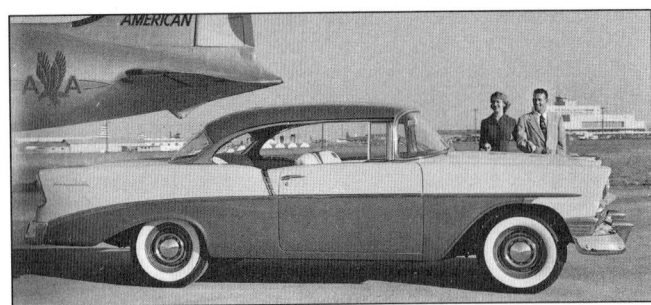
**1956 Two-Ten sport coupe hardtop**

**1957 Bel Air Nomad two-door station wagon**

**1957 Bel Air sport coupe hardtop**

but Chevy's 800,000-plus still beat Ford's 671,000.

Though the Corvette sports car was Chevy's big news for '53 (*see entry*), passenger models got a major facelift. The bottom-end Special series was retitled One-Fifty, DeLuxe became Two-Ten, and Bel Air was applied to a full range of models as the new top of the line. Higher compression brought the Blue Flame Six to 108 bhp with manual transmission or 115 bhp with Powerglide. The figures were 115/125 for 1954, when styling became a bit flashier. Chevy continued to set the production pace. With war restrictions over, volume soared to over 1.3 million units for '53 and to near 1.17 million for '54. But though sound and reliable, Chevys still weren't very exciting. All-new styling and a landmark V-8 would take care of that.

Without question, the new 265 V-8 of 1955 was one of Detroit's milestone engines. Though designed for efficiency and low unit cost, it was really one of those "blue sky" projects that comes along only once or twice in an engineer's career. As principal designer Ed Cole later recalled: "I had worked on V-8 engines all my professional life. I had lived and breathed engines. [Engineer Harry F.] Barr and I were always saying how we would do it if we could ever design a new engine. You just know you want five main bearings—there's no decision to make. We knew that a certain bore/stroke relationship was the most compact. We knew we'd like a displacement of 265 cubic inches . . . And we never changed any of this. We released our engine for tooling direct from the drawing boards. That's how wild and crazy we were."

They had reason to be enthusiastic. The 265 boasted low reciprocating mass allowing high rpm; die-cast heads with integral, interchangeable valve guides; aluminum "slipper" pistons;

a crankshaft of forged pressed-steel instead of alloy iron—and much more. Best of all, it weighed less than the old six yet was far more potent, initially pumping out 162/170 bhp (manual/Powerglide) in standard tune or 180 bhp with optional Power-Pak (four-barrel carburetor and dual exhausts).

Of course, it could give a lot more—and did for '57 when bored to 283 cid and offered with optional fuel injection. Chevrolet developed a new 348-cid "big-block" for 1958 and beyond. It was a good one, but the small-block remains one of the best-known, best-loved engines of all time, earning Chevy a performance reputation the way sixes never could.

At just under $200, Powerglide became an increasingly popular option in the '50s—a smooth operator well-suited to all but high-power models. Standard three-speed manual and extra-cost stick-overdrive were offered throughout the decade, and an all-synchromesh four-speed manual came on board in 1959. Late '57 brought a second automatic option, three-speed Turboglide, but this was complex, costly, and short-lived. Powerglide would be *the* Chevy automatic until the mid-'60s.

The 1955-57 Chevys are coveted collectibles now, and styling has as much to do with this as engineering. Design principals Clare MacKichan (then Chevy studio chief), Carl Renner, Chuck Stebbins, Bob Veryzer, and others worked under Harley Earl's dictum of "Go all the way, then back off." Though the '55 didn't reach showrooms looking like their fanciful renderings, it wasn't far off, wearing Earl's hallmark beltline "dip," wrapped windshield, and a simple eggcrate grille inspired by Ferrari. The last became broader, brighter, and more conventional for '56 in line with buyer tastes.

Other elements in Chevy's winning '55 package included a more-capable suspension, bigger brakes, better steering, more interior and trunk room, better visibility—the list was almost endless. Even the old six was improved: boosted to 123/136 bhp (manual/Powerglide). With all this, plus attractive prices that weren't changed much from '54 (mostly in the $1600-$2260 range), Chevy led the industry in a record Detroit year with over 1.7 million cars, a new make high and a quarter-million better than Ford.

An interesting '55 newcomer was the Bel Air Nomad, America's first "hardtop wagon." A Carl Renner idea adapted from his 1954 Motorama show Corvette, the Nomad didn't sell that well, mainly because two-door wagons were less popular than four-doors, though water leaks were also a problem. Then, too, it was relatively expensive ($2600-$2700). Had anybody else built it, the Nomad probably would have seen minuscule production, but a respectable 8386 were built for 1955, 7886 for '56, and 6103 for 1957.

Chevy called its '55 "The Hot One." Ads said the '56 was even

**1957 Two-Ten Delray club coupe**

**1958 Impala sport coupe hardtop**

**1957 Bel Air convertible coupe**

**1958 Biscayne two-door sedan**

**1958 Bel Air Impala convertible coupe**

**1958 Bel Air sport coupe hardtop**

hotter. It was. The old Stovebolt, now offered with manual shift only, was up to 140 bhp, while the V-8 delivered up to 225 bhp with Power-Pak. A $40-million restyle made all models look more like Cadillacs, and four-door hardtop sport sedans joined the Two-Ten and Bel Air lines. Despite a broad industry retreat, Chevy managed record market penetration of close to 28 percent on just 88 percent of its '55 volume—about 1.5 million units. Ford repeated at around 1.4 million.

Ford (and Plymouth) counterpunched with all-new styling for '57. Chevy had to make do with another substantial facelift, but it was deftly done and quite popular. In fact, this Chevy is still regarded by many as the definitive '50s car. There were now eight engine choices, up three from '56, including no fewer than six 283 V-8s with 185 up to 283 bhp. The last was courtesy of "Ramjet" fuel injection, a new option that found few takers at $500, but enabled the division to claim "1 hp per cu. in." (though Chrysler had achieved that magic figure with its '56 300B). Yet even without the "fuelie," a '57 Chevy could be quite fast. For example, a Bel Air sport sedan with the four-barrel 270-bhp engine could do 0-60 mph in 9.9 seconds, the quarter-mile in 17.5, and over 110 mph flat out.

Properly equipped, the 1955-57 Chevy was a formidable track competitor. Before the Automobile Manufacturers Association voted to withdraw from organized racing in June 1957, Chevy did very well in NASCAR and other stock-car events. At that year's Daytona Speed Weeks, Chevy took the first three places in the two-way flying-mile for Class 4 (213-259 cid); in Class 5 (259-305 cid) it took 33 out of 37 places, the fastest car averaging 131.076 mph. Chevy also won the 1957 Pure Oil Manufacturers Trophy with 574 points against 309 for runner-up Ford.

While the AMA racing "ban" didn't deter Chevy and others from providing under-the-table racing support, it seemed to be reflected in the softer, more-luxurious Chevys of 1958. Riding a new 117.5-inch-wheelbase X-member chassis, they were longer, lower, wider, and heavier, but not really slower than the lighter '57s. Bodies were naturally all-new, too—and shinier, looking more "important" and Cadillac-like than ever. As it turned out, they'd be one-year-only jobs. Not so the new 348 big-block V-8, a modified truck engine (which Chevy was understandably loath to mention) offering 250 to 315 bhp. That year's base V-8 was a 185-bhp 283.

Underscoring all this change was the new line-leading 1958 Impala (a name dreamed up by designer Robert Cadaret), a lush Bel Air subseries offering convertible and sport coupe hardtop with six or V-8 in the $2600-$2800 range. Below was a rearranged model group. One-Fifty was renamed Delray (borrowed from a spiffy 1954-57 Two-Ten two-door sedan), Biscayne replaced Two-Ten, and "Station Wagon" was a separate line with no fewer than five models: two-door Yeoman and four-door Yeoman, Brookwood (in six- and nine-seat form), and Nomad. Unlike the 1955-57 Nomad, the '58 was conventionally styled.

Chevy was now clearly reaching for buyers it had never sought before: solid, substantial Pontiac types who cared more about size and comfort than performance or handling. The division's grasp did not exceed that reach. In a rough year for the economy in general and Detroit in particular, Chevy managed over 1.1 million cars. Impala was a big success, accounting for fully 15 percent of the total.

If Chevrolet showed restraint in bucking tailfins for '58, it more than made up for that the following year with another all-new body bearing huge "cat's-eye" taillamps and a "batwing" rear deck that tester Tom McCahill said was "big enough to land a Piper Cub." It could have been worse. Several 1959 proposals envisioned ugly, Edsel-like vertical grilles. Ford had shaded Chevy in model-year '57 production and came within 12,000

**1959 Impala convertible coupe**

**1959 Bel Air two-door sedan**

**1959 El Camino pickup truck**

**1960 Impala convertible coupe**

**1960 Nomad four-door station wagon**

**1960 Impala hardtop coupe**

# Chevrolet

1961 Impala convertible coupe

1961 Bel Air four-door sedan

1961 Bel Air sport coupe hardtop

1962 Chevy II Nova 400 convertible coupe

1962 Impala sport coupe hardtop

1962 Bel Air sport coupe hardtop

1963 Impala SS convertible coupe

1963 Impala SS sport coupe hardtop

1963 Chevy II Nova 400 SS sport coupe hardtop

1964 Chevelle Malibu SS convertible coupe

1964 Impala convertible coupe

1964 Chevelle Malibu SS sport coupe hardtop

units of doing it again for '59. Dearborn's more-conservative styling no doubt played a part. But future Chevys would be far more-tasteful under William L. Mitchell, who replaced Harley Earl as GM design chief on the latter's retirement in 1958.

Delray disappeared from the '59 line and a new full-range Impala series displaced Bel Air at the top, pushing other non-wagon series down a notch. All models rode a new 119-inch wheelbase, Chevy's longest yet. The growth between 1957 and 1959 was amazing: length up by nearly 11 inches, width by seven inches, weight by 300 pounds. The '59s were the first of the overstuffed "standard" Chevys that would endure for the next 15 years, though they made sense at the time. Buyers demanded ever-bigger cars in the '50s, so even the low-priced three grew to about the size of late-'40s Cadillacs and Lincolns.

Though Chevrolet would mostly follow Ford's marketing initiatives in the '60s, it continued to lead in production, winning every model year except 1961 and 1966. Like its arch rival, Chevy expanded into compacts (Corvair and Chevy II), intermediates (Chevelle), "muscle cars" (Impala SS, Malibu SS) and "ponycars" (Camaro). Each was carefully conceived to fill a specific need, and all succeeded save the singular rear-engine Corvair, which is different enough to merit a separate entry.

Such increasing specialization might imply increasing production, but though Chevy did set some records, its 1969 volume was "only" some 500,000 cars ahead of 1960's despite the introduction of four new model lines. This proliferation reflected a market that had subdivided, generating more "niche" competition than in the '50s. As a result, Chevy often competed less against rivals than against itself or other GM makes.

Its lineup certainly became quite broad by 1969, when it spanned no fewer than five wheelbases: 98 inches for Corvette, 108 for Corvair/Camaro, 111 for Chevy II/Nova, 116 for Chevelle, and 119 inches for full-size Chevrolets. An exception was the post-'67 Chevelle which, like other GM intermediates, went to a 112-inch wheelbase for two-door models and 116 for four-doors, an arrangement that would persist through 1977.

With no change in wheelbase, what became known as the "standard" (full-size) Chevrolet moved from overstyled outrageousness to clean, crisp elegance, though increasing bulk was evident after 1962. The pattern was set immediately, the 1960 edition being a more-subdued version of the wild '59. A taut new package bereft of fins and wrapped windshields bowed for '61, reflecting the first direct influence of Bill Mitchell. For '63 came a bulkier, more-sculptured look. Another complete redesign brought more-flowing lines for '65, followed by even curvier '67s with semifastback hardtop coupes and more-pronounced "Coke bottle" fenders. The '69s had a fuller, squarer look, emphasized by bodyside bulges and elliptical wheel openings. The decade's prettiest big Chevy might well be the '62, with its straight, "correct" lines and, for Impala hardtop coupes, a rear roof sculptured to resemble a raised convertible top.

Nineteen sixty-two also saw Chevy enlarge the 283 small-block V-8 to 327 cid for an initial 250 or 300 bhp in full-size models. But 283s would continue to power a variety of Chevys through 1967, when a stroked 350 more amenable to emission controls began to be phased in.

Biscayne remained Chevy's full-size price leader in the '60s, but buyer interest quickly tapered off. The midpriced Bel Air also waned, but the top-line Impala rapidly became Detroit's single-most-popular model line. Its best sales year in this decade was 1964, when some 889,600 were built.

By far the most-collectible Impala is the performance-bred Super Sport, an option package for mid-1961 and 1968-69, an Impala subseries in other years. Body styles were always limited to convertible and hardtop coupe. The concept was simple: the smooth big Chevy with sporty styling touches and available

1965 Chevelle Malibu SS convertible coupe

1965 Chevy II Nova SS sport coupe hardtop

1965 Impala Super Sport convertible coupe

1965 Impala sport coupe hardtop

1965 Impala sport sedan hardtop

1966 Impala Super Sport convertible coupe

# Chevrolet

performance and handling options. Sixes were available but not often ordered (only 3600 of the '65s, for instance). Typical features ran to special SS emblems, vinyl bucket seats, central shift console, and optional tachometer. A variety of V-8s was offered, including big-blocks, beginning with the famous 409 of 1961, an enlarged 348 delivering 360 horsepower initially and up to 425 bhp by '63.

With options like stiffer springs and shocks, sintered metallic brake linings, four-speed gearbox, and ultra-quick power steering, the SS Impalas were the best-performing big Chevys in history. But they couldn't last forever. Government regulations and the advent of midsize muscle cars combined to do in sporty big cars of all kinds. Yet Impala SS remained exciting right to the end. Even the final 1967-69 models could be ordered with "Mark IV" 427 big-blocks packing 385-425 bhp.

A far-more-lucrative full-size Chevy was the Caprice, an Impala dolled up with the best grades of upholstery and trim. A mid-1965 reply to Ford's quiet-as-a Rolls LTD, Caprice garnered a healthy 181,000 sales for model-year '66, when it became a separate line and the initial hardtop sedan was joined by wagons and a hardtop coupe. Production through the rest of the decade ranged from 115,500 to nearly 167,000. Obviously, Cadillac luxury at a Chevy kind of price still appealed as much in the '60s as it had in the days of the first Impala.

One rung below the full-size Chevy was the intermediate Chevelle, introduced for 1964 in answer to Ford's popular Fairlane. Though conventional in design, Chevelle offered almost as much interior room as Impala within more-sensible exterior dimensions—effectively a return to the ideally proportioned 1955-57 "classic" Chevy. Sales went nowhere but up—

**1966 Caprice Custom coupe hardtop**

**1967 Impala sport coupe**

**1966 Chevelle Super Sport 396 sport coupe hardtop**

**1967 Chevelle SS 396 sport coupe**

**1966 Chevy II Nova Super Sport coupe hardtop**

**1967 Chevy II Nova Super Sport coupe**

**1967 Impala SS convertible coupe**

**1967 Camaro SS 350 hardtop coupe (with RS package)**

# Chevrolet

from 328,400 in the first year to nearly 440,000 by 1969. Helping things along were numerous performance options and bucket-seat Malibu SS convertible and hardtop models.

Third down the size scale was the Chevy II, an orthodox compact rushed out for 1962 to answer Ford's Falcon, which had been handily trimming the radical Corvair. Initial engine choices were a 90-bhp, 153-cid four and a 120-bhp, 194-cid six. (Falcon had only sixes through mid-1963, then added a V-8 option.) It was a good move, but through 1966, Chevy IIs outnumbered Falcons only once: model-year '63. Sales dropped nearly 50 percent for '64, due partly to intramural competition from Chevelle. A spate of Super Sport models didn't help. Nor did a heavy facelift for '66.

What did help was a 1968 Chevy II pumped up to near intermediate size via an all-new 111-inch-wheelbase GM X-body platform. Convertibles, wagons, and hardtop coupes were deleted, leaving four-door sedans and two-door pillared coupes. The latter were available with an SS package option. Backed by a strong ad campaign and competitive prices, Chevy's compact posted soaring sales of 201,000 for '68 and over a quarter-million for 1970, when the name was changed to Nova (originally, the premium Chevy II series).

Adding new spice to Chevy's '67 line was Camaro, which would eventually succeed the ailing Corvair as the division's sporty compact. Despite the beautiful styling and impressive performance of the all-new '65 Corvair, the rear-engine Chevy was no threat to Ford's incredibly successful Mustang in the burgeoning ponycar market. Worse, it was costly to build—entirely different in concept and technology from other Chevys. Six months after the '65s debuted, division managers decided

**1967 El Camino pickup truck**

**1968 Caprice hardtop coupe**

**1968 Chevelle SS 396 sport coupe hardtop**

**1968 Chevy II Nova coupe (sans side-marker lights)**

**1968 Camaro Z-28 Rally Sport prototype**

**1969 Camaro Z-28 sport coupe hardtop**

**1969 Camaro Rally Sport convertible coupe**

**1969 Chevelle SS 396 sport coupe hardtop**

# Chevrolet

1969 Impala Custom coupe hardtop

1969 Kingswood Estate station wagon

1970 Nova coupe

1970 Caprice coupe hardtop

1970 Chevelle SS 396 sport coupe hardtop

1970 Monte Carlo sport coupe hardtop

Corvair would be allowed to fade away in favor of the conventional Camaro, which was deliberately designed as a direct Mustang-fighter.

Created under the omnipresent eye of GM design chief Bill Mitchell, Camaro styling was exactly right: long-hood/short-deck proportions; low, chiseled profile; flowing, slightly "hippy" lines. Like Mustang, Camaro aimed at those who wanted a sporty four-seater that could be equipped as an economy runabout, vivid straight-line performer, or something in-between, so it offered a Mustang-style plethora of options: some 81 factory items and 41 dealer-installed accessories.

Camaro's 1967 prices started at $2466 for the basic hardtop coupe and $2704 for the convertible with standard 140-bhp, 230-cid six. A 155-bhp, 250-cid six cost $26 extra; a 210-bhp 327 V-8 was $106. Next on the list was a 350 V-8 with 295 bhp, exclusive to Camaro in '67 but more-widely available beginning in '68. To get it you had to order a $211 Super Sports package comprising stiffer springs and shocks, D70-14 Firestone Wide-Oval tires, performance hood with extra sound insulation, SS emblems, and "bumblebee" nose stripes. A 396 big-block V-8 became available during the year at nearly $400.

Also tempting '67 Camaro customers were custom carpeting; bucket seats; fold-down rear seat; luxury interior; full instrumentation; and console shifters for the optional Turbo Hydra-Matic, heavy-duty three-speed manual, and four-speed manual. For $105, a Rally Sport package added a hidden-headlight grille, "RS" badges, and other touches. Additional extras ran to tinted glass, radio, heater, air conditioning, clock, cruise control, and a vinyl roof covering for hardtops. Mechanical options included sintered metallic brake linings, ventilated front disc brakes, vacuum brake booster, power steering, fast-ratio manual steering, stiff suspension, Positraction limited-slip differential, and a dozen different axle ratios. With all this, a Camaro could easily be optioned to $5000.

Though two years behind Mustang, Camaro was a big hit. Production topped 220,000 the first year, 235,000 for '68, and 240,000 for '69. There were no major changes through mid-1970. The '68s carried a horizontal grille treatment, ventless side glass, Chevy's new "Astro Ventilation" system, and restyled taillights; the '69s were more-thoroughly face-lifted via a recontoured lower body with front and rear creaselines atop the wheel openings, plus a vee'd grille and new rear styling.

Available for the street but aimed squarely at the track was Camaro RPO (Regular Production Option) Z-28, a tailor-made competition package for hardtops announced during 1967. With it, Camaro won 18 of 25 events in the Sports Car Club of America's new Trans-American road-racing series for production "sedans." Camaro then claimed the class championship in 1968 and '69.

Veteran Chevy engineer Vincent W. Piggins had designed the Z-28 expressly for the Trans-Am—then convinced management to sell it to the public. To meet the prevailing displacement limit, he combined the 327 block with the 283 crankshaft to produce a high-winding 302.4-cid small-block with a nominal 290 bhp—it was more like 350—and 290 pound-feet of torque. Completing the Z-28 package were heavy-duty suspension, 11-inch-diameter clutch, quick steering, hood air ducts feeding big carburetors, close-ratio four-speed gearbox, front disc brakes, metallic rear-brake linings, a "ducktail" rear spoiler, broad dorsal racing stripes, and Rally wheels with wide-tread tires. All this listed for about $400, but actual price was more like $800 because the four-speed, power front discs, special headers, and metallic rear-drum linings were all "mandatory" extras.

Nevertheless, the Z-28 was a whale of high-performance buy. It wasn't for everyone, of course, but production climbed quickly, going from 602 for '67 to 7199 for '68 and then to 20,302 for '69.

# Chevrolet

**1970 Nova coupe**

**1970 Camaro SS 350 hardtop coupe (early series)**

**1970 Camaro Rally Sport coupe (late series)**

**1970 Camaro Rally Sport coupe (late series)**

**1971 Chevelle SS 454 sport coupe hardtop**

**1971 Camaro SS coupe**

**1971 Kingswood Estate station wagon**

**1971 Monte Carlo SS 454 sport coupe hardtop**

All are now coveted collectibles, not only as the first of a great breed, but because, unfortunately, the Z would become less-special in future years.

Chevrolet fielded an all-new Camaro for 1970 and entered the personal-luxury market with the Monte Carlo. A 65-day strike kept the division from outproducing Ford, but its 12-month total of nearly 1.5 million cars was hardly bad. For the model year, Chevy built 1.46 million cars to its arch rival's two million-plus.

A kissin' cousin of Pontiac's all-new '69 Grand Prix, the cleanly styled Monte Carlo rode the Chevelle's 116-inch four-door chassis but came only as a hardtop coupe with the longest hood in Chevy history. A 250-bhp 350 V-8 teamed with Turbo-Hydra-Matic as standard, and all sorts of luxury options were offered. Alternative engines ran to a 300-bhp 350 and a new 400 V-8 with 330 bhp. Base-priced just below $3000, the Monte Carlo sold well: over 145,000 for 1970 (against only 50,000 for Ford's considerably costlier Thunderbird). Among them were a mere 3823 equipped with the optional SS 454 package—an iron fist in a velvet glove if ever there was one.

Listed as RPO Z20, the Monte SS package delivered the division's huge new 454 big-block engine, a stroked 427 tuned for 360 bhp in this application, plus square-tip dual exhausts and a chassis fortified with auto-leveling rear shocks, stiffer front shocks, and power front disc brakes. Discreet badges and black rocker-panel trim were the only clues as to what lay beneath that long hood. Acceleration was vivid: just 7.5 seconds for 0-60 mph. But luxury was this car's forte—after 1919 more in '71, the Monte Carlo wouldn't take another run at performance until years later.

Corvair's demise after 1969 left Nova as Chevy's only compact. The 1970 edition was mildly face-lifted, but saw no substantive change. That year's Chevelle, still on the split-wheelbase 1968 A-body platform, was restyled to look more like full-size Chevys, gaining a divided grille, bulges around each wheel opening, and a more-rounded, massive look. Super Sport packages were again offered for both Nova and Chevelle, the former built around a 350 V-8, the latter around the big-block 454 and 396 (which was actually a 402 now). None saw very high sales, what with rising fuel prices and insurance rates putting a big damper on muscle-car demand throughout Detroit. The big-car sales emphasis was still on the luxurious Impala and Caprice;

# Chevrolet

1971 Chevelle with Heavy Chevy option

1971 Vega 2300 hatchback coupe

1971 Vega 2300 Kammback two-door station wagon

1971 Nova SS coupe

1972 Kingswood Estate station wagon

1972 Chevelle Malibu sport sedan hardtop

1972 Impala Custom coupe

1973 Chevelle Laguna coupe

1973 Chevelle Malibu coupe

1973 Monte Carlo coupe

# Chevrolet

Biscayne and Bel Air were now reduced to just one four-door sedan each.

Arriving in the spring of 1970 was a brilliant new second-generation Camaro ('69s were sold as '70s through the previous December). With dramatic, European-inspired GT styling, it sold nearly 125,000 copies despite the abbreviated 1970 run. The ragtop was no more, another victim of fading demand, but a smooth new coupe offered the usual arm-long list of extras, including two SS packages, like Chevelle's, plus a separate Rally Sport trim group and the still-potent Z28 option. Wheelbase was unchanged, but most everything else was. If the result was heavier and less-efficient, it was also a smoother-riding and better-handling Chevy ponycar.

Chevrolet would remain "USA-1" throughout the '70s despite a few product blunders and the vexing problems that plagued all Detroit in that turbulent decade. In model-year production, it ran second to Ford only in 1970 and '71. After that, Chevy was the consistent industry leader with at least 2 million cars a year except for troubled '75, when depressed big-car demand after the 1973-74 energy crisis dropped the tally to about 1.75 million.

Such strength enabled Chevrolet to endure mistakes that would have crippled most any other brand save Ford. Even the subcompact Vega, long viewed as the division's biggest folly of the period, hung on for seven model years and sold respectably in every one.

Vega certainly seemed a good idea when it bowed for 1971. Riding a 97-inch wheelbase, the shortest in Chevy history, it carried an all-new, 140-cid four with 90 or 110 bhp. Pert styling marked by a Camaro-like front was offered in three practical body styles: two-door notchback sedan, hatchback coupe, and a nifty little two-door "Kammback" wagon.

Chevrolet spent vast sums designing, launching, and promoting this latest attempt at beating back small imports—not to mention Ford's new Pinto—and on a special factory to build it. But like the Corvair, Vega missed its intended target: bought not as basic transport but as a small sporty car, abetted by a GT coupe and wagon. Worse, it quickly became notorious for early, severe body rust, and its alloy-block engine (which made do without cylinder liners) suffered persistent oil leaks and head warping. By 1976, when the even smaller Chevette was ready, Vega was being trounced by a number of domestic and foreign rivals. Though the name was dropped after '77, the basic car—minus the problematic engine—continued through 1979 in the Monza line.

An intriguing Vega offshoot was the Cosworth-Vega of 1975-76, quite "foreign" for a U.S. car and thus something of a collector's item now. Its main attraction was a destroked, 122-cid Vega engine wearing a special 16-valve twincam aluminum cylinder head designed by England's Cosworth Engineering. Fuel was fed by Bendix electronic injection actuated by a glovebox-mounted computer.

Available only as a hatchback coupe, the "CosVeg" initially came only in black with special gold striping and cast-aluminum wheels. Completing the package were wide radial tires, full instrumentation in an engine-turned panel, front/rear anti-roll bars, four-speed gearbox, quick steering, and discreet badges. Unfortunately, the engine yielded only 111 bhp, so this wasn't the BMW-beater Chevy had planned. The '76 version offered any Vega body color and an optional five-speed gearbox, but many were unsold at year's end. Respective production was just 2061 and 1447.

Monza proved a far-more-successful Vega variant. New for '75, it rode the same chassis, but carried a handsome 2+2 coupe body with lift-up rear hatch and a fastback roofline reminiscent of certain Ferraris. A notchback "Towne Coupe" was added during the year. The Vega four was base power, but a new 262-

1974 Caprice convertible coupe

1974 Monte Carlo coupe

1974 Vega Estate Wagon two-door

1974 Nova Custom four-door sedan

1974 Camaro Type LT sport coupe

# Chevrolet

cid small-block V-8 was optional, mildly tuned for 110 bhp. Enthusiasts could opt for several interesting RPOs such as a Z01 performance and handling package and, for 2+2s, a "Spyder" appearance group.

After 1977, the Vega wagon became a Monza, and all three models got a new standard engine: the 151-cid Pontiac "Iron Duke" four (so named to reassure buyers stung by the Vega unit). That same year, the blunt-front Towne Coupe was optionally available with the 2+2's "droop snoot." Monza then saw only minor changes through early 1981, when it departed to make way for an even better small Chevy.

After a mostly stand-pat 1970, the full-size Chevys ballooned to as big as they'd ever get, thanks to 1971's new "fuselage-style" GM B-body and a longer 121.5-inch wheelbase. As ever, promotion focused on Impala and Caprice. The Biscayne and Bel Air sedans were now relegated to the fleet market, and would be discontinued after 1972 and '75, respectively. Mid-price Impala Customs, new for '68, continued finding favor among those who liked, but couldn't quite afford, a Caprice. The Caprice itself was similarly upgraded as more Classic models were added year by year.

Big-Chevy engine choices through 1976 revolved around 350, 400, and 454 V-8s, though a 145-bhp 305 was rushed out as standard for '76 (except on wagons), a post-oil-embargo economy move. Emissions tuning rendered all decreasingly potent, as did the added weight of "crash" bumpers after 1972, plus other federally required measures. Styling became progressively more ornate and "formal," and threatened rollover standards prompted hardtop coupes to be replaced by "pillared" 1974 models with huge rear side windows. For the same reason, the Caprice convertible (an Impala through '72) disappeared after 1975. Despite their limitations, these big Chevys always sold in large numbers—as ever, the epitome of middle-class American motoring.

Then, a revolution: the first wave of GM's corporatewide downsizing program, which saw the 1977 Caprice/Impala trimmed by 5½ inches in wheelbase and 600-800 pounds in gas-wasting bulk. It seemed like a huge gamble then, and Ford tried to take advantage by extolling the "road-hugging weight" of its still-enormous full-sizers. But Chevrolet, as usual, knew exactly what it was doing, and Caprice/Impala sales actually improved (despite the departure of hardtop sedans). And why not? The new models were not only lighter but more-agile, easier on gas and, to some, better-looking.

In the intermediate ranks, Chevelle and Monte Carlo were switched to GM's new "Colonnade" A-body for 1973, which meant fresh styling and no more convertibles or closed pillarless models. The Monte divided into S and plusher Landau offerings, both with rather baroque, "French curve" styling. The blockier Chevelles included base, Malibu and ritzy Malibu Classic coupes and sedans, plus a plethora of wagons in base, Classic, and Classic Estate trim. An interesting 1974-76 concoction was the Laguna S-3 coupe. A cross between a luxury tourer and the now-departed Malibu SS, it sported body-color grille

**1975 Chevelle Malibu Classic coupe**

**1975 Vega LX two-door sedan**

**1975 Nova LN four-door sedan**

**1976 Caprice Classic sport sedan hardtop**

**1975 Monte Carlo coupe**

**1976 Monte Carlo Landau coupe**

# Chevrolet

surround and bumpers, plus a posh vinyl interior available for a time with optional swiveling front seats—a revival of a '50s Chrysler idea.

When the big Chevys shrank to intermediate stature, it was obvious that the midsizers would get smaller, too. They did, for 1978. Chevelles became Malibu, and shared a new 108.1-inch-wheelbase platform with Monte Carlo. The latter retained generally florid looks, but the Malibus were crisp and clean. Again, sales didn't suffer—to Chevy's undoubted relief.

A consistently high seller since its '68 overhaul, the compact Nova saw little change through 1973, when a minor facelift occurred and hatchback two-door sedans arrived in the usual base and Custom trim. An extensive 1975 reskin ushered in new rooflines and more glass, fancy LN ("Luxury Nova") models (renamed Concours for '76), and steering and front suspension borrowed from Camaro. Nova captured 15 percent of Chevy's total 1975 sales to become the year's most-popular American compact. Engine offerings simplified for '76. The "performance" option was now a 305 V-8, a debored 350 replacing both that engine and the little 262. Standard power through 1979 remained the workhorse 250-cid inline six, after which both engine and car were scrubbed in favor of fours and V-6s in a new compact called Citation, "the first Chevy of the '80s."

Unveiled in April 1979, Citation was a runaway success its first year, helped by another fuel crisis. Body styles comprised two- and four-door hatchback sedans and a pillared "slantback" two-door unique among the four versions of this corporate design. On a 104.9-inch wheelbase, Citation's new X-body platform afforded excellent space at moderate weight, which averaged around 2500 pounds. Pontiac's well-proven "Iron Duke" four was standard; the only power option was a new Chevy-built 60-degree V-6 displacing 2.8 liters (173 cid). Both engines were mounted transversely to take advantage of the space-saving front-drive mechanicals. A four-speed manual transaxle was standard, three-speed automatic optional. For a sporty Citation, you ordered either two-door with an X-11 package comprising uprated suspension and other chassis modifications, plus brash exterior graphics. Though it had no more power at first, the X-11 was a capable performer with the V-6.

Like most new designs, however, Citation had a hefty helping of engineering and quality-control problems, and would be recalled many times. But overall balance and livability made it a hot number for awhile, and Chevrolet was hard pressed to meet demand.

Camaro almost expired after 1974 as sales sagged in the wake of the first energy crisis. But a determined effort by enthusiastic GMers saved the striking second generation from a premature end.

The 1971-72 Camaros were much like the inaugural "1970½" models save minor changes dictated by federal regulations. For '73, the macho SS was replaced by a less-pretentious LT (Luxury Touring) model with standard 145-bhp V-8, variable-ratio power steering, and appearance touches like hidden wipers, black rockers, Rally wheels, and woodgrain dash trim.

Prices started to gallop with the '74s, which were face-lifted at each end to accommodate required five-mph impact bumpers. A wraparound rear window marked the '75s, which began Camaro's sales revival after a four-year dry spell. Capitalizing on renewed interest in ponycars, Chevy reinstated the Rally Sport package as a midseason option. This included matte-black hood and front fender tops, special paint, and the further option of color-matched Z28 wheels. The '74 facelift kept going for 1976-77 as Camaro reached, then exceeded, its '60s sales record.

The big Camaro event in 1977 was a revived Z28, only with the emphasis now on refined road manners rather than raw

**1976 Cosworth Vega hatchback coupe**

**1976 Nova coupe**

**1977 Monza Spyder hatchback coupe**

**1977 Caprice Classic four-door sedan**

**1977 Impala coupe**

**1977 Vega GT hatchback coupe**

# Chevrolet

**1978 Monte Carlo coupe**

**1978 Nova Custom four-door sedan**

**1978 Monza two-door wagon**

**1978 Camaro Z28 sport coupe**

**1979 El Camino "Royal Knight" pickup truck**

**1979 Monte Carlo sport coupe**

**1979 Malibu Classic two-door sedan**

**1979 Chevette hatchback sedan**

power. Chassis engineer Jack Turner took a straightforward approach: tighter springs, thicker front antiroll bar, a more-flexible rear bar, larger wheels and tires. New exterior graphics and colors were well suited to the smooth lines. A midyear introduction limited '77 sales, but the reborn Z then zoomed in popularity.

Picking up where Vega left off was Chevette, the smallest Chevrolet ever, announced for bicentennial 1976. Derived from the 1974 German Opel Kadett, the first of GM's "world car" T-body models, it rode a modest 94.3-inch wheelbase, measured 17 inches shorter than Vega, and weighed in at just under a ton. Its mission, of course, was economy, which it delivered: 35 mpg or so on the highway. Engines were small: initially a 1.4-liter/85-cid overhead-cam four with 52 bhp and a 60-bhp 1.6-liter/98-cid version. The former was gone by '78, when the 1.6 was tuned to deliver a slightly more-respectable 63-68 bhp.

Chevette bowed as a single two-door hatchback sedan, but a four-door on a three-inch-longer wheelbase was added for '78. Options were numerous, as the car had been built "down" to a low price. Yet, like so many Chevys before it, Chevette was exactly right for its time, and quite competitive in the increasingly hard-fought subcompact market.

The entire market would be hard-fought in the 1980s. Detroit found itself battling not only a deep national recession early in the decade, but also a horde of Japanese competitors, which had already captured lots of U.S. sales territory with low prices, top-notch workmanship, and superior reliability. Though the economy began recovering after 1982, import penetration reached record levels by mid-decade—some 35-40 percent of the total U.S. car market—despite price increases prompted by a weakening dollar. Much of the Japanese gains came at the expense of AMC, Chrysler, and Ford, but GM had problems of

# Chevrolet

**1980 Citation X-11 notchback**

**1980 Citation hatchback sedan**

**1980 Camaro Z28 coupe**

**1980 Impala sedan**

**1980 Monte Carlo Sport Turbo coupe**

**1980 Citation notchback coupe**

**1980 Malibu Classic Estate wagon**

**1981 Caprice sport coupe**

its own and suffered lower volume, too. Chevrolet's withered to about 1.6 million units for 1981, when the market was still relatively good, then to a bit under 1.4 million for 1985-87.

Meantime, the division had decided to switch rather than fight, and began selling a pair of small Japanese models with bowtie badges. But in domestic production, Chevrolet maintained its traditional number-one rank only through 1987. It was then overhauled by an increasingly aggressive Ford Division, even as Dearborn as a whole out-earned the General for the first time in 40 years—and on only half the volume.

Chevy's mixed fortunes in the '80s certainly weren't for lack of product or canny marketing. GM's long-term downsizing program ushered in a spate of smaller, more-efficient new Chevys, yet old standbys were allowed to carry on so long as sales were decent. Continuing modernization saw fuel injection (both single- and multi-point) replace carburetors on many engines,

which increasingly became V-6s and inline-fours. Yet V-8s were still part of the picture, as were performance cars—once demand for them returned around 1984.

Reflecting these trends were those three division staples of the '80s, the Monte Carlo, Chevette, and Caprice/Impala. The last saw little change following a mild 1980 "aero" reskin that freshened the basic '77 styling even if it did little for mileage as claimed. Hoods were lower, rear decks higher, and coupes exchanged their sharply creased wraparound backlights for flat panes. Sedans used V-6s, either 229-cid Chevy or 231-cid Buick, as base power though 1984, then a 4.3-liter (262-cid) Chevy V-6. There was also a diesel V-8 option, the trouble-prone 350 Olds engine, canceled after '85 as Americans bathed again in a sea of cheap gasoline. Most of these big Chevys carried the reliable 305 small-block V8 (usually standard on wagons). Coupes were dropped for '83, revived for '84, then dropped again four years

# Chevrolet

1981 Chevette hatchback sedan (diesel)

1981 Citation hatchback sedan

1982 Monte Carlo sport coupe

1982 Camaro Z28 sport coupe

1982 Cavalier hatchback coupe

later. The venerable Impala name was gone by '86, as Caprices had proliferated into base, Classic, Classic Brougham, and Classic LS Brougham models.

Chevy was wise to retain big rear-drive cars once Buick, Olds, and for a time, Pontiac dropped them, for they were strong sellers even in the worst of times. And when times got better, so did Caprice/Impala sales, rising from a decade low of about 185,000 units for 1982 to nearly a quarter-million a year for 1983-87. Production then dropped below 200,000, though that was still far from shabby.

The humble Chevette was similarly little changed through the '80s, an increasing sales handicap in the fast-moving small-car sector. Model-year '81 was the production peak—nearly 434,000 units—after which assemblies tapered off steadily each year. Yet even the swan-song '86s managed over 100,000 sales, and the lack of change enabled Chevy to keep the lid on prices. Appearance updates were confined to a full-width grille and square headlamps for '79, bigger taillights for '80. Major mechanical changes were limited to a five-speed manual option from 1983 and an extra-cost four-cylinder diesel (from Isuzu) that was rarely ordered, probably because it made a slow car even slower. Though few mourned its passing, the Chevette had done an able job. It was simply time for better things.

The same could be said of the 1978-vintage Monte Carlo, which departed during 1988. Here, though, there was reason to mourn. A handsome '81 facelift, similar to the big Chevys', was followed at mid-1983 by a revived SS bearing a smoothly raked new nose and a 305 V-8 tuned for 175 bhp (later upped to 180). You also got a beefy suspension with fat raised-white-letter tires, plus bold exterior graphics and trunklid spoiler. Things were pretty plain inside, but luxury options weren't long in coming.

If far removed from late-'60s muscle, this new SS was hardly your typical mid-'80s Monte. In fact, it was the starting point for Chevy's latest racing stockers, which began cleaning up in NASCAR and elsewhere. To help its teams do even better, Chevy released an SS "Aerocoupe" at mid-1986 bearing a huge, compound-curve backlight that allegedly added a few more mph on the long supertracks. It only lasted through 1987, and only some 6200 were built—which only makes this a gilt-edged future collectible.

As ever, the most-popular Montes were the luxury sort; they were even called Luxury Sport from 1986. All sold well: more than 187,000 for '81, over 90,000 for 1982 and '83, an average 120,000 a year thereafter. Chevy might well have kept the decade-old coupe going a little longer but, again, it was time to move on.

"Moving on" at the bottom of the line meant moving to smaller, more-efficient front-drive models. The compact Citation had been the first. Cavalier and Celebrity would follow for the sub-compact and midsize segments, respectively.

Celebrity was one of four GM A-body lines announced for '83 in early 1982. All were essentially X-cars in tailored suits. Inner structure, chassis, even drivetrains were all the same, but squarer, more-formal notchback styling contrived to make Celebrity look more expensive than the slopeback Citation—which it was, by some $1500-$2000. Two- and four-door sedans were the only body styles at first, but an attractive wagon arrived for '84. All could be dressed up with trim packages variously called Custom, CL, and Classic. Also new for '84 was a Eurosport option group, available for any model. A gesture to enthusiasts, this delivered Chevy's firmer F41 handling suspension, plus special emblems, less exterior chrome, and sporty accents inside. It gilded a very middle-class lily, but the result was good enough to beg comparison with much costlier European sports sedans.

# Chevrolet

1982 Celebrity two-door sedan

1983 Celebrity four-door sedan

1984 Monte Carlo SS sport coupe

1983 Cavalier Type 10 hatchback coupe

1983 Camaro Z28 sport coupe

1983 Cavalier Cadet four-door sedan

1984 Citation II hatchback sedan

1984 Cavalier Type 10 convertible coupe

Planned to replace Malibu, Celebrity ran alongside the old rear-drive line through 1983, then soldiered on alone. Not that Chevy needed to worry, for the Celebrity handily surpassed Malibu's peak sales in this decade (278,000 for '80) by averaging 350,000 a year for 1984-87 peaking at nearly 405,000 for '86. Sales dwindled thereafter as the two-door was killed after '88 and the mainstay four-door departed after '89. But this was only because a replacement was at hand. Overall, Celebrity was a winner.

The same could not be said for the Citation that spawned it. Buyers spurned the first front-drive Chevy in rapidly growing numbers amidst a welter of safety recalls, drivability problems, and damaging publicity about weak brakes that locked up too early in panic stops. The division tried to stem the tide for '84 with detail changes and "Citation II" badges, but fooled no one. A high-output, 135-bhp V-6 arrived for the 1982 X-11 package, then became optional for any model, but that didn't help either.

In unit volume, debut 1980 would be Citation's best year: over 811,000. The tally plunged nearly 50 percent for '81, dropped under 166,000 for '82, then fell well below 100,000 through the last-of-the-line '85s. It only seemed to prove what some critics had been saying—that GM left final "shakedown" testing to its unwitting customers.

Far fewer complaints attended the front-drive Cavalier subcompact. Replacing Monza for '82, it rode the new 101.2-inch-wheelbase J-body platform, the first ever offered by all five GM divisions. Cavalier was basically "right" from the start. Nobody much liked the original engine—a new Chevy-built 2.0-liter four with old-fashioned overhead-valve head (some called it the "junkyard engine")—and the four-speed manual transaxle wasn't the slickest around, but that was about it. And there were some tangible strengths: decent room for four, neat styling, initial choice of four body styles—two- and four-door sedans, four-door wagon, and two-door "fasthatch" coupe—and competitive

# Chevrolet

prices, initially less than $6000 base.

Customers responded strongly to Cavalier, snapping up better than 195,000 for the extra-long '82 model year, over 462,000 of the '84s and some 432,000 of the '86s. Steady improvement helped: a five-speed manual option, throttle-body fuel injection, more power, a neat convertible for '83, new frontal styling for '84, "mini-muscle" V-6 Z24 coupes for '85, a major facelift and a Z24 convertible for '88, and detail changes most every year.

Sales continued strong through 1994, last year for the original J-body. Demand throttled back some in the face of fresh competition, yet Cavalier did no worse than 225,000 for 1992. Even the '94s managed almost 274,000, not bad for a basic design in its 13th season. Evolutionary changes helped. Budget-priced VL ("Value Leader") models bowed for 1988. A larger 3.1-liter V-6 making 135 bhp was added in '90. For '91, the pushrod four grew to 2.2 liters and 95 bhp; by '94 it was up to 120 bhp thanks to multipoint fuel injection and other improvements. The '91 Cavs also sported a minor facelift, a more-ergonomic dash, and better-equipped base models tagged RS. Later years brought more cosmetic touchups and extra standard features like larger wheels and tires for some models, plus cupholders, extra instruments, automatic door locks, and GM's ABS VI antilock brake system. Still, starting prices remained comfortably below $10,000, though the natty Z24 convertible was pushing $20,000 by mid-decade.

Succeeding Citation as Chevy's compact were the Corsica sedan and Beretta coupe, introduced in March '87 as early '88 models. Both used a new 103.4-inch-wheelbase L-body platform exclusive to Chevrolet, though with engineering that owed much to the J-car and the front-drive N-body models at Buick, Olds and Pontiac. Among other things, that meant coil-spring suspension with front struts and a twist beam rear axle on trailing arms, rack-and-pinion steering, and front-disc/rear-drum brakes. Standard power at first was the latest Cavalier four, with the division's 130-bhp 2.8 V-6 optional. Styling was also unique to Chevy—and a welcome change from GM's earlier "cloning:" smooth, rounded, aerodynamically efficient. Best of all, these cars reflected Chevy's strongest efforts yet to ensure tight, thorough fit and finish. Corsica/Beretta got off to a strong sales start, with 225,000 built in calendar '87 alone. The "true" '88s saw only running changes. So would most later models.

A Euro-style Corsica called LTZ arrived for 1989, along with a four-door hatchback that was hard to tell from the normal notchback. That same year, Beretta's sporty GT option became a separate model and gained many appearance features of the racy GTU package from mid-'88. The GTU (named for the under-2.0-liter Grand Touring class in the International Motor Sports Association) was distinguished by 16-inch aluminum wheels, "ground effects" lower-body skirting, a five-speed manual gear-box designed by Getrag in Germany, and a tinted

1984 Celebrity Eurosport four-door sedan

1985 Monte Carlo SS sport coupe

1985 Citation II X-11 hatchback coupe

1985 El Camino pickup truck

1985 Camaro IROC-Z sport coupe

1986 Monte Carlo SS "Aerocoupe"

upper-wind-shield band with "Beretta" in big, bold letters. Beretta GT, GTU, and the Corsica LTZ all came with a V-6. A firm Z51 handling option made Berettas corner as slick as they looked. A similar Z52 setup did the same for '91 Corsicas, though it killed the LTZ.

The GTU bids fair as a minor collector's item, being a low-volume short-timer with only 3814 built for '88 and 9813 for '89. Its 1990 replacement was the Beretta GTZ, identified by a neat grilleless face instead of a broad eggcrate. Under the hood sat the High-Output version of Oldsmobile's vaunted new 2.3-liter "Quad-4," a genuine Euro-style twincam engine with four valves per cylinder and an excellent 180 bhp. But though faster than a GTU, the GTZ was far noisier and stiffer-riding. As if to acknowledge its shortcomings, Chevy offered a credit-option V-6 for '91 GTZs, a 140-bhp 3.1-liter unit.

Chevy made an odd bit history by announcing a 1990 Beretta convertible that never made it to showrooms. A handful were built for Indy 500 pace-car duty, but all were prototypes. Like Oldsmobile's new 1990 Cutlass Supreme ragtop, which did see series production, the open Beretta was basically a roofless coupe with a structural metal "hoop" bridging the B-posts. The hoop helped restore some lost torsional rigidity and preserved the coupe's pillar-mounted outside door handles. Chevy dropped Cavalier convertibles to make way for the soft-top Beretta, only to revive them when quality-control problems proved insurmountable on the Beretta. It was a minor but embarrassing episode symbolic of larger troubles.

Spring 1989 ushered in the belated 1990 replacement for Celebrity. Named Lumina, it rode the front-drive GM10 platform first used for 1988 coupes at Buick, Olds, and Pontiac. This time, though, there was no delaying the planned sedan. Base Luminas carried a humble 2.5-liter four—the old "Iron Duke" still hanging on—and offered the 3.1 V-6 at extra cost. The latter was standard for a sporty Euro coupe and sedan with black exterior trim, sport suspension, and wider 16-inch wheels and tires (versus 14s or 15s). All Luminas naturally boasted the GM10's laudable all-independent suspension and four-wheel disc brakes. But the Euro, as *Car and Driver* observed, was really quite "Amero" in ride, handling, performance, and interior treatment.

That wasn't necessarily bad, of course, but Ford's Taurus remained a much more-popular midsize. Even into the '90s, Lumina was handily outsold by Taurus and Japanese rivals Honda Accord and Toyota Camry. Styling was a likely factor. Even Charles M. Jordan, then GM design chief, admitted that Lumina sales suffered because the design sat on a shelf for some seven years before the public saw it, by which time it was no longer "clear" or "up to date."

There were no such problems with Camaro. Effectively face-lifted for 1978, the durable second generation ran three final

**1986 Celebrity Classic four-door sedan**

**1986 El Camino pickup truck**

**1986 Cavalier RS convertible coupe**

**1987 Cavalier Z24 club coupe**

**1986 Camaro Z28 sport coupe**

**1987 IROC-Z convertible coupe**

# Chevrolet

years in four models: base, Rally Sport, Z28 and new-for-'79 luxury Berlinetta (replacing LT). V-6s ousted straight sixes as standard power for 1980, when an interim 267-cid V-8 option joined the 305 and 350 engines. Sales held up well, all things considered: 152,000 for 1980, a bit more than 126,000 for '81.

A smaller Camaro was a foregone conclusion by then, and it duly arrived for 1982 on a trim 101-inch wheelbase. Though retaining the traditional format, the third generation was nearly 10 inches shorter, three inches narrower, and almost 300 pounds lighter, yet looked terrific. Chevy design chief Jerry Palmer precisely tailored styling to the smaller package: chiseled yet obviously aerodynamic. A new liftup rear hatch provided luggage access, and its compound-curve backlight was said to be the largest, most-complex piece of car glasswork ever. Beneath the swoopy new body was a more-modern all-coil suspension with front struts, and rear disc brakes were optionally available to complement the standard front discs.

The Rally Sport temporarily departed as the base '82 sport coupe became the first Camaro with a standard four, the aged 90-bhp "Iron Duke." A 2.8 V-6 was standard for Berlinetta. As ever, the hunky Z28 got the most attention. It packed only 305 V-8s: a four-barrel 150-bhp unit or a 165-bhp version with "Cross Fire" twin-throttle-body electronic fuel injection, as on that year's Corvette. Four-speed manual gearbox was standard except on the 165-bhp 228, where it was three-speed automatic only (optional elsewhere). The base Camaro could be ordered with V-6, Berlinetta with the carbureted 305.

Once again, Chevy scored big with a smaller car, the new Camaro garnering 50,000 more model-year sales than its '81 predecessor. By 1984, it was up past a quarter-million. But 1985-86 production plunged to some 185,000, the '87 tally was 50,000 units below that, and 1988 volume was under 100,000. New competition from all quarters contributed to the decline, but so did indifferent assembly and persistent mechanical troubles.

**1987 Caprice Classic four-door sedan**

**1988 Corsica four-door sedan**

**1988 Beretta GT coupe**

**1988 Camaro IROC-Z sport coupe**

**1988 Cavalier Z24 coupe**

**1989 Camaro RS sport coupe**

**1988 Cavalier Z24 convertible coupe**

**1989 Corsica hatchback sedan**

Nonetheless, the third-generation Camaro—Z28 especially—was very much in the ponycar spirit of the '60s. Changes through 1992 were evolutionary but well timed. For example, a T-bar roof option appeared for '83, when the Z28 switched to a fuel-saving four-speed automatic and other engines became available with a five-speed manual option. The Cross-Fire V-8 disappointed, so a high-output 190-bhp carbureted engine replaced it for '84. That year's Berlinetta acquired a gimmicky dash with hard-to-read electronic digital/graphic instruments and spacey minor controls; thankfully, these didn't last long.

Providing genuine excitement for 1985 was a hot new IROC-Z performance package for Z28, honoring the Camaros used in the revived International Race of Champions "top gun" driver's contests. The H.O. V-8 was exclusive to the IROC and available with five-speed, now standard for all Camaros. More-efficient "Tuned Port Injection" (TPI) yielded a new 215-bhp option for Z28s. IROC hunkered down on 16 × 8 five-spoke aluminum

**1989 Camaro IROC-Z sport coupe**

**1990 Lumina Euro four-door sedan**

**1990 Camaro IROC-Z sport coupe**

**1990 Lumina coupe**

wheels wearing meaty Goodyear Eagle performance tires, came with its own handling suspension and high-effort power steering, and looked ready to race with its full-perimeter lower-body "skirts."

Chevy again turned up the wick for '87. The IROC got the TPI V-8 and could be ordered with the 350 Corvette engine packing 225 bhp (delayed from a promised mid-'86 debut). Z28 returned with standard four-barrel 305. The underpowered four was Berlinetta reverted to being an LT. But the real treat was the first Camaro convertible in 18 years. A mid-'87 arrival, it was quite a head-turner in IROC trim, but could be had in other lines, too. They were crafted "out of house" to Chevy specs, making these "semi-factory" models, but hardly anyone cared when blasting top-down on a winding two-lane.

Then suddenly, the Z28 vanished—a big surprise—though the 1988 sport coupe was much the same thing save a standard V-6. The LT disappeared too. Minor tweaking added five horses to all three V-8s, though you lost 25 on the injected 305 when teamed with automatic. Base prices had risen some $2000-$3000 in five years, a rather modest increase, really. The ragtop IROC was the costliest '88 Camaro with a starting tariff around 18-grand.

The hallowed RS designation returned for 1989 on a V-6 coupe marketed the previous season only in California. It looked a lot like the IROC, but had its own suspension tuning and equipment mix. The RS also came as a convertible with a standard V-8. The IROC itself could now be had with 16-inch wheels and new Z-rated tires certified safe for sustained speeds above 149 mph. Production hit nearly 111,000 for the model year in a modest sales recovery, though there was no particular reason for it.

The 1990 Camaros comprised RS and IROC coupes and convertibles with some extra standard features. Among the goodies: 16-inch wheel/tire package for IROCs, a torquier 3.1-liter V-6 with 140 bhp for RS, and a tilt steering wheel, driver-side airbag and GM "PASS-Key" antitheft ignition for all models. A deliberately shortened model year held production to just under 35,000.

Camaro's 1991 began in the spring of 1990. Z28s took over for IROCs. The reason? Dodge now sponsored the IROC series and owned rights to that name. At least Z coupes could be quicker now with a new 245-bhp 350 option, the extra power reflecting a switch to more-sophisticated sequential multipoint injection. The 305 also got that and rose to 230 bhp. Reworked front and back ends freshened all models, and Z28s wore a higher-flying rear spoiler that looked faintly ludicrous. For all the recent additions to standard equipment, Camaro was still a bargain performance buy, ranging from $12,000 for the RS V-6 coupe to just under $21,000 for ragtop Z28. To Chevrolet's undoubted delight, sales more than tripled, '91 production soaring beyond 100,000.

Volume then faded to 70,000, likely because a new Camaro was known to be coming for 1993. The third generation thus closed out after '92 with only one further change: a $175 "Heritage Appearance" package to mark Camaro's 25th birthday. Available in white, red, or black, it involved only badges and some hood and decklid stripes. It was a feeble gesture, but at least Chevy didn't forget its ponycar's anniversary.

Any chance to celebrate was doubtless welcome by now, for the '80s had not been kind to Chevrolet. True, the division had more models than ever, but it wasn't selling that many more cars. Worse, Ford was entrenched as number one, and seemed destined to remain so.

Nevertheless, Chevrolet was a strong "USA-2" through the mid-'90s, with yearly domestic car sales of around one million units. As with the '80s Nova, the California-built Geo Prizm was counted in those results, but not other Geo cars, which were

# Chevrolet

1991 Caprice Classic four-door sedan

1991 Corsica LT four-door sedan

1991 Lumina Z34 coupe

1991 Beretta GT coupe

classed as imports on the basis of "domestic content" even though some came from Canada instead of Japan.

Chevy had launched the Geo nameplate for 1989 as a marketing umbrella for Japanese-designed models like Prizm. The idea was to distinguish these products from "real" Chevrolets in the minds of those most likely to buy them—what marketing types called "import intenders." But the ploy worked only in the beginning, and Geo sales dropped steadily. A big blow was losing the popular Isuzu-built Storm sporty coupe after model-year '93. By '98 the remaining Geos were badged Chevrolets. The Toyota Corolla-based Prizm was redesigned that year and continued through 2002.

Though Chevy had been "The Heartbeat of America" since 1987 (an ad slogan adopted for the make's 75th anniversary), its mainstream cars of the early '90s offered little to raise anyone's pulse. Indeed, motor-noters began chiding GM for building mostly "rental cars": dependable but dull underachievers compared to class rivals. Nevertheless, the Chevys most-popular with buyers were the least interesting to enthusiasts: Cavalier, Lumina, and Beretta/Corsica, usually in that order. Each was typically good for over 200,000 model-year sales, sometimes a bit more.

Yet there were flashes of interest in this mundane group. The Beretta GTZ was one, as was its 1994 successor, called Z26. Also replacing the Beretta GT, the Z26 was usefully more-refined, thanks to an updated Quad-4 with 170 bhp. In the Lumina line, 1991 introduced a sporty Z34 coupe, named for its new 3.4-liter "Twin Dual Cam" V-6. This engine, the latest version of Chevy's venerable 60-degree pushrod design, delivered a punchy 210 bhp with five-speed manual or 200 with optional four-speed automatic. Also included were firm suspension, fat tires on alloy wheels, a louvered hood, "ground effects" body add-ons and a more-driver-oriented interior. The result was a lively package many enthusiasts could warm to. Lumina sedans from 1992 were similarly entertaining when ordered with the "Euro 3.4" option, though it was limited to automatic.

Otherwise, both these model lines evolved pretty much like Cavalier. Corsica lost its sporty LTZ after 1990 and its four-door body after '91, but both Corsica and Beretta gained progressively stronger 2.2-liter base engines, a more-coherent dash (from '91), larger front brakes with standard antilock control (1992), and more-aggressive "value" pricing. Luminas also benefited from better base engines, as well as ABS, automatic power door locks, and other improvements.

A very different Lumina was the APV ("All Purpose Vehicle"), premiering for 1990 as Chevrolet's first front-drive minivan and one of three "G200" models (the others were Pontiac Trans Sport and Olds Silhouette). Unlike Chevy's rear-drive Astro, APV was a direct reply to the hot-selling Chrysler minivans that owned at least 50 percent of the market, thanks to their carlike convenience and road manners. Accordingly, APV was sized roughly between the standard and extended Chrysler models, riding a 109.8-inch wheelbase and boasting the comfort advantage of all-independent suspension. Body construction was novel, with outer panels of plasticlike composites attached to a steel inner "skeleton," as on Pontiac's late two-seat Fiero. Equally novel was optional "modular" seating for seven, with lightweight individual buckets that could be easily moved or removed to create a variety of useful configurations.

Only Chevy offered a blank-side cargo model, but all GM200s arrived with a 120-bhp 3.1 V-6 and three-speed automatic. That made for weak performance, especially with a full passenger or cargo load, so an optional 3.8-liter Buick V-6 was added for '92, bringing 165 bhp and a more-responsive four-speed automatic. Befitting a Chevy, APV prices were the lowest of the three corporate cousins, initially in a narrow $14,000-$16,000 range.

Unfortunately, APV's pointy-nose styling was too radical for most buyers. Critics typically likened it to an "anteater" or "Dustbuster." Worse, the design dictated a massive dashtop and huge windshield that made for lots of unwanted reflections; a wide extra set of front roof pillars only hampered vision further. The APV also suffered a relatively low-roof interior that compromised both load volume and rear-cabin access.

Hoping to improve sales with an improved product, Chevy bobbed the nose of the '94 APV and offered a new option: a unique power right sliding door (operated by remote control).

# Chevrolet

Chevy also changed the name to Lumina Minivan and capped base prices at $16,800-$17,500. But nothing seemed to help, and the APV/Minivan was no more threat to Chrysler's minivan dominance than the Astro. Sales languished mostly in the 50,000-60,000 area, about a tenth of total Chrysler volume. There seemed nothing to do but try again, and Chevy did for '97 with the conventionally styled all-steel Venture. A competent competitor in the minivan market, it was never a threat to the top-selling Chrysler and Dodge models—or some import-brand rivals.

Minivans had all but eliminated demand for traditional full-size station wagons, so it was rather surprising to see one among the redesigned Caprices of 1991. Even more surprising was the big rear-drive Chevy's new shape. Clean but blimpy, it reminded some of a Step-Down Hudson—and that wasn't meant as a compliment.

There was no denying the new Caprices looked heavier. And they were, the sedan by 200 pounds, the wagon by about 150. Extra sheetmetal was partly to blame, as overall width bulged two inches and overall length added two-three inches. An unchanged wheelbase implied the vintage-'77 B-car chassis was still underneath. It was, but modernized a bit with revised suspension geometry and standard antilock control for the usual front-disc/rear-drum brakes. Returning unchanged was a single powerteam comprising four-speed automatic transmission and a 170-bhp 305 V-8 with throttle-body injection. Inside was a new, if rather uninspired dash with standard driver's airbag, plus a bit more room for heads, legs, and elbows.

The '91 Caprice was an early starter, reaching showrooms in the spring of 1990. Sedans initially offered base and ritzier Classic trim, both six-seaters with a bench front and rear. The wagon was a plain Caprice, but included a roof rack, rear wiper, and a nifty two-way tailgate (swing-out or drop-down) with separate liftup window. An optional foldaway third seat gave eight-passenger capacity. In all, these new Caprices were just old wine in more-contemporary bottles, but they offered a lot of metal for the money at $16,500-$18,000. Perhaps even to Chevy's surprise, model-year sales almost doubled to a over 200,000, though it obviously helped that the '91 run was much longer than usual.

Included in that tally were a relative handful of Classics with a sporty option package, another LTZ. A late addition to the roster at $825, it delivered wider wheels and tires, a firmer suspension than the famous F41 setup (still available), heavy-duty brakes and cooling system, and additional gauges including a digital speedometer to replace the normal strip-type analog device. Most of these items were borrowed from the Caprice police package (law enforcement having become a major sales venue for these cars), but the result wasn't pleasing. Handling was little better than stock, yet ride was stiff to the point of

**1991 Cavalier RS four-door sedan**

**1991 Camaro Z28 convertible**

**1991 Lumina APV minivan**

**1992 Caprice station wagon**

**1992 Lumina Euro four-door sedan**

**1992 Corsica LT four-door sedan**

# Chevrolet

1992 Cavalier RS convertible coupe

1993 Camaro Z28 coupe

1992 Camaro RS coupe

1994 Caprice Classic four-door sedan

1993 Lumina Euro four-door sedan

1994 Lumina Euro four-door sedan

1993 Corsica four-door sedan

1994 Corsica four-door sedan

1993 Cavalier VL coupe

1994 Beretta coupe

irritation. And there was no more power to pull the near two-ton curb weight, so 0-60 proved a leisurely 10.1-second affair in Consumer Guide® tests. Nevertheless, the Caprice LTZ was *Motor Trend's* 1991 "Car of the Year."

Caprice carried into '92 with minor changes: transmission safety interlock (you had to press the brake pedal to get out of Park, as on a growing number of cars), standard tilt steering wheel, and no-cost power rear vent windows for the wagon. Also new for the wagon was an optional 350 V-8; it made only 10 more horses than the 305 but packed an extremely useful 45 extra pound-feet of torque—300 in all. The 350 became an LTZ standard for '93, when base models were retitled Classic and the Classic was tagged LS. At the same time, Chevy answered styling critics by giving sedans a lighter look, achieved with fully radiused wheel openings, broader taillamps and a 1.6-inch wider rear track. Sales eased to just under 100,000.

Just for fun, Chevy displayed a special Caprice sedan at early '93 auto shows. A mean, solid-black thing, it crouched two inches lower on five-spoke 17-inch alloy wheels with fat Goodyear Eagle GS-C tires. Most chrome was erased, a new honeycomb grille installed, and a deft C-pillar insert imparted a jaunty kick-up to the rearmost side glass. Inside were leather-trimmed front bucket seats and center console. Under the hood: the same new 300-bhp LT1 V-8 that powered the latest Corvette. Chevy called it Impala SS, and showgoers went wild. "Build it," they pleaded. Replied Chevy general manager Jim Perkins, "You got it."

The first of the reborn big muscle Chevys rolled off the line in February 1994, thus putting the LTZ to rest. Tires were now Goodrich Comp T/As, ride height was lifted to within an inch of stock Caprice spec, and the LT1 was tuned for 260 bhp but no less torque. Otherwise, the new Impala SS was just like the show car. That included a heavy-duty police chassis with quick-ratio steering, rear disc brakes (with massive 12-inch rotors), rear antiroll bar, uprated body mounts and premium de Carbon gas-pressure shocks. Full power and luxury trim completed another amazing Chevy value in modern performance: $21,290 base, just $327 more than an ordinary Caprice Classic LS at the time of the SS's introduction.

Encouraged by rave "buff book" reviews, demand for the new Super Sport was super-strong. Chevy had planned 4000 of the '94s but ending up selling more than 6000—the most the plant could build. Production was upped to over 20,000 for '95, when dark cherry and green-gray metallic were added to the paint chart. The '96s carried on with a new standard analog tach and console shift (instead of column lever) for the mandatory four-speed automatic. Impala outsold Caprice that year with sales of almost 42,000.

Meantime, Caprices picked up a new dual-airbag dash for '94 (as did the SS). They also got a new 200-bhp base V-8, a 350 cut down to original 1955 size (4.3 liters/265 cid). The '95s were unchanged except that sedans acquired the Impala's kicked-up rear side-window styling—and looked miles better for it.

But by that point, both Caprice and the brawny Impala were doomed. Having decided there was more money to be made with big sport-utility trucks, GM sacrificed the full-size Chevys after 1996 to free up space at their Texas plant for truck production (a move that also claimed the related Buick Roadmaster and Cadillac Fleetwood). Few mourned the Caprice, but it was sad losing the Impala so soon. Though an anachronism in the '90s, it was the kind of car a whole generation understood—a

**1994 Cavalier Z24 coupe**

**1994 Camaro Z28 convertible coupe**

**1995 Monte Carlo LS coupe**

**1995 Cavalier four-door sedan**

**1995 Monte Carlo LS coupe**

**1996 Caprice Classic station wagon**

# Chevrolet

happy throwback to the glory days of Chevy performance.

A ground-up fresh Camaro promised some new glory days. Arriving for '93 in base and Z28 coupe models, it was about the same size as its well-liked predecessor (wheelbase was unchanged) but more-sculptured and futuristically swoopy, patterned on the recent "California Camaro" show car—and not that much more-subdued. Yet the new fourth-generation design was unmistakably Camaro, carefully preserving hallowed appearance "cues" like tunneled headlamps, broad taillights, a low vee'd nose, even optional T-tops for the coupe.

Despite added standard features, the '93 was only some 150 pounds heavier than previous Camaros. One reason was a lighter, yet stronger, unit body/chassis with steel-reinforced composite panels over a steel framework as on GM200 minivans and the small Saturn. The nominal weight gain bode well for performance, especially on the Z28, which now packed a 350 LT1 V-8 with 275 bhp, 30 more than before. The base Camaro also muscled up via a new overhead-valve 3.4-liter V-6 with a creditable 160 horses. Transmission choices comprised standard five-speed manual for the base model, a new six-speed for Z28 (again borrowed from Corvette), and optional four-speed automatic for both. Front suspension reverted to Detroit-traditional twin A-arms, though with unique geometry and premium gas-pressure, coil-over de Carbon shocks. The latter were also featured in back, where the live axle was now located by a torque rod and trailing arms. Each end had a hefty stabilizer bar. Antilock brakes were standard, with rear discs on Z28. A tantalizing new option was RPO 1LE, an ultrastiff performance suspension package for Z28. It was "not recommended for street use" but worked wonders on the track.

With 70 more horses than a Mustang GT and a starting price on the right side of $17-grand, the '93 Z28 was immediately hailed as the new best buy in Detroit performance. That came from "buff books," who typically reported 0-60 at just over five seconds with manual. For buyers of all stripes, Camaro appealed with standards like dual airbags, full instrumentation, and a good sound system (with even better ones available). Options were still fairly numerous but easier to comprehend, being grouped into sensible packages.

A deliberately slow "ramp-up" limited '93 Camaros to just 40,224, all coupes, but they were the tightest, most solid-feeling Camaros in history. Production then hit full stride to pass 125,000 for '94, when promised base and Z28 convertibles went on sale with standard power top; glass backlight; and a low, tidy "top stack." Six-speed Z28s became a bit quicker that year thanks to shorter final gearing (3.42:1 vs. 2.73/3.23). Unhappily, their shifter acquired CAGS, the Computer Aided Gear Selection feature first used on Corvettes. Electronic watchdogs "forced" a short-shift from 1st to 4th at certain speeds and throttle openings, a bit of nonsense prompted by government fuel-economy standards. But enthusiasts found that CAGS could be defeated by pulling a little wire, and many did pull it.

As ever, the torquey Z28 was a prodigious tire-smoker off-the-line, and a standard limited-slip differential was no substitute for modern traction control. Chevy finally obliged for '95 by offering the Corvette's ASR (Acceleration Slip Reduction) as a Z28 option. ASR would restore lost grip by braking a spinning wheel and/or throttling back on engine power as needed—a boon for wet-road control. And when the road was dry, you could switch it off if you wanted. Street racers loved that.

Though a new Mustang had galloped away with the ponycar market, Camaro mostly held its own for 1995, slipping to 110,595. Arriving late that year was a stronger "3800" V-6 option for base models sold in California. This became standard for all '96s, bringing a useful 40 extra horsepower and 25 more pound-feet of torque over the displaced 3.4. With that, a base Camaro

1996 Impala SS four-door sedan

1996 Lumina LS four-door sedan

1996 Monte Carlo Z34 coupe

1996 Corsica four-door sedan

1996 Beretta Z26 coupe

could at least keep up with a Z28 on winding roads, though not on a dragstrip, of course.

Working hard to reclaim "USA-1," Chevy redesigned two of its biggest sellers for 1995. The Lumina sedan got more of a reskin than a total revamping, and a rather conservative one at that, but the similarly restyled coupe resurrected the Monte Carlo name in an effort to stand more-clearly apart. Each offered plain and fancy models: base and LS for Lumina, LS and Z34 for Monte. The usual 3.1 V-6 was standard for all but Z34, whose 210-bhp 3.4-liter twincam engine was optional for Lumina LS. Recalling the "baby Cadillac" Chevys of 1955-57, Monte Carlo looked faintly like Cadillac's latest Eldorado, but even the sporty Z34 wasn't exactly "eye candy." Nor was it that thrilling to drive despite the usual firm chassis and "enthusiast" appointments. At least these Chevys finally had dual airbags (which the market much preferred over motorized "mouse-belts" to meet the government's 1994 mandate for front passive restraints). They were also aggressively priced: as little as $15,500 for a Lumina, about $16,800 for a Monte. Critics initially felt Chevy had done too little with its midsize cars—until the new '96 Ford Taurus came along with controversial looks and much higher prices.

Cavalier was not only way overdue for an overhaul, it needed a very good one to stay competitive in the bruising small-car sales battle. Chevy came through with fresh, clean styling that looked terrific despite being a tad taller and two inches shorter than previous models. Wheelbase grew by 2.8 inches to help open up some extra room inside. Wagons vanished, leaving base coupe and sedan, LS sedan and convertible, and Z24 coupe (the latter two bowing in spring '95). V-6 power was also gone, as Z24 switched to the latest 150-bhp "balance shaft" version of the twincam Quad-4. LS models could be had with this engine. Base Cavs stuck with the familiar pushrod 2.2. Transmissions comprised five-speed manual and optional three-speed automatic (still), but a self-shift four-speed was substituted for '96 Quad-4 cars, which also gained a little displacement and 10 pound-feet of torque (to 2.4 liters and 150). Apart from that, newly standard PASSLock ignition, daytime running lights, and optional low-speed traction control (included with the four-speed automatic), Cavalier was unchanged for '96. Though production snags hampered early sales, output remained quite substantial at well over 229,000 units for calendar '95.

As with arch-rival Ford, trucks loomed ever larger in Chevrolet's total business picture during the 1990s. Indeed, car sales at both makes were eclipsed by demand for light-duty pickups, sport-utility vehicles (SUVs), and minivans as early as 1990. This reflected a sea-change in buyer preferences that would see light trucks surpass cars in total U.S. sales for calendar 2001.

Chevrolet fought the truck wars well. All-new big Chevy pickups released for 1999 under the Silverado banner, followed by a separate new line of more-competitive heavy-duty pickups, tagged Silverado HD, and redesigned Tahoe and Suburban SUVs. For 2002 came a larger new midsize SUV, the TrailBlazer, though some older Blazer models hung on as price-leaders for that segment. Sales steadily waned through the '90s for Chevy's old 1984-vintage Astro minivan, but the compact Tracker SUV, sourced from GM affiliate Suzuki of Japan, did good business, especially once redesigned for 1999.

Trouble was, the rising market clamor for trucks led Chevy to put less apparent effort into its cars—understandable, perhaps, as the car/truck sales gap slowly widened each year. Still, Chevy's replacement car models of the late '90s were often judged underwhelming versus class rivals, and though they generally sold well, they sold more to rental and corporate fleets than retail customers, to the detriment of both image and trade-in value. The same applied to Cavalier and Camaro, which carried into the new millennium with generally minor year-to-year changes.

But a sale is a sale no matter who the customer is, and Chevy was happy to keep moving at least a quarter-million Cavaliers each model year through 2001. Highlights of its later years included the return of a Z24 convertible to replace the LS version for '98, and a mild 2000-model revamp featuring added standard equipment. Collectors may one day note the low yearly production of droptop Cavs, which never broke 10,000 from 1984 through 2001 and was often half that or less (just 4108 of the 1985 Type 10s, 5011 of the '98 Z24s, to cite two examples). Despite continuing benign neglect, Cavalier remained a high-value subcompact with broad appeal, often finishing near the top in industry car sales despite the ever-shifting market landscape of the 1990s.

Two successful newcomers shored up Chevy's position among midsize sedans at the turn of the millennium. Like the recently

**1996 Camaro convertible coupe**

# Chevrolet

reborn Monte Carlo, both revived great names from Chevy's past. Replacing Corsica for '97 was a very different new Malibu, offering front-wheel drive in a sedate looking sedan package sized closer to Lumina than Cavalier. In fact, while Malibu stood 10.5 inches shorter than Lumina, it was only a half-inch trimmer in wheelbase, resulting in a spacious interior. Both the base and LS models came with a good load of expected standard features, plus an optional 155-bhp, 3.1-liter V-6 that most competitors either didn't match or offered at a hefty surcharge. A 150 bhp 2.4-liter Twin Cam four-cylinder was standard, but vanished for 2000 in the face of strong buyer preference for the V-6, which added 15 horses that season. Like Cavalier, the latest Malibu offered no thrills, just honest value at prices in the attractive $16,000-$20,000 range. Buyers responded to the tune of well over 200,000 each model year after shortened inaugural '97.

Though Malibu was arguably a better buy than Lumina, Chevy's older midsize showed surprising sales strength, drawing over 200,000 annual sales through 1999. An interesting new addition for '97 was a sporty LTZ model with front bucket seats, rear disc brakes, and an optional 215-bhp 3.4-liter twincam V-6. Chevy upped its appeal for '98 by substituting a "3800" V-6 with 200 bhp but more usable low-end torque. That same year, Lumina joined Monte Carlo in offering GM's OnStar communications system as a new $895 option. Basically, OnStar linked the car by cell phone and satellite technology to a 24-hour staffed operations center able to provide route guidance and other assistance, including summoning emergency help. OnStar was a boon to owner peace-of-mind, with particularly high appeal for women. It soon spread throughout the Chevy line, cars and trucks alike, as either standard or optional equipment. The LTZ lost its rear disc brakes for '99 but added the 3.8-liter V-6 as standard. Total Lumina sales plunged 33 percent that model year, but that was partly in anticipation of a bigger and better replacement for 2000. Even so, Lumina made one last stand as a single 2000 model aimed mainly at the fleet market.

Lumina's once-and-future replacement was another new Impala, a very different sedan from the rear-drive biggies of a few years before. For starters, it shared a new GM W-body platform with the latest Buick Century/Regal and Oldsmobile's Intrigue, which meant the first Impala with front-wheel drive. That also meant more-rational size, with overall length of 200 inches (about the same, incidentally, as GM's rear-drive 1980s intermediates) and a rangy 110.5-inch wheelbase providing spacious back-seat room and a capacious trunk. Powertrains were familiar fare, with four-speed automatic transmission the only choice. The base Impala used Malibu's 3.4-liter V-6, tuned for 180 bhp; the uplevel LS carried the elderly but still capable 200-bhp "3800" pushrod engine. Both came well equipped with all-disc brakes, 16-inch wheels, air conditioning, and power windows and locks. The LS added antilock brakes, traction control, a firm-ride suspension for tighter handling, and a side airbag for the driver, all of which were available for the base model when optioned with the 3800 engine. The LS also sported front bucket seats in lieu of a three-person bench, and a rear spoiler and other trim options gave it a passing resemblance to the 1994-96 SS.

But that's where the similarities ended. Though much easier to thread along tight, twisty two-lanes, even 3.8-liter Impalas had nowhere near the sizzle of their V-8 predecessors. They were quick enough, thanks to a more-favorable power-to-weight ratio. In fact, Chevy claimed real-world performance suitable for police duty, and even developed a special police package for the new Impala. But John Law wasn't buying. He still preferred the extra perceived ruggedness of the old rear-drive Caprice—enough that one Southern California entrepreneur profited hugely by restoring used squad cars for law-

1997 Malibu four-door sedan

1997 Lumina LTZ four-door sedan

1997 Camaro coupe

1998 Cavalier Z24 convertible

1998 Metro LSi coupe

# Chevrolet

enforcement agencies as a money-saving alternative to new Ford Crown Victoria. The front-drive Impala also took heat for styling, especially the use of two taillamps instead of the traditional three. At least they were round again, not oblong.

Despite such debates, the latest Impala was a modern Chevy success, racking up over 200,000 model year sales in each of its first two years. Like Malibu, it offered solid family transportation at very competitive prices in the Chevrolet tradition.

Arriving in showrooms slightly ahead of the front-drive Impala was a redesigned 2000 Monte Carlo with the same platform, powertrains, general size, and features. The base model was again tagged LS, but the sporty Z34 was retitled SS and given a standard 200-bhp 3800 V-6. Further emphasizing high value, Chevy gave both models standard all-disc ABS brakes, air conditioning, even a tire-pressure monitor. The SS added firmer suspension and performance tires on larger alloy wheels. Styling was made more elaborate, with curved upper-body character lines intended to evoke thoughts of 1973 and later Montes, but it's doubtful that younger folk made the connection. Enthusiasts didn't much connect with the performance or handling, though both were more than capable. Indeed, Consumer Guide® said the "SS shines on twisty roads" and found its ride "compliant enough on bumpy city streets." Summing up, the editors felt the new Monte Carlo "trounces [compact coupes] in size, comfort, and performance, and beats [rival Honda and Toyota] coupes on a features-per-dollar basis. It isn't as polished as those . . . rivals and won't hold its value as well, but this new Chevy does have its own brand of American-car character."

It did not, however, sell better than its immediate predecessor. In fact, production for model-year 2000 fell over 5000 units from the '99 tally, though it recovered to a bit above 71,000 for '01.

The newest Monte saw no significant change through 2002—except for a sad memorial to NASCAR legend Dale Earnhardt, tragically killed just short of the finish line at the 2001 Daytona 500. Honoring the veteran Chevy stock-car ace was the 2002 Dale Earnhardt Signature Edition Monte SS, of which just 3333 were built between October 2001 and March 2002. Like the "Intimidator's" racing Montes, it was finished in black, accented by silver metallic "ground effects" lower-body skirting, "diamond-cut" alloy wheels, and graphics of Dale's signature, his famous No. 3 I.D., and the logo of team owner Richard Childress Racing. The graphics were repeated inside on a commemorative plaque and elsewhere on the dashboard. Also featured inside were ebony seats with pewter leather seating surfaces and embroidered bow-tie emblems on the headrests. Several regular SS options were included as well, such as power moonroof, heated six-way power bucket seats, and free OnStar service for one year. If any turn-of-millennium Monte Carlo stands to be a future collector car, the Earnhardt Signature Edition is it.

Camaro has always had a place in collector affections, so many were surprised, if not shocked, when Chevy announced that 2002 would be the end of the line for its storied ponycar. But industry analysts had expected the move. After all, Ford's Mustang regularly outsold Camaro in the 1990s, and the gap widened each year even though most critics judged the Chevy superior for go-power, handling and, arguably, appearance. Of course, people don't always do what critics say they should, and some sales were likely lost to pickups and SUVs. In any event, Camaro model-year production fell steadily, dropping some two-thirds between 1996 and 2001. By that point, GM was struggling to cut costs and regain market share (then under 30 percent, an historic low). The ailing Camaro was an obvious target for the budgetary axe. (Ditto sibling Pontiac Firebird with its even lower volume.)

Though not fundamentally altered after 1993, Camaro did see several changes with definite collector interest. For example, Z28s added 10 horsepower for '96, and you could up that to 305 via a new SS package available late in the model year. Created and supplied by outside contractor SLP Engineering, the option also included a functional hood scoop (which contributed to the power boost), uprated suspension with bigger wheels and performance tires, a racy rear-deck spoiler, broad dorsal striping and other special trim, all for a reasonable $3000. That year's base models offered a new RS package with spoiler and "aero" lower-body skirts, as well as a performance group comprising the Z28's

**1998 Prizm four-door sedan**

**2000 Impala four-door sedan**

**1999 Lumina LS four-door sedan**

**2000 Monte Carlo LS coupe**

# Chevrolet

limited-slip differential, four-wheel disc brakes, quicker steering and dual-outlet exhaust, provided you ordered optional 16-inch wheels. The RS made a one-year stand as separate coupe and convertible models for '97, when the SS option went to $4000. Priced at just $575 was a special 30th Anniversary Package for Z28s, including SS-equipped models. Recalling 1969, it comprised white paint, orange striping and white alloy wheels, plus white upholstery with houndstooth-check cloth inserts. A reshaped nose updated styling for '98, when V-8 Camaros got a power boost by exchanging their iron-block LT1 engine for the all-aluminum LS1 unit from that year's new "C5" Corvette. Displacement was still 350 cubes, 5.7 liters, but Z28s went to 305 bhp, the SS option to 320. Base models became a bit safer for '99 by offering the optional traction control previously restricted to V-8s. For 2000, all three Camaro engines were retuned to cleaner LEV (Low Emissions Vehicle) standards, a laudable achievement that Chevy topped for '01 by extracting five more horses from each V-8.

But nothing, it seemed, could halt the sales slide. At least Chevy let Camaro live to see a final milestone, observed with a 35th Anniversary Package for 2002 Z28s. Included were the 325-bhp SS engine, Rally Red paint, checkered-flag hood/decklid stripes, anodized brake calipers, unique alloy wheels, and an ebony/pewter leather interior with strategically placed birthday logos. Chevy even threw in an "owner's portfolio" chronicling Camaro history. It was a fairly subdued farewell for one of the most-memorable Chevys ever, a car that kept the performance torch alight during the dark days of 1970s emissions, safety, and fuel-economy woes.

Though a new Camaro isn't likely anytime soon (if ever), some hope the name might return on a different kind of youthful, fun-to-drive Chevy. Something like the 2003 SSR, in fact. A so-called "category-buster" like Chrysler's wildly successful PT Cruiser, the SSR reflects 21st-century market trends by melding attributes of several vehicle types. Outside, it's a "retro-styled" pickup paying homage to Chevy's "Advance Design" trucks of the early post-World War II years. It's also based on a truck chassis, a cut-down version of the well-received 2002 TrailBlazer SUV platform. But the SSR is also two-seat sports car, neo hot rod, and nifty convertible. Coming from a company so long criticized for "blandmobiles," the SSR is a refreshing change, a sign that GM wants to resume its long-time role as Detroit's styling, performance, and innovation leader. Backing that up, the SSR reaches showrooms with surprisingly few changes from its original 1999 concept design, including a hardtop that neatly powers into a well behind the cockpit.

The SSR is rather burly for a "personal" vehicle, striding a 116-inch wheelbase and standing 186 inches long, 62.2 inches tall, and a massive 76.1 inches wide. Fulsome body contours and huge wheels—19-inch diameter front, 20 inches rear—only further the impression. So does the engine: a special aluminum-block version of the modern, stout "Vortec 5300" V-8 that powers full-size Chevy SUVs. Horsepower is in the region of 285, torque about 325 pound-feet—both signifying strong performance.

The same might be said of Chevrolet's immediate future. After some 20 years of so-so products, failed reorganizations, and falling profits and market share, Chevy and the rest of GM seem poised for better times as the new millennium unfolds. Who knows? Chevy might even reclaim its once unassailable position as "USA-1." Whatever coming years may bring, Chevrolet is sure to remain number-one with millions of Americans who just won't have anything else.

2000 Malibu four-door sedan

2001 Impala LS four-door sedan

2002 Camaro Z28 SS convertible 35th Anniversary Edition

2002 Cavalier coupe

2003 SSR

# Chevrolet

## Specifications

### 1930

| AD Universal (wb 107.0) | Wght | Price | Prod |
|---|---|---|---|
| rdstr 2P | 2,195 | 495 | 5,684 |
| spt rdstr 2-4P | 2,250 | 515 | 27,651 |
| phtn 5P | 2,265 | 495 | 1,713 |
| cpe 2P | 2,415 | 565 | 100,373 |
| spt cpe 2-4P | 2,525 | 615 | 45,311 |
| coach 5P | 2,515 | 565 | 255,027 |
| club sdn 5P | 2,575 | 625 | 24,888 |
| sdn 5P | 2,615 | 675 | 135,193 |
| Special sdn 5P | 2,625 | 685 | 35,929 |
| cpe 2P R/S | 2,540 | — | 9,211 |

| 1930 Engine | bore × stroke | bhp | availability |
|---|---|---|---|
| I-6, 194.0 | 3.13 × 3.75 | 50 | S-all |

### 1931

| AE Independence (wb 109.0) | Wght | Price | Prod |
|---|---|---|---|
| rdstr 2P | 2,275 | 475 | 2,939 |
| spt rdstr 2P | 2,330 | 495 | 24,050 |
| DeLuxe phtn 5P | 2,370 | 510 | 852 |
| cpe 2P 3W | 2,490 | 535 | 57,741 |
| spt cpe 2-4P | 2,565 | 575 | 66,029 |
| cpe 2P 5W | 2,490 | 545 | 28,379 |
| coach 5P | 2,585 | 545 | 228,316 |
| sdn 5P | 2,685 | 635 | 52,465 |
| Special sdn 5P | 2,725 | 650 | 109,775 |
| cpe 5P | 2,610 | 595 | 20,297 |
| cab 2-4P | 2,520 | 615 | 23,077 |
| conv sdn 5P | 2,610 | 650 | 5,634 |

| 1931 Engine | bore × stroke | bhp | availability |
|---|---|---|---|
| I-6, 194.0 | 3.13 × 3.75 | 50 | S-all |

### 1932

| BA Confederate (wb 109.0) | Wght | Price | Prod |
|---|---|---|---|
| rdstr 2P | 2,410 | 445 | 1,118 |
| cpe 2P 3W | 2,580 | 490 | 8,874 |
| coach 5P | 2,665 | 495 | 132,109 |
| sdn 5P | 2,750 | 590 | 27,718 |
| spt cpe 2-4P | 2,645 | 535 | 26,623 |
| DeLuxe spt cpe 2-4P | 2,695 | 550 | |
| cpe 2P 5W | 2,580 | 490 | 34,796 |
| DeLuxe cpe 2P 5W | 2,630 | 505 | |
| cpe 5P | 2,700 | 575 | 7,566 |
| DeLuxe cpe 5P | 2,700 | 590 | |
| landau phtn 5P | 2,700 | 625 | 1,602 |
| DeLuxe landau phtn 5P | 2,750 | 640 | |
| DeLuxe phtn 5P | 2,520 | 495 | 419 |
| DeLuxe spt rdstr 2-4P | 2,530 | 500 | 8,552 |
| DeLuxe cpe 2P | 2,630 | 510 | 2,226 |
| DeLuxe coach 5P | 2,715 | 515 | 9,346 |
| DeLuxe Special sdn 5P | 2,850 | 630 | 52,446 |

| 1932 Engine | bore × stroke | bhp | availability |
|---|---|---|---|
| I-6, 194.0 | 3.13 × 3.75 | 60 | S-all |

### 1933

| CA Eagle (wb 110.0) | Wght | Price* | Prod |
|---|---|---|---|
| spt rdstr 2P | 2,675 | 485 | 2,876 |
| phtn 5P | 2,715 | 515 | 543 |
| cpe 2P | 2,715 | 495 | 60,402 |
| spt cpe 2-4P | 2,780 | 535 | 26,691 |
| coach 5P | 2,820 | 515 | 162,629 |
| Town sdn 2d 5P | — | 545 | 30,657 |
| sdn 5P | 2,880 | 565 | 162,361 |
| cab 2-4P | 2,715 | 565 | 4,276 |

* All models $15 extra with 6-wire wheel equipment.

| CC Mercury (wb 107.0) | | | |
|---|---|---|---|
| cpe 2p | 2,335 | 445 | 8,909 |
| cpe 2-4P | 2,395 | 475 | 1,903 |
| coach 5P | 2,425 | 455 | 25,033 |

| 1933 Engines | bore × stroke | bhp | availability |
|---|---|---|---|
| I-6, 181.0 | 3.31 × 3.50 | 60 | S-Mercury series |
| I-6, 206.8 | 3.31 × 4.00 | 65 | S-Eagle series |

### 1934

| DA Master (wb 112.0) | Wght | Price* | Prod |
|---|---|---|---|
| spt rdstr 2-4P | 2,815 | 540 | 1,974 |
| cpe 2P | 2,935 | 560 | 53,018 |
| spt cpe 2-4P | 2,995 | 600 | 18,365 |
| cab 2-4P | 2,990 | 665 | 3,276 |
| coach 5P | 2,995 | 580 | 163,948 |
| sdn 5P | 3,080 | 640 | 124,754 |
| Town sdn 2d 5P | 3,020 | 615 | 49,431 |
| spt sdn 4d 5P | 3,155 | 675 | 37,646 |

| DC Standard (wb 107.0) | | | |
|---|---|---|---|
| spt rdstr 2-4P | 2,380 | 465 | 1,038 |
| phtn 5P | 2,400 | 495 | 234 |
| cpe 2P | 2,470 | 485 | 16,765 |
| sdn 2d | 2,580 | 495 | 69,082 |
| sdn 4d | 2,655 | 540 | 11,840 |

* All DA/DC models exc DC sdn 4d $30 extra with 6-wire wheel equipment.

| 1934 Engines | bore × stroke | bhp | availability |
|---|---|---|---|
| I-6, 181.0 | 3.31 × 3.50 | 60 | S-Standard |
| I-6, 206.8 | 3.31 × 4.00 | 80 | S-Master |

### 1935

| EC Standard (wb 107.0) | Wght | Price | Prod |
|---|---|---|---|
| spt rdstr 2-4P | 2,430 | 465 | 1,176 |
| phtn 5P | 2,495 | 485 | 217 |
| cpe 2P | 2,540 | 475 | 32,193 |
| coach 5P | 2,645 | 485 | 126,138 |
| sdn 5P | 2,700 | 550 | 42,049 |

| ED/EA Master DeLuxe (wb 113.0)* | | | |
|---|---|---|---|
| cpe 2P 5W | 2,910 | 560 | 40,201 |
| spt cpe 2-4P 3W | 2,940 | 600 | 11,904 |
| coach 5P | 3,010 | 580 | 102,996 |
| sdn 5P | 3,055 | 640 | 57,771 |
| Town sdn 2d 5P | 3,055 | 615 | 66,231 |
| spt sdn 4d 5P | 3,130 | 675 | 67,339 |

* ED had no Knee-Action. For EA Knee-Action, add 60 lbs & $20.

| 1935 Engines | bore × stroke | bhp | availability |
|---|---|---|---|
| I-6, 181.0 | 3.31 × 3.50 | 74 | S-Standard |

# Chevrolet

| 1935 Engines | bore × stroke | bhp | availability |
|---|---|---|---|
| I-6, 206.8 | 3.31 × 4.00 | 80 | S-Master DeLuxe |

### 1936

| FC Standard (wb 109.0) | Wght | Price | Prod |
|---|---|---|---|
| cpe 2P | 2,645 | 495 | 59,356 |
| cab 2-4P | 2,745 | 595 | 3,629 |
| coach 5P | 2,750 | 510 | 76,646 |
| sdn 5P | 2,775 | 575 | 11,142 |
| Town sdn 2d 5P | 2,775 | 535 | 220,884 |
| spt sdn 4d 5P | 2,805 | 600 | 46,760 |
| **FD/FA Master DeLuxe (wb 113.0)*** | | | |
| cpe 2P 5W | 2,895 | 560 | 49,319 |
| spt cpe 2-4P | 2,940 | 590 | 10,985 |
| coach 5P | 2,985 | 580 | 40,814 |
| sdn 5P | 3,060 | 640 | 14,536 |
| Town sdn 2d 5P | 3,030 | 605 | 244,134 |
| spt sdn 4d 5P | 3,080 | 665 | 140,073 |

* FD had no Knee-Action. For FA Knee-Action, add 50 lbs & $20.

| 1936 Engine | bore × stroke | bhp | availability |
|---|---|---|---|
| I-6, 206.8 | 3.31 × 4.00 | 79 | S-all |

### 1937

| GB Master (wb 112.3) | Wght | Price | Prod |
|---|---|---|---|
| bus cpe 2P | 2,770 | 619 | 54,683 |
| cab 2-4P | 2,790 | 725 | 1,724 |
| coach 5P | 2,800 | 637 | 15,349 |
| Town sdn 2d 5P T/B | 2,830 | 655 | 178,645 |
| sdn 4d 5P | 2,845 | 698 | 2,755 |
| spt sdn 4d 5P T/B | 2,885 | 716 | 43,240 |
| **GA Master DeLuxe (wb 112.3)** | | | |
| cpe 2P | 2,840 | 685 | 56,166 |
| spt cpe 2-4P | 2,870 | 724 | 8,935 |
| coach 5P | 2,910 | 703 | 7,260 |
| Town sdn 2d 5P T/B | 2,935 | 721 | 300,332 |
| sdn 4d 5P | 2,935 | 770 | 2,221 |
| spt sdn 4d 5P T/B | 2,960 | 788 | 144,110 |

| 1937 Engine | bore × stroke | bhp | availability |
|---|---|---|---|
| I-6, 216.5 | 3.50 × 3.75 | 85 | S-all |

### 1938

| HB Master (wb 112.3) | Wght | Price | Prod |
|---|---|---|---|
| cpe 2P | 2,770 | 648 | 39,793 |
| cab 2-4P | 2,790 | 755 | 2,787 |
| coach 5P | 2,795 | 668 | 3,326 |
| Town sdn 2d T/B | 2,825 | 689 | 95,050 |
| sdn 4d | 2,840 | 730 | 522 |
| spt sdn 4d T/B | 2,845 | 750 | 20,952 |
| **HA Master DeLuxe (wb 112.3)** | | | |
| cpe 2P | 2,840 | 714 | 36,106 |
| spt cpe 4P | 2,855 | 750 | 2,790 |
| coach 5P | 2,900 | 730 | 1,038 |
| Town sdn 2d T/B | 2,915 | 750 | 186,233 |
| sdn 4d | 2,915 | 796 | 236 |
| spt sdn 4d T/B | 2,940 | 817 | 76,323 |

| 1938 Engine | bore × stroke | bhp | availability |
|---|---|---|---|
| I-6, 216.5 | 3.50 × 3.75 | 85 | S-all |

### 1939

| JB Master 85 (wb 112.3) | Wght | Price | Prod |
|---|---|---|---|
| cpe 2P | 2,780 | 628 | 41,770 |
| coach 5P | 2,795 | 648 | 1,404 |
| Town sdn 2d T/B | 2,820 | 669 | 124,059 |
| sdn 4d | 2,805 | 689 | 336 |
| spt sdn 4d T/B | 2,845 | 710 | 22,623 |
| wgn 4d | 3,010 | 848 | 430* |

* 229 with folding end gates, 201 with rear door

| JA Master DeLuxe (wb 112.3) | Wght | Price | Prod |
|---|---|---|---|
| bus cpe 2P | 2,845 | 684 | 33,809 |
| spt cpe 4P | 2,845 | 715 | 20,908 |
| coach 5P | 2,865 | 699 | 180 |
| Town sdn 2d T/B | 2,875 | 720 | 220,181 |
| sdn 4d | 2,875 | 745 | 68 |
| spt sdn 4d T/B | 2,910 | 766 | 110,521 |
| wgn 4d | 3,060 | 883 | 989 |

| 1939 Engine | bore × stroke | bhp | availability |
|---|---|---|---|
| I-6, 216.5 | 3.50 × 3.75 | 85 | S-all |

### 1940

| KB Master 85 (wb 113.0) | Wght | Price | Prod |
|---|---|---|---|
| bus cpe | 2,865 | 659 | 25,734 |
| town sedan 2d, T/B | 2,915 | 699 | 66,431 |
| sport sedan 4d, T/B | 2,930 | 740 | 11,468 |
| wgn 4d, 8P | 3,106 | 903 | 411 |
| **KH Master DeLuxe (wb 113.0)** | | | |
| bus cpe | 2,920 | 684 | 28,090 |
| sport coupe | 2,925 | 715 | 17,234 |
| town sedan 2d, T/B | 2,965 | 725 | 143,125 |
| sport sedan 4d, T/B | 2,990 | 766 | 40,924 |
| **KA Special DeLuxe (wb 113.0)** | | | |
| bus cpe | 2,930 | 720 | 25,537 |
| sport coupe | 2,945 | 750 | 46,628 |
| conv cpe | 3,160 | 898 | 11,820 |
| town sedan 2d, T/B | 2,980 | 761 | 205,910 |
| sport sedan 4d, T/B | 3,010 | 802 | 138,811 |
| wgn 4d, 8P | 3,158 | 934 | 2,493* |

*367 with double rear doors

| 1940 Engine | bore × stroke | bhp | availability |
|---|---|---|---|
| I-6, 216.5 | 3.50 × 3.75 | 85 | S-all |

### 1941

| AG Master DeLuxe (wb 116.0) | Wght | Price | Prod |
|---|---|---|---|
| bus cpe | 3,020 | 712 | 48,763 |
| cpe | 3,025 | 743 | 79,124 |
| town sedan 2d | 3,050 | 754 | 219,438 |
| sport sedan 4d | 3,090 | 795 | 59,538 |
| **AH Special DeLuxe (wb 116.0)** | | | |
| bus cpe | 3,040 | 769 | 17,602 |
| cpe | 3,050 | 800 | 155,889 |
| conv cpe | 3,285 | 949 | 15,296 |
| town sedan 2d | 3,095 | 810 | 228,458 |
| sport sedan 4d | 3,127 | 851 | 148,661 |
| wgn 4d, 8P | 3,410 | 995 | 2,045 |
| Fleetline sdn 4d | 3,130 | 877 | 34,162 |

| 1941 Engine | bore × stroke | bhp | availability |
|---|---|---|---|
| I-6, 216.5 | 3.50 × 3.75 | 90 | S-all |

# Chevrolet

## 1942

| BG Master DeLuxe (wb 116.0) | Wght | Price | Prod |
|---|---|---|---|
| cpe 2P | 3,055 | 760 | 8,089 |
| cpe 5P | 3,060 | 790 | 17,442 |
| town sedan 2d | 3,090 | 800 | 41,872 |
| sport sedan 4d | 3,110 | 840 | 14,093 |
| **BH Special DeLuxe (wb 116.0)** | | | |
| cpe 2P | 3,070 | 815 | 1,716 |
| cpe 5P | 3,085 | 845 | 22,187 |
| conv cpe | 3,385 | 1,080 | 1,182 |
| town sedan 2d | 3,120 | 855 | 39,421 |
| sport sedan 4d | 3,145 | 895 | 31,441 |
| wgn 4d, 8P | 3,425 | 1,095 | 1,057 |
| **BH Fleetline (wb 116.0)** | | | |
| Aerosedan 2d | 3,105 | 880 | 61,855 |
| Sportmaster sdn 4d | 3,165 | 920 | 14,530 |

| 1942 Engine | bore × stroke | bhp | availability |
|---|---|---|---|
| I-6, 216.5 | 3.50 × 3.75 | 90 | S-all |

## 1946

| DJ Stylemaster (wb 116.0) | Wght | Price | Prod |
|---|---|---|---|
| sport sedan 4d | 3,175 | 1,205 | 75,349 |
| town sedan 2d | 3,170 | 1,152 | 61,104 |
| spt cpe | 3,130 | 1,137 | 19,243 |
| bus cpe | 3,105 | 1,098 | 14,267 |
| **DK Fleetmaster (wb 116.0)** | | | |
| sport sedan 4d | 3,225 | 1,280 | 73,746 |
| town sedan 2d | 3,190 | 1,225 | 56,538 |
| spt cpe | 3,145 | 1,212 | 27,036 |
| conv cpe | 3,445 | 1,476 | 4,508 |
| wgn 4d, 8P | 3,465 | 1,712 | 804 |
| **DK Fleetline (wb 116.0)** | | | |
| Sportmaster sdn 4d | 3,240 | 1,309 | 7,501 |
| Aerosedan 2d | 3,165 | 1,249 | 57,932 |

| 1946 Engine | bore × stroke | bhp | availability |
|---|---|---|---|
| I-6, 216.5 | 3.50 × 3.75 | 90 | S-all |

## 1947

| EJ Stylemaster (wb 116.0) | | Wght | Price | Prod |
|---|---|---|---|---|
| 1503 | sport sedan 4d | 3,130 | 1,276 | 42,571 |
| 1502 | town sedan 2d | 3,075 | 1,219 | 88,534 |
| 1524 | spt cpe | 3,060 | 1,202 | 34,513 |
| 1504 | bus cpe | 3,050 | 1,160 | 27,403 |
| **EK Fleetmaster (wb 116.0)** | | | | |
| 2103 | sport sedan 4d | 3,185 | 1,345 | 91,440 |
| 2102 | town sedan 2d | 3,125 | 1,286 | 80,128 |
| 2124 | spt cpe | 3,090 | 1,281 | 59,661 |
| 2134 | conv cpe | 3,390 | 1,628 | 28,443 |
| 2109 | wgn 4d, 8P | 3,465 | 1,893 | 4,912 |
| **EK Fleetline (wb 116.0)** | | | | |
| 2113 | Sportmaster sdn 4d | 3,150 | 1,371 | 54,531 |
| 2144 | Aerosedan 2d | 3,125 | 1,313 | 159,407 |

| 1947 Engine | bore × stroke | bhp | availability |
|---|---|---|---|
| I-6, 216.5 | 3.50 × 3.75 | 90 | S-all |

## 1948

| FJ Stylemaster (wb 116.0) | | Wght | Price | Prod |
|---|---|---|---|---|
| 1502 | town sedan 2d | 3,095 | 1,313 | 70,228 |
| 1503 | sport sedan 4d | 3,115 | 1,371 | 48,456 |
| 1504 | bus cpe | 3,045 | 1,244 | 18,396 |
| 1524 | spt cpe | 3,020 | 1,323 | 34,513 |
| **FK Fleetmaster (wb 116.0)** | | | | |
| 2102 | town sedan 2d | 3,110 | 1,381 | 66,208 |
| 2103 | sport sedan 4d | 3,150 | 1,439 | 93,142 |
| 2109 | wgn 4d, 8P | 3,430 | 2,013 | 10,171 |
| 2124 | spt cpe | 3,050 | 1,402 | 58,786 |
| 2134 | conv cpe | 3,340 | 1,750 | 20,471 |
| **FK Fleetline (wb 116.0)** | | | | |
| 2113 | Sportmaster sdn 4d | 3,150 | 1,492 | 64,217 |
| 2144 | Aerosedan 2d | 3,100 | 1,434 | 211,861 |

| 1948 Engine | bore × stroke | bhp | availability |
|---|---|---|---|
| I-6, 216.5 | 3.50 × 3.75 | 90 | S-all |

## 1949

| GJ Styleline Special (wb 115.0) | | Wght | Price | Prod |
|---|---|---|---|---|
| 1502 | town sedan 2d | 3,070 | 1,413 | 69,398 |
| 1503 | sport sedan 4d | 3,090 | 1,460 | 46,334 |
| 1504 | bus cpe | 3,015 | 1,339 | 20,337 |
| 1524 | spt cpe | 3,030 | 1,418 | 27,497 |
| **GJ Fleetline Special (wb 115.0)** | | | | |
| 1552 | sdn 2d | 3,060 | 1,413 | 58,514 |
| 1553 | sdn 4d | 3,095 | 1,460 | 36,317 |
| **GK Styleline DeLuxe (wb 115.0)** | | | | |
| 2102 | town sedan 2d | 3,100 | 1,492 | 147,347 |
| 2103 | sport sedan 4d | 3,125 | 1,539 | 191,357 |
| 2109 | wgn 4d, wood body | 3,485 | 2,267 | 3,342 |
| 2119 | wgn 4d, steel body | 3,465 | 2,267 | 2,664 |
| 2124 | spt cpe | 3,065 | 1,508 | 78,785 |
| 2134 | conv cpe | 3,375 | 1,857 | 32,392 |
| **GK Fleetline DeLuxe (wb 115.0)** | | | | |
| 2152 | sdn 2d | 3,100 | 1,492 | 180,251 |
| 2153 | sdn 4d | 3,135 | 1,539 | 130,323 |

| 1949 Engine | bore × stroke | bhp | availability |
|---|---|---|---|
| I-6, 216.5 | 3.50 × 3.75 | 90 | S-all |

## 1950

| HJ Styleline Special (wb 115.0) | | Wght | Price | Prod |
|---|---|---|---|---|
| 1502 | town sedan 2d | 3,085 | 1,403 | 89,897 |
| 1503 | sport sedan 4d | 3,120 | 1,450 | 55,644 |
| 1504 | bus cpe | 3,025 | 1,329 | 20,984 |
| 1524 | spt cpe | 3,050 | 1,408 | 28,328 |
| **HJ Fleetline Special (wb 115.0)** | | | | |
| 1552 | sdn 2d | 3,080 | 1,403 | 43,682 |
| 1553 | sdn 4d | 3,115 | 1,450 | 23,277 |
| **HJ Styleline DeLuxe (wb 115.0)** | | | | |
| 2102 | town sedan 2d | 3,100 | 1,482 | 248,567 |
| 2103 | sport sedan 4d | 3,150 | 1,529 | 316,412 |
| 2119 | wgn 4d, steel body | 3,460 | 1,994 | 166,995 |
| 2124 | spt cpe | 3,090 | 1,498 | 81,536 |
| 2134 | conv cpe | 3,380 | 1,847 | 32,810 |
| 2154 | Bel Air htp cpe | 3,225 | 1,741 | 76,662 |
| **HK DeLuxe Fleetline (wb 115.0)** | | | | |
| 2152 | sdn 2d | 3,115 | 1,482 | 189,509 |

# Chevrolet

| HK DeLuxe Fleetline (wb 115.0) | | Wght | Price | Prod |
|---|---|---|---|---|
| 2153 | sdn 4d | 3,145 | 1,529 | 124,287 |
| **1950 Engines** | bore × stroke | bhp | availability | |
| I-6, 216.5 | 3.50 × 3.75 | 92 | S-all | |
| I-6, 235.5 | 3.56 × 3.94 | 105 | S-Powerglide | |

## 1951

| JJ Styleline Special (wb 115.0) | | Wght | Price | Prod |
|---|---|---|---|---|
| 1502 | sdn 2d | 3,095 | 1,540 | 75,566 |
| 1503 | sdn 4d | 3,130 | 1,595 | 63,718 |
| 1504 | bus cpe | 3,040 | 1,460 | 17,020 |
| 1524 | spt cpe | 3,060 | 1,545 | 18,981 |
| **JJ Fleetline Special (wb 115.0)** | | | | |
| 1552 | sdn 2d | 3,090 | 1,540 | 6,441 |
| 1553 | sdn 4d | 3,130 | 1,594 | 3,364 |
| **JK Styleline DeLuxe (wb 115.0)** | | | | |
| 2102 | sdn 2d | 3,110 | 1,629 | 262,933 |
| 2103 | sdn 4d | 3,140 | 1,680 | 380,270 |
| 2119 | wgn 4d | 3,470 | 2,191 | 23,586 |
| 2124 | spt cpe | 3,115 | 1,647 | 64,976 |
| 2134 | conv cpe | 3,380 | 2,030 | 20,172 |
| 2154 | Bel Air htp cpe | 3,225 | 1,914 | 103,356 |
| **JK Fleetline DeLuxe (wb 115.0)** | | | | |
| 2152 | sdn 2d | 3,125 | 1,629 | 131,910 |
| 2153 | sdn 4d | 3,155 | 1,680 | 57,693 |
| **1951 Engines** | bore × stroke | bhp | availability | |
| I-6, 216.5 | 3.50 × 3.75 | 92 | S-all | |
| I-6, 235.5 | 3.56 × 3.94 | 105 | S-Powerglide | |

## 1952

| KJ Styleline Special (wb 115.0) | | Wght | Price | Prod |
|---|---|---|---|---|
| 1502 | sdn 2d | 3,085 | 1,614 | 54,781 |
| 1503 | sdn 4d | 3,115 | 1,670 | 35,460 |
| 1504 | bus cpe | 3,045 | 1,530 | 10,359 |
| 1524 | spt cpe | 3,050 | 1,620 | 8,906 |
| **KK Styleline DeLuxe (wb 115.0)** | | | | |
| 2102 | sdn 2d | 3,110 | 1,707 | 215,417 |
| 2103 | sdn 4d | 3,145 | 1,761 | 319,736 |
| 2119 | wgn 4d | 3,475 | 2,297 | 12,756 |
| 2124 | spt cpe | 3,100 | 1,726 | 36,954 |
| 2134 | conv cpe | 3,380 | 2,128 | 11,975 |
| 2154 | Bel Air htp cpe | 3,215 | 2,006 | 74,634 |
| **KK Fleetline DeLuxe (wb 115.0)** | | | | |
| 2152 | sdn 2d | 3,110 | 1,707 | 37,164 |
| **1952 Engines** | bore × stroke | bhp | availability | |
| I-6, 216.5 | 3.50 × 3.75 | 92 | S-manual shift | |
| I-6, 235.5 | 3.56 × 3.94 | 105 | S-Powerglide | |

## 1953

| 150 Special (wb 115.0) | | Wght | Price | Prod |
|---|---|---|---|---|
| 1502 | sdn 2d | 3,180 | 1,613 | 79,416 |
| 1503 | sdn 4d | 3,215 | 1,670 | 54,207 |
| 1504 | bus cpe | 3,140 | 1,524 | 13,555 |
| 1509 | Handyman wgn 4d | 3,420 | 2,010 | 22,408 |
| 1524 | club cpe | 3,140 | 1,620 | 6,993 |
| **210 DeLuxe (wb 115.0)** | | | | |
| 2102 | sdn 2d | 3,215 | 1,707 | 247,455 |
| 2103 | sdn 4d | 3,250 | 1,761 | 332,497 |
| 2109 | Handyman wgn 4d | 3,450 | 2,123 | 18,258 |
| 2119 | Townsman wgn 4d, 8P | 3,495 | 2,273 | 7,988 |
| 2124 | club cpe | 3,190 | 1,726 | 23,961 |
| 2134 | conv cpe | 3,435 | 2,093 | 5,617 |
| 2154 | htp cpe | 3,295 | 1,967 | 14,045 |
| **240 Bel Air (wb 115.0)** | | | | |
| 2402 | sdn 2d | 3,230 | 1,820 | 144,401 |
| 2403 | sdn 4d | 3,275 | 1,874 | 247,284 |
| 2434 | conv cpe | 3,470 | 2,175 | 24,047 |
| 2454 | htp cpe | 3,310 | 2,051 | 99,028 |
| **1953 Engines** | bore × stroke | bhp | availability | |
| I-6, 235.5 | 3.56 × 3.94 | 108 | S-manual shift | |
| I-6, 235.5 | 3.56 × 3.94 | 115 | S-Powerglide | |

## 1954

| 150 Special (wb 115.0) | | Wght | Price | Prod |
|---|---|---|---|---|
| 1502 | sdn 2d | 3,165 | 1,680 | 64,855 |
| 1503 | sdn 4d | 3,210 | 1,623 | 32,430 |
| 1509 | Handyman wgn 4d | 3,455 | 2,020 | 21,404 |
| 1512 | Utility sdn 2d, 3P | 3,145 | 1,539 | 10,770 |
| **210 DeLuxe (wb 115.0)** | | | | |
| 2102 | sdn 2d | 3,185 | 1,717 | 195,498 |
| 2103 | sdn 4d | 3,230 | 1,771 | 235,146 |
| 2109 | Handyman wgn 4d | 3,470 | 2,133 | 27,175 |
| 2124 | Delray cpe | 3,185 | 1,782 | 66,403 |
| **240 Bel Air (wb 115.0)** | | | | |
| 2402 | sdn 2d | 3,220 | 1,830 | 143,573 |
| 2403 | sdn 4d | 3,255 | 1,884 | 248,750 |
| 2419 | Townsman wgn 4d, 8P | 3,540 | 2,283 | 8,156 |
| 2434 | conv cpe | 3,445 | 2,185 | 19,383 |
| 2454 | sport coupe htp cpe | 3,300 | 2,061 | 66,378 |
| **1954 Engines** | bore × stroke | bhp | availability | |
| I-6, 235.5 | 3.56 × 3.94 | 115 | S-manual | |
| I-6, 235.5 | 3.56 × 3.94 | 125 | S-Powerglide | |

## 1955

| 150 (wb 115.0) | | Wght | Price | Prod |
|---|---|---|---|---|
| 1502 | sdn 2d | 3,145 | 1,685 | 66,416 |
| 1503 | sdn 4d | 3,150 | 1,728 | 29,898 |
| 1512 | Util sdn | 3,070 | 1,593 | 11,196 |
| 1529 | Handyman wgn 4d | 3,275 | 2,030 | 17,936 |
| **210 (wb 115.0)** | | | | |
| 2102 | sdn 2d | 3,130 | 1,775 | 249,105 |
| 2103 | sdn 4d | 3,165 | 1,819 | 317,724 |
| 2109 | Townsman wgn 4d | 3,355 | 2,127 | 82,303 |
| 2124 | Delray cpe | 3,130 | 1,835 | 115,584 |
| 2129 | Handyman wgn 2d | 3,315 | 2,079 | 28,918 |
| 2154 | htp cpe | 3,158 | 1,959 | 11,675 |
| **Bel Air (wb 115.0)** | | | | |
| 2402 | sdn 2d | 3,140 | 1,888 | 168,313 |
| 2403 | sdn 4d | 3,185 | 1,932 | 345,372 |
| 2409 | Beauville wgn 4d | 3,370 | 2,262 | 24,313 |
| 2429 | Nomad wgn 2d | 3,285 | 2,472 | 8,386 |
| 2434 | conv cpe | 3,300 | 2,206 | 41,292 |
| 2454 | sport coupe htp cpe | 3,180 | 2,067 | 185,562 |

# Chevrolet

| 1955 Engines | bore × stroke | bhp | availability |
|---|---|---|---|
| I-6, 235.5 | 3.56 × 3.94 | 123/136 | S-manual/Powerglide |
| V-8, 265.0 | 3.75 × 3.00 | 162 | O-manual |
| V-8, 265.0 | 3.75 × 3.00 | 180 | O-all |

## 1956

| 150 (wb 115.0) | | Wght | Price | Prod |
|---|---|---|---|---|
| 1502 | sdn 2d | 3,154 | 1,826 | 82,384 |
| 1503 | sdn 4d | 3,196 | 1,869 | 51,544 |
| 1512 | Util sdn | 3,117 | 1,734 | 9,879 |
| 1529 | Handyman wgn 2d | 3,299 | 2,171 | 13,487 |
| **210 (wb 115.0)** | | | | |
| 2102 | sdn 2d | 3,167 | 1,912 | 205,545 |
| 2103 | sdn 4d | 3,202 | 1,955 | 283,125 |
| 2109 | Townsman wgn 4d | 3,371 | 2,263 | 113,656 |
| 2113 | Sport htp sdn | 3,252 | 2,117 | 20,021 |
| 2119 | Beauville wgn 4d, 9P | 3,490 | 2,348 | 17,988 |
| 2124 | Delray cpe | 3,172 | 1,971 | 56,382 |
| 2129 | Handyman wgn 2d | 3,334 | 2,215 | 22,038 |
| 2154 | Sport htp cpe | 3,194 | 2,063 | 18,616 |
| **Bel Air (wb 115.0)** | | | | |
| 2402 | sdn 2d | 3,187 | 2,025 | 104,849 |
| 2403 | sdn 4d | 3,221 | 2,068 | 269,798 |
| 2413 | Sport htp sdn | 3,270 | 2,230 | 103,602 |
| 2419 | Beauville wgn 4d, 9P | 3,506 | 2,482 | 13,279 |
| 2429 | Nomad wgn 2d | 3,352 | 2,608 | 7,886 |
| 2434 | conv cpe | 3,330 | 2,344 | 41,268 |
| 2454 | Sport htp cpe | 3,222 | 2,176 | 128,382 |

| 1956 Engines | bore × stroke | bhp | availability |
|---|---|---|---|
| I-6, 235.5 | 3.56 × 3.94 | 140 | S-all |
| V-8, 265.0 | 3.75 × 3.00 | 162/170 | S-manual/Powerglide |
| V-8, 265.0 | 3.75 × 3.00 | 205 | O-all |
| V-8, 265.0 | 3.75 × 3.00 | 225 | O-all |

## 1957

| 150 (wb 115.0) | | Wght | Price | Prod |
|---|---|---|---|---|
| 1502 | sdn 2d | 3,211 | 1,996 | 70,774 |
| 1503 | sdn 4d | 3,236 | 2,048 | 52,266 |
| 1512 | Util sdn 2d | 3,163 | 1,885 | 8,300 |
| 1529 | Handyman wgn 2d | 3,406 | 2,307 | 14,740 |
| **210 (wb 115.0)** | | | | |
| 2102 | sdn 2d | 3,225 | 2,122 | 160,090 |
| 2103 | sdn 4d | 3,270 | 2,174 | 260,401 |
| 2109 | Townsman wgn 4d | 3,461 | 2,456 | 127,803 |
| 2113 | Sport htp sdn | 3,320 | 2,270 | 16,178 |
| 2119 | Beauville wgn 4d | 3,561 | 2,563 | 21,083 |
| 2124 | Delray cpe | 3,220 | 2,162 | 25,644 |
| 2129 | Handyman wgn 2d | 3,406 | 2,402 | 17,528 |
| 2154 | Sport htp cpe | 3,260 | 2,204 | 22,631 |
| **Bel Air (wb 115.0)** | | | | |
| 2402 | sdn 2d | 3,232 | 2,238 | 62,751 |
| 2403 | sdn 4d | 3,276 | 2,290 | 254,331 |
| 2409 | Townsman wgn 4d | 3,460 | 2,580 | 27,375 |
| 2413 | Sport htp sdn | 3,340 | 2,364 | 137,672 |
| 2429 | Nomad wgn 2d | 3,465 | 2,757 | 6,103 |
| 2434 | conv cpe | 3,409 | 2,511 | 47,562 |
| 2454 | Sport htp cpe | 3,278 | 2,299 | 166,426 |

| 1957 Engines | bore × stroke | bhp | availability |
|---|---|---|---|
| I-6, 235.5 | 3.56 × 3.94 | 140 | S-all |
| V-8, 265.0 | 3.75 × 3.00 | 162 | O-all w/manual shift |
| V-8, 283.0 | 3.88 × 3.00 | 185 | S-all w/automatic |
| V-8, 283.0 | 3.88 × 3.00 | 220 | O-all |
| V-8, 283.0 | 3.88 × 3.00 | 245/250 | O-all |
| V-8, 283.0 | 3.88 × 3.00 | 270/283 | O-manual shift |

## 1958

| Delray (wb 117.5)—178,000* built | | Wght | Price | Prod |
|---|---|---|---|---|
| 1121 | Util sdn 2d, I-6 | 3,351 | 2,013 | — |
| 1141 | sdn 2d, I-6 | 3,396 | 2,101 | — |
| 1149 | sdn 4d, I-6 | 3,439 | 2,155 | — |
| 1221 | Util sdn 2d, V-8 | 3,356 | 2,120 | — |
| 1241 | sdn 2d, V-8 | 3,399 | 2,208 | — |
| 1249 | sdn 4d, V-8 | 3,442 | 2,262 | — |
| **Biscayne (wb 117.5)—100,000* built exc 1541** | | | | |
| 1541 | sdn 2d, I-6 | 3,404 | 2,236 | 76,229 |
| 1549 | sdn 4d, I-6 | 3,447 | 2,290 | — |
| 1641 | sdn 2d, V-8 | 3,407 | 2,343 | — |
| 1649 | sdn 4d, V-8 | 3,450 | 2,397 | — |
| **Bel Air (wb 117.5)—592,000* built** | | | | |
| 1731 | Sport htp cpe, I-6 | 3,455 | 2447 | — |
| 1739 | Sport htp sdn, I-6 | 3,511 | 2,511 | — |
| 1741 | sdn 2d, I-6 | 3,424 | 2,386 | — |
| 1747 | Impala htp cpe, I-6 | 3,458 | 2,586 | — |
| 1749 | sdn 4d, I-6 | 3,467 | 2,440 | — |
| 1767 | Impala conv cpe, I-6 | 3,522 | 2,734 | — |
| 1831 | Sport htp cpe, V-8 | 3,458 | 2,554 | — |
| 1839 | Sport htp sdn, V-8 | 3,514 | 2,618 | — |
| 1841 | sdn 2d, V-8 | 3,427 | 2,493 | — |
| 1847 | Impala htp cpe, V-8 | 3,459 | 2,693 | — |
| 1849 | sdn 4d, V-8 | 3,470 | 2,547 | — |
| 1867 | Impala conv cpe, V-8 | 3,523 | 2,841 | — |
| **Station Wagon (wb 117.5)—187,063 built** | | | | |
| 1191 | Yeoman 2d, I-6 | 3,693 | 2,413 | — |
| 1193 | Yeoman 4d, I-6 | 3,740 | 2,467 | — |
| 1291 | Yeoman 2d, V-8 | 3,696 | 2,520 | — |
| 1293 | Yeoman 4d, V-8 | 3,743 | 2,574 | — |
| 1593 | Brookwood 4d, 6P, I-6 | 3,748 | 2,571 | — |
| 1594 | Brookwood 4d, 9P, I-6 | 3,837 | 2,678 | — |
| 1693 | Brookwood 4d, 6P, V-8 | 3,751 | 2,678 | — |
| 1694 | Brookwood 4d, 9P, V-8 | 3,839 | 2,785 | — |
| 1793 | Nomad 4d, I-6 | 3,768 | 2,728 | — |
| 1893 | Nomad 4d, V-8 | 3,771 | 2,835 | — |

* To nearest 100. Impalas approximately 60,000.

| 1958 Engines | bore × stroke | bhp | availability |
|---|---|---|---|
| I-6, 235.5 | 3.56 × 3.94 | 145 | S-six |
| V-8, 283.0 | 3.88 × 3.00 | 185 | S-V-8 |
| V-8, 283.0 | 3.88 × 3.00 | 230/250 | O-all |
| V-8, 283.0 | 3.88 × 3.00 | 290 | O-all w/manual shift |
| V-8, 348.0 | 4.13 × 3.25 | 250 | O-all |
| V-8, 348.0 | 4.13 × 3.25 | 280/315 | O-all |

## 1959

| Biscayne (wb 119.0)—311,800* built | | Wght | Price | Prod |
|---|---|---|---|---|
| 1111 | sdn 2d, I-6 | 3,535 | 2,247 | — |
| 1119 | sdn 4d, I-6 | 3,605 | 2,301 | — |
| 1121 | Util sdn 2d, I-6 | 3,480 | 2,160 | — |
| 1211 | sdn 2d, V-8 | 3,530 | 2,365 | — |

# Chevrolet

| Biscayne (wb 119.0) | | Wght | Price | Prod |
|---|---|---|---|---|
| 1219 | sdn 4d, V-8 | 3,600 | 2,419 | — |
| 1221 | Util sdn 2d, V-8 | 3,490 | 2,278 | — |
| **Bel Air (wb 119.0)—447,100\* built** | | | | |
| 1511 | sdn 2d, I-6 | 3,515 | 2,386 | — |
| 1519 | sdn 4d, I-6 | 3,600 | 2,440 | — |
| 1539 | Sport htp sdn, I-6 | 3,660 | 2,556 | — |
| 1611 | sdn 2d, V-8 | 3,510 | 2,504 | — |
| 1619 | sdn 4d, V-8 | 3,615 | 2,558 | — |
| 1639 | Sport htp sdn, V-8 | 3,630 | 2,674 | — |
| **Impala (wb 119.0)—407,200 built exc 1867** | | | | |
| 1719 | sdn 4d, I-6 | 3,625 | 2,592 | — |
| 1737 | Sport htp cpe, I-6 | 3,570 | 2,599 | — |
| 1739 | Sport htp sdn, I-6 | 3,665 | 2,664 | — |
| 1767 | conv cpe, I-6 | 3,660 | 2,849 | — |
| 1819 | sdn 4d, V-8 | 3,620 | 2,710 | — |
| 1837 | Sport htp cpe, V-8 | 3,580 | 2,717 | — |
| 1839 | Sport htp sdn, V-8 | 3,670 | 2,782 | — |
| 1867 | conv cpe, V-8 | 3,650 | 2,967 | 65,800 |
| **Station Wagon (wb 119.0)—195,583 built\* exc 1215** | | | | |
| 1115 | Brookwood 2d, I-6 | 3,870 | 2,571 | — |
| 1135 | Brookwood 4d, I-6 | 3,955 | 2,638 | — |
| 1215 | Brookwood 2d, V-8 | 3,860 | 2,689 | 18,800 |
| 1235 | Brookwood, 4d, V-8 | 3,955 | 2,756 | — |
| 1535 | Parkwood 4d, I-6 | 3,965 | 2,749 | — |
| 1545 | Kingswood, 4d, 9P, I-6 | 4,020 | 2,852 | — |
| 1635 | Parkwood 4d, V-8 | 3,970 | 2,867 | — |
| 1645 | Kingswood 4d, 9P, V-8 | 4,015 | 2,970 | — |
| 1735 | Nomad 4d, I-6 | 3,980 | 2,891 | — |
| 1835 | Nomad 4d, V-8 | 3,975 | 3,009 | — |

\* To nearest 100.

| 1959 Engines | bore × stroke | bhp | availability |
|---|---|---|---|
| I-6, 235.5 | 3.56 × 3.94 | 135 | S-six |
| V-8, 283.0 | 3.88 × 3.00 | 185 | S-V-8 |
| V-8, 280.0 | 3.88 × 3.00 | 230-290 | O-all |
| V-8, 348.0 | 4.13 × 3.25 | 250-315 | O-all |

## 1960

| Biscayne (wb 119.0)—287,700\* built | | Wght | Price | Prod |
|---|---|---|---|---|
| 1111 | sdn 2d, I-6 | 3,485 | 2,262 | — |
| 1119 | sdn 4d, I-6 | 3,555 | 2,316 | — |
| 1121 | Util sdn 2d, I-6 | 3,455 | 2,175 | — |
| 1211 | sdn 2d, V-8 | 3,500 | 2,369 | — |
| 1219 | sdn 4d, V-8 | 3,570 | 2,423 | — |
| 1221 | Util sdn 2d, V-8 | 3,470 | 2,282 | — |
| **Biscayne Fleetmaster (wb 119.0)—prod included with Biscayne** | | | | |
| 1311 | sdn 2d, I-6 | 3,480 | 2,230 | — |
| 1319 | sdn 4d, I-6 | 3,545 | 2,284 | — |
| 1411 | sdn 2d, V-8 | 3,495 | 2,337 | — |
| 1419 | sdn 4d, V-8 | 3,560 | 2,391 | — |
| **Bel Air (wb 119.0)—381,500\* built** | | | | |
| 1511 | sdn 2d, I-6 | 3,490 | 2,384 | — |
| 1519 | sdn 4d, I-6 | 3,565 | 2,438 | — |
| 1537 | Sport htp cpe, I-6 | 3,515 | 2,489 | — |
| 1539 | Sport htp sdn, I-6 | 3,605 | 2,554 | — |
| 1611 | sdn 2d, V-8 | 3,505 | 2,491 | — |
| 1619 | sdn 4d, V-8 | 3,500 | 2,545 | — |
| 1637 | Sport htp cpe, I-6 | 3,530 | 2,596 | — |
| 1639 | Sport htp sdn, V-8 | 3,620 | 2,661 | — |
| **Impala (wb 119.0)—411,000\* built exc 1867** | | | | |
| 1719 | sdn 4d, I-6 | 3,575 | 2,590 | — |

| Impala (wb 119.0) | | Wght | Price | Prod |
|---|---|---|---|---|
| v1737 | Sport htp cpe, I-6 | 3,530 | 2,597 | — |
| 1739 | Sport htp sdn, I-6 | 3,625 | 2,662 | — |
| 1767 | conv cpe, I-6 | 3,625 | 2,847 | — |
| 1819 | sdn 4d, V-8 | 3,580 | 2,697 | — |
| 1837 | Sport htp cpe, V-8 | 3,540 | 2,704 | — |
| 1839 | Sport htp sdn, V-8 | 3,625 | 2,769 | — |
| 1867 | conv cpe, V-8 | 3,635 | 2,954 | 79,903 |
| **Station Wagon (wb 119.0)—212,700\* built** | | | | |
| 1115 | Brookwood 2d, I-6 | 3,845 | 2,586 | — |
| 1135 | Brookwood 4d, I-6 | 3,935 | 2,653 | — |
| 1215 | Brookwood 2d, V-8 | 3,855 | 2,693 | — |
| 1235 | Brookwood 4d, V-8 | 3,935 | 2,760 | — |
| 1535 | Parkwood 4d, I-6 | 3,945 | 2,747 | — |
| 1545 | Kingswood, 4d, 9P, I-6 | 3,990 | 2,850 | — |
| 1635 | Parkwood 4d, V-8 | 3,950 | 2,854 | — |
| 1645 | Kingswood 4d, 9P, V-8 | 4,000 | 2,957 | — |
| 1735 | Nomad 4d, I-6 | 3,955 | 2,889 | — |
| 1835 | Nomad 4d, V-8 | 3,960 | 2,996 | — |

\* To nearest 100.

| 1960 Engines | bore × stroke | bhp | availability |
|---|---|---|---|
| I-6, 235.5 | 3.56 × 3.94 | 135 | S-six |
| V-8, 283.0 | 3.88 × 3.00 | 170 | S-V-8 |
| V-8, 283.0 | 3.88 × 3.00 | 230 | O-all |
| V-8, 348.0 | 4.13 × 3.25 | 250-335 | O-all |

## 1961

| Biscayne (wb 119.0)—201,000\* built | | Wght | Price | Prod |
|---|---|---|---|---|
| 1111 | sdn 2d, I-6 | 3,415 | 2,262 | — |
| 1121 | Util sdn 2d, I-6 | 3,390 | 2,175 | — |
| 1169 | sdn 4d, I-6 | 3,500 | 2,316 | — |
| 1211 | sdn 2d, V-8 | 3,425 | 2,369 | — |
| 1221 | Util sdn 2d, V-8 | 3,395 | 2,282 | — |
| 1269 | sdn 4d, V-8 | 3,505 | 2,423 | — |
| **Biscayne Fleetmaster (wb 119.0)—3,000\* built** | | | | |
| 1311 | sdn 2d, I-6 | 3,410 | 2,230 | — |
| 1369 | sdn 4d, I-6 | 3,495 | 2,284 | — |
| 1411 | sdn 2d, V-8 | 3,415 | 2,337 | — |
| 1469 | sdn 4d, V-8 | 3,500 | 2,391 | — |
| **Bel Air (wb 119.0)—330,000\* built** | | | | |
| 1511 | sdn 2d, I-6 | 3,430 | 2,384 | — |
| 1537 | Sport htp cpe, I-6 | 3,475 | 2,489 | — |
| 1539 | Sport htp sdn, I-6 | 3,550 | 2,554 | — |
| 1569 | sdn 4d, I-6 | 3,515 | 2,438 | — |
| 1611 | sdn 2d, V-8 | 3,435 | 2,491 | — |
| 1637 | Sport htp cpe, V-8 | 3,480 | 2,596 | — |
| 1639 | Sport htp sdn, V-8 | 3,555 | 2,661 | — |
| 1669 | sdn 4d, V-8 | 3,520 | 2,545 | — |
| **Impala (wb 119.0)—426,400\* built exc 1867** | | | | |
| 1711 | sdn 2d, I-6 | 3,445 | 2,536 | — |
| 1737 | Sport htp cpe, I-6 | 3,485 | 2,597 | — |
| 1739 | Sport htp sdn, I-6 | 3,575 | 2,662 | — |
| 1767 | conv cpe, I-6 | 3,605 | 2,847 | — |
| 1769 | sdn 4d, I-6 | 3,530 | 2,590 | — |
| 1811 | sdn 2d, V-8 | 3,440 | 2,643 | — |
| 1837 | Sport htp cpe, V-8 | 3,480 | 2,704 | — |
| 1839 | Sport htp sdn, V-8 | 3,570 | 2,769 | — |
| 1867 | conv cpe, V-8 | 3,600 | 2,954 | 64,600 |
| 1869 | sdn 4d, V-8 | 3,525 | 2,697 | — |
| **Station Wagon (wb 119.0)—168,900 built\*\*** | | | | |
| 1135 | Brookwood 4d, I-6 | 3,850 | 2,653 | — |

# Chevrolet

| Station Wagon (wb 119.0) | | Wght | Price | Prod |
|---|---|---|---|---|
| 1145 | Brookwood 4d, 9P, I-6 | 3,900 | 2,756 | — |
| 1235 | Brookwood 4d, V-8 | 3,845 | 2,760 | — |
| 1245 | Brookwood 4d, 9P, V-8 | 3,895 | 2,864 | — |
| 1535 | Parkwood 4d, I-6 | 3,865 | 2,747 | — |
| 1545 | Parkwood 4d, 9P, I-6 | 3,910 | 2,850 | — |
| 1635 | Parkwood 4d, V-8 | 3,860 | 2,854 | — |
| 1645 | Parkwood 4d, 9P, V-8 | 3,905 | 2,957 | — |
| 1735 | Nomad 4d, I-6 | 3,885 | 2,889 | — |
| 1745 | Nomad 4d, 9P, I-6 | 3,935 | 2,992 | — |
| 1835 | Nomad 4d, V-8 | 3,880 | 2,996 | — |
| 1845 | Nomad 4d, 9P, V-8 | 3,930 | 3,099 | — |

\* To nearest 100.
\*\* Included with models above.

| 1961 Engines | bore × stroke | bhp | availability |
|---|---|---|---|
| I-6, 235.5 | 3.56 × 3.94 | 135 | S-six |
| V-8, 283.0 | 3.88 × 3.00 | 170 | S-V-8 |
| V-8, 283.0 | 3.88 × 3.00 | 230 | O-all |
| V-8, 348.0 | 4.13 × 3.25 | 250-350 | O-all |
| V-8, 409.0 | 4.31 × 3.50 | 360 | O-Impala SS |

## 1962

| Chevy II 100 (wb 110.0) | | Wght | Price | Prod |
|---|---|---|---|---|
| 0111 | sdn 2d, I-4 | 2,410 | 2,003 | 11,500* |
| 0135 | wgn 4d, I-4 | 2,665 | 2,399 | |
| 0169 | sdn 4d, I-4 | 2,445 | 2,041 | |
| 0211 | sdn 2d, I-6 | 2,500 | 2,063 | 35,500* |
| 0235 | wgn 4d, I-6 | 2,755 | 2,399 | |
| 0269 | sdn 4d, I-6 | 2,535 | 2,101 | |
| **Chevy II 300 (wb 110.0)** | | | | |
| 0311 | sdn 2d, I-4 | 2,425 | 2,084 | — |
| 0345 | wgn 4d, 9P, I-4 | 2,765 | 2,517 | — |
| 0369 | sdn 4d, I-4 | 2,460 | 2,122 | — |
| 0411 | sdn 2d, I-6 | 2,515 | 2,144 | 92,800* |
| 0445 | wgn 4d, 9P, I-6 | 2,855 | 2,577 | |
| 0469 | sdn 4d, I-6 | 2,550 | 2,182 | |
| **Chevy II Nova 400, I-6 (wb 110.0)** | | | | |
| 0435 | wgn 4d | 2,775 | 2,497 | — |
| 0437 | Sport htp cpe | 2,550 | 2,254 | 59,586 |
| 0441 | sdn 2d | 2,540 | 2,198 | 44,390 |
| 0449 | sdn 4d | 2,575 | 2,336 | 139,004 |
| 0467 | conv cpe | 2,745 | 2,475 | 23,741 |
| **Biscayne (wb 119.0)—160,000\*\* built** | | | | |
| 1111 | sdn 2d, I-6 | 3,405 | 2,324 | — |
| 1135 | wgn 4d, I-6 | 3,845 | 2,725 | — |
| 1169 | sdn 4d, I-6 | 3,480 | 2,378 | — |
| 1211 | sdn 2d, V-8 | 3,400 | 2,431 | — |
| 1235 | wgn 4d, V-8 | 3,840 | 2,832 | — |
| 1269 | sdn 4d, V-8 | 3,475 | 2,485 | — |
| **Bel Air (wb 119.0)—365,000\*\* built** | | | | |
| 1511 | sdn 2d, I-6 | 3,410 | 2,456 | — |
| 1535 | wgn 4d, I-6 | 3,845 | 2,819 | — |
| 1537 | Sport htp cpe, I-6 | 3,445 | 2,561 | — |
| 1545 | wgn 4d, 9P, I-6 | 3,895 | 2,922 | — |
| 1569 | sdn 4d, I-6 | 3,480 | 2,510 | — |
| 1611 | sdn 2d, V-8 | 3,405 | 2,563 | — |
| 1635 | wgn 4d, V-8 | 3,840 | 2,926 | — |
| 1637 | Sport htp cpe, V-8 | 3,440 | 2,668 | — |
| 1645 | wgn 4d, 9P, V-8 | 3,890 | 3,029 | — |
| 1669 | sdn 4d, V-8 | 3,475 | 2,617 | — |

| Impala (wb 119.0)—704,900\*\* blt | | Wght | Price | Prod |
|---|---|---|---|---|
| 1735 | wgn 4d, I-6 | 3,870 | 2,961 | — |
| 1739 | Sport htp sdn, I-6 | 3,540 | 2,734 | — |
| 1745 | wgn 4d, 9P, I-6 | 3,925 | 3,064 | — |
| 1747 | Sport htp cpe, I-6 | 3,455 | 2,669 | — |
| 1767 | conv cpe, I-6 | 3,565 | 2,919 | — |
| 1769 | sdn 4d, I-6 | 3,510 | 2,662 | — |
| 1835 | wgn 4d, V-8 | 3,865 | 3,068 | — |
| 1839 | Sport htp sdn, V-8 | 3,535 | 2,841 | — |
| 1845 | wgn 4d, 9P, V-8 | 3,920 | 3,171 | — |
| 1847 | Sport htp cpe, V-8 | 3,450 | 2,776 | — |
| 1867 | conv cpe, V-8 | 3,560 | 3,026 | — |
| 1869 | sdn 4d, V-8 | 3,505 | 2,769 | — |

\* To nearest 100.
\*\* Does not include wagons (187,600 built), but includes SS models.

| 1962 Engines | bore × stroke | bhp | availability |
|---|---|---|---|
| I-4, 153.0 | 3.88 × 3.25 | 90 | S-Chevy II 100, 300 |
| I-6, 194.0 | 3.56 × 3.25 | 120 | S-Chevy II all |
| I-6, 235.5 | 3.56 × 3.94 | 135 | S-Chevrolet I-6 |
| V-8, 283.0 | 3.88 × 3.00 | 170 | S-Chevrolet V-8 |
| V-8, 327.0 | 4.00 × 3.25 | 250/300 | O-V-8-all Chev |
| V-8, 409.0 | 4.31 × 3.50 | 380/409 | O-V-8-all Chev |

## 1963

| Chevy II 100 (wb 110)—50,400\* blt | | Wght | Price | Prod |
|---|---|---|---|---|
| 0111 | sdn 2d, I-4 | 2,430 | 2,003 | — |
| 0135 | wgn 4d, I-4 | 2,725 | 2,338 | — |
| 0169 | sdn 4d, I-4 | 2,455 | 2,040 | — |
| 0211 | sdn 2d, I-6 | 2,520 | 2,062 | — |
| 0235 | wgn 4d, I-6 | 2,810 | 2,397 | — |
| 0269 | sdn 4d, I-6 | 2,545 | 2,099 | — |
| **Chevy II 300 (wb 110.0)—78,800\* built** | | | | |
| 0311 | sdn 2d, I-4 | 2,440 | 2,084 | — |
| 0345 | wgn 4d, 9P, I-4 | 2,810 | 2,516 | — |
| 0369 | sdn 4d, I-4 | 2,470 | 2,121 | — |
| 0411 | sdn 2d, I-6 | 2,530 | 2,143 | — |
| 0445 | wgn 4d, 9P, I-6 | 2,900 | 2,575 | — |
| 0469 | sdn 4d, I-6 | 2,560 | 2,180 | — |
| **Chevy II Nova 400, I-6 (wb 110.0)** | | | | |
| 0435 | wgn 4d | 2,835 | 2,494 | — |
| 0437 | Sport htp cpe | 2,590 | 2,267 | 87,415 |
| 0449 | sdn 4d | 2,590 | 2,235 | 58,862 |
| 0467 | conv cpe | 2,760 | 2,472 | 24,823 |
| **Biscayne (wb 119.0)—186,500\* built** | | | | |
| 1111 | sdn 2d, I-6 | 3,205 | 2,322 | — |
| 1135 | wgn 4d, I-6 | 3,685 | 2,723 | — |
| 1169 | sdn 4d, I-6 | 3,280 | 2,376 | — |
| 1211 | sdn 2d, V-8 | 3,340 | 2,429 | — |
| 1235 | wgn 4d, V-8 | 3,810 | 2,830 | — |
| 1269 | sdn 4d, V-8 | 3,415 | 2,483 | — |
| **Bel Air (wb 119.0)—354,100\* built** | | | | |
| 1511 | sdn 2d, I-6 | 3,215 | 2,454 | — |
| 1535 | wgn 4d, I-6 | 3,685 | 2,818 | — |
| 1545 | wgn 4d, 9P, I-6 | 3,720 | 2,921 | — |
| 1569 | sdn 4d, I-6 | 3,280 | 2,508 | — |
| 1611 | sdn 2d, V-8 | 3,345 | 2,561 | — |
| 1635 | wgn 4d, V-8 | 3,810 | 2,925 | — |
| 1645 | wgn 4d, 9P, V-8 | 3,850 | 3,028 | — |
| 1669 | sdn 4d, V-8 | 3,415 | 2,615 | — |
| **Impala (wb 119)—832,600\* built (includes 153,271 SS models)** | | | | |
| 1735 | wgn 4d, I-6 | 3,705 | 2,960 | — |

219

# Chevrolet

| Impala (wb 119.0) | | Wght | Price | Prod |
|---|---|---|---|---|
| 1739 | Sport htp sdn, I-6 | 3,350 | 2,732 | — |
| 1745 | wgn 4d, 9P, I-6 | 3,745 | 3,063 | — |
| 1747 | Sport htp cpe, I-6 | 3,265 | 2,667 | — |
| 1767 | conv cpe, I-6 | 3,400 | 2,917 | — |
| 1769 | sdn 4d, I-6 | 3,310 | 2,661 | — |
| 1835 | wgn 4d, V-8 | 3,835 | 3,067 | — |
| 1839 | Sport htp sdn, V-8 | 3,475 | 2,839 | — |
| 1845 | wgn 4d, 9P, V-8 | 3,870 | 3,170 | — |
| 1847 | Sport htp cpe, V-8 | 3,390 | 2,774 | — |
| 1867 | conv cpe, V-8 | 3,525 | 3,024 | — |
| 1869 | sdn 4d, V-8 | 3,435 | 2,768 | — |

* To nearest 100; does not include wagons. Total wagons 198,542; Chevy II wagons 75,274.

| 1963 Engines | bore × stroke | bhp | availability |
|---|---|---|---|
| I-4, 153.0 | 3.88 × 3.25 | 90 | S-Chevy II |
| I-6, 194.0 | 3.56 × 3.25 | 120 | S-Chevy II |
| I-6, 230.0 | 3.87 × 3.25 | 140 | S-Chevrolet |
| V-8, 283.0 | 3.88 × 3.00 | 195 | S-Chevrolet |
| V-8, 327.0 | 4.00 × 3.15 | 250-340 | O-Chevrolet |
| V-8, 409.0 | 4.31 × 3.50 | 340-425 | O-Chevrolet |

## 1964

| Chevy II 100 (wb 110)—53,100 built* | | Wght | Price | Prod |
|---|---|---|---|---|
| 0111 | sdn 2d, I-4 | 2,455 | 2,011 | — |
| 0169 | sdn, I-4 | 2,495 | 2,048 | — |
| 0211 | sdn 2d, I-6 | 2,540 | 2,070 | — |
| 0235 | wgn 4d, I-6 | 2,840 | 2,406 | — |
| 0269 | sdn 4d, I-6 | 2,580 | 2,108 | — |
| **Chevy II Nova 400, I-6 (wb 110.0)—102,900* built (includes SS)** | | | | |
| 0411 | sdn 2d | 2,560 | 2,206 | — |
| 0435 | wgn 4d | 2,860 | 2,503 | — |
| 0437 | Sport htp cpe | 2,660 | 2,271 | — |
| 0469 | sdn 4d | 2,595 | 2,243 | — |
| **Chevy II Nova SS, I-6 (wb 110.0)** | | | | |
| 0447 | Sport htp cpe | 2,675 | 2,433 | 10,576 |
| **Chevelle 300 (wb 115.0)—68,300* built** | | | | |
| 5311 | sdn 2d, I-6 | 2,825 | 2,231 | — |
| 5315 | wgn 2d, I-6 | 3,050 | 2,528 | — |
| 5335 | wgn 4d, I-6 | 3,130 | 2,566 | — |
| 5369 | sdn 4d, I-6 | 2,850 | 2,268 | — |
| 5411 | sdn 2d, V-8 | 2,995 | 2,339 | — |
| 5415 | wgn 2d, V-8 | 3,170 | 2,636 | — |
| 5435 | wgn 4d, V-8 | 2,250 | 2,674 | — |
| 5469 | sdn 4d, V-8 | 2,980 | 2,376 | — |
| **Chevelle Malibu (wb 115.0)—149,000* built** | | | | |
| 5535 | wgn 4d, I-6 | 3,140 | 2,647 | — |
| 5537 | Sport htp cpe, I-6 | 2,850 | 2,376 | — |
| 5545 | wgn 4d, 9P, I-6 | 3,240 | 2,744 | — |
| 5567 | conv cpe, I-6 | 2,995 | 2,587 | — |
| 5569 | sdn 4d, I-6 | 2,870 | 2,349 | — |
| 5635 | wgn 4d, V-8 | 3,265 | 2,755 | — |
| 5637 | Sport htp cpe, V-8 | 2,975 | 2,484 | — |
| 5645 | wgn 4d, 9P, V-8 | 3,365 | 2,852 | — |
| 5667 | conv cpe, V-8 | 3,120 | 2,695 | — |
| 5669 | sdn 4d, V-8 | 2,996 | 2,457 | — |
| **Chevelle Malibu SS (wb 115.0)—76,860 built** | | | | |
| 5737 | Sport htp cpe, I-6 | 2,875 | 2,538 | — |
| 5767 | conv cpe, I-6 | 3,020 | 2,749 | — |
| 5837 | Sport htp cpe, V-8 | 3,000 | 2,646 | — |
| 5867 | conv cpe, V-8 | 3,145 | 2,857 | — |

| Biscayne (wb 119.0)—173,900* blt | | Wght | Price | Prod |
|---|---|---|---|---|
| 1111 | sdn 2d, I-6 | 3,230 | 2,363 | — |
| 1135 | wgn 4d, I-6 | 3,700 | 2,763 | — |
| 1169 | sdn 4d, I-6 | 3,300 | 2,417 | — |
| 1211 | sdn 2d, V-8 | 3,365 | 2,471 | — |
| 1235 | wgn 4d, V-8 | 3,820 | 2,871 | — |
| 1269 | sdn 4d, V-8 | 3,430 | 2,524 | — |
| **Bel Air (wb 119.0)—318,100* built** | | | | |
| 1511 | sdn 2d, I-6 | 3,235 | 2,465 | — |
| 1535 | wgn 4d, I-6 | 3,745 | 2,828 | — |
| 1545 | wgn 4d, 9P, I-6 | 3,705 | 2,931 | — |
| 1569 | sdn 4d, I-6 | 3,305 | 2,519 | — |
| 1611 | sdn 2d, V-8 | 3,370 | 2,573 | — |
| 1635 | wgn 4d, V-8 | 3,825 | 2,935 | — |
| 1645 | wgn 4d, 9P, V-8 | 3,865 | 3,039 | — |
| 1669 | sdn 4d, V-8 | 3,440 | 2,626 | — |
| **Impala (wb 119.0)—889,600* built** | | | | |
| 1735 | wgn 4d, I-6 | 3,725 | 2,970 | — |
| 1739 | Sport htp sdn, I-6 | 3,370 | 2,742 | — |
| 1745 | wgn 4d, 9P, I-6 | 3,770 | 3,073 | — |
| — | Sport htp cpe, I-6 | 3,265 | 2,667 | — |
| 1767 | conv cpe, I-6 | 3,400 | 2,927 | — |
| 1769 | sdn 4d, I-6 | 3,340 | 2,671 | — |
| 1835 | wgn 4d, V-8 | 3,850 | 3,077 | — |
| 1839 | Sport htp sdn, V-8 | 3,490 | 2,850 | — |
| 1845 | wgn 4d, 9P, V-8 | 3,895 | 3,181 | — |
| 1847 | Sport htp cpe, V-8 | 3,415 | 2,786 | — |
| 1867 | conv cpe, V-8 | 3,525 | 3,025 | — |
| 1869 | sdn 4d, V-8 | 3,460 | 2,779 | — |
| **Impala SS (wb 119.0)** | | | | |
| 1347 | htp cpe, I-6 | 3,325 | 2,839 | 1,998 |
| 1367 | conv cpe, I-6 | 3,435 | 3,088 | 316 |
| 1447 | Sport htp cpe, V-8 | 3,450 | 2,947 | 97,753 |
| 1467 | conv cpe, V-8 | 3,555 | 3,196 | 19,099 |

* To nearest 100; does not include wagons. Wagon production: Chevy II 35,700; Chevelle 44,000; others 192,800.

| 1964 Engines | bore × stroke | bhp | availability |
|---|---|---|---|
| I-4, 153.0 | 3.88 × 3.25 | 90 | S-Chevy II 100 |
| I-6, 194.0 | 3.56 × 3.25 | 120 | S-Chevy II 100/400, Chevelle |
| I-6, 230.0 | 3.87 × 3.25 | 140 | S-Chevrolet; O-others |
| I-6, 230.0 | 3.87 × 3.25 | 155 | O-all |
| V-8, 283.0 | 3.88 × 3.00 | 195 | S-V-8 Chvlle, Chvrlet; O-Chevy II |
| V-8, 283.0 | 3.88 × 3.00 | 220 | O-Chevelle |
| V-8, 327.0 | 4.00 × 3.25 | 250/300 | O-Chevrolet, Chevelle |
| V-8, 409.0 | 4.31 × 3.50 | 340-425 | O-Chevrolet |

## 1965

| Chevy II 100 (wb 110.0) | | Wght | Price | Prod |
|---|---|---|---|---|
| 11111 | sdn 2d, I-4 | 2,505 | 2,011 | 1,300* |
| 11169 | sdn 4d, I-4 | 2,520 | 2,048 | |
| 11311 | sdn 2d, I-6 | 2,605 | 2,077 | 39,200* |
| 11335 | wgn 4d, I-6 | 2,875 | 2,413 | |
| 11369 | sdn 4d, I-6 | 2,620 | 2,115 | |
| **Chevy II Nova 400, I-6 (wb 110.0)—51,700* built** | | | | |
| 11535 | wgn 4d | 2,880 | 2,510 | — |
| 11537 | htp cpe | 2,645 | 2,270 | — |
| 11569 | sdn 4d | 2,645 | 2,243 | — |

# Chevrolet

| Chevy II Nova SS, I-6 (wb 110.0) | | Wght | Price | Prod |
|---|---|---|---|---|
| 11737 | htp cpe | 2,690 | 2,433 | 9,100 |
| **Chevelle 300 (wb 115.0)—31,600* built (plus 41,600* DeLuxe)** | | | | |
| 13111 | sdn 2d, I-6 | 2,870 | 2,156 | — |
| 13115 | wgn 2d, I-6 | 3,140 | 2,453 | — |
| 13169 | sdn 4d, I-6 | 2,900 | 2,193 | — |
| 13211 | sdn 2d, V-8 | 3,010 | 2,262 | — |
| 13215 | wgn 2d, V-8 | 3,275 | 2,561 | — |
| 13269 | sdn 4d, V-8 | 3,035 | 2,301 | — |
| 13311 | Del sdn 2d, I-6 | 2,870 | 2,231 | — |
| 13335 | Del wgn 4d, I-6 | 3,185 | 2,567 | — |
| 13369 | Del sdn 4d, I-6 | 2,910 | 2,269 | — |
| 13411 | Del sdn 2d, V-8 | 3,010 | 2,339 | — |
| 13435 | Del wgn 4d, V-8 | 3,320 | 2,674 | — |
| 13469 | Del sdn 4d, V-8 | 3,050 | 2,377 | — |
| **Chevelle Malibu (wb 115.0) 152,200* built** | | | | |
| 13535 | wgn 4d, I-6 | 3,225 | 2,647 | — |
| 13537 | htp cpe, I-6 | 2,930 | 2,377 | — |
| 13567 | conv cpe, I-6 | 3,025 | 2,588 | — |
| 13569 | sdn 4d, I-6 | 2,945 | 2,250 | — |
| 13635 | wgn 4d, V-8 | 3,355 | 2,755 | — |
| 13637 | htp cpe, V-8 | 3,065 | 2,485 | — |
| 13667 | conv cpe, V-8 | 3,160 | 2,696 | — |
| 13669 | sdn 4d, V-8 | 3,080 | 2,458 | — |
| **Chevelle Malibu SS (wb 115.0)—101,577 built (201 SS 396)** | | | | |
| 13737 | htp cpe, I-6 | 2,980 | 2,539 | — |
| 13767 | conv cpe, I-6 | 3,075 | 2,750 | — |
| 13837 | htp cpe, V-8 | 3,115 | 2,647 | — |
| 13867 | conv cpe, V-8 | 3,210 | 2,858 | — |
| **Biscayne (wb 119.0)** | | | | |
| 15311 | sdn 2d, I-6 | 3,305 | 2,363 | 107,700* |
| 15335 | wgn 4d, I-6 | 3,765 | 2,764 | |
| 15369 | sdn 4d, I-6 | 3,365 | 2,417 | |
| 15411 | sdn 2d, V-8 | 3,455 | 2,470 | 37,600* |
| 15435 | wgn 4d, V-8 | 3,900 | 2,871 | |
| 15469 | sdn 4d, V-8 | 3,515 | 2,524 | |
| **Bel Air (wb 119.0)** | | | | |
| 15511 | sdn 2d, I-6 | 3,310 | 2,465 | 107,800* |
| 15535 | wgn 4d, I-6 | 3,765 | 2,828 | |
| 15545 | wgn 4d, 9P, I-6 | 3,810 | 2,931 | |
| 15569 | sdn 4d, I-6 | 3,380 | 2,519 | |
| 15611 | sdn 2d, V-8 | 3,460 | 2,573 | 163,600* |
| 15635 | wgn 4d, V-8 | 3,905 | 2,936 | |
| 15645 | wgn 4d, 9P, V-8 | 3,950 | 3,039 | |
| 15669 | sdn 4d, V-8 | 3,530 | 2,626 | |
| **Impala (wb 119.0)—803,400* built (includes Caprice pkg)** | | | | |
| 16335 | wgn 4d, I-6 | 3,825 | 2,970 | 56,600* |
| 16337 | htp cpe, I-6 | 3,385 | 2,678 | |
| 16339 | htp sdn, I-6 | 3,490 | 2,742 | |
| 16345 | wgn 4d, 9P, I-6 | 3,865 | 3,073 | |
| 16367 | conv cpe, I-6 | 3,470 | 2,943 | |
| 16369 | sdn 4d, I-6 | 3,460 | 2,672 | |
| 16435 | wgn 4d, V-8 | 3,960 | 3,078 | 746,800* |
| 16437 | htp cpe, V-8 | 3,525 | 2,785 | |
| 16439 | htp sdn, V-8 | 3,630 | 2,850 | |
| 16445 | wgn 4d, 9P, V-8 | 4,005 | 3,181 | |
| 16467 | conv cpe, V-8 | 3,605 | 3,051 | |
| 16469 | sdn 4d, V-8 | 3,595 | 2,779 | |
| **Impala SS (wb 119.0)—243,114 built** | | | | |
| 16537 | htp cpe, I-6 | 3,435 | 2,839 | — |
| 16567 | conv cpe, I-6 | 3,505 | 3,104 | — |
| 16637 | htp cpe, V-8 | 3,570 | 2,947 | — |

| Impala SS (wb 119.0) | | Wght | Price | Prod |
|---|---|---|---|---|
| 16667 | conv cpe, V-8 | 3,655 | 3,212 | — |

* To nearest 100; does not include wagons. Wagon production: Chevy II, 21,500; Chevelle, 37,600; others, 184,400. Convertible production: Malibu 19,765; Impala SS, 27,842.

| 1965 Engines | bore × stroke | bhp | availability |
|---|---|---|---|
| I-4, 153.0 | 3.88 × 3.25 | 90 | S-Chevy II 100 |
| I-6, 194.0 | 3.56 × 3.25 | 120 | S-Chevy II, Chevelle |
| I-6, 230.0 | 3.87 × 3.25 | 140 | S-Chevrolet; O-others |
| I-6, 250.0 | 3.87 × 3.53 | 150 | O-Chevrolet |
| V-8, 283.0 | 3.88 × 3.00 | 195 | S-Chevrolet, Chevelle; O-Chevy II |
| V-8, 283.0 | 3.88 × 3.00 | 220 | O-all |
| V-8, 327.0 | 4.00 × 3.25 | 250/300 | O-all |
| V-8, 327.0 | 4.00 × 3.25 | 350 | O-Chevelle |
| V-8, 396.0 | 4.09 × 3.75 | 325-425 | O-Chevrolet, Chevelle |
| V-8, 409.0 | 4.31 × 3.50 | 340/400 | O-Chevrolet |

## 1966

| Chevy II 100 (wb 110.0) | | Wght | Price | Prod |
|---|---|---|---|---|
| 11111 | sdn 2d, I-4 | 2,520 | 2,028 | 44,500* |
| 11169 | sdn 4d, I-4 | 2,535 | 2,065 | |
| 11311 | sdn 2d, I-6 | 2,620 | 2,090 | |
| 11335 | wgn 4d, I-6 | 2,855 | 2,430 | |
| 11369 | sdn 4d, I-6 | 2,635 | 2,127 | |
| 11411 | sdn 2d, V-8 | 2,775 | 2,197 | 2,500* |
| 11435 | wgn 4d, V-8 | 2,990 | 2,536 | |
| 11469 | sdn 4d, V-8 | 2,790 | 2,234 | |
| **Chevy II Nova (wb 110.0)** | | | | |
| 11535 | wgn 4d, I-6 | 2,885 | 2,518 | 54,300* |
| 11537 | htp cpe, I-6 | 2,675 | 2,271 | |
| 11569 | sdn 4d, I-6 | 2,640 | 2,245 | |
| 11635 | wgn 4d, V-8 | 3,010 | 2,623 | 19,600* |
| 11637 | htp cpe, V-8 | 2,830 | 2,377 | |
| 11669 | sdn 4d, V-8 | 2,800 | 2,351 | |
| **Chevy II Nova SS (wb 110.0)** | | | | |
| 11737 | htp cpe, I-6 | 2,740 | 2,430 | 6,700* |
| 11837 | htp cpe, V-8 | 2,870 | 2,535 | 16,300* |
| **Chevelle 300 (wb 115.0)** | | | | |
| 13111 | sdn 2d, I-6 | 2,895 | 2,156 | 23,300* |
| 13169 | sdn 4d, I-6 | 2,935 | 2,202 | |
| 13211 | sdn 2d, V-8 | 3,040 | 2,271 | 5,300* |
| 13269 | sdn 4d, V-8 | 3,080 | 2,308 | |
| 13311 | Del sdn 2d, I-6 | 2,910 | 2,239 | 37,600* |
| 13335 | Del wgn 4d, I-6 | 3,210 | 2,575 | |
| 13369 | Del sdn 4d, I-6 | 2,945 | 2,276 | |
| 13411 | Del sdn 2d, V-8 | 3,060 | 2,345 | |
| 13435 | Del wgn 4d, V-8 | 3,350 | 2,681 | |
| 13469 | Del sdn 4d, V-8 | 3,095 | 2,382 | |
| **Chevelle Malibu (wb 115.0)—241,600* built** | | | | |
| 13517 | htp cpe, I-6 | 2,935 | 2,378 | — |
| 13535 | wgn 4d, I-6 | 3,235 | 2,651 | — |
| 13539 | htp sdn, I-6 | 3,035 | 2,458 | — |
| 13567 | conv cpe, I-6 | 3,030 | 2,588 | — |
| 13569 | sdn 4d, I-6 | 2,960 | 2,352 | — |
| 13617 | htp cpe, V-8 | 3,075 | 2,484 | — |
| 13635 | wgn 4d, V-8 | 3,375 | 2,766 | — |
| 13639 | htp sdn, V-8 | 3,180 | 2,564 | — |

# Chevrolet

| Chevelle Malibu | | Wght | Price | Prod |
|---|---|---|---|---|
| 13667 | conv cpe, V-8 | 3,175 | 2,693 | — |
| 13669 | sdn 4d, V-8 | 3,110 | 2,456 | — |
| **Chevelle Malibu SS, V-8 (wb 115.0)—72,300* built** | | | | |
| 13817 | htp cpe | 3,375 | 2,776 | — |
| 13867 | conv cpe, V-8 | 3,470 | 2,984 | — |
| **Biscayne (wb 119.0)** | | | | |
| 15311 | sdn 2d, I-6 | 3,310 | 2,379 | ⎫ |
| 15335 | wgn 4d, I-6 | 3,770 | 2,772 | ⎬ 83,200* |
| 15369 | sdn 4d, I-6 | 3,375 | 2,431 | ⎭ |
| 15411 | sdn 2d, V-8 | 3,445 | 2,484 | ⎫ |
| 15435 | wgn 4d, V-8 | 3,895 | 2,877 | ⎬ 39,200* |
| 15469 | sdn 4d, V-8 | 3,519 | 2,537 | ⎭ |
| **Bel Air (wb 119.0)** | | | | |
| 15511 | sdn 2d, I-6 | 3,315 | 2,479 | ⎫ |
| 15535 | wgn 4d, 2S, I-6 | 3,770 | 2,835 | ⎬ 72,100* |
| 15545 | wgn 4d, 3S, I-6 | 3,815 | 2,948 | |
| 15569 | sdn 4d, I-6 | 3,390 | 2,531 | ⎭ |
| 15611 | sdn 2d, V-8 | 3,445 | 2,584 | ⎫ |
| 15635 | wgn 4d, 2S, V-8 | 3,895 | 2,940 | |
| 15645 | wgn 4d, 9P, V-8 | 3,940 | 3,053 | ⎬ 164,500* |
| 15669 | sdn 4d, V-8 | 3,525 | 2,636 | ⎭ |
| **Impala (wb 119.0)** | | | | |
| 16335 | wgn 4d, 2S, I-6 | 3,805 | 2,971 | ⎫ |
| 16337 | htp cpe, I-6 | 3,430 | 2,684 | |
| 16339 | htp sdn, I-6 | 3,525 | 2,747 | |
| 16345 | wgn 4d, 3S, I-6 | 3,860 | 3,083 | ⎬ 33,100* |
| 16367 | conv cpe, I-6 | 3,484 | 2,935 | |
| 16369 | sdn 4d, I-6 | 3,435 | 2,678 | ⎭ |
| 16435 | wgn 4d, 2S, V-8 | 3,990 | 3,076 | ⎫ |
| 16437 | htp cpe, V-8 | 3,555 | 2,789 | |
| 16439 | htp sdn, V-8 | 3,650 | 2,852 | |
| 16445 | wgn 4d, 3S, V-8 | 4,005 | 3,189 | ⎬ 621,800* |
| 16467 | conv cpe, V-8 | 3,610 | 3,041 | |
| 16469 | sdn 4d, V-8 | 3,565 | 2,783 | ⎭ |
| **Impala SS (wb 119.0)—119,314 built** | | | | |
| 16737 | htp cpe, I-6 | 3,460 | 2,842 | — |
| 16767 | conv cpe, I-6 | 3,505 | 3,093 | — |
| 16837 | htp cpe, V-8 | 3,585 | 2,947 | — |
| 16867 | conv cpe, V-8 | 3,630 | 3,199 | — |
| **Caprice, V-8 (wb 119.0)—181,000* built** | | | | |
| 16635 | wgn 4d, 2S | 3,970 | 3,234 | — |
| 16639 | htp sdn | 3,675 | 3,063 | — |
| 16645 | wgn 4d, 3S | 4,020 | 3,347 | — |
| 16647 | htp cpe | 3,600 | 3,000 | — |

* To nearest 100; does not include wagons. Wagon production: Chevy II, 21,400; Chevelle 31,900; others, 185,500. Impala SS convertible cpe, 15,872.

| 1966 Engines | bore × stroke | bhp | availability |
|---|---|---|---|
| I-4, 153.0 | 3.88 × 3.25 | 90 | S-Chevy II 100 |
| I-6, 194.0 | 3.56 × 3.25 | 120 | S-Chevy II, Chevelle |
| I-6, 230.0 | 3.87 × 3.25 | 140 | O-Chevy II, Chevelle |
| I-6, 250.0 | 3.87 × 3.53 | 155 | S-Chevrolet; O-Chevy II |
| V-8, 283.0 | 3.88 × 3.00 | 195 | S-Chevelle, Chevrolet |
| V-8, 283.0 | 3.88 × 3.00 | 220 | O-Chevrolet |
| V-8, 327.0 | 4.00 × 3.25 | 275/300 | O-all |
| V-8, 327.0 | 4.00 × 3.25 | 350 | O-Chevelle, Chevy II |
| V-8, 396.0 | 4.09 × 3.76 | 325 | S-Chvlle 396; O-Chvrlet, Chvlle |
| V-8, 396.0 | 4.09 × 3.76 | 360/375 | O-Chevelle |
| V-8, 427.0 | 4.25 × 3.76 | 390/425 | O-Chevrolet |

## 1967

| Chevy II 100 (wb 110.0) | | Wght | Price | Prod |
|---|---|---|---|---|
| 11111 | sdn 2d, I-4 | 2,555 | 2,090 | ⎫ |
| 11169 | sdn 4d, I-4 | 2,560 | 2,120 | |
| 11311 | sdn 2d, I-6 | 2,640 | 2,152 | ⎬ 34,200* |
| 11335 | wgn 4d, I-6 | 2,865 | 2,478 | |
| 11369 | sdn 4d, I-6 | 2,650 | 2,182 | ⎭ |
| 11411 | sdn 2d, V-8 | 2,770 | 2,258 | ⎫ |
| 11435 | wgn 4d, V-8 | 2,985 | 2,583 | ⎬ 1,700* |
| 11469 | sdn 4d, V-8 | 2,780 | 2,287 | ⎭ |
| **Chevy II Nova (wb 110.0)** | | | | |
| 11535 | wgn 4d, I-6 | 2,890 | 2,566 | ⎫ |
| 11537 | htp cpe, I-6 | 2,660 | 2,330 | ⎬ 34,400* |
| 11569 | sdn 4d I-6 | 2,660 | 2,298 | ⎭ |
| 11635 | wgn 4d, V-8 | 3,015 | 2,671 | ⎫ |
| 11637 | htp cpe, V-8 | 2,790 | 2,435 | ⎬ 13,200* |
| 11669 | sdn 4d, V-8 | 2,790 | 2,403 | ⎭ |
| **Chevy II Nova SS (wb 110.0)** | | | | |
| 11737 | htp cpe, I-6 | 2,690 | 2,487 | 1,900* |
| 11837 | htp cpe, V-8 | 2,820 | 2,590 | 8,200* |
| **Camaro (wb 108.1) (includes 602 Z28s)** | | | | |
| 12337 | htp cpe, I-6 | 2,770 | 2,466 | ⎫ 58,808 |
| 12367 | conv cpe, I-6 | 3,025 | 2,704 | ⎭ |
| 12437 | htp cpe, V-8 | 2,920 | 2,572 | ⎫ 162,109 |
| 12467 | conv cpe, V-8 | 3,180 | 2,809 | ⎭ |
| **Chevelle 300 (wb 115.0)** | | | | |
| 13111 | sdn 2d, I-6 | 2,935 | 2,221 | ⎫ 19,900* |
| 13169 | sdn 4d, I-6 | 2,955 | 2,250 | ⎭ |
| 13211 | sdn 2d, V-8 | 3,070 | 2,326 | ⎫ 4,800* |
| 13269 | sdn 4d, V-8 | 3,090 | 2,356 | ⎭ |
| 13311 | Del sdn 2d, I-6 | 2,955 | 2,295 | ⎫ |
| 13335 | Del wgn 4d, I-6 | 3,230 | 2,619 | ⎬ 19,300* |
| 13369 | Del sdn 4d, I-6 | 2,980 | 2,324 | ⎭ |
| 13411 | Del sdn 2d, V-8 | 3,090 | 2,400 | ⎫ |
| 13435 | Del wgn 4d, V-8 | 3,360 | 2,725 | ⎬ 7,000* |
| 13469 | Del sdn 4d, V-8 | 3,110 | 2,430 | ⎭ |
| **Chevelle Malibu (wb 115.0)** | | | | |
| 13517 | htp cpe, I-6 | 2,980 | 2,434 | ⎫ |
| 13535 | wgn 4d, I-6 | 3,260 | 2,695 | |
| 13539 | htp sdn, I-6 | 3,065 | 2,506 | |
| 13567 | conv cpe, I-6 | 3,050 | 2,637 | ⎬ 40,600* |
| 13569 | sdn 4d, I-6 | 3,000 | 2,400 | ⎭ |
| 13617 | htp cpe, V-8 | 3,115 | 2,540 | ⎫ |
| 13635 | wgn 4d, V-8 | 3,390 | 2,801 | |
| 13639 | htp sdn, V-8 | 3,200 | 2,611 | ⎬ 187,200* |
| 13667 | conv cpe, V-8 | 3,185 | 2,743 | |
| 13669 | sdn 4d, V-8 | 3,130 | 2,506 | ⎭ |
| **Chevelle Concours (wb 115.0)** | | | | |
| 13735 | wgn 4d, I-6 | 3,270 | 2,827 | 5,900 |
| 13835 | wgn 4d, V-8 | 3,405 | 2,933 | 21,400 |
| **Chevelle Super Sports (wb 115.0)—63,000* built** | | | | |
| 13817 | htp cpe | 3,415 | 2,825 | — |
| 13867 | conv cpe, V-8 | 3,485 | 3,033 | — |
| **Biscayne (wb 119.0)** | | | | |
| 15311 | sdn 2d, I-6 | 3,335 | 2,442 | ⎫ |
| 15335 | wgn 4d, I-6 | 3,765 | 2,817 | ⎬ 54,200* |
| 15369 | sdn 4d, I-6 | 3,395 | 2,484 | |
| 15411 | sdn 2d, V-8 | 3,465 | 2,547 | ⎭ |

# Chevrolet

| Biscayne (wb 119.0) | | Wght | Price | Prod |
|---|---|---|---|---|
| 15435 | wgn 4d, V-8 | 3,885 | 2,923 | 38,600* |
| 15469 | sdn 4d, V-8 | 3,525 | 2,589 | |

| Bel Air (wb 119.0) | | | | |
|---|---|---|---|---|
| 15511 | sdn 2d, I-6 | 3,340 | 2,542 | |
| 15535 | wgn 4d, 2S, I-6 | 3,770 | 2,881 | 41,500* |
| 15545 | wgn 4d, 3S, I-6 | 3,825 | 2,993 | |
| 15569 | sdn 4d, I-6 | 3,410 | 2,584 | |
| 15611 | sdn 2d, V-8 | 3,470 | 2,647 | |
| 15635 | wgn 4d, 2S, V-8 | 3,890 | 2,986 | 138,200* |
| 15645 | wgn 4d, 9P, V-8 | 3,940 | 3,098 | |
| 15669 | sdn 4d, V-8 | 3,535 | 2,689 | |

| Impala (wb 119.0) | | | | |
|---|---|---|---|---|
| 16335 | wgn 4d, 2S, I-6 | 3,805 | 3,016 | |
| 16339 | htp sdn, I-6 | 3,540 | 2,793 | |
| 16345 | wgn 4d, 3S, I-6 | 3,868 | 3,129 | 18,800* |
| 16367 | conv cpe, I-6 | 3,515 | 2,991 | |
| 16369 | sdn 4d, I-6 | 3,455 | 2,723 | |
| 16387 | htp cpe, I-6 | 3,475 | 2,740 | |
| 16435 | wgn 4d, 2S, V-8 | 3,920 | 3,122 | |
| 16439 | htp sdn, V-8 | 3,660 | 2,899 | |
| 16445 | wgn 4d, 3S, V-8 | 3,990 | 3,234 | 556,800* |
| 16467 | conv cpe, V-8 | 3,625 | 3,097 | |
| 16469 | sdn 4d, V-8 | 3,575 | 2,828 | |
| 16487 | htp cpe, V-8 | 3,590 | 2,845 | |

| Impala SS (wb 119.0)—76,055 built (includes 2,124 SS427) | | | | |
|---|---|---|---|---|
| 16767 | conv cpe, I-6 | 3,535 | 3,149 | 400* |
| 16787 | htp cpe, I-6 | 3,500 | 2,898 | |
| 16867 | conv cpe, V-8 | 3,650 | 3,254 | 73,600* |
| 16887 | htp cpe, V-8 | 3,615 | 3,003 | |

| Caprice, V-8 (wb 119.0)—124,500* built | | | | |
|---|---|---|---|---|
| 16635 | wgn 4d, 2S | 3,935 | 3,301 | — |
| 16639 | htp sdn | 3,710 | 3,130 | — |
| 16645 | wgn 4d, 3S | 3,990 | 3,413 | — |
| 16647 | htp cpe | 3,605 | 3,078 | — |

* To nearest 100; does not include wagons. Wagon production: Chevy II 12,900; Chevelle 27,300; others 155,100. Convertible production: Camaro 25,141; Impala SS 9,545.

| 1967 Engines | bore × stroke | bhp | availability |
|---|---|---|---|
| I-4, 153.0 | 3.88 × 3.25 | 90 | S-Chevy II 100 sdns |
| I-6, 194.0 | 3.56 × 3.25 | 120 | S-Chevy II, Chevelle |
| I-6, 230.0 | 3.88 × 3.25 | 140 | S-Camaro |
| I-6, 250.0 | 3.88 × 3.53 | 155 | S-Chevrolet exc Caprice; O-others |
| V-8, 283.0 | 3.88 × 3.00 | 195 | S-all exc Camaro |
| V-8, 302.0 | 4.00 × 3.00 | 290 | O-Camaro (Z28) |
| V-8, 327.0 | 4.00 × 3.25 | 210 | O-Camaro |
| V-8, 327.0 | 4.00 × 3.25 | 275 | O-all |
| V-8, 327.0 | 4.00 × 3.25 | 325 | O-Chevelle |
| V-8, 350.0 | 4.00 × 3.48 | 295 | O-Camaro |
| V-8, 396.0 | 4.09 × 3.76 | 325 | S-Chevelle 396; O-Cam, Chevrolet |
| V-8, 396.0 | 4.09 × 3.76 | 350 | O-Chevelle 396 |
| V-8, 427.0 | 4.25 × 3.76 | 385 | O-Chevrolet |

## 1968

| Chevy II Nova (wb 111)—201,000* built (includes 6,571 SS cps) | | | | |
|---|---|---|---|---|
| | | Wght | Price | Prod |
| 11127 | cpe I-4 | 2,760 | 2,222 | — |
| 11169 | sdn 4d, I-4 | 2,790 | 2,252 | — |
| 11327 | cpe I-6 | 2,860 | 2,284 | — |

| Chevy II Nova (wb 111.0) | | Wght | Price | Prod |
|---|---|---|---|---|
| 11369 | sdn 4d, I-6 | 2,890 | 2,314 | — |
| 11427 | cpe, V-8 | 2,995 | 2,390 | — |
| 11469 | sdn 4d, V-8 | 3,025 | 2,419 | — |

| Camaro (wb 108.1) (includes 7,199 Z28s) | | | | |
|---|---|---|---|---|
| 12337 | htp cpe, I-6 | 2,810 | 2,588 | 50,937 |
| 12367 | conv cpe, I-6 | 3,110 | 2,802 | |
| 12437 | htp cpe, V-8 | 2,955 | 2,694 | 184,178 |
| 12467 | conv cpe, V-8 | 3,245 | 2,908 | |

| Chevelle 300 (wb 112.0; 4d-116.0)(includes 62,785 SS) | | | | |
|---|---|---|---|---|
| 13127 | cpe, I-6 | 3,020 | 2,341 | 2,900* |
| 13135 | Nomad wgn 4d, I-6 | 3,370 | 2,625 | |
| 13227 | cpe, V-8 | 3,155 | 2,447 | 9,700* |
| 13235 | Nomad wgn 4d, V-8 | 3,500 | 2,731 | |
| 13327 | Del cpe, I-6 | 3,035 | 2,415 | |
| 13335 | Cus Nomad wgn 4d, I-6 | 3,415 | 2,736 | 25,500* |
| 13337 | Del htp cpe, I-6 | 3,050 | 2,479 | |
| 13369 | Del sdn 4d, I-6 | 3,105 | 2,445 | |
| 13427 | Del cpe, V-8 | 3,170 | 2,521 | |
| 13435 | Cus Nomad wgn 4d, V-8 | 3,545 | 2,841 | 17,700* |
| 13437 | Del htp cpe, V-8 | 3,185 | 2,584 | |
| 13469 | Del sdn 4d, V-8 | 3,240 | 2,550 | |

| Chevelle Malibu (wb 112.0; 4d-116.0) | | | | |
|---|---|---|---|---|
| 13535 | wgn 4d, I-6 | 3,440 | 2,846 | |
| 13537 | htp cpe, I-6 | 3,070 | 2,558 | |
| 13539 | htp sdn, I-6 | 3,185 | 2,629 | 33,100* |
| 13567 | conv cpe, I-6 | 3,135 | 2,757 | |
| 13569 | sdn 4d, I-6 | 3,125 | 2,524 | |
| 13635 | wgn 4d, V-8 | 3,575 | 2,951 | |
| 13637 | htp cpe, V-8 | 3,204 | 2,663 | |
| 13639 | htp sdn, V-8 | 3,315 | 2,735 | 233,200* |
| 13667 | conv cpe, V-8 | 3,260 | 2,863 | |
| 13669 | sdn 4d, V-8 | 3,255 | 2,629 | |

| Chevelle Concours (wb 116.0) | | | | |
|---|---|---|---|---|
| 13735 | wgn 4d, I-6 | 3,450 | 2,978 | — |
| 13835 | wgn 4d, V-8 | 3,580 | 3,083 | — |

| Chevelle SS 396 (wb 112.0) | | | | |
|---|---|---|---|---|
| 13837 | htp cpe | 3,550 | 2,899 | 60,499 |
| 13867 | conv cpe | 3,570 | 3,102 | 2,286 |

| Biscayne (wb 119.0) | | | | |
|---|---|---|---|---|
| 15311 | sdn 2d, I-6 | 3,400 | 2,581 | |
| 15335 | wgn 4d, I-6 | 3,790 | 2,957 | 44,500* |
| 15369 | sdn 4d, I-6 | 3,465 | 2,623 | |
| 15411 | sdn 2d, V-8 | 3,520 | 2,686 | |
| 15435 | wgn 4d, V-8 | 3,900 | 3,062 | 37,600* |
| 15469 | sdn 4d, V-8 | 3,585 | 2,728 | |

| Bel Air (wb 119.0) | | | | |
|---|---|---|---|---|
| 15511 | sdn 2d, I-6 | 3,405 | 2,681 | |
| 15535 | wgn 4d, 2S, I-6 | 3,800 | 3,020 | 28,800* |
| 15545 | wgn 4d, 3S, I-6 | 3,845 | 3,133 | |
| 15569 | sdn 4d, I-6 | 3,470 | 2,723 | |
| 15611 | sdn 2d, V-8 | 3,525 | 2,786 | |
| 15635 | wgn 4d, 2S, V-8 | 3,910 | 3,125 | 123,400* |
| 15645 | wgn 4d, 3S, V-8 | 3,955 | 3,238 | |
| 15669 | sdn 4d, V-8 | 3,590 | 2,828 | |

| Impala (wb 119.0)—38,210 SS built (includes 1,778 SS427) | | | | |
|---|---|---|---|---|
| 16339 | htp sdn, I-6 | 3,605 | 2,917 | |
| 16369 | sdn 4d, I-6 | 3,520 | 2,846 | 11,400* |
| 16387 | htp cpe, I-6 | 3,250 | 2,863 | |
| 16435 | wgn 4d, 2S, V-8 | 3,850 | 3,245 | |
| 16439 | htp sdn, V-8 | 3,715 | 3,022 | |
| 16445 | wgn 4d, 3S, V-8 | 3,905 | 3,358 | |

223

# Chevrolet

| Impala (wb 119.0) | | Wght | Price | Prod |
|---|---|---|---|---|
| 16447 | Cus htp cpe, V-8 | 3,645 | 3,021 | ⎤ |
| 16467 | conv cpe, V-8 | 3,680 | 3,197 | ⎬ 699,500* |
| 16469 | sdn 4d, V-8 | 3,630 | 2,951 | |
| 16487 | htp cpe, V-8 | 3,630 | 2,968 | ⎦ |
| **Caprice (wb 119.0)—115,500* built** | | | | |
| 16635 | wgn 4d, 2S | 3,950 | 3,458 | — |
| 16639 | htp sdn | 3,755 | 3,271 | — |
| 16645 | wgn 4d, 3S | 4,005 | 3,570 | — |
| 16647 | htp cpe | 3,660 | 3,219 | — |

* To nearest 100; does not include wagons. Wagon production: Chevelle 45,500; others 175,600. Camaro convertible cpe 20,440.

| 1968 Engines | bore × stroke | bhp | availability |
|---|---|---|---|
| I-4, 153.0 | 3.88 × 3.25 | 90 | S-Chevy II |
| I-6, 230.0 | 3.88 × 3.25 | 140 | S-Chevy II, Camaro, Chevelle |
| I-6, 250.0 | 3.88 × 3.53 | 155 | S-Chevrolet; O-Camaro, Chevelle |
| V-8, 302.0 | 4.00 × 3.00 | 290 | O-Camaro (Z28) |
| V-8, 307.0 | 3.88 × 3.25 | 200 | S-Chevy II, Chevelle, Chevrolet |
| V-8, 327.0 | 4.00 × 3.25 | 210 | S-Camaro |
| V-8, 327.0 | 4.00 × 3.25 | 250 | O-Chevelle, Chevrolet |
| V-8, 327.0 | 4.00 × 3.25 | 275 | O-all |
| V-8, 327.0 | 4.00 × 3.25 | 325 | O-Chevelle |
| V-8, 350.0 | 4.00 × 3.48 | 295 | O-Chevy II, Camaro |
| V-8, 396.0 | 4.09 × 3.76 | 325 | S-Chevelle 396; O-Camaro, Chevr |
| V-8, 396.0 | 4.00 × 3.00 | 350/375 | O-Camaro, Chevelle |
| V-8, 427.0 | 4.25 × 3.76 | 385/425 | O-Chevrolet |

## 1969

### Chevy II Nova (wb 111.0)—17,564 SS cpes built

| | | Wght | Price | Prod |
|---|---|---|---|---|
| 11127 | cpe, I-4 | 2,785 | 2,237 | ⎤ 6,100* |
| 11169 | sdn 4d, I-4 | 2,810 | 2,267 | ⎦ |
| 11327 | cpe I-6 | 2,895 | 2,315 | ⎤ 10,200* |
| 11369 | sdn 4d, I-6 | 2,920 | 2,345 | ⎦ |
| 11427 | cpe, V-8 | 3,035 | 2,405 | ⎤ 89,900* |
| 11469 | sdn 4d, V-8 | 3,065 | 2,434 | ⎦ |

### Camaro (wb 108.1) (includes 20,302 Z28s)

| 12337 | htp cpe, I-6 | 3,040 | 2,638 | ⎤ 65,008** |
|---|---|---|---|---|
| 12367 | conv cpe, I-6 | 3,160 | 2,852 | ⎦ |
| 12437 | htp cpe, V-8 | 3,050 | 2,726 | ⎤ 178,087** |
| 12467 | conv cpe, V-8 | 3,295 | 2,940 | ⎦ |

Note: wagon designation "CT" refers to conventional tailgate, opening from top. Most wagons had dual-action tailgates, opening from top or from side, from 1969 onward.

### Chevelle Nomad (wb 116.0)

| 13135 | wgn 4d, CT, I-6 | 3,390 | 2,668 | — |
|---|---|---|---|---|
| 13136 | wgn 4d, I-6 | 3,475 | 2,710 | — |
| 13235 | wgn 4d, CT, V-8 | 3,515 | 2,758 | — |
| 13236 | wgn 4d, V-8 | 3,600 | 2,800 | — |

### Chevelle 300 Del (wb 112.0; 4d-116.0)

| 13327 | cpe, I-6 | 3,035 | 2,458 | ⎤ |
|---|---|---|---|---|
| 13337 | htp cpe, I-6 | 3,075 | 2,521 | ⎬ 11,000* |
| 13369 | sdn 4d, I-6 | 3,100 | 2,488 | ⎦ |
| 13427 | cpe, V-8 | 3,165 | 2,548 | ⎤ |
| 13437 | htp cpe, V-8 | 3,205 | 2,611 | ⎬ 31,000* |
| 13469 | sdn 4d, V-8 | 3,230 | 2,577 | ⎦ |

### Chevelle Greenbrier (wb 116.0)

| | | Wght | Price | Prod |
|---|---|---|---|---|
| 13335 | wgn 4d, CT, I-6 | 3,445 | 2,779 | ⎤ 7,400* |
| 13336 | wgn 4d, I-6 | 3,530 | 2,821 | ⎦ |
| 13435 | wgn 4d, CT, V-8 | 3,585 | 2,869 | ⎤ |
| 13436 | wgn 4d, 2S, V-8 | 3,665 | 2,911 | ⎬ 38,500* |
| 13446 | wgn 4d, 3S, V-8 | 3,740 | 3,020 | ⎦ |

### Chevelle Malibu (wb 112.0; 4d-116.0)(includes 86,307 SS)

| 13537 | htp cpe, I-6 | 3,095 | 2,601 | ⎤ |
|---|---|---|---|---|
| 13539 | htp sdn, I-6 | 3,205 | 2,672 | ⎬ 23,500* |
| 13567 | conv cpe, I-6 | 3,175 | 2,800 | ⎦ |
| 13569 | sdn 4d, I-6 | 3,130 | 2,567 | ⎤ |
| 13637 | htp cpe, V-8 | 3,230 | 2,690 | |
| 13639 | htp sdn, V-8 | 3,340 | 2,762 | ⎬ 343,600* |
| 13667 | conv cpe, V-8 | 3,300 | 2,889 | |
| 13669 | sdn 4d, V-8 | 3,265 | 2,657 | ⎦ |

### Chevelle Concours (wb 116.0)

| 13536 | wgn 4d, I-6 | 3,545 | 2,931 | — |
|---|---|---|---|---|
| 13636 | wgn 4d, 2S, V-8 | 3,685 | 3,021 | — |
| 13646 | wgn 4d, 3S, V-8 | 3,755 | 3,141 | — |
| 13836 | del wgn 4d, 2S, V-8 | 3,680 | 3,153 | — |
| 13846 | del wgn 4d, 3S, V-8 | 3,730 | 3,266 | — |

### Biscayne (wb 119.0)

| 15311 | sdn 2d, I-6 | 3,530 | 2,645 | ⎤ |
|---|---|---|---|---|
| 15336 | Brookwood wgn 4d, I-6 | 4,045 | 3,064 | ⎬ 27,400* |
| 15369 | sdn 4d, I-6 | 3,590 | 2,687 | ⎦ |
| 15411 | sdn 2d, V-8 | 3,670 | 2,751 | ⎤ |
| 15436 | Brookwood wgn 4d, V-8 | 4,170 | 3,169 | ⎬ 41,300* |
| 15469 | sdn 4d, V-8 | 3,725 | 2,793 | ⎦ |

### Bel Air (wb 119.0)

| 15511 | sdn 2d, I-6 | 3,540 | 2,745 | ⎤ 16,000* |
|---|---|---|---|---|
| 15569 | sdn 4d, I-6 | 3,590 | 2,787 | ⎦ |
| 15611 | sdn 2d, V-8 | 3,675 | 2,851 | ⎤ |
| 15636 | Townsman wgn 4d, 2S, V-8 | 4,175 | 3,232 | |
| 15646 | Townsman wgn 4d, 3S, V-8 | 4,230 | 3,345 | ⎬ 139,700* |
| 15669 | sdn 4d, V-8 | 3,725 | 2,893 | ⎦ |

### Impala (wb 119.0)—2,455 SS427 built

| 16337 | htp cpe, I-6 | 3,650 | 2,927 | ⎤ |
|---|---|---|---|---|
| 16339 | htp sdn, I-6 | 3,735 | 2,981 | ⎬ 8,700* |
| 16369 | sdn 4d, I-6 | 3,640 | 2,911 | ⎦ |
| 16436 | Kingswood wgn 4d, 2S, V-8 | 4,225 | 3,352 | ⎤ |
| 16437 | htp cpe, V-8 | 3,775 | 3,033 | |
| 16439 | htp sdn, V-8 | 3,855 | 3,056 | |
| 16446 | Kingswood wgn 4d, 3S, V-8 | 4,285 | 3,465 | ⎬ 768,300* |
| 16447 | Cus htp cpe, V-8 | 3,800 | 3,085 | |
| 16467 | conv cpe, V-8 | 3,835 | 3,261 | |
| 16469 | sdn 4d, V-8 | 3,760 | 3,016 | ⎦ |

### Caprice, V-8 (wb 119.0)—166,900* built

| 16636 | Kingswood Estate wgn 4d, 2S | 4,245 | 3,565 | — |
|---|---|---|---|---|
| 16639 | htp sdn | 3,895 | 3,346 | — |
| 16646 | Kingswood Estate wgn 4d, 3S | 4,300 | 3,678 | — |
| 16647 | htp cpe | 3,815 | 3,294 | — |

* To nearest 100. ** Includes 1970 extension of 1969 model. Wagon production: Chevelle 45,900; others 59,300. Camaro convertible cpe, 17,573.

| 1969 Engines | bore × stroke | bhp | availability |
|---|---|---|---|
| I-4, 153.0 | 3.88 × 3.25 | 90 | S-Chevy II |
| I-6, 230.0 | 3.88 × 3.25 | 140 | S-Chevelle, Chevy II, Camaro |
| I-6, 250.0 | 3.88 × 3.53 | 155 | S-Chvr; O-Chvl, Chev II, Cam |
| V-8, 302.0 | 4.00 × 3.00 | 350 | O-Camaro (Z28) |
| V-8, 307.0 | 3.88 × 3.25 | 200 | S-Chevy II, Chevelle |

# Chevrolet

| 1969 Engines | bore × stroke | bhp | availability |
|---|---|---|---|
| V-8, 327.0 | 4.00 × 3.25 | 210 | S-Camaro |
| V-8, 327.0 | 4.00 × 3.25 | 235 | S-Chevrolet |
| V-8, 350.0 | 4.00 × 3.48 | 255 | O-all |
| V-8, 350.0 | 4.00 × 3.48 | 300 | O-Chevr, Chevl, Nova SS, Cam SS |
| V-8, 396.0 | 4.09 × 3.76 | 265 | S-Chevelle 396; O-Chevrolet |
| V-8, 396.0 | 4.09 × 3.76 | 325 | O-Chevelle 396, Camaro SS |
| V-8, 396.0 | 4.09 × 3.76 | 350/375 | O-Chevelle/Nova/Camaro SS |
| V-8, 427.0 | 4.25 × 3.76 | 335-425 | O-Chevrolet |

Note: Station wagon engines—for wb 116 read Chevelle; for wb 119 read Chevrolet.

## 1970

### Nova (wb 111.0)—254,242 built (incl 19,558 SS models)

| | | Wght | Price | Prod |
|---|---|---|---|---|
| 11127 | htp cpe, I-4 | 2,820 | 2,335 | — |
| 11169 | sdn 4d, I-4 | 2,843 | 2,365 | — |
| 11327 | cpe, I-6 | 2,919 | 2,414 | — |
| 11369 | sdn 4d, I-6 | 2,942 | 2,443 | — |
| 11427 | cpe, V-8 | 3,048 | 2,503 | — |
| 11469 | sdn 4d, V-8 | 3,071 | 2,533 | — |

### Camaro (wb 108.1) (includes 8,733 Z28s)

| 12387 | spt cpe, I-6 | 3,076 | 2,749 | 12,566 |
| 12487 | spt cpe, V-8 | 3,190 | 2,839 | 112,323 |

### Chevelle (wb 112.0; 4d-116.0)—354,855 built (including Malibu)

| 13337 | htp cpe, I-6 | 3,142 | 2,620 | — |
| 13369 | sdn 4d, I-6 | 3,196 | 2,585 | — |
| 13437 | htp cpe, V-8 | 3,260 | 2,710 | — |
| 13469 | sdn 4d, V-8 | 3,312 | 2,679 | — |

### Chev Malibu (wb 112.0; 4d 116.0) (53,599 SS; 3,733 w/454 V-8)

| 13537 | htp cpe, I-6 | 3,197 | 2,719 | — |
| 13539 | htp sdn, I-6 | 3,302 | 2,790 | — |
| 13567 | conv cpe, I-6 | 3,243 | 2,919 | — |
| 13569 | sdn 4d, I-6 | 3,221 | 2,685 | — |
| 13637 | htp cpe, V-8 | 3,307 | 2,809 | — |
| 13639 | htp sdn, V-8 | 3,409 | 2,881 | — |
| 13667 | conv cpe, V-8 | 3,352 | 3,009 | — |
| 13669 | sdn 4d, V-8 | 3,330 | 2,775 | — |

### Station Wagon (wb 116.0)

| 13136 | Nomad 4d, 2S, I-6 | 3,615 | 2,835 | — |
| 13236 | Nomad 4d, 2S, V-8 | 3,718 | 2,925 | — |
| 13336 | Greenbrier 4d, 2S, I-6 | 3,644 | 2,946 | — |
| 13436 | Greenbrier 4d, 2S, V-8 | 3,748 | 3,100 | — |
| 13446 | Greenbrier 4d, 3S, V-8 | 3,794 | 3,213 | — |
| 13536 | Concours 4d, 2S, I-6 | 3,687 | 3,056 | — |
| 13636 | Concours 4d, 2S, V-8 | 3,794 | 3,210 | — |
| 13646 | Concours 4d, 3S, V-8 | 3,836 | 3,323 | — |
| 13836 | Concours del wgn 4d, 2S, V-8 | 3,821 | 3,342 | — |
| 13846 | Concours del wgn 4d, 3S, V-8 | 3,880 | 3,455 | — |

### Biscayne (wb 119.0)

| 15369 | sdn 4d, I-6 | 3,600 | 2,787 | 12,300* |
| 15469 | sdn 4d, V-8 | 3,759 | 2,898 | 23,100* |

### Bel Air (wb 119.0)

| 15569 | sdn 4d, I-6 | 3,604 | 2,887 | 9,000* |
| 15669 | sdn 4d, V-8 | 3,763 | 2,998 | 66,800* |

### Impala (wb 119.0)—495,909 built exc 16467

| | | Wght | Price | Prod |
|---|---|---|---|---|
| 16337 | htp cpe, I-6 | 3,641 | 3,038 | — |
| 16369 | sdn 4d, I-6 | 3,655 | 3,021 | — |
| 16437 | htp cpe, V-8 | 3,788 | 3,149 | — |
| 16439 | htp sdn, V-8 | 3,871 | 3,203 | — |
| 16447 | Cus htp cpe, V-8 | 3,801 | 3,266 | — |
| 16467 | conv cpe, V-8 | 3,843 | 3,377 | 9,562 |
| 16469 | sdn 4d, V-8 | 3,802 | 3,132 | — |

### Caprice (wb 119.0)—92,000* built

| 16639 | htp sdn | 3,905 | 3,527 | |
| 16647 | htp cpe | 3,821 | 3,474 | |

### Monte Carlo (wb 116.0) (inc. 3,823 w/SS454 pkg.)

| 13857 | htp cpe | 3,460 | 3,123 | 145,976 |

### Station Wagon (wb 119.0)

| 15436 | Brookwood 4d, 2S | 4,204 | 3,294 | — |
| 15636 | Townsman 4d, 2S | 4,208 | 3,357 | — |
| 15646 | Townsman 4d, 3S | 4,263 | 3,469 | — |
| 16436 | Kingswood 4d, 2S | 4,269 | 3,477 | — |
| 16446 | Kingswood 4d, 3S | 4,329 | 3,589 | — |
| 16636 | Kingswood del 4d, 2S | 4,295 | 3,753 | — |
| 16646 | Kingswood del 4d, 3S | 4,361 | 3,886 | — |

* To nearest 100; does not include wagons.

| 1970 Engines | bore × stroke | bhp | availability |
|---|---|---|---|
| I-4, 153.0 | 3.88 × 3.25 | 90 | S-Nova |
| I-6, 230.0 | 3.88 × 3.25 | 140 | S-Camaro; O-Nova |
| I-6, 250.0 | 3.88 × 3.53 | 155 | S-Chevrolet exc Caprice & Impala cpe, Chevelle; O-Nova, Camaro |
| V-8, 307.0 | 3.88 × 3.25 | 200 | S-Nova, Camaro; O-Chevelle |
| V-8, 350.0 | 4.00 × 3.48 | 250 | S-Chevr, MC; O-others |
| V-8, 350.0 | 4.00 × 3.48 | 300 | O-Chevr, MC; Chevl, Cam, Nova SS |
| V-8, 350.0 | 4.00 × 3.48 | 360 | O-Camaro (Z28) |
| V-8, 402.0* | 4.13 × 3.76 | 375 | O-Camaro, Chevelle |
| V-8, 402.0* | 4.13 × 3.76 | 350 | O-Camaro, Chevelle |
| V-8, 400.0 | 4.12 × 3.75 | 265 | O-Chevrolet, Monte Carlo |
| V-8, 400.0 | 4.12 × 3.75 | 330 | O-Monte Carlo, Chevelle |
| V-8, 454.0 | 4.25 × 4.00 | 345 | O-Chevrolet |
| V-8, 454.0 | 4.25 × 4.00 | 360 | O-Monte Carlo |
| V-8, 454.0 | 4.25 × 4.00 | 390 | O-Chevrolet |

Note: Station Wagon engines—for wb 116 read Chevelle; for wb 119 read Chevrolet.

* Commonly known as "396," actual displacement 402 cid.

## 1971

### Vega (wb 97.0)

| | | Wght | Price | Prod |
|---|---|---|---|---|
| 14111 | sdn 2d | 2,146 | 2,090 | 58,804 |
| 14177 | htchbk cpe 2d | 2,190 | 2,196 | 168,308 |
| 14115 | Kammback wgn 2d | 2,230 | 2,328 | 42,793 |

### Nova (wb 111.0)

| 11327 | cpe I-6 | 2,952 | 2,376 | 65,891 |
| 11369 | sdn 4d I-6 | 2,976 | 2,405 | 29,037 |
| 11427 | cpe V-8 | 3,084 | 2,471 | 77,344 |
| 11469 | sdn 4d V-8 | 3,108 | 2,501 | 22,606 |

# Chevrolet

| | Camaro (wb 108.1; incl. 4,862 Z28s) | Wght | Price | Prod |
|---|---|---|---|---|
| 12387 | spt cpe I-6 | 3,094 | 2,921 | 11,178 |
| 12487 | spt cpe V-8 | 3,218 | 3,016 | 103,452 |
| | **Chevelle (wb 112.0; 4d-116.0)(includes 19,293 SS454s)** | | | |
| 11337 | htp cpe I-6 | 3,166 | 2,712 | 6,660 |
| 11369 | sdn 4d I-6 | 3,210 | 2,677 | 6,621 |
| 13437 | htp cpe V-8 | 3,296 | 2,807 | 17,117 |
| 13469 | sdn 4d V-8 | 3,338 | 2,773 | 9,042 |
| 13537 | Malibu htp cpe I-6 | 3,212 | 2,885 | 6,220 |
| 13569 | Malibu sdn 4d I-6 | 3,250 | 2,851 | 4,241 |
| 13637 | Malibu htp cpe V-8 | 3,342 | 2,980 | 180,117 |
| 13639 | Malibu htp sdn V-8 | 3,450 | 3,052 | 20,775 |
| 13667 | Malibu conv V-8 | 3,390 | 3,260 | 5,089 |
| 13669 | Malibu sdn 4d V-8 | 3,380 | 2,947 | 37,385 |
| | **Chevelle Wagon (wb 116.0)** | | | |
| 13136 | Nomad 4d 2S I-6 | 3,632 | 2,997 | 2,801 |
| 13236 | Nomad 4d 2S V-8 | 3,746 | 3,097 | 6,528 |
| 13436 | Greenbrier 4d 2S V-8 | 3,820 | 3,228 | 6,128 |
| 13446 | Greenbrier 4d 3S V-8 | 3,882 | 3,340 | 2,129 |
| 13636 | Concours 4d 2S V-8 | 3,864 | 3,337 | 12,716 |
| 13646 | Concours 4d 3S V-8 | 3,908 | 3,450 | 4,276 |
| 13836 | Concours Estate 4d 2S V-8 | 3,892 | 3,514 | 4,502 |
| 13846 | Concours Estate 4d 3S V-8 | 3,944 | 3,626 | 3,219 |
| | **Biscayne (wb 121.5)** | | | |
| 15369 | sdn 4d I-6 | 3,732 | 3,096 | 5,846 |
| 15469 | sdn 4d V-8 | 3,888 | 3,448 | 16,463 |
| | **Bel Air (wb 121.5)** | | | |
| 15569 | sdn 4d I-6 | 3,732 | 3,233 | 3,452 |
| 15669 | sdn 4d V-8 | 3,888 | 3,585 | 38,534 |
| | **Impala (wb 121.5)** | | | |
| 16357 | htp cpe I-6 | 3,742 | 3,408 | 939 |
| 16369 | sdn 4d I-6 | 3,760 | 3,391 | 1,606 |
| 16439 | htp sdn V-8 | 3,978 | 3,813 | 140,300 |
| 16447 | Custom htp cpe V-8 | 3,912 | 3,826 | 139,437 |
| 16457 | htp cpe V-8 | 3,896 | 3,759 | 52,952 |
| 16467 | conv V-8 | 3,960 | 4,021 | 4,576 |
| 16469 | sdn 4d V-8 | 3,914 | 3,742 | 135,334 |
| | **Caprice (wb 121.5)** | | | |
| 16639 | htp sdn 4d | 4,040 | 4,134 | 64,093 |
| 16647 | htp cpe | 3,964 | 4,081 | 46,404 |
| | **Monte Carlo (wb 116.0) (includes 1,919 w/SS454 pkg.)** | | | |
| 13857 | htp cpe | 3,488 | 3,416 | 128,600 |
| | **Chevrolet Wagon (wb 125.0)** | | | |
| 15435 | Brookwood 4d 2S | 4,542 | 3,929 | 5,314 |
| 15635 | Townsman 4d 2S | 4,544 | 4,020 | 12,951 |
| 15645 | Townsman 4d 3S | 4,598 | 4,135 | 6,870 |
| 16435 | Kingswood 4d 2S | 4,588 | 4,112 | 26,638 |
| 16445 | Kingswood 4d 3S | 4,648 | 4,227 | 32,311 |
| 16635 | Kingswood Estate 4d 2S | 4,678 | 4,384 | 11,913 |
| 16645 | Kingswood Estate 4d 3S | 4,738 | 4,498 | 19,010 |

| 1971 Engines | bore × stroke | bhp | availability |
|---|---|---|---|
| I-4, 140.0 | 3.50 × 3.63 | 90 | S-Vega |
| I-4, 140.0 | 3.50 × 3.63 | 110 | O-Vega |
| I-6, 250.0 | 3.88 × 3.53 | 145 | S-Nova, Chevl, Cam, Chevr |
| V-8, 307.0 | 3.88 × 3.25 | 200 | S-Nova, Chevl, Cam |
| V-8, 350.0 | 4.00 × 3.48 | 245 | S-MC, Chevr exc K/Est & Cap; O-Nova, Chevl, Cam |
| V-8, 350.0 | 4.00 × 3.48 | 270 | O-Chevl, Cam, MC, Chevr |
| V-8, 350.0 | 4.00 × 3.48 | 330 | O-Camaro (Z28) |
| V-8, 400.0 | 4.12 × 3.75 | 255 | S-Chevr K/Est & Cap; O-Chevr |
| V-8, 402.0** | 4.13 × 3.76 | 300 | O-Chevl, Cam, MC, Chevr |
| V-8, 454.0 | 4.25 × 4.00 | 365 | O-Chevl, MC, Chevr |
| V-8, 454.0 | 4.25 × 4.00 | 425 | O-Chevl, MC |

Note: "Chevr" for 1971-80 means full-size Chevrolets. In above context, this includes Biscayne, Bel Air, Impala, Caprice, and full-size (125-in. wb) station wagons.
* Commonly known as "396," actual displacement 402 cid.

## 1972

| | Vega (wb 97.0) | Wght | Price | Prod |
|---|---|---|---|---|
| 1V11 | sdn 2d | 2,158 | 2,060 | 55,839 |
| 1V15 | wgn 2d | 2,333 | 2,285 | 71,957 |
| 1V77 | htchbk cpe 2d | 2,294 | 2,160 | 262,682 |
| | **Nova (wb 111.0)** | | | |
| 1X27 | cpe I-6 | 2,949 | 2,351 | 96,740 |
| 1X27 | cpe V-8 | 3,083 | 2,441 | 163,475 |
| 1X69 | sdn 4d I-6 | 2,982 | 2,379 | 43,029 |
| 1X69 | sdn 4d V-8 | 3,116 | 2,469 | 46,489 |
| | **Camaro (wb 108.1; includes 2,575 Z28s)** | | | |
| 1Q87 | spt cpe I-6 | 3,121 | 2,730 | 4,824 |
| 1Q87 | spt cpe V-8 | 3,248 | 2,820 | 63,832 |
| | **Chevelle (wb 112.0; 4d-116.0)** | | | |
| 1C37 | htp cpe I-6 | 3,172 | 2,669 | 6,993 |
| 1C37 | htp cpe V-8 | 3,300 | 2,759 | 22,714 |
| 1C69 | sdn 4d I-6 | 3,204 | 2,636 | 6,764 |
| 1C69 | sdn 4d V-8 | 3,332 | 2,726 | 12,881 |
| 1D37 | Malibu htp cpe I-6 | 3,194 | 2,833 | 4,790 |
| 1D37 | Malibu htp cpe V-8 | 3,327 | 2,923 | 207,598 |
| 1D39 | Malibu htp sdn V-8 | 3,438 | 2,991 | 24,192 |
| 1D67 | Malibu conv V-8 | 3,379 | 3,187 | 4,853 |
| 1D69 | Malibu sdn 4d I-6 | 3,240 | 2,801 | 3,562 |
| 1D69 | Malibu sdn 4d V-8 | 3,371 | 2,891 | 45,013 |
| | **Chevelle Wagon (wb 116.0)** | | | |
| 1B36 | Nomad 4d 2S I-6 | 3,605 | 2,926 | 2,956 |
| 1B36 | Nomad 4d 2S V-8 | 3,732 | 3,016 | 7,768 |
| 1C36 | Greenbrier 4d 2S V-8 | 3,814 | 3,140 | 6,975 |
| 1C46 | Greenbrier 4d 3S V-8 | 3,870 | 3,247 | 2,370 |
| 1D36 | Concours 4d 2S V-8 | 3,857 | 3,244 | 17,968 |
| 1D46 | Concours 4d 3S V-8 | 3,909 | 3,351 | 6,560 |
| 1H36 | Concours Estate 4d 2S V-8 | 3,887 | 3,431 | 5,331 |
| 1H46 | Concours Estate 4d 3S V-8 | 3,943 | 3,538 | 4,407 |
| | **Chevrolet (wb 122.0)** | | | |
| 1K69 | Biscayne sdn 4d I-6 | 3,857 | 3,074 | 1,504 |
| 1K59 | Biscayne sdn 4d V-8 | 4,045 | 3,408 | 19,034 |
| 1L69 | Bel Air sdn 4d I-6 | 3,854 | 3,204 | 868 |
| 1L69 | Bel Air sdn 4d V-8 | 4,042 | 3,538 | 41,020 |
| 1M39 | Impala htp sdn V-8 | 4,150 | 3,771 | 170,304 |
| 1M47 | Impala Custom htp cpe V-8 | 4,053 | 3,787 | 183,493 |
| 1M57 | Impala htp cpe I-6 | 3,864 | 3,385 | 289 |
| 1M57 | Impala htp cpe V-8 | 4,049 | 3,720 | 52,403 |
| 1M67 | Impala conv V-8 | 4,125 | 3,979 | 6,456 |
| 1M69 | Impala sdn 4d I-6 | 3,928 | 3,369 | 1,235 |
| 1M69 | Impala sdn 4d V-8 | 4,113 | 3,708 | 183,361 |
| 1N39 | Caprice htp sdn V-8 | 4,203 | 4,076 | 78,768 |
| 1N47 | Caprice htp cpe V-8 | 4,102 | 4,026 | 65,513 |

# Chevrolet

| | Chevrolet (wb 122.0) | Wght | Price | Prod |
|---|---|---|---|---|
| 1N69 | Caprice sdn 4d | 4,166 | 4,009 | 34,174 |
| **Chevrolet Station Wagon (wb 125.0)** | | | | |
| 1K35 | Brookwood 4d 2S | 4,686 | 3,882 | 8,150 |
| 1L35 | Townsman 4d 2S | 4,687 | 3,969 | 16,482 |
| 1L45 | Townsman 4d 3S | 4,769 | 4,078 | 8,667 |
| 1M35 | Kingswood 4d 2S | 4,734 | 4,056 | 43,152 |
| 1M45 | Kingswood 4d 3S | 4,817 | 4,165 | 40,248 |
| 1N35 | Kingswood Estate 4d 2S | 4,798 | 4,314 | 20,281 |
| 1N45 | Kingswood Estate 4d 3S | 4,883 | 4,423 | 34,723 |
| **Monte Carlo (wb 116.0)** | | | | |
| 1H57 | htp cpe V-8 | 3,506 | 3,362 | 180,819 |

| 1972 Engines | bore × stroke | bhp | availability |
|---|---|---|---|
| I-4, 140.0 | 3.50 × 3.63 | 80 | S-Vega |
| I-4, 140.0 | 3.50 × 3.63 | 90 | O-Vega |
| I-6, 250.0 | 3.88 × 3.53 | 110 | S-Nova, Chevl, Cam, Chevr exc Cap & K/Est |
| V-8, 307.0 | 3.88 × 3.25 | 130 | S-Nova, Chevl & Cam exc Cal |
| V-8, 350.0 | 4.00 × 3.48 | 165 | S-Chevl & Cam in Cal. O-Nova, Chevl, Chevr |
| V-8, 350.0 | 4.00 × 3.48 | 175 | O-Chevl, MC |
| V-8, 350.0 | 4.00 × 3.48 | 200 | O-Cam, Chevr |
| V-8, 350.0 | 4.00 × 3.48 | 255 | O-Camaro (Z28) |
| V-8, 400.0 | 4.12 × 3.75 | 170 | S-Chevr Cap & K/Est; O-Chevr |
| V-8, 402.0 | 4.13 × 3.76 | 210 | O-Chevl |
| V-8, 402.0 | 4.13 × 3.76 | 240 | O-Chevl, Cam, MC |
| V-8, 454.0 | 4.25 × 4.00 | 270 | O-Chevl, MC, Chevr |

## 1973

| | Vega (wb 97.0) | Wght | Price | Prod |
|---|---|---|---|---|
| V11 | sdn 2d | 2,219 | 2,087 | 58,425 |
| V15 | wgn 2d | 2,317 | 2,323 | 102,751 |
| V77 | htchbk cpe 2d | 2,313 | 2,192 | 266,124 |
| **Nova (wb 111.0)** | | | | |
| X17 | htchbk cpe 2d I-6 | 3,145 | 2,528 | 11,005 |
| X17 | htchbk cpe 2d V-8 | 3,274 | 2,618 | 33,949 |
| X27 | cpe I-6 | 3,033 | 2,377 | 54,140 |
| X27 | cpe V-8 | 3,162 | 2,467 | 81,679 |
| X69 | sdn 4d I-6 | 3,065 | 2,407 | 27,440 |
| X69 | sdn 4d V-8 | 3,194 | 2,497 | 32,843 |
| Y17 | Custom htchbk cpe 2d I-6 | 3,152 | 2,701 | 3,172 |
| Y17 | Custom htchbk cpe 2d V-8 | 3,281 | 2,792 | 42,886 |
| Y27 | Custom cpe I-6 | 3,073 | 2,551 | 6,336 |
| Y27 | Custom cpe V-8 | 3,202 | 2,741 | 52,042 |
| Y69 | Custom sdn 4d I-6 | 3,105 | 2,580 | 4,344 |
| Y69 | Custom sdn 4d V-8 | 3,234 | 2,671 | 19,673 |
| **Camaro (wb 108.1; incl. 11,574 Z28s)** | | | | |
| Q87 | spt cpe I-6 | 3,119 | 2,781 | 3,614 |
| Q87 | spt cpe V-8 | 3,238 | 2,872 | 60,810 |
| S87 | Type LT spt cpe V-8 | 3,349 | 3,268 | 32,327 |
| **Chevelle (wb 112.0; 4d-116.0)** | | | | |
| C29 | DeLuxe Colnde sdn 4d I-6 | 3,435 | 2,719 | 5,253 |
| C29 | DeLuxe Colnde sdn 4d V-8 | 3,585 | 2,835 | 15,502 |
| C37 | DeLuxe Colnde cpe I-6 | 3,423 | 2,743 | 6,332 |
| C37 | DeLuxe Colnde cpe V-8 | 3,580 | 2,860 | 15,045 |
| D29 | Malibu Colnde sdn 4d I-6 | 3,477 | 2,871 | 2,536 |
| D29 | Malibu Colnde sdn 4d V-8 | 3,627 | 2,987 | 58,143 |

| | Chevelle (wb 112.0; 4d-116.0) | Wght | Price | Prod |
|---|---|---|---|---|
| D37 | Malibu Colnde cpe I-6 | 3,430 | 2,894 | 3,157 |
| D37 | Malibu Colnde cpe V-8 | 3,580 | 3,010 | 165,627 |
| E29 | Laguna Colnde sdn 4d V-8 | 3,627 | 3,179 | 13,095 |
| E37 | Laguna Colnde cpe V-8 | 3,678 | 3,203 | 42,941 |
| **Chevelle Wagon (wb 116.0)** | | | | |
| C35 | DeLuxe 4d 2S I-6 | 3,849 | 3,106 | 1,870 |
| C35 | DeLuxe 4d 3S V-8 | 4,054 | 3,331 | 1,316 |
| C37 | DeLuxe 4d 2S V-8 | 4,006 | 3,198 | 7,754 |
| D37 | Malibu 4d 3S V-8 | 4,075 | 3,423 | 5,961 |
| D35 | Malibu 4d 2S V-8 | 4,027 | 3,290 | 18,592 |
| G35 | Malibu Estate 4d 3S V-8 | 4,080 | 3,608 | 4,099 |
| G35 | Malibu Estate 4d 2S V-8 | 4,032 | 3,475 | 5,527 |
| E35 | Laguna 4d 3S V-8 | 4,158 | 3,616 | 2,200 |
| E35 | Laguna 4d 2S V-8 | 4,110 | 3,483 | 4,419 |
| H35 | Laguna Estate 4d 3S V-8 | 4,189 | 3,795 | 3,709 |
| H35 | Laguna Estate 4d 2S V-8 | 4,141 | 3,662 | 3,661 |
| **Chevrolet (wb 121.5)** | | | | |
| K69 | Bel Air sdn 4d I-6 | 3,895 | 3,247 | 1,394 |
| K69 | Bel Air sdn 4d V-8 | 4,087 | 3,595 | 40,438 |
| L39 | Impala htp sdn V-8 | 4,162 | 3,822 | 139,143 |
| L47 | Impala Custom cpe V-8 | 4,110 | 3,836 | 176,824 |
| L57 | Impala cpe V-8 | 4,096 | 3,769 | 42,979 |
| L69 | Impala sdn 4d | 4,138 | 3,752 | 190,536 |
| N39 | Caprice Classic htp sdn V-8 | 4,208 | 4,134 | 70,155 |
| N47 | Caprice Classic htp cpe V-8 | 4,103 | 4,082 | 77,134 |
| N67 | Caprice Classic conv cpe V-8 | 4,191 | 4,345 | 7,339 |
| N69 | Caprice Classic sdn 4d V-8 | 4,176 | 4,064 | 58,126 |
| **Chevrolet Station Wagon (wb 125.0)** | | | | |
| K47 | Bel Air 4d 3S | 4,770 | 4,136 | 6,321 |
| K35 | Bel Air 4d 2S | 4,717 | 4,022 | 14,549 |
| L35 | Impala 4d 2S | 4,742 | 4,119 | 46,940 |
| L45 | Impala 4d 3S | 4,807 | 4,233 | 43,664 |
| N35 | Caprice Estate 4d 2S | 4,779 | 4,382 | 22,969 |
| N45 | Caprice Estate 4d 3S | 4,858 | 4,496 | 39,535 |
| **Monte Carlo (wb 116.0)** | | | | |
| H57 | spt cpe | 3,713 | 3,415 | 4,960 |
| H57 | S spt cpe | 3,720 | 3,562 | 177,963 |
| H57 | Landau spt cpe | 3,722 | 3,806 | 107,770 |

| 1973 Engines | bore × stroke | bhp | availability |
|---|---|---|---|
| I-4, 140.0 | 3.50 × 3.63 | 72 | S-Vega |
| I-4, 140.0 | 3.50 × 3.63 | 85 | O-Vega |
| I-6, 250.0 | 3.88 × 3.53 | 100 | S-Nova, Chevl, Cam exc LT Chevr |
| V-8, 307.0 | 3.88 × 3.25 | 115 | S-Nova, Chevl exc Lag, Cam exc LT |
| V-8, 350.0 | 4.00 × 3.48 | 145 | S-Lag, CamLT, MC, Chevr exc Cap; O-Nova, Chevl exc Lag, Cam exc LT, Chevr exc Cap |
| V-8, 350.0 | 4.00 × 3.48 | 175 | O-Nova, Chevl, Cam, MC |
| V-8, 350.0 | 4.00 × 3.48 | 245 | O-Camaro (Z28) |
| V-8, 400.0 | 4.12 × 3.75 | 150 | O-Chevr |
| V-8, 454.0 | 4.25 × 4.00 | 215 | O-Caprice |
| V-8, 454.0 | 4.25 × 4.00 | 245 | O-Chevl, MC, Cap |

## 1974

| | Vega (wb 97.0) | Wght | Price | Prod |
|---|---|---|---|---|
| V11 | sdn 2d | 2,369 | 2,505 | 58,724 |

# Chevrolet

| Vega (wb 97.0) | | Wght | Price | Prod |
|---|---|---|---|---|
| V11 | L× sdn 2d | — | 2,833 | 5,996 |
| V15 | wgn 2d 2S | 2,514 | 2,748 | 88,248 |
| V15 | Estate wgn 2d 2S | — | 2,976 | 27,089 |
| V77 | hatchback cpe | — | — | 276,028 |
| **Nova (wb 111.0)** | | | | |
| X17 | htchbk cpe I-6 | 3,260 | 2,935 | 13,722 |
| X17 | htckbk cpe V-8 | 3,398 | 3,034 | 20,627 |
| X27 | cpe I-6 | 3,150 | 2,811 | 87,399 |
| X27 | cpe V-8 | 3,288 | 2,919 | 72,558 |
| X69 | sdn 4d I-6 | 3,192 | 2,841 | 42,105 |
| X69 | sdn 4d V-8 | 3,330 | 2,949 | 32,017 |
| Y17 | Custom htchbk cpe I-6 | 3,299 | 3,108 | 9,631 |
| Y17 | Custom htchbk cpe V-8 | 3,437 | 3,217 | 36,653 |
| Y27 | Custom cpe I-6 | 3,206 | 2,985 | 11,115 |
| Y27 | Custom cpe V-8 | 3,344 | 3,093 | 39,912 |
| Y69 | Custom sdn 4d I-6 | 3,233 | 3,014 | 7,458 |
| Y69 | Custom sdn 4d V-8 | 3,371 | 3,123 | 17,340 |
| **Camaro (wb 108.1; incl 13,802 Z28s)** | | | | |
| Q87 | spt cpe I-6 | 3,309 | 3,162 | 22,210 |
| Q87 | spt cpe V-8 | 3,450 | 3,366 | 79,835 |
| S87 | Type LT spt cpe V-8 | 3,566 | 3,713 | 48,963 |
| **Chevelle (wb 112.0; 4d-116.0)** | | | | |
| C29 | Malibu sdn Colnde 4d I-6 | 3,638 | 3,049 | 11,399 |
| C29 | Malibu sdn Colnde 4d V-8 | 3,788 | 3,340 | 26,841 |
| C37 | Malibu Colonnade cpe I-6 | 3,573 | 3,054 | 15,790 |
| C37 | Malibu Colonnade cpe V-8 | 3,723 | 3,345 | 37,583 |
| D29 | Malibu Classic Col I-6 | 3,695 | 3,304 | 4,457 |
| D29 | Malibu Classic Col V-8 | 3,845 | 3,595 | 51,468 |
| D37 | Malibu Classic Col I-6 | 3,609 | 3,307 | 4,132 |
| D37 | Malibu Classic Col V-8 | 3,759 | 3,598 | 116,962 |
| D37 | Malibu Classic lan cpe I-6 | — | 3,518 | 351 |
| D37 | Malibu Classic lan cpe V-8 | 3,911 | 3,800 | 27,490 |
| E37 | Laguna S3 Colnde cpe V-8 | 3,951 | 3,723 | 21,902 |
| **Chevelle Wagon (wb 116.0) (all V-8)** | | | | |
| C35 | Malibu 4d 3S | 4,223 | 3,834 | 2,583 |
| C37 | Malibu 4d 2S | 4,191 | 3,701 | 12,408 |
| D35 | Malibu Classic 4d 3S | 4,315 | 4,251 | 4,909 |
| D35 | Malibu Classic 4d 2S | 4,283 | 4,118 | 13,986 |
| G35 | Malibu Classic Estate 4d 3S | 4,338 | 4,424 | 4,742 |
| G35 | Malibu Classic Estate 4d 2S | 4,306 | 4,291 | 5,480 |
| **Chevrolet (wb 121.5)** | | | | |
| K69 | Bel Air sdn 4d | 4,148 | 3,960 | 24,778 |
| L39 | Impala spt sdn 4d | 4,256 | 4,215 | 76,492 |
| L47 | Impala Custom cpe | 4,169 | 4,229 | 98,062 |
| L57 | Impala spt cpe | 4,167 | 4,162 | 50,036 |
| L69 | Impala sdn 4d | 4,205 | 4,135 | 133,164 |
| N39 | Caprice Classic spt sdn 4d | 4,344 | 4,534 | 48,387 |
| N47 | Caprice Classic Custom cpe | 4,245 | 4,483 | 59,484 |
| N67 | Caprice Classic conv cpe | 4,308 | 4,745 | 4,670 |
| N69 | Caprice Classic sdn 4d | 4,294 | 4,465 | 43,367 |
| **Chevrolet Wagon (wb 125.0)** | | | | |
| K35 | Bel Air 4d 2S | 4,829 | 4,464 | 6,437 |
| K45 | Bel Air 4d 3S | 4,884 | 4,578 | 2,913 |
| L35 | Impala 4d 2S | 4,891 | 4,561 | 23,455 |
| L45 | Impala 4d 3S | 4,936 | 4,675 | 23,259 |
| N35 | Caprice Estate 4d 2S | 4,960 | 4,800 | 12,280 |
| N45 | Caprice Estate 4d 3S | 5,004 | 4,914 | 23,063 |
| **Monte Carlo (wb 116.0)** | | | | |
| H57 | S spt cpe | 3,926 | 3,885 | 184,873 |
| H57 | Landau spt cpe | 3,928 | 4,129 | 127,344 |

| 1974 Engines | bore × stroke | bhp | availability |
|---|---|---|---|
| I-4, 140.0 | 3.50 × 3.63 | 75 | S-Vega |
| I-4, 140.0 | 3.50 × 3.63 | 85 | O-Vega |
| I-6, 250.0 | 3.88 × 3.53 | 100 | S-Nova, Chevl, Cam |
| V-8, 350.0 | 4.00 × 3.48 | 145 | S-Nova, Chevl, Cam, MC, Chevr exc Cap |
| V-8, 350.0 | 4.00 × 3.48 | 160 | O-as above |
| V-8, 350.0 | 4.00 × 3.48 | 185 | O-Nova, Camaro |
| V-8, 350.0 | 4.00 × 3.48 | 245 | O-Camaro (Z28) |
| V-8, 400.0 | 4.12 × 3.75 | 150 | S-Caprice exc wgns |
| V-8, 400.0 | 4.12 × 3.75 | 180 | S-wgns; O-Chevl, MC |
| V-8, 454.0 | 4.25 × 4.00 | 235 | O-Chevl, MC, Cap |

## 1975

| Vega (wb 97.0) | | Wght | Price | Prod |
|---|---|---|---|---|
| V11 | sdn 2d | 2,415 | 2,786 | 33,878 |
| V11 | LX sdn 2d | — | 3,119 | 1,255 |
| V15 | wgn 2d 2S | 2,531 | 3,016 | 47,474 |
| V15 | Estate wgn 2d 2S | 2,541 | 3,244 | 8,659 |
| V77 | htchbk cpe | 2,478 | 2,899 | 112,912 |
| V77 | Cosworth htchbk cpe | 2,173 | 5,916 | 2,061 |
| **Monza (wb 97.0)** | | | | |
| M27 | Towne cpe | 2,675 | 3,570 | 69,238 |
| R07 | S htchbk cpe | — | 3,648 | 9,795 |
| R07 | 2+2 htchbk cpe | 2,753 | 3,953 | 57,170 |
| **Nova (wb 111.0)** | | | | |
| X17 | htchbk cpe I-6 | 3,391 | 3,347 | 7,952 |
| X17 | htchbk cpe V-8 | 3,493 | 3,422 | 8,421 |
| X27 | cpe I-6 | 3,276 | 3,205 | 48,103 |
| X27 | S cpe I-6 | — | 3,099 | 16,655 |
| X27 | cpe V-8 | 3,378 | 3,280 | 33,921 |
| X27 | S cpe V-8 | — | 3,174 | 5,070 |
| X69 | sdn 4d I-6 | 3,306 | 3,209 | 43,760 |
| X69 | sdn 4d V-8 | 3,408 | 3,284 | 22,587 |
| Y17 | Custom htckbk cpe I-6 | 3,421 | 3,541 | 3,812 |
| Y17 | Custom htchbk cpe V-8 | 3,523 | 3,616 | 11,438 |
| Y27 | Custom cpe I-6 | 3,335 | 3,402 | 7,214 |
| Y27 | LN Cpe I-6 | — | 3,782 | 1,138 |
| Y27 | Custom cpe V-8 | 3,437 | 3,477 | 19,074 |
| Y27 | LN cpe V-8 | — | 3,857 | 11,395 |
| Y69 | Custom sdn 4d I-6 | 3,367 | 3,415 | 8,959 |
| Y69 | LN sdn 4d I-6 | — | 3,795 | 1,286 |
| Y69 | Custom sdn 4d V-8 | 3,469 | 3,490 | 13,221 |
| Y69 | LN sdn 4d V-8 | — | 3,870 | 8,976 |
| **Camaro (wb 108.1)** | | | | |
| Q87 | spt cpe I-6 | 3,421 | 3,540 | 29,749 |
| Q87 | spt cpe V-8 | 3,532 | 3,685 | 76,178 |
| S87 | Type LT spt cpe V-8 | 3,616 | 4,057 | 39,843 |
| **Chevelle (wb 112.0; 4d-116.0)** | | | | |
| C29 | Malibu sdn 4d I-6 | 3,713 | 3,402 | 12,873 |
| C29 | Malibu sdn 4d V-8 | 3,833 | 3,652 | 24,989 |
| C37 | Malibu cpe I-6 | 3,642 | 3,407 | 13,292 |
| C37 | Malibu cpe V-8 | 3,762 | 3,657 | 23,708 |
| D29 | Malibu Classic sdn 4d I-6 | 3,778 | 3,695 | 1 |
| D29 | Malibu Classic sdn 4d V-8 | 3,898 | 3,945 | 51,070 |
| D37 | Malibu Classic cpe I-6 | 3,681 | 3,698 | 4,330 |
| D37 | Malibu Classic cpe V-8 | 3,801 | 3,948 | 76,607 |

228

# Chevrolet

| Chevelle (wb 112.0; 4d-116.0) | | Wght | Price | Prod |
|---|---|---|---|---|
| D37 | Malibu Classic Landau cpe I-6 | — | 3,930 | 378 |
| D37 | Malibu Classic Landau cpe V-8 | 3,903 | 4,180 | 22,691 |
| E37 | Laguna S3 cpe V-8 | 3,908 | 4,113 | 7,788 |
| **Chevelle Malibu Wagon (wb 116.0)** | | | | |
| C35 | 4d 3S | 4,237 | 4,463 | 2,377 |
| C35 | 4d 2S | 4,207 | 4,318 | 11,600 |
| D36 | Classic 4d 3S | 4,305 | 4,701 | 6,394 |
| D36 | Classic 4d 2S | 4,275 | 4,556 | 15,974 |
| G35 | Classic Estate 4d 3S | 4,331 | 4,893 | 4,600 |
| G35 | Classic Estate 4d 2S | 4,301 | 4,748 | 4,637 |
| **Chevrolet (wb 121.5)** | | | | |
| K69 | Bel Air sdn 4d | 4,179 | 4,345 | 15,871 |
| L39 | Impala spt sdn 4d | 4,265 | 4,631 | 47,125 |
| L47 | Impala Custom cpe | 4,190 | 4,626 | 49,455 |
| L47 | Impala Landau cpe | — | 4,901 | 2,465 |
| L57 | Impala spt cpe | 4,207 | 4,575 | 21,333 |
| L69 | Impala sdn 4d | 4,218 | 4,548 | 91,330 |
| N39 | Caprice Classic spt sdn 4d | 4,360 | 4,891 | 40,482 |
| N47 | Caprice Classic cpe | 4,275 | 4,837 | 36,041 |
| N47 | Caprice Classic Landau cpe | — | 5,075 | 3,752 |
| N67 | Caprice Classic conv cpe | 4,343 | 5,113 | 8,349 |
| N69 | Caprice Classic sdn 4d | 4,311 | 4,819 | 33,715 |
| **Chevrolet Wagon (wb 125.0)** | | | | |
| K35 | Bel Air 4d 2S | 4,856 | 4,878 | 4,032 |
| K45 | Bel Air 4d 3S | 4,913 | 4,998 | 2,386 |
| L35 | Impala 4d 2S | 4,910 | 5,001 | 17,998 |
| L45 | Impala 4d 3S | 4,959 | 5,121 | 19,445 |
| N35 | Caprice Estate 4d 2S | 4,978 | 5,231 | 9,047 |
| N45 | Caprice Estate 4d 3S | 5,036 | 5,351 | 18,858 |
| **Monte Carlo (wb 116.0)** | | | | |
| H57 | S spt cpe | 3,927 | 4,249 | 148,529 |
| H57 | Landau spt cpe | 3,930 | 4,519 | 110,380 |

| 1975 Engines | bore × stroke | bhp | availability |
|---|---|---|---|
| I-4, 122.0 | 3.50 × 3.16 | 111 | S-Cosworth Vega |
| I-4, 140.0 | 3.50 × 3.63 | 78 | S-Vega, Monza exc 2+2 |
| I-4, 140.0 | 3.50 × 3.63 | 87 | S-Monza 2+2; O-Vega |
| I-6, 250.0 | 3.88 × 3.53 | 105 | S-Nova, Chevl, Cam |
| V-8, 262.0 | 3.67 × 3.10 | 110 | O-Nova, Monza |
| V-8, 350.0 | 4.00 × 3.48 | 125 | O-Monza |
| V-8, 350.0 | 4.00 × 3.48 | 145 | S-Nova, Chevl, Cam, MC, Chevr exc wgns |
| V-8, 350.0 | 4.00 × 3.48 | 155 | O-Nova, Chevl, Cam, MC, Chev |
| V-8, 400.0 | 4.12 × 3.75 | 175 | S-Chevr wgns; O-Chevl, MC, Chevr |
| V-8, 454.0 | 4.25 × 4.00 | 235 | O-Chevl, MC, Chevr |

## 1976

| Chevette (wb 94.3) | | Wght | Price | Prod |
|---|---|---|---|---|
| B08 | htchbk sdn 2d | 1,927 | 3,098 | 178,007 |
| J08 | Scooter htchbk sdn 2d | 1,870 | 2,899 | 9,810 |
| **Vega (wb 97.0)** | | | | |
| V11 | sdn 2d | 2,443 | 2,984 | 27,619 |
| V15 | wgn 2d 2S | 2,578 | 3,227 | 46,114 |
| V15 | Estate wgn 2d 2S | — | 3,450 | 7,935 |
| V77 | htchbk cpe | 2,534 | 3,099 | 77,409 |
| V77 | Cosworth htchbk cpe 2d | — | 6,066 | 1,447 |
| **Monza (wb 97.0)** | | | | |
| M27 | Towne cpe | 2,625 | 3,359 | 46,735 |
| R07 | 2+2 htchbk cpe | 2,668 | 3,727 | 34,170 |
| **Nova (wb 111.0)** | | | | |
| X17 | htchbk cpe I-6 | 3,391 | 3,417 | 10,853 |
| X17 | htchbk cpe V-8 | 3,475 | 3,579 | 7,866 |
| X27 | cpe I-6 | 3,188 | 3,248 | 87,438 |
| X27 | cpe V-8 | 3,272 | 3,413 | 44,421 |
| X69 | sdn 4d I-6 | 3,221 | 3,283 | 86,600 |
| X69 | sdn 4d V-8 | 3,305 | 3,448 | 37,167 |
| Y17 | Concours htchbk cpe I-6 | 3,401 | 3,972 | 2,088 |
| Y17 | Concours htchbk cpe V-8 | 3,485 | 4,134 | 5,486 |
| Y27 | Concours cpe I-6 | 3,324 | 3,795 | 6,568 |
| Y27 | Concours cpe V-8 | 3,408 | 3,960 | 15,730 |
| Y69 | Concours sdn 4d I-6 | 3,367 | 3,830 | 10,151 |
| Y69 | Concours sdn 4d V-8 | 3,451 | 3,995 | 20,360 |
| **Camaro (wb 108.1)** | | | | |
| Q87 | spt cpe I-6 | 3,421 | 3,762 | 38,047 |
| Q87 | spt cpe V-8 | 3,511 | 3,927 | 92,491 |
| S87 | Type LT spt cpe V-8 | 3,576 | 4,320 | 52,421 |
| **Chevelle (wb 112.0; 4d-116.0)** | | | | |
| C29 | Malibu sdn 4d I-6 | 3,729 | 3,671 | 13,116 |
| C29 | Malibu sdn 4d V-8 | 3,834 | 4,201 | 25,353 |
| C37 | Malibu cpe I-6 | 3,650 | 3,636 | 12,616 |
| C37 | Malibu cpe V-8 | 3,755 | 4,166 | 17,976 |
| D29 | Malibu Classic sdn 4d I-6 | 3,827 | 4,196 | 4,253 |
| D29 | Malibu Classic sdn 4d V-8 | 3,932 | 4,490 | 73,307 |
| D37 | Malibu Classic cpe I-6 | 3,688 | 3,926 | 5,791 |
| D37 | Malibu Classic cpe V-8 | 3,793 | 4,455 | 76,843 |
| D37 | Malibu Clsc Landau cpe I-6 | — | 4,124 | 672 |
| D37 | Malibu Clsc Landau cpe V-8 | — | 4,640 | 29,495 |
| E37 | Laguna S3 cpe V-8 | 3,978 | 4,621 | 9,100 |
| **Chevelle Malibu Wagon (wb 116.0)** | | | | |
| C35 | 4d 3S | 4,268 | 4,686 | 2,984 |
| C35 | 4d 2S | 4,238 | 4,543 | 13,581 |
| D35 | Classic 4d 3S | 4,330 | 4,919 | 11,617 |
| D35 | Classic 4d 2S | 4,300 | 4,776 | 24,635 |
| G35 | Malibu Clsc Estate 4d 3S | 4,356 | 5,114 | 6,386 |
| G35 | Malibu Clsc Estate 4d 2S | 4,326 | 4,971 | 5,518 |
| **Chevrolet (wb 121.5)** | | | | |
| L39 | Impala spt sdn 4d | 4,245 | 4,798 | 39,849 |
| L47 | Impala Custom cpe | 4,175 | 4,763 | 43,219 |
| L47 | Impala Landau cpe | — | 5,058 | 10,841 |
| L69 | Impala S spt sdn 4d | — | 4,507 | 18,265 |
| L69 | Impala sdn 4d | 4,222 | 4,706 | 86,057 |
| N39 | Caprice Classic spt sdn 4d | 4,314 | 5,078 | 55,308 |
| N47 | Caprice Classic cpe | 4,244 | 5,043 | 28,161 |
| N47 | Caprice Classic Landau cpe | — | 5,284 | 21,926 |
| N69 | Caprice Classic sdn 4d | 4,285 | 5,013 | 47,411 |
| **Chevrolet Wagon (wb 125.0)** | | | | |
| L35 | Impala 4d 2S | 4,912 | 5,166 | 19,657 |
| L45 | Impala 4d 3S | 4,972 | 5,283 | 21,329 |
| N35 | Caprice Estate 4d 2S | 4,948 | 5,429 | 10,029 |
| N45 | Caprice Estate 4d 3S | 5,007 | 5,546 | 21,804 |
| **Monte Carlo (wb 116.0)** | | | | |
| H57 | S spt cpe | 3,907 | 4,673 | 191,370 |
| H57 | Landau spt cpe | — | 4,966 | 161,902 |

| 1976 Engines | bore × stroke | bhp | availability |
|---|---|---|---|
| I-4, 85.0 | 3.23 × 2.61 | 52 | S-Chevt |
| I-4, 97.6 | 3.23 × 2.98 | 60 | O-Chevt |
| I-4, 122.0 | 3.50 × 3.15 | 111 | S-Cosworth Vega |
| I-4, 140.0 | 3.50 × 3.63 | 70 | S-Vega, Monza |

# Chevrolet

| 1976 Engines | bore × stroke | bhp | availability |
|---|---|---|---|
| I-4, 140.0 | 3.50 × 3.63 | 84 | O-Vega, Monza |
| I-6, 250.0 | 3.88 × 3.53 | 105 | S-Nova, Chevl, Cam |
| V-8, 262.0 | 3.67 × 3.10 | 110 | O-Monza |
| V-8, 305.0 | 3.74 × 3.48 | 140 | S-Nova, Chevl, Cam, MC; O-Monza |
| V-8, 305.0 | 3.74 × 3.48 | 145 | S-Chevl wgn, Chevr; O-MC |
| V-8, 350.0 | 4.00 × 3.48 | 165 | O-Nova, Chevl, Cam, MC, Chevr |
| V-8, 400.0 | 4.12 × 3.75 | 175 | S-Chevr wgn; O-Chevl, MC, Chevr |
| V-8, 454.0 | 4.25 × 4.00 | 225 | O-Chevr |

## 1977

| Chevette (wb 94.3) | | Wght | Price | Prod |
|---|---|---|---|---|
| B08 | htchbk sdn 2d | 1,958 | 3,225 | 120,278 |
| J08 | Scooter htchbk sdn 2d | 1,898 | 2,999 | 13,191 |
| **Vega (wb 97.0)** | | | | |
| V11 | sdn 2d | 2,459 | 3,249 | 12,365 |
| V15 | wgn 2d 2S | 2,571 | 3,522 | 25,181 |
| V15 | Estate wgn 2d 2S | — | 3,745 | 3,461 |
| V77 | htchbk cpe | 2,522 | 3,359 | 37,395 |
| **Monza (wb 97.0)** | | | | |
| M27 | Town cpe | 2,580 | 3,560 | 34,133 |
| R07 | 2+2 htchbk cpe | 2,671 | 3,840 | 39,215 |
| **Nova (wb 111.0)** | | | | |
| X17 | htchbk cpe I-6 | 3,217 | 3,646 | 18,048 |
| X17 | htchbk cpe V-8 | 3,335 | 3,766 | |
| X27 | cpe I-6 | 3,139 | 3,482 | 132,833 |
| X27 | cpe V-8 | 3,257 | 3,602 | |
| X69 | sdn 4d I-6 | 3,174 | 3,532 | 141,028 |
| X69 | sdn 4d V-8 | 3,292 | 3,652 | |
| Y17 | Concours htchbk cpe I-6 | 3,378 | 4,154 | 5,481 |
| Y17 | Concours htchbk cpe V-8 | 3,486 | 4,274 | |
| Y27 | Concours cpe I-6 | 3,283 | 3,991 | 28,602 |
| Y27 | Concours cpe V-8 | 3,391 | 4,111 | |
| Y69 | Concours sdn 4d I-6 | 3,329 | 4,066 | 39,272 |
| Y69 | Concours sdn 4d V-8 | 3,437 | 4,186 | |
| **Camaro (wb 108.1)** | | | | |
| Q87 | spt cpe | 3,369 | 4,113 | 131,717 |
| S87 | Type LT spt cpe | 3,422 | 4,478 | 72,787 |
| Q87 | Z28 spt cpe V-8 | — | 5,170 | 14,349 |
| **Chevelle Malibu (wb 112.0; 4d-116.0)** | | | | |
| C29 | sdn 4d I-6 | 3,628 | 3,935 | 39,064 |
| C29 | sdn 4d V-8 | 3,737 | 4,055 | |
| C37 | cpe I-6 | 3,551 | 3,885 | 28,793 |
| C37 | cpe V-8 | 3,650 | 4,005 | |
| D29 | Classic sdn 4d I-6 | 3,725 | 4,475 | 76,776 |
| D29 | Classic sdn 4d V-8 | 3,824 | 4,595 | |
| D37 | Classic cpe I-6 | 3,599 | 4,125 | 73,739 |
| D37 | Classic cpe V-8 | 3,698 | 4,245 | |
| D37 | Classic Landau cpe I-6 | — | 4,353 | 37,215 |
| D37 | Classic Landau cpe V-8 | — | 4,473 | |
| **Chevelle Malibu Wagon (wb 116.0)** | | | | |
| C35 | 4d 3S | 4,169 | 4,877 | 4,014 |
| C35 | 4d 2S | 4,139 | 4,734 | 18,023 |
| D35 | Classic 4d 3S | 4,263 | 5,208 | 19,053 |
| D35 | Classic 4d 2S | 4,233 | 5,065 | 31,539 |
| **Chevrolet (wb 116.0)** | | | | |
| L35 | Impala wgn 4d 3S V-8 | 4,072 | 5,406 | 28,255 |

| Chevrolet (wb 116.0) | | Wght | Price | Prod |
|---|---|---|---|---|
| L35 | Impala wgn 4d 2S V-8 | 4,042 | 5,289 | 37,108 |
| L47 | Impala Custom cpe I-6 | 3,533 | 4,876 | 55,347 |
| L47 | Impala Custom cpe V-8 | 3,628 | 4,996 | |
| L47 | Impala Landau cpe | — | — | 2,745 |
| L69 | Impala sdn 4d I-6 | 3,564 | 4,901 | 196,824 |
| L69 | Impala sdn 4d V-8 | 3,659 | 5,021 | |
| N35 | Caprice Clsc wgn 4d 3S V-8 | 4,118 | 5,734 | 33,639 |
| N35 | Caprice Clsc wgn 4d 2S V-8 | 4,088 | 5,617 | 22,930 |
| N47 | Caprice Clsc cpe I-6 | 3,571 | 5,187 | 62,366 |
| N47 | Caprice Clsc cpe V-8 | 3,666 | 5,307 | |
| N69 | Caprice Clsc sdn 4d I-6 | 3,606 | 5,237 | 212,840 |
| N69 | Caprice Clsc sdn 4d V-8 | 3,701 | 5,357 | |
| N69 | Caprice Landau cpe | — | — | 9,607 |
| **Monte Carlo (wb 116.0)** | | | | |
| H57 | S spt cpe | 3,852 | 4,968 | 224,327 |
| H57 | Landau spt cpe | — | 5,298 | 186,711 |

| 1977 Engines | bore × stroke | bhp | availability |
|---|---|---|---|
| I-4, 85.0 | 3.23 × 2.61 | 57 | S-Chevt |
| I-4, 97.6 | 3.23 × 2.98 | 63 | O-Chevt |
| I-4, 140.0 | 3.50 × 3.15 | 84 | S-Vega, Monza |
| I-6, 250.0 | 3.88 × 3.53 | 110 | S-Nova, Chevl, Cam, Chevr |
| V-8, 305.0 | 3.74 × 3.48 | 145 | S-Nova, Chevl exc Clsc wgn, Cam, MC, Chevr; O-Monza |
| V-8, 350.0 | 4.00 × 3.48 | 170 | S-Chevl Clsc wgn; O-Nova, Chevl, Cam, MC, Chevr |

## 1978

| Chevette (wb 94.3; 4d-97.3) | | Wght | Price | Prod |
|---|---|---|---|---|
| B08 | htchbk sdn 2d | 1,965 | 3,644 | 118,375 |
| B68 | htchbk sdn 4d | 2,035 | 3,764 | 167,769 |
| J08 | Scooter htchbk sdn 2d | 1,932 | 3,149 | 12,829 |
| **Monza (wb 97.0)** | | | | |
| M07 | 2+2 htchbk cpe | 2,732 | 3,779 | 36,227 |
| M15 | wgn 2d | 2,723 | 3,868 | 24,255 |
| M15 | Estate wgn 2d | — | 4,102 | 2,478 |
| M27 | cpe | 2,688 | 3,622 | 37,878 |
| M77 | S htchbk cpe | 2,643 | 3,697 | 2,326 |
| R07 | 2+2 htchbk cpe | 2,777 | 4,247 | 28,845 |
| R27 | spt cpe | 2,730 | 4,100 | 6,823 |
| **Nova (wb 111.0)** | | | | |
| X17 | htchbk cpe I-6 | 3,258 | 3,866 | 12,665 |
| X17 | htchbk cpe V-8 | 3,403 | 4,051 | |
| X27 | cpe I-6 | 3,132 | 3,702 | 101,858 |
| X27 | cpe V-8 | 3,277 | 3,887 | |
| X69 | sdn 4d I-6 | 3,173 | 3,777 | 123,158 |
| X69 | sdn 4d V-8 | 3,318 | 3,962 | |
| Y27 | Custom cpe I-6 | 3,261 | 3,960 | 23,953 |
| Y27 | Custom cpe V-8 | 3,396 | 4,145 | |
| Y69 | Custom sdn 4d I-6 | 3,298 | 4,035 | 26,475 |
| Y69 | Custom sdn 4d V-8 | 3,443 | 4,220 | |
| **Camaro (wb 108.1)** | | | | |
| Q87 | spt cpe | 3,300 | 4,414 | 134,491 |
| Q87 | Rally sport cpe | — | 4,784 | 11,902 |
| S87 | Type LT spt cpe | 3,352 | 4,814 | 65,635 |
| S87 | Type LT Rally sport cpe | — | 5,065 | 5,696 |
| Q87 | Z28 spt cpe V-8 | — | 5,604 | 54,907 |
| **Malibu (wb 108.1)** | | | | |
| T19 | sdn 4d V-6 | 3,006 | 4,276 | 44,426 |

# Chevrolet

| Malibu (wb 108.1) | | Wght | Price | Prod |
|---|---|---|---|---|
| T19 | sdn 4d V-8 | 3,143 | 4,469 | |
| T27 | cpe V-6 | 3,001 | 4,204 | 27,089 |
| T27 | cpe V-8 | 3,138 | 4,394 | |
| T35 | wgn 4d 2S V-6 | 3,169 | 4,516 | 30,850 |
| T35 | wgn 4d 2S V-8 | 3,550 | 4,706 | |
| W19 | Classic sdn 4d V-6 | 3,039 | 4,561 | 102,967 |
| W19 | Classic sdn 4d V-8 | 3,175 | 4,751 | |
| W27 | Classic spt cpe V-6 | 3,031 | 4,461 | 60,992 |
| W27 | Classic spt cpe V-8 | 3,167 | 4,651 | |
| W27 | Classic Landau cpe V-6 | — | 4,684 | 29,160 |
| W27 | Classic Landau cpe V-8 | — | 4,874 | |
| W35 | Classic wgn 4d 2S V-6 | 3,196 | 4,714 | 63,152 |
| W35 | Classic wgn 4d 2S V-8 | 3,377 | 4,904 | |
| **Chevrolet (wb 116.0)** | | | | |
| L35 | Impala wgn 4d 3S V-8 | 4,071 | 5,904 | 28,518 |
| L35 | Impala wgn 4d 2S V-8 | 4,037 | 5,777 | 40,423 |
| L47 | Impala cpe I-6 | 3,511 | 5,208 | 33,990 |
| L47 | Impala cpe V-8 | 3,619 | 5,393 | |
| L47 | Impala Landau cpe I-6 | — | 5,598 | 4,652 |
| L47 | Impala Landau cpe V-8 | — | 5,783 | |
| L69 | Impala sdn 4d I-6 | 3,530 | 5,283 | 183,161 |
| L69 | Impala sdn 4d V-8 | 3,638 | 5,468 | |
| N35 | Caprice Clsc wgn 4d 3S V-8 | 4,109 | 6,151 | 32,952 |
| N35 | Caprice Clsc wgn 4d 2S V-8 | 4,079 | 6,012 | 24,792 |
| N47 | Caprice Clsc cpe I-6 | 3,548 | 5,526 | 37,301 |
| N47 | Caprice Clsc cpe V-8 | 3,656 | 5,711 | |
| N47 | Caprice Landau cpe I-6 | — | 5,830 | 22,771 |
| N47 | Caprice Landau cpe V-8 | — | 6,015 | |
| N69 | Caprice Classic sdn 4d I-6 | 3,578 | 5,628 | 203,837 |
| N69 | Caprice Classic sdn 4d V-8 | 3,686 | 5,811 | |
| **Monte Carlo (wb 108.1)** | | | | |
| Z37 | spt cpe V-6 | 3,040 | 4,785 | 216,730 |
| Z37 | spt cpe V-8 | 3,175 | 4,935 | |
| Z37 | Landau spt cpe V-6 | — | 5,678 | 141,461 |
| Z37 | Landau spt cpe V-8 | — | 5,828 | |

| 1978 Engines | bore × stroke | bhp | availability |
|---|---|---|---|
| I-4, 97.6 | 3.23 × 2.98 | 63 | S-Chevt |
| I-4, 97.6 | 3.23 × 2.98 | 68 | O-Chevt |
| I-4, 151.0 | 4.00 × 3.00 | 85 | S-Monza |
| V-6, 196.0 | 3.50 × 3.40 | 90 | O-Monza |
| V-6, 200.0 | 3.50 × 3.48 | 95 | S-Malibu |
| V-6, 231.0 | 3.80 × 3.40 | 105 | S-MC; O-Malibu, Monza |
| I-6, 250.0 | 3.88 × 3.53 | 110 | S-Nova, Cam exc Z28, Chevr |
| V-8, 305.0 | 3.74 × 3.48 | 145 | S-Nova, Mal, Cam exc Z28, MC, Chevr; O-Monza |
| V-8, 350.0 | 4.00 × 3.48 | 170 | O-Nova, Mal wgns, Cam, Chevr |
| V-8, 350.0 | 4.00 × 3.48 | 185 | S-Camaro Z28 |

## 1979

| Chevette (wb 94.3; 4d-97.3) | | Wght | Price | Prod |
|---|---|---|---|---|
| B08 | htchbk sdn 2d | 1,978 | 3,948 | 136,145 |
| B68 | htchbk sdn 4d | 2,057 | 4,072 | 208,865 |
| J08 | Scooter htchbk sdn 2d | 1,929 | 3,437 | 24,099 |
| **Monza (wb 97.0)** | | | | |
| M07 | 2+2 htchbk cpe | 2,630 | 4,161 | 56,871 |
| M15 | wgn 2d | 2,631 | 4,167 | 15,190 |
| M27 | cpe | 2,577 | 3,850 | 61,110 |

| Monza (wb 97.0) | | Wght | Price | Prod |
|---|---|---|---|---|
| R07 | 2+2 htchbk cpe | 2,676 | 4,624 | 30,662 |
| **Nova (wb 111.0)** | | | | |
| X17 | htchbk cpe I-6 | 3,264 | 4,118 | 4,819 |
| X17 | htchbk cpe V-8 | 3,394 | 4,353 | |
| X27 | cpe I-6 | 3,135 | 3,955 | 36,800 |
| X27 | cpe V-8 | 3,265 | 4,190 | |
| X69 | sdn 4d I-6 | 3,179 | 4,055 | 40,883 |
| X69 | sdn 4d V-8 | 3,309 | 4,290 | |
| Y27 | Custom cpe I-6 | 3,194 | 4,164 | 7,529 |
| Y27 | Custom cpe V-8 | 3,324 | 4,399 | |
| Y69 | Custom sdn 4d I-6 | 3,228 | 4,264 | 7,690 |
| Y69 | Custom sdn 4d V-8 | 3,358 | 4,499 | |
| **Camaro (wb 108.0)** | | | | |
| Q87 | spt cpe | 3,305 | 5,163 | 111,357 |
| Q87 | Rally sport cpe | — | 5,572 | 19,101 |
| S87 | Berlinetta cpe | 3,358 | 5,906 | 67,236 |
| Q87 | Z28 spt cpe V-8 | — | 6,748 | 84,877 |
| **Malibu (wb 108.1)** | | | | |
| T19 | sdn 4d V-6 | 2,988 | 4,915 | 59,674 |
| T19 | sdn 4d V-8 | 3,116 | 5,180 | |
| T27 | cpe V-6 | 2,983 | 4,812 | 41,848 |
| T27 | cpe V-8 | 3,111 | 5,077 | |
| T35 | wgn 2d 2S V-6 | 3,155 | 5,078 | 50,344 |
| T35 | wgn 2d 2S V-8 | 3,297 | 5,343 | |
| W19 | Classic sdn 4d V-6 | 3,024 | 5,215 | 104,222 |
| W19 | Classic sdn 4d V-8 | 3,152 | 5,480 | |
| W27 | Classic cpe V-6 | 3,017 | 5,087 | 60,751 |
| W27 | Classic cpe V-8 | 3,145 | 5,352 | |
| W27 | Classic Landau cpe V-6 | — | 5,335 | 25,213 |
| W27 | Classic Landau cpe V-8 | — | 5,600 | |
| W35 | Classic wgn 4d V-6 | 3,183 | 5,300 | 70,095 |
| W35 | Classic wgn 4d V-8 | 3,325 | 5,565 | |
| **Chevrolet (wb 116.0)** | | | | |
| L35 | Impala wgn 4d 3S V-8 | 4,045 | 6,636 | 28,710 |
| L35 | Impala wgn 4d 2S V-8 | 4,013 | 6,497 | 39,644 |
| L47 | Impala cpe V-6 | 3,495 | 5,828 | 26,589 |
| L47 | Impala cpe V-8 | 3,606 | 6,138 | |
| L47 | Impala Landau cpe I-6 | — | 6,314 | 3,247 |
| L47 | Impala Landau cpe V-8 | — | 6,624 | |
| L69 | Impala sdn 4d I-6 | 3,513 | 5,928 | 172,717 |
| L69 | Impala sdn 4d V-8 | 3,624 | 6,238 | |
| N35 | Caprice Clsc wgn 4d 3S V-8 | 4,088 | 6,960 | 32,693 |
| N35 | Caprice Clsc wgn 4d 2S V-8 | 4,056 | 6,800 | 23,568 |
| N37 | Caprice Classic cpe I-6 | 3,538 | 6,198 | 36,629 |
| N37 | Caprice Classic cpe V-8 | 3,649 | 6,508 | |
| N47 | Caprice Clsc Landau cpe I-6 | — | 6,617 | 21,824 |
| N47 | Caprice Clsc Landau cpe V-8 | — | 6,927 | |
| N69 | Caprice Clsc sdn 4d I-6 | 3,564 | 6,323 | 203,017 |
| N69 | Caprice Clsc sdn 4d V-8 | 3,675 | 6,633 | |
| **Monte Carlo (wb 108.1)** | | | | |
| Z37 | spt cpe V-6 | 3,039 | 5,333 | 225,073 |
| Z37 | spt cpe V-8 | 3,169 | 5,598 | |
| Z37 | Landau spt cpe V-6 | — | 6,183 | 91,850 |
| Z37 | Landau spt cpe V-8 | — | 6,448 | |

| 1979 Engines | bore × stroke | bhp | availability |
|---|---|---|---|
| I-4, 97.6 | 3.23 × 2.98 | 70 | S-Chevt |
| I-4, 97.6 | 3.23 × 2.98 | 74 | O-Chevt |
| I-4, 151.0 | 4.00 × 3.00 | 90 | S-Monza I-4 |
| V-6, 196.0 | 3.50 × 3.40 | 105 | S-Monza V-6 |
| V-6, 200.0 | 3.50 × 3.48 | 94 | S-Malibu, MC |
| V-6, 231.0 | 3.80 × 3.40 | 115 | O-Mal, Monza, MC |
| I-6, 250.0 | 3.88 × 3.53 | 115 | S-Nova, Cam exc |

# Chevrolet

| 1979 Engines | bore × stroke | bhp | availability |
|---|---|---|---|
| V-8, 267.0 | 3.50 × 3.48 | 125 | Z28, Chevr exc wgns S-Malibu, MC |
| V-8, 305.0 | 3.74 × 3.48 | 130 | S-Nova, Cam exc Z28, Chevr; O-Monza |
| V-8, 305.0 | 3.74 × 3.48 | 160 | O-Monte Carlo, Malibu |
| V-8, 350.0 | 4.00 × 3.48 | 170 | O-Nova, Mal, Chevrolet |
| V-8, 350.0 | 4.00 × 3.48 | 175 | S-Camaro Z28; O-Camaro |

## 1980

### Chevette (wb 94.3; 4d-97.3)

| | | Wght | Price | Prod |
|---|---|---|---|---|
| B08 | htchbk sdn 2d | 1,989 | 4,601 | 148,686 |
| B68 | htchbk sdn 4d | 2,048 | 4,736 | 261,477 |
| J08 | Scooter htchbk | 1,935 | 4,057 | 40,998 |

### Monza (wb 97.0)

| | | Wght | Price | Prod |
|---|---|---|---|---|
| M07 | 2+2 htchbk cpe | 2,672 | 4,746 | 53,415 |
| M27 | cpe | 2,617 | 4,433 | 95,469 |
| R07 | Sport 2+2 htchbk cpe | 2,729 | 5,186 | 20,534 |

### Citation (wb 104.9)

| | | Wght | Price | Prod |
|---|---|---|---|---|
| H11 | cpe I-4 | 2,391 | 4,800 | 42,909 |
| H11 | cpe V-6 | 2,428 | 4,925 | |
| X08 | htchbk sdn 2d I-4 | 2,417 | 5,422 | 210,258 |
| X08 | htchbk sdn 2d V-6 | 2,454 | 5,547 | |
| X11 | club cpe I-4 | 2,397 | 5,214 | 100,340 |
| X11 | club cpe V-6 | 2,434 | 5,339 | |
| X68 | htchbk sdn 4d I-4 | 2,437 | 5,552 | 458,033 |
| X68 | htchbk 4d V-6 | 2,474 | 5,677 | |

### Camaro (wb 108.1)

| | | Wght | Price | Prod |
|---|---|---|---|---|
| P87 | spt cpe | 3,218 | 5,843 | 68,174 |
| P87/Z85 | RS cpe | — | 6,086 | 12,015 |
| S87 | Berlinetta cpe | 3,253 | 6,606 | 26,679 |
| P87 | Z28 spt cpe V-8 | — | 7,363 | 45,137 |

### Malibu (wb 108.1)

| | | Wght | Price | Prod |
|---|---|---|---|---|
| T19 | sdn 4d V-6 | 3,001 | 5,617 | 67,696 |
| T19 | sdn 4d V-8 | 3,122 | 5,697 | |
| T27 | spt cpe V-6 | 2,996 | 5,502 | 28,425 |
| T27 | spt cpe V-8 | 3,117 | 5,582 | |
| T35 | wgn 4d 2S V-6 | 3,141 | 5,778 | 30,794 |
| T35 | wgn 4d 2S V-8 | 3,261 | 5,858 | |
| W19 | Classic sdn 4d V-6 | 3,031 | 5,951 | 77,938 |
| W19 | Classic sdn 4d V-8 | 3,152 | 6,031 | |
| W27 | Classic spt cpe V-6 | 3,027 | 5,816 | 28,425 |
| W27 | Classic spt cpe V-8 | 3,148 | 5,896 | |
| W27/Z03 | Classic Landau cpe V-6 | — | 6,009 | 9,342 |
| W27/Z03 | Classic Landau cpe V-8 | — | 6,149 | |
| W35 | Classic wgn 4d 2S V-6 | 3,167 | 6,035 | 35,730 |
| W35 | Classic wgn 4d 2S V-8 | 3,307 | 6,115 | |

### Full-size Chevrolet (wb 116.0)

| | | Wght | Price | Prod |
|---|---|---|---|---|
| L35 | Impala wgn 4d 3S V-8 | 3,924 | 7,186 | 6,767 |
| L35 | Impala wgn 4d 2S V-8 | 3,892 | 7,041 | 11,203 |
| L47 | Impala spt cpe V-6 | 3,344 | 6,535 | 10,756 |
| L47 | Impala spt cpe V-8 | 3,452 | 6,615 | |
| L69 | Impala sdn 4d V-6 | 3,360 | 6,650 | 70,801 |
| L69 | Impala sdn 4d V-8 | 3,468 | 6,730 | |
| N35 | Caprice Clsc wgn 4d 3S V-8 | 3,962 | 7,536 | 13,431 |
| N35 | Caprice Clsc wgn 4d 2S V-8 | 3,930 | 7,369 | 9,873 |

### Full-size Chevrolet (wb 116.0)

| | | Wght | Price | Prod |
|---|---|---|---|---|
| N47 | Caprice Clsc cpe V-6 | 3,376 | 6,946 | 13,919 |
| N47 | Caprice Clsc cpe V-8 | 3,484 | 7,026 | |
| N47/Z03 | Caprice Clsc Lndu cpe V-6 | — | 7,400 | 8,857 |
| N47/Z03 | Caprice Clsc Lndu cpe V-8 | — | 7,480 | |
| N69 | Caprice Clsic sdn 4d V-6/V-8 | — | — | 91,208 |

### Monte Carlo (wb 108.1)

| | | Wght | Price | Prod |
|---|---|---|---|---|
| Z37 | spt cpe V-6 | 3,104 | 6,524 | 116,580 |
| Z37 | spt cpe V-8 | 3,219 | 6,604 | |
| Z37/Z03 | Landau cpe V-6 | — | 6,772 | 32,262 |
| Z37/Z03 | Landau cpe V-8 | — | 6,852 | |

| 1980 Engines | bore × stroke | bhp | availability |
|---|---|---|---|
| I-4, 97.6 | 3.23 × 2.98 | 70 | S-Chevt |
| I-4, 97.6 | 3.23 × 2.98 | 74 | O-Chevt |
| I-4, 151.0 | 4.00 × 3.00 | 86 | S-Monza |
| I-4, 151.0 | 4.00 × 3.00 | 90 | S-Citation |
| V-6, 173.0 | 3.50 × 3.00 | 115 | O-Citation |
| V-6, 229.0 | 3.74 × 3.48 | 115 | S-Mal, Cam, MC, Chevr exc wgn |
| V-6, 231.0 | 3.80 × 3.40 | 110 | O-Cam, Monza, MC, Chevr exc wgn |
| V-6T, 231.0 | 3.80 × 3.40 | 170 | O-MC |
| V-8, 267.0 | 3.50 × 3.48 | 120 | S-Mal, Cam, MC, Chevr |
| V-8, 305.0 | 3.74 × 3.48 | 155 | O-Mal, Cam, MC, Chevr |
| V-8, 350.0 | 4.00 × 3.48 | 190 | S-Camaro Z28; O-other Cam |
| V-8D, 350.0 | 4.06 × 3.39 | 105 | O-Chevr wgn |

## 1981

### Chevette (wb 94.3; 4d-97.3)

| | | Wght | Price | Prod |
|---|---|---|---|---|
| B08 | htchbk sdn 2d | 2,000 | 5,255 | 114,621 |
| B68 | htchbk sdn 4d | 2,063 | 5,394 | 250,616 |
| J08 | Scooter htchbk 2d | 1,945 | 4,695 | 55,211 |
| B08 | Diesel htchbk sdn 2d | — | — | 4,252 |
| B68 | Diesel htchbk sdn 4d | — | — | 8,900 |

### Citation (wb 104.9)

| | | Wght | Price | Prod |
|---|---|---|---|---|
| X08 | htchbk sdn 2d I-4 | 2,404 | 6,270 | 113,983 |
| X08 | htchbk sdn 2d V-6 | 2,459 | 6,395 | |
| X68 | htchbk sdn 4d I-4 | 2,432 | 6,404 | 299,396 |
| X68 | htchbk sdn 4d V-6 | 2,487 | 6,529 | |

### Camaro (wb 108.0)

| | | Wght | Price | Prod |
|---|---|---|---|---|
| P87 | spt cpe V-6 | 3,222 | 6,780 | 62,614 |
| P87 | spt cpe V-8 | 3,392 | 6,830 | |
| S87 | Berlinetta cpe V-6 | 3,275 | 7,576 | 20,253 |
| S87 | Berlinetta cpe V-8 | 3,445 | 7,626 | |
| P87 | Z28 spt cpe V-8 | — | 8,263 | 43,272 |

### Malibu (wb 108.1)

| | | Wght | Price | Prod |
|---|---|---|---|---|
| T69 | sdn 4d V-6 | 3,028 | 6,614 | 60,643 |
| T69 | sdn 4d V-8 | 3,194 | 6,664 | |
| T27 | spt cpe V-6 | 3,037 | 6,498 | 15,834 |
| T27 | spt cpe V-8 | 3,199 | 6,548 | |
| T35 | wgn 4d 2S V-6 | 3,201 | 6,792 | 29,387 |
| T35 | wgn 4d 2S V-8 | 3,369 | 6,842 | |
| W69 | Classic sdn 4d V-6 | 3,059 | 6,961 | 80,908 |
| W69 | Classic sdn 4d V-8 | 3,225 | 7,011 | |
| W27 | Classic spt cpe V-6 | 3,065 | 6,828 | 14,255 |
| W27 | Classic spt cpe V-8 | 3,227 | 6,878 | |
| W27/Z03 | Classic Landau cpe V-6 | — | 7,092 | 4,622 |
| W27/Z03 | Classic Landau cpe V-8 | — | 7,142 | |

# Chevrolet

| Malibu (wb 108.1) | | Wght | Price | Prod |
|---|---|---|---|---|
| W35 | Classic wgn 4d 2S V-6 | 3,222 | 7,069 | 36,798 |
| W35 | Classic wgn 4d 2S V-8 | 3,390 | 7,119 | |
| **Full-size Chevrolet (wb 116.0)** | | | | |
| L35/AQ4 | Impala wgn 4d 3S V-8 | — | 7,765 | 8,462 |
| L35 | Impala wgn 4d 2S V-8 | 3,897 | 7,624 | 11,345 |
| L47 | Impala spt cpe V-6 | 3,326 | 7,129 | 6,067 |
| L47 | Impala spt cpe V-8 | 3,458 | 7,179 | |
| L69 | Impala sdn 4d V-6 | 3,354 | 7,241 | 60,090 |
| L69 | Impala sdn 4d V-8 | 3,486 | 7,291 | |
| N35/AQ4 | Caprice Clsc wgn 4d 3S V-8 | — | 8,112 | 16,348 |
| N35 | Caprice Clsc wgn 4d 2S V-8 | 3,940 | 7,948 | 11,184 |
| N47 | Caprice Clsc cpe V-6 | 3,363 | 7,534 | 9,741 |
| N47 | Caprice Clsc cpe V-8 | 3,495 | 7,584 | |
| N47/Z03 | Caprice Clsc Lndu cpe V-6 | — | 7,990 | 6,615 |
| N47/Z03 | Caprice Clsc Lndu cpe V-8 | — | 8,040 | |
| N69 | Caprice Classic sdn 4d V-6 | 3,400 | 7,667 | 89,573 |
| N69 | Caprice Classic sdn 4d V-8 | 3,532 | 7,717 | |
| **Monte Carlo (wb 108.1)** | | | | |
| Z37 | spt cpe V-6 | 3,102 | 7,299 | 149,659 |
| Z37 | spt cpe V-8 | 3,228 | 7,349 | |
| Z37/Z03 | Landau cpe V-6 | — | 8,006 | 38,191 |
| Z37/Z03 | Landau cpe V-8 | — | 8,056 | |

| 1981 Engines | bore × stroke | bhp | availability |
|---|---|---|---|
| I-4, 97.6 | 3.23 × 2.98 | 70 | S-Chevette |
| I-4D, 111.0 | 3.31 × 3.23 | 51 | O-late Chevette |
| I-4, 151.0 | 4.00 × 3.00 | 84 | S-Citation |
| V-6, 173.0 | 3.50 × 2.99 | 110 | O-Citation |
| V-6, 173.0 | 3.50 × 2.99 | 135 | O-Citation |
| V-6, 229.0 | 3.74 × 3.48 | 110 | S-Cam, Mal, MC, Chevr cpe/sdn |
| V-6, 231.0 | 3.80 × 3.40 | 110 | S-Calif, Cam, Mal, MC, Chevr cpe/sdn |
| V-6T, 231.0 | 3.80 × 3.40 | 170 | O-Monte Carlo |
| V-8, 267.0 | 3.50 × 3.48 | 115 | O-Cam, Mal, MC, Chevr |
| V-8, 305.0 | 3.74 × 3.48 | 150 | S-Chevr wgn; O-Cam, Mal, MC, Chevrolet |
| V-8, 305.0 | 3.74 × 3.48 | 165 | S-Camaro Z28 |
| V-8, 350.0 | 4.00 × 3.48 | 175 | O-Camaro Z28 |
| V-8D, 350.0 | 4.06 × 3.39 | 105 | O-Chevrolet |

## 1982

| Chevette (wb 94.3; 4d-97.3) | | Wght | Price | Prod |
|---|---|---|---|---|
| B08 | htchbk sdn 2d | 2,004 | 5,513 | 51,431 |
| B68 | htchbk sdn 4d | 2,064 | 5,660 | 111,661 |
| J08 | Scooter htchbk 2d | 1,959 | 4,997 | 31,281 |
| J68 | Scooter htchbk 4d | 2,006 | 5,238 | 21,742 |
| B08/Z90 | Diesel htchbk sdn 2d | — | 6,579 | 4,874 |
| B68/Z90 | Diesel htchbk sdn 4d | — | 6,727 | 11,819 |
| **Cavalier (wb 101.2)** | | | | |
| D27 | cpe | 2,318 | 6,966 | 30,245 |
| E77 | htchbk cpe | 2,389 | 7,199 | 22,114 |
| D69 | sdn 4d | 2,372 | 7,137 | 52,941 |
| D35 | wgn 4d | 2,432 | 7,354 | 30,853 |
| D27/Z11 | Cadet cpe | — | 6,278 | 2,281 |
| D69/Z11 | Cadet sdn 4d | — | 6,433 | 9,511 |
| D35/Z11 | Cadet wgn 4d | — | 6,704 | 4,754 |
| D27/Z12 | CL cpe | 2,315 | 7,944 | 6,063 |
| E77/Z12 | CL htchbk cpe | 2,381 | 8,281 | 12,792 |
| D69/Z12 | CL sdn 4d | 2,362 | 8,137 | 15,916 |

| Cavalier (wb 101.2) | | Wght | Price | Prod |
|---|---|---|---|---|
| D35/Z12 | CL wgn 4d | 2,422 | 8,452 | 7,587 |
| **Citation (wb 104.9)** | | | | |
| H11 | cpe I-4 | — | 6,297 | 9,102 |
| H11 | cpe V-6 | — | 6,515 | |
| X08 | htchbk sdn 2d I-4 | 2,442 | 6,754 | 29,613 |
| X08 | htchbk sdn 2d V-6 | — | 6,972 | |
| X68 | htchbk sdn 4d I-4 | 2,409 | 6,899 | 126,932 |
| X68 | htchbk sdn 4d V-6 | — | 7,024 | |
| **Camaro (wb 101.0)** | | | | |
| P87 | spt cpe I-4 | — | 7,631 | 78,761 |
| P87 | spt cpe V-6 | — | 7,755 | |
| P87 | spt cpe V-8 | — | 7,925 | |
| S87 | Berlinetta cpe V-6 | 2,940 | 9,266 | 39,744 |
| S87 | Berlinetta cpe V-8 | — | 9,436 | |
| P87 | Z28 spt cpe V-8 | 2,870 | 9,700 | 63,563 |
| **Celebrity (wb 104.9)** | | | | |
| W27 | cpe I-4 | 2,691 | 8,313 | 19,629 |
| W27 | cpe V-6 | 2,751 | 8,438 | |
| W19 | sdn 4d I-4 | 2,734 | 8,463 | 72,701 |
| W19 | sdn 4d V-6 | 2,794 | 8,588 | |
| **Malibu (wb 108.1)** | | | | |
| W69 | Classic sdn 4d V-6 | 3,091 | 8,137 | 70,793 |
| W69 | Classic sdn 4d V-8 | — | 8,207 | |
| W35 | Classic wgn 4d 2S V-6 | 3,240 | 8,265 | 45,332 |
| W35 | Classic wgn 4d 2S V-8 | — | 8,335 | |
| **Full-size Chevrolet (wb 116.0)** | | | | |
| L35/AQ4 | Impala wgn 4d 3S V-8 | 4,050 | 8,670 | 6,245 |
| L35 | Impala wgn 4d 2S V-8 | 3,930 | 8,516 | 10,654 |
| L69 | Impala sdn 4d V-6 | 3,361 | 7,918 | 47,780 |
| L69 | Impala sdn 4d V-8 | — | 7,988 | |
| N35/AQ4 | Caprice Clsc wgn 4d 3S V-8 | 4,010 | 9,051 | 25,385 |
| N47 | Caprice Clsc spt cpe V-6 | 3,373 | 8,221 | 11,999 |
| N47 | Caprice Clsc spt cpe V-8 | — | 8,291 | |
| N69 | Caprice Classic sdn 4d V-6 | 3,410 | 8,367 | 86,126 |
| N69 | Caprice Classic sdn 4d V-8 | — | 8.437 | |
| **Monte Carlo (wb 108.1)** | | | | |
| Z37 | spt cpe V-6 | 3,190 | 8,177 | 92,392 |
| Z37 | spt cpe V-8 | — | 8,247 | |

| 1982 Engines | bore × stroke | bhp | availability |
|---|---|---|---|
| I-4, 97.6 | 3.23 × 2.98 | 65 | S-Chevette |
| I-4D, 111.0 | 3.36 × 3.28 | 51 | O-Chevette |
| I-4, 112.0 | 3.50 × 2.91 | 88 | S-Cavalier |
| I-4, 151.0 | 4.00 × 3.00 | 90 | S-Cit, Camaro, Celebrity |
| I-4, 122.0 | 3.50 × 2.15 | 90 | O-Cavalier |
| V-6, 173.0 | 3.50 × 2.99 | 112 | O-Citation, Celebrity |
| V-6, 173.0 | 3.50 × 2.99 | 135 | O-Citation |
| V-6, 229.0 | 3.74 × 3.48 | 110 | S-Mal, MC, Chevr cpe/sdn |
| V-6, 231.0 | 3.80 × 3.40 | 110 | S-Calif, Chevrolet |
| V-6D, 262.0 | 4.06 × 3.39 | 85 | O-Malibu, Monte Carlo |
| V-8, 267.0 | 3.50 × 3.48 | 115 | S-Chevr wag; O-Mal, MC, Chevrolet |
| V-8, 305.0 | 3.74 × 3.48 | 150 | S-Cam Z28; O-Cam, Mal, MC, Chevrolet |
| V-8, 305.0 | 3.74 × 3.48 | 165 | O-Camaro Z28 |
| V-8D, 350.0 | 4.06 × 3.39 | 105 | O-Chevr, Malibu, MC |

# Chevrolet

## 1983

### Chevette (wb 94.3; 4d-97.3)

| | | Wght | Price | Prod |
|---|---|---|---|---|
| B08 | htchbk sdn 2d | 2,088 | 5,469 | 37,537 |
| B68 | htchbk sdn 4d | 2,148 | 5,616 | 81,297 |
| J08 | Scooter htchbk 2d | 2,029 | 4,997 | 33,488 |
| J68 | Scooter htchbk 4d | 2,098 | 5,333 | 15,303 |
| B08/Z90 | Diesel htchbk sdn 2d | — | 6,535 | 439 |
| B68/Z90 | Diesel htchbk sdn 4d | — | 6,683 | 1,501 |

### Cavalier (wb 101.2)

| | | Wght | Price | Prod |
|---|---|---|---|---|
| C27 | cpe | 2,384 | 5,888 | 23,028 |
| C69 | sdn 4d | 2,403 | 5,999 | 33,333 |
| C35 | wgn 4d | 2,464 | 6,141 | 27,922 |
| D27 | CS cpe | 2,374 | 6,363 | 22,172 |
| E77 | CS htckbk cpe | 2,440 | 6,549 | 25,869 |
| D69 | CS sdn 4d | 2,425 | 6,484 | 52,802 |
| D35 | CS wgn 4d | 2,486 | 6,633 | 32,834 |
| D27/Z08 | CS conv cpe | — | 10,990 | 627 |

### Citation (wb 104.9)

| | | Wght | Price | Prod |
|---|---|---|---|---|
| H11 | cpe I-4 | 2,471 | 6,333 | 6,456 |
| H11 | cpe V-6 | 2,526 | 6,483 | |
| X08 | htchbk sdn 2d I-4 | 2,463 | 6,788 | 14,323 |
| X08 | htchbk sdn 2d V-6 | 2,518 | 6,938 | |
| X68 | htchbk sdn 4d I-4 | 2,511 | 6,934 | 71,405 |
| X68 | htchbk sdn 4d V-6 | 2,566 | 7,084 | |

### Camaro (wb 101.0)

| | | Wght | Price | Prod |
|---|---|---|---|---|
| P87 | spt cpe I-4 | — | 8,036 | 63,806 |
| P87 | spt cpe V-6 | 2,959 | 8,186 | |
| P87 | spt cpe V-8 | 3,116 | 8,386 | |
| S87 | Berlinetta cpe V-6 | 2,944 | 9,881 | 27,925 |
| S87 | Berlinetta cpe V-8 | 3,136 | 10,106 | |
| P87 | Z28 spt cpe V-8 | 3,061 | 10,336 | 62,100 |

### Celebrity (wb 104.9)

| | | Wght | Price | Prod |
|---|---|---|---|---|
| W27 | cpe I-4 | 2,710 | 8,059 | 19,221 |
| W27 | cpe V-6 | 2,770 | 8,209 | |
| W19 | sdn 4d I-4 | 2,730 | 8,209 | 120,608 |
| W19 | sdn 4d V-6 | 2,790 | 8,359 | |

### Malibu (wb 108.1)

| | | Wght | Price | Prod |
|---|---|---|---|---|
| W69 | Classic sdn 4d V-6 | 3,199 | 8,084 | 61,534 |
| W69 | Classic sdn 4d V-8 | 3,307 | 8,309 | |
| W35 | Classic wgn 4d 2S V-6 | 3,343 | 8,217 | 55,892 |
| W35 | Classic wgn 4d 2S V-8 | 3,470 | 8,442 | |

### Full-size Chevrolet (wb 116.0)

| | | Wght | Price | Prod |
|---|---|---|---|---|
| L69 | Impala sdn 4d V-6 | 3,490 | 8,331 | 45,154 |
| L69 | Impala sdn 4d V-8 | 3,594 | 8,556 | |
| N35 | Caprice Clsc wgn 4d 3S V-8 | 4,092 | 9,518 | 53,028 |
| N69 | Caprice Classic sdn 4d V-6 | 3,537 | 8,802 | 122,613 |
| N69 | Caprice Classic sdn 4d V-8 | 3,641 | 9,027 | |

### Monte Carlo (wb 108.1)

| | | Wght | Price | Prod |
|---|---|---|---|---|
| Z37 | spt cpe V-6 | 3,220 | 8,552 | 91,605 |
| Z37 | spt cpe V-8 | 3,328 | 8,777 | |
| Z37/Z65 | SS spt cpe V-8 | — | 10,474 | 4,714 |

### 1983 Engines

| | bore × stroke | bhp | availability |
|---|---|---|---|
| I-4, 97.6 | 3.23 × 2.98 | 65 | S-Chevette |
| I-4D, 111.0 | 3.31 × 3.23 | 51 | O-Chevette |
| I-4, 121.0 | 3.50 × 3.15 | 88 | S-Cavalier |
| I-4, 151.0 | 4.00 × 3.00 | 92 | S-Cit, Cam, Celeb |
| V-6, 173.0 | 3.50 × 2.99 | 112 | S-Cam Berlinetta; O-Cam, Citation, Celebrity |
| V-6, 173.0 | 3.50 × 2.99 | 135 | O-Citation |
| V-6, 229.0 | 3.74 × 3.48 | 110 | S-Mal, MC, Chevr cpe/sdn |
| V-6, 231.0 | 3.80 × 3.40 | 110 | S-Calif. Chevrolet |
| V-6D, 262.0 | 4.06 × 3.39 | 85 | O-Malibu, MC, Celebrity |
| V-8, 305.0 | 3.74 × 3.48 | 150 | S-Cam Z28, Chevr wgn; O-Cam, Malibu, MC, Chevr |
| V-8, 305.0 | 3.74 × 3.48 | 175 | S-MC SS; O-Cam |
| V-8D, 350.0 | 4.06 × 3.39 | 105 | O-Chevr, Malibu, MC |

## 1984

### Chevette (wb 94.3; 4d-97.3)

| | | Wght | Price | Prod |
|---|---|---|---|---|
| J08 | htchbk sdn 2d | 1,999 | 4,997 | 66,446 |
| J68 | htchbk sdn 4d | 2,051 | 5,333 | 28,466 |
| B08 | CS htchbk 2d | 2,038 | 5,489 | 47,032 |
| B68 | CS htchbk 4d | 2,102 | 5,636 | 94,897 |
| J08/Z90 | Diesel htchbk sdn 2d | — | 5,500 | 1,495 |
| J68/Z90 | Diesel htchbk sdn 4d | — | 5,851 | 1,180 |
| B08/Z90 | CS diesel htchbk sdn 2d | 2,261 | 5,999 | 1,000 |
| B68/Z90 | CS diesel htchbk sdn 4d | 2,320 | 6,161 | 3,384 |

### Cavalier (wb 101.2)

| | | Wght | Price | Prod |
|---|---|---|---|---|
| C69 | sdn 4d | 2,386 | 6,222 | 90,023 |
| C35 | wgn 4d | 2,455 | 6,375 | 50,718 |
| D69 | CS sdn 4d | 2,398 | 6,666 | 110,295 |
| D35 | CS wgn 4d | 2,468 | 6,821 | 58,739 |
| E27 | Type 10 cpe | 2,367 | 6,477 | 103,204 |
| E77 | Type 10 htchbk cpe | 2,418 | 6,654 | 44,146 |
| E27/Z08 | Type 10 conv cpe | 2,583 | 11,299 | 5,486 |

### Citation II (wb 104.9)

| | | Wght | Price | Prod |
|---|---|---|---|---|
| H11 | cpe I-4 | 2,454 | 6,445 | 4,936 |
| H11 | cpe V-6 | 2,529 | 6,695 | |
| X08 | htchbk sdn 2d I-4 | 2,494 | 6,900 | 8,783 |
| X08 | htchbk sdn 2d V-6 | 2,569 | 7,150 | |
| X68 | htchbk sdn 4d I-4 | 2,506 | 7,046 | 83,486 |
| X68 | htchbk sdn 4d V-6 | 2,581 | 7,296 | |

### Camaro (wb 101.0)

| | | Wght | Price | Prod |
|---|---|---|---|---|
| P87 | spt cpe I-4 | 2,899 | 7,995 | 127,292 |
| P87 | spt cpe V-6 | 2,932 | 8,245 | |
| P87 | spt cpe V-8 | 3,112 | 8,545 | |
| S87 | Berlinetta cpe V-6 | 2,944 | 10,895 | 33,400 |
| S87 | Berlinetta cpe V-8 | 3,126 | 11,270 | |
| P87 | Z28 spt cpe V-8 | 3,135 | 10,620 | 100,416 |

### Celebrity (wb 104.9)

| | | Wght | Price | Prod |
|---|---|---|---|---|
| W27 | cpe I-4 | 2,663 | 7,711 | 29,191 |
| W27 | cpe V-6 | 2,781 | 7,961 | |
| W19 | sdn 4d I-4 | 2,703 | 7,890 | 200,259 |
| W19 | sdn 4d V-6 | 2,816 | 8,140 | |
| W35 | wgn 4d 2S I-4 | 2,857 | 8,214 | 48,295 |
| W35 | wgn 4d 2S V-6 | 2,964 | 8,464 | |
| W35/AQ4 | wgn 4d 3S I-4 | — | 8,429 | 31,543 |
| W35/AQ4 | wgn 4d 3S V-6 | — | 8,679 | |

### Full-size Chevrolet (wb 116.0)

| | | Wght | Price | Prod |
|---|---|---|---|---|
| L69 | Impala sdn 4d V-6 | 3,489 | 8,895 | 55,296 |
| L69 | Impala sdn 4d V-8 | 3,628 | 9,270 | |
| N35 | Caprice Clsc wgn 4d 3S V-8 | 4,053 | 10,210 | 65,688 |
| N47 | Caprice Clsc spt cpe V-6 | 3,633 | 9,253 | 19,541 |
| N47 | Caprice Clsc spt cpe V-8 | 3,834 | 9,628 | |
| N69 | Caprice Classic sdn 4d V-6 | 3,532 | 9,400 | 135,970 |
| N69 | Caprice Classic sdn 4d V-8 | 3,662 | 9,775 | |

### Monte Carlo (wb 108.1)

| | | Wght | Price | Prod |
|---|---|---|---|---|
| Z37 | spt cpe V-6 | 3,176 | 8,936 | 112,730 |

# Chevrolet

| Monte Carlo (wb 108.1) | Wght | Price | Prod |
|---|---|---|---|
| Z37   spt cpe V-8 | 3,292 | 9,311 | |
| Z37/Z65 SS spt cpe V-8 | 3,434 | 10,700 | 24,050 |

| 1984 Engines | bore × stroke | bhp | availability |
|---|---|---|---|
| I-4, 97.6 | 3.23 × 2.98 | 65 | S-Chevette |
| I-4D, 111.0 | 3.31 × 3.23 | 51 | O-Chevette |
| I-4, 121.0 | 3.50 × 3.15 | 86 | S-Cavalier |
| I-4, 151.0 | 4.00 × 3.00 | 92 | S-Citation, Camaro, Celeb |
| V-6, 173.0 | 3.50 × 2.99 | 107 | S-Cam Berlinetta; O-Cam |
| V-6, 173.0 | 3.50 × 2.99 | 112 | O-Citation, Celeb |
| V-6, 173.0 | 3.50 × 2.99 | 130/135 | O-Citation, Celeb |
| V-6, 229.0 | 3.74 × 3.48 | 110 | S-MC, Chevr cpe/sdn |
| V-6, 231.0 | 3.80 × 3.40 | 110 | S-Calif. Chevr |
| V-6D, 262.0 | 4.06 × 3.39 | 85 | O-Celebrity |
| V-8, 305.0 | 3.74 × 3.48 | 150 | S-Cam Z28, Chevr wgn; O Cam, Monte Carlo, Chevrolet |
| V-8, 305.0 | 3.74 × 3.48 | 180 | S-Monte Carlo SS |
| V-8, 305.0 | 3.74 × 3.48 | 190 | O-Camaro Z28 |
| V-8D, 350.0 | 4.06 × 3.39 | 105 | O-Chevr, MC |

## 1985

| Chevette (wb 94.3; 4d-97.3) | Wght | Price | Prod |
|---|---|---|---|
| B08   CS htchbk 2d | 2,085 | 5,340 | 57,706 |
| B68   CS htchbk 4d | 2,145 | 5,690 | 65,128 |
| B08/Z90 CS diesel htchbk sdn 2d | 2,261 | 5,850 | 203 |
| B68/Z90 CS diesel htchbk sdn 4d | 2,320 | 6,215 | 462 |

| Cavalier (wb 101.2) | | | |
|---|---|---|---|
| C69   sdn 4d | 2,339 | 6,477 | 86,597 |
| C35   wgn 4d | 2,409 | 6,633 | 34,581 |
| D69   CS sdn 4d | 2,352 | 6,900 | 93,386 |
| D35   CS wgn 4d | 2,420 | 7,066 | 33,551 |
| E27   Type 10 cpe | 2,320 | 6,737 | 106,021 |
| E77   Type 10 htchbk cpe | 2,382 | 6,919 | 25,508 |
| E27/Z08 Type 10 conv cpe | 2,458 | 11,693 | 4,108 |

| Citation II (wb 104.9) | | | |
|---|---|---|---|
| X08   htchbk sdn 2d I-4 | 2,499 | 6,940 | 7,443 |
| X08   htchbk sdn 2d V-6 | 2,568 | 7,200 | |
| X68   htchbk sdn 4d I-4 | 2,535 | 7,090 | 55,279 |
| X68   htchbk sdn 4d V-6 | 2,603 | 7,350 | |

| Camaro (wb 101.0) | | | |
|---|---|---|---|
| P87   spt cpe I-4 | 2,881 | 8,363 | 97,966 |
| P87   spt cpe V-6 | 2,977 | 8,698 | |
| P87   spt cpe V-8 | 3,177 | 8,998 | |
| S87   Berlinetta cpe V-6 | 3,056 | 11,060 | 13,649 |
| S87   Berlinetta cpe V-8 | 3,221 | 11,360 | |
| P87/Z28 Z28 spt cpe V-8 | 3,251 | 11,060 | 47,022 |
| P87/B4Z IROC-Z spt cpe V-8 | 3,319 | 11,739 | 21,177 |

| Celebrity (wb 104.9) | | | |
|---|---|---|---|
| W27   cpe I-4 | 2,689 | 8,102 | 29,010 |
| W27   cpe V-6 | 2,790 | 8,362 | |
| W19   sdn 4d I-4 | 2,722 | 8,288 | 239,763 |
| W19   sdn 4d V-6 | 2,827 | 8,548 | |
| W35   wgn 4d 2S I-4 | 2,857 | 8,479 | 45,602 |
| W35   wgn 4d 2S V-6 | 2,953 | 8,739 | |
| W35/AQ4 wgn 4d 3S I-4 | — | 8,699 | 40,547 |
| W35/AQ4 wgn 4d 3S V-6 | — | 8,959 | |

| Full-size Chevrolet (wb 116.0) | Wght | Price | Prod |
|---|---|---|---|
| L69   Impala sdn 4d V-6 | 3,508 | 9,519 | 53,438 |
| L69   Impala sdn 4d V-8 | 3,634 | 9,759 | |
| N35   Caprice Clsc wgn 4d 3S V-8 | 4,083 | 10,714 | 55,886 |
| N47   Caprice Classic cpe V-6 | 3,525 | 9,888 | 16,229 |
| N47   Caprice Classic cpe V-8 | 3,651 | 10,128 | |
| N69   Caprice Classic sdn 4d V-6 | 3,549 | 10,038 | 139,240 |
| N69   Caprice Classic sdn 4d V-8 | 3,674 | 10,278 | |

| Monte Carlo (wb 108.0) | | | |
|---|---|---|---|
| Z37   spt cpe V-6 | 3,139 | 9,540 | 83,573 |
| Z37   spt cpe V-8 | 3,245 | 9,780 | |
| Z37/Z65 SS spt cpe V-8 | 3,385 | 11,380 | 35,484 |

| 1985 Engines | bore × stroke | bhp | availability |
|---|---|---|---|
| I-4, 97.6 | 3.23 × 2.98 | 65 | S-Chevette |
| I-4D, 111.0 | 3.31 × 3.23 | 51 | O-Chevette |
| I-4, 121.0 | 3.50 × 3.15 | 85 | S-Cavalier |
| I-4, 151.0 | 4.00 × 3.00 | 88/92 | S-Cit, Camaro, Celeb |
| V-6, 173.0 | 3.50 × 2.99 | 112 | O-Citation, Celeb |
| V-6, 173.0 | 3.50 × 2.99 | 125/135 | S-Cam Berlinetta; O-late Cav, Cit, Camaro, Celeb |
| V-6, 262.0 | 4.00 × 3.48 | 130 | S-MC, Chevrolet |
| V-6D, 262.0 | 4.06 × 3.39 | 85 | O-Celeb |
| V-8, 305.0 | 3.74 × 3.48 | 150/165 | S-Cam Z28, Capr wgn; O-Cam, MC, Chevrolet |
| V-8, 305.0 | 3.74 × 3.48 | 180 | S-Monte Carlo SS |
| V-8, 305.0 | 3.74 × 3.48 | 190 | O-Camaro IROC-Z |
| V-8, 305.0 | 3.74 × 3.48 | 215 | O-Camaro Z28/IROC-Z |
| V-8D, 350.0 | 4.06 × 3.39 | 105 | O-Chevr |

## 1986

| Chevette (wb 94.3; 4d-97.3) | Wght | Price | Prod |
|---|---|---|---|
| B08   CS htchbk 2d | 2,080 | 5,645 | 48,756 |
| B68   CS htchbk 4d | 2,140 | 5,959 | 54,164 |
| B08/Z90 CS diesel sdn 2d | 2,261 | 6,152 | 124 |
| B68/Z90 CS diesel sdn 4d | 2,320 | 6,487 | 200 |

| Nova (wb 95.7) | | | |
|---|---|---|---|
| K19   sdn 4d | 2,163 | 7,435 | 124,961* |
| K68   htchbk sdn 4d | 2,205 | 7,669 | 42,788* |

*27,945 additional Novas were built late in the 1985 model year.

| Cavalier (wb 101.2) | | | |
|---|---|---|---|
| C27   cpe I-4 | 2,299 | 6,706 | 57,370 |
| C27   cpe V-6 | — | 7,316 | |
| C69   sdn 4d I-4 | 2,342 | 6,888 | 86,492 |
| C69   sdn 4d V-6 | — | 7,498 | |
| C35   wgn 4d I-4 | 2,412 | 7,047 | 30,490 |
| C35   wgn 4d V-6 | — | 7,657 | |
| D77   CS htchbk cpe I-4 | 2,375 | 7,373 | 8,046 |
| D77   CS htchbk cpe V-6 | — | 7,983 | |
| D69   CS sdn 4d I-4 | 2,355 | 7,350 | 89,168 |
| D69   CS sdn 4d V-6 | — | 7,960 | |
| D35   CS wgn 4d I-4 | 2,423 | 7,525 | 23,101 |
| D35   CS wgn 4d V-6 | — | 8,135 | |
| E27   RS cpe I-4 | 2,325 | 7,640 | 53,941 |
| E27   RS cpe V-6 | — | 8,250 | |
| E77   RS htckbk cpe I-4 | 2,387 | 7,830 | 7,504 |
| E77   RS htckbk cpe V-6 | — | 8,440 | |
| E69   RS sdn 4d I-4 | 2,367 | 7,811 | 17,361 |
| E69   RS sdn 4d V-6 | — | 8,451 | |

235

# Chevrolet

| Cavalier (wb 101.2) | | Wght | Price | Prod |
|---|---|---|---|---|
| E35 | RS wgn 4d I-4 | 2,440 | 7,979 | 6,252 |
| E35 | RS wgn 4d V-6 | — | 8,589 | |
| E67 | RS conv cpe I-4 | 2,444 | 12,530 | 5,785 |
| E67 | RS conv cpe V-6 | 2,642 | 13,140 | |
| F27 | Z24 spt cpe V-6 | 2,519 | 8,878 | 36,365 |
| F77 | Z24 htchbk cpe V-6 | 2,581 | 9,068 | 10,226 |
| **Camaro (wb 101.0)** | | | | |
| P87 | spt cpe I-4 | 2,900 | 8,935 | |
| P87 | spt cpe V-6 | 2,994 | 9,285 | 99,517 |
| P87 | spt cpe V-8 | 3,116 | 9,685 | |
| S87 | Berlinetta cpe V-6 | 3,063 | 11,902 | 4,479 |
| S87 | Berlinetta cpe V-8 | 3,116 | 12,302 | |
| P87/Z28 | Z28 spt cpe V-8 | 3,201 | 11,902 | 38,547 |
| P87/B4Z | IROC-Z spt cpe V-8 | 3,278 | 12,561 | 49,585 |
| **Celebrity (wb 104.9)** | | | | |
| W27 | cpe I-4 | 2,689 | 8,735 | 29,223 |
| W27 | cpe V-6 | 2,794 | 9,170 | |
| W19 | sdn 4d I-4 | 2,719 | 8,931 | 291,760 |
| W19 | sdn 4d V-6 | 2,824 | 9,366 | |
| W35 | wgn 4d 2S I-4 | 2,847 | 9,081 | 36,655 |
| W35 | wgn 4d 2S V-6 | 2,912 | 9,516 | |
| W35/AQ4 | wgn 4d 3S I-4 | 2,850 | 9,313 | 47,245 |
| W35/AQ4 | wgn 4d 3S V-6 | — | 9,748 | |
| **Caprice (wb 116.0)** | | | | |
| L69 | sdn 4d V-6 | 3,535 | 10,243 | 50,751 |
| L69 | sdn 4d V-8 | 3,628 | 10,633 | |
| N35 | Classic wgn 4d 3S V-8 | 4,095 | 11,511 | 45,183 |
| N47 | Classic spt cpe V-6 | 3,546 | 10,635 | 9,869 |
| N47 | Classic spt cpe V-8 | 3,638 | 11,025 | |
| N69 | Classic sdn 4d V-6 | 3,564 | 10,795 | 67,772 |
| N69 | Classic sdn 4d V-8 | 3,656 | 11,185 | |
| N69/B45 | Classic Brgm sdn 4d V-6 | 3,574 | 11,429 | 69,320 |
| N69/B45 | Classic Brgm sdn 4d V-8 | 3,667 | 11,819 | |
| N69/B45 | Classic LS Brgm sdn 4d V-6 | — | — | 2,117 |
| N69/B45 | Classic LS Brgm sdn 4d V-8 | — | — | |
| **Monte Carlo (wb 108.0)** | | | | |
| Z37 | spt cpe V-6 | 3,138 | 10,241 | 50,418 |
| Z37 | spt cpe V-8 | 3,244 | 10,631 | |
| Z37/Z09 | LS cpe V-6 | 3,138 | 10,421 | 27,428 |
| Z76/Z09 | LS cpe V-8 | — | 10,841 | |
| Z37/Z65 | SS spt cpe V-8 | 3,387 | 12,466 | 41,164 |
| Z37/Z65 | SS Aerocoupe V-8 | 3,440 | 14,191 | 200 |

| 1986 Engines | bore × stroke | bhp | availability |
|---|---|---|---|
| I-4, 97.0 | 3.19 × 3.03 | 74 | S-Nova |
| I-4, 97.6 | 3.23 × 2.98 | 65 | S-Chevette |
| I-4D, 111.0 | 3.31 × 3.23 | 51 | O-Chevette |
| I-4, 121.0 | 3.50 × 3.15 | 85 | S-Cavalier |
| I-4, 151.0 | 4.00 × 3.00 | 88/92 | S-Camaro, Celebrity |
| V-6, 173.0 | 3.50 × 2.99 | 112 | O-Celebrity |
| V-6, 173.0 | 3.50 × 2.99 | 120/135 | S-Cam Berlinetta, Cav Z24; O-Cav, Camaro, Celebrity |
| V-6, 262.0 | 4.00 × 3.48 | 140 | S-MC, Caprice |
| V-8, 305.0 | 3.74 × 3.48 | 150/155/165 | S-Cam Z28, Capr wgn; O-Cam, Monte Carlo, Caprice |
| V-8, 305.0 | 3.74 × 3.48 | 180 | S-Monte Carlo SS |
| V-8, 305.0 | 3.74 × 3.48 | 190 | O-Camaro IROC-Z |
| V-8, 305.0 | 3.74 × 3.48 | 215 | O-Camaro Z28/IROC-Z |

## 1987

| Chevette (wb 94.3; 4d-97.3) | | Wght | Price | Prod |
|---|---|---|---|---|
| B08 | CS htchbk 2d | 2,078 | 4,995 | 26,135 |
| B68 | CS htchbk 4d | 2,137 | 5,495 | 20,073 |
| **Nova (wb 95.7)** | | | | |
| K19 | sdn 4d | 2,206 | 8,258 | 123,782 |
| K68 | htchbk sdn 4d | 2,253 | 8,510 | 26,224 |
| **Cavalier (wb 101.2)** | | | | |
| C27 | cpe I-4 | 2,300 | 7,255 | 53,678 |
| C27 | cpe V-6 | — | 7,915 | |
| E27 | RS cpe I-4 | 2,360 | 8,318 | 36,353 |
| E27 | RS cpe V-6 | — | 8,978 | |
| F27 | Z24 spt cpe V-6 | 2,511 | 9,913 | 42,890 |
| D77 | CS htchbk cpe I-4 | 2,359 | 7,978 | 3,480 |
| D77 | CS htchbk cpe V-6 | — | 8,638 | |
| E77 | RS htchbk cpe I-4 | 2,408 | 8,520 | 2,818 |
| E77 | RS htchbk cpe V-6 | — | 9,180 | |
| F77 | Z24 htchbk cpe V-6 | 2,560 | 10,115 | 4,517 |
| C69 | sdn 4d I-4 | 2,345 | 7,449 | 84,445 |
| C69 | sdn 4d V-6 | — | 8,109 | |
| D69 | CS sdn 4d I-4 | 2,355 | 7,953 | 50,625 |
| D69 | CS sdn 4d V-6 | — | 8,613 | |
| E69 | RS sdn 4d I-4 | 2,397 | 8,499 | 15,482 |
| E69 | RS sdn 4d V-6 | — | 9,159 | |
| C35 | wgn 4d I-4 | 2,401 | 7,615 | 25,542 |
| C35 | wgn 4d V-6 | — | 8,275 | |
| D35 | CS wgn 4d I-4 | 2,411 | 8,140 | 15,023 |
| D35 | CS wgn 4d V-6 | — | 8,800 | |
| E35 | RS wgn 4d I-4 | 2,460 | 8,677 | 5,575 |
| E35 | RS wgn 4d V-6 | — | 9,337 | |
| E67 | RS conv cpe I-4 | 2,519 | 13,446 | 5,826 |
| E67 | RS conv cpe V-6 | — | 14,106 | |
| **Camaro (wb 101.0)** | | | | |
| P87 | spt cpe V-6 | 3,062 | 9,995 | 83,890 |
| P87 | spt cpe V-8 | 3,181 | 10,395 | |
| P87 | LT cpe V-6 | — | 11,517 | — |
| P87 | LT cpe V-8 | — | 11,917 | |
| P87/Z28 | Z28 spt cpe V-8 | 3,228 | 12,819 | 52,863 |
| P87/Z28 | IROC-Z spt cpe V-8 | — | 13,488 | |
| P67 | conv cpe V-8 | — | 14,794 | 263 |
| P67/Z28 | Z28 conv cpe V-8 | — | 17,218 | 744 |
| P67/Z28 | IROC-Z conv cpe V-8 | — | 17,917 | |
| **Corsica (wb 103.4)\*—8,973 built** | | | | |
| T69 | sdn 4d I-4 | 2,491 | 8,995 | — |
| T69 | sdn 4d V-6 | 2,609 | 9,655 | — |
| **Beretta (wb 103.4)\*—8,072 built** | | | | |
| V37 | cpe I-4 | 2,550 | 9,555 | |
| V37 | cpe V-6 | 2,648 | 10,215 | — |
| **Celebrity (wb 104.9)** | | | | |
| W27 | cpe I-4 | 2,685 | 9,995 | 18,198 |
| W27 | cpe V-6 | 2,769 | 10,605 | |
| W19 | sdn 4d I-4 | 2,715 | 10,265 | 273,864 |
| W19 | sdn 4d V-6 | 2,799 | 10,875 | |
| W35 | wgn 4d 2S I-4 | 2,847 | 10,425 | 33,894 |
| W35 | wgn 4d 2S V-6 | 2,931 | 11,035 | |
| W35/AQ4 | wgn 4d 3S I-4 | — | 10,672 | 36,568 |
| W35/AQ4 | wgn 4d 3S V-6 | — | 11,382 | |
| **Caprice (wb 116.0)** | | | | |
| L35 | wgn 4d 3S V-8 | 4,114 | 11,995 | 11,953 |
| N35 | Classic wgn 4d 3S V-8 | 4,125 | 12,586 | 28,387 |
| N47 | Classic cpe V-6 | 3,512 | 11,392 | 3,110 |
| N47 | Classic cpe V-8 | 3,605 | 11,802 | |

# Chevrolet

| Caprice (wb 116.0) | | Wght | Price | Prod |
|---|---|---|---|---|
| L69 | sdn 4d V-6 | 3,510 | 10,995 ⎤ | 56,266 |
| L69 | sdn 4d V-8 | 3,603 | 11,435 ⎦ | |
| N69 | Classic sdn 4d V-6 | 3,527 | 11,560 ⎤ | 53,802 |
| N69 | Classic sdn 4d V-8 | 3,620 | 12,000 ⎦ | |
| U69 | Classic Brgm sdn 4d V-6 | 3,576 | 12,549 ⎤ | 51,341 |
| U69 | Classic Brgm sdn 4d V-8 | 3,669 | 12,989 ⎦ | |
| U69/B6N | Classic LS Brgm sdn 4d V-6 | — | 13,805 ⎤ | 23,641 |
| U69/B6N | Classic LS Brgm sdn 4d V-8 | — | 14,245 ⎦ | |

| Monte Carlo (wb 108.0) | | | | |
|---|---|---|---|---|
| Z37 | LS cpe V-6 | 3,283 | 11,306 | |
| Z37 | LS cpe V-8 | 3,389 | 11,746 | 39,794 |
| Z37/Z65 | SS spt cpe V-8 | 3,473 | 13,463 | 33,199 |
| Z37/Z16 | SS Aerocoupe V-8 | 3,526 | 14,838 | 6,052 |

| 1987 Engines | bore × stroke | bhp | availability |
|---|---|---|---|
| I-4, 97.0 | 3.19 × 3.03 | 74 | S-Nova |
| I-4, 97.6 | 3.23 × 2.98 | 65 | S-Chevette |
| I-4, 121.0 | 3.50 × 3.15 | 90 | S-Cav, Corsica, Beretta |
| I-4, 151.0 | 4.00 × 3.00 | 98 | S-Celeb |
| V-6, 173.0 | 3.50 × 2.99 | 125/130 | S-Camaro, Cav Z24; O-Cav, Celebrity, Cors, Beretta |
| V-6, 262.0 | 4.00 × 3.48 | 140/145 | S-MC, Caprice cpe/sdn |
| V-8, 305.0 | 3.74 × 3.48 | 150/170 | S-Cam Z28; O-Cam, MC, Caprice |
| V-8, 305.0 | 3.74 × 3.48 | 180 | S-Monte Carlo SS |
| V-8, 305.0 | 3.74 × 3.48 | 215 | O-Camaro Z28/IROC-Z |
| V-8, 307.0 | 3.80 × 3.38 | 140 | S-Capr wgn |
| V-8, 350.0 | 4.00 × 3.48 | 225 | O-Camaro IROC-Z |

* Corsica and Beretta were actually early 1988 models, introduced during the 1987 model year.

## 1988

| Nova (wb 95.7) | | Wght | Price | Prod |
|---|---|---|---|---|
| K19 | sdn 4d | 2,211 | 8,795 | 87,263 |
| K68 | htchbk sdn 4d | 2,257 | 9,050 | 18,570 |
| L19 | twin-cam sdn 4d | — | 11,395 | 3,300 |

| Cavalier (wb 101.2) | | | | |
|---|---|---|---|---|
| C37 | cpe I-4 | 2,359 | 8,120 | 34,470 |
| C69 | sdn 4d I-4 | 2,363 | 8,195 | 107,438 |
| C35 | wgn 4d I-4 | 2,413 | 8,490 ⎤ | 29,806 |
| C35 | wgn 4d V-6 | — | 9,150 ⎦ | |
| C37/WV9 | VL cpe | — | 6,995 | 43,611 |
| E37 | RS cpe I-4 | 2,371 | 9,175 | 24,359 |
| E69 | RS sdn 4d I-4 | 2,414 | 9,385 | 18,852 |
| F37 | Z24 cpe V-6 | 2,558 | 10,725 | 55,658 |
| F67 | Z24 conv cpe V-6 | 2,665 | 15,990 | 8,745 |

| Camaro (wb 101.0) | | | | |
|---|---|---|---|---|
| P87 | spt cpe V-6 | 3,054 | 10,995 ⎤ | 66,605 |
| P87 | spt cpe V-8 | 3,228 | 11,395 ⎦ | |
| P87/Z28 | IROC-Z spt cpe V-8 | 3,229 | 13,490 | 24,050 |
| P87/Z08 | conv cpe V-8 | 3,350 | 16,255 | 1,859 |
| P87/Z08 | IROC-Z conv cpe V-8 | 3,352 | 18,015 | 3,761 |

| Corsica (wb 103.4)—291,163 built | | | | |
|---|---|---|---|---|
| T69 | sdn 4d I-4 | 2,589 | 9,555 | — |
| T69 | sdn 4d V-6 | 2,688 | 10,215 | — |

| Beretta (wb 103.4) (includes 3,814 GTUs) | | Wght | Price | Prod |
|---|---|---|---|---|
| V37 | cpe I-4 | 2,608 | 10,135 ⎤ | 275,098 |
| V37 | cpe V-6 | 2,707 | 10,795 ⎦ | |

| Celebrity (wb 104.9) | | | | |
|---|---|---|---|---|
| W27 | cpe I-4 | 2,727 | 10,585 ⎤ | 11,909 |
| W27 | cpe V-6 | 2,793 | 11,195 ⎦ | |
| W19 | sdn 4d I-4 | 2,765 | 11,025 ⎤ | 195,205 |
| W19 | sdn 4d V-6 | 2,833 | 11,025 ⎦ | |
| W35/B5E | wgn 4d 2S I-4 | 2,903 | 11,350 ⎤ | 23,759 |
| W35/B5E | wgn 4d 2S V-6 | 2,970 | 11,960 ⎦ | |
| W35/AQ4 | wgn 4d 3S I-4 | — | 11,590 ⎤ | 27,583 |
| W35/AQ4 | wgn 4d 3S V-6 | — | 12,200 ⎦ | |

| Caprice (wb 116.0) | | | | |
|---|---|---|---|---|
| L69 | sdn 4d V-6 | 3,540 | 12,030 ⎤ | 60,900 |
| L69 | sdn 4d V-8 | 3,633 | 12,470 ⎦ | |
| N69 | Classic sdn 4d V-6 | 3,556 | 12,575 ⎤ | 42,292 |
| N69 | Classic sdn 4d V-8 | 3,649 | 13,015 ⎦ | |
| U69 | Classic Brgm sdn 4d V-6 | 3,607 | 13,645 ⎤ | 33,685 |
| U69 | Classic Brgm sdn 4d V-8 | 3,700 | 14,085 ⎦ | |
| U69/B6N | Classic LS Brgm sdn 4d V-6 | — | 14,820 ⎤ | 21,586 |
| U69/B6N | Classic LS Brgm sdn 4d V-8 | — | 15,260 ⎦ | |
| N35 | Classic wgn 4d 3S V-8 | 4,158 | 14,340 | 30,645 |

| Monte Carlo (wb 108.0) | | | | |
|---|---|---|---|---|
| Z37 | LS cpe V-6 | 3,212 | 12,330 ⎤ | 13,970 |
| Z37 | LS cpe V-8 | 3,267 | 12,770 ⎦ | |
| Z37/Z65 | SS cpe V-8 | 3,239 | 14,320 | 16,204 |

| 1988 Engines | bore × stroke | bhp | availability |
|---|---|---|---|
| I-4, 97.0 | 3.19 × 3.03 | 74 | S-Nova |
| I-4, 97.0 | 3.19 × 3.03 | 110 | O-Nova (twin-cam) |
| I-4, 121.0 | 3.50 × 3.15 | 90 | S-Cav, Corsica, Beretta |
| I-4, 151.0 | 4.00 × 3.00 | 98 | S-Celeb |
| V-6, 173.0 | 3.50 × 2.99 | 120/135 | S-Camaro, Cav Z24; O-Cav wgn, Celeb, Cors, Beretta |
| V-6, 262.0 | 4.00 × 3.48 | 140/145 | S-MC, Caprice cpe/sdn |
| V-8, 305.0 | 3.74 × 3.48 | 150/170 | S-Cam IROC-Z; O-Cam, MC, Caprice |
| V-8, 305.0 | 3.74 × 3.48 | 180 | S-MC SS |
| V-8, 305.0 | 3.74 × 3.48 | 220 | O-Camaro IROC-Z |
| V-8, 307.0 | 3.80 × 3.38 | 140 | S-Caprice wgn |
| V-8, 350.0 | 4.00 × 3.48 | 230 | O-Camaro IROC-Z |

## 1989

| Cavalier (wb 101.2) | | Wght | Price | Prod |
|---|---|---|---|---|
| C37 | cpe I-4 | 2,418 | 8,395 | 65,971 |
| C69 | sdn 4d I-4 | 2,423 | 8,595 | 107,569 |
| C35 | wgn 4d I-4 | 2,478 | 8,975 ⎤ | 28,549 |
| C35 | wgn 4d V-6 | 2,566 | 9,635 ⎦ | |
| C37/WV9 | VL cpe I-4 | — | 7,375 | 91,931 |
| F37 | Z24 cpe V-6 | — | 11,325 | 69,531 |
| F67 | Z24 conv cpe V-6 | 2,729 | 16,615 | 13,075 |

| Camaro (wb 101.0) | | | | |
|---|---|---|---|---|
| P87 | RS htchbk cpe V-6 | 3,082 | 11,495 ⎤ | 83,487 |
| P87 | RS htchbk cpe V-8 | 3,285 | 11,895 ⎦ | |
| P87/Z28 | IROC-Z cpe V-8 | 3,264 | 14,145 | 20,067 |
| P67 | RS conv cpe V-8 | 3,116 | 16,995 | 3,245 |
| P67/Z28 | IROC-Z conv cpe V-8 | — | 18,945 | 3,940 |

| Corsica (wb 103.4) | | | | |
|---|---|---|---|---|
| T69 | sdn 4d I-4 | 2,595 | 9,985 | 190,236 |

# Chevrolet

| Corsica (wb 103.4) | | Wght | Price | Prod |
|---|---|---|---|---|
| T69 | sdn 4d V-6 | 2,690 | 10,645 | |
| T68 | htchbk sdn 4d I-4 | 2,648 | 10,375 | 26,578 |
| T68 | htchbk sdn 4d V-6 | — | 11,035 | |
| Z69 | LTZ sdn 4d V-6 | — | 12,825 | 14,353 |
| **Beretta (wb 103.4)** | | | | |
| V37 | cpe I-4 | 2,631 | 10,575 | 91,197 |
| V37 | cpe V-6 | 2,727 | 11,235 | |
| W37 | GT cpe V-6 | — | 12,685 | 89,045 |
| W37 | GTU cpe V-6 | — | — | 9,813 |
| **Celebrity (wb 104.9)** | | | | |
| W19 | sdn 4d I-4 | 2,751 | 11,495 | 162,482 |
| W19 | sdn 4d V-6 | 2,819 | 12,280 | |
| W35/B5E | wgn 4d 2S I-4 | 2,888 | 11,925 | 17,940 |
| W35/B5E | wgn 4d 2S V-6 | 2,928 | 12,710 | |
| W35/AQ4 | wgn 4d 3S I-4 | — | 12,175 | 21,239 |
| W35/AQ4 | wgn 4d 3S V-6 | — | 12,960 | |
| **Caprice (wb 116.0)** | | | | |
| L69 | sdn 4d V-8 | 3,693 | 13,865 | 69,908 |
| N69 | Classic sdn 4d V-8 | — | 14,445 | 42,971 |
| U69 | Classic Brgm sdn 4d V-8 | — | 15,615 | 32,343 |
| U69/B6N | Classic LS Brgm sdn 4d V-8 | — | 16,835 | 28,033 |
| N35 | Classic wgn 4d 3S V-8 | 4,192 | 15,025 | 23,789 |

| 1989 Engines | bore × stroke | bhp | availability |
|---|---|---|---|
| I-4, 121.0 | 3.50 × 3.15 | 90 | S-Cav, Corsica, Beretta |
| I-4, 151.0 | 4.00 × 3.00 | 98 | S-Celebrity |
| V-6, 173.0 | 3.50 × 2.99 | 125/135 | S-Cam RS, Cav Z24; Ber GT/GTU, O-Cav wgn, Celeb, Cors, Ber |
| V-8, 305.0 | 3.74 × 3.48 | 170 | S-Cam RS conv, IROC-Z, Caprice; O-Camaro RS |
| V-8, 305.0 | 3.74 × 3.48 | 220/230 | O-Camaro IROC-Z |
| V-8, 307.0 | 3.80 × 3.38 | 140 | S-Caprice wgn |
| V-8, 350.0 | 4.00 × 3.48 | 230/240 | O-Camaro IROC-Z |

## 1990

| Cavalier (wb 101.2) | | Wght | Price | Prod |
|---|---|---|---|---|
| C37 | cpe I-4 | 2,436 | 8,620 | 35,121 |
| C69 | sdn 4d I-4 | 2,444 | 8,820 | 64,405 |
| C35 | wgn 4d I-4 | — | 9,195 | 13,812 |
| C35 | wgn 4d V-6 | — | 9,880 | |
| C37/WV9 | VL cpe I-4 | — | 7,577 | 111,476 |
| C69/WV9 | VL sdn 4d I-4 | — | 7,777 | 39,429 |
| C35/WV9 | VL wgn 4d I-4 | — | 8,165 | 8,234 |
| F37 | Z24 cpe V-6 | — | 11,505 | 38,474 |
| **Camaro (wb 101.0)** | | | | |
| P87 | RS htchbk cpe V-6 | 3,077 | 10,995 | 28,750 |
| P87 | RS htchbk cpe V-8 | — | 11,345 | |
| P87/Z28 | IROC-Z cpe V-8 | — | 14,555 | 4,213 |
| P67 | RS conv cpe V-8 | 3,263 | 16,880 | 729 |
| P67/Z28 | IROC-Z conv cpe V-8 | — | 20,195 | 1,294 |
| **Corsica (wb 103.4)** | | | | |
| T69 | sdn 4d I-4 | 2,491 | 9,495 | 170,545 |
| T69 | sdn 4d V-6 | — | 10,180 | |
| T68 | htchbk sdn 4d I-4 | 2,609 | 9,895 | 13,001 |
| T68 | htchbk sdn 4d V-6 | — | 10,580 | |
| Z69 | LTZ sdn 4d V-6 | — | 12,795 | 10,975 |

| Beretta (wb 103.4) | | Wght | Price | Prod |
|---|---|---|---|---|
| V37 | cpe I-4 | 3,000 | 10,320 | 46,082 |
| V37 | cpe V-6 | 3,126 | 11,005 | |
| W37 | GT cpe V-6 | — | 12,500 | 35,785 |
| W37 | Indy GT cpe V-6 | — | — | 4,615 |
| Z37 | GTZ cpe I-4 | — | 13,750 | 13,239 |
| **Celebrity (wb 104.9)** | | | | |
| W35/B5E | wgn 4d 2S I-4 | 2,888 | 12,395 | 11,324 |
| W35/B5E | wgn 4d 2S V-6 | — | 13,655 | |
| W35/AQ4 | wgn 4d 3S I-4 | — | 12,645 | 17,881 |
| W35/AQ4 | wgn 4d 3S V-6 | — | 13,305 | |
| **Lumina (wb 107.5)** | | | | |
| L27 | cpe I-4 | 3,042 | 12,140 | 10,209 |
| L27 | cpe V-6 | — | 12,800 | |
| N27 | Euro cpe V-6 | — | 14,040 | 33,703 |
| L69 | sdn 4d I-4 | 3,122 | 12,340 | 164,171 |
| L69 | sdn 4d V-6 | — | 13,000 | |
| N69 | Euro sdn 4d V-6 | — | 14,240 | 86,924 |
| **Caprice (wb 116.0)** | | | | |
| L69 | sdn 4d V-8 | 3,693 | 14,525 | 53,276 |
| N69 | Classic sdn 4d V-8 | — | 15,125 | 15,679 |
| U69 | Classic Brgm sdn 4d V-8 | — | 16,325 | 16,291 |
| U69/B6N | Classic LS Brgm sdn 4d V-8 | — | 17,525 | 11,977 |
| N35 | Classic wgn 4d 3S V-8 | 4,192 | 15,725 | 12,305 |

| 1990 Engines | bore × stroke | bhp | availability |
|---|---|---|---|
| I-4, 133.0 | 3.50 × 3.46 | 95 | S-Cav, Corsica, Beretta |
| I-4, 138.0 | 3.62 × 3.35 | 180 | S-Beretta GTZ |
| I-4, 151.0 | 4.00 × 3.00 | 110 | S-Celebrity, O-Lumina |
| V-6, 191.0 | 3.51 × 3.31 | 135/140 | S-Cam RS, Cav Z24; O-Cav wgn, Celeb, Cors, Beretta, Lumina |
| V-8, 305.0 | 3.74 × 3.48 | 170 | S-Cam RS conv, IROC-Z, Caprice; O-Camaro RS |
| V-8, 305.0 | 3.74 × 3.48 | 220 | O-Camaro IROC-Z |
| V-8, 307.0 | 3.80 × 3.38 | 140 | S-Caprice wgn |
| V-8, 350.0 | 4.00 × 3.48 | 230 | O-Camaro IROC-Z |

## 1991

| Cavalier (wb 101.3) | | Wght | Price | Prod |
|---|---|---|---|---|
| C37/WV9 | VL cpe | 2,480 | 7,995 | 171,759 |
| C37 | RS cpe | 2,465 | 9,065 | |
| F37 | Z24 cpe | 2,688 | 12,050 | |
| C67 | RS conv cpe | 2,753 | 15,214 | 5,882 |
| C69/WV9 | VL sdn 4d | 2,491 | 8,270 | 70,786 |
| C69 | RS sdn 4d | 2,444 | 9,265 | |
| C35/WV9 | VL wgn 4d | 2,587 | 9,225 | 19,685 |
| C35 | RS wgn 4d | 2,587 | 10,270 | |
| **Camaro (wb 101.0)** | | | | |
| P87 | RS cpe | 3,103 | 12,180 | 92,306 |
| P87/Z28 | Z28 cpe | 3,319 | 15,445 | |
| P67 | RS conv cpe | 3,203 | 17,960 | 8,532 |
| P67/Z28 | Z28 conv cpe | 3,400 | 20,815 | |
| **Corsica (wb 103.4)** | | | | |
| T69 | LT sdn 4d | 2,638 | 10,070 | 187,981 |
| T68 | LT htchbk sdn 4d | 2,742 | 10,745 | 2,525 |
| **Beretta (wb 103.4)—69,868 built** | | | | |
| V37 | cpe | 2,649 | 10,365 | — |

# Chevrolet

| Beretta (wb 103.4) | | Wght | Price | Prod |
|---|---|---|---|---|
| W37 | GT cpe | 2,797 | 13,150 | — |
| Z37 | GTZ cpe | 2,795 | 14,550 | — |
| **Lumina (wb 107.5)** | | | | |
| L69 | sdn 4d | 3,192 | 12,870 | 159,482 |
| N69 | Euro sdn 4d | 3,321 | 14,995 | |
| L27 | cpe | 3,111 | 12,670 | 36,345 |
| N27 | Euro cpe | 3,239 | 14,795 | |
| P27 | Z34 cpe | 3,374 | 17,275 | |
| **Caprice (wb 115.9)** | | | | |
| L19 | sdn 4d | 3,907 | 16,515 | 201,880 |
| N19 | Classic sdn 4d | 3,945 | 18,470 | |
| L35 | wgn 4d | 4,354 | 17,875 | 15,582 |

| 1991 Engines | bore × stroke | bhp | availability |
|---|---|---|---|
| I-4, 133.0 | 3.50 × 3.46 | 95 | S-Cavalier, Corsica, Beretta |
| I-4, 138.0 | 3.63 × 3.35 | 180 | O-Beretta (dohc) |
| I-4, 151.0 | 4.00 × 3.00 | 110 | S-Lumina |
| V-6, 191.0 | 3.51 × 3.31 | 140 | S-Camaro, O-Cavalier, Corsica, Beretta, Lumina |
| V-6, 207.0 | 3.62 × 3.31 | 210 | O-Lumina (dohc) |
| V-8, 305.0 | 3.74 × 3.48 | 170 | S-Caprice, O-Camaro |
| V-8, 305.0 | 3.74 × 3.48 | 230 | O-Camaro |
| V-8, 350.0 | 4.00 × 3.48 | 245 | O-Camaro |

## 1992

| Cavalier (wb 101.3) | | Wght | Price | Prod |
|---|---|---|---|---|
| C37/WV9 | VL cpe | 2,465 | 8,899 | 126,117 |
| C37 | RS cpe | 2,436 | 9,999 | |
| F37 | Z24 cpe | 2,689 | 12,995 | |
| C69/WV9 | VL sdn 4d | 2,471 | 8,999 | 70,786 |
| C69 | RS sdn 4d | 2,444 | 10,199 | |
| C35/WV9 | VL wgn 4d | 2,617 | 10,099 | 19,685 |
| C35 | RS wgn 4d | 2,617 | 11,199 | |
| C67 | RS conv cpe | 2,672 | 15,395 | 9,045 |
| F67 | Z24 conv cpe | 2,826 | 18,305 | |
| **Camaro (wb 101.0)** | | | | |
| P87 | RS cpe | 3,103 | 12,075 | 66,191 |
| P87/Z28 | Z28 cpe | 3,319 | 16,055 | |
| P67 | RS conv cpe | 3,203 | 18,055 | 3,816 |
| P67/Z28 | Z28 conv cpe | 3,400 | 21,500 | |
| **Corsica (wb 103.4)** | | | | |
| T69 | LT sdn 4d | 2,638 | 10,999 | 144,833 |
| **Beretta (wb 103.4)—52,451 built** | | | | |
| V37 | cpe | 2,649 | 10,999 | — |
| W37 | GT cpe | 2,749 | 12,575 | — |
| Z37 | GTZ cpe | 2,795 | 15,590 | — |
| **Lumina (wb 107.5)** | | | | |
| L27 | cpe | 3,115 | 13,200 | 38,037 |
| N27 | Euro cpe | 3,224 | 15,600 | |
| P27 | Z34 cpe | 3,402 | 18,400 | |
| L69 | sdn 4d | 3,220 | 13,400 | 198,269 |
| W69/BYP | Euro sdn 4d | 3,328 | 15,800 | |
| **Caprice (wb 115.9)** | | | | |
| L19 | sdn 4d | 3,907 | 17,300 | 103,381 |
| N19 | Classic sdn 4d | 3,951 | 19,300 | |
| N19/B4U | Classic LTZ sdn 4d | 4,080 | 20,125 | |
| L35 | wgn 4d | 4,354 | 18,700 | 13,400 |

| 1992 Engines | bore × stroke | bhp | availability |
|---|---|---|---|
| I-4, 133.0 | 3.50 × 3.46 | 110 | S-Cavalier, Corsica, Beretta |
| I-4, 138.0 | 3.63 × 3.35 | 180 | O-Beretta (dohc) |
| I-4, 151.0 | 4.00 × 3.00 | 105 | S-Lumina |
| V-6, 191.0 | 3.51 × 3.31 | 140 | S-Camaro, O-Cavalier, Corsica, Beretta, Lumina |
| V-6, 207.0 | 3.62 × 3.31 | 210 | O-Lumina (dohc) |
| V-8, 305.0 | 3.74 × 3.48 | 170 | S-Caprice, O-Camaro |
| V-8, 305.0 | 3.74 × 3.48 | 230 | O-Camaro |
| V-8, 350.0 | 4.00 × 3.48 | 180 | O-Caprice |
| V-8, 350.0 | 4.00 × 3.48 | 245 | O-Camaro |

## 1993

| Cavalier (wb 101.3) | | Wght | Price | Prod |
|---|---|---|---|---|
| C37/WV9 | VL cpe | 2,509 | 8,520 | 127,229 |
| C37 | RS cpe | 2,526 | 9,520 | |
| F37 | Z24 cpe | 2,695 | 12,500 | |
| C67 | RS conv cpe | 2,678 | 15,395 | 8,609 |
| F67 | Z24 conv cpe | 2,678 | 18,305 | |
| C69/WV9 | VL sdn 4d | 2,520 | 8,620 | 96,545 |
| C69 | RS sdn 4d | 2,515 | 9,620 | |
| C35/WV9 | VL wgn 4d | 2,623 | 9,735 | 19,207 |
| C35 | RS wgn 4d | 2,698 | 10,785 | |
| **Camaro (wb 101.1)—39,103 built** | | | | |
| P87 | RS cpe | 3,241 | 13,399 | — |
| P87/Z28 | Z28 cpe | 3,373 | 16,779 | — |
| **Corsica (wb 103.4)** | | | | |
| T69 | LT sdn 4d | 2,665 | 11,395 | 148,232 |
| **Beretta (wb 103.4)—42,263 built** | | | | |
| V37 | cpe | 2,649 | 11,395 | — |
| W37 | GT cpe | 2,749 | 12,995 | — |
| Z37 | GTZ cpe | 2,795 | 15,995 | — |
| **Lumina (wb 107.5)** | | | | |
| L27 | cpe | 3,169 | 14,690 | 30,166 |
| N27 | Euro cpe | 3,193 | 15,600 | |
| P27 | Z34 cpe | 3,374 | 18,400 | |
| L69 | sdn 4d | 3,288 | 14,010 | 191,189 |
| W69 | Euro sdn 4d | 3,312 | 15,800 | |
| **Caprice (wb 115.9)** | | | | |
| L19 | sdn 4d | 3,995 | 17,995 | 90,041 |
| N19 | Classic sdn 4d | 3,988 | 19,995 | |
| L35 | wgn 4d | 4,471 | 19,575 | 10,607 |

| 1993 Engines | bore × stroke | bhp | availability |
|---|---|---|---|
| I-4, 133.0 | 3.50 × 3.46 | 110 | S-Cavalier, Corsica, Beretta, Lumina |
| I-4, 138.0 | 3.63 × 3.35 | 175 | O-Beretta (dohc) |
| V-6, 191.0 | 3.51 × 3.31 | 140 | O-Cavalier, Corsica, Beretta, Lumina |
| V-6, 207.0 | 3.62 × 3.31 | 160 | S-Camaro |
| V-6, 207.0 | 3.62 × 3.31 | 210 | O-Lumina (dohc) |
| V-8, 305.0 | 3.74 × 3.48 | 170 | S-Caprice |
| V-8, 350.0 | 4.00 × 3.48 | 180 | O-Caprice |
| V-8, 350.0 | 4.00 × 3.48 | 275 | O-Camaro |

## 1994

| Cavalier (wb 101.3) | | Wght | Price | Prod |
|---|---|---|---|---|
| C37/WV9 | VL cpe | 2,509 | 8,845 | 147,528 |

# Chevrolet

| Cavalier (wb 101.3) | | Wght | Price | Prod |
|---|---|---|---|---|
| C37 | RS cpe | 2,526 | 10,715 | 147,528 |
| F37 | Z24 cpe | 2,695 | 13,995 | |
| C67 | RS conv cpe | 2,678 | 16,995 | 7,932 |
| F67 | Z24 conv cpe | 2,753 | 19,995 | |
| C69/WV9 | VL sdn 4d | 2,520 | 8,995 | 98,966 |
| C69 | RS sdn 4d | 2,515 | 11,315 | |
| C35 | wgn 4d | 2,623 | 11,465 | 18,149 |
| **Camaro (wb 101.1)** | | | | |
| P87 | cpe | 3,247 | 13,399 | 112,529 |
| P87/Z28 | Z28 cpe | 3,436 | 16,779 | |
| P67 | conv cpe | 3,342 | 18,745 | 7,260 |
| P67/Z28 | Z28 conv cpe | 3,524 | 22,075 | |
| **Corsica (wb 103.4)** | | | | |
| D69 | LT sdn 4d | 2,665 | 13,145 | 143,296 |
| **Beretta (wb 103.4)—64,277 built** | | | | |
| V37 | cpe | 2,649 | 12,415 | — |
| W37 | Z26 cpe | 2,795 | 15,310 | — |
| **Lumina (wb 107.5)** | | | | |
| N27 | Euro cpe | 3,269 | 16,875 | 3,860 |
| P27 | Z34 cpe | 3,440 | 19,310 | |
| L69 | sdn 4d | 3,333 | 15,305 | 82,766 |
| W69 | Euro sdn 4d | 3,369 | 16,515 | |
| **Caprice (wb 115.9)** | | | | |
| L19 | Classic sdn 4d | 4,036 | 18,995 | 90,026 |
| N19 | LS sdn 4d | 4,045 | 21,435 | |
| L35 | wgn 4d | 4,541 | 20,855 | 7,719 |
| L19/W×3 | Impala SS sdn 4d | 4,036 | 21,920 | 6,303 |

| 1994 Engines | bore × stroke | bhp | availability |
|---|---|---|---|
| I-4, 133.0 | 3.50 × 3.46 | 120 | S-Cavalier, Corsica, Beretta |
| I-4, 138.0 | 3.63 × 3.35 | 170 | O-Beretta (dohc) |
| V-6, 191.0 | 3.51 × 3.31 | 140 | S-Lumina, O-Cavalier |
| V-6, 191.0 | 3.51 × 3.31 | 160 | O-Corsica, Beretta |
| V-6, 207.0 | 3.62 × 3.31 | 160 | S-Camaro |
| V-6, 207.0 | 3.62 × 3.31 | 200 | O-Lumina (dohc) |
| V-8, 265.0 | 3.74 × 3.00 | 200 | S-Caprice |
| V-8, 350.0 | 4.00 × 3.48 | 260 | S-Impala SS, O-Caprice |
| V-8, 350.0 | 4.00 × 3.48 | 275 | O-Camaro |

## 1995

| Cavalier (wb 104.1) | | Wght | Price | Prod |
|---|---|---|---|---|
| C37 | cpe | 2,617 | 10,060 | 88,909 |
| F37 | Z24 cpe | 2,788 | 13,810 | |
| F67 | LS conv cpe | 2,838 | 17,210 | 6,060 |
| C69 | sdn 4d | 2,676 | 10,265 | 56,700 |
| F69 | LS sdn 4d | 2,736 | 12,465 | |
| **Camaro (wb 101.1)** | | | | |
| P87 | cpe | 3,251 | 14,250 | 115,365 |
| P87/Z28 | Z28 cpe | 3,390 | 17,915 | |
| P67 | conv cpe | 3,342 | 19,495 | 7,360 |
| P67/Z28 | Z28 conv cpe | 3,480 | 23,095 | |
| **Corsica (wb 103.4)** | | | | |
| D69 | LT sdn 4d | 2,745 | 13,890 | 142,073 |
| **Beretta (wb 103.4)—71,762 built** | | | | |
| V37 | cpe | 2,756 | 12,995 | — |
| W37 | Z26 cpe | 2,990 | 16,295 | — |
| **Lumina (wb 107.5)—242,112 built** | | | | |
| L69 | sdn 4d | 3,330 | 15,460 | — |
| N69 | LS sdn 4d | 3,372 | 16,960 | — |
| **Monte Carlo (wb 107.5)—93,150 built** | | | | |
| W27 | LS cpe | 3,306 | 16,760 | — |
| X27 | Z34 cpe | 3,436 | 18,960 | — |
| **Caprice (wb 115.9)** | | | | |
| L19 | Classic sdn 4d | 4,061 | 20,310 | 54,273 |
| L19/WX3 | Impala SS sdn 4d | 4,036 | 22,910 | 21,434 |
| L35 | wgn 4d | 4,473 | 22,840 | 5,030 |

| 1995 Engines | bore × stroke | bhp | availability |
|---|---|---|---|
| I-4, 133.0 | 3.50 × 3.46 | 120 | S-Cavalier, Corsica, Beretta |
| I-4, 138.0 | 3.63 × 3.35 | 150 | O-Cavalier (dohc) |
| V-6, 191.0 | 3.51 × 3.31 | 155 | O-Corsica |
| V-6, 191.0 | 3.51 × 3.31 | 160 | S-Lumina, Monte Carlo, O-Beretta |
| V-6, 207.0 | 3.62 × 3.31 | 160 | S-Camaro |
| V-6, 207.0 | 3.62 × 3.31 | 210 | O-Lumina, Monte Carlo (dohc) |
| V-8, 265.0 | 3.74 × 3.00 | 200 | S-Caprice |
| V-8, 350.0 | 4.00 × 3.48 | 260 | S-Impala SS, O-Caprice |
| V-8, 350.0 | 4.00 × 3.48 | 275 | O-Camaro |

## 1996

| Cavalier (wb 104.1) | | Wght | Price | Prod |
|---|---|---|---|---|
| C37 | cpe | 2,617 | 10,500 | 145,229 |
| F37 | Z24 cpe | 2,788 | 14,200 | |
| F67 | LS conv cpe | 2,838 | 17,500 | 7,073* |
| C69 | sdn 4d | 2,676 | 10,700 | 116,447 |
| F69 | LS sdn 4d | 2,736 | 12,900 | |
| **Camaro (wb 101.1)** | | | | |
| P87 | cpe | 3,306 | 14,990 | 54,525 |
| P87/R7R | RS cpe | — | 17,490 | |
| P87/Z28 | Z28 cpe | 3,466 | 19,390 | |
| P67 | conv cpe | 3,440 | 21,270 | 6,837 |
| P67/R7R | RS conv cpe | — | 22,720 | |
| P67/Z28 | Z28 conv cpe | 3,593 | 24,490 | |
| **Corsica (wb 103.4)** | | | | |
| D69 | LT sdn 4d | 2,745 | 14,385 | 148,652 |
| **Beretta (wb 103.4)—42,476 built** | | | | |
| V37 | cpe | 2,756 | 13,490 | |
| W37 | Z26 cpe | 2,990 | 16,690 | |
| **Lumina (wb 107.5)—224,573 built** | | | | |
| L69 | sdn 4d | 3,330 | 16,355 | — |
| N69 | LS sdn 4d | 3,372 | 18,055 | — |
| **Monte Carlo (wb 107.5)—80,717 built** | | | | |
| W27 | LS cpe | 3,306 | 17,255 | — |
| X27 | Z34 cpe | 3,436 | 19,455 | — |
| **Caprice (wb 115.9)** | | | | |
| L19 | Classic sdn 4d | 4,061 | 19,905 | 27,155 |
| L19/WX3 | Impala SS sdn 4d | 4,036 | 24,405 | 41,941 |
| L35 | wgn 4d | 4,473 | 22,405 | 485 |

| 1996 Engines | bore × stroke | bhp | availability |
|---|---|---|---|
| I-4, 133.0 | 3.50 × 3.46 | 120 | S-Cavalier, Corsica, Beretta |
| I-4, 146.0 | 3.54 × 3.70 | 150 | O-Cavalier (dohc) |
| V-6, 191.0 | 3.51 × 3.31 | 155 | O-Corsica, Beretta |
| V-6, 191.0 | 3.51 × 3.31 | 160 | S-Lumina, Monte Carlo |
| V-6, 207.0 | 3.62 × 3.31 | 215 | O-Lumina, Monte |

# Chevrolet

| 1996 Engines | bore × stroke | bhp | availability |
|---|---|---|---|
| V-6, 231.0 | 3.80 × 3.40 | 200 | S-Camaro |
| V-8, 265.0 | 3.74 × 3.00 | 200 | S-Caprice |
| V-8, 350.0 | 4.00 × 3.48 | 260 | S-Impala SS; O-Caprice |
| V-8, 350.0 | 4.00 × 3.48 | 285** | O-Camaro |

* Cavalier convertible sales figure.  ** 305 horsepower with SS package.

## 1997

| Cavalier (wb 104.1) | | Wght | Price | Prod |
|---|---|---|---|---|
| C37 | cpe | 2,584 | 10,980 | ⎤ |
| C37/WP2 | RS cpe | 2,617 | 12,225 | 171,225 |
| F37 | Z24 cpe | 2,788 | 14,465 | ⎦ |
| F67 | LS conv cpe | 2,899 | 17,765 | 1,108 |
| C69 | sdn 4d | 2,630 | 11,180 | ⎤ 142,803 |
| F69 | LS sdn 4d | 2,729 | 13,380 | ⎦ |

| Camaro (wb 101.1) | | Wght | Price | Prod |
|---|---|---|---|---|
| P87 | cpe | 3,294 | 16,215 | ⎤ |
| P87/R7R | RS cpe | 3,307 | 17,970 | 48,292 |
| P87/Z28 | Z28 cpe | 3,433 | 20,115 | ⎦ |
| P67 | conv cpe | 3,446 | 21,770 | ⎤ |
| P67/R7R | RS conv cpe | 3,455 | 23,170 | 6,680 |
| P67/Z28 | Z28 conv cpe | 3,589 | 25,520 | ⎦ |

| Malibu (wb 107.0)—100,266 built | | Wght | Price | Prod |
|---|---|---|---|---|
| D69 | sdn 4d | 3,051 | 15,470 | — |
| E69 | LS sdn 4d | 3,077 | 18,190 | — |

| Lumina (wb 107.5)—234,626 built | | Wght | Price | Prod |
|---|---|---|---|---|
| L69 | sdn 4d | 3,360 | 16,945 | — |
| N69 | LS sdn 4d | 3,388 | 19,145 | — |
| — | LTZ sdn 4d | — | 19,455 | — |

| Monte Carlo (wb 107.5)—72,555 built | | Wght | Price | Prod |
|---|---|---|---|---|
| W27 | LS cpe | 3,320 | 17,445 | — |
| X27 | Z34 cpe | 3,455 | 19,945 | — |

| 1997 Engines | bore × stroke | bhp | availability |
|---|---|---|---|
| I-4, 133.0 | 3.50 × 3.46 | 120 | S-Cavalier |
| I-4, 146.0 | 3.54 × 3.70 | 150 | S-Malibu, O-Cavalier (dohc) |
| V-6, 191.0 | 3.51 × 3.31 | 160 | S-Lumina, Monte Carlo |
| V-6, 207.0 | 3.62 × 3.31 | 215 | O-Lumina, Monte Carlo (dohc) |
| V-6, 231.0 | 3.80 × 3.40 | 200 | S-Camaro |
| V-8, 350.0 | 4.00 × 3.48 | 285* | O-Camaro |

* 305 horsepower with SS package.

## 1998

| Prizm (wb 97.0)—45,000 built | | Wght | Price | Prod |
|---|---|---|---|---|
| K19 | sdn 4d | 2,359 | 12,045 | — |
| K19/WP2 | LSi 4d | — | 14,615 | — |

| Cavalier (wb 104.1) | | Wght | Price | Prod |
|---|---|---|---|---|
| C37 | cpe | 2,584 | 11,610 | ⎤ 126,599 |
| C37/WP2 | RS cpe | 2,584 | 12,870 | ⎦ |
| F37 | Z24 cpe | 2,749 | 15,710 | 25,879 |
| F67 | Z24 conv cpe | 2,899 | 19,410 | 5,011 |
| C69 | sdn 4d | 2,630 | 11,810 | 117,224 |
| F69 | LS sdn 4d | 2,630 | 14,250 | 55,838 |

| Camaro (wb 101.1) | | Wght | Price | Prod |
|---|---|---|---|---|
| P87 | cpe | 3,331 | 16,625 | ⎤ 49,515 |
| P87/Z28 | Z28 cpe | 3,349 | 20,470 | ⎦ |
| P67 | conv cpe | 3,468 | 22,125 | ⎤ 4,505 |
| P67/Z28 | Z28 conv cpe | 3,574 | 27,450 | ⎦ |

| Malibu (wb 107.0) | | Wght | Price | Prod |
|---|---|---|---|---|
| D69 | sdn 4d | 3,100 | 15,670 | 167,951 |
| E69 | LS sdn 4d | — | 18,470 | 100,537 |

| Lumina (wb 107.5) | | Wght | Price | Prod |
|---|---|---|---|---|
| L69 | sdn 4d | 3,330 | 17,245 | 172,884 |
| N69 | LS sdn 4d | 3,372 | 19,245 | ⎤ 35,743 |
| — | LTZ sdn 4d | 3,420 | 19,745 | ⎦ |

| Monte Carlo (wb 107.5) | | Wght | Price | Prod |
|---|---|---|---|---|
| W27 | LS cpe | 3,239 | 17,795 | 54,395 |
| X27 | Z34 cpe | 3,452 | 20,295 | 14,995 |

| 1998 Engines | bore × stroke | bhp | availability |
|---|---|---|---|
| I-4, 109.5 | 3.11 × 3.60 | 120 | S-Prizm |
| I-4, 133.0 | 3.50 × 3.46 | 115 | S-Cavalier |
| I-4, 146.0 | 3.54 × 3.70 | 150 | S-Malibu, O-Cavalier (dohc) |
| V-6, 191.0 | 3.51 × 3.31 | 150 | O-Malibu |
| V-6, 191.0 | 3.51 × 3.31 | 160 | S-Lumina, Monte Carlo |
| V-6, 231.0 | 3.80 × 3.40 | 200 | S-Camaro, O-Lumina, Monte Carlo |
| V-8, 350.0 | 4.00 × 3.48 | 305 | O-Camaro |
| V-8, 350.0 | 4.00 × 3.48 | 320 | O-Camaro |

## 1999

| Prizm (wb 97.0)—50,000 built | | Wght | Price | Prod |
|---|---|---|---|---|
| K19 | sdn 4d | 2,403 | 12,268 | — |
| K19/WP2 | LSi 4d | — | 14,839 | — |

| Cavalier (wb 104.1) | | Wght | Price | Prod |
|---|---|---|---|---|
| C37 | cpe | 2,617 | 11,871 | ⎤ 116,893 |
| C37/WP2 | RS cpe | — | 13,131 | ⎦ |
| F37 | Z24 cpe | — | 15,791 | 17,432 |
| F67 | Z24 conv cpe | 2,838 | 19,751 | 8,755 |
| C69 | sdn 4d | 2,676 | 11,971 | 101,863 |
| F69 | LS sdn 4d | — | 14,411 | 33,105 |

| Camaro (wb 101.1) | | Wght | Price | Prod |
|---|---|---|---|---|
| P87 | cpe | 3,306 | 16,625 | ⎤ 37,514 |
| P87/Z28 | Z28 cpe | 3,349 | 20,870 | ⎦ |
| P67 | conv cpe | 3,500 | 22,125 | ⎤ 4,584 |
| P67/Z28 | Z28 conv cpe | 3,574 | 27,850 | ⎦ |

| Malibu (wb 107.0) | | Wght | Price | Prod |
|---|---|---|---|---|
| D69 | sdn 4d | 3,051 | 15,950 | 148,691 |
| E69 | LS sdn 4d | 3,077 | 18,910 | 97,924 |

| Lumina (wb 107.5) | | Wght | Price | Prod |
|---|---|---|---|---|
| L69 | sdn 4d | 3,330 | 18,190 | 127,600 |
| N69 | LS sdn 4d | — | 19,920 | ⎤ 11,498 |
| — | LTZ sdn 4d | 3,372 | 20,360 | ⎦ |

| Monte Carlo (wb 107.5) | | Wght | Price | Prod |
|---|---|---|---|---|
| W27 | LS cpe | 3,306 | 18,510 | 49,354 |
| X27 | Z34 cpe | 3,436 | 20,535 | 20,245 |

| 1999 Engines | bore × stroke | bhp | availability |
|---|---|---|---|
| I-4, 109.5 | 3.11 × 3.60 | 120 | S-Prizm |
| I-4, 133.0 | 3.50 × 3.46 | 115 | S-Cavalier |
| I-4, 146.0 | 3.54 × 3.70 | 150 | S-Malibu, O-Cavalier (dohc) |
| V-6, 191.0 | 3.51 × 3.31 | 150 | O-Malibu |

# Chevrolet

| 1999 Engines | bore × stroke | bhp | availability |
|---|---|---|---|
| V-6, 191.0 | 3.51 × 3.31 | 160 | S-Lumina, Monte Carlo |
| V-6, 231.0 | 3.80 × 3.40 | 200 | S-Camaro, O-Lumina, Monte Carlo |
| V-8, 346.0 | 3.90 × 3.62 | 305 | O-Camaro |
| V-8, 346.0 | 3.90 × 3.62 | 320 | O-Camaro |

## 2000

| Prizm (wb 97.0)—38,921 built | | Wght | Price | Prod |
|---|---|---|---|---|
| K19 | sdn 4d | 2,403 | 13,960 | — |
| K19/WP2 | LSi 4d | 2,431 | 16,010 | — |
| **Cavalier (wb 104.1)** | | | | |
| C37 | cpe | 2,584 | 13,160 | 115,751 |
| F37 | Z24 cpe | 2,749 | 16,365 | 26,104 |
| F67 | Z24 conv cpe | 2,899 | 19,830 | 5,293 |
| C69 | sdn 4d | 2,630 | 13,260 | 126,491 |
| F69 | LS sdn 4d | 2,729 | 14,805 | 39,624 |
| **Camaro (wb 101.1)** | | | | |
| P87 | cpe | 3,317 | 17,040 | 39,527 |
| P87/Z28 | Z28 cpe | 3,424 | 21,615 | |
| P67 | conv cpe | 3,454 | 24,340 | 5,934 |
| P67/Z28 | Z28 conv cpe | 3,561 | 28,715 | |
| **Malibu (wb 107.0)** | | | | |
| D69 | sdn 4d | 3,051 | 16,535 | 146,780 |
| E69 | LS sdn 4d | 3,077 | 19,215 | 105,739 |
| **Lumina (wb 107.5)** | | | | |
| L69 | sdn 4d | 3,327 | 18,890 | 37,493 |
| **Impala (wb 110.5)** | | | | |
| F19 | sdn 4d | 3,389 | 18,890 | 141,223 |
| H19 | LS sdn 4d | 3,466 | 22,790 | 79,950 |
| **Monte Carlo (wb 110.5)** | | | | |
| W27 | LS cpe | 3,306 | 19,390 | 31,210 |
| X27 | SS cpe | 3,436 | 21,935 | 33,137 |

| 2000 Engines | bore × stroke | bhp | availability |
|---|---|---|---|
| I-4, 109.5 | 3.11 × 3.60 | 125 | S-Prizm |
| I-4, 133.0 | 3.50 × 3.46 | 115 | S-Cavalier |
| I-4, 146.0 | 3.54 × 3.70 | 150 | O-Cavalier (dohc) |
| V-6, 191.0 | 3.51 × 3.31 | 170 | S-Malibu |
| V-6, 191.0 | 3.51 × 3.31 | 175 | S-Lumina |
| V-6, 205.0 | 3.62 × 3.31 | 180 | S-Impala, Monte Carlo |
| V-6, 231.0 | 3.80 × 3.40 | 200 | S-Camaro, O-Impala, Monte Carlo |
| V-8, 346.0 | 3.90 × 3.62 | 305 | O-Camaro |
| V-8, 346.0 | 3.90 × 3.62 | 320 | O-Camaro |

## 2001

| Prizm (wb 97.0)—50,141 built | | Wght | Price | Prod |
|---|---|---|---|---|
| K19 | sdn 4d | 2,403 | 14,155 | — |
| K19/WP2 | LSi 4d sdn | 2,431 | 16,220 | — |
| **Cavalier (wb 104.1)** | | | | |
| C37 | cpe | 2,617 | 13,260 | 92,232 |
| F37 | Z24 cpe | 2,676 | 16,465 | 18,260 |
| C69 | sdn 4d | 2,676 | 13,360 | 125,476 |
| F69 | LS sdn 4d | 2,729 | 14,955 | 34,597 |
| **Camaro (wb 101.1)** | | | | |
| P87 | cpe | 3,306 | 17,305 | 23,691 |
| P87/Z28 | Z28 cpe | 3,439 | 21,875 | |
| P67 | conv cpe | 3,500 | 24,600 | 5,318 |
| P67/Z28 | Z28 conv cpe | 3,574 | 28,980 | |
| **Malibu (wb 107.0)** | | | | |
| D69 | sdn 4d | 3,051 | 17,150 | 141,819 |
| E69 | LS sdn 4d | 3,077 | 19,410 | 71,189 |
| **Impala (wb 110.5)** | | | | |
| F19 | sdn 4d | 3,466 | 19,269 | 137,143 |
| H19 | LS sdn 4d | 3,466 | 23,345 | 69,845 |
| **Monte Carlo (wb 110.5)** | | | | |
| W27 | LS cpe | 3,340 | 19,690 | 31,988 |
| X27 | SS cpe | 3,391 | 22,520 | 39,280 |

| 2001 Engines | bore × stroke | bhp | availability |
|---|---|---|---|
| I-4, 109.5 | 3.11 × 3.60 | 125 | S-Prizm |
| I-4, 133.0 | 3.50 × 3.46 | 115 | S-Cavalier |
| I-4, 146.0 | 3.54 × 3.70 | 150 | O-Cavalier (dohc) |
| V-6, 191.0 | 3.51 × 3.31 | 170 | S-Malibu |
| V-6, 205.0 | 3.62 × 3.31 | 180 | S-Impala, Monte Carlo |
| V-6, 231.0 | 3.80 × 3.40 | 200 | S-Camaro, O-Impala, Monte Carlo |
| V-8, 346.0 | 3.90 × 3.62 | 310 | O-Camaro |
| V-8, 346.0 | 3.90 × 3.62 | 325 | O-Camaro |

## 2002

| Prizm (wb 97.0) | | Wght | Price | Prod* |
|---|---|---|---|---|
| K19 | sdn 4d | 2,403 | 14,330 | |
| K19/WP2 | LSi 4d | 2,431 | 16,395 | |
| **Cavalier (wb 104.1)** | | | | |
| C37 | cpe | 2,617 | 13,860 | |
| S37 | LS cpe | 2,617 | 14,910 | |
| F37 | Z24 cpe | 2,749 | 16,480** | |
| H37 | LS Sport cpe | 2,676 | 16,280*** | |
| C69 | sdn 4d | 2,676 | 13,960 | |
| F69 | LS sdn 4d | 2,729 | 15,010 | |
| H69 | Z24 sdn 4d | 2,676 | 16,580** | |
| H69 | LS Sport sdn 4d | — | 16,380*** | |
| **Camaro (wb 101.1)** | | | | |
| P87 | cpe | 3,323 | 18,080 | |
| P87/Z28 | Z28 cpe | 3,524 | 22,495 | |
| P67 | conv cpe | 3,524 | 26,075 | |
| P67/Z28 | Z28 conv cpe | 3,577 | 29,590 | |
| **Malibu (wb 107.0)** | | | | |
| D69 | sdn 4d | 3,053 | 17,535 | |
| E69 | LS sdn 4d | 3,077 | 19,740 | |
| **Impala (wb 110.5)** | | | | |
| F19 | sdn 4d | 3,389 | 19,960 | |
| H19 | LS sdn 4d | 3,389 | 23,660 | |
| **Monte Carlo (wb 110.5)** | | | | |
| W27 | LS cpe | 3,340 | 20,060 | |
| X27 | SS cpe | 3,395 | 22,860 | |

| 2002 Engines | bore × stroke | bhp | availability |
|---|---|---|---|
| I-4, 109.5 | 3.11 × 3.60 | 125 | S-Prizm |
| I-4, 133.0 | 3.50 × 3.46 | 115 | S-Cavalier |
| I-4, 134.0 | 3.39 × 3.72 | 140 | O-Cavalier LS Sport (dohc) |
| I-4, 146.0 | 3.54 × 3.70 | 150 | O-Cavalier Z24 (dohc) |
| V-6, 191.0 | 3.51 × 3.31 | 170 | S-Malibu |
| V-6, 205.0 | 3.62 × 3.31 | 180 | S-Impala, Monte Carlo |
| V-6, 231.0 | 3.80 × 3.40 | 200 | S-Camaro, O-Impala, Monte Carlo |
| V-8, 346.0 | 3.90 × 3.62 | 310 | O-Camaro |
| V-8, 346.0 | 3.90 × 3.62 | 325 | O-Camaro |

*Figures not available at time of publication. ** Z24 discontinued early in model year. *** LS Sport replaced Z24.

# Chevrolet Corvair

Corvair was the most-controversial Chevrolet since the abortive "Copper-Cooled" model of 1923. Of course, neither was *supposed* to stir up trouble. Each was merely a response to a particular market situation in its day.

The problem with Corvair was a radical design that made it too costly for its original economy-car mission and too "foreign" for its target audience. Had it not opened up an entirely new market—and almost by accident at that—Corvair wouldn't have lasted even half of the ten years it did hang on. And there's the irony, for it was Corvair's success as a *sporty* compact that spawned the car that ultimately helped do it in: the Ford Mustang. A young lawyer-on-the-make named Ralph Nader did the rest.

Chevrolet's interest in a smaller companion car was evident as early as the late '40s, when it contemplated the Cadet, a prototype 2200-pound four-door sedan of conventional design begun right after World War II. Powered by a short-stroke 133-cid version of the division's famous "Stovebolt Six," this 108-inch-wheelbase compact was intended to sell at rock-bottom prices in anticipation of a postwar recession. Instead, the market boomed, rendering the Cadet unnecessary. What's more, it would have cost as much to build as a regular Chevy, and so was deemed unprofitable at the targeted $1000 retail price. The project was thus canceled in mid-1947.

Things were far different by the late '50s. Led by Volkswagen and Renault, sales of economy imports were becoming too large to ignore, particularly once a national recession hit in mid-1957. American Motors responded with its compact 1958 American, a warmed-over '55 Nash Rambler. Studebaker chimed in with the '59 Lark, a full-size car cut down to compact size. So successful was the Lark that it temporarily halted Studebaker's ultimate slide to oblivion. Both these independent efforts would soon have Big Three rivals. Ford was readying its Falcon and Chrysler its Valiant for model-year 1960. General Motors had peddled its so-called "captive imports," British Vauxhalls and German Opels, in 1958-59. For 1960, GM would rely on Corvair.

Initiated in 1956, the Corvair was largely the brainchild of Chevy chief engineer (and future GM president) Edward N. Cole, who became division general manager in July of that year. It was predictably a technician's car, by far the most-radical of the new Big Three compacts. Perhaps inspired by Cole's interest in airplanes—but more likely by the popular VW Beetle—it was planned around a 140-cid air-cooled flat six developing 80 or 95 horsepower in initial form and—just as uncommon—mounted at the rear ("where an engine belongs," as Corvair ads would claim). It was a relatively complicated engine, with six separate cylinder barrels and a divided crankcase. Yet despite a lightweight aluminum block, it ended up at 366 pounds, some 78 pounds above the target weight, a miscalculation that would have negative consequences for handling.

All-independent suspension and unit construction were equally unusual for a U.S. car. Corvair's trim 108-inch-wheelbase Y-body platform was all new, but its all-coil suspension was perhaps too basic: conventional wishbones in front, VW Beetle-style semitrailing swing axles in back. Antiroll bars were omitted to keep retail price as low as possible, but this saved only $4 a car, and GM was well aware they were needed to achieve acceptable handling with rear swing axles and the tail-heavy weight distribution. This decision, as well as management's desire to standardize assembly, precluded more-sophisticated suspension geometry until 1962, when a Regular Production Option including stiffer springs, shorter rear-axle limit straps, and a front sway bar became available. A major suspension improvement occurred for 1964: a transverse rear camber-compensating spring.

Nevertheless, the initial Corvair suspension of 1960-63 did not create a "dangerous, ill-handling car" as later lawsuits claimed. It did oversteer to be sure, but the tail-wag tendency wasn't severe—*provided* that recommended tire pressures were observed (15 psi front, 26 rear). The problem was that most owners didn't pay attention to that, and some got into trouble. When Ralph Nader found out and wrote *Unsafe at Any Speed*, Corvair handling became a *cause celebre* that wasn't put to rest until a 1972 congressional investigation cleared the 1960-63 models. Of course, this came far too late. Corvair was already three years gone.

Corvair's decade-long model run divides into two design generations: 1960-64 and 1965-69. Initial offerings comprised quite spartan four-door sedans in "500" and more-deluxe "700" trim selling at $2000-$2100. Three-speed floorshift manual transaxle was standard; Chevy's two-speed Powerglide was optional. Two-door 500 and 700 coupes arrived at midseason, but the real attention-getter was the new "900" Monza coupe, which boasted an even spiffier interior with bucket seats.

Bolstered by a newly optional four-speed gearbox for 1961, the Monza caught fire, uncovering a huge latent demand for sporty, fun-to-drive compacts. This was fortunate, because Ford's much simpler and cheaper Falcon was handily outselling other Corvairs in the economy market. From here on, the rear-engine Chevy would aim increasingly at enthusiast drivers.

But it was too late to change some plans, so a brace of Corvair Lakewood station wagons arrived for '61 as scheduled, as did a Monza sedan. The Lakewood offered a surprising amount of cargo space—58 cubic feet behind the front seat, 10 more under the front "hood"—more than other compact wagons and even some larger models. It didn't sell well, though, with first-year production barely topping 25,000. Chevy also issued the interesting Corvair-based Greenbrier window van, Corvan panel, and Rampside pickup, all "forward control" models inspired by VW's Type 2 Microbus and forerunners of today's popular minivans. Finally, the flat six was bored out to 145 cid. Standard power remained at 80, but a $27 "Turbo Air" option lifted that to 98.

For 1962, the 500 series was trimmed to a lone coupe, and the Monza line expanded to include a wagon (no longer called Lakewood) and a new convertible. The Monza wagon was plush, but only about 6000 were built before the body style was dropped entirely to make assembly-line room for the Chevy II, the resolutely orthodox Falcon-style compact rushed out to do what Corvair had failed to in the economy market.

Mid-1962 brought what has become the most highly prized first-generation Corvair: the turbocharged Monza Spyder. Initially, this was a $317 option package for Monza two-doors comprising a 150-bhp engine with lots of chrome dressup, a shorter final drive for sprightlier acceleration, heavy-duty suspension, and a multigauge instrument panel with tachometer and brushed-metal trim. The four-speed and sintered-metallic brake linings were "mandatory" options. The Spyder wasn't cheap—a minimum price of $2600—but it was the next best thing to a Porsche. Total production ran about 40,000 units through 1964.

# Chevrolet Corvair

First-generation Corvair styling saw only minor year-to-year changes, mostly at the front. The original winged Chevy bowtie gave way to a smaller emblem on a slim full-width chrome bar for '61. The '62s substituted dummy air slots. A wide single chevron replaced those for '63. Then came a double-bar version of the '61 treatment. Aside from the aforementioned rear camber compensator, the big news for '64 was a stroked 164-cid engine with 95 or 110 bhp in normally aspirated form. Spyder power was unchanged.

With 1965 came a design revolution. The sleek, second-generation Corvair looked good even from normally unflattering angles, a tribute to the work of GM Design under chief William L. Mitchell. It was something an Italian coachbuilder might do—as Pininfarina did with a specially bodied '64 Corvair of generally similar lines. Not only was the 1965 Corvair nicely shaped, it had just the right amount of chrome trim. Closed models were now pillarless hardtops, and a four-door returned to the 500 series.

The '65s were equally new under their handsome bodies. The turbo six was up to 180 bhp, but the best all-around engine was the new 140-bhp nonturbo version that was standard for the top-line Corsa coupe and convertible, replacing Monza Spyder. Its extra power came from new cylinder heads, redesigned manifolds, and four progressively linked carburetors. The "140"

**1960 700 four-door sedan**

**1961 700 Lakewood four-door station wagon**

**1961 Greenbrier Sports Wagon passenger van**

**1962 900 Monza club coupe**

**1963 900 Monza Spyder convertible coupe**

**1965 Corsa convertible coupe**

**1966 Corvair Corsa sport coupe hardtop**

**1969 Monza sport coupe hardtop**

was an option for lesser Corvairs, which continued with 95 standard and 110 optional bhp.

The 1960 Corvair had been the first mass-produced American car with swing-axle rear suspension. The '65 was the first with fully independent suspension, not counting the '63 Corvette. The sole difference was that where Corvette linked rear wheels with a single transverse leaf spring, Corvair used individual coils. Both systems employed upper and lower control arms at each rear wheel. The uppers were actually the axle halfshafts; the lowers were unequal-length nonparallel trailing arms (two per side). Together, these controlled all wheel motion. Small rubber-mounted rods extended from each lower arm to the main rear crossmember to absorb longitudinal movement at the pivot points.

No question now about tricky behavior "at the limit": Corvair handling was near-neutral with mild initial understeer. With rear wheels nearly vertical at all times, the car could be pushed around corners with fine stability. Attention was also paid to the front suspension, which was tuned to complement the new rear end and provide additional roll stiffness.

Like the Monza Spyder before it, the 1965-66 Corsa was the most-desirable second-generation Corvair—as it still is among collectors. Base-priced at $2519 for the coupe and $2665 as a convertible, it came with full instrumentation, special exterior accents (including a bright rear-panel appliqué for instant recognition), deluxe all-vinyl bucket-seat interior, and the 140-bhp engine. With the $158 turbo-six option, Corsa was squarely in the performance league: less than 11 seconds 0-60 mph, 18 seconds at 80 mph for the standing quarter-mile. Given enough room, a blown Corsa could hit 115 mph.

Unfortunately, Corsa didn't sell well against Ford's instant smash-hit Mustang, which had bowed about six months before and could also better the Chevy's on-road performance. More critical was the decline in Monza sales then setting in. Though the most-popular Corvair rallied slightly for '65, production plunged by some two-thirds the following year. Sales were definitely being affected by Nader's book—and GM's embarrassing admission that it had put Nader under surveillance. But damning charges and damaging publicity were beside the point. GM had already sealed Corvair's fate in April 1965 with an internal memo that said, in effect, "No more development work. Do only enough to meet federal requirements."

When Chevy's true Mustang-fighter, the Camaro, arrived for 1967, Corvair was trimmed to just 500 sedan and coupe and Monza sedan, coupe, and convertible. The turbo engine was also dropped, and hardtop sedans were in their final year.

The 1968-69 models were the rarest Corvairs. Comprising just 500 and Monza hardtops and Monza convertibles, they're readily spotted by federally mandated front side-marker lights—clear on the '68s, amber for '69. Monza convertibles were scarcest of all: respectively, just 1386 and 521 built.

With so little change in light of fast-falling sales, Corvair was looking terminal by 1968, so many were surprised that Chevy even bothered with the '69 models. Some dealers wouldn't sell them and others refused to service them, so the division offered what few buyers remained a $150 credit on the purchase of another Chevy through 1974. With that, the Corvair was dead.

In retrospect, Corvair was a victim of its own success. Had it not been for the Monza, we might not have had the Mustang—and ultimately, the Camaro. Left stillborn by the no-more-development edict was a project dubbed XP-849, which went at least as far as a pair of clay mockups: one apparently a rear-engine design, the other with *front-wheel* drive. Intriguingly, both were badged "Corvair 2." A possible prelude to Chevy's unfortunate 1971 Vega, though likely for overseas consumption, XP-849 would never materialize. But it showed that at least some GMers still remembered the adventuresome spirit of the original Corvair despite years of corporate miscues and public controversy.

## Specifications

### 1960

| 500 (wb 108.0) | | Wght | Price | Prod |
|---|---|---|---|---|
| 0527 | cpe | 2,270 | 1,984 | 14,628 |
| 0569 | sdn 4d | 2,305 | 2,038 | 47,683 |
| **700 (wb 108.0)** | | | | |
| 0727 | cpe | 2,290 | 2,049 | 36,562 |
| 0769 | sdn 4d | 2,315 | 2,103 | 139,208 |
| **900 Monza (wb 108.0)** | | | | |
| 0927 | cpe | 2,280 | 2,238 | 11,926 |

| 1960 Engines | bore × stroke | bhp | availability |
|---|---|---|---|
| flat 6, 140.0 | 3.38 × 2.60 | 80 | S-all |
| flat 6, 140.0 | 3.38 × 2.60 | 95 | O-all |

### 1961

| 500 (wb 108.0) | | Wght | Price | Prod |
|---|---|---|---|---|
| 0527 | cpe | 2,320 | 1,920 | 16,857 |
| 0535 | Lakewood wgn 4d | 2,530 | 2,266 | 5,591 |
| 0569 | sdn 4d | 2,355 | 1,974 | 18,752 |
| **700 (wb 108.0)** | | | | |
| 0727 | cpe | 2,350 | 1,985 | 24,786 |
| 0735 | Lakewood wgn 4d | 2,555 | 2,331 | 20,451 |
| 0769 | sdn 4d | 2,380 | 2,039 | 51,948 |
| **900 Monza (wb 108.0)** | | | | |
| 0927 | cpe | 2,395 | 2,201 | 109,945 |
| 0969 | sdn 4d | 2,420 | 2,201 | 33,745 |

| 1961 Engines | bore × stroke | bhp | availability |
|---|---|---|---|
| flat 6, 145.0 | 3.44 × 2.60 | 80 | S-all |
| flat 6, 145.0 | 3.44 × 2.60 | 98 | O-all |

### 1962

| 500 (wb 108.0) | | Wght | Price | Prod |
|---|---|---|---|---|
| 0527 | cpe | 2,350 | 1,992 | 16,245 |
| **700 (wb 108.0)** | | | | |
| 0727 | cpe | 2,390 | 2,057 | 18,474 |
| 0735 | wgn 4d | 2,590 | 2,407 | 3,716 |
| 0769 | sdn 4d | 2,410 | 2,111 | 35,368 |
| **900 Monza (wb 108.0)** | | | | |
| 0927 | cpe | 2,440 | 2,273 | 144,844 |
| 0927 | Spyder cpe | 2,465 | 2,636 | 6,894 |
| 0935 | wgn 4d | 2,590 | 2,569 | 2,362 |
| 0967 | conv cpe | 2,625 | 2,483 | 13,995 |
| 0967 | Spyder conv cpe | 2,650 | 2,846 | 2,574 |
| 0969 | sdn 4d | 2,455 | 2,273 | 48,059 |

| 1962 Engines | bore × stroke | bhp | availability |
|---|---|---|---|
| flat 6, 145.0 | 3.44 × 2.60 | 80 | S-all exc Spyder |
| flat 6, 145.0 | 3.44 × 2.60 | 102 | O-all exc Spyder |

# Chevrolet Corvair

| 1962 Engines | bore × stroke | bhp | availability |
|---|---|---|---|
| flat 6T, 145.0 | 3.44 × 2.60 | 150 | S-Monza Spyder |

## 1963

| 500 (wb 108.0) | | Wght | Price | Prod |
|---|---|---|---|---|
| 0527 | cpe | 2,330 | 1,992 | 16,680 |
| 700 (wb 108.0) | | | | |
| 0727 | cpe | 2,355 | 2,056 | 12,378 |
| 0769 | sdn 4d | 2,385 | 2,110 | 20,684 |
| 900 Monza (wb 108.0) | | | | |
| 0927 | cpe | 2,415 | 2,272 | 117,917 |
| 0927 | Spyder cpe | 2,440 | 2,589 | 11,627 |
| 0967 | conv cpe | 2,525 | 2,481 | 36,693 |
| 0967 | Spyder conv cpe | 2,550 | 2,798 | 7,472 |
| 0969 | sdn 4d | 2,450 | 2,326 | 31,120 |

| 1963 Engines | bore × stroke | bhp | availability |
|---|---|---|---|
| flat 6, 145.0 | 3.44 × 2.60 | 80 | S-all exc Spyder |
| flat 6, 145.0 | 3.44 × 2.60 | 102 | O-all exc Spyder |
| flat 6T, 145.0 | 3.44 × 2.60 | 150 | S-Monza Spyder |

## 1964

| 500 (wb 108.0) | | Wght | Price | Prod |
|---|---|---|---|---|
| 0527 | cpe | 2,365 | 2,000 | 22,968 |
| 600 Monza Spyder (wb 108.0) | | | | |
| 0627 | cpe | 2,470 | 2,599 | 6,480 |
| 0667 | conv cpe | 2,580 | 2,811 | 4,761 |
| 700 (wb 108.0) | | | | |
| 0769 | sdn 4d | 2,415 | 2,119 | 16,295 |
| 900 Monza (wb 108.0) | | | | |
| 0927 | cpe | 2,445 | 2,281 | 88,440 |
| 0967 | conv cpe | 2,555 | 2,492 | 31,045 |
| 0969 | sdn 4d | 2,470 | 2,335 | 21,926 |

| 1964 Engines | bore × stroke | bhp | availability |
|---|---|---|---|
| flat 6, 164.0 | 3.44 × 2.94 | 95 | S-all exc 600 |
| flat 6, 164.0 | 3.44 × 2.94 | 110 | O-all exc 600 |
| flat 6T, 164.0 | 3.44 × 2.94 | 150 | S-600 |

## 1965

| 500 (wb 108.0) | | Wght | Price | Prod |
|---|---|---|---|---|
| 10137 | htp cpe | 2,385 | 2,066 | 36,747 |
| 10139 | htp sdn | 2,405 | 2,142 | 17,560 |
| Monza (wb 108.0) | | | | |
| 10537 | htp cpe | 2,440 | 2,347 | 88,954 |
| 10539 | htp sdn | 2,465 | 2,422 | 37,157 |
| 10567 | conv cpe | 2,675 | 2,493 | 26,466 |
| Corsa (wb 108.0) | | | | |
| 10737 | htp cpe | 2,475 | 2,519 | 20,291 |
| 10767 | conv cpe | 2,710 | 2,665 | 8,353 |

| 1965 Engines | bore × stroke | bhp | availability |
|---|---|---|---|
| flat 6, 164.0 | 3.44 × 2.94 | 95 | S-all exc Corsa |
| flat 6, 164.0 | 3.44 × 2.94 | 110 | O-all exc Corsa |
| flat 6, 164.0 | 3.44 × 2.94 | 140 | S-Corsa; O-others |
| flat 6T, 164.0 | 3.44 × 2.94 | 180 | O-Corsa |

## 1966

| 500 (wb 108.0) | | Wght | Price | Prod |
|---|---|---|---|---|
| 10137 | htp cpe | 2,400 | 2,083 | 24,045 |
| 10139 | htp sdn | 2,445 | 2,157 | 8,779 |
| Monza (wb 108.0) | | | | |
| 10537 | htp cpe | 2,445 | 2,350 | 37,605 |
| 10539 | htp sdn | 2,495 | 2,424 | 12,497 |
| 10567 | conv cpe | 2,675 | 2,493 | 10,345 |
| Corsa (wb 108.0) | | | | |
| 10737 | htp cpe | 2,485 | 2,519 | 7,330 |
| 10767 | conv cpe | 2,720 | 2,662 | 3,142 |

| 1966 Engines | bore × stroke | bhp | availability |
|---|---|---|---|
| flat 6, 164.0 | 3.44 × 2.94 | 95 | S-all exc Corsa |
| flat 6, 164.0 | 3.44 × 2.94 | 110 | O-all exc Corsa |
| flat 6, 164.0 | 3.44 × 2.94 | 140 | S-Corsa; O-others |
| flat 6T, 164.0 | 3.44 × 2.94 | 180 | O-Corsa |

## 1967

| 500 (wb 108.0) | | Wght | Price | Prod |
|---|---|---|---|---|
| 10137 | htp cpe | 2,435 | 2,128 | 9,257 |
| 10139 | htp sdn | 2,470 | 2,194 | 2,959 |
| Monza (wb 108.0) | | | | |
| 10537 | htp cpe | 2,465 | 2,398 | 9,771 |
| 10539 | htp sdn | 2,515 | 2,464 | 3,157 |
| 10567 | conv cpe | 2,695 | 2,540 | 2,109 |

| 1967 Engines | bore × stroke | bhp | availability |
|---|---|---|---|
| flat 6, 164.0 | 3.44 × 2.94 | 95 | S-all |
| flat 6, 164.0 | 3.44 × 2.94 | 110/140 | O-all |

## 1968

| 500 (wb 108.0) | | Wght | Price | Prod |
|---|---|---|---|---|
| 10137 | htp cpe | 2,470 | 2,243 | 7,206 |
| Monza (wb 108.0) | | | | |
| 10537 | htp cpe | 2,500 | 2,507 | 6,807 |
| 10567 | conv cpe | 2,725 | 2,626 | 1,386 |

| 1968 Engines | bore × stroke | bhp | availability |
|---|---|---|---|
| flat 6, 164.0 | 3.44 × 2.94 | 95 | S-all |
| flat 6, 164.0 | 3.44 × 2.94 | 110/140 | O-all |

## 1969

| 500 (wb 108.0) | | Wght | Price | Prod |
|---|---|---|---|---|
| 10137 | htp cpe | 2,515 | 2,528 | 2,762 |
| Monza (wb 108.0) | | | | |
| 10537 | htp cpe | 2,545 | 2,522 | 2,717 |
| 10567 | conv cpe | 2,770 | 2,641 | 521 |

| 1969 Engines | bore × stroke | bhp | availability |
|---|---|---|---|
| flat 6, 164.0 | 3.44 × 2.94 | 95 | S-all |
| flat 6, 164.0 | 3.44 × 2.94 | 110/140 | O-all |

# Chevrolet Corvette

America's most-enduring sports car debuted in January 1953 as a production-ready Motorama showmobile, the culmination of a 30-month development effort between Harley Earl's Art & Colour Studio and the Chevrolet Division Engineering Staff. Enthusiastic public response prompted management to okay production of the two-seat convertible—a brave decision as sales of import sports cars then amounted to less than one percent of the market. Production commenced June 30 on a small line at Chevy's Flint, Michigan, plant.

All Corvettes through 1962 rode a 102-inch wheelbase, identical with that of the Jaguar XK-120, one of Earl's favorite sports cars. The chassis was initially a cut-down and modified Chevrolet passenger-car frame. Body construction was unique: the first use of fiberglass in a series-production car by a major automaker. Styling was vintage Harley Earl show car: rounded and rather bulbous, with extended pod-type taillights, a toothy grille, and trendy wraparound windshield—hardly timeless, though it looked great at the time.

Ironically, in view of what lay ahead, Corvette almost expired after 1955 due to very low sales. Just 315 were built for '53 (most reserved for promotion and favored VIPs), followed by 3640 for '54—when production was shifted to St. Louis—and a mere 674 of the '55s. Some blamed this disappointing performance on the car's rather odd mix of features. Boulevardier types disliked the plastic side curtains, clumsy cloth top, and the lack of both back seat and exterior door handles. Enthusiasts chided the gimmicky styling and plodding drive-train—two-speed Powerglide automatic and Chevy's 235.5-cubic-inch "Stovebolt Six"—though triple carbs, high-lift cam, higher compression, and other changes brought the aged engine to a commendable 150 horsepower.

Thanks to pleas from Earl and Chevy chief engineer Ed Cole, GM decided in late 1954 to give Corvette a second chance. And Cole had what would prove to be its salvation: the brilliant 265-cid overhead-valve V-8 he'd designed with Harry Barr, John Gordon, and others for Chevy's all-new 1955 passenger cars. Arriving with 195 horsepower, it vastly improved Corvette performance, and almost all the '55 examples were so equipped. A newly optional three-speed floorshift manual gearbox further shifted the car's image from "plastic bathtub" to serious sporting machine.

The restyled '56 did even more, and Chevy rightly billed it as "America's only true sports car." A rounded rump and beautifully sculptured bodysides with curving, concave "coves" just aft of the front-wheel openings marked a stunning improvement over the stubby, slab-sided original. Proper roll-up windows and an optional lift-off hardtop (both previewed on a 1954 Motorama Corvette) made motoring more civilized, as did pushbutton door handles outside. Dropping the six and tuning the V-8 for 210 or 225 horsepower (the latter via high-lift cam, twin four-barrel carburetors, and dual exhausts) made for thrilling performance; adept chassis changes by newly hired engineer Zora Arkus-Duntov made handling more than capable. The close-ratio three-speed manual replaced standard Powerglide, which shifted to the options sheet. The most-potent '56 could nail 60 mph from rest in just 7.5 seconds and top 120 mph.

There was no need to change the handsome styling for '57, but Chevy upped performance by boring the V-8 to 283 cid. This came in five versions offering 220 horsepower up to an amazing 283 horsepower, the latter courtesy of new "Ramjet" fuel injection. A four-speed manual transmission arrived in April at $188 extra, and combined with axle ratios as low as 4.56:1 to make "fuelie" '57s thunderingly fast. Published road tests showed 0-60 in 5.7 seconds, 0-100 mph in 16.8 seconds, the standing quarter-mile in 14.3 seconds at 96 mph, and a maximum speed of 132-plus mph. Unfortunately, mechanical bugs and a steep $500 price limited Ramjet installations to only 1040 units that year. Chevy also offered a $725 "heavy-duty racing suspension" with high-rate springs and shocks, front antiroll bar, quick steering, and ceramic-metallic brake linings with finned drums. With this and one of the high-power engines, a '57 'Vette was virtually ready to race off the showroom floor.

And indeed, Corvette now began making its mark in international competition. Dr. Richard Thompson won the national Sports Car Club of America (SCCA) C-Production championship in 1956, then took the '57 crown in B-Production, where the 'Vette qualified by dint of its larger engine. John Fitch's '56 was the fastest modified car at that year's Daytona Speed Week, a Corvette finished 9th in the grueling 12 Hours of Sebring in '56, and another came home 2nd at Pebble Beach. Chevy's 1957 Sebring assault saw production Corvettes finish 1-2 in the GT class and 12th and 15th overall.

This success was all symbolic of a dramatic metamorphosis. Said one European writer: "Before Sebring . . . the Corvette was regarded as a plastic toy. After Sebring, even the most biased were forced to admit that [it was] one of the world's finest sports cars. . . ." That included buyers, who happily took 3467 of the '56s and 6339 of the '57s. Corvette's future was assured.

Nineteen fifty-eight brought a busier, shinier Corvette measuring 10 inches longer, more than two inches wider, and a few pounds heavier. The basic shape was broadly the same as 1956-57 except for quad headlamps (all the rage that year), a dummy air scoop ahead of each bodyside "cove," simulated hood lou-

**1954 Corvette convertible roadster**

**1955 Corvette Six convertible roadster**

# Chevrolet Corvette

1955 Corvette V-8 convertible roadster

1957 Corvette convertible coupe

1956 Corvette convertible coupe

1958 Corvette with optional hardtop

vers, and equally silly longitudinal chrome strips on the trunklid. Yet there were genuine improvements, including sturdier bumpers and a redesigned cockpit with passenger grab bar, locking glovebox, and all instruments directly ahead of the driver (instead of spread all the way across the panel, as before).

Despite the added heft, performance remained vivid because '58 engines were little changed. In fact, the top fuel-injected 283 gained seven horsepower to reach 290, thus exceeding the hallowed "1 hp per cu. in." benchmark reached the previous year. Inflation plagued the national economy in '58, yet base price remained reasonable at $3631, up just $118 from their debut in '53. Critics generally liked the '58. So did buyers. Model-year production gained 2829 units over the '57 tally as Corvette turned a profit for the first time.

Volume rose another 500 units for '59, when Chevy smoothed out the hood, deleted the chrome trunk trim, and added trailing radius rods (the year's only noteworthy mechanical change) to counteract rear-axle windup in hard acceleration. This basic package carried into 1960 as Corvette production broke the magic 10,000-unit barrier for the first time.

That year brought even higher compression on the top fuelie engine (11.0:1) for an incredible 315 horsepower, plus aluminum clutch housings for manual-shift models. A larger 24-gallon fuel tank was a new extra, and the optional heavy-duty suspension was replaced by a larger front antiroll bar and a new standard rear bar. An extra inch of wheel travel in rebound further contributed to a smoother ride and more-neutral handling. Aluminum radiators were newly offered, but announced cast-aluminum cylinder heads didn't make it.

Though Corvette was fast moving from *pur sang* sports car to plush GT, it was no less a competitor on the track. Highlights include a GT-class win and 12th overall at Sebring '58, national SCCA B-Production championships in 1958-59, fastest sports car at the 1958 Pike's Peak Hill Climb, and a slew of victories by privateers. Thanks to the Automobile Manufacturers Association mid-1957 edict, Chevy was officially "out of racing" now, though not above lending under-the-table support to those campaigning its cars. Among them was sportsman Briggs Cunningham, who gave Corvette one of its finest racing hours when one of his three team cars (driven by John Fitch and Bob Grossman) finished 8th in the 1960 running of the fabled 24 Hours of Le Mans.

The 1960 Corvette might have been very different. Beginning in 1957, Chevy contemplated a smaller, lighter car based on the prototype "Q-model," with rear transaxle, independent rear suspension, and inboard disc brakes. A full-size mockup soon took shape bearing a remarkable resemblance to the production Sting Ray then six years distant, but the project was abandoned because of the '58 recession and the time and money

1958 Corvette convertible coupe

1959 Corvette convertible coupe

# Chevrolet Corvette

1960 Corvette convertible coupe

1961 Corvette convertible coupe

1962 Corvette convertible coupe

1963 Sting Ray "split window" Sport Coupe

1963 Sting Ray with optional hardtop

being expended to bring out Chevy's rear-engine Corvair compact for 1960.

There was nothing to do but soldier on with the existing Corvette while designers and engineers set about creating a less radical replacement. Meantime, GM styling chief Harley Earl had retired in 1958, and his successor, William L. Mitchell, had an idea for breathing new life into the old Corvette.

It took the form of a 1961 model restyled behind the doors along the lines of Mitchell's 1959 Stingray racer (built on the "mule" chassis salvaged from 1957's unsuccessful Corvette SS prototype effort at Sebring). A new flowing "ducktail" not only increased luggage space some 20 percent but mated handsomely with the 1958-60 front, which Mitchell simplified by substituting mesh for the familiar chrome grille "teeth."

Powerteams again stood pat for '61, but Chevy continued to come up with refinements: standard sunvisors, higher-capacity aluminum-core radiator, side-mount expansion tanks, a wider choice of axle ratios. Base price was up to $3934, but that dough got you a lot of go. Even the mildest 283 with Powerglide was good for 7.7 seconds 0-60 mph and nearly 110 mph flat out; figures for the optional 315-bhp "fuelie" and four-speed manual were 5.5 seconds and 130-plus mph. In case anyone still doubted Corvette's track prowess, a near-stock model finished 11th at Sebring '61 against much-costlier and more-exotic racing machinery.

Refinement was again the keynote for '62, but Chevy gave a hint of things to come by offering the next Corvette's engines in the last "traditional" models. There were four in all—one fuelie and three with carburetors—all 283s bored and stroked to 327 cid, good for 250 up to a thumping 360 horsepower. The fuel-injection system was modified, a new 3.08:1 final-drive ratio gave quieter cruising with the two lowest-power engines, and the heavy-duty suspension option returned from '59. Styling was cleaner than ever. Mitchell eliminated the chrome outline around the "coves" and their optional two-toning, blacked-in the grille, and added ribbed aluminum appliques to rocker panels and the dummy reverse front-fender scoops.

Corvette continued its winning ways on the track and in the showroom for '62. Dick Thompson, the "flying dentist," won that year's national A-Production crown in SCCA, Don Yenko the B-P title. More important to GM managers, production was still climbing, from 1961's record 10,000-plus to over 14,500. No question now: The 'Vette was here to stay.

And how. Nineteen sixty-three brought the all-new Sting Ray,

# Chevrolet Corvette

the first complete revision of Chevrolet's sports car in 10 years—a revolution and a revelation. Apart from four wheels and two seats, the only things the new 'Vette shared with the '62 were steering, front suspension, the four 327 V-8s, and fiberglass bodywork. Most everything else was changed—definitely for the better.

Dimensional changes involved slightly shorter overall length, a two-inch narrower rear track, and a wheelbase pared four inches (to 98). Curb weight was also reduced, thanks to a new ladder-type frame (replacing the heavy old X-member affair) and despite a new steel-reinforced "cage" that made for a stronger, safer cockpit. In fact, the Sting Ray had almost twice as much steel support in its main body structure as previous Corvettes, and less fiberglass in its body. Brakes remained drums but were now self-adjusting, and the fronts were wider.

The big mechanical news for '63 was independent rear suspension, a first for a modern U.S. production car. Duntov's clever thinking produced a frame-mounted differential with U-jointed halfshafts acting on a single transverse leaf spring; differential-mounted control arms ran laterally and slightly forward to the hub carriers to limit fore/aft movement, and a pair of trailing radius rods was fitted behind. This arrangement was elegantly simple, relatively cheap, and highly effective. Front/rear weight distribution was now 48/52 percent versus the former 53/47. New recirculating-ball steering combined with a dual-arm, three-link ball-joint front suspension for quicker steering. With all this, Corvette ride and handling were better than ever.

Engines were unchanged from '62, but the '63 versions carried alternators instead of generators, positive crankcase ventilation, and smaller flywheels. Competition options included stiff suspension, metallic brake linings, handsome cast-aluminum wheels with genuine knock-off hubs, and a 36.5-gallon long-distance fuel tank.

Sting Ray styling was equally new and quite dramatic, evolved from the experimental XP-720 coupe of late 1959. The customary convertible gained a sleek fastback coupe companion—a first for Corvette—with rear window split by a vertical divider. Duntov lobbied against the last, saying it hampered outward vision. Mitchell huffed in reply that "if you take that off, you might as well forget the whole thing." Duntov ultimately won, and a one-piece backlight was substituted after '63, leaving the split-window coupe a one-year model—and today all the more highly prized because of it.

Both '63 Sting Rays carried hidden headlights (in rotating pods that fit flush with the pointy nose when the lamps were off), an attractive beltline dip at the doors' trailing edges, humped front and rear fenders, slim L-shape half-bumpers at each end, a slightly different "ducktail," and a sharp full-perimeter "character line" at midbody height. Inside was a new "dual cockpit" dashboard with complete set of big gauges and Corvette's first proper glovebox. Coupe interior access was facilitated by doors cut into the roof. An optional lift-off hardtop was still available for the convertible.

Because of work on the stillborn Q-model, the Sting Ray coupe was developed first, then the convertible. A 2+2 coupe was considered, progressing as far as a full-size mockup, but was rejected as being out of character for Corvette. Prototypes received intensive wind-tunnel testing that resulted in frontal area being trimmed by a square foot. Despite the shorter wheelbase, interior space was at least as good as in previous Corvettes.

The Sting Ray quickly proved the fastest and most-roadable 'Vette, yet. It was also the most popular: 1963 sales were nearly twice the record '62 total, about 10,000 for each body style. Performance had less to do with this than the wider market

1963 Sting Ray convertible coupe

1964 Sting Ray sport coupe

1964 Sting Ray convertible coupe

1965 Sting Ray sport coupe

appeal of new extra-cost creature comforts: leather upholstery, power steering, power brakes (at last), AM/FM radio, air conditioning, and more.

Over the next four years, the Sting Ray was progressively cleaned up, Chevy removing what little nonsense there was or making it functional, as with the fake hood louvers (erased) and coupe rear quarter vents (opened up) for '64. The following year, the sculptured hood was smoothed out and the dummy front-fender slots were made working vents. The design was virtually perfected by 1967, when the only changes were a single oblong backup light above the license plate, bolt-on instead of knock-off aluminum wheels, revised front-fender louvers,

# Chevrolet Corvette

1965 Sting Ray convertible coupe

1966 Sting Ray sport coupe

1967 Sting Ray sport coupe

and an optional vinyl covering for the convertible's accessory hardtop.

Naturally, there were important mechanical improvements in the Sting Ray years. The fuelie 327 was boosted to as high as 375 horsepower for 1964. The following year brought optional four-wheel disc brakes for stopping power to match the steadily escalating performance. Also new for '65 was Corvette's first big-block V-8, the 425-bhp "Mark IV." This was initially sized at 396 cid, then enlarged to 427. To handle its brute force, Chevy specified stiffer suspension, extra-heavy-duty clutch, and larger radiator and fan. With the 4.11:1 rear axle, a '66 Mark IV could do 0-60 in less than five seconds and more than 140 mph flat out—not bad for a civilized, fully equipped machine selling for around $4500. Fuel injection was dropped for the smaller-displacement engines after 1965, mainly due to high production costs and low sales.

But Corvette sales as a whole set new records in all but one of the Sting Ray years, peaking at nearly 28,000 for '66. Horsepower seemed to set yearly records, too. That peak was reached with the stupendous L88 option of 1967: an aluminum-head 427 with 12.5:1 compression, wild cam, and big four-barrel carb, putting out no less than 560 horsepower, but conservatively rated at 430. Only 20 cars were so equipped, but they symbolized how far the 'Vette had come.

Of course, many of the high-power Sting Rays went racing, though they often bowed to Carroll Shelby's stark, super-quick Cobras. Still, there were bright spots. Don Yenko was SCCA national B-Production champ in 1963, a Roger Penske car won its class at Nassau '65, and 1966 saw Sting Rays place 12th overall in the Daytona Continental and 9th at Sebring.

The Sting Ray was a tough act to follow, and not everyone liked its 1968 replacement. Arriving for the first year of federal safety and emissions standards, it combined a new seven-inch-longer body (most of the increase in front overhang) with essentially carryover engines and chassis. Styling, previewed by the 1965 Mako Shark II show car, was all humpy and muscular, with fulsome front and rear fenders housing seven-inch-wide wheels for better roadholding. Flip-up headlamps and modest "lip" spoilers at each end were also featured but, like the Sting Rays, there was still no opening trunklid. And the name wasn't Sting Ray anymore, just Corvette. Coupe and convertible returned, the former a new notchback style with an innovative "T-top" design: twin panels could be removed to create a semiconvertible. Mechanical upgrades were limited to standardizing the previously optional all-disc brakes and substituting General Motors' fine three-speed Turbo Hydra-Matic for the archaic Powerglide.

This third-generation Corvette would have bowed for 1967 had Zora Arkus-Duntov not delayed it to work out some kinks. Still, the '68s had plenty of problems. The most glaring was poor workmanship that led one motor-noter to label his press car "unfit to road test." Other writers judged the new design needlessly gimmicky, with a dashboard awash in winking lights and a trouble-prone pop-up cowl panel hiding the wipers. A narrower cockpit, a penalty of the wasp-waisted styling, and less luggage space didn't win any friends. Neither did inadequate cooling on big-block cars, nor did an average 150 pounds of extra weight. Yet, in spite of all that, the '68 set another Corvette sales record at more than 28,500 units.

The tally was nearly 38,800 for '69, when the Stingray name reappeared—this time as one word on front fenders. Duntov did his best to correct inherent flaws in the year-old design, finding a little more cockpit space (smaller steering wheel, slimmer door panels), adding an override so the wiper panel could be left up in freezing weather, and reworking other assorted bits. Detail styling changes comprised neater outside door handles, black instead of chrome grille bars, and backup lights integrated within the inner taillights. Handling improved via wider wheels, and the frame was stiffened. Emissions considerations prompted lower compression ratios and a small-

# Chevrolet Corvette

block V-8 stroked to 350 cid, while a fourth 427 option appeared with a nominal 430 horsepower and available axle ratios from 4.56:1 to 2.75:1. Even wilder was the all-aluminum ZL-1 big-block, a virtual Can-Am racing engine priced at a formidable $3000. Production? Just two. But Corvette celebrated a production benchmark that year as number 250,000 came off the St. Louis line.

Volume promptly plunged some 50 percent for 1970, thanks to a two-month auto-workers strike. The main news that season was a big-block punched out to 454 cid, again to meet emissions standards that were increasingly sapping power from all Detroit engines. Even so, lower compression left the big-block LS-5 at 390 horsepower. A more-powerful LS-7 version rated at 460 horsepower was advertised and prototype Corvettes so equipped were produced, but the engine was never actually offered for public sale because it couldn't be made "clean" enough. The rest of the car was again little changed—a fine-check grille and front-fender vents provided visual I.D.—but Chevy cleaned up more details and offered a 370-bhp solid-lifter LT-1 small-block as promised, though not delivered, for '69.

Inflation, rising gas prices, and soaring insurance rates were putting a big crimp in performance-car sales. Corvette was no exception, its 1972 volume not even equaling '69's. That year's switch to more-realistic SAE net power ratings made engines seem punier—which they were—and the LS-6 was canceled along with the fiber-optic exterior light monitors available since '68. However, the once-optional antitheft alarm system was now standard, a belated nod to the 'Vette's high "thievability."

The '73s gained a body-color nose of pliable plastic in line with the government's new five-mph impact-protection rule, plus more insulation and new chassis mounts for quietness. The coupe's removable rear window, a feature since '68, went away. So did all engines save a pair of 350s and one 454. Rear-impact standards dictated a matching body-color tail for the '74s, which arrived with the Middle East oil embargo, still higher gas prices, and long lines at the pumps. Yet, while other cars suffered sales drops, Corvette kept climbing.

But it kept slipping, too. Both the LT-1 and the last big-block options were banished after '74, as was the traditional convertible after '75, a victim of steadily falling demand. Changes were few through 1977 (when Stingray badges came off again), yet sales remained strong. The '76 tally broke the 1969 record with over 46,550. The '77s sold an improbable 49,000-plus.

Clearly, Chevy had made a silk purse of the sow's-ear '68 and reaped the rewards. Government's heavy hand made a change in the car's character inevitable, but that was hardly bad. By 1975, the Corvette had become more balanced, less outlandish, and arguably more pleasant. A juvenile straightline screamer had matured into a suave, high-speed gran turismo.

Still, enthusiasts had been long clamoring for an all-new Vette. A pair of 1972 Wankel-engine show cars strongly hinted it could be a midengine design. Perhaps in time for Corvette's silver anniversary in 1978? No, but it came close for 1980. Its basis would have been the Aerovette, the renamed V-8-powered iteration of the four-rotor 1972 experiment. Bill Mitchell lobbied hard for a production version, and GM president Tom Murphy actually approved one very similar to the show-car design. By late '77, Aerovette-style clay models were complete and tooling was ready to be ordered. But the plan foundered when Mitchell retired that year. Zora Duntov, another booster, had retired at the end of '74, and his successor as Corvette chief engineer, David R. McLellan, wanted to keep the "front mid-engine" format for reasons of packaging, manufacturing, performance, and cost.

Indeed, cost finally killed the production Aerovette—never

1968 Corvette convertible coupe

1968 Corvette sport coupe

1969 Stingray coupe

1970 Stingray coupe

mind that midengine designs had not proven the wave of the sports-car future as some predicted back in the '60s. Chevy duly regrouped. By mid-1978, McLellan and company were working on a more-conventional new Corvette.

Meantime, the third generation would have to hold on awhile—no big problem, what with sales still strong. Nevertheless, GM decided to splurge on rejuvenating the old warrior for Corvette's 25th birthday year.

The '78 thus received one big change—a new fastback roofline with a huge compound-curve rear window *a la* Sting Ray—and a host of minor ones (mostly to the cockpit). Corvette was named pace car for that year's Indy 500, and

Chevrolet issued 6200 replicas with special paint, leather interior, and owner-applied pace-car decals. To the division's chagrin, quick-buck artists were quick to convert standard 'Vettes into bogus replicas, creating no little confusion. There was also a Silver Anniversary model, actually a trim package and not all that different from stock. Engine choices were down to two 350s: standard 185-bhp L48 and extra-cost 220-bhp L82.

Corvette mostly marked time for '79. It was now quite plush for a sports car. Power windows, air, tilt steering wheel, power door locks, and AM/FM stereo were all included in a base price swelled by inflation from $9645 to $12,313 in just one year. Despite the cost and poor mileage, sales leaped to over 50,000.

Chevy finally put its sports car on a diet for 1980, removing some 150 pounds via wider use of plastics and by substituting aluminum for steel in the differential housing and front frame crossmember. Aerodynamics improved via a new sloped nose with integral spoiler, plus a faired-in rear spoiler.

More weight-saving occurred for '81, mostly from a fiberglass rear leaf spring and thinner glass for door windows and the optional see-through T-tops. There was now just one 350, a new L81 version with magnesium rocker covers, stainless-steel exhaust manifold, and GM's Computer Command Control engine-management system. Horsepower was unchanged. Government fuel-economy mandates dictated a lockup torque converter for the optional automatic transmission. Inflation pushed base price past $15,000, but that included six-way power driver's seat—and Cadillac-style front cornering lights!

This year saw the historic transfer of production from St. Louis to a new high-tech plant in Bowling Green, Kentucky, built exclusively for Corvette. With it came promises of improved workmanship.

The move to Kentucky also suggested that an all-new Corvette was imminent at last. It was—and sorely needed. Volume had withered since the all-time high of 1979, dropping to the 40,000 level for 1980 and '81. The following year, when the old "shark" design made its 15th and final appearance, production crumbled to a 10-year low of 25,407. A second energy crisis and a deep new national recession hardly helped.

That final "shark" previewed the next-generation drivetrain in a revised L83 engine with fuel injection—the first "fuelie" Corvette since 1965. And for the first time since 1955, there was no manual gearbox, just a new four-speed automatic with torque-converter lockup on all forward gears save first. But the real kicker was another limited-production job tellingly named Collector Edition, with lift-up rear window (belatedly) and unique trim. It was the costliest 'Vette yet at a towering $22,537, a far cry from the $4663 it took to buy a '68. This time, Chevy avoided forgeries by building as many Collectors as customers demanded, which ended up at 6759.

Historians huffed when the much-anticipated fourth generation bowed in early '83 as a 1984 model (a decision made mainly to ease emissions certification)—thus skipping Corvette's 30th model year. Some observers (including former design chief Bill Mitchell) criticized appearance as bland, but most

**1972 Stingray coupe**

**1974 Stingray coupe**

**1975 Stingray coupe**

# Chevrolet Corvette

people liked it. Created under the direction of Jerry Palmer, it was clean, contemporary, recognizably Corvette, and 23.7 percent more aerodynamic—in all, quite a feat. A lift-up hatch window returned from the Collector Edition, but the T-top gave way to a one-piece roof panel, and a new front-hinged "clamshell" hood/fender assembly offered superb engine access.

That engine was a 205-bhp L83 with "Cross-Fire" dual-throttle-body injection, initially mated to four-speed converter-lockup Turbo Hydra-Matic. But the autobox soon became an optional alternative to a new "4+3 Overdrive" manual. The work of 'Vette specialist Doug Nash, this was basically the normal four-speed with a second planetary gearset actuated by engine electronics to provide gas-saving overdrive ratios in all gears but first.

The rest of the '84 was equally new, starting with its "uniframe" construction: a Lotus-like backbone chassis welded to an upper "birdcage." Front suspension was modified with a single transverse plastic leaf spring replacing individual coils. At the rear was new five-link geometry comprising upper and lower longitudinal links, twin lateral strut rods from differential to hub carriers, and the usual tie rods, halfshafts, and transverse plastic leaf spring. Steering switched to rack-and-pinion, and there were new-design disc brakes. Tires were Goodyear's new ultrasticky Eagle VR50s with unidirectional "gatorback" tread, worn on wide cast-alloy wheels.

Weight-saving was again a priority, so the '84 had more lightweight materials than any previous Corvette (including beautiful aluminum forgings for suspension components). Though 150 pounds lighter than the '82, the '84 ended up some 300 pounds heavier than expected despite reductions of two inches in wheelbase (to 96.2) and 8.8 inches in overall length.

Still, the '84 offered more passenger and cargo space, better outward vision, and all the comfort and luxury expected in a thoroughbred GT. Unfortunately, it introduced a dazzling digital/graphic electronic gauge cluster that was hard to read, especially on sunny days. A harsh ride—even harsher with the Z51 handling option—emphasized the new structure's surprising flex. A record base price—$23,360—also drew barbs. But that was about all anyone could fault. Few sports cars could rival the Corvette's performance. Buyers evidently thought it as a good value, for model-year production roared back to near the '79 level, ending at over 51,500.

Chevy tended to details for '85, gaining 25 horsepower by switching from "Cross-Fire" to "Tuned Port" injection, softening both standard and optional suspensions, and adding an oil cooler and gas-pressurized shock absorbers. The '86s were even better. The brakes received standard Bosch antilock control for stopping power to match the now-stupendous cornering power. Though horsepower remained at 230, the evergreen

**1976 Stingray coupe**

**1977 Corvette Coupe**

**1978 Silver Anniversary Corvette coupe**

**1979 Corvette coupe**

**1980 Corvette Coupe**

**1981 Corvette coupe**

# Chevrolet Corvette

1982 Corvette coupe

1984 Corvette Coupe

1984 Corvette Coupe

1985 Corvette Coupe

1986 Corvette Official Pace Car

# Chevrolet Corvette

small-block 350 (now designated L98) received aluminum cylinder heads, higher compression (9.5:1 versus 9.0), and dual exhaust.

But the big event of 1986 was the midseason return of the Corvette convertible after a 10-year absence. To no one's great surprise, it arrived just in time to be selected Indianapolis 500 pace car—which meant another batch of replicas, all yellow ragtops. Because the fourth generation had been designed to be topless, structural stiffening was straightforward: an X-member below the floorpan and reinforcements around the cockpit.

The main change for '87 was roller valve lifters that added another 10 horses for a total of 240. Chevrolet also announced an optional in-cockpit tire-pressure monitoring system, similar to that of the otherworldly Porsche 959, but development problems would delay this until 1989. Seeking still more cornering power, Chevy offered the '88s with optional 17-inch wheels wearing fat P275/40ZR Goodyear Eagle tires. Both these and the standard 16-inch rims were newly styled. Suspension was modified to better resist rear-end squat in hard acceleration and nosedive in panic braking, which was now handled by larger, thicker, all-disc brakes with dual-piston front calipers. Freer-breathing heads and a reprofiled camshaft boosted horsepower to 245.

Another milestone Corvette birthday rolled around in '88—the 35th—and Chevy celebrated with specially trimmed anniversary coupes (actually an optional appearance package, RPO Z01). This was done mostly in white—including interior and even nameplates—accented by black roof pillars and black-tint glass roof panel. Automatic climate system, all-leather cockpit trim, power sports seats, heated rear window and door mirrors, and a Delco/Bose sound system were included, too. Though just 2050 were built, it was a nice way for America's sports car to enter middle age with a 35-year production total approaching 900,000.

But it was only a warm up to 1990's amazing new "King of the Hill" Corvette, a constant subject of "buff book" spy reports since late '87. Though delayed from a planned '89 launch, the ZR1 was well worth waiting for—another Chevy option code destined to make history. Available only in coupe form, it boasted an all-new, all-aluminum V-8 designated LT5, still a 350 but with a smaller bore and longer stroke than the existing L98—plus dual overhead camshafts actuating four valves per cylinder.

LT5 specs read like a competition textbook: forged-steel crank and conrods, diecast pistons, stellite-faced valves, sequential-port fuel injection, "Direct Fire" all-coil ignition, high 11.25:1 compression, and more. The result was 375 horsepower—astounding for a modern emissions-controlled street engine claimed to deliver up to 22.5 mpg. A unique feature was three-stage throttle control providing "stepped" power delivery via the engine's electronic control module. To keep lesser-skilled—or unauthorized—drivers from getting into trouble, the system included a "power mode" that precluded full power at full throttle without a special key. The LT5 was carefully engineered so the engine bay wouldn't need alteration, but the ZR1 was easily spotted from behind by its square taillights and subtly bulged bodywork draped over super-wide tires.

Two ZR1 innovations premiered on '89 Corvettes. One was a six-speed manual gearbox designed by Chevy and Germany's ZF. It had vastly better shift action than the never-liked "4+3" it replaced, but also a rather odd thing called computer-aided gear selection (CAGS) that "forced" a 1-4 shift at light throttle between 12 and 19 mph. Here was another subtle extreme dictated by EPA fuel-economy test procedures and Chevy's desire that Corvette avoid the government's dreaded new gas-guzzler tax. But though CAGS seemed to spoil the fun, it scarcely ever activated in the kind of driving done by most 'Vette owners.

**1986 Corvette convertible "roadster"**

**1987 Corvette coupe**

**1987 Corvette convertible coupe**

Corvette's other '89 innovation was Selective Ride Control (RPO FX3), restricted to cars with the new six-speed and the Z51 handling package. Like some Japanese setups, this electromechanical system provided three selectable damping levels—Touring, Sport, and Competition—via electric motors that varied the size of the proportioning-valve orifice in each shock absorber. Each level also had six progressively firmer settings that automatically cut in with increasing speed, and a high-speed override automatically switched settings for optimum handling. Developed by Bilstein and GM's Delco Division, SRC claimed to improve both ride and cornering, which it did, though not dramatically.

Other '89 developments began with making the 17-inch wheel/tire option and a modified Z52 handling package newly standard for all models. The latter included strengthened front chassis (introduced with the '86 convertible), faster-ratio steering, Delco/Bilstein gas-filled shocks and, for six-speed cars, engine-oil cooler, heavy-duty radiator, and auxiliary cooling fan. Seats were redesigned, and new leather-covered sport lumbar adjustment to the usual six-way positioning. Finally, rearranged top latches made the convertible more-convenient, and Chevy returned to tradition by offering a detachable hardtop for it (priced at $2000).

ZR1 aside, the main 1990 news involved two laudable standard safety features: a driver-side air bag (hidden in the steer-

1988 Corvette coupe

1988 Corvette 35th Anniversary Edition

1989 Corvette with "Convertible Hardtop"

ing-wheel hub) and Bosch "ABS II" antilock braking system. The latter was especially worthwhile on the ZR1, which could do a blistering 4.5 seconds 0-60 and top 175 mph. Not laudable at all was the new "aircraft-inspired" instrument panel given all 1990 Vettes, a planned change that was largely responsible for delaying the ZR1. It was definitely not for the better: a plasticky mish-mash of shapes and colors more outrageous than ergonomic.

On balance, though, the fourth-series Corvette evolved nicely through 1990. The same could not be said for sales after 1984. Model-year production dropped below 40,000 for '85, then sank to less than 31,000 in '87 before bottoming out at fewer than 23,000 for 1988. There was a modest recovery for '89, but the tally was down again for 1990 to some 23,646. The onset of yet another sharp recession played a part, but so did escalating prices. By 1990, the base coupe was $32,000; the convertible over $37,000. Then there was the ZR1, the costliest GM car ever with a delivered retail price of just under $59,000. Rabid speculators and fools with money gladly bid that up to over $100-grand—but not for long. Within 18 months the ZR1 was selling for well under retail amid reports of surplus LT5s and rumors that Chevy would soon kill the "King of the Hill."

In a way, Chevy did precisely that with a 1991 "taillift" for regular 'Vettes. To the outrage of those who'd rushed to buy ZR1s, the standard article now wore a similar convex back panel and square taillights. Though Chevy never explained this move, the likely reason was to boost overall Corvette sales with ZR1 style. If so, the plan backfired, as model-year volume slipped to a little over 20,600. Of these, a mere 2044 were ZR1s, a drop from 3049 the previous season. By the way, the King was now technically a package option, not a separate model, adding $31,683 to the normal coupe's $32,455 base sticker.

Nineteen ninety-one also brought the fourth-generation's first facelift, as all models, ZR1 included, wore a smoother, slimmer nose with wrapped turn-signal/fog-lamp assemblies. In addition, the twin front-fender "gills" gave way to four horizontal "strakes." Mechanical changes were of the detail sort: a standard power-steering cooler, a new Z07 package combining the FX3 and Z51 options, first-time FX3 availability for the convertible, and a new "retained power" feature that allowed operating accessories for a few minutes after shutting off.

Dave Hill took over as Corvette chief engineer in September 1992. He was a good choice, having played the same role for Cadillac's short-lived Allanté. Hill was no less committed than Dave McClelland to traditional 'Vette values, including rear drive and a unique platform. But with two-seater sales increasingly tough—and with GM facing a huge cash crisis—he also knew that Corvette would have to "pull its own weight" as never before. That meant not only improving sales but making each one more profitable by taking cost out of the car—with-

# Chevrolet Corvette

out spoiling it, of course. GM was known to be thinking about spinning future 'Vettes from a higher-volume platform, but Hill wouldn't have that. As he told the press in 1993: "I can assure you, the last thing on our minds is a hot version of the Camaro replacing the Corvette."

As if to signal renewed faith in its sports car, Chevy again reworked the hallowed small-block V-8 for 1992 to give base Corvettes an extra 55 horsepower. The rejuvenated engine, titled LT1, was also quicker to wind and had a higher rev limit, though it wasn't as torquey as the L98, with 330 pound-feet peaking at 4000 rpm (versus 340 at 3200). Nevertheless, the LT1 was cheered by the press and enthusiasts alike, many of whom felt that it rendered the ZR1 almost superfluous. And in fact, with its 5.4-second 0-60 capability, the LT1 wasn't that much slower than the King, especially given the price difference.

The ZR1 itself added front-fender nameplates for '92, but all Corvettes now boasted Acceleration Slip Regulation, a new Bosch-designed traction-control system. Like similar setups at Porsche, BMW, and Mercedes, this one used the ABS sensors to detect wheelspin, in which event it would either brake the offending wheels and/or throttle back power to keep you from slip-sliding away. To back it up, all '92s wore grippier tires, Goodyear's new asymmetric-tread Eagle GS-C.

Those tires grew wider on standard '93s, and wider aft than fore. In fact, they were now close to King size: at the back, 285/40ZR17s on 9.5-inch-wide rims; in front, 255/45ZR17s on 8.5s. Also for '93, the LT1 was retuned for 10 extra pound-feet of torque, but the LT5 was attended to as well, internal changes boosting horsepower to 405 at 5800 rpm (up 30 bhp) and torque to 385 pound-feet at 5200 (up 15). With that, the ZR1 was again the power king of American production cars after bowing to Dodge's spartan new Viper RT/10 in 1991-92.

Unfortunately, the extra muscle didn't do much for the King's 0-60 kick—about 0.2-second at most, according to *Car and Driver*. Top speed, however, was up six mph to a shattering 179, and the new tires improved skidpad cornering from 0.88g to a race-carlike 0.92. Yet all this was quite academic, for ZR1 sales were just a trickle now: a mere 448 for '93, down from 502 the previous model year. On the other hand, overall Corvette sales went up for the first time in four years. Though an improvement of only a little over 1000 units, the '93 upsurge to 21,680 was heartening in Corvette's 40th year.

Yes, it was birthday time again, and as everyone knew it would, Chevrolet issued another anniversary special. A $1455 package option available for any '93, it comprised Ruby Red paint and wheel centers, a color-matched leather-trimmed interior, embroidered "40th" logos on headrests, and corresponding bright insignia on nose, deck, and front fenders. Available separately was a new gadget, the Passive Keyless Entry system. This used a pair of small transmitters to generate a low-power electromagnetic field within a few feet of the car's perimeter; walking up to or away from the car interrupted the field to lock or unlock the doors and hatch. It was a gimmick worthy of Cadillac, Mercedes, or Lexus, but only Corvette had it. Of course, the 'Vette had been picking up such do-dads for years, yet even the posh '93 was still no less the red-blooded all-American sports car loved by millions all over the world.

A good many of those folks got together in September 1994 for a genuine lovefest: the opening of the National Corvette Museum. Located in Bowling Green, not far from the factory, this shrine to America's sports car was built with private funds—and no blessing from Chevy at first. But the division soon recognized it as—ahem—a concrete expression of Corvette fandom and thus a potential gold mine of corporate goodwill. Accordingly, Chevy raided its attic for exhibits, making "permanent loans" of various historic Corvettes, engines

1989 Corvette coupe

1989 Corvette ZR-1 prototype

1990 Corvette with "convertible hardtop"

and other memorabilia, including the '59 Mitchell Sting Ray and the Mako II show car. Zora Duntov was persuaded to attend the museum's opening ceremonies, as was Dave McClelland. Both were doubtless moved by the sight of some 2000 vintage Corvettes driven in from around the U.S. (and a few foreign countries) by loyal owners who just had to be present for a signal moment in automotive history.

Chevy, meantime, cheered a second consecutive gain in Corvette volume, the '94s attracting 23,200 sales despite being little changed. Still, what few changes they had were welcome: a modified dash with knee bolsters and passenger airbag; electronic controls and safety-shift interlock for automatic models; standard heated glass backlight for ragtops; new-design five-spoke wheels for ZR1; softer damping for the FX3 option; a new steering wheel, seats, and door panels. The ZR1 package was downpriced a bit to $31,258, but managed only 448 orders.

The King was belatedly buried after 1995 and a final 448 examples. It would have died sooner, but Chevy was obliged to buy so many LT5 engines from contract builder Mercury Marine, and the condition was only met that year. Happily, other '95 Corvettes got the ZR1's heavy-duty brakes as standard, plus revised fender "gills" and, on automatic models, a transmission-fluid temperature gauge. Base prices were the highest ever, though not exorbitant for the day at $36,785 for the coupe and $43,665 for the ragtop.

# Chevrolet Corvette

A near-stock LT1 convertible paced the 1995 Indy 500, the third such honor for Corvette and the 10th for a Chevrolet. Predictably, the division ran off a few replicas: this time, exactly 527. All were painted Dark Purple Metallic over Arctic White and came with "79th Indianapolis 500" decals for owner application, plus complimentary embroidered logos on the seats.

Magazine testers had been noticing steady improvements in Corvette workmanship and ride comfort, and the '95s were the best yet. Though Chevy couldn't seem to exorcise certain squeaks and rattles, the fourth generation was by now acceptably tight and solid on rough roads, which no longer chattered your teeth so much except with the hard-riding Z51 suspension.

Meantime, the division confirmed what spies were reporting: a brand-new 1997 Corvette that promised to be simpler, lighter, stronger, and more affordable. With that, the fourth series made a final stand for 1996. Signaling the end of this line was another Collector Edition, a $1250 package that dressed a coupe or convertible with pearlescent Sebring Silver paint, bright five-spoke alloys, and special emblems and trim.

More intriguing was a new limited-edition Grand Sport package (RPO Z16), a successor of sorts to the ZR1. Priced at $3250 for coupes and $2880 for convertibles, it delivered the King's wheels and tires, showy black brake calipers, and a pair of red "hashmarks" on the left fender. Coupes also came with tacked-on rear fender flares. A specific color scheme combined Admiral Blue paint with a broad, white dorsal stripe, recalling the trio of original GS Sting Rays raced by John Mecom at Nassau in '63.

But the Grand Sport's big attraction was its new LT4 engine. Optional for other '96s at $1450, it was essentially a higher-output LT1 with wider ports, bigger valves with hollow stems and stronger springs, reshaped pistons giving 10.8:1 compression (versus 10.4), wilder cam, high-flow fuel injectors, and a sturdier crank. The result was 330 horsepower peaking at a higher 5800 rpm, plus five extra pound-feet of torque.

Rounding out GS features were six-way power sport seats with embroidered "Grand Sport" legends and a leather-lined interior in all-black or black and blinding red. Future trivia hounds should note that the coupe's lift-off roof-panel option was *verboten* with the GS group, and that white was the only top color for GS convertibles. Available for all '96s was new "Selective Real-Time Damping," essentially a faster-acting FX3 setup priced at $1695.

GS production was quite low, comprising 810 coupes and just 190 convertibles. That rarity, plus a unique blend of features, implies one of the more collectible 'Vettes of this generation–second only, perhaps, to the mythic ZR1.

Though not widely appreciated, the 'Vette again came close to extinction in the early '90s. The reason was General Motors' huge $4.5 million loss of 1991, which led to a management shakeup that ousted Robert Stempel as company chairman and prompted a temporary freeze on new-model programs through 1996—including a new-generation Corvette. Within days, however, GM's new leaders saw proposals for Chevy's next sports car and gave it the green light, though there was no way it would debut as planned for 1993 in time for Corvette's 40th anniversary.

The new 'Vette was called "C5," (rather inaccurately, we

**1990 Corvette ZR-1 coupe**

**1991 Corvette coupe**

**1991 Corvette convertible**

**1992 Corvette coupe**

**1992 Corvette convertible**

# Chevrolet Corvette

1993 Corvette 40th Anniversary Edition

1994 Corvette convertible

1993 Corvette ZR-1 coupe

1994 Corvette coupe

think) for Corvette fifth generation. This went against the tradition chronology that would have named the new series "C7." But though some four years late, it was well worth waiting for—whatever you called it. For starters, it was the first all-new design in Corvette history, with virtually no borrowed or carry-over components. New it had to be, because Chevy wanted to dramatically expand Corvette's market reach while reducing production costs. Team Corvette succeeded admirably on both counts under Dave Hill. The result was the most technically advanced 'Vette yet—and by most all accounts the best Corvette ever.

Desired gains in passenger space, luggage room, and structural rigidity dictated a clean-sheet design and altered dimensions. Against its predecessor, the C5 was a sizable 8.3 inches longer in wheelbase (a Corvette record at 104.5 inches), nearly three inches wider, and 1.4 inches taller; yet stretched only 1.2 inches longer overall and actually weighed some 80 pounds less in initial hatch coupe form. Beneath the slinky new fiberglass body, which boasted a lower, 0.29 drag factor, was an entirely new structural skeleton built around a much-stiffer frame with a central "backbone" measuring 12 inches high, nine inches wide and four feet long. Immensely rigid, this chassis featured full-length "hydroformed" side rails diecast by a high-pressure water process into stout 4×6-inch members. Providing further reinforcement were a windshield/cowl structure of welded aluminum castings and extrusions, attached to a pair of sturdy rectangular steel members rising from the front frame rails. A cast-magnesium steering column/pedal box added more strength without excess weight. A new steel superstructure provided better support for the coupe's liftup rear window and takeoff roof panel, the latter newly framed in magnesium and attached by convenient latches instead of bolts and a wrench.

Despite the sturdy side rails, sill height was dropped four inches, making for much easier entry/exit than in a C4. Footwells were usefully wider, helped by Corvette's first rear-mounted transmission, which was either four-speed automatic or optional six-speed manual. This wasn't a true rear transaxle, as the differential remained separate, but it didn't impinge on luggage space, which more than doubled in the hatch coupe to 25 cubic feet. More importantly, the tail-mounted tranny helped improve fore/aft weight distribution to 51.5/48.5 percent, all the better for handling.

So, too, the suspension, which applied to new geometry to basic C4 elements. For example, unequal-length A-arms returned up front and an antiroll bar and plastic transverse leaf spring reprised at each end, but all suspension pieces now mounted to noise-isolating cast-aluminum subframes. In addition, rear A-arms with toe-control links relieved the halfshafts of suspension duty, bushings were changed all-round, and shocks were repositioned and revalved for tighter wheel control. Steering changed to GM's new computer-managed "Magnasteer II" system that varied effort according to road speed via electromagnets instead of hydraulics. All-disc antilock brakes returned, slightly smaller in diameter but thicker. In another departure, tires were slightly narrower but larger aft than fore—respectively, P275/40ZR18 and P245/45ZR17. And they were unique to Corvette, being specially developed Goodyear Eagle F1 GS EMTs designed to run safely without air pressure for up to 200 miles, thus eliminating the need for a space-robbing spare tire and jack.

As if all this weren't enough, the C5 got a new engine, too. Dubbed LS1, it looked superficially like an update of the LT1/LT4, with two overhead valves per cylinder and nominal 5.7-liter displacement. In fact, though, only bore spacing was shared. Besides a deeper-skirted new block made of aluminum instead of cast iron, the LS1 boasted new cylinder heads, freer-flow intake and exhaust systems, and Corvette's first "drive-by-wire" throttle. The last replaced the normal mechanical linkage with an electric motor that worked the throttle by computer control according to input from an accelerator position sensor. The throttle was tied through the engine computer to standard cruise and traction control functions for precise power delivery under all conditions, plus fewer parts and easier installation.

At 346 cid, the LS1 has fewer cubes than its iron-block forebears, but was also lighter, physically smaller, and more-potent, turning out 345 horsepower and 350 pound-feet of torque. Even better, it rated slightly higher EPA mileage of 18 mpg city, 28 highway with manual shift. Who said you can't have it all?

Interestingly, the C5 claimed 34 percent fewer parts than a corresponding C4. Team Corvette had overlooked nothing to make their new baby not only more efficient and practical but also easier to build to a high quality standard. But no one's perfect. The first 1400 C5s had to be recalled for rear suspension fixes, and early road tests complained of windows that pushed out from their seals at high speed—and more unwanted squeaks and rattles.

# Chevrolet Corvette

**1995 Corvette Official Pace Car**

**1996 Corvette**

**1996 Corvette Grand Sport**

**1997 Corvette coupe**

**1997 Corvette coupe**

But the rough edges were mostly smoothed out within six months, and did nothing to dampen the C5's enthusiastic reception. Some thought the styling a bit tame, but there was no doubting this new Corvette's ability. Most magazines timed 0-60 at a swift five seconds with manual shift, while praising the near-flat, grippy cornering (0.85g in *Car and Driver's* test); effortless, stable, high-speed cruising; the comfortable new cabin and its refreshingly no-nonsense gauges and controls; greater on-road solidity; and, yes, better workmanship throughout. Best of all, the '97 coupe started at $37,945, just $770 above its '96 counterpart. *Automobile* magazine's David E. David, Jr., aptly summed up the C5 as "a home run in every way, and it could not have come at a more opportune time for Chevrolet and General Motors."

A deliberately slow production build-up held 1997-model output to just 9752 units, but the C5 hit stride the following year with 31,084, the 'Vette's best one-year total since 1986. The C5 was designed as a convertible first, and sun-lovers cheered its return for '98. Thanks to the super-stiff structure, virtually no shoring-up was required, though the convertible was necessarily a tad more willowy than the coupe. Some groused that only a manual top was available, but it was easy to operate and visibly better made. Trunk space was only about half that of the hatch coupe's but double that of the droptop C4. And wonder of wonders, it was accessible from outside via the first proper trunklid on a 'Vette since 1962.

*Car and Driver* proclaimed the latest convertible "the most desirable 'Vette since 1967." Chevrolet got one placed as pace car for the 1998 Indy 500, and again rolled out the expected replicas for retail sale, 1158 in all. *Motor Trend* had passed over the 'Vette for 1997 Car of the Year honors, choosing Chevy's new family Malibu sedan instead, but

# Chevrolet Corvette

made up for it by giving the '98 trophy to the entire Corvette "line."

Two new options arrived: magnesium wheels (soon withdrawn due to supplier problems) and, at midseason, an "Active Handling" antiskid system. The latter supplemented the traction control with additional sensor input allowing more-precise selective braking of individual wheels to keep the car on course. Like the C5 coupe, the convertible offered three suspension choices: base, firm-ride Z51($350), and an evolved F45 "Selective Real-Time Damping" option (a pricey $1695), basically computer-controlled auto-adjusting shock absorbers with driver-selectable Tour, Sport, and Performance modes. Opinions divided on the effectiveness of these setups, but most critics, including ourselves, thought the F45 too harsh on most roads. We preferred the base calibrations, though *Car and Driver* felt the Z51 delivered better handling with only a slight loss in ride comfort, being "nowhere near as punishing as the C4 Z51 was."

That's just as well, because the Z51 was mandatory for 1999's new fixed-roof "hardtop" version of the convertible. This third model was not unexpected, having been rumored in the press and even pictured in Chevrolet publicity for the preceding two years. Originally, the hardtop was supposed to double yearly Corvette sales by offering just the basics (manual cloth seats, smaller footwear, no chip-controlled suspension tricks) at a much lower price, once whispered at around $25,000. But the idea bombed in customer "focus groups," and there was no need for a "stripper" anyway, as Chevy was selling every C5 it could build. Accordingly, the hardtop was recast as a more performance-oriented machine, sold only with manual shift, the Z51 chassis, and few options. Chevy did restore traction control, 18-inch rolling stock, and leather upholstery; but extras were limited to the antiskid system, power driver's seat, and Bose audio.

The hardtop itself was made of fiberglass and bonded to the convertible bodyshell. With that and fewer frills, the new model aimed to be a lighter, stiffer Corvette with consequently better acceleration and handling. Stiffer it was, but it only weighed some 90 pounds less, so it was barely faster than a well-driven manual coupe or convertible. *Car and Driver* reported 0-60 mph at 4.8 seconds, while *Road & Track* scored a rather more believable 5.3. The "buff" magazines loved it. "We had great fun in the hardtop," *C/D* enthused, "[and] we applaud Chevy's tactic of making the quickest Corvette the cheapest." Still, a base price of $38,197 was hardly in budget-car land, and the better-equipped hatchback cost only $400 more.

But the hardtop was a heartening sign that Chevy was again really serious about the Corvette. Another clue was the $3.5 million spent to develop the C5-R, an all-out racing version with a 6.0-liter V-8 making some 600 horsepower for an assault on the fabled 24 Hours of LeMans. For 2000, however, the only Corvettes at the French enduro were a pair of stock-based pace cars, though the C5-R did get a shakedown in several long-distance U.S. races. But Corvette made history in 2001 as a pair of C5-Rs ran 10th and 11th overall in France (first and second in the GTS Class), the first LeMans finish for factory supported 'Vettes in 40 years.

Meantime back in 1999, Chevy introduced more options for the coupe and convertible: a power telescopic steering column and an aircraft-style head-up display (HUD). The latter projected speed and other data onto the windshield at driver eye level. It could be distracting, but it could also be turned off. Buyers were still turned on by the C5, though model-year production rose a scant seven percent to near 33,270.

1998 Corvette coupe

1999 Corvette convertible

1999 Corvette coupe

2000 Corvette convertible

2000 Corvette coupe

# Chevrolet Corvette

**2001 Corvette coupe**

**2001 Corvette Z06 coupe**

**2001 Corvette convertible**

**2002 Corvette coupe**

**2002 Corvette Z06 coupe**

The 2000 total was only 89 units higher, but prices weren't much higher either. The hardtop could now be optioned like other models with the HUD, dual-zone climate control, and fog lamps, but buyers were unmoved, as the model's sales dropped almost 50 percent.

In response, Chevy muscled up the hardtop for 2001, and now it really was the fastest, best-handling Corvette of all. Tagged Z06, recalling the option code of a rare 1963 racing package, it boasted a heavily reworked V-8 reviving another legendary Corvette option number, LS6. Higher compression (10.5:1 vs. 10.1); a hotter cam; new heads; and smoother, higher-capacity intake and exhaust systems helped extract 385 horsepower and 385 pound-feet, up 40 horses and 35 pound-feet from the previous LS1, which got some of the same refinements this year to add 5 horsepower and 25 pound-feet. To match Z06 power, Chevy engineers specified a stronger six-speed gearbox, a firmer FE4 suspension with thicker antiroll bars, and inch-wider wheels wearing 265/40ZR17 tires in front and 295/35ZR18s in back. The beefy tires were purpose-designed Goodyear F1 SCs, but they weren't run-flats, so a small inflator was provided for emergencies. The new wheels and tires shaved some 23 pounds off curb weight. Thinner windshield and rear-window glass erased six pounds more, and mufflers went from aluminum to titanium for a final 18-pound saving. Net curb weight was 3116 pounds, which *Car and Driver* noted was over 50 pounds lighter than the old hardtop and only 77 more than a BMW M3 coupe. Z06 cosmetic alterations were subtle but effective: mesh grille inserts, red-painted brake calipers, a functional brake-cooling duct ahead of each rear wheel, and an arresting black-and-red interior with more heavily bolstered seats.

In most every way, the Z06 was a world-beating performer. Despite a "green" engine, *Car and Driver's* example dispatched 0-60 in just 4.3 seconds, and its 0.98g skidpad tour bested those of a street Viper GTS and Ferrari's 360 Modena. *AutoWeek* reported near-identical acceleration and the shortest stops it had ever recorded. After a few laps on the racetrack, *C/D's* Csaba Csere reported that "the Z06 feels very much like the Corvette showroom-stock endurance cars that several of us raced in the mid-'80s. A smooth touch on the controls was rewarded with beautiful balance and great stability." Yet the Z06 was no high-strung terror on the street. It wasn't exactly quiet, especially at full throttle, but the noise was music to enthusiast ears, the ride firm but not punishing, the engine ever unfussed and supremely tractable. All this for $43,855, just $500 more than a 'Vette ragtop. "When we recall that the old ZR-1 cost about twice as much as a garden-variety Corvette," said Csere, "[the Z06 is] a bargain—and the perfect model to take the Corvette into the 21st century."

Total 'Vette sales improved to 35,537 for '01, but the 5798 souls who bought Z06s were doubtless peeved by the even hotter 2002 edition. Further engine refining added 20 horsepower and 15 pound-feet of torque to reach ZR-1 power levels, and suspension was again retuned for even more predictable handling and a less-agitated rough-road ride. Chevy said some of these improvements weren't ready in time for '01, so those who waited were amply rewarded.

But owning a Corvette has always been its own best reward, and that's sure to continue with the new C6 generation due for model-year 2004. Though this book must end before America's sports car begins another chapter, enthusiasts can be glad that its future seems bright once more. Considering all it's been through, the Corvette has shown remarkable staying power. That's what makes it the icon it is.

# Chevrolet Corvette

## Specifications

### 1953
| 290 (wb 102.0) | | Wght | Price | Prod |
|---|---|---|---|---|
| 2934 | conv rdstr | 2,705 | 3,513 | 315 |

| 1953 Engine | bore × stroke | bhp | availability |
|---|---|---|---|
| I-6, 235.5 | 3.56 × 3.94 | 150 | S-all |

### 1954
| 290 (wb 102.0) | | Wght | Price | Prod |
|---|---|---|---|---|
| 2934 | conv rdstr | 2,705 | 3,523 | 3,640 |

| 1954 Engine | bore × stroke | bhp | availability |
|---|---|---|---|
| I-6, 235.5 | 3.56 × 3.94 | 150/155 | S-all |

### 1955
| 290 (wb 102.0) | | Wght | Price | Prod |
|---|---|---|---|---|
| 2934 | conv rdstr | 2,650 | 2,934 | 674 |

| 1955 Engines | bore × stroke | bhp | availability |
|---|---|---|---|
| I-6, 235.5 | 3.56 × 3.94 | 155 | S-all |
| V-8, 265.0 | 3.75 × 3.00 | 195 | O-all |

### 1956
| 290 (wb 102.0) | | Wght | Price | Prod |
|---|---|---|---|---|
| 2934 | conv rdstr | 2,764 | 3,149 | 3,467 |

| 1956 Engine | bore × stroke | bhp | availability |
|---|---|---|---|
| V-8, 265.0 | 3.75 × 3.00 | 210/225 | S-all |

### 1957
| 290 (wb 102.0) | | Wght | Price | Prod |
|---|---|---|---|---|
| 2934 | conv rdstr | 2,730 | 3,465 | 6,339 |

| 1957 Engines | bore × stroke | bhp | availability |
|---|---|---|---|
| V-8, 283.0 | 3.88 × 3.00 | 220 | S-all |
| V-8, 283.0 | 3.88 × 3.00 | 245/270 | O-all |
| V-8, 283.0 | 3.88 × 3.00 | 250/283 | O-all (FI) |

### 1958
| 290 (wb 102.0) | | Wght | Price | Prod |
|---|---|---|---|---|
| 867 | conv rdstr | 2,793 | 3,631 | 9,168 |

| 1958 Engines | bore × stroke | bhp | availability |
|---|---|---|---|
| V-8, 283.0 | 3.88 × 3.00 | 230 | S-all |
| V-8, 283.0 | 3.88 × 3.00 | 245/270 | O-all |
| V-8, 283.0 | 3.88 × 3.00 | 250/290 | O-all (FI) |

### 1959
| 290 (wb 102.0) | | Wght | Price | Prod |
|---|---|---|---|---|
| 867 | conv rdstr | 2,840 | 3,875 | 9,670 |

| 1959 Engines | bore × stroke | bhp | availability |
|---|---|---|---|
| V-8, 283.0 | 3.88 × 3.00 | 230 | S-all |
| V-8, 283.0 | 3.88 × 3.00 | 245/270 | O-all |
| V-8, 283.0 | 3.88 × 3.00 | 250/290 | O-all (FI) |

### 1960
| 290 (wb 102.0) | | Wght | Price | Prod |
|---|---|---|---|---|
| 0867 | conv rdstr | 2,840 | 3,872 | 10,261 |

| 1960 Engines | bore × stroke | bhp | availability |
|---|---|---|---|
| V-8, 283.0 | 3.88 × 3.00 | 230 | S-all |
| V-8, 283.0 | 3.88 × 3.00 | 245/270 | O-all |
| V-8, 283.0 | 3.88 × 3.00 | 275/315 | O-all (FI) |

### 1961
| 290 (wb 102.0) | | Wght | Price | Prod |
|---|---|---|---|---|
| 0867 | conv rdstr | 2,905 | 3,934 | 10,939 |

| 1961 Engines | bore × stroke | bhp | availability |
|---|---|---|---|
| V-8, 283.0 | 3.88 × 3.00 | 230 | S-all |
| V-8, 283.0 | 3.88 × 3.00 | 245/270 | O-all |
| V-8, 283.0 | 3.88 × 3.00 | 275/315 | O-all (FI) |

### 1962
| 290 (wb 102.0) | | Wght | Price | Prod |
|---|---|---|---|---|
| 0867 | conv rdstr | 2,925 | 4,038 | 14,531 |

| 1962 Engines | bore × stroke | bhp | availability |
|---|---|---|---|
| V-8, 327.0 | 4.00 × 3.25 | 250 | S-all |
| V-8, 327.0 | 4.00 × 3.25 | 300/340 | O-all |
| V-8, 327.0 | 4.00 × 3.25 | 360 | O-all (FI) |

### 1963
| Sting Ray (wb 98.0) | | Wght | Price | Prod |
|---|---|---|---|---|
| 0837 | cpe | 2,859 | 4,252 | 10,594 |
| 0867 | conv rdstr | 2,881 | 4,037 | 10,919 |

| 1963 Engines | bore × stroke | bhp | availability |
|---|---|---|---|
| V-8, 327.0 | 4.00 × 3.25 | 250 | S-all |
| V-8, 327.0 | 4.00 × 3.25 | 300/340 | O-all |
| V-8, 327.0 | 4.00 × 3.25 | 360 | O-all (FI) |

### 1964
| Sting Ray (wb 98.0) | | Wght | Price | Prod |
|---|---|---|---|---|
| 0837 | cpe | 2,960 | 4,252 | 8,304 |
| 0867 | conv rdstr | 2,945 | 4,037 | 13,925 |

| 1964 Engines | bore × stroke | bhp | availability |
|---|---|---|---|
| V-8, 327.0 | 4.00 × 3.25 | 250 | S-all |
| V-8, 327.0 | 4.00 × 3.25 | 300-365 | O-all |
| V-8, 327.0 | 4.00 × 3.25 | 375 | O-all (FI) |

### 1965
| Sting Ray (wb 98.0) | | Wght | Price | Prod |
|---|---|---|---|---|
| 19437 | cpe | 2,975 | 4,321 | 8,186 |

# Chevrolet Corvette

| Sting Ray (wb 98.0) | | Wght | Price | Prod |
|---|---|---|---|---|
| 19467 | conv rdstr | 2,985 | 4,106 | 15,376 |
| **1965 Engines** | **bore × stroke** | **bhp** | **availability** | |
| V-8, 327.0 | 4.00 × 3.25 | 250 | S-all | |
| V-8, 327.0 | 4.00 × 3.25 | 300-365 | O-all | |
| V-8, 327.0 | 4.00 × 3.25 | 375 | O-all (FI) | |
| V-8, 396.0 | 4.09 × 3.75 | 425 | O-all | |

## 1966

| Sting Ray (wb 98.0) | | Wght | Price | Prod |
|---|---|---|---|---|
| 19437 | cpe | 2,985 | 4,295 | 9,958 |
| 19467 | conv rdstr | 3,005 | 4,084 | 17,762 |
| **1966 Engines** | **bore × stroke** | **bhp** | **availability** | |
| V-8, 327.0 | 4.00 × 3.25 | 300 | S-all | |
| V-8, 327.0 | 4.00 × 3.25 | 350 | O-all | |
| V-8, 427.0 | 4.25 × 3.76 | 390/425 | O-all | |

## 1967

| Sting Ray (wb 98.0) | | Wght | Price | Prod |
|---|---|---|---|---|
| 19437 | cpe | 3,000 | 4,353 | 8,504 |
| 19467 | conv rdstr | 3,020 | 4,141 | 14,436 |
| **1967 Engines** | **bore × stroke** | **bhp** | **availability** | |
| V-8, 327.0 | 4.00 × 3.25 | 300 | S-all | |
| V-8, 327.0 | 4.00 × 3.25 | 350 | O-all | |
| V-8, 427.0 | 4.25 × 3.76 | 390-435 | O-all | |

## 1968

| Sting Ray (wb 98.0) | | Wght | Price | Prod |
|---|---|---|---|---|
| 19437 | cpe | 3,055 | 4,663 | 9,936 |
| 19467 | conv rdstr | 3,065 | 4,320 | 18,630 |
| **1968 Engines** | **bore × stroke** | **bhp** | **availability** | |
| V-8, 327.0 | 4.00 × 3.25 | 300 | S-all | |
| V-8, 327.0 | 4.00 × 3.25 | 350 | O-all | |
| V-8, 427.0 | 4.25 × 3.76 | 390-435 | O-all | |

## 1969

| Sting Ray (wb 98.0) | | Wght | Price | Prod |
|---|---|---|---|---|
| 19437 | cpe | 3,140 | 4,781 | 22,154 |
| 19467 | conv rdstr | 3,145 | 4,438 | 16,608 |
| **1969 Engines** | **bore × stroke** | **bhp** | **availability** | |
| V-8, 350.0 | 4.00 × 3.48 | 300 | S-all | |
| V-8, 350.0 | 4.00 × 3.48 | 350 | O-all | |
| V-8, 427.0 | 4.25 × 3.76 | 390-435 | O-all | |

## 1970

| Sting Ray (wb 98.0) | | Wght | Price | Prod |
|---|---|---|---|---|
| 19437 | cpe | 3,184 | 5,192 | 10,668 |
| 19467 | conv rdstr | 3,196 | 4,849 | 6,648 |
| **1970 Engines** | **bore × stroke** | **bhp** | **availability** | |
| V-8, 350.0 | 4.00 × 3.48 | 300 | S-all | |
| V-8, 350.0 | 4.00 × 3.48 | 350/370 | O-all | |
| **1970 Engines** | **bore × stroke** | **bhp** | **availability** | |
| V-8, 454.0 | 4.25 × 4.00 | 390/460* | O-all | |

Note: 1967-70 racing engines not listed. * Advertised but never sold.

## 1971

| Sting Ray (wb 98.0) | | Wght | Price | Prod |
|---|---|---|---|---|
| 19437 | cpe | 3,202 | 5,533 | 14,680 |
| 19467 | conv rdstr | 3,216 | 5,296 | 7,121 |
| **1971 Engines** | **bore × stroke** | **bhp** | **availability** | |
| V-8, 350.0 | 4.00 × 3.48 | 270 | S-all | |
| V-8, 350.0 | 4.00 × 3.48 | 330 | O-all | |
| V-8, 454.0 | 4.25 × 4.00 | 365/425 | O-all | |

## 1972

| Sting Ray (wb 98.0) | | Wght | Price | Prod |
|---|---|---|---|---|
| 1Z37 | cpe | 3,215 | 5,472 | 20,486 |
| 1Z67 | conv rdstr | 3,216 | 5,246 | 6,508 |
| **1972 Engines** | **bore × stroke** | **bhp** | **availability** | |
| V-8, 350.0 | 4.00 × 3.48 | 200 | S-all | |
| V-8, 350.0 | 4.00 × 3.48 | 255 | O-all | |
| V-8, 454.0 | 4.25 × 4.00 | 270 | O-all | |

## 1973

| Sting Ray (wb 98.0) | | Wght | Price | Prod |
|---|---|---|---|---|
| Z37 | cpe | 3,326 | 5,635 | 25,521* |
| Z67 | conv rdstr | 3,333 | 5,399 | 4,943* |
| **1973 Engines** | **bore × stroke** | **bhp** | **availability** | |
| V-8, 350.0 | 4.00 × 3.48 | 190 | S-all | |
| V-8, 350.0 | 4.00 × 3.48 | 250 | O-all | |
| V-8, 454.0 | 4.2534.001 | 275 | O-all | |

## 1974

| Sting Ray (wb 98.0) | | Wght | Price | Prod |
|---|---|---|---|---|
| Z37 | cpe | 3,309 | 6,082 | 32,028 |
| Z67 | conv rdstr | 3,315 | 5,846 | 5,474 |
| **1974 Engines** | **bore × stroke** | **bhp** | **availability** | |
| V-8, 350.0 | 4.00 × 3.48 | 195 | S-all | |
| V-8, 350.0 | 4.00 × 3.48 | 250 | O-all | |
| V-8, 454.0 | 4.25 × 4.00 | 270 | O-all | |

## 1975

| Sting Ray (wb 98.0) | | Wght | Price | Prod |
|---|---|---|---|---|
| Z37 | cpe | 3,433 | 6,797 | 33,836 |
| Z67 | conv rdstr | 3,446 | 6,537 | 4,629 |
| **1975 Engines** | **bore × stroke** | **bhp** | **availability** | |
| V-8, 350.0 | 4.00 × 3.48 | 165 | S-all | |
| V-8, 350.0 | 4.00 × 3.48 | 205 | O-all | |

# Chevrolet Corvette

## 1976

| Sting Ray (wb 98.0) | | Wght | Price | Prod |
|---|---|---|---|---|
| Z37 | cpe | 3,445 | 7,605 | 46,558 |
| **1976 Engines** | **bore × stroke** | **bhp** | **availability** | |
| V-8, 350.0 | 4.00 × 3.48 | 180 | S-all | |
| V-8, 350.0 | 4.00 × 3.48 | 210 | O-all | |

## 1977

| (wb 98.0) | | Wght | Price | Prod |
|---|---|---|---|---|
| Z37 | cpe | 3,448 | 8,648 | 49,213 |
| **1977 Engines** | **bore × stroke** | **bhp** | **availability** | |
| V-8, 350.0 | 4.00 × 3.48 | 180 | S-all | |
| V-8, 350.0 | 4.00 × 3.48 | 210 | O-all | |

## 1978

| (wb 98.0) | | Wght | Price | Prod |
|---|---|---|---|---|
| Z87 | cpe | 3,401 | 9,645 | 41,467* |
| Z87/Z78 | Pace Car Replica cpe | 3,450 | 13,653 | 6,200 |

\* Includes 2,500 Silver Anniversary editions.

| 1978 Engines | bore × stroke | bhp | availability |
|---|---|---|---|
| V-8, 350.0 | 4.00 × 3.48 | 185 | S-all |
| V-8, 350.0 | 4.00 × 3.48 | 220 | O-all |

## 1979

| (wb 98.0) | | Wght | Price | Prod |
|---|---|---|---|---|
| Z87 | cpe | 3,372 | 12,313 | 53,807 |
| **1979 Engines** | **bore × stroke** | **bhp** | **availability** | |
| V-8, 350.0 | 4.00 × 3.48 | 195 | S-all | |
| V-8, 350.0 | 4.00 × 3.48 | 225 | O-all | |

## 1980

| (wb 98.0) | Wght | Price | Prod |
|---|---|---|---|
| Z87 cpe | 3,206 | 13,965 | 40,614 |

| 1980 Engines | bore × stroke | bhp | availability |
|---|---|---|---|
| V-8, 350.0 | 4.00 × 3.48 | 190 | S-all |
| V-8, 350.0 | 4.00 × 3.48 | 230 | O-all |
| V-8, 305.0 | 3.74 × 3.48 | 180 | O-all |

## 1981

| (wb 98.0) | | Wght | Price | Prod |
|---|---|---|---|---|
| Y87 | cpe | 3,179 | 15,248 | 40,606 |
| **1981 Engine** | **bore × stroke** | **bhp** | **availability** | |
| V-8, 350.0 | 4.00 × 3.48 | 190 | S-all | |

## 1982

| (wb 98.0) | | Wght | Price | Prod |
|---|---|---|---|---|
| Y87 | cpe | 3,232 | 18,290 | 18,648 |
| Y07 | Collector Ed htchbk cpe | 3,233 | 22,537 | 6,759 |
| **1982 Engine** | **bore × stroke** | **bhp** | **availability** | |
| V-8, 350.0 | 4.00 × 3.48 | 200 | S-all | |

## 1983

No Corvette model was produced.

## 1984

| (wb 96.2) | | Wght | Price | Prod |
|---|---|---|---|---|
| Y07 | cpe | 3,087 | 23,360 | 51,547 |
| **1984 Engine** | **bore × stroke** | **bhp** | **availability** | |
| V-8, 350.0 | 4.00 × 3.48 | 205 | S-all | |

## 1985

| (wb 96.2) | | Wght | Price | Prod |
|---|---|---|---|---|
| Y07 | htchbk cpe | 3,191 | 24,873 | 39,729 |
| **1985 Engine** | **bore × stroke** | **bhp** | **availability** | |
| V-8, 350.0 | 4.00 × 3.48 | 230 | S-all | |

## 1986

| (wb 96.2) | | Wght | Price | Prod |
|---|---|---|---|---|
| Y07 | htchbk cpe | 3,239 | 27,027 | 27,794 |
| Y67 | conv cpe | — | 32,032 | 7,315 |
| **1986 Engine** | **bore × stroke** | **bhp** | **availability** | |
| V-8, 350.0 | 4.00 × 3.48 | 230 | S-all | |

## 1987

| (wb 96.2) | | Wght | Price | Prod |
|---|---|---|---|---|
| Y07 | htchbk cpe | 3,216 | 27,999 | 20,007 |
| Y67 | conv cpe | 3,279 | 33,172 | 10,625 |
| **1987 Engine** | **bore × stroke** | **bhp** | **availability** | |
| V-8, 350.0 | 4.00 × 3.48 | 240 | S-all | |

## 1988

| (wb 96.2) | | Wght | Price | Prod |
|---|---|---|---|---|
| Y07 | htchbk cpe | 3,229 | 29,480 | 15,382 |
| Y67 | conv cpe | 3,299 | 34,820 | 7,407 |
| **1988 Engine** | **bore × stroke** | **bhp** | **availability** | |
| V-8, 350.0 | 4.00 × 3.48 | 245 | S-all | |

## 1989

| (wb 96.2) | | Wght | Price | Prod |
|---|---|---|---|---|
| Y07 | htchbk cpe | 3,229 | 31,545 | 16,663 |
| Y67 | conv cpe | 3,269 | 36,785 | 9,749 |
| **1989 Engine** | **bore × stroke** | **bhp** | **availability** | |
| V-8, 350.0 | 4.00 × 33.48 | 240/245 | S-base models | |

## 1990

| (wb 96.2) | | Wght | Price | Prod |
|---|---|---|---|---|
| Y67 | conv cpe | 3,263 | 37,264 | 7,630 |
| Y07 | htchbk cpe | 3,223 | 31,979 | 12,967 |
| Z07 | ZR-1 htchbk cpe | 3,465 | 58,995 | 3,049 |
| **1990 Engines** | **bore × stroke** | **bhp** | **availability** | |
| V-8, 350.0 | 4.00 × 3.48 | 245 | S-base models | |
| V-8, 350.0 | 3.90 × 3.66 | 375 | S-ZR1 (dohc) | |

# Chevrolet Corvette

## 1991

| Corvette (wb 96.2) | | Wght | Price | Prod |
|---|---|---|---|---|
| Y07 | htchbk cpe | 3,223 | 32,455 | 12,923 |
| Y67 | conv cpe | 3,263 | 38,770 | 5,762 |
| Z07* | ZR1 htchbk cpe | 3,503 | 64,138 | 2,044 |

| 1991 Engines | bore × stroke | bhp | availability |
|---|---|---|---|
| V-8, 350.0 | 4.00 × 3.48 | 245 | S-base |
| V-8, 350.0 | 3.90 × 3.66 | 375 | O-ZR1 (dohc) |

*Though listed as a separate model, the ZR-1 was technically an option package beginning in 1991.

## 1992

| Corvette (wb 96.2) | | Wght | Price | Prod |
|---|---|---|---|---|
| Y07 | htchbk cpe | 3,223 | 33,635 | 14,102 |
| Y67 | conv cpe | 3,269 | 40,145 | 5,875 |
| Z07 | ZR1 htchbk cpe | 3,503 | 65,318 | 502 |

| 1992 Engines | bore × stroke | bhp | availability |
|---|---|---|---|
| V-8, 350.0 | 4.00 × 3.48 | 300 | S-base |
| V-8, 350.0 | 3.90 × 3.66 | 375 | O-ZR1 (dohc) |

## 1993

| Corvette (wb 96.2) | | Wght | Price | Prod |
|---|---|---|---|---|
| Y07 | htchbk cpe | 3,333 | 34,595 | 15,520 |
| Y67 | conv cpe | 3,383 | 41,195 | 5,712 |
| Z07 | ZR1 htchbk cpe | 3,503 | 66,278 | 448 |

| 1993 Engines | bore × stroke | bhp | availability |
|---|---|---|---|
| V-8, 350.0 | 4.00 × 3.48 | 300 | S-base |
| V-8, 350.0 | 3.90 × 3.66 | 405 | O-ZR1 (dohc) |

## 1994

| Corvette (wb 96.2) | | Wght | Price | Prod |
|---|---|---|---|---|
| Y07 | htchbk cpe | 3,309 | 36,185 | 17,420 |
| Y67 | conv cpe | 3,361 | 42,960 | 5,320 |
| Z07 | ZR1 htchbk cpe | 3,512 | 67,443 | 448 |

| 1994 Engines | bore × stroke | bhp | availability |
|---|---|---|---|
| V-8, 350.0 | 4.00 × 3.48 | 300 | S-base |
| V-8, 350.0 | 3.90 × 3.66 | 385 | O-ZR1 (dohc) |

## 1995

| Corvette (wb 96.2) | | Wght | Price | Prod |
|---|---|---|---|---|
| Y07 | htchbk cpe | 3,203 | 36,785 | 18,788 |
| Y67 | conv cpe | 3,360 | 43,665 | 4,094 |
| Z07 | ZR1 htchbk cpe | 3,512 | 68,043 | 448 |

| 1995 Engines | bore × stroke | bhp | availability |
|---|---|---|---|
| V-8, 350.0 | 4.00 × 3.48 | 300 | S-base |
| V-8, 350.0 | 3.90 × 3.66 | 405 | O-ZR1 (dohc) |

## 1996

| Corvette (wb 96.2) | | Wght | Price | Prod |
|---|---|---|---|---|
| Y07 | htchbk cpe | 3,298 | 37,225 | 16,357 |
| Y07 | GS htchbk cpe | 3,298 | 40,475 | 810 |
| Y67 | conv cpe | 3,360 | 45,060 | 4,179 |
| Y67 | GS conv cpe | 3,360 | 47,940 | 190 |

| 1996 Engines | bore × stroke | bhp | availability |
|---|---|---|---|
| V-8, 350.0 | 4.00 × 3.48 | 300 | S-all |
| V-8, 350.0 | 4.00 × 3.48 | 330 | O-all |

## 1997

| Corvette (wb 104.5) | | Wght | Price | Prod |
|---|---|---|---|---|
| Y07 | htchbk cpe | 3,229 | 37,945 | 9,752 |

| 1997 Engine | bore × stroke | bhp | availability |
|---|---|---|---|
| V-8, 346.0 | 3.90 × 3.62 | 340 | S-all |

## 1998

| Corvette (wb 104.5) | | Wght | Price | Prod |
|---|---|---|---|---|
| Y07 | htchbk cpe | 3,245 | 37,995 | 19,235 |
| Y67 | conv cpe | 3,246 | 44,425 | 11,849 |

| 1998 Engine | bore × stroke | bhp | availability |
|---|---|---|---|
| V-8, 346.0 | 3.90 × 3.62 | 345 | S-all |

## 1999

| Corvette (wb 104.5) | | Wght | Price | Prod |
|---|---|---|---|---|
| Y37 | hrdtp cpe | 3,153 | 38,197 | 4,031 |
| Y07 | htchbk cpe | 3,245 | 38,591 | 18,078 |
| Y67 | conv cpe | 3,246 | 44,999 | 11,161 |

| 1999 Engine | bore × stroke | bhp | availability |
|---|---|---|---|
| V-8, 346.0 | 3.90 × 3.62 | 345 | S-all |

## 2000

| Corvette (wb 104.5) | | Wght | Price | Prod |
|---|---|---|---|---|
| Y37 | hrdtp cpe | 3,173 | 38,705 | 2,113 |
| Y07 | htchbk cpe | 3,245 | 39,280 | 18,246 |
| Y67 | conv cpe | 3,246 | 45,705 | 13,300 |

| 2000 Engine | bore × stroke | bhp | availability |
|---|---|---|---|
| V-8, 346.0 | 3.90 × 3.62 | 345 | S-all |

## 2001

| Corvette (wb 104.5) | | Wght | Price | Prod |
|---|---|---|---|---|
| Y07 | htchbk cpe | 3,214 | 39,830 | 15,563 |
| Y37 | Z06 hrdtp cpe | 3,116 | 46,855 | 5,798 |
| Y67 | conv cpe | 3,210 | 46,355 | 14,176 |

| 2001 Engines | bore × stroke | bhp | availability |
|---|---|---|---|
| V-8, 346.0 | 3.90 × 3.62 | 350 | S-all |
| V-8, 346.0 | 3.90 × 3.62 | 385 | S-Z06 |

## 2002

| Corvette (wb 104.5) | | Wght | Price | Prod* |
|---|---|---|---|---|
| Y07 | htchbk cpe | 3,214 | 41,005 | |
| Y37 | Z06 hrdtp cpe | 3,116 | 49,705 | |
| Y67 | conv cpe | 3,210 | 47,530 | |

| 2002 Engines | bore × stroke | bhp | availability |
|---|---|---|---|
| V-8, 346.0 | 3.90 × 3.62 | 350 | S-all |
| V-8, 346.0 | 3.90 × 3.62 | 405 | S-Z06 |

* Production figures not available at time of publication.

# Chrysler

Walter Percy Chrysler honed his native mechanical skills on the great Midwestern railroads, then learned about cars by tinkering with a $5000 Locomobile he bought in 1908. Within a few years he became plant manager at Buick under Charles W. Nash, then took over for him as Buick president. But Chrysler didn't get along with GM's Billy Durant, so he left to run his own car company (as did Nash). Chrysler was hired to straighten out faltering Maxwell/Chalmers. By 1924, Chrysler had acquired control of the company and introduced a new car under his own name. Thus was born the last of America's "Big Three" automakers (though it wasn't formally incorporated until 1925).

That first Chrysler was the foundation of the company's early success. It was designed with instrumental assistance from three superb engineers: Fred Zeder, Carl Breer, and Owen Skelton, the "Three Musketeers" who would dominate the design of Chrysler Corporation products throughout the '30s. Power came from a high-compression 202-cubic-inch L-head six with seven main bearings and 68 horsepower—0.3 bhp per cubic inch, outstanding for the early '20s. Also featured were four-wheel hydraulic brakes (well ahead of most rivals), full-pressure lubrication, attractive styling, and competitive prices around $1500. It couldn't miss, and it didn't. By 1927, production had soared from 32,000 to some 182,000.

Sixes remained Chrysler's mainstay through 1930, when the make offered four different engines ranging from 195.6 to 309.3 cid. The smallest was the four-main-bearing job in the cheap CJ-Series; the others were derived from the original 1924 design. That year's lineup comprised no fewer than 38 models priced from $795 for the least-costly CJ to $3000-plus for the imposing Imperial.

The Chrysler line then moved rapidly upmarket in price, prestige, and power. The reason was the company's 1928 expansion via the acquisition of Dodge and introduction of DeSoto and Plymouth. Given his GM experience, it's no surprise that Walter Chrysler wanted a similar make "ladder" running from low-priced Plymouths to premium Chryslers to keep customers in his corporate camp. At first, DeSoto, not Dodge, was the step up from Plymouth; their price positions wouldn't be reversed until the mid-'30s.

Imperial had arrived in 1926 to answer Cadillac, though this would always be more of a prestige leader than high money-earner. Also unlike GM's luxury make, Imperials built through 1954 weren't the products of a separate division, just the finest Chryslers, though they usually rivaled Cadillac in most every way. A notable exception is that Imperial didn't try to match Cadillac's costly V-12 and V-16 of the '30s—wise, considering how poorly those sold in the devastated Depression market.

Imperial reached a pinnacle in 1931, when Chrysler introduced its first eights. The largest was naturally reserved for Imperial: a smooth, low-revving 385-cid L-head with nine main bearings and 125 bhp. Despite weighing nearly 5000 pounds, these majestic cars could reach 96 mph and do 0-60 mph in 20 seconds. Styling (heavily influenced by the Cord L-29), was distinctive: long and low, with gracefully curved fenders and a rakish grille. Hard times made sales scarce, but these Imperials provided glorious motoring at relatively modest prices. They remain among the most-beautiful Chryslers ever built—particularly the custom-bodied examples from the likes of Locke, Derham, Murphy, Waterhouse, and especially LeBaron. Though most coachbuilders perished in the Depression, Chrysler hired Ray Dietrich, one of the partners in LeBaron, to head its styling department (such as it was) in the late '30s.

Chrysler also offered an eight-cylinder 1931 CD-Series priced about half as much as Imperials, with engines of 240.3 cid and 82 bhp or 260.8 cid and 90. There was also a DeLuxe Eight with 95 bhp and 282.1 cid. But sixes still anchored the line, as they would through 1954. In the '30s these became progressively larger and more potent, reaching 241.5 cid and 93 bhp by 1934.

Meantime, Chrysler cemented its reputation for advanced engineering with the 1931 debut of "Floating Power" rubber engine mounts. These were standard for all models, as were automatic spark control, free-wheeling, and rustproofed bodies. Welded steel bodies were an innovation from the previous year. To prove their strength, Chrysler persuaded a five-ton elephant to climb atop a sedan at Coney Island in one of the firm's many famous period publicity stunts. Fortunately, the body held.

1930 77 Royal sedan

1931 custom-bodied, close-coupled two-door

1931 Series CG Imperial by LeBaron

# Chrysler

1932 Series CH Imperial town car by LeBaron

1932 Series C16 Six 2/4-passenger roadster

1933 Series CL Imperial convertible sedan

1934 Series CA Six Brougham two-door

1934 Series CX Airflow Imperial Eight four-door sedan

Chrysler also offered an optional four-speed manual transmission, basically a three-speed unit with an extra-low first gear. But hardly anyone used "emergency low," so this was dropped after 1933. Interiors were lavish during these years, especially on Imperials and Chrysler Eights, which came with full instrumentation in a polished walnut panel.

After making few changes through 1933, Chrysler made a major one, summoning the future with the most-radical production car yet attempted by a U.S. maker. Widely recognized as the first truly modern automobile, the 1934 Airflow was an "engineer's" car, which was hardly surprising. What *was* curious is that normally canny Walter Chrysler approved its daring concept without much regard for whether the public would like it.

As the story goes, Carl Breer spotted a squadron of Army Air Corps planes flying overhead in 1927, which inspired him to push with Zeder and Skelton for a streamlined automobile employing aircraft-type design principles. Wind-tunnel tests suggested a modified teardrop shape (and ultimately the Airflow name). Eight-cylinder engines placed over front axles made for considerable passenger space. Seats were an industry-leading 50 inches across, and there was more than enough interior room for even the burly Walter P. Chrysler. What's more, the forward drivetrain positioning enabled all passengers to sit within the wheelbase, thus improving ride comfort for those in back. A beam-and-truss body engineered along aircraft principles provided great strength with less weight. Oliver Clark followed all these dictates with exterior styling that seemed downright strange. The Custom Imperial looked best, its long wheelbase allowing the rounded lines to be stretched out more—and they needed every inch of stretch they could get.

But there was no denying Airflow performance. At the Bonneville Salt Flats a '34 Imperial coupe ran the flying-mile at 95.7 mph, clocked 90 mph for 500 miles, and set 72 new national speed records. Airflows were strong, too. In Pennsylvania, one was hurled off a 110-foot cliff (another publicity stunt); it landed wheels down and was driven away.

Unfortunately, the massive cost and effort of retooling delayed Airflow sales until January 1934 (June for Custom Imperials). Then, jealous competitors—mainly GM—began running "smear" advertising that claimed the cars were unsafe. All this blunted public interest that was initially quite favorable despite the newfangled styling, and prompted rumors that the Airflow was flawed. Save for a group of traditional Series-CA and CB Sixes, the 1934 Chrysler line was all Airflow, and sales were underwhelming. While most makes boosted volume by up to 60 percent from rock-bottom '33, Chrysler rose only 10 percent. It could have been worse—and was for DeSoto, which banked entirely on Airflows that year (all sixes).

Yet the Airflow wasn't nearly the disaster it's long been portrayed to be. Though Chrysler dropped from eighth to tenth in model-year output for 1932, it went no lower through '37, the Airflow's final year, when it rose to ninth. And though the cars did lose money, the losses were far from crippling. The Airflow's most-lasting impact was to discourage Chrysler from fielding anything so adventurous for a very long time. Not until 1955 would the firm again reach for industry design leadership.

There were also two immediate results of the 1934 sales experience. First, planned Airflow-style Dodges and Plymouths were abruptly canceled. Second, Chrysler Division regrouped around more-orthodox "Airstream" Sixes and Eights for 1935 and '36. Though not pure Airflow, this design's pontoon fenders, raked-backed radiators, and

# Chrysler

1936 Series C9 Airflow Eight four-door sedan

1938 Series C19 Imperial four-door sedan

1936 Series C7 Airstream Six business coupe

1938 Series C19 New York Special four-door sedan

1937 Series C16 Royal Six rumble-seat coupe

1939 Chrysler Custom Imperial parade phaeton

1937 Series C17 Airflow Eight four-door sedan

1939 Series C24 Custom Imperial 7-passenger sedan

# Chrysler

teardrop headlamp pods provided a strong family resemblance, yet wasn't so wild that it discouraged customers. Airstreams literally carried Chrysler in those years.

Most 1937 Chryslers and all '38s had transitional styling of the period "potato school," carrying barrel grilles, rounded fenders, and pod-type headlamps. Ornate dashboards grouped gauges in front of the driver on '37s, in a central panel for '38. Offered in both years were revamped non-Airflow models comprising six-cylinder Royals and eight-cylinder standard and Custom Imperials. An interesting 1938 hybrid was the New York Special combining the year's new 119-inch-wheelbase Royal chassis with Imperial's 298.7-cid eight. Distinguished by a color-keyed interior, it came only as a four-door sedan (a business coupe was planned, but it's doubtful any were produced). All eights were now five-main-bearing side-valve engines (the nine-main unit was dropped after '34). Volume recovered from the 1934 low of some 36,000 to over 106,000 by 1937, only to drop by half for recession '38; still Chrysler remained ninth.

The division fell back to eleventh for 1939 despite improved volume of near 72,500—and handsome new Ray Dietrich styling. Headlamps moved stylishly into the fenders above a lower grille composed of vertical bars, and all fenders were lengthened. Adding to the list of Chrysler engineering firsts was "Superfinish," a new process of mirror-finishing engine and chassis components to minimize friction.

Several familiar model names bowed for 1939: Windsor (as a Royal subseries), New Yorker, and Saratoga. The C-22 Royal/Royal Windsor line carried the 241.5-cid six from 1938 and rode an unchanged wheelbase, save for a long sedan and limousine on a 136-inch platform. The 125-inch C-23 Imperial included New Yorker coupes and sedans and a brace of Saratogas. Topping the line was the C-24 Custom Imperial: two long sedans and one limo on a 144-inch-wheelbase. All eight-cylinder offerings used the same 323.5-cid powerplant, with 130-138 brake horsepower depending on the model. Dating from 1934, it would remain in production until the breakthrough hemispherical-head V-8 of 1951.

Walter Chrysler died in August 1940, after turning over the presidency to his chosen successor, K.T. Keller, in 1935. But engineers continued running Chrysler with Keller's wholehearted support. Styling remained conservative, construction sound, value good. Chrysler Division fared well in the immediate prewar years, rising to 10th place on over 92,000 units for 1940, then capturing 8th for '41 with nearly 162,000. Much of this was owed to a now very broad range of models and prices. The 1940 line, for instance, ranged from an $895 Royal Six coupe to a $2445 eight-passenger Crown Imperial limo.

Longer wheelbases accompanied new 1940 Chrysler bodies with notchback profiles, separate fenders, and smooth lines. The result, as one wag said, "wouldn't knock your eyes out, but wouldn't knock your hat off either." Models again grouped into six- and eight-cylinder ranks. Royal and Windsor Sixes rode a 122.5-inch chassis (139.5 for eight-seat sedans and limos). Eights began with the new Traveler, New Yorker, and Saratoga on a 128.5-inch span (the last two also offered formal sedans). A 145.5-inch chassis carried Crown Imperial sedans and limousine. The eight now delivered 135-143 bhp, the six produced 108 or 112 bhp.

Two striking show cars from LeBaron (by then owned by Briggs) appeared during 1940; six of each were built. The Newport, designed by Ralph Roberts, was an Imperial-based dual-cowl phaeton with "melted-butter" streamlining. It paced the 1941 Indianapolis 500. The Thunderbolt was penned by Alex Tremulis of Briggs Manufacturing, Chrysler's longtime body supplier. Built on the New Yorker chassis, it had even sleeker flush-fender styling, plus a three-person bench seat and a novel, fully retracting hard top. Both cars hid their headlamps behind metal doors, a preview of 1942 DeSotos.

The most-interesting 1941 Chrysler was Dave Wallace's unique Town & Country, the make's first station wagon. Unlike other period "woodies," this one was fairly graceful—and functional, with "clamshell" center-opening rear doors. Riding the Royal chassis, the '41 T&C offered six- or nine-passenger seating for a remarkably low $1412/$1492. Still only 997 were built for the model year, mostly the nine-seat type. A new variation on the familiar four-door for '41 was the attractive Town Sedan. Available in each series, it bore rear-roof quarters sans side windows, plus front- instead of rear-hinged back doors.

Wheelbases were trimmed an inch for all '41 Chryslers save Crown Imperial. Grille styling was simpler, taillamps more-ornate. The Traveler departed, but Saratogas expanded to include club and business coupes, two- and four-door sedans, and town sedan. Several interesting new upholstery choices arrived: Highlander, a striking combination of Scots plaid and leatherette; Saran, a woven plastic and leatherette designed for certain open models; and Navajo, a pattern resembling the blankets of those Southwest Indians. The year's main new technical gimmick was optional "Vacamatic" transmission. This was a semiautomatic with two Low and two High gears; you shifted only to go between the ranges. Vacamatic was combined with Fluid Drive (introduced in '39), which allowed the driver to start and stop without using the clutch.

**1940 Series C25 Royal coupe**

**1941 Thunderbolt show car**

**1941 Series C33 Crown Imperial 8-passenger sedan**

# Chrysler

A major facelift achieved a smoother look for '42 by wrapping the horizontal grille bars right around to the front fenders. A sleeker hood opened from the front instead of the sides, and running boards were newly hidden beneath flared door bottoms. Highlander Plaid returned along with a new upholstery option called Thunderbird, also inspired by Indian motifs. Town & Country was upgraded to the Windsor chassis. Increased bore brought the six to 250.6 cid and 120 bhp; the eight cylinder was offered only in a 140-bhp version.

Like other Detroit cars, Chryslers built after January 1, 1942, used painted metal instead of chrome trim per government order. For the same reason, Chrysler ended civilian production in early February 1942 for the duration of World War II. The division built only 5292 cars that calendar year and close to 36,000 for the model year. It then turned out anti-aircraft guns, Wright Cyclone aero engines, land-mine detectors, radar units, marine engines, and "Sea Mule" harbor tugs; tanks were its most-famous wartime product.

When they could during the war, small teams of designers and engineers would work on ideas for postwar Chryslers—largely smoother versions of the 1940-42 models with fully wrapped bumpers and grilles, thinner A- and B-pillars, and skirted rear fenders. But like most every other Detroit producer, Chrysler needed only warmed-over '42s to satisfy the huge seller's market that developed postwar, and that's what it offered through early 1949.

These cars wore less fender brightwork but a new eggcrate grille—one of Detroit's shiniest faces. All prewar offerings returned save Crown Imperial sedans, and engines were slightly detuned. A more-significant change involved the Town & Country, which was no longer a wagon but a separate series of six- and eight-cylinder sedans and convertibles. Chrysler had promised a full line of nonwagon T&Cs, including a two-door brougham sedan and even a true roadster and a hardtop coupe. But only a handful of each were built, all effectively prototypes. Hardtops numbered just seven, created by grafting an elongated coupe roof onto the T&C convertible. All were built in 1946, a good three years before GM began making sales hay with "hardtop convertibles." The eight-cylinder T&C sedan was dropped after '46 and just 100 copies.

Postwar inflation pushed prices up dramatically. For example, a Royal business coupe that had cost a little more than $1000 in 1942 was over $1400 in '46. Prices would continue escalating through decade's end, when a Crown Imperial went for nearly double its 1940 figure. Even so, Chrysler ranked among the top 10 in industry production for 1947-48.

Only detail alterations occurred for 1947: fender trim, wheels/hubcaps, colors, carburetion, instruments, plus low-pressure Goodyear "Super Cushion" tires. The Traveler name returned for a luxurious Windsor utility sedan with special paint and interior and an attractive wood luggage rack. Unlike DeSoto's similar Suburban, it had a separate trunk instead of fold-down triple seats and wood rear floorboards. Also making a belated comeback was the eight-passenger Crown Imperial sedan.

The '48 Chryslers were just carryover '47s, though the six-cylinder T&C sedan was dropped at midyear, leaving the straight-eight convertible to carry on alone. The latter would prove the most-numerous early T&C, with total 1946-48 production of 8380 units. Like all T&Cs through 1950, they've

**1942 New Yorker convertible coupe**

**1942 Series C36N New Yorker with "blackout" trim**

**1946-48 New Yorker "Zippo"**

**1946-48 Saratoga four-door sedan**

**1946-48 Town & Country convertible coupe**

long been bona fide collectibles.

Chrysler wasn't ready with its redesigned Silver Anniversary line in late '48, so existing models—save the ragtop T&C—were sold through March 1949 at unchanged prices, though none of these "first-series" '49s were built that calendar year. Though streamlined styling with integral, skirted fenders had been considered for the all-postwar "second-series" '49s, Keller insisted on bolt-upright bodies with vast interior space. He got them, but with some loss in sales appeal. Output thus fell to some 124,200 for model-year '49, and Chrysler slipped back to 12th place in the industry production race.

Overall, the '49 Chryslers were ornate, with massive chrome-laden grilles, prominent brightwork elsewhere, and curious vertical taillights except on Crown Imperials (which were spared the gaudy devices). Gimmicky names now signaled certain desirable features: "Safety-Level Ride," "Hydra-Lizer" shock absorbers, "Safety-Rim" wheels, "Full-Flow" oil filter, "Cycle-Bonded" brake linings. Wheelbases were generally longer. Royal and Windsor were up to 125.5 inches, with a 139.5-inch chassis continuing for long models; Saratoga, New Yorker, convertible T&C, and an Imperial sedan rode a 131.5-inch chassis; Crowns remained at 145.5. Engines were largely unchanged.

Chrysler-based customs were still around in the late '40s, many built by Derham of Rosemont, Pennsylvania. In 1946-48 Derham offered a Crown Imperial town limousine as well as numerous one-offs such as a dual-cowl Imperial phaeton and a New Yorker coupe that resembled a Lincoln Continental with a Chrysler front end. Derham also tried the padded-top treatment on a handful of '49 New Yorker sedans. Chrysler itself built custom formal sedans, and A. J. Miller of Ohio did a long-wheelbase limousine/hearse. Wildest of all was a promotional 1946-48 New Yorker done up as a giant Zippo lighter.

Chrysler entered the '50s as a lower-medium-price make with seven series and 24 models. By 1959, it was an upper-medium line with 15 models and four series. Styling and engineering improved rapidly, and the dowdy L-head cars of 1950 gave way to exciting high-performance machines by mid-decade. Chrysler also had some of the best-looking tailfins of the age.

Those fins, which premiered as tack-ons for '55, were the work of Virgil M. Exner, who came from Studebaker to head corporate styling in 1949. Exner favored "classic" design elements: upright grilles, circular wheel openings, rakish silhouettes. But the practical, boring boxes of K.T. Keller (then preparing for retirement) weren't selling, and before Exner could get out anything completely new, Chrysler Division's yearly volume had dropped from 180,000 to barely 100,000.

Predictably, the 1950 Chryslers were carryovers of the all-new postwar '49s save the usual trim shuffles and a broader chrome eggcrate smile. A Deluxe Imperial sedan with custom interior arrived, but the big news was Chrysler's first volume hardtop coupe, called Newport, offered as a Windsor, New Yorker, and wood-trimmed T&C (the last replacing the previous convertible).

Six-cylinder Royals were in their last year, selling for $2100-$3100 for 1950. The T&C was no longer needed to glamorize an unglamorous group of cars as it had done in the early postwar period. After '50, T&C would apply only to station wagons. Before leaving, the Town & Country hardtop would pioneer a form of four-wheel disc brakes. Unlike conventional disc brakes, these brakes consisted of two discs expanding inside a drum. Saratoga, another peripheral seller, would

**1949 New Yorker four-door sedan**

**1951 New Yorker Official Pace Car convertible**

**1950 New Yorker Newport hardtop coupe**

**1951 New Yorker four-door sedan**

**1951 New Yorker Newport hardtop coupe**

**1952 Saratoga four-door sedan**

# Chrysler

depart after 1952 (though it would be back). So would the revived Traveler of 1950-51, a Deluxe-trim Windsor utility sedan (something of a contradiction). Standard and Deluxe Windsors and New Yorkers then carried on until 1955's "Hundred Million Dollar Look," when only Deluxes were offered sans remaining long sedans and Imperials; the latter were newly marketed as a separate make (see entry).

With one singular exception, Chryslers didn't change much from 1951 through '54. Wheelbases stayed the same throughout, as did basic styling, though a more-conservative grille marked the '51s. The '52s were all but identical; the firm didn't even keep separate production figures. Taillights are the only way to tell them apart: the '52s had built-in backup lamps. The '53s gained slightly bulkier lower-body sheetmetal, more chrome, and one-piece windshields. The '54s were a little "brighter" still. Body and series assignments also stood pat, though 1953-54 brought a revived Custom Imperial line with sedan and limousine on a 133.5-inch wheelbase, plus a standard-length Newport.

The above-mentioned exception was the new hemispherical-head V-8 of 1951, unquestionably Chrysler's greatest achievement of the decade. Highland Park's early-'50s styling may have been bland, but its engineering was still anything but. The brilliant "Hemi" was simply the latest example. Still, the Chrysler six had long dominated division sales, so its complete disappearance after 1954 surprised some. But it was part of a plan instigated by Keller's successor, Lester Lum "Tex" Colbert. Then, too, the Hemi left fewer buyers for the six: well over 100,000 in 1950, but only some 45,000 by '54.

Colbert took over as company president in 1950 with several goals. The main ones were decentralized division management, a total redesign for all makes as soon as possible, and an ambitious program of plant expansion and financing. Giving the divisions freer reign meant that people close to retail sales would have more say in mapping policy.

The Hemi polished Chrysler's image in a big way, and quickly spread to other Highland Park cars. First offered on the '51 Saratoga, New Yorker, and Imperial, it wasn't really a new idea, but it did have exceptional volumetric efficiency and delivered truly thrilling performance. Despite lower compression that allowed using lower-octane fuel than most other postwar over-head-valve V-8s, the Hemi produced far more power for a given displacement.

And it had plenty of power even in initial 331-cid form. An early prototype recorded 352 bhp on the dynamometer after minor modifications to camshaft, carburetors, and exhaust. Drag racers would later extract up to 1000 bhp. But the Hemi was complex and costly to build, requiring twice as many rocker shafts, pushrods, and rockers; heads were heavy, too. All versions were thus phased out by 1959 in favor of more-conventional "wedge-head" V-8s. But the Hemi was too good to lose, and it would return in Highland Park's great midsize muscle cars of the '60s.

Of course, the Hemi made for some very hot Chryslers in the '50s. By dint of its lighter Windsor chassis, the Hemi Saratoga was the fastest Chrysler up to 1955, able to do 0-60 mph in as little as 10 seconds and close to 110 mph flat-out—right out of the showroom. Bill Sterling's Saratoga won the Stock Class and finished third overall—behind a Ferrari—in the 1951 Mexican Road Race. Chryslers also did well as NASCAR stockers, but were eclipsed by Hudson's "fabulous" Hornets in 1952-54. Meanwhile, though, Briggs Cunningham began building rakish Hemi-powered sports cars for European road races, and his C-5R ran third overall at Le Mans '53 with an average of 104.14 mph (against 105.85 mph for the winning Jaguar C-Type). Then came Chrysler's own

1953 New Yorker DeLuxe Newport hardtop coupe

1953 Custom Imperial Newport hardtop coupe

1954 New Yorker DeLuxe convertible coupe

1954 New Yorker DeLuxe four-door sedan

1955 New Yorker DeLuxe convertible coupe

# Chrysler

1955 C300 hardtop coupe

1955 New Yorker DeLuxe four-door sedan

1955 Windsor DeLuxe four-door sedan

1956 New Yorker convertible coupe

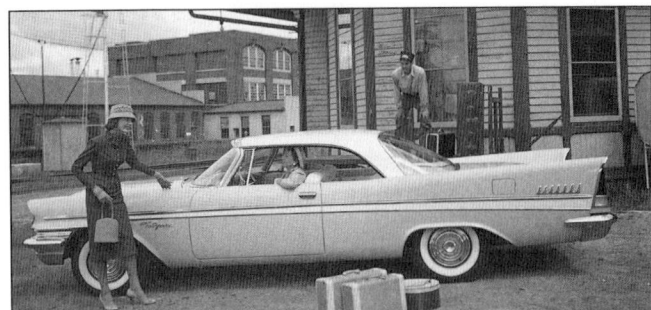
1957 New Yorker hardtop coupe

1957 New Yorker four-door sedan

mighty 1955 C-300 packing a stock Hemi tuned for 300 bhp—the most ever offered on a series-built U.S. car. The 300 dominated NASCAR in 1955-56, and might have continued to do so had the Automobile Manufacturers Association not agreed to de-emphasize racing after 1957.

The 300 was part of the all-new Exner-styled '55 line that cost $100 million to develop, hence the "Hundred Million Dollar Look" advertising hype. But it was worth the expense, boosting model-year volume to over 150,000 units and bringing appearance up to par with performance at last. Evolved from the long early-'50s line of Exner-designed, Ghia-built Chrysler show cars, the '55s were clean and aggressive-looking on a slightly longer 126-inch wheelbase. Windsor DeLuxe was treated to a new 301-cid Hemi with 188 bhp. New Yorker retained a 331 rated at 250 bhp.

The '56s looked even better—rare for a period facelift—and offered even more power. Windsors moved up to the 331 with 225 bhp standard and 250 optional. New Yorker offered 280 bhp via a bored-out 354 Hemi. That year's 300B used the same engine tweaked to 340 bhp; with a hot multicarb option it delivered 355 bhp—making this the first Detroit V-8 to break the magic "1 hp per cu. in." barrier. Chevy would manage the trick for '57, but only with fuel injection.

Exner's work was never better than on the '57 Chryslers: longer, much lower, wider, and sleeker, with modest grilles and graceful fins. They still look good today. That year's 300C was breathtaking: big and powerful yet safe and controllable—and offered as a convertible for the first time. A unique trapezoidal grille set it apart from other models.

Supplementing Newport hardtops for 1955-56 were the Windsor Nassau and New Yorker St. Regis, conservatively two-toned and boasting slightly ritzier interiors than standard Newports. Neither returned for '57, but the previous year's Newport hardtop sedans, a hasty answer to GM, would carry on well into the '70s. The '57 Town & Country wagons, Windsor and New Yorker, seated six, but could hold nine starting in '58, via a novel rear facing third seat.

Saratoga returned as Chrysler's midrange '57 series and promptly sold over 37,000 copies. It again offered a performance premium in its 295-bhp, 354-cid Hemi. Windsors boasted 285 horsepower. New Yorkers moved up to an enlarged 392 with 325 bhp; in the 300C this engine delivered an incredible 375 or 390 bhp. Nobody ran the period "horsepower race" better than Chrysler.

The division had merely caught up in the "transmission race" with fully automatic two-speed PowerFlite, which bowed in late 1953 to replace semiautomatic "Fluid Drive." But Chrysler pulled ahead in mid-'56 by adding three-speed TorqueFlite, one of the finest automatics ever built. Also that year, both transmissions switched to the now-famous—or infamous—pushbutton controls, mounted in a handy pod left of the steering wheel. PowerFlite-equipped '55s used a slender

# Chrysler

1958 300D hardtop coupe

1958 New Yorker hardtop sedan

1958 Windsor "Dartline" hardtop sedan (spring model)

1959 Windsor hardtop coupe

1959 New Yorker Town & Country station wagon

1959 Chrysler 300E hardtop coupe

wand to the right of the helm. Though this looked stiletto-lethal, it crumpled harmlessly on impact.

Chrysler's '57 styling was superb, but offering a second all-new design in three years made for sloppy workmanship and a tendency to early body rust—one reason relatively few of these cars survive today. A series of strikes didn't help. Even so, Chrysler moved close to 125,000 cars for the model year, down from the 128,000 of '56 but still good for 10th in the industry.

No discussion of Chrysler in the '50s is complete without mentioning "Torsion-Aire Ride," a corporate staple from 1957 until the early '80s. Packard had its excellent four-wheel "Torsion Level" system for 1955-56, so the idea wasn't really new. But Torsion-Aire was in far more driveways, and proved once and for all that American cars could be made to handle. Instead of sending road shock into the body structure like coil or leaf springs, torsion bars absorbed most of it by twisting against their anchor points. Chrysler used them only at the front, likely for more engine-compartment space than improved geometry, but it complemented them with a conventional rear end specially calibrated to maximize the bars' effectiveness.

A deep national recession and continuing subpar quality made 1958 a terrible year for Chrysler Division. Volume plunged to less than 64,000, and the make dropped to 11th, still trailing Cadillac (as it had since '56). A mild facelift was generally not for the better except on the 300D, which was all but identical to the '57 C-model. Windsor gained a convertible, but was demoted to the 122-inch Dodge/DeSoto platform. Horsepower kept climbing. Windsors were up to 290 bhp and Saratogas to 310, courtesy of 354-cid Hemis; New Yorkers packed 345 bhp and the 300D a rousing 380/390, all from 392s.

A more-substantial restyle marked the "lion-hearted" '59s. Though less-graceful, they scored close to 70,000 sales in a mild Detroit recovery. Switching to wedgehead V-8s introduced a 383 with 305 bhp for Windsor and 325 for Saratoga; a bigger-bore 413 gave 350 in New Yorker and 380 bhp in the 300E. Though not as efficient as the Hemi, the wedge was much simpler and cheaper to build.

The 300E has been long chided as a weakling next to its Hemi-powered predecessors, but road tests said it was just as quick as a 300D. With 10.1:1 compression, TorqueFlite, and 3.31:1 axle, the E could run 0-60 mph in under 8.5 seconds and reach 90 mph in 17.5. Even so, production was just 550 hardtops and a mere 140 convertibles, a record low that would stand until '63.

After flirting with a GM-style five-division structure in the '50s, Highland Park was back to Dodge and Chrysler-Plymouth by 1960. The firm introduced its first compact that year, the Valiant, but it wasn't badged as a Chrysler. Indeed, C-P repeatedly declared throughout the '60s that there would

# Chrysler

1960 300F hardtop coupe

1960 New Yorker hardtop sedan

1961 300G hardtop coupe

1961 New Yorker hardtop sedan

1961 Newport convertible coupe

never be a small Chrysler. Let Buick, Olds, and Pontiac rush to compacts. Dodge and Plymouth would field—and sometimes suffer with—smaller cars; Chryslers would remain big, brawny, and luxurious. And so they were, right through the mid-'70s.

The 1960-61 models were the last of the outlandishly finned Exner-styled Chryslers and the first to employ full unit construction instead of traditional body-on-frame (even the old Airflow had body panels welded to a separate cage frame). Since "unibodies" were held together more by welds than nuts and bolts, they didn't suffer so much from looseness or rattles. But they were definitely more prone to rust—as many a sad owner found out.

Stylewise, the '60s were highly sculptured but as clean as the deft '57s. Chrome was tastefully handled, superstructures were glassy (especially windshields), and inverted trapezoid grilles conferred an aggressive 300-like appearance. Returning from '59 were optional swiveling front seats that pivoted outward through an automatic latch release when a door was opened.

Chrysler wheelbases and engines stood pat for 1960. The Saratoga was in its last year. Windsor would also depart for good, after '61. Big-inch models were confined to six varieties of luxury New Yorker and the 300F. By decade's end, New Yorker regularly scored over 30,000 annual sales. Prices were just below Imperial's but about equal to those of the larger Buicks from General Motors.

By far the most-exciting 1960 Chrysler was the sixth-edition "letter-series" 300 with a racy yet simple new "cross-hair" grille, four-place bucket-seat interior, road-hugging suspension, and newly optional French-made Pont-a-Mousson four-speed gear-box. The F rode hard, but cornered better than any other car of its size. And it was a flyer. New "ram-induction" manifolding lifted its 413 V-8 to 375 or 400 bhp, good for standing quarter-miles of 16 seconds at 85 mph. A half-dozen different axle ratios were available for even greater speed. With the 3.03 cog plus tuned engine and some streamlining, Andy Granatelli came close to 190 mph in one flying-mile run. The 300F wasn't cheap at $5411 for the hardtop and $5841 for the convertible, but the money bought a lot of style and sizzle.

The '61 line was mostly a repeat of 1960 save somewhat more-contrived styling. Windsor moved up to replace Saratoga; taking its place was a downpriced base series called Newport. The latter immediately became the make's bread-and-butter offering, with competitive pricing of just under $3000 through 1964, a point repeatedly emphasized in Chrysler ads. By 1965, Newport's annual sales were exceeding 125,000. The '61 carried a 265-bhp 361 V-8; Windsor and New Yorker retained their previous engines. That year's 300G didn't offer the four-speed option, but returned to 15-inch wheels (from 14s) for the first time since 1956.

Though Highland Park's fortunes were shaky in these years, Chrysler Division actually improved its volume and industry rank. After sinking to 12th with over 77,000 cars for 1960, it finished 11th on better than 96,000 units for '61.

Nevertheless, the company's general sales difficulties hastened a management shakeup that had an immediate effect on products. At the end of July 1961, a beleaguered "Tex" Colbert retired as president, a role he had resumed in 1960 when William Newberg quit the post after two months amid allegations of having financial interests in several Chrysler suppliers. This ushered in former administrative vice president Lynn A. Townsend, who then became chairman in January 1967, with Virgil Boyd as president through early 1970. These changes also prompted Exner, who bore an

277

# Chrysler

unfair weight of criticism for the '62 styling, to leave in late 1961 after shaping the '63 corporate line. His replacement was Elwood Engel, recruited from Ford and a designer of the elegant '61 Lincoln Continental.

Thus began a new direction for Chrysler styling. For 1962, the division fielded what Exner called the "plucked chickens": a repeat of '61 without fins. The 1963-64s had "the crisp, clean custom look"—chiseled but chunky. For 1965 came Engel's squarish but smooth bodies with fenders edged in bright metal, one of his trademarks.

Among the '62 "plucked chickens" was a four-model group of "nonletter" 300s: convertible, hardtop coupe, and four-doors with and without B-pillars. All carried the same engine as the now-departed Windsor and could be optioned with sporty features like center console and front bucket seats. Save the pillared sedan (only 1801 built, all for export), these 300s were quite popular at prices in the $3300-$3800 range. But they hurt that year's 300H, which cost $1600-$1800 more yet looked almost the same. As a result, letter-series volume dropped from about 1600 for '61 to just 558.

New Yorker was downgraded to the junior 122-inch wheelbase for 1963-64, becoming the same general size as the less-costly Chryslers, yet sales were strong in both years. Arriving as 1963 "spring specials" were a 300 Pace Setter hardtop and convertible and the New Yorker Salon hardtop sedan. The former, commemorating Chrysler's selection as pace car for that year's Indianapolis 500, was identified by crossed checkered-flag emblems and special trim. The Salon came with such standard luxuries as air conditioning; AM/FM radio; "Auto Pilot" speed control; power brakes, steering, seats, and windows; TorqueFlite (of course); and color-keyed wheel covers and vinyl roof. Minus the Pace Setters, this lineup repeated for '64 with largely untouched engines and styling.

The 1963-64 300J/300K (the letter "I" was skipped to avoid confusion with the number "1") were big, solid performance cars in the letter-series tradition. The J came only as a hardtop; the convertible 300 was reinstated with the K. Just 400 Js were built in all, a record low for Chrysler's limited edition, but the K saw a healthy 3600-plus. All ran 413s with 360/390 bhp, down slightly from 300H ratings. The last of the true letter-series cars would be the 300L of 1965. It saw 2845 copies, including a mere 440 convertibles. None of these were quite the stormers that previous 300s were, but they remained the most-roadable Chryslers and among the best-handling of all big Detroiters. Sales lost to the nonletter 300s is what killed them, of course.

Chrysler did very well for 1965, selling over 125,000 Newports, nearly 30,000 nonletter 300s and almost 50,000 New Yorkers. Things were even better for '66: the 300 nearly doubled and Newport climbed by 42,000 units.

The post-1964 Engel Chryslers were shorter than their Exner forebears but just as big inside. Wheelbase was 124

**1962 New Yorker hardtop sedan**

**1963 New Yorker Salon hardtop sedan**

**1962 300H convertible coupe**

**1965 New Yorker hardtop coupe**

**1963 300 hardtop coupe**

**1965 300L hardtop coupe**

# Chrysler

1966 New Yorker hardtop sedan

1967 New Yorker hardtop sedan

1967 Newport Custom hardtop coupe

1968 300 hardtop coupe

1969 Newport Custom hardtop sedan

inches on all models except wagons (121 through '66, then 122 inches). Expanding the '67 line were the Newport Custom two- and four-door hardtop and four-door sedan. Tagged some $200 above comparable standard Newports, Customs were trumpeted as "a giant step in luxury, a tiny step in price." Deluxe interiors were the big attraction: jacquard cloth and textured vinyl, plus pull-down center armrests. Like other '67 Chryslers, the Custom dash sprouted no fewer than eight toggle switches, three thumbwheels, 16 pushbuttons, three sliders, and 12 other assorted controls. Vinyl-covered lift handles appeared on Custom trunklids, and there were "over 1000 chrome accents along the sides, plus 15 gold crown medallions."

Meanwhile, the luxurious New Yorker Town & Country wagon disappeared after 1965 (sales had been slow for years), but six- and nine-passenger Newport wagons continued through '68, after which T&C became a separate wagon series. All typically came with vinyl upholstery instead of the cloth-and-vinyl of Newport sedans.

Spring 1968 brought the interesting $126 "Sportsgrain" option: wagon-type simulated-wood side paneling for the Newport convertible and hardtop coupe. It didn't sell well and thus was dropped after '69, so a Sportsgrain convertible must be rare indeed, as Chrysler built only 2847 ragtop Newports in '68. More-popular '68 offerings were Newport Special two- and four-door hardtops with a turquoise color scheme that later extended to 300s.

Engine choices for '65 involved 270- and 315-bhp 383s for Newport and 300, a 413 with 340 or 360 bhp for New Yorker and 300L. The more-potent 383 gained 10 horses for '66, when a huge new 440 big-block arrived as standard New Yorker power, rated at 350 bhp. This became standard on 300s for 1967, when another version was offered with 375 bhp. The 440s stood pat for 1968-69, but the 383s were retuned to 290 and 330 bhp, this despite the advent of federal emissions standards.

These moves and the conservative Engel styling paid off in vastly higher volume: 206,000-plus for '65 and nearly 265,000 the following year. Though sales dipped to some 219,000 for '67, Chrysler ran tenth in industry output in each of these years, then claimed ninth with 1968 production that just topped the '66 record.

The all-new "fuselage-styled" '69s did almost as well. If not the most-beautiful Chryslers of the decade, they were at least handsome with their great looping bumper/grille combinations, fulsome bodysides, and low rooflines. Despite remaining on the 124-inch wheelbase, all models were bigger than ever: almost 225 inches long and nearly 80 inches wide—about as big as American cars ever got.

Predictably, the 1970 models changed only in detail, but midyear introduced the first Cordobas: a Newport hardtop coupe and sedan with paint, vinyl roof, bodyside moldings, wheels, and grille all in gold, plus unique "Aztec Eagle" upholstery. A well-equipped Newport 440 hardtop also arrived with TorqueFlite, vinyl roof, and other extras as standard.

A reminder, but not a revival, of the great letter-series in 1970 was the 300-H. The "H" stood for Hurst, maker of the floor-mounted shifter used for its automatic gearbox. Performance goodies abounded—special road wheels, white-letter tires, a tuned 440 V-8, heavy-duty suspension—set off by a gold-and-white paint job, custom hood, trunklid spoiler, special grille, pinstriping, and unique interior. Only 501 were built. Also appearing for 1970 were Chrysler's last big convertibles, a Newport and 300 that saw respective production of just 1124 and 1077 units. The 300s are minor collector's items.

# Chrysler

Vast changes in corporate administration were evident by 1969-70. Quality control had become an end in itself as engineers struggled to correct Chrysler Corporation's poor reputation in that area. On the administrative side, Townsend had recentralized Colbert's old decentralized structure and moved to strengthen divisional identities between Dodge vs. Chrysler-Plymouth. Still, the firm would have a very tough road ahead in the '70s.

The Chrysler brand stayed with its basic 1969-70 formula through 1973. Style variations through '72 came via easy-change trim items that became a bit tackier with time. The '73s gained blockier lower-body sheetmetal and a more-conventional front, with bigger bumpers per federal requirement.

New for '71 was a low-priced Newport Royal subseries with standard 255-bhp 360 V-8, an enlarged version of the corporate small-block engine introduced in the mid-'60s. A stroked 400-cid version of the 383, more adaptable to emissions tuning, replaced it for '72, then disappeared with the 360 and all Royal models. Other Chryslers relied on the 440 with added emission controls that sapped horsepower, which was down to 215 bhp by '73—though that was a more-realistic SAE net, not gross, measure. A popular new addition for '72 was the New Yorker Brougham: two hardtops and a sedan with lusher interiors and a $300-$400 price premium over the standard issue.

Overall, Chrysler did fairly well in this period. Sales fell to around 177,000 for 1970-71, but recovered to nearly 205,000 for '72, then to 234,000-plus. Nevertheless, Chrysler still couldn't seem to beat Cadillac, trailing GM's flagship every year in eleventh place.

Sales sank mightily in the wake of the first energy crisis despite a completely redesigned crop of 1974 models, still on a 124-inch wheelbase but about five inches shorter than the "fuselage" generation. Styling was crisper but more slab-sided, and announced by pseudo-classic square grilles, a period fad that Chrysler had studiously avoided. Engine options and horsepower were down: 185/205-bhp 400 V-8s for Newport and Newport Custom, 230/275-bhp 440s for T&C wagons, New Yorker, and New Yorker Brougham. The last was now quite like the Imperial, which was again being marketed as a Chrysler but was still registered as a separate make (and is so treated here). After '75, Imperial actually became a Brougham via the badge-engineering so long practiced by Chrysler—to the confusion of customers up and down the corporate line.

Few in Highland Park had foreseen the energy crisis, which only accelerated the buyer resistance to big cars that had been building as a result of galloping sticker prices. Sales of the record-priced 1974s dropped to 1970 levels, and a two-month backlog quickly piled up, yet chairman Townsend refused to slash prices. Instead, he slashed production. By early November 1974, corporate sales were down 34 percent—not as bad as GM's 43 percent decline, but more serious, as Chrysler's fixed costs were spread over much smaller volume. The results were employee layoffs and an unsold inventory of 300,000 units by early 1975.

Finally, Chrysler did something no one in Detroit had ever done before: instituted cash rebates—essentially paying people to buy. Other producers had little choice but to follow. It amounted to throwing money away in an attempt to lose less on the balance sheets, but it was a necessary, if drastic, step: That big inventory cost Chrysler $300,000 a week.

These sharp reversals prompted a complete rethink that must have seemed quite alien for a make that had once solemnly promised never to build a smaller car. But a new philosophy was emerging that echoed some 1958 remarks of

1970 New Yorker hardtop sedan

1970 Chrysler 300 convertible coupe

1970 Newport hardtop coupe

1972 Town & Country station wagon

1973 New Yorker four-door sedan

then-outgoing president K.T. Keller, who suggested Chrysler should "get back to design for function, with more stress on utility."

The most-visible evidence of the new order was the 1975 Cordoba. Though this personal-luxury coupe broke new ground for the marque, it wasn't all that daring: largely a twin to that year's revamped Dodge Charger, with styling that looked like a cross between the Jaguar XJ6 and Chevrolet Monte Carlo. On a 115-inch wheelbase, this new Cordoba was the shortest Chrysler since the war—and only 2.5 inches longer than the very first 1924 Six.

Cordoba was billed as "the new small Chrysler," which it was, and something of a road car, which it wasn't despite standard antiroll bars and steel-belted radial tires. Reflecting its true character were interiors upholstered in crushed velour or vinyl with brocade cloth. "Fine Corinthian leather," extolled on TV by Ricardo Montalban, cost extra.

The rest of the line was little changed for 1975-76, except for higher prices. The accent was now strictly on luxury with a modicum of "efficiency" thrown in. The opulent New Yorker Brougham boasted standard leather, velour, or brocade upholstery, plus shag carpeting, imitation walnut appliques, and filigree moldings. Economy, such as it was, was boosted with numerically lower rear-axle ratios and a new "Fuel Pacer" option—an intake manifold-pressure sensor hooked to a warning light that glowed during heavy-footed moments.

Chrysler fielded something even smaller for 1977: the midsize, 3500-pound, M-body LeBaron. Cleanly styled in the boxy Mercedes idiom on a 112.7-inch wheelbase, it came in standard and upmarket Medallion trim as either a coupe or four-door sedan. Despite its origins in the workaday A-body Dodge Aspen/Plymouth Volare compacts, it sold extremely well, providing timely sales assistance in a market again gone wild for smaller cars. The full-size line was mildly face-lifted, and Newport Custom departed; Cordoba soldiered on in two little-changed versions.

LeBaron got greater emphasis for 1978 with the addition of downpriced S models and a brace of Town & Countrys, the latter replacing full-size Chrysler wagons. All offered 90- and 110-bhp versions of the firm's veteran 225-cid "Slant Six" as alternatives to optional 140- and 155-bhp 318 V-8s. The slow-selling full-sizers were further reduced by dropping pillared four-doors. The 440 V-8 was still optional for them, but most were ordered with the standard 400. LeBaron had bowed with square headlamps newly approved by Washington. Cordoba now got them, too.

For 1979, Chrysler issued downsized big sedans on a 118.5-inch wheelbase: six and V-8 Newport and V-8-only New Yorker and New Yorker Fifth Avenue. Built on the firm's 1971-vintage intermediate platform, these R-body models were considerably smaller and lighter than the old mastodons, but still managed to look big and heavy—which may explain why sales were underwhelming: about 133,000 in a record Detroit year. The LeBaron line now listed base, Medallion, and new midrange Salon models plus woody-look T&C wagons, none substantially altered. Reviving the spirit of the great letter-series 300 was a midyear option group for Cordoba comprising unique trim, bucket seats, cross-hair grille, and a 195-bhp 360 V-8.

A fast-growing financial crisis was now threatening Chrysler Corporation's very existence. But help was already onboard in the person of newly named chairman Lee A. Iacocca, the recently ousted president of Ford who'd taken the same job at Chrysler in late 1978. He arrived none too soon. Not only was Chrysler near bankruptcy but in "a state of anarchy," as Iacocca wrote later in his best-selling autobiography. "There was no real committee setup, no cement in the organizational chart, no system of meetings to get people talking to each other . . . I took one look at the system and almost threw up. That's when I knew I was in really deep trouble."

"Chrysler had no overall system of financial controls," Iacocca continued. "Nobody in the whole place seemed to fully understand what was going on when it came to financial planning and projecting. I couldn't find out anything. I already knew about the lousy cars, the bad morale, and the deteriorating factories. But I simply had no idea that I wouldn't even be able to get hold of the right numbers so that we could

**1975 New Yorker Brougham hardtop sedan**

**1975 Cordoba coupe**

**1976 New Yorker Brougham hardtop sedan**

**1977 Cordoba coupe with Crown Roof**

# Chrysler

begin to attack some basic problems."

New products to answer some of those problems were nearing completion when Iacocca came in; others were further away. None would have appeared without the federal loan guarantees Iacocca managed to coax from a reluctant Congress in mid-1980.

For the Chrysler line, this situation dictated a holding action for 1980-81, though with a few game attempts at something different. Prime among the latter was a second-generation Cordoba, a crisply reskinned LeBaron coupe on the same 112.7-inch wheelbase. It was a fair success its first year at some 54,000 units, but annual volume then fell to less than half of that through '83, when Cordoba said *adios*. A 185-bhp 360 V-8 was optional for 1980, after which choices thinned to a standard 85-bhp, 225-cid Slant-Six or a 130-bhp 318 V-8. A less-expensive LS edition for 1981-83 again tried to evoke letter-series memories, but few were sold.

The big R-body Newport/New Yorker provided little sales help in this period, and was abandoned after much-reduced 1981 volume of fewer than 11,000 (including a high proportion of taxi and police sales). A much happier fate awaited the M-body LeBaron, which also looked terminal but would run a good deal longer yet. It was face-lifted for 1980 with bolder grilles, more-sharply creased fenders and, save wagons, blockier rooflines. Making room for the downsized Cordoba, LeBaron coupes moved to the 108.7-inch Aspen/Volare wheelbase and gained a more-closely coupled look.

What ultimately prolonged this design appeared as a mid-1980 special called LeBaron Fifth Avenue Edition, a loaded four-door with throwback styling in the image of the like-named R-body New Yorker. When the latter was canceled and a new front-drive LeBaron instituted for '82, this one model

**1977 New Yorker Brougham hardtop sedan**

**1977 Cordoba coupe with Crown roof**

**1977 LeBaron Medallion coupe**

**1978 LeBaron Town & Country station wagon**

**1978 Newport hardtop coupe**

**1978 Cordoba coupe with Crown roof**

**1979 New Yorker Fifth Avenue four-door sedan**

**1979 Cordoba coupe**

# Chrysler

1980 Cordoba Crown coupe

1982 LeBaron four-door sedan

1981 LeBaron Medallion four-door sedan

1982 New Yorker four-door sedan

1981 New Yorker Fifth Avenue four-door sedan

1982 LeBaron Mark Cross convertible coupe

1982 Cordoba LS coupe with Carriage roof

1983 LeBaron Mark Cross Town & Country convertible

1982 Cordoba coupe with Landau roof

1983 New Yorker Fifth Avenue four-door sedan

# Chrysler

1983 Cordoba coupe

1983 E-Class four-door sedan

1984 LeBaron Town & Country station wagon

1984 Laser Turbo coupe

1984 LeBaron convertible coupe

was retained as a badge-engineered "downsized" New Yorker and showed increasing sales strength as the market recovered from its early-decade doldrums. By 1984, it was simply Fifth Avenue and up to over 79,000 produced—a figure that neared 110,000 the next year. Remarkably, the Fifth Avenue was still bringing in over 70,000 orders per year as late as 1987.

There was no mystery in this. A lot of folks still craved traditional rear-drive American luxury. This one offered plenty of standard amenities at attractive prices that began around $13,000 and finished the decade only some $5000 higher. Yes, the Fifth Avenue was terribly outmoded by 1989, but as tooling costs had long been amortized, Chrysler could keep prices reasonable (despite pressures to the contrary), which hardly dampened demand. In all, this car was a pleasant surprise success for Chrysler.

Meanwhile, Iacocca presided over a remarkable resurgence that put Chrysler Corporation solidly back in the black by 1983. This return to prosperity came almost entirely on clever—and seemingly endless—permutations of the front-drive K-car compact, introduced for 1981 as the Dodge Aries/Plymouth Reliant. Chrysler versions followed for '82; by decade's end they'd constitute virtually the entire line.

The first was a smaller LeBaron: base and Medallion coupes and sedans on the 99.9-inch K-car wheelbase. Power came from Chrysler's own newly designed 2.2-liter (135-cid) single-over-head-cam four or an optional 2.6-liter "balancer" four supplied by the firm's longtime Japanese partner, Mitsubishi. A turbocharged 2.2 spinning out 142-146 bhp came in '84 and was relatively popular. Replacing the old M-body LeBarons, these "CV" models were joined at mid-1982 by a woody-look Town & Country wagon and the first American-made convertibles since the mid-'70s. The latter can be fairly credited to Iacocca and were a brilliant stroke, offered in plain and nostalgic T&C trim.

Iacocca also issued CV-based long models recalling the '40s and '50s. These comprised a five-passenger Executive Sedan on a 124-inch chassis and a seven-seat limousine on a 131-inch span—the first "carriage trade" Chryslers since the last Stage-way Imperial limos of 1970. They sold in modest numbers through 1986, mainly to fancy hotels and airport limo services. Chrysler then gave up on them as just so much bother.

The CV LeBarons continued through 1986 with only minor styling and mechanical changes. A stroked 2.5-liter (153-cid) engine with 100 bhp became available that year, a year after TorqueFlite automatic was made standard and the five-speed manual transmission was dropped. The line quickly established itself as Chrysler's top period seller, garnering around 100,000 orders annually. The notchback four-door and T&C wagon lasted through 1988.

Next in the line of K-based Chryslers was a stretched four-door, originally named "Gran LeBaron" but announced for 1983 under the prosaic title of E-Class, a reference to its E-body platform. Though riding a three-inch longer wheelbase, the E-Class was much like the CV LeBaron save revised rear-quarter styling, a roomier back seat, and slightly higher prices. But it failed to catch on—at least as a Chrysler product. After 1984 and some 80,000 examples, it was badge-engineered into Plymouth and Dodge models that sold somewhat better as "new-age" family cars.

A more-successful spinoff was the first front-drive New Yorker. Bowing at mid-1983, this was an E-Class with more class—or what passed for it. Taking a cue from Fifth Avenue sales, stylists gave the E-body a blind-quarter padded vinyl roof, more-upright vertical-bar grille, extra chrome accents,

# Chrysler

1985 New Yorker Turbo four-door sedan

1985 Executive Limousine four-door

1985 LeBaron GTS Turbo hatchback sedan

1985 Fifth Avenue four-door sedan

1986 LeBaron coupe

1986 New Yorker Turbo four-door sedan

1986 LeBaron Town & Country convertible coupe

1986 Laser coupe

1987 LeBaron Town & Country station wagon

1987 LeBaron Turbo convertible coupe

even "opera lamps" (a '70s throwback). There was also a more-uptown interior with Mark Cross leather upholstery (introduced with the LeBaron convertible) and high-tech tricks like an irritating Electronic Voice Alert, a "back-seat driver" with a synthesized voice that nagged you from within the instrument panel. New Yorker wasn't the only Chrysler afflicted by this ill-conceived device, which was soon dropped. The car itself lasted longer, generating some 60,000 sales through 1987, after which it departed for a more-impressive New Yorker.

The two most-interesting Chryslers of the '80s were undoubtedly the Laser coupe and LeBaron GTS sedan. The former, new for '84, was a sleek "fasthatch" on an abbreviated 97.0-inch-wheelbase K-car platform (internally dubbed "G24"). A near-identical twin to the reborn Dodge Daytona introduced alongside it, the Laser was an exciting if somewhat crude performer in turbo form and practical in any guise. But it may have been a little too sporty for most Chrysler types, because the Daytona always outsold it. As Dodge was reasserting its claim as the firm's "performance" division, Chrysler-Plymouth dealers lost the Laser after 1986, though they got something more salable to replace it.

GTS, a 1985 addition, was a very different LeBaron: a smooth hatchback four-door aimed at America's increasingly affluent baby-boomers and their growing preference for premium European sedans. As usual, there was a duplicate Dodge, the Lancer. Both shared the same new H-body and the usual K-car underpinnings on a 103.1-inch wheelbase. Available engines were the now-familiar assortment of Chrysler-built four cylinders teamed with five-speed overdrive manual and TorqueFlite automatic transaxles.

Though no threat to the likes of BMW and Mercedes, the LeBaron GTS was a competent all-around performer, surprisingly roomy and quite versatile (like Laser, its back seat folded down for extra cargo space). Over 135,000 found buyers in the first two years with prices starting at $9000-$11,000. Unfortunately, volume dropped by almost 50 percent for '87, reflecting tough competition from the popular new Ford Taurus/Mercury Sable. For 1989, GTS referred only to a top-spec 2.2 turbo model, the base and midrange offerings becoming just plain LeBarons.

As if buyers weren't already bewildered by so many LeBarons, Chrysler introduced two more for 1987: a new J-body coupe and convertible to replace the previous CV styles. Chrysler's design staff, under new chief Tom Gale, gave them rounded, GTS-type contours, a clean yet dignified hidden-headlamp nose, and a shapely tail with full-width light panel. From the rear, the coupe was nicely reminiscent of Studebaker's Avanti. The convertible looked great from any angle, especially with the top down.

Though the CV wheelbase was retained, the J-model's inner structure related more to Daytona than K-car. By now, corporate planners were seeking to reestablish Chrysler as their premium make, so there were no divisional doubles of these LeBarons. Instead, Chrysler gave up the Laser, and the Daytona continued as a Dodge exclusive. This strategy helped the latter less than the LeBaron Js, which got off to a strong sales start at nearly 83,500 units.

New Yorker figured in another name game for 1988: fully revised on the new 104.3-inch-wheelbase C-body platform shared with Dodge's Dynasty. There were no major chassis innovations at first, but there was a new engine: a smooth 136-bhp 3.0-liter (181-cid) Mitsubishi V-6 with electronic-port fuel injection (now almost universal at Highland Park). Styling was clean but archly conservative—really a cautious update of the Fifth Avenue and, again, reportedly dictated by

1987 LeBaron coupe

1988 New Yorker Landau four-door sedan

1988 New Yorker four-door sedan

1988 Chrysler's TC by Maserati convertible coupe

1988 Fifth Avenue four-door sedan

# Chrysler

1989 Chrysler's TC by Maserati with removable hardtop roof

1989 LeBaron GTS Turbo hatchback sedan

1989 LeBaron GTC Turbo coupe

1989 LeBaron GTC Turbo convertible coupe

1989 Fifth Avenue four-door sedan

1990 New Yorker Fifth Avenue four-door sedan

1990 New Yorker Landau four-door sedan

1990 Town & Country minivan

1990 LeBaron GTC Turbo convertible coupe

1990 LeBaron four-door sedan

# Chrysler

chairman Iacocca himself. Base and better-equipped Landau sedans (the latter with vinyl rear quarter-roof) were listed from around $17,500. A first for Chrysler was availability of antilock brakes, a $1000 option but worth every penny in peace of mind. Handling and performance were nothing special, but these were merely traditional luxury cars of a trimmer, more-efficient sort—really, no bad thing to be.

And Chrysler made them better for 1989 with standard all-disc brakes and a new four-speed automatic transaxle that gave Highland Park another industry first with its fully adaptive electronic shift control. Other new features for the New Yorker nameplate's 50th year included optional antitheft alarm system, power front seatback recliners, two-position "memory" power driver's seat, and a revised electronic instrument cluster.

Plymouth's new 1989 Acclaim compact implied an upscale Chrysler version. Sure enough, it arrived in January 1990 to take over for the departed LeBaron hatchback. A rounded but blocky four-door notchback, it was essentially a gussied-up Acclaim that could look like a pint-size New Yorker with optional bright trim, vinyl-roof toppings, and a standard 141-bhp V-6. The K-car's 2.2-liter four had grown to 2.5 liters and 100 bhp, and it was now standard for all '89 two-door LeBarons. The only option was a 150-bhp turbo version for LeBaron coupes and convertibles. Those J-body cars received a modernized dash for 1990. Designed by Trevor Creed, lately of Citroën, it was flashy, but less than ideal for ergonomics. Also new for the Js was a 2.2-liter "Turbo IV" option with Chrysler's new Variable Nozzle Technology. Power was unchanged from the previous "Turbo II" (174 bhp), but VNT reduced turbo lag by optimizing exhaust-gas flow to the turbocharger with a set of radial vanes whose angle was computer adjusted according to throttle position and engine speed.

Symbolic of Highland Park's 1980s fortunes was its first-ever production two-seater. Awkwardly named Chrysler's TC by Maserati, it was first shown in mid-1986 (as the "Q-coupe") but was delayed by numerous problems to a late-1988 debut as an '89 model. Maserati, of course, is the well-known Italian sports-car maker in which Chrysler had lately acquired a minority interest, but its main role in this joint venture was simply to build Chrysler's design.

Almost too predictably, the TC was yet another K-clone: a shortened 93.3-inch-wheelbase version of that ubiquitous platform topped by a wedgy convertible body looking much like the open LeBaron J (though the TC was actually created first). Powerteams comprised a special 200-bhp turbocharged 2.2 with intercooler, port injection, and a new Maserati-design 16-valve twincam cylinder head, available only with five-speed manual; and a single-cam 160-bhp "Turbo II" engine for buyers preferring three-speed automatic. The customer's only other choice was paint color, since the TC was being sold as a fully equipped "one-price" model. Included were the expected leather upholstery and full power assists, but also all-disc antilock brakes, manual soft top with heated-glass rear window, and a removable hardtop (made of sheet-molding compound). The last had a nostalgic styling touch: rear-quarter portholes, recalling the '56 Thunderbird and the earliest days of Iacocca's career at Ford.

For all this, the TC bombed. Its similarity to the much cheaper LeBaron convertible was too obvious; and handling, refinement, and performance were undistinguished for a car of its price. Adding injury to insult, the announced $30,000 base sticker was hiked $3000 within three months. Thus did trade weekly *Automotive News* name the TC its 1988 "Flop of the Year," the same "honor" it accorded Cadillac's Allanté the

1991 New Yorker Salon four-door sedan

1991 Town & Country minivan

1991 Chrysler TC by Maserati convertible coupe

1991 Imperial four-door sedan

1992 New Yorker Fifth Avenue four-door sedan

# Chrysler

1992 LeBaron convertible coupe

1992 Town & Country minivan

1993 New Yorker Fifth Avenue four-door sedan

1993 Concorde four-door sedan

previous year. The 1990 edition was unchanged save a wood-rimmed steering wheel with airbag and a 3.0-liter Mitsubishi V-6 to replace the Turbo II engine with automatic. Production soon ended at some 7300 total units. A few 1990s were retailed into '91, again at fire-sale prices.

Meanwhile, the old rear-drive M-body Fifth Avenue was finally retired for a new Y-body 1990 model, essentially the latest front-drive New Yorker stretched to a 109.3-inch wheelbase. Styling displayed the usual "formal" cues, though hidden headlamps were a nice change and there were gadgets galore. Under the hood sat a new Chrysler V-6: a 3.3-liter overhead-valve design with port injection and 147 bhp. But the real surprise was yet another reborn Imperial, this one a more-deluxe Fifth Avenue measuring four inches longer (203 overall). An upright grille announced it, and the familiar Imperial eagle badges graced the tail and roof. But prices were stiff for what amounted to luxury K-cars: $21,395 for Fifth Avenue, $25-grand for Imperial. Worse, both were narrower and less-spacious than Cadillac's recently upsized DeVille. And Chrysler charged extra for antilock brakes that Lincoln included on its Continental sedan. With all this, the Y-body twins were not huge sellers. The Fifth Avenue claimed a respectable 44,400 model-year sales, but Imperial managed fewer than 15,000.

There was a new Town & Country for 1990, the first in two years. To no one's surprise, it was a minivan. Chrysler had pioneered this concept with its 1984 Dodge Caravan/Plymouth Voyager, and had kept sales roaring with useful yearly updates, especially the 1987 introduction of extended "Grand" models on a spacious 119.1-inch wheelbase. With every minivan an easy sale—and often loaded with profitable extras—a luxury version was a logical addition to the Chrysler lineup.

The minivan T&C bowed as a single long-chassis model with numerous comfort and convenience features including leather interior. Base price was a bit startling at $25,000, but the only extras were whitewall tires and a front license-plate bracket. A vertical-bar grille and pseudo-wood bodysides distinguished T&C from less-costly Chrysler minivans. The sole powertrain was a 150-bhp 3.3 pushrod V-6 and four-speed automatic, a new option for the 1990 Caravan/Voyager. Though model-year sales were modest at under 3500, Chrysler hoped for better T&C results in the future.

Assuming there was a future, which many were doubting in 1990. Incredibly, Chrysler was again flirting with disaster in a market turned sour once more, but this time there was no question of a government rescue. Chrysler's latest woes were clearly of its own doing.

They stemmed from a mid-'80s spending spree amid windfall earnings, mainly from minivans. Optimistically, Iacocca decided that if GM could profit with Hughes Electronics, Chrysler should buy its own aerospace company—say, Gulfstream Aviation. Trouble was, Chrysler's purchase cost far more than GM's in relation to total assets, and Gulfstream ultimately proved of little direct benefit. Chrysler spent billions more to acquire American Motors in 1987, landing the lucrative Jeep franchise—and assuming a mountain of debt it could ill-afford. Worse, these and other overreaching moves diverted funds that might have been better used to improve Chrysler's own products and plants. As a result, the company was woefully unprepared when a sharp new recession hit in 1990, and sales, earnings, and cash reserves all dropped alarmingly.

As part of its 1980s "diversification," Chrysler split off its vehicle business as a separate Chrysler Motors unit in 1985. But this was an organizational indulgence, and it lasted only five years. In the meantime, the firm began losing the key executives who'd helped engineer its early-'80s comeback, the former Iacocca colleagues from Ford who'd been serving as presidents and chairmen of Chrysler Motors. First to go was minivan "father" Harold Sperlich in 1988; financial whiz Gerald Greenwald and Bennett Bidwell resigned two years later. These departures ushered in Robert Lutz as president of Chrysler Motors in 1988. Three years later, he became overall president of a reunified Chrysler Corporation.

Lutz arrived in the nick of time. A knowledgeable "car guy" with top-level executive experience at Opel, BMW, and Ford Europe, he knew even better than Iacocca that consumer

# Chrysler

tastes had changed dramatically and that Chrysler had to change with them—fast. That not only meant more-contemporary, "international" vehicles but a whole new way of designing, building, and selling them. With Iacocca's endorsement, Chrysler began shedding noncore businesses like Gulfstream while forming "cross-functional platform teams" charged with creating superior cars and trucks—and getting them to market in three years or less instead of the usual four or five.

Under the "team concept," designers, engineers, production experts, and marketing talent would work together from day one to ensure their products were on target with buyers for features, cost, and quality. The idea was to minimize the delays, mistakes, confusion, and "turf battles" that tend to arise when people work on separate pieces of a project. The decision to produce the hot Dodge Viper sports car provided a timely opportunity to test the new approach on a manageably small scale. It worked beautifully, and the team concept was quickly adopted for all future-product programs. Chrysler also began forging much closer alliances with its many suppliers by including them as members of the various teams.

With these and other departures from Detroit tradition, the company liked to say it was "reinventing" itself, hoping to become a "New New Chrysler Corporation" able to make timely, right moves to survive and even thrive in a now vastly changed automotive world. Toward that end, chairman Iacocca was finally persuaded to step down, something he'd resisted for years. Though Lutz was the obvious heir apparent, Iacocca got in one last surprise by handing the job to Robert Eaton in early 1993. Eaton was a shrewd choice. He came directly from GM Europe, which had recently come back strong under his command, and his low-key manner was a nice counterpoint to the up-front Lutz. To his credit, Lutz agreed to stay on and give his all for the new chairman. They made a formidable team.

Of course, massive change doesn't happen overnight, so the early '90s were transition years for the Chrysler line. Existing models were kept on only until replacements were ready, which would be remarkably soon.

Some of the old stuff was treated with "benign neglect." The Y-body, for example, vanished after 1993 and only two interim changes of note: a 3.8-liter V-6 for '91 (standard for Imperial, optional on Fifth Avenue) and a mild Fifth Avenue facelift for '92 year. Sales faded in both cases. Imperial dropped under 12,000 for '91, then to 7600 and about 7000. Fifth Avenue held up better, scoring no worse than just under 30,000 in its last model year. Still, against Cadillac and Lincoln, these cars were only a token luxury presence for the Chrysler brand, and in looks and driving feel they were about as contemporary as a leisure suit.

The same could be said for the C-body New Yorker, which lost its spiffy Landau model for 1991, then got a nearly imperceptible facelift before closing out as a single '93 all but identical with the Dodge Dynasty. Despite base prices that never exceeded $20,000, this New Yorker couldn't match the sales of the costlier Fifth Avenue, managing just 20,000-23,000 a year after 1990.

LeBarons were fiddled with during this period, but not drastically changed. A J-body lineup rearranged for '91 received antilock brakes as a new option for '92, when the A-body sedan expanded to base, LX, and Landau models. Two-doors got a nice facelift for '93, showing new grilles and exposed headlamps. Turbo engines were dropped but the Mitsubishi V-6 was now standard for midline LX and sporty GTC coupes and convertibles. At the same time, the LX sedan departed and the base model was renamed LE. Coupes and four-cylinder power disappeared for '94, leaving the two sedans and one GTC convertible with standard V-6. Only the ragtop returned for '95, after which the LeBaron name was finally put to rest (at least so far). Though sales declined with all models, the J-body two-doors fared a little better.

Heralding Chrysler's next generation was the front-drive Concorde, the 1993 successor to the C-body New Yorker. Though billed as an intermediate, it was really a full-size, standing nearly 17 feet long on a rangy 113-inch wheelbase. All-independent suspension and standard antilock brakes recalled Chrysler's glory days. So did appearance. With its

**1994 New Yorker four-door sedan**

**1995 Cirrus LXi four-door sedan**

**1994 LeBaron GTC convertible coupe**

**1995 Sebring coupe**

# Chrysler

1996 Town & Country LXi minivan

1996 Sebring LX coupe

1996 LHS four-door sedan

1996 Concorde LXi four-door sedan

new "LH" platform (still a "unibody," of course), Concorde introduced "cab forward" sedan styling that made for vast interior space and a sleek, even daring, new look—a refreshing break from boxiness. For the first time in nearly 40 years, Chrysler could claim industry design leadership. Though Concorde's form was shared by divisional sisters Dodge Intrepid and Eagle Vision, Chrysler made sure there were enough differences among the three to avoid the possibility of buyer confusion.

Essentially, cab-forward lengthened the greenhouse and pushed the wheels out closer to the car's corners, resulting in a stubby deck, foreshortened nose, and purposeful wide-track stance (though a longitudinal engine dictated lengthy front overhang). General design thinking had been moving in this direction, so cab-forward was not entirely new or unique to Chrysler. But nobody would it use more. In fact, cab-forward was the company's new design signature.

Concorde bowed in a single, well-equipped model base-priced at $18,341. Included were front bucket seats, shift console, tachometer, dual airbags, full power assists, and other amenities. Power came from one of two V-6s. The pushrod 3.3 was standard, tuned for 153 bhp. Optional was a new 3.5-liter design with dual-overhead camshafts, four valves per cylinder and 214 bhp. Both were mated with four-speed automatic transaxle. Key options included electronic traction control, a firmer "touring" suspension with performance tires, leather interior, and an innovative built-in child safety seat that flipped out from the rear backrest.

Though advertised as "the renaissance of the American car," Concorde was assembled in Canada, as Chrysler was obliged to note in fine print. It was just another sign that the auto world had become a small one after all.

The LH cars had been branded by some as the "Last Hope" for Chrysler's survival. Fortunately, they were the solid success the company needed. Concorde alone scored debut model-year production of 56,218, and its '94 volume was nearly 86,000. The sophomore edition creeped up to $19,500 but gained the touring suspension as standard, revised transmission controls, eight more horses for the 3.3 engine, power steering that increased effort with road speed, and a power moonroof option. No big changes occurred for '95, though trim levels expanded to LX and posher LXi.

Next on the new-model menu were an LH-based New Yorker and a premium companion called LHS, arriving in spring '93 as the 1994 replacements for the starchy Y-body Imperial/Fifth Avenue. Both rode the Concorde wheelbase but stretched nearly five inches longer overall, hence their internal designation "207." Styling was naturally in the wedgy cab-forward mold, but a more-orthodox face and upright rear roofline imparted formality without stuffiness. Graceful reverse-curve C-posts, allegedly inspired by late-'30s Bugattis, combined with a setback rear seat for near-limousine legroom. LHS was the sporty version, aimed at affluent "boomers" with front buckets, shift console, leather interior, touring suspension and a more-"Euro" exterior. New Yorker was for more-conservative folks, delivering a front bench seat, a column shift, cloth trim, softer damping, and a little more outside chrome. Both models carried the twincam 3.5-liter V-6.

At just over $30-grand, the LHS was some $5000 above the new New Yorker, yet outsold it from day one. Combined volume was excellent at nearly 83,000 for debut '94, far above anything the Y-body had managed. Ads playfully admitted that some past Chryslers had been "barges"—but not these two. Like Concorde, the LHS/New Yorker was taut and responsive on twisty roads, peppy enough, smooth and refined (save rather excessive tire noise) and, of course, eminently spacious. Not since the '50s had Chryslers changed so much in just one year—or so much for the better.

The 207s carried into 1995 essentially unchanged. LHS added a power moonroof option as a '94 running change. The '95 New Yorker got a standard premium audio system and touring suspension. With sales running straight in favor of LHS, Chrysler decided to drop the New Yorker after a short 1996-model run, thus ending a veteran American nameplate after 57 long and eventful years.

But Chrysler forged a new link with the past on 1995 models, replacing the corporate pentastar with the make's original "blue ribbon" badge, revived after a 41-year absence. It

# Chrysler

**1997 LHS sedan**

**1997 Sebring convertible**

**1997 Concorde LXi sedan**

**1997 Cirrus LXi sedan**

was a pleasant surprise, but no less so than that year's new Cirrus, the cab-forward replacement for the A-body LeBaron sedan. Once again, Chrysler played fast and loose with semantics, labeling Cirrus a compact even though dimensions were closer to intermediate and even full-size. A 108-inch wheelbase, for example, put Cirrus just 2.8 inches shy of a Buick Park Avenue or Oldsmobile Ninety-Eight. Overall length wasn't that "compact" either at 186 inches.

Nevertheless, Cirrus was relatively vast inside, and it looked even bolder than bigger cab-forwards, though not everyone liked the low, jutting, vertical-bar grille. What people did approve was the taut, assured handling of its new wide-stance "JA" platform, again with all-independent suspension, standard antilock brakes and speed-variable power steering. The powerteam sat transversely here, and four-speed automatic was again mandatory. The only engine for '95 was a Mitsubishi-based 2.5-liter (152-cid) V-6, another twincam multivalve unit, good for 164 bhp. This continued on the posh LXi but was optional for the '96 LX, which switched to a standard twincam four, a new Chrysler-designed 2.4-liter with 150 bhp. Both Cirruses were fully equipped with standard air conditioning, tilt steering wheel, good-quality sound system and power windows/mirrors/door locks. The LXi added power driver's seat in a leather-trimmed interior, remote keyless entry, and antitheft alarm, plus touring suspension with performance tires on alloy wheels. In all, Cirrus was another impressive new Chrysler—and appealing value with base prices in the mid-to-high teens.

A rather different '95 newcomer was the Sebring coupe, a luxury edition of the year-old Dodge Avenger. Replacing the J-body LeBaron coupe, it wasn't technically an American car, as its foundation was the Japanese 1994-98 Mitsubishi Galant sedan platform with 103.7-inch wheelbase. But the snazzy two-door body was styled with Chrysler input, and the base LX model came with a Chrysler-designed 2.0-liter four from the small 1994-95 Dodge/Plymouth Neon. (Mitsubishi's 2.5-liter V-6 featured in the uplevel LXi.) The Sebring coupe was also American-made, built exclusively for the U.S. market at the Illinois factory that Chrysler set up with Mitsubishi in 1989 as Diamond-Star Motors. But sales were never impressive, even though Sebring coupes offered a good many standard features at affordable mid-teens to low-$20,000s prices. A generally shrinking coupe market didn't help, but neither did the few changes that occurred over five model years, the most visible being a modest 1997 facelift. As a result, calendar-year sales ran 25,000-35,000 through 1999, then plunged below 13,000.

More successful was the Sebring convertible that bowed in early 1996 to replace the LeBaron drop top. Unlike the coupe, this Sebring was pure Chrysler, sharing powertrains and a basic platform with the Cirrus sedan. Here, too, cab-forward styling contributed to uncommon interior space, with genuinely comfortable rear seating for two adults, the best of most any affordable ragtop around. Though no sports car, the Sebring convertible was a pleasant tourer on highway and byway alike. There was curiously little difference in power between the two models: 150 bhp from a 2.4-liter four in the base JX, 163 from a 2.5 V-6 in the uplevel JXi. Performance was sedate either way, thanks in part to mandatory automatic transmission, but Chrysler upped the fun quotient a bit for '97 by adding a new "AutoStick" feature to its V-6 models. A separate slot on the selector quadrant allowed the driver to move the gears up and down manually.

Though changed little more year-to-year than the Sebring coupe, the convertible sold better and more consistently, pulling in around 50,000 orders each calendar year through 2000. Like its LeBaron predecessor, a good many went to rental companies in sunbelt areas like Florida, Southern California, and Arizona, so Chrysler retained title to America's most-popular "rent-a-vertible." Among the few noteworthy changes in this period were the addition of a posh LXi Limited version for 1998 with leather-and-wood interior, chrome wheels, V-6, and AutoStick, and Sebring's first traction-control system.

Cirrus, too, seemed stuck in a time warp, its six-year run marked by annual equipment shuffles—including a here today, gone tomorrow four-cylinder engine. An exception was the '99 edition, which sported a larger grille adorned with a broad winged badge in bright chrome, a new Chrysler-brand signature being phased-in throughout the line. Calendar-year sales see-sawed from the low to high 30,000s, a fairly lackluster showing for a mainstream midsize. The related Dodge Stratus did much better business, helped by lower prices and more-aggressive marketing.

We shouldn't forget Town & Country, if only because Chrysler Corporation had become the "minivan company" in more ways than one. Like sister Dodge/Plymouth models, the T&C got a smoother exterior and redesigned dash for '91, plus a standard driver's airbag and exclusive digi-graphic instrumentation (dubious at best). Optional all-wheel drive arrived for 1992, a boon for "snowbelt" mobility that attracted few orders. Only new-design wheels marked the '93s. For '94, the optional 3.8 V-6 became standard and the dash was again modified to include a no-cost passenger airbag. Chrysler also installed door guard beams per new federal rules for side-impact protection, and offered the industry's first integrated child safety seat at extra cost. T&C then carried into '95 with few other changes pending release of redesigned 1996 models. Though base price was then nearing $30,000, T&C sales had also climbed steadily: from just 6400 of the '91s to over 40,000 by middecade, more than respectable for a gilded people-mover.

Adding safety features, especially airbags, only added to sales of all Chrysler minivans in these years. The government may have mandated front "passive restraints," but there were several ways to meet the requirement, and the public showed a marked preference for airbags over motorized front shoulder belts or "passive" three-point harnesses. Chrysler recognized this sooner than Ford or GM, and was quicker to offer airbags throughout its corporate fleet without waiting until model replacement time. It was a particularly shrewd thing to do for minivans, many of which were purchased by parents who naturally wanted the safest possible vehicle for their children. Other makers had no choice but to follow Chrysler's lead, something that hadn't occurred in decades.

Chrysler kept up its product offensive in the late '90s, starting with fully redesigned 1996 T&Cs, Dodge Caravans, and Plymouth Voyagers. Though not a breakthrough like the 1984 originals, the new "NS" models preserved all their winning attributes and added some of their own, including sleeker styling, more available power, and thoughtful family-oriented features like "Easy-Out" second- and third-row seats with built-in rollers and the industry's first driver's-side sliding rear door. The latter proved so popular that the company eventually built all its minivans that way. T&C sales remained steady and fairly strong, running 70,000-76,000 each calendar year through 2000. As ever, minivans remained vital to the health of the Chrysler marque, amounting to 22-40 percent of the brand's total car sales in this period.

Demand for nonminivan Chryslers jumped 25 percent in calendar 1998, and a dramatically redesigned Concorde, a big factor. Wheelbase was not changed, but most everything else was. A wide, Ferrari-like eggcrate grille announced handsome new cab-forward styling that added 7.5 inches to overall length, making a roomy trunk even more so. Yet despite that and a much stiffer structure, the new Concorde weighed about the same as the old, thanks to the use of aluminum for the hood, some rear suspension components, and two new Chrysler-bred V-6s. The base LX model used a 2.7-liter with dual overhead camshafts and 200 bhp, the uplevel LXi a related single-cam 3.2 with 225. Engineers worked hard to reduce the noise, vibration, and harshness criticized in previous LH models, but didn't entirely succeed. And workmanship, though visibly improved, still wasn't up to snuff. Prices held steady, but only with skimping on the quality of some materials, especially inside. Overall, though, the '98 Concorde was an impressive effort—enough that Consumer Guide® named it a Best Buy each year through 2002. But though sales jumped over 67 percent for calendar '98 to nearly 65,000, buyers seemed to lose interest after that, and volume declined to 32,300 by calendar 2001. A much-rougher market was partly to blame, but also some new public-relations problems described further on.

A new Concorde implied a redesigned LHS, and it arrived

**1998 Concorde LXi sedan**

**1998 Cirrus LXi sedan**

**1998 Sebring JXi convertible**

**1999 300M sedan**

# Chrysler

as an early-1999 entry. But the big news was a sportier sister audaciously reviving the famed letter-series 300 line after nearly 35 years. Called 300M, it wore different front and rear styling that made it 10 inches shorter overall. And instead of luxury cruiser like LHS, the M aimed to be a serious driver's car of the "European sports sedan" school. It was even designed for sale in Europe, where regulations dictated the trimmer size. Both models came with front bucket seats and an automatic transmission married to a new single-cam 3.5-liter V-6 with 253 bhp (basically a big-bore version of the Concorde's 3.2), but the 300M added Chrysler's AutoStick manual-shift feature and was noticeably more-athletic off the straight and narrow. An optional $255 Performance and Handling Package made it even more so, delivering higher-effort power steering, firmer damping, uprated all-disc antilock brakes, and stiffer 16-inch tires vs. comfort-oriented 17s (also standard for LHS).

With all this, the 300M was nothing like the "beautiful brutes" of old. Not only was it slower—a so-so 7.7 second 0-60 mph time in *Road & Track*'s test—it was a sedan, not a glam-our-puss convertible or pillarless coupe. But the M could "out-stop" any of its forebears and leave them gasping on a twisty back road. It was also built miles better, if nowhere near as well as the Eurosedans it sought to challenge. Then again, it didn't cost like they did, delivering for a reasonable $30,000 or so, about the same as a like-equipped LHS.

Chrysler was wise to take this two-prong approach with its largest cars, because the 300M way outsold the LHS—by over 2-to-1 in calendar '99 and 2000 with nearly 107,000 units combined. Heeding the market, Chrysler dropped the LHS after 2001, though it gave '02 Concordes a similar nose treatment, plus a top-line Limited model offering most LHS features at a lower price. The 300M maintained its sales pace into calendar 2000, then fell nearly 28 percent in '01. That implied buyers wanted something even sportier, so Chrysler added a 300M Special for 2002 with slightly more power, a few extra frills, the Performance/Handling option, and slim-wall high-speed tires on chunky 18-inch wheels.

The '98 Concorde and '99 LHS/300M rolled out amidst the understandable ballyhoo surrounding Chrysler Corporation's historic marriage to Germany's Daimler-Benz, announced in November 1998 and finalized during '99. Consolidation was then sweeping the industry. Ford had purchased Britain's Jaguar and lately Volvo of Sweden. General Motors controlled several Japanese makers and the automotive operations of Sweden's Saab. With the big fish getting bigger, Chrysler chairman Bob Eaton began seeking a strategic partner to insure his company's survival. The deal was all but sealed when he chanced to mention the notion to D-B's hard-driving chairman, Jurgen Schrempp.

On paper, a Chrysler/Daimler union seemed perfect. Chrysler was then the industry's most-cost-efficient producer, a recognized leader in design and innovation, loaded with talent, and had a strong asset in Jeep. Daimler boasted a formidable image, worldwide resources, and the engineering prowess of Mercedes-Benz. Both companies were profitable, and getting together promised numerous cost-saving "synergies" as well as lots of nifty new cars and trucks.

But what was proclaimed as a "merger of equals" was really a Trojan-horse takeover. Though Eaton and Schrempp were nominal co-chairs of the new DaimlerChrysler, the merger terms clearly favored Daimler, which contributed to a culture clash that delayed combining operations beyond obvious functions like purchasing. Within a year, said some Chrysler hands, the American company was being "Germanized" into a mere division, something Schrempp later conceded was part

1999 LHS sedan

2000 Sebring convertible

2000 Concorde LXi sedan

2000 LHS sedan

2000 Town & Country

# Chrysler

2001 Sebring LX sedan

2001 LHS sedan

2001 PT Cruiser

2002 300M Special sedan

2002 Sebring LX convertible

of his original plan—which only aggravated ill feelings in Michigan. Meantime, a number of Chrysler's best executives, designers, and engineers jumped ship, including manufacturing wizard Dennis Pauley, president Tom Stallkamp, design chief Tom Gale and, tellingly, former president Bob Lutz, who'd largely masterminded Chrysler's early-'90s turnaround and did not favor the merger. Eaton, for his part, said he always believed the merger was of equals, yet he, too, left, stepping down some 18 months before his term expired.

That left Schrempp to tackle a growing pile of vexing problems. First, sales of the cash-cow Jeep Grand Cherokee sport-utility began slipping. Then minivans started lagging, forcing Chrysler to offer more rebates and other costly consumer incentives to clear 2000-model inventories. But that only stole sales that might have gone to the company's redesigned 2001 minivans, which offered more features but cost more to build and thus carried higher prices. That wasn't what buyers wanted, especially as the new models didn't look very different from the old ones. Chrysler dangled more lures to spark sales, but competition was stronger than ever, so the new minivans were a fairly tough sell. With all this and more, DC stock was worth only half as much per share by the end of 2000 as it was at merger time, and some members of the DC board began demanding that Schrempp be fired.

Schrempp dodged the bullet, however, and dispatched a trusted deputy, Dieter Zetsche, to turn things around as the new CEO of what was now called Chrysler Group. Joining him as COO was Wolfgang Bernhard, another Mercedes veteran. Though their recovery program was barely begun at the time of this book's publication, let's hope a future edition records it as an unqualified success.

An early casualty of Chrysler's latest financial crisis was Plymouth, consigned to history after the 2001 model run as a money-saving measure. But the make lived on in spirit for a time, as its Voyager minivans and Prowler neo hot rod were promptly rebadged as Chryslers. Of course, they were still sold by the same dealers, who were fast changing their signs to read Chrysler-Jeep.

Debuting amid all this turmoil was one of the happiest, hippest Chryslers ever, the 2001 PT Cruiser. Beginning sale in mid-2000 after a cagey publicity build-up over the prior 18 months, it was, to quote *Road & Track*, "part street rod, part minivan, totally unlike anything else." Chrysler called it a "category buster," and the PT ("Personal Transportation") was indeed hard to pigeon-hole. Older folks tended to see a practical compact wagon that looked faintly like a late-'30s Ford. The younger crowd simply saw a way-cool ride. The EPA saw it two ways, classifying the Cruiser as a truck for corporate fuel-economy purposes, a car for safety and emissions standards.

But that was the beauty of it. The PT Cruiser could be most anything to most anyone. Not surprisingly, it sold faster than any Chrysler in history, racking up over 273,000 orders through the end of 2001, never mind DaimlerChrysler's mounting, well-publicized troubles. Affordable prices helped: about $16,000 to start, $18,000 "nicely equipped." Not that many early Cruisers sold at sticker, as rabid demand bid up delivered prices by thousands. Chrysler strained to keep up, expanding capacity at the PT plant in Mexico only a few months after sales began.

The PT Cruiser would have been a dandy way to revitalize ailing Plymouth. In fact, its basic concept originated with 1997's Plymouth Pronto show car. A 1998 follow-up, the two-door Pronto Cruzer, previewed the eventual production design, attributed to a young whiz named Brian Nesbitt, working with Bill Dayton and John Bucci.

# Chrysler

Overseeing the project (begun long before the merger) were Tom Gale, then Chrysler's vice president for product development; John Herlitz, then design director; and design execs Trevor Creed (who later replaced Gale) and Neil Walling. Interior design was supervised by veteran designer and respected auto historian Jeff Godshall. But Nesbitt tended to get all the glory, and the PT's instant sales success largely explains why he was soon recruited by Chevrolet, presumably to work similar magic there.

There wasn't much mechanical magic in the Cruiser, just sound, modern engineering. The powerplant, for example, was Chrysler's now-familiar 150-bhp 2.4-liter 16-valve twin-cam four, mated to optional four-speed automatic transmission or a standard five-speed with the tightest, most-precise linkage yet on a front-drive Mopar. Parts of the floorpan and some chassis components originated with the subcompact Neon, but the Cruiser ended up sharing very little with other Chrysler Group vehicles.

Offered in base, Touring, and leather-trimmed Limited versions, the Cruiser scored for its high versatility, funky looks, and obvious potential for personalization. Compact sport-utility size afforded fine room for four adults and all manner of stuff. Chrysler claimed 26 possible configurations for the seats and multiposition rear cargo shelf; the latter could even double as a picnic table. Acceleration was nothing special—around nine seconds 0-60 with manual—but the PT was pleasantly nimble and easy on the bumps. It also belied the notion that Chrysler couldn't deliver quality. Even early examples were solid and well-finished inside and out. Not all people liked the styling, but most did, including a few professional designers. A more-contemporary look was considered, but likely wouldn't have had as much impact. "Some of what we did was very conscious," Gale told *Collectible Automobile* magazine, but "we were not consciously trying to be retro . . . [T]he space and mechanical packages somehow naturally led to the form."

The PT almost begged for hop-up parts and '50s-style customizing, and aftermarket companies obliged with a slew of bolt-on performance components and dress-up accessories. Chrysler joined in for 2002, offering a "flame" decal package, a "Woodie" version with simulated timber on bodysides and liftgate, and a limited-production "Dream Cruiser" with Inca Gold paint, chrome wheels, and a numbered dashboard plaque. A pair of two-door concepts, the 2000 Panel Cruiser and '01 convertible, hint at future possibilities. Speed freaks, meantime, anticipated the turbocharged GT Cruiser with a rumored 215 hp that was almost sure to be added during 2002.

Overshadowed by "PT Mania" were the redesigned midsize Sebrings that bowed for 2001, completing the Chrysler lineup's turn-of-millennium renewal. Body styles now numbered three, as the Cirrus sedan became a Sebring. *Car and Driver* likened it to a scaled-down 300M, though the new four-door didn't aim to be sporty. But it did deliver a beefier, quieter structure; a supple ride; traditional Chrysler trappings; and a safety bonus in available "curtain" side airbags, which deployed from the ceiling just above the windows to protect occupants in a side impact. Styling became more-conservative and less-cab-forward, but interior space remained exceptional for the class. A massaged 2.4-liter four returned as base power, but the optional V-6 was now Chrysler's own twincam 2.7, and the mandatory automatic transmission offered the manually shiftable AutoStick at extra cost. Helped by an extra-long debut season, Sebring sedan sales almost double those of the final Cirrus at over 67,000 through the end of calendar 2001.

**2002 Prowler**

**2002 Concorde LX four-door sedan**

**2002 Sebring LXi coupe**

**2002 PT Cruiser with "Woodie package"**

**Crossfire coupe prototype**

Sebring convertibles were less-visibly changed for '01 despite mostly new outer sheetmetal, but got the same engines as the new sedans and, more important, a thorough structural beefing-up. The result was good enough to finish third in a five-way May 2001 *Car and Driver* convertible test, ahead of a Ford Mustang GT and Toyota Solara. At under $30,000 for their test Limited, "the Sebring emerged as our value champ," said the editors, "and also won as best to behold." About the only thing lacking was enough horsepower to make performance vivid instead of merely brisk. Calendar-year sales slipped to a little over 45,000 units, but that wasn't bad for what proved to be a turbulent year for Chrysler Group and the nation.

Though also redesigned for 2001, Sebring coupes remained more Mitsubishi than Chrysler, sharing the 1999-2000 platform of the Japanese company's latest Galant sedans and sporty Eclipse models. That also meant the V-6 option was a 3.0-liter Mitsubishi engine. Dodge still offered its own versions but now called them Stratus, not Avenger. As with the Sebring line, the aim was to simplify marketing—and maybe reduce buyer confusion at last. For all the changes, however, Sebring coupe sales remained modest at some 16,600 for calendar year 2001, though that was actually a bit above the 2000 tally.

Bringing the Chrysler story up to date is the 2003 Crossfire, a slinky two-passenger coupe aptly termed the first child of the Daimler-Chrysler marriage. Like PT Cruiser and Dodge's Viper, it's patterned on a well-received Chrysler concept (the '01 Crossfire), but much of the engineering is Mercedes-Benz. Indeed, the production Crossfire uses a Mercedes 3.2-liter V-6 with about 215 hp and the German brand's CLK coupe/convertible platform, though with wheelbase trimmed to about 94.5 inches. A five-speed Mercedes automatic is the only transmission, and it drives the rear wheels, not the fronts. Styling is purposeful and aggressive from eggcrate grille through tapered fastback roofline, and belies a fairly compact exterior package measuring some 159 inches long, 69 inches wide and 50.7 inches high. With curb weight of around 3000 pounds, Crossfire promises spirited performance allied with world-class handling and braking. It definitely boasts made-in-Europe cachet, as Germany's famed Karmann works handles production. Yet this is no rare, high-priced exotic, with planned output of at least 20,000 a year and a price on the right side of $40,000. It all adds up to a perfect new "halo" car to replace the Prowler.

Crossfire hadn't fully emerged at this writing, but it suggests a bright new era for the Chrysler marque. Indeed, industry pundits believe future models will follow a similar formula, combining rear-wheel drive and Mercedes-influenced engineering with the kind of trend-setting style that served Chrysler so well in the 1990s. If they're right, future editions of this book may chronicle the best Chryslers ever.

**Crossfire coupe prototype**

# Chrysler

## Specifications

### 1930

| Model CJ6 (wb 109.0) | Wght | Price | Prod* |
|---|---|---|---|
| rdstr 2-4P | 2,390 | 805 | 1,616 |
| touring 5P | 2,455 | 835 | 279 |
| bus cpe 2P | 2,560 | 795 | 2,267 |
| Royal cpe 2-4P | 2,590 | 835 | 3,593 |
| Royal sdn 4d 5P | 2,695 | 845 | 20,748 |
| conv cpe | — | — | 705 |
| chassis | — | — | 31 |

| Model 66 (wb 112.8) | Wght | Price | Prod |
|---|---|---|---|
| rdstr 2-4P | 2,625 | 1,025 | 1,213 |
| phtn 5P | 2,695 | 1,025 | 26 |
| bus cpe 2P | 2,750 | 995 | 2,014 |
| Royal cpe 2-4P | 2,850 | 1,075 | 3,257 |
| brougham 5P | 2,850 | 995 | 2,343 |
| Royal sdn 5P | 2,930 | 1,095 | 3,753 |

| Model 70 (wb 116.5) | Wght | Price | Prod |
|---|---|---|---|
| rdstr 2-4P | 3,205 | 1,345 | 1,431 |
| phtn 5P | 3,235 | 1,295 | 279 |
| bus cpe 2P | 3,410 | 1,345 | 766 |
| Royal cpe 2-4P | 3,490 | 1,395 | 3,135 |
| brougham 5P | 3,490 | 1,345 | 1,204 |
| Royal sdn 5P | 3,590 | 1,445 | 11,213 |
| conv cpe 2-4P | 3,450 | 1,545 | 705 |

| Model 77 (wb 124.0) | Wght | Price | Prod |
|---|---|---|---|
| rdstr 2-4P | 3,370 | 1,665 | 1,729 |
| phtn 5P | 3,495 | 1,795 | 173 |
| bus cpe 2P | 3,560 | 1,395 | 230 |
| Royal cpe 2-4P | 3,615 | 1,495 | 2,954 |
| Crown cpe 4P | 3,580 | 1,575 | 883 |
| conv cpe 2-4P | 3,580 | 1,825 | 418 |
| Royal sdn 5P | 3,750 | 1,495 | 7,211 |
| Town sdn 5P | 3,720 | 1,445 | 436 |
| Crown sdn 5P | 3,760 | 1,595 | 2,654 |

| Imperial (wb 136.0) | Wght | Price | Prod |
|---|---|---|---|
| rdstr 2-4P | 3,955 | 2,995 | — |
| spt phtn 4P | 4,225 | 3,955 | — |
| phtn 7P | 3,925 | 3,195 | 15** |
| cpe 2P | 4,025 | 3,095 | — |
| conv cpe 2-4P | 4,120 | 3,095 | 50** |
| sdn 5P | 4,335 | 3,075 | 300** |
| Town sdn 5P | 4,310 | 3,075 | 100** |
| sdn 7P | 4,460 | 3,195 | 150** |
| sdn limo 7P | 4,510 | 3,575 | — |

* Some figures include later years; see 1931, 1932.
** Estimates based on one-third of 1929-30 model year production.

| 1930 Engines | bore × stroke | bhp | availability |
|---|---|---|---|
| I-6, 195.6 | 3.13 × 4.25 | 62 | S-CJ6 |
| I-6, 195.6 | 3.13 × 4.25 | 65 | S-66s built 1929 |
| I-6, 218.6 | 3.13 × 4.75 | 75 | S-70s built 1929 |
| I-6, 218.6 | 3.13 × 4.75 | 68 | S-66s built 1930 |
| I-6, 268.4 | 3.38 × 5.00 | 93 | S-70s built 1930, 77 |
| I-6, 309.3 | 3.63 × 5.00 | 100 | S-Imperial |

### 1931

**Model CJ6 (wb 109.0)**    Wght   Price   Prod

Production was carried over from 1930, with 1931 model output commencing July 1, 1930. Production figures combined with 1930 CJ6 models. Body styles and weights identical; prices $20-$50 below 1930 prices.

**Model 66 (wb 112.8)**

Production was carried over from 1930 commencing July 1, 1930. Production figures combined with 1930 Model 66. Body styles and weights identical; prices $5 above 1930 prices.

**Model 70 (wb 116.5)**    Wght   Price   Prod

Production was carried over from 1930 commencing July 1, 1930. Production figures combined with 1930 Model 70. Body styles and weights identical. Open car prices unchanged; closed car prices lowered $100 except for Royal sedan, which was lowered $150.

| CM6 New Six (wb 116.0) | Wght | Price | Prod |
|---|---|---|---|
| rdstr 2-4P | 2,565 | 885 | 2,281 |
| cpe 2-4P | 2,700 | 885 | 5,327 |
| sdn 4d | 2,815 | 895 | 28,620 |
| phtn 5P | 2,740 | 915 | 196 |
| bus cpe 2P | 2,730 | 865 | 802 |
| conv cpe 2-4P | 2,750 | 935 | 1,492 |
| chassis | — | — | 99 |

| CD8 New Eight (wb 124.0)* | Wght | Price | Prod |
|---|---|---|---|
| rdstr 2-4P | 3,100 | 1,495 | ⎤ 1,462 |
| spt rdstr 2-4P | 3,225 | 1,595 | ⎦ |
| Royal Standard cpe | 3,235 | 1,495 | ⎤ 3,000 |
| Royal Sport cpe | 3,235 | 1,535 | ⎦ |
| conv cpe 2-4P | 3,195 | 1,665 | 700 |
| Royal Standard sdn | 3,365 | 1,525 | ⎤ 9,000 |
| Royal Special sdn | 3,365 | 1,565 | ⎦ |
| phtn 5P | 3,490 | 1,970 | 85 |
| chassis | — | — | 108 |

*First series commenced July 1930. Second series commenced January 1931; discontinued April 1931 and replaced by Deluxe Eight.

| DeLuxe Eight (wb 124.0) | Wght | Price | Prod |
|---|---|---|---|
| rdstr 2-4P | 3,330 | 1,545 | 511 |
| phtn 5P | 3,545 | 1,970 | 113 |
| cpe 2-4P | 3,525 | 1,525 | 1,506 |
| conv cpe 2-4P | 3,445 | 1,585 | 501 |
| cpe 5P | 3,575 | 1,565 | 500 |
| sdn 5P | 3,640 | 1,565 | 5,843 |
| chassis | — | — | 126 |

| CG Imperial (wb 145.0) | Wght | Price | Prod |
|---|---|---|---|
| Custom rdstr 2-4P | 4,530 | 3,220 | 100 |
| Custom spt phtn 5P | 4,645 | 3,575 | 85 |
| Custom cpe 2-4P | 4,605 | 3,150 | 135 |
| Custom conv cpe | 4,570 | 3,320 | 10 |
| sdn 5P | 4,705 | 2,745 | 909 |
| close-coupled sdn 5P | 4,685 | 2,845 | 1,195 |
| sdn 7P | 4,825 | 2,945 | 403 |
| sdn limo 8P | 4,915 | 3,145 | 271 |
| conv sdn | 4,825 | 3,995 | 25 |
| chassis | — | — | 95 |

| 1931 Engines | bore × stroke | bhp | availability |
|---|---|---|---|
| I-6, 195.6 | 3.13 × 4.25 | 62 | S-CJ6 |
| I-6, 217.8 | 3.25 × 4.38 | 78 | S-CM6 |
| I-6, 218.6 | 3.13 × 4.75 | 68 | S-66 |
| I-6, 268.4 | 3.38 × 5.00 | 93 | S-70 |
| I-8, 240.3 | 3.00 × 4.25 | 82 | S-CD8s built 1930 |
| I-8, 260.8 | 3.13 × 4.25 | 90 | S-CD8s built 1931 |
| I-8, 282.1 | 3.25 × 4.25 | 95 | S-DeLuxe Eight |
| I-8, 384.8 | 3.50 × 5.00 | 125 | S-CG |

### 1932

**Model 70 (wb 116.5)**

Listed by Chrysler for 1932, although production ceased in May 1931. Engine numbers from V-29414. Production combined with 1931 and 1930 (see entries).

**Model CM6 (wb 116.0)**

Production continued from 1931 commencing July 1, ending in December. Engine numbers from CM-30829. Production combined with 1931 (see entry).

# Chrysler

### Model CD DeLuxe Eight (wb 124.0)

Production continued from 1931 commencing July 1, ending in November. Engine numbers from CD-21141. Production combined with 1931 (see entry).

### CG Imperial (wb 145.0)

Production continued from 1931 commencing July 1, ending in December. Engine numbers from CG-3752.

### CI6 "Second Series" Six (wb 116.0)

| | Wght | Price | Prod |
|---|---|---|---|
| rdstr 2-4P | 2,830 | 885 | 474 |
| phtn 5P | 2,905 | 915 | 59 |
| bus cpe 2P | 2,915 | 865 | 354 |
| cpe 2-4P | 3,040 | 885 | 2,913 |
| conv cpe 2-4P | 2,970 | 935 | 1,000 |
| sdn 5P | 3,135 | 895 | 13,772 |
| conv sdn 5P | 3,160 | 1,125 | 322 |
| chassis | — | — | 70 |

### CP8 Eight (wb 125.0)

| | Wght | Price | Prod |
|---|---|---|---|
| cpe 2-4P | 3,735 | 1,435 | 718 |
| conv cpe 2-4P | 3,705 | 1,495 | 396 |
| cpe 5P | 3,810 | 1,475 | 502 |
| sdn 5P | 3,885 | 1,475 | 3,198 |
| conv sdn 5P | 4,090 | 1,695 | 251 |
| chassis | — | — | 48 |

### CH Imperial (wb 135.0)

| | Wght | Price | Prod |
|---|---|---|---|
| cpe 2-4P | 4,480 | 1,925 | 239 |
| sdn 5P | 4,645 | 1,945 | 1,002 |
| conv sdn 5P | 4,890 | 2,195 | 152 |
| chassis | — | — | 9 |

### CL Imperial (wb 146.0)

| | Wght | Price | Prod |
|---|---|---|---|
| conv cpe | 4,930 | 3,295 | 28 |
| phtn 5P | 5,065 | 3,395 | 14 |
| close-coupled sdn 5P | 5,150 | 2,895 | 57 |
| conv sdn 5P | 5,125 | 3,595 | 49 |
| sdn 8P | 5,295 | 2,995 | 35 |
| sdn limo 7P | 5,330 | 3,295 | 32 |
| chassis | — | — | 5 |

### 1932 Engines

| | bore × stroke | bhp | availability |
|---|---|---|---|
| I-6, 217.8 | 3.25 × 4.38 | 78 | S-CM6 |
| I-6, 224.0 | 3.25 × 4.50 | 82 | S-CI6 |
| I-6, 268.4 | 3.38 × 5.00 | 93 | S-70 |
| I-8, 282.1 | 3.25 × 4.25 | 95 | S-CD |
| I-8, 298.6 | 3.25 × 4.50 | 100 | S-CP8 |
| I-8, 384.8 | 3.50 × 5.00 | 125 | S-CG, CH, CL |

## 1933

### CO Six (wb 117.0)

| | Wght | Price | Prod |
|---|---|---|---|
| bus cpe 2P | 2,968 | 745 | 587 |
| cpe 2-4P | 3,018 | 775 | 1,454 |
| conv cpe 2-4P | 3,013 | 795 | 677 |
| brougham 5P | 3,078 | 745 | 1,207 |
| sdn 5P | 3,143 | 785 | 13,264 |
| sdn 7P (special interior) | 3,200 | 845 | 51 |
| conv sdn 5P | 3,212 | 945 | 205 |
| sdn 7P | — | — | 151 |
| chassis | — | — | 267 |

### CT Royal Eight (wb 120.0)

| | Wght | Price | Prod |
|---|---|---|---|
| bus cpe 2P | 3,303 | 895 | 226 |
| cpe 2-4P | 3,343 | 915 | 1,033 |
| conv cpe 2-4P | 3,363 | 945 | 539 |
| sdn 5P | 3,483 | 925 | 7,993 |
| conv sdn 5P | 3,617 | 1,085 | 257 |
| sdn 7P | 3,658 | 1,125 | 246 |
| chassis | — | — | 95 |

### CQ Imperial Eight (wb 126.0)

| | Wght | Price | Prod |
|---|---|---|---|
| cpe 2-4P | 3,734 | 1,275 | 364 |
| conv cpe 2-4P | — | 1,325 | 243 |
| cpe 5P | 3,754 | 1,295 | 267 |
| sdn 5P | 3,864 | 1,295 | 2,584 |
| conv sdn 5P | 4,144 | 1,495 | 364 |
| chassis | — | — | 16 |

### CL Imperial Custom (wb 146.0)

| | Wght | Price | Prod |
|---|---|---|---|
| rdstr 2-4P | 4,910 | 3,295 | 9 |
| phtn 5P | 4,890 | 3,395 | 36 |
| close-coupled sdn 5P | 5,045 | 2,895 | 43 |
| sdn 7P | 5,240 | 2,995 | 21 |
| limo sdn 7P | 5,245 | 3,295 | 22 |
| conv sdn | — | — | 11 |
| stationary cpe | — | — | 3 |
| chassis | — | — | 6 |

### 1933 Engines

| | bore × stroke | bhp | availability |
|---|---|---|---|
| I-6, 224.0 | 3.25 × 4.50 | 83/89 | S-CO |
| I-8, 273.8 | 3.25 × 4.13 | 90/98 | S-CT |
| I-8, 298.7 | 3.25 × 4.50 | 108/100 | S-CQ |
| I-8, 384.8 | 3.50 × 5.00 | 135/125 | S-CL |

## 1934

### CA Six (wb 118.0)

| | Wght | Price | Prod |
|---|---|---|---|
| bus cpe 2P | 2,868 | 740 | 1,650 |
| cpe 2-4P | 2,903 | 815 | 1,875 |
| conv cpe 2-4P | — | 850 | 700 |
| brougham 5P | 3,019 | 760 | 1,575 |
| sdn 5P | 3,123 | 820 | 17,617 |
| chassis | — | — | 385 |

### CB Custom Six (wb 121.0)

| | Wght | Price | Prod |
|---|---|---|---|
| close-coupled sdn 5P | — | 900 | 980 |
| conv sdn 5P | — | 970 | 450 |
| chassis | — | — | 20 |

### CU Airflow Eight (wb 123.0)

| | Wght | Price | Prod |
|---|---|---|---|
| cpe 5P | — | 1,345 | 732 |
| brougham 5P | 3,741 | 1,345 | 306 |
| sdn 6P | 3,760 | 1,345 | 7,226 |
| Town sdn 6P | — | 1,345 | 125 |

### CV Airflow Imperial Eight (wb 128.0)

| | Wght | Price | Prod |
|---|---|---|---|
| cpe 5P | 3,929 | 1,625 | 212 |
| sdn 6P | 3,974 | 1,625 | 1,997 |
| Town sdn 6P | 3,969 | 1,625 | 67 |
| chassis | — | — | 1 |

### CX Airflow Imperial Eight (wb 137.5)

| | Wght | Price | Prod |
|---|---|---|---|
| sdn 5P | 4,154 | 2,245 | 25 |
| Town sdn 5P | 4,160 | 2,245 | 1 |
| sdn limo 8P | 4,299 | 2,345 | 78 |
| Town sdn limo | 4,304 | 2,345 | 2 |

### CW Airflow Imperial Custom Eight (wb 146.0)

| | Wght | Price | Prod |
|---|---|---|---|
| sdn 8P | 5,780 | 5,000 | 17 |
| Town sdn 8P | 5,815 | 5,000 | 28 |
| limo sdn 8P | 5,900 | 5,145 | 20 |
| Town limo sdn 8P | 5,935 | 5,145 | 2 |

### 1934 Engines

| | bore × stroke | bhp | availability |
|---|---|---|---|
| I-6, 241.5 | 3.38 × 4.50 | 93 | S-CA, CB |
| I-6, 241.5 | 3.38 × 4.50 | 100 | O-CA, CB |
| I-8, 298.7 | 3.25 × 4.50 | 122 | S-CU |
| I-8, 323.5 | 3.25 × 4.98 | 130 | S-CV, CX |
| I-8, 384.8 | 3.50 × 5.00 | 150 | S-CW |

# Chrysler

## 1935

| C6 Airstream Six (wb 118.0) | Wght | Price | Prod |
|---|---|---|---|
| bus cpe 2P | 2,863 | 745 | 1,975 |
| cpe 2-4P | 2,953 | 810 | 861 |
| touring brougham 5P | 2,988 | 820 | 1,901 |
| fstbk sdn 4d 5P | 3,013 | 830 | 6,055 |
| touring sdn 5P | 3,048 | 860 | 12,790 |
| fstbk sdn 2d 5P | 2,990 | 820 | 400 |
| chassis | — | — | 476 |

| CZ Airstream Eight (wb 121.0; lwb-133.0) | Wght | Price | Prod |
|---|---|---|---|
| bus cpe 2P | 3,103 | 910 | 100 |
| Deluxe bus cpe 2P | 3,138 | 930 | |
| cpe 2-4P | 3,138 | 935 | 550 |
| Deluxe cpe 2-4P | 3,233 | 955 | |
| touring brougham 2d | 3,203 | 960 | 500 |
| Deluxe touring brougham 2d | 3,293 | 980 | |
| sdn 4d | 3,213 | 975 | 2,958 |
| Deluxe sdn 4d | 3,333 | 985 | |
| touring sdn 4d | 3,263 | 995 | 4,394 |
| Deluxe touring sdn 4d | 3,338 | 1,015 | |
| Deluxe conv cpe 2-4P | 3,298 | 1,015 | 101 |
| Deluxe Traveler sdn 5P | 3,513 | 1,235 | 245 |
| Deluxe lwb sdn 7P | 3,538 | 1,235 | 212 |
| chassis | — | — | 237 |

| C1 Airflow 8 (wb 123.0) | Wght | Price | Prod |
|---|---|---|---|
| bus cpe 2P | 3,823 | 1,245 | 72 |
| cpe 6P | 3,883 | 1,245 | 307 |
| sdn 6P | 3,828 | 1,245 | 4,617 |

| C2 Imperial Airflow 8 (wb 128.0) | Wght | Price | Prod |
|---|---|---|---|
| cpe 6P | 4,003 | 1,475 | 200 |
| sdn 4d 6P | 3,998 | 1,475 | 2,398 |

| C3 Custom Imperial Airflow 8 (wb 137.5) | Wght | Price | Prod |
|---|---|---|---|
| sdn 4d 6P | 4,208 | 2,245 | 69 |
| Town sdn 4d 6P | 4,308 | 2,245 | 1 |
| sdn limo 8P | 4,378 | 2,345 | 53 |
| Town sdn limo 8P | 4,478 | 2,345 | 2 |

| CW Custom Imperial Airflow 8 (wb 146.5) | Wght | Price | Prod |
|---|---|---|---|
| sdn 8P | 4,785 | 5,000 | 15 |
| sdn limo 8P | 5,990 | 5,145 | 15 |
| Town sdn limo 8P | 5,090 | 5,145 | 2 |

| 1935 Engines | bore × stroke | bhp | availability |
|---|---|---|---|
| I-6, 241.5 | 3.38 × 4.50 | 93 | S-C6 |
| I-6, 241.5 | 3.38 × 4.50 | 100 | O-C6 |
| I-8, 273.8 | 3.25 × 4.13 | 105 | S-CZ |
| I-8, 273.8 | 3.25 × 4.13 | 110 | O-CZ |
| I-8, 323.5 | 3.25 × 4.88 | 115 | S-C1 |
| I-8, 323.5 | 3.25 × 4.88 | 120 | O-C1 |
| I-8, 323.5 | 3.25 × 4.88 | 130 | S-C2, C3 |
| I-8, 323.5 | 3.25 × 4.88 | 138 | O-C2, C3 |
| I-8, 384.8 | 3.50 × 5.00 | 150 | S-CW |

## 1936

| C7 Airstream (wb 118.0) | Wght | Price | Prod |
|---|---|---|---|
| bus cpe 2P | 2,963 | 760 | 3,703 |
| cpe 2-4P | 3,037 | 825 | 759 |
| conv cpe 2-4P | 3,053 | 925 | 650 |
| touring brougham 5P | 3,082 | 825 | 3,177 |
| conv sdn 5P | 3,282 | 1,125 | 497 |
| touring sdn 4d | 3,137 | 875 | 34,099 |
| chassis | — | — | 586 |

| C8 Airstream Deluxe (wb 121.0; lwb-133.0) | Wght | Price | Prod |
|---|---|---|---|
| bus cpe 2P | 3,155 | 925 | 520 |
| cpe 2-4P | 3,220 | 995 | 325 |
| conv cpe 2-4P | 3,350 | 1,075 | 240 |
| touring brougham 5P | 3,330 | 995 | 268 |
| conv sdn 5P | 3,495 | 1,265 | 362 |
| touring sdn 4d | 3,345 | 1,045 | 6,547 |
| Traveler sdn 5P | 3,500 | 1,255 | 350 |
| lwb sdn 7P | 3,550 | 1,245 | 619 |
| lwb sdn limo 7P | 3,595 | 1,865 | 67 |
| lwb Town sdn 7P | 3,550 | 4,995 | 8 |
| chassis | — | — | 196 |

| C9 Airflow Eight (wb 123.0) | Wght | Price | Prod |
|---|---|---|---|
| cpe 6P | 3,997 | 1,395 | 110 |
| sdn 4d 6P | 4,102 | 1,345 | 1,590 |

| C10 Airflow Imperial (wb 128.0) | Wght | Price | Prod |
|---|---|---|---|
| cpe 6P | 4,105 | 1,475 | 240 |
| sdn 4d 6P | 4,175 | 1,475 | 4,259 |
| chassis | — | — | 1 |

| C11 Airflow Custom Imperial (wb 137.0; lwb-146.5) | Wght | Price | Prod |
|---|---|---|---|
| sdn 4d 5P | 5,900 | 2,475 | 38 |
| sdn limo 7P | 6,000 | 2,575 | 37 |
| lwb sdn 4d 8P | 6,200* | 5,000* | 10 |
| lwb limo 8P | 6,250* | 5,000* | |

*Estimated

| 1936 Engines | bore × stroke | bhp | availability |
|---|---|---|---|
| I-6, 241.5 | 3.38 × 4.50 | 93 | S-C7 |
| I-6, 241.5 | 3.38 × 4.50 | 100 | O-C7 |
| I-8, 273.8 | 3.25 × 4.13 | 105 | S-C8 |
| I-8, 273.8 | 3.25 × 4.13 | 110 | O-C8 |
| I-8, 323.5 | 3.25 × 4.88 | 115 | S-C9 |
| I-8, 323.5 | 3.25 × 4.88 | 130 | S-C10, C11 |

## 1937

| C16 Royal (wb 116.0; lwb-133.0) | Wght | Price | Prod |
|---|---|---|---|
| bus cpe 2P | 3,049 | 810 | 9,830 |
| cpe 2-4P | 3,099 | 860 | 1,050 |
| conv cpe 2-4P | 3,274 | 1,020 | 767 |
| brougham 5P F/B | 3,114 | 870 | 750 |
| touring brougham 5P | 3,094 | 880 | 7,835 |
| fstbk sdn 4d 5P | 3,124 | 910 | 1,200 |
| touring sdn 4d 5P | 3,134 | 920 | 62,408 |
| conv sdn 5P | 3,484 | 1,355 | 642 |
| lwb sdn 7P | 3,544 | 1,145 | 856 |
| lwb sdn limo 7P | 3,550 | 1,245 | 138 |
| chassis | — | — | 524 |

| C14 Imperial (wb 121.0) | Wght | Price | Prod |
|---|---|---|---|
| bus cpe 2P | 3,374 | 1,030 | 1,075 |
| cpe 2-4P | 3,449 | 1,070 | 225 |
| conv cpe 2-4P | 3,609 | 1,170 | 351 |
| touring brougham 5P | 3,544 | 1,070 | 430 |
| touring sdn 5P | 3,564 | 1,100 | 11,796 |
| conv sdn 5P | 3,824 | 1,500 | 325 |
| chassis | — | — | 118 |

| C17 Airflow (wb 128.0) | Wght | Price | Prod |
|---|---|---|---|
| cpe 6P | 4,225 | 1,610 | 230 |
| sdn 4d 6P | 4,300 | 1,610 | 4,370 |

| C15 Custom Imperial (wb 140.0) | Wght | Price | Prod |
|---|---|---|---|
| sdn 4d | 4,500 | 2,060 | 187 |
| sdn 7P | 4,522 | 2,060 | 721 |
| sdn limo 7P | 4,644 | 2,160 | 276 |
| chassis | — | — | 16 |

# Chrysler

| 1937 Engines | bore × stroke | bhp | availability |
|---|---|---|---|
| I-6, 228.0 | 3.38 × 4.25 | 93 | S-C16 |
| I-6, 228.0 | 3.38 × 4.25 | 100 | O-C16 |
| I-8, 273.8 | 3.25 × 4.13 | 110 | S-C14 |
| I-8, 273.8 | 3.25 × 4.13 | 115 | O-C14 |
| I-8, 323.5 | 3.25 × 4.88 | 130 | S-C17, C15 |
| I-8, 323.5 | 3.25 × 4.88 | 138 | O-C17, C15 |

## 1938

| C18 Royal (wb 119.0; lwb-136.0) | Wght | Price | Prod |
|---|---|---|---|
| bus cpe 2P | 3,090 | 918 | 4,840 |
| cpe 2-4P | 3,135 | 963 | 363 |
| conv cpe 2-4P | 3,250 | 1,085 | 480 |
| fstbk brougham 5P | 3,160 | 963 | 88 |
| touring brougham 5P | 3,165 | 975 | 3,802 |
| fstbk sdn 5P | 3,170 | 998 | 112 |
| touring sdn 5P | 3,180 | 1,010 | 31,991 |
| conv sdn 5P | 3,450 | 1,425 | 177 |
| chassis | — | — | 564 |
| lwb sdn T/B 7P | 3,450 | 1,235 | 722 |
| limo T/B 7P (lwb) | 3,545 | 1,325 | 161 |

| C19 Imperial (wb 125.0; NY Spl-119.0) | Wght | Price | Prod |
|---|---|---|---|
| bus cpe 2P | 3,450 | 1,123 | 766 |
| New York Spl bus cpe 2P | 3,475 | 1,255 | |
| touring sdn 5P | 3,565 | 1,198 | 8,554 |
| New York Spl trng sdn 5P | 3,600 | 1,378 | |
| cpe 2-4P | 3,515 | 1,160 | 80 |
| conv cpe 2-4P | 3,630 | 1,275 | 189 |
| touring brougham 5P | 3,560 | 1,165 | 245 |
| conv sdn 5P | 3,950 | 1,595 | 113 |
| chassis | — | — | 55 |

| C20 Custom Imperial (wb 144.0) | Wght | Price | Prod |
|---|---|---|---|
| sdn 5P | 4,495 | 2,295 | 252 |
| sdn 7P | 4,510 | 2,295 | 122 |
| sdn limo 7P | 4,635 | 2,395 | 145 |
| chassis | — | — | 11 |

| 1938 Engines | bore × stroke | bhp | availability |
|---|---|---|---|
| I-6, 241.5 | 3.38 × 4.50 | 95 | S-C18 |
| I-6, 241.5 | 3.38 × 4.50 | 102 | O-C18 |
| I-8, 298.7 | 3.25 × 4.50 | 110 | S-C19 |
| I-8, 298.7 | 3.25 × 4.50 | 122 | O-C19 |
| I-8, 323.5 | 3.25 × 4.88 | 130 | S-C20 |
| I-8, 323.5 | 3.25 × 4.88 | 138 | O-C20 |

## 1939

| C22 Royal (wb 119.0; lwb-136.0) | Wght | Price | Prod |
|---|---|---|---|
| cpe 2P | 3,120 | 918 | 4,780 |
| Windsor cpe 2P | 3,130 | 983 | |
| Victoria cpe 4P | 3,160 | 970 | 239 |
| Windsor Victoria cpe 4P | 3,165 | 1,065 | |
| brougham 5P | 3,200 | 975 | 4,838 |
| sdn 4d | 3,265 | 1,010 | 45,955 |
| Windsor sdn 4d | 3,275 | 1,075 | |
| Windsor club cpe 5P | 3,245 | 1,185 | 2,983 |
| lwb sdn 7P | 3,520 | 1,235 | 621 |
| lwb sdn limo 7P | 3,625 | 1,325 | 191 |
| chassis | — | — | 394 |

| C23 Imperial/New Yorker/Saratoga (wb 125.0) | Wght | Price | Prod |
|---|---|---|---|
| Imperial bus cpe 2P | 3,520 | 1,123 | 492 |
| Imperial Victoria cpe 4P | 3,555 | 1,160 | 35 |
| Imperial brougham 5P | 3,610 | 1,165 | 185 |
| Imperial sdn 4d | 3,640 | 1,198 | |
| New Yorker sdn 4d | 3,695 | 1,298 | 10,536 |
| Saratoga sdn 4d | 3,720 | 1,443 | |
| New Yorker Victoria cpe 4P | 3,665 | 1,395 | 99 |
| New Yorker bus cpe 2P | 3,540 | 1,223 | 606 |
| New Yorker club cpe 5P | 3,550 | 1,260 | |
| Saratoga club cpe 5P | 3,665 | 1,495 | 134 |
| chassis | — | — | 48 |

| C24 Custom Imperial (wb 144.0) | Wght | Price | Prod |
|---|---|---|---|
| sdn 5P | 4,590 | 2,595 | 88 |
| sdn 7P | 4,620 | 2,595 | 95 |
| sdn limo 7P | 4,665 | 2,695 | 117 |
| chassis | — | — | 7 |

| 1939 Engines | bore × stroke | bhp | availability |
|---|---|---|---|
| I-6, 241.5 | 3.38 × 4.50 | 100 | S-C22 |
| I-6, 241.5 | 3.38 × 4.50 | 107 | O-C22 |
| I-8, 323.5 | 3.25 × 4.88 | 130 | S-C23 |
| I-8, 323.5 | 3.25 × 4.88 | 132 | S-C24 |
| I-8, 323.5 | 3.25 × 4.88 | 138 | O-C24 |

## 1940

| C25 (wb 122.5; 8P-139.5) | Wght | Price | Prod |
|---|---|---|---|
| Royal sdn 4d | 3,175 | 995 | 23,274 |
| Windsor sdn 4d | 3,210 | 1,025 | 28,477 |
| Royal sdn 2d | 3,150 | 960 | 9,851 |
| Windsor sdn 2d | 3,175 | 995 | |
| Royal bus cpe | 3,075 | 895 | 5,117 |
| Windsor bus cpe | 3,095 | 935 | |
| Royal cpe | 3,110 | 960 | 4,315 |
| Windsor cpe | 3,135 | 995 | |
| Windsor Highlander cpe | 3,135 | 1,020 | |
| Windsor conv cpe | 3,360 | 1,160 | 2,275 |
| Windsor HighIndr conv cpe | 3,360 | 1,185 | |
| Royal sdn 4d, 8P | 3,550 | 1,235 | 439 |
| Windsor sdn 4d, 8P | 3,575 | 1,275 | |
| Royal limo | 3,640 | 1,310 | 98 |
| Windsor limo | 3,660 | 1,350 | |
| chassis | — | — | 152 |

| C26 (wb 128.5) | Wght | Price | Prod |
|---|---|---|---|
| Traveler sdn 4d | 3,590 | 1,180 | 14,603 |
| New Yorker sdn 4d | 3,635 | 1,260 | |
| Saratoga sdn 4d | 3,790 | 1,375 | |
| Traveler cpe | 3,525 | 1,150 | 1,117 |
| New Yorker cpe | 3,570 | 1,230 | |
| New Yorker Highlander cpe | 3,570 | 1,255 | |
| Traveler bus cpe | 3,475 | 1,095 | 731 |
| New Yorker bus cpe | 3,490 | 1,175 | |
| Traveler sdn 2d | 3,555 | 1,150 | 275 |
| New Yorker sdn 2d | 3,610 | 1,230 | |
| New Yorker conv cpe | 3,775 | 1,375 | 845 |
| New Yorker Hlndr conv cpe | 3,775 | 1,400 | |

| C27 Crown Imperial (wb 145.5) | Wght | Price | Prod |
|---|---|---|---|
| sdn 4d | 4,340 | 2,245 | 355 |
| sdn 4d, 8P | 4,330 | 2,345 | 284 |
| limo, 8P | 4,365 | 2,445 | 210 |
| chassis | — | — | 1 |

| 1940 Engines | bore × stroke | bhp | availability |
|---|---|---|---|
| I-6, 241.5 | 3.38 × 4.50 | 108 | S-Royal, Windsor |
| I-6, 241.5 | 3.38 × 4.50 | 112 | O-Royal, Windsor |
| I-8, 323.5 | 3.25 × 4.88 | 135 | S-Trav, NY, Saratoga |
| I-8, 323.5 | 3.25 × 4.88 | 143 | O-Trav, NY, Saratoga |
| I-8, 323.5 | 3.25 × 4.88 | 132 | S-Crown Imperial |
| I-8, 323.5 | 3.25 × 4.88 | 143 | O-Crown Imperial |

# Chrysler

## 1941

### C-28S Royal (wb 121.5; 8P-139.5)

|  | Wght | Price | Prod |
|---|---|---|---|
| sdn 4d | 3,300 | 1,091 | 51,378 |
| club cpe | 3,260 | 1,085 | 10,830 |
| luxury brougham 2d | 3,270 | 1,066 | 8,006 |
| bus cpe | 3,170 | 995 | 6,846 |
| town sdn 4d | 3,320 | 1,136 | 1,277 |
| sdn 4d, 8P | 3,650 | 1,345 | 297 |
| limo 8P | 3,695 | 1,415 | 31 |
| chassis | — | — | 3 |
| Town & Country wgn 4d, 6P | 3,540 | 1,412 | 200 |
| Town & Country wgn 4d, 9P | 3,595 | 1,492 | 797 |

### C-28W Windsor (wb 121.5; 8P-139.5)

| | Wght | Price | Prod |
|---|---|---|---|
| sdn 4d | 3,300 | 1,165 | 36,396 |
| club cpe | 3,260 | 1,142 | 8,513 |
| conv cpe | 3,470 | 1,315 | 4,432 |
| luxury brougham 2d | 3,270 | 1,128 | 2,898 |
| town sdn 4d | 3,315 | 1,198 | 2,704 |
| bus cpe | 3,170 | 1,045 | 1,921 |
| sdn 4d, 8P | 3,575 | 1,410 | 116 |
| limo, 8P | 3,660 | 1,487 | 54 |

### C-30K/30N (wb 127.5)

| | Wght | Price | Prod |
|---|---|---|---|
| Saratoga sdn 4d | 3,755 | 1,320 | 15,868 |
| New Yorker sdn 4d | 3,775 | 1,389 | |
| Saratoga club cpe | 3,685 | 1,299 | 2,845 |
| New Yorker club cpe | 3,690 | 1,369 | |
| Saratoga town sdn 4d | 3,750 | 1,350 | 2,326 |
| New Yorker town sdn 4d | 3,785 | 1,399 | |
| Saratoga bus cpe | 3,600 | 1,245 | 771 |
| New Yorker bus cpe | 3,635 | 1,325 | |
| Saratoga lxry brougham 2d | 3,715 | 1,293 | 293 |
| New Yorker luxury broug 2d | 3,745 | 1,369 | |
| New Yorker conv cpe | 3,945 | 1,548 | 1,295 |
| Town & Country wgn 4d | — | proto | 1 |
| chassis | — | — | 9 |

### C-33 Crown Imperial (wb 145.5)

| | Wght | Price | Prod |
|---|---|---|---|
| sdn 4d | 4,435 | 2,595 | 179 |
| sdn 4d, 8P | 4,495 | 2,696 | 205 |
| limo 8P | 4,560 | 2,795 | 316 |
| special town sdn 4d* | 3,900 | 1,760 | 894 |
| chassis | — | — | 1 |

*C-30 body and chassis, C-33 engine and nameplates.

### 1941 Engines

| | bore × stroke | bhp | availability |
|---|---|---|---|
| I-6, 241.5 | 3.38 × 4.50 | 108/112 | S-Royal, Windsor |
| I-6, 241.5 | 3.38 × 4.50 | 115 | O-Royal, Windsor |
| I-8, 323.5 | 3.25 × 4.88 | 137 | S-Saratoga, NY |
| I-8, 323.5 | 3.25 × 4.88 | 140 | O-Saratoga, NY |
| I-8, 323.5 | 3.25 × 4.88 | 143 | S-Crown Imperial |

## 1942

### C-34S Royal (wb 121.5; 8P-139.5)

| | Wght | Price | Prod |
|---|---|---|---|
| bus cpe | 3,331 | 1,075 | 479 |
| club cpe | 3,406 | 1,168 | 779 |
| brougham 2d | 3,431 | 1,154 | 709 |
| sdn 4d | 3,476 | 1,177 | 7,424 |
| town sdn 4d | 3,481 | 1,222 | 73 |
| sdn 4d, 8P | 3,854 | 1,535 | 79 |
| limo 8P | 3,895 | 1,605 | 21 |

### C-34W Windsor (wb 121.5; 8P-139.5)

| | Wght | Price | Prod |
|---|---|---|---|
| bus cpe | 3,351 | 1,140 | 250 |
| club cpe | 3,426 | 1,228 | 1,713 |
| conv cpe | 3,661 | 1,420 | 574 |
| brougham 2d | 3,441 | 1,220 | 317 |

### C-34W Windsor (wb 121.5; 8P-139.5)

| | Wght | Price | Prod |
|---|---|---|---|
| sdn 4d | 3,496 | 1,255 | 10,054 |
| town sdn, 4d | 3,506 | 1,295 | 479 |
| Town & Country wgn 4d, 6P | 3,614 | 1,595 | 150 |
| Town & Country wgn 4d, 9P | 3,699 | 1,685 | 849 |
| sdn 4d, 8P | 3,879 | 1,605 | 29 |
| limo 8P | 3,900 | 1,685 | 12 |

### C-36K Saratoga (wb 127.5)

| | Wght | Price | Prod |
|---|---|---|---|
| bus cpe | 3,703 | 1,325 | 80 |
| club cpe | 3,788 | 1,380 | 193 |
| brougham 2d | 3,798 | 1,365 | 36 |
| sdn 4d | 3,833 | 1,405 | 1,239 |
| town sdn 4d | 3,843 | 1,450 | 46 |
| chassis | — | — | 2 |

### C-36N New Yorker (wb 127.5)

| | Wght | Price | Prod |
|---|---|---|---|
| bus cpe | 3,728 | 1,385 | 158 |
| club cpe | 3,783 | 1,450 | 1,234 |
| conv cpe | 4,033 | 1,640 | 401 |
| brougham 2d | 3,798 | 1,440 | 62 |
| Town & Country wgn 4d, 9P | — | proto | 1 |
| sdn 4d | 3,873 | 1,475 | 7,045 |
| town sdn 4d | 3,893 | 1,520 | 1,648 |

### C-33 Crown Imperial (wb 145.5)

| | Wght | Price | Prod |
|---|---|---|---|
| sdn 4d | 4,565 | 2,815 | 81 |
| sdn 4d, 8P | 4,620 | 2,915 | 152 |
| limo 8P | 4,685 | 3,065 | 215 |
| chassis | — | — | 2 |

### 1942 Engines

| | bore × stroke | bhp | availability |
|---|---|---|---|
| I-6, 250.6 | 3.44 × 4.50 | 120 | S-Royal, Windsor |
| I-8, 323.5 | 3.25 × 4.88 | 140 | S-others |

## 1946

### C-38S Royal (wb 121.5; 8P-139.5)*

| | Wght | Price | Prod |
|---|---|---|---|
| sdn 4d | 3,523 | 1,561 | — |
| sdn 2d | 3,458 | 1,526 | — |
| club cpe | 3,443 | 1,551 | — |
| bus cpe | 3,373 | 1,431 | — |
| sdn 4d, 8P | 3,997 | 1,943 | — |
| limo 8P | 4,022 | 2,063 | — |
| chassis | — | — | — |

### C-38W Windsor (wb 121.5; 8P-139.5)*

| | Wght | Price | Prod |
|---|---|---|---|
| sdn 4d | 3,528 | 1,611 | — |
| sdn 2d | 3,468 | 1,591 | — |
| club cpe | 3,448 | 1,601 | — |
| bus cpe | 3,383 | 1,481 | — |
| conv cpe | 3,693 | 1,861 | — |
| sdn 4d, 8P | 3,977 | 1,993 | — |
| limo 8P | 4,052 | 2,113 | — |
| Traveler sdn 4d | 3,610 | 1,746 | — |

### C-39K Saratoga (wb 127.5)*

| | Wght | Price | Prod |
|---|---|---|---|
| sdn 4d | 3,972 | 1,863 | — |
| sdn 2d | 3,932 | 1,838 | — |
| club cpe | 3,892 | 1,848 | — |
| bus cpe | 3,817 | 1,753 | — |

### C-39N New Yorker (wb 127.5)*

| | Wght | Price | Prod |
|---|---|---|---|
| sdn 4d | 3,973 | 1,963 | — |
| sdn 2d | 3,932 | 1,938 | — |
| club cpe | 3,897 | 1,948 | — |
| bus cpe | 3,837 | 1,853 | — |
| conv cpe | 4,132 | 2,193 | — |
| chassis | — | — | — |

### C-38/39 Town & Country (wb 121.5; I-8-127.5)*

| | Wght | Price | Prod |
|---|---|---|---|
| sdn 4d, I-6 | 3,917 | 2,366 | 124 |

# Chrysler

| C-38/39 T & C (wb 121.5; I-8-127.5)* | Wght | Price | Prod |
|---|---|---|---|
| brougham 2d, I-6 | — | proto | 1 |
| conv cpe, I-6 | — | proto | 1 |
| sdn 4d, I-8 | 4,300 | 2,718 | 100 |
| conv cpe, I-8 | 4,332 | 2,743 | 1,935 |
| htp cpe, I-8 | — | proto | 7 |
| **C-40 Crown Imperial (wb 145.5)*** | | | |
| limo 8P | 4,814 | 3,875 | — |

| 1946 Engines | bore × stroke | bhp | availability |
|---|---|---|---|
| I-6, 250.6 | 3.44 × 4.50 | 114 | S-Royal, Windsor, T&C six |
| I-8, 323.5 | 3.25 × 4.88 | 135 | S-others |

*Factory combined production figures for 1946 through First Series 1949.

## 1947

| C-38S Royal (wb 121.5; 8P-139.5)* | Wght | Price | Prod |
|---|---|---|---|
| sdn 4d | 3,523 | 1,661 | — |
| sdn 2d | 3,458 | 1,626 | — |
| club cpe | 3,443 | 1,651 | — |
| bus cpe | 3,373 | 1,561 | — |
| sdn 4d, 8P | 3,997 | 2,043 | — |
| limo 8P | 4,022 | 2,163 | — |
| **C-38W Windsor (wb 121.5; 8P-139.5)*** | | | |
| sdn 4d | 3,528 | 1,711 | — |
| Traveler sdn 4d | 3,610 | 1,846 | — |
| sdn 2d | 3,468 | 1,691 | — |
| club cpe | 3,448 | 1,701 | — |
| bus cpe | 3,383 | 1,611 | — |
| conv cpe | 3,693 | 2,075 | — |
| sdn 4d, 8P | 3,977 | 2,093 | — |
| limo 8P | 4,052 | 2,213 | — |
| **C-39K Saratoga (wb 127.5)*** | | | |
| sdn 4d | 3,972 | 1,973 | — |
| sdn 2d | 3,900 | 1,948 | — |
| club cpe | 3,930 | 1,958 | — |
| bus cpe | 3,817 | 1,873 | — |
| **C-39N New Yorker (wb 127.5)*** | | | |
| sdn 4d | 3,987 | 2,073 | — |
| sdn 2d | 3,932 | 2,048 | — |
| club cpe | 3,940 | 2,058 | — |
| bus cpe | 3,837 | 1,973 | — |
| conv cpe | 4,132 | 2,447 | — |
| **C-38/39 Town & Country (wb 121.5; I-8-127.5)** | | | |
| sdn 4d, I-6 | 3,955 | 2,713 | 2,651 |
| conv cpe, I-8 | 4,332 | 2,998 | 3,136 |
| **C-40 Crown Imperial (wb 145.5)*** | | | |
| sdn 4d, 8P | 4,865 | 4,205 | — |
| limo 8P | 4,875 | 4,305 | — |

| 1947 Engines | bore × stroke | bhp | availability |
|---|---|---|---|
| I-6, 250.6 | 3.44 × 4.50 | 114 | S-Royal, Windsor, T&C six |
| I-8, 323.5 | 3.25 × 4.88 | 135 | S-others |

*Factory combined production figures for 1946 through First Series 1949.

## 1948-First Series 1949

| C-38S Royal (wb 121.5; 8P-139.5)* | Wght | Price | Prod |
|---|---|---|---|
| sdn 4d | 3,523 | 1,955 | — |
| sdn 2d | 3,485 | 1,908 | — |
| club cpe | 3,475 | 1,934 | — |
| bus cpe | 3,395 | 1,819 | — |
| sdn 4d, 8P | 3,925 | 2,380 | — |
| limo 8P | 4,022 | 2,506 | — |
| **C-38W Windsor (wb 121.5; 8P-139.5)*** | | | |
| sdn 4d | 3,528 | 2,021 | — |
| Traveler sdn 4d | 3,610 | 2,163 | — |
| sdn 2d | 3,510 | 1,989 | — |
| club cpe | 3,475 | 2,000 | — |
| bus cpe | 3,395 | 1,884 | — |
| conv cpe | 3,693 | 2,414 | — |
| sdn 4d, 8P | 3,935 | 2,434 | — |
| limo 8P | 4,035 | 2,561 | — |
| **C-39K Saratoga (wb 127.5)*** | | | |
| sdn 4d | 3,972 | 2,291 | — |
| sdn 2d | 3,900 | 2,254 | — |
| club cpe | 3,930 | 2,265 | — |
| bus cpe | 3,817 | 2,165 | — |
| **C-39N New Yorker (wb 127.5)*** | | | |
| sdn 4d | 3,987 | 2,411 | — |
| sdn 2d | 3,932 | 2,374 | — |
| club cpe | 3,940 | 2,385 | — |
| bus cpe | 3,837 | 2,285 | — |
| conv cpe | 4,132 | 2,815 | — |
| **C-38/39 Town & Country (wb 121.5; I-8-127.5)** | | | |
| sdn 4d, I-6 | 3,955 | 2,860 | 1,175 |
| conv cpe, I-8 | 4,332 | 3,420 | 3,309 |
| **C-40 Crown Imperial (wb 145.5)*** | | | |
| sdn 4d, 8P | 4,865 | 4,662 | — |
| limo 8P | 4,875 | 4,767 | — |

| 1948 Engines | bore × stroke | bhp | availability |
|---|---|---|---|
| I-6, 250.6 | 3.44 × 4.50 | 114 | S-Roy, Win, T&C six |
| I-8, 323.5 | 3.25 × 4.88 | 135 | S-others |

Note: First Series 1949 models sold December 1948 through March 1949; identical in weight/price to 1948 models and comprised about 15% of total production.

* Factory combined production figures for 1946 through First Series 1949; breakdowns are not available from Chrysler archives. However, since the Town & Country figures have been obtained (by historian Donald Narus), it is very likely that breakdowns exist for other models.

## Combined 1946-1949 First Series Production

| C-38S Royal (wb 121.5; 8P-139.5) | Prod |
|---|---|
| sdn 4d | 24,279 |
| sdn 2d | 1,117 |
| club cpe | 4,318 |
| bus cpe | 1,221 |
| sdn 4d, 8P | 626 |
| limo 8P | 169 |
| chassis | 1 |
| **C-38W Windsor (wb 121.5; 8P-139.5)** | |
| sdn 4d | 161,139 |
| Traveler sdn 4d | 4,182 |
| sdn 2d | 4,034 |
| club cpe | 26,482 |
| bus cpe | 1,980 |
| conv cpe | 11,200 |
| sdn 4d, 8P | 4,390 |
| limo 8P | 1,496 |
| **C-39K Saratoga (wb 127.5)** | |
| sdn 4d | 4,611 |
| sdn 2d | 155 |
| club cpe | 765 |
| bus cpe | 74 |

303

# Chrysler

| C-39N New Yorker (wb 127.5) | Prod |
|---|---|
| sdn 4d | 52,036 |
| sdn 2d | 545 |
| club cpe | 10,735 |
| bus cpe | 701 |
| conv cpe | 3,000 |
| chassis | 2 |

| C-38/39 Town & Country (wb 121.5; I-8-127.5) | |
|---|---|
| sdn 4d, I-6 | 4,049 |
| brougham 2d, I-6 (proto) | 1 |
| conv cpe, I-6 (proto) | 1 |
| sdn 4d, I-8 | 100 |
| conv cpe, I-8 | 8,368 |
| htp cpe, I-8 (proto) | 7 |

| C-40 Crown Imperial (wb 145.5) | |
|---|---|
| sdn 4d, 8P | 650 |
| limo 8P | 750 |

## 1949 Second Series

| C-45-1 Royal (wb 125.5; 8P-139.5) | Wght | Price | Prod |
|---|---|---|---|
| sdn 4d | 3,550 | 2,134 | 13,192 |
| club cpe | 3,495 | 2,114 | 4,849 |
| wgn 4d, 9P | 4,060 | 3,121 | 850 |
| sdn 4d, 8P | 4,200 | 2,823 | 185 |

| C-45-2 Windsor (wb 125.5; 8P-139.5) | | | |
|---|---|---|---|
| sdn 4d | 3,681 | 2,329 | 55,879 |
| club cpe | 3,631 | 2,308 | 17,732 |
| conv cpe | 3,845 | 2,741 | 3,234 |
| sdn 4d, 8P | 4,290 | 3,017 | 373 |
| limo 8P | 4,430 | 3,144 | 73 |

| C-46-1 Saratoga (wb 131.5) | | | |
|---|---|---|---|
| sdn 4d | 4,103 | 2,610 | 1,810 |
| club cpe | 4,037 | 2,585 | 465 |

| C-46-2 New Yorker (wb 131.5) | | | |
|---|---|---|---|
| sdn 4d | 4,113 | 2,726 | 18,779 |
| club cpe | 4,048 | 2,700 | 4,524 |
| conv cpe | 4,277 | 3,206 | 1,137 |
| chassis | — | — | 1 |

| C-46-2 Town & Country (wb 131.5) | | | |
|---|---|---|---|
| conv cpe | 4,630 | 3,970 | 1,000 |

| C-46-2 Imperial (wb 131.5) | | | |
|---|---|---|---|
| sdn 4d | 4,300 | 4,665 | 50 |

| C-47 Crown Imperial (wb 145.5) | | | |
|---|---|---|---|
| sdn 4d, 8P | 5,250 | 5,229 | 40 |
| limo 8P | 5,295 | 5,334 | 45 |

| 1949 Engines | bore × stroke | bhp | availability |
|---|---|---|---|
| I-6, 250.6 | 3.44 × 4.50 | 116 | S-Royal, Windsor |
| I-8, 323.5 | 3.25 × 4.88 | 135 | S-others |

## 1950

| C-48-1 Royal (wb 125.5; 8P-139.5) | Wght | Price | Prod |
|---|---|---|---|
| sdn 4d | 3,610 | 2,134 | 17,713 |
| club cpe | 3,540 | 2,114 | 5,900 |
| T&C wgn 4d, wood | 4,055 | 3,163 | 599 |
| T&C wgn 4d, steel | 3,964 | 2,735 | 100 |
| sdn 4d, 8P | 4,190 | 2,855 | 375 |

| C-48-2 Windsor (wb 125.5; 8P-139.5) | | | |
|---|---|---|---|
| sdn 4d | 3,765 | 2,329 | 78,199 |
| Traveler sdn 4d | 3,830 | 2,560 | 900 |
| club cpe | 3,670 | 2,308 | 20,050 |

| C-48-2 Windsor (wb 125.5; 8P-139.5) | Wght | Price | Prod |
|---|---|---|---|
| Newport htp cpe | 3,875 | 2,637 | 9,925 |
| conv cpe | 3,905 | 2,741 | 2,201 |
| sdn 4d, 8P | 4,295 | 3,050 | 763 |
| limo 8P | 4,400 | 3,176 | 174 |
| chassis | — | — | 1 |

| C-49-1 Saratoga (wb 131.5) | | | |
|---|---|---|---|
| sdn 4d | 4,170 | 2,642 | 1,000 |
| club cpe | 4,110 | 2,616 | 300 |

| C-49-2 New Yorker (wb 131.5) | | | |
|---|---|---|---|
| sdn 4d | 4,190 | 2,758 | 22,633 |
| club cpe | 4,110 | 2,732 | 3,000 |
| Newport htp cpe | 4,370 | 3,133 | 2,800 |
| conv cpe | 4,360 | 3,232 | 899 |
| wgn 4d, wood | — | proto | 1 |
| chassis | — | — | 2 |

| C-49-2 Town & Country (wb 131.5) | | | |
|---|---|---|---|
| Newport htp cpe | 4,670 | 4,003 | 700 |

| C-49-2 Imperial (wb 131.5) | | | |
|---|---|---|---|
| sdn 4d | 4,245 | 3,055 | 9,500 |
| Deluxe sdn 4d | 4,250 | 3,176 | 1,150 |

| C-50 Crown Imperial (wb 145.5) | | | |
|---|---|---|---|
| sdn 4d, 8P | 5,235 | 5,229 | 209 |
| limo 8P | 5,305 | 5,334 | 205 |
| chassis | — | — | 1 |

| 1950 Engines | bore × stroke | bhp | availability |
|---|---|---|---|
| I-6, 250.6 | 3.44 × 4.50 | 116 | S-Royal, Windsor |
| I-8, 323.5 | 3.25 × 4.88 | 135 | S-others |

## 1951

| C-51W Windsor (wb 125.5; 8P-139.5) | Wght | Price | Prod |
|---|---|---|---|
| sdn 4d | 3,527 | 2,390 | 10,151* |
| club cpe | 3,570 | 2,368 | 4,243* |
| Town & Country wgn 4d | 3,965 | 3,063 | 1,239* |
| sdn 4d, 8P | 4,145 | 3,197 | 399* |
| ambulance (sp. order) | — | — | 153 |
| Deluxe sdn 4d | 3,775 | 2,608 | 47,573* |
| Deluxe Traveler sdn 4d | 3,890 | 2,867 | 850 |
| Deluxe club cpe | 3,700 | 2,585 | 8,365 |
| Deluxe Newport htp cpe | 3,855 | 2,953 | 6,426* |
| Deluxe conv cpe | 3,945 | 3,071 | 2,646* |
| Deluxe sdn 4d, 8P | 4,295 | 3,416 | 720 |
| Deluxe limo 8P | 4,415 | 3,557 | 152 |

| C-55 Saratoga (wb 125.5; 8P-139.5) | | | |
|---|---|---|---|
| sdn 4d | 4,018 | 3,016 | 22,375* |
| club cpe | 3,948 | 2,989 | 5,355* |
| Newport htp cpe | — | proto | 1 |
| Town & Country wgn 4d | 4,310 | 3,681 | 818* |
| sdn 4d, 8P | 4,465 | 3,912 | 115* |
| ambulance (sp. order) | — | — | 1 |

| C-52 New Yorker (wb 131.5) | | | |
|---|---|---|---|
| sdn 4d | 4,260 | 3,378 | 25,461* |
| club cpe | 4,145 | 3,348 | 3,533 |
| Newport htp cpe | 4,330 | 3,798 | 3,654* |
| conv cpe | 4,460 | 3,916 | 1,386* |
| T&C wgn 4d (4 C51s) | 4,455 | 4,026 | 251 |
| chassis | — | — | 1 |

| C-54 Imperial (wb 131.5) | | | |
|---|---|---|---|
| sdn 4d | 4,350 | 3,674 | 13,678* |
| club cpe | 4,230 | 3,661 | 749* |
| Newport htp cpe | 4,380 | 4,042 | 2,174* |
| conv cpe | 4,570 | 4,402 | 650 |

# Chrysler

| C-53 Crown Imperial (wb 145.5) | Wght | Price | Prod |
|---|---|---|---|
| sdn 4d, 8P | 5,360 | 6,573 | 227* |
| limo 8P | 5,450 | 6,690 | 213* |
| chassis | — | — | 2 |

| 1951 Engines | bore × stroke | bhp | availability |
|---|---|---|---|
| I-6, 250.6 | 3.44 × 4.50 | 116 | S-Windsor |
| V-8, 331.1 | 3.81 × 3.63 | 180 | S-others |

## 1952

| C-51W Windsor (wb 125.5; 8P-139.5) | Wght | Price | Prod |
|---|---|---|---|
| sdn 4d | 3,640 | 2,498 | 5,961* |
| club cpe | 3,550 | 2,475 | 2,492* |
| Town & Country wgn 4d | 4,015 | 3,200 | 728* |
| sdn 4d, 8P | 4,145 | 3,342 | 234* |
| Deluxe sdn 4d | 3,775 | 2,727 | 27,940* |
| Deluxe Newport htp cpe | 3,855 | 3,087 | 3,774* |
| Deluxe conv cpe | 3,990 | 3,210 | 1,554* |

| C-55 Saratoga (wb 125.5; 8P-139.5) | | | |
|---|---|---|---|
| sdn 4d | 4,010 | 3,215 | 13,141* |
| club cpe | 3,935 | 3,187 | 3,145* |
| Town & Country wgn 4d, 8P | 4,345 | 3,925 | 481* |
| sdn 4d, 8P | 4,510 | 4,172 | 68* |

| C-52 New Yorker (wb 131.5) | | | |
|---|---|---|---|
| sdn 4d | 4,205 | 3,530 | 14,954* |
| Newport htp cpe | 4,325 | 3,969 | 2,146* |
| conv cpe | 4,450 | 4,093 | 814* |

| C-54 Imperial (wb 131.5) | | | |
|---|---|---|---|
| sdn 4d | 4,315 | 3,839 | 8,033* |
| club cpe | 4,220 | 3,826 | 440* |
| Newport htp cpe | 4,365 | 4,224 | 1,276* |

| C-53 Crown Imperial (wb 145.5) | | | |
|---|---|---|---|
| sdn rd, 4P | 5,395 | 6,872 | 133* |
| limo 8P | 5,430 | 6,994 | 125* |

| 1952 Engines | bore × stroke | bhp | availability |
|---|---|---|---|
| I-6, 264.5 | 3.44 × 4.75 | 119 | S-Windsor |
| V-8, 331.1 | 3.81 × 3.63 | 180 | S-others |

* As with other corporate makes, Chrysler combined model year production for 1951-52. However, production figures are known for several 1951-only body styles, making production estimates of remaining body styles (spanning both years) more accurate. In the above cases (*), estimates are based on the known percentages of the two-year run: 63% for 1951 and 37% for 1952.

## 1953

| C-60-1 Windsor (wb 125.5; 8P-139.5) | Wght | Price | Prod |
|---|---|---|---|
| sdn 4d | 3,660 | 2,462 | 18,879 |
| club cpe | 3,600 | 2,442 | 11,646 |
| Town & Country wgn 4d | 3,960 | 3,259 | 1,242 |
| sdn 4d, 8P | 4,170 | 3,403 | 425 |

| C-60-2 Windsor Deluxe (wb 125.5) | | | |
|---|---|---|---|
| sdn 4d | 3,775 | 2,691 | 45,385 |
| Newport htp cpe | 3,775 | 2,995 | 5,642 |
| conv cpe | 4,005 | 3,217 | 1,250 |

| C-56-1 New Yorker (wb 125.5; 8P-139.5) | | | |
|---|---|---|---|
| sdn 4d | 4,005 | 3,150 | 37,540 |
| club cpe | 3,925 | 3,121 | 7,749 |
| Newport htp cpe | 4,020 | 3,487 | 2,525 |
| Town & Country wgn 4d | 4,265 | 3,898 | 1,399 |
| sdn 4d, 8P | 4,510 | 4,334 | 100 |

| C-56-2 New Yorker Deluxe (wb 125.5) | | | |
|---|---|---|---|
| sdn 4d | 4,025 | 3,293 | 20,585 |
| club cpe | 3,925 | 3,264 | 1,934 |
| Newport htp cpe | 4,025 | 3,653 | 3,715 |

| C-56-2 New Yorker Deluxe (wb 125.5) | Wght | Price | Prod |
|---|---|---|---|
| conv cpe | 4,295 | 3,945 | 950 |
| chassis | — | — | 21 |

| C-58 Custom Imperial (wb 133.5; htp cpe-131.5) | | | |
|---|---|---|---|
| sdn 4d | 4,305 | 4,225 | 7,793 |
| town limo 6P | 4,525 | 4,762 | 243 |
| Newport htp cpe | 4,290 | 4,525 | 823 |

| C-59 Crown Imperial (wb 145.5) | | | |
|---|---|---|---|
| sdn 4d, 8P | 5,235 | 6,872 | 48 |
| limo 8P | 5,275 | 6,994 | 111 |
| chassis | — | — | 1 |

| 1953 Engines | bore × stroke | bhp | availability |
|---|---|---|---|
| I-6, 264.5 | 3.44 × 4.75 | 119 | S-Windsor |
| V-8, 331.1 | 3.81 × 3.63 | 180 | S-others |

## 1954

| C-62 Windsor Deluxe (wb 125.5; 8P-139.5) | Wght | Price | Prod |
|---|---|---|---|
| sdn 4d | 3,655 | 2,562 | 33,563 |
| club cpe | 3,565 | 2,541 | 5,659 |
| Newport htp cpe | 3,685 | 2,831 | 3,655 |
| conv cpe | 3,915 | 3,046 | 500 |
| Town & Country wgn 4d | 3,955 | 3,321 | 650 |
| sdn 4d, 8P | 4,185 | 3,492 | 500 |

| C-63-1 New Yorker (wb 125.5; 8P-139.5) | | | |
|---|---|---|---|
| sdn 4d | 3,970 | 3,229 | 15,788 |
| club cpe | 3,910 | 3,202 | 2,079 |
| Newport htp cpe | 4,005 | 3,503 | 1,312 |
| Town & Country wgn 4d | 4,245 | 4,024 | 1,100 |
| sdn 4d, 8P | 4,450 | 4,368 | 140 |

| C-63-2 New Yorker Deluxe (wb 125.5) | | | |
|---|---|---|---|
| sdn 4d | 4,065 | 3,433 | 26,907 |
| club cpe | 4,005 | 3,406 | 1,861 |
| Newport htp cpe | 4,095 | 3,707 | 4,814 |
| conv cpe | 4,265 | 3,938 | 724 |
| chassis | — | — | 17 |

| C-64 Custom Imperial (wb 133.5) | | | |
|---|---|---|---|
| sdn 4d | 4,355 | 4,260 | 4,324 |
| town limo 6P | 4,465 | 4,797 | 83 |
| special town limo 6P | 4,475 | — | 2 |
| Newport htp cpe | 4,345 | 4,560 | 1,249 |
| conv cpe | — | proto | 1 |
| chassis | — | — | 2 |

| C-66 Crown Imperial (wb 145.5) | | | |
|---|---|---|---|
| sdn 4d, 8P | 5,220 | 6,922 | 23 |
| limo 8P | 5,295 | 7,044 | 77 |

| 1954 Engines | bore × stroke | bhp | availability |
|---|---|---|---|
| I-6, 264.5 | 3.44 × 4.75 | 119 | S-Windsor Deluxe |
| V-8, 331.1 | 3.81 × 3.63 | 195 | S-NY |
| V-8, 331.1 | 3.81 × 3.63 | 235 | S-others |

## 1955

| C-67 Windsor Deluxe (wb 126.0) | Wght | Price | Prod |
|---|---|---|---|
| sdn 4d | 3,925 | 2,660 | 63,896 |
| Nassau htp cpe | 3,930 | 2,703 | 18,474 |
| Newport htp cpe | 3,925 | 2,818 | 13,126 |
| conv cpe | 4,075 | 3,090 | 1,395 |
| Town & Country wgn 4d | 4,295 | 3,332 | 1,983 |

| C-68 New Yorker Deluxe (wb 126.0) | | | |
|---|---|---|---|
| sdn 4d | 4,160 | 3,494 | 33,342 |
| Newport htp cpe | 4,140 | 3,652 | 5,777 |
| St. Regis htp cpe | 4,125 | 3,690 | 11,076 |

305

# Chrysler

| C-68 New Yorker Deluxe (wb 126.0) | Wght | Price | Prod |
|---|---|---|---|
| conv cpe | 4,285 | 3,924 | 946 |
| Town & Country wgn 4d | 4,430 | 4,209 | 1,036 |
| chassis | — | — | 1 |

| C-68 300 (wb 126.0) | | | |
|---|---|---|---|
| htp cpe | 4,005 | 4,110 | 1,725 |

| 1955 Engines | bore × stroke | bhp | availability |
|---|---|---|---|
| V-8, 301.0 | 3.63 × 3.63 | 188 | S-Windsor Deluxe |
| V-8, 331.1 | 3.81 × 3.63 | 250 | S-NY Deluxe |
| V-8, 331.1 | 3.81 × 3.63 | 300 | S-300 |

## 1956

| C-71 Windsor (wb 126.0) | Wght | Price | Prod |
|---|---|---|---|
| sdn 4d | 3,900 | 2,870 | 53,119 |
| Newport htp sdn | 3,990 | 3,128 | 7,050 |
| Nassau htp cpe | 3,910 | 2,905 | 11,400 |
| Newport htp cpe | 3,920 | 3,041 | 10,800 |
| conv cpe | 4,100 | 3,336 | 1,011 |
| Town & Country wgn 4d | 4,290 | 3,598 | 2,700 |

| C-72 New Yorker (wb 126.0) | | | |
|---|---|---|---|
| sdn 4d | 4,110 | 3,779 | 24,749 |
| Newport htp sdn | 4,220 | 4,102 | 3,599 |
| Newport htp cpe | 4,175 | 3,951 | 4,115 |
| St. Regis htp cpe | 4,175 | 3,995 | 6,686 |
| conv cpe | 4,360 | 4,243 | 921 |
| Town & Country wgn 4d | 4,460 | 4,523 | 1,070 |

| C-72 300B (wb 126.0) | | | |
|---|---|---|---|
| htp cpe | 4,145 | 4,419 | 1,102 |

| 1956 Engines | bore × stroke | bhp | availability |
|---|---|---|---|
| V-8, 331.1 | 3.81 × 3.63 | 225 | S-Windsor |
| V-8, 331.1 | 3.81 × 3.63 | 250 | O-Windsor |
| V-8, 354.0 | 3.94 × 3.63 | 280 | S-NY |
| V-8, 354.0 | 3.94 × 3.63 | 340 | S-300B |
| V-8, 354.0 | 3.94 × 3.63 | 355 | O-300B |

## 1957

| C-75-1 Windsor (wb 126.0) | Wght | Price | Prod |
|---|---|---|---|
| sdn 4d | 3,995 | 3,088 | 17,639 |
| htp sdn | 4,030 | 3,217 | 14,354 |
| htp cpe | 3,925 | 3,153 | 14,027 |
| Town & Country wgn 4d | 4,210 | 3,575 | 2,035 |

| C-75-2 Saratoga (wb 126.0) | | | |
|---|---|---|---|
| sdn 4d | 4,165 | 3,718 | 14,977 |
| htp sdn | 4,195 | 3,832 | 11,586 |
| htp cpe | 4,075 | 3,754 | 10,633 |

| C-76 New Yorker (wb 126.0) | | | |
|---|---|---|---|
| sdn 4d | 4,315 | 4,173 | 12,369 |
| htp sdn | 4,330 | 4,259 | 10,948 |
| htp cpe | 4,220 | 4,202 | 8,863 |
| conv cpe | 4,365 | 4,638 | 1,049 |
| Town & Country wgn 4d | 4,490 | 4,746 | 1,391 |

| C-76 300C (wb 126.0) | | | |
|---|---|---|---|
| htp cpe | 4,235 | 4,929 | 1,918 |
| conv cpe | 4,390 | 5,359 | 484 |

| 1957 Engines | bore × stroke | bhp | availability |
|---|---|---|---|
| V-8, 354.0 | 3.94 × 3.63 | 285 | S-Windsor |
| V-8, 354.0 | 3.94 × 3.63 | 295 | S-Saratoga |
| V-8, 392.0 | 4.00 × 3.90 | 325 | S-NY |
| V-8, 392.0 | 4.00 × 3.90 | 375 | S-300C |
| V-8, 392.0 | 4.00 × 3.90 | 390 | O-300C |

## 1958

| LC-1-L Windsor (wb 122.0) | Wght | Price | Prod |
|---|---|---|---|
| sdn 4d | 3,895 | 3,129 | 12,861 |
| htp sdn | 3,915 | 3,279 | 6,254 |
| htp cpe | 3,860 | 3,214 | 6,205 |
| Town & Country wgn 4d, 9P | 4,245 | 3,803 | 862 |
| Town & Country wgn 4d, 6P | 4,155 | 3,616 | 791 |
| conv cpe | — | — | 2 |

| LC-2-M Saratoga (wb 126.0) | | | |
|---|---|---|---|
| sdn 4d | 4,120 | 3,818 | 8,698 |
| htp sdn | 4,145 | 3,955 | 5,322 |
| htp cpe | 4,045 | 3,878 | 4,466 |

| LC-3-H New Yorker (wb 126.0) | | | |
|---|---|---|---|
| sdn 4d | 4,195 | 4,295 | 7,110 |
| htp sdn | 4,240 | 4,404 | 5,227 |
| htp cpe | 4,205 | 4,347 | 3,205 |
| conv cpe | 4,350 | 4,761 | 666 |
| Town & Country wgn 4d, 9P | 4,445 | 5,083 | 775 |
| Town & Country wgn 4d, 6P | 4,435 | 4,868 | 428 |

| LC-3-S 300D (wb 126.0) | | | |
|---|---|---|---|
| htp cpe | 4,305 | 5,173 | 618 |
| conv cpe | 4,475 | 5,603 | 191 |

| 1958 Engines | bore × stroke | bhp | availability |
|---|---|---|---|
| V-8, 354.0 | 3.94 × 3.63 | 290 | S-Windsor |

| 1958 Engines | bore × stroke | bhp | availability |
|---|---|---|---|
| V-8, 354.0 | 3.94 × 3.63 | 310 | S-Saratoga |
| V-8, 392.0 | 4.00 × 3.90 | 345 | S-NY |
| V-8, 392.0 | 4.00 × 3.90 | 380 | S-300D |
| V-8, 392.0 | 4.00 × 3.90 | 390 | O-300D |

## 1959

| MC-1-L Windsor (wb 122.0) | | Wght | Price | Prod |
|---|---|---|---|---|
| 512 | htp cpe | 3,830 | 3,289 | 6,775 |
| 513 | sdn 4d | 3,800 | 3,204 | 19,910 |
| 514 | htp sdn | 3,735 | 3,353 | 6,084 |
| 515 | conv cpe | 3,950 | 3,620 | 961 |
| 576 | Town & Country wgn 4d, 6P | 4,045 | 3,691 | 751 |
| 577 | Town & Country wgn 4d, 9P | 4,070 | 3,878 | 992 |

| MC-2-M Saratoga (wb 126.0) | | | | |
|---|---|---|---|---|
| 532 | htp cpe | 3,970 | 4,026 | 3,753 |
| 533 | sdn 4d | 4,010 | 3,966 | 8,783 |
| 534 | htp sdn | 4,035 | 4,104 | 4,934 |

| MC-3-H New Yorker (wb 126.0) | | | | |
|---|---|---|---|---|
| 552 | htp cpe | 4,080 | 4,476 | 2,435 |
| 553 | sdn 4d | 4,120 | 4,424 | 7,792 |
| 554 | htp sdn | 4,165 | 4,533 | 4,805 |
| 555 | conv cpe | 4,270 | 4,890 | 286 |
| 578 | Town & Country wgn 6P | 4,295 | 4,997 | 444 |
| 579 | Town & Country wgn 9P | 4,360 | 5,212 | 564 |
| — | chassis | — | — | 3 |

| MC-C-H 300E (wb 126.0) | | | | |
|---|---|---|---|---|
| 592 | htp cpe | 4,290 | 5,319 | 550 |
| 595 | conv cpe | 4,350 | 5,749 | 140 |

| 1959 Engines | bore × stroke | bhp | availability |
|---|---|---|---|
| V-8, 383.0 | 4.03 × 3.75 | 305 | S-Windsor |
| V-8, 383.0 | 4.03 × 3.75 | 325 | S-Saratoga |
| V-8, 413.0 | 4.18 × 3.75 | 350 | S-NY |
| V-8, 413.0 | 4.18 × 3.75 | 380 | S-300E |

## 1960

| PC-1-L Windsor (wb 122.0) | | Wght | Price | Prod |
|---|---|---|---|---|
| 23 | htp cpe | 3,855 | 3,279 | 6,496 |

# Chrysler

| PC-1-L Windsor (wb 122.0) | | Wght | Price | Prod |
|---|---|---|---|---|
| 27 | conv cpe | 3,855 | 3,623 | 1,467 |
| 41 | sdn 4d | 3,815 | 3,194 | 25,152 |
| 43 | htp sdn | 3,850 | 3,343 | 5,897 |
| 46 | Town & Country wgn 4d, 6P | 4,235 | 3,733 | 1,120 |
| 46 | Town & Country wgn 4d, 9P | 4,390 | 3,814 | 1,026 |
| **PC-2-M Saratoga (wb 126.0)** | | | | |
| 23 | htp cpe | 4,030 | 3,989 | 2,963 |
| 41 | sdn 4d | 4,010 | 3,939 | 8,463 |
| 43 | htp sdn | 4,035 | 4,067 | 4,099 |
| **PC-3-H New Yorker (wb 126.0)** | | | | |
| 23 | htp cpe | 4,175 | 4,461 | 2,835 |
| 27 | conv cpe | 4,185 | 4,875 | 556 |
| 41 | sdn 4d | 4,145 | 4,409 | 9,079 |
| 43 | htp sdn | 4,175 | 4,518 | 5,625 |
| 46 | Town & Country wgn, 6P | 4,515 | 5,022 | 624 |
| 46 | Town & Country wgn, 9P | 4,535 | 5,131 | 671 |
| **PC-3-H 300F (wb 126.0)** | | | | |
| 23 | htp cpe | 4,270 | 5,411 | 964 |
| 27 | conv cpe | 4,310 | 5,841 | 248 |

| 1960 Engines | bore × stroke | bhp | availability |
|---|---|---|---|
| V-8, 383.0 | 4.03 × 3.75 | 305 | S-Windsor |
| V-8, 383.0 | 4.03 × 3.75 | 325 | S-Saratoga |
| V-8, 413.0 | 4.18 × 3.75 | 350 | S-NY |
| V-8, 413.0 | 4.18 × 3.75 | 375 | S-300F |
| V-8, 413.0 | 4.18 × 3.75 | 400 | O-300F |

## 1961

| RC-1-L Newport (wb 122.0) | | Wght | Price | Prod |
|---|---|---|---|---|
| 812 | htp cpe | 3,690 | 3,025 | 9,405 |
| 813 | sdn 4d | 3,710 | 2,964 | 34,370 |
| 814 | htp sdn | 3,730 | 3,104 | 7,789 |
| 815 | conv cpe | 3,760 | 3,442 | 2,135 |
| 858 | Town & Country wgn 4d, 6P | 4,070 | 3,541 | 1,832 |
| 859 | Town & Country wgn 4d, 9P | 4,155 | 3,622 | 1,571 |
| **RC-2-M Windsor (wb 122.0)** | | | | |
| 822 | htp cpe | 3,710 | 3,303 | 2,941 |
| 823 | sdn 4d | 3,730 | 3,218 | 10,239 |
| 824 | htp sdn | 3,765 | 3,367 | 4,156 |
| **RC-3-H New Yorker (wb 126.0)** | | | | |
| 832 | htp cpe | 4,065 | 4,175 | 2,541 |
| 833 | sdn 4d | 4,055 | 4,123 | 9,984 |
| 834 | htp sdn | 4,100 | 4,261 | 5,862 |
| 835 | conv cpe | 4,070 | 4,592 | 576 |
| 878 | Town & Country wgn 4d, 6P | 4,425 | 4,764 | 676 |
| 879 | Town & Country wgn 4d, 9P | 4,455 | 4,871 | 760 |
| **RC-4-P 300G (wb 126.0)** | | | | |
| 842 | htp cpe | 4,260 | 5,411 | 1,280 |
| 845 | conv cpe | 4,315 | 5,841 | 337 |

| 1961 Engines | bore × stroke | bhp | availability |
|---|---|---|---|
| V-8, 361.0 | 4.12 × 3.38 | 265 | S-Newport |
| V-8, 383.0 | 4.25 × 3.38 | 305 | S-Windsor |
| V-8, 413.0 | 4.18 × 3.75 | 350 | S-NY |
| V-8, 413.0 | 4.18 × 3.75 | 375 | S-300G |
| V-8, 413.0 | 4.18 × 3.75 | 400 | O-300G |

## 1962

| SC1-L-Newport (wb 122.0) | | Wght | Price | Prod |
|---|---|---|---|---|
| 812 | htp cpe | 3,650 | 3,027 | 11,910 |
| 813 | sdn 4d | 3,690 | 2,964 | 54,813 |
| 814 | htp sdn | 3,715 | 3,106 | 8,712 |
| 815 | conv cpe | 3,740 | 3,399 | 2,051 |
| 858 | Town & Country wgn 4d, 6P | 4,060 | 3,478 | 3,271 |
| 859 | Town & Country wgn 4d, 9P | 4,090 | 3,586 | 2,363 |
| **SC2-M 300 (wb 122.0)** | | | | |
| 822 | htp cpe | 3,750 | 3,323 | 11,341 |
| 823 | sdn 4d | — | 3,258 | 1,801 |
| 824 | htp sdn | 3,760 | 3,400 | 10,030 |
| 825 | conv cpe | 3,815 | 3,883 | 1,848 |
| **SC3-H New Yorker (wb 126.0)** | | | | |
| 833 | sdn 4d | 3,925 | 4,125 | 12,056 |
| 834 | htp sdn | 4,005 | 4,263 | 6,646 |
| 878 | Town & Country 4d, 6P | 4,225 | 4,766 | 728 |
| 879 | Town & Country 4d, 9P | 4,455 | 4,873 | 793 |
| **SC2-M 300H (wb 122.0)** | | | | |
| 842 | htp cpe | 4,010 | 5,090 | 435 |
| 845 | conv cpe | 4,080 | 5,461 | 123 |

| 1962 Engines | bore × stroke | bhp | availability |
|---|---|---|---|
| V-8, 361.0 | 4.12 × 3.38 | 265 | S-Newport |
| V-8, 383.0 | 4.25 × 3.38 | 305 | S-300 |
| V-8, 413.0 | 4.18 × 3.75 | 340 | S-NY |
| V-8, 413.0 | 4.18 × 3.75 | 380 | S-300H |
| V-8, 413.0 | 4.18 × 3.75 | 405 | O-300H |

## 1963

| TC1-L Newport (wb 122.0) | | Wght | Price | Prod |
|---|---|---|---|---|
| 812 | htp cpe | 3,760 | 3,027 | 9,809 |
| 813 | sdn 4d | 3,770 | 2,964 | 49,067 |
| 814 | htp sdn | 3,800 | 3,106 | 8,437 |
| 815 | conv cpe | 3,825 | 3,399 | 2,093 |
| 858 | Town & Country wgn 4d, 6P | 4,200 | 3,478 | 3,618 |
| 859 | Town & Country wgn 4d, 9P | 4,215 | 3,586 | 2,948 |
| **TC2-M 300 (wb 122.0)** | | | | |
| 802 | Pace Setter htp cpe | 3,790 | 3,769 | 306 |
| 822 | htp cpe | 3,790 | 3,430 | 9,423 |
| 805 | Pace Setter conv cpe | 3,840 | 4,129 | 1,861 |
| 825 | conv cpe | 3,845 | 3,790 | 1,535 |
| 823 | sdn 4d | 3,790 | — | 1,625 |
| 824 | htp sdn | 3,815 | 3,400 | 9,915 |
| **TC3-H New Yorker (wb 122.0)** | | | | |
| 833 | sdn 4d | 3,910 | 4,981 | 14,884 |
| 834 | htp sdn | 3,950 | 4,118 | 10,289 |
| 884 | Salon htp sdn | 4,290 | 5,860 | 593 |
| 878 | Town & Country wgn 4d, 6P | 4,350 | 4,708 | 950 |
| 879 | Town & Country wgn 4d, 9P | 4,370 | 4,815 | 1,244 |
| **TC2-M 300J (wb 122.0)** | | | | |
| 842 | htp cpe | 4,000 | 5,184 | 400 |

| 1963 Engines | bore × stroke | bhp | availability |
|---|---|---|---|
| V-8, 361.0 | 4.12 × 3.38 | 265 | S-Newport |
| V-8, 383.0 | 4.25 × 3.38 | 305 | S-300 |
| V-8, 413.0 | 4.19 × 3.75 | 340 | S-NY |
| V-8, 413.0 | 4.19 × 3.75 | 360 | O-300 |
| V-8, 413.0 | 4.19 × 3.75 | 390 | S-300J |

## 1964

| VC1-L Newport (wb 122.0) | | Wght | Price | Prod |
|---|---|---|---|---|
| 812 | htp cpe | 3,760 | 2,962 | 10,579 |
| 813 | sdn 4d | 3,805 | 2,901 | 55,957 |
| 814 | htp sdn | 3,795 | 3,042 | 9,710 |
| 815 | conv cpe | 3,810 | 3,334 | 2,176 |
| 858 | Town & Country wgn 4d, 6P | 4,175 | 3,414 | 3,720 |

# Chrysler

| VC1-L Newport (wb 122.0) | | Wght | Price | Prod |
|---|---|---|---|---|
| 859 | Town & Country wgn 4d, 9P | 4,200 | 3,521 | 3,041 |
| **VC2-M 300 (wb 122.0)*** | | | | |
| 822 | htp cpe | 3,850 | 3,443 | 18,379 |
| 824 | htp sdn | 3,865 | 3,521 | 11,460 |
| 823 | sdn 4d | — | — | 2,078 |
| 825 | conv cpe | 4,120 | 3,803 | 1,401 |
| **VC3-H New Yorker (wb 122.0)** | | | | |
| 832 | htp cpe | — | — | 300 |
| 833 | sdn 4d | 4,015 | 3,994 | 15,443 |
| 834 | htp sdn | 4,035 | 4,131 | 10,887 |
| 878 | Town & Country wgn 4d, 6P | 4,385 | 4,721 | 1,190 |
| 879 | Town & Country wgn 4d, 9P | 4,395 | 4,828 | 1,603 |
| 884 | Salon htp sdn | 4,280 | 5,860 | 1,621 |
| **VC2-M 300K (wb 122.0)*** | | | | |
| 842 | htp cpe | 3,965 | 4,056 | 3,022 |
| 845 | conv cpe | 3,995 | 4,522 | 625 |

*Silver 300 models: 300—2,152; 300K—255.

| 1964 Engines | bore × stroke | bhp | availability |
|---|---|---|---|
| V-8, 361.0 | 4.12 × 3.38 | 265 | S-Newport |
| V-8, 383.0 | 4.25 × 3.38 | 305 | S-300 |
| V-8, 413.0 | 4.19 × 3.75 | 340 | S-NY; O-300 |
| V-8, 413.0 | 4.19 × 3.75 | 360 | S-300K; O-300 |
| V-8, 413.0 | 4.19 × 3.75 | 390 | O-300K |

## 1965

| AC1-L Newport (wb 124; wgns-121) | | Wght | Price | Prod |
|---|---|---|---|---|
| C12 | htp cpe | 4,035 | 3,070 | 23,655 |
| C13 | sdn 4d, 4W | 4,045 | 3,009 | 61,054 |
| C14 | htp sdn | 4,050 | 3,149 | 17,062 |
| C15 | conv cpe | 4,025 | 3,442 | 3,192 |
| C18 | sdn 4d, 6W | 4,000 | 3,146 | 12,411 |
| C56 | Town & Country wgn 4d, 6P | 4,360 | 3,521 | 4,683 |
| C57 | Town & Country wgn 4d, 9P | 4,455 | 3,629 | 3,738 |
| **AC2-M 300 (wb 124.0)** | | | | |
| C22 | htp cpe | 4,085 | 3,551 | 11,621 |
| C24 | htp sdn | 4,150 | 3,628 | 12,452 |
| C25 | conv cpe | 4,140 | 3,911 | 1,418 |
| C28 | sdn 4d, 6W | — | — | 2,187 |
| **AC3-H New Yorker (wb 124.0; wgns-121.0)** | | | | |
| C32 | htp cpe | 4,270 | 4,161 | 9,357 |
| C34 | htp sdn | 4,295 | 4,238 | 21,110 |
| C38 | sdn 4d, 6W | 4,265 | 4,104 | 16,339 |
| C76 | Town & Country wgn 4d, 6P | 4,650 | 4,827 | 1,368 |
| C77 | Town & Country wgn 4d, 9P | 4,745 | 4,935 | 1,697 |
| **AC2-P 300L (wb 124.0)** | | | | |
| C42 | htp cpe | 4,245 | 4,153 | 2,405 |
| C45 | conv cpe | 4,170 | 4,618 | 440 |

| 1965 Engines | bore × stroke | bhp | availability |
|---|---|---|---|
| V-8, 383.0 | 4.25 × 3.38 | 270 | S-Newport; O-300 |
| V-8, 383.0 | 4.25 × 3.38 | 315 | S-300; O-Newport |
| V-8, 413.0 | 4.19 × 3.75 | 340 | S-NY |
| V-8, 413.0 | 4.19 × 3.75 | 360 | S-300L; O-300, NY |

## 1966

| BC1-L Newport (wb 124; wgns-121) | | Wght | Price | Prod |
|---|---|---|---|---|
| 23 | htp cpe | 3,920 | 3,112 | 37,622 |
| 27 | conv cpe | 4,020 | 3,476 | 3,085 |
| 41 | sdn 4d, 4W | 3,875 | 3,052 | 74,964 |
| 42 | sdn 4d, 6W | 3,910 | 3,183 | 9,432 |
| 43 | htp sdn | 4,010 | 3,190 | 24,966 |
| 45 | wgn 4d, 6P | 4,370 | 4,086 | 9,035 |
| 46 | wgn 4d, 9P | 4,550 | 4,192 | 8,567 |
| **BC2-M 300 (wb 124.0)** | | | | |
| 23 | htp cpe | 3,940 | 3,583 | 24,103 |
| 27 | conv cpe | 4,015 | 3,936 | 2,500 |
| 41 | sdn 4d | 3,895 | 3,523 | 2,353 |
| 43 | htp sdn | 4,000 | 3,659 | 20,642 |
| **BC3-H New Yorker (wb 124.0)** | | | | |
| 23 | htp cpe | 4,095 | 4,157 | 7,955 |
| 42 | sdn 4d | 4,100 | 4,101 | 13,025 |
| 43 | htp sdn | 4,140 | 4,233 | 26,599 |

| 1966 Engines | bore × stroke | bhp | availability |
|---|---|---|---|
| V-8, 383.0 | 4.25 × 3.38 | 270 | S-Newport |
| V-8, 383.0 | 4.25 × 3.38 | 325 | S-300; O-Newport |
| V-8, 440.0 | 4.32 × 3.75 | 350 | S-NY |

## 1967

| CC1-E Newport (wb 124; wgns-122) | | Wght | Price | Prod |
|---|---|---|---|---|
| 23 | htp cpe | 3,920 | 3,219 | 26,583 |
| 27 | conv cpe | 3,970 | 3,583 | 2,891 |
| 41 | sdn 4d | 3,955 | 3,159 | 48,945 |
| 43 | htp sdn | 3,980 | 3,296 | 14,247 |
| 45 | wgn 4d, 6P | 4,495 | 4,264 | 7,183 |
| 46 | wgn 4d, 9P | 4,550 | 4,369 | 7,520 |
| **CC1-L Newport Custom (wb 124.0)** | | | | |
| 23 | htp cpe | 3,935 | 3,407 | 14,193 |
| 41 | sdn 4d | 3,975 | 3,347 | 23,101 |
| 43 | htp sdn | 3,995 | 3,485 | 12,728 |
| **CC2-M 300 (wb 124.0)** | | | | |
| 23 | htp cpe | 4,070 | 3,936 | 11,556 |
| 27 | conv cpe | 4,105 | 4,289 | 1,594 |
| 43 | htp sdn | 4,135 | 4,012 | 8,744 |
| **CC3-H New Yorker (wb 124.0)** | | | | |
| 23 | htp cpe | 4,170 | 4,264 | 6,885 |
| 41 | sdn 4d | 4,185 | 4,208 | 10,907 |
| 43 | htp sdn | 4,240 | 4,339 | 21,665 |

| 1967 Engines | bore × stroke | bhp | availability |
|---|---|---|---|
| V-8, 383.0 | 4.25 × 3.38 | 270 | S-Newport |
| V-8, 383.0 | 4.25 × 3.38 | 325 | O-Newport |
| V-8, 440.0 | 4.32 × 3.75 | 350 | S-300, NY; O-wgns |
| V-8, 440.0 | 4.32 × 3.75 | 375 | O-all exc wgns |

## 1968

| DC1-E Newport (wb 124; wgns-122) | | Wght | Price | Prod |
|---|---|---|---|---|
| CE23 | htp cpe* | 3,840 | 3,366 | 36,768 |
| CE27 | conv cpe* | 3,910 | 3,704 | 2,847 |
| CE41 | sdn 4d | 3,850 | 3,306 | 61,436 |
| CE43 | htp sdn | 3,865 | 3,444 | 20,191 |
| CE45 | Town & Country wgn 4d, 6P | 4,340 | 4,418 | 9,908 |
| CE46 | Town & Country wgn 4d, 9P | 4,410 | 4,523 | 12,233 |
| **DC1-L Newport Custom (wb 124.0)** | | | | |
| CL23 | htp cpe | 3,890 | 3,552 | 10,341 |
| CL41 | sdn 4d | 3,855 | 3,493 | 16,915 |
| CL43 | htp sdn | 3,860 | 3,631 | 11,460 |
| **DC2-M 300 (wb 124.0)** | | | | |
| CM23 | htp cpe | 3,985 | 4,010 | 16,953 |
| CM27 | conv cpe | 4,050 | 4,337 | 2,161 |
| CM43 | htp sdn | 4,015 | 4,086 | 15,507 |

# Chrysler

| DC3-H New Yorker (wb 124.0) | | Wght | Price | Prod |
|---|---|---|---|---|
| CH23 | htp cpe | 4,060 | 4,424 | 8,060 |
| CH41 | sdn 4d | 4,055 | 4,367 | 13,092 |
| CH43 | htp sdn | 4,090 | 4,500 | 26,991 |

*Sportsgrain models: htp cpe 965; conv cpe 175.

| 1968 Engines | bore × stroke | bhp | availability |
|---|---|---|---|
| V-8, 383.0 | 4.25 × 3.38 | 290 | S-Newport, T&C |
| V-8, 383.0 | 4.25 × 3.38 | 330 | O-Newport, T&C |
| V-8, 440.0 | 4.32 × 3.75 | 350 | S-300, NY; O-T&C |
| V-8, 440.0 | 4.32 × 3.75 | 375 | O-all exc T&C |

## 1969

| EC-E Newport (wb 124.0)* | | Wght | Price | Prod |
|---|---|---|---|---|
| CE23 | htp cpe | 3,891 | 3,485 | 33,639 |
| CE27 | conv cpe | 4,026 | 3,823 | 2,169 |
| CE41 | sdn 4d | 3,941 | 3,414 | 55,083 |
| CE43 | htp sdn | 4,156 | 3,549 | 20,608 |
| EC-L Newport Custom (wb 124.0) | | | | |
| CL23 | htp cpe | 3,891 | 3,652 | 10,955 |
| CL41 | sdn 4d | 3,951 | 3,580 | 18,401 |
| CL43 | htp sdn | 3,971 | 3,730 | 15,981 |
| EC-P Town & Country (wb 122.0) | | | | |
| CP45 | wgn 4d, 6P | 4,435 | 4,583 | 10,108 |
| CP46 | wgn 4d, 9P | 4,485 | 4,669 | 14,408 |
| EC-M 300 (wb 124.0) | | | | |
| CM23 | htp cpe | 3,965 | 4,104 | 16,075 |
| CM27 | conv cpe | 4,095 | 4,450 | 1,933 |
| CM43 | htp sdn | 4,045 | 4,183 | 14,464 |
| EC-H New Yorker (wb 124.0) | | | | |
| CH23 | htp cpe | 4,070 | 4,539 | 7,537 |
| CH41 | sdn 4d | 4,135 | 4,487 | 12,253 |
| CH43 | htp sdn | 4,165 | 4,615 | 27,157 |

*Sportsgrain models: 195.

| 1969 Engines | bore × stroke | bhp | availability |
|---|---|---|---|
| V-8, 383.0 | 4.24 × 3.38 | 290 | S-Newport, T&C |
| V-8, 383.0 | 4.25 × 3.38 | 330 | O-Newport, T&C |
| V-8, 440.0 | 4.32 × 3.75 | 350 | S-300, NY; O-T&C |
| V-8, 440.0 | 4.32 × 3.75 | 375 | O-all exc T&C |

## 1970

| FC-E Newport (wb 124.0) | | Wght | Price | Prod |
|---|---|---|---|---|
| CE23 | htp cpe* | 4,030 | 3,589 | 21,664 |
| CE27 | conv cpe | 4,085 | 3,925 | 1,124 |
| CE41 | sdn 4d | 4,080 | 3,514 | 39,285 |
| CE43 | htp sdn* | 4,110 | 3,652 | 16,940 |
| FC-L Newport Custom (wb 124.0) | | | | |
| CL23 | htp cpe | 4,035 | 3,781 | 6,639 |
| CL41 | sdn 4d | 4,091 | 3,710 | 13,767 |
| CL43 | htp sdn | 4,125 | 3,861 | 10,873 |
| FC-P Town & Country (wb 122.0) | | | | |
| CP45 | wgn 4d, 6P | 4,490 | 4,738 | 5,686 |
| CP46 | wgn 4d, 9P | 4,555 | 4,824 | 9,583 |
| FC-M 300 (wb 124.0) | | | | |
| CM23 | htp cpe* | 4,135 | 4,234 | 10,084 |
| CM27 | conv cpe | 4,175 | 4,580 | 1,077 |
| CM43 | htp sdn | 4,220 | 4,313 | 9,846 |
| FC-H New Yorker (wb 124.0) | | | | |
| CH23 | htp cpe | 4,235 | 4,681 | 4,917 |
| CH41 | sdn 4d | 4,310 | 4,630 | 9,389 |
| CH43 | htp sdn | 4,335 | 4,761 | 19,903 |

*CE23 includes 1,868 Cordoba htp cpes; CE43 includes 1,873 Cordoba htp sdns; CM23 includes 501 300-H "Hurst" htp cpes.

| 1970 Engines | bore × stroke | bhp | availability |
|---|---|---|---|
| V-8, 383.0 | 4.25 × 3.38 | 290 | S-Newport, T&C |
| V-8, 383.0 | 4.25 × 3.38 | 330 | O-Newport, T&C |
| V-8, 440.0 | 4.32 × 3.75 | 350 | S-NY, 300; O-T&C |
| V-8, 440.0 | 4.32 × 3.75 | 375 | O-all exc T&C |

## 1971

| CE Newport (wb 124.0) | | Wght | Price | Prod |
|---|---|---|---|---|
| 23 | Royal htp cpe | 4,121 | 4,153 | 8,500 |
| 23 | htp cpe | 4,121 | 4,265 | 13,549 |
| 41 | Royal sdn 4d | 4,171 | 4,078 | 19,662 |
| 41 | sdn 4d | 4,171 | 4,190 | 24,834 |
| 43 | Royal htp sdn | 4,191 | 4,216 | 5,188 |
| 43 | htp sdn | 4,191 | 4,265 | 10,800 |
| CP Town & Country (wb 122.0) | | | | |
| 45 | wgn 4d 2S | 4,525 | 4,951 | 5,697 |
| 46 | wgn 4d 3S | 4,580 | 5,037 | 10,993 |
| CL Newport Custom (wb 124.0) | | | | |
| 23 | htp cpe | 4,126 | 4,391 | 5,527 |
| 41 | sdn 4d | 4,181 | 4,319 | 11,254 |
| 43 | htp sdn | 4,211 | 4,471 | 10,207 |
| CS 300 (wb 124.0) | | | | |
| 23 | htp cpe | 4,246 | 4,608 | 7,256 |
| 43 | htp sdn | 4,321 | 4,687 | 6,683 |
| CH New Yorker (wb 124.0) | | | | |
| 23 | htp cpe | 4,250 | 4,961 | 4,485 |
| 41 | sdn 4d | 4,335 | 4,910 | 9,850 |
| 43 | htp sdn | 4,355 | 5,041 | 20,633 |

| 1971 Engines | bore × stroke | bhp | availability |
|---|---|---|---|
| V-8, 360.0 | 4.00 × 3.58 | 255 | S-CE |
| V-8, 383.0 | 4.25 × 3.38 | 275 | S-CL, CP; O-CE Roy |
| V-8, 383.0 | 4.25 × 3.38 | 300 | O-CL, CP, CE Royal |
| V-8, 440.0 | 4.32 × 3.75 | 335 | S-CS, CH; O-all others |
| V-8, 440.0 | 4.32 × 3.75 | 370 | O-all |

## 1972

| CL Newport Royal (wb 124.0) | | Wght | Price | Prod |
|---|---|---|---|---|
| 23 | htp cpe | 4,035 | 4,124 | 22,622 |
| 41 | sdn 4d | 4,095 | 4,051 | 47,437 |
| 43 | htp sdn | 4,100 | 4,186 | 15,185 |
| CM Newport Custom (wb 124.0) | | | | |
| 23 | htp cpe | 4,130 | 4,357 | 10,326 |
| 41 | sdn 4d | 4,185 | 4,435 | 19,278 |
| 43 | htp sdn | 4,195 | 4,435 | 15,457 |
| CP Town & Country (wb 122.0) | | | | |
| 45 | wgn 4d 2S | 4,610 | 5,055 | 6,473 |
| 46 | wgn 4d 3S | 4,665 | 5,139 | 14,116 |
| CH New Yorker (wb 124.0) | | | | |
| 23 | htp cpe | 4,270 | 4,915 | 5,567 |
| 41 | sdn 4d | 4,335 | 4,865 | 7,296 |
| 43 | htp sdn | 4,365 | 4,993 | 10,013 |
| CS New Yorker Brougham (wb 124.0) | | | | |
| 23 | htp cpe | 4,270 | 5,271 | 4,635 |
| 41 | sdn 4d | 4,335 | 5,222 | 5,971 |
| 43 | htp sdn | 4,365 | 5,350 | 20,328 |

| 1972 Engines | bore × stroke | bhp | availability |
|---|---|---|---|
| V-8, 360.0 | 4.00 × 3.58 | 175 | S-CL |
| V-8, 400.0 | 4.34 × 3.38 | 190 | S-CM, CP; O-CL |
| V-8, 440.0 | 4.32 × 3.75 | 225 | S-CH, CS; O-all others |

# Chrysler

## 1973

| CL Newport (wb 124.0) | | Wght | Price | Prod |
|---|---|---|---|---|
| 23 | htp cpe | 4,160 | 4,254 | 27,456 |
| 41 | sdn 4d | 4,200 | 4,181 | 54,147 |
| 43 | htp sdn | 4,210 | 4,316 | 20,175 |
| CM Newport Custom (wb 124.0) | | | | |
| 23 | htp cpe | 4,145 | 4,484 | 12,293 |
| 41 | sdn 4d | 4,200 | 4,419 | 20,092 |
| 43 | htp sdn | 4,225 | 4,567 | 20,050 |
| CP Town & Country (wb 122.0) | | | | |
| 45 | wgn 4d 2S | 4,670 | 5,241 | 5,353 |
| 46 | wgn 4d 3S | 4,725 | 5,266 | 14,687 |
| CH New Yorker (wb 124.0) | | | | |
| 41 | sdn 4d | 4,355 | 4,997 | 7,991 |
| 43 | htp sdn | 4,375 | 5,125 | 7,619 |
| CS New Yorker Brougham (wb 124.0) | | | | |
| 23 | htp cpe | 4,335 | 5,413 | 9,190 |
| 41 | sdn 4d | 4,425 | 5,364 | 8,541 |
| 43 | htp sdn | 4,440 | 5,492 | 26,635 |

| 1973 Engines | bore × stroke | bhp | availability |
|---|---|---|---|
| V-8, 400.0 | 4.34 × 3.38 | 185 | S-CL, CM |
| V-8, 440.0 | 4.32 × 3.75 | 215 | S-CP, CH, CS; O-CL, CM |

## 1974

| CL Newport (wb 124.0) | | Wght | Price | Prod |
|---|---|---|---|---|
| 23 | htp cpe | 4,380 | 4,752 | 13,784 |
| 41 | sdn 4d | 4,430 | 4,677 | 26,944 |
| 43 | htp sdn | 4,440 | 4,816 | 8,968 |
| CM Newport Custom (wb 124.0) | | | | |
| 23 | htp cpe | 4,430 | 5,105 | 7,206 |
| 41 | sdn 4d | 4,480 | 5,038 | 10,569 |
| 43 | htp sdn | 4,500 | 5,190 | 9,892 |
| CP Town & Country (wb 124.0) | | | | |
| 45 | wgn 4d 2S | 4,915 | 5,767 | 2,236 |
| 46 | wgn 4d 3S | 4,970 | 5,896 | 5,958 |
| CH New Yorker (wb 124.0) | | | | |
| 41 | sdn 4d | 4,560 | 5,554 | 3,072 |
| 43 | htp sdn | 4,595 | 5,686 | 3,066 |
| CS New Yorker Brougham (wb 124.0) | | | | |
| 23 | htp cpe | 4,540 | 5,982 | 7,980 |
| 41 | sdn 4d | 4,640 | 5,931 | 4,533 |
| 43 | htp sdn | 4,655 | 6,063 | 13,165 |

| 1974 Engines | bore × stroke | bhp | availability |
|---|---|---|---|
| V-8, 400.0 | 4.34 × 3.38 | 185 | S-CL, CM |
| V-8, 400.0 | 4.34 × 3.38 | 205 | O-CL, CM |
| V-8, 440.0 | 4.32 × 3.75 | 230 | S-CP, CH, CS; O-CL, CM |
| V-8, 440.0 | 4.32 × 3.75 | 275 | O-CH, CS |

## 1975

| SS Cordoba (wb 115.0) | | Wght | Price | Prod |
|---|---|---|---|---|
| 22 | cpe | 3,975 | 5,072 | 150,105 |
| CL Newport (wb 124.0) | | | | |
| 23 | htp cpe | 4,395 | 4,937 | 10,485 |
| 41 | sdn 4d | 4,440 | 4,854 | 24,339 |
| 43 | htp sdn | 4,475 | 5,008 | 6,846 |
| CM Newport Custom (wb 124.0) | | | | |
| 23 | htp cpe | 4,450 | 5,329 | 5,831 |
| 41 | sdn 4d | 4,500 | 5,254 | 9,623 |
| 43 | htp sdn | 4,520 | 5,423 | 11,626 |
| CP Town & Country (wb 124.0) | | | | |
| 45 | wgn 4d 2S | 5,015 | 6,099 | 1,891 |
| 46 | wgn 4d 3S | 5,050 | 6,244 | 4,764 |
| CS New Yorker Brougham (wb 124.0) | | | | |
| 23 | htp cpe | 4,650 | 6,334 | 7,567 |
| 41 | sdn 4d | 4,630 | 6,277 | 5,698 |
| 43 | htp sdn | 4,690 | 6,424 | 12,774 |

| 1975 Engines | bore × stroke | bhp | availability |
|---|---|---|---|
| V-8, 318.0 | 3.91 × 3.31 | 150 | O-SS |
| V-8, 360.0 | 4.00 × 3.58 | 180 | S-SS; O-CL, CM |
| V-8, 360.0 | 4.00 × 3.58 | 190 | O-CL, CM |
| V-8, 400.0 | 4.34 × 3.38 | 165 | O-SS |
| V-8, 400.0 | 4.34 × 3.38 | 175 | S-CL, CM; O-CS |
| V-8, 400.0 | 4.34 × 3.38 | 190 | O-SS |
| V-8, 400.0 | 4.34 × 3.38 | 195 | O-CL, CM, CS |
| V-8, 400.0 | 4.34 × 3.38 | 235 | O-SS |
| V-8, 440.0 | 4.32 × 3.75 | 215 | S-CP, CS; O-others |
| V-8, 440.0 | 4.32 × 3.75 | 260 | O-CP |

## 1976

| SS Cordoba (wb 115.0) | | Wght | Price | Prod |
|---|---|---|---|---|
| 22 | cpe | 4,130 | 5,392 | 120,462 |
| CL Newport (wb 124.0) | | | | |
| 23 | htp cpe | 4,455 | 5,076 | 6,109 |
| 41 | sdn 4d | 4,490 | 4,993 | 16,370 |
| 43 | htp sdn | 4,525 | 5,147 | 5,908 |
| CM Newport Custom (wb 124.0) | | | | |
| 23 | htp cpe | 4,530 | 5,479 | 6,448 |
| 41 | sdn 4d | 4,565 | 5,407 | 11,587 |
| 43 | htp sdn | 4,585 | 5,576 | 9,893 |
| CP Town & Country (wb 124.0) | | | | |
| 45 | wgn 5d 2S | 5,045 | 6,084 | 1,770 |
| 46 | wgn 5d 3S | 5,075 | 6,244 | 3,769 |
| CS New Yorker Brougham (wb 124.0) | | | | |
| 23 | htp cpe | 4,865 | 6,641 | 11,510 |
| 43 | htp sdn | 4,950 | 6,737 | 28,327 |

| 1976 Engines | bore × stroke | bhp | availability |
|---|---|---|---|
| V-8, 318.0 | 3.91 × 3.31 | 150 | O-SS |
| V-8, 360.0 | 4.00 × 3.58 | 170/175 | O-SS, CL, CM |
| V-8, 400.0 | 4.34 × 3.38 | 175 | S-SS, CL, CM; O-CS |
| V-8, 400.0 | 4.34 × 3.38 | 210 | O-all |
| V-8, 400.0 | 4.34 × 3.38 | 240 | O-SS |
| V-8, 440.0 | 4.32 × 3.75 | 205 | S-CP, CS; O-CL, CM |

## 1977

| FH LeBaron (wb 112.7)—54,851 built | | Wght | Price | Prod |
|---|---|---|---|---|
| 22 | cpe | 3,510 | 5,066 | — |
| 41 | sdn 4d | 3,560 | 5,224 | — |
| FP LeBaron Medallion (wb 112.7) Prod. included above. | | | | |
| 22 | cpe | 3,615 | 5,436 | — |
| 41 | sdn 4d | 3,675 | 5,594 | — |
| SS Cordoba (wb 115.0) | | | | |
| SP22 | cpe | — | 5,368 | 183,146 |
| SS22 | cpe | 4,045 | 5,418 | |
| CL Newport (wb 124.0) | | | | |
| 23 | htp cpe | 4,400 | 5,374 | 16,227 |
| 41 | sdn 4d | 4,455 | 5,280 | 39,424 |
| 43 | htp sdn | 4,485 | 5,433 | 20,738 |
| CP Town & Country (wb 124.0) | | | | |
| 45 | wgn 5d 2S | 5,025 | 6,461 | 2,488 |
| 46 | wgn 5d 3S | 5,060 | 6,647 | 6,081 |

# Chrysler

| CS New Yorker Brougham (wb 124.0) | | Wght | Price | Prod |
|---|---|---|---|---|
| 23 | htp cpe | 4,685 | 7,090 | 19,732 |
| 43 | htp sdn | 4,770 | 7,215 | 56,610 |

| 1977 Engines | bore × stroke | bhp | availability |
|---|---|---|---|
| V-8, 318.0 | 3.91 × 3.31 | 135 | O-Cordoba |
| V-8, 318.0 | 3.91 × 3.31 | 145 | S-LeB; O-Crdba |
| V-8, 360.0 | 4.00 × 3.58 | 155 | O-Crdba, Nwpt |
| V-8, 360.0 | 4.00 × 3.58 | 170 | O-Crdba |
| V-8, 400.0 | 4.34 × 3.38 | 190 | S-Crdba, Nwpt; O-T&C, NY |
| V-8, 440.0 | 4.32 × 3.75 | 195 | S-T&C, NY; O-Nwpt |

## 1978

| LeBaron (wb 112.7) | | Wght | Price | Prod |
|---|---|---|---|---|
| FM22 | "S" cpe I-6 | 3,335 | 4,894 | — |
| FM22 | "S" cpe V-8 | 3,415 | 5,080 | — |
| FM41 | "S" sdn 4d I-6 | 3,400 | 5,060 | — |
| FM41 | "S" sdn 4d V-8 | 3,485 | 5,246 | — |
| FH22 | cpe I-6 | 3,420 | 5,144 | 16,273 |
| FH22 | cpe V-8 | 3,505 | 5,330 | |
| FH41 | sdn 4d I-6 | 3,465 | 5,310 | 22,732 |
| FH41 | sdn 4d V-8 | 3,550 | 5,496 | |
| FP22 | Medallion cpe I-6 | 3,495 | 5,526 | 37,138 |
| FP22 | Medallion cpe V-8 | 3,580 | 5,712 | |
| FP41 | Medallion sdn 4d I-6 | 3,550 | 5,692 | 44,291 |
| FP41 | Medallion sdn 4d V-8 | 3,635 | 5,878 | |
| FH45 | T&C wgn 5d 2S I-6 | 3,600 | 5,724 | 22,256 |
| FH45 | T&C wgn 5d 2S V-8 | 3,685 | 5,910 | |

| Cordoba (wb 114.9) | | | | |
|---|---|---|---|---|
| SS22 | cpe | 4,020 | 5,811 | 124,825 |
| SS22 | S cpe | — | 5,611 | |

| Newport (wb 123.9) | | | | |
|---|---|---|---|---|
| CL23 | htp cpe | 4,395 | 5,804 | 8,877 |
| CL43 | htp sdn | 4,460 | 5,888 | 30,078 |

| New Yorker Brougham (wb 123.9) | | | | |
|---|---|---|---|---|
| CS23 | htp cpe | 4,620 | 7,702 | 11,469 |
| CS43 | htp sdn | 4,670 | 7,831 | 33,090 |

| 1978 Engines | bore × stroke | bhp | availability |
|---|---|---|---|
| I-6, 225.0 | 3.40 × 4.12 | 90 | O-LeBaron |
| I-6, 225.0 | 3.40 × 4.12 | 110 | S-LeBaron |
| V-8, 318.0 | 3.91 × 3.31 | 140 | S-LeB; O-Crdba |
| V-8, 318.0 | 3.91 × 3.31 | 155 | O-LeB, Crdba |
| V-8, 360.0 | 4.00 × 3.58 | 155 | S-Crdba S; O-others |
| V-8, 360.0 | 4.00 × 3.58 | 170 | O-all |
| V-8, 400.0 | 4.34 × 3.38 | 190 | S-Crdba, Nwpt, NY; O-Crdba S |
| V-8, 440.0 | 4.32 × 3.75 | 185/195 | O-Nwpt, NY |

## 1979

| LeBaron (wb 112.7) | | Wght | Price | Prod |
|---|---|---|---|---|
| FM22 | cpe I-6 | 3,270 | 5,381 | 10,987 |
| FM22 | cpe V-8 | 3,365 | 5,692 | |
| FM41 | sdn 4d I-6 | 3,330 | 5,479 | 14,297 |
| FM41 | sdn 4d V-8 | 3,425 | 5,790 | |
| FH22 | Salon cpe I-6 | 3,285 | 5,623 | 17,637 |
| FH22 | Salon cpe V-8 | 3,385 | 5,934 | |
| FH41 | Salon sdn 4d I-6 | 3,350 | 5,851 | 18,843 |
| FH41 | Salon sdn 4d V-8 | 3,450 | 6,162 | |
| FP22 | Medallion cpe I-6 | 3,345 | 6,017 | 21,762 |
| FP22 | Medallion cpe V-8 | 3,440 | 6,328 | |
| FP41 | Medallion sdn 4d I-6 | 3,425 | 6,425 | 25,041 |
| FP41 | Medallion sdn 4d V-8 | 3,520 | 6,556 | |
| FH45 | T&C wgn 4d 2S I-6 | 3,585 | 6,331 | 19,932 |
| FH45 | T&C wgn 4d 2S V-8 | 3,675 | 6,642 | |

| Cordoba (wb 114.9) | | | | |
|---|---|---|---|---|
| SS22 | cpe | 3,680 | 6,337 | 88,015 |
| SP22 | "300" cpe | 3,880 | 8,034 | |

| Newport (wb 118.5) | | | | |
|---|---|---|---|---|
| TH42 | sdn 4d I-6 | 3,530 | 6,405 | 78,296 |
| TH42 | sdn 4d V-8 | 3,605 | 6,720 | |

| New Yorker (wb 118.5) | | | | |
|---|---|---|---|---|
| TP42 | sdn 4d | 3,800 | 10,026 | 54,640 |

| 1979 Engines | bore × stroke | bhp | availability |
|---|---|---|---|
| I-6, 225.0 | 3.40 × 4.12 | 100 | S-LeBaron |
| I-6, 225.0 | 3.40 × 4.12 | 110 | S-Nwpt; O-LeB |
| V-8, 318.0 | 3.91 × 3.31 | 135 | S-LeB, Cord, Nwpt; O-NY |
| V-8, 360.0 | 4.00 × 3.58 | 150 | S-NY; O-others |
| V-8, 360.0 | 4.00 × 3.58 | 195 | S-"300"; O-others |

## 1980

| LeBaron (wb 112.7; cpe 108.7) | | Wght | Price | Prod |
|---|---|---|---|---|
| FL41 | Special sdn 4d I-6 | 3,260 | 5,995 | — |
| FM22 | cpe I-6 | 3,220 | 6,362 | 8,181 |
| FM22 | cpe V-8 | 3,300 | 6,457 | |
| FM41 | sdn 4d I-6 | 3,300 | 6,518 | 8,470 |
| FM41 | sdn 4d V-8 | 3,385 | 6,613 | |
| FM45 | wgn 4d 2S I-6 | 3,455 | 6,723 | 1,887 |
| FM45 | wgn 4d 2S V-8 | 3,535 | 6,818 | |
| FH22 | Salon cpe I-6 | 3,230 | 6,643 | 18,538 |
| FH22 | Salon cpe V-8 | 3,310 | 6,738 | |
| FH41 | Salon sdn 4d I-6 | 3,325 | 6,764 | 10,762 |
| FH41 | Salon sdn 4d V-8 | 3,405 | 6,859 | |
| FP22 | Medallion cpe I-6 | 3,285 | 7,185 | 10,448 |
| FP22 | Medallion cpe V-8 | 3,360 | 7,280 | |
| FP41 | Medallion sdn 4d I-6 | 3,400 | 7,329 | 13,079 |
| FP41 | Medallion sdn 4d V-8 | 3,485 | 7,424 | |
| FH45 | T&C wgn 5d 2S I-6 | 3,525 | 7,324 | 11,100 |
| FH45 | T&C wgn 5d 2S V-8 | 3,610 | 7,419 | |

| Cordoba (wb 112.7) | | | | |
|---|---|---|---|---|
| SH22 | cpe I-6 | 3,270 | 6,978 | 31,238 |
| SH22 | cpe V-8 | 3,355 | 7,073 | |
| SP22 | Crown cpe I-6 | 3,320 | 7,428 | |
| SP22 | Crown cpe V-8 | 3,400 | 7,523 | |
| SS22 | LS cpe I-6 | 3,270 | 6,745 | 22,233 |
| SS22 | LS cpe V-8 | 3,365 | 6,840 | |
| SP22 | "300" cpe V-8 | — | — | |

| Newport (wb 118.5) | | | | |
|---|---|---|---|---|
| TH42 | sdn 4d I-6 | 3,545 | 7,247 | 15,061 |
| TH42 | sdn 4d V-8 | 3,630 | 7,343 | |

| New Yorker (wb 118.5) | | | | |
|---|---|---|---|---|
| TP42 | sdn 4d | 3,810 | 10,872 | 13,513 |

| 1980 Engines | bore × stroke | bhp | availability |
|---|---|---|---|
| I-6, 225.0 | 3.40 × 4.12 | 90 | S-all sixes |
| V-8, 318.0 | 3.91 × 3.31 | 120 | S-all V-8s exc "300" |
| V-8, 360.0 | 4.00 × 3.58 | 130 | O-Nwpt, NY |
| V-8, 360.0 | 4.00 × 3.58 | 185 | S-Crdba "300" |

Note: Chrysler production through 1980 includes export models, which makes figures in this book somewhat higher than those quoted elsewhere.

## 1981

| LeBaron (wb 112.7; cpe-108.7) | | Wght | Price | Prod |
|---|---|---|---|---|
| FL45 | Special cpe I-6 | — | 6,672 | 11,890 |
| FL45 | Special cpe V-8 | — | 6,734 | |

# Chrysler

| LeBaron (wb 112.7; cpe-108.7) | | Wght | Price | Prod |
|---|---|---|---|---|
| FL41 | Special sdn 4d I-6 | 3,275 | 6,495 | |
| FL41 | Special sdn 4d V-8 | — | 6,557 | 2,136 |
| FM45 | sdn 4d I-6 | 3,470 | 7,346 | |
| FH22 | Salon cpe I-6 | 3,200 | 7,263 | |
| FH22 | Salon cpe V-8 | 3,325 | 7,325 | |
| FH41 | Salon sdn 4d I-6 | 3,305 | 7,413 | 17,485 |
| FH41 | Salon sdn 4d V-8 | 3,430 | 7,475 | |
| FP22 | Medallion cpe I-6 | 3,255 | 7,768 | |
| FP22 | Medallion cpe V-8 | 3,380 | 7,830 | |
| FP41 | Medallion sdn I-6 | 3,365 | 7,917 | 7,635 |
| FP41 | Medallion sdn V-8 | 3,490 | 7,979 | |
| FH45 | T&C wgn 5d 2S I-6 | 3,545 | 8,008 | 3,987 |
| FH45 | T&C wgn 5d 2S V-8 | 3,665 | 8,070 | |
| **Cordoba (wb 112.7)** | | | | |
| SP22 | cpe I-6 | 3,355 | 7,969 | |
| SP22 | cpe V-8 | 3,495 | 8,033 | 12,978 |
| SS22 | LS cpe I-6 | 3,300 | 7,199 | |
| SS22 | LS cpe V-8 | 3,420 | 7,263 | 7,315 |
| **Newport (wb 118.5)** | | | | |
| TH42 | sdn 4d I-6 | 3,515 | 7,805 | 3,622 |
| TH42 | sdn 4d V-8 | 3,635 | 7,869 | |
| **New Yorker (wb 118.5)** | | | | |
| TP42 | sdn 4d V-8 | 3,805 | 10,463 | 6,548 |

| 1981 Engines | bore × stroke | bhp | availability |
|---|---|---|---|
| I-6, 225.0 | 3.40 × 4.12 | 85 | S-all sixes |
| V-8, 318.0 | 3.91 × 3.31 | 130 | S-all V-8s |
| V-8, 318.0 | 3.91 × 3.31 | 165 | O-Nwpt, NY |

## 1982

| LeBaron (wb 100.3) | | Wght | Price | Prod |
|---|---|---|---|---|
| CH22 | cpe | 2,470 | 8,143 | 14,295 |
| CH41 | sdn 4d | 2,455 | 8,237 | 19,619 |
| CH27 | conv cpe | 2,485 | 11,698 | 3,045 |
| CP22 | Medallion cpe | 2,475 | 8,408 | 12,856 |
| CP41 | Medallion sdn | 2,465 | 8,502 | 22,915 |
| CP27 | Medallion conv cpe | 2,660 | 13,998 | 9,780 |
| CP45 | Town & Country wgn 5d 2S | 2,660 | 9,425 | 7,809 |
| **Cordoba (wb 112.7)** | | | | |
| SP22 | cpe I-6 | 3,370 | 9,197 | |
| SP22 | cpe V-8 | 3,520 | 9,267 | 11,762 |
| SS22 | LS cpe I-6 | 3,315 | 8,258 | |
| SS22 | LS cpe V-8 | 3,465 | 8,328 | 3,136 |
| **New Yorker (wb 112.7)** | | | | |
| FS41 | sdn 4d I-6 | 3,510 | 10,781 | 50,509 |
| FS41 | sdn 4d V-8 | 3,655 | 10,851 | |

| 1982 Engines | bore × stroke | bhp | availability |
|---|---|---|---|
| I-4, 135.0 | 3.44 × 3.62 | 84 | S-LeBaron, exc T&C |
| I-4, 156.0 | 3.59 × 3.86 | 92 | S-LeB T&C; O-LeB |
| I-6, 225.0 | 3.40 × 4.12 | 90 | S-Cordoba, NY sixes |
| V-8, 318.0 | 3.91 × 3.31 | 130 | S-Cordoba, NY V-8s |
| V-8, 318.0 | 3.91 × 3.31 | 165 | S-Calif. Cord, NY V-8 |

## 1983

| LeBaron (wb 100.3) | | Wght | Price | Prod |
|---|---|---|---|---|
| CP22 | cpe | 2,464 | 8,514 | 18,331 |
| CP41 | sdn 4d | 2,531 | 8,790 | 30,869 |
| CP27 | conv cpe | 2,532 | 12,800 | |
| CP27 | Mark Cross conv cpe | — | 14,595 | 9,891 |
| CP27 | Mark Cross T&C conv cpe | — | 15,595 | |
| CP45 | Town & Country wgn 5d 2S | 2,656 | 9,731 | 10,994 |
| **E Class (wb 103.3)** | | | | |
| TH41 | sdn 4d | 2,583 | 9,341 | 39,258 |
| **New Yorker (wb 103.3)** | | | | |
| TP41 | sdn 4d | 2,580 | 10,950 | 33,832 |
| **Cordoba (wb 112.7)** | | | | |
| SP22 | cpe I-6 | 3,467 | 9,580 | 13,471 |
| SP22 | cpe V-8 | 3,605 | 9,805 | |
| **New Yorker Fifth Avenue (wb 112.7)** | | | | |
| FS41 | sdn 4d I-6 | 3,631 | 12,487 | 83,501 |
| FS41 | sdn 4d V-8 | 3,781 | 12,712 | |
| **Executive (wb 124.0; limo 131.0)** | | | | |
| CP48 | sdn 4d | — | 18,900 | — |
| CP49 | limo 4d | — | 21,900 | — |

| 1983 Engines | bore × stroke | bhp | availability |
|---|---|---|---|
| I-4, 135.0 | 3.44 × 3.62 | 94 | S-LeB, E Class, NY |
| I-4, 156.0 | 3.59 × 3.86 | 93 | O-LeB, E Class, NY |
| I-6, 225.0 | 3.40 × 4.12 | 90 | S-Cord, Fifth Ave six |
| V-8, 318.0 | 3.91 × 3.31 | 130 | S-Cord, Fifth Ave V-8 |

## 1984

| Laser (wb 97.0) | | Wght | Price | Prod |
|---|---|---|---|---|
| GCH24 | htchbk cpe 3d | 2,525 | 8,648 | 33,976 |
| GCP24 | XE htchbk cpe 3d | 2,545 | 10,546 | 25,882 |
| **LeBaron (wb 100.3)** | | | | |
| KCP22 | cpe | 2,445 | 8,783 | 24,963 |
| KCP41 | sdn 4d | 2,495 | 9,067 | 47,664 |
| KCP27 | conv cpe | 2,530 | 11,595 | 6,828 |
| KCP27 | Mark Cross conv cpe | — | 15,495 | 8,275 |
| KCP27 | Mark Cross T&C conv cpe | — | 16,495 | 1,105 |
| KCP45 | Town & Country wgn 5d 2S | 2,665 | 9,856 | 11,578 |
| **E Class (wb 103.3)** | | | | |
| ETH41 | sdn 4d | 2,530 | 9,565 | 32,237 |
| **New Yorker (wb 103.3)** | | | | |
| ETP41 | sdn 4d | 2,675 | 12,179 | 60,501 |
| **Fifth Avenue (wb 112.7)** | | | | |
| MFS41 | sdn 4d | 3,660 | 13,990 | 79,441 |
| **Executive (wb 124.0; limo 131.0)** | | | | |
| KCP48 | sdn 4d | 2,945 | 18,975 | 196 |
| KCP49 | limo 4d | — | 21,975 | 594 |

| 1984 Engines | bore × stroke | bhp | availability |
|---|---|---|---|
| I-4, 135.0 | 3.44 × 3.62 | 99 | S-Laser, LeB, E Cl, NY |
| I-4T, 135.0 | 3.44 × 3.62 | 142 | O-Laser, LeB, E Cl, NY |
| I-4, 156.0 | 3.59 × 3.86 | 101 | S-Exec; O-LeB, E Cl, NY |
| V-8, 318.0 | 3.91 × 3.31 | 130 | S-Fifth Ave |

## 1985

| Laser (wb 97.0) | | Wght | Price | Prod |
|---|---|---|---|---|
| GCH24 | htchbk cpe 3d | 2,613 | 8,854 | 32,673 |
| GCP24 | XE htchbk cpe 3d | 2,665 | 10,776 | 18,193 |
| **LeBaron (wb 100.3)** | | | | |
| KCP22 | cpe | 2,533 | 9,460 | 24,970 |
| KCP41 | sdn 4d | 2,559 | 9,309 | 43,659 |
| KCP27 | conv cpe | 2,616 | 11,889 | 9,196 |
| KCP27 | Mark Cross conv cpe | — | 15,994 | 6,684 |
| KCP27 | Mark Cross T&C conv cpe | — | 16,994 | 595 |
| KCP45 | Town & Country wgn 5d 2S | 2,721 | 10,363 | 7,711 |
| **LeBaron GTS (wb 103.1)** | | | | |
| HCH44 | spt sdn 5d | 2,660 | 9,024 | 33,176 |
| HCP44 | LS spt sdn 5d | 2,706 | 9,970 | 27,607 |

# Chrysler

| New Yorker (wb 103.3) | Wght | Price | Prod |
|---|---|---|---|
| ETP41 sdn 4d | 2,583 | 12,865 | 60,700 |
| **Fifth Avenue (wb 112.7)** | | | |
| MFS41 sdn 4d | 3,741 | 13,978 | 109,971 |
| **Limousine (wb 131.3)** | | | |
| KCP49 limo 4d | 3,206 | 26,318 | 759 |

| 1985 Engines | bore × stroke | bhp | availability |
|---|---|---|---|
| I-4, 135.0 | 3.44 × 3.62 | 99 | S-Laser, LeB, GTS |
| I-4T, 135.0 | 3.44 × 3.62 | 146 | O-Laser, LeB, GTS, NY |
| I-4, 156.0 | 3.59 × 3.86 | 101 | S-NY, Limo; O-LeB |
| V-8, 318.0 | 3.91 × 3.31 | 140 | S-Fifth Ave |

## 1986

| Laser (wb 97.0) | Wght | Price | Prod |
|---|---|---|---|
| GCH24 htchbk cpe 3d | 2,547 | 9,364 | 21,123 |
| GCP24 XE htchbk cpe 3d | 2,599 | 11,501 | 8,560 |
| GCP24/AGB XT htchbk cpe 3d | 2,695 | 11,854 | 6,989 |
| **LeBaron (wb 100.3)** | | | |
| KCP22 cpe | 2,525 | 9,977 | 24,761 |
| KCP41 sdn 4d | 2,559 | 10,127 | 40,116 |
| KCP27 conv cpe | 2,625 | 12,695 | 12,578 |
| KCP27 Mark Cross conv cpe | 2,751 | 16,595 | 6,905 |
| KCP27 Mark Cross T&C conv cpe | 2,774 | 17,595 | 501 |
| KCP45 Town & Country wgn 5d 2S | 2,702 | 11,370 | 6,493 |
| **LeBaron GTS (wb 103.1)** | | | |
| HCH44 spt sdn 5d | 2,601 | 9,754 | 42,841 |
| HCP44 Premium spt sdn 5d | 2,647 | 11,437 | 30,716 |
| **New Yorker (wb 103.3)** | | | |
| ETP41 sdn 4d | 2,655 | 13,409 | 51,099 |
| **Fifth Avenue (wb 112.7)** | | | |
| MFS41 sdn 4d | 3,740 | 14,910 | 104,744 |
| **Limousine (wb 131.3)** | | | |
| KCP49 limo 4d | 3,206 | 27,495 | 138 |

| 1986 Engines | bore × stroke | bhp | availability |
|---|---|---|---|
| I-4, 135.0 | 3.44 × 3.62 | 97 | S-Laser, LeB, GTS |
| I-4T, 135.0 | 3.44 × 3.62 | 146 | S-Limo; O-Laser, LeBaron, GTS, NY |
| I-4, 153.0 | 3.44 × 4.09 | 100 | S-Laser XE, LeB T&C wgn, NY; O-Laser, LeB, GTS |
| V-8, 318.0 | 3.91 × 3.31 | 140 | S-Fifth Ave |

## 1987

| LeBaron (wb 100.3) | Wght | Price | Prod |
|---|---|---|---|
| JCH21 cpe | 2,690 | 11,295 | 44,124 |
| JCP21 Premium cpe | 2,731 | 12,288 | 31,291 |
| JCP27 conv cpe | 2,786 | 13,974 | 8,025 |
| KCP41 sdn 4d | 2,582 | 10,707 | 54,678 |
| KCP45 Town & Country wgn 5d 2S | 2,759 | 12,019 | 5,880 |
| **LeBaron GTS (wb 103.1)** | | | |
| HCH44 spt sdn 5d | 2,641 | 9,774 | 23,772 |
| HCP44 Premium spt sdn 5d | 2,709 | 11,389 | 15,278 |
| **New Yorker (wb 103.3)** | | | |
| ETP41 sdn 4d | 2,757 | 14,193 | 68,279 |
| **Fifth Avenue (wb 112.7)** | | | |
| MFS41 sdn 4d | 3,741 | 15,422 | 70,579 |

| 1987 Engines | bore × stroke | bhp | availability |
|---|---|---|---|
| I-4, 135.0 | 3.44 × 3.62 | 97 | S-LeB sdn, GTS |
| I-4T, 135.0 | 3.44 × 3.62 | 146 | S-limo; O-LeB, GTS, NY |
| I-4, 153.0 | 3.44 × 4.09 | 100 | S-LeBaron exc sdn, NY; O-GTS |
| V-8, 318.0 | 3.91 × 3.31 | 140 | S-Fifth Ave |

## 1988

| LeBaron (wb 100.3) | Wght | Price | Prod |
|---|---|---|---|
| JCH21 cpe | 2,769 | 11,473 | 38,733 |
| JCP21 Premium cpe | 2,875 | 13,830 | 9,938 |
| JCH27 conv cpe | 2,860 | 13,959 | 23,150 |
| JCP27 Premium conv cpe | 2,964 | 18,079 | 15,037 |
| KCP41 sdn 4d | 2,559 | 11,286 | 24,452 |
| KCP45 Town & Country wgn 5d 2S | 2,702 | 12,889 | 2,136 |
| **LeBaron GTS (wb 103.1)** | | | |
| HCH44 spt sdn 5d | 2,641 | 10,798 | 9,607 |
| HCP44 Premium spt sdn 5d | 2,709 | 12,971 | 4,604 |
| **New Yorker Turbo (103.3)** | | | |
| ETP41 sdn 4d | 2,826 | 17,373 | 8,805 |
| **New Yorker (wb 104.3)** | | | |
| CCH41 sdn 4d | 3,214 | 17,416 | 23,568 |
| CCS41 Landau sdn 4d | 3,276 | 19,509 | 47,400 |
| **Fifth Avenue (wb 112.7)** | | | |
| MFS41 sdn 4d | 3,759 | 17,243 | 43,486 |

| 1988 Engines | bore × stroke | bhp | availability |
|---|---|---|---|
| I-4, 135.0 | 3.44 × 3.62 | 97 | S-LeB sdn, GTS |
| I-4T, 135.0 | 3.44 × 3.62 | 146 | S-NY Turbo; O-LeB, GTS |
| I-4, 153.0 | 3.44 × 4.09 | 100 | S-LeBaron exc sdn |
| I-4, 153.0 | 3.44 × 4.09 | 96 | S-GTS Prem; O-GTS |
| V-6, 181.4 | 3.59 × 2.99 | 136 | S-NY |
| V-8, 318.0 | 3.91 × 3.31 | 140 | S-Fifth Ave |

## 1989

| LeBaron (wb 100.3)—99,633 built | Wght | Price | Prod |
|---|---|---|---|
| JCH21 Highline cpe | 2,810 | 11,495 | — |
| JCP21 Premium cpe | 2,945 | 14,695 | — |
| JCH27 conv cpe | 2,929 | 13,995 | — |
| JCP27 Premium conv cpe | 3,038 | 18,195 | — |
| JCH21 GT cpe | — | 14,795 | — |
| JCH27 GT conv cpe | — | 17,195 | — |
| JCH21 GTC turbo cpe | — | 17,435 | — |
| JCH27 GTC turbo conv cpe | — | 19,666 | — |
| **LeBaron Sedan (wb 103.1)—6,549 built** | | | |
| HCH44 htchbk spt sdn 5d | 2,714 | 11,495 | — |
| HCP44 Premium htchbk spt sdn 5d | 2,827 | 13,495 | — |
| HCX44 GTS turbo htchbk spt sdn 5d | 2,926 | 17,095 | — |
| **New Yorker (wb 104.3)** | | | |
| CCH41 sdn 4d | 3,214 | 17,416 | 100,461 |
| CCS41 Landau sdn 4d | 3,276 | 19,509 | |
| **Fifth Avenue (wb 112.6)** | | | |
| MFS41 sdn 4d | 3,741 | 18,345 | 17,454 |

| 1989 Engines | bore × stroke | bhp | availability |
|---|---|---|---|
| I-4, 135.0 | 3.44 × 3.62 | 93 | S-LeBaron sdn |
| I-4T 135.0 | 3.44 × 3.62 | 174 | S-LeB GTC, GTS |
| I-4, 153.0 | 3.44 × 4.09 | 100 | S-LeB cpe/conv, prem sdn; O-LeB Sdn |
| I-4T, 153.0 | 3.44 × 4.09 | 150 | O-LeB GTC/GTS |
| V-6, 181.4 | 3.59 × 2.99 | 140 | S-NY |
| V-8, 318.0 | 3.91 × 3.31 | 140 | S-Fifth Ave |

# Chrysler

## 1990

### LeBaron (wb 100.3)—65,220 built

| | | Wght | Price | Prod |
|---|---|---|---|---|
| JCH21 | Highline cpe | 2,810 | 12,495 | — |
| JCP21 | Premium cpe | 2,945 | 16,415 | — |
| JCH27 | conv cpe | 2,929 | 14,995 | — |
| JCP27 | Premium conv cpe | 3,038 | 19,595 | — |
| JCH21 | GT cpe | — | 15,725 | — |
| JCH27 | GT conv cpe | — | 17,799 | — |
| JCH21 | GTC cpe | — | 18,238 | — |
| JCH27 | GTC conv cpe | — | 20,406 | — |

### LeBaron Sedan (wb 103.3)

| | | Wght | Price | Prod |
|---|---|---|---|---|
| | sdn 4d | 2,854 | 15,995 | 8,074 |

### New Yorker (wb 104.3)

| | | Wght | Price | Prod |
|---|---|---|---|---|
| CCH41 | Salon sdn 4d | 3,066 | 16,395 | 41,581 |
| CCS41 | Landau sdn 4d | 3,276 | 18,795 | |

### New Yorker Fifth Avenue (wb 109.3)

| | Wght | Price | Prod |
|---|---|---|---|
| sdn 4d | 3,452 | 21,395 | 44,423 |

### Imperial (wb 109.3)

| | Wght | Price | Prod |
|---|---|---|---|
| sdn 4d | 3,570 | 24,995 | 14,968 |

### 1990 Engines

| | bore × stroke | bhp | availability |
|---|---|---|---|
| I-4T, 135.0 | 3.44 × 3.62 | 174 | S-LeBaron GTC |
| I-4, 153.0 | 3.44 × 4.09 | 100 | S-LeB cpe/conv |
| I-4T, 153.0 | 3.44 × 4.09 | 150 | O-LeBaron cpe/conv |
| V-6, 181.4 | 3.59 × 2.99 | 141 | S-LeB Sdn, LeB Prem/GT cpe/conv |
| V-6, 201.5 | 3.66 × 3.19 | 147 | S-Imperial, NY, NY 5th Ave |

## 1991

### LeBaron (wb 100.3)

| | | Wght | Price | Prod |
|---|---|---|---|---|
| JCH21 | cpe 2d | 2,853 | 12,995 | 7,770 |
| JCP21 | LX cpe 2d | — | 15,520 | |
| JCH21/GTC | GTC cpe 2d | — | 15,595 | |
| JCH27 | conv cpe 2d | 2,991 | 15,976 | 31,979 |
| JCP27 | LX conv cpe 2d | — | 19,226 | |
| JCH27/GTC | GTC conv cpe 2d | — | 18,151 | |

### LeBaron Sedan (wb 103.3)

| | Wght | Price | Prod |
|---|---|---|---|
| sdn 4d | 3,040 | 16,501 | 17,741 |

### New Yorker Salon (wb 104.5)

| | Wght | Price | Prod |
|---|---|---|---|
| sdn 4d | 3,348 | 17,971 | 14,337 |

### New Yorker Fifth Avenue (wb 109.3)

| | Wght | Price | Prod |
|---|---|---|---|
| sdn 4d | 3,452 | 20,875 | 40,892 |

### Imperial (wb 109.3)

| | Wght | Price | Prod |
|---|---|---|---|
| sdn 4d | 3,570 | 26,978 | 10,146 |

### 1991 Engines

| | bore × stroke | bhp | availability |
|---|---|---|---|
| I-4, 153.0 | 3.44 × 4.09 | 100 | S-LeBaron coupe/conv |
| I-4T, 153.0 | 3.44 × 4.09 | 152 | O-LeBaron coupe/conv |
| V-6, 181.4 | 3.59 × 2.99 | 141 | S-Lebaron Sedan; O-LeBaron coupe/conv |
| V-6, 201.5 | 3.66 × 3.19 | 147 | S-New Yorker Salon/Fifth Avenue |
| V-6, 230.5 | 3.78 × 3.42 | 150 | S-Imperial; O-New Yorker/Fifth Avenue |

## 1992

### LeBaron (wb 100.5)

| | | Wght | Price | Prod |
|---|---|---|---|---|
| JCH21 | cpe 2d | 2,863 | 13,488 | 5,595 |
| JCP21 | LX cpe 2d | — | 16,094 | |
| JCH21/GTP | GTC cpe 2d | — | 16,164 | |
| JCH27 | conv cpe 2d | 3,010 | 16,734 | 40,239 |
| JCP27 | LX conv cpe 2d | — | 20,130 | |
| JCH27/GTC | GTC conv cpe 2d | — | 18,985 | |

### LeBaron Sedan (wb 103.5)—33,854 blt

| | Wght | Price | Prod |
|---|---|---|---|
| sdn 4d | 2,972 | 13,998 | — |
| LX sdn 4d | — | 15,287 | — |
| Landau sdn 4d | — | 15,710 | — |

### New Yorker Salon (wb 104.5)

| | Wght | Price | Prod |
|---|---|---|---|
| sdn 4d | 3,346 | 18,849 | 17,231 |

### New Yorker Fifth Avenue (wb 109.5)

| | Wght | Price | Prod |
|---|---|---|---|
| sdn 4d | 3,425 | 21,874 | 34,349 |

### Imperial (wb 109.5)

| | Wght | Price | Prod |
|---|---|---|---|
| sdn 4d | 3,534 | 28,453 | 7,069 |

### 1992 Engines

| | bore × stroke | bhp | availability |
|---|---|---|---|
| I-4, 153.0 | 3.44 × 4.09 | 100 | S-all LeBaron |
| I-4T, 153.0 | 3.44 × 4.09 | 152 | O-LeBaron coupe/conv |
| V-6, 181.4 | 3.59 × 2.99 | 141 | O-all LeBaron |
| V-6, 201.5 | 3.66 × 3.19 | 147 | S-New Yorker Salon/Fifth Avenue |
| V-6, 230.5 | 3.78 × 3.42 | 150 | S-Imperial; O-Fifth Avenue |

## 1993

### LeBaron (wb 100.5 cpe, 100.6 conv)

| | | Wght | Price | Prod |
|---|---|---|---|---|
| JCH21 | cpe 2d | 2,863 | 13,999 | 6,460 |
| JCP21 | LX cpe 2d | — | 16,676 | |
| JCH21/GTP | GTC cpe 2d | — | 16,840 | |
| JCH27 | conv cpe 2d | 3,010 | 17,399 | 28,800 |
| JCP27 | LX conv cpe 2d | — | 21,165 | |
| JCH27/GTP | GTC conv cpe 2d | — | 19,815 | |

### LeBaron Sedan (wb 103.5)—29,454 built

| | Wght | Price | Prod |
|---|---|---|---|
| LE sdn 4d | 2,880 | 14,497 | — |
| Landau sdn 4d | 2,906 | 17,119 | — |

### New Yorker Salon (wb 104.5)

| | Wght | Price | Prod |
|---|---|---|---|
| sdn 4d | 3,273 | 18,705 | 22,323 |

### New Yorker Fifth Avenue (wb 109.6)

| | Wght | Price | Prod |
|---|---|---|---|
| sdn 4d | 3,365 | 21,948 | 29,805 |

### Imperial (wb 109.6)

| | Wght | Price | Prod |
|---|---|---|---|
| sdn 4d | 3,519 | 29,381 | 7,064 |

### Concorde (wb 113.0)

| | | Wght | Price | Prod |
|---|---|---|---|---|
| HLP41 | sdn 4d | 3,327 | 18,341 | 56,218 |

### 1993 Engines

| | bore × stroke | bhp | availability |
|---|---|---|---|
| I-4, 153.0 | 3.44 × 4.09 | 100 | S-all LeBaron |
| V-6, 181.4 | 3.59 × 2.99 | 141 | O-all LeBaron |
| V-6, 201.4 | 3.66 × 3.19 | 147 | S-NY Salon/Fifth Ave |
| V-6, 201.5 | 3.66 × 3.19 | 153 | S-Concorde |
| V-6, 214.7 | 3.78 × 3.19 | 214 | O-Concorde (ohc) |
| V-6, 230.5 | 3.78 × 3.42 | 150 | S-Imperial; O-New Yorker Fifth Avenue |

## 1994

### LeBaron (wb 100.6)

| | | Wght | Price | Prod |
|---|---|---|---|---|
| JCH27 | GTC conv cpe 2d | 3,122 | 16,999 | 37,844 |

### LeBaron Sedan (wb 103.5)—28,678 built

| | Wght | Price | Prod |
|---|---|---|---|
| LE sdn 4d | 2,971 | 16,551 | — |

# Chrysler

| LeBaron (wb 100.6) | Wght | Price | Prod |
|---|---|---|---|
| Landau sdn 4d | — | 17,993 | — |
| **Concorde (wb 113.0)** | | | |
| HLP41 sdn 4d | 3,379 | 19,457 | 85,636 |
| **New Yorker/LHS (wb 113.0)** | | | |
| HCH41 New Yorker sdn 4d | 3,457 | 25,386 | 34,283 |
| HCP41 LHS sdn 4d | 3,483 | 30,283 | 49,335 |

| 1994 Engines | bore × stroke | bhp | availability |
|---|---|---|---|
| V-6, 181.4 | 3.59 × 2.99 | 141 | S-LeBaron conv |
| V-6, 181.4 | 3.59 × 2.99 | 142 | S-LeBaron Sedan |
| V-6, 201.5 | 3.66 × 3.19 | 161 | S-Concorde |
| V-6, 214.7 | 3.78 × 3.19 | 214 | S-New Yorker, LHS; O-Concorde (ohc) |

## 1995

| LeBaron (100.6 conv) | Wght | Price | Prod |
|---|---|---|---|
| JCH27 GTC conv cpe 2d | 3,122 | 17,469 | 36,227 |
| **Sebring (wb 103.7)—20,611 built** | | | |
| JCS22 LX cpe 2d | 2,816 | 15,434 | — |
| JCP22 LXi cpe 2d | 2,980 | 19,029 | — |
| **Cirrus (wb 108.0)—79,275 built** | | | |
| ACP41 LX sdn 4d | 3,145 | 17,435 | — |
| ACP41/K LXi sdn 4d | — | 19,365 | — |
| **Concorde (wb 113.0)** | | | |
| HLP41 sdn 4d | 3,376 | 20,550 | 60,613 |
| **New Yorker/LHS (wb 113.0)** | | | |
| HCH41 New Yorker sdn 4d | 3,592 | 25,596 | 23,624 |
| HCP41 LHS sdn 4d | 3,628 | 29,595 | 32,002 |

| 1995 Engines | bore × stroke | bhp | availability |
|---|---|---|---|
| I-4, 121.8 | 3.44 × 3.27 | 140 | S-Sebring (dohc) |
| V-6, 152.3 | 3.29 × 2.99 | 155 | O-Sebring (ohc) |
| V-6, 152.3 | 3.29 × 2.99 | 164 | S-Cirrus (ohc) |
| V-6, 181.4 | 3.59 × 2.99 | 141 | S-LeBaron |
| V-6, 201.5 | 3.66 × 3.19 | 161 | S-Concorde |
| V-6, 214.7 | 3.78 × 3.19 | 214 | S-New Yorker, LHS; O-Concorde (ohc) |

## 1996

| Sebring (wb cpe 103.7, conv 106) | Wght | Price | Prod |
|---|---|---|---|
| JCS22 LX cpe 2d | 2,908 | 16,441 | 32,527 |
| JCP22 LXi cpe 2d | 3,157 | 20,150 | |
| XCH27 JX conv cpe 2d | 3,340 | 19,490 | 47,809 |
| XCP27 JXi conv cpe 2d | 3,432 | 24,675 | |
| **Cirrus (wb 108.0)** | | | |
| ACP41 LX sdn 4d | 3,148 | 17,560 | 43,367 |
| ACP41/K LXi sdn 4d | 3,153 | 20,430 | |
| **Concorde (wb 113.0)** | | | |
| HLP41 LX sdn 4d | 3,492 | 19,445 | 49,994 |
| HLP41 LXi sdn 4d | — | 24,100 | |
| **New Yorker (wb 113.0)** | | | |
| HCH41 sdn 4d | 3,587 | 27,300 | 3,295 |

| LHS (wb 113.0) | Wght | Price | Prod |
|---|---|---|---|
| HCP41 sdn 4d | 3,596 | 30,255 | 34,900 |

| 1996 Engines | bore × stroke | bhp | availability |
|---|---|---|---|
| I-4, 121.8 | 3.44 × 3.27 | 140 | S-Sebring cpe |
| I-4, 148.2 | 3.44 × 3.98 | 150 | S-Cirrus, Sebring conv |
| V-6, 152.3 | 3.29 × 2.99 | 163 | O-Sebring cpe |
| V-6, 152.3 | 3.29 × 2.99 | 168 | O-Cirrus, Sebring conv |
| V-6, 201.5 | 3.66 × 3.19 | 161 | S-Concorde |
| V-6, 214.7 | 3.78 × 3.19 | 214 | S-New Yorker, LHS; O-Concorde |

## 1997

| Sebring (wb cpe 103.7, conv 106) | Wght | Price | Prod |
|---|---|---|---|
| JCS22 LX cpe 2d | 2,888 | 16,540 | 33,140 |
| JCP22 LXi cpe 2d | 3,197 | 21,020 | |
| XCH27 JX conv cpe 2d | 3,350 | 20,150 | 55,887 |
| XCP27 JXi conv cpe 2d | 3,365 | 24,660 | |
| **Cirrus (wb 108.0)** | | | |
| ACP41 LX sdn 4d | 3,099 | 18,030 | 27,913 |
| ACP41/K LXi sdn 4d | — | 20,365 | |
| **Concorde (wb 113.0)** | | | |
| HLP41 LX sdn 4d | 3,468 | 20,435 | 50,913 |
| HLP41 LXi sdn 4d | — | 24,665 | |
| **LHS (wb 113.0)** | | | |
| HCP41 sdn 4d | 3,625 | 30,255 | 36,525 |

| 1997 Engines | bore × stroke | bhp | availability |
|---|---|---|---|
| I-4, 121.8 | 3.44 × 3.27 | 140 | S-Sebring cpe |
| I-4, 148.2 | 3.44 × 3.98 | 150 | S-Cirrus, Sebring conv |
| V-6, 152.3 | 3.29 × 2.99 | 163 | O-Sebring cpe |
| V-6, 152.3 | 3.29 × 2.99 | 168 | O-Cirrus, Sebring conv |
| V-6, 214.7 | 3.78 × 3.19 | 214 | S-LHS, Concorde |

## 1998

| Sebring (wb cpe 103.7, conv 106) | Wght | Price | Prod |
|---|---|---|---|
| JCS22 LX cpe 2d | 2,888 | 16,840 | 35,010 |
| JCP22 LXi cpe 2d | 3,197 | 20,775 | |
| XCH27 JX conv cpe 2d | 3,344 | 20,575 | 50,814 |
| XCP27 JXi conv cpe 2d | 3,406 | 25,840 | |
| **Cirrus (wb 108.0)** | | | |
| ACP41 LXi sdn 4d | 3,181 | 19,460 | 37,290 |
| **Concorde (wb 113.0)** | | | |
| HLP41 LX sdn 4d | 3,451 | 21,305 | 46,535 |
| HLP41 LXi sdn 4d | 3,531 | 24,220 | |

| 1998 Engines | bore × stroke | bhp | availability |
|---|---|---|---|
| I-4, 121.8 | 3.44 × 3.27 | 140 | S-Sebring cpe |
| I-4, 148.2 | 3.44 × 3.98 | 150 | S-Sebring conv |
| V-6, 152.3 | 3.29 × 2.99 | 163 | O-Sebring cpe |
| V-6, 152.3 | 3.29 × 2.99 | 168 | S-Cirrus; O-Sebring conv |
| V-6, 167.0 | 3.38 × 3.09 | 200 | S-Concorde |
| V-6, 197.0 | 3.62 × 3.19 | 225 | O-Concorde |

# Chrysler

## 1999

### Sebring (wb cpe 103.7, conv 106.0)

|  | Wght | Price | Prod* |
|---|---|---|---|
| JCS22 LX cpe 2d | 2,967 | 17,225 | 24,859 |
| JCP22 LXi cpe 2d | 3,203 | 21,325 | |
| XCH27 JX conv cpe 2d | 3,331 | 23,970 | 55,206 |
| XCP27 JXi conv cpe 2d | 3,382 | 26,285 | |

### Cirrus (wb 108.0)

| | Wght | Price | Prod* |
|---|---|---|---|
| ACP41 LXi sdn 4d | 3,146 | 19,460 | 49,526 |

### Concorde (wb 113.0)—61,403 built

| | Wght | Price | Prod* |
|---|---|---|---|
| HLP41 LX sdn 4d | 3,446 | 21,510 | — |
| HLP41 LXi sdn 4d | 3,556 | 25,235 | — |

### 300M (wb 113.0)

| | Wght | Price | Prod* |
|---|---|---|---|
| HYS41 sdn 4d | 3,567 | 28,700 | 75,191 |

### LHS (wb 113.0)

| | Wght | Price | Prod* |
|---|---|---|---|
| HCP41 sdn 4d | 3,689 | 28,700 | 27,720 |

### 1999 Engines

| | bore × stroke | bhp | availability |
|---|---|---|---|
| I-4, 121.8 | 3.44 × 3.27 | 140 | S-Sebring cpe |
| V-6, 152.3 | 3.29 × 2.99 | 163 | O-Sebring cpe |
| V-6, 152.3 | 3.29 × 2.99 | 168 | S-Cirrus, Sebring conv |
| V-6, 167.0 | 3.38 × 3.09 | 200 | S-Concorde |
| V-6, 197.0 | 3.62 × 3.19 | 225 | O-Concorde |
| V-6, 215.0 | 3.78 × 3.19 | 253 | S-300M, LHS |

## 2000

### Sebring (wb cpe 103.7, conv 106)

| | Wght | Price | Prod* |
|---|---|---|---|
| JCS22 LX cpe 2d | 3,155 | 19,765 | 33,778 |
| JCP22 LXi cpe 2d | 3,203 | 22,100 | |
| XCH27 JX conv cpe 2d | 3,440 | 24,245 | 38,361 |
| XCP27 JXi conv cpe 2d | 3,444 | 26,560 | |

### Cirrus (wb 108.0)

| | Wght | Price | Prod* |
|---|---|---|---|
| ACH41 LX sdn 4d | 2,911 | 16,230 | 40,241 |
| ACP41 LXi sdn 4d | 3,168 | 20,085 | |

### Concorde (wb 113.0)

| | Wght | Price | Prod* |
|---|---|---|---|
| HLP41 LX sdn 4d | 3,452 | 22,145 | 72,352** |
| HLP41 LXi sdn 4d | 3,532 | 26,385 | |

### 300M (wb 113.0)

| | Wght | Price | Prod* |
|---|---|---|---|
| HYS41 sdn 4d | 3,567 | 29,085 | 57,933 |

### LHS (wb 113.0)

| | Wght | Price | Prod* |
|---|---|---|---|
| HCP41 sdn 4d | 3,564 | 28,240 | — |

### 2000 Engines

| | bore × stroke | bhp | availability |
|---|---|---|---|
| I-4, 121.8 | 3.44 × 3.27 | 140 | S-Cirrus |
| V-6, 152.3 | 3.29 × 2.99 | 163 | S-Sebring cpe |
| V-6, 152.3 | 3.29 × 2.99 | 168 | S-Sebring conv; O-Cirrus |
| V-6, 167.0 | 3.38 × 3.09 | 200 | S-Concorde |
| V-6, 197.0 | 3.62 × 3.19 | 225 | O-Concorde |
| V-6, 215.0 | 3.78 × 3.19 | 253 | S-300M, LHS |

*Calendar year production, **Includes LHS

## 2001

### Sebring (wb cpe 103.7, conv 106.0, sdn 108.0)

| | Wght | Price | Prod* |
|---|---|---|---|
| TCS22 LX cpe 2d | 3,155 | 19,910 | 82,108 |
| TCP22 LXi cpe 2d | 3,204 | 21,475 | |
| RCH41 LX sdn 4d | 3,250 | 17,945 | |
| RCP41 LXi sdn 4d | — | 20,830 | |
| RCH27 JX conv cpe 2d | 3,489 | 24,370 | 50,587 |
| RCP27 JXi conv cpe 2d | — | 26,830 | |
| RCS27 Limited conv cpe 2d | — | 28,915 | |

### Concorde (wb 113.0)

| | Wght | Price | Prod* |
|---|---|---|---|
| HCH41 LX sdn 4d | 3,449 | 22,510 | 72,352** |
| HCM41 LXi sdn 4d | 3,548 | 26,755 | |

### 300M (wb 113.0)

| | Wght | Price | Prod* |
|---|---|---|---|
| HYS41 sdn 4d | 3,574 | 29,640 | 37,098 |

### LHS (wb 113.0)

| | Wght | Price | Prod* |
|---|---|---|---|
| HCP41 sdn 4d | 3,557 | 28,680 | — |

### 2001 Engines

| | bore × stroke | bhp | availability |
|---|---|---|---|
| I-4, 143.4 | 3.41 × 3.94 | 142 | S-Sebring cpe |
| I-4, 148.2 | 3.44 × 3.98 | 150 | S-Sebring conv, Sebring sdn |
| V-6, 167.0 | 3.38 × 3.09 | 200 | S-Concorde; O-Sebring sdn, Sebring conv |
| V-6, 181.4 | 3.59 × 2.99 | 200 | O-Sebring cpe |
| V-6, 197.0 | 3.62 × 3.19 | 222 | O-Concorde |
| V-6, 215.0 | 3.78 × 3.19 | 253 | S-300M, LHS |

*Calendar year production, **Includes LHS

## 2002

### Sebring (wb cpe 103.7, conv 106.0, sdn 108.0)

| | Wght | Price | Prod* |
|---|---|---|---|
| TCS22 LX cpe 2d | 3,099 | 20,020 | — |
| TCP22 LXi cpe 2d | 3,183 | 21,710 | — |
| RCH27 LX conv cpe 2d | 3,394 | 23,075 | — |
| RCP27 LXi conv cpe 2d | 3,474 | 26,160 | — |
| RCX27 GTC conv cpe 2d | 3,452 | 25,115 | — |
| RCS27 Limited conv cpe 2d | 3,491 | 28,795 | — |
| RCH41 LX sdn 4d | 3,201 | 17,705 | — |
| RCP41 LXi sdn 4d | 3,273 | 20,280 | — |

### Concorde (wb 113.0)

| | Wght | Price | Prod* |
|---|---|---|---|
| HCH41 LX sdn 4d | 3,479 | 22,370 | — |
| HCM41 LXi sdn 4d | 3,548 | 24,975 | — |
| HCP41 Limited sdn 4d | 3,567 | 27,870 | — |

### 300M (wb 113.0)

| | Wght | Price | Prod* |
|---|---|---|---|
| HYS41 sdn 4d | 3,581 | 28,340 | — |
| HYX41 Special sdn 4d | 3,650 | 31,940 | — |

### Prowler (wb 113.3)

| | Wght | Price | Prod* |
|---|---|---|---|
| RCS27 conv cpe 2d | 2,864 | 44,625 | — |

### 2002 Engines

| | bore × stroke | bhp | availability |
|---|---|---|---|
| I-4, 143.4 | 3.41 × 3.94 | 142 | S-Sebring cpe |
| I-4, 148.2 | 3.44 × 3.98 | 150 | S-Sebring conv, Sebring sdn |
| V-6, 167.0 | 3.38 × 3.09 | 200 | S-Concorde; O-Sebring sdn, Sebring conv |
| V-6, 181.4 | 3.59 × 2.99 | 200 | O-Sebring cpe |
| V-6, 215.0 | 3.78 × 3.19 | 234 | O-Concorde |
| V-6, 215.0 | 3.78 × 3.19 | 250 | O-Concorde |
| V-6, 215.0 | 3.78 × 3.19 | 253 | S-300M, Prowler |

*Production figures not available at time of publication.

# Continental

Officially, the Continental "Marks" of 1956-58 were not Lincolns but the products of a separate division created to establish Ford Motor Company at the very top of the market—even above Cadillac. Only one model was offered for 1956-57: the flawlessly styled, beautifully crafted Mark II, worth every penny of its stratospheric $10,000 price. Yet Ford lost about $1000 on every one, because this was primarily an "image" car—more ego trip than calculated profit-maker. Dearborn then attempted to put Continental in the black with a lower-priced 1958-60 line based on the giant "unibody" Lincoln of those years, but it never sold particularly well.

Dealers and customers had pleaded with Ford to revive the Lincoln Continental since the last of the original line in 1948. But there was no money until 1953, when profits were looking up and Dearborn managers, determined to outflank arch-rival General Motors in every market sector, approved a development program to create a new Continental in the contemporary idiom.

This came under the auspices of a new Special Products Division headed by William Clay Ford, the younger brother of company president Henry Ford II. After calling in five outside consultants, management reviewed 13 different proposals and unanimously selected the one submitted by Special Products.

It was, nevertheless, an excellent choice. Harley F. Copp, Special Products' chief engineer, gave it a unique "cowbelly" chassis dipped low between the front and rear axles to permit high seating without a high roofline. The cabin was thus roomy, as well as starkly simple but also richly appointed in fine broadcloth and nylon or Scottish "Bridge of Weir" leather. The dash echoed locomotive and aircraft motifs with full, brushed-finished instrumentation and large toggle-type switches.

Chosen power was the 368-cubic-inch V-8 destined for the all-new '56 Lincolns, with the same 285 horsepower. However, Mark II units were specially selected and individually adjusted before installation. The same applied to the transmission, Lincoln's three-speed Turbo-Drive automatic, also new for '56, and the 3.07:1 rear axle.

Actually, great pains were taken throughout the assembly process, as Mark IIs were built in a special "go-slow" plant. Bodies, for instance, were first trial-fitted to chassis, then painted, sanded, and polished by hand. Chrome plating exceeded industry standards. Nuts and bolts were torqued by people, not machines. Finally, each car was given a 12-mile preshipment road test, followed by a detailed inspection and correction of any defects.

Appearing on a 126-inch wheelbase, the sleek and timeless Mark II measured 218.5 inches overall and weighed over 4800 pounds. It came only as a hardtop coupe, though the original plan was for a retractable hardtop-convertible (an idea quickly evolved by Ford Division into the 1957-59 Skyliner). The price may have been breathtaking, but it reflected the unusual amount of hand labor and high luxury content. Indeed, air conditioning was the sole option ($740).

The Mark II bowed to thunderous applause from both sides of the Atlantic, and was immediately hailed as a design landmark. But the euphoria didn't last. The Mark II made little impression on the ultra-luxury market. Production came to approximately 2500 of the '56s and a mere 444 of the near-identical '57s. With that, Ford canceled not only the Mark II, but also a beautiful four-door sedan and a convertible that were planned as 1958 "line extensions" (though not before a couple of prototype convertibles were built in 1957).

Years later, one Ford executive declared the Mark II was, on balance, a big mistake. "What we had going for us . . . was liter-

**1956 Mark II hardtop coupe**

# Continental

**1958 Mark III convertible coupe**

ally a revival of the Duesenberg concept. What we ended up with was something much less—and even that didn't last long. It was a project that for a time broke Bill Ford's heart, and I guess you could say that in many ways it broke ours, too."

In line with an upper-management decision, price was cut drastically for 1958's "new" Continental, the Mark III. The result of recommendations from a Mercury cost analyst, this square-rigged Lincoln-based leviathan had a 131-inch wheelbase, elongated fenders, large chrome appliques, canted quad headlamps, a reverse-slant roofline, and a huge new 430-cid V-8 with 375 horsepower. Convertible, four-door sedan, hardtop coupe, and Landau hardtop sedan were offered in the $5800-$6200 range. Closed models sported a rear window that dropped down electrically for flow-through interior ventilation. Standard luxuries abounded once more, but not hand craftsmanship. The Mark III was "built to a price," and those reduced prices increased sales to 12,550 cars—respectable for that difficult, recessionary model year.

But the luxury market had shriveled badly, so Ford canceled Continental as a separate marque after 1958, though a little-changed Mark III returned in the Lincoln line as the 1959 Mark IV. Continental Division was folded into Lincoln-Mercury, which also absorbed the fast-faltering Edsel Division, thus ending Ford's dream of a GM-like five-division hierarchy.

A decade later came a new Mark III, so numbered to signal its "official" status as the Mark II's lineal successor. This was never anything but a Lincoln, however. Also unlike its forebear, it was an immediate sales success. (See Lincoln for the Continental story before and after 1956-58.)

**1958 Mark III Landau hardtop sedan**

## Specifications

### 1956

| Mark II (wb 126.0) | | Wght | Price | Prod |
|---|---|---|---|---|
| 60A | htp cpe | 4,825 | 9,695 | 2,556 |

| 1956 Engine | bore × stroke | bhp | availability |
|---|---|---|---|
| V-8, 368.0 | 4.00 × 3.66 | 285 | S-all |

### 1957

| Mark II (wb 126.0) | | Wght | Price | Prod |
|---|---|---|---|---|
| 60A | htp cpe | 4,800 | 9,966 | 444 |

| 1957 Engine | bore × stroke | bhp | availability |
|---|---|---|---|
| V-8, 368.0 | 4.00 × 3.66 | 300 | S-all |

### 1958

| Mark III (wb 131.0) | | Wght | Price | Prod |
|---|---|---|---|---|
| 54A | sdn 4d | 4,800 | 6,072 | 1,283 |
| 65A | htp cpe | 4,865 | 5,825 | 2,328 |
| 68A | conv cpe | 5,040 | 6,283 | 3,048 |
| 75A | Landau htp sdn | 4,965 | 6,072 | 5,891 |

| 1958 Engine | bore × stroke | bhp | availability |
|---|---|---|---|
| V-8, 430.0 | 4.30 × 3.70 | 375 | S-all |

# Cord

It's been said that one can avoid criticism only by saying nothing, doing nothing, and being nothing. Errett Lobban Cord avoided those pitfalls and was criticized a lot. He jumped from car salesman in 1924, to president and chief stockholder of Auburn in 1926. At age 31, he was the youngest president of an American automaker. By the early '30s he'd also acquired Duesenberg and many other enterprises. His method was only too clear: dump large amounts of common stock until its value was so low that he could buy controlling shares for a song. Cord's empire included aviation, shipping, taxicabs, among other interests. While distracted by these other ventures, Cord's auto companies suffered. Heavy losses forced Cord to sell his holdings in 1937. Auto production was the first to be shut down by the new owners. Some enthusiasts have never really forgiven him for that.

During 10 years of wheeler-dealer success, E.L. Cord was behind some of the most-magnificent cars ever built. In 1928, he ushered in the beautiful Auburn Speedster. The following year introduced the mighty Duesenberg Model J and the Cord L-29. The last proved less than hoped for, but it led to the 1936-37 Cord 810/812, one of the most-memorable and influential cars of all time.

The unbridled optimism of the late '20s prompted many new models and a few new makes to fill specific market niches. E.L. Cord decided to fill the price gap between his eight-cylinder Auburns and exotic Duesenbergs with a rakish new car bearing his own name and the then-novel feature of front-wheel drive.

The resulting L-29 was chiefly engineered by race-car builder Harry Miller and one Cornelius Van Ranst, both avid proponents of "horse-pulls-cart." Its powerplant began as the 298.6-cubic-inch Auburn straight eight, but ended up quite different. For the Cord's front drive it had to be mounted backward so that clutch and transmission could face forward. The cylinder head was altered to put the water outlet up front, and the crankcase was modified for a rear engine mount. According to one Cord authority, the L-29 engine had over 70 unique parts. Advertised at 125 horsepower, its actual output was 115 until 1932 when a larger bore increased horsepower to a truthful 125.

Sending its power to the front wheels was a three-speed sliding-pinion gearbox mounted behind the differential as on a Miller-designed 1927 Indianapolis racer. Brakes were unusual, mounted inboard. Quarter-elliptic leaf springs appeared fore, semielliptics aft, Houdaille-Hershey shock absorbers all around. Driveshafts employed premium Cardan constant-velocity universal joints.

This layout was not without problems. The main one was excessive drivetrain length that dictated a tremendous 137.5-inch wheelbase, yet put more than half of the car's weight over the rear wheels—where it did nothing for traction on hills, icy roads, or gravel surfaces. Worse, the U-joints couldn't stand braking, plus the pounding of wheels that drove as well as steered, and they wore out with merciless frequency. Though these problems could have been licked with time, Cord was adamant that the car debut before 1930 (which it did, though only by six months).

But, oh, what that layout did for looks. The super-long front allowed Auburn chief designer Al Leamy (with help from body engineer John Oswald) to craft a flowing hood/fenders ensemble that only accented that impressive length and the lowness conferred by front-wheel drive. Capping the front end was a sheetmetal grille completely enclosing the radiator—an industry first. In all, the L-29 looked sensational in its four "factory" body types: sedan, brougham, phaeton, and cabriolet, all supplied by subsidiary Cord companies. Numerous celebrities bought L-29s, and coachbuilders at home and abroad created stunning custom bodies. Standard models were fairly priced in the $3100-$3300 range, so the L-29 should have been a success.

It wasn't. Even without the poor traction and U-joint woes, front drive was an unproven commodity and thus a tough sell in the conservative $3000 market. And late 1929 was hardly the best time to launch any car, what with Wall Street types launching themselves out of windows. Furthermore, compared to contemporary Packards, Lincolns, and Cadillacs, the L-29 was a slug. Its 0-60 time was around 25 seconds, top speed barely 75 mph. One writer euphemistically termed this "pleasant tepidity," and it was almost excusable given the brilliant styling.

But there was no way the L-29 could make money. It thus limped along through 1932 with virtually no changes. Total production came to 5010. By 1935, one used-car guide listed the cash value of the L-29 convertible at just $145. Although a fail-

**1930 L-29 convertible sedan**

# Cord

**1930 L-29 Cabriolet 2/4-passenger**

**1937 812 Cabriolet**

▲ 1967 Chevrolet Corvette Sting Ray coupe ▼ 1991 Chevrolet Corvette convertible

▲ 2001 Chevrolet Corvette convertible

▼ 1931 Chrysler Deluxe Series 8 roadster

▲ 1947 Chrysler Town and Country four-door sedan ▼ 1956 Chrysler New Yorker St. Regis two-door hardtop

▲ 1971 Chrysler 300 four-door hardtop ▼ 2002 Chrysler PT Cruiser wagon

▲ 1956 Lincoln Continental Mark II coupe ▼ 1931 Cord L-29 convertible sedan

325

▲ 1937 Cord 812 Supercharged Phaeton convertible ▼ 1947 Crosley pickup truck

▲ 1939 DeSoto S-6 Custom club coupe ▼ 1956 DeSoto Fireflite four-door hardtop

▲ 1934 Dodge convertible coupe

▼ 1948 Dodge Custom convertible

▲ 1957 Dodge Custom Royal Lancer four-door hardtop

▼ 1968 Dodge Charger two-door hardtop

▲ 1970 Dodge Challenger R/T convertible ▼ 1974 Dodge Monaco four-door sedan police car

▲ 2003 Dodge Viper RT/10 convertible ▼ 1930 Duesenberg J convertible sedan

▲ 1930 Duesenberg J two-door convertible   ▼ 1936 Duesenberg SSJ roadster

▲ 1989 Eagle Premier four-door sedan　　　▼ 1958 Edsel Bermuda four-door station wagon

333

▲ 1959 Edsel Corsair convertible

▼ 1960 Edsel Villager four-door station wagon

▲ 1984 Excalibur Series IV roadster ▼ 1985 Excalibur Series IV convertible

▲ 1932 Ford Deluxe roadster

▼ 1940 Ford Deluxe convertible

# Cord

ure in its time, the L-29 has since been widely appreciated—including certification as a Classic by the Classic Car Club of America.

After three years in limbo, the Cord name returned in 1936 on a dashing and predictive new car, the 810. This model retained front-wheel drive, but with a big difference. Where the L-29 had

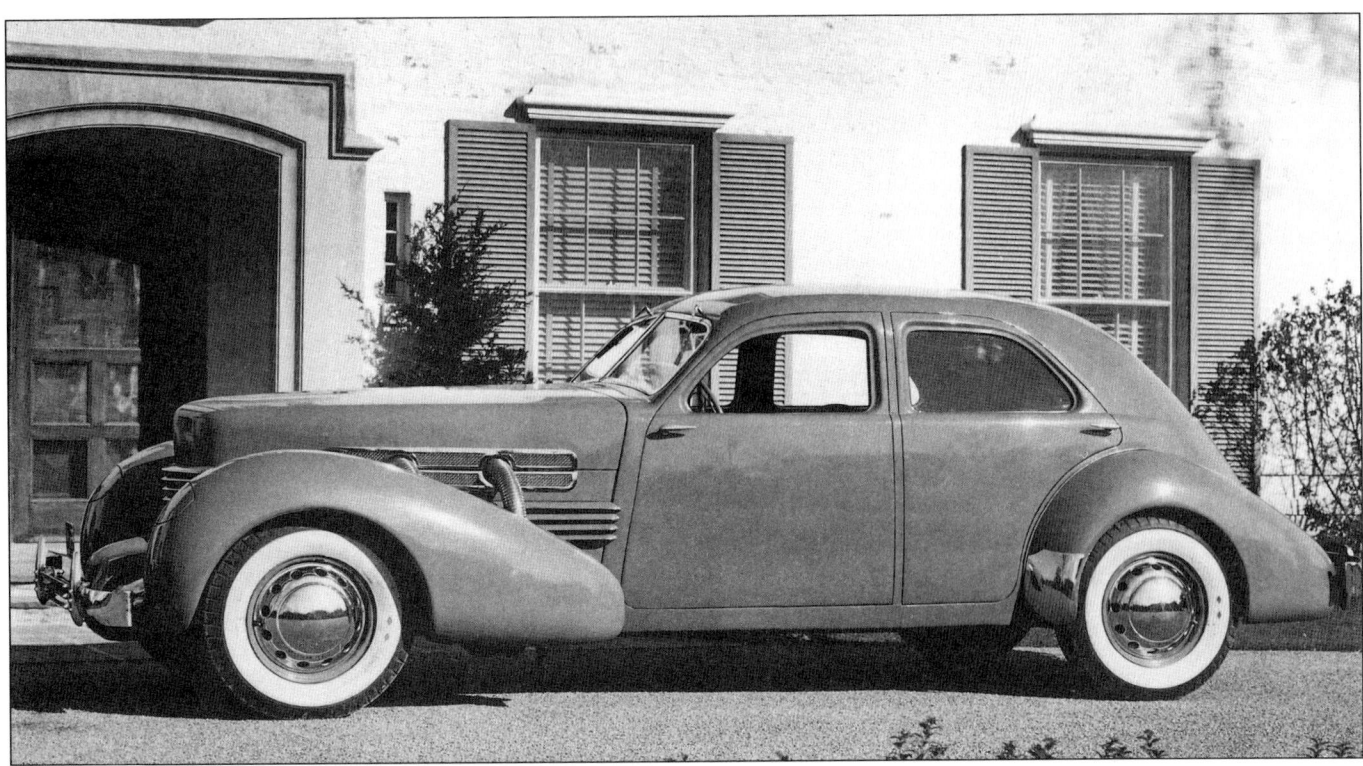

**1937 812 Supercharged Westchester sedan**

**1937 812 Phaeton convertible**

a long straight eight behind the transmission and mounted both far behind the front axle, the 810 used a V-8 that was half as long and could thus sit just aft of the axle; its differential/clutch assembly extended forward to the transmission, which was located slightly ahead of the axle. The results were much better weight distribution and traction than in the L-29, abetted by a trimmer 125-inch wheelbase.

Advanced features abounded in the 810. Front suspension, for instance, comprised independent trailing arms joined by a single transverse leaf spring. The transmission had four forward ratios instead of the usual three, plus Bendix "Electric Hand" preselector. With this, you first chose the desired gear via a switchlike lever on an extension of the steering column, then shifted by stabbing the clutch.

The 810 V-8 was a 288.6-cid unit made by Lycoming, another of Cord's companies. This packed 125 horsepower, which was good, but an available Schwitzer-Cummins centrifugal supercharger (similar to late Auburns) swelled that to an eye-opening 170. The total was soon 190 via a higher-boost blower. Standard 810s would reach 90 mph and run 0-60 in 20 seconds. The supercharged version would do 110 mph and hit 60 in 11-13 seconds—one of the fastest production cars in prewar America.

But performance seems almost secondary next to 810 styling, the work of Gordon Buehrig, assisted by Dale Cosper, Dick Robertson, and Paul Laurenzen. Initially conceived for a stillborn "baby Duesenberg," it was unforgettable: smoothly formed "coffin-nose" hood, striking wraparound horizontal louvers instead of a radiator, minimal trim, pontoon fenders, and, on blown models, racy exposed exhaust pipes. Concealed headlamps flipped up when needed (via manual cranks)—another industry first. Equally futuristic for the time were a unit-body construction, front-opening hood, separate license-plate light, full wheel covers, and concealed gas cap. Inside were a turned-metal dash awash in needle gauges and a ceiling-mounted radio speaker (sedans). Amazingly, Buehrig cobbled up many appearance items from proprietary bits and pieces, including some Auburn leftovers.

Like the L-29, the 810 bowed with four models: Westchester and Beverly sedans (upholstery patterns were the main difference) and two-seat Cabriolet and four-passenger Phaeton Sedan convertibles. Prices, however, were much lower: as little as $2000. Prices were hiked some $500 for 1937's little-changed 812 line, which added two long sedans on a 132-inch wheelbase, the Custom Beverly and Custom Berline, priced at $2,960-$3,575.

Sadly, the 810/812 had even more problems than the L-29. This reflected the fast-fading fortunes of the Cord Corporation that dictated a shoestring budget, cost-cutting engineering in places, and too much hand labor for consistent or even good build quality. Not that any of this mattered in the end. E.L. Cord's empire collapsed in 1937, and the Cord automobile followed Auburn and Duesenberg down the road to oblivion.

Though the L-29 was long ignored by collectors, the 810/812 began appreciating in value almost immediately after production ended (at 1629/1278 units). As with Duesenberg Js and Auburn Speedsters, peerless styling would be a motivation for several postwar revival attempts and shoddy replicas, but none would have even the original's modest success.

## Specifications

### 1930—1,700 registered

| L29 (wb 137.5) | Wght | Price | Prod |
|---|---|---|---|
| cabriolet 2-4P | 4,300 | 3,295 | — |
| sdn 4d 5P | 4,530 | 3,095 | — |
| phaeton sdn 5P | 4,500 | 3,295 | — |
| brougham 5P | 4,500 | 3,095 | — |

| 1930 Engine | bore × stroke | bhp | availability |
|---|---|---|---|
| I-8, 298.6 | 3.25 × 4.50 | 125 | S-all |

### 1931—1,433 built

| L29 (wb 137.5) | Wght | Price | Prod |
|---|---|---|---|
| cabriolet 2-4P | 4,300 | 2,495 | — |
| sdn 4d 5P | 4,530 | 2,395 | — |
| phaeton sdn 5P | 4,500 | 2,595 | — |
| brougham 5P | 4,500 | 2,395 | — |

| 1931 Engine | bore × stroke | bhp | availability |
|---|---|---|---|
| I-8, 298.6 | 3.25 × 4.50 | 125 | all |

### 1932—335 registered*

| L29 (wb 137.5) | Wght | Price | Prod |
|---|---|---|---|
| cabriolet 2-4P | 4,300 | 2,495 | — |
| sdn 4d 5P | 4,560 | 2,395 | — |
| phaeton sdn 5P | 4,500 | 2,595 | — |
| brougham 5P | 4,560 | 2,395 | — |

| 1932 Engine | bore × stroke | bhp | availability |
|---|---|---|---|
| I-8, 322.0 | 3.38 × 4.50 | 125 | all |

*Total L29 production 5,010; began in 1929.

### 1936—1,629 built*

| 810 (wb 125.0) | Wght | Price | Prod |
|---|---|---|---|
| Westchester sdn 4d | 3,715 | 1,995 | — |
| Beverly sdn 4d | 3,740 | 2,095 | — |
| cabriolet | 3,815 | 2,145 | — |
| phaeton | 3,864 | 2,195 | — |

| 1936 Engine | bore × stroke | bhp | availability |
|---|---|---|---|
| V-8, 288.6 | 3.50 × 3.75 | 125 | S-all |

### 1937

| 812 (wb 125.0; Custom-132.0) | Wght | Price | Prod |
|---|---|---|---|
| Westchester sdn 4d | 3,715 | 2,445 | |
| Beverly sdn 4d | 3,800 | 2,545 | |
| cabriolet | 3,815 | 2,595 | 590* |
| phaeton | 3,864 | 2,645 | |
| Custom Beverly sdn 4d | 3,900 | 2,960 | |
| Custom Berline | 4,120 | 3,060 | |

*Estimated

| 812 Supercharged (wb 125.0; Custom-132.0) | Wght | Price | Prod |
|---|---|---|---|
| Westchester sdn 4d | 3,765 | 2,860 | |
| Beverly sdn 4d | 3,850 | 2,960 | |
| cabriolet | 3,865 | 3,010 | 688* |
| phaeton | 3,914 | 3,060 | |
| Custom Beverly sdn 4d | 3,950 | 3,375 | |
| Custom Berline | 4,170 | 3,575 | |

| 1937 Engines | bore × stroke | bhp | availability |
|---|---|---|---|
| V-8, 288.6 | 3.50 × 3.75 | 125 | S-812 |
| V-8, 288.6 | 3.50 × 3.75 | 170/190 | S-Schgd 812 |

*Estimated

# Crosley

Powel Crosley, Jr., built one crude small car while a teenager at the turn of the century, then became a radio and refrigerator magnate in the '20s and '30s. But cars remained his first love, and in 1939 he entered the auto business in a big way with a very small product. Dreaming of an American "volkswagen," he offered a tiny 80-inch-wheelbase two-cylinder job at the lowest price in the land: $325-$350. Measuring just 10 feet long and weighing less than half a ton, it garnered a modest 2017 sales. To buy one, you visited a local hardware store or appliance shop—a novel but shortsighted marketing scheme. Crosley Motors built about 5000 cars by 1942, when the government halted civilian production for the duration of World War II.

There were just two Crosley models for 1939: a two-passenger convertible coupe and a four-passenger convertible sedan. Prices dropped as low as $299 for 1940, when offerings expanded to include standard and DeLuxe convertible sedans, a convertible coupe, a wood-body station wagon, a "covered wagon" with full canvas top, and several commercial types. Styling was little changed and very basic, dominated by low, freestanding fenders and a prominent hood bulged out ahead of small horizontal grilles in the front apron. Headlamps attached to the sides of the hood. Interiors were barren—just a central speedometer flanked by fuel and water gauges.

Crosley power through 1942 came from an air-cooled, two-main-bearing Waukesha twin producing 13½ horsepower from 38.9 cubic inches. Performance wasn't quite as bad as those figures imply, since gearing was ultra-low. Top speed was about 50 miles an hour, though the factory recommended cruising at no more than 40. Crosley claimed up to 60 miles per gallon, though few owners likely exceeded 50 mpg.

Completing this bare-bones package were unsynchronized three-speed gearbox, cable-operated mechanical brakes, six-gallon fuel tank, sliding (instead of roll-down) door windows, a single hand-operated windshield wiper, and petite 4.25×12-inch tires on simple disc wheels. The customary universal joints were eliminated as a further cost-cutting measure, flexible rubber engine mounts supposedly making them unnecessary. But they were necessary, as owners found out. They also discovered that Crosley dealers were far better equipped to fix refrigerators than cars. With this, 1940 volume fell by more than three-fourths despite the expanded lineup.

To fix things up for '41, Crosley called in engineer Paul Klotsch, late of the Briggs Manufacturing Company. Klotsch redesigned the motor mounts, added U-joints to the driveshaft, revised the lubrication system, shortened the stroke, and increased main-bearing surface area—the last two to improve engine durability. The revised engine ended up at 35.3 cid and 12 horsepower, but it powered a greatly improved Crosley and sales went up—to 2289—despite higher prices ($339-$496). The cars were now sold through separate automobile dealers in addition to Crosley's appliance outlets. There were no technical changes for '42, but prices rose again (to $468-$582) and the "covered wagon" was dropped. Crosley built 1029 cars that war-shortened model year.

For a wartime U.S. Navy project, Crosley developed an overhead-cam four-cylinder engine with a block made of brazed copper and sheet steel. Called "CoBra," it was selected to power the first postwar Crosleys. This five-main-bearing unit had been fairly successful in a variety of wartime machinery from truck refrigerators to Mooney Mite airplanes, but was less than happy in a car. The copper-steel block was subject to electrolysis that developed holes in the cylinder bores, thus necessitating early rebuilds. Crosley soon rectified the fault by offering a cast-iron version—called CIBA, for Cast-Iron Block Assembly—of the same 44-cid size and 26.5 horsepower output. Significantly, used-car price guides of the day gave a higher trade-in value for cars with the cast-iron engine, including retrofitted 1946-48 models.

Production of the '46 Crosleys began in June of that year: initially a four-seat closed sedan, then a convertible, too. A wagon returned for '47, a delivery sedan for '48. All were two-door styles. Commercial bodies were also offered. Wheelbase was unchanged, but new styling literally made the cars more "grown up": 28 inches longer than prewar Crosleys. Prices were more than double what they'd been in '39, but the Crosley was still quite inexpensive. A '47 was yours for as little as $888.

For a time, things went well. Production totaled almost 5000 for '46, more than 19,000 for '47, and close to 29,000 for '48. Powel Crosley grandly predicted 80,000 a year in the near future, but his firm would never do so well again. New postwar designs from other independents and the Big Three, plus a nagging reputation for engine problems, caused '49 volume to tumble below 7500.

This was ironic, because the '49 was a much better Crosley. New styling made it look something like a scaled-down '49 Ford, with a smooth hood and integral front fenders bearing sealed-beam headlights. Sedans and convertibles also received remote-control door handles and turn indicators—positively civilized features for a Crosley. In addition, the firm fielded a surprising newcomer: a smart little "bugeye" roadster called Hotshot on an 85-inch wheelbase, priced at just $849.

Seeking to turn things around for 1950, Crosley offered wagon, convertible, and sedan in standard and Super trim, plus the doorless Hotshot and a slightly better-trimmed version called Super Sports, which had conventional doors. Crosley was still in a class by itself on price—$872-$984 that year—and for engineering. Disc brakes, for example, had arrived for 1949-50, a first for series production shared with Chrysler's 1950 Town & Country Newport. Unfortunately, hasty development caused the Crosley brakes to deteriorate quickly after exposure to road salt and grime, causing tremendous service headaches. Since the firm was still smarting from the woes of its unlamented sheetmetal engine, this new problem was the last thing dealers—or customers—needed. Conventional drum brakes were reinstituted for 1951.

Though the little roadsters failed to sell, they were tremendous class competitors in racing. Both could do up to 90 mph, and handling was excellent thanks to a crude but effective semielliptic- and coil-spring front suspension and quarter-elliptic-spring rear suspension. The Hotshot's greatest accomplishment was winning the Index of Performance at Sebring in 1951.

At the other extreme was Crosley's 1950 "FarmORoad," a bare-bones, Jeep-like utility vehicle on a minuscule 63-inch wheelbase. Base price was just $795, and available accessories let it do everything from towing a hay wagon to digging ditches.

But by now, buyers were unmoved by anything Crosley did, so the firm was forced to abandon vehicles in July 1952. It was ultimately acquired by General Tire and Rubber, which disposed of automotive operations after Powel Crosley spent some $3 million trying to save them.

# Crosley

1939 convertible coupe

1939 convertible coupe

1947 convertible sedan

1947 pickup truck

1949 Series CD Four Hotshot roadster

1949-50 Series CD Four two-door sedan

1950 Series CD Four SuperSports roadster

1950 Series CD Four Hotshot with doors

# Crosley

## Specifications

### 1939

| Series 1A (wb 80.0)—2,017 built | Wght | Price | Prod |
|---|---|---|---|
| conv cpe, 2P | 925 | 325 | — |
| conv sdn, 4P | 925 | 350 | — |

| 1939 Engine | bore × stroke | bhp | availability |
|---|---|---|---|
| I-2, 38.9 | 3.00 × 2.75 | 13.5 | S-all |

### 1940

| Series 2A (wb 80.0)—422 built | Wght | Price | Prod |
|---|---|---|---|
| sdn 2d | 975 | 349 | — |
| Deluxe sdn 2d | 975 | 359 | — |
| conv cpe | 950 | 299 | — |
| covered wgn 2d | 1,125 | 399 | — |
| wgn 2d | 1,160 | 450 | — |

| 1940 Engine | bore × stroke | bhp | availability |
|---|---|---|---|
| I-2, 38.9 | 3.00 × 2.75 | 13.5 | S-all |

### 1941

| Series CB41 (wb 80.0)—2,289 built | Wght | Price | Prod |
|---|---|---|---|
| sdn 2d | 975 | 390 | — |
| Deluxe sdn 2d | 975 | 400 | — |
| conv cpe | 950 | 339 | — |
| covered wgn 2d | 1,125 | 441 | — |
| wgn 2d | 1,160 | 496 | — |

| 1941 Engine | bore × stroke | bhp | availability |
|---|---|---|---|
| I-2, 38.9 | 3.00 × 2.75 | 13.5 | S-all |

### 1942

| Series CB42 (wb 80.0)—1,029 built | Wght | Price | Prod |
|---|---|---|---|
| sdn 2d | 975 | 468 | — |
| Deluxe sdn 2d | 1,050 | 516 | — |
| conv cpe | 975 | 413 | — |
| wgn 2d | 1,105 | 582 | — |

| 1942 Engine | bore × stroke | bhp | availability |
|---|---|---|---|
| I-2, 38.9 | 3.00 × 2.75 | 13.5 | S-all |

### 1946

| CC Four (wb 80.0) | Wght | Price | Prod |
|---|---|---|---|
| sdn 2d | 1,145 | 905 | 4,987 |
| conv cpe | 1,150 | proto | 12 |

| 1946 Engine | bore × stroke | bhp | availability |
|---|---|---|---|
| I-4, 44.0 | 2.50 × 2.25 | 26.5 | S-all; O-cast-iron block |

### 1947

| CC Four (wb 80.0) | Wght | Price | Prod |
|---|---|---|---|
| sdn 2d | 1,555 | 888 | 14,090 |
| conv cpe | 1,150 | 949 | 4,005 |
| wgn 2d | 1,305 | 929 | 1,249 |

| 1947 Engine | bore × stroke | bhp | availability |
|---|---|---|---|
| I-4, 44.0 | 2.50 × 2.25 | 26.5 | S-all; O-cast-iron block |

### 1948

| CC Four (wb 80.0) | Wght | Price | Prod |
|---|---|---|---|
| sdn 2d | 1,280 | 869 | 2,760 |
| Sport Utility sdn 2d | 1,160 | 799 | |
| conv cpe | 1,210 | 899 | 2,485 |
| wgn 2d | 1,305 | 929 | 23,489 |

| 1948 Engine | bore × stroke | bhp | availability |
|---|---|---|---|
| I-4, 44.0 | 2.50 × 2.25 | 26.5 | S-all; O-cast-iron block |

### 1949

| CD Four (wb 80.0; rdstr-85.0) | Wght | Price | Prod |
|---|---|---|---|
| DeLuxe sdn 2d | 1,363 | 866 | 2,231 |
| conv cpe | 1,320 | 866 | 645 |
| wgn 4d | 1,403 | 894 | 3,803 |
| Hotshot rdstr | 1,175 | 849 | 752 |

| 1949 Engine | bore × stroke | bhp | availability |
|---|---|---|---|
| I-4, 44.0 | 2.50 × 2.25 | 26.5 | S-all; O-cast-iron block |

### 1950

| CD Four (wb 80.0; rdstr-85.0) | Wght | Price | Prod |
|---|---|---|---|
| sdn 2d | 1,363 | 882 | 1,367 |
| Super sdn 2d | 1,363 | 951 | |
| conv cpe | 1,320 | 882 | 478 |
| Super conv cpe | 1,320 | 954 | |
| wgn 2d | 1,403 | 916 | 4,204 |
| Super wgn 2d | 1,403 | 984 | |
| Hotshot rdstr | 1,175 | 872 | 742 |
| Super Sports rdstr | 1,175 | 925 | |

| 1950 Engine | bore × stroke | bhp | availability |
|---|---|---|---|
| I-4, 44.0 | 2.50 × 2.25 | 26.5 | S-all |

### 1951

| CD Four (wb 80.0; rdstr-85.0) | Wght | Price | Prod |
|---|---|---|---|
| bus cpe | 1,355 | 943 | 1,077 |
| Super sdn 2d | 1,370 | 1,033 | |
| wgn 2d | 1,420 | 1,002 | 4,500 |
| Super wgn 2d | 1,450 | 1,077 | |
| Super conv cpe | 1,310 | 1,035 | 391 |
| Hotshot rdstr | 1,180 | 952 | 646 |
| Super Sports rdstr | 1,180 | 1,029 | |

| 1951 Engine | bore × stroke | bhp | availability |
|---|---|---|---|
| I-4, 44.0 | 2.50 × 2.25 | 26.5 | S-all |

### 1952

| CD Four (wb 80.0; rdstr-85.0) | Wght | Price | Prod |
|---|---|---|---|
| Standard bus cpe | 1,355 | 943 | 216 |
| Super sdn 2d | 1,400 | 1,033 | |
| Standard wgn 2d | 1,430 | 1,002 | 1,355 |
| Super wgn 2d | 1,480 | 1,077 | |
| Super conv cpe | 1,400 | 1,035 | 146 |
| Hotshot rdstr | 1,240 | 952 | 358 |
| Super Sports rdstr | 1,240 | 1,029 | |

| 1952 Engine | bore × stroke | bhp | availability |
|---|---|---|---|
| I-4, 44.0 | 2.50 × 2.25 | 25.5 | S-all |

# DeSoto

Prosperity seemed endless in 1928 when the fast-rising new Chrysler Corporation purchased Dodge and issued its first DeSoto and Plymouth. Though good times soon turned to "hard times," DeSoto would be one of the few pre-Depression "expansion" makes to survive them. DeSoto went on to build its most-exciting cars in the '50s, only to die in late 1960 after a flash recession and sibling rivalry obliterated its narrow, well-defined price niche. In between, DeSoto did good and sometimes great business as the medium-price "bridge" between Dodge and Chrysler, with design and engineering that usually owed more to the latter than the former.

Early DeSotos, though, were pitched just above Plymouth in size, power, and price. The make didn't settle into its long-familiar "middle-middle" role until the late '30s. Even so, DeSoto history generally parallels Chrysler's with one key exception: While Chrysler offered a group of conventionally styled Sixes for 1934, DeSoto relied exclusively on that year's radical new Airflow. The result was a sales disaster that briefly threatened DeSoto's existence.

The 1930-33 DeSotos reflected general Chrysler Corporation trends. Styling was bolt-upright formal through '31, then smoothed a bit with barrel-like grilles. Sixes and eights were available through 1931. All were orthodox side-valve designs with cast-iron construction. The five-main-bearing eight was smoother and quieter than the four-main six, but neither was a powerhouse. Eights cost around $1000, early-'30s Sixes around $800-$850. But Eights appealed to only about one in three buyers, so DeSoto offered nothing but sixes from 1932 until its hemi-head "FireDome" V-8 of 1952. Actually, the six was but a single engine that was periodically enlarged—essentially a smaller version of Chrysler's six.

DeSoto started the '30s in the middle of the industry production pack, but moved upward through 1933 despite building fewer cars each year. Model-year volume totaled some 32,000 for 1930-31, then fell below 25,000 for '32. The tally dropped under 23,000 for 1933, by which time DeSoto had climbed from 15th in a field of 31 makes to 10th out of 26.

Reflecting this sales decline, DeSoto cut prices for 1933: as low as $665 for a standard sedan or coupe and $875 for the top-line Custom convertible sedan. All models carried an 82-horsepower 217.8-cubic-inch six. This became a 100-horsepower, 241.5-cid for 1934-36, after which a destroked 228.1 with 93 or 100 horsepower took over. Though never exciting, DeSoto's six was sturdy and reliable, happily running for long spells with little maintenance other than an occasional quart of oil. It was also fairly thrifty, returning up to 22 mpg with gentle use. These traits made later six-cylinder DeSotos quite popular as taxicabs.

DeSoto first observed a model year with the January 1932 introduction of its SC-Series "All New Six." This wore chunky but attractive styling as a standard sedan, seven-passenger sedan, and Custom sedan, convertible, and phaeton. Additional coupes and a new brougham two-door sedan arrived for '33.

All the pros and cons of the 1934 Chrysler Airflow naturally held for the DeSoto versions, only they came in a single four-model series versus a multiplicity of Chryslers. Output now bottomed out to a prewar low of just under 14,000.

Following Chrysler in a hasty retreat from Airflows, DeSoto introduced more-conventional—and salable—"Airstream" styling for 1935. It appeared on seven companion models bearing a Plymouth-like raked grille, slab sides, and rounded deck.

Sedans were sold with either outside spare tire or "trunkback" styling that enclosed the spare in an integral luggage compartment. There was also a $35 two-tone paint option. Thanks to the Airstreams, production rebounded to 26,800, yet DeSoto dropped to 13th in the wake of Packard's highly successful new medium-priced One Twenty.

DeSoto Division rode out the last half of the '30s with increasingly larger and duller cars. Airflows disappeared after

**1930 Series CF Eight convertible coupe**

**1931 Series SA Six 2/4-passenger roadster**

**1932 Series SC New Six Custom 2/4-passenger roadster**

# DeSoto

1936, a year ahead of Chrysler's, but long sedans and limousines arrived that year on a 130-inch wheelbase; this grew to 136 inches for 1938. The great Ray Dietrich of coachbuilding fame was hired to direct Chrysler's corporate design in this period, so DeSoto looked as conservative as its sister makes, though in tune with contemporary tastes. A national recession limited 1938 output to just under 39,000, but DeSoto still finished 12th. The industry recovered in 1939, but fared much better than DeSoto, which again ran 13th despite higher volume of over 54,000.

The DeSoto line assumed a consistent pattern by 1938: DeLuxe and Custom models selling at around $900 and $1000, respectively. Both rode the same orthodox chassis with standard 119-inch wheelbase. Open styles were conspicuously absent for 1939, though a sliding sunroof was offered on selected closed models. Styling still left something to be desired. A '39 DeSoto looked like a Plymouth with goiter. Dumpy appearance would remain one of the make's sales handicaps until well after World War II.

For 1940 came more-attractive Dietrich styling abetted by

**1933 Series SD 7-passenger sedan**

**1936 Custom Airstream convertible coupe**

**1934 Series SE Airflow 5-passenger coupe**

# DeSoto

longer wheelbases of 122.5 inches standard, 139.5 extended. Chrysler's Fluid Drive, which allowed the driver to start and stop without using the clutch, became available on DeSotos. The Custom convertible coupe was reinstated, but not the convertible sedan. Though model-year output rose some 11,000 units, DeSoto again placed 13th. Like other Chrysler makes, it might have done better had the firm not suffered a crippling strike at the start of 1940 production.

Volume soared for '41, jumping from 65,500 to over 97,000 and moving DeSoto up to tenth—its best placing ever. Much of this success was owed to a heavy facelift that made for good-looking cars with lower hoods and bolder fronts. Grilles smiled with the prominent vertical "teeth" that would remain a DeSoto hallmark through 1955. Standard-chassis models lost an inch in wheelbase but measured 5.5 inches longer overall than the '40s;

they were lower and wider, too. There was a new model: the Custom Town Sedan, a formal but pretty adaptation of the standard issue with closed or "blind" rear-roof quarters, priced about $50 higher. DeSoto wooed buyers with numerous extras including underseat heater, pushbutton radio, and streamlined fender skirts.

A more-extensive restyle for 1942 introduced "Airfoil" hidden headlamps that were "out of sight, except at night." Though not an industry first (the 1936-37 Cord 810/812 had something similar), they were Detroit's only hidden lamps that year, and imparted a cleaner look. Emphasizing them was a grille placed entirely on the lower half of the car's "face." A sculpted lady was introduced as a hood mascot.

Model choices held firm for '42, but there was a "squarer" six, bored out to 236.6 cid. Somewhat detuned and rated at 115

**1936 Series S2 Airflow III 5-passenger coupe**

**1938 Series S5 Six touring sedan**

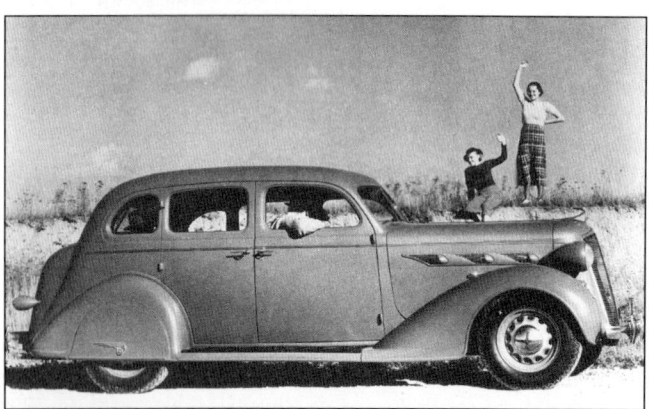
**1936 Series S1 Custom Airstream touring sedan**

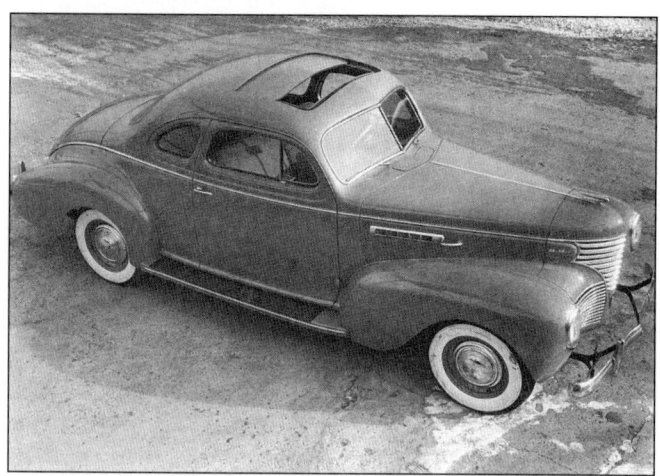
**1939 Series S6 Custom coupe with optional sunroof**

**1937 Series S3 Six 3/5-passenger convertible coupe**

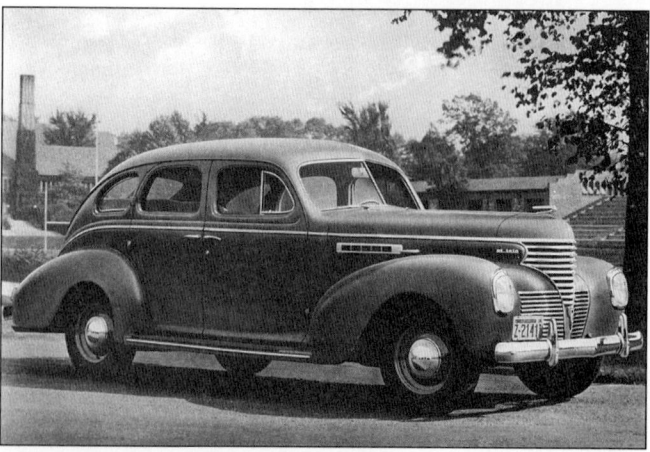
**1939 Series S6 Custom touring sedan**

**1939 Series S6 Custom club coupe**

**1940 Series S-7 DeLuxe 3-passenger coupe**

**1942 Series S-10C Custom four-door sedan**

**1941 Series S-8C Custom four-door sedan**

**1942 Series S-10C Custom club coupe**

horsepower, it would continue through the rest of the decade. There wasn't much time for specials in that war-shortened model year, but DeSoto managed a plush Custom Town Sedan called "Fifth Avenue" (a name much later resurrected at Chrysler). Identified outside only by small nameplates and inside by luxurious leather and Bedford cloth trim, it sold for about $75 more than the regular Town Sedan. Production was low everywhere in Detroit for '42, and DeSoto was no excep-

# DeSoto

tion at less than 25,000—fewer than 1000 of some individual models.

DeSoto returned to civilian sales with an abbreviated 1946 line, though drivetrain and chassis combinations were the same as '42. Cancelation of the long-wheelbase DeLuxe sedan left only three extended-chassis models, all Customs: limousine, seven-seat sedan, and an intriguing newcomer called Suburban. The last was designed for the ultimate in stylish hauling for hotels, airports, and well-heeled individuals. A fold-down rear seat sans trunk partition made for a huge cargo hold. Completing the package was a metal-and-wood roof rack. Not surprisingly, the Suburban was the costliest '46 DeSoto at $2093, a healthy $200 above the seven-seat sedan.

As with all Chrysler makes, the 1947-48 DeSotos were largely the same as the '46s; serial numbers are the only guide to model years. All wore a mild facelift of prewar styling with headlamps reexposed, fenders extended back into the front doors, a wider and heavier-looking grille, and reshuffled medallions and parking lights. Rated horsepower was 109, down six from '42, though this reflected a new rating method, not mechanical changes. Besides "civilian" cars, DeSoto built 11,600 taxicabs in these years—its fifth best-selling model. Suburban production was also quite satisfactory: 7500 for the period.

DeSoto was fully redesigned for '49, as were other Chrysler makes that year. Standard wheelbase was four inches longer at 125.5, but boxy, upright styling hid the fact. This was typical of Chrysler's new postwar look, which was very dull compared to Ford's and GM's. A vertical-bar grille was retained, similar to the 1942-48 design, but the lady mascot was replaced by a bust of Hernando DeSoto. Like any "proper" hood ornament of the time, it glowed when the parking lamps or headlights were on. Horsepower rose by three, to 112. Fluid Drive with "Tip-Toe" semiautomatic shift became standard on Customs and a $121 option for DeLuxes.

The '49 DeSotos arrived in March of that year after a brief run of old-style cars to fill the gap. Among them were some interesting new utility models. Besides a $2959 woody wagon, the DeLuxe line included the all-steel Carry-All, similar to the Custom Suburban but on the standard wheelbase. It was also quite a bit cheaper at $2191. The Suburban itself returned at $3179, up over $500 from '48 (postwar inflation was affecting car prices all over). As before, the Suburban shared the long chassis with an eight-passenger Custom sedan (but not the limo, which was dropped), and offered vast cargo space, rooftop luggage rack, plus rear jump seats giving true nine-passenger capacity. The Carry-All handily sold 2690 copies for the model year, but the wagon did only 850, the Suburban a mere 129. The woody lasted only through 1950, the Suburban and Carry-All through '52.

Overall, 1949 was a less-than-spectacular DeSoto year. Volume remained at the '48 level—about 92,500—and the make again finished 12th. However, Customs outsold DeLuxes by 3-to-1, a sign of growing buyer preference for greater luxury.

The 1950 line arrived with somewhat sleeker rear ends and two new models. DeSoto bowed its first hardtop coupe, the Custom Sportsman, at $2489, and moved the DeLuxe woody wagon up to Custom trim before replacing it with a slightly cheaper all-steel model at midyear. Despite the relative lack of change, model-year production leaped to nearly 134,000 for 1950, a gain of almost 45 percent.

Styling was touched up again for '51, when the venerable L-head six was stroked to 250.6 cid, though that yielded only four extra horses. Chrome was very evident, perhaps more than on any other Chrysler line, especially in those toothy fronts. Production eased to 106,000, dropping DeSoto from 12th to

1946 Custom Suburban 8-passenger sedan

1946 Deluxe sedan

1947 Custom club coupe

1949 Custom convertible coupe

1950 Custom Sportsman hardtop coupe

# DeSoto

1951 Custom four-door sedan

1953 Firedome Sportsman hardtop coupe

1953 Firedome convertible coupe

1954 Firedome four-door sedan

15th, as Kaiser sailed past with its beautiful new '51 design and Hudson did the same with its powerful new six-cylinder Hornets. Government-ordered production cutbacks for the Korean War also played a part.

DeSoto's big event for 1952 was its first-ever V-8. Called "FireDome," it was an overhead-valve hemi-head design—a smaller, 276.1-cid version of the brilliant Chrysler 331 introduced the previous year. Packing 160 horsepower, it put DeSoto firmly in Detroit's escalating "horsepower race."

The FireDome powered a new like-named top-of-the-line 1952 series that duplicated Custom offerings save the Suburban. Though it immediately garnered nearly 50,000 sales, DeSoto as a whole could do no better than 88,000 for the model year. However, it rose a bit in the production ranks, finishing 13th.

For 1953, remaining Custom/DeLuxe models were combined into a new Powermaster Six series that still lagged behind FireDome in sales, this time by a margin of 2-1. Both lines included Sportsman hardtops. The growing influence of newly recruited styling chief Virgil Exner was evident in an update of DeSoto's more-massive '52 look, with new one-piece windshields and more-liberal chrome accents. Model-year volume jumped back to 130,000 and DeSoto moved up to 11th, its best finish since banner '41.

Adding much-needed pizzazz to DeSoto's dour image in 1954 was the interesting Adventurer I, one in the series of Exner-styled show cars begun with the Plymouth XX-500 of 1950. Most were built by Ghia in Italy. Riding a shortened 111-inch wheelbase, Adventurer I was an off-white, close-coupled coupe sporting outside exhausts, wire wheels, and full instrumentation. It came close to production—closer than any other Exner special. "Had it been mass-produced," the designer later said, "it would have been the first four-passenger sports car made in this country. It was better than a 2+2—and, of course, it had the DeSoto Hemi. It was my favorite car." Adventurer II followed in '55, a standard-chassis four-seat fastback shaped more by Ghia than Exner. Painted deep red and lacking bumpers, it was very sleek but not quite as integrated as Adventurer I, and wasn't seriously considered for production.

Meanwhile, the first of Exner's new "Forward Look" production models was due for 1955, so DeSoto's old '49 bodyshell was modestly reworked one last time for '54. The V-8 was tweaked to 170 horsepower, but the big news was the midyear debut of two-speed PowerFlite, Chrysler's first fully automatic transmission. This would be standard on many DeSotos through 1960. Fluid Drive ($130 extra) was on the way out, as was overdrive ($96), long sedans, and the Powermaster Six. Reflecting Chrysler Corporation's 1954 sales nightmare, DeSoto's model-year output dropped below 77,000 and the make fell back to 12th place in the industry.

Much bolder, fully up-to-date new Exner styling and more-powerful engines stood to turn things around for 1955. Firedome (the "d" no longer capitalized) now played "second banana" to a new uplevel Fireflite line. Both shared a 126-inch wheelbase with that year's Chryslers, and carried a Hemi bored out to 291 cid. Rated horsepower was 185 for Firedomes, 200 for Fireflites. No '55 Chrysler product was sedate, but DeSoto looked possibly busiest of all—though still attractive, with a much lower silhouette; wrapped windshield; the last of the toothy grilles; "gullwing" dash; and broad, optional two-toning. This package appealed greatly, boosting division output to nearly 115,000. Still, even that was good for only 13th in a year when most every Detroit car sold very well.

Firedome offered DeSoto's only '55 wagon, along with a detrimmed Special hardtop priced some $110 below its Sportsman counterpart. The plush Coronado sedan, a mid-1954 addition to the Firedome line, returned as a 1955 "spring special" Fireflite at $100 above the $2800 regular sedan. It's now a minor collector's item, mainly for having one of the industry's first three-tone paint jobs (turquoise, black, and white).

# DeSoto

1955 Fireflite Sportsman hardtop coupe

1955 Fireflite Coronado four-door sedan

1956 Firedome Seville hardtop coupe

1955 Fireflite convertible coupe

1957 Fireflite four-door sedan

1956 Fireflite convertible coupe

1957 Fireflite Shopper station wagon

# DeSoto

1957 Fireflite Sportsman hardtop coupe

1957 Firedome convertible coupe

1958 Adventurer hardtop coupe

Convertibles were available in both '55 DeSoto series but saw minuscule sales: just 625 Firedomes and 775 Fireflites.

For 1956, a longer stroke took DeSoto's Hemi to 330.4 cid, lifting Firedome to 230 horsepower and Fireflite to 255. Wire mesh replaced the trademark grille teeth, and unreadable gold-on-white instruments appeared. But as on other Chrysler lines, the big change was tailfins, though they were pretty modest for '56. DeSoto's carried distinctive "tri-tower" taillamps—stacked pairs of round red lenses separated by a matching backup lamp—which would persist through 1959.

Following GM's lead in '55, DeSoto introduced three four-door hardtops for '56: a Sportsman in each series and a low-priced Firedome Seville. A Seville hardtop coupe replaced the previous Firedome Special. (Cadillac's new-for-'56 Eldorado two-door hardtop was also called Seville, but no legal battles ensued.) A midseason highlight was the limited-edition Adventurer hardtop coupe, a supercar awash in gold-anodized aluminum trim. Carrying a new 341-cid, 320-horsepower Hemi, it was part of that year's expanded Highland Park performance squadron along with the Chrysler 300B, Plymouth Fury, and Dodge D-500. DeSoto was selected as the 1956 Indy 500 pace car, and the division celebrated by reeling off about 400 "Pacesetter" replicas, all Fireflite convertibles with Adventurer-style trim, priced at $3615 apiece.

DeSoto shared in the industry's general 1956 retreat, building about 4300 fewer cars. However, it returned to 11th place due to fast-fading sales at Nash and Hudson, Studebaker and Packard. The division finished in that spot again for '57 even though volume jumped to about 110,500—as near as DeSoto ever came to passing Chrysler (ending about 7200 units behind).

No wonder. The '57s were not only all-new for the second time in three years, but superbly engineered and strikingly styled. A low-cost Firesweep series based on the 122-inch Dodge platform joined the line in an effort to extend DeSoto's market territory. It helped. The Firesweep sedan sold for only $2777, where the cheapest Firedome was $2958. Firesweeps also included two-and four-door hardtops and six-seat Shopper and nine-passenger Explorer four-door wagons. Fireflite offered all these plus a convertible; Firedome was the same but had no wagons.

All were big, heavy, powerful cars. The two upper series used the 341 V-8 from the '56 Adventurer with 270 and 295 horsepower, respectively. Firesweeps had the previous year's 330 debored to 325 cid and tuned for 245 horsepower standard, 260 horsepower optional. Last but not least, a soft-top Adventurer joined the hardtop coupe in a separate series above Fireflite. They packed 345 bhp from a modestly bored 345 Hemi.

Virgil Exner's dramatic new styling made finned fantasies of all '57 Chrysler products. DeSoto's version of this second-generation Forward Look was quite handsome: dartlike profile, tri-

# DeSoto

tower taillamps attractively integrated into the soaring rear fenders, simple but pleasant side moldings, prominent bumper/grille, and acres more glass. DeSoto also benefited from Chrysler's corporatewide switch to torsion-bar front suspension, which made these heavyweights uncannily good handlers. Aiding performance was the arrival of quick, responsive three-speed TorqueFlite automatic as an optional alternative to PowerFlite. Also controlled by Highland Park's pushbuttons, it was a great transmission that would way outlive DeSoto.

Indeed, for all this excitement, DeSoto was now threatened again, only this time by an upwardly mobile Dodge and a downward expansion of the Chrysler line. As if on cue, production plunged to 50,000 units the following year—the make's lowest total since 1938. A sharp national recession, poor workmanship after '56, and several marketing mistakes all contributed to a downward spiral from which DeSoto would never recover.

Predictably, the '58 DeSotos were much like the '57s save busier grilles and trim, and standard quad headlights. (Some states hadn't approved "quadrilights" for '57, so DeSoto front fenders were designed to accept one or two lamps each, the latter where law permitted. By '58, four-lamp systems were legal nationwide.) The '58 lineup returned along with a new Firesweep convertible. At $4369, the '58 Adventurer ragtop was the most-expensive DeSoto ever, though Chrysler's convertible 300D cost nearly $1300 more.

Engines and power ratings swelled, but the complex Hemi was ever costly to build, so Chrysler began switching to cheaper wedgehead V-8s for '58. Among them were two new "Turboflash" DeSoto engines. Firesweeps had a 350 with 280 horsepower standard or 295 with optional four-barrel carb. Other models carried a big-bore 361 with 295 bhp in standard Firedome tune, 305 with twin four-barrels in Fireflites (optional on Firedomes), 345 in high-compression Adventurer guise, and a smashing 355 for Adventurers with optional Bendix fuel injection, which was expensive and thus rarely ordered. With all this, the '58 DeSotos were quite quick even without the Hemi, helped by fast-shifting TorqueFlite, now standard on Fireflites and Adventurers. (Firesweeps again came with three-speed manual and offered Firedome's standard PowerFlite at extra cost.) A 305-horsepower Firedome could scale 0-60 in 7.7 seconds, 0-80 mph in 13.5 seconds, and reach 115 mph.

DeSoto claimed its towering tailfins of this era "added stability at speed," but that was pure propaganda. The fins did little from an aerodynamic standpoint under 80 mph. Their main purpose was to make Chrysler products stand out from the crowd—which they most definitely did.

Despite the return of the same broad lineup, 1959 marked the beginning of DeSoto's end. Firesweeps were upgraded to the 361 wedge in just one 295-horsepower version. Other models got an even bigger-bore new 383 with 305 horsepower for Firedome, 325 for Fireflite, and 350 for Adventurer. The last saw slightly improved sales, but total model-year production of just under 46,000 was hardly the sort that had sustained DeSoto earlier in the decade.

Rumors of DeSoto's imminent demise began cropping up in '59, and naturally affected sales. Though calendar-year output was up slightly from '58, volume for both years was less than half that of 1957's near 120,000 units. Plainly, the recession had put DeSoto in the same kind of trouble as Oldsmobile, Buick, and Mercury, but those makes started at higher levels and thus had further to fall. Moreover, all were planning smaller models for 1960-61. Although DeSoto's 1962 plans included "downsized" standard cars, there was no program for a compact.

The real problem, though, was a change in corporate marketing strategy. Previously, company franchises split into

**1959 Fireflite Sportsman hardtop coupe**

**1960 Adventurer hardtop coupe**

**1960 Adventurer four-door sedan**

**1961 hardtop coupe**

**1961 hardtop coupe**

Chrysler-Plymouth, DeSoto-Plymouth, and Dodge-Plymouth dealers. The advent of Imperial as a separate make for 1955 prompted Chrysler Division to expand in the lower end of its price territory, while Dodge moved upward with larger, more-luxurious cars. DeSoto had nowhere to go—except the grave.

At first, Chrysler strongly denied that DeSoto would be terminated, and even staged a 1959 celebration marking production of the two-millionth DeSoto. Press releases noted that almost a million DeSotos were still registered and that $25 million had been earmarked for future models—$7 million for 1960 alone. Officials also said commitments had been made for '61, and that work was underway toward 1962-63. They also pointed out that Chrysler had regularly made a profit on DeSoto.

But then Chrysler combined DeSoto and Plymouth Divisions in 1960, with the new compact Valiant an ostensibly separate make. Valiant sold very well and Plymouth did fairly well, but DeSoto fared badly. Sales in the first two months of 1960 were just 4746—a mere 0.51 percent of the industry—down substantially from the 1959 period (6134 units and 0.72 percent).

DeSoto's 1960 line reflected these developments: cut to just a sedan, hardtop sedan, and hardtop coupe in two series. The upper was called Adventurer, but sold for a few hundred dollars below '59 Fireflites and was much-less-special than previous Adventurers. Fireflite was now in the $3000 area formerly occupied by Firesweep. The year's most-popular DeSoto was the Fireflite sedan, but even it failed to exceed 10,000 units.

All 1960 DeSotos shared a 122-inch wheelbase with that year's Chrysler Windsor and Dodge Matador/Polara. They also adopted the new "unibody" construction that arrived corporate-wide (except on Imperial). Adventurers carried the 305-horsepower 383 from the now-departed Firedome; Fireflites had the 295-horsepower 361 from the '59 Firesweep. Styling was all but identical with the 1960 Chrysler's, announced by a blunt, trapezoidal grille composed of small horizontal bars atop a huge vee'd bumper with rubber-capped guards. Fins flew as high as ever, but performance was down. A 1960 Adventure could stay with a Windsor away from a stoplight, but would lose to a Chrysler Saratoga or the lighter 383 Dodge Dart Phoenix.

DeSoto's appearance for 1961 was brief—token really. Production was understandably low: a mere 3034. There was but one nameless series (the cars were simply "DeSotos"), and four-door pillared sedans were eliminated. Minimal advertising focused on the individual styling. "Odd" was a more-apt adjective—especially in front, where diagonally stacked quad headlights flanked a curious "double" grille with a latticelike lower section; above was a large oval holding the DeSoto name in unreadable stylized letters against a fine mesh. The rest of the effort was equally uninspired.

But DeSoto's fate had long been sealed, so Chrysler wound down production by Christmas 1960, filling what few orders remained with mostly '61 Windsors. Some DeSoto-Plymouth dealers then became Chrysler-Plymouth stores—to the chagrin of existing C-P dealers nearby. Left stillborn were the smaller '62 DeSotos based on the planned new corporate "S-series" platform—though that was no great loss considering their dumpy looks.

It was a sad finale for a marque that had generated much business for Chrysler over more than three decades. And ironically, it was premature. Less than a year later, DeSoto was effectively resurrected at Dodge to bolster sales of its unpopular 1962 standard line, which had been shrunk to near-compact size. Called Custom 880, this reborn full-size Dodge was much like the '61 DeSoto, and even cost about the same, but sold much better with its smoother styling and more model choices. One suspects, then, that DeSoto's rapid decline, like Edsel's, stemmed from a "loser" image as much as from a changed market.

## Specifications

### 1930

| Model K Six (wb 109.0)—29,860 built** | Wght | Price | Prod |
|---|---|---|---|
| rdstr 2-4P | 2,350 | 845 | — |
| touring (phaeton) 5P | 2,445 | 845 | — |
| bus cpe 2P | 2,465 | 845 | — |
| DeLuxe cpe 2-4P | 2,525 | 885 | — |
| sdn 2d 5P | 2,580 | 845 | — |
| sdn 4d 5P | 2,645 | 885 | — |
| DeLuxe sdn 4d 5P | 2,655 | 955 | — |
| **Model CF Eight (wb 114.0)—19,525 built (est.)*** | | | |
| rdstr 2-4P | 2,720 | 985 | 1,457* |
| phaeton 5P | 2,800 | 1,035 | 179* |
| bus cpe 2P | 2,835 | 965 | 1,015* |
| DeLuxe cpe 2-4P | 2,875 | 1,025 | 2,735* |
| conv cpe 2-4P | 2,845 | 1,075 | 524* |
| sdn 4d 5P | 2,965 | 995 | 9,653* |
| DeLuxe sdn 4d 5P | 2,975 | 1,065 | 4,139* |
| chassis | — | — | 373* |
| **Model CK Finer Six (wb 109.0)—7,443 built (est.)*** | | | |
| rdstr 2-4P | 2,385 | 810 | 1,086* |
| DeLuxe rdstr 2-4P | 2,520 | 835 | |
| touring (phaeton) 5P | 2,475 | 830 | 209* |
| bus cpe 2P | 2,515 | 830 | 858* |
| DeLuxe cpe 2-4P | 2,585 | 860 | 1,521* |
| conv cpe 2-4P | 2,540 | 945 | 184* |
| sdn 4d | 2,705 | 875 | 8,248* |
| chassis | — | — | 94* |

* combined 1930-31 individual model exact production

** Available Model K figures include 1929 production. 1930-model production began August 15. Engine number span for 1930: K83241 to K11310. If no engine numbers were skipped, total 1930 Model K production was 29,860. Available Model CF and CK figures include 1931 production. 1930 Model CF production began January 1, 1930. Model CK production began April 29. Sources of serial number spans suggest that of 20,075 Model CFs built, approximately 19,575 were 1930s and 550 1931s. Same sources indicate 7,443 CKs were 1930s and 4,757 1931s.

| 1930 Engines | bore × stroke | bhp | availability |
|---|---|---|---|
| I-6, 174.9 | 3.00 × 4.13 | 57 | S-K |
| I-8, 207.7 | 2.88 × 4.00 | 70 | S-CF |
| I-6, 189.8 | 3.13 × 4.13 | 60 | S-CK |

### 1931

**Model CF Eight (wb 114.0)—550 built (est.)**

Production was carried over from 1930, with 1931-model output commencing July 1. Production figures combined with 1930 CF Eight. Body styles, weights, and prices identical.

**Model CK Finer Six (wb 109.0)—4,757 built (est.)**

Production was carried over from 1930, with 1931-model output commencing July 1. Production figures combined with 1930 CK Finer Six. Body styles, weights, and prices identical.

| Model SA Six (wb 109.0) | Wght | Price | Prod* |
|---|---|---|---|
| rdstr 2-4P | 2,465 | 795 | 1,949 |
| touring (phaeton) 5P | 2,580 | 795 | 100 |
| bus cpe 2P | 2,585 | 740 | 1,309 |
| cpe 2-4P | 2,635 | 775 | 2,663 |
| conv cpe 2-4P | 2,630 | 825 | 638 |
| sdn 2d 5P | 2,680 | 695 | 2,349 |
| sdn 4d 5P | 2,695 | 775 | 17,866 |
| DeLuxe sdn 4d 5P | 2,834 | 825 | 1,450 |
| chassis | — | — | 32 |

# DeSoto

### Model CF Eight Second Series (wb 114.0)

|  | Wght | Price | Prod |
|---|---|---|---|
| rdstr 2-4P | 2,785 | 995 | 73 |
| touring (phaeton) 5P | 2,800 | 1,035 | 22 |
| bus cpe 2P | 2,915 | 965 | 102 |
| DeLuxe cpe 2-4P | 2,970 | 995 | 486 |
| conv cpe 2-4P | 2,970 | 1,075 | 48 |
| sdn 4d 5P | 2,025 | 995 ⎤ | 3,490 |
| DeLuxe sdn 4d 5P | 3,115 | 1,065 ⎦ | |
| chassis | — | — | 3 |

* Model SA and CF Second Series production continued into 1932; production figures are for 1931-32 combined. Approximately one-third of total SA models were 1931s, the rest 1932s. Second Series Model CF production began January 1, 1931.

| 1931 Engines | bore × stroke | bhp | availability |
|---|---|---|---|
| I-8, 207.7 | 2.88 × 4.00 | 70 | S-CF |
| I-6, 189.8 | 3.13 × 4.13 | 60 | S-CF |
| I-6, 205.3 | 3.25 × 4.13 | 67 | S-SK |
| I-8, 220.7 | 2.88 × 4.25 | 77 | S-CF Second Series |

## 1932

### Model SA Six (wb 109.0)

Production was carried over from 1931, with 1932-model output commencing July 23. Production figures combined with 1931 SA Six. Body styles, weights, and prices identical.

### Model SC New Six (wb 112.4)

|  | Wght | Price | Prod |
|---|---|---|---|
| Standard rdstr 2P | 2,725 | 675 ⎤ | 894 |
| Custom rdstr 2-4P | 2,748 | 775 ⎦ | |
| phaeton 5P | NA | 775 | 30 |
| Standard cpe 2P | 2,778 | 695 | 1,691 |
| Standard cpe 2-4P | 2,848 | 735 ⎤ | 2,897 |
| Custom cpe 2-4P | 2,908 | 790 ⎦ | |
| sdn 2d (brougham) | 2,883 | 695 | 3,730 |
| Custom conv cpe 2-4P | 2,848 | 845 | 960 |
| Standard sdn 4d | 2,978 | 775 | 8,924 |
| Custom sdn 4d | 3,018 | 835 | 4,791 |
| Custom conv sdn 5P | 3,175 | 975 | 275 |
| sdn 7P | 3,175 | 925 | 221 |
| chassis | — | — | 83 |

### Model CF Eight Second Series (wb 114.0)

Production was carried over from 1931, with 1932-model output commencing July 23. Production figures combined with 1931 CF Second Series. Body styles, weights, and prices identical.

| 1932 Engines | bore × stroke | bhp | availability |
|---|---|---|---|
| I-6, 205.3 | 3.25 × 4.13 | 67 | S-SA |
| I-8, 220.7 | 2.88 × 4.25 | 77 | S-CF 2nd Series |
| I-6, 211.5 | 3.25 × 4.25 | 75 | S-SC |

## 1933

### Model SD (wb 114.4)

|  | Wght | Price | Prod |
|---|---|---|---|
| bus cpe 2P | 2,930 | 665 | 800 |
| Standard cpe 2-4P | 2,940 | 705 ⎤ | 2,705 |
| Custom cpe 2-4P | 2,995 | 750 ⎦ | |
| Standard sdn 2d | 2,995 | 665 ⎤ | 2,436 |
| Special sdn 2d | 3,000 | 725 ⎦ | |
| Custom conv cpe 2-4P | 2,990 | 775 | 412 |
| Standard sdn 4d | 3,060 | 735 | 7,890 |
| Custom sdn 4d | 3,150 | 795 | 8,133 |
| Custom conv sdn 5P | — | 875 | 132 |
| sdn 7P (export only) | — | — | 104 |
| chassis | — | — | 124 |

| 1933 Engine | bore × stroke | bhp | availability |
|---|---|---|---|
| I-6, 217.8 | 3.25 × 4.38 | 82 | S-all |

## 1934

### Model SE Airflow (wb 115.5)

|  | Wght | Price | Prod |
|---|---|---|---|
| cpe 5P | 3,323 | 995 | 1,584 |
| brougham 6P | 3,323 | 995 | 522 |
| sdn 4d | 3,378 | 995 | 11,713 |
| Town sdn 6P | 3,343 | 995 | 119 |
| chassis | — | — | 2 |

| 1934 Engine | bore × stroke | bhp | availability |
|---|---|---|---|
| I-6, 241.5 | 3.38 × 4.50 | 100 | S-all |

## 1935

### Model SF Airstream Six (wb 116.0)

|  | Wght | Price | Prod |
|---|---|---|---|
| bus cpe 2P | 2,840 | 695 | 1,760 |
| cpe 2-4P | 2,925 | 760 | 900 |
| conv cpe 2-4P | 3,035 | 835 | 226 |
| sdn 2d | 2,915 | 745 | 1,350 |
| touring sdn 2d | 2,960 | 775 | 2,035 |
| sdn 4d | 2,990 | 795 | 5,714 |
| touring sdn 4d | 3,035 | 825 | 8,018 |

### Model SG Airflow Six (wb 115.5)

|  | Wght | Price | Prod |
|---|---|---|---|
| bus cpe 3P | 3,390 | 1,015 | 70 |
| cpe 5P | 3,390 | 1,015 | 418 |
| sdn 4d | 3,390 | 1,015 | 6,269 |
| Town sdn 6P | 3,400 | 1,015 | 40 |

| 1935 Engine | bore × stroke | bhp | availability |
|---|---|---|---|
| I-6, 241.5 | 3.38 × 4.50 | 100 | S-all |

## 1936

### S1 Airstream DeLuxe (wb 118.0)

|  | Wght | Price | Prod |
|---|---|---|---|
| bus cpe 2P | 2,941 | 695 | 2,592 |
| touring brougham 5P | 3,051 | 770 | 2,207 |
| touring sdn 5P | 3,111 | 810 | 13,093 |
| chassis | — | — | 99 |

### S1 Airstream Custom (wb 118; lwb-130.0)

|  | Wght | Price | Prod |
|---|---|---|---|
| bus cpe 2P | — | 745 | 940 |
| cpe 2-4P | — | 795 | 641 |
| conv cpe 2-4P | 3,031 | 895 | 350 |
| touring brougham 5P | 3,031 | 825 | 1,120 |
| touring sdn 4d | 3,126 | 865 | 13,801 |
| conv sdn 5P | — | 1,095 | 215 |
| Traveler sdn 4d* | — | 1,075 | 23 |
| lwb sdn 7P | — | 1,075 | 208 |
| limo 7P (lwb) | — | NA | 10 |

### S2 Airflow II (wb 115.5)

|  | Wght | Price | Prod |
|---|---|---|---|
| cpe 5P | — | 1,095 | 250 |
| sdn 4d | — | 1,095 | 4,750 |

| 1936 Engine | bore × stroke | bhp | availability |
|---|---|---|---|
| I-6, 241.5 | 3.38 × 4.50 | 100 | S-all |

## 1937

### S3 Six (wb 116.0; lwb-133.0)

|  | Wght | Price | Prod |
|---|---|---|---|
| bus cpe 3P | 3,038 | 770 | 11,050 |
| cpe 3-5P | 3,088 | 820 | 1,030 |
| conv cpe 3-5P | 3,225 | 975 | 992 |
| brghm F/B 6P | 3,123 | 830 | 1,200 |
| touring 6P | 3,148 | 840 | 11,660 |
| sdn F/B 4d | 3,123 | 870 | 2,265 |
| touring sdn 4d | 3,148 | 880 | 51,889 |
| conv sdn 5P | 3,441 | 1,300 | 426 |

# DeSoto

| S3 Six (wb 116.0; lwb-133.0) | Wght | Price | Prod |
|---|---|---|---|
| lwb sdn 7P | 3,451 | 1,120 | 695 |
| limo sdn 7P (lwb) | 3,475 | 1,220 | 71 |
| chassis | — | — | 497 |

| 1937 Engine | bore × stroke | bhp | availability |
|---|---|---|---|
| I-6, 228.1 | 3.38 × 4.25 | 93 | S-all |

## 1938

| S5 Six (wb 119.0; lwb-136.0) | Wght | Price | Prod |
|---|---|---|---|
| bus cpe 3P | 3,039 | 870 | 5,160 |
| conv cpe 3-5P | 3,229 | 1,045 | 431 |
| touring brougham 6P | 3,119 | 930 | 5,367 |
| sdn F/B 4d 6P | 3,134 | 958 | 498 |
| touring sdn 4d 6P | 3,139 | 970 | 23,681 |
| conv sdn 5P | 3,394 | 1,375 | 88 |
| lwb sdn 7P | 3,439 | 1,195 | 513 |
| sdn limo 7P (lwb) | 3,524 | 1,285 | 81 |
| Custom Traveler sdn 4d (lwb) | — | — | 2,550 |
| cpe 2-4P | — | — | 38 |
| fstbk brougham | — | — | 11 |
| chassis | — | — | 413 |

| 1938 Engines | bore × stroke | bhp | availability |
|---|---|---|---|
| I-6, 228.1 | 3.38 × 4.25 | 93 | S-all |
| I-6, 228.1 | 3.38 × 4.25 | 100 | O-all |

## 1939

| S6 DeLuxe (wb 119.0; lwb-136.0) | Wght | Price | Prod |
|---|---|---|---|
| bus cpe 2P | 3,064 | 870 | 5,176 |
| cpe A/S 2-4P | 3,089 | 925 | 2,124 |
| touring sdn 2d 5P | 3,129 | 930 | 7,472 |
| touring sdn 4d 5P | 3,174 | 970 | 31,513 |
| lwb touring sdn 7P | 3,454 | 1,195 | 425 |
| sdn limo 7P | 3,549 | 1,285 | 84 |
| chassis | — | — | 154 |

| S6 Custom (wb 119.0; lwb-136.0) | | | |
|---|---|---|---|
| cpe 2P | 3,069 | 923 | 498 |
| cpe A/S 2-4P | 3,094 | 978 | 287 |
| club cpe 4P | 3,164 | 1,145 | 264 |
| touring sdn 2d 5P | 3,134 | 983 | 424 |
| touring sdn 4d 5P | 3,179 | 1,023 | 5,993 |
| lwb touring sdn 7P | 3,459 | 1,248 | 30 |
| sdn limo 7P | 3,554 | 1,338 | 5 |

| 1939 Engines | bore × stroke | bhp | availability |
|---|---|---|---|
| I-6, 228.1 | 3.38 × 4.25 | 93 | S-all |
| I-6, 228.1 | 3.38 × 4.25 | 100 | O-all |

## 1940

| S-7S DeLuxe (wb 122.5; 7P-139.5) | Wght | Price | Prod |
|---|---|---|---|
| bus cpe | 3,001 | 845 | 3,650 |
| cpe, A/S | 3,026 | 905 | 2,098 |
| sdn 2d | 3,066 | 905 | 7,072 |
| sdn 4d | 3,086 | 945 | 18,666 |
| sdn 4d, 7P | 3,490 | 1,175 | 142 |

| S-7C Custom (wb 122.5; 7P-139.5) | | | |
|---|---|---|---|
| bus cpe | 3,024 | 885 | 1,898 |
| pe, A/S | 3,044 | 945 | 2,234 |
| conv cpe | 3,329 | 1,095 | 1,085 |
| sdn 2d | 3,084 | 945 | 3,109 |
| sdn 4d | 3,104 | 985 | 25,221 |
| sdn 4d, 7P | 3,490 | 1,215 | 206 |
| limo 7P | 3,550 | 1,290 | 34 |
| chassis | — | — | 52 |

| 1940 Engines | bore × stroke | bhp | availability |
|---|---|---|---|
| I-6, 228.1 | 3.38 × 4.25 | 100 | S-all |
| I-6, 228.1 | 3.38 × 4.25 | 105 | O-all |

## 1941

| S-8S DeLuxe (wb 121.5; 7P-139.5) | Wght | Price | Prod |
|---|---|---|---|
| bus cpe | 3,134 | 945 | 4,449 |
| club cpe | 3,219 | 1,025 | 5,603 |
| sdn 2d | 3,224 | 1,008 | 9,228 |
| sdn 4d | 3,254 | 1,035 | 26,417 |
| sdn 4d, 7P | 3,629 | 1,270 | 101 |

| S-8C Custom (wb 121.5; 7P-139.5) | | | |
|---|---|---|---|
| bus cpe | 3,144 | 982 | 2,033 |
| club cpe | 3,239 | 1,080 | 6,726 |
| conv cpe | 3,494 | 1,240 | 2,937 |
| brougham 2d | 3,264 | 1,060 | 4,609 |
| sdn 4d | 3,269 | 1,085 | 30,876 |
| town sdn | 3,329 | 1,133 | 4,362 |
| sdn 4d, 7P | 3,649 | 1,310 | 120 |
| limo 7P | 3,700 | 1,390 | 35 |
| chassis | — | — | 1 |

| 1941 Engine | bore × stroke | bhp | availability |
|---|---|---|---|
| I-6, 228.1 | 3.38 × 4.25 | 105 | S-all |

## 1942

| S-10S DeLuxe (wb 121.5; 7P-139.5) | Wght | Price | Prod |
|---|---|---|---|
| bus cpe | 3,190 | 1,010 | 469 |
| club cpe | 3,270 | 1,092 | 1,968 |
| conv cpe | 3,500 | 1,250 | 79 |
| sdn 2d | 3,270 | 1,075 | 1,781 |
| sdn 4d | 3,315 | 1,103 | 6,463 |
| town sdn | 3,335 | 1,147 | 291 |
| sdn 4d, 7P | 3,705 | 1,455 | 49 |

| S-10C Custom (wb 121.5; 7P-139.5) | | | |
|---|---|---|---|
| bus cpe | 3,205 | 1,046 | 120 |
| club cpe | 3,270 | 1,142 | 2,236 |
| conv cpe | 3,510 | 1,317 | 489 |
| sdn 2d | 3,305 | 1,142 | 913 |
| sdn 4d | 3,330 | 1,152 | 7,974 |
| town sdn | 3,365 | 1,196 | 1,084 |
| sdn 4d, 7P | 3,725 | 1,504 | 79 |
| limo 7P | 3,820 | 1,580 | 20 |

| 1942 Engine | bore × stroke | bhp | availability |
|---|---|---|---|
| I-6, 236.6 | 3.44 × 4.25 | 115 | S-all |

## 1946

| S-11S DeLuxe (wb 121.5) | Wght | Price | Prod* |
|---|---|---|---|
| bus cpe | 3,302 | 1,331 | — |
| club cpe | 3,392 | 1,451 | — |
| sdn 2d | 3,397 | 1,426 | — |
| sdn 4d | 3,427 | 1,461 | — |

| S-11C Custom (wb 121.5; 7-8P-139.5)* | | | |
|---|---|---|---|
| club cpe | 3,378 | 1,501 | — |
| conv cpe | 3,618 | 1,761 | — |
| sdn 2d | 3,423 | 1,491 | — |
| sdn 4d | 3,433 | 1,511 | — |
| sdn 4d, 7P | 3,837 | 1,893 | — |
| limo 8P | 3,937 | 2,013 | — |
| Suburban sdn 4d, 8P | 4,012 | 2,093 | — |

# DeSoto

| 1946 Engine | bore × stroke | bhp | availability |
|---|---|---|---|
| I-6, 236.6 | 3.44 × 4.25 | 109 | S-all |

\* Factory combined production figures for 1946 through 1949 First Series.

## 1947

| S-11S DeLuxe (wb 121.5) | Wght | Price | Prod* |
|---|---|---|---|
| bus cpe | 3,323 | 1,451 | — |
| club cpe | 3,413 | 1,541 | — |
| sdn 2d | 3,418 | 1,516 | — |
| sdn 4d | 3,448 | 1,551 | — |
| **S-11C Custom (wb 121.5; 7-8P-139.5)\*** | | | |
| club cpe | 3,398 | 1,591 | — |
| conv cpe | 3,618 | 1,965 | — |
| sdn 2d | 3,443 | 1,581 | — |
| sdn 4d | 3,453 | 1,601 | — |
| sdn 4d, 7P | 3,837 | 1,983 | — |
| limo 7P | 3,995 | 2,013 | — |
| Suburban sdn 4d, 8P | 4,012 | 2,283 | — |

| 1947 Engine | bore × stroke | bhp | availability |
|---|---|---|---|
| I-6, 236.6 | 3.44 × 4.25 | 109 | S-all |

\* Factory combined production figures for 1946 through 1949 First Series.

## 1948

| S-11S DeLuxe (wb 121.5) | Wght | Price | Prod* |
|---|---|---|---|
| bus cpe | 3,285 | 1,699 | — |
| club cpe | 3,385 | 1,815 | — |
| sdn 2d | 3,375 | 1,788 | — |
| sdn 4d | 3,435 | 1,825 | — |
| **S-11C Custom (wb 121.5; 7-9P-139.5)\*** | | | |
| club cpe | 3,389 | 1,874 | — |
| conv cpe | 3,599 | 2,296 | — |
| sdn 2d | 3,399 | 1,860 | — |
| sdn 4d | 3,439 | 1,892 | — |
| sdn 4d, 7P | 3,819 | 2,315 | — |
| limo 7P | 3,995 | 2,442 | — |
| Suburban sdn 4d, 9P | 3,974 | 2,631 | — |

| 1948 Engine | bore × stroke | bhp | availability |
|---|---|---|---|
| I-6, 236.6 | 3.44 × 4.25 | 109 | S-all |

\* Factory combined production figures for 1946 through 1949 First Series.

## 1949 First Series

| S-11S DeLuxe (wb 121.5) | Wght | Price | Prod* |
|---|---|---|---|
| bus cpe | 3,285 | 1,699 | — |
| club cpe | 3,385 | 1,815 | — |
| sdn 2d | 3,375 | 1,788 | — |
| sdn 4d | 3,435 | 1,825 | — |
| **S-11C Custom (wb 121.5; 7-9P-139.5)\*** | | | |
| club cpe | 3,389 | 1,874 | — |
| conv cpe | 3,599 | 2,296 | — |
| sdn 2d | 3,399 | 1,860 | — |
| sdn 4d | 3,439 | 1,892 | — |
| sdn 4d, 7P | 3,819 | 2,315 | — |
| limo 7P | 3,995 | 2,442 | — |
| Suburban 4d, 9P | 3,974 | 2,631 | — |

| 1949(1) Engine | bore × stroke | bhp | availability |
|---|---|---|---|
| I-6, 236.6 | 3.44 × 4.25 | 109 | S-all |

\* Factory combined production figures for 1946 through 1949 First Series.

## Combined 1946-1949 First Series Production:

| S-11S DeLuxe (wb 121.5) | Wght | Price | Prod |
|---|---|---|---|
| bus cpe | | | 1,950 |
| club cpe | | | 8,580 |
| sdn 2d | | | 12,751 |
| sdn 4d | | | 32,213 |
| **S-11C Custom (wb 121.5; 7-9P-139.5)** | | | |
| club cpe | | | 38,720 |
| conv cpe | | | 8,100 |
| sdn 2d | | | 1,600 |
| sdn 4d | | | 126,226 |
| sdn 4d, 7P | | | 3,530 |
| limo 7P | | | 120 |
| Suburban 4d, 8-9P | | | 7,500 |
| chassis | | | 105 |

## 1949 Second Series

| S-13-1 DeLuxe (wb 125.5) | Wght | Price | Prod |
|---|---|---|---|
| club cpe | 3,455 | 1,976 | 6,807 |
| sdn 4d | 3,520 | 1,986 | 13,148 |
| Carry-All sdn 4d, 6P | 3,565 | 2,191 | 2,690 |
| wgn 4d, 9P | 3,915 | 2,959 | 850 |
| **S-13-2 Custom (wb 125.5; 8-9P-139.5)** | | | |
| club cpe | 3,585 | 2,156 | 18,431 |
| conv cpe | 3,785 | 2,578 | 3,385 |
| sdn 4d | 3,645 | 2,174 | 48,589 |
| sdn 4d, 8P | 4,200 | 2,863 | 342 |
| Suburban 4d, 9P | 4,410 | 3,179 | 129 |

| 1949(2) Engine | bore × stroke | bhp | availability |
|---|---|---|---|
| I-6, 236.6 | 3.44 × 4.25 | 112 | S-all |

## 1950

| S-14-1 DeLuxe (wb 125.5; 8P-139.5) | Wght | Price | Prod |
|---|---|---|---|
| club cpe | 3,450 | 1,976 | 10,704 |
| sdn 4d | 3,525 | 1,986 | 18,489 |
| Carry-All sdn 4d, 5P | 3,600 | 2,191 | 3,900 |
| sdn 4d, 8P | 3,995 | 2,676 | 235 |
| chassis | — | — | 1 |
| **S-14-2 Custom (wb 125.5; 8-9P-139.5)** | | | |
| club cpe | 3,575 | 2,156 | 18,302 |
| Sportsman htp cpe | 3,735 | 2,489 | 4,600 |
| conv cpe | 3,815 | 2,578 | 2,900 |
| sdn 4d | 3,640 | 2,174 | 72,664 |
| wgn 4d (wood) | 4,035 | 3,093 | 600 |
| wgn 4d (steel) | 3,900 | 2,717 | 100 |
| sdn 4d, 8P | 4,115 | 2,863 | 734 |
| Suburban 4d, 9P | 4,400 | 3,179 | 623 |
| chassis | — | — | 2 |

| 1950 Engine | bore × stroke | bhp | availability |
|---|---|---|---|
| I-6, 236.6 | 3.44 × 4.25 | 112 | S-all |

## 1951

| S-15-1 DeLuxe (wb 125.5; 8P-139.5) | Wght | Price | Prod* |
|---|---|---|---|
| club cpe | 3,475 | 2,215 | — |
| sdn 4d | 3,570 | 2,227 | — |
| Carry-All sdn 4d | 3,685 | 2,457 | — |
| sdn 4d, 8P | 4,045 | 3,001 | — |
| **S-15-2 Custom (wb 125.5; 8-9P-139.5)** | | | |
| club cpe | 3,585 | 2,418 | — |
| Sportsman htp cpe | 3,760 | 2,761 | — |
| conv cpe | 2,862 | 2,840 | — |
| sdn 4d | 3,685 | 2,438 | — |

# DeSoto

| S-15-2 Custom (wb 125.5;8-9P-139.5) | Wght | Price | Prod* |
|---|---|---|---|
| wgn 4d | 3,960 | 3,047 | — |
| sdn 4d, 8P | 4,122 | 3,211 | — |
| Suburban 4d, 9P | 4,395 | 3,566 | — |

| 1951 Engine | bore × stroke | bhp | availability |
|---|---|---|---|
| I-6, 250.6 | 3.44 × 4.50 | 116 | S-all |

* Factory combined 1951-1952 Deluxe and Custom production figures.

## 1952

| S-15-1 DeLuxe (wb 125.5; 8P-139.5) | Wght | Price | Prod* |
|---|---|---|---|
| club cpe | 3,435 | 2,319 | — |
| sdn 4d | 3,540 | 2,333 | — |
| Carry-All sdn 4d | 3,650 | 2,572 | — |
| sdn 4d, 8P | 4,035 | 3,142 | — |
| **S-15-2 Custom (wb 125.5; 8-9P-139.5)** | | | |
| club cpe | 3,565 | 2,531 | — |
| Sportsman htp cpe | 3,720 | 2,890 | — |
| conv cpe | 3,865 | 2,996 | — |
| sdn 4d | 3,660 | 2,552 | — |
| wgn 4d | 4,020 | 3,189 | — |
| sdn 4d, 8P | 4,155 | 3,362 | — |
| Suburban 4d, 9P | 4,370 | 3,734 | — |
| **S-17 Firedome (wb 125.5; 8P-139.5)** | | | |
| club cpe | 3,675 | 2,718 | 5,699 |
| Sportsman htp cpe | 3,850 | 3,078 | 3,000 |
| conv cpe | 3,950 | 3,183 | 850 |
| sdn 4d | 3,760 | 2,740 | 35,651 |
| wgn 4d | 4,080 | 3,377 | 550 |
| sdn 4d, 8P | 4,325 | 3,547 | 50 |

| 1952 Engines | bore × stroke | bhp | availability |
|---|---|---|---|
| I-6, 250.6 | 3.44 × 4.50 | 116 | S-Deluxe, Custom |
| V-8, 276.1 | 3.63 × 3.34 | 160 | S-Firedome |

* Factory combined 1951-1952 Deluxe and Custom production figures.

### 1951-1952 Deluxe and Custom Production:

| S-15-1 DeLuxe (wb 125.5; 8P-139.5) | Wght | Price | Prod |
|---|---|---|---|
| club cpe | | | 6,100 |
| sdn 4d | | | 13,506 |
| Carry-All sdn 4d | | | 1,700 |
| sdn 4d, 8P | | | 343 |
| **S-15-2 Custom (wb 125.5; 8-9P-139.5)** | | | |
| club cpe | | | 19,000 |
| Sportsman htp cpe | | | 8,750 |
| conv cpe | | | 3,950 |
| sdn 4d | | | 88,491 |
| wgn 4d | | | 1,440 |
| sdn 4d, 8P | | | 769 |
| Suburban 4d, 9P | | | 600 |

## 1953

| S-18 Powermaster (wb 125.5; 8P-139.5) | Wght | Price | Prod |
|---|---|---|---|
| club cpe | 3,480 | 2,334 | 8,063 |
| Sportsman htp cpe | 3,585 | 2,604 | 1,470 |
| sdn 4d | 3,535 | 2,356 | 33,644 |
| wgn 4d | 3,845 | 3,078 | 500 |
| sdn 4d, 8P | 4,080 | 3,251 | 225 |
| **S-16 Firedome (wb 125.5; 8P-139.5)** | | | |
| club cpe | 3,655 | 2,622 | 14,591 |
| Sportsman htp cpe | 3,740 | 2,893 | 4,700 |
| conv cpe | 3,990 | 3,114 | 1,700 |
| sdn 4d | 3,720 | 2,643 | 64,211 |
| wgn 4d | 3,995 | 3,351 | 1,100 |
| sdn 4d, 8P | 4,270 | 3,529 | 200 |

| 1953 Engines | bore × stroke | bhp | availability |
|---|---|---|---|
| I-6, 250.6 | 3.44 × 4.50 | 116 | S-Powermaster |
| V-8, 276.1 | 3.63 × 3.34 | 160 | S-Firedome |

## 1954

| S-20 Powermaster (wb 125.5; 8P-139.5) | Wght | Price | Prod |
|---|---|---|---|
| club cpe | 3,505 | 2,364 | 3,499 |
| Sportsman htp cpe | 3,590 | 2,635 | 250 |
| sdn 4d | 3,570 | 2,386 | 14,967 |
| wgn 4d | 3,855 | 3,108 | 225 |
| sdn 4d, 8P | 4,100 | 3,281 | 263 |
| **S-19 Firedome (wb 125.5; 8P-139.5)** | | | |
| club cpe | 3,735 | 2,652 | 5,762 |
| Sportsman htp cpe | 3,815 | 2,923 | 4,382 |
| conv cpe | 4,015 | 3,144 | 1,025 |
| sdn 4d | 3,790 | 2,673 | 45,095 |
| wgn 4d | 4,045 | 3,381 | 946 |
| sdn 4d, 8P | 4,305 | 3,559 | 165 |
| chassis | — | — | 1 |

| 1954 Engines | bore × stroke | bhp | availability |
|---|---|---|---|
| I-6, 250.6 | 3.44 × 4.50 | 116 | S-Powermaster |
| V-8, 276.1 | 3.63 × 3.34 | 170 | S-Firedome |

## 1955

| S-22 Firedome (wb 126.0) | Wght | Price | Prod |
|---|---|---|---|
| Special htp cpe | 3,801 | 2,541 | ⎱ 28,944 |
| Sportsman htp cpe | 3,805 | 2,654 | ⎰ |
| conv cpe | 4,010 | 2,824 | 625 |
| sdn 4d | 3,870 | 2,498 | 46,388 |
| wgn 4d | 4,185 | 3,170 | 1,803 |
| **S-21 Fireflite (wb 126.0)** | | | |
| Sportsman htp cpe | 3,890 | 2,939 | 10,313 |
| conv cpe | 4,115 | 3,151 | 775 |
| sdn 4d (inc. Coronado) | 3,940 | 2,727 | 26,637 |

| 1955 Engines | bore × stroke | bhp | availability |
|---|---|---|---|
| V-8, 291.0 | 3.72 × 3.34 | 185 | S-Firedome |
| V-8, 291.0 | 3.72 × 3.34 | 200 | S-Fireflite |

## 1956

| S-23 Firedome (wb 126.0) | Wght | Price | Prod |
|---|---|---|---|
| Seville htp cpe | 3,800 | 2,684 | 19,136 |
| Seville htp sdn | 3,920 | 2,833 | 4,030 |
| Sportsman htp cpe | 3,835 | 2,854 | 4,589 |
| Sportsman htp sdn | 3,945 | 2,953 | 1,645 |
| conv cpe | 4,080 | 3,081 | 646 |
| sdn 4d | 3,780 | 2,678 | 44,909 |
| wgn 4d | 4,095 | 3,371 | 2,950 |
| **S-24 Fireflite (wb 126.0)** | | | |
| Sportsman htp cpe | 3,905 | 3,346 | 8,475 |
| Sportsman htp sdn | 3,970 | 3,431 | 3,350 |
| conv cpe | 4,075 | 3,544 | 1,085* |
| Pacesetter conv cpe | 4,070 | 3,615 | 400* |
| sdn 4d | 3,860 | 3,119 | 18,207 |
| Adventurer htp cpe | 3,870 | 3,728 | 996 |

* Estimated; total conv cpes: 1,485.

| 1956 Engines | bore × stroke | bhp | availability |
|---|---|---|---|
| V-8, 330.4 | 3.72 × 3.80 | 230 | S-Firedome |

## DeSoto

| 1956 Engines | bore × stroke | bhp | availability |
|---|---|---|---|
| V-8, 330.4 | 3.72 × 3.80 | 255 | S-Fireflite exc Adventurer |
| V-8, 341.4 | 3.78 × 3.80 | 320 | S-Adventurer |

### 1957

| S-27 Firesweep (wb 122.0) | | Wght | Price | Prod |
|---|---|---|---|---|
| | Sportsman htp cpe | 3,645 | 2,836 | 13,333 |
| | Sportsman htp sdn | 3,720 | 2,912 | 7,168 |
| | sdn 4d | 3,675 | 2,777 | 17,300 |
| | Shopper wgn 4d, 6P | 3,965 | 3,169 | 2,270 |
| | Explorer wgn 4d, 9P | 3,970 | 3,310 | 1,198 |
| S-25 Firedome (wb 126.0) | | | | |
| | Sportsman htp cpe | 3,910 | 3,085 | 12,179 |
| | Sportsman htp sdn | 3,960 | 3,142 | 9,050 |
| | conv cpe | 4,065 | 3,361 | 1,297 |
| | sdn 4d | 3,955 | 2,958 | 23,339 |
| S-26 Fireflite (wb 126.0) | | | | |
| | Sportsman htp cpe | 4,000 | 3,614 | 7,217 |
| | Sportsman htp sdn | 4,125 | 3,671 | 6,726 |
| | conv cpe | 4,085 | 3,890 | 1,151 |
| | sdn 4d | 4,025 | 3,487 | 11,565 |
| | Shopper wgn 4d, 6P | 4,290 | 3,982 | 837 |
| | Explorer wgn 4d, 9P | 4,250 | 4,124 | 934 |
| S-26A Adventurer (wb 126.0) | | | | |
| | htp cpe | 4,040 | 3,997 | 1,650 |
| | conv cpe | 4,235 | 4,272 | 300 |

| 1957 Engines | bore × stroke | bhp | availability |
|---|---|---|---|
| V-8, 325.0 | 3.69 × 3.80 | 245 | S-Firesweep |
| V-8, 325.0 | 3.69 × 3.80 | 260 | O-Firesweep |
| V-8, 341.0 | 3.78 × 3.80 | 270 | S-Firedome |
| V-8, 341.0 | 3.78 × 3.80 | 290 | S-Fireflite |
| V-8, 345.0 | 3.80 × 3.80 | 345 | S-Adventurer |

### 1958

| LS1-L Firesweep (wb 122.0) | | Wght | Price | Prod |
|---|---|---|---|---|
| 23 | Sportsman htp cpe | 3,660 | 2,890 | 5,635 |
| 27 | conv cpe | 3,850 | 3,219 | 700 |
| 41 | sdn 4d | 3,660 | 2,819 | 7,646 |
| 43 | Sportsman htp sdn | 3,720 | 2,953 | 3,003 |
| 45A | Shopper wgn 4d, 6P | 3,955 | 3,266 | 1,305 |
| 45B | Explorer wgn 4d, 9P | 3,980 | 3,408 | 1,125 |
| LS2-M Firedome (wb 126.0) | | | | |
| 23 | Sportsman htp cpe | 3,825 | 3,178 | 4,325 |
| 27 | conv cpe | 4,065 | 3,489 | 519 |
| 41 | sdn 4d | 3,855 | 3,085 | 9,505 |
| 43 | Sportsman htp sdn | 3,920 | 3,235 | 3,130 |
| LS3-H Fireflite (wb 126.0) | | | | |
| 23 | Sportsman htp cpe | 3,920 | 3,675 | 3,284 |
| 27 | conv cpe | 4,105 | 3,972 | 474 |
| 41 | sdn 4d | 3,990 | 3,583 | 4,192 |
| 43 | Sportsman htp sdn | 3,980 | 3,731 | 3,243 |
| 45A | Shopper wgn 4d, 6P | 4,225 | 4,030 | 318 |
| 45B | Explorer wgn 4d, 9P | 4,295 | 4,172 | 609 |
| LS3-S Adventurer (wb 126.0) | | | | |
| 23 | htp cpe | 4,000 | 4,071 | 350 |
| 27 | conv cpe | 4,180 | 4,369 | 82 |

| 1958 Engines | bore × stroke | bhp | availability |
|---|---|---|---|
| V-8, 350.0 | 4.06 × 3.38 | 280 | S-Firesweep |
| V-8, 350.0 | 4.06 × 3.38 | 295 | O-Firesweep |
| V-8, 361.0 | 4.13 × 3.38 | 295 | S-Firedome |
| V-8, 361.0 | 4.13 × 3.38 | 305 | S-Fireflite; O-Firedome |
| V-8, 361.0 | 4.13 × 3.38 | 345 | S-Adventurer |
| V-8, 361.0 | 4.13 × 3.38 | 355 | O-Adventurer |

### 1959

| MS1-L Firesweep (wb 122.0) | | Wght | Price | Prod |
|---|---|---|---|---|
| 23 | Sportsman htp cpe | 3,625 | 2,967 | 5,481 |
| 27 | conv cpe | 3,840 | 3,315 | 596 |
| 41 | sdn 4d | 3,670 | 2,904 | 9,649 |
| 43 | Sportsman htp sdn | 3,700 | 3,038 | 2,875 |
| 45A | Shopper wgn 4d, 6P | 3,950 | 3,366 | 1,054 |
| 45B | Explorer wgn, 4d, 9P | 3,980 | 3,508 | 1,179 |
| MS2-M Firedome (wb 126.0) | | | | |
| 23 | Sportsman htp cpe | 3,795 | 3,341 | 2,862 |
| 27 | conv cpe | 4,015 | 3,653 | 299* |
| 41 | sdn 4d | 3,840 | 3,234 | 9,171* |
| 43 | Sportsman htp sdn | 3,895 | 3,398 | 2,744 |
| MS3-H Fireflite (wb 126.0) | | | | |
| 23 | Sportsman htp cpe | 3,910 | 3,831 | 1,393 |
| 27 | conv cpe | 4,105 | 4,152 | 186 |
| 41 | sdn 4d | 3,920 | 3,763 | 4,480 |
| 43 | Sportsman htp sdn | 3,950 | 3,888 | 2,364 |
| 45A | Shopper wgn 4d, 6P | 4,170 | 4,216 | 271 |
| 45B | Explorer wgn 4d, 9P | 4,205 | 4,358 | 433 |
| MS3-S Adventurer (wb 126.0) | | | | |
| 23 | htp cpe | 3,980 | 4,427 | 590 |
| 27 | conv cpe | 4,120 | 4,749 | 97 |

*Includes Seville htp cpe, conv cpe, sdn 4d, and htp sdn, trim variation introduced in Spring 1959 to mark DeSoto's 30th anniversary.

| 1959 Engines | bore × stroke | bhp | availability |
|---|---|---|---|
| V-8, 361.0 | 4.13 × 3.38 | 295 | S-Firesweep |
| V-8, 383.0 | 4.25 × 3.38 | 305 | S-Firedome |
| V-8, 383.0 | 4.25 × 3.38 | 325 | S-Fireflite |
| V-8, 383.0 | 4.25 × 3.38 | 350 | S-Adventurer; O-others |

### 1960

| PS1-L Fireflite (wb 122.0) | | Wght | Price | Prod |
|---|---|---|---|---|
| 23 | htp cpe | 3,885 | 3,102 | 3,494 |
| 41 | sdn 4d | 3,865 | 3,017 | 9,032 |
| 43 | htp sdn | 3,865 | 3,167 | 1,958 |
| PS3-M Adventurer (wb 122.0) | | | | |
| 23 | htp cpe | 3,945 | 3,663 | 3,092 |
| 41 | sdn 4d | 3,895 | 3,579 | 5,746 |
| 43 | htp sdn | 3,940 | 3,727 | 2,759 |

| 1960 Engines | bore × stroke | bhp | availability |
|---|---|---|---|
| V-8, 361.0 | 4.13 × 3.38 | 295 | S-Fireflite |
| V-8, 383.0 | 4.25 × 3.38 | 305 | S-Adventurer |
| V-8, 383.0 | 4.25 × 3.38 | 325 | O-all |
| V-8, 383.0 | 4.25 × 3.38 | 330 | O-Adventurer |

### 1961

| RS1-L (wb 122.0) | | Wght | Price | Prod |
|---|---|---|---|---|
| 612 | htp cpe | 3,760 | 3,102 | 911 |
| 614 | htp sdn | 3,820 | 3,167 | 2,123 |

| 1961 Engine | bore × stroke | bhp | availability |
|---|---|---|---|
| V-8, 361.0 | 4.13 × 3.38 | 265 | S-all |

# Dodge

The Dodge Brothers Company was 14 years old when it was bought by Walter Chrysler in 1928. As a new division of his corporation, Dodge built 125,000 cars in 1929. Then the Depression turned the nation's economy from sunny to gloomy. Though most makes bottomed out in 1933-34, Dodge averaged a healthy 100,000 cars a year, good for fourth behind Chevrolet, Ford, and sister-make Plymouth.

Brothers John and Horace Dodge were traditionalists who believed in practicality and honest dollar value, so their cars never made any gesture toward sport. This continued under Chrysler, with nothing to suggest the high-performance Dodges to come. Through 1954, Dodges were just solid, reliable, low-to-middle-priced cars. Famed World War I U.S. Army General John J. Pershing did as much as anyone to make "Dodge" synonymous with "dependable" by commanding a fleet of 250 Dodge touring cars during his Mexican border campaign against Pancho Villa in 1916.

Dodge changed rungs on the Chrysler price ladder in the early '30s, sometimes standing above DeSoto, sometimes below. By 1933 it was decided that Dodge should occupy the attractive spot just above Plymouth and below DeSoto. Though the Depression delayed Chrysler's efforts to rebuild Dodge by several years, the division surged in 1935, reaching 159,000 cars for the model year. Dodge then soared to near 264,000 for '36 and reached its prewar peak with over 295,000 for 1937. A deep recession the following year temporarily halted the climb, and Dodge slipped out of the top five, but by 1941 it was back up to 237,000.

The Dodge Brothers (who both died in 1920) and their successors sold only four-cylinder cars through 1928, then announced their first six: 241.5-cubic inch L-head unit making 58-68 horsepower. Chrysler presided over the first Dodge Eight in 1930, which would continue through three different displacements for the next three years. Dodge then offered nothing but inline-sixes through 1952. That engine, a flathead cast-iron design introduced in 1933, ultimately evolved through displacements of 201-230 cid and rated horsepower of 75-138. And it wasn't finished even in 1952; it continued for seven years more.

Dodge styling in the '30s was the most conservative of any Chrysler make, and the division was lucky to escape being saddled with an Airflow, as was planned for 1935. Dodge's long-famous ram hood mascot, a manifestation of the Chrysler

**1930 Series DD New Six four-door sedan**

**1932 Series DK Eight 2/4-passenger coupe**

**1931 Series DH Six station wagon**

**1933 Series DO Eight four-door sedan**

**1932 Series DK Eight four-door sedan**

**1933 Series DP Six Salon Brougham sedan**

# Dodge

takeover, arrived in '32. Lines were four-square through '34 save a slight concession to the "streamlining" craze in a rakish 1933-34 grille. Then came a waterfall grille, skirted fenders, and much-more-rounded lines as part of the companywide "Airstream" look for 1935-36. By 1939, Dodge had acquired extended "pontoon" fenders, elongated rear decks, and a sharp "prow-front" under the direction of company design chief Ray Dietrich, thus falling nicely in line with DeSoto and Chrysler.

Like most makes, and the Depression notwithstanding, Dodge cataloged numerous body types throughout the '30s, including all the popular open styles. Among the latter was a convertible sedan, which was absent for 1935 and then vanished after '38 due to diminishing sales. A long 128-inch-wheelbase chassis appeared for 1936 under seven-passenger sedans and limousines; by 1939 this was up to 134 inches. Dodge also made a strong effort to win custom-body business by selling chassis to hearse, ambulance, and station wagon builders.

Speaking of wheelbases, Dodge did much shuffling there, too. The short-lived Eights started at 114 inches, stretched to 118.5 for '31, then to 122. Sixes ranged from 109 to 120 inches through 1939, but were mostly 114-117 inches. Series names and positions also changed a lot, as did each year's advertising theme. Chrysler would name cars most anything if it helped sales, and it hyped the Dodge line under such prosaic banners as "New Standard" (1934), "New Value" ('35), "Beauty Winner" (1936), and "Luxury Liner" (1939). That last one is still part of auto "journalese," if not popular parlance.

Nineteen thirty-seven brought some of the more innovative period Dodges. Though not vastly altered from the "Air Styled" '36s, they boasted nonsnag door handles, recessed dash knobs, lower driveshaft tunnels, one-piece steel-roof construction (ending fabric inserts at last), and built-in windshield defroster vents. Dodge also claimed an industry first with fully insulated rubber body mounts.

Like other Chrysler products, the '39 Dodges were totally redesigned—fitting for the make's Silver Anniversary year. Also in evident celebration, the division returned to a two-series lineup for the first time since 1934: Special and DeLuxe, differing mainly in interior trim. DeLuxe also offered more models. Long sedans took a year off, but not the sturdy Dodge six: still pumping out 87 horsepower, as it had since '34. A "birthday present" of sorts was a limited-edition five-passenger DeLuxe Town Coupe with Hayes bodywork on the standard 117-inch wheelbase. Hayes built 1000 of these pretty, thin-pillared bodies for use among Dodge, DeSoto, and Chrysler. The Dodge version saw 363 copies of the one-year-only model, and led the "Luxury Liners" in glamour as well as price ($1055).

Continuity was Dodge's hallmark in the '40s, the division retaining its essential 1939 bodyshells all the way through "first-series" 1949 models, though exterior sheetmetal and some internal structure would change along the way. Standard wheelbase throughout was 119.5 inches. A long sedan and limousine

1933 Series DO Eight station wagon

1934 Series DS DeLuxe Six Special convertible sedan

1937 Series D5 convertible sedan

1936 Series D2 Beauty Winner Six two-door trunkback sedan

1936 Series D2 convertible coupe

1937 Series D5 four-door trunkback sedan

# Dodge

1938 Series D8 four-door trunkback sedan

1938 Series D8 convertible coupe

1937 Series D5 two-door sedan

1939 Series D11 Luxury Liner DeLuxe four-door sedan

returned for 1940 on a 139.5-inch chassis, which then shrunk a bit to 137.5. Styling was typical of Highland Park in this era: prominent fenders, increasingly gaudy grilles, and low rooflines with limited glass areas.

The 1940 line repeated '39 offerings: low-priced Special coupe and two- and four-door sedans; the same as DeLuxes plus convertible, five-seater coupe, and the aforementioned seven-place sedan and limousine (the last cost $1170). The upper series accounted for some 120,000 units, about 60 percent of the model-year total—though only 1000 were long models. Running boards were on the way out, now a $10 linewide option. A new 1940 extra was two-tone paint, though with fenders, hood, and deck in the contrasting color, this conferred a taxicab air and was not popular.

A clean facelift livened up looks for '41, announced by parking lights combined with the headlamps in a more horizontal heart-shaped grille. Chrysler's Fluid Drive clutch became optional, and higher compression booted the old-soldier six to 91 bhp. Two-door sedans were now Broughams, DeLuxe designated the inexpensive three-model line, and the upper series was renamed Custom. Expanding the last was a handsome four-door Town Sedan with blank rear-roof quarters. It was a modest success, garnering 16,074 orders. Long models continued selling in small numbers (just 654 this year). Total production divided between 106,000 DeLuxes and 131,000 Customs. Though Dodge had moved from ninth to sixth in the industry for 1940, it fell back a spot for '41. The following year, though, it reclaimed sixth from Oldsmobile.

With Pearl Harbor and America's entry into World War II, the government halted civilian production in February 1942. Dodges weren't as scarce as some other Detroit cars that year, though they're hard enough to come by now. Model-year production was about 68,500. Among standard-chassis models, the Custom convertible was rarest: just 1185 built.

A heavy facelift made the '42 Dodges look good, if not quite as radical as that year's hidden-headlamp DeSotos. Front fenders were broadened to accommodate a more-horizontal grille with a distinct eggcrate texture and bulged center. Optional fender skirts returned from '41 with bright moldings to match rear-fender trim, and five-passenger coupes gained more rakishly angled B-posts. The only mechanical change involved stroking the old six to 230.2 cid and substituting a Carter carb for the previous Stromberg. Horsepower stood at 105.

Sporadic wartime design work in Highland Park produced several interesting prototypes for postwar Dodges. These involved the basic 1940-42 body updated with smoother grilles, wraparound bumpers, thinner door pillars, and fully integrated fenders. But all were rendered stillborn because '42 tooling was far from amortized. Dodge thus resumed civilian production with warmed-over prewar cars for 1946-48, as did most other makes.

The division was especially slow to do so, building only 420 cars by the end of 1945. But output zoomed in calendar '46, and Dodge finished the model year in fourth (behind the low-priced three) with nearly 164,000. The tally was over 243,000 for '47, but Dodge fell to fifth behind an equally resurgent Buick. The make regained fourth the next year, again on slightly more than 243,000 cars.

The facelift for the 1946-48 Dodges—all but identical save serial numbers, like divisional siblings—was created by A.B. "Buzz" Grisinger, John Chika, and Herb Weissinger, a trio soon to win fame at Kaiser-Frazer. Allowed bolt-on alterations only, they opted for a new grille with thick horizontal bars overlaid by thinner vertical ones. Square parking lights sat outboard of the bottom grille corners, and a prominent nameplate graced the hood. Technical improvements included dash-mounted pushbutton starter (replacing a foot pedal), front brakes with double wheel cylinders, revised transmission, inline fuel filter, and "Full-Flo" oil filter.

Like its corporate sisters, Dodge wasn't ready with its first all-new postwar cars in time for a 1949 announcement, so 1948s were sold through April as "first-series" '49s. The "second series" '49s were all-new save a rerated 103-horsepower six, and sold in record numbers: nearly 257,000 for the model year, though that was good for only eighth in industry volume.

Model offerings were considerably revised within two series. The inexpensive group was the 115-inch-wheelbase Wayfarer, comprising a notchback business coupe, a fastback two-door

# Dodge

1940 Series D-14 DeLuxe Luxury Liner four-door sedan

1941 Series D-19 Custom Luxury Liner four-door sedan

1942 Series D-22 DeLuxe business coupe

1946 Series D-24C Custom convertible coupe

sedan, and a novel three-passenger roadster with side curtains. Prices spanned $1611 to $1738. The "volume" models were a new Meadowbrook sedan and top-line Coronet sedan, coupe, convertible, and—new for Dodge—a four-door structural-wood wagon. All rode a 123.5-inch wheelbase and sported better trim and equipment than the spartan Wayfarers. Exclusive to the four-door Coronet was an $85 "Town Sedan" option with luxurious Bedford cord upholstery. The $1848 Meadowbrook sold for about $75 less than the standard Coronet sedan.

As with other Chrysler divisions, Dodge's new '49 styling was very square and slab-sided. A shiny latticework grille bore some resemblance to the 1946-48 affair, but looked more-massive. Bolt-on rear fenders were capped by three-sided taillights, but front fenders were fully flush for the first time. Collectors judge the Wayfarer roadster the most desirable '49 Dodge, and many of the original 5420 have been restored. The Coronet wagon was far less successful: only 800 were produced. After 600 more were built for early 1950, it departed for an all-steel Sierra wagon.

Gyro-Matic semiautomatic transmission became optional. This was an important sales point at a time when people were tiring of manual shifting. Fluid Drive with Gyro-Matic was a complex solution to a simple problem, combining a conventional clutch with a fluid coupling that multiplied torque like a torque converter; electrical shift circuits added to what one writer called a "full range of potential transmission trouble." The coupling performed the usual flywheel functions of storing energy, smoothing power impulses, and meshing the ring gear with the starter pinion. Lacking a clutch-plate contact, a clutch was mounted in tandem. The fluid coupling was a drum filled with low-viscosity mineral oil. Running the engine rotated a set of vanes attached to the inner face that threw oil outward onto a facing runner with another set of vanes. The oil turned the runner to provide a smooth flow of power while avoiding any metal-to-metal contact.

Fluid Drive had two gear positions: Low, governing first and second gears, High for third and fourth. Low was mainly for fast starts or towing. In most other driving you simply shifted into High and pressed the accelerator, then let up at 14 mph, when a "thump" announced the shift from third to fourth. Stops and starts required no clutching or shifting, hence Chrysler's claim that Fluid Drive Gyro-Matic eliminated 95 percent of all shift motions. The clutch was there, but was used only to change between Low and High or to back up.

Unusually for an all-new Detroiter, the '49 Dodge got a heavy facelift for its second season. Coronet now featured Dodge's first hardtop coupe, dubbed Diplomat, and the Wayfarer roadster gained roll-down door glass to become the Sportabout convertible (still with a single bench seat for three). Other offerings returned from '49, including a seven-passenger sedan on a 137.5-inch wheelbase in the Coronet line. This would continue in very small numbers through 1952, mainly for taxi and limousine use.

Dodge fared well in the early '50s despite ho-hum cars and government-ordered caps on civilian production for the Korean War. Division car output was just over 343,000 for 1950 and 290,000 for '51, good for seventh. The division maintained that rank with only 206,000 cars for '52 and a more-satisfying 320,000 for '53, then dropped to eighth on 1954 volume of only 154,000.

Styling became a tad sleeker for 1951-52. Wheelbases were unchanged, but a lower grille opening, clean flanks, and faired-in taillights improved appearance. The most-visible '52 alteration was paint applied to the grille bar just above the bumper.

A revised 1953 lineup put a lone Meadowbrook Suburban wagon and other two-door models on the 114-inch Plymouth wheelbase—thus reviving a stubby look; a 119-inch chassis supported six-cylinder Meadowbrook, Meadowbrook Special, and Coronet sedans and club coupes. But windshields were now one-piece, rooflines restyled, and trim moved around, all of which helped improve what were still slab-sided boxes. As with all '53 Chrysler Corporation cars, this facelift marked the first direct influence of new styling chief Virgil Exner, who'd come to Highland Park from Studebaker a few years before.

But the big news for '53 was the Coronet Eight, a new top-line group that consisted of long-chassis club coupe and sedan and "shorty" convertible, Diplomat hardtop, and two-door Sierra, all powered by Dodge's first-ever performance engine:

the brilliant Red Ram V-8. Arriving at 241.3 cid, it delivered 140 horsepower but was capable of much more. In essence, it was a scaled-down version of 1951's new 331-cid Chrysler Hemi. The company had long experimented with hemispherical combustion chambers and was now cashing in on what it had learned. Against other V-8s, the Hemi offered the inherent advantages of smoother porting and manifold passages, larger valves set farther apart, better thermal efficiency, ample water jacketing, a nearly central spark-plug location, and low heat rejection into coolant. Its main drawback was cost: far more expensive to build than, say, the 1955 Chevrolet 265.

Even so, the Red Ram combined with surprisingly low weight to make the '53 Dodges terrific stormers and fine handlers. They were even frugal with fuel: A Red Ram scored 23.4 miles per gallon in the '53 Mobilgas Economy Run. Other V-8 Dodges broke 196 AAA stock-car records at Bonneville in '53, and Danny Eames drove one to a record 102.62 mph on California's El Mirage dry lake.

Several interesting show cars also contributed to Dodge's now increasingly youthful image. Like others at Chrysler in this period, these were Exner designs built by Ghia in Italy. The first was Firearrow, a nonrunning '53 roadster with a unique frameless windshield; a road-ready version appeared the following year. In late 1954 came the evolutionary Firearrow convertible and sport coupe whose lines inspired the limited-production Dual-Ghia of 1956-58. The coupe proved quite stable aerodynamically, achieving 143.44 mph on the banked oval at the Chrysler Proving Grounds in rural Chelsea, Michigan.

Only detail appearance changes occurred on Dodge's '54 production models, but the Red Ram became available across the board, and a luxurious new top-line Royal V-8 series offered club coupe, sedan, convertible, and Sport hardtop coupe. Meadowbrook now listed six and V-8 sedans and coupes on the 119-inch chassis; Coronet added long-chassis four-door Sierra wagons and short two-door Suburbans, plus convertible and Sport hardtop as before.

Dodge paced the '54 Indy 500, and trumpeted its selection with 701 replica pace-car convertibles called Royal 500. Priced at $2632 apiece, they sported Kelsey-Hayes chrome wire wheels, "continental" outside spare tire, special ornamentation, and a tuned 150-bhp Red Ram. A dealer-installed four-barrel Offenhauser manifold was also available, which must have made this a screamer, though Chrysler never quoted actual horsepower.

The Royal 500 symbolized Dodge's rapid emergence as Chrysler's "performance" outfit. And indeed, the division was rolling up more competition successes. Lincoln is famous for its dominance in the Mexican Road Race of these years. Less widely known is the fact that Dodge overwhelmed the event's Medium Stock class in 1954, finishing 1-2-3-4-6-9.

After suffering poor '54 sales along with sister divisions, Dodge came back with a vengeance. Bearing Exner's first-generation "Forward Look," the all-new '55s were flashy but not overdone, the work of Exner lieutenant Murray Baldwin. They were bigger as well as brighter, with all models on a 120-inch wheelbase. Series comprised six and V-8 Coronets and V-8 Royals and Custom Royals. The last, the new line-topper, offered four-door sedan and three Lancer submodels: sedan (a midyear arrival), convertible, and hardtop coupe. The old six, which had been coaxed to 110 horsepower for '54, now packed 123 horsepower. The Red Ram was bored to 270.1 cid, good for 175/183 bhp; an optional "Power Package" with four-barrel carb delivered 193. Dodge prospered with greatly increased '55 volume of nearly 277,000 cars, but rivals also did well in that record industry year and Dodge couldn't budge from eighth place.

1948 Series D-24C Custom convertible coupe

1949 Coronet four-door sedan

1949 Wayfarer roadster

1950 Coronet four-door sedan

1951 Coronet Diplomat hardtop coupe

# Dodge

1952 Coronet four-door sedan

1952 Wayfarer two-door sedan

1953 Coronet Eight four-door sedan

1954 Royal four-door sedan

1954 Royal sport coupe hardtop

1954 Royal 500 convertible coupe

1954 Royal club coupe

1955 Royal Sierra four-door station wagon

1955 Coronet Six two-door sedan

1955 Coronet V-8 four-door sedan

# Dodge

1955 Custom Royal Lancer hardtop coupe

1955 Custom Royal four-door sedan

1956 Custom Royal Lancer hardtop sedan

1956 Coronet V-8 two-door sedan

1956 Royal Sierra four-door station wagon

1956 Royal Suburban two-door station wagon

1956 Coronet "Texan" Lancer hardtop coupe

1956 Custom Royal La Femme hardtop coupe

1956 Custom Royal four-door sedan

1957 Suburban two-door station wagon

# Dodge

An interesting '55 footnote was "La Femme," a Custom Royal Lancer hardtop coupe painted pink and white. As the name implied, it featured custom accoutrements for m'lady, including a folding umbrella and a fitted handbag in the backs of the front seats. La Femme returned for '56, but response was minimal and few of these cars were produced.

Most '55 Dodge Lancers wore tiny chrome rear-fender trim suggesting fins. For '56 Highland Park offered sharply uplifted fenders, and Dodge wore them as well as any. Two-speed PowerFlite, the firm's first fully automatic transmission, had arrived with lever control in '54. Now it had pushbuttons in a handy pod to the left of the wheel.

Besides revised frontal styling and new interiors, Dodge '56 also advertised a stroked "Super Red Ram" V-8 with 315 cid and 218 horsepower, versus 189 for the returning 270. The evergreen six now offered 131 horses. Available across the board was the first of the now-famous "D-500" options. For '56 this was just a four-barrel carb that provided 230 horsepower. However, a Chrysler historical publication also lists a four-barrel 315 with higher compression (9.25:1 vs. 8.0 elsewhere), good for 260 horsepower. Other '56 developments involved a new Lancer four-door hardtop sedan in each series, and a "spring special" Golden Lancer, a D-500 Custom Royal hardtop coupe with Sapphire White/Gallant Gold exterior and harmonizing white/black/gray interior.

Nineteen fifty-six was a down year for all Detroit, and Dodge built 240,000 cars to again run eighth. But helped by torsion-bar suspension, all-new styling, and more power for '57, Dodge would climb to seventh on volume of nearly 288,000.

Carrying Exner's "second-generation" Forward Look, the '57 Dodges were longer, lower, wider, and more aggressive-looking, with a massive bumper/grille, lots of glass, and high-flying fins (ads called all of this "Swept-Wing" styling). Wheelbase stretched to 122 inches, where it would remain through 1961. The Hemi was again enlarged: bored this time to 325 cid. The result, depending on compression and carbs, was 245-310 bhp. The '57 D-500 option was a 354 from junior Chryslers, tuned for 340 bhp. The old six got another seven horses for its ultimate total of 138.

The D-500 package was Dodge's answer to the limited-edition supercars at sister divisions—available for any model right down to the plain-Jane Coronet two-door. Shocks, springs, and the new-for-'57 front torsion bars were all suitably firmed up for what *Motor Trend* magazine called a "close liaison with the road"—handling that put D-500s at the head of their class. V-8s delivered brisk-to-blistering go. Even the relatively mild 245-bhp mill could scale 0-60 in about 9.5 seconds. The D-500 continued into 1958-59, but with 361- and 383-cid wedgehead V-8s instead of costly Hemis. With the optional Bendix fuel injection offered only for '58, the 361 packed a thrilling 333 horsepower.

A mild facelift with four headlamps and revised trim marked the '58 Dodges. The line was a rerun until February, when a spiffy Regal Lancer hardtop coupe was announced as one of the "spring specials" so long favored by Chrysler marketers. Some of its trim items were also available on lesser Dodges, including lancer-head grille medallion, blackout headlamp trim, and rather contrived bodyside/fin moldings. Sensibly left alone were 1957's new Torsion-Aire Ride and optional three-speed TorqueFlite automatic transmission that had earned near-universal praise—and buyer approval. Both would persist at Dodge and throughout the corporate camp for many years.

Now in its final season, Dodge's 325 Hemi packed 252/265 bhp for '58. The new wedgehead 361 delivered 305, 320, or the aforementioned 333 horsepower. A smaller 350 version offered 295 standard horsepower in Custom Royals and V-8 wagons. Although 1958 was disastrous for every Detroit make, Dodge

1957 Custom Royal Lancer convertible coupe

1957 Custom Royal Lancer hardtop coupe

1957 Custom Royal Lancer hardtop sedan

1957 Custom Sierra four-door station wagon

1957 Custom Royal four-door sedan

1958 Custom Royal Lancer hardtop coupe

1958 Custom Royal Lancer hardtop sedan

1959 Custom Royal Lancer hardtop coupe

1959 Custom Royal four-door sedan

1960 Polara four-door sedan

fared worse than most. Model-year production plunged to 138,000 as the division barely finished ahead of Cadillac.

But Dodge shared in Detroit's modest 1959 recovery, building about 156,000 cars and rebounding from ninth to eighth in the volume stakes. Sales might have been better had it not been for a rather heavy-handed facelift marked by droopy hooded headlamps and misshapen fins above suggestive thrusting taillamps. Revised interiors could be newly furnished with swivel front seats, semibuckets that pivoted outward upon opening a door. The venerable flathead six was in its final year. V-8s, now wedgeheads only, comprised a new 326 with 255 bhp for Coronets; a 305-bhp 361 for other models; and a big new 383 with 320/345 bhp. The last-named was that year's D-500—and not cheap. Both were thirsty, but it was the age of 30-cent-a-gallon gas and the market still craved performance (if not quite as much as before the '58 recession).

The '60s would see Dodge strengthen its position in the high-performance field, push upward into price territory left vacant by DeSoto's cancelation after '61, and diversify with compacts and intermediates. Volume rose rapidly after 1964 to an annual average of over half a million units, and the division set a new record with 633,000 for '66. But competitors were up too, so Dodge's standing in the industry production stakes varied between fifth or sixth in its best years and seventh to ninth in troubled 1961-63.

Taking note of the growing buyer interest in smaller cars prompted by the '58 recession, Dodge entered the '60s with a much broader lineup divided into "junior" and "senior" groups. The former was the new Dart: sixes and V-8s on a 118-inch wheelbase save wagons, which rode a 122. Series were tagged Seneca, Pioneer, and Phoenix in ascending order of price and plush. Phoenix offered a convertible, hardtop coupe and sedan, and pillared four-door; lesser lines were limited to wagons, two- and four-door sedans, and a Pioneer two-door hardtop. The senior line comprised V-8 Matadors and Polaras on the 122-inch wheelbase. All 1960 Dodges employed unit body/chassis construction, new at Chrysler Corporation that year, and wore more-sculptured lines announced by bright, blunt, and busy front ends. Fins were still in evidence, ending well ahead of podlike taillights on Matador/Polara, near the rear of more-conventional fenders on Darts.

Despite appearances, most 1960 Dodges were relatively light and thus offered good performance with reasonable economy. That was even true of base-engine models, which carried the larger, 225-cid version of Chrysler Corporation's new "Slant Six." Initially rated at 145 bhp, this durable workhorse would carry on into the early '80s. Dart's V-8 was the solid, reliable 318 with 230/255 horsepower. Matadors used a 295-bhp Chrysler

# Dodge

1960 Dart Phoenix convertible coupe

1960 Polara hardtop coupe

1961 Dart Phoenix hardtop coupe

1961 Dart Pioneer four-door station wagon

1961 Polara hardtop sedan

1961 Dart Phoenix hardtop coupe

361, optional on Dart Pioneer and Phoenix. Polaras had a standard 383 (available for Phoenix and Matador) with 325/330 horsepower. Helped greatly by the Dart, attractively priced in the $2300-$3000 range, Dodge scored impressively higher sales: up over 200,000 for the model year to nearly 368,000, good for sixth on the industry roster.

Per well-established Chrysler practice, the '61 line included a Dodge version of a Plymouth product: the 106.5-inch-wheelbase Valiant compact, new for 1960. Called Lancer, it shared the Valiant's "unibody" structure and basic styling but stood apart with a horizontal-bar grille and slightly better trim. Also like Valiant, there were two Lancer series, 170 and 770, each with two-door sedan, four-door sedan, and four-door wagon. The 770 added a hardtop coupe that was also new to Valiant for '61, as was the pillared two-door. Power came from the smaller, 170-cid Slant Six with 101 bhp. The 225 Dart engine was optional.

The Dart itself was substantially facelifted for '61, gaining a deeply concave full-width grille cradling quad headlamps, plus curious reverse-slant tailfins. The senior Matador was dropped and remaining Polaras were restyled to be virtual Dart dead-ringers. Engines mostly reprised the 1960 choices. Among these was Dodge's customary D-500 option, now a 383 with twin four-barrel carburetors and ram-induction manifolding (new for '60), good for an outstanding 330 horsepower. In a Dart, that translated to about 10 pounds for each horsepower, a super power-to-weight ratio that meant 120-mph flat out and acceleration to match. Torsionbar suspension and oversized Chrysler brakes made it as roadable as it was quick. It was even quicker when equipped with the Chrysler 413, a ram-induction wedge delivering 350 or 375 bhp as a new Dart option, though price was high and availability quite limited.

However, Dodge sales dropped by over 25 percent for '61, reflecting increased competition and an overall industry downtrend. Lancer didn't sell well, but it was a stopgap anyway. A successor was in the works, so the only notable changes for '62 were a busier grille and a smart bucket-seat GT hardtop (replacing the 770 model).

Meantime, a brand-new 116-inch-wheelbase Dart in base, 330, and 440 series arrived, measuring six inches shorter and 400 pounds lighter than corresponding '61s. Topping the line was a sporty bucket-seat Polara 500 group, offering hardtops with two and four doors, plus convertible. Chrysler design chief Virgil Exner thought that if Americans liked compacts, they'd go for downsized "standard" cars, too. But he was about 15 years ahead of his time, and these cars sold as poorly as the Lancer—aggravated by frankly odd Lancer-like looks.

But performance fans roundly applauded the smaller, lighter Darts, mainly because the big-block 413 returned with more muscle: 365, 380, 410, and a rollicking 420-bhp. Shoehorned into the lightest base-trim two-doors, these cars began terroriz-

# Dodge

1961 Lancer 770 hardtop coupe

1962 Dart 440 hardtop sedan

1962 Polara 500 convertible coupe

1962 Polara 500 hardtop sedan

1962 Lancer GT hardtop coupe

ing the nation's dragstrips, thus renewing Dodge's "hot car" reputation and setting the stage for even wilder doings. In fact, big-inch Dodge intermediates won the National Hot Rod Association Championship in 1962 and would reign supreme for the next few years on literally every quarter-mile. They were also strong contenders at Daytona.

But performance alone doesn't necessarily sell cars, and Dodge's total volume for '62 was down to about 240,500, off some 30,000 in a year when most rivals scored higher sales. Things would have been worse had it not been for the true full-size cars that were reinstated at midyear as the Custom 880. Effectively taking over for the now-departed DeSoto, they looked like the finless '61 Polaras they were, with '62 Chrysler-style "plucked chicken" tails and standard 265-bhp 361 V-8.

While Plymouth struggled on with its related downsized "standards," Dodge increased wheelbase to 119 inches for 1963—and pushed performance. What had been called Dart was now just "Dodge," comprising 330, 440, and Polara series. As before, the last included a swanky bucket-seat 500 convertible and hardtop coupe. Styling was cleaner and more conventional, though the "face" was still pretty odd. Engines remained broadly the same, but a bore job took the 413 wedge to 426 cubes and 370/375 horsepower. But the big news was the "Ramcharger," a super-performance 426 with aluminum pistons and high-lift cam punching out 415/425 horsepower.

Dodge did field a Dart for '63, but it was a very different car: a mostly new compact to replace Lancer. (The name change was a last-minute decision.) It was basically that year's redesigned Valiant with more crisply styled exterior and five extra inches in wheelbase (111 except wagons, still at 106). Sedans and wagons made up the 170 and 270 series, with convertibles offered in 270 and bucket-seat GT guise; there was also a GT hardtop coupe. At the other end of the scale, Custom 880s returned with new lower-priced 880 companions, all bearing grilles with fine vertical bars. With so much new, Dodge surged past Rambler to grab seventh in the industry on record volume of over 446,000 units.

The '64 lineup was much like '63's, with facelifts that continued Dodge's move back to more-orthodox looks. Darts became livelier, as Valiant's new 273-cid small-block V-8 was added to the options list, bringing 180 horsepower. That year's Ramcharger was Chrysler's fabled hemi-head V-8, returning to the performance wars in a new 426 version with 425 horsepower—but only for racing. The top showroom power options remained wedgehead 426s, now with 365 standard horsepower or 415 with high-compression heads. But Hemi-powered Dodge/Plymouth intermediates provided plenty of entertainment anyway, dominating the NASCAR season beginning with a 1-2-3 sweep at the Daytona 500. In the production race, Dodge swept back into sixth for the first time since 1960.

For 1965, the Coronet name returned on a revamped midsize line with more square-cut styling and a 117-inch wheelbase for all models but wagons (116 inches). These were essentially the 1962-64 "standards" logically repositioned to battle popular intermediates like Ford Fairlane and Chevy Chevelle. But there was also a much-altered 115-inch-wheelbase Coronet Hemi-Charger two-door sedan weighing just 3165 pounds. Intended strictly for drag racing and base-priced at $3165, it came with the reborn 426 Hemi, of course, plus heavy-duty springs and shocks, antiroll bar, four-on-the-floor manual transmission, and strong police brakes. Performance was more than ample: 0-60 mph in seven seconds or less. Buyers in less of a hurry flocked to a civilized new buckets-and-console Coronet 500 hardtop and convertible available with wedgehead V-8s up to 426 cubes and 365 horsepower.

Capping the '65 line was a completely redesigned group of

# Dodge

**1962 Custom 880 hardtop sedan**

**1963 Custom 880 hardtop sedan**

**1964 Polara 500 convertible coupe**

**1964 Polara hardtop coupe**

**1964 Custom 880 hardtop coupe**

121-inch wheelbase Polaras and Custom 880s, plus a companion sports/luxury hardtop, the $3355 Monaco. All shared chassis and body structure with that year's Chryslers and full-size Plymouth Furys. Their conservatively square basic shape was dictated by design director Elwood Engel, who'd been recruited from Ford to replace Virgil Exner in 1962. The Dodges were distinguished by a "dumbbell" grille and delta taillamps.

After a modest '65 restyle, Darts squared up for '66, via new front sheetmetal. Coronets returned in standard, Deluxe, 440, and 500 guise, also with blockier fronts as well as curvier rear fenders and wedgy taillights. Custom 880 was renamed Monaco, and the big bucket-seat hardtop became Monaco 500. Monacos and Polaras got wider taillights and crisper lower-body contours, plus Chrysler's new big-block 440 wedgehead with 350 horsepower as the top power option.

A midyear salvo in the division's 1966 "Dodge Rebellion" was Charger, essentially a fastback Coronet hardtop coupe with hidden-headlamp grille, full-width taillights, and a sporty four-seat interior with full-length center console and individual fold-down rear buckets. A mild 318 V-8 was standard, but you could order a mighty 425-bhp "Street Hemi," a new regular production option for all '66 Chrysler intermediates. Also on the Charger option sheet: manual transmission, "Rallye" suspension, and numerous luxury items.

In all, 1966 was a great Dodge year. After easing to 489,000 for '65, volume shot up to its aforementioned decade high, good for fifth in the industry. Dodge wouldn't rank as high again until '88.

For 1967, the Dart got an all-new unit structure on the existing wheelbase and lost its wagons. Styling was a bit curvier and more "important," though still pretty, if rather mainstream. Polara/Monaco also got a new structure: a full-size body/frame platform shared with that year's Chryslers and Plymouth Furys. Styling here was somewhat more contrived: lower and sleeker but with rear decks longer than hoods, plus a complex grille comprising a square vertical-bar section between openings split by horizontal bars. A belated facelift made Coronets look more like the Charger, which continued its '66 appearance but added two 383 V-8 options with 270 and 325 horsepower.

Continuing its performance push, Dodge issued a sportier Coronet for '67. Called R/T, for "Road/Track", it came as a convertible and hardtop coupe with a tuned 375-bhp 440 "Magnum" V-8, heavy-duty suspension, wide tires, and oversize brakes—Dodge's entry in the burgeoning "muscle-car" market uncovered by the Pontiac GTO. A similar package was devised the following year for a new Charger R/T. The 426 Hemi remained

# Dodge

1964 Polara hardtop sedan

1964 Dart GT hardtop coupe

1964 Custom 880 convertible coupe

1965 Dart GT convertible coupe

1965 Monaco hardtop coupe

1965 Coronet 500 hardtop coupe

1966 Polara hardtop sedan

optional for intermediates, still on a limited basis. Despite its appealing '67 line, Dodge fell back to seventh place on model-year volume of nearly 466,000 units.

Dart and full-size Dodges were facelifted for '68, as it was time for Coronet and Charger to be fully revised. The result was the best-looking midsize Dodges yet: long and low, with rounded "fuselage" lines and pleasingly simple grilles. Charger again featured hidden headlamps, but was now a notchback hardtop with a semifastback "flying buttress" roofline.

Sporty models continued multiplying. Dart added a plush GTS hardtop and convertible with standard 340 V-8, an enlarged 273 with 275 horsepower. A big 300-bhp 383 was optional—and bordered on overkill in a compact. Coronet offered the new budget-priced Super Bee, a no-frills two-door muscle coupe with special 335-bhp "Magnum" 383. These and the Coronet and Charger R/Ts made up what Dodge called the "Scat Pack." All wore "bumble-bee" tape stripes on their tails, and ranked among 1968's quickest and most-roadable performance machines.

Along with Chrysler and Plymouth Fury, the '69 Polara/Monaco got "fuselage" styling of their own, but remained on a 122-inch wheelbase. Dart, Coronet, and Charger

# Dodge

**1966 Coronet 500 hardtop coupe**

**1967 Coronet 500 Hemi hardtop coupe**

**1967 Monaco hardtop sedan**

**1967 Coronet R/T hardtop coupe**

**1967 Charger fastback hardtop coupe**

**1967 Polara 500 hardtop coupe**

**1967 Dart GT hardtop coupe**

wore minor facelifts. Dart GTS was joined by a Swinger, a two-door hardtop with special trim, bright grille, and choice of 318 or 340 V-8s.

But the pride of Dodge's '69 fleet was unquestionably the Charger Daytona. Conceived for long-distance NASCAR races like the Daytona 500, it was an exercise in aerodynamics, marked by a unique bullet nose with hidden headlights and "bib" spoiler, plus a flush-window fastback roof and a huge trunklid wing on towering twin stabilizers. All this made the Daytona about 20-percent more "slippery" than previous racing Chargers, which gave it an advantage of 500 yards per lap.

Dodge built only 505—just enough to qualify as "production" under NASCAR rules. A Daytona won the Talladega 500 in September 1969, though that was partly because the Ford contingent didn't show. In 1970, the Daytona's and Plymouth's similar Superbirds won 38 of 48 major NASCAR races. For shorter races, Dodge also had a wingless, blunt-nose Charger 500.

Appearing with Plymouth's third-generation Barracuda for 1970 was a Dodge relative, the division's belated reply to the Ford Mustang, Chevy Camaro, and other ponycars. Fittingly named Challenger, it was offered with a Slant-Six as standard power, plus V-8 options of 318, 383, 440, and even the Hemi.

# Dodge

1968 Coronet R/T hardtop coupe

1969 Coronet 500 hardtop coupe

1968 Charger hardtop coupe

1969 Charger Hemi hardtop coupe

1969 Polara 500 hardtop coupe

1968 Dart GTS hardtop coupe

1969 Charger Daytona hardtop coupe

1968 Monaco 500 hardtop coupe

1969 Dart GT hardtop coupe

# Dodge

Models comprised hardtop coupe and convertible in plain and sporty R/T trim. The hardtop could also be ordered as a Special Edition with padded vinyl roof and a smaller "formal" rear window. Priced attractively in the $3000-$3500 range and cataloging a broad list of options, Challenger sold very well its first year, but then tailed off rapidly. In 1970 sales, sixes outpaced V-8s, while hardtops outsold convertibles. Only about 10,000 SE coupes were built.

Specifications and dimensions for other 1970 Dodges were largely as for '69, but Coronets, Chargers, and Polara/Monaco received large "loop" bumper/grilles; Coronet's divided affair looked a bit swollen. More-massive rear bumpers also adorned the big cars, as well as Darts. Charger offered a six for the first time, while the exotic Daytona, having proven its point, was dropped (leaving Plymouth to carry the colors with its similar Superbird). Ignition/steering-column locks, fiberglass-belted tires, dual-action wagon tailgates, and a long list of federally mandated safety equipment completed the 1970 story. As in 1969, Dodge remained seventh in industry output, though volume fell from 611,000 to 543,000 for the model year.

Dodge's path through the '70s was strewn with the same obstacles that made life difficult for all U.S. automakers in those years: a growing number of ever-stricter government regulations and a dramatically altered business climate stemming from the OPEC oil embargo of 1973-74. The division was ill-prepared for both, its early-decade lines heavy with cars motivated by thirsty V-8s and wallowing on too-soft suspensions. Worse, Chrysler's steadily declining fortunes allowed most of these dinosaurs to hang on too long. Indifferent workmanship only further dampened sales, which culminated in the corporation's near-demise during 1980. But by that point, Dodge was through its trial by fire and building nothing remotely like its early-'70s dinosaurs, save the 118.5-inch-wheelbase St. Regis sedan and the Mirada personal-luxury coupe.

It didn't take much corporate contemplation to dispose of the poor Challenger: clumsy, poorly built, and never a serious sales threat to Camaro/Firebird or even Mustang II (if you call that one a ponycar). The overweight latecomer was put out to pasture after 1974, when only about 16,000 were sold. Collectors have already noted the end of convertibles, R/Ts, and big-inch engines after '71, and have been gathering them in as artifacts of a special era.

With the dawn of the first energy crisis, the brontosauruslike Polara/Monaco also seemed headed for the automotive tar pits, but Dodge tried hard to save them via discounts and cash rebates beginning in 1974, Polara vanished after '73. A blocky new Monaco arrived for '74, similar to that year's redesigned Chrysler but still on a 122-inch wheelbase. In 1977, it became the Royal Monaco—selling in decent numbers only by dint of police and taxi orders—while the Monaco name replaced Coronet on midsize cars.

Given such disappointments, it's no surprise that Dodge increasingly depended on Dart sales through mid-decade. Giving the compact line new appeal for '71 was the fastback Demon, a double to Plymouth's new-for-'70 Valiant Duster with the same 108-inch wheelbase and choice of Slant Six, 318 V-8, and optional 340 V-8. The last was reserved for a sporty Demon 340 decked out with bodyside tape stripes, matte-black hood with dual dummy scoops, and wide tires on special wheels as part of a specially beefed-up chassis.

With its trim size and 275 horsepower, the Demon 340 was nimble yet spirited—really the Dart GTS idea remade for changing times. But the name bothered some people, so Demon was prosaically retitled Dart Sport for '73, when all Darts gained a latticework grille and modest center hood bulge. The Sport 340 became a 360 for 1974-75, Dodge enlarging its small-

1970 Polara hardtop coupe

1970 Coronet 500 hardtop coupe

1970 Challenger hardtop coupe

1970 Dart Swinger 340 hardtop coupe

1970 Charger R/T hardtop coupe

# Dodge

1971 Charger 500 hardtop coupe

1971 Polara Brougham hardtop sedan

1971 Challenger R/T hardtop coupe

1971 Dart Demon "Sizzler" fastback coupe

1971 Monaco hardtop coupe

block V-8 in deference to easier emissions tuning. A memorable Sport option was the "Convertriple," which actually meant two separate extras: fold-down rear seat and sliding-steel sunroof. Ordered together, they made for something vaguely like a "three-way" car. Also making Dart more than just basic transportation were the plush Special Edition sedans and coupes of 1974-76. These offered vinyl tops, special emblems, velour interiors, and other extras for about $3800.

The ultra-reliable Dart remained a sales winner right to the end (mostly on the strength of workaday sedans), but its 1976 replacement was a letdown. This was the Aspen, in essence a slightly larger, roomier, and heavier Dart offering a wider range of luxury options—much like the Granada was to Maverick at Ford. Unfortunately, Aspen soon earned the dubious distinction of being the most-recalled car in history (along with its Volare twin at Plymouth), due to poor workmanship in general and early body rust in particular. (GM's X-cars soon wrested that sorry title.) But performance was good with the extra-cost 360 V-8 listed through '79, and furnishings were nicer than on most Darts. Aspen also revived a compact Dodge wagon, something Dart had lacked since its '67 redesign. There were pseudo-muscle R/T coupes and even a "finish it yourself" 1979 kit-car racer.

Despite its problems, Aspen was important for Dodge sales in the late '70s. It also exemplified one of the few things Detroit began doing well: putting big-car comfort in smaller packages (here, 108.7-inch-wheelbase coupes, 112.7-inch sedans and wagons). Aspen was advertised as the "family car of the future," which was hyperbole worthy of P.T. Barnum, but it would lead to the genuine article.

An unusual Aspen (and Volare) feature was its front suspension, which had torsion bars per Chrysler tradition, but situated crosswise instead of lengthwise. Some critics sneered that this was contrived merely so Chrysler could still advertise front torsion bars—and that it had no real advantage for ride or quietness; a few even claimed it actually hampered handling. Regardless, the transverse bars did allow for better suspension isolation, which made for smoother going than in the Dart. Aspen's mainstay engines, 225 Slant Six and 318 V-8, were by now hoary affairs, but proven. And the thrifty six (which could yield up to 25 mpg on the highway with manual shift) was about as bulletproof as Detroit engines ever got.

If Aspen didn't realize its sales potential, the larger Dodges fared even worse. The midsize Coronet/Monaco became more like the equivalent Plymouth Satellite/Fury with each passing year (all were built nose-to-tail at Chrysler's Lynch Road plant in Detroit) and was hardly a bargain at prices averaging $100 higher. It was also thirsty, and styling was forgettable. The Charger was simply watered down amidst name shuffles. For 1975 it became a twin to Chrysler's posh Cordoba, a car even the *Dukes of Hazzard* wouldn't have recognized.

This midsize generation began with fuselage-style '71 Charger coupes on a 115-inch wheelbase and 117-inch Coronet sedans and wagons. By 1978, they'd been heavily facelifted once—for '75—and trimmed to Charger SE and Magnum XE coupes, plus assorted Monacos and Monaco Broughams.

The reason for thinning those ranks was Diplomat. Launched for 1977, it was much like Chrysler's new LeBaron: a reskinned Aspen/Volare platform with coupes, sedans, and wagons on a 112.7-inch wheelbase. Diplomat sold well from the start, and its more-sensible design made the old-style intermediates unnecessary. The Coronet-turned-Monaco was thus transformed after 1978 into the St. Regis, all but identical with Chrysler's "downsized" R-body Newport/New Yorker sedan. The Cordoba-like Charger vanished at the same time; the related Magnum hung on through '79.

373

# Dodge

Then the smooth Mirada took over as the personal-luxury Dodge. Mounting the Diplomat platform, it was a close cousin of 1980's new second-generation Chrysler Cordoba. One of the few true hardtop coupes left by that time, it bore a striking front end recalling the "coffin nose" of the late-'30s Cord 810/812—and the previous Magnum. Good looks won Mirada a lot of good copy in "buff" magazines. And considering how things had changed since the muscle-car days, it was decently quick—if you ordered the optional 185-bhp 360 V-8, Dodge's hairiest engine that year. Unhappily, this was another one that was just a shade too late to be of any real value, and Mirada's annual production averaged less than 7500 through swan-song 1983.

Capping Dodge's enforced product renewal in the '70s was the L-body Omni, a sensible, front-drive subcompact announced for 1978. It was cut from the trend-setting pattern of the Volkswagen Rabbit, and was even powered at first by a slightly larger version of VW's single-overhead-cam four (also mounted transversely). Omni wasn't quite as much fun to drive, but had the same boxy, four-door hatchback styling and high practicality. Along with Plymouth's near-identical Horizon, Omni was one of the few bright spots in Chrysler's very gloomy sales picture at the time.

For 1979, Omni gained a slick companion coupe on a slight-

**1972 Dart Demon fastback coupe**

**1974 Charger hardtop coupe**

**1972 Charger hardtop coupe**

**1974 Dart S.E. four-door sedan**

**1973 Monaco hardtop coupe**

**1974 Monaco Brougham hardtop sedan**

**1973 Polara hardtop sedan**

**1975 Royal Monaco Brougham, coupe**

# Dodge

1975 Coronet Brougham hardtop coupe

1975 Charger SE (Special Edition) coupe

1976 Royal Monaco Brougham coupe

1976 Coronet Custom four-door sedan

1976 Charger Daytona coupe

1977 Charger Daytona coupe

1977 Monaco Brougham coupe

1977 Monaco Brougham four-door sedan

1977 Diplomat four-door sedan

1977 Aspen R/T coupe

# Dodge

ly shorter chassis (96.7-inch wheelbase versus 99.2). Called 024, it won an immediate following, even managing a few conquest sales among import buyers seeking a sporty and nimble 2+2 that was easy on the pocketbook.

After a quiet 1980, Dodge followed Chrysler-Plymouth in beginning another divisional overhaul, replacing old rear-drive models with smaller, more-efficient front-drive designs, most every one derived from the versatile 100.1-inch wheelbase K-car compact of 1981. Aided by a steadily expanding lineup marketed with a renewed emphasis on sporty performance, Dodge reaped the rewards with higher sales. Division volume rose from 309,000 for 1980 to nearly 341,000 for '81. By 1985, Dodge had achieved its goal of a half-million annual sales.

One model that wouldn't disappear was Diplomat, which got a crisp restyling for 1980, then took over for St. Regis as the traditional full-size Dodge through 1989. Though reduced after 1981 to just a single four-door sedan in two trim levels, Diplomat enjoyed steady, if modest, sales (again mainly to police and taxi fleets). Its standard Slant Six was discontinued after '83, leaving only the veteran 318 V-8.

Aries-K was the literal foundation of Dodge's 1980 line. Replacing Aspen, it was a well-engineered new-wave compact, though no more original than Omni. Design hallmarks included the choice of two transverse-mounted single-overhead-cam fours—Chrysler 2.2 liter (135 cid) or optional Mitsubishi 2.6 (156 cid)—plus rack-and-pinion steering, front-disc/rear-drum brakes, and all-coil suspension with front MacPherson struts and a twist-type rear beam axle doubling as an antiroll bar.

Most Aries were sold with optional TorqueFlite. The standard transaxle was a four-speed floorshift manual; a five-speed option arrived for 1982, then replaced the four-speed for '86, when a 2.5-liter version of the Chrysler "Trans-4" was added. Coupe, sedan, and a neat little five-door wagon were variously available in base, Custom, SE, and LE trim at competitive prices identical with those of Plymouth's twin Reliant. A smooth 1985 facelift made all Ks look more grown-up, and coupes could be ordered with sporty options like 14-inch cast-aluminum road wheels, front bucket seats, and a center console.

Though Aries consistently lagged behind Reliant in sales, it sold consistently well: nearly 181,000 for debut '81, between 125,000 and 150,000 a year thereafter. Progressively improved workmanship, longer warranties (up to 7 years/70,000 miles on drivetrain components by 1987), and sensible product upgrades helped keep it competitive through 1989, when the line was trimmed to make room for the new A-body Spirit. By that time, critics had long chided Chrysler for not building anything truly new since 1981, but many buyers didn't seem to care much. The K sparked Chrysler's renaissance and no little innovation. Few cars can claim as much, let alone one so humble.

Dodge's first K-car derivatives appeared the year after Aries' launch. These were a personal-luxury twosome dubbed 400, a coupe and sedan with a front end like that of the Mirada. A 400 convertible arrived at mid-1982, the first open Dodge since the 1971 Challenger and a deft marketing move by Chrysler chairman Lee Iacocca. Like the LeBaron convertible, the 400 was built at first by an outside contractor, but proved so popular that Chrysler took over production itself. Mechanicals and dimensions for all 400s were nearly identical with Aries'.

Arriving for 1983 was a stretched 400 sedan called 600, using the new K-based 103.1-inch-wheelbase corporate E-body. A 400-like front differentiated it from Chrysler's E-Class and New Yorker. A sporty ES version bid for the burgeoning "EuroSedan" market with black exterior trim, handling package, and five-speed. It didn't win many buyers from Saab, BMW, or Mercedes, but was surprisingly capable, all things considered.

1977 Diplomat coupe

1978 Monaco Brougham four-door sedan

1979 Magnum XE coupe

1979 St. Regis four-door sedan

1979 Diplomat station wagon

# Dodge

**1979 Omni hatchback sedan**

**1979 Omni 024 hatchback coupe**

**1980 Diplomat Medallion four-door sedan**

**1981 Aries two-door sedan**

**1982 Charger 2.2 hatchback coupe**

Shifting gears for 1984, Dodge dropped the 400 sedan and put 600 badges on the CV coupe and convertible. The latter was also newly available in ES trim, tied to the turbo 2.2. It was the raciest Dodge in years, but few were ordered. Still, the new approach helped series sales, which rose from 1983's combined 59,500 to over 72,000 for '84. The following year brought a more prosaic E-body SE sedan, and its strong initial sales pointed the way. After an Aries-like 1986 facelift, the 600 coupe and convertible were canceled, leaving the SE and a detrimmed base four-door to sell just as well all by themselves through 1988.

Dodge dealers bemoaned losing the 600 convertible, but at least their Daytona sports coupe had no more in-house competition from Chrysler's Laser after 1986. Both models had arrived for '84 on a much-modified 97-inch K-car chassis topped by slick, "fasthatch" styling. Corporate finances at the time dictated they be virtually identical, but the Daytona outsold Laser from the start, probably because it was geared more to Dodge's typical clientele. Daytona also had an edge with three models to Laser's two: initially base, Turbo, and the racy Turbo Z, the last distinguished by ground-hugging lower-body extensions, discreet hatchlid spoiler, and big wheels and tires.

With the sort of evolutionary improvements found in all Chrysler products in this decade, the Daytona rocked along at around 50,000 units a year through 1986. By that point it was available with a stroked and fuel-injected 2.5-liter four as base power, plus a T-top option (shared with Laser) and a "C/S" handling package named for Carroll Shelby, the old friend Iacocca had persuaded to "heat up" certain Dodges, as Shelby had done with Mustangs when both worked at Ford back in the '60s.

To compensate for the lost convertible, Dodge dealers got a restyled '87 Daytona. It boasted a smooth, hidden-headlamp "droop-snoot," and was offered in base, luxury Pacifica, and hot-rod Shelby Z models. Pacifica carried the familiar 146-bhp turbo 2.2, the Z a hot 174-bhp "Turbo II" engine; even the base model could be ordered with the 146-bhp unit as part of a C/S performance package. For 1989, Pacifica was replaced by ES and ES Turbo, the latter powered by a new 150-bhp turbocharged 2.5, and the Z was retitled Daytona Shelby. There were several styling and equipment adjustments, including standard four-wheel disc brakes across the board. Of interest to weekend racers was the C/S Competition Package for the base Daytona—basically the Shelby model with special exterior, 2.2-liter "Turbo II" power, and "maximum performance suspension" but few creature comforts so as to realize a 200-pound weight savings. All Daytonas sported a more-ergonomic dashboard and standard driver-side air bag for 1990, when the blown 2.2 received a new Variable Nozzle Technology (VNT) turbocharger that provided no more horsepower but did make driving much smoother. That year's base and ES models also offered Daytona's first V-6: the 3.0-liter (181-cid) 141-bhp Mitsubishi unit fast-spreading throughout the corporate camp.

Though Daytona generated only about a third as many sales as Mustang or Camaro, it symbolized Dodge's return to performance better than anything else in the line. And its sportiest models gave away little in acceleration or handling to those heavier, more-powerful rear-drive ponycars—proof that Chrysler engineering was still to be reckoned with.

Bowing alongside Daytona was a very different '84 Dodge: America's first "garageable" van. Aptly named Caravan, it was essentially a tall K-wagon on a special 112-inch wheelbase. Caravan had a very roomy interior that offered seating options for up to eight. Quick-release anchors made for easy removal of the second and third bench seats for cargo carrying. Front drive and astute packaging conferred a lower ride height than any rear-drive van, which eased entry/exit and contributed to a car-

# Dodge

1982 400 two-door coupe

1982 Diplomat four-door sedan

1983 400 two-door sedan

1984 Caravan LE minivan

1984 600 ES four-door sedan

1984 Daytona Turbo Z hatchback coupe

like driving position. In fact, aside from sitting a little higher and farther forward, driving a Caravan was much like driving an Aries wagon.

This as much as attractive pricing made the Caravan (and Plymouth's twin Voyager) an instant hit, generating upward of 200,000 annual sales. A fair number were windowless Ram Van commercials, but most were passenger models—initially base, SE, and woody-look LE.

Extending Caravan's appeal—literally—was the 1988 addition of 14-inch-longer "Grand" models on a 119.1-inch wheelbase. At the same time, the 3.0 Mitsubishi V-6 joined the options list, bringing 144 horsepower and a welcome gain in towing capacity over the four-cylinder engines. The main 1989 developments were optional availability of Chrysler's new 150-bhp turbocharged 2.5 four on standard-length SE and LE Caravans—somewhat surprising for this sort of rig—and "Ultradrive," a new electronically controlled four-speed automatic option for V-6 LEs and all Grand Caravans.

But Ultradrive had a shaky start, garnering some bad press that it was flawed. Chrysler stonewalled publicly while working quickly and quietly to amend the problems. The next year, Caravans offered a new 3.3-liter overhead-valve V-6 option: the first all-Chrysler engine since the 2.2-liter K-car four and the first in a family of corporate powerplants for the '90s.

Unquestionably, Caravan (and Voyager) was Chrysler's biggest coup of the '80s. For once, Detroit's perennial number-three outfit had delivered the right product at the right time.

Though Dodge canceled the 600 ES sport sedan after 1984, it didn't abandon the idea; it just substituted something better: the H-body Lancer (reviving the early-'60s compact name). This was another new Dodge similar to a new Chrysler, in this case the LeBaron GTS, but Lancer stood apart with the cross-bar grille then being adopted throughout the division (which must have confused Chrysler 300 enthusiasts) and by being offered in a more-overtly sporting ES rendition.

All that may be said of the GTS applies equally to Lancer—except sales, which ran about a third less. One suspects the Chrysler name and its luxury aura did more for GTS than the Dodge name did for Lancer despite similar pricing. Perhaps recognizing this, the division issued a bespoilered Lancer Shelby for 1988 with the 174-bhp "Turbo II" 2.2 and racy body addenda similar to those of the earlier Pacifica and Shelby Lancer limited editions. The '89 ES was sportier, too, gaining the new 150-bhp turbo 2.5 as standard equipment. But the H-body would prove something of a short-timer and would not return for 1990.

More successful was the P-body Shadow, intended to replace the aging Omni but introduced for 1987 as an additional, more-ambitious small sedan. Dodge wanted you to think of it as a junior BMW, but it was really more junior Lancer, with the same

# Dodge

1984 600 ES Turbo convertible coupe

1985 Caravan SE minivan

1985 Omni GLH hatchback sedan

1985 Daytona Turbo hatchback coupe

1985 Diplomat SE four-door sedan

1986 Charger 2.2 hatchback coupe

rounded "aerosedan" styling in three- and five-door notchback body styles on the Daytona wheelbase.

K-car heritage was again evident in the Shadow chassis and drivetrains. The latter initially comprised the usual turbo and "atmospheric" 2.2-liter fours teamed with manual five-speed and automatic TorqueFlite transaxles. Unlike Plymouth with its similar Sundance, Dodge fielded enthusiast-oriented ES models with uprated suspension and a few "Euro" touches. For 1989, the corporate 2.5-liter "balancer-shaft" four was a new option for base models, and the 150-bhp turbo version was standard for ES (replacing the blown 2.2). The latter was also included in a new Daytona-style competition package for three-doors, along with handling suspension, bigger wheels and tires, "aero" body skirting, rear spoiler, and bucket seats. A minor facelift and reworked dashboards arrived for all 1990 Shadows; ES was treated to standard all-disc brakes, and its now-optional Turbo II engine was updated with a VNT blower.

Yet for all the emphasis on sport, it was the workaday Shadows that carried the sales load. And that load was considerable: over 76,000 for the first model year. Plymouth moved a like number of its Sundances.

The reason Omni didn't fade into the Shadow is that it was too good to lose. Despite relatively few changes after 1981, it averaged a remarkable 100,000 sales each year through 1983 and 58,500 or more thereafter.

The turning point was 1981, when the K-car's 2.2-liter "Trans-4" became optional for both Omni and the 024 coupe, improving acceleration and quietness with little or no loss in mileage. A smaller Peugeot-built 1.6-liter (replacing the VW 1.7 for '83) was technically standard through 1986, but almost nobody bought it. Likewise the stripped 1981 "Miser" models, which disappeared after the following year.

Sustaining the L-body line through its 1990 swan-song were an increasingly better-equipped Omni and ever-sportier coupes. The coupes began at mid-1982 with an overdecorated 2.2-liter model reviving the famous Charger name, signaling Dodge's return to interesting cars. The base 024 became a Charger for '83, and the 2.2 was joined at midyear by a dashing Shelby Charger with tuned 107-bhp engine, very stiff suspension, racy body add-ons, silver paint, and big blue stripes evocative of Carroll Shelby's late-'60s Mustang GTs. A wider choice of colors was offered for '84, and other Chargers acquired a nose job and the Shelby's cleaner rear-roof styling. The next year, the Shelby took on the blown, 146-bhp 2.2 to become the Turbo Charger.

But by 1987, a profusion of sporty Daytonas and Shadows were crowding all Chargers out of the market, so production ceased that March. The Shelby Chargers were fairly rare: about 30,000 for the five model years.

Omni, meantime, kept getting better, picking up a more-modern dashboard for '84 and additional standard features most

# Dodge

every year. Workmanship improved too. The aging 1978 design should have been an increasing liability in the marketplace, but Chrysler took advantage of tooling costs long since amortized to keep prices down and sales up.

The company went even further for 1987 by replacing all Omnis with just one fully equipped "America" model, appealingly priced at $5799. Options were limited to reduce overhead and insure higher, more-consistent assembly quality—another cue taken from Europe and Japan. Value-minded shoppers rushed to buy, taking more than 152,000—more sales than the entire Omni/Charger line had ever generated in a single year. Chrysler paid heed and put Aries/Reliant on the "America plan" before closing out the original K-cars after 1989. With that, Omni sales fast declined after '87, but the L-body hung on into model-year 1990, when the America badge was dropped and a driver-side air bag added.

A short-lived exception to such crushing sensibility was the GLH, basically the wolfish Shelby Charger in sheepish Omni dress. The initials, attributed to Ol' Shel, meant "Goes Like Hell." It did. The debut '85 was sprightly enough with its 110-bhp engine, but the turbocharged 146-bhp GLH-S of 1986 was a genuine terror, though it suffered terrible torque-steer; one tester observed the accelerator functioned like a "lane-change switch." Still, like the Shelby Chargers, this Omni was great fun—crude but invigorating in the best muscle-car tradition. And as only a few thousand were built for 1984-86, the GLH/GLH-S bid fair as future collectibles.

Arriving for 1988 was Dynasty, a sort of latterday Diplomat on the front-drive C-body platform of that year's new Chrysler New Yorker. The only body style was a square-lined unibody four-door on a 104.3-inch wheelbase, available in standard and uplevel LE trim levels. Unlike the Chrysler, though, Dynasty's standard engine was the corporate 2.5-liter four with 96 horsepower, a bit weak for the 3000-pound curb weight. Fortunately, the Daytona's 3.0-liter Mitsubishi V-6 was optional. Changes for '89 were confined to a slightly more-powerful, 150-bhp V-6 option teaming with Chrysler's new Ultradrive automatic, plus optional security system, two-position driver-seat "memory" feature, and all-disc antilock brakes (the last phased in during '88). The 150-bhp Japanese option was ousted by Chrysler's own 3.3 V-6 for 1990, when all Dynastys gained standard driver-side airbags.

Billed as a "contemporary family sedan," Dynasty made no gesture toward sport, but it didn't have to. With base prices of $11,500-$12,500, it offered fine value in a roomy, traditional-style car of the sort that still appealed mightily to many people. And numerous they were. Despite its unpretentious nature, Dynasty became Chrysler Corporation's most-popular car line. Model-year '89 production, for example, was close to 138,000—many for rent-a-car companies but a fine showing all the same.

Though Aries was down to two- and four-door Americas for 1989, their heir apparent bowed as the family Dodge for the early '90s. Called Spirit, this notchback sedan was built on the same 103.3-inch-wheelbase A-body platform as Plymouth's new Acclaim, and thus spelled the end for the like-length four-door 600. The now-expected trio of base, luxury LE, and sporty ES models was offered, the last with a standard 2.5-liter turbo four, the others with the nonturbo version of that engine. Dynasty's 3.0-liter V-6 was optional only for ES, again teamed with Ultradrive. Spirit styling echoed Aries', but was smoother and more "grown-up." ES was identified by body-color front- and rear-end caps and rocker extensions, plus integral fog lamps. Spirit returned for 1990 with standard driver-side air bag (Chrysler was now pushing hard with this laudable safety feature), no-cost all-disc

1986 Omni GLH Turbo hatchback sedan

1986 600 ES Turbo convertible coupe

1986 Daytona Turbo Z hatchback coupe

1986 Lancer Pacifica hatchback sedan

1987 Caravan LE minivan (extended wheelbase)

# Dodge

1987 Daytona Shelby Z hatchback coupe

1987 Aries LE two-door sedan

1987 Diplomat SE four-door sedan

1988 Lancer ES Turbo hatchback sedan

1988 Dynasty LE four-door sedan

1988 Shadow ES hatchback sedan

brakes for ES, and numerous detail improvements.

Considering where it began, Dodge fared remarkably well in the '80s, resuming its traditional performance role within Chrysler Corporation while remaining the firm's only "full-line" nameplate and thus its best-selling one. In another return to tradition, Dodge finished the decade a solid sixth in the industry, compared to a lackluster eighth in 1982.

Dodge then retreated to seventh among domestic makes through 1994, passed by Mercury amid new woes for Chrysler Corporation and a timely shift to more salable new products (see Chrysler for more details on early-'90s corporate happenings). Still, sales declined only as far as some 260,000 in 1992 and were back above 342,000 two years later. By 1996, Dodge had replaced every car in its lineup—and many of its trucks, too.

Signaling the start of this product revolution was that stunning 1989 showmobile, the two-seat Viper RT/10 roadster. A stark but potent creature, it was freely created in the image of Carroll Shelby's legendary Cobra. But the real movers behind it were Chrysler president Bob Lutz and chief engineer Francois Castaing, who wanted to show their company was capable of far more than K-cars and minivans.

To no one's surprise, showgoers pleaded for a Viper they could buy. In May 1990, Chrysler said it would oblige them. But more than just an exciting image-booster for Dodge, this low-volume sports car would be the first test for the streamlined "team approach" to vehicle development that Lutz and Castaing wanted to implement companywide. Though the concept car had to be entirely reengineered for production on just $50 million, the showroom Viper was on time and on budget. Sales began in May 1992, just 36 months after project approval, a new record development time for a production MoPar.

If not exactly cheap at $50,000, the Viper cost far less than other contemporary "exotics"—or a genuine Cobra. Raw power and colossal acceleration were its reasons for being. Though based on a forthcoming truck engine, Viper's unusual new all-aluminum V-10 (hence RT/10) was engineered with assistance from Italy's Lamborghini (then owned by Chrysler). It wasn't a sophisticated mill, what with pushrods working two valves per cylinder, but it was huge: no less than 8.0 liters, a massive 488 cid. The result was a mighty 400 horsepower and 450 pound-feet of torque. With mandatory six-speed manual shift and standard limited-slip differential, the Viper could rocket from 0 to 60 mph in about 4.5 seconds and rip through the standing quarter-mile in 13.1 seconds at 108 mph.

Unlike other recent Dodges, Viper had conventional rear-wheel drive and classic all-independent double-wishbone suspension. This was, after all, a "pure sport car," as Shelby called such machines, which also meant few concessions to civility. For example, brakes and steering were powered, but nothing

# Dodge

1989 Spirit ES four-door sedan

1989 Lancer Shelby hatchback sedan

1990 Daytona ES hatchback coupe

1990 Omni hatchback sedan

1990 Shadow ES hatchback coupe

1990 Caravan ES minivan

else. There were no exterior door handles—and no windows, either; just clip-in side-curtains. The top was a rudimentary canvas toupee that didn't ward off rain too well. It did, however, trap much of the V-10's prodigious heat, which was noticed even at speed with the top off and the takeout rear window removed. Trunk space? Barely enough for a gym bag. Yet despite its stark furnishings and lightweight body panels made of plasticlike materials, the Viper ended up a bit heavier than planned at around 3400 pounds, though that partly reflected a very stiff, separate tubular-steel chassis.

But why sweat the details? The Viper was all about fast fun on sunny days—not to mention looking great, as the voluptuous show-car styling survived completely intact. That included a nonstructural "sport bar" behind the cockpit and exposed, functional side exhaust pipes that were wonderfully "retro" but could fry errant legs and sounded quite odd. Huge disc brakes provided terrific stopping power within handsome tri-spoke 17-inch aluminum wheels. Ultra-wide Z-rated tires helped provide super-sticky cornering, though power-sliding oversteer was ever available with a well-timed slam on the hammer. Yet unlike the scary Cobra, the Viper was easy to drive fast and well.

A lot more people wanted Vipers than Dodge could build—which was exactly how Chrysler wanted it. The exoticar market was notoriously fickle, so why build too many Vipers too

soon and risk depressing resale values? Production was slow to start anyway. Seeking top-notch quality for the costliest Dodge ever, Chrysler retooled its Detroit New Mack Avenue plant for turning out Vipers only as needed, which meant mostly by hand. Still, initial quality was somewhat less than world-class, and only 162 Vipers were built as '92 models, all painted bright red. But teething troubles couldn't dim the Viper's luster or the public's lust for Viper.

Viper roared into 1993 with only two changes: black as a second color choice and available dealer-installed air conditioning. Though some 3000 cars were planned that model year, unexpected molding troubles with the big one-piece front end held actual volume to about 1000. But the problems were soon fixed, and '94 production nearly tripled to 2892. Full factory air became optional that year, the transmission got an electric reverse-gear lockout, and color choices expanded to yellow and Emerald Green. The '95 was unchanged except for price, which Chrysler reluctantly raised by a relatively modest $1500.

A Viper paced the 1991 Indy 500, with Carroll Shelby himself driving the prerace parade lap. Though sales were still a year off, Dodge's new hot rod hardly needed this publicity, as "buff" magazines were breathlessly reporting every facet of its show car-to-showroom progress. And in fact, Viper wasn't the first choice. Dodge had bought pace-car privileges to promote its new '91 Stealth, an upscale V-6 sports coupe available with all-wheel drive and up to 300 turbocharged horses. But aside from styling, the Stealth was a Mitsubishi design built in Japan, and a Japanese pace car just wasn't "politically correct" for the premier American race. Dodge relented, prepared a Viper prototype to fill in, and relegated Stealths to the background.

Among other new '91 Dodges was an unexpected high-power edition of the workaday Spirit. Also branded R/T, it was strictly a showroom lure, as only some 1400 were built through 1992. Base price was $17,871, a weighty $4000 above the costliest standard Spirit. Under the hood sat a maxed-out 2.2-liter "Trans-4" with a new twincam cylinder head and other modifications that yielded an amazing (and very peaky) 224 horsepower. Manual five-speed was the only transmission, and Dodge threw in necessary chassis upgrades, including the rear disc brakes newly optional for lesser '91 Spirits. You also got a dechromed exterior in red, white, or black, adorned with subtle decklid spoiler. Though it looked another torque-steer terror, the Spirit R/T handled with fair finesse, if no less noise than an Omni GLH. And it was undeniably quick, with 0-60 times of well under seven seconds. As a rare modern performance Dodge, the Spirit R/T has definite potential as a future collector's item, incongruous though it is.

There was nothing odd about the new '91 Shadow convertible, which carried on from the ragtop 600. This time, though, Dodge left construction chores to American Sunroof Corporation. Cost concerns dictated a manual top, and the conversion slimmed back-seat space, but the regular "Highline" model started at $12,995, and a sporty ES edition sold for very little more. At the other end of the line, Dodge revived the "America" ploy for three- and five-door Shadows priced from just $7699. Power steering was one of their few standard "luxuries," and the only engine offered was the lowly 93-bhp version of the tried and true 2.2.

Like Chrysler's other '91 minivans, Caravan got a timely and very adept update marked by smoother sheetmetal, a new dash (complete with glovebox), and optional all-wheel-drive for 3.3-liter V-6 models. Even more laudable was first-time availability of antilock brakes, initially limited to the upper SE and LE trim levels. Also bolstering Caravan's appeal were a standard driver-side airbag as a '91 running change, followed by America's first integrated child safety seat as a 1992 option. A passenger airbag and side-guard door beams arrived for '94, when LE and ES Grand models could be ordered with a torquier 3.8 V-6 making 162 horsepower. All this did nothing but help sales, which improved from about a quarter-million for 1991 to over 300,000 by '94—and that was just Caravan. Even after 10 years, America still preferred Highland Park's minivans above all others.

There was little left to do for the Daytona, short of a total redesign. With its humble K-car origins and disco-era looks, it was just too old by the early '90s to stand comparison with a host of newer-design rivals for refinement or quality. Still, Dodge tried to inject some of the Viper's venom here, starting with a "High-Torque Turbo I" engine for 1991. Standard for the Shelby and optional in lesser Daytonas, it made only two more horses but a useful 30 extra pound-feet of torque over the previous 2.5 turbo. The raucous VNT 2.2 vanished, but wasn't greatly missed.

A slightly smoother look with exposed headlamps arrived for 1992 Daytonas, as did optional rear disc brakes. Dodge now sponsored the International Race of Champions, so the world's best drivers vied for "top gun" honors in Daytonas instead of Chevy Camaros. A new top-line IROC model was thus no surprise, though its mild 3.0-liter Mitsubishi V-6 arguably was. More interesting was the IROC R/T, a midyear '92 replacement for the Daytona Shelby packing the 224-bhp "Turbo III" engine from the Spirit R/T. Aside from that and deliberately limited production—only some 800 or so—this R/T was much like the regular IROC. But none of this racy stuff could stop Daytona sales from freefalling, and the model was belatedly retired after measly '93 model-year volume of 9677 units.

By this point, Dodge was ready to join C-P Division in introducing a succession of new models to rejuvenate its lineup for the late '90s and beyond. The changeover would be orderly but quite rapid, reflecting the efficient work of the "cross-functional platform teams" recently established in the image of Team Viper. As a result, Spirit, Shadow, and Dynasty were left to fade away with no further changes of note after 1992. All

**1991 Spirit ES four-door sedan**

**1991 Dynasty LE four-door sedan**

**1991 Shadow ES convertible coupe**

**1992 Viper RT/10 roadster**

# Dodge

1992 Spirit R/T four-door sedan

1993 Intrepid ES four-door sedan

1992 Grand Caravan ES minivan

1993 Daytona IROC R/T hatchback coupe

these cars had served Dodge well, but the new stuff was far better. First up was Intrepid, one of the much-discussed 1993 "LH" sedans. Though ostensibly a midsize, it was close to full-size, offering bountiful interior space thanks to a lengthy 113-inch wheelbase and radical "cab forward" styling. The related Chrysler Concorde and Eagle Vision had this too, but they targeted different buyers with their own visual cues and model/equipment mixes.

Intrepid was the most affordable of the LH trio, but also the most-aggressively styled, with a Viper-inspired face, sharper roofline, and a bolder rear end with "Intrepid" writ large on a wide central backup lamp. The base model used the corporate pushrod 3.3 V-6, tuned for 153 horsepower. The sportier ES substituted a new overhead-cam 3.5-liter unit with 24 valves and 214 horsepower. All Intrepids came with four-speed automatic transmission, dual airbags, a wide-track chassis with all-independent suspension, a fair helping of standard amenities, and worthy options like antilock brakes. ES achieved flatter, more-responsive handling with a firm "touring" suspension and wider tires on 16-inch alloy wheels (versus 15-inch steel rims). It was also sportier inside, with shift console and higher-grade trim. Best of all, Intrepid cost about the same as the dull old Dynasty it replaced, the base model arriving at just under $16,000.

With all this, the standard-bearer for the "New Dodge" got off to a strong start, attracting over 81,000 sales for model-year '93. Intrepid jumped above 155,000 for '94 on the strength of standard air conditioning, a newly optional power moonroof, eight more horses for the 3.3 engine, and the advent of speed-variable power steering.

The spotlight then turned to Neon, which bowed in early 1994 to signal the end of Shadow for '95. Plymouth naturally sold it too, as in Omni/Horizon days, only Chrysler didn't bother with separate names, which saved some tooling and marketing money. In fact, Dodge's Neons differed from Plymouth's only in the color of their badges: divisional red instead of blue.

Such clever thinking was a hallmark of Neon's new "PL" platform, and was passed on to consumers as attractively low list prices: as early ads said, "about 95-hundred to start, 12-five nicely loaded." That was for the debut four-door sedan in bare-bones form. The nicer Highline and Sport versions cost a bit more; similarly priced Highline and Sport coupes arrived in the fall. Unfortunately, Chrysler's cost-consciousness also produced rather bargain-basement trim even for an economy car, though it also allowed room in the budget for standard dual airbags and niceties like cupholders and floor console.

Neon continued Chrysler's move to cab-forward styling (as suggested a few years earlier by a Neon concept car). Proportions were scaled down to a 104-inch wheelbase, which was still quite long for a subcompact and thus made for another relatively cavernous interior. Yet there was a winning cuteness to Neon not found in the bigger LH cars, particularly the friendly "face" with oval headlamps and a simple horizontal grille that almost seemed ready to grin. Announcement ads played up this charm with a fetching one-word headline: "Hi!"

Dodge built some 179,000 Neons as '95 models, but close to 131,000 for calendar '94. The latter is perhaps a more-accurate gauge of the car's popularity given its early introduction. The only engine at first was a new 132-bhp 2.0-liter overhead-cam four designed and built by Chrysler. A 16-valve twincam version with 150 horsepower was gradually phased in for Sport models. Transmissions comprised the usual manual five-speed or optional four-speed automatic. Though far from quiet, Neon was great fun to drive, thrifty, pretty reliable, and even speedy: a brisk 8.9 seconds for Consumer Guide®'s base-engine five-speed sedan. In all, Neon was a huge step forward from the old "Omnirizon," proof that Chrysler could still build an appealing small car on its own.

Next on the menu was a Spirit successor called Stratus, which went on sale in early 1995 as a lower-priced version of the new "JA" Chrysler Cirrus sedan introduced some six months before. Hewing to the new corporate formula, Stratus delivered wide-track cab-forward sleekness on a 108-inch wheelbase, plus standard antilock brakes, dual airbags, even air conditioning. Like Intrepid, there were base and sportier ES models. Engine options began with another new all-

Chrysler engine, a twincam multivalve 2.4-liter four with 140 horsepower. ES sported a similar Mitsubishi-based 2.5-liter V-6 with 164 horsepower. Both these engines mated solely with four-speed automatic. The 132-bhp Neon engine with five-speed manual, a combo that proved livelier on the road than it looked on paper, was standard for all Stratus models. Prices were appealingly competitive at just under $14,000 for the standard Stratus and some $17-grand for the better-equipped ES. Roomy, responsive, and rock-solid, Stratus met a very favorable reception, and Dodge happily built over 58,000 for model-year '95.

Though Chrysler was now starting to sever ties with Mitsubishi, its longtime Japanese partner loomed large in the 1995 Avenger. A spiritual successor to Daytona, this was little more than a sporty coupe based on Mitsubishi's midrange Galant family sedan, with rather sedate styling on the same 103.7-inch wheelbase. Most American-market Galants were now built in Illinois, so Avengers were too, even though Chrysler had sold its interest in the plant to Mitsubishi. Chrysler did contribute to Avenger's styling, but though designers tried hard for a cab-forward look, it was less evident here than on the company's all-American products. At least the front maintained a Dodge identity by wearing the make's trademark crossed-bars grille motif. Once again, there were base and ES models. Respective power was the single-cam Neon 2.0-liter and the Mitsubishi V-6 (engines shared with the Stratus ES). The V-6 was limited to four-speed automatic.

At $117,191, the ES cost some $4000 more than the standard Avenger, but the extra money was well spent, bringing anti-lock brakes (optional for the base model), fatter tires on 16-inch alloy wheels, fog lamps, rear spoiler and other goodies. Yet even this Avenger was no excitement machine—just another pleasant, competent, Japanese-style car that bordered on anonymity. Most critics judged Avenger a big step forward from the weary Daytona, but that was surely damning with faint praise.

Dodge finished up its linewide makeover with a brilliant new second-generation Caravan for 1996. Viper had been around only five model years by then, yet was now the oldest car in the fleet. Dodge had indeed remade itself with unusual speed.

Not that Viper was neglected. By 1995, in fact, team leader Roy Sjoberg could claim over 1100 changes to the snaky sports car since the first '92 roadster. New ones joined them for '96, starting with 15 more horsepower (to 415 total) and an extra 23 pound-feet of torque (to 488). Higher compression and a hotter cam were responsible, as was eliminating the distinctive "shin burner" side exhausts for a less-restrictive setup routed beneath the car to a pair of center rear outlets. In addition, curb weight lightened some 60 pounds by changing suspension components from steel to aluminum, a newly optional lightweight hard top afforded much-better weather protection than the skimpy fabric "bikini," and there were new color schemes featuring broad nose and deck stripes hinting at a racing program. Equally significant, production shifted to a new plant on Detroit's Conner Avenue, which promised improved workmanship. Partly because of the move, model-year production was deliberately held to just 500 units.

Another reason was the spring 1996 debut of a fixed-roof Viper fastback as an early '97 entry. Though it looked much like the roadster, the GTS coupe was claimed to be 90 percent new. Standard were power windows, adjustable pedals, air conditioning (at last!), and a redesigned dash incorporating dual airbags, features that also showed up on '97 RT/10s. And there was yet more muscle, as Viper's V-10 was both lightened and fully reengineered to produce 450 horsepower (at 5200 rpm) and a thumping 500 pound-feet of torque (peaking at just 3600 revs).

The racy-looking GTS had obvious competition potential, and Dodge realized it with a squadron of GTS-Rs designed for LeMans and other long-distance events. With factory backing and hard work by several outside teams, these Vipers proved almost unstoppable. In a trio of "three-peats" they claimed the FIA GT2 and GT World Championships in 1997-1999 and class victories at LeMans in 1998-2000. At home, GTS-Rs won the 1999 American LeMans Series (ALMS), scoring a class win in each race they entered, followed in 2000 by overall victory at the 24 Hours of Daytona. Dodge then left international sports-

**1993 Spirit four-door sedan**

**1995 Neon Sport coupe**

**1994 Shadow ES hatchback coupe**

**1995 Stratus four-door sedan**

# Dodge

1995 Neon four-door sedan

1995 Avenger ES coupe

1996 Neon sport coupe

1996 Intrepid sedan

1997 Stratus sedan

car racing to focus anew on NASCAR, but probably not for long.

Meantime, roadgoing Vipers kept evolving nicely. The '99s, for example, exchanged 17-inch wheels for 18s, added power mirrors and aluminum-finish cockpit trim, and offered genuine British Connolly leather upholstery as a new option. Also new that year was an American Club Racer (ACR) package for the GTS with five-point competition seatbelts, special suspension, unique one-piece wheels, and a low-restriction air cleaner that helped liberate an extra 10 horsepower. The option wasn't cheap at $10,000, but weekend warriors loved it on their local racetracks, though they did without air conditioning, audio, and even fog lights Monday through Friday. The package was improved for 2000 with adjustable monotube shock absorbers and a "performance" oil pan providing better lubrication of the mighty engine's innards. For 2001, both roadster and coupe got standard antilock brakes, a great advance for "active" safety, though another step back from Viper's original uncompromising nature. Colors came and went each season through 2002 and the finale of the basic 1992 design. By that point, Viper owners numbered over 14,000, each a happy soul no doubt.

Yet with fewer than 1500 sales per year, Viper was a bit player in the Dodge drama of the 1990s, when minivans, light pickups and sport-utility vehicles (SUVs) increasingly upstaged cars in consumer affections. Indeed, Dodge was then selling way more cars than trucks each year—a record million-plus in 1998-2000, about three times its nontruck volume. The same was true to a lesser degree for Chevrolet and Ford, but Dodge had fewer car models, so its total business depended relatively more on trucks. Though Dodge remained far behind those rivals in truck sales, a series of successful products helped close the gap some. First up was 1994's all-new full-size Ram pickup, whose broad-shouldered styling and available V-10 power (related to Viper's) helped pull in almost three times as many orders as previous models. A further sales boost came in 1998 with the "Quad Cab," an industry first adding two rear-hinged back doors to Ram's extended Club Cab for easier entry/exit. The idea proved so popular that other makers rushed to copy it. Dodge's midsize Dakota pickups also enjoyed much stronger sales after getting a Ram-inspired redesign (for '97) and their own Quad Cabs (for 2000) with four front hinged doors. And after sitting on the sidelines for five years, Dodge launched the Dakota-based Durango for 1998 as a much more-competitive SUV than the ancient '70s-vintage Ramcharger.

As ever, though, Dodge's biggest strength was owning America's favorite minivan, its Caravan line pulling in at least a quarter-million sales each calendar year through 2000. Much of that success stemmed from the full redesign of 1996 that ushered in sleeker looks; roomier, quieter and stronger bodies; larger available engines with more power; and thoughtful new features like "Easy Out" back seats with built-in rollers and sliding rear doors for both sides, not just the right. While the related Plymouth Voyager and Chrysler Town & Country offered all this too, only Dodge tried for a measure of sportiness, fielding ES and Sport models with firmer suspension, youthful styling touches, even a manually shiftable automatic transmission.

Alas, heavy reliance on one product also remained Dodge's biggest weakness, aggravated in the late '90s by a growing public perception of minivans as uncool "soccer mom" transport. But though minivan demand did soften somewhat, Caravan sales weren't seriously affected. What did start to hurt was stronger competition, especially from Honda and Toyota, whose U.S.-bred minivans were stealing Caravan sales with superior workmanship and mechanical finesse. Dodge responded with mostly new 2001 Caravans, but they didn't look that new and were more expensive, in part because Chrysler's controls on production costs, once the envy of Detroit, had become rather lax. With all this, Caravan sales dropped to some 242,000 for calendar '01, still tops in class by far, but the lowest for Dodge in a decade. Then again, 2001 was a tough year for many companies, as the nation's decade-long boom economy ended and a frightening war on terrorism began.

Despite the market's growing preference for trucks, Dodge car sales were consistent and fairly strong in the late 1990s, totaling at least 360,000 each calendar year from '96 through 2000, after which the tally dipped to about 329,000. Leading the pack—though not as much as you might think—was the subcompact Neon, drawing 110,000-112,000 yearly orders through 2000 as a Dodge. Sales of Plymouth-badged Neons ran 25-30 percent lower, partly because of the Plymouth badge, said some analysts.

However, Dodge also did more than Plymouth to woo the younger buyers most attracted to small, low-priced cars. For example, coupes appeared in both lineups for '96, as did an available 150-bhp twincam version of Neon's 2.0-liter four, but only Dodge catered to weekend racers with a Competition Package featuring uprated suspension and tires, all-disc brakes, heavy-duty five-speed gearbox, tachometer, and other go-faster stuff. What's more, it was optional for the workaday sedan (at $1575) as well as the sportier-looking coupe ($1745, including the twincam mill). Dodge followed up for '98 with an R/T Package, again optional in both body styles. This combined the twincam engine and the Competition group's basic chassis bits with more heavily bolstered front bucket seats, a rear spoiler, fog lights, broad dorsal racing stripes, and large "R/T" decals. It didn't make a fire-breather like the big-block R/Ts of old, but it did make a fun ride even more so—and quite popular among said weekend racers.

But those were the highlights in the other uneventful career of the first-generation Neon, which remained rather rough and rowdy next to newer rivals, especially those from Japan. A full redesign for 2000 (arriving in early 1999) strove for wider market appeal, yet failed to address basic shortcomings. The optional automatic, for example, was still an outmoded three-speed unit, and workmanship, though better, remained below par. Coupes were canned—their sales had always disappointed—but so was the twincam engine. Sedans were restyled around little changed dimensions but lost their playful look, and the single-cam engine was scarcely quieter. Buyers must have noticed all this, for Dodge Neon sales dropped to just over 107,000 for calendar '01. Pushing on, Dodge reinstated an R/T package and added an ACR option for 2001, both packing a tuned single-cam 2.0-liter with—you guessed it—150 horsepower. Leather upholstery and front side airbags were newly available too. For 2002 came a four-speed automatic option like most rivals had offered for years. But if still not the most-polished of small cars, the newest Neons could deliver lots of fun for little money. They were, as Consumer Guide®'s Auto 2002 noted, "capable enough to stand comparison with most subcompact competitors."

The full-size Intrepid was more-impressive in its class, earning a string of Consumer Guide® "Best Buy" endorsements following its 1998 redesign. The final first-generation models were CG "Recommended," with the sportier ES gaining more standard power for '96, then Chrysler's new AutoStick manually shiftable automatic transmission for '97. The '98s were something else, however: still "cab-forward" outside and roomy inside, yet sleeker—real "dream car styling" come true. Length and width increased a bit, but wheelbase was

1997 Avenger coupe

1998 Avenger ES coupe

1998 Neon R/T coupe

1998 Dodge Intrepid ES sedan

1999 Avenger coupe

# Dodge

1999 Intrepid ES sedan

2000 Stratus ES sedan

2000 Neon sedan

2001 Neon R/T sedan

unchanged. Unlike before, no exterior body panels were shared with Chrysler's related Concorde. Engines were new, too. The base Intrepid carried a 2.7-liter V-6 with dual overhead camshafts and more ponies than the pushrod 3.3 it replaced. The sportier ES exchanged a single-cam 3.5 for a similar but more-efficient 3.2, also with more power.

Both models came with front buckets and console, but even the ES, which added standard antilock brakes, wasn't the speedy backroads runner its looks implied. Dodge remedied that in early 2000 by adding an Intrepid R/T with broader tires on 17-inch wheels (versus 16s), uprated suspension with larger antiroll bars at each end, and a 3.5-liter V-6 borrowed from Chrysler's vaunted new 300M. Dodge christened the engine "Magnum 3.5," another nod to its famed muscle cars of yore, but corporate planners mandated a detuning that stole 11 ponies and eight pound-feet. Even so, the R/T was a bit lighter than the M, and *Car and Driver* found it a bit quicker, sprinting 0-60 in 7.8 seconds on the way to a 139-mph maximum. Handling? "These large sedans have always behaved like cars weighing and measuring one class smaller," tester Frank Markus reported, "and the R/T provides even crisper turn-in and sharper responsiveness." Summing up, Markus allowed that other Intrepids might be tepid, with engines that "never managed to deliver the performance that the aggressively sporting sheetmetal promised....The R/T fixes that." And at a starting price of just $25,000—excellent value for the day.

Dodge's midsize cars were less successful in this period, partly because they didn't change much despite increasingly stiff class competition. On a calendar-year basis, Avenger coupe sales languished in the low-30,000 area through 1999, then plummeted to a mere 5500 with the year-2000 changeover to redesigned '01 models. The Stratus sedan sold in the mid- to high-90,000s except for 1998, when it topped 106,000, but a good chunk of each year's production went to corporate and rental fleets to the detriment of Stratus' image and resale values on the retail market. Like Neon, these were competent, high-value cars, and Dodge struggled to keep them appealing by juggling trim and minor features each year. Trouble was,

finicky consumers found more to like at other dealerships.

The redesigned 2001 models aimed to lure them back with fresh styling, new features, and a more solid, refined driving experience within little-changed dimensions. Avenger was renamed Stratus coupe, but was still built in Illinois on a Mitsubishi platform, this one borrowed from the Japanese company's 1999-2000 Galant sedan and sporty Eclipse models. Sedans remained purely Chrysler creations, evident in their cab-forward proportions, but production was now centered solely in Michigan (some prior models had been sourced from Mexico). Among the few shared features, other than the Stratus name, were a base 2.4-liter four-cylinder engine and a smooth, rounded nose with Dodge's trademark "cross-hair" grille motif. Models comprised price-leader SE coupes and sedans, a new two-door R/T with Mitsubishi's latest 3.0-liter V-6 (replacing Avenger ES), and a four-door ES packing Chrysler's 2.7-liter V-6. A value-equipped SE Plus sedan was added for '02. Interestingly, both V-6s were rated at 200 horsepower, perhaps to keep peace in the corporate family. Automatic transmission was mandatory for sedans and optional for coupes in lieu of manual five-speed. Enthusiasts were quick to note the V-6/ manual combo, a first for Dodge's midsize coupe and not available in Chrysler's sibling Sebring. Also available for the R/T was Chrysler's AutoStick feature, previously limited to ES sedans.

For all the changes, though, the new Stratuses were just more of the same—noticeably improved in most areas, yet not quite good enough to best the competition's best. Sedans had standard all-disc brakes and offered head-protecting curtain side airbags as a first-time option, but torso side airbags weren't available on any model, and antilock brakes cost extra. And though the manual R/T coupe promised the most-rewarding drive, *Road & Track* damned it with faint initial praise, judging it merely "well equipped to take on the Toyota Solaras and Honda Accord coupes of the world." *Car and Driver* was more-upbeat, finding the R/T "nearly as delightful to flog as its Mitsubishi [Eclipse] cousin."

In any case, the second-generation Stratuses were still

# Dodge

**2001 Stratus sedan**

**2002 Stratus R/T sedan**

**2001 Intrepid R/T sedan**

**2002 Dodge Viper GTS coupe**

young when this book was compiled, so they may yet become more compelling. Dodge certainly has the will to make them so. All it needs is the means, and that depends greatly on the fortunes of DaimlerChrysler, formed from Chrysler Corporation's unpredecented 1998 union with Germany's famed Daimler-Benz (detailed under Chrysler). Though struggling to survive at this writing, DC certainly has the resources to produce exciting new Dodges for tomorrow, more than reason enough to hope for a speedy recovery.

Though we had yet to see any new Dodges created entirely by Daimler-Chrysler, Dodge seems sure to continue pursuing performance as passionately as ever. One obvious sign: a fully redesigned 2003 Viper roadster called SRT/10. A new-generation GTS is only a matter of time. Against the original roadster, the SRT/10 strides a 2.6-inch longer wheelbase (98.8), but is little changed in overall size. Styling remains recognizably Viper, though crisper and, from some angles, more-aggressive. Enhancing appearance is a full manual-fold soft top that dispenses with the fixed rear "sport bar" while improving convenience and weather protection versus the old afterthought "bikini" top. Side exhaust pipes return, but are now integral with the body and shielded to meet noise regulations—not to mention preventing fried legs. Basic construction again involves a steel chassis beneath a composite-plastic body with some aluminum panels. The four-wheel double-wishbone suspension stays roughly the same, too, but wheel diameter goes from 18 to 19 inches, allowing room for larger four-wheel antilock disc brakes. Tires remain Z-rated but are even wider at the rear, with 345/30s replacing 335/30s.

Viper's trademark pushrod aluminum V-10 is pumped up for 2003 to 500 cubic inches, 500 horsepower, and 500 pound-feet of torque, delivered through a fortified six-speed manual gearbox. With that and fractionally less weight, the '03 promises to outperform the final 450-bhp models, which do 0-60 mph in about 4.5 sec. The speedometer now reads to 220 mph, which Dodge says is no accident. Traction control or antiskid system? Nowhere in sight. Viper has always been a chest-thumping "elemental" muscle car, and Dodge isn't about to change that.

Roaring down a very different avenue is the 2003 Neon SRT-4, Dodge's response to that fascinating turn-of-millennium market trend, the "sport compact." A growing number of young urban enthusiasts had been transforming used cars, especially Honda Civics and Acura Integras, into striking custom street racers, creating a huge new market for performance parts and styling accessories. Automakers soon began offering sporty versions of workaday small cars to get in on this lucrative action—and hopefully hook some new buyers for life. Neon was already known as a demon handler, having racked up a number of autocross and road-racing championships. The SRT-4 added lots of sizzle from a turbocharged 2.4-liter twincam four with 205 horsepower. Allied to mandatory heavy-duty five-speed gearbox and a sub-3000-pound curb weight, the intercooled engine delivered 0-60 in only 5.9 seconds, said Dodge, yet starting price was just under $20,000, making SRT-4 the new champ in "bang for the buck," not to mention the second-fastest car in the line (after Viper, of course).

Though planned as an attractive starting point for owner personalizing, SRT-4 was equipped to satisfy right out of the box. There was no doubt about its intent, thanks to a prominent decklid spoiler, fat 17-inch wheels and tires, chrome-tipped exhaust, discreet lower-body cladding, and a bold new nose with functioning hood scoop, a much deeper bumper, and a gaping cross-hair grille. Suspension was lowered and stiffened while a big disc brake stopped each alloy wheel. The interior maintained the performance theme with bolstered bucket seats, turbo-boost/vacuum gauge, satin-finish metal trim for dashboard and pedals, a unique three-spoke steering wheel, and a whimsical "cue ball" shift knob.

While SRT-4 and the new Viper are exceptional cars, they're also exceptions; most future Dodges won't be so extreme. Yet despite corporate ups-and-downs and the challenges of an ever-changing market, the Dodge Boys are still having fun, just like the "good old days," and that's great. It means we have more fun, too.

# Dodge

## Specifications

### 1930

**DA Six (wb 112.0)—15,000 built (est.)***

| | Wght | Price | Prod |
|---|---|---|---|
| rdstr 2-4P | 2,687 | 995 | — |
| phtn 5P | 2,730 | 1,025 | — |
| bus cpe 2P | 2,750 | 945 | — |
| DeLuxe cpe 2-4P | 2,812 | 1,025 | — |
| victoria 4P | 2,846 | 1,025 | — |
| brougham 5P | 2,834 | 995 | — |
| sdn 2d 5P | 2,876 | 925 | — |
| sdn 4d 5P | 2,894 | 995 | — |
| DeLuxe sdn 4d 5P | 2,898 | 1,065 | — |

**DB Six Senior (wb 120.0)—7,000 built (est.)***

| | Wght | Price | Prod |
|---|---|---|---|
| rdstr 2-4P | 3,303 | 1,615 | — |
| cpe 2-4P | 3,426 | 1,595 | — |
| brougham 5P | 3,419 | 1,545 | — |
| sdn 4d | 3,513 | 1,595 | — |
| landau sdn 4d | 3,525 | 1,645 | — |

**DC Eight (wb 114.0)—19,993 built****

| | Wght | Price | Prod |
|---|---|---|---|
| rdstr 2P | 2,802 | 1,095 | 598 |
| phtn 5P | 2,690 | 1,225 | 234 |
| cpe 2-4P | 2,981 | 1,125 | 2,999 |
| conv cpe 2-4P | 2,938 | 1,195 | 728 |
| sdn 4d | 3,043 | 1,145 | 20,315 |
| bus cpe | — | — | 123 |
| chassis | — | — | 253 |

**DD New Six (wb 109.0)—29,651 built*****

| | Wght | Price | Prod |
|---|---|---|---|
| rdstr 2-4P | 2,462 | 855 | 772 |
| phtn 5P | 2,521 | 875 | 542 |
| bus cpe 2P | 2,534 | 835 | 3,877 |
| cpe 2-4P | 2,603 | 855 | 3,363 |
| conv cpe 2-4P | 2,605 | 935 | 620 |
| sdn 4d | 2,668 | 865 | 33,432 |
| chassis | — | — | 899 |

\* Available 1930 figures combined with 1929 production.

\*\* Total based on serial number spans. Individual model totals for 1930-32 combined. Approximately 80 percent of the individual model totals were 1930 models.

\*\*\* Total based on serial number spans. Individual model totals for 1930-32 combined. Approximately 70 percent of the individual model totals were 1930 models.

| 1930 Engines | bore × stroke | bhp | availability |
|---|---|---|---|
| I-6, 208.0 | 3.38 × 3.88 | 63 | S-DA |
| I-6, 241.5 | 3.38 × 4.50 | 78 | S-DB |
| I-6, 189.8 | 3.13 × 4.13 | 61 | S-DD |
| I-8, 220.7 | 2.88 × 4.25 | 75 | S-DC |

### 1931

**DC Eight (wb 114.0)—4,268 built**

Production was carried over from 1930, with 1931-model output commencing July 15. Production figures combined with 1930 DC; total 1931 production based on serial number spans. Body styles and weights identical. Prices $100 less except phaeton, which was $145 less than 1930.

**DD New Six (wb 109.0)—12,854 built**

Production was carried over from 1930, with 1931-model output commencing July 15. Production figures combined with 1930 DD; total 1931 production based on serial number spans. Body styles and weights identical. Prices $100 less than 1930.

**DG Eight (wb 118.5)—9,520 built***

| | Wght | Price | Prod |
|---|---|---|---|
| rdstr 2-4P | 2,936 | 1,095 | 64 |
| cpe 2-4P | 3,094 | 1,095 | 2,181 |
| conv cpe | 3,240 | 1,170 | 500 |
| sdn 4d | 3,175 | 1,135 | 8,937 |
| chassis | — | — | 20 |

**DH Six (wb 114.0)—20,558 built****

| | Wght | Price | Prod |
|---|---|---|---|
| rdstr 2-4P | 2,638 | 825 | 160 |
| bus cpe 2P | 2,661 | 815 | 3,178 |
| cpe 2-4P | 2,745 | 835 | 4,187 |
| sdn 4d | 2,820 | 845 | 33,090 |
| chassis | — | — | 47 |

\* Total based on serial number spans. Individual model totals for 1931-32 combined (see also additional models under 1932). Approximately 80 percent of the individual model totals were 1932 models.

\*\* Total based on serial number spans. Individual model totals for 1931-32 combined (see also additional models under 1932). Approximately 50 percent of the individual model totals were 1931 models.

| 1931 Engines | bore × stroke | bhp | availability |
|---|---|---|---|
| I-8, 220.7 | 2.88 × 4.25 | 75 | S-DC |
| I-6, 189.8 | 3.13 × 4.13 | 61 | S-DD |
| I-8, 240.3 | 3.00 × 4.25 | 84 | S-DG |
| I-6, 211.5 | 3.25 × 4.25 | 68 | S-DH |

### 1932

**DG Eight (wb 118.5)—2,344 built***

| | Wght | Price | Prod |
|---|---|---|---|
| rdstr 2-4P | 2,976 | 1,095 | ** |
| phtn 5P | — | 1,155 | 43** |
| bus cpe 2P | 3,003 | 1,095 | 119** |
| cpe 2-4P | 3,094 | 1,095 | ** |
| conv cpe 5P | 3,240 | 1,145 | ** |
| sdn 4d | 3,175 | 1,135 | ** |
| chassis | — | — | ** |

\* Total production based on serial number spans for 1932.

\*\* Production combined with 1931 except for phaeton (43) and business coupe (119), which were new models for 1932.

**DH Six (wb 114.0)—20,268 built****

| | Wght | Price | Prod |
|---|---|---|---|
| rdstr 2-4P | 2,638 | 850 | ** |
| phtn 5P | 2,655 | 865 | 164 |
| bus cpe 2P | 2,661 | 815 | ** |
| cpe 2-4P | 2,745 | 835 | ** |
| sdn 4d | 2,820 | 845 | ** |
| chassis | — | — | ** |

\* Total production based on serial number spans for 1932.

\*\* Production combined with 1931 except for phaeton (164), which was a new model for 1932.

**DC Eight (wb 114.0)—631 built**

Leftover 1930-31 models sold as 1932s commencing July 1, 1931. Total volume based on serial number spans. Body styles, weights and prices as for 1931.

**DD New Six (wb 109.0)—1,000 built (est.)**

Leftover 1930-31 models sold as 1932s commencing July 1, 1931. Total volume estimated. Body styles, weights and prices as for 1931.

**DL Six (wb 114.3)—21,042 built**

| | Wght | Price | Prod |
|---|---|---|---|
| bus cpe 2P | 2,928 | 795 | 1,963 |
| cpe 2-4P | 2,995 | 835 | 1,815 |
| conv cpe 2-4P | 2,988 | 895 | 224 |
| sdn 4d | 3,094 | 945 | 16,901 |
| conv sdn | — | — | 12 |
| cpe 5P | — | — | 1 |
| chassis | — | — | 126 |

Dodge

| DK Eight (wb 122.0)—6,187 built | Wght | Price | Prod |
|---|---|---|---|
| cpe 2-4P | 3,417 | 1,115 | 821 |
| cpe 5P | 3,504 | 1,145 | 651 |
| conv cpe 2-4P | 3,438 | 1,220 | 126 |
| sdn 4d | 3,527 | 1,145 | 4,422 |
| conv sdn 5P | 3,706 | 1,395 | 88 |
| bus cpe 2P | — | — | 57 |
| chassis | — | — | 22 |

| 1932 Engines | bore × stroke | bhp | availability |
|---|---|---|---|
| I-8, 220.7 | 2.88 × 4.25 | 75 | S-DC |
| I-6, 189.8 | 3.13 × 4.13 | 61 | S-DD |
| I-8, 240.3 | 3.00 × 4.25 | 84 | S-DG |
| I-6, 211.5 | 3.25 × 4.25 | 74 | S-DH |
| I-6, 217.8 | 3.25 × 4.38 | 79 | S-DL |
| I-8, 282.1 | 3.25 × 4.25 | 90 | S-DK |

## 1933

| DP Six (wb 111.3; lwb-115.0) | Wght | Price | Prod |
|---|---|---|---|
| bus cpe 2P | 2,452 | 595 | 11,236 |
| lwb bus cpe 2P | 2,501 | 595 | |
| cpe 2-4P | 2,506 | 640 | 8,875 |
| lwb cpe 2-4P | 2,551 | 640 | |
| conv cpe 2-4P | 2,511 | 695 | 1,563 |
| conv cpe 2-4P | 2,556 | 695 | |
| sdn 2d | 2,591 | 630 | 8,523 |
| lwb sdn 2d | 2,636 | 630 | |
| sdn 4d | 2,632 | 670 | 69,074 |
| lwb sdn 4d | 2,661 | 675 | |
| salon brougham 5P | 2,651 | 660 | 4,200 |
| lwb salon brougham 5P | 2,678 | 660 | |
| chassis | — | — | 980 |

| DO Eight (wb 122.0) | | | |
|---|---|---|---|
| cpe 2-4P | 3,451 | 1,115 | 212 |
| cpe 5P | 3,540 | 1,145 | 159 |
| conv cpe 2-4P | 3,465 | 1,185 | 56 |
| sdn 4d | 3,580 | 1,145 | 1,173 |
| conv sdn 5P | 3,961 | 1,395 | 39 |
| chassis | — | — | 13 |

| 1933 Engines | bore × stroke | bhp | availability |
|---|---|---|---|
| I-6, 201.3 | 3.13 × 4.38 | 75 | S-DP |
| I-8, 282.1 | 3.25 × 4.25 | 92 | S-DO |

## 1934

| DR DeLuxe Six (wb 117.0) | Wght | Price | Prod |
|---|---|---|---|
| bus cpe 2P | 2,695 | 665 | 8,723 |
| cpe 2-4P | 2,745 | 715 | 5,323 |
| conv cpe 2-4P | 2,845 | 765 | 1,239 |
| sdn 2d | 2,855 | 715 | 7,308 |
| sdn 4d | 2,940 | 765 | 53,479 |
| sdns 4d 7P | — | — | 710 |
| chassis | — | — | 1,475 |

| DS DeLuxe Six (wb 121.0) | | | |
|---|---|---|---|
| Special brougham 4d 5P | 2,905 | 845 | 1,397 |
| Special conv sdn 5P | 2,915 | 875 | 350 |
| chassis | — | — | 3 |

| DRXX New Standard Six (wb 117.0) | | | |
|---|---|---|---|
| bus cpe 2P | 2,695 | 645 | 2,284 |
| cpe 2-4P | 2,745 | 690 | 105 |
| sdn 2d | 2,855 | 695 | 3,133 |

| DRXX New Standard Six (wb 117.0) | Wght | Price | Prod |
|---|---|---|---|
| sdn 4d | 2,940 | 745 | 9,481 |
| chassis | — | — | 1 |

| 1934 Engine | bore × stroke | bhp | availability |
|---|---|---|---|
| I-6, 217.8 | 3.25 × 4.38 | 87 | S-all |

## 1935

**DU New Value Six (wb 116.0; lwb-128.0)**

| | Wght | Price | Prod |
|---|---|---|---|
| cpe 2P | 2,731 | 645 | 17,800 |
| cpe 2-4P | 2,801 | 710 | 4,499 |
| conv cpe 2-4P | 2,883 | 770 | 950 |
| fstbk sdn 2d | 2,821 | 690 | 7,891 |
| sdn T/B 2d | 2,868 | 715 | 18,069 |
| fstbk sdn 4d | 2,861 | 735 | 33,118 |
| sdn T/B 4d | 2,868 | 760 | 74,203 |
| Caravan sdn 4d 5P (lwb) | 3,221 | 995 | 193 |
| lwb sdn 4d 7P | 3,118 | 995 | 1,018 |
| chassis | — | — | 1,258 |

| 1935 Engine | bore × stroke | bhp | availability |
|---|---|---|---|
| I-6, 217.8 | 3.25 × 4.38 | 87 | S-all |

## 1936

**D2 Beauty Winner Six (wb 116.0; lwb-128.0)**

| | Wght | Price | Prod |
|---|---|---|---|
| cpe 2P | 2,773 | 640 | 32,952 |
| cpe 2-4P | 2,823 | 695 | 4,317 |
| conv cpe 2-4P | 2,887 | 795 | 1,525 |
| fstbk sdn 2d | 2,903 | 695 | 2,453 |
| sdn T/B 2d | 2,893 | 720 | 37,468 |
| fstbk sdn 4d | 2,923 | 735 | 5,996 |
| sdn T/B 4d | 2,958 | 760 | 174,334 |
| conv sdn 5P | 3,018 | 995 | 750 |
| lwb sdn 4d 7P | 3,238 | 975 | 1,942 |
| chassis | — | — | 1,910 |

| 1936 Engine | bore × stroke | bhp | availability |
|---|---|---|---|
| I-6, 217.8 | 3.25 × 4.38 | 87 | S-all |

## 1937

| D5 (wb 115.0; lwb-132.0) | Wght | Price | Prod |
|---|---|---|---|
| bus cpe 2P | 2,902 | 715 | 41,702 |
| cpe 2-4P | 2,967 | 770 | 3,500 |
| conv cpe 2-4P | 3,057 | 910 | 1,345 |
| fstbk sdn 2d | 2,992 | 780 | 5,302 |
| sdn T/B 2d | 2,997 | 790 | 44,750 |
| fstbk sdn 4d | 2,982 | 820 | 7,555 |
| sdn T/B 4d | 2,997 | 830 | 185,483 |
| conv sdn 5P | 3,262 | 1,230 | 473 |
| lwb sdn 7P | 3,367 | 1,075 | 2,207 |
| limo 7P (lwb) | — | 1,175 | 216 |
| chassis | — | — | 2,514 |

| 1937 Engine | bore × stroke | bhp | availability |
|---|---|---|---|
| I-6, 217.8 | 3.25 × 4.38 | 87 | S-all |

## 1938

| D8 (wb 115.0; lwb-132.0) | Wght | Price | Prod |
|---|---|---|---|
| bus cpe 2P | 2,877 | 808 | 15,552 |
| cpe 2-4P | 2,952 | 858 | 950 |

391

# Dodge

| D8 (wb 115.0; lwb-132.0) | Wght | Price | Prod |
|---|---|---|---|
| conv cpe 2-4P | 3,122 | 960 | 701 |
| fstbk sdn 2d | 2,977 | 858 | 999 |
| sdn T/B 2d | 2,957 | 870 | 17,282 |
| fstbk sdn 4d | 2,977 | 898 | 714 |
| sdn T/B 4d | 2,967 | 910 | 73,417 |
| conv sdn T/B 5P | 3,308 | 1,275 | 132 |
| lwb sdn 7P | 3,332 | 1,095 | 1,953 |
| limo 7P (lwb) | — | 1,185 | 153 |
| wgn 4d | — | — | 375 |
| chassis | — | — | 2,301 |

| 1938 Engine | bore × stroke | bhp | availability |
|---|---|---|---|
| I-6, 217.8 | 3.25 × 4.38 | 87 | S-all |

## 1939

| D11 Luxury Liner Special (wb 117.0) | Wght | Price | Prod |
|---|---|---|---|
| bus cpe 2P | 2,905 | 756 | 12,300 |
| sdn 2d | 2,955 | 815 | 26,700 |
| sdn 4d | 2,955 | 855 | 32,000 |
| **D11 Luxury Liner DeLuxe (wb 117.0)** | | | |
| bus cpe 2P | 2,940 | 803 | 12,800 |
| Town cpe 5P | 3,075 | 1,055 | 363 |
| sdn 2d | 3,010 | 865 | 17,608 |
| sdn 4d | 3,045 | 905 | 80,169 |
| chassis | — | — | 875 |

| 1939 Engine | bore × stroke | bhp | availability |
|---|---|---|---|
| I-6, 217.8 | 3.25 × 4.38 | 87 | S-all |

Note: Many sources also list a 2-4 passenger rumble-seat coupe (2,985 lbs/$860), and a 134-inch wheelbase 7-passenger sedan (3,440 lbs/$1,095) and limousine (3,545 lbs/$1,185). However, Dodge gives no production figures for these models, and their production in 1939 is in doubt.

## 1940

| D-17 Special (wb 119.5) | Wght | Price | Prod |
|---|---|---|---|
| bus cpe | 2,867 | 755 | 12,001 |
| sdn 2d | 2,942 | 815 | 27,700 |
| sdn 4d | 2,997 | 855 | 26,803 |
| **D-14 DeLuxe (wb 119.5; 7P-139.5)** | | | |
| bus cpe | 2,905 | 803 | 12,750 |
| cpe, A/S | 2,973 | 855 | 8,028 |
| conv cpe | 3,190 | 1,030 | 2,100 |
| sdn 2d | 2,990 | 860 | 19,838 |
| sdn 4d | 3,028 | 905 | 84,976 |
| sdn 4d, 7P | 3,460 | 1,095 | 932 |
| limo 7P | 3,500 | 1,170 | 79 |
| chassis | — | — | 298 |

| 1940 Engine | bore × stroke | bhp | availability |
|---|---|---|---|
| I-6, 217.8 | 3.25 × 4.38 | 87 | S-all |

## 1941

| D-19 DeLuxe (wb 119.5) | Wght | Price | Prod |
|---|---|---|---|
| bus cpe | 3,034 | 862 | 22,318 |
| sdn 2d | 3,109 | 915 | 34,566 |
| sdn 4d | 3,149 | 954 | 49,579 |
| **D-19 Custom (wb 119.5; 7P-137.5)** | | | |
| club cpe | 3,154 | 995 | 18,024 |
| conv cpe | 3,384 | 1,162 | 3,554 |
| brougham 2d | 3,169 | 962 | 20,146 |
| sdn 4d | 3,194 | 999 | 72,067 |
| town sdn | 3,234 | 1,062 | 16,074 |
| sdn 4d, 7P | 3,579 | 1,195 | 604 |
| limo 7P | 3,669 | 1,262 | 50 |
| chassis | — | — | 20 |

| 1941 Engine | bore × stroke | bhp | availability |
|---|---|---|---|
| I-6, 217.8 | 3.25 × 4.38 | 91 | S-all |

## 1942

| D-22 DeLuxe (wb 119.5) | Wght | Price | Prod |
|---|---|---|---|
| bus cpe | 3,056 | 895 | 5,257 |
| club cpe | 3,131 | 995 | 3,314 |
| sdn 2d | 3,131 | 958 | 9,767 |
| sdn 4d | 3,171 | 998 | 13,343 |
| **D-22 Custom (wb 119.5; 7P-137.5)** | | | |
| club cpe | 3,171 | 1,045 | 4,659 |
| conv cpe | 3,476 | 1,245 | 1,185 |
| brougham 2d | 3,171 | 1,008 | 4,685 |
| sdn 4d | 3,206 | 1,048 | 22,055 |
| town sdn | 3,256 | 1,105 | 4,047 |
| sdn 4d, 7P | 3,693 | 1,395 | 201 |
| limo 7P | 3,768 | 1,475 | 9 |

| 1942 Engine | bore × stroke | bhp | availability |
|---|---|---|---|
| I-6, 230.2 | 3.25 × 4.63 | 105 | S-all |

## 1946

| D-24S DeLuxe (wb 119.5) | Wght | Price | Prod* |
|---|---|---|---|
| bus cpe | 3,146 | 1,229 | — |
| sdn 2d | 3,236 | 1,299 | — |
| sdn 4d | 3,256 | 1,339 | — |
| **D-24C Custom (wb 119.5; 7P-137.5)** | | | |
| club cpe | 3,241 | 1,384 | — |
| conv cpe | 3,461 | 1,649 | — |
| sdn 4d | 3,281 | 1,389 | — |
| town sdn | 3,331 | 1,444 | — |
| sdn 4d, 7P | 3,757 | 1,743 | — |

| 1946 Engine | bore × stroke | bhp | availability |
|---|---|---|---|
| I-6, 230.2 | 3.25 × 4.63 | 102 | S-all |

* Factory combined production figures for 1946 through First Series 1949.

## 1947

| D-24S DeLuxe (wb 119.5) | Wght | Price | Prod* |
|---|---|---|---|
| bus cpe | 3,146 | 1,347 | — |
| sdn 2d | 3,236 | 1,417 | — |
| sdn 4d | 3,256 | 1,457 | — |
| **D-24C Custom (wb 119.5; 7P-137.5)** | | | |
| club cpe | 3,241 | 1,502 | — |
| conv cpe | 3,461 | 1,871 | — |
| sdn 4d | 3,281 | 1,507 | — |
| town sdn | 3,331 | 1,577 | — |
| sdn 4d, 7P | 3,757 | 1,861 | — |

| 1947 Engine | bore × stroke | bhp | availability |
|---|---|---|---|
| I-6, 230.2 | 3.25 × 4.63 | 102 | S-all |

* Factory combined production figures for 1946 through First Series 1949.

# Dodge

## 1948

| D-24S DeLuxe (wb 119.5) | Wght | Price | Prod* |
|---|---|---|---|
| bus cpe | 3,146 | 1,587 | — |
| sdn 2d | 3,236 | 1,676 | — |
| sdn 4d | 3,256 | 1,718 | — |

| D-24C Custom (wb 119.5; 7P-137.5) | | | |
|---|---|---|---|
| club cpe | 3,241 | 1,774 | — |
| conv cpe | 3,461 | 2,189 | — |
| sdn 4d | 3,281 | 1,788 | — |
| town sdn | 3,331 | 1,872 | — |
| sdn 4d, 7P | 3,757 | 2,179 | — |

| 1948 Engine | bore × stroke | bhp | availability |
|---|---|---|---|
| I-6, 230.2 | 3.25 × 4.63 | 102 | S-all |

* Factory combined production figures for 1946 through First Series 1949.

## 1949 First Series

| D-24S DeLuxe (wb 119.5) | Wght | Price | Prod* |
|---|---|---|---|
| bus cpe | 3,146 | 1,587 | — |
| sdn 2d | 3,236 | 1,676 | — |
| sdn 4d | 3,256 | 1,718 | — |

| D-24C Custom (wb 119.5; 7P-137.5) | | | |
|---|---|---|---|
| club cpe | 3,241 | 1,774 | — |
| conv cpe | 3,461 | 2,189 | — |
| sdn 4d | 3,281 | 1,788 | — |
| town sdn | 3,331 | 1,872 | — |
| sdn 4d, 7P | 3,757 | 2,179 | — |

| 1949(1) Engine | bore × stroke | bhp | availability |
|---|---|---|---|
| I-6, 230.2 | 3.25 × 4.63 | 102 | S-all |

* Factory combined production figures for 1946 through First Series 1949.

Combined 1946-1949 First Series Production:

| D-24S DeLuxe (wb 119.5) | Prod |
|---|---|
| bus cpe | 27,600 |
| sdn 2d | 81,399 |
| sdn 4d | 61,987 |

| D-24C Custom (wb 119.5; 7P-137.5) | |
|---|---|
| club cpe | 103,800 |
| conv cpe | 9,500 |
| sdn 4d | 333,911 |
| town sdn | 27,800 |
| sdn 4d, 7P | 3,698 |
| limo 7P (proto) | 2 |
| chassis | 302 |

## 1949 Second Series

| D-29 Wayfarer (wb 115.0) | Wght | Price | Prod |
|---|---|---|---|
| cpe | 3,065 | 1,611 | 9,342 |
| sdn 2d | 3,180 | 1,738 | 49,058 |
| rdstr | 3,145 | 1,727 | 5,420 |

| D-30 (wb 123.5; 8P-137.5) | | | |
|---|---|---|---|
| Meadowbrook sdn 4d | 3,355 | 1,848 | 144,390 |
| Coronet sdn 4d | 3,380 | 1,927 | |
| Coronet club cpe | 3,325 | 1,914 | 45,435 |
| Coronet conv cpe | 3,570 | 2,329 | 2,411 |
| Coronet sdn 4d, 8P | 4,070 | 2,635 | — |
| Coronet wgn 4d, 9P | 3,830 | 2,865 | 800 |
| chassis | — | — | 1 |

| 1949(2) Engine | bore × stroke | bhp | availability |
|---|---|---|---|
| I-6, 230.2 | 3.25 × 4.63 | 103 | S-all |

## 1950

| D-33 Wayfarer (wb 115.0) | Wght | Price | Prod |
|---|---|---|---|
| bus cpe | 3,095 | 1,611 | 7,500 |
| sdn 2d | 3,200 | 1,738 | 65,000 |
| Sportabout rdstr | 3,155 | 1,727 | 2,903 |

| D-34 (wb 123.5; 8P-137.5) | | | |
|---|---|---|---|
| Meadowbrook sdn 4d | 3,395 | 1,848 | 221,791 |
| Coronet sdn 4d | 3,405 | 1,927 | |
| Coronet sdn 4d, 8P | 4,070 | 2,635 | 1,300 |
| Coronet club cpe | 3,340 | 1,914 | 38,502 |
| Coronet conv cpe | 3,590 | 2,329 | 1,800 |
| Coronet Diplomat htp cpe | 3,515 | 2,223 | 3,600 |
| Coronet wgn 4d (wood) | 3,850 | 2,865 | 600 |
| Coronet Sierra wgn 4d (steel) | 3,726 | 2,485 | 100 |
| chassis | — | — | 1 |

| 1950 Engine | bore × stroke | bhp | availability |
|---|---|---|---|
| I-6, 230.2 | 3.25 × 4.63 | 103 | S-all |

## 1951

| D-41 Wayfarer (wb 115.0) | Wght | Price | Prod* |
|---|---|---|---|
| bus cpe | 3,125 | 1,795 | — |
| sdn 2d | 3,210 | 1,936 | — |
| Sportabout rdstr | 3,175 | 1,924 | 1,002 |

| D-42 (wb 123.5; 8P-137.5) | | | |
|---|---|---|---|
| Meadowbrook sdn 4d | 3,415 | 2,059 | — |
| Coronet sdn 4d | 3,415 | 2,148 | — |
| Coronet club cpe | 3,320 | 2,132 | — |
| Coronet Diplomat htp cpe | 3,515 | 2,478 | — |
| Coronet conv cpe | 3,575 | 2,568 | — |
| Coronet Sierra wgn 4d | 3,750 | 2,768 | — |
| Coronet sdn 4d, 8P | 3,935 | 2,916 | — |

| 1951 Engine | bore × stroke | bhp | availability |
|---|---|---|---|
| I-6, 230.2 | 3.25 × 4.63 | 103 | S-all |

* Factory combined 1951-1952 production.

## 1952

| D-41 Wayfarer (wb 115.0) | Wght | Price | Prod* |
|---|---|---|---|
| bus cpe | 3,053 | 1,886 | — |
| sdn 2d | 3,140 | 2,034 | — |

| D-42 (wb 123.5; 8P-137.5) | | | |
|---|---|---|---|
| Meadowbrook sdn 4d | 3,355 | 2,164 | — |
| Coronet sdn 4d | 3,385 | 2,256 | — |
| Coronet club cpe | 3,290 | 2,240 | — |
| Coronet conv cpe | 3,520 | 2,698 | — |
| Coronet Diplomat htp cpe | 3,475 | 2,602 | — |
| Coronet Sierra wgn 4d | 3,735 | 2,908 | — |
| Coronet sdn 4d, 8P | 3,935 | 3,064 | — |

| 1952 Engine | bore × stroke | bhp | availability |
|---|---|---|---|
| I-6, 230.2 | 3.25 × 4.63 | 103 | S-all |

* Factory combined 1951-1952 production.

### Combined 1951-1952 production:

| D-41 Wayfarer (wb 115.0) | Prod |
|---|---|
| bus cpe | 6,702 |
| sdn 2d | 70,700 |
| Sportabout rdstr (1951 only) | 1,002 |

| D-42 (wb 123.5; 8P-137.5) | |
|---|---|
| Meadowbrook/Coronet sdn 4d | 329,202 |

## Dodge

| D-42 (wb 123.5; 8P-137.5) | Wght | Price | Prod |
|---|---|---|---|
| Coronet club cpe | | | 56,103 |
| Coronet conv cpe | | | 5,550 |
| Coronet Diplomat htp cpe | | | 21,600 |
| Coronet Sierra wgn 4d | | | 4,000 |
| Coronet sdn 4d, 8P | | | 1,150 |

### 1953

| D-46 (wb 119.0) | Wght | Price | Prod |
|---|---|---|---|
| Meadowbrook Special cpe | 3,100 | 1,958 | ⎤ |
| Meadowbrook cpe | 3,085 | 1,958 | 36,766 |
| Coronet cpe | 3,155 | 2,084 | ⎦ |
| Meadowbrook Special sdn 4d | 3,195 | 2,000 | ⎤ |
| Meadowbrook sdn 4d | 3,175 | 2,000 | 84,158 |
| Coronet sdn 4d | 3,220 | 2,111 | ⎦ |
| **D-47 Meadowbrook Suburban (wb 114.0)** | | | |
| wgn 2d | 3,190 | 2,176 | 15,751 |
| **D-44 Coronet Eight (wb 119.0)** | | | |
| club cpe | 3,325 | 2,198 | 32,439 |
| sdn 4d | 3,385 | 2,220 | 124,059 |
| **D-48 Coronet Eight (wb 114.0)** | | | |
| conv cpe | 3,438 | 2,494 | 4,100 |
| Diplomat htp cpe | 3,310 | 2,361 | 17,334 |
| Sierra wgn 2d | 3,425 | 2,503 | 5,400 |
| chassis | — | — | 1 |

| 1953 Engines | bore × stroke | bhp | availability |
|---|---|---|---|
| I-6, 230.2 | 3.25 × 4.63 | 103 | S-D-46, D-47 |
| V-8, 241.3 | 3.44 × 3.25 | 140 | S-D-44, D-48 |

### 1954

| D51-1 Meadowbrook I-6 (wb 119.0) | Wght | Price | Prod |
|---|---|---|---|
| club cpe | 3,120 | 1,983 | 3,501 |
| sdn 4d | 3,195 | 2,025 | 7,894 |
| **D50-1 Meadowbrook V-8 (wb 119.0)** | | | |
| club cpe | 3,335 | 2,154 | 750 |
| sdn 4d | 3,390 | 2,176 | 3,299 |
| **D51-2 Coronet I-6 (wb 119.0)** | | | |
| club cpe | 3,165 | 2,109 | 4,501 |
| sdn 4d | 3,235 | 2,136 | 14,900 |
| **D52 Coronet I-6 (wb 119.0; 2d-114.0)** | | | |
| Suburban wgn 2d | 3,185 | 2,229 | 6,389 |
| Sierra wgn 4d, 6P | 3,430 | 2,719 | 312 |
| Sierra wgn 4d, 8P | 3,435 | 2,790 | |
| **D50-2 Coronet V-8 (wb 119.0)** | | | |
| club cpe | 3,345 | 2,223 | 7,998 |
| sdn 4d | 3,405 | 2,245 | 36,063 |
| **D53-2 Coronet V-8 (wb 114.0; 4d-119.0)** | | | |
| Sport htp cpe | 3,310 | 2,380 | 100 |
| conv cpe | 3,505 | 2,514 | 50 |
| Suburban wgn 2d | 3,400 | 2,517 | 3,100 |
| Sierra wgn 4d, 6P | 3,605 | 2,960 | 988 |
| Sierra wgn 4d, 8P | 3,660 | 3,031 | |
| **D50-3 Royal V-8 (wb 119.0)** | | | |
| club cpe | 3,365 | 2,349 | 8,900 |
| sdn 4d | 3,425 | 2,373 | 50,050 |
| **D53-3 Royal V-8 (wb 114.0)** | | | |
| Sport htp cpe | 3,355 | 2,503 | 3,852 |
| conv cpe (incl. 701 500s) | 3,575 | 2,632 | 2,000 |
| chassis | — | — | 1 |

| 1954 Engines | bore × stroke | bhp | availability |
|---|---|---|---|
| I-6, 230.2 | 3.25 × 4.63 | 110 | S-Coronet 6s |
| V-8, 241.3 | 3.44 × 3.25 | 140 | S-Meadowbrook V-8 |
| V-8, 241.3 | 3.44 × 3.25 | 150 | S-others (Offenhauser manifold available) |

### 1955

| D56-1 Coronet I-6 (wb 120.0) | Wght | Price | Prod |
|---|---|---|---|
| sdn 2d | 3,235 | 2,013 | 13,277 |
| sdn 4d | 3,295 | 2,093 | 15,976 |
| Suburban wgn 2d | 3,410 | 2,349 | 3,248 |
| Suburban wgn 4d, 6P | 3,480 | 2,463 | 1,311 |
| Suburban wgn 4d, 8P | 3,595 | 2,565 | |
| **D55-1 Coronet V-8 (wb 120.0)** | | | |
| sdn 2d | 3,360 | 2,116 | 10,827 |
| club sdn 2d | 3,235 | 2,124 | |
| sdn 4d | 3,395 | 2,196 | 30,098 |
| Lancer htp cpe | 3,375 | 2,281 | 26,727 |
| Suburban wgn 2d | 3,550 | 2,452 | 4,867 |
| Suburban wgn 4d, 6P | 3,590 | 2,566 | 4,641 |
| Suburban wgn 4d, 8P | 3,695 | 2,668 | |
| **D55-2 Royal V-8 (wb 120.0)** | | | |
| sdn 4d | 3,425 | 2,310 | 45,323 |
| Lancer htp cpe | 3,425 | 2,395 | 25,831 |
| Sierra wgn 4d, 6P | 3,655 | 2,659 | 5,506 |
| Sierra wgn 4d, 8P | 3,730 | 2,761 | |
| **D55-3 Custom Royal V-8 (wb 120.0)** | | | |
| sdn 4d | 3,485 | 2,473 | 55,503 |
| Lancer sdn 4d | 3,505 | 2,516 | |
| Lancer htp cpe | 3,480 | 2,543 | 30,499 |
| Lancer conv cpe | 3,610 | 2,748 | 3,302 |

| 1955 Engines | bore × stroke | bhp | availability |
|---|---|---|---|
| I-6, 230.2 | 3.25 × 4.63 | 123 | S-Coronet 6s |
| V-8, 270.1 | 3.63 × 3.25 | 175 | S-Coronet V-8, Royal |
| V-8, 270.1 | 3.63 × 3.25 | 183 | S-Custom Royal |
| V-8, 270.1 | 3.63 × 3.25 | 193 | O-Custom Royal |

### 1956

| D62 Coronet I-6 (wb 120.0)— | Wght | Price | Prod* |
|---|---|---|---|
| sdn 2d | 3,250 | 2,194 | 10,509 |
| sdn 4d | 3,295 | 2,267 | 14,277 |
| Suburban wgn 2d | 3,455 | 2,491 | 2,025 |
| **D63-1 Coronet V-8 (wb 120.0)** | | | |
| club sdn 2d | 3,380 | 2,302 | 24,390 |
| sdn 4d | 3,435 | 2,375 | 50,106 |
| Lancer htp sdn | 3,560 | 2,552 | 3,502 |
| Lancer htp cpe | 3,430 | 2,438 | 21,105 |
| conv cpe | 3,600 | 2,678 | 1,913 |
| Sierra wgn 4d, 6P | 3,600 | 2,716 | 10,241 |
| Sierra wgn 4d, 8P | 3,715 | 2,822 | |
| Suburban wgn 2d | 3,605 | 2,599 | 3,476 |
| **D63-2 Royal V-8 (wb 120.0)** | | | |
| sdn 4d | 3,475 | 2,513 | 26,616 |
| Lancer htp sdn | 3,625 | 2,697 | 3,795 |
| Lancer htp cpe | 3,505 | 2,583 | 11,787 |
| Sierra wgn 4d, 6P | 3,710 | 2,869 | 4,473 |
| Sierra wgn 4d, 8P | 3,800 | 2,974 | |
| Suburban wgn 2d | 3,620 | 2,729 | 1,875 |

# Dodge

| D63-3 Custom Royal V-8 (wb 120.0) | Wght | Price | Prod |
|---|---|---|---|
| sdn 4d | 3,520 | 2,623 | 27,829 |
| Lancer htp sdn | 3,675 | 2,807 | 4,226 |
| Lancer htp cpe | 3,505 | 2,693 | 14,417 |
| conv cpe | 3,630 | 2,913 | 1,378 |

| 1956 Engines | bore × stroke | bhp | availability |
|---|---|---|---|
| I-6, 230.2 | 3.25 × 4.63 | 131 | S-Coronet 6s |
| V-8, 270.1 | 3.63 × 3.25 | 189 | S-Coronet V-8 |
| V-8, 315.0 | 3.63 × 3.80 | 218 | S-Royal, Custom Royal |
| V-8, 315.0 | 3.63 × 3.80 | 230/260 | O-all |

*Includes Canadian exports.

## 1957

| D72 Coronet I-6 (wb 122.0) | Wght | Price | Prod |
|---|---|---|---|
| club sdn 2d | 3,400 | 2,370 | 7,175 |
| sdn 4d | 3,470 | 2,451 | 10,483 |
| **D66 Coronet V-8 (wb 122.0)** | | | |
| club sdn 2d | 3,530 | 2,478 | 21,132 |
| sdn 4d | 3,620 | 2,559 | 60,810 |
| Lancer htp sdn | 3,665 | 2,665 | 13,619 |
| Lancer htp cpe | 3,570 | 2,580 | 44,397 |
| conv cpe | 3,815 | 2,842 | 3,363 |
| **D501 Coronet D-500 V-8 (122.0)** | | | |
| club sdn 2d | 3,885 | 3,314 | 101 |
| conv cpe | 3,975 | 3,670 | |
| **D67-1 Royal V-8 (wb 122.0)** | | | |
| sdn 4d | 3,620 | 2,712 | 19,923 |
| Lancer htp sdn | 3,690 | 2,818 | 8,824 |
| Lancer htp cpe | 3,585 | 2,769 | 12,252 |
| **D67-2 Custom Royal V-8 (wb 122.0)** | | | |
| sdn 4d | 3,690 | 2,881 | 22,548 |
| Lancer htp sdn | 3,750 | 2,991 | 12,068 |
| Lancer htp cpe | 3,670 | 2,920 | 17,629 |
| conv cpe | 3,810 | 3,146 | 2,456 |
| **D70 Station Wagon V-8 (wb 122.0)** | | | |
| Sierra wgn 4d, 6P | 3,930 | 2,946 | 17,352 |
| Sierra wgn 4d, 9P | 4,015 | 3,073 | |
| Suburban wgn 2d | 3,830 | 2,861 | 7,163 |
| **D71 Custom Station Wgn V-8 (wb 122.0)** | | | |
| Sierra wgn 4d, 6P | 3,960 | 3,087 | 7,216 |
| Sierra wgn 4d, 9P | 4,030 | 3,215 | |

| 1957 Engines | bore × stroke | bhp | availability |
|---|---|---|---|
| I-6, 230.2 | 3.25 × 4.63 | 138 | S-D72 |
| V-8, 325.0 | 3.69 × 3.80 | 245 | S-all exc D72, D67, D501 |
| V-8, 325.0 | 3.69 × 3.80 | 260 | S-D67-2 |
| V-8, 325.0 | 3.69 × 3.80 | 285/310 | O-all (D-500) |
| V-8, 354.0 | 3.94 × 3.63 | 340 | O-all (D-500) |

## 1958

| LD-1 Coronet I-6 (wb 122.0) | Wght | Price | Prod |
|---|---|---|---|
| club sdn 2d | 3,360 | 2,449 | 2,922 |
| sdn 4d | 3,410 | 2,530 | 4,592 |
| Lancer htp cpe | 3,400 | 2,572 | 715 |
| **LD-2 Coronet V-8 (wb 122.0)** | | | |
| club sdn 2d | 3,505 | 2,556 | 7,576 |
| sdn 4d | 3,555 | 2,637 | 31,707 |
| Lancer htp sdn | 3,605 | 2,764 | 7,117 |
| Lancer htp cpe | 3,540 | 2,679 | 21,032 |
| Lancer conv cpe | 3,725 | 2,942 | 1,718 |
| **LD-2-M Royal V-8 (wb 122.0)** | | | |
| sdn 4d | 3,570 | 2,797 | 7,515 |
| Lancer htp sdn 4d | 3,640 | 2,915 | 3,332 |
| Lancer htp cpe | 3,565 | 2,854 | 4,318 |
| **LD-3-H Custom Royal V-8 (wb 122.0)** | | | |
| sdn 4d | 3,640 | 3,030 | 9,981 |
| Lancer htp sdn | 3,670 | 3,142 | 5,747 |
| Lancer htp cpe | 3,610 | 3,071 | 7,172 |
| conv cpe | 3,785 | 3,298 | 1,139 |
| Regal Lancer htp cpe | 3,650 | 3,245 | 1,163 |
| **LD-3 Station Wagon V-8 (wb 122.0)** | | | |
| Sierra wgn 4d, 6P | 3,930 | 3,035 | 13,113 |
| Sierra wgn 4d, 9P | 3,990 | 3,176 | |
| Suburban wgn 2d | 3,875 | 2,970 | 1,300 |
| Custom Sierra wgn 4d, 6P | 3,955 | 3,212 | 5,783 |
| Custom Sierra wgn 4d, 9P | 4,035 | 3,354 | |

| 1958 Engines | bore × stroke | bhp | availability |
|---|---|---|---|
| I-6, 230.2 | 3.25 × 4.63 | 138 | S-Coronet 6 |
| V-8, 325.0 | 3.69 × 3.80 | 252 | S-Coronet V-8 |
| V-8, 325.0 | 3.69 × 3.80 | 265 | S-Royal |
| V-8, 350.0 | 4.06 × 3.38 | 295 | S-Cus Royal, wgns |
| V-8, 361.0 | 4.12 × 3.38 | 305-333 | O-all (D-500) |

## 1959

| MD1-L Coronet I-6 (wb 122.0) | | Wght | Price | Prod |
|---|---|---|---|---|
| 21 | club sdn 2d | 3,375 | 2,516 | 5,432 |
| 23 | Lancer htp cpe | 3,395 | 2,644 | 2,151 |
| 41 | sdn 4d | 3,425 | 2,587 | 8,103 |
| **MD2-L Coronet V-8 (wb 122.0)** | | | | |
| 21 | club sdn 2d | 3,565 | 2,636 | 8,002 |
| 23 | Lancer htp cpe | 3,590 | 2,764 | 19,283 |
| 27 | conv cpe | 3,775 | 3,089 | 1,840 |
| 41 | sdn 4d | 3,615 | 2,707 | 43,025 |
| 43 | Lancer htp sdn | 3,620 | 2,842 | 8,946 |
| **MD3-M Royal V-8 (wb 122.0)** | | | | |
| 23 | Lancer htp cpe | 3,625 | 2,990 | 3,483 |
| 41 | sdn 4d | 3,640 | 2,934 | 8,389 |
| 43 | Lancer htp sdn | 3,690 | 3,069 | 2,935 |
| **MD3-H Custom Royal V-8 (wb 122.0)** | | | | |
| 23 | Lancer htp cpe | 3,675 | 3,201 | 6,278 |
| 27 | conv cpe | 3,820 | 3,422 | 984 |
| 41 | sdn 4d | 3,660 | 3,145 | 8,925 |
| 43 | Lancer htp sdn | 3,745 | 3,270 | 5,019 |
| **MD3-L Sierra V-8 (wb 122.0)** | | | | |
| 45A | wgn 4d, 6P | 3,940 | 3,103 | 17,719 |
| 45B | Sierra wgn 4d, 9P | 4,015 | 3,224 | |
| **MD3-H Custom V-8 (wb 122.0)** | | | | |
| 45A | wgn 4d, 6P | 3,980 | 3,318 | 5,871 |
| 45B | wgn 4d, 9P | 4,020 | 3,439 | |

| 1959 Engines | bore × stroke | bhp | availability |
|---|---|---|---|
| I-6, 230.2 | 3.25 × 4.63 | 138 | S-Coronet 6 |
| V-8, 326.0 | 3.95 × 3.31 | 255 | S-Coronet V-8 |
| V-8, 361.0 | 4.12 × 3.38 | 295/305 | S-all exc Coronet |
| V-8, 383.0 | 4.25 × 3.38 | 320/345 | O-all (D-500, Super D-500) |

# Dodge

## 1960

### PD3 Dart I-6 (wb 118.0; wgns-122.0)

| | | Wght | Price | Prod |
|---|---|---|---|---|
| L21 | Seneca sdn 2d | 3,385 | 2,278 | |
| L41 | Seneca sdn 4d | 3,420 | 2,330 | 93,167 |
| L45 | Seneca wgn 4d | 3,805 | 2,695 | |
| M21 | Pioneer sdn 2d | 3,375 | 2,410 | |
| M23 | Pioneer htp cpe | 3,410 | 2,488 | |
| M41 | Pioneer sdn 4d | 3,430 | 2,459 | 36,434 |
| M45A | Pioneer wgn 4d, 6P | 3,820 | 2,787 | |
| M45B | Pioneer wgn 4d, 9P | 3,875 | 2,892 | |
| H23 | Phoenix htp cpe | 3,410 | 2,618 | |
| H27 | Phoenix conv cpe | 3,460 | 2,868 | 6,567 |
| H41 | Phoenix sdn 4d | 3,420 | 2,595 | |
| H43 | Phoenix htp sdn | 3,460 | 2,677 | |

### PD4 Dart V-8 (wb 118.0; wgns-122.0)

| | | Wght | Price | Prod |
|---|---|---|---|---|
| L21 | Seneca sdn 2d | 3,530 | 2,397 | |
| L41 | Seneca sdn 4d | 3,600 | 2,449 | 45,737 |
| L45 | Seneca wgn 4d | 3,975 | 2,815 | |
| M21 | Pioneer sdn 2d | 3,540 | 2,530 | |
| M23 | Pioneer htp cpe | 3,610 | 2,607 | |
| M41 | Pioneer sdn 4d | 3,610 | 2,578 | 74,655 |
| M45A | Pioneer wgn 4d, 6P | 4,000 | 2,906 | |
| M45B | Pioneer wgn 4d, 9P | 4,065 | 3,011 | |
| H23 | Phoenix hpt cpe | 3,605 | 2,737 | |
| H27 | Phoenix conv cpe | 3,690 | 2,988 | 66,608 |
| H41 | Phoenix sdn 4d | 3,610 | 2,715 | |
| H43 | Phoenix htp sdn | 3,655 | 2,796 | |

### PD1-L Matador (wb 122.0)—27,908 built

| | | Wght | Price | Prod |
|---|---|---|---|---|
| 23 | htp cpe | 3,705 | 2,996 | — |
| 41 | sdn 4d | 3,725 | 2,930 | — |
| 43 | htp sdn | 3,820 | 3,075 | — |
| 45A | wgn 4d, 6P | 4,045 | 3,239 | — |
| 44B | wgn 4d, 9P | 4,120 | 3,354 | — |

### PD2-H Polara (wb 122.0)—16,728 built

| | | Wght | Price | Prod |
|---|---|---|---|---|
| 23 | htp cpe | 3,740 | 3,196 | — |
| 27 | conv cpe | 3,765 | 3,416 | — |
| 41 | sdn 4d | 3,735 | 3,141 | — |
| 43 | htp sdn | 3,815 | 3,275 | — |
| 45A | wgn 4d, 6P | 4,085 | 3,506 | — |
| 45B | wgn 4d, 9P | 4,220 | 3,621 | — |

### 1960 Engines

| | bore × stroke | bhp | availability |
|---|---|---|---|
| I-6, 225.0 | 3.40 × 4.13 | 145 | S-Dart 6 |
| V-8, 318.0 | 3.91 × 3.31 | 230 | S-Seneca, Pioneer V-8 |
| V-8, 318.0 | 3.91 × 3.31 | 255 | S-Phoenix V-8 |
| V-8, 361.0 | 4.12 × 3.38 | 295 | S-Matador; O-Pioneer, Phoenix |
| V-8, 383.0 | 4.25 × 3.38 | 325 | S-Polara; O-Matador, Phoenix |
| V-8, 383.0 | 4.25 × 3.38 | 330 | O-Polara, Matador, Phoenix |

## 1961

### RW1-Lancer 170 (wb 106.5)—25,508 built

| | | Wght | Price | Prod |
|---|---|---|---|---|
| 711 | sdn 2d | 2,585 | 1,979 | — |
| 713 | sdn 4d | 2,595 | 2,041 | — |
| 756 | wgn 4d | 2,760 | 2,354 | — |

### RW1-H Lancer 770 (wb 106.5)—49,268 built

| | | Wght | Price | Prod |
|---|---|---|---|---|
| 723 | htp cpe | 2,595 | 2,164 | — |
| 731 | spt cpe | 2,643 | 2,075 | — |
| 733 | sdn 4d | 2,605 | 2,137 | — |
| 776 | wgn 4d | 2,775 | 2,449 | — |

### RD3 Dart I-6 (118.0; wgns-122.0)*

| | | Wght | Price | Prod |
|---|---|---|---|---|
| L411 | Seneca sdn 2d | 3,290 | 2,278 | |
| L413 | Seneca sdn 4d | 3,335 | 2,330 | 60,527 |
| L456 | Seneca wgn 4d | 3,740 | 2,695 | |
| M421 | Pioneer sdn 2d | 3,290 | 2,410 | |
| M422 | Pioneer htp cpe | 3,335 | 2,488 | |
| M423 | Pioneer sdn 4d | 3,335 | 2,459 | 18,214 |
| M466 | Pioneer wgn 4d, 6P | 3,740 | 2,787 | |
| M467 | Pioneer wgn 4d, 9P | 3,825 | 2,892 | |
| H432 | Phoenix htp cpe | 3,325 | 2,618 | |
| H433 | Phoenix sdn 4d | 3,350 | 2,595 | 4,273 |
| H434 | Phoenix htp sdn | 3,385 | 2,677 | |

### RD4 Dart V-8 (wb 118.0; wgns-122.0)

| | | Wght | Price | Prod |
|---|---|---|---|---|
| L511 | Seneca sdn 2d | 3,470 | 2,397 | |
| L513 | Seneca sdn 4d | 3,515 | 2,449 | 27,174 |
| L556 | Seneca wgn 4d | 3,920 | 2,815 | |
| M521 | Pioneer sdn 2d | 3,460 | 2,530 | |
| M522 | Pioneer htp cpe | 3,500 | 2,607 | |
| M523 | Pioneer sdn 4d | 3,510 | 2,578 | 39,054 |
| M566 | Pioneer wgn 4d, 6P | 3,940 | 2,906 | |
| M567 | Pioneer wgn 4d, 9P | 4,005 | 3,011 | |
| H532 | Phoenix htp cpe | 3,520 | 2,737 | |
| H533 | Phoenix sdn 4d | 3,535 | 2,715 | 34,319 |
| H534 | Phoenix htp sdn | 3,555 | 2,796 | |
| H535 | Phoenix conv cpe | 3,580 | 2,988 | |

### RD1-L Polara (wb 122.0)—14,032 built

| | | Wght | Price | Prod |
|---|---|---|---|---|
| 542 | htp cpe | 3,690 | 3,032 | — |
| 543 | sdn 4d | 3,700 | 2,966 | — |
| 544 | htp sdn | 3,740 | 3,110 | — |
| 545 | conv cpe | 3,765 | 3,252 | — |
| 578 | wgn 4d, 6P | 4,115 | 3,294 | — |
| 579 | wgn 4d, 9P | 4,125 | 3,409 | — |

### 1961 Engines

| | bore × stroke | bhp | availability |
|---|---|---|---|
| I-6, 170.0 | 3.40 × 3.13 | 101 | S-Lancer |
| I-6, 225.0 | 3.40 × 4.13 | 145 | S-Dart 6; O-Lancer |
| V-8, 318.0 | 3.91 × 3.31 | 230 | S-Dart V-8 |
| V-8, 318.0 | 3.91 × 3.31 | 260 | O-Dart V-8 |
| V-8, 361.0 | 4.12 × 3.38 | 265 | S-Polara |
| V-8, 361.0 | 4.12 × 3.38 | 305 | O-Dart V-8 (D-500) |
| V-8, 383.0 | 4.25 × 3.38 | 325 | O-Polara (D-500), Dart V-8 |
| V-8, 383.0 | 4.25 × 3.38 | 330 | O-Polara, Dart V-8 (ram ind) |
| V-8, 413.0 | 4.19 × 3.75 | 350/375 | O-Dart |

## 1962*

### SL1-L Lancer 170 (wb 106.5)—19,780 built

| | | Wght | Price | Prod |
|---|---|---|---|---|
| 711 | sdn 2d | 2,495 | 1,951 | — |
| 713 | sdn 4d | 2,525 | 2,011 | — |
| 756 | wgn 4d | 2,685 | 2,306 | — |

### SL1-H Lancer 770 (wb 106.5)—30,888 built

| | | Wght | Price | Prod |
|---|---|---|---|---|
| 731 | sdn 2d | 2,520 | 2,052 | — |
| 733 | sdn 4d | 2,540 | 2,114 | — |
| 776 | wgn 4d | 2,705 | 2,408 | — |

### SL1-P Lancer GT (wb 106.5)

| | | Wght | Price | Prod |
|---|---|---|---|---|
| 742 | htp cpe | 2,560 | 2,257 | 13,683 |

### SD1 Dart I-6 (wb 116.0)

| | | Wght | Price | Prod |
|---|---|---|---|---|
| L401 | Fleet Special sdn 2d | 2,965 | 2,158 | 9,506 |
| L411 | sdn 2d | 2,970 | 2,241 | |
| L403 | Fleet Special sdn 4d | 2,995 | 2,214 | 26,470 |
| L413 | sdn 4d | 3,000 | 2,297 | |
| L456 | wgn 4d | 3,270 | 2,644 | 4,303 |

# Dodge

| SD1 Dart I-6 (wb 116.0) | | Wght | Price | Prod |
|---|---|---|---|---|
| M421 | 330 sdn 2d | 2,965 | 2,375 | 843 |
| M422 | 330 htp cpe | 2,985 | 2,463 | 15,92 |
| M423 | 330 sdn 4d | 3,000 | 2,432 | 6,299 |
| M466 | 330 wgn 4d | 3,275 | 2,739 | 860 |
| H432 | 440 htp cpe | 3,025 | 2,606 | 801 |
| H433 | 440 sdn 4d | 3,045 | 2,584 | 2,338 |
| **SD2 Dart V-8 (wb 116.0)** | | | | |
| L501 | Fleet Special sdn 2d | 3,130 | 2,316 | 2,184 |
| L511 | sdn 2d | 3,135 | 2,348 | |
| L503 | Fleet Special sdn 4d | 3,165 | 2,372 | 10,521 |
| L513 | sdn 4d | 3,170 | 2,404 | |
| L556 | wgn 4d | 3,435 | 2,571 | 4,085 |
| M521 | 330 sdn 2d | 3,135 | 2,482 | 899 |
| M522 | 330 htp cpe | 3,155 | 2,570 | 3,016 |
| M523 | 330 sdn 4d | 3,170 | 2,540 | 13,407 |
| M566 | 330 wgn 4d, 6P | 3,435 | 2,848 | 4,592 |
| M567 | 330 wgn 4d, 9P | 3,500 | 2,949 | 2,896 |
| H532 | 440 htp cpe | 3,185 | 2,713 | 7,119 |
| H533 | 440 sdn 4d | 3,205 | 2,691 | 16,065 |
| H534 | 440 htp sdn | 3,260 | 2,763 | 7,716 |
| H535 | 440 conv cpe | 3,285 | 2,945 | 3,166 |
| H576 | 440 wgn 4d, 6P | 3,460 | 2,989 | 3,606 |
| H577 | 440 wgn 4d, 9P | 3,530 | 3,092 | 3,708 |
| **SD2-P Polara 500 (wb 116.0)** | | | | |
| 542 | htp cpe | 3,315 | 3,019 | 6,834 |
| 544 | htp sdn | 3,360 | 2,960 | 3,345 |
| 545 | conv cpe | 3,430 | 3,268 | 2,089 |
| **SD3-L Custom 880 (wb 122.0)—17,505 built** | | | | |
| 612 | htp cpe | 3,615 | 3,030 | — |
| 613 | sdn 4d | 3,655 | 2,964 | — |
| 614 | htp sdn | 3,680 | 3,109 | — |
| 615 | conv cpe | 3,705 | 3,251 | — |
| 658 | wgn 4d, 6P | 4,025 | 3,292 | — |
| 659 | wgn 4d, 9P | 4,055 | 3,407 | — |

| 1962 Engines | bore × stroke | bhp | availability |
|---|---|---|---|
| I-6, 170.0 | 3.40 × 3.13 | 101 | S-Lancer |
| I-6, 225.0 | 3.40 × 4.13 | 145 | S-Dart 6; O-Lancer |
| V-8, 318.0 | 3.91 × 3.31 | 230 | S-Dart V-8 |
| V-8, 318.0 | 3.91 × 3.31 | 260 | O-Dart V-8 |
| V-8, 361.0 | 4.12 × 3.38 | 265 | S-Custom 880 |
| V-8, 361.0 | 4.12 × 3.38 | 305 | S-Polara 500; O-Dart V-8 |
| V-8, 361.0 | 4.12 × 3.38 | 310 | O-Dart V-8, Polara 500 |
| V-8, 383.0 | 4.25 × 3.38 | 330/335 | O-Dart V-8, Polara 500 |
| V-8, 413.0 | 4.19 × 3.75 | 365/420 | O-Dart V-8, Polara 500 |

*Dart does not include production for Canada/export.

## 1963*

| TL1-L Dart 170 (wb 111.0; wgns-106.0)—58,536 built | | Wght | Price | Prod |
|---|---|---|---|---|
| 711 | sdn 2d | 2,605 | 1,983 | — |
| 713 | sdn 4d | 2,625 | 2,041 | — |
| 756 | wgn 4d | 2,710 | 2,309 | — |
| **TL1-H Dart 270 (wb 110.0; wgns-106.0)—61,159 built** | | | | |
| 731 | sdn 2d | 2,610 | 2,079 | — |
| 733 | sdn 4d | 2,635 | 2,135 | — |
| 735 | conv cpe | 2,740 | 2,385 | — |
| 776 | wgn 4d | 2,735 | 2,433 | — |
| **TL1-P Dart GT (wb 111.0)—34,227 built** | | | | |
| 742 | htp cpe | 2,690 | 2,289 | — |
| 745 | conv cpe | 2,765 | 2,512 | — |
| **TD1-L 330 I-6 (wb 119.0; wgns-116.0)—51,761 built** | | | | |
| 401 | Fleet Special sdn 2d | 3,040 | 2,205 | 10,365 |
| 411 | sdn 2d | 3,050 | 2,245 | |
| 403 | Fleet Special sdn 4d | 3,065 | 2,261 | 29,746 |
| 413 | sdn 4d | 3,070 | 2,301 | |
| 456 | wgn 4d, 2S | 3,320 | 2,648 | 4,554 |
| 457 | wgn 4d, 3S | 3,380 | 2,749 | 942 |
| **TD1-M 440 I-6 (wb 119.0; wgns-116.0)** | | | | |
| 421 | sdn 2d | 3,050 | 2,381 | 1,183 |
| 422 | htp cpe | 3,050 | 2,470 | 1,246 |
| 423 | sdn 4d | 3,075 | 2,438 | 7,434 |
| **TD1-H Polara I-6 (wb 119.0)—68,262 built** | | | | |
| 432 | htp cpe | 3,105 | 2,624 | 623 |
| 433 | sdn 4d | 3,105 | 2,602 | 1,698 |
| **TD2-L 330 V-8 (wb 119.0; wgns-116.0)** | | | | |
| 601 | Fleet Special sdn 2d | 3,310 | 2,313 | 4,654 |
| 611 | sdn 2d | 3,220 | 2,352 | |
| 603 | Fleet Special sdn 4d | 3,335 | 2,369 | 19,330 |
| 613 | sdn 4d | 3,245 | 2,408 | |
| 656 | wgn 4d, 2S | 3,490 | 2,756 | 5,679 |
| 657 | wgn 4d, 3S | 3,550 | 2,857 | 2,332 |
| **TD2-M 440 V-8 (wb 119.0; wgns-116.0)** | | | | |
| 621 | sdn 2d | 3,215 | 2,489 | 1,934 |
| 622 | htp cpe | 3,245 | 2,577 | 5,947 |
| 623 | sdn 4d | 3,250 | 2,546 | 26,247 |
| 666 | wgn 4d, 2S | 3,495 | 2,854 | 7,216 |
| 667 | wgn 4d, 3S | 3,555 | 2,956 | 5,501 |
| **TD2-H Polara V-8 (wb 119.0)** | | | | |
| 632 | htp cpe | 3,255 | 2,732 | 8,234 |
| 633 | sdn 4d | 3,275 | 2,709 | 17,189 |
| 634 | htp sdn | 3,330 | 2,781 | 9,312 |
| 635 | conv cpe | 3,340 | 2,963 | 2,962 |
| **TD2-P Polara 500 V-8 (wb 119.0)** | | | | |
| 642 | htp cpe | 3,375 | 2,965 | 5,676 |
| 645 | conv cpe | 3,455 | 3,196 | 1,580 |
| **TA3 880 V-8 (wb 122.0)** | | | | |
| E503 | sdn 4d | 3,800 | 2,815 | 9,831 |
| E556 | wgn 4d, 6P | 4,145 | 3,142 | |
| E557 | wgn 4d, 9P | 4,175 | 3,257 | |
| L512 | Custom htp cpe | 3,825 | 3,030 | 18,435 |
| L513 | Custom sdn 4d | 3,815 | 2,964 | |
| L514 | Custom htp sdn | 3,840 | 3,109 | |
| L515 | Custom conv cpe | 3,845 | 3,251 | |
| L558 | Custom htp wgn 4d, 2S | 4,160 | 3,292 | |
| L559 | Custom htp wgn 4d, 3S | 4,186 | 3,407 | |

| 1963 Engines | bore × stroke | bhp | availability |
|---|---|---|---|
| I-6, 170.0 | 3.40 × 3.13 | 101 | S-Dart |
| I-6, 225.0 | 3.40 × 4.13 | 145 | S-330/440/Polara 6; O-Dart |
| V-8, 318.0 | 3.91 × 3.31 | 230 | S-330, 440, Polara V-8s |
| V-8, 361.0 | 4.13 × 3.38 | 265 | S-880, Custom 880 |
| V-8, 383.0 | 4.25 × 3.38 | 305 | S-Polara 500; O-others exc Dart |
| V-8, 383.0 | 4.25 × 3.38 | 330 | O-all exc Dart |

# Dodge

| 1963 Engines | bore × stroke | bhp | availability |
|---|---|---|---|
| V-8, 413.0 | 4.19 × 3.75 | 360 | O-880, Custom 880 |
| V-8, 426.0 | 4.25 × 3.75 | 370/425 | O-330, 440, Polara (ram ind) |

*Dart 330/440 and all Polaras do not include production for Canada/export.

## 1964

| | VL1-L Dart 170 (wb 111.0; wgns 106.0) | Wght | Price | Prod* |
|---|---|---|---|---|
| 711 | sdn 2d | 2,615 | 1,988 | 74,625 |
| 713 | sdn 4d | 2,640 | 2,053 | |
| 756 | wgn 4d, 2S | 2,740 | 2,315 | V-8:2,509 |
| | **VL1-H Dart 270 (wb 111.0; wgns-106.0)** | | | |
| 731 | sdn 2d | 2,625 | 2,094 | 58,972 |
| 733 | sdn 4d | 2,645 | 2,160 | |
| 735 | conv cpe | 2,735 | 2,389 | 7,097 |
| 776 | wgn 4d, 2S | 2,745 | 2,414 | |
| | **VL1-P Dart GT (wb 111.0)** | | | |
| 742 | htp cpe | 2,670 | 2,318 | 37,660 |
| 745 | conv cpe | 2,770 | 2,536 | 12,170 |
| | **VD1-L 330 I-6 (wb 119.0; wgns-116.0)** | | | |
| 411 | sdn 2d | 3,115 | 2,264 | 9,514 |
| 413 | sdn 4d | 3,145 | 2,317 | 34,467 |
| 456 | wgn 4d, 2S | 3,400 | 2,654 | 4,111 |
| 457 | wgn 4d, 3S | 3,475 | 2,755 | 1,426 |
| | **VD1-M 440 I-6 (wb 119.0)** | | | |
| 421 | sdn 2d | 3,110 | 2,401 | 886 |
| 422 | htp cpe | 3,120 | 2,483 | 2,163 |
| 423 | sdn 4d | 3,145 | 2,454 | 6,987 |
| | **VD1-H Polara I-6 (wb 119.0)** | | | |
| 432 | htp cpe | 3,135 | 2,637 | 783 |
| 433 | sdn 4d | 3,170 | 2,615 | 1,611 |
| | **VD2-L 330 V-8 (wb 119.0; wgns-116.0)** | | | |
| — | sdn 2d | — | — | 5,195 |
| 613 | sdn 4d | 3,325 | 2,424 | 28,891 |
| 656 | wgn 4d, 2S | 3,570 | 2,762 | 6,961 |
| 657 | wgn 4d, 3S | 3,620 | 2,863 | 2,899 |
| | **VD2-M 440 V-8 (wb 119.0; wgns-116.0)** | | | |
| 621 | sdn 2d | 3,280 | 2,508 | 2,064 |
| 622 | htp cpe | 3,295 | 2,590 | 14,537 |
| 623 | sdn 4d | 3,330 | 2,562 | 32,143 |
| 666 | wgn 4d, 2S | 3,585 | 2,861 | 8,101 |
| 667 | wgn 4d, 3S | 3,640 | 2,962 | 6,673 |
| 667 | wgn 4d, 3S | 3,640 | 2,962 | — |
| | **VD2-H Polara V-8 (wb 119.0)** | | | |
| 632 | htp cpe | 3,320 | 2,745 | 19,689 |
| 633 | sdn 4d | 3,365 | 2,722 | 25,054 |
| 634 | htp sdn | 3,395 | 2,794 | 13,229 |
| 645 | conv cpe | 3,435 | 2,994 | 3,478 |
| | **VD2-P Polara 500 V-8 (wb 119.0)—17,787 built** | | | |
| 642 | htp cpe | 3,340 | 2,978 | 15,163 |
| 645 | conv cpe | 3,550 | 3,227 | 2,624 |
| | **VA3 880 V-8 (wb 122.0)** | | | |
| E513 | sdn 4d | 3,795 | 2,826 | |
| E556 | wgn 4d, 6P | 4,165 | 3,155 | 10,562 |
| E557 | wgn 4d, 9P | 4,185 | 3,270 | |
| L522 | Custom htp cpe | 3,765 | 3,043 | |
| L523 | Custom sdn 4d | 3,825 | 2,977 | |
| L524 | Custom htp sdn | 3,860 | 3,122 | 21,234 |
| L525 | Custom conv cpe | 3,850 | 3,264 | |
| L568 | Custom htp wgn 4d, 2S | 4,155 | 3,305 | |

| | VA3 880 V-8 (wb 122.0) | Wght | Price | Prod |
|---|---|---|---|---|
| L569 | Custom htp wgn 4d, 3S | 4,185 | 3,420 | |

| 1964 Engines | bore × stroke | bhp | availability |
|---|---|---|---|
| I-6, 170.0 | 3.40 × 3.13 | 101 | S-Dart |
| I-6, 225.0 | 3.40 × 4.13 | 145 | S-330/440/Polara 6; O-Dart |
| V-8, 273.5 | 3.63 × 3.31 | 180 | O-Dart |
| V-8, 318.0 | 3.91 × 3.31 | 230 | S-330, 440, Polara V-8 |
| V-8, 361.0 | 4.13 × 3.38 | 265 | S-880, Custom 880 |
| V-8, 383.0 | 4.25 × 3.38 | 305/330 | O-all exc Dart |
| V-8, 426.0 | 4.25 × 3.75 | 365 | O-330, 440, Polara |
| V-8, 426.0 | 4.25 × 3.75 | 415/425 | O-330, 440, Polara (ram ind) |

*Dart 330/440 and all Polaras do not include production for Canada/export.

## 1965

| | AL1-L Dart 170 (wb 111.0; wgns-106.0)—86,013 built | Wght | Price | Prod |
|---|---|---|---|---|
| L11 | sdn 2d | 2,645 | 2,074 | — |
| L13 | sdn 4d | 2,660 | 2,139 | — |
| L56 | wgn 4d | 2,770 | 2,407 | — |
| | **AL1-H Dart 270 (wb 111.0; wgns 106.0)—78,245 built** | | | |
| L31 | sdn 2d | 2,650 | 2,180 | — |
| L32 | htp cpe | 2,675 | 2,274 | — |
| L33 | sdn 4d | 2,670 | 2,247 | — |
| L35 | conv cpe | 2,765 | 2,481 | — |
| L76 | wgn 4d | 2,770 | 2,506 | — |
| | **AL1-P Dart GT (wb 111.0)—45,118 built** | | | |
| L42 | htp cpe | 2,715 | 2,404 | — |
| L45 | conv cpe | 2,795 | 2,628 | — |
| | **AW1-L Coronet I-6 (wb 117.0; wgns-116.0)*** | | | |
| W11 | Deluxe sdn 2d | 3,090 | 2,257 | — |
| W13 | Deluxe sdn 4d | 3,140 | 2,296 | — |
| W21 | sdn 2d | 3,070 | 2,217 | — |
| W23 | sdn 4d | 3,095 | 2,256 | — |
| W56 | Deluxe wgn 4d | 3,390 | 2,592 | — |
| | **AW2-H Coronet 440 I-6 (wb 117.0; wgns-116.0)*** | | | |
| W32 | htp cpe | 3,100 | 2,403 | — |
| W33 | sdn 4d | 3,125 | 2,377 | — |
| W35 | conv cpe | 3,230 | 2,622 | — |
| W76 | wgn 4d | 3,395 | 2,674 | — |
| | **AW2-L Coronet V-8 (wb 117.0; wgns-116.0)*** | | | |
| W01 | Hemi-Charger sdn 2d | 3,165 | — | — |
| W11 | Deluxe sdn 2d | 3,160 | 2,353 | — |
| W13 | Deluxe sdn 4d | 3,210 | 2,392 | — |
| W21 | sdn 2d | 3,145 | 2,313 | — |
| W23 | sdn 4d | 3,195 | 2,352 | — |
| W56 | Deluxe wgn 4d | 3,470 | 2,688 | — |
| | **AW2-H Coronet 440 V-8 (wb 117.0; wgns-116.0)*** | | | |
| W32 | htp cpe | 3,180 | 2,499 | — |
| W33 | sdn 4d | 3,230 | 2,473 | — |
| W35 | conv cpe | 3,295 | 2,718 | — |
| W76 | wgn 4d, 6P | 3,490 | 2,770 | — |
| W77 | wgn 4d, 9P | 3,560 | 2,868 | — |
| | **AW2-P Coronet 500 V-8 (wb 117.0)—32,745 built** | | | |
| W42 | htp cpe | 3,255 | 2,674 | — |
| W45 | conv cpe | 3,340 | 2,894 | — |
| | **AW2-L Polara V-8 (wb 121.0)—12,705 built** | | | |
| D12 | htp cpe | 3,850 | 2,837 | — |

# Dodge

| AW2-L Polara V-8 (wb 121.0)—12,705 built | | Wght | Price | Prod |
|---|---|---|---|---|
| D13 | sdn 4d | 3,905 | 2,806 | — |
| D14 | htp sdn | 3,965 | 2,913 | — |
| D15 | conv cpe | 3,940 | 3,131 | — |
| D23 | sdn 4d (318) | 3,847 | 2,730 | — |
| D56 | wgn 4d, 6P | 4,220 | 3,153 | — |
| D57 | wgn 4d, 9P | 4,255 | 3,259 | — |
| **AD2-H Custom 880 V-8 (wb 121.0)—44,496 built** | | | | |
| D32 | htp cpe | 3,945 | 3,085 | — |
| D34 | htp sdn | 4,155 | 3,150 | — |
| D35 | conv cpe | 3,965 | 3,335 | — |
| D38 | sdn 4d | 3,915 | 3,010 | — |
| D76 | wgn 4d, 6P | 4,270 | 3,422 | — |
| D77 | wgn 4d, 9P | 4,355 | 3,527 | — |
| **AD2-P Monaco V-8 (wb 121.0)** | | | | |
| D42 | htp cpe | 4,000 | 3,355 | 13,096 |

\* Combined I-6 and V-8 production: Coronet 71,880; Coronet 440 104,767.

| 1965 Engines | bore × stroke | bhp | availability |
|---|---|---|---|
| I-6, 170.0 | 3.40 × 3.13 | 101 | S-Dart |
| I-6, 225.0 | 3.40 × 4.13 | 145 | S-Coronet/440 6s; O-Dart |
| V-8, 273.5 | 3.63 × 3.31 | 180 | S-Coronet/440/500 V-8s; O-Dart |
| V-8, 273.5 | 3.63 × 3.31 | 235 | O-Coronet/440/500 V-8s, Dart |
| V-8, 318.0 | 3.91 × 3.31 | 230 | S-Polara 318 sdn; O-Coronet/440/500/V-8s |
| V-8, 361.0 | 4.12 × 3.38 | 265 | O-Coronet/440/500 V-8s |
| V-8, 383.0 | 4.25 × 3.38 | 315 | S-Mo—co; O-Coronets |
| V-8, 383.0 | 4.25 × 3.38 | 270 | S-Polara, Custom 880 |
| V-8, 383.0 | 4.25 × 3.38 | 330 | O-Coronet/440/500 V-8s |
| V-8, 413.0 | 4.19 × 3.75 | 340 | O-Polara, Custom 880, Mo—co |
| V-8, 426.0 | 4.25 × 3.75 | 365 | O-all exc Dart |
| V-8, 426.0 | 4.25 × 3.75 | 425 | S-Hemi-Charger 425 |

## 1966

| BLL Dart (wb 111.0; wgns-106.0)—75,990 built | | | | |
|---|---|---|---|---|
| | | Wght | Price | Prod |
| 1-21 | sdn 2d, I-6 | 2,670 | 2,094 | — |
| 2-21 | sdn 2d, V-8 | 2,860 | 2,222 | — |
| 1-41 | sdn 4d, I-6 | 2,695 | 2,158 | — |
| 2-41 | sdn 4d, V-8 | 2,895 | 2,286 | — |
| 1-45 | wgn 4d, I-6 | 2,780 | 2,436 | — |
| 2-45 | wgn 4d, V-8 | 2,990 | 2,564 | — |
| **BLH Dart 270 (wb 111.0; wgns 106.0)—69,996 built** | | | | |
| 1-23 | htp cpe, I-6 | 2,720 | 2,307 | — |
| 2-23 | htp cpe, V-8 | 2,890 | 2,435 | — |
| 1-27 | conv cpe, I-6 | 2,805 | 2,570 | — |
| 2-27 | conv cpe, V-8 | 2,995 | 2,698 | — |
| 1-21 | sdn 2d, I-6 | 2,665 | 2,214 | — |
| 2-21 | sdn 2d, V-8 | 2,860 | 2,342 | — |
| 1-41 | sdn 4d, I-6 | 2,680 | 2,280 | — |
| 2-41 | sdn 4d, V-8 | 2,895 | 2,408 | — |
| 1-45 | wgn 4d, I-6 | 2,795 | 2,533 | — |
| 2-45 | wgn 4d, V-8 | 3,020 | 2,661 | — |

| BLP Dart GT (wb 111.0)—30,041 built | | Wght | Price | Prod |
|---|---|---|---|---|
| 1-23 | htp cpe, I-6 | 2,735 | 2,417 | — |
| 2-23 | htp cpe, V-8 | 2,915 | 2,545 | — |
| 1-27 | conv cpe, I-6 | 2,830 | 2,700 | — |
| 2-27 | conv cpe, V-8 | 2,995 | 2,828 | — |
| **BWL Coronet (wb 117.0)—66,161 built** | | | | |
| 1-21 | sdn 2d, I-6 | 3,055 | 2,264 | — |
| 2-21 | sdn 2d, V-8 | 3,215 | 2,358 | — |
| 1-41 | sdn 4d, I-6 | 3,077 | 2,306 | — |
| 2-41 | sdn 4d, V-8 | 3,245 | 2,396 | — |
| 1-21 | Deluxe sdn 2d, I-6 | 3,050 | 2,303 | — |
| 2-21 | Deluxe sdn 2d, V-8 | 3,215 | 2,391 | — |
| 1-41 | Deluxe sdn 4d, I-6 | 3,075 | 2,341 | — |
| 2-41 | Deluxe sdn 4d, V-8 | 3,240 | 2,435 | — |
| 1-45 | Deluxe wgn 2d, I-6 | 3,480 | 2,631 | — |
| 2-45 | Deluxe wgn 2d, V-8 | 3,595 | 2,725 | — |
| **BWH Coronet 440 (wb 117.0)—128,998 built** | | | | |
| 1-23 | htp cpe, I-6 | 3,075 | 2,457 | — |
| 1-23 | htp cpe, V-8 | 3,235 | 2,551 | — |
| 1-27 | conv cpe, I-6 | 3,185 | 2,672 | — |
| 2-27 | conv cpe, V-8 | 3,310 | 2,766 | — |
| 1-41 | sdn 4d, I-6 | 3,095 | 2,432 | — |
| 2-41 | sdn 4d, V-8 | 3,220 | 2,526 | — |
| 1-45 | wgn 4d, I-6 | 3,515 | 2,722 | — |
| 2-45 | wgn 4d, 2S, V-8 | 3,585 | 2,816 | — |
| 2-46 | wgn 4d, 3S, V-8 | 3,680 | 2,926 | — |
| **BWP Coronet 500 (wb 117.0)—55,683 built** | | | | |
| 1-23 | htp cpe, I-6 | 3,115 | 2,611 | — |
| 2-23 | htp cpe, V-8 | 3,275 | 2,705 | — |
| 1-27 | conv cpe, I-6 | 3,180 | 2,827 | — |
| 2-27 | conv cpe, V-8 | 3,345 | 2,921 | — |
| 1-41 | sdn 4d, I-6 | 3,120 | 2,586 | — |
| 2-41 | sdn 4d, V-8 | 3,280 | 2,680 | — |
| **BX2-P Charger (wb 117.0)** | | | | |
| 29 | fstbk htp cpe 4P | 3,499 | 3,122 | 37,344 |
| **BD2-L Polara (wb 121.0)—107,832 built** | | | | |
| 23 | htp cpe | 3,820 | 2,874 | — |
| 27 | conv cpe | 3,885 | 3,161 | — |
| 41 | sdn 4d | 3,860 | 2,838 | — |
| 41 | sdn 4d (318) | 3,765 | 2,763 | — |
| 43 | htp sdn | 3,880 | 2,948 | — |
| 45 | wgn 4d, 2S | 4,265 | 3,183 | — |
| 46 | wgn 4d, 3S | 4,295 | 3,286 | — |
| **BD2-H Monaco (wb 121.0)—49,773 built** | | | | |
| 23 | htp cpe | 3,855 | 3,107 | — |
| 41 | sdn 4d | 3,890 | 3,033 | — |
| 43 | htp sdn | 4,835 | 3,170 | — |
| 45 | wgn 4d, 2S | 4,270 | 3,436 | — |
| 46 | wgn 4d, 3S | 4,315 | 3,539 | — |
| **BD2-P Monaco 500 (wb 121.0)** | | | | |
| 23 | htp cpe | 3,895 | 3,604 | 10,840 |

| 1966 Engines | bore × stroke | bhp | availability |
|---|---|---|---|
| I-6, 170.0 | 3.40 × 3.13 | 101 | S-Dart 6s |
| I-6, 225.0 | 3.40 × 4.13 | 145 | S-Coronet 6; O-Dart 6 |
| V-8, 273.5 | 3.63 × 3.31 | 180 | S-Coronet V-8, Dart V-8 |
| V-8, 273.5 | 3.63 × 3.31 | 235 | O-Dart V-8 |
| V-8, 318.0 | 3.91 × 3.31 | 230 | S-Chrgr, Pol 318 sdn; O-Cor V-8 |
| V-8, 361.0 | 4.13 × 3.38 | 265 | O-Charger, Coronet V-8 |

## Dodge

| 1966 Engines | bore × stroke | bhp | availability |
|---|---|---|---|
| V-8, 383.0 | 4.25 × 3.38 | 270 | S-Pol, Mon; O-Mon 500 |
| V-8, 383.0 | 4.25 × 3.38 | 325 | S-Mo—co 500; O-all exc Dart |
| V-8, 426.0 | 4.25 × 3.75 | 425 | O-Charger (max perf cam avail) |
| V-8, 440.0 | 4.32 × 3.75 | 350 | O-Pol, Mon, Mon 500 |

### 1967

| CLL Dart (wb 111.0)—53,043 built | | Wght | Price | Prod |
|---|---|---|---|---|
| 1-21 | sdn 2d, I-6 | 2,710 | 2,187 | — |
| 2-21 | sdn 2d, V-8 | 2,895 | 2,315 | — |
| 1-41 | sdn 4d, I-6 | 2,725 | 2,224 | — |
| 2-41 | sdn 4d, V-8 | 2,910 | 2,352 | — |
| **CLH Dart 270 (wb 111.0)—63,227 built** | | | | |
| 1-23 | htp cpe, I-6 | 2,725 | 2,388 | — |
| 2-23 | htp cpe, V-8 | 2,910 | 2,516 | — |
| 1-41 | sdn 4d, I-6 | 2,735 | 2,362 | — |
| 2-41 | sdn 4d, V-8 | 2,915 | 2,490 | — |
| **CLP Dart GT (wb 111.0)—38,225 built** | | | | |
| 1-23 | htp cpe, I-6 | 2,750 | 2,499 | — |
| 2-23 | htp cpe, V-8 | 2,930 | 2,627 | — |
| 1-27 | conv cpe, I-6 | 2,850 | 2,732 | — |
| 2-27 | conv cpe, V-8 | 3,030 | 2,860 | — |
| **CWE Coronet (wb 117.0)—4,933 built** | | | | |
| 1-45 | wgn 4d, I-6 | 3,485 | 2,622 | — |
| 2-45 | wgn 4d, V-8 | 3,650 | 2,716 | — |
| **CWL Coronet Deluxe (wb 117.0)—29,022 built** | | | | |
| 1-21 | sdn 2d, I-6 | 3,045 | 2,359 | — |
| 2-21 | sdn 2d, V-8 | 3,210 | 2,453 | — |
| 1-41 | sdn 4d, I-6 | 3,070 | 2,397 | — |
| 2-41 | sdn 4d, V-8 | 3,235 | 2,491 | — |
| 1-45 | wgn 2d, I-6 | 3,495 | 2,693 | — |
| 2-45 | wgn 2d, V-8 | 3,625 | 2,787 | — |
| **CWH Coronet 440 (wb 117.0)—106,368 built** | | | | |
| 1-23 | htp cpe, I-6 | 3,065 | 2,500 | — |
| 2-23 | htp cpe, V-8 | 3,235 | 2,594 | — |
| 1-27 | conv cpe, I-6 | 3,140 | 2,740 | — |
| 2-27 | conv cpe, V-8 | 3,305 | 2,834 | — |
| 1-41 | sdn 4d, I-6 | 3,060 | 2,475 | — |
| 2-41 | sdn 4d, V-8 | 3,225 | 2,569 | — |
| 1-45 | wgn 4d, I-6 | 3,495 | 2,771 | — |
| 2-45 | wgn 4d, 2S, V-8 | 3,605 | 2,865 | — |
| 2-46 | wgn 4d, 3S, V-8 | 3,705 | 2,975 | — |
| **CWP Coronet 500 (wb 117.0)—39,260 built (incl. R/T)** | | | | |
| 1-23 | htp cpe, I-6 | 3,115 | 2,679 | — |
| 2-23 | htp cpe, V-8 | 3,280 | 2,773 | — |
| 1-27 | conv cpe, I-6 | 3,190 | 2,919 | — |
| 2-27 | conv cpe, V-8 | 3,355 | 3,013 | — |
| 1-41 | sdn 4d, I-6 | 3,075 | 2,654 | — |
| 2-41 | sdn 4d, V-8 | 3,235 | 2,748 | — |
| **CW2-P Coronet R/T (wb 117.0)** | | | | |
| 23 | htp cpe, V-8 | 3,565 | 3,199 | — |
| 27 | conv cpe, V-8 | 3,640 | 3,438 | — |
| **CW2-P Charger (wb 117.0)** | | | | |
| 29 | fstbk htp cpe 4P, V-8 | 3,480 | 3,128 | 15,788 |
| **CD2-L Polara (wb 122.0)—69,798 built** | | | | |
| 23 | htp cpe | 3,870 | 2,953 | — |
| 27 | conv cpe | 3,930 | 3,241 | — |
| 41 | sdn 4d | 3,885 | 2,915 | — |

| CD2-L Polara | | Wght | Price | Prod |
|---|---|---|---|---|
| 41 | sdn 4d (318) | 3,765 | 2,843 | — |
| 43 | htp sdn | 3,920 | 3,028 | — |
| 45 | wgn 4d, 2S | 4,440 | 3,265 | — |
| 46 | wgn 4d, 3S | 4,450 | 3,368 | — |
| **CD2-M Polara 500 (wb 122.0)—5,606 built** | | | | |
| 23 | htp cpe | 3,880 | 3,155 | — |
| 27 | conv cpe | 3,940 | 3,443 | — |
| **CD2-H Monaco (wb 122.0)—35,225 built** | | | | |
| 23 | htp cpe | 3,885 | 3,213 | — |
| 41 | sdn 4d | 3,895 | 3,138 | — |
| 43 | htp sdn | 3,945 | 3,275 | — |
| 45 | wgn 4d, 2S | 4,425 | 3,543 | — |
| 46 | wgn 4d, 3S | 4,475 | 3,646 | — |
| **CD2-P Monaco 500 (wb 122.0)** | | | | |
| 23 | htp cpe | 3,970 | 3,712 | 5,237 |

| 1967 Engines | bore × stroke | bph | availability |
|---|---|---|---|
| I-6, 170.0 | 3.40 × 3.13 | 115 | S-Dart 6 |
| I-6, 225.0 | 3.40 × 4.13 | 145 | S-Coronet 6; O-Dart 6 |
| V-8, 273.5 | 3.63 × 3.31 | 180 | S-Dart V-8, Coronet V-8 |
| V-8, 273.5 | 3.63 × 3.31 | 235 | O-Dart V-8 |
| V-8, 318.0 | 3.91 × 3.31 | 230 | S-Chrgr, Polara 318; O-Cor V-8 |
| V-8, 383.0 | 4.25 × 3.38 | 270 | S-Polara, Mo—co; O-Cor, Mon 500 |
| V-8, 383.0 | 4.25 × 3.38 | 325 | S-Mon 500; O-Cor, Chgr, Pol, Mon |
| V-8, 426.0 | 4.25 × 3.75 | 425 | O-Coronet R/T, Charger |
| V-8, 440.0 | 4.32 × 3.75 | 350 | O-Polara, Mo—co |
| V-8, 440.0 | 4.32 × 3.75 | 375 | S-Cor R/T; O-Chrgr, Pol, Mon |

### 1968

| DLL Dart (wb 111.0)—60,250 built | | Wght | Price | Prod |
|---|---|---|---|---|
| 1-21 | sdn 2d, I-6 | 2,705 | 2,323 | — |
| 2-21 | sdn 2d, V-8 | 2,875 | 2,451 | — |
| 1-41 | sdn 4d, I-6 | 2,725 | 2,360 | — |
| 2-41 | sdn 4d, V-8 | 2,900 | 2,488 | — |
| **DLH Dart 270 (wb 111.0)—76,497 built** | | | | |
| 1-23 | htp cpe, I-6 | 2,725 | 2,525 | — |
| 2-23 | htp cpe, V-8 | 2,885 | 2,653 | — |
| 1-41 | sdn 4d, I-6 | 2,710 | 2,499 | — |
| 2-41 | sdn 4d, V-8 | 2,900 | 2,627 | — |
| **DLP Dart GT (wb 111.0)—26,280 built** | | | | |
| 1-23 | htp cpe, I-6 | 2,715 | 2,637 | — |
| 2-23 | htp cpe, V-8 | 2,895 | 2,675 | — |
| 1-27 | conv cpe, I-6 | 2,790 | 2,831 | — |
| 2-27 | conv cpe, V-8 | 2,970 | 2,959 | — |
| **DL2-S Dart GTS (wb 111.0)—8,745 built** | | | | |
| 23 | htp cpe, V-8 | 3,065 | 3,189 | — |
| 27 | conv cpe, V-8 | 3,150 | 3,383 | — |
| **DWL Coronet Deluxe (wb 117.0)—46,299 built** | | | | |
| 1-21 | cpe, I-6 | 3,015 | 2,487 | — |
| 2-21 | cpe, V-8 | 3,200 | 2,581 | — |
| 1-41 | sdn 4d, I-6 | 3,035 | 2,525 | — |
| 2-41 | sdn 4d, V-8 | 3,220 | 2,619 | — |
| 1-45 | wgn 4d, I-6 | 3,455 | 2,816 | — |
| 2-45 | wgn 4d, V-8 | 3,590 | 2,910 | — |

# Dodge

### DWH Coronet 440 (wb 117.0)—116,348 built (incl. Super Bee)

| | | Wght | Price | Prod |
|---|---|---|---|---|
| 1-21 | cpe, I-6 | 3,015 | 2,565 | — |
| 2-21 | cpe, V-8 | 3,200 | 2,671 | — |
| 1-23 | htp cpe, I-6 | 3,040 | 2,627 | — |
| 2-23 | htp cpe, V-8 | 3,225 | 2,733 | — |
| 1-41 | sdn 4d, I-6 | 3,035 | 2,603 | — |
| 2-41 | sdn 4d, V-8 | 3,320 | 2,709 | — |
| 1-45 | wgn 4d, I-6 | 3,450 | 2,924 | — |
| 2-45 | wgn 4d, 2S, V-8 | 3,585 | 3,030 | — |
| 2-46 | wgn 4d, 3S, V-8 | 3,680 | 3,140 | — |

### DWH Coronet Super Bee (wb 117.0)

| M-21 | cpe, V-8 | 3,395 | 3,027 | — |
|---|---|---|---|---|

### DW2-P Coronet 500 (wb 117)—40,139 blt

| | | Wght | Price | Prod |
|---|---|---|---|---|
| 23 | htp cpe, V-8 | 3,260 | 2,879 | — |
| 27 | conv cpe, V-8 | 3,360 | 3,036 | — |
| 41 | sdn 4d, V-8 | 3,240 | 2,912 | — |
| 45 | wgn 4d, 2S, V-8 | 3,610 | 3,212 | — |
| 46 | wgn 4d, 3S, V-8 | 3,700 | 3,322 | — |

### DW2-S Coronet R/T (wb 117.0)—10,849 built

| 23 | htp cpe, V-8 | 3,530 | 3,379 | — |
|---|---|---|---|---|
| 27 | conv cpe, V-8 | 3,630 | 3,613 | — |

### DX1-S Charger (wb 117.0)—96,108 built

| 1P-29 | htp cpe 4P, I-6 | 3,100 | 2,934 | — |
|---|---|---|---|---|
| 2P-29 | htp cpe 4P, V-8 | 3,305 | 3,040 | — |
| 2X-29 | R/T htp cpe, 4P, V-8 | 3,575 | 3,506 | — |

### DD2-L Polara (wb 122.0)—99,055 built

| 23 | htp cpe | 3,700 | 3,027 | — |
|---|---|---|---|---|
| 27 | conv cpe | 3,755 | 3,288 | — |
| 41 | sdn 4d | 3,735 | 3,005 | — |
| 43 | htp sdn | 3,755 | 3,100 | — |
| 45 | wgn 4d, 2S | 4,155 | 3,388 | — |
| 46 | wgn 4d, 3S | 4,210 | 3,454 | — |

### DD2-M Polara 500 (wb 122.0)—4,983 built

| 23 | htp cpe | 3,740 | 3,226 | — |
|---|---|---|---|---|
| 27 | conv cpe | 3,780 | 3,487 | — |

### DD2-H Monaco (wb 122.0)—37,412 built

| 23 | htp cpe | 3,845 | 3,369 | — |
|---|---|---|---|---|
| 41 | sdn 4d | 3,885 | 3,294 | — |
| 43 | htp sdn | 3,910 | 3,432 | — |
| 45 | wgn 4d, 2S | 4,295 | 3,702 | — |
| 46 | wgn 4d, 3S | 4,360 | 3,835 | — |

### DD2-P Monaco 500 (wb 122.0)

| 23 | htp cpe | 3,885 | 3,869 | 4,568 |
|---|---|---|---|---|

| 1968 Engines | bore × stroke | bhp | availability |
|---|---|---|---|
| I-6, 170.0 | 3.40 × 3.13 | 115 | S-Dart 6 |
| I-6, 225.0 | 3.40 × 4.13 | 145 | S-Coronet 6; O-Dart 6 |
| V-8, 273.5 | 3.63 × 3.31 | 190 | S-Dart V-8, Coronet V-8 |
| V-8, 318.0 | 3.91 × 3.31 | 230 | S-Chrgr, Pol; O-Dart V-8, Cor V-8 |
| V-8, 340.0 | 4.04 × 3.31 | 275 | S-Dart GTS |
| V-8, 383.0 | 4.25 × 3.38 | 300 | O-Dart GTS |
| V-8, 383.0 | 4.25 × 3.38 | 290 | S-Mon; O-Cor V-8, Chrgr, Pol |
| V-8, 383.0 | 4.25 × 3.38 | 330 | O-Cor V-8, Chrgr, Pol, Mon |
| V-8, 383.0 | 4.25 × 3.38 | 335 | S-Coronet Super Bee |
| V-8, 426.0 | 4.25 × 3.75 | 425 | O-Cor R/T, Chrgr R/T |
| V-8, 440.0 | 4.32 × 3.75 | 350 | O-Polara & Mo—co wgns |
| V-8, 440.0 | 4.32 × 3.75 | 375 | S-Cor R/T, Chrgr R/T; O-Pol, Mon |

## 1969

### LL Dart (wb 111.0)—106,329 built (includes Swinger 340)

| | | Wght | Price | Prod |
|---|---|---|---|---|
| 23 | Swinger htp cpe | 2,795 | 2,400 | — |
| 41 | sdn 4d | 2,810 | 2,413 | — |

### LM Dart Swinger 340 (wb 111.0)

| 23 | htp cpe | 3,097 | 2,836 | — |
|---|---|---|---|---|

### LH Dart Custom (wb 111.0)—63,740 built

| 23 | htp cpe | 2,795 | 2,577 | — |
|---|---|---|---|---|
| 41 | sdn 4d | 2,810 | 2,550 | — |

### LP Dart GT (wb 111.0)—20,914 built

| 23 | htp cpe | 2,800 | 2,672 | — |
|---|---|---|---|---|
| 27 | conv cpe | 2,905 | 2,865 | — |

### LS Dart GTS V-8 (wb 111.0)—6,702 built

| 23 | htp cpe | 3,105 | 3,226 | — |
|---|---|---|---|---|
| 27 | conv cpe | 3,210 | 3,419 | — |

### WL Coronet Deluxe (wb 117.0)—23,988 built

| 21 | cpe | 3,067 | 2,554 | — |
|---|---|---|---|---|
| 41 | sdn 4d | 3,097 | 2,589 | — |
| 45 | wgn 4d | 3,552 | 2,922 | — |

### WH Coronet 440 (wb 117.0)—105,882 built

| 21 | cpe | 3,067 | 2,630 | — |
|---|---|---|---|---|
| 23 | htp cpe | 3,097 | 2,692 | — |
| 41 | sdn 4d | 3,102 | 2,670 | — |
| 45 | wgn 4d, 2S | 3,557 | 3,033 | — |
| 46 | wgn 4d, 3S, V-8 only | 3,676 | 3,246 | — |

### WM Coronet Super Bee V-8 (wb 117.0)—27,846 built

| 21 | cpe | 3,440 | 3,076 | — |
|---|---|---|---|---|
| 23 | htp cpe | 3,470 | 3,138 | — |

### WP Coronet 500 V-8 (wb 117.0)—32,050 built

| 23 | htp cpe | 3,171 | 2,929 | — |
|---|---|---|---|---|
| 27 | conv cpe | 3,306 | 3,069 | — |
| 41 | sdn 4d | 3,206 | 2,963 | — |
| 45 | wgn 4d, 2S | 3,611 | 3,280 | — |
| 46 | wgn 4d, 3S | 3,676 | 3,392 | — |

### WS Coronet R/T (wb 117.0)—7,238 built

| 23 | htp cpe | 3,601 | 3,442 | — |
|---|---|---|---|---|
| 27 | conv cpe | 3,721 | 3,660 | — |

### XP/XS Charger (wb 117.0)

| XP29 | htp cpe, I-6 | 3,103 | 3,020 | 69,142 |
|---|---|---|---|---|
| XP29 | htp cpe, V-8 | 3,256 | 3,126 | |
| XS29 | R/T htp cpe, V-8 | 3,646 | 3,592 | 20,057 |
| — | Daytona htp cpe, V-8 | — | 4,000 | 505 |

### XX Charger 500 V-8 (wb 117.0)

| XX29 | htp cpe | 3,671 | 3,860 | * |
|---|---|---|---|---|

### DL Polara (wb 122.0)—83,122 built

| 23 | htp cpe | 3,646 | 3,117 | — |
|---|---|---|---|---|
| 27 | conv cpe | 3,791 | 3,377 | — |
| 41 | sdn 4d | 3,701 | 3,095 | — |
| 43 | htp sdn | 3,731 | 3,188 | — |
| 45 | wgn 4d, 2S | 4,161 | 3,522 | — |
| 46 | wgn 4d, 3S | 4,211 | 3,629 | — |

## Dodge

| DM Polara 500 (wb 122.0)—5,564 built | | Wght | Price | Prod |
|---|---|---|---|---|
| 23 | htp cpe | 3,681 | 3,314 | — |
| 27 | conv cpe | 3,801 | 3,576 | — |
| **DH Monaco (wb 122.0)—38,566 built** | | | | |
| 23 | htp cpe | 3,811 | 3,528 | — |
| 41 | sdn 4d | 3,846 | 3,452 | — |
| 43 | htp sdn | 3,891 | 3,591 | — |
| 45 | wgn 4d, 2S | 4,306 | 3,917 | — |
| 46 | wgn 4d, 3S | 4,361 | 4,046 | — |

* Production included with XP 29 models

| 1969 Engines | bore × stroke | bhp | availability |
|---|---|---|---|
| I-6, 170.0 | 3.40 × 3.13 | 115 | S-Dart |
| I-6, 225.0 | 3.40 × 4.13 | 145 | S-Coronet Del/440; O-Dart |
| V-8, 273.5 | 3.63 × 3.31 | 190 | S-Dart V-8 exc. GTS, Swinger 340 |
| V-8, 318.0 | 3.91 × 3.31 | 230 | S-Cor Del/440/500, Chgr, Pol; O-Dart |
| V-8, 340.0 | 4.04 × 3.31 | 275 | S-GTS, Swinger 340 |
| V-8, 383.0 | 4.25 × 3.38 | 290 | S-Monaco; O-Polara, Chgr, Coronet |
| V-8, 383.0 | 4.25 × 3.38 | 330 | O-GTS, Cor V-8, Mon, Pol, Chgr |
| V-8, 383.0 | 4.25 × 3.38 | 335 | S-Coronet Super Bee |
| V-8, 426.0 | 4.25 × 3.75 | 425 | O-Coronet R/T, Charger R/T & Daytona |
| V-8, 440.0 | 4.32 × 3.75 | 350 | O-Monaco & Polara wgns |
| V-8, 440.0 | 4.32 × 3.75 | 375 | S-Cor R/T, Chgr R/T & Daytona; O-Pol, Mon exc wagons |
| V-8, 440.0 | 4.32 × 3.75 | 390 | O-Coronet Super Bee |

### 1970

| LL Dart (wb 111.0) | | Wght | Price | Prod |
|---|---|---|---|---|
| 23 | Swinger htp cpe | 2,903 | 2,261 | 119,883 |
| 41 | sdn 4d | 2,900 | 2,308 | 35,499 |
| **LH Dart Custom (wb 111.0)** | | | | |
| 23 | htp cpe | 2,898 | 2,463 | 17,208 |
| 41 | sdn 4d | 2,905 | 2,467 | 23,779 |
| **LM Dart Swinger 340 (wb 111.0)** | | | | |
| 23 | htp cpe | 3,130 | 2,631 | 13,785 |
| **JH Challenger (wb 110.0)** | | | | |
| 23 | htp cpe | 3,028 | 2,851 | 53,337 |
| 27 | conv cpe | 3,103 | 3,120 | 3,173 |
| 29 | S.E. htp cpe | 3,053 | 3,083 | 6,584 |
| **JS Challenger R/T (wb 110.0)** | | | | |
| 23 | htp cpe (incl. T/A) | 3,405 | 3,226 | 14,889 |
| 27 | conv cpe | 3,470 | 3,535 | 1,070 |
| 29 | S.E. htp cpe | 3,440 | 3,498 | 3,979 |
| **WL Coronet Deluxe (wb 117.0)** | | | | |
| 21 | cpe | 3,150 | 2,669 | 2,978 |
| 41 | sdn 4d | 3,188 | 2,704 | 7,894 |
| 45 | wgn 4d | 3,675 | 3,048 | 3,694 |

| WH Coronet 440 (wb 117.0) | | Wght | Price | Prod |
|---|---|---|---|---|
| 21 | cpe | 3,170 | 2,743 | 1,236 |
| 23 | htp cpe | 3,185 | 2,805 | 24,341 |
| 41 | sdn 4d | 3,190 | 2,783 | 33,258 |
| 45 | wgn 4d | 3,673 | 3,156 | 3,964 |
| 46 | wgn 4d | 3,775 | 3,368 | 3,772 |
| **WM Coronet Super Bee (wb 117.0)** | | | | |
| 21 | cpe | 3,500 | 3,012 | 3,966 |
| 23 | htp cpe | 3,535 | 3,074 | 11,540 |
| **WP Coronet 500 (wb 117.0)** | | | | |
| 23 | htp cpe | 3,235 | 3,048 | 8,247 |
| 27 | conv cpe | 3,345 | 3,188 | 924 |
| 41 | sdn 4d | 3,255 | 3,082 | 2,890 |
| 45 | wgn 4d, 2S | 3,715 | 3,404 | 1,657 |
| 46 | wgn 4d, 3S | 3,785 | 3,514 | 1,779 |
| **WS Coronet R/T (wb 117.0)** | | | | |
| 23 | htp cpe | 3,545 | 3,569 | 2,319 |
| 27 | conv cpe | 3,610 | 3,785 | 296 |
| **XH/XP Charger (wb 117.0)** | | | | |
| XH29 | htp cpe | 3,293 | 3,001 | 39,431 |
| XP29 | 500 htp cpe | 3,293 | 3,139 | |
| **XS/XX Charger R/T (wb 117.0)** | | | | |
| XS29 | htp cpe | 3,610 | 3,711 | 10,337 |
| XX29 | Daytona htp cpe | 3,710 | 3,993 | |
| **DE Polara (wb 122.0)*** | | | | |
| 41 | sdn 4d, I-6 | 3,775 | 2,960 | — |
| 45 | wgn 4d, 2S, V-8 | 4,180 | 3,513 | — |
| 46 | wgn 4d, 3S, V-8 | 4,235 | 3,621 | — |
| **DL Polara "Deluxe" V-8 (wb 122.0)*** | | | | |
| 23 | htp cpe | 3,770 | 3,224 | — |
| 27 | conv cpe | 3,830 | 3,527 | 842 |
| 41 | sdn 4d | 3,805 | 3,222 | — |
| 43 | htp sdn | 3,850 | 3,316 | — |
| 45 | wgn 4d, 2S | 4,180 | 3,670 | — |
| 46 | wgn 4d, 3S | 4,235 | 3,778 | — |
| **DM Polara Custom V-8 (wb 122.0)*** | | | | |
| 23 | htp cpe | 4,005 | 3,458 | — |
| 41 | sdn 4d | 3,975 | 3,426 | — |
| 43 | htp sdn | 3,925 | 3,528 | — |
| **DH Monaco (wb 122.0)** | | | | |
| 23 | htp cpe | 3,950 | 3,679 | 3,522 |
| 41 | sdn 4d | 4,010 | 3,604 | 4,721 |
| 43 | htp sdn | 4,045 | 3,743 | 10,974 |
| 45 | wgn 4d, 2S | 4,420 | 4,110 | 2,211 |
| 46 | wgn 4d, 3S | 4,475 | 4,242 | 3,264 |

* Dodge combined production figures for most Polara models. Available figures are:

| | | |
|---|---|---|
| 23 | htp cpe (DL, DM) | 15,243 |
| 27 | conv cpe (DL) | 842 |
| 41 | sdn 4d (DE, DL, DM) | 18,740 |
| 43 | htp sdn (DL, DM) | 19,223 |
| 45 | wgn 4d, 2S (DE, DL) | 3,074 |
| 46 | wgn 4d, 3S (DE, DL) | 3,546 |

| 1970 Engines | bore × stroke | bhp | availability |
|---|---|---|---|
| I-6, 198.0 | 3.40 × 3.64 | 125 | S-Dart |
| I-6, 225.0 | 3.40 × 4.13 | 145 | S-Chal/Cor/Chrgr/Polara 6s; O-Dart |
| V-8, 318.0 | 3.91 × 3.31 | 230 | S-Dart exc Swngr 340, Chal, Cor, Chrgr, Pol |

# Dodge

| 1970 Engines | bore × stroke | bhp | availability |
|---|---|---|---|
| V-8, 340.0 | 4.04 × 3.31 | 275 | S-Swngr 340; O-Chal |
| V-8, 383.0 | 4.25 × 3.38 | 290 | S-Mon, Pol Cus; O-Chal/Cor/Chrgr/Polara V-8s |
| V-8, 383.0 | 4.25 × 3.38 | 330 | O-Chal, Cor, Pol, Pol Cus, Monaco |
| V-8, 383.0 | 4.25 × 3.38 | 335 | S-Super Bee, Chal R/T; O-Chal, Chrgr R/T |
| V-8, 426.0 | 4.25 × 3.75 | 425 | O-Chal, Super Bee, Cor/Chrgr R/Ts |
| V-8, 440.0 | 4.32 × 3.75 | 350 | O-Mo—co, Polara, Polara Custom |
| V-8, 440.0 | 4.32 × 3.75 | 375 | S-Chrgr/Coronet/Challenger R/Ts |
| V-8, 440.0 | 4.32 × 3.75 | 390 | O-Chrgr/Cor/Chal R/Ts, Super Bee |

## 1971

### Dart (wb 111.0; fstbk cpes-108.0)

| | | Wght | Price | Prod |
|---|---|---|---|---|
| LL29 | Demon fstbk cpe | 2,845 | 2,343 | 69,861 |
| LL23 | Swinger Special htp cpe | 2,900 | 2,402 | 13,485 |
| LL41 | sdn 4d | 2,900 | 2,450 | 32,711 |
| LH23 | Swinger htp cpe | 2,900 | 2,561 | 102,480 |
| LH41 | Custom sdn 4d | 2,900 | 2,609 | 21,785 |
| LM29 | Demon fstbk 340 cpe V-8 | 3,165 | 2,721 | 10,098 |

### Challenger (wb 110.0)

| JL23 | cpe | 3,050 | 2,727 | 23,088 |
|---|---|---|---|---|
| JH23 | htp cpe | 3,092 | 2,848 | |
| JH27 | conv cpe | 3,180 | 3,105 | 2,165 |
| JS23 | R/T htp cpe V-8 | 3,495 | 3,273 | 4,630 |

### Coronet (wb 118.0)

| WL41 | sdn 4d | 3,302 | 2,777 | 11,794 |
|---|---|---|---|---|
| WL45 | wgn 4d 2S | 3,778 | 3,101 | 5,470 |
| WH41 | Custom sdn 4d | 3,308 | 2,951 | 37,817 |
| WH45 | Custom wgn 4d 2S | 3,812 | 3,196 | 5,365 |
| WH46 | Custom wgn 4d 3S V-8 | 3,890 | 3,454 | 5,717 |
| WP41 | Brougham sdn 4d V-8 | 3,475 | 3,232 | 4,700 |
| WP45 | Crestwood wgn 4d 2S V-8 | 3,845 | 3,601 | 2,884 |
| WP46 | Crestwood wgn 4d 3S V-8 | 3,900 | 3,682 | 3,981 |

### Charger (wb 115.0)

| WL21 | cpe | 3,270 | 2,707 | 46,183 |
|---|---|---|---|---|
| WH23 | htp cpe | 3,138 | 2,975 | |
| WP23 | 500 htp cpe V-8 | 3,350 | 3,223 | 11,948 |
| WM23 | Super Bee htp cpe V-8 | 3,640 | 3,271 | 5,054 |
| WP29 | SE htp cpe V-8 | 3,375 | 3,422 | 15,811 |
| WS23 | R/T htp cpe V-8 | 3,685 | 3,777 | 3,118 |

### Polara (wb 122.0)

| DE41 | sdn 4d | 3,788 | 3,298 | 16,444 |
|---|---|---|---|---|
| DE23 | htp cpe | 3,755 | 3,319 | 11,500 |
| DE43 | htp sdn V-8 | 3,875 | 3,497 | 2,487 |
| DL41 | Custom sdn 4d V-8 | 3,835 | 3,593 | 13,850 |
| DL43 | Custom htp sdn V-8 | 3,875 | 3,681 | 17,458 |
| DL23 | Custom htp cpe V-8 | 3,805 | 3,614 | 9,682 |
| DL45 | Custom wgn 4d 2S V-8 | 4,280 | 3,992 | 9,682 |
| DL46 | Custom wgn 4d 3S V-8 | 4,335 | 4,098 | |
| DM43 | Brougham htp sdn V-8 | 4,035 | 3,884 | 2,570 |
| DM23 | Brougham htp cpe V-8 | 3,965 | 3,818 | 2,024 |

### Monaco (wb 122.0)

| DH41 | sdn 4d | 4,050 | 4,223 | 16,900 |
|---|---|---|---|---|
| DH43 | htp sdn | 4,080 | 4,362 | |
| DH23 | htp cpe | 4,000 | 4,298 | 3,195 |
| DH45 | wgn 4d 2S | 4,525 | 4,689 | 5,449 |
| DH46 | wgn 4d 3S | 4,585 | 4,821 | |

| 1971 Engines | bore × stroke | bhp | availability |
|---|---|---|---|
| I-6, 198.0 | 3.40 × 3.64 | 125 | S-Dart, Chal JL |
| I-6, 225.0 | 3.40 × 4.13 | 145 | S-Chal JH, Cor, Chrgr, Pol; O-Dart, Chal JL |
| V-8, 318.0 | 3.91 × 3.31 | 230 | S-Chal, Cor, Chrgr, Pol; O-Dart |
| V-8, 340.0 | 4.04 × 3.31 | 275 | S-Demon 340; O-Chal |
| V-8, 360.0 | 4.00 × 3.58 | 275 | O-Polara |
| V-8, 383.0 | 4.25 × 3.38 | 275 | S-Chal R/T, Chrgr Super Bee, Pol B'ham, Mon; O-Chal, Cor, Chrgr, Pol |
| V-8, 383.0 | 4.25 × 3.38 | 300 | O-Chal, Cor, Chrgr, Pol, Mon |
| V-8, 426.0 | 4.25 × 3.75 | 335 | O-Polara, Monaco |
| V-8, 426.0 | 4.25 × 3.75 | 425 | O-Charger, Challenger |
| V-8, 440.0 | 4.32 × 3.75 | 335 | O-Polara, Monaco |
| V-8, 440.0 | 4.32 × 3.75 | 370 | S-Charger R/T; O-Charger |
| V-8, 440.0 | 4.32 × 3.75 | 385 | O-Challenger, Charger |

## 1972

### Dart (wb 111.0; fstbk cpes 108.0)

| | | Wght | Price | Prod |
|---|---|---|---|---|
| LL29 | Demon fstbk cpe | 2,800 | 2,316 | 39,880 |
| LL23 | Swinger Special htp cpe | 2,845 | 2,373 | 19,210 |
| LL41 | sdn 4d | 2,855 | 2,420 | 26,019 |
| LH23 | Swinger htp cpe | 2,835 | 2,528 | 119,618 |
| LH41 | Custom sdn 4d | 2,855 | 2,574 | 49,941 |
| LM29 | Demon 340 fstbk cpe V-8 | 3,125 | 2,759 | 8,750 |

### Challenger (wb 110.0)

| JH23 | cpe | 3,098 | 2,790 | 18,535 |
|---|---|---|---|---|
| JS23 | Rallye htp cpe V-8 | 3,225 | 3,082 | 8,123 |

### Coronet (wb 118.0)

| WL41 | sdn 4d | 3,362 | 2,721 | 11,293 |
|---|---|---|---|---|
| WL45 | wgn 4d 2S V-8 | 3,795 | 3,209 | |
| WH45 | Custom wgn 4d 2S V-8 | 3,800 | 3,382 | 5,452 |
| WH46 | Custom wgn 4d 3S V-8 | 3,840 | 3,460 | |
| WH41 | Custom sdn 4d | 3,370 | 2,998 | 43,132 |
| WP45 | Crestwood wgn 4d 2S V-8 | 3,810 | 3,604 | 6,471 |
| WP46 | Crestwood wgn 4d 3S V-8 | 3,850 | 3,683 | |

### Charger (wb 115.0)

| WL21 | cpe | 3,278 | 2,652 | 7,803 |
|---|---|---|---|---|
| WH23 | htp cpe | 3,292 | 2,913 | 45,361 |
| WP29 | SE htp cpe V-8 | 3,390 | 3,249 | 22,430 |

### Polara (wb 122.0)

| DL41 | sdn 4d | 3,835 | 3,618 | 25,187 |
|---|---|---|---|---|
| DL43 | htp sdn | 3,875 | 3,709 | 8,212 |
| DL23 | htp cpe | 3,800 | 3,641 | 7,000 |
| DM41 | Custom sdn 4d | 3,845 | 3,808 | 19,739 |
| DM43 | Custom htp sdn | 3,890 | 3,898 | 22,505 |
| DM23 | Custom htp cpe | 3,815 | 3,830 | 15,039 |
| DM45 | Custom wgn 4d 2S | 4,320 | 4,262 | 3,497 |

# Dodge

| Polara (wb 122.0) | | Wght | Price | Prod |
|---|---|---|---|---|
| DM46 | Custom wgn 4d 3S | 4,370 | 4,371 | 7,660 |
| **Monaco (wb 122.0)** | | | | |
| DP41 | sdn 4d | 3,980 | 4,095 | 6,474 |
| DP43 | htp sdn | 4,030 | 4,216 | 15,039 |
| DP23 | htp cpe | 3,960 | 4,153 | 7,786 |
| DP45 | wgn 4d 2S | 4,445 | 4,627 | 2,569 |
| DP46 | wgn 4d 3S | 4,490 | 4,756 | 5,145 |

| 1972 Engines | bore × stroke | bhp | availability |
|---|---|---|---|
| I-6, 198.0 | 3.40×3.64 | 100 | S-Dart |
| I-6, 225.0 | 3.40×4.13 | 100 | O-Dart |
| I-6, 225.0 | 3.40×4.13 | 110 | S-Chal, Cor, Chrgr; O-Dart |
| V-8, 318.0 | 3.91×3.31 | 150 | S-Chal, Cor, Chrgr, Pol; O-Dart |
| V-8, 340.0 | 4.04×3.31 | 240 | S-Demon 340, O-Dart, Chal, Chrgr |
| V-8, 360.0 | 4.00×3.58 | 175 | S-Mon; O-Pol |
| V-8, 400.0 | 4.34×3.38 | 190 | O-Chrgr, Pol, Mon |
| V-8, 400.0 | 4.34×3.38 | 250 | O-Pol, Mon |
| V-8, 400.0 | 4.34×3.38 | 255 | O-Charger |
| V-8, 440.0 | 4.32×3.75 | 230 | O-Monaco |
| V-8, 440.0 | 4.32×3.75 | 235 | O-Polara |
| V-8, 440.0 | 4.32×3.75 | 280 | O-Monaco |
| V-8, 440.0 | 4.32×3.75 | 285 | O-Pol, Mon |
| V-8, 440.0 | 4.32×3.75 | 330 | O-Cor, Chrgr |

## 1973

| Dart (wb 111.0; fstbk cpes-108.0) | | Wght | Price | Prod |
|---|---|---|---|---|
| LL29 | Sport fstbk cpe | 2,850 | 2,424 | 68,113 |
| LL23 | Swinger Special htp cpe | 2,895 | 2,462 | 17,480 |
| LL41 | sdn 4d | 2,910 | 2,504 | 21,539 |
| LH23 | Swinger htp cpe | 2,890 | 2,617 | 107,619 |
| LH41 | Custom sdn 4d | 2,910 | 2,658 | 62,626 |
| LM29 | Sport 340 fstbk cpe V-8 | 3,205 | 2,853 | 11,315 |
| **Challenger (wb 110.0)** | | | | |
| JH23 | htp cpe V-8 | 3,155 | 3,011 | 32,596 |
| **Coronet (wb 118.0)** | | | | |
| WL41 | sdn 4d | 3,472 | 2,867 | 14,395 |
| WL45 | wgn 4d 2S V-8 | 3,955 | 3,314 | 4,874 |
| WH41 | Custom sdn 4d | 3,962 | 3,017 | 46,491 |
| WH45 | Custom wgn 4d 2S V-8 | 3,955 | 3,442 | 13,018 |
| WH46 | Custom wgn 4d 3S V-8 | 4,000 | 3,560 | |
| WP45 | Crestwood wgn 4d 2S V-8 | 3,970 | 3,671 | 8,755 |
| WP46 | Crestwood wgn 4d 3S V-8 | 4,005 | 3,791 | |
| **Charger (wb 115.0)** | | | | |
| WL21 | cpe | 3,428 | 2,810 | 11,995 |
| WH23 | htp cpe | 3,465 | 3,060 | 45,415 |
| WP29 | SE htp cpe V-8 | 3,540 | 3,375 | 61,908 |
| **Polara (wb 122.0)** | | | | |
| DL41 | sdn 4d | 3,865 | 3,729 | 15,015 |
| DL23 | htp cpe | 3,835 | 3,752 | 6,432 |
| DL45 | wgn 4d 2S | 4,420 | 4,186 | 3,327 |
| DM41 | Custom sdn 4d | 3,870 | 3,911 | 23,939 |
| DM43 | Custom htp sdn | 3,905 | 4,001 | 29,341 |
| DM23 | Custom htp cpe | 3,835 | 3,928 | 17,406 |
| DM45 | Custom wgn 4d 2S | 4,440 | 4,370 | 3,702 |
| DM46 | Custom wgn 4d 3S | 4,485 | 4,494 | 8,839 |
| **Monaco (wb 122.0)** | | | | |
| DP41 | sdn 4d | 4,020 | 4,218 | 6,316 |
| DP43 | htp sdn | 4,060 | 4,339 | 9,031 |
| DP23 | htp cpe | 3,985 | 4,276 | 6,133 |

| Monaco (wb 122.0) | | Wght | Price | Prod |
|---|---|---|---|---|
| DP45 | wgn 4d 2S | 4,470 | 4,730 | 2,337 |
| DP46 | wgn 4d 3S | 4,515 | 4,859 | 5,579 |

| 1973 Engines | bore × stroke | bhp | availability |
|---|---|---|---|
| I-6, 198.0 | 3.40×3.64 | 95 | S-Dart |
| I-6, 225.0 | 3.40×4.13 | 105 | S-Cor, Chrgr; O-Dart |
| V-8, 318.0 | 3.91×3.31 | 150 | S-Chal, Cor, Chrgr, Pol exc wgns; O-Dart |
| V-8, 340.0 | 4.04×3.31 | 240 | S-Dart Sport 340; O-Chal, Cor, Chrgr |
| V-8, 360.0 | 4.00×3.58 | 170 | S-Pol wgns, Mon; O-Pol |
| V-8, 400.0 | 4.34×3.38 | 175 | O-Coronet, Charger |
| V-8, 400.0 | 4.34×3.38 | 185 | S-Mon wgns; O-Pol, Mon |
| V-8, 400.0 | 4.34×3.38 | 220 | O-Polara, Monaco |
| V-8, 400.0 | 4.34×3.38 | 260 | O-Coronet, Charger |
| V-8, 440.0 | 4.32×3.75 | 220 | O-Polara, Monaco |
| V-8, 440.0 | 4.32×3.75 | 280 | O-Coronet, Charger |

## 1974

| Dart (wb 111.0; fstbk cpes-108.0) | | Wght | Price | Prod |
|---|---|---|---|---|
| LL29 | Sport fstbk cpe | 2,990 | 2,878 | 59,567 |
| LL23 | Swinger Special htp cpe | 3,035 | 2,918 | 16,155 |
| LH23 | Swinger htp cpe | 3,030 | 3,077 | 89,242 |
| LL41 | sdn 4d | 3,055 | 2,961 | 78,216 |
| LH41 | Custom sdn 4d | 3,055 | 3,119 | |
| LM29 | Sport 360 fstbk cpe V-8 | 3,330 | 3,320 | 3,951 |
| LP41 | Special Edition sdn 4d | 3,641 | 3,837 | 12,385 |
| LP23 | Special Edition htp cpe | 3,599 | 3,794 | |
| **Challenger (wb 110.0)** | | | | |
| JH23 | htp cpe V-8 | 3,225 | 3,143 | 16,437 |
| **Coronet (wb 118.0)** | | | | |
| WL41 | sdn 4d | 3,548 | 3,271 | 8,752 |
| WL45 | wgn 4d 2S V-8 | 4,085 | 3,699 | 2,968 |
| WH41 | Custom sdn 4d | 3,538 | 3,374 | 36,021 |
| WH45 | Custom wgn 4d 2S V-8 | 4,090 | 3,882 | 2,975 |
| WH46 | Custom wgn 4d 3S V-8 | 4,130 | 4,196 | 4,950 |
| WP45 | Crestwood wgn 4d 2S V-8 | 4,100 | 4,117 | 1,916 |
| WP46 | Crestwood wgn 4d 3S V-8 | 4,135 | 4,433 | 3,146 |
| **Charger (wb 115.0)** | | | | |
| WL21 | cpe | 3,510 | 3,212 | 8,876 |
| WH23 | htp cpe | 3,528 | 3,412 | 29,101 |
| WP29 | SE htp cpe V-8 | 3,625 | 3,742 | 36,399 |
| **Monaco (wb 122.0; wgns-124.0)** | | | | |
| DM41 | sdn 4d | 4,170 | 4,259 | 9,101 |
| DM23 | htp cpe | 4,150 | 4,283 | 3,347 |
| DM45 | wgn 4d 2S | 4,760 | 4,706 | 1,583 |
| DH41 | Custom sdn 4d | 4,175 | 4,446 | 12,655 |
| DH43 | Custom htp sdn | 4,205 | 4,539 | 10,585 |
| DH23 | Custom htp cpe | 4,155 | 4,464 | 6,649 |
| DH45 | Custom wgn 4d 2S | 4,770 | 4,839 | 1,253 |
| DH46 | Custom wgn 4d 3S | 4,815 | 4,956 | 3,272 |
| DP41 | Brougham sdn 4d | 4,410 | 4,891 | 3,954 |
| DP43 | Brougham htp sdn | 4,445 | 4,999 | 5,649 |
| DP23 | Brougham htp cpe | 4,370 | 4,951 | 4,863 |
| DP45 | Brougham wgn 4d 2S | 4,860 | 5,360 | 1,042 |
| DP46 | Brougham wgn 4d 3S | 4,905 | 5,477 | 2,718 |

| 1974 Engines | bore × stroke | bhp | availability |
|---|---|---|---|
| I-6, 198.0 | 3.40×3.64 | 95 | S-Dart exc SE |
| I-6, 225.0 | 3.40×4.13 | 105 | S-Dart SE, Cor; O-Drt |

# Dodge

| 1974 Engines | bore × stroke | bhp | availability |
|---|---|---|---|
| V-8, 318.0 | 3.91 × 3.31 | 150 | S-Chal, Cor, Chrgr; O-Dart |
| V-8, 360.0 | 4.00 × 3.58 | 180 | S-Mon exc B'ham & wgns; O-Chrgr |
| V-8, 360.0 | 4.00 × 3.58 | 200 | O-Cor, Chrgr, Mon exc Brham & wgns |
| V-8, 360.0 | 4.00 × 3.58 | 245 | S-Dart 360; O-Chal, Chrgr |
| V-8, 400.0 | 4.34 × 3.38 | 185 | S-Mon Brham, wgns; O-Cor, Chrgr |
| V-8, 400.0 | 4.34 × 3.38 | 205 | O-Coronet, Charger |
| V-8, 400.0 | 4.34 × 3.38 | 240 | O-Monaco exc wagons |
| V-8, 400.0 | 4.34 × 3.38 | 250 | O-Coronet, Charger |
| V-8, 440.0 | 4.32 × 3.75 | 230 | O-Monaco exc wagons |
| V-8, 440.0 | 4.32 × 3.75 | 250 | O-Monaco wagons |
| V-8, 440.0 | 4.32 × 3.75 | 275 | O-Coronet, Charger |

## 1975

| Dart (wb 111.0; fstbk cpes-108.0) | Wght | Price | Prod |
|---|---|---|---|
| LL29 Sport fstbk cpe | 2,980 | 3,297 | 50,312 |
| LM29 Sport 360 fstbk cpe V-8 | 3,335 | 4,014 | 1,043 |
| LL23 Swinger Special htp cpe | 3,045 | 3,341 | 9,304 |
| LL41 sdn 4d | 3,060 | 3,269 | 24,193 |
| LH23 Swinger htp cpe | 3,035 | 3,518 | 45,495 |
| LH41 Custom sdn 4d | 3,060 | 3,444 | 60,818 |
| LP23 Special Edition htp cpe | 3,260 | 4,232 | 5,680 |
| LP41 Special Edition sdn 4d | 3,280 | 4,159 | 13,194 |
| **Coronet (wb 117.5; htps-115.0)** | | | |
| WL41 sdn 4d | 3,652 | 3,641 | 8,138 |
| WL21 htp cpe | 3,620 | 3,591 | 6,058 |
| WL45 wgn 4d 2S V-8 | 4,185 | 4,358 | 2,852 |
| WH41 Custom sdn 4d | 3,692 | 3,754 | 26,219 |
| WH23 Custom htp cpe | 3,702 | 3,777 | 18,513 |
| WH45 Custom wgn 4d 2S V-8 | 4,240 | 4,560 | 2,623 |
| WH46 Custom wgn 4d 3S V-8 | 4,290 | 4,674 | 5,052 |
| WP23 Brougham htp cpe V-8 | 3,800 | 4,154 | 10,292 |
| WP45 Crestwood wgn 4d 2S V-8 | 4,230 | 4,826 | 1,784 |
| WP46 Crestwood wgn 4d 3S V-8 | 4,290 | 4,918 | 2,967 |
| **Charger (wb 115.0)** | | | |
| XS22 SE htp cpe | 3,950 | 4,903 | 30,812 |
| **Monaco (wb 121.5; wgns-124.0)** | | | |
| DM41 sdn 4d | 4,280 | 4,605 | 7,097 |
| DM23 htp cpe | 4,225 | 4,631 | 2,116 |
| DH41 Royal sdn 4d | 4,285 | 4,848 | 10,126 |
| DH43 Royal htp sdn | 4,310 | 4,951 | 8,117 |
| DH23 Royal htp cpe | 4,240 | 4,868 | 4,001 |
| DP41 Royal Brougham sdn 4d | 4,455 | 5,262 | 5,126 |
| DP43 Royal Brougham htp sdn | 4,485 | 5,382 | 5,964 |
| DP29 Royal Brougham htp cpe | 4,370 | 5,460 | |
| DM45 wgn 4d 2S | 4,885 | 5,109 | 1,547 |
| DH45 Royal wgn 4d 2S | 4,905 | 5,292 | 1,279 |
| DH46 Royal wgn 4d 3S | 4,945 | 5,415 | 2,666 |
| DP45 Royal Brougham wgn 4d 2S | 4,980 | 5,779 | 1,165 |
| DP46 Royal Brougham wgn 4d 3S | 5,025 | 5,905 | 2,909 |

| 1975 Engines | bore × stroke | bhp | availability |
|---|---|---|---|
| I-6, 225.0 | 3.40 × 4.13 | 95 | S-Dart, Coronet |
| V-8, 318.0 | 3.91 × 3.31 | 135 | O-Charger |
| V-8, 318.0 | 3.91 × 3.31 | 145 | O-Dart |
| V-8, 318.0 | 3.91 × 3.31 | 150 | S-Cor; O-Chrgr, Monaco |
| V-8, 360.0 | 4.00 × 3.58 | 180 | S-Chrgr, Mon exc Brham wgns; O-Cor, Ryl Monaco Brham |
| V-8, 360.0 | 4.00 × 3.58 | 190 | O-Chrgr, Ryl Monaco Brham |
| V-8, 360.0 | 4.00 × 3.58 | 230 | S-Dart 360 |
| V-8, 400.0 | 4.34 × 3.38 | 165/190/235 | O-Coronet, Charger |
| V-8, 400.0 | 4.34 × 3.38 | 175 | S-Ryl Mon Brham; O-Mon |
| V-8, 400.0 | 4.34 × 3.38 | 185 | O-Charger |
| V-8, 400.0 | 4.34 × 3.38 | 195 | O-Monaco |
| V-8, 440.0 | 4.32 × 3.75 | 195 | O-Monaco exc Ryl Brham |
| V-8, 440.0 | 4.32 × 3.75 | 215 | O-all Monaco |

## 1976

| Dart (wb 111.0; fstbk cpe-108.0) | Wght | Price | Prod |
|---|---|---|---|
| LL29 Sport fstbk cpe | 2,990 | 3,258 | 18,873 |
| LL23 Swinger Special htp cpe | 3,050 | 3,337 | 3,916 |
| LL41 sdn 4d | 3,070 | 3,295 | 34,864 |
| LH23 Swinger htp cpe | 3,035 | 3,510 | 10,885 |
| **Aspen (wb 112.7; cpes-108.7)** | | | |
| NL41 sdn 4d | 3,252 | 3,371 | 17,573 |
| NL29 cpe | 3,222 | 3,336 | 27,730 |
| NL45 wgn 5d 2S | 3,605 | 3,658 | 37,642 |
| NH41 Custom sdn 4d | 3,240 | 3,553 | 32,163 |
| NH29 Custom cpe | 3,232 | 3,518 | 23,782 |
| NP41 SE sdn 4d | 3,470 | 4,440 | 24,378 |
| NP29 SE cpe | 3,432 | 4,413 | 21,564 |
| NH45 SE wgn 5d 2S | 3,630 | 3,988 | 34,617 |
| **Coronet (wb 117.5)** | | | |
| WL41 sdn 4d | 3,742 | 3,770 | 15,658 |
| WL45 wgn 4d 2S V-8 | 4,285 | 4,634 | 2,632 |
| WL46 wgn 4d 3S V-8 | 4,350 | 4,776 | 3,336 |
| WH41 Brougham sdn 4d | 3,760 | 4,059 | 15,215 |
| WH45 Crestwood wgn 4d 2S V-8 | 4,285 | 5,023 | 1,725 |
| WH46 Crestwood wgn 4d 3S V-8 | 4,360 | 5,165 | 2,597 |
| **Charger (wb 115.0)** | | | |
| WL23 htp cpe | 3,712 | 3,736 | 9,906 |
| WH23 cpe | 3,718 | 4,025 | 13,826 |
| XS22 SE htp cpe V-8 | 3,945 | 4,763 | 42,168 |
| **Monaco (wb 121.5; wgns-124.0)** | | | |
| DM41 sdn 4d | 4,160 | 4,388 | 6,221 |
| DM45 wgn 4d 2S | 4,910 | 4,948 | 1,116 |
| DH41 Royal sdn 4d | 4,325 | 4,763 | 11,320 |
| DH23 Royal htp cpe | 4,280 | 4,778 | 2,915 |
| DH45 Royal wgn 4d 2S | 4,915 | 5,241 | 923 |
| DH46 Royal wgn 4d 3S | 4,950 | 5,364 | 1,429 |
| DP41 Royal Brougham sdn 4d | 4,520 | 5,211 | 5,111 |
| DP29 Royal Brougham htp cpe | 4,430 | 5,382 | 4,076 |
| DP46 Royal Brougham wgn 4d 3S | 4,995 | 5,869 | 2,480 |

| 1976 Engines | bore × stroke | bhp | availability |
|---|---|---|---|
| I-6, 225.0 | 3.40 × 4.13 | 100 | S-all sixes |
| V-8, 318.0 | 3.91 × 3.31 | 150 | S, Cor exc wgns, Chrgr, Mon exc wgns & Ryl; O-Dart; Asp |
| V-8, 360.0 | 4.00 × 3.58 | 170 | S-Cor wgns, Ryl |

# Dodge

| 1976 Engines | bore × stroke | bhp | availability |
|---|---|---|---|
| V-8, 360.0 | 4.00 × 3.58 | 175 | Mon; O-Asp, Cor, Chrgr, Ryl Mon Brham |
| V-8, 360.0 | 4.00 × 3.58 | 175 | O-Coronet, Charger |
| V-8, 360.0 | 4.00 × 3.58 | 220 | O-Dart, Coronet |
| V-8, 400.0 | 4.34 × 3.38 | 175 | S-Mon wgns/Ryl Brhams; O-Cor, Chrgr, Monaco |
| V-8, 400.0 | 4.34 × 3.38 | 185/240 | O-Coronet, Charger |
| V-8, 400.0 | 4.34 × 3.38 | 210 | O-Monaco |
| V-8, 400.0 | 4.34 × 3.38 | 255 | O-Coronet |
| V-8, 440.0 | 4.32 × 3.75 | 205 | O-Monaco |

## 1977

### Aspen (wb 112.7; cpes-108.7)

| | | Wght | Price | Prod |
|---|---|---|---|---|
| NL41 | sdn 4d | 3,290 | 3,631 | 32,662 |
| NL29 | cpe | 3,235 | 3,582 | 33,102 |
| NL45 | wgn 5d 2S | 3,492 | 3,953 | 67,294 |
| NH41 | Custom sdn 4d | 3,295 | 3,813 | 45,697 |
| NH29 | Custom cpe | 3,240 | 3,764 | 29,946 |
| NP41 | SE sdn 4d | 3,492 | 4,366 | 25,949 |
| NP29 | SE cpe | 3,428 | 4,317 | 19,985 |
| NH45 | SE wgn 5d 2S | 3,518 | 4,283 | 58,011 |

### Charger (wb 115.0)

| | | Wght | Price | Prod |
|---|---|---|---|---|
| XS22 | SE htp cpe V-8 | 3,895 | 5,098 | 42,542 |

### Monaco (wb 117.4; htps-115.0)

| | | Wght | Price | Prod |
|---|---|---|---|---|
| WL41 | sdn 4d | 3,772 | 3,988 | 20,633 |
| WL23 | htp cpe | 3,630 | 3,911 | 14,054 |
| WS23 | Special htp cpe | — | 3,995 | — |
| WL45 | wgn 4d 2S V-8 | 4,335 | 4,724 | 3,896 |
| WL46 | wgn 4d 3S V-8 | 4,395 | 4,867 | 4,594 |
| WH41 | Brougham sdn 4d | 3,782 | 4,217 | 17,224 |
| WH23 | Brougham htp cpe | 3,752 | 4,146 | 14,430 |
| WH45 | Crestwood wgn 4d 2S V-8 | 4,330 | 5,224 | 1,948 |
| WH46 | Crestwood wgn 4d 3S V-8 | 4,405 | 5,367 | 3,301 |

### Diplomat (wb 112.7)

| | | Wght | Price | Prod |
|---|---|---|---|---|
| GH41 | sdn 4d | 3,560 | 5,101 | 9,647 |
| GH22 | cpe | 3,510 | 4,943 | 14,023 |
| GP41 | Medallion sdn 4d | 3,675 | 5,471 | 4,667 |
| GP22 | Medallion cpe | 3,615 | 5,313 | 9,215 |

### Royal Monaco (wb 121.5; wgns-124.0)

| | | Wght | Price | Prod |
|---|---|---|---|---|
| DM41 | sdn 4d | 4,125 | 4,716 | 12,646 |
| DM23 | htp cpe | 4,050 | 4,731 | 3,360 |
| DM45 | wgn 4d 2S | 4,905 | 5,353 | 2,010 |
| DH41 | Brougham sdn 4d | 4,270 | 4,996 | 21,440 |
| DH23 | Brougham htp cpe | 4,205 | 5,011 | 8,309 |
| DH45 | Brougham wgn 4d 2S | 4,900 | 5,607 | 1,418 |
| DH46 | Brougham wgn 4d 3S | 4,935 | 5,730 | 4,251 |

| 1977 Engines | bore × stroke | bhp | availability |
|---|---|---|---|
| I-6, 225.0 | 3.40 × 4.13 | 100 | S-Aspen exc wgns |
| I-6, 225.0 | 3.40 × 4.13 | 110 | S-Asp wgns, Mon; O-Aspen |
| V-8, 318.0 | 3.91 × 3.31 | 145 | S, Dip, Mon exc wgns, Chrgr, Ryl Mon; O-Asp |
| V-8, 318.0 | 3.91 × 3.31 | 135 | O-Mon, Chrgr |
| V-8, 360.0 | 4.00 × 3.58 | 155 | S-Mon wgns, Ryl Mon Brham; O-Asp, Mon, Chrgr, Ryl Mon |
| V-8, 360.0 | 4.00 × 3.58 | 170 | O-Monaco, Charger |
| V-8, 360.0 | 4.00 × 3.58 | 175 | O-Aspen |
| V-8, 400.0 | 4.34 × 3.38 | 190 | S-Ryl Mon wgns; O-Mon, Chrgr, Ryl Mon |
| V-8, 440.0 | 4.32 × 3.75 | 195 | O-Ryl Mon |

## 1978

### Omni (wb 99.2)

| | | Wght | Price | Prod |
|---|---|---|---|---|
| ZL44 | htchbk sdn 5d | 2,145 | 3,976 | 81,611 |

### Aspen (wb 112.7; cpe-108.7)

| | | Wght | Price | Prod |
|---|---|---|---|---|
| NL41 | sdn 4d | 3,235 | 3,911 | 60,191 |
| NL29 | cpe | 3,195 | 3,783 | 75,599 |
| NL45 | wgn 5d 2S | 3,448 | 4,253 | 61,917 |

### Charger/Magnum (wb 114.9)

| | | Wght | Price | Prod |
|---|---|---|---|---|
| XP22 | Charger SE htp cpe V-8 | 3,895 | 5,368 | 2,800 |
| XS22 | Magnum XE htp cpe V-8 | 3,895 | 5,509 | 55,431 |

### Monaco (wb 117.4; cpes-114.9)

| | | Wght | Price | Prod |
|---|---|---|---|---|
| WL41 | sdn 4d | 3,760 | 4,344 | 20,292 |
| SL23 | htp cpe | 3,738 | 4,254 | 10,291 |
| WL45 | wgn 4d 2S V-8 | 4,310 | 5,103 | 2,376 |
| WL46 | wgn 4d 3S V-8 | 4,375 | 5,246 | 2,944 |
| WH41 | Brougham sdn 4d | 3,775 | 4,568 | 8,665 |
| WH23 | Brougham htp cpe | 3,742 | 4,507 | 6,842 |
| WH45 | Crestwood wgn 4d 2S V-8 | 4,305 | 5,549 | 1,329 |
| WH46 | Crestwood wgn 4d 3S V-8 | 4,380 | 5,692 | 2,112 |

### Diplomat (wb 112.7)

| | | Wght | Price | Prod |
|---|---|---|---|---|
| GM41 | S sdn 4d | 3,438 | 4,937 | 1,667 |
| GM22 | S cpe | 3,358 | 4,771 | 1,655 |
| GH41 | sdn 4d | 3,508 | 5,187 | 21,094 |
| GH22 | cpe | 3,462 | 5,021 | 19,000 |
| GH45 | wgn 5d 2S | 3,598 | 5,538 | 11,226 |
| GP41 | Medallion sdn 4d | 3,592 | 5,569 | 11,628 |
| GP22 | Medallion cpe | 3,538 | 5,403 | 12,372 |

| 1978 Engines | bore × stroke | bhp | availability |
|---|---|---|---|
| I-4, 104.7 | 3.13 × 3.40 | 70/75 | S-Omni |
| I-6, 225.0 | 3.40 × 4.13 | 90 | O-Asp exc wgns, Dip |
| I-6, 225.0 | 3.40 × 4.13 | 100 | S-Aspen exc wgns |
| I-6, 225.0 | 3.40 × 4.13 | 110 | S-Asp wgns, Dip; O-Asp, Mon |
| V-8, 318.0 | 3.91 × 3.31 | 140 | S-Asp, Dip, Mag, Mon exc wgns; O-Asp, Dip |
| V-8, 318.0 | 3.91 × 3.31 | 150 | S-Charger |
| V-8, 318.0 | 3.91 × 3.31 | 155 | O-Asp, Dip, Mag, Mon |
| V-8, 360.0 | 4.00 × 3.58 | 155 | S-Mon wgns; O- Asp, Dip, Mag, Mon |
| V-8, 360.0 | 4.00 × 3.58 | 165 | O-Aspen |
| V-8, 360.0 | 4.00 × 3.58 | 170 | O-Dip, Mag, Mon, Chrgr |
| V-8, 360.0 | 4.00 × 3.58 | 175 | O-Aspen, Chrgr |
| V-8, 400.0 | 4.34 × 3.38 | 190 | O-Magnum, Monaco |
| V-8, 400.0 | 4.34 × 3.38 | 175/185/240 | O-Charger |
| V-8, 440.0 | 4.32 × 3.75 | 195 | O-Monaco |

## 1979

### Omni (wb 99.2; 024-96.7)

| | | Wght | Price | Prod |
|---|---|---|---|---|
| ZL44 | htchbk sdn 5d | 2,135 | 4,469 | 84,093 |
| ZL24 | 024 htchbk cpe 3d | 2,195 | 4,864 | 57,384 |

### Aspen (wb 112.7; cpe-108.7)

| | | Wght | Price | Prod |
|---|---|---|---|---|
| NL41 | sdn 4d | 3,175 | 4,516 | 62,568 |

# Dodge

| Aspen (wb 112.7; cpe-108.7) | | Wght | Price | Prod |
|---|---|---|---|---|
| NL29 | cpe | 3,110 | 4,399 | 42,833 |
| NL45 | wgn 5d 2S | 3,380 | 4,838 | 38,183 |
| **Magnum (wb 114.9)** | | | | |
| XS22 | XE htp cpe V-8 | 3,675 | 6,039 | 30,354 |
| **Diplomat (wb 112.7)** | | | | |
| GM41 | sdn 4d | 3,378 | 5,336 | 10,675 |
| GM22 | cpe | 3,318 | 5,234 | 8,733 |
| GH41 | Salon sdn 4d | 3,400 | 5,714 | 5,479 |
| GH22 | Salon cpe | 3,335 | 5,482 | 6,849 |
| GH45 | Salon wgn 5d 2S | 3,588 | 6,127 | 9,511 |
| GP41 | Medallion sdn 4d | 3,472 | 6,198 | 5,995 |
| GP22 | Medallion cpe | 3,392 | 5,966 | 6,637 |
| **St. Regis (wb 118.5)** | | | | |
| EH42 | sdn 4d | 3,602 | 6,532 | 34,972 |

| 1979 Engines | bore × stroke | bhp | availability |
|---|---|---|---|
| I-4, 104.7 | 3.13 × 3.40 | 70 | S-Omni |
| I-6, 225.0 | 3.40 × 4.13 | 100 | S-Aspen, Diplomat |
| I-6, 225.0 | 3.40 × 4.13 | 110 | S-St. Regis; O-Asp, Dip |
| V-8, 318.0 | 3.91 × 3.31 | 135 | S; O-Asp, Dip, St.Regis, Mag |
| V-8, 360.0 | 4.00 × 3.58 | 150 | O-Dip, St. Regis, Magnum |
| V-8, 360.0 | 4.00 × 3.58 | 195 | O-Asp, Dip, St.Regis, Magnum |

## 1980

| Omni (wb 99.2; 024-96.7) | | Wght | Price | Prod |
|---|---|---|---|---|
| ZL44 | htchbk sdn 5d | 2,095 | 5,681 | 76,505 |
| ZL24 | 024 htchbk cpe 3d | 2,135 | 5,526 | 61,650 |
| **Aspen (wb 112.7; cpes-108.7)** | | | | |
| NE41 | Special sdn 4d I-6 | 3,210 | 5,151 | 19,225 |
| NE29 | Special cpe I-6 | 3,155 | 5,151 | 13,166 |
| NL41 | sdn 4d I-6/V-8 | 3,242 | 5,162 | 26,239 |
| NL29 | cpe I-6/V-8 | 3,185 | 5,045 | 11,895 |
| NL45 | wgn 5d 2S I-6/V-8 | 3,410 | 5,434 | 14,944 |
| **Diplomat (wb 112.7; cpes-108.7)** | | | | |
| GL22 | Special spt cpe I-6 | 3,130 | 5,995 | — |
| GM41 | sdn 4d | 3,342 | 6,202 | 7,941 |
| GM22 | spt cpe | 3,260 | 6,048 | 5,884 |
| GM45 | wgn 4d 2S | 3,495 | 6,346 | 2,093 |
| GH41 | Salon sdn 4d | 3,205 | 6,501 | 5,479 |
| GH22 | Salon cpe | 3,270 | 6,372 | 6,849 |
| GH45 | Salon wgn 5d 2S | 3,525 | 7,041 | 2,664 |
| GP41 | Medallion sdn 4d | 3,442 | 7,078 | 2,159 |
| GP22 | Medallion cpe | 3,322 | 6,931 | 2,131 |
| **Mirada (wb 112.7)** | | | | |
| XS22 | S htp cpe | 3,328 | 6,645 | 32,746 |
| XH22 | htp cpe | 3,230 | 6,850 | |
| **St. Regis (wb 118.5)** | | | | |
| EH42 | sdn 4d | 3,608 | 7,129 | 17,068 |

| 1980 Engines | bore × stroke | bhp | availability |
|---|---|---|---|
| I-4, 104.7 | 3.13 × 3.40 | 65 | S-Omni |
| I-6, 225.0 | 3.40 × 4.13 | 90 | S-Asp, Dip, St.Regis, Mirada |
| V-8, 318.0 | 3.91 × 3.31 | 120/155 | O-Asp exc Spcls, Dip, St.Regis, Mirada |
| V-8, 360.0 | 4.00 × 3.58 | 130/185 | O-St. Regis, Mirada |

Note: Dodge production through 1980 includes export models, which makes figures in this book somewhat higher than those reported elsewhere.

## 1981

| Omni (wb 99.1; 024-96.6) | | Wght | Price | Prod |
|---|---|---|---|---|
| ZL44 | htchbk sdn 5d | 2,130 | 5,690 | 41,056 |
| ZE44 | Miser htchbk sdn 5d | 2,060 | 5,299 | |
| ZL24 | 024 htchbk cpe 3d | 2,205 | 6,149 | 35,983 |
| ZE24 | Miser 024 htchbk cpe 3d | 2,137 | 5,299 | |
| **Aries (wb 99.6)** | | | | |
| DL41 | sdn 4d | 2,300 | 5,980 | 47,679 |
| DL21 | sdn 2d | 2,305 | 5,880 | |
| DH41 | Custom sdn 4d | 2,310 | 6,448 | 46,792 |
| DH21 | Custom sdn 2d | 2,315 | 6,315 | |
| DH45 | Custom wgn 5d | 2,375 | 6,721 | 31,380 |
| DP41 | SE sdn 4d | 2,340 | 6,933 | 20,160 |
| DP21 | SE sdn 2d | 2,340 | 6,789 | |
| DP45 | SE wgn 5d | 2,390 | 7,254 | 9,770 |
| **Diplomat (wb 112.7; cpes-108.7)** | | | | |
| GL41 | sdn 4d | 3,337 | 6,672 | 4,608 |
| GL22 | spt cpe | 3,272 | 6,495 | |
| GM45 | wgn 5d 2S | 3,530 | 7,089 | 1,806 |
| GH41 | Salon sdn 4d | 3,367 | 7,268 | 15,023 |
| GH22 | Salon cpe | 3,262 | 7,134 | |
| GH45 | Salon wgn 5d 2S | 3,565 | 7,670 | 1,206 |
| GP41 | Medallion sdn 4d | 3,427 | 7,777 | 1,527 |
| GP22 | Medallion cpe | 3,317 | 7,645 | |
| **Mirada (wb 112.7)** | | | | |
| XS22 | htp cpe | 3,350 | 7,700 | 11,899 |
| **St. Regis (wb 118.5)** | | | | |
| EH42 | sdn 4d | 3,587 | 7,674 | 5,388 |

| 1981 Engines | bore × stroke | bhp | availability |
|---|---|---|---|
| I-4, 104.7 | 3.13 × 3.40 | 63 | S-Omni |
| I-4, 135.0 | 3.44 × 3.62 | 84 | S-Aries; O-Omni |
| I-4, 156.0 | 3.59 × 3.86 | 92 | O-Aries |
| I-6, 225.0 | 3.40 × 4.12 | 85 | S-Diplomat, Mirada, St. Regis |
| V-8, 318.0 | 3.91 × 3.31 | 130/165 | O-Dip, Mir, St. Reg |

## 1982

| Omni (wb 99.1; 024-96.6) | | Wght | Price | Prod |
|---|---|---|---|---|
| ZH44 | Custom htchbk sdn 5d | 2,175 | 5,927 | 14,466 |
| ZE44 | Miser htchbk sdn 5d | 2,110 | 5,499 | 16,105 |
| ZP44 | E-type 5d | 2,180 | 6,636 | 639 |
| ZH24 | 024 htchbk cpe 3d | 2,205 | 6,421 | 11,287 |
| ZE24 | Miser 024 htchbk cpe 3d | 2,180 | 5,799 | 14,947 |
| ZP24 | Charger 2.2 htchbk cpe 3d | 2,315 | 7,115 | 14,420 |
| **Aries (wb 99.9)** | | | | |
| DL41 | sdn 4d | 2,310 | 6,131 | 28,561 |
| DL21 | sdn 2d | 2,315 | 5,990 | 10,286 |
| DH41 | Custom sdn 4d | 2,320 | 7,053 | 19,438 |
| DH21 | Custom sdn 2d | 2,320 | 6,898 | 8,127 |
| DH45 | Custom wgn 5d | 2,395 | 7,334 | 26,233 |
| DP41 | SE sdn 4d | 2,385 | 7,736 | 4,269 |
| DP21 | SE sdn 2d | 2,365 | 7,575 | 1,374 |
| DP45 | SE wgn 5d | 2,470 | 8,101 | 6,375 |
| **400 (wb 99.9)** | | | | |
| VH41 | sdn 4d | 2,423 | 8,137 | 3,595 |
| VH22 | cpe 2d | 2,470 | 8,043 | 12,716 |
| VH27 | conv cpe | 2,485 | 12,300 | 5,541 |
| VP41 | LS sdn 4d | 2,438 | 8,402 | 2,870 |
| VP22 | LS cpe 2d | 2,475 | 8,308 | 6,727 |
| **Diplomat (wb 112.7)** | | | | |
| GL41 | Salon sdn 4d | 3,345 | 7,750 | 19,773 |

407

# Dodge

| Diplomat (wb 112.7) | | Wght | Price | Prod |
|---|---|---|---|---|
| GH41 | Medallion sdn 4d | 3,375 | 8,799 | 3,373 |
| **Mirada (wb 112.7)** | | | | |
| XS22 | htp cpe | 3,380 | 8,619 | 6,818 |

| 1982 Engines | bore × stroke | bhp | availability |
|---|---|---|---|
| I-4, 104.7 | 3.13 × 3.40 | 63 | S-Omni |
| I-4, 135.0 | 3.44 × 3.62 | 84 | S-Aries, 400; O-Omni |
| I-4, 156.0 | 3.59 × 3.86 | 92 | O-Aries, 400 |
| I-6, 225.0 | 3.40 × 4.12 | 90 | S-Diplomat, Mirada |
| V-8, 318.0 | 3.91 × 3.31 | 130/165 | O-Diplomat, Mirada |

## 1983

| Omni (wb 99.1) | | Wght | Price | Prod |
|---|---|---|---|---|
| ZE44 | htchbk sdn 5d | 2,093 | 5,841 | 33,264 |
| ZH44 | Custom htchbk sdn 5d | 2,124 | 6,071 | 9,290 |
| **Charger (wb 96.6)** | | | | |
| ZH24 | htchbk cpe 3d | 2,137 | 6,379 | 22,535 |
| ZP24 | 2.2 htchbk cpe 3d | 2,194 | 7,303 | 10,448 |
| ZS24 | Shelby htchbk cpe 3d | 2,330 | 8,290 | 8,251 |
| **Aries (wb 100.1)** | | | | |
| DL41 | sdn 4d | 2,263 | 6,718 | 51,783 |
| DL21 | sdn 2d | 2,257 | 6,577 | 14,218 |
| DH45 | Custom wgn 5d | 2,372 | 7,636 | 29,228 |
| DH41 | SE sdn 4d | 2,300 | 7,417 | 8,962 |
| DH21 | SE sdn 2d | 2,273 | 7,260 | 4,325 |
| DP45 | SE wgn 5d | 2,424 | 8,186 | 4,023 |
| **400 (wb 100.3)** | | | | |
| VP41 | sdn 4d | 2,482 | 8,490 | 9,560 |
| VP22 | cpe 2d | 2,404 | 8,014 | 11,504 |
| VP27 | conv cpe | 2,473 | 12,500 | 4,888 |
| **600 (wb 103.1)** | | | | |
| EH41 | sdn 4d | 2,524 | 8,841 | 21,065 |
| ES41 | ES sdn 4d | 2,504 | 9,372 | 12,423 |
| **Diplomat (wb 112.7)** | | | | |
| GL41 | Salon sdn 4d | 3,387 | 8,248 | 21,368 |
| GH41 | Medallion sdn 4d | 3,458 | 9,369 | 3,076 |
| **Mirada (wb 112.7)** | | | | |
| XS22 | htp cpe | 3,378 | 9,011 | 5,597 |

| 1983 Engines | bore × stroke | bhp | availability |
|---|---|---|---|
| I-4, 104.7 | 3.13 × 3.40 | 63 | S-Omni, Charger |
| I-4, 97.3 | 3.17 × 3.07 | 62 | S-late Omni, Charger |
| I-4, 135.0 | 3.44 × 3.62 | 94 | S-Chgr 2.2, Aries, 400, 600; O-Omni, Charger |
| I-4, 135.0 | 3.44 × 3.62 | 107 | S-Shelby Charger |
| I-4, 156.0 | 3.59 × 3.86 | 93 | O-Aries, 400, 600 |
| I-6, 225.0 | 3.40 × 4.12 | 90 | S-Diplomat, Mirada |
| V-8, 318.0 | 3.91 × 3.31 | 130 | O-Diplomat, Mirada |

## 1984

| Omni (wb 99.1) | | Wght | Price | Prod |
|---|---|---|---|---|
| ZE44 | htchbk sdn 5d | 2,181 | 5,830 | 54,584 |
| ZH44 | Custom htchbk sdn 5d | 2,249 | 6,148 | 13,486 |
| ZE44/AGBGLH | sdn 5d | — | 7,350 | — |
| **Charger (wb 96.6)** | | | | |
| ZH24 | htchbk cpe 3d | 2,222 | 6,494 | 34,763 |
| ZP24 | 2.2 htchbk cpe 3d | 2,360 | 7,288 | 11,949 |
| ZS24 | Shelby htchbk cpe 3d | 2,388 | 8,541 | 7,552 |
| **Daytona (wb 97.0)** | | | | |
| VH24 | htchbk cpe 3d | 2,528 | 8,308 | 21,916 |
| VS24 | Turbo htchbk cpe 3d | 2,596 | 10,227 | 27,431 |
| VS24/AGSTurbo Z htchbk cpe 3d | | 2,646 | 11,494 | — |
| **Aries (wb 100.3)** | | | | |
| DL41 | sdn 4d | 2,323 | 6,949 | 55,331 |
| DL21 | sdn 2d | 2,317 | 6,837 | 11,921 |
| DH45 | Custom wgn 5d | 2,432 | 7,736 | 31,421 |
| DH41 | SE sdn 4d | 2,360 | 7,589 | 12,314 |
| DH21 | SE sdn 2d | 2,333 | 7,463 | 4,231 |
| DP45 | SE wgn 5d | 2,484 | 8,195 | 4,814 |
| **600 (wb 100.3)** | | | | |
| VP22 | cpe 2d | 2,465 | 8,376 | 13,296 |
| VP27 | conv cpe | 2,533 | 10,595 | 10,960 |
| VP27/AGTTurbo conv cpe | | — | 12,895 | — |
| **600 sedan (wb 103.3)** | | | | |
| EH41 | sdn 4d | 2,564 | 8,903 | 28,646 |
| ES41 | ES sdn 4d | 2,564 | 9,525 | 8,735 |
| **Diplomat (wb 112.7)** | | | | |
| GI-41 | Salon sdn 4d | 3,454 | 9,180 | 16,261 |
| GP41 | SE sdn 4d | 3,584 | 9,828 | 5,902 |

| 1984 Engines | bore × stroke | bhp | availability |
|---|---|---|---|
| I-4, 97.3 | 3.17 × 3.07 | 64 | S-Omni, Charger |
| I-4, 135.0 | 3.44 × 3.62 | 96 | S-Chgr 2.2, Aries, 600 exc sdn; O-Omni, Charger |
| I-4, 135.0 | 3.44 × 3.62 | 99 | S-Daytona, 600 sdn |
| I-4, 135.0 | 3.44 × 3.62 | 110 | S-Shelby; O-Omni, Chgr |
| I-4T, 135.0 | 3.44 × 3.62 | 142 | S-Dayt turbo; O-Dayt, all 600 |
| I-4, 156.0 | 3.59 × 3.86 | 101 | O-Aries, all 600 |
| V-8, 318.0 | 3.91 × 3.31 | 130 | S-Diplomat |

## 1985

| Omni (wb 99.1) | | Wght | Price | Prod |
|---|---|---|---|---|
| LZE44 | htchbk sdn 5d | 2,174 | 5,977 | 54,229 |
| LZH44 | SE htchbk sdn 5d | 2,154 | 6,298 | 13,385 |
| LZE44/AGBGLH htchbk sdn 5d | | 2,222 | 7,620 | 6,513 |
| **Charger (wb 96.5)** | | | | |
| LZH24 | htchbk cpe 3d | 2,215 | 6,584 | 38,203 |
| LZP24 | 2.2 htchbk cpe 3d | 2,366 | 7,515 | 10,645 |
| LZS24 | Shelby htchbk cpe 3d | 2,457 | 9,553 | 7,709 |
| **Daytona (wb 97.0)** | | | | |
| GVH24 | htchbk cpe 3d | 2,611 | 8,505 | 29,987 |
| GVS24 | Turbo htchbk cpe 3d | 2,688 | 10,286 | 9,509 |
| GVS24/AGSTurbo Z htchbk cpe 3d | | 2,744 | 11,620 | 8,023 |
| **Aries (wb 100.3)** | | | | |
| KDL41 | sdn 4d | 2,393 | 7,039 | 39,580 |
| KDL21 | sdn 2d | 2,375 | 6,924 | 9,428 |
| KDM41 | SE sdn 4d | 2,424 | 7,439 | 23,920 |
| KDM21 | SE sdn 2d | 2,390 | 7,321 | 7,937 |
| KDM45 | SE wgn 5d | 2,514 | 7,909 | 22,953 |
| KDH41 | LE sdn 4d | 2,446 | 7,792 | 5,932 |
| KDH21 | LE sdn 2d | 2,414 | 7,659 | 3,706 |
| KDP45 | LE wgn 5d | 2,546 | 8,348 | 4,519 |
| **Lancer (wb 103.1)** | | | | |
| HDH44 | spt sdn 5d | 2,659 | 8,713 | 30,567 |
| HDS44 | ES sdn 5d | 2,726 | 9,690 | 15,286 |
| **600 (wb 100.3; sdn-103.3)** | | | | |
| KVP22 | cpe 2d | 2,539 | 9,060 | 12,670 |
| KVP27 | conv cpe | 2,601 | 10,889 | 8,188 |
| KVP27/AGTES Turbo conv cpe | | — | 13,995 | 5,621 |

# Dodge

| 600 (wb 100.3; sdn-103.3) | Wght | Price | Prod |
|---|---|---|---|
| EEH41 SE sdn 4d | 2,591 | 8,953 | 32,368 |
| **Diplomat (wb 112.7)** | | | |
| MGL41 Salon sdn 4d | 3,558 | 9,399 | 25,398 |
| MGP41 SE sdn 4d | 3,628 | 10,418 | 13,767 |

| 1985 Engines | bore × stroke | bhp | availability |
|---|---|---|---|
| I-4, 97.3 | 3.17 × 3.07 | 64 | S-Omni, Charger |
| I-4, 135.0 | 3.44 × 3.62 | 96 | S-Aries; O-Omni, Charger |
| I-4, 135.0 | 3.44 × 3.62 | 99 | S-Dayt, Lncr, 600; O-Aries |
| I-4, 135.0 | 3.44 × 3.62 | 110 | S-Omni GLH, Chgr 2.2; O-Omni, Charger |
| I-4T, 135.0 | 3.44 × 3.62 | 146 | S-Shelby Charger, Daytona Turbos, 600ES; O-Omni GLH, Dayt, Lancer, 600 |
| I-4, 156.0 | 3.59 × 3.86 | 101 | O-Aries, 600 |
| V-8, 318.0 | 3.91 × 3.31 | 140 | S-Diplomat |

## 1986

| Omni (wb 99.1) | Wght | Price | Prod |
|---|---|---|---|
| LZE44 htchbk sdn 5d | 2,154 | 6,209 | 61,812 |
| LZH44 SE htchbk sdn 5d | 2,174 | 6,558 | 8,139 |
| LZE44/AGBGLH htchbk sdn 5d | 2,341 | 7,918 | 3,629 |
| **Charger (wb 96.5)** | | | |
| LZH24 htchbk cpe 3d | 2,215 | 6,787 | 38,172 |
| LZP24 2.2 htchbk cpe 3d | 2,366 | 7,732 | 4,814 |
| LZS24 Shelby htchbk cpe 3d | 2,382 | 9,361 | 7,669 |
| **Daytona (wb 97.0)** | | | |
| GVH24 htchbk cpe 3d | 2,546 | 9,013 | 26,771 |
| GVS24 Turbo Z htchbk cpe 3d | — | 11,301 | 17,595 |
| **Aries (wb 100.3)** | | | |
| KDL41 sdn 4d | 2,402 | 7,301 | 14,445 |
| KDL21 sdn 2d | 2,395 | 7,184 | 2,437 |
| KDM41 SE sdn 4d | 2,429 | 7,759 | 40,254 |
| KDM21 SE sdn 2d | 2,412 | 7,639 | 9,084 |
| KDM45 SE wgn 5d | 2,513 | 8,186 | 17,757 |
| KDH41 LE sdn 4d | 2,444 | 8,207 | 5,638 |
| KDH21 LE sdn 2d | 2,427 | 8,087 | 2,475 |
| KDH45 LE wgn 5d | 2,549 | 8,936 | 5,278 |
| **Lancer (wb 103.1)** | | | |
| HDH44 htchbk spt sdn 5d | 2,650 | 9,426 | 34,009 |
| HDS44 htchbk ES sdn 5d | 2,702 | 10,332 | 17,888 |
| **600 (wb 100.3; sdn-103.3)** | | | |
| KVP22 cpe 2d | 2,523 | 9,577 | 11,714 |
| KVP27 conv cpe | 2,594 | 11,695 | 11,678 |
| KVP27/AGTES Turbo conv cpe | 2,648 | 14,856 | 4,759 |
| EEM41 sdn 4d | 2,593 | 9,370 | 16,253 |
| EEH41 SE sdn 4d | 2,593 | 10,028 | 15,291 |
| **Diplomat (wb 112.7)** | | | |
| MGL41 Salon sdn 4d | 3,555 | 10,086 | 15,469 |
| MGP41 SE sdn 4d | 3,624 | 11,166 | 11,484 |

| 1986 Engines | bore × stroke | bhp | availability |
|---|---|---|---|
| I-4, 97.3 | 3.17 × 3.07 | 64 | S-Omni, Charger |
| I-4, 135.0 | 3.44 × 3.62 | 96 | O-Omni, Charger |
| I-4, 135.0 | 3.44 × 3.62 | 97 | S-Ar, Dayt, Lncr, 600 |
| I-4, 135.0 | 3.44 × 3.62 | 110 | S-Omni GLH, Chgr 2.2; O-Omni, Chgr |
| I-4T, 135.0 | 3.44 × 3.62 | 146 | S-Shelby, Dayt Turbos 600ES; O-Omni GLH, Dayt, Lncr, 600 |
| I-4, 153.0 | 3.44 × 4.09 | 100 | O-Ar, Dayt, Lncr, 600 |
| V-8, 318.0 | 3.91 × 3.31 | 140 | S-Diplomat |

## 1987

| Omni (wb 99.1) | Wght | Price | Prod |
|---|---|---|---|
| LZE44 America htchbk sdn 5d | 2,237 | 5,499 | 66,907 |
| **Charger (wb 96.5)** | | | |
| LZH24 htchbk cpe 3d | 2,290 | 6,999 | 24,275 |
| LZS24 Shelby htchbk cpe 3d | 2,483 | 9,840 | 2,011 |
| **Daytona (wb 97.0)** | | | |
| GVH24 htchbk cpe 3d | 2,676 | 9,799 | 18,485 |
| GVP24 Pacifica htchbk cpe 3d | 2,862 | 13,912 | 7,467 |
| GVS24 Shelby Z htchbk cpe 3d | 2,812 | 12,749 | 7,152 |
| **Shadow (wb 97.0)** | | | |
| PDH44 htchbk sdn 5d | 2,494 | 7,699 | 37,559 |
| PDH24 htchbk sdn 3d | 2,459 | 7,499 | 38,497 |
| **Aries (wb 100.3)** | | | |
| KDL41 sdn 4d | 2,415 | 7,655 | 4,710 |
| KDM41 SE sdn 4d | 2,484 | 8,134 | 66,506 |
| KDL21 sdn 2d | 2,409 | 7,655 | 204 |
| KDM21 SE sdn 2d | 2,468 | 8,134 | 7,517 |
| KDM45 SE wgn 5d | 2,588 | 8,579 | 20,362 |
| **Lancer (wb 103.1)** | | | |
| HDH44 sdn 5d | 2,645 | 9,474 | 17,040 |
| HDS44 ES htchbk sdn 5d | 2,692 | 10,428 | 9,579 |
| **600 (wb 103.3)** | | | |
| EEM41 sdn 4d | 2,594 | 9,891 | 20,074 |
| EEH41 SE sdn 4d | 2,601 | 10,553 | 20,317 |
| **Diplomat (wb 112.6)** | | | |
| MGL41 Salon sdn 4d | 3,566 | 10,598 | 11,256 |
| MGP41 SE sdn 4d | 3,627 | 11,678 | 9,371 |

| 1987 Engines | bore × stroke | bhp | availability |
|---|---|---|---|
| I-4, 135.0 | 3.44 × 3.62 | 96 | S-Omni, Charger |
| I-4, 135.0 | 3.44 × 3.62 | 97 | S-Aries, Shadow, Lncr, 600 |
| I-4T, 135.0 | 3.44 × 3.62 | 146 | S (auto. trans.), Dayt Pacifica; O-Dayt, Shadow, Lncr, 600 |
| I-4T, 135.0 | 3.44 × 3.62 | 174 | S Shelby Z (man. trans.) |
| I-4, 153.0 | 3.44 × 4.09 | 100 | S-Dayt; O-Aries, Lancer, 600 |
| V-8, 318.0 | 3.91 × 3.31 | 140 | S-Diplomat |

## 1988

| Omni (wb 99.1) | Wght | Price | Prod |
|---|---|---|---|
| LZE44 America htchbk sdn 5d | 2,225 | 5,999 | 59,867 |
| **Daytona (wb 97.0)** | | | |
| GVH24 htchbk cpe 3d | 2,676 | 10,025 | 54,075 |
| GVP24 Pacifica htchbk cpe 3d | 2,862 | 14,513 | 4,752 |
| GVS24 Shelby Z htchbk cpe 3d | 2,812 | 13,394 | 7,580 |
| **Shadow (wb 97.0)** | | | |
| PDH44 htchbk sdn 5d | 2,544 | 8,075 | 55,857 |
| PDH24 htchbk sdn 3d | 2,513 | 7,875 | 36,452 |
| **Aries America (wb 100.3)** | | | |
| KDH41 sdn 4d | 2,485 | 6,995 | 85,613 |

# Dodge

| Aries America (wb 100.3) | Wght | Price | Prod |
|---|---|---|---|
| KDH21 sdn 2d | 2,459 | 6,995 | 6,578 |
| KDH45 wgn 5d | 2,537 | 7,695 | 19,172 |
| **Lancer (wb 103.1)** | | | |
| HDH44 htchbk sdn 5d | 2,646 | 10,482 | 6,580 |
| HDS44 ES htchbk sdn 5d | 2,702 | 12,715 | 2,484 |
| DS44/AFPShelby htchbk sdn 5d | — | — | 279 |
| **600 (wb 103.3)** | | | |
| EEM41 sdn 4d | 2,595 | 10,659 | 10,305 |
| EEH41 SE sdn 4d | 2,633 | 11,628 | 6,785 |
| **Dynasty (wb 104.3)** | | | |
| CDH41 sdn 4d | 2,956 | 11,666 | 26,653 |
| CDP41 LE sdn 4d | 2,966 | 12,226 | 28,897 |
| **Diplomat (wb 112.6)** | | | |
| MGE41 sdn 4d | 3,584 | 12,127 | 444 |
| MGL41 Salon sdn 4d | 3,567 | 11,407 | 12,992 |
| MGP41 SE sdn 4d | 3,634 | 14,221 | 5,737 |

| 1988 Engines | bore × stroke | bhp | availability |
|---|---|---|---|
| I-4, 135.0 | 3.44 × 3.62 | 93 | S-Omni, Aries, Shadow, Lncr, 600 |
| I-4T, 135.0 | 3.44 × 3.62 | 146 | S-Daytona Pacifica; O-Dayt, Shad, Lncr, 600 |
| I-4T, 135.0 | 3.44 × 3.62 | 174 | S-Dayt Shelby Z, Lncr Shelby |
| I-4, 153.0 | 3.44 × 4.09 | 96 | S-Dayt, Dynasty, Lancer ES; O-Aries, Shadow, Lncr, 600 |
| V-6, 181.4 | 3.59 × 2.99 | 136 | O-Dynasty |
| V-8, 318.0 | 3.91 × 3.31 | 140 | S-Diplomat |

## 1989

| Omni (wb 99.1) | Wght | Price | Prod |
|---|---|---|---|
| LZE44 America htchbk sdn 5d | 2,237 | 6,595 | 46,239 |
| **Daytona (wb 97.0)—80,878 built** | | | |
| GVL24 htchbk cpe 3d | 2,751 | 9,295 | — |
| GVH24 ES htchbk cpe 3d | 2,822 | 10,395 | — |
| GVS24 ES turbo cpe 3d | 2,936 | 11,995 | — |
| GVX24 Shelby htchbk cpe 3d | 2,951 | 13,295 | — |
| **Shadow (wb 97.0)—99,743 built** | | | |
| PDH44 htchbk sdn 5d | 2,558 | 8,595 | — |
| PDH24 htchbk cpe 3d | 2,520 | 8,395 | — |
| **Aries America (wb 100.3)—36,932 built** | | | |
| KDH41 sdn 4d | 2,323 | 7,595 | — |
| KDH21 sdn 2d | 2,317 | 7,595 | — |
| **Lancer (wb 103.1)—5,019 built** | | | |
| HDH44 spt sdn 5d | 2,646 | 11,195 | — |
| HDS44 ES sdn 5d | 2,702 | 13,695 | — |
| HDX44 Shelby sdn 5d | 2,838 | 17,395 | — |
| **Spirit (wb 103.3)—68,181 built** | | | |
| ADH41 sdn 4d | 2,765 | 10,485 | — |
| ADP41 ES sdn 4d | 2,842 | 13,145 | — |
| ADX41 LE sdn 4d | 2,901 | 11,845 | — |
| **Dynasty (wb 104.3)—137,718 built** | | | |
| CDH41 sdn 4d | 2,992 | 12,295 | — |
| CDP41 LE sdn 4d | 3,066 | 13,595 | — |
| **Diplomat (wb 112.7)—6,429 built** | | | |
| MGL41 Salon sdn 4d | 3,582 | 11,995 | — |
| MGP41 SE sdn 4d | 3,732 | 14,795 | — |

| 1989 Engines | bore × stroke | bhp | availability |
|---|---|---|---|
| I-4, 135.0 | 3.44 × 3.62 | 93 | S-Omni, Aries, Shdw, Lncr |
| I-4T, 135.0 | 3.44 × 3.62 | 174 | S-Dayt/Lncr Shelby |
| I-4, 153.0 | 3.44 × 4.09 | 100 | S-Dayt, Dynasty, Spirit; O-Aries, Shadow, Lancer |
| I-4T, 153.0 | 3.44 × 4.09 | 150 | S-Spirit ES, Lncr ES; O-Dayt, Lncr, Shadow ES, Sprt |
| V-6, 181.4 | 3.59 × 2.99 | 141 | S-Dyna LE; O-Dyna, Spirit ES |
| V-8, 318.0 | 3.91 × 3.31 | 140 | S-Diplomat |

## 1990

| Omni (wb 99.1) | Wght | Price | Prod |
|---|---|---|---|
| LZE44 htchbk sdn 5d | 2,296 | 6,995 | 16,733 |
| **Daytona (wb 97.0)—43,785 built** | | | |
| GVL24 htchbk cpe 3d | 2,751 | 9,795 | — |
| GVH24 ES htchbk cpe 3d | 2,822 | 10,995 | — |
| GVS24 ES turbo cpe 3d | 2,936 | 12,895 | — |
| GVX24 Shelby htchbk cpe 3d | 2,951 | 14,295 | — |
| **Shadow (wb 97.0)—93,660 built** | | | |
| PDH44 htchbk sdn 5d | 2,642 | 8,935 | — |
| PDH24 htchbk cpe 3d | 2,606 | 8,735 | — |
| **Spirit (wb 103.3)—99,319 built** | | | |
| ADH41 sdn 4d | 2,854 | 10,485 | — |
| ADP41 ES sdn 4d | — | 13,145 | — |
| ADX41 LE sdn 4d | — | 11,845 | — |
| **Dynasty (wb 104.3)—112,833 built** | | | |
| CDH41 sdn 4d | 2,992 | 12,295 | — |
| CDP41 LE sdn 4d | 3,066 | 14,395 | — |

| 1990 Engines | bore × stroke | bhp | availability |
|---|---|---|---|
| I-4, 135.0 | 3.44 × 3.62 | 93 | S-Shadow |
| I-4T, 135.0 | 3.44 × 3.62 | 174 | S-Dayt Shel; O-Shad |
| I-4, 153.0 | 3.44 × 4.09 | 100 | S-Dayt, Dynasty, Spirit; O-Shadow |
| I-4T, 153.0 | 3.44 × 4.09 | 150 | S-Spirit ES; O-Spirit, Shadow, Daytona |
| V-6, 181.4 | 3.59 × 2.99 | 141 | S-Dyna LE; O-Dyna, Spirit, Daytona |
| V-6, 201.5 | 3.66 × 3.19 | 147 | O-Dynasty |

## 1991

| Daytona (wb 97.0)—17,286 built | Wght | Price | Prod |
|---|---|---|---|
| htchbk cpe 3d | 2,777 | 10,500 | — |
| ES htchbk cpe 3d | — | 11,745 | — |
| IROC htchbk cpe 3d | — | 12,940 | — |
| **Shadow (wb 97.0)** | | | |
| America htchbk sdn 3d | 2,615 | 7,699 | ⎤ |
| Highline htchbk sdn 3d | — | 8,948 | 28,344 |
| ES htchbk sdn 3d | — | 10,424 | ⎦ |
| America htchbk sdn 5d | 2,652 | 7,999 | ⎤ |
| Highline htchbk sdn 5d | — | 9,248 | 33,339 |
| ES htchbk sdn 5d | — | 10,724 | ⎦ |
| Highline conv cpe 2d | 2,910 | 12,995 | ⎤ 19,528 |
| ES conv cpe 2d | — | 14,068 | ⎦ |
| **Spirit (wb 103.3)—94,895 built** | | | |
| sdn 4d | 2,801 | 10,976 | — |
| LE sdn 4d | — | 12,976 | — |
| ES sdn 4d | — | 13,760 | — |
| R/T sdn 4d | 3,060 | 17,871 | — |

# Dodge

| Dynasty (wb 104.3)—11,320 built | Wght | Price | Prod |
|---|---|---|---|
| CDH41 sdn 4d | 2,996 | 13,697 | — |
| CDP41 LS sdn 4d | — | 15,137 | — |

| 1991 Engines | bore × stroke | bhp | availability |
|---|---|---|---|
| I-4, 135.0 | 3.44 × 3.62 | 93 | S-Shadow (ohc) |
| I-4T, 135.0 | 3.44 × 3.62 | 224 | S-Spirit R/T (dohc) |
| I-4, 153.0 | 3.44 × 4.09 | 100 | S-Daytona, Spirit, Dynasty O-Shadow (ohc) |
| I-4T, 153.0 | 3.44 × 4.09 | 152 | O-Daytona, Shadow, Spirit |
| V-6, 181.4 | 3.59 × 2.99 | 141 | O-Daytona, Spirit, Dynasty (ohc) |
| V-6, 201.5 | 3.66 × 3.19 | 147 | O-Dynasty (ohv) |

## 1992

| Daytona (wb 97.2)—13,478 built | Wght | Price | Prod |
|---|---|---|---|
| htchbk cpe 3d | 2,779 | 10,469 | — |
| ES htchbk cpe 3d | — | 11,510 | — |
| IROC htchbk cpe 3d | — | 12,805 | — |
| IROC R/T htchbk cpe 3d | — | 19,185 | — |

| Shadow (wb 97.0) | Wght | Price | Prod |
|---|---|---|---|
| America htchbk sdn 3d | 2,615 | 7,869 | 45,786 |
| Highline htchbk sdn 3d | — | 9,246 | |
| ES htchbk sdn 3d | — | 10,912 | |
| America htchbk sdn 5d | 2,652 | 8,269 | 44,201 |
| Highline htchbk sdn 5d | — | 9,646 | |
| ES htchbk sdn 5d | — | 11,234 | |
| Highline conv cpe 2d | 2,910 | 13,457 | 3,152 |
| ES conv cpe 2d | — | 14,685 | |

| Spirit (wb 103.5)—89,697 built | Wght | Price | Prod |
|---|---|---|---|
| sdn 4d | 2,788 | 11,470 | — |
| LE sdn 4d | — | 13,530 | — |
| ES sdn 4d | — | 14,441 | — |
| R/T sdn 4d | 3,089 | 18,674 | — |

| Dynasty (wb 104.5)—96,403 built | Wght | Price | Prod |
|---|---|---|---|
| CDH41 sdn 4d | 3,026 | 14,277 | — |
| CHP41 LS sdn 4d | — | 15,767 | — |

| Viper (96.2) | Wght | Price | Prod |
|---|---|---|---|
| RT/10 conv rdstr 2d | 3476 | 50,000 | 162 |

| 1992 Engines | bore × stroke | bhp | availability |
|---|---|---|---|
| I-4, 135.0 | 3.44 × 3.62 | 93 | S-Shadow (ohc) |
| I-4T, 135.0 | 3.44 × 3.62 | 224 | S-Spirit R/T, Daytona IROC R/T (dohc) |
| I-4, 153.0 | 3.44 × 4.09 | 100 | S-Daytona, Spirit, Dynasty O-Shadow |
| I-4T, 153.0 | 3.44 × 4.09 | 152 | O-Daytona, Shadow, Spirit |
| V-6, 181.4 | 3.59 × 2.99 | 141 | O-Daytona, Shadow, Spirit, Dynasty (ohc) |
| V-6, 201.0 | 3.66 × 3.19 | 147 | O-Dynasty (ohv) |
| V-10, 488.0 | 4.00 × 3.88 | 400 | S-Viper |

## 1993

| Daytona (wb 97.2)—9,677 built | Wght | Price | Prod |
|---|---|---|---|
| htchbk cpe 3d | 2,779 | 10,874 | — |
| ES htchbk cpe 3d | 2,864 | 12,018 | — |
| IROC htchbk cpe 3d | 2,942 | 13,309 | — |
| IROC R/T htchbk cpe 3d | 2,942 | 19,185 | — |

| Shadow (wb 97.0) | Wght | Price | Prod |
|---|---|---|---|
| htchbk sdn 3d | 2,613 | 8,397 | 57,039 |
| ES htchbk sdn 3d | — | 9,804 | |
| htchbk sdn 5d | 2,884 | 8,797 | 52,498 |
| ES htchbk sdn 5d | — | 10,204 | |
| Highline conv cpe 2d | 2,910 | 14,028 | 6,307 |
| ES conv cpe 2d | — | 14,167 | |

| Spirit (wb 103.5)—90,607 built | Wght | Price | Prod |
|---|---|---|---|
| Highline sdn 4d | 2,788 | 11,941 | — |
| ES sdn 4d | — | 14,715 | — |

| Dynasty (wb 104.5)—65,805 built | Wght | Price | Prod |
|---|---|---|---|
| CDH41 sdn 4d | 2,971 | 14,736 | — |
| CDP41 LS sdn 4d | — | 16,267 | — |

| Intrepid (wb 113.0)—81,236 built | Wght | Price | Prod |
|---|---|---|---|
| HDH41 sdn 4d | 3,217 | 15,930 | — |
| HDP41 ES sdn 4d | 3,315 | 17,189 | — |

| Viper (96.2) | Wght | Price | Prod |
|---|---|---|---|
| RDS27 RT/10 conv rdstr 2d | 3,476 | 50,000 | 1,043 |

| 1993 Engines | bore × stroke | bhp | availability |
|---|---|---|---|
| I-4, 135.0 | 3.44 × 3.62 | 93 | S-Shadow (ohc) |
| I-4T, 135.0 | 3.44 × 3.62 | 224 | S-Daytona IROC R/T (dohc) |
| I-4, 153.0 | 3.44 × 4.09 | 100 | S-Daytona, Spirit, Dynasty O-Shadow |
| V-6, 181.4 | 3.59 × 2.99 | 141 | O-Daytona, Shadow, Spirit, Dynasty |
| V-6, 201.0 | 3.66 × 3.19 | 147 | O-Dynasty |
| V-6, 201.4 | 3.66 × 3.19 | 153 | S-Intrepid (ohv) |
| V-6, 214.7 | 3.78 × 3.19 | 214 | O-Intrepid (ohc) |
| V-10, 488.0 | 4.00 × 3.88 | 400 | S-Viper |

## 1994

| Shadow (wb 97.0) | Wght | Price | Prod |
|---|---|---|---|
| htchbk sdn 3d | 2,608 | 8,806 | 50,910 |
| ES htchbk sdn 3d | — | 10,252 | |
| htchbk sdn 5d | 2,643 | 9,206 | 46,953 |
| ES htchbk sdn 5d | — | 10,652 | |

| Spirit (wb 103.5) | Wght | Price | Prod |
|---|---|---|---|
| ADH41 sdn 4d | 2,824 | 12,470 | 82,613 |

| Intrepid (wb 113.0)—155,170 built | Wght | Price | Prod |
|---|---|---|---|
| HDH41 sdn 4d | 3,271 | 17,251 | — |
| HDP41 ES sdn 4d | 3,370 | 19,191 | — |

| Viper (96.2) | Wght | Price | Prod |
|---|---|---|---|
| RDS27 RT/10 conv rdstr 2d | 3,476 | 54,500 | 2,892 |

| 1994 Engines | bore × stroke | bhp | availability |
|---|---|---|---|
| I-4, 135.0 | 3.44 × 3.62 | 93 | S-Shadow |
| I-4, 153.0 | 3.44 × 4.09 | 100 | O-Shadow |
| I-4, 153.0 | 3.44 × 4.09 | 106 | S-Spirit |
| V-6, 181.4 | 3.59 × 2.99 | 142 | O-Shadow, Spirit (ohc) |
| V-6, 201.4 | 3.66 × 3.19 | 161 | S-Intrepid (ohv) |
| V-6, 214.7 | 3.78 × 3.19 | 214 | O-Intrepid (ohc) |
| V-10, 488.0 | 4.00 × 3.88 | 400 | S-Viper |

## 1995

| Neon (wb 104.0) | Wght | Price | Prod |
|---|---|---|---|
| LDL42 sdn 4d | 2,338 | 9,500 | 145,095 |
| LDH42 Highline sdn 4d | 2,405 | 11,240 | |

## Dodge

| Neon (wb 104.0) | Wght | Price | Prod |
|---|---|---|---|
| LDS42 Sport sdn 4d | 2,448 | 13,267 | |
| LDH22 Highline cpe 2d | — | 11,240 | ⎫ 33,808 |
| LDS22 Sport cpe 2d | — | 13,567 | ⎭ |
| **Avenger (wb 103.7)** | | | |
| JDH22 cpe 2d | 2,822 | 13,341 | ⎫ 32,966 |
| JDS22 ES cpe 2d | 3,084 | 17,191 | ⎭ |
| **Spirit (wb 103.5)** | | | |
| ADH41 sdn 4d | 2,863 | 14,323 | 28,412 |
| **Stratus (wb 108.0)** | | | |
| ADH41 sdn 4d | 2,937 | 13,965 | ⎫ 58,550 |
| ADP41 ES sdn 4d | 3,153 | 17,430 | ⎭ |
| **Intrepid (wb 113.0)** | | | |
| HDH41 sdn 4d | 3,310 | 17,974 | ⎫ 178,679 |
| HDP41 ES sdn 4d | 3,372 | 20,884 | ⎭ |
| **Viper (96.2)** | | | |
| RDS27 RT/10 conv rdstr 2d | 3,476 | 56,000 | 1577 |

| 1995 Engines | bore × stroke | bhp | availability |
|---|---|---|---|
| I-4, 121.8 | 3.44 × 3.27 | 132 | S-Neon, Strat (ohc) |
| I-4, 121.8 | 3.44 × 3.27 | 140 | S-Avenger (dohc) |
| I-4, 121.8 | 3.44 × 3.27 | 150 | O-Neon (dohc) |
| I-4, 148.2 | 3.44 × 3.98 | 150 | O-Stratus (dohc) |
| V-6, 152.3 | 3.29 × 2.99 | 155 | O-Avenger (ohc) |
| V-6, 152.3 | 3.29 × 2.99 | 164 | O-Stratus (ohc) |
| I-4, 153.0 | 3.44 × 4.09 | 100 | S-Spirit (ohc) |
| V-6, 181.4 | 3.59 × 2.99 | 142 | O-Spirit (ohc) |
| V-6, 201.4 | 3.66 × 3.19 | 161 | S-Intrepid (ohv) |
| V-6, 214.7 | 3.78 × 3.19 | 214 | O-Intrepid (ohc) |
| V-10, 488.0 | 4.00 × 3.88 | 400 | S-Viper |

### 1996

| Neon (wb 104.0) | Wght | Price | Prod |
|---|---|---|---|
| LDL22 cpe 2d | 2,384 | 9,495 | 34,641 |
| LDH22 Highline cpe 2d | 2,385 | 11,300 | |
| LDS22 Sport cpe 2d | 2,469 | 12,500 | |
| LDL42 sdn 4d | 2,343 | 9,995 | 96,702 |
| LDH42 Highline sdn 4d | 2,416 | 11,500 | |
| LDS42 Sport sdn 4d | 2,456 | 12,700 | |
| **Avenger (wb 103.7)** | | | |
| JDH22 cpe 2d | 2,879 | 14,040 | ⎫ 38,828 |
| JDS22 ES cpe 2d | 3,124 | 16,829 | ⎭ |
| **Stratus (wb 108.0)** | | | |
| ADH41 sdn 4d | 2,899 | 14,460 | ⎫ 98,929 |
| ADP41 ES sdn 4d | 3,117 | 16,110 | ⎭ |
| **Intrepid (wb 113.0)** | | | |
| HDH41 sdn 4d | 3,318 | 18,445 | ⎫ 145,167 |
| HDP41 ES sdn 4d | 3,415 | 22,260 | ⎭ |
| **Viper (wb 96.2)** | | | |
| RDS27 R/T10 conv rdster 2d | 3,445 | 58,600 | 1,234 |
| RDS29 GTS cpe 2d | 3,383 | 66,000 | — |

| 1996 Engines | bore × stroke | bhp | availability |
|---|---|---|---|
| I-4, 121.8 | 3.44 × 3.27 | 132 | S-Neon, Stratus |
| I-4, 121.8 | 3.44 × 3.27 | 140 | S-Avenger (dohc) |
| I-4, 121.8 | 3.44 × 3.27 | 150 | O-Neon (dohc) |
| I-4, 148.2 | 3.44 × 3.98 | 150 | O-Stratus |
| V-6, 152.3 | 3.29 × 2.99 | 163 | O-Avenger |
| V-6, 152.3 | 3.29 × 2.99 | 168 | O-Stratus |
| V-6, 201.5 | 3.66 × 3.19 | 161 | S-Intrepid |
| V-6, 214.7 | 3.78 × 3.19 | 214 | O-Intrepid |
| V-10, 488.0 | 4.00 × 3.88 | 415 | S-Viper |

### 1997

| Neon (wb 104.0) | Wght | Price | Prod |
|---|---|---|---|
| LDL22 cpe 2d | 2,389 | 10,395 | ⎫ 29,551 |
| LDH22 Highline cpe 2d | 2,416 | 12,470 | ⎭ |
| LDL42 sdn 4d | 2,399 | 10,595 | ⎫ 85,559 |
| LDH42 Highline sdn 4d | 2,459 | 12,670 | ⎭ |
| **Avenger (wb 103.7)** | | | |
| JDH22 cpe 2d | 2,822 | 14,620 | ⎫ 32,638 |
| JDS22 ES cpe 2d | 3,084 | 17,490 | ⎭ |
| **Stratus (wb 108.0)** | | | |
| ADH41 sdn 4d | 2,911 | 14,960 | ⎫ 96,757 |
| ADP41 ES sdn 4d | 2,968 | 16,665 | ⎭ |
| **Intrepid (wb 113.0)** | | | |
| HDH41 sdn 4d | 3,349 | 19,405 | ⎫ 151,404 |
| HDP41 ES sdn 4d | 3,440 | 22,910 | ⎭ |
| **Viper (wb 96.2)** | | | |
| RDS27 R/T10 conv rdster 2d | 3,319 | 58,600 | — |
| RDS29 GTS cpe 2d | 3,383 | 66,000 | 954 |

| 1997 Engines | bore × stroke | bhp | availability |
|---|---|---|---|
| I-4, 121.8 | 3.44 × 3.27 | 132 | S-Neon, Stratus |
| I-4, 121.8 | 3.44 × 3.27 | 140 | S-Avenger (dohc) |
| I-4, 121.8 | 3.44 × 3.27 | 150 | O-Neon (dohc) |
| I-4, 148.2 | 3.44 × 3.98 | 150 | O-Stratus |
| V-6, 152.3 | 3.29 × 2.99 | 163 | O-Avenger |
| V-6, 152.3 | 3.29 × 2.99 | 168 | O-Stratus |
| V-6, 201.5 | 3.66 × 3.19 | 161 | S-Intrepid |
| V-6, 214.7 | 3.78 × 3.19 | 214 | O-Intrepid |
| V-10, 488.0 | 4.00 × 3.88 | 415 | S-Viper |

### 1998

| Neon (wb 104.0) | Wght | Price | Prod |
|---|---|---|---|
| LDH22 cpe 2d | 2,470 | 11,155 | 29,886 |
| LDL22 Sport cpe 2d | — | 12,980 | |
| 22 R/T cpe 2d | — | 13,895 | |
| LDH42 sdn 4d | 2,507 | 11,355 | 99,989 |
| LDL42 Sport sdn 4d | — | 13,160 | |
| 42 R/T sdn 4d | — | 14,095 | |
| **Avenger (wb 103.7)** | | | |
| JDH22 cpe 2d | 2,888 | 14,930 | ⎫ 29,603 |
| JDS22 ES cpe 2d | 2,989 | 17,310 | ⎭ |
| **Stratus (wb 108.0)** | | | |
| ADH41 sdn 4d | 2,919 | 14,840 | ⎫ 107,136 |
| ADP41 ES sdn 4d | 2,958 | 17,665 | ⎭ |
| **Intrepid (wb 113.0)** | | | |
| HDH41 sdn 4d | 3,422 | 19,685 | ⎫ 70,266 |
| HDP41 ES sdn 4d | 3,517 | 22,465 | ⎭ |
| **Viper (wb 96.2)** | | | |
| RDS27 R/T10 conv rdster 2d | 3,319 | 64,000 | 74 |
| RDS29 GTS cpe 2d | 3,383 | 66,500 | 848 |

| 1998 Engines | bore × stroke | bhp | availability |
|---|---|---|---|
| I-4, 121.8 | 3.44 × 3.27 | 132 | S-Neon, Stratus |
| I-4, 121.8 | 3.44 × 3.27 | 140 | S-Avenger (dohc) |
| I-4, 121.8 | 3.44 × 3.27 | 150 | O-Neon (dohc) |
| I-4, 148.2 | 3.44 × 3.98 | 150 | O-Stratus |
| V-6, 152.3 | 3.29 × 2.99 | 163 | O-Avenger |
| V-6, 152.3 | 3.29 × 2.99 | 168 | O-Stratus |
| V-6, 167.0 | 3.38 × 3.09 | 200 | S-Intrepid |
| V-6, 197.0 | 3.62 × 3.19 | 225 | O-Intrepid |
| V-10, 488.0 | 4.00 × 3.88 | 450 | S-Viper |

## 1999

| Neon (wb 104.0) 165,229—built | Wght | Price | Prod* |
|---|---|---|---|
| LDH22  cpe 2d | 2,470 | 10,550 | |
| LDL22  Sport cpe 2d | — | 11,225 | |
| 22  R/T cpe 2d | — | 13,365 | |
| LDH42  sdn 4d | 2,507 | 10,750 | |
| LDL42  Sport sdn 4d | — | 11,425 | |
| 42  R/T sdn 4d | — | 13,565 | |

| Avenger (wb 103.7)—15,801 built | Wght | Price | Prod* |
|---|---|---|---|
| JDH22  cpe 2d | 2,897 | 15,370 | |
| JDS22  ES cpe 2d | 2,996 | 17,465 | |

| Stratus (wb 108.0)—100,196 built | Wght | Price | Prod* |
|---|---|---|---|
| ADH41  sdn 4d | 3,007 | 15,140 | |
| ADP41  ES sdn 4d | 3,169 | 18,960 | |

| Intrepid (wb 113.0)—174,607 built | Wght | Price | Prod* |
|---|---|---|---|
| HDH41  sdn 4d | 3,423 | 19,890 | |
| HDP41  ES sdn 4d | 3,518 | 22,640 | |

| Viper (wb 96.2)—1,600 built | Wght | Price | Prod* |
|---|---|---|---|
| RDS27  R/T10 conv rdster 2d | 3,319 | 65,725 | |
| RDS29  GTS cpe 2d | 3,383 | 68,225 | |

| 1999 Engines | bore × stroke | bhp | availability |
|---|---|---|---|
| I-4, 121.8 | 3.44 × 3.27 | 132 | S-Neon, Stratus |
| I-4, 121.8 | 3.44 × 3.27 | 140 | S-Avenger (dohc) |
| I-4, 121.8 | 3.44 × 3.27 | 150 | S-Neon (dohc) |
| I-4, 148.2 | 3.44 × 3.98 | 150 | O-Stratus |
| V-6, 152.3 | 3.29 × 2.99 | 163 | O-Avenger |
| V-6, 152.3 | 3.29 × 2.99 | 168 | O-Stratus |
| V-6, 167.0 | 3.38 × 3.09 | 200 | S-Intrepid |
| V-6, 197.0 | 3.62 × 3.19 | 225 | O-Intrepid |
| V-10, 488.0 | 4.00 × 3.88 | 450 | S-Viper |

*Calendar year.

## 2000

| Neon (wb 105.0) | Wght | Price | Prod* |
|---|---|---|---|
| LDH41  sdn 4d | 2,559 | 12,460 | 179,084 |

| Avenger (wb 103.7) | Wght | Price | Prod* |
|---|---|---|---|
| JDH22  cpe 2d | 3,137 | 18,970 | — |
| JDS22  ES cpe 2d | 3,172 | 21,215 | — |

| Stratus (wb 108.0) | Wght | Price | Prod* |
|---|---|---|---|
| ADH41  SE sdn 4d | 2,940 | 15,930 | 117,178 |
| ADP41  ES sdn 4d | 3,058 | 19,830 | |

| Intrepid (wb 113.0) | Wght | Price | Prod* |
|---|---|---|---|
| HDH41  sdn 4d | 3,471 | 20,545 | 161,599 |
| HDP41  ES sdn 4d | 3,489 | 22,235 | |
| HDX41  R/T sdn 4d | 3,511 | 24,435 | |

| Viper (wb 96.2) | Wght | Price | Prod* |
|---|---|---|---|
| RDS27  R/T10 conv rdster 2d | 3,440 | 67,225 | 1,726 |
| RDS29  GTS cpe 2d | 3,460 | 69,725 | |

| 2000 Engines | bore × stroke | bhp | availability |
|---|---|---|---|
| I-4, 121.8 | 3.44 × 3.27 | 132 | S-Neon, Stratus |
| I-4, 148.2 | 3.44 × 3.98 | 150 | O-Stratus |
| V-6, 152.3 | 3.29 × 2.99 | 163 | S-Avenger |
| V-6, 152.3 | 3.29 × 2.99 | 168 | O-Stratus |
| V-6, 167.0 | 3.38 × 3.09 | 200 | S-Intrepid |
| V-6, 197.0 | 3.62 × 3.19 | 225 | O-Intrepid |
| V-6, 215.0 | 3.78 × 3.19 | 242 | O-Intrepid |
| V-10, 488.0 | 4.00 × 3.88 | 450 | S-Viper |

*Calendar year production.

## 2001

| Neon (wb 105.0) | Wght | Price | Prod* |
|---|---|---|---|
| LDH41  sdn 4d | 2,585 | 12,715 | 145,718 |

| Stratus (wb cpe 103.7, sdn 108.0) | Wght | Price | Prod* |
|---|---|---|---|
| TDH22  SE cpe 2d | 3,012 | 17,810 | 118,871 |
| TDS22  R/T cpe 2d | 3,188 | 20,705 | |
| RDH41  SE sdn 4d | 3,226 | 17,800 | |
| RDP41  ES sdn 4d | 3,297 | 20,435 | |

| Intrepid (wb 113.0) | Wght | Price | Prod* |
|---|---|---|---|
| HDH41  sdn 4d | 3,471 | 20,910 | 120,786 |
| HDP41  ES sdn 4d | 3,493 | 22,605 | |
| HDX41  R/T sdn 4d | 3,563 | 24,975 | |

| Viper (wb 96.2) | Wght | Price | Prod* |
|---|---|---|---|
| RDS27  R/T10 conv rdster 2d | — | 69,225 | 1,887 |
| RDS29  GTS cpe 2d | 3,460 | 72,225 | |

| 2001 Engines | bore × stroke | bhp | availability |
|---|---|---|---|
| I-4, 121.8 | 3.44 × 3.27 | 132 | S-Neon |
| I-4, 121.8 | 3.44 × 3.27 | 150 | O-Neon |
| I-4, 143.4 | 3.41 × 3.94 | 147 | S-Stratus cpe |
| I-4, 148.2 | 3.44 × 3.98 | 150 | S-Stratus sdn |
| V-6, 167.0 | 3.38 × 3.09 | 200 | S-Intrepid, O-Stratus |
| V-6, 181.4 | 3.59 × 2.99 | 200 | O-Stratus cpe |
| V-6, 197.0 | 3.62 × 3.19 | 225 | O-Intrepid |
| V-6, 215.0 | 3.78 × 3.19 | 242 | O-Intrepid |
| V-10, 488.0 | 4.00 × 3.88 | 450 | S-Viper |

*Calendar year production.

## 2002

| Neon (wb 105.0) | Wght | Price | Prod |
|---|---|---|---|
| LDL41  sdn 4d | 2,604 | 12,240 | — |
| LDS41  ACR sdn 4d | 2,566 | 14,305 | — |
| LDH41  SE sdn 4d | 2,645 | 14,015 | — |
| LDP41  ES sdn 4d | 2,662 | 14,545 | — |
| LDX41  R/T sdn 4d | 2,643 | 16,190 | — |

| Stratus (wb cpe 103.7, sdn 108.0) | Wght | Price | Prod |
|---|---|---|---|
| TDH22  SE cpe 2d | 2,949 | 17,920 | — |
| TDS22  R/T cpe 2d | 3,100 | 20,940 | — |
| RDH41  SE sdn 4d | 3,114 | 17,400 | — |
| RDH41  SE Plus sdn 4d | 3,136 | 18,845 | — |
| RDP41  ES sdn 4d | 3,189 | 20,660 | — |
| RDX41  R/T sdn 4d | 3,201 | 21,400 | — |

| Intrepid (wb 113.0) | Wght | Price | Prod |
|---|---|---|---|
| HDH41  sdn 4d | 3,373 | 20,370 | — |
| HDP41  ES sdn 4d | 3,418 | 22,530 | — |
| HDX41  R/T sdn 4d | 3,471 | 26,615 | — |

| Viper (wb 96.2) | Wght | Price | Prod |
|---|---|---|---|
| RDS27  R/T10 conv rdster 2d | 3,340 | 71,725 | — |
| RDS29  GTS cpe 2d | 3,381 | 72,225 | — |

| 2002 Engines | bore × stroke | bhp | availability |
|---|---|---|---|
| I-4, 121.8 | 3.44 × 3.27 | 132 | S-Neon |
| I-4, 121.8 | 3.44 × 3.27 | 150 | O-Neon |
| I-4, 143.4 | 3.41 × 3.94 | 147 | S-Stratus cpe |
| I-4, 148.2 | 3.44 × 3.98 | 150 | S-Stratus sdn |
| V-6, 167.0 | 3.38 × 3.09 | 200 | S-Intrepid, O-Stratus |
| V-6, 181.4 | 3.59 × 2.99 | 200 | O-Stratus cpe |
| V-6, 197.0 | 3.62 × 3.19 | 234 | O-Intrepid |
| V-6, 215.0 | 3.78 × 3.19 | 244 | O-Intrepid |
| V-10, 488.0 | 4.00 × 3.88 | 450 | S-Viper |

Note: Mitsubishi-built captive imports such as the Dodge Colt, Dodge Challenger, and Dodge Stealth, as well as the AMC/Renault-based Dodge Monaco are not included in the above tables.

# Duesenberg

Fred and August Duesenberg built what many still consider the finest American automobiles of all time. Their great skills were evident early on. After the Duesenberg family emigrated from Germany to Iowa in the late 1800s, a twenty-something Fred built racing bicycles renowned for precision craftsmanship. The brothers then moved on to Des Moines and automobiles, where they designed the 1904 Mason, named for their backer. By 1912, they were putting together impressive engines for Mason's competition cars. The following year, they formed Duesenberg Motor Company to build both marine engines and racing cars bearing their name.

In 1917, the brothers set up in a larger plant at Elizabeth, New Jersey, to turn out aircraft and tractor engines as well. But this business was soon overshadowed by new triumphs in automobile racing. In 1919, a special 16-cylinder Duesenberg engine pushed a Land Speed Record car to 158 mph on the sands at Daytona Beach, Florida—astounding for the day. The following year, the brothers built a Bugatti-inspired 180-cubic-inch straight-eight with single overhead camshaft and three valves per cylinder. In 1921, this engine powered the only American car ever to win the French Grand Prix. Duesenberg-powered racers soon came to rival the great racing Millers at Indianapolis, winning the annual 500-miler no less than three times before 1930.

With their vast experience and growing reputation in racing, the Duesenbergs decided to move to Indianapolis and build a road car. Designated Model A, it appeared in late 1921 at the princely price of $6500. A genuine result of lessons learned on the track, it carried a potent 259.6-cid overhead-valve straight-eight that could deliver up to 85 mph. It also boasted a first among American cars: four-wheel hydraulic brakes, a system Fred had devised for racing as early as 1914.

Though brilliantly engineered and fastidiously crafted, the Model A was no style-setter. Nor were the brothers very good businessmen. Thus, after selling fewer than 500 cars through 1926, they sold Duesenberg Motors to the brash Errett Lobban Cord, who also gained control of Auburn that year. Fred and Augie stayed on, however, and in 1927 they built a dozen or so Model A derivatives called Model X. But this was only a stopgap. E.L. Cord wanted something far more exotic.

He got it in the Duesenberg Model J, introduced to universal applause in December 1928. With characteristic immodesty, Cord proclaimed it "the world's finest motor car." And by most any measurement it was, the product of Cord's money and Fred's genius.

Any discussion of Duesenbergs invariably leads to engines and horsepower. The Model J arrived with a 420-cid straight-eight built by Lycoming to Fred's design. Horsepower was advertised as 265, mind-boggling for the time—easily over twice the power of the industry's previous best, Chrysler. Doubters have since argued that the actual figure was closer to 200, but there's evidence the factory didn't exaggerate. Though the stock engine had only 5.2:1 compression, a modified unit with 8:1 ratio allegedly showed 390 horsepower. There was also a fabled Lycoming chart listing a reject Model J engine with 208 horsepower at 3500 rpm, and the late John R. Bond, founder of *Road & Track*, projected 245-250 at the maximum 4250 rpm. So the odds are that production Model Js had at least 250, if not more.

But forget horsepower and consider some of the other specifications. In a day when side valves were usual and overhead valves "modern," the J had overhead camshafts—and not one but two. What's more, they were driven by hefty chains to operate not two but four valves per cylinder—32 in all. The engine itself was enameled in bright green, and fittings were finished in nickel, chrome, or stainless steel. Standard wheelbase was no less than 142.5 inches. Frame rails were a massive 8.5 inches deep and a quarter-inch thick. Brakes were oversized and hydraulic (vacuum-assisted after 1930). Use of aluminum alloy was extensive: in engine, dash, steering column, differential and flywheel housings, crankcase, timing-chain cover, water pump, intake manifold, brake shoes, even the gas tank. So despite their massive size, Model Js didn't weigh much over 5200 pounds. They could thus do a staggering 89 mph in second gear and 112-116 in High.

Interiors were opulent but functional. Instruments were the most numerous yet seen in an automobile: the usual speedometer (calibrated to 150 mph), ammeter, and water-temp and oil-pressure gauges, plus tachometer, brake-pressure gauge, split-second stopwatch, and altimeter/barometer. Warning lights reminded you to add chassis oil (the chassis lubricated itself every 75 miles), change engine oil, or replenish battery water. But all this was only typical of Fred Duesenberg's dedication to excellence—a passion that his cars be superior in every way.

**1930 Model J Sport Berline by Murphy**

**Model J Convertible Victoria (Greta Garbo's car)**

# Duesenberg

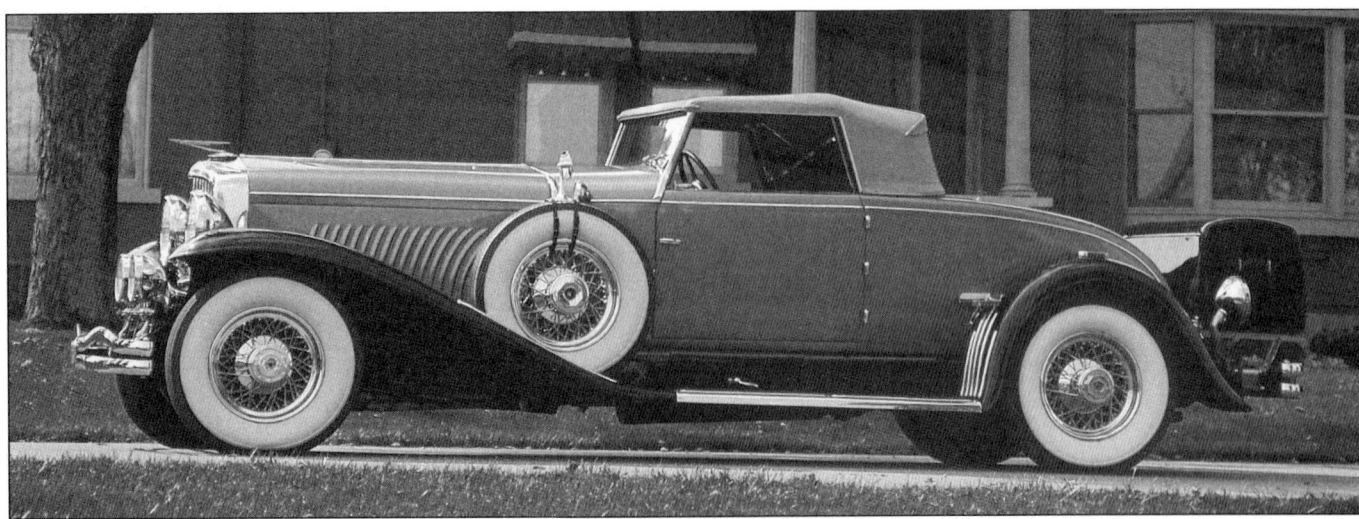

**1930 Model J roadster**

Model J prices have long generated much confusion. Of course, you bought not a finished car but a bare chassis, which listed for a stupendous $8500 in 1929-30, $9500 thereafter. E.L. Cord was aiming only at those wealthy enough to afford such prices—and the lofty extra expense of bodywork custom-designed to presumably discriminating individual tastes. Though standard "factory" styles were announced as low as $2500, the least-costly coupe body, by Murphy of Pasadena, seems to have run at least $3500. Most Model Js originally sold for under $17,000 complete. A few cost up to $20,000, a handful as much as $25,000. In 1929, that was equal to 50 Ford Model As.

Bodies were as regal as the Model J's drivetrain. These were, after all, grand luxe carriages, so only the finest woods, fabrics, and leathers were used. Vanity cases, radios, bars, and rear instrument panels were common owner-specified features. Less common was the town car upholstered in silk and given ebony, silver, and ivory fittings. Another car reportedly got solid-gold hardware and mosaic-wood inlays for the rear compartment. So despite its astonishing performance, the Model J was primarily a super-luxury conveyance able to run in eerie silence, as customers demanded.

And who were those demanding customers? Well, only 470 chassis and 480 engines were built between 1929 and 1936, so the clientele was, at least, exclusive. Some ads emphasized the fact. These contained not a word of hype, nor specifications—not even a picture of the car. Instead, there might be a yachtsman at the helm battling what looked like a 40-knot gale, or a well-dressed tycoon relaxing in a library worthy of a university. Regardless, there was but one line of type: "He Drives a Duesenberg." Not that the ads were chauvinistic. One showed an elegantly attired woman talking to her hat-in-hand gardener in front of an estate that would shame Versailles. Naturally, the

**1935 Model SJ speedster by J. Gurney Nutting**

415

# Duesenberg

**1936 SSJ roadster**

headline declared, "She Drives a Duesenberg."

If the J was imposing, the supercharged SJ was awesome. Only 36 were built, all from 1932 to '35, with chassis priced at a prodigious $11,750. Because the centrifugal blower delivered a five-psi boost at 4000 rpm, conrods were switched from aluminum alloy to sturdier tube-steel types. Early SJs developed no less than 320 horsepower, but Augie Duesenberg wanted more, so he half-heartedly tried a set of "ram's horn" manifolds and was amazed to see 400 horsepower on the dynamometer.

SJ performance is well-documented. A stock example could reach 104 mph in second and top 140. In late 1934, the famed Ab Jenkins drove a lightweight roadster on the Bonneville Salt Flats in Utah for 24 hours; despite no mechanical alterations, the car averaged 135 mph. Jenkins also ran 152 mph for one full hour and clocked one lap at 160! To put it mildly, the SJ was simply incredible.

Yet besides power and luxury, these Duesenbergs had surprising dynamic balance, without the heaviness of so many high-priced contemporaries. Model Js weren't "trucky," did not steer like tanks, and didn't demand huge leg muscles to operate their clutches or brakes. They did understeer, but this was easily checked by exquisitely accurate steering. A wide-open SJ with exhaust cut-out throbbed more than extroverts could endure, but with a closed exhaust cut-out it was little louder than a healthy Cadillac Sixteen.

Only two Model Js could truthfully be called "sports cars," a pair of specials unofficially titled SSJ. Both were built by the Cord-owned Union City Body Company, usually known as La Grande, on "short" 125-inch wheelbases. Both were first driven by movie stars. The first was owned by Gary Cooper. The second was loaned to Clark Gable as a demonstrator, but was not purchased by Gable. Both cars survive today, though as museum pieces, and there's still no definitive information on their performance. But they must have been shattering, what with relatively lean bodies and chassis 17 inches shorter than standard.

Another Model J offshoot was the JN—introduced in 1935. An attempt to give a more-modern look to an aging design, the JN was equipped with smaller 17-inch-diameter wheels (versus 19 inches), skirted fenders, bullet-shaped taillights, and bodies set on the frame rails for a lower look. Supercharged JNs gained the logical SJN designation. But again, confusion reigns. Blowers were later removed from some SJs, while others were added to originally unblown models. Then there's the longtime misconception that any car with pipes snaking out from under its hood has to be supercharged. Like Auburn, Duesenberg built cars with beautiful plumbing outside, but not always connected to a supercharger inside.

Under E.L. Cord, the company wasn't necessarily supposed to make a profit—just magnificent, cost-no-object cars as the flagships of Cord's industrial empire. The plan was for Duesenberg to sell a lot of 500 cars and come out with a new design. The Depression stretched out the time to sell that 500 cars. Cord's empire collapsed in 1937 before a new design was needed.

Sadly, Fred Duesenberg didn't live that long; he had been killed five years earlier in an auto accident—ironically, behind the wheel of an SJ. Brother August continued working, but failed with his plan to revive the marque in 1947. Several subsequent revival attempts proved equally fruitless. Among the more notable was a "modern" Duesenberg sedan floated by Fred's son "Fritz" in 1966 and an abortive 1980 Cadillac-based sedan cooked up by two of the brothers' nephews. There have also been numerous postwar replicas of original models ranging from splendid to schlocky.

But none of these efforts had the heart and soul of Fred himself. As the late Ken Purdy, pioneer automotive journalist, once wrote: "[Fred Duesenberg] died content.... [He] had done what is given few men to do ... chosen a good course and held unswervingly to it.... With his mind and his two good hands he created something new and good and, in its way, immortal. And the creator is, when all is said and done, the most fortunate of men."

# Eagle

Symbolizing power and nobility since Roman times, the name of America's national bird has been used over the years on products ranging from pencils to potato chips—and cars, of course. In fact, no fewer than six different automakers operated under the Eagle flag before World War I, four in the U.S. alone. Durant Motors produced its own Eagle in 1923-24, and Chevrolet used the name for its deluxe models of 1933. In the late '60s, Eagle was a natural choice for the competition cars built by the All-American Racers firm of driving legend Dan Gurney.

As a make, however, the only Eagle pertinent to this book is the one established by Chrysler Corporation from the remains of American Motors Corporation. Chrysler bought AMC from Renault of France in 1987, mainly to gain the lucrative Jeep franchise. But it also inherited the rights to use the Eagle name on cars, which had descended to AMC through a series of mergers and takeovers. This line of succession began with Jeep-builder Willys and its Aero-Eagle passenger cars of 1952-54. Willys (and Jeep) were then bought by Kaiser (*see entry*), which evolved into the Kaiser-Jeep Corporation acquired by AMC in 1970. Later, AMC briefly sold a Jeep Eagle, a fancy CJ-7, then put the Eagle name on its new 1980 line of four-wheel-drive passenger cars (*see* AMC).

Besides this name, Chrysler also inherited AMC's dealer body—which posed a problem. Those dealers were used to selling cars as well as Jeeps, and most still needed cars to sustain their business despite rising Jeep sales. Accordingly, most AMC operations—dealers included—were rolled into a new third Chrysler division called Jeep-Eagle, with Eagle now a full-fledged car make. To avoid "cannibalizing" sales from Dodge and Chrysler-Plymouth, Eagle was to be an upscale brand aimed at the fast-growing import market, where it would presumably win customers from the likes of Toyota, Honda, and Nissan.

Amid grand predictions for early success, Jeep-Eagle opened its doors for model-year '88. There was no question of continuing the outmoded AMC Eagles (which died early in the model year), nor the small, problematic Renault Alliance and Encore that AMC had built in Kenosha since 1983. That left just two remnants of the former Renault regime: the midsize V-6 Premier and the compact four-cylinder Medallion. Both were front-drive Renault designs like Alliance/Encore, but had been rushed to the U.S. just before the Chrysler buyout in a last-ditch effort to reverse sagging AMC sales. Medallion was a French import, basically a "federalized" Renault 21. Premier was a Canadian-built notchback based on the European Renault 30, complete with surprisingly dull styling by Giugiaro of Italy.

Both these cars became 1988 Eagles by the mere substitution of a new (and rather handsome) badge, but they sold no better as such, being conventional for Renaults but still too quirky for most Americans. Workmanship was also wanting, especially on the Medallion, which made a fast exit after 1989. Premier lasted through 1992, but only because Renault insisted that Chrysler keep building the car after taking over AMC. Chrysler tried hard to satisfy this condition, but it was a tough job, and Premier production peaked in calendar '88 at some 59,000 units. Sales then went fast downhill despite the 1990 addition of a Dodge duplicate reviving the Monaco name.

Drawing a tighter bead on "import intenders," Chrysler shifted Eagle to contemporary designs from Japanese partner Mitsubishi. All were "badge-engineered" front-drivers, and all but one were built in Japan—namely the subcompact Summit sedans sold from 1989 (cloned from the Mitsubishi Mirage) and the short-lived early-'90s "mini-minivan" Summit wagon (based on Mitsu's Expo LRV). The one "domestic" in this flock was the sharp Talon sports coupe, which bowed in early 1989 as a spin-off of the new 1990 Mitsubishi Eclipse and Plymouth Laser. All three versions were built in Illinois at the new Diamond-Star Motors plant that Chrysler and Mitsubishi had just set up as a 50/50 joint venture. But though Talon was an enthusiast's delight in top-line all-wheel-drive turbocharged form, it was really a Japanese car and thus another Eagle beyond our scope.

A true American Eagle finally appeared in the new-for-'93 Vision. Though this, too, was built in Canada, it was designed in Detroit as one of the "cab-forward" LH sedans setting a bold new direction for Chrysler styling. Befitting Eagle's mission, Vision was conceived as more "European" than the Chrysler Concorde and Dodge Intrepid, but in the way of corporate cousins it achieved this largely through appropriate styling details and features. Like Intrepid, Vision bowed in regular and premium models, respectively labeled ESi (3.3-liter pushrod V-6) and TSi (twincam 3.5 V-6).

Far more than most home-grown four-doors, Vision was a credible Euro-style sports sedan, though it was no BMW. At best, performance was brisk rather than thrilling, but handling was crisp and responsive thanks to the wide-stance LH chassis with all-independent suspension. The TSi even boasted standard all-disc antilock brakes and, from 1994, speed-variable power steering. Vision also had the appealingly swoopy cab-forward shape that combined with a long 113-inch wheelbase to provide unusually spacious seating for five. Road noise was annoyingly high and some interior trim looked none too classy. Overall though, Vision was an impressive package, earning Consumer Guide® "Best Buy" honors (along with its LH stablemates).

Unfortunately for product planners, Vision sales were disappointingly modest, running a poor third to Concorde on only 30-40 percent of Intrepid's volume. Production was around

**1992 Premier LX four-door sedan**

**1995 Vision TSi four-door sedan**

# Eagle

30,000 for model-year '93 and stubbornly stuck to that level through '95. Price was a likely factor in this lackluster performance. Though Vision was carefully pitched between its LH sisters, Eagle dealers complained it was tough to sell because customers thought it overpriced. Chrysler countered that Visions came with more standard equipment than comparable Intrepids and Concordes, and urged dealers to make sure customers understood that. If buyers did understand, they didn't show it, for production of the 1996-97 models sagged to about 15,500 combined. It also didn't help that the car itself was little changed, though the '96 ESi received two worthy upgrades in standard 16-inch wheels (replacing 15s) and Chrysler's new AutoStick feature that allowed the automatic transmission to be shifted somewhat like a manual. But the '97 Visions were virtual reruns, and Talon sales were languishing, too.

With all this, no one was surprised when Chrysler dropped Vision after '97 and Talon after model year '98, thus ending a nameplate that had seemed a good idea 10 years before, but just didn't pan out. A prime motivation was Chrysler's desire to cut overhead by trimming its dealer body, which it did over the next few years by combining Jeep-Eagle stores with Chrysler-Plymouth outlets wherever practical. It proved a timely move. Sport-utility vehicles were Jeep's stock-in-trade, SUV sales were booming, and Jeep's image was forever golden. As a result, the new Chrysler-Plymouth-Jeep dealers were generally more-profitable than they'd been as either C-P or Jeep-Eagle stores. Company accountants cheered.

In the end, Eagle failed because neither Chrysler nor the public knew quite what to make of it. A hodge-podge lineup and spotty promotion implied Chrysler wasn't fully committed to the nameplate and also left consumers confused about what an Eagle was—if they knew the name at all. The cars were far from losers, yet no model achieved the desirability or clear image of import competitors and even some domestic rivals. Eagle was no Edsel, but Chrysler should have remembered a lesson from that unhappy Ford experience: Respect for any car is always earned, never bestowed.

**1996 Vision sedan**

**1997 Talon TSi coupe**

**1997 Talon ESi coupe**

**1997 Vision TSi sedan**

**1996 Talon ESi coupe**

**1996 Talon TSi coupe**

**1998 Talon TSi coupe**

# Eagle

## Specifications

### 1988

| Eagle (wb 109.3) | Wght | Price | Prod |
|---|---|---|---|
| wag 4d | 3,502 | 12,995 | 2,305 |

| 1988 Engine | bore × stroke | bhp | availability |
|---|---|---|---|
| I-6, 258.0 | 3.75 × 3.90 | 110 | S-all |

### 1990

| Talon (wb 97.2)—32,708 built | Wght | Price | |
|---|---|---|---|
| htchbk cpe | 2,711 | 12,995 | |
| TSi htchbk cpe | 2,777 | 14,753 | |
| TSi AWD htchbk cpe | 3,101 | 16,437 | |

| 1990 Engines | bore × stroke | bhp | availability |
|---|---|---|---|
| I-4, 121.9 | 3.35 × 3.46 | 135 | S-Talon exc TSi |
| I-4T, 121.9 | 3.35 × 3.46 | 190/195 | S-Talon TSi |

### 1991

| Talon (wb 97.2) | Wght | Price | Prod |
|---|---|---|---|
| htchbk cpe | 2,711 | 12,990 | ⎱ 20,080 |
| TSi htchbk cpe | 2,777 | 14,609 | ⎰ |
| TSi AWD htchbk cpe | 3,101 | 16,513 | 12,016 |

| 1991 Engines | bore × stroke | bhp | availability |
|---|---|---|---|
| I-4, 121.9 | 3.35 × 3.46 | 135 | S-Talon exc TSi |
| I-4T, 121.9 | 3.35 × 3.46 | 190/195 | S-Talon TSi |

### 1992

| Talon (wb 97.2) | Wght | Price | Prod |
|---|---|---|---|
| htchbk cpe | 2,712 | 13,631 | ⎱ 21,551 |
| TSi htchbk cpe | 2,791 | 14,963 | ⎰ |
| TSi AWD htchbk cpe | 3,108 | 16,905 | 8,106 |

| 1992 Engines | bore × stroke | bhp | availability |
|---|---|---|---|
| I-4, 121.9 | 3.35 × 3.46 | 135 | S-Talon exc TSi |
| I-4T, 121.9 | 3.35 × 3.46 | 180/195 | S-Talon TSi |

### 1993

| Talon (wb 97.2) | Wght | Price | Prod |
|---|---|---|---|
| DL htchbk cpe | 2,550 | 11,752 | ⎱ |
| ES htchbk cpe | 2,712 | 14,197 | ⎟ 23,291 |
| TSi htchbk cpe | 2,791 | 15,703 | ⎰ |
| TSi AWD htchbk cpe | 3,108 | 17,772 | 2,814 |

| Vision (wb 113.0)—30,676 built | Wght | Price | |
|---|---|---|---|
| HXP41 ESi sdn 4d | 3,290 | 17,387 | |
| HXS41 TSi sdn 4d | 3,422 | 21,104 | |

| 1993 Engines | bore × stroke | bhp | availability |
|---|---|---|---|
| I-4, 107.1 | 3.17 × 3.39 | 92 | S-Talon DL (ohc) |
| I-4, 121.9 | 3.35 × 3.46 | 135 | S-Talon ES (dohc) |
| I-4T, 121.9 | 3.35 × 3.46 | 180/195 | S-Talon TSi (dohc) |
| V-6, 201.4 | 3.66 × 3.19 | 153 | S-Vision ESi (ohv) |
| V-6, 214.7 | 3.78 × 3.19 | 214 | S-Vision TSi (ohc) |

### 1994

| Talon (wb 97.2) | Wght | Price | Prod |
|---|---|---|---|
| DL htchbk cpe | 2,549 | 11,892 | ⎱ |
| ES htchbk cpe | 2,712 | 14,362 | ⎟ 20,545 |
| TSi htchbk cpe | 2,789 | 15,885 | ⎰ |
| TSi AWD htchbk cpe | 3,109 | 17,978 | 635 |

| Vision (wb 113.0)—31,271 built | Wght | Price | |
|---|---|---|---|
| HXP41 ESi sdn 4d | 3,344 | 19,308 | |
| HXS41 TSi sdn 4d | 3,486 | 22,773 | |

| 1994 Engines | bore × stroke | bhp | availability |
|---|---|---|---|
| I-4, 107.1 | 3.17 × 3.39 | 92 | S-Talon DL (ohc) |
| I-4, 121.9 | 3.35 × 3.46 | 135 | S-Talon ES (dohc) |
| I-4T, 121.9 | 3.35 × 3.46 | 180/195 | S-Talon TSi (dohc) |
| V-6, 201.4 | 3.66 × 3.19 | 161 | S-Vision ESi (ohv) |
| V-6, 214.7 | 3.78 × 3.19 | 214 | S-Vision TSi (ohc) |

### 1995

| Talon (wb 98.8) | | Wght | Price | Prod |
|---|---|---|---|---|
| JXH24 | ESi htchbk cpe | 2,756 | 14,362 | ⎱ 17,750 |
| JXP24 | TSi htchbk cpe | 2,866 | 17,226 | ⎰ |
| JFS24 | TSi AWD htchbk cpe | 3,119 | 19,448 | 450 |

| Vision (wb 113.0)—29,821 built | | Wght | Price | |
|---|---|---|---|---|
| HXP41 | ESi sdn 4d | 3,408 | 19,697 | |
| HXS41 | TSi sdn 4d | 3,507 | 22,871 | |

| 1995 Engines | bore × stroke | bhp | availability |
|---|---|---|---|
| I-4, 121.8 | 3.44 × 3.27 | 140 | S-Talon ESi (dohc) |
| I-4T, 121.9 | 3.35 × 3.46 | 205/210 | S-Talon TSi (dohc) |
| V-6, 201.4 | 3.66 × 3.19 | 161 | S-Vision ESi (ohv) |
| V-6, 214.7 | 3.78 × 3.19 | 214 | S-Vision TSi (ohc) |

### 1996

| Talon (wb 98.8)—15,100 built | | Wght | Price |
|---|---|---|---|
| JXL24 | htchbk cpe | 2,789 | 14,059 |
| JXH24 | ESi htchbk cpe | 2,789 | 14,830 |
| JXP24 | TSi htchbk cpe | 2,866 | 18,015 |
| JFS24 | TSi AWD htchbk cpe | 3,120 | 20,271 |

| Vision (wb 113.0)—12,806 built | | Wght | Price |
|---|---|---|---|
| HXP41 | ESi sdn 4d | 3,371 | 19,245 |
| HSX41 | TSi sdn 4d | 3,494 | 23,835 |

| 1996 Engines | bore × stroke | bhp | availability |
|---|---|---|---|
| I-4, 121.8 | 3.44 × 3.27 | 140 | S-Talon base, ESi |
| I-4T, 121.9 | 3.35 × 3.46 | 205/210 | Talon TSi |
| V-6, 201.4 | 3.66 × 3.19 | 161 | S-Vision ESi (ohv) |
| V-6, 214.7 | 3.78 × 3.19 | 214 | S-Vision TSi (ohc) |

### 1997

| Talon (wb 98.8)—9,788 built | | Wght | Price |
|---|---|---|---|
| JXL24 | htchbk cpe | 2,729 | 14,594 |
| JXH24 | ESi htchbk cpe | 2,745 | 15,365 |
| JXP24 | TSi htchbk cpe | 2,899 | 18,550 |
| JFS24 | TSi AWD htchbk cpe | 3,142 | 20,806 |

| Vision (wb 113.0)—5,874 built | | Wght | Price |
|---|---|---|---|
| HXP41 | ESi sdn 4d | 3,439 | 20,305 |
| HSX41 | TSi sdn 4d | 3,535 | 24,485 |

| 1997 Engines | bore × stroke | bhp | availability |
|---|---|---|---|
| I-4, 121.8 | 3.44 × 3.27 | 140 | S-Talon base, ESi |
| I-4T, 121.9 | 3.35 × 3.46 | 210 | S-Talon TSi |
| V-6, 201.4 | 3.66 × 3.19 | 161 | S-Vision ESi (ohv) |
| V-6, 214.7 | 3.78 × 3.19 | 214 | S-Vision TSi (ohc) |

### 1998

| Talon (wb 98.8)—4,308 built | | Wght | Price |
|---|---|---|---|
| JXL24 | htchbk cpe | 2,729 | 14,505 |
| JXH24 | ESi htchbk cpe | 2,745 | 15,275 |
| JXP24 | TSi htchbk cpe | 2,899 | 18,460 |
| JFS24 | TSi AWD htchbk cpe | 3,142 | 20,715 |

| 1997 Engines | bore × stroke | bhp | availability |
|---|---|---|---|
| I-4, 121.8 | 3.44 × 3.27 | 140 | S-Talon base, ESi |
| I-4T, 121.9 | 3.35 × 3.46 | 210 | S-Talon TSi |

# Edsel

A comedy of errors or a good idea at the wrong time? The Edsel was both—proof that what seems sound today may not be so tomorrow. As one historian later wrote: "Its aim was right, but the target moved."

That target was sighted in the heady days of 1954, when Ford Motor Company was strongly recovering from its near-collapse in the late '40s. Led by board chairman Ernest R. Breech, optimistic Dearborn managers, determined to match General Motors model-for-model, laid expansionist plans for a GM-like five-make hierarchy involving a separate new Continental Division (*see entry*) and a second medium-price make to bolster Mercury. The latter made appealing sense at a time when the medium-price market was booming. In record-setting 1955, Pontiac, Buick, and Dodge built nearly two million cars combined.

But with the industry's usual three-year lead times, Edsel didn't arrive until late 1957, by which time the entire market was depressed and the medium-price segment had shriveled from 25 to 18 percent. Hoping to sell 100,000 of its debut '58 models, Edsel Division built only a little over 63,000, though that was fair going for an all-new line in a recession year. But from there it was all downhill. After fewer than 45,000 for '59 and a mere 3000 of the token 1960 models, the make was canceled at the end of November '59.

The name, of course, honored the only son of company founder Henry Ford and the father of then-president Henry Ford II. Not that it was supposed to be the choice. Ford solicited monikers from all over—including free/thinker poet Marianne Moore, who came up with stunners like "Mongoose Civique," "Turcotinga," and "Utopian Turtletop." Ranger, Pacer, Corsair, and Citation were the top finishers among some 6000 names considered by the ad agency, and were ultimately adopted as series designations. But Breech didn't like these or any of the other suggestions. "Edsel" had popped up as an early prospect, probably because the project was widely known as the "E-car." But the Ford family was against it, and even publicly denied that Edsel would ever be used. But when a decision lagged, Breech stepped in. "I'll take care of Henry," he declared. He did, and Edsel it was.

Though originally conceived as a more-expensive and powerful "super Mercury," Edsel was positioned between Ford and Mercury. It was also far from the radical all-new design rumored for some two years before introduction, which might also have affected first-year sales.

The '58 line comprised entry-level Ranger and step-up Pacer series on the 118-inch wheelbase (116 for wagons) of the 1957-58 Ford; further up were Corsair and Citation on the 124-inch Mercury chassis. Bodyshells were similarly shared. Ranger offered two- and four-door sedans and hardtops, two-door Roundup wagon, and four-door Villager wagons with seating for six or nine. Pacer deleted the two-door wagon and sedan but added a convertible; its two wagons were tagged Bermuda. Corsair was confined to two- and four-door hardtops; Citation offered those plus a soft-top model. Prices ranged from $2500 to $3800.

Styling was the '58 Edsel's most unique aspect—and the most controversial, especially the "horse-collar" vertical grille and slim horizontal taillights (which one cynic termed "ingrown toenails"). But fins were mercifully absent, and the package was tastefully restrained next to the glittery '58 Buick and Olds. Typical of the day, gadgets abounded: optional "Teletouch

**1958 Pacer convertible coupe**

**1958 Pacer four-door sedan**

**1959 Corsair convertible coupe**

**1960 Villager 6-passenger station wagon**

Drive" automatic transmission controlled by pushbuttons in the steering-wheel hub, "cyclops eye" rotating-drum speedometer, and power assists for most everything but the rearview mirror.

Power comprised two V-8s from Dearborn's new 1958 "FE-Series" big-block family. The two lower series carried a 361-cubic-incher with 303 horsepower; Corsair/Citation used a massive 410 with 345 horsepower. With that, Edsels were quite rapid, but roadability, braking, and workmanship left much to be desired—also typical of the times.

Disappointing first-year sales dictated a reduced platoon of '59 Edsels on a single 120-inch wheelbase—all basically reskinned Fords. Offerings comprised six- and nine-seater Villager wagons; Corsair convertible; Ranger two-door sedan; and Corsair/Ranger four-door sedans, hardtop coupes, and hardtop sedans. Engines proliferated. Ranger/Villager came with a 200-bhp 292 Ford V-8, but a 145-bhp 223 inline six, also borrowed from Ford, was a new no-charge option, a nod to the market's sudden concern for fuel economy with the '58 recession. Corsairs had a standard 225-bhp 332 V-8, again from Ford Division. The 361 returned unchanged as a $58 linewide option, but in the lighter '59s it delivered 0-60 mph in 10 seconds or less. Styling was toned-down from '58, with grille-mounted headlights, taller windshields, and more-conventional taillights moved into the back panel. Prices were trimmed along with models and weight. The costliest '59, the ragtop Corsair, started at about $3100.

Dearborn halted Edsel production in November 1959 after a halfhearted run of downpriced, "decontented" 1960 models that were even more Ford-like than the '59s. Corsairs and the 361 V-8 disappeared, leaving two Villagers, five Rangers, a 292 V-8 detuned to 185 horsepower, and a new 352 V-8 option with 300 horsepower. Working with that year's all-new Ford design, stylists abandoned the vertical-grille motif for a split-horizontal affair looking suspiciously like that of the '59 Pontiac, though this was pure coincidence. A quartet of vertical ovals housed tail and backup lamps, and slim chrome moldings graced the upper bodysides. Two-speed and three-speed automatic transmissions, power steering, and air conditioning were all still available. The Ranger convertible listed at $3000, but could be optioned up to $3800. The inexpensive Ranger two-door started at $2643.

But everyone knew Edsel was finished, so it's a wonder that any of the '60s got built. Some almost didn't. The ragtop Ranger saw but 76 copies, the nine-passenger Villager a mere 59. Thus ended Detroit's biggest and most public flop since the Tucker.

"Edsel" now shows up in dictionaries as a synonym for "loser"—unfortunate considering the great legacy of Edsel Ford. But though Dearborn reportedly spent $250 million on the project, it wasn't a total loss. Expanding plants for Edsel production left Ford with surplus capacity that came in mighty handy when its new 1960 Falcon immediately ran away with the compact market.

Had it been a truly different car introduced three to five years either side of 1958, the Edsel might be with us yet. Instead, it's become a monument to the cynicism of an age when Detroit thought buyers didn't know—or care—about the difference between style and substance.

## Specifications

### 1958

| Ranger (wb 118.0; wgns-116.0) | | Wght | Price | Prod |
|---|---|---|---|---|
| 21 | sdn 2d | 3,729 | 2,519 | 4,615 |
| 22 | sdn 4d | 3,805 | 2,592 | 6,576 |
| 23 | htp cpe | 3,724 | 2,593 | 5,546 |
| 24 | htp sdn | 3,796 | 2,678 | 3,077 |
| 26 | Roundup wgn 2d | 3,761 | 2,876 | 963 |
| 27 | Villager wgn 4d, 6p | 3,827 | 2,933 | 2,294 |
| 28 | Villager wgn 4d, 9p | 3,900 | 2,990 | 978 |
| **Pacer (wb 118.0; wgns-116.0)** | | | | |
| 42 | sdn 4d | 3,826 | 2,375 | 6,083 |
| 43 | htp cpe | 3,773 | 2,805 | 6,139 |
| 44 | htp sdn | 3,857 | 2,863 | 4,959 |
| 45 | conv cpe | 3,909 | 3,028 | 1,876 |
| 47 | Bermuda wgn 4d, 6p | 3,853 | 3,190 | 1,456 |
| 48 | Bermuda wgn 4d, 9p | 3,919 | 3,247 | 779 |
| **Corsair (wb 124.0)** | | | | |
| 63 | htp cpe | 4,134 | 3,346 | 3,312 |
| 64 | htp sdn | 4,235 | 3,425 | 5,880 |
| **Citation (wb 124.0)** | | | | |
| 83 | htp cpe | 4,136 | 3,535 | 2,535 |
| 84 | htp sdn | 4,230 | 3,615 | 5,112 |
| 85 | conv cpe | 4,311 | 3,801 | 930 |

| 1958 Engines | bore × stroke | bhp | availability |
|---|---|---|---|
| V-8, 361.0 | 4.05 × 3.50 | 303 | S-Ranger, Pacer |
| V-8, 410.0 | 4.20 × 3.70 | 345 | S-Corsair, Citation |

### 1959

| Ranger (wb 120.0) | | Wght | Price | Prod |
|---|---|---|---|---|
| 57F | htp sdn | 3,682 | 2,756 | 2,352 |
| 58D | sdn 4d | 3,774 | 2,684 | 12,814 |
| 63F | htp cpe | 3,591 | 2,691 | 5,474 |
| 64C | sdn 2d | 3,547 | 2,629 | 7,778 |
| **Corsair (wb 120.0)** | | | | |
| 57B | htp sdn | 3,709 | 2,885 | 1,694 |
| 58B | sdn 4d | 3,696 | 2,812 | 3,301 |
| 63B | htp cpe | 3,778 | 2,819 | 2,315 |
| 76E | conv cpe | 3,790 | 3,072 | 1,343 |
| **Station Wagon (wb 120.0)** | | | | |
| 71E | Villager wgn 4d, 9P | 3,930 | 3,055 | 2,133 |
| 71F | Villager wgn 4d, 6P | 3,842 | 2,971 | 5,687 |

| 1959 Engines | bore × stroke | bhp | availability |
|---|---|---|---|
| I-6, 223.0 | 3.62 × 3.60 | 145 | O-Ranger, Station Wagon |
| V-8, 292.0 | 3.75 × 3.30 | 200 | S-Ranger, Station Wagon |
| V-8, 332.0 | 4.00 × 3.30 | 225 | S-Corsair; O-others |
| V-8, 361.0 | 4.05 × 3.50 | 303 | O-all |

### 1960

| Ranger (wb 120.0) | | Wght | Price | Prod |
|---|---|---|---|---|
| 57A | htp sdn | 3,718 | 2,770 | 135 |
| 58A | sdn 4d | 3,700 | 2,697 | 1,288 |
| 63A | htp cpe | 3,641 | 2,705 | 295 |
| 64A | sdn 2d | 3,601 | 2,643 | 777 |
| 76B | conv cpe | 3,836 | 3,000 | 76 |
| **Station Wagon (wb 120.0)** | | | | |
| 71E | Villager wgn 4d, 9P | 4,046 | 3,072 | 59 |
| 71F | Villager wgn 4d, 6P | 4,029 | 2,989 | 216 |

| 1960 Engines | bore × stroke | bhp | availability |
|---|---|---|---|
| I-6, 223.0 | 3.62 × 3.50 | 145 | O-all |
| V-8, 292.0 | 3.75 × 3.30 | 185 | S-all |
| V-8, 352.0 | 4.00 × 3.50 | 300 | O-all |

# Essex

Introduced in 1919, the Hudson-built Essex was a sales winner in its first two years, offering a lively four-cylinder engine and the first closed body types among popular-price mass-production cars. But when Essex adopted a less-reliable six in 1924, its image and popularity suffered accordingly. Though this engine was enlarged and improved in 1930-31, Essex failed to win back its early reputation for ruggedness and durability. Hudson Motor Company might have failed with it except for a happy accident that saved the day.

Roy D. Chapin, one of Hudson's founders, was still active in the company during 1930-32, even though he was working for the Hoover Administration. When Hoover was voted out of office, Chapin immediately returned to Hudson and prepared to make some long-needed changes in the price-leading Essex line. For 1932, he ordered the six enlarged from 160 to 193 cubic inches, which lifted horsepower from 58 to 70. This improved engine initially powered Pacemaker and Challenger models on a 113-inch wheelbase (unchanged since 1930). But at midyear, Chapin dumped it into a new 106-inch-wheelbase series dubbed Terraplane. Said one memorable ad: "In the air, it's aeroplaning; on the water, it's hydroplaning; on the ground, hot diggety dog, that's Terraplaning!"

The Essex Terraplane turned Hudson around in 1932-33. It was fast (up to 80 mph), economical (up to 25 mpg), and cheap (as little as $425). Adding to its appeal was the 1933 option of a 94-bhp 243.9-cid straight eight.

Essex Terraplanes set numerous speed marks, including over 100 stock-car records. The public responded with enthusiasm—so much so that Hudson dropped the Essex name after 1933 to make Terraplane a marque in its own right (*see entry*).

1932 Series E Pacemaker convertible coupe

1930 Challenger Six Sun Sedan two-door

1931 Challenger Six 2-passenger coupe

# Essex

## Specifications

### 1930—68,593 built

| Challenger Six (wb 113.0) | Wght | Price | Prod |
|---|---|---|---|
| rdstr 2-4P | 2,550 | 695 | — |
| phtn 5P | 2,620 | 695 | — |
| cpe 2P | 2,660 | 650 | — |
| cpe 2-4P | 2,700 | 685 | — |
| coach 5P | 2,730 | 650 | — |
| Standard sdn 4d | 2,805 | 715 | — |
| Touring sdn 4d | 2,850 | 775 | — |
| brougham 4d | 2,850 | 795 | — |
| Sun sdn 4d | 2,760 | 695 | — |

| 1930 Engine | bore × stroke | bhp | availability |
|---|---|---|---|
| !-6, 160.0 | 2.75 × 4.50 | 58 | S-all |

### 1931—47,418 built

| Challenger Six (wb 113.0; 7P-119.0) | Wght | Price | Prod |
|---|---|---|---|
| rdstr 2-4P | 2,400 | 725 | — |
| cpe 2P | 2,595 | 595 | — |
| cpe 2-4P | 2,645 | 645 | — |
| Special cpe 2-4P | 2,800 | 725 | — |
| coach 5P | 2,690 | 595 | — |
| Standard sdn 4d | 2,750 | 695 | — |
| Touring sdn 4d | 2,815 | 775 | — |
| Town sdn 4d | 2,815 | 735 | — |
| Special sdn 4d | 2,950 | 855 | — |
| sdn 7P | 2,945 | 895 | — |

| 1931 Engine | bore × stroke | bhp | availability |
|---|---|---|---|
| !-6, 160.0 | 2.75 × 4.50 | 58 | S-all |

### 1932—18,700 built

| Pacemaker (wb 113.0) | Wght | Price | Prod |
|---|---|---|---|
| phtn 5P | — | 765 | — |
| bus cpe 2P | 2,775 | 695 | — |
| cpe 2-4P | 2,840 | 745 | — |
| Special cpe 2-4P | 2,895 | 795 | — |
| conv cpe 2-4P | 2,760 | 845 | — |
| coach 5P | 2,860 | 705 | — |
| Standard sdn 4d | 2,980 | 775 | — |
| Town sdn 4d | 2,950 | 745 | — |
| Special sdn 4d | 3,010 | 845 | — |
| **Standard (wb 113.0)** | | | |
| bus cpe | — | 660 | — |
| cpe 4P | 2,750 | 710 | — |
| coach 5P | 2,785 | 665 | — |
| Standard sdn 4d | 2,870 | 735 | — |
| **Terraplane (wb 106.0)—14,125 built** | | | |
| rdstr 2P | 2,010 | 425 | — |
| phtn 5P | 2,170 | 495 | — |
| bus cpe 2P | 2,135 | 470 | — |
| cpe 2-4P | 2,190 | 510 | — |
| coach 5P | 2,205 | 475 | — |
| Standard sdn 4d | 2,250 | 550 | — |
| Sport rdstr 2-4P | 2,110 | 525 | — |
| Special bus cpe 2P | 2,135 | 510 | — |
| Special cpe 2-4P | 2,190 | 550 | — |
| Special conv cpe 2-4P | 2,145 | 610 | — |

| Terraplane (wb 106.0) | Wght | Price | Prod* |
|---|---|---|---|
| Special coach 5P | 2,205 | 515 | — |
| Special sdn 4d | 2,250 | 590 | — |

| 1932 Engine | bore × stroke | bhp | availability |
|---|---|---|---|
| !-6, 193.0 | 2.94 × 4.75 | 70 | S-all |

### 1933

| Terraplane Six (wb 106.0) | Wght | Price | Prod* |
|---|---|---|---|
| rdstr 2P | 2,135 | 425 | — |
| phtn 5P | 2,260 | 515 | — |
| cpe 2P | 2,220 | 485 | — |
| cpe 2-4P | 2,260 | 535 | — |
| coach 5P | 2,275 | 505 | — |
| sdn 4d | 2,345 | 555 | — |
| Special rdstr 2-4P | 2,220 | 505 | — |
| Special cpe 2-4P | 2,310 | 555 | — |
| Special conv cpe 2-4P | 2,275 | 575 | — |
| Special coach 5P | 2,335 | 525 | — |
| Special sdn 5P | 2,415 | 575 | — |
| **Terraplane Special Six (wb 113.0)** | | | |
| Spt rdstr 2-4P | 2,290 | 505 | — |
| phtn 5P | — | 535 | — |
| bus cpe 2P | 2,320 | 505 | — |
| cpe 2-4P | 2,330 | 555 | — |
| conv cpe 2-4P | — | 575 | — |
| coach 5P | 2,270 | 525 | — |
| sdn 4d | 2,420 | 575 | — |
| **Terraplane DeLuxe Six (wb 113.0)** | | | |
| cpe 2P | 2,395 | 585 | — |
| cpe 2-4P | 2,405 | 635 | — |
| conv cpe 2-4P | 2,395 | 655 | — |
| coach 5P | 2,450 | 605 | — |
| sdn 4d | 2,500 | 655 | — |
| **Terraplane Eight (wb 113.0)** | | | |
| rdstr 2P | 2,410 | 565 | — |
| rdstr 2-4P | 2,455 | 625 | — |
| cpe 2P | 2,485 | 615 | — |
| cpe 2-4P | 2,545 | 655 | — |
| conv cpe 2-4P | 2,495 | 695 | — |
| coach 5P | 2,565 | 615 | — |
| sdn 4d | 2,640 | 675 | — |
| **Terraplane DeLuxe Eight (wb 113.0)** | | | |
| cpe 2P | 2,540 | 685 | — |
| cpe 2-4P | 2,600 | 725 | — |
| conv cpe 2-4P | 2,550 | 765 | — |
| coach 5P | 2,625 | 685 | — |
| sdn 4d | 2,700 | 745 | — |

* Production not available.

| 1933 Engines | bore × stroke | bhp | availability |
|---|---|---|---|
| !-6, 193.0 | 2.94 × 4.75 | 70 | S-all Sixes |
| I-8, 243.9 | 2.94 × 4.50 | 94 | S-all Eights |

Note: Essex production figures shown above are based on serial number spans listed in industry sources and may be presumed reliable, though it is always possible that some numbers were skipped. For comparison, Essex calendar year production, as reported by Don Butler in *The History of Hudson*, was as follows:

| 1930 | 76,158 | 1932 | 34,007 |
| 1931 | 40,338 | 1933 | 38,150 |

See "Terraplane" for 1934-37 models and "Hudson" for 1938-39 Terraplane models.

# Excalibur

Noted industrial designer Brooks Stevens has given us a number of interesting cars, none more exciting than his own Excalibur. The first was actually a series of light race-and-ride roadsters built in 1951 with "vintage-modern" bodywork on a 100-inch-wheelbase Henry J chassis. Though strictly a private effort, these "Excalibur Js" did well enough in competition for Stevens to hope that Kaiser-Frazer might build his design for sale to the public. But K-F had just failed with its fiberglass-bodied Darrin two-seater and would flee the U.S. market after 1955, leaving unfilled Stevens' dream of a new car with classic '30s styling.

The dream got a another chance in 1963 at Studebaker, where Stevens had been a design consultant for four years. Having completed clever, low-cost facelifts on the compact Lark and sporty Hawk coupe, he was asked by company president Sherwood Egbert to devise some 1964 show cars that would bolster Studebaker's public image in the face of steadily declining sales. The firm had just closed its century-old South Bend, Indiana, plant, canceled both the Hawk and Egbert's radical Avanti, and retreated with a reduced Lark line to Hamilton, Ontario. With things looking so terminal, Egbert hoped Stevens' specials would convince people that Studebaker still had a future.

Stevens did his best, but time permitted only a trio of dolled-up Larks that didn't make much of an impression at Chicago in February 1964. But for the next major event, the annual New York Auto Show in April, Stevens was determined to have something that would "get people to come to that damn booth." Though Egbert had departed (stricken by cancer), his successor, Byers Burlingame, agreed to cooperate.

The idea was a "contemporary classic," a new car that looked like the Mercedes SSK that Stevens once owned. "I wanted this to be a replica [for those] who could not play in the collector's market even then [and for those who wanted] a "two-way classic,' something that you can be sure will get you back home...." Stevens duly rendered a dashing neoclassic roadster body, and a Lark Daytona convertible chassis was delivered to his Milwaukee studios with power front-disc brakes and super-charged, 290-horsepower Studebaker 289 V-8. The result, labeled "Studebaker SS," was completed in just six weeks by Stevens and his sons, David and William.

No sooner did it reach New York than Studebaker backed out. A "contemporary classic," said company officials, conflicted with their newly embraced image of the "common-sense car." Undeterred, Stevens arranged to exhibit the SS in a separate space. Luckily, he wound up across from a hot-dog stand, but the cycle-fendered two-seater would have drawn crowds anyway. It was, in fact, a sensation, and dozens of inquiries from would-be owners prompted the Stevens sons to form SS Automobiles in August. By 1966, they had built 56 copies of a mildly modified version bearing the Stevens-registered name Excalibur and also called SS.

Studebaker, meanwhile, had ceased building cars at last, thus ending the availability of its 289 V-8, but General Motors friends Ed Cole and "Bunkie" Knudsen agreed to provide the Stevens family with Chevrolet 327s in 300-bhp Corvette tune. This change made the lithe 2100-pound Excalibur a blistering performer. Even with standard 3.31:1 rear axle, 0-60 mph took less than five seconds, a big improvement over the Studey-powered car's seven seconds. And projected top speed was 160 mph!

Though undeniably old, the 109-inch-wheelbase Studebaker

1964 Studebaker SS roadster (Excalibur prototype)

1965-69 Series I SSK roadster

1966-69 Series I SS phaeton

1970-74 Series II SS phaeton

chassis had several advantages for a "contemporary classic." Unlike newer torque-box designs, it was quite narrow and thus a perfect fit for the slim, '30s-style Excalibur body; and as a convertible platform, it was firmly X-braced. Still, it required considerable reworking to ensure safe handling with such a high power-to-weight ratio.

That task, and many others, fell to David Stevens. The

1975-79 Series III SS roadster

1975-79 Series III phaeton

1980-84 Series IV phaeton

vintage-style cowl, for example, forced a lower steering column and pedals. He also had to decrease spring rates and alter caster and camber, but the result was a car as fast on curves as it was on straights. This modified chassis continued under all "Series I" Excaliburs built through 1969.

Brooks Stevens, of course, was responsible for the styling, which was deliberately planned as an evocative but not line-for-line rendition of the 1928 Mercedes SSK. Interestingly, though, initial sales literature was done in prewar Mercedes style.

Quality was uncompromising from the start, and would continue to distinguish Excalibur from the motley group of "replicars" it inspired. As just one example, Brooks Stevens turned to Mercedes-Benz's original German supplier for the simulated outside exhaust pipes and used French-built freestanding headlamps closely resembling original SSK equipment.

The earliest Excaliburs were bodied in hand-hammered aluminum, but fiberglass was soon substituted. Also for reasons of cost and practicality, the prototype's sheet-brass radiator was exchanged for a cast-aluminum affair. Atop it was Brooks' "sword-in-circle" mascot that simulated, but didn't infringe upon, M-B's jealously guarded three-pointed star. Dominating the cockpit was a full set of white-on-black Stewart-Warner gauges in a vintage-style dash with engine-turned metal appliqué. Seats were modified Studebaker buckets covered in vinyl. With all this, the Excalibur's announced price looked unbelievably low: $7250 for a hand-built car with one of the most-competent chassis in the business.

Encouraged by intense initial interest in the SS—and all the ready buyers for it—the Stevens family added two companion models in 1966: a more-elaborate roadster with full fenders and running boards, and, very late in the year, a four-place "phaeton" convertible. The latter was surprisingly roomy. David Stevens proudly pointed to top-up headroom within an inch of a Cadillac Eldorado's and legroom that was actually greater. Also in 1966, the firm changed its name to Excalibur Automobile Corporation.

Prices inevitably escalated, reaching a $10,000 minimum by '69, but Excaliburs remained a remarkable value. Not until 1976 would they become $20,000 automobiles, and then only because of inflation and the cost of federally mandated safety and emissions equipment. At least the hikes were made less painful by progressively upgraded materials and features. By 1969, no-cost features had expanded to include air conditioning, heater/defroster, variable-ratio power steering with tilt wheel, power front-disc brakes, steel-belted radial tires on chrome-plated wire wheels, the same as twin sidemount spares, luggage rack, AM/FM stereo, leather seats, air horns, driving lights, rear air shocks, "Positraction" limited-slip differential, and self-shift Turbo Hydra-Matic transmission (the last two from GM, of course).

Excalibur production would never be high, but was never intended to be. This was, after all, a labor of love, a gift from the Stevens family to enthusiasts of traditional motoring in the grand Classic manner. After the 56 SS roadsters of 1965 came 90 Series I models in 1966, but production never topped 100 per year through 1972.

Announced in 1970 were Series II Excaliburs with new 111-inch wheelbase and the Corvette's latest 350 V-8. The original roadster was dropped, but the other two models returned at higher $12,000 starting prices. A notable advance was a modern new box-section chassis purpose-designed by David Stevens around Corvette suspension components, thus ousting the old Lark frame (Excalibur's inventory had run out anyway). Turbo Hydra-Matic moved to the options list in favor of a GM "Muncie" four-speed manual gearbox. Independent rear suspension and standard all-disc power brakes combined with Goodyear Polyglas tires on specially designed wire wheels to provide a fine blend of ride comfort and adroit handling. Acceleration was a bit slower despite unchanged horsepower—but not much: A Series II could scale 0-60 in six seconds and reach a genuine 150 mph.

Prices and production began taking off with the Series III, which arrived in 1975 (Excalibur has never adhered to strict model years). This was basically the Series II design modified for tightening safety/emissions rules, but not so much as to compromise styling or roadability that were, by now, Excalibur hallmarks. Besides "shock mounted solid aluminum alloy [bumpers that] meet government standards for absorbing impact," Series IIIs boasted fuller clamshell-type fenders and standard high-back bucket seats covered in leather and made—like most of the car—by Excalibur itself. The main mechanical alteration was switching to Chevy's big-block 454 V-8, which could be emissions-tuned with less loss of power and torque than the small-block 350. Both roadster and phaeton carried identical 1975 starting prices of $18,900, more than double the original figure of a decade before. And prices would go much higher, reaching $28,600 by the end of this series in 1979.

By any standard, Excalibur was still a tiny automaker, but the Stevens brothers would not be rushed. Nor did they want to dilute their market with too much of a good thing. As it had since 1969, the more-practical four-place phaeton continued

# Excalibur

outselling the two-seat roadster, but total volume remained minuscule even for a specialty maker. The Series III saw but 1141 over five years, versus 342 for the Series II and 359 for the original Series I.

Excalibur had traveled far since David and William C. "Steve" Stevens built their first cars (the latter even worked on the assembly line until 1968). Striking evidence of their progress arrived in 1980 with an elegant new Series IV. More luxury tourer than lightweight sports machine, it was the most radically changed Excalibur in history. Wheelbase was stretched to a limousinelike 125 inches, and there were more standard accoutrements than any previous Excalibur. Styling, now by David Stevens, remained firmly "Classic," but was smoother and sleeker in the way that the late-'30s Mercedes 500/540K was evolved from the SS/SSK. The phaeton acquired a lift-off hardtop plus fully powered soft top; the roadster gained a rakish rumble seat.

Most engineering changes came per federal edicts. The most notable was a vastly smaller Chevy V-8, the well-known 5.0-liter/305-cid unit, linked to four-speed overdrive automatic as the sole transmission choice. Excalibur feared a larger engine would have lowered fuel mileage to the point of having to pay fines under Corporate Average Fuel Economy rules, something the tiny firm just couldn't afford. As a result, customers were saddled with a much bigger and heavier Excalibur that was far from exciting on either straights or curves.

With that plus the start of a severe recession and lofty new inflation-fueled prices—initially near $40,000—Excalibur sales nosedived. It couldn't have happened at a worse time for the Stevens family, who faced burdensome new overhead costs from a heavy revamping of their suburban Milwaukee plant (to improve quality). The result was a steadily worsening situation that forced the brothers to file for Chapter 11 bankruptcy in mid-1986. Ironically, this came just after Excalibur marked its 20th anniversary with its first commemoratives: 50 roadsters and 50 phaetons bearing two-tone exteriors with chrome sweepspears and pewter plaques, plus interiors trimmed in walnut and Connolly leather.

But then came help in the form of Henry Warner, president of Acquisition Company of Wisconsin, who bought the Stevens family's interests and reorganized the firm as Excalibur Marketing Corporation. By early 1987, Series IV roadsters and phaetons were again trickling out of Milwaukee as Series V models. Their main difference was a more-potent 350 Chevy V-8 option that partly redressed the weak performance of the standard 305. At midyear, EMC revealed a whopping four-door Touring Sedan on a 144-inch-wheelbase chassis (essentially a 20-inch stretch of the phaeton's square-tube ladder frame). Measuring 224 inches long and weighing 4400 pounds, the Touring Sedan was optimistically priced at the same $65,650 figure applied to both open Series Vs, with which it shared frontal styling. Interiors were opulent. A front bench replaced the phaeton's buckets, and the long wheelbase made for a rear compartment worthy of a '30s Cadillac Sixteen. Also announced was an even-more-extravagant 204-inch-wheelbase "grand limousine." David Stevens had earlier conceived both these closed models as sales-building "line extensions."

But none of this served to boost sales and thus

**1980-84 Series IV phaeton**

**1985 20th Anniversary Signature Series phaeton**

**1985 20th Anniversary Signature Series Roadster**

attract needed capital to offset mounting debts in an economy again gone slack. Nor did a three-year, $9-million lease deal with a Chicago concern involving some 150 cars. As a result, Excalibur went bankrupt again, production ceasing in June 1990.

But Excalibur wasn't quite dead. In November 1991, German Michael Timmer bought the firm for $1.33 million amid charges that the Warner regime engaged in odometer fraud, installed some used parts, failed to meet federal passive-restraint rules, and generally did its best to "kill" the company. Timmer seemed bent on saving it, putting $1 million toward plant improvements with an eye to resuming production by April 1992. There would be four models: Series V roadster, phaeton and sedan, plus, surprisingly, a revived Series III roadster. Prices were targeted for the $50,000-$75,000 range.

Unfortunately, Timmer ran out of money before he could build any cars, so Excalibur was again bankrupt by early '92. But it was still alive, thanks to a new rescue by the German father-and-son team of Udo and

# Excalibur

Jens Geitlinger, who'd made a fortune in real estate. With help from production boss Scott Dennison and some 33 other employees still hanging on from prior regimes, Jens picked up where Timmer left off, issuing an updated Series III roadster called the "Limited Edition 100."

Besides design changes for all the latest safety and emissions standards, including a driver-side air bag, the Geitlinger Series III carried the new 300-bhp Corvette LT1 V-8 teamed with four-speed automatic or optional six-speed ZF manual. Price was set at $89,842. At the same time, the big limo was to get a new dash and GM suspension to sell for a staggering $124,774. The other Series V cars weren't forgotten, being muscled up to L98 Corvette power and starting prices of $74,986 for the roadster and $77,691 for the phaeton. The Geitlingers eyed total first-year production of 60-80 units, and Dennison predicted 120 Excaliburs per year starting in 1993, with some two-thirds earmarked for export.

But the world market had also changed dramatically, and Excalibur could no longer do business as usual. Accordingly, the firm diversified in 1993, first by adding a replica Shelby-Cobra with some interesting deviations from the original, then by becoming a contract supplier of various "accessories" like luggage racks and "aero" cab extensions for trucks. Car production ended in 1997, but accessory production continued.

**1993 Limited Edition roadster**

**1993 Series V phaeton**

**1994 Cobra roadster replica**

## Specifications

### 1965

| Series I (wb 109.0)* | Wght | Price | Prod |
|---|---|---|---|
| SSK rdstr | 2,100 | 7,250 | 56 |

| 1965 Engine | bore × stroke | bhp | availability |
|---|---|---|---|
| V-8, 289.0 | 3.56 × 3.62 | 290 | S-all |

### 1966

| Series I (wb 109.0)* | Wght | Price | Prod |
|---|---|---|---|
| SSK rdstr | 2,100 | 7,250 | 87 |
| rdstr | 2,500 | 8,000 | |
| phtn | 2,500 | 7,950 | 3 |

| 1966 Engine | bore × stroke | bhp | availability |
|---|---|---|---|
| V-8, 327.0 | 4.00 × 3.25 | 300 | S-all |

### 1967

| Series I (wb 109.0)* | Wght | Price | Prod |
|---|---|---|---|
| SSK rdstr | 2,100 | 8,000 | 38 |
| rdstr | 2,500 | 8,500 | |
| phtn | 2,600 | 8,250 | 33 |

# Excalibur

| 1967 Engines | bore × stroke | bhp | availability |
|---|---|---|---|
| V-8, 327.0 | 4.00 × 3.25 | 300 | S-all |
| V-8, 327.0 | 4.00 × 3.25 | 300+ | O-all |

### 1968

| Series I (wb 109.0)* | Wght | Price | Prod |
|---|---|---|---|
| SSK rdstr | 2,300 | 8,650 | ⎤ 37 |
| rdstr | 2,500 | 8,650 | ⎦ |
| phtn | 2,600 | 9,850 | 20 |

| 1968 Engines | bore × stroke | bhp | availability |
|---|---|---|---|
| V-8, 327.0 | 4.00 × 3.25 | 300 | S-all |
| V-8, 327.0 | 4.00 × 3.25 | 300+ | O-all |

### 1969

| Series I (wb 109.0)* | Wght | Price | Prod |
|---|---|---|---|
| SSK rdstr | 2,400 | 9,000 | ⎤ 47 |
| rdstr | 2,550 | 9,000 | ⎦ |
| phtn | 2,650 | 10,000 | 44 |

| 1969 Engines | bore × stroke | bhp | availability |
|---|---|---|---|
| V-8, 327.0 | 4.00 × 3.25 | 300 | S-all |
| V-8, 327.0 | 4.00 × 3.25 | 300+ | O-all |

* Production 1965-69; SSK 168; rdstr 59; phtn 89.

### 1970

| Series II (wb 111.0) | Wght | Price | Prod |
|---|---|---|---|
| SSK rdstr | 2,750 | 12,000 | ⎤ 11 |
| SS rdstr | 2,900 | 12,500 | ⎦ |
| SS phtn | 3,000 | 12,900 | 26 |

| 1970 Engine | bore × stroke | bhp | availability |
|---|---|---|---|
| V-8, 350.0 | 4.00 × 3.48 | 300 | S-all |

### 1971

Excalibur records show no 1971 model production.

### 1972

| Series II (wb 111.0) | Wght | Price | Prod |
|---|---|---|---|
| SS rdstr | 2,900 | 12,500 | 13 |
| SS phtn | 3,000 | 13,500 | 52 |

| 1972 Engine | bore × stroke | bhp | availability |
|---|---|---|---|
| V-8, 454.0 | 4.25 × 4.00 | — | S-all |

### 1973

| Series II (wb 111.0) | Wght | Price | Prod |
|---|---|---|---|
| SS rdstr | 2,900 | 13,500 | 22 |
| SS phtn | 3,000 | 16,000 | 100 |

| 1973 Engine | bore × stroke | bhp | availability |
|---|---|---|---|
| V-8, 454.0 | 4.25 × 4.00 | 270 | S-all |

### 1974

| Series II (wb 111.0) | Wght | Price | Prod |
|---|---|---|---|
| SS rdstr | 2,900 | 17,000 | 26 |
| SS phtn | 3,000 | 17,000 | 92 |

| 1974 Engine | bore × stroke | bhp | availability |
|---|---|---|---|
| V-8, 454.0 | 4.25 × 4.00 | 275 | S-all |

### 1975

| Series III (wb 112.0) | Wght | Price | Prod |
|---|---|---|---|
| SS rdstr | 4,350 | 18,900 | 8 |
| SS phtn | 4,350 | 18,900 | 82 |

| 1975 Engine | bore × stroke | bhp | availability |
|---|---|---|---|
| V-8, 454.0 | 4.25 × 4.00 | 215 | S-all |

### 1976

| Series III (wb 112.0) | Wght | Price | Prod |
|---|---|---|---|
| SS rdstr | 4,350 | 21,500 | 11 |
| SS phtn | 4,350 | 21,500 | 173 |

| 1976 Engine | bore × stroke | bhp | availability |
|---|---|---|---|
| V-8, 454.0 | 4.25 × 4.00 | 215 | S-all |

### 1977

| Series III (wb 112.0) | Wght | Price | Prod |
|---|---|---|---|
| SS rdstr | 4,350 | 23,600 | 15 |
| SS phtn | 4,350 | 23,600 | 222 |

| 1977 Engine | bore × stroke | bhp | availability |
|---|---|---|---|
| V-8, 454.0 | 4.25 × 4.00 | 215 | S-all |

### 1978

| Series III (wb 112.0) | Wght | Price | Prod |
|---|---|---|---|
| SS rdstr | 4,350 | 25,600 | 15 |
| SS phtn | 4,350 | 25,600 | 248 |

| 1978 Engine | bore × stroke | bhp | availability |
|---|---|---|---|
| V-8, 454.0 | 4.25 × 4.00 | 215 | S-all |

### 1979

| Series III (wb 112.0) | Wght | Price | Prod |
|---|---|---|---|
| SS rdstr | 4,350 | 28,600 | 27 |
| SS phtn | 4,350 | 28,600 | 340 |

| 1979 Engine | bore × stroke | bhp | availability |
|---|---|---|---|
| V-8, 350.0 | 4.00 × 3.48 | 180 | S-all |

### 1980

| Series IV (wb 125.0) | Wght | Price | Prod |
|---|---|---|---|
| SS rdstr | 4,300 | — | 0 |
| SS phtn | 4,300 | 37,700 | 93 |

| 1980 Engine | bore × stroke | bhp | availability |
|---|---|---|---|
| V-8, 305.0 | 3.74 × 3.48 | 155 | S-all |

### 1981

| Series IV (wb 125.0) | Wght | Price | Prod |
|---|---|---|---|
| rdstr | 4,400 | 50,000 | 36 |
| phtn | 4,400 | 46,500 | 199 |

| 1981 Engine | bore × stroke | bhp | availability |
|---|---|---|---|
| V-8, 305.0 | 3.74 × 3.48 | 155 | S-all |

### 1982

| Series IV (wb 125.0) | Wght | Price | Prod |
|---|---|---|---|
| rdstr | 4,400 | 57,500 | 60 |
| phtn | 4,400 | 52,000 | 152 |

| 1982 Engine | bore × stroke | bhp | availability |
|---|---|---|---|
| V-8, 305.0 | 3.74 × 3.48 | 155 | S-all |

# Excalibur

### 1983

| Series IV (wb 125.0) | Wght | Price | Prod |
|---|---|---|---|
| rdstr | 4,400 | 59,500 | — |
| phtn | 4,400 | 55,500 | — |

| 1983 Engines | bore × stroke | bhp | availability |
|---|---|---|---|
| V-8, 305.0 | 3.74 × 3.48 | 155 | S-all |

### 1984

| Series IV (wb 125.0) | Wght | Price | Prod |
|---|---|---|---|
| rdstr | 4,400 | 59,500 | — |
| phtn | 4,400 | 57,000 | — |

| 1984 Engine | bore × stroke | bhp | availability |
|---|---|---|---|
| V-8, 305.0 | 3.74 × 3.48 | 155 | S-all |

### 1985

| Signature Series (wb 125.0) | Wght | Price | Prod |
|---|---|---|---|
| rdstr | 4,400 | 62,000 | — |
| phtn | 4,400 | 59,500 | — |

| 1985 Engine | bore × stroke | bhp | availability |
|---|---|---|---|
| V-8, 305.0 | 3.74 × 3.48 | 155 | S-all |

### 1986

| Series IV (wb 125.0) | Wght | Price | Prod |
|---|---|---|---|
| rdstr | — | 65,000 | * |
| phtn | — | 65,000 | * |

| 1986 Engine | bore × stroke | bhp | availability |
|---|---|---|---|
| V-8, 305.0 | 3.74 × 3.48 | 155 | S-all |

* Specifications and prices were announced for 1986, but the Excalibur Company went into bankruptcy. Production resumed in December 1986 with the 1987 models.

### 1987

| (wb 124.0) | Wght | Price | Prod |
|---|---|---|---|
| rdstr | 4,400 | — | — |
| phtn | 4,400 | — | — |

| 1987 Engine | bore × stroke | bhp | availability |
|---|---|---|---|
| V-8, 305.0 | 3.74 × 3.48 | 170 | S-all |

### 1988

| (wb 124.0; Touring Sdn 144.0) | Wght | Price | Prod |
|---|---|---|---|
| rdstr 2d | 4,400 | 65,650 | — |
| phtn 2d | 4,400 | 65,650 | — |
| touring sdn 4d | 4,400 | 65,650 | — |

| 1988 Engines | bore × stroke | bhp | availability |
|---|---|---|---|
| V-8, 305.0 | 3.74 × 3.48 | 170 | S-all |
| V-8, 350.0 | 4.00 × 3.48 | — | O-all |

### 1989

| (wb 124.0; Touring Sdn 144.0) | Wght | Price | Prod |
|---|---|---|---|
| rdstr 2d | 4,400 | 71,865 | — |
| phtn 2d | 4,400 | 71,865 | — |
| touring sdn 4d | 4,400 | 72,325 | — |

| 1989 Engines | bore × stroke | bhp | availability |
|---|---|---|---|
| V-8, 305.0 | 3.74 × 3.48 | 170 | S-all |
| V-8, 350.0 | 4.00 × 3.48 | — | O-all |

### 1990

| (wb 124.0; Touring Sdn 144.0) | Wght | Price | Prod |
|---|---|---|---|
| rdstr 2d | 4,400 | — | — |
| phtn 2d | 4,400 | — | — |
| touring sdn 4d | 4,400 | — | — |

| 1990 Engines | bore × stroke | bhp | availability |
|---|---|---|---|
| V-8, 305.0 | 3.74 × 3.48 | 170 | S-all |
| V-8, 350.0 | 4.00 × 3.48 | — | O-all |

### 1993

| | Wght | Price | Prod |
|---|---|---|---|
| Cobra (wb 94.5) | 2,500 | — | 21 |
| Limited Edition (wb 112.0) | 3,171 | 89,842 | 6 |
| Phaeton (wb 125.1) | 4,389 | 77.691 | 3 |
| Roadster (wb 124.0) | 4,356 | 74,986 | 1 |

| 1993 Engines | bore × stroke | bhp | availability |
|---|---|---|---|
| V-8, 302.0 | 4.00 × 3.00 | 215 | S-Cobra |
| V-8, 350.0 | 4.00 × 3.48 | 245 | S-Phaeton, Roadster |
| V-8, 350.0 | 4.00 × 3.48 | 300 | S-Limited Edition |

### 1994

| | Wght | Price | Prod |
|---|---|---|---|
| Cobra (wb 94.5) | 2,500 | — | 35 |
| Limited Edition (wb 112.0) | 3,171 | — | 14 |
| Roadster (wb 124.0) | 4,356 | — | 2 |

| 1994 Engines | bore × stroke | bhp | availability |
|---|---|---|---|
| V-8, 302.0 | 4.00 × 3.00 | 215 | S-Cobra |
| V-8, 350.0 | 4.00 × 3.48 | 245 | S-Roadster |
| V-8, 350.0 | 4.00 × 3.48 | 300 | S-Limited Edition |

### 1995

| | Wght | Price | Prod |
|---|---|---|---|
| Cobra (wb 94.5) | 2,500 | — | 46 |
| Limited Edition (wb 112.0) | 3,171 | — | 7 |
| Phaeton (wb 125.1) | 4,389 | — | 2 |
| Roadster (wb 124.0) | 4,356 | — | 1 |
| Limousine (wb 172.0) | 5,200 | 124,774 | 1 |

| 1995 Engines | bore × stroke | bhp | availability |
|---|---|---|---|
| V-8, 302.0 | 4.00 × 3.00 | 215 | S-Cobra |
| V-8, 350.0 | 4.00 × 3.48 | 245 | S-Phaeton, Roadster, Limousine |
| V-8, 350.0 | 4.00 × 3.48 | 300 | S-Limited Edition |

### 1996

| | Wght | Price | Prod |
|---|---|---|---|
| Cobra (wb 94.5) | 2,500 | 51,807 | — |
| Limited Edition (wb 112.0) | 3,171 | 74,897 | — |
| Phaeton (wb 125.1) | 4,389 | 98,897 | — |
| Roadster (wb 124.0) | 4,356 | 104,595 | — |
| Limousine (wb 172.0) | 5,200 | 159,000 | — |

| 1996 Engines | bore × stroke | bhp | availability |
|---|---|---|---|
| V-8, 302.0 | 4.00 × 3.00 | 215 | S-Cobra |
| V-8S, 302.0 | 4.00 × 3.00 | 325 | O-Cobra |
| V-8, 350.0 | 4.00 × 3.48 | 245 | S-Phaeton, Roadster, Limousine |
| V-8, 350.0 | 4.00 × 3.48 | 300 | S-Limited Edition |

# Ford

Founded in 1903, Ford Motor Company skyrocketed from obscurity to dominate the American auto industry in less than 12 years. The foundation of this unparalleled success was the world's first mass-produced car: the cheap, simple Model T, whose lovable quirkiness was matched only by that of its creator, company founder Henry Ford. Henry's decision to abandon his treasured "Tin Lizzie" only after 19 years and a staggering 15-million cars—the last not very different from the first—came almost too late, and his company lost a lot in money and goodwill during the long changeover to the belated new Model A.

Yet despite keen competition from an aggressive Chevrolet and newcomer Plymouth, the A was a success, almost perfectly timed for the Depression that began soon after its 1928 debut. Ford built over 1.1 million cars for 1930—almost twice as many as Chevrolet and more than 14 times as many as Plymouth.

The 1930 Model A received a number of changes that seem minor now but were major then. All models retained the "little Lincoln" styling crafted by Henry's artistic son Edsel (whose father named him Ford Motor Company president in 1919), but fenders were lower and wider, the hoodline was higher, and stainless steel replaced nickel plate on radiator and headlight shells. Enhancing the lower look was a switch to balloon tires on smaller 19-inch wheels (replacing 21-inchers). Running changes made during that year included a numerically higher steering ratio for less effort at the wheel, and standardization of vacuum-operated windshield wipers (previously an extra-cost accessory).

As before, the Model A spanned a wide range of body types: coupes, sport coupes, roadsters, and cabriolets with or without rumble seat; "Tudor" and "Fordor" sedans; a surprisingly dignified Town Sedan; and a wood-body station wagon. Most could be had with Standard or DeLuxe trim, the latter typically featuring brighter colors and spiffier interiors. Prices ranged from just $435 for the basic two-seat roadster to $660 for the Town Sedan. There was also a very deluxe Town Car with canvas-covered formal roof. Not many sold at $1200—a mere 96 for the model year. Arriving in June was a $625 DeLuxe two-door phaeton, a jaunty five-seater with standard left-sidemount spare, chrome trunk rack, leather upholstery, and lower steering wheel and windshield. Another new style, bowing in the autumn of 1930, was the Victoria coupe sporting a slanted windshield, soon to be commonplace throughout Detroit.

Little visible change occurred for 1931 save a painted section atop the front of the radiator shell, which made identification easy. Chevrolet was still pushing hard, and Ford yielded the top spot in 1931 model-year volume, though only by some 4100 cars. Ford wouldn't top Chevy again until 1934 despite scoring a coup with America's first low-priced V-8.

Henry Ford had once contemplated a radical X-8 engine for the long-overdue Model T replacement, but ultimately settled for a more-conventional V-8 on which Ford engineers discreetly began work in 1930. But it was delayed by the peculiar con-

**1930 Model A DeLuxe 2-passenger coupe**

**1931 Model A Victoria 5-passenger coupe**

**1931 Model A DeLuxe roadster**

**1931 Model A convertible sedan**

1932 Model 18 V-8 DeLuxe Fordor sedan

1932 Model 18 V-8 sport coupe 2/4 passenger

ditions Henry imposed on his engineers, so the Model A appeared with only four-cylinder power as an interim measure. Model A production ended in autumn 1931, though sales continued through April 1932. Then came a revised four-cylinder car, the Model B. Both this and the new 1932 V-8 Model 18 shared evolutionary styling, a 106.5-inch wheelbase (up three inches from the A's), and the same broad body-style array. The big difference, of course, was under the hood. The V-8 was a tremendous bargain: Standard roadster, coupe, and phaeton all listed below $500. Still, many buyers were wary, so Ford kept four-cylinder cars through 1934.

Ford's first V-8 was that now-famous cast-iron flathead that initially delivered 65 horsepower from 221 cubic inches. That compared with 40/50 horsepower from the 200.5-cid Model A/B four. With a relatively sensational top speed of 78 mph, the peppy V-8 Ford caused a storm of public interest, garnering over 50,000 advance orders. Millions flocked to see it on its March 1932 unveiling.

The old man kept a close watch over the V-8's development, badgering his engineers and telling them what to do. His perceived need for getting the engine to market as soon as possible left insufficient time for durability testing, so troubles surfaced early. Cylinder-head cracks and excessive oil burning were the most common, but some engine mounts worked loose and ignition problems cropped up. Though Ford replaced pistons by the thousands to ease owner worries, the engine difficulties hurt sales. But they'd be cleared up soon enough, and the V-8 became known as a reliable powerplant that could stand considerable "heating up." Hot rodders loved it.

Fords looked more flowing for 1933, reflecting Detroit's swing

1933 Model 40 V-8 DeLuxe Tudor sedan

1935 Model 48 V-8 DeLuxe 2-passenger coupe

1934 Model 40A V-8 convertible coupe

1935 Official Pace Car convertible sedan

# Ford

to streamlining. Edsel Ford had been an important force in Dearborn design for some time, and his tasteful new '33 Ford was universally applauded. The hood now extended back to the windshield, fenders were "skirted" and dipped low in front, sharp corners were rounded off, and rear-hinged doors appeared on closed models. Helping all this was a wheelbase lengthened to 112 inches (where it would remain through 1940) and a wheel diameter shrunk to 17. V-8 durability kept improving, and the frame was completely redesigned. With V-8 production at full strength, Ford's model-year volume rose by 100,000 cars—impressive for difficult 1933, but not enough to beat Chevrolet. Still, the speedy Ford V-8 was attracting a legion of fans. Among them was no less than John Dillinger, who wrote Henry to praise the product—an unsolicited testimonial from Public Enemy Number One.

Appearance became smoother still on 1934's 40A line. The V-8 itself got a new carburetor and manifold that increased advertised horsepower to 85—some claim actual power was 90. By now, most of its early problems were just bad memories. The four-cylinder engine was breathing its last. The Standard two-passenger coupe still sold for little more than $500, while the DeLuxe Fordor cost only $615. Safety glass was newly featured on closed models.

The Ford station wagon, introduced as a 1929 Model A, had a body constructed of birch or maple supplied by the Mingel Company of Kentucky; assembly was by Murray and Briggs in Detroit. Starting in 1935, Ford built these bodies itself in a plant at Iron Mountain on Michigan's Upper Peninsula, an ideal location because of nearby hardwood forests that minimized transportation costs.

A fuller look marked the 1935 Model 48 Fords, with smaller windows and a more prominently vee'd grille than 1933-34. Also new was an integral trunk for sedans. It added a bulky "bustle," but erased the increasingly old-fashioned external trunk rack and spare tire. A new camshaft and better crankcase ventilation further enhanced the lively V-8, and the frame and rear axle were beefed up. Retained from Model T times was an exceedingly simple suspension: just a solid axle on a transverse leaf spring front and rear, an archaic setup that wouldn't be abandoned for another 13 years. This and the use of mechanical brakes through 1939 left Ford distinctly behind the times, but old Henry believed simpler was better, and he was nothing if not stubborn. Still, he did give in to steel wheels, which replaced traditional wires after 1935.

Ford made only minor styling changes for 1936, but they were good ones. The most obvious were a longer, more-pointed hood and a more sharply vee'd grille to match. Industry design trends dictated hiding some previously exposed components, so horns now hooted from behind little covered holes astride the grille. Model choices were still numerous, but Standard and DeLuxe were now distinct series, with the latter listing more body styles.

Offerings expanded for '37 with the addition of a small-bore 136-cid V-8, originally devised for the European market to take advantage of tax laws based on displacement. In America it came to be called the "V-8/60," as it produced that much horsepower. But though it made for cheaper new Model 74 Fords in a year of generally higher car prices, it didn't sell nearly as well as expected. Buyers evidently preferred higher performance over lower retail cost. Economy was supposed to be a strong point, but really wasn't. With this development, the familiar 221 flathead became known as the "V-8/85." For 1937 it benefited from improved cooling via a relocated water pump, plus larger insert bearings, and new cast-alloy pistons. It again powered Standards and DeLuxes now designated Model 78. V-8/60s were Standard-trim only.

**1936 Model 68 V-8 DeLuxe 2/4-passenger roadster**

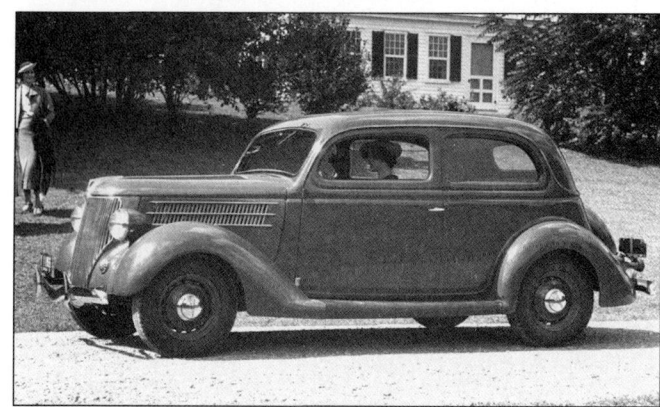
**1936 Model 68 V-8 DeLuxe Tudor sedan**

**1937 Model 78 V-8 DeLuxe Tudor sedan**

Responding to GM's 1936 "Turret-Top" bodies, Ford adopted all-steel construction for 1937 closed models, belatedly discarding the fabric roof inserts of old. But this was easily overshadowed by crisp new bodies with headlamps nestled firmly in the fenders and a prow-type grille composed of fine horizontal bars (stretched rearward at the top). This and a lighter overall look made the '37 Ford one of the prettiest cars of the decade. President Franklin D. Roosevelt liked it enough to buy a convertible sedan for use at his Warm Springs, Georgia, retreat. In a year of questionable styling throughout the industry, Ford was a standout—proof that streamlining didn't necessarily mean an end to distinctive, eye-pleasing automobiles.

The 1938 line ushered in "two-tier styling" for 60-bhp 82A and 85-bhp 81A series. Where Standards used slightly modified 1937 bodies, DeLuxes sported a different new look. The romantic roadster was history, and the equally old-fashioned phaeton (a

# Ford

1938 Model 82A Standard 2-passenger coupe

1939 Model 91A DeLuxe 2-passenger coupe

1938 Model 81A DeLuxe Fordor sedan

1940 DeLuxe Fordor sedan

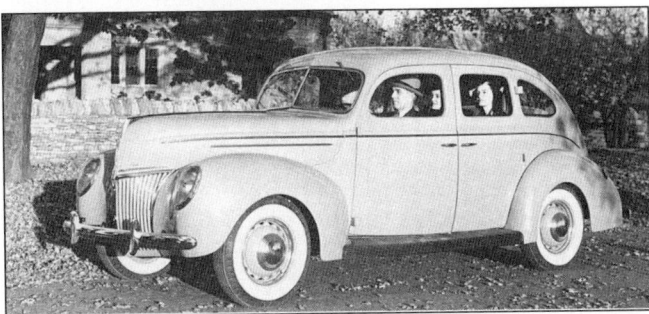
1939 Model 91A DeLuxe Fordor sedan

1941 Super DeLuxe Fordor sedan

throwback to touring-car days) was in its final season. Both body styles had long since lost whatever favor they once had, but Ford was far behind its rivals in realizing this fact (Plymouth's last roadster and phaeton appeared in 1932, Chevrolet's in '35). Closed rumble-seat types were also in their last year. With sales still slow, the V-8/60 line was reduced to just a coupe, Fordor, and Tudor. Styling for all models was a variation on 1937 themes, announced by more-bulbous faces.

DeLuxes were again fully restyled for 1939, bearing a lower vee'd vertical-bar grille and clean front fenders with integral headlamps. As in recent years, this styling was created by E.T. "Bob" Gregorie under Edsel Ford's guidance. By contrast, that year's Ford Standards looked like warmed-over '38 DeLuxes. The convertible sedan made a final bow, again in the DeLuxe line. Prices rose slightly, now covering a $599-$921 spread. Mechanical changes included internal engine enhancements inspired by the new Mercury and hydraulic instead of mechanical brakes. Old Henry had finally given in on the latter point—three years after Chevrolet and 11 years behind Plymouth. But Ford still couldn't match their independent front suspension, and wouldn't until 1949.

Gregorie made Fords even prettier for 1940—so much so that the DeLuxes in particular have long been coveted collectibles. Sealed-beam headlamps arrived, as elsewhere in Detroit, neatly housed in more-upright fender nacelles. The fenders themselves were beautifully curved to complement body contours;

rear fender skirts, long a popular accessory, imparted an even sleeker look. Standards carried a '39 DeLuxe-style vertical-bar grille. DeLuxes bore a chromed horizontal-bar center section flanked by painted subgrilles in the "catwalk" areas between nose and fenders.

Nineteen-forty was the last year for the little-loved V-8/60 and the first for a Standard-trim wood-body Ford wagon. Yet despite a broad model slate, pretty styling, and prices in the $620-$950 range, Ford trailed Chevy in model-year output by a substantial 222,720 cars. Ford had been "USA-1" for 1934-37, then bowed to Chevy by about 55,000 for recession-year '38 (410,200 to 465,000-plus).

Some dealers had been disappointed in Edsel Ford's new Mercury, feeling a six-cylinder Ford would have been a better idea (which was, in fact, the original concept). Edsel promised a six, then had to reckon with his father. But Henry approved it in one of those strange turnabouts for which he was infamous. Edsel went to work, and the new L-head six bowed for 1941. With 226 cid and 90 horsepower, it had five more cubic inches than the V-8 and a like number of extra horsepower—a bit embarrassing.

The '41s were the biggest, flashiest, and heaviest Fords yet. Wheelbase stretched two inches to 114, bodysides ballooned outward, and a stouter frame contributed to an average 100 pounds of added curb weight. Styling was evolutionary, with wider, more-integrated front fenders; a busy vertical-bar grille

# Ford

1942 Super DeLuxe coupe

1942 Super DeLuxe station wagon

1946 Super DeLuxe Sportsman convertible coupe

1946 Super DeLuxe Fordor sedan

walks. The V-8 was pushed up to the same 90 horsepower as the six—likely by the stroke of a engineer's pen. If the V-8 had to cost more, Ford reasoned, it should have at least as much power, even if only on paper. Specials were now sixes only, but the lineup was otherwise unchanged. Prices were hiked about $100 throughout. Ford built just 43,000 cars from January 1 through February 2, when the government ended civilian production for the duration of World War II. At that point, Ford's 1942 model-year total was just shy of 160,500 cars, versus Chevy's quarter-million-plus.

A renowned pacifist during World War I, Henry Ford was in his late 70s when the Japanese attacked Pearl Harbor on December 7, 1941. But he realized that the Second World War was a very different situation, and had already geared his firm to war production. Ford Motor Company duly turned out a variety of military vehicles including Jeeps (with American Bantam and Willys-Overland), and its new mile-long plant in Willow Run, Michigan, near Detroit, produced a variety of bombers through 1945.

Henry finally surrendered control of his company—but not to Edsel, who died a broken man in 1943 at age 49. Despite the end of the war, the doddering mogul stubbornly continued to manage an increasingly troubled Ford Motor Company until his family insisted he step down. That came in 1945, when he handed the reins to grandson Henry Ford II, who would hold them for the next 33 years, most of them successful. The great old man himself passed on in 1947.

Unlike his grandfather, "HFII" consistently sought and encouraged talented managers. However, he just as consistently encouraged their retirement—or fired them—when they reached a certain level of power. Though the Ford family no longer owns a majority of common stock, Ford is still very much a family operation.

Young Henry quickly returned Ford to civilian production after V-J day. Ford Division was again the industry's volume leader for model-year '46, but Chevrolet would be back to full speed the following year and would remain "USA-1" through 1948.

Like most other makes, Ford returned to peacetime with restyled '42 cars, though it bored its V-8 out to 239.4 cid for an extra 10 horsepower. Also, the low-priced Special Sixes were eliminated, leaving six- and eight-cylinder DeLuxe and Super DeLuxe. And there was now a second V-8 convertible, a novel variation on the standard item called Sportsman.

Developed from Bob Gregorie's wartime sketches, the Sportsman featured white ash and mahogany trim over its doors, rear body panels, and deck, as on the Chrysler Town & Country. This was an easy way to give an old design new appeal, and it boosted floor traffic at Ford dealers. But a $500 price premium over the all-steel convertible limited sales to just 1209 for '46, 2250 for '47, and just 28 for '48 (the last actually reserialed '47s).

Appearance alterations for 1947 involved shuffled nameplates and lower-mounted round parking lights. No changes at all occurred for '48, but the six was rerated to 95 horsepower, up five. Postwar inflation had pushed up prices, the increases averaging about $100 for 1947.

But nothing really new was needed in the car-starved early-postwar market, and Ford output exceeded 429,000 units for 1947. The total was only 248,000 the following year, but that only reflected an early end to 1948 production. The reason was the first all-new postwar Fords that went on sale with great anticipation in June 1948.

Styling for these 1949 models was a competitive process, as Ford solicited ideas from freelancers as well as in-house designers. One outside team was headed by George Walker,

with tall center section flanked by low subgrilles; larger rear fenders; and more-rakish coupe rooflines. The lineup expanded, too: low-priced Special, midrange DeLuxe, and new Super DeLuxe, all offered with either six or V-8. Prices ranged from $684 for the six-cylinder Special coupe to $1013 for the V-8 DeLuxe woody wagon—the first factory-built Ford to break the $1000 barrier.

But none of this did much for sales. While Ford's total volume improved to near 691,500, it remained about two-thirds of Chevy's, which went up even more, to slightly over a million.

The 1942 Fords gained a lower, wider, vertical-bar grille surmounted by rectangular parking lamps in the vestigial cat-

1947½ Super DeLuxe Fodor sedan

1948 Super DeLuxe station wagon

1948 Super DeLuxe convertible coupe

1949 Custom convertible coupe

who hired onetime GM and Raymond Loewy employee Richard Caleal to join designers Joe Oros and Elwood Engel. When Caleal became disenchanted with the direction taken by the other members of the Walker team, he was given permission to pursue his own ideas at his home in Indiana. Working in his kitchen with clay modelers Joe Thompson and John Lutz, Caleal shaped his design.

Later, Henry Ford II and other Ford execs gathered at Walker's studio to view design proposals by Caleal, Ford styling head E.T. "Bob" Gregorie, and Oros and Engel. The executives selected Caleal's design, which went into production basically unchanged, except that his vertical taillights were made horizontal and bled into the rear quarter.

Though the '49 Ford was nowhere near as radical as the 1950-51 Studebaker, it sold in numbers Ford hadn't seen since 1930: over 1.1 million for the extra-long model year. Reflecting this and later achievements, Walker was named design chief for all of Ford Motor Company in 1955.

The '49 Ford was crucial to Dearborn's survival. Young Henry II was still scrambling to bring order to the organizational and fiscal chaos he inherited from his grandfather even as the company continued losing money by the bucketful. But the '49 was the most-changed Ford since the Model A, and was as much a hit.

Though wheelbase and engines were unchanged from 1946-48, the '49 was three inches lower, fractionally shorter, and usefully lighter. Even better, it had a modern ladder-type frame with Dearborn's first fully independent front suspension (via coil springs and upper and lower A-arms), plus a modern rear end with open Hotchkiss drive (replacing torque-tube) and parallel longitudinal leaf springs supporting the live axle. It all added up to a sprightly performer that could run circles around rival Chevys and Plymouths. A '49 Ford couldn't quite reach 100 mph, but hopping up the flathead V-8 was still simple, cheap, and easy. Multiple carburetors, headers, dual exhausts, and other "speed parts" were as close as local auto stores.

Though Ford briefly considered retaining it, the low-selling Sportsman was dropped for '49 and other offerings regrouped into Standard and Custom series. The former offered six and V-8 Tudor and Fordor, along with business and club coupes. The better-trimmed V-8-only Custom deleted the business coupe but added a convertible and a new two-door structural-wood wagon (replacing the previous four-door style).

Prices rose again for '49, the range now $1333-$2119. Overdrive was optional across the board at $97. Ford wouldn't have its own automatic transmission until 1951, though it tried to get one earlier. Studebaker had developed an excellent auto-

1949 Custom two-door station wagon

# Ford

matic for 1950 in association with Warner Gear. Ford wanted to buy it for its own cars, but Studebaker refused—much to its later regret.

The '49 Fords suffered handling and noise problems stemming from the rushed design program. Workmanship also suffered for the same reason, and a 24-day auto workers' strike in May 1948 didn't help either. Even so, these were very worthy automobiles—the first tangible evidence that Henry II was firmly in charge. Ably assisting him was the youthful "Whiz Kids" team of executives and engineers he'd recruited, including one Robert S. McNamara.

The stage was set for a smart comeback in the '50s. And indeed, by 1952, Ford Motor Company had passed a faltering Chrysler Corporation to regain the number-two spot in manufacturer volume. The reason? Interesting cars that sold well.

Efforts for 1950 aimed at quashing the bugs from '49. "50 Ways New, 50 Ways Better," blared the ads. And the 1950s were better: tighter and quieter in corners and rough-road driving alike. A new confection was the V-8 Crestliner, a limited-edition Custom Tudor priced $100-$200 above the standard article. It was snazzy, with a padded canvas-covered top and sweeping contrast-color panel on the bodysides, but sales were only fair at 17,601 for 1950 and another 8703 for '51. Crestliner's real purpose was to counter Chevy's true "hardtop-convertible," the 1950 Bel Air.

Otherwise, the 1950 Fords were predictably much like the '49s, though a crest instead of Ford lettering above the "bullet" grille provided instant I.D. Prices held steady, running from $1333 for the DeLuxe business coupe to $2028 for the Squire. Though still without a hardtop and a fully automatic transmission like Chevrolet, Ford bested 1930's imposing model year output, turning out over 1.2 million cars. But Chevrolet managed nearly 1.5-million, and would remain "USA-1" through 1953.

Seeking greater competitiveness, Ford slightly downpriced its '51 models and applied an attractive facelift featuring a new grille with small twin bullets on a thick horizontal bar. The Custom wagon now bore Country Squire script, but would be the last true Ford woody. Ford finally offered a self-shift transmission in Ford-O-Matic Drive—a two-speed automatic to match Chevy's similar Powerglide—and a redesigned dash gave the interior a more upscale look. Also new for '51 was Ford's first hardtop coupe, the Custom V-8 Victoria. Though it, too, was a bit late, the Vicky proved no less popular than Chevy's Bel Air, selling some 110,000 that debut season. Ford's model-year volume declined by about 200,000 cars, but Chevy's fell a similar amount, reflecting new government-ordered restrictions on civilian production prompted by the Korean War.

Model-year '52 introduced a clean, new, square-rigged Ford with a one-piece windshield, simple grille, small round tail-

**1950 Custom Crestliner two-door sedan**

**1950 DeLuxe Six Fordor sedan**

**1951 Custom Fordor sedan**

**1951 Custom Victoria hardtop coupe**

**1951 Custom Country Squire two-door station wagon**

**1952 Crestline Victoria hardtop coupe**

lamps, and an "air scoop" motif on the lower rear flanks. Only detail changes would occur to this basic design through 1954. Wheelbase crept up to 115 inches for a revised model slate that started with a cheap Mainline Tudor/Fordor, business coupe, and two-door Ranch Wagon, followed by Customline sedans, club coupe, and four-door Country Sedan wagon. Topping the range was the V-8 Crestline group of Victoria hardtop, newly named Sunliner convertible, and posh Country Squire four-door wagon. These wagons, by the way, were Ford's first all-steel models (the Squire switching from real wood to wood-look decals). Assisting in their design was Gordon Buehrig, the famed designer of Classic-era Auburns, Cords, and Duesenbergs who'd also had a hand in the '51 Victoria. Doing more with less, Ford introduced a new 215.3-cid overhead-valve six with 101 horsepower as standard for Mainline/Customline. The flathead V-8 was tweaked to 110 horsepower.

Dearborn observed its Golden Anniversary in 1953, proclaimed on Fords by special steering-wheel-hub medallions. But aside from that and a few other cosmetic details, the '53s were basically '52s with higher prices, now ranging from $1400-$2203. With the Korean conflict ended, Ford Division built 1.2 million cars to edge Chevrolet for the model year (Chevy consoled itself with calendar-year supremacy), but only by dumping cars on dealers in a production "blitz" so they could sell for "less than cost." Ironically, Chevrolet wasn't much affected by this onslaught, but Studebaker, American Motors, and Kaiser-Willys were, because they couldn't afford to discount as much. The Ford blitz is generally considered one of the key factors in the independents' mid-'50s decline.

The venerable flathead V-8 was honorably retired for 1954 in favor of a new overhead-valve "Y-block" V-8 (so-called because of its frontal appearance in cross-section). With 130 horsepower, this was easily the year's hottest engine in the low-price field. Together with ball-joint front suspension, also new, the Y-block greatly narrowed the engineering gap between expensive and inexpensive cars. Its initial 239 cid was the same as flathead displacement, but the ohv had different "oversquare" cylinder dimensions. Compression was 7.2:1 in base trim, but could be taken as high as 12:1 if required (which it wasn't).

The rest of the '54 story was basically 1953 save a larger, 223-cid ohv six with 115 bhp. There was also a novel new hardtop called Skyliner, a Crestline Victoria with a transparent, green-tint Plexiglas roof insert over the front seat. This concept, suggested by Buehrig and realized by interior styling director L. David Ash, is a forerunner of today's moonroof. But it cast a strange light on the interior, and heat buildup was a major problem. That and a price identical with the Sunliner convertible's—$2164—held '54 Skyliner sales to 13,344. Only the Country Squire and Mainline business coupe fared worse.

Retaining the 1952-54 shell, the '55 Ford was completely

1952 Crestline Sunliner convertible coupe

1953 Crestline Country Squire Station Wagon

1953 Crestline Sunliner Official Pace Car

1954 Mainline Tudor sedan

1953 Crestline Victoria hardtop coupe

1954 Crestline Skyliner (glasstop) hardtop coupe

# Ford

1955 Fairlane town sedan four-door

1955 Fairlane Crown Victoria hardtop coupe

1955 Fairlane Crown Victoria hardtop coupe

1956 Customline Fordor sedan

1956 Fairlane Sunliner convertible (prototype)

1956 Fairlane Sunliner convertible coupe

1957 Fairlane 500 Skyliner retractable convertible

1957 Custom 300 Tudor sedan

reskinned, emerging colorful if chromey, with a rakish look of motion and a modestly wrapped windshield. Styling was handled by Franklin Q. Hershey, who also gets credit for that year's new two-seat Thunderbird (*see separate entry*). Club coupes were abandoned, wagons grouped in a separate series, and Crestline was renamed Fairlane (after the Ford family estate in Dearborn). With the "horsepower race" at full gallop, the 239 V-8 was ousted for a 272 enlargement, packing 162/182 horsepower as an option for all models. The standard six gained five bhp to deliver 120 total.

Skyliner was also ousted for '55, but Ford had another idea. This was the Fairlane Crown Victoria, a hardtop-style two-door sedan with a bright metal roof band wrapped up and over from steeply angled B-posts. The "tiara" looked like a roll bar, but added no structural strength; a Plexiglas insert rode ahead of it, as on Skyliner. A full steel-roof model was also offered for $70 less than the "bubble-topper"; predictably, it sold much better: 33,000-plus to just 1999. The totals were 9209 and just 603 for '56, after which the Crown Vic was dumped.

But Ford as a whole did spendidly in banner 1955, shattering its postwar record of 1953 by building nearly 1.5 million cars. Still, the division was done in by an all-new Chevy, which tallied better than 1.7 million. Volume for both makes declined in the industry's overall retreat for '56, but Ford dropped by fewer

# Ford

1957 Country Squire 9-passenger station wagon

1957 Ranchero pickup truck (standard model)

1957 Fairlane Victoria hardotp coupe

1957 Fairlane 500 Sunliner convertible coupe

than 50,000 versus Chevy's loss of nearly 200,000.

Ford's '56 line featured the expected mild facelift, plus more-potent engines and two new models: a Customline Victoria and the division's first four-door hardtop, the Fairlane Town Victoria. Ford also began selling "Lifeguard Design" safety features, equipping all models with dished steering wheel, breakaway rearview mirror, and crashproof door locks; padded dash and sunvisors cost $16 extra, factory-installed seatbelts $9. Buyers responded early in the model year, but the rush to seatbelts overtaxed Ford's supplier, so only 20 percent of the '56s got them. Ford continued to stress safety for a few more years, but put more emphasis on performance. Speaking of which, the 272 V-8 delivered 173 horsepower as a '56 Mainline/Customline option. A new 312 "Thunderbird" unit with 215/225 was optional across the board, and a midrange 292 offered 200 horsepower.

The 1957 Fords were all-new, offering a vast array of V-8s from a 190-bhp 272 up to a 245-bhp 312. The 223-cid six was standard for all but one model. There were now two wheelbases and no fewer than five series: 116 inches for Station Wagon and Custom/Custom 300 sedans (replacing Mainline/Customline), 118 inches for Fairlane and the new line-topping Fairlane 500. All were available with six or V-8 power. Both Fairlane series listed two- and four-door Victorias, plus thin-pillar equivalents that looked like hardtops with windows up. The glamorous droptop Sunliner was now a Fairlane 500 and came with the base V-8. Haulers comprised plain and fancier Del Rio two-door Ranch Wagons, a pair of four-door Country Sedans, and the wood-look four-door Squire—Ford's priciest '57 wagon at $2684.

Ford's '57 styling was particularly simple for the period: a blunt face with clean, full-width rectangular grille; tasteful side moldings; and tiny tailfins. More importantly, it was new against Chevy's second facelift in two years. Unfortunately, the Fords had some structural weaknesses (principally roof panels) and were prone to rust, one reason you don't see that many today. But though Plymouth arguably won the styling stakes with its finned "Forward Look," 1957 was a great Ford year. In fact, the division scored a substantial win in model-year output with close to 1.7 million cars to Chevy's 1.5 million. Some statisticians also had Ford ahead in calendar-year volume for the first time since 1935, though the final score showed Chevy ahead by a mere 130 cars.

The Skyliner name returned in mid-1957, but on a very different Ford: the world's first mass-produced retractable hardtop. An addition to the Fairlane 500 series, it stemmed from engineering work done a few years before at Continental Division, which had considered, but didn't produce, the 1956 Mark II as a "retrac." Ford sold 20,766 Skyliners for '57, but demand fast tapered to 14,713 for '58, then to 12,915. The model was duly axed after 1959, a victim of new division chief Bob McNamara's no-nonsense approach to products and profits. Today, the "retracs" are prime collectibles, a monument to an age when Detroit thought it could do anything.

For 1958, Ford countered all-new passenger Chevys and modestly restyled Plymouths with a glittery facelift featuring quad headlamps and taillamps, a massive bumper/grille a la '58 Thunderbird, and more anodized aluminum trim. V-8 choices expanded via two new "FE-series" big-blocks: a 332 offering 240/265 horsepower, and a 300-bhp 352. A deep national recession cut Ford volume to just under 988,000 cars. Chevrolet sold over 1.1 million, but spent much more money to do so.

Chevy then unveiled an all-new line of radical "bat-fin" cars for 1959. Ford replied with more-conservative styling that helped it close the model-year gap to less than 12,000 units. A major reskin of the basic 1957-58 bodyshells brought square lines; simple side moldings; a heavily sculptured "flying-V" back panel; and a low, rectangular grille filled with floating starlike ornaments. All previous models continued, though now on the 118-inch wheelbase. Come midseason, a new Galaxie series of two- and four-door pillared and pillarless sedans generated high buyer interest and strong sales with their square but stylish T-Bird-inspired wide-quarter rooflines. At the same time, the Sunliner convertible and Skyliner retrac gained Galaxie rear-fender script (but retained Fairlane 500 I.D. at the rear). V-8s were down to a 200-bhp 292, 225-bhp 332, and 300-bhp 352. Also carried over from '58 was Cruise-O-Matic, Ford's smooth new three-speed automatic transmission that proved a sales plus against Chevy's Powerglide, if not Plymouth's responsive three-speed TorqueFlite.

# Ford

1958 Custom 300 Tudor sedan

1959 Country Squire 9-passenger station wagon

1958 Fairlane 500 Skyliner retractable hardtop

1959 Fairlane 500 Fordor sedan

1958 Ranchero Custom pickup truck

1959 Fairlane 500 Skyliner retractable hardtop

For Ford Motor Company as a whole, 1959 seemed to justify the strenuous efforts of Henry Ford II and board chairman Ernest R. Breech. Assuming control of a third-rate company in 1945, they'd turned it into something approaching General Motors in less than 15 years.

Ford's path through the '60s closely parallels Chevrolet's. At decade's end, it was also selling only about 400,000 more cars per year than in 1960—despite expansion into important new markets: economy compacts, intermediates, and sportier standard-size models. Also like Chevy, Ford built these diverse types on relatively few wheelbases. (See separate entries for the stories on the personal-luxury T-Bird and the new-for '65 Mustang "ponycar," the two most-specialized Fords of this period.)

Key management changes occurred early on. Lee A. Iacocca took charge as Ford Division general manager in 1960. George Walker left the following year and Eugene Bordinat became Dearborn's design chief. Iacocca soon put an end to the mundane people-movers favored by Bob McNamara, and by 1970 Ford was offering some exciting cars.

Ford also moved from "Chevy-follower" to "Chevy-leader" in the '60s. Its compact Falcon far outsold the rival Corvair, its 1962 midsize Fairlane was two years ahead of Chevelle, and its phenomenally successful Mustang sent Chevrolet racing to draw up the Camaro.

The best way to summarize Fords of the '60s is by size. The smallest was Falcon, which bowed for 1960 as one of the new Big Three compacts (along with Corvair and Chrysler's Valiant). Wheelbase was a trim 109.5 inches through 1965, then 110.9 (113 for wagons). Two- and four-door sedans and four-door wagons were always offered, convertibles and hardtop coupes for 1963-65. All had unit construction.

To some, the pre-'66 Falcons were the ultimate "throwaway" cars: designed to sell at a low price—initially just under $2000—and to be discarded within five years (some said one year). To others, though, Falcon was the Model A reborn: cheap but cheerful, simple but not unacceptably spartan. A conventional suspension and cast-iron six—mostly a 170-cid unit of 101 horsepower—certainly looked dull next to Corvair engineering, but made for friendly, roomy little cars that rode well and delivered 20-25 mpg. Falcons were also easily serviced by "shadetree mechanics" who wouldn't go near the complicated Chevy compact. Though sales gradually declined due to competition from both inside and outside the division, Falcon was always profitable.

Falcon replied to the hot-selling Corvair Monza in the spring of 1961 with the bucket-seat Futura two-door. All Falcons were reskinned for 1964-65 with pointy front fenders and generally square, less-distinctive lines. The prime collector Falcon is the

1960 Galaxie Starliner hardotp coupe

1961 Galaxie club sedan four-door

1960 Galaxie Town Victoria hardtop sedan

1961 Galaxie Starliner hardtop coupe

1960 Falcon two-door sedan (DeLuxe trim)

1961 Falcon Ranchero pickup (standard trim)

Futura Sprint, a pretty convertible and hardtop coupe offered from mid-1963 through 1965. These were available with the lively "Challenger" small-block V-8 from the midsize Fairlane—initially a 260 with 164 horsepower, then a 289 with about 200 horsepower for '65. It was a fine engine, which helps explain why its 302 evolution continued all the way into the 1990s. It completely transformed Falcon performance without greatly affecting mileage. Sprints offered special exterior I.D., vinyl bucket seats, console, and 6000-rpm tachometer. When equipped with optional four-speed manual transmission, they were great fun to drive.

The 1966 Falcons were basically shorter versions of that year's rebodied Fairlanes, with the same sort of curvy GM-like contours and long-hood/short-deck proportions of Mustang. Falcon continued in this form through early 1970. In 1967, its last year before emissions controls, the 289 packed 225 horsepower in "Stage 2" tune with four-barrel carburetor, and made for some very fast Falcons, the sportiest of which was the pillared Futura Sport Coupe. The 289 was detuned to 195 horsepower for '68, when the aforementioned 302 arrived as a new option. This ran on regular gas with a two-barrel carb and delivered 210 bhp; with a four-barrel it made 230 horsepower on premium fuel, though emissions considerations soon put an end to that version.

Mid-1970 brought the final Falcons: a stark wagon and two sedans derived from the intermediate Torino (which had evolved from Fairlane). These could be powered by everything from a 155-bhp 250-cid six to a big-block 429 V-8 with 360-370 horsepower. But the name had outlived its usefulness, and Ford had a new compact, the Maverick, so Falcon was consigned to history.

Back to 1962, Ford broke new ground with the midsize Fairlane, which was basically a bigger Falcon on a 115.5-inch wheelbase. In concept it was much like Virgil Exner's downsized '62 Plymouths and Dodges. But unlike Chrysler, Ford retained full-size Customs and Galaxies—a wise move even though Fairlane sold more than 297,000 units its first year and over 300,000 for '63. Helping the cause were attractive prices in the $2100-$2800 range.

The Fairlane was significant for introducing Ford's brilliant small-block V-8, the basis for some of its hottest '60s cars. Bored out to 289 cid as a '63 option, it packed up to 271 horsepower—almost one horsepower per cubic inch. Powerful and smooth yet surprisingly economical, it was the definitive small V-8. Tuned versions in sports-racers like the Ford GT40 and Shelby Cobra disproved the old adage about there being "no substitute for cubic inches." In fact, the GT40 nearly took the world GT Manufacturers Championship away from Ferrari in 1964, its first full season. Still, it was the big-block Ford GTs that won the Le Mans 24-Hours, the world's most-prestigious sports-car endurance race, two years in a row, 1966-67.

Initially, Fairlane offered two- and four-door sedans in base

# Ford

1962½ Falcon DeLuxe Futura sports coupe

1962 Falcon DeLuxe Futura sports coupe

1962 Galaxie 500/XL Sunliner convertible coupe

1962 Fairlane 500 four-door sedan

1962 Galaxie 500 Sunliner with Starlit top

1963½ Falcon Futura Sprint sports coupe hardtop

1963 300 four door sedan

1963 Galaxie 500/XL "Scatback" hardtop coupe

1964 Fairlane 500 sports coupe hardtop

1964 Falcon Futura Sprint sports coupe hardtop

and sportier 500 trim, plus a bucket-seat 500 Sport Coupe. Four-door Ranch and Squire wagons and a brace of two-door hardtops were added for '63. Beginning with the '64s, Ford offered a growing assortment of handling and performance options, including stiff suspensions and four-speed gearboxes.

Fairlane was completely rebodied for '66 on a 116-inch wheelbase (113 for wagons) gaining a sleek, tailored look via curved side glass and flanks, stacked quad headlamps, and tidy vertical taillights. Heading the line were the bucket-seat 500XL hardtop coupe and convertible in base and GT trim. Standard XLs came with a 120-bhp 200-cid six, but most were ordered with optional 289 V-8s. GTs carried a big-block 390 making a potent 335 horsepower. That engine could be ordered on any Fairlane, and racers were quick to put it in stripped two-door sedans, which earned respect for their competitive prowess.

With no change in wheelbases, Fairlane got another body and styling change for 1968. Joining the base and 500 lines was a new Torino series, Ford's lushest intermediates yet. A 115-bhp 200-cid six was standard for all but the Torino GT convertible, hardtop coupe, and new fastback hardtop (all duplicated in the 500 line), which came with the 210-bhp 302 V-8 as well as buckets-and-console interior, pinstriping, and more performance options than a salesman could memorize.

Ford's '69 midsizers were '68 repeats save for new fastback and notchback Torino hardtops called Cobra (after Carroll Shelby's muscular Ford-powered sports cars). These came with the 335-bhp 428 V-8 that had first appeared in the "1968½" Mercury Cyclone as the "Cobra Jet." A $133 option was "Ram-Air," a fiberglass hood scoop connecting to a special air-cleaner assembly with a valve that ducted incoming air directly into the carb. Four-speed manual gearbox, stiff suspension and racing-style hood locks were all standard. One magazine was actually disappointed when its Cobra ran 0-60 mph in 7.2 seconds and the quarter-mile in 15 seconds at 98.3 miles per hour! But most everyone admitted that of all the '69 "supercars"—Plymouth GTX, Dodge Charger R/T, Pontiac GTO, Chevelle 396, and Buick GS 400—the Torino Cobra was the tightest, best-built, and quietest.

Torino Cobras could be potent racing machines. Ford discovered that the styling of the counterpart Cyclone was slightly more aerodynamic, and thus usually ran the Mercurys in stock-car contests over 250 miles long. Nevertheless, a race-prepped Torino could achieve about 190 mph, and Lee Roy Yarborough drove one to win the '69 Daytona 500.

Ford's biggest cars of the '60s were variously offered as Custom/Custom 500, Fairlane/Fairlane 500 (pre-'62), Galaxie/Galaxie 500, and Station Wagon. Their "standard" wheelbase swelled to 119 inches for 1960, then became 121 after 1968. These were heavy cars (3000-4000 pounds), and most weren't rewarding to drive except on an Interstate, but certain variations were surprisingly capable on winding roads.

What we now call the full-size Fords began the decade with all-new bodyshells that would persist through 1964. The '60s were much longer, lower, wider, and sleeker than the boxy '59s, and even mimicked Chevy's batfins a little, but they looked good with their chrome-edged beltlines and bigger glass areas. The Skyliner was gone, but there was a new fixed-roof Starliner hardtop coupe with sleek semifastback profile. Though less popular than square-roof Galaxies, the Starliner was just the thing for NASCAR racing by dint of its slipperier shape.

Starliner bowed out after 1961, when standards were facelifted via a full-width concave grille (with '59-style insert) and a return to round taillights capped by discreet blades. That year's top engine option was the new 390-cid version of the FE-series big-block. This packed 300 standard horsepower, but was available, though on a very limited basis, as a high-compression

1964 Galaxie 500/XL Sunliner convertible coupe

1965 Falcon Futura hardtop coupe

1965 Galaxie 500/XL hardtop coupe

1965 Ford Galaxie 500/XL convertible coupe

"Interceptor" with 375 and 401 horsepower.

Chunkier, more-"important" styling marked the '62 standards, which regrouped into Galaxie/Galaxie 500/Station Wagon lines spanning roughly the same models. Reflecting the buckets-and-console craze then sweeping Detroit were the midseason 500 XL Victoria hardtop coupe and Sunliner convertible. The "500" stood for the 500-mile NASCAR races the division was winning (Ford won every 500 in '63). "XL" purportedly stood for "Xtra Lively," though the standard powertrain was "just" a 170-bhp 292 V-8 and Cruise-O-Matic. But options could turn this sporty hunk into a real fire-breather. Besides Borg-Warner four-speed manual gearbox and 300-, 340-, 375-, and 401-bhp 390s, there was a larger-bore 406 big-block providing 385/405 horsepower. An even bigger bore for '63 produced a 427-cid powerhouse with 410/425 horsepower. High prices—around $400—made these engines relatively uncommon.

New lower-body sheetmetal gave the '63 "Super-Torque" Galaxies a cleaner, leaner look, announced by a simple concave grille. A pair of cheap "300" sedans was added (renamed Custom/Custom 500 for '64), and there was more midyear excitement in a set of 500 and 500XL sports hardtops with thin-pillar "slantback" rooflines, a bit starchier than the old Starliner but again aimed right at the stock-car ovals.

The last, but most-substantial, restyle on the big 1960 body occurred for '64, bringing heavily sculptured lower-body sheetmetal, a complex grille, and slantback rooflines for all closed models. The entire Ford line won *Motor Trend* magazine's "Car of the Year" award, partly because of the division's ever-widening "Total Performance" campaign. Performance was just what the big Fords had, with available small-block and big-block V-8s offering from 195 up to a rousing 425 horsepower. Even a relatively mild 390 XL could scale 0-60 mph in 9.3 seconds; a 427 reduced that to just over 7 seconds. The one major complaint was a marked tendency to nosedive in "panic" stops, aggravated by overboosted power brakes.

Ford had its best NASCAR year ever in 1965, winning 48 of 55 events, including 32 straight at one point. Luxury, however, got most of the showroom emphasis. All-new except for engines, the '65s were distinguished by simpler, more-linear styling announced by stacked quad headlamps. Underneath was a stronger chassis with a completely new front suspension evolved from NASCAR experience. But arriving at midyear were the poshest big Fords ever, the $3300 Galaxie 500 LTD hardtop coupe and sedan, claimed to be "quiet as a Rolls-Royce." The times were indeed a-changin'. With intermediates taking over in competition, the big Fords no longer needed any sort of "performance" image to support sales.

The '65 platform got a minor touch up for '66, and LTDs gained "7-Litre" companions powered by Thunderbird's big 345-bhp 428 engine. The following year brought new outer sheetmetal

**1965 Fairlane 500 sports coupe hardtop**

**1966 Galaxy 500 LTD limousine (limited production)**

**1966 Ford Galaxie 500 convertible coupe**

**1966 Falcon Futura sports coupe**

**1966 Fairlane 500/XL hardtop coupe**

**1967 Galaxie 500/XL convertible coupe**

with more flowing lines and "faster" rooflines on hardtop coupes. LTD became a separate three-model series, adding four-door sedan but losing the slow-selling 7-Litre models. Hidden-headlamp grilles marked the '68 LTDs and Galaxie XLs as part of a lower-body restyle for all models.

A new bodyshell arrived for '69 with a two-inch longer wheelbase, a "tunneled backlight" for newly named "SportsRoof" fastbacks, and ventless door glass on hardtops and convertibles. LTD sales continued rising. Ford had built nearly 139,000 of the '68s; it built more than twice that number for '69.

Ford kept pace with Chevrolet in the '60s production race, and actually beat it for model years 1961 and '66. Ford would be number one again for 1970 and '71 at slightly over two-million cars to Chevy's 1.5/1.8 million. Ford enjoyed its first two-million-car year in 1965, though that was a great year for all Detroit.

Ford wouldn't lead Chevy again until the late '80s, but it generally fared well in the '70s. Still, Dearborn was the last of the Big Three to abandon traditional full-size cars—and the first to suffer for it. In the wake of the OPEC oil embargo and the first energy crisis, Chrysler pushed compacts while GM went forward with plans to downsize its entire fleet. Ford stubbornly resisted the winds of change, promoting its aging big cars on the basis of greater passenger space and the presumed safety of their "road-hugging weight." But the public didn't buy this cynical line—or as many of the cars.

In large measure, this denial reflected the personal view of chairman Henry Ford II, who decreed there would be no wholesale rush to smaller cars, no vast capital investment in new technology. As a result, Ford greeted 1980 a critical two to three years behind GM in the fuel efficiency and "space" races—and at a critical sales disadvantage next to its domestic foes and a horde of fast-rising Japanese makes. The firm would recover, but not before making drastic product changes.

Leading the 1970 line were modestly facelifted full-size Fords with "poke-through" center grille sections on LTDs and XLs, plus revamped rear ends on all models. Four series were offered: Custom, Galaxie 500, XL, and LTD. The sporty XLs were in their final year. Luxury was further emphasized with a new LTD Brougham hardtop coupe, hardtop sedan, and four-door sedan.

Broughams also featured in the 1970 Torino line, which shared new exterior panels "shaped by the wind" with a three-model Fairlane 500 series. Wheelbase grew an inch; profiles were lower and five inches longer. The Torino Cobra returned as Ford's "budget muscle car" with standard 360/375-bhp 429 V-8. It was a blistering performer and its new hardtop body with concave backlight was distinctive, but hot-car demand was fast-waning everywhere, and only 7675 were built for the model year.

**1967 Fairlane 500/XL GTA convertible coupe**

**1968 LTD hardtop sedan**

**1968 Torino GT fastback hardtop coupe**

**1969 Galaxie 500 fastback hardtop coupe**

**1968 Torino GT 428 Cobra Jet Official Pace Car**

**1969 LTD hardtop sedan**

# Ford

1969 Fairlane Cobra 428 CJ SportsRoof hardtop coupe

1969 Torino GT convertible coupe

1970 Torino GT SportsRoof hardtop coupe

1970½ Falcon two-door sedan

1970 LTD Brougham hardtop sedan

Ford scored much higher 1970 sales with its new compact Maverick, a semifastback two-door on a 103-inch wheelbase. Introduced in early '69, Maverick was much like the original Falcon in size, price, performance, and simplicity; even its basic chassis and powertrain were the same. Arriving just below $2000 and backed by an aggressive but light-hearted ad campaign, this import-fighter scored an impressive 579,000 model-year sales, contributing greatly to Ford's production victory over Chevy.

Bolstering Maverick's appeal for '71 was a notchback four-door on a 109.9-inch wheelbase (almost the same as the original Falcon's), a sportier two-door called Grabber, and a newly optional 302 V-8 as an alternative to the 100-bhp 170 six. With minor changes, Maverick would carry the division's compact sales effort through 1977, which it did tolerably well, though its old-fashioned engineering looked increasingly so with time and the arrival of more-capable domestic and foreign competitors.

Of course, there was little here to interest enthusiasts. The Grabber looked snazzy but was pretty tame even with V-8. And certain requisites like decent instruments and front-disc brakes were either late in coming (the latter didn't arrive until '76) or not available. Maverick's last gesture to the youth market was the Stallion, a 1976 trim package similar to those offered on the Pinto and Mustang II. The Maverick kit, which was strictly for two-doors, included black paint accents, twin door mirrors, styled steel wheels, raised-white-letter tires, and special badging. More popular was the Luxury Decor Option (LDO), a 1973 package available for either body style through the end of the line. It comprised upgraded interior appointments color-keyed to a special paint scheme crowned by a matching vinyl top.

Ford's major 1971 announcement was the four-cylinder Pinto, a 2000-pound, 94.2-inch-wheelbase subcompact with fastback styling in two-door and Runabout three-door hatchback models. A direct reply to Chevrolet's Vega, also new that year, it was smaller, less technically daring, less accommodating, and its performance and fuel economy were nothing special compared to that of many imports. Yet Pinto usually outsold the trouble-prone Vega as well as many overseas contenders. Offered with 98- and 122-cid engines through 1973, then 122- and 140-cid fours, it was progressively dressed-up and civilized with nicer trim and more convenience options. Three-door wagons arrived for 1972, including a woody-look Squire (some called it "Country Squirt"). By 1976, there was also a youthful "Cruising Wagon" with blanked-off side windows and cute little rear portholes. Still, Pinto remained primarily basic transportation throughout its long 10-year life.

Though Pinto served Ford well in a difficult period, it will forever be remembered as what one wag called "the barbecue that seats four." That refers to the dangerously vulnerable fuel tank and filler-neck design of 1971-76 sedan models implicated in a rash of highly publicized (and fatal) fires following rear-end collisions. Sadly, Ford stonewalled in a number of lawsuits all the way to federal court, which severely tarnished its public image, even if Pinto sales didn't seem to suffer much. What really put Pinto out to pasture after 1980 was not bad publicity but relative lack of change—and the advent of a much better small Ford.

The midsize Torino proved exceptionally popular in the early '70s, then fell from favor once fuel economy became a pressing consumer concern. The 14-model 1971 lineup was basically a carryover of the previous year's. The Cobra fastback coupe remained the most-exciting of this bunch, though its standard engine was downgraded to a 285-bhp version of the ubiquitous 351 small-block first seen for 1969. High-power and big-inch engines began disappearing at Ford and throughout Detroit in 1972. By 1980, only a mildly tuned 351 remained as an option

# Ford

1970 Maverick fastback coupe

1971 Torino Cobra SportsRoof coupe

1971 LTD Brougham hardtop coupe

1971 Pinto fastback coupe

1971 Torino Brougham "formal" hardtop coupe

1972 Gran Torino Brougham sedan

1972 Torino Sport fastback hardtop coupe

1972 Galaxie 500 four-door hardtop

for full-size Fords.

Except for engines, the 1972 Torino was all-new—and a big disappointment. Like GM's post-1967 intermediates, models divided along two wheelbases: 114-inch two-door hardtops and fastbacks (including semisporty GT variants) and 118-inch sedans and wagons. Body-on-frame construction appeared for the first time, and dimensions ballooned close to those of late-'60s Galaxies and LTDs. Symbolic of most everything wrong with Detroit at the time, these Torinos were needlessly outsized, overweight, and thirsty, with limited interior room and soggy chassis. Ford tried to make them passably economical, then gave up and simply fitted a larger fuel tank. After getting just 13.5 mpg with a '76, the auto editors of Consumer Guide® decided that "the more buyers learn about the Torino, the more reasons they will find to opt for a Granada."

Equally dismal was the tarted-up Torino bowing at mid-1974 to answer Chevy's popular Monte Carlo. Sharing a coupe bodyshell and running gear with that year's new fat-cat Mercury Cougar, this Grand Torino Elite leaned heavily on "Thunderbird tradition" with most every personal-luxury cliche of the period: overstuffed velour interior, a square "formal" grille, stand-up hood ornament, and a vinyl-covered rear half-roof with dual "opera" windows. Initially priced at $4437, the Elite didn't sell as well as the Monte, though over 366,000 were

# Ford

built through 1976. After that point, a downsized, down-priced T-bird rendered it redundant.

Granada was a far more rational proposition and one of Ford's best-timed ideas of this decade. Introduced during 1975, it was conceived as just a slightly larger Maverick using the same chassis and drivetrains. But when the fuel crunch boosted small-car sales, Ford decided to retain Maverick and launch its erstwhile successor as a more-luxurious compact half a step up in price. This explains why the Granada appeared on the four-door Maverick's 109.9-inch wheelbase.

Adroitly keyed to the changing market, Granada blended American-style luxury with the mock-Mercedes look then in vogue. Buyers wholeheartedly approved, and Granada zoomed from nowhere to become Ford Division's top-seller, outdistancing the full-sizers and swollen Torinos by wide margins. It was soon a familiar sight on American roads. Not that it performed that well on those roads with its untidy cornering response and a roly-poly ride on rough sections. Nevertheless, Granada bridged a big market gap at a crucial time, appealing to both compact buyers with upscale aspirations and big-car owners now energy-conscious for the first time. Offerings through 1980 comprised six and V-8 four-door sedan and opera-window coupe in base and plusher Ghia trim (the last referring to the famed Italian coachbuilder bought by Ford in 1970). There was also a gesture toward sport in the 1978-80 ESS—for "European Sports Sedan"—but it was only a gesture.

Maverick's true successor bowed for 1978 with a name borrowed from Ford's Australian subsidiary: Fairmont. It was undoubtedly Dearborn's single-most-significant new product of the decade, although few knew that outside the company. Why? Because Fairmont's basic engineering would be the foundation for most Ford Motor Company cars introduced through the mid-1980s, including a new-generation Mustang and Thunderbird.

Billed as the first FoMoCo car designed with the aid of computer analysis, the Fairmont (and its Zephyr twin at Mercury) was a common-sense car and pretty conventional. Though conceived around a traditional front-engine/rear-drive format, it was a big improvement over Maverick: clean-lined; sensibly boxy for good interior space on a shorter 105.5-inch wheelbase; lighter and thus thriftier than many expected. Engines were familiar—initially the 140-cid Pinto four, 200-cid six, and 302 V-8—but there was a new all-coil suspension with modified MacPherson-strut front geometry, which mounted the coil springs on lower A-arms. Aside from better handling, this arrangement opened up more underhood space for easier servicing. A front stabilizer bar was standard, as was rack-and-pinion steering, offered at extra cost with variable-ratio power assist, a new item shared with several other Ford models that year.

1973 Pinto Squire two-door station wagon

1973 LTD Brougham hardtop sedan

1974 LTD Brougham sedan

1974 Gran Torino Brougham hardtop coupe

1975 Granada coupe

1975 Maverick fastback coupe

The "Fox" program that produced Fairmont was one of Ford's first projects initiated after the 1973-74 energy crisis, but it wasn't Dearborn's only attempt at downsizing. For 1977, the old Torino was refurbished with cleaner exterior sheetmetal and "badge-engineered" to pass as a new-wave big car. Called LTD II, it was only a little lighter than before, and sales went nowhere. One reason was the simultaneous arrival of a new downsized Thunderbird on this same platform. With much lower prices than before and that magical name, the 'Bird swamped LTD II in sales.

Besides a new Fairmont-based Mustang, 1979 saw the fruition of the "Panther" design project in an LTD that was genuinely downsized. Yet it was less successful than the Fairmont or Mustang—and that was curious. In size and execution this smaller LTD was fully a match for shrunken GM opponents, riding a 114.3-inch wheelbase yet offering more claimed passenger and trunk space than the outsized 1973-78 cars. Styling was boxier and less pretentious, and visibility and fuel economy were better. So were ride and handling, thanks to a new all-coil suspension with more-precise four-bar-link location for the live rear axle. Coupes, sedans, and wagons in two trim levels were offered. With all this, what Ford trumpeted as a "New American Road Car" should have scored even higher output than the 357,000 recorded for '79. The new LTD thus trailed the big Oldsmobiles for second place in full-size car sales and ran far behind Chevy's Caprice/Impala.

Two factors seemed to be at work. One was GM's two-year lead in downsizing. The other was a severe downturn in the national economy—abetted by another fuel crisis—that began in the spring of '79 and put a big crimp in all new-car sales. This LTD would enjoy a sales resurgence, but not before Ford and the U.S. industry passed through three of their bleakest years ever.

Those years—1980-82—saw Ford Division output drop from 1.16 million cars to just under 749,000. But thanks to an economic recovery and an ever-changing line of ever-improving Fords, the division went back above the 1.1-million mark—and would stay there through decade's end. In the process, Ford overhauled Chevrolet, becoming "USA-1" for 1988.

A division mainstay throughout the '80s was the subcompact Escort, the new front-drive 1981 replacement for Pinto. Billed as the first in a promised fleet of Ford "world cars," it was jointly designed by the firm's U.S., British, and German branches under Project "Erika," but the European version ended up sleeker and faster than its American cousin. The practical, low-priced U.S. Escort set a fast sales pace with at least 320,000 copies in each of its first two years. Volume eased to under a quarter million for '85, then returned to at least 363,000 each year through decade's end. The peak was 1986 at over 430,000.

Numerous refinements marked Escort's evolution through

**1976 LTD Landau coupe**

**1976 Maverick Stallion fastback coupe**

**1976 Elite coupe**

**1977 Ford LTD Landau four-door sedan**

**1976 Pinto Stallion Runabout hatchback coupe**

**1977 Pinto Runabout hatchback coupe**

1990. There were always three-door hatchbacks and four-door wagons, plus hatchback sedans after 1981. All rode a 94.2-inch wheelbase and employed transverse-mounted four-cylinder engines—a new "CVH" single-overhead-cam design with hemispherical combustion chambers—initially teamed with four-speed overdrive manual or three-speed automatic transaxles. An optional five-speed manual came along for 1983. All-coil four-wheel independent suspension persisted throughout, with MacPherson struts and lower control arms fore, modified struts on trailing arms and lower control arms aft. Rack-and-pinion steering and front-disc/rear-drum brakes completed the basic specs.

Escort's original 1.6-liter (98-cid) engine had just 69 horsepower, but by 1983 was up to 72/80 horsepower with two-barrel carb or 88 horsepower in optional throttle-body fuel-injected form. The last was standard for a new three-door GT model, which also came with five-speed, firm suspension, and black exterior trim. An optional 2.0-liter (121-cid) 52-bhp diesel four from Mazda arrived for 1984—just in time for the start of a gas glut that quickly killed most all diesel demand in the U.S. That engine duly vanished after '87. A more-exciting 1984 development was a turbocharged 1.6-liter GT with 120 horsepower and a suitably uprated chassis. It was fast and fun but crude and not very quiet. A more-convenient, restyled dash was featured across the line.

A mid-1985 upgrade brought a larger 1.9-liter (113.5 cid) "CVH" with 86 horsepower in carbureted form or 108 with option electronic port fuel injection. The latter was newly standard for GT, which gained its own asymmetric body-color grille, aluminum wheels, bigger tires, rear spoiler, and rocker panel "skirts." All Escorts were mildly facelifted with smoother noses in the "aero" idiom pioneered by the '83 Thunderbird, marked by flush headlamps.

By 1987, Escort's plethora of alphabet series had been sifted down to a stark three-door called Pony, volume-selling GL (all three body styles), and three-door GT. The base engine was treated to throttle-body injection and moved up to 90 horsepower. Styling became smoother in mid-1988: revamped rear quarters for sedans, a new grille and spoiler for GT, and minor cleanups elsewhere. GL was renamed LX, and the dash was restyled a second time. As with previous midyear model revisions, this one carried into 1989 and then 1990 practically without change.

Escort's high success was not matched by an unhappy sporty coupe offshoot, the EXP. New for 1982, it was Ford's first two-seater since the original Thunderbird, but its "frog-eye" styling wasn't in the same league. And though an Escort underneath, it cost considerably more. Still, first-year sales were respectable at over 98,000. But they plunged ominously to under 20,000 for 1983. The following year, EXP picked up the "bubbleback" hatch of its discontinued Mercury twin, the LN7, as well as Escort's new dash and 120-bhp turbo option. Sales recovered to over 23,000. The little-changed '85s sold some 26,400 early into the calendar year, when Ford suspended production. The car then reemerged in mid-1986 as the Escort EXP, with a similar new flush-headlamp front, revamped dash, and 1.9-liter engines for two models: 86-bhp Luxury Coupe and 108-bhp Sport Coupe. Though nearly 31,000 were sold, EXP was still unequal to Japanese two-seaters like the Honda CRX and Toyota MR2. With base and luxury coupe, EXP eased below 26,000 for '87, then was abandoned in 1988 as a bad bet, though this did free up assembly-line space for regular Escorts.

Another constant of Ford's 1980s fleet was the full-size 1979-vintage LTD, which continued beyond 1990 with just minor yearly alterations to equipment, styling, and engines. The changes are easy to chart: standard four-speed overdrive automatic transmission and 255-cid V-8, a new uplevel series reviv-

**1977 Granada with Sports Coupe option**

**1978 Granada ESS (European Sports Sedan)**

**1978 Ranchero GT pickup truck**

**1978 LTD II Brougham coupe**

ing the Crown Victoria name (1980); no more 351 option (1982); standard 302 V-8 with throttle-body fuel injection for all models renamed LTD Crown Victoria (1983); sequential multiport injection for 150 horsepower (versus 140), premium LX series added (1986); two-door coupe canceled, "aero" front and rear styling for remaining four-door sedan and Country Squire wagon (1988); standard driver-side air bag, new-style dash, and revised equipment (1990).

Despite the year-to-year sameness, many buyers still craved big, Detroit-style luxury, and the fact that fewer such cars were available as gas became cheaper again only worked in the Crown Vic's favor. Though sales fluctuated, this line was good for an annual average of well over 118,000—considerably more

1978 Fairmont Squire station wagon

1978 Fairmont Futura coupe

1978 LTD two-door sedan

1979 LTD Country Squire station wagon

1979 Granada ESS four-door sedan

1979 LTD II coupe with Sports Touring package

1979 Pinto Cruising wagon

1980 Granada four-door sedan

in some years. As late as 1990, Crown Vic did a healthy 74,000. By that point, though, the cars themselves were sourced mainly from Canada.

While Fairmont continued carrying Ford's banner in the compact segment, two derivatives served as the division's midsize warriors. First was a new 1981 Granada, basically the two- and four-door Fairmont sedans with a square eggcrate grille, bulkier sheetmetal, and somewhat plusher appointments. Fairmont wagons transferred to this line for '82. This Granada sold respectably: about 120,000 a year. Engines were the same as Fairmont's: standard 2.3-liter four, optional 200-cid six, and "fuel crisis" 255 V-8 (the last eliminated after '81).

For 1983, Granada was transformed into a "small" LTD. This was also an uptown Fairmont, restyled with a sloped nose, airier "six-light" greenhouse, and modestly lipped trunklid. Along with that year's new Thunderbird, it announced Ford's turn to "aero" styling. By 1984, Granada engines were initially carried over along with a new 232-cid V-6. By 1985, only the four, V-6, and an optional 165-bhp 302 V-8 were fielded, the last reserved for a semisporting LX sedan that sold just 3260 copies. Undoubtedly helped by image rub-off from its big sister, the little LTD sold a lot better than Granada: nearly 156,000 for '83 and over 200,000 in 1984 and '85—Ford's second-best-seller after Escort.

# Ford

1981 Escort GLX liftgate wagon with Squire Trim

1980 Fairmont four-door with Exterior Decor Group

1981 Granada GL two-door sedan

1982 EXP 2-passenger hatchback coupe

1981 LTD Country Squire station wagon

1983 LTD Crown Victoria four-door sedan

Fairmont, meantime, finished its run in 1983 after few interim changes from '78. Two sedans, plain and fancy wagons, and a smart "basket-handle-roof" coupe reviving the Futura name were offered through 1981 (after which the wagons became Granadas). Engines were the usual Fox assortment: 2.3-liter four, 200-cid straight six, and small-block V-8s (302 cid for 1978-79, 255 cid for 1980-81). Sales tapered off along with the economy, dropping from the first-year high of nearly 461,000 to less than 81,000 by 1983. Still, that was a fine showing in a turbulent period. The Fairmont had more than done its job.

Filling Fairmont's shoes for 1984 was a new front-drive compact called Tempo, a notchback four-door and coupelike two-door with "jellybean" styling on a 99.9-inch chassis with suspension much like Escort's. Power came from a 2.3-liter four, only it wasn't the Pinto/Fairmont ohc "Lima" unit but a cut-down version of the old overhead-valve Falcon six, rated at 84 horsepower. It didn't work that well, but Ford tried to make it better, fitting throttle-body injection and adding a 100-bhp "H.O." (high-output) option for '85. The latter somehow lost 6 horsepower by '87, then returned to its original rating. Several trim levels were offered, including better-equipped Sport versions with the more powerful engine and firm suspension. Escort's 2.0-liter diesel option was listed through '86, but generated few sales. The standard manual transaxle shifted from a four- to five-speed after '84, with a three-speed automatic optional all years.

Tempo was treated to a mild flush-headlamp facelift for 1986, when it also became one of the first low-priced cars to offer an optional driver-side air bag. The following year brought another interesting new option: all-wheel drive, a part-time "shift-on-the-fly" setup intended for maximum traction on slippery roads, not dry-pavement driving or off-roading. For 1988, Tempo four-doors were reskinned to look like junior versions of the new midsize Taurus, an effective "nip-and-tuck" operation. A new, rather Japanese-looking dash was shared with unchanged coupe models. Offerings now comprised base GL and sporty GLS coupes and sedans, plus four-door all-wheel drive and luxury LX models. Tempo then marked time for 1989-90 aside from price/equipment shuffles.

Despite prosaic mechanicals and increasingly tough compact competition, Tempo proved another fast-selling Ford. It averaged 371,000 buyers in its first two seasons and another 280,000 for 1986-87. Sales then turned strongly upward for 1988-89, breaking the three-quarter-million mark for the two years combined. Dearborn designers and decision-makers evidently had the inside track on what appealed to American buyers.

Yet, even they were likely surprised by the success of Taurus, the front-drive 1986 replacement for the junior LTD in the all-important midsize market. Riding a 106-inch wheelbase, this four-door sedan and four-door wagon were the strongest-ever expressions of Ford's claim to Detroit design leadership: clean,

1983 Escort GT hatchback coupe

1984 Tempo GL coupe

1984 LTD LX four-door sedan

1984 Escort GT hatchback coupe

1984 LTD Crown Victoria with Brougham roof

1985 LTD four-door sedan

smooth, and carefully detailed, yet not lumpy like some other low-drag "aero" cars. Dominating the spacious interiors was an obviously European-inspired dashboard with some controls sensibly copied from the best of BMW, Saab, and Mercedes-Benz.

As expected, Taurus engines mounted transversely in a chassis with all-independent suspension. Sedans used MacPherson struts and coil springs at each corner, supplemented at the rear by parallel control arms. Wagons eschewed rear struts for twin control arms, a system better able to cope with the wider range of load weights wagons carry.

Initial engine choices began with a 2.5-liter 88-bhp four, an enlarged Tempo unit available with standard five-speed manual or, from late '87, optional four-speed overdrive automatic transaxles. Most Tauruses, though, were ordered with the new port-injected 3.0-liter "Vulcan" V-6, a 60-degree overhead-valve design rated at 140 bhp and teamed with automatic only. For 1988, Ford added a reengineered version of its 90-degree 3.8 V-6 as a new option. Horsepower here was also 140, but the 3.8's extra torque provided quicker acceleration than the 3.0.

With its ultramodern styling, good performance, and prices far lower than those of certain coveted German sedans, Taurus charged up the sales chart like a bull in a china shop. Ford sold over 236,000 of the '86s and nearly 375,000 for '87—astounding for what was, after all, a very daring departure for a middle-class American car.

But there were still those who wanted a Taurus with performance and mechanical specifications as sophisticated as its styling. They got one, and 1989 was showtime—or rather SHO time: a new "Super High Output" 3.0 V-6 with overhead-cam cylinder heads and four valves per cylinder (instead of two), plus dual exhausts. Engineered with help from Yamaha, the SHO engine turned out 220 horsepower, good for seven seconds 0-60, according to Ford; Consumer Guide® managed "only" 7.4—still great going. The SHO came only in a sedan with standard antilock all-disc brakes, a handling package with larger antiroll bars, and 15-inch aluminum wheels wearing high-speed V-rated tires. Lending added styling distinction were unique lower-body extensions and inboard front fog lamps. The interior was special too, boasting multi-adjustable front bucket seats, sport cloth upholstery, center console, and, to match the high-winding engine, an 8000-rpm tachometer.

Nevertheless, the SHO was a very slow mover on the sales chart, mainly because there was no automatic option and the mandatory Mazda-supplied manual five-speed suffered balky, high-effort shift action. Production was thus meager through 1990: about 25,000 or so. But Taurus as a whole kept up its initial rip-snorting pace, besting 387,000 for '88, 395,000 for '89, and 333,000 for recession-plagued 1990. Thoughtful yearly upgrades helped. Among the most thoughtful: optional anti-

# Ford

1985 Tempo Sports GL coupe

1986 Taurus station wagon prototype

1986½ EXP 2-passenger sport coupe

1987 Taurus LX four-door sedan

1987 EXP 2-passenger sport coupe

lock brakes for sedans and a standard driver-side air bag for all 1990 models.

We shouldn't leave this decade without mentioning the Probe, new for 1989. A sporty hatchback coupe based on Mazda's MX-6, it was a high point for Dearborn's then 15-year-old partnership with the Japanese automaker. This had been such a success that Ford not only bought a 25-percent stake in Mazda but decided to entrust it with all of Ford's own small-car development for North America. The Probe was the first fruit of that decision.

The original Probe will ever be remembered as the car that almost replaced the Mustang. Ford changed its name only at the last minute amid howls of protest from Mustang loyalists who'd have no truck with a Japanese design—and with "inferior" front drive at that. The name itself came from Ford's exciting early-'80s series of aerodynamic concept cars, but proved to have unexpectedly offensive connotations. To produce the car, Ford and Mazda set up a new factory in Flat Rock, Michigan, not far from historic River Rouge, as part of a joint venture aptly named Auto Alliance. The plant also turned out MX-6s and 626 sedans for Mazda's U.S. dealers.

With all this, the Probe is at best a "half-American" car despite all-Ford styling and availability of the 3.0-liter Taurus V-6 on midrange LX models for 1990-92. (The base GL used a 2.2-liter Mazda four, the top-line GT a turbocharged version). Probe was redesigned for '93 on a new-generation MX-6 platform with 102.9-inch wheelbase (versus 99), again with much more dramatic styling than its cousin. Power was exclusively Mazda: a 2.0-liter four for the base model, a 2.5 V-6 for the sporty GT.

Probe was a timely Ford weapon against sporty Japanese compacts like Toyota Celica, Honda Prelude, Nissan 200SX—and Mazda MX-6. Sales were good at first—over 117,000 by 1990—but then fell victim to a sharp drop in sporty coupe demand. The second-generation Probe was the last—ending in '97.

Despite its ultimate demise, Probe was as much a symbol as Taurus of Ford's strong '80s resurgence, a phoenixlike renaissance engineered by Donald E. Petersen (president from 1980, chairman after 1984) and his young, enthusiastic executive team. From an automaker that was as near to collapse as Chrysler was in 1980, Dearborn remade itself into a trimmer, more-responsive, and vastly more-efficient outfit while fielding aggressive products that were usually right on target. Ford was still the home of "better ideas," but by 1990 it was also home to some of America's most-popular and respected automobiles.

The same was true of trucks—important given the boom in light-truck demand that began in the mid-'80s and continued into the '90s. If anything, Ford was even more successful here than it was with cars. For example, 1982 saw the full-size F-Series pickup begin an unbroken 14-year streak as America's top-selling vehicle of any kind. Ford's Ranger (a 1982 newcomer) became sales king of compact pickups. Dearborn also scored big in the burgeoning sport-utility field with Explorer, the upscale 1991 four-door replacement for the two-door Ranger-based Bronco II. Ford did fumble with minivans, but not seriously. Though its new-for-'86 rear-drive Aerostar was way outpolled by Chrysler's front-drive models, sales were consistent and high enough that Ford stayed the Aerostar's planned 1994 execution, letting the older minivan run alongside the new front-drive Windstar.

By the mid-'90s, these truck successes added to the continuing popularity of Taurus and Escort to make Ford the sales leader in no fewer than five vehicle segments: full-size pickups (F-Series), midsize car (Taurus), sporty-utility vehicles (Explorer), subcompact car (Escort), and compact pickup (Ranger). Moreover, Taurus took over as the country's top-sell-

# Ford

**1988 Taurus LX four-door sedan**

**1989 LTD Crown Victoria LX four-door sedan**

**1989 Taurus LX station wagon**

**1990 Taurus SHO four-door sedan**

**1989 Taurus SHO four-door sedan**

**1990 Escort GT hatchback coupe**

**1989 Probe coupe**

**1990 Probe GT coupe**

ing car line in 1992 to end the Honda Accord's three-year reign, though not without cash rebates and other sales incentives of the kind people had now long taken for granted.

With all this, Ford Division remained "USA-1" in the early '90s, selling well over a million cars a year and a like number of light trucks. Chevy did move about 40,000 more domestic cars in calendar '91, but that was the only time it surpassed Ford in these years.

Two different Dearborn regimes presided over this remarkable sales performance. First, Don Petersen handed over the chairman's gavel in 1990 to his one-time number-two, Harold A. "Red" Poling; at the same time, the president's job was reactivated after a two-year lapse for Phillip Benton, Jr. Both these men were Dearborn veterans, but they were merely a transition team, for late 1993 ushered in the worldly wise Alex Trotman as both president and chairman.

As a veteran of Ford Europe, Trotman brought a more-international outlook to the company's "Glass House" headquarters, which was soon populated by many of his European colleagues. One of their first projects was an ambitious corporate reorganization dubbed "Ford 2000." Announced in 1994, this aimed to mobilize all of the firm's global resources to further improve quality, shorten product development times, and achieve greater manufacturing efficiencies. Though it wouldn't

# Ford

be evident on the road until middecade, Ford 2000 seemed a prudent plan in light of the motor industry's ever increasing globalization.

Meantime, Ford Division had redesigned its Escort for the first time since the 1981 original. Arriving in spring 1990 as an early-'91 premiere, it was another "world car," though in the same way as Probe. Here, Ford applied "mini-Taurus" styling to the latest version of Mazda's small, front-drive 323/Protege to produce a competent Japanese-style subcompact with much greater sales appeal against rival Toyotas, Hondas, and Nissans.

Initial body styles were the same as before. So was the basic "CVH" engine retained for all Escorts save the sporty GT three-door. That one benefited greatly from a new twincam 1.8-liter Mazda four with 16 valves and 127 lively horses. Though the CVH gained sequential-port fuel injection and distributorless electronic ignition, it remained a gruff and noisy slogger with just 88 horsepower. At least it was cheap, and that combined with more efficient production in Mexico as well as Michigan to make for very low list prices: $7976 for the stark three-door Pony to more than $11 grand for the GT. A crisp four-door notchback bowed for 1992 in mid-range LX trim, and there was a sporty LX-E version with the GT's engine and firm suspension, plus rear disc brakes—a kind of pint-size Taurus SHO.

The second-generation Escort would be relatively short-lived, running only through model-year '96 before a new Mazda-based design took over. Changes were evolutionary save the admirable adoption of a passenger air bag for 1995 to supplement the already included driver's restraint; an optional fold-out child safety was also added that year. Sales remained strong despite the yearly sameness. A clever new "one-price" program helped. Begun in 1992, this offered any of the four LX models with several popular options for just $10,899 with five-speed manual transmission or $11,631 with optional four-speed automatic. Ford was copying the no-hassle price policy of GM's Saturn subsidiary, but it was a timely counter to Chevy's Cavalier, which was doing the same thing—not to mention Japanese small cars that were rapidly moving up the scale due to a strengthened yen. Unfortunately, everyday Escorts couldn't match most import competition for pep and refinement, so it's just as well that their '97 successors went on sale in early 1996.

Ford modernized two more of its cars for 1992. First up was a replacement for something even older than the original Escort: the big, vintage-'79 Crown Victoria. Reaching showrooms in March 1991, it was virtually all-new despite retaining the basic rear-drive "Panther" platform and wheelbase. There was new styling, of course: smooth and rounded in Dearborn's now-expected "aero" mold, but not "jellybean" chunky. A grille-less Taurus-type face replaced the dated standup eggcrate. Other passe stuff like vinyl roof covers, opera lights, and wire-wheel covers was rejected, too. So was the LTD name—but also the Crown Vic wagon, Ford having concluded that mini-vans and sport-utility vehicles had now all but replaced traditional full-size wagons in buyer affections. That left a four-door sedan with airy "six-light" roofline in base and uplevel LX trim; a sportier Touring Sedan was added in the fall.

Like its 1990 makeover of the aged Lincoln Town Car, Ford went much further with this new Crown Vic than was absolutely needed to satisfy the market. Where GM was content to merely rebody its largest cars, Ford overhauled the chassis, adding standard all-disc brakes with optional antilock control and making numerous tweaks to steering, springs, shocks, and suspension geometry. The result was surprisingly agile and responsive for a traditional full-size Detroiter and a vast improvement over the old Crown Vic. It was also a more-potent big Ford with adoption of the 4.6-liter overhead-cam V-8 first seen in the '91 Town Car. As the first member of Dearborn's new "modular" engine family, it delivered 190 standard horsepower or 210 with dual exhausts, a gain of 40-50 horsepower over the old pushrod 302. The uprated engine was included in a Handling and Performance package that was standard for the Touring Sedan and optional on other models. As its name implied, this also delivered firmer damping and wider wheels wearing performance tires, as well as ABS and traction control. All models came with a driver-side air bag per Washington's insistence; a passenger-side restraint was also available.

All this plus starting prices in the low $20,000s lit a fire under Crown Victoria sales, which jumped past 152,000 for 1992, the highest since '85. Volume then declined to under 110,000, but remained healthy into the next century. Buyer requests prompted the addition of conventional grille for '93, when the Touring was dropped. The passenger air bag became standard for '94. The '95s got a mild facelift, "gullwing" taillights, revised climate controls and newly standard rear defroster, heated door mirrors, a radio antenna embedded in the rear window, a "battery-saver" feature, and displays for outside temperature and "gal-

1991 Tempo LX four-door sedan

1991 Taurus SHO four-door sedan

1991 Escort LX hatchback sedan

1992 Escort LX-E four-door sedan

lons to empty." Even with all these additions, base price was comfortably below $25,000.

Incidentally, the Crown Vic became an "import" for a few years in the early '90s, built north of the border with a high level of Canadian content. The reason was CAFE, the Corporate Average Fuel Economy law that took effect with model-year '78 but had lately been relaxed some. Still, the Crown Vic had fair thirst (about 17 mpg city, 25 highway, as rated by the Environmental Protection Agency) and was thus a drain on Ford's domestic fleet-average economy. As an "import," the Crown Vic counted in Ford's nondomestic CAFE along with the tiny South Korean-built Festiva, whose really high mileage more than offset the big car's. Later, Ford didn't need such tricks to comply with CAFE, so parts and labor were resourced to make the Crown Vic truly "American" again. Such is the silliness sometimes wrought by well-meaning regulations.

Ford's other '92 freshening involved the top-selling Taurus. With competitors pushing hard, the basic '86 design was now in need of an update, so Ford spent a cool $650 million to give it one. Much of the money was spent on things that didn't show but made a good car even better, particularly in the areas of noise, vibration, and harshness (NVH). Among these were a stiffer unibody, a suspension revised for a smoother ride with no harm to handling, more-responsive power steering, extra sound-deadening in strategic places, engine adjustments for improved drivability, and a more-precise solid-rod shift linkage for the dashing SHO. Ford also dropped the weak four-cylinder engine, which pleased few Taurus buyers apart from rent-a-car companies.

Inside, the '92 Taurus presented a redesigned dash with subtle ergonomic refinements and space for a newly optional passenger airbag. Outside was . . . a disappointment. Though every body panel was new save the doors, the '92 was hard to tell at a glance from previous Tauruses—as critics loved to point out. But buyers just didn't care. As mentioned, Taurus took over America's most-popular car line in '92. Calendar-year sales were smashing at over 397,000, and model-year production was a record 368,000. But that was only a prelude to '93, when model-year output surged to nearly 459,000. The '95 tally was almost as good: just over 410,000.

Ford designers dared to be different once again when styling the new Taurus (and Mercury Sable), but nothing less was expected. Ovoid headlights and a "catfish mouth" grille marked frontal styling. Inside, a central oval panel housed audio and climate controls. Wheelbase gained 2.5 inches (to 108.5). Standard power was a slightly improved pushrod 3.0-liter V-6 in the GL, but LXs came with a new twin-cam "Duratec" V-6 good for 200 horsepower. Prices rose by about $1000 chilling early sales and spurring Ford to add a detrimmed G sedan.

Like Escort, Taurus wouldn't see another major change until middecade. The most-important interim development was standardizing the passenger air bag for 1994. An interesting '95 sedan variation was the SE (Sport Edition), a kind of budget SHO delivering alloy wheels, rear spoiler, sport front seats, and other extras for about $18-grand with base 3.0-liter V-6 or just under $20,000 with the punchier 3.8. Interestingly, the smaller "Vulcan" V-6 got some needed NVH improvements in preparation for the all-new second-generation Taurus of 1996.

Let's not forget the 1992-95 SHO, which gained greater visual distinction from lesser Tauruses with more-aggressive styling front and rear, plus bolder cladding for the lower bodysides. In addition, Ford finally added a four-speed automatic to the SHO's option list for 1993. To maintain performance parity with the five-speed model, the 3.0-liter Yamaha V-6 was enlarged for the shiftless SHO to near 3.2 liters (192 cid), yielding a useful 20 extra pound-feet of torque (220 in all), though no more horse-

**1992 Aerostar Eddie Bauer 4WD extended-length minivan**

**1993 Probe GT coupe**

**1993 Tempo GL four-door sedan**

**1993 Crown Victoria four-door sedan**

**1994 Taurus LX station wagon**

# Ford

1995 Taurus SE four-door sedan

1995 Contour LX four-door sedan

1996 Windstar LX minivan

1996 Taurus LX four-door sedan

power. SHO pricing remained unusually steady in these years, but neither that nor the automatic was much help to sales. With base stickers straddling $25,000, the top-line Taurus still faced a host of formidable foreign sports sedans and usually suffered by comparison. But though eclipsed by those cars for image—and ultimately by its V-8 successor (3.4-liters, 240 bhp) for performance, the V-6 SHO was always a rewarding driver's car with a pleasing blend of American and European characteristics. It's almost certain to draw future collector interest the way that "fuelie" '57 Chevys do now.

Interest value was definitely not a trait of the early-'90s Tempo. Soldiering on with few evident differences from one year to the next, Ford's front-drive compact tended to get lost in the great gray mass of Detroit market-fillers that you were more apt to rent on vacation than want in your driveway. Yet for all its crushing dullness, Tempo remained a decent seller, with steady model-year production of well over 100,000 units through swan-song '94—and the '93s made a surprise spurt to better than 238,000. Tempo's only changes of note in this period were loss of the AWD option after 1991 (when it was called "Four Wheel Drive") and the '92 addition of the 3.0-liter Taurus V-6 as standard for top-line GLS models (which then went away) and an option elsewhere. Base prices remained very attractive, rising no higher than the low $12,000s. While that betrayed an aging design long since paid for, it also helped Ford to keep moving this metal.

Tempo's 1995 replacement stood to be a far easier sell. Called Contour, it was another stab at a "world car," born of "Ford 2000" thinking as an Americanized version of the year-old European Mondeo. But unlike the original compromised U.S. Escort, Contour was very close to its transatlantic cousin, having the same smooth, tightly drawn styling, plus an ultrastiff structure and a sophisicated all-independent suspension that contributed to crisp, taut handling. Even the Mondeo dash was little altered for the States. Unfortunately, so was its snug interior. Despite a wheelbase half-an-inch longer than Taurus', the Contour was frankly cramped in back, with little underseat footroom and marginal knee-, leg-, and headroom.

Still, this was the closest America had yet come to a genuine European sports sedan. It was also a heartening sign of where future Fords were headed under the new Trotman regime. Critics raved. *Road & Track* called Contour "a giant step forward in the compact sedan arena." *Car and Driver* merely termed it "stunningly satisfying." Those verdicts came from road tests of the top-line SE model and its 2.5-liter "Duratec" V-6. A new all-Ford design optional on lesser Contours, this engine made 170 spirited horses—enough for Consumer Guide®'s five-speed car to charge from 0 to 60 mph in just 8.9 seconds. GL and midlevel LX models came with another new engine: a 2.0-liter multivalve twincam four called "Zetec," an outgrowth of Ford Europe's recently introduced "Zeta" family of small, high-efficiency power-plants. In line with a fast-growing Detroit trend, both Contour engines could go 100,000 miles without a tune-up. And, of course, either could drive through an optional four-speed automatic.

Ford spent a record $6 billion to introduce Mondeo, Contour, and Mercury's similar new '95 Mystique. While that was twice the cost of the original Taurus program, it included the high expense of developing two brand-new engines, plus manufacturing facilities and the usual new-model tooling. Even so, Ford had bet heavily on these cars (dubbed "CDW127" in the company's new internal code, the letters denoting "World car" in the "C/D" size class), so it was vital that they succeed.

Contour did succeed, but not as much as Ford might have hoped, scoring debut model-year production just over 175,000. A minor recall slowed early deliveries, but the real problem was "sticker shock." With buyers still flocking to well-equipped Japanese cars, Ford ladled on all kind of standard features (including dual air bags), but this only pushed Contour quite a bit upmarket from the old Tempo, which had been relatively cheap. Thus, many prospects balked when Contour arrived at a minimum of $13,300, over $1000 more than a late loaded Tempo. Opt for an SE with desirable extras like ABS and traction control and you were well over $20,000, which was Taurus money. In short, Ford had underestimated the "price-sensitivity" of Contour's intended market, a telling miscalculation but probably not a serious one.

Ford was more on target with Windstar, which began sales in 1994 for model-year '95. Unlike Mercury's two-year-old Villager, which Ford built in Ohio to a Nissan design, Windstar was Dearborn's own front-drive minivan, using a modified Taurus platform and drivetrains. Ford gave it standard seven-place seating on a 120.7-inch wheelbase—slightly longer than that of Chrysler's extended-length Grand models. Windstar ended up eight inches longer than a Grand and nearly a foot longer than Villager. GL and LX price levels were offered in the $20,000-$24,000 range. Nice looks, a carlike driving feel, high utility, and a full range of passenger-car safety features netted healthy sales—though only about half the volume of Chrysler's minivans, which would be even stiffer competition with their total redesign of 1996.

Ford's real success story of the mid-1990s and beyond had little to do with minvans or, for that matter, much to do with sedans, wagons, or coupes. Sport-utility vehicles were enjoying an incredible—and in many quarters unexpected—surge in popularity, and the Ford Explorer led the field. Redesigned in 1995 and given optional V-8 power the following year, it was the darling of company accountants, piling up the profits in a big way. As befits a star, Explorer was given maximum developmental attention, getting substantial improvements on a yearly basis. When the larger F-150 pickup-based Expedition arrived, followed a couple of years later by the compact Escape, it appeared that Ford's lock on the top spots in the SUV field were secure for years to come.

Though the overall sales and profit picture was impressive, all was not quite as rosy among Ford's mainstream vehicles. The Korean-built Aspire was attracting fewer customers than had been hoped, so whatever future plans the company might have had for its entry-level offering were curtailed in 1997, when only the most minor of trim changes were made, and stopped altogether a year later, when it was deleted from the Ford lineup. As a matter of curiosity, the Aspire was given new life in 2002 under the aegis of Kia, its manufacturer, who offer a warmed-over version, now called Rio, through their own dealer network.

But the lackluster performance of the Aspire wasn't a matter to keep Ford executives awake at night. Tepid buyer response to the Contour was a different matter. Immediate steps to remedy the most-criticized features of the "World Car" were taken, most notably a redesign of the front seatbacks and rear-seat cushion to increase legroom for those riding in back and the addition of a low-price model in 1997. A modest reskin—most evident in the front view—followed a year later, along with the deletion of the two base models. After five years, Ford pulled the plug on Contour while its Mondeo sibling continued in production in Europe.

Contour was something of a conundrum. Driving enthusiasts, including the press (who probably never spent more than a few fleeting miles in the back seat), loved it. Praise for its road manners was unstinting, and only grew in volume when Ford's Special Vehicle Team trotted out its own version. With some subtle interior and exterior alterations, the cream of the

1996 Taurus LX station wagon

1997 Probe GT coupe

1997 Crown Victoria sedan

1997 Aspire hatchback sedan

1997 Taurus LX sedan

# Ford

1997 Escort wagon

1998 Escort ZX2 coupe

1998 Contour SVT sedan

1998 Taurus LX sedan

1999 Contour SVT sedan

standard car's options, a crisp yet comfortable suspension package and a rev-happy 190-bhp (later raised to 195) Duratec engine, the SVT Contour was a performance-sedan-lover's dream. For all that it offered in its brief two-year life, the limited-production SVT (roughly 5000 were built in '98, a like number in '99), was considered a bargain by admirers at $22,665. On the good-news side of Ford's ledger, the Escort remained a best-seller, one that, after a complete makeover for the 1997 model year, seemed to require little in the way of improvements. Available in four-door sedan and station-wagon versions, Escort provided economical yet stylish transportation at a low-price. And that was a formula that worked. Even when fully-loaded with options, Escorts seldom broke the $17,000 barrier, which gave them an edge over some pricier rivals. In some respects, the '97-on Escort was something of a stopgap car, though the public never knew it; at one point, it was intended to be a member of Ford's "World Car" plan, but executives chose a U.S.-developed (with some input from Mazda) version over the Ford of Europe design. In any case, it was already meant to be superceded in North America by the Focus in 2000. In another of those strange quirks that make for fascinating footnotes to mainstream automotive history, the Escort sedan did not die when the Focus arrived; production of the sedan continued through 2002, though sales were made only to fleet operators after the '00 model year ended.

Less than a year after Escort's major redo in '97, Ford rolled out a sporty coupe variant. The '98 Escort ZX2 (the "Escort" prefix was later dropped when the parent model vanished from showrooms) shared much of its architecture and drivetrain with the economy sedan, but wore spunky, distinctive coachwork all its own and replaced the parent model's single-cam inline-four powerplant with a dohc unit also found in the base Contour. The additional 20 ponies (130 bhp versus 110) gave the light (2470-lb) ZX2 frisky, if not neck-snapping, performance. Available initially in "Cool" (base) and "Hot" (upgraded) trim levels, the ZX2 offered good value to budget-minded driving enthusiasts.

And yet the ZX2 didn't exactly take the automotive world by storm. Some testers—including Consumer Guide®—thought its relatively high base price ($12,580 for a '98 sans air conditioning and ABS) made it a less-than-attractive proposition. Some of this criticism was muted a year later when Ford trimmed $1000 off the "Cool" ZX2's price, though CG continued to maintain that "...ZX2 looks sportier than it performs." This must have sounded all too familiar to Ford folks who had memories of a previous Escort-derived coupe, the unlovely and unloved EXP. A more-powerful "SR" package was announced for 2000, but the lure of an extra 13 bhp, tuned suspension, four-wheel disc brakes, alloy wheels carrying "performance" tires and special seats wasn't strong enough to keep that option on the books beyond that year, even though it carried a modest $1495 premium over the base model. By 2002, ZX2 was back to one model with three trim levels, all of which concerned amenities and not performance enhancements, and its days were numbered.

Ford took a major gamble in 2000 by introducing one car meant to replace Escort, ZX2 and Contour. The Focus fell in between its predecessors size-wise, but inside its avant-garde bodyshell it was a masterpiece of space utilization, offering more room for front- and rear-seat passengers (and their luggage) than either the earlier small Fords or most of its rivals. While the two available powerplants (110-bhp sohc and 130-bhp dohc) didn't make road testers' pulses race, the all-independent-suspension system drew raves for delivering both a smooth ride and class-leading handling, as did the spacious interior, overall design, and build quality. In its first year, Focus was offered in three basic forms—three-door hatchback, four-door sedan, and station wagon—each meant to fill a specific market niche. The hatchback was both the entry-level and sporty family member, and had the widest variety in option packages. The sedan and wagon were more-mainstream in appearance, at least from the windshield back; their focus (so to speak) was on comfort and, with the right options, luxury. An award-winner from the start (taking the 2000 North American Car of the Year trophy and gaining CG "Best Buy" status from '01), the Focus quickly became a strong seller. Along with some packaging changes (including a "sport" option for the wagon) two additional models were added to the Focus line in 2002. The first, a four-door hatchback, made the coupe's edgy styling accessible to buyers needing the convenience of rear doors. A sophisticated electronic-stability-control system was made optional on top models. More spectacular was an SVT version of the three-door hatch which finally added at least some of the power critics felt was lacking in other models. The hotter Focus, like other Ford SVT offerings (Mustang Cobra and F-150 Lightning pickup truck), received a substantial upgrading that belied its rather modest $17,505 base price: the engine, though essentially the same dohc unit used in standard Focus models, was given new pistons and a revised cylinder head, variable timing for the intake camshaft, and new intake and exhaust manifolds to raise power to 170 bhp. This free-revving engine drove the SVT's front wheels through a new six-speed manual gearbox. Suspension improvements were also added, as were larger four-wheel disc brakes with ABS (the latter an option on other models) and 17-inch alloy wheels. Exterior and interior features separated the SVT Focus from other models: outside, the SVT received its own front and rear fascias, side sills and a rear spoiler, while the interior was treated to special instrument faces (and two extra gauges), leather/cloth seats with revised padding, aluminum pedal caps and shift knob, and a leather-wrapped steering wheel.

But the impact of the Focus was blunted, at least for a time, by other Ford-generated headlines. A controversy involving Explorers equipped with certain Firestone tires erupted into a major scandal involving congressional hearings, a massive recall program, and the breaking of commercial ties between automaker and tire manufacturer. By the time the dust had settled, the Firestone/Explorer affair had cost Ford an estimated $3 billion-plus and was a major factor in President and CEO Jacques Nasser losing his job. On top of launch woes (mainly involving recalls) for Focus and Thunderbird, and rumors of a decline in Ford vehicles' build quality, the latter days of 2001 were difficult in Dearborn.

While all this was going on the Taurus, in four-door sedan and station wagon forms, continued to play its role as Ford's leading passenger car. A complete redesign in 1996 revived some the car's reputation for leading-edge styling. This sleeker but somewhat unorthodox design was certainly distinctive; perhaps overly so, as it cost the Taurus its Number One position on the U.S. sales charts. Still, the '96 represented a major improvement over past Tauruses in many ways. Powertrain refinement was helped by a new premium engine, the Duratec dohc V-6. In Taurus trim, the 3.0-liter engine produced 200 bhp and was considered by many buyers to be well worth the $500 premium charged. A new version of the SHO featured a 235-bhp dohc V-8 built, like the earlier SHO V-6, by Yamaha in Japan. In many cases, complaints outnumbered compliments. Looks aside, the Taurus fell behind certain rivals (notably the Honda Accord and Toyota Camry) in some important areas such as ride quality.

Some critics and customers also had harsh words for the control layout, which had pushbuttons arranged in an odd curv-

**1999 Crown Victoria sedan**

**1999 Escort ZX2 coupe**

**1999 Taurus sedan**

**2000 Focus ZX3 hatchback coupe**

**2000 Focus SE wagon**

ing fashion within an oval housing in the middle of the dashboard. The new Taurus was also more expensive than the model it replaced. Ford responded by adding a low-priced G model to the existing GL and LX trim levels later in the year. Major improvements had to wait until 2000 when the exterior was toned down, replacing ovoid shapes with more-conventional forms. Changes to the roof panel increased headroom, while the dashboard was made more user-friendly. Safety considerations brought revisions to the air-bag- and seatbelt pretensioner deployment systems. By this time, Taurus was no longer a CG "Best Buy," and had lost its slow-selling SHO flagship model. For all its woes, however, Taurus had regained some of its lost sales ground by 2002 and, if no longer quite the world-beater of yore, had evolved into a most-competent passenger carrier.

Were it not for law-enforcement and taxi fleets, the full-size Crown Victoria sedans might not have made it past the mid-1990s. While many potential buyers and auto-writers scorned the rear-drive, body-on-frame Vic as a dinosaur, its traditional powertrain configuration and rugged construction made it appealing to the high-mileage crowd. Even as late as 2002, the Vic was little different from its 1993 ancestor, save for modest styling changes—a mild brush-up to front and rear ends and roof in 1998 and a number of unseen improvements wrought on engine (horsepower ratings for the Vic's ohc "Modular" V-8 grew from 190 in 1996 to 220 in 2002), suspension and brakes. Strange as it might seem in an era when front-drive has become the norm for most sedans regardless of size, the Vic continued to sell at an annual rate in the low six figures well into the early 2000s.

And, while taxi and police Vics were almost always utilitarian with durable vinyl seats and stiff heavy-duty suspensions, a sizable number of civilian versions tended toward opulence, sporting optional leather interiors, electrically adjustable pedals, and the "Sport and Handling" package—which became the LX Sport model in 2002—consisting of a dual-exhaust system (raising output to 235 bhp), rear air suspension and stiffer front springs, revised shock absorbers and antiroll bars, and handsome 17-inch alloy wheels.

With these goodies in place plus traction control, a full-tilt Vic could cost as much as $35,000, but its unique configuration among American full-size sedans seems to have guaranteed it a place in Ford's future for some time to come. And, despite some punishing bumps in the road, Ford's future seems bright.

The Focus has established itself well, and its popularity should continue, with other model variations—including, possibly, a gas-electric hybrid version—expanding its market niche. Taurus should be replaced by middecade; as of now, it is likely to have two successors, one the "Cross-Trainer" passenger car/SUV announced in early 2002 and the other sharing architecture with an upcoming Volvo. The Crown Victoria just keeps rolling along and just may remain a rear-drive design beyond 2005. Expansion and updating of the SUV fleet is certain to continue, at least as long as the public clamors for big, all-wheel-drive people-haulers. Perhaps most indicative of a new wave of enthusiasm sweeping Ford is the GT40. First introduced as a show car paying tribute to the magnificent GT40 racers of the mid-1960s, the midengine two-seat concept was approved for production in early 2002, with an on-sale date set to coincide with Ford Motor Company's centennial celebration in 2003. Full details had not been released as of this book's press time, but there is little doubt that the low-slung V-8 supercar will serve as an admirable flagship for a company looking toward, and working hard for, a bright future.

2001 Taurus sedan

2001 Taurus SE station wagon

2001 Focus ZTS sedan

2001 ZX2 coupe

2002 Taurus sedan

# Ford

**2002 Crown Victoria sedan**

**2002 ZX2 coupe**

# Ford

2002 Focus SVT hatchback coupe

## Specifications

### 1930

| Model A (wb 103.5) | Wght | Price | Prod |
|---|---|---|---|
| rdstr | 2,155 | 435 | 122,703 |
| rdstr 2-4P | 2,230 | 460 | |
| phtn 5P | 2,212 | 440 | 39,886 |
| Standard cpe 2P | 2,257 | 495 | 232,564 |
| spt cpe 2-4P | 2,283 | 525 | 72,572 |
| cabriolet 2-4P | 2,273 | 625 | 29,226 |
| Tudor sdn 5P | 2,375 | 495 | 425,124 |
| Fordor sdn 2W 5P | 2,441 | 600 | 7,838 |
| Town sdn 5P | 2,475 | 660 | 122,534 |
| Town Car 5P | 2,525 | 1,200 | 96 |
| Standard sdn 3W 5P | 2,462 | 600 | 59,958 |
| DeLuxe rdstr 2-4P | 2,230 | 520 | 11,629 |
| DeLuxe phtn 5P | 2,285 | 625 | 4,635 |
| DeLuxe cpe 2P | 2,265 | 545 | 29,777 |
| victoria 5P | 2,265 | 625 | 6,447 |
| DeLuxe sdn 5P | 2,488 | 640 | 13,710 |
| wgn 4d | — | 650 | 3,799 |
| bus cpe 2P | — | — | 110 |

| 1930 Engine | bore × stroke | bhp | availability |
|---|---|---|---|
| I-4, 200.5 | 3.88×4.25 | 40 | S-all |

### 1931

| Model A (wb 103.5) | Wght | Price | Prod |
|---|---|---|---|
| rdstr 2P | 2,155 | 430 | 7,793 |
| rdstr 2-4P | 2,230 | 455 | |
| phtn 5P | 2,212 | 435 | 11,060 |
| Standard cpe 2P | 2,257 | 490 | 82,885 |

| Model A (wb 103.5) | Wght | Price | Prod |
|---|---|---|---|
| spt cpe 2-4P | 2,283 | 500 | 21,272 |
| cabriolet 2-4P | 2,273 | 595 | 13,706 |
| Tudor sdn 5P | 2,375 | 490 | 170,645 |
| Standard sdn 3W 5P | 2,462 | 590 | 25,720 |
| DeLuxe rdstr 2-4P | 2,230 | 475 | 56,702 |
| DeLuxe phtn 5P | 2,285 | 580 | 2,875 |
| DeLuxe cpe 2P | 2,265 | 525 | 23,653 |
| victoria 5P | 2,265 | 580 | 36,830 |
| DeLuxe Tudor sdn 5P | 2,388 | 525 | 23,490 |
| DeLuxe Fordor sdn 5P | 2,488 | 630 | 4,967 |
| DeLuxe town sdn 5P | 2,475 | 630 | 65,447 |
| conv sdn 5P | 2,360 | 640 | 5,072 |
| wgn 4d | — | 625 | 3,018 |

| 1931 Engine | bore×stroke | bhp | availability |
|---|---|---|---|
| I-4, 200.5 | 3.88×4.25 | 40 | S-all |

### 1932

| Model B (wb 106.5) | Wght | Price | Prod |
|---|---|---|---|
| rdstr 2P | 2,077 | 410 | 948 |
| rdstr 2-4P | 2,119 | 435 | |
| phtn 5P | 2,213 | 445 | 593 |
| cpe 2P | 2,236 | 440 | 20,342 |
| spt cpe 2-4P | 2,261 | 485 | 739 |
| Tudor sdn 5P | 2,353 | 450 | 36,553 |
| Fordor sdn 5P | 2,388 | 540 | 4,116 |
| DeLuxe rdstr 2-4P | 2,153 | 450 | 3,719 |
| DeLuxe phtn 5P | 2,243 | 495 | 281 |
| DeLuxe cpe 2P | 2,339 | 525 | 968 |
| victoria 5P | 2,319 | 550 | 521 |
| cabriolet 2-4P | 2,370 | 560 | 427 |
| DeLuxe Tudor sdn 5P | 2,373 | 500 | 4,077 |
| DeLuxe Fordor sdn 5P | 2,407 | 595 | 2,620 |

# Ford

| Model B (wb 106.5) | Wght | Price | Prod |
|---|---|---|---|
| conv sdn 5P | 2,324 | 600 | 44 |
| wgn 4D | — | — | 1,400* |
| **Model 18 V-8 (wb 106.5)** | | | |
| rdstr | 2,217 | 460 ⎤ | 520 |
| rdstr 2-4P | 2,258 | 485 ⎦ | |
| phtn 5P | 2,344 | 495 | 483 |
| cpe 2P | 2,387 | 490 | 28,904 |
| spt cpe 2-4P | 2,397 | 535 | 1,982 |
| Tudor sdn 5P | 2,487 | 500 | 57,903 |
| Fordor sdn 5P | 2,524 | 590 | 9,320 |
| DeLuxe rdstr 2-4P | 2,283 | 500 | 6,893 |
| DeLuxe phtn 5P | 2,350 | 545 | 923 |
| DeLuxe cpe 2P | 2,477 | 575 | 20,506 |
| victoria 5P | 2,463 | 600 | 7,241 |
| cabriolet 2-4P | 2,390 | 610 | 5,499 |
| DeLuxe Tudor sdn 5P | 2,497 | 550 | 18,836 |
| DeLuxe Fordor sdn 5P | 2,543 | 645 | 18,880 |
| conv sdn 2-4P | 2,455 | 650 | 842 |
| wgn 4d | — | 600 | — |

| 1932 Engines | bore×stroke | bhp | availability |
|---|---|---|---|
| I-4, 200.5 | 3.88×4.25 | 50 | S-Model B |
| V-8, 221.0 | 3.06×3.75 | 65 | S-Model 18 |

*Includes Model 18.

## 1933

| Model 40 I-4 (wb 112.0) | Wght | Price | Prod |
|---|---|---|---|
| rdstr | 2,021 | 425 ⎤ | 107 |
| rdstr 2-4P | 2,064 | 450 ⎦ | |
| phtn 5P | 2,124 | 445 | 457 |
| cpe 3W/5W 2P | 2,147 | 440 | 189 |
| cpe 3W/5W 2-4P | 2,202 | 465 | 2,148 |
| Tudor sdn 5P | 2,418 | 450 | 2,911 |
| Fordor sdn 5P | 2,465 | 510 | 682 |
| DeLuxe rdstr 2-4P | 2,264 | 460 | 101 |
| DeLuxe phtn 5P | 2,154 | 495 | 241 |
| DeLuxe cpe 3W/5W 2P | 2,196 | 490 | 24 |
| DeLuxe cpe 3W/5W 2-4P | 2,202 | 515 | 28 |
| victoria 5P | 2,230 | 545 | 25 |
| cabriolet 2-4P | 2,181 | 535 | 24 |
| DeLuxe Tudor sdn 5P | 2,435 | 500 | 85 |
| DeLuxe Fordor sdn 5P | 2,505 | 560 | 179 |
| wgn 4d | — | 590 | 359 |
| **Model 40 V-8 (wb 112.0)** | **Wght** | **Price** | **Prod** |
| rdstr 2P | 2,337 | 475 ⎤ | 126 |
| rdstr 2-4P | 2,420 | 500 ⎦ | |
| phtn 5P | 2,435 | 495 | 232 |
| cpe 3W/5W 2P | 2,448 | 490 | 6,585 |
| cpe 3W/5W 2-4P | 2,380 | 515 | 31,797 |
| Tudor sdn 5P | 2,536 | 500 | 106,387 |
| Fordor sdn 5P | 2,590 | 560 | 19,602 |
| DeLuxe rdstr 2-4P | 2,376 | 510 | 4,223 |
| DeLuxe phtn 5P | 2,444 | 545 | 1,483 |
| DeLuxe cpe 3W/5W 2P | 2,453 | 540 | 15,894 |
| DeLuxe cpe 3W/5W 2-4P | 2,450 | 565 | 11,244 |
| victoria 5P | 2,510 | 595 | 4,193 |
| cabriolet 2-4P | 2,460 | 585 | 7,852 |
| DeLuxe Tudor sdn 5P | 2,540 | 550 | 48,233 |
| DeLuxe Fordor sdn 5P | 2,599 | 610 | 45,443 |
| wgn 4d | — | 640 | 1,654 |

| 1933 Engines | bore×stroke | bhp | availability |
|---|---|---|---|
| I-4, 200.5 | 3.88×4.25 | 50 | S-Model 40 I-4 |
| V-8, 221.0 | 3.06×3.75 | 75 | S-Model 40 V-8 |

## 1934

| Model 40A Four (wb 112.0) | Wght | Price | Prod |
|---|---|---|---|
| phaeton | — | — | 377 |
| Standard cpe 5W | — | 455 | 20 |
| Tudor sdn 5P | — | 470 | 185 |
| Fordor sdn 5P | — | 525 | 405 |
| DeLuxe rdstr 2-4P | — | 475 | 32 |
| DeLuxe phtn 5P | — | 500 | 412 |
| DeLuxe cpe 3W | — | 495 | 7 |
| DeLuxe cpe 5W | — | 520 | 3 |
| DeLuxe cabriolet 2-4P | — | 540 | 12 |
| DeLuxe Tudor sdn 5P | — | 510 | 12 |
| DeLuxe Fordor sdn 5P | — | 565 | 384 |
| wgn 4d | — | 610 | 95 |
| **Model 40A V-8 (wb 112.0)** | | | |
| roadster 2P | — | — | 4 |
| phaeton | — | — | 373 |
| Standard cpe 5W | 2,448 | 505 | 47,623 |
| Deluxe Victoria 5P | 2,670 | 600 | 20,083 |
| Deluxe cabriolet 2-4P | 2,460 | 590 | 14,496 |
| Tudor sdn 5P | 2,536 | 520 | 124,870 |
| Fordor sdn 5P | 2,590 | 575 | 22,394 |
| DeLuxe rdstr 2-4P | 2,376 | 525 | 5,038 |
| DeLuxe phtn 5P | 2,444 | 550 | 3,128 |
| DeLuxe cpe 3W | 2,453 | 545 | 26,348 |
| DeLuxe cpe 5W | 2,450 | 570 | 26,879 |
| DeLuxe Tudor sdn 5P | 2,540 | 560 | 121,696 |
| DeLuxe Fordor sdn 5P | 2,599 | 615 | 102,268 |
| wgn 4d | 2,695 | 660 | 2,905 |

| 1934 Engines | bore×stroke | bhp | availability |
|---|---|---|---|
| I-4, 200.5 | 3.88×4.25 | 50 | S-Model 40A Four |
| V-8, 221.0 | 3.06×3.75 | 85 | S-Model 40A V-8 |

## 1935

| Model 48 (wb 112.0) | Wght | Price | Prod |
|---|---|---|---|
| cpe 5W 2P | 2,620 | 495 ⎤ | 111,542 |
| DeLuxe cpe 5W 2P | 2,643 | 560 ⎦ | |
| conv cabriolet 2-4P | 2,687 | 625 | 17,000 |
| Tudor sdn 5P | 2,717 | 510 ⎤ | 322,575 |
| DeLuxe Tudor sdn 5P | 2,735 | 575 ⎦ | |
| Tudor touring sdn 5P | 2,772 | 595 | 87,326 |
| Fordor sdn 5P | 2,760 | 575 ⎤ | 124,984 |
| DeLuxe Fordor sdn 5P | 2,767 | 635 ⎦ | |
| Fordor touring sdn 5P | 2,787 | 655 | 105,157 |
| DeLuxe rdstr 2-4P | 2,597 | 550 | 4,896 |
| DeLuxe phtn 5P | 2,667 | 580 | 6,073 |
| DeLuxe cpe 3W 2P | 2,647 | 570 | 31,513 |
| conv sdn 5P | 2,827 | 750 | 4,234 |
| victoria 5P | — | 630 | 235 |
| wgn 4d | — | 670 | 4,536 |
| sdn 7P | — | — | 182 |

| 1935 Engine | bore×stroke | bhp | availability |
|---|---|---|---|
| V-8, 221.0 | 3.06×3.75 | 85 | S-all |

# Ford

## 1936

| Model 68 Standard (wb 112.0) | Wght | Price | Prod |
|---|---|---|---|
| cpe 5W 2P | 2,599 | 510 | 78,534 |
| cpe 5W 2-4P | 2,641 | 535 | |
| Tudor sdn 5P | 2,659 | 520 | 174,770 |
| Tudor T/B sdn 5P | 2,718 | 545 | 165,718 |
| Fordor sdn 5P | 2,699 | 580 | 31,505 |
| Fordor T/B sdn 5P | 2,771 | 605 | 39,607 |
| wgn 4d | 3,020 | 670 | 7,044 |
| **Model 68 DeLuxe (wb 112.0)** | | | |
| rdstr 2-4P | 2,561 | 560 | 3,862 |
| phtn 5P | 2,641 | 590 | 5,555 |
| cpe 3W 2P | 2,621 | 570 | 21,446 |
| cpe 3W 2-4P | 2,656 | 595 | |
| cpe 5W 2P | 2,641 | 555 | 29,938 |
| cpe 5W 2-4P | 2,666 | 580 | |
| cabriolet 2-4P | 2,649 | 625 | 14,068 |
| club cabriolet 2-4P | 2,661 | 675 | 4,616 |
| Tudor sdn 5P | 2,691 | 565 | 20,519 |
| Tudor T/B sdn 5P | 2,789 | 590 | 125,303 |
| Fordor sdn 5P | 2,746 | 625 | 42,867 |
| Fordor T/B sdn 5P | 2,816 | 650 | 159,825 |
| conv sdn 5P | 2,791 | 760 | 5,601 |
| conv sdn T/B 5P | 2,916 | 780 | |

| 1936 Engine | bore×stroke | bhp | availability |
|---|---|---|---|
| V-8, 221.0 | 3.06×3.75 | 85 | S-all |

## 1937

| Model 74 (wb 112.0) | Wght | Price | Prod |
|---|---|---|---|
| cpe 5W 2P | 2,275 | 529 | 43,866 |
| Tudor sdn 5P | 2,405 | 579 | * |
| Tudor T/B sdn 5P | 2,415 | 604 | 51,332 |
| Fordor sdn 5P | 2,435 | 639 | 18,541 |
| Fordor T/B sdn 5P | 2,445 | 664 | 13,976 |
| wgn 4d side curtains | 2,691 | 744 | 193 |
| wgn 4d glass windows | 2,776 | 764 | |
| **Model 78 Standard (wb 112.0)** | | | |
| cpe 5W 2P | 2,496 | 586 | 46,481 |
| Tudor sdn 5P | 2,616 | 611 | 308,446* |
| Tudor T/B sdn 5P | 2,648 | 638 | 78,895 |
| Fordor sdn 5P | 2,649 | 671 | 30,521 |
| Fordor T/B sdn 5P | 2,666 | 696 | 31,555 |
| wgn 4d side curtains | 2,906 | 754 | 9,111 |
| wgn 4d glass curtains | 2,991 | 775 | |
| **Model 78 DeLuxe (wb 112.0)** | | | |
| rdstr 2-4P | 2,576 | 694 | 1,250 |
| phtn 5P | 2,691 | 749 | 3,723 |
| cpe 5W 2P | 2,506 | 659 | 26,783 |
| cabriolet 2-4P | 2,616 | 719 | 10,184 |
| club cpe 5W 5P | 2,616 | 719 | 16,992 |
| club cabriolet 4P | 2,636 | 759 | 8,001 |
| Tudor sdn 5P | 2,656 | 674 | 33,683 |
| Tudor T/B sdn 5P | 2,679 | 699 | 73,690 |
| Fordor sdn 5P | 2,671 | 734 | 22,885 |
| Fordor T/B sdn 5P | 2,696 | 759 | 98,687 |
| conv sdn 5P | 2,861 | 859 | 4,378 |
| sdn 7P | — | — | 521 |

| 1937 Engines | bore×stroke | bhp | availability |
|---|---|---|---|
| V-8, 136.0 | 2.60×3.20 | 60 | S-74 |
| V-8, 221.0 | 3.06×3.75 | 85 | S-78 |

*Combined production.

## 1938

| Model 82A (wb 112.0) | Wght | Price | Prod |
|---|---|---|---|
| cpe 5W 2P | 2,354 | 595 | 13,712 |
| Tudor sdn 5P | 2,455 | 640 | 30,850 |
| Fordor sdn 5P | 2,481 | 685 | 5,878 |
| **Model 81A (wb 112.0)** | | | |
| cpe 5W 2P | 2,575 | 625 | 20,347 |
| Tudor sdn 5P | 2,674 | 665 | 75,267 |
| Fordor sdn 5P | 2,697 | 710 | 24,409 |
| wgn 4d | 2,981 | 825 | 6,944 |
| DeLuxe phtn 5P | 2,748 | 820 | 1,169 |
| DeLuxe cpe 5W 2P | 2,606 | 685 | 22,225 |
| DeLuxe conv cpe 2-4P | 2,679 | 770 | 4,702 |
| DeLuxe club cpe 5P | 2,688 | 745 | 7,171 |
| DeLuxe Tudor sdn 5P | 2,742 | 725 | 101,647 |
| DeLuxe Fordor sdn 5P | 2,773 | 770 | 92,020 |
| DeLuxe conv sdn 5P | 2,883 | 900 | 2,743 |
| DeLuxe sdn 7P | — | — | 449 |

| 1938 Engines | bore×stroke | bhp | availability |
|---|---|---|---|
| V-8, 136.0 | 2.60×3.20 | 60 | S-82A |
| V-8, 221.0 | 3.06×3.75 | 85 | S-81A |

## 1939

| Model 92A (wb 112.0) | Wght | Price | Prod |
|---|---|---|---|
| cpe 5W 2P | 2,463 | 599 | * |
| Tudor sdn 5P | 2,608 | 640 | * |
| Fordor sdn 5P | 2,623 | 686 | * |
| **Model 91A (wb 112.0)** | | | |
| cpe 5W 2P | 2,170 | 640 | * |
| Tudor sdn 5P | 2,830 | 681 | * |
| Fordor sdn 5P | 2,850 | 727 | * |
| wgn 4d | 3,080 | 840 | 3,277 |
| DeLuxe cpe 5W 2P | 2,752 | 702 | 37,326 |
| DeLuxe conv cpe 2-4P | 2,840 | 788 | 10,422 |
| DeLuxe Tudor sdn 5P | 2,867 | 742 | 144,333 |
| DeLuxe Fordor sdn 5P | 2,898 | 788 | 90,551 |
| DeLuxe conv sdn 5P | 2,935 | 921 | 3,561 |
| DeLuxe wgn 4d | 3,095 | 916 | 6,155 |
| DeLuxe sdn 7P | — | — | 192 |

| 1939 Engines | bore×stroke | bhp | availability |
|---|---|---|---|
| V-8, 136.0 | 2.60×3.20 | 60 | S-92A |
| V-8, 221.0 | 3.06×3.75 | 85 | S-91A |

*Production combined by body style as follows:

| | |
|---|---|
| coupe | 38,197 |
| Tudor sdn | 124,866 |
| Fordor sdn | 28,151 |

## 1940

| O1A V-8/85 (wb 112.0) | Wght | Price | Prod |
|---|---|---|---|
| cpe | 2,763 | 660 | * |
| bus cpe | 2,801 | 681 | * |
| Tudor sdn | 2,909 | 701 | * |
| Fordor sdn | 2,936 | 747 | * |
| wgn 4d | 3,249 | 875 | 4,469 |
| DeLuxe cpe | 2,791 | 722 | 27,919 |
| DeLuxe bus cpe | 2,831 | 742 | 20,183 |
| DeLuxe conv cpe | 2,956 | 849 | 23,704 |
| DeLuxe Tudor sdn | 2,927 | 762 | 171,368 |
| DeLuxe Fordor sdn | 2,966 | 808 | 91,756 |

# Ford

| O1A V-8/85 (wb 112.0) | Wght | Price | Prod |
|---|---|---|---|
| DeLuxe wgn 4d | 3,262 | 947 | 8,730 |

| O2A V-8/60 (wb 112.0) | | | |
|---|---|---|---|
| cpe | 2,519 | 619 | * |
| bus cpe | 2,549 | 640 | * |
| Tudor sdn | 2,669 | 660 | * |
| Fordor sdn | 2,696 | 706 | * |

| 1940 Engines | bore×stroke | bhp | availability |
|---|---|---|---|
| V-8, 136.0 | 2.60×3.20 | 60 | S-V-8/60 |
| V-8, 221.0 | 3.06×3.75 | 85 | S-V-8/85 |

*Production combined by body style as follows:

| | |
|---|---|
| cpe | 33,693 |
| bus cpe | 16,785 |
| Tudor sdn | 150,933 |
| Fordor sdn | 25,545 |

## 1941

| 1GA Six (wb 114.0) | Wght | Price | Prod* |
|---|---|---|---|
| Special cpe | 2,870 | 684 | — |
| Special Tudor sdn | 2,975 | 720 | — |
| Special Fordor sdn | 3,020 | 761 | — |
| DeLuxe cpe | 2,947 | 715 | — |
| DeLuxe cpe, A/S | 2,970 | 746 | — |
| DeLuxe Tudor sdn | 3,065 | 756 | — |
| DeLuxe Fordor sdn | 3,100 | 797 | — |
| DeLuxe wgn 4d | 3,395 | 946 | — |
| Super DeLuxe cpe | 2,934 | 761 | — |
| Super DeLuxe cpe, A/S | 2,974 | 792 | — |
| Super DeLuxe sdn cpe | 3,030 | 833 | — |
| Super DeLuxe conv cpe | 3,145 | 931 | — |
| Super DeLuxe Tudor sdn | 3,096 | 802 | — |
| Super DeLuxe Fordor sdn | 3,131 | 843 | — |
| Super DeLuxe wgn 4d | 3,400 | 998 | — |

| 11A V-8 (wb 114.0) | | | |
|---|---|---|---|
| Special cpe | 2,878 | 700 | 9,823 |
| Special Tudor sdn | 2,983 | 736 | 27,189 |
| Special Fordor sdn | 3,033 | 777 | 3,838 |
| DeLuxe cpe | 2,953 | 730 | 33,598 |
| DeLuxe cpe, A/S | 2,981 | 761 | 12,844 |
| DeLuxe Tudor sdn | 3,095 | 772 | 177,018 |
| DeLuxe Fordor sdn | 3,121 | 813 | 25,928 |
| DeLuxe wgn 4d | 3,412 | 962 | 6,116 |
| Super DeLuxe cpe | 2,969 | 777 | 22,878 |
| Super DeLuxe cpe, A/S | 3,001 | 807 | 10,796 |
| Super DeLuxe sdn cpe | 3,052 | 849 | 45,977 |
| Super DeLuxe conv cpe | 3,187 | 946 | 30,240 |
| Super DeLuxe Tudor sdn | 3,110 | 818 | 185,788 |
| Super DeLuxe Fordor sdn | 3,146 | 859 | 88,053 |
| Super DeLuxe wgn 4d | 3,419 | 1,013 | 9,485 |

| 1941 Engines | bore×stroke | bhp | availability |
|---|---|---|---|
| I-6, 226.0 | 3.30×4.40 | 90 | S-Six |
| V-8, 221.0 | 3.06×3.75 | 85 | S-V-8 |

*11A V-8 includes 1GA Six.

## 1942

| 2GA Six (wb 114.0) | | Wght | Price | Prod |
|---|---|---|---|---|
| 70C | Special Tudor sdn | 3,053 | 815 | 3,187 |
| 73C | Special Fordor sdn | 3,093 | 850 | 27,189 |
| 77C | Special cpe | 2,910 | 780 | 1,606 |

| 2GA Six (wb 114.0) | | Wght | Price | Prod |
|---|---|---|---|---|
| 70A | DeLuxe Tudor sdn | 3,122 | 840 | — |
| 72A | DeLuxe sdn cpe | 3,045 | 865 | — |
| 73A | DeLuxe Fordor sdn | 3,141 | 875 | — |
| 77A | DeLuxe cpe | 2,958 | 805 | — |
| 79A | DeLuxe wgn 4d, 8P | 3,405 | 1,035 | — |
| 70B | Super DeLuxe Tudor sdn | 3,136 | 885 | — |
| 72B | Super DeLuxe sdn cpe | 3,109 | 910 | — |
| 73B | Super DeLuxe Fordor sdn | 3,179 | 920 | — |
| 76 | Super DeLuxe conv cpe | 3,218 | 1,080 | — |
| 77B | Super DeLuxe cpe | 3,030 | 850 | — |
| 79B | Super DeLuxe wgn 4d, 8P | 3,453 | 1,115 | — |

| 21A V-8 (wb 114.0) | | Wght | Price | Prod |
|---|---|---|---|---|
| 70A | DeLuxe Tudor sdn | 3,141 | 850 | 27,302* |
| 72A | DeLuxe sdn cpe | 3,065 | 875 | 5,419* |
| 73A | DeLuxe Fordor sdn | 3,161 | 885 | 5,127* |
| 77A | DeLuxe cpe | 2,978 | 815 | 5,936* |
| 79A | DeLuxe wgn 4d, 8P | 3,420 | 1,090 | 567* |
| 70B | Super DeLuxe Tudor sdn | 3,159 | 895 | 37,189* |
| 72B | Super DeLuxe sdn cpe | 3,120 | 920 | 13,543* |
| 73B | Super DeLuxe Fordor sdn | 3,200 | 930 | 24,846* |
| 76 | Super DeLuxe conv cpe | 3,238 | 1,090 | 2,920* |
| 77B | Super DeLuxe cpe | 3,050 | 860 | 5,411* |
| 79B | Super DeLuxe wgn 4d, 8P | 3,468 | 1,125 | 5,483* |

| 1942 Engines | bore×stroke | bhp | availability |
|---|---|---|---|
| I-6, 226.0 | 3.30×4.40 | 90 | S-Six |
| V-8, 221.0 | 3.06×3.75 | 90 | S-V-8 |

*Includes 2GA Six.

## 1946

| 6GA Six (wb 114.0)* | | Wght | Price | Prod |
|---|---|---|---|---|
| 70A | DeLuxe Tudor sdn | 3,157 | 1,136 | — |
| 73A | DeLuxe Fordor sdn | 3,187 | 1,198 | — |
| 77A | DeLuxe cpe | 3,007 | 1,074 | — |
| 70B | Super DeLuxe Tudor sdn | 3,157 | 1,211 | — |
| 72B | Super DeLuxe cpe sdn | 3,107 | 1,257 | — |
| 73B | Super DeLuxe Fordor sdn | 3,207 | 1,273 | — |
| 77B | Super DeLuxe cpe | 3,007 | 1,148 | — |
| 79B | Super DeLuxe wgn 4d | 3,457 | 1,504 | — |

| 69A V-8 (wb 114.0)* | | Wght | Price | Prod |
|---|---|---|---|---|
| 70A | DeLuxe Tudor sdn | 3,190 | 1,185 | — |
| 73A | DeLuxe Fordor sdn | 3,220 | 1,248 | — |
| 77A | DeLuxe cpe | 3,040 | 1,123 | — |
| 70B | Super DeLuxe Tudor sdn | 3,190 | 1,260 | — |
| 71 | Super DLx Sprtsmn conv | 3,340 | 1,982 | 1,209 |
| 72B | Super DeLuxe cpe sdn | 3,140 | 1,307 | — |
| 73B | Super DeLuxe Fordor sdn | 3,240 | 1,322 | — |
| 76 | Super DeLuxe conv cpe | 3,240 | 1,488 | — |
| 77B | Super DeLuxe cpe | 3,040 | 1,197 | — |
| 79B | Super DeLuxe wgn 4d, 8P | 3,490 | 1,533 | — |

*Model year production by body style (Six/V-8):

| DeLuxe (wb 114.0) | Prod |
|---|---|
| Tudor sdn | 74,954 |
| Fordor sdn | 9,246 |
| cpe | 10,670 |
| chassis | 86 |

| Super DeLuxe (wb 114.0) | |
|---|---|
| Tudor sdn | 163,370 |
| Fordor sdn | 92,056 |
| sdn cpe | 70,826 |
| conv cpe | 16,359 |

# Ford

| Super DeLuxe (wb 114.0) | | | Prod |
|---|---|---|---|
| cpe | | | 12,249 |
| wgn 4d | | | 16,960 |
| chassis | | | 37 |

| 1946 Engines | bore×stroke | bhp | availability |
|---|---|---|---|
| I-6, 226.0 | 3.30×4.40 | 90 | S-Six |
| V-8, 239.4 | 3.19×3.75 | 100 | S-V-8 |

## 1947

| 7GA Six (wb 114.0)* | Wght | Price | Prod |
|---|---|---|---|
| DeLuxe Fordor sdn | 3,213 | 1,270 | — |
| DeLuxe Tudor sdn | 3,183 | 1,212 | — |
| DeLuxe cpe | 3,033 | 1,154 | — |
| Super DeLuxe Fordor sdn | 3,233 | 1,372 | — |
| Super DeLuxe Tudor sdn | 3,183 | 1,309 | — |
| Super DeLuxe cpe sdn | 3,133 | 1,330 | — |
| Super DeLuxe cpe | 3,033 | 1,251 | — |
| Super DeLuxe wgn 4d, 8P | 3,487 | 1,893 | — |

| 79A V-8 (wb 114.0)* | Wght | Price | Prod |
|---|---|---|---|
| DeLuxe Fordor sdn | 3,246 | 1,346 | — |
| DeLuxe Tudor sdn | 3,216 | 1,288 | — |
| DeLuxe cpe | 3,066 | 1,230 | — |
| Super DeLuxe Fordor sdn | 3,266 | 1,440 | — |
| Super DeLuxe Tudor sdn | 3,216 | 1,382 | — |
| Super DeLuxe cpe sdn | 3,166 | 1,409 | — |
| Super DeLuxe conv cpe | 3,266 | 1,740 | 22,159 |
| Super DLx Sprtsmn conv | 3,366 | 2,282 | 2,250 |
| Super DeLuxe wgn 4d, 8P | 3,520 | 1,972 | — |

*Model year production by body style (Six/V-8):

| DeLuxe (wb 114.0) | | | Prod |
|---|---|---|---|
| Tudor sdn | | | 44,523 |
| Fordor sdn | | | 20 |
| cpe | | | 10,872 |
| chassis | | | 23 |

| Super DeLuxe (wb 114.0) | | | Prod |
|---|---|---|---|
| Tudor sdn | | | 136,126 |
| Fordor sdn | | | 116,744 |
| cpe sdn | | | 80,830 |
| wgn 4d, 8P | | | 16,104 |
| chassis | | | 23 |

| 1947 Engines | bore×stroke | bhp | availability |
|---|---|---|---|
| I-6, 226.0 | 3.30×4.40 | 90 | S-Six |
| V-8, 239.4 | 3.19×3.75 | 100 | S-V-8 |

## 1948

| 87HA Six (wb 114.0)* | Wght | Price | Prod |
|---|---|---|---|
| 70A DeLuxe Tudor sdn | 3,183 | 1,212 | — |
| 77A DeLuxe cpe | 3,033 | 1,154 | — |
| 70B Super DeLuxe Tudor sdn | 3,183 | 1,309 | — |
| 72B Super DeLuxe cpe sdn | 3,133 | 1,330 | — |
| 73B Super DeLuxe Fordor sdn | 3,233 | 1,372 | — |
| 79B Super DeLuxe wgn 4d, 8P | 3,487 | 1,893 | — |

| 89A V-8 (wb 114.0)* | Wght | Price | Prod |
|---|---|---|---|
| 70A DeLuxe Tudor sdn | 3,216 | 1,288 | — |
| 77A DeLuxe cpe | 3,066 | 1,230 | — |
| 70B Super DeLuxe Tudor sdn | 3,216 | 1,382 | — |
| 71B Super DLx Sprtsmn conv | 3,366 | 2,282 | 28 |
| 72B Super DeLuxe cpe sdn | 3,166 | 1,409 | — |
| 73B Super DeLuxe Fordor sdn | 3,266 | 1,440 | — |
| 76B Super DeLuxe conv cpe | 3,266 | 1,740 | 12,033 |
| 79B Super DeLuxe wgn 4d, 8P | 3,520 | 1,972 | — |

*Model year production by body style (Six/V-8):

| DeLuxe (wb 114.0) | | | Prod |
|---|---|---|---|
| Tudor sdn | | | 23,356 |
| cpe | | | 5,048 |

| Super DeLuxe (wb 114.0) | | | Prod |
|---|---|---|---|
| Tudor sdn | | | 82,161 |
| Fordor sdn | | | 71,358 |
| cpe sdn | | | 44,826 |
| wgn 4d, 8P | | | 8,912 |

| 1948 Engines | bore×stroke | bhp | availability |
|---|---|---|---|
| I-6, 226.0 | 3.30×4.40 | 95 | S-Six |
| V-8, 239.4 | 3.19×3.75 | 100 | S-V-8 |

## 1949

| Standard (wb 114.0) | | Wght | Price | Prod |
|---|---|---|---|---|
| 70A | Tudor sdn | 2,965 | 1,425 | 126,770 |
| 72A | club cpe | 2,945 | 1,415 | 4,170 |
| 72C | bus cpe | 2,891 | 1,333 | 28,946 |
| 73A | Fordor sdn | 3,010 | 1,472 | 44,563 |
| — | chassis | — | — | 1 |

| Custom V-8 (wb 114.0) | | Wght | Price | Prod |
|---|---|---|---|---|
| 70B | Tudor sdn | 2,968 | 1,511 | 433,316 |
| 72B | club cpe | 2,948 | 1,511 | 150,254 |
| 73B | Fordor sdn | 3,013 | 1,559 | 248,176 |
| 76 | conv cpe | 3,254 | 1,886 | 51,133 |
| 79 | wgn 2d, 8P | 3,543 | 2,119 | 31,412 |
| — | chassis | — | — | 18 |

| 1949 Engines | bore×stroke | bhp | availability |
|---|---|---|---|
| I-6, 226.0 | 3.30×4.40 | 95 | S-Six |
| V-8, 239.4 | 3.19×3.75 | 100 | O-V-8 |

## 1950

| DeLuxe (wb 114.0) | | Wght | Price | Prod |
|---|---|---|---|---|
| D70 | Tudor sdn | 3,007 | 1,424 | 275,360 |
| D72C | bus cpe | 2,949 | 1,333 | 35,120 |
| D73 | Fordor sdn | 3,064 | 1,472 | 77,888 |

| Custom (wb 114.0) | | Wght | Price | Prod |
|---|---|---|---|---|
| C70 | Tudor sdn | 3,015 | 1,511 | 398,060 |
| C70C | Crestliner sdn 2d | 3,050 | 1,711 | 17,601 |
| C72 | club cpe | 2,981 | 1,511 | 85,111 |
| C73 | Fordor sdn | 3,078 | 1,558 | 247,181 |
| C76 | conv cpe | 3,263 | 1,948 | 50,299 |
| C79 | Country Squire wgn 2d | 3,511 | 2,028 | 22,929 |

| 1950 Engines | bore×stroke | bhp | availability |
|---|---|---|---|
| I-6, 226.0 | 3.30×4.40 | 95 | S-all exc C70C, C76 |
| V-8, 239.4 | 3.19×3.75 | 100 | S-C70C, C76; O-others |

## 1951

| DeLuxe (wb 114.0) | | Wght | Price | Prod |
|---|---|---|---|---|
| 70 | Tudor sdn | 3,043 | 1,417 | 146,010 |
| 72C | bus cpe | 2,979 | 1,324 | 20,343 |

# Ford

| | DeLuxe (wb 114.0) | Wght | Price | Prod |
|---|---|---|---|---|
| 73 | Fordor sdn | 3,102 | 1,465 | 54,265 |
| | **Custom (wb 114.0)** | | | |
| 60 | Victoria htp cpe | 3,188 | 1,925 | 110,286 |
| 70 | Tudor sdn | 3,043 | 1,505 | 317,869 |
| 70C | Crestliner sdn 2d | 3,065 | 1,595 | 8,703 |
| 72 | club cpe | 3,015 | 1,505 | 53,263 |
| 73 | Fordor sdn | 3,102 | 1,553 | 232,691 |
| 76 | conv cpe | 3,268 | 1,949 | 40,934 |
| 79 | Country Squire wgn 2d | 3,530 | 2,029 | 29,017 |

| 1951 Engines | bore×stroke | bhp | availability |
|---|---|---|---|
| I-6, 226.0 | 3.30×4.40 | 95 | S-all exc 60, 70C, 76 |
| V-8, 239.4 | 3.19×3.75 | 100 | S-60, 70C, 76; O-others |

## 1952

| | Mainline (wb 115.0) | Wght | Price | Prod |
|---|---|---|---|---|
| 59A | Ranch Wagon 2d | 3,212 | 1,832 | 32,566 |
| 70A | sdn 2d | 3,111 | 1,485 | 79,931 |
| 72C | bus cpe | 3,035 | 1,389 | 10,137 |
| 73A | sdn 4d | 3,190 | 1,530 | 41,227 |
| | **Customline (wb 115.0)** | | | |
| 70B | sdn 2d | 3,111 | 1,570 | 175,762 |
| 72B | club cpe | 3,116 | 1,579 | 26,550 |
| 73B | sdn 4d | 3,190 | 1,615 | 188,303 |
| 79C | Country Sedan wgn 4d, 6P | 3,617 | 2,060 | 11,927 |
| | **Crestline (wb 115.0)** | | | |
| 60B | Victoria htp cpe | 3,274 | 1,925 | 77,320 |
| 76B | Sunliner conv cpe | 3,339 | 2,027 | 22,534 |
| 79B | Country Squire wgn 4d, 8P | 3,640 | 2,186 | 5,426 |

| 1952 Engines | bore×stroke | bhp | availability |
|---|---|---|---|
| I-6, 215.3 | 3.56×3.60 | 101 | S-all exc 79C, Crestline (ohv) |
| V-8, 239.4 | 3.19×3.75 | 110 | S-79C, Crestline; O-others |

## 1953

| | Mainline (wb 115.0) | Wght | Price | Prod |
|---|---|---|---|---|
| 59A | Ranch Wagon 2d | 3,406 | 1,917 | 66,976 |
| 70A | sdn 2d | 3,092 | 1,497 | 152,995 |
| 72C | bus cpe | 3,018 | 1,400 | 16,280 |
| 73A | sdn 4d | 3,138 | 1,542 | 69,463 |
| | **Customline (wb 115.0)** | | | |
| 70B | sdn 2d | 3,100 | 1,582 | 305,433 |
| 72B | club cpe | 3,084 | 1,591 | 43,999 |
| 73B | sdn 4d | 3,154 | 1,628 | 374,487 |
| 79B | Country Sedan wgn 4d, 6P | 3,539 | 2,076 | 37,743 |
| | **Crestline (wb 115.0)** | | | |
| 60B | Victoria htp cpe | 3,250 | 1,941 | 128,302 |
| 76B | Sunliner conv cpe | 3,334 | 2,043 | 40,861 |
| 79C | Country Squire wgn 4d, 8P | 3,609 | 2,203 | 11,001 |
| — | chassis | — | — | 2 |

| 1953 Engines | bore×stroke | bhp | availability |
|---|---|---|---|
| I-6, 215.3 | 3.56×3.60 | 101 | S-all exc 79B, Crestline |
| V-8, 239.4 | 3.19×3.75 | 110 | S-79B, Crestline; O-others |

## 1954

| | Mainline (wb 115.5) | Wght | Price | Prod |
|---|---|---|---|---|
| 59A | Ranch Wagon 2d | 3,399 | 2,029 | 44,315 |
| 70A | sdn 2d | 3,147 | 1,651 | 123,329 |
| 72C | bus cpe | 3,082 | 1,548 | 10,665 |
| 73A | sdn 4d | 3,203 | 1,701 | 55,371 |
| | **Customline (wb 115.5)** | | | |
| 59B | Ranch Wagon 2d | 3,405 | 2,122 | 36,086 |
| 70B | sdn 2d | 3,160 | 1,744 | 293,375 |
| 72B | club cpe | 3,141 | 1,753 | 33,951 |
| 73B | sdn 4d | 3,216 | 1,793 | 262,499 |
| 79B | Country Sedan wgn 4d, 6P | 3,574 | 2,202 | 48,384 |
| | **Crestline (wb 115.5)** | | | |
| 60B | Victoria htp cpe | 3,245 | 2,055 | 95,464 |
| 60F | Skyliner htp cpe | 3,265 | 2,164 | 13,344 |
| 73C | sdn 4d | 3,220 | 1,898 | 99,677 |
| 76B | Sunliner conv cpe | 3,292 | 2,164 | 36,685 |
| 79C | Country Squire wgn 4d, 8P | 3,624 | 2,339 | 12,797 |

| 1954 Engines | bore×stroke | bhp | availability |
|---|---|---|---|
| I-6, 223.0 | 3.62×3.60 | 115 | S-all exc 79B |
| V-8, 239.4 | 3.50×3.10 | 130 | S-79B; O-others (ohv) |

## 1955

| | Mainline (wb 115.5) | Wght | Price | Prod |
|---|---|---|---|---|
| 70A | sdn 2d | 3,119 | 1,707 | 76,698 |
| 70D | bus cpe | 3,081 | 1,606 | 8,809 |
| 73A | sdn 4d | 3,161 | 1,753 | 41,794 |
| | **Customline (wb 115.5)** | | | |
| 70B | sdn 2d | 3,139 | 1,801 | 236,575 |
| 73B | sdn 4d | 3,181 | 1,845 | 235,417 |
| | **Fairlane (wb 115.5)** | | | |
| 60B | Victoria htp cpe | 3,251 | 2,095 | 113,372 |
| 64A | Crown Victoria htp cpe | 3,313 | 2,202 | 33,165 |
| 64B | Crwn Vic htp cpe, glass top | 3,321 | 2,272 | 1,999 |
| 70C | club sdn 2d | 3,155 | 1,914 | 173,311 |
| 73C | Town Sedan | 3,201 | 1,960 | 254,437 |
| 76B | Sunliner conv cpe | 3,315 | 2,224 | 49,966 |
| | **Station Wagon (wb 115.5)** | | | |
| 59A | Ranch 2d, 6P | 3,376 | 2,043 | 40,493 |
| 59B | Custom Ranch 2d, 6P | 3,394 | 2,109 | 43,671 |
| 79B | Country Sedan 4d, 8P | 3,536 | 2,287 | 53,209 |
| 79C | Country Squire 4d, 8P | 3,538 | 2,392 | 19,011 |
| 79D | Country Sedan 4d, 6P | 3,460 | 2,156 | 53,075 |

| 1955 Engines | bore×stroke | bhp | availability |
|---|---|---|---|
| I-6, 223.0 | 3.62×3.60 | 120 | S-all |
| V-8, 272.0 | 3.62×3.30 | 162 | O-all |
| V-8, 272.0 | 3.62×3.30 | 182 | O-all |
| V-8, 292.0 | 3.75×3.30 | 198 | O-Fairlane, stn wgn |

## 1956

| | Mainline (wb 115.5) | Wght | Price | Prod |
|---|---|---|---|---|
| 70A | sdn 2d | 3,143 | 1,850 | 106,974 |
| 70D | bus sdn 2d | 3,088 | 1,748 | 8,020 |
| 73A | sdn 4d | 3,183 | 1,895 | 49,448 |
| | **Customline (wb 115.5)** | | | |
| 64D | Victoria htp cpe | 3,202 | 1,985 | 33,130 |
| 70B | sdn 2d | 3,163 | 1,939 | 164,828 |

# Ford

| Customline (wb 115.5) | | Wght | Price | Prod |
|---|---|---|---|---|
| 73B | sdn 4d | 3,203 | 1,985 | 170,695 |
| **Fairlane (wb 115.5)** | | | | |
| 57A | Victoria htp sdn | 3,369 | 2,249 | 32,111 |
| 64A | Crown Victoria htp cpe | 3,289 | 2,337 | 9,209 |
| 64B | Crwn Vic htp cpe, glass top | 3,299 | 2,407 | 603 |
| 64C | Victoria htp cpe | 3,274 | 2,194 | 177,735 |
| 70C | club sdn 2d | 3,179 | 2,047 | 142,629 |
| 73C | Town Sedan | 3,219 | 2,093 | 224,872 |
| 76B | Sunliner conv cpe | 3,384 | 2,359 | 58,147 |
| **Station Wagon (wb 115.5)** | | | | |
| 59A | Ranch 2d, 6P | 3,402 | 2,185 | 48,348 |
| 59B | Custom Ranch 2d, 6P | 3,417 | 2,249 | 42,317 |
| 59C | Parklane 2d | 3,432 | 2,428 | 15,186 |
| 79B | Country Sedan 4d, 8P | 3,555 | 2,428 | 85,374 |
| 79C | Country Squire 4d, 8P | 3,566 | 2,533 | 23,221 |

| 1956 Engines | bore×stroke | bhp | availability |
|---|---|---|---|
| I-6, 223.0 | 3.62×3.60 | 137 | S-all |
| V-8, 272.0 | 3.62×3.30 | 173 | O-Mainline, Customline |
| V-8, 292.0 | 3.75×3.30 | 200 | O-Fairlane wgn, (202 bhp w/auto) |
| V-8, 312.0 | 3.80×3.44 | 215 | O-all (225 bhp w/auto) |

## 1957

| Custom (wb 116.0) | | Wght | Price | Prod |
|---|---|---|---|---|
| 70A | sdn 2d | 3,211 | 1,991 | 116,963 |
| 70D | bus sdn 2d | 3,202 | 1,879 | 6,888 |
| 73A | sdn 4d | 3,254 | 2,042 | 68,924 |
| **Custom 300 (wb 116.0)** | | | | |
| 70B | sdn 2d | 3,224 | 2,105 | 160,360 |
| 73B | sdn 4d | 3,269 | 2,157 | 194,877 |
| **Fairlane (wb 118.0)** | | | | |
| 57B | Victoria htp sdn | 3,411 | 2,357 | 12,695 |
| 58A | Town Sedan 4d | 3,376 | 2,286 | 52,060 |
| 63B | Victoria htp cpe | 3,366 | 2,293 | 44,127 |
| 64A | club sdn 2d | 3,331 | 2,235 | 39,843 |
| **Fairlane 500 (wb 118.0)** | | | | |
| 51A | Skyliner retrac conv cpe | 3,916 | 2,942 | 20,766 |
| 57A | Victoria htp sdn | 3,426 | 2,404 | 68,550 |
| 58B | Town Sedan 4d | 3,384 | 2,286 | 193,162 |
| 63A | Victoria htp cpe | 3,381 | 2,339 | 183,202 |
| 64B | club sdn 2d | 3,346 | 2,281 | 93,756 |
| 76B | Sunliner conv cpe | 3,536 | 2,505 | 77,726 |
| **Station Wagon (wb 116.0)** | | | | |
| 59A | Ranch 2d, 6P | 3,455 | 2,301 | 60,486 |
| 59B | Del Rio 2d, 6P | 3,462 | 2,397 | 46,105 |
| 79C | Country Sedan 4d, 9P | 3,614 | 2,556 | 49,638 |
| 79D | Country Sedan 4d, 6P | 3,525 | 2,451 | 137,251 |
| 79E | Country Squire 4d, 9P | 3,628 | 2,684 | 27,690 |

| 1957 Engines | bore×stroke | bhp | availability |
|---|---|---|---|
| I-6, 223.0 | 3.62×3.60 | 144 | S-all exc 51A |
| V-8, 272.0 | 3.62×3.30 | 190 | S-51A; O-others |
| V-8, 292.0 | 3.75×3.30 | 212 | O-Fairlane, Fairlane 500, wgns |
| V-8, 312.0 | 3.80×3.44 | 245 | O-all |

## 1958

| Custom (wb 116.0) | | Wght | Price | Prod |
|---|---|---|---|---|
| 70A | sdn 2d | 3,250 | 2,055 | 36,272 |
| 70D | bus sdn | 3,227 | 1,967 | 4,062 |
| 73A | sdn 4d | 3,278 | 2,109 | 27,811 |
| **Custom 300 (wb 116.0)** | | | | |
| 70B | sdn 2d | 3,300 | 2,305 | 137,169 |
| 73B | sdn 4d | 3,328 | 2,159 | 135,557 |
| **Fairlane (wb 118.0)** | | | | |
| 57B | Victoria htp sdn | 3,450 | 2,419 | 5,868 |
| 58A | Town Sedan 4d | 3,427 | 2,275 | 57,490 |
| 63B | Victoria htp cpe | 3,373 | 2,354 | 16,416 |
| 64A | club sdn 2d | 3,375 | 2,221 | 38,366 |
| **Fairlane 500 (wb 118.0)** | | | | |
| 51A | Skyliner retrac conv cpe | 4,069 | 3,163 | 14,713 |
| 57A | Victoria htp sdn | 3,488 | 2,499 | 36,509 |
| 58B | sdn 4d | 3,452 | 2,428 | 105,698 |
| 63A | Victoria htp cpe | 3,390 | 2,435 | 80,439 |
| 64B | club sdn 2d | 3,380 | 2,374 | 34,041 |
| 76B | Sunliner conv | 3,556 | 2,650 | 35,029 |
| **Station Wagon (wb 116.0)** | | | | |
| 59A | Ranch 2d, 6P | 3,552 | 2,397 | 34,578 |
| 59B | Del Rio 2d, 6P | 3,734 | 2,503 | 12,687 |
| 79A | Ranch 4d, 6P | 3,608 | 2,451 | 32,854 |
| 79C | Country Sedan 4d, 9P | 3,682 | 2,664 | 20,702 |
| 79D | Country Sedan 4d, 6P | 3,614 | 2,557 | 68,772 |
| 79E | Country Squire 4d, 9P | 3,718 | 2,794 | 15,020 |

| 1958 Engines | bore×stroke | bhp | availability |
|---|---|---|---|
| I-6, 223.0 | 3.62×3.60 | 145 | S-all exc 51A |
| V-8, 292.0 | 3.75×3.30 | 205 | S-51A; O-others |
| V-8, 332.0 | 4.00×3.30 | 240 | O-wgns (265 bhp w/auto) |
| V-8, 332.0 | 4.00×3.30 | 265 | O-all |
| V-8, 352.0 | 4.00×3.50 | 300 | O-all |

## 1959

| Custom 300 (wb 118.0) | | Wght | Price | Prod |
|---|---|---|---|---|
| 58E | sdn 4d | 3,436 | 2,273 | 249,553 |
| 64F | sdn 2d | 3,360 | 2,219 | 228,573 |
| 64G | bus sdn | 3,334 | 2,132 | 4,084 |
| **Fairlane (wb 118.0)** | | | | |
| 58A | Town Sedan 4d | 3,466 | 2,411 | 64,663 |
| 64A | club sdn 2d | 3,382 | 2,357 | 35,126 |
| **Fairlane 500 (wb 118.0)** | | | | |
| 57A | Victoria htp sdn | 3,502 | 2,602 | 9,308 |
| 58B | sdn 4d | 3,468 | 2,530 | 35,670 |
| 63A | Victoria htp cpe | 3,416 | 2,537 | 23,892 |
| 64B | club sdn 2d | 3,388 | 2,476 | 10,141 |
| **Galaxie (wb 118.0)** | | | | |
| 51A | Skyliner retrac htp cpe | 4,064 | 3,346 | 12,915 |
| 54A | sdn 4d | 3,456 | 2,582 | 183,108 |
| 64H | club sdn 2d | 3,388 | 2,528 | 52,848 |
| 65A | Victoria htp cpe | 3,428 | 2,589 | 121,869 |
| 75A | Victoria htp sdn | 3,544 | 2,654 | 47,728 |
| 76B | Sunliner conv cpe | 3,578 | 2,839 | 45,868 |
| **Station Wagon (wb 118.0)** | | | | |
| 59C | Ranch 2d, 6P | 3,640 | 2,567 | 45,588 |
| 59D | Del Rio 2d, 6P | 3,664 | 2,678 | 8,663 |
| 71E | Country Sedan 4d, 9P | 3,818 | 2,829 | 28,811 |
| 71F | Country Sedan 4d, 6P | 3,768 | 2,745 | 94,601 |

# Ford

| Station Wagon (wb 118.0) | | Wght | Price | Prod |
|---|---|---|---|---|
| 71G | Country Squire 4d, 9P | 3,808 | 2,958 | 24,336 |
| 71H | Ranch 4d, 6P | 3,736 | 2,634 | 67,339 |

| 1959 Engines | bore×stroke | bhp | availability |
|---|---|---|---|
| I-6, 223.0 | 3.62×3.60 | 145 | S-all exc 51A |
| V-8, 292.0 | 3.75×3.30 | 200 | S-51A; O-others |
| V-8, 332.0 | 4.00×3.30 | 225 | O-all |
| V-8, 352.0 | 4.00×3.50 | 300 | O-all |

## 1960

| Falcon (wb 109.5) | | Wght | Price | Prod |
|---|---|---|---|---|
| 58A | sdn 4d | 2,288 | 1,974 | 167,896 |
| 59A | wgn 2d | 2,540 | 2,225 | 27,552 |
| 64A | sdn 2d | 2,259 | 1,912 | 193,470 |
| 71A | wgn 4d | 2,575 | 2,287 | 46,758 |

| Custom 300 (wb 119.0) | | | | |
|---|---|---|---|---|
| 58F | sdn 4d | 3,576 | 2,284 | 572 |
| 64H | sdn 2d | 3,465 | 2,230 | 302 |

| Fairlane (wb 119.0) | | | | |
|---|---|---|---|---|
| 58E | sdn 4d | 3,656 | 2,311 | 109,801 |
| 64F | sdn 2d | 3,582 | 2,257 | 93,256 |
| 64G | bus sdn | 3,555 | 2,170 | 1,733 |

| Fairlane 500 (wb 119.0) | | | | |
|---|---|---|---|---|
| 58A | Town Sedan 4d | 3,663 | 2,388 | 153,234 |
| 64A | club sdn 2d | 3,586 | 2,334 | 91,041 |

| Galaxie (wb 119.0) | | | | |
|---|---|---|---|---|
| 54A | Town Sedan 4d | 3,684 | 2,603 | 104,784 |
| 62A | club sdn 2d | 3,603 | 2,549 | 31,866 |
| 63A | Starliner htp cpe | 3,617 | 2,610 | 68,461 |
| 75A | Victoria htp sdn | 3,692 | 2,675 | 39,215 |
| 76B | Sunliner conv cpe | 3,791 | 2,860 | 44,762 |

| Station Wagon (wb 119.0) | | | | |
|---|---|---|---|---|
| 59C | Ranch 2d, 6P | 3,881 | 2,586 | 27,136 |
| 71E | Country Sedan 4d, 9P | 4,058 | 2,837 | 19,277 |
| 71F | Country Sedan 4d, 6P | 4,012 | 2,752 | 59,302 |
| 71G | Country Squire 4d, 6P | 4,072 | 2,967 | 22,237 |
| 71H | Ranch 4d, 6P | 3,998 | 2,656 | 43,872 |

| 1960 Engines | bore×stroke | bhp | availability |
|---|---|---|---|
| I-6, 144.3 | 3.50×2.50 | 90 | S-Falcon only |
| I-6, 223.0 | 3.62×3.60 | 145 | S-all exc Falcon |
| V-8, 292.0 | 3.75×3.30 | 185 | O-all exc Falcon |
| V-8, 352.0 | 4.00×3.50 | 235 | O-all exc Falcon |
| V-8, 352.0 | 4.00×3.50 | 300/360 | O-all exc Falcon |

## 1961

| Falcon (wb 109.5) | | Wght | Price | Prod |
|---|---|---|---|---|
| 58A | sdn 4d | 2,289 | 1,976 | 159,761 |
| 59A | wgn 2d | 2,525 | 2,227 | 32,045 |
| 62A | Futura sdn 2d | 2,322 | 2,162 | 44,470 |
| 64A | sdn 2d (inc 50 Econ sdns) | 2,254 | 1,914 | 150,032 |
| 71A | wgn 4d | 2,558 | 2,270 | 87,933 |

| Custom 300 (wb 119.0) | | | | |
|---|---|---|---|---|
| 58F | sdn 4d | 3,516 | — | 303 |
| 64H | sdn 2d | 3,405 | — | 49 |

| Fairlane (wb 119.0) | | | | |
|---|---|---|---|---|
| 58E | sdn 4d | 3,634 | 2,317 | 96,602 |
| 64F | sdn 2d | 3,536 | 2,263 | 66,875 |

| Fairlane 500 (wb 119.0) | | Wght | Price | Prod |
|---|---|---|---|---|
| 58A | sdn 4d | 3,642 | 2,432 | 98,917 |
| 64A | sdn 2d | 3,551 | 2,378 | 42,468 |

| Galaxie (wb 119.0) | | | | |
|---|---|---|---|---|
| 54A | sdn 4d | 3,619 | 2,592 | 141,823 |
| 62A | sdn 2d | 3,537 | 2,538 | 27,780 |
| 63A | Starliner htp cpe | 3,566 | 2,599 | 29,669 |
| 65A | Victoria htp cpe | 3,594 | 2,599 | 75,437 |
| 75A | Victoria htp sdn | 3,637 | 2,664 | 30,342 |
| 76B | Sunliner conv cpe | 3,743 | 2,849 | 44,614 |

| Station Wagon (wb 119.0) | | | | |
|---|---|---|---|---|
| 59C | Ranch 2d, 6P | 3,865 | 2,588 | 12,042 |
| 71E | Country Sedan 4d, 9P | 4,011 | 2,858 | 16,356 |
| 71F | Country Sedan 4d, 6P | 3,983 | 2,754 | 46,311 |
| 71G | Country Squire 4d, 9P | 4,015 | 3,013 | 14,657 |
| 71H | Ranch 4d, 6P | 3,960 | 2,658 | 30,292 |
| 71J | Country Squire 4d, 6P | 3,969 | 2,943 | 16,961 |

| 1961 Engines | bore×stroke | bhp | availability |
|---|---|---|---|
| I-6, 144.3 | 3.50×2.50 | 85 | S-Falcon |
| I-6, 170.0 | 3.50×2.94 | 101 | S-Fairlane; O-Falcon |
| I-6, 223.0 | 3.62×3.30 | 135 | S-all exc Falcon, Fairlane |
| V-8, 292.0 | 3.75×3.30 | 175 | S-all exc Falcon |
| V-8, 352.0 | 4.00×3.50 | 220 | O-all exc Falcon |
| V-8, 390.0 | 4.05×3.78 | 300 | O-all exc Falcon |
| V-8, 390.0 | 4.05×3.78 | 375/401 | O-all exc Falcon (limited) |

## 1962

| Falcon (wb 109.5) | | Wght | Price | Prod |
|---|---|---|---|---|
| 58A | sdn 4d | 2,279 | 2,047 | 126,041 |
| 58B | Deluxe sdn 4d | 2,285 | 2,133 | |
| 59A | wgn 2d | 2,539 | 2,298 | 20,025 |
| 59B | Deluxe wgn 2d | 2,545 | 2,384 | |
| 62C | Futura sdn 2d | 2,343 | 2,273 | 17,011 |
| 64A | sdn 2d | 2,243 | 1,985 | 143,650 |
| 64B | Deluxe sdn 2d | 2,249 | 2,071 | |
| 71A | wgn 4d | 2,575 | 2,341 | 66,819 |
| 71B | Deluxe wgn 4d | 2,581 | 2,427 | |
| 71C | Squire wgn 4d | 2,591 | 2,603 | 22,583 |

| Series 30 Fairlane (wb 115.5) | | | | |
|---|---|---|---|---|
| 54A | sdn 4d | 2,848 | 2,216 | 45,342 |
| 62A | sdn 2d | 2,815 | 2,154 | 34,264 |

| Series 40 Fairlane 500 (wb 115.5) | | | | |
|---|---|---|---|---|
| 54B | 500 sdn 4d | 2,865 | 2,304 | 129,258 |
| 62B | 500 sdn 2d | 2,832 | 2,242 | 68,624 |
| 62C | 500 spt cpe | 2,928 | 2,403 | 19,628 |

| Galaxie (wb 119.0) | | | | |
|---|---|---|---|---|
| 54B | sdn 4d | 3,636 | 2,507 | 115,594 |
| 62B | sdn 2d | 3,554 | 2,453 | 54,930 |

| Galaxie 500 (wb 119.0) | | | | |
|---|---|---|---|---|
| 54A | sdn 4d | 3,650 | 2,667 | 174,195 |
| 62A | sdn 2d | 3,568 | 2,613 | 27,824 |
| 65A | Victoria htp cpe | 3,568 | 2,674 | 87,562 |
| 65B | XL Victoria htp cpe | 3,672 | 2,268 | 28,412 |
| 75A | Victoria htp sdn | 3,640 | 2,739 | 30,778 |
| 76A | Sunliner conv cpe | 3,730 | 2,924 | 42,646 |
| 76B | XL Sunliner conv cpe | 3,831 | 3,518 | 13,183 |

# Ford

| Station Wagon (wb 119.0) | | Wght | Price | Prod |
|---|---|---|---|---|
| 71A | Country Squire 4d, 9P | 4,022 | 3,088 | 15,666 |
| 71B | Country Sedan 4d, 6P | 3,992 | 2,829 | 47,635 |
| 71C | Country Sedan 4d, 9P | 4,010 | 2,933 | 16,562 |
| 71D | Ranch 4d, 6P | 3,968 | 2,733 | 33,674 |
| 71E | Country Squire 4d, 6P | 4,006 | 3,018 | 16,114 |

| 1962 Engines | bore×stroke | bhp | availability |
|---|---|---|---|
| I-6, 144.3 | 3.50×2.50 | 85 | S-Falcon |
| I-6, 170.0 | 3.50×2.94 | 101 | S-Fairlane; O-Falcon |
| I-6, 223.0 | 3.62×3.60 | 138 | S-all exc Falcon, Fairlane |
| V-8, 221.0 | 3.50×2.87 | 145 | O-Fairlane |
| V-8, 260.0 | 3.80×2.87 | 164 | O-Fairlane |
| V-8, 292.0 | 3.75×3.30 | 170 | S-76B; O-all exc Falcon, Fairlane |
| V-8, 352.0 | 4.00×3.50 | 220 | O-all exc Falcon, Fairlane |
| V-8, 390.0 | 4.05×3.78 | 300/340 | O-all exc Falcon, Fairlane |
| V-8, 390.0 | 4.05×3.78 | 375/401 | O-all exc Falcon, Fairlane |
| V-8, 406.0 | 4.13×3.78 | 385/405 | O-all exc Falcon, Fairlane |

## 1963

| Series 0 Falcon (wb 109.5) | | Wght | Price | Prod |
|---|---|---|---|---|
| 54A | sdn 4d | 2,337 | 2,047 | 62,365 |
| 62A | sdn 2d | 2,300 | 1,985 | 70,630 |
| Series 10 Falcon Futura (wb 109.5) | | | | |
| 54B | sdn 4d | 2,345 | 2,161 | 31,736 |
| 62B | sdn 2d | 2,308 | 2,116 | 27,018 |
| 63B | htp cpe | 2,455 | 2,198 | 28,496 |
| 63C | Sprint htp cpe | 2,490 | 2,603 | 10,479 |
| 76A | conv cpe | 2,655 | 2,470 | 31,192 |
| 76B | Sprint conv cpe | 2,690 | 2,837 | 4,602 |
| Series 20 Falcon Wagon (wb 109.5) | | | | |
| 59A | wgn 2d | 2,580 | 2,298 | 7,322 |
| 59B | Deluxe wgn 2d | 2,586 | 2,384 | 4,269 |
| 71A | wgn 4d | 2,617 | 2,341 | 18,484 |
| 71B | Deluxe wgn 4d | 2,623 | 2,427 | 23,477 |
| 71C | Squire wgn 4d | 2,639 | 2,603 | 8,269 |
| Series 30 Fairlane (wb 115.5) | | | | |
| 54A | sdn 4d | 2,930 | 2,216 | 44,454 |
| 62A | sdn 2d | 2,890 | 2,154 | 28,984 |
| 71D | Ranch Wagon 4d | 3,281 | 2,525 | 24,006 |
| Series 40 Fairlane 500 (wb 115.5) | | | | |
| 54B | sdn 4d | 2,945 | 2,304 | 104,175 |
| 62B | sdn 2d | 2,905 | 2,242 | 34,764 |
| 65A | htp cpe | 2,923 | 2,324 | 41,641 |
| 65B | htp cpe, bkt sts | 2,923 | 2,504 | 28,268 |
| 71B | Cus Ranch Wagon 4d | 3,298 | 2,613 | 29,612 |
| 71E | Squire Wagon 4d | 3,295 | 2,781 | 7,983 |
| Series 50 300 (wb 119.0) | | | | |
| 54E | sdn 4d | 3,627 | 2,378 | 44,142 |
| 62E | sdn 2d | 3,547 | 2,324 | 26,010 |
| Series 50 Galaxie (wb 119.0) | | | | |
| 54B | sdn 4d | 3,647 | 2,507 | 82,419 |
| 62B | sdn 2d | 3,567 | 2,453 | 30,335 |

| Series 60 Galaxie 500 (wb 119.0) | | Wght | Price | Prod |
|---|---|---|---|---|
| 54A | sdn 4d | 3,667 | 2,667 | 205,722 |
| 62A | sdn 2d | 3,587 | 2,613 | 21,137 |
| 63B | XL htp cpe, fstbk | 3,772 | 2,674 | 134,370 |
| 65A | htp cpe | 3,599 | 2,674 | 49,733 |
| 75A | htp sdn | 3,679 | 2,739 | 39,154 |
| 76A | Sunliner conv cpe | 3,757 | 2,924 | 29,713 |
| Series 70 Station Wagon (wb 119.0) | | | | |
| 71A | Country Squire 4d, 9P | 4,003 | 3,088 | 19,567 |
| 71B | Country Sedan 4d, 6P | 3,977 | 2,829 | 64,954 |
| 71C | Country Sedan 4d, 9P | 3,989 | 2,933 | 22,250 |
| 71E | Country Squire 4d, 6P | 3,991 | 3,018 | 20,359 |

| 1963 Engines | bore×stroke | bhp | availability |
|---|---|---|---|
| I-6, 144.3 | 3.50×2.50 | 85 | S-Falcon |
| I-6, 170.0 | 3.50×2.94 | 101 | S-Fairlane; O-Falcon |
| I-6, 200.0 | 3.68×3.13 | 116 | O-Fairlane |
| I-6, 223.0 | 3.62×3.60 | 138 | S-all exc Falc, Fair |
| V-8, 221.0 | 3.50×2.87 | 145 | O-Fairlane |
| V-8, 260.0 | 3.80×2.87 | 164 | S-Falcon Sprint; O-others |
| V-8, 289.0 | 4.00×2.87 | 271 | O-Fairlane |
| V-8, 352.0 | 4.00×3.50 | 220 | O-all exc Falcon, Fairlane |
| V-8, 390.0 | 4.05×3.78 | 300/330 | O-all exc Falcon, Fairlane |
| V-8, 406.0 | 4.13×3.78 | 385/405 | O-all exc Falcon, Fairlane |
| V-8, 427.0 | 4.23×3.78 | 410/425 | O-all exc Falcon, Fairlane |

## 1964

| Series 0 Falcon (wb 109.5) | | Wght | Price | Prod |
|---|---|---|---|---|
| 01 | sdn 2d | 2,365 | 1,996 | 36,441 |
| 01 | Deluxe sdn 2d | 2,380 | 2,039 | 28,411 |
| 02 | sdn 4d | 2,400 | 2,058 | 27,722 |
| 02 | Deluxe sdn 4d | 2,420 | 2,101 | 26,532 |
| Series 10 Falcon Futura (wb 109.5) | | | | |
| 11 | htp cpe, bkt seats | 2,545 | 2,325 | 8,607 |
| 12 | conv cpe, bkt seats | 2,735 | 2,597 | 2,980 |
| 13 | Sprint htp cpe | 2,813 | 2,436 | 13,830 |
| 14 | Sprint conv cpe | 3,008 | 2,671 | 4,278 |
| 15 | conv cpe | 2,710 | 2,481 | 13,220 |
| 16 | sdn 4d | 2,410 | 2,176 | 38,032 |
| 17 | htp cpe | 2,515 | 2,209 | 32,608 |
| 19 | sdn 2d | 2,375 | 2,127 | 16,833 |
| Series 20 Falcon Wagon (wb 109.5) | | | | |
| 21 | wgn 2d | 2,660 | 2,326 | 6,034 |
| 22 | wgn 4d | 2,695 | 2,360 | 17,779 |
| 24 | Deluxe wgn 4d | 2,715 | 2,446 | 20,697 |
| 26 | Squire wgn 4d | 2,720 | 2,622 | 6,766 |
| Series 30 Fairlane (wb 115.5) | | | | |
| 31 | sdn 2d | 2,855 | 2,194 | 20,421 |
| 32 | sdn 4d | 2,895 | 2,235 | 36,693 |
| 38 | Ranch wgn 4d | 3,290 | 2,531 | 20,980 |
| Series 40 Fairlane 500 (wb 115.5) | | | | |
| 41 | sdn 2d | 2,863 | 2,276 | 23,447 |
| 42 | sdn 4d | 2,910 | 2,317 | 86,919 |
| 43 | htp cpe | 2,925 | 2,341 | 42,733 |
| 47 | htp cpe, bkt sts | 2,945 | 2,502 | 21,431 |
| 48 | Ranch Cus wgn 4d | 3,310 | 2,612 | 24,962 |

# Ford

| Series 50 Custom (wb 119.0) | | Wght | Price | Prod |
|---|---|---|---|---|
| 51 | 500 sdn 2d | 3,559 | 2,464 | 20,619 |
| 52 | 500 sdn 4d | 3,659 | 2,518 | 68,828 |
| 53 | sdn 2d | 3,529 | 2,361 | 41,359 |
| 54 | sdn 4d | 3,619 | 2,415 | 57,964 |
| **Series 60 Galaxie 500 (wb 119.0)** | | | | |
| 60 | XL htp sdn | 3,722 | 3,298 | 14,661 |
| 61 | sdn 2d | 3,574 | 2,624 | 13,041 |
| 62 | sdn 4d | 3,674 | 2,678 | 198,805 |
| 64 | htp sdn | 3,689 | 2,750 | 49,242 |
| 66 | htp cpe | 3,584 | 2,685 | 206,998 |
| 65 | Sunliner conv cpe | 3,759 | 2,947 | 37,311 |
| 68 | XL htp cpe | 3,622 | 3,233 | 58,306 |
| 69 | XL conv cpe | 3,687 | 3,495 | 15,169 |
| **Series 70 Station Wagon (wb 119.0)** | | | | |
| 72 | Country Sedan 4d, 6P | 3,973 | 2,840 | 68,578 |
| 74 | Country Sedan 4d, 9P | 3,983 | 2,944 | 25,661 |
| 76 | Country Squire 4d, 6P | 3,988 | 3,029 | 23,570 |
| 78 | Country Squire 4d, 9P | 3,998 | 3,099 | 23,120 |

| 1964 Engines | bore×stroke | bhp | availability |
|---|---|---|---|
| I-6, 144.3 | 3.50×2.50 | 85 | S-Flcn exc conv, Sprnt, Del wgns |
| I-6, 170.0 | 3.50×2.94 | 101 | S-Flcn conv, Sprnt, Del wgn, Fairlane; O-other Flcn |
| I-6, 200.0 | 3.68×3.13 | 116 | O-Fairlane, Falcon |
| I-6, 223.0 | 3.62×3.60 | 138 | S-all exc Fairlane, Falcon |
| V-8, 260.0 | 3.80×2.87 | 164 | S-Flcn Sprnt; O-Other Flcn, Fair |
| V-8, 289.0 | 4.00×2.87 | 195/271 | S-60, 68, 69; O-all |
| V-8, 352.0 | 4.00×3.50 | 250 | O-all exc Falcon, Fairlane |
| V-8, 390.0 | 4.05×3.78 | 300/330 | O-all exc Falcon, Fairlane |
| V-8, 427.0 | 4.23×3.78 | 410/425 | O-all exc Falcon, Fairlane |

## 1965

| Series 0 Falcon (wb 109.5) | | Wght | Price | Prod |
|---|---|---|---|---|
| 01 | sdn 2d | 2,366 | 2,020 | 35,858 |
| 01 | Deluxe sdn 2d | 2,381 | 2,120 | 13,824 |
| 02 | sdn 4d | 2,406 | 2,082 | 30,186 |
| 02 | Deluxe sdn 4d | 2,426 | 2,182 | 13,850 |
| **Series 10 Falcon Futura (wb 109.5)** | | | | |
| 13 | Sprint htp cpe | 2,749 | 2,437 | 2,806 |
| 14 | Sprint conv cpe | 2,971 | 2,671 | 300 |
| 15 | conv cpe | 2,673 | 2,481 | 6,315 |
| 16 | sdn 4d | 2,413 | 2,192 | 33,985 |
| 17 | htp cpe | 2,491 | 2,226 | 25,754 |
| 19 | sdn 2d | 2,373 | 2,144 | 11,670 |
| **Series 20 Falcon Wagon (wb 109.5)** | | | | |
| 21 | wgn 2d | 2,611 | 2,333 | 4,891 |
| 22 | wgn 4d | 2,651 | 2,367 | 14,911 |
| 24 | Deluxe wgn 4d (Futura) | 2,667 | 2,506 | 12,548 |
| 26 | Squire wgn 4d | 2,669 | 2,665 | 6,703 |
| **Series 30 Fairlane (wb 116.0)** | | | | |
| 31 | sdn 2d | 2,902 | 2,230 | 13,685 |
| 32 | sdn 4d | 2,954 | 2,271 | 25,378 |

| Series 30 Fairlane (wb 116.0) | | Wght | Price | Prod |
|---|---|---|---|---|
| 38 | wgn 4d | 3,279 | 2,567 | 13,911 |
| **Series 40 Fairlane 500 (wb 116.0)** | | | | |
| 41 | sdn 2d | 2,901 | 2,312 | 16,092 |
| 42 | sdn 4d | 2,959 | 2,353 | 77,836 |
| 43 | htp cpe | 2,973 | 2,377 | 41,405 |
| 47 | htp cpe, bkt sts | 2,984 | 2,538 | 15,141 |
| 48 | wgn 4d | 3,316 | 2,648 | 20,506 |
| **Series 50 Custom (wb 119.0)** | | | | |
| 51 | sdn 2d | 3,306 | 2,313 | 49,034 |
| 52 | sdn 4d | 3,378 | 2,366 | 96,393 |
| 53 | 500 sdn 2d | 3,336 | 2,464 | 19,603 |
| 54 | 500 sdn 4d | 3,408 | 2,518 | 71,727 |
| **Series 60 Galaxie 500 (wb 119.0)** | | | | |
| 60 | LTD htp sdn | 3,578 | 3,313 | 68,038 |
| 62 | sdn 4d | 3,440 | 2,678 | 181,183 |
| 64 | htp sdn | 3,480 | 2,765 | 49,982 |
| 65 | conv cpe | 3,592 | 2,950 | 31,930 |
| 66 | htp cpe | 3,380 | 2,685 | 157,284 |
| 67 | LTD htp cpe | 3,486 | 3,233 | 37,691 |
| 68 | XL htp cpe | 3,497 | 3,233 | 28,141 |
| 69 | XL conv cpe | 3,665 | 3,498 | 9,849 |
| **Series 70 Station Wagon (wb 119.0)** | | | | |
| 71 | Ranch 4d, 6P | 3,869 | 2,763 | 30,817 |
| 72 | Country Sedan 4d, 6P | 3,879 | 2,855 | 59,693 |
| 74 | Country Sedan 4d, 9P | 3,893 | 2,959 | 32,344 |
| 76 | Country Squire 4d, 6P | 3,925 | 3,104 | 24,308 |
| 78 | Country Squire 4d, 9P | 3,937 | 3,174 | 30,502 |

| 1965 Engines | bore×stroke | bhp | availability |
|---|---|---|---|
| I-6, 170.0 | 3.50×2.94 | 101 | S-Flcn exc Futura, Squire until 9/25/64 |
| I-6, 200.0 | 3.68×3.13 | 120 | S-Futura/Squire, Fairlane; O-Flcn |
| I-6, 240.0 | 4.00×3.18 | 150 | S-all exc Flcn, Fairlane, LTD, XL |
| V-8, 289.0 | 4.00×2.87 | 200/271 | S-LTD, XL; O-others |
| V-8, 352.0 | 4.00×3.50 | 250 | O-all exc Falcon, Fairlane |
| V-8, 390.0 | 4.05×3.78 | 300/330 | O-all exc Falcon, Fairlane |
| V-8, 427.0 | 4.23×3.78 | 425 | O-all exc Falcon, Fairlane |

## 1966

| Series 0 Falcon (wb 110.9; wgn-113.0) | | Wght | Price | Prod |
|---|---|---|---|---|
| 01 | club cpe | 2,519 | 2,060 | 41,432 |
| 02 | sdn 4d | 2,559 | 2,114 | 34,685 |
| 06 | wgn 4d | 3,037 | 2,442 | 16,653 |
| **Series 10 Falcon Futura (wb 110.9; wgn-113.0)** | | | | |
| 11 | club cpe | 2,527 | 2,183 | 21,997 |
| 12 | sdn 4d | 2,567 | 2,237 | 34,039 |
| 13 | spt cpe | 2,597 | 2,328 | 20,289 |
| 16 | wgn 4d | 3,045 | 2,553 | 13,574 |
| **Series 30 Fairlane (wb 116; wgn-113.0)** | | | | |
| 31 | club cpe | 2,832 | 2,240 | 13,498 |
| 32 | sdn 4d | 2,877 | 2,280 | 26,170 |
| 38 | wgn 4d | 3,267 | 2,589 | 12,379 |
| **Series 40 Fairlane 500 (wb 116; wgn-113.0)** | | | | |
| 40 | XL GT htp cpe, V-8 | 3,493 | 2,843 | 33,015 |
| 41 | club cpe | 2,839 | 3,317 | 14,118 |

# Ford

| Series 40 Fairlane 500 | | Wght | Price | Prod |
|---|---|---|---|---|
| 42 | sdn 4d | 2,884 | 2,357 | 68,635 |
| 43 | htp cpe | 2,941 | 2,378 | 75,947 |
| 44 | XL GT conv cpe | 3,070 | 3,068 | 4,327 |
| 45 | conv cpe | 3,169 | 2,603 | 9,299 |
| 46 | XL conv cpe | 3,184 | 2,768 | 4,560 |
| 47 | XL htp cpe | 2,969 | 2,533 | 23,942 |
| 48 | Deluxe wgn 4d | 3,277 | 2,665 | 19,826 |
| 49 | Squire wgn 4d | 3,285 | 2,796 | 11,558 |
| **Series 50 Custom (wb 119.0)** | | | | |
| 51 | 500 sdn 2d | 3,397 | 2,481 | 28,789 |
| 52 | 500 sdn 4d | 3,466 | 2,533 | 109,449 |
| 53 | sdn 2d | 3,355 | 2,380 | 32,292 |
| 54 | sdn 4d | 3,455 | 2,432 | 72,245 |
| **Series 60 Galaxie 500 (wb 119.0)** | | | | |
| 60 | LTD htp sdn | 3,649 | 3,278 | 69,400 |
| 61 | 7-Litre htp cpe | 3,914 | 3,621 | 8,705 |
| 62 | sdn 4d | 3,478 | 2,677 | 171,886 |
| 63 | 7-Litre conv cpe, V-8 | 4,059 | 3,872 | 2,368 |
| 64 | htp sdn | 3,548 | 2,762 | 54,884 |
| 65 | conv cpe | 3,655 | 2,934 | 27,454 |
| 66 | htp cpe | 3,459 | 2,685 | 198,532 |
| 67 | LTD htp cpe | 3,601 | 3,201 | 31,696 |
| 68 | XL htp cpe | 3,616 | 3,231 | 25,715 |
| 69 | XL conv cpe | 3,761 | 3,480 | 6,360 |
| **Series 70 Station Wagon (wb 119.0)** | | | | |
| 71 | Ranch 4d | 3,941 | 2,793 | 33,306 |
| 72 | Country Sedan 4d, 6P | 3,956 | 2,882 | 55,616 |
| 74 | Country Sedan 4d, 9P | 3,997 | 2,999 | 36,633 |
| 76 | Country Squire 4d, 6P | 4,026 | 3,182 | 27,645 |
| 78 | Country Squire 4d, 9P | 4,040 | 3,265 | 41,953 |

| 1966 Engines | bore×stroke | bhp | availability |
|---|---|---|---|
| I-6, 170.0 | 3.50×2.94 | 105 | S-Falcon |
| I-6, 200.0 | 3.68×3.13 | 120 | S-Flcn Futura/wgn, Fair exc GT, GTA; O-Flcn |
| I-6, 240.0 | 4.00×3.18 | 150 | S-all exc Flcn, Fair; O-Flcn wgns |
| V-8, 289.0 | 4.00×2.87 | 200/225 | S-XL, LTD; O-Flcn, Fair exc GT, GTA; 50, 60, 70 exc 7L |
| V-8, 352.0 | 4.00×3.50 | 250 | O-all exc 7L, Fairlane, Falcon |
| V-8, 390.0 | 4.05×3.78 | 265 | O-all exc 7L, Fair GT/GTA, Flcn |
| V-8, 390.0 | 4.05×3.78 | 315 | O-all exc 7L, Fairlane, Falcon |
| V-8, 390.0 | 4.05×3.78 | 335 | S-Fair GT/GTA; O-other Fair |
| V-8, 427.0 | 4.23×3.78 | 410/425 | O-all exc 7L, 70, Fairlane, Flcn |
| V-8, 428.0 | 4.13×3.98 | 345 | S-7L; O-others exc Fairlane, Falcon |

## 1967

| Falcon (wb 110.9; wgn-113.0) | | Wght | Price | Prod |
|---|---|---|---|---|
| 10 | sdn 2d | 2,520 | 2,118 | 16,082 |
| 11 | sdn 4d | 2,551 | 2,167 | 13,554 |
| 12 | wgn 4d | 3,030 | 2,497 | 5,553 |

| Falcon Futura (wb 110.9; wgn-113.0) | | Wght | Price | Prod |
|---|---|---|---|---|
| 20 | club cpe | 2,528 | 2,280 | 6,287 |
| 21 | sdn 4d | 2,559 | 2,322 | 11,254 |
| 22 | spt cpe | 3,062 | 2,437 | 7,053 |
| 23 | Squire wgn 4d | 2,556 | 2,609 | 4,552 |
| **Fairlane (wb 116.0; wgns-113.0)** | | | | |
| 30 | sdn 2d | 2,832 | 2,297 | 10,628 |
| 31 | sdn 4d | 2,867 | 2,339 | 19,740 |
| 32 | Ranch wgn 4d | 3,283 | 2,643 | 10,881 |
| 33 | 500 club cpe | 2,840 | 2,377 | 8,473 |
| 34 | 500 sdn 4d | 2,887 | 2,417 | 51,522 |
| 35 | 500 htp cpe | 2,927 | 2,439 | 70,135 |
| 36 | 500 conv cpe | 3,244 | 2,664 | 5,428 |
| 37 | Deluxe wgn 4d | 3,291 | 2,718 | 15,902 |
| 38 | Country Squire wgn 4d | 3,302 | 2,902 | 8,348 |
| **Fairlane 500XL (wb 116.0)** | | | | |
| 40 | htp cpe | 2,955 | 2,724 | 14,871 |
| 41 | conv cpe | 3,272 | 2,950 | 1,943 |
| 42 | GT htp cpe | 3,301 | 2,839 | 18,670 |
| 43 | GT conv cpe | 3,607 | 3,064 | 2,117 |
| **Series 50 Custom (wb 119.0)** | | | | |
| 50 | sdn 2d | 3,430 | 2,441 | 18,107 |
| 51 | sdn 4d | 3,488 | 2,496 | 41,417 |
| 52 | 500 sdn 2d | 3,482 | 2,553 | 18,146 |
| 53 | 500 sdn 4d | 3,490 | 2,595 | 82,260 |
| **Galaxie 500 (wb 119.0)** | | | | |
| 54 | sdn 4d | 3,500 | 2,732 | 130,063 |
| 55 | htp cpe | 3,503 | 2,755 | 197,388 |
| 56 | htp sdn | 3,571 | 2,808 | 57,087 |
| 57 | conv cpe | 3,682 | 3,003 | 19,068 |
| 58 | XL htp sdn | 3,594 | 3,243 | 18,174 |
| 59 | XL conv cpe | 3,794 | 3,493 | 5,161 |
| **LTD (wb 119.0)** | | | | |
| 62 | htp cpe | 3,626 | 3,362 | 46,036 |
| 64 | sdn 4d | 3,795 | 3,298 | 12,491 |
| 66 | htp sdn | 3,676 | 3,363 | 51,978 |
| **Station Wagon (wb 119.0)** | | | | |
| 70 | Ranch 4d, 6P | 3,930 | 2,836 | 23,932 |
| 71 | Country Sedan 4d, 6P | 3,943 | 2,935 | 50,818 |
| 72 | Country Sedan 4d, 9P | 4,023 | 3,061 | 34,377 |
| 73 | Country Squire 4d, 6P | 3,990 | 3,234 | 25,600 |
| 74 | Country Squire 4d, 9P | 4,030 | 3,359 | 44,024 |

| 1967 Engines | bore×stroke | bhp | availability |
|---|---|---|---|
| I-6, 170.0 | 3.50×2.94 | 105 | S-Falcon exc Futura, wagons |
| I-6, 200.0 | 3.68×3.13 | 120 | S-Flcn Futura/wgns, Fair exc GTs |
| I-6, 240.0 | 4.00×3.18 | 150 | S-all exc Falcon, Fairlane |
| V-8, 289.0 | 4.00×2.87 | 200 | S-Fair GT, Gal 500XL LTD; O-others |
| V-8, 289.0 | 4.00×2.87 | 225 | O-Falcon |
| V-8, 390.0 | 4.05×3.78 | 270 | O-Fairlane |
| V-8, 390.0 | 4.05×3.78 | 315 | O-Cus, Gal, LTD, Station Wgn |
| V-8, 390.0 | 4.05×3.78 | 320 | O-Fairlane |
| V-8, 427.0 | 4.23×3.78 | 410/425 | O-all exc Falcon |
| V-8, 428.0 | 4.13×3.98 | 345 | O-all exc Falcon, Fairlane |

# Ford

## 1968

| Falcon (wb 110.9; wgn-113.0) | | Wght | Price | Prod |
|---|---|---|---|---|
| 10 | sdn 2d | 2,680 | 2,252 | 29,166 |
| 11 | sdn 4d | 2,714 | 2,301 | 36,443 |
| 12 | wgn 4d | 3,123 | 2,617 | 15,576 |
| **Falcon Futura (wb 110.9; wgn-113.0)** | | | | |
| 20 | sdn 2d | 2,685 | 2,415 | 10,633 |
| 21 | sdn 4d | 2,719 | 2,456 | 18,733 |
| 22 | spt cpe | 2,713 | 2,541 | 10,077 |
| 23 | wgn 4d | 3,123 | 2,728 | 10,761 |
| **Fairlane (wb 116.0; wgn-113.0)** | | | | |
| 30 | htp cpe | 3,028 | 2,456 | 44,683 |
| 31 | sdn 4d | 2,986 | 2,464 | 18,146 |
| 32 | wgn 4d | 3,333 | 2,770 | 14,800 |
| 33 | 500 htp cpe | 3,066 | 2,591 | 33,282 |
| 34 | 500 sdn 4d | 3,024 | 2,543 | 42,930 |
| 35 | 500 fstbk htp cpe | 3,080 | 2,566 | 32,452 |
| 36 | 500 conv cpe | 3,226 | 2,822 | 3,761 |
| 37 | 500 wgn 4d | 3,377 | 2,880 | 10,190 |
| **Torino (wb 116.0; wgn-113.0)** | | | | |
| 38 | Squire wgn 4d | 3,425 | 3,032 | 14,773 |
| 40 | htp cpe | 3,098 | 2,710 | 35,964 |
| 41 | sdn 4d | 3,062 | 2,688 | 17,962 |
| 42 | GT fstbk htp cpe | 3,208 | 2,747 | 74,135 |
| 43 | GT conv cpe | 3,352 | 3,001 | 5,310 |
| 44 | GT htp cpe | 3,194 | 2,772 | 23,939 |
| **Custom (wb 119.0)** | | | | |
| 50 | sdn 2d | 3,471 | 3,584 | 18,485 |
| 51 | sdn 4d | 3,498 | 2,642 | 45,980 |
| 52 | 500 sdn 2d | 3,460 | 2,669 | 8,983 |
| 53 | 500 sdn 4d | 3,511 | 2,741 | 49,398 |
| **Galaxie 500 (wb 119.0)** | | | | |
| 54 | sdn 4d | 3,516 | 2,864 | 117,877 |
| 55 | fstbk htp cpe | 3,534 | 2,881 | 69,760 |
| 56 | htp sdn | 3,562 | 2,936 | 55,461 |
| 57 | conv cpe | 3,679 | 3,108 | 11,832 |
| 58 | htp cpe | 3,540 | 2,916 | 84,332 |
| 60 | XL fstbk htp cpe | 3,588 | 2,985 | 50,048 |
| 61 | XL conv cpe | 3,745 | 3,214 | 6,066 |
| **LTD (wb 119.0)** | | | | |
| 62 | htp cpe | 3,679 | 3,153 | 54,163 |
| 64 | sdn 4d | 3,596 | 3,135 | 22,834 |
| 66 | htp sdn | 3,642 | 3,206 | 61,755 |
| **Station Wagon (wb 119.0)** | | | | |
| 70 | Ranch 4d, 6P | 3,925 | 3,000 | 18,237 |
| 71 | Ranch 500 4d, 6P | 3,935 | 3,063 | 18,181 |
| 72 | Ranch 500 4d, 9P | 3,981 | 3,176 | 13,421 |
| 73 | Country Sedan 4d, 6P | 3,944 | 3,184 | 39,335 |
| 74 | Country Sedan 4d, 9P | 4,001 | 3,295 | 29,374 |
| 75 | Country Squire 4d, 6P | 4,013 | 3,539 | 33,994 |
| 76 | Country Squire 4d, 9P | 4,059 | 3,619 | 57,776 |

| 1968 Engines | bore×stroke | bhp | availability |
|---|---|---|---|
| I-6, 170.0 | 3.50×2.94 | 100 | S-base Falcon cpes, sdns |
| I-6, 200.0 | 3.68×3.13 | 115 | S-Fair, Tor, Flcn Fut wgn; O-Flcn |
| I-6, 240.0 | 4.00×3.18 | 150 | S-all exc Futura, Tor GT, LTD |
| V-8, 289.0 | 4.00×2.87 | 195 | O-Falcon |
| V-8, 302.0 | 4.00×3.00 | 210 | S-LTD, Tor GT, O-all |
| V-8, 302.0 | 4.00×3.00 | 230 | O-Falcon, Fairlane, Torino |
| V-8, 390.0 | 4.05×3.78 | 265 | O-all exc Falcon |
| V-8, 390.0 | 4.05×3.78 | 315 | O-all exc Falcon, Fairlane |
| V-8, 390.0 | 4.05×3.78 | 335 | O-Fairlane |
| V-8, 427.0 | 4.23×3.78 | 390 | O-Fairlane/Torino htps |
| V-8, 428.0 | 4.13×3.98 | 340 | O-all exc Falcon, Fairlane |

## 1969

| Falcon (wb 110.9; wgn-113.0) | | Wght | Price | Prod |
|---|---|---|---|---|
| 10 | sdn 2d | 2,700 | 2,283 | 29,262 |
| 11 | sdn 4d | 2,735 | 2,333 | 22,719 |
| 12 | wgn 4d | 3,100 | 2,660 | 11,568 |
| **Falcon Futura (wb 110.9; wgn-113.0)** | | | | |
| 20 | sdn 2d | 2,715 | 2,461 | 6,482 |
| 21 | sdn 4d | 2,748 | 2,498 | 11,850 |
| 22 | spt cpe | 2,738 | 2,598 | 5,931 |
| 23 | wgn 4d | 3,120 | 2,771 | 7,203 |
| **Fairlane (wb 116.0; wgn-113.0)** | | | | |
| 30 | htp cpe | 3,079 | 2,499 | 85,630 |
| 31 | sdn 4d | 3,065 | 2,488 | 27,296 |
| 32 | wgn 4d | 3,441 | 2,841 | 10,882 |
| 33 | 500 htp cpe | 3,090 | 2,626 | 28,179 |
| 34 | 500 sdn 4d | 3,082 | 2,568 | 40,888 |
| 35 | 500 fstbk htp cpe | 3,137 | 2,601 | 29,849 |
| 36 | 500 conv cpe | 3,278 | 2,851 | 2,264 |
| 37 | 500 wgn 4d | 3,469 | 2,951 | 12,869 |
| **Torino (wb 116.0; wgn-113.0)** | | | | |
| 38 | Squire wgn 4d | 3,503 | 3,107 | 14,472 |
| 40 | htp cpe | 3,143 | 2,754 | 20,789 |
| 41 | sdn 4d | 3,128 | 2,733 | 11,971 |
| 42 | GT fstbk htp cpe | 3,220 | 2,840 | 61,319 |
| 43 | GT conv cpe | 3,356 | 3,090 | 2,552 |
| 44 | GT htp cpe | 3,173 | 2,865 | 17,951 |
| 45 | Cobra htp cpe | 3,490 | 3,164 | * |
| 46 | Cobra fstbk htp cpe | 3,537 | 3,189 | * |
| **Custom (wb 121.0)** | | | | |
| 50 | sdn 2d | 3,605 | 2,649 | 15,439 |
| 51 | sdn 4d | 3,628 | 2,691 | 45,653 |
| 52 | 500 sdn 2d | 3,590 | 2,748 | 7,585 |
| 53 | 500 sdn 4d | 3,640 | 2,790 | 45,761 |
| 70 | Ranch wgn 4d | 4,089 | 3,091 | 17,489 |
| 71 | 500 wgn 4d, 6P | 4,102 | 3,155 | 16,432 |
| 72 | 500 wgn 4d, 9P | 4,152 | 3,268 | 11,563 |
| **Galaxie 500 (wb 121.0)** | | | | |
| 54 | sdn 4d | 3,690 | 2,914 | 104,606 |
| 55 | fstbk htp cpe | 3,700 | 2,930 | 63,921 |
| 56 | htp sdn | 3,725 | 2,983 | 64,031 |
| 57 | conv cpe | 3,860 | 3,159 | 6,910 |
| 58 | htp cpe | 3,655 | 2,982 | 71,920 |
| 73 | Country Sedan wgn 4d, 6P | 4,087 | 3,274 | 36,387 |
| 74 | Country Sedan wgn 4d, 9P | 4,112 | 3,390 | 27,517 |
| **XL (wb 121.0)** | | | | |
| 60 | fstbk htp cpe | 3,805 | 3,069 | 54,557 |
| 61 | conv cpe | 3,955 | 3,297 | 7,402 |
| **LTD (wb 121.0)** | | | | |
| 62 | htp cpe | 3,745 | 3,251 | 111,565 |
| 64 | sdn 4d | 3,745 | 3,209 | 63,709 |

# Ford

| LTD (wb 121.0) | | Wght | Price | Prod |
|---|---|---|---|---|
| 66 | htp sdn | 3,840 | 3,278 | 113,168 |
| 75 | Country Squire wgn 4d, 6P | 4,202 | 3,661 | 46,445 |
| 76 | Country Squire wgn 4d, 9P | 4,227 | 3,738 | 82,790 |

| 1969 Engines | bore×stroke | bhp | availability |
|---|---|---|---|
| I-6, 170.0 | 3.50×2.94 | 100 | S-Falcon exc Futura |
| I-6, 200.0 | 3.68×3.13 | 115 | S-Futura |
| I-6, 240.0 | 4.00×3.18 | 150 | S-all exc Flcn, Fair, Tor GT, LTD |
| I-6, 250.0 | 3.68×3.91 | 155 | S-Fairlane, Tor exc GT, Cobra |
| V-8, 302.0 | 4.00×3.00 | 220 | S-LTD, Tor GT; O-others |
| V-8, 351.0 | 4.00×3.50 | 250 | O-Fairlane, Tor exc Cobra |
| V-8, 351.0 | 4.00×3.50 | 290 | O-Fairlane, Tor exc Cobra |
| V-8, 390.0 | 4.05×3.78 | 265 | O-full size |
| V-8, 390.0 | 4.05×3.78 | 320 | O-Fairlane, Tor exc Cobra |
| V-8, 428.0 | 4.13×3.98 | 335** | S-Tor Cobra; O-Fairlane |
| V-8, 429.0 | 4.36×3.59 | 320/360 | O-full size |

*Included with Torino GT models. **Available in standard and Ram Air versions.

## 1970

| Maverick (wb 103.0) | | Wght | Price | Prod |
|---|---|---|---|---|
| 91 | sdn 2d | 2,411 | 1,995 | 578,914 |

| Falcon (wb 110.9, wgn-113.0) | | | | |
|---|---|---|---|---|
| 10 | sdn 2d | 2,708 | 2,390 | 4,373 |
| 11 | sdn 4d | 2,753 | 2,438 | 5,301 |
| 12 | wgn 4d | 3,155 | 2,767 | 1,624 |

| Falcon Futura (wb 110.9; wgn-113.0) | | | | |
|---|---|---|---|---|
| 20 | sdn 2d | 2,727 | 2,542 | 1,129 |
| 21 | sdn 4d | 2,764 | 2,579 | 2,262 |
| 23 | wgn 4d | 3,191 | 2,878 | 1,005 |

| "1970½" Falcon (wb 117.0; wgn-114.0)* | | | | |
|---|---|---|---|---|
| 26 | sdn 2d | 3,100 | 2,460 | 26,071 |
| 27 | sdn 4d | 3,116 | 2,500 | 30,443 |
| 40 | wgn 4d | 3,483 | 2,801 | 10,539 |

| Fairlane 500 (wb 117.0; wgn-114.0) | | | | |
|---|---|---|---|---|
| 28 | sdn 4d | 3,166 | 2,627 | 25,780 |
| 29 | htp cpe | 3,178 | 2,660 | 70,636 |
| 41 | wgn 4d | 3,558 | 2,957 | 13,613 |

| Torino (wb 117.0; wgn-114.0) | | | | |
|---|---|---|---|---|
| 30 | htp cpe | 3,223 | 2,722 | 49,826 |
| 31 | sdn 4d | 3,208 | 2,689 | 30,117 |
| 32 | htp sdn | 3,239 | 2,795 | 14,312 |
| 33 | Brougham htp cpe | 3,293 | 3,006 | 16,911 |
| 34 | fstbk htp cpe | 3,261 | 2,899 | 12,490 |
| 35 | GT htp cpe | 3,366 | 3,105 | 56,819 |
| 36 | Brougham htp sdn | 3,309 | 3,078 | 14,543 |
| 37 | GT conv cpe | 3,490 | 3,212 | 3,939 |
| 38 | Cobra fstbk htp cpe | 3,774 | 3,270 | 7,675 |
| 42 | wgn 4d | 3,603 | 3,164 | 10,613 |
| 43 | Squire wgn 4d | 3,673 | 3,379 | 13,166 |

| Custom (wb 121.0) | | | | |
|---|---|---|---|---|
| 51 | sdn 4d | 3,545 | 2,850 | 42,849 |
| 52 | 500 htp cpe | 3,510 | 2,918 | 2,677 |
| 53 | 500 sdn 4d | 3,585 | 2,872 | 41,261 |

| Custom (wb 121.0) | | Wght | Price | Prod |
|---|---|---|---|---|
| 70 | Ranch wgn 4d | 4,079 | 3,305 | 15,086 |
| 71 | 500 wgn 4d, 6P | 4,049 | 3,368 | 15,304 |
| 72 | 500 wgn 4d, 9P | 4,137 | 3,481 | 9,943 |

| Galaxie 500 (wb 121.0) | | | | |
|---|---|---|---|---|
| 54 | sdn 4d | 3,601 | 3,026 | 101,784 |
| 55 | fstbk htp cpe | 3,610 | 3,043 | 50,825 |
| 56 | htp sdn | 3,672 | 3,096 | 53,817 |
| 58 | htp cpe | 3,611 | 3,094 | 57,059 |
| 73 | Country Sedan wgn 4d, 6P | 4,089 | 3,488 | 32,209 |
| 74 | Country Sedan wgn 4d, 9P | 4,112 | 3,600 | 22,645 |

| XL (wb 121.0) | | | | |
|---|---|---|---|---|
| 60 | fstbk htp cpe | 3,750 | 3,293 | 27,251 |
| 61 | conv cpe | 3,983 | 3,501 | 6,348 |

| LTD (wb 121.0) | | | | |
|---|---|---|---|---|
| 62 | htp cpe | 3,727 | 3,356 | ⎤ 96,324 |
| 62 | Brougham htp cpe | 3,855 | 3,537 | ⎦ |
| 64 | sdn 4d | 3,701 | 3,307 | ⎤ 78,306 |
| 64 | Brougham sdn | 3,829 | 3,502 | ⎦ |
| 66 | htp sdn | 3,771 | 3,385 | ⎤ 90,390 |
| 66 | Brougham htp sdn | 4,029 | 3,579 | ⎦ |
| 75 | Country Squire wgn 4d, 6P | 4,139 | 3,832 | 39,837 |
| 76 | Country Squire wgn 4d, 9P | 4,185 | 3,909 | 69,077 |

| 1970 Engines | bore×stroke | bhp | availability |
|---|---|---|---|
| I-6, 170.0 | 3.50×2.94 | 105 | S-Maverick |
| I-6, 200.0 | 3.68×3.13 | 120 | S-Falcon; O-Maverick |
| I-6, 240.0 | 4.00×3.18 | 150 | S-full size exc XL, LTD |
| I-6, 250.0 | 3.68×3.91 | 155 | S-Tor exc GT, Brghm, Squire, Cobra |
| V-8, 302.0 | 4.00×3.00 | 220 | S-Tor GT/Brghm/Squire Cobra; O-others |
| V-8, 351.0 | 4.00×3.50 | 250 | S-XL, LTD, full-size wgns; O-all exc Flcn, Cobra |
| V-8, 351.0 | 4.00×3.50 | 300 | O-Torino exc Cobra |
| V-8, 390.0 | 4.05×3.78 | 265 | O-all full size |
| V-8, 429.0 | 4.36×3.59 | 320 | O-all full size |
| V-8, 429.0 | 4.36×3.59 | 360 | S-Tor Cobra; O-full-size, Torino |
| V-8, 429.0 | 4.36×3.59 | 370** | O-Torino exc wgns |
| V-8, 429.0 | 4.36×3.59 | 375 | O-Torino, Cobra |

*Replaced Fairlane 500. **Available in standard and Ram Air versions.

| 1970½ Engines | bore×stroke | bhp | availability |
|---|---|---|---|
| I-6, 250.0 | 3.68×3.91 | 155 | S-Falcon |
| V-8, 302.0 | 4.00×3.00 | 220 | O-Falcon |
| V-8, 351.0 | 4.00×3.50 | 250/300 | O-Falcon |
| V-8, 429.0 | 4.36×3.59 | 360 | O-Falcon |
| V-8, 429.0 | 4.36×3.59 | 370 | O-Falcon (w/o Ram Air) |

## 1971

| Pinto (wb 94.2) | | Wght | Price | Prod |
|---|---|---|---|---|
| 10 | fstbk sdn 2d | 1,949 | 1,919 | 288,606 |
| 11 | Runabout htchbk sdn 2d | 1,993 | 2,062 | 63,796 |

| Maverick (wb 103.0; 4d-109.9) | | | | |
|---|---|---|---|---|
| 91 | fstbk sdn 2d | 2,546 | 2,175 | 159,726 |
| 92 | sdn 4d | 2,641 | 2,234 | 73,208 |

# Ford

| Maverick (wb 103.0; 4d-109.9) | | Wght | Price | Prod |
|---|---|---|---|---|
| 93 | Grabber fstbk sdn 2d | 2,601 | 2,354 | 38,963 |
| **Torino (wb 117.0; wgns-114.0)** | | | | |
| 25 | formal htp cpe | 3,168 | 2,706 | 37,518 |
| 27 | sdn 4d | 3,163 | 2,672 | 29,501 |
| 40 | wgn 4d | 3,514 | 3,023 | 21,570 |
| 30 | 500 formal htp cpe | 3,170 | 2,887 | 89,966 |
| 31 | 500 sdn 4d | 3,160 | 2,855 | 35,650 |
| 32 | 500 htp sdn | 3,196 | 2,959 | 12,724 |
| 34 | 500 fstbk htp cpe | 3,179 | 2,943 | 11,150 |
| 42 | 500 wgn 4d | 3,514 | 3,170 | 23,270 |
| 33 | Brghm formal htp cpe V-8 | 3,209 | 3,175 | 8,593 |
| 36 | Brghm formal htp sdn V-8 | 3,256 | 3,248 | 4,408 |
| 43 | Squire wgn 4d V-8 | 3,583 | 3,560 | 15,805 |
| 35 | GT fstbk htp cpe V-8 | 3,287 | 3,150 | 31,641 |
| 37 | GT conv V-8 | 3,428 | 3,408 | 1,613 |
| 38 | Cobra fstbk htp cpe | 3,525 | 3,295 | 3,054 |
| **Ford (wb 121.0)** | | | | |
| 51 | Custom sdn 4d | 3,700 | 3,288 | 41,062 |
| 70 | Custom Ranch Wgn 4d V-8 | 4,222 | 3,890 | 16,696 |
| 53 | Custom 500 sdn 4d | 3,705 | 3,426 | 33,765 |
| 72 | C500 Rnch Wgn 4d 2S V-8 | 4,231 | 3,982 | 25,957 |
| 72 | C500 Rnch Wgn 4d 3S V-8 | 4,281 | 4,097 | |
| 54 | Galaxie 500 sdn 4d | 3,782 | 3,594 | 98,130 |
| 56 | Galaxie 500 htp sdn | 3,838 | 3,665 | 46,595 |
| 58 | Galaxie 500 htp cpe | 3,783 | 3,628 | 117,139 |
| 74 | G500 Ctry Sdn wgn 4d 2S V-8 | 4,246 | 4,074 | 60,487 |
| 74 | G500 Ctry Sdn wgn 4d 3S V-8 | 4,296 | 4,188 | |
| 61 | LTD conv V-8 | 4,053 | 4,094 | 5,750 |
| 62 | LTD htp cpe V-8 | 3,919 | 3,923 | 103,896 |
| 63 | LTD sdn 4d V-8 | 3,981 | 3,931 | 92,260 |
| 64 | LTD htp sdn V-8 | 3,976 | 3,969 | 48,166 |
| 76 | Cntry Squire wgn 4d 2S V-8 | 4,306 | 4,380 | 130,644 |
| 76 | Cntry Squire wgn 4d 3S V-8 | 4,356 | 4,496 | |
| 66 | LTD Brougham sdn 4d V-8 | 4,111 | 4,094 | 26,186 |
| 67 | LTD Brougham htp sdn V-8 | 4,016 | 4,140 | 27,820 |
| 68 | LTD Brougham htp cpe V-8 | 3,945 | 4,097 | 43,303 |

| 1971 Engines | bore×stroke | bhp | availability |
|---|---|---|---|
| I-4, 98.6 | 3.19×3.06 | 75 | S-Pinto |
| I-4, 122.0 | 3.58×3.03 | 100 | O-Pinto |
| I-6, 170.0 | 3.50×2.94 | 100 | S-Maverick |
| I-6, 200.0 | 3.68×3.13 | 115 | O-Maverick |
| I-6, 240.0 | 4.00×3.18 | 140 | S-Ford Customs |
| I-6, 250.0 | 3.68×3.91 | 145 | S-Tor exc GT Cobra; O-Mav |
| V-8, 302.0 | 4.00×3.00 | 210 | S-Mav, Ford Cus, Tor exc Cobra |
| V-8, 351.0 | 4.00×3.50 | 240 | S-Ford exc Cus |
| V-8, 351.0 | 4.00×3.50 | 285 | S-Tor Cobra; O-Torino |
| V-8, 400.0 | 4.00×4.00 | 260 | O-Ford |
| V-8, 429.0 | 4.36×3.59 | 320/360 | O-Ford |
| V-8, 429.0 | 4.36×3.59 | 370 | O-Torino |

## 1972

| Pinto (wb 94.2) | | Wght | Price | Prod |
|---|---|---|---|---|
| 10 | fstbk sdn 2d | 2,061 | 1,960 | 181,002 |
| 11 | Runabout htchbk sdn 2d | 2,099 | 2,078 | 197,290 |
| 12 | wgn 2d | 2,283 | 2,265 | 101,483 |
| **Maverick (wb 103.0; 4d-109.9)** | | | | |
| 91 | fstbk sdn 2d | 2,654 | 2,140 | 145,931 |
| 92 | sdn 4d | 2,751 | 2,195 | 73,686 |
| 93 | Grabber fstbk sdn 2d | 2,708 | 2,309 | 35,347 |
| **Torino (wb 118.0; 2d-114.0)** | | | | |
| 25 | formal htp cpe | 3,374 | 2,673 | 33,530 |
| 27 | sdn 4d | 3,442 | 2,641 | 33,486 |
| 40 | wgn 4d | 3,840 | 2,955 | 22,204 |
| 30 | Gran Torino formal htp cpe | 3,410 | 2,878 | 132,284 |
| 31 | Gran Torino sdn 4d | 3,484 | 2,856 | 102,300 |
| 42 | Gran Torino wgn 4d | 3,874 | 3,096 | 45,212 |
| 35 | GT Sport fstbk htp cpe V-8 | 3,470 | 3,094 | 60,794 |
| 38 | Grn Torino frml htp cpe V-8 | 3,466 | 3,094 | 31,239 |
| 43 | Squire wgn 4d V-8 | 3,938 | 3,486 | 35,595 |
| **Ford (wb 121.0)** | | | | |
| 51 | Custom sdn 4d | 3,742 | 3,246 | 33,014 |
| 70 | Custom Ranch wgn 5d V-8 | 4,304 | 3,852 | 13,064 |
| 53 | Custom 500 sdn 4d | 3,808 | 3,377 | 24,870 |
| 72 | C500 Ranch wgn 4d 2S V-8 | 4,314 | 3,941 | 16,834 |
| 72 | C500 Ranch wgn 4d 3S V-8 | 4,364 | 4,051 | |
| 54 | Galaxie 500 sdn 4d | 3,848 | 3,537 | 104,167 |
| 56 | Galaxie 500 htp sdn | 3,910 | 3,604 | 28,939 |
| 58 | Galaxie 500 htp cpe | 3,852 | 3,572 | 80,855 |
| 74 | G500 Ctry wgn 4d 2S V-8 | 4,349 | 4,028 | 55,238 |
| 74 | G500 Ctry wgn 4d 3S V-8 | 4,399 | 4,136 | |
| 62 | LTD htp cpe V-8 | 3,999 | 3,882 | 101,048 |
| 63 | LTD sdn 4d V-8 | 4,065 | 3,890 | 104,167 |
| 64 | LTD htp sdn V-8 | 4,060 | 3,925 | 33,742 |
| 61 | LTD conv V-8 | 4,165 | 4,057 | 4,234 |
| 76 | LTD Ctry wgn 4d 2S V-8 | 4,393 | 4,318 | 121,419 |
| 76 | LTD Ctry wgn 4d 3S V-8 | 4,443 | 4,430 | |
| 66 | LTD Brougham sdn 4d V-8 | 4,095 | 4,031 | 36,909 |
| 67 | LTD Brougham htp sdn V-8 | 4,090 | 4,074 | 23,364 |
| 68 | LTD Brhm frml htp cpe V-8 | 4,031 | 4,034 | 50,409 |

| 1972 Engines | bore×stroke | bhp | availability |
|---|---|---|---|
| I-4, 98.6 | 3.19×3.06 | 54 | S-Pinto exc wgn |
| I-4, 122.0 | 3.58×3.03 | 86 | S-Pinto wgn; O-Pinto |
| I-6, 170.0 | 3.50×2.94 | 82 | S-Maverick |
| I-6, 200.0 | 3.68×3.13 | 91 | O-Maverick |
| I-6, 240.0 | 4.00×3.18 | 103 | S-Ford exc wgn |
| I-6, 250.0 | 3.68×3.91 | 95 | S-Torino exc GT |
| I-6, 250.0 | 3.68×3.91 | 98 | O-Maverick |
| V-8, 302.0 | 4.00×3.00 | 140 | O-Torino, Ford Cus V-8 |
| V-8, 302.0 | 4.00×3.00 | 143 | O-Maverick |
| V-8, 351.0 | 4.00×3.50 | 153 | S-Ford wgn; O-Ford |
| V-8, 351.0 | 4.00×3.50 | 161 | O-Torino |
| V-8, 351.0 | 4.00×3.50 | 248 | O-Torino |
| V-8, 400.0 | 4.00×4.00 | 168 | O-Torino |
| V-8, 400.0 | 4.00×4.00 | 172 | O-Ford |
| V-8, 429.0 | 4.36×3.59 | 205 | O-Torino |
| V-8, 429.0 | 4.36×3.59 | 208 | O-Ford |

## 1973

| Pinto (wb 94.2) | | Wght | Price | Prod |
|---|---|---|---|---|
| 10 | fstbk sdn 2d | 2,115 | 2,021 | 116,146 |
| 11 | Runabout htchbk sdn 2d | 2,145 | 2,144 | 150,603 |
| 12 | wgn 2d | 2,386 | 2,343 | 217,763 |
| **Maverick (wb 103.0; 4d-109.9)** | | | | |
| 91 | fstbk sdn 2d | 2,730 | 2,248 | 148,943 |
| 92 | sdn 4d | 2,844 | 2,305 | 110,382 |
| 93 | Grabber fstbk sdn 2d | 2,770 | 2,427 | 32,350 |

# Ford

| Torino (wb 118.0; 2d-114.0) | | Wght | Price | Prod |
|---|---|---|---|---|
| 25 | htp cpe | 3,548 | 2,732 | 28,005 |
| 27 | sdn 4d | 3,620 | 2,701 | 37,524 |
| 40 | wgn 4d V-8 | 4,063 | 3,198 | 23,982 |
| 30 | Gran Torino htp cpe | 3,591 | 2,921 | ⎤ 138,962 |
| 30 | Gran Torino Brham htp cpe | 3,598 | 3,071 | ⎦ |
| 31 | Gran Torino sdn 4d | 3,675 | 2,890 | ⎤ 98,404 |
| 31 | Gran Torino Brham sdn 4d | 3,690 | 3,051 | ⎦ |
| 42 | Gran Torino wgn 4d V-8 | 4,097 | 3,344 | 60,738 |
| 43 | Grn Tor Squire wgn 4d V-8 | 4,129 | 3,559 | 40,023 |
| 35 | Gm Tor Spt fstbk htp cpe V-8 | 3,664 | 3,154 | 51,853 |
| 38 | Grn Tor formal htp cpe V-8 | 3,650 | 3,154 | 17,090 |

| Ford (wb 121.0) | | | | |
|---|---|---|---|---|
| 53 | Custom 500 sdn 4d | 4,059 | 3,606 | 42,549 |
| 72 | C500 Ranch Wagon 4d 2S | 4,529 | 4,050 | ⎤ 22,432 |
| 72 | C500 Ranch Wagon 4d 3S | 4,579 | 4,164 | ⎦ |
| 54 | Galaxie 500 sdn 4d | 4,086 | 3,771 | 85,654 |
| 56 | Galaxie 500 htp sdn | 4,102 | 3,833 | 25,802 |
| 58 | Galaxie 500 htp cpe | 4,034 | 3,778 | 70,808 |
| 74 | G500 Cntry Sdn Wgn 4d 2S | 4,555 | 4,146 | ⎤ 51,290 |
| 74 | G500 Cntry Sdn Wgn 4d 3S | 4,605 | 4,260 | ⎦ |
| 62 | LTD htp cpe | 4,059 | 3,950 | 120,864 |
| 63 | LTD sdn 4d | 4,107 | 3,958 | 122,851 |
| 64 | LTD htp sdn | 4,123 | 4,001 | 28,606 |
| 76 | LTD Cntry Squire wgn 4d 2S | 4,579 | 4,401 | ⎤ 142,983 |
| 76 | LTD Cntry Squire wgn 4d 3S | 4,629 | 4,515 | ⎦ |
| 66 | LTD Brougham sdn 4d | 4,130 | 4,113 | 49,553 |
| 67 | LTD Brougham htp sdn | 4,148 | 4,157 | 22,268 |
| 68 | LTD Brougham htp cpe | 4,077 | 4,107 | 68,901 |

| 1973 Engines | bore×stroke | bhp | availability |
|---|---|---|---|
| I-4, 98.6 | 3.19×3.06 | 54 | S-Pinto exc wgn |
| I-4, 122.0 | 3.58×3.03 | 83 | S-Pinto wgn; O-Pinto |
| I-6, 200.0 | 3.68×3.13 | 84 | S-Maverick |
| I-6, 250.0 | 3.68×3.91 | 88 | O-Maverick |
| I-6, 250.0 | 3.68×3.91 | 92 | O-Torino |
| V-8, 302.0 | 4.00×3.00 | 137/138 | S-Torino 35 & wgns; O-other Torino |
| V-8, 351.0 | 4.00×3.50 | 158/159 | S-Ford; O-Torino |
| V-8, 351.0 | 4.00×3.50 | 246 | O-Torino cpe |
| V-8, 400.0 | 4.00×4.00 | 168 | O-Torino, Ford |
| V-8, 429.0 | 4.36×3.59 | 201 | O-Torino, Ford |
| V-8, 460.0 | 4.36×3.85 | 202 | O-Ford |

## 1974

| Pinto (wb 94.2) | | Wght | Price | Prod |
|---|---|---|---|---|
| 10 | fstbk sdn 2d | 2,372 | 2,527 | 132,061 |
| 11 | Runabout htchbk sdn 2d | 2,406 | 2,676 | 174,754 |
| 12 | wgn 2d | 2,576 | 2,771 | 237,394 |

| Maverick (wb 103.0; 4d-109.9) | | | | |
|---|---|---|---|---|
| 91 | fstbk sdn 2d | 2,739 | 2,790 | 139,818 |
| 92 | sdn 4d | 2,932 | 2,824 | 137,728 |
| 93 | Grabber fstbk sdn 2d | 2,868 | 2,923 | 23,502 |

| Torino (wb 118.0; 2d-114.0) | | | | |
|---|---|---|---|---|
| 25 | htp cpe | 3,709 | 3,236 | 22,738 |
| 27 | sdn 4d | 3,793 | 3,239 | 31,161 |
| 40 | wgn 4d | 4,175 | 3,818 | 15,393 |
| 30 | Gran Torino htp cpe | 3,742 | 3,411 | 76,290 |
| 31 | Gran Torino sdn 4d | 3,847 | 3,454 | 72,728 |
| 42 | Gran Torino wgn 4d | 4,209 | 4,017 | 29,866 |
| 32 | Gran Torino Brham htp cpe | 3,794 | 3,975 | 26,402 |
| 33 | Gran Torino Brham sdn 4d | 3,887 | 3,966 | 11,464 |
| 43 | Gran Torino Squire wgn 4d | 4,250 | 4,300 | 22,837 |
| 38 | Gran Torino Sport htp cpe | 3,771 | 3,824 | 23,142 |
| 21 | Gran Torino Elite htp cpe | — | 4,437 | 96,604 |

| Ford (wb 121.0) | | | | |
|---|---|---|---|---|
| 53 | Custom 500 sdn 4d | 4,180 | 3,982 | 28,941 |
| 72 | C500 Ranch Wagon 4d 2S | 4,654 | 4,488 | ⎤ 12,104 |
| 72 | C500 Ranch Wagon 4d 3S | 4,687 | 4,608 | ⎦ |
| 54 | Galaxie 500 sdn 4d | 4,196 | 4,164 | 49,661 |
| 56 | Galaxie 500 htp sdn | 4,212 | 4,237 | 11,526 |
| 58 | Galaxie 500 htp cpe 4d | 4,157 | 4,211 | 34,214 |
| 74 | G500 Cntry Sdn wgn 4d 2S | 4,690 | 4,584 | ⎤ 22,400 |
| 74 | G500 Cntry Sdn wgn 4d 3S | 4,722 | 4,704 | ⎦ |
| 62 | LTD htp cpe | 4,215 | 4,389 | 73,296 |
| 63 | LTD sdn 4d | 4,262 | 4,370 | 72,251 |
| 64 | LTD htp sdn | 4,277 | 4,438 | 12,375 |
| 76 | LTD Cntry Squire wgn 4d 2S | 4,752 | 4,898* | ⎤ 64,047 |
| 76 | LTD Cntry Squire wgn 4d 3S | 4,785 | 5,018* | ⎦ |
| 66 | LTD Brougham sdn 4d | 4,292 | 4,647 | 30,203 |
| 67 | LTD Brougham htp sdn | 4,310 | 4,717 | 11,371 |
| 68 | LTD Brougham htp cpe | 4,247 | 4,669 | 39,084 |

*Prices with optional woodgrain bodyside trim. Nonwoodgrain version $136 less.

| 1974 Engines | bore×stroke | bhp | availability |
|---|---|---|---|
| I-4, 122.0 | 3.58×3.03 | 80 | S-Pinto |
| I-4, 140.0 | 3.78×3.13 | 82 | O-Pinto |
| I-6, 200.0 | 3.68×3.13 | 84 | S-Maverick |
| I-6, 250.0 | 3.68×3.91 | 91 | S-Torino, O-Maverick |
| V-8, 302.0 | 4.00×3.00 | 140 | O-Maverick, Torino |
| V-8, 351.0 | 4.00×3.50 | 162 | S-Ford exc 76; O-Torino |
| V-8, 400.0 | 4.00×4.00 | 170 | S-Ford 76; O-Torino Other Ford |
| V-8, 460.0 | 4.36×3.85 | 220 | O-Torino, Ford |

## 1975

| Pinto (wb 94.4; wgns-94.7) | | Wght | Price | Prod |
|---|---|---|---|---|
| 10 | fstbk sdn 2d | 2,495 | 2,769 | 64,081 |
| 11 | Runabout htchbk sdn 3d | 2,528 | 2,984 | 68,919 |
| 12 | wgn 2d | 2,692 | 3,153 | 90,763 |

| Maverick (wb 103.0; 4d-109.9) | | | | |
|---|---|---|---|---|
| 91 | fstbk sdn 2d | 2,896 | 3,025 | 90,695 |
| 92 | sdn 4d | 3,018 | 3,061 | 63,404 |
| 93 | Grabber fstbk sdn 2d | 2,903 | 3,282 | 8,473 |

| Granada (wb 109.9) | | | | |
|---|---|---|---|---|
| 81 | sdn 4d | 3,279 | 3,756 | 118,168 |
| 82 | sdn 2d | 3,230 | 3,698 | 100,810 |
| 83 | Ghia sdn 4d | 3,392 | 4,283 | 43,652 |
| 84 | Ghia sdn 2d | 3,342 | 4,225 | 40,028 |

| Torino (wb 118.0; 2d-114.0) | | | | |
|---|---|---|---|---|
| 25 | htp cpe | 3,981 | 3,954 | 13,394 |
| 27 | sdn 4d | 4,053 | 3,957 | 22,928 |
| 40 | wgn 4d | 4,406 | 4,336 | 13,291 |
| 30 | Gran Torino htp cpe | 3,992 | 4,314 | 35,324 |
| 31 | Gran Torino sdn 4d | 4,084 | 4,338 | 53,161 |
| 42 | Gran Torino wgn 4d | 4,450 | 4,673 | ⎤ 23,951 |
| 43 | Gran Torino Squire wgn 4d | 4,490 | 4,952 | ⎦ |
| 32 | Gran Torino Brham htp cpe | 4,081 | 4,805 | 4,849 |
| 33 | Gran Torino Brham sdn 4d | 4,157 | 4,837 | 5,929 |
| 38 | Gran Torino Sport htp cpe | 4,038 | 4,790 | 5,126 |

# Ford

| Torino (wb 118.0; 2d-114.0) | | Wght | Price | Prod |
|---|---|---|---|---|
| 21 | Elite htp cpe | 4,154 | 4,767 | 123,372 |
| **Ford (wb 121.0)** | | | | |
| 53 | Custom 500 sdn 4d | 4,377 | 4,477 | 31,043 |
| 72 | Cstm 500 Ranch Wagon 4d | 4,787 | 5,067 | 6,930 |
| 62 | LTD htp cpe | 4,359 | 4,753 | 47,432 |
| 63 | LTD sdn 4d | 4,408 | 4,712 | 82,382 |
| 74 | LTD wgn 4d 2S | 4,803 | 5,158 ⎤ | 22,936 |
| 74 | LTD wgn 4d 3S | 4,836 | 5,283 ⎦ | |
| 66 | LTD Brougham sdn 4d | 4,419 | 5,099 | 32,327 |
| 68 | LTD Brougham sdn 2d | 4,391 | 5,133 | 24,005 |
| 76 | LTD Cntry Squire wgn 4d 2S | 4,845 | 5,440 ⎤ | 41,550 |
| 76 | LTD Cntry Squire wgn 4d 3S | 4,878 | 5,565 ⎦ | |
| 64 | LTD Landau sdn 4d | 4,446 | 5,453 | 32,506 |
| 65 | LTD Landau sdn 2d | 4,419 | 5,484 | 26,919 |

| 1975 Engines | bore×stroke | bhp | availability |
|---|---|---|---|
| I-4, 140.0 | 3.78×3.13 | 83 | S-Pinto |
| V6, 170.0 | 3.66×2.70 | 97 | O-Pinto 11, 12 |
| I-6, 200.0 | 3.68×3.13 | 75 | S-Mav, Granada exc Ghia |
| I-6, 250.0 | 3.68×3.91 | 72 | S-Granada Ghia; O-Mav, Grnda |
| V-8, 302.0 | 4.00×3.00 | 122 | S-Maverick, Granada |
| V-8, 351.0 | 4.00×3.50 | 143 | O-Granada |
| V-8, 351.0 | 4.00×3.50 | 148/150 | S-Torino |
| V-8, 400.0 | 4.00×4.00 | 144/158 | S-Ford 74, 76; O-Torino, other Ford |
| V-8, 460.0 | 4.36×3.85 | 216 | O-Torino, Ford |

## 1976

| Pinto (wb 94.4; wgns-94.7) | | Wght | Price | Prod |
|---|---|---|---|---|
| 10 | Pony MPG fstbk sdn 2d I-4 | 2,450 | 2,895 ⎤ | |
| 10 | MPG fstbk sdn 2d I-4 | 2,452 | 3,025 | 92,264 |
| 10 | sdn 2d V6 | 2,590 | 3,472 ⎦ | |
| 11 | MPG htchbk sdn 2d I-4 | 2,482 | 3,200 ⎤ | |
| 11 | Squire MPG htchbk sdn 2d I-4 | 2,518 | 3,505 | 92,540 |
| 11 | Runabout htchbk sdn 2d V6 | 2,620 | 3,647 | |
| 11 | Squire htchbk sdn 2d V6 | 2,656 | 3,952 ⎦ | |
| 12 | MPG wgn 2d I-4 | 2,635 | 3,365 ⎤ | |
| 12 | Squire MPG wgn 2d I-4 | 2,672 | 3,671 | 105,328 |
| 12 | wgn 2d V6 | 2,773 | 3,865 | |
| 12 | Squire wgn 2d V6 | 2,810 | 4,171 ⎦ | |
| **Maverick (wb 109.9; 2d-103.0)** | | | | |
| 91 | fstbk sdn 2d | 2,846 | 3,117 | 60,611 |
| 92 | sdn 4d | 2,956 | 3,189 | 79,076 |
| **Granada (wb 109.9)** | | | | |
| 81 | sdn 4d | 3,222 | 3,798 | 187,923 |
| 82 | sdn 2d | 3,172 | 3,707 | 161,618 |
| 83 | Ghia sdn 4d | 3,392 | 4,355 | 52,457 |
| 84 | Ghia sdn 2d | 3,334 | 4,265 | 46,786 |
| **Torino (wb 118.0; 2d-114.0)** | | | | |
| 25 | htp cpe | 3,976 | 4,172 | 34,518 |
| 27 | sdn 4d | 4,061 | 4,206 | 17,394 |
| 30 | Gran Torino htp cpe | 3,999 | 4,461 | 23,939 |
| 31 | Gran Torino sdn 4d | 4,081 | 4,495 | 40,568 |
| 32 | Gran Torino Brham htp cpe | 4,063 | 4,883 | 3,183 |
| 33 | Gran Torino Brham sdn 4d | 4,144 | 4,915 | 4,473 |
| 40 | wgn 4d | 4,409 | 4,521 | 17,281 |
| 42 | Gran Torino wgn 4d | 4,428 | 4,769 | 30,596 |
| 43 | Gran Torino Squire wgn 4d | 4,454 | 5,083 | 21,144 |

| Elite (wb 114.0) | | Wght | Price | Prod |
|---|---|---|---|---|
| 21 | htp cpe | 4,169 | 4,879 | 146,475 |
| **Ford (wb 121.0)** | | | | |
| 52 | Custom 500 sdn 2d | — | — | 7,037 |
| 53 | Custom 500 sdn 4d | 4,298 | 4,493 | 23,447 |
| 72 | Cst 500 Ranch Wgn 4d | 4,737 | 4,918 | 4,633 |
| 62 | LTD sdn 2d | 4,257 | 4,780 | 62,844 |
| 63 | LTD sdn 4d | 4,303 | 4,752 | 108,168 |
| 74 | LTD wgn 4d 2S | 4,752 | 5,207 ⎤ | 30,237 |
| 74 | LTD wgn 4d 3S | 4,780 | 5,333 ⎦ | |
| 66 | LTD Brougham sdn 4d | 4,332 | 5,245 | 32,917 |
| 68 | LTD Brougham sdn 2d | 4,299 | 5,299 | 20,863 |
| 76 | LTD Cntry Squire wgn 4d 2S | 4,809 | 5,523 ⎤ | 47,379 |
| 76 | LTD Cntry Squire wgn 4d 3S | 4,837 | 5,649 ⎦ | |
| 64 | LTD Landau sdn 4d | 4,394 | 5,560 | 35,663 |
| 65 | LTD Landau sdn 2d | 4,346 | 5,613 | 29,673 |

| 1976 Engines | bore×stroke | bhp | availability |
|---|---|---|---|
| I-4, 140.0 | 3.78×3.13 | 92 | S-Pinto |
| V6, 170.8 | 3.66×2.70 | 103 | O-Pinto |
| I-6, 200.0 | 3.68×3.13 | 81 | S-Mav, Granada exc Ghia |
| I-6, 250.0 | 3.68×3.91 | 90 | S-Granada Ghia; O-Mav, Gran |
| V-8, 302.0 | 4.00×3.00 | 134/138 | O-Granada, Maverick |
| V-8, 351.0 | 4.00×3.50 | 152/154 | S-Tor, Elite, Ford exc wgns; O-Granada |
| V-8, 400.0 | 4.00×4.00 | 180 | S-Ford wgns; O-Torino, Ford, Elite |
| V-8, 460.0 | 4.36×3.85 | 202 | O-Torino, Ford, Elite |

## 1977

| Pinto (wb 94.4; wgns-94.7) | | Wght | Price | Prod |
|---|---|---|---|---|
| 10 | Pony sdn 2d I-4 | 2,313 | 3,099 ⎤ | 48,863* |
| 10 | sdn 2d | 2,376 | 3,237 ⎦ | |
| 11 | Runabout htchbk sdn 3d | 2,412 | 3,353 | 74,237* |
| 12 | wgn 2d | 2,576 | 3,548 ⎤ | 79,499* |
| 12 | Squire wgn 2d | 2,614 | 3,891 ⎦ | |
| **Maverick (wb 109.9; 2d-103.0)** | | | | |
| 91 | fstbk sdn 2d | 2,864 | 3,322 | 40,086 |
| 92 | sdn 4d | 2,970 | 3,395 | 58,420 |
| **Granada (wb 109.9)** | | | | |
| 81 | sdn 4d | 3,222 | 4,118 | 163,071 |
| 82 | sdn 2d | 3,172 | 4,022 | 157,612 |
| 83 | Ghia sdn 4d | 3,276 | 4,548 | 35,730 |
| 84 | Ghia sdn 2d | 3,222 | 4,452 | 34,166 |
| **LTD II (wb 118.0; 2d-114.0)** | | | | |
| 25 | S htp cpe | 3,789 | 4,528 | 9,531 |
| 27 | S sdn 4d | 3,894 | 4,579 | 18,775 |
| 30 | htp cpe | 3,789 | 4,785 | 57,449 |
| 31 | sdn 4d | 3,904 | 4,870 | 57,704 |
| 32 | Brougham htp cpe | 3,898 | 5,121 | 20,979 |
| 33 | Brougham sdn 4d | 3,930 | 5,206 | 18,851 |
| 40 | S wgn 4d 2S | 4,393 | 4,806 ⎤ | 9,636 |
| 40 | S wgn 4d 3S | 4,410 | 4,906 ⎦ | |
| 42 | wgn 4d 2S | 4,404 | 5,064 ⎤ | 23,237 |
| 42 | wgn 4d 3S | 4,421 | 5,164 ⎦ | |
| 43 | Squire wgn 4d 2S | 4,430 | 5,335 ⎤ | 17,162 |
| 43 | Squire wgn 4d 3S | 4,447 | 5,435 ⎦ | |

# Ford

### LTD (wb 121.0)

| | | Wght | Price | Prod |
|---|---|---|---|---|
| 52 | Custom 500 sdn 2d | — | — | 4,139 |
| 53 | Custom 500 sdn 4d | — | — | 5,582 |
| 62 | LTD sdn 2d | 4,190 | 5,128 | 73,637 |
| 63 | LTD sdn 4d | 4,240 | 5,152 | 160,255 |
| 64 | LTD Landau sdn 4d | 4,319 | 5,742 | 65,030 |
| 65 | LTD Landau sdn 2d | 4,270 | 5,717 | 44,396 |
| 72 | Custom 500 Ranch Wgn 4d | — | — | ⎫ 1,406 |
| 74 | LTD wgn 5d 2S | 4,635 | 5,415 | ⎫ |
| 74 | LTD wgn 5d 3S | 4,679 | 5,541 | ⎬ 90,711 |
| 74 | Country Squire wgn 4d 2S | 4,674 | 5,866 | |
| 74 | Country Squire sgn 4d 3S | 4,718 | 5,992 | ⎭ |

| 1977 Engines | bore×stroke | bhp | availability |
|---|---|---|---|
| I-4, 140.0 | 3.78×3.13 | 89 | S-Pinto |
| V6, 170.8 | 3.66×2.70 | 93 | O-Pinto, exc Pony |
| I-6, 200.0 | 3.68×3.13 | 96 | S-Maverick, Granada exc Ghia |
| I-6, 250.0 | 3.68×3.91 | 98 | S-Gran Ghia; O-Mav, Gran |
| V-8, 302.0 | 4.00×3.00 | 122 | O-Granada |
| V-8, 302.0 | 4.00×3.00 | 130 | S-LTD II exc wgns |
| V-8, 302.0 | 4.00×3.00 | 137 | O-Maverick |
| V-8, 351.0 | 4.00×3.50 | 135 | O-Granada |
| V-8, 351.0 | 4.00×3.50 | 149 | S-LTD II wgns; O-other LTD II |
| V-8, 351.0 | 4.00×3.50 | 161 | S-LTD exc wgns; O-LTD II wgns |
| V-8, 400.0 | 4.00×4.00 | 173 | S-LTD wgns; O-LTD II, other LTD |
| V-8, 460.0 | 4.36×3.85 | 197 | O-LTD |

* incl. some units produced as 1978 models but sold as 1977 models.

### 1978*

#### Pinto (wb 94.4; wgns-94.7)

| | | Wght | Price | Prod |
|---|---|---|---|---|
| 10 | Pony sdn 2d I-4 | 2,321 | 3,139 | ⎫ 62,317 |
| 10 | sdn 2d | 2,400 | 3,629 | ⎭ |
| 11 | Runabout htchbk sdn 2d | 2,444 | 3,744 | 74,313 |
| 12 | wgn 2d | 2,579 | 4,028 | ⎫ 52,269 |
| 12 | Squire wgn 2d | 2,614 | 4,343 | ⎭ |

#### Fairmont (wb 105.5)

| 91 | sdn 2d | 2,590 | 3,624 | 78,776 |
|---|---|---|---|---|
| 92 | sdn 4d | 2,632 | 3,710 | 136,849 |
| 93 | Futura cpe | 2,626 | 4,103 | 116,966 |
| 94 | wgn 4d | 2,740 | 4,063 | ⎫ 128,390 |
| 94 | Squire wgn 4d | 2,748 | 4,428 | ⎭ |

#### Granada (wb 109.9)

| 81 | sdn 2d | 3,132 | 4,300 | ⎫ |
|---|---|---|---|---|
| 81 | Ghia sdn 2d | 3,192 | 4,685 | ⎬ 110,481 |
| 81 | ESS sdn 2d | 3,190 | 4,872 | ⎭ |
| 82 | sdn 4d | 3,167 | 4,390 | ⎫ |
| 82 | Ghia sdn 4d | 3,275 | 4,776 | ⎬ 139,305 |
| 82 | ESS sdn 4d | 3,225 | 4,962 | ⎭ |

#### LTD II (wb 118.0; 2d-114.0)

| 25 | S htp cpe | 3,746 | 4,850 | 9,004 |
|---|---|---|---|---|
| 27 | S sdn 4d | 3,836 | 4,935 | 21,122 |
| 30 | htp cpe | 3,773 | 5,112 | ⎫ 76,285 |
| 30 | Brougham htp cpe | 3,791 | 5,448 | ⎭ |
| 31 | sdn 4d | 3,872 | 5,222 | ⎫ 64,133 |
| 31 | Brougham sdn 4d | 3,901 | 5,558 | ⎭ |

#### LTD (wb 121.0)

| 62 | htp cpe | 3,972 | 5,398 | 57,466 |
|---|---|---|---|---|
| 63 | sdn 4d | 4,032 | 5,483 | 112,392 |
| 64 | LTD Landau htp cpe | 4,029 | 5,970 | 27,305 |
| 65 | LTD Landau sdn 4d | 4,081 | 6,055 | 39,836 |
| 74 | wgn 4d 2S | 4,532 | 5,885 | ⎫ |
| 74 | wgn 4d 3S | 4,567 | 6,028 | ⎬ 71,285 |
| 74 | Country Squire wgn 4d 2S | 4,576 | 6,304 | |
| 74 | Country Squire wgn 4d 3S | 4,601 | 6,447 | ⎭ |

*Fiesta not included (import).

| 1978 Engines | bore×stroke | bhp | availability |
|---|---|---|---|
| I-4, 140.0 | 3.78×3.13 | 88 | S-Pinto, Fairmont |
| V6, 170.0 | 3.66×2.70 | 90 | O-Pinto, exc Pony |
| I-6, 200.0 | 3.68×3.13 | 85 | O-Fairmont |
| I-6, 250.0 | 3.68×3.91 | 97 | S-Granada |
| V-8, 302.0 | 4.00×3.00 | 134 | S-LTD II, LTD exc wgns |
| V-8, 302.0 | 4.00×3.00 | 139 | S-Granada; O-Fairmont |
| V-8, 351.0 | 4.00×3.50 | 144/145 | S-LTD wgns; O-LTD II, other LTD |
| V-8, 351.0 | 4.00×3.50 | 152 | O-LTD II |
| V-8, 400.0 | 4.00×4.00 | 166 | O-LTD II, LTD |
| V-8, 460.0 | 4.36×3.85 | 202 | O-LTD |

### 1979

#### Pinto (wb 94.4; wgns-94.7)

| | | Wght | Price | Prod |
|---|---|---|---|---|
| 10 | Pony fstbk sdn 2d I-4 | 2,329 | 3,434 | ⎫ 75,789 |
| 10 | fstbk sdn 2d | 2,396 | 3,939 | ⎭ |
| 11 | Runabout htchbk sdn 2d | 2,442 | 4,055 | 69,383 |
| 12 | Pony wgn 2d I-4 | — | 3,899 | ⎫ |
| 12 | wgn 2d | 2,571 | 4,338 | ⎬ 53,846 |
| 12 | Squire wgn 2d | 2,607 | 4,654 | ⎭ |

#### Fairmont (wb 105.5)

| 91 | sdn 2d | 2,524 | 4,102 | 54,798 |
|---|---|---|---|---|
| 92 | sdn 4d | 2,578 | 4,220 | 133,813 |
| 93 | Futura cpe | 2,580 | 4,463 | 106,065 |
| 94 | wgn 4d | 2,708 | 4,497 | ⎫ 100,691 |
| 94 | Squire wgn 4d | — | 4,856 | ⎭ |

#### Granada (wb 109.9)

| 81 | sdn 2d | 3,088 | 4,678 | ⎫ |
|---|---|---|---|---|
| 81 | Ghia sdn 2d | 3,124 | 5,051 | ⎬ 76,850 |
| 81 | ESS sdn 2d | 3,140 | 5,211 | ⎭ |
| 82 | sdn 4d | 3,134 | 4,782 | ⎫ |
| 82 | Ghia sdn 4d | 3,168 | 5,157 | ⎬ 105,526 |
| 82 | ESS sdn 4d | 3,210 | 5,317 | ⎭ |

#### LTD II (wb. 118.0; 2d-114.0)

| 25 | S htp cpe | 3,781 | 5,561 | 834 |
|---|---|---|---|---|
| 27 | S sdn 4d | 3,844 | 5,661 | 9,649 |
| 30 | htp cpe | 3,797 | 5,799 | ⎫ 18,300 |
| 30 | Brougham htp cpe | 3,815 | 6,135 | ⎭ |
| 31 | sdn 4d | 3,860 | 5,924 | ⎫ 19,781 |
| 31 | Brougham sdn 4d | 3,889 | 6,259 | ⎭ |

#### LTD (wb 114.3)

| 62 | sdn 2d | 3,421 | 6,184 | 54,005 |
|---|---|---|---|---|
| 63 | sdn 4d | 3,463 | 6,284 | 117,730 |
| 64 | Landau sdn 2d | 3,472 | 6,686 | 42,314 |
| 65 | Landau sdn 4d | 3,527 | 6,811 | 74,599 |
| 74 | wgn 4d 2S | 3,678 | 6,550 | ⎫ 37,955 |
| 74 | wgn 4d 3S | — | 6,699 | ⎭ |
| 76 | Country Squire wgn 4d 2S | 3,719 | 7,006 | ⎫ 29,932 |
| 76 | Country Squire wgn 4d 3S | — | 7,155 | ⎭ |

▲ 1950 Ford two-door club coupe ▼ 1956 Ford two-door Crown Victoria

▲ 1966 Ford LTD four-door hardtop    ▼ 1972 Ford Gran Torino hardtop coupe

▲ 2000 Ford Focus coupe ▼ 1965 Ford Mustang GT convertible

▲ 1969 Ford Mustang Mach I fastback coupe ▼ 1973 Ford Mustang notchback coupe

▲ 2000 Ford Mustang Cobra R coupe ▼ 1957 Ford Thunderbird convertible

▲ 1959 Ford Thunderbird convertible

▼ 1964 Ford Thunderbird convertible

▲ 1983 Ford Thunderbird coupe ▼ 2002 Ford Thunderbird convertible

▲ 1949 Frazer Manhattan four-door sedan

▼ 1951 Frazer Manhattan hardtop sedan

▲ 1939 Graham four-door sedan ▼ 1941 Graham Hollywood sedan

▲ 1951 Henry J Deluxe two-door sedan         ▼ 1937 Hudson Country Club four-door sedan

▲ 1954 Hudson Hornet club coupe ▼ 1956 Hudson Hornet Hollywood hardtop coupe

▲ 1932 Hupmobile 222F sport coupe

▼ 1955 Imperial Newport two-door hardtop

▲ 1960 Imperial Crown convertible ▼ 1968 Imperial Crown four-door hardtop

493

▲ 1947 Kaiser Special four-door sedan   ▼ 1951 Kaiser Golden Dragon four-door sedan

▲ 1954 Kaiser-Darrin convertible

▼ 1955 Kaiser Manhattan two-door sedan

▲ 1930 LaSalle 340 convertible

▼ 1939 LaSalle opera coupe

# Ford

| 1979 Engines | bore×stroke | bhp | availability |
|---|---|---|---|
| I-4, 140.0 | 3.78×3.13 | 88 | S-Pinto, Fairmont |
| V6, 170.0 | 3.66×2.70 | 102 | O-Pinto exc Pony |
| I-6, 200.0 | 3.68×3.13 | 85 | O-Fairmont |
| I-6, 250.0 | 3.68×3.91 | 97 | S-Granada |
| V-8, 302.0 | 4.00×3.00 | 129 | S-LTD |
| V-8, 302.0 | 4.00×3.00 | 133 | S-LTD II |
| V-8, 302.0 | 4.00×3.00 | 137 | O-Granada |
| V-8, 302.0 | 4.00×3.00 | 140 | O-Fairmont |
| V-8, 351.0 | 4.00×3.50 | 142 | O-LTD |
| V-8, 351.0 | 4.00×3.50 | 151 | O-LTD II, LTD |

## 1980

| | Pinto (wb 94.4; wgns-94.7) | Wght | Price | Prod |
|---|---|---|---|---|
| 10 | Pony fstbk sdn 2d | 2,377 | 4,117 | 84,053 |
| 10 | fstbk sdn 2d | 2,385 | 4,605 | |
| 11 | Runabout htchbk sdn 2d | 2,426 | 4,717 | 61,842 |
| 12 | Pony wgn 2d | 2,545 | 4,627 | |
| 12 | wgn 2d | 2,553 | 5,004 | 39,159 |
| 12/604 | Squire wgn 2d | 2,590 | 5,320 | |

| | Fairmont (wb 105.5) | | | |
|---|---|---|---|---|
| 91 | sdn 2d | 2,576 | 4,894 | 45,074 |
| 92 | sdn 4d | 2,610 | 5,011 | 137,812 |
| 92 | Futura sdn 4d | — | 5,390 | 5,306 |
| 93 | Futura cpe | 2,623 | 5,325 | 51,878 |
| 94 | wgn 4d | 2,735 | 5,215 | 77,035 |

| | Granada (wb 109.9) | | | |
|---|---|---|---|---|
| 81 | sdn 2d | 3,135 | 5,541 | |
| 81/602 | Ghia sdn 2d | 3,168 | 5,942 | 60,872 |
| 81/933 | ESS sdn 2d | 3,199 | 6,031 | |
| 82 | sdn 4d | 3,168 | 5,664 | |
| 82/602 | Ghia sdn 4d | 3,209 | 6,065 | 29,557 |
| 82/933 | ESS sdn 4d | 3,240 | 6,154 | |

| | LTD (wb 114.3) | | | |
|---|---|---|---|---|
| | S sdn 2d | — | — | 553 |
| 61 | S sdn 4d | 3,464 | 6,875 | 19,283 |
| 62 | sdn 2d | 3,447 | 7,003 | 15,333 |
| 63 | sdn 4d | 3,475 | 7,117 | 51,360 |
| 64 | Crown Victoria sdn 2d | 3,482 | 7,628 | 7,725 |
| 65 | Crown Victoria sdn 4d | 3,524 | 7,763 | 21,962 |
| 72 | S wgn 4d 2S | 3,707 | 7,198 | |
| 72 | S wgn 4d 3S | 3,748 | 7,344 | 3,490 |
| 74 | wgn 4d 2S | 3,717 | 7,463 | |
| 74 | wgn 4d 3S | 3,758 | 7,609 | 11,718 |
| 76 | Crown Victoria wgn 4d 2S | 3,743 | 7,891 | |
| 76 | Crown Victoria wgn 4d 3S | 3,784 | 8,042 | 9,868 |

| 1980 Engines | bore×stroke | bhp | availability |
|---|---|---|---|
| I-4, 140.0 | 3.78×3.13 | 88 | S-Pinto, Fairmont |
| I-6, 200.0 | 3.68×3.13 | 91 | O-Fairmont |
| I-6, 250.0 | 3.68×3.91 | 90 | S-Granada |
| V-8, 255.0 | 3.68×3.00 | 119 | O-Fairmont, Granada |
| V-8, 302.0 | 4.00×3.00 | 130 | S-LTD |
| V-8, 302.0 | 4.00×3.00 | 134 | O-Granada |
| V-8, 351.0 | 4.00×3.50 | 140 | O-LTD |

## 1981

| | Escort (wb 94.2) | Wght | Price | Prod |
|---|---|---|---|---|
| 05 | htchbk sdn 2d | 1,962 | 5,158 | |
| 05/60Q | L htchbk sdn 2d | 1,964 | 5,494 | |
| 05/60Z | GL htchbk sdn 2d | 1,987 | 5,838 | |
| 05/602 | GLX htchbk sdn 2d | 2,029 | 6,476 | 192,554 |
| 05/936 | SS htchbk sdn 2d | 2,004 | 6,139 | |
| 08 | htchbk sdn 4d | 2,074 | 5,731 | |
| 08/60Q | L htchbk sdn 4d | 2,075 | 5,814 | |
| 08/60Z | GL htchbk sdn 4d | 2,094 | 6,178 | 128,173 |
| 08/602 | GLX htchbk sdn 4d | 2,137 | 6,799 | |
| 08/936 | SS htchbk sdn 4d | 2,114 | 6,464 | |

| | Fairmont (wb 105.5) | | | |
|---|---|---|---|---|
| 20 | S sdn 2d | — | 5,701 | — |
| 20 | sdn 2d | 2,590 | 6,032 | 23,066 |
| 21 | sdn 4d | 2,640 | 6,151 | |
| 21/605 | Futura sdn 4d | 2,674 | 6,361 | 104,883 |
| 22 | Futura cpe | 2,645 | 6,347 | 24,197 |
| 23 | wgn 4d | 2,754 | 6,384 | |
| 23/605 | Futura wgn 4d | 2,788 | 6,616 | 59,154 |

| | Granada (wb 105.5) | | | |
|---|---|---|---|---|
| 26 | L sdn 2d | 2,752 | 6,474 | |
| 26/602 | GL sdn 2d | 2,773 | 6,875 | 35,057 |
| 26/933 | GLX sdn 2d | 2,777 | 6,988 | |
| 27 | L sdn 4d | 2,795 | 6,633 | |
| 27/602 | GL sdn 4d | 2,822 | 7,035 | 86,284 |
| 27/933 | GLX sdn 4d | 2,829 | 7,148 | |

| | LTD (wb 114.3) | | | |
|---|---|---|---|---|
| 31 | S sdn 4d | 3,490 | 7,527 | 17,490 |
| 32 | sdn 2d | 3,496 | 7,607 | 6,279 |
| 33 | sdn 4d | 3,538 | 7,718 | 35,932 |
| 34 | Crown Victoria sdn 2d | 3,496 | 8,251 | 11,061 |
| 35 | Crown Victoria sdn 4d | 3,538 | 8,384 | 39,139 |
| 37 | S wgn 4d 2S | 3,717 | 7,942 | 2,465 |
| 38 | wgn 4d 2S | 3,719 | 8,180 | 10,554 |
| 39 | Country Squire wgn 4d 2S | 3,737 | 8,640 | 9,443 |

| 1981 Engines | bore×stroke | bhp | availability |
|---|---|---|---|
| I-4, 97.6 | 3.15×3.13 | 69 | S-Escort |
| I-4, 140.0 | 3.78×3.13 | 88 | S-Fairmont, Granada |
| I-6, 200.0 | 3.68×3.13 | 88 | O-Fairmont, Granada |
| V-8, 255.0 | 3.68×3.00 | 115/120 | S-LTD; O-Fmont, Granada |
| V-8, 302.0 | 4.00×3.00 | 130 | O-LTD |
| V-8, 351.0 | 4.00×3.50 | 145 | O-LTD |

## 1982

| | Escort (wb 94.2) | Wght | Price | Prod |
|---|---|---|---|---|
| 05 | htchbk sdn 2d | 1,920 | 5,462 | |
| 05 | L htchbk sdn 2d | 1,926 | 6,046 | |
| 05 | GL htchbk sdn 2d | 1,948 | 6,406 | 165,660 |
| 05 | GLX htchbk sdn 2d | 1,987 | 7,086 | |
| 05 | GT htchbk sdn 2d | 1,963 | 6,706 | |
| 06 | htchbk sdn 4d | 1,926 | 5,668 | |
| 06 | L htchbk sdn 4d | 2,003 | 6,263 | |
| 06 | GL htchbk sdn 4d | 2,025 | 6,622 | 130,473 |
| 06 | GLX htchbk sdn 4d | 2,064 | 7,302 | |
| 08 | L wgn 4d | 2,023 | 6,461 | |
| 08 | GL wgn 4d | 2,043 | 6,841 | 88,999 |
| 08 | GLX wgn 4d | 2,079 | 7,475 | |

| | EXP (wb 94.2) | | | |
|---|---|---|---|---|
| 01 | htchbk cpe | 2,146 | 7,387 | 98,256 |

# Ford

| Fairmont Futura (wb 105.5) | | Wght | Price | Prod |
|---|---|---|---|---|
| 20 | sdn 2d | 2,616 | 5,985 | 8,222 |
| 21 | sdn 4d | 2,664 | 6,419 | 101,666 |
| 22 | spt cpe | 2,640 | 6,517 | 17,851 |
| **Granada (wb 105.5)** | | | | |
| 26 | L sdn 2d | 2,732 | 7,126 | ⎤ |
| 26 | GL sdn 2d | 2,758 | 7,543 | 12,802 |
| 26 | GLX sdn 2d | 2,776 | 7,666 | ⎦ |
| 27 | L sdn 4d | 2,764 | 7,301 | ⎤ |
| 27 | GL sdn 4d | 2,794 | 7,718 | 62,339 |
| 27 | GLX sdn 4d | 2,812 | 7,840 | ⎦ |
| 28 | L wgn 4d I-6 | 2,965 | 7,983 | ⎤ 45,182 |
| 28 | GL wgn 4d I-6 | 2,995 | 8,399 | ⎦ |
| **LTD (wb 114.3)** | | | | |
| 31 | S sdn 4d | 3,522 | 8,312 | 22,182 |
| 32 | sdn 2d | 3,496 | 8,455 | 3,510 |
| 33 | sdn 4d | 3,526 | 8,574 | 29,776 |
| 34 | Crown Victoria sdn 2d | 3,523 | 9,149 | 9,287 |
| 35 | Crown Victoria sdn 4d | 3,567 | 9,294 | 41,405 |
| 37 | S wgn 4d 2S | 3,725 | 8,783 | 2,973 |
| 38 | wgn 4d 2S | 3,741 | 9,073 | 9,294 |
| 39 | Country Squire wgn 4d 2S | 3,741 | 9,580 | 9,626 |

| 1982 Engines | bore×stroke | bhp | availability |
|---|---|---|---|
| I-4, 97.6 | 3.15×3.13 | 70 | S-Escort, EXP |
| I-4, 97.6 | 3.15×3.13 | 80 | O-late Escort, EXP |
| I-4, 140.0 | 3.78×3.13 | 86 | S-Fairmont, Granada |
| I-6, 200.0 | 3.68×3.13 | 87 | S-Gran wgn; O-Fmont, Granada |
| V-6, 232.0 | 3.80×3.40 | 112 | O-Granada |
| V-8, 255.0 | 3.68×3.00 | 122 | S-LTD; O-Fmont (police) |
| V-8, 302.0 | 4.00×3.00 | 132 | S-LTD wgn; O-LTD |
| V-8, 351.0 | 4.00×3.50 | 165 | S-LTD (police only) |

## 1983

| Escort (wb 94.2) | | Wght | Price | Prod |
|---|---|---|---|---|
| 04 | L htchbk sdn 2d | 2,016 | 5,639 | ⎤ |
| 05 | GL htchbk sdn 2d | 1,959 | 6,384 | 151,386 |
| 06 | GLX htchbk sdn 2d | 1,993 | 6,771 | |
| 07 | GT htchbk sdn 2d | 2,020 | 7,339 | ⎦ |
| 13 | L htchbk sdn 4d | 2,078 | 5,846 | ⎤ |
| 14 | GL htchbk sdn 4d | 2,025 | 6,601 | 84,649 |
| 15 | GLX htchbk sdn 4d | 2,059 | 6,988 | ⎦ |
| 09 | L wgn 4d | 2,117 | 6,052 | ⎤ |
| 10 | GL wgn 4d | 2,052 | 6,779 | 79,335 |
| 11 | GLX wgn 4d | 2,083 | 7,150 | ⎦ |
| **EXP (wb 94.2)—19,697 built** | | | | |
| 01 | htchbk cpe | 2,156 | 6,426 | — |
| 01/301B | HO htchbk cpe | — | 7,004 | — |
| 01/302B | HO sport htchbk cpe | — | 7,794 | — |
| 01/303B | Luxury htchbk cpe | — | 8,225 | — |
| 01/304B | GT htchbk cpe | — | 8,739 | — |
| **Fairmont Futura (wb 105.5)** | | | | |
| 35 | sdn 2d | 2,890 | 6,444 | ⎤ 3,664 |
| 35/41K | S sdn 2d | 2,628 | 5,985 | ⎦ |
| 36 | sdn 4d | 2,933 | 6,590 | ⎤ 69,287 |
| 36/41K | S sdn 4d | 2,672 | 6,125 | ⎦ |
| 37 | spt cpe | 2,908 | 6,666 | 7,882 |
| **LTD (wb 105.6)** | | | | |
| 39 | L sdn 4d | 2,912 | 7,777 | ⎤ 111,813 |

| LTD (wb 105.6) | | Wght | Price | Prod |
|---|---|---|---|---|
| 39/60H | Brougham sdn 4d | 2,845 | 8,165 | ⎦ |
| 40 | wgn 4d I-6 | 3,092 | 8,577 | 43,945 |
| **LTD Crown Victoria (wb 114.3)** | | | | |
| 43 | sdn 4d | 3,748 | 10,094 | ⎤ 81,859 |
| 43/41K | S sdn 4d | 3,732 | 9,130 | ⎦ |
| 42 | sdn 2d | 3,732 | 10,094 | 11,414 |
| 44 | Country Squire wgn 4d 2S | 3,901 | 10,253 | ⎤ |
| 44/41E | wgn 4d 2S | 3,895 | 10,003 | 20,343 |
| 44/41K | S wgn 4d 2S | 3,891 | 9,444 | ⎦ |

| 1983 Engines | bore×stroke | bhp | availability |
|---|---|---|---|
| I-4, 97.6 | 3.15×3.13 | 72 | S-Escort, EXP |
| I-4, 97.6 | 3.15×3.13 | 80 | O-Escort, EXP |
| I-4, 97.6 | 3.15×3.13 | 88 | S-Escort GT; O-Escort, EXP |
| I-4, 140.0 | 3.78×3.13 | 90 | S-Fairmont, LTD |
| I-4P, 140.0 | 3.78×3.13 | — | O-LTD (propane) |
| I-6, 200.0 | 3.68×3.13 | 92 | S-LTD wgn; O-Fmont, other LTD |
| V-6, 232.0 | 3.80×3.40 | 110 | O-LTD |
| V-8, 302.0 | 4.00×3.00 | 130 | S-Crown Vic; O-LTD |
| V-8, 302.0 | 4.00×3.00 | 145 | O-Crown Vic |
| V-8, 351.0 | 4.00×3.50 | 165 | S-Crown Vic (police only) |

## 1984

| Escort (wb 94.2) | | Wght | Price | Prod |
|---|---|---|---|---|
| 04 | htchbk sdn 2d | 2,016 | 5,629 | ⎤ |
| 04 | L htchbk sdn 2d | 2,080 | 5,885 | |
| 05 | GL htchbk sdn 2d | 2,122 | 6,382 | 184,323 |
| 07 | GT htchbk sdn 2d | 2,170 | 7,593 | |
| 07/935 | GT turbo sdn 2d | — | 8,680 | ⎦ |
| 13 | htchbk sdn 4d | 2,078 | 5,835 | ⎤ |
| 13 | L htchbk sdn 4d | 2,146 | 6,099 | 99,444 |
| 14 | GL htchbk sdn 4d | 2,188 | 6,596 | |
| 15 | LX htchbk sdn 4d | 2,222 | 7,848 | ⎦ |
| 09 | L wgn 4d | 2,176 | 6,313 | ⎤ |
| 10 | GL wgn 4d | 2,216 | 6,773 | 88,756 |
| 11 | LX wgn 4d | 2,249 | 7,939 | ⎦ |
| **EXP (wb 94.2)—23,016 built** | | | | |
| 01/A80 | htchbk cpe | 2,212 | 6,653 | — |
| 01/A81 | Luxury htchbk cpe | 2,235 | 7,539 | — |
| 01/A82 | Turbo htchbk cpe | 2,243 | 9,942 | — |
| **Tempo (wb 99.9)** | | | | |
| 18 | L sdn 2d | 2,286 | 6,936 | ⎤ |
| 19 | GL sdn 2d | — | 7,159 | 107,065 |
| 20 | GLX sdn 2d | — | 7,621 | ⎦ |
| 21 | L sdn 4d | 2,348 | 6,936 | ⎤ |
| 22 | GL sdn 4d | — | 7,159 | 295,149 |
| 23 | GLX sdn 4d | — | 7,621 | ⎦ |
| **LTD (wb 105.6)** | | | | |
| 39 | sdn 4d | 2,830 | 8,605 | ⎤ |
| 39/60H | Brougham sdn 4d | — | 9,980 | 154,173 |
| 39/93B | LX sdn 4d V-8 | — | 11,098 | ** |
| 40 | wgn 4d I-6 | 3,123 | 9,102 | 59,569 |
| **LTD Crown Victoria (wb 114.3)** | | | | |
| 43 | sdn 4d | 3,730 | 10,954 | ⎤ 130,164 |
| 43/41K | S sdn 4d | 3,728 | 9,826 | ⎦ |
| 42 | sdn 2d | 3,689 | 10,954 | 12,522 |
| 44 | Country Squire wgn 4d 2S | 3,936 | 11,111 | ⎤ |
| 44/41E | wgn 4d 2S | 3,931 | 10,861 | 30,803 |

# Ford

| LTD Crown Victoria (wb 114.3) | | Wght | Price | Prod |
|---|---|---|---|---|
| 44/41K | S wgn 4d 2S | 3,880 | 10,136 | |

** 3,260 LTD LX models built in 1984-85 model years combined.

| 1984 Engines | bore×stroke | bhp | availability |
|---|---|---|---|
| I-4, 97.6 | 3.15×3.13 | 70 | S-Escort exc LX, GT |
| I-4, 97.6 | 3.15×3.13 | 80 | S-EXP; O-Escort |
| I-4, 97.6 | 3.15×3.13 | 84 | S-Escort LX, GT; O-Escort, EXP |
| I-4T, 97.6 | 3.15×3.13 | 120 | S-Escort GT/EXP Turbo |
| I-4D, 121.0 | 3.39×3.39 | 52 | O-Escort, Tempo |
| I-4, 140.0 | 3.70×3.30 | 84 | S-Tempo |
| I-4, 140.0 | 3.78×3.13 | 88 | S-LTD exc LX |
| I-4P, 140.0 | 3.78×3.13 | — | O-LTD (propane) |
| V-6, 232.0 | 3.80×3.40 | 120 | S-LTD wgn; O-LTD |
| V-8, 302.0 | 4.00×3.00 | 140 | S-Crown Vic exc wgn |
| V-8, 302.0 | 4.00×3.00 | 155 | S-Crown Vic wgn |
| V-8, 302.0 | 4.00×3.00 | 165 | S-LTD LX |

## 1985

| Escort First Series (wb 94.2) | | Wght | Price | Prod |
|---|---|---|---|---|
| 04/41P | htchbk sdn 2d | 1,990 | 5,620 | |
| 04 | L htchbk sdn 2d | 1,979 | 5,876 | |
| 05 | GL htchbk sdn 2d | 2,047 | 6,374 | 112,406* |
| 07 | GT htchbk sdn 2d | 2,140 | 7,585 | |
| 07/935 | GT turbo htchbk sdn 2d | 2,172 | 8,680 | |
| 13 | htchbk sdn 4d | 2,078 | 5,835 | |
| 13/41P | L htchbk sdn 4d | 2,055 | 5,827 | 62,709* |
| 14 | GL htchbk sdn 4d | 2,114 | 6,588 | |
| 15 | LX htchbk sdn 4d | 2,175 | 7,840 | |
| 09 | L wgn 4d | 2,071 | 6,305 | |
| 10 | GL wgn 4d | 2,139 | 6,765 | 45,740* |
| 11 | LX wgn 4d | 2,198 | 7,931 | |

* Estimated totals

| Escort Second Series 1985½ (wb 94.2) | | Wght | Price | Prod |
|---|---|---|---|---|
| 31 | htchbk sdn 2d | 2,142 | 5,856 | |
| 31 | L htchbk sdn 2d | — | 6,127 | 100,554 |
| 32 | GL htchbk sdn 2d | — | 6,642 | |
| 36 | L htchbk sdn 4d | 2,195 | 6,341 | 48,676 |
| 37 | GL htchbk sdn 4d | — | 6,855 | |
| 34 | L wgn 4d | 2,223 | 6,622 | 36,998 |
| 35 | GL wgn 4d | — | 7,137 | |

| EXP (wb 94.2)—26,462 built | | | | |
|---|---|---|---|---|
| 01/A80 | htchbk cpe | 2,098 | 6,697 | — |
| 01/A81 | Luxury htchbk cpe | 2,124 | 7,585 | — |
| 01/A82 | Turbo htchbk cpe | 2,232 | 9,997 | — |

| Tempo (wb 99.9) | | | | |
|---|---|---|---|---|
| 18 | L sdn 2d | 2,271 | 7,052 | |
| 19 | GL sdn 2d | 2,302 | 7,160 | 72,311 |
| 20 | GLX sdn 2d | 2,372 | 8,253 | |
| 21 | L sdn 4d | 2,328 | 7,052 | |
| 22 | GL sdn 4d | 2,358 | 7,160 | 266,776 |
| 23 | GLX sdn 4d | 2,428 | 8,302 | |

| LTD (wb 105.6) | | | | |
|---|---|---|---|---|
| 39 | sdn 4d I-4/V-6 | 2,852 | 8,874 | |
| 39/60H | Brougham sdn 4d I-4/V-6 | 2,857 | 9,262 | 162,884 |
| 39/938 | LX sdn 4d V-8 | 2,904 | 11,421 | ** |
| 40 | wgn 4d V-6 | 2,990 | 9,384 | 42,642 |

| LTD Crown Victoria (wb 114.3) | | | | |
|---|---|---|---|---|
| 43 | sdn 4d | 3,588 | 11,627 | |
| 43/41K | S sdn 4d | 3,709 | 10,609 | 154,612 |
| 42 | sdn 2d | 3,552 | 11,627 | |
| 44 | Country Squire wgn 4d 2S | 3,763 | 11,809 | |
| 44/41E | wgn 4d 2S | 3,758 | 11,559 | 30,825 |
| 44/41K | S wgn 4d 2S | 3,883 | 10,956 | |

** 3,260 LTD LX models built in 1984-85 model years combined.

| 1985 Engines | bore×stroke | bhp | availability |
|---|---|---|---|
| I-4, 97.6 | 3.15×3.13 | 70 | S-Escort exc LX, GT |
| I-4, 97.6 | 3.15×3.13 | 80 | S-EXP; O-Escort |
| I-4, 97.6 | 3.15×3.13 | 84 | S-Escort LX, GT; O-Escort |
| I-4T, 97.6 | 3.15×3.13 | 120 | S-Escort/EXP Turbo |
| I-4, 113.5 | 3.23×3.46 | 86 | S-late Escort |
| I-4D, 121.0 | 3.39×3.39 | 52 | O-Escort, Tempo |
| I-4, 140.0 | 3.70×3.30 | 86 | S-Tempo |
| I-4, 140.0 | 3.70×3.30 | 100 | O-Tempo |
| I-4, 140.0 | 3.78×3.13 | 88 | S-LTD exc wgn |
| I-4P, 140.0 | 3.78×3.13 | — | O-LTD (propane) |
| V-6, 232.0 | 3.80×3.40 | 120 | S-LTD wgn; O-other LTD |
| V-8, 302.0 | 4.00×3.00 | 140 | S-Crown Vic |
| V-8, 302.0 | 4.00×3.00 | 155 | O-Crown Vic |
| V-8, 302.0 | 4.00×3.00 | 165 | S-LTD LX |
| V-8, 351.0 | 4.00×3.50 | 180 | S-Crown Vic (police only) |

## 1986

| Escort (wb 94.2) | | Wght | Price | Prod |
|---|---|---|---|---|
| 31/41P | Pony htchbk sdn 2d | 2,159 | 6,052 | |
| 31 | L htchbk sdn 2d | 2,153 | 6,327 | 228,013 |
| 32 | LX htchbk sdn 2d | 2,238 | 7,234 | |
| 33 | GT htchbk sdn 2d | 2,364 | 8,112 | |
| 36 | L htchbk sdn 4d | 2,201 | 6,541 | 117,300 |
| 37 | LX htchbk sdn 4d | 2,281 | 7,448 | |
| 34 | L wgn 4d | 2,233 | 6,822 | 84,740 |
| 35 | LX wgn 4d | 2,311 | 7,729 | |

| EXP (wb 94.2)—30,978 built | | | | |
|---|---|---|---|---|
| 01 | htchbk cpe | 2,311 | 7,186 | — |
| 01/931 | Luxury htchbk cpe | 2,413 | 8,235 | — |

| Tempo (wb 99.9) | | | | |
|---|---|---|---|---|
| 19 | GL sdn 2d | 2,339 | 7,358 | 69,101 |
| 20 | GLX sdn 2d | 2,461 | 8,578 | |
| 22 | GL sdn 4d | 2,398 | 7,508 | 208,570 |
| 23 | GLX sdn 4d | 2,522 | 8,777 | |

| Taurus (wb 106.0) | | | | |
|---|---|---|---|---|
| 29 | L sdn 4d I-4/V-6 | 2,979 | 9,645 | |
| 29/934 | MT5 sdn 4d I-4 | 2,878 | 10,276 | 178,737 |
| 29/60D | GL sdn 4d V-6 | 3,009 | 11,322 | |
| 29/60H | LX sdn 4d V-6 | 3,109 | 13,351 | |
| 30 | L wgn 4d V-6 | 3,184 | 10,763 | |
| 30/934 | MT5 wgn 4d I-4 | 3,076 | 10,741 | 57,625 |
| 30/60D | GL wgn 4d V-6 | 3,214 | 11,790 | |
| 30/60H | LX wgn 4d V-6 | 3,306 | 13,860 | |

| LTD (wb 105.6) | | | | |
|---|---|---|---|---|
| 39 | sdn 4d | 3,001 | 10,032 | 58,270 |
| 39/60H | Brougham sdn 4d | 3,009 | 10,420 | |
| 40 | wgn 4d | 3,108 | 10,132 | 14,213 |

# Ford

| LTD Crown Victoria (wb 114.3) | | Wght | Price | Prod |
|---|---|---|---|---|
| 43 | sdn 4d | 3,748 | 12,562 | ⎤ |
| 43/60H | LX sdn 4d | 3,781 | 13,784 | 97,314 |
| 43/41K | S sdn 4d | 3,715 | 12,188 | ⎦ |
| 42 | sdn 2d | 3,708 | 13,022 | ⎤ 6,559 |
| 42/60H | LX sdn 2d | 3,754 | 13,752 | ⎦ |
| 44 | Country Squire wgn 4d 2S | 3,937 | 12,655 | ⎤ |
| 44/60H | LX Cntry Squire wgn 4d 2S | 3,829 | 13,817 | |
| 44/41E | wgn 4d 2S | 3,930 | 12,405 | 20,164 |
| 44/41E | LX wgn 4d 2S | 3,821 | 13,567 | |
| 44/41K | S wgn 4d 2S | 3,921 | 12,468 | ⎦ |

| 1986 Engines | bore×stroke | bhp | availability |
|---|---|---|---|
| I-4, 113.5 | 3.23×3.46 | 86 | S-Escort exc GT, EXP |
| I-4, 113.5 | 3.23×3.46 | 108 | S-Escort GT; O-Escort, EXP |
| I-4D, 121.0 | 3.39×3.39 | 52 | O-Escort, Tempo |
| I-4, 140.0 | 3.70×3.30 | 86 | S-Tempo |
| I-4, 140.0 | 3.70×3.30 | 100 | O-Tempo |
| I-4, 153.0 | 3.70×3.60 | 88 | S-Taurus I-4 |
| V-6, 182.0 | 3.50×3.15 | 140 | S-Taurus LX, wgn; O-other Taurus |
| V-6, 232.0 | 3.80×3.40 | 120 | S-LTD |
| V-8, 302.0 | 4.00×3.00 | 150 | S-Crown Vic |
| V-8, 351.0 | 4.00×3.50 | 180 | S-Crown Vic (police only) |

## 1987

| Escort (wb 94.2) | | Wght | Price | Prod |
|---|---|---|---|---|
| 20 | Pony htchbk sdn 2d | 2,180 | 6,436 | ⎤ |
| 21 | GL htchbk sdn 2d | 2,187 | 6,801 | 206,729 |
| 23 | GT htchbk sdn 2d | 2,516 | 8,724 | ⎦ |
| 25 | GL htchbk sdn 4d | 2,222 | 7,022 | 102,187 |
| 28 | GL wgn 4d | 2,274 | 7,312 | 65,849 |

| EXP (wb 94.2)—25,888 built | | | | |
|---|---|---|---|---|
| 18 | sport htchbk cpe | 2,388 | 8,831 | — |
| 17 | Luxury htchbk cpe | 2,291 | 7,622 | — |

| Tempo (wb 99.9) | | | | |
|---|---|---|---|---|
| 31 | GL sdn 2d | 2,462 | 8,043 | ⎤ |
| 32 | LX sdn 2d | 2,562 | 9,238 | 70,164 |
| 33 | Spt GL sdn 2d | 2,667 | 8,888 | |
| 34 | AWD (4WD) sdn 2d | 2,667 | 9,984 | ⎦ |
| 36 | GL sdn 4d | 2,515 | 8,198 | ⎤ |
| 37 | LX sdn 4d | 2,617 | 9,444 | 212,468 |
| 38 | Spt GL sdn 4d | 2,270 | 9,043 | |
| 39 | AWD (4WD) sdn 4d | 2,720 | 10,138 | ⎦ |

| Taurus (wb 106.0) | | | | |
|---|---|---|---|---|
| 50 | L sdn 4d I-4/V-6 | 2,982 | 10,491 | ⎤ |
| 51 | MT5 sdn 4d I-4 | 2,886 | 11,966 | |
| 52 | GL sdn 4d I-4/V-6 | 3,045 | 11,498 | 278,562 |
| 53 | LX sdn 4d V-6 | 3,113 | 14,613 | ⎦ |
| 55 | L wgn 4d V-6 | 3,186 | 11,722 | ⎤ |
| 56 | MT5 wgn 4d I-4 | 3,083 | 12,534 | 96,201 |
| 57 | GL wgn 4d V-6 | 3,242 | 12,688 | |
| 58 | LX wgn 4d V-6 | 3,309 | 15,213 | ⎦ |

| LTD Crown Victoria (wb 114.3) | | | | |
|---|---|---|---|---|
| 73 | sdn 4d | 3,741 | 14,355 | ⎤ |
| 72 | S sdn 4d | 3,708 | 13,860 | 105,789 |
| 74 | LX sdn 4d | 3,788 | 15,454 | ⎦ |
| 70 | cpe 2d | 3,724 | 14,727 | ⎤ 5,527 |
| 71 | LX cpe 2d | 3,735 | 15,421 | ⎦ |
| 78 | Country Squire wgn 4d | 3,920 | 14,507 | ⎤ |

| LTD Crown Victoria (wb 114.3) | | Wght | Price | Prod |
|---|---|---|---|---|
| 76 | wgn 4d | 3,920 | 14,235 | ⎤ |
| 75 | S wgn 4d | 3,894 | 14,228 | 17,562 |
| 79 | LX Country Squire wgn 4d | 4,000 | 15,723 | |
| 77 | LX wgn 4d | 4,000 | 15,450 | ⎦ |

| 1987 Engines | bore×stroke | bhp | availability |
|---|---|---|---|
| I-4, 113.5 | 3.23×3.46 | 90 | S-Escort exc GT, EXP Luxury |
| I-4, 113.5 | 3.23×3.46 | 115 | S-Esc GT, EXP spt; O-other Esc |
| I-4D, 121.0 | 3.39×3.39 | 58 | O-Escort |
| I-4, 140.0 | 3.70×3.30 | 86 | S-Tempo exc 4WD |
| I-4, 140.0 | 3.70×3.30 | 94 | S-Tempo AWD; O-Tempo |
| I-4, 153.0 | 3.70×3.60 | 90 | S-Taurus I-4 |
| V-6, 182.0 | 3.50×3.15 | 140 | S-Taurus LX, wgn; O-other Taurus |
| V-8, 302.0 | 4.00×3.00 | 150 | S-Crown Vic |
| V-8, 351.0 | 4.00×3.50 | 180 | S-Crown Vic (police only) |

## 1988

| Escort First Series (wb 94.2) | | Wght | Price | Prod |
|---|---|---|---|---|
| 20 | Pony htchbk sdn 2d | 2,180 | 6,632 | ⎤ |
| 21 | GL htchbk sdn 2d | 2,187 | 6,949 | 251,911 |
| 23 | GT htchbk sdn 2d | 2,516 | 9,055 | ⎦ |
| 25 | GL htchbk sdn 4d | 2,222 | 7,355 | ⎤ 113,470 |
| 28 | GL wgn 4d | 2,274 | 7,938 | ⎦ |

| Escort Second Series 1988 1/2 (wb 94.2)* | | | | |
|---|---|---|---|---|
| 90 | Pony htchbk sdn 2d | — | 6,747 | — |
| 91 | LX htchbk sdn 2d | 2,258 | 7,127 | — |
| 93 | GT htchbksdn 2d | — | 9,093 | — |
| 95 | LX htchbk sdn 4d | 2,295 | 7,457 | — |
| 98 | LX wgn 4d | 2,307 | 8,058 | — |

| EXP First Series (wb 94.2) | | | | |
|---|---|---|---|---|
| 17 | Luxury htchbk cpe | 2,291 | 8,037 | |

| EXP Second Series 1988½ (wb 94.2) | | | | |
|---|---|---|---|---|
| 88 | Luxury htchbk cpe | 2,359 | 8,201 | — |

| Tempo (wb 99.9) | | | | |
|---|---|---|---|---|
| 31 | GL sdn 2d | 2,536 | 8,658 | ⎤ 49,930 |
| 33 | GLS sdn 2d | 2,552 | 9,249 | ⎦ |
| 36 | GL sdn 4d | 2,585 | 8,808 | 163,409 |
| 37 | LX sdn 4d | 2,626 | 9,737 | ⎤ |
| 38 | GLS sdn 4d | 2,601 | 9,400 | 263,332 |
| 39 | AWD (4WD) sdn 4d | 2,799 | 10,413 | ⎦ |

| Taurus (wb 106.0) | | | | |
|---|---|---|---|---|
| 50 | L sdn 4d I-4/V-6 | 3,005 | 11,699 | ⎤ |
| 51 | MT5 sdn 4d I-4 | 2,882 | 12,835 | 284,576 |
| 52 | GL sdn 4d I-4/V-6 | 3,049 | 12,200 | |
| 53 | LX sdn 4d V-6 | 3,119 | 15,295 | ⎦ |
| 55 | L wgn 5d V-6 | 3,182 | 12,884 | ⎤ |
| 57 | GL wgn 4d V-6 | 3,215 | 13,380 | 93,001 |
| 58 | LX wgn 4d V-6 | 3,288 | 15,905 | ⎦ |

| LTD Crown Victoria (wb 114.3) | | | | |
|---|---|---|---|---|
| 73 | sdn 4d | 3,779 | 15,218 | ⎤ |
| 72 | S sdn 4d | 3,742 | 14,653 | 110,249 |
| 74 | LX sdn 4d | 3,820 | 16,134 | ⎦ |
| 78 | Crown Squire wgn 4d | 3,998 | 15,613 | ⎤ |
| 76 | wgn 4d | 3,991 | 15,180 | 14,940 |
| 79 | LX Country Squire wgn 4d | 4,070 | 16,643 | ⎦ |

# Ford

| LTD Crown Victoria (wb 114.3) | | Wght | Price | Prod |
|---|---|---|---|---|
| 77 | LX wgn 4d | 3,972 | 16,210 | |

*Prod included in Escort First Series

| 1988 Engines | bore×stroke | bhp | availability |
|---|---|---|---|
| I-4, 113.5 | 3.23×3.46 | 90 | S-Escort exc GT, EXP |
| I-4, 113.5 | 3.23×3.46 | 115 | S-Escort GT |
| I-4, 140.0 | 3.70×3.30 | 98 | S-Tempo exc AWD, GLS |
| I-4, 140.0 | 3.70×3.30 | 100 | S-Tempo AWD, GLS |
| I-4, 153.0 | 3.70×3.60 | 90 | S-Taurus I-4 |
| V-6, 182.0 | 3.50×3.15 | 140 | S-Taurus LX, wgn; O-other Taurus |
| V-6, 232.0 | 3.80×3.40 | 140 | O-Taurus |
| V-8, 302.0 | 4.00×3.00 | 150 | S-Crown Vic |
| V-8, 351.0 | 4.00×3.50 | 180 | S-Crown Vic (police only) |

## 1989

| Escort (wb 94.2) | | Wght | Price | Prod |
|---|---|---|---|---|
| 90 | Pony htchbk sdn 2d | 2,235 | 6,964 | 210,795 |
| 91 | LX htchbk sdn 2d | 2,242 | 7,349 | |
| 93 | GT htchbk sdn 2d | 2,442 | 9,315 | |
| 95 | LX htchbk sdn 4d | 2,313 | 7,679 | 119,582 |
| 98 | LX wgn 4d | 2,312 | 8,280 | 32,745 |

| Probe (wb 99.0)—133,650 built* | | | | |
|---|---|---|---|---|
| 20 | GL htchbk cpe | 2,715 | 10,660 | — |
| 21 | LX htchbk cpe | 2,715 | 11,644 | — |
| 22 | GT htchbk cpe | 2,870 | 13,794 | — |

| Tempo (wb 99.9) | | | | |
|---|---|---|---|---|
| 31 | GL sdn 2d | 2,529 | 9,057 | 27,705 |
| 33 | GLS sdn 2d | 2,545 | 9,697 | |
| 36 | GL sdn 4d | 2,587 | 9,207 | 261,080 |
| 37 | LX sdn 4d | 2,628 | 10,156 | |
| 38 | GLS sdn 4d | 2,603 | 9,848 | |
| 39 | AWD (4WD) sdn 4d | 2,787 | 10,860 | |

| Taurus (wb 106.0) | | | | |
|---|---|---|---|---|
| 50 | L sdn 4d I-4/V-6 | 3,001 | 11,778 | 284,605 |
| 52 | GL sdn 4d I-4/V-6 | 3,046 | 12,202 | |
| 53 | LX sdn 4d V-6 | 3,076 | 15,282 | |
| — | SHO sdn 4d V-6 | 3,078 | 19,739 | 16,561 |
| 55 | L wgn 5d V-6 | 3,172 | 13,143 | 94,095 |
| 57 | GL wgn 5d V-6 | 3,189 | 13,544 | |
| 58 | LX wgn 5d V-6 | 3,220 | 16,524 | |

| LTD Crown Victoria (wb 114.3) | | | | |
|---|---|---|---|---|
| 73 | sdn 4d | 3,730 | 15,851 | 120,741 |
| 74 | LX sdn 4d | 3,770 | 16,767 | |
| 78 | Country Squire wgn 4d | 3,935 | 16,527 | 13,362 |
| 76 | wgn 4d | 3,941 | 16,209 | |
| 79 | LX Country Squire wgn 4d | 4,013 | 17,556 | |
| 77 | LX wgn 4d | 3,915 | 17,238 | |

*Calendar year

| 1989 Engines | bore×stroke | bhp | availability |
|---|---|---|---|
| I-4, 113.5 | 3.23×3.46 | 90 | S-Escort exc GT |
| I-4, 113.5 | 3.23×3.46 | 115 | S-Escort GT |
| I-4, 133.0 | 3.39×3.70 | 110 | S-Probe GL/LX |
| I-4T, 133.0 | 3.39×3.70 | 145 | S-Probe GT |
| I-4, 140.0 | 3.70×3.30 | 98 | S-Tempo exc AWD, GLS |
| I-4, 140.0 | 3.70×3.30 | 100 | S-Tempo AWD, GLS |
| I-4, 153.0 | 3.70×3.60 | 90 | S-Taurus I-4 |
| V-6, 182.0 | 3.50×3.15 | 140 | S-Taurus V-6 exc SHO, LX wgn |
| V-6, 182.0 | 3.50×3.15 | 220 | S-Taurus SHO |
| V-6, 232.0 | 3.80×3.40 | 140 | S-Taurus LX wgn; O-other Taurus |
| V-8, 302.0 | 4.00×3.00 | 150 | S-Crown Vic |
| V-8, 351.0 | 4.00×3.50 | 180 | S-Crown Vic (police only) |

## 1990

| Escort (wb 94.2) | | Wght | Price | Prod |
|---|---|---|---|---|
| 90 | Pony htchbk sdn 2d | 2,242 | 7,402 | 110,534 |
| 91 | LX htchbk sdn 2d | — | 7,806 | |
| 93 | GT htchbk sdn 2d | — | 9,804 | |
| 95 | LX htchbk sdn 4d | 2,310 | 8,136 | 70,016 |
| 98 | LX wgn 4d | 2,313 | 8,737 | 15,760 |

| Probe (wb 99.0)—109,898 built | | | | |
|---|---|---|---|---|
| 20 | GL htchbk cpe | 2,731 | 11,470 | — |
| 21 | LX htchbk cpe | — | 13,006 | — |
| 22 | GT htchbk cpe | — | 14,726 | — |

| Tempo (wb 99.9) | | | | |
|---|---|---|---|---|
| 31 | GL sdn 2d | 2,462 | 9,483 | 9,805 |
| 33 | GLS sdn 2d | — | 10,300 | |
| 36 | GL sdn 4d | 2,515 | 9,633 | 256,088 |
| 37 | LX sdn 4d | — | 10,605 | |
| 38 | GLS sdn 4d | — | 10,448 | |
| 39 | AWD (4WD) sdn 4d | 2,720 | 11,331 | |

| Taurus (wb 106.0) | | | | |
|---|---|---|---|---|
| 50 | L sdn 4d I-4/V-6 | 2,956 | 12,640 | 242,197 |
| 52 | GL sdn 4d I-4/V-6 | — | 13,113 | |
| 53 | LX sdn 4d V-6 | — | 16,180 | |
| — | SHO sdn 4d V-6 | — | 21,633 | 8,609 |
| 55 | L wgn 4d V-6 | 3,244 | 14,272 | 82,195 |
| 57 | GL wgn 4d V-6 | — | 14,722 | |
| 58 | LX wgn 4d V-6 | — | 17,771 | |

| LTD Crown Victoria (wb 114.3) | | | | |
|---|---|---|---|---|
| 73 | sdn 4d | 3,821 | 117,257 | 68,187 |
| 74 | LX sdn 4d | — | 17,894 | |
| 78 | Country Squire wgn 4d | 3,941 | 17,921 | 6,419 |
| 76 | wgn 4d | 3,941 | 17,668 | |
| 79 | LX Country Squire wgn 4d | — | 18,761 | |
| 77 | LX wgn 4d | — | 18,418 | |

| 1990 Engines | bore×stroke | bhp | availability |
|---|---|---|---|
| I-4, 113.5 | 3.23×3.46 | 90 | S-Escort exc GT |
| I-4, 113.5 | 3.23×3.46 | 110 | S-Escort GT |
| I-4, 133.0 | 3.39×3.70 | 110 | S-Probe GL |
| I-4T, 133.0 | 3.39×3.70 | 145 | S-Probe GT |
| I-4, 140.0 | 3.70×3.30 | 98 | S-Tempo exc AWD, GLS |
| I-4, 140.0 | 3.70×3.30 | 100 | S-Tempo AWD, GLS |
| I-4, 153.0 | 3.70×3.60 | 90 | S-Taurus I-4 |
| V-6, 182.0 | 3.50×3.15 | 140 | S-Probe LX, Taur LX sdn; O-other Taurus |
| V-6, 182.0 | 3.50×3.15 | 220 | S-Taurus SHO |
| V-6, 232.0 | 3.80×3.40 | 140 | S-Taurus LX wgn; O-other Taurus |
| V-8, 302.0 | 4.00×3.00 | 150 | S-Crown Vic |
| V-8, 351.0 | 4.00×3.50 | 180 | S-Crown Vic (police only) |

# Ford

Note: Full-size (Crown Victoria) station wagons in the 1980s could have an optional dual-facing rear seat. Base prices of 1983-87 Escort and Tempo diesel models were higher than amounts shown.

## 1991

| Escort (98.4) | | Wght | Price | Prod |
|---|---|---|---|---|
| 61/BM | Pony htchbk sdn 2d | 2,287 | 7,976 | 136,157 |
| 61/AI | LX htchbk sdn 2d | 2,312 | 8,667 | |
| 61/AX | GT htchbk sdn 2d | 2,364 | 11,484 | 58,201 |
| 58 | LX htchbk sdn 4d | 2,355 | 9,095 | 126,579 |
| 74 | LX wgn 4d | 2,411 | 9,680 | 62,513 |

| Probe (wb 99.0)—93,737 built | | | | |
|---|---|---|---|---|
| AF | GL htchbk cpe | 2,730 | 11,691 | — |
| AI | LX htchbk cpe | 3,000 | 13,229 | — |
| AX | GT htchbk cpe | 2,970 | 14,964 | — |

| Tempo (wb 99.9) | | | | |
|---|---|---|---|---|
| 66/HVB | GL sdn 2d | 2,532 | 9,541 | 8,585 |
| 66/HVD | GLS sdn 2d | 2,601 | 10,358 | |
| 54/HVB | GL sdn 4d | 2,600 | 9,691 | |
| 54/HVD | GLS sdn 4d | 2,659 | 10,506 | 211,756 |
| 54/HVC | LX sdn 4d | 2,626 | 10,663 | |
| 39 | AWD (4WD) sdn 4d | 2,587 | 11,390 | |

| Taurus (106.0) | | | | |
|---|---|---|---|---|
| FC/HVS | L sdn 4d | 3,049 | 13,352 | 224,344 |
| FC/HVD | GL sdn 4d | — | 13,582 | |
| FC/HVB | LX sdn 4d | — | 17,373 | |
| FC/HVE | SHO sdn 4d | — | 22,071 | 9,136 |
| FF/HVS | L wgn 4d | 3,276 | 14,784 | 69,092 |
| FF/HVD | GL wgn 4d | — | 14,990 | |
| FF/HVB | LX wgn 4d | — | 18,963 | |

| Crown Victoria (wb 114.3) | | | | |
|---|---|---|---|---|
| FC/AB | sdn 4d | 3,822 | 18,227 | 81,667 |
| FC/AI | LX sdn 4d | — | 18,863 | |
| | wgn 4d | 4,028 | 18,083 | |
| | LX wgn 4d | — | 18,883 | 3,865 |
| | Country Squire wgn 4d | — | 18,335 | |
| | LX Country Squire wgn 4d | — | 19,085 | |

| 1991 Engines | bore×stroke | bhp | availability |
|---|---|---|---|
| I-4, 109.0 | 3.27×3.35 | 127 | S-Escort GT (dohc) |
| I-4, 114.0 | 3.23×3.46 | 88 | S-Escort |
| I-4, 133.3 | 3.39×3.70 | 110 | S-Probe GL/LX |
| I-4T, 133.3 | 3.39×3.70 | 145 | S-Probe GT |
| I-4, 141.0 | 3.70×3.30 | 98 | S-Tempo |
| I-4, 141.0 | 3.70×3.30 | 100 | O-Tempo |
| I-4, 153.0 | 3.70×3.60 | 105 | S-Taurus exc SHO |
| V-6, 182.0 | 3.50×3.15 | 140 | O-Taurus exc SHO |
| V-6, 182.0 | 3.50×3.10 | 145 | O-Probe |
| V-6, 182.0 | 3.50×3.15 | 220 | S-Taurus SHO (dohc) |
| V-6, 232.0 | 3.80×3.40 | 140 | O-Taurus exc SHO |
| V-8, 302.0 | 4.00×3.00 | 150 | S-Crown Victoria |
| V-8, 302.0 | 4.00×3.00 | 160 | O-Crown Victoria |
| V-8, 351.0 | 4.00×3.50 | 180 | O-Crown Victoria (police only) |

## 1992

| Escort (98.4) | | Wght | Price | Prod |
|---|---|---|---|---|
| 61/BM | Pony htchbk sdn 2d | 2,287 | 8,355 | 36,568 |
| 61/AI | LX htchbk sdn 2d | 2,312 | 9,055 | |
| 61/AX | GT htchbk sdn 2d | 2,458 | 11,871 | 14,241 |
| 54/AI | LX sdn 4d | 2,364 | 9,795 | 37,400 |
| 54/AX | LX-E sdn 4d | 2,464 | 11,933 | 6,771 |
| 58/AI | LX htchbk sdn 4d | 2,355 | 9,483 | 34,880 |
| 74/AI | LX wgn 4d | 2,411 | 10,067 | 39,749 |

| Probe (wb 99.0)—50,517 built | | | | |
|---|---|---|---|---|
| AF | GL htchbk cpe | 2,730 | 12,257 | — |
| AI | LX htchbk cpe | 3,000 | 13,257 | — |
| AX | GT htchbk cpe | 2,970 | 14,857 | — |

| Tempo (wb 99.9) | | | | |
|---|---|---|---|---|
| 66/HVB | GL sdn 2d | 2,532 | 9,987 | 37,364 |
| 66/HVD | GLS sdn 2d | 2,601 | 12,652 | |
| 54/HVB | GL sdn 4d | 2,600 | 10,137 | |
| 54/HVD | GLS sdn 4d | 2,659 | 12,800 | 301,606 |
| 54/HVC | LX sdn 4d | 2,626 | 11,115 | |

| Taurus (106.0) | | | | |
|---|---|---|---|---|
| FC/HVS | L sdn 4d | 3,111 | 14,980 | 286,090 |
| FC/HVD | GL sdn 4d | 3,117 | 15,280 | |
| FC/HVB | LX sdn 4d | 3,193 | 17,775 | |
| FC/HVE | SHO sdn 4d | 3,309 | 23,889 | 8,000 |
| FF/HVS | L wgn 4d | 3,262 | 16,013 | 73,964 |
| FF/HVD | GL wgn 4d | 3,264 | 16,290 | |
| FF/HVB | LX wgn 4d | 3,388 | 19,464 | |

| Crown Victoria (wb 114.3)—152,373 built | | | | |
|---|---|---|---|---|
| FC/AB | sdn 4d | 3,748 | 19,563 | — |
| FC/AI | LX sdn 4d | 3,769 | 20,887 | — |
| FC/A3 | Touring Sedan sdn 4d | 3,850 | 23,832 | — |

| 1992 Engines | bore×stroke | bhp | availability |
|---|---|---|---|
| I-4, 109.0 | 3.27×3.35 | 127 | S-Escort GT (dohc) |
| I-4, 114.0 | 3.23×3.46 | 88 | S-Escort |
| I-4, 133.3 | 3.39×3.70 | 110 | S-Probe GL/LX |
| I-4T, 133.3 | 3.39×3.70 | 145 | S-Probe GT (ohc) |
| I-4, 141.0 | 3.70×3.30 | 98 | S-Tempo exc GLS |
| I-4, 153.0 | 3.70×3.60 | 105 | S-Taurus exc SHO |
| V-6, 182.0 | 3.50×3.15 | 140 | O-Taurus exc SHO |
| V-6, 182.0 | 3.50×3.10 | 135 | S-Tempo GLS, O-other Tempo |
| V-6, 182.0 | 3.50×3.10 | 145 | O-Probe |
| V-6, 182.0 | 3.50×3.15 | 220 | S-Taurus SHO (dohc) |
| V-6, 232.0 | 3.80×3.40 | 140 | O-Taurus exc SHO |
| V-8, 281.0 | 3.60×3.60 | 190 | S-Crown Victoria |
| V-8, 281.0 | 3.60×3.60 | 210 | O-Crown Victoria |

## 1993

| Escort (98.4) | | Wght | Price | Prod |
|---|---|---|---|---|
| 61/BM | Std. htchbk sdn 2d | 2,285 | 8,355 | 104,827 |
| 61/AI | LX htchbk sdn 2d | 2,306 | 9,364 | |
| 61/AX | GT htchbk sdn 2d | 2,440 | 11,871 | |
| 54/AI | LX sdn 4d | 2,359 | 10,041 | 78,905 |
| 54/AX | LX-E sdn 4d | 2,440 | 11,933 | |
| 58/AI | LX htchbk sdn 4d | 2,354 | 9,797 | 66,021 |
| 74/AI | LX wgn 4d | 2,403 | 10,367 | 175,354 |

| Probe (wb 102.9)—89,701 built | | | | |
|---|---|---|---|---|
| AB | htchbk cpe | 2,619 | 12,845 | — |
| AX | GT htchbk cpe | 2,815 | 15,174 | — |

| Tempo (wb 99.9) | | | | |
|---|---|---|---|---|
| 66/HVB | GL sdn 2d | 2,511 | 10,267 | 56,250 |
| 54/HVB | GL sdn 4d | 2,569 | 10,267 | 182,043 |
| 54/HVC | LX sdn 4d | 2,613 | 12,135 | |

# Ford

| Taurus (106.0) | Wght | Price | Prod |
|---|---|---|---|
| FC/HVD GL sdn 4d | 3,083 | 15,491 | ⎤ 350,487 |
| FC/HVB LX sdn 4d | 3,201 | 18,300 | ⎦ |
| FC/HVE SHO sdn 4d | 3,354 | 24,829 | 21,991 |
| FF/HVDGL wgn 4d | 3,255 | 16,656 | ⎤ 86,231 |
| FF/HVBLX wgn 4d | 3,368 | 19,989 | ⎦ |

**Crown Victoria (wb 114.4)—108,201 built**

| | | | |
|---|---|---|---|
| FC/AB sdn 4d | 3,793 | 19,972 | — |
| FC/AI LX sdn 4d | 3,799 | 21,559 | — |

| 1993 Engines | bore×stroke | bhp | availability |
|---|---|---|---|
| I-4, 109.0 | 3.27×3.35 | 127 | S-Escort GT (dohc) |
| I-4, 114.0 | 3.23×3.46 | 88 | S-Escort |
| I-4, 122.0 | 3.27×3.62 | 115 | S-Probe (dohc) |
| I-4, 141.0 | 3.70×3.30 | 96 | S-Tempo |
| V-6, 153.0 | 3.33×2.92 | 164 | S-Probe GT (dohc) |
| V-6, 182.0 | 3.50×3.15 | 140 | S-Taurus exc SHO |
| V-6, 182.0 | 3.50×3.10 | 135 | O-Tempo |
| V-6, 182.0 | 3.50×3.15 | 220 | S-Taurus SHO (manual) (dohc) |
| V-6, 195.0 | 3.60×3.15 | 220 | S-Taurus SHO (automatic) (dohc) |
| V-6, 232.0 | 3.80×3.40 | 140 | O-Taurus exc SHO |
| V-8, 281.0 | 3.60×3.60 | 190 | S-Crown Victoria |
| V-8, 281.0 | 3.60×3.60 | 210 | O-Crown Victoria |

## 1994

| Escort (98.4) | Wght | Price | Prod* |
|---|---|---|---|
| 61/BM Std. htchbk sdn 2d | 2,304 | 9,035 | ⎤ |
| 61/AI LX htchbk sdn 2d | 2,325 | 9,890 | ⎥ 96,434 |
| 61/AX GT htchbk sdn 2d | 2,447 | 12,300 | ⎦ |
| 54/AK LX sdn 4d | 2,371 | 10,550 | 50,786 |
| 61/AI LX htchbk sdn 4d | 2,419 | 10,325 | 116,321 |
| 74/AI LX wgn 4d | 2,419 | 10,880 | 47,278 |

**Probe (wb 102.8)—83,872 built**

| AB | htchbk cpe | 2,690 | 13,685 | — |
|---|---|---|---|---|
| AX | GT htchbk cpe | 2,921 | 16,015 | — |

**Tempo (wb 99.9)**

| 66/HVB GL sdn 2d | 2,511 | 10,735 | 35,445 |
|---|---|---|---|
| 54/HVB GL sdn 4d | 2,569 | 10,735 | ⎤ 145,625 |
| 54/HVC LX sdn 4d | 2,613 | 12,560 | ⎦ |

**Taurus (106.0)**

| FC/HVD GL sdn 4d | 3,104 | 16,140 | ⎤ 225,532 |
|---|---|---|---|
| FC/HVB LX sdn 4d | 3,177 | 18,785 | ⎦ |
| FC/HVE SHO sdn 4d | 3,395 | 24,715 | 13,698 |
| FF/HVDGL wgn 4d | 3,272 | 17,220 | ⎤ 70,966 |
| FF/HVBLX wgn 4d | 3,349 | 20,400 | ⎦ |

**Crown Victoria (wb 114.4)—109,545 built**

| FC/AB sdn 4d | 3,786 | 19,300 | — |
|---|---|---|---|
| FC/AI LX sdn 4d | 3,794 | 20,715 | — |

*Includes production for export.

| 1994 Engines | bore×stroke | bhp | availability |
|---|---|---|---|
| I-4, 109.0 | 3.27×3.35 | 127 | S-Escort GT (dohc) |
| I-4, 114.0 | 3.23×3.46 | 88 | S-Escort |
| I-4, 122.0 | 3.27×3.62 | 115 | S-Probe (dohc) |
| I-4, 141.0 | 3.70×3.30 | 96 | S-Tempo |
| V-6, 153.0 | 3.33×2.92 | 164 | S-Probe GT (dohc) |
| V-6, 182.0 | 3.50×3.15 | 140 | S-Taurus exc SHO |
| V-6, 182.0 | 3.50×3.10 | 135 | O-Tempo exc SHO |
| V-6, 182.0 | 3.50×3.15 | 220 | S-Taurus SHO (manual) (dohc) |
| V-6, 195.0 | 3.60×3.15 | 220 | S-Taurus SHO (automatic) (dohc) |
| V-6, 232.0 | 3.80×3.40 | 140 | O-Taurus exc SHO |
| V-8, 281.0 | 3.60×3.60 | 190 | S-Crown Victoria |
| V-8, 281.0 | 3.60×3.60 | 210 | O-Crown Victoria |

## 1995

| Escort (98.4) | Wght | Price | Prod |
|---|---|---|---|
| P10 Std. htchbk sdn 2d | 2,316 | 9,580 | ⎤ |
| P11 LX htchbk sdn 2d | 2,355 | 10,435 | ⎥ 91,785 |
| P12 GT htchbk sdn 2d | 2,459 | 12,720 | ⎦ |
| P13 LX sdn 4d | 2,385 | 11,040 | 62,713 |
| P14 LX htchbk sdn 4d | 2,404 | 10,870 | 50,233 |
| P15 LX wgn 4d | 2,451 | 11,425 | 115,960 |

**Probe (wb 102.8)—52,226 built**

| T20 | htchbk cpe | 2,690 | 14,180 | — |
|---|---|---|---|---|
| T22 | GT htchbk cpe | 2,921 | 16,545 | — |

**Contour (wb 106.5)—178,832 built**

| P65 | GL sdn 4d | 2,769 | 13,310 | — |
|---|---|---|---|---|
| P66 | LX sdn 4d | — | 13,995 | — |
| P67 | SE sdn 4d | 3,040 | 15,695 | — |

**Taurus (106.0)**

| P52 GL sdn 4d | 3,118 | 17,585 | ⎤ |
|---|---|---|---|
| P52/SE SE sdn 4d | — | 18,630 | ⎥ 345,244 |
| P53 LX sdn 4d | — | 19,400 | ⎥ |
| P54 SHO sdn 4d | — | 25,140 | ⎦ |
| P57 GL wgn 4d | 3,285 | 18,680 | ⎤ 50,494 |
| P58 LX wgn 4d | — | 21,010 | ⎦ |

**Crown Victoria (wb 114.4)—98,309 built**

| P73 | sdn 4d | 3,762 | 20,160 | — |
|---|---|---|---|---|
| P74 | LX sdn 4d | — | 21,970 | — |

| 1995 Engines | bore×stroke | bhp | availability |
|---|---|---|---|
| I-4, 109.0 | 3.27×3.35 | 127 | S-Escort GT (dohc) |
| I-4, 114.0 | 3.23×3.46 | 88 | S-Escort |
| I-4, 121.0 | 3.34×3.46 | 125 | S-Cntr GL/LX(dohc) |
| I-4, 122.0 | 3.27×3.62 | 118 | S-Probe (dohc) |
| V-6, 153.0 | 3.33×2.92 | 164 | S-Probe GT (dohc) |
| V-6, 155.0 | 3.24×3.13 | 170 | S-Contour SE (dohc); O-Contour LX |
| V-6, 182.0 | 3.50×3.15 | 140 | S-Taurus exc SHO |
| V-6, 182.0 | 3.50×3.15 | 220 | S-Taurus SHO (manual) (dohc) |
| V-6, 195.0 | 3.60×3.15 | 220 | S-Taurus SHO (automatic) (dohc) |
| V-6, 232.0 | 3.80×3.40 | 140 | O-Taurus exc SHO |
| V-8, 281.0 | 3.60×3.60 | 190 | S-Crown Victoria |
| V-8, 281.0 | 3.60×3.60 | 210 | O-Crown Victoria |

## 1996

| Escort (wb 98.4) | Wght | Price | Prod |
|---|---|---|---|
| P10 htchbk sdn 2d | 2,323 | 10,065 | ⎤ |
| P11 LX htchbk sdn 2d | 3,356 | 10,910 | ⎥ 71,626 |
| P12 GT htchbk sdn 2d | 2,455 | 13,205 | ⎦ |
| P13 LX sdn 4d | 2,378 | 11,515 | 17,019 |
| P14 LX htchbk sdn 4d | 2,398 | 11,345 | 15,056 |

# Ford

| Escort (wb 98.4) | | Wght | Price | Prod |
|---|---|---|---|---|
| P15 | LX wgn sdn 4d | 2,444 | 11,900 | 42,708 |
| **Probe (wb 102.8)—30,125 built** | | | | |
| T20 | SE htchbk cpe | 2,690 | 13,930 | — |
| T22 | GT htchbk cpe | 2,921 | 16,450 | — |
| **Contour (wb 106.5)—186,263 built** | | | | |
| P65 | GL sdn 4d | 2,769 | 13,785 | — |
| P66 | LX sdn 4d | 2,815 | 14,470 | — |
| P67 | SE sdn 4d | 3,040 | 16,170 | — |
| **Taurus (wb 108.5)** | | | | |
| P51 | G sdn 4d | 3,329 | 17,995 | |
| P52 | GL sdn 4d | 3,326 | 18,600 | |
| P53 | LX sdn 4d | 3,358 | 20,980 | 378,577 |
| P54 | SHO sdn 4d | 3,544 | 25,140 | |
| P57 | GL wgn 4d | 3,480 | 19,680 | 60,672 |
| P58 | LX wgn 4d | 3,531 | 22,000 | |
| **Crown Victoria (wb 114.4)—115,547 built** | | | | |
| P73 | sdn 4d | 3,780 | 20,955 | |
| P74 | LX sdn 4d | 3,791 | 22,675 | |

| 1996 Engines | bore × stroke | bhp | availability |
|---|---|---|---|
| I-4, 109.0 | 3.27 × 3.35 | 127 | S-Escort GT (dohc) |
| I-4, 114.0 | 3.23 × 3.46 | 88 | S-Escort |
| I-4, 121.0 | 3.34 × 3.46 | 125 | S-Contour GL, LX |
| I-4, 122.0 | 3.27 × 3.62 | 118 | S-Probe |
| V-6, 153.0 | 3.33 × 2.92 | 164 | S-Probe GT |
| V-6, 155.0 | 3.24 × 3.13 | 170 | S-Contour SE |
| V-6, 181.0 | 3.50 × 3.10 | 200 | S-Taurus LX (dohc) |
| V-6, 182.0 | 3.50 × 3.15 | 145 | S-Taurus G, GL |
| V-8, 207.0 | 3.20 × 3.10 | 240 | S-Taurus SHO |
| V-8, 281.0 | 3.60 × 3.60 | 190 | S-Crown Victoria |
| V-8, 281.0 | 3.60 × 3.60 | 210 | O-Crown Victoria |

## 1997

| Escort (wb 98.4) | | Wght | Price | Prod |
|---|---|---|---|---|
| P10 | sdn 4d | 2,457 | 11,015 | 251,894 |
| P13 | LX sdn 4d | 2,503 | 11,515 | |
| P15 | LX wgn sdn 4d | 2,571 | 12,065 | 71,610 |
| **Probe (wb 102.8)—16,821 built** | | | | |
| T20 | htchbk cpe | 2,690 | 14,280 | — |
| T22 | GT htchbk cpe | 2,921 | 16,780 | — |
| **Contour (wb 106.5)—79,951 built** | | | | |
| P65 | sdn 4d | 2,769 | 13,460 | — |
| P65 | GL sdn 4d | 2,769 | 14,285 | — |
| P66 | LX sdn 4d | 2,769 | 14,915 | — |
| P67 | SE sdn 4d | 2,994 | 16,615 | — |
| **Taurus (wb 108.5)** | | | | |
| P51 | G sdn 4d | 3,329 | 17,995 | |
| P52 | GL sdn 4d | 3,329 | 18,985 | |
| P53 | LX sdn 4d | 3,326 | 21,610 | 384,844 |
| P54 | SHO sdn 4d | 3,440 | 26,460 | |
| P57 | GL wgn 4d | 3,480 | 20,195 | 13,958 |
| P58 | LX wgn 4d | 3,480 | 22,715 | |
| **Crown Victoria (wb 114.4)—123,833 built** | | | | |
| P73 | sdn 4d | 3,776 | 21,475 | — |
| P74 | LX sdn 4d | 3,780 | 23,195 | — |

| 1997 Engines | bore × stroke | bhp | availability |
|---|---|---|---|
| I-4, 121.0 | 3.34 × 3.46 | 110 | S-Escort |
| I-4, 121.0 | 3.34 × 3.46 | 125 | S-Cntr exc SE (dohc) |
| I-4, 122.0 | 3.27 × 3.62 | 118 | S-Probe |
| V-6, 153.0 | 3.33 × 2.92 | 164 | S-Probe GT |
| V-6, 155.0 | 3.24 × 3.13 | 170 | S-SE; O-Cntr GL/LX |
| V-6, 181.0 | 3.50 × 3.10 | 200 | S-Taurus LX (dohc) |
| V-6, 182.0 | 3.50 × 3.15 | 145 | S-Taurus G, GL |
| V-8, 207.0 | 3.20 × 3.10 | 235 | S-Taurus SHO |
| V-8, 281.0 | 3.60 × 3.60 | 190 | S-Crown Victoria |

## 1998

| Escort (wb 98.4)—331,860 built | | Wght | Price | Prod* |
|---|---|---|---|---|
| P10 | LX sdn 4d | 2,468 | 11,280 | — |
| P13 | SE sdn 4d | — | 12,580 | — |
| P15 | LX wgn sdn 4d | 2,531 | 13,780 | — |
| P11 | ZX2 Cool cpe 2d | 2,478 | 12,580 | — |
| P11 | ZX2 Hot cpe 2d | — | 13,080 | — |
| **Contour (wb 106.5)—147,783 built** | | | | |
| P66 | LX sdn 4d | 2,811 | 14,460 | — |
| P67 | SE sdn 4d | 3,030 | 15,785 | — |
| P68 | SVT sdn 4d | 3,068 | 22,405 | — |
| **Taurus (wb 108.5)—400,652 built** | | | | |
| P52 | LX sdn 4d | 3,353 | 18,245 | — |
| P52/60E | SE sdn 4d | 3,294 | 19,445 | — |
| P54 | SHO sdn 4d | — | 28,920 | — |
| P57 | SE wgn 4d | 3,457 | 21,105 | — |
| **Crown Victoria (wb 114.4)—134,905 built** | | | | |
| P73 | sdn 4d | 3,917 | 20,935 | — |
| P74 | LX sdn 4d | — | 23,135 | — |

| 1998 Engines | bore × stroke | bhp | availability |
|---|---|---|---|
| I-4, 121.0 | 3.34 × 3.46 | 110 | S-Escort exc ZX2 |
| I-4, 121.0 | 3.34 × 3.46 | 125 | S-Cont exc SVT (dohc) |
| I-4, 121.0 | 3.34 × 3.46 | 130 | S-Escort ZX2 (dohc) |
| V-6, 155.0 | 3.24 × 3.13 | 170 | O-Contour exc SVT |
| V-6, 155.0 | 3.24 × 3.13 | 195 | S-Contour SVT |
| V-6, 181.0 | 3.50 × 3.10 | 200 | O-Taurus exc SHO (dohc) |
| V-6, 182.0 | 3.50 × 3.15 | 145 | S-Taurus exc SHO |
| V-8, 207.0 | 3.20 × 3.10 | 235 | S-Taurus SHO |
| V-8, 281.0 | 3.60 × 3.60 | 200 | S-Crown Victoria |
| V-8, 281.0 | 3.60 × 3.60 | 215 | O-Crown Victoria |

*Calendar year production.

## 1999

| Escort (wb 98.4)—114,171 built | | Wght | Price | Prod* |
|---|---|---|---|---|
| P10 | LX sdn 4d | 2,468 | 11,455 | — |
| P13 | SE sdn 4d | — | 12,935 | — |
| P15 | LX wgn sdn 4d | 2,531 | 14,135 | — |
| P11 | ZX2 Cool cpe | 2,478 | 11,610 | — |
| P11 | ZX2 Hot cpe | — | 13,290 | — |
| **Contour (wb 106.5)—110,146 built** | | | | |
| P66 | LX sdn 4d | 2,769 | 14,460 | — |
| P67 | SE sdn 4d | — | 15,955 | — |
| P68 | SVT sdn 4d | — | 22,665 | — |
| **Taurus (wb 108.5)—380,337 built** | | | | |
| P52 | LX sdn 4d | 3,329 | 17,745 | — |
| P52/60E | SE sdn 4d | 3,353 | 18,445 | — |
| P54 | SHO sdn 4d | — | 29,000 | — |
| P57 | SE wgn 4d | 3,480 | 19,445 | — |
| **Crown Victoria (wb 114.4)—125,624 built** | | | | |
| P73 | sdn 4d | 3,917 | 21,905 | — |
| P74 | LX sdn 4d | 3,927 | 23,925 | — |

| 1999 Engines | bore × stroke | bhp | availability |
|---|---|---|---|
| I-4, 121.0 | 3.34 × 3.46 | 110 | S-Escort exc ZX2 |

# Ford

| 1999 Engines | bore × stroke | bhp | availability |
|---|---|---|---|
| I-4, 121.0 | 3.34 × 3.46 | 125 | S-Cont exc SVT (dohc) |
| I-4, 121.0 | 3.34 × 3.46 | 130 | S-Escort ZX2 (dohc) |
| V-6, 155.0 | 3.24 × 3.13 | 170 | O-Contour exc SVT |
| V-6, 155.0 | 3.24 × 3.13 | 200 | S-Contour SVT |
| V-6, 181.0 | 3.50 × 3.10 | 200 | O-Taurus exc SHO (dohc) |
| V-6, 182.0 | 3.50 × 3.15 | 145 | S-Taurus exc SHO |
| V-8, 207.0 | 3.20 × 3.10 | 235 | S-Taurus SHO |
| V-8, 281.0 | 3.60 × 3.60 | 200 | S-Crown Victoria |
| V-8, 281.0 | 3.60 × 3.60 | 215 | O-Crown Victoria |

*Calendar year production.

## 2000

| Escort (wb 98.4)—107,005 built | | Wght | Price | Prod* |
|---|---|---|---|---|
| P13 | sdn 4d | 2,468 | 12,070 | — |
| P11 | ZX2 cpe | 2,478 | 11,760 | — |
| **Focus (wb 103.0)** | | | | |
| P31 | ZX3 htchbk cpe | 2,551 | 11,865 | 63,538 |
| P33 | LX sdn 4d | 2,564 | 12,125 | |
| P34 | SE sdn 4d | 2,564 | 13,565 | 325,879 |
| P38 | ZTS sdn 4d | — | 15,165 | |
| P36 | SE wgn 4d | 2,717 | 15,380 | |
| **Contour (wb 106.5)—17,410 built** | | | | |
| P66 | Sport sdn 4d | 2,603 | 16,845 | — |
| P68 | SVT sdn 4d | 3,065 | 22,905 | — |
| **Taurus (wb 108.5)—440,678 built** | | | | |
| P52 | LX sdn 4d | 3,326 | 17,885 | — |
| P53 | SE sdn 4d | 3,355 | 18,935 | — |
| P55 | SES sdn 4d | 3,392 | 19,810 | — |
| P56 | SEL sdn 4d | 3,408 | 21,085 | — |
| P57 | SE wgn 4d | 3,519 | 20,090 | — |
| **Crown Victoria (wb 114.4)—102,911 built** | | | | |
| P73 | sdn 4d | 3,946 | 22,005 | — |
| P74 | LX sdn 4d | 3,968 | 24,120 | — |

| 2000 Engines | bore × stroke | bhp | availability |
|---|---|---|---|
| I-4, 121.0 | 3.34 × 3.46 | 110 | S-Esc sdn, Foc LX/SE |
| I-4, 121.0 | 3.34 × 3.46 | 130 | S-Escrt ZX2, Foc ZX3, ZTS; O-other Foc (dohc) |
| V-6, 155.0 | 3.24 × 3.13 | 170 | S-Contour Sport |
| V-6, 155.0 | 3.24 × 3.13 | 200 | S-Contour SVT |
| V-6, 181.0 | 3.50 × 3.10 | 200 | O-Taurus (dohc) |
| V-6, 182.0 | 3.50 × 3.15 | 155 | S-Taurus |
| V-8, 281.0 | 3.60 × 3.60 | 200 | S-Crown Victoria |
| V-8, 281.0 | 3.60 × 3.60 | 215 | O-Crown Victoria |

*Calendar year production.

## 2001

| ZX2 (wb 98.4) | | Wght | Price | Prod* |
|---|---|---|---|---|
| P11 | cpe 2d | 2,478 | 12,050 | 89,850 |
| **Focus (wb 103.0)** | | | | |
| P31 | ZX3 htchbk cpe | 2,551 | 12,125 | 55,529 |
| P33 | LX sdn 4d | 2,564 | 12,385 | |
| P34 | SE sdn 4d | 2,564 | 14,040 | 249,879 |
| P38 | ZTS sdn 4d | — | 15,260 | |
| P36 | SE wgn 4d | 2,717 | 16,235 | |
| **Taurus (wb 108.5)—350,076 built** | | | | |
| P52 | LX sdn 4d | 3,326 | 18,260 | — |
| P53 | SE sdn 4d | 3,355 | 19,035 | — |
| P55 | SES sdn 4d | 3,392 | 20,050 | — |

| Taurus (wb 108.5)—350,076 built | | Wght | Price | Prod |
|---|---|---|---|---|
| P56 | SEL sdn 4d | 3,408 | 21,535 | — |
| P57 | SE wgn 4d | 3,519 | 20,190 | — |
| **Crown Victoria (wb 114.4)—101,409 built** | | | | |
| P73 | sdn 4d | 3,946 | 22,005 | — |
| P74 | LX sdn 4d | 3,968 | 24,120 | — |

| 2001 Engines | bore × stroke | bhp | availability |
|---|---|---|---|
| I-4, 121.0 | 3.34 × 3.46 | 110 | S-Focus LX/SEs |
| I-4, 121.0 | 3.34 × 3.46 | 130 | S-ZX2, Focus ZX3, ZTS; O-other Foc (dohc) |
| V-6, 181.0 | 3.50 × 3.10 | 200 | O-Taurus (dohc) |
| V-6, 182.0 | 3.50 × 3.15 | 155 | S-Taurus (ohc) |
| V-8, 281.0 | 3.60 × 3.60 | 220 | S-Crown Victoria |
| V-8, 281.0 | 3.60 × 3.60 | 235 | O-Crown Victoria |

*Calendar year production.

## 2002

| ZX2 (wb 98.4) | | Wght | Price | Prod* |
|---|---|---|---|---|
| P11 | Deluxe cpe 2d | — | 13,545 | |
| P11 | Premium cpe 2d | — | 14,000 | |
| **Focus (wb 103.0)** | | | | |
| P31 | ZX3 htchbk cpe | 2,551 | 12,445 | |
| P31 | ZX3 Premium htchbk cpe | — | 13,540 | |
| P31 | ZX3 Power Premium htchbk cpe | — | 14,480 | |
| P39 | SVT htchbk cpe | 2,770 | 17,505 | |
| P33 | LX sdn 4d | 2,551 | 12,760 | |
| P33 | LX Premium sdn 4d | — | 13,605 | |
| P34 | SE sdn 4d | — | 14,350 | |
| P34 | SE Comfort sdn 4d | — | 14,695 | |
| P34 | SE Comfort/Zetec sdn 4d | — | 14,945 | |
| P38 | ZTS sdn 4d | — | 15,270 | |
| P37 | ZX5 htchbk sdn 4d | 2,600 | 15,645 | |
| P36 | SE wgn 4d | 2,551 | 16,555 | |
| P36 | SE Comfort wgn 4d | — | 16,900 | |
| P36 | ZTW wgn 4d | — | 17,735 | |
| **Taurus (wb 108.5)** | | | | |
| P52 | LX sdn 4d | 3,326 | 18,750 | |
| P53 | SE sdn 4d | 3,355 | 19,560 | |
| P55 | SES Standard sdn 4d | 3,392 | 20,575 | |
| P55 | SES Deluxe sdn 4d | — | 21,675 | |
| P56 | SEL Deluxe sdn 4d | 3,408 | 22,445 | |
| P56 | SEL Premium sdn 4d | — | 23,015 | |
| P58 | SE Standard wgn 4d | 3,519 | 21,495 | |
| P58 | SE Deluxe wgn 4d | — | 22,120 | |
| P58 | SE Premium wgn 4d | — | 22,810 | |
| P59 | SEL Deluxe wgn 4d | — | 22,695 | |
| **Crown Victoria (wb 114.4)** | | | | |
| P73 | sdn 4d | 3,942 | 22,855 | |
| P74 | LX sdn 4d | — | 26,445 | |
| P74 | LX Sport sdn 4d | — | 28,060 | |

| 2002 Engines | bore × stroke | bhp | availability |
|---|---|---|---|
| I-4, 121.0 | 3.34 × 3.46 | 110 | S-Focus LX/SE |
| I-4, 121.0 | 3.34 × 3.46 | 130 | S-ZX2, Focus ZX3, ZTS, ZTW; O-Foc (dohc) |
| I-4, 121.0 | 3.34 × 3.46 | 170 | S-Focus SVT (dohc) |
| V-6, 181.0 | 3.50 × 3.10 | 200 | O-Taurus (dohc) |
| V-6, 182.0 | 3.50 × 3.15 | 155 | S-Taurus |
| V-8, 281.0 | 3.60 × 3.60 | 220 | S-Crown Victoria |
| V-8, 281.0 | 3.60 × 3.60 | 235 | O-Crown Victoria |

*Figures not available at time of publication.

# Ford Mustang

Mustang, the original "ponycar," was Detroit's greatest single success of the '60s. Announced six months ahead of model-year 1965, it lifted Ford volume by well over half a million units and set an all-time record for first-year new-model sales. No fewer than 680,989 were sold between the April 1964 introduction (at the New York World's Fair) and August 1965 (when production switched to '66 models). Truckers accidentally drove through showroom windows while staring at them, housewives entered contests to win them, and dealers auctioned them off because demand initially exceeded supply by 15-to-1. No doubt about it: Everyone loved the Mustang.

Spearheading this remarkable achievement was Lee A. Iacocca, the plain-talking car salesman who in five years worked his way from an obscure Ford outpost in Pennsylvania to vice president and general manager of Ford Division. In 1970, he became president of Ford Motor Company, only to be fired eight years later by chairman Henry Ford II. As is now well known, that celebrated debacle sent Iacocca off to take over as board chairman at Chrysler Corporation, where he'd become a legend all over again.

The Mustang idea was simplicity itself: a low-cost "personal car" derived from a high-volume compact. People had pleaded with Ford to revive the two-seat Thunderbird ever since its demise in 1957. Iacocca and company briefly considered doing that very thing with the "XT-Bird" prototype proposed by the Budd Company in 1961. Ultimately, though, they opted for a new young-person's car that would seat four, be inexpensive to build, peppy, sporty-looking, and priced to sell for less than $2500. Projected volume was modestly pegged at 100,000 units a year.

The very first Mustang was a low, two-seat fiberglass roadster with a 90-inch wheelbase and midmounted 2.0-liter German Ford V-4 developing 90 horsepower. This experiment was pretty but impractical. After looking at those who drooled over it at auto shows, Iacocca concluded, "That's sure not the car we want to build, because it can't be a volume car. It's too far out." So dozens more prototypes were drawn, developed, and debated, culminating in the conventional, 108-inch-wheelbase production Mustang of "1964½." From a marketing standpoint, it couldn't have been better.

Through 1973, Mustang was offered as a hardtop coupe, convertible, and fastback coupe. Convertible sales started at the 100,000-unit annual level but dropped to less than 15,000 by 1969. The crisp notchback hardtop was the best-seller by far. The fastback, initially a seminotch style called 2+2, arrived in autumn 1964 with the rest of the '65 Ford line. It soon outsold the convertible, averaging about 50,000 a year through 1970.

Standard power at first came from the Falcon's sturdy and simple 170-cubic-inch 101-horsepower straight six; optional was the lively 260-cid "Challenger" V-8 from Ford's midsize Fairlane, good for 164 horsepower. After the first six months of production, engines switched to standard 200-cid six with 120 horsepower and bored-out 289 V-8 options with 200-271 horsepower. Increasingly hairy big-block engines were offered before government rules put an end to Ford's "Total Performance" program: for 1967 a 320-horsepower 390; for 1968 a 427 with 390 horsepower; for 1969 a 335-horsepower 428.

Much of Mustang's appeal stemmed from the myriad options allowing customers to personalize the car to taste. Depending on use of the order form, you could have a stylish economy car, a thunderingly fast drag racer, a deceptively nimble sporty car, or a small luxury liner. Transmission choices comprised automatic, three- and four-speed manuals, and stick-overdrive. Handling packages, power steering, front-disc brakes, air conditioning, and tachometer were all available. So was a bench seat in lieu of the standard front buckets, though few buyers opted for it. A GT package option delivered a pleasant assortment of goodies including firm suspension, full-gauge instru-

**1965 convertible coupe**

# Ford Mustang

**1965 GT 2+2 fastback coupe**

**1965 GT 2+2 fastback coupe**

ment panel, and special badges. A variety of interior trims was available, as were exterior accent stripes and special moldings.

The original Mustang was an inspired piece of design, the work of Joe Oros, L. David Ash, and Gale L. Halderman of the Ford Division styling studio. Its long-hood/short-deck proportions quickly became Detroit de rigueur, particularly for the imitators that soon became known, in Mustang's honor, as "ponycars." The basic '65 styling saw careful refinement in the first four years. The '66s changed only in detail. A deeper grille and sculptured side panels ending in twin simulated air scoops marked the '67s, when the 2+2 adopted a full-fastback roofline. The '68s had a revised grille with a bright inner ring around the galloping-horse emblem.

This relative sameness, plus increasing competition and a steady decline in ponycar demand took its toll in Mustang production. After an impressive 607,500 units for '66, volume dropped to 472,000 in 1967, then to 317,000 for '68.

Mustang was more extensively revised for 1969, becoming lower, longer, wider, and more-exaggerated. New features included ventless side glass, quad headlamps, and a more-imposing dash. A new Mach 1 fastback with firm suspension and standard 250-horsepower 351 V-8 joined the line at $3139. It stood apart from the standard "SportsRoof" via a special grille with driving lamps, matte-black center hood section with functional air scoop, quick-fill gas cap, and black honeycomb rear appliqué. Catering to the luxury market was a new Grandé hardtop priced at $2866 with standard six-cylinder engine and offering landau-style black or white vinyl roof, racing-type mirrors, special I.D., and bright wheel-well moldings.

Making an even bigger splash for mid-1969 was the fastback Boss 302, a $3588 roadgoing version of the Mustangs then cleaning up in the Sports Car Club of America's Trans-American racing series. Its exclusive 302 small-block delivered an alleged 290 horsepower, but actual output was more like 350. Only 1934 were built for '69, another 6319 for 1970. All had special striping, front "chin" spoiler, Mach 1-style rear wing, and distinctive rear-window louvers.

A horse of a different color was the big-block Boss 429. Tagged at $4798, it was stuffed full of Ford's "Cobra Jet" big-block wearing aluminum heads with semihemispherical combustion chambers. Only 858 were built for '69 and another 498 to 1970 specs. All were largely custom-crafted, as the front end required considerable reworking to accommodate the bulky 429.

The '69 package was mildly facelifted for 1970 with recessed taillamps and a return to dual headlamps, plus standard high-back bucket seats for all models (as on the '69 Mach 1). As before, available Mach 1 V-8s ran from a 351 to a four-barrel 428 with optional "Ram Air" induction. Convertibles were becoming quite scarce by now thanks to growing buyer preference for air conditioning and closed body styles. This year's total was off nearly 50 percent from 1969's, dropping from 14,700 to about 7700. Overall Mustang volume was down, too. The '69s garnered just under 300,000 sales; the '70s sank to a bit less than 191,000.

In late 1970, Ford abandoned most of its Trans-Am, USAC, NASCAR, and international competition efforts. Meantime, future Mustangs were being planned with an eye to the plunging market for hot cars in general, and ponycars in particular.

But that wasn't evident in the third-generation Mustang of 1971, conceived in the ponycar's late-'60s heyday. Heavily influenced by Semon E. "Bunkie" Knudsen, the GM executive who briefly served as Ford Motor Company president, it was intended to answer a frequent criticism of early ponycars—namely insufficient passenger room. The result was the most-changed Mustang yet: larger, heavier, and thirstier—as fat as Mustang would ever get. Though wheelbase grew only an inch, the '71 was eight inches longer overall, six inches wider, and close to

**1966 hardtop coupe**

**1966 convertible coupe**

# Ford Mustang

1967 convertible coupe

1967 GTA 2+2 fastback coupe

1967 hardtop coupe

1968 GT/SC (later California Special)

600 pounds heavier than the '65 original. Styling was more-massive, too, with busier sheetmetal; aggressive noses; and a sweeping, near-horizontal roofline on the "SportsRoof" 2+2 inspired by Ford's international GT endurance racers.

There was now plenty of room for big-block V-8s, so the performance-oriented Mach 1 now offered an optional 429 Cobra Jet packing 370 horsepower. But with the market's growing preference for luxury and convenience, this engine could now be ordered with air conditioning, power steering, tilt wheel, and other niceties. Yet a '71 Mustang could be blindingly quick. With automatic and 3.25:1 final drive, the 429 Mach 1 could do 0-60 mph in 6.5 seconds and the standing quarter-mile in 14.5 seconds.

A more-balanced '71 performer was the new Boss 351 fastback, replacing both previous Boss models. Though its efficient, highly tuned small-block delivered 330 horsepower and ample go, high price—$4124, nearly $1000 more than a Mach 1—limited sales and the model vanished after one year.

Other Mustangs fared little better. Total 1971 production dropped below 150,000 units, with the compact Maverick and other Ford products cannibalizing some sales. The '72s were little changed, but engine options were fewer, horsepower and performance were down, and Ford turned to promoting new colors and fabrics. One new package was the Sprint decor option sporting white paint set off by broad blue racing stripes edged in red; complementary colors were used inside, and mag wheels, raised-white-letter tires, and competition suspension were all available. But nothing seemed to help much, and production bottomed out at a bit over 125,000.

Mustang remained its hefty self for one more year and again saw little change. But Ford was well along on a more-practical successor by 1973—and more willing to admit its error. Said design vice president Eugene Bordinat: "We started out with a secretary's car and all of a sudden we had a behemoth." Most '73 changes were prompted by the latest federal regulations: 5-mph front bumpers (optional color-keyed covers helped keep them from looking like clumsy afterthoughts), rubber-sheathed control knobs, flame-retardant upholstery, and exhaust-gas recirculation to help curb emissions. Volume recovered to nearly 135,000 units, the increase perhaps coming from buyers who'd heard that a "downsized" Mustang was due and feared what it might be like.

Yet the all-new Mustang II of 1974 was a turning point for the original ponycar. Much trimmer and thriftier than the 1971-73 generation, it couldn't have been better timed, arriving just as the nation was being rocked by its first energy crisis. Sales boomed. With model-year production of nearly 400,000, the II came within 10 percent of equaling the original Mustang's first-year record.

Taking note of the growing popularity of sporty import coupes, Iacocca specified that the Mustang II have a wheelbase of 96-100 inches—it ended up at 96.2—plus a scaled-down version of the familiar long-hood/short-deck styling. Compared to the "fat" Mustangs, the II was 20 inches shorter, four inches narrower, an inch lower and a sizable 400-500 pounds lighter. Mustang II shared components with the subcompact Pinto and the Pinto gained some of Mustang's upgrades. Both had unit construction and a conventional short/long-arm coil-spring front suspension. But instead of being bolted directly to the main structure, the Mustang's lower arms attached to a rubber-mounted subframe that supported the rear of the engine/transmission assembly. This added to production costs, but was deemed necessary to provide more-precise steering and a smoother, quieter ride than Pinto. Also, Mustang II's rear leaf springs were longer than Pinto's, and its shock absorbers were staggered for better handling and grip. These and other refinements made for what Iacocca called "the little jewel."

There was no Mustang II convertible, but notchback and fastback coupe body styles continued. The former was now a fixed-pillar style, the latter a hatchback. And for the first time, there was no V-8, initial engine offerings being limited to a 2.3-liter inline four of 88 horsepower and a 2.8-liter V-6 (sourced from Ford Germany) with 105 horsepower (like other makes, Ford was by now quoting horsepower in more realistic SAE net measure, rather than gross). The V-6 was standard for a new hatchback Mach 1, which could do 0-60 mph in 13-14 seconds and reach 100 mph with the standard four-speed gearbox.

The Mustang II continued for five years without significant change. The Mach 1 as well as luxury four-cylinder and V-6 Ghia notchbacks were available throughout. So were numerous options, per Mustang tradition. Air conditioning, power steering and brakes, a raft of sound equipment, fancier trim, a vinyl top for notchbacks, sunroof, and forged-aluminum wheels were among the available items. For 1975, a sliding-glass moonroof and a luxury package became optional for the already posh Ghia.

Subsequent Mustang II sales never came near the 1974 level, but were a lot better than 1971-73. The total fell by over half for '75, to just short of 189,000, then held steady.

Ford made a gesture toward performance by reviving a V-8 option for '75. This was the workhorse 302 small-block, initially rated at 122 horsepower. Following at mid-'76 was a "Cobra

1969 Boss 302 fastback hardtop coupe prototype

1970 Boss 302 fastback hardtop coupe

1969 Mach 1 CJ 428 fastback hardtop coupe

1971 Boss 351 fastback hardtop coupe

1969 Grandé hardtop coupe

# Ford Mustang

1972 Sprint fastback hardtop coupe

1973 convertible coupe

1972 hardtop coupe

1973 Mach 1 fastback hardtop coupe

1974 Mustang II Mach 1 hatchback coupe

# Ford Mustang

II" trim package for hatchbacks. This comprised sports steering wheel, dual remote-control door mirrors, brushed-aluminum dash and door-panel appliqués, black grille, styled steel wheels, flip-out rear side windows with add-on louvers, front airdam, rear spoiler, and simulated hood scoop. Cobra II was first available only with blue stripes against white paint, then offered additional color combinations. It was flashy, but a far cry from the great Shelby Mustang it tried to ape. Ford again tried "paint-on performance" with the 1978 King Cobra. This package had many Cobra II items, plus a gaudy snake decal on the hood and tape stripes from stem to stern. You also got the 302, power steering, and a handling suspension with 70-series radial tires. A 17-second quarter-mile didn't make this a really hot car, but it was decent for its day.

Then came a new-generation Mustang for 1979, in many ways the best car ever to wear the galloping-horse emblem. From some angles, it looked vaguely like a BMW—clean, taut, and tight—and its surface execution, downswept nose, ample glass area, and lack of needless ornamentation combined the best of contemporary American and European design. It was the sort of restrained, efficient, and elegant ponycar Ford had built in the first place.

Many styling proposals were considered for the '79. The one that went into production originated with a team headed by Jack Telnack, then executive director of Ford North American Light Truck and Car Design, later corporate design chief. Greater use of lightweight materials—mainly plastics, low-alloy steel, and aluminum—made the '79 roughly 200 pounds lighter than a comparable Mustang II, despite the fact that the new car was larger in almost every dimension. A wheelbase lengthened to 100.4 inches upped rear legroom by five inches. Other interior measurements gained too: for example, shoulder room by 3.5/5.0 inches front/rear, cargo volume by two cubic feet.

The '79's new suspension was borrowed from the compact Fairmont/Zephyr, which meant modified MacPherson-strut geometry in front, four-bar-link live rear axle, antisway bars at both ends, and coil springs all around. A handling package with firmer springs and shocks and stiffer bushings was available with mandatory 14-inch tires. There was also a premium setup for maximum roadability via Michelin TRX tires, specially sized forged-aluminum wheels, and appropriately tuned chassis pieces. The 1979 engine lineup was expanded with a 140-horsepower turbocharged version of the standard four, good for 0-60 times of 10 seconds or so and fuel economy in the low to mid-20s. Late in the model year, the 200-cid six returned to supplant the V-6, which Ford's German subsidiary couldn't supply in adequate numbers.

Mustang paced the 1979 Indianapolis 500, and a pace-car replica was duly issued at midyear. For 1980, this model's slatted grille showed up on a revived Cobra package offering front and rear spoilers, integral fog lamps, nonfunctional hood scoop, and the TRX suspension. The 302 vanished, but a debored 255 small-block option with 118 horsepower was available for all models.

**1974 Mustang II "Grandé" prototype**

**1977 Mustang II hatchback coupe**

**1975 Mustang II Ghia V-8 notchback coupe**

**1978 Mustang II Ghia V-8 notchback coupe**

**1976 Mustang II Stallion hatchback coupe**

**1978 Mustang II King Cobra hatchback coupe**

# Ford Mustang

**1979 Cobra Turbo hatchback coupe**

**1979 Ghia notchback coupe**

Because the market was strong and Ford's ponycar all-new, Mustang's '79 volume was substantially above 1978's, soaring to just almost 370,000. After losing almost 100,000 for 1980, sales remained healthy through the Eighties in spite of difficult market conditions that loomed early and late in the decade, because Mustang only became more exciting as the '80s progressed, leading the way to the renaissance in Detroit performance we still enjoy at this writing.

Announcing this trend was a revived Mustang GT for 1982, a hatchback packing a reborn 302 with 157 horsepower. Looking much like the Cobra it replaced, though without the cartoonish body decoration, the GT came only with four-speed manual and was one of Detroit's hotter 1982 items. Arrayed below were L, GL, and GLX notchbacks and hatchbacks, all with carryover power save the turbo-four, which temporarily vanished. A five-speed overdrive manual, announced at mid-1980, remained optional with the normally aspirated base four.

Ford turned up the wick again for '83. A pretty facelift brought bigger taillamps and a more-aggressive face, but the big news was the first Mustang convertible in 10 years, offered only in top GLX trim. Performance fans applauded a more-potent 302 with a big four-barrel carb (instead of two-barrel) that boosted horsepower to 175. An improved blown four offered 142 horsepower in a new GT Turbo hatchback, but was nowhere near as satisfying as the smooth, torquey V-8 GT, so sales were very low. The nonturbo four and a new 232-cid V-6 (replacing the old straight six) were offered for slow-laners. Unlike some other reborn ragtops of these years, the Mustang was a "factory" job from the first, built by Ford itself. It was also quite practical for a convertible, with standard features like power top, glass rear window, and roll-down rear side windows.

Perhaps as a hedge against another energy crisis, Ford massaged its turbo-four even more for 1984, wrapping the result in a new performance Mustang, the SVO. Named for the company's Special Vehicle Operations unit, which engineered it, the SVO boasted 175 horsepower via electronic-port fuel injection and turbo intercooler, plus standard four-wheel disc brakes—a first for Mustang—and a fortified suspension with 16-inch wheels and meaty 225-section tires. Outside were a special grilleless nose and a "biplane" double-wing rear spoiler, which proved controversial. However, the SVO was much fussier to drive than the V-8 GT; worse, it was also a little slower yet cost over $5000 more, so demand was predictably limited. Ford per-

**1979 Cobra hatchback coupe**

sisted with the SVO through 1986, when the engine was coaxed to an impressive 200 horsepower, then gave up after total production of just 9844.

The rest of the '84 line was rearranged into two- and three-door L and LX models (the latter merging the previous GL and GLX) plus hatchback and convertible V-8 and Turbo GTs. The Turbos succumbed to slow sales a couple years before the SVO, disappearing after 1984. A second 302 with fuel injection and 165 horsepower was newly available for non-GTs or with automatic. Ford halfheartedly observed Mustang's 20th birthday with a modest paint-and-tape special called, for no particular reason, GT-350. Carroll Shelby, who by now had joined Lee Iaccoca at Chrysler, had used the title for his first modified Mustangs of 1965, and made a fuss over Ford's using it here.

For 1985, the cheap L models were dropped and remaining LX and GT Mustangs acquired new nose styling similar to the SVO. The high-output GT V-8 was booted to 210 horsepower via a wilder camshaft and low-friction roller valve lifters; similar changes lifted the injected 302 to 180 horsepower. The GT remained five-speed only, with revised internal ratios enhancing performance even further. Though a GT now cost some three times more in raw dollars than its predecessor of 20 years before, it was a far more-balanced performer. Better equipped, too. This year, for instance, it acquired beefier 60-series "gatorback" tires on seven-inch-wide cast-aluminum wheels, plus gas-pressurized front shocks.

The 1986 Mustang was little changed from the previous year. The main change was adoption of port fuel injection and lower compression for a single 302 V-8 rated at 200 horsepower and available with either five-speed or automatic. Ford's continuing attention to details was evident in such practical matters as a longer anticorrosion warranty, increased sound-deadening, and a single-key lock system.

The clean fifth-generation Mustang got its first major facelift for 1987 in Ford's by-now customary "aero" idiom, announced by new Euro-style flush-mounted headlamps. GT appearance ended up rather busy, with heavily sculptured rocker-panel extensions and multislot tail panel. The more-sedate-looking LXs could be ordered with most important GT features, including V-8 and handling suspension. The venerable 302 was more potent than ever, new cylinder heads and manifolding bringing an additional 25 horsepower. Strangely, the midrange V-6 option was canceled, leaving the old four as the only other engine choice. Still standard for LXs, this now had port injection, too. But with only 90 horsepower, it left a huge gap with V-8 performance.

Though Mustang ended the decade with no further changes of great consequence, offerings expanded for '89 to include a new "LX 5.0L" series—notchback, hatchback, and convertible that amounted to GTs in conservative LX dress. But wait: 1989 marked Mustang's 25th birthday. Time for another commemorative special, right? Well, no. Ford considered one, but was distracted by several issues—including Mustang enthusiasts who objected to the new domestically built Mazda-based 1989 Probe, which was originally devised to replace Mustang. But Ford didn't neglect the original ponycar, ponying up $200 million that year to upgrade the Mustang assembly plant in Dearborn.

And there was a commemorative of sorts in 3800 special Emerald Green V-8 LX convertibles offered from mid-January 1990—appropriate, as Ford always regarded the first Mustang as a '65 model, not a "1964½." It was a poor substitute for the

**1980 Cobra hatchback coupe**

**1984 SVO hatchback coupe**

**1982 GT 5.0 hatchback coupe**

**1986 GT 5.0 convertible coupe**

# Ford Mustang

**1988 GT 5.0 hatchback coupe**

**1990 LX 5.0 hatchback coupe**

much hotter Silver Anniversary special that had been rumored, but at least the Mustang we knew and loved was still alive—and destined for a ground-up redesign come 1994.

Meantime, Ford kept on upgrading the venerable fifth generation. The 1990 models gained a driver-side air bag in the steering-wheel hub to meet a new federal rule for front "passive restraints," plus door map pockets, clearcoat paint, and newly optional leather interior trim (as on the commemorative convertibles). Prices remained attractive: under $9500 for a four-cylinder LX two-door, less than $19,000 for the GT ragtop. Even so, production plunged to just over 128,000. The reason had less to do with Mustang's advancing age as a national economy being crippled again by recession.

Sales dropped under 99,000 for 1991, the lowest Mustang figure anyone could remember. Changes were again few. The anemic four was boosted to 105 horsepower via a new eight-plug cylinder head, but only rental-car fleet managers really cared. Convertible tops were redesigned to fold closer to the body, and the automatic transmission met another new federal edict by adding a safety interlock that required pushing the brake pedal to move the shifter out of Park. Prices rose a bit, the base LX two-door going just beyond $10,000, but V-8 convertibles again stickered below $20,000.

A few more details were changed for '92, when Mustang sales hit an all-time model-year low of 79,280. An optional four-way power driver's seat arrived, but extra-cost whitewalls and wire-wheel covers departed, a blow for good taste.

With the economy perking up by model-year '93, Mustang sales rebounded to around 114,200—which was a bit surprising. For one thing, GM had a swoopy new Camaro/Firebird with 275 horsepower from the latest 5.7-liter Corvette V-8, while Ford had to downgrade the Mustang V-8 to more "realistic" ratings of 205 horsepower and 275 pound-feet Even without that, the fifth generation should have lost sales in this final year. Perhaps the arrival of the new '94 was an incentive to buy for all the many folks who still loved the old warhorse.

Ford provided its own incentive with a hot hatchback that might have appeared with 25th Anniversary badges. But it wore the Cobra name and snake insignia of Carroll Shelby's legendary '60s sports cars, mainly so Ford could keep its legal claim to both from expiring for lack of use. *Road & Track* called it the "best of an aging breed," and by most measures it was. Developed by Dearborn's new Special Vehicle Team (SVT, successor to SVO), the '93 Cobra packed 235 horsepower from a tweaked 302 with special big-port "GT40" heads, tuned-runner intake manifold, revised cam, and other muscle-building improvements. Torque, a stout 280 pound-feet, was delivered by a beefier (and mandatory) manual five-speed and massive 245/45ZR17 performance tires. Standard rear disc brakes were a first for a volume Mustang, and there was more "balanced"

suspension tuning that went against conventional wisdom with softer damping and a smaller front stabilizer. Outside were a neater nose, taillamps from the late SVO, seven-blade alloy wheels, oversized rear spoiler—and, finally, the return of the nostalgic running-horse grille emblem. In all, it was a speedy, sophisticated package.

Did we say speedy? *R&T*'s Cobra clocked 5.9 seconds 0-60 mph, 14.5 at 98 mph in the standing quarter-mile, and under 16 seconds 0-100. As for sophisticated, *Car and Driver*'s Don Schroeder termed this "a nicer-riding, more-supple car [than the GT]. Although it can feel less buttoned down . . . the Cobra makes better use of its tires and rewards coordinated hands and feet with clearly higher limits and cornering speeds. . . ."

Although cynics viewed the '93 Cobra as a ploy to keep Ford's old ponycar from being overshadowed by GM's new ones, it was grand send-off for the grand old fifth generation. And with only some 5000 built, the Cobra stands to be the most collectible of this long-lived breed.

Except for exactly 107 Cobra R models. Recalling a 1965-66 Shelby variation, the "R" meant "racing." Upgrades involved competition-grade front brakes, cooling system and chassis tuning, plus bigger wheels and tires, and strategic structural reinforcements. Omitting the stock Cobra's back seat, air conditioning, and power accessories saved 60 pounds—not much on the road but critical on the track. Ford sold every R-model for the full $25,692 sticker price, versus about $20-grand for a regular Cobra, itself a bona fide bargain.

But it was finally time to move on, and a mostly new Mustang rode in for 1994 on a tidal wave of anticipation and nostalgia. Announcement ads pictured it with the classic '65 to declare, "It is what it was." Actually, it almost wasn't at all.

The uproar over the Probe had shown that ponycar diehards wouldn't take a Japanese-style substitute. Trouble was, demand for "real" ponycars was lagging again by the early '90s, leading some in Dearborn to question if another new Mustang might ever be needed. Even if it were, Ford had more-profitable product fish to fry, and the refurbished old Mustangs were still selling decently well, so why rush? With that, planning floundered for a good two years while the car's future was debated. Then Ford learned GM was abandoning a planned front-drive Camaro/Firebird for a new rear-drive 1993 concept. Corporate pride demanded a proper reply, and Ford authorized work on a new Mustang in 1991.

Because Ford had become a much leaner outfit, and with the "team concept" now gospel in Detroit, SN95 (as the project was dubbed) developed quite differently from earlier Mustangs. The big departure was forming a fairly small, independent multidiscipline group to herd the new pony from drawing board to showroom. Money matters dictated a slim $700 million budget, with only $200 million for design and engineering. The deadline was equally tight: just 36 months.

Echoing earlier Mustangs was the trio of mock-ups considered for production styling. All had the requested "retro" appearance cues, including a big galloping steed for the grille, plus a smooth, muscular, slightly wedgy shape in Ford's now-expected "aero" idiom. Tamest of the three was the "Bruce Jenner," a "trim, athletic" design that scored low in clinics for looking too "soft." At the other extreme was "Rambo," an aggressively exaggerated version that failed as such. This left the in-between "Arnold Schwarzenegger" proposal to carry the day. All three finalists were modeled as notchback coupes. Though a new convertible was never in doubt, Americans no longer cared much for hatchbacks, so that body style was forgotten despite its importance to fifth-generation Mustang sales.

Interior designers also strove for a "classic" feel while building in new government-mandated safety features like dual air bags and anti-intrusion door beams. What emerged was the usual 2+2 package with a wildly sculpted "twin-cowl" instrument panel paying faint homage to the '60s. Body engineers worked hard to increase rigidity without appreciable weight gain, and they largely succeeded. Against the previous notchback, the SN95 coupe was some 56-percent stiffer in bending and 44 percent in torsion; comparable convertible numbers were 76 percent and an amazing 150 percent. Despite these impressive improvements, curb weights were only some 280 pounds higher than for equivalent '93 models.

Time and money precluded a new chassis, so SN95 made do with a much-modified version of the old '79 platform dubbed "Fox-4" with somewhat softer damping, numerous geometry changes, and an extra 1.8 inches in wheelbase. Wheel/tire packages were upgraded. So were brakes, with larger front discs, newly standard rear discs, a bigger booster, and Bosch antilock control as a first-time option. Powerteams were familiar fare. Base models, no longer called LX, lost the anemic four in favor of the 3.8-liter V-6 last offered in '86 Mustangs, though tuned for 145 horsepower. The LX 5.0L package was also dropped, leaving V-8 power the sole property of GT models. Though the venerable small-block was little changed from '93, it somehow gained 10 horsepower and a like number of pound-feet of torque, probably by the stroke of an engineer's pen. Transmissions again comprised five-speed manual or optional four-speed automatic, but the latter was Ford's latest "AOD-E" unit with electronic shift control.

Overall, the '94 Mustang seemed the same kind of thorough makeover already accorded the big Crown Victoria and Lincoln Town Car. Still, some were disappointed that the long-awaited new model wasn't all-new, especially as prices were higher to the point of "sticker shock." The base coupe, for instance, rose $2646 to $13,365, though that included a bigger engine, better brakes and dual air bags, plus a tilt steering wheel and power driver-side seat, both options before. The GT coupe was up $1533 to $17,280, though it, too, boasted all the '94 improvements, plus expected standards like fog lights, rear spoiler, and sport seats. At least the base convertible looked a fine value at $20,160, and the GT edition was a reasonable $21,970. Both ragtops were again factory-built with standard power roof and glass rear window, which now included a rear defogger. An optional 80-pound lift-off hardtop was announced as a $1500 convertible option, but was never actually sold due to production glitches.

To Ford's undoubted dismay, the rejuvenated Mustang earned decidedly mixed reviews. While road-testers rightly lauded the many improvements, there was general head-scratching over the GT's 60-horsepower deficit with the latest Camaro Z28 and Firebird Trans Am. "The carryover power may challenge the loyalty of some...fans," mused Car and Driver, "[though] with substantial improvements in braking and body structure, the Mustang [GT still] offers tremendous performance for the dollar." As if to prove the point, C/D's five-speed coupe clocked 0-60 mph in just 6.1 seconds and the standing quarter-mile in 14.9 at 93 mph—not bad for a 30-year-old engine. The automatic version was no slouch either, Consumer Guide®'s coupe doing 0-60 in a brisk 7.4 seconds.

Still, the power/performance gap with GM suggested sights had not been set very high. Indeed, Dearborn admitted the '94 was designed mainly to please the 6.1 million people who'd

**1991 LX 5.0L convertible**

**1995 Cobra R coupe**

**1993 Cobra hatchback coupe**

**1996 Cobra coupe**

# Ford Mustang

bought Mustangs since day one. From a sales viewpoint, that wasn't a bad plan. As *Motor Trend* observed: "Mustang fans have been deprived of a new platform for so long they would've accepted almost anything with a chrome horse on it." And of course, they did accept it—certainly more enthusiastically than some of the press. And why not? They had, after all, helped design it. As a thank you, Ford hosted regional parties for Mustang clubs on Sunday, April 17, 1994, exactly 30 years since the original Mustang's smash debut.

But the celebrating didn't end there. Again recalling '60s doings, Ford got a special Cobra convertible named the '94 Indianapolis 500 pace car. Sure enough, Dearborn wasn't conceding the power issue entirely to GM, and by model year's end it had built 6009 new-design Cobras, 5009 coupes, and 1000 ragtops—the latter sold as replica Pace Cars.

Another SVT project, the '94 Cobra wore a unique front fascia, low-profile rear spoiler, chrome 17-inch five-spoke wheels with ultrawide Z-rated tires, discreet front-fender snake emblems, and a leather-lined interior with snazzy white-faced gauges. Underneath were bigger brakes with twin front calipers and standard ABS, a GT suspension again made slightly softer for "controlled compliance" handling, and a 302 V-8 massaged for . . . 240 horsepower. Motor-noters heaved more sighs. Even this new Cobra was still 35 horses shy of a V-8 Camaro/Firebird.

*Car and Driver* found the performance gap narrowed, but not much. Though its five-speed coupe turned 5.9 seconds 0-60 and the standing-quarter in 14.7 at 96 mph, both times were a good half-second adrift of a Z28's. The Cobra "is undoubtedly the most muscular Mustang available," *C/D* declared, "and at $21,240 for the coupe and $24,010 for the convertible, the most expensive. At those prices . . . we have a hard time imagining that a new breed of customers will be flocking into SVT showrooms [some 750 carefully selected Ford dealers]."

But if Mustang remained runner-up in a drag race, it still easily won the sales race. In fact, with model-year output of just over 137,000, the '94 Mustang came close to outselling Camaro and Firebird combined. Ford also built more ponycars for the calendar year: some 199,000 versus GM's 192,000. Only a bit less impressive, Mustang's showing represented a 16-percent gain on 1993, itself a good year despite the new GM competition.

Mustang showed no real changes for '95, but the lineup expanded at midyear with the GTS, essentially a GT coupe with base-model trimmings and a friendlier $16,910 price. The year also saw a revival of the Cobra R. A 351-cid V-8 (last used in Mustangs in '73) good for 300 horsepower and 365 pound-feet of torque under a domed hood announced the 250 or so built primarily for competition.

Underhood changes grabbed the Mustang headlines in 1996. The GT's long-serving pushrod V-8, an evolution of the engine that had been used in Mustangs from the beginning, was replaced by Ford's 4.6-liter "modular" sohc unit. No changes to horsepower or torque figures were reported, so the GT's overall performance with the new iron-block, aluminum-head engine remained on par with the '95 version. The new powerplant was noticeably smoother than its predecessors, however. At the same time, the base V-6 engine received a five-horsepower boost, bringing it up to 150 horsepower. A mesh insert in the front air intake and new taillamps, said to evoke memories of the original Mustang's vertical three-segment lights, were the sole exterior changes.

The SVT Cobra models received a derivative of the "modular" V-8 as well, using an aluminum block and a forged crankshaft. Twincam cylinder heads were fitted, making for a well-filled engine bay. The resulting 305 horsepower (a gain of 90 ponies over the sohc GT and 65 more than the '95 Cobra) and

**1996 GT convertible**

**1997 Cobra coupe**

**1997 GT convertible**

**1998 Cobra coupe**

**1999 35th Anniversary Edition convertible**

# Ford Mustang

1999 Cobra convertible

1999 coupe

2000 convertible

2000 Cobra convertible

2001 GT coupe

300 pound-feet of torque brought SVT's pony level with the hottest Camaros and Firebirds. Something of a character transformation was involved here; the dohc Cobra thrived on high rpm—"Anything under about 3500 rpm is bogging-down territory," wrote one tester—with a consequent need to make more use of the 5-speed transmission.

Despite a few moans from the automotive press about the lack of noticeable gains from the engine swap, the standard Mustang retained its popularity with customers, as it would continue to do, even without any substantial mechanical or design changes, during the next two model years. Engineers pulled an extra 10 horsepower out of the 4.6 engine for the '98 GT without tangible results, and SVT began to offer what were called "Off-highway" parts—including a supercharger kit—to speed-seeking customers through Ford dealers, but that was about all.

For 1999, Mustang was given a brand-new skin. Described as "Ford's New Edge goes retro" by *Road & Track*, the freshened exterior combined traditional Mustang styling cues with design elements then being applied to other cars in the Ford family. Hitherto-rounded corners were sharpened to knife-edge crispness, air inlets whether real (the grille and intake below the front bumper) or fake (on the hood and in front of the rear wheel arches) were emphasized. Head and taillamps were reshaped to suit. Almost everything save the galloping-horse emblem in the grill got a makeover.

To their credit, the Mustang crew didn't blow their entire budget on the visuals. Fully boxed chassis rails increased structural stiffness, while rerated coil springs improved the GT version's handling. More power was on the agenda for '99, and in useful doses: the V-6 got a wake-up call; a new intake manifold, freer-flowing cylinder heads, and reduced-friction pistons contributed to the 3.8-liter engine's 190-horsepower rating. A balance shaft was also added to the base powerplant, and this was almost as welcome for its contributions to smoothness as the other mods were for their power boost.

Revisions to the GT's engine included improvements to induction and exhaust systems and new camshafts, boosting it to 260 horsepower. Electronic traction control, a combination of rear-brake application and engine-power reduction to minimize wheel spin joined the GT's optional-equipment list.

Reaction to the new Mustang echoed sentiments expressed in 1994, though fewer mutterings were heard about a lack of power. The new exterior was polarizing; critics were vocal about the design's shortcomings but, once again, the public kept on buying. That, as usual, was what counted.

SVT added its own bit of wizardry to the reskinned pony. Independent rear suspension had been on and off of the Mustang rumor circuit since 1965. For the '99 Cobra it became a reality with a coil-spring/locating-arm setup that was a triumph of inventiveness over budgeting: only the addition of two bolt holes with "weld nuts" were needed to incorporate it into the existing floor pan and body structure. Preassembled, the unit could be installed on the regular Mustang assembly line. Half-shafts and locating arms were Mustang-specific, while the differential and its housing were sourced from the discontinued Lincoln Mark VIII.

Handling benefits were subtle, and best-appreciated during hard driving, something for which the Cobra was well-suited. Paradoxically, the SVT Mustang continued to offer a slightly softer and more-compliant ride than the standard GT, as it had since the first examples were introduced in 1993. In all, the Mustang was celebrating its 35th anniversary in style.

The only damper on the celebration was the Cobra's engine. Some Cobras put out far less than the rated 230 horsepower, which was caused by faulty intake parts. As a result, no Cobras

# Ford Mustang

(except Cobra Rs) were built for 2000, and Ford repaired the '99s at no charge. The R was a lightened Cobra packing a 385-horsepower 5.4-liter V-8. Only 300 were built, all in red, starting at $54,995.

Changes for 2000 were minimal. Base models were finally granted an appearance package that gave them most of the look (as well as the wheels and tires) of the GT mode. ABS was made standard on the GT.

A healthy Cobra was back for 2001 and a "Bullitt" package was available for that year. The 6500 Dark Highland Park Green (or, for the less sentimental, blue or black) cars were an homage to the 1968 movie of the same name in which Steve McQueen, driving a dark-green Mustang 390 fastback, participated in one of the most-exciting car chases ever recorded on film. Bullitt was more than an appearance package: beneath the understated exterior (no rear wing, a minimum of trim, unique—though still fake—side scoops, special C-pillar and rocker-panel moldings, and a brushed-aluminum fuel-filler door) and interior (special seats trimmed in leather, brushed-aluminum shift knob, special door-sill plates, aluminum pedal covers and unique instrument graphics) were some particularly nice powertrain and chassis upgrades.

A larger throttle body, cast-aluminum intake manifold, small accessory-drive pulleys, and a free-flowing exhaust system added 10 horses to the GT's 260-horsepower rating while broadening the torque curve noticeably. Improvements to the engine's sound and feel were subtle, but noticeable. The Bullitt's ride height was lowered three-quarters of an inch. Unique strut/shock absorber units, antiroll bars, and what Ford termed "frame rail connectors" gave the Bullitt ride and handling qualities that were easily the best of any non-Cobra Mustangs. Thirteen-inch front brake discs with red-painted calipers gave impressive stopping power. Dealers reportedly had no trouble selling the entire Bullitt production run at (or above) the $26,830 sticker price. Cobra disappeared again for 2002, in preparation for an early release of the 2003. An Eaton supercharger with intercooler is expected to push the Cobra's power output to 390 horsepower at 6000 rpm. Torque goes up as well, to 390 pound-feet at 3500 rpm. For durability reasons, the engine block reverts to cast-iron instead of aluminum, and other internal improvements will be made to cope with increased pressure. A 6-speed manual transmission will be standard in all '03 Cobras.

Few major changes are expected for the standard and GT Mustangs before the current version is replaced—said to be in 2006, at which time the venerable Fox-based platform shared by all Mustangs since 1979 will finally disappear.

As the original ponycar heads toward its 40th year of production, its last two direct competitors—the Chevrolet Camaro and Pontiac Firebird—are due to be retired at the end of the 2002 model year. Try as they might, the GM duo were never able to topple Mustang from its perch as the premier American sporty car. Even without opposition, Ford seems determined not to let their icon wither away. Let's hope the enthusiasm, both within Ford and among Mustang's loyal and ever-increasing cadre of fans, continues.

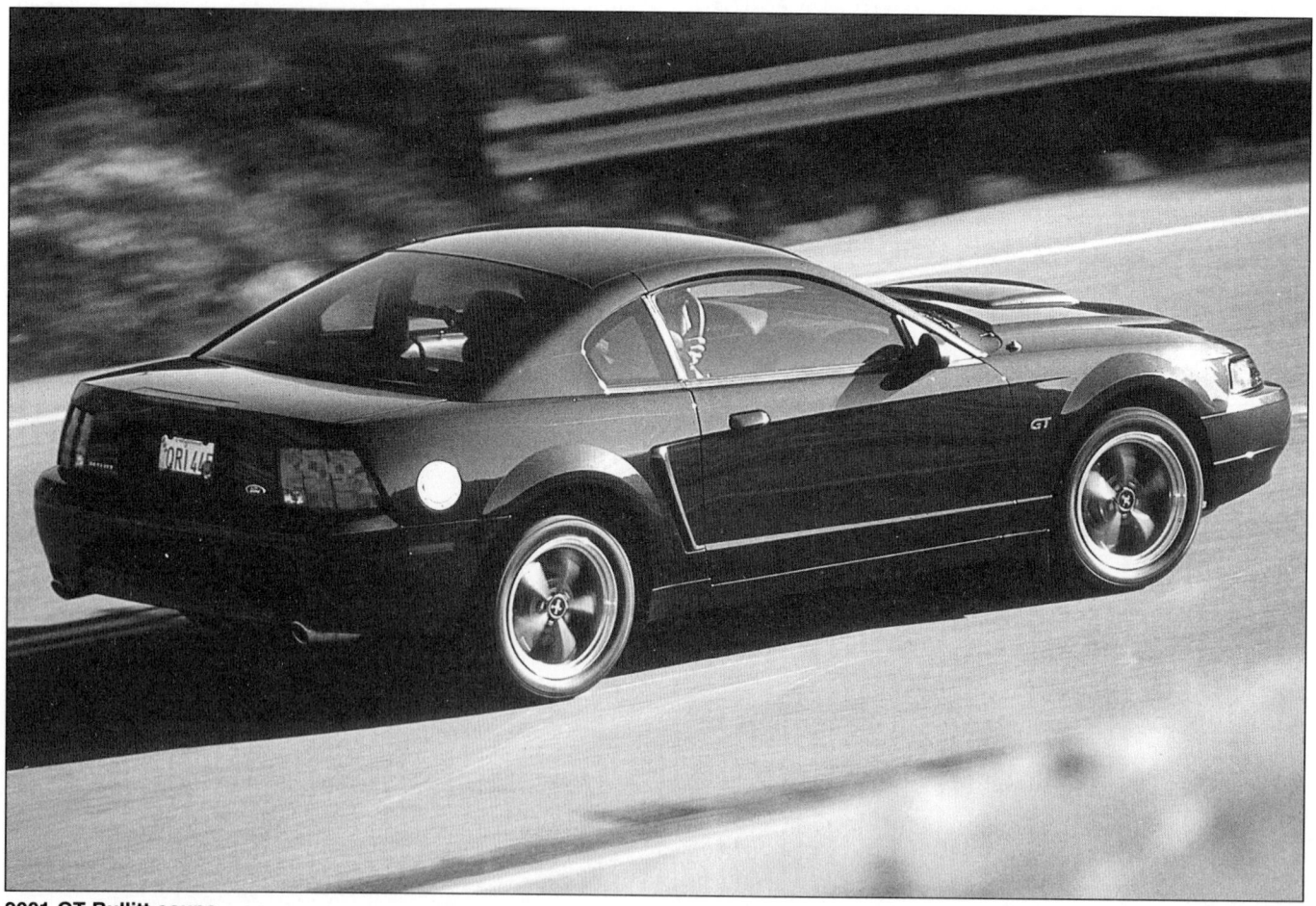

**2001 GT Bullitt coupe**

# Ford Mustang

**2002 coupe**

**2002 GT convertible**

## Specifications

### 1965

| (wb 108.0) | | Wght | Price | Prod |
|---|---|---|---|---|
| 07 | htp cpe | 2,583 | 2,372 | 501,965 |
| 08 | conv cpe | 2,789 | 2,614 | 101,945 |
| 09 | fstbk cpe | 2,633 | 2,589 | 77,079 |

| 1965 Engines | bore × stroke | bhp | availability |
|---|---|---|---|
| I-6, 170.0 | 3.50 × 2.94 | 101 | S-all through 9/24/64 |
| I-6, 200.0 | 3.68 × 3.13 | 120 | S-all after 9/24/64 |
| V-8, 260.0 | 3.80 × 2.87 | 164 | O-all through 9/24/64 |
| V-8, 289.0 | 4.00 × 2.87 | 200 | O-all after 9/24/64 |
| V-8, 289.0 | 4.00 × 2.87 | 225/271 | O-all |

Note: 1965 production totals include 121,538 early (1964½) models.

### 1966

| (wb 108.0) | | Wght | Price | Prod |
|---|---|---|---|---|
| 01 | htp cpe | 2,488 | 2,416 | 499,751 |
| 02 | fstbk cpe | 2,519 | 2,607 | 35,698 |
| 03 | conv cpe | 2,650 | 2,653 | 72,119 |

| 1966 Engines | bore × stroke | bhp | availability |
|---|---|---|---|
| I-6, 200.0 | 3.68 × 3.13 | 120 | S-all |
| V-8, 289.0 | 4.00 × 2.87 | 200 | O-all |
| V-8, 289.0 | 4.00 × 2.87 | 225/271 | O-all |

### 1967

| (wb 108.0) | | Wght | Price | Prod |
|---|---|---|---|---|
| 01 | htp cpe | 2,568 | 2,461 | 356,271 |
| 02 | fstbk cpe | 2,605 | 2,592 | 71,042 |
| 03 | conv cpe | 2,738 | 2,698 | 44,808 |

| 1967 Engines | bore × stroke | bhp | availability |
|---|---|---|---|
| I-6, 200.0 | 3.68 × 3.13 | 120 | S-all |
| V-8, 289.0 | 4.00 × 2.87 | 200 | O-all |
| V-8, 289.0 | 4.00 × 2.87 | 225/271 | O-all |
| V-8, 390.0 | 4.05 × 3.78 | 320 | O-all |

### 1968

| (wb 108.0) | | Wght | Price | Prod |
|---|---|---|---|---|
| 01 | htp cpe | 2,635 | 2,602 | 249,447 |
| 02 | fstbk cpe | 2,659 | 2,712 | 42,581 |
| 03 | conv cpe | 2,745 | 2,814 | 25,376 |

| 1968 Engines | bore × stroke | bhp | availability |
|---|---|---|---|
| I-6, 200.0 | 3.68 × 3.13 | 115 | S-all |
| I-6, 250.0 | 3.68 × 3.91 | 155 | O-all (late) |
| V-8, 289.0 | 4.00 × 2.87 | 195 | O-all |
| V-8, 302.0 | 4.00 × 3.00 | 220 | O-all |
| V-8, 390.0 | 4.05 × 3.78 | 335 | O-all |
| V-8, 427.0 | 4.23 × 3.78 | 390 | O-all |
| V-8, 428.0 | 4.13 × 3.98 | 335 | O-all (late) |

### 1969

| (wb 108.0) | | Wght | Price | Prod |
|---|---|---|---|---|
| 01 | htp cpe | 2,798 | 2,635 | 128,458 |
| 02 | fstbk cpe | 2,822 | 2,635 | 60,046 |
| 02 | Boss 302 fstbk cpe, V-8 | 3,210 | 3,588 | 1,934 |
| 02 | Boss 429 fstbk cpe, V-8 | — | 4,798 | 858 |
| 03 | conv cpe | 2,908 | 2,849 | 14,746 |
| 04 | Grandé htp cpe | 2,873 | 2,866 | 22,182 |
| 05 | Mach 1 fstbk cpe | 3,175 | 3,139 | 72,458 |

| 1969 Engines | bore × stroke | bhp | availability |
|---|---|---|---|
| I-6, 200.0 | 3.68 × 3.13 | 115 | S-all exc Mach 1, Boss |
| I-6, 250.0 | 3.68 × 3.91 | 155 | O-all exc Mach 1, Boss |
| V-8, 302.0 | 4.00 × 3.00 | 220 | O-all exc Mach 1, Boss |
| V-8, 302.0 | 4.00 × 3.00 | 290 | S-Boss 302 |
| V-8, 351.0 | 4.00 × 3.50 | 250 | S-Mach 1; O-others exc Boss |
| V-8, 351.0 | 4.00 × 3.50 | 290 | O-all |
| V-8, 390.0 | 4.05 × 3.78 | 320 | O-all |
| V-8, 428.0 | 4.13 × 3.98 | 335 | O-Mach 1 (Ram Air avail) |
| V-8, 429.0 | 4.36 × 3.59 | 360/375 | S-Boss 429 |

### 1970

| (wb 108.0) | | Wght | Price | Prod |
|---|---|---|---|---|
| 01 | htp cpe | 2,822 | 2,721 | 82,569 |
| 02 | fstbk cpe | 2,846 | 2,771 | 39,316 |
| 02 | Boss 302 fstbk cpe, V-8 | 3,227 | 3,720 | 6,319 |
| 02 | Boss 429 fstbk cpe, V-8 | — | 4,798 | 498 |
| 03 | conv cpe | 2,932 | 3,025 | 7,673 |
| 04 | Grandé htp cpe | 2,907 | 2,926 | 13,581 |
| 05 | Mach 1 cpe | 3,240 | 3,271 | 40,970 |

# Ford Mustang

| 1970 Engines | bore × stroke | bhp | availability |
|---|---|---|---|
| I-6, 200.0 | 3.68 × 3.13 | 115 | S-all exc Mach 1, Boss |
| I-6, 250.0 | 3.68 × 3.91 | 155 | O-all exc Mach 1, Boss |
| V-8, 302.0 | 4.00 × 3.00 | 220 | O-all exc Mach 1, Boss |
| V-8, 302.0 | 4.00 × 3.00 | 290 | S-Boss 302 |
| V-8, 351.0 | 4.00 × 3.50 | 250 | S-Mach 1; O-others exc Boss |
| V-8, 351.0 | 4.00 × 3.50 | 300 | O-all exc Boss |
| V-8, 428.0 | 4.13 × 3.98 | 335 | O-Mach 1 (Ram Air avail) |
| V-8, 429.0 | 4.36 × 3.59 | 375 | S-Boss 429, O-Mach 1 |

## 1971

| (wb 109.0) | | Wght | Price | Prod |
|---|---|---|---|---|
| 01 | htp cpe | 2,982 | 2,911 | 65,696 |
| 02 | fstbk cpe | 2,950 | 2,973 | 23,956 |
| 02 | Boss 351 fstbk cpe V-8 | 3,281 | 4,124 | |
| 03 | conv | 3,102 | 3,227 | 6,121 |
| 04 | Grandé htp cpe | 3,006 | 3,117 | 17,406 |
| 05 | Mach 1 fstbk cpe V-8 | 3,220 | 3,268 | 36,499 |

| 1971 Engines | bore × stroke | bhp | availability |
|---|---|---|---|
| I-6, 250.0 | 3.68 × 3.91 | 145 | S-all exc Mach 1, Boss 351 |
| V-8, 302.0 | 4.00 × 3.00 | 210 | O-all exc Boss 351 |
| V-8, 351.0 | 4.00 × 3.50 | 240 | O-all exc Boss 351 |
| V-8, 351.0 | 4.00 × 3.50 | 285 | O-all exc Boss 351 |
| V-8, 351.0 | 4.00 × 3.50 | 330 | S-Boss 351; O-others |
| V-8, 429.0 | 4.36 × 3.59 | 370 | O-all |

## 1972

| (wb 109.0) | | Wght | Price | Prod |
|---|---|---|---|---|
| 01 | htp cpe | 2,983 | 2,729 | 57,350 |
| 02 | fstbk cpe | 2,952 | 2,786 | 15,622 |
| 03 | conv | 3,099 | 3,015 | 6,401 |
| 04 | Grandé htp cpe | 3,008 | 2,915 | 18,045 |
| 05 | Mach 1 fstbk cpe V-8 | 3,046 | 3,053 | 27,675 |

| 1972 Engines | bore × stroke | bhp | availability |
|---|---|---|---|
| I-6, 250.0 | 3.68 × 3.91 | 99 | S-all exc Mach 1 |
| V-8, 302.0 | 4.00 × 3.00 | 141 | S-Mach 1; O-others |
| V-8, 351.0 | 4.00 × 3.50 | 177/275 | O-all |

## 1973

| (wb 109.0) | | Wght | Price | Prod |
|---|---|---|---|---|
| 01 | htp cpe | 3,040 | 2,760 | 51,480 |
| 02 | fstbk cpe | 3,053 | 2,820 | 10,820 |
| 03 | conv | 3,171 | 3,102 | 11,853 |
| 04 | Grandé htp cpe | 3,059 | 2,946 | 25,274 |
| 05 | Mach 1 fstbk cpe V-8 | 3,115 | 3,088 | 35,440 |

| 1973 Engines | bore × stroke | bhp | availability |
|---|---|---|---|
| I-6, 250.0 | 3.68 × 3.91 | 95 | S-all exc Mach 1 |
| V-8, 302.0 | 4.00 × 3.00 | 136 | S-Mach 1; O-others |
| V-8, 351.0 | 4.00 × 3.50 | 154/156 | O-all |

## 1974

| II (wb 96.2) | | Wght | Price | Prod |
|---|---|---|---|---|
| 02 | cpe 2d | 2,654 | 3,134 | 177,671 |
| 03 | htchbk cpe 3d | 2,734 | 3,328 | 74,799 |
| 04 | Ghia cpe 2d | 2,820 | 3,480 | 89,477 |
| 05 | Mach 1 htchbk cpe 3d V-6 | 2,778 | 3,674 | 44,046 |

| 1974 Engines | bore × stroke | bhp | availability |
|---|---|---|---|
| I-4, 140.0 | 3.78 × 3.13 | 88 | S-all exc Mach 1 |
| V-6, 170.0 | 3.66 × 2.70 | 105 | S-Mach 1; O-others |

## 1975

| II (wb 96.2) | | Wght | Price | Prod |
|---|---|---|---|---|
| 02 | cpe 2d | 2,718 | 3,529 | 85,155 |
| 03 | htchbk cpe 3d | 2,754 | 3,818 | 30,038 |
| 04 | Ghia cpe 2d | 2,762 | 3,938 | 52,320 |
| 05 | Mach 1 htchbk cpe 3d V-6 | 2,879 | 4,188 | 21,062 |

| 1975 Engines | bore × stroke | bhp | availability |
|---|---|---|---|
| I-4, 140.0 | 3.78 × 3.13 | 83 | S-all exc Mach 1 |
| V-6, 170.0 | 3.66 × 2.70 | 97 | S-Mach 1; O-others |
| V-8, 302.0 | 4.00 × 3.00 | 122 | O-all |

## 1976

| II (wb 96.2) | | Wght | Price | Prod |
|---|---|---|---|---|
| 02 | cpe 2d | 2,717 | 3,525 | 78,508 |
| 03 | htchbk cpe 3d | 2,745 | 3,781 | 62,312 |
| 04 | Ghia cpe 2d | 2,768 | 3,859 | 37,515 |
| 05 | Mach 1 htchbk cpe V-6 3d | 2,822 | 4,209 | 9,232 |

| 1976 Engines | bore × stroke | bhp | availability |
|---|---|---|---|
| I-4, 140.0 | 3.78 × 3.13 | 92 | S-all exc Mach 1 |
| V-6, 170.0 | 3.66 × 2.70 | 103 | S-Mach 1; O-others |
| V-8, 302.0 | 4.00 × 3.00 | 134 | O-all |

## 1977

| II (wb 96.2) | | Wght | Price | Prod |
|---|---|---|---|---|
| 02 | cpe 2d | 2,688 | 3,702 | 67,783 |
| 03 | htchbk cpe 3d | 2,734 | 3,901 | 49,161 |
| 04 | Ghia cpe 2d | 2,728 | 4,119 | 29,510 |
| 05 | Mach 1 htchbk cpe V-6 3d | 2,785 | 4,332 | 6,719 |

| 1977 Engines | bore × stroke | bhp | availability |
|---|---|---|---|
| I-4, 140.0 | 3.78 × 3.13 | 89 | S-all exc Mach 1 |
| V-6, 170.0 | 3.66 × 2.70 | 93 | S-Mach 1; O-others |
| V-8, 302.0 | 4.00 × 3.00 | 139 | O-all |

## 1978

| II (wb 96.2) | | Wght | Price | Prod |
|---|---|---|---|---|
| 02 | cpe 2d | 2,656 | 3,555 | 81,304 |
| 03 | htchbk cpe 3d | 2,702 | 3,798 | 68,408 |
| 04 | Ghia cpe 2d | 2,694 | 3,972 | 34,730 |
| 05 | Mach 1 htchbk cpe V-6 3d | 2,733 | 4,253 | 7,968 |

| 1978 Engines | bore × stroke | bhp | availability |
|---|---|---|---|
| I-4, 140.0 | 3.78 × 3.13 | 88 | S-all exc Mach 1 |
| V-6, 170.0 | 3.66 × 2.70 | 90 | S-Mach 1; O-others |
| V-8, 302.0 | 4.00 × 3.00 | 139 | O-all |

# Ford Mustang

### 1979

| (wb 100.4) | | Wght | Price | Prod |
|---|---|---|---|---|
| 02 | cpe 2d | 2,471 | 4,071 | 156,666 |
| 03 | htchbk cpe 3d | 2,491 | 4,436 | 120,535 |
| 04 | Ghia cpe 2d | 2,579 | 4,642 | 56,351 |
| 05 | Ghia htchbk cpe 3d | 2,588 | 4,824 | 36,384 |

| 1979 Engines | bore × stroke | bhp | availability |
|---|---|---|---|
| I-4, 140.0 | 3.78 × 3.13 | 88 | S-all |
| I-4T, 140.0 | 3.78 × 3.13 | 140 | O-all |
| V-6, 170.0 | 3.66 × 2.70 | 109 | O-all |
| I-6, 200.0 | 3.68 × 3.13 | 91 | O-all (late) |
| V-8, 302.0 | 4.00 × 3.00 | 140 | O-all |

### 1980

| (wb 100.4) | | Wght | Price | Prod |
|---|---|---|---|---|
| 02 | cpe 2d | 2,514 | 4,884 | 128,893 |
| 03 | htchbk cpe 3d | 2,548 | 5,194 | 98,497 |
| 04 | Ghia cpe 2d | 2,582 | 5,369 | 23,647 |
| 05 | Ghia htchbk cpe 3d | 2,606 | 5,512 | 20,285 |

| 1980 Engines | bore × stroke | bhp | availability |
|---|---|---|---|
| I-4, 140.0 | 3.78 × 3.13 | 88 | S-all |
| I-4T, 140.0 | 3.78 × 3.13 | 140 | O-all |
| I-6, 200.0 | 3.68 × 3.13 | 91 | O-all |
| V-8, 255.0 | 2.68 × 3.00 | 118 | O-all |

### 1981

| (wb 100.4) | | Wght | Price | Prod |
|---|---|---|---|---|
| 10 | cpe 2d | 2,537 | 6,171 | 77,458 |
| 15 | htchbk cpe 3d | 2,557 | 6,408 | 77,399 |
| 12 | Ghia cpe 2d | 2,571 | 6,645 | 13,422 |
| 13 | Ghia htchbk cpe 3d | 2,606 | 6,729 | 14,273 |

| 1981 Engines | bore × stroke | bhp | availability |
|---|---|---|---|
| I-4, 140.0 | 3.78 × 3.13 | 88 | S-all |
| I-4T, 140.0 | 3.78 × 3.13 | 140 | O-all |
| I-6, 200.0 | 3.68 × 3.13 | 88/94 | O-all |
| V-8, 255.0 | 3.68 × 3.00 | 115 | O-all |

### 1982

| (wb 100.4) | | Wght | Price | Prod |
|---|---|---|---|---|
| 10 | L cpe 2d | 2,568 | 6,345 | 45,316 |
| 10 | GL cpe 2d | 2,585 | 6,844 | |
| 16 | GL htchbk cpe 3d | 2,622 | 6,979 | 45,901 |
| 16 | GT htchbk cpe 3d V-8 | 2,597 | 8,308 | 23,447 |
| 12 | GLX cpe 2d | 2,600 | 6,980 | 5,828 |
| 13 | GLX htchbk cpe 3d | 2,636 | 7,101 | 9,926 |

| 1982 Engines | bore × stroke | bhp | availability |
|---|---|---|---|
| I-4, 140.0 | 3.78 × 3.13 | 88 | S-all |
| I-6, 200.0 | 3.68 × 3.13 | 88 | O-all |
| V-8, 255.0 | 3.68 × 3.00 | 120 | O-all |
| V-8, 302.0 | 4.00 × 3.00 | 157 | S-GT; O-all |

### 1983

| (wb 100.4) | | Wght | Price | Prod |
|---|---|---|---|---|
| 26 | L cpe 2d | 2,684 | 6,727 | |
| 26/60C | GL cpe 2d | 2,743 | 7,264 | 33,201 |
| 26/602 | GLX cpe 2d | 2,760 | 7,398 | |
| 28/60C | GL htchbk cpe 3d | 2,788 | 7,439 | |
| 28/602 | GLX htchbk cpe 3d | 2,801 | 7,557 | 64,234 |
| 28/932 | GT htchbk cpe 3d V-8 | 2,969 | 9,328 | |
| 28/932 | Turbo GT htchbk cpe 3d | — | 9,714 | |
| 27/602 | GLX conv cpe V-6 | 2,807 | 12,467 | 23,438 |
| 27/932 | GT conv cpe V-8 | — | 13,479 | |

| 1983 Engines | bore × stroke | bhp | availability |
|---|---|---|---|
| I-4, 140.0 | 3.78 × 3.13 | 90 | S-all exc conv, GTs |
| I-4T, 140.0 | 3.78 × 3.13 | 142 | S-Turbo GT |
| V-6, 232.0 | 3.80 × 3.40 | 112 | S-conv; O-all exc GTs |
| V-8, 302.0 | 4.00 × 3.00 | 175 | S-GT; O-others exc Turbo GT |

### 1984

| (wb 100.4) | | Wght | Price | Prod |
|---|---|---|---|---|
| 26 | L cpe 2d | 2,736 | 7,098 | 37,780 |
| 26/602 | LX cpe 2d | 2,757 | 7,290 | |
| 28 | L htchbk cpe 3d | 2,782 | 7,269 | |
| 28/602 | LX htchbk cpe 3d | 2,807 | 7,496 | |
| 28/932 | GT htchbk cpe 3d V-8 | 3,013 | 9,578 | 86,200 |
| 28/932 | Turbo GT htchbk cpe 3d | 2,869 | 9,762 | |
| 28/939 | SVO turbo htchbk cpe 3d | 2,992 | 15,596 | |
| 27/602 | LX conv cpe V-6 | 3,020 | 11,849 | |
| 27/932 | GT conv cpe V-8 | 3,124 | 13,051 | 17,600 |
| 27/932 | Turbo GT conv cpe | 3,004 | 13,245 | |

| 1984 Engines | bore × stroke | bhp | availability |
|---|---|---|---|
| I-4, 140.0 | 3.78 × 3.13 | 88 | S-all exc conv, GTs/SVO |
| I-4T, 140.0 | 3.78 × 3.13 | 145 | S-Turbo GT |
| I-4T, 140.0 | 3.78 × 3.13 | 175 | S-SVO |
| V-6, 232.0 | 3.80 × 3.40 | 120 | S-conv; O-all exc GTs, SVO |
| V-8, 302.0 | 4.00 × 3.00 | 165 | O-all exc GTs, SVO |
| V-8, 302.0 | 4.00 × 3.00 | 175 | S-GT |

### 1985

| (wb 100.4) | | Wght | Price | Prod |
|---|---|---|---|---|
| 26/602 | LX cpe 2d | 2,657 | 6,885 | 56,781 |
| 28/602 | LX htchbk cpe 3d | 2,729 | 7,345 | |
| 28/932 | GT htchbk cpe 3d V-8 | 3,063 | 9,885 | 84,623 |
| 28/939 | SVO turbo htchbk cpe 3d | 2,991 | 14,521 | |
| 27/602 | LX conv cpe V-6 | 2,907 | 11,985 | 15,110 |
| 27/932 | GT conv cpe V-8 | 3,165 | 13,585 | |

| 1985 Engines | bore × stroke | bhp | availability |
|---|---|---|---|
| I-4, 140.0 | 3.78 × 3.13 | 88 | S-all exc conv, GT, SVO |
| I-4T, 140.0 | 3.78 × 3.13 | 175 | S-SVO |
| V-6, 232.0 | 3.80 × 3.40 | 120 | S-conv; O-all exc GT, SVO |
| V-8, 302.0 | 4.00 × 3.00 | 180 | O-all exc SVO |
| V-8, 302.0 | 4.00 × 3.00 | 210 | S-GT |

### 1986

| (wb 100.4) | | Wght | Price | Prod |
|---|---|---|---|---|
| 26 | LX cpe 2d | 2,795 | 7,189 | 106,720 |
| 27 | LX conv cpe V-6 | 3,044 | 12,821 | |
| 27 | GT conv cpe V-8 | 3,269 | 14,523 | |
| 28 | LX htchbk cpe 3d | 2,853 | 7,744 | 117,690 |
| 28 | GT htchbk cpe V-8 | 3,139 | 10,691 | |
| 28/937 | SVO turbo htchbk cpe 3d | 3,140 | 15,272 | |

# Ford Mustang

| 1986 Engines | bore × stroke | bhp | availability |
|---|---|---|---|
| I-4, 140.0 | 3.78 × 3.13 | 88 | S-all exc conv, GTs, SVO |
| I-4T, 140.0 | 3.78 × 3.18 | 200 | S-SVO |
| V-6, 232.0 | 3.80 × 3.40 | 120 | S-conv; O-all exc GT, SVO |
| V-8, 302.0 | 4.00 × 3.00 | 200 | S-GT |

## 1987

| (wb 100.5)—159,145 built | | Wght | Price | Prod |
|---|---|---|---|---|
| 40 | LX cpe 2d | 2,862 | 8,043 | 64,704* |
| 44 | LX conv cpe | 3,059 | 12,840 | |
| 45 | GT conv cpe V-8 | 3,214 | 15,724 | |
| 41 | LX htchbk cpe 3d | 2,920 | 8,474 | 94,441* |
| 42 | GT htchbk cpe V-8 | 3,080 | 11,835 | |

*Some industry sources state that 58,100 two-doors, 80,717 hatchbacks, and 20,328 convertibles were built.

| 1987 Engines | bore × stroke | bhp | availability |
|---|---|---|---|
| I-4, 140.0 | 3.78 × 3.13 | 90 | S-LX |
| V-8, 302.0 | 4.00 × 3.00 | 225 | S-GT; O-LX |

## 1988

| (wb 100.4)—211,225 built | | Wght | Price | Prod |
|---|---|---|---|---|
| 40 | LX cpe 2d | 2,894 | 8,726 | — |
| 44 | LX conv cpe | 3,081 | 13,702 | — |
| 45 | GT conv cpe V-8 | 3,341 | 16,610 | — |
| 41 | LX htchbk cpe 3d | 2,961 | 9,221 | — |
| 42 | GT htchbk cpe V-8 | 3,193 | 12,745 | — |

| 1988 Engines | bore × stroke | bhp | availability |
|---|---|---|---|
| I-4, 140.0 | 3.78 × 3.13 | 90 | S-LX |
| V-8, 302.0 | 4.00 × 3.00 | 225 | S-GT; O-LX |

## 1989

| (wb 100.4)—209,769 built* | | Wght | Price | Prod |
|---|---|---|---|---|
| 40 | LX cpe 2d I-4 | 2,754 | 9,050 | — |
| 40 | LX 5.0L cpe 2d V-8 | 3,045 | 11,410 | — |
| 44 | LX conv cpe I-4 | 2,966 | 14,140 | — |
| 44 | LX 5.0L conv cpe V-8 | 3,257 | 17,001 | — |
| 45 | GT conv cpe V-8 | 3,333 | 17,512 | — |
| 41 | LX htchbk cpe 3d I-4 | 2,819 | 9,556 | — |
| 41 | LX 5.0L htchbk 3d V-8 | 3,110 | 12,265 | — |
| 42 | GT htchbk cpe V-8 | 3,194 | 13,272 | — |

*Total includes 42,244 convertibles.

| 1989 Engines | bore × stroke | bhp | availability |
|---|---|---|---|
| I-4, 140.0 | 3.78 × 3.13 | 90 | S-LX |
| V-8, 302.0 | 4.00 × 3.00 | 225 | S-GT, LX 5.0L |

## 1990

| (wb 100.4)—128,189 built* | | Wght | Price | Prod |
|---|---|---|---|---|
| 40 | LX cpe 2d I-4 | 2,759 | 9,456 | — |
| 40 | LX 5.0L cpe 2d V-8 | — | 12,164 | — |
| 44 | LX conv cpe I-4 | 2,960 | 15,141 | — |
| 44 | LX 5.0L conv cpe V-8 | — | 18,183 | — |
| 45 | GT conv cpe V-8 | — | 18,805 | — |
| 41 | LX htchbk cpe 3d I-4 | 2,824 | 9,962 | — |
| 41 | LX 5.0L htchbk 3d V-8 | — | 13,007 | — |
| 42 | GT htchbk cpe V-8 | — | 13,986 | — |

*Total includes 26,958 convertibles.

| 1990 Engines | bore × stroke | bhp | availability |
|---|---|---|---|
| I-4, 140.0 | 3.78 × 3.13 | 88 | S-LX |
| V-8, 302.0 | 4.00 × 3.00 | 225 | S-GT, LX 5.0L |

## 1991

| (wb 100.5) | Wght | Price | Prod |
|---|---|---|---|
| 66/HVS LX cpe 2d | 2,759 | 10,157 | 19,447 |
| 66/HVS LX 5.0L cpe 2d | — | 13,270 | |
| 61/HVS LX cpe 3d | 2,824 | 10,663 | 57,777 |
| 61/HVS LX 5.0L cpe 3d | — | 14,055 | |
| 61/HVB GT cpe 3d | — | 15,034 | |
| 66/HVS (B2L) LX conv cpe 2d | 2,960 | 16,222 | 21,513 |
| 66/HVS (B2I) LX 5.0L conv cpe 2d | — | 19,242 | |
| 66/HVS (B2L) GT conv cpe 2d | — | 19,864 | |

| 1991 Engines | bore × stroke | bhp | availability |
|---|---|---|---|
| I-4, 140.0 | 3.78 × 3.12 | 105 | S-LX |
| V-8, 302.0 | 4.00 × 3.00 | 225 | S-LX 5.0, GT |

## 1992

| (wb 100.5) | Wght | Price | Prod |
|---|---|---|---|
| 66/HVS LX cpe 2d | 2,775 | 10,215 | 15,717 |
| 66/HVS LX 5.0L cpe 2d | 3,010 | 13,422 | |
| 61/HVS LX cpe 3d | 2,834 | 10,721 | 40,093 |
| 61/HVS LX 5.0L cpe 3d | 3,069 | 14,207 | |
| 61/HVB GT cpe 3d | 3,144 | 15,243 | |
| 66/HVS (B2L) LX conv cpe 2d | 2,996 | 16,899 | 23,470 |
| 66/HVS (B2I) LX 5.0L conv cpe 2d | 3,231 | 19,644 | |
| 66/HVS (B2L) GT conv cpe 2d | 3,365 | 20,199 | |

| 1992 Engines | bore × stroke | bhp | availability |
|---|---|---|---|
| I-4, 140.0 | 3.78 × 3.12 | 105 | S-LX |
| V-8, 302.0 | 4.00 × 3.00 | 225 | S-LX 5.0, GT |

## 1993

| (wb 100.5) | Wght | Price | Prod |
|---|---|---|---|
| 66/HVS LX cpe 2d | 2,751 | 10,719 | 24,851 |
| 66/HVS LX 5.0L cpe 2d | 3,035 | 13,926 | |
| 61/HVS LX cpe 3d | 2,812 | 11,224 | 56,978 |
| 61/HVS LX 5.0L cpe 3d | 3,096 | 14,710 | |
| Cobra cpe 3d | 3,255 | 19,990 | 5,099 |
| 61/HVB GT cpe 3d | 3,144 | 15,747 | |
| 66/HVS (B2L) LX conv cpe 2d | 2,973 | 17,548 | 27,300 |
| 66/HVS (B2I) LX 5.0L conv cpe 2d | 3,259 | 20,293 | |
| 66/HVS (B2L) GT conv cpe 2d | 3,365 | 20,848 | |

| 1993 Engines | bore × stroke | bhp | availability |
|---|---|---|---|
| I-4, 140.0 | 3.78 × 3.12 | 105 | S-LX |
| V-8, 302.0 | 4.00 × 3.00 | 205 | S-LX 5.0, GT |
| V-8, 302.0 | 4.00 × 3.00 | 235 | S-Cobra |

## 1994

| (wb 101.3) | | Wght | Price | Prod |
|---|---|---|---|---|
| 63 | cpe 2d | 3,065 | 13,365 | 84,010 |
| 63 | GT cpe 2d | 3,276 | 17,280 | |
| | Cobra cpe 2d | 3,365 | 20,765 | 5,009 |
| 76 | conv cpe 2d | 3,245 | 20,160 | 47,055 |
| 76 | GT conv cpe 2d | 3,452 | 21,970 | |
| | Cobra conv cpe 2d | 3,567 | 23,535 | 1,000 |

| 1994 Engines | bore × stroke | bhp | availability |
|---|---|---|---|
| V-6, 232.0 | 3.80 × 3.40 | 145 | S-base |
| V-8, 302.0 | 4.00 × 3.00 | 215 | S-GT |
| V-8, 302.0 | 4.00 × 3.00 | 240 | S-Cobra |

# Ford Mustang

## 1995

| (wb 101.3) | | Wght | Price | Prod |
|---|---|---|---|---|
| P40 | cpe 2d | 3,077 | 14,330 | |
| P44 | conv cpe 2d | 3,257 | 20,795 | |
| — | GTS cpe 2d | | 16,910 | 167,880 |
| P42 | GT cpe 2d | 3,280 | 17,905 | |
| P45 | GT conv cpe 2d | 3,451 | 22,595 | |
| P42 | Cobra cpe 2d | 3,354 | 21,300 | 4,005 |
| P45 | Cobra conv cpe 2d | 3,524 | 25,605 | 1,003 |

| 1995 Engines | bore × stroke | bhp | availability |
|---|---|---|---|
| V-6, 232.0 | 3.80 × 3.40 | 145 | S-base |
| V-8, 302.0 | 4.00 × 3.00 | 215 | S-GT |
| V-8, 302.0 | 4.00 × 3.00 | 240 | S-Cobra |

## 1996

| (wb 101.3) | | Wght | Price | Prod |
|---|---|---|---|---|
| P40 | cpe 2d | 3,065 | 15,180 | |
| P42 | GT cpe 2d | 3,278 | 17,610 | 99,947 |
| P42 | Cobra cpe 2d | 3,393 | 24,810 | |
| P44 | conv cpe 2d | 3,264 | 21,060 | 33,173 |
| P45 | GT conv cpe 2d | 3,471 | 23,495 | |
| P45 | Cobra conv cpe 2d | 3,565 | 27,580 | 2,500 |

| 1996 Engines | bore × stroke | bhp | availability |
|---|---|---|---|
| V-6, 232.0 | 3.80 × 3.40 | 150 | S-base |
| V-8, 281.0 | 3.60 × 3.60 | 215 | S-GT |
| V-8, 281.0 | 3.60 × 3.60 | 305 | S-Cobra (dohc) |

## 1997

| (wb 101.3) | | Wght | Price | Prod |
|---|---|---|---|---|
| P40 | cpe 2d | 3,084 | 15,355 | 75,760 |
| P42 | GT cpe 2d | 3,288 | 18,000 | |
| P44 | conv cpe 2d | 3,264 | 20,755 | 24,490 |
| P45 | GT conv cpe 2d | 3,422 | 23,895 | |
| P42 | Cobra cpe 2d | 3,404 | 25,335 | 7,475 |
| P45 | Cobra conv cpe 2d | 3,540 | 28,135 | 2,525 |

| 1997 Engines | bore × stroke | bhp | availability |
|---|---|---|---|
| V-6, 232.0 | 3.80 × 3.40 | 150 | S-base |
| V-8, 281.0 | 3.60 × 3.60 | 215 | S-GT |
| V-8, 281.0 | 3.60 × 3.60 | 305 | S-Cobra (dohc) |

## 1998

| (wb 101.3)—149,129 built* | | Wght | Price | Prod |
|---|---|---|---|---|
| P40 | cpe 2d | 3,065 | 15,970 | — |
| P42 | GT cpe 2d | 3,227 | 19,970 | — |
| P44 | conv cpe 2d | 3,210 | 20,470 | — |
| P45 | GT conv cpe 2d | 3,400 | 23,970 | — |
| P42 | Cobra cpe 2d | 3,364 | 26,400 | — |
| P45 | Cobra conv cpe 2d | 3,506 | 30,200 | — |

| 1998 Engines | bore × stroke | bhp | availability |
|---|---|---|---|
| V-6, 232.0 | 3.80 × 3.40 | 150 | S-base |
| V-8, 281.0 | 3.60 × 3.60 | 225 | S-GT |
| V-8, 281.0 | 3.60 × 3.60 | 305 | S-Cobra (dohc) |

*Calendar-year production.

## 1999

| (wb 101.3)—192,889 built* | | Wght | Price | Prod |
|---|---|---|---|---|
| P40 | cpe 2d | 3,069 | 16,470 | — |
| P42 | GT cpe 2d | — | 20,870 | — |
| P44 | conv cpe 2d | 3,211 | 21,070 | — |
| P45 | GT conv cpe 2d | — | 24,870 | — |
| P42 | Cobra cpe 2d | — | 27,470 | — |
| P45 | Cobra conv cpe 2d | — | 31,470 | — |

| 1999 Engines | bore × stroke | bhp | availability |
|---|---|---|---|
| V-6, 232.0 | 3.80 × 3.40 | 190 | S-base |
| V-8, 281.0 | 3.60 × 3.60 | 260 | S-GT |
| V-8, 281.0 | 3.60 × 3.60 | 320 | S-Cobra (dohc) |

*Calendar-year production.

## 2000

| (wb 101.3)—181,209 built* | | Wght | Price | Prod |
|---|---|---|---|---|
| P40 | cpe 2d | 3,066 | 16,805 | — |
| P42 | GT cpe 2d | 3,241 | 22,440 | — |
| P44 | conv cpe 2d | 3,208 | 22,220 | — |
| P45 | GT conv cpe 2d | 3,479 | 26,695 | — |

| 2000 Engines | bore × stroke | bhp | availability |
|---|---|---|---|
| V-6, 232.0 | 3.80 × 3.40 | 190 | S-base |
| V-8, 281.0 | 3.60 × 3.60 | 260 | S-GT |

*Calendar-year production.

## 2001

| (wb 101.3)—160,964 built* | | Wght | Price | Prod |
|---|---|---|---|---|
| P40 | cpe 2d | 3,066 | 16,805 | — |
| P42 | GT cpe 2d | 3,241 | 22,440 | — |
| P44 | conv cpe 2d | 3,208 | 22,220 | — |
| P45 | GT conv cpe 2d | 3,379 | 26,695 | — |
| P42 | Cobra cpe 2d | — | 28,605 | — |
| P45 | Cobra conv cpe 2d | — | 32,605 | — |

| 2001 Engines | bore × stroke | bhp | availability |
|---|---|---|---|
| V-6, 232.0 | 3.80 × 3.40 | 190 | S-base |
| V-8, 281.0 | 3.60 × 3.60 | 260/275 | S-GT/Bullitt |
| V-8, 281.0 | 3.60 × 3.60 | 320 | S-Cobra (dohc) |

*Calendar-year production.

## 2002

| (wb 101.3) | | Wght | Price | Prod* |
|---|---|---|---|---|
| P40 | Standard cpe 2d | 3,066 | 17,305 | — |
| P40 | Deluxe cpe 2d | — | 17,910 | — |
| P40 | Premium cpe 2d | — | 19,025 | — |
| P42 | GT Deluxe cpe 2d | 3,241 | 22,965 | — |
| P42 | GT Premium cpe 2d | — | 24,135 | — |
| P44 | Deluxe conv cpe 2d | 3,208 | 22,745 | — |
| P44 | Premium conv cpe 2d | — | 25,330 | — |
| P45 | GT Deluxe conv cpe 2d | 3,379 | 27,220 | — |
| P45 | GT Premium conv cpe 2d | — | 28,390 | — |

| 2002 Engines | bore × stroke | bhp | availability |
|---|---|---|---|
| V-6, 232.0 | 3.80 × 3.40 | 190 | S-base |
| V-8, 281.0 | 3.60 × 3.60 | 260 | S-GT |

*Figures not available at time of publication.

# Ford Thunderbird

Legend says the Thunderbird was born in October 1951, when Ford Division general manager Louis Crusoe visited the Paris Auto Show with styling consultant George Walker. America had a love affair with European sports cars in the early postwar years, and both men were taken by what they saw in Paris—especially the curvy Jaguar XK-120 and GM's experimental two-seat LeSabre. "Why don't we have something like that?" Crusoe asked. "Oh, but we do!" replied Walker—who then hurried to phone Dearborn to get his troops cracking.

But like many apocryphal stories, this one isn't true. Frank Hershey, who headed the team that styled the original '55 T-Bird, said Ford had been conjuring two-seaters well before this, but never felt rushed to build one because sports-car sales only amounted to a minuscule 0.27 percent of the total U.S. market. But in January 1953, GM threw down a gauntlet Ford couldn't ignore: the Chevrolet Corvette. Barely a month later, Ford was hard at work on the car that would ultimately be named for the god worshiped by America's Southwest Native Americans as the bringer of rain and prosperity.

First displayed as a wood mock-up at the Detroit show in early 1954, the Thunderbird was a "personal" car, not a pure sports car. It rode the same wheelbase as the first-generation Corvette—102 inches—but was far more luxurious and practical. In place of creaking fiberglass and clumsy side curtains was a sturdy steel body with convenient roll-up windows. Instead of an ill-fitting soft top was a snug convertible top, a detachable hardtop, or both. And there was no plodding six-cylinder engine but a burly 292-cubic-inch Mercury V-8 delivering 193 bhp with stickshift or 198 bhp with optional self-shift Ford-O-Matic.

Bill Burnett supervised the engineering, which relied heavily on passenger-Ford components. Styling, conceived by Walker lieutenant Hershey and executed by a young Bill Boyer, couldn't have been better: simple and smooth yet clearly Ford, with rakish long-hood/short-deck proportions recalling the classic early-'40s Lincoln Continental.

With European style and American comfort, convenience, and go, the Thunderbird proved well-nigh irresistible at just under $3000 without options. It whipped the rival Chevy in 1955 production by nearly 24-to-1—16,155 for the model year.

You don't mess with success in Detroit, and Ford didn't with the '56 T-Bird. Changes were limited to a larger 312 V-8 option with 215/225 bhp (nonoverdrive stickshift cars retained the 292, now up to 202 bhp), plus exterior-mounted spare (answering

**1955 2-passenger convertible coupe**

**1955 convertible coupe**

**1956 2-passenger convertible coupe**

# Ford Thunderbird

**1957, with and without removable hardtop**

cries for more trunk space), softer suspension (for a smoother ride), and no-cost portholes for the hardtop (a Boyer idea inspired by vintage coachwork). Porthole hardtops heavily outsold the nonporthole kind in 1956, and virtually all '57 Thunderbirds had them. Production eased to 15,631, but was still five times Corvette's. Trouble was, Robert S. McNamara, who'd replaced Crusoe as head of Ford Division, wanted much higher volume. Also, market surveys indicated much greater demand for a four-seater. So for 1958 and beyond, that's what the T-Bird would be.

The '57 was thus the last two-seat 'Bird—and arguably the best. A handsome facelift brought a prominent bumper/grille and a longer deck (again enclosing the spare) wearing modest bladelike tailfins. There was more power than ever. Stickshift models still had a 292, but uprated to 212 bhp, and there was now a trio of 312s offering 245, 270, or 285 bhp, the last being a

**1957 2-passenger convertible with hardtop**

**1957 2-passenger convertible with hardtop**

**1958 convertible coupe**

525

# Ford Thunderbird

**1958 hardtop coupe**

twin-four-barrel version with 10.0:1 compression. Ford also built 208 supercharged "F-Birds" with 300/340 bhp courtesy of Paxton-McCulloch blowers, mainly for racing.

And race the early 'Birds did, though with limited success. A '55 sponsored by *Mechanix Illustrated* magazine's Tom McCahill swept the production sports-car class at that year's Daytona Speed Weeks, Joe Ferguson clocking a two-way average of 124.633 mph to best every Austin-Healey, Porsche, and all but one Jaguar XK-120. Chuck Daigh did even better in '56 with a 'Bird prepped by Pete DePaolo; he did 88.779 mph in the standing mile, though a 'Vette modified by Zora Arkus-Duntov proved faster (at 89.735 mph). Daigh returned in '57 to score 93.312 mph, and a privately entered 'Bird ran the flying-mile at 146.282 mph one way, 138.775 mph both ways. Then the Automobile Manufacturers Association issued its infamous racing "ban" and development stopped.

With a base price still under $3500 for '57, the T-Bird remained an attractive buy. Production ran through the end of the calendar year, so production was the highest for the three two-seater years at 21,380.

As expected, the all-new four-seater arrived for 1958 (though Ford briefly considered retaining a two-seater with updated styling). A dramatic design with unibody construction; all-coil suspension; and a low, rakish stance, the second-generation Thunderbird rode a compact 113-inch wheelbase, yet had ample interior room. Only one engine was available, a new 300-bhp 352 big-block V-8, linked to Ford Division's three-speed Cruise-O-Matic self-shift transmission, also new that year. Joining the familiar convertible was a fixed-roof hardtop that popularized the square "formal-look" wide-quarter roofline that would soon spread throughout the Ford line—and to other automakers. (A rumored retractable hardtop like the 1957-59 Ford Skyliner was canceled in the design stage. The '59 convertible used a similar top-stowing arrangement in that the power top folded beneath a rear-hinged decklid.) A new interior feature—a central control console atop the transmission

**1959 convertible coupe**

**1960 hardtop coupe with sunroof**

**1960 hardtop coupe**

**1961 hardtop coupe**

# Ford Thunderbird

**1961 convertible coupe**

tunnel—would also be widely imitated.

With all this, the '58 Thunderbird was a solid hit despite higher base prices of $3600-$3900. Nearly 38,000 were built for the model year, about twice as many as any of the previous two-seaters. The '59s changed only in detail: a honeycomb, instead of horizontal-bar, motif for grille; nonfunctional hood air-scoop and taillight appliqué; "bullet" moldings on the sculptured lower-body "bombs"; reworked Thunderbird script; a bird emblem instead of a round emblem on hardtop C-pillars. Lincoln's huge 350-bhp 430 V-8, listed the previous year but likely never installed, became a full-fledged Thunderbird option. Owing to production over a full model year, the '59 bested the '58 at some 67,500 units.

The 1960 edition marked the end of the planned three-year "squarebird" styling cycle. Though substantially the same as its predecessor, it wore a new grille with a main horizontal bar bisecting three vertical bars ahead of a fine grid, plus triple taillights (replacing dual-lamp clusters), and detail-trim changes. Engines were untouched. Returning to U.S. production for the first time before World War II was a slide-back metal sunroof as a new hardtop option. Volume continued climbing, reaching nearly 91,000 units. Included were 2536 limited-edition hardtops with gold-color roofs and other special touches. Hardtops as a whole, outsold convertibles nearly 8-to-1, suggesting that T-Bird buyers wanted luxury first and sportiness second.

A new third-generation 'Bird bowed for 1961 on an unchanged wheelbase and would see mostly minor alterations through 1963. Distinctive styling was highlighted by severely pointed front profiles, modest "blade" tailfins, big circular taillamps (a sometimes Ford hallmark), and outward-curving bodysides bereft of sheetmetal sculpturing. There was again just one engine: Ford Division's new 390 V-8, a stroked 352 but delivering the same 300 horsepower. An optional power package offered 40 more bhp for 1962-63. With minor alterations, the 390 would be the basic Thunderbird powerplant through 1968, joined by big-block options beginning with '66. Base prices for '61 stood at $4172 for the hardtop and $4639 for the ragtop.

Third-generation engineering was conservative but sound. Ford had contemplated front-wheel drive, but felt it too unorthodox for this market. Instead, engineers stressed quality control, solid construction, high ride comfort, and minimum noise at speed. Extensive use of rubber bushings for the coil-spring independent front and leaf-spring rear suspensions made the 1961-63 Thunderbirds among the best-riding cars of the day.

Two derivative models were added for '62: the Sports Roadster and the Landau. The former was the only production four-seat car to become a two-seater. (Of course, there are many examples of the opposite—including the '58 T-Bird.) It was okayed by new Ford Division chief Lee A. Iacocca largely because dealers had been besieged with requests for a car like

**1962 Sports Roadster convertible coupe**

**1963 Sports Roadster convertible coupe**

527

# Ford Thunderbird

1964 convertible coupe

1965 convertible coupe

1965 convertible coupe

1966 Landau hardtop coupe

the 1955-57 'Bird. While Iacocca knew there was no significant market for anything like that, he felt a semisports model couldn't hurt.

The designer most responsible for the Sports Roadster was Bud Kaufman, who developed a fiberglass tonneau to cover the normal convertible's rear seat, thus creating a "two-seater." When installed, the cover formed twin headrests for the front seats and blended neatly with the rear deck. Kaufman overcame fitting problems so that the soft top could be raised and lowered with the tonneau in place. Completing the package were Kelsey-Hayes chrome wire wheels with knock-off hubs that dictated omitting the stock rear fender skirts (due to inadequate clearance).

But stunning though it was, the Sports Roadster didn't sell. The problem was price: initially $5439, a hefty $650 above the standard convertible. Ford built only 1427 of the '62s and just 455 of the '63s before canceling the model. Ford dealers offered a similar tonneau and wire wheels as accessories for 1964 convertibles, but these are even scarcer today.

The Landau was far more popular. At $4398 it cost only $77 more than the standard hardtop, yet delivered a vinyl-covered roof with a fake landau or "S" bar on each rear pillar, plus a spiffier interior. Despite these minor touches, buyers flocked to the Landau. By 1966, it was outselling the plain hardtop; three years after that it was generating the bulk of T-Bird sales. There were also 2000 examples of a Limited Edition 1963 Landau. Introduced in the spring of that year, it came with a special numbered plaque on the console, plus all-white interior, special paint, and spinner wheel covers.

Though Thunderbird production was down in these years, it remained far higher than in the two-seater days. The respective totals for model years 1961-63 were 73,000, 78,000, and about 63,300.

Following the now customary three-year cycle, and with wheelbase again unchanged, the 1964 Thunderbird arrived with completely new sheetmetal highlighted (if that's the word) by busy bodyside sculpturing. This fourth design generation would carry on without major change through 1966. Quiet, refined luxury was again increasingly emphasized as convertible sales declined markedly. The open 'Bird, which accounted for only 7.5 percent of production in '66, didn't return for '67. The '64s set a T-Bird production record with close to 92,500 units. Volume eased to around 75,000 for '65, then to just over 69,000.

Among features introduced with this generation were a cockpit-style passenger compartment and "Silent-Flo" ventilation (1964); standard front-disc brakes (1965); full-width taillight housings, including backup lights and sequential turn signals, and a "Town" (formal) roofline for the Landau and hardtop (all for '66). A popular accessory offered since 1961 was the "Swing-Away" steering wheel. With the transmission in Park, it could be shifted about 10 inches inboard to facilitiate driver

1967 Landau four-door sedan

# Ford Thunderbird

**1968 Landau hardtop coupe**

**1968 Landau four-door sedan**

**1969 Landau hardtop coupe**

entry/exit. The 300-bhp 390 remained the only engine through 1965, after which it gained 15 horsepower, plus an alternative 428 big-block option rated at 345 bhp.

The pros and cons of offering a Thunderbird sedan were debated by Ford officials throughout the '60s. By middecade, Iacocca was satisfied that sporty-car buyers were being catered to by other Fords—namely the new Mustang and an attractive array of Falcons and Fairlanes. Market studies indicated that the T-Bird, now firmly entrenched as a personal-luxury car, no longer needed even a semisporting image.

Reflecting this conclusion was a completely restyled group of 1967 Thunderbirds headlined by a new $4825 four-door Landau on a 117.2-inch wheelbase. The hardtop and two-door Landau continued on a 114.7-inch span, priced at $4600/$4700. Front ends featured a handsome recessed loop grille with honeycomb insert, plus headlamps covered by matching flip-up sections; a hefty bumper wrapped underneath. Rear-quarter windows on two-doors now retracted horizontally into the roof pillars. Engines were unchanged.

This fifth-generation series would continue through 1971 despite sales that trended mostly downward as prices went upward (reaching $5500 for the '71 four-door). The Landau sedan wasn't very practical—especially its rear-hinged back doors, a throwback to the '30s—and it declined from almost 25,000 sales for '67 to just over 8400 by 1970. Volume as a whole sank from 78,000 to just above 49,000 for '69, then recovered to just over 50,000.

Styling changes were minor through decade's end. The '68s bore narrowed rocker moldings and an eggcrate grille pattern. For '69, the grille was composed of horizontal louvers and three vertical dividers, the full-width taillamp ensemble gave way to divided units, and rear-quarter windows were eliminated on the Landau coupe. Returning for the first time since 1960 was a sliding sunroof, albeit electrically operated, as an option for any vinyl-top model.

In its first departure from a three-year design cycle, Thunderbird received a heavy facelift of its '67 shell for 1970, marked by a more-prominent thrust-forward snout. Radio antenna and windshield wipers were newly concealed (the latter via an extended hood) and two-door models had a "faster" roofline. The customary three-model lineup returned for '71 with wheel covers, grille insert, and minor trim the only revisions. However, two-door Landaus were newly available sans the dummy S-bars (a 'Bird emblem substituted).

Big-block V-8s were the order of the day but very mildly tuned, the 'Bird no longer having a performance image to uphold. For 1968, the optional 428 gave way to Ford's new 429. Rated at 360 bhp, it was more easily adaptable to the new emissions standards that took effect that year. It would be standard T-Bird power from 1969 through 1973.

Following a '71 sales slide to some 36,000, Thunderbird was completely redesigned for 1972. Riding a new 120.4-inch wheelbase, it was larger and heavier than any 'Bird before—or since. The plain coupe and slow-selling sedans were dropped, leaving a single Landau hardtop to share basic structure with that year's new Continental Mark IV. Besides list prices starting around $5300, some $2500 below Lincoln, a big selling point for this bigger 'Bird was a plusher-riding, new all-coil suspension with four-bar-link location for the live rear axle.

Not surprisingly, greater size and weight conspired with more-restrictive emissions tuning to hurt both performance and economy. This explains why a second engine option returned: the big Lincoln 460, though it was scarcely more powerful than the still-standard 429: 224 bhp versus 212, both in newly proscribed SAE net measure. Either way, the '72 'Bird needed 12 seconds for the 0-60 sprint and returned a dismal

# Ford Thunderbird

1969 Landau hardtop coupe with sunroof

1970 hardtop coupe

1971 Landau hardtop coupe

1972 Landau hardtop coupe

11-12 miles per gallon of increasingly more-expensive gas.

Yet buyers apparently didn't care. Perhaps because of its closer similarity with the prestigious Mark, the '72 posted a healthy 60-percent sales gain, followed by over 87,000 for '73—the 'Bird's third-best yearly total yet. Then came the Middle East oil embargo, which put a big dent in big-car sales. Thunderbird was no exception, dropping below 59,000 for '74, then to just under 43,000. The last of this generation, the '76, managed a slight recovery—to near 53,000—mainly because the economy had mostly recovered from the 1973-74 gas crisis.

Yet if these figures were disheartening to Ford, the 'Bird at least maintained a solid lead over the rival Buick Riviera and Olds Toronado.

Relatively few changes attended the heavyweight sixth-generation 'Bird. Federal bumper standards took effect for 1973, which meant withstanding a 5-mph frontal impact (and a 5-mph rear shunt for '74s) without damage to safety-related components. The 'Bird met this requirement with bigger bumpers that only aggravated its weight problem. Styling changes involved headlights set in square chrome bezels, a gaudy eggcrate instead of horizontal bars for the grille, a stand-up hood ornament, and, instead of dummy landau irons, optional "opera" windows—contrived little oblong panes in the still ultrawide rear-roof pillars.

The '74 had to be the least pleasant of all Thunderbirds to live with. The infamous, short-lived seatbelt interlock system, mandated by the feds, forced strapping in anything on the right front seat—even a bag of groceries—before the car could be started. Heftier rear bumpers added to overall length with no gain in interior space. With weight up and emissions standards stricter, the whopping Lincoln 460 V-8 with 220 bhp became standard that year, along with vinyl roof, opera windows, solid-state ignition, AM radio, air conditioning, power windows, and tinted glass. There were eight variations of metalflake paint available, and a glass moonroof appeared as an optional alternative to the steel sunroof.

Aside from details, such as segmented taillights for 1974, this series saw few appearance changes after '73. Emissions tuning continued to strangle the big 460 V-8. Rated horsepower was 218/202 for 1975-76—ridiculously low for such a large engine, and this despite adoption of the catalytic converter. Ford went all-out to promote the '75 as "the best luxury car buy," trumpeting "new softness, new ease, with ample room for six . . . rich, lavish fabrics . . . 24-oz. cut-pile carpeting . . . woodtone appliques." More-practical options included four-wheel disc brakes (available since '72), "Sure-Track" antilock braking system (ditto), and a fuel-monitor warning light. The last was really needed, because these 'Birds were among the thirstiest cars ever seen from Dearborn.

Ford had long since become a master at keeping interest alive in an aging model via special editions, and the mid-'70s Thunderbird offered its share. An optional gold-tint moonroof was announced at mid-1974, along with Burgundy and White-and-Gold Luxury Groups color-keyed to a fare-thee-well inside and out. Copper and Silver Luxury Groups replaced them for '75, each offering velour or leather upholstery; a Jade LG was added in April. All of these wore a padded vinyl rear half-roof with opera windows, the latter being deleted when a moonroof was specified. The '76 LGs were Creme-and-Gold, Bordeaux, and "Lipstick." The last was actually far less gaudy than its name implied.

For 1977, Thunderbird marked a first in its history by being smaller than it was the year before. This "downsized" model was nothing more than a new derivative of Ford's existing mid-size platform as suggested by the 1974-76 Gran Torino Elite, which tested whether the public would accept a Thunderbird sized like Chevy's Monte Carlo. Though the Elite had sold quite well, this "new" 'Bird would put it in the shade.

Compared to the 1972-76 models, the '77 was lighter and more-economical, reflecting big reductions in almost every dimension: nearly 10 inches in overall length, 6.4 inches in wheelbase (to 114), three in width—and up to 900 pounds of "road-hugging weight." There were big reductions in price, too: some $2700 for the base model, which now started at just over $5000. Of course, the old big-blocks were gone. Standard power was now a 130-bhp version of the trusty 302 V-8—except for

# Ford Thunderbird

**1973 coupe**

**1974 coupe**

**1974 coupe**

**1975 coupe with Copper Luxury Group**

**1976 coupe with power glass Moonroof**

California, where only a 135-bhp 351 was sold. Optional was a 400 V-8, rated at 173 bhp for '77 and 166 bhp the following year, after which it was canceled.

Downsizing the 'Bird this way was expedient given that Washington's new corporate average fuel economy standards (CAFE) would be in force for 1978. But it was that much lower price and the Thunderbird name that sent sales soaring; better fuel efficiency was merely incidental. Thunderbird thus enjoyed 300,000-unit years for 1977 and '78—better than three times the previous model-year record set in distant 1960. And it easily outsold its sibling LTD II (see Ford) despite far fewer model choices.

Though the '77 was smaller and less-singular than previous 'Birds, it had many of the same style overtones and brash trim touches. Prices soon started climbing to where they had been.

January 1977 brought a new top-line Town Landau with a near $8000 base price and numerous standard luxuries, plus a dubious brushed-aluminum "tiara" roof band echoing the old mid-'50s Crown Victoria.

There was little change for 1978, but a Diamond Jubilee edition was issued to commemorate Ford Motor Company's 75th anniversary. Tagged at close to $10,000, it was painted in Diamond Blue or Ember metallics and came with the owner's initials near the outside door handles and on a 22-carat-gold dashboard nameplate. This package proved so popular that Ford retained it for 1979 as the Heritage, finished in either special maroon or light blue. There were few other changes that year except for volume, which was down again but hardly bad at about 284,000 units.

Thunderbird was further downsized, and in much the same

531

# Ford Thunderbird

1977 coupe

1977 Town Landau coupe

1978 coupe with T-Roof Convertible option

1978 coupe with Sports Decor Group

1978 coupe

manner, for 1980. Instead of an intermediate, its foundation this time was a compact, the practical "Fox" platform developed for the 1978 Ford Fairmont/Mercury Zephyr. But the size reductions for this eighth generation were just as dramatic as they'd been for the seventh: 16 inches in overall length, 4.5 inches in width, 5.6 inches in wheelbase (now 108.4). Next to the '76, the 1980 looked positively tiny: two feet shorter, eight inches narrower, a foot less between wheel centers, and nearly a ton lighter. Yet it was no less comfortable or luxurious than its immediate predecessors.

The adoption of the Fox platform returned Thunderbird from body-on-frame to unitized construction for the first time since 1966, which contributed to both weight efficiency and interior-space utilization. The interior blended opulence and convenience, and a split front-bench seat, buckets, and purpose-designed Recaro bucket seats were all available. The 302 V-8, now rated at 131 bhp, shifted to the options column and its debored 255-cid relative moved in as standard with 115 bhp. At midmodel year, Ford made its 200-cid six available as a credit option, the first six in Thunderbird history.

Other 1980 developments included a new four-speed overdrive automatic transmission, providing the traditional economy benefit of OD without the hassle of shifting; rack-and-pinion steering, for precision unknown in previous 'Birds; and the all-coil suspension system so well-proven in the Fairmont/Zephyr. A midyear offering expected in that 25th Thunderbird year was a Silver Anniversary special, again featuring a tiara roof appliqué plus a standard 302, the overdrive automatic, and gray-and-silver upholstery with complementing paintwork.

This more-efficient T-Bird should have sold well, but the market turned sour as another energy crisis began in late '79; then too, the boxy, overdecorated 1980 styling did not appeal to potential buyers. As a result, production slid below 157,000, then dropped by 50 percent a year for the 1981s and '82s.

But help was on the way for '83 in the form of a stunning new ninth-generation 'Bird that announced a new direction for Dearborn styling: the clean, no-frills "aero look." Though still built on the faithful Fox platform, the '83 employed a new 104-inch-wheelbase "S-shell" whose rounded "organic" shape cheated the wind with a rakish 60-degree windshield angle and a three-inch reduction in overall width, reducing the drag coefficient to a slick 0.35. The only vestige of recent Thunderbirds was a modest eggcrate grille curved snugly on the nose.

The startlingly different and handsome 1983 'Bird arrived in base and upmarket Heritage models with a choice of Ford's aluminum-head 232-cid "Essex" V-6 or an equally new 140-bhp 302 V-8 with single-point fuel injection. But the real surprise came at midmodel year with the Turbo Coupe, the sportiest T-Bird in 20 years. As the name implied, it carried a reengineered 142-bhp version of Mustang's 2.3-liter turbo-four from recent Mustangs, now with port fuel injection among numerous improvements. Initially, it linked exclusively to a five-speed overdrive manual gearbox. A standard handling package, optional for other '83s, brought high-rate springs and shocks; a second pair of rear shocks, horizontally mounted to resist axle patter (Ford termed this "Quadra-Trac"); "Traction-Lok" limited-slip differential; and beefy performance radials on handsome aluminum wheels. Completing this enthusiasts' T-Bird were black exterior moldings, fog lamps, and a well-furnished interior with shapely multiadjustable front bucket seats featuring variable thigh and lumbar supports.

Roundly applauded by "buff books" and even Consumer Guide®, the Turbo Coupe was a bit crude mechanically, but the most-roadable T-Bird anyone could remember. It was quick, too: 0-60 mph took 9.6 seconds. Yet it could return an honest 23 mpg in city/suburban driving—impressive for a 3000-pound lux-

# Ford Thunderbird

**1979 Heritage coupe**

**1979 coupe with T-Roof**

**1980 Town Landau coupe**

**1980 Town Landau coupe with Exterior Decor Group**

**1981 coupe**

**1981 Heritage coupe**

**1982 Town Landau coupe**

**1983 coupe**

ury midsize. Workmanship was also better than anyone could recall (or dared to). All the '83s were tight and solid, thoroughly detailed, and beautifully finished.

Buyers were quick to recognize the excellence of what Ford had wrought, snapping up nearly 122,000 of the 1983 Thunderbirds—a sensational 250 percent gain over depressed 1982-model sales. The Turbo Coupe made up only about 10 percent of Thunderbird sales but, as T-Birds always have, lured many people into showrooms who left in one of the tamer versions or another Ford model.

Indeed, the market was fast pulling out of its early-decade slump, and T-Bird shared in the renewed prosperity with some 170,500 sales for 1984. Changes that year were modest but useful. The V-6 discarded its carburetor for throttle-body injection that gave a slight power increase, and both it and the 302 V-8 took on Ford's EEC-IV electronic control system, as already used on the Turbo Coupe engine. The TC itself was unchanged save newly available three-speed automatic transmission. Heritage was renamed Elan, and a new Fila "designer" model was added with special colors and trim inspired by the Italian sportswear maker.

More refinements followed for '85: altered grille texture, full-width wraparound taillamps, counterbalanced hood (thus banishing a cheap, awkward prop-rod), restyled dash with new fully electronic instrumentation (one of the more-informative and legible such setups) and wider standard tires (meaty

# Ford Thunderbird

**1983½ Turbo coupe**

**1983½ Turbo coupe**

**1984 Fila coupe**

**1985 30th Anniversary coupe**

**1985 Turbo coupe**

**1986 coupe**

**1987 Turbo coupe**

**1988 coupe**

225/60VR-15s on Turbo Coupe, 205/70-14s elsewhere). Model-year volume remained healthy at close to 152,000.

The '86 figure was even better, reflecting the fact that it was one of Detroit's strongest sales years of the decade. The Fila model was dropped, but sequential-port injection and friction-reducing internal changes lifted the 302 V-8 to 150 bhp. A power moonroof was newly optional. Gas was again cheap, so the V-8 was ordered in the bulk of that year's nearly 164,000 Thunderbirds in spite of its so-so 20-mpg thirst. Judicious use of the options sheet made it possible to order the V-8 with most Turbo Coupe features. Many buyers did just that, enjoying more-relaxed performance and far greater refinement. Even in the late '80s, there was still no substitute for cubic inches.

Recognizing this trend, Ford issued a rearranged group of '87 Thunderbirds with all-new sheetmetal. The reskin didn't much change silhouette, but did make a slick car look even slicker. Glass areas were larger (though not the actual window openings) and both headlamps and side glass were fully flush-mounted to further reduce air drag. The Turbo Coupe wore twin functional hood scoops behind a unique grilleless nose. Other models displayed a rather gaudy chrome eggcrate between the headlamps. Replacing Elan were two new offerings: luxury LX and the Sport. The latter combined the V-8 with a TC-style chassis, interior and exterior, but was otherwise equipped like the base 'Bird. At just over $15,000, it cost some $1800 less than a Turbo Coupe, which made it a terrific performance buy—second only perhaps to the Mustang GT.

The '87s had mechanical and equipment improvements aplenty. The TC acquired the intercooled four of the recently departed Mustang SVO, here rated at 190 bhp. Even more laudable were its newly standard four-wheel disc brakes with electronic antilock control (developed by Ford with the German Alfred Teves company), plus a new variable-rate shock-absorber system (called Automatic Ride Control) and standard 225/60VR-16 unidirectional performance tires. Air conditioning and tinted glass were standard across the Thunderbird board, and the overdrive automatic took over entirely for the less-efficient three-speeder. Yet for all this, volume dipped, sinking to near 128,000.

The same lineup—V-6 base and LX, V-8 Sport and four-cylinder Turbo Coupe—sold somewhat better for '88: over 147,000. The V-6 was heavily revised, gaining 20 horsepower via multi-point injection, plus a "balancer" shaft mounted in the vee between cylinder banks to help quell secondary vibrations. TC appointments were slightly upgraded, and the Sport changed from digital/graphic to analog gauges as standard.

A striking new 10th-generation Thunderbird was Ford's big attraction for 1989. And new it was: smoother, slightly wider and lower, and nearly 3.5 inches shorter on a wheelbase stretched to 113 inches—longer than that of even the overblown early-'70s cars. Overall appearance reminded some of BMW's classic 6-Series coupe, but it nevertheless managed to be distinctively Ford—proving, perhaps, that the '83 'Bird and the equally striking '86 Taurus sedan weren't flukes after all.

Surprisingly, both the V-8 and turbo-four were gone, replaced by a brace of reworked 232 V-6s. The familiar 140-bhp unit with sequential-port injection continued in the base Thunderbird and luxury LX, offered only with automatic. But all eyes were on the hot new Super Coupe with a supercharged and intercooled 210-bhp V-6, teamed with standard five-speed manual (automatic was optional). The engine-driven supercharger was a '30s idea which enjoyed a revival at several European and Japanese automakers. With the SC, Ford joined them in offering its well-known advantages over the exhaust-driven turbocharger—mainly smoother, more-progressive power delivery at a slight sacrifice in noise and efficiency.

Chassis engineering was equally new. Though the front suspension retained MacPherson-style coil-over-shock units, geometry now involved an A-arm atop each strut and a transverse arm at the base connected by a long, sickle-shaped member integrated with the hub carrier. Rear suspension was fully independent—a first for Thunderbird—and quite compact with variable-rate coil springs sandwiched between an upper lateral link and a wide H-shaped lower member. Vertical shocks rode ahead of the hub carriers. Steering remained power rack-and-pinion, but with new speed-sensitive variable assist as standard. Though base and LX carried front-disc/rear-drum power brakes, they offered the SC's all-disc ABS system as a first-time option. The SC itself came with a more-sophisticated version of the Turbo Coupe's electronic variable-damping system.

Inside the '89s was a logically ordered, very "Euro-looking" instrument panel with digital/graphic or analog instruments (the latter standard on Super Coupe). Maintaining tradition was a functional center console on all models.

But no car is perfect, and the '89 T-Birds ended up much too heavy in the opinion of many critics: a minimum of 3500 pounds. As a result, an unblown LX took a sluggish 10.4 seconds in Consumer Guide®'s 0-60 test. The magazine's five-speed SC was far livelier at just 7.8, but would have been faster still without so many extra pounds. The '89 also ended up way over budget, prompting Ford to fire some development engineers.

1988 Turbo coupe

1989 Super Coupe (SC)

1989 Super Coupe (SC)

1989 LX coupe

1989 LX coupe

# Ford Thunderbird

**1990 Super Coupe (SC)**

**1990 Super Coupe (SC)**

More disturbing for an all-new model, certainly for company accountants, production dropped again. The '89 total was below 115,000, and the little-changed 1990 models were 1000 units under that. Higher prices undoubtedly played a part: some $15,000 for the base 1990, over $20,000 for the Super Coupe. The deep new national recession that began in 1990 didn't help. Still, those production numbers were respectable given a worsening economy and a far more crowded luxury-performance field.

T-Bird volume became even less respectable for '91, then sank to just under 78,000 for model-year '92 before turning up again along with the economy. Only one notable change occurred: the return of V-8 power as a 1991 option for base and LX models. Of course, it was the familiar pushrod 5.0-liter last offered for 1988, but it now made 200 bhp, a whopping 45 more than before. On the other hand, that was 25 less than the same engine in a '91 Mustang or Lincoln Mark VII, the result of a more-restrictive exhaust system. Still, the V-8 was welcome, being slower, but less-thirsty, than the supercharged V-6, and it quickly accounted for the bulk of 'Bird sales. Two minor '91 improvements involved automatic climate control as a new linewide option and availability of the SC's analog gauges for base and LX.

Expanding the '92 lineup was a revived Sport model. This time, it was a slightly detrimmed Super Coupe with the V-8 and narrower tires (but on unique alloy wheels). Price was attractive at $18,611, a good $3500 below that year's blown 'Bird. All '92s wore full-width taillamps nestled under a reshaped "gull-wing" trunklid, and both the Sport and LX adopted the SC's distinctive aero front-bumper and driving lamps as standard equipment.

Only the LX and SC returned for '93. The former lost a few standard frills to undercut the previous base model by over $500. It was all for sales, of course, and it worked, T-Bird model-year volume nearly doubling to over 133,000. To no one's surprise, the vast majority were LXs. The SC was lowered a token $16 that year, which only underscored how good a value it was at $22,030 to start. But affordable luxury was now overwhelmingly preferred to high-tech potency, and the Super Coupe continued to decline as a percentage of total 'Bird sales.

The LX and SC looked nearly identical for 1994, when a timely freshening occurred, starting with a minor facelift announced by large oval cutouts in the front bumper. The dash was revised to contain a passenger air bag. Dual cupholders were added, too, but electronic gauges were deleted. The big news was in the engine room. Internal changes boosted the blown V-6 to 230 bhp, a gain of 20, while the LX switched optional V-8s, ditching the pushrod 5.0-liter for Ford's new 4.6-liter "modular" unit with single overhead camshaft.

Reduced V-8 displacement implied reduced V-8 torque. Sure

**1991 LX coupe**

**1992 Sport coupe**

**1993 LX coupe**

**1994 Super Coupe (SC)**

# Ford Thunderbird

enough, the 4.6 made 10 fewer pound-feet than the 5.0, 265 in all, though it did bring a nominal gain of five horsepower. It did not, however, bring a noticeable improvement in smoothness or quietness, and performance was predictably little changed, Consumer Guide® clocking 0-60 mph in a decent 8.8 seconds. Like the old V-8, the new one teamed exclusively with four-speed automatic, which gained an overdrive lockout button (to give better around-town performance at the driver's discretion) and electronic shift control. The latter was noticeable, but mostly in the negative, as it made some shifts slurred, others sharp, and both often tardy.

Despite such fumbles, Thunderbird output eased only a little for '94, dropping some 7000 units to just over 126,000. Continued aggressive pricing certainly helped stem the loss in a rougher-than-ever market where buyers often "cross-shopped" the 'Bird against luxury sedans. In that light, the $22,240 SC looked an even better buy in luxury-performance, its base price having risen only $2400 over five model years. The LX was up to $16,830, less than $1900 higher than the less-well-equipped base model of 1990. Unfortunately, the basic '89 design was showing its age, and little was done to freshen it in '95. Sales continued to decline. Even new bumper fascias front and rear, headlamps, hood and taillamp clusters, and spark plugs guaranteed to last 100,000 miles couldn't spark much interest from the public. If the picture was bleak in '96, it grew positively dismal when the '97 'Birds were introduced. The only change of any consequence was the deletion of two gauges from the instrument panel. Rumors swirled through the industry that a new 'Bird was imminent, perhaps a smaller, lighter 'Bird with front-wheel drive. Such speculation certainly didn't help dealers shift their remaining '97s.

And then there were none. No '98 'Birds appeared, except in the hands of racing teams in the NASCAR Winston Cup series; they were allowed to run their '97-bodied cars for an extra season while Ford developed a new racer for stock-car racing's premier series. When the substitute finally appeared, it was a two-door Taurus, a mythical beast with no analogue available to the public. And the front-drive 'Bird? While the idea may have been given serious consideration—and some sources suggested it was a definite possibility at one point—what emerged in 1998 (for the '99 model year) was a redesigned Mercury Cougar based on the Ford Contour/Mercury Mystique floorpan. At last, T-Bird and Cougar were separated.

Few if any observers believed that Ford would let so significant a nameplate vanish altogether, so few were surprised to see a Thunderbird "concept car" on the Ford stand at the Detroit Auto Show in January 1999. No one who had seen the '55 original needed to see the badges on this stunning showpiece. Given the constraints placed on them by modern safety regulations and other considerations unknown 44 years before, the designers of the new 'Bird had done a masterful job. No, it wasn't a line-for-line lift of the old shape; bumpers were integrated into the body, there were no "eyebrows" over the headlamps, and chrome trim played only the most minor of decorative roles, but the flavor of the first 'Bird had been captured. Except, that is, for the tailfins which, for some reason, a younger crop of stylists just couldn't bring themselves to include.

While the word "retro" was heard from many quarters when the design was discussed, Ford was careful to term the show-'Bird's shape "modern heritage." The name didn't matter. What was important was that a new generation at Ford embraced the two-seater form that had previously been the object of scorn. Of course times, and manufacturing processes, have changed.

It was now reckoned that a car like this 'Bird could profitably be produced in limited quantities by drawing mechanical and structural hardware from high-volume models. If, said Ford spokespeople, the 'Bird was to be built at all in this form.

A little over a year later, journalists' suspicions that the show car looked a little too production-ready to be a mere design exercise were confirmed when it was announced that a two-seat 'Bird would go on sale in 2001 as an '02 model. Under its skin, it would share engine, transmission, and four-wheel independent suspension components with the Lincoln LS/Jaguar S-Type cars, and would use a shortened version of their structure. Unlike the two sedans, it would be offered only with the 3.9-liter dohc V-8 engine, rated at the same 252 bhp as the LS unit. The sole transmission would be a five-speed automatic.

**1995 LX coupe**

**1997 LX coupe**

**1996 LX coupe**

**2002 Premium convertible coupe with removable hardtop**

# Ford Thunderbird

Not long after, it was announced that the first production 'Birds would leave the Wixom, Michigan, assembly plant at the end of July 2001. But first Neiman Marcus customers had the chance to snap up 200 advance copies. In a arrangement with the upscale department store, a specially trimmed $41,995 NM Edition Thunderbird was introduced in August 2000 at the 50th annual Concours d'Elegance in Pebble Beach, California. Listed in the Neiman Marcus "Christmas Book," the car was offered for sale on September 23, 2000. All of the black and silver cars were sold in a phone blitz that lasted a little over two hours.

As it happened, normal deliveries didn't begin until September, delayed by a need to fix problems that were cropping up in preproduction examples. Cooling-system and other woes required replacement of components previously assumed to be acceptable. This, on top of the recent Ford Explorer/Firestone tire debacle and a rash of recalls that plagued early examples of the Focus subcompact, brought on a wave of negative publicity that might have seriously damaged a car of lesser pedigree. But the 'Bird's engineers persevered, and full production began in the autumn of 2001. Eager customers, some of whom had put down deposits even before the official announcement that the car would be built, were finally able to put their new 'Birds on the road.

First impressions were generally positive. Some critics complained that the new 'Bird didn't measure up to sports-car standards in the ride and handling department but that was beside the point; it was billed from the start as a comfortable, sporty car, a latter-day version of the '55 "Personal Car." Viewed in that light, it was excellent, with more than enough performance to make it fun to drive. In fact, the driving experience was eerily like being behind the wheel of an original 'Bird, once allowances were made for modern improvements in brakes and steering. Like many convertibles, it suffered a little from cowl shake over rough surfaces, despite the addition of three sturdy cross-braces to the platform, and was a little claustrophobic with the top up. But it would have been a winner based strictly on style, whether judged for its sleek exterior or comfortable interior. The interior drew heavily on LS components (the dashboard being the most notable of these), but was most attractive. Optional exterior-color accent trim, which covered dashboard, seat inserts, door panels, and center console, was a nice retro ("modern heritage") touch. Another tie with past was the turquoise pointer used on the instruments, an homage to the use of the same color on the original 'Bird's badges.

Considering the limited production volume, the '02 'Bird had a reasonable base price of $34,965, with the uplevel model costing $1000 more. The removable hardtop, another echo of the past with its porthole side windows, added $2500 to the price of either model. These prices did not reflect the markups some dealers were demanding.

Given the cyclical nature of the automotive business, it would be foolish to predict the Thunderbird's future. It might once again expand into a four-seat car as it did in 1958, or it might get additional variants, among which a high-performance 'Bird, possibly using the supercharged V-8 from Jaguar. If the latter happens, it would not be surprising to see a fixed hardtop and/or considerable added chassis bracing as part of the package, along with stiffened suspension.

Whatever direction future 'Birds take, the current two-seater is a home run, and a positive sign of an emerging push-the-envelope attitude at Ford.

**2002 Neiman Marcus Edition convertible coupe with hardtop**

# Ford Thunderbird

**2002 convertible coupe with hardtop**

## Specifications

### 1955

| (wb 102.0) | | Wght | Price | Prod |
|---|---|---|---|---|
| 40A | conv 2S | 2,980 | 2,944 | 16,155 |

| 1955 Engines | bore × stroke | bhp | availability |
|---|---|---|---|
| V-8, 292.0 | 3.75 × 3.30 | 193 | S-stickshift |
| V-8, 292.0 | 3.75 × 3.30 | 198 | S-automatic |

### 1956

| (wb 102.0) | | Wght | Price | Prod |
|---|---|---|---|---|
| 40A | conv 2S | 3,038 | 3,151 | 15,631 |

| 1956 Engines | bore × stroke | bhp | availability |
|---|---|---|---|
| V-8, 292.0 | 3.75 × 3.30 | 202 | S-3-speed trans |
| V-8, 312.0 | 3.80 × 3.44 | 215 | S-overdrive |
| V-8, 312.0 | 3.80 × 3.44 | 225 | S-automatic |

### 1957

| (wb 102.0) | | Wght | Price | Prod |
|---|---|---|---|---|
| 40 | conv 2S | 3,145 | 3,408 | 21,380 |

| 1957 Engines | bore × stroke | bhp | availability |
|---|---|---|---|
| V-8, 292.0 | 3.75 × 3.30 | 212 | S-3-speed trans |
| V-8, 312.0 | 3.80 × 3.44 | 245 | S-overdrive, automatic |
| V-8, 312.0 | 3.80 × 3.44 | 270/285 | O-all(3-speed briefly) |
| V-8S, 312.0 | 3.80 × 3.44 | 300/340 | O-auto; few od/3sp |

### 1958

| (wb 113.0) | | Wght | Price | Prod |
|---|---|---|---|---|
| 63A | htp cpe | 3,876 | 3,631 | 35,758 |
| 76A | conv cpe | 3,944 | 3,929 | 2,134 |

| 1958 Engines | bore × stroke | bhp | availability |
|---|---|---|---|
| V-8, 352.0 | 4.00 × 3.50 | 300 | S-all |
| V-8, 430.0 | 4.30 × 3.70 | 350 | O-prod questionable |

### 1959

| (wb 113.0) | | Wght | Price | Prod |
|---|---|---|---|---|
| 63A | htp cpe | 3,813 | 3,696 | 57,195 |
| 76A | conv cpe | 3,903 | 3,979 | 10,261 |

| 1959 Engines | bore × stroke | bhp | availability |
|---|---|---|---|
| V-8, 352.0 | 4.00 × 3.50 | 300 | S-all |
| V-8, 430.0 | 4.30 × 3.70 | 350 | O-all |

### 1960

| (wb 113.0) | | Wght | Price | Prod |
|---|---|---|---|---|
| 63A | htp cpe | 3,799 | 3,755 | 76,447 |
| 63B | htp cpe, gold top | 3,799 | 3,900* | 2,536 |
| 76A | conv cpe | 3,897 | 4,222 | 11,860 |

| 1960 Engines | bore × stroke | bhp | availability |
|---|---|---|---|
| V-8, 352.0 | 4.00 × 3.50 | 300 | S-all |
| V-8, 430.0 | 4.30 × 3.70 | 350 | O-all |

* Estimated

### 1961

| (wb 113.0) | | Wght | Price | Prod |
|---|---|---|---|---|
| 63A | htp cpe | 3,958 | 4,172 | 62,535 |
| 76A | conv cpe | 4,130 | 4,639 | 10,516 |

| 1961 Engine | bore × stroke | bhp | availability |
|---|---|---|---|
| V-8, 390.0 | 4.05 × 3.78 | 300 | S-all |

### 1962

| (wb 113.0) | | Wght | Price | Prod |
|---|---|---|---|---|
| 63A | htp cpe | 4,132 | 4,321 | 69,554* |
| 63B | Landau htp cpe | 4,144 | 4,398 | |

# Ford Thunderbird

| (wb 113.0) | | Wght | Price | Prod |
|---|---|---|---|---|
| 76A | conv cpe | 4,370 | 4,788 | 7,030* |
| 76B | Sports Roadster conv cpe | 4,471 | 5,439 | 1,427* |

* Some sources list total of 68,127 hardtops/Landaus and 9,884 convertibles.

| 1962 Engines | bore × stroke | bhp | availability |
|---|---|---|---|
| V-8, 390.0 | 4.05 × 3.78 | 300 | S-all |
| V-8, 390.0 | 4.05 × 3.78 | 340 | O-all |

## 1963

| Series 80 (wb 113.0) | | Wght | Price | Prod |
|---|---|---|---|---|
| 63A | htp cpe | 4,195 | 4,445 | 42,806* |
| 63B | Landau htp cpe | 4,203 | 4,548 | 14,139* |
| 76A | conv cpe | 4,322 | 4,912 | 5,913* |
| 76B | Sports Roadster conv cpe | 4,396 | 5,563 | 455* |

* Some sources list total of 59,000 hardtops/Landaus and 5,457 convertibles. Model 63B includes 2,000 Limited Edition Landaus with special trim; model 76B includes 37 units with 340-bhp engine.

| 1963 Engines | bore × stroke | bhp | availability |
|---|---|---|---|
| V-8, 390.0 | 4.05 × 3.78 | 300 | S-all |
| V-8, 390.0 | 4.05 × 3.78 | 340 | O-all |

## 1964

| Series 80 (wb 113.2) | | Wght | Price | Prod |
|---|---|---|---|---|
| 83 | htp cpe | 4,431 | 4,486 | 60,552 |
| 85 | conv cpe | 4,586 | 4,953 | 9,198 |
| 87 | Landau htp cpe | 4,441 | 4,589 | 22,715 |

| 1964 Engine | bore × stroke | bhp | availability |
|---|---|---|---|
| V-8, 390.0 | 4.05 × 3.78 | 300 | S-all |

## 1965

| Series 80 (wb 113.2) | | Wght | Price | Prod |
|---|---|---|---|---|
| 83 | htp cpe | 4,470 | 4,486 | 42,652 |
| 85 | conv cpe | 4,588 | 4,953 | 6,846 |
| 87 | Landau htp cpe | 4,478 | 4,589 | 20,974 |
| 87 | Limited Ed Special Landau | 4,500 | 4,639 | 4,500 |

| 1965 Engine | bore × stroke | bhp | availability |
|---|---|---|---|
| V-8, 390.0 | 4.00 × 3.78 | 300 | S-all |

## 1966

| Series 80 (wb 113.2) | | Wght | Price | Prod |
|---|---|---|---|---|
| 81 | Town Hardtop cpe | 4,359 | 4,483 | 15,633 |
| 83 | htp cpe | 4,386 | 4,426 | 13,389 |
| 85 | conv cpe | 4,496 | 4,879 | 5,049 |
| 87 | Landau htp cpe | 4,367 | 4,584 | 35,105 |

| 1966 Engines | bore × stroke | bhp | availability |
|---|---|---|---|
| V-8, 390.0 | 4.00 × 3.78 | 315 | S-all |
| V-8, 428.0 | 4.13 × 3.98 | 345 | O-all |

## 1967

| Series 80 (wb 114.7; 4d-117.2) | | Wght | Price | Prod |
|---|---|---|---|---|
| 81 | htp cpe | 4,248 | 4,603 | 15,567 |
| 82 | Landau htp cpe | 4,256 | 4,704 | 37,422 |
| 84 | Landau sdn 4d | 4,348 | 4,825 | 24,967 |

| 1967 Engines | bore × stroke | bhp | availability |
|---|---|---|---|
| V-8, 390.0 | 4.00 × 3.78 | 315 | S-all |
| V-8, 428.0 | 4.13 × 3.98 | 345 | O-all |

## 1968

| Series 80 (wb 114.7; 4d-117.2) | | Wght | Price | Prod |
|---|---|---|---|---|
| 83 | htp cpe | 4,366 | 4,716 | 9,977 |
| 84 | Landau htp cpe | 4,372 | 4,845 | 33,029 |
| 87 | Landau sdn 4d | 4,458 | 4,924 | 21,925 |

| 1968 Engines | bore × stroke | bhp | availability |
|---|---|---|---|
| V-8, 390.0 | 4.00 × 3.78 | 315 | S-all |
| V-8, 429.0 | 4.36 × 3.59 | 360 | O-all |

## 1969

| Series 80 (wb 114.7; 4d-117.2) | | Wght | Price | Prod |
|---|---|---|---|---|
| 83 | htp cpe | 4,348 | 4,824 | 5,913 |
| 84 | Landau htp cpe | 4,360 | 4,964 | 27,664 |
| 87 | Landau sdn 4d | 4,460 | 5,043 | 15,695 |

| 1969 Engine | bore × stroke | bhp | availability |
|---|---|---|---|
| V-8, 429.0 | 4.36 × 3.59 | 360 | S-all |

## 1970

| Series 80 (wb 114.7; 4d-117.2) | | Wght | Price | Prod |
|---|---|---|---|---|
| 83 | htp cpe | 4,354 | 4,961 | 5,116 |
| 84 | Landau htp cpe | 4,630 | 5,104 | 36,847 |
| 87 | Landau sdn 4d | 4,464 | 5,182 | 8,401 |

| 1970 Engine | bore × stroke | bhp | availability |
|---|---|---|---|
| V-8, 429.0 | 4.36 × 3.59 | 360 | S-all |

## 1971

| Series 80 (wb 115.0; 4d-118.0) | | Wght | Price | Prod |
|---|---|---|---|---|
| 83 | htp cpe | 4,399 | 5,295 | 9,146 |
| 84 | Landau htp cpe | 4,370 | 5,438 | 20,356 |
| 87 | Landau sdn 4d | 4,509 | 5,516 | 6,553 |

| 1971 Engine | bore × stroke | bhp | availability |
|---|---|---|---|
| V-8, 429.0 | 4.36 × 3.59 | 360 | S-all |

## 1972

| Series 80 (wb 120.4) | | Wght | Price | Prod |
|---|---|---|---|---|
| 87 | htp cpe | 4,420 | 5,293 | 57,814 |

| 1972 Engines | bore × stroke | bhp | availability |
|---|---|---|---|
| V-8, 429.0 | 4.36 × 3.59 | 212 | S-all |
| V-8, 460.0 | 4.36 × 3.85 | 224 | O-all |

## 1973

| Series 80 (wb 120.4) | | Wght | Price | Prod |
|---|---|---|---|---|
| 87 | htp cpe | 4,505 | 6,437 | 87,269 |

| 1973 Engines | bore × stroke | bhp | availability |
|---|---|---|---|
| V-8, 429.0 | 4.36 × 3.59 | 208 | S-all |
| V-8, 460.0 | 4.36 × 3.85 | 219 | O-all |

## 1974

| Series 80 (wb 120.4) | | Wght | Price | Prod |
|---|---|---|---|---|
| 87 | htp cpe | 4,825 | 7,330 | 58,443 |

| 1974 Engine | bore × stroke | bhp | availability |
|---|---|---|---|
| V-8, 460.0 | 4.36 × 3.85 | 220 | S-all |

## 1975

| Series 80 (wb 120.4) | | Wght | Price | Prod |
|---|---|---|---|---|
| 87 | htp cpe | 4,893 | 7,701 | 42,685 |

# Ford Thunderbird

| 1975 Engine | bore × stroke | bhp | availability |
|---|---|---|---|
| V-8, 460.0 | 4.36 × 3.85 | 218 | S-all |

### 1976

| Series 80 (wb 120.4) | | Wght | Price | Prod |
|---|---|---|---|---|
| 87 | htp cpe | 4,808 | 7,790 | 52,935* |

| 1976 Engine | bore × stroke | bhp | availability |
|---|---|---|---|
| V-8, 460.0 | 4.36 × 3.85 | 202 | S-all |

* includes 30 commemorative editions.

### 1977

| (wb 114.0) | | Wght | Price | Prod |
|---|---|---|---|---|
| 87 | htp cpe | 3,907 | 5,063 | 318,140 |
| 87 | Town Landau cpe | 4,104 | 7,990 | |

| 1977 Engines | bore × stroke | bhp | availability |
|---|---|---|---|
| V-8, 302.0 | 4.00 × 3.00 | 130 | S-all |
| V-8, 351.0 | 4.00 × 3.50 | 135 | S-in Calif.; O-all |
| V-8, 400.0 | 4.00 × 4.00 | 173 | O-all |

### 1978

| (wb 114.0) | | Wght | Price | Prod |
|---|---|---|---|---|
| 87 | htp cpe | 3,907 | 5,411 | 333,757 |
| 87 | Town Landau cpe | 4,104 | 8,420 | |
| 87 | Diamond Jubilee cpe | 4,200 | 10,106 | 18,994 |

| 1978 Engines | bore × stroke | bhp | availability |
|---|---|---|---|
| V-8, 302.0 | 4.00 × 3.00 | 134 | S-all |
| V-8, 351.0 | 4.00 × 3.50 | 152 | O-all |
| V-8, 400.0 | 4.00 × 4.00 | 166 | O-all |

### 1979

| (wb 114.0) | | Wght | Price | Prod |
|---|---|---|---|---|
| 87 | cpe | 3,893 | 5,877 | 284,141 |
| 87/607 | Town Landau cpe | 4,284 | 8,866 | |
| 87/603 | Heritage cpe | 4,178 | 10,687 | |

| 1979 Engines | bore × stroke | bhp | availability |
|---|---|---|---|
| V-8, 302.0 | 4.00 × 3.00 | 133 | S-all |
| V-8, 351.0 | 4.00 × 3.50 | 135/151 | O-all |

### 1980

| (wb 108.4) | | Wght | Price | Prod |
|---|---|---|---|---|
| 87 | cpe | 3,118 | 6,432 | 156,803 |
| 87/607 | Town Landau cpe | 3,357 | 10,036 | |
| 87/603 | Silver Anniversary cpe | 3,225 | 11,679 | |

| 1980 Engines | bore × stroke | bhp | availability |
|---|---|---|---|
| I-6, 200.0 | 3.68 × 3.13 | 88 | O-all(late) |
| V-8, 255.0 | 3.68 × 3.00 | 115 | S-all |
| V-8, 302.0 | 4.00 × 3.00 | 131 | S-Sil. Ann.; O-others |

### 1981

| (wb 108.4) | | Wght | Price | Prod |
|---|---|---|---|---|
| 42 | cpe | 3,064 | 7,551 | 86,693 |
| 42/60T | Town Landau cpe | 3,127 | 8,689 | |
| 42/607 | Heritage cpe V-8 | 3,303 | 11,355 | |

| 1981 Engines | bore × stroke | bhp | availability |
|---|---|---|---|
| I-6, 200.0 | 3.68 × 3.13 | 88 | S-all exc Heritage |
| V-8, 255.0 | 3.68 × 3.00 | 115 | S-Heritage; O-others |
| V-8, 302.0 | 4.00 × 3.00 | 130 | O-all |

### 1982

| (wb 108.4) | | Wght | Price | Prod |
|---|---|---|---|---|
| 42 | cpe I-6/V-8 | 3,068 | 8,492 | 45,142 |
| 42/60T | Town Landau cpe I-6/V-8 | 3,131 | 9,703 | |
| 42/607 | Heritage cpe V-6/V-8 | 3,303 | 12,742 | |

| 1982 Engines | bore × stroke | bhp | availability |
|---|---|---|---|
| I-6, 200.0 | 3.68 × 3.13 | 88 | S-all exc Heritage |
| V-6, 232.0 | 3.80 × 3.40 | 112 | O-all exc Heritage |
| V-8, 255.0 | 3.68 × 3.00 | 120 | S-Heritage; O-others |

### 1983

| (wb 104.0) | | Wght | Price | Prod |
|---|---|---|---|---|
| 46 | cpe V-6/V-8 | 3,076 | 9,197 | 121,999 |
| 46/607 | Heritage cpe V-6/V-8 | 3,076 | 12,228 | |
| 46/934 | Turbo cpe I-4T | — | 11,790 | |

| 1983 Engines | bore × stroke | bhp | availability |
|---|---|---|---|
| I-4T, 140.0 | 3.78 × 3.13 | 142 | S-turbo cpe |
| V-6, 232.0 | 3.80 × 3.40 | 110 | S-all exc turbo cpe |
| V-8, 302.0 | 4.00 × 3.00 | 140 | O-all exc turbo cpe |

### 1984

| (wb 104.0) | | Wght | Price | Prod |
|---|---|---|---|---|
| 46 | cpe V-6/V-8 | 3,155 | 9,633 | 170,553 |
| 46/607 | Elan cpe V-6/V-8 | 3,221 | 12,661 | |
| 46/606 | Fila cpe V-6/V-8 | 3,326 | 14,471 | |
| 46/934 | Turbo cpe I-4T | 3,073 | 12,330 | |

| 1984 Engines | bore × stroke | bhp | availability |
|---|---|---|---|
| I-4T, 140.0 | 3.78 × 3.13 | 145 | S-turbo cpe |
| V-6, 232.0 | 3.80 × 3.40 | 120 | S-all exc turbo cpe |
| V-8, 302.0 | 4.00 × 3.00 | 140 | O-all exc turbo cpe |

### 1985

| (wb 104.0) | | Wght | Price | Prod |
|---|---|---|---|---|
| 46 | cpe V-6/V-8 | 3,004 | 10,249 | 151,851 |
| 46/607 | Elan cpe V-6/V-8 | 3,041 | 11,916 | |
| 46/606 | Fila cpe V-6/V-8 | 3,108 | 14,974 | |
| 46/934 | Turbo cpe I-4T | 2,990 | 13,365 | |

| 1985 Engines | bore × stroke | bhp | availability |
|---|---|---|---|
| I-4T, 140.0 | 3.78 × 3.13 | 155 | S-turbo cpe |
| V-6, 232.0 | 3.80 × 3.40 | 120 | S-all exc turbo cpe |
| V-8, 302.0 | 4.00 × 3.00 | 140 | O-all exc turbo cpe |

### 1986

| (wb 104.0) | | Wght | Price | Prod |
|---|---|---|---|---|
| 46 | cpe V-6/V-8 | 3,182 | 11,020 | 163,965 |
| 46 | Elan cpe V-6/V-8 | 3,238 | 12,554 | |
| 46 | Turbo cpe I-4T | 3,172 | 14,143 | |

| 1986 Engines | bore × stroke | bhp | availability |
|---|---|---|---|
| I-4T, 140.0 | 3.78 × 3.13 | 145/155 | S-turbo cpe |
| V-6, 232.0 | 3.80 × 3.40 | 120 | S-all exc turbo cpe |
| V-8, 302.0 | 4.00 × 3.00 | 150 | O-all exc turbo cpe |

# Ford Thunderbird

## 1987

| (wb 104.2)—128,135 built | | Wght | Price | Prod |
|---|---|---|---|---|
| 60 | cpe V-6/V-8 | 3,202 | 12,972 | |
| 61 | Sport cpe V-8 | 3,346 | 15,079 | 128,135 |
| 62 | LX cpe V-6/V-8 | 3,245 | 15,383 | |
| 64 | Turbo cpe I-4T | 3,380 | 16,805 | |

| 1987 Engines | bore × stroke | bhp | availability |
|---|---|---|---|
| I-4T, 140.0 | 3.78 × 3.13 | 190 | S-turbo cpe |
| I-4T, 140.0 | 3.78 × 3.13 | 150 | S-turbo cpe (automatic) |
| V-6, 232.0 | 3.80 × 3.40 | 120 | S-all exc turbo cpe |
| V-8, 302.0 | 4.00 × 3.00 | 150 | O-all exc turbo cpe |

## 1988

| (wb 104.2) | | Wght | Price | Prod |
|---|---|---|---|---|
| 60 | cpe V-6/V-8 | 3,280 | 13,599 | |
| 61 | Sport cpe V-8 | 3,450 | 16,030 | 147,243 |
| 62 | LX cpe V-6/V-8 | 3,324 | 15,585 | |
| 64 | Turbo cpe I-4T | 3,415 | 17,250 | |

| 1988 Engines | bore × stroke | bhp | availability |
|---|---|---|---|
| I-4T, 140.0 | 3.78 × 3.13 | 190 | S-turbo cpe |
| I-4T, 140.0 | 3.78 × 3.13 | 150 | S-turbo cpe (automatic) |
| V-6, 232.0 | 3.80 × 3.40 | 140 | S-all exc turbo cpe |
| V-8, 302.0 | 4.00 × 3.00 | 155 | S-spt; O-all exc turbo cpe |

## 1989

| (wb 113.0) | | Wght | Price | Prod |
|---|---|---|---|---|
| — | cpe V-6 | 3,542 | 14,612 | |
| — | LX cpe V-6 | 3,554 | 16,817 | 101,906 |
| — | Super cpe S/C V-6 | 3,701 | 19,823 | 12,962 |

| 1989 Engines | bore × stroke | bhp | availability |
|---|---|---|---|
| V-6, 232.0 | 3.80 × 3.40 | 140 | S-all exc Super cpe |
| V-6S, 232.0 | 3.80 × 3.40 | 210 | S-Super cpe |

## 1990

| (wb 113.0) | | Wght | Price | Prod |
|---|---|---|---|---|
| — | cpe V-6 | 3,581 | 14,980 | |
| — | LX cpe V-6 | — | 17,283 | 90,247 |
| — | Super cpe S/C V-6 | — | 20,390 | 23,710 |

| 1990 Engines | bore × stroke | bhp | availability |
|---|---|---|---|
| V-6, 232.0 | 3.80 × 3.40 | 140 | S-all exc Super cpe |
| V-6S, 232.0 | 3.80 × 3.40 | 210 | S-Super cpe |

## 1991

| (wb 113.0) | | Wght | Price | Prod |
|---|---|---|---|---|
| 63/HVD | cpe 2d | 3550 | 15,318 | |
| — | LX cpe 2d | — | 17,374 | 75,547 |
| 63/HVC | SC cpe 2d | — | 20,999 | 7,267 |

| 1991 Engines | bore × stroke | bhp | availability |
|---|---|---|---|
| V-6, 232.0 | 3.80 × 3.40 | 140 | S-Base, LX |
| V-6S, 232.0 | 3.80 × 3.40 | 210 | S-Super Coupe |
| V-8, 302.0 | 4.00 × 3.00 | 200 | O-Base, LX |

## 1992

| (wb 113.0) | | Wght | Price | Prod |
|---|---|---|---|---|
| BA/VS-AB | cpe 2d | 3,772 | 16,345 | |
| BA/VS | Sport cpe 2d | 3,738 | 18,611 | 73,175 |
| BA/VS-AI | LX cpe 2d | 3,719 | 18,778 | |
| BA/VS-BB/SC | cpe 2d | 3,686 | 22,046 | 4,614 |

| 1992 Engines | bore × stroke | bhp | availability |
|---|---|---|---|
| V-6, 232.0 | 3.80 × 3.40 | 140 | S-Base, LX |
| V-6S, 232.0 | 3.80 × 3.40 | 210 | S-Super Coupe |
| V-8, 302.0 | 4.00 × 3.00 | 200 | O-Base, LX |

## 1993

| (wb 113.0) | | Wght | Price | Prod |
|---|---|---|---|---|
| BA/VS-AI | LX cpe 2d | 3,536 | 15,797 | 128,931 |
| BA/VS-BB | SC cpe 2d | 3,760 | 22,030 | 4,178 |

| 1993 Engines | bore × stroke | bhp | availability |
|---|---|---|---|
| V-6, 232.0 | 3.80 × 3.40 | 140 | S-LX |
| V-6S, 232.0 | 3.80 × 3.40 | 210 | S-Super Coupe |
| V-8, 302.0 | 4.00 × 3.00 | 200 | O-LX |

## 1994

| (wb 113.0) | | Wght | Price | Prod |
|---|---|---|---|---|
| BA/VS-AI | LX cpe 2d | 3,570 | 16,830 | 123,283 |
| BA/VS-BB | SC cpe 2d | 3,758 | 22,240 | 2,973 |

| 1994 Engines | bore × stroke | bhp | availability |
|---|---|---|---|
| V-6, 232.0 | 3.80 × 3.40 | 140 | S-LX |
| V-6S, 232.0 | 3.80 × 3.40 | 230 | S-Super Coupe |
| V-8, 281.0 | 3.60 × 3.60 | 205 | O-LX |

## 1995

| (wb 113.0) | | Wght | Price | Prod |
|---|---|---|---|---|
| P62 | LX cpe 2d | 3,536 | 17,400 | 115,165 |
| P64 | SC cpe 2d | — | 22,910 | |

| 1995 Engines | bore × stroke | bhp | availability |
|---|---|---|---|
| V-6, 232.0 | 3.80 × 3.40 | 140 | S-LX |
| V-6S, 232.0 | 3.80 × 3.40 | 230 | S-Super Coupe |
| V-8, 281.0 | 3.60 × 3.60 | 205 | O-LX |

## 1996

| (wb 113.0) | | Wght | Price | Prod |
|---|---|---|---|---|
| P62 | LX cpe 2d | 3,536 | 17,485 | 86,549 |

| 1996 Engines | bore × stroke | bhp | availability |
|---|---|---|---|
| V-6, 232.0 | 3.80 × 3.40 | 140 | S-LX |
| V-8, 281.0 | 3.60 × 3.60 | 205 | O-LX |

## 1997

| (wb 113.0) | | Wght | Price | Prod |
|---|---|---|---|---|
| P62 | LX cpe 2d | 3,561 | 17,885 | 73,814 |

| 1996 Engines | bore × stroke | bhp | availability |
|---|---|---|---|
| V-6, 232.0 | 3.80 × 3.40 | 145 | S-LX |
| V-8, 281.0 | 3.60 × 3.60 | 205 | O-LX |

## 2002

| (wb 107.2) | | Wght | Price | Prod* |
|---|---|---|---|---|
| P60 | Deluxe conv cpe 2d | 3,775 | 34,965 | |
| P60 | Premium conv cpe 2d | — | 35,965 | |

| 2002 Engines | bore × stroke | bhp | availability |
|---|---|---|---|
| V-8, 241.0 | 3.39 × 3.35 | 252 | S-all |

*Figures not available at time of publication.

# Franklin

Franklin has the special distinction in being one of the few U.S. automakers to achieve real success with air-cooled power. It was featured on the very first Franklins of 1902, which immediately won a reputation for high quality and innovation that would carry on right to the end of the company in 1934.

Weight-saving construction received particular emphasis. In an age when cast iron was the standard stuff of engine blocks, pistons, and cylinder heads, Franklin used high-grade, light-weight aluminum. Equally unusual were the cars' all-around full-elliptic springs, which provided a smoother ride and much reduced tire wear than most competitors' half-elliptic suspensions. A flexible wood frame also softened the ride. By 1920, other advanced technical features such as full-pressure lubrication, automatic spark control, and electric choke were long-familiar Franklin fare. So too were six-cylinder engines; Franklin abandoned fours after 1914.

Franklin's commitment to "aircooling" got a boost when Charles A. Lindbergh made his historic transatlantic flight in 1927. After all, the *Spirit of St. Louis* had an air-cooled engine, and Franklin advertising eagerly pointed up the parallel. The company then began using the name "Airman" on some 1928 models to honor the Lone Eagle. All Franklins that year adopted four-wheel Lockheed hydraulic brakes and a steel chassis. Standard "silent second" synchromesh was further innovation for 1929.

Like many Detroit producers, Franklin entered the '30s with optimism despite Wall Street's recent, ominous crash. That was understandable. The company had enjoyed record sales in 1929, and interest in both aviation and air-cooling was at an all-time high.

Reflecting Franklin's rosy outlook was its 1930 line of "145" and "147" models with new styling and power on respective wheelbases of 125 and 132 inches. Both were announced by a handsome new radiator, which Franklin always termed a "hood front," believing that a conventional radiator was essential to sales. This now had shutters governing the amount of incoming air, with shutter opening controlled automatically by a thermostat connected to the number-one cylinder. Per company tradition, the new engine had six individually cast cylinders and overhead valves, but differed in having cooling air directed to the sides of the block from left to right—an arrangement soon known as "side-blast" cooling. The supercharged six delivered 95 horsepower from 274 cubic inches.

Franklin had always been a luxury make, so its chassis were a logical basis for many custom bodies, typically by Derham, Dietrich, Locke, and Brunn. Among the more memorable 1930 open styles was Dietrich's four-door Pirate, available as either a five-passenger phaeton or seven-seater touring. Its most striking feature was running boards fully concealed by flared door bottoms. Also new that year was the Pursuit, a dual-cowl phaeton that lacked external door handles in the interest of cleaner appearance. Upholstery in the Pursuit's front compartment wrapped up and over the outer edge of the doors *a la* aircraft cockpits of the day. Dietrich also conjured a popular four-door, four-seat speedster with an abbreviated body ending midway over the rear wheels. Most of these were closed styles with permanent canvas tops, but a full-convertible option was offered at extra cost.

As you might expect, famous pioneer aviators like Lindbergh, Amelia Earhart, and Frank Hawks chose Franklins as their personal cars, something else the company was only too eager to publicize. But though Franklin had its sporty models, it never sold cars on that basis. Most of its customers were physicians, attorneys, business executives, and other professionals, so paint colors were usually conservative and blackwall tires were the norm. Franklin had pioneered closed cars by offering sedans before 1920, and these remained the models of choice in the '30s. Franklins may thus be described as conservative, elegant, and fairly expensive. The owners were loyal, and Franklin had many repeat customers.

Franklin claimed its share of the "fine car business" was up 100 percent in the first quarter of 1930 versus the comparable 1928 period. Trouble was, the Great Depression had all but killed the "fine car business," so Franklin's 1930 calendar-year sales came to less than half its 1929 total. Seeking desperately to maintain production levels, Franklin introduced the "Transcontinent Six" (Series 141) in May 1930. Like the "145," it offered a closed coupe, convertible coupe, victoria brougham, and four-door sedan on the 125-inch chassis. The sedan was the cheapest car Franklin had ever offered, but even its $2395 price was four times the cost of a new Model A Ford. In those days, remember, such sums equaled a nice annual salary. With all this, model-year production was dismal: just 5744.

Offerings were promptly pared for 1931. Transcontinent returned with its previous body styles at prices trimmed to just $1800-$1900. Up in the $2400-$2700 area was the

**1930 Series 147 Six Town Car by Derham**

**1930 Series 147 Six Pirate dual-cowl phaeton**

# Franklin

1930 Series 147 Six Pirate 7-passenger phaeton

1931 Series 153 DeLuxe Six Pirate touring

1931 Series 153 DeLuxe Six Speedster sedan

1932 Airman Six convertible coupe

1933 Series 18 Olympic four-door sedan

1933 Series 17-A Twelve four-door sedan

DeLuxe Six, a four-model group sporting rakish clamshell fenders and beautiful flowing body lines by Ray Dietrich on the 132-inch wheelbase. The blown six was coaxed up to 100 brake horsepower for all models. Advertising continued to stress engineering links with aviation via florid phrases such as "riding like gliding." But the Great Depression had set in with a vengeance, and Franklin's model-year production withered to 2851.

Then Franklin hatched a startling idea: an air-cooled V-12—a mighty thing with 398 cid and 150 bhp. Franklin advertised its V-12 as "supercharged," but in reality it had a ram-air effect, courtesy of a duct from the cooling fan. The Twelve was originally planned for the 1931 DeLuxe Six chassis, but was delayed to '32 by financial problems. Franklin had failed to meet payment on certain notes, and the banks sent in managers to protect their investment. Company president Edwin McEwan also decided some changes were needed, so the Twelve bowed as an entirely new and larger car for 1932.

It resembled previous Franklins only in being air-cooled. The traditional full-elliptics and tubular front axle gave way to semi-elliptics and an I-beam. Instead of bodies built by Walker of Massachusetts, Franklin's longtime supplier, Twelve coach-work was hand-crafted at the company's own Syracuse factory. LeBaron was responsible for the styling, distinguished by a sharply vee'd "hood cover" extending back to a jaunty angled windshield. By the standards of 1932, the Franklin Twelve was truly exotic and magnificent to the eye. On a 144-inch wheelbase, its size alone was impressive.

But sales were far from that: an estimated 200 for the model year, plus another 1700 or so six-cylinder Airmans on the 132-inch chassis. Franklin's situation was now quite desperate.

Accordingly, the firm issued an even cheaper line for 1933. Dubbed Olympic, it resulted from a hasty agreement with Reo (*see entry*), another automaker facing imminent demise. Basically it was Reo's new 118-inch-wheelbase Flying Cloud with a Franklin six installed by Franklin in Syracuse, New York. Reo shipped 30 bodies a day from its Lansing, Michigan, factory; a like number of Olympics rolled out of Syracuse the following day. Franklin's investment was modest, so the Olympic's retail price was attractively low: $1385 for either the coupe or sedan, and $1500 for a convertible coupe.

The Olympic was a very good car, but it was too late to save Franklin. Just 1218 were built for 1933, and a mere 109 for swan-song '34. Franklin also offered mechanically unchanged Twelves and Airman Sixes in those final two years, each with four body styles, but production was minuscule. Combined totals were only 98 and 468 units, respectively.

# Franklin

## Specifications

### 1930—5,744 built

| 145 Six (wb 125.0) | Wght | Price | Prod |
|---|---|---|---|
| cpe 3-5P | 3,880 | 2,610 | — |
| conv cpe 3-5P | 3,790 | 2,710 | — |
| victoria brougham 4-6P | 3,790 | 2,695 | — |
| sdn 4d | 3,930 | 2,585 | — |
| **147 Six (wb 132.0)** | | | |
| rdstr 2-4P | 3,950 | 2,885 | — |
| Pirate phtn 5P | 4,120 | 2,885 | — |
| Pirate touring 7P | 4,050 | 2,885 | — |
| Salon spdstr sdn 5P | 4,130 | 2,715 | — |
| sdn 7P | 4,230 | 2,875 | — |
| Pursuit phtn | 4,120 | 2,885 | — |
| **141 Transcontinent Six (wb 125.0)*** | | | |
| cpe 3-5P | 3,850 | 2,445 | — |
| conv cpe 3-5P | 3,775 | 2,495 | — |
| victoria brougham 4P | 3,845 | 2,495 | — |
| sdn 4d | 3,930 | 2,395 | — |

* Production combined with 1931 Series 151.

| 1930 Engine | bore × stroke | bhp | availability |
|---|---|---|---|
| I-6, 274.0 | 3.50 × 4.75 | 95 | S-all |

### 1931—2,851 built

| 151 Transcontinent Six (wb 125.0)* | Wght | Price | Prod |
|---|---|---|---|
| cpe 3-5P | 3,850 | 1,845 | — |
| conv cpe 3-5P | 3,775 | 1,895 | — |
| victoria brougham 4P | 3,845 | 1,895 | — |
| sdn 4d | 3,930 | 1,795 | — |
| **153 DeLuxe Six (wb 132.0)** | | | |
| Custom conv spdstr 4P | 4,110 | 2,695 | — |
| conv cpe 3-5P | 4,185 | 2,465 | — |
| victoria brougham 5P | 4,200 | 2,495 | — |
| sdn 4d | 4,220 | 2,395 | — |

* Includes 1930 Series 141.

| 1931 Engine | bore × stroke | bhp | availability |
|---|---|---|---|
| I-6, 274.0 | 3.50 × 4.75 | 100 | S-all |

### 1932

| 16 Airman Six (wb 132.0)—1,700 built* | | | |
|---|---|---|---|
| | Wght | Price | Prod |
| cpe 3-5P | 4,210 | 2,345 | — |
| conv cpe 3-5P | 4,285 | 2,390 | — |
| victoria brougham 4P | 4,390 | 2,445 | — |
| sdn 4d | 4,420 | 2,345 | — |
| **17 Twelve (wb 144.0)—200 built*** | | | |
| sdn 4d | 5,600 | 3,885 | — |
| club brougham | 5,515 | 3,885 | — |
| sdn 7P | 5,900 | 3,985 | — |
| limo 7P | 5,890 | 4,185 | — |

* estimated.

| 1932 Engines | bore × stroke | bhp | availability |
|---|---|---|---|
| I-6, 274.0 | 3.50 × 4.75 | 100 | S-16 |
| V-12, 398.0 | 3.25 × 4.00 | 150 | S-17 |

### 1933

| 18 Olympic (wb 118.0)—889 built | Wght | Price | Prod |
|---|---|---|---|
| cpe 3-5P | 3,500 | 1,385 | — |
| conv cpe 3-5P | 3,425 | 1,500 | — |
| sdn 4d | 3,625 | 1,385 | — |
| **16-B Airman Six (wb 132.0)—171 built** | | | |
| sdn 4d | 4,420 | 1,936 | — |
| Oxford sdn 4d | 4,420 | 1,995 | — |
| club sdn 5P | 4,425 | 1,985 | — |
| sdn 7P | 4,500 | 2,135 | — |
| **17-A Twelve (wb 144.0)—98 built*** | | | |
| sdn 4d | 5,630 | 2,885 | — |
| club brougham 5P | 5,515 | 2,885 | — |
| sdn 7P | 5,900 | 2,985 | — |
| limo 7P | 5,890 | 3,185 | — |
| **18-B Olympic (wb 118.0)—329 built** | | | |
| cpe 3-5 P | 3,500 | 1,435 | — |
| conv cpe 3-5P | 3,425 | 1,550 | — |
| sdn 4d | 3,625 | 1,435 | — |

* incl. 1934 Series 17-B.

| 1933 Engines | bore × stroke | bhp | availability |
|---|---|---|---|
| I-6, 274.0 | 3.50 × 4.75 | 100 | S-18, 18-B, 16-B |
| V-12, 398.0 | 3.25 × 4.00 | 150 | S-17-B |

### 1934

| 18-C Olympic (wb 118.0)—109 built | Wght | Price | Prod |
|---|---|---|---|
| cpe 3-5P | 3,500 | 1,435 | — |
| conv cpe 3-5P | 3,425 | 1,550 | — |
| sdn 4d | 3,625 | 1,435 | — |
| **19A Airman (wb 132.0)—186 built** | | | |
| cpe 3-5P | 4,270 | 2,185 | — |
| sdn 4d | 4,500 | 2,185 | — |
| club sdn 5P | 4,610 | 2,285 | — |
| sdn 7P | 4,710 | 2,385 | — |
| **19-B Airman (wb 132.0)—111 built** | | | |
| cpe 3-5P | 4,270 | 2,185 | — |
| sdn 4d | 4,500 | 2,185 | — |
| club sdn 5P | 4,610 | 2,285 | — |
| sdn 7P | 4,710 | 2,385 | — |
| **17-B Twelve (wb 144.0)—98 built*** | | | |
| sdn 4d | 5,630 | 2,885 | — |
| club brougham 5P | 5,515 | 2,885 | — |
| sdn 7P | 5,900 | 2,985 | — |
| limo 7P | 5,890 | 3,185 | — |

* Includes 1933 Series 17-A.

| 1934 Engines | bore × stroke | bhp | availability |
|---|---|---|---|
| I-6, 274.0 | 3.50 × 4.75 | 100 | S-18-C, 19, 19-B |
| V-12, 398.0 | 3.25 × 4.00 | 150 | S-17-B |

# Frazer

**1948 Standard four-door sedan**

Frazer was one of the few genuinely new post World War II American cars, but managed only a short, somewhat unhappy life. The name honored Joseph Washington Frazer, the high-born aristocrat (descended from the Virginia Washingtons) who loved motorcars and became a super-salesman through stints at Packard, Pierce-Arrow, and General Motors. Frazer also worked with Walter P. Chrysler in the 1920s and resuscitated moribund Willys-Overland in the late '30s.

In the early '40s, Frazer was looking to build a new postwar car, an idea that also occurred to Henry J. Kaiser, the West Coast metals and construction tycoon who'd turned out wartime Liberty ships double-quick. Frazer and Kaiser met, hit it off, and formed Kaiser-Frazer Corporation in July 1945, with Frazer as president, Kaiser as board chairman. It seemed a match made in automotive heaven: Joe's redoubtable sales acumen married to Henry J.'s vast manufacturing resources.

After considering several proposals (including a radical front-drive design), they settled on a conventional rear-drive four-door sedan with modern flush-fender styling by renowned custom-body designer Howard A. "Dutch" Darrin. The end product wasn't all Darrin's work—nor entirely to his satisfaction—but it was smooth and fairly stylish for the period, with the arguable exception of the high blunt hood.

Two versions were planned: a medium-price Kaiser and a luxury Frazer. Henry J, thinking big as usual, geared up for Kaisers by buying Ford's huge, wartime bomber plant at Willow Run, Michigan. Frazers were to be built by Graham-Paige in Detroit, lately acquired by Joe and his associates. But G-P was foundering and sold out to K-F in 1947, so all but the earliest Frazers were built alongside Kaisers.

Both makes began production in June 1946 (for model-year '47). Each offered basic and upmarket models. Frazers were nameless "Standards" and Manhattans. There was only one engine: a long-stroke 226.2-cubic-inch flathead six, basically the Continental "Red Seal" design improved upon and mostly built by K-F. Frazer advertised it as the "Supersonic Six," but with only 100/110 horsepower to push over 3300 pounds, no K-F car acted jet-propelled. At least the "Darrin-styled" body offered exceptional passenger room—including the industry's widest front seat—64 inches—and the rugged box-section chassis boasted modern front-coil/rear-leaf suspension.

Initially, K-F built two Kaisers to each Frazer, reflecting the latter's higher $2295 starting price—close to Cadillac territory. The Manhattan was some $400 more, but also elegantly upholstered in nylon and fine Bedford cord cloth keyed to

**1949-50 Manhattan convertible sedan**

**1949-50 Manhattan four-door sedan**

exterior colors, which were typically two-tones. Full leather upholstery was also available. Unfortunately, this Cadillac price rival lacked an automatic transmission of any kind, let alone one to match ultrasmooth Hydra-Matic: just a three-speed manual or the same with optional Borg-Warner overdrive ($80).

Yet despite the stiff prices, lack of automatic, and no eight-cylinder engine in sight, K-F enjoyed strong initial sales to earn the press sobriquet of "postwar wonder company." Still, some observers doubted the dynamic managerial duo. Henry Kaiser, they said, didn't know an automobile from a motorboat, while Frazer had only sold cars, not built them.

Even so, K-F succeeded despite postwar materials shortages, forming a crack team of expediters who foraged the country for everything from sheet steel to copper wire. They usually got what they wanted—though at a price, the main reason the cars cost so much. Still, K-F racked up the highest output of any independent in 1947-48, with total volume sufficient for ninth place in the production race.

And why not? Both the Kaiser and Frazer had the advantage of being all-new cars with no prewar links, and both were readily available (though competitors were fast returning to prewar production levels). They also looked good: very clean, with modest horizontal grilles (Frazer's was a bit more ornate than Kaiser's) and little decorative chrome or sculptured sheetmetal, reflecting Darrin's design ideals. A long 123.5-inch wheelbase provided a smooth ride, and the six-cylinder engine, though plodding, delivered excellent fuel economy. But this was a heady age when buyers wanted all the performance and chrome they could get. Though Frazer ultimately got around to optional hood ornaments and more-glittery interiors, the lack of eight-cylinder power would prove an increasing sales liability for the prices charged.

In fact, the Frazer never really went much beyond its original formula. Indeed, the '48 models changed only in detail yet cost even more: $2483-$2746. So though the postwar seller's market was still in full swing, Frazer volume dropped ominously for model-year '48, from 68,775 to 48,071.

Then, a gross miscalculation. Knowing his firm could field only facelifts against all-new models from the Big Three and Nash, Joe Frazer recommended cutting 1949 production, then coming back with all-new designs for 1950. But Henry Kaiser wouldn't hear of it, declaring, "The Kaisers never retrench!" Predictably, Henry won. In protest, Joe stepped down to the meaningless position of board vice-chairman, and Henry appointed his own son, Edgar, as president. K-F duly tooled for 200,000 cars, but ended up selling just 58,000 for '49. A long downhill slide had begun.

The '49 Frazers took on an eggcrate grille, prominent rectangular parking lamps, and large two-lens vertical taillamps. There was also a new four-door Manhattan convertible, but it was a makeshift job at best. Directed to do or die, engineers John Widman and Ralph Isbrandt sheared the top off a sedan, retained B-pillars with little inset glass panes, and purchased

**1949 Standard prototype (with Kaiser hubcaps)**

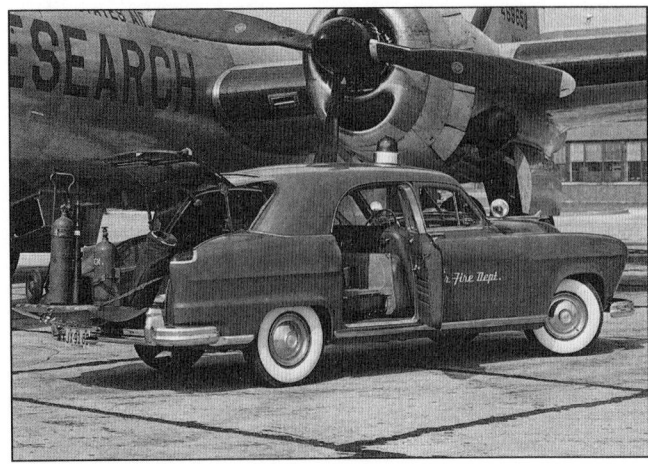
**1951 Standard Vagabond utility sedan**

# Frazer

1951 Standard four-door sedan

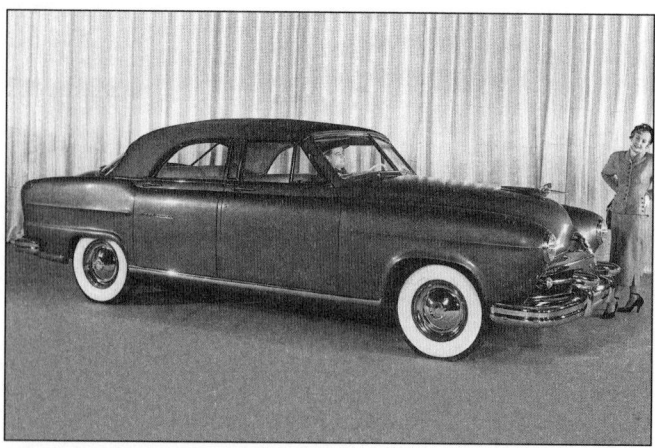

1951 Manhattan hardtop sedan

beefed-up X-member frames at an inordinate price. But at over $3000, the four-door flop-top Frazer simply couldn't sell in viable numbers.

Nor could any '49 Frazer. As a result, some 5000 '49 leftovers were reserialed for a brief 1950 run that ended in the spring of that year. Production for the two seasons came to just under 25,000 units, including a mere 70 Manhattan convertibles. It's estimated that only 15 percent of the total were sold as 1950 models.

Frazer's 1951 was abbreviated, too, but the cars looked startlingly different, thanks to an effective front and rear redo by Herb Weissinger of K-F Styling. The intent was to use up remaining 1949-50 bodyshells. Thus, leftover Kaiser Vagabond utility sedans (with double hatchback and folding rear seat) became standard-trim '51 Frazer Vagabonds, while Kaiser Virginian four-door "hardtops" were made into '51 Frazer Manhattans. Pillared sedans were assigned to Frazer's standard line, but trimmed like 1950 Manhattans. Encouraged by the belated arrival of Hydra-Matic as a $159 option, dealers ordered 55,000 of the '51 Frazers, but received only 10,214. The Frazer was dead.

K-F stylists had created numerous renderings for future Frazers based on Darrin's sleek and low 1951 "Anatomic" Kaiser. But these and other plans were rendered stillborn when Joe Frazer left the company in early '49. Two years later, the Kaisers were busy with their new small car, the Henry J—and leftover '51 Kaisers. In retrospect, they really should have listened to Joe.

## Specifications

### 1947

| Standard (wb 123.5) | Wght | Price | Prod |
|---|---|---|---|
| F47   sdn 4d | 3,340 | 2,295 | 36,120 |
| **Manhattan (wb 123.5)** | | | |
| F47C   sdn 4d | 3,375 | 2,712 | 32,655 |

| 1947 Engines | bore × stroke | bhp | availability |
|---|---|---|---|
| I-6, 226.2 | 3.31 × 4.38 | 100 | S-all |
| I-6, 226.2 | 3.31 × 4.38 | 112 | O-Manhattan |

### 1948

| F485 Standard (wb 123.5) | Wght | Price | Prod |
|---|---|---|---|
| 4851   sdn 4d | 3,340 | 2,483 | 29,480 |
| **F486 Manhattan (wb 123.5)** | | | |
| 4861   sdn 4d | 3,375 | 2,746 | 18,591 |

| 1948 Engines | bore × stroke | bhp | availability |
|---|---|---|---|
| I-6, 226.2 | 3.31 × 4.38 | 100 | S-all |
| I-6, 226.2 | 3.31 × 4.38 | 112 | O-Manhattan |

### 1949-50

| F495/505 Standard (wb 123.5) | Wght | Price | Prod |
|---|---|---|---|
| 4951/5051   sdn 4d | 3,386 | 2,395 | 14,700* |
| **F496/506 Manhattan (wb 123.5)** | | | |
| 4961/5051   sdn 4d | 3,391 | 2,595 | 9,950* |
| 4962/5052   conv sdn | 3,726 | 3,295 | 70* |

* Estimated: actual total 24,923. Years were combined by factory; estimated breakdown 85% 1949, 15% 1950.

| 1949-50 Engine | bore × stroke | bhp | availability |
|---|---|---|---|
| I-6, 226.2 | 3.31 × 4.38 | 112 | S-all |

### 1951

| F515 Standard (wb 123.5) | Wght | Price | Prod |
|---|---|---|---|
| 5151   sdn 4d | 3,456 | 2,359 | 6,900* |
| 5155   Vagabond util sdn 4d | 3,556 | 2,399 | 3,000* |
| **F516 Manhattan (wb 123.5)** | | | |
| 5161   htp sdn | 3,771 | 3,075 | 152 |
| 5162   conv sdn | 3,941 | 3,075 | 131 |

* Estimated from actual total of 9,931.

| 1951 Engine | bore × stroke | bhp | availability |
|---|---|---|---|
| I-6, 226.2 | 3.31 × 4.38 | 115 | S-all |

# Graham

Brothers Joseph, Robert, and Ray Graham were "Indiana sharpies," to quote auto historian Jeffrey Godshall—farm boys with "dreams beyond the bucolic life." Sharp they were. After starting a glassmaking business that grew to become Libbey-Owens-Ford in 1930, the brothers built trucks for Dodge. They did so well that by 1926 they were running Dodge's entire truck organization. Then, suddenly, they left and bought the declining Paige Motor Company in 1927 to build their own cars. The first appeared the following year under the Graham-Paige banner, which continued through 1930. The name was then changed to simply Graham, though Paige remained in the company name and on its commercial vehicles.

The Grahams prospered with cars as quickly as they had with trucks, volume soaring to more than 77,000 in calendar 1929. By that time they'd set up a vast new factory in Dearborn, plus facilities in Indiana and Florida. However, 1929 would be the firm's production peak.

Graham's 1930 line was expansive, comprising Standard and Special Sixes on a 115-inch wheelbase and Standard, Special, and Custom Eights on spans of 122, 134, 127, and 137 inches. Engines were conventional L-heads: 207- and 224-cubic-inch inline-sixes with 66/76 horsepower as well as 298.6- and 322-cid straight-eights with 100/120 bhp. Among numerous body styles were beautiful long-wheelbase Custom Eight town cars and limousines by the LeBaron studios at Briggs Manufacturing Company. All models featured Graham-Paige's famous four-speed transmission.

This basic lineup continued through early 1932, joined in the spring of 1931 by the hopefully named "Prosperity Six," a cheap four-model series priced as low as $785. But the Depression was on, and Graham-Paige failed to prosper. Model-year 1930 car production sank to about 24,000, then slid to 20,000 for '31.

Undaunted, the Grahams came back for 1932 with the Blue Streak Eight. This mounted a generous 123-inch wheelbase that perfectly suited magnificent new styling by Amos Northup of the Murray Corporation. Northup had just created the 1931 Reo Royale and was also responsible for the earlier Hupp Century. The Blue Streak was no less stunning. Smooth, ultraclean bodies hid unsightly chassis components, windshields tilted jauntily back, a radiator with tapered vertical bars and no cap fit flush with the hood, and fenders were artfully drawn down to hug the wheels—the "skirted" treatment was a first for a production car.

The Blue Streak bowed with only a coupe, four-door sedan, and convertible coupe. All carried a 90-bhp 245.4-cid eight with an aluminum head and pistons. Beneath the trend-setting bodies was an equally advanced chassis with straight side rails, outboard rear springs, and "banjo" rear-axle mounting. The result was exceptional handling stability combined with great ride comfort, abetted by adjustable shock absorbers and, a bit later, low-pressure tires. Standard and Deluxe trim was offered at attractively low prices ranging from $1095 to $1270.

In good times, the Blue Streak would have sold well. But 1932 wasn't a good year for anyone in Detroit, and Graham's calendar-year volume slid to 12,967. Most were Blue Streaks and conventionally styled Sixes.

The Blue Streak was renamed Custom Eight for 1933, when its little-changed basic design spread to all "second-series" Grahams. Competitors' styling began mimicking the Blue Streak, so Graham proclaimed itself "the most imitated car on the road." With almost every '33 American car wearing fender skirts, they were right. Below the Custom were a new 113-inch-wheelbase Standard Six and 119-inch Standard Eight. All models rode stronger frames with front K-brace and sported gracefully vee'd front bumpers. Yet for all this quality and appeal, Graham-Paige production sank again, hitting 11,000 for the calendar year, though the firm somehow eked out a tiny $67,000 profit.

Still hoping for better times, Graham sprang a surprise for

**1932 Model 57 Blue Streak Eight 3-window coupe**

# Graham

1932 Model 57 Blue Streak Eight four-door sedan

1933 Model 64 Standard Eight four-door sedan (Second Series)

1933 Model 65 Standard Six four-door sedan (Second Series)

1934 Model 67 Standard Eight trunkback sedan (Second Series)

1934: the Supercharged Custom Eight. Tagged as low as $1295, it was America's first moderate-cost supercharged car. Boosting its newly bored 265.4-cid engine was a Graham-built centrifugal blower that helped deliver 135 bhp—good for lively midrange urge and 90 mph all-out. Daredevil driver "Cannonball" Baker drove a Supercharged Custom cross-country in 53 hours, 30 minutes; a solo record that would stand until 1975. Baker's feat also testified to the utter reliability of the Graham blower. Over the next six years, Graham would build more supercharged cars than any company ever had before.

Other Grahams saw little change through the "first-series" 1935 models, though the lineup was juggled several times and built-in trunks were a notable new option for sedans (at $35). With calender 1934 output rising to 15,745 cars, things seemed to be looking up.

Offerings shuffled again for 1935's "second series." Coupes and convertibles looked much as before, but sedans began backing away from Blue Streak styling, which was becoming a bit dated anyway. A smaller new Standard Six arrived with a 60-bhp, 169.6-cid engine and Blue Streak styling on a trim 111-inch wheelbase. It lacked some big-Graham technical features, but sold well. A good thing, as eight-cylinder sales declined sharply. So even though model-year volume went up to near 18,500, Graham was now feeling a severe financial pinch.

Accordingly, the firm abandoned Eights for 1936 but offered America's first supercharged six: a 217.8-cid unit that would be Graham's mainstay engine right to the end. It arrived in 115-inch-wheelbase Supercharged and unblown Cavalier series sharing Hayes-built coupe, sedan, and convertible bodies with Reo's 1935-36 Flying Cloud, an arrangement worked out during 1935. The two companies never "married," but Graham used Reo bodies through 1937, which resulted in some very ordinary looking cars. Graham's price-leading 1936-37 Crusader used 1935 tooling, which was later sold to Nissan of Japan to bring in needed cash. And Graham needed that, losing $1 million in 1936 despite higher calendar-year sales of over 16,400.

Hoping for a miracle, Graham unleashed the radical "Spirit of Motion" for 1938, a blown and unblown four-door sedan with a sharply undercut front that soon earned the dubious nickname "sharknose." It was Northup's last design before his untimely death in 1936. (Ray Graham had passed away in 1932; he was only 45.) Graham was trying to be the style leader it had been with the Blue Streak, but the public didn't buy it—literally, as model-year production ended at 5020. A "sharknose" two-door sedan and "Combination" club coupe

1935 Model 69 Supercharged Custom Eight sedan (First Series)

arrived for 1939, when running boards were eliminated. Horsepower remained 116 supercharged, 90 unblown, and all models offered Deluxe and better Custom trim. Despite impressive supercharged performance (10.9 seconds 0-50) and fuel economy of up to 25 mpg, the "sharknose" remained a poor seller. It thus departed after 1940, seeing little further change save slight horsepower gains (to 120 and 93). Respective 1939-40 model-year production was 5392 and an estimated 1000.

By now, company president Joseph Graham had spent a half-million dollars of his own money to keep his firm going. He needed something new, but how to pay for it? The answer came in 1939 with Norman De Vaux, who'd failed with automobiles marketed under his own name. De Vaux had bought up the tooling for the late 1936-37 Cord 810/812 Westchester sedan, and had talked equally struggling Hupp Motors into building a modified version with rear-wheel drive instead of front drive. Joe Graham proposed building the bodies, provided his company could sell its own version of the car with Graham power. Aside from that and minor trim differences, the resulting Graham Hollywood and Hupp Skylark were identical. The Skylark was announced first, in April 1939 at the New York World's Fair, though that proved premature. Gearing up for production took longer than expected, so neither model was built in significant numbers until May 1940.

Like Hupp, Graham planned to offer a sedan and convertible, but only one Hupp convertible was ever built and maybe up to five Grahams. Production Hollywoods carried Graham's own 120-bhp supercharged six, and thus cost a bit more than Hupp's unblown Skylark: initially $1250 versus $1145. Both models rode a 115-inch wheelbase, 10 inches shorter than the parent Cord's. To fit their tall engine beneath the Cord's lower hoodline, Graham engineers offset both carburetor and air cleaner. Both versions wore a handsomely reworked face (by the renowned John Tjaarda) with a double grille (fully chromed on Hollywoods), exposed bullet headlamps, and nicely shaped front fenders.

Unfortunately, the old tooling was simply unsuitable for volume production—the same thing that had tripped up the Cord. The roof alone comprised seven separate panels. Joe Graham hoped to simplify matters, but was distracted when he agreed to take over Skylark production, which necessitated a complete overhaul of Graham's assembly line and added further cost and delay.

Though Hupp called it quits in the summer of 1940, Graham pressed on for '41, adding an unblown Hollywood priced at just $968 and cutting the price of the supercharged model to $1065. Horsepower was upped slightly on both engines. But it was all to no avail, and Graham finally gave up the auto business, too, in September 1940.

**1935 Model 75 Supercharged Eight four-door sedan**

**1936 Series 110 Supercharged touring sedan two-door**

**1937 Series 120 Custom Supercharged business coupe**

**1939 Series 96 Special Combination coupe**

**1940 Series 107 Supercharged Custom four-door sedan**

**1941 Custom Hollywood Supercharged four-door sedan**

# Graham

Ironically, departing the car business proved quite timely, as Graham prospered through World War II on $20 million of government defense contracts. Joseph W. Frazer then bought the firm in 1944. His namesake Frazer car was built as a "Graham-Paige" product in 1946-47, though at Kaiser's Willow Run factory rather than G-P's old Dearborn plant. In early 1947, Graham-Paige sold its remaining automotive interests to Kaiser-Frazer, and in 1952 quit farm equipment as well. G-P then dropped "Motors" from its name and became a closed investment corporation. It later operated Madison Square Garden and owned several professional New York athletic teams. All these endeavors proved far more profitable than carmaking had ever been.

## Specifications

Note: All production figures approximate, based on assigned serial number spans.

### 1930

| Standard Six (wb 115)—18,000 built | Wght | Price | Prod |
|---|---|---|---|
| rdstr 2-4P | 2,865 | 995 | — |
| phtn 5P | 2,910 | 1,015 | — |
| cpe 2P | 2,940 | 845 | — |
| cpe 2-4P | 2,995 | 895 | — |
| cabriolet 2-4P | 2,950 | 1,065 | — |
| sdn 2d | 3,015 | 895 | — |
| Universal sdn 3W 5P | 3,160 | 895 | — |
| DeLuxe sdn 3W 5P | 3,175 | 995 | — |
| Town sdn 2W 5P | 3,145 | 845 | — |
| DeLuxe cpe 2P | 2,940 | 895 | — |
| DeLuxe cpe 2-4P | 2,995 | 945 | — |
| DeLuxe Town sdn 5P | 3,145 | 945 | — |

| Special Six (wb 115.0)—2,600 built | | | |
|---|---|---|---|
| cpe 2P | 3,230 | 1,195 | — |
| cpe 2-4P | 3,355 | 1,225 | — |
| sdn 4d | 3,390 | 1,225 | — |

| Standard Eight (wb 122.0; 7P-134.0)—925 built | | | |
|---|---|---|---|
| cpe 2-4P | 3,735 | 1,445 | — |
| sdn 4d | 3,795 | 1,445 | — |
| conv sdn 5P | 3,725 | 1,985 | — |
| sdn 7P | 4,040 | 1,745 | — |

| Special Eight (wb 122.0; 7P-134.0)—2,025 built | | | |
|---|---|---|---|
| cpe 2-4P | 3,805 | 1,595 | — |
| sdn 4d | 3,875 | 1,595 | — |
| conv sdn 5P | 3,785 | 2,085 | — |
| sdn 7P | 4,120 | 1,845 | — |

| Custom Eight (wb 127.0; lwb-137.0)—575 built | | | |
|---|---|---|---|
| rdstr 2-4P | 4,009 | 2,225 | |
| phtn 5P | 3,975 | 2,295 | |
| cpe 2-4P | 4,105 | 2,225 | 250 |
| cabriolet 2-4P | 4,075 | 2,245 | |
| sdn 4d | 4,300 | 2,025 | |
| lwb phtn 7P | 4,200 | 2,295 | |
| lwb sdn 4d | 4,405 | 2,445 | |
| Town sdn 4d (lwb) | 4,465 | 2,455 | |
| lwb sdn 7P | 4,340 | 2,525 | 325 |
| limo 7P (lwb) | 4,590 | 2,595 | |
| LeBaron limo sdn 7P (lwb) | 4,535 | 3,940 | |
| LeBaron town car 7P (lwb) | 4,545 | 4,255 | |
| LeBaron limo 7P (lwb) | 4,545 | 4,505 | |

| 1930 Engines | bore × stroke | bhp | availability |
|---|---|---|---|
| I-6, 207.0 | 3.13 × 4.50 | 66 | S-Standard 6 |
| I-6, 224.0 | 3.25 × 4.50 | 76 | S-Special 6 |
| I-8, 298.6 | 3.25 × 4.50 | 100 | S-Standard 8, Sp 8 |
| I-8, 322.0 | 3.38 × 4.50 | 120 | S-Custom 8 |

### 1931

| Standard Six (wb 115)—9,000 built | Wght | Price | Prod |
|---|---|---|---|
| rdstr 2-4P | 2,865 | 995 | — |
| phtn 5P | 2,910 | 1,015 | — |
| bus cpe 2P | 2,940 | 845 | — |
| cpe 2-4P | 2,995 | 895 | — |
| spt cpe 2-4P | 2,995 | 1,045 | — |
| sdn 2d | 3,015 | 895 | — |
| Town sdn 5P | 3,145 | 845 | — |
| Univ sdn 5P | 3,160 | 895 | — |
| DeLuxe sdn 5P | 3,175 | 995 | — |
| DeLuxe Town sdn 5P | 3,145 | 945 | — |

| Special Six (wb 115.0)—1,400 built | | | |
|---|---|---|---|
| bus cpe 2P | 3,230 | 1,195 | — |
| cpe 2-4P | 3,355 | 1,225 | — |
| sdn 5P | 3,390 | 1,225 | — |

| 621 Six (wb 121.0) | | | |
|---|---|---|---|
| rdstr 2-4P | 3,835 | 1,795 | — |
| phtn 5P | 3,805 | 1,865 | — |
| victoria cpe 4P | 3,905 | 1,595 | — |
| cpe 2-4P | 3,935 | 1,795 | — |
| sdn 5P | 4,130 | 1,595 | — |

| Standard Eight (wb 122.0; lwb-134.0) | | | |
|---|---|---|---|
| cpe 2-4P | 3,735 | 1,445 | — |
| sdn 5P | 3,795 | 1,445 | — |
| conv sdn 5P | 3,725 | 1,985 | — |
| lwb sdn 7P | 4,040 | 1,745 | — |
| lwb sdn 5P | 3,980 | 1,695 | — |
| limo 7P (lwb) | 4,090 | 1,945 | — |

| Special Eight (wb 122.0; lwb-134.0)—2,025 built | | | | |
|---|---|---|---|---|
| 822 | cpe 2-4P | 3,805 | 1,595 | |
| 822 | sdn 5P | 3,875 | 1,635 | 1,125 |
| 822 | conv sdn 5P | 3,785 | 1,635 | |
| | lwb sdn 7P | 4,120 | 1,845 | |
| | lwb sdn 5P | 4,060 | 1,795 | 900 |
| | limo 7P (lwb) | 4,110 | 2,045 | |

| Custom Eight (wb 127.0; lwb-137.0) | | | |
|---|---|---|---|
| rdstr 2-4P | 4,005 | 2,225 | — |
| phtn 5P | 3,975 | 2,295 | — |
| victoria cpe 4P | 4,075 | 2,025 | — |
| cabriolet 2-4P | 4,075 | 2,245 | — |
| sdn 5P | 4,300 | 2,025 | — |
| lwb phtn 7P | 4,270 | 2,595 | — |
| lwb sdn 5P | 4,470 | 2,455 | — |
| LeBaron limo 7P (lwb) | 4,620 | 4,505 | — |

| 1931 Engines | bore × stroke | bhp | availability |
|---|---|---|---|
| I-6, 207.0 | 3.13 × 4.50 | 66 | S-Standard 6 |
| I-6, 224.0 | 3.25 × 4.50 | 76 | S-Special 6 |
| I-6, 228.0 | 3.50 × 5.00 | 97 | S-621 |
| I-8, 298.6 | 3.25 × 4.50 | 100 | S-Standard 8, Special 8 |
| I-8, 322.0 | 3.38 × 4.50 | 120 | S-Custom 8 |

### 1931 Second Series (Production began Jan. 1, 1931)

| Standard Six (wb 115)—11,600 built | Wght | Price | Prod |
|---|---|---|---|
| rdstr 2-4P | 2,930 | 895 | — |
| sdn 5P | 3,265 | 955 | — |
| bus cpe 2P | 3,120 | 845 | — |

# Graham

| Standard Six (wb 115) | Wght | Price | Prod |
|---|---|---|---|
| cpe 2-4P | 3,170 | 895 | — |
| Town sdn 5P | 3,220 | 895 | — |
| **Special Six (wb 115.0)—2,000 built** | | | |
| bus cpe 2P | 3,175 | 925 | — |
| cpe 2-4P | 3,235 | 975 | — |
| sdn 4d | 3,330 | 1,035 | — |
| Town sdn 5P | 3,270 | 975 | — |
| **820 Special Eight (wb 120.0)—2,800 built** | | | |
| bus cpe 2P | 3,445 | 1,155 | — |
| cpe 2-4P | 3,500 | 1,195 | — |
| spt sdn 5P | 3,565 | 1,195 | — |
| sdn 5P | 3,560 | 1,245 | — |
| **834 Custom Eight (wb 134.0)—200 built** | | | |
| sdn 4d | 4,100 | 1,845 | — |
| sdn 7P | 4,190 | 1,895 | — |
| limo 7P | 4,245 | 2,095 | — |
| **Prosperity Six (wb 113.0)—1,000 built** | | | |
| cpe 2P | 3,015 | 785 | — |
| cpe 2-4P | 3,070 | 825 | — |
| sdn 5P | 3,100 | 825 | — |
| Town sdn 5P | 3,100 | 795 | — |

| 1931(2) Engines | bore × stroke | bhp | availability |
|---|---|---|---|
| I-6, 207.0 | 3.13 × 4.50 | 70 | S-Prosperity Six |
| I-6, 224.0 | 3.25 × 4.50 | 76 | S-Std 6, Sp 6 |
| I-8, 245.4 | 3.13 × 4.50 | 85 | S-820 |
| I-8, 298.6 | 3.25 × 4.50 | 100 | S-834 |

## 1932

| Prosperity Six (wb 113)—700 built | Wght | Price | Prod |
|---|---|---|---|
| cpe 2P | 3,015 | 785 | — |
| cpe 2-4P | 3,070 | 825 | — |
| sdn 5P | 3,100 | 825 | — |
| Town sdn 5P | 3,100 | 795 | — |
| **Standard Six (wb 115.0)** | | | |
| rdstr 2-4P | 2,930 | 945 | — |
| bus cpe 2P | 3,120 | 934 | — |
| cpe 2-4P | 3,170 | 985 | — |
| sdn 5P | 3,265 | 995 | — |
| Town sdn 5P | 3,220 | 975 | — |
| **Special Six (wb 115.0)** | | | |
| rdstr 2-4P | 2,995 | 985 | — |
| bus cpe 2P | 3,175 | 985 | — |
| cpe 2-4P | 3,235 | 1,025 | — |
| sdn 4d | 3,330 | 1,035 | — |
| Town sdn 5P | 3,270 | 1,015 | — |
| **820 Special Eight (wb 120.0)** | | | |
| bus cpe 2P | 3,445 | 1,185 | — |
| cpe 2-4P | 3,500 | 1,225 | — |
| spt sdn 5P | 3,565 | 1,235 | — |
| sdn 5P | 3,560 | 1,285 | — |
| **822 Special Eight (wb 122.0)** | | | |
| sdn 5P | 3,875 | 1,635 | — |
| conv sdn 5P | 3,785 | 1,635 | — |
| **834 New Custom Eight (wb 134.0)** | | | |
| sdn 4d | 4,100 | 1,895 | — |
| sdn 7P | 4,190 | 1,945 | — |
| limo 7P | 4,245 | 2,145 | — |
| **57 Blue Streak Eight (wb 123.0)—9,714 built** | | | |
| cpe 2P | 3,600 | 1,095 | — |
| cpe 2-4P | 3,675 | 1,145 | — |

| 57 Blue Streak Eight (wb 123.0) | Wght | Price | Prod |
|---|---|---|---|
| sdn 5P | 3,665 | 1,145 | — |
| DeLuxe cpe 2P | 3,620 | 1,170 | — |
| DeLuxe cpe 2-4P | 3,685 | 1,220 | — |
| DeLuxe conv cpe | 3,730 | 1,270 | — |
| DeLuxe sdn 5P | 3,690 | 1,220 | — |
| **Six (wb 113.0)—700 built** | | | |
| sdn 5P | 3,205 | 795 | — |
| Town sdn 5P | 3,190 | 765 | — |

| 1932 Engines | bore × stroke | bhp | availability |
|---|---|---|---|
| I-6, 207.0 | 3.13 × 4.50 | 70 | S-Six, Prosp Six |
| I-6, 224.0 | 3.25 × 4.50 | 76 | S-Standard 6, Special 6 |
| I-8, 245.4 | 3.13 × 4.50 | 85 | S-820 |
| I-8, 245.4 | 3.13 × 4.50 | 90 | S-57 |
| I-8, 298.6 | 3.25 × 4.50 | 100 | S-822, 834 |

## 1933

| Six(a) (wb 118.0) | Wght | Price | Prod |
|---|---|---|---|
| bus cpe 2P | 3,480 | 825 | — |
| cpe 2-4P | 3,545 | 875 | — |
| conv cab 2-4P | 3,590 | 895 | — |
| sdn 5P | 3,570 | 875 | — |
| **Six(b) (wb 113.0)** | | | |
| sdn 5P | 3,205 | 710 | — |
| Town sdn 5P | 3,190 | 680 | — |
| **57A Eight (wb 123.0)** | | | |
| cpe 2P | 3,600 | 925 | — |
| cpe 2-4P | 3,675 | 975 | — |
| sdn 5P | 3,665 | 975 | — |
| DeLuxe cpe 2P | 3,620 | 1,000 | — |
| DeLuxe 2-4P | 3,685 | 1,050 | — |
| DeLuxe conv cpe 2-4P | 3,730 | 1,070 | — |
| DeLuxe sdn 5P | 3,690 | 1,050 | — |
| **65 Standard Six (wb 113.0)—4,000 built** | | | |
| bus cpe 2P | 3,230 | 745 | — |
| cpe 2-4P | 3,295 | 795 | — |
| conv cpe 2-4P | 3,255 | 835 | — |
| sdn 5P | 3,265 | 795 | — |
| **64 Standard Eight (wb 119.0)—2,000 built** | | | |
| bus cpe 2P | 3,455 | 845 | — |
| cpe 2-4P | 3,510 | 895 | — |
| conv cpe 2-4P | 3,470 | 935 | — |
| sdn 5P | 3,500 | 895 | — |
| **57A Custom Eight (wb 123.0)—1,000 built** | | | |
| cpe 2P | 3,625 | 1,045 | — |
| cpe 2-4P | 3,680 | 1,095 | — |
| sdn 5P | 3,695 | 1,095 | — |

| 1933 Engines | bore × stroke | bhp | availability |
|---|---|---|---|
| I-6, 207.0 | 3.13 × 4.50 | 70 | S-Six(b) |
| I-6, 224.0 | 3.25 × 4.50 | 80 | S-Six(a) |
| I-6, 224.0 | 3.25 × 4.50 | 85 | S-Std Six |
| I-8, 245.4 | 3.13 × 4.50 | 90 | S-57A Eight |
| I-8, 245.4 | 3.13 × 4.50 | 95 | S-64, 57A Custom Eight |

## 1934

| 65 Standard Six (wb 113)—6,000 built | Wght | Price | Prod |
|---|---|---|---|
| cpe 2P | 3,205 | 745 | — |
| cpe 2-4P | 3,275 | 795 | — |
| conv cpe 2-4P | 3,230 | 835 | — |
| sdn 5P | 3,240 | 795 | — |

# Graham

| 64 Standard Eight (wb 119)—3,000 blt | Wght | Price | Prod |
|---|---|---|---|
| cpe 2P | 3,415 | 845 | — |
| cpe 2-4P | 3,485 | 895 | — |
| conv cpe 2-4P | 3,430 | 935 | — |
| sdn 5P | 3,460 | 895 | — |
| **57A Custom Eight (wb 123.0)—4,000 built** | | | |
| cpe 2P | 3,600 | 1,045 | — |
| cpe 2-4P | 3,640 | 1,095 | — |
| sdn 5P | 3,670 | 1,095 | — |
| **68 Six (wb 116.0)—8,550 built** | | | |
| Standard bus cpe 2P | 3,135 | 695 | |
| Standard cpe 2-4P | 3,190 | 765 | |
| Standard sdn 5P | 3,165 | 775 | |
| Standard sdn T/B 5P | 3,260 | 810 | |
| DeLuxe bus cpe 2P | 3,165 | 805 | 5,320 |
| DeLuxe cpe 2-4P | 3,210 | 855 | |
| DeLuxe conv cpe 2-4P | 3,195 | 845 | |
| DeLuxe sdn 5P | 3,215 | 855 | |
| DeLuxe sdn T/B 5P | 3,300 | 890 | |
| **later production (from April 1934)** | | | |
| Standard bus cpe 2P | 3,100 | 745 | |
| Standard cpe 2-4P | 3,165 | 795 | |
| Standard conv cpe 2-4P | 3,165 | 845 | 3,230 |
| Standard sdn 5P | 3,120 | 795 | |
| Standard sdn T/B 5P | 3,210 | 830 | |
| **67 Eight (wb 123.0)—915 built** | | | |
| Special bus cpe 2P | 3,365 | 875 | — |
| Special cpe 2-4P | 3,450 | 925 | — |
| Special sdn 5P | 3,490 | 925 | — |
| Special sdn T/B 5P | 3,500 | 960 | — |
| Standard bus cpe 2P | 3,415 | 965 | — |
| Standard cpe 2-4P | 3,475 | 1,015 | — |
| Standard conv cpe 2-4P | 3,445 | 995 | — |
| Standard sdn 5P | 3,470 | 1,015 | — |
| Standard sdn T/B 5P | 3,555 | 1,050 | — |
| **69 Custom Eight (wb 123.0)—89 built** | | | |
| bus cpe 2P | 3,505 | 1,245 | — |
| cpe 2-4P | 3,590 | 1,295 | — |
| conv cpe 2-4P | 3,535 | 1,295 | — |
| sdn 5P | 3,600 | 1,295 | — |
| sdn T/B 5P | 3,660 | 1,330 | — |
| **71 Custom Eight (wb 138.0)** | | | |
| sdn 7P | — | 1,695 | — |
| sdn T/B 7P | — | 1,730 | — |

| 1934 Engines | bore × stroke | bhp | availability |
|---|---|---|---|
| I-6, 224.0 | 3.25 × 4.50 | 85 | S-65, 68 |
| I-8, 245.4 | 3.13 × 4.50 | 95 | S-57A, 64, 67 |
| I-8, 265.4 | 3.25 × 4.50 | 135 | S-69, 71 |

## 1935

| 68 Standard Six (wb 116)—4,000 blt | Wght | Price | Prod |
|---|---|---|---|
| bus cpe 3P | 3,105 | 695 | — |
| cpe 3-5P | 3,165 | 765 | — |
| conv cpe 3-5P | 3,155 | 845 | — |
| sdn 6P | 3,135 | 775 | — |
| sdn T/B 6P | 3,225 | 810 | — |
| **67 Special Eight (wb 123.0)** | | | |
| cpe 3P | 3,365 | 875 | — |
| cpe 3-5P | 3,450 | 925 | — |
| conv cpe 3-5P | 3,445 | 995 | — |
| sdn 6P | 3,385 | 925 | — |
| sdn T/B 6P | 3,480 | 960 | — |
| **69 Special Eight (wb 123)—2,419 blt** | | | |
| bus cpe 3P | 3,445 | 1,045 | — |
| cpe 3-5P | 3,505 | 1,095 | — |
| conv cpe 3-5P | 3,490 | 1,165 | — |
| sdn 6P | 3,475 | 1,095 | — |
| sdn T/B 6P | 3,560 | 1,130 | — |
| **69 Supercharged Custom Eight (wb 123.0)—1,862 built** | | | |
| cpe 3P | 3,505 | 1,245 | — |
| cpe 3-5P | 3,590 | 1,295 | — |
| conv cpe 3-5P | 3,535 | 1,295 | — |
| sdn 6P | 3,560 | 1,295 | — |
| sdn T/B 6P | 3,640 | 1,330 | — |
| **74 Standard Six (wb 111.0)—11,470 built** | | | |
| touring sdn 2d | 2,620 | 595 | — |
| touring sdn 4d | 2,655 | 635 | — |
| DeLuxe touring sdn 2d | 2,645 | 645 | — |
| DeLuxe touring sdn 4d | 2,680 | 685 | — |
| **73 Special Six (wb 116.0)—4,903 built** | | | |
| cpe 2P | 3,130 | 795 | — |
| cpe 2-4P | 3,215 | 845 | — |
| conv cpe 2-4P | 3,190 | 915 | — |
| touring sdn 4d | 3,265 | 845 | — |
| **72 Eight (wb 123.0)—1,020 built** | | | |
| cpe 2P | 3,385 | 925 | — |
| cpe 2-4P | 3,445 | 975 | — |
| conv cpe 2-4P | 3,425 | 1,045 | — |
| touring sdn 4d | 3,530 | 975 | — |
| **75 Supercharged Eight (wb 123.0)—1,252 built** | | | |
| cpe 2P | 3,480 | 1,095 | — |
| cpe 2-4P | 3,585 | 1,145 | — |
| conv cpe 2-4P | 3,545 | 1,215 | — |
| touring sdn 4d | 3,640 | 1,145 | — |

| 1935 Engines | bore × stroke | bhp | availability |
|---|---|---|---|
| I-6, 169.6 | 3.00 × 4.00 | 60 | S-74 |
| I-6, 224.0 | 3.25 × 4.50 | 85 | S-68, 73 |
| I-8, 245.4 | 3.13 × 4.50 | 95 | S-67, 72 |
| I-8, 265.4 | 3.25 × 4.50 | 135 | S-69 Sp 8 |
| I-8, 265.4 | 3.25 × 4.50 | 140 | S-69 S'chgd, 75 |

## 1936

| 80/80A Crusader (wb 111)—3,220 blt | Wght | Price | Prod |
|---|---|---|---|
| touring sdn 2d | 2,665 | 640 | — |
| touring sdn 2d T/B | 2,690 | 655 | — |
| touring sdn 4d | 2,700 | 680 | — |
| touring sdn 4d T/B | 2,735 | 695 | — |
| **90 Cavalier (wb 115.0)—2,755 built** | | | |
| bus cpe 3P | 2,815 | 725 | — |
| cpe 3-5P | 2,880 | 710 | — |
| conv cpe 3-5P | 2,960 | 775 | — |
| touring sdn 2d | 2,930 | 720 | — |
| touring sdn 2d T/B | 2,930 | 825 | — |
| touring sdn 4d | 3,015 | 750 | — |
| touring sdn 4d T/B | 3,015 | 825 | — |
| **90A Cavalier (wb 115.0)—7,750 built** | | | |
| bus cpe 3P | 2,730 | 750 | — |
| cpe 3-5P | 2,795 | 735 | — |
| conv cpe 3-5P | 2,875 | 800 | — |
| touring sdn 2d | 2,785 | 745 | — |
| touring sdn 2d T/B | 2,785 | 850 | — |
| touring sdn 4d | 2,870 | 775 | — |
| touring sdn 4d T/B | 2,870 | 850 | — |

# Graham

| 110 Supercharged (wb 115)—5,500 blt | Wght | Price | Prod |
|---|---|---|---|
| bus cpe 2P | 2,930 | 865 | — |
| cpe 2-4P | 2,995 | 875 | — |
| conv cpe 3-5P | 3,075 | 910 | — |
| touring sdn 2d | 3,060 | 850 | — |
| touring sdn 2d T/B | 3,060 | 880 | — |
| touring sdn 4d | 3,080 | 895 | — |
| touring sdn 4d T/B | 3,080 | 925 | — |
| Custom touring sdn 4d T/B | 3,200 | 1,170 | — |

| 1936 Engines | bore × stroke | bhp | availability |
|---|---|---|---|
| I-6, 169.6 | 3.00 × 4.00 | 70 | S-80/80A |
| I-6, 199.1 | 3.25 × 4.00 | 80 | S-90A |
| I-6, 217.8 | 3.25 × 4.38 | 85 | S-90 |
| I-6, 217.8 | 3.25 × 4.38 | 112 | S-110 |

## 1937

| 85 Crusader (wb 111)—4,218 built | Wght | Price | Prod |
|---|---|---|---|
| touring sdn 2d | 2,660 | 690 | — |
| touring sdn 2d T/B | 2,675 | 720 | — |
| touring sdn 4d | 2,695 | 770 | — |
| touring sdn 4d T/B | 2,715 | 795 | — |

| 95 Cavalier (wb 116.0)—8,250 built | | | |
|---|---|---|---|
| bus cpe 3P | 2,815 | 850 | — |
| cpe 3-5P | 2,880 | 900 | — |
| conv cpe 3-5P | 2,960 | 945 | — |
| touring sdn 2d | 2,930 | 875 | — |
| touring sdn 2d T/B | 2,930 | 905 | — |
| touring sdn 4d | 2,960 | 905 | — |
| touring sdn 4d T/B | 2,945 | 935 | — |

| 116 Supercharged (wb 116.0)—5,551 built | | | |
|---|---|---|---|
| bus cpe 3P | 2,975 | 1,015 | — |
| cpe 3-5P | 3,040 | 1,045 | — |
| conv cpe 3-5P | 3,120 | 1,080 | — |
| touring sdn 2d | 3,105 | 1,020 | — |
| touring sdn 2d T/B | 3,105 | 1,050 | — |
| touring sdn 4d | 3,125 | 1,050 | — |
| touring sdn 4d T/B | 3,125 | 1,080 | — |

| 120 Custom Supercharged (wb 116.0; lwb-120.0)—200 built | | | |
|---|---|---|---|
| bus cpe 3P | 3,020 | 1,105 | — |
| cpe 3-5P | 3,055 | 1,135 | — |
| conv cpe 3-5P | 3,135 | 1,170 | — |
| lwb touring sdn 4d | 3,200 | 1,160 | — |
| lwb touring sdn 4d T/B | 3,200 | 1,190 | — |

| 1937 Engines | bore × stroke | bhp | availability |
|---|---|---|---|
| I-6, 169.6 | 3.00 × 4.00 | 70 | S-85 |
| I-6, 199.1 | 3.25 × 4.00 | 85 | S-95 |
| I-6, 199.1 | 3.25 × 4.00 | 106 | S-116 |
| I-6, 217.8 | 3.25 × 4.38 | 116 | S-120 |

## 1938

| 96 Six (wb 120.0)—2,610 built | Wght | Price | Prod |
|---|---|---|---|
| Standard sdn 4d T/B | 3,250 | 1,025 | — |
| Special sdn 4d T/B | 3,275 | 1,075 | — |

| 97 Supercharged (wb 120.0)—2,410 built | | | |
|---|---|---|---|
| sdn 4d T/B | 3,345 | 1,198 | — |
| Custom sdn 4d T/B | 3,350 | 1,320 | — |

| 1938 Engines | bore × stroke | bhp | availability |
|---|---|---|---|
| I-6, 217.8 | 3.25 × 4.38 | 90 | S-96 |
| I-6, 217.8 | 3.25 × 4.38 | 116 | S-97 |

## 1939

| 96 Special (wb 120.0)—2,913 built* | Wght | Price | Prod |
|---|---|---|---|
| Combination cpe 5P | 3,185 | 940 | — |
| sdn 2d T/B | 3,230 | 940 | — |
| sdn 4d T/B | 3,240 | 965 | — |
| Custom Combination cpe 5P | 3,200 | 1,070 | — |
| Custom sdn 2d T/B | 3,245 | 1,070 | — |
| Custom sdn 4d T/B | 3,255 | 1,095 | — |

| 97 Supercharged (wb 120.0)—2,479 built* | | | |
|---|---|---|---|
| Combination cpe 5P | 3,260 | 1,070 | — |
| sdn 2d T/B | 3,285 | 1,070 | — |
| sdn 4d T/B | 3,295 | 1,095 | — |
| Custom Combination cpe 5P | 3,290 | 1,200 | — |
| Custom sdn 2d T/B | 3,315 | 1,200 | — |
| Custom sdn 4d T/B | 3,325 | 1,225 | — |

| 1939 Engines | bore × stroke | bhp | availability |
|---|---|---|---|
| I-6, 217.8 | 3.25 × 4.38 | 90 | S-96 |
| I-6, 217.8 | 3.25 × 4.38 | 116 | S-97; O-96 Custom |

* Production totals based on published serial number spans. Total calendar-year production: 3,876.

## 1940

| 107 Supercharged (wb 120.0)—est. 1,000 built (includes Standard) | Wght | Price | Prod |
|---|---|---|---|
| Deluxe cpe | 3,245 | 1,160 | — |
| Deluxe sdn 2d | 3,250 | 1,135 | — |
| Deluxe sdn 4d | 3,250 | 1,160 | — |
| Custom cpe | 3,370 | 1,295 | — |
| Custom sdn 2d | 3,365 | 1,265 | — |
| Custom sdn 4d | 3,370 | 1,295 | — |

| 108 Standard (wb 120.0) | | | |
|---|---|---|---|
| Deluxe cpe | 3,190 | 1,020 | — |
| Deluxe sdn 2d | 3,195 | 995 | — |
| Deluxe sdn 4d | 3,195 | 1,015 | — |
| Custom cpe | 3,315 | 1,160 | — |
| Custom sdn 2d | 3,315 | 1,135 | — |
| Custom sdn 4d | 3,320 | 1,160 | — |

| Hollywood Custom Supercharged (wb 115.0) | | | |
|---|---|---|---|
| sdn 4d | 2,965 | 1,250 | * |
| conv cpe (prototype) | 3,075 | — | 1-2 |

| 1940 Engines | bore × stroke | bhp | availability |
|---|---|---|---|
| I-6, 217.8 | 3.25 × 4.38 | 93 | S-unsupercharged |
| I-6, 217.8 | 3.25 × 4.38 | 120 | S-supercharged |

*Total 1940-41 Hollywood production: 1,859 (some sources claim 1,597).

## 1941

| 109 Hollywood Custom Supercharged (wb 115) | Wght | Price | Prod |
|---|---|---|---|
| sdn 4d | 2,965 | 1,065 | * |

| 113 Custom Hollywood (wb 115.0) | | | |
|---|---|---|---|
| sdn 4d | 2,915 | 968 | * |

| 1941 Engines | bore × stroke | bhp | availability |
|---|---|---|---|
| I-6, 217.8 | 3.25 × 4.38 | 95 | S-unsupercharged |
| I-6, 217.8 | 3.25 × 4.38 | 124 | S-supercharged |

*Total 1940-41 Hollywood production: 1,859 (some sources claim 1,597).

# Henry J

Kaiser-Frazer went from being the "postwar wonder" of 1947-48 to looking like a postwar blunder in 1949, falling from ninth to fourteenth in Detroit production. Determined to press on, chairman Henry J. Kaiser borrowed $44 million from the Reconstruction Finance Corporation to maintain inventories, then tooled up for new models. One result was the abrupt departure of co-founder Joseph W. Frazer. Kaiser promised the RFC that part of its money would go toward a new small car that any American could afford. With no little modesty, he named it the Henry J.

Designer Howard A. "Dutch" Darrin had proposed a short-wheelbase compact derived from his beautiful 1951 Kaiser, which was already locked up during Henry J planning. But the head man, wanting something all-new, went with a proposal from American Metal Products, a Detroit supplier of frames and springs for car seats. Darrin reluctantly tried to improve this ungainly little two-door fastback sedan, applying his trademark "dip" to beltline, windshield, and rear window—plus little tailfins. Though the result was still pretty weird, The New York Fashion Academy named Henry J its 1951 "Fashion Car of the Year."

Power was provided by Willys L-head engines: a 134 cubic-inch four and a 161-cid six. Incredible economy was promised for the 68-horsepower Four. The 80-horsepower Six turned out to be something of a hot rod, with 0-60 times of around 14 seconds, helped largely by low curb weight (around 2300 pounds). Though built on a compact 100-inch wheelbase, the Henry J could handle four passengers along with a considerable amount of luggage.

K-F began its '51 model year in March 1950. For awhile, the Henry J was quite popular, and nearly 82,000 were sold for the model year. But that evidently satisfied demand, for sales went down sharply through 1952. One reason was price. At $1363, even the four-cylinder model was only $200 cheaper than a full-size six-cylinder Chevrolet—and far more basic. The Henry J Six offered "DeLuxe" trim starting at $1499, but was only slightly less stark.

A mild facelift gave 1952-54 models a smart new full-width grille, taillights moved from the body to the fins, and nicer interiors. An interim '52 measure designed to use up leftover stock was the Vagabond—a '51 wearing "continental" outside spare tire, identifying script, and a hood ornament of black plastic and chrome. After this, Henry Js were called Corsair or Corsair DeLuxe, priced around $1400 for the four, $1560 with the six.

But nothing seemed to work, so the Henry J departed in 1954. An estimated 1100 were sold that year, all of which were reserialed '53 leftovers. Some 30,000 were built altogether. Left stillborn were plans for a hardtop, wagon, four-door sedan, and even a convertible.

Many felt the original approach was wrong. Lacking gloveboxes, trunklids, and other expected features, the '51s were simply too plain for most buyers. As Joe Frazer later comment-

**1951 Standard two-door fastback sedan**

**1953 Corsair DeLuxe two-door fastback sedan**

**1951 DeLuxe two-door fastback sedan**

**1953 Corsair two-door fastback sedan**

# Henry J

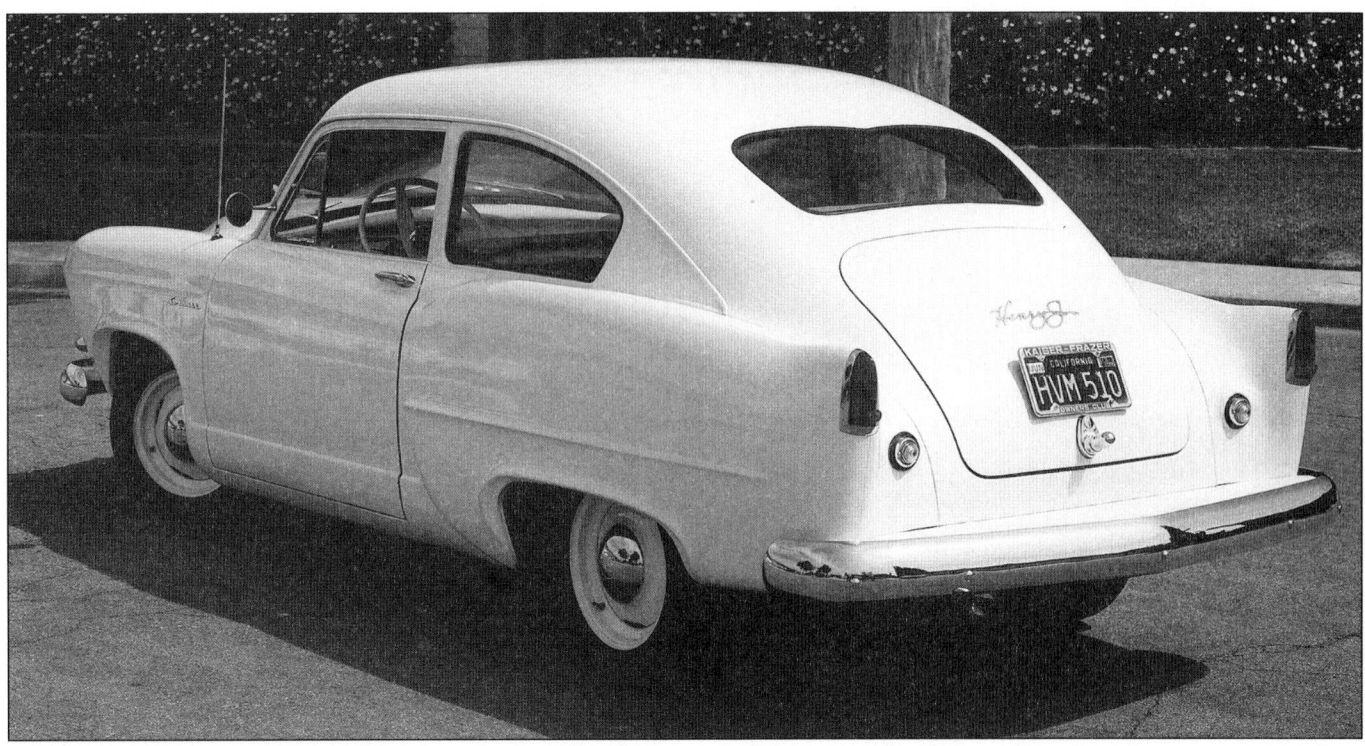

**1953 Corsair two-door fastback sedan**

ed: "I would have brought it out dressed up." And indeed, that's what Sears did with its short-lived Allstate derivative (*see* Allstate). Then, too, the market wasn't quite ready for compacts (though it soon would be), and K-F was looking increasingly terminal, which surely kept some buyers away.

In all, this was a classic case of too little, too soon. Like Hudson's equally ill-starred Jet, the Henry J was the wrong car at the wrong time.

## Specifications

### 1951

| K513 Standard (wb 100.0) | | Wght | Price | Prod |
|---|---|---|---|---|
| 5134 | sdn 2d | 2,293 | 1,363 | 38,500* |
| **K514 DeLuxe (wb 100.0)** | | | | |
| 5144 | sdn 2d | 2,341 | 1,499 | 43,400* |
| **1951 Engines** | **bore × stroke** | **bhp** | **availability** | |
| I-4, 134.2 | 3.13 × 4.38 | 68 | S-K513 | |
| I-6, 161.0 | 3.13 × 3.50 | 80 | S-K514 | |

### 1952

| K523 Vagabond (wb 100.0) | | Wght | Price | Prod |
|---|---|---|---|---|
| 5234 | sdn 2d | 2,365 | 1,407 | 3,000* |
| **K524 Vagabond DeLuxe (wb 100.0)** | | | | |
| 5244 | sdn 2d | 2,385 | 1,552 | 4,000* |
| **K523 Corsair (wb 100.0)** | | | | |
| 5234 | sdn 2d | 2,370 | 1,517 | 7,600* |
| **K524 Corsair DeLuxe (wb 100.0)** | | | | |
| 5244 | sdn 2d | 2,405 | 1,664 | 8,900* |
| **1952 Engines** | **bore × stroke** | **bhp** | **availability** | |
| I-4, 134.2 | 3.13 × 4.38 | 68 | S-K523 | |
| I-6, 161.0 | 3.13 × 3.50 | 80 | S-K524 | |

### 1953

| K533 Corsair (wb 100.0) | | Wght | Price | Prod |
|---|---|---|---|---|
| 5334 | sdn 2d | 2,395 | 1,399 | 8,500* |
| **K534 Corsair DeLuxe (wb 100.0)** | | | | |
| 5344 | sdn 2d | 2,445 | 1,561 | 8,100* |
| **1953 Engines** | **bore × stroke** | **bhp** | **availability** | |
| I-4, 134.2 | 3.13 × 4.38 | 68 | S-K533 | |
| I-6, 161.0 | 3.13 × 3.50 | 80 | S-K534 | |

### 1954

| K543 Corsair (wb 100.0) | | Wght | Price | Prod |
|---|---|---|---|---|
| 5434 | sdn 2d | 2,405 | 1,404 | 800* |
| **K544 Corsair DeLuxe (wb 100.0)** | | | | |
| 5444 | sdn 2d | 2,455 | 1,566 | 300* |
| **1954 Engines** | **bore × stroke** | **bhp** | **availability** | |
| I-4, 134.2 | 3.13 × 4.38 | 68 | S-K543 | |
| I-6, 161.0 | 3.13 × 3.50 | 80 | S-K544 | |

* Estimates based on highest serial numbers found. Total model-year production:

| 1951 all | 81,942 |
|---|---|
| 1952 Vagabond | 7,017 |
| 1952 Corsair | 23,568 |
| 1953 all | 16,672 |
| 1954 all | 1,123 |

# Hudson

Eight Detroit businessmen pooled resources to found the Hudson Motor Car Company in February 1909. Among them was retailing magnate Joseph L. Hudson. Another was Roy D. Chapin, Sr., who led the new firm to high prosperity as its president from 1910 to 1923.

Hudson built some of America's fleetest and finest cars during its 48-year history and was often among the industry's sales leaders through 1950. A key early success was the low-priced four-cylinder Essex introduced in 1919. By 1925, it had boosted Hudson to third place behind Ford and Chevrolet. Hudson then ran third, fourth, or fifth on volume that reached 300,000 cars by 1929. Unfortunately, total sales fell sharply in the devastated Depression market. Had it not been for the speedy, inexpensive Essex Terraplane (*see* Essex and Terraplane), Hudson might have folded by 1940.

The firm forged an enviable reputation in the '20s largely with its Super and Special Sixes: big, smooth, solid cars offering good performance for the money and fine reliability. But with the advent of an Essex Six in 1924, Hudson decided to move upmarket. The result was a single 1930 line called Great Eight. Great it wasn't. At 213.5 cubic inches, its engine was actually smaller than previous Hudson sixes, had just 80 horsepower to move a heavy chassis, and wasn't as sturdy. It did boast an integrally cast block and crankcase, and was the first straight eight with counterweighted crankshaft, but its splash lubrication system was outmoded. Hudson stayed with this engine for the optimistically named Greater Eights of 1931-32—in retrospect a mistake for a depressed market where sixes would surely have sold better. Displacement was increased each year: first to 233.7 cid and 87 bhp, then to 254 cid and 101 bhp.

Another 1930 setback was the Depression-related closure of Biddle and Smart, Hudson's longtime supplier of magnificent open bodies. The company thus turned to Murray and Briggs for phaeton and speedster bodies. A few eight-cylinder Hudsons of this period also sported dashing coachwork by the renowned firm LeBaron.

Through 1933, Hudson Eights offered numerous body styles on wheelbases of 119-132 inches: roadsters, Victorias, convertibles, sedans, town sedans, coupes, and Broughams (two-door sedans). It was an attractive line that would have done justice to far-costlier brands, but it wasn't successful. The Greater Eight managed only 22,250 sales for 1931. The '32 total was below 8000, despite unchanged prices and lush new Sterling and Major series.

Seeing the error of its ways, Hudson launched a new Super Six for its 1933 "Pacemaker" line—the car was essentially the 73-bhp 193-cid Essex Terraplane engine in the 113-inch Hudson chassis. That year's Eights comprised four 119-inch-wheelbase standard models and five luxurious Majors on a 132-inch platform. But production bottomed out at under 3000. Interestingly, Eights outsold Sixes nearly 2-to-1. For 1934, Hudson again abandoned sixes, reserving them for the new Terraplane line that replaced Essex as the firm's "companion" marque.

Like most other Detroit producers in the early '30s, Hudson began moving away from classic four-square styling, rooted in Greek architecture, to embrace streamlining. The 1934-35s were transitional: still rather boxy but less-angular, helped by skirted front fenders. The all-new '36s looked something like the previous year's Chrysler/DeSoto Airstreams: modern, but

1930 Great Eight four-door town sedan

1931 Greater Eight Brougham DeLuxe four-door

1931 Greater Eight convertible sedan by Murphy

1932 Greater Eight Major Brougham four-door sedan

not Airflow-radical. Highlights included tall, rounded, Plymouth-like diecast grilles and all-steel bodies with rather dowdy lines. Engines remained dowdy, too. The straight eight was little changed through 1936, variously sold in Standard, DeLuxe, and Custom series. For '35 came a new six: a 212.1-cid unit that made 93 bhp through 1936, then 101/107. The 1937-38 Eights delivered 122/128 bhp.

A reduced 1935-36 market share suggests Hudson was late in shifting to the popular "potato look." Though the firm managed 85,000 units and fifth place for 1934, some two-thirds were low-priced Terraplanes. Output then rose to average 100,000 units per year in 1935-37, but that was good for only eighth—and Terraplane still garnered the lion's share of sales. Worse, Hudson likely cut prices below the profit point, as it kept losing money despite this increased volume. From less than $1 million in earnings for 1937, Hudson lost nearly $5 million in recession 1938.

After serving in the Hoover Administration, Roy Chapin returned as Hudson president in 1933. He departed again three years later after making some key product decisions inaugurated under his successor, A. E. Barit. These involved a consolidated line emphasizing economy rather than performance. Thus, after four years as a separate marque, Terraplane was put back under the Hudson banner for 1938. Bowing that same year was a new low-priced senior series, the "112" (named for its wheelbase length). With only a small 175-cid six making just 83 bhp, the 112 was sluggish next to the speedy 96-bhp Terraplane: 35 seconds 0-60 mph, top speed barely 70 mph. But it returned up to 24 mpg and was attractively priced as low as $700. The 212 Terraplane engine also powered that year's Custom Six, again tuned for 101/107 bhp. An unchanged eight was reserved for a single Custom line.

The national economy was looking up by 1939, when Hudson dropped Terraplane, trimmed the 112 to a single DeLuxe series, and unveiled new 101-bhp Pacemaker and Country Club Sixes on respective wheelbases of 118 and 122 inches. The 212 six also returned in large, comfortable five- and seven-passenger sedans curiously tagged "Big Boy." Custom Eight became Country Club Eight, but power and wheelbases were untouched. This was the final year for Hudson's 1936 bodies, and some deft design work alleviated much of their former bulkiness. Long-chassis models were especially graceful, but all '39s wore more-horizontal grilles with thick bars that made for a nicer "face" than the controversial "waterfall" ensemble of 1937-38.

Hudson's 1940 line was rearranged, rebodied, and restyled. Though not innovative, the new look was pleasing and clean, with little side ornamentation and a trendy "prow front" dividing a lower horizontal-bar grille. Hudson added another page to its book of durability triumphs by running over 20,000

1934 DeLuxe Eight 2/4 passenger coupe

1935 Custom Eight Brougham four-door sedan

1936 Custom Six Touring Brougham two-door

1937 Custom Eight convertible Brougham

1938 Custom Eight Country Club touring sedan

1939 Pacemaker Six touring sedan

# Hudson

miles at an average 70.5 mph—a new American Automobile Association record.

Offerings spanned seven series, three wheelbases, and three engines. Smallest were the new 113-inch Traveler and DeLuxe: coupes, Victoria coupes, two- and four-door sedans, a convertible, and convertible sedan. All carried the 175-cid six, now rated at 92 bhp. The 212 engine with 98/102 bhp powered the Country Club Six and a new 118-inch-wheelbase Super Six, plus the two Big Boys. The old 254 straight-eight was still around, now producing 128 bhp. Standard Eights shared the Super Six chassis and full range of body styles. Country Club Eights remained on the 125-inch span but were down to one six-passenger and two seven-passenger sedans. Yet for all this, Hudson volume changed little—just under 88,000 for the model year—and red ink flowed again with a calendar-year loss of some $1.5 million.

A mild facelift was performed for 1941, when wheelbases were juggled once more: 116 inches for DeLuxe and new entry-level Traveler Sixes, 121 and 128 for Super Six and new Commodore Six and Eight. All series listed two coupes and two sedans. DeLuxe, Super Six, and Commodores also offered convertible sedans. Hudson had held onto that body style longer than most makes, but buyers didn't much want it anymore, and only 200 or so were built this year in each series. Rarer still were the new Super Six and Commodore Eight wagons, Hudson's first: only about 100 of each. Prices ranged from $754 for the Traveler coupe to $1537 for the long-wheelbase Commodore Eight seven-place sedan. As it had for many years, Hudson continued selling a fair number of commercial vehicles. Among seven offerings for '41 was a car-style pickup that now inherited the Big Boy name.

Perhaps because many people suspected war was coming, Hudson recorded 1941-model production of close to 92,000 cars, good for nearly $4 million in earnings. But that profit came mainly from defense contracts, which began materializing in early '41—a badly needed breather.

The 1942 models arrived in August 1941 looking smoother, if chubbier. Running boards were newly hidden, the grille was again lowered and simpler, and fenders became more stylishly fulsome. Hudson's famous white-triangle logo graced each side of the prow, and lit up with the headlamps to aid after-dark identification. Offerings were broadly the same, but wagons were departing, and a new Commodore Custom Eight listed a lush 121-inch-wheelbase coupe and 128-inch six-seater sedan in the $1300-$1400 range. All prices nudged upward, the minimum now above $800. The government-ordered turn to war production in February 1942 ended the firm's model-year car output at just under 41,000. Among them were a handful of Hudson's last four-door convertibles.

Hudson's contributions to winning World War II included

**1939 Country Club Eight convertible Brougham**

**1940 Eight two-door convertible sedan**

**1941 Super Six four-door station wagon**

**1941 Commodore Eight two-door convertible sedan**

**1941 Super Six four-door touring sedan**

**1942 Commodore Eight four-door sedan**

# Hudson

1942 Commodore Six convertible

1946 Commodore Eight four-door sedan

1947 Commodore Eight four-door sedan

1948 Commodore Six four-door sedan

1948 Commander convertible

"Helldiver" aircraft, "Invader" landing-craft engines, sections for B-29 bombers and Aircobra helicopters, and a variety of naval munitions. The company made small wartime profits, then quickly resumed production after V-J Day. A total of 4735 cars put Hudson fifth for calendar 1945, a spot it hadn't held since 1934—and would not hold again.

Like most other Detroit cars, the 1946-47 Hudsons were just '42s with new wrinkles—mainly a less-elegant front sans prow. However, the small 175-cid six was forgotten, and a vastly simplified lineup offered fewer models spread among Super and Commodore Six and Eight, all on a 121-inch chassis. But there were no fewer than three transmission options: $88 stick/overdrive, $40 "Vacumotive Drive," and $98 "Drive-Master" (with Vacumotive). Vacumotive operated the clutch automatically, while Drive-Master eliminated both clutch and shift motions. By putting the shifter in third gear, the car would start in second gear and upshift to third when the accelerator was lifted. Slowing to a stop, Drive-Master would shift to second again. Hudson built over 91,000 of its '46 models, two-thirds of which were Super Sixes.

The 1947s were unchanged save details like a chrome trunk-lid nameplate, right- and left-side exterior door locks, and a small lip on the housing of the prominent triangle medallion above the grille. Hudson produced some 92,000 cars for the model year, but fell from ninth to 11th on the industry board. Other makes were doing better in the unprecedented postwar seller's market. Still, Hudson sales exceeded $120 million in 1946, and the firm netted over $2.3 million. Two years later, Hudson made more money than it ever would again, earning $13.2 million on gross sales of $274 million.

The reason was a brand-new car, the now-famous "Step-Down." Named for its innovative recessed or dropped floorpan, it completely surrounded passengers with strong frame girders in one of the safest packages of the day—maybe one of the safest ever. It also offered rattle-free unitized construction and a radically low center of gravity that made for great handling. The long 124-inch wheelbase provided a smooth ride and king-size interior space. The Step-Down was even beautiful in its way: a long "torpedo" with clean flush-fender sides, modest taillamps, fully skirted rear wheels, and a low, horizontal grille. The design evolved from wartime doodles of aerodynamic forms by a team under Frank Spring, who went way back with Hudson and was way ahead of the times with the Step-Down.

Though Hudson stuck with a four-series lineup for 1948-49, it violated an old Detroit caution about not restyling and re-engineering in the same year. Thus, Super and Commodore Sixes carried a new 262-cid inline six-cylinder engine with 121 bhp, only seven less than the unchanged 254-cid straight eight. It had only four main bearings instead of five, but was as smooth and durable as the eight. It also delivered surprising performance: 0-40 mph in 12 seconds with Drive-Master; stick-shift cars were even faster. With this gutsy new six in the advanced Step-Down platform, Hudson was transformed almost overnight from an also-ran performer into one of America's quickest, most-roadworthy cars.

Dealers cheered the Step-Down upon its mid-1948 introduction. Here was precisely what they needed for great sales in a heady market where customers sometimes outnumbered available cars. Sure enough, Hudson surged not only in profits but also in production, selling 117,200 of the '48s and 159,100 of the near-identical '49s (only the serial numbers were different).

But there was one big problem. As a unitized design, the Step-Down couldn't be greatly changed without great expense, and Hudson sales wouldn't be sufficient to cover the cost once the postwar seller's market ended in 1950. A slow-selling 1953-54 compact only accelerated the depletion of cash reserves. As a result, the Step-Down wouldn't be updated much until 1954, by which time it was way too late, forcing Hudson to seek refuge with Nash under the American Motors banner. Nor would Hudson be able to afford a station wagon or V-8 engine, two very popular '50s commodities. In fact, Hudson offered only sixes in 1953-54, and though the "fabulous" Hornet engine dominated stock-car racing in that period, sixes were a tough sell in the mostly eight-cylinder medium-price field where Hudson competed.

Sales executive Roy D. Chapin, Jr., the son of the famous Hudson founders (and a future chairman of American Motors), later explained things this way: "If you don't have enough money to do something . . . and if you haven't learned to specialize in a given thing . . . sooner or later you find you just can't do everything. [Hudson was] usually reacting, rather than anticipating." To a large extent, Hudson's postwar plight was shared by all the independents: too little money for enough changes to keep buyers interested, resulting in fewer sales and even less money for new products.

Hudson entered the '50s in excellent shape, selling over 120,000 Step-Downs for the model year. A big hit—over 39,000 orders—was the new low-priced Pacemaker with a 119-inch wheelbase and a destroked 232-cid Super Six. Though horsepower was only 112, performance was as good as that of Nash's top-line Ambassador and well ahead of most similarly priced rivals.

Both Pacemaker and the 1950 Super Six offered fastback four-door sedans, long-deck club coupe, and a convertible and fastback two-door sedan called Brougham. Pacemaker also listed a three-passenger coupe, the 1950 price-leader at $1807. Other standard Pacemakers cost under $2000 except the convertible ($2428). A few dollars more bought a Pacemaker DeLuxe in the same body types save the long-deck coupe. These used the 262 Super Six engine, which was a bit more potent now at 123 bhp. Commodore Six and Eight deleted two-door sedans, Super Eight the convertible. The main appearance change from 1948-49 involved adding twin diagonal grille bars—the make's traditional triangle motif.

Hudson also added yet another transmission choice for 1950. Though called Supermatic, this was just a semiautomatic like Drive-Master. Supermatic added an overdrive that automatically engaged at 22 mph when selected by a dashboard button. Price was $199, versus $105 for Drive-Master. Of course, neither was a proper substitute for a fully automatic transmission, which belatedly arrived for 1951: a proprietary GM Hydra-Matic at $158. At that point, Supermatic was dropped.

But Hudson's big '51 news was the powerful six-cylinder Hornet, a four-model line priced the same as Commodore Eight ($2543-$3099). At 308 cubic inches, the Hornet engine was the largest L-head six ever offered, and though it made just 145 bhp in initial form, it was capable of far more in the hands of precision tuners.

Undoubtedly the most famous of Hudson wrench-spinners was Marshall Teague, who claimed he could get 112 mph from an AAA- or NASCAR-certified stock Hornet. An enthusiastic cadre of Hudson engineers helped by conjuring a raft of "severe usage" options—thinly disguised racing parts. By late 1953, they'd cooked up a hot "7-X" racing engine with about 220 bhp via 0.020 overbored cylinders, special cam and head, larger valves, higher compression, and "Twin-H Power" with dual carbs and manifolds—which Hudson claimed were the first twin manifolds on a six.

The Hornet proved near-invincible in stock-car racing.

1950 Pacemaker four-door sedan

1950 Commodore Eight Custom convertible Brougham

1951 Hornet convertible Brougham

1951 Commodore Eight Custom Hollywood hardtop coupe

1951 Commodore Eight Custom Hollywood hardtop coupe

# Hudson

1952 Hornet four-door sedan

1952 Pacemaker Brougham two-door sedan

1952 Hornet club coupe

1952 Wasp convertible Brougham

1952 Hudson Wasp Hollywood hardtop coupe

1953 Super Wasp four-door sedan

Teague finished his 1952 AAA season with a 1000-point lead over his closest rival, winning 12 of the 13 scheduled events. NASCAR aces Herb Thomas, Dick Rathmann, Al Keller, and Frank Mundy drove Hornets to 27 victories in 1952, another 21 in '53, and 17 in '54.

Hornets kept on winning after that, but none of their competition successes affected production Hudsons, and sales continued to fall. Though the company kept adding and subtracting series through 1954, it couldn't alter styling much, nor add new body styles after the Hollywood hardtop coupe bowed as a Hornet, Super Six, and Commodore Six/Eight for 1951. Super Eight and the standard Pacemaker were dropped that year, when another facelift brought more-massive, full-width grilles, plus larger rear windows for nonhardtop closed models.

More trim was shuffled for '52, when Super Six was renamed Wasp and gained a slightly more-potent 127-bhp 262 engine that it shared with Commodore Six. Pacemaker and both Commodores vanished for '53, leaving 119-inch-wheelbase Wasp coupe and sedans, the same plus Hollywood and convertible in new upmarket Super Wasp trim, and four Hornets on the 124-inch platform. One bright spot: The Hornet six was now offered in a 160-bhp version, and the 170-bhp Twin-H Power (7-X) mill was a regular factory option.

But Step-Down production diminished in each of these years, falling from about 93,000 in '51 to 45,000 in 1953. Though government-ordered Korean War cutbacks didn't help civilian sales, military contracts earned Hudson an $8.3 million profit in 1952. Unfortunately, that was more than wiped out by staggering 1953 losses totaling more than $10.4 million.

Part of that was reflected in the $12 million bill for Hudson's first compact, the ill-fated 1953 Jet. Bowing as a standard-trim notchback four-door and nicer "Super Jet" two- and four-door sedans, the Jet carried a 202-cid inline six carved from the old Commodore eight. Only 104 bhp was standard, but optional "Twin-H" and high-compression head improved that to 114, which made the little 105-inch-wheelbase Hudsons fairly speedy. Jets were also as roadable and well-built as any Hudson, but they were not pretty. Over the objections of chief designer Spring, company president A.E. Barit insisted on bolt-upright, slab-sided styling that failed to impress. Hudson tried harder for 1954, adding a cheap Family club sedan at $1621 and luxury Jet-Liners at around $2050. Still, sales went from bad to worse, dropping from 21,143 to only 14,224.

But the Jet did spark a project that might have become the much-needed Step-Down replacement. Called Italia, this was a four-place *gran turismo* designed by Spring and bodied on the Jet chassis by Carrozzeria Touring of Milan. Advanced

# Hudson

features abounded: *de rigueur* wrapped windshield, doors cut into the roof, fender scoops that fed cooling air to the brakes, flow-through ventilation, form-fitting leather seats, and a 10-inch lower stance than '54 Step-Downs. But the Italia was too heavy for the 114-bhp Jet inline six-cylinder engine, and its aluminum bodywork was fragile. Of course, these problems might have been licked if Hudson had the money, but by now it didn't. As a result, only 25 "production" Italias were built, plus the prototype and an experimental four-door derivative called X-161 (Spring's 161st design project, evidently intended for '57). Project sales manager Roy Chapin, Jr., booted Italias out the door as fast as he could at $4800 apiece. "I got rid of them," he said later, "[but] it wasn't one of my greatest accomplishments."

Nor, for that matter, was the last-gasp Step-Down of 1954. Somehow, Hudson found money for a one-piece windshield and a below-the-belt reskin that imparted fashionable GM squareness—and an unfortunate resemblance to the dumpy Jet. Cheap Hornet Specials—club coupe and two fastback four-doors—were added at around $2600, but the Step-Down was just too old to sell anymore. Model-year production ended at 36,436.

The 1954 Hudsons had bowed amid rumors of a Hudson-Nash merger. The talk was true, and Nash couldn't have come calling at a better time. From January 1, 1954, to its demise as an independent in April, Hudson lost over $6 million on sales of just $28.7 million. However, Nash president George Mason insisted on one condition: The Jet had to go. Hudson chief A. E. Barit resisted, but not for long. He was in no position to bargain.

The merger amounted to a Nash takeover. Mason had hoped to add just-married Studebaker and Packard to make his new American Motors Corporation into Detroit's "Big Fourth," but that was forever forestalled by his untimely death in October 1954. Mason lieutenant George Romney succeeded to the president's chair, and soon put all of AMC's eggs into the compact basket.

Meantime, Hudson's Detroit plant was closed and the Nash factory in Kenosha, Wisconsin, retooled for an "all-new" '55 Hudson. Of course, everyone knew what it was: a restyled Nash. Still, it wasn't all bad. Hudson could not only continue to tout unit construction but also Nash's all-coil suspension in lighter, trimmer cars that promised better fuel economy.

AMC stylists hid the Nash origins well, giving Hudsons a handsome eggcrate grille, distinct trim, a different rear end, full front-wheel openings (instead of semiskirted), plus Nash's new '55 wrapped windshield. One direct link to the Step-Down: 1954 gauges.

Offerings began with Wasp Super and Custom sedans and Custom Hollywood hardtop with 114.3-inch Nash Statesman wheelbase and a 202 "Hi-Torque" six from the now-departed Jet. Hornet Six rode Nash's 121.3-inch Ambassador platform and offered the same three models with 160/170-bhp 308-cid engines. Topping the line were a trio of 208-bhp Hornets powered by Packard's new 320-cid V-8 (a legacy of Mason's planned four-way merger). Twin-H Power was again available for sixes, and Nash's tiny Metropolitans and compact Ramblers gained Hudson badges to give the make broader market coverage. Yet for all this—and a banner Detroit sales year—big-Hudson volume continued sliding, reaching just over 20,000.

Fewer models and horrendous "V-Line Styling" arrived for '56. AMC design chief Edmund E. Anderson gets blamed for the ugliest Hudsons in a generation. These really did look like a "Hash," as some latterday wags refer to post-'54 Hudsons. The Hornet Six was otherwise unchanged, but the Wasp was

1954 Italia coupe

1954 Super Jet club sedan

1954 Wasp four-door sedan

1955 Hornet Custom Hollywood hardtop coupe

1955 Wasp Custom four-door sedan

# Hudson

1955 Wasp Custom Hollywood hardtop coupe

1956 Wasp four-door sedan

1956 Hornet V-8 Hollywood hardtop coupe

1957 Hornet V-8 Hollywood hardtop coupe

down to a lone four-door, and Hornet V-8s gave way in March to downpriced Hornet Specials with AMC's own new 250-cid V-8—which had only 190 bhp. An anemic engine and terrible looks only depressed demand, and AMC built just 10,671 non-Rambler '56 Hudsons.

Styling didn't improve in '57, but horsepower did. The AMC V-8 was newly bored to 327 cid, netting a more-respectable 255 bhp for a four-Hudson line of Hornet Super and Custom sedans and Hollywoods. But buyers had long since branded Hudson a loser, and all but 3876 stayed away from the '57s. With that, Hudson was put out of its misery, as was Nash. In

their place for '58 was a new Rambler Ambassador line with cleaner new styling originally intended for Hudson and Nash.

In retrospect, dropping these venerable makes was just common sense. As Roy Chapin, Jr., later recalled: ". . .[T]he decision really was one that said we've got to spend our money and our effort and our concentration on the Rambler . . . ." Thus expired two once-great names, with Hudson perhaps the greater, sadder loss. Given the Hornet's great performance record and the Step-Down's engineering legacy, one can only guess what Hudson might have become had things been different.

1957 Hornet four-door sedan

# Hudson

## Specifications

### 1930

| Great Eight (wb 119.0; lwb-126.0) | Wght | Price | Prod |
|---|---|---|---|
| rdstr 2-4P | 2,870 | 995 | |
| phtn 5P | 2,940 | 965 | |
| cpe 2P | 3,010 | 885 | |
| cpe 2-4P | 3,060 | 925 | 74,891 |
| coach 5P | 3,080 | 895 | |
| sdn 4d | 3,200 | 1,025 | |
| Sun sdn 5P | 3,100 | 1,045 | |
| lwb phtn 7P | 3,080 | 1,160 | |
| lwb Brougham 4d | 3,210 | 1,195 | 10,516 |
| lwb touring sdn 5P | 3,270 | 1,145 | |
| lwb sdn 7P | 3,385 | 1,295 | |

| 1930 Engine | bore × stroke | bhp | availability |
|---|---|---|---|
| I-8, 213.5 | 2.75 × 4.50 | 80 | S-all |

### 1931

| Great Eight (wb 119.0; lwb-126.0) | Wght | Price | Prod |
|---|---|---|---|
| rdstr 2-4P | 2,675 | 995 | |
| phtn 5P | 2,745 | 1,095 | |
| cpe 2P | 3,865 | 875 | |
| cpe 2-4P | 2,955 | 925 | |
| coach 5P | 2,975 | 895 | 16,477 |
| Town sdn 5P | 3,055 | 945 | |
| Standard sdn 4d | 3,115 | 995 | |
| spt cpe 2-4P | 3,145 | 1,065 | |
| lwb phtn 7P | 3,055 | 1,295 | |
| lwb touring sdn 5P | 3,190 | 1,145 | |
| lwb Family sdn 5-7P | 3,230 | 1,195 | |
| lwb Brougham 5P | 3,190 | 1,225 | 5,769 |
| lwb club sdn 5P | 3,225 | 1,445 | |
| lwb sdn 7P | 3,305 | 1,450 | |
| lwb DeLuxe Brougham 5P | 3,480 | 1,375 | |
| lwb Special sdn 5P | 3,430 | 1,325 | |

| 1931 Engine | bore × stroke | bhp | availability |
|---|---|---|---|
| I-8, 233.7 | 2.88 × 4.50 | 87 | S-all |

### 1932 (Total calendar-year production: 7,777)

| Greater Eight—Standard (wb 119.0)—5,933 built | Wght | Price | Prod |
|---|---|---|---|
| cpe 2P | 3,145 | 995 | — |
| cpe 2-4P | 3,175 | 1,045 | — |
| conv cpe 2-4P | 3,085 | 1,195 | — |
| Special cpe 2-4P | 3,215 | 1,195 | — |
| coach 5P | 3,190 | 1,025 | — |
| Town sdn 5P | 3,270 | 1,050 | — |
| Std sdn 5P | 3,285 | 1,095 | — |

| Greater Eight—Sterling (wb 126.0) | | | |
|---|---|---|---|
| Suburban 5P | 3,350 | 1,275 | — |
| Special sdn 5P | 3,415 | 1,295 | — |

| Greater Eight—Major (wb 132.0)—1,116 built | | | |
|---|---|---|---|
| phtn 7P | 3,350 | 1,395 | — |
| touring sdn 5P | 3,475 | 1,445 | — |
| club sdn 5P | 3,555 | 1,495 | — |
| Brougham 5P | 3,560 | 1,495 | — |
| sdn 7P | 3,590 | 1,595 | — |

| 1932 Engine | bore × stroke | bhp | availability |
|---|---|---|---|
| I-8, 254.5 | 3.00 × 4.50 | 101 | S-all |

### 1933

| Super Six Pacemaker (wb 113.0)—962 blt | Wght | Price | Prod |
|---|---|---|---|
| phtn 5P | 2,700 | 765 | — |
| bus cpe 2P | 2,780 | 695 | — |
| cpe 2-4P | 2,845 | 735 | — |
| conv cpe 2-4P | — | 845 | — |
| coach 5P | 2,900 | 695 | — |
| sdn 4d | 2,980 | 765 | — |

| Pacemaker Eight (wb 119.0; Major-132.0)—1,890 built | | | |
|---|---|---|---|
| Standard cpe 2-4P | 3,190 | 995 | — |
| Standard conv cpe 2-4P | 3,145 | 1,145 | — |
| Standard coach 5P | 3,245 | 975 | — |
| Standard sdn 4d | 3,345 | 1,045 | — |
| Major phtn 7P | — | 1,250 | — |
| Major sdn 4d T/B | 3,485 | 1,250 | — |
| Major Brougham 5P | 3,650 | 1,350 | — |
| Major club sdn 5P | 3,630 | 1,350 | — |
| Major sdn 7P | 3,605 | 1,350 | — |

| 1933 Engines | bore × stroke | bhp | availability |
|---|---|---|---|
| I-6, 193.1 | 2.94 × 4.75 | 73 | S-Six |
| I-8, 254.5 | 3.00 × 4.50 | 101 | S-Eight |
| I-8, 254.5 | 3.00 × 4.50 | 110 | O-Eight |

### 1934

| LT/LU Eight (wb 116.0)—18,679 built | Wght | Price | Prod |
|---|---|---|---|
| Special bus cpe 2P | 2,720 | 695 | — |
| Special cpe 2P | 2,750 | 725 | — |
| Special cpe 2-4P | 2,795 | 775 | — |
| Special conv cpe 2-4P | 2,815 | 835 | — |
| Special comp Victoria 5P | 2,880 | 785 | — |
| Special coach 5P | 2,855 | 745 | — |
| Special sdn 4d | 2,905 | 805 | — |
| Special sdn 4d T/B | 2,930 | 845 | — |
| DeLuxe cpe 2P | 2,805 | 815 | — |
| DeLuxe cpe 2-4P | 2,850 | 855 | — |
| DeLuxe comp Victoria 5P | 2,895 | 875 | — |
| DeLuxe coach 5P | 2,870 | 835 | — |
| DeLuxe sdn 4d | 2,930 | 895 | — |
| DeLuxe sdn 4d T/B | 2,955 | 935 | — |

| LL/LLU Major Eight (wb 123.0)—4,158 built | | | |
|---|---|---|---|
| Special sdn 4d touring | 2,950 | 970 | — |
| Special sdn 4d T/B touring | 2,975 | 1,000 | — |
| DeLuxe club sdn 4P | 3,085 | 1,070 | — |
| DeLuxe 5P Brougham | 3,075 | 1,145 | — |
| DeLuxe club sdn 4P T/B | 3,110 | 1,125 | — |

| LTS Challenger Eight (wb 116.0)—4,217 built | | | |
|---|---|---|---|
| cpe 2P | 2,720 | 685 | — |
| cpe 2-4P | 2,765 | 735 | — |
| conv cpe 2-4P | 2,785 | 800 | — |
| coach 5P | 2,860 | 705 | — |
| sdn 4d | 2,910 | 765 | — |

| 1934 Engines | bore × stroke | bhp | availability |
|---|---|---|---|
| I-8, 254.5 | 3.00 × 4.50 | 108 | S-Eight, Challenger |
| I-8, 254.5 | 3.00 × 4.50 | 113 | S-Major |
| I-8, 254.5 | 3.00 × 4.50 | 121 | O-All |

### 1935

| GH Big Six (wb 116.0)—7,624 built | Wght | Price | Prod |
|---|---|---|---|
| cpe 2P | 2,600 | 695 | — |
| cpe 2-4P | 2,665 | 740 | — |
| conv cpe 2-4P | 2,640 | 790 | — |
| touring Brougham 5P | 2,735 | 742 | — |

# Hudson

| GH Big Six (wb 116.0) | | Wght | Price | Prod |
|---|---|---|---|---|
| | coach 5P | 2,720 | 710 | — |
| | sdn 4d | 2,780 | 770 | — |
| | Suburban sdn 5P | 2,795 | 802 | — |
| **Eight (wb 117.0)** | | | | |
| HT | Special cpe 2P | 2,740 | 760 | |
| HT | Special cpe 2-4P | 2,810 | 810 | |
| HT | Special conv cpe 2-4P | 2,765 | 860 | |
| HT | Special touring B'ham 5P | 2,855 | 812 | 7,150 |
| HT | Special coach 5P | 2,840 | 780 | |
| HT | Special sdn 4d | 2,890 | 840 | |
| HT | Suburban sdn 5P | 2,905 | 872 | |
| HU | DeLuxe cpe 2P | 2,790 | 845 | |
| HU | DeLuxe cpe 2-4P | 2,855 | 895 | |
| HU | DeLuxe conv cpe 2-4P | 2,805 | 955 | |
| HU | DeLuxe touring B'ham 5P | 2,895 | 907 | 3,097 |
| HU | DeLuxe coach 5P | 2,880 | 875 | |
| HU | DeLuxe sdn 4d | 2,945 | 935 | |
| HU | DeLuxe Suburban sdn 5P | 2,960 | 967 | |
| **HHU Custom Eight (wb 124.0)—1,460 built** | | | | |
| | Brougham 5P | 3,055 | 1,095 | — |
| | touring Brougham 5P | 3,070 | 1,127 | — |
| | club sdn 5P | 3,130 | 1,025 | — |
| | Suburban sdn 5P | 3,145 | 1,057 | — |
| **Eight (wb 124.0)** | | | | |
| HTL | Special Brougham 5P | 2,995 | 930 | |
| HTL | Special touring B'ham 5P | 3,010 | 962 | 968 |
| HTL | club sdn 5P | 2,975 | 880 | |
| HTL | Special Suburban sdn 5P | 2,990 | 912 | |
| HUL | DeLuxe Brougham 5P | 3,055 | 1,025 | |
| HUL | DeLuxe touring B'ham 5P | 3,070 | 1,057 | 721 |
| HUL | DeLuxe club sdn 5P | 3,015 | 975 | |
| HUL | DeLuxe Suburban sdn 5P | 3,030 | 1,007 | |

| 1935 Engines | bore × stroke | bhp | availability |
|---|---|---|---|
| I-6, 212.0 | 3.00 × 5.00 | 93 | S-Big Six |
| I-6, 212.0 | 3.00 × 5.00 | 100 | O-Big Six |
| I-8, 254.5 | 3.00 × 4.50 | 113 | S-all Eights |
| I-8, 254.5 | 3.00 × 4.50 | 124 | O-all Eights |

## 1936

| 63 Custom Six (wb 120)—9,720 built | | Wght | Price | Prod |
|---|---|---|---|---|
| 63 | cpe 2P | 2,730 | 710 | — |
| 63 | cpe 2-4P | 2,810 | 755 | — |
| 63 | conv cpe 2-4P | 2,870 | 810 | — |
| 63 | Brougham 2d 5P | 2,830 | 730 | — |
| 63 | touring 2d 5P | 2,830 | 755 | — |
| 63 | sdn 4d | 2,880 | 785 | — |
| 63 | touring sdn 4d | 2,880 | 810 | — |
| **64/66 DeLuxe Eight (wb 120.0; lwb-127.0)*** | | | | |
| 64 | cpe 2P | 2,865 | 760 | — |
| 64 | cpe 2-4P | 2,965 | 810 | — |
| 64 | conv cpe 2-4P | 3,000 | 875 | — |
| 64 | Brougham 2d 5P | 2,985 | 790 | — |
| 64 | touring Brougham 2d 5P | 2,985 | 815 | — |
| 64 | sdn 4d | 3,045 | 830 | — |
| 64 | touring sdn 4d | 3,045 | 855 | — |
| 66 | lwb sdn 4d | 3,110 | 855 | — |
| 66 | lwb touring sdn 4d | 3,110 | 880 | — |
| **65/67 Custom Eight (wb 120.0; lwb-127.0)*** | | | | |
| 65 | cpe 2P | 2,915 | 845 | — |
| 65 | cpe 2-4P | 3,000 | 895 | — |
| 65 | conv cpe 2-4P | 3,045 | 970 | — |
| 65 | Brougham 2d 5P | 3,034 | 885 | — |
| 65 | touring Brougham 2d 5P | 3,034 | 910 | — |
| 65 | sdn 4d | 3,075 | 925 | — |
| 65 | touring sdn 4d | 3,075 | 950 | — |
| 67 | lwb sdn 4d | 3,140 | 950 | — |
| 67 | lwb touring sdn 4d | 3,140 | 975 | — |

* Total Eight production: 16,627

| 1936 Engines | bore × stroke | bhp | availability |
|---|---|---|---|
| I-6, 212.0 | 3.00 × 5.00 | 93 | S-63 |
| I-6, 212.0 | 3.00 × 5.00 | 100 | O-63 |
| I-8, 254.5 | 3.00 × 4.50 | 113 | S-Eights |
| I-8, 254.5 | 3.00 × 4.50 | 124 | O-Eights |

## 1937

| 73 Custom Six (wb 122)—6,813 built | | Wght | Price | Prod |
|---|---|---|---|---|
| 73 | bus cpe 2P | 2,760 | 865 | — |
| 73 | cpe 3P | 2,805 | 905 | — |
| 73 | Victoria cpe 3P | 2,865 | 950 | — |
| 73 | conv cpe 2P | 2,870 | 1,005 | — |
| 73 | Brougham 2d 5P | 2,925 | 930 | — |
| 73 | touring Brougham 2d 5P | 2,925 | 955 | — |
| 73 | sdn 4d | 2,990 | 980 | — |
| 73 | touring sdn 4d | 2,990 | 1,005 | — |
| 73 | conv Brougham 4P | 2,945 | 1,000 | — |
| **74/76 DeLuxe (wb 122.0; lwb-129.0)** | | | | |
| 74 | cpe 3P | 3,010 | 950 | |
| 74 | Victoria cpe 3P | 3,055 | 1,015 | |
| 74 | conv cpe 2P | 3,020 | 1,080 | |
| 74 | Brougham 2d 5P | 3,105 | 1,000 | 5,628 |
| 74 | touring Brougham 2d 5P | 3,105 | 1,025 | |
| 74 | sdn 4d | 3,135 | 1,040 | |
| 74 | touring sdn 4d | 3,135 | 1,065 | |
| 74 | conv Brougham 4P | 3,125 | 1,165 | |
| 76 | lwb sdn 4d | 3,205 | 1,065 | 1,097 |
| 76 | lwb touring sdn 4d | 3,205 | 1,090 | |
| **75/77 Custom Eight (wb 122.0; lwb-129.0)** | | | | |
| 75 | cpe 3P | 3,055 | 1,050 | |
| 75 | Victoria cpe 3P | 3,085 | 1,100 | |
| 75 | conv cpe 2p | 3,070 | 1,175 | |
| 75 | Brougham 2d 5P | 3,135 | 1,090 | 3,274 |
| 75 | touring Brougham 2d 5P | 3,135 | 1,115 | |
| 75 | sdn 4d | 3,195 | 1,140 | |
| 75 | touring sdn 4d | 3,195 | 1,165 | |
| 75 | conv Brougham 4P | 3,160 | 1,260 | |
| 77 | lwb sdn 5P | 3,260 | 1,165 | 3,652 |
| 77 | lwb touring sdn 5P | 3,260 | 1,190 | |

| 1937 Engines | bore × stroke | bhp | availability |
|---|---|---|---|
| I-6, 212.0 | 3.00 × 5.00 | 101 | S-73 |
| I-6, 212.0 | 3.00 × 5.00 | 107 | O-73 |
| I-8, 254.5 | 3.00 × 4.50 | 122 | S-Eights |
| I-8, 254.5 | 3.00 × 4.50 | 128 | O-Eights |

## 1938

| 80/88 Terraplane Six (wb 117; lwb-124) | | Wght | Price | Prod |
|---|---|---|---|---|
| 80 | Util cpe 3P | 2,840 | 789 | — |
| 80 | Util coach 6P | 2,835 | 779 | — |
| 80 | Util touring cabriolet 6P | 2,840 | 799 | — |
| 80 | Util wgn 4d | 3,055 | 965 | — |
| 88 | lwb sdn 6P | 2,965 | 974 | — |
| 88 | lwb touring sdn 6P | 2,970 | 995 | — |
| **81 Terraplane DeLuxe Six (wb 117.0)** | | | | |
| 81 | cpe 3P | 2,725 | 789 | |
| 81 | Victoria cpe 3-5P | 2,775 | 835 | |

# Hudson

| 81 Terraplane DeLuxe Six (wb 117.0) | | Wght | Price | Prod |
|---|---|---|---|---|
| 81 | conv cpe 3P | 2,780 | 926 | — |
| 81 | Brougham 6P | 2,820 | 822 | — |
| 81 | touring Brougham 6P | 2,825 | 843 | — |
| 81 | sdn 6P | 2,885 | 864 | — |
| 81 | touring sdn 6P | 2,890 | 884 | — |
| 81 | conv Brougham 6P | 2,860 | 990 | — |
| **82 Terraplane Super Six (wb 117.0)** | | | | |
| 82 | cpe 3P | 2,755 | 845 | — |
| 82 | Victoria cpe 3-5P | 2,805 | 886 | — |
| 82 | conv cpe 3P | 2,835 | 971 | — |
| 82 | Brougham 6P | 2,865 | 878 | — |
| 82 | touring Brougham 6P | 2,870 | 899 | — |
| 82 | sdn 6P | 2,925 | 915 | — |
| 82 | touring sdn 6P | 2,930 | 935 | — |
| 82 | conv Brougham 6P | 2,880 | 1,034 | — |
| **89 "112" Six (wb 112.0)** | | | | |
| | Standard cpe 3P | 2,500 | 694 | |
| | Standard Victoria cpe 4P | 2,540 | 740 | |
| | Standard conv cpe 3P | 2,545 | 835 | |
| | Standard Brougham 6P | 2,595 | 724 | |
| | Standard touring B'ham 6P | 2,600 | 743 | |
| | Standard sdn 4d | 2,600 | 755 | ⎤ 24,475 |
| | Standard touring sdn 5d | 2,625 | 775 | |
| | Standard conv B'ham 6P | 2,610 | 886 | |
| | Utility cpe 3P | 2,660 | 724 | |
| | Utility coach 6P | 2,600 | 697 | |
| | Utility coach T/B 6P | 2,605 | 716 | ⎦ |
| | Deluxe cpe 3P | 2,500 | 704 | — |
| | Deluxe Victoria cpe 4P | 2,540 | 750 | — |
| | Deluxe conv cpe 3P | 2,545 | 840 | — |
| | Deluxe Brougham 6P | 2,595 | 734 | — |
| | Deluxe touring B'ham 6P | 2,600 | 753 | — |
| | Deluxe sdn 4d | 2,620 | 765 | — |
| | Deluxe touring sdn 4d | 2,625 | 785 | — |
| | Deluxe conv Brougham 6P | 2,610 | 891 | — |
| **83 Custom Six (wb 122.0)** | | | | |
| | cpe 3P | 2,825 | 909 | — |
| | Victoria cpe 3-5P | 2,880 | 955 | — |
| | conv cpe 3P | 2,895 | 1,041 | — |
| | Brougham 6P | 2,935 | 948 | — |
| | touring Brougham 6P | 2,940 | 968 | — |
| | sdn 4d | 3,005 | 984 | — |
| | touring sdn 4d | 3,010 | 1,005 | — |
| | conv Brougham 6P | 2,975 | 1,104 | — |
| **84 Deluxe Eight (wb 122.0)** | | | | |
| | cpe 3P | 3,010 | 990 | — |
| | Victoria cpe 3-5P | 3,060 | 1,031 | — |
| | conv cpe 3P | 3,060 | 1,121 | — |
| | Brougham 6P | 3,115 | 1,028 | — |
| | touring Brougham 6P | 3,120 | 1,049 | — |
| | sdn 4d | 3,155 | 1,060 | — |
| | touring sdn 4d | 3,160 | 1,080 | — |
| | conv Brougham 6P | 3,140 | 1,185 | — |
| **85/87 Custom Eight (wb 122.00; lwb-129.0)** | | | | |
| 85 | cpe 3P | 3,020 | 1,080 | — |
| 85 | Victoria cpe 3-5P | 3,080 | 1,131 | — |
| 85 | Brougham 6P | 3,140 | 1,134 | — |
| 85 | touring Brougham 6P | 3,145 | 1,155 | — |
| 85 | sdn 4d | 3,190 | 1,171 | — |
| 85 | touring sdn | 3,195 | 1,191 | — |
| 87 | Country Club sdn 4d (lwb) | 3,270 | 1,199 | — |
| 87 | Country Club vic sdn 4d (lwb) | 3,275 | 1,299 | — |

| 1938 Engines | bore × stroke | bhp | availability |
|---|---|---|---|
| I-6, 175.0 | 3.00 × 4.13 | 83 | S-89 |
| I-6, 212.0 | 3.00 × 5.00 | 96 | S-80, 81, 88 |
| I-6, 212.0 | 3.00 × 5.00 | 101 | S-82, 83 |
| I-6, 212.0 | 3.00 × 5.00 | 107 | O-83 |
| I-8, 254.5 | 3.00 × 4.50 | 122 | S-84, 85, 87 |

**1939** (Total calendar-year production: 81,521)

| 90 "112" Deluxe Six (wb 112.0) | Wght | Price | Prod |
|---|---|---|---|
| Traveler cpe 3P | 2,544 | 695 | — |
| cpe 3P | 2,587 | 745 | — |
| Victoria cpe 4P | 2,622 | 791 | — |
| conv cpe 3P | 2,627 | 886 | — |
| touring Brougham 6P | 2,682 | 775 | — |
| conv Brougham 6P | 2,732 | 936 | — |
| touring sdn 4d | 2,712 | 806 | — |
| Utility coach 6P | 2,634 | 725 | — |
| Utility cpe 3P | 2,714 | 750 | — |
| Utility wgn 4d | 2,880 | 931 | — |
| **91 Pacemaker Six (wb 118.0)** | | | |
| cpe 3P | 2,717 | 793 | — |
| Victoria cpe 5P | 2,752 | 844 | — |
| touring Brougham 6P | 2,832 | 823 | — |
| touring sdn 4d | 2,867 | 854 | — |
| **92 Six (wb 118.0)** | | | |
| cpe 3P | 2,757 | 833 | — |
| Victoria cpe 5P | 2,787 | 879 | — |
| conv cpe 3P | 2,782 | 982 | — |
| touring Brougham 6P | 2,847 | 866 | — |
| conv Brougham 6P | 2,892 | 1,042 | — |
| touring sdn 4d | 2,897 | 908 | — |
| **93 Country Club Six (wb 122.0)** | | | |
| cpe 3P | 2,848 | 919 | — |
| Victoria cpe 5P | 2,893 | 967 | — |
| conv cpe 3P | 2,898 | 1,052 | — |
| touring Brougham 6P | 2,968 | 960 | — |
| conv Brougham 6P | 2,983 | 1,115 | — |
| touring sdn 4d | 3,023 | 995 | — |
| **98 Big Boy Six (wb 119.0)** | | | |
| sdn 4d | 2,909 | 884 | — |
| sdn 7P | 3,022 | 1,114 | — |

| 95/97 Country Club Eight (wb 122.0; lwb-129.0) | | | | |
|---|---|---|---|---|
| 95 | cpe 3P | 3,003 | 1,009 | — |
| 95 | Victoria cpe 5P | 3,053 | 1,051 | — |
| 95 | conv cpe 3P | 3,033 | 1,138 | — |
| 95 | touring Brougham 6P | 3,138 | 1,049 | — |
| 95 | conv Brougham 6P | 3,123 | 1,201 | — |
| 95 | touring sdn 4d | 3,193 | 1,079 | — |
| 97 | lwb touring sdn 4d | 3,268 | 1,174 | — |
| 97 | lwb sdn 7P | 3,378 | 1,430 | — |

| 1939 Engines | bore × stroke | bhp | availability |
|---|---|---|---|
| I-6, 175.0 | 3.00 × 4.13 | 86 | S-90, 98 sdn 4d |
| I-6, 212.0 | 3.00 × 5.00 | 96/101 | S-91, 92, 93, 98 sdn 7P |
| I-8, 254.5 | 3.00 × 4.50 | 122 | S-95, 97 |

**1940** (Total model-year production: 87,915; Sixes: 77,295; Eights: 10,620)

| 40-T Traveler (wb 113.0) | Wght | Price | Prod |
|---|---|---|---|
| cpe 3P | 2,800 | 670 | — |
| Victoria cpe 4P | 2,830 | 750 | — |
| sdn 2d | 2,895 | 735 | — |
| sdn 4d | 2,940 | 763 | — |

# Hudson

| 40-P Deluxe (wb 113.0) | Wght | Price | Prod |
|---|---|---|---|
| cpe 3P | 2,840 | 745 | — |
| Victoria cpe 4P | 2,865 | 791 | — |
| conv cpe | 2,860 | 930 | — |
| sdn 2d | 2,930 | 775 | — |
| sdn 4d | 2,965 | 808 | — |
| conv sdn | 2,920 | 955 | — |
| **41 Super (wb 118.0)** | | | |
| cpe 3P | 2,950 | 809 | — |
| Victoria cpe 4P | 2,980 | 860 | — |
| conv cpe | 2,980 | 995 | — |
| sdn 2d | 3,020 | 839 | — |
| sdn 4d | 3,050 | 870 | — |
| conv sdn 2d | 3,020 | 1,030 | — |
| **43 Country Club (wb 125.0)** | | | |
| sdn 4d | 3,240 | 1,018 | — |
| Special sdn 4d | 3,240 | 1,044 | — |
| sdn 4d, 7P | 3,355 | 1,230 | — |
| **44 Eight (wb 118.0)** | | | |
| cpe 3P | 3,040 | 860 | — |
| Victoria cpe 4P | 3,075 | 942 | — |
| conv cpe | 3,065 | 1,087 | — |
| sdn 2d | 3,140 | 918 | — |
| sdn 4d | 3,185 | 952 | — |
| conv sdn 2d | 3,130 | 1,122 | — |
| **47 Country Club Eight (wb 125.0)** | | | |
| sdn 4d | 3,285 | 1,118 | — |
| Special sdn 4d | 3,285 | 1,144 | — |
| sdn 4d, 7P | 3,400 | 1,330 | — |
| **48 Big Boy (wb 125.0)** | | | |
| Carry-all sdn 4d | 3,245 | 989 | — |
| sdn 4d, 7P | 3,140 | 1,095 | — |

| 1940 Engines | bore × stroke | bhp | availability |
|---|---|---|---|
| I-6, 175.0 | 3.00 × 4.13 | 92 | S-40 |
| I-6, 212.0 | 3.00 × 5.00 | 98 | S-48 |
| I-6, 212.0 | 3.00 × 5.00 | 102 | S-41, 43 |
| I-8, 254.5 | 3.00 × 4.50 | 128 | S-44, 47 |

## 1941 (Total model-year production: 91,769; Sixes: 82,051; Eights: 9,718)

| 10-T Traveler (wb 116.0) | Wght | Price | Prod |
|---|---|---|---|
| cpe 3P | 2,790 | 695 | — |
| club cpe 4P | 2,840 | 788 | — |
| sdn 2d | 2,850 | 765 | — |
| sdn 4d | 2,900 | 793 | — |
| **10-P Deluxe (wb 116.0)** | | | |
| cpe 3P | 2,840 | 801 | — |
| club cpe 4P | 2,895 | 848 | — |
| sdn 2d | 2,900 | 822 | — |
| sdn 4d | 2,950 | 856 | — |
| conv sdn 2d | 2,980 | 1,063 | 140 est |
| **11 Super (wb 121.0)** | | | |
| cpe 3P | 2,935 | 881 | — |
| club cpe 4P | 2,980 | 936 | — |
| sdn 2d | 3,000 | 901 | — |
| sdn 4d | 3,050 | 932 | — |
| conv sdn 2d | 3,125 | 1,156 | 300 est |
| wgn 4d | 3,315 | 1,297 | 100 est |
| **12 Commodore Six (wb 121.0)** | | | |
| cpe 3P | 3,000 | 935 | — |
| club cpe 4P | 3,045 | 997 | — |
| sdn 2d | 3,050 | 966 | — |
| sdn 4d | 3,100 | 994 | — |
| conv sdn 2d | 3,160 | 1,204 | 200 est |
| **14 Commodore Eight (wb 121.0)** | | | |
| cpe 3P | 3,135 | 978 | — |
| club cpe 4P | 3,210 | 1,040 | — |
| sdn 2d | 3,210 | 1,003 | — |
| sdn 4d | 3,260 | 1,035 | — |
| conv sdn | 3,350 | 1,254 | 200 est |
| wgn 4d | 3,400 | 1,383 | 80 est |
| **15-17 Commodore Eight (wb 128.0; cpe-121.0)** | | | |
| 15 cpe 3P | 3,185 | 1,064 | — |
| 15 club cpe 4P | 3,235 | 1,127 | — |
| 17 sdn 4d | 3,370 | 1,232 | — |
| 17 sdn 4d 7P | 3,440 | 1,438 | — |
| **18 Big Boy (wb 128.0)** | | | |
| sdn 4d, 7P | 3,155 | 1,223 | |

| 1941 Engines | bore × stroke | bhp | availability |
|---|---|---|---|
| I-6, 175.0 | 3.00 × 4.13 | 92 | S-10 |
| I-6, 212.0 | 3.00 × 5.00 | 98 | S-18 |
| I-6, 212.0 | 3.00 × 5.00 | 102 | S-11, 12 |
| I-8, 254.5 | 3.00 × 4.50 | 128 | S-14, 15, 17 |

## 1942 (Total model-year production: 40,661; Sixes: 34,069; Eights: 6,592)

| 20T Traveler (wb 116.0) | Wght | Price | Prod |
|---|---|---|---|
| cpe 3P | 2,795 | 893 | — |
| club cpe 4P | 2,845 | 965 | — |
| sdn 2d | 2,895 | 945 | — |
| sdn 4d | 2,940 | 973 | — |
| **20P Deluxe (wb 116.0)** | | | |
| cpe 3P | 2,845 | 981 | — |
| club cpe 4P | 2,900 | 1,034 | — |
| sdn 2d | 2,935 | 1,012 | — |
| sdn 4d | 2,975 | 1,045 | — |
| conv sdn | 3,140 | 1,292 | — |
| **21 Super (wb 121.0)** | | | |
| cpe 3P | 2,950 | 1,102 | — |
| club cpe 4P | 3,010 | 1,159 | — |
| sdn 2d | 3,035 | 1,132 | — |
| sdn 4d | 3,080 | 1,162 | — |
| conv sdn 2d | 3,200 | 1,414 | — |
| wgn 4d | 3,315 | 1,486 | — |
| **22 Commodore Six (wb 121.0)** | | | |
| cpe 3P | 2,995 | 1,176 | — |
| club cpe 5P | 3,090 | 1,239 | — |
| sdn 2d | 3,090 | 1,216 | — |
| sdn 4d | 3,145 | 1,246 | — |
| conv sdn | 3,280 | 1,481 | — |
| **24 Commodore Eight (wb 121.0)** | | | |
| cpe 3P | 3,130 | 1,220 | — |
| club cpe 5P | 3,205 | 1,282 | — |
| sdn 2d | 3,230 | 1,252 | — |
| sdn 4d | 3,280 | 1,291 | — |
| conv sdn 2d | 3,400 | 1,533 | — |
| **25 Commodore Custom Eight (wb 121.0)** | | | |
| cpe 3p | 3,160 | 1,318 | — |
| club cpe 4P | 3,235 | 1,380 | — |
| **27 Commodore Custom Eight (wb 128.0)** | | | |
| sdn 4d, 8P | 3,395 | 1,510 | — |

| 1942 Engines | bore × stroke | bhp | availability |
|---|---|---|---|
| I-6, 175.0 | 3.00 × 4.13 | 92 | S-20 |

# Hudson

| 1942 Engines | bore × stroke | bhp | availability |
|---|---|---|---|
| I-6, 212.0 | 3.00 × 5.00 | 102 | S-21, 22 |
| I-8, 254.5 | 3.00 × 4.50 | 128 | S-24, 25, 27 |

## 1946

### 51 Super Six (wb 121)—61,787 built

| | Wght | Price | Prod |
|---|---|---|---|
| sdn 4d | 3,085 | 1,555 | — |
| Brougham sdn 2d | 3,030 | 1,511 | — |
| club cpe | 3,015 | 1,553 | — |
| cpe 3P | 2,950 | 1,481 | — |
| Brougham conv cpe | 3,195 | 1,879 | 1,035* |

### 52 Commodore Six (wb 121.0)—17,685 built

| | | | |
|---|---|---|---|
| sdn 4d | 3,150 | 1,699 | — |
| club cpe | 3,065 | 1,693 | — |

### 53 Super Eight (wb 121.0)—3,961 built

| | | | |
|---|---|---|---|
| sdn 4d | 3,235 | 1,668 | — |
| club cpe | 3,065 | 1,664 | — |

### 54 Commodore Eight (wb 121.0)—8,193 built

| | | | |
|---|---|---|---|
| sdn 4d | 3,305 | 1,774 | — |
| club cpe | 3,235 | 1,760 | — |
| Brougham conv cpe | 3,410 | 2,050 | 140* |

* Estimated; total convertibles: 1,177

| 1946 Engines | bore × stroke | bhp | availability |
|---|---|---|---|
| I-6, 212.0 | 3.00 × 5.00 | 102 | S-51, 52 |
| I-8, 254.5 | 3.00 × 4.50 | 128 | S-53, 54 |

## 1947

### 171 Super Six (wb 121)—49,276 built

| | Wght | Price | Prod |
|---|---|---|---|
| sdn 4d | 3,110 | 1,749 | — |
| Brougham sdn 2d | 3,055 | 1,704 | — |
| club cpe | 3,040 | 1,744 | — |
| cpe 3P | 2,975 | 1,628 | — |
| Brougham conv cpe | 3,220 | 2,021 | 1,460* |

### 172 Commodore Six (wb 121.0)—25,138 built

| | | | |
|---|---|---|---|
| sdn 4d | 3,175 | 1,896 | — |
| club cpe | 3,090 | 1,887 | — |

### 173 Super Eight (wb 121.0)—5,076 built

| | | | |
|---|---|---|---|
| sdn 4d | 3,260 | 1,862 | — |
| club cpe | 3,210 | 1,855 | — |

### 174 Commodore Eight (wb 121.0)—12,593 built

| | | | |
|---|---|---|---|
| sdn 4d | 3,330 | 1,972 | — |
| club cpe | 3,260 | 1,955 | — |
| Brougham conv cpe | 3,435 | 2,196 | 360* |

* Estimated; total convertibles: 1,823

| 1947 Engines | bore × stroke | bhp | availability |
|---|---|---|---|
| I-6, 212.0 | 3.00 × 5.00 | 102 | S-171, 172 |
| I-8, 254.5 | 3.00 × 4.50 | 128 | S-173, 174 |

## 1948

### 481 Super Six (wb 124)—49,388 built

| | Wght | Price | Prod |
|---|---|---|---|
| sdn 4d | 3,500 | 2,222 | — |
| Brougham sdn 2d | 3,470 | 2,172 | — |
| club cpe | 3,480 | 2,219 | — |
| cpe 3P | 3,460 | 2,069 | — |
| Brougham conv cpe | 3,750 | 2,836 | 88* |

### 482 Commodore Six (wb 124.0)—27,159 built

| | | | |
|---|---|---|---|
| sdn 4d | 3,540 | 2,399 | — |
| club cpe | 3,550 | 2,374 | — |
| Brougham conv cpe | 3,780 | 3,057 | 48* |

### 483 Super Eight (wb 124.0)—5,338 blt

| | Wght | Price | Prod |
|---|---|---|---|
| sdn 4d | 3,525 | 2,343 | — |
| club cpe | 3,495 | 2,340 | — |

### 484 Commodore Eight (wb 124.0)—35,315 built

| | | | |
|---|---|---|---|
| sdn 4d | 3,600 | 2,514 | — |
| club cpe | 3,570 | 2,490 | — |
| Brougham conv cpe | 3,800 | 3,138 | 64* |

* Estimated; total convertibles: 200

| 1948 Engines | bore × stroke | bhp | availability |
|---|---|---|---|
| I-6, 262.0 | 3.56 × 4.38 | 121 | S-481, 482 |
| I-8, 254.5 | 3.00 × 4.50 | 128 | S-483, 484 |

## 1949

### 491 Super Six (wb 124)—91,333 built

| | Wght | Price | Prod |
|---|---|---|---|
| sdn 4d | 3,555 | 2,207 | — |
| Brougham sdn 2d | 3,515 | 2,156 | — |
| club cpe | 3,480 | 2,203 | — |
| cpe 3P | 3,485 | 2,053 | — |
| Brougham conv cpe | 3,750 | 2,799 | 1,870* |

### 492 Commodore Six (wb 124.0)—32,715 built

| | | | |
|---|---|---|---|
| sdn 4d | 3,625 | 2,383 | — |
| club cpe | 3,585 | 2,359 | — |
| Brougham conv cpe | 3,780 | 2,952 | 655* |

### 493 Super Eight (wb 124.0)—6,365 built

| | | | |
|---|---|---|---|
| sdn 4d | 3,565 | 2,296 | — |
| Brougham sdn 2d | 3,545 | 2,245 | — |
| club cpe | 3,550 | 2,292 | — |

### 494 Commodore Eight (wb 124.0)—28,687 built

| | | | |
|---|---|---|---|
| sdn 4d | 3,650 | 2,472 | — |
| club cpe | 3,600 | 2,448 | — |
| Brougham conv cpe | 3,800 | 3,041 | 595* |

* Estimated; total convertibles: 3,119

| 1949 Engines | bore × stroke | bhp | availability |
|---|---|---|---|
| I-6, 262.0 | 3.56 × 4.38 | 121 | S-491, 492 |
| I-8, 254.5 | 3.00 × 4.50 | 128 | S-493, 494 |

## 1950

### 500 Pacemaker (wb 119)—39,455 built

| | Wght | Price | Prod |
|---|---|---|---|
| sdn 4d | 3,510 | 1,933 | — |
| Brougham sdn 2d | 3,475 | 1,912 | — |
| club cpe | 3,460 | 1,933 | — |
| cpe 3P | 3,445 | 1,807 | — |
| Brougham conv cpe | 3,655 | 2,428 | 1,100* |

### 50A Pacemaker Deluxe (wb 119.0)—22,297 built

| | | | |
|---|---|---|---|
| sdn 4d | 3,520 | 1,959 | — |
| Brougham sdn 2d | 3,485 | 1,928 | — |
| club cpe | 3,470 | 1,959 | — |
| Brougham conv cpe | 3,665 | 2,444 | 630* |

### 501 Super Six (wb 124.0)—17,246 built

| | | | |
|---|---|---|---|
| sdn 4d | 3,590 | 2,105 | — |
| Brougham sdn 2d | 3,565 | 2,068 | — |
| club cpe | 3,555 | 2,102 | — |
| Brougham conv cpe | 3,750 | 2,629 | 465* |

### 502 Commodore Six (wb 124.0)—24,605 built

| | | | |
|---|---|---|---|
| sdn 4d | 3,655 | 2,282 | — |
| club cpe | 3,640 | 2,257 | — |
| Brougham conv cpe | 3,840 | 2,809 | 700* |

### 503 Super Eight (wb 124.0)—1,074 built

| | | | |
|---|---|---|---|
| sdn 4d | 3,605 | 2,189 | — |
| Brougham sdn 2d | 3,575 | 2,152 | — |
| club cpe | 3,560 | 2,186 | — |

# Hudson

| 504 Commodore Eight (wb 124.0)—16,731 blt | Wght | Price | Prod |
|---|---|---|---|
| sdn 4d | 3,675 | 2,366 | — |
| club cpe | 3,655 | 2,341 | — |
| Brougham conv cpe | 3,865 | 2,893 | 425* |

\* Estimated; total convertibles: 3,322

| 1950 Engines | bore × stroke | bhp | availability |
|---|---|---|---|
| I-6, 232.0 | 3.56 × 3.88 | 112 | S-500 |
| I-6, 262.0 | 3.56 × 4.38 | 123 | S-50A, 501, 502 |
| I-8, 254.5 | 3.00 × 4.50 | 128 | S-503, 504 |

## 1951

| 4A Pacemaker Custom (wb 119.0)—34,495 blt | Wght | Price | Prod |
|---|---|---|---|
| sdn 4d | 3,460 | 2,145 | — |
| Brougham sdn 2d | 3,430 | 2,102 | — |
| club cpe | 3,410 | 2,145 | — |
| cpe 3P | 3,380 | 1,965 | — |
| Brougham conv cpe | 3,600 | 2,642 | 430* |

| 5A Super Six Custom (wb 124.0)—22,532 built | Wght | Price | Prod |
|---|---|---|---|
| sdn 4d | 3,565 | 2,287 | — |
| Brougham sdn 2d | 3,535 | 2,238 | — |
| club cpe | 3,525 | 2,287 | — |
| Hollywood htp cpe | 3,590 | 2,605 | 1,100* |
| Brougham conv cpe | 3,720 | 2,827 | 280* |

| 6A Commodore Six Custom (wb 124.0)—16,979 built | Wght | Price | Prod |
|---|---|---|---|
| sdn 4d | 3,600 | 2,480 | — |
| club cpe | 3,585 | 2,455 | — |
| Hollywood htp cpe | 3,640 | 2,780 | 820* |
| Brougham conv cpe | 3,785 | 3,011 | 210* |

| 7A Hornet (wb 124.0)—43,656 built | Wght | Price | Prod |
|---|---|---|---|
| sdn 4d | 3,600 | 2,568 | — |
| club cpe | 3,580 | 2,543 | — |
| Hollywood htp cpe | 3,630 | 2,869 | 2,100* |
| Brougham conv cpe | 3,780 | 3,099 | 550* |

| 8A Commodore Eight Custom (wb 124.0)—14,243 built | Wght | Price | Prod |
|---|---|---|---|
| sdn 4d | 3,620 | 2,568 | — |
| club cpe | 3,600 | 2,543 | — |
| Hollywood htp cpe | 3,650 | 2,869 | 670* |
| Brougham conv cpe | 3,800 | 3,099 | 180* |

\* Estimated; total convertibles: 1,651; total hardtops: 4,689

| 1951 Engines | bore × stroke | bhp | availability |
|---|---|---|---|
| I-6, 232.0 | 3.56 × 3.88 | 112 | S-Pacemaker |
| I-6, 262.0 | 3.56 × 4.38 | 123 | S-Supr & Comdr Six |
| I-6, 308.0 | 3.81 × 4.50 | 145 | S-Hornet |
| I-8, 254.5 | 3.00 × 4.50 | 128 | S-Commo Eight |

## 1952

| 4B Pacemaker (wb 119)—7,486 built | Wght | Price | Prod |
|---|---|---|---|
| sdn 4d | 3,390 | 2,311 | — |
| Brougham sdn 2d | 3,355 | 2,264 | — |
| club cpe | 3,335 | 2,311 | — |
| cpe 3P | 3,305 | 2,116 | — |

| 5B Wasp (wb 119.0)—21,876 built | Wght | Price | Prod |
|---|---|---|---|
| sdn 4d | 3,485 | 2,466 | — |
| Brougham sdn 2d | 3,470 | 2,413 | — |
| club cpe | 3,435 | 2,466 | — |
| Hollywood htp cpe | 3,525 | 2,812 | 1,320* |
| Brougham conv cpe | 3,635 | 3,048 | 220* |

| 6B Commodore Six (wb 124.0)—1,592 built | Wght | Price | Prod |
|---|---|---|---|
| sdn 4d | 3,595 | 2,674 | — |
| club cpe | 3,550 | 2,647 | — |
| Hollywood htp cpe | 3,625 | 3,000 | 100* |
| Brougham conv cpe | 3,750 | 3,247 | 20* |

| 7B Hornet (wb 124.0)—35,921 blt | Wght | Price | Prod |
|---|---|---|---|
| sdn 4d | 3,600 | 2,769 | — |
| club cpe | 3,550 | 2,742 | — |
| Hollywood htp cpe | 3,630 | 3,095 | 2,160* |
| Brougham conv cpe | 3,750 | 3,342 | 360* |

| 8B Commodore Eight (wb 124.0)—3,125 built | Wght | Price | Prod |
|---|---|---|---|
| sdn 4d | 3,630 | 2,769 | — |
| club cpe | 3,580 | 2,742 | — |
| Hollywood htp cpe | 3,660 | 3,095 | 190* |
| Brougham conv cpe | 3,770 | 3,342 | 30* |

\* Estimated; total convertibles: 636; total hardtops: 3,777

| 1952 Engines | bore × stroke | bhp | availability |
|---|---|---|---|
| I-6, 232.0 | 3.56 × 3.88 | 112 | S-Pacemaker |
| I-6, 262.0 | 3.56 × 4.38 | 127 | S-Wasp, Commodore Six |
| I-6, 308.0 | 3.81 × 4.50 | 145 | S-Hornet |
| I-8, 254.5 | 3.00 × 4.50 | 128 | S-Commodore Eight |

## 1953

| 1C Jet (wb 105.0)—21,143 built (includes Super Jet) | Wght | Price | Prod |
|---|---|---|---|
| sdn 4d | 2,650 | 1,858 | — |

| 2C Super Jet (wb 105.0) | | | |
|---|---|---|---|
| sdn 4d | 2,700 | 1,954 | — |
| sdn 2d | 2,695 | 1,933 | — |

| 4C Wasp (wb 119.0)—17,792 built (includes Super Wasp) | Wght | Price | Prod |
|---|---|---|---|
| sdn 4d | 3,380 | 2,311 | — |
| sdn 2d | 3,350 | 2,264 | — |
| club cpe | 3,340 | 2,311 | — |

| 5C Super Wasp (wb 119.0) | | | |
|---|---|---|---|
| sdn 4d | 3,480 | 2,466 | — |
| sdn 2d | 3,460 | 2,413 | — |
| club cpe | 3,455 | 2,466 | — |
| Hollywood htp cpe | 3,525 | 2,812 | 590* |
| Brougham conv cpe | 3,655 | 3,048 | 50* |

| 7C Hornet (wb 124.0)—27,208 built | | | |
|---|---|---|---|
| sdn 4d | 3,570 | 2,769 | — |
| club cpe | 3,530 | 2,742 | — |
| Hollywood htp cpe | 3,610 | 3,095 | 910* |
| Brougham conv cpe | 3,760 | 3,342 | — |

\* Estimated; total hardtops: 1,501

| 1953 Engines | bore × stroke | bhp | availability |
|---|---|---|---|
| I-6, 202.0 | 3.00 × 4.75 | 104 | S-Jet |
| I-6, 202.0 | 3.00 × 4.75 | 106/114 | O-Jet |
| I-6, 232.0 | 3.56 × 3.88 | 112 | S-Wasp |
| I-6, 262.0 | 3.56 × 4.38 | 127 | S-Super Wasp |
| I-6, 308.0 | 3.81 × 4.50 | 145 | S-Hornet |
| I-6, 308.0 | 3.81 × 4.50 | 160 | O-Hornet |
| I-6, 308.0 | 3.81 × 4.50 | 170 | O-Hornet (7-X) |

## 1954

| 1D Jet (wb 105.0)—14,224 built (includes Super Jet and Jet-Liner) | Wght | Price | Prod |
|---|---|---|---|
| sdn 4d | 2,675 | 1,858 | — |
| Utility sdn 2d | 2,715 | 1,837 | — |
| Family club sdn 2d | 2,635 | 1,621 | — |

| 2D Super Jet (wb 105.0) | | | |
|---|---|---|---|
| sdn 4d | 2,725 | 1,954 | — |
| club sdn 2d | 2,710 | 1,933 | — |

| 3D Jet-Liner (wb 105.0) | | | |
|---|---|---|---|
| sdn 4d | 2,760 | 2,057 | — |

# Hudson

| 3D Jet-Liner (wb 105.0) | Wght | Price | Prod |
|---|---|---|---|
| club sdn 2d | 2,740 | 2,046 | — |
| **4D Wasp (wb 119.0)—11,603 built (includes Super Wasp)** | | | |
| sdn 4d | 3,440 | 2,256 | — |
| club sdn 2d | 3,375 | 2,209 | — |
| club cpe | 3,360 | 2,256 | — |
| **5D Super Wasp (wb 119.0)** | | | |
| sdn 4d | 3,525 | 2,466 | — |
| club sdn 2d | 3,490 | 2,413 | — |
| club cpe | 3,475 | 2,466 | — |
| Hollywood htp cpe | 3,570 | 2,704 | — |
| Brougham conv cpe | 3,680 | 3,004 | — |
| **6D Hornet Special (wb 124.0)—24,833 built (includes Hornet)** | | | |
| Brougham conv cpe | 3,680 | 3,004 | — |
| sdn 4d | 3,560 | 2,619 | — |
| club sdn 2d | 3,515 | 2,571 | — |
| club cpe | 3,505 | 2,619 | — |
| **7D Hornet (wb 124.0)** | | | |
| sdn 4d | 3,620 | 2,769 | — |
| club cpe | 3,570 | 2,742 | — |
| Hollywood htp cpe | 3,655 | 2,988 | — |
| Brougham conv cpe | 3,800 | 3,288 | — |
| **Italia (wb 105.0)** | | | |
| cpe | 2,710 | 4,800 | 26 |

| 1954 Engines | bore × stroke | bhp | availability |
|---|---|---|---|
| I-6, 202.0 | 3.00 × 4.75 | 104 | S-Jet |
| I-6, 202.0 | 3.00 × 4.75 | 106/114 | S-Italia; O-Jet |
| I-6, 232.0 | 3.56 × 3.88 | 126 | S-Wasp |
| I-6, 262.0 | 3.56 × 4.38 | 140 | S-Super Wasp |
| I-6, 308.0 | 3.81 × 4.50 | 160 | S-Hornet |
| I-6, 308.0 | 3.81 × 4.50 | 170 | O-Hornet (Twin-H) |

## 1955

| 54 Metropolitan (wb 85)—3,000* blt | Wght | Price | Prod |
|---|---|---|---|
| 1 conv cpe 3P | 1,803 | 1,469 | — |
| 2 htp cpe | 1,843 | 1,445 | — |
| **55 Rambler (wb 100.0)** | | | |
| 12 Deluxe bus sdn | 2,400 | 1,457 | 34 |
| 14-1 Super Suburban wgn 2d | 2,532 | 1,869 | 1,335 |
| 16-1 Super club sdn | 2,450 | 1,683 | 2,970 |
| 17-2 Custom Cntry Club htp cpe | 2,518 | 2,098 | 1,601 |
| **55 Rambler (wb 108.0)** | | | |
| 15 Deluxe sdn 4d | 2,567 | 1,695 | ⎫ |
| 15-1 Super sdn 4d | 2,570 | 1,798 | ⎬ 7,210 |
| 15-2 Custom sdn 4d | 2,606 | 1,989 | ⎭ |
| 18-1 Super Cross Cntry wgn 4d | 2,675 | 1,975 | ⎱ 12,023 |
| 18-2 Custom Cross Cntry wgn 4d | 2,685 | 1,995 | ⎰ |
| **3554 Wasp (wb 114.3)** | | | |
| 5-1 Super sdn 4d | 3,254 | 2,290 | ⎱ 5,551 |
| 5-2 Custom sdn 4d | 3,347 | 2,460 | ⎰ |
| 7-2 Custom Hollywood htp cpe | 3,362 | 2,570 | 1,640 |
| **3556 Hornet 6 (wb 121.3)** | | | |
| 5-1 Super sdn 4d | 3,495 | 2,565 | ⎱ 5,357 |
| 5-2 Custom sdn 4d | 3,562 | 2,760 | ⎰ |
| 7-2 Custom Hollywood htp cpe | 3,587 | 2,880 | 1,554 |
| **3558 Hornet V-8 (wb 121.3)** | | | |
| 5-1 Super sdn 4d | 3,806 | 2,825 | ⎱ 4,449 |
| 5-2 Custom sdn 4d | 3,846 | 3,015 | ⎰ |
| 7-2 Custom Hollywood htp cpe | 3,878 | 3,145 | 1,770 |

| Italia (wb 105.0) | Wght | Price | Prod |
|---|---|---|---|
| cpe | 2,710 | 4,800 | 5 |

*Estimated; total Nash & Hudson, 3,849.

| 1955 Engines | bore × stroke | bhp | availability |
|---|---|---|---|
| I-4, 73.2 | 2.56 × 3.50 | 42 | S-Metropolitan |
| I-6, 195.6 | 3.13 × 4.25 | 90 | S-Rambler |
| I-6, 195.6 | 3.13 × 4.25 | 100 | S-Rambler fleet model |
| I-6, 202.0 | 3.00 × 4.75 | 110 | S-Wasp |
| I-6, 202.0 | 3.00 × 4.75 | 114 | S-Italia |
| I-6, 202.0 | 3.00 × 4.75 | 120 | O-Wasp |
| I-6, 308.0 | 3.81 × 4.50 | 160 | S-Hornet 6 |
| I-6, 308.0 | 3.81 × 4.50 | 170 | O-Hornet 6 (Twin-H) |
| V-8, 320.0 | 3.81 × 3.50 | 208 | S-Hornet V-8 |

## 1956

| 54 Metropolitan (wb 85)—3,000* blt | Wght | Price | Prod |
|---|---|---|---|
| 1 conv cpe 3P | 1,803 | 1,469 | — |
| 2 htp cpe 3P | 1,843 | 1,445 | — |
| **56 Rambler DeLuxe (wb 108.0)—5,000 blt (includes Super and Custom)** | | | |
| 15 sdn 4d | 2,891 | 1,829 | — |
| **56 Rambler Super (wb 108.0)** | | | |
| 15-1 sdn 4d | 2,096 | 1,939 | — |
| 18-1 Cross Cntry wgn 4d | 2,992 | 2,233 | — |
| **56 Rambler Custom (wb 108.0)** | | | |
| 13-2 Cross Cntry htp wgn 4d | 3,095 | 2,494 | — |
| 15-2 sdn 4d | 2,929 | 2,059 | — |
| 18-2 Cross Cntry wgn 4d | 3,110 | 2,329 | — |
| 19-2 htp sdn | 2,990 | 2,224 | — |
| **3564 Wasp (wb 114.3)** | | | |
| 5-1 sdn 4d | 3,264 | 2,216 | 2,519 |
| **3565 Hornet Special (wb 114.3)** | | | |
| 5-1 sdn 4d | 3,467 | 2,626 | 1,528 |
| 7-1 Hollywood htp cpe | 3,486 | 2,741 | 229 |
| **3566 Hornet 6 (wb 121.3)** | | | |
| 5-1 Super sdn 4d | 3,545 | 2,777 | ⎱ 3,022 |
| 5-2 Custom sdn 4d | 3,636 | 3,019 | ⎰ |
| 7-2 Hollywood htp cpe | 3,646 | 3,136 | 358 |
| **3568 Hornet V-8 (wb 121.3)** | | | |
| 5-2 sdn 4d | 3,862 | 3,286 | 1,962 |
| 7-2 Hollywood htp cpe | 3,872 | 3,429 | 1,053 |

*Estimated; total Nash & Hudson: 7,645

| 1956 Engines | bore × stroke | bhp | availability |
|---|---|---|---|
| I-4, 73.2 | 2.56 × 3.50 | 42 | S-Metropolitan |
| I-6, 195.6 | 3.13 × 4.25 | 120 | S-Rambler |
| I-6, 202.0 | 3.00 × 4.75 | 120 | S-Wasp |
| I-6, 202.0 | 3.00 × 4.75 | 130 | O-Wasp (Twin-H) |
| I-6, 308.0 | 3.81 × 4.50 | 165 | S-Hornet 6 |
| V-8, 352.0 | 4.00 × 3.50 | 220 | S-Hornt V-8 (thru 3/56) |
| V-8, 250.0 | 3.50 × 3.25 | 190 | S-Hornt Spcl (3/56 on) |

## 1957

| 357-1 Hornet Super (wb 121.3) | Wght | Price | Prod |
|---|---|---|---|
| sdn 4d | 3,631 | 2,821 | 1,103 |
| Hollywood htp cpe | 3,655 | 2,911 | 266 |
| **357-2 Hornet Custom (wb 121.3)** | | | |
| sdn 4d | 3,678 | 3,011 | 2,256 |
| Hollywood htp cpe | 3,693 | 3,101 | 483 |

| 1957 Engine | bore × stroke | bhp | availability |
|---|---|---|---|
| V-8, 327.0 | 4.00 × 3.25 | 255 | S-all |

# Hupmobile

Robert C. Hupp was an engineer who worked with Ransom Eli Olds and Henry Ford before setting up his own car company in November 1909. His first product, developed with help from several colleagues he hired away from Olds, was the Model 20, a little 16.9-horsepower four-cylinder job on an 86-inch wheelbase. Hupp priced it at a modest $750, a full $75 below Ford's recently introduced Model T. With features like high-tension magneto and two-speed sliding-gear transmission, this first Hupmobile garnered 1618 sales. By 1913, Hupp production was over 12,000.

Hupp left in a huff during 1911 (his next venture would be the unsuccessful RCH), but Hupp Motor Car Company prospered through the Teens and '20s. A straight-eight debuted in 1925, and six-cylinder models replaced fours in 1926. By that point the firm had inked a favorable contract with the Murray Body Corporation, and the considerable talents of its chief designer, Amos Northup, were evident by 1928 in Hupp's stylish new Century line of Sixes and Eights. Buyers responded, and registrations that year totaled some 55,500.

But that would be the peak, and Hupp never built more than 9500 cars a year after 1932. Though its post-1933 "Aerodynamic" cars were among the better examples of period streamlining, the public didn't go for them. As a result, Hupp closed down midway through 1936, reopened to produce a handful of 1937-38 cars, then struggled on without much success into 1939.

After a second straight year of healthy sales, Hupp volume plunged to 22,183 for 1930. That year's line began with the six-cylinder S, a six-model line with 111-inch wheelbase and a 70-bhp, 211.6-cubic-inch engine. Prices were $995-$1160, which made it a medium-priced car. Then came three straight-eight series designated C, H, and U, which were assembled in Detroit; the S was produced in Cleveland at the former Chandler plant that Hupp had acquired. The S and C were Hupp's bread-and-butter cars. The latter mounted a 121-inch chassis and carried a 268.6-cid engine with 100 bhp. H and U used a larger 365.6-cid eight with 133 bhp and included some luxurious limousines on a 137-inch wheelbase.

The next year brought more of the same, plus a new L-series Century Eight with a 90-bhp 240.2-cid engine. A two-door victoria, one of the most-handsome Hupps ever, arrived in the U-Series, and freewheeling was a sales point across the line. With the Depression exerting its death grip, Hupp flew buyers to Detroit and Cleveland to help stimulate orders, but sales remained sluggish at 17,456 for the model year.

For 1932, Hupp series codes indicated model year and wheelbase. That year's B-216 thus rode a 116-inch wheelbase; it also carried a new 75-bhp 228.1-cid engine. Hupp now secured the services of designer Raymond Loewy, who styled the eight-cylinder F-222 and I-226 with tire-hugging, cycle-type fenders; vee'd radiators; sloped windshields; and chrome wheel discs. Fs had 250.7- or 261.5-cid engines with about 95 bhp. A 103-bhp, 279.9-cid unit powered the I-models. These graceful, handsome cars (issued after a brief run of "first-series" '31 carry-overs) won many awards for Loewy but few sales for Hupp, and production dropped again, this time to just under 10,500.

The 1933 Hupps were essentially '32 reruns, with a more-sloping grille the most obvious visual change. The 250 eight departed, while the 279 engine was bored out to 303.2 cid and 109 bhp for the I-326. Expanding the line were a cycle-fendered Six, the K-321, plus a cheaper K-321A with stationary hood louvers and single windshield wiper and taillight. But none of this helped, and Hupp's total volume dropped to just 7316.

For 1934, Hupp hitched its falling star to the radical Loewy-designed J-421 Six and T-427 Eight. Advertised as the "Hupp Aerodynamic," these wore three-piece windshields with mild wraparound effect, headlights neatly faired-in between radiator and front fenders, and flush-mounted spare tire. More-orthodox looks graced the W-417 Six, which had a good many body parts borrowed from Ford. Power came from a small 224-cid engine with just 80 bhp. J-models introduced a 245.3-cid engine with 93 bhp, while the T-Series offered 116 horses from an improved 303 eight. This overall formula had evident appeal, for sales rose to 9420. It continued with little change for 1935. However, Hupp enhanced it by introducing the D-518 Aerodynamic Six with flat windshield and 101-bhp 245 engine, and the O-521 Eight with a 120-bhp 303. Production recovered to 1932 levels, nearing 10,800.

But the big news about Hupp in this period concerned a fight for company control. Archie Andrews, promoter of the unsuccessful front-drive 1930 Ruxton, gained control of Hupp in late 1934. He was forced out a year later, but not before the firm was in ruins. Hupp was thus obliged to close its doors in early 1936, keeping them shut for over 18 months. Hupp returned for 1938 with 245 and 303 engines in conventionally styled E-822 Six and H-825 Eight models—just in time for a brief but sharp national recession. As a result, model-year production came to just 2001 units.

Meanwhile, Norman De Vaux had become Hupp general manager, and had just purchased the body tooling from the late front-drive Cord 810/812. Offering a rear-drive version in fair numbers would revive Hupp—or so he thought. And indeed, De Vaux reportedly took 6000 advance orders for what was announced in 1939 as the "Junior Six," later renamed Skylark. But with funds critically low, Hupp wasn't able to move the project beyond 35 prototypes, all hand-built before year's end.

Undaunted, De Vaux approached Graham-Paige president Joseph Graham, who agreed to produce Skylark bodies if G-P could sell its own version of the car. This deal gave Hupp a ready supplier and Graham a new model to supplement its languishing "sharknose" line. Hupp president J.W. Drake said it did "not mean a merger of the two corporations. The Hupp-Graham contract is a most favorable one for both of us, as careful checking of all production costs demonstrated that great savings could be made." In reality, this was a partnership born of desperation.

Like Graham's Hollywood, the Hupp Skylark was identical to the defunct Cord from the cowl back, but wheelbase was

**1930 Model C Standard Eight rumble-seat coupe**

# Hupmobile

trimmed 10 inches, to 115, via a new front end designed by John Tjaarda. Both versions wore a double grille and "bullet" headlamps nestled inboard of the front fenders, but the upper grille was painted on Skylarks, chromed on Hollywoods. Each firm naturally used its own engines. For Skylark this meant the 101-bhp, 245 six from 1935. Hollywoods carried a 217.8-cid Graham six with 120 bhp supercharged or 95 unsupercharged. The Skylark was thus a bit livelier than an unblown Hollywood, but slower than the blown model. It was also a bit cheaper: $1145 to the Graham's initial $1250.

But the Skylark/Hollywood was delayed by the same tooling problems and cost overruns that had plagued the Cord. Worse, a full nine months were lost in transferring Skylark tools to the Graham assembly line in Dearborn, which had to be reconfigured for the "new" models, so production didn't begin in earnest until May 1940—by which time most of the advance orders had been canceled. Graham, which grabbed the publicity spotlight with its blown engine, ended up building six times as many of these cars. Hupp gave up at the end of July 1940, just three weeks after the start of '41-model production. Only some 300 Skylarks were built in all.

Hupp recovered somewhat with military contracts during World War II, but elected not to return to the auto manufacturing business when peace returned. Eventually, Hupp began making accessories for other auto companies as well as kitchen and electronics equipment.

1932 Series F-222 Eight sport coupe with rumble seat

1934 Series J-421 Six "Aerodynamic" four-door sedan

1936 Series O-621 Eight DeLuxe touring sedan

1938 Series E-822 Six four-door sedan

1940 Skylark Custom four-door sedan

1941 Skylark Custom four-door sedan

# Specifications

### 1930—22,183 built
| S Standard Six (wb 111.0) | Wght | Price | Prod |
|---|---|---|---|
| phaeton 5P | 2,690 | 1,135 | — |
| bus cpe 2P | 2,710 | 995 | — |
| cabriolet 2-4P | 2,690 | 1,110 | — |
| sdn 4d | 2,885 | 1,095 | — |
| cpe 2-4P | 2,740 | 1,095 | — |
| DeLuxe sdn 4d | — | 1,160 | — |
| **C Standard Eight (wb 121.0)** | | | |
| touring div sdn 7P | 3,600 | 1,785 | — |
| cpe 2-4P | 3,560 | 1,695 | — |
| cabriolet 2-4P | 3,500 | 1,770 | — |
| victoria cpe 5P | 3,535 | 1,715 | — |
| sdn 4d | 3,640 | 1,695 | — |
| Town div sdn 5P | — | 1,805 | — |
| **H Standard Eight (wb 125.0)** | | | |
| touring div sdn 7P | 3,870 | 2,190 | — |
| cpe 2-4P | 3,915 | 2,080 | — |
| cabriolet 2-4P | 3,880 | 2,155 | — |
| victoria cpe 5P | 3,830 | 2,100 | — |
| sdn 4d | 3,995 | 2,080 | — |
| Town div sdn 4d | 3,995 | 2,190 | — |
| **U Standard Eight (wb 137.0)** | | | |
| sdn 7P | 4,225 | 2,495 | — |
| sdn limo 7P | 4,390 | 2,645 | — |

| 1930 Engines | bore × stroke | bhp | availability |
|---|---|---|---|
| I-6, 211.6 | 3.25 × 4.25 | 70 | S-S |
| I-8, 268.6 | 3.00 × 4.75 | 100 | S-C |
| I-8, 365.6 | 3.50 × 4.75 | 133 | S-H, U |

### 1931—17,456 built
| S Century Six (wb 114.0) | Wght | Price | Prod |
|---|---|---|---|
| rdstr 2-4P | 2,855 | 1,075 | — |
| phtn 5P | 2,900 | 1,050 | — |
| comp cpe 2P | 2,825 | 995 | — |
| cpe 2-4P | 2,865 | 995 | — |
| cabriolet 2-4P | 2,855 | 1,050 | — |
| sdn 4d | 2,985 | 995 | — |
| **L Century Eight (wb 118.0)** | | | |
| rdstr 2-4 P | 3,055 | 1,375 | — |
| phaeton 5P | 3,330 | 1,350 | — |
| cpe 2P | 3,100 | 1,295 | — |
| cpe 2-4P | 3,165 | 1,295 | — |
| cabriolet 2-4P | 3,125 | 1,350 | — |
| sdn 4d | 3,275 | 1,295 | — |
| **C Standard Eight (wb 121.0)** | | | |
| touring sdn 7P | 3,715 | 1,685 | — |
| cpe 2-4P | 3,650 | 1,595 | — |
| cabriolet 2-4P | 3,610 | 1,595 | — |
| victoria cpe 5P | 3,695 | 1,615 | — |
| cpe 4P | 3,695 | 1,615 | — |
| sdn 4d | 3,730 | 1,595 | — |
| Town sdn 4d | 3,785 | 1,705 | — |
| **H Standard Eight (wb 125.0)** | | | |
| touring sdn 7P | 3,975 | 2,005 | — |
| cpe 2-4P | 4,015 | 1,895 | — |
| cabriolet 2-4P | 3,975 | 1,895 | — |
| victoria cpe 5P | 4,010 | 1,915 | — |

| H Standard Eight (wb 125.0) | Wght | Price | Prod |
|---|---|---|---|
| cpe 4P | 4,010 | 1,915 | — |
| sdn 4d | 4,095 | 1,895 | — |
| Town sdn 4d | 4,230 | 2,005 | — |
| **U Standard Eight (wb 137.0)—474 built** | | | |
| victoria cpe 5P | 4,165 | 2,295 | — |
| sdn 7P | 4,360 | 2,295 | — |
| sdn limo 7P | 4,400 | 2,445 | — |

| 1931 Engines | bore × stroke | bhp | availability |
|---|---|---|---|
| I-6, 211.6 | 3.25 × 4.25 | 70 | S-S |
| I-8, 240.2 | 2.88 × 4.63 | 90 | S-L |
| I-8, 268.6 | 3.00 × 4.75 | 100 | S-C |
| I-8, 365.6 | 3.50 × 4.75 | 133 | S-H, U |

### 1932 First Series
| S "214" Six (wb 114.0)—2,210 built | Wght | Price | Prod |
|---|---|---|---|
| rdstr 2-4P | 2,855 | 875 | — |
| phaeton 5P | 2,900 | 850 | — |
| cpe 2P | 2,825 | 795 | — |
| cpe 2-4P | 2,865 | 795 | — |
| cabriolet 2-4P | 2,855 | 850 | — |
| sdn 4d | 2,985 | 795 | — |
| **L "218" Eight (wb 118.0)—1,096 built** | | | |
| rdstr 2-4P | 3,055 | 1,075 | — |
| phaeton 5P | 3,330 | 1,050 | — |
| cpe 2P | 3,100 | 995 | — |
| cpe 2-4P | 3,165 | 995 | — |
| cabriolet 2-4P | 3,125 | 1,050 | — |
| sdn 4d | 3,275 | 995 | — |
| **C "221" Eight (wb 121.0)—675 built** | | | |
| phaeton 7P | 3,715 | 1,305 | — |
| cpe 2-4P | 3,650 | 1,195 | — |
| cpe 4P | 3,695 | 1,215 | — |
| victoria cpe 5P | 3,695 | 1,215 | — |
| sdn 4d | 3,730 | 1,195 | — |
| Town sdn 4d | 3,825 | 1,195 | — |
| **H "225" Eight (wb 125.0)—446 built** | | | |
| phaeton 7P | 3,985 | 1,585 | — |
| cpe 2-4P | 4,015 | 1,455 | — |
| cpe 4P | 4,010 | 1,475 | — |
| victoria cpe 5P | 4,010 | 1,475 | — |
| sdn 4d | 4,095 | 1,455 | — |
| Town sdn 4d | 4,300 | 1,430 | — |
| **U "237" Eight (wb 137.0)—132 built** | | | |
| victoria cpe | 4,165 | 1,795 | — |
| sdn 7P | 4,360 | 1,895 | — |
| limo 7P | 4,400 | 1,955 | — |

| 1932(1) Engines | bore × stroke | bhp | availability |
|---|---|---|---|
| I-6, 211.6 | 3.25 × 4.25 | 70 | S-S |
| I-8, 240.2 | 2.88 × 4.63 | 90 | S-L |
| I-8, 268.6 | 3.00 × 4.75 | 100 | S-C |
| I-8, 365.6 | 3.50 × 4.75 | 133 | S-H, U |

### 1932 Second Series (from Jan. 1)
| B "216" Six (wb 116.5)—3,500 built | Wght | Price | Prod |
|---|---|---|---|
| rdstr 2-4P | 2,825 | 795 | — |
| phaeton 5P | 2,925 | 795 | — |

# Hupmobile

| B "216" Six (wb 116.5)—3,500 built | Wght | Price | Prod |
|---|---|---|---|
| cpe 2-4P | 2,975 | 895 | — |
| cpe 2P | 2,935 | 895 | — |
| conv cabriolet 2-4P | 2,985 | 895 | — |
| sdn 4d | 3,095 | 895 | — |
| **F "222" Eight (wb 122.0)—3,755 built** | | | |
| rdstr cab 2-4P | 3,415 | 1,395 | — |
| cpe 2-4P | 3,505 | 1,295 | — |
| victoria cpe | 3,585 | 1,360 | — |
| sdn 4d | 3,550 | 1,295 | — |
| **I "226" Eight (wb 126.0)—713 built** | | | |
| rdstr cab 2-4P | 3,650 | 1,695 | — |
| cpe 2-4P | 3,740 | 1,595 | — |
| victoria cpe 5P | 3,820 | 1,660 | — |
| sdn 4d | 3,785 | 1,595 | — |

| 1932(2) Engines | bore × stroke | bhp | availability |
|---|---|---|---|
| I-6, 228.1 | 3.38 × 4.25 | 75 | S-B |
| I-8, 250.7 | 2.94 × 4.63 | 93 | S-F thru #6905 |
| I-8, 261.5 | 3.00 × 4.63 | — | S-F from #6906 |
| I-8, 279.9 | 3.06 × 4.75 | 103 | S-I |

## 1933

| B "316" Six (wb 116.0)—1,463 built | Wght | Price | Prod |
|---|---|---|---|
| rdstr 2P | 2,825 | 795 | — |
| phaeton 5P | 2,925 | 795 | — |
| cpe 2P | 2,935 | 895 | — |
| cpe 2-4P | 2,975 | 895 | — |
| cabriolet 2-4P | 2,965 | 895 | — |
| sdn 4d | 3,095 | 895 | — |
| **K "321" Six (wb 121.0)—4,600 built** | | | |
| cab rdstr 2-4P | 3,235 | 1,095 | — |
| cpe 2-4P | 3,235 | 995 | — |
| victoria cpe 5P | 3,250 | 1,060 | — |
| sdn 4d | 3,290 | 995 | — |
| **F "322" Eight (wb 122.0)—700 built** | | | |
| cab rdstr 2-4P | 3,600 | 1,295 | — |
| cpe 2-4P | 3,545 | 1,195 | — |
| victoria cpe 5P | 3,605 | 1,260 | — |
| sdn 4d | 3,650 | 1,195 | — |
| **I "326" Eight (wb 126.0)—250 built** | | | |
| cab rdstr 2-4P | 3,810 | 1,545 | — |
| cpe 2-4P | 3,795 | 1,445 | — |
| victoria cpe 5P | 3,830 | 1,510 | — |
| sdn 4d | 3,845 | 1,445 | — |
| **KK "321-A" Six (wb 121.0)—300 built** | | | |
| cpe 2-4P | 3,135 | 895 | — |
| victoria cpe 5P | 3,150 | 960 | — |
| sdn 4d | 3,190 | 895 | — |

| 1933 Engines | bore × stroke | bhp | availability |
|---|---|---|---|
| I-6, 228.1 | 3.38 × 4.25 | 75 | S-B |
| I-6, 228.1 | 3.38 × 4.25 | 90 | S-K, KK |
| I-8, 261.5 | 3.00 × 4.63 | 96 | S-F |
| I-8, 303.2 | 3.19 × 4.75 | 109 | S-I |

## 1934—9,420 built

| KK "421-A" Six (wb 121)—300 built | Wght | Price | Prod |
|---|---|---|---|
| cpe 2-4P | 3,160 | 795 | — |
| victoria cpe 5P | 3,165 | 860 | — |
| sdn 4d | 3,200 | 795 | — |
| **K "421" Six (wb 121.0)** | | | |
| rdstr cab 2-4P | 3,235 | 895 | — |
| cpe 2-4P | 3,250 | 795 | — |
| victoria cpe 5P | 3,255 | 860 | — |
| sdn 4d | 3,290 | 895 | — |
| **F "422" Eight (wb 122.0)** | | | |
| rdstr cab 2-4P | 3,600 | 1,045 | — |
| cpe 2-4P | 3,545 | 945 | — |
| victoria cpe 5P | 3,630 | 1,010 | — |
| sdn 4d | 3,665 | 1,045 | — |
| **I "426" Eight (wb 126.0)** | | | |
| rdstr cab 2-4P | 3,810 | 1,145 | — |
| cpe 2-4P | 3,795 | 1,045 | — |
| victoria cpe 5P | 3,830 | 1,110 | — |
| sdn 4d | 3,845 | 1,145 | — |
| **W "417" Six (wb 117.0)** | | | |
| cpe 2-4P | 2,940 | 795 | — |
| sdn 4d | 3,040 | 795 | — |
| touring sdn 4d T/B | 3,075 | 845 | — |
| DeLuxe cpe 2-4P | 2,940 | 845 | — |
| DeLuxe sdn 4d | 3,040 | 845 | — |
| DeLuxe touring sdn 4d T/B | 3,075 | 895 | — |
| **J "421" Six (wb 121.0)** | | | |
| cpe 3-5P | 3,230 | 1,195 | — |
| victoria cpe 5P | 3,325 | 1,195 | — |
| sdn 4d | 3,325 | 1,095 | — |
| **T "427" Eight (wb 127.0)** | | | |
| cpe 3-5P | 3,675 | 1,345 | — |
| victoria cpe 5P | 3,700 | 1,265 | — |
| sdn 4d | 3,700 | 1,245 | — |

| 1934 Engines | bore × stroke | bhp | availability |
|---|---|---|---|
| I-6, 224.0 | 3.50 × 3.88 | 80 | S-W |
| I-6, 228.1 | 3.38 × 4.25 | 90 | S-K, KK |
| I-6, 245.3 | 3.50 × 4.25 | 93 | S-J |
| I-8, 261.5 | 3.00 × 4.63 | 96 | S-F |
| I-8, 303.2 | 3.19 × 4.75 | 109 | S-I |
| I-8, 303.2 | 3.19 × 4.75 | 116 | S-T |

## 1935

| W "517" Six (wb 117.0)—2,586 built | Wght | Price | Prod |
|---|---|---|---|
| cpe 2P | 2,900 | 695 | — |
| cpe 2-4P | 2,940 | 695 | — |
| sdn 4d | 3,040 | 695 | — |
| touring sdn 5P | 3,075 | 745 | — |
| DeLuxe cpe 2P | 2,900 | 745 | — |
| DeLuxe cpe 2-4P | 2,940 | 745 | — |
| DeLuxe sdn 4d | 3,040 | 745 | — |
| DeLuxe touring sdn 4d | 3,075 | 795 | — |
| **D "518" Six (wb 118.0)—5,900 built** | | | |
| sdn 4d | 2,930 | 795 | — |
| touring sdn 4d | 2,945 | 845 | — |
| DeLuxe sdn 4d | 2,930 | 835 | — |
| DeLuxe touring sdn 4d | 2,945 | 885 | — |
| **J "521" Six (wb 121.0)—993 built** | | | |
| cpe 3-5P | 3,230 | 1,095 | — |

# Hupmobile

| J "521" Six (wb 121.0)—993 built | Wght | Price | Prod |
|---|---|---|---|
| victoria sdn 4d | 3,325 | 1,095 | — |
| sdn 4d | 3,325 | 1,095 | — |
| DeLuxe cpe 3-5P | 3,230 | 1,170 | — |
| DeLuxe vic sdn 4d | 3,325 | 1,170 | — |
| DeLuxe sdn 4d | 3,325 | 1,170 | — |

| T "527" Eight (wb 127.0)—902 built | Wght | Price | Prod |
|---|---|---|---|
| cpe 3-5P | 3,625 | 1,395 | — |
| victoria sdn 4d | 3,700 | 1,395 | — |
| sdn 4d | 3,700 | 1,395 | — |
| DeLuxe cpe 3-5P | 3,625 | 1,445 | — |
| DeLuxe vic sdn 4d | 3,700 | 1,445 | — |
| DeLuxe sdn 4d | 3,700 | 1,445 | — |

| O "521" Eight (wb 121.0)—400 built | Wght | Price | Prod |
|---|---|---|---|
| cpe 3-5P | 3,300 | 1,195 | — |
| victoria cpe 5P | 3,432 | 1,195 | — |
| sdn 4d | 3,432 | 1,195 | — |
| touring vic cpe 5P | 3,447 | 1,195 | — |
| touring sdn 4d | 3,447 | 1,195 | — |
| DeLuxe cpe 3-5P | 3,330 | 1,245 | — |
| DeLuxe vic cpe 5P | 3,432 | 1,245 | — |
| DeLuxe sdn 4d | 3,432 | 1,245 | — |
| DeLuxe touring vic 5P | 3,447 | 1,245 | — |
| DeLuxe touring sdn 4d | 3,447 | 1,245 | — |

| 1935 Engines | bore × stroke | bhp | availability |
|---|---|---|---|
| I-6, 224.0 | 3.50 × 3.88 | 91 | S-W |
| I-6, 245.3 | 3.50 × 4.25 | 101 | S-D, J |
| I-8, 303.2 | 3.19 × 4.75 | 120 | S-T, O |

## 1936

| D "618" Six (wb 118.0)—1,873 built | Wght | Price | Prod |
|---|---|---|---|
| sdn 4d | 2,930 | 795 | — |
| touring sdn 4d | 2,945 | 845 | — |
| DeLuxe sdn 4d | 2,930 | 835 | — |
| DeLuxe touring sdn 4d | 2,945 | 885 | — |

| O "621" Eight (wb 121.0)—298 built | Wght | Price | Prod |
|---|---|---|---|
| cpe 3-5P | 3,330 | 1,195 | — |
| victoria 5P | 3,432 | 1,195 | — |
| sdn 4d | 3,432 | 1,195 | — |
| touring victoria 5P | 3,447 | 1,195 | — |
| touring sdn 4d | 3,447 | 1,195 | — |
| DeLuxe cpe 3-5P | 3,330 | 1,245 | — |
| DeLuxe victoria 5P | 3,432 | 1,245 | — |
| DeLuxe sdn 4d | 3,432 | 1,245 | — |
| DeLuxe touring victoria 5P | 3,447 | 1,245 | — |
| DeLuxe touring sdn 4d | 3,447 | 1,245 | — |

| 1936 Engines | bore × stroke | bhp | availability |
|---|---|---|---|
| I-6, 245.3 | 3.50 × 4.25 | 101 | S-D |
| I-8, 303.2 | 3.19 × 4.75 | 120 | S-O |

## 1937

Note: Hupp closed in early 1936 and remained closed for 18 months. Most sources state no 1937 models were produced, but industry records do quote the following model listings (production based on announced serial number spans):

| G Six (wb 118.0)—199 built | Wght | Price | Prod |
|---|---|---|---|
| bus cpe 3P | 3,010 | 795 | — |
| cpe 3-5P | 3,060 | 840 | — |
| sdn 2d | 2,980 | 815 | — |
| touring sdn 2d | 3,030 | 850 | — |

| G Six (wb 118.0)—199 built | Wght | Price | Prod |
|---|---|---|---|
| sdn 4d | 3,000 | 855 | — |
| touring sdn 4d | 3,040 | 890 | — |

| N Eight (wb 121.0)—39 built | Wght | Price | Prod |
|---|---|---|---|
| cpe 3-5P | 3,565 | 1,035 | — |
| sdn 2d | 3,535 | 995 | — |
| touring sdn 2d | 3,565 | 1,035 | — |
| sdn 4d | 3,535 | 1,035 | — |
| touring sdn 4d | 3,550 | 1,075 | — |

| 1937 Engines | bore × stroke | bhp | availability |
|---|---|---|---|
| I-6, 245.3 | 3.50 × 4.25 | 101 | S-G |
| I-8, 303.2 | 3.19 × 4.75 | 120 | S-N |

## 1938

| E "822" (wb 122.0)—1,804 built | Wght | Price | Prod |
|---|---|---|---|
| Standard sdn 4d T/B | 3,320 | 1,045 | — |
| Regular sdn 4d T/B | 3,370 | 1,180 | — |
| DeLuxe sdn 4d T/B | 3,400 | 1,222 | — |
| Custom sdn 4d T/B | 3,440 | 1,340 | — |

| H "825" (wb 125.0)—197 built | Wght | Price | Prod |
|---|---|---|---|
| Regular sdn 4d T/B | 3,955 | 1,325 | — |
| DeLuxe sdn 4d T/B | 4,085 | 1,365 | — |
| Custom sdn 4d T/B | 4,125 | 1,485 | — |

| 1938 Engines | bore × stroke | bhp | availability |
|---|---|---|---|
| I-6, 245.3 | 3.50 × 4.25 | 101 | S-E |
| I-8, 303.2 | 3.19 × 4.75 | 120 | S-H |

## 1939

| E "922" Senior Six (wb 122)—800 built | | Wght | Price | Prod |
|---|---|---|---|---|
| EQ | DeLuxe touring sdn 4d | 3,400 | 995 | — |
| EQD | Custom touring sdn 4d | 3,440 | 1,095 | — |

| H "925" Senior Eight (wb 125.0)—200 built | | Wght | Price | Prod |
|---|---|---|---|---|
| HQ | DeLuxe touring sdn 4d | 4,085 | 1,145 | — |
| HQD | Custom touring sdn 4d | 4,215 | 1,245 | — |

| Skylark (wb 115.0) | | Wght | Price | Prod |
|---|---|---|---|---|
| | Custom sdn 4d | 3,000 | 1,145 | 35* |

* handbuilt prototypes

| 1939 Engines | bore × stroke | bhp | availability |
|---|---|---|---|
| I-6, 245.3 | 3.50 × 4.25 | 101 | S-922, Skylark |
| I-8, 303.2 | 3.19 × 4.75 | 120 | S-925 Eight |

Note: 1939 production estimates are based on published serial number spans. Total calendar-year production: 1,400.

## 1940

| R-015 Skylark Custom (wb 115.0) | | Wght | Price | Prod* |
|---|---|---|---|---|
| RQK | sdn 4d | 3,000 | 1,145 | — |

| 1940 Engine | bore × stroke | bhp | availability |
|---|---|---|---|
| I-6, 245.3 | 3.50 × 4.25 | 101 | S-all |

## 1941

| R-115 Skylark Custom (wb 115.0) | | Wght | Price | Prod* |
|---|---|---|---|---|
| RQK | sdn 4d | 3,000 | 1,095 | — |

| 1941 Engine | bore × stroke | bhp | availability |
|---|---|---|---|
| I-6, 245.3 | 3.50 × 4.25 | 101 | S-all |

*Total 1940-41 Skylark production: 319. Total registrations: 211 in 1940, 103 in 1941.

# Imperial

Imperial became a distinct make for 1955 and continued as such for the next 20 years. The name, of course, had been familiar since the late '20s on the most-luxurious Chryslers (*see entry*)—and that was a problem. Somehow, Imperial could never shake its image as a Chrysler, and it was this, more than any other factor, that hampered sales in the prestige-conscious luxury field.

Nevertheless, some of Imperial's best years as a separate make were its first. The beautiful 1955 models, based extensively on Virgil Exner's period Parade Phaeton show cars, are still regarded as the most-desirable Imperials of all. Elegantly trimmed inside and out, this big 130-inch-wheelbase sedan and Newport hardtop coupe wore a distinctive split grille, unique "gunsight" taillights, modestly wrapped windshield, and circular rear-wheel openings, making them among the best-looking of Chrysler Corporation's all-new '55 fleet. Chrome was abundant but tastefully applied; two-toning was limited to the roof.

Naturally, the '55s inherited the brilliant 331-cubic-inch Chrysler hemi-head V-8 used since 1951, now with 250 brake horsepower and mated to the firm's new fully automatic two-speed PowerFlite transmission. At nearly 11,500 units for the model year, volume was about double that of the 1954 Chrysler Imperial, an auspicious beginning. Still, Cadillac's '55 output was 10 times as great, Lincoln's five times as high.

Wheelbase was stretched three inches for 1956. (It would shrink back to 129 inches for '57.) The Newport was renamed Southampton and joined by a pillarless four-door. Still topped by "gunsights," rear fenders were raised into fins, but no other Chrysler product that year wore them more attractively. Frontal styling was unchanged. Following Chrysler, the Hemi was bored to 354 cid for a gain of 30 bhp (helped by higher 9:1 compression), and the Power-Flite switched from a dashboard lever to pushbutton control, which would be featured on Chrysler automatics through 1963. Though not in the same league as a Chrysler 300, the 1955-56 Imperials were lively performers yet surprisingly thrifty, winning luxury-class laurels in the Mobilgas Economy Runs. They were also impeccably built—really the last Imperials that could make that claim. The one major option in these years was air conditioning, priced at $567. List prices ranged from the mid-$4000s to just over $5000.

Also available in 1955-56 were long-wheelbase Crown Imperial sedans and limousines. Built in Detroit, these took over for the long, eight-seat Dodge, DeSoto, and Chrysler sedans offered through '54. Styling and engineering followed that of standard Imperials, but prices were much higher—$7100-$7700—and availability was limited. Just 172 were built for '55; another 226 for '56. Reflecting the industry's general decline from record-setting '55, Imperial's 1956 volume dropped to just below 11,000 units.

Imperial was all-new for 1957, bearing second-generation "Forward Look" styling from design chief Exner, marked by huge tailfins (with vestigial gunsights in the trailing edges), airier rooflines with curved side glass (an industry first), a finely checked full-width grille, and, where law allowed, quad headlamps in lieu of conventional dual units (where law didn't allow). The last was not a first, however,

**1955 four-door sedan**

**1956 four-door sedan**

**1955 Newport hardtop coupe**

**1957 Crown convertible coupe**

# Imperial

**1958 Crown Southampton hardtop sedan**

**1958 LeBaron four-door sedan**

**1959 Crown Southampton hardtop coupe**

**1960 Crown convertible coupe**

**1960 LeBaron Southampton hardtop sedan**

as that year's Chrysler, DeSoto, Nash, Lincoln, and Cadillac Eldorado Brougham also offered "quadrilights." Seeking higher sales, Imperial expanded from one series to three, adding more elaborately trimmed Crown and LeBaron versions of the standard pillared sedan and Southampton hardtops. The Crown also offered the line's only convertible—the first soft-top Imperial since 1951. Arriving in January was a pair of LeBaron models, recalling the famed prewar coachworks closely associated with Chrysler—a pillared sedan and four-door Southampton. Both new series were priced considerably higher than the standard Imperials: $5400-$5600 for Crown, and $5743 for either LeBaron.

Standard for '57 Imperials was Chrysler's superb new three-speed TorqueFlite automatic transmission, plus a Hemi enlarged to 392 cid for 325 bhp with 9.25:1 compression. Also shared with other '57 Highland Park cars was torsion-bar front suspension (called "Torsion-Aire Ride"). It made for fine roadability, the best in the luxury field. With all this, Imperial showed surprising sales strength. Volume more than tripled from '56, reaching near 35,000 units. That was still far behind Cadillac's 122,000.

Though the Crown Imperial sedan vanished for '57, the limo returned at a breathtaking $15,075—which largely stemmed from the fact that the car was now built by Ghia in Turin, Italy. With such low sales, Chrysler could no longer justify the time and space necessary to build such cars itself, especially with projected tooling costs of some $3.3 million.

Each Ghia Crown limo began as an unfinished two-door hardtop body mounted on the more-rigid convertible chassis and shipped with all body panels intact. Ghia cut the car apart, added 20.5 inches to the wheelbase, reworked the structure above the beltline, fitted and trimmed the luxurious interior, and finished off the exterior with 150 pounds of lead filler. Each car took a month to complete, and initial delays made the Crown Imperial a very late '57 introduction. Sales were not impressive: only 132 Ghia Crowns would be built by the time production was ended in 1965, but all were impeccably tailored. Exactly 36 were built to '57 specifications, followed by 31 of the '58s and only 7 for '59.

A predictably minor facelift was ordained for '58. The main differences were circular parking lights, standard quad headlamps (by now legal everywhere), and a simpler grille. Prices were marginally higher across an unchanged lineup, and the 392 was tweaked to 345 brake horsepower. Reflecting Exner's fondness for "Classic" styling themes was an optional round decklid hump suggesting a spare tire, a 1957 option that continued to find favor in '58. But this proved a poor year for the industry in general and Chrysler in particular, so only about 16,000 Imperials were built for the model year. To the frustration of dealers, people still thought of these cars as "Chrysler Imperials"—and a Chrysler, though prestigious, didn't have the charisma of a Cadillac.

For 1959 came a more-extensive facelift of the basic '57 styling, highlighted—for some, anyway—by a toothy grille and broad brushed-finish appliqués on the lower rear flanks. Standard models finally got a name—Custom—but the lineup was otherwise again unchanged. As at other Highland Park divisions, Imperial switched from Hemi to wedgehead V-8s: a new 350-bhp 413-cid unit shared with '59 Chrysler New Yorkers. It provided comparable performance, but was more economical to build and maintain than the fabled Hemi. Production inched up to about 17,000.

579

# Imperial

1961 Crown Southampton four-door hardtop sedan

1963 Crown Imperial limousine by Ghia

1962 LeBaron Southampton four-door hardtop sedan

1963 Crown four-door hardtop sedan

1962 Custom hardtop coupe

1964 Crown convertible coupe

Imperial would outsell Lincoln in 1959 and '60, but would never do so again.

After 1960, Imperial was strictly an also-ran among the Big Three luxury makes. As ever, Cadillac was the overwhelming sales leader, Lincoln a distant second, Imperial an even more-distant third.

Though other Highland Park cars adopted "unibody" construction for 1960, Imperial retained a separate body and frame, mainly because it was more amenable to isolation from noise and road shock, necessary for the level of smoothness and silence luxury buyers demanded. Returning unchanged was a lone 413 wedgehead V-8, whose 10:1 compression required premium fuel.

Imperial model choices were also unchanged, but styling became cartoonish for 1960, with swollen fins, a florid grille, and an even larger windshield. Interiors were ornate, dominated by an impressively bright, complicated dash with a plethora of pushbuttons; a squarish steering wheel was merely odd. Emphasizing comfort was a new high-back driver's seat padded in thick foam rubber. Options by now had grown to include adjustable "spot" air conditioning, six-way power seat with single rotary control, "Auto-Pilot"

cruise control, and automatic headlamp dimmer. Customs were upholstered in pretty crown-pattern nylon. Upholstery for Crown was wool, leather, or nylon and vinyl. Wool broadcloth lined LeBarons. Model-year production held at the '59 level.

The new 1960 bodyshell was considerably changed for 1961—and not for the better. Fins were the most blatant ever to appear on an Imperial—high and gull-like, with the trademark gunsight taillamps suspended from them. And there was a new gimmick: freestanding headlamps, individual chrome bullets on tiny pedestals pocketed in severely concave front fenders—another of Exner's "classic" throwbacks. This strange idea would persist through 1963, but rear styling became much more tasteful. Four-door pillared sedans were eliminated for '61, but other offerings returned along with an unchanged powerteam. Sci-fi styling; Chrysler's now-widespread reputation for indifferent workmanship; and a handsome, more-compact new Lincoln Continental conspired to dampen demand, and model-year production dropped to around 12,250—less than half of Lincoln's total.

Exner left Chrysler during 1961, but not before fashion-

580

ing a completely new, truncated "S-Series" Imperial as part of an entirely downsized corporate line for 1962. It didn't reach production, which was fortunate because his downsized Dodges and Plymouths did—and met a poor reception. Instead, the '61 Imperial was reissued but with the ugly fins planed off, leaving straight-top rear fenders capped by cigarlike gunsights. The 413 was detuned by 10 bhp, and would continue in this form through 1965. Production rose to a bit over 14,250, but was still only about 50 percent of Lincoln's. Cadillac remained far ahead of both.

Another facelift gave the '63s a new grille insert composed of elongated rectangles, plus a crisper rear roofline and restyled rear deck. The stylist responsible for much of this revision was Elwood Engel, who'd come over from Ford—where he designed the aforementioned Continental—to replace Exner in mid-1961. The lineup was again unchanged, and model-year production was about the same as for '62.

Clean, all-new Engel styling completely banished the old Exner silhouette for 1964 as Imperial became very much like his square-lined Continental. The beltline was edged with full-length bright moldings, a divided grille appeared (recalling 1955-56), and the freestanding headlamps gave way to integral units within the grille. One Exner touch remained, however: the simulated trunklid spare, though it was also squarish now, carried down into the bumper as on the 1956-57 Continental Mark II. A less-contrived dash with strong horizontal format was featured inside. Modelwise, the slow-selling Custom was eliminated along with the Southampton name for pillarless styles, leaving Crown convertible and hardtops, LeBaron hardtop sedan, and the Ghia Crown limo. Model-year sales were exceedingly good at over 23,000, a level that wouldn't be approached again until 1969.

Good sales and the big '64 redesign dictated a stand-pat 1965. The only significant changes were prominent crossed grille bars on a mesh background, glass-covered headlights, and prices bumped up $100-$200. Displayed at that year's New York Auto Show was the exotic LeBaron D'Or, a customized hardtop coupe. The "D'Or" part referred to gold-tint exterior striping and interior embellishments, as well as special "Royal Essence Laurel Gold" paint.

Ghia stopped building Crown limousines in 1965, but 10 more were constructed in Spain using '66 grilles and rear decks. When Imperial finally went to unit construction for '67, Chrysler worked out a limousine program with Stageway Coaches of Fort Smith, Arkansas. Built through 1971 at the rate of about six per year, these cars, simply called LeBaron, were much larger, riding an unbelievable 163-inch wheelbase, by far the longest in the American industry. Prices ranged from $12,000 to $15,000, depending on equipment.

Regular Imperials again saw mostly detail changes for 1966. The grille now carried an eggcrate motif, each "crate" containing tiny elongated rectangles, and the decklid was cleaned up by deleting the fake spare tire. A literal big change involved boring the wedge V-8 to 440 cid, which returned horsepower to 350. Model-year production went the other way, though, dropping from 1965's 18,500—itself a considerable decline from '64—to fewer than 13,750.

The '67 Imperials were all-new. Chrysler engineers were by now sufficiently experienced with unit construction to use it for their most-expensive product, and newer technology allowed computerized stress testing of a given shape before it was ever built. Unibody construction also

1965 Crown Imperial limousine by Ghia

1966 Crown convertible coupe

1967 convertible coupe

1968 Crown hardtop sedan

1969 LeBaron hardtop sedan

# Imperial

1970 LeBaron hardtop coupe

1971 LeBaron hardtop sedan

1972 LeBaron hardtop coupe

1973 LeBaron hardtop sedan

1974 LeBaron hardtop sedan

promised weight savings. And indeed, the '67s were about 100 pounds lighter than comparable '66s.

But the real reason for this switch was lackluster sales that had made a completely separate Imperial platform just too costly to sustain. Thus, as before 1960, Imperial again shared basic architecture with Chrysler in the interest of reduced production costs.

Still, this was not readily apparent from 1967 styling. Up front was a high grille with a prominent nameplate, flanked by squarish Lincolnesque fenders containing the parking lights. The rear bumper was a broad U below a full-width taillamp panel with a large Imperial eagle medallion in a central circle. Sides were still flat, but relieved a little by full-length moldings above the rocker panels. Wheelbase contracted to 127 inches, though that was still three inches longer than Chrysler's. A four-door pillared sedan returned without a series name at $5374, the most-affordable '67 Imperial. Other models soldiered on. Sales moved up to near 18,000, but Imperial was still far adrift of Lincoln, let alone Cadillac.

Volume dropped below 15,400 the following year and prompted a far-reaching decision: From 1969, Imperial would share most Chrysler sheetmetal as well as structure. One casualty of this move was the Crown convertible, which made its last appearance as a '68. Style changes from '67 were slight: A new grille wrapped around the fenders to enclose parking and cornering lights; side marker lights front and rear, newly required by Washington; narrow paint stripes along the beltline; dual lower-bodyside moldings. Newly optional dual exhausts and twin-snorkel air cleaner coaxed 360 bhp from the 440 V-8, but only for this one year.

The Chrysler-like 1969-70 models were among the tidiest Imperials ever, with rounded, low-roof "fuselage styling" announced by a full-width eggcrate face with newly concealed headlamps (behind flip-up doors matched to grille texture). Ventless side glass was featured on air-conditioned coupes. Overall length stretched by five inches with no change in wheelbase, yet curb weights ran about 100 pounds less. Model choices were pared to a hardtop coupe and sedan in Crown and LeBaron trim, plus a pillared Crown sedan priced identically to the Crown hardtop. LeBaron was no longer the $7000 semicustom it had once been, its list price being slashed by about $800 to the $5900-$6100 level. Despite fewer models, LeBaron bested the Crown in sales for the first time. The overall '69 total exceeded 22,000 units, the third-best showing in Imperial history.

However, the return to a close resemblance with Chrysler and increasing buyer preference for more-manageable cars contributed to a sales decline that would end Imperial's life as a separate make. As if to forecast the bitter days ahead, 1970-model production dropped by almost half from '69, to about 11,800.

Imperial retained its basic '69 design through 1973. Styling modifications were confined to easy-change items like grilles, taillamps, and minor trim, plus modest sheetmetal alterations at each end and year-to-year price/equipment shuffles. Offerings slimmed to just the pair of LeBarons after 1971. Emissions tuning dropped the big 440 V-8 to 335 bhp for '71, then to 225 bhp—in newly adopted SAE *net* measure—and ultimately to 215 bhp. Horsepower recovered to 230 for 1974 with the adoption of catalytic converters. A laudable new '71 exclusive was a Bendix antiskid brake system, priced at $250; it was extended to the entire Chrysler line for 1972.

# Imperial

**1975 LeBaron hardtop coupe**

**1975 LeBaron four-door hardtop sedan**

**1981 coupe**

**1981 coupe**

**1982 Frank Sinatra Edition coupe**

Not surprisingly, Imperial suffered more than its rivals from the effects of the first energy crisis. The brand-new 1974 models had crisper lines and bold upright grillework, plus a three-inch shorter wheelbase and about 100 pounds less weight. But these modest reductions had less to do with the fuel shortage—which Chrysler hadn't dreamed of—than the need to realize further economies of scale through even closer sharing with that year's redesigned New Yorker.

Still, these Imperials were good-looking in their way, and distinctly different from the Chryslers. But with prices rapidly moving upward—now $7700-$7800—they were none too successful. At just over 14,000, model-year volume for '74 was the lowest since '71; the following year it sank to fewer than 10,000. Seeking to cut losses, Chrysler decided it was time to forget Imperial, and the last '75 Imperial left the Jefferson Avenue plant in Detroit on June 12, 1975: a LeBaron hardtop sedan bearing serial number YM43-T5C-182947. But only the nameplate vanished immediately, for the basic '75 package continued through 1978 as the Chrysler New Yorker Brougham.

By 1980, however, Chrysler thought it time for another stab at a separate luxury line. Though facing imminent bankruptcy, and having staked their future on the sensible front-drive K-car compacts and planned derivatives, Chrysler executives led by president (and soon-to-be-chairman) Lee Iacocca felt a new flagship would assure the public that Chrysler had a future.

The result appeared for 1981 in a revived Imperial that amounted to little more than the world's most-expensive Dodge Aspen/Plymouth Volare. Actually, it was a reskinned version of Chrysler's second-generation 1980 Cordoba coupe, built on the same 112.7-inch-wheelbase "M-body" platform, complete with odd transverse-torsion-bar front suspension and an ordinary live rear axle on longitudinal leaf springs. The company's veteran 318 V-8 was inevitable, but Imperial received a newly developed fuel-injected version as an exclusive, with mild 8.5:1 compression and a modest 140 bhp. It naturally teamed with the TorqueFlite automatic.

Styling was handsome. Up front was a square, Lincoln-like vertical-bar grille flanked by concealed headlamps inboard of knife-edge fenders. A distinctive "bustleback" rear end evoked razor-edge British custom coachwork from the early '50s—and Cadillac's second-generation Seville, which had arrived the previous year with something very similar. Of course, there was no way Chrysler could have "stolen" the Cadillac's treatment, and the Imperial's bustle was arguably more attractive, but the sameness was still a bit embarrassing.

Chrysler marketed the reborn Imperial as what it called a "one-price" car. Standard equipment was predictably lavish—but then the base price was a steep $18,311. Still, you got clearcoat paint, choice of Mark Cross leather or rich velour upholstery, electronic digital instruments (a dubious feature), full power equipment, and various choices of tires and factory sound systems. The sole option was an electric sliding sunroof priced at a hefty $1044. Production was assigned to Chrysler's Windsor, Ontario, plant, which took pains to ensure that quality would rank with the world's best. Among special measures taken were several post-assembly checks, plus a 5.5-mile road test and a final polish before shipment. Chrysler announced first-year production would be limited to "just" 25,000 units, also in the interest of high quality—not to mention snob appeal.

Unfortunately, the new Imperial got lost in Highland

# Imperial

**1983 coupe**

Park's much-publicized financial crisis and an equal amount of ballyhoo surrounding the make-or-break K-cars. Promotional funds were limited. Frank Sinatra helped his friend Iacocca by singing "It's time for Imperial" in television commercials, but even Ol' Blue Eyes couldn't persuade buyers, and model-year production ended up at just 7225 cars.

The following year brought no changes save an "FS" package option—special emblems outside, a set of tapes with Frankie's greatest hits inside—and a base price hiked to nearly $21,000. Though the Imperial still cost thousands less than the rival Cadillac Eldorado and Lincoln Mark VI, sales remained tough, so despite heavy dealer discounts, production sank to just 2329. The '83s were also little changed—the Sinatra option was dropped, price lowered to $18,688—and fared even worse: just 1427. Having now turned the financial corner, but in no need of money-losers, Chrysler put Imperial out to pasture a second time.

Imperial came back, in a way, as the 1990-93 Chrysler Imperial (see Chrysler). This was a luxury version of the Chrysler New Yorker sedan. The name died a third time when the LH platform sedans of '93 didn't include an Imperial.

It's unlikely there will be another Imperial revival, but one can still hope a Chrysler concept car will someday bear the Imperial eagle.

## Specifications

### 1955

| C69 (wb 130.0) | Wght | Price | Prod |
|---|---|---|---|
| sdn 4d | 4,565 | 4,483 | 7,840 |
| Newport htp cpe | 4,490 | 4,720 | 3,418 |
| conv cpe (proto) | 4,600 | — | 1 |
| chassis | — | — | 1 |
| **C70 Crown Imperial (wb 149.5)** | | | |
| sdn 4d, 8P | 5,180 | 6,973 | 45 |
| limo 4d | 5,230 | 7,095 | 127 |

| 1955 Engine | bore × stroke | bhp | availability |
|---|---|---|---|
| V-8, 331.0 | 3.81 × 3.63 | 250 | S-all |

### 1956

| C73 (wb 133.0) | Wght | Price | Prod |
|---|---|---|---|
| sdn 4d | 4,575 | 4,832 | 6,821 |
| Southampton htp sdn | 4,680 | 5,225 | 1,543 |
| Southampton htp cpe | 4,555 | 5,094 | 2,094 |
| **C70 Crown Imperial (wb 149.5)** | | | |
| sdn 4d, 8P | 5,145 | 7,603 | 51 |
| limo 4d | 5,205 | 7,737 | 175 |

| 1956 Engine | bore × stroke | bhp | availability |
|---|---|---|---|
| V-8, 354.0 | 3.94 × 3.63 | 280 | S-all |

### 1957

| IM1-1 (wb 129.0) | Wght | Price | Prod |
|---|---|---|---|
| sdn 4d | 4,640 | 4,838 | 5,569 |
| Southampton htp sdn | 4,780 | 4,838 | 7,157 |
| Southampton htp cpe | 4,640 | 4,736 | 4,595 |
| **IM1-2 Crown (wb 129.0)** | | | |
| sdn 4d | 4,740 | 5,406 | 3,472 |
| Southampton htp sdn | 4,920 | 5,406 | 7,429 |
| Southampton htp cpe | 4,755 | 5,269 | 3,888 |
| conv cpe | 4,830 | 5,598 | 1,167 |
| **IM1-4 LeBaron (wb 129.0)** | | | |
| sdn 4d | 4,765 | 5,743 | 1,659 |
| Southampton htp sdn | 4,900 | 5,743 | 821 |
| **Crown Imperial (wb 149.5)** | | | |
| limo 4d | 5,960 | 15,075 | 36 |

| 1957 Engine | bore × stroke | bhp | availability |
|---|---|---|---|
| V-8, 392.0 | 4.00 × 3.90 | 325 | S-all |

### 1958

| LY1-L (wb 129.0) | | Wght | Price | Prod |
|---|---|---|---|---|
| 23 | Southampton htp cpe | 4,640 | 4,839 | 1,801 |
| 41 | sdn 4d | 4,590 | 4,945 | 1,926 |
| 43 | Southampton htp sdn | 4,795 | 4,945 | 3,336 |
| **LY1-M Crown (wb 129.0)** | | | | |
| 23 | Southampton htp cpe | 4,730 | 5,388 | 1,939 |
| 27 | conv cpe | 4,820 | 5,729 | 675 |
| 41 | sdn 4d | 4,755 | 5,632 | 1,240 |
| 43 | Southampton htp sdn | 4,915 | 5,632 | 4,146 |
| **LY1-H LeBaron (wb 129.0)** | | | | |
| 41 | sdn 4d | 4,780 | 5,969 | 501 |
| 43 | Southampton htp sdn | 4,940 | 5,969 | 538 |
| **Crown Imperial (wb 149.5)** | | | | |
| | limo 4d | 5,960 | 15,075 | 31 |

| 1958 Engines | bore × stroke | bhp | availability |
|---|---|---|---|
| V-8, 392.0 | 4.00 × 3.90 | 345 | S-all exc Crown Imperial |
| V-8, 392.0 | 4.00 × 3.90 | 325 | S-Crown Imperial |

### 1959

| MY1-L Custom (wb 129.0) | | Wght | Price | Prod |
|---|---|---|---|---|
| 612 | Southampton htp cpe | 4,675 | 4,910 | 1,743 |
| 613 | sdn 4d | 4,735 | 5,016 | 2,071 |
| 614 | Southampton htp sdn | 4,745 | 5,016 | 3,984 |
| **MY1-M Crown (wb 129.0)** | | | | |
| 632 | Southampton htp cpe | 4,810 | 5,403 | 1,728 |

# Imperial

| MY1-M Crown (wb 129.0) | Wght | Price | Prod |
|---|---|---|---|
| 633  sdn 4d | 4,830 | 5,647 | 1,335 |
| 634  Southampton htp sdn | 4,840 | 5,647 | 4,714 |
| 635  conv cpe | 4,850 | 5,774 | 555 |
| **MY1-H LeBaron (wb 129.0)** | | | |
| 653  sdn 4d | 4,865 | 6,103 | 510 |
| 654  Southampton htp sdn | 4,875 | 6,103 | 622 |
| **Crown Imperial (wb 149.5)** | | | |
| limo 4d | 5,960 | 15,075 | 7 |

| 1959 Engines | bore × stroke | bhp | availability |
|---|---|---|---|
| V-8, 413.0 | 4.18 × 3.75 | 350 | S-all exc Crown Imperial |
| V-8, 392.0 | 4.00 × 3.90 | 325 | S-Crown Imperial |

## 1960

| PY1-L Custom (wb 129.0) | Wght | Price | Prod |
|---|---|---|---|
| 912  Southampton htp cpe | 4,655 | 4,923 | 1,498 |
| 913  sdn 4d | 4,700 | 5,029 | 2,335 |
| 914  Southampton htp sdn | 4,760 | 5,029 | 3,953 |
| **PY1-M Crown (wb 129.0)** | | | |
| 922  Southampton htp cpe | 4,720 | 5,403 | 1,504 |
| 923  sdn 4d | 4,770 | 5,647 | 1,594 |
| 924  Southampton htp sdn | 4,765 | 5,647 | 4,510 |
| 925  conv cpe | 4,820 | 5,774 | 618 |
| **PY1-H LeBaron (wb 129.0)** | | | |
| 933  sdn 4d | 4,860 | 6,318 | 692 |
| 934  Southampton htp sdn | 4,835 | 6,318 | 999 |
| **Crown Imperial (wb 149.5)** | | | |
| limo 4d | 5,960 | 16,500 | 16 |

| 1960 Engine | bore × stroke | bhp | availability |
|---|---|---|---|
| V-8, 413.0 | 4.18 × 3.75 | 350 | S-all |

## 1961

| RY1-L Custom (wb 129.0) | Wght | Price | Prod |
|---|---|---|---|
| 912  Southampton htp cpe | 4,715 | 4,923 | 889 |
| 914  Southampton htp sdn | 4,740 | 5,109 | 4,129 |
| **RY1-M Crown (wb 129.0)** | | | |
| 922  Southampton htp cpe | 4,790 | 5,403 | 1,007 |
| 924  Southampton htp sdn | 4,855 | 5,647 | 4,769 |
| 925  conv cpe | 4,865 | 5,774 | 429 |
| **RY1-H LeBaron (wb 129.0)** | | | |
| 934  Southampton htp sdn | 4,875 | 6,426 | 1,026 |
| **Crown Imperial (wb 149.5)** | | | |
| limo 4d | 5,960 | 16,500 | 9 |

| 1961 Engine | bore × stroke | bhp | availability |
|---|---|---|---|
| V-8, 413.0 | 4.18 × 3.75 | 350 | S-all |

## 1962

| SY1-L Custom (wb 129.0) | Wght | Price | Prod |
|---|---|---|---|
| 912  Southampton htp cpe | 4,540 | 4,920 | 826 |
| 914  Southampton htp sdn | 4,620 | 5,106 | 3,587 |
| **SY1-M Crown (wb 129.0)** | | | |
| 922  Southampton htp cpe | 4,650 | 5,400 | 1,010 |
| 924  Southampton htp sdn | 4,680 | 5,644 | 6,911 |
| 925  conv cpe | 4,765 | 5,770 | 554 |
| **SY1-H LeBaron (wb 129.0)** | | | |
| 934  Southampton htp sdn | 4,725 | 6,422 | 1,449 |

| 1962 Engine | bore × stroke | bhp | availability |
|---|---|---|---|
| V-8, 413.0 | 4.18 × 3.75 | 340 | S-all |

## 1963

| TY1-L Custom (wb 129.0) | Wght | Price | Prod |
|---|---|---|---|
| 912  Southampton htp cpe | 4,640 | 5,058 | 749 |
| 914  Southampton htp sdn | 4,690 | 5,243 | 3,264 |
| **TY1-M Crown (wb 129.0)** | | | |
| 922  Southampton htp cpe | 4,720 | 5,412 | 1,067 |
| 924  Southampton htp sdn | 4,740 | 5,656 | 6,960 |
| 925  conv cpe | 4,795 | 5,782 | 531 |
| **TY1-H LeBaron (wb 129.0)** | | | |
| 934  Southampton htp sdn | 4,830 | 6,434 | 1,537 |
| **Crown Imperial (wb 149.5)** | | | |
| limo 4d | 6,100 | 18,500 | 13 |

| 1963 Engine | bore × stroke | bhp | availability |
|---|---|---|---|
| V-8, 413.0 | 4.18 × 3.75 | 340 | S-all |

## 1964

| VY1-M Crown (wb 129.0) | Wght | Price | Prod |
|---|---|---|---|
| 922  htp cpe | 4,950 | 5,739 | 5,233 |
| 924  htp sdn | 4,970 | 5,581 | 14,181 |
| 925  conv cpe | 5,185 | 6,003 | 922 |
| **VY1-H LeBaron (wb 129.0)** | | | |
| 934  htp sdn | 5,005 | 6,455 | 2,949 |
| **Crown Imperial (wb 149.5)** | | | |
| limo 4d | 6,100 | 18,500 | 10 |

| 1964 Engine | bore × stroke | bhp | availability |
|---|---|---|---|
| V-8, 413.0 | 4.18 × 3.75 | 340 | S-all |

## 1965

| AY1-M Crown (wb 129.0) | Wght | Price | Prod |
|---|---|---|---|
| 922  htp cpe | 5,075 | 5,930 | 3,974 |
| 924  htp sdn | 5,015 | 5,772 | 11,628 |
| 925  conv cpe | 5,345 | 6,194 | 633 |
| **AY1-H LeBaron (wb 129.0)** | | | |
| 934  htp sdn | 5,080 | 6,596 | 2,164 |
| **Crown Imperial (wb 149.5)** | | | |
| limo 4d | 6,100 | 18,500 | 10 |

| 1965 Engine | bore × stroke | bhp | availability |
|---|---|---|---|
| V-8, 413.0 | 4.18 × 3.75 | 340 | S-all |

## 1966

| BY3-M Crown (wb 129.0) | Wght | Price | Prod |
|---|---|---|---|
| 23  htp cpe | 5,000 | 5,887 | 2,373 |
| 27  conv cpe | 5,315 | 6,164 | 514 |
| 43  htp sdn | 4,990 | 5,733 | 8,977 |
| **BY3-H LeBaron (wb 129.0)** | | | |
| 43  htp sdn | 5,090 | 6,540 | 1,878 |

| 1966 Engine | bore × stroke | bhp | availability |
|---|---|---|---|
| V-8, 440.0 | 4.32 × 3.75 | 350 | S-all |

# Imperial

## 1967

### CY1-M (wb 127.0)

| | | Wght | Price | Prod |
|---|---|---|---|---|
| 23 | Crown htp cpe | 4,780 | 6,011 | 3,235 |
| 27 | conv cpe | 4,815 | 6,244 | 577 |
| 41 | sdn 4d | 4,830 | 5,374 | 2,193 |
| 43 | Crown htp sdn | 4,860 | 5,836 | 9,415 |

### CY1-H LeBaron (wb 127.0)

| | | Wght | Price | Prod |
|---|---|---|---|---|
| 43 | htp sdn | 4,970 | 6,661 | 2,194 |

### LeBaron, Stageway body (wb 163.0)

| | | Wght | Price | Prod |
|---|---|---|---|---|
| | limo 4d | 6,300 | 15,000 | 6 |

| 1967 Engine | bore × stroke | bhp | availability |
|---|---|---|---|
| V-8, 440.0 | 4.32 × 3.75 | 350 | S-all |

## 1968

### YM Crown (wb 127.0)

| | | Wght | Price | Prod |
|---|---|---|---|---|
| 23 | htp cpe | 4,660 | 5,722 | 2,656 |
| 27 | conv cpe | 4,795 | 6,497 | 474 |
| 41 | sdn 4d | 4,685 | 5,654 | 1,887 |
| 43 | htp sdn | 4,715 | 6,115 | 8,492 |

### YH LeBaron (wb 127.0)

| | | Wght | Price | Prod |
|---|---|---|---|---|
| 43 | htp sdn | 4,815 | 6,940 | 1,852 |

### LeBaron, Stageway body (wb 163.0)

| | | Wght | Price | Prod |
|---|---|---|---|---|
| | limo 4d | 6,300 | 15,000 | 6 |

| 1968 Engines | bore × stroke | bhp | availability |
|---|---|---|---|
| V-8, 440.0 | 4.32 × 3.75 | 350 | S-all |
| V-8, 440.0 | 4.32 × 3.75 | 360 | O-all (dual exhaust) |

## 1969

### Crown (wb 127.0)

| | | Wght | Price | Prod |
|---|---|---|---|---|
| YL23 | htp cpe | 4,555 | 5,592 | 224 |
| YL43 | htp sdn | 4,690 | 5,770 | 823 |
| YM41 | sdn 4d | 4,620 | 5,770 | 1,617 |

### LeBaron (wb 127.0)

| | | Wght | Price | Prod |
|---|---|---|---|---|
| YM23 | htp cpe | 4,610 | 5,898 | 4,592 |
| YM43 | htp sdn | 4,710 | 6,131 | 14,821 |

### LeBaron, Stageway body (wb 163.0)

| | | Wght | Price | Prod |
|---|---|---|---|---|
| | limo 4d | 6,300 | 16,000 | 6 est |

| 1969 Engine | bore × stroke | bhp | availability |
|---|---|---|---|
| V-8, 440.0 | 4.32 × 3.75 | 350 | S-all |

## 1970

### YL Crown (wb 127.0)

| | | Wght | Price | Prod |
|---|---|---|---|---|
| 23 | htp cpe | 4,610 | 5,779 | 254 |
| 43 | htp sdn | 4,735 | 5,956 | 1,333 |

### YM LeBaron (wb 127.0)

| | | Wght | Price | Prod |
|---|---|---|---|---|
| 23 | htp cpe | 4,660 | 6,095 | 1,803 |
| 43 | htp sdn | 4,805 | 6,328 | 8,426 |

### LeBaron, Stageway body (wb 163.0)

| | | Wght | Price | Prod |
|---|---|---|---|---|
| | limo 4d | 6,500 | 16,500 | 6 est |

| 1970 Engine | bore × stroke | bhp | availability |
|---|---|---|---|
| V-8, 440.0 | 4.32 × 3.75 | 350 | S-all |

## 1971

### YM LeBaron (wb 127.0)

| | | Wght | Price | Prod |
|---|---|---|---|---|
| 23 | htp cpe | 4,800 | 6,632 | 1,442 |
| 43 | htp sdn | 4,950 | 6,864 | 10,116 |

| 1971 Engine | bore × stroke | bhp | availability |
|---|---|---|---|
| V-8, 440.0 | 4.32 × 3.75 | 335 | S-all |

## 1972

### YM LeBaron (wb 127.0)

| | | Wght | Price | Prod |
|---|---|---|---|---|
| 23 | htp cpe | 4,790 | 6,550 | 2,322 |
| 43 | htp sdn | 4,955 | 6,778 | 13,472 |

| 1972 Engine | bore × stroke | bhp | availability |
|---|---|---|---|
| V-8, 440.0 | 4.32 × 3.75 | 225 | S-all |

## 1973

### YM LeBaron (wb 127.0)

| | | Wght | Price | Prod |
|---|---|---|---|---|
| 23 | htp cpe | 4,905 | 6,829 | 2,563 |
| 43 | htp sdn | 5,035 | 7,057 | 14,166 |

| 1973 Engine | bore × stroke | bhp | availability |
|---|---|---|---|
| V-8, 440.0 | 4.32 × 3.75 | 215 | S-all |

## 1974

### YM LeBaron (wb 124.0)

| | | Wght | Price | Prod |
|---|---|---|---|---|
| 23 | htp cpe | 4,825 | 7,673 | 3,850 |
| 43 | htp sdn | 4,965 | 7,804 | 10,576 |

| 1974 Engine | bore × stroke | bhp | availability |
|---|---|---|---|
| V-8, 440.0 | 4.32 × 3.75 | 230 | S-all |

## 1975

### YM LeBaron (wb 124.0)

| | | Wght | Price | Prod |
|---|---|---|---|---|
| 23 | htp cpe | 4,965 | 8,698 | 2,728 |
| 43 | htp sdn | 5,065 | 8,844 | 6,102 |

| 1975 Engine | bore × stroke | bhp | availability |
|---|---|---|---|
| V-8, 440.0 | 4.32 × 3.75 | 215 | S-all |

Note: Chrysler built no cars under the Imperial name from 1975 to 1980.

## 1981—7,225 built

### (wb 112.7)

| | | Wght | Price | Prod |
|---|---|---|---|---|
| YS22 | cpe | 3,968 | 18,311 | — |

| 1981 Engine | bore × stroke | bhp | availability |
|---|---|---|---|
| V-8, 318.0 | 3.91 × 3.31 | 140 | S-all |

## 1982—2,329 built

### (wb 112.7)

| | | Wght | Price | Prod |
|---|---|---|---|---|
| YS22 | cpe | 3,945 | 20,988 | — |

| 1982 Engine | bore × stroke | bhp | availability |
|---|---|---|---|
| V-8, 318.0 | 3.91 × 3.31 | 140 | S-all |

## 1983—1,427 built

### (wb 112.7)

| | | Wght | Price | Prod |
|---|---|---|---|---|
| YS22 | cpe | 4,019 | 18,688 | — |

| 1983 Engine | bore × stroke | bhp | availability |
|---|---|---|---|
| V-8, 318.0 | 3.91 × 3.31 | 140 | S-all |

# Kaiser

Henry J. Kaiser and Joseph W. Frazer literally parted company in 1949, but they'd been at loggerheads once before. In 1942, Kaiser was experimenting with plastic-bodied cars, hinting that he just might sell them for $400-$600 once World War II was over. He also suggested that auto companies announce their postwar plans immediately. Industry-veteran Frazer was incensed: "I resent a West Coast shipbuilder asking us if we have the courage to plan postwar automobiles when the President has asked us to forego all work which would take away from the war effort. Kaiser has done a great job as a shipbuilder... but I think his challenge to automobile men is as half-baked as some of his other statements... I think the public is being misled by all these pictures of plastic models with glass tops, done by artists who probably wouldn't want to sit under those tops in the summer and sweat."

This public brouhaha was long forgotten by July 1945, when Henry and Joe joined forces to form Kaiser-Frazer. Both men compromised, and their relationship was amicable, at least for a time. Though Henry discovered that his plastic car for the common man was just so much wishful thinking, he had high hopes for a more-radical Kaiser than what ultimately emerged.

It would have stemmed from the 1946 K-85 prototype, which looked like the conventional Frazer then already locked up, but employed unit construction on a shorter 117-inch wheelbase. Suspension and the "Packaged Power" drivetrain, worked out by engineer Henry C. McCaslin, were very different. For one thing, an 85-horsepower Continental six drove the front wheels, not the rears. A conventional three-speed transmission sent power via a helical-gear transfer case to a front differential, then to the wheels by U-jointed halfshafts. Equally novel was four-wheel independent "Torsionetic" suspension: a pair of longitudinal torsion bars, each 1.3 inches thick by 44.5 inches long. The steel bars twisted to provide spring action like conventional coils or semiellipitics. McCaslin wanted unit construction because "we needed to use more of the operation in the plant. We had the welding equipment but lacked large dies and cranes. It was a compromise to get the car into production."

But the front-drive K-85 didn't have a chance. Aside from exorbitant tooling expense, technical problems such as heavy steering, gear whine, and wheel shimmy proved insurmountable. With so much weight over the front wheels, the K-85 would have needed power steering and that would have added $900 to the retail price. So in May 1946, K-F decided to abandon this idea for a conventional rear-drive Kaiser priced below the Frazer.

Production for both new makes began that June at the huge wartime bomber plant in Willow Run, Michigan, near Detroit, that Henry had purchased from Ford. Like the Frazer, the new Kaiser Special was a 1947 model. Initial price was $1868, though postwar inflation quickly boosted it above $2000.

**1947½-48 Special four-door sedan**

**1949 DeLuxe Vagabond utility sedan**

**1949 DeLuxe "Glass Green" four-door sedan**

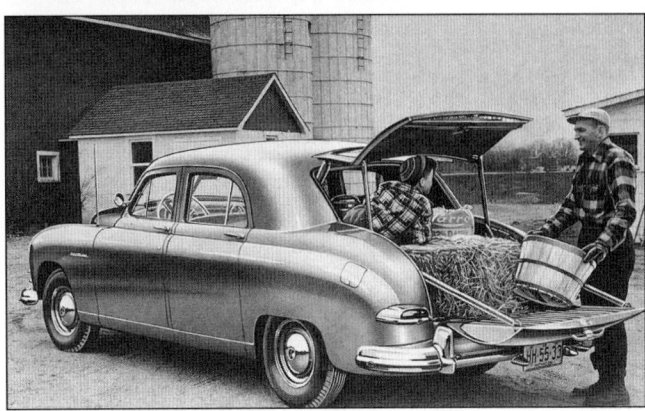
**1949-50 Special Traveler utility sedan**

# Kaiser

1949-50 DeLuxe Virginian hardtop sedan

1949 DeLuxe four-door sedan prototype

It was very much like the Frazer, of course: a roomy flush-fender four-door sedan with 123.5-inch wheelbase, styling by the eminent Howard A. "Dutch" Darrin, and a "stroker" six making 100 bhp from 226 cubic inches. The Kaiser wore a multipiece grille that was cheaper to make than the Frazer's because the pieces were smaller. Furnishings were naturally more-basic, in line with the lower price. Perhaps inevitably, a fancier Kaiser Custom was added late in the model year at about $350 above the Special and $150 more than the standard Frazer, but some $250 less than the top-line Frazer Manhattan. A bit later, Customs were offered with optional dual intake and exhaust manifolds that boosted bhp to 112. But Kaiser would have no automatic transmission through 1950 (after which proprietary GM Hydra-Matic was offered); only a standard three-speed manual available with overdrive as an $80 option.

Though plans called for building two Kaisers to every Frazer, the 1947 ratio was 1:1 so as to fill initial orders. Both lines were basically unchanged for 1948, when very few Customs were built, though Kaiser volume far outpaced Frazer's. These were outstanding years for what came to be called the "postwar wonder company." Kaiser production totaled more than 70,000 for '47 and nearly 92,000 for '48. All told, K-F made a healthy $30 million profit on 1947-48 volume that put it ninth in Detroit production—the highest among the independents.

A scheduled facelift gave the 1949 Kaisers a broader, shinier grille and larger taillights. Custom was retitled DeLuxe, and gained the 112-bhp engine as standard. Four new models arrived. Two were utility sedans, an idea from Henry Kaiser himself. They were much like the standard article save a double-door rear hatch and fold-down back seat. The economical Special Traveler arrived at $2088, the leather-upholstered Custom Vagabond at $200 more. In effect, these were a cost-saving substitute for a true station wagon, one of many things K-F never would get around to building.

Kaiser's other two '49 newcomers were a four-door convertible and the Virginian four-door hardtop, the first postwar use of those body types. Both were richly appointed DeLuxe offerings with excellent visibility thanks to the lack of steel B-posts, though both retained vestigial pillars with glass panes. The convertible also carried fixed side-window frames and a heavily braced X-member frame for added structural strength. Unfortunately, both Kaisers cost as much as some Cadillacs—$3000-$3200—so only a handful were produced: an estimated 946 Virginians and just 54 convertible sedans. Those that didn't sell as '49s were given new serial numbers for 1950.

From the first, K-F offered an unusually wide range of paint, trim, and upholstery variations. This was the work of Carleton Spencer, who took some initial cues from research on home interiors done by *House & Garden* magazine. The results were hues like Indian Ceramic (a vivid pink), Crystal Green, Caribbean Coral, and Arena Yellow. These and other color names were actually written in chrome script on the front fenders of '49 Kaiser Customs. Detroit, as a whole, listed 218 exterior colors for '49; 37 were K-F's. Of the industry's 150 different 1949 interior fabrics, K-F owned 62.

The original Kaiser dashboard was an inexpensive design with horizontal gauges. For 1949, this gave way to a more-ornate panel with a giant speedometer ahead of the driver and a matching clock on the passenger's side. DeLuxe dashboards sparkled with chrome, stainless steel, and a massive ivory steering wheel with a big semicircular chrome horn ring. Such flash combined with colorful paint and fashion upholstery did much to doll up what was otherwise an unchanged and surprisingly fast-aging design.

And therein lay the seeds of disaster. Chairman Henry Kaiser boldly tooled up for 1949 volume of 200,000 cars—against the advice of his marketwise partner. Joe Frazer realized the company couldn't sell nearly that many against all-new 1949 Big Three competition, and had urged a holding action until K-F released its own new models, then scheduled for 1950. But Henry wouldn't have it. "The Kaisers never retrench," he stormed. By now, Kaiser's people had far more influence in company affairs than Frazer's, so Joe yielded the presidency to Kaiser's son Edgar, remaining on the board only for appearance sake. By year's end, he was gone.

Henry should have listened. Instead, K-F's 1949 sales were barely half the number planned: only some 101,000. About 20 percent couldn't be sold, and were thus recycled with new serial numbers as 1950 models. Though it's impossible to separate model-year "production," 1949 units account for about 84 percent of the total, according to expert estimates.

Meantime, Dutch Darrin and K-F Styling had prepared a real blockbuster: a slender, beautiful new Kaiser with "Anatomic Design." Though scheduled for 1950, it didn't arrive until March of that year as a 1951 offering (delayed until those '49 leftovers were cleared). But it sold like no

1951 DeLuxe two-door sedan

# Kaiser

1952 Manhattan four-door sedan

1953 "Hardtop" Dragon four-door sedan

1953 Carolina two-door sedan

1954 Kaiser-Darrin roadster

1954 Special four-door sedan

1955 Manhattan four-door sedan

Kaiser before: close to 140,000 for the model year. From 17th in Detroit for '49, Kaiser promptly shot up to 12th.

Looking unlike any other car of its day, the '51 Kaiser boasted 700 square inches more glass area than its nearest competitor and a lower beltline than any Detroit car offered through 1956. Though wheelbase slimmed to 118.5 inches, the '51 looked miles sleeker than first-generation Kaisers. Complementing its artful styling was another bewildering array of bright exterior colors and high-fashion interiors by "color engineer" Spencer.

The '51 Kaiser was also the first car that actually sold at least partly on safety features: offering a padded dash, recessed gauges and controls, slim roof pillars for outstanding visibility, and a windshield that popped out if struck with a force of more than 35 pounds per square inch. Though chief engineers John Widman and Ralph Isbrandt shunned unit construction, they designed a very rigid separate body for a strong frame weighing but 200 pounds. They also provided a low center of gravity that ensured fine handling, and a suspension that delivered a terrific ride despite curb weights averaging only some 3100 pounds. Said one Chrysler engineer who later sampled a '51 Kaiser: "It rides like one of our 4500-pound cars."

Still in the lower medium-price field, Kaiser's '51 prices ranged from just under $2000 to a bit over $2400. Special and DeLuxe series returned, each offering regular and utility Traveler sedans with two or four doors, plus long-deck club coupe; there was also a stripped Special business coupe. But hardtops, convertibles, and station wagons were conspicuously absent, as was a V-8. Though K-F had plans for all of these, it would never have the money to market them. The old six was lifted to 115 bhp via two-barrel carburetor and dual exhausts, but the missing V-8 would prove an increasing sales liability.

A scheduled 1952 facelift wasn't quite ready on time, so Virginian models, basically leftover '51s with "Continental kits," were sold in the interim—about 5500 in all. The "real" '52s arrived with bulbous taillights and a more-prominent, heavier-looking grille. Two-door Travelers and the business coupe departed, Specials became DeLuxes, and previous DeLuxes—a coupe and two sedans—were now retitled Manhattan (borrowing the old Frazer name). The "second-series" '52s are fairly rare: only 7500 DeLuxes and 19,000 Manhattans.

Kaiser had pitched the "fashion market" in 1951 with its $125 Dragon trim options: limited-edition four-door sedans available in Golden, Silver, Emerald, and Jade editions. All sported alligator-look "Dragon" vinyl inside and color-keyed exteriors with padded vinyl tops.

This idea was tried again with 1953's "Hardtop" Dragon

589

sedan, the most-luxurious Kaiser of all. It was easily spotted by a gold-plated hood ornament, badges, and even keyhole covers, plus a padded roof usually covered in "bambu" vinyl—a tough, oriental-style material that also adorned the dash and parts of seats and door panels. Seat inserts were done in "Laguna" cloth, a fabric with an oblong pattern created by fashion consultant Marie Nichols. Standard amenities were plentiful: tinted glass, Hydra-Matic Drive, whitewalls, twin-speaker radio, and Calpoint custom carpet. The finishing touch was a gold-plated dash plaque engraved with the owner's name. The Dragon was spectacular, but a high $3924 price—nearly as much as a Cadillac Coupe de Ville—limited sales to just 1277, and a few of those almost had to be given away.

Otherwise, the '53 Kaisers were little changed. A pair of stripped Carolina sedans was fielded in the $2300 range, an effort to build showroom traffic, but only 1800 were sold. Club coupes were eliminated, the six was persuaded up to 118 bhp, and power steering bowed late in the season as a $122 option.

But Kaiser sales were falling fast: only 32,000 for '52 and just 28,000 for '53. The compact Henry J (*see entry*) had squandered development funds that would have been better spent on new styling, new body types, or a V-8. Cash reserves were further depleted in 1954 when Henry Kaiser decided to buy Willys-Overland, which was no better off.

Seeking to slash overhead, Kaiser transferred production from Willow Run to W-O's Toledo, Ohio, facilities, and hoped for a sales miracle with a clever facelift by stylist Arnott "Buzz" Grisinger. From the front, the '54 Kaisers looked much like the Buick XP-300 show car (a favorite of company president Edgar Kaiser), with a wide concave grille, dummy hood scoop, and headlights "floating" within oval housings. Out back were "Safety-Glo" taillights: the existing units given little finned housings with a lighted strip run forward atop the fenders.

Remaining Travelers were canceled for '54, but Manhattans were booted to a maximum 140 bhp by bolting on a McCulloch centrifugal supercharger that cut in at full throttle. Also offered that year were unsupercharged Specials in two "series." The first involved '53 Manhattans warmed over with '54 front ends—yet another effort to use up leftovers. Second-series Specials were genuine '54s with wrapped rear windows, as on all of that year's Manhattans.

But sales refused to improve, and 1954 Kaiser production was a dismal 8539, including 4110 Manhattans, 3500 "early" Specials, and a paltry 929 "late" Specials. With that, only Manhattans returned for '55, distinguished by a higher fin on the hood scoop and little else. Just 270 were sold. Another 1021 were exported, most to Argentina, where Kaiser Motors hoped to continue production for South America at a subsidiary plant. It's a tribute to the durability of this basic design that the '55 was built there through 1962 as the little-altered Kaiser Carabella.

A memorable last-gasp U.S. effort was the 1954 Kaiser-Darrin sliding-door sports car. Dutch had designed it in late 1952 for the 100-inch-wheelbase Henry J chassis, and talked Henry Kaiser into selling it for $3668. Only 435 were built before Kaiser ceased U.S. production.

The Darrin was beautifully styled, and still looks good today. Besides a then-novel fiberglass body, it boasted unique sliding doors, a patented Darrin idea first tried on an unrelated 1946 prototype. The DKF-161 (the official designation) also offered a three-position landau convertible top with intermediate half-up position, plus full instrumentation and, usually, a three-speed floorshift transmission with overdrive. This plus the 90 bhp of the Henry J's 161-cid Willys six gave economy of around 30 mpg, but also 0-60 sprints of about 13 seconds and near-100 mph flat out.

But the Kaiser-Darrin affair greatly disappointed Dutch, who bought about 100 leftovers, fitted many with Cadillac V-8s, and sold them for $4350 apiece at his Los Angeles showroom. The V-8 Darrins were potent indeed, capable of some 140 mph.

Kaiser came to an end in America during 1955 after 10 years and $100 million in losses. They were usually good cars and often innovative, but they never seemed to make it with the public. Edgar Kaiser liked to say, "Slap a Buick nameplate on it and it would sell like hotcakes." He was probably right.

## Specifications

### 1947

| K100 Special (wb 123.5) | | Wght | Price | Prod |
|---|---|---|---|---|
| 1005 | sdn 4d | 3,295 | 2,104 | 65,062 |
| **K101 Custom (wb 123.5)** | | | | |
| 1015 | sdn 4d | 3,295 | 2,456 | 5,412 |
| **1947 Engines** | **bore × stroke** | **bhp** | **availability** | |
| I-6, 226.2 | 3.31 × 4.38 | 100 | S-all | |
| I-6, 226.2 | 3.31 × 4.38 | 112 | O-Custom | |

### 1948

| K481 Special (wb 123.5) | | Wght | Price | Prod |
|---|---|---|---|---|
| 4815 | sdn 4d | 3,295 | 2,244 | 90,588 |
| **K482 Custom (wb 123.5)** | | | | |
| 4825 | sdn 4d | 3,295 | 2,466 | 1,263 |
| **1948 Engines** | **bore × stroke** | **bhp** | **availability** | |
| I-6, 226.2 | 3.31 × 4.38 | 100 | S-all | |
| I-6, 226.2 | 3.31 × 4.38 | 112 | O-Custom | |

### 1949-50

| K491 Special (wb 123.5) | | Wght | Price | Prod |
|---|---|---|---|---|
| 4911 | sdn 4d | 3,311 | 1,995 | 29,000* |
| 4915 | Traveler util sdn 4d | 3,456 | 2,088 | 22,000* |
| **K492 DeLuxe (wb 123.5)** | | | | |
| 4921 | sdn 4d | 3,341 | 2,195 | 38,250* |
| 4922 | conv sdn | 3,726 | 3,195 | 54* |
| 4923 | Virginian htp sdn | 3,541 | 2,995 | 946* |
| 4925 | Vagabond util sdn 4d | 3,501 | 2,288 | 4,500* |

\* 1949-50 production combined by factory; approximate breakdown 84-percent 1949, 16-percent 1950. Estimates for body styles based on body numbers in extant vehicles. Actual 1949-50 production: 95,175.

# Kaiser

| 1949-50 Engines | bore × stroke | bhp | availability |
|---|---|---|---|
| I-6, 226.2 | 3.31 × 4.38 | 100 | S-Special |
| I-6, 226.2 | 3.31 × 4.38 | 112 | S-DeLuxe |

## 1951

| K511 Special (wb 118.5) | | Wght | Price | Prod |
|---|---|---|---|---|
| 5110 | Traveler util sdn 2d | 3,210 | 2,265 | 1,500* |
| 5111 | sdn 4d | 3,126 | 2,212 | 43,500* |
| 5113 | bus cpe | 3,061 | 1,992 | 1,500* |
| 5114 | sdn 2d | 3,106 | 2,160 | 10,000* |
| 5115 | Traveler util sdn 4d | 3,270 | 2,317 | 2,000* |
| 5117 | club cpe | 3,066 | 2,058 | 1,500* |
| **K512 DeLuxe (wb 118.5)** | | | | |
| 5120 | Traveler util sdn 2d | 3,285 | 2,380 | 1,000* |
| 5121 | sdn 4d | 3,171 | 2,328 | 70,000* |
| 5124 | sdn 2d | 3,151 | 2,275 | 11,000* |
| 5125 | Traveler util sdn 4d | 3,345 | 2,433 | 1,000* |
| 5127 | club cpe | 3,111 | 2,296 | 6,000* |

* Estimates based on extant vehicles. Actual total model-year production: 139,452.

| 1951 Engine | bore × stroke | bhp | availability |
|---|---|---|---|
| I-6, 226.2 | 3.31 × 4.38 | 115 | S-all |

## 1952

| K521 Virginian Special (wb 118.5)* | | Wght | Price | Prod |
|---|---|---|---|---|
| 5110 | Traveler util sdn 2d | 3,210 | 2,085 | — |
| 5111 | sdn 4d | 3,126 | 2,036 | — |
| 5113 | bus cpe | 3,061 | 1,832 | — |
| 5114 | sdn 2d | 3,106 | 1,988 | — |
| 5115 | Traveler util sdn 4d | 3,270 | 2,134 | — |
| **K522 Virginian DeLuxe (wb 118.5)*** | | | | |
| 5120 | Traveler util sdn 2d | 3,285 | 2,192 | — |
| 5121 | sdn 4d | 3,171 | 2,143 | — |
| 5124 | sdn 2d | 3,151 | 2,095 | — |
| 5125 | Traveler util sdn 4d | 3,345 | 2,241 | — |
| 5127 | club cpe | 3,111 | 2,114 | — |
| **K521 DeLuxe (wb 118.5)** | | | | |
| 5211 | sdn 4d | 3,195 | 2,537 | 5,000** |
| 5214 | sdn 2d | 3,145 | 2,484 | 2,000** |
| 5215 | Traveler util sdn 4d | 3,369 | 2,643 | *** |
| 5217 | club cpe | 3,045 | 2,296 | 500** |
| **K522 Manhattan (wb 118.5)** | | | | |
| 5221 | sdn 4d | 3,220 | 2,654 | 16,500** |
| 5224 | sdn 2d | 3,185 | 2,601 | 2,000** |
| 5227 | club cpe | 3,185 | 2,622 | 500** |

* Total Virginian production: 5,579.
** Estimates based on extant vehicles. Total DeLuxe/Manhattan production: 26,552.
*** Actual production questionable.

| 1952 Engine | bore × stroke | bhp | availability |
|---|---|---|---|
| I-6, 226.2 | 3.31 × 4.38 | 115 | S-all |

## 1953

| K530 "Hardtop" Dragon (wb 118.5) | | Wght | Price | Prod |
|---|---|---|---|---|
| 5301 | sdn 4d | 3,320 | 3,924 | 1,277 |
| **K531 DeLuxe (wb 118.5)** | | Wght | Price | Prod |
| 5311 | sdn 4d | 3,200 | 2,513 | 5,800* |
| 5314 | sdn 2d | 3,150 | 2,459 | 1,500* |
| 5315 | Traveler util sdn 4d | 3,315 | 2,619 | 1,000* |
| **K532 Manhattan (wb 118.5)** | | | | |
| 5321 | sdn 4d | 3,265 | 2,650 | 15,450* |
| 5324 | sdn 2d | 3,235 | 2,597 | 2,500* |
| 5325 | Traveler util sdn 4d | 3,371 | 2,755 | ** |
| **K538 Carolina (wb 118.5)** | | | | |
| 5381 | sdn 4d | 3,185 | 2,373 | 1,400* |
| 5384 | sdn 2d | 3,135 | 2,313 | 400* |

| 1953 Engine | bore × stroke | bhp | availability |
|---|---|---|---|
| I-6, 226.2 | 3.31 × 4.38 | 118 | S-all |

* Estimates based on extant vehicles. Model-year production:

| K531 | DeLuxe | 7,883 |
|---|---|---|
| K532 | Manhattan | 17,957 |
| K538 | Carolina | 1,182 |

** One example found; volume production questionable.

## 1954

| 161 Darrin (wb 100.0) | | Wght | Price | Prod |
|---|---|---|---|---|
| 161 | conv rdstr | 2,175 | 3,668 | 435 |
| **K542 Manhattan (wb 118.5)** | | | | |
| 5421 | sdn 4d | 3,375 | 2,670 | 3,860* |
| 5424 | sdn 2d | 3,265 | 2,334 | 250* |
| **K545 Special, early (wb 118.5)** ** | | | | |
| 5451 | sdn 4d | 3,265 | 2,389 | 3,000* |
| 5454 | sdn 2d | 3,235 | 2,334 | 500* |
| **K545 Special, late (wb 118.5)** | | | | |
| 5451 | sdn 4d | 3,305 | 2,389 | 800* |
| 5454 | sdn 2d | 3,265 | 2,334 | 125* |

| 1954 Engines | bore × stroke | bhp | availability |
|---|---|---|---|
| I-6, 161.0 | 3.13 × 3.50 | 90 | S-Darrin |
| I-6, 226.2 | 3.31 × 4.38 | 118 | S-Special |
| I-6S, 226.2 | 3.31 × 4.38 | 140 | S-Manhattan |

* Estimates based on extant vehicles. Model year production:

| K542 | Manhattan | 4,110 |
|---|---|---|
| K545 | Special, early** | 3,500 |
| K545 | Special, late | 929 |

** Converted leftover 1953 Manhattans.

## 1955

| Manhattan (wb 118.5) | | Wght | Price | Prod |
|---|---|---|---|---|
| 51363 | sdn 4d (export) | 3,350 | — | 1,021 |
| 51367 | sdn 4d | 3,375 | 2,670 | 226 |
| 51467 | sdn 2d | 3,335 | 2,617 | 44 |

| 1955 Engine | bore × stroke | bhp | availability |
|---|---|---|---|
| I-6S, 226.2 | 3.31 × 4.38 | 140 | S-all |

# LaSalle

Cadillac's romantic companion make stemmed from the desire of legendary General Motors president Alfred P. Sloan to offer a car for every pocketbook, the basic philosophy that made GM the giant it is today. In the mid-'20s, Sloan detected a price gap between Buick and Cadillac, and assigned the latter to fill it with a second model line. The division chose the name LaSalle, honoring another French explorer like Cadillac, and introduced its junior series in 1927 on a wheelbase shorter than that of its senior cars. It was all part of the great period of expansion that brought forth a host of such cars to satisfy a market that looked like it would grow forever.

A big attraction of that first LaSalle was elegant body design by Harley Earl, a talented young West Coast designer reared in the "carriage trade," whom Sloan hired specifically to shape the new line. LaSalle amply fulfilled GM's hopes, and launched Earl on an illustrious 30-year career as the company's dean of design. In its first year, LaSalle accounted for 25 percent of Cadillac sales. By 1929, it was outselling its big sister.

In the Depression-racked '30s, LaSalle provided the sales volume that helped Cadillac survive. Though the division's total yearly production rarely exceeded Packard's, LaSalle's share was often substantial and sometimes critical. In rock-bottom

**1931 Series 345A town sedan**

**1933 Series 345C town coupe**

**1931 Series 345A sedan for five passengers**

**1935 Series 50 two-door touring sedan**

**1932 Series 345B convertible coupe**

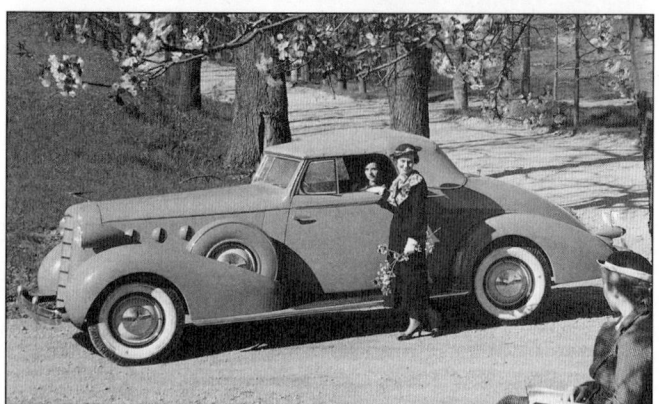
**1935 Series 50 convertible coupe for two passengers**

# LaSalle

1936 Series 50 four-door touring sedan

1937 Series 50 four-door touring sedan

1940 Special touring sedan

1940 Series 52 Special convertible sedan

two coupes, two four-door sedans, a convertible coupe, and a pair of seven-passenger sedans in the $2500-$3000 range. Up in the $2400-$4000 area were six semicustom styles by Fleetwood, another respected GM-acquired coachbuilder: a roadster, two phaetons, a seven-seat touring, and two five-passenger sedans. By comparison, 1930 Cadillac prices started at $3295 and went to more than $10,800.

Not surprisingly for a Cadillac product, LaSalle bowed with a V-8, a 303-cubic-inch unit making close to 80 horsepower. This was bored out for 1928 to 328 cid and 86 bhp. To match the increased size and weight of the 1930 models, the V-8 was enlarged once more, this time to 340 cid, good for 90 bhp.

LaSalle styling in 1930 still owed much to Earl's original 1927 concepts: low silhouette, long and sweeping "clamshell" fenders, a tall and round-shouldered radiator inspired by that of the fabled Hispano-Suiza, and two-tone paint, then a novelty. The most obvious change for 1930 was a taller radiator that enhanced an already impressive styling package. The public continued to buy, and LaSalle recorded model-year production of some 15,000. Though that was about 75 percent of Cadillac's volume, it was nonetheless respectable in the aftermath of the Wall Street crash.

The fast-deepening Depression forced Cadillac to adopt cost-cutting measures for 1931-33. As a result, the 1931 Series 345A gained the senior line's 95-bhp 353 V-8, while that year's Cadillac Eights were put on the LaSalle chassis. Power improved to 115 for 1932-33. Model choices remained broadly the same for '31, then reduced for the 345B- and C-series of 1932-33, when seven-passenger sedans were upgraded to a 136-inch chassis and standard models were demoted to a 130-inch platform.

LaSalle prices were also reduced in 1931-33—down to $2200-$2800. Though that was about $500 below Cadillac Eights, the latter evidently looked like better buys, for they matched LaSalle in sales and actually beat the junior line in '31. LaSalle volume was well down anyway, dropping from 10,000 to just under 3400 for '32; the 1933 total was scarcely better.

Seeking to turn things around, Cadillac issued an all-new 1934 Series 350 with a look exclusive to LaSalle. Prices were again slashed, this time to $1000 under the senior Eights. Models were also slashed, leaving just a coupe, four-door sedan, club sedan, and convertible coupe. All rode a trim 119-inch wheelbase shared with Oldsmobile, as were basic bodyshells. Still cutting costs, Cadillac replaced LaSalle's V-8 with a 240.3-cid Olds L-head straight eight, albeit with Cadillac-supplied aluminum pistons and other changes. Still, horsepower withered to 95. But "Knee-Action" independent front suspension was a new talking point, and a first at GM (shared with Olds). Stylewise, the transitional 1933 look gave way to full streamlining, highlighted by a rounded grille and curious portholes on the hood sides.

This design/price formula persisted for two more years, but it didn't work well enough and sales remained well below those of rival junior editions. Still, LaSalle improved from just under 7200 for 1934 to over 8600 for the eight-model 1935 range, then to 13,000 for 1936, when offerings were again trimmed to four. Prices for '36 were the lowest ever: $1175 for the two-passenger coupe, $1255 for the convertible coupe. Interim changes included a 105-bhp 248 option for '35 that was made standard for '36, plus the phasing-in of "trunkback" sedans to replace outmoded trunkless styles. All LaSalles were designated Series 50 from 1935 to '39.

Cadillac tried a new formula for 1937, making LaSalles much like its 1936 Series 60—predictable perhaps, given the high success of that low-priced senior line. Power came from the same new 125-bhp 322 "monobloc" V-8, and deftly revised styling on

1933, for example, Cadillac's model-year output slid to 6700 units, but LaSalle accounted for fully half of it. In 1937, when Cadillac built 46,000 cars, 32,000 were LaSalles. Even so, LaSalle sales never really satisfied GM managers, who wanted much more.

The 1930 LaSalles, designated Series 340, followed general industry thinking of the times in being longer, heavier, and more expensive than the 1929 offerings. Wheelbase was now 134 inches as all models were put on the "long" chassis, and the original 125-inch "standard" platform was dropped. As before, the mainstay sellers carried bodies from the Fisher Brothers concern acquired by GM some years earlier. These comprised

# LaSalle

a unique 124-inch wheelbase made LaSalles arguably more attractive than that year's Caddys. Buyers responded, and LaSalle sales reached a record 32,000 for the model year. Few major changes occurred for 1938, but a four-door sedan with a sliding-steel "Sunshine Turret Roof" joined the existing two-and four-door sedans, convertible sedan, and rumble-seat coupe and convertible. Sadly, a short but sharp recession shrank sales by half, to the chagrin of GM accountants. LaSalle was floundering, yet its cars were still bargains at 1938 prices of $1300-$1900.

But Cadillac was determined, so LaSalle was completely reworked for 1939. The V-8 was untouched, but a new midrange GM B-body brought a smart new shape with greater glass area and no running boards (except on convertibles, where they were optional). Wheelbase, which was shared with senior Oldsmobiles, was trimmed to 120 inches (as for '36). Despite all this, output was disappointing once more: only about 21,000 for the model year.

The 1940 model year brought modified styling that marked a high point in LaSalle's 14-year history, plus the make's first two-series lineup in a decade. The design leader was the plush new Series 52 Special bearing Harley Earl's latest "torpedo" look. While Cadillacs retained bullet-pod headlamps on the hood sides, the 52's new sealed beams (shared with other 1940 Detroiters) moved down into the fenders. Body lines were gently rounded and clean, interiors were more spacious on a three-inch longer wheelbase, and windows became even larger. The trademark LaSalle grille arguably reached its pinnacle: still slimmer than Cadillac's but artfully shaped. Like the '39s, the 1940 models wore vertical brightwork in the "catwalk" areas between grille and headlamps (another Earl idea), but the catwalks were now wider and fully integrated with the fenders.

Along with the 1940 Series 50, the new 52 Special offered a coupe and four-door sedan, now with fully integral trunks. The 50s, which included a two-door sedan, retained the basic '39 appearance. Though boxy next to the new Specials, they were nonetheless attractive, with the longer wheelbase and smoother front. The season's most-elegant LaSalles were unquestionably the Special convertible coupe and sedan that arrived midyear. Minor changes added five horsepower to the 322 L-head V-8, lifting output to 130.

But by now, LaSalle had been crowded out of its once-exclusive price niche. True, its 1940 spread was fairly broad, running from the $1240 Series 50 coupe to the $1895 Special convertible sedan. But a genuine Series 62 Cadillac could be had for as little as $1685 that year; Buicks listed at $895-$2199. And although LaSalle accounted for almost two-thirds of Cadillac's total 1940 volume—24,130 out of some 37,000—it ranked only slightly ahead of Lincoln and remained far behind Packard. It now seemed more logical to offer a lower-priced Cadillac rather than a junior line with less prestige. The division did precisely that for 1941, replacing LaSalle with the new entry-level Cadillac, Series 61.

The decision to drop LaSalle ultimately proved correct. Spanning a $1350-$1535 range, the Series 61 sold 29,250 copies its first year, then was gradually outpaced by the costlier 62s. But the 61 remained in premium-price territory to prevent a cheapening of Cadillac's image. Postwar prosperity rendered it unnecessary after 1951. By that point, Cadillac had become America's luxury sales leader by far.

Before the decision to drop LaSalle, GM Styling had prepared a prototype 1941 design. A torpedo-style fastback four-door sedan, it was a pretty car with the traditional slim grille and "catwalk" fender trim, plus thin horizontal parking lights, spinner hubcaps, and a revival of the early LaSalle radiator badge—an "LaS" monogram in a circle.

Memories of LaSalle's distinction, refinement, and class continued to exert considerable magic within GM Design long after World War II, and the name popped up in connection with several projects that led some to believe a revival was imminent. The first of these were the "LaSalle II" hardtop sedan and two-seat roadster created for the 1955 Motorama. Though strictly for show, they wore grilles composed of vertical slats reminiscent of the 1940 catwalks, plus traditional LaSalle heraldry. The name surfaced again for what became the 1963 Buick Riviera, and only at the last minute was LaSalle rejected for Seville as the moniker for Cadillac's new compact sedan of mid-1975.

Will LaSalle ever be reborn? Probably not, but it's a nice thought.

## Specifications

### 1930—14,986 built

| 340 Fisher (wb 134.0) | Wght | Price | Prod |
|---|---|---|---|
| cpe 2P | 4,465 | 2,490 | — |
| conv cpe 2P | 4,435 | 2,590 | — |
| cpe 5P | 4,485 | 2,590 | — |
| sdn 4d | 4,465 | 2,565 | — |
| Town sdn 4d | 4,660 | 2,590 | — |
| sdn 7P | 4,745 | 2,775 | — |
| Imperial sdn 7P | 4,820 | 2,925 | — |
| **340 Fleetwood Custom (wb 134.0)** | | | |
| rdstr 2P | 4,340 | 2,450 | — |
| phtn 5P | 4,380 | 2,385 | — |
| touring 7P | 4,435 | 2,525 | — |
| phtn A/W 5P | 4,670 | 3,995 | — |
| sdnt cab 5P | 4,600 | 3,725 | — |
| sdnt 5P | 4,600 | 3,825 | — |

| 1930 Engine | bore × stroke | bhp | availability |
|---|---|---|---|
| V-8, 340.0 | 3.31 × 4.94 | 90 | S-all |

### 1931—10,095 built

| 345A (wb 134.0) | Wght | Price | Prod |
|---|---|---|---|
| rdstr 2-4P | 4,345 | 2,245 | — |
| touring 7P | 4,440 | 2,345 | — |
| cpe 2P | 4,470 | 2,195 | — |
| conv cpe 2P | 4,440 | 2,295 | — |
| cpe 5P | 4,490 | 2,295 | — |
| sdn 4d | 4,650 | 2,295 | — |
| Town sdn 4d | 4,665 | 2,345 | — |
| phtn A/W 5P | 4,675 | 3,245 | — |
| sdn 7P | 4,750 | 2,475 | — |
| Imperial sdn 7P | 4,825 | 2,595 | — |
| sdnt cab 5P | 4,675 | 3,245 | — |
| sdnt 5P | 4,650 | 3,245 | — |

| 1931 Engine | bore × stroke | bhp | availability |
|---|---|---|---|
| V-8, 353.0 | 3.38 × 4.94 | 95 | S-all |

### 1932—3,386 built

| 345B (wb 130.0); lwb-136.0 | Wght | Price | Prod |
|---|---|---|---|
| cpe 2P | 4,660 | 2,395 | — |

# LaSalle

| 345B (wb 130.0); lwb-136.0) | Wght | Price | Prod |
|---|---|---|---|
| conv cpe 2P | 4,630 | 2,545 | — |
| Town cpe 5P | 4,695 | 2,545 | — |
| sdn 4d | 4,840 | 2,495 | — |
| Town sdn 4d (lwb) | 4,895 | 2,645 | — |
| lwb sdn 7P | 5,025 | 2,645 | — |
| Imp 7P (lwb) | 5,065 | 2,795 | — |

| 1932 Engine | bore × stroke | bhp | availability |
|---|---|---|---|
| V-8, 353.0 | 3.38 × 4.94 | 115 | S-all |

## 1933—3,482 built

| 345C (wb 130.0; lwb-136.0) | Wght | Price | Prod |
|---|---|---|---|
| cpe 2P | 4,730 | 2,245 | — |
| conv cpe 2P | 4,675 | 2,395 | — |
| Town cpe 5P | 4,695 | 2,395 | — |
| sdn 4d | 4,805 | 2,245 | — |
| Town sdn 4d (lwb) | 4,915 | 2,495 | — |
| lwb sdn 7P | 4,990 | 2,495 | — |
| Imperial sdn 7P | 5,020 | 2,645 | — |

| 1933 Engine | bore × stroke | bhp | availability |
|---|---|---|---|
| V-8, 353.0 | 3.38 × 4.94 | 115 | S-all |

## 1934—7,195 built

| 350 (wb 119.0) | | Wght | Price | Prod |
|---|---|---|---|---|
| 6330S | sdn 4d | 3,960 | 1,695 | — |
| 633S | club sdn 5 | 3,960 | 1,695 | — |
| 6335 | conv cpe 2-4P | 3,780 | 1,695 | — |
| 6376 | cpe 2P | 3,815 | 1,595 | — |

| 1934 Engine | bore × stroke | bhp | availability |
|---|---|---|---|
| I-8, 240.3 | 3.00 × 4.25 | 95 | S-all |

## 1936—13,004 built

| Series 50 (wb 120.0) | | Wght | Price | Prod |
|---|---|---|---|---|
| 5011 | sdn 2d T/B | 3,605 | 1,185 | — |
| 5019 | sdn 4d T/B | 3,635 | 1,225 | — |
| 5067 | conv cpe 2-4P | 3,540 | 1,255 | — |
| 5077 | cpe 2P | 3,460 | 1,175 | — |

| 1936 Engine | bore × stroke | bhp | availability |
|---|---|---|---|
| I-8, 248.0 | 3.00 × 4.38 | 105 | S-all |

## 1935—8,651 built

| Series 50 (wb 119.0) | | Wght | Price | Prod |
|---|---|---|---|---|
| 6330S | sdn 4d | 3,960 | 1,545 | — |
| 633S | club sdn 5P | 3,960 | 1,545 | — |
| 6335 | conv cpe 2-4P | 3,780 | 1,545 | — |
| 6376 | cpe 2P | 3,185 | 1,445 | — |
| 35-5011 | sdn 2d T/B | 3,620 | 1,255 | — |
| 35-5019 | sdn 4d T/B | 3,650 | 1,295 | — |
| 35-5067 | conv cpe 2-4P | 3,510 | 1,325 | — |
| 35-5077 | cpe 2P | 3,475 | 1,225 | — |

| 1935 Engines | bore × stroke | bhp | availability |
|---|---|---|---|
| I-8, 240.3 | 3.00 × 4.25 | 95 | S-6300 series |
| I-8, 248.0 | 3.00 × 4.38 | 105 | S-5000 series |

## 1937—32,000 built*

| Series 50 (wb 124.0) | | Wght | Price | Prod |
|---|---|---|---|---|
| 5011 | sdn 2d T/B | 3,780 | 1,275 | — |
| 5019 | sdn 4d T/B | 3,810 | 1,320 | — |
| 5027 | cpe 2-4P opt seats | 3,675 | 1,155 | — |
| 5049 | conv sdn 5P | 3,850 | 1,680 | — |
| 5067 | conv cpe 2-4P | 3,715 | 1,350 | — |

* includes some commercial chassis on 160.0" wheelbase and some CKD.

| 1937 Engine | bore × stroke | bhp | availability |
|---|---|---|---|
| V-8, 322.0 | 3.38 × 4.50 | 125 | S-all |

## 1938

| Series 50 (wb 124.0) | | Wght | Price | Prod |
|---|---|---|---|---|
| 5011 | sdn 2d T/B | 3,800 | 1,345 | 700 |
| 5019 | sdn 4d T/B | 3,830 | 1,385 | 9,993 |
| 5019A | Sunroof sdn 4d T/B | 3,850 | 1,435 | 72 |
| 5027 | cpe 2-4P opt seats | 3,745 | 1,295 | 2,710 |
| 5029 | conv sdn 5P | 3,870 | 1,825 | 265 |
| 5067 | conv cpe 2-4P | 3,735 | 1,420 | 855 |
|  | chassis | — | — | 80 |

| 1938 Engine | bore × stroke | bhp | availability |
|---|---|---|---|
| V-8, 322.0 | 3.38 × 4.50 | 125 | S-all |

## 1939

| Series 50 (wb 120.0) | | Wght | Price | Prod |
|---|---|---|---|---|
| 5011 | sdn 2d T/B | 3,710 | 1,280 | 977 |
| 5011A | Sunroof sdn 2d T/B | 3,780 | 1,320 | 23 |
| 5019 | sdn 4d T/B | 3,740 | 1,320 | 15,928 |
| 5019A | Sunroof sdn 4d T/B | 3,810 | 1,380 | 404 |
| 5027 | cpe 2-4P, opt seats | 3,635 | 1,240 | 2,525 |
| 5029 | conv sdn 5P | 3,780 | 1,800 | 185 |
| 5067 | conv cpe 2-4P | 3,715 | 1,395 | 1,056 |
|  | chassis | — | — | 29 |

| 1939 Engine | bore × stroke | bhp | availability |
|---|---|---|---|
| V-8, 322.0 | 3.38 × 4.50 | 125 | S-all |

## 1940

| 40-50 (wb 123.0) | | Wght | Price | Prod |
|---|---|---|---|---|
| 5011 | sdn 2d | 3,760 | 1,280 | 375 |
| 5019 | sdn 4d | 3,790 | 1,320 | 6,722 |
| 5027 | cpe, A/S | 3,700 | 1,240 | 1,527 |
| 5029 | conv sdn | 4,000 | 1,800 | 125 |
| 5067 | conv cpe | 3,805 | 1,395 | 599 |
| 50 | chassis | — | — | 1,032 |

| 40-52 Special (wb 123.0) | | Wght | Price | Prod |
|---|---|---|---|---|
| 5219 | sdn 4d | 3,900 | 1,440 | 10,250 |
| 5227 | cpe | 3,810 | 1,380 | 3,000 |
| 5229 | conv sdn | 4,110 | 1,895 | 75 |
| 5267 | conv cpe | 3,915 | 1,535 | 425 |

| 1940 Engine | bore × stroke | bhp | availability |
|---|---|---|---|
| V-8, 322.0 | 3.38 × 4.50 | 130 | S-all |

# Lincoln

Lincoln and Cadillac had a common founder: the stern, patrician Henry Martyn Leland, "Master of Precision." Leland and his associates formed Cadillac in 1902 from the remains of the Henry Ford Company—which is why his first Cadillac and the first production Ford, both named Model A, are so similar. William C. Durant bought Cadillac in 1909 for his burgeoning General Motors. Leland, meantime, went off to build Liberty aircraft engines during World War I. Then, with son Wilfred, he returned to the car business by forming Lincoln—named for the U.S. president, one of his heroes. When this enterprise ran into financial trouble, Leland came full circle by selling out to Henry Ford in 1922.

At first, Ford Motor Company did little to alter or update the Lincoln Model L that Leland had designed around 1920. Powered by a 385-cid V-8 with 90 horsepower, it was beautifully built and handsomely furnished. But by 1930 it was an anachronism: unfashionably upright and sluggish next to contemporary Cadillacs, Packards, and Chrysler Imperials.

Then Henry and son Edsel brought forth the 1931 Model K (why they went backward in the alphabet remains a mystery).

Its new 145-inch-wheelbase chassis carried a modernized, 120-bhp V-8 that retained "fork-and-blade" rods and three-piece cast-iron block/crankcase assembly, Leland engineering features that let ads dwell lovingly on its "precision-built" quality.

The new chassis was massive, with nine-inch-deep side rails and six cross members with cruciform bracing. Like the L, the K employed torque-tube drive and a floating rear axle. Other features included worm and roller steering, hydraulic shocks by Houdaille, and mechanical brakes by Bendix. Stylewise, a slightly peaked radiator led a far longer hood, punctuated by twin-trumpet horns and bowl-shaped headlamps. The K was also longer, lower, and sleeker than the L, and it offered an improved ride, greater stability and, with its extra power, faster acceleration and higher top speed.

The K-chassis had been designed for an all-new V-12 that arrived for 1932 in a new KB-Series. This was a smooth 448-cid engine with 150 bhp—Ford's answer to the 12- and 16-cylinder giants from Cadillac, Packard, and others. The V-12 provided better performance than the K's V-8, yet KBs sold for slightly less and came in a wider range of body types. A magnificent

**1930 Series L 3-window town sedan**

**1931 Series K sport phaeton**

**1932 Series KB convertible sedan by Dietrich**

**1933 Series KB 2-window Berline by Judkins**

**1935 3-window Berline by Judkins**

**1935 Series K convertible sedan by Brunn**

# Lincoln

1936 Series K 3-window four-door sedan

1936 Lincoln-Zephyr four-door sedan

1939 Continental ("Special Lincoln-Zephyr")

1939 Series K LeBaron convertible sedan

1940 Lincoln-Zephyr Continental cabriolet

around-town car and a fast open-road tourer, the KB was an extraordinary machine that stood far above most contemporary cars.

Accompanying the 1932 V-12 was the V-8 KA-Series on a 136-inch wheelbase. Its chassis was dimensionally the same as the old Model L's but structurally equal to the new KB's. The bodies were less lavishly furnished than on 12-cylinder models, but the KA was high-class, not a middle-priced product. Still, this V-8 wasn't as smooth as the engines from Cadillac, Packard, or Pierce-Arrow.

That changed the following year when the KA received a smaller bore 381.7-cid V-12 with the same 125 bhp as the departed V-8. This was also installed in the shorter Lincoln chassis, topped by Murray-built bodies made of wood, steel, and aluminum. KB continued as the senior line.

Meantime, the artistic Edsel Ford had been transforming Lincoln styling, updating the standard factory-built bodies, and securing a plethora of custom and semicustom styles from the cream of America's coachbuilders, including Brunn, Dietrich, Judkins, LeBaron, Murphy, and Willoughby. The result was some of the finest expressions of Classic-era design. A cautious move toward streamlining, begun with the 1932 models, was more evident on the '33s, which wore a rakish vee'd radiator with a chrome grille concealing vertical shutters. Also new that year were hood louvers (replacing shutters), drawn-down "skirted" fenders, vee'd front bumper, and redesigned trunk racks.

With sales slow in the Depression-ravaged market, Lincoln consolidated for 1934 around a single 414-cid V-12, a bored-out KA unit with the same 150 bhp as the old 448. Differences included aluminum cylinder heads and 6.3:1 compression. The latter was unheard of at the time, but made possible by the advent of 70-octane gasoline, which was nearly as potent as contemporary aviation fuel.

Most 1934 Lincolns could reach 95 mph, helped by the 414's wider rev range compared to the 448. Chassis specs were virtually unchanged, but Murray custom bodies were eliminated and radiators were now lacquered in body color. Smaller headlamps, parking lamps, and color-matched metal spare-tire covers helped clean up the appearance. Sedans and limousines also received sloped tails, fairly radical for the day. Like Pierce, Packard, and Stutz, Lincoln was reluctant to abandon the graceful "oh gee" fenders so characteristic of the period—but it would after 1935.

By that point, big-Lincoln engineering was in the essential form it would carry through 1940. The slightly smoother-looking 1935s were all called Model K and a vast array of body types was still available on the previous two wheelbases. Semi-teardrop fenders appeared for '36, along with a simpler radiator, new disc wheels, and larger hubcaps.

The 1937s emphasized absolute styling simplicity, possibly influenced by the Cord 810. Headlamps were integrated into the fenders, belt moldings were erased, and doors were extended down almost to the running boards. Spare tires lived within new built-in trunk compartments (unless sidemounts were ordered), and factory bodies received their first vee'd windshields. As ever, standard Model K interiors were done with rich broadcloth and curly-maple garnish moldings; rarer woods and fabrics were available in custom styles. The V-12 gained hydraulic lifters and moved further forward, which improved ride. Nominal horsepower remained 150, but post-1936 models probably had more because of a different cam contour. A synchromesh transmission was also new for '37.

The lush luxury-car market of the '20s had long since dried up in the economic drought of the '30s, and Lincoln suffered as much as any premium make. Sales hovered around 3500 annu-

# Lincoln

ally from 1930 through '33, dropping by about half in 1934. After '34, the K-Series would see no more than 2000 units per year; by 1940 it was available only by special order, built on chassis completed during 1939. (The largest of these, the 160-inch-wheelbase "Sunshine Special," served as the parade car of presidents Roosevelt and Truman.)

What pulled Lincoln through the Depression was the Zephyr. It burst on the scene for 1936 as a medium-price product of the sort Cadillac and Packard also relied upon for survival but was far more advanced. Its major design concepts evolved from a series of radical unit-body prototypes designed by John Tjaarda along aircraft principles and built with help from Briggs Manufacturing Company, eager to win some volume body business from Lincoln. Tjaarda's original design featured a rear-engine layout, but this was switched to a conventional front-engine/rear-drive format.

The rest of the Zephyr was unconventional. Tjaarda claimed it was the first car in which aircraft-type stress analysis proved the superiority of unit construction. Indeed, at around 3300 pounds, the Zephyr emerged lighter than Chrysler's body-on-frame Airflow yet was much stiffer. Best of all, unit construction offered important cost savings.

A modified Ford flathead V-8 with about 100 bhp was initially slated, but company president Edsel Ford decided that, as a Lincoln, the Zephyr had to have a V-12. As the existing 414 was too large for this smaller package, engineer Frank Johnson, one the ablest in the industry, was told to add four cylinders to the Ford V-8. But because of cost pressures, the resulting V-12 was not outstanding. A four-main-bearing L-head unit with 267 cid, it employed a "monobloc" casting similar to the V-8s, with an exhaust cored between the cylinders. The initial horsepower was not that impressive at only 110. The rest of the drivetrain was also derived from Ford V-8 components.

Production Zephyr styling was similar to that of Tjaarda's prototypes, but a pointy rear-hinged "alligator" hood and matching vee'd radiator were grafted on under Edsel's direction by Ford stylist E. T. "Bob" Gregorie. The changes made for a much prettier car than either Tjaarda's prototypes or the curved-nose Airflow, yet the essential shape remained more slippery than the Airflow's even though it wasn't "styled in the wind tunnel" like portions of the Chrysler design.

Briggs built most of the Zephyr. Ford only installed the drivetrain, added front sheetmetal, and saw to trimming and painting. Edsel laughingly told Tjaarda that Briggs might as well build the whole thing, as the Zephyr assembly line was only 40 feet long!

Designated Model H, the Zephyr bowed as a two- and four-door sedan on a 122-inch wheelbase. Prices were attractive at around $1300 and performance was at least decent. Top speed was over 87 mph, and a 4.33:1 rear axle, chosen for low-end acceleration over all-out speed, made for 0-50 mph in 10.8 seconds and 30-50 mph in six seconds flat. Yet mileage consistently averaged 16-18 miles per gallon. With all this, the Zephyr was an immediate hit. Nearly 15,000 were sold for '36, better than 80 percent of Lincoln's total model-year output. That boosted the make to 18th on the industry production card—the first time Lincoln broke into the top 20. Sales for the 1937 HB models came to nearly 30,000 despite few changes, though a three-passenger coupe and division-window Town Limousine were added.

The 1938 Zephyrs bowed with a three-inch-longer wheelbase and revised styling announced by a "mouth organ" grille that beat everyone to the next design trend: the horizontal front-end format. Model offerings expanded again with new two- and four-door convertibles. A Custom interior option provided additional variations for 1939. A deep recession limited 1938 sales

1940 Lincoln-Zephyr 3-passenger coupe

1941 Continental cabriolet

1942 Custom limousine 8-passenger

1942 Continental cabriolet

1947 Continental club coupe

# Lincoln

1947 Continental club coupe

1950 Lincoln sport sedan four-door

1947 Lincoln convertible coupe

1951 Cosmopolitan sport sedan four-door

1949 Cosmopolitan convertible coupe

1951 Lincoln sport sedan four-door

1949 Cosmopolitan town sedan fastback

1951 Cosmopolitan Capri coupe

1950 Cosmopolitan sport sedan four-door

1951 Lincoln Lido coupe

# Lincoln

to just over 19,000—though that was still some 5500 more than Cadillac managed with LaSalle. The '39 total was more encouraging at nearly 21,000, but might have been higher had it not been for intramural competition from the new medium-priced Mercury.

Zephyr mechanical alterations before 1940 followed those of other Ford Motor Company cars. Old Henry's stubbornness precluded hydraulic brakes until '39. An optional two-speed Columbia rear axle came along, reducing engine speed 28 percent in its higher cruising ratio. The V-12 was modified to cure several persistent problems. Water passages, for example, proved inadequate, leading to overheating, bore warpage, and excessive ring wear. Inadequate crankcase ventilation created oil sludge buildup, and oil flow was poor. Yet despite the addition of hydraulic valve lifters for 1938 and cast-iron heads after '41, the powerplant never shed its poor reliability image. Had World War II not intervened, it might have been fully reengineered. But it wasn't, and many collector/owners have since replaced the V-12 with L-head or later overhead-valve V-8s.

With no change in wheelbase or basic appearance, Zephyr was fully rebodied for 1940, gaining sealed-beam headlamps, larger windows and trunk, bodysides that bulged out to cover running boards, and a more-conventional dash. A larger bore brought the V-12 to 292 cid and 120 bhp. The slow-selling convertible sedan was discarded. Among Custom-interior closed models was a special five-passenger "town limousine," a four-door sedan conversion by Briggs. Brunn also built 10 Zephyr town cars in 1940-41 (three of which went to the Ford family); all were heavy-looking rigs with rooflines that didn't match well with the chiseled lower body. Zephyr production again inched upward, reaching just over 21,750.

But Lincoln had bigger 1940 news. It was, of course, the Zephyr-based Continental, one of the most-stunning automobiles of all time. Though executed by Gregorie, its styling was conceived by Edsel Ford, who directed him to make it "thoroughly continental," complete with outside spare tire—hence the name. It originated in a one-off convertible that Edsel used on his annual winter vacation in Palm Beach during 1938-39. Everyone who saw it thought it sensational, which encouraged Ford to offer production models scarcely a year later. A coupe and cabriolet debuted at about $2850 and brought customers into Lincoln dealerships by the thousands.

Continental was thus duly broken out from the Zephyr line for 1941, and received its own badges. Model-year production increased from 404 to 1250. Meantime, Lincoln maintained a semblance of K-Series coachbuilt tradition with a Zephyr-based Custom sedan and limousine on a 138-inch wheelbase. But at about $2800, only 650 were called for. The Briggs town limo was scratched for '41, but other Zephyrs returned with minor mechanical improvements, including power tops for convertibles and optional Borg-Warner overdrive in place of the two-speed Columbia axle. Styling changes were slight: fender-mounted parking/turn-indicator lights and, for Continentals, pushbutton exterior door releases (replacing handles). In all, Lincoln built about 18,250 cars for the last full model year before World War II.

War-shortened 1942 brought significant engineering and design changes. A more-reliable V-12 bored out to 305 cid yielded 10 additional horsepower, and a flashy facelift forecast immediate postwar styling. All models now had longer and higher fenders, a busy two-tier horizontal-bar grille, and headlamps flanked by parking lights on either side. Overall height was a bit lower, curb weights a bit higher. Lincoln built 6547 of these cars by early February 1942, when the government ordered a halt to civilian production for the duration.

Despite the dictates of war, Ford stylists found time to experiment with postwar designs in hundreds of renderings and dozens of scale models. Most involved the "bathtub" look that materialized on several makes for 1948-49. Some Lincoln concepts bordered on the grotesque. Many looked as if they'd been "carved out of a bar of soap," as one stylist put it.

Like most other makes, Lincoln resumed peacetime production with warmed-over '42 models that would not change much through 1948. However, the prewar Customs and three-passenger coupe did not come back, and the Zephyr name was abandoned for just plain Lincoln. Curiously, the V-12 reverted to its pre-1942 displacement, but produced only five fewer horses (125). Custom interiors were still available for closed standard-model Lincolns.

The main design difference between 1946 and '42 was grillework composed of vertical and horizontal bars, with a Lincoln emblem in the upper segment, plus a new winged-globe hood ornament. The 1947s carried "Lincoln" lettering on the hubcaps, plus pullout door handles, "pocket" interior armrests, and a hood ornament with a longer wing. There were no changes for 1948.

Lincoln's first new postwar cars arrived in mid-1948, but a Continental wasn't among them. One had been planned but was shelved due to low projected sales. It would have been ponderous anyway, and some Ford designers, respectful of the late Edsel Ford (who died in 1943) were thankful it didn't appear.

Concentrating instead on high-volume models, Lincoln issued two series for 1949: a 121-inch-wheelbase standard line and the costlier 125-inch Cosmopolitan. The former, sharing basic bodyshells with that year's new Mercury, comprised sedan, coupe, and convertible body styles; Cosmo added a Town Sedan, a massive six-window fastback. The aged V-12 was replaced at last by a 152-bhp 337-cid L-head V-8 originally designed for Ford trucks. Overdrive was a $96 extra.

Dearborn's original '49 planning called for a 118-inch-wheelbase Ford and a 121-inch Mercury. What emerged as the Cosmopolitan was conceived as a Zephyr. At the last minute, Ford's policy committee, led by Ernest Breech and Harold Youngren, mandated a smaller 114-inch-wheelbase Ford, so the proposed Mercury became the '49 standard Lincoln and the 118-inch Ford was made a Mercury—hence the latter's change from "senior Ford" to "junior Lincoln" in this period. The ex-Mercury Lincolns were thus much cheaper than the Cosmos, spanning a $2500-$3100 range versus $3200-$3950.

Predictably, given its wartime design exercises, Lincoln's '49 styling was of the "bar-of-soap" school but clean and dignified nonetheless. Fadeaway front fenderlines marked base models; Cosmos had fully flush fenders plus one-piece (instead of two-piece) windshields, broad chrome gravel deflectors over the front wheel arches, and thin window frames. All models wore conservative grilles, sunken headlamps (glass covers were planned), and "frenched" taillamps. Model-year volume set a record at 73,507 units.

Lincoln's first new postwar generation continued for the next two years with no major alteration. However, offerings were shuffled for 1950, as the standard convertible and the fat-looking Cosmo Town Sedan were deleted. This left a notchback coupe and a four-door Sport Sedan (with throwback "suicide" rear doors) in each series, plus a Cosmopolitan convertible. There were also two newcomers for 1950: the $2721 Lido and $3406 Cosmo Capri. These were limited-edition coupes with custom interiors and padded canvas tops offered in lieu of a true pillarless hardtop like Cadillac's 1949 Coupe de Ville. Few were sold through 1951. All 1950 Lincolns sported a restyled dashboard by chief designer Tom Hibbard. It was an attractive rolled design with an oblong instrument cluster, a format that would continue through 1957. A self-shifting Hydra-Matic trans-

1952 Capri hardtop coupe

1955 Capri hardtop coupe

1953 Capri hardtop coupe

1955 Capri sedan with air conditioning

1954 Capri convertible coupe

1955 Capri convertible coupe

mission, bought from arch rival GM, arrived as a new 1950 option; it would be standard in 1952-54. The '51 models were spruced up by longer rear fenders with upright taillamps (versus the previous round units), plus a simpler grille and different wheel covers.

While not known for performance, Lincoln had enough of the right stuff to place ninth in the 1950 *Carrera Panamericana*—the first of the legendary Mexican Road Races. Lincoln then won the 1951 Mobilgas Economy Run at an average 25.5 mpg. Neither of these feats helped sales, which were well down from the record in '49. The totals were just over 28,000 for 1950 and a more gratifying 32,500 for '51.

All Ford Motor Company cars were completely new for '52 but though sales rose—to nearly 41,000 by '53—Lincoln was still miles behind Cadillac. One problem may have been sedate, square styling through 1955: again very much like Mercury—and also Ford. Uniformity may have caused trouble, too, with the same five models through '54. Cosmopolitan became the lower series in this period, Capri the upper. Both listed four-door sedan and a belated hardtop coupe (three years behind Cadillac's); Capri added a convertible.

Nevertheless, 1952-54 was a significant period in Lincoln history. The most notable mechanical development was the make's first overhead-valve V-8: a new short-stroke design of 318 cid, good for 160 bhp at first and 205 bhp for 1953-54. It was superior in many ways. Its crankshaft, for example, had eight counterweights versus most competitors' six. Intake valves were oversized for better breathing and higher specific output. (Among '53 engines, it produced 0.64 bhp per cubic inch against 0.63 for Cadillac and 0.54 for the Chrysler Hemi.) The crankcase extended below the crankshaft centerline to form an extremely stiff shaft support, hence this engine's family nickname: "Y-block."

The 1952 model year also brought ball-joint front suspension to Lincoln. Together with the new V-8, it made for taut, powerful road machines that would dominate their class in the Mexican Road Race. Other new features included recirculating-ball power steering, oversized drum brakes, liberal sound insulation, optional four-way power seat and, with the extra-cost factory air conditioning, flow-through ventilation (when the compressor was idle). Fabrics, leathers, and fit and finish were of a level that far exceeded conventional Ford products.

Despite a rather short 123-inch wheelbase, the 1952-54 Lincolns were roomier inside than previous models—and some later ones. Visibility was better than on any other contemporary U.S. car save Kaiser, and exteriors were notably free of period excesses. Fluted taillamps shed water and dirt, just like those Mercedes would adopt in the '70s.

Lincoln turned in some spectacular performances at the *Carrera Panamericana*—virtually unrivaled in the International Standard Class. Lincolns took the first five places in 1952, the top four in '53, and first and second in 1954. Major credit for race preparation goes to Clay Smith, a gifted mechanic who was tragically killed in a pit accident in 1954. Of great

# Lincoln

help were publicity-conscious Dearborn engineers who supplied stiff "export" suspension pieces, Ford truck camshafts, mechanical valve lifters, special front spindles and hubs, and rear-axle ratios that enabled a "stock" Lincoln to top 130 mph. The 1952 race winner, Chuck Stevenson, finished the 2000-mile grind from Juarez to the Guatemala border nearly an hour ahead of the Ferrari that had won the year before.

Lincoln wasn't ready with a total redesign for 1955, so its cars were among the most conservative in that banner Detroit sales year despite an extensive facelift. Still, they were crisp, clean, and elegant. Though the wrapped windshield held sway most everywhere else, the '55 Lincolns didn't have one, and were thus more practical. Interiors remained luxurious combinations of high-quality fabrics and top-grain leather.

Wheelbase was unchanged for '55, but the restyle added extra sheetmetal (mostly in back) and 50-100 pounds in curb weight. A good thing, then, that the V-8 was bored to 341 cid and gained 20 horsepower. Elsewhere, Cosmopolitan was retagged Custom, and Lincoln finally offered its own automatic, called Turbo Drive. It was basically the four-year-old Ford/Merc-O-Matic transmission enlarged and strengthened to withstand the greater torque of Lincoln's V-8. But likely because its '55s weren't "new" enough, Lincoln was one of the few makes to suffer in Detroit's best sales season of the decade, dropping from nearly 37,000 for '54 to a bit over 27,000.

The '56s were new—really new. Though ads proclaimed them "Unmistakably Lincoln," there was scarcely a trace of the trim '55s. Wheelbase grew three inches, overall length seven inches, width three inches. Capri now signified the lower series, Premiere the costlier one. Body-style assignments were unchanged, though pillared four-doors were made to look much like hardtops. Styling, partly previewed by the 1954 Mercury XM-800 show car, was fully up to date, with wrapped windshield, clean grille, and peaked headlamps. Rakish vertical taillights capped long exhaust ports located on either side of a "grille" motif that duplicated the design of the front. Ornamentation was simple, with two-toning confined to the roof.

Matching the new '56 styling was a bigger engine, a Y-block enlarged to 368 cid and 285 bhp. "True power," blared the ads, "that works for your safety at every speed." Despite their greater bulk, the '56s didn't weigh much more than the '55s. But they cost a whopping $500-$700 more, the range thus running from $4120 to about $4750. Yet as the only make with a major restyle instead of a mere facelift, Lincoln did well for '56, moving more than 50,000 cars. Still, even that was only about a third of Cadillac's total.

Prices rose another $500-$700 for 1957, when Lincoln joined a popular Detroit trend by offering its first four-door hardtops, dubbed "Landau," one in each series. Huge tailfins sprouted, and the front gained "Quadra-Lites": conventional seven-inch-diameter headlamps above 5¾-inch "road" lamps. Though not a true four-light system, it put Lincoln ahead of most rivals. Compression went to 10:1, horsepower to 300. Overall, 1957 was a good, but not great, Lincoln year. At just over 41,000, model-year volume was slightly higher than Imperial's but less than a third of Cadillac's.

Lincoln pinned hopes for 1958 on yet another all-new design. But '58 proved to be a horrible year for Detroit and a devastating one for Ford's finest, considering the millions invested in new tooling. A flash recession sent the economy reeling and buyers rushing off to buy more-economical cars as industry sales fell 50 percent from 1957. Ford trailed Chevrolet by a quarter-million units, Edsel began its rapid slide to nowhere, and Mercury ran 46 percent behind its '57 pace. Lincoln's new '58s were longer, lower, and wider in a year when even luxury-

1956 Premiere hardtop coupe

1956 Premiere four-door sedan with air conditioning

1957 Capri four-door sedan

1957 Premiere convertible coupe

1958 Capri Landau hardtop sedan

# Lincoln

**1959 Premiere four-door sedan**

**1960 Lincoln Landau hardtop sedan**

**1960 Continental Mark V hardtop sedan**

**1961 Continental four-door sedan**

**1961 Continental convertible sedan**

car buyers were starting to think about more-sensible size. As a result, model-year production tumbled.

At the bottom of this avalanche was a square-lined unibody giant on a 131-inch wheelbase stretching six inches longer overall than the '57 Lincoln. It was easily recognized, for there was nothing else like it: heavily sculptured sides, a wide grille flanked by true quad headlamps in garish slanted recesses, and gigantic flared bumpers. Under a hood not much smaller than a Ping-Pong table was 1958's largest American passenger-car engine: a new big-block 430-cid V-8 making 375 bhp.

Of course, this package had been conceived in the far healthier market of 1955. And recession or not, most luxury buyers still wanted big cars like this. What's more, despite appearances and 2½-ton curb weights, the '58 Lincolns were surprisingly quick in a straight line and not that clumsy in curves. But they were too big and ornate for a public that had suddenly turned against such blatant excess. Cadillac attracted more customers with a heavy facelift, and Imperial gained sales with a mild restyle of its finned wonders from '57. Both rivals also had lately expanded offerings, and comparable '58 Cadillacs cost several hundred dollars less than Lincolns. No wonder 1958 was a debacle for Dearborn's prestige make. At least it ushered in a three-year program that would culminate in a more-compact—and vastly more-successful—new Lincoln for 1961.

Meantime, there was nothing to do but offer more of the same, so both Lincolns and Continentals changed little for '59. The Premiere convertible had been transferred to the related but distinct 1958 Continental Mark III line, leaving a four-door sedan and two- and four-door hardtops in the Capri and Premiere series. All returned for '59, when Continental was absorbed as a Lincoln subseries and the Capri name was changed to simply Lincoln.

It bears mentioning that although the 1956-57 Mark II and 1958 Mark III were products of a separate Continental Division, and thus "non-Lincolns," all later Marks and Continentals are properly regarded as Lincolns. The reason is the collapse of Ford's grand plan for a GM-like five-division structure following the '58 recession, and the particular failure of Edsel and the Mark II to make their hoped-for market impressions. The Continental marque was thus merged with Lincoln for the 1959 model year. In January of 1958, both Edsel and Mercury Divisions were folded in to form a short-lived M-E-L structure as a cost-cutting move. Ford's upper division then reverted to its original status as just plain Lincoln-Mercury, which it retains to this day.

The '59 Mark IV was just a facelifted Mark III but offered a new formal-roof Town Car and limousine priced about the same as the short-lived $10,000 Mark II. Likewise, '59 Lincolns were lightly touched-up '58s. Horsepower was reduced to 350 for all models in a faint sop to a now mileage-minded public. Though the division desperately held prices close to previous levels—$4900-$5500 for Lincolns and Premieres, $6600-$7000 for standard Marks—Imperial surged ahead in 1959 model-year volume—and would win again the following year. Lincoln's '59 total was dismal at 15,780, plus 11,126 Mark IVs.

Lincoln and Continental styling was touched up again for 1960. Grilles gained new inserts, the massive front bumper guards moved inboard of the canted headlamps, and rear ends were reworked. Lincolns also sported a reshaped roofline and rear window, plus new full-length upper-body moldings. Horsepower dropped to 315. Prices stayed much the same, and standard equipment was as comprehensive as ever, but Lincoln sales withered to just under 14,000, though Continental held steady at about 11,000.

A much happier chapter opened for 1961 with an all-new "downsized" Continental. Replacing all the old behemoths, it

# Lincoln

bowed in just two models: a thin-pillar four-door sedan and America's first four-door convertible since the abortive Frazer Manhattan model of a decade before. Both rode a 123-inch wheelbase, same as on the trim mid-'50s Lincolns, and featured a '30s throwback in rear-hinged "suicide" back doors. Prices were in the middle of what had been Mark V territory: an announced $6067 for the hardtop, $6713 for the convertible.

With its classic beauty and superb engineering, the '61 was arguably the most-satisfying Lincoln since the V-12 K-Series. It was certainly one of the '60s best Detroit automobiles. Enhancing both its image and sales was fortuitous timing, arriving just as a youthful new First Family was occupying the White House. The new Continentals were soon seen in newspaper and magazine photos as the new Administration's transport of choice, personal and official, which is why these cars have since become known by some as the "Kennedy Lincolns."

Their chiseled good looks reflected the efforts of seven Ford stylists: Eugene Bordinat (corporate design chief), Don DeLaRossa, Elwood P. Engel, Gale L. Halderman, John Najjar, Robert M. Thomas, and George Walker. They were collectively honored by an award from the Industrial Design Institute—unusual, as the IDI rarely bothers with cars. But the '61 Lincoln, it said, was an "outstanding contribution of simplicity and design elegance." Interestingly, the basic cowl structure was shared with that year's revamped Ford Thunderbird, which halved tooling costs for two low-volume models even though the 'Bird was very different aft of the cowl and rode a 113-inch wheelbase.

The '61 introduced a basic Lincoln look that would continue into the late '80s. The original was naturally the purest: smooth, gently curved bodysides topped by straight-through fenderlines edged in bright metal; a modest grille with outboard horizontal quad headlamps; a simple tail (not unlike the Mark II's) with a back panel repeating the grille texture and taillamps set in the trailing edges of the fenders. All corners were easily seen from behind the wheel, handy for parking. Side windows that curved inward toward the top were a first for mass production, matched by a greenhouse with the greatest degree of "tumble-home" yet seen on a large American luxury car. Door glass would remain curved through '63, became flat for 1964-70, then became curved again. Unlike the old Frazer, the convertible sedan's window frames slid completely out of sight. So did its top, via 11 relays connecting mechanical and hydraulic linkages. (Much of that design stemmed from Ford engineering for the 1957-59 Skyliner "retrac" hardtops and 1958-60 Thunderbird convertibles.

Styling aside, these Lincolns were renowned for quality. This was mostly due to the efforts of Harold C. MacDonald, then chief engineer of Ford's Car and Truck Group. The '61s had the most-rigid unit body/chassis ever produced, the best sound insulation and shock damping in series production, and extremely close machining tolerances. The model year also brought an unprecedented number of long-life components, including a completely sealed electrical system, and superior rust and corrosion protection.

They also were the most thoroughly tested cars in Detroit history. Each engine—still a 430 V-8, though now detuned to 300 bhp—was run three hours on a dynamometer at 3500 rpm (equal to about 98 mph), torn down for inspection, then reassembled. Automatic transmissions were tested for 30 minutes before installation. Each car was given a final 12-mile road test and checked for nearly 200 individual items, after which an ultraviolet light was used to visualize a fluorescent dye in lubricants as a check for leaks. Backing these measures was an

1962 Continental convertible sedan

1964 Continental convertible sedan

1963 Continental convertible sedan

1965 Continental four-door sedan

unprecedented two-year, 24,000-mile warranty.

Response to the '61s was immediate and satisfying. Sales exceeded 25,000, and Lincoln surged ahead of Imperial for keeps. Styling changes for the second and third year were minimal, Lincoln having promised to concentrate on functional improvements, at least for awhile. The '62s had a tidier grille with narrowed central crossbar and headlamps no longer recessed; the '63s gained a finely checked grille, matching backpanel appliqué, and increased trunk space, plus engine tuning that yielded 20 additional horsepower.

Wheelbase grew to 126 inches for 1964, where it would stay through '69. But the essential look was unchanged. The main alterations, aside from the aforementioned flat door glass, were a slightly convex vertical-bar grille, broader rear window, and a lower-profile convertible top. The '65s received a horizontal grille motif, parking/turn-signal lights in the front fenders, and ribbed taillamps.

A body change for 1966 ushered in a revived two-door hardtop as Lincoln sought higher volume, the convertible having accounted for only 10 percent of sales. Body lines became less rectilinear as a slightly larger fender "hop-up" appeared just ahead of larger rear-wheel cutouts. An extended front added some five inches to overall length, the grille acquired fine horizontal bars and a bulged center section (carried through in the sheetmetal above), and the front bumper wrapped all the way back to the front wheel openings. The V-8 was bored and stroked to 462 cid and 340 bhp.

All this plus lower prices—as low as $5485 for the hardtop coupe—pushed 1966 Lincoln sales to nearly 55,000 cars, though that was still only 25 percent of Cadillac's model-year volume. A segmented grille, shuffled emblems and taillamps, and a spring-loaded hood emblem appeared for '67, when the convertible sedan made a final bow with only 2276 copies sold. Overall production remained strong, however, at over 45,500 for the model year.

Lincoln's most-intriguing development for 1968 was the $6585 Continental Mark III. This wasn't a revival of the leviathan '58 but the lineal successor to the matchless 1956-57 Mark II. It bore the personal stamp of company president Henry Ford II, just as his brother, William Clay, had influenced the Mark II and their father, Edsel, had hatched the original 1940 "Mark I." Why "Mark III" instead of the expected "Mark VI?" Because HF II didn't view the heavyweight 1958-60 Mark III/IV/V as true Continentals.

But this new one was true to its heritage, at least in spirit. The project had begun in late 1965 as a personal-luxury coupe with long-hood/short-deck proportions in the Continental tradition. Exterior styling was naturally supervised by corporate design chief Gene Bordinat. Hermann Brunn, scion of the great coachbuilding family and a member of Bordinat's staff, was chiefly responsible for the interior, endowing it with large, comfortable bucket seats and a woodgrained dash with easy-to-reach controls. Henry Ford II himself selected both the interior and exterior designs from numerous proposals submitted in early 1966.

The result was actually a structural cousin to the new-for-'67 Thunderbird sedan, set on the same 117.2-inch wheelbase (some nine inches shorter than the Mark II's). Overall length was identical with that of Cadillac's new 1967 front-drive Eldorado. Though slightly baroque, the Mark III was handsome, helped by America's longest hood—more than six feet. It also offered a wide choice of luxury interiors and 26 exterior colors, including four special "Moondust" metallic paints. The 1969-71 models cost a fair bit more: ultimately over $8800. Standard equipment ran to Select-Shift Turbo-Drive automatic, power brakes (discs in front, drums in back), concealed headlamps,

1966 Continental coupe hardtop

1966 Continental convertible sedan

1967 Continental four-door sedan

ventless door windows, power seats and windows, flow-through ventilation, and 150 pounds of sound insulation. Beneath that long hood lurked a new 460 cid V-8—one of Detroit's largest—with 10.5:1 compression and 365 bhp. Also adopted for standard '68 Continentals, it would remain Lincoln's mainstay powerplant for the next 10 years.

Because of a late introduction (in April), the Mark III saw only 7770 units for model-year '68. But there was no question that it was right for its market. As proof—and despite no major change—more than 23,000 were sold for '69, another 21,432 for 1970, and over 27,000 for '71. The front-drive Eldorado may have been more technically advanced, but the Mark III evidently had more magic, for it nearly matched Eldorado sales each year through 1971 and never trailed by more than 2000. This was a great achievement considering Lincoln's annual volume had never come close to Cadillac's.

Aside from the larger engine, the '68 Continental sedan and hardtop updated their basic '66 look with a new horizontal grille texture and matching rear-panel applique, beefier bumpers, and large "star" ornaments on the nose and trunklid. A multifunction lamp at each corner imparted a cleaner look by combining turn signals, side-marker lamps (newly required by Washington), and parking lamps (front) or brake/taillamps. Also new were a government-required dual hydraulic brake system with warning light, a four-way emergency flasher, and an energy-absorbing steering column and instrument panel.

# Lincoln

1968 Continental Executive Limousine by Lehmann-Peterson

1968 Continental coupe hardtop

1969 Continental coupe hardtop

1969 Continental Mark III hardtop coupe

1970 Continental four-door sedan

1971 Continental coupe

Model-year volume for this line totaled more than 39,000.

Announcing the 1969 Continentals was a square, finely checked vee'd grille more-distinct from the headlamps. A new Town Car interior option for the sedan provided "unique, super-puff leather-and-vinyl seats and door panels, luxury wood-tone front seat back and door trim inserts, extra plush carpeting and special napped nylon headlining." Series production eased once again, settling at about 38,300.

The 1970 Continentals carried new bodies on a torque-box chassis inspired by Mercury, with coil-link rear suspension (Lincoln's first since 1959) and an inch-longer wheelbase and wider rear track. Styling was updated with hidden headlamps, a more prominently bulged slat grille, plus ventless front-door glass, concealed wipers, and full-width taillamps—all popular period features. Less obvious were wider doors, with the rears now front-hinged on sedans, and a slightly smaller fuel tank (though ample at 24.1 gallons). The hardtop, still advertised as the Coupe, gained a sweeping roofline with massive C-pillars that made over-the-shoulder vision dodgy. The powertrain was essentially a carryover. Prices were still about what they'd been back in 1961: $5976 for the hardtop, $6211 for the sedan.

This heavier, bulkier-looking Lincoln continued through 1974 with relatively few changes—most dictated by federal, not market, requirements. Prices did change, pushed by inflation past $7000 for 1971 and a little beyond $8000 by 1974. Horsepower numbers changed, too, but only because more-realistic SAE *net* measures replaced gross figures after 1971. Thus, the big 460 V-8 suffered a paper drop from 365 gross bhp to 212/224 (Mark/Continental). An even bigger Continental arrived for '75 with a fractionally longer wheelbase and some eight inches more overall length. Curb weight, though, was slightly lower at around 5000 pounds.

Continental styling remained resolutely blocky and formal throughout the '70s as Ford designers sought to establish a closer family resemblance with the Mark. Sales moved smartly up for 1972—to nearly 95,000, including Marks—then to a record 128,000-plus for '73. A decline followed in the wake of the OPEC oil embargo, but it was only temporary. Along with other big Detroiters, the big Lincoln rallied in 1975. By 1977, output was more than 190,000, another all-time Lincoln high, though still only slightly more than half of Cadillac's.

Longer-lower-wider was the formula that had traditionally worked well for luxury makes, and it worked well for Lincoln with the new Continental Mark IV of 1972. Sales nearly doubled over those of the '71 Mark III and would average 50,000 or so each year through the final 1976 models. Remarkably, the Mark IV offered less passenger room than the III and was predictably thirstier and less agile. It, too, shared its basic structure and wheelbase (here, 120.4 inches) with the concurrent Ford Thunderbird, but it wasn't immediately apparent.

Lincoln enjoyed good success with Continental's Town Car option. The 1970 package consisted of special leather inserts

1971 Continental four-door sedan

1974 Continental Mark IV coupe

1972 Continental Town Car four-door sedan

1974 Continental Town Car four-door sedan

1973 Continental Mark IV coupe

1975 Continental Town coupe

and vinyl bolsters for seats, woodlike panels on the backs of the front seats, deeper cut-pile carpeting and a soft nylon headliner, all color-keyed in a choice of five hues. For 1971, Lincoln offered an extra-special Town Car with dash and front-fender nameplates plus a set of keys and door-mounted owner initials all done in 22-carat gold—which made for a Golden Anniversary Continental to celebrate Lincoln's 50th birthday. For 1972, the Town Car became a Continental submodel. The hardtop got the same treatment for 1973 to become the Town Coupe.

Lincoln marked time in 1974. The only noteworthy news was heavier bumpers at the rear to match the beefier front units adopted the previous year per federal mandate, plus a brace of Luxury Group interior/exterior packages for the Mark. The revamped big-car line for '75 brought the end of pure "hardtop styling" and the beginning of "opera window" rooflines with fixed B-posts and heavily padded vinyl coverings. These models continued largely intact through 1979.

For 1977, the Mark IV was restyled inside and out to become the Mark V, distinguished by a crisper, lighter appearance. And appearances were not deceiving. Though it rode the same wheelbase and was little changed mechanically, the Mark V weighed some 500 pounds less than the Mark IV. It also boasted 21 percent more trunk space—which seems a large gain only because the IV had so little. Engineers paid belated attention to fuel economy by standardizing the corporate 400-cid V-8 with 179 net bhp. The old reliable 460 continued as an option except in California, where it couldn't meet the state's tougher emissions hurdles.

Model-year 1977 also saw Lincoln move into the luxury-compact class, its first response to the radically changed market left behind by the first energy crisis. Called Versailles, this was a hastily contrived reply to Cadillac's remarkably successful Seville. It was little more than an everyday Ford Granada/Mercury Monarch carrying a Continental-style square grille, a stand-up hood ornament and humped trunklid, and more standard equipment. Established Lincoln buyers looked askance at its plebeian origins (which the press never failed to mention), while buyers balked at the $11,500 price. You can only fool some of the people some of the time, and Lincoln didn't fool many with this one. Versailles' 1977-model sales were a mere 15,434, a fraction of Seville's.

This basic three-car lineup held the fort for 1978-79 while Lincoln prepared a troop of downsized 1980 models. Amazingly, the big cars continued to sell well, defying the combined threat of further fuel shortages and a fleet of luxury intermediates from lesser makes. Part of this was due to circumstance. By 1979, anyone who wanted a truly large luxury car—a "traditional-size" car, as Lincoln called it—had precious few choices.

One of Lincoln's most-successful marketing ploys in the '70s was its Designer Series. American Motors had already tried something similar with Gucci Hornets and Pierre Cardin

# Lincoln

1975 Continental Mark IV coupe

1975 Continental Town Car four-door sedan

1977 Continental Mark V with Gold/Cream Luxury Group

1977 Continental Town coupe

1978 Continental Mark V Diamond Jubilee Edition coupe

1979 Versailles four-door sedan

Javelins. But as a luxury make, Lincoln was in a better position to cash in on the snob appeal of *haute couture* names. First seen for 1976, these extra-cost packages were decorated inside and out with colors and materials specified by well-known high-fashion designers. The schemes varied somewhat from package to package and year to year, but the results were invariably striking and usually pleasing. Perhaps the most consistently tasteful was the Bill Blass edition, a nautically inspired blend of navy-blue paint and eggshell-white vinyl top outside, and navy velour or dark blue-and-cream leather upholstery inside. There also were versions by Givenchy (generally turquoise or jade), Emilio Pucci (maroon and gunmetal grey), and Cartier (champagne/grey). The last, of course, honored not a designer but the famous jeweler.

Following a spate of limited-edition 1978 trim packages to mark Ford Motor Company's 75th anniversary, Lincoln devised a "Collector Series" option group for the '79 Continental and Mark. Both were adorned with appropriate nameplates, gold grille accents, special midnight-blue metallic paint, and a host of "custom" accoutrements such as color-keyed umbrella and leather-bound owner's manual and tool kit. It was a telling development: The era of oversized Lincolns was over.

So, too, it seemed, any real distinction between the Continental and the Mark. For 1980, they became much more alike, but also much more sensible. Lincoln now adopted the "Panther" platform introduced with the '79 Ford LTD and Mercury Marquis as the basis for a substantially downsized Continental and an upmarket twin, the Mark VI, thus resuming its 1958-60 practice of fielding two versions of a single basic design. Compared to their immediate predecessors, these cars were up to 10 inches shorter between the wheels and significantly lighter. Yet they were nearly as spacious, thanks to only marginal reductions in width, plus taller, boxier styling.

Each line retained its usual appearance cues, but not the usual big-block engines. Standard for both was the corporate 302-cid small-block V-8 in new 129-bhp fuel-injected form; a 140-bhp 351 was the only option. It was all for the sake of economy, as was Ford Motor Company's new four-speed overdrive automatic transmission, basically a three-speed unit with a super-tall fourth gear added (0.67:1). Handling was more competent courtesy of a revised suspension, and refinement was emphasized with retuned body mounts and suspension bushings, plus standard high-pressure radial tires, which also helped eke out slightly more mpg. A pillared four-door Mark returned for the first time since 1960, and the various designer editions were bolstered by a new Signature Series much like the previous Collector option.

A second fuel shock occurred in 1979, touching off a deep national recession that drastically reduced 1980 volume throughout the industry. Lincoln suffered more than most, its model-year total skidding to just under 75,000—nearly 115,000 below '79. The underwhelming Versailles was in its final year

# Lincoln

1979 Continental Collector's Series four-door sedan

1979 Continental Mark V Bill Blass Edition coupe

1980 Versailles four-door sedan

1980 Continental Town Car four-door sedan

1980 Continental Town coupe

and found fewer than 5000 buyers.

The 1981 result was even worse, falling to about 69,500, but that would be the decade low. Lincoln followed the general market in making a strong recovery. By 1985, it was up to some 166,500. Output dipped the following two years, then rebounded to levels over 215,000 units through 1990. More important to proud division managers, Lincoln passed Cadillac in 1988, then lost that position, but remained competitive with its arch rival—even though it offered only three distinct models to Cadillac's five.

Remarkably, much of this success was owed to a single 1980-vintage four-door that saw only one major change through 1989: a rounded-corner "aero" facelift for 1985. Called Town Car after 1980, it soldiered on following cancellation of the 114.3-inch-wheelbase Town Coupe after '81 and the Mark VI duo after '83. The 129-bhp throttle-body fuel-injected 302 V-8 was the only engine available after 1980, but it was upgraded along the way; to 130 bhp in '81, 140 in '84. In 1985, it gained a more-sophisticated multi-point fuel-injection system, which lifted horsepower to 155. Trim and equipment shuffles were the only alterations most years.

But it didn't matter: At 50,000-100,000 units annually, this series outsold other Lincolns by margins of 2-to-1 or more—sometimes upwards of 5-to-1. Yes, the Town Car was smaller than its late-'70s predecessor, but it proved that traditional Detroit biggies still had a place in the '80s. As Mark Twain would have said, reports of their demise (in the wake of "Energy Crisis II") were greatly exaggerated.

It's interesting that a large, relatively old-fashioned product should do so well. Though Cadillac remained the luxury sales leader, its lead over Lincoln dwindled as the '80s unfolded. One reason: an increasing portion of Cadillac sales depended on smaller "big" cars that looked too much like cheaper GM models and lacked the Town Car's sheer presence. Lincoln was quick to play up its rival's "lookalike" problem in snobbish TV commercials—and just as quick to cash in with a growing number of "conquest" sales. Chrysler, of course, had nothing remotely like a traditional full-size car after 1981, though its midsize Fifth Avenue found a steady market for the same reasons the Town Car did: plentiful creature comforts in a package more "mature" buyers could relate to, all at reasonable prices. Of course, stickers swelled a lot on all cars from 1981 to '89. In the Town Car's case from about $14,000 to about $25,000. But relatively speaking, this Lincoln remained a good buy, and the public's "pocketbook vote" confirmed it.

If the late-'70s Versailles was a hasty reply to Cadillac's Seville, the new compact Continental sedan of 1982 was a more-considered response. It even had "bustleback" styling similar to the 1980 front-drive Seville's, plus a Mark-type grille and the usual base, Signature Series, and designer-edition trim and equipment variations.

Underneath, though, it was just a heavily modified Ford Fairmont, riding an extended 108.7-inch-wheelbase (later 108.5) version of the rear-drive "Fox" platform and really none the worse for it—except, perhaps, in rear-seat room, which was limited at best. A 232-cid V-6 was offered in the debut '82s but proved not potent enough for the 3700-pound curb weight, so most left the factory with injected 302 V-8s of 130, 140, or 150 bhp (the last adopted after 1985). The front and rear ends were smoothed out for '84 *a la* Town Car, the only appearance change for this design generation.

A noteworthy mechanical development was an antilock brake system (ABS), a 1985 option that became standard equipment for all Lincolns the following year. Developed jointly by Ford and the German company Alfred Teves, ABS greatly improved steering control in panic stops and shortened stop-

# Lincoln

ping distances on slick surfaces, a laudable safety advance.

Lincoln had better luck with the Continental than the Versailles, selling an average 21,000-26,000 a year through 1987. If not a vast styling improvement over Versailles, the bustleback sedan was more roadable and enjoyable, well put together, and as posh as any Lincoln. And at $21,000-$26,000, it, too, represented good luxury value.

After years of oversized excess, Lincoln's premium coupe took a surprising new direction for 1984 with the dramatic Mark VII. Though built on the same chassis as the bustleback Continental, this swoopy semifastback coupe was derived from the new-for-'83 Ford Thunderbird/Mercury Cougar. The result was smooth, distinctive, and more-slippery styling than any previous Mark. A humped trunklid, modest taillamps in the rear fender trailing edges, and a toned-down Mark grille were stylistic links with the past, but the car was clearly aimed at a very different clientele: younger, affluent buyers who'd been defecting to high-dollar, high-status imports, a group Lincoln had never courted before. It was also an end-run around Cadillac's Eldorado, which was still relatively overblown.

The Mark VII was an instant critical success, especially the performance-oriented LSC (Luxury Sport Coupe)—the fabled "Hot Rod Lincoln" come to life. Enthusiast magazines fell all over themselves comparing it to the BMW 6-Series and Mercedes-Benz SEC. No wonder. Where the base and Designer models had a soft-riding chassis and traditional appointments, the LSC rode a firm suspension with fat performance tires on handsome cast-aluminum wheels, and came with multi-adjustable sports bucket seats and Lincoln's best cloth or leather upholstery. For 1985, it adopted the Mustang GT's high-output V-8 with 165 bhp (versus 140 for other models). The '86 got an even hotter port-injected version with 200 bhp (versus 150 bhp on other models), plus standard four-wheel disc brakes with antilock control and a nice set of analog gauges (replacing the digital/graphic electronic display retained for its linemates). Engine refinements gave another 25 bhp for 1988-90.

With all this, the LSC was the most overtly sporting Lincoln since the first Continental and the most-roadable Lincoln since the mid-'50s "Mexican Road Race" cars. It was also one terrific buy at initial prices of $23,700—about half the cost of erstwhile German competitors. Lincoln-Mercury planners thought lesser VIIs would outsell it, but buyers confounded them by ordering more LSCs—to the point that by 1988, the original four variations were down to just LSC and Bill Blass. Overall sales were good: 30,000-plus in its first season 15,000-38,000 thereafter. Prices inevitably escalated, reaching the $27,000 level by decade's end, but standard equipment also kept growing even as trim variations thinned. The 1990 models boasted an important new safety feature in a standard driver-side air bag, which also brought a reworked, slightly more ergonomic dash.

Perhaps even more daring than the Mark VII was the all-new Continental sedan that bowed for 1988. Essentially a stretched version of the excellent midsize Ford Taurus/Mercury Sable, it was the first Lincoln with front-wheel drive and the first with all-independent suspension, both of which contributed to a noticeable increase in cabin room despite a wheelbase only half an inch longer than its bustleback predecessor's (109 inches). In appearance, which L-M described as "aero limousine," this new Continental departed even more from tradition than the Mark VII: squarish but carefully detailed for good airflow "management." The old humped trunklid was abandoned at last, leaving a vertical-bar grille to echo the past—and even that was low and smoothly curved to match the nose, flanked by flush-fit Euro-style headlamps.

Powering the new Continental was the 140-bhp 3.8-liter V-6 made optional for the '88 Taurus/Sable, mounted transversely

1980 Continental Mark VI Signature Series coupe

1983 Continental Signature Series with Carriage Roof

1983 Continental Givenchy Designer Series sedan

1983 Town Car Cartier Designer Series sedan

1984 Continental Mark VII coupe

(in typical front-drive fashion) and teamed with a four-speed overdrive automatic transaxle. It didn't provide much snap in the heavier Conti (which was little lighter than its rear-drive forebear), and even L-M officials later admitted the car was underpowered for its class. At least quietness was a strength. A MacPherson-strut suspension employing dual-rate shock absorbers and LSC-style air springs, both computer-controlled, sounded great on paper. Unfortunately, this complicated design failed to provide a truly outstanding ride/handling balance in the real world. The standard all-disc brakes with ABS were superb, however, and interior decor was a blend of Euro-modern and American traditional. For 1989, the dash and steering wheel were redesigned to accommodate dual front air bags. A single air bag for the driver would have satisfied the federal government's new passive-restraint rule, but Lincoln got the jump on Cadillac by providing air bags on both sides.

Arriving at dealers in December 1987, the front-drive Continental proved a strong seller, thanks partly to an attractive $26,000 base price—again, thousands less than similar European sedans. Model-year production totaled about 41,000 for '88, rose to 57,775 for '89, then climbed to over 64,000 for 1990. The Continental wouldn't fare as well afterward, but the mere fact that Lincolns could now stand comparison with high-buck foreigners spoke volumes about how far Lincoln had come in the '80s and where it would go in the '90s.

A faint hint of that future arrived for 1990 in the first fully restyled Town Car in a decade. Actually, it was little more than the old model in new aerodynamic clothes. Dimensions, weight, and powertrain were all little changed. Not everyone liked the much-more-rounded new look—but then, Lincoln had the unenviable task of needing to make its top-seller look more modern without making it look too different.

Indeed, designers tried hard to satisfy Town Car loyalists by retaining opera windows and a square "formal" grille, though both were tastefully muted, as well as lush interiors with cushy bench seats, tufted upholstery, pseudo-wood dash trim and power everything. Base, Signature, and Cartier models were also still available to ease the minds of troubled traditionalists. Yet the 1990 model had laudable improvements, including speed-sensitive power steering, self-leveling rear air springs, and air bags for both driver and front passenger—all standard at base prices in the $27,000-$32,000 range. Antilock brakes were optional at $936.

With all this, the updated Town Car was another sales hit on a lengthening Dearborn list. Model-year volume topped 147,000, a healthy gain of almost 20,000 over the still-popular '89. L-M must have heaved a big sigh of relief, for the Town Car still accounted for more than 60 percent of total Lincoln sales. For 1990, it outpolled the four-door Continental by over 2-to-1 and the Mark VIII by almost 7-to-1. It was thus a key factor in

**1985 Continental Mark VII LSC coupe**

**1985 Continental four-door sedan**

**1985 Town Car four-door sedan**

**1986 Continental four-door sedan**

**1987 Mark VII LSC coupe**

**1987 Continental Givenchy Designer Series sedan**

# Lincoln

boosting Lincoln volume so much closer to Cadillac's.

But "closer" can still leave an unbridgeable gap, and Lincoln sales continued trailing Cadillac's into the early '90s by 22,000 to 78,000 cars. Cadillac should have enjoyed even bigger margins, though, with its much-broader lineup. Lincoln did very well in running so consistently close with just three models. Evidently, a good many buyers agreed with the make's ad slogan of the time: "What a Luxury Car Should Be."

Even so, a sharp new recession and increasing luxury competition diminished Lincoln's yearly volume after 1990, pushing it into the 160,000-197,000 range through middecade. But the Town Car kept rolling on, accounting for fewer buyers in this period but an even bigger piece of Lincoln's total sales pie, accounting for two-thirds of sales.

Considered improvements played a big part in this performance. The biggest one occurred for 1991, when Town Car introduced the first in a new Dearborn family of modern overhead-cam engines: the so-called "modular" (sometimes "mod") V-8. The name referred to a basic block that could also be used for V-6s and even slant-fours built on the same tooling and assembly lines. The core V-8 allotted to Town Car was a single-cam 4.6-liter unit with electronic multiport fuel injection and cast-iron block and heads. Standard horsepower was 190, up 40 from the ousted pushrod 5.0-liter, or 210 bhp with optional dual exhausts. Though not a huge advance for smoothness or quietness, the "mod" V-8 was more easily tuned than the old 302 for the even tighter emissions limits then coming on the scene.

The '91 Town Car also boasted a revised front suspension for slightly crisper handling, plus better stopping ability via standard four-wheel disc brakes (versus rear drums). A new option also enhanced "active safety." Called Traction Assist, it was a simple form of traction control that relied on the ABS wheel-speed sensors and was thus tied to the optional antilock brakes. When the sensors detected wheel slip, the system would automatically apply gentle brake pressure to the rear wheels until grip was restored. Other Lincolns would get this feature, too.

Town Car then stood pat, though there were notable minor changes. For example, 1992 brought more-responsive electronic shift control to the four-speed automatic transmission, plus a safety interlock that prevented shifting from Park without depressing the brake pedal, a legacy of the recent furor over "unintended acceleration." Subtle grille and taillight revisions arrived for '93, as did a handling package option with somewhat firmer damping and wider tires on alloy wheels. The latter was welcome, if rather a paradox for such a big cruiser. There was also a new "designer edition" for '93, this one inspired by golfing great Jack Nicklaus. It was offered only this one year for the midline Signature Series. The dual-exhaust engine became standard for '94, as did high-tech "solar-tint" glass for all windows. The '95s got a few cosmetic touchups, and the Signature and top-line Cartier gained a new three-mode power steering system that allowed choosing low, medium, or high steering effort with the push of a dashboard button.

If the Town Car was relatively static in this period, prices weren't, rising to a minimum $41,200 for the 1995 Cartier. Despite this, sales held up well at some 125,000 for '91, over 113,000 for '92, and 117,000-118,000 for 1993-94. Though not a sales factor, Town Car was affected by a shortage of air bags in 1991-92, owing to tight supplies of air bag propellant. Indeed, some '91s had to be built without the planned passenger-side restraint. However, Lincoln did the right thing when supplies improved by retrofitting air bags to those cars at no cost.

The Mark VII also marked time before closing out after 1992. The only interim change was upgrading the Bill Blass model to the same steering, suspension, tires and alloy wheels as the

1988 Mark VII LSC coupe

1988 Continental Signature Series four-door sedan

1990 Town Car Cartier Designer Series four-door sedan

1990 Continental Signature Series four-door sedan

1990 Mark VII LSC coupe

sporty LSC. Sales nosedived from over 22,000 for model-year 1990 to just 15,000 for 1991-92 combined. There were two reasons for this. First, the VII had been around nearly a decade—and looked it. Second, a brand-new Mark was waiting in the wings.

Arriving for 1993 as a single well-equipped coupe, the Mark VIII was the most-exciting Lincoln yet. Sleek, smooth, and obviously "aero," it made the VII seem almost stodgy. Styling nodded to Mark tradition with a vertical-bar grille and trunklid tire hump, but both were sized and shaped to blend in naturally with the overall design. Though not everyone liked some elements of the new look (the "predented" bodyside concavities were particularly debated), the Mark VIII was unmistakably Lincoln and unlike anything else on the road.

Structurally, the Mark VIII owed much to the latest MN12 Thunderbird/Cougar, but it was different enough to merit its own internal code, FN10. Compared to the Mark VII, it stood 4.5 inches longer in wheelbase (on the 113-inch T-Bird/Cougar span), 4.1 inches longer overall and 3.7 inches wider, yet was actually 30 pounds lighter at the curb thanks to careful weight-watching; in spite of added features like dual air bags. Engineering was more sophisticated than ever with all-independent air-spring suspension *a la* Continental, speed-variable power steering and optional Traction Assist. Under the hood lurked a potent new engine: the promised twincam version of the "mod" V-8. Displacement was still 4.6 liters (281 cid), but a 32-valve aluminum cylinder head helped deliver a smashing 280 bhp and a thumping 285 pound-feet of torque. A four-speed automatic remained the only transmission, but was now blessed with electronic control. And for the first time, Mark drivers worked the shifter from a center console, part of a sweeping new "cockpit" dash that wrapped in from the center to give a definite "fighter plane" feel behind the wheel.

The Mark VIII could certainly fly like a jet. Despite giving away 15 horses to Cadillac's Northstar-powered Eldorado Touring Coupe, the Lincoln proved decisively quicker in Consumer Guide® tests, posting a 0-60 time of just 6.9 seconds versus 7.7 for the Eldo. But more than just straightline go, the new Mark set a new high for Lincoln roadability. Cornering was flat and stable, steering fast and informative, braking swift and sure. About the only things not to like were certain ergonomic details and less passenger and cargo space than expected in a car of this bulk.

In all, the Mark VIII was a revelation: fast, supremely capable, quiet, luxurious, and comfortable. It was naturally a very different Mark, but it was also the first to invite comparison with the pricey likes of BMW, Mercedes, and Japanese upstart Lexus. Speaking of price, Lincoln's latest was a real eye-opener at well under $37,000 to start, thousands less than comparable *grand luxe* import coupes. Buyers responded by taking nearly 32,400 of the '93s and 28,000-plus for '94. The '95 tally was lower, but so was overall demand for luxury coupes.

Perhaps to perk up that market, Lincoln revived the LSC moniker for an even hotter Mark VIII. This was announced for 1995 but not actually made available until model-year '96. Dual exhausts gave it 290 bhp, while a firmer chassis gave even more tenacious handling and roadholding. If this wasn't the "Hot Rod Lincoln" fabled in song, it was certainly the next best thing.

After making its debut to generally good reviews, the Mark stumbled in the sales race. Perhaps it was the competition, perhaps it was a general decline in demand for expensive coupes; all that can really be said for certain is that too many customers went elsewhere. Lincoln put in some serious effort to make the Mark more appealing, instituting a host of changes for the 1997 model year. A new grille (flanked by high-intensity gas-discharge headlamps) and hood tilted the visual balance from "aero" to "formal," and a redesigned tail received a full-width neon light bar in place of ordinary taillamps. Inside, the seats were reshaped, a power tilt-telescope function was added to the steering column, instrument-panel lighting was brightened and wood trim—somewhat at odds with the high-tech character the car was originally meant to have—was applied. The chassis received its share of attention as well, getting firmer shock absorbers and larger antiroll bars. Traction control was made standard as well. But these changes weren't as noticeable at first glance as a sharp reduction in the Mark's base price.

Once again, the restorative measures failed to produce results. Neither the standard Mark or its LSC variant could bring in buyers. This even though the LSC got an additional 10 bhp (290 total) and sportier suspension calibrations to revive the "Hot Rod Lincoln" image (which it didn't). The Mark finally faded away after the 1998 model, unmourned, after putting up sales numbers ranging from 13,600 to 18,400 from 1995 to '97 and eventually falling to only 6100 in its final year. Perhaps it was a victim of certain innate problems—most notably the lack of interior space considering the Mark's overall size—or the overwhelmingly positive response to rival Lexus SC400.

The Continental sedan carried through 1994 with considered yearly improvements but no great alterations to the successful front-drive formula of 1988. The base model was renamed Executive Series for '91, when the pushrod 3.8 V-6 gained standard dual exhausts and 10 more horsepower for a total of 155. Another five bhp arrived the following year via internal-engine changes. Like Town Car, the Continental picked up electronic transmission control ('91), shift interlock ('92), the expected trim and appearance shuffles, a few extra standard features, and new optional items like front bucket seats (for Executive from '93) and remote keyless entry system. Also prevailing here were spotty passenger-side air bag availability on 1990-92 models, and steady price escalation that lifted base stickers into the mid-$30,000 range by 1994. Production went the other way through '93, when it was down to 26,798, less than half the 1990

**1992 Town Car Signature Series four-door sedan**

**1993 Mark VIII coupe**

# Lincoln

total—which made the '94 result of over 52,000 a real surprise.

An even nicer surprise was the all-new 1995 Continental appearing just ahead of Lincoln's 75th birthday. Though still front-drive, it was rather like a Mark VIII in more-conservative four-door dress. It even had the same twincam V-8, though transverse mounting and a more-restrictive exhaust robbed 20 horses to leave "just" 260. Wheelbase was unchanged, and width and height were up only an inch apiece, but weight ballooned nearly 400 pounds despite the use of plasticlike sheet-molding compound to replace steel in the hood, trunklid, and fenders. Some of the extra pounds reflected a stiffer unitized structure with more sound-deadening. Others came from added standard features like full automatic climate control with pollen microfilter. Dual air bags and ABS were again included, and there was a no-cost choice of front seating: three-place bench with column shift or buckets with console shift.

Trying more than most cars to be all things to all people, the '95 Continental came with a dazzling bit of electronic trickery called the "Memory Profile System" (MPS). This provided "his and her" memory settings for a host of functions including position of power mirrors, driver's seat, and steering wheel (the last an electric tilt/telescopic affair), radio presets, power window and alarm operation, and—most novel of all—suspension and steering.

Like the previous Continental, the '95 rode an all-independent air-spring suspension, but a second, horizontal pair of shock absorbers was added in back, and all shocks were electronically controlled, like the air springs. With this, Ford decided to rig the system to allow choosing between Firm, Normal, or Plush damping via the new MPS. The power steering was now electronic, too. Though assist still decreased as road speed increased, overall effort could now be varied by selecting Low, Medium, or High on the MPS display. Wisely, Dearborn's computer nerds prohibited combining Plush damping with Low steering effort, but the differences among the settings weren't that great. In fact, the car felt best in the Normal/Medium "default" mode. Firm/High only made the ride more fidgety and helm work more tiring.

With all its new gadgetry, the '95 Continental cost a good $5000 more than the last of the V-6 generation, the lone sedan running higher up in the "near luxury" market at $40,750. Options were restricted to chrome wheels, voice-activated cellular phone (complete with a dash display for signal strength and call duration), power moonroof, all-speed traction control, CD changer, and a novel wheeled "cart" that moved back and forth in the trunk and could be partitioned for carrying smaller items without them tipping over.

And so the battle was joined: front-drive V-8 Lincoln versus front-drive V-8 Cadillacs. On paper, the Continental covered all the bases—the company's marketers had even adopted a snappy name ("InTech") for the dohc engine used in Continental and Mark VIII in response to Cadillac's "Northstar" moniker. The only question was one of customer preference—would buyers go for Continental's rounded, sleek styling or the more-formal sharp-edged look in favor at Cadillac?

Answers came quickly. Continental sales started off slow, about 45,000 in 1995, and continued at a modest pace that was well below expectations. During the first full year of production, a Personal Security Package was added; this two-part option brought with it Lincoln's RESCU System—a cellular phone link to a dedicated emergency operator—and Michelin run-flat tires. But that didn't turn the tide, and neither did the next year's substantial price cuts which took nearly $4600 off the car's previous $41,800 sticker, even though the previously optional traction control system was made standard. It was clear to all concerned that stronger measures needed to be taken, and in 1998 they were.

A major 1998 redesign made substantial changes to the Continental's character. Realizing that the dramatic, heavily sculptured look was proving no more successful here than on parent Ford's Taurus, Lincoln designers opted for a "formal" appearance, giving the car conventional rounded sides and a more-upright frontal aspect emphasizing Lincoln's "corporate" grille design. The front and rear overhangs were shortened as well. The driver-adjustable suspension was relegated to the options list; unless it was ordered, the buyer got conventional shock absorbers and a more-basic self-leveling system in the rear, though the adjustable power-steering system remained standard. Production jumped by 4000 units, from 32,000 to 36,000 in '98, with the new design, but that wasn't enough. A horsepower increase (from 260 to 275 bhp) came along in 2001, but that and some minor fiddling with color schemes and minor options was effectively the end of the Continental story. By 2001, production was down to under 18,000, and the decision was made to take it out of production at the end of the following model year.

It can't be said that the Continental was a bad car; in reality, it was a very competent luxury sedan that just didn't strike a responsive chord with buyers. Whether because of styling, price (at least initially) or the lukewarm reviews it received from testers (". . . worth considering only if you can get a big discount," said Consumer Guide® on more than one occasion) Lincoln's first, and so far only, front-drive sedan was a weak player in its class from the start, and none of the changes made throughout its life helped.

In the mid-1990s, Lincoln decided to enter the sport-utility market. Since developing and tooling up a completely unique vehicle was out of the question, the fullsize Ford Expedition

**1995 Town Car Signature Series four-door sedan**

**1996 Continental four-door sedan**

# Lincoln

1997 Town Car four-door sedan

1998 Continental four-door sedan

1998 Town Car four-door sedan

1999 Continental four-door sedan

2000 Continental four-door sedan

was chosen as a base. When introduced in 1997, the Lincoln Navigator was essentially a retrimmed (but fully loaded) Expedition with some new exterior paneling and interior features to set it apart. Navigator was an immediate hit, zooming up to the number two slot on the Lincoln sales charts, and allaying whatever fears executives may have had about asking $10,000 more for what at first blush appeared to be a warmed-over Ford. "At least we won't be out too much money if it doesn't work," one Lincoln honcho said privately. Continued customer demand paved the way for additional improvements, including replacing the Expedition's 260-bhp sohc V-8 with 300-bhp's-worth of dohc "InTech" V-8. In 2002, Navigator was joined by the Blackwood, a limited-edition machine that was essentially a mating of the Navigator with a Ford F-150 Super Crew pickup, with the addition of a novel powered cover over the load bed. Excessive, perhaps, but novel.

In another rather dramatic development, Lincoln management made a cross-country move in 1999, settling down in Irvine, California. That was about as far away from the Dearborn-based parent company as one could get without crossing an ocean. The intent was to give Lincoln (and Mercury, which moved as well) a separate identity, both in the minds of employees and the general public. California, so the reasoning went, was fertile ground for cutting-edge automotive developments, and Lincoln wanted to gain maximum benefit from that. At the same time, a major corporate restructuring placed Lincoln in Ford's new Premier Automotive Group, a quasi-independent entity that combined Lincoln, Mercury, Jaguar, Aston Martin, Volvo, and Land Rover. All of the U.S. management personnel ended up together, but somewhat independent, in a new Irvine facility by late 2001.

Jaguar had been a Ford subsidiary since 1990, and was doing well. But Ford's mandate to Jaguar was to increase sales volume, and the only way to do that was to add new models priced below the existing XJ-series sedans and XK-series sports cars. The first new program instituted for that purpose dovetailed neatly with Lincoln's need to expand its own product line. Working in tandem, the two companies developed a compact rear-wheel drive platform that would carry either Jaguar's existing all-alloy dohc V-8 engine or a Ford-based dohc V-6. Jaguar and Lincoln would have considerable freedom in exterior and interior design and chassis tuning, but essential hardware would be shared. For Jaguar, the end result was the S-Type, which has indeed increased the company's sales volume considerably.

Lincoln's LS turned out to be a low-key winner as well, with production topping 60,000 in its first year. Less flamboyant than the English equivalent, it brought to market a conservative but handsome shape, with a long wheelbase, short front and rear overhangs, and an airy greenhouse. In front, of course, the signature grille dominated, but that was the only retro element in a classic, muscular design. The inside was done up to match, with all the wood and leather that buyers in the near-luxury class expect. With ample room for four adults and above-average build quality, the LS seemed a bargain—the base model listed for $30,915 at introduction—with prices nearly $10,000 below those of the equivalent Jaguar models. Within two years, the marketing strategy changed a bit, and the initial three-model lineup of V-6 with manual transmission, V-6 automatic, and V-8 with automatic swelled to eight permutations, based on powertrain and amenity content, though this move did keep the options list short.

For many drivers, the LS's dynamics were most impressive. The V-6 engine (Ford's 3.0 liter Duratec, rated at 220 bhp) was

# Lincoln

perhaps not as refined as many would have wished, but it was the only choice for customers who insisted on a manual transmission. On the other hand, the Jaguar V-8 (3.9 liters, 252 bhp) worked quite happily with a five-speed automatic, and delivered a balanced blend of performance and refinement. With either engine, the suspension worked very well, blending European-style handling and a smooth ride. The primary complaint of most testers had to do with tire noise at speed; it was noticeable but not really obtrusive. LS offered an effective electronic antiskid system, though this was an optional addition to its basic traction control system rather than a standard fitting, as it might have been on more-expensive sport sedans. Thanks to its mix of low price, excellent build quality, and European-style performance and handling, the LS rapidly became a welcome and profitable presence in Lincoln showrooms.

But the number one spot on the roster was, as it had been for many years, the evergreen Town Car. Sports writers sometimes refer to "franchise players," those gifted all-around achievers who can make the right play when the going gets rough. That was the role Town Car played for Lincoln. Many scorned it as a dinosaur, a relic of more-wasteful times, but it continued to bring home the bacon for the dealers. Like any other car, it had its good and bad selling days, but, ultimately, Town Car turned out to be a very durable product, surviving and thriving on a basic structure first introduced in 1980. It had been freshened after a decade, and benefited from numerous advances in technology, but the old wine and its newer bottle still had something going for them. And that advantage was an adherence to the traditional body-on-frame, rear-wheel-drive concept. General Motors abandoned them for passenger cars after 1996, effectively handing the custom limousine business—especially when adding length to create "stretch" limos was involved—to Lincoln. It was far easier and far more economical for an aftermarket company to splice extra footage onto a separate frame than to rework a unitized structure, so Town Car came to rule a fairly sizable market unopposed. With a healthy "modular" V-8 engine to pull it along, even the longest of oversized limousines could roll along at a more-than-reasonable pace.

But the Town Car needed to keep up with the times, so it was redesigned again in 1998. This time, the renovations were major, as three inches of overall length and 200 pounds were lopped off. The boxy look that had lasted nearly two decades was gone as well, replaced by a rounded massive form that was not universally loved, at least by critics; one described it as looking like "a bloated copy of a [early 1950s] Mark IX Jaguar." Far from high praise. The new cabin fared better, being lauded for roomy accommodations and a return of traditional analog gauges. Suspension improvements brought a better-controlled (but still plushy) ride. Prices for the three versions—Executive, Signature, and Cartier Editions—were lowered as well. Leather, pile carpet, and wood trim were lavished on the interiors. Everything from ABS and traction control to eight-way power seats were standard, making the options list brief. Production topped 110,000 units in its first year, but fell steadily for the next three, with a 2001 low just over 67,000.

Road testers complained about the negative effect the wide rear pillars had on rearward vision, and Consumer Guide®'s writer delighted in nautical allusions ("It's still a big vessel" and "its road manners are less aquatic") as did another who simply dismissed it as a "tuna boat." But in a way, both missed the point: a Town Car owner generally wasn't too worried about looking back, as that was the chauffeur's job. And no sensible person would ever take a Town Car for a Porsche hunt on a mountain road. Still, Lincoln did add stiffer suspension to its Signature Touring Sedan in 2000, as well as a dual-exhaust system that upped horsepower to 220. The extra power was also offered to Cartier buyers, leaving only Executives to ride along behind the standard 200 horses, at least until 2002, when 220 became the base rating and the upgrade was 235 bhp. Private owners and limousine services alike seemed to be pleased.

The first years of the new century saw Lincoln weathering more than one storm. There was, in some quarters, a sense of confusion over the marque's place in the Premier Automotive Group, and fears that its identity might be diluted. Lincoln also experienced rough sales periods. But Lincoln's core strengths remained: The Town Car, improved for 2003, and the LS appeared to have real staying power, while the Navigator and Blackwood brought the Lincoln name into new arenas. A smaller SUV, the Aviator, based on the Ford Explorer but using the 300-bhp "InTech" V-8 for power, expanded the nameplate's reach into yet another part of that market for the 2003 model year. As the LS matures, it is sure to receive enhancements that will add to its appeal. And no one believes that the storied Continental name is gone for good; rumors have it returning on an all-new car middecade. All of which augurs well for the continuing prosperity of a historic name.

**2001 Town Car Cartier L four-door sedan**

**2001 LS four-door sedan**

**2002 LS four-door sedan**

# Lincoln

2002 Continental four-door sedan

## Specifications

### 1930

| Model L (wb 136.0) | Wght | Price | Prod |
|---|---|---|---|
| conv rdstr 2-4P | 4,740 | 4,500 | 12 |
| spt phtn 4P | 4,840 | 4,200 | 53 |
| spt phtn 4P, tonneau-cowl | 4,850 | 4,400 | 90 |
| spt touring 7P | 4,940 | 4,200 | 79 |
| cpe 5P | 4,940 | 4,400 | 275 |
| Town sdn 2W 4P | 5,010 | 4,400 | 169 |
| Town sdn 3W 4P | 5,010 | 4,400 | 285 |
| sdn 4d 2-3W | 5,180 | 4,500 | 541 |
| sdn 7P | 5,245 | 4,700 | 458 |
| limo 7P | 5,190 | 4,900 | 329 |
| chassis | — | 3,500 | 47 |
| *Custom bodies:* | | | |
| Locke spt rdstr | — | — | 15 |
| Judkins cpe 2P | 4,790 | 5,000 | 65 |
| Judkins berline 4P 2W | 5,280 | 5,600 | 72 |
| Judkins berline 4P 3W | 4,930 | 5,600 | 100 |
| Brunn brougham A/W 7P | 5,045 | 7,000 | 68 |
| Brunn cab s.c. A/W 7P | 4,985 | 7,200 | 44 |
| LeBaron conv rdstr | — | — | 100 |
| LeBaron cab 7P | 5,370 | 7,200 | NA |
| LeBaron A/W cab 7P | 5,045 | 6,900 | 29 |
| LeBaron cab 7P semi-clpsble | 5,190 | 7,100 | 20 |
| LeBaron cpe-sdn 4P | 5,030 | 5,300 | 8 |
| Willoughby limo 6P | 5,180 | 5,900 | 244 |
| Willoughby brougham A/W | 5,900 | NA | 5 |
| Dietrich conv cpe 4P | 5,180 | 6,200 | 42 |
| Dietrich conv sdn 5P | 5,235 | 6,600 | 40 |
| Derham conv cpe 4P | 4,850 | 6,400 | 1 |
| Derham phaeton | 6,000 | NA | 21 |

| 1930 Engine | bore × stroke | bhp | availability |
|---|---|---|---|
| V-8, 385.0 | 3.50 × 5.00 | 90 | S-all |

### 1931

| 201 Model K (wb 145.0) | | Wght | Price | Prod |
|---|---|---|---|---|
| 202A | dual-cowl spt phaeton 5P | 4,970 | 4,600 | 77 |
| 202B | spt phaeton 5P | 4,960 | 4,400 | 60 |
| 203 | spt tourer 7P | 5,060 | 4,400 | 45 |
| 204A | Town sdn 5P 2W | 5,130 | 4,600 | 195 |
| 204B | Town sdn 5P 3W | 5,130 | 4,600 | 447 |
| 205 | sdn 5P | 5,300 | 4,700 | 552 |
| 206 | cpe 5P | 5,060 | 4,600 | 225 |
| 207A | sdn 7P | 5,365 | 4,900 | 521 |
| 207B/C | limo 7P | 5,310 | 5,100 | 401 |
| 208A | Brunn cab A/W | 5,280 | 7,400 | 30 |
| 209 | Brunn brougham A/W | 5,165 | 7,200 | 34 |
| 210 | Dietrich conv cpe 4P | 5,300 | 6,400 | 25 |
| 211 | Dietrich sdn 4d | 5,355 | 6,800 | 65 |
| 212 | Derham phtn 4P | 4,970 | 6,200 | 11 |
| 213A | Judkins berline 4P 3W | 5,050 | 5,800 | 171 |
| 214 | LeBaron conv rdstr 2-4P | 4,860 | 4,700 | 275 |
| 215 | Willoughby limo 6P | 5,300 | 6,100 | 151 |
| 216 | Willoughby panel b'ham 7P | 5,340 | 7,400 | 15 |
| 217A | LeBaron Cab A/W 7P | 5,165 | 7,100 | 21 |
| 217B | LeBaron Cab 7P semi-clpsble | 5,100 | 7,300 | |
| 218 | Judkins cpe 2P | 4,910 | 5,200 | 86 |
| 219 | Dietrich cpe 2P | 5,050 | — | 35 |
| 201 | chassis, 145" wb | — | — | 61 |
| 220 | chassis, 150" wb | — | — | 3 |
| 221 | chassis, 155" wb | — | — | 3 |
| — | misc. specials | — | — | 47 |

| 1931 Engine | bore × stroke | bhp | availability |
|---|---|---|---|
| V-8, 385.0 | 3.50 × 5.00 | 120 | S-all |

### 1932

| 501 Model KA (wb 136.0) | | Wght | Price | Prod |
|---|---|---|---|---|
| 502A | cpe 2P | 5,335 | 3,200 | 86 |
| 502B | cpe 2-4P | 5,205 | 3,245 | |

617

# Lincoln

| 501 Model KA (wb 136.0) | | Wght | Price | Prod |
|---|---|---|---|---|
| 504 | Town sdn 5P | 5,330 | 3,100 | 147 |
| 505 | sdn 4d | 5,300 | 3,200 | 921 |
| 506 | victoria 5P | 5,345 | 3,200 | 265 |
| 507A | sdn 7P | 5,435 | 3,300 | 508 |
| 507B | limo 7P | 5,520 | 3,350 | 122 |
| 508 | phaeton | 5,270 | 3,000 | 29 |
| 510A | rdstr 2P | 5,050 | 2,900 | 12 |
| 510B | rdstr 2-4P | 5,180 | 2,945 | |
| 501 | chassis | — | — | 7 |
| — | misc. & unaccounted for | — | — | 127 |

| 231 Model KB (wb 145.0) | | Wght | Price | Prod |
|---|---|---|---|---|
| 232A | Murphy dual-cowl spt phtn 4P | 5,625 | 4,500 | 30 |
| 232B | Murphy spt phaeton 4P | 5,250 | 4,300 | 13 |
| 233 | spt touring 7P | 5,720 | 4,300 | 24 |
| 234A | Town sdn 5P 2W | 5,740 | 4,500 | 123 |
| 234B | Town sdn 5P 3W | 5,740 | 4,500 | 200 |
| 235 | sdn 4d | 5,975 | 4,600 | 216 |
| 236 | cpe 5P | 5,600 | 4,400 | 83 |
| 237A | sdn 7P | 5,975 | 4,700 | 266 |
| 237B | limo 7P | 5,990 | 4,900 | 41 |
| 237C | limo 7P | 5,900 | 4,000 | 135 |
| 238 | Brunn cab A/W 5P | 5,855 | 7,200 | 14 |
| 239 | Brunn brougham A/W 7P | 5,920 | 7,000 | 13 |
| 240 | Dietrich spt berline 5P | 5,605 | 6,500 | 8 |
| 241 | Dietrich conv sdn 5P | 5,720 | 6,400 | 20 |
| 242A | Dietrich cpe 2-4P | 5,745 | 5,150 | 17 |
| 242B | Dietrich cpe 2P | 5,710 | 5,000 | |
| 243A | Judkins berline 5P 2W | 5,860 | 5,700 | 74 |
| 243B | Judkins berline 5P 3W | 5,860 | 5,700 | |
| 244A | Judkins cpe 2-4P | 5,610 | 5,350 | 23 |
| 244B | Judkins cpe 2P | 5,595 | 5,100 | |
| 245 | Willoughby limo 7P | 5,950 | 5,900 | 64 |
| 246 | Willoughby panel brham 4P | 5,855 | 7,100 | 4 |
| 247 | Waterhouse conv victoria 5P | 5,470 | 5,900 | 10 |
| 248 | LeBaron rdstr 2-4P | 5,535 | 4,600 | 112 |
| 249 | Murphy spt rdstr 2P | 5,605 | 6,800 | 3 |
| 231 | chassis, 145" wb | — | — | 18 |
| 250 | chassis, 150" wb | — | — | 1 |
| — | misc. specials | — | — | 13 |

| 1932 Engines | bore × stroke | bhp | availability |
|---|---|---|---|
| V-8, 385.0 | 3.50 × 5.00 | 125 | S-KA |
| V-12, 448.0 | 3.25 × 4.50 | 150 | S-KB |

## 1933

| 511 Model KA (wb 136.0) | | Wght | Price | Prod |
|---|---|---|---|---|
| 512A | cpe 2-4P | 4,929 | 3,145 | 44 |
| 512B | cpe 2P | 4,909 | 3,100 | |
| 513A | conv rdstr 2-4P | 4,769 | 3,200 | 85 |
| 514 | Town sdn 5P | 4,954 | 3,100 | 201 |
| 515 | sdn 4d | 4,989 | 3,200 | 320 |
| 516 | victoria 5P | 4,919 | 3,200 | 109 |
| 517A | sdn 7P | 5,159 | 3,300 | 190 |
| 517B | limo 7P | 5,184 | 3,350 | 111 |
| 518A | dual-cowl phaeton 5P | 4,759 | 3,200 | 12 |
| 518B | phaeton 5P | 4,749 | 3,000 | 12 |
| 519 | phaeton 7P | 4,759 | 3,200 | 10 |
| 520A | rdstr 2-4P | 4,739 | 2,745 | 12 |
| 520B | rdstr 2P | 4,719 | 2,700 | |
| 511 | chassis | — | — | 7 |
| — | misc. specials | — | — | 5 |

| 251 Model KB (wb 145.0) | | | | |
|---|---|---|---|---|
| 252A | dual-cowl phaeton 5P | 5,310 | 4,400 | 9 |

| 251 Model KB (wb 145.0) | | Wght | Price | Prod |
|---|---|---|---|---|
| 252B | spt phaeton 4P | 5,220 | 4,200 | 6 |
| 253 | spt touring 7P | 5,310 | 4,300 | 6 |
| 254A | Town sdn 2W | 5,401 | 4,400 | 39 |
| 254B | Town sdn 3W | 5,401 | 4,400 | 41 |
| 255 | sdn 4d | 5,491 | 4,500 | 52 |
| 256 | victoria cpe 5P | 5,511 | 4,300 | 18 |
| 257A | sdn 7P | 5,521 | 4,600 | 110 |
| 257B | limo 7P | 5,571 | 4,800 | 105 |
| 258C | Brunn cab 5P | 5,685 | 6,900 | 8 |
| 258D | Brunn cab semi-clpsble 5P | 5,386 | 6,900 | |
| 259B | Brunn brougham 7P | 5,431 | 6,900 | 13 |
| 260 | Brunn conv cpe 5P | 5,171 | 5,700 | 15 |
| 260 | Dietrich spt berline 5P | — | — | — |
| 261 | Dietrich conv sdn 5P | 5,410 | 6,100 | 15 |
| 263A | Judkins berline 2W 4P | 5,411 | 5,500 | 36 |
| 263B | Judkins berline 3W 4P | 5,411 | 5,500 | |
| 264D | Judkins cpe 2P | 5,530 | 5,000 | 12 |
| 265B | Willoughby limo 7P | 5,541 | 5,700 | 40 |
| 267B | LeBaron conv rdstr 2-4P | 5,191 | 4,500 | 37 |
| 2197 | Dietrich cpe 2P | — | 4,900 | 8 |
| 251 | chassis | — | — | 4 |
| — | chassis, 155" wb | — | — | 1 |
| — | misc. specials | — | — | 19 |

| 1933 Engines | bore × stroke | bhp | availability |
|---|---|---|---|
| V-12, 381.7 | 3.00 × 4.50 | 125 | S-KA |
| V-12, 448.0 | 3.25 × 4.50 | 150 | S-KB |

## 1934

| 521 Model KA (wb 136.0) | | Wght | Price | Prod |
|---|---|---|---|---|
| 522A | cpe 2-4P | 4,879 | 3,250 | 60 |
| 522B | cpe 2P | 5,210 | 3,200 | |
| 523 | conv rdstr 2-4P | 5,050 | 3,400 | 75 |
| 524 | Town sdn 5P | 5,140 | 3,450 | 450 |
| 525 | sdn 4d | 5,044 | 3,400 | 425 |
| 526 | victoria cpe 5P | 5,029 | 3,400 | 115 |
| 527A | sdn 7P | 5,203 | 3,500 | 275 |
| 527B | limo 7P | 5,228 | 3,550 | 175 |
| 531 | conv sdn phtn 5P | 5,029 | 3,900 | 75 |
| 521 | chassis | — | — | 21 |
| — | misc. specials | — | — | 8 |

| 271 Model KB (wb 145.0) | | Wght | Price | Prod |
|---|---|---|---|---|
| 273 | touring 7P | 5,720 | 4,200 | 20 |
| 277A | sdn 7P | 5,510 | 4,500 | 210 |
| 277B | limo 7P | 5,570 | 4,700 | 215 |
| 278A | Brunn cab 5P semi-clpsble | 5,315 | 6,800 | 13 |
| 278B | Brunn cab 5P | 5,615 | 6,800 | |
| 279 | Brunn brougham 7P | 5,480 | 6,800 | 15 |
| 280 | Brunn conv cpe 5P | 5,045 | 5,600 | 25 |
| 281 | Dietrich conv sdn 5P | 5,330 | 5,600 | 25 |
| 282 | Judkins sdn limo 7P | 5,570 | 5,700 | 27 |
| 283A | Judkins berline 4P 2W | 5,710 | 5,400 | 37 |
| 283B | Judkins berline 4P 3W | 5,710 | 5,400 | 17 |
| 285 | Willoughby limo 7P | 5,605 | 5,600 | 77 |
| 287 | LeBaron conv rdstr 2-4P | 5,085 | 4,400 | 45 |
| 271 | chassis | — | — | 12 |
| — | misc. specials | — | — | 14 |

| 1934 Engine | bore × stroke | bhp | availability |
|---|---|---|---|
| V-12, 414.0 | 3.13 × 4.50 | 150 | S-all |

## 1935

| 541 Model K (wb 136.0) | | Wght | Price | Prod |
|---|---|---|---|---|
| 542 | LeBaron conv rdstr 2-4P | 5,030 | 4,600 | 30 |

# Lincoln

| 541 Model K (wb 136.0) | | Wght | Price | Prod |
|---|---|---|---|---|
| 543 | sdn 4d 2W | 5,385 | 4,300 | 170 |
| 544 | sdn 4d 3W | 5,375 | 4,300 | 278 |
| 545 | cpe 5P | 5,230 | 4,200 | 44 |
| 546 | LeBaron conv sdn phtn 5P | 5,360 | 5,000 | 20 |
| 547 | Brunn conv victoria 5P | 5,135 | 5,500 | 15 |
| 548 | LeBaron cpe 2P | 5,030 | 4,600 | 23 |
| 541 | chassis | — | — | 1 |
| — | misc. specials | — | — | 5 |
| **301 Model K (wb 145.0)** | | | | |
| 302 | touring 7P | 5,225 | 4,200 | 15 |
| 303A | sdn 7P | 5,535 | 4,600 | 351 |
| 303B | limo 7P | 5,630 | 4,700 | 282 |
| 304A | Brunn cab 5P | 5,505 | 6,600 | 13 |
| 304B | Brunn cab 5P semi-clpsble | 5,415 | 6,700 | 13 |
| 305 | Brunn brougham 7P | 5,530 | 6,700 | 10 |
| 307 | LeBaron conv sdn 5P | 5,325 | 5,500 | 20 |
| 308 | Judkins limo 7P | 5,645 | 5,700 | 18 |
| 309A | Judkins berline 2W | 5,545 | 5,500 | 34 |
| 309B | Judkins berline 3W | 5,555 | 5,500 | 13 |
| 310 | Willoughby limo 7P | 5,695 | 5,700 | 40 |
| 311 | Willoughby spt sdn | 5,075 | 6,800 | 5 |
| 301 | chassis | — | — | 8 |
| — | misc. specials | — | — | 26 |

| 1935 Engine | bore × stroke | bhp | availability |
|---|---|---|---|
| V-12, 414.0 | 3.13 × 4.50 | 150 | S-all |

## 1936

| Series H Zephyr (wb 122.0) | | Wght | Price | Prod |
|---|---|---|---|---|
| 902 | sdn 4d | 3,349 | 1,320 | 13,180 |
| 903 | sdn 2d | 3,289 | 1,275 | 1,814 |
| **Model K (wb 136.0)** | | | | |
| 324A | sdn 5P 2W | 5,426 | 4,300 | 103 |
| 324B | sdn 5P 3W | 5,476 | 4,300 | 297 |
| 326 | cpe 5P | 5,266 | 4,200 | 36 |
| 328 | Brunn conv victoria 5P | 5,176 | 5,500 | 10 |
| 330 | LeBaron conv rdstr 2-4P | 5,136 | 4,700 | 20 |
| 332 | LeBaron cpe 2-4P | 4,700 | 5,126 | 25 |
| 334 | LeBaron conv sdn phtn 5P | 5,296 | 5,000 | 15 |
| **Model K (wb 145.0)** | | | | |
| 323 | touring 7P | 5,276 | 4,200 | 8 |
| 327A | sdn 7P | 5,591 | 4,600 | 368 |
| 327B | limo 7P | 5,641 | 4,700 | 370 |
| 329A | Brunn cab 5P | 5,511 | 6,600 | 10 |
| 329B | Brunn cab 5P semi-clpsble | 5,491 | 6,700 | 10 |
| 331 | Brunn brougham 7P | 5,571 | 6,700 | 20 |
| 333 | LeBaron conv sdn 5P | 5,381 | 5,500 | 30 |
| 335 | Judkins sdn limo 7P | 5,671 | 5,800 | 26 |
| 337A | Judkins berline 5P 2W | 5,561 | 5,500 | 51 |
| 337B | Judkins berline 5P 3W | 5,581 | 5,600 | 13 |
| 339 | Willoughby limo 7P | 5,661 | 5,700 | 62 |
| 341 | Willoughby spt sdn | 5,561 | 6,800 | 11 |
| 321 | chassis | — | — | 9 |
| — | misc. specials | — | — | 30 |
| 322 | chassis | — | — | 6 |
| — | misc. specials | — | — | 4 |

| 1936 Engines | bore × stroke | bhp | availability |
|---|---|---|---|
| V-12, 267.3 | 2.75 × 3.75 | 110 | S-Zephyr |
| V-12, 414.0 | 3.13 × 4.50 | 150 | S-K |

## 1937

| Series HB Zephyr (wb 122.0) | | Wght | Price | Prod |
|---|---|---|---|---|
| 700 | cpe sdn | 3,289 | 1,245 | 1,500 |
| 720 | cpe | 3,323 | 1,165 | 5,199 |
| 730 | sdn 4d | 3,349 | 1,265 | 23,159 |
| 737 | Town sdn | 3,507 | 1,425 | 139 |
| **Model K (wb 136.0; lwb-145.0)** | | | | |
| 353 | Willoughby touring 7P (lwb) | 5,950 | 5,550 | 7 |
| 354A | sdn 5P 2W | 5,700 | 4,450 | 48 |
| 354B | sdn 5P 3W | 5,700 | 4,450 | 136 |
| 356 | Willoughby cpe 5P | 5,790 | 5,550 | 6 |
| 357A | lwb sdn 7P | 5,905 | 4,750 | 212 |
| 357B | limo 7P (lwb) | 5,905 | 4,850 | 248 |
| 358 | Brunn conv vic 5P | 5,660 | 5,550 | 13 |
| 359A | Brunn lwb cab 5P | — | 6,650 | 10 |
| 359B | Brunn lwb cab semiclpsble 5P | 5,960 | 6,750 | 7 |
| 360 | LeBaron conv rdstr 2-4P | 5,490 | 4,950 | 15 |
| 361 | Brunn lwb brougham 7P | 5,995 | 6,750 | 29 |
| 362 | LeBaron cpe 2P | 5,380 | 4,950 | 24 |
| 363A | LeBaron lwb conv sdn/partition | 5,880 | 5,650 | 37 |
| 363B | LeBaron lwb conv sdn | 5,980 | 5,850 | 12 |
| 365 | Judkins sdn limo 7P (lwb) | 5,940 | 5,950 | 27 |
| 367A | Judkins lwb berline 5P 2W | 5,880 | 5,650 | 47 |
| 367B | Judkins lwb berline 5P 3W | 5,890 | 5,750 | 19 |
| 369 | Willoughby limo 7P (lwb) | 6,115 | 5,850 | 60 |
| 371 | Willoughby lwb spt sdn 5P | 5,915 | 6,850 | 6 |
| 373 | Willoughby pnl brham 7P (lwb) | — | 7,050 | 4 |
| 375 | Brunn lwb touring cab 5P | 6,020 | 6,950 | 10 |

| 1937 Engines | bore × stroke | bhp | availability |
|---|---|---|---|
| V-12, 267.3 | 2.75 × 3.75 | 110 | S-Zephyr |
| V-12, 414.0 | 3.13 × 4.50 | 150 | S-K |

## 1938

| Series 86H Zephyr (wb 125.0) | | Wght | Price | Prod |
|---|---|---|---|---|
| 700 | cpe sdn | 3,409 | 1,355 | 800 |
| 720 | cpe 3P | 3,294 | 1,295 | 2,600 |
| 730 | sdn 4d | 3,444 | 1,375 | 14,520 |
| 737 | Town limo | 3,474 | 1,550 | 130 |
| 740 | conv sdn 5P | 3,724 | 1,790 | 461 |
| 760B | conv cpe 3P | 3,489 | 1,700 | 600 |
| **Model K (wb 136.0; lwb-145.0)** | | | | |
| 403 | Willoughby lwb touring 7P | 5,557 | 5,900 | 5 |
| 404A | sdn 5P 2W | 5,527 | 4,900 | 9 |
| 404B | sdn 5P 3W | 5,532 | 4,900 | 49 |
| 406 | Willoughby cpe 5P | 5,407 | 5,900 | 4 |
| 407A | lwb sdn 7P | 5,672 | 5,100 | 78 |
| 407B | limo 7P (lwb) | 5,762 | 5,200 | 91 |
| 408 | Brunn conv victoria 5P | 5,322 | 5,900 | 8 |
| 409A | Brunn cab 5P | 5,696 | 6,900 | 6 |
| 409B | Brunn cab 5P semiclpsble (lwb) | 5,716 | 7,000 | 5 |
| 410 | LeBaron conv rdstr 2-4P | 5,297 | 5,300 | 8 |
| 411 | Brunn lwb brougham 7P | 5,806 | 7,000 | 13 |
| 412 | LeBaron cpe 2P | 5,462 | 5,300 | 12 |
| 413A | LeBaron lwb conv sdn/partition | 5,572 | 5,800 | 15 |
| 413B | LeBaron lwb conv sdn | 5,572 | 6,000 | 7 |
| 415 | Judkins lwb sdn limo 7P | 5,742 | 6,300 | 11 |
| 417A | Judkins lwb berline 5P 2W | 5,562 | 6,000 | 19 |
| 417B | Judkins lwb berline 5P 3W | 5,632 | 6,100 | 11 |
| 419 | Willoughby limo 7P (lwb) | 5,826 | 6,200 | 46 |
| 421 | Willoughby lwb spt sdn 5P | 5,716 | 7,000 | 4 |
| 423 | Willoughby panel brham 7P | — | 7,400 | 6 |
| 425 | Brunn lwb touring cab 5P | 5,662 | 7,200 | 9 |

| 1938 Engines | bore × stroke | bhp | availability |
|---|---|---|---|
| V-12, 267.3 | 2.75 × 3.75 | 110 | S-Zephyr |

# Lincoln

| 1938 Engines | bore × stroke | bhp | availability |
|---|---|---|---|
| V-12, 414.0 | 3.13 × 4.50 | 150 | S-K |

## 1939

| Series 96H Zephyr (wb 125.0) | | Wght | Price | Prod |
|---|---|---|---|---|
| 700 | cpe sdn | 3,600 | 1,369 | 800 |
| 720 | cpe 3P | 3,520 | 1,358 | 2,500 |
| 730 | sdn 4d | 3,620 | 1,399 | 16,663 |
| 737 | Town limo | 3,670 | 1,747 | 95 |
| 740 | conv sdn 5P | 3,900 | 1,839 | 302 |
| 760B | conv cpe 2-4P | 3,790 | 1,747 | 640 |

| Model K (wb 136.0; lwb-145.0) | | | | |
|---|---|---|---|---|
| 403 | Willoughby lwb touring 7P | 5,870 | 5,932 | 1 |
| 404A | sdn 5P 2W | 5,735 | 4,905 | 2 |
| 404B | sdn 5P 3W | 5,740 | 4,905 | 12 |
| 406 | Willoughby cpe 5P | 5,615 | 5,926 | 1 |
| 407A | lwb sdn 7P | 5,880 | 5,109 | 25 |
| 407B | limo 7P (lwb) | 5,970 | 5,211 | 58 |
| 408 | Brunn conv vic 5P | 5,530 | 5,926 | 2 |
| 409A | Brunn lwb cab 5P | 6,010 | 6,947 | 1 |
| 409B | Brunn lwb cab 5P semiclpsble | 6,030 | 7,049 | 1 |
| 410 | LeBaron conv rdstr 2-4P | 5,050 | 5,313 | 2 |
| 411 | Brunn lwb brougham 7P | 6,120 | 7,049 | 2 |
| 412 | LeBaron cpe 2P | 5,435 | 5,313 | 4 |
| 413A | LeBaron lwb conv sdn | 5,670 | 5,828 | 3 |
| 413B | LeBaron lwb conv sdn/partition | 5,780 | 6,028 | 6 |
| 415 | Judkins sdn limo 7P (lwb) | 5,950 | 6,334 | 2 |
| 417A | Judkins lwb berline 5P 2W | 5,770 | 6,028 | 2 |
| 417B | Judkins lwb berline 5P 3W | 5,840 | 6,130 | 1 |
| 419 | Willoughby limo 7P (lwb) | 6,140 | 6,232 | 4 |
| 421 | Willoughby lwb spt sdn 5P | 6,300 | 7,049 | 1 |
| 423 | Willoughby panel brham 7P | — | — | 1 |
| 425 | Brunn lwb touring cab 5P | 5,870 | 7,253 | 2 |

| 1939 Engines | bore × stroke | bhp | availability |
|---|---|---|---|
| V-12, 267.3 | 2.75 × 3.75 | 110 | S-Zephyr |
| V-12, 414.0 | 3.13 × 4.50 | 150 | S-Model K |

## 1940

| 06H Zephyr (wb 125.0) | | Wght | Price | Prod |
|---|---|---|---|---|
| 56 | Continental conv cpe | 3,740 | 2,916 | 350 |
| 57 | Continental club cpe | 3,850 | 2,783 | 54 |
| 72A | cpe 3P | 3,500 | 1,399 | ⎤ 1,256 |
| 72A | cpe 3P, Custom interior | 3,500 | 1,506 | ⎦ |
| 72B | cpe, A/S | 3,480 | 1,429 | 316 |
| 73 | sdn 4d | 3,660 | 1,439 | ⎤ 15,764 |
| 73 | sdn 4d, Custom interior | 3,660 | 1,547 | ⎦ |
| 76 | conv cpe | 3,760 | 1,818 | 700 |
| 77 | club cpe | 3,590 | 1,439 | ⎤ 3,500 |
| 77 | club cpe, Custom interior | 3,590 | 1,547 | ⎦ |
| 22 | Custom Town Limousine | 3,700 | 1,787 | 4 |
| 26 | Custom Town Car | 3,650 | 1,750 | 4 |

| K Series (wb 136.0)* | | | | |
|---|---|---|---|---|
| 404A | sdn 4d | 5,735 | 4,905 | — |
| 406 | Willoughby cpe | 5,615 | 5,926 | — |
| 408 | Brunn conv Victoria | 5,530 | 5,926 | — |
| 410 | LeBaron rdstr | 5,505 | 5,313 | — |
| 412 | LeBaron stationary cpe | 5,415 | 5,313 | — |

| K Series (wb 145.0)* | | | | |
|---|---|---|---|---|
| 407A | sdn 4d, 7P | 5,880 | 5,109 | — |
| 407B | limo | 5,970 | 5,211 | — |
| 409 | Brunn cabriolet | 6,010 | 6,947 | — |
| 411 | Brunn brougham 7P | 6,120 | 7,049 | — |
| 413 | LeBaron conv sdn | 5,670 | 5,823 | — |
| 415 | Judkins sdn limo 7P | 5,950 | 6,334 | — |
| 417A | Judkins berline 2W | 5,770 | 6,028 | — |
| 417B | Judkins berline 3W | 5,840 | 6,130 | — |
| 419 | Willoughby limo | 6,140 | 6,232 | — |
| 421 | Willoughby spt sdn | 6,300 | 7,049 | — |
| 425 | Brunn cabriolet 2P | 5,870 | 7,253 | — |

*Total K Series model-year production: 133.

| 1940 Engines | bore × stroke | bhp | availability |
|---|---|---|---|
| V-12, 292.0 | 2.88 × 3.75 | 120 | S-Zephyr |
| V-12, 414.0 | 3.13 × 4.50 | 150 | S-K Series |

## 1941

| 16H Zephyr (wb 125.0) | | Wght | Price | Prod |
|---|---|---|---|---|
| 72A | cpe 3P | 3,560 | 1,478 | ⎤ 972 |
| 72A | cpe 3P, Custom interior | 3,560 | 1,557 | ⎦ |
| 72B | cpe 5P | 3,580 | 1,464 | 178 |
| 73 | sdn 4d | 3,710 | 1,541 | ⎤ 14,469 |
| 73 | sdn 4d, Custom interior | 3,710 | 1,641 | ⎦ |
| 76 | conv cpe | 3,840 | 1,858 | 725 |
| 77 | club cpe | 3,640 | 1,541 | ⎤ 3,750 |
| 77 | club cpe, Custom interior | 3,640 | 1,541 | ⎦ |

| 16H Continental (wb 125.0) | | | | |
|---|---|---|---|---|
| 56 | conv cpe ("cabriolet") | 3,860 | 2,865 | 400 |
| 57 | club cpe | 3,890 | 2,812 | 850 |

| 168H Custom (wb 138.0) | | | | |
|---|---|---|---|---|
| 31 | sdn 4d 8P | 4,250 | 2,704 | 355 |
| 32 | limo | 4,270 | 2,836 | 295 |

| 1941 Engine | bore × stroke | bhp | availability |
|---|---|---|---|
| V-12, 292.0 | 2.88 × 3.75 | 120 | S-all |

## 1942

| 26H Zephyr (wb 125.0) | | Wght | Price | Prod |
|---|---|---|---|---|
| 72A | cpe 3P | 3,730 | 1,650 | ⎤ 273 |
| 72A | cpe 3P, Custom interior | 3,730 | 1,735 | ⎦ |
| 73 | sdn 4d | 3,920 | 1,700 | ⎤ 4,418 |
| 73 | sdn 4d, Custom interior | 3,920 | 1,795 | ⎦ |
| 76 | conv cpe | 4,130 | 2,150 | 191 |
| 77 | club cpe | 3,810 | 1,700 | ⎤ 1,236 |
| 77 | club cpe, Custom interior | 3,810 | 1,795 | ⎦ |

| 26H Continental (wb 125.0) | | | | |
|---|---|---|---|---|
| 56 | conv cpe ("cabriolet") | 4,020 | 3,000 | 136 |
| 57 | club cpe | 4,000 | 3,000 | 200 |

| 268H Custom (wb 125.0) | | | | |
|---|---|---|---|---|
| 31 | sdn 4d 8P | 4,380 | 2,950 | 47 |
| 32 | limo | 4,400 | 3,075 | 66 |

| 1942 Engine | bore × stroke | bhp | availability |
|---|---|---|---|
| V-12, 305.0 | 2.94 × 3.75 | 130 | S-all |

## 1946

| 66H (wb 125.0)—16,179 built | | Wght | Price | Prod |
|---|---|---|---|---|
| 73 | sdn 4d | 3,980 | 2,337 | — |
| 73 | sdn 4d, Custom interior | 3,980 | 2,486 | — |
| 76 | conv cpe | 4,210 | 2,883 | — |
| 77 | club cpe | 3,915 | 2,318 | — |

# Lincoln

| 66H (wb 125.0) | | Wght | Price | Prod |
|---|---|---|---|---|
| 77 | club cpe, Custom interior | 3,915 | 2,467 | — |
| **66H Continental (wb 125.0)** | | | | |
| 56 | conv cpe ("cabriolet") | 4,090 | 4,474 | 201 |
| 57 | club cpe | 4,100 | 4,392 | 265 |

| 1946 Engines | bore × stroke | bhp | availability |
|---|---|---|---|
| V-12, 292.0 | 2.88 × 3.75 | 120 | S-all late |
| V-12, 305.0 | 2.94 × 3.50 | 130 | S-all early |

## 1947

| 76H (wb 125.0)—19,891 built | | Wght | Price | Prod |
|---|---|---|---|---|
| 73 | sdn 4d | 4,015 | 2,554 | — |
| 73 | sdn 4d, Custom interior | 4,015 | 2,722 | — |
| 76 | conv cpe | 4,245 | 3,142 | — |
| 77 | club cpe | 3,915 | 2,533 | — |
| 77 | club cpe, Custom interior | 3,915 | 2,701 | — |
| **76H Continental (wb 125.0)** | | | | |
| 56 | conv cpe ("cabriolet") | 4,135 | 4,746 | 738 |
| 57 | club cpe | 4,125 | 4,662 | 831 |

| 1947 Engine | bore × stroke | bhp | availability |
|---|---|---|---|
| V-12, 292.0 | 2.88 × 3.75 | 125 | S-all |

## 1948

| 876H (wb 125.0)—6,470 built | | Wght | Price | Prod |
|---|---|---|---|---|
| 73 | sdn 4d | 4,015 | 2,554 | — |
| 73 | sdn 4d, Custom interior | 4,015 | 2,722 | — |
| 76 | conv cpe | 4,245 | 3,142 | — |
| 77 | club cpe | 3,915 | 2,533 | — |
| 77 | club cpe, Custom interior | 3,915 | 2,701 | — |
| **876H Continental (wb 125.0)** | | | | |
| 56 | conv cpe ("cabriolet") | 4,135 | 4,746 | 452 |
| 57 | club cpe | 4,125 | 4,662 | 847 |

| 1948 Engine | bore × stroke | bhp | availability |
|---|---|---|---|
| V-12, 292.0 | 2.88 × 3.75 | 125 | S-all |

## 1949

| 9EL (wb 121.0)—38,384 built | Wght | Price | Prod |
|---|---|---|---|
| cpe | 3,959 | 2,527 | — |
| Sport Sedan 4d | 4,009 | 2,575 | — |
| conv cpe | 4,224 | 3,116 | — |
| **9EH Cosmopolitan (wb 125.0)—35,123 built** | | | |
| cpe | 4,194 | 3,186 | — |
| Sport Sedan 4d | 4,259 | 3,238 | — |
| Town sdn 4d | 4,272 | 3,238 | — |
| conv cpe | 4,419 | 3,948 | — |

| 1949 Engine | bore × stroke | bhp | availability |
|---|---|---|---|
| V-8, 336.7 | 3.50 × 4.38 | 152 | S-all |

## 1950

| OEL (wb 121.0) | | Wght | Price | Prod |
|---|---|---|---|---|
| L-72 | cpe | 4,090 | 2,529 | ⎤ 5,748 |
| L-72C | Lido cpe | 4,145 | 2,721 | ⎦ |
| L-74 | Sport Sedan 4d | 4,115 | 2,576 | 11,741 |
| **OEH Cosmopolitan (wb 125.0)** | | | | |
| H-72 | cpe | 4,375 | 3,187 | ⎤ 1,824 |
| H-72C | Capri cpe | 4,385 | 3,406 | ⎦ |
| H-74 | Sport Sedan 4d | 4,410 | 3,240 | 8,341 |
| H-76 | conv cpe | 4,640 | 3,950 | 536 |

| 1950 Engine | bore × stroke | bhp | availability |
|---|---|---|---|
| V-8, 336.7 | 3.50 × 4.38 | 152 | S-all |

## 1951

| 1EL (wb 121.0) | | Wght | Price | Prod |
|---|---|---|---|---|
| L-72B | cpe | 4,065 | 2,505 | ⎤ 4,482 |
| L-72C | Lido cpe | 4,100 | 2,702 | ⎦ |
| L-74 | Sport Sedan 4d | 4,130 | 2,553 | 12,279 |
| **1EH Cosmopolitan (wb 125.0)** | | | | |
| H-72B | cpe | 4,340 | 3,129 | ⎤ 2,727 |
| H-72C | Capri cpe | 4,360 | 3,350 | ⎦ |
| H-74 | Sport Sedan 4d | 4,415 | 3,182 | 12,229 |
| H-76 | conv cpe | 4,615 | 3,891 | 857 |

| 1951 Engine | bore × stroke | bhp | availability |
|---|---|---|---|
| V-8, 336.7 | 3.50 × 4.38 | 154 | S-all |

## 1952

| 2H Cosmopolitan (wb 123.0) | | Wght | Price | Prod |
|---|---|---|---|---|
| 60C | Spt htp cpe | 4,155 | 3,293 | 4,545 |
| 73A | sdn 4d | 4,125 | 3,198 | * |
| **2H Capri (wb 123.0)** | | | | |
| 60A | htp cpe | 4,235 | 3,518 | 5,681 |
| 73B | sdn 4d | 4,140 | 3,331 | * |
| 76A | conv cpe | 4,350 | 3,665 | 1,191 |

* Combined sedan production: 15,854.

| 1952 Engine | bore × stroke | bhp | availability |
|---|---|---|---|
| V-8, 317.5 | 3.80 × 3.50 | 160 | S-all |

## 1953

| 8H Cosmopolitan (wb 123.0) | | Wght | Price | Prod |
|---|---|---|---|---|
| 60C | Sport htp cpe | 4,155 | 3,322 | 6,562 |
| 73A | sdn 4d | 4,135 | 3,226 | 7,560 |
| **8H Capri (wb 123.0)** | | | | |
| 60A | htp cpe | 4,165 | 3,549 | 12,916 |
| 73B | sdn 4d | 4,150 | 3,453 | 11,352 |
| 76A | conv cpe | 4,310 | 3,699 | 2,372 |

| 1953 Engine | bore × stroke | bhp | availability |
|---|---|---|---|
| V-8, 317.5 | 3.80 × 3.50 | 205 | S-all |

## 1954

| Cosmopolitan (wb 123.0) | | Wght | Price | Prod |
|---|---|---|---|---|
| 60C | Sport htp cpe | 4,155 | 3,625 | 2,994 |
| 73A | sdn 4d | 4,135 | 3,522 | 4,447 |
| **Capri (wb 123.0)** | | | | |
| 60A | htp cpe | 4,250 | 3,869 | 14,003 |
| 73B | sdn 4d | 4,245 | 3,711 | 13,598 |
| 76A | conv cpe | 4,310 | 4,031 | 1,951 |

| 1954 Engine | bore × stroke | bhp | availability |
|---|---|---|---|
| V-8, 317.5 | 3.80 × 3.50 | 205 | S-all |

## 1955

| Custom (wb 123.0) | | Wght | Price | Prod |
|---|---|---|---|---|
| 60C | Sport htp cpe | 4,185 | 3,666 | 1,362 |

# Lincoln

| Custom (wb 123.0) | | Wght | Price | Prod |
|---|---|---|---|---|
| 73A | sdn 4d | 4,235 | 3,563 | 2,187 |
| **Capri (wb 123.0)** | | | | |
| 60A | htp cpe | 4,305 | 3,910 | 11,462 |
| 73B | sdn 4d | 4,245 | 3,752 | 10,724 |
| 76A | conv cpe | 4,415 | 4,072 | 1,487 |

| 1955 Engine | bore × stroke | bhp | availability |
|---|---|---|---|
| V-8, 341.0 | 3.94 × 3.50 | 225 | S-all |

## 1956

| Capri (wb 126.0) | | Wght | Price | Prod |
|---|---|---|---|---|
| 60E | Sport htp cpe | 4,305 | 4,119 | 4,355 |
| 73A | sdn 4d | 4,315 | 4,212 | 4,436 |
| **Premiere (wb 126.0)** | | | | |
| 60B | htp cpe | 4,357 | 4,601 | 19,619 |
| 73B | sdn 4d | 4,347 | 4,601 | 19,465 |
| 76B | conv cpe | 4,452 | 4,747 | 2,447 |

| 1956 Engine | bore × stroke | bhp | availability |
|---|---|---|---|
| V-8, 368.0 | 4.00 × 3.66 | 285 | S-all |

## 1957

| Capri (wb 126.0) | | Wght | Price | Prod |
|---|---|---|---|---|
| 57A | Landau htp sdn | 4,460 | 4,794 | 1,451 |
| 58A | sdn 4d | 4,349 | 4,794 | 1,476 |
| 60A | htp cpe | 4,373 | 4,649 | 2,973 |
| **Premiere (wb 126.0)** | | | | |
| 57B | Landau htp sdn | 4,538 | 5,294 | 11,223 |
| 58B | sdn 4d | 4,527 | 5,294 | 5,139 |
| 60B | htp cpe | 4,451 | 5,149 | 15,185 |
| 76B | conv cpe | 4,676 | 5,381 | 3,676 |

| 1957 Engine | bore × stroke | bhp | availability |
|---|---|---|---|
| V-8, 368.0 | 4.00 × 3.66 | 300 | S-all |

## 1958

| Capri (wb 131.0) | | Wght | Price | Prod |
|---|---|---|---|---|
| 53A | sdn 4d | 4,799 | 4,951 | 1,184 |
| 57A | Landau htp sdn | 4,810 | 4,951 | 3,084 |
| 63A | htp cpe | 4,735 | 4,803 | 2,591 |
| **Premiere (wb 131.0)** | | | | |
| 53B | sdn 4d | 4,802 | 5,505 | 1,660 |
| 57B | Landau htp sdn | 4,798 | 5,505 | 5,572 |
| 63B | htp cpe | 4,734 | 5,318 | 3,043 |

| 1958 Engine | bore × stroke | bhp | availability |
|---|---|---|---|
| V-8, 430.0 | 4.30 × 3.70 | 375 | S-all |

## 1959

| (wb 131.0) | | Wght | Price | Prod |
|---|---|---|---|---|
| 53A | sdn 4d | 4,823 | 5,090 | 1,312 |
| 57A | Landau htp sdn | 4,824 | 5,090 | 4,417 |
| 63A | htp cpe | 4,741 | 4,902 | 2,200 |
| **Premiere (wb 131.0)** | | | | |
| 53B | sdn 4d | 4,887 | 5,594 | 1,282 |
| 57B | Landau htp sdn | 4,880 | 5,594 | 4,606 |
| 63B | htp cpe | 4,798 | 5,347 | 1,963 |
| **Continental Mark IV (wb 131.0)** | | | | |
| 23A | limo | 5,061 | 10,230 | 49 |
| 23B | formal sdn | 5,190 | 9,208 | 78 |
| 54A | sdn 4d | 5,061 | 6,845 | 955 |
| 65A | htp cpe | 4,967 | 6,598 | 1,703 |
| 68A | conv cpe | 5,076 | 7,056 | 2,195 |
| 75A | htp sdn | 5,050 | 6,845 | 6,146 |

| 1959 Engine | bore × stroke | bhp | availability |
|---|---|---|---|
| V-8, 430.0 | 4.30 × 3.70 | 350 | S-all |

## 1960

| (wb 131.0) | | Wght | Price | Prod |
|---|---|---|---|---|
| 53A | sdn 4d | 5,016 | 5,441 | 1,093 |
| 57A | Landau htp sdn | 5,012 | 5,441 | 4,397 |
| 63A | htp cpe | 4,917 | 5,253 | 1,670 |
| **Premiere (wb 131.0)** | | | | |
| 53B | sdn 4d | 5,064 | 5,945 | 1,010 |
| 57B | Landau htp sdn | 5,060 | 5,945 | 4,200 |
| 63B | htp cpe | 4,965 | 5,696 | 1,365 |
| **Continental Mark V (wb 131.0)** | | | | |
| 23A | limo | 5,481 | 10,230 | 34 |
| 23B | formal sdn | 5,272 | 9,208 | 136 |
| 54A | sdn 4d | 5,143 | 6,845 | 807 |
| 65A | htp cpe | 5,044 | 6,598 | 1,461 |
| 68A | conv cpe | 5,180 | 7,056 | 2,044 |
| 75A | Landau htp sdn | 5,139 | 6,845 | 6,604 |

| 1960 Engine | bore × stroke | bhp | availability |
|---|---|---|---|
| V-8, 430.0 | 4.30 × 3.70 | 315 | S-all |

## 1961

| Continental (wb 123.0) | | Wght | Price | Prod |
|---|---|---|---|---|
| 53A | htp sdn | 4,927 | 6,067 | 22,303 |
| 57C | htp sdn, special model | — | — | 4 |
| 74A | conv sdn | 5,215 | 6,713 | 2,857 |

| 1961 Engine | bore × stroke | bhp | availability |
|---|---|---|---|
| V-8, 430.0 | 4.30 × 3.70 | 300 | S-all |

## 1962

| Continental (wb 123.0) | | Wght | Price | Prod |
|---|---|---|---|---|
| 53A | htp sdn | 4,966 | 6,074 | 27,849 |
| 74A | conv sdn | 5,370 | 6,720 | 3,212 |

| 1962 Engine | bore × stroke | bhp | availability |
|---|---|---|---|
| V-8, 430.0 | 4.30 × 3.70 | 300 | S-all |

## 1963

| Continental (wb 123.0) | | Wght | Price | Prod |
|---|---|---|---|---|
| 53A | htp sdn | 4,936 | 6,270 | 28,095 |
| 74A | conv sdn | 5,340 | 6,916 | 3,138 |

| 1963 Engine | bore × stroke | bhp | availability |
|---|---|---|---|
| V-8, 430.0 | 4.30 × 3.70 | 320 | S-all |

## 1964

| Continental (wb 126.0) | | Wght | Price | Prod |
|---|---|---|---|---|
| 82 | htp sdn | 5,055 | 6,292 | 32,969 |
| 86 | conv sdn | 5,393 | 6,938 | 3,328 |

| 1964 Engine | bore × stroke | bhp | availability |
|---|---|---|---|
| V-8, 430.0 | 4.30 × 3.70 | 320 | S-all |

# Lincoln

## 1965

| Continental (wb 126.0) | | Wght | Price | Prod |
|---|---|---|---|---|
| 82 | htp sdn | 5,075 | 6,292 | 36,824 |
| 86 | conv sdn | 5,475 | 6,938 | 3,356 |

| 1965 Engine | bore × stroke | bhp | availability |
|---|---|---|---|
| V-8, 430.0 | 4.30 × 3.70 | 320 | S-all |

## 1966

| Continental (wb 126.0) | | Wght | Price | Prod |
|---|---|---|---|---|
| 82 | sdn 4d | 5,085 | 5,750 | 35,809 |
| 86 | conv sdn | 5,480 | 6,383 | 3,180 |
| 89 | htp cpe | 4,985 | 5,485 | 15,766 |

| 1966 Engine | bore × stroke | bhp | availability |
|---|---|---|---|
| V-8, 462.0 | 4.38 × 3.83 | 340 | S-all |

## 1967

| Continental (wb 126.0) | | Wght | Price | Prod |
|---|---|---|---|---|
| 82 | sdn 4d | 5,049 | 5,795 | 32,331 |
| 86 | conv sdn | 5,505 | 6,449 | 2,276 |
| 89 | htp cpe | 4,940 | 5,553 | 11,060 |

| 1967 Engine | bore × stroke | bhp | availability |
|---|---|---|---|
| V-8, 462.0 | 4.38 × 3.83 | 340 | S-all |

## 1968

| Continental (wb 126.0) | | Wght | Price | Prod |
|---|---|---|---|---|
| 81 | htp cpe | 4,883 | 5,736 | 9,415 |
| 82 | sdn 4d | 4,978 | 5,970 | 29,719 |

| Continental Mark III (wb 117.2) | | | | |
|---|---|---|---|---|
| 89 | htp cpe | 4,739 | 6,585 | 7,770 |

| 1968 Engines | bore × stroke | bhp | availability |
|---|---|---|---|
| V-8, 462.0 | 4.38 × 3.83 | 340 | S-all early |
| V-8, 460.0 | 4.36 × 3.85 | 365 | S-all late |

## 1969

| Continental (wb 126.0) | | Wght | Price | Prod |
|---|---|---|---|---|
| 81 | htp cpe | 4,910 | 5,830 | 9,032 |
| 82 | sdn 4d | 5,005 | 6,063 | 29,258 |

| Continental Mark III (wb 117.2) | | | | |
|---|---|---|---|---|
| 89 | htp cpe | 4,762 | 6,758 | 23,088 |

| 1969 Engine | bore × stroke | bhp | availability |
|---|---|---|---|
| V-8, 460.0 | 4.36 × 3.85 | 365 | S-all |

## 1970

| Continental (wb 126.0) | | Wght | Price | Prod |
|---|---|---|---|---|
| 81 | htp cpe | 4,669 | 5,976 | 9,073 |
| 82 | sdn 4d | 4,719 | 6,211 | 28,622 |

| Continental Mark III (wb 117.2) | | | | |
|---|---|---|---|---|
| 89 | htp cpe | 4,675 | 7,281 | 21,432 |

| 1970 Engine | bore × stroke | bhp | availability |
|---|---|---|---|
| V-8, 460.0 | 4.36 × 3.85 | 365 | S-all |

## 1971

| Continental (wb 127.0) | | Wght | Price | Prod |
|---|---|---|---|---|
| 81 | htp cpe | 5,032 | 7,172 | 8,205 |
| 82 | sdn 4d | 5,072 | 7,419 | 27,346 |

| Continental Mark III (wb 117.2) | | Wght | Price | Prod |
|---|---|---|---|---|
| 89 | htp cpe | 5,003 | 8,813 | 27,091 |

| 1971 Engine | bore × stroke | bhp | availability |
|---|---|---|---|
| V-8, 460.0 | 4.36 × 3.85 | 365 | S-all |

## 1972

| Continental (wb 127.0) | | Wght | Price | Prod |
|---|---|---|---|---|
| 81 | htp cpe | 4,906 | 7,068 | 10,408 |
| 82 | sdn 4d | 4,958 | 7,302 | 36,561 |

| Continental Mark IV (wb 120.4) | | | | |
|---|---|---|---|---|
| 89 | htp cpe | 4,792 | 8,640 | 48,591 |

| 1972 Engines | bore × stroke | bhp | availability |
|---|---|---|---|
| V-8, 460.0 | 4.36 × 3.85 | 224 | S-81, 82 |
| V-8, 460.0 | 4.36 × 3.85 | 212 | S-89 |

## 1973

| Continental (wb 127.0) | | Wght | Price | Prod |
|---|---|---|---|---|
| 81 | htp cpe | 5,016 | 7,230 | 13,348 |
| 82 | sdn 4d | 5,049 | 7,474 | 45,288 |

| Continental Mark IV (wb 120.4) | | | | |
|---|---|---|---|---|
| 89 | htp cpe | 4,908 | 8,984 | 69,437 |

| 1973 Engines | bore × stroke | bhp | availability |
|---|---|---|---|
| V-8, 460.0 | 4.36 × 3.85 | 219 | S-81, 82 |
| V-8, 460.0 | 4.36 × 3.85 | 208 | S-89 |

## 1974

| Continental (wb 127.2) | | Wght | Price | Prod |
|---|---|---|---|---|
| 81 | htp cpe | 5,366 | 8,053 | 7,318 |
| 82 | sdn 4d | 5,361 | 8,238 | 29,351 |

| Continental Mark IV (wb 120.4) | | | | |
|---|---|---|---|---|
| 89 | htp cpe | 5,362 | 10,194 | 57,316 |

| 1974 Engines | bore × stroke | bhp | availability |
|---|---|---|---|
| V-8, 460.0 | 4.36 × 3.85 | 215 | S-81, 82 |
| V-8, 460.0 | 4.36 × 3.85 | 220 | S-89 |

## 1975

| Continental (wb 127.2) | | Wght | Price | Prod |
|---|---|---|---|---|
| 81 | cpe | 5,219 | 9,214 | 21,185 |
| 82 | sdn 4d | 5,229 | 9,656 | 33,513 |

| Continental Mark IV (wb 120.4) | | | | |
|---|---|---|---|---|
| 89 | htp cpe | 5,145 | 11,082 | 47,145 |

| 1975 Engines | bore × stroke | bhp | availability |
|---|---|---|---|
| V-8, 460.0 | 4.36 × 3.85 | 206 | S-81, 82 |
| V-8, 460.0 | 4.36 × 3.85 | 194 | S-89 |

## 1976

| Continental (wb 127.2) | | Wght | Price | Prod |
|---|---|---|---|---|
| 81 | cpe | 5,035 | 9,142 | 24,663 |
| 82 | sdn 4d | 5,083 | 9,293 | 43,983 |

| Continental Mark IV (wb 120.4) | | | | |
|---|---|---|---|---|
| 89 | htp cpe | 5,051 | 11,060 | 56,110 |

| 1976 Engines | bore × stroke | bhp | availability |
|---|---|---|---|
| V-8, 460.0 | 4.36 × 3.85 | 202 | S-all |

# Lincoln

## 1977

| Versailles (wb 109.9) | | Wght | Price | Prod |
|---|---|---|---|---|
| 84 | sdn 4d | 3,800 | 11,500 | 15,434 |
| **Continental (wb 127.2)** | | | | |
| 81 | cpe | 4,836 | 9,474 | 27,440 |
| 82 | sdn 4d | 4,880 | 9,636 | 68,160 |
| **Continental Mark V (wb 120.4)** | | | | |
| 89 | htp cpe | 4,652 | 11,396 | 80,321 |

| 1977 Engines | bore × stroke | bhp | availability |
|---|---|---|---|
| V-8, 351.0 | 4.00 × 3.50 | 135 | S-Versailles |
| V-8, 400.0 | 4.00 × 4.00 | 179 | S-81, 82, 89 |
| V-8, 460.0 | 4.36 × 3.85 | 208 | O-81, 82, 89 |

## 1978

| Versailles (wb 109.0) | | Wght | Price | Prod |
|---|---|---|---|---|
| 84 | sdn 4d | 3,759 | 12,529 | 8,931 |
| **Continental (wb 127.2)** | | | | |
| 81 | cpe | 4,659 | 9,974 | 20,977 |
| 82 | sdn 4d | 4,660 | 10,166 | 67,110 |
| **Continental Mark V (wb 120.4)** | | | | |
| 89 | htp cpe | 4,567 | 12,099 | 72,602 |

| 1978 Engines | bore × stroke | bhp | availability |
|---|---|---|---|
| V-8, 302.0 | 4.00 × 3.00 | 133 | S-Versailles |
| V-8, 400.0 | 4.00 × 4.00 | 166 | S-81, 82, 89 |
| V-8, 460.0 | 4.36 × 3.85 | 210 | O-81, 82, 89 |

## 1979

| Versailles (wb 109.9) | | Wght | Price | Prod |
|---|---|---|---|---|
| 84 | sdn 4d | 3,684 | 12,939 | 21,007 |
| **Continental (wb 127.2)** | | | | |
| 81 | cpe | 4,639 | 10,985 | 16,142 |
| 82 | sdn 4d | 4,649 | 11,200 | 76,458 |
| **Continental Mark V (wb 120.4)** | | | | |
| 89 | htp cpe | 4,589 | 13,067 | 75,939 |

| 1979 Engines | bore × stroke | bhp | availability |
|---|---|---|---|
| V-8, 302.0 | 4.00 × 3.00 | 130 | S-Versailles |
| V-8, 400.0 | 4.00 × 4.00 | 159 | S-81, 82, 89 |

## 1980

| Versailles (wb 109.9) | | Wght | Price | Prod |
|---|---|---|---|---|
| 84 | 4d | 3,661 | 14,674 | 4,784 |
| **Continental (wb 117.3; 2d-114.3)** | | | | |
| 81 | cpe | 3,843 | 12,555 | 7,177 |
| 82 | sdn 4d | 3,919 | 12,884 | 24,056 |
| **Continental Mark VI (wb 117.3; 2d-114.3)—38,891 built** | | | | |
| 89 | sdn 2d | 3,892 | 15,424 | — |
| 90 | sdn 4d | 3,988 | 15,824 | 38,891 |
| 96 | Signature sdn 2d | 3,896 | 20,940 | — |
| 96 | Signature sdn 4d | 3,993 | 21,309 | — |

| 1980 Engines | bore × stroke | bhp | availability |
|---|---|---|---|
| V-8, 302.0 | 4.00 × 3.00 | 132 | S-Versailles |
| V-8, 302.0 | 4.00 × 3.00 | 129 | S-Contl, Mk VI |
| V-8, 351.0 | 4.00 × 3.50 | 140 | O-Contl, Mk VI |

## 1981

| Town Car (wb 117.3) | | Wght | Price | Prod |
|---|---|---|---|---|
| 93 | sdn 2d | 3,884 | 13,707 | 4,935 |
| 94 | sdn 4d | 3,958 | 14,068 | 27,904 |
| **Continental Mark VI (wb 117.3; 2d-114.3)** | | | | |
| 95 | cpe 2d | 3,899 | 16,858 | ⎤ 18,740 |
| 95 | Signature cpe 2d | 3,990 | 22,463 | ⎦ |
| 96 | sdn 4d | 3,944 | 17,303 | ⎤ 17,958 |
| 96 | Signature sdn 4d | 4,035 | 22,838 | ⎦ |

| 1981 Engines | bore × stroke | bhp | availability |
|---|---|---|---|
| V-8, 302.0 | 4.00 × 3.00 | 130 | S-all |

## 1982

| Continental (wb 108.5)—23,908 built | | Wght | Price | Prod |
|---|---|---|---|---|
| 98 | sdn 4d | 3,512 | 21,302 | — |
| 98/603 | Signature sdn 4d | 3,610 | 24,456 | — |
| 98/60H | Givenchy sdn 4d | 3,610 | 24,803 | — |
| **Mark VI (wb 117.3; 2d-114.3)** | | | | |
| 95 | cpe 2d | 3,879 | 19,452 | ⎤ |
| 95/603 | Signature cpe 2d | 3,888 | 22,252 | ⎥ 11,532 |
| 95/60M | Givenchy cpe 2d | 3,910 | 22,722 | ⎥ |
| 95/60N | Bill Blass cpe 2d | 3,910 | 23,594 | ⎦ |
| 96 | sdn 4d | 3,976 | 19,924 | ⎤ |
| 96/603 | Signature sdn 4d | 3,985 | 22,720 | ⎥ 14,804 |
| 96/60P | Pucci sdn 4d | 3,970 | 23,465 | ⎦ |
| **Town Car (wb 117.3)—35,069 built** | | | | |
| 94 | sdn 4d | 3,936 | 16,100 | — |
| 94/60U | Signature sdn 4d | 3,952 | 17,394 | — |
| 94/605 | Cartier sdn 4d | 3,944 | 18,415 | — |

| 1982 Engines | bore × stroke | bhp | availability |
|---|---|---|---|
| V-6, 232.0 | 3.80 × 3.40 | 112 | O-Continental |
| V-8, 302.0 | 4.00 × 3.00 | 130 | S-Continental |
| V-8, 302.0 | 4.00 × 3.00 | 134 | S-Mark, Town Car |

## 1983

| Continental (wb 108.5)—16,831 built | | Wght | Price | Prod |
|---|---|---|---|---|
| 97 | sdn 4d | 3,719 | 20,985 | — |
| 98/60R | Valentino sdn 4d | 3,757 | 22,576 | — |
| 97/60M | Givenchy sdn 4d | 3,757 | 22,576 | — |
| **Mark VI (wb 117.3; 2d-114.3)** | | | | |
| 98 | cpe 2d | 4,004 | 20,229 | ⎤ |
| 98/603 | Signature cpe 2d | 4,013 | 23,124 | ⎥ 12,743 |
| 98/60N | Bill Blass cpe 2d | 4,035 | 24,533 | ⎥ |
| 98/60P | Pucci cpe 2d | NA | 24,345 | ⎦ |
| 99 | sdn 4d | 4,105 | 20,717 | ⎤ |
| 99/603 | Signature sdn 4d | 4,114 | 23,612 | ⎥ 18,113 |
| 99/60P | Pucci sdn 4d | 4,099 | 24,407 | ⎦ |
| **Town Car (wb 117.3)—53,381 built** | | | | |
| 96 | sdn 4d | 4,062 | 16,923 | — |
| 96/60U | Signature sdn 4d | 4,078 | 18,265 | — |
| 96/605 | Cartier sdn 4d | 4,070 | 19,601 | — |

| 1983 Engines | bore × stroke | bhp | availability |
|---|---|---|---|
| V-8, 302.0 | 4.00 × 3.00 | 130 | S-all |
| V-8, 302.0 | 4.00 × 3.00 | 145 | O-Mark |

## 1984

| Continental (wb 108.5)—30,468 built | | Wght | Price | Prod |
|---|---|---|---|---|
| 97 | sdn 4d | 3,750 | 21,769 | — |

# Lincoln

| Continental (wb 108.5) | Wght | Price | Prod |
|---|---|---|---|
| 97/60R Valentino sdn 4d | — | 24,217 | — |
| 97/60M Givenchy sdn 4d | — | 24,242 | — |
| **Mark VII (wb 108.5)—33,344 built** | | | |
| 98 cpe 2d | 3,625 | 21,707 | — |
| 98/938 LSC cpe 2d | — | 23,706 | — |
| 98/60N Bill Blass cpe 2d | — | 24,807 | — |
| 98/60P Versace cpe 2d | — | 24,406 | — |
| **Town Car (wb 117.3)—93,622 built** | | | |
| 96 sdn 4d | 4,062 | 18,071 | — |
| 96/60U Signature sdn 4d | 4,078 | 20,040 | — |
| 96/605 Cartier sdn 4d | 4,070 | 21,706 | — |

| 1984 Engines | bore × stroke | bhp | availability |
|---|---|---|---|
| I-6TD, 149.0 | 3.15 × 3.19 | 115 | O-Cont, Mark VII |
| V-8, 302.0 | 4.00 × 3.00 | 140 | S-all |
| V-8, 302.0 | 4.00 × 3.00 | 155 | O-Town Car |

## 1985

| Continental (wb 108.5)—28,253 built | Wght | Price | Prod |
|---|---|---|---|
| 97/850A sdn 4d | 3,790 | 22,573 | — |
| 97/865A Valentino sdn 4d | — | 26,078 | — |
| 97/860A Givenchy sdn 4d | — | 25,783 | — |
| **Mark VII (wb 108.5)—18,355 built** | | | |
| 98/800A cpe 2d | 3,615 | 22,399 | — |
| 98/805A LSC cpe 2d | — | 24,332 | — |
| 98/810A Bill Blass cpe 2d | — | 26,659 | — |
| 98/815A Versace cpe 2d | — | 26,578 | — |
| **Town Car (wb 117.3)—119,878 built** | | | |
| 96/700A sdn 4d | 4,027 | 19,047 | — |
| 96/705A Signature sdn 4d | — | 22,130 | — |
| 96/710A Cartier sdn 4d | — | 23,637 | — |

| 1985 Engines | bore × stroke | bhp | availability |
|---|---|---|---|
| I-6TD, 149.0 | 3.15 × 3.19 | 115 | O-Cont, Mark VII |
| V-8, 302.0 | 4.00 × 3.00 | 140 | S-all exc LSC |
| V-8, 302.0 | 4.00 × 3.00 | 155 | O-Town Car |
| V-8, 302.0 | 4.00 × 3.00 | 165 | S-Mark VII LSC |

Note: 1984-85 Lincolns with turbodiesel engine were priced higher than amounts shown.

## 1986

| Continental (wb 108.5)—19,012 built | Wght | Price | Prod |
|---|---|---|---|
| 97/850A sdn 4d | 3,778 | 24,556 | — |
| 97/860A Givenchy sdn 4d | 3,808 | 26,837 | — |
| **Mark VII (wb 108.5)—20,056 built** | | | |
| 98/800A cpe 2d | 3,667 | 22,399 | — |
| 98/805B LSC cpe 2d | 3,718 | 23,857 | — |
| 98/810B Bill Blass cpe 2d | 3,732 | 23,857 | — |
| **Town Car (wb 117.3)—117,771 built** | | | |
| 96/700B sdn 4d | 4,038 | 20,764 | — |
| 96/705B Signature sdn 4d | 4,121 | 29,972 | — |
| 96/710B Cartier sdn 4d | 4,093 | 25,235 | — |

| 1986 Engines | bore × stroke | bhp | availability |
|---|---|---|---|
| V-8, 302.0 | 4.00 × 3.00 | 150 | S-all exc LSC |
| V-8, 302.0 | 4.00 × 3.00 | 200 | S-Mark VII LSC |

## 1987

| Continental (wb 108.5)—17,597 built | Wght | Price | Prod |
|---|---|---|---|
| 97 sdn 4d | 3,799 | 26,402 | — |
| 98 Givenchy sdn 4d | 3,826 | 28,902 | — |
| **Mark VII (108.5)—15,286 built** | | | |
| 91 cpe 2d | 3,722 | 24,216 | — |
| 93 LSC cpe 2d | 3,772 | 25,863 | — |
| 92 Bill Blass cpe 2d | 3,747 | 25,863 | — |
| **Town Car (wb 117.3)—76,483 built** | | | |
| 81 sdn 4d | 4,051 | 22,549 | — |
| 82 Signature sdn 4d | 4,106 | 25,541 | — |
| 83 Cartier sdn 4d | 4,086 | 26,868 | — |

| 1987 Engines | bore × stroke | bhp | availability |
|---|---|---|---|
| V-8, 302.0 | 4.00 × 3.00 | 150 | S-all exc LSC |
| V-8, 302.0 | 4.00 × 3.00 | 200 | S-Mark VII LSC |

## 1988

| Continental (wb 109.0)—41,287 built | Wght | Price | Prod |
|---|---|---|---|
| 97 sdn 4d | 3,628 | 26,078 | — |
| 98 Signature sdn 4d | 3,618 | 27,944 | — |
| **Mark VII (wb 108.5)—38,259 built** | | | |
| 93 LSC cpe 2d | 3,772 | 25,016 | — |
| 92 Bill Blass cpe 2d | 3,747 | 25,016 | — |
| **Town Car (wb 117.3)—201,113 built** | | | |
| 81 sdn 4d | 4,093 | 23,126 | — |
| 82 Signature sdn 4d | 4,119 | 25,990 | — |
| 83 Cartier sdn 4d | 4,107 | 27,273 | — |

| 1988 Engines | bore × stroke | bhp | availability |
|---|---|---|---|
| V-6, 232.0 | 3.80 × 3.40 | 140 | S-Continental |
| V-8, 302.0 | 4.00 × 3.00 | 150 | S-Town Car |
| V-8, 302.0 | 4.00 × 3.00 | 225 | S-Mark VII |

## 1989

| Continental (wb 109.0)—57,775 built | Wght | Price | Prod |
|---|---|---|---|
| 97 sdn 4d | 3,635 | 27,468 | — |
| 98 Signature sdn 4d | 3,633 | 29,334 | — |
| **Mark VII (wb 108.5)—29,658 built** | | | |
| 93 LSC cpe 2d | 3,743 | 27,218 | — |
| 92 Bill Blass cpe 2d | 3,783 | 27,218 | — |
| **Town Car (wb 117.3)—128,533 built** | | | |
| 81 sdn 4d | 4,044 | 25,205 | — |
| 82 Signature sdn 4d | 4,070 | 28,206 | — |
| 83 Cartier sdn 4d | 4,059 | 29,352 | — |
| — Gucci sdn 4d | 4,059 | — | — |

| 1989 Engines | bore × stroke | bhp | availability |
|---|---|---|---|
| V-6, 232.0 | 3.80 × 3.40 | 140 | S-Continental |
| V-8, 302.0 | 4.00 × 3.00 | 150 | S-Town Car |
| V-8, 302.0 | 4.00 × 3.00 | 225 | S-Mark VII |

## 1990

| Continental (wb 109.0)—64,257 built | Wght | Price | Prod |
|---|---|---|---|
| 97 sdn 4d | 3,663 | 29,258 | — |
| 98 Signature sdn 4d | — | 31,181 | — |
| **Mark VII (wb 108.5)—22,313 built** | | | |
| 93 LSC cpe 2d | 3,779 | 29,437 | — |
| 92 Bill Blass cpe 2d | — | 29,215 | — |
| **Town Car (wb 117.3)—147,160 built** | | | |
| 81 sdn 4d | 4,025 | 27,315 | — |

# Lincoln

| Town Car (wb 117.3) | | Wght | Price | Prod |
|---|---|---|---|---|
| 82 | Signature sdn 4d | — | 30,043 | — |
| 83 | Cartier sdn 4d | — | 32,137 | — |

| 1990 Engines | bore × stroke | bhp | availability |
|---|---|---|---|
| V-6, 232.0 | 3.80 × 3.40 | 140 | S-Continental |
| V-8, 302.0 | 4.00 × 3.00 | 150 | S-Town Car |
| V-8, 302.0 | 4.00 × 3.00 | 225 | S-Mark VII |

## 1991

| Continental (wb 109.0)—53,109 built | Wght | Price | Prod |
|---|---|---|---|
| 54/HVS Executive sdn 4d | 3,633 | 30,211 | — |
| 54/HVB Signature sdn 4d | 3,635 | 32,120 | — |

| Mark VII (wb 108.5)—9,299 built | Wght | Price | Prod |
|---|---|---|---|
| 63/HVC Bill Blass cpe 2d | 3,782 | 30,238 | — |
| 63/HVB LSC cpe 2d | 3,807 | 30,362 | — |

| Town Car (wb 117.4)—124,919 built | Wght | Price | Prod |
|---|---|---|---|
| AB/FC sdn 4d | 4,035 | 29,458 | — |
| BR/FC Signature sdn 4d | — | 32,416 | — |
| BS/FC Cartier sdn 4d | — | 34,504 | — |

| 1991 Engines | bore × stroke | bhp | availability |
|---|---|---|---|
| V-6, 232.0 | 3.80 × 3.40 | 155 | S-Continental |
| V-8, 281.0 | 3.60 × 3.60 | 190 | S-Town Car (ohc) |
| V-8, 281.0 | 3.60 × 3.60 | 210 | O-Town Car (ohc) |
| V-8, 302.0 | 4.00 × 3.00 | 225 | S-Mark VII |

## 1992

| Continental (wb 109.0)—40,822 built | Wght | Price | Prod |
|---|---|---|---|
| 54/HVS Executive sdn 4d | 3,628 | 32,263 | — |
| 54/HVB Signature sdn 4d | 3,623 | 34,253 | — |

| Mark VII (wb 108.5)—5,732 built | Wght | Price | Prod |
|---|---|---|---|
| 63/HVC Bill Blass cpe 2d | 3,768 | 32,032 | — |
| 63/HVB LSC cpe 2d | 3,781 | 32,156 | — |

| Town Car (wb 117.4)—113,458 built | Wght | Price | Prod |
|---|---|---|---|
| AB/FC sdn 4d | 4,024 | 31,211 | — |
| BR/FC Signature sdn 4d | 4,025 | 34,252 | — |
| BS/FC Cartier sdn 4d | 4,035 | 36,340 | — |

| 1992 Engines | bore × stroke | bhp | availability |
|---|---|---|---|
| V-6, 232.0 | 3.80 × 3.40 | 160 | S-Continental |
| V-8, 281.0 | 3.60 × 3.60 | 190 | S-Town Car (ohc) |
| V-8, 281.0 | 3.60 × 3.60 | 210 | O-Town Car (ohc) |
| V-8, 302.0 | 4.00 × 3.00 | 225 | S-Mark VII |

## 1993

| Continental (wb 109.0)—26,798 built | Wght | Price | Prod |
|---|---|---|---|
| 54/HVS Executive sdn 4d | 3,595 | 33,328 | — |
| 54/HVB Signature sdn 4d | 3,634 | 35,319 | — |

| Mark VIII (wb 113.0) | Wght | Price | Prod |
|---|---|---|---|
| 63/HVB cpe 2d | 3,752 | 36,640 | 32,370 |

| Town Car (wb 117.4)—118,040 built | Wght | Price | Prod |
|---|---|---|---|
| AB/FC Executive sdn 4d | 4,040 | 34,190 | — |
| BR/FC Signature sdn 4d | 4,046 | 35,494 | — |
| BS/FC Cartier sdn 4d | 4,084 | 37,581 | — |

| 1993 Engines | bore × stroke | bhp | availability |
|---|---|---|---|
| V-6, 232.0 | 3.80 × 3.40 | 160 | S-Continental |
| V-8, 281.0 | 3.60 × 3.60 | 190 | S-Town Car (ohc) |
| V-8, 281.0 | 3.60 × 3.60 | 210 | O-Town Car (ohc) |
| V-8, 281.0 | 3.60 × 3.60 | 280 | S-Mark VIII (dohc) |

## 1994

| Continental (wb 109.0)—52,107 built | Wght | Price | Prod |
|---|---|---|---|
| 54/HVS Executive sdn 4d | 3,576 | 33,750 | — |
| 54/HVB Signature sdn 4d | 3,613 | 35,600 | — |

| Mark VIII (wb 113.0) | Wght | Price | Prod |
|---|---|---|---|
| 63/HVB cpe 2d | 3,768 | 38,050 | 28,164 |

| Town Car (wb 117.4) | Wght | Price | Prod |
|---|---|---|---|
| AB/FC Executive sdn 4d | 4,039 | 34,750 | 62,865 |
| BS/FC Cartier sdn 4d | 4,095 | 38,100 | |
| BR/FC Signature sdn 4d | 4,057 | 36,050 | 54,583 |

| 1994 Engines | bore × stroke | bhp | availability |
|---|---|---|---|
| V-6, 232.0 | 3.80 × 3.40 | 160 | S-Continental |
| V-8, 281.0 | 3.60 × 3.60 | 210 | S-Town Car (ohc) |
| V-8, 281.0 | 3.60 × 3.60 | 280 | S-Mark VIII (dohc) |

## 1995

| Continental (wb 109.0) | Wght | Price | Prod |
|---|---|---|---|
| M97 sdn 4d | 3,969 | 40,750 | 44,854 |

| Mark VIII (wb 113.0 | Wght | Price | Prod |
|---|---|---|---|
| M91 cpe 2d | 3,768 | 38,800 | 18,390 |

| Town Car (wb 117.4)—119,109 built | Wght | Price | Prod |
|---|---|---|---|
| M81 Executive sdn 4d | 4,031 | 36,400 | — |
| M82 Signature sdn 4d | — | 38,500 | — |
| M83 Cartier sdn 4d | — | 41,200 | — |

| 1995 Engines | bore × stroke | bhp | availability |
|---|---|---|---|
| V-8, 281.0 | 3.60 × 3.60 | 210 | S-Town Car (ohc) |
| V-8, 281.0 | 3.60 × 3.60 | 260 | S-Continental (dohc) |
| V-8, 281.0 | 3.60 × 3.60 | 280 | S-Mark VIII (dohc) |

## 1996

| Continental (wb 109.0) | Wght | Price | Prod |
|---|---|---|---|
| M97 sdn 4d | 3,911 | 41,800 | 29,455 |

| Mark VIII (wb 113.0) | Wght | Price | Prod |
|---|---|---|---|
| M91 cpe 2d | 3,768 | 39,650 | 13,625 |

| Town Car (wb 117.4)—93,616 built | Wght | Price | Prod |
|---|---|---|---|
| M81 Executive sdn 4d | 4,040 | 36,910 | — |
| M82 Signature sdn 4d | 4,040 | 38,960 | — |
| M83 Cartier sdn 4d | 4,103 | 41,960 | — |

| 1996 Engines | bore × stroke | bhp | availability |
|---|---|---|---|
| V-8, 281.0 | 3.60 × 3.60 | 210 | S-Town Car |
| V-8, 281.0 | 3.60 × 3.60 | 260 | S-Continental (dohc) |
| V-8, 281.0 | 3.60 × 3.60 | 280 | S-Mark VIII (dohc) |
| V-8, 281.0 | 3.60 × 3.60 | 290 | O-Mark VIII (dohc) |

## 1997

| Continental (wb 109.0) | Wght | Price | Prod |
|---|---|---|---|
| M97 sdn 4d | 3,884 | 37,280 | 32,245 |

| Mark VIII (wb 113.0)—16,365 built | Wght | Price | Prod |
|---|---|---|---|
| M91 cpe 2d | 3,765 | 37,280 | — |
| M92 LSC cpe 2d | 3,785 | 38,880 | — |

| Town Car (wb 117.4)—104,533 built | Wght | Price | Prod |
|---|---|---|---|
| M81 Executive sdn 4d | 3,997 | 37,280 | — |

## Lincoln

| Town Car (wb 117.4)—104,533 built | | Wght | Price | Prod |
|---|---|---|---|---|
| M82 | Signature sdn 4d | 3,977 | 39,640 | — |
| M83 | Cartier sdn 4d | 3,977 | 43,200 | — |

| 1997 Engines | bore × stroke | bhp | availability |
|---|---|---|---|
| V-8, 281.0 | 3.60 × 3.60 | 210 | S-Town Car |
| V-8, 281.0 | 3.60 × 3.60 | 260 | S-Continental (dohc) |
| V-8, 281.0 | 3.60 × 3.60 | 280 | S-Mark VIII (dohc) |
| V-8, 281.0 | 3.60 × 3.60 | 290 | O-Mark VIII (dohc) |

### 1998

| Continental (wb 109.0) | | Wght | Price | Prod* |
|---|---|---|---|---|
| M97 | sdn 4d | 3,868 | 37,830 | 36,328 |
| **Mark VIII (wb 113.0)—6,103 built** | | | | |
| M91 | cpe 2d | 3,765 | 37,830 | — |
| M92 | LSC cpe 2d | 3,785 | 39,320 | — |
| **Town Car (wb 117.7)—110,718 built** | | | | |
| M81 | Executive sdn 4d | 3,860 | 37,830 | — |
| M82 | Signature sdn 4d | — | 39,480 | — |
| M83 | Cartier sdn 4d | — | 41,830 | — |

| 1998 Engines | bore × stroke | bhp | availability |
|---|---|---|---|
| V-8, 281.0 | 3.60 × 3.60 | 200 | S-Town Car |
| V-8, 281.0 | 3.60 × 3.60 | 220 | O-Town Car |
| V-8, 281.0 | 3.60 × 3.60 | 260 | S-Continental (dohc) |
| V-8, 281.0 | 3.60 × 3.60 | 280 | S-Mark VIII (dohc) |
| V-8, 281.0 | 3.60 × 3.60 | 290 | O-Mark VIII (dohc) |

*Calendar-year production.

### 1999

| Continental (wb 109.0) | | Wght | Price | Prod* |
|---|---|---|---|---|
| M97 | sdn 4d | 3,868 | 38,325 | 27,682 |
| **Town Car (wb 117.7)—83,235 built** | | | | |
| M81 | Executive sdn 4d | 4,015 | 38,325 | — |
| M82 | Signature sdn 4d | — | 40,325 | — |
| M83 | Cartier sdn 4d | — | 42,825 | — |

| 1999 Engines | bore × stroke | bhp | availability |
|---|---|---|---|
| V-8, 281.0 | 3.60 × 3.60 | 200 | S-Town Car |
| V-8, 281.0 | 3.60 × 3.60 | 220 | O-Town Car |
| V-8, 281.0 | 3.60 × 3.60 | 275 | S-Continental (dohc) |

*Calendar-year production.

### 2000

| LS (wb 114.5)—60,066 built | | Wght | Price | Prod* |
|---|---|---|---|---|
| M86 | V-6 automatic sdn 4d | 3,593 | 30,915 | — |
| M86 | V-6 manual sdn 4d | 3,598 | 31,715 | — |
| M87 | V-8 sdn 4d | 3,692 | 34,690 | — |
| **Continental (wb 109.0)** | | | | |
| M97 | sdn 4d | 3,868 | 38,880 | 23,440 |
| **Town Car (wb 117.7)—83,517 built** | | | | |
| M81 | Executive sdn 4d | 4,015 | 38,630 | — |
| M82 | Signature sdn 4d | — | 40,630 | — |
| M83 | Cartier sdn 4d | — | 43,130 | — |

| 2000 Engines | bore × stroke | bhp | availability |
|---|---|---|---|
| V-6, 181.0 | 3.50 × 3.13 | 210 | S-LS (dohc) |
| V-8, 240.0 | 3.39 × 3.35 | 252 | O-LS (dohc) |
| V-8, 281.0 | 3.60 × 3.60 | 200 | S-Town Car (ohc) |
| V-8, 281.0 | 3.60 × 3.60 | 220 | O-Town Car (ohc) |
| V-8, 281.0 | 3.60 × 3.60 | 275 | S-Continental (dohc) |

*Calendar-year production.

### 2001

| LS (wb 114.5)—38,946 built | | Wght | Price | Prod* |
|---|---|---|---|---|
| M86 | V-6 automatic sdn 4d | 3,593 | 31,665 | — |
| M86 | V-6 manual sdn 4d | 3,598 | 33,445 | — |
| M87 | V-8 sdn 4d | 3,692 | 35,695 | — |
| **Continental (wb 109.0)** | | | | |
| M97 | sdn 4d | 3,848 | 39,380 | 17,873 |
| **Town Car (wb 117.7, L-123.7)—67,380 built** | | | | |
| M81 | Executive sdn 4d | 4,015 | 39,145 | — |
| M82 | Signature sdn 4d | 4,020 | 41,315 | — |
| M83 | Cartier sdn 4d | 4,095 | 43,700 | — |
| M85 | Cartier L sdn 4d | 4,215 | 48,510 | — |

| 2001 Engines | bore × stroke | bhp | availability |
|---|---|---|---|
| V-6, 181.0 | 3.50 × 3.13 | 210 | S-LS (dohc) |
| V-8, 240.0 | 3.39 × 3.35 | 252 | O-LS (dohc) |
| V-8, 281.0 | 3.60 × 3.60 | 225 | S-Town Car (ohc) |
| V-8, 281.0 | 3.60 × 3.60 | 240 | O-Town Car (ohc) |
| V-8, 281.0 | 3.60 × 3.60 | 275 | S-Continental (dohc) |

*Calendar-year production.

### 2002

| LS (wb 114.5) | | Wght | Price | Prod* |
|---|---|---|---|---|
| M86 | V-6 auto sdn 4d | 3,593 | 33,045 | |
| M86 | V-6 Convenience auto sdn 4d | — | 34,230 | |
| M86 | V-6 Sport auto sdn 4d | — | 35,030 | |
| M86 | V-6 Sport man sdn 4d | — | 35,055 | |
| M86 | V-6 Premium auto sdn 4d | — | 36,335 | |
| M87 | V-8 sdn 4d | 3,692 | 37,220 | |
| M87 | V-8 Sport sdn 4d | — | 38,075 | |
| M87 | V-8 Premium sdn 4d | — | 39,395 | |
| **Continental (wb 109.0)** | | | | |
| M97 | sdn 4d | 3,848 | 38,010 | |
| M97 | Driver Select sdn 4d | — | 38,615 | |
| M97 | Personal Security sdn 4d | — | 39,600 | |
| M97 | Luxury Appearance sdn 4d | — | 39,720 | |
| **Town Car (wb 117.7, L-123.7)** | | | | |
| M81 | Executive sdn 4d | 4,015 | 39,995 | |
| M82 | Signature sdn 4d | 4,020 | 42,165 | |
| M82 | Signature Touring sdn 4d | — | 42,875 | |
| M82 | Signature Premium sdn 4d | — | 44,295 | |
| M82 | Signature Prem Touring sdn 4d | — | 45,005 | |
| M83 | Cartier sdn 4d | 4,095 | 44,550 | |
| M83 | Cartier Premium sdn 4d | — | 46,680 | |
| M85 | Cartier L sdn 4d | 4,215 | 49,060 | |

| 2002 Engines | bore × stroke | bhp | availability |
|---|---|---|---|
| V-6, 181.0 | 3.50 × 3.13 | 220 | S-LS (dohc) |
| V-8, 240.0 | 3.39 × 3.35 | 252 | O-LS (dohc) |
| V-8, 281.0 | 3.60 × 3.60 | 225 | S-Town Car (ohc) |
| V-8, 281.0 | 3.60 × 3.60 | 235 | O-Town Car (ohc) |
| V-8, 281.0 | 3.60 × 3.60 | 275 | S-Continental (dohc) |

*Figures not available at time of publication.

# Marmon

Howard Marmon was a mechanical genius who strove to build the perfect automobile. By some accounts, he did exactly that with his magnificent 1931-33 Sixteen. But the Depression was not a time for perfectionists or super-expensive luxury giants, so Marmon Motor Car Company went out in a blaze of V-16 glory after only a few years of significant production.

Marmon grew up around his father's Indianapolis milling-machine business, Nordyke and Marmon, said to be the world's largest by the turn of the century. In 1902, after earning a mechanical-engineering degree from the University of California at Berkeley, Howard returned to the family firm as its chief engineer. He was only 26. That same year, he tinkered up his first car: an air-cooled V-twin with pressure lubrication, then a revolutionary development.

Following in 1904 was the 50-cubic-inch V-4 Model A, another air-cooled ohv design but with an embryonic form of independent front suspension. Only six were built. The next year brought a similar Model B, a 2000-pound four-seater with a 90-inch wheelbase. Marmon sold 25 of those at $2500 each. After the derivative C35 and D36 came the ambitious M37 of 1906, a $5000 seven-seat touring car with a 128-inch wheelbase and a 65-horsepower air-cooled V-8 with a massive 707 cid. Yet the car scaled a svelte 3500 pounds, reflecting Howard's passion for low weight through extensive use of aluminum and various alloys.

The M37 didn't sell at all, so Marmon turned to conventional water-cooled inline-fours in 1909. At the same time, he devised his first Six, the Model 32. Marmon had already discovered the sales value of racing, but the 32 propelled him to the publicity pinnacle when a modified version called the "Wasp" won the first Indianapolis 500 in 1911. (Other racing Marmons racked up 51 competition victories in 1909-12.) This encouraged Howard to sell a road version, which arrived as the 1913 Model 48. But it sold poorly at $5000—then a king's ransom. So, too, did the successor 41 of 1914-15. Then came the advanced 1916 Model 34. Its 340-cid six was virtually all-aluminum, as were the transmission and differential housings, body, fenders, hood, even the radiator. The 34 was an outstanding performer and its balanced chassis gave good handling. Durable, too. Driven by a relay team, one trekked from New York to San Francisco in only five days to break Cannonball Baker's record run in a Cadillac by a substantial 41 hours. Sales more than tripled.

Nordyke and Marmon was contracted to build 5000 Liberty aircraft engines during World War I. Howard, meantime, joined the Army Air Corps, rising to the rank of lieutenant-colonel. He then returned home to usher in an improved Model 34, but sales were difficult due to the 1924 economic downturn. With that, Howard's older brother, Walter, resigned as company president in 1924 (to become board chairman) and hired George M. Williams to put the firm back on its feet. New president Williams thought the solution was lower-priced Marmons with conventional small-displacement straight-eights. He was right: Sales improved through 1926, when Nordyke and Marmon became Marmon Motor Company. By 1929, volume had risen to 22,300. Meanwhile, Howard set up a "front" firm called Midwest Aircraft, where he developed a V-16.

Marmon Motors continued with Williams' Eights, issuing new examples of that engine type almost yearly. This activity peaked in 1930 with a facelifted Marmon-Roosevelt, revised straight-eight models designated 69 and 79, and a luxurious new Big Eight with 315 cid and 125 bhp. Prices now stretched from $995 to $3170. But this expansion was too soon and too rapid, and Marmon's image became confused. The Roosevelt (named for President Teddy) was a low-priced "junior edition" typical of the optimistic late '20s, but it failed to sell well and also tarnished the high-class aura of senior Marmons. As a result, registrations plunged nearly 50 percent to 12,369.

Amid this bad news came one result of five years' research and dreaming by Howard Marmon: the unbelievable 1931 Sixteen. Packing 200 bhp from 490.8 cid, this amazing giant was guaranteed to do 100 mph. But it carried a giant-size price: $5100-$5400. Worse, the Cadillac Sixteen, which had arrived a year earlier—much to Howard's dismay—was draining off what little demand still existed for such extraordinary machines in extraordinarily hard times.

Marmon advertised the Sixteen as "The World's Most Advanced Car," and not without reason. Beside overhead valves actuated by pushrods from a single camshaft, the engine employed all-aluminum construction that was a triumph of the foundry art. Both the block and crankcase were cast as a single unit, the block actually being a "Y" in section. One dual-throat downdraft carburetor fed the fuel, and a single cast manifold served both cylinder banks. Despite its size, the engine weighed a relatively light 930 pounds fully dressed, some 370 pounds less than Cadillac's slightly smaller V-16. This contributed to a weight-to-power ratio of just 4.65 pound-horsepower, a figure likely rivaled only by Duesenberg.

Howard's passion for minimal weight was naturally evident elsewhere. The hood, front and rear splash aprons, running-board aprons, spare-wheel mounts, headlamp and taillamp brackets, and even the fuel-filler pipe were all made of aluminum. Because of this, few cars could approach the Marmon for sheer speed or through-the-gears acceleration. It accelerated faster than even the mighty Duesenberg Model J, though the Duesie had a higher top speed due to the superior breathing of its twin-cam engine. But while the Marmon was certainly pricey, it cost little more than half as much as a Duesenberg *chassis*.

The body design caused as much stir as the engine. This wasn't Howard's work, but he deserves credit for hiring an industrial designer at a time when that profession was in its infancy. The designer was 47-year-old Walter Dorwin Teague, Sr., though he admitted that his son did all the original sketches and drawings, as well as the full-size renderings and some interior concepts, including the unusual aircraft-type instrument panel. W. D. Teague, Jr., then a student at MIT, completed these tasks on weekends and in summer school. Since the name of the youngster's father carried considerably more prestige, Marmon publicity gave credit to Teague, Sr. Indeed, he handled the contract work with Marmon and translated the concept into production form.

With no resemblance to any previous Marmon, the Sixteen looked modern but not radical. A raked vee'd radiator devoid of ornament or badge led to a hood concealing the water filler. The doors extended down almost to the running boards. The fenders were designed to hide chassis components. Further accenting a low-slung profile were a prominent beltline that ran absolutely straight around the body, a windshield raked to match the radiator, and ultralow rooflines.

The Sixteen was touted as a "new concept in fine cars," with styling and engineering given equal emphasis. All but three of the 390 Sixteens ultimately built carried "standard" bodies built by LeBaron: five sedans, two coupes, and a victoria. The only custom bodies known are two Waterhouse tourers and a very individual victoria built by Hayes to a design by Alexis de Sakhnoffsky. These were likely artifacts of Howard's plan to offer 32 "regular" custom styles by the likes of Murphy, Waterhouse, and Judkins: town cars, all-weather phaetons, limos, speedsters, and "sunshine-roof" sedans. Minuscule sales precluded this grand idea (announced in September 1931).

As if the Sixteen weren't enough, Marmon offered five different Eights in two 1931 series. The first series, announced in August 1930, comprised the 120-inch wheelbase Model 79 with the 110-bhp, 303.2-cid engine; the 114-inch Model 69 with an 84-bhp, 211.2-cid engine; and the 136-inch Big Eight, still with a 125-bhp, 315.2-cid powerplant. The last became the Model 88 for the "second series" issued in January 1931, and was reduced some $450 to spark sales—which it didn't. At the same time came a new Model 70 to replace both the model 79 and the 69; it used the 69's engine but sold for $950-$1045, far less than its predecessors.

Despite this weeding out of less-popular models, Marmon sales dropped by over half. Registrations (the only reliable figures available) totaled 5687 for calendar '31, good for only 25th in the industry between LaSalle and struggling Reo. Sixteen sales were hobbled by a long delay. Prototypes attracted much attention at the winter auto shows, but deliveries didn't begin until April 1931. By that point, most prospects had opted for a Cadillac Sixteen or something less conspicuous. As a result, Cadillac's Sixteen outsold Marmon's 10-to-1.

Besides plummeting sales, Marmon was also now contending with wracking internal problems. The engineering department split into two warring camps, production people had trouble getting out the Sixteens, and the sales force was

**1932 Sixteen Touring Cabriolet**

struggling to overcome the Roosevelt's low-bucks image.

Retrenchment seemed the only course, so the 1932 line was pared to just the Sixteen, the 70, and the 125. The last was a two-model line offered on a 125-inch wheelbase to replace the Big Eight/88, and it gave away nothing but a shorter distance between the wheel centers and many dollars in price. Both the sedan and coupe listed for just $1420 versus $2220-$2920 for comparable predecessor models. Yet for all this, registrations were the lowest yet, just 1365.

Those price and model reductions left some feeling that Marmon was about to leave the fine-car field. Actually, it was preparing to do just the opposite. For 1933, the Sixteen was the only Marmon you could buy, and you could get one for about $1000 less on average. The coupe and sedan dropped to $4825, the seven-passenger sedan fell to $4975, and the convertible sedan eased to $5075. Specifications were unchanged.

The price cuts didn't solve the big problem. Marmon Motor Car Company was broke. It was duly sold in January 1934 to the American Automotive Corporation, organized and backed by Harry Miller, the famed Indy race-car designer, and a hot-shot promoter named Preston Tucker, whose own postwar car would win both fame and infamy. But they couldn't get things moving again, so Marmon was liquidated by receivers in 1937. The new company produced Marmon-Herrington trucks into the Eighties and truck components after that.

**1932 Sixteen close-coupled four-door sedan**

# Marmon

Left stillborn was a revolutionary V-12 car designed by Howard Marmon and chassis engineer George Freers. This envisioned a cut-down Sixteen with 4-wheel independent suspension, tubular "backbone" frame, and an aluminum body with new Teague styling highlighted by slab sides, pontoon fenders, and integral headlamps and trunk. A prototype was built for $160,000, financed out of necessity from Howard's personal fortune, but it never had a chance. It was stored on the Marmon estate in North Carolina until Howard's death in 1943, then made its way to industrial designer Brooks Stevens' automotive museum in Mequon, Wisconsin.

Like so many other makes, Marmon fell victim to the Depression for lack of corporate strength and a strong market base. All it had was brilliant engineering and bold visions. Too bad they weren't enough for any car company in those very hard times.

## Specifications

### 1930

| Big Eight (wb 136.0) | Wght | Price | Prod |
|---|---|---|---|
| touring 7P | 4,200 | 3,170 | 37 |
| cpe 2-4P | 4,100 | 2,850 | 123 |
| sdn 4d | 4,210 | 2,720 | 473 |
| sdn 7P | 4,307 | 2,920 | 270 |
| **Model 79 (wb 120.0)** | | | |
| spdstr phtn 5P | 3,800 | 2,020 | 40 |
| cpe 2-4P | 3,805 | 1,995 | 124 |
| sdn 4d | 3,900 | 2,020 | 958 |
| **Model 69 (wb 114.0)** | | | |
| spdstr phtn 5P | 3,025 | 1,610 | 32 |
| cpe 2-4P | 3,011 | 1,495 | 196 |
| sdn 4d | 3,100 | 1,520 | 1,605 |
| **Roosevelt (wb 112.8)—9,000 built*** | | | |
| sdn 4d | 2,695 | 995 | — |
| cpe | — | — | — |
| Victoria 2d | — | — | — |
| conv cpe | — | — | — |

*Approximate

| 1930 Engines | bore × stroke | bhp | availability |
|---|---|---|---|
| I-8, 201.9 | 2.75 × 4.25 | 72 | S-Roosevelt |
| I-8, 211.2 | 2.81 × 4.25 | 84 | S-69 |
| I-8, 303.2 | 3.19 × 4.75 | 110 | S-79 |
| I-8, 315.2 | 3.25 × 4.75 | 125 | S-Big Eight |

### 1931

| Big Eight (wb 136.0) | Wght | Price | Prod* |
|---|---|---|---|
| touring 7P | 4,200 | 3,170 | — |
| cpe 2-4P | 4,100 | 2,850 | — |
| sdn 4d | 4,210 | 2,720 | — |
| sdn 7P | 4,307 | 2,920 | — |
| **Model 79 (wb 120.0)** | | | |
| phtn 5P | 3,800 | 2,020 | — |
| cpe 2-4P | 3,805 | 1,995 | — |
| brougham 5P | 3,884 | 2,070 | — |
| sdn 4d | 3,900 | 2,020 | — |
| **Model 69 (wb 114.0)** | | | |
| phtn 5P | 3,025 | 1,610 | — |
| cpe 2-4P | 3,011 | 1,495 | — |
| brougham 4d | 3,153 | 1,565 | — |
| sdn 4d | 3,103 | 1,520 | — |
| **Model 70 (wb 112.8)—second series** | | | |
| cpe 2-4P | 2,694 | 950 | — |
| conv cpe 2-4P | 2,586 | 1,045 | — |
| victoria cpe 2-4P | 2,678 | 995 | — |
| sdn 4d | 2,823 | 995 | — |
| **Model 88 (wb 130.0; lwb-136.0)—second series** | | | |
| cpe 2-4P | 4,290 | 2,275 | — |

| Model 88 | Wght | Price | Prod* |
|---|---|---|---|
| sdn 4d | 4,375 | 2,220 | — |
| club sdn 5P | 4,398 | 2,345 | — |
| lwb sdn 7P | 4,504 | 2,495 | — |
| **Sixteen (wb 145.0)**\*\* | | | |
| cpe 2-4P | 5,090 | 5,220 | — |
| sdn, cl coupled 4d | 5,335 | 5,270 | — |
| sdn 4d | 5,360 | 5,200 | — |
| sdn 7P | 5,440 | 5,400 | — |

| 1931 Engines | bore × stroke | bhp | availability |
|---|---|---|---|
| I-8, 211.2 | 2.81 × 4.25 | 84 | S-69, 70 |
| I-8, 303.2 | 3.19 × 4.75 | 110 | S-79 |
| I-8, 315.2 | 3.25 × 4.75 | 125 | S-Big Eight, 88 |
| V-16, 490.8 | 3.13 × 4.00 | 200 | S-Sixteen |

### 1932

| Model 70 (wb 112.8) | Wght | Price | Prod* |
|---|---|---|---|
| cpe 2-4P | 2,694 | 950 | — |
| sdn 4d | 2,823 | 995 | — |
| **Model 125 (wb 125.0)** | | | |
| cpe 2-4P | 3,625 | 1,420 | — |
| sdn 4d | 3,653 | 1,420 | — |
| **Sixteen (wb 145.0)**\*\* | | | |
| cpe 2-4P | 5,090 | 5,700 | — |
| sdn 4d, close-coupled | 5,335 | 5,800 | — |
| sdn 4d | 5,360 | 5,700 | — |
| sdn 7P | 5,440 | 5,900 | — |

| 1932 Engines | bore × stroke | bhp | availability |
|---|---|---|---|
| I-8, 211.2 | 2.81 × 4.25 | 84 | S-70 |
| I-8, 315.2 | 3.25 × 4.75 | 125 | S-125 |
| V-16, 490.8 | 3.13 × 4.00 | 200 | S-Sixteen |

### 1933

| Sixteen (wb 145.0)** | Wght | Price | Prod* |
|---|---|---|---|
| cpe 2-4P | 5,090 | 4,825 | — |
| sdn 4d | 5,360 | 4,825 | — |
| conv sdn 5P | 5,285 | 5,075 | — |
| sdn 7P | 5,440 | 4,975 | — |

| 1933 Engine | bore × stroke | bhp | availability |
|---|---|---|---|
| V-16, 490.8 | 3.13 × 4.00 | 200 | S-all |

*Because of its size and limited volume, Marmon did not record model year production per se. Calendar year registrations were as follows:

| | |
|---|---|
| 1930: | 12,369 |
| 1931: | 5,687 |
| 1932: | 1,365 |
| 1933: | 86 |

(source: *The Production Figure Book for U.S. Cars*)

**Total 1931-33 Sixteen production: 390

# Mercury

Mercury was conceived largely by Edsel Ford, who saw a place for it in the Ford Motor Company line some time before his father Henry did. It arrived for 1939 in the same price league as the Pontiac Eight but somewhat below Oldsmobile—precisely where Edsel wanted it and Dearborn needed it. While Mercury would take many years to approach those GM makes in volume, it was successful from the start. Production averaged about 80,000 per year in the early '40s, good for 12th or 13th in the industry, thus winning important new business for Dearborn by covering the market between Ford and the Lincoln Zephyr.

The original Mercury engine would remain in production through 1948. A 239-cubic-inch L-head V-8, it was a slightly larger version of the Ford "V-8/85," having the same stroke but a larger bore. Horsepower was 95 through 1941, then 100. Mercury quickly gained a reputation for performance appropriate to its name (after the winged messenger god in Greek mythology). Well-tuned stock models were quicker than V-8 Fords, usually capable of turning close to 100 mph.

Mercury bowed on a 116-inch wheelbase, four inches longer than the '39 Ford's and sufficient to give its similar styling a "more-important" look. A dashboard with strip-type instruments was also like Ford's, but Mercury's column-mounted gearshift was a talking point at the time. Styling for 1939-40 featured a crisply pointed "prow," beautifully curved fenders, and rounded body lines. Initial offerings comprised two- and four-door "beetleback" sedans, a notchback sedan coupe, and a convertible coupe spanning a price range of $916-$1018. A $1212 convertible sedan was added for 1940, that year's heaviest and most-expensive Mercury. But four-door ragtops had waned in popularity, so this one was dropped for 1941. Only about 1150 units were built.

Models expanded to seven for '41 with a two/four-passenger coupe, business coupe, and wood-bodied station wagon. Styling, again in the Ford mold, was chunkier and less graceful despite a two-inch longer wheelbase; with higher, bulkier fenders; a divider-bar grille; and fender-top parking lights.

Mercury tried harder for 1942 with a serious facelift, the aforementioned 100-bhp engine, and a new extra-cost semi-automatic transmission called "Liquamatic." The last proved

**1939 Series 99A convertible coupe**

**1940 Series 09A convertible coupe**

**1941 Series 19A 3-passenger coupe**

**1942 Series 29A four-door station wagon**

**1946 Series 69M Sportsman convertible coupe**

**1947½ 69M four-door station wagon**

# Mercury

very troublesome, though, and was quickly canceled. America's entry into World War II limited model-year production to below 23,000 units. Chrome was "in," at least before the government diverted it to war use. All '42 Mercs wore a broad, glittery two-section horizontal-bar grille, double chrome bands on each fender, and a bright full-perimeter molding at the beltline. Parking lights shifted inboard to flank a still-pointy hood. The general effect was busier than '41, which had been busier than 1940. Like other '42s, the mostly chromeless, late-production "blackout" Mercurys are especially prized by collectors.

At war's end, Henry Ford II, Edsel's son and old Henry's grandson, returned from the Navy to run Ford Motor Company. Edsel had died in 1943 of complications due to stomach cancer. Henry II quickly began civilian production, and Mercury placed tenth in the 1946 industry race with about 86,600 units. As Dearborn delayed its first all-new postwar models to 1949, interim Mercurys were similar to the '42 models. The inboard parking lights and two-band fender moldings remained, but the hood was blunted above a new vertical-bar grille carrying a large "Mercury Eight" nameplate. Mechanicals were unchanged except Liquamatic didn't return. Ford's adoption of the 239 V-8 for 1946 was hardly to Mercury's advantage.

Mercury's prewar model offerings also carried over into 1946 with a singular exception: The business coupe was replaced by the novel Sportsman convertible. Comparable to the like-named Ford model, it was adorned with maple or yellow birch framing mahogany inserts. The wood was structural, not merely decorative. This created a problem at the rear, where the standard production fenders wouldn't fit. Both Sportsmans thus used 1941 sedan delivery fenders and wood structure shaped to suit. The solid-wood framing was beautifully mitred and finished with multiple coats of varnish. But with only 205 sold, Mercury's Sportsman was dropped after '46. The likely reason for the low sales was high price: $2209, some $200 more than Ford's version, which did more satisfying business and continued into 1948.

Ford's most-important 1947 corporate development was the organization of the Lincoln-Mercury Division. Henry II decided that the two makes could be more competitive as an autonomous operation *a la* the various General Motors units. That year's Mercurys used more of the raw materials that had been scarce during wartime: mainly aluminum (for pistons and hood ornament) and chrome (interior hardware and grille frame). Belt moldings now ended just ahead of the cowl. Postwar inflation boosted prices an average $450, lifting the range to $1450-$2200. Production of the 1947 models didn't begin until February of that year, so Mercury's output was about the same as its 1946 tally.

Except for serial numbers and deletion of the two-door sedan, the '48s were unchanged. The '48s sold from November 1947

1949 Series 9CM two-door station wagon

1951 Series 1CM two-door station wagon

1949 Series 9CM convertible coupe

1952 Series 2M four-door station wagon

1950 Series 0CM convertible coupe

1952 Series 2M Custom sport coupe hardtop

# Mercury

1953 Monterey convertible coupe

1954 Monterey Sun Valley hardtop coupe

1955 Montclair hardtop coupe

1955 Montclair convertible coupe

1956 Medalist phaeton hardtop sedan

through mid-April 1948, when the '49s appeared. As a result, model-year production ended at only about 50,250.

The '49 Mercurys bowed with flush-fender "inverted bathtub" styling like that of the 1948-49 Packards and Hudsons; Mercury's stemmed from sporadic wartime work by Dearborn designers. The wheelbase was unchanged, but bodyshells were shared with a new standard Lincoln line instead of Ford, the result of a last-minute change in postwar plans. Styling was good: massive yet clean and streamlined. The grille looked something like the '48 affair but lower and wider. A single bright molding ran full-length at midflank. As before, a single series offered four body styles: coupe, four-door Sport Sedan (with "suicide" rear-hinged back doors), convertible, and a new two-door wagon with less structural wood than the superseded four-door style.

Like Ford, the '49 Mercury was treated to a new chassis with fully independent front suspension, weight-saving Hotchkiss drive (replacing torque-tube), and a live axle on modern parallel longitudinal leaf springs instead of old Henry's cherished single transverse leaf. Resuming its power lead over Ford, Mercury got a stroked V-8 with 255.4 cid, dual downdraft Holley carburetors and 110 bhp to become a genuine 100-mph performer for the first time. Also introduced was an automatic-overdrive option priced at $97, teamed with a 4.27:1 rear axle instead of the standard 3.90:1.

The 1949 Mercury was an attractive buy with its Lincoln styling, lower prices ($1979-$2716), and a V-8 more-potent than Ford's (necessary to offset some 100 extra pounds in curb weight). Buyers responded by taking over 301,000 of the '49s—more than three times the volume of Mercury's previous best year and good for sixth in the industry, another all-time high.

Despite few major changes, sales continued strong for the next two seasons: close to 294,000 for 1950 and a record-setting 310,000-plus for '51, when Mercury again claimed sixth. The 1950 models gained a hood-front chrome molding bearing the Mercury name; the '51s combined this with a large semicircular crest and also sported more-prominent grille bars, larger parking lights (swept back to the front wheel wells), and longer rear fenders with rounded corners and vertical trailing edges. Horsepower rose a nominal two for '51, when a significant new option arrived in Merc-O-Matic Drive. This was, of course, the new three-speed fully automatic transmission developed with the Warner Gear Division of Borg-Warner (and also offered for '51 by Ford as Ford-O-Matic).

A couple of new models were added for 1950: a stripped price-leader coupe ($1875) and the interesting Monterey. The latter was a spiffy limited edition with upgraded interior and a top covered in canvas or leather. At around $2150, it cost some $160 more than the standard coupe, but it wasn't the costliest 1950-51 Merc: The wagon was over $400 more. Monterey's purpose, as with the Ford Crestliner and Lincoln Lido/Capri of those years, was to stand in for the pillarless "hardtop-convertibles" being offered by GM and Chrysler rivals.

Hardtops arrived in force for 1952, when Ford Motor Company was the only Big Three maker with all-new styling. Mercury got a pair of hardtops: a Sport Coupe and a more-deluxe Monterey version (*sans* covered roof). Monterey also offered a convertible and a four-door sedan (now minus "suicide" doors). Following an industry trend, wagons were all-steel four-doors with simulated wood trim. Base-trim two- and four-door sedans completed the lineup. Bodyshells were again shared with Ford, though Mercury retained a three-inch longer wheelbase, all of it ahead of the cowl. Also shared with Ford was tight, clean styling, though the resemblance with that year's equally new Lincoln didn't hurt. Higher compression boosted the flathead V-8 to 125 bhp on unchanged displace-

# Mercury

1956 Medalist hardtop coupe

1957 Montclair hardtop coupe

1957 Turnpike Cruiser four-door hardtop

1958 Montclair Turnpike Cruiser hardtop coupe

1958 Colony Park hardtop station wagon

1959 Colony Park Country Cruiser hardtop station wagon

1959 Montclair Cruiser hardtop coupe

1960½ Comet four-door sedan

ment. The Korean war limited 1952 production throughout Detroit, so Mercury built only 172,087 cars to finish eighth in the annual race.

Mercury bowed its first formal two-series line for 1953: the Custom series included a hardtop and two- and four-door sedans, while the Monterey line came as a convertible, hardtop, wagon, or four-door sedan. Retained from '52 was a trendy dashboard with big aircraft-type levers flanking a large half-moon gauge cluster. Business picked up with the end of Korean war restrictions, and Mercury moved nearly 305,000 cars, though it again ran eighth. Prices ranged from $2000 for the Custom two-door to nearly $2600 for the Monterey wagon.

A significant engineering change for 1954 was Mercury's first overhead-valve V-8, a bigger version of the new "Y-Block" design featured on that year's Ford. Though little larger than Mercury's previous L-head—256 cid—the ohv had modern short-stroke dimensions, a five-main-bearing crankshaft, and much more horsepower—161 with the standard four-barrel carburetor. With a low 3.90 rear axle and standard transmission, the V-8 made any '54 Merc quick off the line. Equally noteworthy was a ball-joint front suspension, another development shared with Ford.

Styling improved for '54 via wraparound taillights and a clean but more-aggressive grille with larger bullet guards. Joining

# Mercury

1960 Montclair Cruiser hardtop sedan

1962 Monterey Custom convertible coupe

1961 Monterey convertible coupe

1963 Comet Custom Sportster hardtop coupe

1962 Meteor Custom four-door sedan

1963 Meteor S-33 hardtop coupe

previous models was a new top-line hardtop, the Monterey Sun Valley (a name that must have amused Californians), which is more famous now than it was then. An outgrowth of Dearborn's experiments with plastic-topped cars (as was Ford's similar '54 Skyliner), the Sun Valley was nice in theory: the airiness of a convertible combined with closed-car comfort and practicality. In practice, though, it was something else. Though the Plexiglas front half-roof was tinted and a snap-in shade was provided for hot weather, customers complained the interior heated up like a sauna. Sales were unimpressive: just 9761 of the '54s and a mere 1787 for the 1955 Montclair followup.

At about 260,000 units in all, 1954 wasn't Mercury's greatest sales year, but hopes were high for '55. With colorful new styling on the basic 1952-54 shell, Mercury's first wheelbase increase since 1941—to 119 inches except on wagons, which remained at 118—and a more-potent V-8, the '55s couldn't miss. They didn't: Model-year production was a record 329,000-plus.

Topping the '55 fleet was the new Montclair line: four-door sedan, hardtop, convertible, and Sun Valley. All wore a slim contrast-color panel outlined in bright metal beneath the side windows. A step below were the Monterey sedan, hardtop, and wagon, followed by the Custom series with the same body styles plus a two-door sedan. Common to all were Mercury's first wrapped windshield, an evolutionary form of the '54 grille, hooded headlamps, and eye-catching surface ornamentation. A Y-block V-8 swelled to 292 cid was offered in two forms: 188 bhp for Custom and Monterey and 198 bhp for Montclair. The higher output version was also available as an option for lesser models with the optional Merc-O-Matic.

Four-door Phaeton hardtops arrived for 1956's "Big M" line, which represented an ambitious expansion into somewhat uncharted territory. To stay competitive in the face of rising prices, Mercury fielded a cut-rate group of Medalist two- and four-door hardtops and sedans at the bottom end of the medium-price ladder. But inflation made these "low-price" Mercs more expensive than 1955 Customs ($2250-$2460)—and not that much cheaper than the better-trimmed '56 Customs ($2350-$2800). Dealers pushed hard with two-door sedans, but Medalist sales came to only 45,812 in all. Custom, Monterey, and Montclair all beat the price-leader by more than 2-to-1. With that, Medalist was duly dropped, only to resurface for '58, when it interfered in a price bracket that should have been reserved exclusively for the new Edsel.

Mercury's '56 styling was a good update of its '55 look. All models save Medalists wore jazzy single Z-shaped side moldings that delineated the contrast color area with optional two-toning (the area below was generally matched to the roof). Monterey and Montclair added Phaeton hardtop sedans at mid-season, replacements for their low-roof pillared Sport Sedans held over from mid-1955. Mercury also offered a second con-

635

# Mercury

1963 Monterey Custom "Breezeway" hardtop sedan

1965 Comet Caliente hardtop coupe

1964 Comet Cyclone hardtop coupe

1965 Park Lane Marauder hardtop coupe

1964 Montclair Marauder hardtop sedan

1965 Montclair Marauder hardtop coupe

vertible for the first time, in the Custom group. The Y-block was enlarged again, this time to 312 cid, good for 210 bhp that could be tuned to 235; the latter was standard for Monterey and Montclair.

Though 1956 was a "breather" for the industry as a whole, Mercury was an exception with some 328,000 cars, slightly off its '55 pace. An encouraging sign was the premium Montclair, which managed to sell almost as well as it had in frantic '55. The midline Monterey was still the big breadwinner, though.

The '57s were all-new, trumpeted as "a dramatic expression of dream car design." They were inspired by the XM-Turnpike Cruiser show car of 1956, which also had direct showroom counterparts in the new top-line Turnpike Cruiser two- and four-door hardtops.

The Turnpike Cruiser had glitz and gimmicks galore: "skylight dual curve windshield," drop-down reverse-slant rear window, and dual air intakes over the A-posts housing little horizontal antennae. If that wasn't enough, there was optional "Seat-O-Matic," which automatically powered the front seat to one of 49 possible positions at the twist of two dials. Mercury also joined Chrysler in offering pushbutton automatic transmission controls, another "space-age" Cruiser standard. Arriving late in the season was a Convertible Cruiser, honoring Mercury's selection as the 1957 Indy 500 pace car, and supplied with replica regalia decals. Yet for all their gadgets—and likely because of them—

the Cruisers failed miserably. They were not just expensive—$3760-$3850 for the hardtops, $4100 for the ragtop—they were too far out even for that gilded age.

1957's major redesign gave Mercury its own bodyshells and a new 122-inch-wheelbase chassis—the first time it was neither "senior Ford" nor "junior Lincoln." Like the all-new '57 Ford, this was done partly to prepare for the '58 Edsel line that borrowed some from both makes. Monterey and Montclair were bereft of station wagons, which were now a separate series with six models. Offered, from the top, were a woody-look Colony Park, four-door nine-seater; metal-sided two- and four-door Voyagers; and three Commuters with the various seat and door combinations. All had pillarless hardtop styling, the new rage in Big Three wagons.

Styling matched the "Big M's" more-expansive new '57 dimensions, looking square, heavy, and contrived. Up front, a massive dual-oblong bumper nestled beneath a slim concave grille of vertical bars. Headlights were quads where legal, regular duals otherwise. Long scallops, typically contrast-colored, carried the beltline from midbody through the upper rear fenders to huge pie-slice taillamps. Weight was up, but so was horsepower. A 255-bhp 312 was newly standard except on Cruisers, which carried a 290-bhp, 368-cid Lincoln V-8 that was optional elsewhere.

Mercury did fairly well for '57 but not as well as in '56. Volume

# Mercury

1966 Colony Park station wagon

1966 Comet Caliente convertible coupe

1967 Monterey hardtop coupe

1967 Comet Cylcone GT hardtop coupe

1967 Cougar hardtop coupe

dropped to about 286,000 and the make's production rank fell from seventh to eighth—not encouraging for an all-new design in a fairly strong sales year.

A minor facelift yielded slightly quieter styling for 1958, but that year was a disaster, production falling to 153,000. The Convertible Cruiser was abandoned (after only 1265 of the '57s) and the two closed Cruisers became Montclair submodels. Lower prices failed to perk up sales (barely 6400 between them). The cheap Medalist returned for a brief encore with two- and four-door sedans but, again, proved disappointing: Only 18,732 were sold. Topping the line was the new Park Lane series of two hardtops and a convertible (also available as Montclairs and Montereys). These were ostensibly Cruiser replacements with less hoke and a giant 430-cid V-8 with 360 bhp that was shared with that year's Lincolns. A new automatic called Multi-Drive debuted (basically Ford Division's new Cruise-O-Matic), as did a 383-cid V-8—the same size as one of Chrysler's new '58 wedgehead engines but with more-over-square dimensions. The 383 was standard for all '58 Mercs, save Medalists (which came with a 235-bhp 312) and Park Lane, and delivered 312 or 330 bhp depending on the model.

Although the bottom dropped out of the medium-price market in '58, Mercury remained eighth despite building only 40 percent of its 1957 volume. But significantly, Rambler passed the Big M in sales and was fast gaining on Pontiac, Olds, and Buick. Mercury would join the rush to compacts and intermediates soon enough. In the meantime, it could only offer more of the same.

More the '59 Mercurys definitely had, with even bigger bodies on a four-inch longer wheelbase. Styling was still square but more-sculpted, marked by a mile-wide grille, huge bumpers at each end, enormous windshields and rear windows, and a more sharply creased version of the odd 1957-58 rear-fender scallops. The Medalist and Turnpike Cruiser were forgotten, and Montclair and wagons each slimmed from six models to four. Engines were detuned in a faint nod to a newly economy-conscious public. The '59 slate listed a 210-bhp 312 for Monterey, a 345-bhp 430 for Park Lane, and 280- and 322-bhp 383s for others. Despite the retrenchment, model-year volume failed to top 150,000 units—hardly the hoped-for recovery.

Looking back, Mercury sales stumbled after 1956 at least in part because the fleet, good-looking cars of earlier years were abandoned for shiny, begadgeted behemoths that couldn't hope to sell well in a down economy. But the make would return to "hot cars" in the '60s and, with them, achieve new success.

Indeed, volume went up substantially for 1960—to 271,000-plus—though that was owed mainly to the new compact Comet. The four-series big-car line (which might have been offered as Edsels had things gone better there) remained two-ton heavyweights with huge compound-curve windshields, but a handsome facelift removed a little chrome and added a tidier concave grille and more-discreet "gullwing" rear fenders. Model choices were mostly as before: Cruiser two- and four-door hardtops in each series, four-door Monterey/Montclair sedans, Monterey two-door sedan, Park Lane convertible, and, still broken out, four-door Commuter and wood-sided Colony Park hardtop wagons.

Mercury offered three V-8s for 1960, all with lower compression for the sake of economy (such as it was). The 312 was cut to 205 bhp for Monterey and Commuter, the 383 returned as a single 280-bhp option, and a 310-bhp Lincoln 430 was standard elsewhere. Production rose slightly to some 155,000.

The "Big M" shrunk noticeably in both size and price for 1961. In fact, it was again a "deluxe Ford," though on an inch-longer 120-inch wheelbase. This was done in the interest of production economies as well as fuel economy, and the resulting cars

# Mercury

were indeed lighter, thriftier, and more-maneuverable. Of course, this also ended four years of unique Mercury chassis and bodyshells, reflecting the collapse of Dearborn's grand mid-'50s "divisionalization," the stab at a GM-style five-make structure that had spawned the Edsel and Continental Divisions. Dismal sales since '57 had rendered a separate Mercury platform unacceptably expensive, hence this return to the make's original concept.

Beginning with the 1960 Comet, Mercury followed the rest of the industry trend of spinning off additional models in new sizes, with name changes sometimes confusing buyers. The latter was perhaps symbolic of the make's mixed fortunes in the '60s. Still, Comet and Monterey spanned the entire decade. A new name was Meteor, long the brand of a Canadian-made Mercury derivative, which appeared on two quite different U.S. models.

The first of these arrived at the low end of the 1961 full-size line: two- and four-door sedans and hardtops in "600" and nicer "800" trim offered at vastly reduced prices beginning at $2535. In effect, they filled the gap left by Edsel's demise the previous year. Monterey was again the premium Mercury, listing a four-door sedan and hardtop, a two-door hardtop, and a convertible. The separate Station Wagon series reverted to conventional pillared four-doors: six- and nine-passenger Commuters and Colony Parks. Styling was even more conservative than in 1960. The grille remained concave and fins vestigial, but flanks were rounded and '50s gimmicks were mere memories. Meteors carried a standard 223-cid Ford six with 135 bhp; the optional V-8, included on Montereys, was a 175-bhp 292. Across-the-board options comprised a 220-bhp 352 and new big-block 390s with 300 or 330 bhp.

Although Meteor actually outsold Monterey, sales were not spectacular. Accordingly, the line was replaced for '62 by a "Monterey 6," and the name moved to Mercury's version of the new intermediate Ford Fairlane.

Most everything said about the 1962-63 Fairlane (*see* Ford) applies equally to that second Meteor. Its styling was busier and model names were different, but bodies were shared. So were powertrains, including Ford's fine new small-block V-8 with 221 cid and 145 bhp or 260 cid and 164 bhp. Custom denoted the upmarket midsize Meteors, S-33 the sportier bucket-seaters—a two-door sedan for '62, a hardtop coupe for '63. Wagons—woody-look Country Cruiser and plain-sided Villagers (a name transferred from the Edsel line)—joined hardtops as new 1963 arrivals. For all this, the Meteor didn't sell nearly as well as the Fairlane, and Mercury dropped it for 1964 in favor of an extensively upgraded Comet.

Once planned as an Edsel, the first Comet was basically Ford's hugely successful 1960 Falcon compact with squared-up rooflines, a double-row concave grille, and an extended stern with canted fins and oval taillamps. Wheelbase was 114 inches on two- and four-door sedans; wagons used Falcon's 109.5-inch span. It wasn't exciting, but it sold well: over 116,000 for the abbreviated debut season. Sales set a record for '61 at 197,000 and were strong for '62, which hurt Meteor. In fact, one reason Meteor didn't sell well is that Comet was comparably sized yet more-affordable. Mercury was thus wise to make Comet its only small car after '63. Sales jumped by 55,000 units for '64 and remained high into '67.

Early Comets ran less than $100 higher than comparable Falcons yet were more-elaborately trimmed. S-22, a $2300 bucket-seat two-door sedan, responded to the sporty-compact craze beginning in 1961, when all Comets gained an optional 101-bhp six. Custom sedans and wagons and a posh Villager wagon with imitation wood trim aided '62 sales. The following year brought Custom and S-22 convertibles and Sportster hardtop coupes. A

1967 Cougar XR-7 hardtop coupe

1968 Park Lane convertible coupe

1968 Cougar XR-7 7.0 Litre GT-E hardtop coupe

1968 Montego MX station wagon

1968 Cyclone fastback hardtop coupe

# Mercury

**1969 Cougar CJ 428 hardtop coupe**

**1969 Marquis Brougham hardtop sedan**

**1969 Marauder X-100 hardtop coupe**

**1970 Montego MX Brougham hardtop sedan**

**1970 Cougar hardtop coupe**

**1970 Cyclone Spoiler 429 hardtop coupe**

**1971 Cougar XR-7 hardtop coupe**

**1972 Monterey Custom hardtop coupe**

squarish facelift arrived for 1964, when S-22 was renamed Caliente and any Comet could be ordered with the outstanding 260-cid small-block. A midseason Caliente offshoot, the $2655 Cyclone hardtop, offered even higher performance from a standard 210-bhp 289.

Comet received its first major overhaul for 1966, going from compact to intermediate by shifting to that year's new Fairlane platform. This underlined a basic marketing assumption: Mercury buyers were wealthier than Ford's, and thus probably wanted a compact larger than Falcon.

This 116-inch-wheelbase platform continued on Comets through 1969, but sales waned along with the name, which by 1967 applied only to a pair of very basic "202" sedans. The rest of that year's line comprised Capri (borrowed from Lincoln to replace "404"), Caliente, Cyclone, and Station Wagon. All gave way for 1968 to a three-series Montego line on the same wheelbase. This offered a standard sedan and hardtop coupe; MX sedan, hardtop coupe, convertible, and wagon; and top-line MX Brougham sedan and hardtop. The last was furnished with a high-quality cloth interior and other luxuries. Comet was retained for one price-leading two-door hardtop, then was temporarily shelved after 1969.

Mercury jumped into the midsize muscle market with both feet and won several racing laurels. Model-year 1966 brought a

639

# Mercury

smooth Cyclone GT hardtop coupe and convertible powered by Ford's 335-bhp 390 and offered with a variety of useful suspension upgrades. The '67 was even more thrilling with optional 427s delivering 410-425 bhp.

Similar street racers were available for '68, though the 427 was detuned to 390 bhp. Besides Montego, that year's midsize line included new base and GT Cyclone hardtop coupes with the same curvy new lower-body contours and racy full-fastback rooflines *a la* Ford Mustang/Torino. There was also a one-year-only GT notchback hardtop. For 1969, Mercury unleashed the Cyclone CJ with Ford's 428-cid big-block Cobra Jet engines. GTs and CJs had black grilles, special emblems, bodyside paint stripes, and unique rear-end styling. CJs carried a functional hood scoop when equipped with optional Ram-Air induction. Although Ford won the 1968-69 NASCAR championship, Cyclones turned in some of the most-notable performances. A highlight was Cale Yarborough's win in the '68 Daytona 500 at an average speed of 143.25 mph.

For all its activity in compacts and intermediates, big cars remained Mercury's bread-and-butter in the '60s. Annual production averaged around 100,000, though there were back-to-back records for 1965-66—over 165,000 each year. Of all the big Merc model names, only Monterey stayed the entire time. The upper-echelon Montclair and Park Lane returned for 1964-68, then vanished again, replaced by a full-range Marquis line.

With Meteor an intermediate, the 1962 full-size line was regrouped into Monterey, Monterey Custom, and Station Wagon. The lone convertible shifted to the Custom series. Joining Mercury's bucket-seat brigade at midyear were the S-55 hardtop coupe and convertible. Styling was busier on all the big '62s, with tunneled taillights and a complex convex grille. All V-8s returned, as did the faithful big six as standard power for base Montereys and Commuter wagons.

A similar array on the same 120-inch wheelbase returned for 1963, when a heavy reskin introduced "Breezeway Styling" for nonwagon closed models: reverse-slant rear windows that dropped down for ventilation as on the old Turnpike Cruiser (and 1958-60 Continental Marks). Wagons were pared to a pair of Colony Parks. Joining the S-55 subseries at midyear was a handsome "slantback" two-door like Ford's Galaxie sports hardtop. Engines remained V-8s: 390s with 250-330 bhp, a new 406-cid enlargement packing 385/405 bhp, and, as a late-season option, a high-performance 427 with 410 bhp.

Tradition returned for Silver Anniversary 1964 in a revived four-series line of Monterey, Montclair, Park Lane, and Commuter/Colony Park wagons. The first three included Breezeway two- and four-door hardtops and four-door sedans (Monterey still included a pillared two-door), plus slantback "Marauder" hardtop coupes and sedans. A toothy convex grille replaced the concave '63 design. The previous 390 V-8s continued, but the 406s didn't, giving way to 427s with 410/425 optional bhp for all models save wagons. Big-inch Marauders were awesome performers.

The record 1965 model year brought a larger full-size body with crisp, rectilinear lines "in the Lincoln Continental tradition," as well as a new "torque box" frame (tuned for each body to minimize noise, vibration, and harshness). Wagons now rode the 119-inch Ford wheelbase; other models were up to 123. Breezeways thinned to a trio of four-door sedans, all hardtops were now slantbacks, and the Marauder name was de-emphasized amid calls for greater automotive safety. V-8s now comprised a quartet of 390s with 250-330 bhp, plus a single 425-bhp 427. The basic '65 look carried into 1966 with a new diecast "electric-shaver" grille and, for hardtop coupes, a "sweep-style roof" with a concave backlight.

More-rounded bodysides mixed well with sharp-edged fenders

1972 Cougar XR-7 hardtop coupe

1972 Montego MX hardtop coupe prototype

1973 Cougar XR-7 hardtop coupe

1974 Marquis Brougham four-door pillared hardtop

1974 Cougar XR-7 coupe

▲ 1932 Lincoln KB four-door sedan ▼ 1940 Lincoln Continental coupe

641

▲ 1956 Lincoln Premiere convertible ▼ 1961 Lincoln Continental four-door convertible

▲ 1998 Lincoln Town Car four-door sedan   ▼ 1940 Mercury convertible club coupe

▲ 1946 Mercury four-door station wagon ▼ 1957 Mercury Commuter two-door station wagon

▲ 1963 Mercury Comet Custom four-door station wagon ▼ 1967 Mercury Monterey S-55 two-door hardtop

▲ 2002 Mercury Mountaineer wagon ▼ 1954 Muntz Jet two-door hardtop coupe

▲ 1932 Nash two-door coupe ▼ 1948 Nash Ambassador Brougham convertible

▲ 1950 Nash Ambassador Super four-door sedan ▼ 1957 Nash Ambassador Country Club hardtop coupe

648

▲ 1939 Oldsmobile 70 business coupe ▼ 1942 Oldsmobile 98 four-door sedan

▲ 1958 Oldsmobile Dynamic 88 two-door hardtop ▼ 1965 Oldsmobile 4-4-2 two-door coupe

▲ 1967 Oldsmobile Toronado hardtop coupe ▼ 2002 Oldsmobile Bravada wagon

▲ 1935 Packard V-12 sport phaeton ▼ 1938 Packard Super 8 coupe roadster

▲ 1941 Packard 120 four-door station wagon ▼ 1952 Packard 250 convertible

▲ 1956 Packard Caribbean two-door hardtop ▼ 1933 Pierce-Arrow Silver Arrow four-door sedan

▲ 1935 Pierce-Arrow Silver Arrow V-12 two-door coupe ▼ 1934 Plymouth two-door coupe

▲ 1947 Plymouth Special Deluxe business coupe ▼ 1955 Plymouth Belvedere four-door sedan for '67. Sedans adopted conventional rooflines but still offered an optional drop-down backlight. Hardtop coupes received "faster" profiles. Three new limited-production line-toppers arrived: Marquis, a two-door hardtop with broad C-pillars and standard vinyl-roof covering, a similar Park Lane Brougham hardtop sedan, and a Park Lane Brougham Breezeway four-door sedan. Intermediates were waging Mercury's sporty-car wars, so the bucket-seat S-55 ragtop and hardtop were in their final year—and just a Monterey option package now. Respective production was minuscule: just 145 and 570.

After a minor '68 facelift, the big Mercs were fully revised for 1969. Wheelbases grew to 121 inches on wagons and 124 on other models, sizes that would persist until their first downsizing in 1979. Series regrouped around base Monterey, revived Monterey Custom, and a full Marquis line comprising Colony Park wagon, convertible, and standard and Brougham sedans, hardtop coupes, and hardtop sedans. Riding the shorter wheelbase was a new Marauder, a high-performance "tunnelback" hardtop that garnered 14,666 sales. Offered in standard and spiffier X-100 trim, it shared Marquis' hidden-headlamp front and the ventless side glass used by most other models. V-8s comprised the usual 390s and a new 429-cid big-block with 360 bhp, the latter being standard for Marauder X-100, optional elsewhere. The 1970s were basically reruns save minor trim and equipment revisions. Sporty big cars had mostly disappeared by now, and so would the Marauder after just 6043 sales that model year.

One of Mercury's most-interesting and desirable '60s products was Cougar, an upscale edition of Ford's highly successful Mustang ponycar, premiering for 1967 as a lone two-door hardtop in three basic permutations. Convertibles were added for 1969. Striding a three-inch-longer wheelbase than Mustang—111 in all—Cougar offered more luxury and standard power for about $200 additional (prices started at $2851). Where Mustang's base engine was a six, Cougar's was a livelier 200-bhp 289-cid V-8. The big 335-bhp, 428-cid CJ became an extra-cost option for 1969-70.

The 1967-68 Cougars arguably looked best with their crisply tailored lines, hidden headlamps in an electric-shaver grille, and a matching back panel with sequential turn signals, a gimmick borrowed from Ford's Thunderbird. Length and width increased on the '69s, which sported Buick-like sweepspear bodyside contours, ventless side glass, less-distinctive "faces," and full-width taillights. The '70s adopted a divided vertical-bar grille with a slightly bulged, separate nose.

Early Cougars came in several forms. The most-luxurious was the XR-7, boasting a rich interior with leather accents and full instrumentation in a simulated walnut dashboard. A GT option

**1975 Monarch Ghia four-door sedan**

**1976 Marquis Brougham four-door station wagon**

**1976 Monarch Ghia coupe**

**1976 Cougar XR-7 coupe**

**1975 Bobcat Villager two-door station wagon**

**1976 Montego MX Brougham four-door sedan**

# Mercury

delivered a firmer suspension for more-capable roadholding and a standard 320-bhp 390 V-8 for extra go. For 1968 came a GTE package with several unique appearance features and a 390-bhp 427. The hottest '69 Cougar was the Eliminator hardtop, with 428 power and a standard rear-deck spoiler. Convertibles saw very low sales: fewer than 10,000 total for 1969 and less than 4300 for 1970.

Cougar never approached Mustang in sales, though it was more solid and elegant, and just as roadable. Production was still more than respectable: 150,000 in the first year, about 114,000 in '68, close to 100,000 in '69, then about 72,000 in '70. All are now collector's items.

Cougar was the crowning touch to a decade that saw Mercury move into luxury cars rivaling Lincoln even as it recaptured the performance aura it established in the late '40s and early '50s. But the good times of the '60s couldn't last. As the '70s rolled along, Mercurys became more like Ford equivalents, while government mandates and the vagaries of petroleum power-politics conspired to sacrifice performance on the twin altars of safety and fuel economy. By 1980, Mercury had once again resumed its original role as a plusher, costlier, and sometimes larger Ford. The only differences were that the parallel model lines encompassed five or six different-size classes, instead of one or two, and that Mercury styling more often related to Lincoln's than Ford's.

The ponycar field was one area where the Ford and L-M divisions parted company in the '70s. Actually, Cougar began diverging from Mustang as early as 1971, when both models were redesigned. The Mercury jumped two inches in wheelbase instead of one (to 113 inches) and looked considerably bulkier. Standard and XR-7 convertibles remained through the end of this generation in 1973, and have become minor collector's items, primarily by dint of low annual production: fewer than 2000 of each type, except for the 3165 XR-7s in '73.

Of course, this only reflected the general abrupt drop in demand for all ponycars after 1970, and it prompted Mercury to chart a new course for Cougar. While Mustang became a smaller, lighter, Pinto-based sporty car for 1974, Cougar grew into a kind of ersatz Thunderbird, adopting the 114-inch-wheelbase two-door platform of the intermediate Montego line. Oddly, L-M had created the design chosen for the production Mustang II. But rather than field a badge-engineered clone of that car, the division opted to continue with the German-built Ford Capri it had been selling successfully since 1970—a "mini ponycar" like Mustang II but better-built and more-roadable.

The T-Bird-like Cougar continued through 1976 as Mercury's marker in the midsize personal-luxury segment dominated by the Chevrolet Monte Carlo and Pontiac Grand Prix. The name was diluted for 1977 when it replaced Montego for the entire intermediate line, with the XR-7 label reserved for a single top-

1977 Bobcat Runabout with Sports Accent Group

1978 Zephyr ES two-door sedan

1977 Cougar Villager four-door station wagon

1978 Cougar XR-7 with Midnight/Chamois Decor Group

1977 Cougar XR-7 coupe

1978 Zephyr Z-7 coupe

# Mercury

1978 Zephyr four-door sedan

1979 Monarch coupe

1979 Marquis Brougham Colony Park station wagon

1979 Capri RS hatchback coupe

1979 Cougar XR-7 coupe

shelf coupe. Things were temporarily sorted out again for 1980, only Cougar really *was* a Thunderbird now, a twin to that year's new downsized model on a special 108.4-inch version of the compact "Fox" platform.

In between, Ford again redesigned the Mustang, and this time Mercury wanted in. The result was a new American-made Capri for 1979. The direct descendent of the genuine Cougar ponycar, it was virtually identical with the new-generation Mustang (*see entry*) save somewhat busier styling based on the Ford's three-door hatch coupe body style. The '79 Capri offered the same four engines as that year's Mustang in base and luxury Ghia models (the latter honoring the famed Italian coachbuilder that Ford purchased in 1970). More enthusiastic types could order a sporty RS package that was roughly equivalent to the Mustang Cobra (Mercury never called it "Rally Sport," likely for fear of objection from Chevrolet).

One of the last cars of this era with a distinctly Mercury character was the Cyclone, which bowed out after 1971. Offered that year with standard 351 and optional 429-cid V-8s, this muscular midsize was as impressively fast as ever. Swoopier sheet-metal set it clearly apart from its run-of-the-mill Montego line-mates and Ford's corresponding Torino GT and Cobra, particularly the protruding nose and "gunsight" grille that appeared with the midsize line's 1970-71 facelift. Reflecting the muscle-car market's sad state of affairs at the time, Cyclone sold poorly in its farewell season, especially the desirable low-production Spoiler hardtop (just 353 of the '71s were built).

Elsewhere, Mercury's new-model development story in the '70s was primarily one of badge engineering. It began when the Comet name was revived for a restyled version of Ford's new 1970 compact Maverick, distinguished mainly by a Montego-style nose. Announced for 1971, this Comet soldiered on through '74 as the division's sole representative in a size and price sector that took on urgent new importance in the wake of the 1973-74 Middle East oil embargo.

Help arrived for 1975 in the form of two new entries. One was the Comet's once-and-future replacement, the slightly larger Granada-based Monarch. The other was Mercury's belated, if inevitable, rendition of the subcompact Ford Pinto, bearing the cute Bobcat name and a pretentious little stand-up grille. Ford replaced Maverick with the more-able Fairmont for 1978, so Mercury got a look-alike derivative, the Zephyr. If none of these moves was exactly original, they at least combined to leave Mercury much more competitive in a market that had been forever changed by an unprecedented combination of forces.

As with Buick and Oldsmobile, intermediate and full-size cars remained Mercury's mainstay through the '70s, and it was here that the changes were most dramatic—and most needed. Mercury's midsize contender was a near duplicate of the Ford Torino/LTD II, under the Montego name for 1972-76, then, as noted, with the Cougar badge from 1977 through the last of this body-on-frame design for 1979. Like the Fords, there was little praiseworthy about them, though the Mercurys arguably looked nicer.

Up in what was loosely called the "standard" class sat the big two-ton Marquis and Monterey. Neither changed much through 1978. Model names centered on Marquis exclusively after 1974, and styling became progressively more like that of the big Lincoln Continental, particularly up front. These Mercs were mammoths, but good ones: smooth and reliable, powered by reasonably potent V-8s (400s, 429s, and Lincoln 460s), and fully equipped (if not always tasteful). Pillarless hardtops gave way to pillared styling after 1974. Like Ford's LTD, the Marquis underwent the "big shrink" for '79, losing 10 inches in wheel-base and about 700 pounds in curb weight.

In retrospect, the '70s weren't particularly good for Mercury.

# Mercury

1980 Zephyr Z-7 turbo sports coupe

1980 Grand Marquis four-door sedan

1980 Cougar XR-7 coupe

1980 Cougar XR-7 coupe

1981 Lynx LS hatchback coupe

1982 LN7 2-passenger hatchback coupe

The make again lost its performance image, and not all the fault lay with Washington and OPEC. A succession of heavier, clumsier Cougars and confusingly named intermediates hardly helped, while moves into the compact and subcompact arenas were blunted by higher prices on cars that offered little more than the Fords they so obviously were. Meantime, Mercury's traditional big-car foundation was rocked by the new economic order of a more energy-conscious world. Yet by 1980, Mercury was turning the corner with cars like the exciting Capri, the practical Zephyr, and reborn Cougar and Marquis.

Mercury decisively completed that maneuver in the '80s, benefiting from the same astute management and timely product introductions that made Ford Motor Company the industry's profit leader by 1986. Though no one Mercury line was among Detroit's top-selling nameplates, the make's total production rose rapidly from a low of 347,700 for 1980 to a decade high of nearly half a million U.S.-built cars for '84—an impressive recovery, though still far below record '79 (669,000-plus). On the model-year tote board, Mercury sat anywhere from sixth to ninth, as it had since the '50s, but managed fifth for 1983, its best finish ever.

As before, the Mercury line continued to parallel Ford's annual offerings except for somewhat higher prices and different model/equipment mixes. Styling also remained similar through 1982, but the following year saw the return of a more-distinctive Mercury look. Much sooner than GM, Dearborn had correctly concluded that too many clones spoil the sales broth. With the 1983 models, Mercurys again began standing more clearly apart from equivalent Fords—and GM rivals—to the undoubted benefit of sales.

Still, volume throughout the '80s remained much lower than Ford's model-for-model, and Mercury didn't have the same relative success with some of the same products. The Capri ponycar was one telling example. Like Mustang, it received almost annual power increases and higher performance, commencing with 1982's high-output 157-bhp 302-cid V-8. But then Mustang got a handsome facelift and a revived convertible, while Capri soldiered on for '83 with just a hatchback coupe and its basic '79 appearance except for a huge "bubbleback" rear window of dubious aesthetic merit. It's almost as if L-M was ashamed of Capri, and it showed in half-hearted promotion that aggravated the lack of overt change. Production thus steadily waned, from nearly 80,000 for 1980 to only some 18,500 of the '85s (compared with over 156,000 Mustangs). At that level, Capri was too costly to sustain, and it was banished after '86.

The same fate awaited another "bubbleback" Merc: the two-seat LN7, introduced in early 1982 alongside the related Ford EXP. Both were sporty coupes derived from the front-drive Ford Escort/Mercury Lynx subcompacts, which had scored big sales since replacing the old Pinto/Bobcat twins for 1981.

# Mercury

1982 Capri RS 5.0 hatchback coupe

1983 Marquis Brougham four-door sedan

1983 Zephyr four-door sedan

1983 LN7 2-passenger hatchback coupe

1984 Topaz LS four-door sedan

1983 Cougar LS coupe

Unfortunately, the coupes were anything but lovely, and no match for a number of Japanese competitors in performance, refinement, or workmanship. Perhaps buyers didn't expect a two-seater in L-M showrooms, for the LN7 attracted a middling 40,000 sales before being retired after 1983. A facelifted EXP then took on its bulbous backlight and proved somewhat more popular.

Lynx was Mercury's entry into the increasingly tough small-car market in 1981, and it sold respectably, racking up over 100,000 units in its first two seasons and about 85,000 a year thereafter. Like Escort, it began with a three-door hatchback sedan and a neat five-door wagon in trim levels from plain to fancy. These were bolstered for 1982 by five-door sedans, a sporty three-door RS, and a posh five-door LTS (for Luxury Touring Sedan).

Through mid-'85, Lynx was powered by the Escort's 1.6-liter "CVH" four, also offered in H.O. and turbocharged guises. In mid-'85, both of the latter were dropped and a normal-tune 1.9-liter enlargement took over. A 2.0-liter diesel four supplied by Mazda in Japan was also offered beginning with the '84s, though it attracted few buyers as gas prices fell in an improving national economy. The appearance was cleaned up for "1985½" with a smoother nose and flush headlamps in line with Dearborn's strong turn to aerodynamic styling. An even sportier three-door, called XR3, bowed the following year.

But here, too, Ford planners would conclude that one clone was one too many. However, a falling dollar and lower offshore production costs also figured in the decision to drop Lynx during 1987 in favor of the Mexican-built Tracer, a badge-engineered version of Mazda's similarly sized 323. Yet despite generating less than half of Escort's volume in most years, the Lynx must be judged a success, as it rung up crucial business for L-M dealers during some very difficult times.

The same holds for Mercury's compacts and intermediates of this decade. For 1981-82 these comprised the familiar (and largely unchanged) Zephyr line and a new upmarket Cougar sedan series, both built on the proven rear-drive "Fox" platform of 1978. Weighing some 350-400 pounds less than the Monarchs they replaced, these Cougars were twins to Ford's reborn '81 Granadas. Styling was similarly squared up and more-formal than Zephyr's, appropriate for the higher prices. Though the origins of these models were obvious, there was evidently some magic left in the Cougar name. Between them, Cougar and Zephyr netted well over 80,000 annual sales in 1981-82, not bad considering the then-sorry state of the market.

Mercury did somewhat better by replacing the Fox-platform Cougars with a new small Marquis for 1983. This was yet another Fairmont/Zephyr variation, but its cleaner styling was a big improvement, even if it looked rather too much like the downsized 1983 LTD that took over for Granada at Ford. Still,

# Mercury

1983 Capri GS hatchback coupe

1984 Topaz LS coupe with TR Performance Group

1984 Cougar XR-7 coupe

1985 Capri RS 5.0 hatchback coupe

1986 Sable LS four-door station wagon

1986 Sable LS four-door sedan

the name link with a full-size Merc didn't hurt, and by 1984 Marquis sales totaled some 108,000, half again as much as the previous Cougar series.

To avoid confusion, the biggest Mercurys were renamed Grand Marquis after 1982, one of their few important changes during the entire decade. Not that many changes were needed. Roomy, quiet, and comfortable, they remained traditional V-8 American family cruisers whose sales rebounded strongly once the economy began recovering and an oil glut pushed gas prices down to more-reasonable levels. Chrysler Corporation and the Buick, Olds, and Pontiac divisions of GM lent a helping hand by canceling most of their old rear-drive biggies by 1985, leaving the Grand Marquis all but alone in the medium-price full-size field.

Grand Marquis thus journeyed through the '80s with only the barest of updates. Two-door coupes were dropped after 1985, the mainstay four-door sedan and wagon gained smoother noses and tails for 1988, and fuel injection replaced carburetors on the 302 V-8, but that was about it. Once their original '79 tooling was amortized, the big Mercurys (and Fords) became the darlings of corporate accountants and dealers alike, earning more profit per unit than any other model in the line. Consumers kept on buying despite the lack of change. Grand Marquis sales totaled nearly 96,000 for '83, over 148,000 for '84, then 110,000-160,000 each year all the way through 1989.

Obviously, the "Big M" still offered what a lot of folks wanted.

Cougar was Mercury's most-dramatic success of these years—not the aforementioned sedan series but L-M's version of the Ford Thunderbird. Blocky and ornate, the downsized XR-7 was little changed through 1982, and laid a gigantic sales egg, dropping below 20,000 units. But then came 1983's handsome aerodynamic redesign, and volume more than tripled, reaching nearly 76,000 units. Sales rose by another 55,000 for '84, then held above 100,000 through 1988.

This Cougar had almost everything the latest T-Bird did—which was plenty. Aiming for a more-conservative clientele, Mercury gave it a more-traditional, nearly vertical backlight and offered a standard 232-cid V-6 or optional 302 V-8. The essential Fox chassis of 1980-82 was retained, but more finely tuned for a better ride/handling balance, and interiors could be downright luxurious with just a modicum of options. No XR-7 model was offered at first, but it returned for '84 as a counterpart to the Thunderbird Turbo Coupe, with the same hyperaspirated 145-cid four, appropriately beefed-up suspension, and standard five-speed manual transmission. The last was an item that hadn't been seen on Cougars since the '60s.

In all, it was a most-pleasing package, made even more so by an interim facelift for '87, Cougar's 20th anniversary. This involved larger-appearing windows and a shapelier nose bearing flush headlamps and a more-rakish grille. At the same time,

# Mercury

1986 Lynx XR3 hatchback coupe

1986 Cougar XR-7 coupe

1986 Sable GS four-door station wagon

1987 Cougar LS coupe

1987 Sable LS four-door sedan

the XR-7's turbo-four was dropped and a new fuel-injected 302 with 155 horses became standard. New for '88 were a hot XR-7 with monochrome exterior, dual exhausts for the V-8, and 20 more horsepower for the base V-6 (now at 140 total).

But all this was merely a warm-up for the spectacular all-new '89 Cougar. Again, it was based on a new T-Bird, emerging lower and wider but no longer despite a 113-inch wheelbase (previously 104.2). Styling was even more smoothly aerodynamic, but the vertical backlight and more-formal grille that had set Cougar apart from the 'Bird were still evident.

The new Cougar followed the '89 Thunderbird in forsaking both a V-8 and the old turbo-four for a pair of fuel-injected 232 V-6s: a normally aspirated 140-bhp unit for the LS model and a 210-bhp supercharged version with intercooler for the high-performance XR-7—America's first supercharged six since the 1954-55 Kaiser Manhattan. It was mounted in a sophisticated new chassis with all-independent suspension, variable-rate shock absorbers, and other technical features that made the new Cougar a road car worthy of comparison with premium European coupes.

No doubt about it: Cougar had been fully transformed in a satisfying way. Sales remained satisfying too, though volume was down somewhat: to about 97,000 for '89, then to a more-worrisome 81,500. Higher prices were undoubtedly a factor: nearly $16,000 for the 1990 LS, a bit over $20,000 for the XR-7. Still, those price tags looked reasonable against the far loftier stickers of imported sports-luxury coupes.

Mercury was well represented in the hard-fought compact and midsize battles of the '80s, its respective warriors being the Topaz and Sable. Topaz, arriving for 1984 as the front-drive replacement for Zephyr, was a predictable kissin' cousin of Ford's new Tempo and thus evolved in parallel with it. Included in developments through decade's end were an available high-output 2.3-liter four, sporty two-doors, 1987's new all-wheel-drive option, a stem-to-stern makeover for 1988 sedans, and an optional driver-side air bag starting in 1986 (one of the earliest domestic cars to offer that feature). Dearborn designers tried to make Topaz look somewhat different from Tempo at each end and by deleting the Tempo sedan's rearmost side windows—not huge distinctions, but another sign that Mercurys were becoming individual once more.

A pleasant and capable compact, though not state-of-the-art, Topaz followed Lynx in generating lower volume than its Ford counterpart: 80,000-128,000 a year, about half of Tempo's sales. But again, that volume was helpful to L-M dealers.

Sable, replacing the little Marquis, was far more helpful. Arriving with base prices in the $11,000-$13,000 range, it immediately commanded almost 96,000 sales for debut '86, then shot up to over 121,000 for '87 and a resounding 130,000-plus for 1989. Sable was Mercury's version of the acclaimed front-drive Ford Taurus, and thus shared most of its widely praised basic design. There were exceptions, though. Where Taurus had three trim levels, Sable offered two: GS and upmarket LS. Mercury also decided it didn't need Ford's small 2.5-liter four after '86—wise, as most Taurus buyers decided they didn't need it either. This left 3.0-liter and, from 1988, 3.8-liter "Vulcan" V-6s. Both produced 140 bhp, but the 3.8 was the engine of choice for all-around driving due to its larger displacement and commensurately greater torque (215 pound-feet vs. 160). Sable also had more simulated wood on the dash and door panels.

But the real distinction was outside. Where the four-door Taurus sedan wore a "six-light" roof treatment, the Sable version had a rear window wrapped fully around to the rear-door trailing edges for a smooth hidden-pillar effect. Also, Sable's rear wheel arches were flat-topped, versus rounded on Taurus. Even more dramatic was Sable's unique front "light bar," a set

# Mercury

of running lights behind a wide central white lens that illuminated with the headlamps to make both sedans and the five-door wagons unmistakable at night. The net effect of these simple but clever differences was to give Sable an identity quite apart from that of Taurus. Seldom in recent times had a Mercury been more its "own car"—or more handsome.

Sable didn't get anything like the high-performance '89 Taurus SHO, but this was a reasonable marketing decision given Mercury's more luxury-oriented clientele. And those folks no doubt appreciated useful upgrades for 1990 that included optional antilock brakes for sedans, a standard driver-side air bag for all Sables, a dash reworked to be more ergonomic, and new features like an optional compact-disc player and standard tilt steering wheel.

With a stunning new Cougar to carry the performance banner, plus the updated Topaz, evergreen Grand Marquis, and strong-selling Sable, Mercury could take justifiable pride during Golden Anniversary 1989, when total domestic volume (excluding off-shore products like Tracer) approached a smashing 500,000. Despite occasional mistakes and some rough periods in its first 50 years, Mercury had produced some of America's most-memorable automobiles. Now, on the eve of its second

1987 Cougar LS coupe

1989 Cougar XR7 coupe

1988 Grand Marquis LS four-door sedan

1990 Grand Marquis Colony Park LS station wagon

1988 Cougar XR-7 coupe

1990 Cougar LS coupe

1988 Cougar XR-7 coupe

1991 Capri 2+2 convertible coupe

# Mercury

half-century, it was doing so again.

But Mercury's calendar-year domestic sales plunged to around 309,000 in 1991, reflecting the onset of a deep new national recession that would last a good three years. Even so, Mercury was able to claim sixth from Dodge the following year, then held the spot on steadily rising volume that reached nearly 387,000 units in 1994. It was a quite credible performance considering that Mercury had only two products in this period not shared with Ford—and that only one was a real success.

The product in question was the new Villager, arriving for 1993 as Mercury's first minivan. At first glance, it seemed just a belated copy of the Dodge Caravan/Plymouth Voyager that had been around for a decade and still dominated minivan sales by a wide margin. Indeed, Villager followed their lead by being a front-drive design sized about halfway between their standard and extended Grand models, riding a 112.2-inch wheelbase and stretching 189.9 inches overall.

But Villager had its attractions, starting with neat, trim styling that was arguably more-fashionable than Chrysler's, plus standard (instead of optional) four-wheel antilock brakes. Mercury also dispensed with the sham of price-leader models with four-cylinder power and manual transmission, opting for GS and luxury LS editions with a 3.0-liter 150-bhp single-overhead-cam V-6 and four-speed overdrive automatic. Villager's chassis was more-sophisticated, too—its modern all-coil suspension making for even more carlike ride and handling than Chrysler had. It even had a clever novelty in a sliding three-place third-row bench seat that could be moved up on built-in floor tracks to substitute for the removable two-place middle bench; it could also be slid halfway up to open up extra cargo space behind.

Trouble was (if that's the word), Villager was all but identical with Nissan's new Quest, built to the same design that borrowed liberally from the Japanese firm's Maxima sedan. The Mercury differed only in having an illuminated front "light bar" *a la* Sable, plus minor trim and equipment distinctions. At least these twins were built in the U.S., produced under Ford auspices at Avon Lake, Ohio. It was another joint venture of the sort now common in the industry, but Ford's influence was confined to minor areas like switchgear and interior materials.

Fortunately for L-M, buyers weren't at all bothered by Villager's Asian origins, especially with high-value base prices of $16,500-$22,000. In fact, thanks to a deliberate production bias in Mercury's favor, Villager outsold Quest by more than 2-to-1 for debut '93—and those sales were nearly 109,000. While that was only about a quarter of combined Caravan/Voyager sales, it was hardly bad for such a Johnny-come-lately. And, of course, it was all "plus" business for L-M dealers.

For 1994, Villager added a spiffy top-line Nautica model with standard leather interior, front and middle "captain's chair" bucket seats and a specific blue/cream color scheme inspired by Nautica sportswear. Nissan was accorded more Quests that season, which partly explains why Villager volume dropped to just under 62,000 for the model year. Both versions added a standard driver-side air bag, but still lacked a passenger-side restraint like Chrysler's minivans. Production sank a bit further for 1995, reflecting stiffer price and product competition in this fast-moving market.

Mercury wasn't at all successful with its other unique product of this period, which was American only in name. This was the Australian-built two-seat convertible that appeared in mid-1990 as yet another Capri. Like Tracer, it was based on the small 323 platform from Japanese affiliate Mazda, with the same proven front-drive mechanicals plus four-wheel-disc brakes, independent rear suspension, driver-side air bag, and an optional liftoff hardtop. A 1.6-liter four delivered 100 bhp in the base model or 132 turbocharged ponies in the uplevel XR2. Yet despite open-

1991 Topaz GS four-door sedan

1991 Cougar LS coupe

1991 Sable LS station wagon

1992 Grand Marquis LS four-door sedan

1992 Sable GS four-door sedan

# Mercury

1992 Capri XR2 convertible coupe

1992 Tracer LTS four-door sedan

1993 Topaz GS four-door sedan

1993 Tracer four-door sedan

1993 Villager minivan

air allure and affordable pricing in the $13,000-$15,000 range, this Capri just didn't sell. Dumpy styling hurt as much as indifferent workmanship, and Mazda's own Miata offered a prettier, "more-authentic" sports car with superior Japanese build quality for not many more dollars. With all this, Capri sales peaked at about 21,200 for calendar '91, then plummeted to nowhere. Mercury gave up after 1994, when it instituted a mild facelift and standard passenger-side air bag. Perhaps the Capri name had been cursed.

As ever, other Mercs of the early-'90s generally evolved like counterpart Fords. Thus, the subcompact Tracer aped Escort with a full redesign for 1991, while '92 brought a Grand Marquis revamped like Crown Victoria and a Sable reworked *a la* Taurus.

But Mercury didn't follow Ford in every way. The '91 Tracer, for example, offered no hatchback sedans, just a five-door wagon and a four-door notchback. The latter was a full year ahead of Escort's, though, and was used for the sporting model, here called LTS. Though it had twincam Mazda power like the Escort GT, LTS stood apart by wearing the front "light bar" motif ushered in by Sable as a Mercury hallmark, though it didn't light up on this lower-cost car. Base models got this and other LTS appearance cues for 1993, when Tracer followed Escort to "one-price" marketing: base models with air conditioning and automatic transmission selling at $11,665. Also like Escort, Tracer added a driver-side air bag for '94 and optional ABS for the LTS. The following year brought a standard passenger air bag, plus a low-cost "Trio" trim package that added a rear spoiler and alloy wheels to the base sedan. One thing Mercury couldn't seem to change was relative sales, and Tracer volume remained only a fraction of Escort's. Then again, with so many small cars to choose from, some buyers likely forgot that L-M dealers even had one.

Sable sales held generally steady, both in absolute numbers and as a proportion of Taurus', but Mercury's midsize was quicker than Ford's to offer a passenger-side air bag: first as an option with the '92 redesign, then standard. Though Sable still had no counterpart to the high-power Taurus SHO, Mercury did offer front buckets and console as new '93 extras for the uplevel LS sedan. These became standard for the '94 version, which was joined late in the year by a sportier LTS sedan with leather inside and a "more-Euro" look outside. Overall Sable production remained strong in this period, running 116,000-137,000 in all years save recessionary '91, when sales dipped to just above 96,000.

The full-size Grand Marquis showed surprising sales strength with its '92 redesign, accounting for much of Mercury's increased overall volume through middecade. In fact, the newly aerodynamic "Big M" outpolled its Ford sister in '92 model-year production by some 10,000 units with a relatively amazing 163,000-plus. It then settled down to around 100,000 yearly sales except for 1993 (a bit over 90,000).

Grand Marquis still eschewed any pretense of sport, but its '92 makeover was the same considered update accorded Crown Victoria. Highlights included Dearborn's new 4.6-liter "modular" V-8, standard all-disc brakes, available ABS, a thoroughly reworked rear-drive chassis, and a firm-ride Handling and Performance option with dual exhausts adding 20 bhp to the regular 190. Like Ford, Mercury bailed out of big wagons, but the GS and uplevel LS sedans were nicely tailored to stand more clearly apart from Crown Vics. Differences included a modest grille from day one, a conventional "four-light" roofline, and Sable-inspired taillight treatment. Considering the conservative character of both the car and its clientele, the rejuvenated Grand Marquis showed a lot of sales life in the early '90s.

The same could not be said for Cougar, which lost interest value after 1990—and a lot of customers. In a way, this was

# Mercury

1994 Capri XR2 convertible coupe

1994 Cougar XR7 coupe

1994 Grand Marquis LS sedan

1995 Tracer station wagon

probably inevitable. Like Thunderbird buyers, Cougar prospects were now mainly those who cared less about sporty performance than getting the most luxury per buck. Since there was no point in giving people something they didn't want, Mercury swapped engines for the uplevel '91 XR7, yanking out the supercharged V-6 (and its five-speed manual transmission) for a good old 5.0-liter V-8 with 200 bhp (and mandatory automatic). At the same time, the V-8 became a first-time option for the base LS, replacing its unblown (and unchanged) 3.8 V-6. Both Cougars also wore a minor facelift involving the hood, headlamps, grille, and back panel.

Cougar changed little for 1992, a disappointing way for the model to observe its 25th anniversary. So was the midseason birthday special based not on the XR7 but the everyday LS, with distinctions limited to just a monochrome exterior and fancy BBS alloy wheels. Model-year sales plunged by more than 13,000 to just over 49,000, which was only about half of what Cougar had tallied with its 1989 redesign. Then again, Mercury wasn't pushing the car too hard, and there were other, more-tempting coupes available in Cougar's $16,000-$22,000 price bracket. All the more surprising, then, that sales leaped to near 81,500 for 1993 despite only a single, little-changed XR7 without so much as a driver-side air bag.

A substantial '94 freshening made the XR7 look a bit different at each end without really improving it. But there were genuine improvements elsewhere: standard dual air bags within a reworked dash, newly optional traction control (with ABS required), and a switch in V-8 options from pushrod 5.0-liter to new single-cam 4.6 "mod." Even with all this, the base price was held to just $16,260—which must have angered all those folks who'd bought '93s. But fewer folks bought '94s, model-year output easing to around 76,000, and fewer still opted for the little-changed '95s, which were pared down to just the XR7. By that point, Cougar again looked like just another stray cat in the personal-luxury jungle, with little of substance to separate it from the competitive herd. It was certainly a long way from the exciting luxury ponycar of the '60s.

Excitement was never a trait of Mercury's compact Topaz, and still wasn't when the line ended after 1994. The high point, such as it was, came with '92, when all Topazes got a Sable-type "light bar" face and the sporty LTS sedan and XR5 coupe got the Sable's 3.0-liter 135-bhp V-6 standard (optional elsewhere). But the V-6 didn't do that much for performance, and a lack of buyer interest finally killed the useful all-wheel-drive option that year. Topaz was further diluted for '93, down to just a two-door and four-door GS with "value" pricing but little standard equipment. Even a driver-side air bag cost extra, and then only with the base four and optional automatic transmission (the V-6 remained available). Like Ford's related Tempo, this Mercury had come to have more appeal for rental fleets than retail buyers, which might well explain why sales for 1990-93 were relatively spectacular at 80,000 to 100,000 a year. Like vanilla ice cream, the Topaz was far from memorable, but offered enough to satisfy many people.

A much tastier small Mercury arrived for 1995. Called Mystique, it was essentially that year's new Ford Contour with a slightly more-conservative look and somewhat higher prices. The last stemmed from the inclusion of several features that were optional on the Ford. Thus, the $13,855 Mystique GS cost $545 more than the counterpart Contour GL, but gave buyers a full console, tachometer, and power mirrors without asking. The uplevel LS boasted nicer trim, a few more goodies, and a starting price of $15,230.

To its credit, L-M Division didn't monkey with the basic design originated by Ford's European Mondeo, so this front-drive Merc had a genuine "sports sedan" mystique. That was particularly true for handling and roadholding, which set new standards for small domestic four-doors, but workmanship was also in a higher league: tight, solid, and thorough. Performance was rather tame with the base 2.0-liter 125-bhp four, but was almost exhilarating with the optional 170-bhp 2.5-liter twincam V-6. The back seat was tight enough for grown-ups to feel like sardines, but that was about the only serious complaint. Overall, Mystique was vast improvement on the tepid Topaz. Just as important, it charted a refreshing new course for other Mercurys to follow.

But there were rough seas ahead for Mystique. Despite positive initial reviews, buyers just weren't queuing up for

# Mercury

Mercury's new compact. It was an instant replay of what was happening to the Contour but on a smaller scale. The company did what it could, revising front seatbacks and rear seat cushions to add a precious inch of rear legroom—not quite enough—and putting a brave new face with a distinctive headlamp treatment on the '99 version. But the changes, allied with a revised front suspension that more closely approximated that of the European Mondeo on which Mystique and Contour were based, weren't enough to keep the line alive. The last Mystiques came off the assembly line in 2000. Hindsight suggests that nothing could have saved the little Mercury, not even an analogue to Contour's peppy SVT model; it appears to have been a doomed effort from the start.

Mercury's other compact offering, the Tracer, was on the downward portion of its development curve as well. The redesigned '97 model was a handsome, efficient little car, nicely equipped and sensibly priced. Like its near-twin, the Ford Escort, Tracer offered both sedan and wagon models, very good road manners, and was finished to a higher standard than many rivals. Its 110-bhp sohc inline-four powerplant performed well in the little lightweight, even with the optional four-speed automatic transmission. But Tracer's ultimate fate was tied to events at Ford, and when Escort was cut back to a single model in 2000, no Tracer equivalent was offered and the last sub-$15,000 Mercury was gone.

The same fate had befallen the sporty Cougar three years before. The Thunderbird-based coupe had been cut back to a single model for '97, and, in base form, it was not particularly appealing. The standard 145-bhp V-6 engine lacked the urge needed to push a 3500-lb coupe along with any alacrity, and it was singularly unrefined. Fortunately, the optional sohc V-8 did have enough suds (at 205 bhp) to do the job, and it was available in a package that included several other desirable amenities for a mere $1345. This gave it a nice performance edge on its six-cylinder rivals from General Motors, and there were still customers who preferred the driving characteristics of a traditional front-engine/rear-drive layout. Not many, though, and not enough to keep either Cougar or T-Bird alive.

This time, Mercury had a replacement waiting in the wings, and it was a stand-alone design with no Ford equivalent. When the Cougar nameplate returned in 1999, it was appended to a new front-drive coupe based on the Contour/Mystique platform. Sporting the most-adventuresome styling seen from Mercury in many years, the Cougar opened to mixed reviews but benefited from fortuitous timing, as the market for small performance coupes was expanding rapidly. A longer wheelbase than its direct rivals gave it a decent ride, and suspension calibrations aimed at the enthusiast driver made it nimble. Though a base model with a 2.0-liter dohc inline-four engine was available, the optional 170-bhp dohc V-6 proved far more

**1996 Grand Marquis LS four-door sedan**

**1999 Cougar V-6 coupe**

**1997 Mystique four-door sedan**

**2001 Grand Marquis four-door sedan**

**1997 Sable GS four-door sedan**

**2002 Sable station wagon**

popular, and not just because it delivered excellent performance; it added a mere $500 to the $16,195 base price, which made it more attractive to budget buyers than some Japanese competitors. Not everyone was thrilled: Consumer Guide®, for one, found plenty of details to criticize, but others reacted more favorably.

Initial plans called for a high-performance version with, perhaps, a 195-bhp V-6 underhood, that would have made its debut in 2000. As sales began to soften, however, this idea was shelved, and a mild restyling, confined to front and rear soft fascias and the instrument panel, distinguished the '01 model. The list of extra-cost items remained much as before—a Sport Group package, for example, jazzed up the V-6 Cougars with 16-inch wheels, four-wheel disc brakes, grippier seats, and other amenities—with the notable addition of side airbags. By this time, even a reasonable price wasn't enough to keep interest in the Cougar alive. This was not entirely the fault of the basic package; new arrivals such as the Acura RSX raised the compact sports-coupe bar considerably, and only substantial changes, which Mercury was unable to provide, could have stopped declining sales. For '02, alterations were cosmetic only (with the exception of moving four-wheel disc brakes to the standard-equipment list), consisting of two new trim packages, one of which (XR) added 17-inch wheels and some body add-ons attributed to Ford associate Jack Roush. This last-ditch effort couldn't keep Cougar from extinction, and the plug was pulled at the end of '02 model-year production.

Another dropout in '02 was Mercury's Villager minivan. Between its 1993 introduction and the '98 model year, the Villager, a twin to the Nissan Quest, got along without major changes. The '99 model received a near-total makeover, gaining length (4.5 inches) and weight (140 lbs) as well as a second (left-side) rear sliding door. A new 170-bhp V-6, available only with four-speed automatic transmission, offset the weight gain, but the fact was that Villager was now only six inches shorter—and actually heavier—than the more-modern and space-efficient Ford Windstar and the best-selling Chrysler minivans. Details, such as power sliding doors and front-seat side airbags, that either weren't common or hadn't yet become expected features in the class back when Nissan (with some input from Mercury designers) created the original Village/Quest didn't make it into the new version either. In the end, the once-praised Villager was considered an also-ran by testers, and the public wasn't any kinder. The "young families" Mercury was wooing had plenty of other choices.

In the 1990s, it seemed as if no manufacturer could exist without an SUV in its catalog. Mercury's entry into this rapidly expanding market came in 1997 with the Mountaineer, a four-door Ford Explorer with revisions to some exterior body panels and interior trim. The Mercury iteration was initially available only with a 5.0-liter V-8 engine, though either two- or four-wheel drive could be ordered. When Ford introduced a new sohc version of Explorer's 3.8-liter V-6 and teamed it with a five-speed automatic transmission (the latter a first for the class) in 1998, that 205-bhp powerplant became standard for Mountaineer, with the V-8 optional. Both Explorer and Mountaineer were redone for 2002; Mountaineer was given its own visual identity with a bold new face incorporating a large "waterfall" grille and front bumper with inset driving lights. The V-6 engine continued, but V-8 buyers got the 4.6-liter sohc "modular" engine. Like Explorer, Mountaineer benefited from new four-wheel independent suspension.

On the Sable front, changes came in lockstep with the near-identical Ford Taurus. Taurus' complete redesign of 1996 was daring and modernistic, but somewhat less so for Sable. Sable had a little brightwork up front to soften the effect of the oval air inlet, a conventional rear window shape in place of Taurus' rounded back glass, and a different taillamp treatment. The new and bold forms were equally dramatic on both the sedan and wagon. Inside, a new dashboard continued the ovoid exterior themes. Numerous functional changes were made as well, including a new uplevel engine, the 200-bhp Duratec dohc V-6, which was far more refined than the previous 3.8-liter V-6. As before, the base powerplant was a conventional pushrod 3.0-liter V-6, now rated at 145 bhp. Over the next two years, the base engine's power rating would go up (to 155 bhp), most likely due to changes in measurement methods rather than any substantial alterations. All in all, this heavily sculptured new Sable didn't go over well with Mercury buyers, a situation not improved until 2000, when the exterior was reworked to impart a more-traditional look, complete with a distinctive grille to replace the chrome-trimmed snout. The interior was revised as well, becoming less oval. As before, customers were offered a choice between five- and six-passenger seating in sedans; when the latter was chosen, a steering-column-mounted gearshift lever replaced the floor shift. Station wagons offered accommodations for either six or eight passengers, depending on whether or not the optional third seat was supplied.

The evolution of yet another Mercury, the fullsize Grand Marquis, was also tied closely to the fortunes of its mirror-image Ford. While the Crown Victoria captured an increasing share of the taxi, fleet, and police-car markets as its rivals dropped their body-on-frame rear-drive platforms, the Grand Marquis was forced to rely largely on retail customers for survival. A few modest styling revisions, including a subtle reworking of the front and rear ends and roof in 1998, and a number of internal changes to the engine (increasing horsepower from 190 in 1996 to 220 in 2002), suspension, and brakes were made between 1993 and 2002. These, it would seem, were sufficient to keep the biggest Mercury's appeal alive. While luxury was always at the forefront of the Grand's packaging and marketing efforts, a mild undercurrent of performance was always present. In addition to the expected premium option groups—full of such goodies as automatic climate control, leather upholstery, digital instrumentation, a gold-trim package, and the like—buyers could order a "handling package" which included alloy wheels, firmer suspension, automatic rear self-leveling, and a dual-exhaust system, which brought the 4.6-liter ohc V-8 engine's output up to first 215, then 235 bhp.

Enough customers called for the performance upgrades to suggest that a hotter Grand might be in order and, for '03, Mercury added a Marauder model to the line. With lowered suspension, wide blackwall tires on alloy wheels, some specific interior- and exterior-trim items, and, best of all, a 300-bhp dohc version of the 4.6-liter V-8, Marauder made a strong statement about the versatility of the Grand Marquis concept and the potential breadth of its market.

Amid confusion and rumors that it might vanish, Mercury continues to look ahead. Its membership in the Premier Automotive Group virtually guarantees that future Mercury products will benefit from a wider choice of platforms and powertrains to share. Moreover, Mercury's management has announced ambitious plans for future products to appear by middecade, including a new minivan (possibly developed with a PAG partner), at least one new sedan, and a hybrid gasoline/electric vehicle. It is also rumored that a new Cougar will return to the model's historic roots by coming from a Mustang base. A two-door convertible based on the Marauder—already seen during the '02 auto show season—may see limited production as a niche product. If even some of these new vehicles make it to market, Mercury may yet shed its image of being Ford's sometimes-neglected stepchild.

# Mercury

## Specifications

### 1939—75,000 built*

| Series 99A (wb 116.0) | Wght | Price | Prod |
|---|---|---|---|
| conv club cpe 5P | 2,995 | 1,018 | — |
| sdn 2d 5P | 2,997 | 916 | — |
| cpe sdn 2d 5P | 3,000 | 957 | — |
| Town Sedan 4d 5P | 3,103 | 957 | — |

| 1939 Engine | bore × stroke | bhp | availability |
|---|---|---|---|
| V-8, 239.4 | 3.19 × 3.75 | 95 | S-all |

*Estimated.

### 1940

| Series 09A (wb 116.0)—81,128 built* | Wght | Price | Prod |
|---|---|---|---|
| conv cpe | 3,107 | 1,079 | — |
| sdn 2d | 3,068 | 946 | — |
| cpe-sdn 2d 5P | 3,030 | 978 | — |
| town sedan 4d | 3,103 | 987 | — |
| conv sdn | 3,249 | 1,212 | — |

*Estimated (see note below 1942).

| 1940 Engine | bore × stroke | bhp | availability |
|---|---|---|---|
| V-8, 239.4 | 3.19 × 3.75 | 95 | S-all |

### 1941

| Series 19A (wb 118.0)—82,391* built | Wght | Price | Prod |
|---|---|---|---|
| 67 cpe, A/S | 3,049 | 936 | — |
| 70 sdn 2d | 3,184 | 946 | — |
| 72 cpe-sdn 2d 5P | 3,118 | 977 | — |
| 73 town sedan 4d | 3,221 | 987 | — |
| 76 conv cpe | 3,222 | 1,100 | — |
| 77 cpe 3P | 3,008 | 910 | — |
| 79 wgn 4d | 3,468 | 1,141 | — |

*Estimate (see note below 1942).

| 1941 Engine | bore × stroke | bhp | availability |
|---|---|---|---|
| V-8, 239.4 | 3.19 × 3.75 | 95 | S-all |

### 1942

| Series 29A (wb 118.0)—22,186 built* | Wght | Price | Prod |
|---|---|---|---|
| 70 sdn 2d | 3,228 | 1,030 | — |
| 72 cpe-sdn 2d 5P | 3,148 | 1,055 | — |
| 73 town sedan 4d | 3,263 | 1,065 | — |
| 76 conv cpe | 3,288 | 1,215 | — |
| 77 cpe 3P | 3,073 | 995 | — |
| 79 wgn 4d 8P | 3,528 | 1,260 | — |

* Estimate (see below).

| 1942 Engine | bore × stroke | bhp | availability |
|---|---|---|---|
| V-8, 239.4 | 3.19 × 3.75 | 100 | S-all |

Note: Factory records provide only calendar-year production during 1940-41. Estimates are calculated by adding 25% of previous year's calendar production to 75% of current year's production. Model-year production began in October each year.

### 1946

| Series 69M (wb 118.0) | Wght | Price | Prod |
|---|---|---|---|
| 70 sdn 2d | 3,240 | 1,448 | 13,108 |
| 71 Sportsman conv cpe | 3,407 | 2,209 | 205 |
| 72 cpe-sdn 2d 5P | 3,190 | 1,495 | 24,163 |
| 73 town sedan 4d | 3,270 | 1,509 | 40,280 |
| 76 conv cpe | 3,340 | 1,711 | 6,044 |
| 79 wgn 4d | 3,540 | 1,729 | 2,797 |
| — chassis | — | — | 11 |

| 1946 Engine | bore × stroke | bhp | availability |
|---|---|---|---|
| V-8, 239.4 | 3.19 × 3.75 | 100 | S-all |

### 1947

| Series 79M (wb 118.0) | Wght | Price | Prod |
|---|---|---|---|
| 70 sdn 2d | 3,268 | 1,592 | 34 |
| 72 cpe-sdn 2d 5P | 3,218 | 1,645 | 29,284 |
| 73 town sedan 4d | 3,298 | 1,660 | 43,281 |
| 76 conv cpe | 3,368 | 2,002 | 10,221 |
| 79 wgn 4d | 3,571 | 2,207 | 3,558 |
| — chassis | — | — | 5 |

| 1947 Engine | bore × stroke | bhp | availability |
|---|---|---|---|
| V-8, 239.4 | 3.19 × 3.75 | 100 | S-all |

### 1948

| Series 89M (wb 118.0) | Wght | Price | Prod |
|---|---|---|---|
| 72 cpe-sdn 2d 5P | 3,218 | 1,645 | 16,476 |
| 73 town sedan 4d | 3,298 | 1,660 | 24,283 |
| 76 conv cpe | 3,368 | 2,002 | 7,586 |
| 79 wgn 4d | 3,571 | 2,207 | 1,889 |
| — chassis | — | — | 34 |

| 1948 Engine | bore × stroke | bhp | availability |
|---|---|---|---|
| V-8, 239.4 | 3.19 × 3.75 | 100 | S-all |

### 1949

| Series 9CM (wb 118.0) | Wght | Price | Prod |
|---|---|---|---|
| 72 cpe | 3,321 | 1,979 | 120,616 |
| 74 sport sedan 4d | 3,386 | 2,031 | 155,882 |
| 76 conv cpe | 3,591 | 2,410 | 16,765 |
| 79 wgn 2d, 8P | 3,626 | 2,716 | 8,044 |
| — chassis | — | — | 12 |

| 1949 Engine | bore × stroke | bhp | availability |
|---|---|---|---|
| V-8, 255.4 | 3.19 × 4.00 | 110 | S-all |

### 1950

| Series OCM (wb 118.0) | Wght | Price | Prod |
|---|---|---|---|
| M-72A cpe (economy) | 3,345 | 1,875 | ⎤ |
| M-72B club cpe | 3,430 | 1,980 | |
| M-72C Monterey cpe, canvas top | 3,480 | 2,146 | ⎬ 151,489 |
| M-72C Monterey cpe, vinyl top | 3,480 | 2,157 | ⎦ |
| M-74 sport sedan 4d | 3,470 | 2,032 | 132,082 |
| M-76 conv cpe | 3,710 | 2,412 | 8,341 |
| M-79 wgn 2d 8P | 3,755 | 2,561 | 1,746 |

| 1950 Engine | bore × stroke | bhp | availability |
|---|---|---|---|
| V-8, 255.4 | 3.19 × 4.00 | 110 | S-all |

### 1951

| Series 1CM (wb 118.0) | Wght | Price | Prod |
|---|---|---|---|
| M-72B cpe | 3,485 | 1,947 | ⎤ |
| M-72C Monterey cpe, canvas top | 3,485 | 2,116 | ⎬ 142,168 |
| M-72C Monterey cpe, vinyl top | 3,485 | 2,127 | ⎦ |
| M-74 sport sedan 4d | 3,550 | 2,000 | 157,648 |
| M-76 conv cpe | 3,760 | 2,380 | 6,759 |
| M-79 wgn 2d 8P | 3,800 | 2,530 | 3,812 |

# Mercury

| 1951 Engine | bore × stroke | bhp | availability |
|---|---|---|---|
| V-8, 255.4 | 3.19 × 4.00 | 112 | S-all |

## 1952

| Series 2M (wb 118.0) | | Wght | Price | Prod |
|---|---|---|---|---|
| 60B | Monterey htp cpe | 3,520 | 2,225 | 24,453 |
| 60E | sport coupe htp | 3,435 | 2,100 | 30,599 |
| 70B | sdn 2d | 3,335 | 1,987 | 25,812 |
| 73B | sdn 4d | 3,390 | 2,040 | 83,475 |
| 73C | Monterey sdn 4d | 3,375 | 2,115 | |
| 76B | Monterey conv cpe | 3,635 | 2,370 | 5,261 |
| 79B | wgn 4d 6P | 3,795 | 2,525 | 2,487 |
| 79D | wgn 4d 8P | 3,795 | 2,570 | |

| 1952 Engine | bore × stroke | bhp | availability |
|---|---|---|---|
| V-8, 255.4 | 3.19 × 4.00 | 125 | S-all |

## 1953

| 3M Custom (wb 118.0) | | Wght | Price | Prod |
|---|---|---|---|---|
| 60E | sport coupe htp | 3,465 | 2,117 | 39,547 |
| 70B | sdn 2d | 3,405 | 2,004 | 50,183 |
| 73B | sdn 4d | 3,450 | 2,057 | 59,794 |
| **3M Monterey (wb 118.0)** | | | | |
| 60B | htp cpe | 3,465 | 2,244 | 76,119 |
| 73C | sdn 4d | 3,425 | 2,133 | 64,038 |
| 76B | conv cpe | 3,585 | 2,390 | 8,463 |
| 79B | wgn 4d 8P | 3,765 | 2,591 | 7,719 |

| 1953 Engine | bore × stroke | bhp | availability |
|---|---|---|---|
| V-8, 255.4 | 3.19 × 4.00 | 125 | S-all |

## 1954

| Custom (wb 118.0) | | Wght | Price | Prod |
|---|---|---|---|---|
| 60E | sport coupe htp | 3,485 | 2,315 | 15,234 |
| 70B | sdn 2d | 3,435 | 2,194 | 37,146 |
| 73B | sdn 4d | 3,480 | 2,251 | 32,687 |
| **Monterey (wb 118.0)** | | | | |
| 60B | htp cpe | 3,520 | 2,452 | 79,533 |
| 60F | Sun Valley htp cpe | 3,535 | 2,582 | 9,761 |
| 73C | sdn 4d | 3,515 | 2,333 | 65,995 |
| 76B | conv cpe | 3,620 | 2,610 | 7,293 |
| 79B | wgn 4d 8P | 3,735 | 2,776 | 11,656 |

| 1954 Engine | bore × stroke | bhp | availability |
|---|---|---|---|
| V-8, 256.0 | 3.62 × 3.10 | 161 | S-all |

## 1955

| Custom (wb 119.0; wgn-118.0) | | Wght | Price | Prod |
|---|---|---|---|---|
| 60E | htp cpe | 3,480 | 2,341 | 7,040 |
| 70B | sdn 2d | 3,395 | 2,218 | 31,295 |
| 73B | sdn 4d | 3,450 | 2,277 | 21,219 |
| 79B | wgn 4d | 3,780 | 2,686 | 14,134 |
| **Monterey (wb 119.0; wgn-118.0)** | | | | |
| 60B | htp cpe | 3,510 | 2,465 | 69,093 |
| 73C | sdn 4d | 3,500 | 2,400 | 70,392 |
| 79C | wgn 4d | 3,770 | 2,844 | 11,968 |
| **Montclair (wb 119.0)** | | | | |
| 58A | sdn 4d | 3,600 | 2,685 | 20,624 |
| 64A | htp cpe | 3,490 | 2,631 | 71,588 |
| 64B | Sun Valley htp cpe | 3,560 | 2,712 | 1,787 |
| 76B | conv cpe | 3,685 | 2,712 | 10,668 |

| 1955 Engines | bore × stroke | bhp | availability |
|---|---|---|---|
| V-8, 292.0 | 3.75 × 3.30 | 188 | S-Custom, Monterey |
| V-8, 292.0 | 3.75 × 3.30 | 198 | S-Montclair; O-others |

## 1956

| Medalist (wb 119.0) | | Wght | Price | Prod |
|---|---|---|---|---|
| 57D | Phaeton htp sdn | 3,530 | 2,458 | 6,685 |
| 64E | Sport htp cpe | 3,545 | 2,398 | 11,892 |
| 70C | sdn 2d | 3,430 | 2,254 | 20,582 |
| 73D | sdn 4d | 3,500 | 2,313 | 6,653 |
| **Custom (wb 119.0; wgn-118.0)** | | | | |
| 57C | Phaeton htp sdn | 3,550 | 2,555 | 12,187 |
| 64D | Sport htp cpe | 3,560 | 2,485 | 20,857 |
| 70B | sdn 2d | 3,505 | 2,351 | 16,343 |
| 73B | sdn 4d | 3,520 | 2,410 | 15,860 |
| 76A | conv cpe | 3,665 | 2,712 | 2,311 |
| 79B | wgn 4d 8P | 3,860 | 2,819 | 9,292 |
| 79D | wgn 4d 6P | 3,790 | 2,722 | 8,478 |
| **Monterey (wb 119.0; wgn-118.0)** | | | | |
| 57B | Phaeton htp sdn | 3,800 | 2,700 | 10,726 |
| 58B | sport sedan 4d | 3,550 | 2,652 | 11,765 |
| 64C | Sport htp cpe | 3,590 | 2,630 | 42,863 |
| 73C | sdn 4d | 3,570 | 2,555 | 26,735 |
| 79C | wgn 4d 8P | 3,885 | 2,977 | 13,280 |
| **Montclair (wb 119.0)** | | | | |
| 57A | Phaeton htp sdn | 3,640 | 2,835 | 23,493 |
| 58A | sport sedan 4d | 3,610 | 2,786 | 9,617 |
| 64A | Sport htp cpe | 3,620 | 2,765 | 50,562 |
| 76B | conv cpe | 3,725 | 2,900 | 7,762 |

| 1956 Engines | bore × stroke | bhp | availability |
|---|---|---|---|
| V-8, 312.0 | 3.80 × 3.44 | 210 | S-all (manual trans.) |
| V-8, 312.0 | 3.80 × 3.44 | 225 | S-all (auto trans.) |
| V-8, 312.0 | 3.80 × 3.44 | 235 | O-all (auto trans.) |

## 1957

| Monterey (wb 122.0) | | Wght | Price | Prod |
|---|---|---|---|---|
| 57A | Phaeton htp sdn | 3,915 | 2,763 | 22,475 |
| 58A | sdn 4d | 3,890 | 2,645 | 53,839 |
| 63A | Phaeton htp cpe | 3,870 | 2,693 | 42,199 |
| 64A | sdn 2d | 3,875 | 2,576 | 33,982 |
| 76A | Phaeton conv cpe | 4,035 | 3,005 | 5,033 |
| **Montclair (wb 122.0)** | | | | |
| 57B | Phaeton htp sdn | 3,925 | 3,317 | 21,567 |
| 58B | sdn 4d | 3,905 | 3,188 | 19,836 |
| 63B | Phaeton htp cpe | 3,900 | 3,236 | 30,111 |
| 76B | Phaeton conv cpe | 4,010 | 3,430 | 4,248 |
| **Turnpike Cruiser (wb 122.0)** | | | | |
| 65A | htp cpe | 4,005 | 3,758 | 7,291 |
| 75A | htp sdn | 4,015 | 3,849 | 8,305 |
| 76S | conv cpe | 4,125 | 4,103 | 1,265 |
| **Station Wagon (wb 122.0)** | | | | |
| 56A | Commuter 2d 6P | 4,115 | 2,903 | 4,885 |
| 56B | Voyager 2d 6P | 4,240 | 3,403 | 2,283 |

# Mercury

| Station Wagon (wb 122.0) | | Wght | Price | Prod |
|---|---|---|---|---|
| 77A | Commuter 4d 6P | 4,195 | 2,973 | 11,990 |
| 77B | Colony Park 4d 9P | 4,165 | 3,677 | 7,386 |
| 77C | Commuter 4d 9P | 4,155 | 3,070 | 5,752 |
| 77D | Voyager 4d 9P | 4,280 | 3,570 | 3,716 |

| 1957 Engines | bore × stroke | bhp | availability |
|---|---|---|---|
| V-8, 312.0 | 3.80 × 3.44 | 255 | S-all exc Turnpike Cruiser |
| V-8, 368.0 | 4.00 × 3.66 | 290 | S-Turnpike Cruiser; O-others |

## 1958

| Medalist (wb 122.0) | | Wght | Price | Prod |
|---|---|---|---|---|
| 58C | sdn 4d | 3,875 | 2,617 | 10,982 |
| 64B | sdn 2d | 3,790 | 2,547 | 7,750 |

| Monterey (wb 122.0) | | Wght | Price | Prod |
|---|---|---|---|---|
| 57A | Phaeton htp sdn | 4,150 | 2,840 | 6,909 |
| 58A | sdn 4d | 4,160 | 2,721 | 28,892 |
| 63A | Phaeton htp cpe | 4,075 | 2,769 | 13,693 |
| 64A | sdn 2d | 4,080 | 2,652 | 10,526 |
| 76A | conv cpe | 4,225 | 3,081 | 2,292 |

| Montclair (wb 122.0) | | Wght | Price | Prod |
|---|---|---|---|---|
| 57B | Phaeton htp sdn | 4,165 | 3,365 | 3,609 |
| 58B | sdn 4d | 4,155 | 3,236 | 4,801 |
| 63B | Phaeton htp cpe | 4,085 | 3,284 | 5,012 |
| 65A | Turnpike Cruiser htp cpe | 4,150 | 3,498 | 2,864 |
| 75A | Turnpike Cruiser htp sdn | 4,230 | 3,577 | 3,543 |
| 76B | conv cpe | 4,295 | 3,536 | 844 |

| Park Lane (wb 125.0) | | Wght | Price | Prod |
|---|---|---|---|---|
| 57C | Phaeton htp sdn | 4,390 | 3,944 | 5,241 |
| 63C | Phaeton htp cpe | 4,280 | 3,867 | 3,158 |
| 76C | conv cpe | 4,405 | 4,118 | 853 |

| Station Wagon (wb 122.0) | | Wght | Price | Prod |
|---|---|---|---|---|
| 56A | Commuter 2d 6P | 4,400 | 3,035 | 1,912 |
| 56B | Voyager 2d 6P | 4,435 | 3,535 | 568 |
| 77A | Commuter 4d 6P | 4,485 | 3,105 | 8,601 |
| 77B | Colony Park 4d 6-9P | 4,605 | 3,775 | 4,474 |
| 77C | Commuter 4d 9P | 4,525 | 3,201 | 4,227 |
| 77D | Voyager 4d 6-9P | 4,540 | 3,635 | 2,520 |

| 1958 Engines | bore × stroke | bhp | availability |
|---|---|---|---|
| V-8, 312.0 | 3.80 × 3.44 | 235 | S-Medalist |
| V-8, 383.0 | 4.30 × 3.30 | 312 | S-Monterey, Commuter |
| V-8, 383.0 | 4.30 × 3.30 | 330 | S-Montclair, Voyager, Col Park |
| V-8, 430.0 | 4.30 × 3.70 | 360 | S-Park Lane; O-others |
| V-8, 430.0 | 4.30 × 3.70 | 400 | O-all, exc. Medalist |

## 1959

| Monterey (wb 126.0) | | Wght | Price | Prod |
|---|---|---|---|---|
| 57A | Cruiser htp sdn | 4,013 | 2,918 | 11,355 |
| 58A | sdn 4d | 3,985 | 2,832 | 43,570 |
| 63A | Cruiser htp cpe | 3,932 | 2,854 | 17,232 |
| 64A | sdn 2d | 3,914 | 2,768 | 12,694 |
| 76A | conv cpe | 4,074 | 3,150 | 4,426 |

| Montclair (wb 126.0) | | Wght | Price | Prod |
|---|---|---|---|---|
| 57B | Cruiser htp sdn | 4,234 | 3,437 | 6,713 |
| 58B | sdn 4d | 4,205 | 3,308 | 9,514 |
| 63B | Cruiser htp cpe | 4,146 | 3,357 | 7,375 |

| Park Lane (wb 128.0) | | Wght | Price | Prod |
|---|---|---|---|---|
| 57C | Cruiser htp sdn | 4,386 | 4,031 | 7,206 |
| 63C | Cruiser htp cpe | 4,311 | 3,955 | 4,060 |
| 76C | conv cpe | 4,455 | 4,206 | 1,257 |

| Station Wagon (wb 126.0) | | Wght | Price | Prod |
|---|---|---|---|---|
| 56A | Commuter 2d 6P | 4,334 | 3,145 | 1,051 |
| 77A | Commuter 4d 6P | 4,405 | 3,215 | 15,122 |
| 77B | Colony Park 4d 6P | 4,535 | 3,932 | 5,929 |
| 77D | Voyager 4d 6P | 4,483 | 3,793 | 2,496 |

| 1959 Engines | bore × stroke | bhp | availability |
|---|---|---|---|
| V-8, 312.0 | 3.80 × 3.44 | 210 | S-Monterey |
| V-8, 383.0 | 4.30 × 3.30 | 280 | S-Commuter; O-Monterey |
| V-8, 383.0 | 4.30 × 3.30 | 322 | S-Montclair, Voyager, Col Park |
| V-8, 430.0 | 4.30 × 3.70 | 345 | S-Park Lane |

## 1960

| Comet (wb 114.0; wgn-109.5) | | Wght | Price | Prod |
|---|---|---|---|---|
| 54A | sdn 4d | 2,432 | 2,053 | 47,416 |
| 59A | wgn 2d | 2,548 | 2,310 | 5,115 |
| 62A | sdn 2d | 2,399 | 1,998 | 45,374 |
| 71A | wgn 4d | 2,581 | 2,365 | 18,426 |

| Monterey (wb 126.0) | | Wght | Price | Prod |
|---|---|---|---|---|
| 57A | Cruiser htp sdn | 4,011 | 2,845 | 9,536 |
| 58A | sdn 4d | 3,981 | 2,730 | 49,594 |
| 63A | Cruiser htp cpe | 3,931 | 2,781 | 15,790 |
| 64A | sdn 2d | 3,901 | 2,631 | 21,557 |
| 76A | conv cpe | 4,131 | 3,077 | 6,062 |

| Montclair (wb 126.0) | | Wght | Price | Prod |
|---|---|---|---|---|
| 57B | Cruiser htp sdn | 4,285 | 3,394 | 5,548 |
| 58B | sdn 4d | 4,255 | 3,280 | 8,510 |
| 63B | Cruiser htp cpe | 4,205 | 3,331 | 5,756 |

| Park Lane (wb 126.0) | | Wght | Price | Prod |
|---|---|---|---|---|
| 57F | Cruiser htp sdn | 4,380 | 3,858 | 5,788 |
| 63F | Cruiser htp cpe | 4,300 | 3,794 | 2,974 |
| 76D | conv cpe | 4,500 | 4,018 | 1,525 |

| Station Wagon (wb 126.0) | | Wght | Price | Prod |
|---|---|---|---|---|
| 77A | Commuter 4d 6-9P | 4,301 | 3,127 | 14,949 |
| 77B | Colony Park 4d 9P | 4,558 | 3,837 | 7,411 |

| 1960 Engines | bore × stroke | bhp | availability |
|---|---|---|---|
| I-6, 144.3 | 3.50 × 2.50 | 90 | S-Comet |
| V-8, 312.0 | 3.80 × 3.44 | 205 | S-Monterey, Commuter |
| V-8, 383.0 | 4.30 × 3.30 | 280 | O-Monterey, Commuter |
| V-8, 430.0 | 4.30 × 3.70 | 310 | S-Montclair, P Lane, Col Park |

## 1961

| Comet (wb 114.0; wgn-109.5) | | Wght | Price | Prod |
|---|---|---|---|---|
| 54A | sdn 4d | 2,411 | 2,055 | 85,332 |
| 59A | wgn 2d | 2,548 | 2,312 | 4,199 |

# Mercury

| Comet (wb 114.0; wgn-109.5) | | Wght | Price | Prod |
|---|---|---|---|---|
| 62A | sdn 2d | 2,376 | 2,000 | 71,563 |
| 62C | S-22 sdn 2d | 2,441 | 2,284 | 14,004 |
| 71A | wgn 4d | 2,581 | 2,355 | 22,165 |
| **Meteor (wb 120.0)** | | | | |
| 58A | 600 sdn 4d | 3,714 | 2,589 | ⎤ 18,117 |
| 64A | 600 sdn 2d | 3,647 | 2,535 | ⎦ |
| 54A | 800 sdn 4d | 3,762 | 2,767 | ⎤ |
| 62A | 800 sdn 2d | 3,680 | 2,713 | ⎥ 35,005 |
| 65A | 800 htp cpe | 3,694 | 2,774 | ⎥ |
| 75A | 800 htp sdn | 3,780 | 2,839 | ⎦ |
| **Monterey (wb 120.0)** | | | | |
| 54B | sdn 4d | 3,777 | 2,871 | 22,881 |
| 65B | htp cpe | 3,709 | 2,878 | 10,942 |
| 75B | htp sdn | 3,795 | 2,943 | 9,252 |
| 76A | conv cpe | 3,872 | 3,128 | 7,053 |
| **Station Wagon (wb 120.0)** | | | | |
| 71A | Commuter 4d 6P | 4,115 | 2,924 | 8,945 |
| 71B | Colony Park 4d 6P | 4,131 | 3,120 | ⎤ 7,887 |
| 71B | Colony Park 4d 9P | 4,171 | 3,191 | ⎦ |
| 71C | Commuter 4d 9P | 4,155 | 2,994 | 6 |

| 1961 Engines | bore × stroke | bhp | availability |
|---|---|---|---|
| I-6, 144.3 | 3.50 × 2.50 | 85 | S-Comet |
| I-6, 170.0 | 3.50 × 2.94 | 101 | O-Comet |
| I-6, 223.0 | 3.62 × 3.60 | 135 | O-Meteor, Commuter |
| V-8, 292.0 | 3.75 × 3.30 | 175 | S-all exc Comet |
| V-8, 352.0 | 4.00 × 3.50 | 220 | O-all exc Comet |
| V-8, 390.0 | 4.05 × 3.78 | 300 | O-Meteor 800, Monterey |
| V-8, 390.0 | 4.05 × 3.78 | 330 | O-all exc Comet |

## 1962

| Comet (wb 114.0; wgn-109.5) | | Wght | Price | Prod |
|---|---|---|---|---|
| 54A | sdn 4d | 2,457 | 2,139 | ⎤ 70,227 |
| 54B | Custom sdn 4d | 2,648 | 2,226 | ⎦ |
| 59A | wgn 2d | 2,626 | 2,396 | ⎤ 2,121 |
| 59B | Custom wgn 2d | 2,642 | 2,483 | ⎦ |
| 62A | sdn 2d | 2,420 | 2,084 | ⎤ |
| 62B | Custom sdn 2d | 2,431 | 2,170 | ⎥ 73,880 |
| 62C | S-22 sdn 2d | 2,458 | 2,368 | ⎦ |
| 71A | wgn 4d | 2,662 | 2,439 | ⎤ 16,759 |
| 71B | Custom wgn 4d | 2,679 | 2,526 | ⎦ |
| 71C | Villager wgn 4d | 2,712 | 2,710 | 2,318 |
| **Meteor (wb 116.5)** | | | | |
| 54A | sdn 4d | 2,956 | 2,340 | 18,708 |
| 54B | Custom sdn 4d | 2,964 | 2,428 | 23,484 |
| 62A | sdn 2d | 2,922 | 2,278 | 11,550 |
| 62B | Custom sdn 2d | 2,930 | 2,366 | 9,410 |
| 62C | S-33 sdn 2d | 2,960 | 2,509 | 5,900 |
| **Monterey (wb 120.0)** | | | | |
| 54A | sdn 4d | 3,772 | 2,726 | 18,975 |
| 62A | sdn 4d | 3,695 | 2,672 | 5,117 |
| 65A | htp cpe | 3,712 | 2,733 | 5,328 |
| 75A | htp sdn | 3,781 | 2,798 | 2,691 |
| **Monterey Custom (wb 120.0)** | | | | |
| 54B | sdn 4d | 3,836 | 2,965 | 27,591 |
| 65B | htp cpe | 3,772 | 2,972 | 10,814 |
| 65C | S-55 htp cpe | 4,802 | 3,488 | 2,772 |
| 75B | htp sdn | 3,851 | 3,037 | 8,932 |

| Monterey Custom (wb 120.0) | | Wght | Price | Prod |
|---|---|---|---|---|
| 76A | conv cpe | 3,938 | 3,222 | 5,489 |
| 76B | S-55 conv cpe | 3,968 | 3,738 | 1,315 |
| **Station Wagon (wb 120.0)** | | | | |
| 71A | Commuter 4d 6P | 4,120 | 2,920 | ⎤ 8,389 |
| 71C | Commuter 4d 9P | 4,132 | 2,990 | ⎦ |
| 71B | Colony Park 4d 6P | 4,186 | 3,219 | ⎤ 9,596 |
| 71D | Colony Park 4d 9P | 4,198 | 3,289 | ⎦ |

| 1962 Engines | bore × stroke | bhp | availability |
|---|---|---|---|
| I-6, 144.3 | 3.50 × 2.50 | 85 | S-Comet |
| I-6, 170.0 | 3.50 × 2.94 | 101 | S-Meteor; O-Comet |
| I-6, 223.0 | 3.62 × 3.60 | 138 | S-Monterey, Commuter |
| V-8, 221.0 | 3.50 × 2.87 | 145 | O-Meteor |
| V-8, 260.0 | 3.80 × 2.87 | 164 | O-Meteor |
| V-8, 292.0 | 3.75 × 3.30 | 170 | S-Custom, Col Park; O-Mntry, Cmmtr |
| V-8, 352.0 | 4.00 × 3.50 | 220 | O-all except Comet, Meteor |
| V-8, 390.0 | 4.05 × 3.78 | 300 | S-S55; O-all exc Comet, Meteor |
| V-8, 390.0 | 4.05 × 3.78 | 330 | O-all exc Comet, Meteor |
| V-8, 406.0 | 4.13 × 3.78 | 385 | O-all exc Comet, Meteor |

## 1963

| Comet (wb 114.0; wgn-109.5) | | Wght | Price | Prod |
|---|---|---|---|---|
| 54A | sdn 4d | 2,499 | 2,139 | 24,230 |
| 54B | Custom sdn 4d | 2,508 | 2,206 | 27,498 |
| 59A | wgn 2d | 2,644 | 2,440 | 623 |
| 59B | Custom wgn 2d | 2,659 | 2,527 | 272 |
| 62A | sdn 2d | 2,462 | 2,084 | 24,351 |
| 62B | Custom sdn 2d | 2,471 | 2,171 | 11,897 |
| 62C | S-22 sdn 2d | 2,512 | 2,368 | 6,303 |
| 63B | Custom Sportster htp cpe | 2,572 | 2,605 | 9,432 |
| 63C | S-22 htp cpe | 2,613 | 2,635 | 5,807 |
| 71A | wgn 4d | 2,681 | 2,483 | 4,419 |
| 71B | Custom wgn 4d | 2,696 | 2,570 | 5,151 |
| 71C | Villager wgn 4d | 2,736 | 2,754 | 1,529 |
| 76A | Custom conv cpe | 2,784 | 2,557 | 7,354 |
| 76B | S-22 conv cpe | 2,825 | 2,710 | 5,757 |
| **Meteor (wb 116.5; wgn-115.5)** | | | | |
| 54A | sdn 4d | 3,025 | 2,340 | 9,183 |
| 54B | Custom sdn 4d | 3,031 | 2,428 | 14,498 |
| 62A | sdn 2d | 2,986 | 2,278 | 3,935 |
| 62B | Custom sdn 2d | 2,992 | 2,366 | 2,704 |
| 65A | Custom htp cpe | 3,010 | 2,448 | 7,565 |
| 65B | S-33 htp cpe | 3,030 | 2,628 | 4,865 |
| 71B | wgn 4d 6P | 3,303 | 2,631 | 2,904 |
| 71D | Country Cruiser wgn 4d 6-9P | 3,319 | 2,886 | 1,485 |
| 71E | Custom wgn 4d 6-9P | 3,311 | 2,719 | 3,636 |
| **Monterey (120.0)** | | | | |
| 54A | sdn 4d | 3,944 | 2,887 | 18,177 |
| 62A | sdn 2d | 3,854 | 2,834 | 4,640 |
| 65A | htp cpe | 3,869 | 2,930 | 3,879 |
| 75A | htp sdn | 3,959 | 2,995 | 1,692 |
| **Monterey Custom (wb 120.0)** | | | | |
| 54B | sdn 4d | 3,956 | 3,075 | 39,542 |
| 63B | Marauder fstbk htp cpe | 3,887 | 3,083 | 7,298 |

# Mercury

| Monterey Custom (wb 120.0) | | Wght | Price | Prod |
|---|---|---|---|---|
| 63C | S-55 Marauder fstbk htp cpe | 3,900 | 3,650 | 2,319 |
| 65B | htp cpe | 3,881 | 3,083 | 10,693 |
| 65C | S-55 htp cpe | 3,894 | 3,650 | 3,863 |
| 75B | htp sdn | 3,971 | 3,148 | 8,604 |
| 75C | S-55 htp sdn | 3,984 | 3,715 | 1,203 |
| 76A | conv cpe | 4,043 | 3,333 | 3,783 |
| 76B | S-55 conv cpe | 4,049 | 3,900 | 1,379 |
| **Station Wagon (wb 120.0)** | | | | |
| 71B | Colony Park 4d 6P | 4,306 | 3,295 | 6,447 |
| 71D | Colony Park 4d 9P | 4,318 | 3,365 | 7,529 |

| 1963 Engines | bore × stroke | bhp | availability |
|---|---|---|---|
| I-6, 144.3 | 3.50 × 2.50 | 85 | S-Comet early |
| I-6, 170.0 | 3.50 × 2.94 | 101 | S-Comet later, Meteor |
| I-6, 200.0 | 3.68 × 3.15 | 116 | O-Meteor |
| V-8, 221.0 | 3.50 × 2.87 | 145 | O-Comet, Meteor |
| V-8, 260.0 | 3.80 × 2.87 | 164 | O-Meteor Cus, S-33, Comet |
| V-8, 390.0 | 4.05 × 3.78 | 250 | S-all full-size except S-55 |
| V-8, 390.0 | 4.05 × 3.78 | 300 | S-S55; O-other full size |
| V-8, 390.0 | 4.05 × 3.78 | 330 | O-all full size |
| V-8, 406.0 | 4.13 × 3.78 | 385 | O-Monterey, Monterey Custom |
| V-8, 406.0 | 4.13 × 3.78 | 405 | O-Monterey, Monterey Custom |
| V-8, 427.0 | 4.23 × 3.78 | 410 | O-late Monterey, Mont Custom |

| Park Lane (wb 120.0) | | Wght | Price | Prod |
|---|---|---|---|---|
| 62 | sdn 4d | 4,035 | 3,348 | 6,230 |
| 63 | htp cpe | 3,960 | 3,359 | 1,786 |
| 64 | htp sdn | 4,050 | 3,413 | 2,402 |
| 65 | conv cpe | 4,066 | 3,549 | 1,967 |
| 67 | Marauder fstbk htp cpe | 3,966 | 3,359 | 2,721 |
| 68 | Marauder fstbk htp sdn | 4,056 | 3,413 | 4,505 |
| **Station Wagon (wb 120.0)** | | | | |
| 72 | Commuter 4d 6P | 4,259 | 3,236 | 3,484 |
| 72 | Commuter 4d 9P | 4,271 | 3,306 | 1,839 |
| 76 | Colony Park 4d 6P | 4,275 | 3,434 | 4,234 |
| 76 | Colony Park 4d 9P | 4,287 | 3,504 | 5,624 |

| 1964 Engines | bore × stroke | bhp | availability |
|---|---|---|---|
| I-6, 170.0 | 3.50 × 2.94 | 101 | S-Comet |
| I-6, 200.0 | 3.68 × 3.15 | 116 | O-Comet |
| V-8, 260.0 | 3.80 × 2.87 | 164 | O-Comet |
| V-8, 289.0 | 4.00 × 2.87 | 210 | S-Cyclone; O-other Comet |
| V-8, 390.0 | 4.05 × 3.78 | 250 | S-all exc Comet, Park Lane |
| V-8, 390.0 | 4.05 × 3.78 | 266 | O-all exc Comet, Park Lane |
| V-8, 390.0 | 4.05 × 3.78 | 300 | S-Park Lane |
| V-8, 390.0 | 4.05 × 3.78 | 330 | O-Park Lane |
| V-8, 427.0 | 4.23 × 3.78 | 410 | O-Monterey, Montclair, P Lane |
| V-8, 427.0 | 4.23 × 3.78 | 425 | O-Monterey, Montclair, P Lane |

## 1964

| Comet 202 (wb 114.0; wgn-109.5) | | Wght | Price | Prod |
|---|---|---|---|---|
| 01 | sdn 2d | 2,539 | 2,126 | 33,824 |
| 02 | sdn 4d | 2,580 | 2,182 | 29,147 |
| 32 | wgn 4d | 2,727 | 2,463 | 5,504 |
| **Comet 404 (wb 114.0; wgn-109.5)** | | | | |
| 11 | sdn 2d | 2,551 | 2,213 | 12,512 |
| 12 | sdn 4d | 2,588 | 2,269 | 25,136 |
| 34 | Custom wgn 4d | 2,741 | 2,550 | 6,918 |
| 36 | Villager wgn 4d | 2,745 | 2,734 | 1,980 |
| **Comet Caliente (wb 114.0)** | | | | |
| 22 | sdn 4d | 2,668 | 2,350 | 27,218 |
| 23 | htp cpe | 2,688 | 2,375 | 31,204 |
| 25 | conv cpe | 2,861 | 2,636 | 9,039 |
| **Comet Cyclone (wb 114.0)** | | | | |
| 27 | htp cpe | 2,860 | 2,655 | 7,454 |
| **Monterey (wb 120.0)** | | | | |
| 41 | sdn 2d | 3,895 | 2,819 | 3,932 |
| 42 | sdn 4d | 3,985 | 2,892 | 20,234 |
| 43 | htp cpe | 3,910 | 2,884 | 2,926 |
| 45 | conv cpe | 4,027 | 3,226 | 2,592 |
| 47 | Marauder fstbk htp cpe | 3,916 | 2,884 | 8,760 |
| 48 | Marauder fstbk htp sdn | 3,914 | 2,957 | 4,143 |
| **Montclair (wb 120.0)** | | | | |
| 52 | sdn 4d | 3,996 | 3,116 | 15,520 |
| 53 | htp cpe | 3,921 | 3,127 | 2,329 |
| 57 | Marauder fstbk htp cpe | 3,927 | 3,127 | 6,459 |
| 58 | Marauder fstbk htp sdn | 4,017 | 3,181 | 8,655 |

## 1965

| Comet 202 (wb 114.0; wgn-109.5) | | Wght | Price | Prod |
|---|---|---|---|---|
| 01 | sdn 2d | 2,584 | 2,154 | 32,425 |
| 02 | sdn 4d | 2,624 | 2,210 | 23,501 |
| 32 | wgn 4d | 2,784 | 2,491 | 4,814 |
| **Comet 404 (wb 114.0; wgn-109.5)** | | | | |
| 11 | sdn 2d | 2,594 | 2,241 | 10,900 |
| 12 | sdn 4d | 2,629 | 2,294 | 18,628 |
| 34 | Custom wgn 4d | 2,789 | 2,578 | 5,226 |
| 36 | Villager wgn 4d | 2,789 | 2,762 | 1,592 |
| **Comet Caliente (wb 114.0)** | | | | |
| 22 | sdn 4d | 2,659 | 2,378 | 20,337 |
| 23 | htp cpe | 2,684 | 2,403 | 29,247 |
| 25 | conv cpe | 2,869 | 2,664 | 6,035 |
| **Comet Cyclone (wb 114.0)** | | | | |
| 27 | htp cpe | 2,994 | 2,683 | 12,347 |
| **Monterey (wb 123.0)** | | | | |
| 42 | Breezeway sdn 4d | 3,898 | 2,904 | 19,569 |
| 43 | sdn 2d | 3,788 | 2,767 | 5,775 |
| 44 | sdn 4d | 3,853 | 2,839 | 23,363 |
| 45 | conv cpe | 3,928 | 3,230 | 4,762 |
| 47 | htp cpe | 3,823 | 2,902 | 16,857 |
| 48 | htp sdn | 3,893 | 2,978 | 10,047 |
| **Montclair (wb 123.0)** | | | | |
| 52 | Breezeway sdn 4d | 3,933 | 3,137 | 18,924 |
| 57 | htp cpe | 3,848 | 3,135 | 9,645 |
| 58 | htp sdn | 3,928 | 3,210 | 16,977 |
| **Park Lane (wb 123.0)** | | | | |
| 62 | Breezeway sdn 4d | 3,988 | 3,369 | 8,335 |
| 65 | conv cpe | 4,013 | 3,599 | 3,006 |

# Mercury

| Park Lane (wb 123.0) | | Wght | Price | Prod |
|---|---|---|---|---|
| 67 | htp cpe | 3,908 | 3,367 | 6,853 |
| 68 | htp sdn | 3,983 | 3,442 | 14,211 |
| **Station Wagon (wb 119.0)** | | | | |
| 72 | Commuter 4d 6P | 4,178 | 3,235 | 5,453 |
| 72 | Commuter 4d 9P | 4,213 | 3,312 | 2,628 |
| 76 | Colony Park 4d 6P | 4,228 | 3,434 | 6,910 |
| 76 | Colony Park 4d 9P | 4,263 | 3,511 | 8,384 |

| 1965 Engines | bore × stroke | bhp | availability |
|---|---|---|---|
| I-6, 200.0 | 3.68 × 3.15 | 120 | S-Comet |
| V-8, 289.0 | 4.00 × 2.87 | 200 | S-Cyclone; O-other Comet |
| V-8, 289.0 | 4.00 × 2.87 | 225 | O-Comet |
| V-8, 390.0 | 4.05 × 3.78 | 250 | S-Monterey, Commuter |
| V-8, 390.0 | 4.05 × 3.78 | 266 | S-Montclair, Colony Park |
| V-8, 390.0 | 4.05 × 3.78 | 300 | S-Park Lane; O-all exc Comet |
| V-8, 390.0 | 4.05 × 3.78 | 330 | O-all exc Comet |
| V-8, 427.0 | 4.23 × 3.78 | 425 | O-all exc Comet |

| Park Lane (wb 123.0) | | Wght | Price | Prod |
|---|---|---|---|---|
| 68 | fstbk htp sdn | 4,070 | 3,460 | 19,204 |
| **Station Wagon (wb 119.0)** | | | | |
| 72 | Commuter 4d 6P | 4,280 | 3,240 | 3,970 |
| 72 | Commuter 4d 9P | 4,331 | 3,336 | 2,877 |
| 76 | Colony Park 4d 6P | 4,332 | 3,502 | 7,190 |
| 76 | Colony Park 4d 9P | 4,383 | 3,598 | 11,704 |

| 1966 Engines | bore × stroke | bhp | availability |
|---|---|---|---|
| I-6, 200.0 | 3.68 × 3.15 | 120 | S-Comet exc Cyclone |
| V-8, 289.0 | 4.00 × 2.87 | 200 | S-Cyclone; O-other Comet |
| V-8, 390.0 | 4.05 × 3.78 | 265 | S-Cyclone GT, full-size w/man |
| V-8, 390.0 | 4.05 × 3.78 | 275 | S-full-size w/auto; O-Cyclone GT |
| V-8, 390.0 | 4.05 × 3.78 | 335 | O-Cyclone GT |
| V-8, 410.0 | 4.05 × 3.98 | 330 | S-Park Lane; O-other full-size, exc. S55 |
| V-8, 428.0 | 4.13 × 3.98 | 345 | S-S55; O-other full-size |

## 1966

| Comet 202 (wb 116.0; wgn-113.0) | | Wght | Price | Prod |
|---|---|---|---|---|
| 01 | sdn 2d | 2,864 | 2,206 | 35,964 |
| 02 | sdn 4d | 2,908 | 2,263 | 20,440 |
| 06 | Voyager wgn 4d | 3,282 | 2,553 | 7,595 |
| **Comet Capri (wb 116.0; wgn-113.0)** | | | | |
| 12 | sdn 4d | 2,928 | 2,378 | 15,635 |
| 13 | htp cpe | 2,960 | 2,400 | 15,031 |
| 16 | Villager wgn 4d | 3,319 | 2,790 | 3,880 |
| **Comet Caliente (wb 116.0)** | | | | |
| 22 | sdn 4d | 2,930 | 2,453 | 17,933 |
| 23 | htp cpe | 2,966 | 2,475 | 25,862 |
| 25 | conv cpe | 3,228 | 2,735 | 3,922 |
| **Comet Cyclone (wb 116.0)** | | | | |
| 27 | htp cpe | 3,078 | 2,700 | 6,889 |
| 27 | GT htp cpe | 3,315 | 2,891 | 13,812 |
| 29 | conv cpe | 3,321 | 2,961 | 1,305 |
| 29 | GT conv cpe | 3,595 | 3,152 | 2,158 |
| **Monterey (wb 123.0)** | | | | |
| 42 | Breezeway sdn 4d | 3,966 | 2,917 | 14,174 |
| 43 | sdn 2d | 3,835 | 2,783 | 2,487 |
| 44 | sdn 4d | 3,903 | 2,854 | 18,998 |
| 45 | conv cpe | 4,039 | 3,237 | 3,279 |
| 47 | fstbk htp cpe | 3,885 | 2,915 | 19,103 |
| 48 | fstbk htp sdn | 3,928 | 2,990 | 7,647 |
| **S-55 (wb 123.0)** | | | | |
| 46 | conv cpe | 4,148 | 3,614 | 669 |
| 49 | fstbk htp cpe | 4,031 | 3,292 | 2,916 |
| **Montclair (wb 123.0)** | | | | |
| 54 | sdn 4d | 3,921 | 3,087 | 11,856 |
| 57 | fstbk htp cpe | 3,887 | 3,144 | 11,290 |
| 58 | fstbk htp sdn | 3,971 | 3,217 | 15,767 |
| **Park Lane (wb 123.0)** | | | | |
| 62 | Breezeway sdn 4d | 4,051 | 3,389 | 8,696 |
| 65 | conv cpe | 4,148 | 3,608 | 2,546 |
| 67 | fstbk htp cpe | 3,971 | 3,387 | 8,354 |

## 1967

| Comet 202 (wb 116.0) | | Wght | Price | Prod |
|---|---|---|---|---|
| 01 | sdn 2d | 2,868 | 2,284 | 14,251 |
| 02 | sdn 4d | 2,906 | 2,336 | 10,281 |
| **Comet Capri (wb 116.0)** | | | | |
| 06 | sdn 4d | 2,940 | 2,436 | 9,292 |
| 07 | htp cpe | 2,970 | 2,459 | 11,671 |
| **Comet Caliente (wb 116.0)** | | | | |
| 10 | sdn 4d | 2,952 | 2,535 | 9,153 |
| 11 | htp cpe | 2,982 | 2,558 | 9,966 |
| 12 | conv cpe | 3,250 | 2,818 | 1,539 |
| **Comet Station Wagon (wb 113.0)** | | | | |
| 03 | Voyager 4d | 3,310 | 2,604 | 4,930 |
| 08 | Villager 4d | 3,332 | 2,841 | 3,140 |
| **Comet Cyclone (wb 116.0)** | | | | |
| 15 | htp cpe | 3,075 | 2,737 | 2,682 |
| 15 | GT htp cpe | 3,372 | 3,372 | 3,419 |
| 16 | conv cpe | 3,632 | 2,997 | 431 |
| 16 | GT conv cpe | 3,350 | 3,632 | 378 |
| **Cougar (wb 111.0)** | | | | |
| 91 | htp cpe | 2,988 | 2,851 | 116,260 |
| 91 | GT htp cpe | 3,000 | 3,175 | 7,412 |
| 93 | XR-7 htp cpe | 3,015 | 3,081 | 27,221 |
| **Monterey (wb 123.0)** | | | | |
| 44 | sdn 4d | 3,798 | 2,904 | 15,177 |
| 44 | Breezeway sdn 4d | 3,847 | 2,967 | 5,910 |
| 45 | conv cpe | 3,943 | 3,314 | 2,673 |
| 46 | S-55 conv cpe | 3,960 | 3,837 | 145 |
| 47 | htp cpe | 3,820 | 2,985 | 16,910 |
| 48 | htp sdn | 3,858 | 3,059 | 8,013 |
| 49 | S-55 fstbk htp cpe | 3,837 | 3,511 | 570 |
| **Montclair (wb 123.0)** | | | | |
| 54 | sdn 4d | 3,863 | 3,187 | 5,783 |
| 54 | Breezeway sdn 4d | 3,881 | 3,250 | 4,151 |
| 57 | htp cpe | 3,848 | 3,244 | 4,118 |

# Mercury

| Montclair (wb 123.0) | | Wght | Price | Prod |
|---|---|---|---|---|
| 58 | htp sdn | 3,943 | 3,316 | 5,870 |
| **Park Lane (wb 123.0)** | | | | |
| 61 | Brougham Breezeway sdn 4d | 3,980 | 3,896 | 3,325 |
| 62 | Brougham htp sdn | 4,000 | 3,986 | 4,189 |
| 64 | Breezeway sdn 4d | 4,011 | 3,736 | 4,163 |
| 65 | conv cpe | 4,114 | 3,984 | 1,191 |
| 67 | htp cpe | 3,947 | 3,752 | 2,196 |
| 68 | htp sdn | 3,992 | 3,826 | 5,412 |
| **Marquis (wb 123.0)** | | | | |
| 69 | htp cpe | 3,995 | 3,989 | 6,510 |
| **Station Wagon (wb 119.0)** | | | | |
| 72 | Commuter 4d 6P | 4,178 | 3,289 | 3,447 |
| 72 | Commuter 4d 9P | 4,297 | 3,384 | 4,451 |
| 76 | Colony Park 4d 6P | 4,258 | 3,657 | 5,775 |
| 76 | Colony Park 4d 9P | 4,294 | 3,752 | 12,915 |

| 1967 Engines | bore × stroke | bhp | availability |
|---|---|---|---|
| I-6, 200.0 | 3.68 × 3.15 | 120 | S-Comet exc Cyclone |
| V-8, 289.0 | 4.00 × 2.87 | 200 | S-Cougar, Cycl; O-other Comet |
| V-8, 289.0 | 4.00 × 2.87 | 225 | O-Cougar |
| V-8, 390.0 | 4.05 × 3.78 | 270 | S-Mntry, Mntclr, S Wgn; O-Comet |
| V-8, 390.0 | 4.05 × 3.78 | 320 | S-Cycl/Cougar GT; O-other Cougar |
| V-8, 410.0 | 4.05 × 3.98 | 330 | S-Park Lane, Marquis; O-Monterey, Montclair |
| V-8, 427.0 | 4.23 × 3.78 | 410 | O-Comet htps and 2d sedans |
| V-8, 427.0 | 4.23 × 3.78 | 425 | O-Comet htps and 2d sedans |
| V-8, 428.0 | 4.13 × 3.98 | 345 | S-S55; O-other full-size |

## 1968

| Comet (wb 116.0) | | Wght | Price | Prod |
|---|---|---|---|---|
| 01 | htp cpe | 3,166 | 2,477 | 16,693 |
| **Montego (wb 116.0; wgn-113.0)** | | | | |
| 06 | sdn 4d | 3,062 | 2,504 | 18,492 |
| 07 | htp cpe | 3,138 | 2,552 | 15,002 |
| 08 | MX wgn 4d | 3,460 | 2,876 | 9,328 |
| 10 | MX sdn 4d* | 3,088 | 2,657 | 18,413 |
| 11 | MX htp cpe* | 3,162 | 2,676 | 25,827 |
| 12 | MX conv cpe | 3,374 | 2,935 | 3,248 |
| **Cyclone (wb 116.0)** | | | | |
| 15 | fstbk htp cpe | 3,407 | 2,768 | 6,165 |
| 15 | GT fstbk htp cpe | 3,430 | 2,936 | 6,105 |
| 17 | htp cpe | 3,361 | 2,768 | 1,034 |
| 17 | GT htp cpe | 3,380 | 2,936 | 334 |
| **Cougar (wb 111.0)\*\*** | | | | |
| 91 | htp cpe | 3,134 | 2,933 | 81,014 |
| 93 | XR-7 htp cpe | 3,174 | 3,232 | 32,712 |
| **Monterey (wb 123.0)** | | | | |
| 44 | sdn 4d | 3,895 | 3,052 | 30,727 |
| 45 | conv cpe | 3,977 | 3,436 | 1,515 |
| 47 | htp cpe | 3,854 | 3,133 | 18,845 |

| Monterey (wb 123.0) | | Wght | Price | Prod |
|---|---|---|---|---|
| 48 | htp sdn | 3,892 | 3,207 | 8,927 |
| **Montclair (wb 123.0)** | | | | |
| 54 | sdn 4d | 3,897 | 3,331 | 7,255 |
| 57 | htp cpe | 3,882 | 3,387 | 3,497 |
| 58 | htp sdn | 3,907 | 3,459 | 4,008 |
| **Park Lane (wb 123.0)** | | | | |
| 64 | sdn 4d* | 4,019 | 3,552 | 6,408 |
| 65 | conv cpe | 4,122 | 3,822 | 1,112 |
| 67 | htp cpe | 3,955 | 3,575 | 2,584 |
| 68 | htp sdn* | 4,000 | 3,647 | 10,390 |
| **Marquis (wb 123.0)** | | | | |
| 69 | htp cpe | 3,987 | 3,685 | 3,965 |
| **Station Wagon (wb 119.0)** | | | | |
| 72 | Commuter 4d 6P | 4,212 | 3,441 | 3,497 |
| 72 | Commuter 4d 9P | 4,331 | 3,569 | 5,191 |
| 76 | Colony Park 4d 6P | 4,259 | 3,460 | 5,674 |
| 76 | Colony Park 4d 6P | 4,295 | 3,888 | 15,505 |

*Includes cars with Brougham trim option.
**Includes cars with GT and GTE package options.

| 1968 Engines | bore × stroke | bhp | availability |
|---|---|---|---|
| I-6, 200.0 | 3.68 × 3.15 | 115 | S-Comet, Montego |
| V-8, 289.0 | 4.00 × 2.87 | 195 | S-base Cougar; O-Comet |
| V-8, 302.0 | 4.00 × 3.00 | 210 | S-Cougar XR-7, Cyclone, O-Montego |
| V-8, 302.0 | 4.00 × 3.00 | 230 | O-Cougar, Montego |
| V-8, 390.0 | 4.05 × 3.78 | 265 | S-full size w/man; O-Montego, Cyclone |
| V-8, 390.0 | 4.05 × 3.78 | 280 | S-full-size w/auto; O-Cougar |
| V-8, 390.0 | 4.05 × 3.78 | 315 | S-P Lane, Marquis; O-other full-size |
| V-8, 390.0 | 4.05 × 3.78 | 325 | S-Cougar GT; O-Montego exc MX wgn, Cyclone, Cougar (exc. GTE) |
| V-8, 390.0 | 4.05 × 3.78 | 335 | O-Montego exc wgn, Cyclone |
| V-8, 427.0 | 4.23 × 3.78 | 390 | S-Cgr GTE; O-Cycln, Mntgo htps |
| V-8, 428,0 | 4.13 × 3.98 | 335 | O-Montego, Cyclone, Cougar |
| V-8, 428.0 | 4.13 × 3.98 | 340 | O-full size only |

## 1969

| Comet (wb 116.0) | | Wght | Price | Prod |
|---|---|---|---|---|
| 01 | htp cpe | 3,175 | 2,532 | 14,104 |
| **Montego (wb 116.0; wgn-113.0)** | | | | |
| 06 | sdn 4d | 3,140 | 2,556 | 21,950 |
| 07 | htp cpe | 3,154 | 2,605 | 17,785 |
| 08 | MX wgn 4d | 3,504 | 2,979 | 10,590 |
| 10 | MX sdn 4d | 3,174 | 2,718 | 16,148 |
| 10 | MX Brougham sdn 4d | 3,198 | 2,808 | 1,590 |
| 11 | MX htp cpe | 3,186 | 2,736 | 23,160 |
| 11 | MX Brougham htp cpe | 3,210 | 2,826 | 1,226 |
| 12 | MX conv cpe | 3,356 | 2,979 | 1,725 |
| **Cyclone (wb 116.0)** | | | | |
| 15 | fstbk htp cpe | 3,273 | 2,771 | 5,882 |
| 16 | CJ fstbk htp cpe | 3,634 | 3,224 | 3,261 |

# Mercury

| Cougar (wb 111.0) | | Wght | Price | Prod |
|---|---|---|---|---|
| 91 | htp cpe | 3,219 | 3,016 | 66,331 |
| 92 | conv cpe | 3,343 | 3,382 | 5,796 |
| 93 | ×R-7 htp cpe | 3,221 | 3,315 | 23,918 |
| 94 | ×R-7 conv cpe | 3,343 | 3,595 | 4,024 |
| — | Eliminator htp cpe | 3,250 | — | — |
| **Monterey (wb 124.0, wgn-121.0)** | | | | |
| 44 | sdn 4d | 3,948 | 3,158 | 23,009 |
| 45 | conv cpe | 4,093 | 3,540 | 1,297 |
| 46 | htp cpe | 3,970 | 3,237 | 9,865 |
| 48 | htp sdn | 4,008 | 3,313 | 6,066 |
| 72 | wgn 4d 6-9P | 4,277 | 3,536 | 5,844 |
| **Monterey Custom (wb 124.0; wgn-121.0)** | | | | |
| 54 | sdn 4d | 4,013 | 3,377 | 7,103 |
| 56 | htp cpe | 3,998 | 3,459 | 2,898 |
| 58 | htp sdn | 4,023 | 3,533 | 2,827 |
| 74 | wgn 4d 6-9P | 4,342 | 3,757 | 1,920 |
| **Marauder (wb 121.0)** | | | | |
| 60 | htp cpe | 4,044 | 3,368 | 9,031 |
| 61 | X-100 htp cpe | 4,191 | 4,091 | 5,635 |
| **Marquis (wb 124.0; wgn-121.0)** | | | | |
| 63 | sdn 4d | 4,226 | 3,857 | 16,787 |
| 63 | Brougham sdn 4d | 4,195 | 4,129 | 14,601 |
| 65 | conv cpe | 4,359 | 4,124 | 2,319 |
| 66 | htp cpe | 4,192 | 3,919 | 9,907 |
| 66 | Brougham htp cpe | 4,215 | 4,191 | 8,395 |
| 68 | htp sdn | 4,237 | 3,990 | 14,423 |
| 68 | Brougham htp sdn | 4,436 | 4,262 | 14,966 |
| 76 | Colony Park wgn 4d 6-9P | 4,376 | 3,895 | 25,604 |

| 1969 Engines | bore × stroke | bhp | availability |
|---|---|---|---|
| I-6, 250.0 | 3.68 × 3.91 | 155 | S-Comet, Montego |
| V-8, 302.0 | 4.00 × 3.00 | 220 | S-Cyclone; O-Comet, Montego |
| V-8, 302.0 | 4.00 × 3.00 | 290 | O-Cougar (Elim) |
| V-8, 351.0 | 4.00 × 3.50 | 250 | S-Coug; O-Montego, Comet, Cyclone |
| V-8, 351.0 | 4.00 × 3.50 | 290 | O-Coug, Comet, Cyc, Montego |
| V-8, 390.0 | 4.05 × 3.78 | 265 | S-Mntry, Mrdr, SW w/man |
| V-8, 390.0 | 4.05 × 3.78 | 280 | O-Mntry, Mrdr, SW w/man |
| V-8, 390.0 | 4.05 × 3.78 | 320 | O-Coug, Montego, Cyc, Comet |
| V-8, 428.0 | 4.13 × 3.98 | 335 | S-Cyclone CJ; O-Cougar; Montego exc Brghm, SW, conv/sdns with 4 spd |
| V-8, 428.0 | 4.13 × 3.98 | 335 | O-Coug, Cyc, Cyc CJ (ram air) |
| V-8, 429.0 | 4.36 × 3.59 | 320 | S-Marquis; O-other full-size |
| V-8, 429.0 | 4.36 × 3.59 | 360 | S-X100; O-other full-size |

## 1970

| Montego (wb 117.0; wgn-114.0) | | Wght | Price | Prod |
|---|---|---|---|---|
| 01 | htp cpe | 2,859 | 2,645 | 21,298 |
| 02 | sdn 4d | 3,208 | 2,631 | 13,988 |
| 06 | MX sdn 4d | 3,215 | 2,728 | 16,708 |
| 07 | MX htp cpe | 3,228 | 2,740 | 15,533 |
| 08 | MX wgn 4d 6P | 3,653 | 3,091 | 5,094 |

| Montego (wb 117.0; wgn-114.0) | | Wght | Price | Prod |
|---|---|---|---|---|
| 10 | MX Brougham sdn 4d | 3,238 | 2,896 | 3,315 |
| 11 | MX Brougham htp cpe | 3,248 | 2,915 | 8,074 |
| 12 | MX Brougham htp sdn | 3,268 | 3,037 | 3,685 |
| 18 | MX Brghm wgn 4d 6P | 3,668 | 3,304 | 2,682 |
| **Cyclone (wb 117.0)** | | | | |
| 15 | htp cpe | 3,721 | 3,238 | 1,695 |
| 16 | GT htp cpe | 3,462 | 3,226 | 10,170 |
| 17 | Spoiler htp cpe | 3,773 | 3,759 | 1,631 |
| **Cougar (wb 111.1)** | | | | |
| 91 | htp cpe* | 3,285 | 3,114 | 49,479 |
| 92 | conv cpe | 3,382 | 3,480 | 2,322 |
| 93 | XR-7 htp cpe | 3,311 | 3,413 | 18,565 |
| 94 | XR-7 conv cpe | 3,408 | 3,692 | 1,977 |
| **Monterey (wb 124.0; wgn-121.0)** | | | | |
| 44 | sdn 4d | 3,926 | 3,248 | 29,432 |
| 45 | conv cpe | 4,071 | 3,668 | 581 |
| 46 | htp cpe | 3,890 | 3,329 | 9,359 |
| 48 | htp sdn | 3,961 | 3,406 | 5,032 |
| 72 | wgn 4d 6P | 4,235 | 3,682 | 1,657 |
| 72 | wgn 4d 9P | 4,327 | 3,774 | 3,507 |
| **Monterey Custom (wb 124.0)** | | | | |
| 54 | sdn 4d | 3,931 | 3,520 | 4,823 |
| 56 | htp cpe | 3,992 | 3,600 | 1,357 |
| 58 | htp sdn | 3,973 | 3,676 | 1,194 |
| **Marauder (wb 121.0)** | | | | |
| 60 | htp cpe | 3,972 | 3,503 | 3,397 |
| 61 | X100 htp cpe | 4,128 | 4,136 | 2,646 |
| **Marquis (wb 124.0; wgn-121.0)** | | | | |
| 62 | Brougham sdn 4d | 4,166 | 4,367 | 14,920 |
| 63 | sdn 4d | 4,121 | 4,052 | 14,394 |
| 64 | Brougham htp cpe | 4,119 | 4,428 | 7,113 |
| 65 | conv cpe | 4,337 | 4,318 | 1,233 |
| 66 | htp cpe | 4,072 | 4,113 | 6,229 |
| 67 | Brougham htp sdn | 4,182 | 4,500 | 11,623 |
| 68 | htp sdn | 4,141 | 4,185 | 8,411 |
| 74 | wgn 4d 6P | 4,347 | 3,930 | 959 |
| 74 | wgn 4d 9P | 4,393 | 4,022 | 1,429 |
| 76 | Colony Park wgn 4d 6P | 4,442 | 4,123 | 4,655 |
| 76 | Colony Park wgn 4d 9P | 4,488 | 4,215 | 14,549 |

| 1970 Engines | bore × stroke | bhp | availability |
|---|---|---|---|
| I-6, 250.0 | 3.68 × 3.91 | 155 | S-Montego |
| V-8, 302.0 | 4.00 × 3.00 | 220 | O-Montego |
| V-8, 302.0 | 4.00 × 3.00 | 290 | O-Cougar Eliminator |
| V-8, 351.0 | 4.00 × 3.50 | 250 | S-Cyclone, Cougar exc. Elim; O-Montego |
| V-8, 351.0 | 4.00 × 3.50 | 300 | S-Cgr Elim; O-Coug, Montego |
| V-8, 390.0 | 4.05 × 3.78 | 265 | S-Monterey, Marauder, C Park w/man |
| V-8, 390.0 | 4.05 × 3.78 | 280 | S-above models w/auto |
| V-8, 428.0 | 4.13 × 3.98 | 335 | O-Cougar |
| V-8, 429.0 | 4.36 × 3.59 | 320 | S-Marquis exc Colony Park |
| V-8, 429.0 | 4.36 × 3.59 | 360 | S-Cyc exc Spoiler, Mrdr X100; O-Mntg, Mntry, Mrdr, C Park |
| V-8, 429.0 | 4.36 × 3.59 | 370 | S-Spoiler; O-Cyclone, GT** |
| V-8, 429.0 | 4.36 × 3.59 | 375 | O-all Cyclone |

# Mercury

| 1970 Engines | bore × stroke | bhp | availability |
|---|---|---|---|
| V-8, 429.0 | 4.36 × 3.59 | 375 | O-all Cyclone, Cougar Elim ("Boss") |

*Includes models with Eliminator performance option.
**Available in Ram Air and non-Ram Air versions.

## 1971

| Comet (wb 109.9; 2d-103.0) | | Wght | Price | Prod |
|---|---|---|---|---|
| 30 | sdn 4d | 2,789 | 2,446 | 28,116 |
| 31 | fstbk sdn 2d | 2,700 | 2,387 | 54,884 |
| **Montego (wb 117.0; wgns-114.0)** | | | | |
| 01 | htp cpe | 3,229 | 2,893 | 9,623 |
| 02 | sdn 4d | 3,228 | 2,888 | 5,718 |
| 06 | MX sdn 4d | 3,235 | 2,994 | 13,559 |
| 07 | MX htp cpe | 3,236 | 3,007 | 13,719 |
| 08 | MX wgn | 3,651 | 3,331 | 3,698 |
| 10 | MX Brougham sdn 4d | 3,258 | 3,189 | 1,565 |
| 11 | MX Brougham htp cpe | 3,275 | 3,201 | 2,851 |
| 12 | MX Brougham htp sdn | 3,302 | 3,273 | 1,156 |
| 18 | MX Villager wgn | 3,666 | 3,572 | 2,121 |
| **Cyclone (wb 117.0)** | | | | |
| 15 | fstbk htp cpe | 3,595 | 3,369 | 444 |
| 16 | GT fstbk htp cpe | 3,492 | 3,680 | 2,287 |
| 17 | Spoiler fstbk htp cpe | 3,585 | 3,801 | 353 |
| **Cougar (wb 113.0)** | | | | |
| 91 | htp cpe | 3,331 | 3,289 | 34,008 |
| 92 | conv | 3,461 | 3,681 | 1,723 |
| 93 | XR-7 htp cpe | 3,360 | 3,629 | 25,416 |
| 94 | XR-7 conv | 3,480 | 3,877 | 1,717 |
| **Monterey (wb 124.0; wgns-121.0)** | | | | |
| 44 | sdn 4d | 4,029 | 3,858 | 22,744 |
| 46 | htp cpe | 3,959 | 3,900 | 9,099 |
| 48 | htp sdn | 4,024 | 3,968 | 2,483 |
| 72 | wgn 3S | 4,451 | 4,410 | 4,160 |
| 72 | wgn 2S | 4,401 | 4,283 | |
| 54 | Custom sdn 4d | 4,144 | 4,030 | 12,411 |
| 56 | Custom htp cpe | 4,074 | 4,113 | 4,508 |
| 58 | Custom htp sdn | 4,140 | 4,185 | 1,397 |
| **Marquis (wb 124.0; wgns-121.0)** | | | | |
| 63 | sdn 4d | 4,346 | 4,474 | 16,030 |
| 66 | htp cpe | 4,276 | 4,557 | 7,726 |
| 68 | htp sdn | 4,341 | 4,624 | 5,491 |
| 74 | wgn 3S | 4,501 | 4,674 | 2,158 |
| 74 | wgn 2S | 4,451 | 4,547 | |
| 62 | Brougham sdn 4d | 4,346 | 4,880 | 25,790 |
| 64 | Brougham htp cpe | 4,276 | 4,963 | 14,570 |
| 67 | Brougham htp sdn | 4,341 | 5,033 | 13,781 |
| 76 | Colony Park wgn 3S | 4,562 | 4,933 | 20,004 |
| 76 | Colony Park wgn 2S | 4,512 | 4,806 | |

| 1971 Engines | bore × stroke | bhp | availability |
|---|---|---|---|
| I-6, 170.0 | 3.50 × 2.94 | 100 | S-Comet |
| I-6, 200.0 | 3.68 × 3.13 | 115/155 | O-Comet |
| I-6, 250.0 | 3.68 × 3.91 | 145 | S-Montego |
| V-8, 302.0 | 4.00 × 3.00 | 210 | O-Comet, Montego, Cyclone |
| V-8, 351.0 | 4.00 × 3.50 | 240 | S-Cyclone GT, Cougar, Cougar XR-7, Monterey exc Custom and sta wag; O-Montego, Cyclone |
| V-8, 351.0 | 4.00 × 3.50 | 280 | O-Cougar |
| V-8, 351.0 | 4.00 × 3.50 | 285 | S-Cyclone exc GT, Monterey; O-Montego, Cougar |
| V-8, 400.0 | 4.00 × 4.00 | 260 | S-Monterey Custom and sta wag; O-Marquis, Monterey |
| V-8, 429.0 | 4.36 × 3.59 | 320 | S-Marquis; O-Monterey |
| V-8, 429.0 | 4.36 × 3.59 | 360 | O-Marquis, Monterey |
| V-8, 429.0 | 4.36 × 3.59 | 370 | O-Montego, Cyclone, Marquis, Monterey |
| V-8, 429.0 | 4.36 × 3.59 | 375 | O-Montego, Cyclone, Cougar |

## 1972

| Comet (wb 109.9; 2d-103.0) | | Wght | Price | Prod |
|---|---|---|---|---|
| 30 | sdn 4d | 2,674 | 2,398 | 29,092 |
| 31 | fstbk sdn 2d | 2,579 | 2,342 | 53,267 |
| **Montego (wb 118.0; 2d-114.0)** | | | | |
| 02 | sdn 4d | 3,454 | 2,843 | 8,658 |
| 03 | htp cpe | 3,390 | 2,848 | 9,963 |
| 04 | MX sdn 4d | 3,485 | 2,951 | 23,387 |
| 07 | MX htp cpe | 3,407 | 2,971 | 25,802 |
| 08 | MX wgn | 3,884 | 3,264 | 6,268 |
| 10 | MX Brougham sdn 4d | 3,512 | 3,127 | 17,540 |
| 11 | MX Brougham htp cpe | 3,433 | 3,137 | 28,417 |
| 18 | MX Villager wgn | 3,907 | 3,438 | 9,237 |
| 16 | GT fstbk htp cpe | 3,517 | 3,346 | 5,820 |
| **Cougar (wb 113.0)** | | | | |
| 91 | htp cpe | 3,282 | 3,016 | 23,731 |
| 92 | conv | 3,412 | 3,370 | 1,240 |
| 93 | XR-7 htp cpe | 3,298 | 3,323 | 26,802 |
| 94 | XR-7 conv | 3,451 | 3,547 | 1,929 |
| **Monterey (wb 124.0; wgns-121.0)** | | | | |
| 44 | sdn 4d | 4,136 | 3,793 | 19,012 |
| 46 | htp cpe | 4,086 | 3,832 | 6,731 |
| 48 | htp sdn | 4,141 | 3,896 | 1,416 |
| 72 | wgn 3S | 4,545 | 4,334 | 4,644 |
| 72 | wgn 2S | 4,495 | 4,212 | |
| 54 | Custom sdn 4d | 4,225 | 3,956 | 16,879 |
| 56 | Custom htp cpe | 4,175 | 4,035 | 5,910 |
| 58 | Custom htp sdn | 4,230 | 4,103 | 1,583 |
| **Marquis (wb 124.0; wgns-121.0)** | | | | |
| 63 | sdn 4d | 4,386 | 4,493 | 14,122 |
| 66 | htp cpe | 4,236 | 4,572 | 5,507 |
| 68 | htp sdn | 4,391 | 4,637 | 1,583 |
| 74 | wgn 3S | 4,589 | 4,567 | 2,085 |
| 74 | wgn 2S | 4,539 | 4,445 | |
| 62 | Brougham sdn 4d | 4,436 | 4,890 | 38,242 |
| 64 | Brougham htp cpe | 4,386 | 4,969 | 20,064 |
| 67 | Brougham htp sdn | 4,441 | 5,034 | 12,841 |
| 76 | Colony Park wgn 3S | 4,629 | 4,672 | 20,192 |
| 76 | Colony Park wgn 2S | 4,579 | 4,550 | |

# Mercury

| 1972 Engines | bore × stroke | bhp | availability |
|---|---|---|---|
| I-6, 170.0 | 3.50 × 2.94 | 82 | S-Comet |
| I-6, 200.0 | 3.68 × 3.13 | 91 | O-Comet |
| I-6, 250.0 | 3.68 × 3.91 | 95 | O-Montego |
| I-6, 250.0 | 3.68 × 3.91 | 98 | O-Comet |
| V-8, 302.0 | 4.00 × 3.00 | 140 | S-Montego |
| V-8, 302.0 | 4.00 × 3.00 | 143 | S-Comet |
| V-8, 351.0 | 4.00 × 3.50 | 161 | O-Montego |
| V-8, 351.0 | 4.00 × 3.50 | 163 | S-Mntry exc Cus wgn |
| V-8, 351.0 | 4.00 × 3.50 | 164 | S-Cougar |
| V-8, 351.0 | 4.00 × 3.50 | 262/266 | O-Cougar |
| V-8, 400.0 | 4.00 × 4.00 | 168 | O-Montego |
| V-8, 400.0 | 4.00 × 4.00 | 172 | S-Mntry Cus & Marq wgns |
| V-8, 429.0 | 4.36 × 3.59 | 205 | O-Montego |
| V-8, 429.0 | 4.36 × 3.59 | 208 | S-Marquis exc wgn |
| V-8, 460.0 | 4.36 × 3.85 | 224 | O-Monterey, Marquis |

| 1973 Engines | bore × stroke | bhp | availability |
|---|---|---|---|
| I-6, 200.0 | 3.68 × 3.13 | 84 | S-Comet 6 |
| I-6, 250.0 | 3.68 × 3.91 | 88 | O-Comet 6 |
| I-6, 250.0 | 3.68 × 3.91 | 92 | O-Montego |
| V-8, 302.0 | 4.00 × 3.00 | 137/138 | S-Montego, Comet |
| V-8, 351.0 | 4.00 × 3.50 | 159/161 | S-Mntry exc Cus/wgn; O-Mntgo |
| V-8, 351.0 | 4.00 × 3.50 | 168 | S-Cougar |
| V-8, 351.0 | 4.00 × 3.50 | 246 | O-Montego cpes |
| V-8, 351.0 | 4.00 × 3.50 | 264 | O-Cougar (CJ) |
| V-8, 400.0 | 4.00 × 4.00 | 168/171 | S-Mntry Cus/wgn; O-Mntgo |
| V-8, 429.0 | 4.36 × 3.59 | 171 | S-Marquis exc wgn; O-Marquis wgn |
| V-8, 429.0 | 4.36 × 3.59 | 198/200 | O-Monterey, Montego |
| V-8, 460.0 | 4.36 × 3.85 | 202/267 | O-Monterey, Marquis |

## 1973

| | Comet (wb 109.9; 2d-103.0) | Wght | Price | Prod |
|---|---|---|---|---|
| 30 | sdn 4d | 2,904 | 2,489 | 28,984 |
| 31 | fstbk sdn 2d | 2,813 | 2,432 | 55,707 |
| | **Montego (wb 118.0; 2d-114.0)** | | | |
| 02 | sdn 4d | 3,719 | 2,916 | 7,459 |
| 03 | htp cpe | 3,653 | 2,926 | 7,082 |
| 04 | MX sdn 4d | 3,772 | 3,009 | 25,300 |
| 07 | MX htp cpe | 3,683 | 3,041 | 27,812 |
| 08 | MX wgn | 4,124 | 3,417 | 7,012 |
| 10 | MX Brougham sdn 4d | 3,813 | 3,189 | 24,329 |
| 11 | MX Brougham htp cpe | 3,706 | 3,209 | 40,951 |
| 18 | MX Villager wgn | 4,167 | 3,606 | 12,396 |
| 16 | GT fstbk htp cpe | 3,662 | 3,413 | 4,464 |
| | **Cougar (wb 113.0)** | | | |
| 91 | htp cpe | 3,396 | 3,372 | 21,069 |
| 92 | conv | 3,524 | 3,726 | 1,284 |
| 93 | XR-7 htp cpe | 3,416 | 3,679 | 35,110 |
| 94 | XR-7 conv | 3,530 | 3,903 | 3,165 |
| | **Monterey (wb 124.0; wgns-121.0)** | | | |
| 44 | sdn 4d | 4,225 | 3,961 | 16,622 |
| 46 | htp cpe | 4,167 | 4,004 | 6,452 |
| 72 | wgn 3S | 4,673 | 4,501 | 4,275 |
| 72 | wgn 2S | 4,623 | 4,379 | |
| 54 | Custom sdn 4d | 4,295 | 4,124 | 20,873 |
| 56 | Custom htp cpe | 4,239 | 4,207 | 6,962 |
| | **Marquis (wb 124.0; wgns-121.0)** | | | |
| 63 | sdn 4d | 4,477 | 4,648 | 15,250 |
| 66 | htp cpe | 4,411 | 4,727 | 5,973 |
| 68 | htp sdn | 4,453 | 4,782 | 2,185 |
| 74 | wgn 3S | 4,745 | 4,730 | 2,464 |
| 74 | wgn 2S | 4,695 | 4,608 | |
| 62 | Brougham sdn 4d | 4,547 | 5,072 | 46,624 |
| 64 | Brougham htp cpe | 4,475 | 5,151 | 22,770 |
| 67 | Brougham htp sdn | 4,565 | 5,206 | 10,613 |
| 76 | Colony Park wgn 3S | 4,780 | 4,835 | 23,283 |
| 76 | Colony Park wgn 2S | 4,730 | 4,713 | |

## 1974

| | Comet (wb 109.9; 2d-103.0) | Wght | Price | Prod |
|---|---|---|---|---|
| 30 | sdn 4d | 2,969 | 3,042 | 60,944 |
| 31 | fstbk sdn 2d | 2,861 | 3,008 | 64,751 |
| | **Montego (wb 118.0; 2d-114.0)** | | | |
| 02 | sdn 4d | 4,062 | 3,360 | 5,674 |
| 03 | htp cpe | 3,977 | 3,327 | 7,645 |
| 04 | MX sdn 4d | 4,092 | 3,478 | 19,446 |
| 07 | MX htp cpe | 3,990 | 3,443 | 20,957 |
| 08 | MX wgn | 4,426 | 4,083 | 4,085 |
| 10 | MX Brougham sdn 4d | 4,143 | 3,680 | 13,467 |
| 11 | MX Brougham htp cpe | 4,010 | 3,646 | 20,511 |
| 18 | MX Villager wgn | 4,463 | 4,307 | 6,234 |
| | **Cougar (wb 114.0)** | | | |
| 93 | XR-7 htp cpe | 4,255 | 4,706 | 91,670 |
| | **Monterey (wb 124.0; wgns-121.0)** | | | |
| 44 | sdn 4d | 4,559 | 4,367 | 6,185 |
| 46 | htp cpe | 4,506 | 4,410 | 2,003 |
| 72 | wgn 3S | 4,966 | 4,853 | 1,669 |
| 72 | wgn 2S | 4,916 | 4,731 | |
| 54 | Custom sdn 4d | 4,561 | 4,480 | 13,113 |
| 56 | Custom htp cpe | 4,504 | 4,523 | 4,510 |
| | **Marquis (wb 124.0; wgns-121.0)** | | | |
| 63 | sdn 4d | 4,757 | 5,080 | 6,910 |
| 66 | htp cpe | 4,698 | 5,080 | 2,633 |
| 68 | htp sdn | 4,753 | 5,080 | 784 |
| 74 | wgn 3S | 5,023 | 5,082 | 1,111 |
| 74 | wgn 2S | 4,973 | 4,960 | |
| 62 | Brougham sdn 4d | 4,833 | 5,519 | 24,477 |
| 64 | Brougham htp cpe | 4,762 | 5,519 | 10,207 |
| 67 | Brougham htp sdn | 4,853 | 5,519 | 4,189 |
| 76 | Colony Park wgn 3S | 5,056 | 5,188 | 10,802 |
| 76 | Colony Park wgn 2S | 5,006 | 5,066 | |

| 1974 Engines | bore × stroke | bhp | availability |
|---|---|---|---|
| I-6, 200.0 | 3.68 × 3.13 | 84 | S-Comet |
| I-6, 250.0 | 3.68 × 3.91 | 91 | O-Comet |
| V-8, 302.0 | 4.00 × 3.00 | 140 | S-Comet, Montego |
| V-8, 351.0 | 4.00 × 3.50 | 162 | S-Cougar; O-Montego |

# Mercury

| 1974 Engines | bore × stroke | bhp | availability |
|---|---|---|---|
| V-8, 351.0 | 4.00 × 3.50 | 246/264 | O-Montego, Cougar (CJ) |
| V-8, 400.0 | 4.00 × 4.00 | 170 | S-Mntry; O-Mntgo, Cgr |
| V-8, 460.0 | 4.36 × 3.85 | 195 | S-Marquis; O-Mntgo, Mntry |
| V-8, 460.0 | 4.36 × 3.85 | 220 | O-Cougar |
| V-8, 460.0 | 4.36 × 3.65 | 275 | O-Monterey, Marquis |

## 1975

| | | Wght | Price | Prod |
|---|---|---|---|---|
| **Bobcat (wb 94.5; wgn-94.8)** | | | | |
| 20 | Runabout htchbk sdn 2d | 2,535 | 3,189 | 20,651 |
| 22 | Villager wgn 2d | 2,668 | 3,481 | 13,583 |
| **Comet (wb 109.9; 2d-103.0)** | | | | |
| 30 | sdn 4d | 3,193 | 3,270 | 31,080 |
| 31 | fstbk sdn 2d | 3,070 | 3,236 | 22,768 |
| **Monarch (wb 109.9)** | | | | |
| 34 | sdn 4d | 3,195 | 3,822 | 34,307 |
| 35 | sdn 2d | 3,142 | 3,764 | 29,151 |
| 37 | Ghia sdn 4d | 3,281 | 4,349 | 22,723 |
| 37 | Grand sdn 4d | 3,432 | 5,375 | |
| 38 | Ghia sdn 2d | 3,231 | 4,291 | 17,755 |
| **Montego (wb 118.0; 2d-114.0)** | | | | |
| 02 | sdn 4d | 4,066 | 4,128 | 4,142 |
| 03 | htp cpe | 4,003 | 4,092 | 4,051 |
| 04 | MX sdn 4d | 4,111 | 4,328 | 16,033 |
| 07 | MX htp cpe | 4,030 | 4,304 | 13,666 |
| 08 | MX wgn | 4,464 | 4,674 | 4,508 |
| 10 | MX Brougham sdn 4d | 4,130 | 4,498 | 8,235 |
| 11 | MX Brougham htp cpe | 4,054 | 4,453 | 8,791 |
| 18 | MX Villager wgn | 4,522 | 4,909 | 5,754 |
| **Cougar (wb 114.0)** | | | | |
| 93 | XR-7 htp cpe | 4,108 | 5,218 | 62,987 |
| **Marquis (wb 124.0; wgns-121.0)** | | | | |
| 63 | sdn 4d | 4,513 | 5,115 | 20,058 |
| 66 | htp cpe | 4,470 | 5,049 | 6,807 |
| 74 | wgn 3S | 4,930 | 5,538 | 1,904 |
| 74 | wgn 2S | 4,880 | 5,411 | |
| 62 | Brougham sdn 4d | 4,799 | 6,037 | 19,667 |
| 64 | Brougham htp cpe | 4,747 | 5,972 | 7,125 |
| 60 | Grand Marquis sdn 4d | 4,815 | 6,469 | 12,307 |
| 61 | Grand Marquis htp cpe | 4,762 | 6,403 | 4,945 |
| 76 | Colony Park wgn 2S | 5,003 | 5,725 | 11,652 |
| 76 | Colony Park wgn 2S | 4,953 | 5,598 | |

| 1975 Engines | bore × stroke | bhp | availability |
|---|---|---|---|
| I-6, 140.0 | 3.78 × 3.13 | 83 | S-Bobcat |
| V-6, 170.8 | 3.66 × 2.70 | 97 | O-Bobcat |
| I-6, 200.0 | 3.68 × 3.13 | 75 | S-Comet, Mnrch exc Ghia |
| I-6, 250.0 | 3.68 × 3.91 | 72 | S-Mnrch Ghia; O-Cmt, Mntry |
| V-8, 302.0 | 4.00 × 3.00 | 122 | O-Comet |
| V-8, 302.0 | 4.00 × 3.00 | 129 | O-Monarch |
| V-8, 351.0 | 4.00 × 3.50 | 148/150 | S-Cougar, Montego |
| V-8, 351.0 | 4.00 × 3.50 | 143 | O-Monarch |

| 1975 Engines | bore × stroke | bhp | availability |
|---|---|---|---|
| V-8, 400.0 | 4.00 × 4.00 | 158 | S-Marq exc wgn & B'ham; O-Mntgo, Cgr |
| V-8, 460.0 | 4.36 × 3.85 | 216 | S-Grand Marq, wgn & Marq Brghm; O-Montgo, Cgr, Marq |

## 1976

| | | Wght | Price | Prod |
|---|---|---|---|---|
| **Bobcat (wb 94.5; wgn-94.8)** | | | | |
| 20 | MPG Runabout htchbk sdn 2d | 2,535 | 3,338 | 28,905 |
| 22 | MPG Villager wgn 2d | 2,668 | 3,643 | 18,731 |
| **Comet (wb 109.9; 2d-103.0)** | | | | |
| 30 | sdn 4d | 3,058 | 3,465 | 21,006 |
| 31 | fstbk sdn 2d | 2,952 | 3,398 | 15,068 |
| **Monarch (wb 109.9)** | | | | |
| 34 | sdn 4d | 3,195 | 3,864 | 56,351 |
| 35 | sdn 2d | 3,142 | 3,773 | 47,466 |
| 37 | Ghia sdn 4d | 3,218 | 4,422 | 27,056 |
| 37 | Grand sdn 4d | 3,432 | 5,740 | |
| 38 | Ghia sdn 2d | 3,231 | 4,331 | 14,950 |
| **Montego (wb 118.0; 2d-114.0)** | | | | |
| 02 | sdn 4d | 4,133 | 4,343 | 3,403 |
| 03 | htp cpe | 4,057 | 4,299 | 2,287 |
| 04 | MX sdn 4d | 4,133 | 4,498 | 12,666 |
| 07 | MX htp cpe | 4,085 | 4,465 | 12,367 |
| 08 | MX wgn | 4,451 | 4,778 | 5,012 |
| 10 | MX Brougham sdn 4d | 4,150 | 4,670 | 5,043 |
| 11 | MX Brougham htp cpe | 4,097 | 4,621 | 3,905 |
| 18 | MX Villager wgn | 4,478 | 5,065 | 6,412 |
| **Cougar (wb 114.0)** | | | | |
| 93 | XR-7 htp cpe | 4,168 | 5,125 | 83,765 |
| **Marquis (wb 124.0; wgns-121.0)** | | | | |
| 63 | sdn 4d | 4,460 | 5,063 | 28,212 |
| 66 | htp cpe | 4,436 | 5,063 | 10,450 |
| 62 | Brougham sdn 4d | 4,693 | 6,035 | 22,411 |
| 64 | Brougham htp cpe | 4,652 | 5,955 | 10,431 |
| 60 | Grand Marquis sdn 4d | 4,723 | 6,528 | 17,650 |
| 61 | Grand Marquis htp cpe | 4,679 | 6,439 | 9,207 |
| 74 | wgn 3S | 4,824 | 5,401 | 2,493 |
| 74 | wgn 2S | 4,796 | 5,275 | |
| 76 | Colony Park wgn 3S | 4,906 | 5,716 | 15,114 |
| 76 | Colony Park wgn 2S | 4,878 | 5,590 | |

| 1976 Engines | bore × stroke | bhp | availability |
|---|---|---|---|
| I-4, 140.0 | 3.78 × 3.13 | 92 | S-Bobcat |
| V-6, 170.8 | 3.66 × 2.70 | 100 | O-Bobcat |
| I-6, 200.0 | 3.68 × 3.13 | 81 | S-Mnrch exc Ghia; O-Comet |
| I-6, 250.0 | 3.68 × 3.91 | 90 | S-Mnrch Ghia; O-Cmt, Mnrch |
| V-8, 302.0 | 4.00 × 3.00 | 143 | O-Monarch |
| V-8, 302.0 | 4.00 × 3.00 | 138 | O-Comet |
| V-8, 351.0 | 4.00 × 3.50 | 154 | S-Montego exc wgn |
| V-8, 351.0 | 4.00 × 3.50 | 152 | S-Mntgo wgn, Cgr; O-Mnrch |
| V-8, 400.0 | 4.00 × 4.00 | 180 | S-Marq; O-Mntgo, Cgr |
| V-8, 460.0 | 4.36 × 3.85 | 202 | O-Mntgo, Cgr, Marquis |

# Mercury

## 1977

| Bobcat (wb 94.5; wgn-94.8) | | Wght | Price | Prod |
|---|---|---|---|---|
| 20 | Runabout htchbk sdn 2d | 2,369 | 3,438 | 18,405* |
| 22 | wgn 2d | 2,505 | 3,629 | 13,047* |
| 22 | Villager wgn 2d | — | 3,771 | |

| Comet (wb 109.9; 2d-103.0) | | | | |
|---|---|---|---|---|
| 30 | sdn 4d | 3,065 | 3,617 | 12,436 |
| 31 | fstbk sdn 2d | 2,960 | 3,544 | 9,109 |

| Monarch (wb 109.9) | | | | |
|---|---|---|---|---|
| 34 | sdn 4d | 3,250 | 4,154 | 55,952 |
| 35 | sdn 2d | 3,200 | 4,076 | 44,509 |
| 37 | Ghia sdn 4d | 3,382 | 4,722 | 16,545 |
| 38 | Ghia sdn 2d | 3,321 | 4,643 | 11,051 |

| Cougar (wb 118.0; 2d-114.0) | | | | |
|---|---|---|---|---|
| 90 | sdn 4d | 3,893 | 4,832 | 15,256 |
| 91 | htp cpe | 3,811 | 4,700 | 15,910 |
| 92 | wgn | 4,434 | 5,104 | 4,951 |
| 93 | XR-7 htp cpe | 3,909 | 5,274 | 124,799 |
| 94 | Brougham sdn 4d | 3,946 | 5,230 | 16,946 |
| 95 | Brougham htp cpe | 3,852 | 4,990 | 8,392 |
| 96 | Villager wgn | 4,482 | 5,363 | 8,569 |

| Marquis (wb 124.0; wgns-121.0) | | | | |
|---|---|---|---|---|
| 63 | sdn 4d | 4,326 | 5,496 | 36,103 |
| 66 | htp cpe | 4,293 | 5,496 | 13,242 |
| 62 | Brougham sdn 4d | 4,408 | 6,324 | 29,411 |
| 64 | Brougham htp cpe | 4,350 | 6,229 | 12,237 |
| 60 | Grand Marquis htp sdn | 4,572 | 6,975 | 31,231 |
| 61 | Grand Marquis htp cpe | 4,516 | 6,880 | 13,445 |
| 74 | wgn 3S | 4,678 | 5,794 | 20,363 |
| 74 | wgn 2S | 4,628 | 5,631 | |

| 1977 Engines | bore × stroke | bhp | availability |
|---|---|---|---|
| I-4, 140.0 | 3.78 × 3.13 | 89 | S-Bobcat |
| V-6, 170.8 | 3.66 × 2.70 | 93 | O-Bobcat |
| I-6, 200.0 | 3.68 × 3.13 | 96 | S-Monarch exc Ghia; O-Cmt |
| I-6, 250.0 | 3.68 × 3.91 | 98 | S-Mnrch Ghia; O-Mnrch, Cmt |
| V-8, 302.0 | 4.00 × 3.00 | 122/134 | O-Monarch |
| V-8, 302.0 | 4.00 × 3.00 | 130 | S-Cougar exc wgn |
| V-8, 302.0 | 4.00 × 3.00 | 137 | O-Comet |
| V-8, 351.0 | 4.00 × 3.50 | 149 | O-Cougar exc wgn |
| V-8, 351.0 | 4.00 × 3.50 | 161 | S-Cgr wgn; O-Monarch Ghia |
| V-8, 400.0 | 4.00 × 4.00 | 173 | S-Marq exc Grand; O-Cgr |
| V-8, 460.0 | 4.36 × 3.85 | 197 | S-Grand Marquis; O-Marquis |

*Includes some cars built as 1978 models but sold as 1977 models.

## 1978

| Bobcat (wb 94.5; wgn-94.8) | | Wght | Price | Prod |
|---|---|---|---|---|
| 20 | Runabout htchbk sdn 2d | 2,389 | 3,830 | 23,428 |
| 22 | wgn 2d | 2,532 | 4,112 | 8,840 |
| 22 | Villager wgn 2d | — | 4,244 | |

| Zephyr (wb 105.5) | | | | |
|---|---|---|---|---|
| 31 | sdn 2d | 2,594 | 3,777 | 27,673 |
| 32 | sdn 4d | 2,636 | 3,863 | 47,334 |
| 35 | Z-7 spt cpe | 2,630 | 4,154 | 44,569 |
| 36 | wgn | 2,744 | 4,216 | 32,596 |

| Monarch (wb 109.9) | | | | |
|---|---|---|---|---|
| 33 | sdn 2d | 3,094 | 4,366 | 38,939 |
| 34 | sdn 4d | 3,138 | 4,457 | 52,775 |

| Cougar (wb 114.0; 4d-118.0) | | | | |
|---|---|---|---|---|
| 91 | htp cpe | 3,761 | 5,052 | 21,398 |
| 92 | sdn 4d | 3,848 | 5,179 | 25,364 |
| 93 | XR-7 htp cpe | 3,865 | 5,720 | 166,508 |

| Marquis (wb 124.0; wgns-121.0) | | | | |
|---|---|---|---|---|
| 61 | htp cpe | 4,296 | 5,897 | 27,793 |
| 62 | sdn 4d | 4,328 | 5,949 | 11,176 |
| 63 | Brougham htp cpe | 4,317 | 6,525 | 10,368 |
| 64 | Brougham sdn 4d | 4,346 | 6,638 | 26,030 |
| 65 | Grand Marquis htp cpe | 4,342 | 7,290 | 15,624 |
| 66 | Grand Marquis sdn 4d | 4,414 | 7,399 | 37,753 |
| 74 | wgn 3S | 4,606 | 6,292 | 16,883 |
| 74 | wgn 2S | 4,578 | 6,106 | |

| 1978 Engines | bore × stroke | bhp | availability |
|---|---|---|---|
| I-4, 140.0 | 3.78 × 3.13 | 88 | S-Bobcat, Zephyr |
| V-6, 170.6 | 3.66 × 2.70 | 90 | O-Bobcat |
| I-6, 200.0 | 3.68 × 3.13 | 85 | O-Zephyr |
| I-6, 250.0 | 3.68 × 3.91 | 97 | S-Monarch |
| V-8, 302.0 | 4.00 × 3.00 | 134 | S-Cougar |
| V-8, 302.0 | 4.00 × 3.00 | 139 | O-Zephyr, Monarch |
| V-8, 351.0 | 4.00 × 3.50 | 144/145 | O-Cougar, S-Marquis |
| V-8, 351.0 | 4.00 × 3.50 | 152 | O-Cougar |
| V-8, 400.0 | 4.00 × 4.00 | 160 | O-Marquis |
| V-8, 400.0 | 4.00 × 4.00 | 166 | O-Cougar |
| V-8, 460.0 | 4.36 × 3.85 | 202 | O-Marquis |

## 1979

| Bobcat (wb 94.5; wgn-94.8) | | Wght | Price | Prod |
|---|---|---|---|---|
| 20 | Runabout htchbk sdn 2d | 2,424 | 4,104 | 35,667 |
| 22 | wgn 2d | 2,565 | 4,410 | 9,119 |
| 22 | Villager wgn 2d | — | 4,523 | |

| Capri (wb 100.4) | | | | |
|---|---|---|---|---|
| 14 | htchbk cpe | 2,548 | 4,872 | 92,432 |
| 16 | Ghia htchbk cpe | 2,645 | 5,237 | 17,712 |

| Zephyr (wb 105.5) | | | | |
|---|---|---|---|---|
| 31 | sdn 2d | 2,518 | 4,253 | 15,920 |
| 32 | sdn 4d | 2,582 | 4,370 | 41,316 |
| 35 | Z-7 spt cpe | 2,553 | 4,504 | 42,923 |
| 36 | wgn | 2,683 | 4,647 | 25,218 |

| Monarch (wb 109.9) | | | | |
|---|---|---|---|---|
| 33 | sdn 2d | 3,110 | 4,735 | 28,285 |
| 34 | sdn 4d | 3,151 | 4,841 | 47,594 |

| Cougar (wb 114.0; 4d-118.0) | | | | |
|---|---|---|---|---|
| 91 | htp cpe | 3,792 | 5,379 | 2,831 |
| 92 | sdn 4d | 3,843 | 5,524 | 5,605 |
| 93 | XR-7 htp cpe | 3,883 | 6,430 | 163,716 |

# Mercury

| Marquis (wb 114.3) | | Wght | Price | Prod |
|---|---|---|---|---|
| 61 | htp cpe | 3,507 | 6,292 | 10,035 |
| 62 | sdn 4d | 3,557 | 6,387 | 32,289 |
| 63 | Brougham htp cpe | 3,540 | 6,986 | 10,627 |
| 64 | Brougham sdn 4d | 3,605 | 7,176 | 24,682 |
| 65 | Grand Marquis htp cpe | 3,592 | 7,721 | 11,066 |
| 66 | Grand Marquis sdn 4d | 3,659 | 7,909 | 32,349 |
| 74 | wgn 3S | 3,825 | 6,894 | 5,994 |
| 74 | wgn 2S | 3,775 | 6,701 | |
| 76 | Colony Park wgn 3S | 3,850 | 7,688 | 13,758 |
| 76 | Colony Park wgn 2S | 3,800 | 7,495 | |

| 1979 Engines | bore × stroke | bhp | availability |
|---|---|---|---|
| I-4, 140.0 | 3.78 × 3.13 | 88 | S-Bobcat, Zephyr, Capri |
| I-4T, 140.0 | 3.78 × 3.13 | 140 | O-Capri (Turbo RS) |
| V-6, 170.6 | 3.66 × 2.70 | 102 | O-Bobcat |
| V-6, 170.6 | 3.66 × 2.70 | 109 | O-Capri |
| I-6, 200.0 | 3.68 × 3.13 | 85 | O-Zephyr |
| I-6, 250.0 | 3.68 × 3.91 | 97 | S-Monarch |
| V-8, 302.0 | 4.00 × 3.00 | 129/133 | S-Marquis, Cougar |
| V-8, 302.0 | 4.00 × 3.00 | 137 | O-Monarch |
| V-8, 302.0 | 4.00 × 3.00 | 140 | O-Capri, Zephyr |
| V-8, 351.0 | 4.00 × 3.50 | 135 | S-Cougar XR-7 |
| V-8, 351.0 | 4.00 × 3.50 | 138 | O-Marquis |
| V-8, 351.0 | 4.00 × 3.50 | 151 | O-Cougar |

## 1980

| Bobcat (wb 94.5; wgn-94.8) | | Wght | Price | Prod |
|---|---|---|---|---|
| 20 | Runabout htchbk sdn 2d | 2,445 | 4,764 | 28,103 |
| 22 | wgn 2d | 2,573 | 5,070 | 5,547 |
| 22 | Villager wgn 2d | — | 5,183 | |
| **Capri (wb 100.4)** | | | | |
| 14 | htchbk cpe | 2,566 | 5,672 | 72,009 |
| 16 | Ghia htchbk cpe | 2,651 | 5,968 | 7,975 |
| **Zephyr (wb 105.5)** | | | | |
| 31 | sdn 2d | 2,607 | 5,041 | 10,977 |
| 32 | sdn 4d | 2,649 | 5,158 | 40,399 |
| 35 | Z-7 spt cpe | 2,646 | 5,335 | 19,486 |
| 36 | wgn | 2,771 | 5,364 | 20,341 |
| **Monarch (wb 109.9)** | | | | |
| 33 | sdn 2d | 3,126 | 5,628 | 8,772 |
| 34 | sdn 4d | 3,180 | 5,751 | 21,746 |
| **Cougar (wb 108.4)** | | | | |
| 93 | XR-7 cpe | 3,191 | 7,045 | 58,028 |
| **Marquis (wb 114.3)** | | | | |
| 61 | sdn 2d | 3,450 | 7,075 | 2,521 |
| 62 | sdn 4d | 3,488 | 7,185 | 13,018 |
| 63 | Brougham sdn 2d | 3,476 | 7,860 | 2,353 |
| 64 | Brougham sdn 4d | 3,528 | 8,057 | 8,819 |
| 65 | Grand Marquis sdn 2d | 3,504 | 8,631 | 3,434 |
| 66 | Grand Marquis sdn 4d | 3,519 | 8,824 | 15,995 |
| 74 | wgn 3S | 3,747 | 7,782 | 2,407 |
| 74 | wgn 2S | 3,697 | 7,583 | |
| 76 | Colony Park wgn 3S | 3,793 | 8,676 | 5,781 |
| 76 | Colony Park wgn 2S | 3,743 | 8,477 | |

| 1980 Engines | bore × stroke | bhp | availability |
|---|---|---|---|
| I-4, 140.0 | 3.78 × 3.13 | 88 | S-Bobcat, Zphr, Capri |
| I-4T, 140.0 | 3.78 × 3.13 | 140 | O-Capri, Zephyr* |
| I-6, 200.0 | 3.68 × 3.13 | 91 | O-Capri, Zephyr |
| I-6, 250.0 | 3.68 × 3.91 | 90 | S-Monarch |
| V-8, 255.0 | 3.68 × 3.00 | 115 | S-Cougar |
| V-8, 255.0 | 3.68 × 3.00 | 118/119 | O-Capri, Zephyr, Monarch |
| V-8, 302.0 | 4.00 × 3.00 | 130/131 | S-Marquis; O-Cougar |
| V-8, 302.0 | 4.00 × 3.00 | 134 | O-Monarch |
| V-8, 351.0 | 4.00 × 3.50 | 140 | O-Marquis |

*Withdrawn for Zephyr after announcement; production doubtful.

## 1981

| Lynx (wb 94.2) | | Wght | Price | Prod |
|---|---|---|---|---|
| 63 | htchbk sdn 2d | — | 5,603 | 72,786 |
| 63 | L htchbk sdn 2d | 1,935 | 5,665 | |
| 63/60Z | GL htchbk sdn 2d | 1,957 | 5,903 | |
| 63/602 | GS htchbk sdn 2d | 1,996 | 6,642 | |
| 63/603 | LS htchbk sdn 2d | 2,004 | 7,127 | |
| 63/936 | RS htckbk sdn 2d | 1,980 | 6,223 | |
| 65 | htchbk 4d | — | 5,931 | 39,192 |
| 65 | L htchbk 4d | 2,059 | 6,070 | |
| 65/60Z | GL htchbk 4d | 2,074 | 6,235 | |
| 65/602 | GS htchbk 4d | 2,114 | 6,914 | |
| 65/936 | RS htchbk 4d | 2,098 | 6,563 | |
| **Capri (wb 100.4)** | | | | |
| 67 | htchbk cpe | 2,589 | 6,685 | 51,786 |
| 68 | GS htchbk cpe | 2,636 | 6,867 | 7,160 |
| **Zephyr (wb 105.5)** | | | | |
| 70 | sdn 2d | 2,558 | 6,103 | 5,814 |
| — | S sdn 2d | — | 5,769 | — |
| 71 | sdn 4d | 2,623 | 6,222 | 34,334 |
| 73 | wgn | 2,698 | 6,458 | 16,283 |
| 72 | Z-7 cpe | 2,610 | 6,252 | 10,078 |
| **Cougar (wb 105.5; XR-7-108.4)** | | | | |
| 76 | sdn 2d | 2,727 | 6,535 | 10,793 |
| 77 | sdn 4d | 2,771 | 6,694 | 42,860 |
| 90 | XR-7 cpe | 3,068 | 7,799 | 37,275 |
| **Marquis (wb 114.3)** | | | | |
| 81 | sdn 4d | 3,493 | 7,811 | 10,392 |
| 82 | Brougham sdn 2d | 3,513 | 8,601 | 2,942 |
| 83 | Brougham sdn 4d | 3,564 | 8,800 | 11,744 |
| 84 | Grand Marquis sdn 2d | 3,533 | 9,228 | 4,268 |
| 85 | Grand Marquis sdn 4d | 3,564 | 9,459 | 23,780 |
| 87 | wgn 2S | 3,745 | 8,309 | 2,219 |
| 88 | Colony Park 4d 2S | 3,800 | 9,304 | 6,293 |

| 1981 Engines | bore × stroke | bhp | availability |
|---|---|---|---|
| I-4, 97.6 | 3.15 × 3.13 | 65 | S-Lynx |
| I-4, 140.0 | 3.78 × 3.13 | 88 | S-Capri, Zephyr, Cougar |
| I-4T, 140.0 | 3.78 × 3.13 | — | O-Capri |
| I-6, 200.0 | 3.68 × 3.13 | 88/95 | S-XR-7; O-Capri, Zphyr, other Cgr |
| V-8, 255.0 | 3.68 × 3.00 | 115/120 | S-Marq; O-Capri, Zphyr, Cgr |
| V-8, 302.0 | 4.00 × 3.00 | 130 | O-Cougar XR-7, Marquis |

# Mercury

| 1981 Engines | bore × stroke | bhp | availability |
|---|---|---|---|
| V-8, 351.0 | 4.00 × 3.50 | 145 | O-Marquis |
| V-8, 351.0 | 4.00 × 3.50 | 165 | S-Marquis (police only) |

| 1982 Engines | bore × stroke | bhp | availability |
|---|---|---|---|
| V-8, 302.0 | 4.00 × 3.00 | 132 | S-Marq B'ham, Grand Marquis 4d; O-Marquis |
| V-8, 302.0 | 4.00 × 3.00 | 157 | O-Capri |
| V-8, 351.0 | 4.00 × 3.50 | 165 | S-Marquis (police only) |

## 1982

| Lynx (wb 94.2) | | Wght | Price | Prod |
|---|---|---|---|---|
| 63 | htchbk sdn 2d | 1,924 | 5,502 | |
| 63 | L htchbk sdn 2d | 1,927 | 6,159 | |
| 63/60Z | GL htchbk sdn 2d | 1,950 | 6,471 | |
| 63/602 | GS htchbk sdn 2d | 1,987 | 7,257 | 54,611 |
| 63/603 | LS htchbk sdn 2d | 1,952 | 7,762 | |
| 63/936 | RS htchbk sdn 2d | 1,961 | 6,790 | |
| 64 | htchbk sdn 4d | 1,984 | 5,709 | |
| 64 | L htchbk sdn 4d | 1,989 | 6,376 | |
| 64/60Z | GL htchbk sdn 4d | 2,012 | 6,688 | 40,713 |
| 64/602 | GS htchbk sdn 4d | 2,049 | 7,474 | |
| 64/603 | LS htchbk sdn 4d | 2,014 | 7,978 | |
| 65 | L wgn | 2,028 | 6,581 | |
| 65/60Z | GL wgn | 2,049 | 6,899 | 23,835 |
| 65/602 | GS wgn | 2,087 | 7,594 | |
| 65/603 | LS wgn | 2,052 | 8,099 | |

| LN7 (wb 94.2) | | | | |
|---|---|---|---|---|
| 61 | htchbk cpe | 2,059 | 7,787 | 35,147 |

| Capri (wb 100.4)—36,134 built | | | | |
|---|---|---|---|---|
| 67 | htchbk cpe | 2,554 | 6,711 | — |
| 67 | L htchbk cpe | 2,627 | 7,245 | — |
| 67 | Black Magic cpe 2d | — | 7,946 | — |
| 67 | RS htchbk cpe V-8 | — | 8,107 | — |
| 68 | GS htckbk cpe 2d | 2,637 | 7,432 | — |

| Zephyr (wb 105.5) | | | | |
|---|---|---|---|---|
| 71 | sdn 4d | 2,690 | 6,411 | 31,698 |
| 71/602 | GS sdn 4d | 2,703 | 6,734 | |
| 72/Z-7 | spt cpe | 2,687 | 6,309 | 7,394 |
| 72/602 | Z-7 GS spt cpe | 2,697 | 6,670 | |

| Cougar (wb 105.5) | | | | |
|---|---|---|---|---|
| 76 | GS sdn 2d | 2,939 | 7,983 | 6,984 |
| 76 | LS sdn 2d | 2,974 | 8,415 | |
| 77 | GS sdn 4d | 2,981 | 8,158 | 30,672 |
| 77 | LS sdn 4d | 3,023 | 8,587 | |
| 78 | GS wgn | 3,114 | 8,216 | 19,294 |

| Cougar XR-7 (wb 108.4)—16,867 built | | | | |
|---|---|---|---|---|
| 90 | GS cpe | 3,220 | 9,094 | — |
| 90/60H | LS cpe | 3,229 | 9,606 | — |

| Marquis (wb 114.3) | | | | |
|---|---|---|---|---|
| 81 | sdn 4d | 3,734 | 8,674 | 9,454 |
| 82 | Brougham sdn 2d | 3,693 | 9,490 | 2,833 |
| 83 | Brougham sdn 4d | 3,776 | 9,767 | 15,312 |
| 84 | Grand Marquis sdn 2d | 3,724 | 10,188 | 6,149 |
| 85 | Grand Marquis sdn 4d | 3,809 | 10,456 | 32,918 |
| 87 | wgn 2S | 3,880 | 9,198 | 2,487 |
| 88 | Colony Park wgn 2S | 3,890 | 10,252 | 8,004 |

| 1982 Engines | bore × stroke | bhp | availability |
|---|---|---|---|
| I-4, 97.6 | 3.15 × 3.13 | 70 | S-Lynx, LN7 |
| I-4, 140.0 | 3.78 × 3.13 | 86 | S-Capri, Zephyr |
| I-6, 200.0 | 3.68 × 3.13 | 87 | S-Cgr, XR-7; O-Capri, Zphyr |
| V-6, 232.0 | 3.80 × 3.40 | 112 | O-Cougar, XR-7 |
| V-8, 255.0 | 3.68 × 3.00 | 120-122 | S-Marquis; O-Capri, XR-7, Zphyr |

## 1983

| Lynx (wb 94.2) | | Wght | Price | Prod |
|---|---|---|---|---|
| 54 | L htchbk sdn 2d | 1,922 | 5,751 | |
| 55 | GS htchbk sdn 2d | 1,948 | 6,476 | 40,142 |
| 58 | LS htchbk sdn 2d | 1,950 | 7,529 | |
| 57 | RS htchbk sdn 2d | 1,997 | 7,370 | |
| 55 | L htchbk sdn 4d | 1,984 | 5,958 | |
| 66 | GS htchbk sdn 4d | 2,010 | 6,693 | 28,461 |
| 68 | LS htchbk sdn 4d | 2,012 | 7,746 | |
| 65/934 | LTS htchbk sdn 4d | 1,920 | 7,334 | |
| 60 | L wgn | 2,026 | 6,166 | |
| 61 | GS wgn | 2,050 | 6,872 | 19,192 |
| 63 | LS wgn | 2,050 | 7,909 | |

| LN7 (wb 94.2)—4,528 built | | | | |
|---|---|---|---|---|
| 51/A80 | htchbk cpe | 2,076 | 7,398 | — |
| 51/A8C | RS htchbk cpe | — | 8,765 | — |
| 51/A8A | Sport htchbk cpe | — | 8,084 | — |
| 51/ABB | Grand Sport cpe 2d | — | 8,465 | — |

| Capri (wb 100.4)—25,376 built | | | | |
|---|---|---|---|---|
| 79/41P | htchbk cpe | 2,643 | 7,156 | — |
| 79 | L htchbk cpe | 2,669 | 7,711 | — |
| 79 | Black Magic cpe 2d | 2,651 | 8,629 | — |
| 79 | Crimson Cat cpe 2d | — | 8,525 | — |
| 79/602 | GS htckbk cpe 2d | — | 7,914 | — |
| 79 | RS htchbk cpe | — | 9,241 | — |

| Cougar (wb 104.0)—75,743 built | | | | |
|---|---|---|---|---|
| 92 | cpe | 2,997 | 9,521 | — |
| 92/603 | LS cpe | 2,911 | 10,850 | — |

| Zephyr (wb 105.5) | | | | |
|---|---|---|---|---|
| 86 | sdn 4d | 2,690 | 6,545 | 21,732 |
| 86/602 | GS sdn 4d | 2,756 | 7,311 | |
| 87 | Z-7 spt cpe | 2,687 | 6,442 | 3,471 |
| 87/602 | Z-7 GS spt cpe | 2,750 | 7,247 | |

| Marquis (wb 105.5) | | | | |
|---|---|---|---|---|
| 89 | sdn 4d | 2,778 | 7,893 | 50,169 |
| 89 | Brougham sdn 4d | — | 8,202 | |
| 90 | wgn | 2,978 | 8,693 | 17,189 |
| 90 | Brougham wgn | — | 8,974 | |

| Grand Marquis (wb 114.3) | | | | |
|---|---|---|---|---|
| 93 | sdn 2d | 3,607 | 10,654 | 11,117 |
| 93/60H | LS sdn 2d | 3,607 | 11,209 | |
| 95 | sdn 4d | 3,761 | 10,718 | 72,207 |
| 95/60H | LS sdn 4d I-6 | 3,761 | 11,273 | |
| 94 | Colony Park wgn 2S I-6 | 3,788 | 10,896 | 12,394 |

| 1983 Engines | bore × stroke | bhp | availability |
|---|---|---|---|
| I-4, 97.6 | 3.15 × 3.13 | 70 | S-Lynx, LN7 |
| I-4, 97.6 | 3.15 × 3.13 | 80 | O-Lynx, LN7 |
| I-4, 97.6 | 3.15 × 3.13 | 88 | O-Lynx, LN7 |
| I-4, 140.0 | 3.78 × 3.13 | 90 | S-Capri, Zephyr, Marquis sdns |
| I-4T, 140.0 | 3.78 × 3.13 | 142 | O-Capri |

683

# Mercury

| 1983 Engines | bore × stroke | bhp | availability |
|---|---|---|---|
| I-4P, 140.0 | 3.78 × 3.13 | — | O-Marquis (propane) |
| I-6, 200.0 | 3.68 × 3.13 | 92 | S-Marquis wgns; O-Zephyr, Marquis sdns |
| V-6, 232.0 | 3.80 × 3.40 | 110-112 | S-Cougar; O-Capri, Marq |
| V-8, 302.0 | 4.00 × 3.00 | 130 | S-Grand Marq; O-Cougar |
| V-8, 302.0 | 4.00 × 3.00 | 145 | O-Grand Marquis |
| V-8, 302.0 | 4.00 × 3.00 | 175 | O-Capri |
| V-8, 351.0 | 4.00 × 3.50 | 165 | S-Grand Marq (police only) |

| 1984 Engines | bore × stroke | bhp | availability |
|---|---|---|---|
| I-4, 140.0 | 3.70 × 3.30 | 84 | S-Topaz |
| I-4, 140.0 | 3.78 × 3.13 | 88 | S-Capri GS, Marquis |
| I-4T, 140.0 | 3.78 × 3.13 | 145 | S-Cougar XR-7 |
| I-4T, 140.0 | 3.78 × 3.13 | 175 | S-Capri RS Turbo |
| I-4P, 140.0 | 3.78 × 3.13 | — | O-Marquis (propane) |
| V-6, 232.0 | 3.80 × 3.40 | 120 | S-Cougar, Marq wgn; O-Capri GS, Marquis |
| V-8, 302.0 | 4.00 × 3.00 | 140 | S-Grand Marq; O-Cougar |
| V-8, 302.0 | 4.00 × 3.00 | 155 | O-Grand Marquis |
| V-8, 302.0 | 4.00 × 3.00 | 165/175 | O-Capri GS/RS |
| V-8, 351.0 | 4.00 × 3.50 | 180 | S-Grand Marq (police only) |

## 1984

| Lynx (wb 94.2) | | Wght | Price | Prod |
|---|---|---|---|---|
| 54 | htchbk sdn 2d | 2,176 | 5,758 | |
| 54 | L htchbk sdn 2d | 2,087 | 6,019 | |
| 55 | GS htchbk sdn 2d | 2,128 | 6,495 | 38,208 |
| 57 | RS htchbk sdn 2d | 2,177 | 7,641 | |
| 57 | RS Turbo htchbk sdn 2d | 1,997 | 8,728 | |
| 65 | htchbk sdn 4d | 2,241 | 5,965 | |
| 65 | L htchbk sdn 4d | 2,152 | 6,233 | 21,090 |
| 66 | GS htchbk sdn 4d | 2,193 | 6,709 | |
| 68/934 | LTS htchbk sdn 4d | — | 7,879 | |
| 60 | L wgn | 2,181 | 6,448 | 16,142 |
| 61 | GS wgn | 2,220 | 6,887 | |

| Topaz (wb 99.9) | | | | |
|---|---|---|---|---|
| 72 | GS sdn 2d | 2,357 | 7,477 | 32,749 |
| 73 | LS sdn 2d | — | 7,880 | |
| 75 | GS sdn 4d | 2,415 | 7,477 | 96,505 |
| 76 | LS sdn 4d | 2,447 | 7,880 | |

| Capri (wb 100.5)—20,642 built | | | | |
|---|---|---|---|---|
| 79 | GS htchbk cpe I-4/V-6 | 2,827 | 7,758 | — |
| 79 | RS htchbk cpe V-8 | — | 9,638 | — |
| 79 | RS Turbo htchbk cpe I-4T | 2,775 | 9,822 | — |

| Cougar (wb 104.0)—131,190 built | | | | |
|---|---|---|---|---|
| 92 | cpe | 3,151 | 9,978 | — |
| 92/603 | LS cpe | 3,180 | 11,265 | — |
| 92/934 | XR-7 cpe I-4T | 3,053 | 13,065 | — |

| Marquis (wb 105.5) | | | | |
|---|---|---|---|---|
| 89 | sdn 4d | 2,966 | 8,727 | 91,808 |
| 89 | Brougham sdn 4d | — | 9,003 | |
| 90 | wgn V-6 | 3,128 | 9,224 | 16,004 |
| 90 | Brougham wgn V-6 | — | 9,498 | |

| Grand Marquis (wb 114.3) | | | | |
|---|---|---|---|---|
| 93 | sdn 2d | 3,734 | 11,576 | 13,657 |
| 93/60H | LS sdn 2d | — | 12,131 | |
| 95 | sdn 4d | 3,780 | 11,640 | 117,739 |
| 95/60H | LS sdn 4d | — | 12,195 | |
| 94 | Colony Park wgn 2S | 3,981 | 11,816 | 17,421 |

| 1984 Engines | bore × stroke | bhp | availability |
|---|---|---|---|
| I-4, 97.6 | 3.15 × 3.13 | 70 | S-Lynx exc RS Turbo |
| I-4, 97.6 | 3.15 × 3.13 | 80 | O-Lynx exc RS Turbo |
| I-4, 97.6 | 3.15 × 3.13 | 88 | S-Lynx RS Turbo; O-Lynx |
| I-4D, 121.0 | 3.39 × 3.39 | 52 | O-Lynx, Topaz |

## 1985

| Lynx (wb 94.2) | | Wght | Price | Prod |
|---|---|---|---|---|
| 54/41P | htchbk sdn 2d | 1,980 | 5,750 | |
| 54 | L htchbk sdn 2d | 2,000 | 6,170 | 26,653* |
| 55 | GS htchbk sdn 2d | 2,070 | 6,707 | |
| 65 | L htchbk sdn 4d | 2,060 | 6,384 | 11,658* |
| 66 | GS htchbk sdn 4d | 2,125 | 6,921 | |
| 60 | L wgn | 2,080 | 6,508 | 7,948* |
| 61 | GS wgn | 2,155 | 6,973 | |

*Estimated totals for First Series.

| Lynx Second Series 1985½ (wb 94.2) | | | | |
|---|---|---|---|---|
| 51 | htchbk sdn 2d | 2,158 | 5,986 | 20,515 |
| 51 | L htchbk sdn 2d | — | 6,272 | |
| 52 | GS htchbk sdn 2d | — | 6,962 | |
| 63 | L htchbk sdn 4d | 2,206 | 6,486 | 11,297 |
| 64 | GS htchbk sdn 4d | — | 7,176 | |
| 58 | L wgn | — | 6,767 | 6,721 |
| 59 | GS wgn | — | 7,457 | |

| Topaz (wb 99.9) | | | | |
|---|---|---|---|---|
| 72 | GS sdn 2d | 2,395 | 7,767 | 18,990 |
| 73 | LS sdn 2d | 2,445 | 8,931 | |
| 75 | GS sdn 4d | 2,450 | 7,767 | 82,366 |
| 76 | LS sdn 4d | 2,500 | 8,980 | |

| Capri (wb 100.5)—18,657 built | | | | |
|---|---|---|---|---|
| 79 | GS htchbk cpe I-4/V-6 | 2,885 | 7,944 | — |
| 79 | RS/5.0L htchbk cpe V-8 | 3,290 | 10,223 | — |

| Cougar (wb 104.0)—117,274 built | | | | |
|---|---|---|---|---|
| 92 | cpe 2d | 3,010 | 10,650 | — |
| 92/603 | LS cpe 2d | 3,040 | 11,850 | — |
| 92/934 | XR-7 cpe 2d I-4T | 2,978 | 13,599 | — |

| Marquis (wb 105.6) | | | | |
|---|---|---|---|---|
| 89 | sdn 4d | 2,915 | 8,996 | 91,465 |
| 89/60H | Brougham sdn 4d | 2,923 | 9,323 | |
| 90 | wgn V-6 | 2,993 | 9,506 | 12,733 |
| 90/60H | Brougham wgn V-6 | 3,000 | 9,805 | |

| Grand Marquis (wb 114.3) | | | | |
|---|---|---|---|---|
| 93 | sdn 2d | 3,619 | 12,240 | 10,900 |
| 93/60H | LS sdn 2d | — | 12,789 | |
| 95 | sdn 4d | 3,657 | 12,305 | 136,239 |
| 95/60H | LS sdn 4d | — | 12,854 | |
| 94 | Colony Park wgn 2S | 3,828 | 12,511 | 14,119 |

# Mercury

| 1985 Engines | bore × stroke | bhp | availability |
|---|---|---|---|
| I-4, 97.6 | 3.15 × 3.13 | 70 | S-Lynx base, L |
| I-4, 97.6 | 3.15 × 3.13 | 80 | S-Lynx GS; O-Lynx |
| I-4, 113.0 | 3.23 × 3.46 | 86 | S-late Lynx |
| I-4D, 121.0 | 3.39 × 3.39 | 52 | O-Lynx, Topaz |
| I-4, 140.0 | 3.70 × 3.30 | 86 | S-Topaz |
| I-4, 140.0 | 3.70 × 3.30 | 100 | O-Topaz |
| I-4, 140.0 | 3.78 × 3.13 | 88 | S-Capri GS, Marquis |
| I-4T, 140.0 | 3.78 × 3.13 | 155 | S-Cougar XR-7 |
| V-6, 232.0 | 3.80 × 3.40 | 120 | S-Cougar; O-Capri, Marq |
| V-8, 302.0 | 4.00 × 3.00 | 140 | S-Grand Marq; O-Cougar |
| V-8, 302.0 | 4.00 × 3.00 | 155 | O-Grand Marquis |
| V-8, 302.0 | 4.00 × 3.00 | 180 | O-Capri GS |
| V-8, 302.0 | 4.00 × 3.00 | 210 | S-Capri RS; O-Capri GS |

## 1986

| Lynx (wb 94.2) | | Wght | Price | Prod |
|---|---|---|---|---|
| 51 | htchbk sdn 2d | 2,156 | 6,182 | |
| 51 | L htchbk sdn 2d | 2,158 | 6,472 | 45,880 |
| 52 | GS htchbk sdn 2d | 2,246 | 7,162 | |
| 53 | XR3 htchbk sdn 2d | 2,374 | 8,193 | |
| 63 | L htchbk sdn 4d | 2,206 | 6,686 | 26,512 |
| 64 | GS htchbk sdn 4d | 2,289 | 7,376 | |
| 58 | L wgn | 2,238 | 6,967 | 13,580 |
| 59 | GS wgn | 2,312 | 7,657 | |
| **Topaz (wb 99.9)** | | | | |
| 72 | GS sdn 2d | 2,377 | 8,085 | 15,757 |
| 73 | LS sdn 2d | 2,464 | 9,224 | |
| 75 | GS sdn 4d | 2,440 | 8,235 | 62,640 |
| 76 | LS sdn 4d | 2,531 | 9,494 | |
| **Capri (wb 100.5)—20,869 built** | | | | |
| 79 | GS htchbk cpe I-4/V-6 | 2,877 | 8,331 | — |
| 79 | 5.0L htchbk cpe V-8 | 3,183 | 10,950 | — |
| **Cougar (wb 104.0)—135,909 built** | | | | |
| 92 | GS cpe 2d | 3,178 | 11,421 | — |
| 92 | LS cpe 2d | 3,214 | 12,757 | — |
| 92 | XR-7 cpe 2d I-4T | 3,158 | 14,377 | — |
| **Marquis (wb 105.6)** | | | | |
| 89 | sdn 4d | 2,969 | 9,660 | 24,121 |
| 89/60H | Brougham sdn 4d | 2,994 | 10,048 | |
| 90 | wgn V-6 | 3,112 | 10,254 | 4,461 |
| 90/60H | Brougham wgn V-6 | 3,139 | 10,613 | |
| **Sable (wb 106.0)** | | | | |
| 87 | GS sdn 4d I-4/V-6 | 2,983 | 10,700 | 71,707 |
| 87 | LS sdn 4d V-6 | 3,135 | 12,574 | |
| 88 | GS wgn V-6 | 3,210 | 11,776 | 23,931 |
| 88 | LS wgn V-6 | 3,225 | 13,068 | |
| **Grand Marquis (wb 114.3)** | | | | |
| 93 | sdn 2d | 3,782 | 13,480 | 5,610 |
| 93/60H | LS sdn 2d | 3,782 | 13,929 | |
| 95 | sdn 4d | 3,818 | 13,504 | 93,919 |
| 95/60H | LS sdn 4d | 3,818 | 13,952 | |
| 94 | Colony Park wgn 2S | 3,993 | 13,724 | 9,891 |

| 1986 Engines | bore × stroke | bhp | availability |
|---|---|---|---|
| I-4, 113.5 | 3.23 × 3.46 | 86 | S-Lynx exc XR3 |
| I-4, 113.5 | 3.23 × 3.46 | 108 | S-Lynx XR3; O-other Lynx |
| I-4D, 121.0 | 3.39 × 3.39 | 52 | O-Lynx, Topaz |
| I-4, 140.0 | 3.70 × 3.30 | 86 | S-Topaz |
| I-4, 140.0 | 3.70 × 3.30 | 100 | O-Topaz |
| I-4, 140.0 | 3.78 × 3.13 | 88 | S-Capri GS, Marquis |
| I-4T, 140.0 | 3.78 × 3.13 | 145/155 | S-Cougar XR-7 |
| I-4, 153.0 | 3.70 × 3.60 | 88 | S-late Sable GS sdn |
| V-6, 182.0 | 3.50 × 3.15 | 140 | S-Sable, LS/wgn; O-other Sable |
| V-6, 232.0 | 3.80 × 3.40 | 120 | S-Cougar, Marq wgn; O-Capri GS, Marquis |
| V-8, 302.0 | 4.00 × 3.00 | 150 | S-Grand Marq; O-Cougar GS |
| V-8, 302.0 | 4.00 × 3.00 | 200 | S-Capri 5.0L |

## 1987

| Lynx (wb 94.2) | | Wght | Price | Prod |
|---|---|---|---|---|
| 20 | L htchbk sdn 2d | 2,183 | 6,569 | |
| 21 | GS htchbk sdn 2d | 2,202 | 6,951 | 20,930 |
| 23 | XR3 htchbk sdn 2d | 2,396 | 8,808 | |
| 25 | GS htchbk sdn 4d | 2,258 | 7,172 | 12,124 |
| 28 | GS wgn | 2,277 | 7,462 | 6,985 |
| **Topaz (wb 99.9)** | | | | |
| 31 | GS sdn 2d | 2,503 | 8,562 | 19,738 |
| 33 | GS Spt sdn 2d | 2,565 | 9,308 | |
| 36 | GS sdn 4d | 2,557 | 8,716 | |
| 38 | GS Spt sdn 4d | 2,621 | 9,463 | 78,692 |
| 76 | LS sdn 4d | 2,631 | 10,213 | |
| **Cougar (wb 104.2)—104,526 built** | | | | |
| 60 | LS cpe | 3,202 | 13,595 | — |
| 62 | XR-7 cpe V-8 | 3,355 | 15,832 | — |
| **Sable (wb 106.0)** | | | | |
| 50 | GS sdn 4d | 3,054 | 12,240 | 91,001 |
| 53 | LS sdn 4d | 3,138 | 14,522 | |
| 55 | GS wgn | 3,228 | 12,793 | 30,312 |
| 58 | LS wgn | 3,311 | 15,054 | |
| **Grand Marquis (wb 114.3)** | | | | |
| 72 | LS sdn 2d | 3,764 | 15,323 | 4,904 |
| 74 | GS sdn 4d | 3,794 | 15,198 | 115,599 |
| 75 | LS sdn 4d | 3,803 | 15,672 | |
| 78 | Colony Park GS wgn 2S | 3,975 | 15,462 | 10,691 |
| 79 | Colony Park LS wgn 2S | 4,015 | 16,010 | |

| 1987 Engines | bore × stroke | bhp | availability |
|---|---|---|---|
| I-4, 113.5 | 3.23 × 3.46 | 90 | S-Lynx exc. XR3 |
| I-4, 113.5 | 3.23 × 3.46 | 115 | S-Lynx XR3 |
| I-4D, 121.0 | 3.39 × 3.39 | 58 | O-Lynx |
| I-4, 140.0 | 3.70 × 3.30 | 86 | S-Topaz exc Sport |
| I-4, 140.0 | 3.70 × 3.30 | 94 | O-other Topaz |
| V-6, 182.0 | 3.50 × 3.15 | 140 | S-Sable |
| V-6, 232.0 | 3.80 × 3.40 | 120 | S-Cougar LS |
| V-8, 302.0 | 4.00 × 3.00 | 150/155 | S-XR-7, Grand Marq; O-Cougar LS |

## 1988

| Topaz (wb 99.9) | | Wght | Price | Prod |
|---|---|---|---|---|
| 31 | GS sdn 2d | 2,565 | 9,166 | 16,001 |
| 33 | XR5 sdn 2d | 2,560 | 10,058 | |

# Mercury

| Topaz (wb 99.9) | Wght | Price | Prod |
|---|---|---|---|
| 36  GS sdn 4d | 2,608 | 9,323 | ⎫ |
| 37  LS sdn 4d | 2,651 | 10,591 | ⎬ 95,885 |
| 38  LTS sdn 4d | 2,660 | 11,541 | ⎭ |

| Cougar (wb 104.2)—119,162 built | | | |
|---|---|---|---|
| 60  LS cpe | 3,314 | 14,134 | — |
| 62  XR-7 cpe V-8 | 3,485 | 16,266 | — |

| Sable (wb 106.0) | | | |
|---|---|---|---|
| 50  GS sdn 4d V-6 | 3,097 | 14,145 | ⎫ 94,694 |
| 53  LS sdn 4d V-6 | 3,165 | 15,138 | ⎭ |
| 55  GS wgn V-6 | 3,208 | 14,665 | ⎫ 26,591 |
| 58  LS wgn V-6 | 3,268 | 15,683 | ⎭ |

| Grand Marquis (wb 114.3) | | | |
|---|---|---|---|
| 74  GS sdn 4d | 3,828 | 16,100 | ⎫ 11,611 |
| 75  LS sdn 4d | 3,839 | 16,612 | ⎭ |
| 78  Colony Park GS wgn 2S | 4,019 | 16,341 | ⎫ 9,456 |
| 79  Colony Park LS wgn 2S | 4,025 | 16,926 | ⎭ |

| 1988 Engines | bore × stroke | bhp | availability |
|---|---|---|---|
| I-4, 140.0 | 3.70 × 3.30 | 98/100 | S-Topaz |
| V-6, 182.0 | 3.50 × 3.15 | 140 | S-Sable |
| V-6, 232.0 | 3.80 × 3.40 | 140 | S-Cougar LS; O-Sable |
| V-8, 302.0 | 4.00 × 3.00 | 150/155 | S-XR-7, Grand Marq; O-Cougar LS |

## 1989

| Topaz (wb 99.9) | Wght | Price | Prod |
|---|---|---|---|
| 31  GS sdn 2d | 2,567 | 9,577 | ⎫ 10,015 |
| 33  XR5 sdn 2d | 2,544 | 10,498 | ⎭ |
| 36  GS sdn 4d | 2,606 | 9,734 | ⎫ |
| 37  LS sdn 4d | 2,647 | 11,030 | ⎬ 118,120 |
| 38  LTS sdn 4d | 2,706 | 11,980 | ⎭ |

| Sable (wb 106.0) | | | |
|---|---|---|---|
| 50  GS sdn 4d | 3,054 | 14,101 | ⎫ 102,571 |
| 53  LS sdn 4d | 3,168 | 15,094 | ⎭ |
| 55  GS wgn | 3,228 | 14,804 | ⎫ 28,086 |
| 58  LS wgn | 3,252 | 15,872 | ⎭ |

| Cougar (wb 113.0) | | | |
|---|---|---|---|
| 60  LS cpe | 3,553 | 15,448 | 92,163 |
| 60  XR7 cpe | 3,710 | 19,650 | 5,149 |

| Grand Marquis (wb 114.3) | | | |
|---|---|---|---|
| 74  GS sdn 4d | 3,763 | 16,701 | ⎫ |
| 75  LS sdn 4d | 3,774 | 17,213 | ⎬ 130,248 |
|     50th anniversary sdn 4d | 3,887 | — | ⎭ |
| 78  Colony Park GS wgn 2S | 3,995 | 17,338 | ⎫ 8,665 |
| 79  Colony Park LS wgn 2S | 3,913 | 17,922 | ⎭ |

| 1989 Engines | bore × stroke | bhp | availability |
|---|---|---|---|
| I-4, 140.0 | 3.70 × 3.30 | 98/100 | S-Topaz |
| V-6, 182.0 | 3.50 × 3.15 | 140 | S-Sable |
| V-6, 232.0 | 3.80 × 3.40 | 140 | S-Cougar LS; O-Sable |
| V-6S, 232.0 | 3.80 × 3.40 | 210 | S-Cougar XR7 |
| V-8, 302.0 | 4.00 × 3.00 | 150 | S-Grand Marquis |

## 1990

| Topaz (wb 99.9) | Wght | Price | Prod |
|---|---|---|---|
| 31  GS sdn 2d | 2,567 | 10,027 | ⎫ 2,512 |
| 33  XR5 sdn 2d | — | 10,988 | ⎭ |
| 36  GS sdn 4d | 2,602 | 10,184 | ⎫ |
| 37  LS sdn 4d | — | 11,507 | ⎬ 104,367 |
| 38  LTS sdn 4d | — | 12,514 | ⎭ |

| Sable (wb 106.0) | | | |
|---|---|---|---|
| 50  GS sdn 4d | 3,131 | 15,009 | ⎫ 80,423 |
| 53  LS sdn 4d | — | 16,011 | ⎭ |
| 55  GS wgn | 3,260 | 15,711 | ⎫ 23,326 |
| 58  LS wgn | — | 16,789 | ⎭ |

| Cougar (wb 113.0) | | | |
|---|---|---|---|
| 60  LS cpe | 3,608 | 15,911 | 76,174 |
| 60  XR7 cpe | — | 20,217 | 5,246 |

| Grand Marquis (wb 114.3) | | | |
|---|---|---|---|
| 74  GS sdn 4d | 3,833 | 17,633 | ⎫ 72,945 |
| 75  LS sdn 4d | — | 18,133 | ⎭ |
| 78  Colony Park GS wgn 2S | 4,006 | 18,348 | ⎫ 4,450 |
| 79  Colony Park LS wgn 2S | — | 18,920 | ⎭ |

| 1990 Engines | bore × stroke | bhp | availability |
|---|---|---|---|
| I-4, 140.0 | 3.70 × 3.30 | 98/100 | S-Topaz |
| V-6, 182.0 | 3.50 × 3.15 | 140 | S-Sable |
| V-6, 232.0 | 3.80 × 3.40 | 140 | S-Cougar LS; O-Sable |
| V-6S, 232.0 | 3.80 × 3.40 | 210 | S-Cougar XR7 |
| V-8, 302.0 | 4.00 × 3.00 | 150 | S-Grand Marquis |

Note: 1981-89 Colony Park wagons could have optional dual-facing rear seats. Base prices of 1984-87 Lynx and Tempo models with diesel engines were higher than figures shown above.

## 1991

| Tracer (wb 98.4) | Wght | Price | Prod |
|---|---|---|---|
| 54/AB    sdn 4d | 2,356 | 9,386 | ⎫ 59,825 |
| 54/AK    LTS sdn 4d | 2,464 | 11,636 | ⎭ |
| 74/AB    wgn | 2,468 | 10,407 | 13,999 |

| Topaz (wb 99.9) | | | |
|---|---|---|---|
| 66/HVB GS sdn 2d | 2,546 | 10,065 | ⎫ 2,789 |
| 66/HVD XR5 sdn 2d | — | 11,064 | ⎭ |
| 54/HVB GS sdn 4d | 2,602 | 10,222 | ⎫ |
| 54/HVE LS sdn 4d | — | 11,601 | ⎬ 77,663 |
| 54/HVC LTS sdn 4d | — | 12,626 | ⎭ |

| Sable (wb 106.0) | | | |
|---|---|---|---|
| FC/HVS GS sdn 4d | 3,131 | 15,311 | ⎫ 77,471 |
| FC/HVB LS sdn 4d | — | 16,154 | ⎭ |
| FF/HVS GS wgn | 3,260 | 16,256 | ⎫ 18,806 |
| FF/HVB LS wgn | — | 17,124 | ⎭ |

| Cougar (113.0) | | | |
|---|---|---|---|
| BA/VS-AJ LS cpe | 3,587 | 15,629 | 59,329 |
| BA/VS-AW XR7 cpe | — | 20,905 | 3,104 |

| Grand Marquis (wb 114.3) | | | |
|---|---|---|---|
| 74  GS sdn 4d | 3,836 | 18,741 | ⎫ 79,329 |
| 75  LS sdn 4d | — | 19,241 | ⎭ |
| 78  Colony Park GS wgn | 4,032 | 18,918 | ⎫ 3,104 |
| 79  Colony Park LS wgn | — | 19,490 | ⎭ |

| 1991 Engines | bore × stroke | bhp | availability |
|---|---|---|---|
| I-4, 109.0 | 3.27 × 3.35 | 127 | S-Tracer LTS (dohc) |
| I-4, 114.0 | 3.23 × 3.46 | 88 | S-Tracer (ohc) |
| I-4, 141.0 | 3.70 × 3.30 | 98 | S-Topaz |
| I-4, 141.0 | 3.70 × 3.30 | 100 | O-Topaz |

# Mercury

| 1991 Engines | bore × stroke | bhp | availability |
|---|---|---|---|
| V-6, 182.0 | 3.50 × 3.15 | 140 | S-Sable |
| V-6, 232.0 | 3.80 × 3.40 | 140 | S-Cougar LS, O-Sable |
| V-8, 302.0 | 4.00 × 3.00 | 150 | S-Grand Marquis |
| V-8, 302.0 | 4.00 × 3.00 | 225 | S-Cougar XR7; O-Cougar LS |

## 1992

| Tracer (wb 98.4) | Wght | Price | Prod |
|---|---|---|---|
| 54/AB sdn 4d | 2,356 | 9,773 | 21,060 |
| 54/AK LTS sdn 4d | 2,464 | 12,023 | |
| 74/AB wgn | 2,468 | 10,794 | 4,660 |
| **Topaz (wb 99.9)** | | | |
| 66/HVB GS sdn 2d | 2,544 | 10,512 | 20,567 |
| 66/HVD XR5 sdn 2d | 2,608 | 13,452 | |
| 54/HVB GS sdn 4d | 2,600 | 10,678 | 80,655 |
| 54/HVE LS sdn 4d | 2,625 | 12,057 | |
| 54/HVC LTS sdn 4d | 2,763 | 14,244 | |
| **Sable (wb 106.0)** | | | |
| FC/HVS GS sdn 4d | 3,147 | 16,418 | 104,054 |
| FC/HVB LS sdn 4d | 3,186 | 17,368 | |
| FF/HVS GS wgn | 3,292 | 17,396 | 23,476 |
| FF/HVB LS wgn | 3,331 | 18,395 | |
| **Cougar (113.0)** | | | |
| BA/VS-AJ LS cpe | 3,587 | 16,460 | 47,821* |
| BA/VS-AW XR7 cpe | 3,800 | 22,054 | 1,433 |
| **Grand Marquis (wb 114.3)—163,262 built** | | | |
| FA/AG GS sdn 4d | 3,768 | 20,216 | — |
| FA/AJ LS sdn 4d | 3,780 | 20,644 | — |

*Includes 4,800 Cougar 25th Anniversary models.

| 1992 Engines | bore × stroke | bhp | availability |
|---|---|---|---|
| I-4, 109.0 | 3.27 × 3.35 | 127 | S-Tracer LTS (dohc) |
| I-4, 114.0 | 3.23 × 3.46 | 88 | S-Tracer (ohc) |
| I-4, 141.0 | 3.70 × 3.30 | 98 | S-Topaz |
| V-6, 182.0 | 3.50 × 3.15 | 135 | S-Topaz XR5, LTS O-other Topaz |
| V-6, 182.0 | 3.50 × 3.15 | 140 | S-Sable |
| V-6, 232.0 | 3.80 × 3.40 | 140 | S-Cougar LS, O-Sable |
| V-8, 281.0 | 3.60 × 3.60 | 190 | S-Grand Marquis (ohc) |
| V-8, 281.0 | 3.60 × 3.60 | 210 | O-Grand Marquis (ohc) |
| V-8, 302.0 | 4.00 × 3.00 | 200 | S-Cougar XR7, O-Cougar LS |

## 1993

| Tracer (wb 98.4) | Wght | Price | Prod |
|---|---|---|---|
| 54/AB sdn 4d | 2,348 | 10,155 | 53,985 |
| 54/AK LTS sdn 4d | 2,460 | 12,023 | |
| 74/AB wgn | 2,462 | 10,982 | 24,162 |
| **Topaz (wb 99.9)** | | | |
| 66/HVB GS sdn 2d | 2,546 | 9,831 | 20,400 |
| 54/HVB GS sdn 4d | 2,602 | 10,976 | 78,305 |
| **Sable (wb 106.0)** | | | |
| FC/HVS GS sdn 4d | 3,122 | 17,480 | 114,457 |
| FC/HVB LS sdn 4d | 3,165 | 18,430 | |
| FF/HVS GS wgn | 3,271 | 18,459 | 22,876 |
| FF/HVB LS wgn | 3,314 | 19,457 | |
| **Cougar (113.0)** | | | |
| BA/VS-AW XR7 sdn 2d | 3,512 | 14,855 | 81,450 |
| **Grand Marquis (wb 114.3)—90,367 built** | | | |
| FA/AG GS sdn 4d | 3,794 | 21,973 | — |
| FA/AJ LS sdn 4d | 3,805 | 22,500 | — |

| 1993 Engines | bore × stroke | bhp | availability |
|---|---|---|---|
| I-4, 109.0 | 3.27 × 3.35 | 127 | S-Tracer LTS (dohc) |
| I-4, 114.0 | 3.23 × 3.46 | 88 | S-Tracer (ohc) |
| I-4, 141.0 | 3.70 × 3.30 | 98 | S-Topaz |
| V-6, 182.0 | 3.50 × 3.15 | 135 | O-Topaz |
| V-6, 182.0 | 3.50 × 3.15 | 140 | S-Sable |
| V-6, 232.0 | 3.80 × 3.40 | 140 | S-Cougar, O-Sable |
| V-8, 281.0 | 3.60 × 3.60 | 190 | S-Grand Marquis (ohc) |
| V-8, 281.0 | 3.60 × 3.60 | 210 | O-Grand Marquis (ohc) |
| V-8, 302.0 | 4.00 × 3.00 | 200 | O-Cougar |

## 1994

| Tracer (wb 98.4)* | Wght | Price | Prod |
|---|---|---|---|
| 54/AB sdn 4d | 2,393 | 10,250 | 31,632 |
| 54/AK LTS sdn 4d | 2,458 | 12,560 | |
| 74/AB wgn | 2,476 | 10,520 | 14,701 |
| **Topaz (wb 99.9)** | | | |
| 66/HVB GS sdn 2d | 2,531 | 11,270 | 12,344 |
| 54/HVB GS sdn 4d | 2,588 | 11,270 | 69,615 |
| **Sable (wb 106.0)** | | | |
| FC/HVS GS sdn 4d | 3,126 | 17,740 | 98,536 |
| FC/HVB LS sdn 4d | 3,177 | 20,000 | |
| FF/HVS GS wgn | 3,275 | 18,900 | 17,915 |
| FF/HVB LS wgn | 3,323 | 21,110 | |
| **Cougar (113.0)** | | | |
| BA/VS-AW XR7 cpe | 3,564 | 16,260 | 75,792 |
| **Grand Marquis (wb 114.3)—107,894 built** | | | |
| FA/AG GS sdn 4d | 3,787 | 20,330 | — |
| FA/AJ LS sdn 4d | 3,796 | 21,500 | — |

| 1994 Engines | bore × stroke | bhp | availability |
|---|---|---|---|
| I-4, 109.0 | 3.27 × 3.35 | 127 | S-Tracer LTS (dohc) |
| I-4, 114.0 | 3.23 × 3.46 | 88 | S-Tracer (ohc) |
| I-4, 141.0 | 3.70 × 3.30 | 96 | S-Topaz |
| V-6, 182.0 | 3.50 × 3.15 | 135 | O-Topaz |
| V-6, 182.0 | 3.50 × 3.15 | 140 | S-Sable |
| V-6, 232.0 | 3.80 × 3.40 | 140 | S-Cougar, O-Sable |
| V-8, 281.0 | 3.60 × 3.60 | 190 | S-Grand Marquis |
| V-8, 281.0 | 3.60 × 3.60 | 205 | O-Cougar (ohc) |
| V-8, 281.0 | 3.60 × 3.60 | 210 | O-Grand Marquis |

*Includes production for export.

# Mercury

## 1995

| Tracer (wb 98.4)—44,682 built* | | Wght | Price | Prod |
|---|---|---|---|---|
| M10 | sdn 4d | 2,418 | 11,280 | — |
| M15 | wgn | 2,498 | 11,800 | — |
| M14 | LTS sdn 4d | 2,472 | 13,140 | — |
| **Mystique (wb 106.5)—66,742 built** | | | | |
| M65 | GS sdn 4d | 2,824 | 13,855 | — |
| M66 | LS sdn 4d | 3,040 | 15,230 | — |
| **Sable (wb 106.0)** | | | | |
| M50 | GS sdn 4d | 3,144 | 18,210 | ⎤ |
| M53 | LS sdn 4d | — | 20,470 | ⎬ 90,197 |
| M53 | LTS sdn 4d | — | 21,715 | ⎦ |
| M55 | GS wgn | 3,292 | 19,360 | ⎤ 12,300 |
| M58 | LS wgn | — | 21,570 | ⎦ |
| **Cougar (113.0)** | | | | |
| M62 | XR7 cpe | 3,533 | 16,860 | 60,201 |
| **Grand Marquis (wb 114.3)—94,202 built** | | | | |
| M74 | GS sdn 4d | 3,761 | 21,270 | — |
| M75 | LS sdn 4d | — | 22,690 | — |

| 1995 Engines | bore × stroke | bhp | availability |
|---|---|---|---|
| I-4, 109.0 | 3.27 × 3.35 | 127 | S-Tracer LTS (dohc) |
| I-4, 114.0 | 3.23 × 3.46 | 88 | S-Tracer (ohc) |
| I-4, 121.0 | 3.34 × 3.46 | 125 | S-Mystique (dohc) |
| V-6, 155.0 | 3.24 × 3.13 | 170 | O-Mystique (dohc) |
| V-6, 182.0 | 3.50 × 3.15 | 140 | S-Sable |
| V-6, 232.0 | 3.80 × 3.40 | 140 | S-Cougar, O-Sable |
| V-8, 281.0 | 3.60 × 3.60 | 190 | S-Grand Marquis |
| V-8, 281.0 | 3.60 × 3.60 | 205 | O-Cougar |
| V-8, 281.0 | 3.60 × 3.60 | 210 | O-Grand Marquis |

*Tracer calender-year production.

## 1996

| Tracer (wb 98.4) | | Wght | Price | Prod |
|---|---|---|---|---|
| M10 | sdn 4d | 2,409 | 11,755 | ⎤ 10,790 |
| M14 | LTS sdn 4d | 2,460 | 13,625 | ⎦ |
| M15 | wgn | 2,485 | 12,285 | 2,500 |
| **Mystique (wb 106.5)—62,207 built** | | | | |
| M65 | GS sdn 4d | 2,833 | 14,330 | — |
| M66 | LS sdn 4d | 2,855 | 15,075 | — |
| **Sable (wb 108.5)** | | | | |
| M51 | G sdn 4d | — | 18,360 | ⎤ |
| M50 | GS sdn 4d | 3,358 | 18,995 | ⎬ 121,203 |
| M53 | LS sdn 4d | 3,359 | 21,295 | ⎦ |
| M55 | GS wgn | 3,502 | 20,015 | ⎤ 17,211 |
| M58 | LS wgn | 3,525 | 22,355 | ⎦ |
| **Cougar (wb 113.0)** | | | | |
| M62 | XR7 cpe | 3,559 | 17,430 | 39,749 |
| **Grand Marquis (wb 114.3)** | | | | |
| M74 | GS sdn 4d | 3,796 | 21,975 | ⎤ 104,433 |
| M75 | LS sdn 4d | — | 23,385 | ⎦ |

| 1996 Engines | bore × stroke | bhp | availability |
|---|---|---|---|
| I-4, 109.0 | 3.27 × 3.35 | 127 | S-Tracer LTS (dohc) |
| I-4, 114.0 | 3.23 × 3.46 | 88 | S-Tracer (ohc) |
| I-4, 121.0 | 3.34 × 3.46 | 125 | S-Mystique |
| V-6, 155.0 | 3.24 × 3.13 | 170 | O-Mystique |
| V-6, 181.0 | 3.50 × 3.10 | 200 | O-Sable (dohc) |
| V-6, 182.0 | 3.50 × 3.15 | 145 | S-Sable (ohv) |
| V-6, 232.0 | 3.80 × 3.40 | 145 | S-Cougar |
| V-8, 281.0 | 3.60 × 3.60 | 190 | S-Grand Marquis |
| V-8, 281.0 | 3.60 × 3.60 | 205 | O-Cougar |
| V-8, 281.0 | 3.60 × 3.60 | 210 | O-Grand Marquis |

## 1997

| Tracer (wb 98.4) | | Wght | Price | Prod |
|---|---|---|---|---|
| M10 | GS sdn 4d | 2,457 | 11,145 | ⎤ 58,662 |
| M14 | LS sdn 4d | 2,503 | 11,950 | ⎦ |
| M15 | LS wgn | 2,569 | 12,605 | 7,250 |
| **Mystique (wb 106.5)—23,321 built** | | | | |
| M65 | sdn 4d | — | 13,960 | — |
| M65 | GS sdn 4d | 2,861 | 14,775 | — |
| M66 | LS sdn 4d | 2,884 | 16,150 | — |
| **Sable (wb 108.5)** | | | | |
| M51 | G sdn 4d | — | 18,505 | ⎤ |
| M50 | GS sdn 4d | 3,333 | 19,495 | ⎬ 89,108 |
| M53 | LS sdn 4d | 3,360 | 22,080 | ⎦ |
| M55 | GS wgn | 3,476 | 19,495 | ⎤ 25,132 |
| M58 | LS wgn | 3,502 | 22,080 | ⎦ |
| **Cougar (wb 113.0)** | | | | |
| M62 | XR7 cpe | 3,536 | 17,830 | 35,267 |
| **Grand Marquis (wb 114.3)—127,949 built** | | | | |
| M74 | GS sdn 4d | 3,792 | 22,495 | 127,949 |
| M75 | LS sdn 4d | 3,796 | 23,905 | |

| 1997 Engines | bore × stroke | bhp | availability |
|---|---|---|---|
| I-4, 121.0 | 3.34 × 3.46 | 110 | S-Tracer |
| I-4, 121.0 | 3.34 × 3.46 | 125 | S-Mystique (dohc) |
| V-6, 155.0 | 3.24 × 3.13 | 170 | O-Mystique |
| V-6, 181.0 | 3.50 × 3.10 | 200 | O-Sable (dohc) |
| V-6, 182.0 | 3.50 × 3.15 | 145 | S-Sable |
| V-6, 232.0 | 3.80 × 3.40 | 145 | S-Cougar |
| V-8, 281.0 | 3.60 × 3.60 | 190 | S-Grand Marquis |
| V-8, 281.0 | 3.60 × 3.60 | 205 | O-Cougar |

## 1998

| Tracer (wb 98.4)—29,616 built | | Wght | Price | Prod* |
|---|---|---|---|---|
| M10 | GS sdn 4d | 2,469 | 11,355 | — |
| M14 | LS sdn 4d | — | 12,710 | — |
| M15 | LS wgn | 2,532 | 14,205 | — |
| **Mystique (wb 106.5)—47,128 built** | | | | |
| M65 | GS sdn 4d | 2,808 | 16,235 | — |
| M66 | LS sdn 4d | — | 17,645 | — |
| **Sable (wb 108.5)—111,676 built** | | | | |
| M50 | GS sdn 4d | 3,299 | 19,445 | — |
| M50/60 | LS sdn 4d | — | 20,445 | — |
| M55 | LS wgn | 3,462 | 22,285 | — |
| **Grand Marquis (wb 114.3)—134,155 built** | | | | |
| M74 | GS sdn 4d | 3,917 | 21,890 | — |
| M75 | LS sdn 4d | 3,922 | 23,790 | — |

# Mercury

| 1998 Engines | bore × stroke | bhp | availability |
|---|---|---|---|
| I-4, 121.0 | 3.34 × 3.46 | 110 | S-Tracer |
| I-4, 121.0 | 3.34 × 3.46 | 125 | S-Mystique (dohc) |
| V-6, 155.0 | 3.24 × 3.13 | 170 | O-Mystique |
| V-6, 181.0 | 3.50 × 3.10 | 200 | O-Sable (dohc) |
| V-6, 182.0 | 3.50 × 3.15 | 145 | S-Sable |
| V-8, 281.0 | 3.60 × 3.60 | 200 | S-Grand Marquis |
| V-8, 281.0 | 3.60 × 3.60 | 215 | O-Grand Marquis |

*Calendar-year production.

## 1999

| Tracer (wb 98.4)—14,691 built | | Wght | Price | Prod* |
|---|---|---|---|---|
| M10 | GS sdn 4d | 2,469 | 11,530 | — |
| M14 | LS sdn 4d | — | 13,070 | — |
| M15 | LS wgn | 2,532 | 14,275 | — |
| **Mystique (wb 106.5)—36,791 built** | | | | |
| M65 | GS sdn 4d | 2,805 | 16,390 | — |
| M66 | LS sdn 4d | — | 17,745 | — |
| **Sable (wb 108.5)—110,700 built** | | | | |
| M50 | GS sdn 4d | 3,302 | 18,445 | — |
| M50/60 | LS sdn 4d | — | 19,545 | — |
| M55 | LS wgn | 3,470 | 20,645 | — |
| **Cougar (wb 106.4)** | | | | |
| T60 | htchbk cpe I-4 | 2,892 | 16,195 | — |
| T61 | htchbk cpe V-6 | — | 16,695 | — |
| **Grand Marquis (wb 114.3)—142,372 built** | | | | |
| M74 | GS sdn 4d | 3,917 | 22,220 | — |
| M75 | LS sdn 4d | — | 24,120 | — |

| 1999 Engines | bore × stroke | bhp | availability |
|---|---|---|---|
| I-4, 121.0 | 3.34 × 3.46 | 110 | S-Tracer |
| I-4, 121.0 | 3.34 × 3.46 | 125 | S-Mystique, Cougar |
| I-4, 121.0 | 3.34 × 3.46 | 130 | O-Tracer (dohc) |
| V-6, 155.0 | 3.24 × 3.13 | 170 | O-Mystique, Cougar |
| V-6, 181.0 | 3.50 × 3.10 | 200 | O-Sable (dohc) |
| V-6, 182.0 | 3.50 × 3.15 | 145 | S-Sable |
| V-8, 281.0 | 3.60 × 3.60 | 200 | S-Grand Marquis |
| V-8, 281.0 | 3.60 × 3.60 | 215 | O-Grand Marquis |

*Calendar-year production.

## 2000

| Mystique (wb 106.5)—5006 built | | Wght | Price | Prod* |
|---|---|---|---|---|
| M65 | GS sdn 4d | 2,805 | 16,145 | — |
| M66 | LS sdn 4d | — | 17,445 | — |
| **Sable (wb 108.5)—114,511 built** | | | | |
| M50 | GS sdn 4d | 3,302 | 18,845 | — |
| M53 | LS sdn 4d | — | 19,545 | — |
| M55 | LS Premium sdn 4d | — | 21,245 | — |
| M58 | GS wgn | 3,470 | 20,835 | — |
| M59 | LS Premium wgn | 3,470 | 22,345 | — |
| **Cougar (wb 106.4)** | | | | |
| T60 | htchbk cpe I-4 | 2,892 | 16,195 | — |
| T61 | htchbk cpe V-6 | — | 16,695 | — |
| **Grand Marquis (wb 114.3)—132,870 built** | | | | |
| M74 | GS sdn 4d | 3,917 | 22,220 | — |
| M75 | LS sdn 4d | — | 24,120 | — |

| 2000 Engines | bore × stroke | bhp | availability |
|---|---|---|---|
| I-4, 121.0 | 3.34 × 3.46 | 125 | S-Mystique, Cougar |
| V-6, 155.0 | 3.24 × 3.13 | 170 | O-Mystique, Cougar |
| V-6, 181.0 | 3.50 × 3.10 | 200 | O-Sable (dohc) |
| V-6, 182.0 | 3.50 × 3.15 | 153 | S-Sable |
| V-8, 281.0 | 3.60 × 3.60 | 200 | S-Grand Marquis |
| V-8, 281.0 | 3.60 × 3.60 | 215 | O-Grand Marquis |

*Calendar-year production.

## 2001

| Sable (wb 108.5)—97,366 built | | Wght | Price | Prod* |
|---|---|---|---|---|
| M50 | GS sdn 4d | 3,302 | 19,185 | — |
| M53 | LS sdn 4d | — | 20,285 | — |
| M55 | LS Premium sdn 4d | — | 21,585 | — |
| M58 | GS wgn | 3,470 | 20,985 | — |
| M59 | LS Premium wgn | — | 22,685 | — |
| **Cougar (wb 106.4)** | | | | |
| T60 | htchbk cpe I-4 | 2,861 | 16,700 | — |
| T61 | htchbk cpe V-6 | 3,013 | 17,200 | — |
| **Grand Marquis (wb 114.3)—100,774 built** | | | | |
| M74 | GS sdn 4d | 3,957 | 22,805 | — |
| M75 | LS sdn 4d | 3,970 | 24,705 | — |

| 2001 Engines | bore × stroke | bhp | availability |
|---|---|---|---|
| I-4, 121.0 | 3.34 × 3.46 | 125 | S-Cougar (dohc) |
| V-6, 155.0 | 3.24 × 3.13 | 170 | O-Cougar |
| V-6, 181.0 | 3.50 × 3.10 | 200 | O-Sable (dohc) |
| V-6, 182.0 | 3.50 × 3.15 | 155 | S-Sable |
| V-8, 281.0 | 3.60 × 3.60 | 220 | S-Grand Marquis |
| V-8, 281.0 | 3.60 × 3.60 | 235 | O-Grand Marquis |

*Calendar-year production.

## 2002

| Sable (wb 108.5) | | Wght | Price | Prod* |
|---|---|---|---|---|
| M50 | GS sdn 4d | 3,366 | 19,630 | — |
| M50 | GS Plus sdn 4d | — | 20,690 | — |
| M55 | LS Premium sdn 4d | — | 22,055 | — |
| M58 | GS wgn | 3,531 | 21,040 | — |
| M58 | GS Plus wgn | — | 21,930 | — |
| M59 | LS Premium wgn | — | 23,220 | — |
| **Cougar (wb 106.4)** | | | | |
| T60 | htchbk cpe I-4 | 2,861 | 16,520 | — |
| T61 | htchbk cpe V-6 | 3,013 | 17,020 | — |
| T61 | Sport htchbk cpe | — | 17,520 | — |
| T61 | Sport Premium htchbk cpe | — | 18,520 | — |
| T61 | Sport Ultimate htchbk cpe | — | 19,920 | — |
| **Grand Marquis (wb 114.3)** | | | | |
| M74 | GS sdn 4d | 3,966 | 23,645 | — |
| M74 | GS Convenience sdn 4d | — | 24,065 | — |
| M75 | LS Premium sdn 4d | 3,988 | 27,120 | — |
| M75 | LS Ultimate sdn 4d | — | 28,300 | — |
| M75 | LS Ultimate sdn 4d | — | 28,300 | — |
| M75 | LSE sdn 4d | — | 28,625 | — |

| 2002 Engines | bore × stroke | bhp | availability |
|---|---|---|---|
| I-4, 121.0 | 3.34 × 3.46 | 125 | S-Cougar (dohc) |
| V-6, 155.0 | 3.24 × 3.13 | 170 | O-Cougar |
| V-6, 181.0 | 3.50 × 3.10 | 200 | O-Sable (dohc) |
| V-6, 182.0 | 3.50 × 3.15 | 155 | S-Sable |
| V-8, 281.0 | 3.60 × 3.60 | 220 | S-Grand Marquis |
| V-8, 281.0 | 3.60 × 3.60 | 235 | O-Grand Marquis |

*Figures not available at time of publication.

# Muntz

The Muntz Jet was one of those interesting "shoestring" cars that sprang up in the late '40s and early '50s, when many believed that a dream and a little money were all it took to make it big in the auto business. The dreamer here was Earl "Madman" Muntz, an irrepressible radio/television manufacturer whose wild-and-woolly advertising also made him Southern California's largest—and most-flamboyant—used-car dealer.

Muntz's car actually originated with Frank Kurtis, the famed designer of winning race cars (especially dirt-track midgets) who turned his enormous talent to a street sports car in 1948. The resulting Kurtis Sport was a slab-sided two-seat convertible that was unusual for the day in having a unit body/chassis with just ten outer panels, all aluminum except for a fiberglass hood and rear deck. Appearance was bulbous but pleasing on a tight 100-inch wheelbase. Side windows were clumsy, clip-in Plexiglas affairs, but a removable rigid top was provided along with the soft top.

Like interior hardware, the Kurtis' suspension and running gear were mostly proprietary components, though Frank Kurtis tuned spring and damper rates for optimum handling and roadholding. The powerteam was anything the buyer wanted, though 239-cid Ford flathead V-8s with Edelbrock manifolds were fitted to most examples. The Sport was also offered as a kit at $1495-$3495, depending on completeness.

Light weight gave the Sport good acceleration despite the flathead's meager 100 horsepower, and reviewers loved the car's nimbleness and stability. But Kurtis-Kraft was a small company building cars mostly by hand, so sales were as slow and sparse as profits. Thus, after building just 36 Sports through 1950, Kurtis sold his Glendale, California, operation to the "Madman" for $200,000.

Muntz set about making the Sport more salable, retaining its basic styling but adding 13 inches to the wheelbase, a back seat, and more conveniences. This meant extra weight, so Cadillac's new 160-horsepower, 331-cid overhead-valve V-8 was substituted for the Ford flathead. The result was America's first high-performance personal-luxury car. Muntz called it the Jet.

Working out of the former Kurtis plant, Muntz built 28 Jets before moving operations to his hometown of Evanston, Illinois, just north of Chicago, and making more substantial changes. The aluminum body—"It would dent if you leaned against it," he told Collectible Automobile® magazine in 1985—gave way to a steel shell on a new 116-inch wheelbase. Curiously, the modern Cadillac V-8 was ditched for Lincoln's old 336.7-cid flathead, albeit modified to produce 154 bhp via solid lifters (replacing hydraulics) from the Ford truck version. GM Hydra-Matic transmission was made standard, though Borg-Warner stick-overdrive was optionally available.

"We tooled that car for $75,000," Muntz recalled. But labor costs were a monumental $2000 per car because body panels had to be carefully fitted, then leaded-in. Meticulous detailing was required elsewhere.

The Evanston cars weighed 3780 pounds, about 400 more than the Glendale Jets, but were more durable. Both versions were fairly quick. Lincoln-powered models could do 0-60 in a tick over 12 seconds and see nearly 108 mph. Toward the end, Muntz switched to fiberglass fenders and Lincoln's 317.5-cid ohv V-8, which began at 160 bhp and was later rated at 205 bhp.

Unfortunately, Muntz lost money from the start on his cars, and when his television business hit hard times in 1954, he shut down his car-manufacturing business.

Even the "Madman" didn't know for sure, but it's estimated that 394 Jets were built; of these, at least 49 survive today.

## Specifications

### 1951

| Jet (wb 113.0) | | Wght | Price | Prod |
|---|---|---|---|---|
| conv cpe | | 3,380* | 5,500* | ** |
| **1951 Engine** | bore × stroke | bhp | availability | |
| V-8, 331.0 | 3.81 × 3.63 | 160 | S-all | |

### 1952

| Jet (wb 116.0) | | Wght | Price | Prod |
|---|---|---|---|---|
| conv cpe | | 3,780* | 5,500* | ** |
| **1952 Engine** | bore × stroke | bhp | availability | |
| V-8, 336.7 | 3.50 × 4.38 | 154 | S-all | |

### 1953

| Jet (wb 116.0) | | Wght | Price | Prod |
|---|---|---|---|---|
| conv cpe | | 3,780* | 5,500* | ** |
| **1953 Engine** | bore × stroke | bhp | availability | |
| V-8, 336.7 | 3.50 × 4.38 | 154 | S-all | |

### 1954

| Jet (wb 116.0) | | Wght | Price | Prod |
|---|---|---|---|---|
| conv cpe | | 3,700* | 5,500* | ** |
| **1954 Engine** | bore × stroke | bhp | availability | |
| V-8, 317.5 | 3.80 × 3.50 | 205 | S-all | |

Note: Chassis and engine changes did not necessarily occur on a model-year basis, so some vehicles of a given model year may have different engines or specifications than those listed.

\* Approximate figures

\*\* First-series Jet production with Cadillac V-8 is estimated at 28; total 1951-54 Jet production is estimated at 394.

**1951-54 Muntz Jet convertible coupe**

# Nash

Crusty Charles W. Nash resigned as president of General Motors in 1916 to build a car under his own name. Two years later, he bought the Thomas B. Jeffery Company of Kenosha, Wisconsin, which manufactured the slow-selling Jeffery and an earlier model called Rambler. Renamed Nash Motors, the firm charged up the sales charts, reaching as high as eighth place in industry production during the 1920s. Along the way, Nash introduced the low-cost six-cylinder Ajax and expanded by absorbing Mitchell and LaFayette. But none of these marques were as successful as the Nash itself and were gone by 1930.

Nash suffered in the general economic malaise following the 1929 Wall Street crash but found financial salvation by merging with the Kelvinator appliance company in 1937. Kelvinator president George Mason, a burly man described by many as "cigar-chomping," continued as president of the new concern; Charles Nash was chairman of the board. By 1940, Nash-Kelvinator had turned the corner and was profitable once more.

Many early-'30s Nashes were sumptuous, beautifully styled automobiles with numerous special features. But the firm also sold low-priced cars with an ordinary side-valve six. For 1930-32, this was a 201.3-cubic-inch engine with 60-70 horsepower; for 1933, it grew to 217.8 cid and 75 bhp. Series were variously titled Single Six (1930), 660 (1931), 960 (1932), and Big Six (1932-33). Prices started at around $1000 in 1930 but were later lowered to the $800-$900 range to spur sales in the Depression-crushed market. A side-valve straight eight was added for the 870/970 of 1931-32, with 227.2 cid and 78 bhp. In 1932-33 came a bored-out 247.4-cid engine with 85 bhp for Standard and Special Eights (Series 1070/1080), listing at $1000-$1500. The smaller eights generally sold for just below $1000.

More interesting were Nash's "Twin Ignition" cars, also variously titled. As the name implied, these employed two sets of spark plugs and points plus dual condensers and coils, all operating from a single distributor. The Twin Ignition Six arrived in 1928 as a 242-cid engine with 74 bhp. It continued through 1930, then stepped aside for a 240-cid straight eight with 88-94 bhp. The Twin Ignition Eight arrived for 1930, delivering 100-115 bhp from 298.6 cid. That powerplant persisted through 1932, when it was bracketed by new 260.8- and 322-cid engines with respective bhp of 100 and 125. The 322 was canceled after 1934, but the 260.8 would carry on all the way through 1942.

Charlie Nash was president of Buick in 1910-11, a make that espoused overhead valves, so it wasn't surprising that all these Nash engines were ohv too. The eights also boasted nine main bearings for smooth operation. Cost factors and rising public demand for greater fuel economy prompted Nash to abandon eights after 1942; they wouldn't return until 1955.

Nash persisted with classically upright styling through 1934 even though other makes were shifting to a rounder streamlined look. Body styles in all early-'30s series encompassed the most-popular period types: closed sedans, touring car, victoria, rumble-seat coupe, roadster, and convertible cabriolet. Seven-passenger sedans and limousines on wheelbases of 133 and 142 inches were cataloged for the six- and eight-cylinder Twin Ignition lines. A notable addition for 1932 was the Ambassador—a nicely proportioned, luxuriously trimmed five-seat sedan priced at $1855. A four-door brougham sedan was also offered, as were two seven-seaters priced $100-$200 higher. Additional choices arrived for 1933.

Charles Nash believed in offering a lot for the money, and his cars bristled with innovations. The Twin Ignition Eight, for example, sported cowl ventilation, a dashboard starter button, shatter-proof glass, and automatic radiator vents in 1930; downdraft carburetors and Bijur automatic chassis lubrication for '31; "Syncro-Safety Shift" (with a dash-mounted gearlever) and optional freewheeling for 1932 (a device built into the transmission that allowed the car to coast when the driver's foot was off the accelerator; it was ultimately determined to be dangerous because it eliminated engine braking); ignition/steering-wheel lock for '33; and aircraft-type instruments for '34. Many of these features also appeared on the cheaper side-valve Eights.

Like most automakers, Nash was damaged badly by the Depression. Though it regularly built over 100,000 cars a year in the late '20s, it wouldn't repeat that figure in the '30s, and thus ranked 11th, 12th, or 13th in industry production, with the exception of 1932, when it placed seventh in a down year for the industry. Also like many others, Nash hit bottom in 1933, output totaling less than 15,000. With a new approach desperately needed, a planned 1934 restyle was postponed a year while Nash pinned its hopes—and resources—on new low-priced LaFayettes.

Nash built its millionth car in 1934 while trying to summon better times with a drastically reduced line consisting of the 116-inch-wheelbase Big Six, 121-inch Advanced Eight, and 133/142-inch Ambassador Eight, all with ohv Twin Ignition engines. But production didn't improve much, and Nash lost over $1.6 million. Hydraulic brakes arrived for 1935 models, reduced to just a four-door sedan and six-passenger victoria in each series. Ambassador also lost its smooth 322-cid engine, sharing the Advanced Eight's 260.8-cid unit.

**1930 Twin Ignition Eight Touring 7-passenger (lwb)**

**1931 Series 880 two-door convertible sedan**

1933 Advanced Eight convertible roadster

1934 LaFayette touring sedan two-door

1935 Ambassador Eight four-door sedan

1936 400 New Six touring sedan trunkback

1937 Ambassador Eight trunkback sedan

1938 Lafayette DeLuxe trunkback sedan

But the belated restyle appeared that year as "Aeroform Design," and it was good. Highlights included sweeping skirted fenders, a handsome vee'd radiator, and a louvered hood. Prices spanned a range of $825-$1220. Happily for Nash, sales turned up. Registrations for the calendar year went from just under 24,000 to a bit over 35,000. Things were even better for 1936, reaching 43,000 with the help of new low-priced six-cylinder "400" models, standard and Deluxe. That year's Ambassadors comprised two Sixes and one eight-cylinder "trunkback" sedan, all on a 125-inch wheelbase. Prices were $835-$995. Sixes shared the "400" engine: the 234.8-cid unit introduced back in '34, now with 90 or 93 bhp.

Hopes for the revived LaFayette weren't entirely realized. An ostensibly separate make, it was, of course, planned as a junior-edition Depression-beater. Trouble was, the Great Depression was easing by the time the car debuted in 1934, which made the line far less necessary. Indeed, LaFayette attracted only 5000 first-year buyers and another 9400 for '35 before unexpectedly sky-rocketing to 27,860. They had ordinary styling on a 113-inch wheelbase, and popular body styles were offered at $585-$715. But the cars were "built down" to achieve those prices. Their powerplant, for instance, was the old 75-83 bhp 217.8-cid six from 1931-33.

Accordingly, LaFayette was made the lowest-priced 1937 Nash, taking over an unchanged chassis from the previous year's "400s." The Ambassador Six returned on a 121-inch platform and was increased to 105 bhp. Ambassador Eight continued with its 125-inch chassis and a 260.8-cid Twin Ignition eight that now made 115 bhp. This range of engines and wheelbases continued through decade's end. Styling was cautious, even imitative. The '37s, for instance, were much like Chrysler/DeSoto Airstreams: slightly lumpy, with similar barrel grilles. But they seemed to satisfy buyers. Nash had its best year of the decade in 1937, building 77,000 cars to earn $3.4 million.

Kenosha lost some of this hard-won sales ground as 1938 production stumbled to 41,543 cars and the new Nash-Kelvinator Corporation lost $7.7 million. A severe facelift changed Nash resemblance from Chrysler to the dumpier GM products, but the sales drop was primarily due to that year's sharp recession. A noteworthy innovation was the "Weather-Eye" heating/ventilation system, a pioneering "climatizer" that would remain one of the best in Detroit for the next 20 years.

A total 1939 restyle ushered in handsome Ford-like styling announced by flush-fit headlamps astride a narrow prow bearing horizontal bars; fine vertical bars adorned the "catwalks" on either side. The rest of the package was neat, trim, and coherent, combining all the best elements of late "art-deco" design. Production rebounded strongly to 63,000 cars. Significantly, LaFayette accounted for over 50 percent of production. Although Nash-Kelvinator lost $1.6 million in 1939,

# Nash

1939 LaFayette DeLuxe four-door sedan

1940 Ambassador Eight All-Purpose cabriolet

1941 600 DeLuxe trunkback four-door sedan

1942 600 trunkback four-door sedan

1946 Ambassador fastback four-door sedan

its future looked brighter than it had in a decade.

LaFayette made its final appearance for 1940, when all models were cautiously facelifted, mainly via applied trim. The veteran 234.8-cid six, as smooth and quiet as ever with its seven main bearings, was up to 99 horsepower for LaFayette. Ambassador Sixes still offered 105 bhp from the same engine, plus a four-inch-longer wheelbase, for about $110 more model-for-model. Ambassador Eights again delivered 115 bhp, as they had since 1937. Body styles were the same in all three series: business coupe, two- and four-door fastback sedans, trunkback four-door, and "All-Purpose" coupe and cabriolet. Model-year output was down slightly from '39 but still fairly healthy at 62,131.

For 1941, Nash joined future partner Hudson in advocating "single-unit" construction with the new 600, which signified 600 miles on a 20-gallon tank of gas. A handsome package on a 112-inch wheelbase, the 600 offered eight models powered by a new 75-bhp, 172.6-cid six. These included sedans and coupes in Special or Deluxe trim, all priced remarkably low. The Special fastback four-door, for instance, cost $805, less than a comparable Ford V-8. *Time* magazine called the 600 "the only completely new car in 1941," and demand was strong. Styling, evolved from the '40 look, was shared by senior Nashes, which also gained new unitized bodies, though the Ambassador Eight was demoted to the shorter chassis of its six-cylinder sister. More-horizontal front styling was featured across the board. Altogether, 1941 proved very profitable for Nash-Kelvinator, which closed the fiscal year with $4.6 million in earnings on total volume of just over 84,000 cars.

Production slimmed to only 31,780 for war-shortened 1942. Following an industry trend, Nash heavily facelifted with a low wraparound grille composed of three horizontal bars, a motif repeated as fender trim on some models. A slightly blunted prow hood rode above a small upper grille with four short horizontal bars, and parking lights appeared atop the front fenders. The same three series continued, but with fewer body and trim variations. Nash-Kelvinator then dug in for war production, turning out $600 million worth of aircraft engines and parts, munitions, cargo trailers, and other goods.

Despite severe postwar materials shortages, Nash returned to civilian operations earlier than most automakers and built 6148 cars during late 1945. That was good for third in the calendar-year race, but amounted to only four months of production. For 1946, the first full postwar model year, Nash built about 94,000 cars to finish eighth. Its 1947-48 totals were 101,000 and 110,000, good for only tenth and 11th. Still, these were good years, with strong profits. As if to celebrate, Nash opened a new 204-acre proving grounds near Burlington, Wisconsin, in 1946.

In June 1948, Nash president George Mason became board chairman, succeeding the venerable Charles Nash, who died that month at age 84. Nash was able to share in the 1946 celebration of the auto industry's Golden Jubilee, one of only a dozen pioneers still living at the time.

Mason was among the postwar industry's most visionary executives, certainly the most prophetic outside the Big Three. Believing the independents would have to merge for survival against the Detroit giants, he soon began working to put Nash together with Hudson and hoped to combine with Studebaker and Packard as well. More immediately, he presided over the development of a radical all-new Nash for 1949.

In the interim, Nash followed most other makes by fielding renovated 1942 models for 1946-48. Ambassador Eights were dropped, the 600's horsepower was boosted to 82, and the

# Nash

1947 Ambassador Suburban four-door sedan

1948 Ambassador Super four-door sedan

1948 Ambassador 6-passenger Brougham

1949 Ambassador Custom fastback four-door sedan

Ambassador Six was pushed to 112 bhp. Styling alterations were relatively minor, yet the cars managed to appear fresh enough. The 1946-47s had inboard parking lamps; the '47s gained a wider upper grille and raised-center hubcaps. For '48, Nash erased the side moldings below the beltline, a cheap change that inadvertently made for a higher, less-streamlined appearance.

The postwar 600 line comprised fastback and trunkback four-door sedans and a notchback Brougham two-door. The lineup was expanded for '48 with the addition of DeLuxe, Super, and Custom trim variations, Nash anticipating a major sales upsurge that year. Ambassador Six offered the same choices save for DeLuxe-trim '48s.

Unique to Ambassador was the Sedan Suburban, lavishly trimmed in wood like the contemporary Chrysler Town & Country and Ford/Mercury Sportsman. Extensive hand labor necessitated stiff prices ($1929-$2227), so Nash built only 272 Suburbans for '46, 595 for '47, and a mere 130 of the '48s (which came only with Super trim). But they played the same role as the nonwagon Ford and Chrysler woodies, attracting buyers to showrooms with the promise of something new. Suburbans are now coveted collectibles, mainly because only 10-15 are thought to survive. Only slightly less rare was the Custom-trim cabriolet added to the 1948 Ambassador line. It was the first open Nash since the war, but only 1000 or so were built. (Nash also built a small number of trucks with sedan-type front ends beginning with the 1947 model year, but most were exported.)

Meantime, Nash's independent rivals had restyled for 1947-48, as had Olds and Cadillac. Remaining Big Three makes targeted 1949 for their first all-new postwar models. But so had Nash, and it weighed in with a stunner: the radical Airflyte. Continued through '51, it looks rather strange now, yet in its day the Airflyte was one of the most-advanced cars on the road. It was unquestionably the boldest Nash ever.

The Airflyte was cooked up during World War II by engineers Ted Ulrich and Nash veteran Nils Erik Wahlberg. Ulrich had worked on the prewar "600" while at The Budd Company, and was hired by Wahlberg on the strength of its success. The way-out "bathtub" styling was the work of Holden "Bob" Koto, who, with partner Ted Pietsch in 1943, had shown Wahlberg a small scale model much like the eventual production Airflyte. Wahlberg must have liked it, for he'd already experimented with streamlined cars in wind-tunnel tests. The Airflyte was thus very slick aerodynamically, with only 113 pounds of drag at 60 mph versus up to 171 pounds for the similar-looking '49 Packard.

Maintaining Nash's two-series lineup, the '49 Airflyte came as a "600," still on a 112-inch wheelbase, and as a 121-inch Ambassador (with the extra wheelbase length again entirely ahead of the firewall). Each series listed two- and four-door sedans and Brougham club coupes, all bulbous fastbacks. Engines were unchanged from 1946-48. Novelties abounded: one-piece curved windshield, "Uniscope" gauge cluster (in a pod atop the steering column), dual inward-facing rear seats on Broughams (separated by a "card table" armrest) and, after '49, optional seatbelts and reclining right-front seat (dealers sold pneumatic mattresses as accessories). Those seats, plus the acclaimed "Weather-Eye" system, made Airflytes the most habitable long-distance cars in America.

With the postwar seller's market still strong, the Airflyte sold very well—better than any big Nashes had before. Some 135,000 were built for '49, rocketing Nash into the industry's top ten. The 1950 total was over 160,000—a company record, and that didn't include Nash's new compact Rambler introduced that year.

Optional Hydra-Matic Drive (purchased from GM) arrived for 1950, when the 600 was renamed Statesman. The rear windows were enlarged to improve visibility, though it was still pretty poor. Prices remained competitive: under $2000 for Statesmans, $2060-$2200 for Ambassadors. New for '51 were extended and raised rear fenders that softened the "beetle-back" look, plus new grilles and three more horsepower for each engine. As in 1950, trim levels comprised base DeLuxe, midrange Super, and top-shelf Custom, an arrangement Nash would keep for most of the rest of its days. Prices again changed little, but the public was tiring of "bathtubs", so production eased to about 153,000, again minus Rambler.

1950 Rambler Custom Landau convertible coupe

1951 Rambler Custom Country Club hardtop coupe

1952 Ambassador Custom Country Club hardtop coupe

1953 Rambler Custom Country Club hardtop coupe

1953 Ambassador Custom Country Club hardtop coupe

The new 100-inch-wheelbase 1950 Rambler was the very antithesis of the huge Airflyte. Though several Detroit automakers had attempted smaller cars before World War II, Rambler was the first to sell in significant numbers. Interestingly, Ford and Chevrolet briefly considered compacts after the war, but their concepts were quite different from Nash's. As George Romney, then Mason's top assistant, once said: "It's one thing for a small company—a marginal firm—to pioneer a new concept like that and really push it. But it's another thing for people who already have a big slice to begin pushing something that undercuts their basic market." Still, the Rambler's early sales success didn't go unnoticed at the Big Three, who would follow Nash's lead—though they'd take ten years to do so.

Small cars fascinated George Mason, who knew that the independents couldn't hope to survive in the postwar market without offering types of cars that the Big Three didn't. Together with chief engineer Meade Moore, Mason hammered away until the Rambler (and later the Metropolitan) was a reality. It arrived just as the sell-anything era was ending, and it would keep Nash's head above water through its 1954 merger with Hudson. Three years later, the resulting American Motors Corporation would be selling Ramblers almost exclusively.

The 1950 Rambler saw little change through 1952. Only two models were offered initially: a Custom two-door wagon and the interesting Custom Landau convertible with fixed side-window frames. A pretty hardtop coupe called Country Club was added for '51, but most sales came from the practical, attractive wagons (called Suburban after '51). In those early days of all-steel models, Rambler accounted for 22 percent of total U.S. wagon sales. All these Ramblers carried Nash's smaller 82-bhp L-head six, good for a claimed 25-30 mpg. The '52s maintained the 1950-51 sales pace, recording just over 53,000.

Quotable road-tester Tom McCahill of *Mechanix Illustrated* magazine once wrote that Mason and Nash were "busier than a mouse in a barrel of hungry cats." As proof, Mason busied himself with a sports car in these years. Called Nash-Healey, it started with a chance meeting aboard the *Queen Elizabeth* between Mason and famed British sports-car builder Donald Healey, then looking to buy American engines. Their meeting led directly to a low, slab-sided, two-seat roadster appearing in 1951 with a 102-inch wheelbase, British-crafted aluminum body, and an Ambassador six tuned for 125 bhp. Healey built it at his small works in Warwick, England.

The Nash-Healey perfectly expressed Mason's "be different or die" attitude, but it cost a bunch—over $4000 at first—and thus didn't sell well: 104 of the '51s, 150 of '52, 162 of the '53s, and just 90 for '54 (including a few leftovers reserialed as '55 models). Even so, the N-H became better as it went along. Handsome steel bodywork shaped by Italy's Pinin Farina bowed for 1952. The next year brought a six-inch longer wheelbase for a companion coupe called Le Mans (honoring high N-H finishes at the French 24-hour race in 1951-52). Nash also offered a 140-bhp dual-carburetor option, but canceled the roadster after '53. The high cost of transatlantic shipping pushed the price over $6000 by the end, but every Nash-Healey was a genuine dual-purpose sports car: quick and nimble on the road, yet strong enough for the track.

Mason so liked Farina's N-H restyle that he asked the designer to shape a new big Nash for 1952. Farina submitted two proposals, but the end product was mostly the doing of Nash's own Edmund A. Anderson. The only surviving Farina elements were a simple, square grille and a three-element wraparound rear window. Still, the 1952 Statesmans and

# Nash

Ambassadors were good-looking notchbacks that wore "Pinin Farina" badges, just like post-'51 Nash-Healeys. Nash called them "Golden Airflytes," honoring the firm's 50th birthday that year. Unfortunately, integral front-fender skirts, as on the 1949-51 "bathtubs," made for huge turning circles and difficult tire-changing.

Big-Nash offerings for '52 comprised Super and Custom two- and four-door sedans plus a new Custom Country Club hardtop in each line. Statesmans now rode a 114.3-inch wheelbase and carried a stroked 195.6-cid six with 88 bhp. Prices moved up: $2150-$2400 for Statesmans, $2520-$2830 for Ambassadors.

The '53s were identified only by small chrome spacers on their cowl air scoops (part of "Weather-Eye"). Nash still billed itself as "America's travel car" with things like a drawer-type glovebox and a full-width parcel net above the windshield, but those were just masks for tepid performance. To perk things up for '53, Nash boosted the Statesman to 100 bhp and offered the Ambassadors with dual carburetors and a high-compression aluminum head in a 140-bhp "Le Mans" option *a la* Nash-Healey.

An attractive new "floating" grille appeared for '54, when Custom two-door sedans were scratched and the Statesman got its own dual-carb engine: a 110-bhp setup dubbed "Dual Powerflyte." That surely raised eyebrows at Chrysler, which had a new PowerFlite automatic transmission that year, but Nash probably got away with it because sales had been steadily dropping: from about 143,000 for '52, to 109,000 for '53, and finally 77,000 for '54. More ominously, the low-profit Ramblers—nicely updated for '53 via a clean single-bar grille—accounted for a continuously growing percentage of this dwindling pie.

And Nash had something even smaller for '54: a tiny two-seater on an 85-inch wheelbase. Called Metropolitan, it originated in a prototype by freelance designer Bill Flajole that was displayed to select audiences during 1950 as the NXI (for "Nash Xperimental International"). Response was favorable, but Mason didn't arrange for production until late 1953. The bodies were contracted to the well-known Fisher & Ludlow works in Birmingham, England, and final assembly to Austin in Longbridge, England. Austin also donated a four-cylinder engine from its A40 model, an elderly long-stroke bit of ironmongery that extracted 42 bhp from 73.8 cid.

The Metropolitan arrived in hardtop and convertible models priced around $1450. Weight was just over 1800 pounds, so mileage was good: up to 40 mpg. At first, sales were pretty good too, Austin shipping 13,095 through late '54. But demand fell to just under 6100 the next year, prompting some changes for '56.

Mason achieved a portion of his goal on May 1, 1954, when Nash and Hudson merged, forming American Motors Corporation (AMC). He still wanted Studebaker and Packard to join the fold so the resulting company could enjoy the economies of scale of the Big Three, and therefore be competitive with them. Studebaker and Packard did merge with each other (also in '54), but Mason died late that year, and his dream of a large company made up of several independents was never realized.

Meanwhile, the big "Farina" Nashes were facelifted for 1955, acquiring raised front wheel arches at last, plus a wrapped windshield and a smart new oval grille encircling the headlights. Cooperation between the new AMC and Studebaker-Packard (another '54 merger) gave Nash its first eight-cylinder cars since 1942: Ambassadors with a new 208-bhp Packard-built V-8 of 320 cid. The Ambassador Eight was much quicker than the Six, but cost $300 more. Remaining two-door sedans

1952-53 Nash-Healey roadster by Pinin Farina

1954 Statesman Custom two-door sedan

1955½ Rambler Custom Cross Country station wagon

1955 Ambassador Eight Custom Country Club hardtop coupe

1956 Ambassador Eight Custom four-door sedan

1956 Rambler Custom hardtop sedan

1957 Ambassador Custom Country Club hardtop coupe

1957 Rambler V-8 Custom Cross Country hardtop wagon

1957 Rambler Rebel hardtop sedan

1958 Metropolitan convertible coupe

departed, but other models stayed. As in '54, Statesmans had 100 standard bhp, Ambassador Sixes 130, and both again offered power-packs adding 10 bhp.

Rambler got exposed front wheels for '55, plus an eggcrate grille and its first four-doors: sedans and Cross Country *wagons* on a new 108-inch platform (unitized, of course). Two-doors retained the original 100-inch chassis. All body styles offered a choice of Deluxe, Super, and Custom trim. Rambler had adopted larger six-cylinder engines in '53: the old 184- and 195.6-cid engines with 85 and 90 bhp, respectively. The smaller engine disappeared for 1955, but the larger one now came in 90- and 100-bhp guises.

With Ramblers still popular and Nash newly married to moribund Hudson, the 1955 Ramblers were sold through both dealer chains—with appropriate badges, naturally. The same would apply to 1955-56 Metropolitans. But this tended to obscure the fact that the big Nashes were failing as much as the big Hudsons. In a model year when almost every Detroit make did well, Statesman/Ambassador managed only slightly over 40,000 sales—lower even than the '54 tally.

Accordingly, Rambler got all the emphasis for '56 under new AMC president Romney (who took over upon Mason's death). A full outer-body reskin brought a wrapped windshield, squared eggcrate grille with inboard headlamps, blocky body lines, and colorful exteriors with optional two-tone and even three-tone paint. What's more, all Ramblers were now on the 108-inch wheelbase and had four doors. Some lacked B-posts, though, as airy hardtop sedans and Detroit's first hardtop wagons were added. Horsepower was boosted to 120 across the board. Prices were higher too, but still reasonable: $1830-$2330. Once more, Ramblers wore Nash or Hudson badges depending on which network they were sold through. About 10,000 were built for the model year, after which Rambler became a separate make (*see* Rambler).

An improved Metropolitan, the 1500, was introduced in mid-'56. That referred to the metric displacement of a 90.9-cid Austin four churning out 52 bhp, 24 percent more than the old "1200." Where early Mets did only about 70 mph tops, the 1500 could approach 80, though it was still hardly a sports car. Styling was updated by a mesh grille with a prominent new "M" medallion, a hood shorn of its dummy air scoop, and zigzag side moldings that delineated loud two-tone paint schemes. Though prices were hiked to $1500-$1600, the Met would continue to find favor through decade's end. Sales averaged 14,000 a year for 1957-58, then jumped to 22,300 for '59. But that would prove the peak. Sales dropped to 13,000 for 1960, then plunged below 1000. The Met thus departed in 1962, when a mere 412 were sold—all leftovers (production ceased in mid-1960). These cute little cars have since become "cult collectibles." Who would have thought it?

Far less unthinkable in 1956 was the end of the big Nash. That year's lineup was cut to Statesman and Ambassador Six Super sedans, plus V-8 Ambassador Super and Custom sedans and Custom Country Club. The V-8s retained Packard power through April, then became Ambassador Specials by switching to AMC's own new 250-cid with 190 bhp. Ed Anderson devised big "lollipop" taillights, extra chrome for the sides and front, and splashy duo-tone and tri-tone paint schemes, but they were little help. Model-year production plunged by two-thirds.

Nash got one more chance, but 1957 was anticlimactic. Side trim was shuffled, and headlamps not only moved back to the fenders but multiplied to stack in pairs astride a busy oval grille. Models were limited to Super and Custom Ambassador sedans and Country Clubs, with Customs often heroically overcolored. All carried a 327-cid V-8 lifted to 255 bhp by a

# Nash

four-barrel carb, dual exhausts, and 9:1 compression.

But the bell had been tolling for some time, so after 1957 production of under 3600 big cars, Nash was laid to rest alongside Hudson. It was purely a survival move. AMC was still digging out from the debts incurred with the Nash-Hudson merger, and the Rambler name had become a far more salable commodity—to say nothing of the cars. At least the Ambassador didn't die, returning as a 1958 line of stretched Ramblers once planned for Nash and Hudson.

## Specifications

### 1930

| 450 Single Six (wb 114.3)—33,118 blt | | Wght | Price | Prod |
|---|---|---|---|---|
| 456 | rdstr 2-4P | 2,550 | 975 | — |
| 458 | touring 5P | 2,650 | 995 | — |
| 452 | cpe 2P | 2,650 | 940 | — |
| 452R | cpe 2-4P | 2,700 | 980 | — |
| 451 | cabriolet 2-4P | 2,600 | 1,005 | — |
| 453 | sdn 2d | 2,750 | 935 | — |
| 450 | sdn 4d | 2,850 | 1,005 | — |
| 457 | Deluxe sdn 4d | 2,900 | 1,095 | — |
| 455 | landaulet | 2,900 | 1,155 | — |
| **480 Twin Ignition Six (wb 118.0; lwb-128.3)—17,346 built** | | | | |
| 486 | rdstr 2-4P | 3,250 | 1,365 | — |
| 488S | touring, d.c. 5P | 3,540 | 1,595 | — |
| 488 | lwb touring 7P | 3,450 | 1,475 | — |
| 482 | cpe 2P | 3,400 | 1,345 | — |
| 482R | cpe 2-4P | 3,450 | 1,395 | — |
| 481 | cabriolet 2-4P | 3,350 | 1,385 | — |
| 489 | victoria 4P | 3,400 | 1,410 | — |
| 483 | sdn 2d | 3,500 | 1,325 | — |
| 480 | sdn 4d | 3,535 | 1,415 | — |
| 484 | lwb sdn 7P | 3,750 | 1,745 | — |
| 485 | limo 7P (lwb) | 3,760 | 1,920 | — |
| **490 Twin Ignition Eight (wb 124.0; lwb-133.0)—12,801 built** | | | | |
| 498 | lwb touring 7P | 3,770 | 1,845 | — |
| 498S | lwb touring, d.c. 5P | 3,840 | 1,975 | — |
| 492 | lwb coupe 2P | 3,900 | 1,915 | — |
| 4012R | lwb coupe 2-4P | 3,945 | 1,975 | — |
| 401 | lwb cabriolet 2-4P | 3,840 | 1,875 | — |
| 493 | sdn 2d | 3,950 | 1,675 | — |
| 490 | sdn 4d | 4,000 | 1,795 | — |
| 492 | Ambassador lwb sdn | 4,050 | 2,095 | — |
| 497B | lwb Amb. Brghm trpdo sdn | 4,050 | 2,095 | — |
| 494 | lwb sedan 7P | 4,170 | 2,195 | — |
| 495 | limo 7P (lwb) | 4,210 | 2,385 | — |
| 499 | lwb victoria 5P | 3,950 | 2,045 | — |

| 1930 Engines | bore × stroke | bhp | availability |
|---|---|---|---|
| I-6, 201.3 | 3.13 × 4.38 | 60 | S-Single Six |
| I-6, 242.0 | 3.38 × 4.50 | 74 | S-T.I. Six |
| I-8, 298.6 | 3.25 × 4.50 | 100 | S-T.I. Eight |

### 1931

| 660 (wb 114.3)—12,241 built | | Wght | Price | Prod |
|---|---|---|---|---|
| 662 | cpe 2d | 2,600 | 795 | — |
| 662R | cpe 2-4P | 2,650 | 825 | — |
| 663 | sdn 2d | 2,740 | 795 | — |
| 660 | sdn 4d | 2,800 | 845 | — |
| 668 | touring 5P | 2,640 | 895 | — |
| **870 (wb 116.3)—12,116 built** | | | | |
| 872 | cpe 2P | 2,870 | 945 | — |

| 870 (wb 116.3) | | Wght | Price | Prod |
|---|---|---|---|---|
| 872R | cpe 2-4P | 2,920 | 975 | — |
| 870 | sdn 4d | 3,000 | 995 | — |
| 877 | Special sdn 4d | 3,000 | 955 | — |
| 871 | conv sdn 2d | 2,950 | 1,075 | — |
| **880 (wb 121.0)—6,830 built** | | | | |
| 882 | cpe 2P | 3,200 | 1,245 | — |
| 882R | cpe 2-4P | 3,250 | 1,285 | — |
| 880 | sdn 4d | 3,360 | 1,295 | — |
| 887 | Town sdn 4d | 3,400 | 1,375 | — |
| 881 | conv sdn 2d | 3,275 | 1,325 | — |
| **890 (wb 124.0; lwb-133.0)—6,199 built** | | | | |
| 892 | cpe 2P | 3,900 | 1,695 | — |
| 892R | cpe 2-4P | 3,950 | 1,745 | — |
| 891 | cabriolet 2-4P | 3,850 | 1,695 | — |
| 890 | lwb sedan 4d | 4,000 | 1,565 | — |
| 897 | Ambassador sdn 4d | 4,050 | 1,825 | — |
| 894 | lwb sdn 7P | 4,170 | 1,925 | — |
| 895 | limo 7P (lwb) | 4,210 | 2,025 | — |
| 899 | victoria 5P | 3,950 | 1,765 | — |
| 898 | lwb touring 7P | 3,880 | 1,595 | — |

| 1931 Engines | bore × stroke | bhp | availability |
|---|---|---|---|
| I-6, 201.3 | 3.13 × 4.38 | 65 | S-660 |
| I-8, 227.2 | 2.88 × 4.38 | 78 | S-870 |
| I-8, 240.0 | 3.00 × 4.25 | 88 | S-880 (T. Ign.) |
| I-8, 298.6 | 3.25 × 4.50 | 115 | S-890 (T. Ign.) |

### 1932

| 960 (wb 114.3)—5,787 built | | Wght | Price | Prod |
|---|---|---|---|---|
| 968 | phaeton 5P | 2,640 | 895 | — |
| 962 | cpe 2P | 2,600 | 795 | — |
| 962R | cpe 2-4P | 2,650 | 825 | — |
| 963 | sdn 2d | 2,740 | 795 | — |
| 960 | sdn 4d | 2,800 | 845 | — |
| **970 (wb 116.3)—8,201 built** | | | | |
| 972 | cpe 2P | 2,870 | 945 | — |
| 972R | cpe 2-4P | 2,920 | 975 | — |
| 970 | sdn 4d | 3,000 | 995 | — |
| 977 | Special sdn 4d | 3,000 | 955 | — |
| 971 | conv sdn 2d | 2,950 | 1,075 | — |
| **980 (wb 121.0)—5,204 built** | | | | |
| 982 | cpe 2P | 3,200 | 1,245 | — |
| 982R | cpe 2-4P | 3,250 | 1,285 | — |
| 980 | sdn 4d | 3,360 | 1,295 | — |
| 987 | Town sdn 4d | 3,400 | 1,375 | — |
| 981 | conv sdn 2d | 3,275 | 1,325 | — |
| **990 (wb 124.0; lwb 133.0)—3,900 built** | | | | |
| 998 | lwb touring 7P | 3,880 | 1,595 | — |
| 992 | cpe 2P | 3,900 | 1,695 | — |
| 992R | cpe 2-4P | 3,950 | 1,745 | — |
| 991 | cabriolet 2-4P | 3,840 | 1,695 | — |
| 999 | victoria 5P | 3,950 | 1,765 | — |
| 990 | lwb sdn 4d | 4,000 | 1,565 | — |

# Nash

| 990 (wb 124.0; lwb 133.0) | | Wght | Price | Prod |
|---|---|---|---|---|
| 996 | sdn 4d | 4,100 | 1,825 | — |
| 997 | Ambassador sdn 4d | 4,050 | 1,825 | — |
| 994 | lwb sdn 7P | 4,170 | 1,925 | — |
| 995 | limo 7P (lwb) | 4,210 | 2,025 | — |
| **1060 Big Six (wb 116.0)—6,564 built** | | | | |
| 1061 | conv rdstr 2-4P | 3,120 | 895 | — |
| 1062 | cpe 2P | 3,050 | 777 | — |
| 1062R | cpe 2-4P | 3,100 | 825 | — |
| 1060 | sdn 4d | 3,200 | 840 | — |
| 1063 | conv sdn 2d | 3,125 | 935 | — |
| 1067 | Town sdn 4d | 3,150 | 825 | — |
| **1070 Standard Eight (wb 121.0)—4,069 built** | | | | |
| 1071 | conv rdstr 2-4P | 3,270 | 1,055 | — |
| 1072 | cpe 2P | 3,250 | 1,072 | — |
| 1072R | cpe 2-4P | 3,300 | 1,015 | — |
| 1070 | sdn 4d | 3,400 | 1,015 | — |
| 1073 | conv sdn 2d | 3,275 | 1,095 | — |
| 1077 | Town sdn 4d | 3,400 | 975 | — |
| **1080 Special Eight (wb 128.0)—3,221 built** | | | | |
| 1081 | conv rdstr 2-4P | 3,750 | 1,395 | — |
| 1082 | cpe 2P | 3,710 | 1,270 | — |
| 1082R | cpe 2-4P | 3,800 | 1,320 | — |
| 1089 | victoria cpe 2d | 3,840 | 1,395 | — |
| 1080 | sdn 4d | 3,870 | 1,320 | — |
| 1083 | conv sdn 4d | 4,000 | 1,475 | — |
| **1090 Advanced Eight (wb 133.0)—1,891 built*** | | | | |
| 1091 | conv rdstr 2-4P | 4,270 | 1,795 | — |
| 1092R | cpe 2-4P | 4,300 | 1,695 | — |
| 1099 | victoria cpe 2d | 4,300 | 1,785 | — |
| 1090 | sdn 4d | 4,350 | 1,595 | — |
| 1093 | conv sdn 4d | 4,470 | 1,875 | — |
| **1090 Ambassador Eight (wb 142.0)*** | | | | |
| 1096 | sdn 4d | 4,510 | 1,855 | — |
| 1097 | brougham 4d | 4,470 | 1,855 | — |
| 1094 | sdn 7P | 4,600 | 1,955 | — |
| 1095 | limo 7P | 4,650 | 2,055 | — |

*Includes Ambassador Eight.

| 1932 Engines | bore × stroke | bhp | availability |
|---|---|---|---|
| I-6, 201.3 | 3.13 × 4.38 | 65 | S-960 |
| I-6, 201.3 | 3.13 × 4.38 | 70 | S-1060 |
| I-8, 227.2 | 2.88 × 4.38 | 78 | S-970 |
| I-8, 240.0 | 3.00 × 4.25 | 94 | S-980 (T. Ign.) |
| I-8, 247.4 | 3.00 × 4.38 | 85 | S-1070 |
| I-8, 260.8 | 3.13 × 4.25 | 100 | S-1080 (T. Ign.) |
| I-8, 298.6 | 3.25 × 4.50 | 115 | S-990 (T. Ign.) |
| I-8, 322.0 | 3.38 × 4.50 | 125 | S-1090 (T. Ign.) |

## 1933

| 1120 Big Six (wb 116.0)—4,600 built | | Wght | Price | Prod |
|---|---|---|---|---|
| 1120 | sdn 4d | 3,125 | 745 | — |
| 1121 | conv rdstr 2-4P | 3,000 | 810 | — |
| 1122 | cpe 2P | 3,000 | 725 | — |
| 1122R | cpe 2-4P | 3,050 | 745 | — |
| 1127 | Town sdn 4d | 3,125 | 695 | — |
| **1130 Standard Eight (wb 116.0)*** | | | | |
| 1130 | sdn 4d | 3,200 | 845 | — |
| 1131 | conv rdstr 2-4P | 3,050 | 900 | — |
| 1132 | cpe 2P | 3,050 | 830 | — |

| 1130 Standard Eight (wb 116.0)* | | Wght | Price | Prod |
|---|---|---|---|---|
| 1132R | cpe 2-4P | 3,100 | 845 | — |
| 1137 | Town sdn 4d | 3,175 | 830 | — |
| **1170 Special Eight (wb 121.0)*** | | | | |
| 1170 | sdn 4d | 3,400 | 1,015 | — |
| 1171 | conv rdstr 2-4P | 3,270 | 1,055 | — |
| 1172 | cpe 2P | 3,250 | 965 | — |
| 1172R | cpe 2-4P | 3,300 | 1,015 | — |
| 1173 | conv sdn 2d | 3,275 | 1,095 | — |
| 1177 | Town sdn 4d | 3,400 | 975 | — |
| **1180 Advanced Eight (wb 128.0)—780 built** | | | | |
| 1180 | sdn 4d | 3,870 | 1,320 | — |
| 1181 | conv rdstr 2-4P | 3,750 | 1,395 | — |
| 1182 | cpe 2P | 3,710 | 1,255 | — |
| 1182R | cpe 2-4P | 3,800 | 1,275 | — |
| 1183 | conv sdn 4d | 4,000 | 1,575 | — |
| 1189 | victoria 5P | 3,840 | 1,395 | — |
| **1190 Ambassador Eight (wb 133.0; lwb 142.0)—610 built** | | | | |
| 1190 | sdn 4d | 4,350 | 1,575 | — |
| 1191 | conv rdstr 2-4P | 4,270 | 1,645 | — |
| 1192R | cpe 2-4P | 4,300 | 1,545 | — |
| 1193 | conv sdn 4d | 4,470 | 1,875 | — |
| 1194 | lwb sdn 7P | 4,600 | 1,955 | — |
| 1195 | limo 7P (lwb) | 4,650 | 2,055 | — |
| 1196 | lwb sdn 4d | 4,510 | 1,855 | — |
| 1197 | lwb brougham 4d | 4,470 | 1,820 | — |
| 1199 | victoria 5P | 4,300 | 1,785 | — |

* Production not available.

| 1933 Engines | bore × stroke | bhp | availability |
|---|---|---|---|
| I-6, 217.8 | 3.25 × 4.38 | 75 | S-1120 |
| I-8, 247.4 | 3.00 × 4.38 | 80 | S-1130 |
| I-8, 247.4 | 3.00 × 4.38 | 85 | S-1170 |
| I-8, 260.8 | 3.13 × 4.25 | 100 | S-1180 (T. Ign.) |
| I-8, 322.0 | 3.38 × 4.50 | 125 | S-1190 (T. Ign.) |

## 1934—23,616 built*

| 1220 Big Six (wb 116.0) | | Wght | Price | Prod |
|---|---|---|---|---|
| 1220 | sdn 4d | 3,370 | 755 | — |
| 1222 | cpe 2P | 3,290 | 735 | — |
| 1222R | cpe 2-4P | 3,340 | 755 | — |
| 1223 | brougham 5P T/B | 3,400 | 745 | — |
| 1227 | Town sdn 4d | 3,370 | 715 | — |
| 1228 | brougham 5P | 3,400 | 785 | — |
| **1280 Advanced Eight (wb 121.0)** | | | | |
| 1280 | sdn 4d | 3,540 | 995 | — |
| 1282 | cpe 2P | 3,460 | 965 | — |
| 1285R | cpe 2-4P | 3,510 | 985 | — |
| 1283 | brougham 5P T/B | 3,570 | 995 | — |
| 1287 | Town sdn 4d | 3,540 | 965 | — |
| 1288 | brougham 5P | 3,370 | 1,025 | — |
| **1290 Ambassador Eight (wb 133.0; lwb-142.0)** | | | | |
| 1290 | sdn 4d | 4,330 | 1,475 | — |
| 1293 | sdn 4d T/B | 4,360 | 1,505 | — |
| 1294 | lwb sdn 7P | 4,590 | 1,805 | — |
| 1295 | limo 7P (lwb) | 4,640 | 1,905 | — |
| 1297 | lwb brougham 5P | 4,460 | 1,670 | — |

| 1934 Engines | bore × stroke | bhp | availability |
|---|---|---|---|
| I-6, 234.0 | 3.38 × 4.38 | 88 | S-1220 (T. Ign.) |
| I-8, 260.8 | 3.13 × 4.25 | 100 | S-1280 (T. Ign.) |
| I-8, 322.0 | 3.38 × 4.50 | 125 | S-1290 (T. Ign.) |

* Calendar-year registrations.

# Nash

## 1935—35,184 built*

| 3520 Advanced Six (wb 120.0) | Wght | Price | Prod |
|---|---|---|---|
| 3520 sdn 4d 6W | 3,630 | 875 | — |
| 3525 victoria 6P | 3,540 | 825 | — |
| **3580 Advanced Eight (wb 125.0)** | | | |
| 3580 sdn 4d 6W | 3,750 | 1,095 | — |
| 3585 victoria 6P | 3,660 | 1,045 | — |
| **3580 Ambassador Eight (wb 125.0)** | | | |
| 3588 sdn 4d 6W | 3,750 | 1,220 | — |
| 3589 victoria 6P | 3,660 | 1,170 | — |

| 1935 Engines | bore × stroke | bhp | availability |
|---|---|---|---|
| I-6, 234.8 | 3.38 × 4.38 | 90 | S-3520 |
| I-8, 260.8 | 3.13 × 4.25 | 102 | S-3580 (T. Ign.) |

*Calendar-year registrations.

## 1936—43,070 built*

| 3640 "400" New Six (wb 117.0) | Wght | Price | Prod |
|---|---|---|---|
| 3640 sdn 4d | 2,970 | 765 | — |
| 3642 bus cpe 3P | 2,900 | 675 | — |
| 3642R cpe 3-5P | 2,960 | 725 | — |
| 3643 touring victoria 6P T/B | 2,970 | 745 | — |
| 3645 victoria 6P | 2,950 | 715 | — |
| 3648 touring sdn 4d T/B | 3,000 | 790 | — |
| **3640A "400" Deluxe (wb 117.0)** | | | |
| 3640A sdn 4d | 3,020 | 765 | — |
| 3641A special cab 3-5P | 3,800 | 800 | — |
| 3642A bus cpe 3P | 2,950 | 675 | — |
| 3642A-R cpe 3-5P | 3,010 | 725 | — |
| 3643A touring victoria 6P T/B | 3,020 | 745 | — |
| 3645A victoria 5P | 3,000 | 715 | — |
| 3648 sdn 4d T/B | 3,050 | 790 | — |
| **3620 Ambassador Six (wb 125.0)** | | | |
| 3620 sdn 4d T/B | 3,710 | 885 | — |
| 3625 victoria 6P | 3,710 | 835 | — |
| **3680 Ambassador Super Eight (wb 125.0)** | | | |
| 3680 sdn 4d T/B | 3,820 | 995 | — |

| 1936 Engines | bore × stroke | bhp | availability |
|---|---|---|---|
| I-6, 234.8 | 3.38 × 4.38 | 90 | S-3640, 3640A |
| I-8, 234.8 | 3.38 × 4.38 | 93 | S-3620 |
| I-8, 260.8 | 3.13 × 4.25 | 102 | S-3680 (T. Ign.) |

*Calendar-year registrations

## 1937—85,949 built

| 3710 Lafayette 400 (wb 117.0) | Wght | Price | Prod |
|---|---|---|---|
| 3711 cabriolet 3-5P | 3,180 | 885 | — |
| 3712 bus cpe 3P | 3,140 | 740 | — |
| 3712A All-Purpose cpe | 3,160 | 805 | — |
| 3712R cpe 3-5P | 3,190 | 795 | — |
| 3713 victoria 2d 6P | 3,200 | 800 | — |
| 3718 sdn 4d T/B | 3,240 | 845 | — |
| **3720 Ambassador Six (wb 121.0)** | | | |
| 3721 cabriolet 3-5P | 3,320 | 1,040 | — |
| 3722 bus cpe 3P | 3,290 | 935 | — |
| 3722A All-Purpose cpe | 3,310 | 990 | — |
| 3722R cpe 3-5P | 3,320 | 975 | — |
| 3723 victoria 2d 6P | 3,380 | 975 | — |
| 3728 sdn 4d T/B | 3,400 | 1,025 | — |
| **3780 Ambassador Eight (wb 125.0)** | | | |
| 3781 cabriolet 3-5P | 3,640 | 1,180 | — |
| 3782 bus cpe 3P | 3,590 | 1,075 | — |
| 3782A All-Purpose cpe | 3,610 | 1,130 | — |
| 3782R cpe 3-5P | 3,640 | 1,115 | — |
| 3783 victoria 2d 6P | 3,690 | 1,115 | — |
| 3788 sdn 4d T/B | 3,720 | 1,165 | — |

| 1937 Engines | bore × stroke | bhp | availability |
|---|---|---|---|
| I-6, 234.8 | 3.38 × 4.38 | 90 | S-3710 |
| I-6, 234.8 | 3.38 × 4.38 | 105 | S-3720 |
| I-8, 260.8 | 3.13 × 4.25 | 115 | S-3780 (T. Ign.) |

## 1938—32,017 built

| 3810 Lafayette (wb 117.0) | Wght | Price | Prod |
|---|---|---|---|
| 3811 Deluxe cab 3-5P | 3,240 | 940 | — |
| 3812 Deluxe All-Purpose cpe | 3,230 | 860 | — |
| 3813 Deluxe victoria 6P | 3,290 | 855 | — |
| 3814 Deluxe bus cpe 2P | 3,160 | 820 | — |
| 3815 Master bus cpe 3P | 3,120 | 770 | — |
| 3816 Master victoria 2d 6P | 3,190 | 805 | — |
| 3817 Master sdn 4d T/B | 3,200 | 850 | — |
| 3818 Deluxe sdn 4d T/B | 3,300 | 900 | — |
| **3820 Ambassador Six (wb 121.0)** | | | |
| 3821 cabriolet 3-5P | 3,340 | 1,099 | — |
| 3822 All-Purpose cpe | 3,360 | 1,015 | — |
| 3823 victoria 6P | 3,450 | 1,000 | — |
| 3825 bus cpe 3P | 3,300 | 970 | — |
| 3828 sdn 4d T/B | 3,460 | 1,050 | — |
| **3880 Ambassador Eight (wb 125.0)** | | | |
| 3881 cabriolet 3-5P | 3,620 | 1,240 | — |
| 3882 All-Purpose cpe | 3,640 | 1,165 | — |
| 3883 victoria 6P | 3,780 | 1,150 | — |
| 3885 bus cpe 3P | 3,580 | 1,120 | — |
| 3888 sdn 4d T/B | 3,790 | 1,200 | — |

| 1938 Engines | bore × stroke | bhp | availability |
|---|---|---|---|
| I-6, 234.8 | 3.38 × 4.38 | 95 | S-3810 |
| I-6, 234.8 | 3.38 × 4.38 | 105 | S-3820 |
| I-8, 260.8 | 3.13 × 4.25 | 115 | S-3880 (T. Ign.) |

## 1939

| 3910 Lafayette (wb 117.0)—37,302 blt* | Wght | Price | Prod |
|---|---|---|---|
| 3910 Deluxe sdn 4d T/B | 3,350 | 885 | — |
| 3911 Deluxe All-Purpose cab 5P | 3,340 | 950 | — |
| 3912 Deluxe All-Purpose cpe 5P | 3,260 | 860 | — |
| 3913 Deluxe sdn 2d | 3,320 | 855 | — |
| 3914 Deluxe bus cpe 3P | 3,270 | 825 | — |
| 3915 Special bus cpe 3P | 3,200 | 770 | — |
| 3916 Special sdn 2d | 3,250 | 810 | — |
| 3917 Special sdn 4d | 3,290 | 840 | — |
| 3918 Deluxe sdn 4d | 3,350 | 855 | — |
| 3919 Special sdn 4d I/B | 3,285 | 840 | — |
| **3920 Ambassador Six (wb 121.0)—8,500 built*** | | | |
| 3920 sdn 4d T/B | 3,470 | 985 | — |
| 3921 All-Purpose cab 5P | 3,430 | 1,050 | — |
| 3922 All-Purpose cpe 5P | 3,360 | 960 | — |
| 3923 sdn 2d | 3,420 | 955 | — |
| 3925 bus cpe 3P | 3,370 | 925 | — |
| 3928 sdn 4d | 3,450 | 985 | — |
| **3980 Ambassador Eight (wb 125.0)—17,052 built*** | | | |
| 3980 sdn 4d T/B | 3,820 | 1,235 | — |

# Nash

| 3980 Ambassador Eight (wb 125.0) | Wght | Price | Prod |
|---|---|---|---|
| 3981 All-Purpose cab 5P | 3,740 | 1,295 | — |
| 3982 All-Purpose cpe 5P | 3,710 | 1,210 | — |
| 3983 sdn 2d | 3,770 | 1,205 | — |
| 3985 bus cpe 3P | 3,720 | 1,175 | — |
| 3988 sdn 4d | 3,800 | 1,235 | — |

| 1939 Engines | bore × stroke | bhp | availability |
|---|---|---|---|
| I-6, 234.8 | 3.38 × 4.38 | 99 | S-3910 |
| I-6, 234.8 | 3.38 × 4.38 | 105 | S-3920 |
| I-8, 260.8 | 3.13 × 4.25 | 115 | S-3980 (T. Ign.) |

\* Maximum possible production, derived from published serial-number spans.

## 1940—62,131 built

| Lafayette (wb 117.0) | Wght | Price | Prod |
|---|---|---|---|
| 4010 T/B sdn 4d | 3,280 | 875 | — |
| 4011 All-Purpose cabriolet | 3,310 | 975 | — |
| 4012 All-Purpose cpe | 3,190 | 850 | — |
| 4013 fstbk sdn 2d | 3,235 | 845 | — |
| 4014 bus cpe | 3,190 | 795 | — |
| 4018 fstbk sdn 4d | 3,275 | 875 | — |

| Ambassador Six (wb 121.0) | Wght | Price | Prod |
|---|---|---|---|
| 4020 T/B sdn 4d | 3,385 | 985 | — |
| 4021 All-Purpose cabriolet | 3,410 | 1,085 | — |
| 4022 All-Purpose cpe | 3,295 | 960 | — |
| 4023 fstbk sdn 2d | 3,350 | 955 | — |
| 4025 bus cpe | 3,290 | 925 | — |
| 4028 fstbk sdn 4d | 3,380 | 985 | — |

| Ambassador Eight (wb 125.0) | Wght | Price | Prod |
|---|---|---|---|
| 4080 T/B sdn 4d | 3,660 | 1,195 | — |
| 4081 All-Purpose cabriolet | 3,640 | 1,295 | — |
| 4082 All-Purpose cpe | 3,575 | 1,170 | — |
| 4083 fstbk sdn 2d | 3,260 | 1,165 | — |
| 4085 bus cpe | 3,555 | 1,135 | — |
| 4088 fstbk sdn 4d | 3,655 | 1,195 | — |

| 1940 Engines | bore × stroke | bhp | availability |
|---|---|---|---|
| I-6, 234.8 | 3.38 × 4.38 | 99 | S-Lafayette |
| I-6, 234.8 | 3.38 × 4.38 | 105 | S-Ambassador Six |
| I-8, 260.8 | 3.13 × 4.25 | 115 | S-Ambassador Eight |

## 1941—84,007 built

| 600 (wb 112.0) | Wght | Price | Prod |
|---|---|---|---|
| 4140 DeLuxe T/B sdn 4d | 2,655 | 860 | — |
| 4142 DeLuxe bus cpe | 2,500 | 783 | — |
| 4143 DeLuxe Brougham 2d | 2,575 | 810 | — |
| 4145 Special bus cpe | 2,490 | 731 | — |
| 4146 Special fstbk cpe | 2,630 | 745 | — |
| 4147 Special fstbk sdn 4d | 2,615 | 780 | — |
| 4148 DeLuxe fstbk sdn 4d | 2,630 | 810 | — |
| 4149 DeLuxe fstbk sdn 2d | 2,640 | 777 | — |

| Ambassador Six (wb 121.0) | Wght | Price | Prod |
|---|---|---|---|
| 4160 T/B sdn 4d | 3,300 | 1,065 | — |
| 4161 All-Purpose cabriolet | 3,430 | 1,130 | — |
| 4162 bus cpe | 3,180 | 940 | — |
| 4163 Brougham 2d | 3,235 | 1,009 | — |
| 4165 Special bus cpe | 3,310 | 890 | — |
| 4167 Special fstbk sdn 4d | 3,300 | 970 | — |
| 4168 fstbk sdn 4d | 3,300 | 1,020 | — |
| 4169 Special sdn 2d | 3,320 | 933 | — |

| Ambassador Eight (wb 121.0) | Wght | Price | Prod |
|---|---|---|---|
| 4180 T/B sdn 4d | 3,475 | 1,186 | — |
| 4181 All-Purpose cabriolet | 3,580 | 1,250 | — |
| 4183 DeLuxe Brougham 2d | 3,400 | 1,116 | — |
| 4187 Special fstbk sdn 4d | 3,465 | 1,091 | — |
| 4188 DeLuxe fstbk sdn 4d | 3,455 | 1,141 | — |

| 1941 Engines | bore × stroke | bhp | availability |
|---|---|---|---|
| I-6, 172.6 | 3.13 × 3.75 | 75 | S-600 |
| I-6, 234.8 | 3.38 × 4.38 | 105 | S-Ambassador Six |
| I-8, 260.8 | 3.13 × 4.25 | 115 | S-Ambassador Eight |

## 1942—31,780 built

| 600 (wb 112.0) | Wght | Price | Prod |
|---|---|---|---|
| 4240 T/B sdn 4d | 2,655 | 993 | — |
| 4242 bus cpe | 2,540 | 918 | — |
| 4243 Brougham 2d | 2,580 | 958 | — |
| 4248 fstbk sdn 4d | 2,650 | 968 | — |
| 4249 fstbk sdn 2d | 2,605 | 948 | — |

| Ambassador Six (wb 121.0) | Wght | Price | Prod |
|---|---|---|---|
| 4260 T/B sdn 4d | 3,335 | 1,069 | — |
| 4262 bus cpe | 3,200 | 994 | — |
| 4263 Brougham 2d | 3,230 | 1,034 | — |
| 4268 fstbk sdn 4d | 3,335 | 1,044 | — |
| 4269 sdn 2d | 3,285 | 1,024 | — |

| Ambassador Eight (wb 121.0) | Wght | Price | Prod |
|---|---|---|---|
| 4280 T/B sdn 4d | 3,485 | 1,119 | — |
| 4282 bus cpe | 3,350 | 1,035 | — |
| 4283 Brougham 2d | 3,385 | 1,084 | — |
| 4288 fstbk sdn 4d | 3,485 | 1,094 | — |
| 4289 fstbk sdn 2d | 3,435 | 1,065 | — |

| 1942 Engines | bore × stroke | bhp | availability |
|---|---|---|---|
| I-6, 172.6 | 3.13 × 3.75 | 75 | S-600 |
| I-6, 234.8 | 3.38 × 4.38 | 105 | S-Ambassador Six |
| I-8, 260.8 | 3.13 × 4.25 | 115 | S-Ambassador Eight |

## 1946

| 600 (wb 112.0) | Wght | Price | Prod |
|---|---|---|---|
| 4640 T/B sdn 4d | 2,740 | 1,342 | 7,300 |
| 4643 Brougham 2d | 2,685 | 1,293 | 8,500 |
| 4648 fstbk sdn 4d | 2,780 | 1,298 | 42,300 |

| Ambassador (wb 121.0) | Wght | Price | Prod |
|---|---|---|---|
| 4660 T/B sdn 4d | 3,335 | 1,511 | 3,875 |
| 4663 Brougham 2d | 3,260 | 1,453 | 4,825 |
| 4664 Suburban sdn 4d | 3,470 | 1,929 | 275 |
| 4668 fstbk sdn 4d | 3,360 | 1,469 | 26,925 |

| 1946 Engines | bore × stroke | bhp | availability |
|---|---|---|---|
| I-6, 172.6 | 3.13 × 3.75 | 82 | S-600 |
| I-6, 234.8 | 3.38 × 4.38 | 112 | S-Ambassador |

## 1947

| 600 (wb 112.0) | Wght | Price | Prod |
|---|---|---|---|
| 4740 T/B sdn 4d | 2,740 | 1,464 | 21,500 |
| 4743 Brougham 2d | 2,685 | 1,415 | 12,100 |
| 4748 fstbk sdn 4d | 2,780 | 1,420 | 27,700 |

# Nash

| Ambassador (wb 121.0) | | Wght | Price | Prod |
|---|---|---|---|---|
| 4760 | T/B sdn 4d | 3,335 | 1,809 | 15,927 |
| 4763 | Brougham 2d | 3,260 | 1,751 | 8,673 |
| 4764 | Suburban sdn 4d | 3,420 | 2,227 | 595 |
| 4788 | fstbk sdn 4d | 3,360 | 1,767 | 14,505 |

| 1947 Engines | bore × stroke | bhp | availability |
|---|---|---|---|
| I-6, 172.6 | 3.13 × 3.75 | 82 | S-600 |
| I-6, 234.8 | 3.38 × 4.38 | 112 | S-Ambassador |

## 1948

| 600 (wb 112.0) | | Wght | Price | Prod |
|---|---|---|---|---|
| 4840 | Super T/B sdn 4d | 2,786 | 1,587 | 25,103 |
| 4842 | DeLuxe bus cpe | 2,635 | 1,478 | 925 |
| 4843 | Super Brougham 2d | 2,731 | 1,538 | 11,530 |
| 4848 | Super fstbk sdn 4d | 2,826 | 1,543 | 25,044 |
| 4850 | Custom T/B sdn 4d | 2,786 | 1,776 | 346 |
| 4853 | Custom Brougham 2d | 2,731 | 1,727 | 170 |
| 4858 | Custom fstbk sdn 4d | 2,826 | 1,732 | 332 |

| Ambassador (wb 121.0) | | | | |
|---|---|---|---|---|
| 4860 | Super T/B sdn 4d | 3,387 | 1,916 | 14,248 |
| 4863 | Super Brougham 2d | 3,312 | 1,858 | 7,221 |
| 4864 | Super Suburban sdn 4d | 3,522 | 2,239 | 130 |
| 4868 | Super fstbk sdn 4d | 3,412 | 1,874 | 14,777 |
| 4870 | Custom T/B sdn 4d | 3,387 | 2,105 | 4,102 |
| 4871 | Custom cabriolet (conv) | 3,465 | 2,345 | 1,000 |
| 4873 | Custom Brougham 2d | 3,312 | 2,047 | 929 |
| 4878 | Custom fstbk sdn 4d | 3,412 | 2,063 | 4,143 |

| 1948 Engines | bore × stroke | bhp | availability |
|---|---|---|---|
| I-6, 172.6 | 3.13 × 3.75 | 82 | S-600 |
| I-6, 234.8 | 3.38 × 4.38 | 112 | S-Ambassador |

## 1949

| 600 (wb 112.0) | | Wght | Price | Prod |
|---|---|---|---|---|
| 4923 | Super Special Brham 2d | 2,960 | 1,846 | 2,564 |
| 4928 | Super Special sdn 4d | 2,950 | 1,849 | 23,606 |
| 4929 | Super Special sdn 2d | 2,935 | 1,824 | 9,605 |
| 4943 | Super Brougham 2d | 2,960 | 1,808 | 2,954 |
| 4948 | Super sdn 4d | 2,950 | 1,811 | 31,194 |
| 4949 | Super sdn 2d | 2,935 | 1,786 | 17,006 |
| 4953 | Custom Brougham 2d | 2,970 | 1,997 | 17 |
| 4958 | Custom sdn 4d | 2,985 | 2,000 | 199 |
| 4959 | Custom sdn 2d | 2,985 | 1,975 | 29 |

| Ambassador (wb 121.0) | | | | |
|---|---|---|---|---|
| 4963 | Super Brougham 2d | 3,390 | 2,191 | 1,541 |
| 4968 | Super sdn 4d | 3,385 | 2,195 | 17,960 |
| 4969 | Super sdn 2d | 3,365 | 2,170 | 4,602 |
| 4973 | Custom Brougham 2d | 3,415 | 2,359 | 1,837 |
| 4978 | Custom sdn 4d | 3,415 | 2,363 | 6,539 |
| 4979 | Custom sdn 2d | 3,400 | 2,338 | 691 |
| 4993 | Super Special Brham 2d | 3,390 | 2,239 | 807 |
| 4998 | Super Special sdn 4d | 3,385 | 2,243 | 6,777 |
| 4999 | Super Special sdn 2d | 3,365 | 2,218 | 2,072 |

| 1949 Engines | bore × stroke | bhp | availability |
|---|---|---|---|
| I-6, 172.6 | 3.13 × 3.75 | 82 | S-600 |
| I-6, 234.8 | 3.38 × 4.38 | 112 | S-Ambassador |

## 1950

| Rambler (wb 100.0) | | Wght | Price | Prod |
|---|---|---|---|---|
| 5021 | Custom Landau conv cpe | 2,430 | 1,808 | 9,330 |
| 5024 | Custom wgn 2d | 2,515 | 1,808 | 1,712 |

| Statesman (wb 112.0) | | | | |
|---|---|---|---|---|
| 5032 | DeLuxe bus cpe | 2,830 | 1,633 | 1,198 |
| 5043 | Super club cpe | 2,940 | 1,735 | 1,489 |
| 5048 | Super sdn 4d | 2,965 | 1,738 | 60,090 |
| 5049 | Super sdn 2d | 2,930 | 1,713 | 34,196 |
| 5053 | Custom club cpe | 2,965 | 1,894 | 132 |
| 5058 | Custom sdn 4d | 2,990 | 1,897 | 11,500 |
| 5059 | Custom sdn 2d | 2,950 | 1,872 | 2,693 |

| Ambassador (wb 121.0) | | | | |
|---|---|---|---|---|
| 5063 | Super club cpe | 3,335 | 2,060 | 716 |
| 5068 | Super sdn 4d | 3,350 | 2,064 | 27,523 |
| 5069 | Super sdn 2d | 3,325 | 2,039 | 7,237 |
| 5073 | Custom club cpe | 3,385 | 2,219 | 108 |
| 5078 | Custom sdn 4d | 3,390 | 2,223 | 12,427 |
| 5079 | Custom sdn 2d | 3,365 | 2,198 | 1,045 |

| 1950 Engines | bore × stroke | bhp | availability |
|---|---|---|---|
| I-6, 172.6 | 3.13 × 3.75 | 82 | S-Rambler |
| I-6, 184.0 | 3.13 × 4.00 | 82 | S-Statesman |
| I-6, 234.8 | 3.38 × 4.38 | 112 | S-Ambassador |

## 1951

| Rambler (wb 100.0) | | Wght | Price | Prod |
|---|---|---|---|---|
| 5114 | Super Suburban wgn 2d | 2,515 | 1,885 | 5,569 |
| 5121 | Custom conv cpe | 2,430 | 1,993 | 15,259 |
| 5124 | Custom wgn 2d | 2,515 | 1,993 | 28,618 |
| 5127 | Custom Cntry Club htp cpe | 2,420 | 1,968 | 19,317 |

| Statesman (wb 112.0) | | | | |
|---|---|---|---|---|
| 5132 | DeLuxe bus cpe | 2,835 | 1,841 | 52 |
| 5143 | Super club cpe | 2,935 | 1,952 | 152 |
| 5148 | Super sdn 4d | 2,970 | 1,955 | 52,325 |
| 5149 | Super sdn 2d | 2,930 | 1,928 | 22,261 |
| 5153 | Custom club cpe | 2,950 | 2,122 | 38 |
| 5158 | Custom sdn 4d | 2,990 | 2,125 | 18,846 |
| 5159 | Custom sdn 2d | 2,940 | 2,099 | 2,141 |

| Ambassador (wb 121.0) | | | | |
|---|---|---|---|---|
| 5163 | Super club cpe | 3,370 | 2,326 | 40 |
| 5168 | Super sdn 4d | 3,410 | 2,330 | 34,935 |
| 5169 | Super sdn 2d | 3,370 | 2,304 | 4,382 |
| 5173 | Custom club cpe | 3,395 | 2,496 | 37 |
| 5178 | Custom sdn 4d | 3,445 | 2,501 | 21,071 |
| 5179 | Custom sdn 2d | 3,380 | 2,474 | 1,118 |

| 1951 Engines | bore × stroke | bhp | availability |
|---|---|---|---|
| I-6, 172.6 | 3.13 × 3.75 | 82 | S-Rambler |
| I-6, 184.0 | 3.13 × 4.00 | 85 | S-Statesman |
| I-6, 234.8 | 3.38 × 4.38 | 115 | S-Ambassador |

## 1952

| Rambler (wb 100.0) | | Wght | Price | Prod |
|---|---|---|---|---|
| 5214 | Super Suburban wgn 2d | 2,515 | 2,003 | 2,970 |
| 5221 | Custom conv cpe | 2,430 | 2,119 | 3,108 |
| 5224 | Custom wgn 2d | 2,515 | 2,119 | 19,889 |
| 5227 | Custom Cntry Club htp cpe | 2,420 | 2,094 | 25,784 |

| Statesman (wb 114.3) | | | | |
|---|---|---|---|---|
| 5245 | Super sdn 4d | 3,045 | 2,178 | 27,304 |
| 5246 | Super sdn 2d | 3,025 | 2,144 | 6,795 |

## Nash

| Statesman (wb 114.3) | | Wght | Price | Prod |
|---|---|---|---|---|
| 5255 | Custom sdn 4d | 3,070 | 2,332 | 13,660 |
| 5256 | Custom sdn 2d | 3,050 | 2,310 | 1,872 |
| 5257 | Custom Cntry Club htp cpe | 3,095 | 2,433 | 869 |
| **Ambassador (wb 121.3)** | | | | |
| 5265 | Super sdn 4d | 3,430 | 2,557 | 16,838 |
| 5266 | Super sdn 2d | 3,410 | 2,521 | 1,871 |
| 5275 | Custom sdn 4d | 3,480 | 2,716 | 19,585 |
| 5276 | Custom sdn 2d | 3,450 | 2,695 | 1,178 |
| 5277 | Custom Cntry Club htp cpe | 3,550 | 2,829 | 1,228 |

| 1952 Engines | bore × stroke | bhp | availability |
|---|---|---|---|
| I-6, 172.6 | 3.13 × 3.75 | 82 | S-Rambler |
| I-6, 195.6 | 3.13 × 4.25 | 88 | S-Statesman |
| I-6, 252.6 | 3.50 × 4.38 | 120 | S-Ambassador |

### 1953

| Rambler (wb 100.0) | | Wght | Price | Prod |
|---|---|---|---|---|
| 5314 | Super Suburban wgn 2d | 2,555 | 2,003 | 1,114 |
| 5321 | Custom conv cpe | 2,590 | 2,150 | 3,284 |
| 5324 | Custom wgn 2d | 2,570 | 2,119 | 10,571 |
| 5327 | Custom Cntry Club htp cpe | 2,550 | 2,125 | 16,809 |
| **Statesman (wb 114.3)** | | | | |
| 5345 | Super sdn 4d | 3,045 | 2,178 | 28,445 |
| 5346 | Super sdn 2d | 3,025 | 2,143 | 7,999 |
| 5355 | Custom sdn 4d | 3,070 | 2,332 | 11,476 |
| 5356 | Custom sdn 2d | 3,050 | 2,310 | 1,305 |
| 5357 | Custom Cntry Club htp cpe | 3,095 | 2,433 | 7,025 |
| **Ambassador (wb 121.3)** | | | | |
| 5365 | Super sdn 4d | 3,430 | 2,557 | 12,489 |
| 5366 | Super sdn 2d | 3,410 | 2,521 | 1,273 |
| 5375 | Custom sdn 4d | 3,480 | 2,716 | 12,222 |
| 5376 | Custom sdn 2d | 3,450 | 2,695 | 428 |
| 5377 | Custom Cntry Club htp cpe | 3,550 | 2,829 | 6,438 |

| 1953 Engines | bore × stroke | bhp | availability |
|---|---|---|---|
| I-6, 184.0 | 3.13 × 4.00 | 85 | S-Rambler manual |
| I-6, 195.6 | 3.13 × 4.25 | 90 | S-Rambler automatic |
| I-6, 195.6 | 3.13 × 4.25 | 100 | S-Statesman |
| I-6, 252.6 | 3.50 × 4.38 | 120 | S-Ambassador |
| I-6, 252.6 | 3.50 × 4.38 | 140 | O-Ambassador |

### 1954

| Rambler (wb 100.0; 4d-108.0) | | Wght | Price | Prod |
|---|---|---|---|---|
| 5406 | DeLuxe sdn 2d | 2,425 | 1,550 | 7,273 |
| 5414 | Super Suburban wgn 2d | 2,520 | 1,800 | 504 |
| 5415 | Super sdn 4d | 2,570 | 1,795 | 4,313 |
| 5416 | Super sdn 2d | 2,425 | 1,700 | 300 |
| 5417 | Super Cntry Club htp cpe | 2,465 | 1,800 | 1,071 |
| 5421 | Custom conv cpe | 2,555 | 1,980 | 221 |
| 5424 | Custom wgn 2d | 2,535 | 1,950 | 2,202 |
| 5425 | Custom sdn 4d | 2,630 | 1,965 | 7,640 |
| 5427 | Custom Cntry Club htp cpe | 2,515 | 1,950 | 3,612 |
| 5428 | Cus Cross Cntry wgn 4d | 2,715 | 2,050 | 9,039 |
| **Statesman (wb 114.3)** | | | | |
| 5445 | Super sdn 4d | 3,045 | 2,158 | 11,401 |
| 5446 | Super sdn 2d | 3,025 | 2,110 | 1,855 |
| 5455 | Custom sdn 4d | 3,095 | 2,332 | 4,219 |
| — | Custom sdn 2d | 3,050 | 2,310 | 24 |
| 5457 | Custom Cntry Club htp cpe | 3,120 | 2,423 | 2,276 |

| Ambassador (wb 121.3) | | Wght | Price | Prod |
|---|---|---|---|---|
| 5465 | Super sdn 4d | 3,430 | 2,417 | 7,433 |
| 5466 | Super sdn 2d | 3,410 | 2,365 | 283 |
| 5475 | Custom sdn 4d | 3,505 | 2,600 | 10,131 |
| 5477 | Custom Cntry Club htp cpe | 3,575 | 2,735 | 3,581 |

| 1954 Engines | bore × stroke | bhp | availability |
|---|---|---|---|
| I-6, 184.0 | 3.13 × 4.00 | 85 | S-Rambler 2dr manual |
| I-6, 195.6 | 3.13 × 4.25 | 90 | S-Rambler 4dr, 2dr automatic |
| I-6, 195.6 | 3.13 × 4.25 | 110 | S-Statesman |
| I-6, 252.6 | 3.50 × 4.38 | 130 | S-Ambassador |
| I-6, 252.6 | 3.50 × 4.38 | 140 | O-Ambassador |

### 1955

| Rambler (wb 100.0; 4d-108.0)-56,000 blt* | | Wght | Price | Prod |
|---|---|---|---|---|
| 5512 | Fleet bus sdn 2d | 2,400 | — | — |
| 5514 | DeLuxe Suburban wgn 2d | 2,528 | 1,771 | — |
| 5514-1 | Super Suburban wgn 2d | 2,532 | 1,869 | — |
| 5515 | DeLuxe sdn 4d | 2,567 | 1,695 | — |
| 5515-1 | Super sdn 4d | 2,570 | 1,798 | — |
| 5515-2 | Custom sdn 4d | 2,606 | 1,989 | — |
| 5516 | DeLuxe sdn 2d | 2,432 | 1,585 | — |
| 5516-1 | Super sdn 2d | 2,450 | 1,683 | — |
| 5517-2 | Custom Cntry Club htp cpe | 2,518 | 1,995 | — |
| 5518-1 | Fleet Cross Cntry wgn 4d | 2,675 | — | — |
| 5518-2 | Cus Cross Cntry wgn 4d | 2,685 | 2,098 | — |
| 2504 | Fleet util wgn 2d | 2,500 | — | — |
| **Statesman (wb 114.3)—14,300 built*** | | | | |
| 5545-1 | Super sdn 4d | 3,134 | 2,215 | — |
| 5545-2 | Custom sdn 4d | 3,204 | 2,385 | — |
| 5547-2 | Custom Cntry Club htp cpe | 3,220 | 2,495 | — |
| **Ambassador Six (wb 121.3)—15,200 built*** | | | | |
| 5565-1 | Super sdn 4d | 3,538 | 2,480 | — |
| 5565-2 | Custom sdn 4d | 3,576 | 2,675 | — |
| 5567-2 | Cus Cntry Club htp cpe | 3,593 | 2,795 | — |
| **Ambassador Eight (wb 121.3)—10,600 built*** | | | | |
| 5585-1 | Super sdn 4d | 3,795 | 2,775 | — |
| 5585-2 | Custom sdn 4d | 3,827 | 2,965 | — |
| 5587-2 | Custom Cntry Club htp cpe | 3,839 | 3,095 | — |

*To nearest 100.

| 1955 Engines | bore × stroke | bhp | availability |
|---|---|---|---|
| I-6, 195.6 | 3.13 × 4.25 | 90 | S-Rambler exc Fleet |
| I-6, 195.6 | 3.13 × 4.25 | 100 | S-Rambler Fleet, Statesman manual |
| I-6, 195.6 | 3.13 × 4.25 | 110 | S-Statesman auto |
| I-6, 252.6 | 3.50 × 4.38 | 130 | S-Ambassador Six |
| I-6, 252.6 | 3.50 × 4.38 | 140 | O-Ambassador Six |
| V-8, 320.0 | 3.81 × 3.50 | 208 | S-Ambassador Eight |

### 1956

| Rambler (wb 108.0)* | | Wght | Price | Prod |
|---|---|---|---|---|
| 5613-2 | Cus Crs Cntry htp wgn 4d | 3,095 | 2,494 | — |
| 5615 | DeLuxe sdn 4d | 2,891 | 1,829 | — |
| 5615-1 | Super sdn 4d | 2,906 | 1,939 | — |
| 5615-2 | Custom sdn 4d | 2,929 | 2,059 | — |
| 5618-1 | Super Cross Cntry wgn 4d | 2,992 | 2,233 | — |
| 5618-2 | Cus Cross Cntry wgn 4d | 3,110 | 2,329 | — |

703

# Nash

| Rambler (wb 108.0)* | | Wght | Price | Prod |
|---|---|---|---|---|
| 5619-1 | Custom htp sdn | 2,990 | 2,224 | — |
| **Statesman (wb 114.3)*** | | | | |
| 5645-1 | Super sdn 4d | 3,134 | 2,139 | — |
| **Ambassador Special (wb 114.3)—4,145 built*** | | | | |
| 5657-1 | sdn 4d | 3,397 | 2,355 | — |
| 5657-2 | Country Club htp cpe | 3,418 | 2,462 | — |
| 5657-3 | Custom sdn 4d | 3,567 | 2,541 | — |
| **Ambassador Six (wb 121.3)*** | | | | |
| 5665-1 | Super sdn 4d | 3,555 | 2,425 | — |
| **Ambassador Eight (wb 121.3)*** | | | | |
| 5685-1 | Super sdn 4d | 3,748 | 2,716 | — |
| 5685-2 | Custom sdn 4d | 3,846 | 2,939 | — |
| 5687-2 | Cus Cntry Club htp cpe | 3,854 | 3,072 | — |

*Estimated Rambler production: 10,000; total Statesman/Ambassador: 14,352.

| 1956 Engines | bore × stroke | bhp | availability |
|---|---|---|---|
| I-6, 195.6 | 3.13 × 4.25 | 120 | S-Rambler, Statesman |
| I-6, 252.6 | 3.50 × 4.38 | 130 | S-Ambassador Six |
| I-6, 252.6 | 3.50 × 4.38 | 140 | O-Ambassador Six |
| V-8, 250.0 | 3.50 × 3.25 | 190 | S-Ambassador Special |
| V-8, 352.0 | 4.00 × 3.33 | 200 | S-Ambassador Eight |

## 1957*

| Ambassador Super (wb 121.3) | | Wght | Price | Prod |
|---|---|---|---|---|
| 5785-1 | sdn 4d | 3,639 | 2,586 | — |
| 5787-1 | Country Club htp cpe | 3,655 | 2,670 | — |
| **Ambassador Custom (wb 121.3)** | | | | |
| 5785-2 | sdn 4d | 3,701 | 2,763 | — |
| 5787-2 | Country Club htp cpe | 3,722 | 2,847 | — |

* Approximate model-year production: 3,600.

| 1957 Engine | bore × stroke | bhp | availability |
|---|---|---|---|
| V-8, 327.0 | 4.00 × 3.25 | 255 | S-all |

Note: See Rambler listing for 1957 and later models.

## Nash Metropolitan Specifications

### 1954

| Series 54 (wb 85.0)—11,198 built* | | Wght | Price | Prod |
|---|---|---|---|---|
| 541 | conv cpe 3P | 1,803 | 1,469 | — |
| 542 | cpe 3P | 1,843 | 1,445 | — |

* Includes 571 shipments in 1953.

| 1954 Engine | bore × stroke | bhp | availability |
|---|---|---|---|
| I-4, 73.8 | 2.56 × 3.50 | 42 | S-all |

### 1955

| Series 54 (wb 85.0)—3,849 built | | Wght | Price | Prod |
|---|---|---|---|---|
| 541 | conv cpe 3P | 1,803 | 1,469 | — |
| 542 | cpe 3P | 1,843 | 1,445 | — |

| 1955 Engine | bore × stroke | bhp | availability |
|---|---|---|---|
| I-4, 73.8 | 2.56 × 3.50 | 42 | S-all |

### 1956—7,645 built

| Series 54 (wb 85.0) | | Wght | Price | Prod |
|---|---|---|---|---|
| 541 | conv cpe 3P | 1,803 | 1,469 | — |
| 542 | cpe 3P | 1,843 | 1,445 | — |
| **Series 56 "1500" (wb 85.0)** | | | | |
| 561 | conv cpe 3P | 1,803 | 1,551 | — |
| 562 | cpe 3P | 1,843 | 1,527 | — |

| 1956 Engines | bore × stroke | bhp | availability |
|---|---|---|---|
| I-4, 73.8 | 2.56 × 3.50 | 42 | S-Series 54 (1200) |
| I-4, 90.9 | 2.88 × 3.50 | 52 | S-Series 56 (1500) |

### 1957

| Series 56 "1500" (wb 85.0)—13,425 blt | | Wght | Price | Prod |
|---|---|---|---|---|
| 561 | conv cpe 3P | 1,803 | 1,591 | — |
| 562 | cpe 3P | 1,843 | 1,567 | — |

| 1957 Engine | bore × stroke | bhp | availability |
|---|---|---|---|
| I-4, 90.9 | 2.88 × 3.50 | 52 | S-all |

### 1958

| Series 56 "1500" (wb 85.0)—11,951 blt | | Wght | Price | Prod |
|---|---|---|---|---|
| 561 | conv cpe 3P | 1,835 | 1,650 | — |
| 562 | cpe 3P | 1,875 | 1,626 | — |

| 1958 Engine | bore × stroke | bhp | availability |
|---|---|---|---|
| I-4, 90.9 | 2.88 × 3.50 | 52 | S-all |

### 1959

| Series 56 "1500" (wb 85.0)—20,435 blt | | Wght | Price | Prod |
|---|---|---|---|---|
| 561 | conv cpe 3P | 1,835 | 1,650 | — |
| 562 | cpe 3P | 1,875 | 1,626 | — |

| 1959 Engine | bore × stroke | bhp | availability |
|---|---|---|---|
| I-4, 90.9 | 2.88 × 3.50 | 55/52 | S-all |

### 1960

| Series 56 "1500" (wb 85.0)—13,103 blt | | Wght | Price | Prod |
|---|---|---|---|---|
| 561 | conv cpe 3P | 1,850 | 1,697 | — |
| 562 | cpe 3P | 1,890 | 1,673 | — |

| 1960 Engine | bore × stroke | bhp | availability |
|---|---|---|---|
| I-4, 90.9 | 2.88 × 3.50 | 55/52 | S-all |

### 1961

| Series 56 "1500" (wb 85.0)—853 blt | | Wght | Price | Prod |
|---|---|---|---|---|
| 561 | conv cpe 3P | 1,850 | 1,697 | — |
| 562 | cpe 3P | 1,890 | 1,673 | — |

| 1961 Engine | bore × stroke | bhp | availability |
|---|---|---|---|
| I-4, 90.9 | 2.88 × 3.50 | 55/52 | S-all |

### 1962

| Series 56 "1500" (wb 85.0)—412 blt | | Wght | Price | Prod |
|---|---|---|---|---|
| 561 | conv cpe 3P | 1,850 | 1,697 | — |
| 562 | cpe 3P | 1,890 | 1,673 | — |

| 1962 Engine | bore × stroke | bhp | availability |
|---|---|---|---|
| I-4, 90.9 | 2.88 × 3.50 | 55/52 | S-all |

Note: Metropolitans were built in England but marketed by American Motors as Nash and Hudson models. See 1955-57 Hudson listings for additional Metropolitan models. Sold with "Metropolitan" badge 1958-62.

# Oldsmobile

There was a time when Oldsmobile, not Chevy or Ford, was America's leading car producer. That time was 1903-05, when Lansing rolled to success with Ransom Eli Olds' little curved-dash runabout, which was then selling in the thousands annually. Ransom had cobbled up his first car in 1891, strictly as an experiment. But regular production got under way in 1897, the same year the Olds Motor Vehicle Company was formed. (The concern was reorganized as Olds Motor Works two years later.) Ultimately, Oldsmobile became the only American automaker founded in the 19th century to survive into the 21st.

A decline set in soon after Ransom left to form Reo in 1904 (see Reo). General Motors bought Olds Motor Works four years later, but that didn't help sales right way. Not until its side-valve V-8 of 1916 did Oldsmobile again do healthy business. The make's best pre-Depression years were 1919, 1921, and 1929, when it finished ninth on the industry chart. Its worst model year during the Depression was 1932: only 18,846 cars. But the division recovered rapidly, notching more than 191,000 sales for 1936. A recession cut 1938 output to 85,000, but Olds rallied quickly, then reached a new high with 1941 domestic volume of nearly 266,000. It would do far better in the '50s, '60s, and '70s.

Innovation was an Olds hallmark in the '30s, the make (among others) pioneering Dubonnet-type "Knee-Action" independent front suspension for '34, a semiautomatic transmission for 1937-39, and a full-shifting Hydra-Matic Drive for '40 models. It was these features that earned Olds its longtime reputation as GM's "experimental" division, a role it would play through the late '60s.

Much of Oldsmobile's technical daring in the '30s was spurred by Charles L. McCuen, who had been chief engineer before becoming division general manager in 1933. To take his place as chief engineer he recruited another innovator, Harold T. Youngren. Working under him were experimental engineering manager Jack Wolfram and dynamometer wizard Harold Metzel. The last two became division chiefs in later years. Youngren left in 1946 to help develop Ford's engineering department.

Oldsmobile suffered less from the Depression than most other makes, thanks to conservative but salable styling and a fairly consistent lineup of six- and eight-cylinder models. Its

1930 Series F-30 DeLuxe Six four-door sedan

1932 Series L-32 Eight four-door sedan

1930 Viking Eight DeLuxe convertible coupe

1933 Series F-33 Six four-door sedan

1931 Series F-31 DeLuxe convertible roadster

1934 Series F-34 Six sport coupe 2/4 passenger

# Oldsmobile

L-head six began the decade at 197.5 cubic inches and 62-65 horsepower. Olds' first straight-eight, another orthodox sidevalve design, arrived for 1932 with 240 cubic inches and 87 bhp. These smooth, quiet, and reliable powerplants received important improvements as the decade wore on, such as aluminum pistons for 1936. The eight was otherwise unchanged, but the six grew to 213.3 cid and 74 bhp for 1932.

A major redesign for 1937 took the six to 230 cid and 95 bhp, the eight to 257 cid and 110 bhp. Additional changes that year comprised full-length water jackets, stiffer piston skirts and crankshaft, stronger cams and valve lifters, and longer valve guides. So modified, the eight continued in this form through 1948, after which time it was honorably retired for the history-making overhead-valve "Rocket" V-8. The six would remain unchanged through 1940.

Oldsmobile's 1930s styling followed general industry trends: classically square through '32; slightly streamlined, with angled radiator and skirted fenders for 1933-34; "potato" shapes for 1935-36. After that, the pace of change picked up. Though the division used the same GM B-body as Cadillac's junior-edition LaSalle and the smaller Buicks, its cars managed to look quite individual. More-massive fronts with cross-hatched or horizontal-bar grilles appeared for 1937; the 1938-39s had GM design chief Harley Earl's flanking "catwalk" auxiliary grilles, plus headlamp pods partly faired into the front-fender aprons.

**1935 Series F-35 Six four-door station wagon**

**1936 Series F-36 Six 2/4 passenger convertible coupe**

**1937 Series F-37 Six 2/4 passenger convertible coupe**

Prices in these years were carefully contrived to target a precise area above Pontiac and below Buick and LaSalle. The range was $900-$1100 through 1932, after which Depression-prompted cuts lowered Sixes to as little as $650 by '34. Prices then inched upward again, returning to the initial spread by '38.

Beside choices in wheelbase, engine, and trim, Olds offered styling options such as sidemount spare tires and—a bit ahead of most rivals—trunkless or "trunkback" sedans starting in 1933. Two notable body innovations were Fisher's "No-Draft" front-door ventwing windows from 1934 and all-steel "Turret-Top" roof construction from 1935. Convertible coupes were always low-production items. Oddly enough, considering its pioneer ways, Olds was relatively slow to abandon sidemounts and rumble-seat body styles, persisting doggedly with both through 1938.

Lansing's 1930-31 line comprised popular period styles in Standard, Special, and Deluxe trim, all on a 113.5-inch wheelbase. Trim variations then disappeared for 1932, when the Eight arrived and wheelbase grew to 116.5 inches across the board. Thereafter, Eights were mounted on chassis of 119 inches (1933-34), 121 inches (1935-36), and 124 inches (1937-38). Sixes rode a 115-inch platform from 1933 through 1936 except for '34, when they mysteriously lost an inch; they then graduated to a 117-inch length.

The two transmission innovations noted earlier deserve special comment. The first was "Automatic Safety Transmission" for 1937. This was a semiautomatic four-speed unit for eight-cylinder models that worked like, but was not mechanically identical to, Chrysler's subsequent Fluid Drive. Before moving off, the driver depressed the usual clutch pedal and selected Low or High range. The transmission then shifted between first and second in Low; or first, third, and fourth in High. Changes within each range were automatic via oil pressure and two planetary gearsets. Shift points were preset according to vehicle speed.

Olds said AST delivered up to 15-percent-better gas mileage than regular manual shift, but that was due to the numerically lower rear-axle ratio specified. The "safety" aspect referred to the claim that with less shifting to do, the driver could keep both hands on the wheel more of the time. AST became an option for all 1938-39 Oldsmobiles, and some 28,000 were installed. But its real significance led to Hydra-Matic for 1940.

Though Hydra-Matic also had four speeds, it was, of course, fully automatic, using a fluid coupling and a complex system of clutches and brake bands. It arrived at only $57 extra. That surely didn't reflect its true manufacturing or development costs, but both would be offset by high volume. Indeed, by the early '50s, Hydra-Matic had become not only a popular Olds option, but was also being offered by Cadillac and Pontiac as well as Lincoln and independents Nash, Hudson, and Kaiser-Frazer.

Oldsmobile's 1939 line boasted newly styled bodies in three groups: 115-inch-wheelbase Series 60, new 120-inch Series 70, and the similarly sized eight-cylinder Series 80. The 70 was powered by the 230 six, but a 90 bhp 216-cid six drove the 60. All three listed business and club coupes and two- and four-door sedans, the latter available in the two upper lines with "Sunshine Turret Top," an optional sliding-metal sunroof that saw few installations. The 70 and 80 also included a convertible coupe. Prices ranged from $777 to $1119.

This basic lineup repeated for 1940 with slightly higher prices, reassigned wheelbases, somewhat smoother looks, and two new models. The 60 now rode a 116-inch platform, adopted the 230-cube six, and included a structural-wood station wagon bodied by Hercules. Replacing the 80 was a new 124-inch-wheelbase Series 90 that included Oldsmobile's first convertible sedan—called "phaeton" per GM practice—an odd latecomer, considering this body type was fast waning at other outfits. At $1570, the Series 90 phaeton was the costliest 1940 Olds, and production was predictably limited: just 50 in all. Styling throughout the line was typical of GM that year, with wider grilles and front fenders, semi-integrated headlights, and, on the 90s, smoother tails and rear rooflines.

A more-massive look arrived for 1941. Grillework was lower and wider, and headlights now firmly resided within even wider front fenders that blended more smoothly into the bodysides. Series doubled as Olds offered both six and straight-eight models in two trim levels spanning a narrower $852-$1575 price range. Series designations denoted cylinders. The low-end Special 66 and 68 rode a new 119-inch wheelbase, while the Dynamic Cruiser 76 and 78 shared a 125-inch chassis with the top-line Custom Cruiser 96 and 98. The six was bored out to 238.1 cid for 100 bhp.

Though Olds repeated body styles for '41, all but one were now available with either engine. The sole exception was the phaeton convertible sedan, which came only as a Custom Cruiser 98. Its production was again minuscule at only 119 for the model year, after which the division followed everyone else by dropping four-door convertibles. Fastback styling bowed in new Dynamic Cruiser four-door and club sedans. Four-door Custom Cruiser sedans again sported a handsome notchback profile with semiclosed rear-roof quarters. In March, the 66/68 expanded by adding a four-door town sedan with styling like the Series 90 model. Despite record model-year production, Olds finished sixth in the annual industry race. Though the division had risen as high as fifth for '36, it would usually run sixth or seventh into the mid-'50s.

Olds slipped to seventh for war-shortened 1942, but enjoyed respectable volume of just under 68,000 units. Styling for this year's "B-44" line featured "Fuselage Fenders"—elongated pontoon types faired into the front doors—and a busy, two-tier "double-duty" grille bisected by a prominent horizontal bar. Longer back fenders tapered beyond the rear deck, but remained bolt-on components. Engines stayed the same, but not models. The six-cylinder 96 departed and the remaining 98 was cut to convertible coupe, club sedan, and four-door sedan on a new 127-inch wheelbase. All series now offered torpedo-style club sedans, with plain and Deluxe versions for 76/78.

To help win World War II, Oldsmobile turned out 350,000 precision aero-engine parts, 175 million pounds of gun forgings, 140,000 machine guns, and millions of rounds of ammunition. It officially became the Oldsmobile Division of General Motors on New Year's Day 1942, thus ousting the Olds Motor Works title that dated from 1899.

Like most everyone else, Olds returned to peacetime with warmed-over prewar cars. Business was good in the sell-any-

**1938 Series L-38 Eight trunkback touring sedan**

**1940 Series 90 convertible phaeton**

**1939 Series 70 2/4-passenger club coupe**

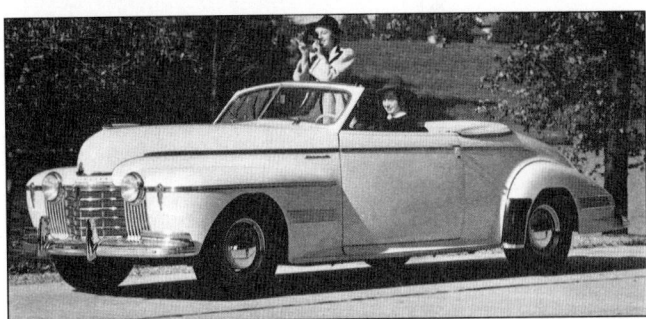
**1941 Custom Cruiser Series 90 convertible**

**1940 Series 60 four-door station wagon**

**1941 Series 78 Dynamic Cruiser two-door club sedan**

# Oldsmobile

thing market of the day—close to 118,000 for 1946 and about 200,000 for '47—yet Olds again ran seventh. Most '42 offerings immediately returned with no changes in wheelbase, engines, or body styles. An exception was the Series 68, which wasn't reinstated until 1947. Prices did change in a big way, thanks to postwar inflation. The cheapest '47 Olds, the 66 club coupe, sold for $1407, and the 98 convertible topped the line at more than $2000.

Styling was cleaned up via a four-bar grille shaped like a wide, upside-down U; a shield-type hood medallion rode above it. Front fender moldings were enlarged for '47. Hydra-Matic was increasingly popular, and Olds began producing more self-shift cars as a percentage of total volume than any other make.

Though called "Dynamic," the '48 Oldsmobiles saw only detail changes: round hood medallion, "Oldsmobile" spelled in block letters below, and full-length chrome rocker-panel moldings. Then, in February, Olds got a jump on most rivals with the "Futuramic" 98, arriving simultaneously with similar styling from Cadillac as GM's first all-new postwar models. Both were created by Harley Earl's Art & Colour staff with inspiration from the Lockheed P-38 fighter aircraft (well-known for having prompted Cadillac's new 1948 tailfins). The 98s comprised a convertible, four-door sedan, and fastback club sedan that were beautifully shaped to look longer and lower despite a slightly trimmer new 125-inch wheelbase. Sedans offered a choice of standard and deluxe trim. Prices ranged from $1920 for the base two-door to $2466 for the Deluxe-only convertible. The public responded strongly to the '48 Oldsmobiles, particularly the 98s, which saw better than 65,000 sales. More than half were four-door sedans.

Olds followed up with Futuramic styling for all 1949 models, plus two new innovations. One was the landmark overhead-valve "Rocket" V-8 designed by Gilbert Burrell. Again, Olds shared honors with Cadillac, which also had a new high-compression V-8 that year, though it was developed independently of Lansing's. Both divisions had been encouraged to outdo each other, and Cadillac actually raised displacement to maintain a "proper distance" from Oldsmobile's V-8. The Rocket arrived at 303.7 cid; Cadillac had started at 309, then went to 331 cid.

A five-main-bearing unit with oversquare cylinder dimensions, the Rocket was initially rated at 135 bhp. Putting it in the lighter 119.5-inch chassis of the six-cylinder 76 created a new Futuramic 88 with power-to-weight ratios of about 22.5 pound/horsepower—quite good for the time. Torque was also impressive at 263 pound-feet. Initial compression was a mild 7.25:1, but the Rocket was designed for ratios as high as 12:1. Engineers had anticipated postwar fuels with ultrahigh octane, though levels never became quite high enough to make such ratios practical.

Management had originally planned the Rocket only for the 98, but dropping it into the smaller B-body was a natural move, and the 88 soon began rewriting the stock-car racing record

1942 Series 68 Special two-door club sedan

1946 Series F-46 Special 66 convertible coupe

1947 Series L-47 Custom Cruiser 98 convertible coupe

1947 Series J-47 Dynamic Cruiser 76 two-door club sedan

1948 Futuramic 98 DeLuxe convertible coupe

1948 Futuramic 98 DeLuxe four-door sedan

book. Meanwhile, the Olds six was enlarged to the old eight's 257.1 cid for 105 bhp. It continued through 1950, after which Olds offered nothing but V-8s.

Oldsmobile's other '49 innovation was the 98 Holiday, a new $2973 pillarless coupe that bowed alongside the Buick Riviera and Cadillac Coupe de Ville as America's first volume-production "hardtop convertibles." Foretelling another trend was Lansing's first all-steel station wagon, offered in 76 and 88 guise. As at Chevy and Pontiac, it appeared at midyear to replace the existing part-wood wagon, and looked much like it. Not predictive at all were fastback town sedan four-doors added to the 76 and 88 lines. None sold that well, and would be dropped after this one year.

With so much new, Olds had a rollicking 1949, with home-market production soaring from the 172,500 of 1948 to a record 288,000-plus. The 1950 tally was nearly 408,000, helped by new 76 and 88 Holidays.

Weighing 300-500 pounds less than a comparable 98, the Rocket-engine 88 wowed race-goers in 1949. Oldsmobile was the winningest make in NASCAR that year, winning five of eight races. Red Byron won the '49 NASCAR "Strictly Stock" title driving an 88. In 1950, an 88 broke the class speed record at Daytona with a two-way average of 100.28 mph. That same year, an 88 won the first Mexican Road Race, besting such formidable competitors as Alfa Romeo, Cadillac, and Lincoln. Back on the stock-car ovals, Olds won 10 of 19 NASCAR contests in 1950 (when young Olds pilot Bill Rexford copped the driving title) and 20 of 41 in '51. Though displaced by Hudson's amazing six-cylinder Hornets in 1952-54, 88s continued to show their mettle. Paul Frere, for example, drove one to victory in a 1952 stock-car race at Spa in Belgium, and a 1950 model nicknamed "Roarin' Relic" was still winning the occasional modified race as late as 1959.

Such goings-on kept sales going strong even after the post-war seller's market went bust around 1950. Olds tapered off to 213,500 for '52, but was back up to 354,000 by 1954, when it finished fifth in the model-year production race. Interestingly, Olds managed these triumphs with only three basic series and no station wagons for 1951-56.

Not content to rest on its styling laurels, Olds took advantage of GM's new 1950 B-body to give 98s a one-piece windshield plus a general look that was again lower and more-massive despite another wheelbase cut, this time to 122 inches. The junior 88 and 76 lines received a mild update of their new '49 styling and were granted Holiday hardtops of their own. Fastback sedans were in their final year. Curiously, the lower level Olds ragtops—76 and 88—were now offered in standard trim only.

The big event of 1951 was the Super 88 with a new 120-inch wheelbase and a styling resemblance to that year's facelifted 98. Prices were in the $2200-$2700 bracket. Canceling the 76 left the 88 as the entry-level Olds; models were pared to just two- and four-door sedans, each around $2000. Those repeated as Super 88s along with a notchback club coupe, convertible, and Holiday hardtop. The 98 was trimmed to a Deluxe sedan and convertible and standard/Deluxe Holidays. The Futuramic label was abandoned as styling became more "important," though the grille was formed by simple bars and side decoration was minimal. This basic appearance continued for '52, when the 88 became a detrimmed Super with a retuned 145-bhp Rocket V-8; horsepower on other models moved up to 160. Also, the 98 now had its name spelled out: "Ninety-Eight."

Along with the Cadillac Eldorado and Buick Skylark, 1953 brought a limited-production Olds convertible, the Fiesta, a $5717 midyear addition to the Ninety-Eight line. Custom leather interior, wraparound "panoramic" windshield, and a special

1949 Futuramic 98 DeLuxe Holiday hardtop coupe

1950 Futuramic 98 Deluxe Holiday hardtop coupe

1950 Futuramic 88 DeLuxe Holiday hardtop coupe

1951 98 Holiday DeLuxe four-door sedan

170-bhp V-8 distinguished it from the normal Ninety-Eight ragtop. Hydra-Matic, power brakes and steering, and hydraulic servos for windows and seat were all standard. So were distinctive "spinner" wheel covers soon copied by most every accessory house, appearing on scores of hot rods and custom cars. Though only 458 were built for this one model year, the Fiesta did serve as a styling preview of the next-generation Olds.

That duly arrived for 1954 on a new B-body bearing squared-up below-the-belt sheetmetal, fully wrapped windshields, curved back windows, and distinctive L-shaped bodyside moldings that delineated contrast color areas on some two-tone

# Oldsmobile

1951 Super 88 convertible coupe

1952 88 DeLuxe two-door sedan

1953 Ninety-Eight Holiday hardtop coupe

1953 Ninety-Eight Fiesta convertible coupe

power was bumped to 185 and 202 for 1955, then to 230 and 240 bhp for '56.

Olds set another record by building about 40 percent more cars for '55 than '54—some 583,000—and held onto fifth in a booming industry. A substantial facelift gave the '55s a bold oval grille and jazzier two-toning. The '56s gained a large, "gaping-mouth" front like that of the 1953 Starfire show car. Despite a general industry retreat, the division did quite well to turn out some 485,000 of its '56s.

Another new body arrived for 1957 with sleeker styling and the first Olds wagons since 1950. Called Fiesta, the revived haulers comprised a pillared 88 four-door and pillarless 88 and Super 88 models, the latter reflecting the public's passion for hardtop styling. Both 88 lines were subtitled Golden Rocket (after a 1956 show car) to mark Oldsmobile's 60th anniversary; Ninety-Eights gained Starfire as a first name. The Rocket enlarged again, now at 371.1 cid and 277 bhp. Also new was a three-by-two-barrel carburetor option called J-2, good for 300 bhp. With the high-profile exception of driver Lee Petty, Olds was by now largely absent from stock-car tracks, but the J-2 made it a force to be reckoned with on the street: A J-2 88 could do 0-60 mph in less than eight seconds.

Priced in the $2700-$4200 range, the '57 Oldsmobiles were rather cleanly styled for GM cars that year. The wide-mouth grille was mildly reshaped; windshield pillars were more rakishly angled; a broad, stainless-steel sweepspear dropped down from the middle of the belt, then shot straight back to the tail, thus defining a two-toning area; and there were finless rear fenders ending in peaked, elliptic taillamps. But GM styling was beginning to seem a bit passé next to Virgil Exner's "Forward Look" at Chrysler; Harley Earl's reign as America's automotive styling arbiter was coming to a close. Still, Olds built nearly 385,000 U.S.-market cars for the model year to finish fifth once again.

While most makes faltered badly in recessionary 1958, Olds slipped into fourth, though on reduced volume near the 315,000 mark. Model offerings stood pat except that two-door sedans were now restricted to the base series, renamed Dynamic 88. Wheelbases stretched a nominal half-inch on all models. Styling, as most observers concluded, was atrocious. Ford designer Alex Tremulis satirized Oldsmobile's four horizontal rear-fender chrome strips by drawing in a clef and a few notes of music on a photograph. And indeed, Dearborn's '58s looked somewhat better than GM's, while Chrysler's modestly face-lifted cars were in another league entirely. Yet for all the over-chromed dazzle, Oldsmobiles sold pretty well for '58—aided, no doubt, by more power choices: 265 bhp for 88s (a nod to buyers suddenly concerned with fuel economy), 305 bhp standard on Supers and Ninety-Eights, and a 312-bhp J-2 setup optional for all.

The '59s might have looked even worse, but GM responded to Chrysler's 1957 initiative with a crash restyling program that produced generally cleaner cars than first envisioned—plus a significant divisional body realignment. Chevy and Pontiac would now share the corporate A-body, the junior Buicks and Oldsmobiles a new B-body, and senior models a slightly different C-body with Cadillac. Olds and Buick wheelbases were set at 123 and 126.3 inches; Pontiac's was slightly shorter, Chevy's shorter still. This program had repercussions. Chevy and Pontiac, for example, had to drop their all-new '58 platforms after only a year; Olds, Buick, and Cadillac after two years. Still, this change helped hold down production costs, thus enabling the company to put that much more time and money into developing a squadron of new compacts.

As ever, divisional styling strived for distinct looks, though the '59 Olds ended up more like Pontiac than Lansing might

models. This was arguably the most-attractive Olds of the decade. Happily, its basic look would persist through 1956.

So would body styles: 88 and Super 88 two- and four-door sedans and hardtop coupe; Super 88 convertible; Ninety-Eight Holiday, Deluxe Holiday, Deluxe sedan, and Starfire convertible. Holiday four-door hardtops bowed in all three lines at mid-1955, half a year ahead of other make's offerings save the Buick Special and Century (introduced along with Oldsmobile's). Wheelbases shifted to 122 inches for 88/Super 88 and 126 for Ninety-Eight. The Rocket was bored out for '54 to 324 cid, good for 170 bhp in 88s, 185 in Super 88s and Ninety-Eights. But the "horsepower race" was escalating throughout Detroit, so

# Oldsmobile

1954 Ninety-Eight DeLuxe Holiday hardtop coupe

1954 88 four-door sedan

1955 Ninety-Eight DeLuxe Holiday hardtop sedan

1955 Ninety-Eight Starfire convertible coupe

1955 Super 88 four-door sedan

1956 Super 88 Holiday hardtop sedan

1957 Golden Rocket 88 Holiday hardtop coupe

1957 Super 88 Fiesta station wagon prototype

1957 Golden Rocket Super 88 convertible coupe

1958 Ninety-Eight convertible coupe

# Oldsmobile

have liked. With a new emphasis on "Wide-Track" handling, Pontiac outpaced Olds in production, something it hadn't done since 1953.

But Lansing's '59s were hardly slim, swelling nine inches in width on a new "Guard-Beam" chassis. They were also 10 inches longer. Naturally they shared basic elements of the new corporate styling: vastly enlarged "Vista-Panoramic" windshields, curving nondogleg A-posts, big rear windows (fully wrapped on new Holiday sport sedan hardtops), thin-section coupe rooflines, narrow pillars, and fuller lower body sheetmetal. To this Olds added a simple dumbbell-shaped grille with four widely spaced headlights and straight-topped rear fenders with teeny fins above elliptical taillights. Division ad types called all this "The Linear Look."

No matter: The '59s were a vast improvement on the sparkly '58s. But there were still gadgets aplenty, including "New-Matic Ride," Lansing's year-old version of air suspension that was costly, unpopular, and about to disappear. At least power was still plentiful. Dynamic 88s retained a 371 V-8 with 270 bhp standard, 300 optional. New for Ninety-Eights and Super 88s was a bored-out 394 making 315 bhp with four-barrel carb but slightly reduced compression (9.75:1). Not at all obvious were many internal changes made to this year's Rocket as well as the "Jet-Away" Hydra-Matic long ordered by most Olds customers. For 1959, buyers could choose from a convertible, two- and four-door Holidays, and a pillared Celebrity sedan in each line, plus Dynamic 88 two-door sedan, and four-door Dynamic and Super Fiesta wagons. Prices were higher than ever. Only three Dynamics started below $3000, while the Ninety-Eight convertible was now close to $4400.

Even so, 1959 was a good Olds year on balance, the division notching another fifth-place finish on slightly improved volume of nearly 383,000. Though its cars had come a long way from the first 88s, Olds still retained something of a performance image (aided by Lee Petty's photo-finish win in the first Daytona 500), which it would shine anew to great success in the '60s.

The market began fragmenting soon after the new decade's dawn, and Lansing responded along with other makes by issuing a variety of new models. Most sold very well. The division never fell below seventh in industry output during these years and ran as high as fourth, rising from about 347,000 cars produced for 1960 to 635,000 by decade's end.

Olds jumped on the 1961 bandwagon for upscale compacts by fielding the F-85, which together with its later Cutlass variations saw progressively higher annual production through 1968. This reflected an astute matching of customer tastes with new products: small V-8s for 1961-62, larger compacts with an optional V-6 for 1964-65, and the high-performance 4-4-2 series for 1964. Each year's junior Olds line was invariably right on the money. The division's standard-size cars also sold consistently well.

F-85 was one of GM's "second-wave" compacts, evolved along with the Buick Special and Pontiac Tempest from Chevy's rear-engine 1960 Corvair. All thus shared the first-generation Corvair's basic Y-body platform, albeit reworked for an orthodox front-engine/rear-drive format. Tempest, with its curved driveshaft and rear transaxle, was the most radical of the B-O-P trio. Special and F-85 were resolutely conventional. Both carried an all-new, all-aluminum Buick-built V-8 of 215 cid and 155 bhp, which gave reasonable go (typical 0-60 mph: 13 seconds) and economy (18 mpg). In appearance, the Olds was a bit cleaner than the Buick, with a simpler front end (a small-scale rendition of that year's big-Olds face) but the same sculptured bodysides and crisp roofline.

Naming the F-85 had been a small problem. Starfire was the

**1958 Super 88 Fiesta hardtop station wagon**

**1959 Dynamic 88 hardtop coupe**

**1960 Super 88 convertible coupe**

**1961 F-85 Cutlass DeLuxe sports coupe**

first choice, but seemed to denote a big sporty car, as it had in the past (and ultimately would again in '61.) "Rockette" was rejected for projecting an unwanted image of the Radio City Music Hall dancers. The final choice looked to the Corvette-like F-88 show car of 1954, with "85" selected to avoid confusion with the big 88s.

F-85 initially offered a four-door sedan and hatchback four-door wagon in standard and Deluxe trim spanning a $2300-$2900 price spread. All rode a trim 112-inch wheelbase. At midyear came a pair of coupes, including a $2621 job with bucket seats and luxury interior called Cutlass, a name that would eventually supplant F-85. Base and Cutlass convertibles arrived for 1962.

All '62 Cutlasses offered a 185-bhp "Power-Pack" V-8, but greater interest surrounded yet another new derivation. This was the turbocharged Jetfire hardtop coupe, which shares honors with Chevy's 1962 Corvair Monza Spyder as America's first high-volume turbocar. With blower, the Jetfire V-8 churned out a healthy 215 bhp—the long-hallowed "1 hp per cu. in." ideal—but carbon buildup with certain grades of fuel necessitated an unusual water-injection system (actually, a water/alcohol mix).

While the Jetfire was remarkably fast (0-60 mph: about 8.5 seconds; top speed: 107 mph), the water-injection proved unreliable. As a result, Olds abandoned turbos for 1964 in favor of a conventional 330-cid V-8 of 230-290 bhp; at the same time, Buick's new 155-bhp 225-cid V-6 became base power for the F-85 line.

The compact Oldsmobiles grew to intermediate size after 1963, GM taking note of the huge sales generated by Ford's 1962-63 Fairlane. Wheelbase went to 115 inches, when Cutlass Holiday hardtop coupes were added. For '68, the line was split into 112-inch two-door models and 116-inch-wheelbase four-doors. Styling improved over time. The original look became squarer and more "important" for '63. The '64s were bulkier but still very clean, with an even closer resemblance to big Oldsmobiles. Straight beltlines yielded to more-flowing "Coke-bottle "contours for '66, when models again expanded via hard-top sedans in Cutlass and F-85 Deluxe trim. Appearance began getting cluttered again after '68, with busier grilles and sometimes clumsy vinyl tops.

The most-exciting F-85s were called 4-4-2, which meant four speeds (or 400 cubic inches beginning in '65), four-barrel carburetor, and dual exhausts. The debut 1964 edition was a package option for any F-85 except wagons comprising a 310-bhp 330 V-8, heavy-duty suspension, and four-speed manual gearbox. The '65 (now confined to two-door cars) was hotter still with a 345-bhp 400—a debored version of the full-size cars' then-new 425-cid V-8—plus heavy-duty wheels, shocks, springs, rear axle, driveshaft, engine mounts, steering and frame; front/rear stabilizer bars; fat tires; special exterior and interior trim; 11-inch clutch; and a 70-amp battery—all for about $250. Performance was terrific: 0-60 in 7.5 seconds, the standing quarter-mile in 17 seconds at 85 mph, top speed of 125 mph. The 4-4-2 proved, as *Motor Trend* magazine said, "that Detroit can build cars that perform, handle, and stop, without sacrificing road comfort."

Each year's 4-4-2 was eagerly awaited. Though the 400 V-8 wasn't pushed much beyond 350 bhp, Oldsmobile's hot middleweights remained handsome, fast, and fun. They were also better-balanced overall than rival muscle machines that had too much power for their chassis. The '69s wore large "4-4-2" numerals on front fenders, rear deck, and on a body-color vertical divider ahead of a black-finish grille, plus a unique "bi-level" hood with contrasting paint stripes. If a bit outlandish, the '69 was no less a performance car than the first 4-4-2. It was also a fine value at base prices as low as $3141.

Debuting for 1966 was the most-innovative Olds in a generation. This, of course, was the intriguing front-wheel-drive Toronado, a hardtop coupe offered in $4617 standard guise or as a nicer Deluxe model priced $200 higher. Toronado represented a clean break with the past—and a commitment to front

**1961 Super 88 Starfire convertible coupe**

**1962 F-85 DeLuxe Jetfire sports coupe hardtop**

**1961 Ninety-Eight Holiday sport sedan hardtop**

**1963 F-85 DeLuxe Jetfire sports coupe hardtop**

**1962 Starfire hardtop coupe**

**1963 Starfire hardtop coupe**

# Oldsmobile

drive that would be corporatewide by 1980. It was also a big turnabout for a company that had once panned the front-drive Cord, but GM had planned it well.

The goals for Toronado were traditional American power combined with outstanding handling and traction. Its 425 V-8 came from full-size Oldsmobiles but delivered an extra 10 horsepower—385 total—and teamed with a new "split" automatic transmission. A torque converter mounted behind the engine connected via chain drive and sprocket to a Turbo Hydra-matic transmission located remotely under the left cylinder bank. The chain drive, flexible yet virtually unbreakable, saved weight and cut costs. It also resulted in a very compact drivetrain that opened up extra cabin room. (The long 119-inch wheelbase helped, too.) Most previous front-drive systems had put the engine behind a transmission slung out ahead of the axle. Toronado's split transmission allowed the engine to be placed directly over the front wheels for a front/rear weight distribution of 54/46 percent, good for a big front-driver that some said could never work simply because it was so big and heavy (more than 4300 pounds).

Toronado styling was as sophisticated as its engineering. The C-pillars spilled gently down from the roof, there was no beltline "break" behind the rear side windows, the rakish fastback roofline terminated in a neatly cropped tail, the curved fuselage was set off by boldly flared wheel arches, and there was a distinctive front end with hidden headlamps. *Automobile Quarterly* editor Don Vorderman termed the result "logical, imaginative, and totally unique."

It was just as superb on the road. Understeer wasn't excessive for a front-driver, 100 mph was a quiet business, and top speed was near 135 mph even with the fairly rangy standard final-drive ratio. Unquestionably, Toronado was the most outstanding single Olds of the '60s. It would also prove to be the last truly innovative product that Lansing could call its own.

Toronado improved for '67 by offering optional front-disc power brakes and radial tires. Save detail changes, styling was mercifully left alone. Sales, unfortunately, took a big dive, dropping from 41,000 to about 21,800.

The 1968 Toro looked heavier in front, gaining a simple but massive combination bumper/grille. The following year brought added rear-end sheetmetal, an apparent effort to create a more-conventional notchback appearance. The same reasoning prompted an optional vinyl roof cover that didn't work at all well with the clean C-pillar lines. Horsepower declined by 10 for '68 despite a switch to the giant new 455 V-8 offered in that year's full-size Olds line. However, an optional W-34 version served up an even 400 bhp thanks to dual exhausts, special cam, and other modifications. Little else but exposed headlamps distinguished the 1970 model, last of the first-generation Toros. Sales were erratic in these years. The total was near

1963 Ninety-Eight convertible coupe

1965 Cutlass 4-4-2 convertible coupe

1964 Starfire hardtop coupe

1965 Jetstar 1 sports coupe

1964 Cutlass Holiday hardtop coupe

1966 Cutlass 4-4-2 Holiday hardtop coupe

# Oldsmobile

1966 Cutlass 4-4-2 Holiday hardtop coupe

1966 Toronado DeLuxe hardtop coupe

1966 Toronado hardtop coupe

1966 Starfire hardtop coupe

1967 Ninety-Eight Holiday hardtop coupe

1967 Delta 88 Custom Holiday hardtop coupe

26,500 for '68, an encouraging gain over dismal '67, then rose to almost 28,500 before easing back to 25,400 for 1970.

Despite the likes of Toronado and 4-4-2, big cars remained Oldsmobile's stock-in-trade in the '60s. The 1960 models were basically the expansive "Linear Look" '59s with simpler, more-dignified lines courtesy of a below-the-belt reskin. Pointy "rocket" rear fenders and busier bodysides marked the '61s, followed by more-involved grilles and rear-end treatments for '62. Wheelbases and series remained unchanged: 123 inches for price-leader Dynamic 88 and extra-performance Super 88, 126.3 for the luxury Ninety-Eight. A 1961 newcomer was the bucket-seat Starfire convertible on the Super 88 chassis. A companion hardtop coupe was added for '62.

Further full-size expansion occurred for 1964, when the Dynamic moved up a notch in price to make room for new Jetstar 88s. Among them was the bucket-seat Jetstar I sports coupe with a concave backlight *a la* Pontiac's contemporary Grand Prix. Super 88 was renamed Delta 88 for 1965; two years later, Dynamics and standard Jetstars were rolled into a single Delmont 88 series. But Delmont would be short-lived, giving way for 1969 to standard, Custom, and Royale Deltas, all on a 124-inch wheelbase. That year's Ninety-Eight moved up to a 127-inch platform.

Despite complete body changes for 1961, '65, and '69, big-Olds styling was remarkably consistent throughout the decade.

The "dumbbell" grille shape persisted through 1966, after which the first of Oldsmobile's split grilles appeared. Lines were crisp and straight through 1964, then progressively curvier and bulkier. Body styles were the usual assortment through '64, after which big station wagons were dropped in deference to new F-85/Cutlass-based haulers, including the Vista Cruiser with a raised, glassed-in rear superstructure (shared by Buick's contemporary Skylark-based Sportwagons) and a 120-inch wheelbase. For 1968, the Vista Cruiser chassis grew to 121 inches, though lesser Cutlass wagons were five inches shorter.

After a carryover 1960, big-Olds power through 1964 was provided by 394 V-8s delivering from 250 bhp in base 88s to 345 bhp in the 1962-64 Starfire. The low-priced '64 Jetstar used the F-85's 330 V-8. The 394 was stroked to 425 cid for 1965, and power rose gradually, reaching 375 bhp by 1967. A still longer stroke created 1968's massive 455, but it made only 365 bhp, with some power lost to the advent of emission controls and necessary detuning. The '67 Delmont offered both the 425- and 330-cid engines. The latter was boosted to 350 cid and 250 bhp for 1968.

Of Oldsmobile's two big bucket-seat performance cars, only the Starfire had any success. Production zoomed from 7600 for debut '61 to almost 42,000 for '62. But that would be the peak, output tapering fast through the end of the series in 1966. Jetstar I was the same idea at a more-popular price, but it didn't catch on; only about 22,600 were built for 1964-65.

# Oldsmobile

1967 4-4-2 Holiday hardtop coupe

1967 Toronado Deluxe hardtop coupe

1968 Toronado Custom hardtop coupe

1968 4-4-2 Holiday hardtop coupe

1969 4-4-2 Holiday hardtop coupe

1969 Ninety-Eight Luxury Sedan four-door

Though neither was anything like a true sports car (despite Oldsmobile's claims), they were distinctive and handled well for their size.

Like its sister GM divisions, Oldsmobile's responses to the tumultuous events of the 1970s were quick and usually correct. The 1973-74 OPEC oil embargo and the resulting energy crisis dramatically highlighted the need for smaller, thriftier cars in every size and price range, and Olds needed them as much as any medium-price make. At the start of the decade, its smallest models were two-door intermediates. Yet by 1980, it was offering no fewer than three model lines on wheelbases of less than 110 inches, plus more sensibly sized full-size cars and the trimmest Toronado yet. However, GM's decision to downsize its entire fleet came well in advance of the fuel shortage. That the first of the new breed appeared barely two years after the crisis had passed was merely happy coincidence.

But Oldsmobile's great sales success in the '70s was no coincidence; rather, it was the result of canny, calculated marketing. In fact, Olds usually ranked third behind Ford and Chevrolet—remarkable considering its products were basically corporate designs available under other nameplates for the same or less money. What undoubtedly attracted buyers was the extra prestige of the Olds badge on more nicely trimmed cars priced only a little upstream of comparable Chevys and Pontiacs but slightly below equivalent Buicks. The full-size B-body Delta 88 and the midsize A-body Cutlass were far and away the division's biggest money spinners in these years.

Cutlass firmly established itself in the '70s as one of America's favorites, often topping the individual model-line sales charts. Although it remained essentially an upmarket Chevy Chevelle/Malibu, Cutlass always offered a broad range of model and trim choices at competitively attractive prices. Another plus was more-august Oldsmobile styling.

Among the most popular of this popular line was the posh range-topping Cutlass Supreme, which debuted as a single 1966 hardtop sedan, then expanded into a separate full-range series (bolstered by a convertible for 1970-72). By 1973, the two-door alone accounted for nearly 220,000 sales, greater than the combined total for all other Cutlasses. Most buyers specified V-8s, especially early in the decade, though sixes were available beginning with the '75s. Coupes far outsold sedans and wagons in most years.

Given this popularity, the downsized 108.1-inch-wheelbase Cutlass/Cutlass Supreme of 1978 seemed very brave at the time, but buyers took to it with no less enthusiasm. The sole exception was the 1978-80 "aeroback" two- and four-door sedans, which were too dumpy-looking even for Oldsmobile's basically conservative clientele. Conventional notchback styling was thus applied to the four-door after '79, and was greeted with immediate acceptance.

# Oldsmobile

1969 Delta 88 Royale Holiday hardtop coupe

1969 Vista Cruiser station wagon

1970 Toronado Custom hardtop coupe

1970 4-4-2 Official Pace Car convertible

1971 Toronado hardtop coupe

The enthusiast's Cutlass fell on hard times in the '70s, as did every other Detroit muscle car. The last of the traditional high-power 4-4-2s appeared for 1971, a convertible and Holiday hardtop coupe packing the division's big 455 V-8. Sales dropped fast: from 19,000 for 1970 to less than 7600. After this, the 4-4-2 was reduced to a mere option package and a shadow of its original performance self. With GM's redesigned "Colonnade" intermediates of 1973, Olds tried a new approach in the Cutlass Salon, an American-style sporty sedan series somewhat akin to Pontiac's Grand Am. Though it failed to catch on, the name kept popping up on later midsize and compact models. As for the 4-4-2, you could still get a car so badged in 1979, but it was far more show than go.

Olds followed Buick back to compacts in 1973—and with the same basic car. Omega was Lansing's version, one of three badge-engineered derivatives of the 111-inch-wheelbase X-body platform introduced with the 1968 Chevy Nova. Though it managed a respectable 60,000 first-season sales, Omega was never a big winner. Sales actually fell for 1975 despite a handsome new outer skin and an improved chassis. When the X-body was shrunk around more space-efficient front-drive mechanicals for 1980, Omega vied with Pontiac's counterpart Phoenix for low spot on the sales totem pole, though an avalanche of highly publicized reliability and safety problems severely hurt all of these corporate cousins.

A similar fate befell another "company car," the subcompact Starfire. Introduced for 1975, this was Oldsmobile's edition of the Vega-based Chevrolet Monza 2+2, with the same hatchback coupe body and the 231-cid V-6 used in Buick's near-identical Skyhawk. Though the name once attached to Lansing's largest and most-opulent cars, this 97-inch-wheelbase Starfire was the smallest Olds in living memory, and thus should have done well in the post-energy crisis market. But big-car sales were on the rise again, and Starfire captured a mere six percent of division sales in its first season. It wouldn't do much better through the final 1980 models.

Upper-middle-class luxury remained Oldsmobile's mainstay in the '70s, and its big cars never strayed from it. What they did stray from, eventually, was needless bulk, which had become an increasing liability in the more-energy-conscious climate of late decade. GM bowed the largest full-size cars in its history for 1971, so Oldsmobile's B-body Delta 88 and C-body Ninety-Eight acquired extra inches and pounds on wheelbases unchanged from '69. Big-block 455 V-8s prevailed, but were progressively detuned to meet ever-stricter emissions standards. Wagons in this design generation had an interesting "clamshell" rear window/tailgate that retracted electrically into the body like a rolltop desk. The big Chevy, Pontiac, and Buick wagons all had it too, but it worked none too well.

As with Cutlass, the full-size Olds lost none of its appeal when downsized for 1977. If anything, these smaller big cars sold even better than the bigger old ones, doubtlessly due to improved fuel economy and maneuvering ease with no sacrifice in passenger room and ride comfort. Wheelbases contracted to 116 inches for Delta 88 and the Custom Cruiser wagon, and to 119 for Ninety-Eight, sizes that would persist through the mid '80s. Substantial weight reductions allowed the use of 350- and 403-cid V-8s without compromising performance. Diesel V-8s and Buick's 231 gas V-6 were offered as standard or optional from 1978 on. Model choices changed several times, but sedans and coupes usually ran to base, Royale, and Royale Brougham Deltas, and Luxury and Regency Ninety-Eights. The Custom Cruiser hung on in this form all the way through 1990, mainly because GM elected not to replace it with a smaller front-drive model that would have been less-useful as a full-size wagon.

The personal-luxury Toronado evolved through the '70s more

# Oldsmobile

or less in step with the full-size Oldsmobiles. For 1971, it also became as large as it would ever be, changing from mild sportiness to outsized opulence on a 123-inch wheelbase. Styling also changed—mostly for the worse—becoming more contrived and Cadillac-like through the end of this second generation in 1978.

Two Toronado styling developments in these years bear mention. One was a throwback to the early-postwar Studebaker Starlight coupes: a huge rear window wrapped around to the sides in a near unbroken sweep on the XS model of 1977. More laudable was a second set of brake lights just below the rear window, the precursor to an idea that would later be mandated by Washington for all cars sold in the U.S.

Despite its innovative engineering, the Toronado had no direct technical bearing on GM's linewide switch to front drive that began with the 1980 X-body compacts. In fact, it would probably have sold just as well with rear drive—as indeed did Buick's Riviera, which used a rear-drive version of the Toronado platform after 1965 but was always more popular. Save 1973, when sales neared 56,000, second-series Toronado volume was hardly exceptional: about 23,000 in most years.

The new downsized generation of 1979 was smaller than even the 1966 original, with a new 114-inch-wheelbase E-body platform and adequately potent small-block V-8s. It immediately garnered a bit more than 50,000 orders, then from 34,000 to 48,000 a year through 1985.

Oldsmobile's fortunes in the '80s were decidedly mixed. Lansing had sold a record 1.14 million cars for '77 and nearly as many for '78 and '79. With the second energy crisis that began in late '79 came a deep national recession that held division sales well below the 1-million mark through 1983. But then Olds bounced back to set another record: a smashing 1.17 million for 1985. In the yearly production derby the division continued to run its usual third, just ahead of Buick, but it also managed to beat Ford for second spot in 1983 and '85. Yet by 1987, Olds was down below 671,000, its worst total since the mid-'70s, and Pontiac had regained third. The decline continued, Olds averaging but 534,000 for 1988-89, then dipping under half a million for 1990.

What happened? One problem was that Oldsmobile's image became confused with Buick's—no surprise given similar

**1971 Delta 88 Royale hardtop coupe**

**1971 4-4-2 convertible coupe**

**1972 Delta 88 Royale hardtop coupe**

**1972 Toronado Custom hardtop coupe**

**1973 Cutlass Supreme Colonnade coupe**

**1973 Ninety-Eight Luxury Coupe hardtop**

**1973 Omega hatchback coupe**

**1973 Toronado hardtop coupe**

model lines that had evolved pretty much in lockstep since the mid-'70s at least. Another problem was Pontiac, which in the early '80s began offering the kind of performance-oriented machinery that had served it so well in the '60s. By that point, Oldsmobile's one real marketing asset seemed to be the Cutlass name, and even that had lost much of its appeal by being indiscriminately tacked onto too many models. Olds also suffered from GM's policies of "identicar" styling and divisional duplicates of most every platform in the corporate stable.

Then, too, there was the wholesale corporate reorganization hatched by chairman Roger Smith in 1984. This was a well-intentioned attempt at addressing many ills, including blurred divisional identities, but it only squandered valuable time and untold employee morale. Compounding this confusion was Smith's headlong rush to buy Hughes Electronics and the Electronic Data Systems company of one H. Ross Perot, in the mistaken belief that expensive computerized-manufacturing systems would increase both productivity and profitability. Instead, the acquisitions only sapped funds that would have been more wisely spent on much-needed new models. Meantime, the hastily installed automation only worsened the build quality of existing products. Symbolic of the near-chaos that once reigned was the highly touted "Poletown" plant opened in the mid-'80s in Hamtramck, near Detroit, where robots painted each other instead of cars and driverless parts carts scurried around aimlessly.

A final problem, and perhaps the most-telling, was the inability—or was it the refusal?—of top GM managers to see that they had any problems at all. Of course, some executives were quite insulated by GM's size, and their "business-as-usual" attitude was not harmful as long as the market remained healthy. But when the market turned weak in 1990, GM began hemorrhaging cash like it hadn't done even in its earliest days. Huge losses continued to pile up over the next three years. By that point, rumors had started that Oldsmobile—then about to celebrate its 95th anniversary—might have to be sacrificed as part of saving the corporation.

With all this, the decade of the 1980s was not one of Oldsmobile's happiest. For a time, Lansing tried swapping roles with Flint, emphasizing sporty luxury as a sort of "American BMW" while Buick reasserted its traditional blend of substantial size and smooth-riding softness in what it now called "premium American motorcars." But this game plan worked only for Buick. By decade's end, Olds seemed hopelessly lost and increasingly unnecessary, squeezed by an aggressive Pontiac from below and a resurgent Buick from above. It was all eerily reminiscent of what happened to DeSoto in the late '50s—and, come to that, the Edsel.

The cars that carried Olds to this uncertain state of affairs were workaday intermediates and full-size models. Surprisingly

**1973 Ninety-Eight Luxury coupe**

**1973 Hurst/Olds W-30 Official Pace Car**

**1974 Ninety-Eight Regency coupe**

**1975 Hurst/Olds W-30 T-top coupe**

**1976 Delta 88 Royale Crown Landau hardtop coupe**

**1976 Toronado Brougham coupe**

719

# Oldsmobile

perhaps, given the difficult early-'80s market, the big rear-drive Delta 88 and Ninety-Eight took over as the division's top-sellers through middecade. Together, they attracted a quarter-million buyers a year through 1982 and more than 340,000 in 1983 and '84. Both were soon put on smaller front-drive platforms (except, as noted, the Custom Cruiser wagon) as part of a second-wave GM downsizing program. The 1985 Ninety-Eight was thus put on a new C-body, shared with Buick's Electra; the 88 was similarly transformed for '86 on the related new H-body also used for the Buick LeSabre and Pontiac Bonneville. Like the first-wave '77s, these smaller big cars sold just as well as their predecessors. But aside from styling and equipment details, all these Oldsmobiles, rear-drive and front-drive, differed little from counterpart Buicks.

Number-two on Lansing's 1980s hit parade was the midsize Cutlass, which involved two distinct lines: continuations of the 1978-vintage rear-drive series and its perceived front-drive successor, the A-body Cutlass Ciera, new for '82. Each accounted for upward of 200,000-300,000 sales in their best years. Rear-drive Cutlass coupes received a sloped-nose "aero" facelift for 1981 (similar to the full-size cars' 1980 redo). Model years 1983 and '87 saw the end of Cutlass wagons and sedans, respectively. Two-doors adopted flush-mounted "composite" headlamps for '86. Signaling the imminent arrival of a new front-drive Cutlass Supreme, the rear-drive '88s—produced in a short run—were renamed Supreme Classic.

Of interest to collectors is the trio of low-volume, period muscle-car revivals based on the rear-drive Cutlass coupe: a 15th anniversary Hurst/Olds commemorative for 1983, a similar 1984 followup, and a reborn 4-4-2 option package offered for 1985-87. The H/Os wore special badging and modest decklid spoilers. All three packed a four-barrel, 180-bhp version of Oldsmobile's 307-cid small-block V-8 (170 in 1987) and were quite fast. Their mild engine tuning would have seemed laughable in the '60s, but nobody had to be concerned with corporate average fuel economy (CAFE) in those days.

CAFE was a definite motivation for the smaller midsize Olds, the Cutlass Ciera. It was, predictably, much like Buick's new-wave Century, derived from the front-drive X-car design and initially offered as a notchback coupe and sedan; glass-hatch wagons arrived for 1984. Engine choices included a standard Pontiac-built 151-cid four-cylinder, 181-cube gas V-6, and a 262 diesel V-6. For mid-1986, the Ciera coupe gained a smoother, slightly abbreviated roofline. Sedans got a similarly rounded backlight for 1989, when a new 160-bhp 3.3-liter V-6 replaced the 231-cid Buick V-6 optional since '85.

The rear-drive Cutlass and front-drive Ciera typically offered a choice of plain and fancy trim (the latter usually dubbed Brougham). There were also sporting versions: GT and Euro-style ES Cieras through 1987; Calais and Salon Cutlass coupes—

**1976 Cutlass S 4-4-2 coupe (option W-29)**

**1976 Starfire GT hatchback coupe**

**1977 Cutlass S 4-4-2 coupe**

**1977 Toronado XS coupe**

**1977 Delta 88 Royale town sedan four-door**

**1978 Cutlass Calais coupe**

# Oldsmobile

1978 Starfire GT hatchback coupe

1979 Cutlass Salon sedan diesel

1979 Delta 88 Royale sedan

1979 Starfire Firenza hatchback coupe

1979 Cutlass Salon 4-4-2 fastback coupe

all with fortified suspensions and less traditional interiors. From 1988, the enthusiast's Ciera was retitled International Series, but retained the usual black-finish exterior trim, bigger wheel/tire package, and special body addenda (front and rear spoilers, later matched by rocker-panel skirts).

Somehow, Oldsmobile was less successful with small cars than Buick, let alone Chevrolet. Perhaps they weren't sufficiently different enough, or maybe Oldsmobile customers just couldn't resist the bigger jobs. Whatever the reason, Lansing's smallest cars were slow movers. The front-drive X-body Omega, for example, peaked at nearly 148,000 for 1981, then tailed off to less than 54,000 by '83. Lack of change didn't help, and it was summarily dismissed after 1984.

Firenza fared even worse. Arriving in March 1982 to replace Starfire, Lansing's version of the front-drive 101.2-inch-wheelbase J-body corporate car failed to attract more than about 45,000 customers in most years—except for 1984, when it garnered a creditable 82,500—even though Olds tried most everything it could think of to sell it. By 1988 the Firenza had offered all the J-body types, sporty GT and SX variants, overhead-valve and overhead-cam fours, optional V-6, and a confusing procession of price-leader and luxury models. But nothing seemed to work, and Olds gave up after '88.

Firenza was no great loss, though, because 1985 brought a more-salable small Olds in the new N-body Calais, called Cutlass Calais after 1988. Sized between Firenza and Omega on a 103.4-inch wheelbase, it bowed as a rounded, short-deck coupe in two versions: base and—just to confuse things—Supreme. Four-door sedans were added for 1986. There was a lot of J-car engineering under the "modern formal" styling, and initial engine choices were the Ciera's familiar Pontiac-built four and 3.0-liter Buick V-6. Even so, customers generally liked this new bottle of old wine, snapping up 100,000-plus in the first year and better than 150,000 of the '86s—about midway between the volume of the similar Pontiac Grand Am and Buick Skylark/Somerset.

For 1988, Calais coupes and sedans grouped into base, luxury SL, and sporty International Series (the last replacing a GT package option), but the big news was the first twincam, 16-valve four-cylinder engine in American production, the Quad-4. Designed and built by Olds and offered as an across-the-board Calais option, it delivered 150 rather rough and noisy horses, but was claimed capable of much more. Olds proved it by adding a tuned 180-bhp version for 1989. A more-useful option that year was the new 3.3-liter derivative of the 173-cid Chevy V-6. Replacing the Buick 3.0, it also produced 160 bhp—and more torque than even the "High Output" Quad-4. To fill in for the departed Firenza, prosaically named Value Leader Calais models appeared for '89 with less standard equipment and restricted options but lower prices.

Enthusiasts surely shuddered when the 442 returned (*sans* hyphens) as a performance option for the base 1990 Calais coupe. Olds said the once-great designation now stood for "Quad-4, 4 valves per cylinder and 2 camshafts." Included in the $1667 package were the 180-horse Quad-4, five-speed manual transaxle, a specific version of Oldsmobile's now-familiar FE3 sport suspension, meaty 215/60R14 performance tires on alloy wheels, full instrumentation, a cute rear-deck spoiler, and bold "442" exterior I.D. "Buff books" gave this latest 442 a lot of ink, but customers mostly gave it the cold shoulder. Even a hallowed name on an honestly speedy little car couldn't convince many that Olds still specialized in high performance as it had in the '50s and '60s.

Olds observed 20 years of Toronados with a new fourth-generation design for 1986, which should have been cause for celebration. In many ways it was: 18 inches trimmer and 550

721

# Oldsmobile

pounds slimmer on a new 108-inch wheelbase; just as quick despite switching from V-8s to the Buick 231-cid V-6 (making it the first Toro without eight cylinders); clean and contemporary styling, with hidden headlamps for the first time since 1969. Beginning in early '87, there was even a new companion model aimed straight at enthusiasts: the Trofeo (pronounced tro-FAY-oh, "trophy" in Spanish and Italian), with a more-subdued exterior, leather interior, and FE3 "handling" suspension.

Yet for all that, buyers didn't respond. Toronado had long been eclipsed in sales by its Buick Riviera and Cadillac Eldorado cousins. The '86 was no different, except that sales were less than half of what they had been: fewer than 16,000 in the debut season versus 42,000-plus for the last of the third-generation cars. The Riv and Eldo fared little better. Critics blamed this poor performance on styling that was uncomfortably close to that of the much cheaper Calais, and a package that had been downsized a little too far for most personal-luxury buyers.

Sadly, there was little Olds could do to improve matters right away. The '87s thus received only new engine mounts plus roller valve lifters that helped lift the V-6 from 140 to 150 bhp. A revised "3800" engine gave the '88s another 15 bhp, a new antilock brake system (ABS) devised by GM and the German Alfred Teves company became optional, and there were minor mechanical and ergonomic changes. More details were attended to for '89 and the Trofeo came with more standard equipment, including ABS.

Cadillac and Buick had made their E-bodies more-impressive looking in 1988 and '89. For 1990, Olds was finally able to do the same for Toronado, adding 12.4 inches to overall length, mainly at the rear, complemented by minor facial surgery. The result was handsome, and the extra length yielded an extra 2.5 cubic feet of trunk space. Olds also threw in a standard driver-side airbag and larger wheels and tires for both the Toro and Trofeo (the latter now increasingly marketed as a separate model). Nevertheless, sales remained a fraction of what they'd once been, although the 1990 total of just over 15,000 was a heartening gain on the previous year's dismal 9900.

By now, GM had learned the folly of fielding too many cars that looked too much like each other. The all-new front-drive Cutlass Supreme that bowed in '88 was striking proof. Though it shared the W-body/GM10 platform with that year's Buick Regal and Pontiac Grand Prix, this newest Supreme had its own roofline and outer sheetmetal so it would not be confused with the others (nor they with Supreme). Hallmarks included a low, tapered nose; slim Olds-trademark split grille; curvy flanks; large wheel openings; crisply clipped tail; and a glassy notchback superstructure with semiconcealed C-posts and slim A- and B-pillars.

The front-drive Supreme's initial powerteam was a five-speed manual transaxle driven by the workhorse 173-cid Chevy V-6 in 125-bhp port-injected form; for 1989, cars with optional automatic received a 3.1-liter/191-cid enlargement boasting 135 bhp. At the same time, optional ABS arrived to fortify the standard all-disc brakes. Model choices through '89 comprised Oldsmobile's now-usual range of base, SL, and sporty International Series—all coupes. The I-Series came with quick-ratio power steering, tuned exhaust, full instrumentation, and, for '89, cassette tape player, power door mirrors, and central locking.

Buyers by now had been conditioned to expect rebates or low-interest financing offers even on new models. The front-drive Supreme bowed without those, and thus got off to a relatively slow sales start: a little less than 95,000 made despite the extra-long 1988 model year. Olds took the hint, offered incentives, and watched sales pass 100,000 for '89, then 119,000 for '90. But what really made the difference was the belated 1990 arrival of four-door Supremes, which critics said should have

1980 Omega Brougham four-door sedan

1981 Cutlass Supreme Brougham coupe

1981 Toronado Custom Brougham coupe

1982 Omega Brougham four-door sedan

1982 Cutlass Ciera Brougham two-door sedan

# Oldsmobile

1982 Firenza SX hatchback coupe

1984 Firenza GT hatchback coupe

1984 Calais Hurst/Olds coupe

1984 Toronado Caliente coupe

1985 Ninety-Eight Regency Brougham two-door sedan

been introduced first. At the same time, the engine lineup was curiously rejuggled. Base power with five-speed manual was now the 180-bhp H.O. Quad-4, with the 160-bhp version reserved for cars with optional three-speed automatic. The 3.1 V-6 again teamed solely with extra-cost four-speed automatic, but that combination was no longer offered for the I-Series, which could have used it just as much.

A happier 1990 surprise was the first Supreme convertible in 18 years. Inspired by a one-off ragtop that paced the 1988 Indianapolis 500, it was announced at $20,995 with SL trim and, sensibly, the 3.1 V-6 and four-speed autobox. What Olds called a "structural top bar" partly made up for lost rigidity in what was basically a roofless Supreme coupe. The bar did not add rollover protection, as PR types hastened to note, but it did make for a clumsy top-down appearance. Actually, this evil was necessary because of the W-body coupe's B-pillar-mounted exterior door handles, which would have cost too much to change given the convertible's low planned production. Also, the bar was needed to provide proper, convenient anchors for the mandatory front shoulder belts. At least the Supreme came with a power top, which was more than a Cadillac Allanté or convertible Corvette could claim, and lowering the top automatically lowered all four side windows with it, another boon for convenience. Also featured were a glass rear window with electric defroster and a low, tidy top stack.

These and other engineering details reflected the expertise of noted convertible converter C&C, Inc., of Brighton, Michigan, which was tapped to build the reborn sunny-days Supreme. Brochures said it was "the first Oldsmobile that can go from zero to wide-open in 12 seconds." Deliveries, however, took considerably longer, as C&C didn't begin production until April, mainly in the interest of highest possible workmanship. As a result, fewer than 500 of the 1990s were built.

Convertibles are always nice, but Olds looked to be in big trouble by now, partly because GM was, too. Where Ford and Chrysler had taken painful steps in the '80s to become leaner and more efficient, GM merely redrew its organizational chart to enter the '90s with the highest overhead and lowest per-unit profit in the U.S. industry. Then the bottom dropped out of the market in a deep new recession, and GM began gushing red ink. By 1993, it piled up a towering four-year net loss of $18 billion—a U.S. business record. With cost-cutting imperative, some thought GM might take the easy way out and eliminate its weakest division, hence a spate of rumors that Olds would be killed. (Ultimately, the rumors weren't wrong—just premature.)

Apart from corporate pride, losing Olds was unthinkable given the political impact of laying off its thousands of workers—and putting some 3000 Olds dealers out of business. Also, there were far less drastic ways to save money, even if chairman Bob Stempel wasn't moving fast enough in those areas to satisfy an increasingly worried GM board. In fact, after just two years in office, Stempel was ousted in an unprecedented 1992 "palace coup." This set the stage for yet another reorganization under John Smale, the one-time CEO of Proctor & Gamble who became the first GM chairman not chosen from company ranks. John F. "Jack" Smith returned from GM Europe to take over as president. This dynamic new duo achieved fast results, and GM was making money again by 1994.

Finally, Olds may have been wounded in this period, but it was far from dead. Granted, calendar-year sales slid fast after 1989, going from more than a half-million to only 381,000 in 1993. And yes, Olds sustained these losses despite entering the two hottest segments of the market: minivans, with the 1990 Silhouette, and sport-utility vehicles, with the '91 Bravada. Yet as grim as all this was, Olds ran a consistent fifth in domestic output (behind Ford, Chevy, Pontiac, and Buick) and sixth

# Oldsmobile

among all U.S.-based producers (after American Honda). What's more, model-year output turned solidly upward for 1994 to 478,872 units. The '95 tally was better still at nearly 481,000 vehicles. Though even that was a long way from the million-car years of the '70s and '80s, Olds was still generating sizable business that GM couldn't afford to give up.

Important to the future of that business was John D. Rock, who took over as division general manager in 1992 after a successful stint heading GMC Truck. A brawny, straight-talking "cowboy" type, Rock worked feverishly to restore sagging employee morale and improve the confused, yet generally stodgy, Olds image that was hurting sales as much as all those rumors about the make's imminent demise. He also began implementing some successful ideas borrowed from GM's new Saturn subsidiary, including "no-haggle" pricing (you paid what the sticker said) and "kid-gloves" customer service. At the same time, Olds looked beyond its historic 100th birthday in 1997 with the "Centennial Plan," a business and product map through the year 2005.

Rock wanted nothing less than to "completely re-create" Olds, a task he likened to "overhauling the engines of a 747 in midflight . . . [T]here's no place at the GM table for the 'old' Oldsmobile. No place for a division hell-bent on being a 'Me-Too Pontiac' or a 'Buick-Lite.'"

**1986 Cutlass Salon coupe**

**1988 Toronado coupe**

**1986 Toronado Brougham coupe**

**1988 Cutlass Supreme Official Pace Car convertible**

**1987½ Toronado Trofeo coupe**

**1988 Cutlass Supreme Classic Brougham coupe**

**1988 Cutlass Ciera International Series coupe**

**1988 Cutlass Supreme coupe**

1990 Silhouette minivan

1990 Cutlass Supreme convertible coupe

1990 Cutlass Supreme International Series coupe

1990 Toronado Trofeo coupe

Unfortunately, Rock couldn't do much about existing models and a couple of new ones in the pipeline. Thus, the Toronado and its Trofeo offshoot were left to languish through 1992, then dropped for lack of sales (a mere 6436 that last season). Both finished out with the improved "3800" V-6 and electronic transmission controls adopted for '91, when antilock brakes became standard for Toro as well Trofeo. It was a sad end for a car once so innovative and compelling.

Likewise, the big Custom Cruiser vanished after 1992 and a two-year stand as a clone of Chevy's restyled '91 Caprice wagon. Just slightly more than 12,000 were made. Nineteen-ninety marked the last use of the 307 V-8 descended from the original '49 "Rocket." It was another sad ending for Olds, but the engine was simply no longer needed. With GM down to a handful of rear-drive cars, economics dictated that all but the Cadillacs use Chevy power. And in fact, Chevy's 5.0-liter V-8 was made standard, and its 180-bhp 5.7-liter V-8 was added as a '92 Custom Cruiser option. It was too late to help sales, but the bigger engine's bountiful torque and 10 extra bhp were appreciated in the weighty wagon.

The Ninety-Eight observed its 50th anniversary with a substantial makeover for 1991. Wheelbase was unchanged, but the new four-door styling was handsome in its chunky way. Both the touring sedan and new Regency Elite boasted ample interior space, all kinds of no-cost amenities, and a smooth new "3800" V-6 with 170 bhp. Like Toronado, however, sales were but an echo of Oldsmobile's best days. Though some 55,000 buyers were persuaded for '91, demand tapered off despite the '92 addition of a lower-priced standard Regency (at $24,595) and a 205-bhp supercharged option for the touring sedan. By 1994, sales were down around 26,600.

The Eighty-Eight got its own redesign for 1992. Coupes were gone, but Royale and uplevel Royale LS sedans wore attractive new styling to stand crisply apart from H-body cousins Buick LeSabre and Pontiac Bonneville. Here, too, was a "3800" V-6 and, for LS, newly optional traction control. Arriving in the spring was the suave LSS (Luxury Sport Sedan) option package with front bucket seats and a handling-oriented chassis with 16-inch wheels and performance tires. Overall sales were good: some 115,000 for the model year.

All Eighty-Eights got a bit more torque for '93, plus standard antilock brakes (formerly optional). The '94s sported minor cosmetic changes and a tidier dash with a passenger-side air bag to complement the already included driver-side restraint. For '95 came an improved "Series II" V-6 with 35 extra bhp, and the LSS was available with a supercharged "Series I" with 225 bhp. Sales see-sawed despite the rising technical progress, falling to about 62,400 for '93, then swinging up past 82,000 before easing back to some 75,400. But this was still one of the most-pleasant and practical of family cars, and the Eighty-Eight remained the third-most-popular Olds after Cutlasses Ciera and Supreme.

Once the country's best-selling car line, the Supreme wasn't even in the top 25 after 1989, a huge comedown for a mainstream midsize. There were two likely reasons: the increasingly negative image of the Olds name and wave after wave of new, highly aggressive competitors. Regardless, Supreme hit a modern sales low with model-year '93 and barely 83,000 units—at best, only a fourth of what it had done as recently as the mid-'80s. Lansing was thus surely relieved when volume went solidly over the 100,000 level for 1994 and '95.

In a way, it's a wonder sales didn't fall further, for aside from a mild '92 facelift and annual powertrain shuffles, the Supreme saw no notable change through middecade. At least the convertible was still around as a customer lure. Though it was always peripheral to overall sales, production climbed steadily, reaching 1515 for '91, then zooming to 4306 for '92 and 6751 for troubled '93. The recovery year of '94 saw a healthy 8638 units, but even that wasn't enough for GM accountants, so the sunshine Supreme was dropped after 1995 and a final 4490 examples. Many dealers were sad to see it go; it had done much to brighten Olds showrooms during a dreary time.

An interesting new standard engine arrived for Supreme's 1991 I-Series coupe and sedan: a 3.4-liter V-6 with dual overhead camshafts and four-valve cylinder heads. Quaintly named "Twin Dual Cam," it delivered 210 bhp with five-speed manual or 200 with optional four-speed automatic. Though a much

# Oldsmobile

more satisfying performer than any Quad-4, it didn't act nearly as racy as its specifications implied. The following year's restyle was a good one, announced by a tidier version of the trademark split-theme Olds grille. New "mini-quad" headlamps flanked square parking lights for a Pontiac-like "six-lamp" visage, and more body-color components gave some Supremes a more-integrated look. Sensibly, the Quad-4 was axed for '92, and no one missed it. A car of this class with four-cylinder power, no matter how "advanced" on paper, just wasn't what the market wanted. Also that year, the I-Series got an aircraft-type Head-Up Display (HUD): Readouts of speed and other information projected onto the windshield for easy viewing. Olds offered this as an option in the search for "a difference to sell." Like the Quad-4, though, it mainly drew blank stares.

Supreme marked time for '93, though the 3.4 V-6 was now optional for the ragtop and all models gained automatic power door locks and a front cupholder. The '94s benefited from a standard driver-side airbag and antilock brakes, but the I-Series vanished and SL trim became a package option as Olds turned to emphasizing value with a new "one-price" Special Edition coupe and sedan starting at $16,995. Internal improvements added 20 bhp to the mainstay 3.1 pushrod V-6 (still hanging on). Besides a swan-song soft top, the '95 lineup offered just SL coupe and sedan (replacing S) in "Series I" and "Series II" trim/equipment levels. Prices again spanned a narrow $1000 range (here $17,500-$18,500), with the convertible way upstream at $25,460. A more-ergonomic dash with standard dual airbags then carried Supreme through a quiet 1996, after which both car and name finally stepped aside for a new and better midsize Olds called Intrigue.

Lansing's most-popular car of the early '90s was something far older than the W-body Supreme. Against all odds, it was the hoary Cutlass Ciera, whose surprising sales stamina was probably as much an embarrassment to Olds as it was a relief. This was, after all, a very old car by now and quite at odds with the more "with it" image Olds was trying to forge. But Olds needed every sale it could get, and every Ciera made money, as GM had long since amortized the cost of the vintage-'82 design.

What kept Ciera going were steadily improved quality and dollar value. The former reflected a gradual but wholesale reengineering effort that put this Olds (and Buick's related Century) near the top of GM's internal quality audits by 1993—and on a few independent surveys, too. As for value, Ciera discarded its I-Series after 1990 and coupes after '91 to focus on workaday sedans and wagons in basic S or better SL guise. SLs alone carried on for '94 "one-price" Special Editions as part of the effort. A decent supply of standard features included driver-side airbag (optional before) and GM's low-cost "ABS VI" antilock brake system. By that point, Ciera had exchanged the old "Iron Duke" base four for a 2.2-liter Chevy engine with 120 bhp; for '94, the 3.3 Buick V-6 gave way to a similar 3.1 Chevy unit with 160 bhp. Respective transmissions were three- and four-speed automatics. The game plan changed for '95, when the SLs returned in Series I and V-6 Series II price levels.

Despite inflationary pressures, Ciera prices rose only as far as $17,000 by middecade, making this Olds a tempting buy even for a relic of a bygone age. Volume fell substantially after 1990, but the old soldier resounded with 140,000 or more per year for 1992-'94. Though more rental car than driveway dream, the Ciera did more than its share to pull Olds through some very rough years.

There was far less help from Achieva, the redesigned 1992 replacement for Cutlass Calais. The new name was a last-minute decision prompted by surveys showing that buyers had become confused by three different cars called Cutlass. Besides, Achieva had a modern upscale ring to it—just what

1991 Cutlass Ciera SL four-door sedan

1991 Ninety-Eight Touring sedan

1992 Toronado Trofeo coupe

1992 Eighty-Eight Royale LS four-door sedan

1992 Achieva SC coupe

# Oldsmobile

1992 Cutlass Supreme International Series coupe

1993 Silhouette minivan

1993 Ninety-Eight Touring sedan

1993 Cutlass Supreme convertible coupe

1994 Achieva SL four-door sedan

Olds wanted.

Unfortunately, Lansing's new N-body was something less than its name implied. Like cousins Buick Skylark and Pontiac Grand Am (also redesigned that year), Achieva owed much to Chevy's L-body Corsica/Beretta, using the same floorpan, inner structure, and suspension. Each model had its own styling, though. Achieva was cautiously inoffensive: more-conservative than Grand Am, far less weird than Skylark. Four-door sedans were rather "junior Ninety-Eight," but coupes were disappointingly GM-generic, with elements of Chevy Cavalier and even the new Saturn SC. At the 11th hour, designers decided the Achieva two-door looked better with rounded rear wheel arches instead of the sedan's flat-top openings, a change that delayed the start of sales for the entire line by some three months to January 1992.

Like Calais, Achieva emphasized Quad-4 power, including a cheaper new version of this Olds design with a single-cam eight-valve cylinder head. Oddly named Quad OHC, it provided 120 bhp as the standard engine in entry-level S models. Midrange SLs had the familiar twincam Quad-4 with 160 bhp, while the 180-bhp H.O. unit was reserved for manual-shift versions of a sportier coupe prosaically titled SC. Optional across this board was Buick's 160-bhp 3.3 V-6. Added a bit later was the even hotter SCX. Like the previous Calais Quad 442, this delivered a 190-bhp Quad-4, close-ratio manual five-speed, unique 14-inch alloy wheels, rear spoiler, and suitable exterior I.D., plus standard ABS VI as on other models.

Olds pushed Achieva hard, pitting it against the popular Honda Accord and Toyota Camry in a splashy 100,000-mile consumer-comparison test. The SCX provided bonus publicity by scoring major victories in IMSA and SCCA road racing. Yet for all the horn-blowing, Achieva didn't achieve its hoped-for sales. The '92 total was fair at just shy of 80,000 (including a few exports), but Pontiac moved far more Grand Ams, and Olds managed only some 48,000 for 1993 despite adding value-priced Special Editions. Achieva did share in the division's '94 recovery by surging to 62,000 but none were SCXs, as that model was dropped after just 1146 of the '92s and a mere 500 of the '93s.

Achieva really retrenched for 1995, listing just an S coupe and sedan in Series I and II equipment levels respectively tagged at $13,500 and $15,200. The OHC and H.O. engines were dismissed too, but the surviving twincam finally got what it had always needed: twin "balance shafts" to quell inherent rock-and-roll roughness. The result was a somewhat-smoother, slightly quieter Quad-4 with five fewer bhp. Another belated drivetrain improvement was a four-speed automatic transmission to replace the outmoded nonoverdrive three-speed as standard with the V-6 (by now a 155-bhp 3.1 liter) and optional with the four. Olds naturally thought all these changes would help sales, but they didn't, and Achieva model-year output sagged to a bit over 57,000.

As a minivan, Lansing's front-drive Silhouette should have sold like crazy, but it, too, didn't live up to expectations. Befitting an Olds, this was a more-luxurious version of the new plastic-paneled "GM200" design used for the Pontiac Trans Sport and Chevy Lumina APV. The Olds cost the most at an initial $17,195, but came with the novel seven-passenger seating package that was optional on the others, with light, easily movable middle- and third-row buckets. There was even a hint of "grand touring" in an available FE3 handling package. But the 3.1-liter V-6 was a thrashy plodder, and the shared "anteater" styling proved a real turnoff for many buyers. Standard ABS and a 3.8-liter V-6 option didn't turn them on for 1992, nor did a unique power-sliding right-door as a new '94 extra. Thus, after finding slightly more than 28,000 buyers for debut 1990, Silhouette settled into the 17,000-26,000 range

# Oldsmobile

1996 Ninety-Eight Regency Elite four-door sedan

1996 Cutlass Supreme SL coupe

1996 Achieva SL four-door sedan

1997 Regency sedan

through middecade—not great when Plymouth and Dodge each sold more than 200,000 minivans a year. There was nothing to do but start over, and Olds would with a new all-steel 1997 replacement bearing a more-conventional shape.

Announcing a new direction for future Oldsmobiles was the all-new 1995 Aurora, the most-exciting car from Lansing in 20 years. Originally planned as the next Toronado, it was built on the same new G-body platform as Buick's latest Riviera coupe, but boldly aimed at upscale sports sedans with unique four-door styling, state-of-the-art V-8 power, a taut front-drive chassis, and loads of luxury, all for less than $32,000 to start.

Aurora's engine wasn't brand-new. A smaller-bore 4.0-liter version of Cadillac's two-year-old "Northstar" 4.6, it was even built in the Cadillac plant. But it was a good, strong contemporary V-8 with 250 bhp, so despite fair heft (nearly two tons at the curb), Aurora clocked 0-60 mph at a brisk 8.2 seconds in Consumer Guide® tests. A computer-controlled four-speed automatic was the only transmission, and options were limited to power moonroof, cloth upholstery (a no-cost alternative to standard leather), heated front seats, and an "Autobahn" package with firm shocks, high-speed tires, and slightly tighter final gearing.

As the first of a new generation for GM's most-troubled division, Aurora naturally drew lots of media interest, and Olds confidently sent out preproduction examples for press drives more than a year before sales began. Initial verdicts were generally quite positive. Enthused *Motor Trend*: "The new Aurora has us believing miracles can still happen." *Car and Driver* called it a "combination of value and sophistication that will make an ideal birthright for the new Oldsmobile," while Consumer Guide®'s *Auto '95* termed Aurora a "huge step in a new and better direction for Oldsmobile. It's competitive with Japanese and European sedans that cost thousands more...."

How odd, then, that Aurora wore a new stylized "A" logo but almost no Olds I.D., perhaps a tacit admission of how tarnished the old Rocket badge had become. Then again, Aurora was intended to stand somewhat above the rest of the line as a more-exclusive "halo" car. Indeed, the model was sold by only two-thirds of Olds dealers, the ones who met rigid new divisional standards for everything from showroom display to technical proficiency in the service department. Of course, that was only right for an image-building flagship, and it paid off with strong debut model-year sales of close to 48,000, tops among premium sedans.

But that would be the peak. Aurora sales plunged about 50 percent for model-year '96 and stayed at roughly that level until 1999, when fewer than 20,000 were built. Why the sudden fall? A big factor was tougher-than-ever luxury-class competition, especially from Japanese rivals Acura and Lexus. Aurora, by contrast, got but one major innovation in its first five years: GM's new OnStar communications and assistance service as a dealer-installed option for '98. While Olds had promised no gratuitous changes, hindsight suggests it might have done more to keep Aurora fresh. Then again, this flagship was never intended to be a high-volume moneymaker. Not so the cars that would follow in its image, with nothing less than Oldsmobile's future riding on their success.

GM had its own troubles, saddled with too many models that cost too much to build yet weren't selling as expected. As a result, GM's total market was down to less than 34 percent by 1995, and would go lower still. But GM began cutting costs and was soon making money again, helped by a tech-driven boom economy that fueled an upsurge in demand for profitable trucks. Meanwhile, Olds still struggled. GM bean counters were particularly dismayed by the continuing slide in Olds sales, which were now barely a third of record 1985's nearly 1.2 million units.

The total was even lower when Oldsmobile's centennial rolled around on August 21, 1997—100 years to the day since the formal incorporation of the Olds Motor Vehicle Company. Despite the dreary sales situation, Lansing happily welcomed thousands of celebrants from all over the country, many of whom brought vintage Oldsmobiles for a memorable birthday parade comprising nearly 100 vehicles. Also highlighting the festivities were the next Centennial Plan models, all bearing a "soaring rocket" emblem instituted under John Rock, who felt the old '60s-vintage logo resembled a "chicken track."

Two of the newcomers went on sale before the birthday bash as '97 entries. Though not central to this book, the second-generation Silhouette bears mention for offering more-conventional minivan looks and construction in regular-length and new extended models. All boasted seating for seven, dual sliding rear side doors (the left one optional at first, later standard), a torquier 3.4-liter V-6, and more-upscale furnishings and features than sisters Chevrolet Venture and Pontiac Trans Sport. It all added up to a big improvement. Performance was just adequate, but handling was tops among minivans, with standard antilock brakes and available traction control enhancing "dynamic safety." Versatility, convenience, and value earned high marks, too. But Silhouette and its siblings were visibly narrower than most minivans, and that turned off many buyers. As a result, they never threatened the sales-leading Chrysler Corporation minivans. Of the GM trio, Silhouette was the most-expensive and, thus, the least-popular.

Oldsmobile's other '97 debutante was yet another Cutlass, a replacement for the long-serving Ciera. Though just a dressier version of Chevy's new Malibu sedan, it fit neatly between the compact Achieva and midsize Cutlass Supreme in size and price. Differences from Malibu were confined to Aurora-look wheels, minor trim, and a standard instead of optional V-6. Both the base Cutlass (later GL) and uptown GLS offered good value, delivering for $20,000 or less with air conditioning, ABS, and other expected amenities. An unexpected bonus was the "Oldsmobile Edge," the comprehensive customer-service program launched a few years earlier for all Olds models. One of its provisions allowed a dissatisfied buyer to return a car within 30 days or 1500 miles for a full refund. That might have won a few sales, but it wasn't nearly enough. Though this Cutlass was a match in most ways for the popular Honda Accord and Toyota Camry it targeted, production was less than 20,000 for '97, poor even discounting the short model year. The '98 tally was also underwhelming at some 52,600. With that, Oldsmobile's junior midsize was buried, taking the once-magical Cutlass name with it.

The Centennial Plan envisioned "more-international" Oldsmobiles designed with high appeal for the younger, more-affluent customers who typically bought imports. If the Malibu-like Cutlass didn't quite fit that template, the Cutlass Supreme was an even bigger mismatch. Accordingly, the Supreme departed after 1997 with no further changes of substance. A decent car to the end, with Consumer Guide® "Recommended" labels to prove it, the W-body Supreme had simply grown too old to be as competitive as Olds needed it to be. Achieva, never that competitive in the hard-fought compact class, also vanished after '97, though Olds ran off some 27,000 carefully equipped 1998 sedans for the rental market—anything to make a sale.

Even less relevant to the emerging new Olds order, the Ninety-Eight was quietly dropped after '96—no great loss, as model-year volume was down to just 15,000, less than even the Aurora's. But Olds was reluctant to abandon traditional full-size luxury, so it retained the old Regency name for a top-line 1997 addition to the Eighty-Eight line. This offered similarly posh trappings and even a bright grille reminiscent of the last Ninety-Eights, but drew only about half as many orders despite a slightly lower price. To no one's surprise, the Eighty-Eight Regency vanished after just two seasons in another money-saving move aimed at breaking completely with the past.

Other Eighty-Eights got a mild makeover for '96, including a slim twin nostril grille, reshaped front fenders, and new headlights and taillamps. The sporty LSS became even more so, gaining more-supportive Aurora-style front bucket seats and a massaged supercharged V-6 option with an extra 15 bhp, 240 in all. For 1999, Olds marked a half-century of Eighty-Eights with a limited-production 50th Anniversary Edition, a specially equipped version of the mainstay LS priced $2245 higher. But this gesture soon looked very hollow, because the Eighty-Eight would not be back. Dealers howled once they found out, saying a full-size family car was still vital to their business, but their protests went unheeded.

One reason is that GM had discovered something that seemed sure to cure all its ills. "Brand management" wasn't a

**1997 Achieva sedan**

**1997 LSS sedan**

**1997 Cutlass Supreme sedan**

**1998 Regency sedan**

**1998 Aurora sedan**

**1998 Cutlass sedan**

# Oldsmobile

new business practice, but it was new to the auto industry. It assumes that products of a given type are all pretty much the same, so consumers tend to choose one over another based on their perception of the label or brand; the better the image of a brand, the better the sales of the products that wear it. Chairman John Smale was a strong believer. So was Jack Smith, Jr., who succeeded him in 1996. Ditto G. Richard Wagoner, Jr., who replaced Smith as president in 1998. But the real push for brand management came from Ronald Zarrella, recruited from optics maker Bausch & Lomb to succeed Wagoner as president of GM's North American operations in 1999. Under Zarrella, GM reorganized—again—and greatly expanded marketing staff and budgets. At the same time, overlapping or underperforming models were pruned from "product portfolios," hence the deaths of the Ninety-Eight and Eighty-Eight. But critics said cars don't sell in the same way as "commodity products" like soap or eyeglasses, and in time they were proved right. Not only did brand management do little to improve GM's fortunes, it actually added cost, time, and complexity in getting out new models, which tended to wind up as overly cautious, even bland products.

We mention all this because brand management was bad news for Olds, reducing the make to just three car lines by 2000. The most commercially promising was Intrigue, a new import-flavored midsize sedan arriving in May '97 as the 1998 replacement for Cutlass Supreme. Though related to the latest Pontiac Grand Prix and Buick Regal, it was arguably Detroit's strongest challenger yet to the all-conquering Accord and Camry. Intrigue rode a 109-inch wheelbase, the same as the Regal but shorter than the GP. Styling, previewed by the 1995 Antares concept, was clean and understated, with more than a hint of Aurora. The interior, also tastefully restrained, featured clear, well-placed gauges and controls; plus comfortable space for four adults, five in a pinch. Roadability was another asset. Said *Car and Driver:* "What's genuinely surprising is how the Intrigue's chassis mimics the behavior and feel of the imports— European imports at that. The structure always feels solid and tight [and] the suspension keeps a very tight rein on body motions." The only engine at first was GM's decidedly un-European "3800" pushrod V-6, but its 195 bhp made for brisk acceleration (just under eight seconds 0-60) despite a mandatory four-speed automatic. For 1999, Olds phased in a new 3.5-liter twincam V-6 derived from the all-aluminum Olds/Cadillac Northstar V-8. Dubbed the "shortstar" by some, it made 215 bhp despite less displacement, but it had little more torque, so performance was comparable. Even so, the 3.5 was quicker to rev, sounded neat, and backed up Intrigue's credentials as a serious alternative to imports.

Intrigued bowed in plain and fancier GL trim, as well as a late-arriving, leather-upholstered GLS. All came with premium features like front buckets and console, all-disc antilock brakes, traction control, and 16-inch wheels and tires at low- to mid-$20,000 prices, the heart of the market. A worthy new option for 2000 was an antiskid Precision Control System, which helped the keep the car on course if it started to slide.

*Consumer Guide®* welcomed Intrigue as "more sophisticated than the brash Grand Prix and more nimble and poised than the Ford Taurus or Camry V-6. If you're looking for a midsize car with a thoughtful blend of features and performance, don't decide until you've driven this pleasant and surprising new Olds." Yet despite that and many other endorsements, Intrigue sales tapered off right away, going from nearly 108,000 for extra long model-year '98 to just under 94,000, then to about 80,500 for 2000. But this wasn't the car's fault. Other factors were at work, as we'll see.

Complementing Intrigue for 1999 was a more-competitive

1998 Intrigue sedan

1999 Cutlass GLS sedan

1999 Alero GLS coupe

1999 Aurora sedan

1999 Eighty-Eight 50th Anniversary Edition sedan

# Oldsmobile

1999 LSS sedan

2000 Alero coupe

2000 Intrigue sedan

2000 Silhouette Premiere minivan

2000 Bravada wagon

2001 Aurora sedan

2001 Alero coupe

2001 Silhouette minivan

2002 Bravada wagon

2002 Silhouette minivan

# Oldsmobile

Olds compact, the Alero. Pontiac's redesigned Grand Am used the same platform and powertrains, but Alero was very much a junior Intrigue, with similarly handsome Aurora-inspired styling inside and out. A 107-inch wheelbase, rangy for compacts, served sedan and jaunty coupe body styles, each offering GX, GL, and top-drawer GLS trim. A 170-hp 3.4-liter twincam V-6 (with roots in 1980, by the way) was standard for GLS models and available for GLs in lieu of a 150-bhp 2.4-liter "Twin Cam" four-cylinder, a more-civilized version of the Quad-4 and one of the few carryover items from the last Achievas. Like Intrigues, all Aleros had standard all-disc antilock brakes, but also traction control (albeit a simpler setup). GL and GLS added a handy electronic tire-pressure monitor, and a firmer Performance Suspension Package was available for GLS coupes. Alero tilted even more toward sportiness for 2000, when a five-speed manual transmission—supplied by the renowned Getrag of Germany, no less—replaced the four-speed automatic as standard for some four-cylinder models. Olds shuffled prices and some features that year and again for 2001. Otherwise, Alero was little changed in its first three seasons.

Predictably, perhaps, Alero met the same warm welcome as Intrigue. *Car and Driver* judged its V-6 GLS coupe "downright world-class." *Road & Track*, after testing a similar car, praised "expressive styling, a lively chassis, and . . . satisfying torque." Being smaller and lighter than Intrigues, V-6 Aleros posted slightly quicker 0-60 times and were even more nimble. Four-cylinder performance was slower but adequate, though also rather noisier. But if not perfect—what car is?—Alero gave value-minded shoppers another compelling reason to visit their local Olds dealer. As Consumer Guide® observed: "This new Olds comes across as a refined car that's not embarrassed by a twisting road. Alero feels more mature than [Grand Am], and with a long list of standard features and competitive prices, shapes up as a good value."

Despite the impressive one-two punch of Intrigue and Alero, Olds sales kept sliding. Buyers were hardly reassured by journalists' doubts about Oldsmobile's future, a chorus that only grew louder once Chrysler announced termination of once-mighty Plymouth after model-year 2001. Nothing, it seemed, was sacred in Detroit at the turn of the millennium, not even America's oldest surviving nameplate.

Heavy symbolic freight thus attached to the all-new 2001 Aurora that reached dealers in spring 2000. Actually, there were two now: a 4.0-liter V-8 model and a more-affordable companion motivated by Intrigue's snappy 3.5 V-6. Both were slightly smaller in most dimensions than the original Aurora and looked more-conservative, but the trusty G-body platform was reengineered to be stiffer and thus more-protective in a crash, as well as quieter. Options were few, as both models were lavishly equipped with standard leather-and-wood interior, automatic climate control, antilock all disc brakes, GM's OnStar system, and much more. V-8s added 17-inch wheels instead of 16s and the antiskid Precision Control System.

At just over $30,000 to start, the V-6 Aurora was basically a stand-in for the departed Eighty-Eight, bringing distinctive style and surprising performance to the family-car market. The uplevel V-8 was arguably less-special than its predecessor, but it also cost a few thousand less. And true to the Centennial

**2002 Intrigue GLS sedan**

Plan, each was a fine road car. Said *Motor Trend:* "This fresh Aurora is a fun-to-drive, remarkably well-executed sport sedan that nicely balances the luxury-comfort and responsive-agile sides of the driving equation at a reasonable price. Less can be more, after all."

But not for GM managers, who by now were more pressured than ever to boost the company's bottom line and, especially, stock price. Olds wasn't the only GM unit in the red, but estimated losses of $120 million a year made it a prime target for cost-cutters. Thus, barely two weeks before Christmas 2000, GM announced plans to phase out the Olds nameplate over the next several years. Future-model development was stopped (it already had been in some cases) and advertising and marketing were cut to the bone.

Dealers were stunned, not to mention angry. So were some within Oldsmobile itself. As it happened, the death notice came during the press preview of a new and better 2002 Bravada sport-utility, where it took Olds designers, engineers, and marketers completely by surprise. In another poignant irony, Olds car sales finally turned up for 2001, the first year-to-year increase since 1994. It wasn't a big gain—less than five percent on a model-year basis—but it did suggest a nascent turnaround. As Zarella told *AutoWeek*: "Our strategy [with Olds] was starting to work—we ended up with a lot of positive demographics. The problem is, there just weren't enough of them." Veteran Olds public relations director Gus Buenz put it more succinctly: "We've got good product, but not enough people know about it."

At first, GM planned to keep building the various Oldsmobiles "until the end of their current life cycles or as long as they remain economically viable." By September 2001, however, GM had decided that "Oldsmobile production has remained unprofitable," so the end would come no later than model-year 2004. Intrigue and the V-6 Aurora died much sooner (in June 2002), with the V-8 Aurora slated to follow (May 2003).

**2002 Alero sedan**

**2002 Aurora sedan**

# Oldsmobile

## Specifications

### 1930

**F-30 Standard Six (4 wood wheels) (wb 113.5)**

|  | Wght | Price | Prod |
|---|---|---|---|
| conv rdstr 4P | 2,665 | 995 | 822 |
| w/5 wire wheels | 2,735 | 1,050 | 364 |
| phtn 5P | 2,655 | 965 | 17 |
| w/5 wire wheels | 2,735 | 1,020 | 5 |
| cpe 2P | 2,755 | 895 | 3,726 |
| w/5 wire wheels | 2,835 | 950 | 343 |
| spt cpe 4P | 2,810 | 965 | 2,214 |
| w/5 wire wheels | 2,890 | 1,020 | 584 |
| sdn 2d | 2,840 | 895 | 9,295 |
| w/5 wire wheels | 2,920 | 950 | 1,357 |
| sdn 4d | 2,940 | 995 | 11,841 |
| w/5 wire wheels | 3,020 | 1,050 | 1,242 |
| Patrician sdn 4d | 2,945 | 1,060 | 1,015 |
| w/5 wire wheels | 3,025 | 1,140 | 303 |

**F-30 Special Six (wb 113.5)**

|  | Wght | Price | Prod |
|---|---|---|---|
| conv rdstr 4P | 2,745 | 1,070 | 233 |
| phtn 5P | 2,730 | 1,040 | 5 |
| cpe 2P | 2,820 | 970 | 633 |
| spt cpe 4P | 2,895 | 1,040 | 478 |
| sdn 2d | 2,920 | 970 | 1,598 |
| sdn 4d | 3,020 | 1,070 | 3,031 |
| Patrician sdn 4d | 3,025 | 1,135 | 426 |

**F-30 DeLuxe Six (wb 113.5)**

|  | Wght | Price | Prod |
|---|---|---|---|
| conv rdstr 4P | 2,815 | 1,125 | 1,560 |
| phtn 5P | 2,800 | 1,095 | 76 |
| cpe 2P | 2,900 | 1,025 | 306 |
| spt cpe 4P | 2,960 | 1,095 | 1,594 |
| sdn 2d | 2,990 | 1,025 | 615 |
| sdn 4d | 3,080 | 1,125 | 2,973 |
| Patrician sdn 4d | 3,090 | 1,190 | 2,525 |

**Export Production:**

|  | Prod |
|---|---|
| conv rdstr 4P | 27 |
| phtn 5P | 9 |
| cpe 2P | 5 |
| sdn 2d | 47 |
| sdn 4d | 95 |
| Patrician sdn 4d | 31 |

| 1930 Engine | bore × stroke | bhp | availability |
|---|---|---|---|
| I-6, 197.5 | 3.19 × 4.13 | 62 | S-all |

### 1931

**F-31 Standard Six (wb 113.5)**

|  | Wght | Price | Prod |
|---|---|---|---|
| conv rdstr 4P | 2,800 | 935 | 357 |
| cpe 2P | 2,750 | 845 | 2,423 |
| spt cpe 2-4P | 2,825 | 895 | 1,545 |
| sdn 2d | 2,855 | 845 | 5,323 |
| sdn 4d | 2,935 | 925 | 6,736 |
| Patrician sdn 4d | 2,950 | 960 | 958 |

**F-31 DeLuxe Six (wb 113.5)**

|  | Wght | Price | Prod |
|---|---|---|---|
| conv rdstr 4P | 2,875 | 1,000 | 3,144 |
| cpe 2P | 2,815 | 910 | 1,277 |
| spt cpe 2-4P | 2,905 | 960 | 3,355 |
| sdn 2d | 2,925 | 910 | 3,833 |
| sdn 4d | 3,000 | 990 | 10,486 |
| Patrician sdn 4d | 3,020 | 1,025 | 7,840 |

Note: Prices in both series were the same for either wire or wood wheels (five on Standards, six on DeLuxes). In addition, a few Standards were built with disc wheels: sdn 2d (1), sdn 4d (26), Patrician sdn (5). Distribution of wire and wood wheels was approximately equal.

| 1931 Engine | bore × stroke | bhp | availability |
|---|---|---|---|
| I-6, 197.5 | 3.19 × 4.13 | 65 | S-all |

### 1932

**F-32 Six (wb 116.5) (5 wheels)**

|  | Wght | Price | Prod |
|---|---|---|---|
| conv rdstr 2-4P | 2,870 | 955 | 141 |
| cpe 2P | 2,845 | 875 | 760 |
| spt cpe 2-4P | 2,925 | 925 | 366 |
| sdn 2d | 2,960 | 875 | 1,829 |
| sdn 4d | 3,035 | 955 | 2,603 |
| Patrician sdn 4d | 3,040 | 990 | 236 |

**F-32 Six (wb 116.5) (6 wheels)**

|  | Wght | Price | Prod |
|---|---|---|---|
| conv rdstr 2-4P | 2,975 | 1,000 | 582 |
| for export, RHD | — | — | 21 |
| spt cpe 2-4P | 3,025 | 970 | 809 |
| sdn 2d | 3,060 | 920 | 975 |
| sdn 4d | 3,135 | 1,000 | 3,297 |
| Patrician sdn 4d | 3,155 | 1,035 | 1,878 |

**D-32 Eight (wb 116.5) (5 wheels)**

|  | Wght | Price | Prod |
|---|---|---|---|
| conv rdstr 2-4P | 2,995 | 1,055 | 47 |
| cpe 2P | 2,970 | 975 | 89 |
| spt cpe 2-4P | 3,045 | 1,025 | 84 |
| sdn 2d | 3,080 | 975 | 122 |
| sdn 4d | 3,165 | 1,055 | 525 |
| Patrician sdn 4d | 3,165 | 1,090 | 181 |

**L-32 Eight (wb 116.5) (6 wheels)**

|  | Wght | Price | Prod |
|---|---|---|---|
| conv rdstr 2-4P | 3,100 | 1,100 | 347 |
| cpe 2P | 3,075 | 1,020 | 127 |
| spt cpe 2-4P | 3,145 | 1,070 | 392 |
| sdn 2d | 3,180 | 1,020 | 149 |
| sdn 4d | 3,260 | 1,100 | 1,205 |
| Patrician sdn 4d | 3,275 | 1,135 | 2,081 |

| 1932 Engines | bore × stroke | bhp | availability |
|---|---|---|---|
| I-6, 213.3 | 3.31 × 4.13 | 74 | S-Six |
| I-8, 240.0 | 3.00 × 4.25 | 87 | S-Eight |

### 1933

**F-33 Six (wb 115.0)**

|  | Wght | Price | Prod |
|---|---|---|---|
| bus cpe 2P | 2,945 | 745 | 1,547 |
| spt cpe 2P | 3,010 | 780 | 1,740 |
| conv cpe 2P | 2,970 | 825 | 317 |
| cpe 5P | 3,025 | 745 | 4,070 |
| touring cpe 5P | 3,090 | 775 | 5,464 |
| sdn 4d | 3,105 | 825 | 7,194 |
| touring sdn 4d | 3,165 | 855 | 5,720 |

**L-33 Eight (wb 119.0)**

|  | Wght | Price | Prod |
|---|---|---|---|
| bus cpe 2P | 3,090 | 845 | 396 |
| spt cpe 2P | 3,160 | 880 | 827 |
| conv cpe 2P | 3,110 | 925 | 267 |
| cpe 5P | 3,190 | 845 | 203 |
| touring cpe 5P | 3,230 | 875 | 1,901 |
| sdn 4d | 3,255 | 925 | 2,639 |
| touring sdn 4d | 3,305 | 955 | 4,357 |

| 1933 Engines | bore × stroke | bhp | availability |
|---|---|---|---|
| I-6, 221.4 | 3.38 × 4.13 | 80 | S-Six |
| I-8, 240.3 | 3.00 × 4.25 | 90 | S-Eight |

### 1934

**F-34 Six (wb 114.0)**

|  | Wght | Price | Prod |
|---|---|---|---|
| bus cpe 2P | 2,970 | 650 | 3,934 |
| spt cpe 2-4P | 3,030 | 695 | 2,370 |
| cpe 5P | 3,040 | 695 | 4,679 |
| touring cpe 5P | 3,095 | 725 | 12,306 |

# Oldsmobile

| F-34 Six (wb 114.0) | Wght | Price | Prod |
|---|---|---|---|
| sdn 4d | 3,100 | 755 | 7,014 |
| sdn 4d T/B | 3,160 | 785 | 20,781 |
| **L-34 Eight (wb 119.0)** | | | |
| bus cpe 2P | 3,320 | 885 | 900 |
| spt cpe 2-4P | 3,370 | 920 | 1,278 |
| conv cpe 2-4P | 3,325 | 975 | 915 |
| cpe 5P | 3,400 | 895 | 649 |
| touring cpe 5P | 3,440 | 925 | 4,291 |
| sdn 4d | 3,470 | 965 | 4,187 |
| sdn 4d T/B | 3,520 | 995 | 12,272 |

| 1934 Engines | bore × stroke | bhp | availability |
|---|---|---|---|
| I-6, 213.3 | 3.31 × 4.13 | 84 | S-Six |
| I-8, 240.3 | 3.00 × 4.25 | 90 | S-Eight |

## 1935

| F-35 Six (wb 115.0) | Wght | Price | Prod |
|---|---|---|---|
| bus cpe 2P | 3,110 | 675 | 8,468 |
| spt cpe 2-4P | 3,150 | 725 | 2,905 |
| conv cpe 2-4P | 3,155 | 800 | 1,598 |
| cpe 5P | 3,225 | 725 | 12,785 |
| touring cpe 5P T/B | 3,225 | 755 | 18,821 |
| sdn 4d | 3,285 | 790 | 13,009 |
| touring sdn 4d T/B | 3,285 | 820 | 32,647 |
| **L-35 Eight (wb 121.0)** | | | |
| bus cpe 2P | 3,335 | 860 | 1,226 |
| spt cpe 2-4P | 3,380 | 895 | 959 |
| conv cpe 2-4P | 3,390 | 950 | 910 |
| cpe 5P | 3,480 | 870 | 870 |
| touring cpe 5P | 3,485 | 900 | 4,868 |
| sdn 4d | 3,530 | 940 | 2,976 |
| touring sdn 4d T/B | 3,530 | 970 | 18,058 |

| 1935 Engines | bore × stroke | bhp | availability |
|---|---|---|---|
| I-6, 213.3 | 3.31 × 4.13 | 90 | S-Six |
| I-8, 240.3 | 3.00 × 4.25 | 100 | S-Eight |

## 1936

| F-36 Six (wb 115.0) | Wght | Price | Prod |
|---|---|---|---|
| bus cpe 2P | 3,019 | 665 | 19,346 |
| spt cpe 2-4P | 3,054 | 730 | 2,838 |
| conv cpe 2-4P | 3,109 | 805 | 2,136 |
| cpe 5P | 3,144 | 730 | 11,143 |
| touring cpe 5P T/B | 3,144 | 755 | 45,391 |
| sdn 4d | 3,179 | 795 | 4,082 |
| touring sdn 4d T/B | 3,194 | 820 | 66,714 |
| **L-36 Eight (wb 121.0)** | | | |
| bus cpe 2P | 3,231 | 810 | 2,181 |
| spt cpe 2-4P | 3,261 | 845 | 959 |
| conv cpe 2-4P | 3,321 | 935 | 931 |
| cpe 5P | 3,376 | 845 | 232 |
| touring cpe 5P T/B | 3,376 | 870 | 6,626 |
| sdn 4d | 3,401 | 910 | 395 |
| touring sdn 4d T/B | 3,421 | 935 | 28,373 |

| 1936 Engines | bore × stroke | bhp | availability |
|---|---|---|---|
| I-6, 213.3 | 3.31 × 4.13 | 90 | S-Six |
| I-8, 240.3 | 3.00 × 4.25 | 100 | S-Eight |

## 1937

| F-37 Six (wb 117.0) | Wght | Price | Prod |
|---|---|---|---|
| bus cpe 2P | 3,220 | 810 | 13,958 |
| club cpe 2-4P | 3,210 | 870 | 7,426 |
| conv cpe 2-4P | 3,350 | 965 | 1,619 |
| sdn 2d | 3,275 | 860 | 9,664 |
| sdn 2d T/B | 3,275 | 895 | 38,048 |

| F-37 Six (wb 117.0) | Wght | Price | Prod |
|---|---|---|---|
| sdn 4d | 3,310 | 920 | 4,020 |
| sdn 4d T/B | 3,295 | 945 | 62,933 |
| **L-37 Eight (wb 124.0)** | | | |
| bus cpe 2P | 3,395 | 925 | 2,060 |
| club cpe 2-4P | 3,405 | 985 | 2,302 |
| conv cpe 2-4P | 3,530 | 1,080 | 728 |
| sdn 2d | 3,480 | 985 | 398 |
| sdn 2d T/B | 3,480 | 1,010 | 5,818 |
| sdn 4d | 3,510 | 1,035 | 496 |
| sdn 4d T/B | 3,495 | 1,060 | 30,365 |

| 1937 Engines | bore × stroke | bhp | availability |
|---|---|---|---|
| I-6, 230.0 | 3.44 × 4.13 | 95 | S-Six |
| I-8, 257.0 | 3.25 × 3.88 | 110 | S-Eight |

## 1938

| F-38 Six (wb 117.0) | Wght | Price | Prod |
|---|---|---|---|
| bus cpe 2P | 3,205 | 873 | 6,538 |
| club cpe 2-4P | 3,195 | 929 | 3,632 |
| conv cpe 2-4P | 3,360 | 1,046 | 1,184 |
| sdn 2d | 3,275 | 919 | 3,975 |
| touring sdn 2d T/B | 3,265 | 944 | 17,390 |
| sdn 4d | 3,285 | 970 | 1,477 |
| touring sdn 4d T/B | 3,290 | 995 | 30,914 |
| **L-38 (wb 124.0)** | | | |
| bus cpe 2P | 3,400 | 989 | 1,098 |
| club cpe 2-4P | 3,385 | 1,035 | 1,136 |
| conv cpe 2-4P | 3,530 | 1,163 | 475 |
| sdn 2d | 3,475 | 1,030 | 137 |
| touring sdn 2d T/B | 3,465 | 1,056 | 1,950 |
| sdn 4d | 3,490 | 1,081 | 200 |
| touring sdn 4d T/B | 3,480 | 1,107 | 14,939 |

| 1938 Engines | bore × stroke | bhp | availability |
|---|---|---|---|
| I-6, 230.0 | 3.44 × 4.13 | 95 | S-Six |
| I-8, 257.0 | 3.25 × 3.88 | 110 | S-Eight |

## 1939

| F-39 Series 60 (wb 115.0) | Wght | Price | Prod |
|---|---|---|---|
| bus cpe 2P | 2,870 | 777 | 5,575 |
| club cpe 2-4P | 2,915 | 833 | 2,273 |
| sdn 2d | 2,965 | 838 | 16,910 |
| sdn 4d | 3,000 | 889 | 15,958 |
| **G-39 Series 70 (wb 120.0)** | | | |
| bus cpe 2P | 3,040 | 840 | 5,211 |
| club cpe 2-4P | 3,080 | 891 | 4,795 |
| conv cpe 2-4P | 3,230 | 1,045 | 1,714 |
| sdn 2d (incl. 17 Sun sdns) | 3,140 | 901 | 19,442 |
| sdn 4d (incl. 81 Sun sdns) | 3,180 | 952 | 38,224 |
| **L-39 Series 80 (wb 120.0)** | | | |
| bus cpe 2P | 3,190 | 920 | 738 |
| club cpe 2-4P | 3,230 | 971 | 1,147 |
| conv cpe 2-4P | 3,390 | 1,119 | 472 |
| sdn 2d (incl. 7 Sun sdns) | 3,290 | 992 | 1,571 |
| sdn 4d (incl. 85 Sun sdns) | 3,340 | 1,043 | 13,197 |

| 1939 Engines | bore × stroke | bhp | availability |
|---|---|---|---|
| I-6, 216.0 | 3.44 × 3.88 | 90 | S-60 |
| I-6, 230.0 | 3.44 × 4.13 | 95 | S-70 |
| I-8, 257.1 | 3.25 × 3.88 | 110 | S-80 |

## 1940

| F-40 Series 60 (wb 116.0) | Wght | Price | Prod |
|---|---|---|---|
| bus cpe | 3,030 | 807 | 2,752 |
| club cpe | 3,015 | 848 | 7,664 |
| conv cpe | 3,110 | 1,021 | 1,347 |

# Oldsmobile

| F-40 Series 60 (wb 116.0) | Wght | Price | Prod |
|---|---|---|---|
| sdn 2d | 3,065 | 853 | 27,220 |
| sdn 4d | 3,100 | 899 | 24,422 |
| wgn 4d | 3,255 | 1,042 | 633 |
| **G-40 Series 70 (wb 120.0)** | | | |
| bus cpe | 3,100 | 865 | 4,337 |
| club cpe | 3,105 | 901 | 8,505 |
| conv cpe | 3,240 | 1,045 | 1,070 |
| sdn 2d | 3,170 | 912 | 21,486 |
| sdn 4d | 3,220 | 963 | 41,467 |
| **L-40 Series 90 (wb 124.0)** | | | |
| club cpe | 3,440 | 1,069 | 10,836 |
| conv cpe | 3,590 | 1,222 | 290 |
| sdn 4d | 3,555 | 1,131 | 33,075 |
| conv phaeton 4d | 3,750 | 1,570 | 50 |

| 1940 Engines | bore × stroke | bhp | availability |
|---|---|---|---|
| I-6, 230.0 | 3.44 × 4.13 | 95 | S-60, 70 |
| I-8, 257.1 | 3.25 × 3.88 | 110 | S-90 |

## 1941 Production includes exports

| 66 Special 6 (wb 119.0) | Wght | Price | Prod |
|---|---|---|---|
| bus cpe | 3,299 | 852 | 6,455 |
| club cpe | 3,335 | 893 | 24,027 |
| conv cpe | 3,503 | 1,048 | 2,897 |
| sdn 2d | 3,338 | 898 | 30,506 |
| sdn 4d | 3,384 | 945 | 27,125 |
| town sedan 4d | 3,377 | 945 | 11,963 |
| wgn 4d | 3,692 | 1,104 | 609 |
| chassis | — | 642 | 644 |
| **68 Special 8 (wb 119.0)** | | | |
| bus cpe | 3,429 | 893 | 188 |
| club cpe | 3,461 | 935 | 2,703 |
| conv cpe | 3,633 | 1,089 | 789 |
| sdn 2d | 3,471 | 940 | 500 |
| sdn 4d | 3,512 | 987 | 3,885 |
| town sedan 4d | 3,511 | 987 | 2,193 |
| wgn 4d | 3,790 | 1,217 | 96 |
| chassis | — | 683 | 2 |
| **76 Dynamic Cruiser 6 (wb 125.0)** | | | |
| bus cpe | 3,418 | 908 | 353 |
| club sdn | 3,466 | 954 | 47,098 |
| sdn 4d | 3,527 | 1,010 | 41,409 |
| chassis | — | 737 | 3 |
| **78 Dynamic Cruiser 8 (wb 125.0)** | | | |
| bus cpe | 3,525 | 944 | 51 |
| club sdn | 3,571 | 989 | 13,641 |
| sdn 4d | 3,637 | 1,045 | 15,702 |
| **96 Custom Cruiser 6 (wb 125.0)** | | | |
| club cpe | 3,475 | 1,043 | 2,196 |
| conv cpe | 3,677 | 1,191 | 332 |
| sdn 4d | 3,558 | 1,099 | 4,248 |
| **98 Custom Cruiser 8 (wb 125.0)** | | | |
| club cpe | 3,575 | 1,079 | 6,372 |
| conv cpe | 3,786 | 1,227 | 1,300 |
| conv sdn 4d | 3,939 | 1,575 | 125 |
| sdn 4d | 3,668 | 1,135 | 22,509 |
| chassis | — | 822 | 127 |

| 1941 Engines | bore × stroke | bhp | availability |
|---|---|---|---|
| I-6, 238.1 | 3.50 × 4.13 | 100 | S-66, 76, 96 |
| I-8, 257.1 | 3.25 × 3.88 | 110 | S-68, 78, 98 |

## 1942 Production includes exports

| 66 Special 6 (wb 119.0) | Wght | Price | Prod |
|---|---|---|---|
| bus cpe | 3,385 | 972 | 1,085 |
| club cpe | 3,410 | 1,015 | 3,803 |
| conv cpe | 3,714 | 1,257 | 669 |
| club sdn | 3,421 | 1,030 | 9,493 |
| sdn 2d | 3,436 | 1,020 | 3,557 |
| sdn 4d | 3,469 | 1,068 | 7615 |
| town sedan 4d | 3,460 | 1,068 | 3,253 |
| wgn 4d | 3,875 | 1,356 | 744 |
| **68 Special 8 (wb 119.0)** | | | |
| bus cpe | 3,519 | 1,015 | 90 |
| club cpe | 3,550 | 1,057 | 477 |
| conv cpe | 3,850 | 1,299 | 211 |
| club sdn | 3,566 | 1,073 | 1,357 |
| sdn 2d | 3,571 | 1,063 | 137 |
| sdn 4d | 3,603 | 1,110 | 1,054 |
| town sedan 4d | 3,596 | 1,110 | 707 |
| wgn 4d | 3,995 | 1,398 | 56 |
| **76 Dynamic Cruiser 6 (wb 125.0)** | | | |
| club sdn | 3,549 | 1,073 | 10,142 |
| sdn 4d | 3,610 | 1,131 | 8,871 |
| **78 Dynamic Cruiser 8 (wb 125.0)** | | | |
| club sdn | 3,685 | 1,116 | 3,674 |
| sdn 4d | 3,736 | 1,174 | 4,129 |
| **98 Custom Cruiser 8 (wb 127.0)** | | | |
| conv cpe | 4,124 | 1,536 | 230 |
| club sdn | 3,806 | 1,294 | 1,795 |
| sdn 4d | 3,885 | 1,351 | 4,799 |
| chassis | — | — | 51 |

| 1942 Engines | bore × stroke | bhp | availability |
|---|---|---|---|
| I-6, 238.1 | 3.50 × 4.13 | 100 | S-66, 76 |
| I-8, 257.1 | 3.25 × 3.88 | 110 | S-68, 78, 98 |

## 1946 Production includes exports

| Special 66 (wb 119.0) | Wght | Price | Prod |
|---|---|---|---|
| conv cpe | 3,697 | 1,327 | 1,409 |
| club cpe | 3,436 | 1,108 | 4,537 |
| club sdn 2d | 3,455 | 1,134 | 11,721 |
| sdn 4d | 3,488 | 1,169 | 11,053 |
| wgn 4d | 3,892 | 1,795 | 140 |
| chassis | — | — | 1,695 |
| **Dynamic Cruiser 76 (wb 125.0)** | | | |
| club sdn 2d | 3,570 | 1,184 | 30,929 |
| Deluxe club sdn 2d | — | 1,284 | 1,923 |
| sdn 4d | 3,665 | 1,234 | 18,425 |
| Deluxe sdn 4d | — | 1,334 | 2,179 |
| **Dynamic Cruiser 78 (wb 125.0)** | | | |
| club sdn 2d | 3,704 | 1,264 | 8,723 |
| Deluxe club sdn 2d | — | 1,364 | 2,188 |
| sdn 4d | 3,780 | 1,313 | 7,103 |
| Deluxe sdn 4d | — | 1,413 | 2,939 |
| **Custom Cruiser 98 (wb 127.0)** | | | |
| club sdn 2d | 3,837 | 1,442 | 2,459 |
| conv cpe | 4,185 | 1,840 | 874 |
| sdn 4d | 3,933 | 1,492 | 11,031 |
| chassis | — | — | 51 |

| 1946 Engines | bore × stroke | bhp | availability |
|---|---|---|---|
| I-6, 238.1 | 3.50 × 4.13 | 100 | S-66, 76 |
| I-8, 257.1 | 3.25 × 3.88 | 110 | S-78, 98 |

# Oldsmobile

**1947** Production includes exports

| Special 66 (wb 119.0) | Wght | Price | Prod |
|---|---|---|---|
| club sdn 2d | 3,330 | 1,433 | 13,960 |
| club cpe | 3,315 | 1,407 | 11,699 |
| conv cpe | 3,520 | 1,742 | 3,947 |
| sdn 4d | 3,375 | 1,471 | 21,015 |
| wgn 4d | 3,715 | 2,319 | 968 |
| chassis | — | 1,075 | 134 |
| **Special 68 (wb 119.0)** | | | |
| club sdn 2d | 3,405 | 1,490 | 6,759 |
| club cpe | 3,390 | 1,463 | 2,996 |
| conv cpe | 3,595 | 1,798 | 2,581 |
| sdn 4d | 3,450 | 1,527 | 5,128 |
| wgn 4d | — | 2,375 | 492 |
| **Dynamic Cruiser 76 (wb 125.0)** | | | |
| club sdn 2d | 3,460 | 1,497 | 28,067 |
| sdn 4d | 3,525 | 1,568 | 21,644 |
| **Dynamic Cruiser 78 (wb 125.0)** | | | |
| club sdn 2d | 3,535 | 1,554 | 16,782 |
| sdn 4d | 3,600 | 1,624 | 17,181 |
| **Custom Cruiser 98 (wb 127.0)** | | | |
| club sdn | 3,690 | 1,762 | 8,475 |
| conv cpe | 3,765 | 2,188 | 3,940 |
| sdn 4d | 3,775 | 1,812 | 24,733 |

| 1947 Engines | bore × stroke | bhp | availability |
|---|---|---|---|
| I-6, 238.1 | 3.50 × 4.13 | 100 | S-66, 76 |
| I-8, 257.1 | 3.25 × 3.88 | 110 | S-68, 78, 98 |

**1948** Production includes exports

| Dynamic 66 (wb 119.0) | Wght | Price | Prod |
|---|---|---|---|
| club sdn 2d | 3,439 | 1,513 | 19,029 |
| club cpe | 3,386 | 1,488 | 7,159 |
| conv cpe | 3,695 | 1,845 | 1,801 |
| sdn 4d | 3,471 | 1,556 | 16,614 |
| wgn 4d | 3,653 | 2,456 | 840 |
| Deluxe wgn 4d | — | — | 553 |
| chassis | — | 1,134 | 808 |
| **Dynamic 68 (wb 119.0)** | | | |
| club sdn 2d | 3,570 | 1,572 | 6,672 |
| club cpe | 3,519 | 1,546 | 2,415 |
| conv cpe | 3,818 | 1,903 | 2,091 |
| sdn 4d | 3,602 | 1,614 | 4,379 |
| wgn 4d | 3,880 | 2,514 | 760 |
| Deluxe wgn 4d | — | — | 554 |
| **Dynamic 76 (wb 125.0)** | | | |
| club sdn 2d | 3,571 | 1,584 | 14,945 |
| sdn 4d | 3,634 | 1,659 | 14,222 |
| **Dynamic 78 (wb 125.0)** | | | |
| club sdn 2d | 3,701 | 1,643 | 10,227 |
| sdn 4d | 3,764 | 1,717 | 10,424 |
| **Futuramic 98 (wb 125.0)** | | | |
| club sdn 2d | 3,795 | 1,920 | 2,311 |
| Deluxe club sdn 2d | — | 2,024 | 11,949 |
| sdn 4d | 3,866 | 1,993 | 5,605 |
| Deluxe sdn 4d | — | 2,098 | 32,456 |
| conv cpe | 4,185 | 2,466 | 12,914 |
| chassis | — | 1,441 | 1 |

| 1948 Engines | bore × stroke | bhp | availability |
|---|---|---|---|
| I-6, 238.1 | 3.50 × 4.13 | 100 | S-66, 76 |
| I-8, 257.1 | 3.25 × 3.88 | 110 | S-68, 78 |
| I-8, 257.1 | 3.25 × 3.88 | 115 | S-98 |

**1949**

| Futuramic 76 (wb 119.5) | Wght | Price | Prod |
|---|---|---|---|
| club sdn 2d | 3,290 | 1,758 | 23,059 |
| Deluxe club sdn 2d | 3,355 | 1,900 | 8,960 |
| club cpe | 3,260 | 1,732 | 9,403 |
| Deluxe club cpe | 3,315 | 1,873 | 3,280 |
| conv cpe | 3,580 | 2,148 | 5,338 |
| town sedan 4d | 3,335 | 1,821 | 3,741 |
| Deluxe town sedan 4d | 3,400 | 1,963 | 2,725 |
| sdn 4d | 3,340 | 1,832 | 23,631 |
| Deluxe sdn 4d | 3,375 | 1,974 | 13,874 |
| Deluxe wgn 4d | 3,680 | 2,895 | 1,545* |
| **Futuramic 88 (wb 119.5)** | | | |
| club sdn 2d | 3,585 | 2,170 | 16,887 |
| Deluxe club sdn 2d | 3,615 | 2,301 | 11,820 |
| club cpe | 3,550 | 2,143 | 6,562 |
| Deluxe club cpe | 3,590 | 2,274 | 4,999 |
| conv cpe | 3,845 | 2,559 | 5,434 |
| town sedan 4d | 3,625 | 2,233 | 2,859 |
| Deluxe town sedan 4d | 3,665 | 2,364 | 2,974 |
| sdn 4d | 3,615 | 2,244 | 23,342 |
| Deluxe sdn 4d | 3,645 | 2,375 | 23,044 |
| Deluxe wgn 4d | 3,945 | 3,296 | 1,355* |
| **Futuramic 98 (wb 125.0)** | | | |
| club sdn | 3,835 | 2,426 | 3,849 |
| Deluxe club sdn | 3,840 | 2,520 | 16,200 |
| sdn 4d | 3,890 | 2,500 | 8,820 |
| Deluxe sdn 4d | 3,925 | 2,594 | 49,001 |
| Deluxe Holiday htp cpe | 4,000 | 2,973 | 3,006 |
| Deluxe conv cpe | 4,200 | 2,973 | 12,602 |

| 1949 Engines | bore × stroke | bhp | availability |
|---|---|---|---|
| I-6, 257.1 | 3.53 × 4.38 | 105 | S-76 |
| V-8, 303.7 | 3.75 × 3.44 | 135 | S-88, 98 |

*Includes part-wood and all-steel (midyear) models

**1950**

| Futuramic 76 (wb 119.5) | Wght | Price | Prod |
|---|---|---|---|
| club sdn 2d | 3,280 | 1,745 | 3,186 |
| Deluxe club sdn 2d | 3,285 | 1,813 | 1,919 |
| club cpe | 3,260 | 1,719 | 2,238 |
| Deluxe club cpe | 3,280 | 1,787 | 1,126 |
| conv cpe | 3,585 | 2,135 | 973 |
| Holiday htp cpe | 3,335 | 2,003 | 144 |
| Deluxe Holiday htp cpe | 3,385 | 2,108 | 394 |
| sdn 4d | 3,320 | 1,819 | 7,396 |
| Deluxe sdn 4d | 3,340 | 1,887 | 9,159 |
| sdn 2d | 3,290 | 1,761 | 3,865 |
| Deluxe sdn 2d | 3,295 | 1,829 | 2,489 |
| wgn 4d | 3,610 | 2,362 | 121 |
| Deluxe wgn 4d | 3,615 | 2,504 | 247 |
| **Futuramic 88 (wb 119.5)** | | | |
| club sdn 2d | 3,475 | 1,904 | 14,705 |
| Deluxe club sdn 2d | 3,486 | 1,982 | 16,388 |
| club cpe | 3,435 | 1,878 | 10,684 |
| Deluxe club cpe | 3,455 | 1,956 | 10,772 |
| conv cpe | 3,745 | 2,294 | 9,127 |
| Holiday htp cpe | 3,510 | 2,162 | 1,366 |
| Deluxe Holiday htp cpe | 3,565 | 2,267 | 11,316 |
| sdn 4d | 3,515 | 1,978 | 40,301 |
| Deluxe sdn 4d | 3,520 | 2,056 | 100,810 |
| sdn 2d | 3,485 | 1,920 | 23,889 |
| Deluxe sdn 2d | 3,500 | 1,998 | 26,672 |
| wgn 4d | 3,775 | 2,520 | 1,830 |
| Deluxe wgn 4d | 3,780 | 2,662 | 552 |

# Oldsmobile

| Futuramic 98 (wb 122.0) | Wght | Price | Prod |
|---|---|---|---|
| club sdn 2d | 3,685 | 2,225 | 2,270 |
| Deluxe club sdn 2d | 3,705 | 2,319 | 9,719 |
| Deluxe conv cpe | 4,150 | 2,772 | 3,925 |
| Holiday htp cpe | 3,775 | 2,383 | 317 |
| Deluxe Holiday htp cpe | 3,840 | 2,641 | 7,946 |
| town sedan 4d | 3,710 | 2,267 | 255 |
| Deluxe town sedan 4d | 3,755 | 2,361 | 1,523 |
| sdn 4d | 3,765 | 2,299 | 7,499 |
| Deluxe sdn 4d | 3,775 | 2,393 | 72,766 |

| 1950 Engines | bore × stroke | bhp | availability |
|---|---|---|---|
| I-6, 257.1 | 3.53 × 4.38 | 105 | S-76 |
| V-8, 303.7 | 3.75 × 3.44 | 135 | S-88, 98 |

## 1951

| 88 (wb 119.5) | Wght | Price | Prod |
|---|---|---|---|
| sdn 4d | 3,542 | 2,111 | 22,848 |
| sdn 2d | 3,507 | 2,049 | 11,792 |

| Super 88 (wb 120.0) | | | |
|---|---|---|---|
| club cpe | 3,557 | 2,219 | 7,328 |
| sdn 4d | 3,636 | 2,328 | 90,131 |
| sdn 2d | 3,579 | 2,265 | 34,963 |
| conv cpe | 3,831 | 2,673 | 3,854 |
| Holiday htp cpe | 3,743 | 2,558 | 14,180 |

| 98 (wb 122.0) | | | |
|---|---|---|---|
| Deluxe sdn 4d | 3,787 | 2,610 | 78,122 |
| Holiday htp cpe | 3,762 | 2,545 | 3,917 |
| Deluxe Holiday htp cpe | 3,857 | 2,882 | 14,012 |
| Deluxe conv cpe | 4,107 | 3,025 | 4,468 |

| 1951 Engine | bore × stroke | bhp | availability |
|---|---|---|---|
| V-8, 303.7 | 3.75 × 3.44 | 135 | S-all |

## 1952

| 88 Deluxe (wb 120.0) | Wght | Price | Prod |
|---|---|---|---|
| sdn 4d | 3,608 | 2,327 | 12,215 |
| sdn 2d | 3,565 | 2,262 | 6,402 |

| Super 88 (wb 120.0) | | | |
|---|---|---|---|
| club cpe | 3,597 | 2,345 | 2,050 |
| sdn 4d | 3,649 | 2,462 | 70,606 |
| sdn 2d | 3,603 | 2,395 | 24,963 |
| conv cpe | 3,867 | 2,853 | 5,162 |
| Holiday htp cpe | 3,640 | 2,673 | 15,777 |

| Ninety-Eight (wb 124.0) | | | |
|---|---|---|---|
| sdn 4d | 3,765 | 2,786 | 58,550 |
| conv cpe | 4,111 | 3,229 | 3,544 |
| Holiday htp cpe | 3,874 | 3,022 | 14,150 |

| 1952 Engines | bore × stroke | bhp | availability |
|---|---|---|---|
| V-8, 303.7 | 3.75 × 3.44 | 145 | S-88 |
| V-8, 303.7 | 3.75 × 3.44 | 160 | S-Super 88, 98 |

## 1953

| 88 Deluxe (wb 120.0) | Wght | Price | Prod |
|---|---|---|---|
| sdn 4d | 3,642 | 2,327 | 20,400 |
| sdn 2d | 3,603 | 2,262 | 12,400 |

| Super 88 (wb 120.0) | | | |
|---|---|---|---|
| sdn 4d | 3,673 | 2,462 | 119,317 |
| sdn 2d | 3,628 | 2,395 | 36,824 |
| conv cpe | 3,905 | 2,853 | 8,310 |
| Holiday htp cpe | 3,661 | 2,673 | 36,881 |

| Ninety-Eight (wb 124.0) | | | |
|---|---|---|---|
| sdn 4d | 3,779 | 2,786 | 64,431 |
| conv cpe | 4,119 | 3,229 | 7,521 |
| Holiday htp cpe | 3,893 | 3,022 | 27,920 |

| Ninety-Eight (wb 124.0) | Wght | Price | Prod |
|---|---|---|---|
| Fiesta conv cpe | 4,453 | 5,717 | 458 |

| 1953 Engines | bore × stroke | bhp | availability |
|---|---|---|---|
| V-8, 303.7 | 3.75 × 3.44 | 150 | S-88 |
| V-8, 303.7 | 3.75 × 3.44 | 165 | S-Super 88, 98 |
| V-8, 303.7 | 3.75 × 3.44 | 170 | S-Fiesta |

## 1954

| 88 (wb 122.0) | Wght | Price | Prod |
|---|---|---|---|
| sdn 4d | 3,719 | 2,337 | 29,028 |
| sdn 2d | 3,699 | 2,272 | 18,013 |
| Holiday htp cpe | 3,721 | 2,449 | 25,820 |

| Super 88 (wb 122.0) | | | |
|---|---|---|---|
| sdn 4d | 3,780 | 2,477 | 111,326 |
| sdn 2d | 3,729 | 2,410 | 27,882 |
| conv cpe | 4,003 | 2,868 | 6,452 |
| Deluxe Holiday htp cpe | 3,775 | 2,688 | 42,155 |

| Ninety-Eight (wb 126.0) | | | |
|---|---|---|---|
| Deluxe sdn 4d | 3,895 | 2,806 | 47,972 |
| Holiday htp cpe | 3,851 | 2,826 | 8,865 |
| Deluxe Holiday htp cpe | 3,938 | 3,042 | 29,688 |
| Starfire conv cpe | 4,193 | 3,249 | 6,800 |

| 1954 Engines | bore × stroke | bhp | availability |
|---|---|---|---|
| V-8, 324.3 | 3.88 × 3.44 | 170 | S-88 |
| V-8, 324.3 | 3.88 × 3.44 | 185 | S-Super 88, 98 |

## 1955

| 88 (wb 122.0) | Wght | Price | Prod |
|---|---|---|---|
| sdn 4d | 3,707 | 2,362 | 57,777 |
| sdn 2d | 3,688 | 2,297 | 37,507 |
| Holiday htp sdn | 3,768 | 2,548 | 41,310 |
| Holiday htp cpe | 3,707 | 2,474 | 85,767 |

| Super 88 (wb 122.0) | | | |
|---|---|---|---|
| sdn 4d | 3,762 | 2,503 | 111,316 |
| sdn 2d | 3,720 | 2,436 | 11,950 |
| conv cpe | 3,983 | 2,894 | 9,007 |
| Deluxe Holiday htp sdn | 3,825 | 2,788 | 47,385 |
| Deluxe Holiday htp cpe | 3,765 | 2,714 | 62,534 |

| Ninety-Eight (wb 126.0) | | | |
|---|---|---|---|
| sdn 4d | 3,864 | 2,833 | 39,847 |
| Starfire conv cpe | 4,159 | 3,276 | 9,149 |
| Deluxe Holiday htp sdn | 3,976 | 3,140 | 31,267 |
| Deluxe Holiday htp cpe | 3,924 | 3,069 | 38,363 |

| 1955 Engines | bore × stroke | bhp | availability |
|---|---|---|---|
| V-8, 324.3 | 3.88 × 3.44 | 185 | S-88 |
| V-8, 324.3 | 3.88 × 3.44 | 202 | S-Super 88, 98; O-88 |

## 1956

| 88 (wb 122.0) | Wght | Price | Prod |
|---|---|---|---|
| sdn 4d | 3,748 | 2,487 | 57,092 |
| sdn 2d | 3,691 | 2,422 | 31,949 |
| Holiday htp sdn | 3,797 | 2,671 | 52,239 |
| Holiday htp cpe | 3,741 | 2,599 | 74,739 |

| Super 88 (wb 122.0) | | | |
|---|---|---|---|
| sdn 4d | 3,768 | 2,640 | 59,728 |
| sdn 2d | 3,717 | 2,574 | 5,465 |
| Holiday htp sdn | 3,869 | 2,881 | 61,192 |
| Holiday htp cpe | 3,771 | 2,808 | 43,054 |
| conv cpe | 4,033 | 3,031 | 9,561 |

| Ninety-Eight (wb 126.0) | | | |
|---|---|---|---|
| sdn 4d | 4,028 | 3,298 | 20,105 |
| Holiday htp sdn | 4,167 | 3,551 | 42,320 |

# Oldsmobile

| Ninety-Eight (wb 126.0) | Wght | Price | Prod |
|---|---|---|---|
| Holiday htp cpe | 4,080 | 3,480 | 19,433 |
| Starfire conv cpe | 4,325 | 3,740 | 8,581 |

| 1956 Engines | bore × stroke | bhp | availability |
|---|---|---|---|
| V-8, 324.3 | 3.88 × 3.44 | 230 | S-88 |
| V-8, 324.3 | 3.88 × 3.44 | 240 | S-Super 88, 98; O-88 |

## 1957

| Golden Rocket 88 (wb 122.0) | | Wght | Price | Prod |
|---|---|---|---|---|
| 3611 | sdn 2d | 3,942 | 2,733 | 18,477 |
| 3637 | Holiday htp cpe | 3,963 | 2,854 | 49,187 |
| 3639 | Holiday htp sdn | 4,052 | 2,932 | 33,830 |
| 3667TX | conv cpe | 4,232 | 3,182 | 6,423 |
| 3669 | sdn 4d | 4,000 | 2,798 | 53,923 |
| 3693 | Fiesta wgn 4d | 4,281 | 3,202 | 5,052 |
| 3695 | Fiesta htp wgn 4d | 4,314 | 3,313 | 5,767 |

| Golden Rocket Super 88 (wb 122.0) | | Wght | Price | Prod |
|---|---|---|---|---|
| 3637SD | Holiday htp cpe | 4,010 | 3,180 | 31,155 |
| 3639SD | Holiday htp sdn | 4,117 | 3,257 | 39,162 |
| 3667DTX | conv cpe | 4,283 | 3,447 | 7,128 |
| 3669D | sdn 4d | 4,044 | 3,030 | 42,629 |
| 3695SD | Fiesta htp wgn 4d | 4,364 | 3,541 | 8,981 |
| 3611D | sdn 2d | 4,001 | 2,968 | 2,983 |

| Starfire Ninety-Eight (wb 126.0) | | Wght | Price | Prod |
|---|---|---|---|---|
| 3037SDX | Holiday htp cpe | 4,296 | 3,937 | 17,791 |
| 3039SDX | Holiday htp sdn | 4,385 | 4,013 | 32,099 |
| 3067DX | conv cpe | 4,572 | 4,217 | 8,278 |
| 3069D | sdn 4d | 4,322 | 3,741 | 21,525 |

| 1957 Engines | bore × stroke | bhp | availability |
|---|---|---|---|
| V-8, 371.1 | 4.00 × 3.69 | 277 | S-all |
| V-8, 371.1 | 4.00 × 3.69 | 300 | O-all (J-2) |

## 1958

| Dynamic 88 (wb 122.5) | | Wght | Price | Prod |
|---|---|---|---|---|
| 3611 | sdn 2d | 3,961 | 2,772 | 11,833 |
| 3637 | Holiday htp cpe | 3,972 | 2,893 | 35,036 |
| 3639 | Holiday htp sdn | 4,035 | 2,971 | 28,241 |
| 3667TX | conv cpe | 3,987 | 3,221 | 4,456 |
| 3669 | sdn 4d | 3,985 | 2,837 | 60,429 |
| 3693 | Fiesta wgn 4d | 4,258 | 3,284 | 3,249 |
| 3695 | Fiesta htp wgn 4d | 4,297 | 3,395 | 3,323 |

| Super 88 (wb 122.5) | | Wght | Price | Prod |
|---|---|---|---|---|
| 3637SD | Holiday htp cpe | 4,000 | 3,262 | 18,653 |
| 3639SD | Holiday htp sdn | 4,073 | 3,339 | 27,521 |
| 3667DTX | conv cpe | 4,010 | 3,529 | 3,799 |
| 3669D | sdn 4d | 4,008 | 3,112 | 33,844 |
| 3695SD | Fiesta htp wgn 4d | 4,334 | 3,623 | 5,175 |

| Ninety-Eight (wb 126.5) | | Wght | Price | Prod |
|---|---|---|---|---|
| 3037SDX | Holiday htp cpe | 4,329 | 4,020 | 11,012 |
| 3039SDX | Holiday htp sdn | 4,391 | 4,096 | 27,603 |
| 3067DX | conv cpe | 4,318 | 4,300 | 5,605 |
| 3069D | sdn 4d | 4,316 | 3,824 | 16,595 |

| 1958 Engines | bore × stroke | bhp | availability |
|---|---|---|---|
| V-8, 371.1 | 4.00 × 3.69 | 265 | S-88 |
| V-8, 371.1 | 4.00 × 3.69 | 305 | S-Super 88, 98; O-88 |
| V-8, 371.1 | 4.00 × 3.69 | 312 | O-all (J-2) |

## 1959

| Dynamic 88 (wb 123.0) | | Wght | Price | Prod |
|---|---|---|---|---|
| 3211 | sdn 2d | 4,040 | 2,837 | 16,123 |
| 3219 | Celebrity sdn 4d | 4,130 | 2,902 | 70,995 |
| 3235 | Fiesta wgn 4d | 4,465 | 3,365 | 11,298 |
| 3237 | Holiday SceniCoupe htp | 4,085 | 2,958 | 38,488 |
| 3239 | Holiday sport sedan htp | 4,165 | 3,036 | 48,707 |
| 3267 | conv cpe | 4,120 | 3,286 | 8,491 |

| Super 88 (wb 123.0) | | Wght | Price | Prod |
|---|---|---|---|---|
| 3519 | Celebrity sdn 4d | 4,135 | 3,178 | 37,024 |
| 3535 | Fiesta wgn 4d | 4,485 | 3,669 | 7,015 |
| 3537 | Holiday SceniCoupe htp | 4,090 | 3,328 | 20,259 |
| 3539 | Holiday sport sedan htp | 4,185 | 3,405 | 38,467 |
| 3567 | conv cpe | 4,135 | 3,595 | 4,895 |

| Ninety-Eight (wb 126.3) | | Wght | Price | Prod |
|---|---|---|---|---|
| 3819 | Celebrity sdn 4d | 4,390 | 3,890 | 23,106 |
| 3837 | Holiday SceniCoupe htp | 4,360 | 4,086 | 13,669 |
| 3839 | Holiday sport sedan htp | 4,450 | 4,162 | 36,813 |
| 3867 | conv cpe | 4,360 | 4,366 | 7,514 |

| 1959 Engines | bore × stroke | bhp | availability |
|---|---|---|---|
| V-8, 371.1 | 4.00 × 3.69 | 270 | S-88 |
| V-8, 371.1 | 4.00 × 3.69 | 300 | O-88 |
| V-8, 394.0 | 4.13 × 3.69 | 315 | S-Super 88, 98 |

## 1960

| Dynamic 88 (wb 123.0) | | Wght | Price | Prod |
|---|---|---|---|---|
| 3211 | sdn 2d | 4,026 | 2,835 | 13,545 |
| 3219 | Celebrity sdn 4d | 4,091 | 2,900 | 76,377 |
| 3235 | Fiesta wgn 4d 6P | 4,449 | 3,363 | 8,834 |
| 3237 | Holiday SceniCoupe htp | 4,049 | 2,956 | 29,368 |
| 3239 | Holiday sport sedan htp | 4,139 | 3,034 | 43,761 |
| 3245 | Fiesta wgn 4d 8P | 4,470 | 3,471 | 5,708 |
| 3267 | conv cpe | 4,101 | 3,284 | 12,271 |

| Super 88 (wb 123.0) | | Wght | Price | Prod |
|---|---|---|---|---|
| 3519 | Celebrity sdn 4d | 4,128 | 3,176 | 35,094 |
| 3535 | Fiesta wgn 4d 6P | 4,483 | 3,665 | 3,765 |
| 3537 | Holiday SceniCoupe htp | 4,086 | 3,325 | 16,464 |
| 3539 | Holiday sport sedan htp | 4,182 | 3,402 | 33,285 |
| 3545 | Fiesta wgn 4d 8P | 4,506 | 3,773 | 3,475 |
| 3567 | conv cpe | 4,134 | 3,592 | 5,830 |

| Ninety-Eight (wb 126.3) | | Wght | Price | Prod |
|---|---|---|---|---|
| 3819 | Celebrity sdn 4d | 4,360 | 3,887 | 17,188 |
| 3837 | Holiday SceniCoupe htp | 4,322 | 4,083 | 7,635 |
| 3839 | Holiday sport sedan htp | 4,431 | 4,159 | 27,257 |
| 3867 | conv cpe | 4,349 | 4,362 | 7,284 |

| 1960 Engines | bore × stroke | bhp | availability |
|---|---|---|---|
| V-8, 371.1 | 4.00 × 3.69 | 240 | S-88 |
| V-8, 371.1 | 4.00 × 3.69 | 260 | O-88 |
| V-8, 394.0 | 4.13 × 3.69 | 315 | S-Super 88, 98 |

## 1961

| F-85 (wb 112.0) | | Wght | Price | Prod |
|---|---|---|---|---|
| 3019 | sdn 4d | 2,541 | 2,384 | 19,765 |
| 3027 | club cpe | 2,549 | 2,330 | 2,336 |
| 3035 | wgn 4d 6P | 2,716 | 2,681 | 6,677 |
| 3045 | wgn 4d 8P | 2,800 | 2,762 | 10,087 |

| F-85 Deluxe (wb 112.0) | | Wght | Price | Prod |
|---|---|---|---|---|
| 3117 | Cutlass spt cpe | 2,664 | 2,621 | 9,935 |
| 3119 | sdn 4d | 2,547 | 2,519 | 26,311 |
| 3135 | wgn 4d 6P | 2,731 | 2,816 | 526 |
| 3145 | wgn 4d 8P | 2,822 | 2,897 | 757 |

| Dynamic 88 (wb 123.0) | | Wght | Price | Prod |
|---|---|---|---|---|
| 3211 | sdn 2d | 3,966 | 2,835 | 4,920 |
| 3235 | wgn 4d 6P | 4,354 | 3,363 | 5,374 |
| 3237 | Holiday htp cpe | 3,981 | 2,956 | 19,878 |
| 3239 | Holiday htp sdn | 4,074 | 3,034 | 51,562 |

# Oldsmobile

| Dynamic 88 (wb 123.0) | | Wght | Price | Prod |
|---|---|---|---|---|
| 3245 | wgn 4d 8P | 4,428 | 3,471 | 4,013 |
| 3267 | conv cpe | 4,068 | 3,284 | 9,049 |
| 3269 | Celebrity sdn 4d | 4,031 | 2,900 | 42,584 |
| **Super 88 (wb 123.0)** | | | | |
| 3535 | wgn 4d 6P | 4,382 | 3,665 | 2,761 |
| 3537 | Holiday htp cpe | 4,024 | 3,325 | 7,009 |
| 3539 | Holiday htp sdn | 4,099 | 3,402 | 23,272 |
| 3545 | wgn 4d 8P | 4,445 | 3,773 | 2,170 |
| 3567 | conv cpe | 4,099 | 3,592 | 2,624 |
| 3569 | Celebrity sdn 4d | 4,065 | 3,176 | 15,328 |
| 3667 | Starfire conv cpe | 4,330 | 4,647 | 7,600 |
| **Ninety-Eight (wb 126.3)** | | | | |
| 3819 | town sdn 4d | 4,208 | 3,887 | 9,087 |
| 3829 | Holiday htp sdn | 4,269 | 4,021 | 13,331 |
| 3837 | Holiday htp cpe | 4,187 | 4,083 | 4,445 |
| 3839 | sport sedan htp | 4,319 | 4,159 | 12,343 |
| 3867 | conv cpe | 4,225 | 4,362 | 3,804 |

| 1961 Engines | bore × stroke | bhp | availability |
|---|---|---|---|
| V-8, 215.0 | 3.50 × 2.80 | 155 | S-F-85 |
| V-8, 394.0 | 4.13 × 3.69 | 250 | S-88 |
| V-8, 394.0 | 4.13 × 3.69 | 325 | S-Super 88, 98; O-88 |
| V-8, 394.0 | 4.13 × 3.69 | 330 | S-Starfire |

## 1962

| F-85 (wb 112.0) | | Wght | Price | Prod |
|---|---|---|---|---|
| 3019 | sdn 4d | 2,599 | 2,457 | 8,074 |
| 3027 | club cpe | 2,607 | 2,403 | 7,909 |
| 3035 | wgn 4d 6P | 2,780 | 2,754 | 3,204 |
| 3045 | wgn 4d 8P | 2,852 | 2,835 | 1,887 |
| 3067 | conv cpe | 2,790 | 2,760 | 3,660 |
| **F-85 Deluxe (wb 112.0)** | | | | |
| 3117 | Cutlass spt cpe | 2,651 | 2,694 | 32,461 |
| 3119 | sdn 4d | 2,634 | 2,592 | 18,736 |
| 3135 | wgn 4d 6P | 2,812 | 2,889 | 4,974 |
| 3167 | Cutlass conv cpe | 2,830 | 2,971 | 9,893 |
| 3147 | Jetfire htp cpe | 2,739 | 3,049 | 3,765 |
| **Dynamic 88 (wb 123.0)** | | | | |
| 3235 | Fiesta wgn 4d 6P | 4,392 | 3,460 | 8,527 |
| 3239 | Holiday htp sdn | 4,080 | 3,131 | 53,438 |
| 3245 | Fiesta wgn 4d 8P | 4,428 | 3,568 | 6,417 |
| 3247 | Holiday htp cpe | 3,992 | 3,054 | 39,676 |
| 3267 | conv cpe | 4,104 | 3,381 | 12,212 |
| 3269 | Celebrity sdn 4d | 4,038 | 2,997 | 68,467 |
| **Super 88 (wb 123.0)** | | | | |
| 3535 | Fiesta wgn 4d 6p | 4,412 | 3,762 | 3,837 |
| 3539 | Holiday htp sdn | 4,117 | 3,499 | 21,175 |
| 3547 | Holiday htp cpe | 4,022 | 3,422 | 9,010 |
| 3569 | Celebrity sdn 4d | 4,069 | 3,273 | 24,125 |
| **Starfire (wb 123.0)** | | | | |
| 3647 | htp cpe | 4,213 | 4,131 | 34,839 |
| 3667 | conv cpe | 4,334 | 4,744 | 7,149 |
| **Ninety-Eight (wb 126.0)** | | | | |
| 3819 | town sedan 4d | 4,258 | 3,984 | 12,167 |
| 3829 | Holiday htp sdn | 4,306 | 4,118 | 7,653 |
| 3839 | sport sedan htp | 4,337 | 4,256 | 33,095 |
| 3847 | Holiday htp cpe | 4,231 | 4,180 | 7,546 |
| 3867 | conv cpe | 4,298 | 4,459 | 3,693 |

| 1962 Engines | bore × stroke | bhp | availability |
|---|---|---|---|
| V-8, 215.0 | 3.50 × 2.80 | 155 | S-F-85 exc Cutlass, Jetfire |
| V-8, 215.0 | 3.50 × 2.80 | 185 | S-F-85 Ctls; O-F-85 |
| V-8T, 215.0 | 3.50 × 2.80 | 215 | S-F-85 Jetfire |
| V-8, 394.0 | 4.13 × 3.69 | 260 | O-88 |
| V-8, 394.0 | 4.13 × 3.69 | 280 | S-88 |
| V-8, 394.0 | 4.13 × 3.69 | 330 | S-Super 88, 98 |
| V-8, 394.0 | 4.13 × 3.69 | 345 | S-Starfire |

## 1963

| F-85 (wb 112.0) | | Wght | Price | Prod |
|---|---|---|---|---|
| 3019 | sdn 4d | 2,629 | 2,457 | 8,937 |
| 3027 | club cpe | 2,599 | 2,403 | 11,276 |
| 3035 | wgn 4d 6P | 2,812 | 2,754 | 3,348 |
| **F-85 Deluxe (wb 112.0)** | | | | |
| 3117 | Cutlass club cpe | 2,679 | 2,694 | 41,343 |
| 3119 | sdn 4d | 2,659 | 2,592 | 29,269 |
| 3135 | wgn 4d 6P | 2,833 | 2,889 | 6,647 |
| 3147 | Jetfire htp cpe | 2,774 | 3,048 | 5,842 |
| 3167 | Cutlass conv cpe | 2,858 | 2,971 | 12,149 |
| **Dynamic 88 (wb 123.0)** | | | | |
| 3235 | wgn 4d 6P | 4,322 | 3,459 | 9,615 |
| 3239 | Holiday htp sdn | 4,059 | 3,130 | 62,351 |
| 3245 | wgn 4d 8P | 4,354 | 3,566 | 7,116 |
| 3247 | Holiday htp cpe | 3,839 | 3,052 | 39,071 |
| 3267 | conv cpe | 4,039 | 3,379 | 12,551 |
| 3269 | Celebrity sdn 4d | 3,998 | 2,995 | 68,611 |
| **Super 88 (wb 123.0)** | | | | |
| 3535 | Fiesta wgn 4d 6P | 4,347 | 3,748 | 3,878 |
| 3539 | Holiday htp sdn | 4,083 | 3,473 | 25,387 |
| 3547 | Holiday htp cpe | 3,966 | 3,408 | 8,930 |
| 3569 | Celebrity sdn 4d | 4,027 | 3,246 | 24,575 |
| **Starfire (wb 123.0)** | | | | |
| 3657 | htp cpe | 4,172 | 4,129 | 21,148 |
| 3667 | conv cpe | 4,293 | 4,742 | 4,401 |
| **Ninety-Eight (wb 126.0)** | | | | |
| 3819 | town sedan 4d | 4,240 | 3,982 | 11,053 |
| 3829 | Luxury htp sdn 6W | 4,362 | 4,332 | 19,252 |
| 3839 | sport sedan htp 4W | 4,347 | 4,258 | 23,330 |
| 3847 | Holiday Sport htp | 4,215 | 4,178 | 4,984 |
| 3867 | conv cpe | 4,272 | 4,457 | 4,267 |
| 3947 | Custom coupe htp | 4,285 | 4,381 | 7,422 |

| 1963 Engines | bore × stroke | bhp | availability |
|---|---|---|---|
| V-8, 215.0 | 3.50 × 2.80 | 155 | S-F-85 exc Cutlass, Jetfire |
| V-8T, 215.0 | 3.50 × 2.80 | 185 | S-F-85 Cutlass; O-F-85 |
| V-8, 215.0 | 3.50 × 2.80 | 215 | S-F-85 Jetfire |
| V-8, 394.0 | 4.13 × 3.69 | 260 | O-88 |
| V-8, 394.0 | 4.13 × 3.69 | 280 | S-88 |
| V-8, 394.0 | 4.13 × 3.69 | 330 | S-Super 88, 98 exc Custom |
| V-8, 394.0 | 4.13 × 3.69 | 345 | S-Starfire, 98 Custom |

## 1964

| F-85 (wb 115.0; Vista Crsr-120.0) | | Wght | Price | Prod |
|---|---|---|---|---|
| 3027 | club cpe* | 2,980 | 2,343 | 16,298 |
| 3035 | wgn 4d 2S | 3,274 | 2,689 | 4,047 |
| 3055 | Vista Cruiser wgn 4d 2S | 3,652 | 2,938 | 1,305 |
| 3065 | Vista Cruiser wgn 4d 3S | 3,729 | 3,072 | 2,089 |
| 3069 | sdn 4d* | 3,025 | 2,397 | 12,106 |
| 3127 | Deluxe sports coupe* | 2,824 | 2,537 | 6,594 |
| 3135 | Deluxe wgn 4d 2S | 3,304 | 2,797 | 909 |
| 3169 | Deluxe sdn 4d * | 3,055 | 2,505 | 7,428 |

# Oldsmobile

| Cutlass (wb 115.0) | | Wght | Price | Prod |
|---|---|---|---|---|
| 3227 | sports coupe* | 3,141 | 2,644 | 15,440 |
| 3237 | Holiday htp cpe* | 3,180 | 2,784 | 36,153 |
| 3255 | Custom wgn 4d 2S | 3,714 | 3,146 | 3,320 |
| 3265 | Custom wgn 4d 3S | 3,781 | 3,270 | 7,286 |
| 3267 | conv cpe* | 3,263 | 2,984 | 12,822 |
| **Jetstar 88 (wb 123.0)** | | | | |
| 3339 | Holiday htp sdn | 3,783 | 3,069 | 19,325 |
| 3347 | Holiday htp cpe | 3,701 | 2,992 | 14,663 |
| 3367 | conv cpe | 3,754 | 3,318 | 3,903 |
| 3369 | Celebrity sdn 4d | 3,729 | 2,935 | 24,614 |
| **Dynamic 88 (123.0)** | | | | |
| 3435 | wgn 4d 2S | 4,286 | 3,468 | 10,747 |
| 3439 | Holiday htp sdn | 4,012 | 3,139 | 50,327 |
| 3445 | wgn 4d 3S | 4,324 | 3,576 | 6,599 |
| 3447 | Holiday htp cpe | 3,924 | 3,062 | 32,369 |
| 3457 | Jetstar I spt cpe | 4,019 | 3,603 | 16,084 |
| 3467 | conv cpe | 3,996 | 3,389 | 10,042 |
| 3469 | Celebrity sdn 4d | 3,966 | 3,005 | 57,590 |
| **Super 88 (wb 123.0)** | | | | |
| 3539 | Holiday htp sdn | 4,069 | 3,486 | 17,778 |
| 3569 | Celebrity sdn 4d | 4,009 | 3,256 | 19,736 |
| **Starfire (wb 123.0)** | | | | |
| 3657 | htp cpe | 4,167 | 4,138 | 13,753 |
| 3667 | conv cpe | 4,253 | 4,753 | 2,410 |
| **Ninety-Eight (wb 126.0)** | | | | |
| 3819 | town sedan 4d | 4,234 | 3,993 | 11,380 |
| 3829 | Luxury htp sdn 4d | 4,337 | 4,342 | 17,346 |
| 3839 | Holiday sports sedan htp | 4,323 | 4,265 | 24,791 |
| 3847 | Holiday sports coupe | 4,205 | 4,118 | 6,139 |
| 3867 | conv cpe | 4,255 | 4,468 | 4,004 |
| 3947 | Custom sports coupe htp | 4,271 | 4,391 | 4,594 |

| 1964 Engines | bore × stroke | bhp | availability |
|---|---|---|---|
| V-6, 225.0 | 3.75 × 3.40 | 155 | S-F-85 exc Vista Crsr |
| V-8, 330.0 | 3.94 × 3.38 | 230 | S-Vista Crsr; O-F-85, Jetstar 88 |
| V-8, 330.0 | 3.94 × 3.38 | 245 | S-Jetstar 88 |
| V-8, 330.0 | 3.94 × 3.38 | 290 | S-Cutlass; O-F-85, Jetstar 88 |
| V-8, 330.0 | 3.94 × 3.38 | 310 | O-F-85/Ctls (4-4-2 pkg.) |
| V-8, 394.0 | 4.13 × 3.69 | 260 | O-Dynamic 88 |
| V-8, 394.0 | 4.13 × 3.69 | 280 | S-Dynamic 88 |
| V-8, 394.0 | 4.13 × 3.69 | 330 | S-Super 88, 98; O-Dynamic 88 |
| V-8, 394.0 | 4.13 × 3.69 | 345 | S-Jetstar I, Starfire, 98 Cust; O-Super 88, 98 |

*Production includes models with 4-4-2 performance package.

## 1965

| F-85 (wb 115.0; Vista Crsr-120.0) | | Wght | Price | Prod |
|---|---|---|---|---|
| 3327 | club cpe V-6 | 2,940 | 2,344 | 5,289 |
| 3335 | wgn 4d V-6 | 3,252 | 2,689 | 714 |
| 3369 | sdn 4d V-6 | 2,991 | 2,398 | 3,089 |
| 3427 | club cpe V-8 | 3,146 | 2,415 | 7,720* |
| 3435 | wgn 4d V-8 | 3,457 | 2,760 | 2,496 |
| 3455 | Vista Crsr wgn 6P V-8 | 3,732 | 2,937 | 2,110 |
| 3465 | Vista Crsr wgn 8P V-8 | 3,809 | 3,072 | 3,335 |
| 3469 | sdn 4d V-8 | 3,174 | 2,469 | 5,661 |
| **F-85 Deluxe (wb 115.0; Vista Crsr-120.0)** | | | | |
| 3527 | sports coupe V-6 | 2,980 | 2,538 | 6,141* |
| 3535 | wgn 4d V-6 | 3,262 | 2,797 | 659 |

| F-85 Deluxe | | Wght | Price | Prod |
|---|---|---|---|---|
| 3569 | sdn 4d V-6 | 3,016 | 2,505 | 4,989 |
| 3635 | wgn 4d V-8 | 3,459 | 2,868 | 10,365 |
| 3669 | sdn 4d V-8 | 3,218 | 2,576 | 47,767 |
| 3855 | Cus Vista Crsr wgn 4d 6P V-8 | 3,762 | 3,146 | 9,335 |
| 3865 | Cus Vista Crsr wgn 4d 8P V-8 | 3,864 | 3,270 | 17,205 |
| **Cutlass (wb 115.0)** | | | | |
| 3827 | sports coupe V-8 | 3,221 | 2,643 | 26,441* |
| 3837 | Holiday htp cpe V-8 | 3,245 | 2,784 | 46,138* |
| 3867 | conv cpe V-8 | 3,338 | 2,983 | 12,628* |
| **Jetstar 88 (wb 123.0)** | | | | |
| 5237 | Holiday htp cpe | 3,688 | 2,995 | 13,911 |
| 5239 | Holiday htp sdn | 3,775 | 3,072 | 15,922 |
| 5267 | conv cpe | 3,741 | 3,337 | 2,879 |
| 5269 | Celebrity sdn 4d | 3,726 | 2,938 | 22,725 |
| **Jetstar I (wb 123.0)** | | | | |
| 5457 | sports coupe | 3,982 | 3,602 | 6,552 |
| **Dynamic 88 (wb 123.0)** | | | | |
| 5637 | Holiday htp cpe | 3,873 | 3,065 | 24,746 |
| 5639 | Holiday htp sdn | 3,961 | 3,143 | 38,889 |
| 5667 | conv cpe | 3,946 | 3,408 | 8,832 |
| 5669 | Celebrity sdn 4d | 3,908 | 3,008 | 47,030 |
| **Delta 88 (wb 123.0)** | | | | |
| 5837 | Holiday htp cpe | 3,924 | 3,253 | 23,194 |
| 5839 | Holiday htp sdn | 4,011 | 3,330 | 37,358 |
| 5869 | Celebrity sdn 4d | 3,940 | 3,158 | 29,915 |
| **Starfire (wb 123.0)** | | | | |
| 6657 | htp cpe | 4,152 | 4,138 | 13,024 |
| 6667 | conv cpe | 4,247 | 4,778 | 2,236 |
| **Ninety-Eight (wb 126.0)** | | | | |
| 8437 | Holiday sports coupe htp | 4,178 | 4,197 | 12,166 |
| 8439 | Holiday htp sdn | 4,286 | 4,273 | 28,480 |
| 8467 | conv cpe | 4,250 | 4,493 | 4,903 |
| 8469 | town sedan 4d | 4,186 | 4,001 | 13,266 |
| 8669 | Luxury sdn 4d | 4,285 | 4,351 | 33,591 |

| 1965 Engines | bore × stroke | bhp | availability |
|---|---|---|---|
| V-6, 225.0 | 3.75 × 3.40 | 155 | V-6 |
| V-8, 330.0 | 3.94 × 3.38 | 250/260 | S-F-85 V-8 exc Cutlass, Jetstar 88 |
| V-8, 330.0 | 3.94 × 3.38 | 315 | S-Cutlass |
| V-8, 400.0 | 4.00 × 3.98 | 320 | O-Cutlass |
| V-8, 400.0 | 4.00 × 3.98 | 345 | O-F-85 (4-4-2 pkg.) |
| V-8, 425.0 | 4.13 × 3.98 | 310 | S-Dlt 88, Dyn 88; O-98 |
| V-8, 425.0 | 4.13 × 3.98 | 360 | S-98; O-other full-size |
| V-8, 425.0 | 4.13 × 3.98 | 370 | S-Jetstar I, Starfire; O-full-size |

*Production includes models with 4-4-2 performance packages.

## 1966

| F-85 (wb 115.0) | | Wght | Price | Prod |
|---|---|---|---|---|
| 33307 | club cpe I-6 | 2,951 | 2,348 | 6,341 |
| 33335 | wgn 4d I-6 | 3,246 | 2,695 | 508 |
| 33369 | sdn 4d I-6 | 3,001 | 2,401 | 2,862 |
| 33407 | club cpe V-8 | 3,153 | 2,418 | 4,923* |
| 33435 | wgn 4d V-8 | 3,431 | 2,764 | 1,652 |
| 33469 | sdn 4d V-8 | 3,187 | 2,471 | 3,754 |
| **F-85 Deluxe (wb 115.0)** | | | | |
| 33517 | Holiday htp cpe I-6 | 2,990 | 2,513 | 2,974 |
| 33535 | wgn 4d I-6 | 3,273 | 2,793 | 434 |
| 33539 | Holiday htp sde I-6 | 3,077 | 2,629 | 1,002 |
| 33569 | sdn 4d I-6 | 3,023 | 2,497 | 3,568 |
| 33617 | Holiday htp cpe V-8 | 3,196 | 2,583 | 13,141* |

# Oldsmobile

| F-85 Deluxe (wb 115.0) | | Wght | Price | Prod |
|---|---|---|---|---|
| 33635 | wgn 4d V-8 | 3,453 | 2,862 | 8,058 |
| 33639 | Holiday htp sde V-8 | 3,272 | 2,699 | 6,911 |
| 33669 | sdn 4d V-8 | 3,210 | 2,567 | 27,452 |
| **Cutlass (wb 115.0)** | | | | |
| 33807 | sports coupe | 3,219 | 2,633 | 13,518* |
| 33817 | Holiday htp cpe | 3,243 | 2,770 | 34,580* |
| 33389 | Supreme htp sdn | 3,296 | 2,846 | 30,871 |
| 33867 | conv cpe | 3,349 | 2,965 | 9,410* |
| 33869 | Celebrity sdn 4d | 3,240 | 2,673 | 9,017 |
| **Vista Cruiser (wb 120.0)** | | | | |
| 33455 | wgn 4d 2S | 3,735 | 2,935 | 1,660 |
| 33465 | wgn 4d 3S | 3,806 | 3,087 | 1,869 |
| 33855 | Custom wgn 4d 2S | 3,765 | 3,137 | 8,910 |
| 33865 | Custom wgn 4d 3S | 3,861 | 3,278 | 14,167 |
| **4-4-2 (wb 115.0)** | | | | |
| 33407 | cpe | 3,454 | 2,604 | 1,430* |
| 33617 | htp cpe | 3,502 | 2,769 | 3,827* |
| 33807 | sports coupe | 3,506 | 2,786 | 3,937* |
| 33817 | Holiday htp cpe | 3,523 | 2,923 | 10,053* |
| 33867 | conv cpe | 3,629 | 3,118 | 2,750* |
| **Jetstar 88 (wb 123.0)** | | | | |
| 35237 | Holiday htp cpe | 3,727 | 2,983 | 8,575 |
| 35239 | Holiday htp sdn | 3,823 | 3,059 | 7,938 |
| 35269 | Celebrity sdn 4d | 3,776 | 2,927 | 13,734 |
| **Dynamic 88 (wb 123.0)** | | | | |
| 35637 | Holiday htp cpe | 3,899 | 3,069 | 20,768 |
| 35639 | Holiday htp sdn | 3,982 | 3,144 | 30,784 |
| 35667 | conv cpe | 3,971 | 3,404 | 5,540 |
| 35669 | Celebrity sdn 4d | 3,930 | 3,013 | 38,742 |
| **Delta 88 (wb 123.0)** | | | | |
| 35837 | Holiday htp cpe | 3,944 | 3,253 | 20,857 |
| 35839 | Holiday htp sdn | 4,026 | 3,328 | 33,326 |
| 35867 | conv cpe | 4,010 | 3,588 | 4,303 |
| 35869 | Celebrity sdn 4d | 3,963 | 3,160 | 30,140 |
| **Starfire (wb 123.0)** | | | | |
| 35457 | htp cpe | 4,013 | 3,564 | 13,019 |
| **Ninety-Eight (wb 126.0)** | | | | |
| 38437 | Holiday htp cpe | 4,165 | 4,158 | 11,488 |
| 38439 | Holiday htp sdn | 4,266 | 4,233 | 23,048 |
| 38467 | conv cpe | 4,233 | 4,443 | 4,568 |
| 38469 | town sedan 4d | 4,177 | 3,966 | 10,892 |
| 38669 | Luxury Sedan 4d | 4,271 | 4,308 | 38,123 |
| **Toronado (wb 119.0)** | | | | |
| 39487 | htp cpe | 4,311 | 4,617 | 6,333 |
| 39687 | Deluxe htp cpe | 4,366 | 4,812 | 34,630 |

*Production combined; numbers given are proportional to production of same models in F-85 and Cutlass lines. Total 4-4-2 production: 21,997.

| 1966 Engines | bore × stroke | bhp | availability |
|---|---|---|---|
| I-6, 250.0 | 3.88 × 3.53 | 155 | S-F-85 I-6 |
| V-8, 330.0 | 3.94 × 3.38 | 250 | S-F-85 V-8, Vista Crsr; O-Jetstar 88 |
| V-8, 330.0 | 3.94 × 3.38 | 260 | S-Jetstar 88 |
| V-8, 330.0 | 3.94 × 3.38 | 310 | O-F85/Cutlass V-8, Vista Crsr |
| V-8, 330.0 | 3.94 × 3.38 | 320 | S-Cutlass; O-Jetstr 88, F-85, Vista Crsr |
| V-8, 400.0 | 4.00 × 3.98 | 350 | S-442 |
| V-8, 425.0 | 4.13 × 3.98 | 300 | O-Delt 88, Dyn 88 |
| V-8, 425.0 | 4.13 × 3.98 | 310 | S-Delt 88, Dynamic 88 |
| V-8, 425.0 | 4.13 × 3.98 | 365 | S-98; O-Delta 88, Dynamic 88 |
| V-8, 425.0 | 4.13 × 3.98 | 375 | S-Star; O-98, Delt 88 |
| V-8, 425.0 | 4.13 × 3.98 | 385 | S-Toronado |

## 1967

| F-85 (wb 115.0) | | Wght | Price | Prod |
|---|---|---|---|---|
| 33307 | club cpe I-6 | 3,014 | 2,410 | 5,349 |
| 33335 | wgn 4d I-6 | 3,295 | 2,749 | 2,749 |
| 33369 | town sedan 4d I-6 | 3,031 | 2,457 | 2,458 |
| 33407 | club cpe V-8 | 3,184 | 2,480 | 6,700 |
| 33435 | wgn 4d V-8 | 3,463 | 2,818 | 1,625 |
| 33469 | town sedan 4d V-8 | 3,469 | 2,527 | 5,126 |
| **Cutlass (wb 115.0)** | | | | |
| 33517 | Holiday htp cpe I-6 | 3,033 | 2,574 | 2,564 |
| 33535 | wgn 4d I-6 | 3,308 | 2,848 | 365 |
| 33539 | Holiday htp sdn I-6 | 3,125 | 2,683 | 644 |
| 33567 | conv cpe I-6 | 3,125 | 2,770 | 567 |
| 33569 | town sedan 4d I-6 | 3,055 | 2,552 | 2,219 |
| 33617 | Holiday htp cpe V-8 | 3,216 | 2,644 | 29,799 |
| 33635 | wgn 4d V-8 | 3,473 | 2,917 | 8,130 |
| 33639 | Holiday htp sdn V-8 | 3,292 | 2,753 | 7,344 |
| 33667 | conv cpe V-8 | 3,306 | 2,839 | 3,777 |
| 33669 | town sedan 4d V-8 | 3,223 | 2,622 | 29,062 |
| **Cutlass Supreme (wb 115.0)** | | | | |
| 33807 | sports coupe | 3,238 | 2,694 | 13,041* |
| 33817 | Holiday htp cpe | 3,262 | 2,831 | 41,344* |
| 33839 | Holiday htp sdn | 3,346 | 2,900 | 22,571 |
| 33867 | conv cpe | 3,867 | 3,026 | 7,793* |
| 33869 | town sedan 4d | 3,258 | 2,726 | 8,346 |
| **4-4-2 (wb 115.0)** | | | | |
| 33807 | sports coupe | 3,540 | 2,788 | 5,215* |
| 33817 | Holiday htp cpe | 3,568 | 3,015 | 16,514* |
| 33867 | conv cpe | 4,047 | 3,210 | 3,104* |
| **Vista Cruiser (wb 120.0)** | | | | |
| 33465 | wgn 4d 3S | 3,836 | 3,136 | 2,748 |
| 33855 | Custom wgn 4d 2S | 3,796 | 3,228 | 9,513 |
| 33865 | Custom wgn 4d 3S | 3,907 | 3,369 | 15,293 |
| **Delmont 88 "330" (wb 123.0)** | | | | |
| 35239 | Holiday htp sdn | 3,932 | 3,139 | 10,600 |
| 35269 | town sedan 4d | 3,867 | 3,008 | 15,076 |
| 35287 | Holiday htp cpe | 3,819 | 3,063 | 10,786 |
| **Delmont 88 "425" (wb 123.0)** | | | | |
| 35639 | Holiday htp sdn | 4,007 | 3,202 | 22,980 |
| 35667 | conv cpe | 4,010 | 3,462 | 3,525 |
| 35669 | town sedan 4d | 3,968 | 3,071 | 28,690 |
| 35687 | Holiday htp cpe | 3,914 | 3,126 | 16,699 |
| **Delta 88 (wb 123.0)** | | | | |
| 35839 | Holiday htp sdn | 4,053 | 3,386 | 21,909 |
| 35867 | conv cpe | 4,039 | 3,646 | 2,447 |
| 35869 | town sedan 4d | 3,986 | 3,218 | 22,770 |
| 35887 | Holiday htp cpe | 3,956 | 3,310 | 14,471 |
| **Delta 88 Custom (wb 123.0)** | | | | |
| 35439 | Holiday htp sdn | 4,081 | 3,582 | 14,306 |
| 35487 | Holiday htp cpe | 3,994 | 3,522 | 12,192 |
| **Ninety-Eight (wb 126.0)** | | | | |
| 38439 | Holiday htp sdn | 4,323 | 4,276 | 17,533 |
| 38457 | Holiday htp cpe | 4,221 | 4,214 | 10,476 |
| 38467 | conv cpe | 4,271 | 4,498 | 3,769 |
| 38469 | town sedan 4d | 4,242 | 4,009 | 8,900 |
| 38669 | Luxury Sedan 4d | 4,309 | 4,351 | 35,511 |

# Oldsmobile

| Toronado (wb 119.0) | Wght | Price | Prod |
|---|---|---|---|
| 39487 htp cpe | 4,310 | 4,674 | 1,770 |
| 39687 Deluxe htp cpe | 4,362 | 4,869 | 20,020 |

\* Production combined; numbers given are proportional to production of same models in Cutlass Supreme line. Total 4-4-2 production: 24,833.

| 1967 Engines | bore × stroke | bhp | availability |
|---|---|---|---|
| I-6, 250.0 | 3.88 × 3.53 | 155 | S-F-85/Cutlass I-6 |
| V-8, 330.0 | 3.94 × 3.38 | 250 | S-F-85 V-8, Vst Crsr, Delm 330 man; O-Delm auto |
| V-8, 330.0 | 3.94 × 3.38 | 260 | S-Delmont 330 w/auto |
| V-8, 330.0 | 3.94 × 3.38 | 310 | O-Supreme, Cutls, F-85, VC |
| V-8, 330.0 | 3.94 × 3.38 | 320 | S-Sprme; O-Delm 330, VC, F-85, Cutls |
| V-8, 400.0 | 4.00 × 3.98 | 300 | O-Sprme cpe & conv |
| V-8, 400.0 | 4.00 × 3.98 | 350 | S-442; O-Sprme cpe & conv |
| V-8, 425.0 | 4.13 × 3.98 | 300 | S-all 88 man; O-all 88 auto |
| V-8, 425.0 | 4.13 × 3.98 | 310 | S-all 88 automatic |
| V-8, 425.0 | 4.13 × 3.98 | 365 | S-98; O-Delta 88, Delmont 425 |
| V-8, 425.0 | 4.13 × 3.98 | 375 | O-98, Delta 88, Delmont 425 |
| V-8, 425.0 | 4.13 × 3.98 | 385 | S-Toronado |

## 1968

| F-85 (wb 116.0; 2d-112.0) | Wght | Price | Prod |
|---|---|---|---|
| 33169 town sedan 4d I-6 | 3,108 | 2,560 | 1,847 |
| 33177 club cpe I-6 | 3,062 | 2,512 | 4,052 |
| 33269 town sedan 4d V-8 | 3,304 | 2,665 | 3,984 |
| 33277 club cpe V-8 | 3,255 | 2,618 | 5,426 |
| **Cutlass (wb 116.0; 2d-112.0)** | | | |
| 33535 wgn 4d 2S, I-6 | 3,473 | 2,969 | 354 |
| 33539 Holiday htp sdn I-6 | 3,193 | 2,804 | 265 |
| 33567 conv cpe I-6 | 3,161 | 2,949 | 410 |
| 33569 town sedan 4d I-6 | 3,143 | 2,674 | 1,305 |
| 33577 sports coupe I-6 | 3,064 | 2,632 | 1,181 |
| 33587 Holiday htp cpe I-6 | 3,108 | 2,696 | 1,492 |
| 33635 wgn 4d 2S, V-8 | 3,649 | 3,075 | 9,291 |
| 33639 Holiday htp sdn V-8 | 3,374 | 2,910 | 7,839 |
| 33667 conv cpe V-8 | 3,342 | 3,055 | 13,667 |
| 33669 town sedan 4d V-8 | 3,325 | 2,779 | 25,994 |
| 33677 sport coupe V-8 | 3,271 | 2,738 | 14,586 |
| 33687 Holiday htp cpe V-8 | 3,282 | 2,801 | 59,577 |
| **Cutlass Supreme (wb 116.0; 2d-112.0)** | | | |
| 34239 Holiday htp sdn | 3,421 | 3,057 | 15,067 |
| 34269 town sedan 4d | 3,372 | 2,884 | 5,524 |
| 34287 Holiday htp cpe | 3,312 | 2,982 | 33,518 |
| **4-4-2 (wb 112.0)\*** | | | |
| 34467 conv cpe | 3,580 | 3,341 | 5,142 |
| 34477 sports coupe | 3,502 | 3,087 | 4,282 |
| 34487 Holiday htp cpe | 3,512 | 3,150 | 24,183 |
| **Vista Cruiser (wb 121.0)** | | | |
| 34855 Custom wgn 4d 2S | 3,917 | 3,367 | 13,375 |
| 34865 Custom wgn 4d 3S | 4,027 | 3,508 | 22,768 |
| **Delmont 88 (wb 123.0)\*\*** | | | |
| 35439 Holiday htp sdn | 3,928 | 3,278 | 21,056 |
| 35467 conv cpe | 3,916 | 3,515 | 2,812 |
| 35469 town sedan 4d | 3,873 | 3,146 | 24,365 |

| Delmont 88 (wb 123.0)\*\* | Wght | Price | Prod |
|---|---|---|---|
| 35487 Holiday htp cpe | 3,844 | 3,202 | 18,391 |
| **Delta 88 (wb 123.0)\*\*** | | | |
| 36439 Holiday htp sdn | 4,038 | 3,525 | 30,048 |
| 36469 town sedan 4d | 3,979 | 3,357 | 33,689 |
| 36487 Holiday htp cpe | 3,950 | 3,449 | 18,501 |
| 36639 Custom Holiday htp sdn | 4,059 | 3,721 | 10,727 |
| 36687 Custom Holiday htp cpe | 3,982 | 3,661 | 9,540 |
| **Ninety-Eight (wb 126.0)** | | | |
| 38439 Holiday htp sdn | 4,278 | 4,422 | 21,147 |
| 38457 Holiday htp cpe | 4,185 | 4,360 | 15,319 |
| 38467 conv cpe | 4,264 | 4,618 | 3,942 |
| 38469 town sedan 4d | 4,197 | 4,155 | 10,584 |
| 38669 Luxury Sedan 4d | 4,273 | 4,497 | 40,755 |
| **Toronado (wb 119.0)** | | | |
| 39487 htp cpe | 4,322 | 4,750 | 3,957 |
| 39687 Custom htp cpe | 4,374 | 4,945 | 22,497 |

\* 4-4-2 production includes 515 Hurst/Olds models.

\*\* Factory records also indicate 54,794 Dynamic 88s, although other sources do not include these models.

| 1968 Engines | bore × stroke | bhp | availability |
|---|---|---|---|
| I-6, 250.0 | 3.88 × 3.53 | 155 | S-F-85/Cutlass I-6 |
| V-8, 350.0 | 4.06 × 3.38 | 250 | S-Dlmnt, Vst Crsr; O-Ctls, F-85 |
| V-8, 350.0 | 4.06 × 3.38 | 310 | S-Supreme; O-F-85, Ctls, Vista Cruiser, Dlmnt auto |
| V-8, 400.0 | 4.00 × 3.98 | 290 | O-442 auto, Vista Cruiser auto |
| V-8, 400.0 | 4.00 × 3.98 | 325 | S-442 auto; O-Vista Cruiser auto |
| V-8, 400.0 | 4.00 × 3.98 | 350 | S-442 manual |
| V-8, 400.0 | 4.00 × 3.98 | 360 | O-442 all |
| V-8, 455.0 | 4.13 × 4.25 | 310 | S-Delta/Cust; O-Delm |
| V-8, 455.0 | 4.13 × 4.25 | 320 | O-above models w/automatic |
| V-8, 455.0 | 4.13 × 4.25 | 365 | S-98; O-all 88 w/automatic |
| V-8, 455.0 | 4.13 × 4.25 | 375 | S-Toronado |
| V-8, 455.0 | 4.13 × 4.25 | 390 | O-442 (Hurst/Olds) |
| V-8, 455.0 | 4.13 × 4.25 | 400 | O-Toronado |

## 1969

| F-85 (wb 112.0) | Wght | Price | Prod |
|---|---|---|---|
| 33177 sports coupe I-6 | 3,082 | 2,561 | 2,899 |
| 33277 sports coupe V-8 | 3,281 | 2,672 | 5,541 |
| **Cutlass (wb 116.0; 2d-112.0)** | | | |
| 33535 wgn 4d 2S, I-6 | 3,537 | 3,055 | 180 |
| 33539 Holiday htp sdn I-6 | 3,212 | 2,853 | 236 |
| 33567 S conv cpe I-6 | 3,188 | 2,998 | 236 |
| 33569 town sedan 4d I-6 | 3,155 | 2,722 | 137 |
| 33577 S sports coupe I-6 | 3,093 | 2,681 | 483 |
| 33587 S Holiday htp cpe I-6 | 3,118 | 2,745 | 566 |
| 33635 wgn 4d 2S, V-8 | 3,736 | 3,165 | 8,559 |
| 33639 Holiday htp sdn V-8 | 3,407 | 2,964 | 7,046 |
| 33667 S conv cpe V-8 | 3,386 | 3,109 | 13,498 |
| 33669 town sedan 4d V-8 | 3,356 | 2,833 | 24,521 |
| 33677 S sports coupe V-8 | 3,293 | 2,792 | 10,682 |
| 33687 S Holiday htp cpe V-8 | 3,316 | 2,855 | 66,495 |
| **Cutlass Supreme (wb 116; 2d-112.0)** | | | |
| 34239 Holiday htp sdn | 3,421 | 3,111 | 8,714 |
| 34269 town sedan 4d | 3,361 | 2,938 | 4,522 |

743

# Oldsmobile

| Cutlass Supreme (wb 116; 2d-112.0) | | Wght | Price | Prod |
|---|---|---|---|---|
| 34287 | Holiday htp cpe | 3,331 | 3,036 | 24,193 |
| **4-4-2 (wb 112.0)*** | | | | |
| 34467 | conv cpe | 3,580 | 3,395 | 4,295 |
| 34477 | sports coupe | 3,502 | 3,141 | 2,475 |
| 34487 | Holiday htp cpe | 3,512 | 3,204 | 19,587 |

*Includes 914 Hurst/Olds models (2 convertibles).

| Vista Cruiser (wb 121.0) | | | | |
|---|---|---|---|---|
| 34855 | wgn 4d 2S | 3,952 | 3,457 | 11,879 |
| 34865 | wgn 4d 3S | 4,052 | 3,600 | 21,508 |
| **Delta 88 (wb 124.0)** | | | | |
| 35437 | Holiday htp cpe | 3,812 | 3,277 | 41,947 |
| 35439 | Holiday htp sdn | 3,901 | 3,353 | 42,690 |
| 35467 | conv cpe | 3,892 | 3,590 | 5,294 |
| 35469 | town sedan 4d | 3,859 | 3,222 | 49,995 |
| 36437 | Custom Holiday htp cpe | 3,927 | 3,525 | 22,083 |
| 36439 | Custom Holiday htp sdn | 4,009 | 3,600 | 36,502 |
| 36469 | Custom town sedan 4d | 3,962 | 3,432 | 31,012 |
| 36647 | Royale Holiday htp cpe | 3,935 | 3,836 | 22,564 |
| **Ninety-Eight (wb 127.0)** | | | | |
| 38439 | Holiday htp sdn | 4,260 | 4,523 | 17,294 |
| 38457 | Holiday htp cpe | 4,150 | 4,461 | 27,041 |
| 38467 | conv cpe | 4,223 | 4,719 | 4,288 |
| 38469 | town sedan 4d | 4,150 | 4,255 | 11,169 |
| 38639 | Luxury Sedan htp | 4,288 | 4,692 | 25,973 |
| 38669 | Luxury Sedan 4d | 4,245 | 4,598 | 30,643 |
| **Toronado (wb 119.0)** | | | | |
| 39487 | htp cpe | 4,316 | 4,835 | 3,421 |
| 39687 | Custom htp cpe | 4,368 | 5,030 | 25,073 |

| 1969 Engines | bore × stroke | bhp | availability |
|---|---|---|---|
| I-6, 250.0 | 3.88 × 3.53 | 155 | S-F-85/Cutlass I-6 |
| V-8, 350.0 | 4.06 × 3.38 | 250 | S-F-85/Cutlass V-8, Delta 88 base, Vst Crsr; O-Supreme |
| V-8, 350.0 | 4.06 × 3.38 | 310 | S-Supreme; O-F-85/Cutlass V-8, Vst Crsr |
| V-8, 350.0 | 4.06 × 3.38 | 325 | O-Cutlass S, F-85 |
| V-8, 400.0 | 4.00 × 3.98 | 325 | S-442 auto, Vista Cruiser auto |
| V-8, 400.0 | 4.00 × 3.98 | 350 | S-442 manual |
| V-8, 400.0 | 4.00 × 3.98 | 360 | O-442 |
| V-8, 455.0 | 4.13 × 4.25 | 310 | S-Delta Cus/Royale; O-other Delta |
| V-8, 455.0 | 4.13 × 4.25 | 365 | S-98; O-all Delta 88 |
| V-8, 455.0 | 4.13 × 4.25 | 375 | S-Toronado |
| V-8, 455.0 | 4.13 × 4.25 | 380 | O-442 (Hurst/Olds) |
| V-8, 455.0 | 4.13 × 4.25 | 390 | O-all Delta 88 |
| V-8, 455.0 | 4.13 × 4.25 | 400 | O-Toronado |

## 1970

| F-85 (wb 112.0) | | Wght | Price | Prod |
|---|---|---|---|---|
| 33177 | sports coupe I-6 | 3,190 | 2,676 | 2,836 |
| 33277 | sports coupe V-8 | 3,401 | 2,787 | 8,274 |
| **Cutlass (wb 116.0; 2d-112.0)** | | | | |
| 33535 | wgn 4d 2S, I-6 | 3,630 | 3,234 | 85 |
| 33539 | Holiday htp sdn I-6 | 3,326 | 2,968 | 238 |
| 33569 | town sedan 4d I-6 | 3,257 | 2,837 | 1,171 |
| 33577 | S sports coupe I-6 | 3,201 | 2,796 | 484 |
| 33587 | S Holiday htp cpe I-6 | 3,238 | 2,859 | 729 |
| 33635 | wgn 4d 2S, V-8 | 3,837 | 3,344 | 7,686 |
| 33639 | Holiday htp sdn V-8 | 3,523 | 3,079 | 9,427 |

| Cutlass (wb 116.0; 2d-112.0) | | Wght | Price | Prod |
|---|---|---|---|---|
| 33669 | town sedan V-8 | 3,468 | 2,948 | 35,239 |
| 33677 | S sports coupe V-8 | 3,416 | 2,907 | 10,677 |
| 33687 | S Holiday htp cpe V-8 | 3,452 | 2,970 | 88,578 |
| **Cutlass Supreme (wb 116; 2d-112.0)** | | | | |
| 34239 | Holiday htp sdn | 3,558 | 3,226 | 10,762 |
| 34257 | Holiday htp cpe | 3,471 | 3,151 | 68,309 |
| 34267 | conv cpe | 3,510 | 3,335 | 11,354 |
| **4-4-2 (wb 112.0)** | | | | |
| 34467 | conv cpe | 3,740 | 3,567 | 2,933 |
| 34477 | sports coupe | 3,667 | 3,312 | 1,688 |
| 34487 | Holiday htp cpe | 3,713 | 3,376 | 14,709 |
| **Vista Cruiser (wb 121.0)** | | | | |
| 34855 | wgn 4d 2S | 4,064 | 3,636 | 10,758 |
| 34865 | wgn 4d 3S | 4,166 | 3,778 | 23,336 |
| **Delta 88 (wb 124.0)** | | | | |
| 35437 | Holiday htp cpe | 3,900 | 3,590 | 33,017 |
| 35439 | Holiday htp sdn | 3,986 | 3,666 | 37,695 |
| 35467 | conv cpe | 3,985 | 3,903 | 3,095 |
| 35469 | town sedan 4d | 3,944 | 3,534 | 47,067 |
| 36437 | Custom Holiday htp cpe | 3,999 | 3,848 | 16,149 |
| 36439 | Custom Holiday htp sdn | 4,087 | 3,924 | 28,432 |
| 36469 | Custom town sedan 4d | 4,040 | 3,755 | 24,727 |
| 36647 | Royale Holiday htp cpe | 4,002 | 4,159 | 13,249 |
| **Ninety-Eight (wb 127.0)** | | | | |
| 38439 | Holiday htp sdn | 4,329 | 4,582 | 14,098 |
| 38457 | Holiday htp cpe | 4,257 | 4,656 | 21,111 |
| 38467 | conv cpe | 4,289 | 4,914 | 3,161 |
| 38469 | town sedan 4d | 4,263 | 4,451 | 9,092 |
| 38639 | Luxury Sedan htp | 4,400 | 4,888 | 19,377 |
| 38669 | Luxury Sedan 4d | 4,356 | 4,793 | 29,005 |
| **Toronado (wb 119.0)** | | | | |
| 39487 | htp cpe | 4,331 | 5,023 | 2,351 |
| 39687 | Custom htp cpe | 4,386 | 5,216 | 23,082 |

| 1970 Engines | bore × stroke | bhp | availability |
|---|---|---|---|
| I-6, 250.0 | 3.88 × 3.53 | 155 | S- F-85/Cutlass I-6 |
| V-8, 350.0 | 4.06 × 3.38 | 250 | S- F-85/Cutlass V-8, Vst Crsr; O-Supreme |
| V-8, 350.0 | 4.06 × 3.38 | 310 | S-Supreme; O-Vst Crsr, F-85, Cutlass |
| V-8, 350.0 | 4.06 × 3.38 | 325 | O-F-85, Cutlass S auto or 4 spd |
| V-8, 455.0 | 4.13 × 4.25 | 310 | S-Delta 88 manual |
| V-8, 455.0 | 4.13 × 4.25 | 320 | O-Cutlass w/auto |
| V-8, 455.0 | 4.13 × 4.25 | 365 | S-442, 98; O-Supreme, 88/Vst Crsr manual |
| V-8, 455.0 | 4.13 × 4.25 | 370 | O-442 w/auto or close-ratio 4 spd |
| V-8, 455.0 | 4.13 × 4.25 | 375 | S-Toronado |
| V-8, 455.0 | 4.13 × 4.25 | 390 | O-Delta 88 |
| V-8, 455.0 | 4.13 × 4.25 | 400 | O-Toronado |

## 1971

| F-85 (wb 116.0) | | Wght | Price | Prod |
|---|---|---|---|---|
| 33169 | town sedan 4d I-6 | 3,226 | 2,885 | 769 |
| 33269 | town sedan 4d V-8 | 3,424 | 3,006 | 3,650 |
| **Cutlass (wb 116.0; 2d-112.0)** | | | | |
| 33187 | Holiday htp cpe I-6 | 3,292 | 2,901 | 1,345 |
| 33536 | wgn 4d 2S I-6 | 3,732 | 3,454 | 47 |
| 33569 | town sedan 4d I-6 | 3,252 | 2,999 | 618 |
| 33287 | htp cpe V-8 | 3,398 | 3,022 | 32,278 |

# Oldsmobile

| Cutlass (wb 116.0; 2d-112.0) | | Wght | Price | Prod |
|---|---|---|---|---|
| 33636 | wgn 4d 2S V-8 | 3,927 | 3,575 | 6,742 |
| 33669 | town sdn 4d V-8 | 3,438 | 3,120 | 31,904 |
| 33577 | S sports coupe I-6 | 3,196 | 2,958 | 113 |
| 33587 | S htp cpe I-6 | 3,228 | 3,021 | 169 |
| 33677 | S sports coupe V-8 | 3,392 | 3,079 | 4,339 |
| 33687 | S htp cpe V-8 | 3,398 | 3,142 | 63,145 |
| **Cutlass Supreme (wb 116.0; 2d-112.0)** | | | | |
| 34239 | htp sdn | 3,541 | 3,398 | 10,458 |
| 34257 | htp cpe | 3,429 | 3,323 | 60,599 |
| 34267 | conv | 3,513 | 3,507 | 10,255 |
| **4-4-2 (wb 112.0)** | | | | |
| 34467 | conv cpe | 3,731 | 3,743 | 1,304 |
| 34487 | cpe | 3,688 | 3,552 | 6,285 |
| **Vista Cruiser (wb 121.0)** | | | | |
| 34856 | wgn 4d 2S | 4,163 | 3,866 | 5,980 |
| 34866 | wgn 4d 3S | 4,251 | 4,008 | 20,566 |
| **Delta 88 (wb 124.0; wgns-127.0)** | | | | |
| 35439 | sdn 4d | 4,202 | 4,103 | 31,420 |
| 35457 | htp cpe | 4,122 | 4,041 | 27,031 |
| 35469 | town sedan 4d | 4,150 | 3,985 | 38,298 |
| 36439 | Custom htp sdn | 4,237 | 4,366 | 26,593 |
| 36457 | Custom cpe | 4,179 | 4,291 | 24,251 |
| 36469 | Custom town sedan 4d | 4,202 | 4,198 | 22,209 |
| 36647 | Royale htp cpe | 4,221 | 4,549 | 8,397 |
| 36667 | Royale conv | 4,296 | 4,557 | 2,883 |
| 36835 | Custom Cruiser wgn 4d 2S | 4,880 | 4,776 | 4,049 |
| 36845 | Custom Cruiser wgn 4d 3S | 5,000 | 4,917 | 9,932 |
| **Ninety-Eight (wb 127.0)** | | | | |
| 38437 | htp cpe | 4,382 | 4,790 | 8,335 |
| 38439 | htp sdn | 4,467 | 4,852 | 15,025 |
| 38637 | Luxury Coupe htp | 4,418 | 5,065 | 14,876 |
| 38639 | Luxury Sedan htp | 4,504 | 5,159 | 45,055 |
| **Toronado (wb 123.0)** | | | | |
| 39657 | htp cpe | 4,522 | 5,457 | 28,980 |

| 1971 Engines | bore × stroke | bhp | availability |
|---|---|---|---|
| I-6, 250.0 | 3.88 × 3.53 | 145 | S-F-85/Cutlass I-6 |
| V-8, 350.0 | 4.06 × 3.38 | 240 | S-F-85/Cutlass V-8 Delta, VC |
| V-8, 350.0 | 4.06 × 3.38 | 260 | S-Supreme, O-F-85, Cutlass, VC |
| V-8, 455.0 | 4.13 × 4.25 | 280 | O-Delta |
| V-8, 455.0 | 4.13 × 4.25 | 320 | S-98; O-442, F-85, Ctls, VC, Dlta |
| V-8, 455.0 | 4.13 × 4.25 | 340 | S-442; O-F-85, Cutlass, VC |
| V-8, 455.0 | 4.13 × 4.25 | 350 | S-Toronado |

## 1972

| F-85 (wb 116.0) | | Wght | Price | Prod |
|---|---|---|---|---|
| 3D69 | sdn 4d | 3,420 | 2,958 | 3,792 |
| **Cutlass (wb 116.0; 2d-112.0)** | | | | |
| 3F87 | cpe | 3,379 | 2,973 | 37,790 |
| 3G36 | Cruiser wgn 4d 2S | 3,919 | 3,498 | 7,979 |
| 3G69 | town sedan 4d | 3,443 | 3,066 | 38,893 |
| 3G77 | S spt cpe | 3,387 | 3,027 | 4,141 |
| 3G87 | S htp cpe | 3,404 | 3,087 | 78,461 |
| 3J39 | Supreme htp sdn | 3,530 | 3,329 | 14,955 |
| 3J57 | Supreme htp cpe | 3,395 | 3,258 | 105,087 |
| 3J67 | Supreme conv | 3,528 | 3,433 | 11,571 |
| **Vista Cruiser (wb 121.0)** | | | | |
| 3K56 | wgn 4d 2S | 4,150 | 3,774 | 10,573 |
| 3K66 | wgn 4d 3S | 4,241 | 3,908 | 21,340 |
| **Delta 88 (wb 124.0)** | | | | |
| 3L39 | sdn 4d | 4,235 | 4,060 | 35,538 |
| 3L57 | htp cpe | 4,133 | 4,001 | 32,036 |
| 3L69 | town sedan 4d | 4,187 | 3,948 | 46,092 |
| 3N39 | Royale sdn 4d | 4,263 | 4,238 | 42,606 |
| 3N57 | Royale htp cpe | 4,184 | 4,179 | 34,345 |
| 3N67 | Royale conv | 4,257 | 4,387 | 3,900 |
| 3N69 | Royale town sedan 4d | 4,198 | 4,101 | 34,150 |
| 3R35 | Custom Cruiser wgn 4d 2S | 4,947 | 4,700 | 6,907 |
| 3R45 | Custom Cruiser wgn 4d 3S | 5,040 | 4,834 | 18,087 |
| **Ninety-Eight (wb 127.0)** | | | | |
| 3U37 | htp cpe | 4,372 | 4,748 | 13,111 |
| 3U39 | htp sdn | 4,448 | 4,807 | 17,572 |
| 3V37 | Luxury Coupe htp | 4,428 | 5,009 | 24,453 |
| 3V39 | Luxury Sedan htp | 4,533 | 5,098 | 69,920 |
| **Toronado (wb 122.0)** | | | | |
| 3Y57 | Custom htp cpe | 4,544 | 5,341 | 48,900 |

| 1972 Engines | bore × stroke | bhp | availability |
|---|---|---|---|
| V-8, 350.0 | 4.06 × 3.38 | 160 | S-F-85, Ctls, Dlta exc wgns |
| V-8, 350.0 | 4.06 × 3.38 | 180 | S-Supreme; O-Ctls, F-85, VC, Delta exc wgn |
| V-8, 455.0 | 4.13 × 4.25 | 225 | S-Dlta wgn, 98; O-other Dlta |
| V-8, 455.0 | 4.13 × 4.25 | 250 | S-Toro; O-Delta, 98 |
| V-8, 455.0 | 4.13 × 4.25 | 270/300 | O-Ctls cpe/conv (Hurst/Olds) |

Note: A total of 629 Hurst/Olds packages were installed on Cutlass models.

## 1973

| Omega (wb 111.0) | | Wght | Price | Prod |
|---|---|---|---|---|
| B17 | htchbk cpe | 3,329 | 2,762 | 21,433 |
| B27 | cpe | 3,217 | 2,613 | 26,126 |
| B69 | sdn 4d | 3,280 | 2,641 | 12,804 |
| **Cutlass (wb 116.0; 2d-112.0)** | | | | |
| G29 | Colonnade sdn 4d | 3,786 | 3,137 | 35,578 |
| F37 | Colonnade coupe | 3,713 | 3,049 | 22,022 |
| G37 | Colonnade S coupe | 3,721 | 3,159 | 77,558 |
| J29 | Supreme Colonnade sdn 4d | 3,808 | 3,395 | 26,099 |
| J57 | Supreme Colonnade cpe | 3,694 | 3,324 | 219,857 |
| **Vista Cruiser (wb 116.0)** | | | | |
| J35 | wgn 4d 2S | 4,240 | 3,789 | 10,894 |
| J45 | wgn 4d 3S | 4,290 | 3,902 | 13,531 |
| **Delta 88 (wb 124.0)** | | | | |
| L39 | htp sdn | 4,270 | 4,108 | 27,986 |
| L57 | htp cpe | 4,192 | 4,047 | 27,096 |
| L69 | town sedan 4d | 4,243 | 3,991 | 42,476 |
| N39 | Royale htp sdn | 4,296 | 4,293 | 49,145 |
| N57 | Royale htp cpe | 4,206 | 4,221 | 27,096 |
| N67 | Royale conv | 4,298 | 4,442 | 7,088 |
| N69 | Royale town sedan 4d | 4,255 | 4,156 | 42,672 |
| Q35 | Custom Cruiser wgn 4d 2S | 4,997 | 4,630 | 5,275 |
| Q45 | Custom Cruiser wgn 4d 3S | 5,061 | 4,769 | 7,341 |
| R35 | Custom Cruiser wgn 4d 2S | 4,999 | 4,785 | 7,142 |
| R45 | Custom Cruiser wgn 4d 3S | 5,063 | 4,924 | 19,163 |
| **Ninety-Eight (wb 127.0)** | | | | |
| T37 | htp cpe | 4,435 | 4,799 | 7,850 |
| T39 | htp sdn | 4,522 | 4,860 | 13,989 |
| V37 | Luxury Coupe htp | 4,471 | 5,071 | 26,925 |
| V39 | Luxury Sedan htp | 4,560 | 5,164 | 55,695 |
| X39 | Regency htp sdn | 4,594 | 5,418 | 34,009 |

# Oldsmobile

| Toronado (wb 122.0) | | Wght | Price | Prod |
|---|---|---|---|---|
| Y57 | htp cpe | 4,654 | 5,441 | 55,921 |

| 1973 Engines | bore × stroke | bhp | availability |
|---|---|---|---|
| I-6, 250.0 | 3.88 × 3.53 | 100 | S-Omega |
| V-8, 350.0 | 4.06 × 3.38 | 160 | S-Delta exc wgns |
| V-8, 350.0 | 4.06 × 3.38 | 180 | S-Omega, Cutls, VC |
| V-8, 455.0 | 4.13 × 4.25 | 225 | S-Dlta wgns, 98; O-other Dlta |
| V-8, 455.0 | 4.13 × 4.25 | 250 | S-Toronado, O-Cutlass, VC |

## 1974

| Omega (wb 111.0) | | Wght | Price | Prod |
|---|---|---|---|---|
| B17 | htchbk cpe | 3,423 | 3,166 | 12,449 |
| B27 | cpe | 3,319 | 3,043 | 27,075 |
| B69 | sdn 4d | 3,367 | 3,071 | 10,756 |
| **Cutlass (wb 116.0; 2d-112.0)** | | | | |
| F37 | Colonnade cpe | 3,868 | 3,793 | 16,063 |
| G29 | Colonnade sdn 4d | 3,924 | 3,868 | 25,718 |
| G37 | Colonnade S coupe | 3,883 | 3,890 | 50,860 |
| J29 | Supreme Colonnade sdn 4d | 3,969 | 4,142 | 12,525 |
| J57 | Supreme Colonnade cpe | 3,872 | 4,085 | 172,360 |
| H35 | Supreme Cruiser wgn 4d 2S | 4,369 | 4,289 | 3,437 |
| H45 | Supreme Cruiser wgn 4d 3S | 4,406 | 4,402 | 3,101 |
| **Vista Cruiser (wb 116.0)** | | | | |
| J35 | wgn 4d 2S | 4,380 | 4,499 | 4,191 |
| J45 | wgn 4d 3S | 4,417 | 4,612 | 7,013 |
| **Delta 88 (wb 124.0)** | | | | |
| L39 | htp sdn | 4,428 | 4,490 | 11,941 |
| L57 | htp cpe | 4,375 | 4,429 | 11,615 |
| L69 | town sedan 4d | 4,396 | 4,373 | 17,939 |
| N39 | Royale htp sdn | 4,462 | 4,650 | 26,363 |
| N57 | Royale htp cpe | 4,397 | 4,584 | 27,515 |
| N67 | Royale conv | 4,454 | 4,799 | 3,716 |
| N69 | Royale town sedan 4d | 4,414 | 4,513 | 22,504 |
| Q35 | Cust Cruiser wgn 4d 2S | 5,120 | 4,981 | 1,481 |
| Q45 | Cust Cruiser wgn 4d 3S | 5,182 | 5,120 | 2,528 |
| R35 | Cust Cruiser wgn 4d 2S (wdgrain) | 5,123 | 5,136 | 2,960 |
| R45 | Cust Cruiser wgn 4d 3S (wdgrain) | 5,184 | 5,275 | 8,947 |
| **Ninety-Eight (wb 127.0)** | | | | |
| T39 | htp sdn | 4,699 | 5,303 | 4,395 |
| V37 | Luxury Coupe htp | 4,638 | 5,514 | 9,236 |
| V39 | Luxury Sedan htp | 4,730 | 5,607 | 21,896 |
| X37 | Regency cpe | 4,664 | 5,776 | 10,719 |
| X39 | Regency htp sdn | 4,759 | 5,869 | 24,310 |
| **Toronado (wb 122.0)** | | | | |
| Y57 | htp cpe | 4,698 | 5,933 | 27,582 |

| 1974 Engines | bore × stroke | bhp | availability |
|---|---|---|---|
| I-6, 250.0 | 3.88 × 3.53 | 100 | S-Omega |
| V-8, 350.0 | 4.06 × 3.38 | 180 | S-Omega, Ctls, VC, Delta exc wgns |
| V-8, 350.0 | 4.06 × 3.38 | 200 | O-Ctls, VC, Delta exc wgns |
| V-8, 455.0 | 4.13 × 4.25 | 210 | S-Delta wgns, 98; O-other Delta |
| V-8, 455.0 | 4.13 × 4.25 | 230 | S-Toro; O-all exc Omega |
| V-8, 455.0 | 4.13 × 4.25 | 275 | O-Cutlass, VC |

## 1975

| Starfire (wb 97.0) | | Wght | Price | Prod |
|---|---|---|---|---|
| D37 | htchbk cpe | 2,914 | 4,144 | 31,081 |
| T07 | htchbk cpe 2d | 2,889 | 3,873 | |

| Omega (wb 111.0) | | Wght | Price | Prod |
|---|---|---|---|---|
| S27 | F-85 htchbk cpe | 3,250 | 3,203 | 15,979 |
| B27 | cpe | 3,390 | 3,422 | |
| B17 | htchbk cpe | 3,482 | 3,546 | 6,287 |
| B69 | sdn 4d | 3,436 | 3,450 | 13,971 |
| C17 | Salon htchbk cpe | 3,566 | 4,298 | 1,694 |
| C27 | Salon cpe | 3,476 | 4,148 | 2,176 |
| C69 | Salon sdn 4d | 3,526 | 4,192 | 1,758 |
| **Cutlass (wb 116.0; 2d-112.0)** | | | | |
| F37 | Colonnade cpe | 3,684 | 3,742 | 12,797 |
| G29 | Colonnade sdn 4d | 3,806 | 3,818 | 30,144 |
| G37 | Colonnade S cpe | 3,740 | 3,840 | 42,921 |
| J29 | Supreme Colonnade sdn 4d | 3,852 | 4,092 | 15,517 |
| J57 | Supreme Colonnade cpe | 3,754 | 4,035 | 150,874 |
| K29 | Salon Colonnade sdn 4d V-8 | 4,008 | 4,713 | 5,810 |
| K57 | Salon Colonnade cpe V-8 | 3,915 | 4,641 | 39,050 |
| H35 | Supreme Cruiser wgn 4d 2S V-8 | 4,376 | 4,665 | 8,329 |
| H45 | Supreme Cruiser wgn 4d 3S V-8 | 4,413 | 4,778 | 3,096 |
| J35 | Visa Cruiser wgn 4d 2S V-8 | 4,380 | 4,875 | 7,089 |
| J45 | Vista Cruiser wgn 4d 3S V-8 | 4,417 | 4,988 | 7,101 |
| **Delta 88 (wb 124.0)** | | | | |
| L39 | htp sdn | 4,404 | 4,891 | 9,283 |
| L57 | htp cpe | 4,343 | 4,830 | 8,522 |
| L69 | town sedan 4d | 4,356 | 4,778 | 16,112 |
| N39 | Royale htp sdn | 4,454 | 5,051 | 32,481 |
| N57 | Royale htp cpe | 4,386 | 4,985 | 23,465 |
| N67 | Royale conv | 4,455 | 5,200 | 21,038 |
| N69 | Royale town sedan 4d | 4,385 | 4,914 | 7,181 |
| Q35 | Custom Cruiser wgn 4d 2S | 5,095 | 5,413 | 6,008 |
| R35 | Cust Cruiser wgn 4d 2S (wdgrain) | 5,107 | 5,568 | |
| Q45 | Custom Cruiser wgn 4d 3S | 5,146 | 5,552 | 10,060 |
| R45 | Cust Cruiser wgn 4d 3S (wdgrain) | 5,161 | 5,707 | |
| **Ninety-Eight (wb 127.0)** | | | | |
| V37 | Luxury Coupe | 4,591 | 5,950 | 8,798 |
| V39 | Luxury Sedan htp | 4,743 | 6,091 | 18,091 |
| X37 | Regency cpe | 4,621 | 6,212 | 16,697 |
| X39 | Regency htp sdn | 4,755 | 6,353 | 35,264 |
| **Toronado (wb 122.0)** | | | | |
| Y57 | Custom htp cpe | 4,647 | 6,523 | 4,419 |
| Z57 | Brougham htp cpe | 4,691 | 6,753 | 18,882 |

| 1975 Engines | bore × stroke | bhp | availability |
|---|---|---|---|
| V-6, 231.0 | 3.80 × 3.40 | 110 | S-Starfire |
| I-6, 250.0 | 3.88 × 3.53 | 105 | S-Omega, Ctls exc wgns |
| V-8, 260.0 | 3.50 × 3.39 | 110 | S-Omega, Ctls exc wgns |
| V-8, 350.0 | 4.06 × 3.38 | 145 | O-Omega |
| V-8, 350.0 | 4.06 × 3.38 | 165 | O-Omega |
| V-8, 350.0 | 4.06 × 3.38 | 170 | S-Ctls wgns, Delta exc wgns; O-other Ctls |
| V-8, 400.0 | 4.12 × 3.75 | 185 | O-Delta, 98 |
| V-8, 455.0 | 4.13 × 4.25 | 190 | S-Delta wgns, 98; O-Ctls, other Delta |
| V-8, 455.0 | 4.13 × 4.25 | 215 | S-Toronado |

## 1976

| Starfire (wb 97.0) | | Wght | Price | Prod |
|---|---|---|---|---|
| D07 | SX htchbk cpe | 2,864 | 4,062 | 20,854 |
| T07 | htchbk cpe | 2,857 | 3,882 | 8,305 |

| Omega (wb 111.0) | | Wght | Price | Prod |
|---|---|---|---|---|
| S27 | F-85 cpe | 3,246 | 3,390 | 3,918 |
| B17 | htchbk cpe | 3,322 | 3,627 | 4,497 |
| B27 | cpe | 3,248 | 3,485 | 15,347 |

# Oldsmobile

| Omega (wb 111.0) | | Wght | Price | Prod |
|---|---|---|---|---|
| B69 | sdn 4d | 3,270 | 3,514 | 20,221 |
| E17 | Brougham htchbk cpe | 3,332 | 3,817 | 1,235 |
| E27 | Brougham cpe | 3,252 | 3,675 | 5,363 |
| E69 | Brougham sdn 4d | 3,286 | 3,704 | 7,587 |
| **Cutlass (wb 116.0; cpe-112.0)** | | | | |
| G29 | S Colonnade sdn 4d | 3,772 | 4,033 | 34,994 |
| G37 | S Colonnade | 3,690 | 3,999 | 59,179 |
| J29 | Supreme Colonnade sdn 4d | 3,812 | 4,415 | 37,112 |
| J57 | Supreme Colonnade cpe | 3,718 | 4,291 | 186,647 |
| M57 | Supreme Brougham cpe | 3,750 | 4,580 | 91,312 |
| K29 | Salon Colonnade sdn 4d V-8 | 3,949 | 4,965 | 7,921 |
| K57 | Salon Colonnade cpe V-8 | 3,829 | 4,890 | 48,440 |
| H35 | Sprme Crusr wgn 4d 2S V-8 | 4,298 | 4,923 | 13,964 |
| H35 | Sprme Crusr wgn 4d 3S V-8 | 4,350 | 5,056 | |
| J35 | Vista Cruiser wgn 4d 2S V-8 | 4,304 | 5,041 | 20,560 |
| J35 | Vista Cruiser wgn 4d 3S V-8 | 4,350 | 5,174 | |
| **Delta 88 (wb 124.0; wgns-127.0)** | | | | |
| L39 | sdn 4d | 4,336 | 5,038 | 9,759 |
| L57 | cpe 2d | 4,243 | 4,975 | 7,204 |
| L69 | town sedan 4d | 4,279 | 4,918 | 17,115 |
| N39 | Royale sdn 4d | 4,268 | 5,217 | 52,103 |
| N57 | Royale cpe 2d | 4,263 | 5,146 | 33,364 |
| N69 | Royale town sdn 4d | 4,294 | 5,078 | 33,268 |
| Q35 | Cust Cruiser wgn 4d 2S | 4,987 | 5,563 | 2,572 |
| Q45 | wgn 4d 3S | 5,060 | 5,705 | 3,626 |
| R35 | wgn 4d 2S (woodgrain) | 5,009 | 5,719 | 3,849 |
| R45 | CC wgn 4d 3S (woodgrain) | 5,071 | 5,861 | 12,269 |
| **Ninety-Eight (wb 127.0)** | | | | |
| V37 | Luxury Coupe | 4,501 | 6,271 | 6,056 |
| V39 | Luxury Sedan htp | 4,633 | 6,419 | 16,802 |
| X37 | Regency cpe | 4,535 | 6,544 | 26,282 |
| X39 | Regency htp sdn | 4,673 | 6,691 | 55,339 |
| **Toronado (wb 122.0)** | | | | |
| Y57 | Custom htp cpe | 4,694 | 6,891 | 2,555 |
| Z57 | Brougham htp cpe | 4,729 | 7,137 | 21,749 |

| 1976 Engines | bore × stroke | bhp | availability |
|---|---|---|---|
| V-6, 231.0 | 3.80 × 3.40 | 105 | S-Starfire |
| I-6, 250.0 | 3.88 × 3.53 | 105 | S-Omga,Ctls exc Salon |
| V-8, 260.0 | 3.50 × 3.39 | 110 | S-Omega, Ctls Salon; O-other Ctls |
| V-8, 350.0 | 3.80 × 3.85 | 140/155 | O-Omega |
| V-8, 350.0 | 4.06 × 3.38 | 170 | S-Delta exc wgn; O-Ctls, Salon |
| V-8, 455.0 | 4.13 × 4.25 | 190 | S-Delta wgn, 98; O-Ctls, other Delta |
| V-8, 455.0 | 4.13 × 4.25 | 215 | S-Toronado |

## 1977

| Starfire (wb 97.0) | | Wght | Price | Prod |
|---|---|---|---|---|
| D07 | SX htchbk cpe | 2,836 | 4,140 | 14,181 |
| T07 | htchbk cpe | 2,808 | 3,942 | 4,910 |
| **Omega (wb 111.0)** | | | | |
| S27 | F-85 cpe | 3,184 | 3,653 | 2,241 |
| B17 | htchbk cpe | 3,270 | 3,905 | 4,739 |
| B27 | cpe | 3,202 | 3,740 | 18,611 |
| B69 | sdn 4d | 3,236 | 3,797 | 21,723 |
| E17 | Brougham htchbk cpe | 3,302 | 4,105 | 1,189 |
| E27 | Brougham cpe | 3,226 | 3,934 | 6,478 |
| E67 | Brougham sdn 4d | 3,262 | 3,994 | 9,003 |
| **Cutlass (wb 116.0; 2d-112.0)** | | | | |
| G29 | S sdn 4d | 3,690 | 4,387 | 42,923 |
| G37 | S cpe | 3,608 | 4,351 | 70,155 |
| J29 | Supreme sdn 4d | 3,438 | 4,734 | 37,929 |
| J57 | Supreme cpe | 3,638 | 4,670 | 242,874 |
| M29 | Supreme Brougham sdn 4d | 3,764 | 5,033 | 16,738 |
| M57 | Supreme Brougham cpe | 3,656 | 4,969 | 124,712 |
| K57 | Salon cpe V-8 | 3,787 | 5,269 | 56,757 |
| H35 | Supreme Cruiser wgn 4d V-8 | 4,218 | 5,243 | 14,838 |
| H35 | Vista Cruiser wgn 4d V-8 | 4,255 | 5,395 | 25,816 |
| **Delta (wb 116.0)** | | | | |
| L37 | cpe | 3,496 | 5,145 | 8,788 |
| L69 | sdn 4d | 3,537 | 5,205 | 26,084 |
| N37 | Royale cpe | 3,505 | 5,363 | 61,138 |
| N69 | Royale sdn 4d | 3,561 | 5,433 | 117,571 |
| Q35 | Custom Cruiser wgn 4d 2S V-8 | 4,064 | 5,923 | 32,827 |
| Q35 | Custom Cruiser wgn 4d 3S V-8 | 4,095 | 6,098 | |
| **Ninety-Eight (wb 119.0)** | | | | |
| V37 | Luxury cpe | 3,753 | 6,609 | 5,058 |
| V69 | Luxury sdn 4d | 3,807 | 6,786 | 14,323 |
| X37 | Regency cpe | 3,767 | 6,949 | 32,072 |
| X69 | Regency sdn 4d | 3,840 | 7,133 | 87,970 |
| **Toronado (wb 122.0)** | | | | |
| W57 | XS htp cpe | 4,688 | 10,684 | 2,714* |
| Z57 | Brougham htp cpe | 4,634 | 8,134 | 31,371 |

*Includes one XSR prototype.

| 1977 Engines | bore × stroke | bhp | availability |
|---|---|---|---|
| I-4, 140.0 | 3.50 × 3.63 | 84 | S-Starfire |
| V-6, 231.0 | 3.80 × 3.40 | 105 | S-Omega, Ctls, exc Salon/wgns, Delta; O-Strfre |
| V-8, 260.0 | 3.50 × 3.39 | 110 | S-Ctls Salon; O-Omega, other Cutlass, Delta |
| V-8, 305.0 | 3.74 × 3.48 | 145 | O-Omega |
| V-8, 350.0 | 4.06 × 3.38 | 160 | O-Delta |
| V-8, 350.0 | 4.06 × 3.38 | 170 | S-Ctls wgns, CC wgns, 98; O-other Ctls, Delta |
| V-8, 403.0 | 4.35 × 3.38 | 185 | O-Ctls, Delta, 98 |
| V-8, 403.0 | 4.35 × 3.38 | 200 | S-Toronado |

## 1978

| Starfire (wb 97.0) | | Wght | Price | Prod |
|---|---|---|---|---|
| D07 | SX htchbk cpe | 2,790 | 4,306 | 9,265 |
| T07 | htchbk cpe 2d | 2,786 | 4,095 | 8,056 |
| **Omega (wb 111.0)** | | | | |
| B17 | htchbk cpe | 3,250 | 4,173 | 4,084 |
| B27 | cpe 2d | 3,184 | 4,009 | 15,632 |
| B69 | sdn 4d | 3,236 | 4,094 | 19,478 |
| E27 | Brougham cpe 2d | 3,204 | 4,215 | 3,798 |
| E69 | Brougham sdn 4d | 3,246 | 4,300 | 7,125 |
| **Cutlass (wb 108.1)** | | | | |
| G09 | Salon sdn 4d | 3,136 | 4,543 | 29,509 |
| G87 | Salon cpe | 3,122 | 4,433 | 21,198 |
| J09 | Salon Brougham sdn 4d | 3,186 | 4,828 | 21,902 |
| J87 | Salon Brougham cpe | 3,082 | 4,717 | 10,741 |
| R47 | Supreme cpe | 3,228 | 4,873 | 240,917 |
| K47 | Calais cpe | 3,212 | 5,231 | 40,842 |
| M47 | Supreme Brougham cpe | 3,204 | 5,287 | 117,880 |
| H35 | Cruiser wgn 4d 2S | 3,308 | 5,287 | 44,617 |
| **Delta 88 (wb 116.0)** | | | | |
| L37 | cpe | 3,496 | 5,549 | 17,469 |
| L67 | sdn 4d | 3,541 | 5,634 | 25,322 |
| N37 | Royale cpe | 3,507 | 5,778 | 68,469 |

# Oldsmobile

| Delta 88 (wb 116.0) | | Wght | Price | Prod |
|---|---|---|---|---|
| N69 | Royale sdn 4d | 3,569 | 5,888 | 131,430 |
| Q35 | Custom Cruiser wgn 4d 2S V-8 | 4,045 | 6,419 | 34,491 |
| Q35 | Custom Cruiser wgn 4d 3S V-8 | 4,075 | 6,605 | |
| **Ninety-Eight (wb 119.0)** | | | | |
| V37 | Luxury cpe | 3,753 | 7,170 | 2,956 |
| V69 | Luxury sdn 4d | 3,805 | 7,351 | 9,136 |
| X37 | Regency cpe | 3,767 | 7,538 | 28,573 |
| X69 | Regency sdn 4d | 3,836 | 7,726 | 78,100 |
| **Toronado (wb 122.0)** | | | | |
| Z57 | Brougham cpe | 4,624 | 9,412 | 22,362 |
| W57 | XSC cpe | 4,627 | — | 2,453 |

| 1978 Engines | bore × stroke | bhp | availability |
|---|---|---|---|
| I-4, 151.0 | 4.00 × 3.00 | 85 | S-Starfire |
| V-6, 231.0 | 3.80 × 3.40 | 105 | S-Omega, Ctls, Delta; O-Starfire |
| V-8, 260.0 | 3.50 × 3.39 | 110 | O-Cutlass, Delta |
| V-8, 305.0 | 3.74 × 3.48 | 145 | O-Strfre, Omega, Ctls |
| V-8, 305.0 | 3.74 × 3.48 | 165 | O-Cutlass |
| V-8D, 350.0 | 4.06 × 3.38 | 120 | O-Delta, 98 |
| V-8, 350.0 | 4.06 × 3.38 | 170 | O-Delta, 98, O-Omega, Ctls |
| V-8, 403.0 | 4.35 × 3.38 | 185/190 | S-Toro; O-Delta, 98 |

## 1979

| Starfire (wb 97.0) | | Wght | Price | Prod |
|---|---|---|---|---|
| D07 | SX htchbk cpe 2d | 2,703 | 4,475 | 7,155 |
| T07 | htchbk cpe 2d | 2,690 | 4,275 | 13,144 |
| **Omega (wb 111.0)** | | | | |
| B17 | htchbk cpe | 3,222 | 4,345 | 956 |
| B27 | cpe | 3,145 | 4,181 | 4,806 |
| B69 | sdn 4d | 3,183 | 4,281 | 5,826 |
| E27 | Brougham cpe | 3,156 | 4,387 | 1,078 |
| E69 | Brougham sdn 4d | 3,214 | 4,487 | 2,145 |
| **Cutlass (wb 108.1)** | | | | |
| G09 | Salon sdn 4d | 3,138 | 5,038 | 20,266 |
| G87 | Salon cpe | 3,118 | 4,938 | 8,399 |
| J09 | Salon Brougham sdn | 3,185 | 5,352 | 18,714 |
| J87 | Salon Brougham cpe | 3,158 | 5,227 | 3,617 |
| R47 | Supreme cpe | 3,148 | 5,390 | 277,944 |
| K47 | Calais cpe | 3,180 | 5,828 | 43,780 |
| M47 | Supreme Brougham cpe | 3,174 | 5,829 | 137,323 |
| G35 | Cruiser wgn 4d 2S | 3,281 | 5,223 | 10,755 |
| H35 | Cruiser B'ham wgn 4d 2S | 3,325 | 5,775 | 42,953 |
| **Delta 88 (wb 116.0)** | | | | |
| L37 | cpe | 3,550 | 6,112 | 16,202 |
| L69 | sdn 4d | 3,576 | 6,212 | 25,424 |
| N37 | Royale cpe | 3,560 | 6,399 | 60,687 |
| N69 | Royale sdn 4d | 3,602 | 6,524 | 152,526 |
| Q35 | Custom Cruiser wgn 4d 2S V-8 | 4,042 | 7,201 | 36,648 |
| Q35 | Custom Cruiser wgn 4d 3S V-8 | 4,092 | 7,394 | |
| **Ninety-Eight (wb 119.0)** | | | | |
| V37 | Luxury cpe | 3,806 | 8,614 | 2,104 |
| V69 | Luxury sdn 4d | 3,850 | 8,795 | 6,720 |
| X37 | Regency cpe | 3,810 | 9,236 | 29,965 |
| X69 | Regency sdn 4d | 3,885 | 9,424 | 91,962 |
| **Toronado (wb 114.0)** | | | | |
| Z57 | Brougham cpe | 3,731 | 10,709 | 50,056 |

| 1979 Engines | bore × stroke | bhp | availability |
|---|---|---|---|
| I-4, 151.0 | 4.00 × 3.00 | 85 | O-Starfire |
| I-4, 151.0 | 4.00 × 3.00 | 90 | S-Starfire |
| V-6, 231.0 | 3.80 × 3.40 | 115 | S-Omega, Ctls, Dlta; O-Strfre |
| V-8D, 260.0 | 3.50 × 3.39 | 90 | O-Cutlass |
| V-8, 260.0 | 3.50 × 3.39 | 105 | S-Ctls, Delta exc wgn |
| V-8, 301.0 | 4.00 × 3.00 | 135 | O-Delta exc wgn |
| V-8, 305.0 | 3.74 × 3.48 | 130 | O-Starfire, Omega |
| V-8, 305.0 | 3.74 × 3.48 | 160 | O-Cutlass |
| V-8, 350.0 | 4.06 × 3.28 | 160 | S-Delta wagons |
| V-8D, 350.0 | 4.06 × 3.38 | 125 | O-Ctls, Delta, 98, Toronado |
| V-8, 350.0 | 4.06 × 3.38 | 160 | S-98 |
| V-8, 350.0 | 4.06 × 3.38 | 165 | S-Toro; O-Omega, Ctls wgn |
| V-8, 403.0 | 4.35 × 3.38 | 175 | O-Delta wgns, 98 |

## 1980

| Starfire (wb 97.0) | | Wght | Price | Prod |
|---|---|---|---|---|
| D07 | SX htchbk cpe | 2,668 | 4,950 | 8,237 |
| T07 | htchbk cpe | 2,656 | 4,750 | |
| **Omega (wb 104.9)** | | | | |
| B37 | cpe | 2,420 | 5,501 | 28,267 |
| B69 | sdn 4d | 2,446 | 5,672 | 42,172 |
| E37 | Brougham cpe | 2,452 | 5,858 | 21,595 |
| E69 | Brougham sdn 4d | 2,478 | 6,013 | 42,289 |
| **Cutlass (wb 108.1)** | | | | |
| G69 | sdn 4d | 3,144 | 6,124 | 36,923 |
| G87 | Salon cpe | 3,140 | 5,764 | 3,429 |
| J87 | Salon Brougham cpe | 3,140 | 6,054 | 965 |
| R47 | Supreme cpe | 3,264 | 6,655 | 169,597 |
| R69 | LS sdn 4d | 3,254 | 6,780 | 86,868 |
| K47 | Calais cpe | 3,276 | 7,119 | 26,269 |
| M47 | Supreme Brougham cpe | 3,276 | 7,094 | 77,875 |
| M69 | Supreme Brougham sdn 4d | 3,280 | 7,219 | 52,462 |
| G35 | Cruiser wgn 4d 2S | 3,343 | 6,572 | 7,815 |
| H35 | Cruiser Brougham wgn 4d 2S | 3,380 | 6,809 | 22,791 |
| **Delta 88 (wb 116.0)** | | | | |
| L37 | cpe | 3,395 | 6,808 | 6,845 |
| L69 | sdn 4d | 3,428 | 6,905 | 15,285 |
| N37 | Royale cpe | 3,403 | 7,076 | 39,303 |
| N69 | Royale sdn 4d | 3,406 | 7,228 | 87,178 |
| P35 | Custom Cruiser wgn 4d 2S V-8 | 3,910 | 7,820 | 17,067 |
| P35 | Custom Cruiser wgn 4d 3S V-8 | 3,940 | 8,028 | |
| **Ninety-Eight (wb 119.0)** | | | | |
| V69 | Luxury sdn 4d | 3,789 | 9,517 | 2,640 |
| X37 | Regency cpe | 3,811 | 10,035 | 12,391 |
| X69 | Regency sdn 4d | 3,832 | 10,159 | 58,603 |
| **Toronado (wb 114.0)** | | | | |
| Z57 | cpe | 3,627 | 11,934 | 43,440 |

| 1980 Engines | bore × stroke | bhp | availability |
|---|---|---|---|
| I-4, 151.0 | 4.00 × 3.00 | 85/90 | S-Starfire, Omega |
| V-6, 173.0 | 3.50 × 3.00 | 115 | O-Omega |
| V-6, 231.0 | 3.80 × 3.40 | 110 | S-Ctls, Delta exc wgns; O-Starfire |
| V-8, 260.0 | 3.50 × 3.39 | 105 | S-Cutlass |
| V-8, 265.0 | 3.75 × 3.00 | 120 | S-Delta exc wgns |
| V-8, 305.0 | 3.74 × 3.48 | 155 | O-Cutlass |
| V-8, 307.0 | 3.80 × 3.38 | 150 | S-Delta wgns, 98, Toro; O-Delta |
| V-8D, 350.0 | 4.06 × 3.38 | 105 | O-Ctls, Delta, 98, Toro |
| V-8, 350.0 | 4.06 × 3.38 | 160 | O-Ctls, Delta, 98, Toronado |

# Oldsmobile

## 1981

### Omega (wb 104.9)
| | | Wght | Price | Prod |
|---|---|---|---|---|
| B37 | cpe 2d | 2,439 | 6,343 | 27,323 |
| B69 | sdn 4d | 2,469 | 6,514 | 51,715 |
| E37 | Brougham cpe 2d | 2,462 | 6,700 | 19,260 |
| E69 | Brougham sdn 4d | 2,499 | 6,855 | 49,620 |

### Cutlass (wb 108.1)
| | | | | |
|---|---|---|---|---|
| G69 | sdn 4d | 3,205 | 6,955 | 25,580 |
| R47 | Supreme cpe | 3,213 | 7,484 | 187,875 |
| R69 | LS sdn 4d | 3,236 | 7,652 | 84,272 |
| K47 | Calais cpe | 3,227 | 8,004 | 4,105 |
| M47 | Supreme Brougham cpe | 3,238 | 7,969 | 93,855 |
| M69 | Supreme Brougham sdn 4d | 3,242 | 8,100 | 53,952 |
| G35 | Cruiser wgn 4d 2S | 3,369 | 7,418 ⎤ | 31,926 |
| H35 | Cruiser Brougham wgn 4d 2S | 3,367 | 7,725 ⎦ | |

### Delta 88 (wb 116.0)
| | | | | |
|---|---|---|---|---|
| L37 | cpe | 3,485 | 7,429 | 3,330 |
| L69 | sdn 4d | 3,501 | 7,524 | 10,806 |
| N37 | Royale cpe | 3,489 | 7,693 ⎤ | 41,682 |
| Y37 | Royale Brougham cpe | 3,519 | 8,058 ⎦ | |
| N69 | Royale sdn 4d | 3,530 | 7,842 ⎤ | 104,124 |
| Y69 | Royale Brougham sdn 4d | 3,564 | 8,141 ⎦ | |
| P35 | Custom Cruiser wgn 4d 2S V-8 | 3,950 | 8,452 | 18,956 |

### Ninety-Eight (wb 119.0)
| | | | | |
|---|---|---|---|---|
| V69 | Luxury sdn 4d | 3,741 | 9,951 | 1,957 |
| X37 | Regency cpe | 3,735 | 10,440 | 13,696 |
| X69 | Regency sdn 4d | 3,794 | 10,558 | 74,017 |

### Toronado (wb 114.0)
| | | | | |
|---|---|---|---|---|
| Z57 | cpe | 3,631 | 12,148 | 42,604 |

### 1981 Engines
| | bore × stroke | bhp | availability |
|---|---|---|---|
| I-4, 151.0 | 4.00 × 3.00 | 90 | S-Omega |
| V-6, 173.0 | 3.50 × 3.00 | 110 | O-Omega |
| V-6, 231.0 | 3.80 × 3.40 | 110 | S-Ctls, Delta exc wgns |
| V-6, 252.0 | 3.97 × 3.40 | 125 | S-98, Toronado |
| V-8, 260.0 | 3.50 × 3.39 | 105 | O-Cutlass, Delta 88 |
| V-8, 307.0 | 3.80 × 3.39 | 140 | S-Delta wgn; O-Cutlass wgn, Delta, 98, Toro |
| V-8D, 350.0 | 4.06 × 3.39 | 105 | O-Ctls, Delta, 98, Toro |

## 1982

### Firenza (wb 101.2)
| | | Wght | Price | Prod |
|---|---|---|---|---|
| C77 | S htchbk cpe | 2,344 | 7,413 | 8,894 |
| C69 | sdn 4d | 2,345 | 7,448 | 9,256 |
| D77 | SX htchbk cpe | 2,379 | 8,159 | 6,017 |
| D69 | LX sdn 4d | 2,370 | 8,080 | 5,941 |

### Omega (wb 104.9)
| | | | | |
|---|---|---|---|---|
| B37 | cpe | 2,506 | 7,388 | 12,140 |
| B69 | sdn 4d | 2,538 | 7,574 | 29,548 |
| E37 | Brougham cpe | 2,529 | 7,722 | 9,430 |
| E69 | Brougham sdn 4d | 2,569 | 7,891 | 26,351 |

### Cutlass Ciera (wb 104.9)
| | | | | |
|---|---|---|---|---|
| G27 | cpe | 2,618 | 8,847 | 5,185 |
| G19 | sdn 4d | 2,637 | 8,997 | 9,717 |
| J27 | LS cpe | 2,618 | 8,968 | 10,702 |
| J19 | LS sdn 4d | 2,624 | 9,157 | 29,322 |
| M27 | Brougham cpe | 2,620 | 9,397 | 12,518 |
| M19 | Brougham sdn 4d | 2,626 | 9,599 | 33,876 |

### Cutlass (wb 108.1)
| | | | | |
|---|---|---|---|---|
| R47 | Supreme cpe | 3,231 | 8,588 | 89,617 |
| R69 | sdn 4d | 3,292 | 8,712 | 60,053 |
| K47 | Calais cpe | 3,304 | 9,379 | 17,109 |

### Cutlass (wb 108.1)
| | | Wght | Price | Prod |
|---|---|---|---|---|
| M47 | Supreme Brougham cpe | 3,258 | 9,160 | 59,592 |
| M69 | Supreme Brougham sdn 4d | 3,317 | 9,255 | 34,717 |
| H35 | Cruiser wgn 4d 2S | 3,433 | 8,905 | 20,363 |

### Delta 88 (wb 116.0)
| | | | | |
|---|---|---|---|---|
| L69 | sdn 4d | 3,557 | 8,603 | 8,278 |
| N37 | Royale cpe | 3,534 | 8,733 ⎤ | 41,382 |
| Y37 | Royale Brougham cpe | 3,572 | 9,202 ⎦ | |
| N69 | Royale sdn 4d | 3,572 | 8,894 ⎤ | 105,184 |
| Y69 | Royale Brougham sdn 4d | 3,608 | 9,293 ⎦ | |
| P35 | Custom Cruiser wgn 4d 2S V-8 | 4,026 | 9,614 | 19,367 |

### Ninety-Eight (wb 119.0)
| | | | | |
|---|---|---|---|---|
| X37 | Regency cpe | 3,785 | 12,117 | 11,832 |
| X69 | Regency sdn 4d | 3,842 | 12,294 ⎤ | 79,135 |
| W69 | Regency Brougham sdn 4d | 3,890 | 13,344 ⎦ | |

### Toronado (wb 114.0)
| | | | | |
|---|---|---|---|---|
| Z57 | Brougham cpe | 3,695 | 14,462 | 33,928 |

### 1982 Engines
| | bore × stroke | bhp | availability |
|---|---|---|---|
| I-4, 112.0 | 3.50 × 2.91 | 88 | S-Firenza |
| I-4, 121.0 | 3.50 × 3.15 | 90 | O-Firenza |
| I-4, 151.0 | 4.00 × 3.00 | 90 | S-Omega, Ctls Ciera |
| V-6, 173.0 | 3.50 × 3.00 | 112 | O-Omega |
| V-6, 173.0 | 3.50 × 3.00 | 130 | O-Omega |
| V-6, 181.0 | 3.80 × 2.66 | 110 | O-Cutlass Ciera |
| V-6, 231.0 | 3.80 × 3.40 | 110 | S-Ctls Supreme, Delta exc wgns |
| V-6, 252.0 | 3.97 × 3.40 | 125 | S-98, Toronado |
| V-8, 260.0 | 3.50 × 3.39 | 100 | O-Ctls Supreme, Delta exc wgns |
| V-6D, 262.0 | 4.06 × 3.39 | 85 | O-Ctls Ciera, Suprme |
| V-8, 307.0 | 3.80 × 3.39 | 140 | S-Delta wgn; O-Ctls Supreme, other Delta, 98, Toro |
| V-8D, 350.0 | 4.06 × 3.39 | 105 | O-Supreme, Delta, 98, Toro |

## 1983

### Firenza (wb 101.2)
| | | Wght | Price | Prod |
|---|---|---|---|---|
| C77 | S htchbk cpe | 2,440 | 7,007 | 8,208 |
| C69 | sdn 4d | 2,418 | 7,094 | 11,278 |
| D77 | SX htchbk cpe | 2,478 | 7,750 | 3,767 |
| D69 | LX sdn 4d | 2,438 | 7,646 | 5,067 |
| C35 | Cruiser wgn 4d | 2,496 | 7,314 | 7,460 |
| D35 | LX Cruiser wgn 4d | 2,520 | 7,866 | 4,972 |

### Omega (wb 104.9)
| | | | | |
|---|---|---|---|---|
| B37 | cpe | 2,531 | 7,478 | 6,448 |
| B69 | sdn 4d | 2,569 | 7,676 | 24,287 |
| E37 | Brougham cpe | 2,562 | 7,767 | 5,177 |
| E69 | Brougham sdn 4d | 2,594 | 7,948 | 18,014 |

### Cutlass Ciera (wb 104.9)
| | | | | |
|---|---|---|---|---|
| J27 | LS cpe | 2,732 | 8,703 | 12,612 |
| J19 | LS sdn 4d | 2,765 | 8,892 | 66,731 |
| M27 | Brougham cpe | 2,754 | 9,183 | 17,088 |
| M19 | Brougham sdn 4d | 2,789 | 9,385 | 73,219 |

### Cutlass (wb 108.1)
| | | | | |
|---|---|---|---|---|
| R47 | Supreme cpe | 3,340 | 8,950 | 107,946 |
| R69 | sdn 4d | 3,382 | 9,103 | 56,347 |
| M47 | Supreme Brougham cpe | 3,377 | 9,589 | 60,025 |
| M69 | Supreme Brougham sdn 4d | 3,416 | 9,719 | 28,451 |
| K47 | Calais cpe | 3,357 | 9,848 | 16,660 |
| K47/W40 | Calais Hurst/Olds cpe V-8 | — | 12,069 | 3,001 |
| H35 | Cruiser wgn 4d 2S | 3,529 | 9,381 | 22,037 |

749

# Oldsmobile

| Delta 88 (wb 116.0) | | Wght | Price | Prod |
|---|---|---|---|---|
| L69 | sdn 4d | 3,644 | 9,084 | 8,297 |
| N37 | Royale cpe | 3,632 | 9,202 | 54,771 |
| Y37 | Royale Brougham cpe | 3,648 | 9,671 | |
| N69 | Royale sdn 4d | 3,679 | 9,363 | 132,683 |
| Y69 | Royale Brougham sdn 4d | 3,689 | 9,762 | |
| P35 | Custom Cruiser wgn 4d 2S V-8 | 4,202 | 10,083 | 25,243 |

| Ninety-Eight (wb 119.0) | | | | |
|---|---|---|---|---|
| X37 | Regency cpe | 3,910 | 12,943 | 13,816 |
| X69 | Regency sdn 4d | 3,964 | 13,120 | 105,948 |
| W69 | Regency Brougham sdn 4d | 4,006 | 14,170 | |

| Toronado (wb 114.0) | | | | |
|---|---|---|---|---|
| Z57 | Brougham cpe | 3,816 | 15,252 | 39,605 |

| 1983 Engines | bore × stroke | bhp | availability |
|---|---|---|---|
| I-4, 112.0 | 3.34 × 3.13 | 84 | O-Firenza |
| I-4, 121.0 | 3.50 × 3.15 | 86 | S-Firenza |
| I-4, 151.0 | 4.00 × 3.00 | 90 | S-Omega, Ctls Ciera |
| V-6, 173.0 | 3.50 × 3.00 | 112 | O-Omega |
| V-6, 173.0 | 3.50 × 3.00 | 130 | O-Omega |
| V-6, 181.0 | 3.80 × 2.66 | 110 | O-Cutlass Ciera |
| V-6, 231.0 | 3.80 × 3.40 | 110 | S-Ctls Supreme, Delta exc wgns |
| V-6, 252.0 | 3.97 × 3.40 | 125 | S-98, Toronado |
| V-6D, 262.0 | 4.06 × 3.39 | 85 | O-Ctls Ciera, Suprme |
| V-8, 307.0 | 3.80 × 3.39 | 140 | S-Delta wgn; O-Ctls Supreme, other Delta, 98, Toro |
| V-8, 307.0 | 3.80 × 3.39 | 180 | S-Calais Hurst/Olds |
| V-8D, 350.0 | 4.06 × 3.39 | 105 | O-Supreme, Delta, 98, Toro |

## 1984

| Firenza (wb 101.2) | | Wght | Price | Prod |
|---|---|---|---|---|
| C77 | S htchbk cpe | 2,457 | 7,214 | 13,811 |
| C69 | sdn 4d | 2,461 | 7,301 | 34,564 |
| D77 | SX htchbk cpe | 2,505 | 7,957 | 4,179 |
| D69 | LX sdn 4d | 2,505 | 7,853 | 11,761 |
| C35 | Cruiser wgn 4d | 2,507 | 7,521 | 12,389 |
| D35 | LX Cruiser wgn 4d | 2,525 | 8,073 | 5,771 |

| Omega (wb 104.9) | | | | |
|---|---|---|---|---|
| B37 | cpe | 2,539 | 7,634 | 5,242 |
| B69 | sdn 4d | 2,572 | 7,832 | 21,571 |
| E37 | Brougham cpe | 2,556 | 7,923 | 5,870 |
| E69 | Brougham sdn 4d | 2,593 | 8,104 | 20,303 |

| Cutlass Ciera (wb 104.9) | | | | |
|---|---|---|---|---|
| J27 | LS cpe | 2,742 | 9,014 | 14,887 |
| J19 | LS sdn 4d | 2,762 | 9,203 | 99,182 |
| M27 | Brougham cpe | 2,768 | 9,519 | 22,687 |
| M19 | Brougham sdn 4d | 2,788 | 9,721 | 102,667 |
| J35 | LS Cruiser wgn 4d | 2,957 | 9,551 | 41,816 |

| Cutlass (wb 108.1)* | | | | |
|---|---|---|---|---|
| R47 | Supreme cpe | 3,301 | 9,376 | 132,913 |
| R69 | sdn 4d | 3,344 | 9,529 | 62,136 |
| M47 | Supreme Brougham cpe | 3,340 | 10,015 | 87,207 |
| M69 | Supreme Brougham sdn 4d | 3,374 | 10,145 | 37,406 |
| K47 | Calais cpe | 3,377 | 10,274 | 21,393 |
| K47/W40 | Calais Hurst/Olds cpe V-8 | — | 12,644 | 3,500 |

* Cutlass totals include Canadian production for the U.S. market.

| Delta 88 (wb 116.0) | | | | |
|---|---|---|---|---|
| N37 | Royale cpe | 3,585 | 9,939 | 23,387 |
| Y37 | Royale Brougham cpe | 3,619 | 10,408 | 41,913 |
| N69 | Royale sdn 4d | 3,624 | 10,051 | 87,993 |

| Delta 88 (wb 116.0) | | Wght | Price | Prod |
|---|---|---|---|---|
| Y69 | Royale Brougham sdn 4d | 3,654 | 10,499 | 89,450 |
| V69 | Royale B'ham LS sdn 4d V-8 | 3,853 | 13,854 | 17,064 |
| P35 | Custom Cruiser wgn 4d 2S V-8 | 4,128 | 10,839 | 34,061 |

| Ninety-Eight (wb 119.0) | | | | |
|---|---|---|---|---|
| G37 | Regency cpe | 4,090 | 13,974 | 7,855 |
| G69 | Regency sdn 4d | 4,126 | 14,151 | 26,919 |
| H69 | Regency brougham sdn 4d | 4,177 | 15,201 | 42,059 |

| Toronado (wb 114.0) | | | | |
|---|---|---|---|---|
| Z57 | Brougham cpe | 3,795 | 16,107 | 48,100 |

| 1984 Engines | bore × stroke | bhp | availability |
|---|---|---|---|
| I-4, 112.0 | 3.34 × 3.13 | 82 | O-Firenza |
| I-4, 121.0 | 3.50 × 3.15 | 88 | S-Firenza |
| I-4, 151.0 | 4.00 × 3.00 | 92 | S-Omega, Ctls Ciera |
| V-6, 173.0 | 3.50 × 3.00 | 112 | O-Omega |
| V-6, 173.0 | 3.50 × 3.00 | 130 | O-Omega |
| V-6, 181.0 | 3.80 × 2.66 | 110 | O-Cutlass Ciera |
| V-6, 231.0 | 3.80 × 3.40 | 110 | S-Ctls Supreme, Delta exc wgns |
| V-6, 252.0 | 3.97 × 3.40 | 125 | S-Toronado |
| V-6D, 262.0 | 4.06 × 3.39 | 85 | O-Ctls Ciera, Suprme |
| V-8, 307.0 | 3.80 × 3.39 | 140 | S-Delta wgn, 98; O-Ctls Supreme, other Delta, Toro |
| V-8, 307.0 | 3.80 × 3.39 | 180 | S-Calais Hurst/Olds |
| V-8D, 350.0 | 4.06 × 3.39 | 105 | O-Supreme, Delta, 98, Toro |

## 1985

| Firenza (wb 101.2) | | Wght | Price | Prod |
|---|---|---|---|---|
| C77 | S htchbk cpe | 2,388 | 7,588 | 5,842 |
| C69 | sdn 4d | 2,385 | 7,679 | 25,066 |
| D77 | SX htchbk cpe | 2,438 | 8,395 | 1,842 |
| D69 | LX sdn 4d | 2,441 | 8,255 | 7,563 |
| C35 | Cruiser wgn 4d | 2,450 | 7,898 | 6,291 |
| D35 | LX Cruiser wgn 4d | 2,487 | 8,492 | 2,436 |

| Calais (wb 103.4) | | | | |
|---|---|---|---|---|
| F27 | cpe | 2,545 | 8,499 | 49,545 |
| T27 | Supreme cpe | 2,547 | 8,844 | 56,695 |

| Cutlass Ciera (wb 104.9) | | | | |
|---|---|---|---|---|
| J27 | LS cpe | 2,763 | 9,307 | 13,396 |
| J19 | LS sdn 4d | 2,802 | 9,497 | 118,575 |
| M27 | Brougham cpe | 2,784 | 9,787 | 20,476 |
| M19 | Brougham sdn 4d | 2,825 | 9,998 | 112,441 |
| J35 | LS Cruiser wgn 4d | 2,962 | 9,858 | 38,225 |

| Cutlass (wb 108.1) | | | | |
|---|---|---|---|---|
| R47 | Supreme cpe | 3,277 | 9,797 | 75,045 |
| R69 | sdn 4d | 3,321 | 9,961 | 43,085 |
| M47 | Supreme Brougham cpe | 3,308 | 10,468 | 58,869 |
| M69 | Supreme sdn 4d | 3,341 | 10,602 | 28,741 |
| K47 | Salon cpe | 3,308 | 10,770 | 14,512 |
| K47/W42 | Salon 4-4-2 cpe V-8 | — | 12,435 | 3,500 |

| Delta 88 (wb 116.0) | | | | |
|---|---|---|---|---|
| N37 | Royale cpe | 3,584 | 10,488 | 15,002 |
| Y37 | Royale Brougham cpe | 3,584 | 10,968 | 31,891 |
| N69 | Royale sdn 4d | 3,616 | 10,596 | 69,641 |
| Y69 | Royale Brougham sdn 4d | 3,616 | 11,062 | 72,103 |
| V69 | Royale B'ham LS sdn 4d V-8 | 3,515 | 14,331 | 30,239 |
| P35 | Custom Cruiser wgn 4d 2S V-8 | 4,085 | 11,627 | 22,889 |

| Ninety-Eight (wb 110.8) | | | | |
|---|---|---|---|---|
| X11 | Regency cpe | 3,261 | 14,725 | 4,734 |
| X69 | Regency sdn 4d | 3,297 | 14,665 | 43,697 |

# Oldsmobile

| Ninety-Eight (wb 110.8) | | Wght | Price | Prod |
|---|---|---|---|---|
| W11 | Regency Brougham cpe | 3,261 | 15,932 | 9,704 |
| W69 | Rgncy Brougham sdn 4d | 3,297 | 15,864 | 111,297 |
| **Toronado (wb 114.0)** | | | | |
| Z57 | Brougham cpe | 3,853 | 16,798 | 42,185 |

| 1985 Engines | bore × stroke | bhp | availability |
|---|---|---|---|
| I-4, 112.0 | 3.34 × 3.13 | 82 | O-Firenza |
| I-4, 121.0 | 3.50 × 3.15 | 88 | S-Firenza |
| I-4, 151.0 | 4.00 × 3.00 | 92 | S-Calais, Ctls Ciera |
| V-6, 173.0 | 3.50 × 3.00 | 130 | O-Firenza |
| V-6, 181.0 | 3.80 × 2.66 | 110 | S-98 exc B'ham; O-Cutlass Ciera |
| V-6, 181.0 | 3.80 × 2.66 | 125 | O-Calais |
| V-6, 231.0 | 3.80 × 3.40 | 110 | S-Ctls, Supreme, Delta exc LS/wgns |
| V-6, 231.0 | 3.80 × 3.40 | 125 | S-98 B'ham; O-Ciera, 98 |
| V-6D, 262.0 | 4.06 × 3.39 | 85 | O-Ciera, Supreme, 98 |
| V-8, 307.0 | 3.80 × 3.39 | 140 | S-Delta LS/wgn, Toro; O-Ctls Supreme, other Delta |
| V-8, 307.0 | 3.80 × 3.39 | 180 | S-Salon 4-4-2 |
| V-8D, 350.0 | 4.06 × 3.39 | 105 | O-Supreme, Delta, Toronado |

## 1986

| Firenza (wb 101.2) | | Wght | Price | Prod |
|---|---|---|---|---|
| C27 | cpe 2d | 2,344 | 7,782 | 12,003 |
| D27 | LC cpe 2d | 2,396 | 8,611 | 2,867 |
| C77 | S htchbk cpe | 2,396 | 7,941 | 2,531 |
| D77 | GT htchbk cpe V-6 | 2,445 | 9,774 | 1,032 |
| C69 | sdn 4d | 2,397 | 8,035 | 18,437 |
| D69 | LX sdn 4d | 2,428 | 8,626 | 4,415 |
| C35 | Cruiser wgn 4d | 2,454 | 8,259 | 5,416 |
| **Calais (wb 103.4)** | | | | |
| F27 | cpe | 2,531 | 9,283 | 52,726 |
| F69 | sdn 4d | 2,598 | 9,478 | 40,393 |
| T27 | Supreme cpe | 2,542 | 9,668 | 33,060 |
| T69 | Supreme sdn 4d | 2,601 | 9,863 | 25,128 |
| **Cutlass Ciera (wb 104.9)** | | | | |
| J27 | LS cpe | 2,761 | 10,153 | 9,233 |
| J37 | S cpe | 2,757 | 10,619 | 16,281 |
| J19 | LS sdn 4d | 2,805 | 10,354 | 144,466 |
| M27 | Brougham cpe | 2,778 | 10,645 | 11,534 |
| M37 | Brougham SL cpe | 2,800 | 11,154 | 12,525 |
| M19 | Brougham sdn 4d | 2,834 | 10,868 | 123,027 |
| J35 | LS Cruiser wgn 4d | 2,964 | 10,734 | 35,890 |
| **Cutlass (wb 108.1)** | | | | |
| R47 | Supreme cpe | 3,277 | 10,698 | 79,654 |
| R69 | sdn 4d | 3,320 | 10,872 | 41,973 |
| M47 | Supreme Brougham cpe | 3,307 | 11,408 | 55,275 |
| M69 | Supreme Brougham sdn 4d | 3,341 | 11,551 | 24,646 |
| K47 | Salon cpe | 3,340 | 11,728 | 9,608 |
| K47/W42 | Salon 4-4-2 cpe V-8 | — | 14,343 | |
| **Delta 88 (wb 110.8)** | | | | |
| N37 | Royale cpe | 3,141 | 12,760 | 13,696 |
| N69 | Royale sdn 4d | 3,186 | 12,760 | 88,564 |
| Y37 | Royale Brougham cpe | 3,170 | 13,461 | 23,697 |
| Y69 | Royale Brougham sdn 4d | 3,211 | 13,461 | 108,344 |
| **Custom Cruiser (wb 116.0)** | | | | |
| P35 | wgn 4d 2S V-8 | 4,085 | 13,416 | 21,073 |

| Ninety-Eight (wb 110.8) | | Wght | Price | Prod |
|---|---|---|---|---|
| X11 | Regency cpe | 3,268 | 16,062 | 803 |
| X69 | Regency sdn 4d | 3,304 | 15,989 | 23,717 |
| W11 | Regency Brougham cpe | 3,285 | 17,052 | 5,007 |
| W69 | Regency Brougham sdn 4d | 3,320 | 16,979 | 95,045 |
| **Toronado (wb 108.0)** | | | | |
| Z57 | cpe | 3,304 | 19,418 | 15,924 |

| 1986 Engines | bore × stroke | bhp | availability |
|---|---|---|---|
| I-4, 112.0 | 3.34 × 3.13 | 84 | O-Firenza exc GT |
| I-4, 121.0 | 3.50 × 3.15 | 88 | S-Firenza exc GT |
| I-4, 151.0 | 4.00 × 3.00 | 92 | S-Calais, Ctls Ciera |
| V-6, 173.0 | 3.50 × 3.00 | 112 | O-Cutlass Ciera |
| V-6, 173.0 | 3.50 × 3.00 | 130 | S-Firenza GT |
| V-6, 181.0 | 3.80 × 2.66 | 125 | S-Delta; O-Calais |
| V-6, 231.0 | 3.80 × 3.40 | 110 | S-Ctls Supreme |
| V-6, 231.0 | 3.80 × 3.40 | 140 | S-98, Toronado |
| V-6, 231.0 | 3.80 × 3.40 | 150 | O-Ciera, Delta |
| V-8, 307.0 | 3.80 × 3.39 | 140 | S-Cus Cruiser; O-Supreme |
| V-8, 307.0 | 3.80 × 3.39 | 180 | S-Salon 4-4-2 |

## 1987

| Firenza (wb 101.2) | | Wght | Price | Prod |
|---|---|---|---|---|
| C27 | cpe 2d | 2,327 | 8,541 | 5,335 |
| D27 | LC cpe 2d | 2,379 | 9,639 | 874 |
| C77 | S htchbk cpe | 2,380 | 8,976 | 991 |
| D77 | GT htchbk cpe V-6 | 2,576 | 11,034 | 783 |
| C69 | sdn 4d | 2,381 | 8,499 | 12,597 |
| D69 | LX sdn 4d | 2,412 | 9,407 | 2,388 |
| C35 | Cruiser wgn 4d | 2,438 | 9,146 | 2,860 |
| **Calais (wb 103.4)** | | | | |
| F27 | cpe | 2,516 | 9,741 | 52,286 |
| F69 | sdn 4d | 2,584 | 9,741 | 35,169 |
| T27 | Supreme cpe | 2,529 | 10,397 | 17,883 |
| T69 | Supreme sdn 4d | 2,595 | 10,397 | 11,676 |
| **Cutlass Ciera (wb 104.9)** | | | | |
| J37 | S cpe | 2,811 | 10,940 | 21,904 |
| J19 | sdn 4d | 2,775 | 10,940 | 140,334 |
| M37 | Brougham SL cpe | 2,822 | 11,747 | 11,960 |
| M19 | Brougham sdn 4d | 2,846 | 11,747 | 94,764 |
| J35 | Cruiser wgn 4d | 2,975 | 11,433 | 20,556 |
| M35 | Brougham Cruiser wgn 4d | 2,975 | 12,095 | 7,770 |
| **Cutlass (wb 108.1)** | | | | |
| R47 | Supreme cpe | 3,293 | 11,539 | 46,343 |
| R47/W42 | Supreme 4-4-2 cpe V-8 | — | 14,706 | 4,210 |
| R69 | sdn 4d | 3,345 | 11,539 | 21,379 |
| M47 | Supreme Brougham cpe | 3,252 | 12,378 | 28,607 |
| M69 | Supreme Brougham sdn 4d | 3,427 | 12,378 | 17,383 |
| K47 | Salon cpe | 3,293 | 12,697 | 8,862 |
| **Delta 88 (wb 110.8)** | | | | |
| N37 | Royale cpe | 3,176 | 13,639 | 4,287 |
| N69 | Royale sdn 4d | 3,216 | 13,639 | 66,214 |
| Y37 | Royale Brougham cpe | 3,204 | 14,536 | 7,907 |
| Y69 | Royale Brougham sdn 4d | 3,237 | 14,536 | 75,129 |
| **Custom Cruiser (wb 116.0)** | | | | |
| P35 | wgn 4d 2S V-8 | 4,136 | 14,420 | 17,742 |
| **Ninety-Eight (wb 110.8)** | | | | |
| X69 | Regency sdn 4d | 3,307 | 17,371 | 18,600 |
| W11 | Regency Brougham cpe | 3,285 | 18,388 | 4,207 |
| W69 | Rgncy Brougham sdn 4d | 3,320 | 18,388 | 58,199 |
| **Toronado (wb 108.0)** | | | | |
| Z57 | cpe | 3,352 | 19,938 | 15,040 |

# Oldsmobile

| 1987 Engines | bore × stroke | bhp | availability |
|---|---|---|---|
| I-4, 121.0 | 3.50 × 3.15 | 90 | S-Firenza exc GT |
| I-4, 121.0 | 3.50 × 3.15 | 102 | O-Firenza exc GT |
| I-4, 151.0 | 4.00 × 3.00 | 98 | S-Calais, Ctls Ciera |
| V-6, 173.0 | 3.50 × 3.00 | 125 | S-Frnza GT; O-other Frnza, Ciera |
| V-6, 181.0 | 3.80 × 2.66 | 125 | O-Calais |
| V-6, 231.0 | 3.80 × 3.40 | 110 | S-Cutlass Supreme |
| V-6, 231.0 | 3.80 × 3.40 | 150 | S-Delta, 98, Toro; O-Ciera |
| V-8, 307.0 | 3.80 × 3.39 | 140 | S-Cus Cruiser; O-Supreme |
| V-8, 307.0 | 3.80 × 3.39 | 170 | S-Supreme 4-4-2 |

## 1988

### Firenza (wb 101.2)—12,260 built

| | | Wght | Price | Prod |
|---|---|---|---|---|
| C27 | cpe 2d | 2,327 | 9,295 | |
| C69 | sdn 4d | 2,381 | 9,295 | |
| C35 | Cruiser wgn 4d | 2,438 | 9,995 | |

### Calais (wb 103.4)—110,276 built

| F27 | cpe | 2,500 | 10,320 | |
|---|---|---|---|---|
| F69 | sdn 4d | 2,571 | 10,320 | |
| T27 | SL cpe | 2,518 | 11,195 | |
| T69 | SL sdn 4d | 2,583 | 11,195 | |
| K27 | International cpe I-4 | 2,757 | 13,695 | |
| K69 | International sdn 4d I-4 | 2,830 | 13,695 | |

### Cutlass Ciera (wb 104.9)—21,620 built

| J37 | cpe | 2,805 | 10,995 | |
|---|---|---|---|---|
| J19 | sdn 4d | 2,769 | 11,656 | |
| M37 | Brougham SL cpe | 2,816 | 11,845 | |
| M19 | Brougham sdn 4d | 2,840 | 12,625 | |
| S37 | International cpe V-6 | 2,958 | 14,995 | |
| S19 | International sdn 4d V-6 | 1,913 | 15,825 | |
| J35 | Cruiser wgn 4d | 2,968 | 12,320 | |
| M35 | Brougham Cruiser wgn 4d | 3,039 | 12,995 | |

### Cutlass Supreme FWD (wb 107.7)—94,723 built

| H47 | cpe | 2,958 | 12,846 | |
|---|---|---|---|---|
| S47 | SL cpe | — | 13,495 | |
| R47 | International cpe | — | 15,644 | |

### Cutlass Supreme Classic RWD (wb 108.1)—27,678 built

| R47 | cpe | 3,180 | 13,163 | |
|---|---|---|---|---|
| M47 | Brougham cpe | 3,233 | 13,995 | |

### Delta 88 (wb 110.8)—160,913 built

| N37 | Royale cpe | 3,172 | 14,498 | |
|---|---|---|---|---|
| N69 | Royale sdn 4d | 3,216 | 14,498 | |
| Y37 | Royale Brougham cpe | 3,187 | 15,451 | |
| Y69 | Royale Brougham sdn 4d | 3,220 | 15,451 | |

### Custom Cruiser RWD (wb 116.0)

| P35 | wgn 4d 2S V-8 | 4,136 | 15,655 | 11,114 |
|---|---|---|---|---|

### Ninety-Eight (wb 110.8)—79,935 built

| X69 | Regency sdn 4d | 3,300 | 17,995 | |
|---|---|---|---|---|
| W69 | Regency Brougham sdn 4d | 3,316 | 19,371 | |
| V69 | Touring sdn 4d | 3,421 | 24,470 | |

### Toronado (wb 108.0)—16,496 built

| Z57 | cpe | 3,364 | 20,598 | |
|---|---|---|---|---|
| V57 | Trofeo cpe | 3,426 | 22,695 | |

| 1988 Engines | bore × stroke | bhp | availability |
|---|---|---|---|
| I-4, 121.0 | 3.50 × 3.15 | 90 | S-Firenza |
| I-4, 121.0 | 3.50 × 3.15 | 96 | O-Firenza |
| I-4, 138.0 | 3.62 × 3.35 | 150 | S-Calais Int'l; O-Calais (dohc) |
| I-4, 151.0 | 4.00 × 3.00 | 98 | S-Calais, Ctls Ciera |
| V-6, 173.0 | 3.50 × 3.00 | 125 | S-Ctls Supreme; O-Ciera |
| V-6, 181.0 | 3.80 × 2.66 | 125 | O-Calais |
| V-6, 231.0 | 3.80 × 3.40 | 150 | S-Ciera Int'l, Delta; O-Ciera |
| V-6, 231.0 | 3.80 × 3.40 | 165 | S-98, Toro; O-Delta |
| V-8, 307.0 | 3.80 × 3.39 | 140 | S-Cus Crsr; O-Supreme Classic |

## 1989

### Cutlass Calais (wb 103.4)

| | | Wght | Price | Prod |
|---|---|---|---|---|
| L27 | VL cpe | 2,512 | 9,995 | 11,432 |
| L69 | VL sdn 4d | 2,573 | 9,995 | 14,506 |
| F27 | S cpe | 2,512 | 10,895 | 33,633 |
| F69 | S sdn 4d | 2,573 | 10,995 | 25,592 |
| T27 | SL cpe | 2,538 | 11,895 | 10,350 |
| T69 | SL sdn 4d | 2,597 | 11,995 | 9,443 |
| K27 | International cpe I-4 | 2,740 | 14,395 | 3,345 |
| K69 | International sdn 4d I-4 | 2,804 | 14,495 | 1,590 |

### Cutlass Ciera (wb 104.9)

| J37 | cpe | 2,736 | 11,695 | 7,221 |
|---|---|---|---|---|
| J69 | sdn 4d | 2,764 | 12,195 | 140,264 |
| M37 | SL cpe | 2,767 | 12,695 | 2,548 |
| M69 | SL sdn 4d | 2,791 | 13,495 | 65,725 |
| S37 | International cpe V-6 | — | 15,995 | 1,913 |
| S69 | International sdn 4d V-6 | — | 16,795 | 5,132 |
| J35 | Cruiser wgn 4d | 2,913 | 12,995 | 12,368 |
| M35 | Brougham Cruiser wgn 4d | 2,938 | 13,995 | 4,431 |

### Cutlass Supreme (wb 107.7)

| H47 | cpe | 3,084 | 14,295 | 49,895 |
|---|---|---|---|---|
| S47 | SL cpe | — | 15,195 | 32,015 |
| R47 | International cpe | — | 16,995 | 18,116 |

### Eighty-Eight (wb 110.8)

| N37 | Royale cpe | 3,215 | 15,195 | 1,927 |
|---|---|---|---|---|
| N69 | Royale sdn 4d | 3,265 | 15,295 | 81,512 |
| Y37 | Royale Brougham cpe | 3,236 | 16,295 | 3,024 |
| Y69 | Royale Brougham sdn 4d | 3,285 | 16,395 | 65,576 |

### Custom Cruiser (wb 116.0)

| P35 | wgn 4d 2S V-8 | 4,221 | 16,795 | 8,929 |
|---|---|---|---|---|

### Ninety-Eight (wb 110.8)

| X69 | Regency sdn 4d | 3,329 | 19,295 | 17,184 |
|---|---|---|---|---|
| W69 | Regency Brougham sdn 4d | 3,353 | 20,495 | 48,726 |
| V69 | Touring sdn 4d | 3,494 | 25,995 | 7,193 |

### Toronado (wb 108.0)

| Z57 | cpe | 3,361 | 21,995 | 3,734 |
|---|---|---|---|---|
| V57 | Trofeo cpe | 3,428 | 24,995 | 6,143 |

| 1989 Engines | bore × stroke | bhp | availability |
|---|---|---|---|
| I-4, 138.0 | 3.62 × 3.35 | 150 | S-Calais Int'l; O-Calais (dohc) |
| I-4, 138.0 | 3.62 × 3.35 | 180 | O-late Calais |
| I-4, 151.0 | 4.00 × 3.00 | 110 | S-Calais, (dohc) Ciera |
| V-6, 173.0 | 3.50 × 3.00 | 125 | O-Ciera |
| V-6, 173.0 | 3.50 × 3.00 | 130 | S-Supreme |
| V-6, 191.0 | 3.30 × 3.27 | 135 | O-late Supreme |
| V-6, 204.0 | 3.70 × 3.16 | 160 | S-Ciera Int'l; O-Cal, Ciera |

# Oldsmobile

| 1989 Engines | bore × stroke | bhp | availability |
|---|---|---|---|
| V-6, 231.0 | 3.80 × 3.40 | 165 | S-88, 98, Toronado |
| V-8, 307.0 | 3.80 × 3.39 | 140 | S-Custom Cruiser |

## 1990

| Cutlass Calais (wb 103.4) | | Wght | Price | Prod |
|---|---|---|---|---|
| L27 | VL cpe | 2,518 | 9,995 | 15,846 |
| L69 | VL sdn 4d | 2,585 | 9,995 | 41,018 |
| F27 | S cpe | — | 10,895 | 12,839 |
| F69 | S sdn 4d | — | 10,995 | 12,207 |
| T27 | SL cpe | — | 13,195 | 2,503 |
| T69 | SL sdn 4d | — | 13,295 | 3,971 |
| K27 | International cpe I-4 | — | 14,895 | 1,454 |
| K69 | International sdn 4d I-4 | — | 14,995 | 877 |
| **Cutlass Ciera (wb 104.9)** | | | | |
| L69 | sdn 4d | 2,764 | 11,995 | 46,933 |
| J37 | S cpe | 2,767 | 12,395 | 2,203 |
| J69 | S sdn 4d | 2,791 | 12,995 | 54,549 |
| M69 | SL sdn 4d | — | 14,695 | 33,229 |
| S37 | International cpe V-6 | — | 15,995 | 411 |
| S69 | International sdn 4d V-6 | — | 16,795 | 959 |
| J35 | Cruiser S wgn 4d | 2,913 | 13,395 | 3,321 |
| M35 | Cruiser SL wgn 4d | 2,938 | 15,295 | 5,576 |
| **Cutlass Supreme (wb 107.7)** | | | | |
| H47 | cpe | 3,133 | 14,495 | 15,848 |
| H69 | sdn 4d | 3,221 | 14,595 | 47,043 |
| S47 | SL cpe | — | 16,095 | 10,076 |
| S69 | SL sdn 4d | — | 16,195 | 32,798 |
| R47 | International cpe | — | 17,995 | 5,602 |
| R69 | International sdn 4d | — | 17,995 | 7,474 |
| T67 | conv cpe | 3,501 | 20,995 | 464 |
| **Eighty-Eight (wb 110.8)** | | | | |
| N37 | Royale cpe | 3,248 | 15,895 | 1,127 |
| N69 | Royale sdn 4d | 3,293 | 15,995 | 65,800 |
| Y37 | Royale Brougham cpe | — | 17,295 | 1,585 |
| Y69 | Royale Brougham sdn 4d | — | 17,395 | 48,311 |
| **Custom Cruiser (wb 116.0)** | | | | |
| P35 | wgn 4d 2S V-8 | 4,221 | 17,595 | 3,890 |
| **Ninety-Eight (wb 110.8)** | | | | |
| X69 | Regency sdn 4d | 3,325 | 19,995 | 17,914 |
| W69 | Brougham sdn 4d | — | 21,595 | 38,915 |
| V69 | Touring sdn 4d | — | 26,795 | 5,566 |
| **Toronado (wb 108.0)** | | | | |
| Z57 | cpe | 3,462 | 21,995 | 5,596 |
| V57 | Trofeo cpe | — | 24,995 | 9,426 |

| 1990 Engines | bore × stroke | bhp | availability |
|---|---|---|---|
| I-4, 138.0 | 3.62 × 3.35 | 160 | S-Calais SL; O-Calais, Supreme (dohc) |
| I-4, 138.0 | 3.62 × 3.35 | 180 | S-Calais Int'l, Supreme (dohc) |
| I-4, 151.0 | 4.00 × 3.00 | 110 | S-Calais, Ciera |
| V-6, 191.0 | 3.30 × 3.27 | 135 | S-Supreme SL/conv.; O-Supreme |
| V-6, 204.0 | 3.70 × 3.16 | 160 | S-Ciera SL/Int'l; O-Cal, Ciera |
| V-6, 231.0 | 3.80 × 3.40 | 165 | S-88, 98, Toronado |
| V-8, 307.0 | 3.80 × 3.39 | 140 | S-Custom Cruiser |

## 1991

| Cutlass Calais (wb 103.4) | | Wght | Price | Prod |
|---|---|---|---|---|
| L27 | cpe | 2,553 | 10,295 | 14,978 |
| L69 | sdn 4d | 2,616 | 10,295 | 41,746 |
| F27 | S cpe | 2,548 | 11,495 | 6,906 |
| F69 | S sdn 4d | 2,613 | 11,595 | 7,267 |
| T27 | SL cpe | 2,665 | 15,095 | 1,030 |
| T69 | SL sdn 4d | 2,725 | 15,195 | 2,437 |
| K27 | I Series cpe | 2,729 | 16,295 | 671 |
| K69 | I Series sdn 4d | 2,798 | 16,395 | 379 |
| **Cutlass Ciera (104.9)** | | | | |
| L69 | sdn 4d | 2,771 | 12,459 | 63,888 |
| J37 | S sdn 2d | 2,771 | 13,395 | 1,665 |
| J69 | S sdn 4d | 2,813 | 12,995 | 29,307 |
| M69 | SL sdn 4d | 2,958 | 15,895 | 13,700 |
| J35 | Cruiser S wgn 4d | 2,975 | 13,895 | 3,977 |
| M35 | Cruiser SL wgn 4d | 3,160 | 19,595 | 3,247 |
| **Cutlass Supreme (wb 107.7)** | | | | |
| H47 | cpe | 3,187 | 14,995 | 16,766 |
| H69 | sdn 2d | 3,228 | 15,095 | 52,241 |
| S47 | SL cpe | 3,260 | 16,895 | 4,253 |
| S69 | SL sdn 4d | 3,355 | 16,995 | 15,653 |
| R47 | I Series cpe | 3,517 | 19,695 | 2,304 |
| R69 | I Series sdn 4d | 3,597 | 19,795 | 7,357 |
| T67 | conv cpe | 3,602 | 20,995 | 1,515 |
| **Eighty-Eight (wb 110.8)** | | | | |
| H37 | Royale cpe | 3,248 | 17,095 | 234 |
| N69 | Royale sdn 4d | 3,292 | 17,195 | 33,690 |
| Y37 | Brougham cpe | 3,276 | 18,695 | 458 |
| Y69 | Brougham sdn 4d | 3,303 | 18,795 | 21,865 |
| **Ninety-Eight (wb 110.8)** | | | | |
| X69 | Regency Elite sdn 4d | 3,580 | 23,695 | 50,625 |
| V69 | touring sedan 4d | 3,654 | 28,595 | 4,280 |
| **Custom Cruiser (wb 115.9)** | | | | |
| P35 | wgn 4d | 4,435 | 20,495 | 7,663 |
| **Toronado (wb 108.0)** | | | | |
| Z57 | cpe | 3,455 | 23,795 | 2,705 |
| V57 | Trofeo cpe | 3,526 | 26,495 | 5,348 |

| 1991 Engines | bore × stroke | bhp | availability |
|---|---|---|---|
| I-4, 138.0 | 3.63 × 3.94 | 160 | S-Supreme; O-Calais (dohc) |
| I-4, 138.0 | 3.63 × 3.94 | 180 | O-Calais (dohc) |
| I-4, 138.0 | 3.63 × 3.94 | 190 | O-Calais (dohc) |
| I-4, 151.0 | 4.00 × 3.00 | 110 | S-Calais, Ciera |
| V-6, 191.0 | 3.50 × 3.30 | 140 | O-Supreme |
| V-6, 204.0 | 3.70 × 3.16 | 160 | O-Calais, Ciera |
| V-6, 207.0 | 3.62 × 3.30 | 200 | S-Supreme I-Series (dohc) |
| V-6, 207.0 | 3.62 × 3.30 | 210 | S-Supreme I-Series (dohc) |
| V-6, 231.0 | 3.80 × 3.40 | 165 | S-Eighty-Eight |
| V-6, 231.0 | 3.80 × 3.40 | 170 | S-Ninety-Eight, Toronado |
| V-8, 305.0 | 3.74 × 3.48 | 170 | S-Custom Cruiser |

## 1992

| Achieva (wb 103.4) | | Wght | Price | Prod |
|---|---|---|---|---|
| L37 | S cpe | 2,696 | 12,715 | 24,719* |
| L69 | S sdn 4d | 2,778 | 12,815 | 38,171 |
| F37 | SL cpe | 2,795 | 14,495 | 2,892 |
| F69 | SL sdn 4d | 2,868 | 14,595 | 11,674 |

# Oldsmobile

| Cutlass Ciera (104.9) | | Wght | Price | Prod |
|---|---|---|---|---|
| J69 | S sdn 4d | 2,886 | 12,995 | 123,243 |
| M69 | SL sdn 4d | 3,048 | 15,895 | 8,867 |
| J35 | Cruiser S wgn 4d | 2,992 | 13,895 | 5,861 |
| M35 | Cruiser SL wgn 4d | 3,226 | 19,595 | 1,932 |
| **Cutlass Supreme (wb 107.7)** | | | | |
| H47 | S cpe | 3,221 | 15,695 | 20,700 |
| H69 | S sdn 4d | 3,375 | 15,795 | 63,692 |
| R47 | I Series cpe | 3,385 | 21,795 | 1,181 |
| R69 | I Series sdn 4d | 3,498 | 21,895 | 2,066 |
| T67 | conv cpe | 3,589 | 21,995 | 4,306 |
| **Eighty-Eight (wb 110.8)** | | | | |
| N69 | sdn 4d | 3,404 | 18,495 | 75,182 |
| Y69 | LS sdn 4d | 3,468 | 21,395 | 40,142 |
| **Ninety-Eight (wb 110.8)** | | | | |
| X69 | Regency sdn 4d | 3,593 | 24,595 | 20,076 |
| W69 | Regency Elite sdn 4d | — | 26,195 | 24,713 |
| V69 | touring sedan 4d | 3,697 | 28,995 | 2,795 |
| **Custom Cruiser (wb 115.9)** | | | | |
| P35 | wgn 4d | 4,378 | 20,995 | 4,347 |
| **Toronado (wb 108.0)** | | | | |
| Z57 | cpe | 3,467 | 24,695 | 1,239 |
| V57 | Trofeo cpe | 3,528 | 27,295 | 5,197 |

*Includes 1,146 SC× models.

| 1992 Engines | bore × stroke | bhp | availability |
|---|---|---|---|
| I-4, 138.0 | 3.63 × 3.94 | 120 | S-Achieva |
| I-4, 138.0 | 3.63 × 3.94 | 160 | O-Achieva (dohc) |
| I-4, 138.0 | 3.63 × 3.94 | 180 | O-Achieva (dohc) |
| I-4, 138.0 | 3.63 × 3.94 | 190 | S-Achieva SCX (dohc) |
| I-4, 151.0 | 4.00 × 3.00 | 110 | S-Ciera |
| V-6, 191.0 | 3.50 × 3.30 | 140 | S-Supreme |
| V-6, 204.0 | 3.70 × 3.16 | 160 | O-Achieva, Ciera |
| V-6, 207.0 | 3.62 × 3.30 | 200 | S-Supreme I-Series (dohc) |
| V-6, 207.0 | 3.62 × 3.30 | 210 | O-Supreme I-Series (dohc) |
| V-6, 231.0 | 3.80 × 3.40 | 170 | S-Eighty-Eight, Ninety-Eight, Toronado |
| V-6S, 231.0 | 3.80 × 3.40 | 205 | O-Ninety-Eight V69 |
| V-8, 305.0 | 3.74 × 3.48 | 170 | S-Custom Cruiser |
| V-8, 350.0 | 4.00 × 3.48 | 180 | O-Custom Cruiser |

## 1993

| Achieva (wb 103.4) | | Wght | Price | Prod |
|---|---|---|---|---|
| L37 | S cpe | 2,716 | 13,409 | 13,525* |
| L69 | S sdn 4d | 2,779 | 13,149 | 30,837 |
| F37 | SL cpe | — | 14,849 | 590 |
| F69 | SL sdn 4d | — | 14,949 | 3,283 |
| **Cutlass Ciera (104.9)** | | | | |
| J69 | S sdn 4d | 2,886 | 14,859 | 142,552 |
| M69 | SL sdn 4d | 3,048 | 18,559 | 4,304 |
| J35 | Cruiser S wgn 4d | 2,992 | 15,559 | 5,785 |
| M35 | Cruiser SL wgn 4d | 3,226 | 19,059 | 1,084 |
| **Cutlass Supreme (wb 107.7)** | | | | |
| H47 | S cpe | 3,243 | 15,695 | 23,544 |
| H69 | sdn 4d | 3,354 | 15,795 | 51,678 |
| R47 | I Series cpe | 3,376 | 22,799 | 395 |
| R69 | I Series sdn 4d | 3,479 | 22,899 | 645 |
| T67 | conv cpe | 3,651 | 22,699 | 6,751 |
| **Eighty-Eight (wb 110.8)** | | | | |
| N69 | sdn 4d | 3,404 | 19,549 | 47,428 |
| Y69 | LS sdn 4d | 3,468 | 21,949 | 14,903 |
| **Ninety-Eight (wb 110.8)** | | | | |
| X69 | Regency sdn 4d | 3,512 | 24,999 | 8,906 |
| W69 | Regency Elite sdn 4d | 3,527 | 26,999 | 9,900 |
| V69 | touring sedan 4d | 3,697 | 29,699 | 1,885 |

*Includes 500 SCX models.

| 1993 Engines | bore × stroke | bhp | availability |
|---|---|---|---|
| I-4, 133.0 | 3.50 × 3.46 | 110 | S-Ciera S |
| I-4, 138.0 | 3.63 × 3.94 | 115 | S-Achieva |
| I-4, 138.0 | 3.63 × 3.94 | 155 | O-Achieva (dohc) |
| I-4, 138.0 | 3.63 × 3.94 | 175 | O-Achieva (dohc) |
| I-4, 138.0 | 3.63 × 3.94 | 185 | S-Achieva SCX (dohc) |
| V-6, 191.0 | 3.50 × 3.30 | 140 | S-Supreme |
| V-6, 204.0 | 3.70 × 3.16 | 160 | S-Ciera SL; O-Achieva, Ciera S |
| V-6, 207.0 | 3.62 × 3.30 | 200 | S-Supreme I-Series (dohc) |
| V-6, 231.0 | 3.80 × 3.40 | 170 | S-Eighty-Eight, Ninety-Eight, |
| V-6S, 231.0 | 3.80 × 3.40 | 205 | O-Ninety-Eight V69 |

## 1994

| Achieva (wb 103.4) | | Wght | Price | Prod |
|---|---|---|---|---|
| L37 | S cpe | 2,716 | 14,075 | 15,668 |
| L69 | S sdn 4d | 2,779 | 14,175 | 43,329 |
| F37 | SC cpe | — | 17,475 | 1,555 |
| F69 | SL sdn 4d | — | 17,475 | 1,540 |
| **Cutlass Ciera (104.9)** | | | | |
| G69 | SL sdn 4d | 2,833 | 15,675 | 132,351 |
| J35 | Cruiser SL wgn 4d | 3,086 | 17,175 | 9,809 |
| **Cutlass Supreme (wb 107.7)** | | | | |
| H47 | S cpe | 3,307 | 17,375 | 35,757 |
| H69 | S sdn 4d | 3,405 | 17,475 | 77,861 |
| T67 | conv cpe | 3,638 | 25,275 | 8,638 |
| **Eighty-Eight (wb 110.8)** | | | | |
| N69 | sdn 4d | 3,439 | 20,875 | 60,362 |
| Y69 | LS sdn 4d | 3,469 | 22,875 ⎤ | |
| Y69/R7C | LSS sdn 4d | — | 22,995 ⎦ | 21,664 |
| **Ninety-Eight (wb 110.8)** | | | | |
| X69 | Regency sdn 4d | 3,509 | 25,875 | 20,171 |
| W69 | Regency Elite sdn 4d | 3,585 | 27,975 | 6,463 |

| 1994 Engines | bore × stroke | bhp | availability |
|---|---|---|---|
| I-4, 133.0 | 3.50 × 3.46 | 120 | S-Ciera |
| I-4, 138.0 | 3.63 × 3.94 | 115 | S-Achieva |
| I-4, 138.0 | 3.63 × 3.94 | 155 | O-Achieva (dohc) |
| I-4, 138.0 | 3.63 × 3.94 | 170 | O-Achieva (dohc) |
| V-6, 191.0 | 3.50 × 3.30 | 160 | S-Supreme; O-Achieva, Ciera |
| V-6, 207.0 | 3.62 × 3.30 | 210 | O-Supreme (dohc) |
| V-6, 231.0 | 3.80 × 3.40 | 170 | S-Eighty-Eight, Ninety-Eight |
| V-6S, 231.0 | 3.80 × 3.40 | 225 | O-Ninety-Eight |

## 1995

| Achieva (wb 103.4) | | Wght | Price | Prod |
|---|---|---|---|---|
| L37/R7B | S cpe (Series I) | 2,716 | 13,500 ⎤ | |
| L37/R7C | S cpe (Series II) | — | 15,200 ⎦ | 16,078 |

# Oldsmobile

| Achieva (wb 103.4) | Wght | Price | Prod |
|---|---|---|---|
| L69/R7B S sdn 4d (Series I) | 2,779 | 13,500 | 41,185 |
| L69/R7C S sdn 4d (Series II) | — | 15,200 | |
| **Cutlass Ciera (104.9)** | | | |
| J69/R7B SL sdn 4d (Series I) | 2,722 | 14,460 | 126,244 |
| G69/R7C SL sdn 4d (Series II) | — | 16,060 | |
| J35 SL wgn 4d | 2,934 | 17,060 | 9,102 |
| **Cutlass Supreme (wb 107.7)** | | | |
| H47/R7B SL cpe (Series I) | 3,243 | 17,460 | 24,809 |
| H47/R7C SL cpe (Series II) | — | 18,460 | |
| H69/R7B SL sdn 4d (Series I) | 3,354 | 17,460 | 83,933 |
| H69/R7C SL sdn 4d (Series II) | — | 18,460 | |
| T67 conv cpe | 3,651 | 25,460 | 4,490 |
| **Eighty-Eight (wb 110.8)** | | | |
| N69 sdn 4d | 3,404 | 20,410 | 56,862 |
| Y69 LS sdn 4d | — | 22,710 | 7,106 |
| Y69/R7C LSS sdn 4d | — | 24,010 | 11,513 |
| **Ninety-Eight (wb 110.8)—25,444 built** | | | |
| X69/R7B Reg Elite sdn 4d (Series I) | 3,593 | 26,060 | |
| X69/R7C Reg Elite sdn 4d (Series II) | — | 27,160 | |
| **Aurora (wb 113.0)** | | | |
| R29 sdn 4d | 4,000 | 31,370 | 47,831 |

| 1995 Engines | bore × stroke | bhp | availability |
|---|---|---|---|
| I-4, 133.0 | 3.50 × 3.46 | 120 | S-Ciera |
| I-4, 138.0 | 3.63 × 3.94 | 150 | S-Achieva (dohc) |
| V-6, 191.0 | 3.50 × 3.30 | 155 | O-Achieva |
| V-6, 191.0 | 3.50 × 3.30 | 160 | S-Supreme; O-Ciera |
| V-6, 207.0 | 3.62 × 3.30 | 210 | O-Supreme (dohc) |
| V-6, 231.0 | 3.80 × 3.40 | 205 | S-Eighty-Eight, Ninety-Eight |
| V-6S, 231.0 | 3.80 × 3.40 | 225 | O-Eighty-Eight, Ninety-Eight, LSS |
| V-8, 244.0 | 3.42 × 3.31 | 250 | S-Aurora (dohc) |

## 1996

| Achieva (wb 103.4) | Wght | Price | Prod |
|---|---|---|---|
| L37/1SA SC cpe (Series I) | 2,751 | 13,495 | 1,437 |
| L37/1SB SC cpe (Series II) | — | 14,495 | 6,496 |
| L37/1SC SC cpe (Series III) | — | 16,495 | 2,286 |
| L69/1SA SL sdn 4d (Series I) | — | — | 34 |
| L69/1SB SL sdn 4d (Series II) | 2,813 | 14,495 | 9,833 |
| L69/1SC SL sdn 4d (Series III) | — | 16,495 | 17,661 |
| **Cutlass Ciera (104.9)** | | | |
| J69/1SA sdn 4d | — | — | 6,710 |
| J69/1SB sdn 4d (Series I) | 2,924 | 14,455 | 23,744 |
| J69/1SC sdn 4d (Series II) | 3,059 | 16,455 | 86,721 |
| J35/1SA wgn 4d | — | — | 1,851 |
| J35/1SB wgn 4d | 3,229 | 17,455 | 7,156 |
| **Cutlass Supreme (wb 107.7)** | | | |
| H47/1SA cpe (Series I) | 3,283 | 17,455 | 5,597 |
| H69/1SA sdn 4d (Series I) | 3,388 | 17,455 | 9,541 |
| H47/1SB cpe (Series II) | — | 18,455 | 7,194 |
| H69/1SB sdn 4d (Series II) | — | 18,455 | 15,876 |
| H47/1SC cpe (Series III) | — | 18,960 | 9,548 |
| H69/1SC sdn 4d (Series III) | — | 18,960 | 13,597 |
| H47/1SD cpe (Series IV) | — | 20,160 | 8,256 |
| H69/1SD sdn 4d (Series IV) | — | 20,160 | 9,986 |

| Eighty-Eight (wb 110.8) | Wght | Price | Prod |
|---|---|---|---|
| N69/1SA sdn 4d | 3,455 | 20,405 | 12,528 |
| N69/1SB LS sdn 4d | 3,459 | 22,810 | 33,017 |
| Y69/1SA LSS sdn 4d | 3,502 | 26,010 | 12,074 |
| Y69/1SB LSS sdn 4d | — | — | 1 |
| **Ninety-Eight (wb 110.8)** | | | |
| X69/1SB Reg Elite sdn 4d (Series I) | 3,515 | 28,160 | 5,638 |
| X69/1SC Reg Elite sdn 4d (Series II) | — | 29,260 | 9,469 |
| **Aurora (wb 113.8)** | | | |
| R29 sdn 4d | 3,967 | 34,360 | 24,133 |

| 1996 Engines | bore × stroke | bhp | availability |
|---|---|---|---|
| I-4, 133.0 | 3.50 × 3.46 | 120 | S-Ciera |
| I-4, 146.0 | 3.54 × 3.70 | 150 | S-Achieva (dohc) |
| V-6, 191.0 | 3.50 × 3.30 | 155 | O-Achieva |
| V-6, 191.0 | 3.50 × 3.30 | 160 | S-Supreme, O-Ciera |
| V-6, 207.0 | 3.62 × 3.30 | 215 | O-Supreme (dohc) |
| V-6, 231.0 | 3.80 × 3.40 | 205 | S-Eighty-Eight, Ninety-Eight |
| V-6S, 231.0 | 3.80 × 3.40 | 240 | O-Eighty-Eight LSS |
| V-8, 244.0 | 3.42 × 3.31 | 250 | S-Aurora |

## 1997

| Achieva (wb 103.4) | Wght | Price | Prod |
|---|---|---|---|
| L37/1SA SC cpe (Series I) | 2,886 | 15,425 | 4,951 |
| L37/1SB SC cpe (Series II) | — | 16,975 | |
| L69/1SA SL sdn 4d (Series I) | 2,917 | 15,225 | 47,593 |
| L69/1SB SL sdn 4d (Series II) | — | 16,775 | |
| **Cutlass (107.0)** | | | |
| J69 sdn 4d | 2,982 | 17,325 | 9,973 |
| G69 GLS sdn 4d | — | 19,225 | 8,139 |
| **Cutlass Supreme (wb 107.7)** | | | |
| H47/1SA cpe (Series I) | 3,286 | 18,950 | 10,197 |
| H47/1SB cpe (Series II) | — | 19,850 | |
| H47/1SC cpe (Series III) | — | 20,750 | |
| H69/1SA sdn 4d (Series I) | 3,388 | 18,950 | 49,327 |
| H69/1SB sdn 4d (Series II) | — | 19,850 | |
| H69/1SC sdn 4d (Series III) | — | 20,750 | |
| **Eighty-Eight (wb 110.8)** | | | |
| N69 sdn 4d | 3,465 | 22,495 | 51,183 |
| N69 LS sdn 4d | — | 23,795 | |
| Y69 LSS sdn 4d | 3,547 | 27,695 | 11,101 |
| C69 Regency sdn 4d | — | 27,995 | 8,219 |
| **Aurora (wb 113.8)** | | | |
| R29 sdn 4d | 3,967 | 35,795 | 27,927 |

| 1997 Engines | bore × stroke | bhp | availability |
|---|---|---|---|
| I-4, 146.0 | 3.54 × 3.70 | 150 | S-Achieva (dohc) |
| V-6, 191.0 | 3.50 × 3.310 | 155 | S-Cutlass, O-Achieva |
| V-6, 191.0 | 3.50 × 3.30 | 160 | S-Cutlass Supreme |
| V-6, 231.0 | 3.80 × 3.40 | 205 | S-Eighty-Eight |
| V-6S, 231.0 | 3.80 × 3.40 | 240 | O-Eighty-Eight LSS |
| V-8, 244.0 | 3.42 × 3.31 | 250 | S-Aurora |

## 1998

| Achieva (wb 103.4) | Wght | Price | Prod |
|---|---|---|---|
| L69 SL sdn 4d | 2,917 | — | 26,922 |

# Oldsmobile

| Cutlass (107.0) | | Wght | Price | Prod |
|---|---|---|---|---|
| B69 | GL sdn 4d | 2,982 | 17,800 | 21,428 |
| G69 | GLS sdn 4d | — | 19,425 | 31,256 |
| **Intrigue (wb 109.0)** | | | | |
| H69 | sdn 4d | 3,455 | 20,700 | 43,840 |
| S69 | GL sdn 4d | — | 22,100 | 59,525 |
| X69 | GLS sdn 4d | — | 24,110 | 4,303 |
| **Eighty-Eight (wb 110.8)** | | | | |
| N69 | sdn 4d | 3,455 | 22,795 | 20,000 |
| N69 | LS sdn 4d | — | 24,195 | 34,075 |
| Y69 | LSS sdn 4d | 3,502 | 28,095 | 5,283 |
| C69 | Regency sdn 4d | 3,813 | 28,295 | 7,958 |
| **Aurora (wb 113.8)** | | | | |
| R29 | sdn 4d | 3,967 | 35,960 | 25,721 |

| 1998 Engines | bore × stroke | bhp | availability |
|---|---|---|---|
| I-4, 146.0 | 3.54 × 3.70 | 150 | S-Achieva (dohc) |
| V-6, 191.0 | 3.51 × 3.31 | 150 | S-Cutlass |
| V-6, 191.0 | 3.51 × 3.31 | 155 | O-Achieva |
| V-6, 231.0 | 3.80 × 3.40 | 195 | S-Intrigue |
| V-6, 231.0 | 3.80 × 3.40 | 205 | S-Eighty-Eight |
| V-6S, 231.0 | 3.80 × 3.40 | 240 | O-Eighty-Eight LSS |
| V-8, 244.0 | 3.42 × 3.31 | 250 | S-Aurora |

## 1999

| Alero (wb 107.0) | | Wght | Price | Prod |
|---|---|---|---|---|
| — | GX cpe | 2,960 | 16,325 | 8,730 |
| — | GL cpe | — | 18,655 | 22,302 |
| — | GLS cpe | — | 20,875 | 11,273 |
| — | GX sdn 4d | 3,020 | 16,325 | 5,711 |
| — | GL sdn 4d | — | 18,220 | 71,944 |
| — | GLS sdn 4d | — | 20,875 | 22,302 |
| **Intrigue (wb 109.0)** | | | | |
| H69 | GX sdn 4d | 3,465 | 21,175 | 38,553 |
| S69 | GL sdn 4d | — | 22,575 | 39,321 |
| X69 | GLS sdn 4d | — | 24,945 | 16,041 |
| **Eighty-Eight (wb 110.8)** | | | | |
| — | sdn 4d | — | 23,555 | 11,546 |
| — | LS sdn 4d | 3,455 | 25,105 | 24,091 |
| — | LSS sdn 4d | 3,500 | 29,105 | 597 |
| — | 50th Anniv. sdn 4d | — | 27,350 | 4,719 |
| **Aurora (wb 113.8)** | | | | |
| R29 | sdn 4d | 3,965 | 36,229 | 19,635 |

| 1999 Engines | bore × stroke | bhp | availability |
|---|---|---|---|
| I-4, 146.0 | 3.54 × 3.70 | 150 | S-Alero (dohc) |
| V-6, 207.0 | 3.62 × 3.31 | 170 | S-Alero GLS; O-Alero GL |
| V-6, 212.0 | 3.52 × 3.62 | 215 | O-Intrigue (dohc) |
| V-6, 231.0 | 3.80 × 3.40 | 195 | S-Intrigue |
| V-6, 231.0 | 3.80 × 3.40 | 205 | S-Eighty-Eight |
| V-6S, 231.0 | 3.80 × 3.40 | 240 | O-Eighty-Eight LSS |
| V-8, 244.0 | 3.42 × 3.31 | 250 | S-Aurora |

## 2000

| Alero (wb 107.0) | | Wght | Price | Prod |
|---|---|---|---|---|
| K37 | GX cpe | 3,027 | 15,675 | 6,506 |
| L37 | GL cpe | 3,038 | 17,650 | 19,378 |
| F37 | GLS cpe | 3,051 | 21,365 | 8,422 |
| K69 | GX sdn 4d | 3,078 | 15,675 | 11,937 |
| L69 | GL sdn 4d | 3,089 | 17,650 | 71,624 |
| F69 | GLS sdn 4d | 3,102 | 21,635 | 19,273 |
| **Intrigue (wb 109.0)** | | | | |
| H69 | GX sdn 4d | 3,426 | 22,090 | 43,249 |
| S69 | GL sdn 4d | 3,452 | 23,720 | 21,564 |
| X69 | GLS sdn 4d | 3,433 | 25,720 | 15,698 |

| 2000 Engines | bore × stroke | bhp | availability |
|---|---|---|---|
| I-4, 146.0 | 3.54 × 3.70 | 150 | S-Alero (dohc) |
| V-6, 207.0 | 3.62 × 3.31 | 170 | O-Alero |
| V-6, 212.0 | 3.52 × 3.62 | 215 | S-Intrigue (dohc) |

## 2001

| Alero (wb 107.0) | | Wght | Price | Prod |
|---|---|---|---|---|
| K37 | GX cpe | 2,973 | 17,210 | 5,026 |
| L37 | GL cpe | 2,997 | 18,620 | 17,044 |
| F37 | GLS cpe | 3,060 | 22,190 | 4,795 |
| K69 | GX sdn 4d | 3,026 | 17,210 | 13,902 |
| L69 | GL sdn 4d | 3,046 | 18,620 | 75,895 |
| F69 | GLS sdn 4d | 3,108 | 21,965 | 13,064 |
| **Intrigue (wb 109.0)** | | | | |
| H69 | GX sdn 4d | 3,493 | 22,395 | 26,637 |
| S69 | GL sdn 4d | 3,420 | 24,150 | 12,926 |
| X69 | GLS sdn 4d | 3,434 | 26,615 | 5,104 |
| **Aurora (wb 112.2)** | | | | |
| R29 | V-6 sdn 4d | 3,686 | 30,469 | 37,397 |
| S29 | V-8 sdn 4d | 3,803 | 34,644 | 16,243 |

| 2001 Engines | bore × stroke | bhp | availability |
|---|---|---|---|
| I-4, 146.0 | 3.54 × 3.70 | 150 | S-Alero (dohc) |
| V-6, 207.0 | 3.62 × 3.31 | 170 | O-Alero |
| V-6, 212.0 | 3.52 × 3.62 | 215 | S-Intrigue, Aurora V-6 (dohc) |
| V-8, 244.0 | 3.42 × 3.31 | 250 | S-Aurora V-8 |

## 2002

| Alero (wb 107.0) | | Wght | Price | Prod |
|---|---|---|---|---|
| K37 | GX cpe 2d | 2,946 | 17,470 | — |
| L37 | GL1 cpe 2d | 2,961 | 19,680 | — |
| L37 | GL2 cpe 2d | 3,042 | 20,580 | — |
| F37 | GLS cpe 2d | 3,085 | 22,315 | — |
| K69 | GX sdn 4d | 3,021 | 17,470 | — |
| L69 | GL1 sdn 4d | 3,016 | 19,455 | — |
| L69 | GL2 sdn 4d | 3,103 | 20580 | — |
| F69 | GLS sdn 4d | 3,0147 | 22090 | — |
| **Intrigue (wb 109.0)** | | | | |
| H69 | GX sdn 4d | 3,393 | 22,817 | — |
| S69 | GL sdn 4d | 3,420 | 24,402 | — |
| X69 | GLS sdn 4d | 3,434 | 27,892 | — |
| **Aurora (wb 112.2)** | | | | |
| R29 | V6 sdn 4d | 3,686 | 30,995 | — |
| S29 | V8 sdn 4d | 3,803 | 34,990 | — |

| 2002 Engines | bore × stroke | bhp | availability |
|---|---|---|---|
| I-4, 134.0 | 3.38 × 3.72 | 140 | S-Alero (dohc) |
| V-6, 207.0 | 3.62 × 3.31 | 170 | O-Alero |
| V-6, 212.0 | 3.52 × 3.62 | 215 | S-Intrigue, Aurora V-6 (dohc) |
| V8, 244.0 | 3.42 × 3.31 | 250 | S-Aurora V-8 |

# Packard

For many people, Packard was, in its heyday, "the supreme combination of all that is fine in motor-cars." It may not have always been the technical "Standard of the World," but it was the social Standard of America, even for millions of would-be buyers who could never afford one. In 1929, more people owned stock in Packard than any other company save General Motors, and there were far more Packard stockholders than Packard owners.

Packard got its start in Warren, Ohio, in 1899, when James Ward Packard figured he could build a better car than the Winton he had purchased. His first was a small one-cylinder model with automatic spark advance. James B. Joy took over the concern in 1901 and moved it to Detroit in 1903, the year of the first four-cylinder Packard.

The car that moved Packard firmly into the industry's front rank was its 48-horsepower Six of 1912. Packard then leap-frogged Cadillac's new 1915 V-8 with a V-12 the following year—the fabled "Twin Six," though that only lasted until 1923. A new straight-eight arrived soon afterward. Packard did introduce a less-prestigious Six in 1921, but that was dropped well before 1930. The make then maintained its reputation mainly with eight-cylinder engines right on through its sad death in 1958.

For an automaker so single-mindedly devoted to luxury, Packard compiled a remarkable production record. It regularly outproduced Cadillac in 1925-30, even though its GM rival had help from LaSalle beginning in 1927. Except for 1931, '32, and '34, Packard continued to out-build Cadillac/LaSalle until World War II.

Like other luxury makes, Packard relied on middle-priced products to survive the Depression, most notably the One Twenty, new for 1935. This, together with the companion One Ten, enabled Packard not only to endure "hard times" but to grow rapidly from low-volume luxury to true mass-market producer. Unfortunately, the firm was far slower to abandon medium-price products after World War II than either Cadillac or Lincoln, thus sowing the seeds of its ultimate demise.

In 1923, Packard began using a "series" number to designate each year's model line, a practice it continued into the '50s. Historians have since converted these to model years for ease of recognition. Thus the Seventh Series, for example, coincides with 1930.

That hierarchy began with a standard Eight, which had the least-pretentious bodies on relatively short wheelbases of 127.5 and 134.5 inches. Power came from a 320-cubic-inch inline engine making 90 bhp. Next up was the dashing Speedster Eight, offering lithe boattail and standard roadsters, plus phaeton, victoria, and sedan, all on a 134-inch chassis. Speedsters cost the world—$5200-$6000—so only 150 were built before the series was canceled after 1930. A 385-cid eight delivered 125-145 bhp in Speedsters. A 106-bhp version powered Custom and DeLuxe Eights on respective wheelbases of 140.5 and 145.5 inches. These were generally built with closed bodies, but were also available in phaeton, roadster, and convertible styles by Packard and various custom coach-builders. Prices here weren't quite the world, ranging from $3200 to over $5000. Then again, such sums bought a rather nice house at the time.

The 1931 Eighth Series comprised standard, Custom, and DeLuxe Eights. The standard line now offered "Individual Customs" on the 134.5-inch chassis. Included were a Dietrich convertible sedan and victoria, plus Packard's own cabriolet, town car, and landaulet styles. Standard models retained the 320 engine, now 10 bhp richer; Custom and DeLuxe again carried the 385 unit, now with 120 bhp. The extra power came from modified intake and exhaust passages similar to those on the 1930 Speedsters. Other linewide mechanical changes included automatic Bijur chassis-lubrication system and a new quick-shift mechanism for the four-speed gearbox to reduce effort.

For 1932's Ninth Series came a more-conventional three-speed all-synchromesh transmission, plus lower, more-streamlined styling that was nonetheless similar to upright 1930-31 appearance. But the big news occurred at the top and bottom of the line. Leading the fleet was a new Twin Six, which was renamed Twelve after this one year. It bore no relationship to the 1916-23 original, with a new 445.5-cid V-12 that had actually been planned for an aborted front-drive chassis. Though a fairly low numerical axle ratio was available, most of these cars got gearsets of 4.41:1 or higher. The result was smooth, relatively shift-free motoring rather than high performance. The factory claimed a sustained 100 mph was well within the new V-12's capabilities, but that was under test conditions; the 160-bhp engine usually ran out of breath at about 90 mph in stock tune. At 60 or 70 mph, though, it was whisper quiet and highly refined.

The 1932-34 V-12s shared the same two wheelbases and most bodies with the upper Eight series, which was again called DeLuxe for '32, then Super. In all cases, the longer chassis was reserved for Individual Customs and a standard seven-passenger sedan and limousine. Despite their prestige as the ultimate Packards, the V-12s arrived at only $100-$200 above counterpart DeLuxes with factory bodywork, but the gap grew as time passed, especially between the various custom-body models. In 1935, when "senior" production was consolidated to make room for the new high-volume One Twenty, the Twelve gained a stroked 473-cid engine with 175 bhp, and shifted to 139- and 144-inch wheelbases. Super Eights offered similar body styles on those same chassis, as well as a trim 132-inch platform. Custom bodies thinned quickly as coachbuilders either went bankrupt or were bought out, but a few were always listed right on through 1942.

As an independent, Packard couldn't face the Depression with solid financial backing from a big parent, so it tried medium-price cars well before Cadillac or Lincoln. Its first was the 1932 Light Eight, appearing two years ahead of a smaller, cheaper LaSalle and four years ahead of Lincoln's advanced Zephyr. A quality product built with the same meticulous care as other Packards, the Light Eight was true to its name. It rode a lighter, trimmer 127.8-inch chassis mounting the standard Eight's 320 engine, rated that year at 110 bhp. The Light Eight was thus faster than its bigger sisters. Body styles comprised four-door sedan, five-passenger coupe-sedan, and rumble-seat roadster and coupe.

But the Light Eight looked chunkier than other '32 Packards because it was shorter overall, and its attractively affordable pricing—around $2000—was more liability than asset. A Light Eight cost almost as much to build as a corresponding standard Eight yet sold for $500-$850 less, so Packard was lucky to break even on any Light Eight sold. The line was accordingly dropped after this one year.

Packard lost $7 million in 1932, much of it on the Light Eight, so company president Alvan Macauley began searching the ranks of GM executives for someone wise in the ways of volume production who could help the firm develop a profitable middle-priced car. Ironically, the firm netted $500,000 with 1933 sales that amounted to 38 percent of the high-priced market—well above Cadillac's share. Trouble was, the high-priced market was virtually gone.

But Macauley's search was about to pay big dividends. Soon coming aboard were Max Gilman, "that hardboiled guy in New York" (he'd started as a Brooklyn truck salesman in 1919), and George T. Christopher, a production whiz enticed out of retirement from GM. (Gilman replaced Macauley as president in 1938, when the latter became chairman; Christopher replaced Gilman in 1942.) While Gilman astutely set the publicity stage, Christopher modern-

# Packard

1932 900 Series Light 8 cabriolet

1936 One Twenty four-door sedan

1935 One Twenty four-door sedan

1938 Twelve 7-passenger limousine

1935 One Twenty sport coupe 2/4-passenger

1938 Eight two-door touring sedan

ized Packard's plant end-to-end for much higher volume. The fruit of their combined labors was unveiled on January 6, 1935, as the One Twenty.

It was a dramatic departure for Packard. Bowing in seven models, the One Twenty cost a little more than half as much as the unmourned Light Eight—$1000-$1100—perfect for those who'd always wanted a Packard but had never been able to afford one. There were traditional hallmarks like "ox-yoke" radiator and red hexagon wheel-hub emblems, but styling was fully updated, emerging conservative but contemporary with rounded contours, "potato-shape" windows, fullsome fenders, and a radiator raked 30 degrees from vertical—all pretty daring for Packard.

Designed largely by former GM people, the One Twenty engine was a straightforward L-head eight of 257.2 cid and 110 bhp. Features included a heavily ribbed block, individual exhaust ports, ample water jackets, five main bearings, and counterweighted overlapping journals. It was a smooth engine, easy on gas, and granite strong. After 1935, a longer stroke yielded 282 cid and 120 bhp. Most One Twentys could reach 85 mph and do 0-60 in less than 20 seconds—pretty decent for a 3500-pound prewar car.

For 1936, the One Twenty added a convertible sedan bearing "Dietrich" body plates, though Ray Dietrich personally had nothing to do with it; his name had been owned by the Murray Body Company since the early '30s. The following year brought a station wagon, three DeLuxe closed models, and a 138-inch wheelbase sedan and limousine. The '37 Senior Packards joined the One Twenty in offering independent front suspension, grease fittings (instead of the Bijur automatic chassis-lube system), and hydraulic brakes. For 1938, when the One Twenty was simply called Eight—and that year only—standard wheelbase lengthened to 127 inches.

Though long and unfairly criticized as "cheap," the One Twenty was a genuine Packard in appearance, road behavior, and workmanship. To no one's surprise, it sold like nickel hot dogs. As a result, Packard rocketed to 12th in industry production for 1935, leaping from 8000 to nearly 32,000. And it kept right on soaring, reaching about 61,000 in '36 and 122,000 in '37. A sharp recession held 1938 volume to some 56,000, but the firm soon recovered, and output remained healthy until World War II.

Contributing to that 1937 record was an even less-expensive line, the new Six, called One-Ten for 1940-42. Arriving on a 115-inch wheelbase, it used what was basically an over-bored One Twenty eight with two fewer cylinders, which made for a 237-cid six with 100 bhp. Wheelbase stretched to 122 inches for 1938-39, when displacement went up to 245 cid, though horsepower was unchanged. Offerings basically duplicated the One Twenty's, but prices averaged some $150 lower, so the One Ten outsold the One Twenty by 13-to-10 in 1937. Though its six wasn't as smooth or potent as the One Twenty eight, it did offer excellent mileage and adequate performance.

The One Ten completed Packard's transformation from a purveyor of virtually handmade luxury cars to one of Detroit's top-10

# Packard

1939 One Twenty four-door touring sedan

1940 Darrin convertible sedan

1940 Darrin victoria convertible

1940 One Twenty four-door touring sedan

1941 One Eighty four-door touring sedan

producers. Of course, the firm still sold regular and Super Eights and opulent Twelves through decade's end, but at a rate of only some 6000 a year. The One Twenty was far and away the breadwinning eight, costing some $1200 less than a standard Eight. Testifying to its success, the Super Eight lost its 385 engine after 1936, demoted to the 320 unit of the standard Eight, which itself disappeared after 1937, though not in name.

But the rather small and dumpy One Ten/Six was by no means a Packard in the traditional sense. Perhaps the firm had become too greedy for sales, blinded by George Christopher's push for ever-higher production. Regardless, by the end of the '30s, Cadillac was in firm charge as the sales and prestige leader of the high-dollar class. Many people who previously wouldn't have been seen in a Caddy now bought them instead of big Packards, which had been upstaged by the low-cost One Ten/One Twenty that looked almost the same, at least in front.

A definite factor in Cadillac's leap to luxury-league supremacy was its more-modern Harley Earl styling. True to tradition, Packard maintained a tall, formal look that seemed quite stuffy by 1939, not least because it hadn't changed much since the great design overhaul of four years before.

The line was again anchored for '39 by the Six (soon to be called One Ten), priced as low as $1000 for the business coupe. (Fords and Chevys cost $600-$900 that year.) The One Twenty name returned on entry-level eight-cylinder models, with 127- and 148-inch wheelbases; prices were $1245-$1700. Super Eights offered the same two chassis, but models were reduced to cover a $1650-$2300 spread. The Twelve, however, still ran a very broad gamut of models and prices ($4155-$8355), including custom styles by Rollston and Brunn. However, the magnificent Twelve was in its final year; the Depression had rendered it an unnecessary anachronism. Only 5744 were built during its eight-year reign as queen of the line (including 1932 Twin Sixes).

More major styling adjustments occurred for 1940, when a new 160-bhp 356-cid engine bowed in an expanded Super Eight line divided between One Sixty and Custom One Eighty models. These spanned wheelbases of 127, 138, and 148 inches and a price band of $1500-$2900 with standard bodywork. The new 356 was impressively quiet, what with nine main bearings and a crankshaft that weighed 105 pounds. It was also potent enough to push the lighter models to well over 100 mph. The 356 would power Supers through 1947 and Customs through 1950. Another new feature for 1940 was air conditioning. Packard was the first production car to offer it, though it was bulky and not as effective as later units.

Meantime, the low-priced Six was again a One Ten for 1940, but neither it nor the One Twenty was much changed mechanically. However, rumble-seat models were eliminated, and the One Twenty extended its coverage with four new DeLuxe-trim models: a sedan, club coupe and sedan, and convertible coupe in the $1160-$1300 price range.

A stunning exception to Packard's more-competitive 1940 price structure was a new quartet of rakish custom-built Darrin models, the work of renowned designer Howard A. "Dutch" Darrin. Effectively filling the glamour gap left by the departed Twelve, these comprised a One Twenty convertible victoria, a Custom Super Eight One Eighty version on the same short wheelbase, and a long-chassis Custom Super convertible sedan and closed Sport Sedan. All boasted ground-hugging silhouettes enhanced by the complete absence of running boards (Dutch detested running boards, though they were fast-fading anyway). The victorias were simply exquisite: smooth, low, ideally proportioned, yet with just the right amount of proper Packard dignity.

The Darrin-Packards evolved from a handful of 1938-39 specials that Dutch had built at his Hollywood works for various celebrities, including actor/crooner Dick Powell. Strong response encouraged Dutch to convince Packard to catalog such wares on a special-order

# Packard

basis. In a clever ploy to do just that, he got the Powell car parked at the Packard Proving Grounds in the summer of 1939, where it was roundly cheered by dealers attending their annual sales meeting.

Save sectioned radiators and hoods, the Darrins wore unique body panels. The Sport Sedan was a handsome "gentleman's" car with a semblance of Bill Mitchell's 1938 Cadillac Sixty Special in its curved, blind-quarter roof, chrome-edged windows, and sharp beltline. But the real eye-catcher was the sleek victoria, with cut-down windshield and an abrupt kickup to the rear flanks from a gradually sloped doorline—the famous "Darrin notch."

The Darrins were naturally Packard's priciest 1940s—$3819 for the One Twenty victoria, $6332 for the Custom Super convertible sedan—so sales were naturally minuscule. Then, too, planned production (at the old Auburn plant in Connersville, Indiana) was deliberately limited. Only 50 victorias were built for 1940 and a mere 12 convertible sedans (of which nine survive today). The Sport Sedan was announced as "virtually a request car—built for those who look to Packard to . . . create the newest, the finest, the most luxurious in motorcar transportation." But it never got going, dropped after only two were completed at Dutch's shop. Packard itself built two "Darrinized" sedans with stock 1940 front ends, but they weren't nearly as pretty and led nowhere. As you might expect, all the Darrin-Packards have long been deemed "Classics" by the Classic Car Club of America (CCCA).

Also offered for 1940 were an all-weather cabriolet and town car by Rollston, priced at $4473 and $4599, respectively. Only a handful were built. But even some regular models were quite scarce. Of the 98,000 Packards built for 1940, only 5662 were Super Eights and just 1900 were Customs. The rest were One Tens and One Twentys.

Packard finally rebodied its entire line for 1941, though it wasn't blindingly obvious. The main visual clues were slightly larger windows and—in a big styling innovation for Packard—headlamps set firmly within the front fenders. Wheelbases were unchanged, but floors were lowered, suspension was suitably revised, motor mounts were enlarged, and engines benefited from steel-backed rod bearings and an oil-bath air cleaner. These changes also applied to Darrins, but there was only one now: a Custom Super Eight One Eighty Victoria. This retained its general 1940 appearance save minor trim, a slightly different "notch" treatment, and the flush headlamps. One other difference: Its production was transferred to Cincinnati, where ambulance/hearse builder Sayers and Scoville crafted 35 as '41 models and another 15 to little-changed 1942 specifications. Overdrive was still optionally available throughout the Packard line, but for 1941 it could team with a new $37.50 "Electromatic" clutch. This disengaged by manifold vacuum upon releasing the accelerator to permit "clutchless" driving in second gear, which covered most day-to-day use; the pedal could still be floored to select first.

But Packard saved its biggest '41 news for midseason, when it unveiled the Clipper, a single four-door sedan priced at $1420, squarely between the One Twenty and One Sixty. Though built on the One Twenty chassis, it looked like no Packard before: smooth and utterly modern—a bold, unexpected bid for industry design leadership. The Clipper bore the unmistakable Darrin touch but was actually a joint project, with contributions from Packard's own stylists under Werner Gubitz, plus several stellar consultants. Still, it was mostly Darrin, seen in the descending beltline, tapered tail, and long prow-front with the slimmest Packard radiator yet. Predicting postwar styling at Packard and elsewhere was a nearly flush-sided "envelope" body with front fenders "swept-through" into the doors—and width that exceeded height.

Dutch had dashed off the Clipper in just 10 days to meet Packard's deadline, but never got a promised $10,000 fee. That was poor form, for the Clipper alone garnered some 16,000 sales—22 percent of Packard's total '41 volume, which was down some 25,000 from 1940. Still, this performance encouraged Packard to proceed with making

1941 One Twenty four-door station wagon

1947 Custom Super Clipper club sedan

1950 Eight DeLuxe four-door sedan

1952 Patrician 400 four-door sedan

"Clipper styling" virtually linewide for 1942. The sole exceptions were commercial vehicles, One Sixty/One Eighty convertible coupes, and custom bodies. The last again included the Rollston styles as well as new LeBaron-built long sedans and limousines and a beautifully formal Sport Brougham. Like other makes, Packard's 1942 production was cut short by America's entry into World War II, the total ending just shy of 34,000, mostly Clipper-styled 110/120 and One Sixty/One Eighty models.

After building Rolls-Royce Merlin aero engines and power units for military vehicles and PT boats, Packard returned to peacetime as the only independent completely free of debt. But then came a decision that would ultimately prove fatal. Instead of reverting to luxury cars alone, Packard continued to stress medium-price models in the One Twenty tradition. While such cars had been vital during the Depression, they simply weren't needed in the hectic sell-everything postwar economy, and they severely squandered what remained of Packard's grand-luxe image.

Still, disaster was a long way off in 1946, when Packard followed most other Detroit makes in reprising its final prewar line, though abbreviated. That year's low-priced Clipper Six sedan and coupe looked exactly like the Clipper Eight models, which included DeLuxe versions. All used the familiar 120-inch wheelbase. Clipper Super and Custom sedans and coupes had the equally familiar 127-inch chassis save the seven-passenger Custom sedan and limo (which had a 148-inch wheelbase). Basic Eights retained the prewar 282 engine with 125 bhp, Supers and Customs kept the 165-bhp 356 from '42, and the Six continued with its 105-bhp 245. Overdrive and Electromatic clutch returned as options. Customs were trimmed with plush broadcloth and leather upholstery, special carpeting, and beautiful imitation wood paneling. Packard moved more than 30,000 cars in 1946 and over 50,000 of the '47s, which were identical except for serial numbers.

There was just one problem. Most automakers were able to stretch their prewar tooling through 1948, then issue all-new postwar designs that were ahead of the Clipper in style. But Packard, despite its postwar financial health, couldn't afford to junk its prewar dies so soon because they hadn't been amortized over sufficient production. Accordingly, Packard stylists loaded on heavy chunks of sheetmetal to give the Clipper a modern "flow-through-fender" effect. It also added 200 needless pounds in curb weight. The result looked fatter too, aggravated by a short, squat grille—eggcrate on Customs, bar-type on other models—that was far-less-elegant than the slim prow of 1941-47. All this moved auto writer Tom McCahill to pronounce the '48 Packard fit for "a dowager in a Queen Mary hat." Many simply called it a "pregnant elephant."

Still, in 1948 it didn't matter whether a Packard looked trim or tubby or cost $2500 or $4500. Like most everyone else in the postwar seller's market, Packard could sell every car it built, and it sold a respectable number: some 92,000 for model-year '48 and about 116,000 of the similar '49s—two of its best years ever.

Engine and chassis assignments altered somewhat for the '48 line of standard, DeLuxe, Super, and Custom Eights. Customs retained their 160-bhp 356 engine, but Supers got a new 327 unit with five main bearings and 145 bhp; standard Eights used a much squarer new 288 engine with 130 bhp. These powerplants carried through to May 1949 in the Twenty-Second Series. Then the Twenty-Third series appeared with horsepower raised to 135 for standards and to 150 for Supers.

As before, sedans and coupes were Packard's mainstays in 1948-50. Standards, DeLuxes, and Supers kept to 120-inch wheelbases, Customs to a 127-inch chassis; a 141-inch platform supported four new Super Eight long sedans and limos, while a 148-inch chassis continued under counterpart Customs. Packard also crafted a few long Custom commercial chassis, plus some six-cylinder 1948 platforms for taxi and export use.

Also new for '48 were Custom and Super convertibles and the novel four-door Station Sedan in the standard Eight series. The last, priced at $3425, had a wagonlike body made almost entirely of steel, though it employed structural wood at the tailgate and decorative timber on the doors. It was rather unusual for a Packard, which may be why it didn't sell too well: just 3864 copies through 1950. The Custom Eight convertible was Packard's priciest standard model tagged at $4295 for 1948-49, then $4520.

Ushered in with the Twenty-Third series of mid-1949 was Ultramatic, the only automatic transmission developed by an independent without outside help. This combined a torque converter with multiple-disc and direct-drive clutches, plus forward/reverse bands. The car started from rest using the torque converter, then shifted into direct mechanical drive at about 15 miles an hour. Though much smoother than GM's rival Hydra-Matic, Ultramatic provided only leisurely acceleration, and frequent use of Low range for faster starts caused premature wear.

Also arriving with the Twenty-Third series was a mild facelift distinguished by a beltline spear on most models, plus new Deluxe-trim Eight and Super Eight sedans and coupes. The Super versions carried a 327-cid engine and the same eggcrate grille as corresponding Customs but cost about $1000 less, so Custom sales suffered mightily. So did Packard as a whole. The seller's market was ending, and production showed it, plunging to just under 42,400 units for the model year.

Packard finally managed a total redesign for 1951, adopting John Reinhart's squarish, but praiseworthy, "high-pockets" notchback shape—a complete break with the "elephants." A new 122-inch chassis supported a "200" series of standard and DeLuxe two- and four-door sedans, plus a spiffy "250" convertible and Mayfair hardtop coupe, the latter body style a first for Packard. A 127-inch platform was used for "300" and Patrician 400 sedans. Like the old One Ten, the 200s weren't traditional Packards even though they carried the same 288 engine as the previous standard Eight. The line even included a $2302 business coupe, $529 less than the cheapest '51 Cadillac. But with the seller's market ended, the 200s couldn't hope to do well against established price rivals, and they didn't.

The "real" Packards of 1951 were the 250s, which did sell pretty well, and the regal 300 and Patrician. At just under $3700, the Patrician effectively replaced the broad Custom Eight line. But though very smooth and utterly reliable, the Custom's 356 engine cost too much to build in light of expected sales, so Packard's biggest '51 engine was the destroked 327, previously the middle powerplant and with nearly as much horsepower: 155 for Patricians and Ultramatic 250/300s, 150 otherwise.

Overall, Packard's new '51 package fared quite well—probably because it was new in a year when little else was. Model-year production ended at 101,000—more than twice the dismal 1950 total. (Packard also built 401 "300" chassis that year for the professional car market and what remained of its once-thriving custom-body business.)

Unfortunately, 1952 production was down substantially, sliding to just under 63,000 units. Changes were few. The 200 business coupe was dropped, power brakes arrived as a (postwar) first-time option, and there were colorful new interiors in high-quality fabric and leather by fashion designer Dorothy Draper. Styling was virtually untouched, however. The most-obvious change was a different wing position for the traditional "pelican" hood ornament.

A far more significant change occurred in the executive suite during 1952. In May, aging president Hugh Ferry (who'd replaced George Christopher in 1949) stepped down in favor of James J. Nance, a marketwise hotshot recruited from Hotpoint to turn Packard around. That was sorely needed. By the time Nance arrived, Packard's Detroit plant was working at only 50 percent capacity. Incredibly, several long-time executives felt that was good enough, but Nance saw then what we all see now: At that pace, Packard was doomed.

Nance blew in like a tornado, aggressively seeking new military business while declaring that the firm's continued emphasis on medium-price cars was "bleeding the Packard name white." Accordingly, he made the 200/250 into new Packard Clipper models for 1953, stage-one of his plan to divorce the cheaper cars from the rest of the line in both fact and name. Packard, he decreed, would henceforth build nothing but luxury cars, including the long-wheelbase formal sedans and limousines it had lately neglected.

Lack of time and money precluded a linewide makeover for '53, but Nance did see to the inclusion of an eight-place Executive Sedan and "Corporation Limousine" on a massive 149-inch chassis, priced around $7000. He also contracted with the Derham Body Company

# Packard

1953 Caribbean convertible coupe

1954 Clipper DeLuxe Sportster coupe

1953 Patrician four-door sedan

1955 Four Hundred two-door hardtop

for a few formal Patricians with leather-covered tops, tiny rear windows, and $6531 price tags.

Also for the top of the '53 line, Nance pushed out the Caribbean, a glamorous convertible on the short wheelbase with colorful styling by Richard A. Teague. Inspired by Richard Arbib's 1952 Packard Pan American show car (built by Henney), the Caribbean carried a 180-bhp 327, rakish circular rear-wheel cutouts, jaunty "Continental kit" outside spare tire, and chrome wire wheels, plus most every optional amenity in the book. It cost a lofty $5210 and was deliberately limited to 750 copies—for snob appeal—but the Caribbean was as well-received as Cadillac's new '53 Eldorado.

Anchoring the '53 line were Nance's Clippers: two- and four-door sedans in standard and DeLuxe guise powered by unchanged 288 and 327 engines. Included in the standard group was a snazzy hardtop-styled pillared two-door called Sportster, attractively priced at $2805. The 250-series was defunct, but the Mayfair and standard convertible returned; the cheapest long-wheelbase '53 was a single sedan called Cavalier, replacing the 300 model.

Nance had hoped for all-new '54 Packards, but time and money were again lacking, so a look-alike interim series was fielded with rimmed headlamps and integrated backup lights the only visible differences. The 327 engine was enlarged to 359 cid and 212 bhp for Patrician, Caribbean and standard convertibles, commercial chassis, and a hardtop named Pacific. Air conditioning now returned for the first time since the war. But 1954 was a terrible Packard year, with production of only 31,000 cars. Of these, some 23,000 were Clippers: Specials and DeLuxes as before, plus new Super sedans and a Super Panama hardtop coupe. Specials again used the 288 engine, but the DeLuxe's 327 was bumped up five bhp; the latter also powered Supers. The Cavalier sedan used a 185-bhp version. Chassis production came to 335.

The revolutionary new model Nance wanted for '54 was postponed to '55 partly by the so-called Studebaker-Packard merger, which was actually a Packard buyout. What Nance didn't know when he signed the papers was that Studebaker had huge productivity problems in its high-overhead South Bend, Indiana plant, with a breakeven point somewhere over 250,000 cars. Contrary to many accounts, Packard was still a fairly healthy company at this point, but Studebaker was sinking and would eventually drag Packard down with it.

As the all-new '55s neared production, another smoldering problem burst into flame. Back in 1940, Packard had stopped building its own bodies, contracting the work to Briggs Manufacturing Company. But Packard lost this supplier when Chrysler bought Briggs in 1954, and thus had to build its own bodies again. Inexplicably, it settled for a cramped body plant on Conner Avenue in Detroit. Never large enough, this facility caused big production tie-ups and quality-control problems that hampered sales of the '55 Packards and forced immediate cancellation of long models. Though Packard built some 55,000 cars for prosperous '55, it would have done better to assign body production to its old, but adequate, main plant on Detroit's East Grand Boulevard.

Despite these woes, the 1955 Packard was a technological marvel. Prime among its wonders was "Torsion-Level" suspension: long torsion bars connecting front and rear wheels on each side. A complex electrical system enabled the suspension to correct for load weight, and effectively interlinked all four wheels for truly extraordinary ride and handling despite two-ton bulk. And there was more: powerful new short-stroke ohv V-8s, ousting the old-fashioned flathead straight-eights at last. Clipper DeLuxes and Supers (now shorn of two-door sedans) used a 320-cid version with 225 bhp. A bored-out 352 delivered 245 bhp in new Clipper Customs (a sedan and Constellation hardtop), 275 bhp in Caribbeans (via twin four-barrel carbs) and 260 bhp in Patrician sedans and new "Four Hundred" hardtop coupes. Ultramatic was suitably modified to handle the higher V-8 torque.

The engines, improved Ultramatic, and Torsion-Level gave the '55 Packards a fine chassis. Despite their heft, these were impressively fast and roadable cars—real Packards in every sense. Styling was equally impressive. Dick Teague's clever facelift of the old '51 body produced "cathedral" taillights; peaked front fenders; an ornate grille; and that '55 must-have, a wrapped windshield. Clippers gained their own special grille and retained 1954-style taillights.

Production problems at the Conner plant were finally licked, but not in time for '56, when customers were scared away by Stude-

# Packard

1955 Caribbean convertible coupe

1956 Clipper Super hardtop coupe

1957 Town Sedan four-door

1958 hardtop coupe

1958 Hawk hardtop coupe

baker's desperate struggle as well as the '55 Packards' notorious quality and service problems. Ironically, the '56s were better built.

Nance's "divorce action" reached fruition that year in an entirely separate Clipper line. Besides registering the name as a distinct make, he decreed separate Clipper and Packard dealer signs, and changed Packard Division to the Packard-Clipper Division of Studebaker-Packard Corporation. As a final touch, "Packard" appeared nowhere on '56 Clippers except for tiny decklid script—and some didn't even have that.

Nevertheless, the line again offered five models: DeLuxe, Super, and Custom four-door sedans and Super and Custom Constellation hardtops. Wheelbase was unchanged, but horsepower was lifted to 275 for Customs and 240 for other models. Torsion-Level was again featured too, although a conventional suspension was available on the DeLuxe. Options included overdrive manual transmission ($110), Ultramatic ($199), power steering, power brakes, and air conditioning.

These Clippers were luxuriously trimmed and nicely styled, but sales weren't sufficient to help floundering S-P. The DeLuxe sedan was the most popular, attracting 5715 buyers. Least popular was the handsome Custom Constellation hardtop, garnering under 1500 sales. Though still obvious Packard relatives, the '56 Clippers retained their own grille and taillamp designs, made even more different in line with Nance's aims.

The Packard line still listed Clipper-type models in the 1956 Executive, a sedan and hardtop coupe announced at midyear to bridge the price gap with Clipper. Executives even shared the Clipper's chassis, 275-bhp 352 V-8, and pointy taillights, but wore "senior" '56 front-end styling, plus higher prices in the $3500-$3600 range. The longer 127-inch chassis returned for Patrician, Four Hundred, and two Caribbeans: the familiar convertible and a new hardtop, both with unique seat covers that could be reversed from fabric to leather. All these models were upgraded to a bored-out 374 V-8 packing a mighty 310 bhp in Caribbeans and 290 bhp elsewhere. But none of this helped, and only 10,353 Packards were built for '56, including just 263 Caribbean hardtops and 276 convertibles.

Packard was now sinking fast, being pulled down with Studebaker. Including Clipper, 1956 production totaled 28,835 cars, just slightly more than half of '55 volume.

Studebaker-Packard had planned an all-new 1957 corporate line that included a shared bodyshell but totally different looks for Studebaker and Clipper, plus a much larger separate platform for a group of high-luxury Packards styled in the image of Dick Teague's 1956 Packard Predictor show car. But S-P was on the ropes, so no financial backing could be found, leading Nance to resign in August 1956. (He soon resurfaced at another ill-fated outfit: the new Edsel Division of Ford Motor Company.) Salvation finally arrived in the form of Curtiss-Wright Corporation, which picked up Studebaker-Packard as a dalliance and/or tax write-off. C-W's Roy Hurley began directing S-P's affairs. One of his first decisions was to end Packard production in Detroit and substitute Studebaker-based models built in South Bend.

Thus appeared a new Packard Clipper for 1957: the infamous "Packardbaker," as many have since called it. Though a very good Studebaker, it was hardly in the same league with the 1955-56 Packards. It came in just two models: four-door Town Sedan and Country Sedan station wagon (the latter name must have irked Ford). The sedan was on Studebaker's longer 120.5-inch chassis while the wagon was on a 116.5-inch chassis. A supercharged Studebaker 289-cid V-8 delivered the same 275 bhp as on '55 Caribbeans and '56 Executives, but Ultramatic, Torsion-Level, and other "real Packard" features were gone. Styling, at least, played on Packard themes. Prices were higher than for comparable Studeys: $3212/$3384. But everyone recognized this as a charade, and only about 5000 of the '57s, mostly sedans, were called for.

A big-Packard revival was still theoretically possible as the '58s

# Packard

were planned, so S-P again tried a holding action. This time there were four "Packardbakers" priced as high as $3995. Studebaker's shorter 116.5-inch platform carried a two-door hardtop and four-door wagon, the 120-inch chassis a sedan and the Packard Hawk. The last, perhaps the most-famous of this series, was a more-luxurious version of Studebaker's Golden Hawk.

All featured full-leather interiors and bizarre styling announced by low, "fish-mouth" grilles. In defense of stylist Duncan McRae, the Hawk was really built only because of Roy Hurley, who also dictated its long, bolt-on fiberglass nose and gaudy gold-mylar tailfins.

McRae, however, gets the blame for the Hawk's outside "armrests" and styling on the other three models: also garishly finned, and with hastily contrived four-headlight systems to keep up with an industry trend. Only the Hawk was supercharged. Other '58 Packards used a stock 289 with 210 bhp. Production was uniformly low: 159 wagons, 588 Hawks, 675 hardtops, and 1200 sedans.

With that, there was no point in going on, and once-proud Packard vanished from the scene (though its name continued in the corporate title until 1962). It was a great loss, but it did give Studebaker a new lease on life, though that make, too, would soon expire.

## Specifications

### 1930

| 726 Eight (wb 127.5) | | Wght | Price | Prod |
|---|---|---|---|---|
| 403 | sdn 4d | 4,265 | 3,275 | 15,731 |
| **733 Eight (wb 134.5)—12,531 built** | | | | |
| 400 | touring 7P | 4,055 | 2,525 | — |
| 401 | phtn 4P | 3,935 | 2,425 | — |
| 402 | rdstr 2-4P | 3,945 | 2,425 | — |
| 404 | sdn 7P | 4,500 | 2,675 | — |
| 405 | sdn limo 7P | 4,555 | 2,775 | — |
| 406 | club sdn 5P | 4,325 | 2,675 | — |
| 407 | cpe 5P | 4,255 | 2,675 | — |
| 408 | cpe 2-4P | 4,180 | 2,525 | — |
| 409 | conv cpe 2-4P | 4,100 | 2,550 | — |
| 431 | spt phtn 4P | 4,130 | 2,725 | — |
| **734 Speedster Eight (wb 134.0)—113 built** | | | | |
| 422 | boattail rdstr 2P | 4,295 | 5,210 | — |
| 443 | sdn 5P | 4,660 | 6,000 | — |
| 445 | phtn 4P | 4,300 | 5,200 | — |
| 447 | cpe victoria 5P | 4,525 | 6,000 | — |
| 452 | rdstr 2-4P | 4,435 | 5,200 | — |
| **740 Custom Eight (wb 140.5)—6,200 built** | | | | |
| 410 | touring 7P | 4,345 | 3,325 | — |
| 411 | phtn 4P | 4,250 | 3,190 | — |
| 412 | rdstr 2-4P | 4,245 | 3,190 | — |
| 413 | sdn 4d 5P | 4,560 | 3,585 | — |
| 414 | sdn 7P | 4,765 | 3,785 | — |
| 415 | sdn limo 7P | 4,810 | 3,885 | — |
| 416 | club sdn 5P | 4,580 | 3,750 | — |
| 417 | cpe 5P | 4,555 | 3,650 | — |
| 418 | cpe 2-4P | 4,500 | 3,295 | — |
| 419 | conv cpe 2-4P | 4,425 | 3,350 | — |
| 441 | spt phtn | 4,450 | 3,490 | — |
| **745 DeLuxe Eight (wb 145.5)—1,789 built** | | | | |
| 420 | touring 7P | 4,745 | 4,585 | — |
| 421 | phtn 4P | 4,645 | 4,585 | — |
| 422 | rdstr 2-4P | 4,695 | 4,585 | — |
| 423 | sdn 4d 5P | 4,805 | 4,985 | — |
| 424 | sdn 7P | 5,095 | 5,185 | — |
| 425 | sdn limo 7P | 5,140 | 5,350 | — |
| 426 | club sdn 5P | 5,000 | 5,150 | — |
| 427 | cpe 5P | 4,995 | 5,100 | — |
| 428 | cpe 2-4P | 4,875 | 4,785 | — |
| 429 | conv cpe 2-4P | 4,665 | 4,885 | — |
| 451 | spt phtn 4P | 4,845 | 4,885 | — |

| 1930 Engines | bore × stroke | bhp | availability |
|---|---|---|---|
| I-8, 320.0 | 3.19 × 5.00 | 90 | S-726, 733 |
| I-8, 384.8 | 3.50 × 5.00 | 106 | S-740, 745 |
| I-8, 384.8 | 3.50 × 5.00 | 125/145 | S-734 |

### 1931

| 826 Eight (wb 127.5) | | Wght | Price | Prod |
|---|---|---|---|---|
| 463 | sdn 4d 5P | 4,479 | 2,385 | 6,009 |
| **833 Eight (wb 134.5)—6,096 built** | | | | |
| 460 | touring 7P | 4,256 | 2,525 | — |
| 461 | phtn 4P | 4,185 | 2,425 | — |
| 462 | rdstr 2-4P | 4,140 | 2,425 | — |
| 464 | sdn 7P | 4,665 | 2,785 | — |
| 465 | sdn limo 7P | 4,695 | 2,885 | — |
| 466 | club sdn 5P | 4,488 | 2,675 | — |
| 467 | cpe 5P | 4,308 | 2,675 | — |
| 468 | cpe 2-4P | 4,360 | 2,525 | — |
| 469 | conv cpe 2-4P | 4,290 | 2,550 | — |
| 481 | spt phtn 4P | 4,285 | 2,725 | — |
| 483 | conv sdn 5P | 4,555 | 3,465 | — |
| *Individual custom:* | | | | |
| 1879 | Dietrich conv victoria 4P | 4,186 | 4,275 | — |
| 1881 | Dietrich conv sdn 4P | 4,442 | 4,375 | — |
| 3000 | A/W cab 7P | 4,684 | 4,850 | — |
| 3001 | A/W landaulet 7P | 4,684 | 5,050 | — |
| 3002 | A/W town car 7P | 4,744 | 4,975 | — |
| 3003 | A/W landaulet town car 7P | 4,744 | 5,175 | — |
| 3004 | sdn cab limo 6P | 4,485 | 4,490 | — |
| 3008 | A/W spt cab 7P | 4,614 | 4,850 | — |
| 3009 | A/W spt landaulet 7P | 4,614 | 5,050 | — |
| **840 Custom Eight (wb 140.5)—2,035 built** | | | | |
| 470 | touring 7P | 4,507 | 3,595 | — |
| 471 | phtn 4P | 4,439 | 3,490 | — |
| 472 | rdstr 2-4P | 4,383 | 3,490 | — |
| 473 | sdn 4d 5P | 4,955 | 3,795 | — |
| 476 | club sdn 5P | 4,720 | 3,950 | — |
| 477 | cpe 5P | 4,673 | 3,850 | — |
| 478 | cpe 2-4P | 4,592 | 3,545 | — |
| 479 | conv cpe 2-4P | 4,523 | 3,595 | — |
| 491 | spt phtn 4P | 4,535 | 3,790 | — |
| *Individual custom:* | | | | |
| 1879 | Dietrich conv victoria 4P | 4,418 | 5,175 | — |
| 1881 | Dietrich conv sdn 4P | 4,674 | 5,275 | — |
| 3000 | A/W cab 7P | 4,916 | 5,750 | — |
| 3001 | A/W landaulet 7P | 4,976 | 5,950 | — |
| 3002 | A/W town car 7P | 4,976 | 5,875 | — |
| 3003 | A/W landaulet town car 7P | 4,976 | 6,075 | — |
| 3008 | A/W spt cab 7P | 4,846 | 5,750 | — |
| 3009 | A/W spt landaulet 7P | 4,846 | 5,950 | — |
| **845 DeLuxe Eight (wb 145.5)—1,310 built** | | | | |
| 474 | sdn 7P | 5,010 | 4,150 | — |
| 475 | sdn limo 7P | 5,080 | 4,285 | — |

| 1931 Engines | bore × stroke | bhp | availability |
|---|---|---|---|
| I-8, 320.8 | 3.19 × 5.00 | 100 | S-826, 833 |
| I-8, 384.8 | 3.50 × 5.00 | 120 | S-840, 845 |

## 1932

### 900 Light Eight (wb 127.8)

| | | Wght | Price | Prod |
|---|---|---|---|---|
| 553 | sdn 4d | 4,115 | 1,895 | 4,850* |
| 558 | cpe 2-4P | 3,990 | 1,940 | 510* |
| 559 | cpe-rdstr 2-4P | 3,930 | 1,940 | 1,060* |
| 563 | cpe-sdn 5P | 4,060 | 1,940 | 330* |

### 901 Eight (wb 129.5)

| | | | | |
|---|---|---|---|---|
| 503 | sdn 4d 5P | 4,570 | 2,485 | 3,922 |

### 902 Eight (wb 136.5)—3,737 built

| | | | | |
|---|---|---|---|---|
| 500 | touring 7P | 4,345 | 2,775 | — |
| 501 | phtn 4P | 4,300 | 2,650 | — |
| 504 | sdn 7P | 4,735 | 2,885 | — |
| 505 | sdn limo 7P | 4,770 | 2,985 | — |
| 506 | club sdn 5P | 4,555 | 2,775 | — |
| 507 | cpe 5P | 4,505 | 2,795 | — |
| 508 | cpe 2-4P | 4,475 | 2,675 | — |
| 509 | cpe rdstr 2-4P | 4,420 | 2,650 | — |
| 521 | spt phtn 5P | 4,400 | 2,950 | — |
| 523 | conv sdn 5P | 4,573 | 3,445 | — |
| 527 | conv victoria 5P | 4,317 | 3,395 | — |
| 543 | sdn 4d 5P | 4,590 | 3,685 | — |

### 903 DeLuxe Eight (wb 142.5)—955 built

| | | | | |
|---|---|---|---|---|
| 510 | touring 7P | 4,760 | 3,795 | — |
| 511 | phtn 4P | 4,715 | 3,690 | — |
| 513 | sdn 4d 5P | 5,045 | 3,845 | — |
| 516 | club sdn 5P | 5,000 | 3,890 | — |
| 517 | cpe 5P | 4,985 | 3,850 | — |
| 518 | cpe 2-4P | 4,890 | 3,725 | — |
| 519 | cpe rdstr 2-4P | 4,825 | 3,750 | — |
| 531 | spt phtn 4P | 4,795 | 3,990 | — |
| 533 | conv sdn 5P | 4,985 | 4,550 | — |
| 537 | conv victoria 5P | 4,727 | 4,495 | — |

### 904 DeLuxe Eight (wb 147.5)—700 built

| | | | | |
|---|---|---|---|---|
| 514 | sdn 7P | 5,195 | 4,150 | — |
| 515 | sdn limo 7P | 5,240 | 4,285 | — |
| | *Individual custom:* | | | |
| 2060 | Dietrich stationary cpe 2-4P | 5,000 | 5,900 | — |
| 2069 | Dietrich spt phtn 4P | 4,800 | 5,800 | — |
| 2070 | Dietrich conv sdn 5P | 5,100 | 6,250 | — |
| 2071 | Dietrich conv cpe 2-4P | 4,965 | 6,050 | — |
| 2072 | Dietrich conv victoria 4P | 4,815 | 6,150 | — |
| 4000 | A/W cab 7P | 5,250 | 6,850 | — |
| 4001 | A/W landaulet 7P | 5,250 | 7,250 | — |
| 4002 | A/W town car 7P | 5,310 | 6,850 | — |
| 4003 | A/W landaulet town car 7P | 5,310 | 7,250 | — |
| 4004 | limo sdn cabriolet 6P | 5,050 | 6,850 | — |
| 4005 | spt sdn 4d 5P | 5,030 | 6,850 | — |
| 4006 | A/W brougham 7P | 5,293 | 6,850 | — |
| 4007 | Dietrich limousine sdn 6P | 5,075 | 6,850 | — |
| 4008 | A/W spt cab 7P | 5,180 | 6,850 | — |
| 4009 | A/W spt landaulet 7P | 5,180 | 7,250 | — |

### 905 Twin Six (wb 142.5)—311 built

| | | | | |
|---|---|---|---|---|
| 570 | touring 7P | 5,315 | 3,895 | — |
| 571 | phtn 4P | 5,275 | 3,790 | — |
| 573 | sdn 4d 5P | 5,635 | 3,745 | — |
| 576 | club sdn 5P | 5,585 | 3,895 | — |
| 577 | cpe 5P | 5,485 | 3,850 | — |
| 578 | cpe 2-4P | 5,425 | 3,650 | — |
| 579 | cpe rdstr 2-4P | 5,350 | 3,750 | — |
| 581 | spt phtn 4P | 5,375 | 4,090 | — |
| 583 | conv sdn 5P | 5,255 | 4,395 | — |
| 587 | conv victoria 5P | 5,180 | 4,325 | — |

### 906 Twin Six (wb 147.5)—238 blt

| | | Wght | Price | Prod |
|---|---|---|---|---|
| 574 | sdn 7P | 5,765 | 3,995 | — |
| 575 | sdn limo 7P | 5,830 | 4,195 | — |
| | *Individual custom:* | | | |
| 2068 | Dietrich cpe 2-4P | 5,180 | 6,600 | — |
| 2069 | Dietrich spt phtn 4P | 4,980 | 6,500 | — |
| 2070 | Dietrich conv sdn 5P | 5,280 | 6,950 | — |
| 2071 | Dietrich conv cpe 2-4P | 5,145 | 6,750 | — |
| 2072 | Dietrich conv victoria 4P | 4,995 | 6,850 | — |
| 4000 | A/W cabriolet 7P | 5,430 | 7,550 | — |
| 4001 | A/W landaulet 7P | 5,430 | 7,950 | — |
| 4002 | A/W town car 7P | 5,490 | 7,550 | — |
| 4003 | A/W town car landaulet 7P | 5,490 | 7,950 | — |

* Estimates based on serial number analysis by Jack Triplett (*The Packard Cormorant*, Spring 1979).

### 1932 Engines

| | bore × stroke | bhp | availability |
|---|---|---|---|
| I-8, 320.0 | 3.19 × 5.00 | 110 | S-900, 901, 902 |
| I-8, 384.8 | 3.50 × 5.00 | 135 | S-903, 904 |
| V-12, 445.5 | 3.44 × 4.00 | 160 | S-905, 906 |

## 1933

### 1001 Eight (wb 127.5)

| | | Wght | Price | Prod |
|---|---|---|---|---|
| 602 | cpe sdn 5P | 4,245 | 2,190 | 73* |
| 603 | sdn 4d 5P | 4,335 | 2,150 | 1,465* |
| 608 | cpe 2-4P | 4,200 | 2,160 | 120* |
| 609 | cpe rdstr 2-4P | 4,150 | 2,250 | 215* |
| — | chassis | — | — | 9* |

### 1002 Eight (wb 136.0)—1,099 built

| | | | | |
|---|---|---|---|---|
| 610 | touring 7P | 4,275 | 2,390 | — |
| 611 | phtn 5P | 4,270 | 2,370 | — |
| 613 | sdn 4d 5P | 4,590 | 2,385 | — |
| 614 | sdn 7P | 4,640 | 2,455 | — |
| 615 | limo 7P | 4,725 | 2,550 | — |
| 616 | club sdn 5P | 4,545 | 2,390 | — |
| 617 | cpe 5P | 4,500 | 2,440 | — |
| 618 | cpe 2-4P | 4,455 | 2,350 | — |
| 623 | conv sdn 5P | 4,515 | 2,890 | — |
| 627 | conv victoria 5P | 4,540 | 2,780 | — |
| 5613 | formal sdn 4d 5P | 4,900 | 3,085 | — |

### 1003 Super Eight (wb 135.0)

| | | | | |
|---|---|---|---|---|
| 653 | sdn 4d 5P | 4,815 | 2,750 | 512 |

### 1004 Super Eight (wb 142.0)—788 built

| | | | | |
|---|---|---|---|---|
| 650 | touring 7P | 4,610 | 2,980 | — |
| 651 | phtn 5P | 4,490 | 2,890 | — |
| 654 | sdn 7P | 4,965 | 3,090 | — |
| 655 | limo 7P | 5,025 | 3,280 | — |
| 656 | club sdn 5P | 4,795 | 2,975 | — |
| 657 | cpe 5P | 4,780 | 2,980 | — |
| 658 | cpe 2-4P | 4,670 | 2,780 | — |
| 659 | cpe rdstr 2-4P | 4,625 | 2,870 | — |
| 661 | spt phtn 2-4P | 4,690 | 3,150 | — |
| 663 | conv sdn 5P | 4,840 | 3,590 | — |
| 667 | conv victoria 5P | 4,795 | 3,440 | — |
| 673 | formal sdn 4d 5P | 5,155 | 3,600 | — |

### 1005 Twelve (wb 142.0)—244 built

| | | | | |
|---|---|---|---|---|
| 631 | phtn 5P | 5,095 | 3,790 | — |
| 633 | sdn 4d 5P | 5,385 | 3,860 | — |
| 636 | club sdn 5P | 5,400 | 3,880 | — |
| 637 | cpe 5P | 5,300 | 3,890 | — |
| 638 | cpe 2-4P | 5,255 | 3,720 | — |
| 639 | cpe rdstr 2-4P | 5,160 | 3,850 | — |
| 641 | spt phtn 5P | 5,175 | 4,090 | — |
| 643 | conv sdn 5P | 5,405 | 4,650 | — |

# Packard

| 1005 Twelve (wb 142.0) | | Wght | Price | Prod |
|---|---|---|---|---|
| 647 | conv victoria 5P | 5,225 | 4,490 | — |
| 5633 | formal sdn 5P | 5,690 | 4,560 | — |
| **1006 Twelve (wb 147.0)—276 built** | | | | |
| 634 | sdn 7P | 5,600 | 4,085 | — |
| 635 | limo 7P | 5,650 | 4,285 | — |
| *Individual custom:* | | | | |
| 3068 | Dietrich stationary cpe 2-4P | 5,360 | 6,000 | — |
| 3069 | Dietrich spt phtn 4P | 5,160 | 5,875 | — |
| 3070 | Dietrich conv sdn 5P | 5,460 | 6,570 | — |
| 3071 | Dietrich conv runabout 2-4P | 5,325 | 6,085 | — |
| 3072 | Dietrich conv victoria 4P | 5,175 | 6,070 | — |
| 3182 | Dietrich form sdn 7P | 5,735 | 7,000 | — |
| 758 | LeBaron A/W cab 7P | 5,610 | 7,000 | — |
| 759 | LeBaron A/W town car 7P | 5,670 | 7,000 | — |
| 4000 | A/W cab 7P | 5,650 | 6,030 | — |
| 4001 | A/W landaulet 7P | 5,650 | 6,250 | — |
| 4002 | A/W town car 7P | 5,610 | 6,080 | — |
| 4003 | landaulet town car 7P | 5,610 | 6,250 | — |
| 4004 | landaulet limo 7P | 5,650 | 6,000 | — |
| 4005 | spt sdn 4d 5P | 5,330 | 6,000 | — |
| 4007 | limo 7P | 5,650 | 6,045 | — |

* Estimate based on serial number analysis by Jack Triplett (*The Packard Cormorant*, Spring 1979).

| 1933 Engines | bore × stroke | bhp | availability |
|---|---|---|---|
| I-8, 320.0 | 3.19 × 5.00 | 120 | S-1001, 1002 |
| I-8, 384.8 | 3.50 × 5.00 | 145 | S-1003, 1004 |
| V-12, 445.5 | 3.44 × 4.00 | 160 | S-1005, 1006 |

## 1934

| 1100 Eight (wb 129.0)* | | Wght | Price | Prod |
|---|---|---|---|---|
| 703 | sdn 4d 5P | 4,640 | 2,350 | — |
| **1101 Eight (wb 136.0)*** | | | | |
| 710 | touring 7P | 4,400 | 2,590 | — |
| 711 | phtn 4P | 4,359 | 2,570 | — |
| 712 | formal sdn 5P | 4,760 | 3,285 | — |
| 713 | sdn 4d 5P | 4,660 | 2,585 | — |
| 716 | club sdn 5P | 4,730 | 2,670 | — |
| 717 | cpe 5P | 4,580 | 2,640 | — |
| 718 | cpe 2-4P | 4,580 | 2,640 | — |
| 719 | cpe rdstr 2-4P | 4,430 | 2,580 | — |
| 721 | spt phtn 4P | 4,430 | 2,830 | — |
| 723 | conv sdn 5P | 4,680 | 3,090 | — |
| 727 | conv victoria 5P | 4,710 | 2,980 | — |
| **1102 Eight (wb 141.0)*** | | | | |
| 714 | sdn 7P | 4,945 | 2,655 | — |
| 715 | limo sdn 7P | 5,000 | 2,790 | — |
| **1103 Super Eight (wb 135.0)** ** | | | | |
| 753 | sdn 4d 5P | 4,890 | 2,950 | — |
| **1104 Super Eight (wb 142.0)** ** | | | | |
| 750 | touring 7P | 4,720 | 3,180 | — |
| 751 | phtn 4P | 4,645 | 3,090 | — |
| 752 | formal sdn 5P | 5,010 | 3,800 | — |
| 756 | club sdn 5P | 4,985 | 3,255 | — |
| 757 | cpe 5P | 4,885 | 3,180 | — |
| 758 | cpe 2-4P | 4,800 | 2,980 | — |
| 759 | cpe rdstr 2-4P | 4,680 | 3,070 | — |
| 761 | spt phtn 4P | 4,740 | 3,350 | — |
| 763 | conv sdn 5P | 4,930 | 3,790 | — |
| 767 | conv victoria 5P | 4,875 | 3,640 | — |
| 773 | sdn 4d 5P | 4,910 | 3,200 | — |

| 1105 Super Eight (wb 147.0)** | | Wght | Price | Prod |
|---|---|---|---|---|
| 754 | sdn 7P | 5,245 | 3,290 | — |
| 755 | sdn limo 7P | 5,275 | 3,480 | — |
| *Individual custom:* | | | | |
| 280 | LeBaron phtn 4P | 4,755 | 7,065 | — |
| 858 | LeBaron A/W cab 7P | 5,205 | 5,450 | — |
| 859 | LeBaron A/W town car 7P | 5,265 | 5,450 | — |
| 4068 | Dietrich stationary cpe 2-4P | 4,955 | 5,445 | — |
| 4070 | Dietrich conv sdn 5P | 5,055 | 5,800 | — |
| 4071 | Dietrich runabout conv 2-4P | 4,920 | 5,365 | — |
| 4072 | Dietrich conv victoria 4P | 4,770 | 5,345 | — |
| 4182 | Dietrich spt sdn 5P | 5,380 | 6,295 | — |
| **1106 Twelve (wb 135.0)**** | | | | |
| 275 | LeBaron spdstr runabout 2P | 5,400 | 7,746 | |
| **1107 Twelve (wb 142.0)**** | | | | |
| 730 | touring 7P | 5,415 | 3,980 | — |
| 731 | phtn 4P | 5,325 | 3,890 | — |
| 732 | formal sdn 5P | 5,630 | 4,660 | — |
| 733 | sdn 4d 5P | 5,530 | 3,960 | — |
| 736 | club sdn 5P | 5,660 | 4,060 | — |
| 737 | cpe 5P | 5,530 | 3,990 | — |
| 738 | cpe 2-4P | 5,585 | 3,820 | — |
| 739 | cpe rdstr 2-4P | 5,330 | 3,850 | — |
| 741 | spt phtn 4P | 5,400 | 4,190 | — |
| 743 | conv sdn 5P | 5,470 | 4,750 | — |
| 747 | conv victoria 5P | 5,440 | 4,590 | — |
| **1108 Twelve (wb 147.0)**** | | | | |
| 734 | sdn 7P | 5,700 | 4,185 | — |
| 735 | sdn limo 7P | 5,750 | 4,385 | — |
| *Individual custom:* | | | | |
| 280 | LeBaron spt phtn 4P | 5,130 | 7,065 | — |
| 858 | Lebaron A/W cab 7P | 5,655 | 6,155 | — |
| 859 | LeBaron A/W town car 7P | 5,655 | 6,155 | — |
| 4002 | Dietrich A/W town car 7P | 5,715 | 5,695 | — |
| 4068 | Dietrich stationary cpe 2-4P | 5,405 | 6,185 | — |
| 4069 | Dietrich spt phtn 4P | 5,400 | 5,180 | — |
| 4070 | Dietrich conv sdn 5P | 5,505 | 6,555 | — |
| 4071 | Dietrich conv runabout 2-4P | 5,370 | 6,100 | — |
| 4072 | Dietrich conv victoria 4P | 5,220 | 6,080 | — |
| 4182 | Dietrich spt sdn 5P | 5,130 | 7,060 | — |

*Total 1100/1101/1102 production: 5,120  **Total Super Eight production: 1,920
***Total Twelve production: 960

| 1934 Engines | bore × stroke | bhp | availability |
|---|---|---|---|
| I-8, 320.0 | 3.19 × 5.00 | 120 | S-Eight |
| I-8, 384.8 | 3.50 × 5.00 | 145 | S-Super Eight |
| V-12, 445.5 | 3.44 × 4.00 | 160 | S-Twelve |

## 1935

| 120A One Twenty (wb 120)—24,995 blt | | Wght | Price | Prod |
|---|---|---|---|---|
| 892 | touring sdn 4d | 3,550 | 1,095 | — |
| 893 | sdn 4d | 3,510 | 1,060 | — |
| 894 | touring cpe 5P | 3,455 | 1,025 | — |
| 895 | spt cpe 2-4P | 3,435 | 1,020 | — |
| 896 | club sdn 5P | 3,515 | 1,085 | — |
| 898 | bus cpe 2P | 3,400 | 980 | — |
| 899 | conv cpe 2-4P | 3,385 | 1,070 | — |
| **1200 Eight (wb 127.0)*** | | | | |
| 803 | sdn 4d | 4,780 | 2,385 | — |
| **1201 Eight (wb 134.0)*** | | | | |
| 195 | LeBaron A/W cab 7P | 5,185 | 5,240 | — |
| 807 | conv victoria 5P | 4,835 | 3,100 | — |
| 811 | phtn 5P | 4,475 | 2,670 | — |
| 812 | formal sdn 4d 5P | 5,035 | 3,285 | — |

# Packard

| 1201 Eight (wb 134.0)* | | Wght | Price | Prod |
|---|---|---|---|---|
| 813 | sdn 4d 5P | 4,935 | 2,585 | — |
| 816 | club sdn 5P | 4,845 | 2,580 | — |
| 817 | cpe 5P | 4,700 | 2,560 | — |
| 818 | cpe 2-4P | 4,625 | 2,475 | — |
| 819 | conv cpe 2-4P | 4,555 | 2,580 | — |
| **1202 Eight (wb 139.0)*** | | | | |
| 194 | LeBaron A/W town car 7P | 5,225 | 5,385 | — |
| 810 | touring 7P | 4,400 | 3,170 | — |
| 814 | comm sdn 8P | 4,985 | 2,630 | — |
| 815 | limo 7P | 5,125 | 2,890 | — |
| 815 | comm limo 8P | 5,150 | 2,765 | — |
| 863 | conv sdn 5P | 4,800 | 3,200 | — |
| **1203 Super Eight (wb 132.0)**** | | | | |
| 843 | sdn 4d | 4,985 | 2,990 | — |
| **1204 Super Eight (wb 139.0)**** | | | | |
| 195 | LeBaron A/W cab 7P | 5,300 | 5,670 | — |
| 841 | spt phtn 5P | 4,875 | 3,450 | — |
| 847 | conv victoria 5P | 5,000 | 3,760 | — |
| 851 | phtn 5P | 4,775 | 3,190 | — |
| 852 | formal sdn 5P | 5,150 | 3,800 | — |
| 856 | club sdn 5P | 5,100 | 3,170 | — |
| 857 | cpe 5P | 5,015 | 3,080 | — |
| 858 | cpe 2-4P | 4,920 | 2,880 | — |
| 859 | conv cpe 2-4P | 4,800 | 3,070 | — |
| **1205 Super Eight (wb 144.0)**** | | | | |
| 194 | LeBaron A/W town car 7P | 5,525 | 5,815 | — |
| 850 | touring 7P | 4,729 | 3,690 | — |
| 854 | sdn 7P | 5,375 | 3,390 | — |
| 854 | comm sdn 8P | 5,320 | 3,265 | — |
| 855 | limo 7P | 5,400 | 3,580 | — |
| 855 | comm limo 8P | 5,380 | 3,455 | — |
| 883 | conv sdn 5P | 5,050 | 3,910 | — |
| **1206 Twelve (wb 132.0)***** | | | | |

The "06" series of short-wheelbase Twelve sedans was omitted by Packard for this and subsequent years; there is some conjecture on whether minor production occurred, but this has not been confirmed to date.

| 1207 Twelve (wb 139.0)*** | | | | |
|---|---|---|---|---|
| 195 | LeBaron A/W cab 7P | 5,930 | 6,290 | — |
| 821 | spt phtn 5P | 5,550 | 4,290 | — |
| 827 | conv victoria 5P | 5,590 | 4,790 | — |
| 831 | phtn 5P | 5,470 | 3,990 | — |
| 832 | formal sdn 7P | 5,780 | 4,660 | — |
| 833 | sdn 5P | 5,700 | 3,960 | — |
| 836 | club sdn 5P | 5,800 | 4,060 | — |
| 837 | cpe 5P | 5,680 | 3,990 | — |
| 838 | cpe 2-4P | 5,635 | 3,820 | — |
| 839 | conv cpe 2-4P | 5,480 | 3,850 | — |
| **1208 Twelve (wb 144.0)***** | | | | |
| 194 | LeBaron A/W town car 7P | 5,950 | 6,535 | — |
| 830 | touring 7P | 5,415 | 4,490 | — |
| 834 | sdn 7P | 5,800 | 4,285 | — |
| 835 | limo 7P | 5,900 | 4,485 | — |
| 873 | conv sdn 5P | 5,620 | 4,950 | — |

*Total Eight production: 4,781  **Total Super Eight production: 1,392
***Total Twelve production: 721

| 1935 Engines | bore × stroke | bhp | availability |
|---|---|---|---|
| I-8, 257.2 | 3.25 × 3.88 | 110 | S-120A |
| I-8, 320.0 | 3.19 × 5.00 | 130 | S-1200, 1201, 1202 |
| I-8, 384.8 | 3.50 × 5.00 | 150 | S-1203, 1204, 1205 |
| V-12, 473.0 | 3.44 × 4.25 | 175 | S-1207, 1208 |

## 1936

| 120B One Twenty (wb 120)—55,042 blt | | Wght | Price | Prod |
|---|---|---|---|---|
| 992 | touring sdn 5P | 3,560 | 1,115 | — |
| 993 | sdn 4d 5P | 3,505 | 1,075 | — |
| 994 | touring cpe 5P | 3,575 | 1,040 | — |
| 995 | spt cpe 2-4P | 3,455 | 1,030 | — |
| 996 | club sdn 5P | 3,495 | 1,090 | — |
| 997 | conv sdn 5P | 3,660 | 1,395 | — |
| 998 | bus cpe 2P | 3,380 | 990 | — |
| 999 | conv cpe 2-4P | 3,525 | 1,110 | — |
| **1400 Eight (wb 127.0)*** | | | | |
| 903 | sdn 4d 5P | 4,815 | 2,385 | — |
| **1401 Eight (wb 134.0)*** | | | | |
| 294 | LeBaron A/W cab 7P | 5,185 | 5,240 | — |
| 907 | conv victoria 5P | 4,810 | 3,200 | — |
| 911 | phtn 4P | 4,890 | 3,020 | — |
| 912 | formal sdn 7P | 5,030 | 3,285 | — |
| 913 | sdn 4d 5P | 4,978 | 2,585 | — |
| 916 | club sdn 5P | 4,815 | 2,580 | — |
| 917 | cpe 5P | 4,745 | 2,560 | — |
| 918 | cpe 2-4P | 4,735 | 2,470 | — |
| 919 | cpe rdstr 2-4P | 4,740 | 2,730 | — |
| **1402 Eight (wb 139.0)*** | | | | |
| 295 | LeBaron A/W town car 7P | 5,225 | 5,385 | — |
| 910 | touring 7P | 5,060 | 3,270 | — |
| 914 | sdn 7P | 4,955 | 2,755 | — |
| 914 | bus sdn 8P | 4,985 | 2,630 | — |
| 915 | limo 7P | 5,045 | 2,890 | — |
| 915 | bus limo 8P | 5,150 | 2,765 | — |
| 963 | conv sdn 5P | 5,140 | 3,400 | — |
| **1403 Super Eight (wb 132.0)**** | | | | |
| 943 | sdn 4d | 5,080 | 2,990 | — |
| **1404 Super Eight (wb 139.0)**** | | | | |
| 294 | LeBaron A/W cab 7P | 5,300 | 5,670 | — |
| 941 | spt phtn 5P | 5,200 | 3,650 | — |
| 947 | conv victoria 5P | 5,122 | 3,860 | — |
| 951 | phtn 5P | 5,080 | 3,390 | — |
| 952 | formal sdn 5P | 5,245 | 3,800 | — |
| 956 | club sdn 5P | 5,178 | 3,170 | — |
| 957 | cpe 5P | 5,010 | 3,080 | — |
| 958 | cpe 2-4P | 4,933 | 2,880 | — |
| 959 | cpe rdstr 2-4P | 4,993 | 3,070 | — |
| **1405 Super Eight (wb 144.0)**** | | | | |
| 295 | LeBaron A/W town car 7P | 5,525 | 5,815 | — |
| 950 | touring 7P | 5,200 | 3,690 | — |
| 954 | sdn 7P | 5,300 | 3,390 | — |
| 954 | bus sdn 8P | 5,320 | 3,265 | — |
| 955 | limo 7P | 5,380 | 3,580 | — |
| 955 | bus limo 8P | 5,380 | 3,455 | — |
| 983 | conv sdn 5P | 5,390 | 4,010 | — |
| **1407 Twelve (wb 139.0)***** | | | | |
| 294 | LeBaron A/W cab 7P | 5,900 | 6,290 | — |
| 921 | spt phtn 5P | 5,785 | 4,490 | — |
| 927 | conv victoria 5P | 5,585 | 4,890 | — |
| 931 | phtn 5P | 5,480 | 4,190 | — |
| 932 | formal sdn 5P | 5,735 | 4,660 | — |
| 933 | sdn 5P | 5,695 | 3,960 | — |
| 936 | clb sdn 5P | 5,640 | 4,060 | — |
| 937 | cpe 5P | 5,495 | 3,990 | — |
| 938 | cpe 2-4P | 5,495 | 3,820 | — |
| 939 | cpe rdstr 2-4P | 5,495 | 3,850 | — |

# Packard

| 1408 Twelve (wb 144.0) | | Wght | Price | Prod |
|---|---|---|---|---|
| 295 | LeBaron A/W town car 7P | 5,950 | 6,435 | — |
| 934 | sdn 7P | 5,790 | 4,285 | — |
| 935 | limo 7P | 5,890 | 4,483 | — |
| 930 | touring 7P | 5,460 | 4,490 | — |
| 973 | conv sdn 5P | 5,945 | 5,050 | — |

*Total Eight production: 3,973  **Total Super Eight production: 1,330
***Total Twelve production: 682

| 1936 Engines | bore × stroke | bhp | availability |
|---|---|---|---|
| I-8, 282.0 | 3.25 × 4.25 | 120 | S-120B |
| I-8, 320.0 | 3.19 × 5.00 | 130 | S-1400, 1401, 1402 |
| I-8, 384.8 | 3.50 × 5.00 | 150 | S-1403, 1404, 1405 |
| V-12, 473.0 | 3.44 × 4.25 | 175 | S-1407, 1408 |

## 1937

| 115C Six (wb 115.0)—65,400 built | | Wght | Price | Prod |
|---|---|---|---|---|
| 1060 | wgn 4d 8P | 3,380 | 1,295 | — |
| 1082 | touring sdn 5P | 3,310 | 910 | — |
| 1083 | sdn 4d 5P | 3,265 | 895 | — |
| 1084 | touring cpe 5P | 3,235 | 860 | — |
| 1085 | spt cpe 2-4P | 3,215 | 840 | — |
| 1086 | club sdn 5P | 3,275 | 900 | — |
| 1088 | bus cpe 2P | 3,140 | 795 | — |
| 1089 | conv cpe 2-4P | 3,285 | 910 | — |

| 120C/CD One Twenty (wb 120.0)* | | | | |
|---|---|---|---|---|
| 1070 | wgn 4d 8P | 3,590 | 1,485 | — |
| 1092 | touring sdn 5P | 3,520 | 1,060 | — |
| 1093 | sdn 4d 5P | 3,465 | 1,045 | — |
| 1094 | touring cpe 5P | 3,435 | 1,010 | — |
| 1095 | spt cpe 2-4P | 3,415 | 990 | — |
| 1096 | club sdn 5P | 3,455 | 1,050 | — |
| 1097 | conv sdn 5P | 3,630 | 1,355 | — |
| 1098 | bus cpe 2P | 3,340 | 945 | — |
| 1099 | conv cpe 2-4P | 3,485 | 1,060 | — |
| 1094CD | touring cpe 5P | 3,465 | 1,220 | — |
| 1096CD | club sdn 5P | 3,485 | 1,260 | — |
| 1098CD | touring sdn 4d | 3,550 | 1,270 | — |

| 138CD One Twenty (wb 138.0)* | | | | |
|---|---|---|---|---|
| 1090CD | touring limo 7P | 3,900 | 1,840 | — |
| 1091CD | touring sdn 7P | 3,835 | 1,690 | — |

| 1500 Super Eight (wb 127.0)** | | | | |
|---|---|---|---|---|
| 1003 | touring sdn 5P | 4,530 | 2,335 | — |

| 1501 Super Eight (wb 134.0)** | | | | |
|---|---|---|---|---|
| L394 | LeBaron A/W cab 7P | 4,965 | 4,850 | — |
| 1007 | victoria 5P | 4,650 | 3,150 | — |
| 1012 | formal sdn 5P | 4,795 | 3,235 | — |
| 1013 | touring sdn 5P | 4,670 | 2,535 | — |
| 1016 | club sdn 5P | 4,600 | 2,530 | — |
| 1017 | cpe 5P | 4,595 | 2,510 | — |
| 1018 | cpe 2-4P | 4,585 | 2,420 | — |
| 1019 | conv cpe 2-4P | 4,580 | 2,680 | — |

| 1502 Super Eight (wb 139.0)** | | | | |
|---|---|---|---|---|
| L395 | LeBaron A/W town car 7P | 5,360 | 4,990 | — |
| 1014 | touring sdn 7P | 4,700 | 2,705 | — |
| 1014B | bus sdn 8P | 4,755 | 2,580 | — |
| 1015 | touring limo 7P | 4,815 | 2,840 | — |
| 1015B | bus limo 8P | 4,925 | 2,715 | — |
| 1063 | conv sdn 5P | 4,945 | 3,350 | — |

| 1506 Twelve (wb 132.0)*** | | | | |
|---|---|---|---|---|
| 1023 | touring sdn 5P | 5,335 | 3,490 | — |

| 1507 Twelve (wb 139.0)*** | | | | |
|---|---|---|---|---|
| L394 | LeBaron A/W cab 7P | 5,740 | 5,700 | — |
| 1027 | victoria 5P | 5,345 | 4,490 | — |
| 1032 | formal sdn 5P | 5,550 | 4,260 | — |
| 1033 | touring sdn 4d | 5,525 | 3,560 | — |
| 1036 | club sdn 5P | 5,520 | 3,660 | — |
| 1037 | cpe 5P | 5,415 | 3,590 | — |
| 1038 | cpe 2-4P | 5,255 | 3,420 | — |
| 1039 | conv cpe 2-4P | 5,255 | 3,450 | — |

| 1508 Twelve (wb 144.0)*** | | | | |
|---|---|---|---|---|
| L395 | LeBaron A/W town car 7P | 5,790 | 5,900 | — |
| 1034 | touring sdn 7P | 5,600 | 3,885 | — |
| 1035 | touring limo 7P | 5,660 | 4,085 | — |
| 1073 | conv sdn 5P | 5,680 | 4,650 | — |

*Total One Twenty production: 50,100  **Total Super Eight production: 5,793
***Total Twelve production: 1,300

| 1937 Engines | bore × stroke | bhp | availability |
|---|---|---|---|
| I-6, 237.0 | 3.44 × 4.25 | 100 | S-Six |
| I-8, 282.0 | 3.25 × 4.25 | 120 | S-One Twenty |
| I-8, 320.0 | 3.19 × 5.00 | 135 | S-Super Eight |
| V-12, 473.0 | 3.44 × 4.25 | 175 | S-Twelve |

## 1938

| 1600 Six (wb 122.0)—30,050 built | | Wght | Price | Prod |
|---|---|---|---|---|
| 1182 | touring sdn 4d | 3,525 | 1,175 | — |
| 1184 | touring sdn 2d | 3,475 | 1,145 | — |
| 1185 | club cpe 2-4P | 3,425 | 1,120 | — |
| 1188 | bus cpe 2P | 3,450 | 1,075 | — |
| 1189 | conv cpe 2-4P | 3,500 | 1,235 | — |

| 1601 Eight (wb 127.0)* | | | | |
|---|---|---|---|---|
| 1192 | touring sdn 4d | 3,650 | 1,525 | — |
| 1194 | touring sdn 2d | 3,600 | 1,295 | — |
| 1195 | club cpe 2-4P | 3,550 | 1,270 | — |
| 1197 | conv sdn 5P | 3,775 | 1,650 | — |
| 1198 | bus cpe 2P | 3,570 | 1,225 | — |
| 1199 | conv cpe 2-4P | 3,625 | 1,365 | — |
| 1172 | DeLuxe touring sdn 4d | 3,685 | 1,540 | — |

| 1601 Eight (wb 139.0)* | | | | |
|---|---|---|---|---|
| 1665 | Rollston A/W cabriolet 7P | — | 4,810 | — |
| 1668 | Rollston A/W brougham 4P | — | 5,100 | — |
| 1669 | Rollston A/W town car 7P | — | 4,885 | — |

| 1602 Eight (wb 148.0)* | | | | |
|---|---|---|---|---|
| 1190 | limo 7P | 4,245 | 1,955 | — |
| 1191 | touring sdn 7P | 4,195 | 2,110 | — |

| 1603 Super Eight (wb 127.0)** | | | | |
|---|---|---|---|---|
| 1103 | touring sdn 4d | 4,530 | 2,790 | — |

| 1604 Super Eight (wb 134.0)** | | | | |
|---|---|---|---|---|
| 1107 | victoria 5P | 4,650 | 3,670 | — |
| 1112 | formal sdn 5P | 4,795 | 3,710 | — |
| 1113 | touring sdn 4d | 4,670 | 2,995 | — |
| 1116 | club sdn 5P | 4,600 | 2,990 | — |
| 1117 | cpe 5P | 4,595 | 2,965 | — |
| 1118 | cpe 2-4P | 4,585 | 2,925 | — |
| 1119 | conv cpe 4P | 4,580 | 3,210 | — |

| 1605 Super Eight (wb 139.0)** | | | | |
|---|---|---|---|---|
| 494 | Rollston A/W cab 7P | 4,945 | 5,790 | — |
| 495 | Rollston A/W town car 7P | 4,940 | 5,890 | — |
| 1114 | bus sdn 7P | 4,815 | 3,165 | — |
| 1115 | bus limo 7P | 4,815 | 3,305 | — |
| 1143 | conv sdn 5P | 4,945 | 3,970 | — |
| 3086 | Brunn touring cabriolet 7P | 4,990 | 7,475 | — |
| 3087 | Brunn A/W cabriolet 7P | 4,995 | 7,475 | — |

# Packard

| 1607 Twelve (wb 134.0)*** | | Wght | Price | Prod |
|---|---|---|---|---|
| 1127 | victoria 5P | 5,345 | 5,230 | — |
| 1132 | formal sdn 5P | 5,550 | 4,865 | — |
| 1133 | touring sdn 4d | 5,525 | 4,155 | — |
| 1136 | club sdn 5P | 5,520 | 4,255 | — |
| 1137 | cpe 5P | 5,415 | 4,185 | — |
| 1138 | cpe 2-4P | 5,255 | 4,135 | — |
| 1139 | conv cpe 2-4P | 5,255 | 4,370 | — |
| **1608 Twelve (wb 139.0)*** | | | | |
| 494 | Rollston A/W cab 7P | 5,740 | 6,730 | — |
| 495 | Rollston A/W town car 7P | 5,735 | 6,880 | — |
| 1134 | touring sdn 7P | 5,600 | 4,485 | — |
| 1135 | touring limo 7P | 5,600 | 4,485 | — |
| 1153 | conv sdn 5P | 5,680 | 5,390 | — |
| 3086 | Brunn touring cabriolet 7P | 5,725 | 8,510 | — |
| 3087 | Brunn A/W cabriolet 7P | 5,730 | 8,510 | — |

*Total Eight production: 22,624  **Total Super Eight production: 2,478
***Total Twelve production: 566

| 1938 Engines | bore × stroke | bhp | availability |
|---|---|---|---|
| I-6, 245.0 | 3.50 × 4.25 | 100 | S-Six |
| I-8, 282.0 | 3.25 × 4.25 | 120 | S-Eight |
| I-8, 320.0 | 3.19 × 5.00 | 130 | S-Super Eight |
| V-12, 473.0 | 3.44 × 4.25 | 175 | S-Twelve |

## 1939

| 1700 Six (wb 122.0)—24,350 built | | Wght | Price | Prod |
|---|---|---|---|---|
| 1282 | touring sdn 4d | 3,400 | 1,095 | — |
| 1283 | wgn 4d 7P | 3,652 | 1,404 | — |
| 1284 | touring sdn 2d | 3,390 | 1,065 | — |
| 1285 | club cpe 2-4P | 3,365 | 1,045 | — |
| 1288 | bus cpe 2P | 3,295 | 1,000 | — |
| 1289 | conv cpe 2-4P | 3,385 | 1,092 | — |
| **1701 One Twenty (wb 127.0)*** | | | | |
| 1292 | touring sdn 4d | 3,605 | 1,295 | — |
| 1293 | wgn 4d 7P | 3,850 | 1,636 | — |
| 1294 | touring sdn 2d | 3,595 | 1,265 | — |
| 1295 | club cpe 2-4P | 3,535 | 1,245 | — |
| 1297 | conv sdn 5P | 3,780 | 1,700 | — |
| 1298 | bus cpe 2P | 3,490 | 1,200 | — |
| 1299 | conv cpe 2-4P | 3,545 | 1,390 | — |
| **1702 One Twenty (wb 148.0)*** | | | | |
| 1290 | touring limo 7P | 4,185 | 1,955 | — |
| 1291 | touring sdn 7P | 4,100 | 1,805 | — |
| **1703 Super Eight (wb 127.0)** | | | | |
| 1272 | touring sdn 4d | 3,930 | 1,732 | — |
| 1275 | club cpe 2-4P | 3,860 | 1,650 | — |
| 1277 | conv sdn 5P | 4,005 | 2,130 | — |
| 1279 | conv cpe 2-4P | 3,870 | 1,875 | — |
| **1705 Super Eight (wb 148.0)** | | | | |
| 1270 | touring limo 7P | 4,510 | 2,294 | — |
| 1271 | touring sdn 7P | 4,425 | 2,156 | — |
| **1707 Twelve (wb 134.0)** | | | | |
| 594 | Rollston A/W cab 7P | 4,950 | 6,730 | — |
| 1227 | victoria 5P | 5,570 | 5,230 | — |
| 1232 | formal sdn 5P | 5,745 | 4,865 | — |
| 1233 | touring sdn 4d | 5,670 | 4,155 | — |
| 1236 | club cpe 5P | 5,590 | 4,255 | — |
| 1237 | cpe 5P | 5,425 | 4,185 | — |
| 1238 | cpe 2-4P | 5,400 | 4,185 | — |
| 1239 | conv cpe 2-4P | 5,540 | 4,375 | — |
| **1708 Twelve (wb 139.0)*** | | | | |
| 595 | Rollston A/W town car 7P | 5,075 | 6,880 | — |

| 1708 Twelve (wb 139.0)*** | | Wght | Price | Prod |
|---|---|---|---|---|
| 1234 | touring sdn 7P | 5,750 | 4,485 | — |
| 1235 | touring limo 7P | 5,825 | 4,690 | — |
| 1253 | conv sdn 5P | 5,890 | 5,395 | — |
| 4086 | Brunn touring cabriolet 5P | 5,845 | 8,355 | — |
| 4087 | Brunn A/W cabriolet 6P | 5,845 | 8,355 | — |

*Total One Twenty production: 17,647  **Total Super Eight production: 3,962
***Total Twelve production: 446

| 1939 Engines | bore × stroke | bhp | availability |
|---|---|---|---|
| I-6, 245.0 | 3.50 × 4.25 | 100 | S-Six |
| I-8, 282.0 | 3.25 × 4.25 | 120 | S-One Twenty |
| I-8, 320.0 | 3.19 × 5.00 | 130 | S-Super Eight |
| V-12, 473.0 | 3.44 × 4.25 | 175 | S-Twelve |

## 1940

| 1800 One Ten (wb 122)—62,300 built | | Wght | Price | Prod |
|---|---|---|---|---|
| 1382 | sdn 4d | 3,200 | 996 | — |
| 1383 | wgn 4d, 8P | 3,380 | 1,200 | — |
| 1384 | sdn 2d | 3,190 | 964 | — |
| 1385 | club cpe | 3,165 | 940 | — |
| 1388 | bus cpe | 3,120 | 867 | — |
| 1389 | conv cpe | 3,200 | 1,104 | — |
| **1801 One Twenty (wb 127.0)—28,138 built** | | | | |
| 700 | conv vic by Darrin | 3,826 | 3,819 | — |
| 1392 | sdn 4d | 3,520 | 1,166 | — |
| 1393 | wgn 4d, 8P | 3,590 | 1,404 | — |
| 1394 | sdn 2d | 3,510 | 1,135 | — |
| 1395 | club cpe | 3,450 | 1,111 | — |
| 1396 | club sdn | 3,520 | 1,239 | — |
| 1397 | conv sdn | 3,710 | 1,573 | — |
| 1398 | bus cpe | 3,340 | 1,038 | — |
| 1399 | conv cpe | 3,540 | 1,277 | — |
| DE 1392 | Deluxe sdn 4d | 3,495 | 1,246 | — |
| DE 1395 | Deluxe club cpe | 3,400 | 1,161 | — |
| DE 1396 | Deluxe club sdn | 3,480 | 1,314 | — |
| DE 1399 | Deluxe conv cpe | 3,470 | 1,318 | — |
| **1803 Super Eight One Sixty** (wb 127.0)—5,662 blt (includes all One Sixtys) | | | | |
| 1372 | sdn 4d | 3,855 | 1,655 | — |
| 1375 | club cpe | 3,760 | 1,614 | — |
| 1376 | club sdn | 3,855 | 1,740 | — |
| 1377 | conv sdn | 4,000 | 2,075 | — |
| 1378 | bus cpe | 3,735 | 1,524 | — |
| 1379 | conv cpe | 3,825 | 1,797 | — |
| **1804 Super Eight One Sixty (wb 138.0)** | | | | |
| 1362 | sdn 4d | 4,165 | 1,919 | — |
| **1805 Super Eight One Sixty (wb 148.0)** | | | | |
| 1370 | limo 7P | 4,500 | 2,179 | — |
| 1371 | sdn 4d, 7P | 4,425 | 2,051 | — |
| **1806 Custom Super Eight One Eighty** (wb 127.0)—1,900 built (includes all One Eightys) | | | | |
| 700 | conv vic by Darrin | 4,121 | 4,593 | — |
| 1356 | club sdn | 3,900 | 2,243 | — |
| **1807 Custom Super Eight One Eighty (wb 138.0)** | | | | |
| 694 | A/W cabriolet by Rollston | 4,050 | 4,473 | — |
| 710 | conv sdn by Darrin | 4,050 | 6,332 | — |
| 1332 | formal sdn | 4,210 | 2,855 | — |
| 1342 | sdn 4d | 4,210 | 2,422 | — |
| **1808 Custom Super Eight One Eighty (wb 148.0)** | | | | |
| 695 | A/W town car by Rollston | 4,175 | 4,599 | — |
| 1350 | limo 7P | 4,585 | 2,683 | — |
| 1351 | sdn 4d, 7P | 4,510 | 2,554 | — |

# Packard

| 1940 Engines | bore × stroke | bhp | availability |
|---|---|---|---|
| I-6, 245.3 | 3.50 × 4.25 | 100 | S-One Ten |
| I-8, 282.0 | 3.25 × 4.25 | 120 | S-One Twenty |
| I-8, 356.0 | 3.50 × 4.63 | 160 | S-Spr/Cust Spr Eghts |

## 1941

### 1900 One Ten (wb 122)—34,700 blt (est.)

| | | Wght | Price | Prod |
|---|---|---|---|---|
| 1482 | sdn 4d | 3,260 | 1,076 | — |
| 1483 | wgn 4d, 8P | 3,460 | 1,251 | — |
| 1484 | sdn 2d | 3,250 | 1,010 | — |
| 1485 | club cpe | 3,230 | 1,020 | — |
| 1488 | bus cpe | 3,190 | 927 | — |
| 1489 | conv cpe | 3,260 | 1,195 | — |
| 1463DE | Deluxe wgn 4d, 8P | 3,470 | 1,236 | — |
| 1482DE | Deluxe sdn 4d | 3,280 | 1,136 | — |
| 1484DE | Deluxe sdn 2d | 3,270 | 1,070 | — |
| 1485DE | Deluxe club cpe | 3,250 | 1,058 | — |
| 1489DE | Deluxe conv cpe | 3,280 | 1,229 | — |

### 1901 One Twenty (wb 127.0)—17,000 built (estimate)

| | | Wght | Price | Prod |
|---|---|---|---|---|
| 1473 | Deluxe wgn 4d, 8P | 3,730 | 1,541 | — |
| 1492 | sdn 4d | 3,535 | 1,291 | — |
| 1493 | wgn 4d, 8P | 3,720 | 1,466 | — |
| 1494 | sdn 2d | 3,525 | 1,260 | — |
| 1495 | club cpe | 3,470 | 1,235 | — |
| 1497 | conv sdn | 3,725 | 1,753 | — |
| 1498 | bus cpe | 3,360 | 1,142 | — |
| 1499 | conv cpe | 3,570 | 1,407 | — |

### 1951 Clipper (wb 127.0)

| | | Wght | Price | Prod |
|---|---|---|---|---|
| 1401 | sdn 4d | 3,725 | 1,420 | 16,600 |

### 1903 Super Eight One Sixty (wb 127.0)—3,525 built (includes all One Sixtys)

| | | Wght | Price | Prod |
|---|---|---|---|---|
| 1472 | sdn 4d | 3,995 | 1,795 | — |
| 1475 | club cpe | 3,900 | 1,754 | — |
| 1477 | conv sdn | 4,140 | 2,225 | — |
| 1478 | bus cpe | 3,875 | 1,639 | — |
| 1479 | conv cpe | 3,965 | 1,937 | — |
| 1477DE | Deluxe conv sdn | 4,160 | 2,450 | — |
| 1479DE | Deluxe conv cpe | 3,985 | 2,112 | — |

### 1904 Super Eight One Sixty (wb 138.0)

| | | Wght | Price | Prod |
|---|---|---|---|---|
| 1462 | sdn 4d | 4,305 | 2,054 | — |

### 1905 Super Eight One Sixty (wb 148.0)

| | | Wght | Price | Prod |
|---|---|---|---|---|
| 1470 | limo 7P | 4,570 | 2,334 | — |
| 1471 | sdn 4d 7P | 4,495 | 2,206 | — |

### 1906 Custom Super Eight One Eighty (wb 127.0)—930 built (includes all One Eightys)

| | | Wght | Price | Prod |
|---|---|---|---|---|
| 1429 | conv vic by Darrin | 4,040 | 4,595 | — |

### 1907 Custom Super Eight One Eighty (wb 138.0)

| | | Wght | Price | Prod |
|---|---|---|---|---|
| 794 | A/W cabriolet by Rollston | 4,075 | 4,695 | — |
| 1422 | spt sdn by Darrin | 4,490 | 4,795 | — |
| 1432 | form sdn | 4,350 | 3,090 | — |
| 1442 | sdn 4d | 4,350 | 2,632 | — |
| 1452 | Sprt Brougham by LeBaron | 4,450 | 3,545 | — |

### 1908 Custom Super Eight One Eighty (wb 148.0)

| | | Wght | Price | Prod |
|---|---|---|---|---|
| 795 | A/W town car by Rollston | 4,200 | 4,820 | — |
| 1420 | limo 7P by LeBaron | 4,850 | 5,595 | — |
| 1421 | sdn 4d, 7P by LeBaron | 4,740 | 5,345 | — |
| 1450 | limo 7P | 4,650 | 2,913 | — |
| 1451 | sdn 4d, 7P | 4,590 | 2,769 | — |

| 1941 Engines | bore × stroke | bhp | availability |
|---|---|---|---|
| I-6, 245.3 | 3.50 × 4.25 | 100 | S-One Ten |
| I-8, 282.0 | 3.25 × 4.25 | 120 | S-One Twenty |
| I-8, 282.0 | 3.25 × 4.25 | 125 | S-Clipper |
| I-8, 356.0 | 3.50 × 4.63 | 160 | S-One Sixtys, One Eightys |

## 1942

### 2000 Clipper 110 Special (wb 120.0)—11,325 blt (includes all 110s)

| | | Wght | Price | Prod |
|---|---|---|---|---|
| 1582 | sdn 4d | 3,435 | 1,232 | — |
| 1585 | club sdn | 3,415 | 1,199 | — |
| 1588 | bus cpe | 3,365 | 1,166 | — |

### 2010 Clipper 110 Custom (wb 120.0)

| | | Wght | Price | Prod |
|---|---|---|---|---|
| 1502 | sdn 4d | 3,460 | 1,299 | — |
| 1505 | club sdn | 3,440 | 1,266 | — |

### 2020 Clipper 110 (wb 122.0)

| | | Wght | Price | Prod |
|---|---|---|---|---|
| 1589 | conv cpe | 3,315 | 1,375 | — |

### 2001 Clipper 120 Special (wb 120.0)—19,199 built (includes all 120s)

| | | Wght | Price | Prod |
|---|---|---|---|---|
| 1592 | sdn 4d | 3,560 | 1,275 | — |
| 1595 | club sdn | 3,540 | 1,241 | — |
| 1598 | bus cpe | 3,490 | 1,208 | — |

### 2011 Clipper 120 Custom (wb 120.0)

| | | Wght | Price | Prod |
|---|---|---|---|---|
| 1512 | sdn 4d | 3,585 | 1,341 | — |
| 1515 | club sdn | 3,565 | 1,308 | — |

### 2021 Clipper 120 (wb 127.0)

| | | Wght | Price | Prod |
|---|---|---|---|---|
| 1599 | conv cpe | 3,585 | 1,469 | — |

### 2003 Clipper One Sixty (wb 127.0)—2,580 blt (includes all One Sixtys)

| | | Wght | Price | Prod |
|---|---|---|---|---|
| 1572 | sdn 4d | 4,005 | 1,688 | — |
| 1575 | club sdn | 3,985 | 1,630 | — |

### 2023 Clipper One Sixty (wb 127.0)

| | | Wght | Price | Prod |
|---|---|---|---|---|
| 1579 | conv cpe | 3,905 | 1,786 | — |

### 2004 Clipper One Sixty (wb 138.0)

| | | Wght | Price | Prod |
|---|---|---|---|---|
| 1562 | sdn 4d | 4,090 | 1,893 | — |

### 2005 Clipper One Sixty (wb 148.0)

| | | Wght | Price | Prod |
|---|---|---|---|---|
| 1570 | limo 7P | 4,445 | 2,156 | — |
| 1571 | sdn 4d, 7P | 4,325 | 2,034 | — |

### 2055 Clipper One Sixty (wb 148.0)

| | | Wght | Price | Prod |
|---|---|---|---|---|
| 1590 | bus limo 7P | 4,435 | 2,010 | — |
| 1591 | bus sdn 4d, 7P | 4,315 | 1,888 | — |

### 2006 Clipper One Eighty (wb 127.0)—672 built (includes all One Eightys)

| | | Wght | Price | Prod |
|---|---|---|---|---|
| 1522 | sdn 4d | 4,030 | 2,196 | — |
| 1525 | club sdn | 4,010 | 2,099 | — |
| 1529 | conv vic by Darrin | 3,920 | 4,519 | — |

### 2007 Clipper One Eighty (wb 138.0)

| | | Wght | Price | Prod |
|---|---|---|---|---|
| 894 | A/W cabriolet by Rollston | 4,075 | 4,792 | — |
| 1532 | form sdn | 4,390 | 3,011 | — |
| 1542 | sdn 4d | 4,280 | 2,440 | — |

### 2008 Clipper One Eighty (wb 148.0)

| | | Wght | Price | Prod |
|---|---|---|---|---|
| 895 | A/W town car by Rollston | 4,200 | 4,889 | — |
| 1520 | limo 7P by LeBaron | 4,850 | 5,690 | — |
| 1521 | sdn 4d, 7P by LeBaron | 4,740 | 5,446 | — |
| 1550 | limo 7P | 4,540 | 2,645 | — |
| 1551 | sdn 4d, 7P | 4,525 | 2,523 | — |

| 1942 Engines | bore × stroke | bhp | availability |
|---|---|---|---|
| I-6, 245.3 | 3.50 × 4.25 | 105 | S-Clipper 110 |
| I-8, 282.0 | 3.25 × 4.25 | 125 | S-Clipper 120 |
| I-8, 356.0 | 3.50 × 4.63 | 165 | S-Clipper One Sixty, One Eighty |

## 1946

### 2100 Clipper Six (wb 120)—15,892 blt

| | | Wght | Price | Prod |
|---|---|---|---|---|
| 1682 | sdn 4d | 3,495 | 1,730 | — |
| 1685 | club sdn | 3,450 | 1,680 | — |

# Packard

| 2101 Clipper Eight (wb 120.0) | | Wght | Price | Prod |
|---|---|---|---|---|
| 1692 | sdn 4d | 3,630 | 1,802 | 1,500 |
| **2111 Clipper Deluxe Eight (wb 120.0)—5,714 built** | | | | |
| 1612 | sdn 4d | 3,670 | 1,869 | — |
| 1615 | club sdn | 3,625 | 1,817 | — |
| **2103 Super Clipper (wb 127.0)—4,924 built** | | | | |
| 1672 | sdn 4d | 3,995 | 2,290 | — |
| 1675 | club sdn | 3,950 | 2,241 | — |
| **2106 Custom Super Clipper (wb 127.0)—1,472 built** | | | | |
| 1622 | sdn 4d | 4,060 | 3,047 | — |
| 1625 | club sdn | 4,000 | 2,913 | — |
| **2126 Custom Super Clipper (wb 148.0)—1,291 built** | | | | |
| 1650 | limo 7P | 4,900 | 4,496 | — |
| 1651 | sdn 4d, 7P | 4,870 | 4,332 | — |

| 1946 Engines | bore × stroke | bhp | availability |
|---|---|---|---|
| I-6, 245.3 | 3.50 × 4.25 | 105 | S-Clipper Six |
| I-8, 282.0 | 3.25 × 4.25 | 125 | S-Clipper Eight/DeLuxe Eight |
| I-8, 356.0 | 3.50 × 4.63 | 165 | S-Super/Custom Super Clipper |

## 1947

| 2100 Clipper Six (wb 120)—14,949 blt | | Wght | Price | Prod |
|---|---|---|---|---|
| 2182 | sdn 4d | 3,520 | 1,937 | — |
| 2185 | club sdn | 3,475 | 1,912 | — |
| **2111 Clipper DeLuxe Eight (wb 120.0)—23,855 built** | | | | |
| 2112 | sdn 4d | 3,695 | 2,149 | — |
| 2115 | club sdn | 3,650 | 2,124 | — |
| **2103 Super Clipper (wb 127.0)—4,802 built** | | | | |
| 2172 | sdn 4d | 4,025 | 2,772 | — |
| 2175 | club sdn | 3,980 | 2,747 | — |
| **2106 Custom Super Clipper (wb 127.0)—7,480 built (includes model 2126)** | | | | |
| 2122 | sdn 4d | 4,090 | 3,449 | — |
| 2125 | club sdn | 3,384 | 2,125 | — |
| **2126 Custom Super Clipper (wb 148.0)** | | | | |
| 2150 | limo 7P | 4,920 | 4,668 | — |
| 2151 | sdn 4d, 7P | 4,890 | 4,504 | — |

| 1947 Engines | bore × stroke | bhp | availability |
|---|---|---|---|
| I-6, 245.0 | 3.50 × 4.25 | 105 | S-Clipper Six |
| I-8, 282.0 | 3.25 × 4.25 | 125 | S-Clipper Eight/DeLuxe Eight |
| I-8, 356.0 | 3.50 × 4.63 | 165 | S-Super/Custom Super Clipper |

## 1948

| 2201 Eight (wb 120)—12,782 built | | Wght | Price | Prod |
|---|---|---|---|---|
| 2292 | sdn 4d | 3,815 | 2,275 | — |
| 2293 | Station Sedan wgn 4d | 4,075 | 3,425 | * |
| 2295 | club sdn | 3,755 | 2,250 | — |
| **2211 DeLuxe Eight (wb 120.0)—47,807 built** | | | | |
| 2262 | sdn 4d | 3,840 | 2,543 | — |
| 2265 | club sdn | 3,770 | 2,517 | — |
| **2202 Super Eight (wb 120.0)—12,921 built** | | | | |
| 2272 | sdn 4d | 3,855 | 2,827 | — |
| 2275 | club sdn | 3,790 | 2,802 | — |
| **2222 Super Eight (wb 141.0)—1,766 built** | | | | |
| 2270 | DeLuxe limo 7P | 4,610 | 4,000 | — |
| 2271 | Deluxe sdn 4d, 7P | 4,590 | 3,850 | — |
| 2276 | limo 7P | 4,525 | 3,650 | — |
| 2277 | sdn 4d, 7P | 4,460 | 3,500 | — |
| **2232 Super Eight (wb 120.0)** | | | | |
| 2279 | conv cpe | 4,025 | 3,250 | 7,763 |
| **2206 Custom Eight (wb 127.0)—5,936 built** | | | | |
| 2252 | sdn 4d | 4,175 | 3,750 | — |
| 2255 | club sdn | 4,110 | 3,700 | — |
| **2226 Custom Eight (wb 148.0)—230 built** | | | | |
| 2250 | limo 7P | 4,880 | 4,868 | — |
| 2251 | sdn 4d, 7P | 4,860 | 4,704 | — |
| **2313 Custom Eight (wb 148.0)** | | | | |
| — | chassis | — | — | 1,941 |
| **2233 Custom Eight (wb 127.0)** | | | | |
| 2259 | conv cpe | 4,380 | 4,295 | 1,105 |

| 1948 Engines | bore × stroke | bhp | availability |
|---|---|---|---|
| I-8, 288.0 | 3.50 × 3.75 | 130 | S-Eight, DLxe Eight |
| I-8, 327.0 | 3.50 × 4.25 | 145 | S-Super Eight |
| I-8, 356.0 | 3.50 × 4.63 | 160 | S-Custom Eight |

\* See note following 1950.

## 1949 First Series

| 2201 Eight (wb 120)—13,553* blt | | Wght | Price | Prod |
|---|---|---|---|---|
| 2292-9 | sdn 4d | 3,815 | 2,275 | — |
| 2293-9 | Station Sedan wgn 4d | 4,075 | 3,425 | * |
| 2295-9 | club sdn | 3,755 | 2,250 | — |
| **2211 DeLuxe Eight (wb 120.0)—27,422 built** | | | | |
| 2262-9 | sdn 4d | 3,840 | 2,543 | — |
| 2265-9 | club sdn | 3,770 | 2,517 | — |
| **2202 Super Eight (wb 120.0)—5,879 built** | | | | |
| 2272-9 | sdn 4d | 3,855 | 2,827 | — |
| 2275-9 | club sdn | 3,790 | 2,802 | — |
| **2222 Super Eight (wb 141.0)—867 built** | | | | |
| 2270-9 | DeLuxe limo 7P | 4,610 | 4,000 | — |
| 2271-9 | DeLuxe sdn 4d, 7P | 4,590 | 3,850 | — |
| 2276-9 | limo 7P | 4,525 | 3,650 | — |
| 2277-9 | sdn 4d, 7P | 4,460 | 3,500 | — |
| **2232 Super Eight (wb 120.0)** | | | | |
| 2279-9 | conv cpe | 4,025 | 3,250 | 1,237 |
| **2206 Custom Eight (wb 127.0)—2,990 built** | | | | |
| 2252-9 | sdn 4d | 4,175 | 3,750 | — |
| 2255-9 | club sdn | 4,110 | 3,700 | — |
| **2226 Custom Eight (wb 148.0)—50 built** | | | | |
| 2250-9 | limo 7P | 4,880 | 4,868 | — |
| 2251-9 | sdn 4d, 7P | 4,860 | 4,704 | — |
| **2213 Custom Eight (wb 148.0)** | | | | |
| — | chassis | — | — | 220 |
| **2233 Custom Eight (wb 127.0)** | | | | |
| 2259-9 | conv cpe | 4,380 | 4,295 | 213 |

\* See note following 1950.

## 1949 Second Series

| 2301 Eight (wb 120)—53,168* blt | | Wght | Price | Prod |
|---|---|---|---|---|
| 2362 | DeLuxe sdn 4d | 3,840 | 2,383 | — |
| 2365 | DeLuxe club sdn | 3,770 | 2,358 | — |
| 2392 | sdn 4d | 3,815 | 2,249 | — |
| 2393 | Station Sedan wgn 4d | 4,075 | 3,449 | * |
| 2395 | club sdn | 3,740 | 2,224 | — |
| **2302 Super Eight (wb 127.0)—8,759 built** | | | | |
| 2372 | DeLuxe sdn 4d | 3,925 | 2,919 | — |
| 2375 | DeLuxe club sdn | 3,855 | 2,894 | — |
| 2382 | sdn 4d | 3,870 | 2,633 | — |

## Packard

| 2302 Super Eight (wb 127.0) | | Wght | Price | Prod |
|---|---|---|---|---|
| 2385 | club sdn | 3,800 | 2,608 | — |
| **2322 Super Eight (wb 141.0)—4 built** | | | | |
| 2370 | DeLuxe limo 7P | 4,620 | 4,100 | — |
| 2371 | DeLuxe sdn 4d, 7P | 4,600 | 3,950 | — |
| **2332 Super Eight (wb 127.0)** | | | | |
| 2332 | DeLuxe conv cpe | 4,260 | 3,350 | 685 |
| **2306 Custom Eight (wb 127.0)** | | | | |
| 2352 | sdn 4d | 4,310 | 3,750 | 973 |
| **2313 Custom Eight (wb 148.0)** | | | | |
| — | chassis | — | — | 160 |
| **2333 Custom Eight (wb 127.0)** | | | | |
| 2359 | conv cpe | 4,530 | 4,295 | 68 |

| 1949 Engines | bore × stroke | bhp | availability |
|---|---|---|---|
| I-8, 288.0 | 3.50 × 3.75 | 135 | S-Eight, DLux Eight |
| I-8, 327.0 | 3.50 × 4.25 | 150 | S-Super/Super DeLuxe Eight |
| I-8, 356.0 | 3.50 × 4.63 | 160 | S-Custom Eight |

* See note following 1950.

### 1950

| 2301 Eight (wb 120)—36,471 built | | Wght | Price | Prod |
|---|---|---|---|---|
| 2362-5 | DeLuxe sdn 4d | 3,840 | 2,383 | — |
| 2365-5 | DeLuxe club sdn | 3,770 | 2,358 | — |
| 2392-5 | sdn 4d | 3,815 | 2,249 | — |
| 2393-5 | Station Sedan wgn 4d | 4,075 | 3,449 | * |
| 2395-5 | club sdn | 3,740 | 2,224 | — |
| **2302 Super Eight (wb 127.0)—4,528 built** | | | | |
| 2372-5 | DeLuxe sdn 4d | 3,925 | 2,919 | — |
| 2375-5 | club sdn | 3,855 | 2,894 | — |
| 2382-5 | sdn 4d | 3,870 | 2,633 | — |
| 2385-5 | club sdn | 3,800 | 2,608 | — |
| **2332 Super Eight (wb 127.0)** | | | | |
| 2379-5 | conv cpe | 4,110 | 3,350 | 600 |
| **2306 Custom Eight (wb 127.0)** | | | | |
| 2352-5 | sdn 4d | 4,310 | 3,975 | 707 |
| **2313 Custom Eight (wb 148.0)** | | | | |
| — | chassis | — | — | 244 |
| **2333 Custom Eight (wb 127.0)** | | | | |
| 2359-5 | conv cpe | 4,530 | 4,520 | 77 |

*See 1950.

| 1950 Engines | bore × stroke | bhp | availability |
|---|---|---|---|
| I-8, 288.0 | 3.50 × 3.75 | 135 | S-Eight, DLux Eight |
| I-8, 327.0 | 3.50 × 4.25 | 150 | S-Super/Super DeLuxe Eight |
| I-8, 356.0 | 3.50 × 4.63 | 160 | S-Custom Eight |

* Although Packard did not break down model-year production by body style, some calendar-year figures exist for the Station Sedan. These are: 126 in 1947, 3,266 in 1948, and 472 in 1949, for a total of 3,864. An estimated 75 percent were 1948 models.

### 1951

| 2401 200 (wb 122.0) | | Wght | Price | Prod |
|---|---|---|---|---|
| 2462 | DeLuxe sdn 4d | 3,660 | 2,616 | ⎤ |
| 2465 | DeLuxe club sdn | 3,605 | 2,563 | ⎦ 47,052 |
| 2492 | sdn 4d | 3,665 | 2,469 | ⎤ |
| 2495 | club sdn | 3,600 | 2,416 | ⎥ 24,310 |
| 2498 | bus cpe | 3,550 | 2,302 | ⎦ |

| 2401 250 (wb 122.0)—4,640 built | | Wght | Price | Prod |
|---|---|---|---|---|
| 2467 | Mayfair htp cpe | 3,820 | 3,234 | — |
| 2469 | conv cpe | 4,040 | 3,391 | — |
| **2402 300 (wb 127.0)** | | | | |
| 2472 | sdn 4d | 3,875 | 3,034 | 15,309 |
| **2413 300 (wb 127.0)** | | | | |
| — | chassis | — | — | 401 |
| **2406 Patrician 400 (wb 127.0)** | | | | |
| 2452 | sdn 4d | 4,115 | 3,662 | 9,001 |

| 1951 Engines | bore × stroke | bhp | availability |
|---|---|---|---|
| I-8, 288.0 | 3.50 × 3.75 | 135 | S-200 |
| I-8, 327.0 | 3.50 × 4.25 | 150 | S-250/300 manual |
| I-8, 327.0 | 3.50 × 4.25 | 155 | S-Patrician 400, 250/300 auto |

### 1952

| 2501 200 (wb 122.0)—46,720 built | | Wght | Price | Prod |
|---|---|---|---|---|
| 2562 | DeLuxe sdn 4d | 3,685 | 2,695 | — |
| 2565 | DeLuxe club sdn | 3,660 | 2,641 | — |
| 2592 | sdn 4d | 3,680 | 2,548 | — |
| 2595 | club sdn | 3,640 | 2,494 | — |
| **2531 250 (wb 122.0)—5,201 built** | | | | |
| 2577 | Mayfair htp cpe | 3,805 | 3,318 | — |
| 2579 | conv cpe | 4,000 | 3,476 | — |
| **2502 300 (wb 127.0)** | | | | |
| 2572 | sdn 4d | 3,380 | 3,116 | 6,705 |
| **2513 300 (wb 127.0)** | | | | |
| — | chassis | — | — | 320 |
| **2506 Patrician 400 (wb 127.0)** | | | | |
| 2552 | sdn 4d | 4,100 | 3,797 | 3,975 |

| 1952 Engines | bore × stroke | bhp | availability |
|---|---|---|---|
| I-8, 288.0 | 3.50 × 3.75 | 135 | S-200 |
| I-8, 327.0 | 3.50 × 4.25 | 150 | S-250/300 manual |
| I-8, 327.0 | 3.50 × 4.25 | 155 | S-Patrician 400, 250/300 auto |

### 1953

| 2601 Clipper (wb 122.0) | | Wght | Price | Prod |
|---|---|---|---|---|
| 2692 | sdn 4d | 3,730 | 2,598 | 23,126 |
| 2695 | club sdn | 3,700 | 2,544 | 6,370 |
| 2697 | Sportster cpe | 3,720 | 2,805 | 3,672 |
| — | chassis | — | — | 1 |
| **2611 Clipper DeLuxe (wb 122.0)** | | | | |
| 2662 | sdn 4d | 3,760 | 2,745 | 26,037 |
| 2665 | club sdn | 3,720 | 2,691 | 4,678 |
| **2633 Clipper commercial (wb 122.0)** | | | | |
| — | chassis (Henney bodies) | — | — | 380 |
| **2631 (wb 122.0)** | | | | |
| 2677 | Mayfair htp cpe | 3,905 | 3,278 | 5,150 |
| 2678 | Caribbean conv cpe | 4,265 | 5,210 | 750 |
| 2679 | conv cpe | 4,125 | 3,486 | 1,518 |
| **2602 Cavalier (wb 127.0)** | | | | |
| 2672 | sdn 4d | 3,975 | 3,244 | 10,799 |
| **2613 Packard commercial (wb 127.0)** | | | | |
| — | chassis (Henney bodies) | — | — | 166 |

# Packard

| 2606 Patrician (wb 127.0) | | Wght | Price | Prod |
|---|---|---|---|---|
| 2652 | sdn 4d | 4,190 | 3,740 | 7,456 |
| 2653 | formal sdn by Derham | 4,335 | 6,531 | 25* |
| **2626 (wb 149.0)** | | | | |
| 2650 | Corporation limo 8P | 4,720 | 7,100 | 50 |
| 2651 | Executive sdn 4d, 8P | 4,650 | 6,900 | 100 |
| **2602-2606-2631** | | | | |
| — | chassis | — | — | 9 |

* Constructed from finished Patricians.

| 1953 Engines | bore × stroke | bhp | availability |
|---|---|---|---|
| I-8, 288.0 | 3.50 × 3.75 | 150 | S-2601 |
| I-8, 327.0 | 3.50 × 4.25 | 160 | S-2611 |
| I-8, 327.0 | 3.50 × 4.25 | 180 | S-2602, 2631 (5 main bearing) |
| I-8, 327.0 | 3.50 × 4.25 | 180 | S-2606, 2626 (9 main bearing) |

## 1954

| 5400 Clipper Special (wb 122.0) | | Wght | Price | Prod |
|---|---|---|---|---|
| 5482 | sdn 4d | 3,650 | 2,594 | 970 |
| 5485 | club sdn | 3,585 | 2,544 | 912 |
| **5401 Clipper DeLuxe (wb 122.0)** | | | | |
| 5492 | sdn 4d | 3,660 | 2,695 | 7,610 |
| 5495 | club sdn | 3,650 | 2,645 | 1,470 |
| 5497 | Sportster cpe | 3,595 | 2,830 | 1,336 |
| **5411 Clipper Super (wb 122.0)** | | | | |
| 5462 | sdn 4d | 3,695 | 2,815 | 6,270 |
| 5465 | club sdn | 3,610 | 2,765 | 887 |
| 5467 | Panama htp cpe | 3,765 | 3,125 | 3,618 |
| **5433 Clipper commercial (wb 122.0)** | | | | |
| — | chassis (Henney bodies) | — | — | 120 |
| **5402 Cavalier (wb 127.0)** | | | | |
| 5472 | sdn 4d | 3,955 | 3,344 | 2,580 |
| **5413 Packard commercial (wb 127.0)** | | | | |
| — | chassis (Henney bodies) | — | — | 205 |
| **5431 (wb 122.0)** | | | | |
| 5477 | Pacific htp cpe | 4,065 | 3,827 | 1,189 |
| 5478 | Caribbean conv cpe | 4,660 | 6,100 | 400 |
| 5479 | convertible cpe | 4,290 | 3,935 | 863 |
| — | chassis | — | — | 1 |
| **5406 Patrician (wb 127.0)** | | | | |
| 5452 | sdn 4d | 4,190 | 3,890 | 2,760 |
| **5426 (wb 149.0)** | | | | |
| 5450 | Corporation limo 8P | 4,720 | 5,960 | 35 |
| 5451 | Executive sdn 4d, 8P | 4,650 | 5,610 | 65 |

| 1954 Engines | bore × stroke | bhp | availability |
|---|---|---|---|
| I-8, 288.0 | 3.50 × 3.75 | 150 | S-5400 |
| I-8, 327.0 | 3.50 × 4.25 | 165 | S-5401, 5411 |
| I-8, 327.0 | 3.50 × 4.25 | 185 | S-5402 |
| I-8, 359.0 | 3.56 × 4.50 | 212 | S-5406, 5426, 5431 (9 main bearing) |

## 1955

| 5540 Clipper (wb 122.0) | | Wght | Price | Prod |
|---|---|---|---|---|
| 5522 | DeLuxe sdn 4d | 3,680 | 2,586 | 8,309 |
| | | Wght | Price | Prod |
| 5542 | Super sdn 4d | 3,670 | 2,686 | 7,979 |
| 5547 | Super Panama htp cpe | 3,700 | 2,776 | 7,016 |

| 5560 Clipper Custom (wb 122.0) | | Wght | Price | Prod |
|---|---|---|---|---|
| 5562 | sdn 4d | 3,885 | 2,926 | 8,708 |
| 5567 | Constellation htp cpe | 3,865 | 3,076 | 6,672 |
| **5580 (wb 127.0)** | | | | |
| 5582 | Patrician sdn 4d | 4,275 | 3,890 | 9,127 |
| 5587 | Four Hundred htp cpe | 4,250 | 3,930 | 7,206 |
| 5588 | Caribbean conv cpe | 4,755 | 5,932 | 500* |

| 1955 Engines | bore × stroke | bhp | availability |
|---|---|---|---|
| V-8, 320.0 | 3.81 × 3.50 | 225 | S-Clipper DeLuxe/Super |
| V-8, 352.0 | 4.00 × 3.50 | 245 | S-Clipper Custom |
| V-8, 352.0 | 4.00 × 3.50 | 260 | S-Packard exc Caribbean |
| V-8, 352.0 | 4.00 × 3.50 | 275 | S-Caribbean |

* Estimated

## 1956

| Clipper (wb 122.0)* | Wght | Price | Prod |
|---|---|---|---|
| DeLuxe sdn 4d | 3,745 | 2,733 | 5,715 |
| Super sdn 4d | 3,800 | 2,866 | 5,173 |
| Super Panama htp cpe | 3,825 | 2,916 | 3,999 |
| Custom sdn 4d | 3,860 | 3,069 | 2,129 |
| Custom Constellation htp cpe | 3,860 | 3,164 | 1,466 |

| 5670 Executive (wb 122.0) | | Wght | Price | Prod |
|---|---|---|---|---|
| 5672 | sdn 4d | 4,185 | 3,465 | 1,784 |
| 5677 | htp cpe | 4,185 | 3,560 | 1,031 |
| **5680 (wb 127.0)** | | | | |
| 5682 | Patrician sdn 4d | 4,045 | 4,160 | 3,775 |
| 5687 | Four Hundred htp cpe | 4,080 | 4,190 | 3,224 |
| **5688 Caribbean (wb 127.0)** | | | | |
| 5697 | htp cpe | 4,590 | 5,495 | 263 |
| 5699 | conv cpe | 4,960 | 5,995 | 276 |

| 1956 Engines | bore × stroke | bhp | availability |
|---|---|---|---|
| V-8, 352.0 | 4.00 × 3.50 | 240 | S-Clipper |
| V-8, 352.0 | 4.00 × 3.50 | 275 | S-Executive, Clipper Custom |
| V-8, 374.0 | 4.13 × 3.50 | 290 | S-Patrician, Four Hundred |
| V-8, 374.0 | 4.13 × 3.50 | 310 | S-Caribbean |

*Clipper was marketed as a separate make for 1956.

## 1957

| 57L (wb 120.5; wgn-116.5) | | Wght | Price | Prod |
|---|---|---|---|---|
| Y8 | Town Sedan 4d | 3,570 | 3,212 | 3,940 |
| P8 | Country Sedan wgn 4d | 3,650 | 3,384 | 869 |

| 1957 Engine | bore × stroke | bhp | availability |
|---|---|---|---|
| V-8, 289.0 | 3.56 × 3.63 | 275 | S-all (supercharged) |

## 1958

| 58L (wb 120.5; wgn/htp-116.5) | | Wght | Price | Prod |
|---|---|---|---|---|
| J8 | sdn 4d | 3,505 | 3,212 | 1,200 |
| Y8 | htp cpe | 3,480 | 3,262 | 675 |
| K9 | Hawk htp cpe | 3,470 | 3,995 | 588 |
| P8 | wgn 4d | 3,555 | 3,384 | 159 |

| 1958 Engines | bore × stroke | bhp | availability |
|---|---|---|---|
| V-8, 289.0 | 3.56 × 3.63 | 275 | S-Hawk (superchgd) |
| V-8, 289.0 | 3.56 × 3.63 | 210 | S-Others |

Note: Final (1957-58) Packards were based on Studebaker models, following the 1954 merger of the two companies.

# Panoz

A true "family affair," Panoz Auto Development Company was founded in late 1988 by sports-car and racing enthusiast Daniel Panoz with backing from his billionaire father Donald. The elder Panoz (pronounced "PAY-nose") made his fortune with two pharmaceutical companies, one of which developed the enormously lucrative transdermal patch familiar to many cigarette smokers.

Danny Panoz wanted to the put the family crest on a high-performance low-production sports car in the mold of Caroll Shelby's hallowed Cobra, but aimed to keep it affordable and practical by using off-the-shelf Ford components that could be easily serviced most anywhere. While setting up a small new factory near the family estate outside Atlanta, he worked with engineer John Leverett to develop a spartan two-seat roadster from an earlier British design, though the eventual Panoz Roadster was entirely new. That included classic cycle-fender styling on a steel frame with a pushrod 5.0-liter Mustang V-8, five-speed manual transmission, solid rear axle, 16-inch wheels, and 98.5-inch wheelbase. All were sold at a suggested price of $43,495, including canvas top and side curtains.

In late 1996 Panoz invited *Car and Driver* to test an improved version dubbed A.I.V.—"Aluminum Intensive Vehicle." The term referred to a stout new "twin tier" spaceframe chassis made of extruded aluminum. There were many other changes, including a six-inch longer wheelbase, independent rear suspension (with unequal-length A-arms and coil-over shocks as up front), 18-inch wheels, fatter tires, and a big hood air scoop for clearing a taller engine, the 4.6-liter twincam V-8 from the latest Mustang SVT Cobra. *Car and Driver* clocked 4.8 seconds 0-60 and a standing quarter-mile of 13.6 seconds at 101 mph. "It's like driving a Lotus 7 but with fewer rattles, twice the room, and twice the thrust," enthused tester John Phillips.

Despite its elemental nature, the A.I.V. was beautifully crafted. Each took 350 man-hours to build, a big reason why price eventually reached $63,000, a bit less than a Dodge Viper RT/10. Even so, the Panoz came with a three-year/36,000-mile warranty, generous by "exoticar" standards. And appropriate for the price, the factory would send out a person to work with a local body shop on a car unlucky enough to be crunched.

In 1996, Don Panoz and his son formed Panoz Motor Sports and tapped famed constructor Adrian Reynard to develop two prototype-class coupes for the 1997 LeMans 24 Hours. Neither of those cars finished, but a Panoz GTR-1 did complete the 1998 event, placing an impressive seventh overall. A similar car won the team prize in that year's U.S. Road Racing Championship. Meanwhile, Don purchased the famed Road Atlanta track, set up a Panoz Racing School for drivers, and helped instigate two new long-distance series, the Petit LeMans and the American LeMans Series (ALMS), where his racers could show their stuff. Fittingly, a special open-top Panoz LMP 1 Roadster S won both the Team and Manufacturers titles in the 1999 ALMS, beating full-on entries from BMW and Audi.

The Panoz racers were a thrilling preview of a new roadgoing sports car that looked much like them. Named Esperante, it was publicly unveiled at the April 2000 New York Auto Show but didn't enter production until August, delaying initial deliveries until 2001. A luxurious two-seat convertible, Esperante was sized close to the Roadster and used a similar suspension, but featured an all-new spaceframe conceived by Leverett and fellow engineer William McClendon. The design comprised five extruded-aluminum modules that bolted and bonded together instead of being welded or riveted. Panoz claimed extraordinary strength for this chassis while hinting that its modular nature would make additional models that much easier to realize.

Initial base price was $79,950, which included 24-hour roadside assistance and a 3/36 warranty. Unlike the Roadsters, Esperante was fully equipped, boasting dual dashboard airbags, antilock brakes (again big discs all-around), electronic traction control, power steering, power driver-side seat, power windows/locks/mirrors, cruise control, and a "semirigid" manual top with a folding-fabric rear section and a hard liftoff panel above the seats. Under the hood was the latest Mustang Cobra V-8 with 320 bhp, but hand-assembled by SVT especially for Panoz. Five-speed manual was again the only transmission.

*Road & Track* dubbed Esperante "the gentleman's LeMans racer," but no magazine was able to do a full test immediately. The right way was still the only way for Danny Panoz, and Esperante production was slow to get started, though ambitiously targeted at 300-500 cars per year, thanks to a major plant expansion. Even so, the factory's performance numbers seemed entirely credible: 0-60 mph in 5.1 seconds, 0-100 in 12.6, the standing quarter-mile in 13.7 seconds at 103.5 mph.

The Panoz saga is still unfolding, but it bears the hallmarks of a long-running story filled with more high adventure on the track and more high performance for the street. Future editions of this book will no doubt have many exciting new tales to tell.

## Specifications

### 1990-96

| Roadster (wb 98.5) | | Wght | Price | Prod |
|---|---|---|---|---|
| conv 2d | | 2,316 | 43,495 | 60 |

| 1990-96 Engine | bore × stroke | bhp | availability |
|---|---|---|---|
| V-8, 302.0 | 4.00 × 3.00 | 205 | S-all |

### 1997-2000

| A.I.V. Roadster (wb 104.5) | | Wght | Price | Prod |
|---|---|---|---|---|
| conv 2d | | 2,698 | 57,980-62,500 | 250 |

| 1997-2000 Engine | bore × stroke | bhp | availability |
|---|---|---|---|
| V-8, 281.0 | 3.55 × 3.54 | 305 | S-all |

### 2000-2002

| Esperante (wb 106.0) | | Wght | Price | Prod |
|---|---|---|---|---|
| conv 2d | | 2,800-3,200 | 79,950-88,950 | 65* |

| 2000-2002 Engine | bore × stroke | bhp | availability |
|---|---|---|---|
| V-8, 281.0 | 3.55 × 3.54 | 320 | S-all |

*2001 production.

**1999 Panoz A.I.V. Roadster**

# Pierce-Arrow

Of all the great American classics, none is more famous for meticulous craftsmanship or refined luxury than the noble Pierce-Arrow. Along with Packard and Peerless, it was one of the fabled "three Ps" of U.S. automotive royalty.

Pierce-Arrow Motor Car Company started out in 1901 as an outgrowth of the George N. Pierce Company of Buffalo, New York, a bicycle manufacturer and, earlier, a birdcage maker. By 1918, it reached the pinnacle of preeminence with cars like the Model 66A. This mounted a giant 147.5-inch wheelbase, carried a huge 824.7-cubic-inch T-head six, and sold for upward of $8000 at a time when a Model T Ford cost a paltry $525; even the costliest 1918 Packard, the Twin Six Imperial limousine, seemed modest at $5850. But staunch conservatism led to stagnation, and by the mid-'20s, Pierce-Arrows were technically passé. The firm was soon awash in red ink, its cars hopelessly outdated if still ardently admired.

That Pierce survived to build any cars in the '30s was owed to Albert R. Erskine, the accountant-turned-president of Studebaker who wanted a prestige nameplate for the automotive empire he hoped to erect in South Bend. Thus, after months of negotiating, Studebaker acquired Pierce in 1928 through a stock transfer. Pierce remained ostensibly independent with its own general manager, Arthur J. Chanter, though Erskine named himself president. More importantly, Buffalo and not South Bend would retain responsibility for developing new Pierce-Arrows.

Pierce sold its traditional big sixes through 1928. Its first Eight of 1929 did much to restore the make's flagging reputation. Against the Sixes it was better looking, better handling, faster, lower slung—and, remarkably enough, lower priced. As a result, Pierce enjoyed its best-ever sales year: some 9700 for calendar 1929, more than double the 1928 tally.

Eights comprised the entire 1930 lineup, which was quite broad for such a low-volume producer. A vast array of body types covered three series, four wheelbases—132, 134, 139, and a regal 144 inches—and three nine-main-bearing inline engines: a 115-horsepower 340 cid, a 125-bhp 366, and a 132-bhp 385. Prices were stiff, ranging from $2700 for the short-chassis Model C club brougham to over $5000 for the long Model A seven-passenger salon town car.

Still, Pierce sales remained healthy through spring despite the stock market crash. Though demand began flagging in the second quarter, there was no immediate concern, for 1930 would be the firm's second-best year despite much-reduced sales of 6795. Once again, Pierce viewed a worsening market with a combination of arrogance and naïveté.

The firm forged ahead with an even broader line for 1931. Engines stood pat, but wheelbases shifted: 134/137 inches for the least-expensive Model 43s, 142 for the midrange 42s, and 147 for the top-line Model 41s. The last now included five semi-custom "catalog" styles by LeBaron; and Derham, Dietrich, and Brunn contributed special bodies on a few individual chassis. But calendar-year sales withered to just 4522, a worrisome 46 percent below the high-water mark of just two years before.

Determined to improve sales and prove its mettle, Pierce cut back on Eights for 1932 but cut loose with two new V-12s. Flagship of the fleet was the Model 52, offering five body types on 142- and 147-inch wheelbases at prices in the $4295-$4800 range. All carried a new 150-bhp 429-cid V-12. Designed by chief engineer Karl M. Wise, this was a super-smooth, super-quiet engine with an 80-degree cylinder-bank angle, seven main bearings, and dual downdraft carburetors. A smaller-bore 398 version with 140 bhp powered the Model 53, which listed more choices on 137- and 142-inch wheelbases for some $500 less than comparable 52s. Anchoring the line was the Model 54, essentially the 53 with an improved 366 straight-eight. Common to all '32 Pierce-Arrows were ultrasteady eight-point engine mounting, stronger frames, and "fingertip" adjustable shock absorbers. Yet despite all these worthy developments, sales skidded to a disheartening 2234 units and Pierce posted a $3 million loss.

Save skirted fenders, the 1933s showed slight external change. Series rose to four: straight-eight Model 836 and V-12 Models 1236, 1242, and 1247. The smaller twelve was axed for want of performance, the eight gained 10 bhp for 135 total, and the 429 V-12 went to 160 bhp for the 1236 series. The top-line 1242/1247 carried a bored-out 452 V-12 with higher-compression heads giving a majestic 175 bhp. All engines featured hydraulic valve tappets for quiet operation and less maintenance—an industry first.

Test driver Ab Jenkins took to the Bonneville Salt Flats in September 1932 with a stripped 452 V-12 roadster prototype that had already done 33,000 miles. It promptly ran 2710 miles in 24 hours at an average speed of 112.91 mph. Jenkins commented: "The car was stable at all speeds, more like a racing chassis." The car was stable enough that Jenkins could write notes to spectators and toss them out at speeds over 110. No mechanical problems were experienced during the run. Fenders, windshield, and other road equipment reinstalled for the 2000 mile drive back to Buffalo—a convincing demonstration of Pierce-Arrow stamina. Jenkins returned to Utah in 1933 with a modified 207-bhp car that set 79 world speed records over 25½ hours, running as high as 128 mph. The road and weather conditions were more-difficult than the first trip, but neither car nor driver seemed to mind. Ab managed to shave during the final laps.

But speed records, multicylinder engines, and high-priced luxury were not enough to survive "hard times," as Cadillac, Marmon, Packard, and Stutz were learning. Pierce had grossly underestimated both the depth and breadth of the Depression, just like its Studebaker owner. Extensive advertising didn't help. By 1933, both firms were dangerously overextended, yet Studebaker continued pumping money into Pierce-Arrow. The two companies soon agreed to standardize several manufacturing processes for their vastly dissimilar cars, but this didn't save much money. Still, Pierce was able to reduce some operating costs in light of its fast-dwindling sales.

Late 1932 brought a new sales manager in Roy Faulkner, the dynamic former president of Auburn, which lent credence to rumors of an impending Pierce/Auburn merger. One of his first acts was the revolutionary Silver Arrow that was displayed at the 1933 Chicago World Fair. Designed by Phil Wright, it was the product of numerous wind-tunnel tests yet a striking aesthetic success. Said company literature: "It gives you in 1933 the car of 1940."

Actually, the Silver Arrow wasn't a literal forecast of future Pierce styling, but it was truly futuristic. A four-door sedan on the 139-inch chassis of the model 1236, it bore a handsomely vee'd radiator flanked by Pierce's trademark faired-in headlamps now fully integrated with flush-sided fenders. Running boards were absent, and pronounced pontoon rear fenders set off a radically tapered "beetle back" with a narrow vee'd slit for

# Pierce-Arrow

1931 Model 42 convertible

1933 Silver Arrow four-door show car

1934 Silver Arrow fastback coupe

a rear window. Pierce claimed the Silver Arrow capable of 115 mph, but with over 5700 pounds of heft, even the 175-bhp V12 would be hard pressed to get much over 100. At an announced $10,000 (Faulker evidently planned limited regular sales) this dream car would remain just that for most, and only five were built.

Faulkner, the Silver Arrow, and Jenkin's speed runs briefly lifted Pierce fortunes in early 1933. Twelve-cylinder sales were up by 200 percent in January and by 130 percent in February; even through October they ran 55 percent ahead of the previous year's pace. But this recovery was dashed by strikes at tool-and-die makers, and Pierce lost 300-400 orders late in the year. As a result, calendar-1933 sales came to 2152. Worse, Studebaker went bankrupt in the spring of 1933, leading Erskine to commit suicide that July. Studebaker's receivers ordered Pierce to be sold, so in August the firm passed to a group of Buffalo-area businessmen and bankers who paid $1 million for a chance to turn things around. Faulkner returned to Indiana.

With this, Pierce-Arrow was independent again and, ironically, healthier than Studebaker. With debts canceled, the new owners hoped to break even at 3000 annual sales and to make $1 million at 4000. To achieve that they installed Chanter as president, who began planning for higher volume.

Somehow, Pierce managed a total restyle for 1934, adopting a more-streamlined look that would continue for '35. Offerings were trimmed, but not drastically. The standard 1934 Eight offered four models with a 136-inch wheelbase and 135-bhp 366 engine in the $2500-$2700 range. A new long-stroke 385 eight with 140 bhp powered a more-extensive DeLuxe Eight line on 139- and 144-inch chassis shared with Salon Twelves. Both Salons and that year's 147-inch Custom Twelves carried an unchanged 462 engine. The DeLuxe Eight covered a $2800-$5000 price range. Twelves sold for $3200-$4500 with standard bodywork; six long-wheelbase Brunn "town" models listed for as high as $7000. A notable newcomer was a 144-inch-wheelbase two-door fastback in the image of the Silver Arrow, available as a DeLuxe Eight or Salon Twelve. Other closed bodies sported draft-free ventwing front-door windows, adjustable rear seats, and more head room.

Yet for all this, sales refused to improve, and Pierce kept bleeding cash: $861,000 for the first half of 1934, another $176,000 in July alone. The very next month, Pierce filed for bankruptcy after futile merger talks with Auburn and Reo. Though Chanter managed to raise $1 million from the Buffalo community and New York banks, Pierce had to slash its workforce some 70 percent. With the new capital, a leaner, reorganized company called Pierce-Arrow Motor Corporation began operations in May 1935.

Despite a threadbare budget, Pierce managed an attractive redesign for 1936. Advertised as "The World's Safest Car," it

# Pierce-Arrow

boasted over 30 significant improvements: more fashionably rounded lines with built-in trunks on sedans; standard vacuum brake booster; added cruciform frame member; engines and radiators moved farther forward; and a steering box mounted ahead of the front axle with a trailing drag link. Pierces had always been surprisingly easy to drive, but improved steering, brakes, suspension, and weight distribution gave the 1936s outstanding roadability despite the near three-ton bulk of some models. The previous three wheelbases returned for a reduced line of Eights and Twelves downpriced to $3100-$5600. The 366 eight was dropped, but new high-compression aluminum cylinder heads added ten horsepower to the other two engines.

Registrations climbed 25 percent in the first four months of 1936, suggesting Pierce had finally turned the corner, but calendar-year sales ended below the meager 1935 level: just 787. Pierce bravely carried on with little-changed 1937 models, but sold only 166 before suspending production. Though new financing was simply unavailable now, the company announced 1938 models in October '37, but built fewer than 40. Their only visual changes were a plastic-rim "banjo" steering wheel, new license-plate lamp, and relocated emergency brake handle.

The success of medium-priced cars at Packard and Lincoln prompted a final reorganization attempt, Pierce announcing a $10.7-million stock issue in August 1937 to produce 25,000 medium-priced cars, 1200 luxury models, and 4800 trailers. It also planned to tap Postmaster General James A. Farley, then about to leave the Roosevelt Administration, as new general manager. But none of this came to pass. Farley had received similar offers from Studebaker and Willys that he also rejected because they meant using his Washington connections, presumably to obtain contract work or federal loans.

Thus, Pierce again filed for bankruptcy in December 1937 after losing nearly $250,000 in the 17 months that followed July 1936. The firm was declared insolvent the following April; a month later, it was summarily liquidated. It was a sad end for a once-great American marque.

## Specifications

### 1930

| Model A (wb 144.0)—335 built | Wght | Price | Prod |
|---|---|---|---|
| touring 7P | 4,510 | 3,975 | — |
| conv cpe 2P | 4,540 | 3,975 | — |
| sedan 7P | 4,820 | 4,485 | — |
| salon sdn 7P | 4,900 | 4,835 | — |
| salon town car 7P | 5,040 | 5,035 | — |

| Model B (wb 134.0; lwb-139.0) | Wght | Price | Prod |
|---|---|---|---|
| rdstr 2P | 4,290 | 3,125 | |
| touring 4-5P | 4,375 | 3,300 | |
| dual-cowl spt phtn 4-5P | 4,470 | 3,600 | 110 |
| conv cpe 2-4P | 4,420 | 3,350 | |
| lwb victoria cpe 5P | 4,590 | 3,475 | |
| lwb sdn 4d | 4,720 | 3,495 | |
| lwb salon sdn 4d | 4,780 | 3,795 | |
| lwb salon club sdn 4d | 4,770 | 3,795 | |
| lwb salon club berline 5P | 4,840 | 3,995 | |
| lwb club sdn 5P | 4,730 | 3,670 | 1,228 |
| lwb club berline 7P | 4,790 | 3,870 | |
| lwb sdn 7P | 4,790 | 3,625 | |
| limo 7P (lwb) | 4,820 | 3,825 | |
| lwb salon sdn 7P | 4,840 | 3,925 | |
| lwb salon limo 7P | 4,860 | 4,125 | |

| Model C (wb 132.0)—1,082 built | Wght | Price | Prod |
|---|---|---|---|
| cpe 2-4 | 4,450 | 2,865 | — |
| club brougham 5P | 4,460 | 2,695 | — |
| sdn 4d | 4,525 | 2,875 | — |

* Production estimated where possible. Calendar-year registrations: 6,795.

| 1930 Engines | bore × stroke | bhp | availability |
|---|---|---|---|
| I-8, 340.0 | 3.38 × 4.75 | 115 | S-C |
| I-8, 366.0 | 3.50 × 4.75 | 125 | S-B |
| I-8, 385.0 | 3.50 × 5.00 | 132 | S-A |

### 1931*

| Model 41 (wb 147.0) | Wght | Price | Prod |
|---|---|---|---|
| touring 7P | 4,786 | 4,275 | — |
| conv cpe 2-4P | 4,740 | 4,275 | — |
| sdn 7P | 5,100 | 4,785 | — |
| limo 7P | 5,157 | 4,985 | — |
| LeBaron cpe 2-4P | — | 5,100 | — |
| LeBaron victoria cpe 5P | — | 5,100 | — |
| LeBaron conv sdn 5P | — | 5,200 | — |
| LeBaron spt sdn 5P | — | 5,375 | — |
| LeBaron limo 7P | — | 5,975 | — |
| town brougham 7P | 5,206 | 6,250 | — |
| town car 7P | 5,211 | 6,250 | — |
| town landau 7P | — | 6,400 | — |

| Model 42 (wb 142.0)—700 built* | Wght | Price | Prod |
|---|---|---|---|
| spt roadster 2-4P | 4,565 | 3,450 | — |
| touring 5P | 4,605 | 3,450 | — |
| dual-cowl spt phtn 4P | 4,734 | 3,750 | — |
| conv cpe 2-4P | 4,698 | 3,650 | — |
| sdn 4d | 4,980 | 3,695 | — |
| club sdn 5P | 4,929 | 3,745 | — |
| sdn 7P | 5,046 | 3,825 | — |
| club berline 5P | 4,953 | 3,945 | — |
| limo 7P | 5,075 | 3,995 | — |

| Model 43 (wb 134.0; lwb-137.0)—2,500 built* | Wght | Price | Prod |
|---|---|---|---|
| rdstr 2-4P | 4,332 | 2,895 | — |
| touring 5P | 4,372 | 2,895 | — |
| cpe 2-4P | 4,528 | 2,685 | — |
| lwb sdn 4d | 4,638 | 2,685 | — |
| lwb club sdn 5P | 4,654 | 2,835 | — |
| lwb sdn 7P | 4,717 | 2,995 | — |
| limo (lwb) 7P | 4,819 | 3,145 | — |
| lwb conv sdn 5P | — | 3,650 | — |

* Calendar-year registration: 4,522.

| 1931 Engines | bore × stroke | bhp | availability |
|---|---|---|---|
| I-8, 366.0 | 3.50 × 4.75 | 125 | S-43 |
| I-8, 385.0 | 3.50 × 5.00 | 132 | S-41, 42 |

### 1932*

| Model 54 (wb 137.0; lwb-142.0) | Wght | Price | Prod |
|---|---|---|---|
| conv rdstr 2-4P | 4,650 | 3,100 | |
| touring 4P | — | 3,150 | |
| spt phtn 4P | — | 3,350 | 1550 |
| cpe 2-4P | 4,735 | 2,985 | |
| club 5P brougham | 4,745 | 2,850 | |
| sdn 4d | 4,819 | 2,985 | |

# Pierce-Arrow

| Model 54 (wb 137.0; lwb-142.0) | Wght | Price | Prod |
|---|---|---|---|
| club sdn 5P | — | 3,150 | |
| conv sdn 5P | 4,961 | 3,450 | |
| club berline 5P | — | 3,350 | |
| lwb touring 7P | — | 3,450 | |
| lwb sdn 7P | 5,024 | 3,185 | 237 |
| limo (lwb) 7P | 5,071 | 3,450 | |

| Model 51/52 (wb 142.0; lwb-147.0) | | | |
|---|---|---|---|
| 52 sdn 4d | 5,395 | 4,295 | |
| 52 club sdn 5P | — | 4,400 | 61 |
| 52 club berline 5P | — | 4,600 | |
| 51 lwb sdn 7P | 5,465 | 4,535 | 138 |
| 51 limo 7P (lwb) | 5,506 | 4,800 | |

| Model 53 (wb 137.0; lwb-142.0) | | | |
|---|---|---|---|
| conv rdstr 2-4P | — | 3,900 | |
| touring 4P | — | 3,950 | |
| spt phtn 4P | — | 4,150 | |
| cpe 2-4P | — | 3,785 | |
| club brougham 5P | 5,042 | 3,650 | 187 |
| sdn 4d | 5,080 | 3,785 | |
| club sdn 5P | 5,244 | 3,950 | |
| conv sdn 5P | — | 4,250 | |
| club berline 5P | — | 4,150 | |
| lwb touring 7P | — | 4,250 | |
| lwb sdn 7P | 5,301 | 3,985 | 61 |
| limo 7P (lwb) | 5,366 | 4,250 | |

* Calendar-year registrations: 2,481.

| 1932 Engines | bore × stroke | bhp | availability |
|---|---|---|---|
| I-8, 366.0 | 3.50 × 4.75 | 125 | S-54 |
| V-12, 398.0 | 3.25 × 4.00 | 140 | S-53 |
| V-12, 429.0 | 3.38 × 4.00 | 150 | S-51/52 |

## 1933*

### Model 836 (wb 136.0; lwb-139.0)—1,527 built

| | Wght | Price | Prod |
|---|---|---|---|
| conv rdstr 2-4P | 4,618 | 3,100 | |
| cpe 2-4P | 4,663 | 2,795 | |
| club brougham 5P | 4,622 | 2,385 | |
| sdn 4d | 4,660 | 2,575 | |
| club sdn 5P | 4,681 | 2,695 | |
| conv sdn 5P | 4,958 | 2,975 | |
| lwb sdn 7P | 4,780 | 2,850 | |
| limo 7P (lwb) | 4,819 | 2,975 | |
| salon conv rdstr 2-4P | 4,643 | 3,265 | |
| salon cpe 2-4P | 4,688 | 2,960 | |
| salon club brougham 5P | 4,647 | 2,550 | |
| salon sdn 4d | 4,685 | 2,740 | |
| salon club sdn 5P | 4,706 | 2,860 | |
| salon conv sdn 7P | 4,983 | 3,140 | |
| lwb salon sdn 7P | 4,805 | 3,015 | |
| salon limo lwb 7P | 4,844 | 3,140 | |

### Model 1236 (wb 136.0; lwb-139.0)—505 built

| | Wght | Price | Prod |
|---|---|---|---|
| conv rdstr 2-4P | 4,729 | 3,500 | |
| cpe 2-4P | 4,922 | 3,195 | |
| club brougham 5P | 4,854 | 2,785 | |
| sdn 4d | 4,892 | 2,975 | |
| club sdn 5P | 4,929 | 3,095 | |
| conv sdn 5P | — | 3,375 | |
| lwb sdn 7P | 5,027 | 3,250 | |
| limo 7P (lwb) | 5,088 | 3,375 | |
| salon conv rdstr 2-4P | 4,754 | 3,665 | |
| salon cpe 2-4P | 4,947 | 3,360 | |
| salon club brougham 5P | 4,879 | 2,950 | |
| salon sdn 4d | 4,917 | 3,140 | |

| Model 1236 (wb 136.0; lwb-139.0) | Wght | Price | Prod |
|---|---|---|---|
| salon club sdn 5P | 4,954 | 3,260 | |
| salon conv sdn 5P | — | 3,540 | |
| lwb salon sdn 7P | 5,052 | 3,415 | |
| salon limo 7P (lwb) | 5,113 | 3,540 | |

| Model 1242 (wb 137.0; lwb-142.0) | | | |
|---|---|---|---|
| conv cpe rdstr | 5,107 | 3,900 | |
| touring 5P | 5,256 | 3,950 | |
| spt phtn 5P | 5,296 | 4,150 | |
| cpe 2-4P | — | 3,785 | |
| club brougham 5P | 5,198 | 3,650 | 45 |
| sdn 4d | — | 3,785 | |
| club sdn 5P | 5,361 | 3,950 | |
| conv sdn 5P | 5,438 | 4,250 | |
| club berline 5P | — | 4,150 | |
| lwb touring 7P | — | 4,250 | |
| lwb sdn 7P | — | 3,985 | 73 |
| limo 7P (lwb) | 5,507 | 4,250 | |

| Model 1247 (wb 142.0; lwb-147.0)—143 built | | | |
|---|---|---|---|
| sdn 4d | — | 4,295 | — |
| club sdn 5P | 5,417 | 4,400 | — |
| club berline 5P | 5,421 | 4,600 | — |
| lwb LeBaron cpe metal-back 2P | 5,286 | 5,300 | — |
| lwb LeBaron cpe leather-back 2P | 5,286 | 5,600 | — |
| lwb LeBaron conv vic 5P | 5,198 | 5,200 | — |
| lwb LeBaron conv sdn 5P | 5,466 | 5,700 | — |
| lwb LeBaron conv sdn/partition 5P | — | 6,100 | — |
| lwb LeBaron club sdn | 5,391 | 5,700 | — |
| lwb LeBaron sdn 7P | 5,550 | 4,535 | — |
| limo 7P (lwb) | 5,550 | 4,800 | — |
| LeBaron limo 7P (lwb) | 5,778 | 6,200 | — |
| lwb Brunn town brougham | — | 6,700 | — |
| lwb Brunn cab | — | 7,200 | — |
| lwb Brunn town car | 5,768 | 6,700 | — |
| lwb Brunn brougham | — | 7,200 | — |

| Silver Arrow (wb 139.0) | | | |
|---|---|---|---|
| sdn 4d | 5,729 | 10,000 | 5 |

* Calendar-year registrations: 1,776.

| 1933 Engines | bore × stroke | bhp | availability |
|---|---|---|---|
| I-8, 366.0 | 3.50 × 4.75 | 135 | S-836 |
| V-12, 429.0 | 3.38 × 4.00 | 160 | S-1236 |
| V-12, 462.0 | 3.50 × 4.00 | 175 | S-1242, 1247, S Arrow |

## 1934*

| 836A Eight (wb 136.0)—700+ built | Wght | Price | Prod |
|---|---|---|---|
| club brougham 5P | 4,780 | 2,495 | |
| club brougham salon 5P | 4,797 | 2,595 | |
| sdn 4d | 4,923 | 2,595 | |
| salon sdn 4d | 4,940 | 2,695 | |

| 840A DeLuxe Eight (wb 139.0; lwb-144.0) | | | |
|---|---|---|---|
| conv rdstr | 4,817 | 2,995 | |
| cpe 4P | 4,913 | 2,895 | |
| club brougham 5P | 4,906 | 2,795 | 439 |
| sdn 4d | 4,964 | 2,895 | |
| club sdn 5P | 5,042 | 2,995 | |
| Silver Arrow sdn 4d (lwb) | 5,046 | 3,495 | |
| lwb sdn 7P | 5,107 | 3,200 | |
| limo 7P (lwb) | 5,183 | 3,350 | 219 |
| Brunn metro | — | — | |
| town brougham 5P (lwb) | 5,228 | 4,995 | |

| 1240A Salon Twelve (wb 139.0; lwb-144.0) | | | |
|---|---|---|---|
| conv rdstr 4P | 5,072 | 3,395 | |
| cpe 4P | 5,168 | 3,295 | |

# Pierce-Arrow

| 1240A Salon Twelve (wb 139.0; lwb:144.0) | Wght | Price | Prod |
|---|---|---|---|
| club brougham 5P | 5,152 | 3,195 | 167 |
| sdn 4d | 5,227 | 3,295 | |
| club sdn 5P | 5,315 | 3,395 | |
| Silver Arrow sdn 4d (lwb) | 5,347 | 3,895 | 120 |
| lwb sdn 7P | 5,381 | 3,600 | |
| limo 7P (lwb) | 5,442 | 3,750 | |
| Brunn metro town brougham 7P (lwb) | 5,529 | 5,395 | |

| 1248A Custom Twelve (wb 147.0)—90 built | | | |
|---|---|---|---|
| sdn 7P | — | 4,295 | — |
| limo 7P | 5,494 | 4,495 | — |
| Brunn limo 7P | — | 6,000 | — |
| Brunn town brougham 7P | — | 6,500 | — |
| Brunn town cab 7P | — | 7,000 | — |
| Brunn town car 7P | — | 6,500 | — |
| Brunn brougham 7P | — | 7,000 | — |

\* Calendar-year registrations: 1,740.

| 1934 Engines | bore × stroke | bhp | availability |
|---|---|---|---|
| I-8, 366.0 | 3.50 × 4.75 | 135 | S-836A |
| I-8, 385.0 | 3.50 × 5.00 | 140 | S-840A |
| V-12, 462.0 | 3.50 × 4.00 | 175 | S-1240A, 1248A |

## 1935*

| 845 Eight (wb 139.0; lwb-144.0) | Wght | Price | Prod |
|---|---|---|---|
| conv rdstr 2-4P | — | 2,995 | |
| cpe 2-4P | — | 2,895 | |
| club brougham 5P | — | 2,795 | 360 |
| sdn 4d | 4,964 | 2,895 | |
| club sdn 5P | — | 2,995 | |
| Silver Arrow sdn 4d (lwb) | — | 3,495 | |
| lwb sdn 7P | — | 3,200 | 163 |
| limo 7P (lwb) | — | 3,350 | |
| Brunn metro town brougham 5P (lwb) | — | 4,995 | |

| 1245 Twelve (wb 139.0; lwb-144.0) | | | |
|---|---|---|---|
| conv rdstr 2-4P | — | 3,395 | |
| cpe 2-4P | — | 3,295 | |
| club brougham 5P | — | 3,195 | 90 |
| sdn 4d | 5,433 | 3,295 | |
| club sdn 5P | — | 3,395 | |
| Silver Arrow sdn 4d (lwb) | — | 3,895 | |
| lwb sdn 7P | — | 3,600 | 54 |
| limo 7P (lwb) | — | 3,750 | |
| Brunn town brougham 5P (lwb) | — | 5,395 | |

| 1255 Twelve (wb 147.0)—60 built | | | |
|---|---|---|---|
| sdn 7P | — | 4,295 | — |
| limo 7P | — | 4,495 | — |

\* Calendar-year registrations: 875.

| 1935 Engines | bore × stroke | bhp | availability |
|---|---|---|---|
| I-8, 366.0 | 3.50 × 4.75 | 135 | S-836A |
| I-8, 385.0 | 3.50 × 5.00 | 140 | S-845 |
| V-12, 462.0 | 3.50 × 4.00 | 175 | S-1245, 1255 |

## 1936*

| 1601 Eight (wb 139.0, 144.0, 147.0) | Wght | Price | Prod |
|---|---|---|---|
| 438C | cpe 2P, 139" | — | 3,115 | |
| 438E | club berline 5P, 139" | 5,600 | 3,495 | |
| 438N | club sdn 5P, 139" | 5,600 | 3,295 | 403 |
| 438P | conv rdstr cpe 2P, 139" | 5,590 | 3,295 | |
| 438S | sdn 4d, 139" | — | 3,195 | |
| 444L | limo 7P, 144" | — | 3,650 | 207 |
| 444M | sdn 7P, 144" | — | 3,500 | |
| 447L | limo 7P, 147" | — | — | 26 |
| 447M | sdn 7P, 147" | — | — | |

| 1602 Twelve (wb 139.0; lwb-144.0)—135 built** | | | |
|---|---|---|---|
| 538 | sdn 4d | — | 3,900 | — |
| 544 | lwb sdn 7P | — | 4,050 | — |
| 538 | conv rdstr cpe, 2P | 5,800 | 3,695 | — |
| 538 | club sdn 5P | 5,850 | 3,795 | — |

| 1603 Twelve (wb 147.0)—71 built | | | |
|---|---|---|---|
| sdn 7P | — | 4,795 | — |
| limo 7P | 6,145 | 4,995 | — |
| Brunn metro town car 7P | — | 5,795 | — |

\* Calendar-year registrations: 787.
\*\* Includes additional styles as per 1601 "438" and "444."

| 1936 Engines | bore × stroke | bhp | availability |
|---|---|---|---|
| I-8, 385.0 | 3.50 × 5.00 | 150 | S-Eight |
| V-12, 462.0 | 3.50 × 4.00 | 185 | S-Twelve |

## 1937*

| 1701 (wb 139.0, 144.0, 147.0) | Wght | Price | Prod |
|---|---|---|---|
| cpe 2P, 139" | — | 3,195 | |
| club berline 5P, 139" | 5,600 | 3,495 | |
| club sdn 5P, 139" | 5,600 | 3,295 | |
| conv rdstr cpe 2P, 139" | 5,590 | 3,295 | 50 |
| sdn 4d, 139" | — | 3,195 | |
| conv sdn 5P, 139" | — | — | |
| formal sdn 4d, 139" | — | — | |
| limo 7P, 144" | — | 3,650 | 61 |
| sdn 7P, 144" | — | 3,500 | |
| limo 7P, 147" | — | — | 10 |
| sdn 7P, 147" | — | — | |

| 1702 Twelve (wb 139.0; lwb-144.0) | | | |
|---|---|---|---|
| sdn 4d | — | 3,900 | |
| conv rdstr cpe 2P | 5,800 | 3,695 | |
| club sdn 5P | 5,850 | 3,795 | 20 |
| club berline 5P | 5,850 | 3,945 | |
| conv sdn 5P | 5,920 | 4,650 | |
| formal sdn 4d | — | — | |
| lwb sdn 7P | — | 4,050 | 23 |

| 1703 Twelve (wb 147.0)—28 built | | | |
|---|---|---|---|
| sdn 7P | 6,065 | 4,845 | — |
| limo 7P | 6,145 | 4,995 | — |
| town car 7P | 6,100 | 6,500 | — |
| Brunn metro town car 7P | 6,085 | 5,795 | — |

\* Calendar-year registrations: 166.

| 1937 Engines | bore × stroke | bhp | availability |
|---|---|---|---|
| I-8, 385.0 | 3.50 × 5.00 | 150 | S-Eight |
| V-12, 462.0 | 3.50 × 4.00 | 185 | S-Twelve |

## 1938

| 1801 Eight (wb 138.0, 144.0, 147.0) | Wght | Price | Prod |
|---|---|---|---|
| Body Styles similar to 1937 "1701" | — | — | 12* |

| 1802 Twelve (wb 139.0; lwb-144.0) | | | |
|---|---|---|---|
| Body styles similar to 1937 "1702" | — | — | 12* |

| 1803 Twelve (wb 147.0) | | | |
|---|---|---|---|
| Body Styles similar to 1937 "1703" | — | — | 12* |

\* Estimated; actual model-year production less than 40.

| 1938 Engines | bore × stroke | bhp | availability |
|---|---|---|---|
| I-8, 385.0 | 3.50 × 5.00 | 150 | S-Eight |
| V-12, 462.0 | 3.50 × 4.00 | 185 | S-Twelve |

# Plymouth

When Walter P. Chrysler decided to launch a low-priced car in 1928, his sales manager, Joseph W. Frazer, suggested the name Plymouth, after the storied Massachusetts rock where the Pilgrims landed. WPC wasn't sure people would make that connection, so Frazer mentioned another product well known to the ex-farmboy. That was all Chrysler needed. "Every goddam farmer in America's heard of Plymouth Binder Twine," he replied—so Plymouth it was.

Plymouth was a success from day one. Though it was first sold only through Chrysler dealers, demand was so strong that franchises were extended to Dodge and DeSoto agents by 1930. The strategy was an excellent one that vastly increased the number of Plymouth dealers while insulating them from the Depression-era sales reversals suffered by costlier Chrysler makes.

Yet despite those "hard times"—or perhaps because of them—Plymouth prospered in the '30s on a formidable combination of low price, attractive styling, and engineering often more advanced than that of Ford or Chevrolet. Though Plymouth never outproduced those rivals, it was firmly established as America's number-three seller as early as 1932, a spot it would hold well into the '50s.

Many key features figured in this meteoric rise: all-steel construction (per Chrysler practice) in an age of wood-framed bodies; four-wheel hydraulic brakes some years before Ford and Chevy had them; "Floating Power" rubber engine mounts that gave the 1931 models "the smoothness of an eight and the economy of a four"; independent coil-spring front suspension for 1934, again beating Ford (and matching Chevrolet); rubber body isolators (1936); standard safety glass, recessed controls, concealed heater blower and defroster vents (1937).

Reflecting these and other pluses, Plymouth was one of the few makes to score higher production in 1930-31 than in the pre-Depression period. It also gained in 1933, one of the roughest industry years on record. Output peaked at nearly 552,000 for 1937, dropped to about 279,000 for recession-year 1938, then recovered beyond the half-million mark by 1941.

A "New Finer Plymouth" was announced in April 1930, but it was much like the 1928-29 Models Q and U, with the same 109-inch wheelbase and a competitive lineup in the $600-$700 range. The big difference was a four-cylinder engine enlarged for the third time in as many years, reaching 196 cid (versus 170 for '28 and 175.4 for 1929). Horsepower stood at 48, up three. Like the Model U, the 30U carried into the succeeding calendar year, but saw lower total production of 76,950 versus 108,350. A likely factor was Ford's enormously popular new Model A.

Plymouth responded in May 1931 with a car that was genuinely new, the fruit of a $2.5-million development program. Designated PA, it kept to the same wheelbase but boasted "Floating Power," as mentioned, plus eight more horses to go with it. There was also a broader lineup with a dashing new sport phaeton and rumble-seat roadster. But mindful of the Depression, Plymouth also fielded two cheap "Thrift" sedans at $495 and $575. Despite the general economic gloom, model-year production soared to nearly 107,000.

Bowing in February 1932 was the last four-cylinder domestic Plymouth for the next 46 years. Styling wasn't greatly altered, but the new PB was more expansive on a three-inch longer standard wheelbase. A convertible sedan was added, Chrysler evidently feeling confident enough to dabble with less-popular body styles even in its price-leader line. Also new was a seven-seat sedan on a 121-inch chassis. That model found only 2200 buyers and was duly dropped—but not for long. Horsepower kept climbing, reaching 65, but prices stayed put. Sales fell sharply in this first year of Ford's milestone V-8, but were still respectable at just under 84,000.

Plymouth offered better value by switching to a six for 1933. The project cost $9 million, but was worth every penny in extra sales, which leaped beyond 298,000 for the model year. No wonder, for the new Six sold for as little as $445, over $300 less than the original 1928 Four. The six naturally had more horses, but from fewer cubic inches. Arriving with 189.8 cid and 70 bhp, it was stroked to 201.3 cid and 77 bhp for 1934. Save an interim push to 82 bhp for 1935, this sturdy four-main-bearing L-head would remain that size through 1941, when it was spinning out 87 bhp.

Like other makes, Plymouth continued "splitting" model years by offering two 1933 series. The first, titled PC, was built from October 1932 through March 1933 in five models on a 107-inch wheelbase. Then came a two-series PD line of standard and DeLuxe Sixes on respective wheelbases of 108 and 112 inches. A convertible coupe was exclusive to DeLuxe. Following another industry trend, Plymouth began a cautious move from four-square to streamlined styling, adopting fully skirted fenders and a rounder hood/radiator ensemble. A winged-lady hood mascot arrived as a new accessory.

Styling was smoother still for 1934, when Plymouth made its aforementioned moves to independent front suspension and a larger six. Offerings grouped into PF Standard and PE DeLuxe, the latter on a still-longer 114-inch wheelbase. A second Standard series designated PG arrived in March with three cheap models priced around $500. DeLuxes now featured safety glass as well as "artillery" steel wheels, which were gaining favor over traditional wires that looked old-hat on streamlined cars. The winged-lady mascot was replaced by an image of the good ship *Mayflower*, reminding buyers of the Plymouth Rock connection.

Though a factory Plymouth station wagon wouldn't arrive until 1938, U.S. Body & Forge of Tell City, Indiana, built wagon bodies on

**1932 Series PA 2/4-passenger convertible coupe**

**1932 Series PB convertible sedan two-door**

# Plymouth

1933 Series PC Six four-door sedan

1934 Series PE DeLuxe four-door sedan

1935 Series PJ DeLuxe Six 2/4-passenger convertible coupe

1936 Series P-1 Business Series 2-passenger coupe

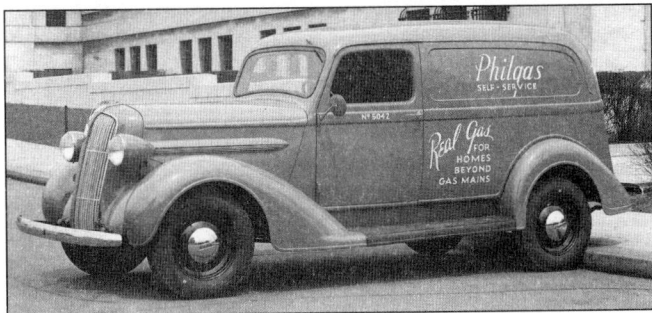

1937 Series PT-50 commercial sedan

modified 1934 Plymouth Standard chassis. The resulting Westchester Suburban was a four-door model made mostly of wood from the cowl back; it thus demanded lots of upkeep. Only 119 were built that year. On August 10, Chrysler built its one-millionth Plymouth, and Walter Chrysler was pleased by even higher model-year volume of over 321,000.

Lumpy but modern "potato" streamlining identified the fully redesigned 1935 PJ Plymouths, which included new "trunkback" two- and four-door Touring sedans with integral luggage compartments. Standard and DeLuxe continued, but now shared a single 113-inch wheelbase. The one exception was the new DeLuxe Traveler, a five-passenger four-door sedan on its own 128-inch chassis. Only 77 were sold that year. All models boasted new "Chair-Height" seats, improved engine cooling via full-length water jackets, an extra five horsepower, and better handling via a new front stabilizer bar and improved weight distribution. Helped by prices as low as $510, Plymouth moved up in model-year production: nearly 327,500.

Despite relatively few changes, the 1936 Plymouths broke the half-million mark, a first for the make. The long chassis was trimmed three inches between wheel centers, and the Standard line was prosaically retitled Business. The main styling distinction was a fulsome barrellike radiator with thin vertical bars.

Plymouth achieved its decade production high with rebodied 1937 models bearing reduced window areas but standard safety glass on all models. Also as mentioned, Plymouth offered recessed interior knobs, plus a rounded dash bottom and a padded front-seat top, all for safety's sake. Oddly, a right-hand windshield wiper still cost extra. Crank-open windshields were in their final year, but 1937 was the first time Plymouth prices exceeded $1000. That applied to a new seven-seat DeLuxe limousine, which shared a long wheelbase, stretched seven inches from '36, with a similar sedan. Other models lost an inch between wheel centers.

Styling became dumpy for 10th Anniversary 1938; a near-oval radiator didn't help. Models and specifications were mostly carryovers, though there were some changes. For example, a high-compression head was newly optional, lifting bhp to 86, up four from standard. Also available, as it had been since 1936, was a low-compression 65-bhp "economy" engine, a no-charge lure offered to Depression-weary buyers. On the model front, the Business line became the Roadking in March 1938, but was no less spartan for it. A four-door DeLuxe station wagon, the Suburban, bowed as Plymouth's first such "catalog" model, though U.S. Body & Forge built its coachwork, as it had done back in '34. Like some other contemporary wagons, this came with front-door glass only; glazing behind cost extra. There was no rear bumper either, but a tailgate-mounted spare tire provided some protection.

A refreshing facelift arrived for 1939, the work of Raymond H. Dietrich, the great coachbuilder who then headed Chrysler styling. Hallmarks included a strongly peaked "prow" front, perhaps inspired by the Lincoln Zephyr's, plus a vee'd two-piece windshield instead of the previous single pane. Headlights, now rectangular, nestled within the front fenders, and the gearshift moved from floor to steering column. The canvas convertible top could be power-operated for the first time in any car, a definite selling point—especially in the low-price arena. Offerings largely reprised the '38 line, but Roadking added a Suburban and two-door utility sedan. The former saw just 97 copies. Plymouth's long models were equally slow sellers: only about 2000 for the model year. Such cars would be a Chrysler specialty for many years to come, but none would sell well. Making a final stand in the DeLuxe series was the rumble-seat convertible coupe and a 117-inch-wheelbase five-seat convertible sedan. The latter was a Plymouth exclusive at Chrysler Corporation for '39, revived for a 12-month stand. After a big dip below 280,000 for recessionary '38, Plymouth recovered nicely with 1939 volume of over 417,000.

# Plymouth

1938 Series S-6 DeLuxe Westchester Suburban wagon

1939 Series P-8 DeLuxe convertible coupe

1940 Series P-10 DeLuxe convertible coupe

1941 Series P20-12 Special DeLuxe station wagon

1942 Series P-14C Special DeLuxe convertible coupe

1942 Series P-14C Special DeLuxe four-door sedan

A full body change for 1940 introduced "speedline" fenders and better proportions on three-inch-longer wheelbases. Sealed-beam headlamps appeared, as elsewhere in Detroit, and simple horizontal-bar grilles flanked a less-prominent prow. Sedans were now solely trunked fastbacks, though with more luggage space than the superseded "trunkbacks." Though 1940 prices began as low as $645, Plymouths remained a bit costlier than equivalent Fords. They also remained noticeably slower than Dearborn's V-8/85s despite a token two extra horsepower for 1940. Yet if no speedway threat, the Plymouth six still provided reliable cruising at over 65 mph, and was well-known for economy. A notable manufacturing advance was Chrysler "Superfinish," a special process of giving certain internal engine parts a mirror-smooth surface for reduced friction and decreased wear.

After healthy 1940-model production of 423,000, Plymouth scored a robust 546,000 for '41, thanks mainly to heavy output in the closing months of 1940. Calendar-year figures reflected the turn toward defense work at the end of 1941, running some 50,000 units behind Ford.

The 1941 Plymouths wore an adroit facelift featuring a simple, almost heart-shaped grille and modest bright-metal side accents. Six cheap standard-trim models were added, Roadking became DeLuxe, and the old DeLuxe was now Special DeLuxe. The slow-selling limousine was axed after just 24 were built. Other '41 rarities were the DeLuxe club coupe (204) and the standard club coupe (994), utility sedan (468), and Suburban (217). All models boasted another Chrysler engineering first: the Safety-Rim wheel, with a beaded circumference to prevent tire loss in a blowout. The battery moved under the hood for the first time, and Plymouth offered "Powermatic" shift, a vacuum-transmission assist.

War-shortened 1942 introduced a more-massive look via a wider grille and front fenders, plus door sheetmetal extended to cover the running boards. The six was enlarged for the first time since 1934, bored out to 217.8 cid and 95 bhp; it wouldn't be touched again until 1949. Standard-trim models departed, and Special DeLuxe expanded with the Town Sedan, a new period Chrysler style with more-formal, closed-in rear roof quarters.

Plymouth Division's 1942 output was close to 152,500 when the government halted civilian auto production in February for the duration of World War II. While all '42 Detroit cars are quite scarce today, some of these Plymouths are especially so. For example, only 80 utility sedans, 1136 wagons, and 2806 convertibles were built.

While Plymouth manufactured munitions and military engines during the war, stylists like A. B. "Buzz" Grisinger, John Chika, and Herb Weissinger worked on postwar ideas whenever they could. Typical of Chrysler thinking at the time, these involved smooth, flush-fender bodies with thin door pillars and wraparound grilles. But like most everyone else, Plymouth resumed civilian operations with mildly modified '42s, which the booming seller's market hap-

# Plymouth

pily consumed into model-year '49. The first all-new postwar Plymouths bowed in March '49 as squarer and more-upright than any wartime study. Plymouth built just 770 cars between V-J Day and the end of 1945, then quickly picked up the pace, reaching near 265,000 for 1946 and over half a million by '49.

Plymouth's 1946-48 facelift involved a more-modest grille with alternating thick/thin horizontal bars, rectangular parking lights beneath the headlamps, wide front-fender moldings, a new hood ornament, and reworked rear fenders. DeLuxe and Special DeLuxe returned, but without utility models. No styling or mechanical changes would occur through early '49, so serial numbers are the only clue as to model year.

Postwar inflation boosted 1946 prices by some $270 over 1942. The '47s ran about $250 more than the '46s, and the '48s were up to $300 costlier than the '47s. While Plymouth readied its first all-new postwar models for spring introduction, the '48s were sold as "interim" '49s with inch-smaller wheels and tires (15s versus 16s), plus other minor alterations, but still at '48 prices.

When the "real" '49s arrived, Grisinger and Weissinger had departed for Kaiser-Frazer and a new styling philosophy was in force. It reflected the tastes of K. T. Keller, who'd taken over as company president following Walter Chrysler's death in 1940. No fan of low "torpedos," Keller preferred what designers termed "three-box styling—one box on top of two others," believing in function over form. "Cars should accommodate people rather than the ideas of far-out designers," he said. What he failed to grasp was how much postwar buyers wanted the long, low look—never mind the reduced headroom or ground clearance. In time, Keller's practical bent would severely hurt company sales.

But the seller's market was at its height in 1949, most everything sold no matter what it looked like, and the new Plymouth offered an efficient, comfortable, and roomy package with good visibility. Wheelbase stretched to 118.5 inches for a DeLuxe notchback coupe and sedan priced in the $1500s, and for Special DeLuxe

**1946-48 Series P-15C Special DeLuxe convertible coupe**

**1946-48 Special DeLuxe four-door sedan**

**1946-48 DeLuxe coupe**

**1949 Series P-19 DeLuxe Suburban two-door station wagon**

**1950 Series P-20 Special DeLuxe convertible coupe**

**1951 Series P-23 Cranbrook four-door sedan**

# Plymouth

coupe, sedan, convertible, and wood-trimmed wagon covering a $1600-$2400 spread. A shorter 111-inch chassis supported a DeLuxe fastback two-door, business coupe, and new all-steel Suburban wagon.

Plymouth liked to credit its '49 Suburban as the first "modern" wagon, but Chevy, Olds, and Pontiac also issued all-steel haulers during 1949. Still, the Suburban cost only $1840, quite a bit less than the GM models, and thus sold well: nearly 20,000 for '49. Buyers evidently loved wagons that didn't require costly, time-consuming upkeep. Within four years, other Chrysler makes and the rest of Detroit had put "woodys" to rest. Plymouth kept its wood-framed wagon through 1950.

Oldsmobile's 1949 "Rocket" 88 fired the gun for a "horsepower race" that turned all manner of staid cars into stylish sizzlers. Plymouth was one of them. But even more than Chevrolet, Pontiac, or sister Dodge, Plymouth reinvented itself because it had to. Although the make spent most of the early '50s still entrenched as number-three, it sold fewer and fewer cars after 1949, bottoming to fifth in calendar-year sales by 1954.

As continuations of the new '49 models, the 1950-54 Plymouths were well-engineered, solid, and reliable; but square, stubby-looking, and none too fast. The ancient L-head six was raised to 97 bhp for '49 and would remain there through 1952, after which it went to 100 bhp (probably by the stroke of an ad writer's pen). Plymouths were still thrifty (20-23 mpg wasn't uncommon), but hard-pressed to beat 80 mph. However, automatic electric choke and combined ignition/starter switch arrived as important innovations for the low-priced field.

The 1950 line was basically a '49 reprise. An effective facelift brought a simpler square grille with large horizontal bar, slightly

**1952 Series P-23 Cranbrook Belvedere hardtop coupe**

**1953 Series P24-2 Cranbrook club coupe**

**1954 Belvedere sport coupe hardtop**

1955 Belvedere Six sport coupe hardtop

1955 Belvedere Suburban four-door station wagon

1956 Plaza club sedan with Sportone two-tone

longer rear decks (to relieve the boxiness), and taillights placed low within reworked fenders. The Special outsold the plain DeLuxe by about 7-to-5.

After some 611,000 of its 1950s, Plymouth built about the same number of its 1951 models, which gained a modified hood and a lower, wider grille that made frontal appearance a little less blunt. New model names accompanied the fresh face. Short-wheelbase DeLuxes were retitled Concord and now included a two-door Savoy wagon besides the Suburban. The long-chassis DeLuxe and Special DeLuxe were now Cambridge and Cranbrook, respectively. The latter listed a convertible and Plymouth's first hardtop coupe, the Belvedere, which typically wore "saddleback" two-toning with the roof and rear body (but not rear fenders) in a contrast color. Ford also offered its first hardtop for '51, but it, too, was a year behind Chevrolet's Bel Air. The Belvedere trailed both in sales by wide margins, but was still pretty popular, with 51,266 built for 1951-52.

Chrysler didn't bother to separate 1951 and '52 production, mainly because its cars changed so little. Plymouth was no exception, though a rear nameplate integrated with the trunk-handle (replacing separate script) was a small spotter's point. Overdrive arrived for '52 as a new option, and all Plymouths continued with an important 1951 improvement: Oriflow shock absorbers, a Chrysler hydraulic-type designed to improve ride and handling. But dumpy looks, a weak old six, and lack of full automatic transmission put Plymouth at a sales disadvantage in '52, when output slid by a substantial 204,000 units to below 400,000, aggravated by government-ordered civilian production cutbacks for the Korean War.

The '53s addressed some of the competitive deficits, starting with an outer-body reskin that brought flow-through fenderlines, a one-piece windshield, and a more-aggressive grille. A single new 114-inch wheelbase was used for a revived two-series lineup minus Concord (Cambridge expanded to embrace the business coupe and wagons). Another ploy to boost sales was the midyear introduction of semiautomatic "Hy-Drive," a manual transmission with torque converter that eliminated most clutch work, though you still had to clutch between forward and reverse.

But the '53s still looked small, and so did the facelifted '54s, which were as uninspired as any Chrysler product. Volume dwindled from the previous year's 650,000-plus to around 463,000—less than half of Ford/Chevy output. Models were regrouped again, this time into cheap Plaza, midline Savoy, and top-shelf Belvedere series covering a $1600-$2300 price spread. Plaza and Savoy each listed a club coupe, sedans with two or four doors, and a Suburban wagon; there was also a Plaza business coupe. Belvedere comprised four-door sedan, convertible, Suburban, and Sport Coupe hardtop.

Two important mechanical changes occurred during '54. The old six was enlarged for the first time since 1942, a longer stroke swelling displacement to 230.2 cid and horsepower to 110. Also at about midyear came a fully automatic two-speed PowerFlite transmission as a new option. It would prove very popular.

Plymouth repeated this basic lineup for 1955, but with a dramatic difference: all-new styling hatched by Chrysler design chief Virgil Exner and executed under his assistant, Maury Baldwin. Suddenly, Plymouths looked exciting. What's more, they had performance to match, thanks to the first V-8 in Plymouth history—and a new polyspherical design, at that.

Called "Hy-Fire," this new V-8 was an excellent overhead-valve unit in the small-block tradition begun with Studebaker's 232 of 1951. It premiered in two sizes: 241 cid and 157 bhp, and a 260 with 167 standard bhp or 177 with an optional "Power-Pak" of four-barrel carb and dual exhausts. Outstanding features ran to lightweight aluminum pistons and carburetor, and chrome-plated top piston rings for longer life and better oil control. Tuning changes brought the old six, now called "PowerFlow," to 117 bhp.

Other highlights for '55 included suspended foot pedals, tubeless tires, front shocks enclosed within the front coil springs, and dashboard lever control for the PowerFlite automatic. There were also several options new to Plymouth: factory air conditioning, power windows, and power front seat.

But Plymouth's most-visible '55 attraction was its crisp new styling: pointed front and rear fenders, smooth flanks, shapely tail, a bright but not gaudy grille. Two-toning was confined to the roof and, via optional moldings, broad bodyside sweep panels. Four-door wagons returned for the first time since 1948 as Plaza and Belvedere Suburbans. The line-topping Belvedere convertible came only with V-8, as it would through the end of the decade.

Ads proclaimed the '55 a "great new car for the young in heart." It was certainly a clean break from Plymouth's plodding past. Customers rushed to buy—encouraged by prices little higher than in '54—but production lagged and Plymouth dropped to sixth for the model year at 401,000 units. But volume for calendar '55 was a rousing 742,991 (including some '56s, of course)—a record that would stand well into the '60s.

Plymouth reclaimed fourth for model-year '56s, which introduced "The Forward Look"—essentially tailfins, achieved by raising rear fenderlines a little. Engineers brought forth push-button PowerFlite, a 12-volt electrical system, and an optional "Highway Hi-Fi" record player that used special platters and a tone arm designed to stay in the groove—which it typically did not on bumpy roads. Suburbans became a separate line with two-door Deluxe, two- and four-door Customs, and four-door Sport models respectively trimmed like Plaza, Savoy, and Belvedere. A Sport Sedan four-door hardtop expanded Belvedere models, and a two-door hardtop did likewise for Savoy. Both Hy-Fire V-8s were larger and more-potent, comprising a base 270-cid version with 180 bhp, and a pair of 277s packing 187 and 200 bhp.

An even hotter Plymouth arrived at mid-'56: the limited-edition Fury. An attractive hardtop coupe, it came only in white, set off by bodyside sweepspears of gold anodized aluminum. Power was supplied by a special 303 V-8 with 240 bhp via 9.25:1 compression, solid lifters, stronger valve springs, dual exhausts, and a Carter four-barrel carb. A stock Fury could do 0-60 mph in about 10 seconds and reach 110 mph, though one modified example approached 145 mph on the sands of Daytona Beach. The Fury gave a big boost to Plymouth's growing performance image, and 4485 of the '56s were sold—not bad for the $2866 price, some $600 above the Belvedere hardtop.

After record-shattering production of nearly 553,000, Plymouth zoomed to better than 762,000 with its stunning all-new '57 line. Ads said, "Suddenly, It's 1960"—and not without reason. Next to its rivals, Plymouth did seem "three full years ahead," with the lowest beltline and highest tailfins of the Low-Priced Three. Wheelbases lengthened to 122 inches for wagons and to 118 inches for other models. Offerings were unchanged through midyear, when a Savoy Sport Sedan hardtop was added.

The PowerFlow six had been coaxed up to 132 bhp by 1957, when Plymouth listed no fewer than five V-8s: 197- and 235-bhp 277s, new 301s with 215/235 bhp, and the Fury's even larger new wedgehead 318 with 290 bhp. TorqueFlite, Chrysler's excellent new three-speed automatic, was an optional alternative to PowerFlite. Also shared with other '57 Chrysler cars was new torsion-bar front suspension, whose superior geometry made for the best-handling Plymouth ever.

It's hard to remember how truly different Plymouth seemed in 1957: low and wide with distinctive "shark" fins, a graceful grille, a front bumper raised over a vertically slotted center panel, two-toning on the roof and tasteful bodyside color panels (sometimes the roof alone), huge glass areas (the convertible windshield curved at the top as well as the sides), and a delicate-looking thin-section roofline on hardtop coupes. Suburbans gained load space

# Plymouth

1956 Belvedere convertible coupe

1956 Fury sport coupe hardtop

1957 Belvedere two-door sedan

1957 Belvedere four-door sedan

1957 Fury hardtop coupe

1958 Belvedere sport coupe hardtop

1958 Belvedere sport sedan hardtop

1959 Sport Fury convertible coupe

1959 Sport Fury hardtop coupe

1960 Fury hardtop sedan

# Plymouth

1960 Fury hardtop coupe

1960 Valiant V-200 four-door sedan

1960 Valiant V-100 four-door station wagon

with an upright spare tire mounted in the right-rear fender, an idea borrowed from the 1956 Plymouth Plainsman show car. The '57 Plymouths were indeed memorable, but their tendency to early rust—reflecting a rushed development program and a consequent decline in quality control—makes good examples fairly rare today.

A predictably mild facelift for '58 brought quad headlamps, a horizontal-bar grille insert (repeated in the under-bumper modesty panel), and small round taillights at the base of the fins (bright metal filled the space above). A trio of 318 V-8s offered 225-290 bhp (the latter standard for Fury), and a newly optional 350 "Golden Commando" wedgehead packed 305 bhp or, with that year's ultra-rare fuel-injection option, 315 bhp. A deep national recession held production to just under 444,000, but most everyone built fewer cars for '58.

Plymouth shared in the industry's modest '59 recovery, turning out a bit more than 458,000 cars that were heavily restyled—and heavy-handed: longer and higher fins, garish eggcrate grille, headlamps with odd "siamesed" eyelids, more-prominent bumpers, more-plentiful bright trim, and abstract pilgrim-ship emblems. The Plaza vanished and Savoy and Belvedere moved down a notch in price; Fury became a top-line series with two- and four- door hardtops and a four-door sedan in the $2700-$2800 range. Plymouth's high performer was the new Sport Fury, offering a convertible as well as hardtop coupe for around $3000, including a 260-bhp 318 V-8. That year's regular 318 delivered 230 bhp. Fuel injection was no longer offered, but a new 361 "Golden Commando" V-8 with 305 bhp arrived as an $87 extra.

The division's '59 convertibles and hardtop coupes could be ordered with a simulated spare tire on the decklid, a lump of add-on tin reflecting Virgil Exner's love of "classic" design elements. It's since acquired the unflattering nickname "toilet seat." Typical of the gimmick-mad 1950s—and increasingly of Chrysler—was Sport Fury's standard "swivel-action" front seats: individual affairs (separated by a pull-down armrest) that turned outward at the touch of a lever to ease getting in and out. Sturdy latches kept them from swiveling while in use.

Also gimmicky, if occasionally predictive, were the several interesting Plymouth-branded show cars of the 1950s. They started with Ghia's 1950 XX-500, a pretty sedan that won Exner's patronage for the Italian coachworks to build later show cars and limousines. The 1954 Explorer, another Ghia-built Exner design, was a smoothly styled grand tourer. Also in 1954, Briggs Manufacturing, the body maker purchased by Chrysler that year, contributed the two-seat Belmont roadster. The car was supposed to spur Plymouth into offering something similar for the showroom—with Briggs-supplied bodies, of course—thus answering Chevy's Corvette and the Ford Thunderbird. A minuscule sports-car market precluded that, however, which was just as well: The Belmont wasn't much of a looker. The glassy '56 Plainsman, mentioned above, was followed by the even-glassier 1958 Cabana "dream wagon," which sported four-door hardtop styling that would make it to showrooms on 1960-62 Chrysler wagons, but not Plymouth's.

Plymouth built its hottest cars in the '60s—and also began the long slow slide to its demise. Though Plymouth ran its usual third for 1960, it would not do so again for another 11 years. It dropped to eighth for 1962, knocked out by Rambler, Pontiac, and Olds—and its own slow-selling line of smaller big cars with no full-size alternatives. Though it began to recover the next year, Plymouth wouldn't dislodge Pontiac from third until 1971, settling for fourth instead. Much of this trouble reflected management's repeated failure to gauge the market correctly and have the right products at the right time.

Trouble was apparent right away, with 1960 volume easing to just under 448,000 despite support from the compact Valiant, which arrived at Chrysler-Plymouth dealers as an ostensibly separate make. Sport Fury departed but other Plymouths returned with Highland Park's new "Unibody" construction on an unchanged wheelbase. "Misshapen" described the styling. Tailfins strained to mimic the outlandish appendages of '59 Cadillacs, and headlamp hoods stretched awkwardly down and around from a blunt front to the front wheel openings.

Good news began with a new 225-cid ohv "Slant Six" with 145 bhp, essentially a larger version of the Valiant's 170 unit to replace the old L-head six as base power. Exceptionally strong and reliable, this fine engine would be a corporate mainstay for the next 20 years. V-8s were largely '59 reruns and all "wedge-heads": 318s with 230/260 bhp for Savoys and low-line Suburban wagons; 361s with 260/305/310 bhp for Belvederes and midline Suburbans; and top-dog Golden Commando 383 with new "Ram-Induction" manifolding and 330 bhp for Fury/Sport Suburban. Though Rambler's more-conservative styling and thriftier sixes scored 2000 more sales for calendar 1960, Plymouth won the model-year race by a substantial 25,000-plus, though that included 194,292 Valiants.

The compact Valiant got Plymouth badges for 1961, and the standard line just got weird. A drastic restyle of the year-old Unibody eliminated fins and Fury's extra-cost "toilet seat," but taillights became ponderous bullets attached to scalloped fenders, while the pinched grille was eerily reminiscent of an old Graham "sharknose." A V-8 reshuffle cut the 260-bhp, while a hotter one arrived with 340 bhp. Chrysler's biggest V-8, the mighty 413 wedge, came to Plymouth with 350/375 bhp. But Plymouth's odd "plucked chicken"

# Plymouth

styling combined with still-mediocre workmanship to boost Rambler into third, with Plymouth behind on model-year volume of just over 350,000.

Then came the division's worst mistake of the '60s. Anticipating strong demand for smaller "standard" cars, Exner sliced standard Plymouths eight inches in overall length, trimmed two inches from wheelbase, slashed curb weights by up to 550 pounds, and applied strange, Valiant-like styling. Existing models returned, and Sport Fury was reborn at midseason as a sporty bucket-seat convertible and hardtop coupe.

These lighter, more-maneuverable '62 Plymouths could get away with a smaller standard engine. The 225 Slant Six became the powerplant for more models. Previous V-8s returned, though horsepower ratings fluctuated somewhat. Most significant was the boost given to the big 413, which now packed a whopping 410/420 bhp, making these Plymouths (and sister Dodges) the cars to beat at the dragstrip. But mainstream buyers, not enthusiasts, were what mattered, and they still hungered for "full-size" cars. Ford and Chevrolet had them, and thus prospered as Plymouth's model-year volume plunged below 340,000 (again including Valiant). At least that would be the decade low.

Beating a hasty retreat, Plymouth issued more-conservative, squared-up styling for '63, then a Chevy-like '64 facelift. Both were crafted under Ford alumnus Elwood Engel, who replaced Exner in 1962. But this didn't help much. Plymouth rebounded to fourth for '63 mainly on continuing strong demand for Valiants rather than appreciable gains in its "big-car" sales.

Engines in these years stood pretty much pat save a notable '63 newcomer. This was a wedgehead 426, a bored-out 413 with ultra-high compression—11:1 up to 13.5:1—packing 370/375 bhp with twin four-barrel carburetors or 415/425 with Ram Induction. Driver Richard Petty gave Plymouth a big morale boost by winning the '64 NASCAR championship hands down, driving a Fury hardtop whose new "slantback" rear roofline undoubtedly aided aerodynamics on the long-distance "super-tracks." But this triumph came with a 426 hemi-head V-8 available only to racers, not the general public. Still, it was heartening to see Chrysler's famed '50s muscle mill revived for a new "horsepower race" that was already well underway.

A full-scale Plymouth renaissance was evident for 1965, largely because the make returned to the full-size fold with big, blocky Furys on a new 119-inch wheelbase (121 for wagons). Fury I and II offered two sedans and a wagon; Fury III added two- and four-door hardtops and a convertible; at the top were a bucket-seat Sport Fury convertible and hardtop coupe. They were the largest Plymouths ever, and naturally far roomier than the '64s. Yet prices were amazingly reasonable: $2400-$3200. Unit construction continued, but a bolt-on subframe carried engine and front suspension. Powerplants ran from 225 Slant Six through 318, 361, 383, and wedgehead 426 V-8s producing 230-365 bhp.

Meantime, the advent of intermediates begun with Ford's 1962 Fairlane suggested a new role for the 116-inch-wheelbase "standard" Plymouth of 1962-64. With a blocky reskin to resemble the big Fury, it returned for '65 as the "new midsize" Belvedere and met strong buyer approval. Offerings ran to Belvedere I sedans and wagon; Belvedere II four-door sedan, wagon, hardtop coupe, and convertible; bucket-seat V-8-only Satellite hardtop and convertible; and a much-altered drag-oriented two-door hardtop aptly named Super Stock. A wedgehead 426 with 365/425 bhp was standard on S/S and optional for other Belvederes. S/S rode a special 115-inch chassis and weighed just 3170 pounds, so performance was mighty: 120 mph all out, 0-60 in eight seconds. But it was neither cheap at $4671, nor readily available. Normal Belvederes cost $2200-$2700 and offered mostly the same engines as Furys, though their base V-8 was a new small-block 273 rated at 180 bhp. This was actually a debored cousin of the 318, which was reengineered for '65 to save

1961 Fury hardtop coupe

1961 Valiant V-200 hardtop coupe

1962 Sport Fury convertible coupe

weight, yet the result was no less durable or potent.

Scoring points with performance-minded youngbloods, Plymouth finally took the incredible Hemi from track to showroom as a limited-production option for the 1966 Belvedere II/Satellite. Heavy-duty suspension and oversize brakes were included to cope with its awesome power, which was 425 advertised but closer to 500 actual. Transmission was initially limited to four-speed manual, but three-speed TorqueFlite automatic was soon added.

Surprisingly docile at low "touring" speeds, Street Hemi Belvederes were electrifying demons when pushed. Correctly set up with proper tires and axle ratio, they could reach 100 mph in 12-13 seconds, making them prime quarter-mile competitors in the National Hot Rod Association's A/Stock and AA/Stock classes, along with Dodge's similar Coronet-based Hemi-Chargers. Chrysler's mighty "B-body" middleweights continued doing well in NASCAR. David Pearson won the '66 championship for Dodge; Richard Petty again did the honors for Plymouth in '67.

Belvedere/Satellite's crisp-lined '66 styling continued with only detail changes for 1967, the last year for the original '62 "standard" platform. Topping the line was the new Belvedere GTX, a lush hardtop coupe ($3178) and convertible ($3418) equipped with a 375-bhp version of the big-block 440 wedge (evolved from the 426) introduced on Chrysler Corporation's full-size '66s. Plymouth reserved its '67 Street Hemi option exclusively for GTX, which was easily

# Plymouth

1963 Fury hardtop sedan

1964 Fury convertible coupe

1963 Valiant Signet 200 convertible coupe

1965 Fury III hardtop coupe

1963 Valiant Signet 200 hardtop coupe

1965 Valiant Signet V-8 convertible coupe

spotted: silver-and-black grille and back panel, simulated hood air intakes, sport striping, and dual exhausts.

A new B-body with no change in wheelbases gave Plymouth's 1968 intermediates a more-rounded look that was just as pretty. Belvedere was reduced to a low-line coupe, sedan, and wagon. Satellite was now the full-range volume series, and Sport Satellite denoted a top-line wagon, convertible, and hardtop coupe priced just below GTX ($2800-$3240).

Plymouth scored a marketing coup with the 1968 Road Runner, a budget-priced no-frills muscle machine with ingenious tie-ins to the beloved Warner Bros. cartoon character. It bowed as a pillared coupe, but unexpected popularity (2500 first-year sales forecast, almost 45,000 actual) prompted adding a two-door hardtop at mid-year. Exterior badging comprised RR nameplates and cartoon-bird decals inside and out, along with side-facing dummy hood scoops that could be made functional for a little extra money. Power came from a 335-bhp 383 with intake manifold and big-port heads from the 440. The Street Hemi was available, as was a slew of comfort and cosmetic goodies; beefy suspension, four-speed, and a cute "beep-beep" horn were standard. Dynamite on street or track, this finely tuned package of power and performance cost only $2800-$3100—an extraordinary bargain for the day.

The midsize Plymouths continued through 1970 with only minor interim changes. A convertible and more standard equipment bolstered Road Runner's appeal for 1969, though higher prices didn't ($3000-$3300). The ragtop GTX disappeared after '69 and a mere 700 copies.

Following a mild '66 facelift, the big Furys received crisp new lower-body sheetmetal that added inches to length and width. Wheelbases and engines stayed largely the same, with the big-block 440 option returning from '66 with 350/375 bhp. Fury's standard V-8 remained a 230-bhp 318; a brace of optional 383s offered 270/325 bhp. The 225 slant six continued as base power for all models.

Plymouth joined Ford and Chevy in the move up to medium-price territory with the 1966 Fury VIP, a hardtop coupe and sedan offering standard 318 V-8, vinyl top, richly appointed interior, and special badging for around $3100. VIP returned as a separate series for '67 with the same two body styles although the hardtop switched from notchback to that year's "Fast Top" styling, with a slanted backlight and very wide C-pillars that also showed up on a second Sport Fury hardtop. Pillarless Fury coupes offered the same choice of rooflines for 1968, when another mild facelift occurred.

If not exactly head-turners, late-'60s Furys gave away nothing in appearance to rival Fords and Chevys. The 1965-66 models wore conservative full-width grilles, stacked quad headlamps, minimal side decoration, and simple taillights. Sheetmetal was more-sculptured for 1967-68—crisper yet somehow more-imposing than before.

For 1969, the big Plymouths adopted the smoother, more-

# Plymouth

1966 Barracuda Formula S fastback hardtop coupe

1967 Barracuda hardtop coupe

1966 Valiant Signet four-door sedan

1967 Satellite Hemi hardtop coupe

1967 Valiant Signet four-door sedan

1967 VIP hardtop sedan

massive "fuselage styling" then in vogue at Chrysler. Beltlines were higher, which made windows shallower, and lower-body contours were more-flowing and heavier-looking. Squarish fenderlines were links with the past, but headlamps reverted to horizontal pairs. Model offerings again stood pat, with nonwagon styles on an inch-longer 120-inch wheelbase. Plymouth's big ragtops were now fast-waning sellers. The Fury III saw only 4129 copies for '69, the Sport fury a mere 1579. The latter then disappeared, leaving the bench-seat job as Plymouth's last big convertible; only 1952 of the 1970 models were built.

The car that pulled Plymouth through its early-'60s troubles was Valiant, one of the Big Three's original 1960 compacts. The first design generation ran through 1962: ruggedly built Unibody cars with Exner styling marked by square grilles, pronounced "blade" fenderlines, and short decks adorned by dummy spare tires, all on a 106.5-inch wheelbase. A four-door sedan and wagon were initially offered in V100 and V200 trim for $2000-$2500—cheaper than Chevy's Corvair but quite a bit upstream of Ford's runaway-hit Falcon. A V100 two-door sedan and V200 hardtop coupe arrived for '61. With bucket seats and spiffy trim, the hardtop became 1962's Signet 200, perhaps the most-collectible early Valiant.

A strong point of most every Valiant ever built was its robust Slant Six, so named because the block canted right to permit lower hoodlines, though engineers also claimed certain manufacturing and operational benefits. The initial 170-cid version produced 101 bhp; a 1960-61 four-barrel option called "Hyper-Pack" raised that to 148 bhp. The larger 225 unit from the big Plymouths became optional from 1962.

Exner's departure left Elwood Engel to shape the '63 Valiant, which emerged as clean, rounded, and conventional, if a bit stodgy. Bolstered by appealing new Signet and V200 convertibles, Valiant picked up sales, rising from about 157,000 for '62 to over 225,000. The '64s sold even better, thanks in part to optional availability of the new 273 small-block V-8, which made these sprightly cars indeed.

After two facelift years, Valiant was completely redesigned for 1967, adopting a 108-inch wheelbase and four-square lines reminiscent of some midsize European sedans. Wagons were dropped—they hadn't been huge sellers anyway—as were hardtops and convertibles, leaving two- and four-door sedans in "100" and Signet trim. Yet despite this, and aggressive new Ford and Chevy competition, Valiant remained one of Detroit's most-popular compacts. Except for some interesting interim developments, the basic '67 design would persist through the final Valiants of 1976.

The reason Valiant lost its sporty models was the success of Chevy's Corvair Monza, which prompted Plymouth to refocus its sights on the sporty-compact market. The result was Barracuda, launched in mid-1964 as a '65 model. This was not a direct reply to Ford's Mustang "ponycar," though some observers thought otherwise, as the two models appeared almost simultaneously. Actually,

# Plymouth

1968 Satellite convertible coupe

1968 Barracuda Formula S hardtop coupe

1968 Sport Satellite hardtop coupe

1968 Sport Barracuda Formula S fastback coupe

1968 Barracuda Formula S hardtop coupe

Barracuda was the existing Valiant with a new superstructure: a cleverly conceived fastback hardtop coupe with a huge compound-curve backlight and stubby trunklid. A fold-down back seat, then a novelty for Detroit, could be used to create a seven-foot-long cargo deck for hauling things like surfboards and hero sandwiches. Despite its obvious workaday origins, Barracuda offered a pleasing combination of sporty looks, good handling, utility, and room for four. Close to 65,000 were sold for model-year '65—far adrift of Mustang's near 681,000, but welcome added business all the same. And unlike Mustang, Barracuda didn't "cannibalize" sales from sister models.

Predictably, the 225 slant six was standard for the 1964-65 Barracuda, with the 180-bhp 273 V-8 optional. However, a high-performance 235-bhp 273 was also offered with a high-lift, high-overlap camshaft, domed pistons, solid lifters, dual-contact breaker points, unsilenced air cleaner, and a sweet-sounding, low-restriction exhaust system. With "Rallye Suspension" (heavy-duty front torsion bars and antisway bars, stiff rear leaf springs), "Firm-Ride" shocks, and a four-speed gearbox, the 235-bhp job could do 0-60 mph in eight seconds flat.

After a debatable '66 facelift featuring a squarish front (shared with Valiant) and two-piece eggcrate grille, Barracuda was handsomely redesigned for '67. Wheelbase was stretched two inches, overall length five inches, and a shapelier fastback (without the "glassback") was joined by a new convertible and notchback hardtop coupe (the latter with a rather odd, "kinked" rear roofline). A newly available four-barrel 383 with 280 bhp provided better straightline performance, but hurt handling by adding up to 300 extra pounds at the front. The 273 remained the best choice for all-around roadability. As for '66, a Formula S package was offered comprising heavy-duty suspension, tachometer, wide-oval tires, and special stripes and badges.

Happily, the '67 Barracudas continued without drastic change through 1969—except, of course, for the feds' new safety and emissions equipment then appearing on all Detroit cars. A vertical-bar grille insert and small round side-market lights identified the '68s; the '69s gained a checked insert, revamped taillights, and square side-markers. In both years, Plymouth fielded muscle-market "'Cuda" versions offering a choice of Chrysler's new 340 small-block with 275 bhp or the big-block 383 with 300 bhp for '68 and 330 bhp for '69.

Appearing for 1970 was a fully redesigned third-generation Barracuda that donated its basic structure to a new Dodge double, the Challenger. Against the 1967-69 Barracudas, the '70 was two inches lower, three inches wider, a tad shorter, much heavier, and somehow more-conventional-looking. Wheelbase remained at 108 inches, but the new "widebody" design had plenty of room for every big-block V-8 in the Chrysler stable, up to and including the 426 Hemi and a new six-barrel 440 that was conservatively rated at 390 bhp. Those two were available with a special "shaker" hood, so-called because a functional scoop attached directly to the carb housing poked through the panel and could be seen a-shakin'. The trademark fastback was no more, but hardtop and convertible returned in three forms: base, performance-oriented 'Cuda, and luxury Gran Coupe (which in ragtop form was thus a Gran Coupe convertible).

Perhaps the most-interesting 1970 Barracuda was the racy, mid-year AAR, named for and inspired by the Dan Gurney All-American Racers team cars that contested that year's Trans-Am series in Sports Car Club of America competition. Based on the 'Cuda 340 hardtop, the AAR was easily spotted by its bold body-side "strobe" stripes, wide tires, matte-black fiberglass hood with functional scoop, rear spoiler, and long exhaust trumpets peeking out from beneath the rocker panels. The last also made the thing unmistakable to the ear. A modified 340 V-8 carried an Edelbrock intake manifold mounting three two-barrel carbs, plus special heads and

# Plymouth

1969 GTX hardtop coupe

1970 Barracuda 'Cuda Hemi hardtop coupe

1969 Barracuda 383-S Sports fastback coupe

1970 Barracuda AAR 'Cuda hardtop coupe

1970 Road Runner Superbird hardtop coupe

1970 Fury III hardtop sedan

1970 Valiant Duster 340 coupe

1970 Fury Gran Coupe two-door

a fortified block and valvetrain. Heavy-duty suspension was also included. Planned production was 2800, but the final figure is estimated at no more than 1500.

Giving Valiant a lift for 1970 was a new semifastback pillared coupe called Duster, a pleasant little car of good quality that attracted more than 217,000 first-year sales. Several thousand sported a "Gold Duster" option package with gold accents on grille, body, and interior, plus bucket seats, whitewall tires, and special wheel covers. The Duster 340 was a racy derivation with a mechanical package similar to the 'Cuda 340's. Equipment ran to the 275-bhp small-block, three-speed floor-shift, front disc brakes, wide tires, and tuned suspension.

Among 1970 Plymouth intermediates was a startling newcomer: the Superbird. Part of the Road Runner series, it was an evolution of Dodge's 1969 Charger Daytona, with a similar hidden-headlamp "droop-snoot" and huge struts carrying a stabilizer wing high above the rear deck. The Superbird looked fast—and was: Racing versions recorded over 220 mph. Street models came with a four-barrel 440 and TorqueFlite automatic, but the 440 "Six Pak," 426 Street Hemi, and four-speed manual transmission were all optionally available. Dodge built some 500 Charger Daytonas to qualify it as "production" for NASCAR events; then the sanctioning body increased its minimum to 1500. That was no problem for Plymouth, which ended up building 1920 Superbirds.

# Plymouth

1971 GTX hardtop coupe

1971 Barracuda 'Cuda 340 hardtop coupe

1971 Sport Fury hardtop coupe

1971 Road Runner 440+6 hardtop coupe

1971 Valiant Duster 340 coupe

1971 Valiant Scamp hardtop coupe

The Superbird's greatest moment came at the 1970 Daytona 500, when Pete Hamilton romped home at an average speed of nearly 150 mph to best every Dodge and every Ford. Superbirds then went on to take 21 of Chrysler's 38 Grand National wins that year. But NASCAR changed the rules again for 1971, thus ending the Superbird's dominance on the high-speed ovals—and the car itself.

Full-size Plymouths got their own dose of extra performance for 1970. Most notable was the new Sport Fury GT, a hardtop coupe carrying a 350-bhp 440, heavy-duty suspension, and long-legged rear axle ratios (up to 2.76:1). Also new to the Sport Fury line was the S/23 hardtop. Its standard 230-bhp 318 wasn't in the GT's league, but you did get a tuned chassis and modest "strobe" body stripes. Other Sport Furys were upgraded to take over from the now-departed luxury VIP, and all versions now hid their headlamps within a big new loop bumper/grille worn by all full-size Plymouths. Arriving in February was a plush Gran Coupe pillared two-door boasting most every comfort and convenience feature in the book at $3833 without air conditioning or $4216 with A/C.

For two brief shining moments, 1971 and '74, Plymouth again finished its traditional third in the industry production race. But after that, it never ran higher than fourth. By decade's end Plymouth had sunk to ninth, even though 1979 was a very healthy Detroit year. By the early '80s, the make was all but invisible.

Several factors contributed to this sorry decline: more wrong products at wrong times, indifferent workmanship even on the few models that were well timed, dwindling public confidence in Chrysler Corporation generally, and decreased styling distinction with related Dodges. Plymouth also suffered from a growing dullness that stemmed from the '60s consolidation of Chrysler's five divisions into two (Dodge and Chrysler-Plymouth). Because this eliminated the need to put all nameplates on all major platforms, glamour assignments like Cordoba went to Chrysler while Dodge increasingly got sportier models all to itself. By 1978, Plymouth was back to peddling basic family transportation—just as it had started out doing 50 years before.

Yet few could have forseen this diminished role in 1970, when Plymouth countered Ford and Chevy with five separate car lines spanning 44 individual models and about 70 basic variations (counting trim levels and engines). Valiant, the lone survivor of the original Big Three compacts, dominated its market right on through swan-song '76. A key factor was the Duster coupe, which chalked up well over a quarter-million sales for 1974 alone. It was conventional but cute and well-engineered, and at least as well-built as comparable GM and Ford products.

Plymouth kept Duster desirable with a stream of extra-cost packages. The 1971-74 "Twister" option included matte-black hood, Duster 340-type black grille, bodyside tape stripes, and Rallye wheels. The Gold Duster continued through 1975 with a color-keyed pebble-grain vinyl roof. The "Space Duster" of 1973-74 was Plymouth's equivalent of Dodge's Dart Sport "Convertriple," with a

# Plymouth

1972 Barracuda 'Cuda 340 hardtop coupe

1972 Satellite Sebring Plus hardtop coupe

1972 Fury Gran Coupe hardtop

1973 Road Runner coupe with metal sunroof

1973 Barracuda hardtop coupe

1973 Road Runner coupe

wagon-style fold-down rear seatback that gave a 6½-foot-long carpeted cargo deck. (Shades of the original Barracuda.) Even at the end of the line there was a special "Silver Duster" (a handsome combination of silver, red, and black) as well as a "Feather Duster." The latter, a reply to Ford's "MPG" models, had an economy-tuned 225 Slant Six with aluminum intake manifold, plus aluminum instead of steel inner panels for hood and decklid. With a manual-overdrive gearbox, which had an aluminum case, the Feather Duster was surprisingly frugal for its size; a prudent driver could nurse one up to 30 mpg.

Further bolstering the Valiant line were the performance-oriented V-8 Duster 340 (through '73) and 360 (1974-75); the 1974-76 Brougham luxury option for sedans and two-door hardtops, offering opulence not usually found in compacts; and the Scamp hardtop, which was new for 1971. Altogether, Valiant and Dodge's similar Dart were impressive sellers right to the end. In some years Valiant gave Chrysler the compact lead over Ford and Chevy.

Unveiled for mid-'76 was Volare, a more-upscale Plymouth compact that replaced Valiant entirely the following year. Though only a bit larger outside, Volare (and its Dodge Aspen cousin) had been designed for maximum interior space, which was quite good for the day. Workmanship, however, was anything but good. Still, this very real problem didn't surface for a few years. Trim levels comprised base, mid-range Custom, and high-line Premier; the last offering unexpected luxury for around $4500. Volare also came as a five-door wagon in addition to the expected coupe and sedan—Plymouth's first compact wagon since 1966.

The Volare was right on target, racking up almost 400,000 sales for '77. Most examples had a 225 Slant Six or 318 V-8, both able veterans of some two decades. Though no trend-setter, Volare appealed mainly for its restrained styling and a decent performance/economy compromise.

Compacts were Plymouth's only real success in the '70s; its intermediates and full-size cars fared poorly. So, too, did the Barracuda, which was of no significance in the steadily declining ponycar market. The all-new 1970 design was warmed over for '71, gaining quad headlamps and a none-too-pretty vee'd grille with vertical slats. A low-priced pillared hardtop replaced the convertible Gran Coupe and promptly took the lion's share of drastically reduced sales. Convertibles and big-block power were scrubbed for '72, leaving standard and 'Cuda V-8 coupes. These carried on for two more seasons before Plymouth gave up. Low production has lately thrust 'Cudas and Gran Coupes into the collector limelight—especially convertibles. The '71 droptop 'Cuda saw just 374 copies, and the standard convertible was almost as rare at 1014.

Midsize Plymouths consolidated under the Satellite name for 1971 and were completely revamped, shedding their relatively square 1968-70 look for more radically sculptured sheetmetal and large loop bumper/grilles. In line with a Detroit trend, coupes rode

# Plymouth

1973 Fury Gran Coupe hardtop

1973 Satellite Sebring Plus hardtop coupe

1974 Barracuda hardtop coupe

1974 Fury Gran Sedan hardtop

1974 Valiant four-door sedan

a shorter wheelbase than sedans and wagons (115 vs. 117 inches). Convertibles vanished here too, but Road Runner and GTX were still around, and there was a smart new sports-luxury hardtop called Sebring Plus.

Unfortunately, these Plymouths suffered the same fate as most '70s intermediates, becoming ever-more ponderous, thirsty, and ugly. The GTX was dumped after '71 for lack of sales, and the Road Runner, still ostensibly a separate model, wasn't nearly as fast on its feet as before. An attempt to regroup for 1975 brought the "small Fury," basically the existing platform with squared-up outer sheetmetal and a new name, but sales continued to languish. The last of these cars rolled out the door in 1978.

The big full-size Furys vanished after 1977, but for 1971-73 they were restyled continuations of the 1969-70 "fuselage" body/chassis design. They retained the same four-series lineup of top-drawer Sport Fury and three lower trim levels designated by Roman numerals. Plymouth began whittling away at this group for '72, with Gran Fury taking over at the top and economy Fury I offerings cut from four to one. Meanwhile, Chrysler Corporation was preparing a brand-new design for all its full-size cars, scheduled well in advance of the brewing Middle East oil crisis.

Nevertheless, the hulkier new 1974 Fury (and the corresponding Dodge Monaco and Chrysler Newport/New Yorker) seemed incredibly ill-timed. They were not only heavier, but looked it: square and undistinguished on wheelbases stretched two inches. A Slant Six was available in some models, but made them grossly underpowered. V-8s were the now-usual assortment of 318, 360, midrange 400, and big-block 440. Significantly, sales didn't improve even after gas supplies eased and big-car sales began recovering.

After 1974, the full-size Fury was called Gran Fury to avoid confusion with Plymouth's renamed '75 intermediate Furys. But somehow, Chrysler never seemed to understand that badge shifting seldom (if ever) makes any difference in sales. It sure didn't here. Except for the midrange Custom sedan, not a single Gran Fury model scored more than 10,000 sales for 1976, and production of some Brougham and wagon models was laughably low for a traditional high-volume make.

Hoping to cut such losses, Plymouth trimmed big-car offerings for '76 and again for '77—mainly hardtop sedans and some trim variations. But the losses continued, and Plymouth temporarily fled the full-size field. It halfheartedly returned for 1980 with a bargain-basement version of the pseudo-downsized R-body Chrysler Newport, again bearing the Gran Fury name and intended mainly for the fleet market. But sales, at less than 19,000 for the model year, were disappointing.

The shape of Plymouth's future arrived with the all-new 1978 Horizon, a five-door subcompact sedan whose 99.2-inch wheelbase made it the smallest Plymouth in history. It was virtually identical to Dodge's Omni except for grille insert, taillights, and badges, and thus shared distinction as America's first domestically built frontdrive small car.

Horizon sold briskly from the start despite later ill-founded charges that handling wasn't all it should be. In fact, roadability was one of Horizon's strengths. So was fine economy, courtesy of a 70-bhp, Volkswagen-based 104.7-cid four-cylinder engine. Another plus was the practical, space-efficient hatchback body. A sleek 2+2 "fasthatch" coupe called TC3, riding a 96.7-inch wheelbase, added some spice to the line for '79.

But by that point, Plymouth was a mere shadow of its former self, down to just Horizons, TC3s, and Volares. Management tried fostering the illusion that this was still a "full-line" make by slapping Plymouth nameplates on various "captive imports" from Mitsubishi of Japan. These included the little Arrow hatch-back coupe (1976-80), the larger and more-luxurious notchback Sapporo (1978-82, sold with a Dodge double reviving the Challenger name), and the front-drive Champ economy hatchback (new for '79 and duplicat-

# Plymouth

1975 Gran Fury Brougham coupe

1975 Valiant Duster 360 coupe

1975 Fury Sport hardtop coupe

1976 Gran Fury Brougham four-door sedan

1976 Volare Premier four-door sedan

1977 Gran Fury Brougham coupe

1978 Horizon hatchback with Premium Woodgrain package

1978 Volare Road Runner coupe

ed as the Dodge Colt). The badging was a good marketing move, providing vital sales support at a crucial time, but it only underscored how low once-prominent Plymouth had fallen.

Though more salable new domestic products soon appeared, Plymouth's record in the '80s was pretty sorry for what used to be Detroit's perennial number-three. After moving slightly more than 500,000 American-made cars for 1977 and again for '78, Plymouth wouldn't exceed 400,000 in any one year through 1986—and was well below 300,000 for 1980, '82, and '83.

Though having fewer domestic models was a definite sales handicap, Plymouth's also-ran status in the '80s stemmed as much from a conscious decision to change its role within the corporate lineup.

Planners decreed that Chrysler would cater to luxury buyers, per tradition, while Dodge would again go after the performance crowd. This left Plymouth with nothing to emphasize except reliable value-for-money cars that duplicated Dodges but were often less interesting and fewer in number.

The Plymouth product story in the '80s is thus basically the same as for the duller Dodges. And a short one it is, too, because the make missed out on reborn convertibles, luxury models, and a latterday ponycar like the front-drive Dodge Daytona. With that, most Plymouth sales came from just two model lines: the L-body Horizon and derivative TC3 coupe (retitled Turismo for 1983-87), and the seminal K-body Reliant, which ousted Volare as the divi-

# Plymouth

1978 Fury Salon four-door sedan

1978 Horizon TC3 2+2 hatchback coupe

1981 Reliant Special Edition two-door sedan

1981 Gran Fury four-door sedan

1982 Turismo TC3 hatchback coupe

sion's compact for 1981. In yearly styling and engineering changes they parallel Dodge's near-identical Omni/Charger and Aries, respectively, except for minor trim and, in line with Plymouth's solid-citizen role, no Shelby-tuned subcompacts.

In most years, Reliant earned honors as Chrysler's single best-selling model line. Wagons departed after 1989, but coupes and sedans finished out Reliant's run as value-equipped "America" models priced at $7595. Plymouth's L-bodies also outsold Dodge's, though not by much, averaging 150,000 per year except for about 90,000 managed for 1982-83.

Badge-engineering gave the make token representation in the full-size and intermediate ranks. For the former, Plymouth was doled a "downsized" 1982 Gran Fury, a near-twin of the 112.7-inch-wheelbase M-body Dodge Diplomat to replace the slow-selling R-body GF of 1980-81. This also sputtered along as a four-door sedan with few interim changes through swan-song 1989. Engines were the expected Slant Six and 318 V-8 (V-8 only after '83), and trim levels were restricted to only one or two. Of course, this was nothing like previous Gran Furys, being the original Aspen/Volare compact as evolved through the midsize 1977 Diplomat/Chrysler LeBaron. Most sold to police and taxi fleets, where the M-body's aging but proven rear-drive design was an asset.

Canadians were offered an M-body Plymouth before 1982 as the Caravelle. For 1985 this name came to the U.S. on a restyled, down-priced version of what had been the Chrysler E-Class. All but a copy of Dodge's 103.3-inch-wheelbase 600 four-door sedan, this front-drive Caravelle was nominally Plymouth's midsize family car, and sold in plain and uplevel SE trim at a respectable 35,000-45,000 a year until its 1988 retirement when sales dropped to 17,000. Unlike Dodge with the 600 ES, Plymouth was not allowed a more-sporty model or even a five-speed transaxle, but for a time the 146-bhp turbocharged edition of Chrysler's 2.2-liter (135-cid) "Trans-4" engine was optional. Most Caravelles had either a 2.6-liter (156-cid) Mitsubishi "balancer" four or, after debut-model 1985, the 2.5-liter (153-cid) enlargement of Chrysler's 2.2. All carried TorqueFlite automatic.

Like Dodge, Plymouth's other big winner in this decade was the practical K-based T-115 minivan, new for '84. The name here was Voyager (retained from Dodge-clone big-Plymouth vans of the '70s), but that and a different grille were about all that separated it from Dodge's Caravan. Added to the K-cars' success, the fast-selling T-wagons were a big reason why Chrysler Corporation enjoyed record profits by middecade, a mere five years after nearly tumbling into the financial abyss. Because the industry counts minivans as trucks rather than cars, Voyagers don't figure in the Plymouth production totals cited here.

Plymouth got in on the new-for-'87 P-body, the more-upscale subcompact originally intended to replace Omni/Horizon. That replacement didn't happen immediately, though, as strong demand for the high-value "America" models announced for 1987 prompted Chrysler to keep the L-bodies through 1990. A surprising number of changes occurred that final year: new dash, standard driver-side air bag, and no America tag. Identically priced at $6995 for 1990, the Omni/Horizon went out as outstanding value for the money.

Plymouth's name for the erstwhile successor P-body was Sundance (recalling an early-'70s Satellite trim option). Though predictably all but identical to Dodge's Shadow, Sundance aimed more at luxury-minded small-car shoppers, offering three- and five-door notchback sedans with only one well-equipped trim level and a suspension tuned more for ride than handling.

But Highland Park hadn't entirely forgotten Plymouth's performance past, because the 1988 Sundance offered a new RS package option with sportier appointments that included integral fog lamps, two-tone paint, wider tires on racier wheels, special bucket seats, and leather-rim steering wheel. An optional 2.2-liter port-injected turbo-four with 146 bhp backed up this brag, then gave way to a

# Plymouth

blown 150-bhp 2.5 the next year. Also available through 1990 were standard 93-bhp 2.2 and optional 96-bhp 2.5, both normally aspirated engines with electronic throttle-body injection. All could be teamed with standard five-speed manual or optional TorqueFlite transaxles. A new face with flush headlamps cleaned up Sundance's 1989 appearance. The 1990s added a driver-side air bag in the steering-wheel hub as a worthy safety advance.

Like Shadow, Sundance generated nearly 76,000 sales in its first year. Production then settled at around the 80,000-100,000 unit level through 1990. This suggested that Chrysler could still reach small-car buyers, but not nearly as many per year as in Valiant days. Still, many things had changed, and Sundance was arguably just as right for its time and market.

That also applied to the new-for-'89 Acclaim. Like Sundance, this was conceived to replace an older Plymouth, the remarkable Reliant, but the K-car's continuing sales strength prompted corporate planners to let the new and the old run side-by-side that year, as Volare and Valiant did in '76. More immediately, Acclaim replaced Caravelle as Plymouth's midsize sedan. Riding the same wheelbase but sharing the latest corporate A-body with that year's new Dodge Spirit. There was still lots of Reliant in Acclaim styling, but the look was more contemporary: formal yet smooth, and carefully detailed for good aerodynamic efficiency.

Again, Plymouth marketed a shared package less aggressively than Dodge, announcing Acclaim in base, midrange LE, and luxury LX guises with few sporting touches. Engine choices were naturally the same: blown and unblown 2.5 fours and a new 3.0-liter (181-cid) Mitsubishi V-6 with 141 bhp. The last was reserved for LX and teamed only with Chrysler's first four-speed overdrive automatic transaxle, called Ultradrive. Of course, certain sporty features were available, including bucket seats and, for 1990, a Rallye Sport option with uprated chassis, enthusiast-oriented interior, and subtle exterior badging.

But this was only a nod to Plymouth's performance past, and fully 85 percent of Acclaim buyers opted for the workaday base model. That wasn't necessarily bad, of course. After all, Plymouth's value-for-money marketing emphasis stood to pay off big once the economy turned down again in 1990. But two domestic cars and a smattering of rebadged Japanese imports (still from Chrysler affiliate Mitsubishi) were no substitute for the full-range lineup Plymouth had lacked for so long, especially as none of its cars was really tops in class. As a result, Plymouth became an even weaker also-ran in the early '90s, finishing next to last in domestic model-year car sales through middecade. The low point came with 1993, when Plymouth moved some 141,300 domestic cars, after which volume picked up to just over 178,000 for '94. While the make's overall volume in this period wasn't exactly puny at between 365,000 and 424,000, more than half of each year's total came from Voyager minivans, making Plymouth more of a "truck" producer than a carmaker for the first time in its history.

It was just as well, for Plymouth might have died sooner without Voyager's consistently high yearly sales. At one point in late '91, Chrysler was said to be on the verge of killing Plymouth so as to free up funds for its new upscale Eagle line, of which great things were expected (see entry). But where Eagle generated only a third to a sixth of Plymouth's volume (to run dead last in the industry race), Plymouth still accounted for no less than 40 percent of total company sales, thanks mainly to Voyager. On realizing that, management decided Plymouth deserved another chance and approved a heavy infusion of product and promotion money in an attempt to rejuvenate a name that had slipped in public awareness to somewhere between fuzzy and unknown. They even plumped for a nostalgic new Plymouth logo: a stylized sailing vessel reminiscent of the Good Ship *Mayflower* that would be in place by 1996.

Money was one thing, however, and mission quite another. Though any attention was welcome after some 20 years of not-so-

**1981 Reliant Custom four-door sedan prototype**

**1982 Horizon Custom hatchback sedan**

**1982 Gran Fury four-door sedan**

**1982 Reliant Custom two-door sedan**

**1983 Turismo coupe**

# Plymouth

1984 Voyager Limited Edition minivan

1987 Grand Voyager LE minivan

1985 Caravelle four-door sedan

1987 Caravelle SE four-door sedan

1986 Turismo Duster hatchback coupe

1988 Sundance RS Turbo Liftback coupe

1986 Gran Fury sedan with Police Package

1989 Acclaim LX four-door sedan

1987 Horizon America hatchback sedan

1990 Acclaim LX four-door sedan

# Plymouth

benign neglect, Plymouth still had no place in the corporate scheme except as a "value" brand with a limited selection of low-priced, largely low-profile cars. No surprise, then, that Plymouth continued in the '90s exactly as it had in the '80s, except that offerings declined to three with the complete elimination of imports after 1994. This reflected the decision (at the time) of a newly resurgent Chrysler to sever long-standing product and manufacturing ties with Mitsubishi. Among the casualties was arguably the most-interesting Plymouth of this era, the Laser sport coupe, a "badge-engineered" Mitsubishi Eclipse built in the same Illinois plant (as was an Eagle version, the Talon).

Voyager, meantime, kept doing land-office business, helped by the same thoughtful changes accorded Dodge's Caravan. Highlights began with a deft exterior makeover for 1991, which also introduced antilock brakes as a first-time extra, plus a revised dash and, with the optional 3.3-liter V-6, available all-wheel drive. A standard driver-side air bag was added as a '91 running change, followed by the industry's first integrated child safety seat as a 1992 option. For '94 came a standard passenger air bag in another revised dash, plus side-guard door beams and an optional 3.3 V-6 converted to run on compressed natural gas. Environmentalists loved it, even if a $1700 price severely tested their convictions. The basic '84-vintage Voyager then put in a final year. Though Plymouth still trailed Dodge in passenger minivan sales, Voyager volume remained significant after 1990 at well over 200,000 per model year.

By contrast, Acclaim and Sundance mostly withered in both sales and interest value, giving little evidence that Plymouth had ever offered anything so exciting as a Hemi 'Cuda or Superbird. With product plans now dictated by marketing goals and sales trends, Plymouth's midsize line was reduced for 1992 to a single base-trim sedan with an exhaustingly long list of option packages but only two engine choices: 100-bhp 2.5-liter four and 141-bhp 3.0-liter V-6. An eggcrate grille was the main visual change for '93, when an interesting "flex fuel" version of the four became optional. Sold only to fleets for '93 but available to retail customers for '94, this could run on any combination of gasoline or "M85" methanol (an 85-percent methanol/gasoline mix). Also for '94, Acclaim gained a motorized right-front-shoulder belt to meet that year's federal man-date for dual front "passive restraints." The A-body Plymouth then made a last stand with a shortened options list omitting automatic, ABS, and the flex-fuel engine. Production declined steadily after 1991's respectable 97,000-plus, finishing just above 12,000 for the token '95 model run.

Sundance was treated to a few more yearly changes than Acclaim, but not many. Predictably, most were shared with Dodge's Shadow. Sundance never got a convertible like its P-body sister, but it did add budget-priced three- and five-door America models for 1991. Though you could get one for as little as $7699, you had to make do with less sound insulation, fewer options, no cargo area carpeting, and just a 93-bhp version of the veteran 2.2-liter inline four. For '92, Sundance dropped its sporty RS option in favor of a new confection reviving the Duster name from Valiant days. Available for both body styles at about $2100 above base-trim spec, this package delivered sporty paint, applied tape graphics, a slightly firmer suspension, cast aluminum wheels, more-aggressive standard tires, and—the big attraction—the same 3.0-liter V-6 available in Acclaim. Ordering the Duster also opened up a new optional transmission: the first four-speed automatic available in a Chrysler subcompact. Though 141 bhp implied a certain speediness, this Duster was no whirlwind, but it was pleasantly swifter than any four-banger Sundance save the rough and raucous turbo models.

Duster stayed on for '93, but America and Highline trim disappeared in favor of a single price level equipped with elements of both. Antilock brakes were newly optional, a laudable addition. Like Acclaim, Sundance added a right front "mouse-belt" to meet 1994's requirement for dual passive restraints, but five-doors exited

1990 Horizon hatchback sedan

1991 Acclaim LX four-door sedan

1991 Sundance America hatchback coupe

1992 Grand Voyager LE minivan

1992 Acclaim four-door sedan

▲ 1962 Plymouth Fury convertible ▼ 1970 Plymouth Barracuda 'Cuda Hemi two-door hardtop

▲ 1971 Plymouth Road Runner two-door hardtop

▼ 2001 Plymouth Neon four-door sedan

▲ 1934 Pontiac Eight two-door coupe ▼ 1941 Pontiac Deluxe Six Torpedo two-door coupe

▲ 1950 Pontiac Chieftain Eight Catalina two-door hardtop ▼ 1957 Pontiac Safari two-door station wagon

▲ 1962 Pontiac Catalina convertible ▼ 1974 Pontiac Grand Prix SJ two-door coupe

▲ 2001 Pontiac Firebird Trans Am WS6 Ram Air coupe ▼ 1959 Rambler Ambassador four-door station wagon

▲ 1963 Rambler Classic 770 two-door coupe ▼ 1936 Reo Flying Cloud two-door sedan

▲ 1994 Saturn SC1 two-door coupe ▼ 1997 Saturn SL2 four-door sedan

▲ 2001 Saturn SC2 three-door coupe ▼ 1964 (AC) Shelby Cobra roadster

▲ 1969 Shelby GT 500 convertible ▼ 1988 Dodge Shelby Shadow two-door coupe

▲ 1931 Studebaker President 80R roadster ▼ 1941 Studebaker Commander two-door coupe

▲ 1948 Studebaker Commander convertible

▼ 1956 Studebaker Golden Hawk hardtop coupe

▲ 1961 Studebaker Lark VI convertible ▼ 1963 Studebaker Avanti two-door coupe

▲ 1932 Stutz DV-32 convertible coupe ▼ 1934 Terraplane K Special touring convertible sedan

▲ 1948 Tucker Torpedo four-door sedan ▼ 1935 Willys Model 77 two-door coupe

▲ 1941 Willys Americar two-door coupe ▼ 1954 Willys Aero-Lark two-door hardtop

# Plymouth

**1992 Sundance America hatchback coupe**

**1993 Acclaim four-door sedan**

**1992 Laser RS Turbo AWD hatchback coupe**

**1994 Grand Voyager LE minivan**

**1992 Acclaim four-door sedan**

**1994 Sundance Duster hatchback coupe**

**1995 Neon coupe**

817

# Plymouth

in January, leaving three-doors to finish out the last model year. Considering its elderly K-car origins and lack of real pizzazz, Sundance sold quite well in this period, falling no further than 62,800 for model-year '91 and hitting nearly 86,000 for '93.

The reason Sundance lost its five-door models early was the advent of a much better small Plymouth, the Neon. Of course, it was all but identical with the 1995 Dodge Neon that arrived at the same time, so everything said about that version applies to this one—save for badges done in Plymouth blue instead of Dodge red. As with minivans, Plymouth's Neon didn't sell quite as well as Dodge's, yet C-P dealers moved some 121,400 Neons for the '95 season. This was strong public acceptance recalling that of Plymouth's first front-drive car, the 1978-79 Horizon, yet Neon was far superior, offering spunky performance, taut handling, and surprising interior room thanks to scaled-down "cab-forward" styling that managed to be winsomely cute. Low prices also spurred sales: under $10,000 to start. About all that needed fixing were undue engine and road noise, patchy workmanship, and obviously low-buck interior materials. Overall, though, Neon represented impressive value, and competitors lost sleep trying to figure out how Chrysler could deliver so much small car for the money. Even vaunted Toyota was moved to take one apart to learn its secrets.

Speaking of cab-forward, Plymouth was denied the car that pioneered the look, Chrysler's full-size LH sedan of 1993—and more's the pity. One suspects a new LH-based "Fury" would have sold well. But Plymouth was always in the loop for the new midsize JA platform, even if its 1996 Breeze was a year behind the similar Chrysler Cirrus and Dodge Stratus.

Per Plymouth's ongoing mission, Breeze was the cheapest of the JA trio, appealingly base-priced at $14,060, about $300 below the last Acclaim. Though inevitably less lavish than its sister "cloud cars," Breeze was no stripper, boasting standard dual air bags, air conditioning, AM/FM stereo radio, tilt steering wheel, tinted glass, and fold-down back seat. An eggcrate grille echoed Acclaim, but attached to a much slicker cab-forward sedan body on a rangy 108-inch wheelbase that again made for relatively generous passenger and cargo space. As the most-affordable JA, Breeze offered the fewest options, though the short list included important items like antilock brakes; integrated child safety seat; and power windows, mirrors, and door locks.

Price reasons also dictated but one engine: the new 2.0-liter overhead-cam inline four designed and built by Chrysler for the Neon. Though its 132 bhp promised slow going in the larger, heavier JA, the Breeze proved surprisingly able, running 0-60 in 10 seconds with standard five-speed manual and about 11.5 with optional four-speed automatic—decent if not exactly, er, breezy. Even nicer perhaps, Consumer Guide® found this Plymouth a very tight and solid car by any standard, a real revelation for a low-priced Detroiter. And, of course, Breeze was no less fun to drive than a Cirrus or Stratus, inheriting their crisp, responsive front-drive handling; stable, well-planted wide-stance cornering poise; precise power steering; and delightfully "tossable" feel.

For 1998, Chrysler's well-known 2.4-liter four with 150 bhp became optional for Breeze. Automatic was mandatory, so the bigger engine delivered little more zip than the smaller one with manual, but it did reduce driver stress in the daily grind and used little more gas. Any Breeze was more comfortable for '99, thanks to softer damping providing a more-absorbent ride.

Together with Neon and an all-new crop of superbly redesigned 1996 Voyagers, the Breeze gave reason to be optimistic about Plymouth's future. So did Chrysler's stated commitment to the make, symbolized by a handsome new "Mayflower" logo. Marketing efforts were stepped up to "reintroduce" Plymouth to those who still remembered, while hammering home the "high value" message to younger folks who didn't. One of the more-novel initiatives involved setting up computerized "Plymouth Place" kiosks in selected major shopping malls, where prospective buyers could learn about the various models and even price one to order without fear of being set upon by some salesperson. Chrysler also staked out some cyberspace for Plymouth on the burgeoning Internet, and returned to forceful advertising of more-conventional kinds with the slogan "One clever idea after another."

For sheer impact, though, nothing could match the 1997 Prowler, the most-exciting Plymouth in a generation. It was unlike anything ever offered by a mainstream automaker, being a modern reincarnation of the iconic American hot rod. Like the Dodge Viper before it, Prowler began as a concept, premiering at the 1993 Detroit Auto Show amid rabid pleas to "Build it!" Once more, Chrysler president Bob Lutz gave his full endorsement to a fairly outrageous automobile aimed squarely at car buffs like himself. Again sharing his enthusiasm were design chief Tom Gale, long an active hot rod hobbyist, and Advanced Design director Neil Walling, who oversaw the concept's development from an idea suggested by a staffer at the company's California design outpost, Chrysler Pacifica. Though hardly the sort of car expected of a "value brand," Prowler promised to do for Plymouth what Viper had for Dodge—namely, get people talking and change their minds. Indeed, Chrysler viewed its two-seat retro roadster has having just the right "shock value" for resuscitating Plymouth's moribund image and low "brand awareness" among consumers.

There was high-tech seriousness beneath the hot-rod fun, as Prowler became Chrysler's low-volume laboratory for nontraditional construction and materials. For example, aluminum was used not only for an all-independent suspension but the entire chassis and much of the body. In fact, Prowler packed more aluminum than any car in Chrysler history—some 900 pounds of it—construction rivaled only by the exotic Honda-built Acura NSX sports car. The result was a lean machine with about the same length as a Porsche 911 but weighing well under 2900 pounds. Other weight-watching measures included a lateral dashboard brace made of costly magnesium, the industry's first cast aluminum brake rotors (rear only; front discs were iron Voyager parts), and plasticlike sheet molding to shape the quarter panels, vintage cycle-type front fenders, and a pointy nose skimming just 4.5 inches above the pavement.

Helped by a sharp raked-forward profile and broad 76.5-inch

**1997 Prowler roadster**

**1998 Neon Expresso four-door sedan**

818

beam, the Prowler turned heads like nothing else on the street. The only changes from the stunning concept were more-prominent front "bumperettes" and headlights, both to satisfy the feds. Wheels were handsome five-spoke alloys measuring 17 × 7.5 inches fore and a massive 20 × 10 aft, and you could have any color at first so long as it was vivid Prowler Purple. The manual top, a black fabric affair, stowed easily beneath a rear-hinged trunklid—and most always was. Prowler, after all, was about lookin' good. There was no room for introverts.

Or much of anything else. The front-tapering '30s-style body left footwells uncomfortably narrow (though wider than on the concept). Standard run-flat tires eliminated the need for a spare, but the trunk was nearly useless, squeezed from below by the fuel tank (itself laughably small at 12 gallons) and a rear transaxle, also new for Chrysler. The latter contributed to front/rear weight distribution of 45/55 percent, making Prowler quite nimble on dry roads despite a long 113-inch wheelbase. And for times when you had to carry more than a couple of pizzas, Chrysler offered a small accessory trailer, shaped like the tail, for about five-grand. But the fat tires with their ultrastiff sidewalls "find every bump," as *Car and Driver* noted, and could be way too slippery in the rain. And like Viper, antilock brakes and traction control weren't available, yet a number of luxuries were standard: air conditioning, power windows and mirrors, leather upholstery, high-power sound system, even a gee-whiz tire-pressure monitor.

Hot-rod purists also shook their heads at Prowler's powertrain: a 3.5-liter V-6 sending a modest 214 bhp through a four-speed automatic transmission. Like much of the interior, these were off-the-shelf components used to keep price reasonable, which it was at an initial $38,300. Yet despite that, the lowish weight and standard AutoStick manual-shift feature, Prowler was nowhere near as fast as it looked. *Car and Driver*'s results were typical: 0-60 in 7 seconds flat, a standing quarter-mile of 15.6 at 87 mph—pretty tame.

Overall, *C/D* viewed Prowler as "awash in contradictions. Hot rods have V-8s and manual gearboxes. The Prowler offers neither. Hot rods are supposed to ride badly and handle badly, then set fire to the dragstrip. Instead, the Prowler handles almost like a sports car but is a relative flatliner on the dragstrip. Hot rods are supposed to have individualized exteriors...[not] one level of trim. Hot rods customarily sport spartan, handmade interiors. The Prowler's is more plush and option laden than a BMW Z3's." On the other hand, "It's a convertible, the drivetrain is dead reliable, it can be driven [every day] as long as there's no snow, there's a three-year/36,000-mile warranty, and the vehicle regularly twists the needle right off...the gawk meter."

Predictably, Chrysler's latest piece of eye candy was always in short supply. Though the long wait from concept to reality stoked demand to a fever pitch, Chrysler wouldn't rush. After all, Prowler was Plymouth's important new image-leader, and thus needed to be well-made and glitch-free from day one. Besides, why risk diluting the car's mystique—and driving down resale values—by building too many too fast? All this echoed Viper experience, and Chrysler sensibly assigned Prowler production to the Viper plant on Detroit's Conner Avenue, which was geared to build semi-custom machines at a measured pace with considerable hand labor. As it happened, though, Prowlers didn't begin reaching dealers until August 1997, delayed by last-minute production glitches. As a result, model-year output was only 312 units instead of the 2000-3000 planned, and a bidding war broke out among would-be owners.

Prowler skipped model-year '98 for an early start on 1999. Red, black, and a vibrant yellow expanded the color palette, but the big news was an aluminum-block version of the single-cam 3.5 V-6. Horsepower swelled by 39 to 253, peaking at 6400 rpm instead of 5850. Torque rose by a useful 34 pound-feet to 255, and maxed out at more-accessible 3100 rpm (versus 3950). *Car and Driver* lopped a second off the 0-60 dash and timed quarter-mile acceleration at 14.7 seconds at 90 mph. Other magazine tests showed less-dramatic improvements, but the '99 was stronger by most accounts. And though the traditional hot-rod exhaust burble was still missing, so

**2000 Breeze four-door sedan**

# Plymouth

were some of the '97 model's unwanted cowl shake and body quivering. Base price went up $1000, but nobody complained.

Yet for all its high-profile pizzazz, Prowler did nothing to spur sales of workaday Plymouths, and that spelled trouble once Germany's Daimler-Benz absorbed Chrysler Corporation in late 1998. The new DaimlerBenz was troubled from the start, and the mostly German top brass were far more concerned with "shareholder value" than any value Plymouth might have for their American "division." Thus, in late October 1999, after months of mounting rumors, DC's American-born president, James Holden, announced that Plymouth would be terminated after model-year 2001 as irrelevant to the company's new "global growth stategy." It was a sad day for many car lovers, but industry analysts (and even Chrysler-Plymouth dealers) weren't surprised. After all, Prowler was only the first Plymouth since the '69 Barracuda with no direct Dodge duplicate, and Dodge always did better with shared products.

But *C/D*'s Pat Bedard, himself a former Chrysler engineer, begged to differ. In a March 2000 epitaph, he noted that Plymouth sales might still be sliding, but were "hardly dead...Voyager sales not only outnumbered Plymouth cars in 1998, they outgunned the combined minivan efforts of the Chevrolet Venture and Pontiac Montana...There's something odd, too, about DC's notion of global growth. Yeah, Plymouth is only a U.S. brand. So what?...Low-priced brands always slump when people have the dough to buy higher on the status ladder. [When they don't], a trusted budget brand makes a great lifeboat [for an automaker]. Building a fresh one, as GM did with Saturn, costs billions...I think DaimlerChrysler is walking away from sales."

Maybe so, but losing Plymouth was easy for DC, and customers could be steered to other company brands. With that, Breeze was dropped with the 2001 redesign of its Dodge and Chrysler siblings (which would then presumably take up the slack), and rebadging created Chrysler Voyagers even before the company's new minivans arrived, also for '01. The second-generation 2000 Neon was sold as Plymouth, but only for about 18 months and without the sporty options Dodge offered.

Prowler, too, became a Chrysler, swapping nameplates during model-year 2001, but hung on through '02. The 2000 edition got revised damping and adjustable shock absorbers for a more-pliant ride, plus a few minor feature additions. Otherwise, only colors were changed.

Left behind in Plymouth's demise was the intriguing Howler concept. Basically a Prowler with a handsome new squared-off tail, it offered usable luggage space at last, achieved by exchanging the rear transaxle for a conventional front-mounted transmission. Even better, though, that gearbox was a five-speed manual bolted to a V-8, a torquey 250 4.7-liter borrowed from the Jeep Grand Cherokee. Enthusiasts cheered, but there was no hope for Howler, a strictly what-if dream unveiled only weeks before Plymouth's announced execution.

Plymouth wasn't Detroit's only historic nameplate to be killed off by new-century corporate tactics. Oldsmobile went to the gallows barely a year later. But there's an ironic footnote in that the 2001 PT Cruiser was once planned for Plymouth, as product chief Tom Gale told us. Considering its huge sales success as a low-priced Chrysler, the versatile, "way-cool" Cruiser could have been just the comeback car Plymouth needed, setting the stage for more Plymouth-only models and a true revival of the make. A pity Chrysler walked away from that, too.

**2001 Prowler Black Tie Edition roadster**

# Plymouth

## Specifications

### 1930

| Model U (wb 109.0) | Wght | Price | Prod* |
|---|---|---|---|
| rdstr 2-4P | 2,265 | 610 | — |
| phaeton 5P | 2,355 | 625 | — |
| cpe 2P | 2,380 | 590 | — |
| Deluxe cpe 2-4P | 2,415 | 625 | — |
| sdn 2d | 2,475 | 610 | — |
| sdn 4d | 2,555 | 625 | — |
| Deluxe sdn 4d | 2,590 | 675 | — |
| **Model 30U (wb 109.0)** | | | |
| spt rdstr 2-4P | 2,280 | 610 | — |
| phaeton 5P | 2,340 | 625 | — |
| cpe 2P | 2,420 | 590 | — |
| cpe 2-4P | 2,510 | 625 | — |
| sdn 4d | 2,595 | 625 | — |
| Deluxe sdn 4d | 2,590 | 745 | — |
| conv cpe 2-4P | 2,450 | 695 | — |
| chassis | — | — | — |

| 1930 Engines | bore × stroke | bhp | availability |
|---|---|---|---|
| I-4, 175.4 | 3.63 × 4.25 | 45 | S-Model U |
| I-4, 196.0 | 3.63 × 4.75 | 48 | S-Model 30U |

* 1930 model-year production was confused by the overlapping of the Model U into 1929 and the Model 30U into 1931.

For the Model U, no serial number spans are recorded for 1929 or 1930, but 1929 calendar-year production was 93,592, and total 1929-30 Model U production was 108,350.

For the 1930-31 Model 30U, total production was 76,950. The 1930-model 30U carried serial numbers 1500001 to 1530244 (30,244 cars), while 1931 models carried serial numbers 1530245 to 1570300 (40,055 cars). This does not add up to the 76,950 total figure, but may serve to provide an approximate breakdown between the two model years. Individual factory production figures for Model 30U body styles are given under 1931. Note that the business roadster and both two-door sedans were not offered during model year 1930.

### 1931

| Model 30U (wb 109.0) | Wght | Price | Pro |
|---|---|---|---|
| bus rdstr 2P | 2,245 | 535 | 1,609 |
| sdn 2d | 2,497 | 565 | 7,980 |
| commercial sdn 2d | 2,450 | 750 | 80 |
| spt rdstr 2-4P | 2,280 | 610 | 2,884* |
| spt phaeton 5P | 2,340 | 625 | 632* |
| cpe 2P | 2,420 | 565 | 9,189* |
| cpe 2-4P | 2,510 | 625 | 5,850* |
| sdn 4d | 2,595 | 625 | 47,152* |
| conv cpe 2-4P | 2,450 | 695 | 1,272* |
| chassis | — | — | 302* |

* Combined production for 1930-31 models. For approximate breakdown, take 57% of total shown for 1931, 43% for 1930. See also production notes under 1930.

| 1931 Engine | bore × stroke | bhp | availability |
|---|---|---|---|
| I-4, 196.0 | 3.63 × 4.75 | 48 | S-all |

### 1932

| Model PA (wb 109.0) built 5/31-2/32 | Wght | Price | Prod |
|---|---|---|---|
| bus rdstr 2P | 2,440 | 535 | 2,000 |
| spt rdstr 2-4P | 2,470 | 595 | 2,680 |
| spt phaeton 5P | 2,545 | 595 | 528 |
| cpe 2P | 2,600 | 565 | 1,279 |
| cpe 2-4P | 2,645 | 610 | 9,696 |
| conv cpe 2-4P | 2,615 | 645 | 2,783 |
| sdn 2d | 2,650 | 575 | 23,038 |
| sdn 4d | 2,730 | 635 | 49,465 |
| Deluxe sdn 4d | 2,795 | 690 | 4,384 |
| Thrift sdn 2d | 2,690 | 495 | |
| **Model PA (wb 109.0) built 5/31-2/32** | | | |
| Thrift sdn 4d | 2,745 | 575 | * |
| chassis and taxicabs | — | — | 243 |
| **Model PB (wb 112.0; lwb-121.0) built 2/32-9/32** | | | |
| bus rdstr 2P | 2,550 | 495 | 3,225 |
| spt rdstr 2-4P | 2,600 | 595 | 2,163 |
| spt phaeton 5P | 2,660 | 595 | 259 |
| cpe 2P | 2,700 | 565 | 11,126 |
| cpe 2-4P | 2,755 | 610 | 8,159 |
| conv cpe 2-4P | 2,735 | 645 | 4,853 |
| sdn 2d | 2,830 | 575 | 13,031 |
| sdn 4d | 2,875 | 635 | 38,066 |
| conv sdn 5P | 2,925 | 785 | 690 |
| lwb sdn 7P | 3,075 | 725 | 2,179 |
| chassis and taxicabs | — | — | 159 |

* Production included with 2d and 4d sedans. Total production of Thrift models was 4,894.

| 1932 Engines | bore × stroke | bhp | availability |
|---|---|---|---|
| I-4, 196.1 | 3.63 × 4.75 | 56 | S-PA |
| I-4, 196.1 | 3.63 × 4.75 | 65 | S-PB |

### 1933

| PC Six (wb 107.0) | Wght | Price | Prod |
|---|---|---|---|
| cpe 2P | 2,418 | 495 | 10,853 |
| cpe 2-4P | 2,473 | 525 | 8,894 |
| conv cpe 2-4P | 2,483 | 565 | 2,034 |
| sdn 2d | 2,498 | 505 | 4,008 |
| sdn 4d | 2,553 | 545 | 33,815 |
| chassis | — | — | 396 |
| **PCXX Standard Six (wb 108.0)** | | | |
| bus cpe 2P | 2,353 | 445 | 9,200 |
| cpe 2-4P | 2,423 | 485 | 2,497 |
| sdn 2d | 2,443 | 464 | 17,736 |
| sdn 4d | 2,523 | 510 | 13,661 |
| chassis | — | — | 309 |
| **PD DeLuxe Six (wb 112.0)** | | | |
| cpe 2P | 2,485 | 495 | 30,728 |
| cpe 2-4P | 2,545 | 545 | 20,821 |
| conv cpe 2-4P | 2,530 | 595 | 4,596 |
| sdn 2d | 2,560 | 525 | 49,826 |
| sdn 4d | 2,645 | 575 | 88,404 |
| chassis | — | — | 779 |

| 1933 Engines | bore × stroke | bhp | availability |
|---|---|---|---|
| I-6, 189.8 | 3.13 × 4.14 | 70 | S-PC |
| I-6, 189.8 | 3.13 × 4.14 | 76 | S-PCXX, PD |

### 1934

| PE DeLuxe (wb 114.0) | Wght | Price | Prod |
|---|---|---|---|
| bus cpe 2P | 2,668 | 595 | 28,433 |

# Plymouth

| PE DeLuxe (wb 114.0) | Wght | Price | Prod |
|---|---|---|---|
| cpe 2-4P | 2,733 | 630 | 15,658 |
| conv cpe 2-4P | 2,698 | 685 | 4,482 |
| sdn 2d | 2,773 | 610 | 58,535 |
| sdn 4d | 2,848 | 660 | 108,407 |
| town sdn 4d 5P | 2,898 | 695 | 7,049 |
| sdn 7P | — | — | 891 |
| chassis | — | — | 2,362 |

| PF Standard (wb 108.0) | Wght | Price | Prod |
|---|---|---|---|
| bus cpe 2P | 2,513 | 540 | 6,980 |
| cpe 2-4P | 2,573 | 570 | 2,061 |
| sdn 2d | 2,603 | 560 | 12,562 |
| sdn 4d | 2,693 | 600 | 16,789 |
| chassis | — | — | 1,152 |

| PFXX Special (wb 108.0) | Wght | Price | Prod |
|---|---|---|---|
| bus cpe 2P | 2,563 | 560 | 3,721 |
| cpe 2-4P | 2,608 | 590 | 1,746 |
| sdn 2d | 2,658 | 580 | 12,497 |
| sdn 4d | 2,708 | 620 | 16,760 |
| town sdn 4d 5P | 2,783 | 655 | 574 |

| PG Standard (wb 108.0) | Wght | Price | Prod |
|---|---|---|---|
| bus cpe 2P | 2,438 | 485 | 7,844 |
| sdn 2d | 2,538 | 510 | 12,603 |
| sdn 4d | — | — | 62 |
| chassis | — | — | 3 |

| 1934 Engines | bore × stroke | bhp | availability |
|---|---|---|---|
| I-6, 201.3 | 3.13 × 4.38 | 77 | S-all |
| I-6, 201.3 | 3.13 × 4.38 | 82 | O-all |

## 1935

| PJ Six (wb 113.0) | Wght | Price | Prod |
|---|---|---|---|
| bus cpe 2P | 2,625 | 510 | 16,691 |
| bus sdn 2d | 2,670 | 535 | 29,942 |
| bus sdn 4d | 2,720 | 570 | 15,761 |
| bus commercial sdn 2d | 2,735 | 635 | 1,142 |
| cpe 2P | 2,665 | 565 | 6,664 |
| sdn 2d | 2,685 | 615 | 7,284 |

| PJ DeLuxe Six (wb 113.0; lwb-128.0) | Wght | Price | Prod |
|---|---|---|---|
| bus cpe 2P | 2,675 | 575 | 29,190 |
| cpe 2-4P | 2,730 | 630 | 12,118 |
| conv cpe 2-4P | 2,830 | 695 | 2,308 |
| sdn 2d | 2,720 | 625 | 12,424 |
| touring sdn 2d T/B | 2,780 | 650 | 45,203 |
| sdn 4d | 2,790 | 660 | 66,083 |
| touring sdn 4d T/B | 2,815 | 685 | 82,068 |
| Traveler lwb sdn 5P | — | 895 | 77 |
| lwb sdn 7P | 3,130 | 895 | 350 |
| Westchester Sub wgn 4d | — | 765 | 119 |
| chassis (lwb) | — | — | 24 |

| 1935 Engine | bore × stroke | bhp | availability |
|---|---|---|---|
| I-6, 201.3 | 3.13 × 4.13 | 82 | S-all |

## 1936

| P1 Business Series (wb 113.0) | Wght | Price | Prod |
|---|---|---|---|
| cpe 2P | 2,650 | 510 | 26,856 |
| sdn 2d | 2,720 | 545 | 39,516 |

| P1 Business Series (wb 113.0) | Wght | Price | Prod |
|---|---|---|---|
| sdn 4d | 2,750 | 590 | 19,104 |
| wgn 4d | 2,920 | 765 | 309 |
| commercial sdn 2d | — | 605 | 3,527 |
| touring sdn 4d T/B | — | — | 1,544 |
| touring sdn 2d T/B | — | — | 768 |
| chassis | — | — | 1,211 |

| P2 DeLuxe Series (wb 113.0; lwb-125.0) | Wght | Price | Prod |
|---|---|---|---|
| cpe 2P | 2,705 | 580 | 54,601 |
| cpe 2-4P | 2,775 | 620 | 9,663 |
| conv cpe 2-4P | 2,830 | 725 | 3,297 |
| sdn 2d | 2,785 | 625 | 6,149 |
| touring sdn 2d T/B | 2,815 | 645 | 99,373 |
| sdn 4d | 2,820 | 660 | 10,001 |
| touring sdn 4d T/B | 2,850 | 680 | 240,136 |
| touring sdn 7P T/B (lwb) | 3,155 | 895 | 1,504 |
| chassis | — | — | 2,775 |

| 1936 Engines | bore × stroke | bhp | availability |
|---|---|---|---|
| I-6, 201.3 | 3.13 × 4.38 | 82 | S-all |
| I-6, 201.3 | 3.13 × 4.38 | 65 | O-all |

## 1937

| P3 Business Series (wb 112.0) | Wght | Price | Prod |
|---|---|---|---|
| cpe 2P | 2,771 | 580 | 18,202 |
| cpe 2-4P | 2,841 | 620 | 540 |
| sdn 2d | 2,841 | 620 | 28,685 |
| touring sdn 2d T/B | 2,871 | 640 | 1,350 |
| sdn 4d | 2,841 | 665 | 16,000 |
| touring sdn 4d T/B | 2,871 | 685 | 7,842 |
| chassis | — | — | 1,025 |

| P4 DeLuxe Series (wb 112.0; lwb-132.0) | Wght | Price | Prod |
|---|---|---|---|
| cpe 2P | 2,839 | 650 | 67,144 |
| cpe 2-4P | 2,884 | 700 | 6,877 |
| conv cpe 2-4P | 2,994 | 830 | 3,110 |
| sdn 2d | 2,899 | 715 | 7,926 |
| touring sdn 2d T/B | 2,914 | 725 | 111,099 |
| sdn 4d | 2,914 | 745 | 9,000 |
| touring sdn 4d T/B | 2,944 | 755 | 269,062 |
| lwb sdn 7P | 3,333 | 995 | 1,840 |
| sdn limo 7P (lwb) | 3,400 | 1,095 | 63 |
| chassis and taxicabs | — | — | 2,229 |

| 1937 Engines | bore × stroke | bhp | availability |
|---|---|---|---|
| I-6, 201.3 | 3.13 × 4.38 | 82 | S-all |
| I-6, 201.3 | 3.13 × 4.38 | 65 | O-all |

## 1938

| P5 Business/Roadking* (wb 112.0) | Wght | Price | Prod |
|---|---|---|---|
| cpe 2P | 2,739 | 645 | 15,932 |
| sdn 2d | 2,764 | 685 | 15,393 |
| sdn 4d | 2,809 | 730 | 6,459 |
| touring sdn 2d T/B | 2,779 | 701 | 16,413 |
| touring sdn 4d T/B | 2,824 | 746 | 18,664 |
| cpe 2-4P | 2,809 | 695 | 338 |
| chassis | — | — | 1,586 |

*Name changed to Roadking March 31, 1938, and touring sedans introduced.

# Plymouth

| P6 DeLuxe (wb 112.0; lwb-132.0) | Wght | Price | Prod |
|---|---|---|---|
| cpe 2P | 2,804 | 730 | 27,181 |
| cpe 2-4P | 2,864 | 770 | 2,000 |
| conv cpe 2-4P | 3,009 | 850 | 1,900 |
| sdn 2d | 2,874 | 773 | 1,222 |
| touring sdn 2d T/B | 2,864 | 785 | 46,669 |
| sdn 4d | 2,894 | 803 | 1,446 |
| touring sdn 4d T/B | 2,874 | 815 | 119,669 |
| Suburban wgn 4d 8P | 3,039 | 880 | 555 |
| lwb sdn 7P T/B | 3,289 | 1,005 | 1,824 |
| sdn limo 7P (lwb) | 3,300 | 1,095 | 75 |
| chassis and taxicabs | — | — | 2,062 |

| 1938 Engines | bore × stroke | bhp | availability |
|---|---|---|---|
| I-6, 201.3 | 3.13 × 4.38 | 82 | S-all |
| I-6, 201.3 | 3.13 × 4.38 | 65 | O-all |
| I-6, 201.3 | 3.13 × 4.38 | 86 | O-all |

## 1939

| P7 Roadking (wb 114.0) | Wght | Price | Prod |
|---|---|---|---|
| cpe 2P | 2,724 | 645 | 22,537 |
| cpe 2-4P | 2,784 | 695 | 222 |
| sdn 2d | 2,824 | 685 | 7,499 |
| touring sdn 2d T/B | 2,824 | 699 | 42,186 |
| sdn 4d | 2,839 | 726 | 2,553 |
| touring sdn 4d T/B | 2,829 | 740 | 23,047 |
| util sdn 2d | 2,844 | 685 | 341 |
| commercial sdn | — | — | 2,270 |
| Suburban wgn 4d | — | — | 97 |
| chassis | — | — | 1,616 |

| P8 DeLuxe (wb 114.0; conv sdn-117.0; lwb-134.0) | Wght | Price | Prod |
|---|---|---|---|
| cpe 2P | 2,789 | 725 | 41,924 |
| cpe 2-4P | 2,874 | 755 | 1,322 |
| conv cpe 2-4P | 3,044 | 895 | 5,976 |
| sdn 2d | 2,889 | 761 | 2,653 |
| touring sdn 2d T/B | 2,894 | 775 | 80,981 |
| sdn 4d | 2,909 | 791 | 2,279 |
| touring sdn 4d T/B | 2,919 | 885 | 175,054 |
| conv sdn 4d | 3,209 | 1150 | 387 |
| Suburban wgn 4d 8P (side curtains) | 3,089 | 930 | 1,680 |
| Suburban wgn 4d 8P (glass encl) | 3,189 | 970 | |
| util sd 2d | — | — | 13 |
| lwb sdn 7P T/B | 3,374 | 1,005 | 1,837 |
| sdn limo 7P (lwb) | 3,440 | 1,095 | 98 |
| chassis and taxicabs | — | — | 947 |

| 1939 Engine | bore × stroke | bhp | availability |
|---|---|---|---|
| I-6, 201.3 | 3.13 × 4.38 | 82 | S-all |
| I-6, 201.3 | 3.13 × 4.38 | 86 | O-all |
| I-6, 201.3 | 3.13 × 4.38 | 65 | O-all |

## 1940

| P9 Roadking (wb 117.5) | Wght | Price | Prod |
|---|---|---|---|
| bus cpe | 2,769 | 645 | 26,745 |
| sdn 2d | 2,834 | 699 | 55,092 |
| sdn 4d | 2,869 | 740 | 20,076 |
| util sdn | 2,769 | 699 | 589 |
| club cpe | 2,814 | 699 | 360 |
| wgn 4d | 3,089 | 925 | 80 |
| chassis | — | — | 907 |

| P10 DeLuxe (wb 117.5; 7P-137.0) | Wght | Price | Prod |
|---|---|---|---|
| bus cpe | 2,804 | 725 | 32,244 |
| sdn 2d | 2,889 | 775 | 76,781 |
| sdn 4d | 2,924 | 805 | 173,351 |
| util sdn | 2,824 | 775 | 4 |
| club cpe | 2,849 | 770 | 22,174 |
| conv cpe | 3,049 | 950 | 6,986 |
| wgn 4d | 3,144 | 970 | 3,126 |
| sdn 4d 7P | 3,359 | 1,005 | 1,179 |
| limo 7P | 3,409 | 1,080 | 68 |
| chassis | — | — | 503 |

| 1940 Engines | bore × stroke | bhp | availability |
|---|---|---|---|
| I-6, 201.3 | 3.13 × 4.38 | 84 | S-all |
| I-6, 201.3 | 3.13 × 4.38 | 87 | O-all |
| I-6, 201.3 | 3.13 × 4.38 | 65 | O-all |

## 1941

| P11 DeLuxe (wb 117.5) | Wght | Price | Prod |
|---|---|---|---|
| bus cpe | 2,809 | 720 | 23,754 |
| sdn 2d | 2,859 | 769 | 46,646 |
| sdn 4d | 2,889 | 800 | 21,175 |
| util sdn | 2,794 | 760 | 468 |
| club cpe | 2,819 | 764 | 994 |
| wgn 4d | 3,139 | 1,006 | 217 |
| DeLuxe bus cpe | 2,839 | 760 | 15,862 |
| DeLuxe sdn 2d | 2,899 | 809 | 46,138 |
| DeLuxe sdn 4d | 2,924 | 845 | 32,336 |
| DeLuxe club cpe | 2,859 | 804 | 204 |
| DeLuxe util sdn | — | proto | 1 |
| chassis | — | — | 676 |

| P12 Special DeLuxe (wb 117.5; 7P-137.0) | Wght | Price | Prod |
|---|---|---|---|
| bus cpe | 2,859 | 795 | 23,851 |
| sdn 2d | 2,934 | 845 | 84,810 |
| sdn 4d | 2,959 | 877 | 190,513 |
| util sdn | — | proto | 2 |
| club cpe | 2,934 | 842 | 37,352 |
| conv cpe | 3,166 | 1,007 | 10,545 |
| wgn 4d | 3,194 | 1,031 | 5,594 |
| sdn 4d, 7P | 3,379 | 1,078 | 1,127 |
| limo, 7P | 3,429 | 1,153 | 24 |
| chassis | — | — | 321 |

| 1941 Engines | bore × stroke | bhp | availability |
|---|---|---|---|
| I-6, 201.3 | 3.13 × 4.38 | 87 | S-all |
| I-6, 201.3 | 3.13 × 4.38 | 92 | O-all |

## 1942

| P14S DeLuxe (wb 117.5) | Wght | Price | Prod |
|---|---|---|---|
| bus cpe | 2,906 | 812 | 3,783 |
| sdn 2d | 2,961 | 850 | 9,350 |
| sdn 4d | 3,001 | 889 | 11,973 |
| util sdn | 2,906 | 842 | 80 |
| club cpe | 2,966 | 885 | 2,458 |
| chassis | — | — | 1 |

# Plymouth

| P14C Special DeLuxe (wb 117.5) | Wght | Price | Prod |
|---|---|---|---|
| bus cpe | 2,931 | 855 | 7,258 |
| sdn 2d | 2,996 | 895 | 24,142 |
| sdn 4d | 3,036 | 935 | 68,924 |
| Town Sedan | 3,061 | 980 | 5,821 |
| club cpe | 3,011 | 928 | 14,685 |
| conv cpe | 3,231 | 1,078 | 2,806 |
| wgn 4d | 3,371 | 1,145 | 1,136 |
| chassis | — | — | 10 |

| 1942 Engine | bore × stroke | bhp | availability |
|---|---|---|---|
| I-6, 217.8 | 3.25 × 4.38 | 95 | S-all |

**1946*** See note following 1949 First Series.

| P15S DeLuxe (wb 117.5) | Wght | Price | Prod |
|---|---|---|---|
| bus cpe | 2,977 | 1,089 | — |
| sdn 2d | 3,047 | 1,124 | — |
| sdn 4d | 3,082 | 1,164 | — |
| club cpe | 3,037 | 1,159 | — |
| chassis | — | — | — |
| **P15C Special DeLuxe (wb 117.5)** | | | |
| bus cpe | 2,982 | 1,159 | — |
| sdn 2d | 3,062 | 1,199 | — |
| sdn 4d | 3,107 | 1,239 | — |
| club cpe | 3,057 | 1,234 | — |
| conv cpe | 3,282 | 1,439 | — |
| wgn 4d | 3,402 | 1,539 | — |
| chassis | — | — | — |

| 1946 Engine | bore × stroke | bhp | availability |
|---|---|---|---|
| I-6, 217.8 | 3.25 × 4.38 | 95 | S-all |

**1947*** See note following 1949 First Series.

| P15S DeLuxe (wb 117.5) | Wght | Price | Prod |
|---|---|---|---|
| bus cpe | 2,977 | 1,139 | — |
| sdn 2d | 3,047 | 1,164 | — |
| sdn 4d | 3,082 | 1,214 | — |
| club cpe | 3,037 | 1,189 | — |
| chassis | — | — | — |
| **P15C Special DeLuxe (wb 117.5)** | | | |
| bus cpe | 2,982 | 1,209 | — |
| sdn 2d | 3,062 | 1,239 | — |
| sdn 4d | 3,107 | 1,289 | — |
| club cpe | 3,057 | 1,264 | — |
| conv cpe | 3,282 | 1,565 | — |
| wgn 4d | 3,402 | 1,765 | — |
| chassis | — | — | — |

| 1947 Engine | bore × stroke | bhp | availability |
|---|---|---|---|
| I-6, 217.8 | 3.25 × 4.38 | 95 | S-all |

**1948*** See note following 1949 First Series.

| P15S DeLuxe (wb 117.5) | Wght | Price | Prod |
|---|---|---|---|
| bus cpe | 2,955 | 1,346 | — |
| sdn 2d | 2,995 | 1,383 | — |
| sdn 4d | 3,030 | 1,441 | — |
| club cpe | 3,005 | 1,409 | — |
| chassis | — | — | — |
| **P15C Special DeLuxe (wb 117.5)** | | | |
| bus cpe | 2,950 | 1,440 | — |
| sdn 2d | 3,030 | 1,471 | — |
| sdn 4d | 3,045 | 1,529 | — |
| club cpe | 3,020 | 1,503 | — |
| conv cpe | 3,225 | 1,857 | — |
| wgn 4d | 3,320 | 2,068 | — |
| chassis | — | — | — |

| 1948 Engine | bore × stroke | bhp | availability |
|---|---|---|---|
| I-6, 217.8 | 3.25 × 4.38 | 95 | S-all |

**1949 First Series*** See note following 1949 First Series.

| P15S DeLuxe (wb 117.5) | Wght | Price | Prod |
|---|---|---|---|
| bus cpe | 2,955 | 1,346 | — |
| sdn 2d | 2,995 | 1,383 | — |
| sdn 4d | 3,030 | 1,441 | — |
| club cpe | 3,005 | 1,409 | — |
| chassis | — | — | — |
| **P15C Special DeLuxe (wb 117.5)** | | | |
| bus cpe | 2,950 | 1,440 | — |
| sdn 2d | 3,030 | 1,471 | — |
| sdn 4d | 3,045 | 1,529 | — |
| club cpe | 3,020 | 1,503 | — |
| conv cpe | 3,225 | 1,857 | — |
| wgn 4d | 3,320 | 2,068 | — |
| chassis | — | — | — |

| 1949(1) Engine | bore × stroke | bhp | availability |
|---|---|---|---|
| I-6, 217.8 | 3.25 × 4.38 | 95 | S-all |

*Factory combined production figures for 1946 through 1949 First Series.

**Combined 1946-1949 First Series Production**

| P15S DeLuxe (wb 117.5) | Prod |
|---|---|
| bus cpe | 16,117 |
| sdn 2d | 49,918 |
| sdn 4d | 120,757 |
| club cpe | 10,400 |
| chassis | 10 |
| **P15C Special DeLuxe (wb 117.5)** | |
| bus cpe | 31,399 |
| sdn 2d | 125,704 |
| sdn 4d | 514,986 |
| club cpe | 156,629 |
| conv cpe | 15,295 |
| wgn 4d | 12,913 |
| chassis | 5,361 |

**1949 Second Series**

| P17 DeLuxe (wb 111.0) | Wght | Price | Prod |
|---|---|---|---|
| bus cpe | 2,825 | 1,371 | 13,715 |

# Plymouth

| P17 DeLuxe (wb 111.0) | Wght | Price | Prod |
|---|---|---|---|
| sdn 2d | 2,951 | 1,492 | 28,516 |
| Suburban wgn 2d | 3,105 | 1,840 | 19,220 |
| chassis | — | — | 4 |
| **P18 DeLuxe (wb 118.5)** | | | |
| sdn 4d | 3,059 | 1,551 | 61,021 |
| club cpe | 3,034 | 1,519 | 25,687 |
| **P18 Special DeLuxe (wb 118.5)** | | | |
| sdn 4d | 3,079 | 1,629 | 252,878 |
| club cpe | 3,046 | 1,603 | 99,680 |
| conv cpe | 3,323 | 1,982 | 15,240 |
| wgn 4d | 3,341 | 2,372 | 3,443 |
| chassis | — | — | 981 |

| 1949(2) Engine | bore × stroke | bhp | availability |
|---|---|---|---|
| I-6, 217.8 | 3.25 × 4.38 | 97 | S-all |

## 1950

| P19 DeLuxe (wb 111.0) | Wght | Price | Prod |
|---|---|---|---|
| bus cpe | 2,872 | 1,371 | 16,861 |
| sdn 2d | 2,946 | 1,492 | 67,584 |
| Suburban wgn 2d | 3,116 | 1,840 | 34,457 |
| Suburban Special wgn 2d | 3,155 | 1,946 | |
| chassis | — | — | 1 |
| **P20 DeLuxe (wb 118.5)** | | | |
| sdn 4d | 3,068 | 1,551 | 87,871 |
| club cpe | 3,040 | 1,519 | 53,890 |
| **P20 Special DeLuxe (wb 118.5)** | | | |
| sdn 4d | 3,072 | 1,629 | 234,084 |
| club cpe | 3,041 | 1,603 | 99,361 |
| conv cpe | 3,295 | 1,982 | 12,697 |
| wgn 4d | 3,353 | 2,372 | 2,057 |
| chassis | — | — | 2,091 |

| 1950 Engine | bore × stroke | bhp | availability |
|---|---|---|---|
| I-6, 217.8 | 3.25 × 4.38 | 97 | S-all |

## 1951** See note following 1952.

| P22 Concord (wb 111.0) | Wght | Price | Prod |
|---|---|---|---|
| bus cpe | 2,919 | 1,537 | — |
| sdn 2d | 2,969 | 1,673 | — |
| Savoy wgn 2d | 3,184 | 2,182 | — |
| Suburban wgn 2d | 3,124 | 2,064 | — |
| **P23 Cambridge (wb 118.5)** | | | |
| sdn 4d | 3,104 | 1,739 | — |
| club cpe | 3,059 | 1,703 | — |
| **P23 Cranbrook (wb 118.5)** | | | |
| sdn 4d | 3,109 | 1,826 | — |
| club cpe | 3,074 | 1,796 | — |
| conv cpe | 3,294 | 2,222 | — |
| Belvedere htp cpe | 3,182 | 2,114 | — |

| 1951 Engine | bore × stroke | bhp | availability |
|---|---|---|---|
| I-6, 217.8 | 3.25 × 4.38 | 97 | S-all |

## 1952** See note following 1952.

| P22 Concord (wb 111.0) | Wght | Price | Prod |
|---|---|---|---|
| bus cpe | 2,893 | 1,610 | 14,255 |
| sdn 2d | 2,959 | 1,753 | 49,139 |
| Savoy wgn 2d | 3,165 | 2,287 | 76,520 |
| Suburban wgn 2d | 3,145 | 2,163 | |
| **P23 Cambridge (wb 118.5)** | | | |
| sdn 4d | 3,068 | 1,822 | 179,417 |
| club cpe | 3,030 | 1,784 | 101,784 |
| **P23 Cranbrook (wb 118.5)** | | | |
| sdn 4d | 3,088 | 1,914 | 388,735 |
| club cpe | 3,046 | 1,883 | 126,725 |
| Belvedere htp cpe | 3,105 | 2,216 | 51,266 |
| conv cpe | 3,256 | 2,329 | 15,650 |
| chassis | — | — | 4,171 |

| 1952 Engine | bore × stroke | bhp | availability |
|---|---|---|---|
| I-6, 217.8 | 3.25 × 4.38 | 97 | S-all |

**Factory combined 1951 and 1952 production figures.

## 1953

| P24-1 Cambridge (wb 114.0) | Wght | Price | Prod |
|---|---|---|---|
| bus cpe | 2,888 | 1,618 | 6,975 |
| sdn 2d | 2,943 | 1,727 | 56,800 |
| sdn 4d | 2,983 | 1,765 | 93,585 |
| club cpe | 2,950 | 1,725 | 1,050 |
| Suburban wgn 2d | 3,129 | 2,064 | 43,545 |
| **P24-2 Cranbrook (wb 114.0)** | | | |
| sdn 4d | 3,023 | 1,873 | 298,976 |
| club cpe | 2,971 | 1,843 | 92,102 |
| Belvedere htp cpe | 3,027 | 2,064 | 35,185 |
| conv cpe | 3,193 | 2,220 | 6,301 |
| Savoy wgn 2d | 3,170 | 2,207 | 12,089 |
| chassis | — | — | 843 |

| 1953 Engine | bore × stroke | bhp | availability |
|---|---|---|---|
| I-6, 217.8 | 3.25 × 4.38 | 100 | S-all |

## 1954

| P25-1 Plaza (wb 114.0) | Wght | Price | Prod |
|---|---|---|---|
| bus cpe | 2,889 | 1,618 | 5,000 |
| club cpe | 2,950* | 1,700* | 1,275 |
| sdn 4d | 3,004 | 1,765 | 43,077 |
| sdn 2d | 2,943 | 1,727 | 27,976 |
| Suburban wgn 2d | 3,122 | 2,064 | 35,937 |
| chassis | — | — | 1 |
| **P25-2 Savoy (wb 114.0)** | | | |
| club cpe | 2,982 | 1,843 | 30,700 |
| sdn 4d | 3,036 | 1,873 | 139,383 |
| sdn 2d | 2,986 | 1,835 | 25,396 |
| chassis | — | — | 3,588 |
| **P25-3 Belvedere (wb 114.0)** | | | |
| sdn 4d | 3,050 | 1,953 | 106,601 |
| Sport Coupe htp | 3,038 | 2,145 | 25,592 |
| conv cpe | 3,273 | 2,301 | 6,900 |
| Suburban wgn 2d | 3,186 | 2,288 | 9,241 |
| chassis | — | — | 2,031 |

*Estimated.

# Plymouth

| 1954 Engines | bore × stroke | bhp | availability |
|---|---|---|---|
| I-6, 217.8 | 3.25 × 4.38 | 100 | S-all to engine #P25-243000 |
| I-6, 230.2 | 3.25 × 4.63 | 110 | S-all from engine #P25-243001 |

## 1955

| P26-1 Plaza, I-6 (wb 115.0) | Wght | Price | Prod |
|---|---|---|---|
| sdn 4d | 3,129 | 1,781 | 68,826 |
| club cpe | 3,089 | 1,738 | 45,561 |
| Suburban wgn 2d | 3,261 | 2,077 | 23,319 |
| Suburban wgn 4d | 3,282 | 2,158 | 10,594 |
| bus cpe | 3,025 | 1,639 | 4,882 |
| **P27-1 Plaza, V-8 (wb 115.0)** | | | |
| sdn 4d | 3,246 | 1,884 | 15,330 |
| club cpe | 3,202 | 1,841 | 8,049 |
| Suburban wgn 2d | 3,389 | 2,180 | 8,469 |
| Suburban wgn 4d | 3,408 | 2,262 | 4,828 |
| **P26-3 Savoy, I-6 (wb 115.0)** | | | |
| sdn 4d | 3,154 | 1,880 | 93,716 |
| club cpe | 3,109 | 1,837 | 45,438 |
| chassis | — | — | 1 |
| **P27-3 Savoy, V-8 (wb 115.0)** | | | |
| sdn 4d | 3,265 | 1,983 | 69,025 |
| club cpe | 3,224 | 1,940 | 29,442 |
| **P26-2 Belvedere, I-6 (wb 115.0)** | | | |
| sdn 4d | 3,159 | 1,979 | 69,128 |
| club cpe | 3,129 | 1,936 | 19,471 |
| Sport Coupe htp | 3,330 | 2,113 | 13,942 |
| Suburban wgn 4d | 3,312 | 2,322 | 6,197 |
| **P27-2 Belvedere V-8 (wb 115.0)** | | | |
| sdn 4d | 3,262 | 2,082 | 91,856 |
| club cpe | 3,228 | 2,039 | 22,174 |
| Sport Coupe htp | 3,261 | 2,217 | 33,433 |
| conv cpe | 3,409 | 2,351 | 8,473 |
| Suburban wgn 4d | 3,475 | 2,425 | 12,291 |

| 1955 Engines | bore × stroke | bhp | availability |
|---|---|---|---|
| I-6, 230.2 | 3.25 × 4.63 | 117 | S-all I-6 |
| V-8, 241.0 | 3.44 × 3.25 | 157 | O-all V-8 |
| V-8, 260.0 | 3.56 × 3.25 | 167 | S-all V-8 |
| V-8, 260.0 | 3.56 × 3.25 | 177 | O-all V-8 |

## 1956

| P28/29-1 Plaza (wb 115.0) | Wght | Price | Prod |
|---|---|---|---|
| bus cpe | 3,100 | 1,784 | 3,728 |
| sdn 4d | 3,210 | 1,926 | 60,197 |
| club sdn | 3,175 | 1,883 | 43,022 |
| **P28/29-2 Savoy (wb 115.0)** | | | |
| sdn 4d | 3,228 | 2,025 | 151,762 |
| club sdn | 3,190 | 1,982 | 57,927 |
| Sport Coupe htp | 3,200 | 2,130 | 16,473 |
| **P28/29-3 Belvedere (wb 115.0)** | | | |
| sdn 4d | 3,248 | 2,109 | 84,218 |
| club sdn 2d | 3,285 | 2,170 | 19,057 |
| Sport Sedan htp | 3,343 | 2,281 | 17,515 |
| Sport Coupe htp | 3,243 | 2,214 | 24,723 |
| conv cpe V-8 | 3,435 | 2,478 | 6,735 |
| **P28/29 Suburban (wb 115.0)** | | | |
| DeLuxe wgn 2d | 3,373 | 2,196 | 23,866 |
| Custom wgn 2d | 3,418 | 2,267 | 9,489 |
| Custom wgn 4d | 3,470 | 2,314 | 33,333 |
| Sport wgn 4d | 3,513 | 2,484 | 15,104 |
| **P29-3 Fury (wb 115.0)** | | | |
| htp cpe | 3,650 | 2,866 | 4,485 |

| 1956 Engines | bore × stroke | bhp | availability |
|---|---|---|---|
| I-6, 230.2 | 3.25 × 4.38 | 125 | S-all exc Fury, Belv conv |
| I-6, 230.2 | 3.25 × 4.38 | 131 | O-all exc Fury, Belv conv |
| V-8, 270.0 | 3.63 × 3.26 | 180 | O-Plaza, Savoy, Belvedere |
| V-8, 277.0 | 3.75 × 3.13 | 187 | S-Belv conv; O-Belv, Savoy, Plaza |
| V-8, 277.0 | 3.75 × 3.13 | 200 | O-all exc Fury |
| V-8, 303.0 | 3.82 × 3.31 | 240 | S-Fury |

## 1957

| P30/31-1 Plaza (wb 118.0) | Wght | Price | Prod |
|---|---|---|---|
| bus cpe | 3,235 | 1,899 | 2,874 |
| sdn 4d | 3,333 | 2,050 | 70,248 |
| sdn 2d | 3,245 | 2,009 | 49,137 |
| **P30/31-2 Savoy (wb 118.0)** | | | |
| sdn 4d | 3,340 | 2,194 | 153,093 |
| Sport Sedan htp | 3,428 | 2,317 | 7,601 |
| sdn 2d | 3,263 | 2,147 | 55,590 |
| Sport Coupe htp | 3,335 | 2,229 | 31,373 |
| **P30/31-3 Belvedere (wb 118.0)** | | | |
| sdn 4d | 3,373 | 2,310 | 110,414 |
| Sport Sedan htp | 3,428 | 2,419 | 37,446 |
| sdn 2d | 3,288 | 2,264 | 55,590 |
| Sport Coupe htp | 3,348 | 2,349 | 67,268 |
| conv cpe V-8 | 3,585 | 2,638 | 9,866 |
| **P30/31 Suburban (wb 122.0)** | | | |
| DeLuxe wgn 2d | 3,620 | 2,330 | 20,111 |
| Custom wgn 2d | 3,668 | 2,440 | 11,196 |
| Custom wgn 4d, 6P | 3,753 | 2,494 | 40,227 |
| Custom wgn 4d, 9P | 3,800 | 2,649 | 9,357 |
| Sport wgn 4d, 6P | 3,748 | 2,622 | 15,414 |
| Sport wgn 4d, 9P | 3,795 | 2,777 | 7,988 |
| **P31 Fury (wb 118.0)** | | | |
| htp cpe | 3,595 | 2,925 | 7,438 |

| 1957 Engines | bore × stroke | bhp | availability |
|---|---|---|---|
| I-6, 230.2 | 3.25 × 4.63 | 132 | S-all exc Fury, Belv conv |
| V-8, 277.0 | 3.75 × 3.13 | 197 | O-Plaza |
| V-8, 301.0 | 3.91 × 3.13 | 215 | O-Plaz, Savoy, Belv |
| V-8, 301.0 | 3.91 × 3.13 | 235 | O-all exc Fury |
| V-8, 318.0 | 3.91 × 3.31 | 290 | S-Fury |

## 1958

| LP1/2-L Plaza (wb 118.0) | | Wght | Price | Prod |
|---|---|---|---|---|
| 21 | club sdn | 3,253 | 2,118 | 39,062 |

# Plymouth

| LP1/2-L Plaza (wb 118.0) | | Wght | Price | Prod |
|---|---|---|---|---|
| 22 | bus cpe | 3,245 | 2,028 | 1,472 |
| 41 | sdn 4d | 3,335 | 2,169 | 54,194 |
| **LP1/2-M Savoy (wb 118.0)** | | | | |
| 21 | club sdn | 3,290 | 2,254 | 17,624 |
| 23 | Sport Coupe htp | 3,320 | 2,329 | 19,500 |
| 41 | sdn 4d | 3,310 | 2,305 | 67,933 |
| 43 | Sport Sedan htp | 3,393 | 2,400 | 5,060 |
| **LP1/2H Belvedere (wb 118.0)** | | | | |
| 21 | club sdn | 3,305 | 2,389 | 4,229 |
| 23 | Sport Coupe htp | 3,325 | 2,457 | 36,043 |
| 27 | conv cpe V-8 | 3,545 | 2,762 | 9,941 |
| 41 | sdn 4d | 3,343 | 2,440 | 49,124 |
| 43 | Sport Sedan htp | 3,425 | 2,528 | 18,194 |
| **LP1/2 Suburban (wb 122.0)** | | | | |
| — | DeLuxe wgn 4d | 3,660 | 2,486 | 15,535 |
| 25 | DeLuxe wgn 2d | 3,560 | 2,432 | 15,625 |
| 25 | Custom wgn 2d | 3,630 | 2,553 | 5,925 |
| 45A | Custom wgn 4d, 6P | 3,665 | 2,607 | 38,707 |
| 45B | Custom wgn 4d, 9P | 3,763 | 2,747 | 17,158 |
| 45A | Sport wgn 4d, 6P | 3,680 | 2,760 | 10,785 |
| 45B | Sport wgn 4d, 9P | 3,758 | 2,900 | 12,385 |
| **LP2-H Fury (wb 118.0)** | | | | |
| 23 | htp cpe | 3,510 | 3,067 | 5,303 |

| 1958 Engines | bore × stroke | bhp | availability |
|---|---|---|---|
| I-6, 230.2 | 3.25 × 4.63 | 132 | S-all exc Fury, Belv conv |
| V-8, 318.0 | 3.91 × 3.31 | 225 | O-all exc Fury |
| V-8, 318.0 | 3.91 × 3.31 | 250 | O-all exc Fury |
| V-8, 318.0 | 3.91 × 3.31 | 290 | S-Fury |
| V-8, 350.0 | 4.06 × 3.38 | 305 | O-all |
| V-8, 350.0 | 4.06 × 3.38 | 315 | O-all (fuel injection) |

## 1959

| MP1/2-L Savoy (wb 118.0) | | Wght | Price | Prod |
|---|---|---|---|---|
| 21 | club sdn | 3,333 | 2,222 | 46,979 |
| 22 | bus cpe | 3,130 | 2,143 | 1,051 |
| 41 | sdn 4d | 3,333 | 2,283 | 84,272 |
| **MP1/2-M Belvedere (wb 118.0)** | | | | |
| 21 | club sdn | 3,310 | 2,389 | 13,816 |
| 23 | htp cpe | 3,318 | 2,461 | 23,469 |
| 27 | conv cpe | 3,580 | 2,814 | 5,063 |
| 41 | sdn 4d | 3,353 | 2,440 | 67,980 |
| 43 | htp sdn 4d | 3,335 | 2,525 | 5,713 |
| **MP2-H Fury (wb 118.0)** | | | | |
| 23 | htp cpe | 3,435 | 2,714 | 21,494 |
| 41 | sdn 4d | 3,455 | 2,691 | 30,149 |
| 43 | htp sdn | 3,505 | 2,771 | 13,614 |
| **MP2-P Sport Fury (wb 118.0)** | | | | |
| 23 | htp cpe | 3,475 | 2,927 | 17,867 |
| 27 | conv cpe | 3,670 | 3,125 | 5,990 |
| **MP1/2 Suburban (wb 122.0)** | | | | |
| 25 | DeLuxe wgn 2d | 3,625 | 2,694 | 15,074 |
| 25 | Custom wgn 2d, 6P | 3,690 | 2,814 | 1,852 |
| 45A | DeLuxe wgn 4d | 3,675 | 2,761 | 35,086 |
| 45A | Custom wgn 4d, 6P | 3,678 | 2,881 | 35,024 |
| 45B | Custom wgn 4d, 9P | 3,775 | 2,991 | 16,993 |
| 45A | Sport wgn 4d, 6P | 3,760 | 3,021 | 7,224 |
| 45B | Sport wgn 4d, 9P | 3,805 | 3,131 | 9,549 |

| 1959 Engines | bore × stroke | bhp | availability |
|---|---|---|---|
| I-6, 230.2 | 3.25 × 4.63 | 132 | S-all exc Fury, Sport Fury, Del/Cus Sub |
| V-8, 318.0 | 3.91 × 3.31 | 230 | S-Fury, Cus Sub; O-other exc Sprt Fury |
| V-8, 318.0 | 3.91 × 3.31 | 260 | S-Sport Fury; O-others |
| V-8, 361.0 | 4.12 × 3.38 | 305 | O-all |

## 1960

| V100 Valiant (wb 106.5) | | Wght | Price | Prod |
|---|---|---|---|---|
| 110 | sdn 4d | 2,635 | 2,053 | 52,788 |
| 140 | wgn 4d, 6P | 2,815 | 2,365 | 12,018 |
| — | wgn 4d, 9P | 2,845 | 2,488 | 1,928 |
| **V200 Valiant (wb 106.5)** | | | | |
| 130 | sdn 4d | 2,655 | 2,130 | 106,515 |
| 170 | wgn 4d, 6P | 2,855 | 2,443 | 16,368 |
| — | wgn 4d, 9P | 2,860 | 2,566 | 4,675 |
| **PP1/2-L Savoy (wb 118.0)** | | | | |
| 21 | club sdn | 3,410 | 2,260 | 26,820 |
| 41 | sdn 4d | 3,433 | 2,310 | 51,384 |
| **PP1/2-M Belvedere (wb 118.0)** | | | | |
| 21 | club sdn | 3,423 | 2,389 | 6,529 |
| 23 | htp cpe | 3,438 | 2,641 | 14,085 |
| 41 | sdn 4d | 3,448 | 2,439 | 42,130 |
| **PP1/2-H Fury (wb 118.0)** | | | | |
| 23 | htp cpe | 3,465 | 2,599 | 18,079 |
| 27 | conv cpe | 3,630 | 2,967 | 7,080 |
| 41 | sdn 4d | 3,475 | 2,575 | 21,292 |
| 43 | htp sdn | 3,528 | 2,656 | 9,036 |
| **PP1/2 Suburban (wb 122.0)** | | | | |
| 25 | DeLuxe wgn 2d | 3,375 | 2,721 | 5,503 |
| 45 | DeLuxe wgn 4d | 3,815 | 2,787 | 18,484 |
| 45 | Custom wgn 4d, 6P | 3,890 | 2,880 | 17,308 |
| 45 | Custom wgn 4d, 9P | 3,875 | 2,990 | 8,116 |
| 45 | Sport wgn 4d, 6P | 3,895 | 3,024 | 3,333 |
| 45 | Sport wgn 4d, 9P | 4,020 | 3,134 | 4,253 |

| 1960 Engines | bore × stroke | bhp | availability |
|---|---|---|---|
| I-6, 170.0 | 3.40 × 3.13 | 101 | S-Valiant |
| I-6, 170.0 | 3.40 × 3.13 | 148 | O-Valiant |
| I-6, 225.0 | 3.40 × 4.13 | 145 | S-full-size |
| V-8, 318.0 | 3.91 × 3.31 | 230/260 | S-full-size V-8 (PP2) |
| V-8, 361.0 | 4.12 × 3.38 | 305/310 | O-all full-size (PP2) |
| V-8, 383.0 | 4.25 × 3.38 | 330 | O-full-size (PP2) |

## 1961

| V100 Valiant (wb 106.5) | | Wght | Price | Prod |
|---|---|---|---|---|
| 111 | sdn 2d | 2,565 | 1,955 | 22,230 |
| 113 | sdn 4d | 2,590 | 2,014 | 25,695 |
| 156 | wgn 4d | 2,745 | 2,327 | 6,717 |
| **V200 Valiant (wb 106.5)** | | | | |
| 132 | htp cpe | 2,605 | 2,137 | 18,586 |
| 133 | sdn 4d | 2,600 | 2,110 | 59,056 |
| 176 | wgn 4d | 2,770 | 2,423 | 10,794 |
| **RP1/2-L Savoy (wb 118.0)** | | | | |
| 211 | sdn 2d, I-6 | 3,300 | 2,260 | 18,729 |

# Plymouth

| RP1/2-L Savoy (wb 118.0) | | Wght | Price | Prod |
|---|---|---|---|---|
| 311 | sdn 2d, V-8 | 3,440 | 2,379 | |
| 213 | sdn 4d, I-6 | 3,310 | 2,310 | 44,913 |
| 313 | sdn 4d, V-8 | 3,465 | 2,430 | |
| **RP1/2-M Belvedere (wb 118.0)** | | | | |
| 221 | sdn 2d, I-6 | 3,300 | 2,389 | 4,740 |
| 321 | sdn 2d, V-8 | 3,450 | 2,508 | |
| 222 | htp cpe, I-6 | 3,320 | 2,461 | 9,591 |
| 322 | htp cpe, V-8 | 3,460 | 2,580 | |
| 223 | sdn 4d, I-6 | 3,315 | 2,439 | 40,090 |
| 323 | sdn 4d, V-8 | 3,470 | 2,559 | |
| **RP1/2-H Fury (wb 118.0)** | | | | |
| 232 | htp cpe, I-6 | 3,330 | 2,599 | 16,141 |
| 332 | htp cpe, V-8 | 3,520 | 2,718 | |
| 233 | sdn 4d, I-6 | 3,350 | 2,575 | 22,169 |
| 333 | sdn 4d, V-8 | 3,515 | 2,694 | |
| 234 | htp sdn, I-6 | 3,390 | 2,656 | 8,507 |
| 334 | htp sdn V-8 | 3,555 | 2,775 | |
| 335 | conv cpe, V-8 | 3,535 | 2,967 | 6,948 |
| **RP1/2 Suburban (wb 122.0)** | | | | |
| 255 | DeLuxe wgn 2d, I-6 | 3,675 | 2,602 | 2,464 |
| 355 | DeLuxe wgn 2d, V-8 | 3,845 | 2,721 | |
| 256 | DeLuxe wgn 4d, I-6 | 3,715 | 2,668 | 12,980 |
| 356 | DeLuxe wgn 4d, V-8 | 3,885 | 2,788 | |
| 266 | Custom wgn 4d, I-6 | 3,730 | 2,761 | |
| 366 | Custom wgn 4d, V-8 | 3,885 | 2,880 | 13,553 |
| 367 | Custom wgn 4d, 9P, V-8 | 3,985 | 2,990 | |
| 376 | Sport wgn 4d, 6P, V-8 | 3,890 | 3,024 | 2,844 |
| 377 | Sport wgn 4d, 9P, V-8 | 3,995 | 3,134 | 3,088 |

| 1961 Engines | bore × stroke | bhp | availability |
|---|---|---|---|
| I-6, 170.0 | 3.40 × 3.13 | 101 | S-Valiant |
| I-6, 170.0 | 3.40 × 3.13 | 148 | O-Valiant |
| I-6, 225.0 | 3.40 × 4.13 | 145 | S-full-size |
| V-8, 318.0 | 3.91 × 3.31 | 230 | S-full-size V-8 (RP2) |
| V-8, 318.0 | 3.91 × 3.31 | 260 | O-full-size with TorqueFlite |
| V-8, 361.0 | 4.12 × 3.38 | 305 | O-full-size exc PowerFlite or a/c |
| V-8, 383.0 | 4.25 × 3.38 | 325-340 | O-full-size exc PowerFlite or a/c |
| V-8, 413.0 | 4.19 × 3.75 | 350/375 | O-full-size |

## 1962

| SV1-L Valiant V100 (wb 106.5) | | Wght | Price | Prod |
|---|---|---|---|---|
| 111 | sdn 2d | 2,480 | 1,930 | 19,679 |
| 113 | sdn 4d | 2,500 | 1,991 | 33,769 |
| 156 | wgn 4d | 2,660 | 2,285 | 5,932 |
| **SV1-H Valiant V200 (wb 106.5)** | | | | |
| 131 | sdn 2d | 2,500 | 2,026 | 8,484 |
| 133 | sdn 4d | 2,510 | 2,087 | 55,789 |
| 176 | wgn 4d | 2,690 | 2,381 | 8,055 |
| **SV1-P Valiant Signet (wb 106.5)** | | | | |
| 142 | htp cpe | 2,515 | 2,230 | 25,586 |
| **SP1/2-L Savoy (wb 115.0)** | | | | |
| 211 | sdn 2d, I-6 | 2,930 | 2,206 | 18,825 |
| 311 | sdn 2d, V-8 | 3,080 | 2,313 | |
| 213 | sdn 4d, I-6 | 2,960 | 2,262 | 49,777 |
| 313 | sdn 4d, V-8 | 3,115 | 2,369 | |
| **SP1/2-M Belvedere (wb 116.0)** | | | | |
| 221 | sdn 2d, I-6 | 2,930 | 2,342 | 3,128 |

| SP1/2-M Belvedere (wb 116.0) | | Wght | Price | Prod |
|---|---|---|---|---|
| 321 | sdn 2d, V-8 | 3,070 | 2,450 | |
| 222 | htp cpe, I-6 | 2,945 | 2,431 | 5,086 |
| 322 | htp cpe, V-8 | 3,075 | 2,538 | |
| 223 | sdn 4d, I-6 | 2,960 | 2,399 | 31,263 |
| 323 | sdn 4d, V-8 | 3,095 | 2,507 | |
| **SP1/2-H Fury (wb 116.0)** | | | | |
| 232 | htp cpe, I-6 | 2,960 | 2,585 | 9,589 |
| 332 | htp cpe, V-8 | 3,105 | 2,693 | |
| 233 | sdn 4d, I-6 | 2,990 | 2,563 | 17,531 |
| 333 | sdn 4d, V-8 | 3,125 | 2,670 | |
| 334 | htp sdn, V-8 | 3,190 | 2,742 | 5,995 |
| 335 | conv cpe, V-8 | 3,210 | 2,924 | 4,349 |
| **SP2-P Sport Fury (wb 116.0)** | | | | |
| 342 | htp cpe, V-8 | 3,195 | 2,851 | 4,039 |
| 345 | conv cpe, V-8 | 3,295 | 3,082 | 1,516 |
| **SP1/2 Station Wagon (wb 116.0)*** | | | | |
| 256 | Savoy wgn 4d, I-6 | 3,225 | 2,609 | 12,710 |
| 356 | Savoy wgn 4d, V-8 | 3,390 | 2,717 | |
| 266 | Belvedere wgn 4d, 6P, I-6 | 3,245 | 2,708 | 9,781 |
| 366 | Belvedere wgn 4d, 6P, V-8 | 3,390 | 2,815 | |
| 367 | Belvedere wgn 4d, 9P, V-8 | 3,440 | 2,917 | 4,168 |
| 376 | Fury wgn 4d, 6P, V-8 | 3,395 | 2,968 | 2,352 |
| 377 | Fury wgn 4d, 9P, V-8 | 3,455 | 3,071 | 2,411 |

*Due to factory numbering in 1962, model names such as "Savoy" were listed as body style names. This practice occurred in 1962 only.

| 1962 Engines | bore × stroke | bhp | availability |
|---|---|---|---|
| I-6, 170.0 | 3.40 × 3.13 | 101 | S-Valiant |
| I-6, 225.0 | 3.40 × 4.13 | 145 | S-SP1; O-Valiant |
| V-8, 318.0 | 3.91 × 3.31 | 230 | S-all SP2 exc Sport Fury |
| V-8, 318.0 | 3.91 × 3.31 | 260 | O-all SP2 exc Sport Fury |
| V-8, 361.0 | 4.12 × 3.38 | 305 | S-Sport Fury; O-other SP2 exc w/PowerFlite or A/C |
| V-8, 383.0 | 4.25 × 3.38 | 330/335 | O-SP2 |
| V-8, 413.0 | 4.19 × 3.75 | 365/380/410 | O-Fury, Sprt Fury |

## 1963

| TV1-Valiant V100 (wb 106.0) | | Wght | Price | Prod |
|---|---|---|---|---|
| 111 | sdn 2d | 2,515 | 1,910 | 32,761 |
| 113 | sdn 4d | 2,535 | 1,973 | 54,617 |
| 156 | wgn 4d | 2,700 | 2,268 | 11,864 |
| **TV1-H Valiant V200 (wb 106.0)** | | | | |
| 131 | sdn 2d | 2,515 | 2,035 | 10,605 |
| 133 | sdn 4d | 2,555 | 2,097 | 57,029 |
| 135 | conv cpe | 2,640 | 2,340 | 7,122 |
| 176 | wgn 4d | 2,715 | 2,392 | 11,147 |
| **TV1-P Valiant Signet 200 (wb 106.0)** | | | | |
| 142 | htp cpe | 2,570 | 2,230 | 30,857 |
| 145 | conv cpe | 2,675 | 2,454 | 9,154 |
| **TP1/2-L Savoy (wb 116.0)** | | | | |
| 211 | sdn 2d, I-6 | 2,980 | 2,206 | 20,281 |
| 311 | sdn 2d, V-8 | 3,200 | 2,313 | |
| 213 | sdn 4d, I-6 | 3,020 | 2,262 | 56,313 |
| 313 | sdn 4d, V-8 | 3,220 | 2,369 | |
| 256 | wgn 4d, 6P, I-6 | 3,325 | 2,609 | 12,874 |
| 356 | wgn 4d, 6P, V-8 | 3,475 | 2,717 | |

# Plymouth

| TP1/2-L Savoy (wb 116.0) | | Wght | Price | Prod |
|---|---|---|---|---|
| 257 | wgn 4d, 9P, I-6 | 3,375 | 2,710 ⎤ | 4,342 |
| 357 | wgn 4d, 9P, V-8 | 3,560 | 2,818 ⎦ | |
| **TP1/2-M Belvedere (wb 116.0)** | | | | |
| 221 | sdn 2d, I-6 | 3,000 | 2,342 ⎤ | 6,218 |
| 321 | sdn 2d, V-8 | 3,215 | 2,450 ⎦ | |
| 222 | htp cpe, I-6 | 3,025 | 2,431 ⎤ | 9,204 |
| 322 | htp cpe, V-8 | 3,190 | 2,538 ⎦ | |
| 223 | sdn 4d, I-6 | 3,020 | 2,399 ⎤ | 54,929 |
| 323 | sdn 4d, V-8 | 3,235 | 2,507 ⎦ | |
| 366 | wgn 4d, 6P, V-8 | 3,490 | 2,815 | 10,297 |
| 367 | wgn 4d, 9P, V-8 | 3,585 | 2,917 | 4,012 |
| **TP1/2-H Fury (wb 116.0)** | | | | |
| 232 | htp cpe, I-6 | 3,030 | 2,585 ⎤ | 13,832 |
| 332 | htp cpe, V-8 | 3,215 | 2,693 ⎦ | |
| 233 | sdn 4d, I-6 | 3,075 | 2,563 ⎤ | 31,891 |
| 333 | sdn 4d, V-8 | 3,265 | 2,670 ⎦ | |
| 334 | htp sdn, V-8 | 3,295 | 2,742 | 11,887 |
| 335 | conv cpe, V-8 | 3,340 | 2,924 | 5,221 |
| 376 | wgn 4d, 6P, V-8 | 3,545 | 2,968 | 3,304 |
| 377 | wgn 4d, 9P, V-8 | 3,590 | 3,071 | 3,368 |
| **TP2-P Sport Fury (wb 116.0)** | | | | |
| 342 | htp cpe, V-8 | 3,235 | 2,851 | 11,483 |
| 345 | conv cpe, V-8 | 3,385 | 3,082 | 3,836 |

| 1963 Engines | bore × stroke | bhp | availability |
|---|---|---|---|
| I-6, 170.0 | 3.40 × 3.13 | 101 | S-Valiant |
| I-6, 225.0 | 3.40 × 4.13 | 145 | S-all TP1; O-Valiant |
| V-8, 318.0 | 3.91 × 3.31 | 230 | S-all TP2 |
| V-8, 361.0 | 4.12 × 3.38 | 265 | O-all TP2 |
| V-8, 383.0 | 4.25 × 3.38 | 320/330 | O-all TP2 |
| V-8, 426.0 | 4.25 × 3.75 | 370/425 | O-TP2 |

## 1964

| VV1-L Valiant V100 (wb 106.0) | | Wght | Price | Prod |
|---|---|---|---|---|
| 111 | sdn 2d | 2,540 | 1,921 | 35,403 |
| 113 | sdn 4d | 2,575 | 1,992 | 44,208 |
| 156 | wgn 4d | 2,725 | 2,273 | 10,759 |
| **VV1-H Valiant V200 (wb 106.0)** | | | | |
| 131 | sdn 2d | 2,545 | 2,044 | 11,013 |
| 133 | sdn 4d | 2,570 | 2,112 | 63,828 |
| 135 | conv cpe | 2,670 | 2,349 | 5,856 |
| 176 | wgn 4d | 2,730 | 2,388 | 11,146 |
| **VV1-P Valiant Signet 200 (wb 106.0)** | | | | |
| 142 | htp cpe | 2,600 | 2,256 | 37,736 |
| 145 | conv cpe | 2,690 | 2,473 | 7,636 |
| 149 | Barracuda fstbk htp cpe | 2,740 | 2,365 | 23,443 |
| **VP1/2-L Savoy (wb 116.0)** | | | | |
| 211 | sdn 2d, I-6 | 2,990 | 2,224 ⎤ | 21,326 |
| 311 | sdn 2d, V-8 | 3,205 | 2,332 ⎦ | |
| 213 | sdn 4d, I-6 | 3,040 | 2,280 ⎤ | 51,024 |
| 313 | sdn 4d, V-8 | 3,210 | 2,388 ⎦ | |
| 256 | wgn 4d, 6P, I-6 | 3,345 | 2,620 ⎤ | 12,401 |
| 356 | wgn 4d, 6P, V-8 | 3,495 | 2,728 ⎦ | |
| 257 | wgn 4d, 9P, I-6 | 3,400 | 2,721 ⎤ | 3,242 |
| 357 | wgn 4d, 9P, V-8 | 3,600 | 2,829 ⎦ | |
| **VP1/2-M Belvedere (wb 116.0)** | | | | |
| 221 | sdn 2d, I-6 | 3,000 | 2,359 ⎤ | 5,364 |
| 321 | sdn 2d, V-8 | 3,210 | 2,466 ⎦ | |
| 222 | htp cpe, I-6 | 3,010 | 2,444 ⎤ | 16,334 |
| 322 | htp cpe, V-8 | 3,190 | 2,551 ⎦ | |

| VP1/2-M Belvedere (wb 116.0) | | Wght | Price | Prod |
|---|---|---|---|---|
| 223 | sdn 4d, I-6 | 3,065 | 2,417 ⎤ | 57,307 |
| 323 | sdn 4d, V-8 | 3,225 | 2,524 ⎦ | |
| 366 | wgn 4d, 6P, V-8 | 3,510 | 2,826 | 10,317 |
| 367 | wgn 4d, 9P, V-8 | 3,605 | 2,928 | 4,207 |
| **VP1/2-H Fury (wb 116.0)** | | | | |
| 232 | htp cpe, I-6 | 3,040 | 2,598 ⎤ | 26,303 |
| 332 | htp cpe, V-8 | 3,212 | 2,706 ⎦ | |
| 233 | sdn 4d, I-6 | 3,045 | 2,573 ⎤ | 34,901 |
| 333 | sdn 4d, V-8 | 3,230 | 2,680 ⎦ | |
| 334 | htp sdn, V-8 | 3,300 | 2,752 | 13,713 |
| 335 | conv cpe, V-8 | 3,345 | 2,937 | 5,173 |
| 376 | wgn 4d, 6P, V-8 | 3,530 | 2,981 | 3,646 |
| 377 | wgn 4d, 9P, V-8 | 3,630 | 3,084 | 4,482 |
| **VP2-P Sport Fury (wb 116.0)** | | | | |
| 342 | htp cpe, V-8 | 3,270 | 2,864 | 23,695 |
| 345 | conv cpe, V-8 | 3,405 | 3,095 | 3,858 |

| 1964 Engines | bore × stroke | bhp | availability |
|---|---|---|---|
| I-6, 170.0 | 3.40 × 3.13 | 101 | S-Valiant |
| I-6, 225.0 | 3.40 × 4.13 | 145 | S-VP1; O-Valiant |
| V-8, 273.0 | 3.62 × 3.31 | 180 | O-Valiant |
| V-8, 318.0 | 3.91 × 3.31 | 230 | S-all VP2 |
| V-8, 361.0 | 4.12 × 3.38 | 265 | O-all exc Valiant |
| V-8, 383.0 | 4.25 × 3.38 | 305/330 | O-all exc Valiant |
| V-8, 426.0 | 4.25 × 3.75 | 365 | O-all exc Valiant |
| V-8, 426.0 | 4.25 × 3.75 | 415/425 | O-VP2 (Super Stock/Street) |

## 1965

| AV1-L Valiant 100 (wb 106.0)* | | Wght | Price | Prod |
|---|---|---|---|---|
| V11 | sdn 2d | 2,560 | 2,004 | 40,434 |
| V13 | sdn 4d | 2,590 | 2,075 | 42,857 |
| V56 | wgn 4d | 2,750 | 2,361 | 10,822 |
| **AV1-H Valiant 200 (wb 106.0)*** | | | | |
| V31 | sdn 2d | 2,570 | 2,127 | 8,919 |
| V33 | sdn 4d | 2,605 | 2,195 | 41,642 |
| V35 | conv cpe | 2,695 | 2,437 | 2,769 |
| V78 | wgn 4d | 2,755 | 2,476 | 6,133 |
| **AV-1P Valiant Signet (wb 106.0)*** | | | | |
| V42 | htp cpe | 2,620 | 2,340 | 10,999 |
| V45 | conv cpe | 2,725 | 2,561 | 2,578 |
| **AV1-P Barracuda (wb 106.0)*** | | | | |
| V89 | fstbk htp cpe | 2,725 | 2,487 | 64,596 |
| **AR1/2-L Belvedere I (wb 116.0; SS-115.0)** | | | | |
| R01 | Super Stock htp cpe | 3,170 | 4,671 | — |
| R11 | sdn 2d | 3,088 | 2,226 | 12,536 |
| R13 | sdn 4d | 3,153 | 2,265 | 35,968 |
| R56 | wgn 4d | 3,423 | 2,562 | 8,338 |
| **AR1/2-H Belvedere II (wb 116.0)** | | | | |
| R32 | htp cpe | 3,123 | 2,378 | 29,924 |
| R33 | sdn 4d | 3,128 | 2,352 | 41,445 |
| R35 | conv cpe | 3,230 | 2,597 | 1,921 |
| R76 | wgn 4d, 6P | 3,425 | 2,649 | 5,908 |
| R77 | wgn 4d, 9P | 3,488 | 2,747 | 3,294 |
| **AR2-P Satellite (wb 116.0)** | | | | |
| R42 | htp cpe | 3,220 | 2,649 | 23,341 |
| R45 | conv cpe | 3,325 | 2,869 | 1,860 |
| **AP1/2-L Fury I (wb 119.0; wgns-121.0)** | | | | |
| P11 | sdn 2d | 3,518 | 2,376 | 17,294 |

# Plymouth

| AP1/2-L Fury I (wb 119.0; wgns-121.0) | | Wght | Price | Prod |
|---|---|---|---|---|
| P13 | sdn 4d | 3,573 | 2,430 | 48,575 |
| P56 | wgn 4d | 4,030 | 2,776 | 13,360 |
| **AP1/2-M Fury II (wb 119.0; wgn-121.0)** | | | | |
| P21 | sdn 2d | 3,525 | 2,478 | 4,109 |
| P23 | sdn 4d | 3,573 | 2,532 | 43,350 |
| P66 | wgn 4d, 6P | 4,135 | 2,948 | 12,853 |
| P67 | wgn 4d, 9P | 4,160 | 3,051 | 6,445 |
| **AP1/2-H Fury III (wb 119.0; wgns-121.0)** | | | | |
| P32 | htp cpe | 3,563 | 2,691 | 43,251 |
| P33 | sdn 4d | 3,595 | 2,684 | 50,725 |
| P34 | htp sdn | 3,690 | 2,863 | 21,367 |
| P35 | conv cpe | 3,710 | 3,048 | 5,524 |
| P76 | wgn 4d, 6P | 4,140 | 3,090 | 8,931 |
| P77 | wgn 4d, 9P | 4,200 | 3,193 | 9,546 |
| **AP2-P Sport Fury (wb 119.0)** | | | | |
| P42 | htp cpe | 3,715 | 2,960 | 38,348 |
| P45 | conv cpe | 3,755 | 3,209 | 6,272 |

*Factory quoted only V-8 Valiant prices this year, which are given along with V-8 weights. For sixes, deduct approximately $128.

| 1965 Engines | bore × stroke | bhp | availability |
|---|---|---|---|
| I-6, 170.0 | 3.40 × 3.13 | 101 | S-Valiant |
| I-6, 225.0 | 3.40 × 4.13 | 145 | S-Barracuda, all AR1/AP1; O-Valiant |
| V-8, 273.0 | 3.62 × 3.31 | 180 | S-all AR2; O-Valiant, Barracuda, |
| V-8, 273.0 | 3.62 × 3.31 | 235 | O-Valiant, Barracuda |
| V-8, 318.0 | 3.91 × 3.31 | 230 | S-AP2; O-AR2 |
| V-8, 361.0 | 4.12 × 3.38 | 265 | O-AR2 |
| V-8, 383.0 | 4.25 × 3.38 | 270 | O-AP2 |
| V-8, 383.0 | 4.25 × 3.38 | 330 | O-AR2, AP2 |
| V-8, 426.0 | 4.25 × 3.75 | 365 | S-Belv I SS; O-Sat, Sport Fury |
| V-8, 426.0 | 4.25 × 3.75 | 425 | O-Belv I SS (hemi) |

## 1966

| BV1/2-L Valiant 100 (wb 106.0) | | Wght | Price | Prod |
|---|---|---|---|---|
| 21 | sdn 2d | 2,700 | 2,025 | 35,787 |
| 41 | sdn 4d | 2,725 | 2,095 | 36,031 |
| 45 | wgn 4d | 2,648 | 2,387 | 6,838 |
| **BV1/2-H Valiant 200 (wb 106.0)** | | | | |
| 41 | sdn 4d | 2,728 | 2,226 | 39,392 |
| 45 | wgn 4d | 2,883 | 2,502 | 4,537 |
| **BV1/2-H Valiant Signet (wb 106.0)** | | | | |
| 23 | htp cpe | 2,735 | 2,261 | 13,045 |
| 27 | conv cpe | 2,830 | 2,527 | 2,507 |
| **BV1/2-P Barracuda (wb 106.0)** | | | | |
| 29 | fstbk htp cpe | 2,865 | 2,556 | 38,029 |
| **BR1/2-L Belvedere I (wb 116.0; wgn-117.0)** | | | | |
| 21 | sdn 2d | 3,095 | 2,277 | 9,381 |
| 41 | sdn 4d | 3,125 | 2,315 | 31,063 |
| 45 | wgn 4d | 3,523 | 2,605 | 8,200 |
| **BR1/2-H Belvedere II (wb 116.0; wgn-117.0)** | | | | |
| 23 | htp cpe | 3,123 | 2,430 | 36,644 |
| 27 | conv cpe | 3,200 | 2,644 | 2,502 |
| 41 | sdn 4d | 3,115 | 2,405 | 49,941 |
| 45 | wgn 4d, 6P | 3,525 | 2,695 | 8,667 |
| 46 | wgn 4d, 9P | 3,618 | 2,804 | 4,726 |

| BR2-P Satellite (wb 116.0) | | Wght | Price | Prod |
|---|---|---|---|---|
| 23 | htp cpe | 3,255 | 2,695 | 35,399 |
| 27 | conv cpe | 3,320 | 2,910 | 2,759 |
| **BP1/2-L Fury I (wb 119.0; wgn-121.0)** | | | | |
| 21 | sdn 2d | 3,518 | 2,426 | 12,538 |
| 41 | sdn 4d | 3,570 | 2,479 | 39,698 |
| 45 | wgn 4d | 4,048 | 2,836 | 9,690 |
| **BP1/2-M Fury II (wb 119.0; wgn-121.0)** | | | | |
| 21 | sdn 2d | 3,530 | 2,526 | 2,503 |
| 41 | sdn 4d | 3,573 | 2,579 | 55,016 |
| 45 | wgn 4d, 6P | 4,145 | 2,986 | 10,718 |
| 46 | wgn 4d, 9P | 4,175 | 3,087 | 5,580 |
| **BP1/2-H Fury III (wb 119.0; wgn-121.0)** | | | | |
| 23 | htp cpe | 3,578 | 2,724 | 41,869 |
| 27 | conv cpe | 3,720 | 3,074 | 4,326 |
| 41 | sdn 4d | 3,217 | 2,718 | 46,505 |
| 43 | htp sdn | 3,730 | 2,893 | 33,922 |
| 45 | wgn 4d, 6P | 4,155 | 3,115 | 9,239 |
| 46 | wgn 4d, 9P | 4,165 | 3,216 | 10,886 |
| **BP2-P Sport Fury (wb 119.0)** | | | | |
| 23 | htp cpe | 3,730 | 3,006 | 32,523 |
| 27 | conv cpe | 3,755 | 3,251 | 3,418 |
| **VP2-H VIP (wb 119.0)*** | | | | |
| 23 | htp cpe | 3,700 | 3,069 | — |
| 43 | htp sdn | 3,780 | 3,133 | — |

*Included with Fury III.

| 1966 Engines | bore × stroke | bhp | availability |
|---|---|---|---|
| I-6, 170.0 | 3.40 × 3.13 | 101 | S-Valiant |
| I-6, 225.0 | 3.40 × 4.13 | 145 | S-Barracuda, all BR1, BP1; O-Val |
| V-8, 273.0 | 3.62 × 3.31 | 180 | S-BR2, Brcda, Val |
| V-8, 273.0 | 3.62 × 3.31 | 235 | O-Brcda, Val Signet |
| V-8, 318.0 | 3.91 × 3.31 | 230 | S-all BP2; O-BR2 |
| V-8, 361.0 | 4.12 × 3.38 | 265 | O-Belvedere, Satellite |
| V-8, 383.0 | 4.25 × 3.38 | 325 | O-BR2, BP2 |
| V-8, 426.0 | 4.25 × 3.75 | 425 | O-BR2 (hemi) exc wgn |
| V-8, 440.0 | 4.32 × 3.75 | 365 | O-VIP, Sport Fury |

## 1967

| CV1/2-L Valiant 100 (wb 108.0) | | Wght | Price | Prod |
|---|---|---|---|---|
| 21 | sdn 2d | 2,738 | 2,117 | 29,093 |
| 41 | sdn 4d | 2,753 | 2,163 | 46,638 |
| **CV1/2-H Valiant Signet (wb 108.0)** | | | | |
| 21 | sdn 2d | 2,765 | 2,262 | 6,843 |
| 41 | sdn 4d | 2,750 | 2,308 | 26,395 |
| **CV1/2-P Barracuda (wb 108.0)** | | | | |
| 23 | htp cpe | 2,793 | 2,449 | 28,196 |
| 27 | conv cpe | 2,903 | 2,779 | 4,228 |
| 29 | fstbk htp cpe | 2,878 | 2,639 | 30,110 |
| **CR1/2-E Belvedere (wb 117.0)** | | | | |
| 45 | wgn 4d | 3,543 | 2,579 | 5,477 |
| **CR1/2-L Belvedere I (wb 116.0; wgn-117.0)** | | | | |
| 21 | sdn 2d | 3,095 | 2,318 | 4,718 |
| 41 | sdn 4d | 3,125 | 2,356 | 13,988 |
| 45 | wgn 4d | 3,553 | 2,652 | 3,172 |
| **CR1/2-H Belvedere II (wb 116.0; wgn-117.0)** | | | | |
| 23 | htp cpe | 3,130 | 2,457 | 34,550 |
| 27 | conv cpe | 3,205 | 2,695 | 1,552 |
| 41 | sdn 4d | 3,118 | 2,434 | 42,694 |
| 45 | wgn 4d, 6P | 3,553 | 2,729 | 5,583 |

# Plymouth

| CR1/2-H Belvedere II (wb 116.0; wgn-117.0) | | Wght | Price | Prod |
|---|---|---|---|---|
| 46 | wgn 4d, 9P | 3,595 | 2,836 | 3,968 |
| **CR2-P Satellite (wb 116.0)** | | | | |
| 23 | htp cpe | 3,265 | 2,747 | 30,328 |
| 27 | conv cpe | 3,335 | 2,986 | 2,050 |
| **CR2-P Belvedere GTX (wb 116.0)*** | | | | |
| 23 | htp cpe | 3,545 | 3,178 | — |
| 27 | conv cpe | 3,615 | 3,418 | — |
| **CP1/2E Fury I (wb 119.0; wgn-122.0)** | | | | |
| 21 | sdn 2d | 3,493 | 2,473 | 6,647 |
| 41 | sdn 4d | 3,533 | 2,517 | 29,354 |
| 45 | wgn 4d | 4,000 | 2,884 | 6,067 |
| **CP1/2L Fury II (wb 119.0; wgn-122.0)** | | | | |
| 21 | sdn 2d | 3,490 | 2,571 | 2,783 |
| 41 | sdn 4d | 3,526 | 2,614 | 45,673 |
| 45 | wgn 4d, 6P | 4,045 | 3,021 | 10,736 |
| 46 | wgn 4d, 9P | 4,110 | 3,122 | 5,649 |
| **CP1/2-M Fury III (wb 119.0; wgn-122.0)** | | | | |
| 23 | htp cpe | 3,535 | 2,872 | 37,448 |
| 27 | conv cpe | 3,670 | 3,118 | 4,523 |
| 41 | sdn 4d | 3,555 | 2,746 | 52,690 |
| 43 | htp sdn | 3,650 | 2,922 | 43,614 |
| 45 | wgn 4d, 6P | 4,080 | 3,144 | 9,270 |
| 46 | wgn 4d, 9P | 4,135 | 3,245 | 12,533 |
| **CP2-H Sport Fury (wb 119.0)** | | | | |
| 23 | htp cpe | 3,630 | 3,033 | 28,448 |
| 23 | fstbk htp cpe | 3,705 | 3,062 | |
| 27 | conv cpe | 3,645 | 3,279 | 3,133 |
| **CP2-P VIP (wb 119.0)** | | | | |
| 23 | htp cpe | 3,705 | 3,182 | 7,912 |
| 43 | htp sdn | 3,660 | 3,117 | 10,830 |

* Included with Satellite.

| 1967 Engines | bore × stroke | bhp | availability |
|---|---|---|---|
| I-6, 170.0 | 3.40 × 3.13 | 115 | S-Valiant |
| I-6, 225.0 | 3.40 × 4.13 | 145 | S-Barracuda, CR1, CP1; O-Val |
| V-8, 273.0 | 3.62 × 3.31 | 180 | S-Brcda, Val, CR2 exc GTX |
| V-8, 273.0 | 3.62 × 3.31 | 235 | O-Val, Barracuda |
| V-8, 318.0 | 3.91 × 3.31 | 230 | S-CP2,CR2 exc GTX |
| V-8, 383.0 | 4.25 × 3.38 | 270 | O-CP2, CR2, exc GTX |
| V-8, 383.0 | 4.25 × 3.38 | 280 | O-Barracuda |
| V-8, 383.0 | 4.25 × 3.38 | 325 | O-Barracuda, Furys, Belv exc GTX |
| V-8, 426.0 | 4.25 × 3.75 | 425 | O-Belv GTX (hemi) |
| V-8, 440.0 | 4.32 × 3.75 | 350 | O-Fury wgns |
| V-8, 440.0 | 4.32 × 3.75 | 375 | S-GTX, O-Furys exc wgns |

## 1968

| VL Valiant 100 (wb 108.0)* | | Wght | Price | Prod |
|---|---|---|---|---|
| 21 | sdn 2d | 2,733 | 2,254 | 31,178 |
| 41 | sdn 4d | 2,763 | 2,301 | 49,446 |
| **VH Valiant Signet (wb 108.0)** | | | | |
| 21 | sdn 2d | 2,745 | 2,400 | 6,265 |
| 41 | sdn 4d | 2,768 | 2,447 | 23,906 |
| **VH Barracuda (wb 108.0)** | | | | |
| 23 | htp cpe | 2,810 | 2,605 | 19,997 |
| 27 | conv cpe | 2,923 | 2,907 | 2,840 |
| **VL Valiant 100 (wb 108.0)*** | | | | |
| 29 | fstbk htp cpe | 2,895 | 2,762 | 22,575 |
| **RL Belvedere (wb 116.0; wgn-117.0)** | | | | |
| 21 | cpe | 3,050 | 2,444 | 15,702 |
| 41 | sdn 4d | 3,080 | 2,483 | 17,214 |
| 45 | wgn 4d | 3,553 | 2,773 | 8,982 |
| **RH Satellite (wb 116.0; wgn-117.0)** | | | | |
| 23 | htp cpe | 3,070 | 2,594 | 46,539 |
| 27 | conv cpe | 3,188 | 2,824 | 1,771 |
| 41 | sdn 4d | 3,080 | 2,572 | 42,309 |
| 45 | wgn 4d, 6P | 3,605 | 2,891 | 12,097 |
| 46 | wgn 4d, 9P | 3,625 | 2,998 | 10,883 |
| **RP Sport Satellite (wb 116.0; wgn-117.0)** | | | | |
| 23 | htp cpe | 3,155 | 2,822 | 21,014 |
| 27 | conv cpe | 3,285 | 3,036 | 1,523 |
| 45 | wgn 4d, 6P | 3,610 | 3,131 | ** |
| 46 | wgn 4d, 9P | 3,685 | 3,239 | ** |
| **RM Road Runner (wb 116.0)** | | | | |
| 21 | cpe | 3,440 | 2,896 | 29,240 |
| 23 | htp cpe | 3,455 | 3,034 | 15,359 |
| **RS GTX (wb 116.0)** | | | | |
| 23 | htp cpe | 3,470 | 3,355 | 17,914 |
| 27 | conv cpe | 3,595 | 3,590 | 1,026 |
| **PE Fury I (wb 119.0)** | | | | |
| 21 | sdn 2d | 3,480 | 2,617 | 5,788 |
| 41 | sdn 4d | 3,653 | 2,660 | 23,208 |
| **PL Fury II (wb 119.0)** | | | | |
| 21 | sdn 2d | 3,488 | 2,715 | 3,112 |
| 41 | sdn 4d | 3,533 | 2,757 | 49,423 |
| **PM Fury III (wb 119.0)** | | | | |
| 23 | htp cpe | 3,538 | 2,912 | 60,472 |
| 23 | fstbk htp cpe "PX" | 3,528 | 2,932 | |
| 27 | conv cpe | 3,680 | 3,236 | 4,483 |
| 41 | sdn 4d | 3,545 | 2,890 | 57,899 |
| 43 | htp sdn | 3,635 | 3,067 | 45,147 |
| **PH Sport Fury (wb 119.0)** | | | | |
| 23 | htp cpe | 3,620 | 3,206 | 6,642 |
| 23 | fstbk htp cpe "PS" | 3,615 | 3,225 | 17,073 |
| 27 | conv cpe | 3,710 | 3,425 | 2,489 |
| **PP VIP (wb 119.0)** | | | | |
| 23 | fstbk htp cpe | 3,615 | 3,260 | 6,768 |
| 43 | htp sdn | 3,655 | 3,326 | 10,745 |
| **DP Suburban (wb 122.0)** | | | | |
| 45 | wgn 4d | 3,990 | 3,048 | 6,749 |
| 45 | Custom wgn 4d, 6P | 4,045 | 3,252 | 17,078 |
| 46 | Custom wgn 4d, 9P | 4,090 | 3,353 | 9,954 |
| 45 | Sport wgn 4d, 6P | 4,055 | 3,442 | 9,203 |
| 46 | Sport wgn 4d, 9P | 4,100 | 3,543 | 13,224 |

* Includes "Valiant 200" trim option.
** Sport Satellite wagon included with Satellite wagon.

| 1968 Engines | bore × stroke | bhp | availability |
|---|---|---|---|
| I-6, 170.0 | 3.40 × 3.13 | 115 | S-Valiant |
| I-6, 225.0 | 3.40 × 4.13 | 145 | S-Brcda, Belv, Sat, FI/II, FIII sdn/htps, Suburban; O-Val |
| V-8, 273.0 | 3.62 × 3.31 | 190 | O-Val, Belv, Sat, Spt Sat wgn |
| V-8, 318.0 | 3.91 × 3.31 | 230 | S-Spt Sat, Fury III; O-Val, Brcda, Belv, Sat, Spt Sat wgn |

# Plymouth

| 1968 Engines | bore × stroke | bhp | availability |
|---|---|---|---|
| V-8, 340.0 | 4.04 × 3.31 | 275 | S-Brcda Formula S |
| V-8, 383.0 | 4.25 × 3.38 | 290 | O-Belv, Sat, Spt Sat, Furys |
| V-8, 383.0 | 4.25 × 3.38 | 300 | O-Brcda Formula S |
| V-8, 383.0 | 4.25 × 3.38 | 330 | O-Belv, Satellite, Furys, Suburbans |
| V-8, 383.0 | 4.25 × 3.38 | 335 | S-Road Runner |
| V-8, 426.0 | 4.25 × 3.75 | 425 | O-Rd Rnr, GTX (hemi) |
| V-8, 440.0 | 4.32 × 3.75 | 375 | S-GTX; O-Fury exc DP |
| V-8, 440.0 | 4.32 × 3.75 | 350 | O-Suburban |

## 1969

| | | Wght | Price | Prod |
|---|---|---|---|---|
| **VL Valiant 100 (wb 108.0)*** | | | | |
| 21 | sdn 2d | 2,740 | 2,094 | 29,672 |
| 41 | sdn 4d | 2,760 | 2,154 | 49,409 |
| **VH Valiant Signet (wb 108.0)** | | | | |
| 21 | sdn 2d | 2,740 | 2,253 | 6,645 |
| 41 | sdn 4d | 2,760 | 2,313 | 21,492 |
| **VH Barracuda (wb 108.0)** | | | | |
| 23 | htp cpe | 2,815 | 2,780 | 12,757 |
| 27 | conv cpe | 2,940 | 3,082 | 1,442 |
| 29 | fstbk htp cpe | 2,902 | 2,813 | 17,788 |
| **RL Belvedere (wb 116.0; wgn-117.0)** | | | | |
| 21 | cpe | 3,052 | 2,509 | 7,063 |
| 41 | sdn 4d | 3,082 | 2,548 | 12,914 |
| 45 | wgn 4d | 3,540 | 2,879 | 7,038 |
| **RH Satellite (wb 116.0; wgn-117.0)** | | | | |
| 23 | htp cpe | 3,080 | 2,659 | 38,323 |
| 27 | conv cpe | 3,200 | 2,875 | 1,137 |
| 41 | sdn 4d | 3,087 | 2,635 | 35,296 |
| 45 | wgn 4d, 6P | 3,540 | 2,997 | 5,837 |
| 46 | wgn 4d, 9P | 3,612 | 3,106 | 4,730 |
| **RP Sport Satellite (wb 116.0; wgn-117.0)** | | | | |
| 23 | htp cpe | 3,156 | 2,883 | 15,807 |
| 27 | conv cpe | 3,276 | 3,081 | 818 |
| 41 | sdn 4d | 3,196 | 2,911 | 5,836 |
| 45 | wgn 4d, 6P | 3,596 | 3,241 | 3,221 |
| 46 | wgn 4d, 9P | 3,666 | 3,350 | 3,152 |
| **RM Road Runner (wb 116.0)** | | | | |
| 21 | cpe | 3,435 | 2,945 | 33,743 |
| 23 | htp cpe | 3,450 | 3,083 | 48,549 |
| 27 | conv cpe | 3,790 | 3,313 | 2,128 |
| **RS GTX (wb 116.0)** | | | | |
| 23 | htp cpe | 3,465 | 3,416 | 14,902 |
| 27 | conv cpe | 3,590 | 3,635 | 700 |
| **PE Fury I (wb 120.0)** | | | | |
| 21 | sdn 2d | 3,501 | 2,701 | 4,971 |
| 41 | sdn 4d | 3,533 | 2,744 | 18,771 |
| **PL Fury II (wb 120.0)** | | | | |
| 21 | sdn 2d | 3,506 | 2,813 | 3,268 |
| 41 | sdn 4d | 3,536 | 2,841 | 41,047 |
| **PM Fury III (wb 120.0)** | | | | |
| 23 | htp cpe | 3,516 | 3,000 | 44,168 |
| 27 | conv cpe | 3,704 | 3,324 | 4,129 |
| 29 | formal htp cpe | 3,601 | 3,020 | 22,738 |
| 41 | sdn 4d | 3,541 | 2,979 | 72,747 |
| **PM Fury III (wb 120.0)** | | | | |
| 43 | htp sdn | 3,643 | 3,155 | 68,818 |
| **PH Sport Fury (wb 120.0)** | | | | |
| 23 | htp cpe | 3,603 | 3,283 | 14,120 |
| 27 | conv cpe | 3,729 | 3,502 | 1,579 |
| 29 | formal htp cpe | 3,678 | 3,303 | 2,169 |
| **PP VIP (wb 120.0)** | | | | |
| 23 | htp cpe | 3,583 | 3,382 | 4,740 |
| 29 | formal htp cpe | 3,668 | 3,402 | 1,059 |
| 43 | htp sdn | 3,663 | 3,433 | 7,982 |
| **EP Suburban (wb 122.0)** | | | | |
| 45 | wgn 4d | 4,056 | 3,231 | 6,424 |
| 45 | Custom wgn 4d, 6P | 4,103 | 3,436 | 15,976 |
| 46 | Custom wgn 4d, 9P | 4,148 | 3,527 | 10,216 |
| 45 | Sport wgn 4d, 6P | 4,123 | 3,651 | 8,201 |
| 46 | Sport wgn 4d, 9P | 4,173 | 3,718 | 13,502 |

*Includes "Valiant 200" trim option.

| 1969 Engines | bore × stroke | bhp | availability |
|---|---|---|---|
| I-6, 170.0 | 3.40 × 3.13 | 115 | S-Valiant |
| I-6, 225.0 | 3.40 × 4.13 | 145 | S-Brcda, Belv, Sat, Fury I/II; O-Valiant |
| V-8, 273.0 | 3.62 × 3.31 | 190 | O-Valiant |
| V-8, 318.0 | 3.91 × 3.31 | 230 | S-Brcda, Spt Sat, Fury III, Spt Fury, VIP, Suburban |
| V-8, 340.0 | 4.04 × 3.31 | 275 | O-Barracuda |
| V-8, 383.0 | 4.25 × 3.38 | 290 | O-Belv, Sat, Spt Sat, Furys, VIP |
| V-8, 383.0 | 4.25 × 3.38 | 330 | O-Brcda, Belv, Sat, Spt Sat, Furys, VIP |
| V-8, 383.0 | 4.25 × 3.38 | 335 | S-Road Runner |
| V-8, 426.0 | 4.25 × 3.75 | 425 | O-Rd Rnr, GTX (hemi) |
| V-8, 440.0 | 4.32 × 3.75 | 375 | S-GTX; O-Furys exc EP |
| V-8, 440.0 | 4.32 × 3.75 | 350 | O-Suburban |

## 1970

| | | Wght | Price | Prod |
|---|---|---|---|---|
| **VL Valiant (wb 108.0)** | | | | |
| 29 | Duster fstbk cpe | 2,830 | 2,172 | 192,375 |
| 41 | sdn 4d | 2,835 | 2,250 | 50,810 |
| **VS Valiant Duster 340 (wb 108.0)** | | | | |
| 29 | fstbk cpe | 3,110 | 2,547 | 24,817 |
| **BH Barracuda (wb 108.0)** | | | | |
| 23 | htp cpe | 2,905 | 2,764 | 25,651 |
| 27 | conv cpe | 3,071 | 3,034 | 1,554 |
| **BP Barracuda Gran Coupe (wb 108.0)** | | | | |
| 23 | htp cpe | 3,015 | 2,934 | 8,183 |
| 27 | conv cpe | 3,090 | 3,160 | 596 |
| **BS 'Cuda (wb 108.0)** | | | | |
| 23 | htp cpe | 3,395 | 3,164 | 18,880 |
| 27 | conv cpe | 3,480 | 3,433 | 635 |
| **RL Belvedere (wb 116.0; wgn-117.0)** | | | | |
| 21 | cpe | 3,095 | 2,603 | 4,717 |
| 41 | sdn 4d | 3,130 | 2,641 | 13,945 |
| 45 | wgn 4d | 3,655 | 3,075 | 5,584 |
| **RH Satellite (wb 116.0; wgn-117.0)** | | | | |
| 23 | htp cpe | 3,105 | 2,765 | 28,200 |

# Plymouth

| RH Satellite (wb 116.0; wgn-117.0) | | Wght | Price | Prod |
|---|---|---|---|---|
| 27 | conv cpe | 3,225 | 3,006 | 701 |
| 41 | sdn 4d | 3,125 | 2,741 | 30,377 |
| 45 | wgn 4d, 6P | 3,637 | 3,101 | 4,204 |
| 46 | wgn 4d, 9P | 3,747 | 3,211 | 3,277 |
| **RP Sport Satellite (wb 116.0; wgn-117.0)** | | | | |
| 23 | htp cpe | 3,170 | 2,988 | 8,749 |
| 41 | sdn 4d | 3,205 | 3,017 | 3,010 |
| 45 | wgn 4d, 6P | 3,675 | 3,345 | 1,975 |
| 46 | wgn 4d, 9P | 3,750 | 3,455 | 2,161 |
| **RM Road Runner (wb 116.0)** | | | | |
| 21 | cpe | 3,450 | 2,896 | 15,716 |
| 23 | htp cpe | 3,475 | 3,034 | 24,944 |
| 23 | Superbird htp cpe | 3,785 | 4,298 | 1,920 |
| 27 | conv cpe | 3,550 | 3,289 | 824 |
| **RS GTX (wb 116.0)** | | | | |
| 23 | htp cpe | 3,515 | 3,535 | 7,748 |
| **PE Fury I (wb 120.0)** | | | | |
| 21 | sdn 2d | 3,603 | 2,790 | 2,353 |
| 41 | sdn 4d | 3,640 | 2,825 | 14,813 |
| **PL Fury II (wb 120.0)** | | | | |
| 21 | sdn 2d | 3,583 | 2,903 | 21,316 |
| 41 | sdn 4d | 3,643 | 2,922 | 27,694 |
| **PM Fury III (wb 120.0)** | | | | |
| 23 | htp cpe | 3,610 | 3,091 | 21,373 |
| 27 | conv cpe | 3,770 | 3,415 | 1,952 |
| 29 | formal htp cpe | 3,645 | 3,217 | 12,367 |
| 41 | sdn 4d | 3,645 | 3,069 | 50,876 |
| 43 | htp sdn | 3,690 | 3,246 | 47,879 |
| **PH Sport Fury (wb 120.0)** | | | | |
| 23 | htp cpe | 3,630 | 3,313 | |
| 23 | S/23 htp cpe "PS" | 3,660 | 3,379 | 8,018 |
| 23 | GT htp cpe "PP" | 3,925 | 3,898 | |
| 29 | formal htp cpe | 3,645 | 3,333 | 5,688 |
| 41 | sdn 4d | 3,680 | 3,291 | 5,135 |
| 43 | htp sdn | 3,705 | 3,363 | 6,854 |
| **PL Fury Gran Coupe (wb 120.0)** *Included with Fury II sdn 2d | | | | |
| 21 | sdn 2d | 3,864 | 3,833 | See note* |
| **FP Suburban (wb 122.0)** | | | | |
| 45 | wgn 4d, 6P | 4,125 | 3,303 | 5,300 |
| 46 | wgn 4d, 9P | 4,205 | 3,518 | 2,250 |
| 45 | Custom wgn 4d, 6P | 4,155 | 3,527 | 8,898 |
| 46 | Custom wgn 4d, 9P | 4,215 | 3,603 | 6,792 |
| 45 | Sport wgn 4d, 6P | 4,200 | 3,725 | 4,403 |
| 46 | Sport wgn 4d, 9P | 4,260 | 3,804 | 9,170 |

| 1970 Engines | bore × stroke | bhp | availability |
|---|---|---|---|
| I-6, 198.0 | 3.40 × 3.64 | 125 | S-Valiant VL |
| I-6, 225.0 | 3.40 × 4.13 | 145 | S-Brcda, Belv, Sat, Fury I/II; O-Val VL |
| V-8, 318.0 | 3.91 × 3.31 | 230 | S-Spt Sat, Fury III, Spt Fury, Gran Coupe, Suburban |
| V-8, 340.0 | 4.04 × 3.31 | 275 | S-Duster 340; O-'Cuda |
| V-8, 383.0 | 4.25 × 3.38 | 290 | O-all exc Valiant |
| V-8, 383.0 | 4.25 × 3.38 | 330 | O-all exc Valiant |
| V-8, 383.0 | 4.25 × 3.38 | 335 | S-Rd Rnr, 'Cuda |
| V-8, 426.0 | 4.25 × 3.75 | 425 | O-Rd Rnr, 'Cuda, GTX (hemi) |
| V-8, 440.0 | 4.32 × 3.75 | 350 | S-Spt Fury GT; O-other Fury |
| V-8, 440.0 | 4.32 × 3.75 | 375 | S-GTX, O-'Cuda |
| V-8, 440.0 | 4.32 × 3.75 | 390 | O-'Cuda, RR, GTX, PH23 |

## 1971

| Valiant (wb 108.0; Scamp-111.0) | | Wght | Price | Prod |
|---|---|---|---|---|
| VL29 | Duster fstbk cpe | 2,825 | 2,313 | 173,592 |
| VL41 | sdn 4d | 2,831 | 2,392 | 42,660 |
| VH23 | Scamp htp cpe | 2,900 | 2,561 | 48,253 |
| VS29 | Duster 340 fstbk cpe | 3,140 | 2,703 | 12,886 |
| **Barracuda (wb 108.0)** | | | | |
| VH21 | cpe 2d | 3,040 | 2,654 | 9,459 |
| VH23 | htp cpe | 3,075 | 2,766 | |
| VH27 | conv | 3,145 | 3,023 | 1,014 |
| VP23 | Gran Coupe htp cpe V-8 | 3,105 | 3,029 | 1,615 |
| VS23 | 'Cuda htp cpe V-8 | 3,475 | 3,155 | 6,228 |
| VS27 | 'Cuda conv cpe V-8 | 3,550 | 3,412 | 374 |
| **Satellite (wb 117.0; 2d-115.0)** | | | | |
| RL41 | sdn 4d | 3,294 | 2,734 | 11,059 |
| RL21 | cpe | 3,230 | 2,663 | 46,807 |
| RH23 | Sebring htp cpe | 3,256 | 2,931 | |
| RL45 | wgn 4d, 2S | 3,770 | 3,058 | 7,138 |
| RH41 | Custom sdn 4d | 3,286 | 2,908 | 30,773 |
| RH45 | Custom wgn 4d, 2S | 3,776 | 3,235 | 5,045 |
| RH46 | Custom wgn 4d, 3S | 3,846 | 3,315 | 4,626 |
| RM23 | Road Runner htp cpe V-8 | 3,640 | 3,147 | 14,218 |
| RP23 | Sebring Plus htp cpe V-8 | 3,300 | 3,179 | 16,253 |
| RP41 | Brougham sdn 4d, V-8 | 3,330 | 3,189 | 3,020 |
| RP45 | Regent wgn 4d, 2S, V-8 | 3,815 | 3,558 | 2,161 |
| RP46 | Regent wgn 4d, 3S, V-8 | 3,885 | 3,638 | 2,985 |
| RS23 | GTX htp cpe V-8 | 3,675 | 3,733 | 2,942 |
| **Fury (wb 120.0; wgn-122.0)** | | | | |
| PE41 | I sdn 4d | 3,742 | 3,163 | 16,395 |
| PE41 | I Custom sdn 4d | 3,742 | 3,241 | |
| PE21 | I sdn 2d | 3,708 | 3,113 | 5,152 |
| PE21 | I Custom sdn 2d | 3,708 | 3,208 | |
| PL23 | II htp cpe | 3,710 | 3,283 | 7,859 |
| PL41 | II sdn 4d | 3,746 | 3,262 | 20,098 |
| PL45 | II Sub wgn 4d, 2S, V-8 | 4,245 | 3,758 | 4,877 |
| PL46 | II Sub wgn 4d, 3S, V-8 | 4,290 | 3,869 | 2,662 |
| PM23 | III htp cpe | 3,716 | 3,458 | 21,319 |
| PM41 | III sdn 4d | 3,752 | 3,437 | 44,244 |
| PM29 | III formal htp cpe V-8 | 3,750 | 3,600 | 24,465 |
| PM43 | III htp sdn V-8 | 3,820 | 3,612 | 55,356 |
| PM45 | III Cus Sub wgn 4d, 2S, V-8 | 4,240 | 3,854 | 10,874 |
| PM46 | III Cus Sub wgn 4d, 3S, V-8 | 4,300 | 3,930 | 11,702 |
| **Sport Fury (wb 120.0; wgn-122.0)** | | | | |
| PH23 | htp cpe V-8 | 3,805 | 3,677 | 3,912 |
| PH29 | formal htp cpe V-8 | 3,810 | 3,710 | 3,957 |
| PH41 | sdn 4d, V-8 | 3,845 | 3,656 | 2,823 |
| PH43 | htp sdn V-8 | 3,865 | 3,724 | 4,813 |
| PH45 | Sport Sub wgn 4d, 2S, V-8 | 4,290 | 4,071 | 5,103 |
| PH46 | Sport Sub wgn 4d, 3S, V-8 | 4,370 | 4,146 | 13,021 |
| PP23 | GT htp cpe V-8 | 4,090 | 4,111 | 375 |

| 1971 Engines | bore × stroke | bhp | availability |
|---|---|---|---|
| I-6, 198.0 | 3.40 × 3.64 | 125 | S-Val, Brcda cpe |
| I-6, 225.0 | 3.40 × 4.13 | 145 | S-Brcda exc cpe, Sat, Fury exc GT; O-Val, Brcda cpe |

# Plymouth

| 1971 Engines | bore × stroke | bhp | availability |
|---|---|---|---|
| V-8, 318.0 | 3.91 × 3.31 | 230 | S-Sat, Fury; O-Val, Barracuda |
| V-8, 340.0 | 4.04 × 3.31 | 275 | S-Dstr 340, 'Cuda; O-Barracuda |
| V-8, 360.0 | 4.00 × 3.58 | 255 | O-Fury |
| V-8, 383.0 | 4.25 × 3.38 | 275 | O-Brcda, Rd Runner, Fury |
| V-8, 383.0 | 4.25 × 3.38 | 300 | S-'Cuda, Rd Rnr; O-Barracuda, Fury |
| V-8, 426.0 | 4.25 × 3.75 | 425 | O-Barracuda (hemi) |
| V-8, 440.0 | 4.32 × 3.75 | 335 | O-Fury |
| V-8, 440.0 | 4.32 × 3.75 | 370 | S-GTX, Fury GT; O-Fury |
| V-8, 440.0 | 4.32 × 3.75 | 385 | O-Barracuda |

## 1972

| Valiant (wb 108.0; Scamp-111.0) | | Wght | Price | Prod |
|---|---|---|---|---|
| VL29 | Duster fstbk cpe | 2,780 | 2,287 | 212,331 |
| VL41 | sdn 4d | 2,800 | 2,363 | 52,911 |
| VH23 | Scamp htp cpe | 2,825 | 2,528 | 49,470 |
| VS29 | Duster 340 fstbk cpe | 3,100 | 2,742 | 15,681 |
| **Barracuda (wb 108.0)** | | | | |
| VH23 | htp cpe | 3,185 | 2,710 | 10,622 |
| VS23 | 'Cuda htp cpe V-8 | 3,195 | 3,029 | 7,828 |
| **Satellite (wb 117.0; 2d-115.0)** | | | | |
| RL21 | cpe | 3,272 | 2,609 | 10,507 |
| RL41 | sdn 4d | 3,312 | 2,678 | 12,794 |
| RL45 | wgn 4d 2S V-8 | 3,785 | 3,167 | 7,377 |
| RH23 | Sebring htp cpe | 3,282 | 2,871 | 34,353 |
| RH41 | Custom sdn 4d | 3,318 | 2,848 | 34,973 |
| RH45 | Custom wgn 2S V-8 | 3,825 | 3,340 | 5,485 |
| RH46 | Custom wgn 4d 3S V-8 | 3,780 | 3,418 | 5,637 |
| RP23 | Sebring Plus htp cpe V-8 | 3,320 | 3,127 | 21,399 |
| RP45 | Regent wgn 4d 2S V-8 | 3,790 | 3,562 | 1,893 |
| RP46 | Regent wgn 4d 3S V-8 | 3,830 | 3,640 | 2,907 |
| RM23 | Road Runner htp cpe V-8 | 3,495 | 3,095 | 7,628 |
| **Fury (wb 120.0; wgn-122.0)** | | | | |
| PL41 | I sdn 4d | 3,840 | 3,464 | 14,006 |
| PM23 | II htp cpe | 3,790 | 3,605 | 7,515 |
| PM41 | II sdn 4d | 3,830 | 3,583 | 20,051 |
| PM45 | II Suburban wgn 4d 2S | 4,315 | 4,024 | 5,368 |
| PM46 | II Suburban wgn 4d 3S | 4,360 | 4,139 | 2,773 |
| PH23 | III htp cpe | 3,790 | 3,785 | 21,204 |
| PH29 | III formal htp cpe | 3,790 | 3,818 | 9,036 |
| PH41 | III sdn 4d | 3,830 | 3,763 | 46,731 |
| PH43 | III htp sdn | 3,855 | 3,829 | 48,618 |
| PH45 | III Cus Suburban wgn 4d 2S | 4,315 | 4,123 | 11,067 |
| PH46 | III Cus Suburban wgn 4d 3S | 4,365 | 4,201 | 14,041 |
| PP23 | Gran Fury htp cpe | 3,735 | 3,941 | 15,840 |
| PP29 | Gran Fury formal htp cpe | 3,805 | 3,974 | 8,509 |
| PP43 | Gran Fury htp sdn | 3,865 | 3,987 | 17,551 |
| PP45 | Sport Suburban wgn 4d 2S | 4,335 | 4,389 | 4,971 |
| PP46 | Sport Suburban wgn 4d 3S | 4,395 | 4,466 | 15,628 |

| 1972 Engines | bore × stroke | bhp | availability |
|---|---|---|---|
| I-6, 198.0 | 3.40 × 3.64 | 100 | S-Valiant |
| I-6, 225.0 | 3.40 × 4.13 | 110 | S-Brcda, Sat; O-Val |
| V-8, 318.0 | 3.91 × 3.31 | 150 | S-Sat, Fury; O-Val, Barracuda |
| V-8, 340.0 | 4.04 × 3.31 | 240 | S-Duster 340, 'Cuda, Rd Runner; O-Barracuda |
| V-8, 360.0 | 4.00 × 3.58 | 170 | O-Fury |
| V-8, 400.0 | 4.34 × 3.38 | 190/250 | O-Fury |
| V-8, 440.0 | 4.32 × 3.75 | 230/285 | O-Fury |

## 1973

| Valiant (wb 108.0; Scamp-111.0) | | Wght | Price | Prod |
|---|---|---|---|---|
| VL29 | Duster fstbk cpe | 2,830 | 2,376 | 249,243 |
| VL41 | sdn 4d | 2,865 | 2,447 | 61,826 |
| VH23 | Scamp htp cpe | 2,885 | 2,617 | 53,792 |
| VS29 | Duster 340 fstbk cpe | 3,175 | 2,822 | 15,731 |
| **Barracuda (wb 108.0)** | | | | |
| VH23 | htp cpe | 3,140 | 2,935 | 11,587 |
| VS23 | 'Cuda htp cpe | 3,235 | 3,120 | 10,626 |
| **Satellite (wb 117.0; 2d-115.0)** | | | | |
| RL21 | cpe | 3,408 | 2,755 | 13,570 |
| RL41 | sdn 4d | 3,482 | 2,824 | 14,716 |
| RL45 | wgn 4d 2S V-8 | 3,950 | 3,272 | 6,906 |
| RH23 | Sebring htp cpe | 3,425 | 2,997 | 51,575 |
| RH41 | Custom sdn 4d | 3,478 | 2,974 | 46,748 |
| RH45 | Custom wgn 4d 2S V-8 | 3,945 | 3,400 | 6,733 |
| RH46 | Custom wgn 4d 3S V-8 | 3,990 | 3,518 | 7,705 |
| RP23 | Sebring Plus htp cpe V-8 | 3,455 | 3,258 | 43,628 |
| RP45 | Regent wgn 4d 2S V-8 | 3,950 | 3,621 | 2,781 |
| RP46 | Regent wgn 4d 3S V-8 | 4,010 | 3,740 | 4,786 |
| **Satellite (wb 117.0; 2d-115.0)** | | | | |
| RM21 | Road Runner cpe V-8 | 3,525 | 3,115 | 19,056 |
| **Fury (wb 120.0; wgn-122.0)** | | | | |
| PL41 | I sdn 4d | 3,865 | 3,575 | 17,365 |
| PM41 | II sdn 4d | 3,845 | 3,694 | 21,646 |
| PM45 | II Suburban wgn 4d 2S | 4,410 | 4,150 | 5,206 |
| PH23 | III htp cpe | 3,815 | 3,883 | 34,963 |
| PH41 | III sdn 4d | 3,860 | 3,866 | 51,742 |
| PH43 | III htp sdn | 3,880 | 3,932 | 51,215 |
| PH45 | III Cus Sub wgn 4d 2S | 4,420 | 4,246 | 9,888 |
| PH46 | III Cus Sub wgn 4d 3S | 4,465 | 4,354 | 15,671 |
| PP23 | Gran Fury htp cpe | 3,845 | 4,064 | 18,127 |
| PP43 | Gran Fury htp sdn | 3,890 | 4,110 | 14,852 |
| PP45 | Sport Sub wgn 4d 2S | 4,435 | 4,497 | 4,832 |
| PP46 | Sport Sub wgn 4d 3S | 4,495 | 4,599 | 15,680 |

| 1973 Engines | bore × stroke | bhp | availability |
|---|---|---|---|
| I-6, 198.0 | 3.40 × 3.64 | 100 | S-Valiant |
| I-6, 225.0 | 3.40 × 4.13 | 110 | S-Barracuda, Sat; O-Valiant |
| V-8, 318.0 | 3.91 × 3.31 | 150 | S-Sat, Fury; O-Val, Barracuda |
| V-8, 340.0 | 4.04 × 3.31 | 240 | S-Duster 340, 'Cuda, Rd Runner; O-Barracuda |
| V-8, 360.0 | 4.00 × 3.58 | 175 | O-Fury |
| V-8, 400.0 | 4.34 × 3.38 | 190/250 | O-Fury |
| V-8, 440.0 | 4.32 × 3.75 | 230/285 | O-Fury |

## 1974

| Valiant (wb 110.0; fstbk-108.0) | | Wght | Price | Prod |
|---|---|---|---|---|
| VL29 | Duster fstbk cpe | 2,975 | 2,829 | 277,409 |
| VS29 | Duster 360 fstbk cpe | 3,315 | 3,288 | |

# Plymouth

| Valiant (wb 110.0; fstbk-108.0) | | Wght | Price | Prod |
|---|---|---|---|---|
| VL41 | sdn 4d | 3,035 | 2,942 | 127,430 |
| VP41 | Brougham sdn 4d | 3,195 | 3,819 | |
| VP23 | Brougham htp cpe | 3,180 | 3,794 | 2,545 |
| VH23 | Scamp htp cpe | 3,010 | 3,077 | 51,699 |
| **Barracuda (wb 108.0)** | | | | |
| VH23 | htp cpe | 3,210 | 3,067 | 6,745 |
| VS23 | 'Cuda htp cpe | 3,300 | 3,252 | 4,989 |
| **Satellite (wb 117.0; 2d-115.0)** | | | | |
| RL21 | cpe | 3,470 | 3,155 | 10,634 |
| RL41 | sdn 4d | 3,555 | 3,226 | 12,726 |
| RL45 | wgn 4d 2S V-8 | 4,065 | 3,654 | 4,622 |
| RH23 | Sebring htp cpe | 3,490 | 3,353 | 31,980 |
| RH41 | Custom sdn 4d | 3,550 | 3,329 | 45,863 |
| RH45 | Custom wgn 4d 2S V-8 | 4,065 | 3,839 | 4,354 |
| RH46 | Custom wgn 4d 3S V-8 | 4,110 | 4,152 | 5,591 |
| RP45 | Regent wgn 4d 2S V-8 | 4,065 | 4,066 | 2,026 |
| RP46 | Regent wgn 4d 3S V-8 | 4,130 | 4,381 | 3,132 |
| RP23 | Sebring Plus htp cpe V-8 | 3,555 | 3,621 | 18,480 |
| RM21 | Road Runner cpe V-8 | 3,615 | 3,545 | 11,555 |
| **Fury (wb 120.0; wgn-124.0)** | | | | |
| PL41 | I sdn 4d | 4,185 | 4,101 | 8,162 |
| PM41 | II sdn 4d | 4,165 | 4,223 | 11,649 |
| PM45 | II Suburban wgn 4d 2S | 4,745 | 4,669 | 2,490 |
| PH23 | III htp cpe | 4,125 | 4,418 | 14,167 |
| PH41 | III sdn 4d | 4,180 | 4,400 | 27,965 |
| PH43 | III htp sdn | 4,205 | 4,268 | 18,778 |
| PH45 | III Cus Sub wgn 4d 2S | 4,755 | 4,767 | 3,877 |
| PH46 | III Cus Sub wagon 4d 3S | 4,800 | 4,878 | 5,628 |
| PP23 | Gran Fury htp cpe | 4,300 | 4,627 | 9,617 |
| PP43 | Gran Fury htp sdn | 4,370 | 4,675 | 8,191 |
| PP45 | Sport Sub wgn 4d 2S | 4,795 | 5,025 | 1,712 |
| PP46 | Sport Sub wgn 4d 3S | 4,850 | 5,130 | 6,047 |

| 1974 Engines | bore × stroke | bhp | availability |
|---|---|---|---|
| I-6, 198.0 | 3.40 × 3.64 | 95 | S-Valiant exc Brham |
| I-6, 225.0 | 3.40 × 4.13 | 105 | S-Val, Brham, Sat; O-Val |
| V-8, 318.0 | 3.91 × 3.31 | 150 | S-Brcda, Sat; O-Val |
| V-8, 318.0 | 3.91 × 3.31 | 170 | S-Road Runner |
| V-8, 360.0 | 4.00 × 3.58 | 180 | S-Fury exc wgn/Gran Fury |
| V-8, 360.0 | 4.00 × 3.58 | 200 | O-Sat, Fury exc wgn/Gran Fury |
| V-8, 360.0 | 4.00 × 3.58 | 245 | S-Duster 360; O-Val |
| V-8, 400.0 | 4.34 × 3.38 | 185 | S-Gran Fury, Fury wgns; O-Fury |
| V-8, 400.0 | 4.34 × 3.38 | 205 | O-Satellite, Fury |
| V-8, 400.0 | 4.34 × 3.38 | 240 | O-Fury |
| V-8, 400.0 | 4.34 × 3.38 | 250 | O-Satellite |
| V-8, 440.0 | 4.32 × 3.75 | 230/250 | O-Fury |
| V-8, 440.0 | 4.32 × 3.75 | 275 | O-Satellite |

## 1975

| Valiant (wb 111.0; fstbk-108.0) | | Wght | Price | Prod |
|---|---|---|---|---|
| VL29 | Duster fstbk cpe | 2,970 | 3,243 | 79,384 |
| VH29 | Duster Custom fstbk cpe | 2,970 | 3,418 | 38,826 |
| VL41 | sdn 4d | 3,040 | 3,247 | 44,471 |
| VH41 | Custom sdn 4d | 3,040 | 3,422 | 56,258 |
| VH23 | Scamp htp cpe | 3,020 | 3,518 | 23,581 |
| VS29 | Duster 360 fstbk cpe V-8 | 3,315 | 3,979 | 1,421 |
| **Valiant (wb 111.0; fstbk-108.0)** | | | | |
| VP23 | Brougham htp cpe | 3,240 | 4,232 | 5,781 |
| VP41 | Brougham sdn 4d | 3,250 | 4,139 | 17,803 |
| **Fury (wb 117.5; 2d-115.0)** | | | | |
| RL21 | cpe | 3,612 | 3,542 | 8,398 |
| RL41 | sdn 4d | 3,642 | 3,591 | 11,432 |
| RL45 | wgn 4d V-8 | 4,180 | 4,309 | 4,468 |
| RH23 | Custom cpe | 3,692 | 3,711 | 27,486 |
| RH41 | Custom wgn 4d | 3,692 | 3,704 | 31,080 |
| RH45 | Custom wgn 4d 2S V-8 | 4,230 | 4,512 | 3,890 |
| RH46 | Custom wagon 4d 3S V-8 | 4,285 | 4,632 | 4,285 |
| RP23 | Sport htp cpe V-8 | 3,790 | 4,105 | 17,782 |
| RP45 | Sport Sub wgn 4d 2S V-8 | 4,230 | 4,770 | 1,851 |
| RP46 | Sport Sub wgn 4d 3S V-8 | 4,295 | 4,867 | 3,107 |
| **Gran Fury (wb 122.0; wgn-124.0)** | | | | |
| PM41 | sdn 4d | 4,260 | 4,565 | 8,185 |
| PM45 | wgn 4d 2S | 4,855 | 5,067 | 2,295 |
| PH23 | Custom htp cpe | 4,205 | 4,781 | 6,041 |
| PH41 | Custom sdn 4d | 4,260 | 4,761 | 19,043 |
| PH43 | Custom htp sdn | 4,290 | 4,837 | 11,292 |
| PH45 | Custom wgn 4d 2S | 4,870 | 5,176 | 3,155 |
| PH46 | Custom wgn 4d 3S | 4,915 | 5,294 | 4,500 |
| PP29 | Brougham htp cpe | 4,310 | 5,146 | 6,521 |
| PP43 | Brougham htp sdn | 4,400 | 5,067 | 5,521 |
| PP45 | Sport Sub wgn 4d 2S | 4,885 | 5,455 | 1,508 |
| PP46 | Sport Sub wgn 4d 3S | 4,930 | 5,573 | 4,740 |

| 1975 Engines | bore × stroke | bhp | availability |
|---|---|---|---|
| I-6, 225.0 | 3.40 × 4.13 | 90 | S-Valiant |
| I-6, 225.0 | 3.40 × 4.13 | 95 | S-Fury |
| V-8, 318.0 | 3.91 × 3.31 | 135 | O-Fury, Valiant |
| V-8, 318.0 | 3.91 × 3.31 | 150 | S-Fury; O-G Fury exc wgn/Brham |
| V-8, 360.0 | 4.00 × 3.58 | 180 | S-Gran Fury exc wgn/Brham; O-Fury, G.F. wgn/Brham |
| V-8, 360.0 | 4.00 × 3.58 | 190 | O-Fury, Gran Fury |
| V-8, 360.0 | 4.00 × 3.58 | 230 | S-Duster 360 |
| V-8, 400.0 | 4.34 × 3.38 | 165/185 | O-Fury |
| V-8, 400.0 | 4.34 × 3.38 | 175 | S-Gran Fury Brougham wgn; O-other |
| V-8, 400.0 | 4.34 × 3.38 | 190/235 | O-Fury |
| V-8, 400.0 | 4.34 × 3.38 | 195 | O-Gran Fury |
| V-8, 440.0 | 4.32 × 3.75 | 215 | O-Gran Fury |

## 1976

| Valiant (wb 111.0; fstbk-108.0) | | Wght | Price | Prod |
|---|---|---|---|---|
| VL23 | Scamp Special htp cpe | 3,020 | 3,337 | 4,018 |
| VL29 | Duster fstbk cpe | 2,975 | 3,241 | 34,681 |
| VL41 | sdn 4d | 3,050 | 3,276 | 40,079 |
| VH23 | Scamp htp cpe | 3,020 | 3,510 | 6,908 |
| **Volare (wb 112.5; cpe-108.5)** | | | | |
| HL29 | cpe | 3,222 | 3,324 | 37,024 |
| HL41 | sdn 4d | 3,252 | 3,359 | 23,058 |
| HL45 | wgn 5d | 3,622 | 3,646 | 46,065 |
| HH29 | Custom cpe | 3,232 | 3,506 | 31,252 |
| HH41 | Custom sdn 4d | 3,262 | 3,541 | 36,407 |
| HP29 | Premier cpe | 3,438 | 4,402 | 31,475 |
| HP41 | Premier sdn 4d | 3,472 | 4,389 | 37,131 |
| HH45 | Premier wgn 5d | 3,628 | 3,976 | 49,507 |

# Plymouth

| Fury (wb 117.5; 2d-115.0) | | Wght | Price | Prod |
|---|---|---|---|---|
| RL23 | htp cpe | 3,708 | 3,699 | 16,415 |
| RL41 | sdn 4d | 3,742 | 3,733 | 22,654 |
| RL45 | wgn 4d 2S V-8 | 4,285 | 4,597 | 4,624 |
| RL46 | wgn 4d 3S V-8 | 4,350 | 4,739 | 4,412 |
| RH23 | Sport htp cpe | 3,712 | 3,988 | 28,851 |
| RH41 | Salon sdn 4d | 3,762 | 4,022 | 20,234 |
| RH45 | Sport Sub wgn 2S V-8 | 4,285 | 4,986 | 2,175 |
| RH46 | Sport Sub wgn 3S V-8 | 4,360 | 5,128 | 3,482 |
| **Gran Fury (wb 122.0; wgn-124.0)** | | | | |
| PM41 | sdn 4d | 4,140 | 4,349 | 8,928 |
| PM45 | wgn 4d 2S | 4,880 | 4,909 | 1,587 |
| PH23 | Custom htp cpe | 4,265 | 4,730 | 2,733 |
| PH41 | Custom sdn 4d | 4,305 | 4,715 | 14,738 |
| PH45 | Cust Suburban wgn 4d 2S | 4,895 | 5,193 | 1,433 |
| PH46 | Cust Suburban wgn 4d 3S | 4,940 | 5,316 | 1,998 |
| PP29 | Brougham htp cpe | 4,400 | 5,334 | 2,619 |
| PP41 | Brougham sdn 4d | 4,435 | 5,162 | 2,990 |
| PP46 | Sport Suburban wgn 4d 3S | 4,975 | 5,761 | 2,484 |

| 1976 Engines | bore × stroke | bhp | availability |
|---|---|---|---|
| I-6, 225.0 | 3.40 × 4.13 | 100 | S-Val, Vol, Fury exc wagon |
| V-8, 318.0 | 3.91 × 3.31 | 150 | S-Fury exc wgn, Gran Fury sdn; O-Valiant, Volare |
| V-8, 360.0 | 4.00 × 3.58 | 170 | S-Fury wagon, G. Fury Cus; O-Val, Vol, Fury, Gran Fury exc Cus/Brougham |
| V-8, 360.0 | 4.00 × 3.58 | 220 | O-Volare, Fury |
| V-8, 400.0 | 4.34 × 3.38 | 175 | S-GF wgn/Brham; O-Fury |
| V-8, 400.0 | 4.34 × 3.38 | 200/240 | O-Gran Fury |
| V-8, 440.0 | 4.32 × 3.75 | 205 | O-Gran Fury |

## 1977

| Volare (wb 112.7; cpe-108.7) | | Wght | Price | Prod |
|---|---|---|---|---|
| HL29 | cpe | 3,235 | 3,570 | 42,455 |
| HL41 | sdn 4d | 3,290 | 3,619 | 44,550 |
| HL45 | wgn 4d | 3,500 | 3,941 | 80,180 |
| HH29 | Custom cpe | 3,240 | 3,752 | 34,196 |
| HH41 | Custom sdn 4d | 3,295 | 3,801 | 50,859 |
| HP29 | Premier cpe | 3,430 | 4,305 | 21,979 |
| HP41 | Premier sdn 4d | 3,496 | 4,354 | 31,443 |
| HP45 | Premier wgn 5d | 3,505 | 4,271 | 76,756 |
| **Fury (wb 117.5; 2d-115.0)** | | | | |
| RL23 | htp cpe | 3,742 | 3,893 | 16,410 |
| RL41 | sdn 4d | 3,772 | 3,944 | 25,172 |
| RL45 | Suburban wgn 4d 2S V-8 | 4,335 | 4,687 | 6,765 |
| RL46 | Suburban wgn 4d 3S V-8 | 4,390 | 4,830 | 5,556 |
| RH23 | Sport htp cpe | 3,748 | 4,132 | 30,075 |
| RH41 | Salon sdn 4d | 3,782 | 4,185 | 25,617 |
| RH45 | Sport Sub wgn 4d 2S V-8 | 4,330 | 5,192 | 2,502 |
| RH46 | Sport Sub wgn 4d 3S V-8 | 4,400 | 5,335 | 4,065 |
| **Gran Fury (wb 122.0; wgn-124.0)** | | | | |
| PM23 | cpe | 4,070 | 4,692 | 2,772 |
| PM41 | sdn 4d | 4,145 | 4,677 | 14,242 |
| PM45 | Suburban wgn 4d 2S | 4,885 | 5,315 | 2,055 |
| PH23 | Brougham cpe | 4,190 | 4,963 | 4,846 |
| PH41 | Brougham sdn 4d | 4,250 | 4,948 | 17,687 |

| Gran Fury (wb 122.0; wgn-124.0) | | Wght | Price | Prod |
|---|---|---|---|---|
| PH45 | Sport Suburban wgn 4d 2S | 4,880 | 5,558 | 1,631 |
| PH46 | Sport Suburban wgn 4d 3S | 4,925 | 5,681 | 4,319 |

| 1977 Engines | bore × stroke | bhp | availability |
|---|---|---|---|
| I-6, 225.0 | 3.40 × 4.13 | 100 | S-Volare exc wgns |
| I-6, 225.0 | 3.40 × 4.13 | 110 | S-Vol wgns; Fury exc wgns |
| V-8, 318.0 | 3.91 × 3.31 | 145 | S-Gran Fury exc Brham wgn; O-Vol, other Fury |
| V-8, 360.0 | 4.00 × 3.58 | 155 | S-Fury wgns, Gran Fury Brham; O-Volare, Fury, other Gran Fury |
| V-8, 360.0 | 4.00 × 3.58 | 170 | O-Fury, Gran Fury |
| V-8, 400.0 | 4.34 × 3.38 | 190 | S-GF wgns; O-Fury, Gran Fury |
| V-8, 440.0 | 4.32 × 3.75 | 185/195 | O-Gran Fury |

## 1978

| Horizon (wb 99.2) | | Wght | Price | Prod |
|---|---|---|---|---|
| ML44 | htchbk sdn 4d | 2,145 | 3,976 | 106,772 |
| **Volare (wb 112.7; cpe-108.7)** | | | | |
| HL29 | cpe | 3,200 | 3,771 | 74,818 |
| HL41 | sdn 4d | 3,235 | 3,899 | 100,718 |
| HL45 | wgn 5d | 3,465 | 4,241 | 81,242 |
| **Fury (wb 117.5; 2d-115.0)** | | | | |
| RL23 | htp cpe | 3,725 | 4,236 | 13,276 |
| RL41 | sdn 4d | 3,760 | 4,326 | 83,649 |
| RL45 | Suburban wgn 4d 2S V-8 | 4,310 | 5,084 | 4,522 |
| RL46 | Suburban sgn 4d 3S V-8 | 4,370 | 5,227 | 3,889 |
| RH23 | Sport htp cpe | 3,735 | 4,483 | 13,031 |
| RH41 | Salon sdn 4d | 3,770 | 4,568 | 14,964 |
| RH45 | Sport Sub wgn 4d 2S V-8 | 4,300 | 5,545 | 1,720 |
| RH46 | Sport Sub wgn 4d 3S V-8 | 4,375 | 5,688 | 2,528 |

| 1978 Engines | bore × stroke | bhp | availability |
|---|---|---|---|
| I-4, 104.7 | 3.13 × 3.40 | 70 | S-Horizon |
| I-6, 225.0 | 3.40 × 4.13 | 90 | O-Volare exc wgn |
| I-6, 225.0 | 3.40 × 4.13 | 100 | S-Volare exc wgn |
| I-6, 225.0 | 3.40 × 4.13 | 110 | S-Volare wgn, Fury |
| V-8, 318.0 | 3.91 × 3.31 | 140 | S-Volare, Fury exc wgns |
| V-8, 318.0 | 3.91 × 3.31 | 155 | O-Volare, Fury exc wgns |
| V-8, 360.0 | 4.00 × 3.58 | 155 | S-Fury wgns; O-Vol, other Fury |
| V-8, 360.0 | 4.00 × 3.58 | 165/175 | O-Volare |
| V-8, 360.0 | 4.00 × 3.58 | 170 | O-Fury |
| V-8, 400.0 | 4.34 × 3.38 | 190 | O-Fury |

## 1979

| Horizon (wb 99.2; TC3-96.6) | | Wght | Price | Prod |
|---|---|---|---|---|
| ML24 | TC3 htchbk cpe | 2,195 | 4,864 | 63,715 |
| ML44 | htchbk sdn 4d | 2,135 | 4,469 | 99,048 |

# Plymouth

| Volare (wb 112.7; cpe-108.7) | | Wght | Price | Prod |
|---|---|---|---|---|
| HL29 | cpe | 3,110 | 4,387 | 63,620 |
| HL41 | sdn 4d | 3,175 | 4,504 | 95,383 |
| HL45 | wgn 5d | 3,435 | 5,110 | 50,683 |

| 1979 Engines | bore × stroke | bhp | availability |
|---|---|---|---|
| I4, 104.7 | 3.13 × 3.40 | 70 | S-Horizon |
| I-6, 225.0 | 3.40 × 4.13 | 100 | S-Volare |
| I-6, 225.0 | 3.40 × 4.13 | 110 | O-Volare |
| V-8, 318.0 | 3.91 × 3.31 | 135 | O-Volare |
| V-8, 360.0 | 4.00 × 3.58 | 195 | O-Volare |

## 1980

| Horizon (wb 99.2; TC3-96.6) | | Wght | Price | Prod |
|---|---|---|---|---|
| ML24 | TC3 htchbk cpe | 2,135 | 5,681 | 67,738 |
| ML44 | htchbk sdn 4d | 2,095 | 5,526 | 94,740 |

| Volare (wb 112.7; cpes-108.7) | | Wght | Price | Prod |
|---|---|---|---|---|
| HE29 | Special cpe 16 | 3,155 | 5,151 | 16,475 |
| HE41 | Special sdn 4d I-6 | 3,210 | 5,151 | 25,509 |
| HL29 | cpe | 3,170 | 5,033 | 17,781 |
| HL41 | sdn 4d | 3,225 | 5,150 | 30,097 |
| HL45 | wgn 4d | 3,540 | 5,422 | 19,910 |

| Gran Fury (wb 118.5) | | Wght | Price | Prod |
|---|---|---|---|---|
| JL42 | sdn 4d | 3,562 | 6,741 | 15,469 |
| JH42 | Salon sdn 4d | 3,438 | 7,116 | 3,255 |

| 1980 Engines | bore × stroke | bhp | availability |
|---|---|---|---|
| I-4, 104.7 | 3.13 × 3.40 | 65 | S-Horizon |
| I-6, 225.0 | 3.40 × 4.13 | 90 | S-Volare, Gran Fury |
| V-8, 318.0 | 3.91 × 3.31 | 120 | S-Gran Fury, O-Volare exc Spcl |
| V-8, 360.0 | 4.00 × 3.58 | 130 | O-Gran Fury |

Note: Plymouth production totals through 1980 include export models, which makes figures in this book higher than some quoted elsewhere.

## 1981

| Horizon (wb 99.1; TC3-96.6) | | Wght | Price | Prod |
|---|---|---|---|---|
| ML24 | TC3 htchbk cpe | 2,205 | 6,149 | 36,312 |
| ME24 | Miser TC3 htchbk cpe | 2,137 | 5,299 | |
| ML44 | htchbk sdn 4d | 2,130 | 5,690 | 58,547 |
| ME44 | Miser htchbk sdn 4d | 2,060 | 5,299 | |

| Reliant (wb 99.6) | | Wght | Price | Prod |
|---|---|---|---|---|
| PL21 | sdn 2d | 2,305 | 5,880 | 58,093 |
| PL41 | sdn 4d | 2,300 | 5,980 | |
| PH21 | Custom sdn 2d | 2,315 | 6,315 | 13,587 |
| PH41 | Custom sdn 4d | 2,310 | 6,448 | |
| PH45 | Custom wgn 5d | 2,375 | 6,721 | 40,830 |
| PP21 | SE sdn 2d | 2,340 | 6,789 | 28,457 |
| PP41 | SE sdn 4d | 2,340 | 6,933 | |
| PP45 | SE wgn 5d | 2,390 | 7,254 | 10,670 |

| Gran Fury (wb 118.5) | | Wght | Price | Prod |
|---|---|---|---|---|
| L42 | sdn 4d | 3,547 | 7,387 | 7,719 |

| 1981 Engines | bore × stroke | bhp | availability |
|---|---|---|---|
| I-4, 104.7 | 3.13 × 3.40 | 63 | S-Horizon |
| I-4, 135.0 | 3.44 × 3.62 | 84 | S-Relnt, late TC3; O-Horiz |
| I-4, 156.0 | 3.59 × 3.86 | 92 | O-Reliant |
| I-6, 225.0 | 3.40 × 4.12 | 85 | S-Gran Fury |
| V-8, 318.0 | 3.91 × 3.31 | 130 | O-Gran Fury |
| V-8, 318.0 | 3.91 × 3.31 | 165 | O-Gran Fury (Calif.) |

## 1982

| TC3 (wb 96.6) | | Wght | Price | Prod |
|---|---|---|---|---|
| MH24 | Custom htchbk cpe | 2,205 | 6,421 | 12,889 |
| ME24 | Miser htchbk cpe | 2,180 | 5,799 | 18,359 |
| MP24 | Turismo htchbk cpe | 2,285 | 7,115 | 6,608 |

| Horizon (wb 99.1) | | Wght | Price | Prod |
|---|---|---|---|---|
| MH44 | htchbk sdn 4d | 2,175 | 5,927 | 17,315 |
| ME44 | Miser htchbk sdn 4d | 2,110 | 5,499 | 19,102 |
| MP44 | Euro-Sedan sdn 4d | 2,285 | 6,636 | 779 |

| Reliant (wb 99.6) | | Wght | Price | Prod |
|---|---|---|---|---|
| PL21 | sdn 2d | 2,315 | 5,990 | 12,026 |
| PL41 | sdn 4d | 2,310 | 6,131 | 37,488 |
| PH21 | Custom sdn 2d | 2,320 | 6,898 | 12,403 |
| PH41 | Custom sdn 4d | 2,320 | 7,053 | 29,980 |
| PH45 | Custom wgn 5d | 2,395 | 7,334 | 32,501 |
| PP21 | SE sdn 2d | 2,365 | 7,575 | 2,536 |
| PP41 | SE sdn 4d | 2,385 | 7,736 | 4,578 |
| PP45 | SE wgn 5d | 2,470 | 8,101 | 7,711 |

| Gran Fury (wb 112.7) | | Wght | Price | Prod |
|---|---|---|---|---|
| BL41 | sdn 4d | 3,345 | 7,750 | 18,111 |

| 1982 Engines | bore × stroke | bhp | availability |
|---|---|---|---|
| I-4, 104.7 | 3.13 × 3.40 | 63 | S-TC3, Horizon |
| I-4, 135.0 | 3.44 × 3.62 | 84 | S-Reliant, TC3 Turismo; O-TC3, Horizon |
| I-4, 156.0 | 3.59 × 3.86 | 92 | O-Reliant |
| I-6, 225.0 | 3.40 × 4.12 | 90 | S-Gran Fury |
| V-8, 318.0 | 3.91 × 3.31 | 130 | O-Gran Fury |
| V-8, 318.0 | 3.91 × 3.31 | 165 | O-Gran Fury (Calif.) |

## 1983

| Turismo (wb 96.6) | | Wght | Price | Prod |
|---|---|---|---|---|
| MH | htchbk cpe | 2,226 | 6,379 | 22,527 |
| MP | 2.2 htchbk cpe | 2,363 | 7,303 | 9,538 |

| Horizon (wb 99.1) | | Wght | Price | Prod |
|---|---|---|---|---|
| ME44 | htchbk sdn 4d | 2,175 | 5,841 | 35,796 |
| MH | Custom htchbk sdn 4d | 2,206 | 6,071 | 10,675 |

| Reliant (wb 100.1) | | Wght | Price | Prod |
|---|---|---|---|---|
| PL21 | sdn 2d | 2,317 | 6,577 | 16,109 |
| PL41 | sdn 4d | 2,323 | 6,718 | 69,112 |
| PH45 | Custom wgn 5d | 2,372 | 7,636 | 38,264 |
| PH21 | SE sdn 2d | 2,333 | 7,260 | 5,852 |
| PH41 | SE sdn 4d | 2,360 | 7,417 | 13,434 |
| PP45 | SE wgn 5d | 2,432 | 8,186 | 3,791 |

| Gran Fury (wb 112.7) | | Wght | Price | Prod |
|---|---|---|---|---|
| BL41 | Salon sdn 4d | 3,478 | 8,248 | 15,739 |

# Plymouth

| 1983 Engines | bore × stroke | bhp | availability |
|---|---|---|---|
| I-4, 97.3 | 3.17 × 3.07 | 62 | S-late Turismo, Horizon |
| I-4, 104.7 | 3.13 × 3.40 | 63 | S-early Turismo, Horizon |
| I-4, 135.0 | 3.44 × 3.62 | 94 | S-Reliant, Turismo 2.2; O-Turismo, Horizon |
| I-4, 156.0 | 3.59 × 3.86 | 93 | O-Reliant |
| I-6, 225.0 | 3.40 × 4.12 | 90 | S-Gran Fury |
| V-8, 318.0 | 3.91 × 3.31 | 130 | O-Gran Fury |

## 1984

| Turismo (wb 96.6) | | Wght | Price | Prod |
|---|---|---|---|---|
| MH24 | htchbk cpe | 2,220 | 6,494 | 38,835 |
| MP24 | 2.2 htchbk cpe | 2,327 | 7,288 | 10,881 |
| **Horizon (wb 99.1)** | | | | |
| ME44 | htchbk sdn 4d | 2,151 | 5,830 | 62,903 |
| MH44 | SE htchbk sdn 4d | 2,180 | 6,148 | 15,661 |
| **Reliant (wb 100.3)** | | | | |
| PL21 | sdn 2d | 2,354 | 6,837 | 14,533 |
| PL41 | sdn 4d | 2,361 | 6,949 | 72,595 |
| PH45 | Custom wgn 5d | 2,450 | 7,736 | 39,207 |
| PH21 | SE sdn 2d | 2,364 | 7,463 | 5,287 |
| PH41 | SE sdn 4d | 2,394 | 7,589 | 16,223 |
| PP45 | SE wgn 5d | 2,501 | 8,195 | 4,338 |
| **Gran Fury (wb 112.7)** | | | | |
| BL41 | Salon sdn 4d | 3,558 | 9,180 | 14,516 |

| 1984 Engines | bore × stroke | bhp | availability |
|---|---|---|---|
| I-4, 97.3 | 3.17 × 3.07 | 64 | S-Turismo, Horizon |
| I-4, 135.0 | 3.44 × 3.62 | 96 | S-Reliant; O-Trsmo, Horizon |
| I-4, 135.0 | 3.44 × 3.62 | 101 | S-Turismo 2.2 |
| I-4, 135.0 | 3.44 × 3.62 | 110 | O-Turismo, Horizon |
| I-4, 156.0 | 3.59 × 3.86 | 101 | O-Reliant |
| V-8, 318.0 | 3.91 × 3.31 | 130 | S-Gran Fury |

## 1985

| Turismo (wb 96.6) | | Wght | Price | Prod |
|---|---|---|---|---|
| LMH24 | htchbk cpe | 2,215 | 6,584 | 44,377 |
| LMP24 | 2.2 htchbk cpe | 2,366 | 7,515 | 7,785 |
| **Horizon (wb 99.1)** | | | | |
| LME44 | htchbk sdn 4d | 2,154 | 5,977 | 71,846 |
| LMH44 | SE htchbk sdn 4d | 2,174 | 6,342 | 16,165 |
| **Reliant (wb 100.3)** | | | | |
| KPL21 | sdn 2d | 2,375 | 6,924 | 11,317 |
| KPL41 | sdn 4d | 2,393 | 7,039 | 46,972 |
| KPM21 | SE sdn 2d | 2,390 | 7,321 | 9,530 |
| KPM41 | SE sdn 4d | 2,424 | 7,439 | 27,231 |
| KPH45 | SE wgn 5d | 2,514 | 7,909 | 27,489 |
| KPH21 | LE sdn 2d | 2,414 | 7,659 | 4,110 |
| KPH41 | LE sdn 4d | 2,446 | 7,792 | 7,072 |
| KPP45 | LE wgn 5d | 2,546 | 8,348 | 4,017 |
| **Caravelle (wb 103.3)** | | | | |
| EJH41 | SE sdn 4d | 2,593 | 9,007 | 39,971 |
| **Gran Fury (wb 112.7)** | | | | |
| MBL41 | Salon sdn 4d | 3,553 | 9,658 | 19,102 |

| 1985 Engines | bore × stroke | bhp | availability |
|---|---|---|---|
| I-4, 97.3 | 3.17 × 3.07 | 64 | S-Turismo, Horizon |
| I-4, 135.0 | 3.44 × 3.62 | 96 | S-Reliant, O-Trsmo, Horizon |
| I-4, 135.0 | 3.44 × 3.62 | 99 | S-Caravelle |
| I-4, 135.0 | 3.44 × 3.62 | 110 | S-Turismo 2.2 |
| I-4T, 135.0 | 3.44 × 3.62 | 146 | O-Caravelle |
| I-4, 156.0 | 3.59 × 3.86 | 101 | O-Reliant, Caravelle |
| V-8, 318.0 | 3.91 × 3.31 | 140 | S-Gran Fury |

## 1986

| Turismo (wb 96.6) | | Wght | Price | Prod |
|---|---|---|---|---|
| LMH24 | htchbk cpe | 2,215 | 6,787 | 41,899 |
| LMP24 | 2.2 htchbk cpe | 2,366 | 7,732 | 4,488 |
| **Horizon (wb 99.1)** | | | | |
| LME44 | htchbk sdn 4d | 2,154 | 6,209 | 76,458 |
| LMH44 | SE htchbk sdn 4d | 2,174 | 6,558 | 8,050 |
| **Reliant (wb 100.3)** | | | | |
| KPL21 | sdn 2d | 2,395 | 7,184 | 2,573 |
| KPL41 | sdn 4d | 2,402 | 7,301 | 26,220 |
| KPM21 | SE sdn 2d | 2,412 | 7,639 | 10,707 |
| KPM41 | SE sdn 4d | 2,429 | 7,759 | 47,827 |
| KPM45 | SE wgn 5d | 2,513 | 8,186 | 22,154 |
| KPH21 | LE sdn 2d | 2,427 | 8,087 | 2,482 |
| KPH41 | LE sdn 4d | 2,444 | 8,207 | 5,941 |
| KPH45 | LE wgn 5d | 2,549 | 8,936 | 5,101 |
| **Caravelle (wb 103.3)** | | | | |
| EJM41 | sdn 4d | 2,589 | 9,241 | 18,698 |
| EJH41 | SE sdn 4d | 2,589 | 9,810 | 15,654 |
| **Gran Fury (wb 112.7)** | | | | |
| MBL41 | Salon sdn 4d | 3,550 | 9,947 | 14,761 |

| 1986 Engines | bore × stroke | bhp | availability |
|---|---|---|---|
| I-4, 97.3 | 3.17 × 3.07 | 64 | S-Turismo, Horizon |
| I-4, 135.0 | 3.44 × 3.62 | 96 | O-Turismo, Horizon |
| I-4, 135.0 | 3.44 × 3.62 | 97 | S-Reliant, Caravelle |
| I-4, 135.0 | 3.44 × 3.62 | 110 | S-Turismo 2.2 |
| I-4T, 135.0 | 3.44 × 3.62 | 146 | O-Caravelle |
| I-4, 153.0 | 3.44 × 4.09 | 100 | O-Reliant, Caravelle |
| V-8, 318.0 | 3.91 × 3.31 | 140 | S-Gran Fury |

## 1987

| Turismo (wb 96.6) | | Wght | Price | Prod |
|---|---|---|---|---|
| LMH24 | htchbk cpe | 2,290 | 7,199 | 24,104 |
| **Horizon (wb 99.1)** | | | | |
| LME44 | America htchbk sdn 4d | 2,237 | 5,799 | 79,449 |
| **Sundance (wb 97.0)** | | | | |
| PPH24 | htchbk sdn 2d | 2,527 | 7,599 | 35,719 |
| PPH44 | htchbk sdn 4d | 2,565 | 7,799 | 39,960 |

# Plymouth

| Reliant (wb 100.3) | Wght | Price | Prod |
|---|---|---|---|
| KPL21 sdn 2d | 2,409 | 7,655 | 204 |
| KPL41 sdn 4d | 2,415 | 7,655 | 5,142 |
| KPM21 LE sdn 2d | 2,468 | 8,134 | 9,127 |
| KPM41 LE sdn 4d | 2,484 | 8,134 | 66,575 |
| KPM45 LE wgn 5d | 2,588 | 8,579 | 22,905 |
| **Caravelle (wb 103.3)** | | | |
| EJM41 sdn 4d | 2,589 | 9,762 | 23,132 |
| EJH41 SE sdn 4d | 2,596 | 10,355 | 19,333 |
| **Gran Fury (wb 112.7)** | | | |
| MBL41 Salon sdn 4d | 3,599 | 10,598 | 10,377 |

| 1987 Engines | bore × stroke | bhp | availability |
|---|---|---|---|
| I-4, 135.0 | 3.44 × 3.62 | 96 | S-Turismo, Horizon |
| I-4, 135.0 | 3.44 × 3.62 | 97 | S-Sundance, Reliant, Carav |
| I-4T, 135.0 | 3.44 × 3.62 | 146 | O-Sundance, Caravelle |
| I-4, 153.0 | 3.44 × 4.09 | 100 | O-Reliant, Caravelle |
| V-8, 318.0 | 3.91 × 3.31 | 140 | S-Gran Fury |

## 1988

| Horizon (wb 99.1) | Wght | Price | Prod |
|---|---|---|---|
| LME44 America htchbk sdn 4d | 2,225 | 5,999 | 61,715 |
| **Sundance (wb 97.0)** | | | |
| PPH24 htchbk sdn 2d | 2,513 | 7,975 | 34,827 |
| PPH44 htchbk sdn 4d | 2,544 | 8,175 | 53,521 |
| **Reliant (wb 100.3)** | | | |
| KPH21 America sdn 2d | 2,459 | 6,995 | 8,543 |
| KPH41 America sdn 4d | 2,485 | 6,995 | 95,551 |
| KPH45 America wgn 5d | 2,537 | 7,695 | 21,213 |
| **Caravelle (wb 103.3)** | | | |
| EJM41 sdn 4d | 2,594 | 10,659 | 9,718 |
| EJH41 SE sdn 4d | 2,632 | 11,628 | 7,171 |
| **Gran Fury (wb 112.7)** | | | |
| MBE41 sdn 4d | 3,576 | 12,127 | 238 |
| MBL41 Salon sdn 4d | 3,588 | 11,407 | 11,183 |

| 1988 Engines | bore × stroke | bhp | availability |
|---|---|---|---|
| I-4, 135.0 | 3.44 × 3.62 | 93 | S-Hrzn, Sundance, Reliant, Caravelle |
| I-4T, 135.0 | 3.44 × 3.62 | 146 | O-Sundance, Caravelle |
| I-4, 153.0 | 3.44 × 4.09 | 96 | O-Sundance, Reliant, Caravelle |
| V-8, 318.0 | 3.91 × 3.31 | 140 | S-Gran Fury |

## 1989

| Horizon (wb 99.1) | Wght | Price | Prod |
|---|---|---|---|
| LME44 America htchbk sdn 4d | 2,237 | 6,595 | 45,341 |
| **Sundance (wb 97.0)—104,150 built** | | | |
| PPH24 htchbk sdn 2d | 2,520 | 8,395 | — |
| PPH44 htchbk sdn 4d | 2,558 | 8,595 | — |
| **Reliant (wb 100.3)—36,012 built** | | | |
| KPH21 America sdn 2d | 2,317 | 7,595 | — |
| KPH41 America sdn 4d | 2,323 | 7,595 | — |
| **Acclaim (wb 103.3)—77,752 built** | | | |
| APJ41 sdn 4d | 2,753 | 9,920 | — |
| APP41 LE sdn 4d | 2,827 | 11,295 | — |
| APX41 LX sdn 4d | 2,968 | 13,195 | — |
| **Gran Fury (wb 112.7)** | | | |
| MBL41 Salon sdn 4d | 3,599 | 11,995 | 4,985 |

| 1989 Engines | bore × stroke | bhp | availability |
|---|---|---|---|
| I-4, 135.0 | 3.44 × 3.62 | 93 | S-Horizon, Sndnce, Reliant |
| I-4, 153.0 | 3.44 × 4.09 | 100 | S-Acclaim exc LX; O-Sndnce, Rlnt |
| I-4T, 153.0 | 3.44 × 4.09 | 150 | O-Sundance, Acclaim |
| V-6, 181.0 | 3.59 × 2.99 | 141 | S-Acclaim LX |
| V-8, 318.0 | 3.91 × 3.31 | 140 | S-Gran Fury |

## 1990

| Horizon (wb 99.1) | Wght | Price | Prod |
|---|---|---|---|
| LME44 htchbk sdn 4d | 2,296 | 6,995 | 16,397 |
| **Sundance (wb 97.0)—79,562 built** | | | |
| PPH24 htchbk sdn 2d | 2,513 | 8,795 | — |
| PPH44 htchbk sdn 4d | 2,544 | 8,995 | — |
| **Acclaim (wb 103.3)—110,330 built** | | | |
| APJ41 sdn 4d | 2,854 | 10,385 | — |
| APP41 LE sdn 4d | — | 11,815 | — |
| APX41 LX sdn 4d | — | 13,805 | — |

| 1990 Engines | bore × stroke | bhp | availability |
|---|---|---|---|
| I-4, 135.0 | 3.44 × 3.62 | 93 | S-Horizon, Sndnce |
| I-4, 153.0 | 3.44 × 4.09 | 100 | S-Acclaim exc LX; O-Sndnce |
| I-4T, 153.0 | 3.44 × 4.09 | 150 | O-Sundance, Acclaim |
| V-6, 181.0 | 3.59 × 2.99 | 141 | S-Acclaim LX |

## 1991

| Sundance (wb 97.0) | Wght | Price | Prod |
|---|---|---|---|
| PPH24 America htchbk sdn 2d | 2,617 | 7,699 | 27,909 |
|     Highline htchbk sdn 2d | — | 8,899 | |
|     RS htchbk sdn 2d | — | 10,099 | |
| PPH44 America htchbk sdn 4d | 2,654 | 7,999 | 34,911 |
|     Highline htchbk sdn 4d | — | 9,199 | |
|     RS htchbk sdn 4d | — | 10,425 | |
| **Acclaim (wb 103.3)—97,146 built** | | | |
| APJ41 sdn 4d | 2,789 | 10,825 | — |
| APP41 LE sdn 4d | — | 12,880 | — |
| APX41 LX sdn 4d | — | 14,380 | — |
| **Laser (wb 97.2)—30,720 built** | | | |
| htchbk cpe | 2,524 | 10,864 | |
| RS htchbk cpe | — | 12,770 | |
| RS Turbo htchbk cpe | 2,745 | 13,954 | |

# Plymouth

| 1991 Engines | bore × stroke | bhp | availability |
|---|---|---|---|
| I-4, 107.1 | 3.17 × 3.39 | 92 | S-Laser (ohc) |
| I-4, 122.0 | 3.35 × 3.46 | 135 | O-Laser (dohc) |
| I-4T, 122.0 | 3.35 × 3.46 | 190 | O-Laser (dohc) |
| I-4, 135.0 | 3.44 × 3.62 | 93 | S-Sundance (ohc) |
| I-4T, 135.0 | 3.44 × 3.62 | 152 | O-Sundance (ohc) |
| I-4, 153.0 | 3.44 × 4.09 | 100 | S-Acclaim; O-Sundance (ohc) |
| V-6, 181.4 | 3.66 × 3.19 | 141 | O-Acclaim (ohc) |

## 1992

| Sundance (wb 97.0) | Wght | Price | Prod |
|---|---|---|---|
| PPH24 America htchbk sdn 2d | 2,617 | 7,984 | |
| Highline htchbk sdn 2d | — | 9,246 | 29,951 |
| Duster htchbk sdn 2d | — | 9,849 | |
| PPH44 America htchbk sdn 4d | 2,654 | 8,384 | |
| Highline htchbk sdn 4d | — | 9,646 | 36,606 |
| Duster htchbk sdn 4d | — | 10,249 | |
| **Acclaim (wb 103.3)** | | | |
| APH41 sdn 4d | 2,784 | 11,470 | 77,105 |
| **Laser (wb 97.2)—25,019 built** | | | |
| htchbk cpe | 2,531 | 11,206 | — |
| RS htchbk cpe | 2,690 | 13,101 | — |
| RS Turbo htchbk cpe | 2,756 | 14,392 | — |
| RS Turbo AWD htchbk cpe | 3,073 | 16,368 | — |

| 1992 Engines | bore × stroke | bhp | availability |
|---|---|---|---|
| I-4, 107.1 | 3.17 × 3.39 | 92 | S-Laser (ohc) |
| I-4, 122.0 | 3.35 × 3.46 | 135 | O-Laser (dohc) |
| I-4T, 122.0 | 3.35 × 3.46 | 195 | O-Laser (dohc) |
| I-4, 135.0 | 3.44 × 3.62 | 93 | S-Sndnce exc Dustr |
| I-4, 153.0 | 3.44 × 4.09 | 100 | S-Acclaim; O-Sundance (ohc) exc Duster |
| V-6, 181.4 | 3.66 × 3.19 | 141 | S-Duster; O-Acclaim (ohc) |

## 1993

| Sundance (wb 97.0) | Wght | Price | Prod |
|---|---|---|---|
| PPH24 htchbk sdn 2d | 2,613 | 8,397 | |
| Duster htchbk sdn 2d | — | 10,498 | 42,020 |
| PPH44 htchbk sdn 4d | 2,884 | 8,797 | |
| Duster htchbk sdn 4d | — | 10,898 | 43,736 |
| **Acclaim (wb 103.5)** | | | |
| APH41 sdn 4d | 2,784 | 11,910 | 55,531 |
| **Laser (wb 97.2)—17,178 built** | | | |
| htchbk cpe | 2,531 | 11,406 | — |
| RS htchbk cpe | 2,690 | 13,749 | — |
| RS Turbo htchbk cpe | 2,756 | 15,267 | — |
| RS Turbo AWD htchbk cpe | 3,073 | 17,371 | — |

| 1993 Engines | bore × stroke | bhp | availability |
|---|---|---|---|
| I-4, 107.1 | 3.17 × 3.39 | 92 | S-Laser (ohc) |
| I-4, 122.0 | 3.35 × 3.46 | 135 | O-Laser (dohc) |
| I-4T, 122.0 | 3.35 × 3.46 | 180 | O-Laser (dohc) |
| I-4T, 122.0 | 3.35 × 3.46 | 195 | O-Laser (dohc) |
| I-4, 135.0 | 3.44 × 3.62 | 93 | S-Sundance (ohc) |
| I-4, 153.0 | 3.44 × 4.09 | 100 | S-Acclaim; O-Sundance (ohc) |
| V-6, 181.4 | 3.66 × 3.19 | 141 | O-Acclaim, Sundance (ohc) |

## 1994

| Sundance (wb 97.0) | Wght | Price | Prod |
|---|---|---|---|
| PPH24 htchbk sdn 2d | 2,608 | 8,806 | |
| Duster htchbk sdn 2d | — | 10,946 | 33,599 |
| PPH44 htchbk sdn 4d | 2,643 | 9,206 | |
| Duster htchbk sdn 4d | — | 11,346 | 36,839 |
| **Acclaim (wb 103.5)** | | | |
| APH41 sdn 4d | 2,831 | 12,470 | 40,294 |
| **Laser (wb 97.2)—5,067 built** | | | |
| htchbk cpe | 2,531 | 11,542 | — |
| RS htchbk cpe | 2,690 | 13,910 | — |
| RS Turbo htchbk cpe | 2,756 | 15,444 | — |
| RS Turbo AWD htchbk cpe | 3,073 | 17,572 | — |

| 1994 Engines | bore × stroke | bhp | availability |
|---|---|---|---|
| I-4, 107.1 | 3.17 × 3.39 | 92 | S-Laser (ohc) |
| I-4, 122.0 | 3.35 × 3.46 | 135 | O-Laser (dohc) |
| I-4T, 122.0 | 3.35 × 3.46 | 180 | O-Laser (dohc) |
| I-4T, 122.0 | 3.35 × 3.46 | 195 | O-Laser (dohc) |
| I-4, 135.0 | 3.44 × 3.62 | 93 | S-Sundance (ohc) |
| I-4, 153.0 | 3.44 × 4.09 | 100 | S-Acclaim; O-Sundance (ohc) |
| V-6, 181.4 | 3.66 × 3.19 | 141 | O-Sundance (ohc) |
| V-6, 181.4 | 3.66 × 3.19 | 142 | O-Acclaim (ohc) |

## 1995

| Neon (wb 104.0) | Wght | Price | Prod |
|---|---|---|---|
| LPL42 sdn 4d | 2,338 | 9,500 | |
| LPH42 Highline sdn 4d | 2,405 | 11,240 | 93,187 |
| LPS42 Sport sdn 4d | 2,448 | 13,267 | |
| LPH22 Highline sdn 2d | — | 11,240 | |
| LPS22 Sport sdn 2d | — | 13,567 | 28,187 |
| **Acclaim (wb 103.5)** | | | |
| APH41 sdn 4d | 2,862 | 14,323 | 12,331 |

| 1995 Engines | bore × stroke | bhp | availability |
|---|---|---|---|
| I-4, 121.8 | 3.44 × 3.27 | 132 | S-Neon (ohc) |
| I-4, 121.8 | 3.44 × 3.27 | 150 | O-Neon (dohc) |
| I-4, 153.0 | 3.44 × 4.09 | 100 | S-Acclaim (ohc) |
| V-6, 181.4 | 3.66 × 3.19 | 142 | O-Acclaim (ohc) |

## 1996

| Neon (wb 104.0) | Wght | Price | Prod |
|---|---|---|---|
| LPL42 sdn 4d | 2,338 | 9,995 | 75,684 |

# Plymouth

| Neon (wb 104.0) | Wght | Price | Prod |
|---|---|---|---|
| LPH42 Highline sdn 4d | 2,405 | 11,500 | |
| LPS42 Sport sdn 4d | 2,448 | 12,700 | |
| LPL22 sdn 2d | — | 9,495 | 28,129 |
| LPH22 Highline sdn 2d | — | 11,300 | |
| LPS22 Sport sdn 2d | — | 12,500 | |
| **Breeze (wb 108.0)** | | | |
| APH41 sdn 4d | 2,931 | 14,060 | 46,355 |

| 1996 Engines | bore × stroke | bhp | availability |
|---|---|---|---|
| I-4, 121.8 | 3.44 × 3.27 | 132 | S-Neon, Breeze |
| I-4, 121.8 | 3.44 × 3.27 | 150 | O-Neon (dohc) |

## 1997

| Neon (wb 104.0) | Wght | Price | Prod |
|---|---|---|---|
| LPL42 sdn 4d | 2,399 | 10,595 | 60,713 |
| LPH42 Highline sdn 4d | 2,459 | 12,670 | |
| LPL22 cpe 2d | 2,389 | 10,395 | 22,108 |
| LPH22 Highline cpe 2d | 2,416 | 12,470 | |
| **Breeze (wb 108.0)** | | | |
| APH41 sdn 4d | 2,931 | 14,795 | 70,549 |
| **Prowler (wb 113.0)** | | | |
| RPS27 conv rdstr 2d | 2,800 | 38,300 | 463* |

| 1997 Engines | bore × stroke | bhp | availability |
|---|---|---|---|
| I-4, 121.8 | 3.44 × 3.27 | 132 | S-Neon, Breeze |
| I-4, 121.8 | 3.44 × 3.27 | 150 | O-Neon (dohc) |
| V-6, 215.0 | 3.78 × 3.19 | 214 | S-Prowler |

*Calendar-year production.

## 1998

| Neon (wb 104.0) | Wght | Price | Prod |
|---|---|---|---|
| LPL42 Highline sdn 4d | 2,507 | 11,355 | 68,521 |
| LPH42 Expresso sdn 4d | 2,459 | 13,160 | |
| LPH42 Style sdn 4d | — | 14,095 | |
| LPL22 Highline cpe 2d | 2,470 | 11,155 | 18,545 |
| LPH22 Expresso cpe 2d | — | 12,980 | |
| **Breeze (wb 108.0)** | | | |
| APH41 sdn 4d | 2,929 | 14,675 | 66,620 |
| **Prowler (wb 113.0)** | | | |
| RPS27 conv rdstr 2d | — | — | 2,124* |

| 1998 Engines | bore × stroke | bhp | availability |
|---|---|---|---|
| I-4, 121.8 | 3.44 × 3.27 | 132 | S-Neon, Breeze |
| I-4, 121.8 | 3.44 × 3.27 | 150 | O-Neon (dohc) |
| I-4, 148.0 | 3.44 × 3.98 | 150 | O-Breeze |
| V-6, 215.0 | 3.78 × 3.19 | 214 | S-Prowler |

*Calendar-year production. Titled as 1997 or 1999.

## 1999

| Neon (wb 104.0)—63,216 built | Wght | Price | Prod* |
|---|---|---|---|
| LPL42 Highline sdn 4d | 2,507 | 11,820 | |
| LPH42 Expresso sdn 4d | — | 12,825 | |
| LPH42 Style sdn 4d | — | 13,960 | |
| LPL22 Highline cpe 2d | 2,470 | 11,735 | |
| LPH22 Expresso cpe 2d | — | 12,740 | |
| **Breeze (wb 108.0)** | | | |
| APH41 sdn 4d | 2,929 | 15,115 | 47,911 |
| **Prowler (wb 113.0)** | | | |
| RPS27 conv rdstr 2d | 2,838 | 39,300 | 2,868 |

| 1999 Engines | bore × stroke | bhp | availability |
|---|---|---|---|
| I-4, 121.8 | 3.44 × 3.27 | 132 | S-Neon, Breeze |
| I-4, 121.8 | 3.44 × 3.27 | 150 | O-Neon (dohc) |
| I-4, 148.0 | 3.44 × 3.98 | 150 | O-Breeze |
| V-6, 215.0 | 3.78 × 3.19 | 253 | S-Prowler |

*Calendar-year production.

## 2000

| Neon (wb 105.0) | Wght | Price | Prod* |
|---|---|---|---|
| LPH41 sdn 4d | 2,559 | 12,490 | 43,181 |
| **Breeze (wb 108.0)** | | | |
| APH41 sdn 4d | 2,945 | 16,080 | 2,030 |
| **Prowler (wb 113.0)** | | | |
| RPS27 conv rdstr 2d | 2,838 | 42,800 | 2,890 |

| 1998 Engines | bore × stroke | bhp | availability |
|---|---|---|---|
| I-4, 121.8 | 3.44 × 3.27 | 132 | S-Neon, Breeze |
| I-4, 148.0 | 3.44 × 3.98 | 150 | O-Breeze |
| V-6, 215.0 | 3.78 × 3.19 | 253 | S-Prowler |

*Calendar-year production

## 2001

| Neon (wb 105.0) | Wght | Price | Prod* |
|---|---|---|---|
| LPH41 sdn 4d | 2,559 | 12,715 | 21,600 |
| **Prowler (wb 113.0)** | | | |
| RPS27 conv rdstr 2d | 2,838 | 44,225 | 3,002 |

| 2001 Engines | bore × stroke | bhp | availability |
|---|---|---|---|
| I-4, 121.8 | 3.44 × 3.27 | 132 | S-Neon |
| I-4, 121.8 | 3.44 × 3.27 | 150 | O-Neon (dohc) |
| V-6, 215.0 | 3.78 × 3.19 | 253 | S-Prowler |

*Calendar-year production.

# Pontiac

Of the four "companion" makes introduced by General Motors in the 1920s, Pontiac was the only one to survive past 1940. Yet its future was far from certain in the early Depression years. The first Pontiac, the 1926 Six, quickly invigorated the popularity of its Oakland parent, pushing combined sales beyond 250,000 within three years. But sales plummeted with the Great Crash, as elsewhere in Detroit, and Oakland was ditched after 1931 and just 13,408 cars. Pontiac bottomed out in 1932 at a bit over 45,000.

What saved Pontiac was the calm, confident policies of GM president Alfred P. Sloan, who combined Pontiac's manufacturing with Chevrolet's in early 1932, thus saving vast sums in tooling costs through increased sharing of bodies, chassis, and other major components. At the same time he merged Buick, Oldsmobile, and Pontiac sales operations, requiring dealers for each make to sell the other two as well—albiet usually unwillingly. These belt-tightening measures continued through mid-1933, effectively reducing GM to three divisions: Cadillac, Chevrolet, and B-O-P.

The well-styled 1933 Eight turned Pontiac around completely, with production that model year recovering to more than 90,000. By 1937, the division was back over 200,000, and Pontiac went on to rank among the top five or six Detroit producers well into the '50s. A group of highly competent people contributed mightily to this resurgence. Among the most notable: former Ford executive William S. "Big Bill" Knudsen, division general manager in 1932-33 and GM president in 1937-40; chief engineer Benjamin H. Anibal, father of the Pontiac eight; and division design chief Franklin Q. Hershey, creator of the handsome 1933 and subsequent models.

Pontiac's 1930-31 cars were virtually unchanged mechanically from the popular 1929 "Big Six" models, retaining an orthodox inline L-head engine with 200 cubic inches and 60 horsepower. Offerings comprised the usual open and closed styles on a 110-inch wheelbase (upped two inches for '31) spread over a $665-$785 price range. Sedans and coupes sold best. For 1932, the rough-running V-8 Oakland became a 117-inch-wheelbase Pontiac, but met with no more success: outsold more than 6-to-1 by "The Chief of the Sixes" on a new 114-inch chassis.

Wheelbase increased to 115 inches for 1933, when Anibal's new straight-eight arrived in a slimmer model group down-priced to the $585-$695 area. Though smaller at 223.4 cid, the inline eight was much smoother than the 85-bhp 251-cid Oakland V-8, and thus far more salable. Horsepower climbed for 1934 from 77 to 84, then to 87 with a bored-out 232 replacement for 1936. The straight-eight was further enlarged for '37, and would continue at that 249-cid size through 1949. A highly reliable engine, it would remain a Pontiac staple until the division's first modern high-compression V-8 of 1955.

Pontiac styling followed industry trends in these years. The 1930-32s were boxy and undistinguished, but the transitional '33s and the more fully streamlined '34s were among the prettiest medium-price cars of the era. The latter jumped to a new 117.5-inch chassis and boasted a notable innovation in GM's "Knee-Action" independent front suspension. This was featured on 1934 Chevrolets as well, but components were not interchangeable between the two models.

Many other parts were shared by then, thanks to Sloan's cor-

**1930 Series 6-29A Big Six sport roadster**

**1933 Series 601 Economy Eight two-door sedan**

**1931 Series 401 Fine Six two-door sedan**

**1934 Series 603 Eight 2/4-passenger sport coupe**

porate reorganization, yet the 1933-34 Pontiacs looked unique. Credit Hershey and chief body engineer Roy Milner. Hershey convinced GM styling director Harley Earl of the need for more-streamlined Pontiacs, and accordingly designed a Bentley-type radiator and skirted front fenders with horizontal "speed streaks." Milner gave open models (including Pontiac's last roadsters in '33) a smooth deck and beltline moldings different from Chevrolet's. With this, Knee-Action, and Anibal's straight-eight, the Pontiac Eight was a pleasing package. Though it couldn't quite keep pace with a Ford V-8 or Hudson Terraplane, it didn't lag by much. Pontiac's future was now secure.

After two years of nothing but eight-cylinder cars, and with the market still sluggish, Pontiac reinstated sixes for 1935: Standard and DeLuxe on a 112-inch wheelbase. Sized at 208 cid, their "new" six was really just a bigger-bore version of the old 200. Surprisingly, it made only four fewer horsepower than that year's eight: 80 in all. Standard Sixes cost about $100 less than comparable Eights, which was a lot in those days, and for the rest of the decade they outsold the senior models by a wide margin. Eights were demoted to a slightly shorter 116.6-inch chassis for '35, and all Pontiacs boasted GM's new all-steel "Turret Top" construction that eliminated traditional fabric roof inserts.

"Trunkback" sedans with integral luggage compartments had appeared for 1934. These returned for '35, but bodies were entirely new. Styling was new also, by now of the rounded "potato" school. Pontiac gained added distinction with "Silver Streak" trim, bright-metal bands running forward from the cowl, over the hood, and down the front of the radiator. This has been variously credited to Hershey, "Big Bill" Knudsen, and a young designer named Virgil Exner, who would figure in early-postwar Studebakers and Chrysler's mid-'50s "Forward Look." No matter: Silver Streaks made Pontiacs unmistakable, and would continue as a make hallmark for the next 20 years.

After a mostly stand-pat 1936, Pontiac issued new styling for a trimmer 1937 line of DeLuxe Sixes and Eights on the GM "B" body. Respective wheelbases lengthened five and six inches, which made for better proportions, and a racy reshaped nose recalled the late Auburn Speedster, but the vertical streaks overlaid a more massive wrapped radiator, yielding a rather busy "face." A bore-and-stroke job swelled the six to 222.7 cid, where it would stay through 1940; horsepower stood at 85. The eight was stroked to achieve its aforementioned 249 cid, good for 100 bhp.

After five years of mostly steady gains, sales eased to just over 97,000 in recessionary 1938, pushing Pontiac from fifth to sixth behind Dodge. A four-door station wagon debuted in the DeLuxe Six series. Ads bubbled about all models' "New Silver Streak Beauty," but that was no more than a facelift consisting mainly of a barrellike radiator with thick horizontal bars and

**1935 Series 605 Eight touring sedan**

**1936 Series 6BA DeLuxe Silver Streak Six cabriolet**

**1937 Series 8CA DeLuxe Eight four-door touring sedan**

**1938 Series 6DA DeLuxe Six two-door touring sedan**

**1939 Series 6EB DeLuxe Six four-door touring sedan**

**1940 Series 29HB Torpedo Eight four-door sedan**

# Pontiac

vertical instead of horizontal hood vents.

The rebodied '39s were prettier, with wider "pontoon" fenders, reduced overall height, larger glass areas, and smaller pod-style headlamps well inboard of the front-fender crowns. Pontiac's face remained a bit confused, however, as Harley Earl applied his favored "catwalk" vertical trim between the fenders and a radiator bearing four groups of horizontal chrome bands overlaid with Silver Streaks. Still, there was no mistaking Pontiac for Chevrolet.

Rumble-seat styles and four-door convertibles were absent for '39, but there was one more series. Anchoring the line was the 115-inch-wheelbase Quality Six. It shared bodies with Chevrolet and came as coupes, sedans, and a wood-body wagon in the $760-$990 range. Some $55 more bought the same models (except the wagon) in new DeLuxe 120 guise: a six-cylinder version of that year's 120-inch-wheelbase DeLuxe Eight. Both DeLuxe lines included a convertible. As ever, Pontiac's six was thrifty and reliable, its eight a bit thirstier but more-refined and potent enough. One English magazine opined that a Pontiac Eight "might be borne along by the wind" because it was so impressively quiet and smooth. Depression gloom was lifting, though only because American industry was gearing up for anticipated war production. Still, Pontiac moved a creditable 144,000 cars in the improving 1939 economy to retain sixth behind Chevy, Ford, Plymouth, Buick, and Dodge.

Series expanded to four for 1940: Special and DeLuxe Sixes and DeLuxe and Torpedo Eights. All listed four-passenger coupes and four-door sedans; Special and the DeLuxes added a business coupe and two-door sedan. There were also DeLuxe "cabriolet" convertibles and a Special wagon. All wore a heavy facelift announced by a more-coherent face with a painted prow, still Silver Streaked, dividing a lower-profile horizontal-bar grille. Also in evidence were wider front fenders with fully integrated sealed-beam headlamps. Wheelbase extended to 117 inches for Special; DeLuxes returned at 120. Smoothest of all were the new Torpedo coupe and sedan on a 122-inch chassis. Sixes gained two horsepower via light engine modifications. Volume moved up substantially, reaching 217,000 for the model year.

A corporatewide restyle for 1941 gave Pontiacs higher, wider, crisper fenders embellished with additional Silver Streaks, plus a near full-width horizontal-bar grille with prominent center bulge. Running boards were newly concealed via flared door bottoms (except on wagons). Pontiac's six took the form it would retain through 1954, being bored out to 239.2 cid for 90 bhp. The veteran straight-eight was tweaked to 103 bhp in 1940, where it would remain through '47.

Series now numbered six, all called Torpedo: six- and eight-cylinder DeLuxe, Streamliner, and Custom. DeLuxes, which garnered 155,000 sales, shared a new 119-inch-wheelbase GM A-body platform with Chevrolet and thus offered the most body styles. Among them was the attractive midseason Metropolitan

**1941 Series 29JC Custom Torpedo Eight four-door sedan**

**1941 Custom Torpedo Eight station wagon**

**1942 Series 27KA Torpedo Eight four-door sedan**

**1946 Streamliner Eight four-door sedan**

**1947 Streamliner Eight sedan coupe**

**1948 Torpedo Eight DeLuxe convertible coupe**

# Pontiac

1949 Chieftain Eight DeLuxe convertible coupe

1949 Chieftain Eight DeLuxe four-door sedan

1950 Streamliner Eight DeLuxe sedan coupe fastback

1950 Chieftan Eight DeLuxe convertible coupe

1951 Chieftain Eight DeLuxe Catalina hardtop coupe

sedan patterned after the previous four-door Torpedo, with "formal" closed rear-roof quarters. Streamliners and Customs used the same 122-inch B-body as junior Buicks and Oldsmobiles, and included new fastback four-door sedans and two-door "sedan coupes." Convertibles, again DeLuxes, had a top without rear side windows, a design that recalled certain Packards but made for awful top-up visibility.

Ever the next step up from Chevy on the GM price/prestige ladder, Pontiac was less luxurious than a Buick or Olds but carefully built to very competitive prices. Its cheapest model cost just $783 in 1940 and only $828 in '41; the costliest was the $1250 Custom Torpedo Eight station wagon of 1941.

After record volume of more than 330,000, Pontiac built about 83,500 of its heavily facelifted '42s, all but 15,400 in the closing months of 1941. Styling again followed GM trends: a gaudy grille, longer front fenders swept back into the front doors, and rounded "drop-off" rear fenders. Series were reduced to four: 122-inch Streamliner and 119-inch Torpedo, each offered as a Six and Eight. The '41 Streamliners had been divided into standard and Super submodels. The '42s came in standard and Chieftain guise, each offering fastback "sedan coupe," fastback four-door sedan, and "woody" wagon. Chieftains cost $50 more than standards, which ran slightly above corresponding Torpedos. Eights delivered for only $25 more than Sixes, yet production split about 50/50.

Like most other makes, Pontiac issued warmed-over '42 models for 1946-48, but stylists made each succeeding version a little different. The '46s, which began streaming from Pontiac, Michigan, in September 1945, had a big bell-shaped grille of vertical and horizontal bars. The grille was simplified for '47, then became busier again on the '48s, which adopted round taillights and were the first Pontiacs to carry Silver Streak nameplates.

Otherwise, the 1946-47 Pontiacs were entirely prewar in design and specifications. A three-speed manual remained the only transmission available. Chieftain submodels did not return, though other prewar models did. Eights cost about $30 more than Sixes for 1946, and postwar inflation pushed all prices steadily upward through '48, when the spread reached $1500-$2500. A DeLuxe Torpedo ragtop bowed for 1947 at $1853 with the six, $1900 with the eight.

Though still basically '42s, the '48 Pontiacs had some interesting distinctions. A DeLuxe trim option for most models included chrome fender moldings, gravel guards, wheel discs (except on wagons), and other embellishments for $78-$90. Also, the eight was inexplicably uprated by one bhp. But the big news that year was the introduction of Hydra-Matic Drive as a $185 option. This was a key factor in boosting Pontiac's model-year volume to near 235,500 because it so well-suited the eight-cylinder models that buyers increasingly preferred. Indeed, Eights outsold Sixes for the first time in 1947, and were far ahead for '48, when Hydra-Matic was ordered on 64 percent of Sixes but 77 percent of Eights.

This activity suggested that Pontiac would grow from a "big Chevy" into a lusher medium-price car—and so it did. Along the way, Pontiacs were transformed from ho-hum to hot.

But this was still some years off when Pontiac unwrapped its 1949 models, which fared quite well in GM's first postwar redesign. All-new A-bodies, now on a single 120-inch wheelbase, were attractively styled under Harley Earl's ever-watchful eye. Highlights began with a lower full-width grille bisected by a modest single horizontal bar above little vertical teeth. Silver Streaks still adorned hood and rear deck, but front fenders were now flush with the bodysides and the pontoon rear fenders snugged in closer. Body types divided between Chieftain and Streamliner, the latter with fastback rather than notchback styles, plus four-door wagons. Exclusive to Chieftain were a

# Pontiac

business coupe, long-deck sedan coupe (or club coupe), and convertible. Both lines offered the usual six- or eight-cylinder power and standard or DeLuxe trim, except the DeLuxe-only convertible.

DeLuxes wore extra chrome headlamp rings, side moldings, fender gravel guards, and full wheel covers. Newly optional high-compression heads lofted the six to 93 bhp and the eight to 106. Overall performance was little changed, as the '49s weighed a bit more than the '48s.

Continuing postwar inflation pushed prices considerably higher for 1949. The Chieftain DeLuxe Eight convertible jumped by $134; the woody wagon cost more than $2600. As at Chevrolet, the Pontiac wagon switched from part-structural wood to more-practical all-steel construction at mid-'49, though there was no change in price and little change in appearance. Despite the heftier price tags, model-year volume rose to nearly 305,000, the second-highest total in Pontiac history.

Except for larger, taller grille teeth and reshuffled trim, the 1950 models were predictably much like the '49s. However, the long-running eight was bored to 268.4 cid, good for 108 bhp standard or 113 with high-compression head. Chieftain gained an important new body style in Pontiac's first "hardtop-convertible." Called Catalina and sold in DeLuxe or new Super DeLuxe trim, it accounted for 42,305 sales, nine percent of the division's total model-year volume. As in past years, an illuminated countenance of Chief Pontiac continued as a hood mas-

**1952 Chieftain Eight DeLuxe convertible coupe**

**1954 Star Chief Custom four-door sedan**

**1952 Chieftain Eight DeLuxe four-door station wagon**

**1955 Star Chief convertible coupe**

**1953 Chieftain Eight DeLuxe convertible coupe**

**1955 Star Chief Custom Catalina hardtop coupe**

**1954 Star Chief Custom Catalina hardtop coupe**

**1955 Star Chief Custom Safari two-door station wagon**

cot; like other such devices of the day, it glowed when the headlights were on. Production rose again, smashing the 1941 record at more than 446,000. Still, Pontiac ran fifth overall, as it had since '48, and would not finish higher until 1959.

Volume sank to about 370,000 for 1951 as all Detroit began feeling the effects of the Korean War, yet that was Pontiac's second-best total ever. Fastbacks were fading from favor, so the Streamliner four-door was dropped, soon followed by the sedan coupe. The most noticeable change was a "gullwing" grille bar below a prominent medallion. Engines were tweaked: the six to 96/100 bhp, the eight to 116/120 bhp.

A busier grille and new DeLuxe side trim were the main alterations for 1952. Horsepower crept up, too. Korean War restrictions and a nationwide steel strike limited model-year output to 271,000.

A major reskin of the '49 A-body and a two-inch longer wheelbase gave 1953's new all-Chieftain line a more "important" look. Once more, buying patterns had prompted these and other changes. Catalina hardtops, for example, now accounted for nearly 20 percent of sales, and automatic transmission installations had climbed to 75 percent. The '53s were shinier and larger in most every dimension. Chief features of the new look were kicked-up rear fenders, a lower grille, more-prominent bumpers, and a one-piece windshield.

Newly optional power steering made the '53s easier to park; more horsepower made them faster. The six now delivered 115 bhp with manual transmission or 118 with Hydra-Matic; corresponding eight-cylinder outputs were 118/122. A lowish rear axle ratio of 3.08:1 was specified for smooth top-gear performance with Hydra-Matic. A mid-1953 fire in the Hydra-Matic plant hampered supplies, however, so 18,499 Pontiacs were fitted with Chevrolet Powerglide in 1953-54. Overall production remained strong at nearly 419,000.

Nineteen fifty-four brought a minor facelift of 1953's major one. Rearranged side moldings and a narrow oval in the central grille bar were the main changes. The big news was Star Chief, a top-line eight-cylinder hardtop, convertible, and four-door sedan on a new 124-inch chassis. These were the plushest Pontiacs yet—and the priciest ($2300-$2600), another sign of the make's steady push upmarket. Star Chiefs sold well, but Pontiac's total volume slipped to just below 288,000, suggesting it was time for something different.

The all-new '55s were precisely that. Among their claimed 109 new features were fully up-to-date styling, an improved chassis, and—the really hot item—a modern overhead-valve V-8, Pontiac's first. Dubbed "Strato-Streak," the new engine bowed at 287.2 cid, but could grow much larger and soon did. Standard horsepower was 173/180 (manual/automatic); an optional four-barrel carburetor yielded an even 200. A strong oversquare design with five main bearings, the Strato-Streak was somewhat related to Chevy's all-new 1955 "Turbo-Fire" V-8. Though not quite as advanced, it would serve Pontiac admirably for more than a quarter-century.

As on other '55 GM cars, Pontiac styling was rather boxy but quite trendy, especially the wrapped "Panoramic" windshield taken from recent Harley Earl showmobiles. Equally *au courant* were cowl ventilation; bright solid colors and two-tones; and a longer, lower look despite unchanged wheelbases. A blunt face was the one dubious aspect. As before, Pontiac shared its A-body with Chevrolet, but maintained distinct wheelbases. The shorter one again carried two Chieftain lines: low-priced "860" and midrange "870" sedans and wagons, plus an "870" Catalina hardtop. Star Chief returned on its extended chassis with base-trim convertible and four-door sedan and a Custom sedan and Catalina.

Mounting the Chieftain chassis but officially a Star Chief was

1956 Star Chief DeLuxe convertible coupe

1957 Star Chief convertible coupe

1957 Bonneville convertible coupe

1957 Star Chief Custom Safari "Transcontinental" wagon

an exotic new wagon, the Custom Safari, a "hardtop-style" two-door based on Chevy's new '55 Nomad. Chevy designer Carl Renner recalled that "when Pontiac saw [the Nomad] they felt they could do something with it.... Management wanted it for the Pontiac line, so it worked out." Like Nomad, the original '55 Safari continued with successive facelifts only through 1957, after which both names were applied to conventional four-door wagons. Two-door Safaris naturally cost more than Nomads—for '55, a stiff $2962—and thus sold in fewer numbers: 3760, followed by 4042 for '56, and a final 1292.

On balance, 1955 was a vintage Pontiac year. Its cars were a solid hit with dealers and public alike, and the division built about 554,000 of them, a new record. But some rough times lay ahead, and Pontiac wouldn't better this figure until 1963, after which it set new records. At least three factors figured in the interim slump. Buick's Special and the base Olds 88 were priced more aggressively; demand for lower-medium cars shrank as import sales expanded in the late '50s; and the 1956-58 Pontiacs weren't particularly exciting, though they were competitive in most ways and faster than ever.

The '56s were mildly restyled, and four-door Catalina hardtops arrived in each series. Styling was less distinctive—tester

# Pontiac

1958 Bonneville Custom convertible coupe

1958 Bonneville Custom hardotp coupe

1959 Star Chief Vista hardtop sedan

1959 Catalina Vista hardtop sedan

1960 Bonneville Custom Safari four-door station wagon

1961 Bonneville convertible coupe

1961 Bonneville Vista hardtop sedan

1961 Tempest sport coupe

Tom McCahill said the '56 looked like "it was born on its nose"—and the ride was not so easy. A bore job took the V-8 to 316.6 cid, but didn't yield much more power: only up to 205 for Chieftains and 227 bhp for Star Chiefs (though at midyear, a 285-bhp option was offered). Pontiac settled for '56 volume that was well down on record-shattering '55, declining to 405,500 and a sixth-place industry finish.

July 1956 ushered in a new Pontiac general manager who would prove crucial to the make's near-term fortunes. This was Semon E. "Bunkie" Knudsen, son of '30s division chief "Big Bill" and the youngest leader in Pontiac history. GM brass told Bunkie to do what he could with the existing design for '57, and he hustled, instituting longer rear springs in rubber shackles, 14-inch wheels and tires (ousting 15-inchers), pedal parking brake, and a V-8 stroked to 347 cid for 227-290 bhp. Stylewise, the grille became a massive bucktooth affair; two-toning switched from 1955-56's half-car pattern to bodyside sweep-spears; and Bunkie did the unthinkable by banishing Silver Streak trim as old-hat (it did, after all, hark to his dad's day). Series were regrouped into low-end Chieftain and new mid-price Super Chief on the shorter chassis and Star Chief on the longer 124-inch wheelbase.

Where Bunkie really made his mark was the Bonneville, a flashy Star Chief-based convertible launched in mid-'57. Packing 310 bhp via a bore job (to 370 cid), fuel injection, and aggressive cam, this $5782 limited edition was the costliest Pontiac yet. Unfortunately, a hefty curb weight of nearly 4300 pounds dulled performance somewhat. Still it was no slouch: A Bonnie was timed at 18 seconds in the quarter-mile.

Because it was basically a promotional piece for dealers, the '57 Bonneville saw only 630 copies. But it gave Pontiac a whole new performance image even as the Auto Manufacturers Association came down against factory-sponsored racing. (Several '57 "Ponchos" did run well in NASCAR, but they were strictly private entries.) Yet the lack of race wins didn't hamper sales. While Chevy, Olds, and Buick all lost sales to rival 1957 Chrysler products, Pontiac built some 333,500 cars to move within 51,000 units of fifth-place Olds.

Expansive new styling should have helped the '58s sell even better, but a sharp national recession held demand to some 217,000. Unlike some '58 GM cars, Pontiac was reasonably tasteful, with a simple mesh grille, quad headlights, and side-

# Pontiac

1962 Tempest Le Mans convertible coupe

1962 Grand Prix sport coupe hardtop

1963 Bonneville convertible coupe

1962 Catalina Vista hardtop sedan

1963 Grand Prix sport coupe hardtop

spears made wider and concave toward the rear. Bodies were lower but not much longer or wider; wheelbases were unchanged. Offerings now included no fewer than seven Catalina hardtops with two or four doors. Bonneville became a regular series, and sold 12,240 convertibles and hardtop coupes. The 370 V-8 was now standard across the board, delivering 240 bhp in stickshift Chieftains/Super Chiefs, and up to 285 in Hydra-Matic Star Chiefs and Bonnevilles. Optional across the board were a 300-bhp triple-carb "Tri-Power" unit and a 310-bhp "fuelie."

Then came the first Pontiacs to fully reflect Bunkie's boldness. The '59s were not just startlingly new; they established the performance pattern that would carry Pontiac to undreamed-of glory in the 1960s. Crisp styling on a brand-new body introduced the split-grille theme that remains a Pontiac hallmark to this day, plus modest twin-fin rear fenders and minimal side trim. Wheelbases were again unchanged, but the wheels spread farther apart on a new "Wide-Track" chassis that made Pontiacs among the most-roadable cars in America.

The V-8 was again enlarged, the cube count rising to 389, a number destined for greatness. Horsepower ranged from 345 with Tri-Power down to 245. There was also a detuned 215-bhp "Tempest 420E" for economy-minded buyers, capable of up to 20 mpg. Ridding Pontiac of "that Indian concept" was still part of Bunkie's plan, so Chieftain and Super Chief gave way to a new Catalina line on the shorter wheelbase; Bonneville again shared the longer chassis with Star Chief, which would hang on a good long while. Bonneville, bolstered by new Safari wagons and Vista hardtop sedans, garnered some 82,000 sales. Total volume for the model year rose to near 383,000, boosting Pontiac into fourth place for the first time.

Pontiac show cars of the '50s were always interesting and often predictive. The smooth 1954 Strato Streak previewed the pillarless four-doors of '56. Also shown in '54 was the first Bonneville, a Corvette-like two-seater with canopy-type cockpit on a 100-inch wheelbase. Both cars carried straight eights. The 1955 Strato Star was a two-door four-seat hardtop forecasting 1956 styling. Wildest of all was the 1956 Club de Mer, with "twin-pod" seating and dual-bubble windshields. Standing only 38.4 inches high, its aluminum body was painted Cerulean blue, one of Harley Earl's favorite colors.

From mostly "also-ran" in the '50s, Pontiac became a consistent front-runner in the '60s, finishing third in the industry race every year from 1962 to 1970. Much of this was owed to three enthusiastic general managers: Knudsen through 1961, then Elliot M. "Pete" Estes (GM president in 1974-81), and finally John Z. DeLorean in 1965-69. These and numerous other "car guys" made Pontiac synonymous with high performance, great looks, superb roadability, innovation, and tasteful, comfortable luxury. No wonder Pontiac did so well.

A minor exception to that was the compact 1961-63 Tempest, significant for having GM's first postwar four-cylinder engine, a flexible driveshaft, and a rear transaxle (transmission in unit with the differential) allied to independent link-type suspension. One buff magazine called Tempest "a prototype of the American car for the '60s," but no other U.S. make has yet copied its radical driveline (though Porsche used something similar on its 928 of 1977). The 1961-63 Tempests were fairly popular, but Pontiac felt a more-orthodox design would sell far better. This appeared for 1964, and it did. At that point, the original Tempest's 195-cid four, basically half a 389 V-8, was abandoned for an inline six—sensibly cost-effective, but hardly daring.

Like a speedometer cable, the 1961-63 Tempest's "rope" driveshaft carried rotary motion through a gentle curve: a long bar bent slightly beneath the floor. Thin, but lightly stressed within

# Pontiac

a steel case, it was mounted on bearings and was permanently lubed. The slight sag reduced the height of the transmission tunnel in front, though not in back; it also eliminated the need for U-joints and permitted softer engine mounts for better interior isolation. The rear transaxle, a first for Detroit if not the world, made Tempest less nose-heavy than conventional cousins Olds F-85 and Buick Special. But though its independent rear suspension was ostensibly superior, it tended to induce sudden oversteer that could be alarming, especially on wet roads. Still, the Tempest handled well—more so than Chevy's aft-engine Corvair, even though both used tricky rear swing axles.

The initial 112-inch-wheelbase Tempests used a unitized Y-body structure adapted from the first Corvairs, as did the F-85 and Special. Its standard slant-four teamed with manual and automatic transaxles, and was offered in tunes to suit regular or premium gas. By 1963, horsepower was up to 115-166 (from 110/130 in '61). Optionally available for 1961-62 was the Special's 215-cid aluminum V-8 with 155/185 bhp. This gave way for '63 to a debored 326-cid version of the Pontiac 389 packing 260 bhp. So equipped, any Tempest was able to scale 0-60 mph in 9.5 seconds and reach 115 mph.

Tempest bowed as a single series with standard- and Custom-trim four-door notchback sedans and four-door Safari wagons with one-piece rear "liftgate." Coupes arrived at midseason with bench- or bucket-seat interiors, the latter christened LeMans. Custom and LeMans convertibles were added for '62 and proved quite popular, prompting a separate LeMans series for '63. Styling didn't change much. A twin-oval grille was used for '61, a full-width three-section affair for '62, a different split grille and squarer body lines for '63. Prices also didn't change much, with most models in the $2200-$2500 region.

For 1964, GM lengthened the B-O-P compacts to a 115-inch wheelbase, which made them intermediates. Pontiac's new Tempest wore taut, "geometric" lines on the resulting new A-body shared with Chevrolet's new Chevelle, the Olds F-85/Cutlass, and Buick's Special/Skylark. But the real excitement came with the midseason debut of the Tempest GTO, the first "muscle car." That nickname was apt, because with the right options, a GTO packed unprecedented performance for a six-passenger automobile.

Most GTOs were "built" from the order form. For 1964, you started with a Tempest coupe, hardtop coupe, or convertible, then checked off the GTO option: floorshift, 325-horse 389, quick steering, stiff shocks, dual exhaust, and premium tires, all for about $300. From there you ad-libbed: four-speed gearbox ($188); metallic brake linings, heavy-duty radiator, and limited-slip differential ($75 the lot); 348-bhp 389 ($115). Then all you needed was a lead foot and lots of gas.

Sports-car purists took umbrage at Pontiac's use of GTO—for gran turismo omologato, a hallowed Italian term for an approved production-based racing car—but the outspoken *Car and Driver* bravely answered them by comparing Pontiac's GTO with Ferrari's GTO. A good Pontiac, they said, would trim the Ferrari in a drag race and lose on a road course. But "with the addition of NASCAR road racing suspension, the Pontiac will take the measure of any Ferrari other than prototype racing cars. . . . The Ferrari costs $20,000. With every conceivable option on a GTO, it would be difficult to spend more than $3800. That's a bargain."

The successful LeMans/Tempest formula saw relatively little change through 1967. Vertical headlights, crisper styling, and three-inch-longer bodies arrived for '65. The '66s had smoother contours, including hopped-up "Coke-bottle" rear fenders and, on coupes and hardtops, "flying buttresses" astride recessed backlights. Standard for the 1967 GTO was a new 400-cid exten-

1963 Tempest Le Mans convertible coupe

1964 Catalina 2+2 sport coupe hardtop

1964 Bonneville convertible coupe

1964 Grand Prix sport coupe hardtop

1964 Tempest GTO sport coupe

# Pontiac

1965 Tempest Le Mans GTO convertible coupe

1965 Grand Prix sport coupe hardtop

1965 Catalina 2+2 421 sport coupe hardtop

1965 Bonneville convertible coupe

1966 Tempest GTO convertible coupe

1966 Grand Prix sport coupe hardtop

1967 Firebird hardtop coupe

1967 Catalina 2+2 428 sport coupe hardtop

1967 Grand Prix convertible coupe

1967 Tempest GTO hardtop coupe

# Pontiac

1968 Tempest GTO hardtop coupe

1968 Bonneville convertible coupe

1969 Tempest GTO hardtop coupe with Ram Air IV

1969 Grand Prix Model J hardtop coupe

1969 Firebird Trans Am hardtop coupe

sion of the 389 pumping out 335 bhp; 360 bhp was optional via "Ram-Air," a functional hood scoop.

For 1968 came a new A-body with dual wheelbases—116 inches on four-doors, 112 on two-doors—plus a full redesign that continued to display big-Pontiac design elements such as a large bumper/grille and, on hardtop coupes, more-rakish rooflines with flush rear windows. GTO also featured a neatly integrated new energy-absorbing front bumper covered in color-keyed Endura plastic that resisted dings and dents. One TV commercial pointed out its virtues by showing a group of white-coated Pontiac "engineers" happily hammering the proboscis to absolutely no ill effect.

The midsize Pontiacs continued in this basic form through 1972. Among the mildly facelifted '69s was a hotter GTO: "The Judge," actually an option package with colorful striping, loud paint, a 366-bhp Ram-Air V-8, and three-speed manual gearbox with Hurst floorshift. The 1970s received clumsier front ends, bigger rear bumpers, and pronounced longitudinal bodyside bulges above the wheel openings. The result was a heavier-looking Tempest, GTO, LeMans, and LeMans Sport. Collectors have since tended to prefer the tidier 1964-69 models.

The base engine on 1964-65 Tempests was a 215-cid inline six rated at 140 bhp. For 1966 came a surprising replacement engine, a European-style overhead-cam six developed by Pontiac. Sized at 230 cid, it delivered 165 standard bhp or 207 in "Sprint" guise (via Rochester Quadra-Jet carburetor, hotter valve timing, and double valve springs). The crankshaft had seven main bearings. The camshaft was driven by a fiberglass-reinforced notched belt rather than the usual chain or gears.

With that, the '66 Tempest Sprint was a satisfying performer, if hardly in the GTO's league. The typical example could do 0-60 in 10 seconds and reach 115 mph. With options like bucket seats, console, and four-on-the-floor, the clean-lined Sprint had the look and feel of a European grand-touring machine. A longer stroke took the ohc engine to 250 cid for 1968, good for 175 bhp or, in Sprint trim, 215 bhp (230 bhp for '69). Sadly, it proved less than reliable and, echoing the Tempest four before it, departed after 1969 in favor of a conventional overhead-valve Chevy engine of the same displacement.

With Pontiac's performance image secure by middecade, division managers knew their Firebird "ponycar" had to be special—especially as it used the same 108.1-inch-wheelbase F-body structure as Chevrolet's new-for-'67 Camaro. But the Firebird was special, sporting a divided grille of the sort now expected on Pontiacs, and offering a "400" model with a 325-bhp V-8 of that size. The base-tune ohc six was initially standard; the optional Sprint version made for a sprightly, yet economical, Firebird Sprint.

Making its debut about five months behind Camaro, Firebird wasn't modified much for 1968. A change of engines made the 326 model a 350, and side-marker lights were added in accordance with new government decree. The '69s were restyled below the belt and gained a host of federally ordered safety items. Convertibles continued until "1970½," when an all-new coupe-only second generation was introduced.

The hottest and most-memorable early Firebird was the '69 Trans Am, a $725 option package announced in March. It was loosely inspired by the Firebirds then half-heartedly contesting the Sports Car Club of America's Trans-American road-racing series. Special badges, white paint, twin blue dorsal racing stripes, and a decklid spoiler identified it. A 335-bhp Ram Air III 400 gave great performance, and a heavily fortified chassis and brakes made for superb roadability. Only 697 of the '69s were built, including a mere eight convertibles and just nine cars with the optional 345-bhp "Ram Air IV" engine. But the T/A was destined for far greater sales very soon.

Meantime, Pontiac was building some of the best-looking, best-handling standard cars in all of '60s Detroit. The public loved them. Sales were both strong and consistent, starting at about 396,000 for 1960 and reaching near half a million by '65.

Pontiac began the decade with facelifted versions of the successful "Wide Track" '59s, bearing high "twin-tube" taillamps and a vee'd, full-width horizontal-bar grille. A fourth series was added that year, the Catalina-based Ventura, a hardtop coupe and Vista hardtop sedan priced just below Star Chief at around $3000. Ventura was dropped for '62 in favor of the bucket-seat Grand Prix, an elegantly tailored $3500 hardtop coupe, also on the Catalina chassis. GP sales flirted with the 73,000 mark in 1963, then gradually eased off through '68 with the exception of a tiny spike in 1967, when a convertible was added. Offered only that year, the ragtop is now a minor collector's item, as only 5856 were built.

Big-Pontiac styling kept improving, at least through '66, thanks to the efforts of William L. Mitchell, who'd replaced the legendary Harley Earl as GM design chief back in 1958. Pontiac's distinctive split grille returned to stay for 1961, along with crisp new styling on shorter wheelbases: 119 inches for Catalina/Ventura and all wagons, 123 for Star Chief/Bonneville. Catalina added an inch for '62. Even cleaner machines with stacked quad headlamps and narrow, split grilles were issued for 1963-64. The '65s were well-executed but massive, with a bulging front and billowy bodysides. Wheelbase was lengthened to 121 inches for Catalina/GP/wagons and to 124 for Star Chief/Bonneville. The forceful looks were slightly muted for '66.

Regrettably, the '67s had a heavy look highlighted by bulky, curved rear fenders. The '68 model year brought a huge bumper/grille with a prominent vertical center bulge and a return to horizonal headlamps. The snout was toned down for '69, when another inch was tacked on to wheelbases. The following year brought an upright twin-element grille faintly reminiscent of the '30s, but far less graceful.

Full-size model choices were as consistent as Pontiac sales in these years. Catalinas in all the usual body styles persisted throughout, as did the midrange Star Chief sedan, hardtop sedan, and—from '66—hardtop coupe. The latter three types plus convertible and four-door Safaris made up top-line Bonnevilles. (A four-door sedan joined in 1968.) A bucket-seat "2+2" option package bowed for 1964 on the Catalina convertible and two-door hardtop; it became a distinct series for '66, then vanished after 1967 in the fast-fading market for sporty full-sizers. One change involved Star Chief: It tacked on the name Executive for '66, which then replaced Star Chief through 1970.

Big-Pontiac V-8s were equally consistent in the '60s, with numerous horsepower variations in just four basic sizes—two large and two "small"—all based on the original '55 block. The small ones were a 389 available through 1966 and a bored-out

**1970 GTO "The Judge" hardtop coupe**

**1971 Le Mans T-37 hardtop coupe**

**1970 Grand Prix Model SJ hardtop coupe**

**1971 Firebird Trans Am coupe**

**1970½ Firebird Formula 400 coupe**

**1971 Bonneville hardtop sedan**

# Pontiac

400 from '67. These were base power for all full-size models, and power ranged from 215 to 350, with the latter standard on Grand Prix starting in '67. The larger mills, optional on most models, were a 421 for 1963-66 and a 428 for 1967-69, after which a huge 455 took over. Horsepower peaked at 390 for 1968-69, then began waning with federally mandated emission controls. A mere handful of "Super-Duty" 421s appeared in drag-oriented lightweight Catalinas in 1961. For a few years starting in '62, this engine would become a bit easier to obtain. Output topped 400 bhp.

The 1970s would prove one of Pontiac's most difficult decades. A decision to outproduce and "out-price" Chevy (generally credited to DeLorean) while simultaneously reaching into Buick/Oldsmobile territory led to a startling slip in workmanship. These policies also contributed to a confusing succession of models that left many buyers wondering just what a Pontiac was. Not surprisingly, sales sagged. After falling to fourth in the '71 rankings, Pontiac finished fourth or fifth, usually behind Olds, most every year through 1986. Even Buick was often a threat, closing to within 27,000 units for 1972. By 1980, Pontiac trailed both: Buick by nearly 84,000 and Oldsmobile by more than 140,000.

But not all was gloom. Given the ponycar market's rapid decline after 1969, Firebird was a surprising bright spot, the Trans Am in particular. The brilliant second-generation design of mid-1970 was good enough to last all the way through 1981 with just three styling updates, for 1974, '77, and '79. Through it all, the Trans Am kept Pontiac's "hot car" image simmering—to the point where, as the division later admitted, Trans Am had higher name recognition than Pontiac.

Like Camaro, Firebird almost died after 1972 due to GM's doubts about the future of performance cars, aggravated by a strike that severely cut that year's production. But Pontiac kept the faith and reaped the rewards. While Chevy dropped its hottest Camaro, the Z28, for 1975-76, Pontiac retained the T/A as the most-serious model in the line. As a result, the T/A soon moved from peripheral seller (only 1286 for '72) to become the most-popular Firebird of all (more than 117,000 for '79).

Pontiac also helped Firebird sales by fielding the same four models each year—base coupe, luxury Esprit, roadworthy Formula, and T/A. (Chevy continually fiddled with the Camaro lineup in these years.) Formula and T/A went on a horsepower diet for 1978 in light of corporate average fuel economy mandates (CAFE) that took effect that year, but they never relinquished their V-8s and never failed to deliver lively motoring. An optional turbocharged 301, issued for 1980, had a bit less go than the big-blocks of old, but was somewhat easier on gas.

Higher-than-ever fuel prices were but one legacy of the 1973-74 oil embargo, though gas was becoming costlier well before that. Renewed buyer interest in thrifty compacts—and Pontiac's lack of same—prompted the division to put a different nose on Chevrolet's 111-inch-wheelbase Nova to create the

**1971 Catalina hardtop coupe**

**1972 Grand Prix Model J hardtop coupe**

**1972 Le Mans GTO hardtop coupe**

**1973 Ventura Custom coupe with Sprint package**

**1973 Grand Am SD-455 Colonnade coupe**

**1973 Firebird Esprit coupe**

1973 Le Mans Sport Colonnade coupe with GTO option

1973 Grand Ville convertible coupe

1973 Firebird Trans Am SD-455 coupe

1974 Ventura coupe with GTO package

1974 Le Mans Colonnade coupe with GT package

Ventura II. Launched in March 1971, it evolved parallel with Nova through 1979 (minus the Roman numeral after '72), but always saw lower volume. One interesting difference is that the hallowed GTO became a Ventura variation for 1974—actually a $195 option package for the workaday pillared two-door comprising hood scoop, different grille, chassis enhancements, and standard 350 V-8. Purists moaned, but Pontiac moved 7058 of these pretenders before ringing the curtain down on a great tradition—a year too late.

In line with sister X-body compacts, Ventura adopted a more European look for 1975—and promptly withered on the sales vine. Inept marketing and mediocre build quality were as much to blame as competition from within the Pontiac line and elsewhere. An upmarket version called Phoenix arrived for mid-1977, with plusher interiors and a busier front end; the Ventura name vanished the following year. Unhappily, Phoenix was an also-ran, too, and remained so even after it switched to GM's front-drive X-body for 1980.

Another "lend-lease" deal with Chevrolet produced the subcompact Astre, arriving in the U.S. for 1975 after being marketed in Canada from mid-1973. This was little more than a modestly restyled twin of Chevy's ill-starred Vega, and thus inherited most of its faults. Pontiac varied the model program a bit with base and semisporty SJ hatchbacks and wagons. (A budget S series, which also included a notchback sedan, was added during '75.) There was also a GT package option combining the low-line interior with the SJ's performance and handling. Astres were confined to a single series in 1976-77. A swan-song '77 arrival was Pontiac's then-new 151-cid (2.5-liter) "Iron Duke" four, a nickname chosen partly to counter the horrendous durability reputation of the all-aluminum Vega engine.

Chevy had introduced its sporty Vega-based Monza coupe for 1975, and Pontiac got into this act as well a year later with the Sunbird. But unlike other editions of this corporate H-Special design, the new Sunbird arrived only as a notchback two-door akin to Chevy's Monza Towne Coupe. The 2+2 fastback was added for 1977 as the Sunbird Sport Hatch, followed in '78 by the little three-door wagon from the deceased Astre line. Bolstered by various option groups, including a sporty Formula package, Sunbird eventually became Pontiac's top seller. By then it was getting old, however. It carried on with few changes through 1981; the final cars sold were actually 1980 leftovers.

The story of the larger Pontiacs of the 1970s is about as exciting as rust, which is what many of them quickly did. Basic designs were inevitably shared with sister GM intermediates and standards, but workmanship often seemed half a notch below. By late decade, though, both the LeMans/Grand LeMans and Catalina/Bonneville had evolved into more-sensible, solid, and salable cars much better suited to the times than the aging hulks that Chrysler and Ford still peddled.

Intermediate Pontiacs quickly turned from their assured roadability of the 1960s to an emphasis on luxury and convenience. One bright exception was the Grand Am. Introduced as part of the new 1973 line with "Colonnade" styling, this LeMans-based coupe and sedan was billed as combining Grand Prix luxury with Trans Am performance, hence the name. The idea was largely owed to assistant chief engineer Bill Collins, who'd been heavily involved with the original GTO, and chassis wizard John Seaton. Their aim was to approximate European sedans like the Mercedes 250/280 and the BMW Bavaria at a third to half the money.

While some features strained at mimicry—a Mercedes-like jumbo-hub steering wheel, for instance—the "G/A" was, on balance, one of the most-impressive big Detroiters in a generally dull Detroit decade. But it failed to make a real impression in a market where most buyers looked for either everyday transport

# Pontiac

or as much glitz as their money would buy. Grand Am garnered only some 43,000 sales in its debut year—mainly coupes—then plunged to 17,000 for '74 and only 11,000 or so for '75. To no one's surprise, it subsequently disappeared. Curiously, the name resurfaced on a coupe and sedan in the downsized 1978 LeMans line, but these were nowhere near as special and would prove similarly short-lived, the sedan being dropped after '79, the coupe a year later. But as we'll see, the Grand Am was far from finished.

Rivaling Firebird's '70s success was that of the personal-luxury Grand Prix—in some years Pontiac's best-selling single model. It was reborn for 1969 as a lighter, quicker midsize car on a new 118-inch-wheelbase "A-Special" chassis. Offered with both 400 and 428 (later 455) V-8s, it was a handsome brute, with short-deck notchback roofline and a distinctly Pontiac face ahead of a mile-long hood. Inside was an innovative curved instrument cluster bringing all controls within easy driver reach. Cribbing Model J and SJ nomenclature from the revered Duesenberg was a vain attempt at cachet, but the public applauded this Grand Prix, snapping up nearly 112,500 of the '69s. Sales were healthy through the end of this design generation in 1972, when just under 92,000 were retailed. Styling didn't change much, and although horsepower went down a bit after 1970, big-block performance remained quite good.

Pontiac continued this successful formula through GM's 1973-77 Colonnade intermediates, when the GP went to the same 116-inch wheelbase as Chevy's imitative Monte Carlo. A vertical grille and a roof with a '67 Eldorado-like crease through the backlight set these GPs apart. Interestingly, Grand Prix notched a new all-time sales record for 1977, close to 288,500. The '78, unfortunately, was much more like LeMans, downsized to the same new 108.1-inch platform and looking less distinctive, yet sales weren't vastly affected: some 228,000 for the model year. Clearly, the GP had succeeded in a way that various gussied-up Luxury and Grand LeMans variations couldn't. Without it, Pontiac wouldn't have weathered the ups and downs of the '70s nearly as well.

As the 1980s dawned, Pontiac's troubles were far from over. Workmanship still wasn't all it should have been, and increased model-sharing with Chevrolet had only made Pontiac's confused image even fuzzier. Adding insult to these injuries were the deep national recession and accompanying sharp downturn in auto sales that began in late 1979 when the Shah of Iran was deposed, triggering a second "energy crisis." Pontiac suffered as much as any Detroit make. In two years, division output plunged by nearly a third, to around 620,500 for '81, then slipped below 500,000 two years later—a sorry situation for a make that had averaged better than 700,000 cars a year since the midpoint of the 1960s.

But better times were at hand. Having floundered under four general managers since '69, the division got back on course under William Hoglund, who took over the helm in 1980. Taking

**1974 Catalina coupe**

**1974 Firebird Trans Am coupe**

**1975 Grand Ville Brougham convertible coupe**

**1975 Grand Am Colonnade coupe**

**1975 Grand Le Mans Safari four-door station wagon**

**1976 Firebird Formula coupe**

a cue from history, Hoglund and a bright young team of designers and engineers began steering Pontiac back toward the sort of driver-oriented cars that had been the foundation of its high success in the '60s. Events played right into their hands. The economy recovered, the gas shortage became a gas glut, and the market went crazy again for performance. Proclaiming "We Build Excitement," Pontiac turned the corner, and by 1984 it was solidly back over the half-million mark.

Hoglund left in 1984 to head GM's developing Saturn Division, but Pontiac kept picking up steam under new captain J. Michael Losh. For 1986, it sailed past 750,000 and then, a year later, surpassed a bumbling Olds Division to grab third place for the first time in 17 years. Pontiac repeated the performance for '87. The 1989 tally was an impressive 801,600, nearly 300,000 better than a recovering Buick.

The amazing part of Pontiac's resurgence is that it was managed mainly with compacts, intermediates, and the Firebird. Unlike Buick and Olds, big cars were never significant to Pontiac sales in the '80s. In fact, the division's 1982 lineup had no traditional full-size cars at all.

Catalina and Bonneville had been redesigned for 1977 as part of GM's first-wave downsizing program, but didn't sell as well as their B-body cousins at Buick, Olds, and Chevy. Believing buyers were ready to foresake even these smaller biggies in another fuel crunch, Pontiac canceled the line after '81 and substituted a restyled LeMans sedan and wagon called Bonneville Model G (the letter denoting a redesignated A-body platform). But what looked like a smart idea in 1980 seemed just bad timing once big-car sales turned up again, so Pontiac decided to revive its B-body during 1983. As there was no longer any production room stateside, U.S. dealers got a slightly modified Canadian version—which had never been dropped—under its north-of-the-border name, Parisienne.

If these moves recalled the great Dodge/Plymouth debacle of 20 years before, they weren't nearly so disastrous. But they weren't that successful, either. Bonneville G peaked at about 82,800 sales in '83, then tailed off to around 41,000 for its final appearance in 1986. Parisienne averaged about 83,000 for 1985-86, after which the sedan departed (the B-body two-door hadn't returned) and annual sales ran below 13,200 for the lone Safari wagon marketed through 1989. Design, engineering, and yearly changes for both these lines virtually duplicated those for counterpart Chevys, the intermediate Malibu and full-size Caprice/Impala.

Another up-north idea was the subcompact T1000, a Chevette clone by way of Pontiac Canada's Acadian model. Announced in April 1981, it immediately attracted 70,000 buyers, then fell to an annual average of 25,000 or so after 1982, when it was called just plain 1000. Black window frames and a prominent arrowhead grille emblem were the main design elements that set it apart from the littlest Chevy. Naturally, the 1000 evolved in parallel with Chevette through 1987, then gave way to a new front-drive LeMans (which is beyond the scope of this book, being a Korean-built sister of a German Opel Kadett). The 1000 was just a token nod to the econocar market and never a big money-spinner.

The second-generation Phoenix was the least popular of GM's four front-drive X-body compacts, likely because the same package was available with more model/trim choices as a Chevy Citation or with more nameplate prestige as a Buick Skylark or Olds Omega. Pontiac tried to make the Phoenix appealing by offering two-door notchback and four-door hatchback sedans in plain, luxury LJ, and sporty SJ trim (the latter two called LE and SE in '84). But nothing seemed to work, and demand fell off rapidly when numerous mechanical bugs began surfacing, with recalls to fix them. Phoenix never sold better

1976 Astre hatchback coupe

1976 Grand Prix coupe

1977 Le Mans Sport Coupe with Can Am package

1977 Catalina coupe

1977 Grand Prix SJ coupe

# Pontiac

1977½ Phoenix four-door sedan

1978 Firebird Trans Am Special Edition coupe

1979 Firebird Trans Am coupe

1979 Sunbird Formula hatchback coupe

1980 Phoenix LJ hatchback sedan

than in its extra-long 1980 debut year: 178,000-plus. Volume dipped below 50,000 for '82 and was under 23,000 by the 1984 finale.

Yet Phoenix was successful in a way, because it spawned a more rational and popular midsize Pontiac, the front-drive 6000. Arriving for the '82 model year, it was closely related to the new A-body Buick Century, Chevy Celebrity, and Oldsmobile Cutlass Ciera, but with crisper, more "important" sheetmetal over the X-car inner structure. Initial offerings comprised base and LE coupe and sedan, but Pontiac went a big step further with the STE (Special Touring Edition). Announced for the 1983 season, this enthusiast-oriented four-door represented a new Pontiac challenge to premium European sports sedans from the likes of Audi, BMW, Mercedes, Saab, and Volvo.

The STE proved itself a surprisingly capable challenger. Quick-ratio steering and a fortified suspension with air-adjustable rear shocks and upgraded wheels and tires made the car supremely roadable. Appointments were tastefully understated, and equipment was generous (including even a leather-bound roadside emergency kit). All it lacked was sparkling acceleration; the mandatory three-speed automatic transaxle strained the 135 horses of the standard high-output, 173-cid Chevy-built V-6. But the STE served notice that Pontiac was not only back to building driver's cars but could compete on a "best-in-class" basis against many comers.

Other 6000s bathed in the STE's glow, and by 1984 this line was Pontiac's best-selling larger car, bolstered that year by the addition of station wagons. Worthy improvements came almost annually: electronic fuel injection for the base 2.5-liter four (throttle-body, 1983) and V-6 (multipoint for all models by 1987); a more-versatile and efficient four-speed automatic for selected models (1986); an S/E sedan and wagon offering much of the STE's sportiness and performance for less money (1987); an all-wheel-drive option (AWD) with 3.1-liter V-6 for an extensively reengineered STE, plus optional five-speed manual (1988).

Two-doors were dropped for 1988. For '89, Pontiac gave four-doors a restyled rear greenhouse and offered STE only with AWD. The optional 3.1 V-6 picked up five extra horses for 140 total. By that point, the S/E was what STE had been, yet was more price-competitive against comparable Japanese sedans at $16,000-$17,000. For 1990, the AWD became an S/E extra. Amazingly, the 6000 was still around for '91, though that was its final year. It had served exceptionally well.

Vying with the 6000 for divisional sales leadership was Pontiac's version of the front-drive J-body subcompact, which succeeded the old rear-drive Sunbird in 1982. At first, the name seemed to change more than the car, which debuted as J2000, then evolved as the 2000 (1983), 2000 Sunbird (1984), and finally just Sunbird again. Pontiac had gotten into "alphamumer-ic"designations under Hoglund's immediate predecessor, Robert C. Stempel (named GM president in 1987 and chairman in 1990), but eventually backed away from them after fearing buyers found them confusing.

There was no confusion about the cars, which were much like Chevy's Cavaliers down to the same body styles—including a convertible from 1983. Though Chevy's 2.0-liter overhead-valve four was available for a time, Pontiac emphasized an Opel-designed overhead-cam engine imported from GM of Brazil. That engine became standard for 1983, with throttle-body injection and 84 bhp from 1.8 liters (109 cid), followed by a 150-bhp turbocharged option with port injection. Both versions grew to 2.0 liters for 1987, good for respective horsepower of 96 and 165.

Three trims were offered through 1985: base, plush LE, and

1980 Bonneville Brougham four-door sedan

1982 Grand Prix Brougham Landau coupe

1982 J2000 hatchback coupe

1982 Firebird S/E coupe

1983 Firebird S/E coupe

1984 Fiero Official Pace Car coupe

sporty SE. The LE was canceled for '86, when turbocharged GTs arrived with a new front end highlighted by hidden headlamps. The 1988 GTs were trimmed to just convertible and coupe, the latter a restyled slantback two-door also offered in SE form. A new dashboard was the big event for '89. By 1990, Sunbird and Cavalier were the only two J-cars left from the original five, and neither showed signs of going away. Pontiac kept Sunbird going with a handsome restyle featuring a smoother hidden-headlamp nose and various lower-body addenda for SE and GT coupes; the 1990 convertible came only as a cheaper but less-sporting LE. With so much variety, plus attractive prices only a bit above Cavalier's, the 2000/Sunbird garnered well more than 100,000 sales in most years, including a record 170,000-plus for '84. Demand remained healthy right through 1990, when output totaled just under 145,000.

As at Buick and Olds, the J-car was the basis for a new compact Pontiac to replace the unloved X-body after 1984. Resurrecting the Grand Am name, this rendition of the 103.4-inch-wheelbase N-body design promptly outsold its divisional cousins by emphasizing handling options and sporty appointments in the European mold. Demand was strong: more than 82,500 of the debut 1985 coupes, a stunning 223,000 coupes and sedans for 1986. This Grand Am was the lifeblood of Pontiac dealers, accounting for better than 235,000 orders each model year through 1989 despite a constant stream of new competition. Not until the market turned difficult in 1990 did Grand Am sales dip below 200,000—and then not by much.

Again seeking individuality, Pontiac proffered a more overtly sporting SE in addition to the expected plain and luxury Grand Ams. The division also varied engines, making Sunbird's turbo-four a 1987 option, then replacing the original 3.0-liter Buick V-6 option with GM's new 150-bhp "Quad-4," America's first postwar production engine with dual overhead cams and four valves per cylinder.

Buyers seeking a smaller sports sedan had every reason to look closely at Grand Am SE. Its monochrome exterior with color-keyed wheels, front spoiler, and perimeter lower-body extensions was aggressive but not childish. A well-planned cockpit, assured handling, comfortable ride, and brisk performance completed the package. As with the STE, Pontiac again seemed able to do more with a shared platform than either Buick or Olds, at least as far as enthusiasts were concerned.

The same could be said for the first front-drive Bonneville, unveiled for 1987 on the 110.8-inch-wheelbase H-body platform of the previous year's new Buick LeSabre and Olds Delta 88. Pontiac designers strove mightily to make this one different, too, and succeeded handsomely. There wasn't much they could do about the boxy roofline, but much smoother front and rear ends set Bonneville clearly and cleanly apart from its corporate cousins.

Here, too, there was a sporty SE, an option package with

# Pontiac

1984 Fiero two-passenger coupe

1984 Grand Prix coupe

1985 6000 STE four-door sedan

1985 Bonneville Brougham four-door sedan

1985 Firebird Trans Am coupe

1986 Grand Prix Brougham coupe

uprated suspension, larger wheels and tires, mellow-sounding exhaust, less exterior chrome, console-mounted floorshift for the mandatory four-speed automatic transaxle, a shorter final drive for snappier step-off, and a full set of large, legible gauges, including tachometer. With all this, you might forget that the SE had the same 150-bhp 3.8-liter (231-cid) V-6 as the base and LE models.

An improved 165-bhp engine arrived for 1988, when Pontiac went a bit over the top with a new top-line Bonneville SSE. It was visually contrived, with body-color wheels, grille, decklid spoiler, and rocker skirting set off by a gaudy grille medallion trimmed in gold. More-worthy standards ran to GM/Teves antilock brakes (optional on other Bonnevilles for 1989-90), an electronic variable-damping system, and a leather-lined interior with multiadjustable power bucket seats. Still, most critics felt the more-modestly trimmed SE a better buy: less costly, smoother-riding, slightly quieter to both ears and eyes. The public generally agreed, but liked all the new Bonnies to the tune of some 120,000 sales in 1987 and 108,000 in 1988—not far behind LeSabre and Delta despite lacking their coupe body style. Only detail changes occurred for 1990, but the market was down and so Bonneville demand skidded to just under 86,000 for the model year, down from some 109,000.

Firebird showed surprising sales strength in this decade, averaging about 100,000 each year through 1986. But that only reflected the renewed interest in performance cars that began around 1982, making that year's all-new Firebird exceedingly well-timed. Inevitably, it bowed with the same 101-inch wheelbase F-body design as a new-generation Chevy Camaro. Though these ponycars were more alike than ever, Pontiac stylists under John Schinella again maintained the Firebird's distinctive look, via a low-riding nose with shallow twin grilles and hidden headlamps—the latter a first for Firebird—plus full-width taillamps with a smoked lens on some models for a "custom" blackout effect.

Initially, the third-series Firebird was limited to base, midrange S/E, and racy Trans Am—all "glassback" hatch coupes—but the Formula was revived as an option package for 1987, along with the "big" 350 V-8 of bygone years. That V-8 powered an even meaner-looking Trans Am called GTA. Other developments largely paralleled Camaro's except that Pontiac wouldn't field a Firebird convertible until 1992; it also continued offering specific chassis tuning and trim/equipment mixes. Styling was good enough to last through 1990 with only minor annual tweaks, many of which were exclusive to the Trans Am. Most noticeable was a grilleless "bottom-breather" nose for '84.

Recalling 1976's Limited-Edition T/A (for Pontiac's 50th birthday) and 1979's Tenth Anniversary Trans Am was yet another celebratory Firebird for 1989: the 20th Anniversary Trans Am. This involved a 1500-unit run of special GTAs powered by the turbocharged 231 V-6 from Buick's recently depart-

# Pontiac

1986 Grand Prix 2+2 "aero" coupe

1986 Firebird Trans Am coupe

1986 Grand Am LE four-door sedan

1986 1000 hatchback sedan

1986 6000 STE four-door sedan

ed GNX. Though sold only with four-speed overdrive automatic, it was the most-potent T/A in more than a decade, packing a quoted 250 bhp and an imposing 340 pound-feet torque (versus the V-8 GTA's 225 bhp and 330 pound-feet). You could have any color as long as it was white, just like the '69 original; no racing stripes, though, just subtle "20th Anniversary" cloisonné emblems and "Turbo Trans Am" badges. Performance was straight from "the good old days"—better, really. Would you believe 0-60 in 5.4 seconds? Believe it: This Firebird was the 1989 Indianapolis 500 pace car, and it performed the duty with no engine modifications. Price was reasonable, all told, about $25,000 with included T-top roof and pace-car decals. In all, this was a glorious reminder that nobody in Detroit still cared more about hot cars than Pontiac.

Unfortunately, Firebird fell on hard times after 1986, with production fading to some 80,000 for '87, then to an average 63,000 a year through '89. The situation grew even more grim for 1990, when fewer than 21,000 were sold. A little-changed basic design and fast-rising prices were mainly to blame (a new F-body wouldn't appear until 1993), but so were intensified import competition, rising hot-car insurance rates (Camaros and Firebirds were long notorious as frequent theft targets), and continuing lackluster workmanship.

By far the most interesting 1980s Pontiac was the innovative but ill-starred Fiero. New for 1984, it was Detroit's first mid-engine production car and the first new series-built U.S. two-seater since the original Ford Thunderbird. Fiero was broached in 1978 as a low-cost, high-mileage "commuter," but that was just a ruse to convince management that the project would help GM fulfill its CAFE obligations. The urge toward something sportier was irresistible, since the plan called for transplanting the front-drive X-body powertrain behind the cockpit to drive the rear wheels.

GM president Elliot Estes approved the concept in 1978, perhaps for sentimental reasons: He had pleaded for a two-seat Pontiac while he was division chief back in the '60s. Corporate cash-flow problems almost killed the Fiero program several times in 1980-82, but engineering director Hulki Aldikacti somehow persuaded decision makers that this new "P-car" not only made financial sense but could also improve Pontiac's image.

What emerged was definitely sporty; a smooth but chunky notchback coupe on a 93.4-inch wheelbase, evolved under Ron Hill in GM's Advanced Design III section and finalized by John Schinella's production studio. A fully drivable steel space-frame chassis served as a skeleton that supported body panels made of various plastics—but not fiberglass—thus making style changes cheap, quick, and easy. To minimize production costs and retail price, steering, front suspension, and brakes were borrowed from the humble Chevy Chevette; rear suspension and disc brakes were retained with the X-car power package.

Announced at base prices carefully pitched in the $8000-$9600 range, the Fiero predictably generated lots of excitement. The division's Pontiac, Michigan, home plant, fully retooled as Fiero's exclusive production center, happily cranked out nearly 137,000 of the '84s. But Fiero was flawed—heavy and thus sluggish with the standard 92-bhp, 151-cid four; little faster with the optional 173-cid V-6; low, cramped, noisy, and hard to see out of; hard to shift; stiff-riding; indifferently put together. As it had with the X-cars, GM shot itself in the foot by selling a car before it was fully developed.

Word got around quickly. Fiero sales crumbled by more than 40 percent in the second model year, recovered to near 84,000 for '86, then fell by nearly half for '87. A further blow came in September 1987, when a spate of engine fires implicating some 20 percent of the '84 models occasioned a government-ordered

# Pontiac

**1986 Grand Prix 2+2 coupe**

**1987 Sunbird SE coupe**

**1987 Fiero GT two-passenger coupe**

**1987 Firebird Formula coupe**

**1987 Firebird Trans Am GTA coupe**

**1988 Firebird Trans Am GTA coupe**

**1987 Bonneville four-door sedan**

**1988 Grand Prix LE coupe**

recall. With all this, plus a sharp drop in two-seater demand due to soaring insurance rates, GM announced in early 1988 that Fiero was dead, lamely claiming itself unable to make a profit at 50,000 units a year. Ironically, Pontiac had just spent $30 million for an all-new suspension that greatly improved handling on the '88 Fieros. Left stillborn were plans for a 1989 Quad-4 option and the more-distant prospect of a lighter aluminum space-frame that would have done wonders for performance.

As it is, the V-6 S/E and GT models rate as the most-collectible Fieros. And collected they will be. The GT bowed for 1985 with a sleek nose inspired by the '84 Indy 500 pace car (of which a few thousand replicas were sold). Standard rear spoiler, "ground effects" body addenda, uprated suspension, and a deep-voiced exhaust made it a sort of minimuscle car. Without the V-6, this package became the midrange S/E model for 1986, bolstered at midseason by a restyled GT with modified rear flanks and "flying buttress" fastback roofline. Arriving in June that year was a five-speed manual transaxle, long promised as an optional alternative to the standard four-speed and extra-cost three-speed automatic. The main '87 changes involved a reshaped nose for base and S/E, plus a larger fuel tank.

Though a compromise in many ways and a relative commercial failure, the Fiero symbolized Pontiac's renewed commitment to interesting automobiles. A more successful expression was the all-new front-drive Grand Prix that replaced one of Detroit's dullest cars for 1988.

Pontiac

**1988 Bonneville SSE four-door sedan**

**1988 Fiero GT two-passenger coupe**

**1988 Sunbird GT Turbo coupe**

**1989 Firebird Trans Am Turbo Official Pace Car**

**1989 Grand Prix Turbo coupe**

Pontiac's personal-luxury coupe had become almost invisible since its '78 downsizing, limping along after 1981 with somewhat smoother but still uninspired styling that strained at marrying "aero modern" with "middle-class traditional." Engines were equally uninspired, mostly Buick V-6s and Chevy smallblock V-8s, all economy-tuned. The trouble-prone Olds 350 diesel V-8 offered in GPs from 1981 to '84 only heightened the old-fogey aura of a car that was less important on the street than on NASCAR circuits (thanks to Richard Petty, and others).

But its role as stock-car standard-bearer did lead to an interesting limited edition reviving the 2+2 handle. Introduced at mid-1986, this wore a wind-cheating body-color front instead of the usual stand-up brightwork, plus a huge "glassback" deck designed for smoother airflow to a bespoilered tail. GM Design concocted this configuration to counter Ford's more-slippery new Thunderbirds in long-distance races. As ever, NASCAR approval depended on building a set number of street models, hence this Pontiac and Chevy's similar Monte Carlo SS Aerocoupe. Showroom 2+2s carried a four-barrel, 165-bhp Chevy 305 V-8 (fair enough considering all GM competitors in NASCAR in this period ran Chevy-based engines). This is likely to be the only GP built between 1978 and '87 that will interest future collectors.

The all-new '88 Grand Prix was a different story. Though it premiered with the same W-body/GM10 coupe platform as the newest Olds Cutlass Supreme and Buick Regal, its looks were pure Pontiac: sleek, purposeful, and obviously more "aero" than its blocky predecessor. It was more sophisticated, too, with standard all-disc brakes and four-wheel independent suspension. Though 7.8 inches shorter overall than the '87, the '88 GP rode a wheelbase only 0.5-inch shorter. This, plus a transverse drivetrain (nearly universal with front drive), made for a much-roomier interior than before.

For the base and intermediate LE models, that drivetrain involved a 130-bhp 173 Chevy V-6 with port fuel injection driving a four-speed automatic transaxle; a five-speed manual designed by Getrag of Germany was optional. The five-speed was standard on the sporty SE, which came with a beefed-up suspension and more-comprehensive instruments set in a very busy dash. Automatic GPs were upgraded to a stroked 3.1-liter (191-cid) V-6 during 1989, but the big thrill was a McLaren Turbo model powered by a blown 3.1 producing 200 bhp.

The "McTurbo" was another limited edition, developed with ASC/McLaren and planned for only 2000 copies. Finished in monochrome red or black with gold accents, it rolled on sizable 16-inch lacy-spoke wheels fitted with Z-rated high-performance tires (safe at over 149 mph). Wheel openings were suitably flared for clearance via specific lower-body panels with front and rear "spats" at each wheel, plus a grooved rub strip carried into the bumpers at each end. Like Ford with its '83 Thunderbird, Pontiac had come up with a car to revitalize a tired name. The McLaren was arguably the best GP yet for all-around performance.

Workaday Grand Prixs got off to a good sales start with model-year '88 output of about 86,000. The '89s fared even better at just under 137,000, though optional antilock brakes were a new inducement to buy. The 1990 total was a bit lower at 128,000—disturbing, as that included two new sedans, an LE and a reincarnated STE. Both were shapely, but the STE was both sporty and lush; features included standard antilock brakes, handling suspension, upgraded rolling stock, analog gauges (instead of contrived digi-graphic), buckets-and-console interior, and an available 205-bhp 3.1 turbo V-6 (offered on a Turbo coupe as well). Bodyside cladding made for a cluttered appearance, a bank of running lights between the headlamps looked me-too against the Mercury Sable (which had it first),

# Pontiac

1989 6000 STE All-Wheel-Drive four-door sedan

1990 Trans Sport SE minivan

1989 Sunbird GT Turbo convertible

1990 Firebird Trans Am GTA coupe

and the standard powertrain teamed the unexciting 140-bhp 3.1 V-6 with mandatory four-speed automatic. Still, it was heartening to see the STE continue, and the LE was a fitting successor to the 6000 as Pontiac's mainstream family four-door.

Of course, front-drive Grand Prixs, Grand Ams, and Bonnevilles were light years removed from their great 1960s namesakes, but they suggested the spirit of those cars was still infused the folks in Pontiac, Michigan. The feeling would carry on into the '90s where, aside from a slip in '92, Pontiac would remain third in domestic output.

Pontiac entered the '90s well entrenched as GM's "excitement" division. A spate of turbocharged cars with aggressive body addenda had fueled this image as the '80s wound to a close, but performance in the following decade would increasingly rely on a combination of multivalve engines, supercharging, and good old cubic inches.

Sunbird lost its turbo engine for 1991, offering in its place a 140-horsepower 3.1-liter V-6. It was standard in the GT coupe, which retained its distinctive front end incorporating partially hidden headlights. Carried over in LE trim were coupe, sedan, and convertible body styles; the SE coupe also returned with much of the GT's sporting appeal but at a lower price. All besides the GT came standard with the old 2.0-liter four, offering the V-6 as an option. New to the lineup were a base coupe and sedan, which listed at nearly $800 less than comparable LE models but offered a very limited choice of options—the V-6 not among them.

Sunbird was a virtual rerun for '92 save for newly standard antilock brakes, the addition of automatic door locks, a shift interlock for the automatic transmission, and some shuffling of trim designations. The two base models disappeared—at least in name—replaced by LE badges. SEs now comprised coupe, sedan, and convertible body styles, while the GT again came only as a coupe. A new fuel-injection system added 15 horsepower to the 2.0-liter four, bringing the total to 111. Once again, the V-6 was standard on the GT, optional on the midline SEs. As before, both engines could be backed by either a five-speed manual transmission or three-speed automatic.

The same lineup returned for '93, though SE coupes gained an optional Sport Appearance Package that offered the GT's partially hidden headlight front end and body cladding at a cheaper price. Aside from losing one horsepower on the 2.0-liter four (now 110), powertrains remained the same, as did Sunbirds in general. Not much changed for '94 either, though the line was condensed into LE coupe, sedan, and convertible, along with a sole SE coupe boasting the Sport Appearance Package and V-6 engine as standard equipment—essentially the former GT with a lower price (and, perhaps, lower insurance premiums).

Even though it was generally good for at least about 100,000 units annually in the early '90s, Sunbird was looking terribly long in the tooth compared to its imported rivals, and not just because it shunned air bags for antiquated "automatic deploying" door-mounted seat belts. No, the Sunbird was just plain old—it had served with little in the way of substantive updates since its debut in 1982.

What greeted Pontiac buyers for 1995 was not only a new car, but also a new name. "Sunbird" was perhaps judged too wimpy for Pontiac's hard-earned performance image, so the subcompact's moniker was changed to "Sunfire." Like its Cavalier sister over at Chevrolet, the Sunfire boasted curvy new sheetmetal, but the two cars came out looking more-distinct from one another than they ever had in the past—particularly the coupes. Both exhibited a steeply sloping roofline, but where the Cavalier's had thin pillars running into a high, squared-off tail, the Sunfire had squared-off rear quarter windows and a drooping tail. The revived GT version of the Sunfire carried a decklid spoiler mounted at the cut line between the roof and trunk. Front ends were just as unique, and even the side trim differed.

Two new engines were offered in the Sunfire, both gleaned from other car lines. The former 2.0-liter overhead-cam base engine was replaced by the 2.2-liter overhead-valve four that had been used in the Cavalier for years. Base horsepower increased with the switch, going up by 10 to 120. Substituting for the V-6 was GM's 150-horsepower 2.3-liter Quad 4, which had seen service in various corporate compacts and intermediates. A five-speed manual was standard on both engines, and while the 2.2 offered an optional three-speed automatic, the Quad 4 could be mated to an extra-cost four-speed automatic.

At Sunfire's fall 1994 introduction, only an SE coupe and sedan were present, with the GT coupe coming at midyear and an SE convertible with power top the following summer. GTs predictably came standard with the Quad 4, which was optional on SE coupes. Chief among Sunfire's selling points were standard dual air bags (at last) and antilock brakes, while those with the Quad 4 and four-speed automatic included traction control in the bargain. Initially, only coupes could get the Quad 4; sedans had to make do with the 2.2, which meant no four-speed automatic and no traction control—a disappointment for those seeking a sporty family hauler. With prices starting at a reasonable $11,074 for an SE coupe, a buyer could get a sporty little ride with dual air bags, antilock brakes, air conditioning, a potent Quad 4, four-speed automatic, and traction control, all for about $13,000.

As might be expected, Sunfire saw few changes for 1996. The Quad 4 was renamed the Twin Cam as it grew slightly to 2.4 liters and gained internal refinements, but the changes produced no more horsepower so the rating stayed at 150. The lack of a "sport sedan" offering was addressed by allowing SE four-doors to be equipped with the new Twin Cam engine, yet even the base 2.2-liter four could now be mated to the four-speed automatic, which still came with traction control.

Since its introduction in 1985, the compact Grand Am had been a strong sales performer for Pontiac, often topping the line. In order to maintain the momentum with a car that had changed little over the years, Pontiac added a lower-cost base model for 1991, along with standard antilock brakes on the top-line SE version—which was claimed to be the lowest-priced car in America with standard ABS, despite stickers that had risen more than $1300 that year to $16,000-plus. Other revisions to the lineup aimed mostly at offering sportier editions of current models at lower prices. LEs, now the midline offerings, offered a new Sport Performance Package that brought the looks of an SE along with the potent H.O. Quad 4 engine.

Powertrains carried over from 1990, meaning a standard "Iron Duke" 2.5-liter four with 110 horsepower in base and LE models, the Quad 4 in SEs (optional on LEs) with 160 when tied to a three-speed automatic, 180 when mated to the five-speed manual.

Grand Am's first redesign came for 1992 when it switched to a new N-body platform based on the one used for Chevrolet's Corsica/Beretta (and was again shared by Buick and Oldsmobile sisters). Wheelbase remained at 103.4 inches, but length grew by more than half a foot. Two-door coupes and four-door sedans were offered in SE and GT trim. Despite the general industry move to air bags to meet the government's passive restraint law, Grand Am held steadfastly to door-mounted automatic safety belts, promoting its newly standard antilock brakes instead.

Though an all-new design, styling carried on the traditional Grand Am look, from the BMW-like split grille to the squarish taillights. Rear roof pillars on sedans were thicker and sloped a bit more than the staunchly upright posts found on the previous generation, but coupes got a different roofline altogether with thin rear pillars set at a decidedly sportier rake. Headlights took on a "cat's eye" shape, and GT versions wore aggressive lower-body cladding with fog lamps faired into an "open mouth" front spoiler.

There were new powertrain choices as well. The 2.5-liter Iron Duke four was finally retired from Grand Am duty, its place being taken by a single-cam version of the Quad 4 called the Quad OHC. Like the Quad 4, the Quad OHC was sized at 2.3 liters, but horsepower was down to 120—though that was still

1991 Sunbird GT coupe

1991 Firebird Trans Am convertible coupe

1991 Bonneville SSE four-door sedan

1991 Grand Prix STE four-door sedan

1992 Grand Am GT coupe

1992 SSEi four-door sedan

1992 Firebird Trans Am convertible coupe

1993 Grand Am SE four-door sedan

1993 Grand Prix LE four-door sedan

1993 Sunbird SE convertible coupe

10 more than the old Iron Duke could muster. The 160/180-horse Quad 4 returned unchanged, but a V-6 was made available for the first time since 1987: a 3.3-liter with overhead valves and the same 160 horsepower as the "automatic version" of the Quad 4, but with greater torque at lower speeds that made it a better match to Grand Am's three-speed automatic transmission—which indeed was the only one offered with the V-6.

The new look and optional V-6 engine spurred Grand Am sales to even greater heights, from 1991's impressive 178,000 to about 208,500 for '92—and that figure would go even higher in subsequent years, nearing 255,000 by '94. Furthermore, those gains were accomplished with little in the way of revisions. For '93, a remote keyless entry system was added as an option and all four-cylinder engines were revised slightly for quieter performance, but they were still rather unrefined powerplants and all lost five horsepower in the bargain. Battery rundown protection was a new standard feature, but there was little else that Pontiac could brag about—except for another increase in sales.

By contrast, 1994's changes were almost monumental. Grand Am finally got a driver-side air bag—just as most others in the class were boasting dual air bags—and a four-speed automatic transmission joined the powertrain lineup along with a 155-horsepower 3.1-liter V-6 to replace the former 160-horse 3.3. Leather upholstery was added as an option, and the sometimes-hated automatic door locks could now be set to unlock automatically as well (previously, riders had to flick the power lock switch in order to get out).

After a short three-year run, the Quad OHC engine was dropped for 1995, making a 150-horsepower Quad 4 the base powerplant. While it got new internal balance shafts to make it run smoother, it lost its H.O. (High Output) variant, so the only optional engine was the 155-horse 3.1-liter V-6. It didn't matter. Despite being a virtual carryover otherwise, Grand Am sales continued to get even stronger, nudging past 291,000 for the model year.

A new base engine, slightly revised styling, dual air bags, and available traction control graced the 1996 edition of the Grand Am. The base Quad 4 engine grew to 2.4 liters and changed its name to Twin Cam; and though horsepower stayed the same at 150, internal revisions made it smoother and quieter. The three-speed automatic was dropped, the remaining four-speed automatic bringing traction control along as a bonus. Adding the passenger-side air bag prompted a redesigned dashboard that calmed some of the swoopy lines of the previous edition, while external revisions were limited to a mild recontouring of the famous split grille and clenched-fist taillights. It looked to be yet another banner year for the Grand Am, which of late had not only been Pontiac's best-seller, but the second-most-popular car among all GM offerings.

Another surprising sales performer in the Pontiac line was the midsize Grand Prix, which enjoyed far greater popularity than its sister W-body cars over at Buick and Oldsmobile, if not quite up to the level of the bargain-priced Chevrolet Lumina.

Replacing the former Turbo coupe for 1991 were GT and GTP coupes, the latter a "model option" dressed in aggressive body cladding and alloy wheels; sedans remained available in LE, SE, and STE guise. While enthusiasts bemoaned the demise of the turbocharged engine, Pontiac consoled them with GM's new 3.4-liter Twin Dual Cam V-6, a 24-valve engine rated at 210 horsepower with the five-speed manual or 200 even with the new four-speed automatic introduced that year. Standard on the GTP coupe, this engine was optional on all Grand Prixs save the LE sedan. Other engine choices included a 140-horsepower 3.1-liter V-6 and 160-horsepower 2.3-liter Quad 4. LE sedans also missed out on the antilock brakes that

# Pontiac

1993 Firebird Trans Am coupe

1994 Sunbird SE coupe

1994 Grand Am GT coupe

1994 Firebird Trans Am coupe with 25th Anniversary package

were a new option elsewhere in the line.

The Quad 4 dropped out for 1992, leaving the 140-horse 3.1-liter V-6 as the standard engine. Antilock brakes were made standard on top-line models, optional on the rest. All sedans took on the front light bar previously reserved for the STE.

There were even fewer changes for 1993. Pontiac ad writers were hard pressed for material, the most newsworthy item being the addition of automatic door locks. But the buying public didn't seem to mind, as the Grand Prix topped nearly 117,000 shopping lists.

Grander news headlined the 1994 models, as dual air bags arrived in a redesigned interior. Oddly, Grand Prix was the only one of the W-body family to get dual bags that year, the rest making due with just a driver-side air bag. But even the Grand Prix was behind on this score, as the majority of competitors had already been offering dual air bags for years. With the lineup trimmed to a single SE trim level in both coupe and sedan form, all Grand Prixs boasted a relatively high level of standard equipment (including a revised 3.1-liter V-6 with 160 horsepower, 20 more than before), but the options list was rife with antilock brakes, custom interior groups, performance packages with sporting features, and the 3.4-liter Twin Dual Cam V-6, now rated solely at 210 horsepower. Gone, however, was the five-speed manual transmission, the lone gearbox being the newly standard four-speed automatic.

After all those exhausting changes for '94, Grand Prix took another breather for '95. A standard transmission-shift interlock was the most noteworthy new feature, though some nifty five-spoke alloys replaced the previous cross-lace wheels in the performance packages. But Pontiac announced some bigger news at midyear.

Introduced at the Detroit Auto Show in January 1995 was the 300 GPX, a four-door concept car touted as being "very close" to the redesigned Grand Prix sedan due as a 1997 model. And indeed it was; save for some exaggerated fender flares, it was nearly identical to the 1997 Grand Prix sedan previewed at Detroit the following year, with its coupe counterpart debuting at the Chicago Auto Show in February 1996.

With redesigned versions on the way, the 1996 editions of the Grand Prix predictably changed little, with equipment shuffling and dressier trim packages being the order of the day. The optional 3.4-liter Twin Dual Cam V-6 gained five horsepower (to 215) in its final appearance in the Grand Prix.

With its SE and SSE variants establishing the Bonneville as a sports sedan of large—if rather boxy—proportions, Pontiac's full-size front-driver marched into 1991 with few changes, as a complete makeover was scheduled for the following year.

Visitors to Chicago's 1991 auto show were given a sneak peek at the new car, and what they saw caused a sensation: Abandoned were the squared-off, conservative lines of its predecessor, as the redesigned Bonneville boasted flowing contours set off with cat's-eye headlights and a BMW-style kickup at the rear window. Inside was a similarly curvy dashboard, while underneath the hood of the top-line SSEi model there lurked a supercharged version of the 3.8-liter V-6.

Upon its official arrival that fall, three models were offered, all with a standard driver-side air bag: SE, SSE (which added antilock brakes, bucket seats with console, and alloy wheels), and SSEi. The last was priced at a dizzying $28,045, but that included a lengthy list of standard equipment comprising a passenger-side air bag, automatic climate control, 12-way power front seats, and head-up instrument display that projected a digital speed reading onto the windshield. Also included was a new traction control system that helped tame the 205 frenzied horsepower served up by its supercharged version of the 3.8-liter V-6. Those who had criticized the previous SSE as a family car in sport-sedan clothing fell silent; the SSEi could compete with European performance sedans costing far more.

For 1993, some of the SSEi's high-tech equipment floated downstream. The supercharged V-6 could be ordered in place of the standard 170-horse 3.8 in the SSE, as could a passenger-side air bag and head-up display. Antilock brakes were now standard on the base SE, which also gained an optional SLE package that included an SSEi-styled grille and body addenda, along with 16-inch crosslace wheels and other amenities.

The SSEi was dropped as a separate model for 1994, but most of its equipment—including a stronger 225-horsepower supercharged V-6—was offered in an SSEi option package for the surviving SSE. If that didn't make complete sense, at least the standardization of dual air bags across the line did. SEs could again be optioned with an SLE appearance package, and a specially priced version for the California market offered the SLE package along with other added equipment and the destination charge—about a $4500 value—for just $1371 over the SE's base price of $20,424. Newly optional for the SSE was GM's Computer Command Ride (CCR) suspension, which automatically adjusted from soft to firm when cornering or braking.

Bonneville's base 3.8-liter V-6 was pumped up to 205 horsepower for 1995, and even the SE could get its supercharged brother, still rated at 225, though the SLE package had to be ordered as well.

Save for some variation in wheel designs, styling hadn't been altered since the Bonneville's transformation in 1992, so the minor facelift that was applied to the '96 models was perhaps overdue. Grilles took on a different ovoid shape and front facias were changed slightly, as were the taillights and rear facia. Overall, however, the modifications could best be described as subtle. Less subtle was an increase of 15 horsepower for the supercharged V-6, now rated at 240.

As with its other car lines, Pontiac had taken a decidedly sportier approach with the Bonneville than was applied to its LeSabre and Eighty-Eight sisters over at Buick and Oldsmobile. While LeSabre continually topped the trio in volume, Bonneville was always a strong second ahead of the hapless Eighty-Eight, and undoubtedly served to further Pontiac's claim that "We build Excitement."

But the car that delivered the most Pontiac excitement was the Firebird, which received a facelift when the '91s debuted about six months early in the spring of 1990. The chiseled front end gave way to a smoother-looking snout reminiscent of Pontiac's Banshee show car, and engineers managed to find five more horsepower in Firebird's hotter V-8 engines. Base, Formula, Trans Am, and GTA versions continued, with a new Sport Appearance Package being offered for the base Firebird that gave it the show—but not the go—of a Trans Am. Engines ranged from the pedestrian 140-horsepower 3.1-liter V-6 to a 240-horsepower 5.7-liter V-8. A driver-side air bag remained standard, but antilock brakes weren't offered.

Then, just as it looked as though the Firebird was going to coast until its scheduled redesign for '93, Pontiac pulled an ace from its sleeve: the first Firebird convertible in more than two decades. Arriving midway through the 1991 model year, it was very similar to the Camaro convertible introduced in 1987, but it helped spur Firebird sales that had been sagging of late. There were no more surprises in store for 1992, as the Firebird repeated virtually unchanged.

Though the new Firebird that debuted in the spring of 1992 as a '93 model rode the same 101-inch wheelbase as before, little else was carried over. Offerings were trimmed to just base, Formula, and Trans Am hatchbacks, convertibles being temporarily discontinued. Many of the components contributing to Firebird's flowing contours were molded from dent-resistant fiberglasslike material, including the front and rear fascias, front fenders, doors, roof, and rear hatch lid. Powertrain choices were also trimmed, with base models matching a new 160-horsepower 3.4-liter V-6 with either a five-speed manual or four-speed automatic transmission, while the Formula and Trans Am shared a revised 5.7-liter LT1 V-8 churning out 275 horsepower through a standard six-speed manual or an optional four-speed automatic. Assembly was moved from Van Nuys, California, to north of the border in St. Therese, Quebec, Canada.

The new Firebirds came standard with dual air bags and antilock brakes, rare features in this price class. Aside from the obvious advantages, it was hoped that these safety features would appease the insurance industry, which had saddled most sporty cars with high rates that were at least partially to blame for a slump in sales. Of course, those items also contributed to a rather substantial jump in prices: A base Firebird previously listed at $12,505, which included an automatic transmission; the '93 came standard with a manual trans, and the price of entry had climbed to $13,995.

No matter. In 1994, the new Firebird's first model year with production in full stride, sales topped 51,000. Some minor changes were incorporated for '94 that placed a new Trans Am GT at the top rung of the ladder, "demoting" the regular Trans

1995 Firebird Trans Am coupe

1995 Grand Am GT coupe

1995 Sunfire SE four-door sedan

1995 Bonneville SSE four-door sedan with SSEi package

1996 Trans Sport SE minivan

1996 Sunfire SE four-door sedan

1996 Grand Am GT four-door sedan

1996 Bonneville SE four-door sedan with SLE package

1996 Firebird Trans Am coupe with Ram Air package

Am by scaling down its list of standard equipment—and its price. Also, the six-speed manual standard on V-8 versions gained the CAGS (Computer Aided Gear Selection) feature that had been introduced on Corvettes earlier, a widely disdained addition that forced a first-to-fourth shift under light throttle for better fuel economy. In reality it wasn't all that intrusive, and allowed the substitution of a lower rear axle ratio (now 3.42 versus 3.23) for even better jump off the line.

Midyear saw the return of the Firebird convertible, which unlike the previous edition, was assembled entirely in-house, and featured a power-operated top. Also appearing was a 25th Anniversary Trans Am boasting a blue dorsal stripe on a white exterior, monogrammed white leather seats, unique body-colored five-spoke wheels, and, of course, special identifying logos. Only about 1500 were built in all: a limited number of coupes along with an even-more-limited number of convertibles. The package added only $995 to the cost of a Trans Am GT, making the coupe $22,504, the convertible $27,474—not bad for cars destined to become classics.

Though originally promised for late 1994, traction control did not become available until 1995. Priced at $450, it was offered only on V-8 models, which had come to mean just Formula and Trans Am—no more Trans Am GT. Late in the model year, a new V-6 engine joined the options list for the base Firebird: a Series II 3.8-liter bringing with it a stout 200 horsepower, 40 more than the standard 3.4-liter, though it was initially offered only in concert with the four-speed automatic transmission.

That changed in 1996, when the 3.8 became the standard Firebird engine, available with five-speed manual or four-speed automatic. V-8 models also saw a power increase, the 5.7 being boosted to 285 horsepower in standard form, a whopping 305 with the new Ram Air package that included (naturally) a big air scoop incorporated into the hood, along with larger tires on five-spoke alloy wheels.

A rather odd addition to Pontiac's line came with the 1990 introduction of the Trans Sport minivan, a family oriented front-wheel-drive entry that shared its design with the Chevy Lumina minivan and Olds Silhouette. All boasted unique construction that placed composite body panels over a steel skeleton, similar to the technique used on the departed Fiero. Equally unique was a profile headed by a long pointed snout that prompted wags to deride them as "dustbusters." Aside from rendering them "aesthetically challenged," the design resulted in a dashtop that seemed to stretch out to the horizon before meeting with the windshield, leaving the front corners of the vehicle invisible to the driver. Furthermore, the steep windshield required the addition of an "A-plus" pillar on each side, which did nothing to aid visibility or tame the odd feel from the cockpit.

Trans Sport emerged as the sportiest of the entries, yet all were offered only with a 3.1-liter V-6 tied to a three-speed automatic transmission. Unlike the port-fuel-injected versions of this engine used in various GM car lines, the ones in the minivans relied on less-efficient throttle-body injection, with a resulting drop in horsepower output from 140 to 120—hardly a selling point for a vehicle that could potentially be loaded with seven passengers and/or lots of cargo.

Changes to the original design came steadily. Antilock brakes and an available 165-horsepower 3.8-liter V-6 were valuable additions for '92. A pop-up sunroof, leather upholstery, steering-wheel-mounted auxiliary radio controls, and five more horsepower for the 3.8-liter V-6 arrived in '93, while the following year brought a driver-side air bag, automatic door locks, an optional power sliding side door, and a blunted nose that pared 2.3 inches from overall length. Late in the year, traction control was added to the options list. Progress slowed as the planned

# Pontiac

**1997 Bonneville SSEi four-door sedan**

**1997 Sunfire GT coupe**

**1998 Grand Am GT coupe**

**1998 Grand Prix GTP four-door sedan**

**1999 30th Anniversary Trans Am coupe**

1997 redesign drew near; just a shift interlock for '95, and a new 180-horsepower 3.4-liter V-6 as the sole engine offering for '96.

Pontiac sales and production remained relatively strong and steady into the new millenium, with yearly totals of 450,000 to well more than 600,000 units. This showing was remarkable in being achieved almost entirely with cars at a time when light trucks, especially sport-utility vehicles (SUVs), were siphoning off more and more car sales throughout the industry.

Taking note of that trend, General Motors merged Pontiac with the GMC truck division to form a "full-line" franchise like Chevrolet. The announcement was made in February 1996 by Ronald Zarrella, recruited four years earlier from optics maker Bausch & Lomb to be GM's group executive for North American vehicle sales, service and marketing. In a press release, Zarrella touted the new Pontiac-GMC Division as part of GM's "continuing effort . . . to configure our organization to achieve the most effective, efficient results for our customers, dealers, and stockholders. Both Pontiac and GMC have long recognized the complimentary [sic] nature of their businesses . . . and the advantages inherent in a dual franchise." Indeed, some 55 percent of Pontiac dealers already handled GMC at the time. The new division began with 3736 outlets and combined calendar-year sales of more than 1 million units.

Zarrella, named president of GM North America in 1999, espoused "brand management," long a staple at consumer-products companies like Proctor & Gamble. GM chairman John Smale, who once headed P&G, and president John F. "Jack" Smith were believers, too. Smale and Smith came to power in the board-instigated 1992 "palace coup" that ignominiously removed chairman Bob Stempel and president Lloyd Reuss, GM veterans who came to be blamed for continuing losses in company market share and earnings. Zarrella's mission was to help turn things around. Under brand management, that meant sharpening the image of each GM make for higher customer appeal and reduced intramural competition, as well as weeding out similar and underperforming models throughout the corporate fleet.

But Zarrella's efforts, however well-intentioned, produced mixed results. Though recovery was evident at GM by mid-decade, it was due more to a tech-driven boom economy and fast-growing demand for profitable trucks than fancy ads and design increasingly dictated by consumer focus groups. At the end of 2001, Zarella, realizing he'd never make CEO at GM, returned to Bausch & Lomb to be CEO there. Taking over his GM job was none other than former Chrysler Corporation president Bob Lutz, a genuine "car guy" who immediately began dismantling brand management and the confusing, costly, time-wasting bureaucracy it had spawned. Ironically, Zarrella might have done the same had he stayed, having learned, as he admitted to reporters shortly before his departure, that good product maybe is more important to a successful car company than good marketing.

Pontiac was less affected by brand-management antics than any other GM make save Saturn, which was in its own orbit anyway. In fact, the Pontiac brand was being well managed even before Zarrella came aboard, long liked and well respected for symbolizing sporty, driver-oriented cars in line with the "We Build Excitement!" ad slogan. All Pontiac needed to do was more of the same—which it did, as the above sales figures attest.

Grand Am and Grand Prix remained the most-popular Pontiacs in this period, but Sunfire contributed important volume of more than 100,000 units each model year through 2001. This, too, was remarkable, considering how little the car itself changed. The '98s, for example, were virtual reruns of the 1995-97 models, while the main news for '99 was shifting the convertible from SE to sportier GT trim. Modestly freshened 2000 Sunfires arrived in early '99. The longer model year yielded higher production on that basis, but calendar-year orders declined. The ragtop, never a strong seller, was phased out during the year. Sunfire's next notable changes didn't come until 2002. The passé three-speed automatic option was finally dropped (the four-speed continued, of course), and GTs switched to a tuned version of the SE models' 2.2-liter four-cylinder. The new engine made 10 fewer horses than the Quad-4-based Twin Cam, but provided similar real-world performance—and, sad to say, about the same mechanical refinement.

Sunfire and sister Chevy Cavalier would have been all-new for 2000 or 2001, but the prototype bombed in consumer focus groups and was duly shelved. By the time designers and engineers returned from their drawing boards, Sunfire was deemed unnecessary. So although some makes would have been overjoyed to pull 100,000 yearly sales, Sunfire was destined to be history by 2004.

Pontiac's minivan sold only half as well as Sunfire despite becoming more competitive for 1997. Like that year's Olds Silhouette and new Chevy Venture, Trans Sport was fully redesigned, with all-steel construction replacing dent- and rust-resistant plastic panels over an internal space frame. That looked a retrograde step to some, as did retaining an undistinguished front-drive powertrain. But the controversial "Dustbuster" profile gave way to attractive, mainstream styling peppered with Pontiac hallmarks, and there was a choice of regular and extended bodies on separate wheelbases, a nod to the sales-leading Chrysler minivans, themselves overhauled for '96. Also aping Chrysler's latest was an available left-side sliding rear door, which later became standard and could be electrically operated like the power right-side door GM had pioneered. All the new GM models were widely judged the best-handling minivans. Trans Sport went further with a Montana Package comprising tighter suspension, alloy wheels and traction control, plus jazzy two-tone exterior. Reasonably priced at around $1000-$1200 depending on model, this option proved so popular that Montana replaced the Trans Sport name for '99 (except in Canada), with most previous Montana features regrouped into a new Performance and Handling option.

This new blend of minivan practicality, fun-to-drive Pontiac flair, and affordable low-$20,000 prices more than doubled Trans Sport sales in 1997, but volume went little higher afterward. Dodge moved over four times as many Caravans each year. Though all minivans were increasingly seen as un cool "soccer mom" vehicles, with a consequent softening in overall demand, GM's entries had another problem in being visibly narrower than their rivals, reflecting a basic design created partly for the tight streets of Europe, where it was sold as the Opel/Vauxhall Sintra. Most Americans didn't want minivans so skinny, and shopped elsewhere. And like Sunfire, Trans Sport/Montana stayed mostly the same each year despite ever-tougher competition. The only changes of note after '97 were an optional "MontanaVision" rear-seat video system (1999); standard GM OnStar communications/assistance (2001); and available fold-flat third-row seat, "Versatrak" all-wheel-drive, and ultrasonic rear-obstacle-warning system (2002). The benign neglect was unfortunate. Like other GM efforts of these years, Trans Sport/Montana was a good vehicle, but not quite what the market wanted.

Buyers all but shunned the Aztek, Pontiac's response to the soaring late-decade popularity of carlike SUVs. An early 2001 debut, it was basically a short-wheelbase Montana transformed into "active lifestyle" vehicle. To that end, Aztek introduced optional Versatrak all-wheel drive, GM's clever new way of adding four-wheel traction to a front-drive powerteam without added complexity or weight. Instead of a rear propshaft and extra differentials, an electronically controlled clutch pack at each rear wheel could lock up as needed to redirect torque from the front. This also brought a bonus in independent rear suspension to replace the normal twist-beam axle, plus rear disc brakes instead of drums.

Still, no Aztek was a serious off-roader. Pontiac rightly called it a "sport recreational vehicle," meaning it was designed for hauling up to five people and their gear to activities not too far off the beaten path. Naturally, Aztek drove much like its minivan parent, with adequate acceleration and safe—but ponderous—handling, plus standard antilock brakes as on Montanas.

**2000 Bonneville SSEi four-door sedan**

**2000 Sunfire GT coupe**

**2001 Aztek GT wagon**

**2001 Grand Prix GTP Special Edition four-door sedan**

# Pontiac

Its big attraction was a versatile interior with many novel touches. For example, a totable drinks cooler/CD box locked in between the front seats, and a slide out rear storage tray could double as a table for "tailgate" parties or folded out into a rollaway cart. Also available were separate stereo controls and speakers for the cargo bay, washable seat covers, and a camper package with a fitted air mattress and a tent for slipping over the raised rear hatch.

Trouble was, these nifty ideas came wrapped in some pretty odd styling. *Motor Trend* described Aztek as "minivan meets creature from the black lagoon." The *Los Angeles Times* simply wondered, "Who let the dog out?" Said *Road & Track*: Aztek is trying way too hard to be hip. That's understandable if you're trying to hide its minivan roots, [but] Pontiac has gone to extremes. The overall length was shortened and the rear hatch chopped into a fastback while the hood was raised and sliding doors were replaced with conventional portals. . . . The styling [is] ungainly [despite] hood nostrils that recall the Ram Air look of the Trans Am and enough body cladding for a fleet of surfboards." There were kinder, gentler reviews, but hardly anyone bought an Aztek for its looks.

Early sales suggested as much. Pontiac planned on moving 60,000 Azteks every 12 months, but retailed just slightly more than 38,000 during the 18 months of the extended 2001 model year. Beyond questionable styling, some also faulted Aztek as too pricey for the younger buyers it targeted. Pontiac addressed both issues for 2002. Body-color cladding without molded-in "speed streaks" cleaned up the exterior, and making some standard features optional allowed cutting base prices by a few thousand dollars to about $20,000 minimum. Even so, Aztek was already a symbol for everything wrong with GM's brand-managed approach to design and engineering. No wonder Bob Lutz came in vowing such things would never happen again.

Styling excesses were evident at Pontiac even before the Aztek, but weren't nearly so looney. On the contrary, the redesigned '97 Grand Prix was one of the handsomest Ponchos since the '60s: purposeful, curvy, near frippery-free. The new sedan showed particularly dramatic change in its new coupe-like profile. Even better, "Wide Track" was back, as ads proclaimed. Like Buick's latest Regal, built off the same new W-body front-drive platform, the GP was little longer than before despite a three-inch longer wheelbase, but Pontiac went for a broader stance, upping track width by two inches fore, three inches aft.

Grand Prix offered three V-6 models for '97: a mom-and-pop 3.1-liter SE sedan with 160 bhp and enthusiast-oriented GT sedan and coupe with GM's ever-improving "3800" engine and 195 standard bhp. For real excitement, an optional GTP package supercharged the 3800 to 240 strong horses. It also included a beefier four-speed automatic transmission, slightly firmer suspension, stickier tires, modest decklid spoiler, and discreet identification. All models boasted all-disc antilock brakes and traction control as standard, though the latter was denied GTPs until 1998, when a stouter system was adopted across the board.

*Car and Driver* had good things to say about its '97 GTP sedan. Topping the list were strong 0-60 performance of just 6.8 seconds, fine skidpad grip (0.79g), safe and predictable front-drive moves, a roomy and comfortable cabin with generally sound ergonomics, and lots of features for only about $25,000 delivered. There were a few faults, to be sure, but C/D dismissed them as "relatively minor carping. We were expecting the 1997 Grand Prix to be a better car than the previous model, but we weren't expecting it to be this much better."

Buyers responded to the '97 GP, snapping up about 159,000 for the model year. Though an extra-long debut season helped pump up the volume, it was the GP's best model-year performance in two decades. Demand was lower for '98 at a bit over 142,000, but the '99 tally was 155,000, and model-year 2000 production was nearly 173,000. Interim changes helped keep buyers interested. The GTP proved popular enough to earn separate model status for '99, when the base 3800 engine added five bhp. For 2000, GM's worthy OnStar communications and assistance system became available, the base V-6 got 15 more horses of its own, and all models gained a standard engine immobilizer that disabled the ignition if starting was attempted by devious means. Grand Prix was chosen as the 2000 Daytona 500 pace car, and Pontiac reeled off 2000 replica coupes, all silver GTPs with unique 16-inch aluminum wheels, functional hood vents, special interior, and Daytona insignia inside and out. A similar package appeared for 2002 to mark the 40th anniversary of the Grand Prix name at Pontiac. Available for any GT or GTP, this option delivered Dark Cherry paint, special red/grey interior, rear spoiler, hood ducts, and chrome wheels.

Following the new Grand Prix for 1999 was a redesigned version of Pontiac's top seller. Though arguably less impressive, it proved somewhat more popular than recent Grand Ams. Again, a new Pontiac jumped the model-year gun, with sales commencing in early '98. Coupes and sedans continued, but the lineup was more confusing, with each body style offered in base SE, SE1, and SE2 versions, plus sportier GT and GT1 models. Wheelbase stretched 3.6 inches to a relatively rangy 107, and width swelled almost three inches (to 70.4). Overall length was little changed. Alas, so were powertrains. SE2s and all GTs came with GM's hoary 3.4-liter pushrod V-6; others used the 2.4-liter Twin Cam until 2002, when they followed Sunbird to the newer 2.2-liter "L850" corporate four-cylinder. Four-speed automatic remained the only transmission until 2000, after which four-cylinder models got a standard five-speed manual supplied by respected German gearbox specialist Getrag.

The '99 Grand Ams looked like smaller Grand Prixs, but with lots of gimcracks larded on. *Car and Driver* judged the styling "overwrought and exaggerated," especially on GTs. "Only the roof panel is devoid of scoops, spoilers, strakes and other 'character' lines. . . . Even the GT's five-spoke alloys are cluttered with little cartoonish speedline indentations on each spoke. One or two of these cues might be acceptable, but together they're too much."

The rest of the car wasn't quite enough. Despite a performance sapping automatic, *C/D*'s test GT sedan ran 0-60 in a brisk 7.7 seconds and scored well for handling, but lacked the poise and polish of most import rivals. Ride was generally judged good on any model, but noise levels were only average and workmanship needed, well, work. Value was an asset, but didn't erase the deficits for Consumer Guide®. Said CG's Auto 2000 issue: "Unless sporty looks are your top priority in a family compact, you'd be well advised to scout the competition." Fortunately for Pontiac, many people bought Grand Ams anyway.

CG still liked the full-size Bonneville, but demoted it to "Recommended" status after 1997, conferring "Best Buy" class honors on an attractive new Dodge Intrepid and Chrysler Concorde, LHS, and 300M. With stronger competition on all fronts, plus few further changes of consequence, Bonneville sales gradually declined, bottoming out at just a little more than 54,000 for model-year '99.

A brand-new 2000 Bonneville stood to do better, being designed on the latest version of the GM G-car platform that made the Olds Aurora such a roadable big four-door. Like the latest GP and Grand Am, Bonneville grew a bit longer in wheelbase. It was also a tad taller and heavier. Styling was visibly bolder, with a more steeply raked windshield, newly downsloped hood, and wheels pushed further toward the corners on slightly wider tracks. Pontiac's plastics factory supplied more flashy lower-body cladding, and Grand Am-type "speed streaks" popped up inside as well as outside. Not everyone liked this look, but it would seem quite tasteful once the Aztek appeared.

There were three Bonnevilles for Y2K: volume-selling SE, semi-sporty SLE, and supercharged SSEi. Powertrains were broadly the same as before, though internal refinements made the 3800 V-6 a tad smoother and quieter, and the G-platform, GM's stiffest ever, provided a solid driving feel. Predictably, the hot-shot SSEi was the focus of most "buff book" reviews, which were generally quite positive. *Car and Driver* clocked 0-60 in 7.8 seconds, which beat Chrysler's Euro-inspired 300M, and the magazine judged the ride/handling compromise just about right for a sporty big domestic. The dashboard was something else. "Whoever designed it," *C/D* said, "seemed to have an obsession with gray plastic buttons and knobs—from the driver's seat, we counted 70 of them." For passengers, though, the interior was roomy and comfortable, a pleasant place to while away the miles.

If overdone in places, the 2000 was a clearly better Bonneville, and model-year sales rose nearly 13 percent from the '99 level. Changes for 2001 included the return of GM OnStar as standard for SLE and SSEi, standard traction control for the top model, and optional heated front seats for all models, not just the SSEi. As Pontiac expected, the value-priced SE accounted for more than half of Bonneville sales. What Pontiac didn't expect was the steep 27-percent drop in '01 model-year volume to less than 45,500, marginal even for a high-profit full-size. By 2002, Detroit's rumor mill was predicting that Bonneville would not get another redesign, having become too costly to continue and out of step with future product plans.

Sadly, those same factors conspired to do in the Firebird after 2002. It seemed unthinkable that Pontiac would kill off the best expression of its "Excitement" mantra, but the decision was strictly business. Big-engine trucks were the new icons of performance, and Firebird sales were still dwindling, ever behind those of sister Chevy Camaro, never mind the Ford Mustang that was now consistently outselling both GM cars combined.

But true to form, the F-Bird did not go quietly. Like V-8 Camaros, the '98 Formula and Trans Am got the sterling new aluminum-block LS1 engine from Chevy's C5 Corvette. In the ponycars it made 305 bhp, up 20 from the final iron-block LT1; Pontiac's optional WS6 Ram Air package upped the count to 320. At the same time, the six-speed manual gearbox became a no-cost option to four-speed automatic for V-8 models. All '98 Firebirds wore a modest facelift featuring honeycomb-pattern taillights and a slightly shorter, more-rounded front; a pair of aggressive nasal air slots distinguished Trans Ams—four nostrils on Ram-Air cars. Changes for '99 were few but appreciated. V-8s adopted a more-effective Torsen limited-slip differential, traction control was now optional for base V-6 Firebirds as well as V-8s, and all models got a slightly larger fuel tank.

Trans Am had another birthday party in 1999, observed with a 30th Anniversary Package comprising the WS engine, manual or automatic transmission, Arctic White paint, wide blue dorsal striping, unique 17-inch alloy wheels—and, yes, "Screaming Chicken" decals, albeit much less blatant than in the old days. Also included was the expected logo-decorated interior, this one with a numbered commemorative plaque for the console. Production was naturally as limited as with past anniversary T/As: 1065 "targa" coupes (65 reserved for Canada), 535 convertibles (35 for up north).

Otherwise, the final chapter of the Firebird saga was a tale of year to-year equipment shuffles and sales that wouldn't stop sliding. By 2001, model-year volume was down to around 21,500, barely a third the 1995 figure. There was one last special Trans Am, actually a 2002 option package tellingly named Collector Edition. This, too, delivered the WS6 engine and its snarky snout, plus bright yellow paint with black accents, and unique wheels and trim. Then, just like that, it was over. But Firebird, and the T/A in particular, had served Pontiac well through some very trying times. It was tough to lose, but it left a good many highly collectible models that are sure to keep the memories strong in coming years.

Firebird may be history, but there will be more Pontiacs to carry on its tradition with a style and character all their own. Pointing the way is the 2003 Vibe, a compact "sportwagon" engineered with Toyota and built at the respected GM-Toyota plant in California. That's appropriate, as Vibe is a very "California" car: good-looking, fun-to-drive, versatile, very easy on gasoline and the atmosphere.

Also providing a new definition of Pontiac performance were the shapely two-seater Solstice concepts presented at the 2002 North American International Auto Show in Detroit. Developed as both roadster and fastback coupe, Solstice went from drawing-board dream to drivable reality in less four months, helped by liberal use of components from throughout the global GM empire—and hearty encouragement from Bob Lutz, who knows a winner when he sees it. But even if the Solstice never reaches showrooms, it suggests a new can-do spirit is now taking hold, bringing with it the promise of more great Pontiacs.

## Specifications

### 1930

| 6-29 Big Six (wb 110.0) | Wght | Price | Prod* |
|---|---|---|---|
| rdstr 4P | 2,394 | 775 | — |
| phaeton 5P | 2,407 | 825 | — |
| std cpe 2P | 2,532 | 745 | — |
| sdn 2d | 2,595 | 745 | — |
| sdn 4d | 2,717 | 845 | — |
| **6-30 Big Six (wb 110.0)** | | | |
| rdstr 2-4P | 2,410 | 665 | — |
| phaeton 5P | 2,475 | 695 | — |
| std cpe 2P | 2,580 | 665 | — |
| spt cpe 2-4P | 2,655 | 725 | — |
| sdn 2d | 2,695 | 665 | — |
| sdn 4d | 2,745 | 725 | — |

| 6-30 Big Six (wb 110.0) | Wght | Price | Prod |
|---|---|---|---|
| Custom sdn 4d | 2,785 | 785 | — |

*Total 1930 production: 62,888. Pontiac does not state whether this is model or calendar year.

| 1930 Engine | bore × stroke | bhp | availability |
|---|---|---|---|
| I-6, 200.0 | 3.31 × 3.88 | 60 | S-all |

### 1931

| 401 Six (wb 112.0) | Wght | Price | Prod* |
|---|---|---|---|
| cpe 2P | 2,670 | 675 | — |
| spt cpe 2-4P | 2,730 | 715 | — |
| conv cpe 2-4P | 2,710 | 745 | — |
| sdn 2d | 2,765 | 675 | — |
| sdn 4d | 2,845 | 745 | — |
| Custom sdn 4d | 2,855 | 785 | — |

# Pontiac

*Total 1931 production: 84,708. Pontiac does not state whether this is model or calendar year.

| 1931 Engine | bore × stroke | bhp | availability |
|---|---|---|---|
| I-6, 200.0 | 3.31 × 3.88 | 60 | S-all |

## 1932

### 402 Six (wb 114.0)—39,059 built

| | Wght | Price | Prod |
|---|---|---|---|
| std cpe 2P | 2,765 | 635 | — |
| spt cpe 2-4P | 2,810 | 715 | — |
| conv cpe 2-4P | 2,770 | 765 | — |
| sdn 2d | 2,870 | 645 | — |
| sdn 4d | 2,960 | 725 | — |
| Custom sdn 4d | 2,965 | 795 | — |

### 302 V-8 (wb 117.0)—6,281 built

| | Wght | Price | Prod |
|---|---|---|---|
| std cpe 2P | 3,145 | 845 | — |
| spt cpe 2-4P | 3,205 | 925 | — |
| conv cpe 2-4P | 3,165 | 945 | — |
| sdn 2d | 3,225 | 845 | — |
| sdn 4d | 3,310 | 945 | — |
| Custom sdn 4d | 3,335 | 1,025 | — |

| 1932 Engines | bore × stroke | bhp | availability |
|---|---|---|---|
| I-6, 200.0 | 3.31 × 3.88 | 65 | S-402 |
| V-8, 251.0 | 3.44 × 3.38 | 85 | S-302 |

## 1933

### 601 Eight (wb 115.0)—90,198 built

| | Wght | Price | Prod |
|---|---|---|---|
| rdstr 2-4P | 2,675 | 585 | — |
| cpe 2P | 2,865 | 635 | — |
| spt cpe 2-4P | 2,930 | 670 | — |
| conv cpe 2-4P | 2,905 | 695 | — |
| touring sdn 4d | 2,995 | 675 | — |
| sdn 2d | 2,945 | 635 | — |
| sdn 4d | 3,020 | 695 | — |

| 1933 Engine | bore × stroke | bhp | availability |
|---|---|---|---|
| I-8, 223.4 | 3.19 × 3.50 | 77 | S-all |

## 1934

### 603 Eight (wb 117.5)—78,859 built

| | Wght | Price | Prod |
|---|---|---|---|
| cpe 2P | 3,185 | 675 | — |
| spt cpe 2-4P | 3,260 | 725 | — |
| cabriolet 2-4P | 3,225 | 765 | — |
| sdn 2d | 3,280 | 705 | — |
| sdn 2d T/B | 3,300 | 745 | — |
| sdn 4d | 3,350 | 765 | — |
| sdn 4d T/B | 3,405 | 805 | — |

| 1934 Engine | bore × stroke | bhp | availability |
|---|---|---|---|
| I-8, 223.4 | 3.19 × 3.50 | 84 | S-all |

## 1935

### 701-B Standard Six (wb 112.0)—48,302 built

| | Wght | Price | Prod |
|---|---|---|---|
| cpe 2P | 3,065 | 615 | — |
| sdn 2d T/B | 3,195 | 695 | — |
| sdn 2d | 3,195 | 665 | — |
| touring sdn 4d T/B | 3,245 | 745 | — |
| sdn 4d | 3,245 | 715 | — |

### 701-A DeLuxe Six (wb 112.0)—36,032 built

| | Wght | Price | Prod |
|---|---|---|---|
| cpe 2P | 3,125 | 675 | — |
| spt cpe 2-4P | 3,150 | 725 | — |
| cabriolet 2-4P | 3,180 | 775 | — |
| sdn 2d T/B | 3,245 | 745 | — |
| sdn 2d | 3,245 | 715 | — |
| touring sdn 4d T/B | 3,300 | 795 | — |
| sdn 4d | 3,300 | 765 | — |

### 605 Eight (wb 116.6)—44,134 built

| | Wght | Price | Prod |
|---|---|---|---|
| cpe 2P | 3,260 | 730 | — |
| spt cpe 2-4P | 3,290 | 780 | — |
| cabriolet 2-4P | 3,305 | 840 | — |
| sdn 2d T/B | 3,400 | 805 | — |
| sdn 2d | 3,400 | 775 | — |
| touring sdn 4d T/B | 3,450 | 860 | — |
| sdn 4d | 3,450 | 830 | — |

| 1935 Engines | bore × stroke | bhp | availability |
|---|---|---|---|
| I-6, 208.0 | 3.38 × 3.88 | 80 | S-Sixes |
| I-8, 223.4 | 3.19 × 3.50 | 84 | S-Eight |

## 1936

### 6BB Master Six (wb 112.0)—93,475 built

| | Wght | Price | Prod |
|---|---|---|---|
| cpe 2P | 3,085 | 615 | — |
| spt cpe 2-4P | 3,120 | 675 | — |
| cabriolet 2-4P | 3,125 | 760 | — |
| sdn 2d | 3,195 | 675 | — |
| touring sdn 2d T/B | 3,195 | 700 | — |
| sdn 4d | 3,235 | 720 | — |
| touring sdn 4d T/B | 3,245 | 745 | — |

### 6BA DeLuxe Six (wb 112.0)—44,040 built

| | Wght | Price | Prod |
|---|---|---|---|
| cpe 2P | 3,130 | 665 | — |
| spt cpe 2-4P | 3,165 | 720 | — |
| cabriolet 2-4P | 3,200 | 810 | — |
| sdn 2d | 3,265 | 720 | — |
| touring sdn 2d T/B | 3,270 | 745 | — |
| sdn 4d | 3,300 | 770 | — |
| touring sdn 4d T/B | 3,300 | 795 | — |

### 8BA DeLuxe Eight (wb 116.0)—38,755 built

| | Wght | Price | Prod |
|---|---|---|---|
| cpe 2P | 3,250 | 730 | — |
| spt cpe 2-4P | 3,285 | 785 | — |
| cabriolet 2-4P | 3,335 | 855 | — |
| sdn 2d | 3,390 | 770 | — |
| touring sdn 2d T/B | 3,390 | 795 | — |
| sdn 4d | 3,415 | 815 | — |
| touring sdn 4d T/B | 3,420 | 840 | — |

| 1936 Engines | bore × stroke | bhp | availability |
|---|---|---|---|
| I-6, 208.0 | 3.38 × 3.88 | 80 | S-Sixes |
| I-8, 232.3 | 3.25 × 3.50 | 87 | S-Eight |

## 1937

### 6CA DeLuxe Six (wb 117.0)—179,244 built

| | Wght | Price | Prod |
|---|---|---|---|
| cpe 2P | 3,165 | 781 | — |
| spt cpe 2-4P | 3,165 | 853 | — |
| cabriolet 2-4P | 3,250 | 945 | — |
| sdn 2d | 3,240 | 830 | — |
| touring sdn 2d T/B | 3,240 | 855 | — |
| sdn 4d | 3,265 | 881 | — |
| touring sdn 4d T/B | 3,275 | 906 | — |
| conv sdn 5P | 3,375 | 1,197 | — |
| wgn 4d | 3,340 | 992 | — |

### 8CA DeLuxe Eight (wb 122.0)—56,945 built

| | Wght | Price | Prod |
|---|---|---|---|
| cpe 2P | 3,305 | 857 | — |
| spt cpe 2-4p | 3,305 | 913 | — |
| cabriolet 2-4P | 3,360 | 985 | — |
| sdn 2d | 3,385 | 893 | — |
| touring sdn 2d T/B | 3,380 | 919 | — |
| sdn 4d | 3,410 | 939 | — |
| touring sdn 4d T/B | 3,400 | 965 | — |
| conv sdn 5P | 3,505 | 1,235 | — |

# Pontiac

| 1937 Engines | bore × stroke | bhp | availability |
|---|---|---|---|
| I-6, 222.7 | 3.44 × 4.00 | 85 | S-Six |
| I-8, 248.9 | 3.25 × 3.75 | 100 | S-Eight |

## 1938

### 6DA DeLuxe Six (wb 117.0)—77,713 built

| | Wght | Price | Prod |
|---|---|---|---|
| cpe 2P | 3,190 | 835 | — |
| spt cpe 2-4P | 3,200 | 891 | — |
| cabriolet 2-4P | 3,285 | 993 | — |
| sdn 2d | 3,265 | 865 | — |
| touring sdn 2d T/B | 3,265 | 891 | — |
| sdn 4d | 3,295 | 916 | — |
| touring sdn 4d T/B | 3,280 | 942 | — |
| conv sdn 5P | 3,410 | 1,310 | — |
| wgn 4d | 3,420 | 1,110 | — |

### 8DA DeLuxe Eight (wb 122.0)—19,426 built

| | Wght | Price | Prod |
|---|---|---|---|
| cpe 2P | 3,320 | 898 | — |
| spt cpe 2-4P | 3,325 | 955 | — |
| cabriolet 2-4P | 3,390 | 1,057 | — |
| sdn 2d | 3,395 | 934 | — |
| touring sdn 2d T/B | 3,385 | 960 | — |
| sdn 4d | 3,415 | 980 | — |
| touring sdn 4d T/B | 3,410 | 1,006 | — |
| conv sdn 5P | 3,530 | 1,353 | — |

| 1938 Engines | bore × stroke | bhp | availability |
|---|---|---|---|
| I-6, 222.7 | 3.44 × 4.00 | 85 | S-Six |
| I-8, 248.9 | 3.25 × 3.75 | 100 | S-Eight |

## 1939

### 6EA Quality Six (wb 115.0)—55,736 built

| | Wght | Price | Prod |
|---|---|---|---|
| cpe 3P | 2,875 | 758 | — |
| spt cpe 5P | 2,920 | 809 | — |
| touring sdn 2d T/B | 2,965 | 820 | — |
| touring sdn 4d T/B | 3,000 | 866 | — |
| wgn 4d | 3,175 | 990 | — |

### 6EB DeLuxe Six (wb 120.0)—53,830 built

| | Wght | Price | Prod |
|---|---|---|---|
| cpe 3P | 3,020 | 814 | — |
| spt cpe 5P | 3,055 | 865 | — |
| conv cpe 5P | 3,155 | 993 | — |
| touring sdn 2d T/B | 3,115 | 871 | — |
| touring sdn 4d T/B | 3,165 | 922 | — |

### 8EA DeLuxe Eight (wb 120.0)—34,774 built

| | Wght | Price | Prod |
|---|---|---|---|
| cpe 3P | 3,105 | 862 | — |
| spt cpe 5P | 3,165 | 913 | — |
| conv cpe 5P | 3,250 | 1,046 | — |
| touring sdn 2d T/B | 3,225 | 919 | — |
| touring sdn 4d T/B | 3,265 | 970 | — |

| 1939 Engines | bore × stroke | bhp | availability |
|---|---|---|---|
| I-6, 222.7 | 3.44 × 4.00 | 85 | S-Sixes |
| I-8, 248.9 | 3.25 × 3.75 | 100 | S-Eight |

## 1940

### 25HA Special Six (wb 117.0)—106,892 built

| | Wght | Price | Prod |
|---|---|---|---|
| cpe 3P | 3,060 | 783 | — |
| spt cpe 4P | 3,045 | 819 | — |
| sdn 2d | 3,095 | 830 | — |
| wgn 4d, 8P | 3,295 | 1,015 | — |
| sdn 4d | 3,125 | 876 | — |

### 26HB DeLuxe Six (wb 120.0)—58,452 built

| | Wght | Price | Prod |
|---|---|---|---|
| cpe 3P | 3,115 | 835 | — |
| spt cpe 4P | 3,105 | 876 | — |
| cabriolet (conv cpe) | 3,190 | 1,003 | — |
| sdn 2d | 3,170 | 881 | — |
| sdn 4d | 3,210 | 932 | — |

### 28HA DeLuxe Eight (wb 120.0)—20,433 built

| | Wght | Price | Prod |
|---|---|---|---|
| cpe 3P | 3,180 | 875 | — |
| spt cpe 4P | 3,195 | 913 | — |
| cabriolet (conv cpe) | 3,280 | 1,046 | — |
| sdn 2d | 3,250 | 919 | — |
| sdn 4d | 3,300 | 970 | — |

### 29HB Torpedo Eight (wb 122.0)—31,224 built

| | Wght | Price | Prod |
|---|---|---|---|
| spt cpe 4P | 3,390 | 1,016 | — |
| sdn 4d | 3,475 | 1,072 | — |

| 1940 Engines | bore × stroke | bhp | availability |
|---|---|---|---|
| I-6, 222.7 | 3.44 × 4.00 | 87 | S-Sixes |
| I-8, 248.9 | 3.25 × 3.75 | 100 | S-DeLuxe Eight |
| I-8, 248.9 | 3.25 × 3.75 | 103 | S-Torpedo Eight |

## 1941

### 25JA DeLuxe Torpedo Six (wb 119.0)—117,976 built

| | Wght | Price | Prod |
|---|---|---|---|
| cpe 3P | 3,145 | 828 | — |
| sdn cpe | 3,180 | 864 | — |
| conv cpe | 3,335 | 1,023 | — |
| sdn 2d | 3,190 | 874 | — |
| sdn 4d 6W | 3,235 | 921 | — |
| Metropolitan sdn 4d 4W | 3,230 | 921 | — |

### 26JB Streamliner Torpedo Six (wb 122.0)—82,527 built

| | Wght | Price | Prod |
|---|---|---|---|
| sdn cpe | 3,305 | 923 | — |
| Super sdn cpe | 3,320 | 969 | — |
| sdn 4d | 3,365 | 980 | — |
| Super sdn 4d | 3,400 | 1,026 | — |

### 24JC Custom Torpedo Six (wb 122.0)—8,257 built

| | Wght | Price | Prod |
|---|---|---|---|
| sdn cpe | 3,260 | 995 | — |
| sdn 4d | 3,355 | 1,052 | — |
| wgn 4d, 8P | 3,650 | 1,175 | — |
| DeLuxe wgn 4d 8P | 3,665 | 1,225 | — |

### 27JA DeLuxe Torpedo Eight (wb 119.0)—37,823 built

| | Wght | Price | Prod |
|---|---|---|---|
| cpe 3P | 3,220 | 853 | — |
| sdn cpe | 3,250 | 889 | — |
| conv cpe | 3,390 | 1,048 | — |
| sdn 2d | 3,250 | 899 | — |
| sdn 4d 6W | 3,285 | 946 | — |
| Metropolitan sdn 4d 4W | 3,295 | 946 | — |

### 28JB Streamliner Torpedo Eight (wb 122.0)—66,287 built

| | Wght | Price | Prod |
|---|---|---|---|
| sdn cpe | 3,370 | 948 | — |
| Super sdn cpe | 3,385 | 994 | — |
| sdn 4d | 3,425 | 1,005 | — |
| Super sdn 4d | 3,460 | 1,051 | — |

### 29JC Custom Torpedo Eight (wb 122.0)—17,191 built

| | Wght | Price | Prod |
|---|---|---|---|
| sdn cpe | 3,325 | 1,020 | — |
| sdn 4d | 3,430 | 1,077 | — |
| wgn 4d, 8P | 3,715 | 1,200 | — |
| DeLuxe wgn 4d, 8P | 3,730 | 1,250 | — |

| 1941 Engines | bore × stroke | bhp | availability |
|---|---|---|---|
| I-6, 239.2 | 3.56 × 4.00 | 90 | S-Sixes |
| I-8, 248.9 | 3.25 × 3.75 | 103 | S-Eights |

## 1942

### 25KA Torpedo Six (wb 119.0)—29,886 built

| | Wght | Price | Prod |
|---|---|---|---|
| cpe 3P | 3,210 | 895 | — |
| sdn cpe | 3,255 | 950 | — |
| spt cpe | 3,260 | 935 | — |
| conv cpe | 3,535 | 1,165 | — |
| sdn 2d | 3,265 | 940 | — |
| sdn 4d 6W | 3,305 | 985 | — |

# Pontiac

| 25KA Torpedo Six (wb 119.0) | Wght | Price | Prod |
|---|---|---|---|
| Metropolitan sdn 4d 4W | 3,295 | 985 | — |
| **26KB Streamliner Six (wb 122.0)** | | | |
| sdn cpe | 3,355 | 980 | ⎫ |
| sdn 4d | 3,415 | 1,035 | ⎬ 10,284 |
| wgn 4d, 8P | 3,810 | 1,265 | ⎭ |
| Chieftain sdn cpe | 3,400 | 1,030 | ⎫ |
| Chieftain sdn 4d | 3,460 | 1,085 | ⎬ 2,458 |
| Chieftain wgn 4d 6P | 3,785 | 1,315 | ⎭ |
| **27KA Torpedo Eight (wb 119.0)—14,421 built** | | | |
| cpe 3P | 3,270 | 920 | — |
| sdn cpe | 3,320 | 975 | — |
| spt cpe | 3,320 | 960 | — |
| conv cpe | 3,605 | 1,190 | — |
| sdn 2d | 3,325 | 965 | — |
| sdn 4d 6W | 3,360 | 1,010 | — |
| Metropolitan sdn 4d 4W | 3,355 | 1,010 | — |
| **28KB Streamliner Eight (wb 122.0)** | | | |
| sdn cpe | 3,430 | 1,005 | ⎫ |
| sdn 4d | 3,485 | 1,060 | ⎬ 15,465 |
| wgn 4d, 8P | 3,885 | 1,290 | ⎭ |
| Chieftain sdn cpe | 3,460 | 1,055 | ⎫ |
| Chieftain sdn 4d | 3,515 | 1,110 | ⎬ 11,041 |
| Chieftain wgn 4d 6P | 3,865 | 1,340 | ⎭ |

| 1942 Engines | bore × stroke | bhp | availability |
|---|---|---|---|
| I-6, 239.2 | 3.56 × 4.00 | 90 | S-Sixes |
| I-8, 248.9 | 3.25 × 3.75 | 103 | S-Eights |

## 1946

### 25LA Torpedo Six (wb 119.0)—26,636 built

| | Wght | Price | Prod |
|---|---|---|---|
| sdn 4d | 3,361 | 1,427 | — |
| sdn 2d | 3,326 | 1,368 | — |
| sdn cpe | 3,326 | 1,399 | — |
| spt cpe | 3,311 | 1,353 | — |
| cpe 3P | 3,261 | 1,307 | — |
| conv cpe | 3,591 | 1,631 | — |
| **26LB Streamliner Six (wb 122.0)—43,430 built** | | | |
| sdn 4d | 3,490 | 1,510 | — |
| sdn cpe | 3,435 | 1,438 | — |
| wgn 4d 8P | 3,790 | 1,942 | — |
| DeLuxe wgn 4d 8P | 3,735 | 2,019 | — |
| **27LA Torpedo Eight (wb 119.0)—18,273 built** | | | |
| sdn 4d | 3,436 | 1,455 | — |
| sdn 2d | 3,396 | 1,395 | — |
| sdn cpe | 3,391 | 1,428 | — |
| spt cpe | 3,376 | 1,381 | — |
| cpe 3P | 3,331 | 1,335 | — |
| conv cpe | 3,651 | 1,658 | — |
| **28LB Streamliner Eight (wb 122.0)—49,301 built** | | | |
| sdn 4d | 3,550 | 1,538 | — |
| sdn cpe | 3,495 | 1,468 | — |
| wgn 4d 8P | 3,870 | 1,970 | — |
| DeLuxe wgn 4d 8P | 3,850 | 2,047 | — |

| 1946 Engines | bore × stroke | bhp | availability |
|---|---|---|---|
| I-6, 239.2 | 3.56 × 4.00 | 90 | S-Sixes |
| I-8, 248.9 | 3.25 × 3.75 | 103 | S-Eights |

## 1947

### 6MA Torpedo Six (wb 119.0)—67,125 built

| | Wght | Price | Prod |
|---|---|---|---|
| sdn 4d | 3,320 | 1,512 | — |

| 6MA Torpedo Six (wb 119.0) | Wght | Price | Prod |
|---|---|---|---|
| sdn 2d | 3,295 | 1,453 | — |
| sdn cpe | 3,300 | 1,484 | — |
| spt cpe | 3,295 | 1,438 | — |
| cpe 3P | 3,245 | 1,387 | — |
| conv cpe | 3,560 | 1,811 | — |
| DeLuxe conv cpe | 3,560 | 1,853 | — |
| **6MB Streamliner Six (wb 122.0)—42,336 built** | | | |
| sdn 4d | 3,450 | 1,598 | — |
| sdn cpe | 3,400 | 1,547 | — |
| wgn 4d 8P | 3,775 | 2,235 | — |
| DeLuxe wgn 4d 8P | 3,715 | 2,312 | — |
| **8MA Torpedo Eight (wb 119.0)—34,815 built** | | | |
| sdn 4d | 3,405 | 1,559 | — |
| sdn 2d | 3,370 | 1,500 | — |
| sdn cpe | 3,370 | 1,531 | — |
| spt cpe | 3,360 | 1,485 | — |
| cpe 3P | 3,310 | 1,434 | — |
| conv cpe | 3,635 | 1,854 | — |
| DeLuxe conv cpe | 3,635 | 1,900 | — |
| **8MB Streamliner Eight (wb 122.0)—86,324 built** | | | |
| sdn 4d | 3,515 | 1,645 | — |
| sdn cpe | 3,455 | 1,595 | — |
| wgn 4d 8P | 3,845 | 2,282 | — |
| DeLuxe wgn 4d 8P | 3,790 | 2,359 | — |

| 1947 Engines | bore × stroke | bhp | availability |
|---|---|---|---|
| I-6, 239.2 | 3.56 × 4.00 | 90 | S-Six |
| I-8, 248.9 | 3.25 × 3.75 | 103 | S-Eight |

## 1948

| 6PA Torpedo Six (wb 119.0)—39,262 built | Wght | Price | Prod |
|---|---|---|---|
| sdn 4d | 3,320 | 1,641 | — |
| sdn 2d | 3,280 | 1,583 | — |
| sdn cpe | 3,275 | 1,614 | — |
| spt cpe | 3,220 | 1,552 | — |
| bus cpe | 3,230 | 1,500 | — |
| DeLuxe sdn 4d | 3,340 | 1,731 | — |
| DeLuxe sdn cpe | 3,275 | 1,704 | — |
| DeLuxe spt cpe | 3,230 | 1,641 | — |
| DeLuxe conv cpe | 3,525 | 2,025 | — |
| **6PB Streamliner Six (wb 122.0)—37,742 built** | | | |
| sdn 4d | 3,450 | 1,727 | — |
| sdn cpe | 3,365 | 1,677 | — |
| wgn 4d 8P | 3,755 | 2,364 | — |
| DeLuxe sdn 4d | 3,455 | 1,817 | — |
| DeLuxe sdn cpe | 3,370 | 1,766 | — |
| DeLuxe wgn 4d 6P | 3,695 | 2,442 | — |
| **8PA Torpedo Eight (wb 119.0)—35,300 built** | | | |
| sdn 4d | 3,395 | 1,689 | — |
| sdn 2d | 3,360 | 1,630 | — |
| sdn cpe | 3,340 | 1,661 | — |
| spt cpe | 3,295 | 1,599 | — |
| bus cpe | 3,295 | 1,548 | — |
| DeLuxe sdn 4d | 3,395 | 1,778 | — |
| DeLuxe sdn cpe | 3,340 | 1,751 | — |
| DeLuxe spt cpe | 3,305 | 1,689 | — |
| DeLuxe conv cpe | 3,600 | 2,072 | — |
| **8PB Streamliner Eight (wb 122.0)—123,115 built** | | | |
| sdn 4d | 3,525 | 1,775 | — |
| sdn cpe | 3,425 | 1,724 | — |
| wgn 4d 8P | 3,820 | 2,412 | — |
| DeLuxe sdn 4d | 3,530 | 1,864 | — |
| DeLuxe sdn cpe | 3,455 | 1,814 | — |
| DeLuxe wgn 4d 6P | 3,765 | 2,490 | — |

# Pontiac

| 1948 Engines | bore × stroke | bhp | availability |
|---|---|---|---|
| I-6, 239.2 | 3.56 × 4.00 | 90 | S-Six |
| I-8, 248.9 | 3.25 × 3.75 | 103 | S-Eight |

## 1949

### 6R Streamliner Six (wb 120.0)—69,654 built (includes 6R Chieftain)

| | Wght | Price | Prod |
|---|---|---|---|
| sdn 4d | 3,385 | 1,740 | — |
| sdn cpe | 3,360 | 1,689 | — |
| wgn 4d 8P wood body | 3,745 | 2,543 | — |
| wgn 4d 8P metal body | 3,650 | 2,543 | — |
| DeLuxe sdn 4d | 3,415 | 1,835 | — |
| DeLuxe sdn cpe | 3,375 | 1,784 | — |
| Dlx wgn 4d 6P wood body | 3,730 | 2,622 | — |
| Dlx wgn 4d 6P metal body | 3,580 | 2,622 | — |

### 6R Chieftain Six (wb 120.0)

| | | | |
|---|---|---|---|
| sdn 4d | 3,385 | 1,761 | — |
| sdn 2d | 3,355 | 1,710 | — |
| sdn cpe | 3,330 | 1,710 | — |
| bus cpe | 3,280 | 1,587 | — |
| DeLuxe sdn 4d | 3,415 | 1,856 | — |
| DeLuxe sdn 2d | 3,360 | 1,805 | — |
| DeLuxe sdn cpe | 3,345 | 1,805 | — |
| DeLuxe conv cpe | 3,600 | 2,138 | — |

### 8R Streamliner Eight (wb 120.0)—235,165 built (includes 8R Chieftain)

| | | | |
|---|---|---|---|
| sdn 4d | 3,470 | 1,808 | — |
| sdn cpe | 3,435 | 1,758 | — |
| wgn 4d 8P wood body | 3,835 | 2,611 | — |
| wgn 4d 8P metal body | 3,690 | 2,611 | — |
| DeLuxe sdn 4d | 3,500 | 1,903 | — |
| DeLuxe sdn cpe | 3,445 | 1,853 | — |
| Dlx wgn 4d 6P wood body | 3,800 | 2,690 | — |
| Dlx wgn 4d 6P metal body | 3,640 | 2,690 | — |

### 8R Chieftain Eight (wb 120.0)

| | | | |
|---|---|---|---|
| sdn 4d | 3,475 | 1,829 | — |
| sdn 2d | 3,430 | 1,779 | — |
| sdn cpe | 3,390 | 1,779 | — |
| bus cpe | 3,355 | 1,656 | — |
| DeLuxe sdn 4d | 3,480 | 1,924 | — |
| DeLuxe sdn 2d | 3,430 | 1,874 | — |
| DeLuxe sdn cpe | 3,415 | 1,874 | — |
| DeLuxe conv cpe | 3,670 | 2,206 | — |

| 1949 Engines | bore × stroke | bhp | availability |
|---|---|---|---|
| I-6, 239.2 | 3.56 × 4.00 | 90 | S-Sixes |
| I-6, 239.2 | 3.56 × 4.00 | 93 | O-Sixes |
| I-8, 248.9 | 3.25 × 3.75 | 104 | S-Eights |
| I-8, 248.9 | 3.25 × 3.75 | 106 | O-Eights |

## 1950

### 6T Streamliner Six (wb 120.0)—115,542 built (includes 6T Chieftain)

| | Wght | Price | Prod |
|---|---|---|---|
| fstbk sdn 4d | 3,414 | 1,724 | — |
| fstbk sdn cpe | 3,379 | 1,673 | — |
| wgn 4d 8P | 3,714 | 2,264 | — |
| DeLuxe fstbk sdn 4d | 3,419 | 1,819 | — |
| DeLuxe fstbk sdn cpe | 3,399 | 1,768 | — |
| DeLuxe wgn 4d 6P | 3,649 | 2,343 | — |

### 6T Chieftain Six (wb 120.0)

| | | | |
|---|---|---|---|
| sdn 4d | 3,409 | 1,745 | — |
| sdn 2d | 3,384 | 1,694 | — |
| sdn cpe | 3,359 | 1,694 | — |
| bus cpe | 3,319 | 1,571 | — |
| DeLuxe sdn 4d | 3,414 | 1,840 | — |

### 6T Chieftain Six (wb 120.0)

| | Wght | Price | Prod |
|---|---|---|---|
| DeLuxe sdn 2d | 3,389 | 1,789 | — |
| DeLuxe sdn cpe | 3,364 | 1,789 | — |
| DeLuxe Catalina htp cpe | 3,469 | 2,000 | — |
| DeLuxe conv cpe | 3,624 | 2,122 | — |
| Super Dlx Catalina htp cpe | 3,469 | 2,058 | — |

### 8T Streamliner Eight (wb 120.0)—330,997 built (includes 8T Chieftain)

| | | | |
|---|---|---|---|
| fstbk sdn 4d | 3,499 | 1,792 | — |
| fstbk sdn cpe | 3,464 | 1,742 | — |
| wgn 4d 8P | 3,799 | 2,332 | — |
| DeLuxe fstbk sdn 4d | 3,509 | 1,887 | — |
| DeLuxe fstbk sdn cpe | 3,469 | 1,837 | — |
| DeLuxe wgn 4d 6P | 3,739 | 2,411 | — |

### 8T Chieftain Eight (wb 120.0)

| | | | |
|---|---|---|---|
| sdn 4d | 3,494 | 1,813 | — |
| sdn 2d | 3,454 | 1,763 | — |
| sdn cpe | 3,444 | 1,763 | — |
| bus cpe | 3,399 | 1,640 | — |
| DeLuxe sdn 4d | 3,499 | 1,908 | — |
| DeLuxe sdn 2d | 2,464 | 1,858 | — |
| DeLuxe sdn cpe | 3,454 | 1,858 | — |
| DeLuxe Catalina htp cpe | 3,549 | 2,069 | — |
| DeLuxe conv cpe | 3,704 | 2,190 | — |
| Super Dlx Catalina htp cpe | 3,549 | 2,127 | — |

| 1950 Engines | bore × stroke | bhp | availability |
|---|---|---|---|
| I-6, 239.2 | 3.56 × 4.00 | 90 | S-Sixes |
| I-6, 239.2 | 3.56 × 4.00 | 93 | O-Sixes |
| I-8, 268.4 | 3.38 × 3.75 | 108 | S-Eights |
| I-8, 268.4 | 3.38 × 3.75 | 113 | O-Eights |

## 1951

### 6U Streamliner Six (wb 120.0)—53,748 built (includes 6U Chieftain)

| | | | |
|---|---|---|---|
| fstbk sdn cpe | 3,363 | 1,824 | — |
| wgn 4d 8P | 3,718 | 2,470 | — |
| DeLuxe fstbk sdn cpe | 3,378 | 1,927 | — |
| DeLuxe wgn 4d 6P | 3,638 | 2,556 | — |

### 6U Chieftain Six (wb 120.0)

| | | | |
|---|---|---|---|
| sdn 4d | 3,388 | 1,903 | — |
| sdn 2d | 3,358 | 1,848 | — |
| sdn cpe | 3,338 | 1,848 | — |
| bus cpe | 3,308 | 1,713 | — |
| DeLuxe sdn 4d | 3,388 | 2,006 | — |
| DeLuxe sdn 2d | 3,358 | 1,951 | — |
| DeLuxe sdn cpe | 3,343 | 1,951 | — |
| DeLuxe Catalina htp cpe | 3,458 | 2,182 | — |
| DeLuxe conv cpe | 3,603 | 2,314 | — |
| Super Dlx Catalina htp cpe | 3,468 | 2,244 | — |

### 8U Streamliner Eight (wb 120.0)—316,411 built (includes 8U Chieftain)

| | | | |
|---|---|---|---|
| fstbk sdn cpe | 3,458 | 1,900 | — |
| wgn 4d 8P | 3,813 | 2,544 | — |
| DeLuxe fstbk sdn cpe | 3,463 | 2,003 | — |
| DeLuxe wgn 4d 6P | 3,743 | 2,629 | — |

### 8U Chieftain Eight (wb 120.0)

| | | | |
|---|---|---|---|
| sdn 4d | 3,478 | 1,977 | — |
| sdn 2d | 3,443 | 1,922 | — |
| sdn cpe | 3,418 | 1,922 | — |
| bus cpe | 3,388 | 1,787 | — |
| DeLuxe sdn 4d | 3,488 | 2,081 | — |
| DeLuxe sdn 2d | 3,448 | 2,026 | — |
| DeLuxe sdn cpe | 3,433 | 2,026 | — |
| DeLuxe Catalina htp cpe | 3,543 | 2,257 | — |
| DeLuxe conv cpe | 3,683 | 2,388 | — |
| Super Dlx Catalina htp cpe | 3,548 | 2,320 | — |

# Pontiac

| 1951 Engines | bore × stroke | bhp | availability |
|---|---|---|---|
| I-6, 239.2 | 3.56 × 4.00 | 96 | S-Sixes |
| I-6, 239.2 | 3.56 × 4.00 | 100 | S-Sixes |
| I-8, 268.4 | 3.38 × 3.75 | 116 | S-Eights |
| I-8, 268.4 | 3.38 × 3.75 | 120 | S-Eights |

### 1952
#### 6W Chieftain Six (wb 120.0)—19,809 built

| | Wght | Price | Prod |
|---|---|---|---|
| sdn 4d | 3,403 | 2,014 | — |
| sdn 2d | 3,378 | 1,956 | — |
| wgn 4d 8P | 3,718 | 2,615 | — |
| DeLuxe sdn 4d | 3,403 | 2,119 | — |
| DeLuxe sdn 2d | 3,378 | 2,060 | — |
| DeLuxe Catalina htp cpe | 3,483 | 2,304 | — |
| DeLuxe conv cpe | 3,603 | 2,444 | — |
| DeLuxe wgn 4d 6P | 3,653 | 2,699 | — |
| Super Dlx Catalina htp cpe | 3,493 | 2,370 | — |

#### 8W Chieftain Eight (wb 120.0)—251,564 built

| | Wght | Price | Prod |
|---|---|---|---|
| sdn 4d | 3,503 | 2,090 | — |
| sdn 2d | 3,458 | 2,031 | — |
| wgn 4d 8P | 3,813 | 2,689 | — |
| DeLuxe sdn 4d | 3,503 | 2,194 | — |
| DeLuxe sdn 2d | 3,458 | 2,136 | — |
| DeLuxe Catalina htp cpe | 3,568 | 2,380 | — |
| DeLuxe conv cpe | 3,683 | 2,518 | — |
| DeLuxe wgn 4d 6P | 3,758 | 2,772 | — |
| Super Dlx Catalina htp cpe | 3,573 | 2,446 | — |

| 1952 Engines | bore × stroke | bhp | availability |
|---|---|---|---|
| I-6, 239.2 | 3.56 × 4.00 | 100/102 | S-Six man/auto |
| I-8, 268.4 | 3.38 × 3.75 | 118/122 | S-Eight man/auto |

### 1953
#### 6X Chieftain Six (wb 122.0)—38,914 built

| | Wght | Price | Prod |
|---|---|---|---|
| sdn 4d | 3,506 | 2,015 | — |
| sdn 2d | 3,466 | 1,956 | — |
| wgn 4d 6P | 3,713 | 2,450 | — |
| wgn 4d 6P (woodgrain) | 3,713 | 2,530 | — |
| wgn 4d 8P | 3,791 | 2,505 | — |
| wgn 4d 8P (woodgrain) | 3,791 | 2,585 | — |
| DeLuxe sdn 4d | 3,521 | 2,119 | — |
| DeLuxe sdn 2d | 3,481 | 2,060 | — |
| DeLuxe Catalina htp cpe | 3,546 | 2,304 | — |
| DeLuxe conv cpe | 3,696 | 2,444 | — |
| DeLuxe wgn 4d 6P | 3,751 | 2,590 | — |
| DeLuxe 4d 6P (woodgrain) | 3,751 | 2,670 | — |
| Custom Catalina htp cpe | 3,546 | 2,370 | — |

#### 8X Chieftain Eight (wb 122.0)—379,705 built

| | Wght | Price | Prod |
|---|---|---|---|
| sdn 4d | 3,581 | 2,090 | — |
| sdn 2d | 3,546 | 2,031 | — |
| wgn 4d 6P | 3,811 | 2,525 | — |
| wgn 4d 6P (woodgrain) | 3,811 | 2,605 | — |
| wgn 4d 8P | 3,881 | 2,580 | — |
| wgn 4d 8P (woodgrain) | 3,881 | 2,660 | — |
| DeLuxe sdn 4d | 3,596 | 2,194 | — |
| DeLuxe sdn 2d | 3,561 | 2,136 | — |
| DeLuxe Catalina htp cpe | 3,621 | 2,380 | — |
| DeLuxe conv cpe | 3,751 | 2,518 | — |
| DeLuxe wgn 4d 6P | 3,841 | 2,664 | — |
| Dlx wgn 4d 6P (woodgrain) | 3,841 | 2,744 | — |
| Custom Catalina htp cpe | 3,621 | 2,446 | — |

| 1953 Engines | bore × stroke | bhp | availability |
|---|---|---|---|
| I-6, 239.2 | 3.56 × 4.00 | 115 | S-Six man |
| I-6, 239.2 | 3.56 × 4.00 | 118 | S-Six auto |
| I-8, 268.4 | 3.38 × 3.75 | 118 | S-Eight man |
| I-8, 268.4 | 3.38 × 3.75 | 122 | S-Eight auto |

### 1954
#### 6Z Chieftain Six (wb 122.0)—22,670 built

| | Wght | Price | Prod |
|---|---|---|---|
| Special sdn 4d | 3,391 | 2,027 | — |
| Special sdn 2d | 3,331 | 1,968 | — |
| Special wgn 4d 8P | 3,691 | 2,419 | — |
| Special wgn 4d 6P | 3,601 | 2,364 | — |
| DeLuxe sdn 4d | 3,406 | 2,131 | — |
| DeLuxe sdn 2d | 3,351 | 2,072 | — |
| DeLuxe Catalina htp cpe | 3,421 | 2,316 | — |
| DeLuxe wgn 4d 6P | 3,646 | 2,504 | — |
| Custom Catalina htp cpe | 3,421 | 2,382 | — |

#### 8Z Chieftain Eight (wb 122.0)—149,986 built

| | Wght | Price | Prod |
|---|---|---|---|
| Special sdn 4d | 3,451 | 2,102 | — |
| Special sdn 2d | 3,396 | 2,043 | — |
| Special wgn 4d 8P | 3,771 | 2,494 | — |
| Special wgn 4d 6P | 3,676 | 2,439 | — |
| DeLuxe sdn 4d | 3,466 | 2,206 | — |
| DeLuxe sdn 2d | 3,416 | 2,148 | — |
| DeLuxe Catalina htp cpe | 3,491 | 2,392 | — |
| DeLuxe wgn 4d 6P | 3,716 | 2,579 | — |
| Custom Catalina htp cpe | 3,491 | 2,458 | — |

#### 8Z Star Chief (wb 124.0)—115,088 built

| | Wght | Price | Prod |
|---|---|---|---|
| DeLuxe sdn 4d | 3,536 | 2,301 | — |
| DeLuxe conv cpe | 3,776 | 2,630 | — |
| Custom sdn 4d | 3,536 | 2,394 | — |
| Custom Catalina htp cpe | 3,551 | 2,557 | — |

| 1954 Engines | bore × stroke | bhp | availability |
|---|---|---|---|
| I-6, 239.2 | 3.56 × 4.00 | 115 | S-Six man |
| I-6, 239.2 | 3.56 × 4.00 | 118 | S-Six auto |
| I-8, 268.4 | 3.38 × 3.75 | 122 | S-Eights |
| I-8, 268.4 | 3.38 × 3.75 | 127 | S-Eights |

### 1955
#### 860 Chieftain (wb 122.0)

| | Wght | Price | Prod |
|---|---|---|---|
| sdn 4d | 3,511 | 2,164 | 65,155 |
| sdn 2d | 3,476 | 2,105 | 58,654 |
| wgn 4d 8P | 3,686 | 2,518 | 6,091 |
| wgn 2d 6P | 3,626 | 2,434 | 8,620 |

#### 870 Chieftain (wb 122.0)

| | Wght | Price | Prod |
|---|---|---|---|
| sdn 4d | 3,511 | 2,268 | 91,187 |
| sdn 2d | 3,476 | 2,209 | 28,950 |
| Catalina htp cpe | 3,521 | 2,335 | 72,608 |
| wgn 4d 6P | 3,676 | 2,603 | 19,439 |

#### Star Chief (wb 124.0; wgn-122.0)

| | Wght | Price | Prod |
|---|---|---|---|
| sdn 4d | 3,556 | 2,362 | 44,800 |
| conv cpe | 3,791 | 2,691 | 19,762 |
| Custom sdn 4d | 3,557 | 2,455 | 35,153 |
| Custom Catalina htp cpe | 3,566 | 2,499 | 99,629 |
| Custom Safari wgn 2d 6P | 3,636 | 2,962 | 3,760 |

| 1955 Engines | bore × stroke | bhp | availability |
|---|---|---|---|
| V-8, 287.2 | 3.75 × 3.25 | 173 | S-all (manual) |
| V-8, 287.2 | 3.75 × 3.25 | 180 | S-all (automatic) |
| V-8, 287.2 | 3.75 × 3.25 | 200 | O-all |

### 1956
#### 860 Chieftain (wb 122.0)

| | Wght | Price | Prod |
|---|---|---|---|
| sdn 4d | 3,512 | 2,298 | 41,987 |
| Catalina htp sdn | 3,577 | 2,443 | 35,201 |
| sdn 2d | 3,452 | 2,240 | 41,908 |
| Catalina htp cpe | 3,512 | 2,370 | 46,335 |
| wgn 4d 9P | 3,707 | 2,653 | 12,702 |
| wgn 2d 6P | 3,612 | 2,569 | 6,099 |

# Pontiac

| 870 Chieftain (wb 122.0) | Wght | Price | Prod |
|---|---|---|---|
| sdn 4d | 3,512 | 2,413 | 22,082 |
| Catalina htp sdn | 3,577 | 2,534 | 25,372 |
| Catalina htp cpe | 3,512 | 2,840 | 24,744 |
| wgn 4d 6P | 3,657 | 2,749 | 21,674 |
| **Star Chief (wb 124.0; wgn-122.0)** | | | |
| sdn 4d | 3,577 | 2,527 | 18,346 |
| conv cpe | 3,797 | 2,857 | 13,510 |
| Custom Catalina htp sdn | 3,647 | 2,735 | 48,035 |
| Custom Catalina htp cpe | 3,567 | 2,665 | 43,392 |
| Custom Safari wgn 2d 6P | 3,642 | 3,129 | 4,042 |

| 1956 Engines | bore × stroke | bhp | availability |
|---|---|---|---|
| V-8, 316.6 | 3.94 × 3.25 | 192 | O-Chieftain |
| V-8, 316.6 | 3.94 × 3.25 | 205 | S-Chieftain |
| V-8, 316.6 | 3.94 × 3.25 | 216 | O-Str Chf, Chftns |
| V-8, 316.6 | 3.94 × 3.25 | 227 | S-Str Chf; O-Chftns |
| V-8, 316.6 | 3.94 × 3.25 | 285 | O-all |

## 1957

| Chieftain (wb 122.0) | Wght | Price | Prod |
|---|---|---|---|
| sdn 4d | 3,560 | 2,527 | 35,671 |
| Catalina htp sdn | 3,635 | 2,614 | 40,074 |
| sdn 2d | 3,515 | 2,463 | 21,343 |
| Catalina htp cpe | 3,555 | 2,529 | 51,017 |
| Safari wgn 4d 9P | 3,835 | 2,898 | 11,536 |
| Safari wgn 2d 6P | 3,690 | 2,841 | 2,934 |
| **Super Chief (wb 122.0)** | | | |
| sdn 4d | 3,585 | 2,664 | 15,153 |
| Catalina htp sdn | 3,640 | 2,793 | 19,758 |
| Catalina htp cpe | 3,570 | 2,735 | 15,494 |
| Safari wgn 4d 6P | 3,765 | 3,021 | 14,095 |
| **Star Chief (wb 124.0; wgn-122.0)** | | | |
| sdn 4d | 3,630 | 2,839 | 3,774 |
| conv cpe | 3,860 | 3,105 | 12,789 |
| Custom sdn 4d | 3,645 | 2,896 | 8,874 |
| Custom Catalina htp sdn | 3,710 | 2,975 | 44,283 |
| Custom Catalina htp cpe | 3,640 | 2,901 | 32,862 |
| Custom Safari wgn 4d 6P | 3,810 | 3,636 | 1,894 |
| Custom Safari wgn 2d 6P* | 3,750 | 3,481 | 1,292 |
| **Bonneville (wb 124.0)** | | | |
| conv cpe | 4,285 | 5,782 | 630 |

*All 1957 Pontiac wagons were called Safari. The model indicated is the "hardtop-styled" Safari offered 1955-1957 only.

| 1957 Engines | bore × stroke | bhp | availability |
|---|---|---|---|
| V-8, 347.0 | 3.94 × 3.56 | 227 | S-Chieftain man |
| V-8, 347.0 | 3.94 × 3.56 | 252 | S-Chieftain auto |
| V-8, 347.0 | 3.94 × 3.56 | 244 | S-Super, Star Chief man |
| V-8, 347.0 | 3.94 × 3.56 | 270 | S-Spr Chf, Str Chf auto |
| V-8, 347.0 | 3.94 × 3.56 | 290 | O-all exc Bonneville |
| V-8, 370.0 | 4.06 × 3.56 | 310 | S-Bonneville (fuel inj) |

## 1958

| Chieftain (wb 122.0) | | Wght | Price | Prod |
|---|---|---|---|---|
| 2567 | conv cpe | 3,850 | 3,019 | 7,359 |
| 2731 | Catalina htp cpe | 3,650 | 2,707 | 26,003 |
| 2739 | Catalina htp sdn | 3,785 | 2,792 | 17,946 |
| 2741 | sdn 2d | 3,640 | 2,573 | 17,394 |
| 2749 | sdn 4d | 3,735 | 2,638 | 44,999 |
| 2793 | Safari wgn 4d 6P | 4,025 | 3,019 | 9,701 |
| 2794 | Safari wgn 4d 9P | 4,070 | 3,088 | 5,417 |

| Super Chief (wb 124.0) | | Wght | Price | Prod |
|---|---|---|---|---|
| 2831D | Catalina htp cpe | 3,690 | 2,880 | 7,236 |
| 2839D | Catalina htp sdn | 3,810 | 2,961 | 7,886 |
| 2849D | sdn 4d | 3,770 | 2,834 | 12,006 |
| **Star Chief (wb 124.0; wgn-122.0)** | | | | |
| 2793SC | Custom Safari wgn 4d 6P | 4,065 | 3,350 | 2,905 |
| 2831SD | Catalina htp cpe | 3,735 | 3,122 | 13,888 |
| 2839SD | Catalina htp sdn | 3,850 | 3,210 | 21,455 |
| 2849SD | Custom sdn 4d | 3,825 | 3,071 | 10,547 |
| **Bonneville (wb 122.0)** | | | | |
| 2547SD | Sport Coupe htp | 3,710 | 3,481 | 9,144 |
| 2567SD | conv cpe | 3,925 | 3,586 | 3,096 |

| 1958 Engines | bore × stroke | bhp | availability |
|---|---|---|---|
| V-8, 370.0 | 4.06 × 3.56 | 240 | S-Chieftain/Super Chief man |
| V-8, 370.0 | 4.06 × 3.56 | 255 | S-Str Chf/Bnville man |
| V-8, 370.0 | 4.06 × 3.56 | 270 | S-Chieftain/Super Chief auto |
| V-8, 370.0 | 4.06 × 3.56 | 285 | S-Str Chf/Bnville auto |
| V-8, 370.0 | 4.06 × 3.56 | 300 | O-all (Tri-Power) |
| V-8, 370.0 | 4.06 × 3.56 | 310 | O-all (fuel injection) |

## 1959

| Catalina (wb 122.0) | | Wght | Price | Prod |
|---|---|---|---|---|
| 2111 | Sport sdn 2d | 3,870 | 2,633 | 26,102 |
| 2119 | sdn 4d | 3,955 | 2,704 | 72,377 |
| 2135 | Safari wgn 4d 6P | 4,345 | 3,101 | 21,162 |
| 2137 | Sport Coupe htp | 3,900 | 2,768 | 38,309 |
| 2139 | Vista Sedan htp | 4,005 | 2,844 | 45,012 |
| 2145 | Safari wgn 4d 9P | 4,405 | 3,209 | 14,084 |
| 2167 | conv cpe | 3,970 | 3,080 | 14,515 |
| **Star Chief (wb 124.0)** | | | | |
| 2411 | Sport sdn 2d | 3,930 | 2,934 | 10,254 |
| 2419 | sdn 4d | 4,005 | 3,005 | 27,872 |
| 2439 | Vista Sedan htp | 4,055 | 3,138 | 30,689 |
| **Bonneville (wb 124.0; wgn-122.0)** | | | | |
| 2735 | Custom Safari wgn 4d 6P | 4,370 | 3,532 | 4,673 |
| 2837 | Sport Coupe htp | 3,985 | 3,257 | 27,769 |
| 2839 | Vista Sedan htp | 4,085 | 3,333 | 38,696 |
| 2867 | conv cpe | 4,070 | 3,478 | 11,426 |

| 1959 Engines | bore × stroke | bhp | availability |
|---|---|---|---|
| V-8, 389.0 | 4.06 × 3.75 | 215 | O-all auto |
| V-8, 389.0 | 4.06 × 3.75 | 245 | S-Catalina/Star Chief man |
| V-8, 389.0 | 4.06 × 3.75 | 260 | S-Bonneville manual |
| V-8, 389.0 | 4.06 × 3.75 | 280 | S-Catal/Str Chf auto |
| V-8, 389.0 | 4.06 × 3.75 | 300 | S-Bonneville auto |
| V-8, 389.0 | 4.06 × 3.75 | 300/303 | O-all (4bbl) |
| V-8, 389.0 | 4.06 × 3.75 | 315/345 | O-all (Tri-Power) |

## 1960

| Catalina (wb 122.0) | | Wght | Price | Prod |
|---|---|---|---|---|
| 2111 | Sport sdn 2d | 3,835 | 2,631 | 25,504 |
| 2119 | sdn 4d | 3,935 | 2,702 | 72,650 |
| 2135 | Safari wgn 4d 6P | 4,310 | 3,099 | 21,253 |
| 2137 | Sport Coupe htp | 3,850 | 2,766 | 27,496 |
| 2139 | Vista Sedan htp | 3,990 | 2,842 | 32,710 |
| 2145 | Safari wgn 4d 9P | 4,365 | 3,207 | 14,149 |
| 2167 | conv cpe | 3,940 | 3,078 | 17,172 |
| **Ventura (wb 122.0)** | | | | |
| 2337 | Sport Coupe htp | 3,865 | 2,971 | 27,577 |
| 2339 | Vista Sedan htp | 3,990 | 3,047 | 28,700 |

# Pontiac

| | Star Chief (wb 124.0) | Wght | Price | Prod |
|---|---|---|---|---|
| 2411 | Sport sdn 2d | 3,910 | 2,932 | 5,797 |
| 2419 | sdn 4d | 3,995 | 3,003 | 23,038 |
| 2439 | Vista Sedan htp | 4,040 | 3,136 | 14,856 |
| | **Bonneville (wb 124.0; wgn-122.0)** | | | |
| 2735 | Custom Safari wgn 4d 6P | 4,360 | 3,530 | 5,163 |
| 2837 | Sport Coupe htp | 3,965 | 3,255 | 24,015 |
| 2839 | Vista Sedan htp | 4,065 | 3,331 | 39,037 |
| 2867 | conv cpe | 4,030 | 3,476 | 17,062 |

| 1960 Engines | bore × stroke | bhp | availability |
|---|---|---|---|
| V-8, 389.0 | 4.06 × 3.75 | 215 | O-all auto |
| V-8, 389.0 | 4.06 × 3.75 | 245 | S-Str Chf/Cat/Vent man |
| V-8, 389.0 | 4.06 × 3.75 | 283 | S-Str Chf/Cat/Vent auto |
| V-8, 389.0 | 4.06 × 3.75 | 281 | S-Bonneville man |
| V-8, 389.0 | 4.06 × 3.75 | 303 | S-Bonneville auto |
| V-8, 389.0 | 4.06 × 3.75 | 318/348 | O-all (Tri-Power) |

## 1961

| | Tempest (wb 112.0) | Wght | Price | Prod |
|---|---|---|---|---|
| 2117 | Custom spt cpe | 2,795 | 2,297 | 7,455 |
| 2119 | sdn 4d | 2,800 | 2,167 | 22,557 |
| 2120 | Custom sdn 4d | 2,810 | 2,351 | 40,082 |
| 2127 | spt cpe | 2,785 | 2,113 | 7,432 |
| 2135 | Safari wgn 4d | 2,980 | 2,438 | 7,404 |
| 2136 | Custom Safari wgn 4d | 2,990 | 2,622 | 15,853 |
| | **Catalina (wb 119.0)** | | | |
| 2311 | Sport sdn 2d | 3,650 | 2,631 | 9,846 |
| 2335 | Safari wgn 4d 6P | 4,135 | 3,099 | 12,595 |
| 2337 | Sport Coupe htp | 3,680 | 2,766 | 14,524 |
| 2339 | Vista Sedan htp | 3,785 | 2,842 | 17,589 |
| 2345 | Safari wgn 4d 9P | 4,175 | 3,207 | 7,783 |
| 2367 | conv cpe | 3,805 | 3,078 | 12,379 |
| 2369 | sdn 4d | 3,725 | 2,702 | 38,638 |
| | **Ventura (wb 119.0)** | | | |
| 2537 | Sport Coupe htp | 3,685 | 2,971 | 13,297 |
| 2539 | Vista Sedan htp | 3,795 | 3,047 | 13,912 |
| | **Star Chief (wb 123.0)** | | | |
| 2639 | Vista Sedan htp | 3,870 | 3,136 | 13,557 |
| 2669 | sdn 4d | 3,840 | 3,003 | 16,024 |
| | **Bonneville (wb 123.0; wgn-119.0)** | | | |
| 2735 | Custom Safari wgn 4d | 4,185 | 3,530 | 3,323 |
| 2837 | Sport Coupe htp | 3,810 | 3,255 | 16,906 |
| 2839 | Vista Sedan htp | 3,895 | 3,331 | 30,830 |
| 2867 | conv cpe | 3,905 | 3,476 | 18,264 |

| 1961 Engines | bore × stroke | bhp | availability |
|---|---|---|---|
| I-4, 194.5 | 4.06 × 3.75 | 110 | S-Tempest man |
| I-4, 194.5 | 4.06 × 3.75 | 130 | S-Tempest auto |
| V-8, 215.0 | 3.50 × 2.80 | 155 | O-Tempest |
| V-8, 389.0 | 4.06 × 3.75 | 215 | S-Str Chf/Cat/Vent man |
| V-8, 389.0 | 4.06 × 3.75 | 230 | O-all auto exc Tmpst |
| V-8, 389.0 | 4.06 × 3.75 | 235 | S-Bonneville man; O-other man |
| V-8, 389.0 | 4.06 × 3.75 | 267 | S-Cat/Vntra auto |
| V-8, 389.0 | 4.06 × 3.75 | 283 | S-Star Chief auto |
| V-8, 389.0 | 4.06 × 3.75 | 287 | O-Cat/Vntra auto |
| V-8, 389.0 | 4.06 × 3.75 | 303 | S-Bonneville auto; O-Star Chief auto |
| V-8, 389.0 | 4.06 × 3.75 | 318/348 | O-all exc Tempest (Tri-Power) |
| V-8, 389.0 | 4.06 × 3.75 | 333 | O-full-size (4bbl) |
| V-8, 421.0 | 4.09 × 4.00 | 363/373 | O-all (Supr Duty ltd) |

## 1962

| | Tempest (wb 112.0)* | Wght | Price | Prod |
|---|---|---|---|---|
| 2117 | spt cpe | 2,800 | 2,294 | 51,981 |
| 2119 | sdn 4d | 2,815 | 2,240 | 37,430 |
| 2127 | cpe | 2,785 | 2,186 | 15,473 |
| 2135 | Safari wgn 4d | 2,995 | 2,511 | 17,674 |
| 2167 | conv cpe | 2,955 | 2,564 | 20,635 |
| | **Catalina (wb 120.0; wgn-119.0)** | | | |
| 2311 | Sport sdn 2d | 3,705 | 2,725 | 14,263 |
| 2335 | Safari wgn 4d 6P | 4,180 | 3,193 | 19,399 |
| 2339 | Vista Sedan htp | 3,825 | 2,936 | 29,251 |
| 2345 | Safari wgn 4d 9P | 4,220 | 3,301 | 10,716 |
| 2347 | Sport Coupe htp | 3,730 | 2,860 | 46,024 |
| 2367 | conv cpe | 3,855 | 3,172 | 16,877 |
| 2369 | sdn 4d | 3,765 | 2,796 | 68,124 |
| | **Star Chief (wb 123.0)** | | | |
| 2639 | Vista Sedan htp | 3,925 | 3,230 | 18,882 |
| 2669 | sdn 4d | 3,875 | 3,097 | 27,760 |
| | **Bonneville (wb 123.0; wgn-119.0)** | | | |
| 2735 | Custom Safari wgn 4d | 4,255 | 3,624 | 4,527 |
| 2839 | Vista Sedan htp | 4,005 | 3,425 | 44,015 |
| 2847 | Sport Coupe htp | 3,900 | 3,349 | 31,629 |
| 2867 | conv cpe | 4,005 | 3,570 | 21,582 |
| | **Grand Prix (wb 120.0)** | | | |
| 2947 | htp cpe | 3,835 | 3,490 | 30,195 |

*Tempest includes DeLuxe and LeMans trim options. Factory records include the following production breakdowns:

| | Standard | Deluxe | LeMans |
|---|---|---|---|
| cpe | 15,473 | — | — |
| spt cpe | — | 12,319 | 39,662 |
| sdn 4d | 16,057 | 21,373 | — |
| Safari wgn 4d | 6,504 | 11,170 | — |
| conv cpe | — | 5,076 | 15,559 |

| 1962 Engines | bore × stroke | bhp | availability |
|---|---|---|---|
| I-4, 194.5 | 4.06 × 3.75 | 110 | S-Tempest man |
| I-4, 194.5 | 4.06 × 3.75 | 115 | S-Tempest auto |
| V-8, 215.0 | 3.50 × 2.80 | 185 | O-Tempest |
| V-8, 389.0 | 4.06 × 3.75 | 215 | S-Cat/Str Chf man |
| V-8, 389.0 | 4.06 × 3.75 | 230 | O-all full-size |
| V-8, 389.0 | 4.06 × 3.75 | 235 | S-Bonn man; O-Cat/Str Chf man |
| V-8, 389.0 | 4.06 × 3.75 | 267 | S-Catalina auto |
| V-8, 389.0 | 4.06 × 3.75 | 283 | S-Star Chief auto |
| V-8, 389.0 | 4.06 × 3.75 | 303 | S-Bonn auto, GP; O-others |
| V-8, 389.0 | 4.06 × 3.75 | 318 | O-all full-size (Tri-Power) |
| V-8, 389.0 | 4.06 × 3.75 | 333 | O-all full-size (4bbl) |
| V-8, 389.0 | 4.06 × 3.75 | 348 | O-all full-size (Tri-Power) |
| V-8, 421.0 | 4.09 × 4.00 | 405 | O-all (Super Duty) |

## 1963

| | Tempest (wb 112.0) | Wght | Price | Prod |
|---|---|---|---|---|
| 2117 | DeLuxe spt cpe | 2,820 | 2,294 | 13,157 |
| 2119 | sdn 4d (incl DeLuxe) | 2,835 | 2,241 | 28,221 |
| 2127 | cpe | 2,810 | 2,188 | 13,307 |
| 2135 | Safari wgn 4d (incl DeLuxe) | 2,995 | 2,512 | 10,135 |
| 2167 | DeLuxe conv cpe | 2,980 | 2,564 | 5,012 |
| | **Tempest LeMans (wb 112.0)** | | | |
| 2217 | spt cpe | 2,865 | 2,418 | 45,701 |
| 2267 | conv cpe | 3,035 | 2,742 | 15,957 |

# Pontiac

| Catalina (wb 120.0; wgn-119.0) | | Wght | Price | Prod |
|---|---|---|---|---|
| 2311 | Sport sdn 2d | 3,685 | 2,725 | 14,091 |
| 2335 | Safari wgn 4d 6P | 4,175 | 3,193 | 18,446 |
| 2339 | Vista Sedan htp | 3,815 | 2,934 | 31,256 |
| 2345 | Safari wgn 4d 9P | 4,230 | 3,300 | 11,751 |
| 2347 | Sport Coupe htp | 3,725 | 2,859 | 60,795 |
| 2367 | conv cpe | 3,835 | 3,179 | 18,249 |
| 2369 | sdn 4d | 3,755 | 2,795 | 79,961 |
| **Star Chief (wb 123.0)** | | | | |
| 2639 | Vista Sedan htp | 3,915 | 3,229 | 12,448 |
| 2669 | sdn 4d | 3,885 | 3,096 | 28,309 |
| **Bonneville (wb 123.0; wgn-119.0)** | | | | |
| 2835 | Custom Safari wgn 4d 6P | 4,245 | 3,623 | 5,156 |
| 2839 | Vista Sedan htp | 3,985 | 3,423 | 49,929 |
| 2847 | Sport Coupe htp | 3,895 | 3,348 | 30,995 |
| 2865 | conv cpe | 3,970 | 3,568 | 23,459 |
| **Grand Prix (wb 120.0)** | | | | |
| 2957 | htp cpe | 3,915 | 3,489 | 72,959 |

| 1963 Engines | bore × stroke | bhp | availability |
|---|---|---|---|
| I-4, 194.5 | 4.06 × 3.75 | 115 | S-Tempest |
| I-4, 194.5 | 4.06 × 3.75 | 120 | O-Tempest man |
| I-4, 194.5 | 4.06 × 3.75 | 140 | O-Tempest auto |
| I-4, 194.5 | 4.06 × 3.75 | 166 | O-Tempest |
| V-8, 326.0 | 3.72 × 3.75 | 260 | O-Tempest |
| V-8, 389.0 | 4.06 × 3.75 | 215 | S-Cat/Str Chf man |
| V-8, 389.0 | 4.06 × 3.75 | 230 | O-all full-size auto |
| V-8, 389.0 | 4.06 × 3.75 | 235 | S-Bonn man; O-Cat/Str Chf man |
| V-8, 389.0 | 4.06 × 3.75 | 267 | S-Catalina man |
| V-8, 389.0 | 4.06 × 3.75 | 283 | S-Star Chief man |
| V-8, 389.0 | 4.06 × 3.75 | 303 | S-GP, Bonn auto; O-SC/Cat auto |
| V-8, 389.0 | 4.06 × 3.75 | 318 | O-all full-size (Tri-Power) |
| V-8, 421.0 | 4.09 × 4.00 | 353 | O-all full-size |
| V-8, 421.0 | 4.09 × 4.00 | 370 | O-all full-size |
| V-8, 421.0 | 4.09 × 4.00 | 390/410 | O-all (Super Duty) |

## 1964

| Tempest (wb 115.0) | | Wght | Price | Prod |
|---|---|---|---|---|
| 2027 | spt cpe | 2,930 | 2,259 | 6,365 |
| 2035 | Safari wgn 4d | 3,245 | 2,605 | 6,834 |
| 2069 | sdn 4d | 2,970 | 2,313 | 19,427 |
| 2127 | Custom spt cpe | 2,955 | 2,345 | 25,833 |
| 2135 | Custom Safari wgn 4d | 3,260 | 2,691 | 10,696 |
| 2167 | Custom conv cpe | 3,075 | 2,641 | 7,987 |
| 2169 | Custom sdn 4d | 2,990 | 2,399 | 29,948 |
| 2227 | LeMans spt cpe | 2,975 | 2,491 | 31,317 |
| 2237 | LeMans htp cpe | 2,995 | 2,556 | 31,310 |
| 2267 | LeMans conv cpe | 3,125 | 2,796 | 17,559 |
| **Tempest G.T.O. (wb 115.0)** | | | | |
| 2227 | spt cpe | 3,000 | 3,200 | 7,384 |
| 2237 | htp cpe | 3,020 | 3,250 | 18,422 |
| 2267 | conv cpe | 3,150 | 3,500 | 6,644 |
| **Catalina (wb 120.0; wgn-119.0)*** | | | | |
| 2311 | sdn 2d | 3,695 | 2,735 | 12,480 |
| 2335 | Safari wgn 4d 6P | 4,190 | 3,203 | 20,356 |
| 2339 | Vista Sedan htp | 3,835 | 2,945 | 33,849 |
| 2345 | Safari wgn 4d 9P | 4,235 | 3,311 | 13,140 |
| 2347 | Sport Coupe htp* | 3,750 | 2,869 | 74,793 |
| 2367 | conv cpe* | 3,825 | 3,181 | 18,693 |
| 2369 | sdn 4d | 3,770 | 2,806 | 84,457 |
| **Star Chief (wb 123.0)** | | | | |
| 2639 | Vista Sedan htp | 3,945 | 3,239 | 11,200 |
| 2669 | sdn 4d | 3,885 | 3,107 | 26,453 |
| **Bonneville (wb 123.0; wgn-119.0)** | | | | |
| 2835 | Custom Safari wgn 4d | 4,275 | 3,633 | 5,844 |
| 2839 | Vista Sedan htp | 3,995 | 3,433 | 57,630 |
| 2847 | Sport Coupe htp | 3,920 | 3,358 | 34,769 |
| 2867 | conv cpe | 3,985 | 3,578 | 22,016 |
| **Grand Prix (wb 120.0)** | | | | |
| 2957 | htp cpe | 3,930 | 3,499 | 63,810 |

*Includes models equipped with 2+2 option package.

| 1964 Engines | bore × stroke | bhp | availability |
|---|---|---|---|
| I-6, 215.0 | 3.75 × 3.25 | 140 | S-Tempest exc GTO |
| V-8, 326.0 | 3.72 × 3.75 | 250 | O-Tempest |
| V-8, 326.0 | 3.72 × 3.75 | 280 | O-Tempest |
| V-8, 389.0 | 4.06 × 3.75 | 230 | O-all full-size auto |
| V-8, 389.0 | 4.06 × 3.75 | 235 | S-Cat/Str Chf man |
| V-8, 389.0 | 4.06 × 3.75 | 267 | S-Cat/Str Chf auto |
| V-8, 389.0 | 4.06 × 3.75 | 283 | S-Cat 2+2 option; O-Cat/SC auto |
| V-8, 389.0 | 4.06 × 3.75 | 303 | S-GP/Bonn auto; O-Cat/SC auto |
| V-8, 389.0 | 4.06 × 3.75 | 306 | S-GP/Bonn man; O-Cat/SC man |
| V-8, 389.0 | 4.06 × 3.75 | 325 | S-GTO; O-Tempest |
| V-8, 389.0 | 4.06 × 3.75 | 330 | O-full-size |
| V-8, 389.0 | 4.06 × 3.75 | 348 | O-GTO |
| V-8, 421.0 | 4.09 × 4.00 | 320/350 | O-full-size |
| V-8, 421.0 | 4.09 × 4.00 | 370 | O-full size |

## 1965

| 233 Tempest (wb 115.0) | | Wght | Price | Prod |
|---|---|---|---|---|
| 27 | spt cpe | 2,930 | 2,260 | 18,198 |
| 35 | Safari wgn 4d | 3,220 | 2,605 | 5,622 |
| 69 | sdn 4d | 2,975 | 2,313 | 15,705 |
| **235 Tempest Custom (wb 115.0)** | | | | |
| 27 | spt cpe | 2,975 | 2,346 | 18,367 |
| 35 | Safari wagn 4d | 3,215 | 2,691 | 10,792 |
| 37 | htp cpe | 2,975 | 2,411 | 21,906 |
| 67 | conv cpe | 3,080 | 2,641 | 8,346 |
| 69 | sdn 4d | 2,980 | 2,400 | 25,242 |
| **237 Tempest LeMans (wb 115.0)** | | | | |
| 27 | spt cpe | 3,020 | 2,491 | 18,881 |
| 27 | G.T.O. spt cpe | 3,468 | 2,751 | 8,319 |
| 37 | htp cpe | 3,030 | 2,556 | 60,548 |
| 37 | G.T.O. htp cpe | 3,478 | 2,816 | 55,722 |
| 67 | conv cpe | 3,115 | 2,797 | 13,897 |
| 67 | G.T.O. conv cpe | 3,563 | 3,057 | 11,311 |
| 69 | sdn 4d | 3,020 | 2,551 | 14,227 |
| **252 Catalina (wb 121.0)** | | | | |
| 11 | sdn 2d | 3,695 | 2,734 | 9,526 |
| 35 | Safari wgn 4d 6P | 4,165 | 3,202 | 22,399 |
| 37 | Sport Coupe htp* | 3,750 | 2,868 | 92,009 |
| 39 | Vista Sedan htp | 3,855 | 2,945 | 34,814 |
| 45 | Safari wgn 4d 9P | 4,210 | 3,309 | 15,110 |
| 67 | conv cpe* | 3,815 | 3,196 | 18,347 |
| 69 | sdn 4d | 3,750 | 2,805 | 78,853 |
| **256 Star Chief (wb 124.0)** | | | | |
| 39 | Vista Sedan htp | 3,925 | 3,238 | 9,132 |
| 69 | sdn 4d | 3,860 | 3,106 | 22,183 |

# Pontiac

| 262 Bonneville (wb 124.0; wgn-121.0) | | Wght | Price | Prod |
|---|---|---|---|---|
| 35 | Custom Safari wgn 4d | 4,310 | 3,632 | 6,460 |
| 37 | Sport Coupe htp | 3,890 | 3,357 | 44,030 |
| 39 | Vista Sedan htp | 3,990 | 3,433 | 62,480 |
| 67 | conv cpe | 3,950 | 3,594 | 21,050 |
| **266 Grand Prix (wb 121.0)** | | | | |
| 57 | htp cpe | 3,940 | 3,498 | 57,881 |

*Includes models equipped with 2+2 option package.

| 1965 Engines | bore × stroke | bhp | availability |
|---|---|---|---|
| I-6, 215.0 | 3.75 × 3.25 | 140 | S-Tempest exc GTO |
| V-8, 326.0 | 3.72 × 3.75 | 250 | O-Tempest |
| V-8, 326.0 | 3.72 × 3.75 | 285 | O-Tempest |
| V-8, 389.0 | 4.06 × 3.75 | 256 | S-Cat/SC man; O-other full-size |
| V-8, 389.0 | 4.06 × 3.75 | 290 | S-Cat/Str Chf auto |
| V-8, 389.0 | 4.06 × 3.75 | 325 | S-Bonn/GP auto |
| V-8, 389.0 | 4.06 × 3.75 | 333 | S-Bonn/GP man |
| V-8, 389.0 | 4.06 × 3.75 | 335 | S-GTO |
| V-8, 389.0 | 4.06 × 3.75 | 360 | O-GTO |
| V-8, 421.0 | 4.09 × 4.00 | 338 | S-Cat 2+2; O-other full-size |
| V-8, 421.0 | 4.09 × 4.00 | 356 | O-all full-size |
| V-8, 421.0 | 4.09 × 4.00 | 376 | O-all full-size |

## 1966

| 233 Tempest (wb 115.0) | | Wght | Price | Prod |
|---|---|---|---|---|
| 07 | spt cpe | 3,040 | 2,278 | 22,266 |
| 35 | Safari wgn 4d | 3,340 | 2,624 | 4,095 |
| 69 | sdn 4d | 3,075 | 2,331 | 17,392 |
| **235 Tempest Custom (wb 115.0)** | | | | |
| 07 | spt cpe | 3,060 | 2,362 | 17,182 |
| 17 | htp cpe | 3,075 | 2,426 | 31,322 |
| 35 | Safari wgn 4d | 3,355 | 2,709 | 7,614 |
| 39 | htp sdn | 3,195 | 2,547 | 10,996 |
| 67 | conv cpe | 3,170 | 2,665 | 5,557 |
| 69 | sdn 4d | 3,100 | 2,415 | 23,988 |
| **237 LeMans (wb 115.0)** | | | | |
| 07 | spt cpe | 3,090 | 2,505 | 16,654 |
| 17 | htp cpe | 3,125 | 2,568 | 78,109 |
| 39 | htp sdn | 3,195 | 2,701 | 13,897 |
| 67 | conv cpe | 3,220 | 2,806 | 13,080 |
| **242 Tempest G.T.O (wb 115.0)** | | | | |
| 07 | spt cpe | 3,445 | 2,783 | 10,363 |
| 17 | htp cpe | 3,465 | 2,847 | 73,785 |
| 67 | conv cpe | 3,555 | 3,082 | 12,798 |
| **252 Catalina (wb 121.0)** | | | | |
| 11 | sdn 2d | 3,715 | 2,762 | 7,925 |
| 35 | Safari wgn 4d 6P | 4,250 | 3,217 | 21,082 |
| 37 | Sport Coupe htp | 3,835 | 2,893 | 79,013 |
| 39 | Vista Sedan htp | 3,910 | 2,968 | 38,005 |
| 45 | Safari wgn 4d 9P | 4,315 | 3,338 | 12,965 |
| 67 | conv cpe | 3,860 | 3,219 | 14,837 |
| 69 | sdn 4d | 3,785 | 2,831 | 80,483 |
| **254 2+2 (wb 121.0)—6,383 built*** | | | | |
| 37 | Sport Coupe htp | 4,005 | 3,298 | — |
| 67 | conv cpe | 4,030 | 3,602 | — |
| **256 Star Chief Executive (wb 124.0)** | | | | |
| 37 | Sport Coupe htp | 3,920 | 3,170 | 10,140 |
| 39 | Vista Sedan htp | 3,980 | 3,244 | 10,583 |
| 69 | sdn 4d | 3,920 | 3,114 | 24,489 |

| 262 Bonneville (wb 124.0; wgn-121.0) | | Wght | Price | Prod |
|---|---|---|---|---|
| 37 | Sport Coupe htp | 4,020 | 3,354 | 42,004 |
| 39 | Vista Sedan htp | 4,070 | 3,428 | 68,646 |
| 45 | Custom Safari wgn 4d 3S | 4,390 | 3,747 | 8,452 |
| 67 | conv cpe | 4,015 | 3,586 | 16,299 |
| **266 Grand Prix (wb 121.0)** | | | | |
| 57 | htp cpe | 4,015 | 3,492 | 36,757 |

*Included with equivalent Catalina body styles.

| 1966 Engines | bore × stroke | bhp | availability |
|---|---|---|---|
| I-6, 230.0 | 3.88 × 3.25 | 165 | S-Tempest, LeMans |
| I-6, 230.0 | 3.88 × 3.25 | 207 | O-Tempest, LeMans |
| V-8, 326.0 | 3.72 × 3.75 | 250 | O-Tempest, LeMans |
| V-8, 326.0 | 3.72 × 3.75 | 285 | O-Tempest, LeMans |
| V-8, 389.0 | 4.06 × 3.75 | 256 | S-Cat/SC man; O-other full-size |
| V-8, 389.0 | 4.06 × 3.75 | 290 | O-Cat, Star Chief |
| V-8, 389.0 | 4.06 × 3.75 | 325 | S-Bonn/GP auto; O-Cat, Star Chief |
| V-8, 389.0 | 4.06 × 3.75 | 333 | S-Bonn/GP man, GTO |
| V-8, 389.0 | 4.06 × 3.75 | 360 | O-GTO |
| V-8, 421.0 | 4.09 × 4.00 | 338 | S-2+2; O-other full-size |
| V-8, 421.0 | 4.09 × 4.00 | 356 | O-all full-size |
| V-8, 421.0 | 4.09 × 4.00 | 376 | O-all full-size |

## 1967

| 223 Firebird (wb 108.1) | | Wght | Price | Prod |
|---|---|---|---|---|
| 37 | htp cpe | 2,955 | 2,666 | 67,032 |
| 67 | conv cpe | 3,247 | 2,903 | 15,528 |
| **233 Tempest (wb 115.0)** | | | | |
| 07 | cpe | 3,110 | 2,341 | 17,978 |
| 35 | wgn 4d | 3,370 | 2,666 | 3,495 |
| 69 | sdn 4d | 3,140 | 2,388 | 13,136 |
| **235 Tempest Custom (wb 115.0)** | | | | |
| 07 | cpe | 3,130 | 2,437 | 12,469 |
| 17 | htp cpe | 3,140 | 2,494 | 30,512 |
| 35 | wgn 4d | 3,370 | 2,760 | 5,324 |
| 39 | htp sdn | 3,240 | 2,608 | 5,493 |
| 67 | conv cpe | 3,240 | 2,723 | 4,082 |
| 69 | sdn 4d | 3,145 | 2,482 | 17,445 |
| **237 LeMans (wb 115.0)** | | | | |
| 07 | cpe | 3,155 | 2,586 | 10,693 |
| 17 | htp cpe | 3,155 | 2,648 | 75,965 |
| 39 | htp sdn | 3,265 | 2,771 | 8,424 |
| 67 | conv cpe | 3,250 | 2,881 | 9,820 |
| **239 Tempest Safari (wb 115.0)** | | | | |
| 35 | wgn 4d | 3,390 | 2,936 | 4,511 |
| **242 Tempest G.T.O. (wb 115.0)** | | | | |
| 07 | cpe | 3,425 | 2,871 | 7,029 |
| 17 | htp cpe | 3,430 | 2,935 | 65,176 |
| 67 | conv cpe | 3,515 | 3,165 | 9,517 |
| **252 Catalina (wb 121.0)** | | | | |
| 11 | sdn 2d | 3,735 | 2,807 | 5,633 |
| 35 | wgn 4d 6P | 4,275 | 3,252 | 18,305 |
| 39 | htp sdn | 3,960 | 3,020 | 37,256 |
| 45 | wgn 4d 9P | 4,340 | 3,374 | 11,040 |
| 67 | conv cpe* | 3,910 | 3,276 | 10,033 |
| 69 | sdn 4d | 3,825 | 2,866 | 80,551 |
| 87 | htp cpe* | 3,860 | 2,951 | 77,932 |
| **256 Executive (wb 124.0; wgn-121.0)** | | | | |
| 35 | wgn 4d 6P | 4,290 | 3,600 | 5,903 |

# Pontiac

| 256 Executive (wb 124.0; wgn-121.0) | | Wght | Price | Prod |
|---|---|---|---|---|
| 39 | htp sdn | 4,020 | 3,296 | 8,699 |
| 45 | wgn 4d 9P | 4,370 | 3,722 | 5,593 |
| 69 | sdn 4d | 3,955 | 3,165 | 19,861 |
| 87 | htp cpe | 3,925 | 3,227 | 6,931 |
| 262 Bonneville (wb 124.0; wgn-121.0) | | | | |
| 39 | htp sdn | 4,110 | 3,517 | 56,307 |
| 45 | wgn 4d 9P | 4,415 | 3,819 | 6,771 |
| 67 | conv cpe | 4,010 | 3,680 | 8,902 |
| 87 | htp cpe | 3,975 | 3,448 | 31,016 |
| 266 Grand Prix (wb 121.0) | | | | |
| 57 | htp cpe | 4,005 | 3,549 | 37,125 |
| 67 | conv cpe | 4,040 | 3,813 | 5,856 |

*Includes models equipped with 2+2 option package.

| 1967 Engines | bore × stroke | bhp | availability |
|---|---|---|---|
| I-6, 230.0 | 3.88 × 3.25 | 165 | S-Firebird, LeMans, Temp exc GTO |
| I-6, 230.0 | 3.88 × 3.25 | 215 | O-Firebird, LeMans, Temp exc GTO |
| V-8, 326.0 | 3.72 × 3.75 | 250 | O-Firebird, LeMans, Temp exc GTO |
| V-8, 326.0 | 3.72 × 3.75 | 285 | O-Fbd, LeM, Temp exc Temp Sfr wgn |
| V-8, 400.0 | 4.12 × 3.75 | 255 | O-GTO auto |
| V-8, 400.0 | 4.12 × 3.75 | 265 | S-Cat/Exc man; O-auto |
| V-8, 400.0 | 4.12 × 3.75 | 290 | S-Cat/Exec auto |
| V-8, 400.0 | 4.12 × 3.75 | 325 | S-Bonn auto, Fbd 400; O-Cat, Exec |
| V-8, 400.0 | 4.12 × 3.75 | 333 | S-Bonn man; O-Cat, Exec |
| V-8, 400.0 | 4.12 × 3.75 | 335 | S-GTO |
| V-8, 400.0 | 4.12 × 3.75 | 350 | S-Grand Prix |
| V-8, 400.0 | 4.12 × 3.75 | 360 | O-GTO |
| V-8, 428.0 | 4.12 × 4.00 | 360 | S-2+2; O-Cat, Exec, Bonn, Grand Prix |
| V-8, 428.0 | 4.12 × 4.00 | 376 | O-Catalina, Exec, Bonn, Grand Prix |

## 1968

| 223 Firebird (wb 108.1) | | Wght | Price | Prod |
|---|---|---|---|---|
| 37 | htp cpe | 3,061 | 2,781 | 90,152 |
| 67 | conv cpe | 3,346 | 2,996 | 16,960 |
| 233 Tempest (wb 116.0; 2d-112.0) | | | | |
| 27 | spt cpe | 3,242 | 2,461 | 19,991 |
| 69 | sdn 4d | 3,309 | 2,509 | 11,590 |
| 235 Tempest Custom (wb 116.0; 2d-112.0) | | | | |
| 27 | spt cpe | 3,252 | 2,554 | 10,634 |
| 35 | wgn 4d | 3,667 | 2,906 | 8,253 |
| 37 | htp cpe | 3,277 | 2,614 | 40,574 |
| 39 | htp sdn | 3,384 | 2,728 | 6,147 |
| 67 | conv cpe | 3,337 | 2,839 | 3,518 |
| 69 | sdn 4d | 3,297 | 2,602 | 17,304 |
| 237 LeMans (wb 116.0; 2d-112.0) | | | | |
| 27 | spt cpe | 3,287 | 2,724 | 8,439 |
| 37 | htp cpe | 3,302 | 2,786 | 110,036 |
| 39 | htp sdn | 3,407 | 2,916 | 9,002 |
| 67 | conv cpe | 3,377 | 3,015 | 8,820 |
| 239 Tempest Safari (wb 116.0) | | | | |
| 35 | wgn 4d | 3,677 | 3,107 | 4,414 |
| 242 Tempest G.T.O (wb 112.0) | | | | |
| 37 | htp cpe | 3,506 | 3,101 | 77,704 |
| 67 | conv cpe | 3,590 | 3,227 | 9,980 |

| 252 Catalina (wb 121.0) | | Wght | Price | Prod |
|---|---|---|---|---|
| 11 | sdn 2d | 3,839 | 2,945 | 5,247 |
| 35 | wgn 4d 6P | 4,327 | 3,390 | 21,848 |
| 39 | htp sdn | 4,012 | 3,158 | 41,727 |
| 45 | wgn 4d 9P | 4,408 | 3,537 | 13,363 |
| 67 | conv cpe | 3,980 | 3,391 | 7,339 |
| 69 | sdn 4d | 3,888 | 3,004 | 94,441 |
| 87 | htp cpe | 3,943 | 3,089 | 92,217 |
| 256 Executive (wb 124.0; wgn-121.0) | | | | |
| 35 | wgn 4d 6P | 4,378 | 3,744 | 6,195 |
| 39 | htp sdn | 4,077 | 3,439 | 7,848 |
| 45 | wgn 4d 9P | 4,453 | 3,890 | 5,843 |
| 69 | sdn 4d | 4,022 | 3,309 | 18,869 |
| 87 | htp cpe | 3,975 | 3,371 | 5,880 |
| 262 Bonneville (wb 124.0; wgn-121.0) | | | | |
| 39 | htp sdn | 4,171 | 3,660 | 57,055 |
| 45 | wgn 4d 9P | 4,485 | 3,987 | 6,926 |
| 67 | conv cpe | 4,090 | 3,800 | 7,358 |
| 69 | sdn 4d | 4,122 | 3,530 | 3,499 |
| 87 | htp cpe | 4,054 | 3,592 | 29,598 |
| 266 Grand Prix (wb 121.0) | | | | |
| 57 | htp cpe | 4,075 | 3,697 | 31,711 |

| 1968 Engines | bore × stroke | bhp | availability |
|---|---|---|---|
| I-6, 250.0 | 3.88 × 3.53 | 175 | S-Frbrd exc Sprint, LeM, Tmpst exc GTO |
| I-6, 250.0 | 3.88 × 3.53 | 215 | S-Frbrd Sprint; O-as above exc wgns |
| V-8, 350.0 | 3.88 × 3.75 | 265 | S-Frbrd 350; O-Tmpst exc GTO, LeM |
| V-8, 350.0 | 3.88 × 3.75 | 320 | S-Frbrd HO; O-Temp, LeM exc wgns |
| V-8, 400.0 | 4.12 × 3.75 | 265 | O-GTO, all full-size |
| V-8, 400.0 | 4.12 × 3.75 | 290 | S-Catalina, Exec |
| V-8, 400.0 | 4.12 × 3.75 | 330 | S-Firebird 400 |
| V-8, 400.0 | 4.12 × 3.75 | 335 | O-Frbd 400 (Ram-Air) |
| V-8, 400.0 | 4.12 × 3.75 | 340 | S-Bonn; O-Cat, Exec |
| V-8, 400.0 | 4.12 × 3.75 | 350 | S-Grand Prix, GTO |
| V-8, 400.0 | 4.12 × 3.75 | 360 | O-GTO |
| V-8, 428.0 | 4.12 × 4.00 | 375 | O-Cat, Exc, Bonn, GP |
| V-8, 428.0 | 4.12 × 4.00 | 390 | O-Cat, Exec, Bonn, GP (HO) |

## 1969

| 223 Firebird (wb 108.0)* | | Wght | Price | Prod |
|---|---|---|---|---|
| 37 | htp cpe | 3,080 | 2,821 | 76,059 |
| 67 | conv cpe | 3,330 | 3,045 | 11,649 |
| 233 Tempest (wb 116.0; 2d-112.0) | | | | |
| 27 | spt cpe | 3,180 | 2,510 | 17,181 |
| 69 | sdn 4d | 3,250 | 2,557 | 9,741 |
| 235 Tempest Custom (wb 116.0; 2d-112.0) | | | | |
| 27 | spt cpe | 3,210 | 2,603 | 7,912 |
| 35 | wgn 4d | 3,595 | 2,956 | 6,963 |
| 37 | htp cpe | 3,220 | 2,663 | 46,886 |
| 39 | htp sdn | 3,315 | 2,777 | 3,918 |
| 67 | conv cpe | 3,265 | 2,888 | 2,379 |
| 69 | sdn 4d | 3,235 | 2,651 | 16,532 |
| 237 LeMans (wb 116.0; 2d-112.0) | | | | |
| 27 | spt cpe | 3,225 | 2,773 | 5,033 |
| 37 | htp cpe | 3,245 | 2,835 | 82,817 |
| 67 | conv cpe | 3,290 | 3,064 | 5,676 |
| 69 | htp sdn | 3,360 | 2,965 | 6,475 |

## Pontiac

| 239 LeMans Safari (wb 116.0) | | Wght | Price | Prod |
|---|---|---|---|---|
| 36 | wgn 4d | 3,690 | 3,198 | 4,115 |
| **242 Tempest G.T.O. (wb 112.0)** | | | | |
| 37 | htp cpe | 3,503 | 3,156 | 64,851 |
| 67 | conv cpe | 3,553 | 3,382 | 7,436 |
| **252 Catalina (wb 122.0)** | | | | |
| 36 | wgn 4d 6P | 4,455 | 3,519 | 20,352 |
| 37 | htp cpe | 3,925 | 3,174 | 84,006 |
| 39 | htp sdn | 4,005 | 3,244 | 38,819 |
| 46 | wgn 4d 9P | 4,520 | 3,664 | 13,393 |
| 67 | conv cpe | 3,985 | 3,476 | 5,436 |
| 69 | sdn 4d | 3,945 | 3,090 | 84,590 |
| **256 Executive (wb 125.0; wgn-122.0)** | | | | |
| 36 | wgn 4d 6P | 4,475 | 3,872 | 6,411 |
| 37 | htp cpe | 3,970 | 3,456 | 4,492 |
| 39 | htp sdn | 4,065 | 3,525 | 6,522 |
| 46 | wgn 4d 9P | 4,545 | 4,017 | 6,805 |
| 69 | sdn 4d | 4,045 | 3,394 | 14,831 |
| **262 Bonneville (wb 125.0; wgn-122.0)** | | | | |
| 37 | htp cpe | 4,080 | 3,688 | 27,773 |
| 39 | htp sdn | 4,180 | 3,756 | 50,817 |
| 46 | wgn 4d 9P | 4,600 | 4,104 | 7,428 |
| 67 | conv cpe | 4,130 | 3,896 | 5,438 |
| 69 | sdn 4d | 4,180 | 3,626 | 4,859 |
| **276 Grand Prix (wb 118.0)** | | | | |
| 57 | htp cpe | 3,715 | 3,866 | 112,486 |

*Production includes 689 Trans Am hardtop coupes, 8 convertibles.

| 1969 Engines | bore × stroke | bhp | availability |
|---|---|---|---|
| I-6, 250.0 | 3.88 × 3.53 | 175 | S-Frbrd, LeM, Tmpst exc GTO (ohc) |
| I-6, 250.0 | 3.88 × 3.53 | 230 | S-Frbrd Sprint; O-LeM, Tmpst exc GTO (ohc) |
| V-8, 350.0 | 3.88 × 3.75 | 265 | S-Frbrd 350; O-Tempest, LeMans |
| V-8, 350.0 | 3.88 × 3.75 | 325 | S-Firebird 350 HO |
| V-8, 350.0 | 3.88 × 3.75 | 330 | O-Frbrd, Tmpst, LeM exc wgns/GTO |
| V-8, 400.0 | 4.12 × 3.75 | 265 | O-GTO/full-size auto |
| V-8, 400.0 | 4.12 × 3.75 | 290 | S-Cat, Vntra, Exec |
| V-8, 400.0 | 4.12 × 3.75 | 330 | S-Firebird 400 |
| V-8, 400.0 | 4.12 × 3.75 | 335 | O-Frbrd 400 (Ram Air) |
| V-8, 400.0 | 4.12 × 3.75 | 345 | O-Frbrd 400 (Ram Air) |
| V-8, 400.0 | 4.12 × 3.75 | 350 | S-GTO, Grand Prix |
| V-8, 400.0 | 4.12 × 3.75 | 366 | O-GTO (Ram Air) |
| V-8, 400.0 | 4.12 × 3.75 | 370 | O-GTO (Ram Air) |
| V-8, 428.0 | 4.12 × 4.00 | 370/390 | O-GP, full size |

### 1970

| 223 Firebird (wb 108.0) | | Wght | Price | Prod |
|---|---|---|---|---|
| 87 | cpe | 3,140 | 2,875 | 18,874 |
| 87 | Formula 400 cpe | 3,470 | 3,370 | 7,708 |
| 87 | Trans Am cpe | 3,550 | 4,305 | 3,196 |
| 87 | Esprit cpe | 3,435 | 3,241 | 18,961 |
| **233 Tempest (wb 116.0; 2d-112.0)** | | | | |
| 27 | cpe | 3,225 | 2,623 | 11,977 |
| 37 | htp cpe | 3,250 | 2,683 | 20,883 |
| 69 | sdn 4d | 3,295 | 2,670 | 9,187 |
| **235 LeMans (wb 116.0; 2d-112.0)** | | | | |
| 27 | cpe | 3,240 | 2,735 | 5,565 |

| 235 LeMans (wb 116.0; 2d-112.0) | | Wght | Price | Prod |
|---|---|---|---|---|
| 35 | wgn 4d | 3,585 | 3,092 | 7,165 |
| 37 | htp cpe | 3,265 | 2,795 | 52,304 |
| 39 | htp sdn | 3,385 | 2,921 | 3,872 |
| 69 | sdn 4d | 3,315 | 2,782 | 15,255 |
| **237 LeMans Sport (wb 116.0; 2d-112.0)** | | | | |
| 27 | cpe | 3,265 | 2,891 | 1,673 |
| 36 | wgn 4d | 3,775 | 3,328 | 3,823 |
| 37 | htp cpe | 3,290 | 2,953 | 58,356 |
| 39 | htp sdn | 3,405 | 3,083 | 3,657 |
| 67 | conv cpe | 3,330 | 3,182 | 4,670 |
| **242 G.T.O. (wb 112.0)*** | | | | |
| 37 | htp cpe | 3,641 | 3,267 | 36,366 |
| 67 | conv cpe | 3,691 | 3,492 | 3,783 |
| **252 Catalina (wb 122.0)** | | | | |
| 36 | wgn 4d 6P | 4,517 | 3,646 | 16,944 |
| 37 | htp cpe | 3,952 | 3,249 | 70,350 |
| 39 | htp sdn | 4,042 | 3,319 | 35,155 |
| 46 | wgn 4d 9P | 4,607 | 3,791 | 12,450 |
| 67 | conv cpe | 4,027 | 3,604 | 3,686 |
| 69 | sdn 4d | 3,997 | 3,164 | 84,795 |
| **256 Executive (wb 125.0; wgn-122.0)** | | | | |
| 36 | wgn 4d 6P | 4,552 | 4,015 | 4,861 |
| 37 | htp cpe | 4,042 | 3,600 | 3,499 |
| 39 | htp sdn | 4,132 | 3,669 | 5,376 |
| 46 | wgn 4d 9P | 4,632 | 4,160 | 5,629 |
| 69 | sdn 4d | 4,087 | 3,538 | 13,061 |
| **262 Bonneville (wb 125.0; wgn-122.0)** | | | | |
| 37 | htp cpe | 4,111 | 3,832 | 23,418 |
| 39 | htp sdn | 4,226 | 3,900 | 44,241 |
| 46 | wgn 4d 9P | 4,686 | 4,247 | 7,033 |
| 67 | conv cpe | 4,161 | 4,040 | 3,537 |
| 69 | sdn 4d | 4,181 | 3,770 | 3,802 |
| **276 Grand Prix (wb 118.0)** | | | | |
| 57 | htp cpe | 3,784 | 3,985 | 65,750 |

*Includes models equipped with "The Judge" option (3,629 coupes and 168 convertibles).

| 1970 Engines | bore × stroke | bhp | availability |
|---|---|---|---|
| I-6, 250.0 | 3.88 × 3.53 | 155 | S-Tempest, LeMans, Firebird (ohv) |
| V-8, 350.0 | 3.88 × 3.75 | 255 | S-Firebird Esprit; O-above models, Cat exc conv and wgns |
| V-8, 400.0 | 4.12 × 3.75 | 265 | O-all auto exc GTO, Bonn |
| V-8, 400.0 | 4.12 × 3.75 | 290 | S-Cat conv/wgn, Exec; O-other Cat |
| V-8, 400.0 | 4.12 × 3.75 | 330 | S-Frbrd 400; O-Tmpst/LeM/Cat/Exec auto |
| V-8, 400.0 | 4.12 × 3.75 | 345 | S-Frbrd Trans Am; O-Tmpst/LeM man |
| V-8, 400.0 | 4.12 × 3.75 | 350 | S-GTO, Grand Prix |
| V-8, 400.0 | 4.12 × 3.75 | 366 | S-GTO Judge; O-GTO (Ram Air) |
| V-8, 400.0 | 4.12 × 3.75 | 370 | O-GTO (Ram Air); O-GTO Judge |
| V-8, 455.0 | 4.15 × 4.21 | 360 | S-Bonn; O-Cat, Exec, GTO |
| V-8, 455.0 | 4.15 × 4.21 | 370 | S-Bonn wgn, Grand Prix SJ; O-GP J, Cat, Exec, Bonn |

## Pontiac

### 1971

| Ventura II (wb 111.0) | | Wght | Price | Prod |
|---|---|---|---|---|
| 21327 | cpe | 3,010 | 2,458 | 34,681 |
| 21369 | sdn 4d | 3,050 | 2,488 | 13,803 |
| **Firebird (wb 108.0)** | | | | |
| 22387 | cpe | 3,292 | 3,047 | 23,021 |
| 22487 | Esprit cpe V-8 | 3,423 | 3,416 | 20,185 |
| 22687 | Formula 400 cpe V-8 | 3,473 | 3,445 | 7,802 |
| 22887 | Trans Am cpe V-8 | 3,578 | 4,595 | 2,116 |
| **LeMans (wb 116.0; 2d-112.0)** | | | | |
| 23327 | T-37 cpe | 3,317 | 2,747 | 7,184 |
| 23337 | T-37 htp cpe | 3,322 | 2,807 | 29,466 |
| 23369 | T-37 sdn 4d | 3,347 | 2,795 | 8,336 |
| 23527 | cpe | 3,327 | 2,877 | 2,374 |
| 23536 | wgn 4d 2S | 3,867 | 3,353 | 6,311 |
| 23537 | htp cpe | 3,327 | 2,938 | 40,966 |
| 23539 | htp sdn | 3,442 | 3,064 | 3,186 |
| 23546 | wgn 4d 3S | 3,917 | 3,465 | 4,363 |
| 23569 | sdn 4d | 3,357 | 2,925 | 11,979 |
| 23737 | Sport htp cpe | 3,327 | 3,125 | 34,625 |
| 23739 | Sport htp sdn | 3,442 | 3,255 | 2,451 |
| 23767 | Sport conv cpe | 3,417 | 3,359 | 3,865 |
| 24237 | GTO htp cpe V-8 | 3,619 | 3,446 | 9,497 |
| 24237 | GTO Judge htp cpe | 3,650 | 3,840 | 357 |
| 24267 | GTO conv cpe | 3,664 | 3,676 | 661 |
| 24267 | GTO Judge conv cpe | 3,700 | 4,070 | 17 |
| **Catalina (wb 123.5; wgn-127.0)** | | | | |
| 25235 | Safari wgn 4d 2S | 4,815 | 4,315 | 10,332 |
| 25239 | htp sdn | 4,107 | 3,939 | 22,333 |
| 25245 | Safari wgn 4d 3S | 4,905 | 4,462 | 9,283 |
| 25257 | htp cpe | 4,042 | 3,870 | 46,257 |
| 25267 | conv cpe | 4,081 | 4,156 | 2,036 |
| 25269 | sdn 4d | 4,077 | 3,770 | 59,355 |
| 25839 | Brougham htp sdn | 4,179 | 4,154 | 9,001 |
| 25857 | Brougham htp cpe | 4,119 | 4,084 | 8,823 |
| 25869 | Brougham sdn 4d | 4,149 | 4,000 | 6,069 |
| **Bonneville (wb 126.0; wgn-127.0)** | | | | |
| 26235 | Grand Safari wgn 4d 2S | 4,843 | 4,643 | 3,613 |
| 26239 | htp sdn | 4,273 | 4,340 | 16,393 |
| 26245 | Grand Safari wgn 4d 3S | 4,913 | 4,790 | 5,972 |
| 26257 | htp cpe | 4,188 | 4,272 | 8,778 |
| 26269 | sdn 4d | 4,213 | 4,210 | 6,513 |
| **Grand Ville (wb 126.0)** | | | | |
| 26847 | htp cpe | 4,223 | 4,497 | 14,017 |
| 26849 | htp sdn | 4,303 | 4,566 | 30,524 |
| 26867 | conv cpe | 4,266 | 4,706 | 1,789 |
| | chassis | — | — | 194 |
| **Grand Prix (wb 118.0)** | | | | |
| 27657 | htp cpe | 3,863 | 4,557 | 58,325 |

| 1971 Engines | bore × stroke | bhp | availability |
|---|---|---|---|
| I-6, 250.0 | 3.88 × 3.53 | 145 | S-LeM exc GTO; Fbd exc Fmla & T/A |
| I-6, 250.0 | 3.88 × 3.53 | 185 | S-Ventura |
| V-8, 307.0 | 3.88 × 3.25 | 235 | O-Ventura |
| V-8, 350.0 | 3.88 × 3.75 | 250 | S-Cat exc Br/Saf; O-LeM exc GTP, Fbd exc T/A |
| V-8, 400.0 | 4.12 × 3.75 | 265 | S-Cat Br/Saf; O-Fbd exc Frmla & T/A, Catalina |
| V-8, 400.0 | 4.12 × 3.75 | 300 | S-GTO, Fbd Frmla, GP; O-LeMans, Fbd Esprit |
| V-8, 455.0 | 4.15 × 4.21 | 280 | S-Bonn; O-Catalina |
| V-8, 455.0 | 4.15 × 4.21 | 325 | S-GV; O-LeM, Fbd T/A, Catalina, GP |
| V-8, 455.0 | 4.15 × 4.21 | 335 | S-Trans Am; O-LeMans |

### 1972

| Ventura II (wb 111.0) | | Wght | Price | Prod |
|---|---|---|---|---|
| 2Y27 | cpe | 3,019 | 2,426 | 51,203 |
| 2Y69 | sdn 4d | 3,054 | 2,454 | 21,584 |
| **Firebird (wb 108.0)** | | | | |
| 2S87 | cpe | 3,263 | 2,828 | 12,000 |
| 2T87 | Esprit cpe V-8 | 3,359 | 3,194 | 11,415 |
| 2U87 | Formula cpe V-8 | 3,424 | 3,221 | 5,250 |
| 2V87 | Trans Am cpe V-8 | 3,564 | 4,256 | 1,286 |
| **LeMans (wb 116.0; 2d-112.0)*** | | | | |
| 2D27 | cpe | 3,402 | 2,722 | 6,855 |
| 2D36 | wgn 4d 2S | 3,907 | 3,271 | 8,332 |
| 2D37 | htp cpe | 3,342 | 2,851 | 80,383 |
| 2D46 | wgn 4d 3S | 3,947 | 3,378 | 5,266 |
| 2D67 | conv cpe | 3,392 | 3,228 | 3,438 |
| 2D69 | sdn 4d | 3,377 | 2,814 | 19,463 |
| 2G37 | Luxury htp cpe V-8 | 3,488 | 3,196 | 37,615 |
| 2G39 | Luxury htp sdn V-8 | 3,638 | 3,319 | 8,641 |
| **Catalina (wb 123.5; wgn-127.0)** | | | | |
| 2L35 | Safari wgn 4d 2S | 4,743 | 4,232 | 14,536 |
| 2L39 | htp sdn | 4,879 | 3,874 | 28,010 |
| 2L45 | Safari wgn 4d 3S | 4,818 | 4,372 | 12,766 |
| 2L57 | htp cpe | 4,129 | 3,808 | 60,233 |
| 2L67 | conv cpe | 4,204 | 4,080 | 2,399 |
| 2L69 | sdn 4d | 4,154 | 3,713 | 83,004 |
| 2M39 | Brougham htp sdn | 4,238 | 4,062 | 8,762 |
| 2M57 | Brougham htp cpe | 4,158 | 3,996 | 10,545 |
| 2M69 | Brougham sdn 4d | 4,188 | 3,916 | 8,007 |
| **Bonneville (wb 126.0; wgn-127.0)** | | | | |
| 2N35 | Grand Safari wgn 4d 2S | 4,918 | 4,581 | 5,675 |
| 2N39 | htp sdn | 4,338 | 4,293 | 15,806 |
| 2N45 | Grand Safari wgn 4d 3S | 4,938 | 4,721 | 8,540 |
| 2N57 | htp cpe | 4,238 | 4,228 | 10,568 |
| 2N69 | sdn 4d | 4,288 | 4,169 | 9,704 |
| **Grand Ville (wb 126.0)** | | | | |
| 2P47 | htp cpe | 4,262 | 4,442 | 19,852 |
| 2P49 | htp sdn | 4,378 | 4,507 | 41,346 |
| 2P67 | conv cpe | 4,333 | 4,640 | 2,213 |
| | chassis | — | — | 320 |
| **Grand Prix (wb 118.0)** | | | | |
| 2K57 | htp cpe | 3,898 | 4,472 | 91,961 |

*Production includes models with Sport ($164), GTO ($344), and GT ($231) option packages. GTO production: 5,807.

| 1972 Engines | bore × stroke | bhp | availability |
|---|---|---|---|
| I-6, 250.0 | 3.88 × 3.53 | 110 | S-Vntra, LeM, Fbd exc T/A |
| V-8, 307.0 | 3.88 × 3.25 | 130 | O-Ventura exc Calif. |
| V-8, 350.0 | 3.88 × 3.75 | 160 | S-Cat exc Saf, Br; O-Vntra (Cal.), LeM, Fbd exc T/A |
| V-8, 400.0 | 4.12 × 3.75 | 175 | S-Cat Saf, Br; O-LeM, Cat, Firebird exc T/A |
| V-8, 400.0 | 4.12 × 3.75 | 250 | S-GP; O-Fbd exc T/A |

# Pontiac

| 1972 Engines | bore × stroke | bhp | availability |
|---|---|---|---|
| V-8, 455.0 | 4.15 × 4.21 | 185 | S-Bonn, GV, GSaf; O-Cat |
| V-8, 455.0 | 4.15 × 4.21 | 220 | O-Bonn, GV, GSaf, Cat |
| V-8, 455.0 | 4.15 × 4.21 | 230 | O-LeMans |
| V-8, 455.0 | 4.15 × 4.21 | 250 | O-LeMans, Grand Prix |
| V-8, 455.0 | 4.15 × 4.21 | 300 | S-Fbd T/A; O-LeM, Fbd |

## 1973

### Ventura (wb 111.0)

| | | Wght | Price | Prod |
|---|---|---|---|---|
| Y17 | htchbk cpe | 3,276 | 2,603 | 26,335 |
| Z17 | Custom htchbk cpe | 3,309 | 2,759 | |
| Y27 | cpe | 3,170 | 2,452 | 49,153 |
| Z27 | Custom cpe | 3,203 | 2,609 | |
| Y69 | sdn 4d | 3,230 | 2,481 | 21,012 |
| Z69 | Custom sdn 4d | 3,263 | 2,638 | |

### Firebird (wb 108.0)

| | | Wght | Price | Prod |
|---|---|---|---|---|
| S87 | cpe | 3,270 | 2,895 | 14,096 |
| T87 | Esprit cpe V-8 | 3,309 | 3,249 | 17,249 |
| U87 | Formula cpe V-8 | 3,318 | 3,276 | 10,166 |
| V87 | Trans Am cpe V-8 | 3,504 | 4,204 | 4,802 |

### LeMans (wb 116.0; 2d-112.0)

| | | Wght | Price | Prod |
|---|---|---|---|---|
| D29 | Colonnade sdn 4d | 3,713 | 2,918 | 26,554 |
| D35 | Safari wgn 4d 2S | 4,064 | 3,296 | 10,446 |
| D37 | Colonnade sdn 2d | 3,687 | 2,920 | 68,230 |
| D45 | Safari wgn 4d 3S | 4,101 | 3,429 | 6,127 |
| F37 | Sport Colonnade sdn 2d* | 3,702 | 3,008 | 50,999 |
| G29 | Luxury Col sdn 4d V-8 | 3,867 | 3,344 | 9,377 |
| G37 | Luxury Col sdn 2d V-8 | 3,799 | 3,274 | 33,916 |

### Grand Am (wb 116.0; 2d-112.0)

| | | Wght | Price | Prod |
|---|---|---|---|---|
| H29 | Colonnade sdn 4d V-8 | 4,018 | 4,353 | 8,691 |
| H37 | Colonnade sdn 2d V-8 | 3,992 | 4,264 | 34,445 |

### Catalina (wb 124.0; wgn-127.0)

| | | Wght | Price | Prod |
|---|---|---|---|---|
| L35 | Safari wgn 4d 2S | 4,791 | 4,311 | 15,762 |
| L39 | htp sdn | 4,270 | 3,938 | 31,663 |
| L45 | Safari wgn 4d 3S | 4,873 | 4,457 | 14,654 |
| L57 | htp cpe | 4,190 | 3,869 | 74,394 |
| L69 | sdn 4d | 4,234 | 3,770 | 100,592 |

### Bonneville (wb 124.0)

| | | Wght | Price | Prod |
|---|---|---|---|---|
| N39 | htp sdn | 4,369 | 4,292 | 17,202 |
| N57 | htp cpe | 4,292 | 4,225 | 13,866 |
| N69 | sdn 4d | 4,333 | 4,163 | 15,830 |

### Grand Ville/Grand Safari (wb 126.0/127.0)

| | | Wght | Price | Prod |
|---|---|---|---|---|
| P35 | Grand Safari wgn 4d 2S | 4,823 | 4,674 | 6,894 |
| P45 | Grand Safari wgn 4d 3S | 4,925 | 4,821 | 10,776 |
| P47 | Grand Ville htp cpe | 4,321 | 4,524 | 23,963 |
| P49 | Grand Ville htp sdn | 4,376 | 4,592 | 44,092 |
| P67 | Grand Ville conv | 4,339 | 4,766 | 4,447 |
| | chassis | — | — | 240 |

### Grand Prix (wb 116.0)

| | | Wght | Price | Prod |
|---|---|---|---|---|
| K57 | htp cpe | 4,025 | 4,583 | 153,899 |

Production includes models with GT ($246) and GTO ($368) option packages. GTO production: 4,806.

| 1973 Engines | bore × stroke | bhp | availability |
|---|---|---|---|
| I-6, 250.0 | 3.88 × 3.53 | 100 | S-Vntra, LeM, Fbd exc T/A |
| V-8, 350.0 | 3.88 × 3.75 | 150 | S-Cat exc wgn; O-Vntra, LeM, Fbd exc T/A |
| V-8, 350.0 | 3.88 × 3.75 | 175 | O-Vntra, LeM, Fbd exc T/A |
| V-8, 400.0 | 4.12 × 3.75 | 170 | S-GA, Bonn, Cat wgn; O-LeMans, other Catalina |
| V-8, 400.0 | 4.12 × 3.75 | 185 | O-GA, LeM, Bonn, Cat |
| V-8, 400.0 | 4.12 × 3.75 | 200 | S-Grand Saf |
| V-8, 400.0 | 4.12 × 3.75 | 230 | S-GA, LeM, Fbd exc T/A, GSaf, Cat, Bonn |
| V-8, 400.0 | 4.12 × 3.75 | 250 | S-Grand Prix |
| V-8, 455.0 | 4.15 × 4.21 | 215 | S-GV; O-GSaf, Cat, Bonn |
| V-8, 455.0 | 4.15 × 4.21 | 250 | S-Fbd T/A; O-Fbd, GSaf, GV, Bonn, GP |
| V-8, 455.0 | 4.15 × 4.21 | 310 | O-Firebird |

## 1974

### Ventura (wb 111.0)

| | | Wght | Price | Prod |
|---|---|---|---|---|
| Y17 | htchbk cpe | 3,372 | 3,018 | 16,694 |
| Z17 | Custom htchbk cpe | 3,376 | 3,176 | |
| Y27 | cpe* | 3,262 | 2,892 | 47,782 |
| Z27 | Custom cpe* | 3,298 | 3,051 | |
| Y69 | sdn 4d | 3,284 | 2,921 | 17,323 |
| Z69 | Custom sdn 4d | 3,332 | 3,080 | |

### Firebird (wb 108.0)

| | | Wght | Price | Prod |
|---|---|---|---|---|
| S87 | cpe | 3,394 | 3,335 | 26,372 |
| T87 | Esprit cpe V-8 | 3,540 | 3,687 | 22,583 |
| U87 | Formula cpe V-8 | 3,548 | 3,659 | 14,519 |
| V87 | Trans Am cpe V-8 | 3,655 | 4,446 | 10,255 |

### LeMans (wb 116.0; 2d-112.0)

| | | Wght | Price | Prod |
|---|---|---|---|---|
| D29 | Colonnade sdn 4d | 3,736 | 3,236 | 17,266 |
| D37 | Colonnade sdn 2d | 3,660 | 3,216 | 37,061 |
| D35 | Safari wgn 4d 2S V-8 | 4,333 | 4,052 | 4,743 |
| D45 | Safari wgn 4d 3S V-8 | 4,371 | 4,186 | 3,004 |
| F37 | Sport Colonnade cpe | 3,688 | 3,300 | 37,955 |
| G35 | Lux Safari wgn 4d 2S V-8 | 4,363 | 4,326 | 952 |
| G29 | Luxury Col sdn 4d V-8 | 3,904 | 3,759 | 4,513 |
| G37 | Luxury Col cpe V-8 | 3,808 | 3,703 | 25,882 |
| G45 | Lux Safari wgn 4d 3S V-8 | 4,401 | 4,459 | 1,178 |

### Grand Am (wb 116.0; 2d-112.0)

| | | Wght | Price | Prod |
|---|---|---|---|---|
| H29 | Colonnade sdn 4d | 4,073 | 4,623 | 3,122 |
| H37 | Colonnade cpe | 3,992 | 4,534 | 13,961 |

### Catalina (wb 124.0; wgn-127.0)

| | | Wght | Price | Prod |
|---|---|---|---|---|
| L35 | Safari wgn 4d 2S | 4,973 | 4,692 | 5,662 |
| L39 | htp sdn | 4,352 | 4,347 | 11,769 |
| L45 | Safari wgn 4d 3S | 5,037 | 4,834 | 6,486 |
| L57 | htp cpe | 4,279 | 4,278 | 40,657 |
| L69 | sdn 4d | 4,294 | 4,190 | 46,025 |

### Bonneville (wb 124.0)

| | | Wght | Price | Prod |
|---|---|---|---|---|
| N39 | htp sdn | 4,444 | 4,639 | 6,151 |
| N57 | htp cpe | 4,356 | 4,572 | 7,639 |
| N69 | sdn 4d | 4,384 | 4,510 | 6,770 |

### Grand Ville/Grand Safari (wb 124.0/127.0)

| | | Wght | Price | Prod |
|---|---|---|---|---|
| P35 | Grand Safari wgn 4d 2S | 5,011 | 5,099 | 2,894 |
| P45 | Grand Safari wgn 4d 3S | 5,112 | 5,256 | 5,255 |
| P47 | Grand Ville htp cpe | 4,432 | 4,871 | 11,631 |
| P49 | Grand Ville htp sdn | 4,515 | 4,939 | 21,714 |
| P67 | Grand Ville conv | 4,476 | 5,113 | 3,000 |
| | chassis | — | — | 113 |

## Pontiac

| Grand Prix (wb 116.0) | | Wght | Price | Prod |
|---|---|---|---|---|
| K57 | htp cpe | 4,096 | 4,936 | 99,817 |

\* GTO option package ($195) for Ventura coupe only. GTO production: 7,058.

| 1974 Engines | bore × stroke | bhp | availability |
|---|---|---|---|
| I-6, 250.0 | 3.88 × 3.53 | 100 | S-Ventura, LeMans, Firebird S87 |
| V-8, 350.0 | 3.88 × 3.75 | 155 | S-Fbd T87; O-Vntra, LeMans, Fbd S87 |
| V-8, 350.0 | 3.88 × 3.75 | 170 | S-Firebird U87; O-LeMans |
| V-8, 350.0 | 3.88 × 3.75 | 200 | O-LeMans |
| V-8, 400.0 | 4.12 × 3.75 | 175 | S-GA, Cat, Bonn, GSaf, GV |
| V-8, 400.0 | 4.15 × 3.75 | 190 | O-Grand Am |
| V-8, 400.0 | 4.12 × 3.75 | 200 | O-Cat, Bonn, GSaf, GV |
| V-8, 400.0 | 4.12 × 3.75 | 225 | S-Fbd T/A, GP; O-GA, other Fbd |
| V-8, 455.0 | 4.15 × 4.21 | 215 | S-GV; O-GA, Cat, Bonn |
| V-8, 455.0 | 4.15 × 4.21 | 250 | O-GA, Fbd T/A, GP |
| V-8, 455.0 | 4.15 × 4.21 | 255 | O-all full-size |
| V-8, 455.0 | 4.15 × 4.21 | 290 | O-Fbd Formula/Trans Am |

### 1975

| Astre (wb 97.0) | | Wght | Price | Prod |
|---|---|---|---|---|
| C11 | S sdn 2d | 2,416 | 2,841 | 8,339 |
| C15 | S Safari wgn 2d | 2,519 | 3,071 | |
| V15 | Safari wgn 2d | 2,545 | 3,175 | 15,322 |
| X15 | SJ Safari wgn 2d | 2,602 | 3,686 | |
| C77 | S htchbk cpe | 2,487 | 2,954 | |
| V77 | htchbk cpe | 2,499 | 3,079 | 40,809 |
| X77 | SJ htchbk cpe | 2,558 | 3,610 | |
| **Ventura (wb 111.1)** | | | | |
| E27 | S cpe | 3,360 | 3,162 | |
| Y27 | cpe | 3,382 | 3,293 | 34,023 |
| Z27 | Custom cpe | 3,442 | 3,449 | |
| B27 | SJ cpe | 3,424 | 3,829 | |
| Y17 | htchbk cpe | 3,466 | 3,432 | |
| Z17 | Custom htchbk cpe | 3,482 | 3,593 | 10,463 |
| B17 | SJ htchbk cpe | 3,484 | 3,961 | |
| Y69 | sdn 4d | 3,418 | 3,304 | |
| Z69 | Custom sdn 4d | 3,462 | 3,464 | 22,068 |
| B69 | SJ sdn 4d | 3,454 | 3,846 | |
| **Firebird (wb 108.0)** | | | | |
| S87 | cpe | 3,498 | 3,713 | 22,293 |
| T87 | Esprit cpe | 3,543 | 3,958 | 20,826 |
| U87 | Formula cpe V-8 | 3,631 | 4,349 | 13,670 |
| W87 | Trans Am cpe V-8 | 3,716 | 4,740 | 27,274 |
| **LeMans (wb 116.0; 2d-112.0)** | | | | |
| D29 | Colonnade sdn 4d | 3,838 | 3,612 | 15,065 |
| D35 | wgn 4d 2S V-8 | 4,401 | 4,555 | 3,988 |
| D37 | Colonnade sdn 2d | 3,766 | 3,590 | 20,636 |
| D45 | wgn 4d 3S V-8 | 4,439 | 4,688 | 2,393 |
| F37 | Sport cpe | 3,978 | 3,708 | 23,817 |
| G35 | Grand wgn 4d 2S V-8 | 4,462 | 4,749 | 1,393 |
| G29 | Grand Colonnade sdn 4d | 3,896 | 4,157 | 4,906 |
| G37 | Grand Colonnade sdn 2d | 3,832 | 4,101 | 19,310 |
| G45 | Grand wgn 4d 3S V-8 | 4,500 | 4,882 | 1,501 |

| Grand Am (wb 116.0; 2d-112.0) | | Wght | Price | Prod |
|---|---|---|---|---|
| H29 | Colonnade sdn 4d | 4,055 | 4,976 | 1,893 |
| H37 | Colonnade sdn 2d | 4,008 | 4,887 | 8,786 |
| **Catalina (wb 124.0; wgn-127.0)** | | | | |
| L35 | Safari wgn 4d 2S | 4,933 | 5,149 | 3,964 |
| L45 | Safari wgn 4d 3S | 5,000 | 5,295 | 4,992 |
| L57 | cpe | 4,334 | 4,700 | 21,644 |
| L69 | sdn 4d | 4,347 | 4,612 | 40,398 |
| **Bonneville (wb 124.0; wgn-127.0)** | | | | |
| P35 | Grand Safari wgn 4d 2S | 5,035 | 5,433 | 2,568 |
| P45 | Grand Safari wgn 4d 3S | 5,090 | 5,580 | 4,752 |
| P47 | cpe | 4,370 | 5,085 | 7,854 |
| P49 | htp sdn | 4,503 | 5,153 | 12,641 |
| **Grand Ville Brougham (wb 126.0)** | | | | |
| R47 | cpe | 4,404 | 5,729 | 7,477 |
| R49 | htp sdn | 4,558 | 5,896 | 15,686 |
| R67 | conv | 4,520 | 5,858 | 4,519 |
| | chassis | — | — | 60 |
| **Grand Prix (wb 116.0)** | | | | |
| K57 | cpe | 4,032 | 5,296 | 86,582 |

| 1975 Engines | bore × stroke | bhp | availability |
|---|---|---|---|
| I-4, 140.0 | 3.50 × 3.63 | 78 | S-Astre exc SJ |
| I-4, 140.0 | 3.50 × 3.63 | 87 | S-Astre SJ; O-Astre |
| I-6, 250.0 | 3.88 × 3.53 | 105 | S-Vntra, LeM exc Saf, GA, Firebird S87/T87 |
| V-8, 260.0 | 3.50 × 3.39 | 110 | O-Ventura |
| V-8, 350.0 | 3.88 × 3.75 | 145/165 | O-Ventura |
| V-8, 350.0 | 3.88 × 3.75 | 155 | S-LeM exc Saf; Fbd S87/T87 |
| V-8, 350.0 | 3.88 × 3.75 | 175 | S-Fbd U87; O-LeM exc Saf |
| V-8, 400.0 | 4.12 × 3.75 | 170 | S-LeM Saf, GA, exc wgn; O-LeM, GP |
| V-8, 400.0 | 4.12 × 3.75 | 185 | S-T/A, Cat wgn; GSaf, GV; O-LeM, GA, U87 |
| V-8, 455.0 | 4.15 × 4.21 | 200 | O-all exc Ast, Vntra |

### 1976

| Astre (wb 97.0) | | Wght | Price | Prod |
|---|---|---|---|---|
| C11 | sdn 2d | 2,439 | 3,064 | 18,143 |
| C15 | Safari wgn 2d | 2,545 | 3,306 | 13,125 |
| C77 | htchbk cpe | 2,505 | 3,179 | 19,116 |
| **Sunbird (wb 97.0)** | | | | |
| M27 | cpe | 2,653 | 3,431 | 52,031 |
| **Ventura (wb 111.1)** | | | | |
| Y17 | htchbk cpe | 3,428 | 3,503 | 6,428 |
| Z17 | SJ htchbk cpe | 3,460 | 3,775 | 1,823 |
| Y27 | cpe | 3,358 | 3,326 | 28,473 |
| Z27 | SJ cpe | 3,370 | 3,612 | 4,815 |
| Y69 | sdn 4d | 3,350 | 3,361 | 27,773 |
| Z69 | SJ sdn 4d | 3,406 | 3,637 | 4,804 |
| **Firebird (wb 108.0)** | | | | |
| S87 | cpe | 3,473 | 3,906 | 21,209 |
| T87 | Esprit cpe | 3,521 | 4,162 | 22,252 |
| U87 | Formula cpe V-8 | 3,625 | 4,566 | 20,613 |
| W87 | Trans Am cpe V-8 | 3,640 | 4,987 | 46,701 |
| **LeMans (wb 116.0; 2d-112.0)** | | | | |
| D29 | sdn 4d | 3,848 | 3,813 | 22,199 |

## Pontiac

| LeMans (wb 116.0; 2d-112.0) | | Wght | Price | Prod |
|---|---|---|---|---|
| D37 | sdn 2d | 3,738 | 3,768 | 21,130 |
| D35 | Safari wgn 4d 2S V-8 | 4,336 | 4,687 | 3,988 |
| D45 | Safari wgn 4d 3S V-8 | 4,374 | 4,820 | 2,393 |
| F37 | Sport cpe | 3,756 | 3,916 | 15,582 |
| G29 | Grand LeMans sdn 4d | 3,948 | 4,433 | 8,411 |
| G37 | Grand LeMans sdn 2d | 3,834 | 4,330 | 14,757 |
| G35 | Gd LeM Saf wgn 5d 2S V-8 | 4,389 | 4,928 | 1,393 |
| G45 | Gd LeM Saf wgn 5d 3S V-8 | 4,427 | 5,061 | 3,964 |
| **Catalina (wb 124.0; wgn-127.0)** | | | | |
| L35 | Safari wgn 4d 2S | 4,944 | 5,324 | 4,735 |
| L45 | Safari wgn 4d 3S | 5,000 | 5,473 | 5,513 |
| L57 | cpe | 4,256 | 4,844 | 15,262 |
| L69 | sdn 4d | 4,276 | 4,767 | 47,235 |
| **Bonneville (wb 124.0; wgn-127.0)** | | | | |
| P35 | Grand Safari wgn 4d 2S | 5,035 | 5,746 | 3,462 |
| P45 | Grand Safari wgn 4d 3S | 5,091 | 5,895 | 6,176 |
| P47 | cpe | 4,308 | 5,246 | 9,189 |
| P49 | htp sdn 4d | 4,460 | 5,312 | 14,942 |
| R47 | Brougham cpe | 4,341 | 5,734 | 10,466 |
| R49 | Brougham htp sdn 4d | 4,514 | 5,906 | 20,236 |
| **Grand Prix (wb 116.0)** | | | | |
| J57 | cpe | 4,048 | 4,798 | 110,814 |
| — | LJ cpe* | — | — | 29,045 |
| K57 | SJ cpe | 4,052 | 5,223 | 88,232 |

*Option package ($625) for J57.

| 1976 Engines | bore × stroke | bhp | availability |
|---|---|---|---|
| I-4, 140.0 | 3.50 × 3.63 | 70 | S-Astre, Sunbird |
| I-4, 140.0 | 3.50 × 3.63 | 84 | O-Astre, Sunbird |
| V-6, 231.0 | 3.80 × 3.40 | 105 | O-Sunbird |
| I-6, 250.0 | 3.88 × 3.53 | 110 | S-Vntra, LeM, Fbd exc T/A |
| V-8, 260.0 | 3.50 × 3.39 | 110 | O-Ventura, LeMans |
| V-8, 350.0 | 3.88 × 3.75 | 140/155 | O-Ventura |
| V-8, 350.0 | 3.88 × 3.75 | 160 | S-Fbd exc T/A, GP exc SJ; O-LeM |
| V-8, 350.0 | 3.88 × 3.75 | 165 | O-LeM, Fbd exc T/A, GP exc SJ |
| V-8, 400.0 | 4.12 × 3.75 | 170 | S-all G LeMans, Cat, Bonn |
| V-8, 400.0 | 4.12 × 3.75 | 185 | S-Fbd T/A, GP SJ; O-LeM, Fbd, Cat, Bonn, GP |
| V-8, 455.0 | 4.15 × 4.21 | 200 | S-Cat/Bonn wgns; O-LeM, Fbd T/A, Cat, Bonn, GP |

### 1977

| Astre (wb 97.0) | | Wght | Price | Prod |
|---|---|---|---|---|
| C11 | sdn 2d | 2,480 | 3,305 | 10,327 |
| C15 | Safari wgn 2d | 2,608 | 3,595 | 10,341 |
| C77 | htchbk cpe | 2,573 | 3,430 | 12,120 |
| **Ventura (wb 111.1)** | | | | |
| Y17 | htchbk cpe | 3,292 | 3,792 | 4,015 |
| Y27 | cpe | 3,170 | 3,596 | 26,675 |
| Y69 | sdn 4d | 3,210 | 3,650 | 27,089 |
| Z17 | SJ htchbk cpe | 3,336 | 4,165 | 1,100 |
| Z27 | SJ cpe | 3,248 | 3,985 | 3,418 |
| Z69 | SJ sdn 4d | 3,278 | 4,012 | 4,339 |
| **Sunbird (wb 97.0)—55,398 built** | | | | |
| M07 | Sport Hatch cpe | 2,693 | 3,784 | — |
| M27 | cpe | 2,662 | 3,659 | — |

| Phoenix (wb 111.1) | | Wght | Price | Prod |
|---|---|---|---|---|
| X27 | cpe | 3,283 | 4,075 | 10,489 |
| X69 | sdn 4d | 3,331 | 4,122 | 13,639 |
| **Firebird (wb 108.0)** | | | | |
| S87 | cpe | 3,306 | 4,270 | 30,642 |
| T87 | Esprit cpe | 3,354 | 4,551 | 34,548 |
| U87 | Formula cpe V-8 | 3,411 | 4,977 | 21,801 |
| W87 | Trans Am cpe V-8 | 3,526 | 5,456 | 68,745 |
| **LeMans (wb 116.0; 2d-112.0)** | | | | |
| D29 | sdn 4d | 3,680 | 4,105 | 23,060 |
| D37 | cpe | 3,592 | 4,057 | 16,038 |
| D35 | wgn 4d 2S V-8 | 4,135 | 4,889 | 10,081 |
| D35 | wgn 4d 3S V-8 | 4,167 | 5,041 | |
| F37 | Sport cpe | 3,600 | 4,216 | 12,277 |
| G29 | Grand LeMans sdn 4d | 3,782 | 4,742 | 5,584 |
| G37 | Grand LeMans cpe | 3,630 | 4,614 | 7,581 |
| G35 | Gd LeMans wgn 4d 2S V-8 | 4,179 | 5,144 | 5,393 |
| G35 | Gd LeMans wgn 4d 3S V-8 | 4,211 | 5,296 | |
| **Catalina (wb 124.0; wgn-127.0)** | | | | |
| L37 | cpe | 3,521 | 5,053 | 14,752 |
| L69 | sdn 4d | 3,555 | 5,050 | 46,926 |
| L35 | Safari wgn 4d 2S V-8 | 4,024 | 5,492 | 13,058 |
| L35 | Safari wgn 4d 3S V-8 | 4,056 | 5,657 | |
| **Bonneville (wb 124.0; wgn-127.0)** | | | | |
| N35 | Grand Safari wgn 4d 2S | 4,066 | 5,772 | 18,304 |
| N35 | Grand Safari wgn 4d 3S | 4,098 | 5,937 | |
| N37 | cpe | 3,579 | 5,411 | 37,817 |
| N69 | sdn 4d | 3,616 | 5,457 | 13,697 |
| Q37 | Brougham cpe | 3,617 | 5,897 | 15,901 |
| Q69 | Brougham sdn 4d | 3,680 | 5,992 | 47,465 |
| **Grand Prix (wb 116.0)** | | | | |
| J57 | cpe | 3,804 | 5,120 | 168,247 |
| K57 | LJ cpe | 3,815 | 5,483 | 66,741 |
| H57 | SJ cpe | 3,976 | 5,753 | 53,442 |

| 1977 Engines | bore × stroke | bhp | availability |
|---|---|---|---|
| I-4, 140.0 | 3.50 × 3.63 | 84 | S-Astre sdn |
| I-4, 151.0 | 4.00 × 3.00 | 87 | S-Ast wgn/htchbk, Sbd; O-Astre sdn, Phnx, Vntra |
| V-6, 231.0 | 3.80 × 3.40 | 105 | S-Phnx, Vntra, LeM, Fbd exc T/A, Cat; O-Sunbird |
| V-8, 301.0 | 4.00 × 3.00 | 135 | S-Vntra, LeM, Fbd exc T/A, Cat, Bonn, GP exc SJ |
| V-8, 305.0 | 3.74 × 3.48 | 145 | S-Phnx, Vntra, Fbd exc T/A |
| V-8, 350.0 | 3.88 × 3.75 | 170 | O-Phnx, Vntra, LeM, Fbd exc T/A, GP |
| V-8, 400.0 | 4.12 × 3.75 | 180/200 | S-Fbd T/A, GP SJ; O-LeM, Sbd, GP |
| V-8, 350.0 | 3.88 × 3.75 | 180 | O-Cat, Bonn |
| V-8, 403.0 | 4.36 × 3.39 | 185 | O-Fbd, Cat, Bonn |

### 1978

| Sunbird (wb 97.0) | | Wght | Price | Prod |
|---|---|---|---|---|
| E27 | cpe | 2,662 | 3,590 | 20,413 |
| M07 | Sport Hatch cpe | 2,694 | 3,962 | 25,380 |
| M15 | Safari wgn 2d | 2,610 | 3,741 | 8,424 |
| M27 | Sport Coupe | 2,662 | 3,823 | 32,572 |
| **Phoenix (wb 111.1)** | | | | |
| Y17 | htchbk cpe | 3,250 | 4,103 | 3,252 |

# Pontiac

| Phoenix (wb 111.1) | | Wght | Price | Prod |
|---|---|---|---|---|
| Y27 | cpe | 3,167 | 3,907 | 26,143 |
| Y69 | sdn 4d | 3,217 | 3,992 | 32,529 |
| Z27 | LJ cpe | 3,276 | 4,399 | 6,210 |
| Z69 | LJ sdn 4d | 3,325 | 4,484 | 8,393 |
| **Firebird (wb 108.0)** | | | | |
| S87 | cpe | 3,316 | 4,593 | 32,672 |
| T87 | Esprit cpe | 3,346 | 4,897 | 36,926 |
| U87 | Formula cpe V-8 | 3,452 | 5,533 | 24,346 |
| W87 | Trans Am cpe V-8 | 3,511 | 5,889 | 93,341 |
| **LeMans (wb 108.1)** | | | | |
| D19 | sdn 4d | 3,108 | 4,512 | 22,728 |
| D27 | cpe | 3,098 | 4,427 | 20,581 |
| D35 | Safari wgn 4d | 3,298 | 4,980 | 15,714 |
| F19 | Grand LeMans sdn 4d | 3,158 | 4,915 | 21,252 |
| F27 | Grand Lemans cpe | 3,130 | 4,801 | 18,433 |
| F35 | G.LeM Safari wgn 4d | 3,316 | 5,310 | 11,125 |
| G19 | Grand Am sdn 4d V-8 | 3,239 | 5,634 | 2,841 |
| G27 | Grand Am cpe V-8 | 3,209 | 5,520 | 7,767 |
| **Catalina (wb 116.0)** | | | | |
| L35 | Safari wgn 4d 2S V-8 | 3,976 | 6,011 | 12,819 |
| L37 | cpe | 3,498 | 5,439 | 9,224 |
| L69 | sdn 4d | 3,530 | 5,484 | 39,707 |
| **Bonneville (wb 116.0)** | | | | |
| N35 | Grand Safari wgn 4d 2S | 4,002 | 6,319 | 13,847 |
| N37 | cpe | 3,581 | 5,913 | 22,510 |
| N69 | sdn 4d | 3,637 | 6,023 | 48,647 |
| Q37 | Brougham cpe | 3,611 | 6,674 | 17,948 |
| Q69 | Brougham sdn 4d | 3,667 | 6,784 | 36,192 |
| **Grand Prix (wb 108.1)** | | | | |
| J37 | cpe V-6/V-8 | 3,162 | 4,880 | 127,253 |
| K37 | LJ cpe V-8 | 3,216 | 5,815 | 65,122 |
| H37 | SJ cpe V-8 | 3,229 | 6,088 | 36,069 |

| 1978 Engines | bore × stroke | bhp | availability |
|---|---|---|---|
| I-4, 151.0 | 4.00 × 3.00 | 85 | S-Sbd; O-Phnx |
| V-6, 231.0 | 3.80 × 3.40 | 105 | S-Phnx, LeM exc GA, Fbd S87/T87, Cat, GP J37; O-Sbd |
| V-8, 301.0 | 4.00 × 3.00 | 140 | S-LeM GA, Cat, Bonn, GP LJ |
| V-8, 301.0 | 4.00 × 3.00 | 150 | O-LeM GA, GP SJ |
| V-8, 305.0 | 3.74 × 3.48 | 145 | S-Fbd Fmla; O-Sbd, Phnx, LeM, Fbd exc U/W87 |
| V-8, 350.0 | 3.80 × 3.85 | 160 | O-Phoenix, Firebird |
| V-8, 350.0 | 3.80 × 3.85 | 155/170 | O-Catalina, Bonn |
| V-8, 400.0 | 4.12 × 3.75 | 180 | S-Fbd T/A; O-Fbd Fmla, Cat, Bonn |
| V-8, 403.0 | 4.36 × 3.38 | 185 | O-Fbd, Cat, Bonn |

## 1979

| Sunbird (wb 97.0) | | Wght | Price | Prod |
|---|---|---|---|---|
| M07 | cpe | 2,642 | 3,899 | 24,221 |
| M15 | Safari spt wgn 2d | 2,651 | 4,321 | 2,902 |
| M27 | Sport Coupe | 2,774 | 4,148 | 30,087 |
| E27 | Sport Hatch cpe | 2,774 | 4,248 | 40,560 |
| **Phoenix (wb 111.1)** | | | | |
| Y17 | htchbk cpe | 3,319 | 4,239 | 923 |
| Y27 | cpe | 3,236 | 4,089 | 9,233 |
| Y69 | sdn 4d | 3,286 | 4,189 | 10,565 |
| Z27 | LJ cpe | 3,345 | 4,589 | 1,826 |
| Z69 | LJ sdn 4d | 3,394 | 4,689 | 2,353 |
| **Firebird (wb 108.0)** | | | | |
| S87 | cpe | 3,294 | 5,260 | 38,642 |
| T87 | Esprit cpe | 3,324 | 5,638 | 30,853 |
| U87 | Formula cpe V-8 | 3,460 | 6,564 | 24,851 |
| W87 | Trans Am cpe V-8 | 3,551 | 6,883 | 109,609 |
| X87 | T/A Limited Edition | 3,551 | 10,620 | 7,500 |
| **LeMans (wb 108.1)** | | | | |
| D19 | sdn 4d | 3,082 | 5,134 | 26,958 |
| D27 | cpe | 3,076 | 5,031 | 14,197 |
| D35 | Safari wgn | 3,240 | 5,587 | 27,517 |
| F19 | Grand LeMans sdn 4d | 3,126 | 5,430 | 28,577 |
| F27 | Grand LeMans cpe | 3,098 | 5,302 | 13,020 |
| F35 | Grand LeM Safari wgn | 3,274 | 5,931 | 20,783 |
| G19 | Grand Am sdn 4d | 3,124 | 5,529 | 1,865 |
| G27 | Grand Am cpe | 3,120 | 5,530 | 4,021 |
| **Catalina (wb 116.0)** | | | | |
| L35 | Safari wgn 4d 2S V-8 | 3,997 | 6,681 | 13,353 |
| L35 | Safari wgn 4d 3S V-8 | 4,029 | 6,864 | |
| L37 | cpe | 3,534 | 6,020 | 5,410 |
| L69 | sdn 4d | 3,566 | 6,076 | 28,121 |
| **Bonneville (wb 116.0)** | | | | |
| N35 | Safari wgn 4d 2S | 4,022 | 7,050 | 16,925 |
| N35 | Safari wgn 4d 3S | 4,054 | 7,233 | |
| N37 | cpe | 3,616 | 6,593 | 34,127 |
| Q37 | Brougham cpe | 3,659 | 7,395 | 39,094 |
| N69 | sdn 4d | 3,672 | 6,718 | 71,906 |
| Q69 | Brougham sdn 4d | 3,726 | 7,584 | 17,364 |
| **Grand Prix (wb 108.1)** | | | | |
| J37 | cpe | 3,166 | 5,454 | 124,815 |
| K37 | LJ cpe V-8 | 3,285 | 6,555 | 61,175 |
| H37 | SJ cpe V-8 | 3,349 | 6,814 | 24,060 |

| 1979 Engines | bore × stroke | bhp | availability |
|---|---|---|---|
| I-4, 151.0 | 4.00 × 3.00 | 85 | S-Sunbd; O-Phnx |
| V-6, 231.0 | 3.74 × 3.48 | 115 | S-Phoenix, Firebird S87/T87, LeM, GP exc SJ, Catalina; O-Sunbird |
| V-8, 301.0 | 4.00 × 3.00 | 140 | S-Bonn, GP exc SJ; O-Phnx, LeM, Fbd S87/T87, Cat |
| V-8, 301.0 | 3.80 × 3.85 | 150 | S-Fbd Fmla, GP SJ; O-Phoenix, Firebird S87/T87, LeMans, Catalina, Bonn |
| V-8, 305.0 | 3.80 × 3.85 | 145 | O-Sunbird, Phoenix, LeM, Fbd S/T87 |
| V-8, 350.0 | 3.88 × 3.75 | 160 | O-Phoenix, Firebird |
| V-8, 350.0 | 3.88 × 3.75 | 155/170 | O-Catalina, Bonn |
| V-8, 400.0 | 4.12 × 3.75 | 180 | S-Fbd T/A; O-Fbd Fmla, Cat, Bonn |
| V-8, 400.0 | 4.12 × 3.75 | 220 | O-Fbd Formula, T/A |
| V-8, 403.0 | 4.36 × 3.38 | 185 | O-Fbd, Formula |

Note: Because 350-cid V-8s from several GM divisions were used in the late 1970s, bore/stroke may differ from dimensions shown.

## 1980

| Sunbird (wb 97.0) | | Wght | Price | Prod |
|---|---|---|---|---|
| E07 | htchbk cpe | 2,651 | 4,808 | 27,910 |
| M07 | Sport Hatch cpe | 2,657 | 4,731 | 25,042 |
| E27 | cpe | 2,603 | 4,371 | 105,847 |
| M27 | Sport Coupe | 2,609 | 4,620 | 29,180 |

# Pontiac

| Phoenix (wb 104.9) | | Wght | Price | Prod |
|---|---|---|---|---|
| Y37 | cpe | 2,516 | 5,465 | 49,485 |
| Y67 | htchbk sdn 4d | 2,558 | 5,656 | 72,875 |
| Z37 | LJ cpe | 2,550 | 5,936 | 23,674 |
| Z68 | LJ htchbk sdn 4d | 2,610 | 6,127 | 32,257 |
| **Firebird (wb 108.0)** | | | | |
| S87 | cpe | 3,306 | 5,948 | 29,811 |
| T87 | Esprit cpe | 3,360 | 6,311 | 17,277 |
| V87 | Formula cpe V-8 | 3,410 | 7,256 | 9,356 |
| W87 | Trans Am cpe V-8 | 3,429 | 7,480 | 50,896 |
| **LeMans (wb 108.0)** | | | | |
| D19 | sdn 4d | 3,080 | 5,758 | 20,485 |
| D27 | cpe | 3,064 | 5,652 | 9,110 |
| D35 | Safari wgn 4d | 3,296 | 6,257 | 12,912 |
| F19 | Grand LeMans sdn 4d | 3,129 | 6,120 | 18,561 |
| F27 | Grand LeMans cpe | 3,090 | 5,947 | 6,477 |
| F35 | Gd LeMans Safari wgn 4d | 3,328 | 6,682 | 14,832 |
| G27 | Grand Am cpe V-8 | 3,299 | 7,504 | 1,647 |
| **Catalina (wb 116.0)** | | | | |
| L35 | Safari wgn 4d 2S V-8 | 3,939 | 7,362 | 2,931 |
| L35 | Safari wgn 4d 3S V-8 | 3,961 | 7,561 | |
| L37 | cpe | 3,448 | 6,703 | 3,319 |
| L69 | sdn 4d | 3,474 | 6,761 | 10,408 |
| **Bonneville (wb 116.0)** | | | | |
| N35 | Safari wgn 4d 2S V-8 | 3,939 | 7,958 | 5,309 |
| N35 | Safari wgn 4d 3S V-8 | 3,981 | 8,157 | |
| N37 | cpe | 3,486 | 7,034 | 16,771 |
| R37 | Brougham cpe | 3,525 | 7,968 | 12,374 |
| N69 | sdn 4d | 3,532 | 7,167 | 26,112 |
| R69 | Brougham sdn 4d | 3,610 | 8,160 | 21,249 |
| **Grand Prix (wb 108.1)** | | | | |
| J37 | cpe | 3,201 | 6,621 | 72,659 |
| K37 | LJ cpe | 3,342 | 7,000 | 34,968 |
| H37 | SJ cpe V-8 | 3,291 | 7,597 | 7,087 |

| 1980 Engines | bore × stroke | bhp | availability |
|---|---|---|---|
| I-4, 151.0 | 4.00 × 3.00 | 90 | S-Sunbird, Phoenix |
| V-6, 173.0 | 3.50 × 3.00 | 115 | O-Phoenix |
| V-6, 229.0 | 3.74 × 3.48 | 115 | S-LeMans |
| V-6, 231.0 | 3.80 × 3.40 | 110/115 | S-Fbd S/T87, Cat/Bonn exc wgn, GP; O-Sbd |
| V-8, 265.0 | 3.75 × 3.00 | 120 | O-LeM |
| V-8, 301.0 | 4.00 × 3.00 | 140 | S-GA, Fbd V/W, Cat/Bonn wgn, GP SJ; O-LeM, Fbd, other Cat/Bonn, other GP |
| V-8T, 301.0 | 4.00 × 3.00 | 210 | O-Fbd V/W |
| V-8, 305.0 | 3.70 × 3.48 | 150 | O-LeM, Fbd S/T, GP |
| V-8D, 350.0 | 3.88 × 3.75 | 105 | O-Cat, Bonn wgn/Brham |
| V-8, 350.0 | 4.06 × 3.39 | 155/160 | O-Catalina, Bonn |

## 1981

| T1000 (wb 94.3; 4d-97.3) | | Wght | Price | Prod |
|---|---|---|---|---|
| M08 | htchbk sdn 2d | 2,058 | 5,358 | 26,415 |
| M68 | htchbk sdn 4d | 2,122 | 5,504 | 43,779 |
| **Phoenix (wb 104.9)** | | | | |
| Y37 | cpe | 2,477 | 6,307 | 31,829 |
| Y68 | htchbk sdn 4d | 2,524 | 6,498 | 62,693 |
| Z37 | LJ cpe | 2,519 | 6,778 | 11,975 |
| Z68 | LJ htchbk sdn 4d | 2,579 | 6,969 | 21,372 |
| **Firebird (wb 108.2)** | | | | |
| S87 | cpe | 3,312 | 6,901 | 20,541 |
| T87 | Esprit cpe | — | 7,645 | 10,938 |
| V87 | Formula cpe | — | 7,854 | 5,927 |
| W87 | Trans Am cpe V-8 | — | 8,322 | 33,493 |
| X87 | Trans Am turbo SE cpe | — | 12,257 | |
| **LeMans (wb 108.1)** | | | | |
| D27 | cpe | 3,093 | 6,689 | 2,578 |
| D69 | sdn 4d | 3,110 | 6,797 | 22,186 |
| D69/Y83 | LJ sdn 4d | — | 7,100 | |
| D35 | Safari wgn 4d | 3,313 | 7,316 | 13,358 |
| F27 | Grand LeMans cpe | 3,121 | 6,976 | 1,819 |
| F69 | Grand LeMans sdn 4d | 3,166 | 7,153 | 25,241 |
| F35 | Gd LeMans Safari wgn 4d | 3,352 | 7,726 | 16,683 |
| **Catalina (wb 116.0)** | | | | |
| L35 | Safari wgn 4d 2S V-8 | 3,924 | 8,666 | 2,912 |
| L37 | cpe | 3,480 | 7,367 | 1,074 |
| L69 | sdn 4d | 3,488 | 7,471 | 6,456 |
| **Bonneville (wb 116.0)** | | | | |
| N35 | Safari wgn 4d 2S V-8 | 3,949 | 9,205 | 6,855 |
| N37 | cpe | 3,502 | 7,649 | 14,940 |
| R37 | Brougham cpe | 3,502 | 8,580 | 14,317 |
| N69 | sdn 4d | 3,520 | 7,776 | 32,056 |
| R69 | Brougham sdn 4d | 3,520 | 8,768 | 23,395 |
| **Grand Prix (wb 108.1)** | | | | |
| J37 | cpe | 3,226 | 7,424 | 74,786 |
| K37 | LJ cpe | 3,255 | 7,803 | 46,842 |
| P37 | Brougham cpe | 3,281 | 8,936 | 26,083 |

| 1981 Engines | bore × stroke | bhp | availability |
|---|---|---|---|
| I-4, 97.6 | 3.23 × 2.98 | 70 | S-T1000 |
| I-4, 151.0 | 4.00 × 3.00 | 84 | S-Phoenix |
| V-6, 173.0 | 3.50 × 3.00 | 110 | O-Phoenix |
| V-6, 231.0 | 3.80 × 3.40 | 110 | S-Fbd S/T, LeM, Cat, Bonn, GP |
| V-8, 265.0 | 3.75 × 3.00 | 120 | S-Fbd Formula; O-Fbd S/T, LeM, Cat, Bonn, GP |
| V-8, 301.0 | 4.00 × 3.00 | 135 | O-Fbd S/T, Cat, Bonn, LeM wgn |
| V-8, 301.0 | 4.00 × 3.00 | 150 | S-Fbd T/A; O-Fbd |
| V-8T, 301.0 | 4.00 × 3.00 | 200 | O-Fbd Formula, Trans Am |
| V-8, 305.0 | 3.74 × 3.48 | 145 | O-Fbd Formula, Trans Am |
| V-8, 307.0 | 3.80 × 3.39 | 145 | S-Bonn/Cat wgn; O-Cat, Bon |
| V-8D, 350.0 | 4.06 × 3.39 | 105 | O-Cat, Bon, Safari, GP |

## 1982

| T1000 (wb 94.3; 4d-97.3) | | Wght | Price | Prod |
|---|---|---|---|---|
| L08 | htchbk sdn 2d | 2,034 | 5,782 | 21,053 |
| L68 | htchbk sdn 4d | 2,098 | 5,945 | 23,416 |
| **J2000 (wb 101.2)** | | | | |
| B27 | cpe | 2,295 | 6,999 | 15,865 |
| B77 | htchbk cpe | 2,353 | 7,275 | 21,219 |
| B69 | sdn 4d | 2,347 | 7,203 | 29,920 |
| B35 | wgn 4d | 2,418 | 7,448 | 16,014 |
| E27 | S cpe | 2,295 | 6,734 | 2,722 |
| E69 | S sdn 4d | 2,353 | 6,902 | 2,760 |
| E35 | S wgn 4d | 2,355 | 7,208 | 1,245 |

# Pontiac

| J2000 (wb 101.2) | | Wght | Price | Prod |
|---|---|---|---|---|
| C27 | LE cpe | 2,302 | 7,372 | 6,313 |
| C69 | LE sdn 4d | 2,353 | 7,548 | 14,268 |
| D77 | SE htchbk cpe | 2,362 | 7,654 | 8,533 |
| **Firebird (wb 101.0)** | | | | |
| S87 | htchbk cpe I-4/V-6 | — | 7,996 | ⎫ 41,683 |
| S87 | htchbk cpe V-8 | — | 8,291 | ⎭ |
| X87 | S/E htchbk cpe V-6/V-8 | — | 9,624 | 21,719 |
| W87 | Trans Am htchbk cpe V-8 | — | 9,658 | 52,960 |
| **Phoenix (wb 104.9)** | | | | |
| Y37 | cpe | 2,395 | 6,964 | 12,282 |
| Y68 | htchbk sdn 4d | 2,503 | 7,172 | 24,026 |
| Z37 | LJ cpe | 2,494 | 7,449 | 4,436 |
| Z68 | LJ htchbk sdn 4d | 2,527 | 7,658 | 7,161 |
| T37 | SJ cpe V-6 | 2,562 | 8,723 | 994 |
| T68 | SJ htchbk sdn 4d V-6 | 2,612 | 8,884 | 268 |
| **6000 (wb 104.9)** | | | | |
| F27 | cpe | 2,531 | 8,729 | 6,505 |
| F19 | sdn 4d | 2,676 | 8,890 | 17,751 |
| G27 | LE cpe | 2,636 | 9,097 | 7,025 |
| G19 | LE sdn 4d | 2,682 | 9,258 | 26,253 |
| **Bonneville G (wb 108.1)** | | | | |
| N69 | sdn 4d | 3,203 | 8,527 | 44,378 |
| R69 | Brougham sdn 4d | 3,213 | 8,985 | 20,035 |
| N35 | wgn 4d | 3,380 | 8,694 | 16,100 |
| **Grand Prix (wb 108.1)** | | | | |
| J37 | cpe | 3,226 | 8,333 | 37,672 |
| K37 | LJ cpe | 3,248 | 8,788 | 29,726 |
| P37 | Brougham cpe | 3,264 | 9,209 | 12,969 |

| 1982 Engines | bore × stroke | bhp | availability |
|---|---|---|---|
| I-4, 97.6 | 3.23 × 2.98 | 70 | S-T1000 |
| I-4, 112.0 | 3.50 × 2.91 | 88 | S-J2000 (ohc) |
| I-4, 151.0 | 4.00 × 3.00 | 90 | S-Phoenix exc SJ, Firebird, 6000 |
| V-6, 173.0 | 3.50 × 3.00 | 105 | S-Fbd S/E; O-Fbd |
| V-6, 173.0 | 3.50 × 3.00 | 112 | O-Phnx exc SJ, 6000 |
| V-6, 173.0 | 3.50 × 3.00 | 135 | O-Phoenix SJ |
| V-6, 231.0 | 3.80 × 3.40 | 110 | S-Bonn, Grand Prix |
| V-6, 252.0 | 3.96 × 3.40 | 125 | O-Bonn, Grand Prix |
| V-6D, 262.0 | 4.06 × 3.39 | 85 | O-6000, Bonneville |
| V-8, 305.0 | 3.74 × 3.48 | 145 | S-Fbd Trans Am; O-Firebird |
| V-8, 305.0 | 3.74 × 3.48 | 165 | O-Fbd Trans Am |
| V-8D, 350.0 | 4.06 × 3.39 | 105 | O-Bonneville, Grand Prix |

## 1983

| 1000 (wb 94.3; 4d-97.3) | | Wght | Price | Prod |
|---|---|---|---|---|
| L08 | htchbk sdn 2d | 2,081 | 5,582 | 13,171 |
| L68 | htchbk sdn 4d | 2,130 | 5,785 | 12,806 |
| **2000 (wb 101.2)** | | | | |
| B27 | cpe | 2,353 | 6,499 | 22,063 |
| B77 | htchbk cpe | 2,413 | 6,809 | 7,331 |
| B69 | sdn 4d | 2,412 | 6,621 | 24,833 |
| B35 | wgn 4d | 2,487 | 6,926 | 10,214 |
| C27 | LE cpe | 2,385 | 7,020 | 2,690 |
| C67 | LE conv cpe | — | — | 626 |
| C69 | LE sdn 4d | 2,436 | 7,194 | 6,957 |
| C35 | LE wgn 4d | 2,517 | 7,497 | 1,780 |
| D77 | SE htchbk cpe | 2,470 | 8,393 | 1,835 |

| Firebird (wb 101.0) | | Wght | Price | Prod |
|---|---|---|---|---|
| S87 | htchbk cpe I-4/V-6 | 2,937 | 8,399 | ⎫ 32,020 |
| S87 | htchbk cpe V-8 | 3,117 | 8,774 | ⎭ |
| X87 | S/E htchbk cpe V-6/V-8 | 3,055 | 10,322 | 10,934 |
| W87 | Trans Am htchbk cpe V-8 | 3,107 | 10,396 | 31,930 |
| **Phoenix (wb 104.9)** | | | | |
| Y37 | cpe | 2,512 | 6,942 | 7,205 |
| Y68 | htchbk sdn 4d | 2,569 | 7,087 | 13,377 |
| Z37 | LJ cpe | 2,553 | 7,489 | 2,251 |
| Z68 | LJ htchbk sdn 4d | 2,601 | 7,698 | 3,635 |
| T37 | SJ cpe V-6 | 2,581 | 8,861 | 853 |
| T68 | SJ htchbk sdn 4d V-6 | 2,642 | 8,948 | 172 |
| **6000 (wb 104.9)** | | | | |
| F27 | cpe | 2,719 | 8,399 | 3,524 |
| F19 | sdn 4d | 2,757 | 8,569 | 20,267 |
| G27 | LE cpe | 2,732 | 8,837 | 4,278 |
| G19 | LE sdn 4d | 2,771 | 8,984 | 33,676 |
| H19 | STE sdn 4d V-6 | 2,823 | 13,572 | 6,719 |
| **Bonneville (wb 108.1)** | | | | |
| N69 | sdn 4d | 3,252 | 8,899 | 47,003 |
| R69 | Brougham sdn 4d | 3,248 | 9,399 | 19,335 |
| N35 | wgn 4d | 3,313 | 9,112 | 17,551 |
| **Grand Prix (wb 108.1)** | | | | |
| J37 | cpe | 3,261 | 8,698 | 41,511 |
| K37 | LJ cpe | — | 9,166 | 33,785 |
| P37 | Brougham cpe | — | 9,781 | 10,502 |
| **Parisienne (wb 115.9)** | | | | |
| L69 | sdn 4d | 3,409 | 9,609 | 9,279 |
| T69 | Brougham sdn 4d | — | 9,779 | 5,139 |
| L35 | wgn 4d V-8 | 3,963 | 9,927 | 3,027 |

| 1983 Engines | bore × stroke | bhp | availability |
|---|---|---|---|
| I-4, 97.6 | 3.23 × 2.98 | 65 | S-1000 |
| I-4, 109.0 | 3.34 × 3.13 | 84 | S-2000 (ohc) |
| I-4D, 111.0 | 3.31 × 3.23 | 51 | O-1000 |
| I-4, 121.0 | 3.50 × 3.15 | 88 | O-2000 (ohv) |
| I-4, 151.0 | 4.00 × 3.00 | 90 | S-Phoenix, Fbd, 6000 |
| V-6, 173.0 | 3.50 × 3.00 | 107/112 | O-Phnx, Fbd S87, 6000 |
| V-6, 173.0 | 3.50 × 3.00 | 125/135 | S-Phnx SJ, Fbd S/E, 6000 STE |
| V-6, 231.0 | 3.80 × 3.40 | 110 | S-Bonn, GP, Parisienne |
| V-6D, 262.0 | 4.06 × 3.39 | 85 | O-6000 |
| V-8, 305.0 | 3.74 × 3.48 | 150 | S-Fbd T/A; O-other Fbd, Bonn, GP |
| V-8, 305.0 | 3.74 × 3.48 | 175 | O-Firebird Trans Am |
| V-8D, 350.0 | 4.06 × 3.39 | 105 | O-Bonn, GP, Parisienne |

## 1984

| Fiero (wb 93.4) | | Wght | Price | Prod |
|---|---|---|---|---|
| E37 | cpe | 2,437 | 7,999 | 7,099 |
| M37 | Sport Coupe | 2,465 | 8,499 | 62,070 |
| F37 | SE cpe | 2,465 | 9,599 | 67,671 |
| **1000 (wb 94.3; 4d-97.3)** | | | | |
| L08 | htchbk sdn 2d | 2,078 | 5,621 | 19,628 |
| L68 | htchbk sdn 4d | 2,138 | 5,824 | 17,118 |
| **2000 Sunbird (wb 101.2)** | | | | |
| B27 | cpe | 2,347 | 6,675 | 53,070 |

# Pontiac

| 2000 Sunbird (wb 101.2) | | Wght | Price | Prod |
|---|---|---|---|---|
| B77 | htchbk cpe | 2,424 | 6,995 | 12,245 |
| B69 | sdn 4d | 2,406 | 6,799 | 59,312 |
| B35 | wgn 4d | 2,483 | 7,115 | 15,143 |
| C27 | LE cpe | 2,384 | 7,333 | 5,189 |
| C67 | LE conv cpe | 2,514 | 11,749 | 5,458 |
| C69 | LE sdn 4d | 2,436 | 7,499 | 11,183 |
| C35 | LE wgn 4d | 2,504 | 7,819 | 2,011 |
| D27 | SE cpe | 2,469 | 9,019 | 2,141 |
| D77 | SE htchbk cpe | 2,477 | 9,489 | 2,165 |
| D69 | SE sdn 4d | 2,528 | 9,185 | 1,373 |
| **Firebird (wb 101.0)** | | | | |
| S87 | htchbk cpe I-4/V-6 | 2,955 | 8,349 ⎤ | 62,621 |
| S87 | htchbk cpe V-8 | 3,157 | 9,024 ⎦ | |
| X87 | S/E htchbk cpe V-6/V-8 | 3,072 | 10,649 | 10,309 |
| W87 | Trans Am htchbk cpe V-8 | 3,189 | 10,699 | 55,374 |
| **Phoenix (wb 104.9)** | | | | |
| Y37 | cpe | 2,518 | 7,090 | 7,461 |
| Y68 | htchbk sdn 4d | 2,587 | 7,165 | 11,545 |
| Z37 | LE cpe | 2,578 | 7,683 | 1,357 |
| Z68 | LE htchbk sdn 4d | 2,615 | 7,816 | 1,783 |
| T37 | SE cpe V-6 | 2,681 | 9,071 | 701 |
| **6000 (wb 104.9)** | | | | |
| F27 | cpe | 2,707 | 8,699 | 4,171 |
| F19 | sdn 4d | 2,748 | 8,873 | 35,202 |
| G27 | LE cpe | 2,731 | 9,142 | 4,731 |
| G19 | LE sdn 4d | 2,772 | 9,292 | 41,218 |
| F35 | wgn 4d | 2,909 | 9,221 | 8,423 |
| G35 | LE wgn 4d | 2,924 | 9,612 | 9,211 |
| H19 | STE sdn 4d V-6 | 2,990 | 14,437 | 19,236 |
| **Bonneville (wb 108.1)** | | | | |
| N69 | sdn 4d | 3,213 | 9,131 | 40,908 |
| R69 | Brougham sdn 4d | 3,247 | 9,835 | 15,030 |
| S69 | LE sdn 4d | 3,221 | 9,358 | 17,451 |
| **Grand Prix (wb 108.1)** | | | | |
| J37 | cpe | 3,258 | 9,145 | 36,893 |
| K37 | LE cpe | 3,278 | 9,624 | 31,037 |
| P37 | Brougham cpe | 3,319 | 10,299 | 9,514 |
| **Parisienne (wb 115.9)** | | | | |
| L69 | sdn 4d | 3,535 | 9,881 | 18,713 |
| T69 | Brougham sdn 4d | 3,575 | 10,281 | 25,212 |
| L35 | wgn 4d V-8 | 4,080 | 10,394 | 16,599 |

| 1984 Engines | bore × stroke | bhp | availability |
|---|---|---|---|
| I-4, 97.6 | 3.23 × 2.98 | 65 | S-1000 |
| I-4, 109.0 | 3.34 × 3.13 | 84 | S-2000 (ohc) |
| I-4T, 109.0 | 3.34 × 3.13 | 150 | O-2000 (ohc) |
| I-4, 121.0 | 3.50 × 3.15 | 88 | O-2000 (ohv) |
| I-4, 151.0 | 4.00 × 3.00 | 92 | S-Fiero, Phoenix, Fbd, 6000 |
| V-6, 173.0 | 3.50 × 3.00 | 107/112 | O-Phoenix, Fbd, 6000 |
| V-6, 173.0 | 3.50 × 3.00 | 125/130 | S-Phnx SE, Firebird S/E, 6000 STE; O-Phoenix |
| V-6, 231.0 | 3.80 × 3.40 | 110 | S-Bonn, GP, Parisienne |
| V-6D, 262.0 | 4.06 × 3.39 | 85 | O-6000 |
| V-8, 305.0 | 3.74 × 3.48 | 150 | S-Trans Am, Paris wgn; O-other Fbd, Bonn, GP, Parisnne |
| V-8, 305.0 | 3.74 × 3.48 | 190 | O-Firebird Trans Am |
| V-8D, 350.0 | 4.06 × 3.39 | 105 | O-Bonn, GP, Parisienne |

## 1985

| Fiero (wb 93.4) | | Wght | Price | Prod |
|---|---|---|---|---|
| E37 | cpe | 2,454 | 8,495 | 5,280 |
| M37 | Sport Coupe | 2,500 | 8,995 | 23,823 |
| F37 | SE cpe | 2,525 | 9,995 | 24,734 |
| G37 | GT cpe | — | 11,795 | 22,534 |
| **1000 (wb 94.3; 4d-97.3)** | | | | |
| L08 | htchbk sdn 2d | 2,083 | 5,445 | 8,647 |
| L68 | htchbk sdn 4d | 2,142 | 5,695 | 8,216 |
| **Sunbird (wb 101.2)** | | | | |
| B27 | cpe | 2,316 | 6,875 | 39,721 |
| B77 | htchbk cpe | 2,392 | 7,215 | 5,235 |
| B69 | sdn 4d | 2,372 | 6,995 | 44,553 |
| B35 | wgn 4d | 2,446 | 7,335 | 7,371 |
| C27 | LE cpe | 2,349 | 7,555 | 3,424 |
| C67 | LE conv cpe | 2,534 | 12,035 | 2,114 |
| C69 | LE sdn 4d | 2,435 | 7,725 | 6,287 |
| C35 | LE wgn 4d | 2,468 | 8,055 | 1,036 |
| D27 | SE cpe I-4T | 2,422 | 9,295 | 965 |
| D77 | SE htchbk cpe I-4T | 2,500 | 9,765 | 535 |
| D69 | SE sdn 4d I-4T | 2,479 | 9,455 | 658 |
| **Firebird (wb 101.0)** | | | | |
| S87 | htchbk cpe I-4/V-6 | 2,933 | 8,763 ⎤ | 46,644 |
| S87 | htchbk cpe V-8 | 3,135 | 9,357 ⎦ | |
| X87 | SE htchbk cpe V-6/V-8 | 3,124 | 11,063 | 5,208 |
| W87 | Trans Am htchbk cpe V-8 | 3,213 | 11,113 | 44,028 |
| **Grand Am (wb 103.4)** | | | | |
| E27 | cpe | 2,575 | 7,995 | 40,275 |
| V27 | LE cpe | 2,595 | 8,485 | 42,269 |
| **6000 (wb 104.9)** | | | | |
| F27 | cpe | 2,766 | 8,899 | 4,493 |
| F19 | sdn 4d | 2,809 | 9,079 | 54,424 |
| G27 | LE cpe | 2,777 | 9,385 | 3,777 |
| G19 | LE sdn 4d | 2,821 | 9,539 | 54,284 |
| F35 | wgn 4d | 2,931 | 9,435 | 8,491 |
| G35 | LE wgn 4d | 2,937 | 9,869 | 8,025 |
| H19 | STE sdn 4d V-6 | 3,065 | 14,829 | 22,728 |
| **Bonneville (wb 108.1)** | | | | |
| N69 | sdn 4d | 3,267 | 9,549 | 34,466 |
| R69 | Brougham sdn 4d | 3,308 | 10,280 | 8,425 |
| S69 | LE sdn 4d | 3,281 | 9,789 | 10,503 |
| **Grand Prix (wb 108.1)** | | | | |
| J37 | cpe | 3,276 | 9,569 | 30,365 |
| K37 | LE cpe | 3,296 | 10,049 | 21,195 |
| P37 | Brougham cpe | 3,314 | 10,749 | 8,223 |
| **Parisienne (wb 116.0)** | | | | |
| I69 | sdn 4d | 3,573 | 10,395 | 25,638 |
| T69 | Brougham sdn 4d | 3,586 | 11,125 | 38,831 |
| L35 | wgn 4d V-8 | 4,095 | 10,945 | 17,638 |

| 1985 Engines | bore × stroke | bhp | availability |
|---|---|---|---|
| I-4, 97.6 | 3.23 × 2.98 | 65 | S-1000 |
| I-4, 109.0 | 3.34 × 3.13 | 82 | S-Sunbird (ohc) |
| I-4T, 109.0 | 3.34 × 3.13 | 150 | S-Sunbird SE (ohc) |
| I-4, 121.0 | 3.50 × 3.15 | 88 | O-Sunbird (ohv) |
| I-4, 151.0 | 4.00 × 3.00 | 88/92 | S-Fiero, G Am, Fbd, 6000 exc STE |
| V-6, 173.0 | 3.50 × 3.00 | 112 | O-6000 exc STE |
| V-6, 173.0 | 3.50 × 3.00 | 125/135 | S-Firebird S/E, 6000 STE; O-Fiero, other Firebird, 6000 |
| V-6, 181.0 | 3.80 × 2.70 | 125 | O-Grand Am |
| V-6, 231.0 | 3.80 × 3.40 | 110 | S-Bonn, Grand Prix |

# Pontiac

| 1985 Engines | bore × stroke | bhp | availability |
|---|---|---|---|
| V-6, 262.0 | 4.00 × 3.48 | 130 | S-Parisienne |
| V-6D, 262.0 | 4.06 × 3.39 | 85 | O-6000 |
| V-8, 305.0 | 3.74 × 3.48 | 165 | S-TA, Paris wgn; O-other Fbd, Bonn, GP, Paris |
| V-8, 305.0 | 3.74 × 3.48 | 190/205 | O-Firebird Trans Am |
| V-8D, 350.0 | 4.06 × 3.39 | 105 | O-Parisienne |

## 1986

### Fiero (wb 93.2)

| | | Wght | Price | Prod |
|---|---|---|---|---|
| E37 | cpe I-4 | 2,490 | 8,949 | 9,143 |
| M37 | Sport Coupe I-4 | 2,504 | 9,449 | 24,866 |
| F37 | SE cpe I-4/V-6 | 2,531 | 10,595 | 32,305 |
| G97 | GT fstbk cpe V-6 | 2,696 | 12,875 | 17,660 |

### 1000 (wb 94.3; 4d-97.3)

| L08 | htchbk sdn 2d | 2,076 | 5,749 | 12,266 |
|---|---|---|---|---|
| L68 | htchbk sdn 4d | 2,135 | 5,969 | 9,423 |

### Sunbird (wb 101.2)

| B69 | sdn 4d | 2,383 | 7,495 | 60,080 |
|---|---|---|---|---|
| B35 | wgn 4d | 2,456 | 7,879 | 7,445 |
| D27 | SE cpe | 2,365 | 7,469 | 37,526 |
| D77 | SE htchbk cpe | 2,405 | 7,829 | 3,822 |
| D67 | SE conv cpe | 2,549 | 12,779 | 1,598 |
| U27 | GT cpe | 2,488 | 9,459 | 18,118 |
| U67 | GT conv cpe | 2,645 | 14,399 | 1,268 |
| U77 | GT htchbk cpe | 2,564 | 9,819 | 2,442 |
| U69 | GT sdn 4d | 2,540 | 9,499 | 2,802 |

### Firebird (wb 101.0)

| S87 | htchbk cpe I-4/V-6 | 2,909 | 9,279 | 59,334 |
|---|---|---|---|---|
| S87 | htchbk cpe V-8 | 2,995 | 10,029 | |
| X87 | SE htchbk cpe V-6/V-8 | 2,991 | 11,995 | 2,259 |
| W87 | Trans Am htchbk cpe V-8 | 3,227 | 12,395 | 48,870 |

### Grand Am (wb 103.4)

| E27 | cpe | 2,529 | 8,549 | 69,545 |
|---|---|---|---|---|
| E69 | sdn 4d | 2,605 | 8,749 | 49,166 |
| V27 | LE cpe | 2,565 | 9,079 | 48,530 |
| V69 | LE sdn 4d | 2,631 | 9,279 | 31,790 |
| W27 | SE cpe V-6 | 2,686 | 11,499 | 15,506 |
| W69 | SE sdn 4d V-6 | 2,756 | 11,749 | 8,957 |

### 6000 (wb 104.9)

| F27 | cpe | 2,781 | 9,549 | 4,739 |
|---|---|---|---|---|
| F19 | sdn 4d | 2,817 | 9,729 | 81,531 |
| G27 | LE cpe | 2,799 | 10,049 | 4,803 |
| G19 | LE sdn 4d | 2,836 | 10,195 | 67,697 |
| E19 | SE sdn 4d V-6 | 2,914 | 11,179 | 7,348 |
| F35 | wgn 4d | 2,954 | 10,095 | 10,094 |
| G35 | LE wgn 4d | 2,972 | 10,579 | 7,556 |
| E35 | SE wgn 4d V-6 | 3,067 | 11,825 | 1,308 |
| H19 | STE sdn 4d V-6 | 3,122 | 15,949 | 26,299 |

### Bonneville (wb 108.1)

| N69 | sdn 4d | 3,276 | 10,249 | 27,801 |
|---|---|---|---|---|
| R69 | Brougham sdn 4d | 3,305 | 11,079 | 5,941 |
| S69 | LE sdn 4d | 3,285 | 10,529 | 7,179 |

### Grand Prix (wb 108.1)

| J37 | cpe | 3,283 | 10,259 | 21,668 |
|---|---|---|---|---|
| J37 | 2+2 cpe V-8 | 3,530 | 18,214 | 1,118 |
| K37 | LE cpe | 3,305 | 10,795 | 13,918 |
| P37 | Brougham cpe | 3,328 | 11,579 | 4,798 |

### Parisienne (wb 116.0)

| L69 | sdn 4d | 3,639 | 11,169 | 27,078 |
|---|---|---|---|---|
| T69 | Brougham sdn 4d | 3,667 | 11,949 | 43,540 |
| L35 | wgn 4d V-8 | 4,102 | 11,779 | 14,464 |

| 1986 Engines | bore × stroke | bhp | availability |
|---|---|---|---|
| I-4, 97.6 | 3.23 × 2.98 | 65 | S-1000 |
| I-4, 109.0 | 3.34 × 3.13 | 84 | S-Sunbird (ohc) |
| I-4, 109.0 | 3.34 × 3.13 | 150 | S-Sunbird GT (ohc) |
| I-4T, 109.0 | 3.34 × 3.13 | 88/92 | S-Fiero, GA, Fbd, 6000 |
| I-4, 151.0 | 4.00 × 3.00 | | |
| V-6, 173.0 | 3.50 × 3.00 | 112 | O-6000 |
| V-6, 173.0 | 3.50 × 3.00 | 130/140 | S-Firebird SE, 6000 STE, Fiero GT; O-Fiero SE, Firebird |
| V-6, 181.0 | 3.80 × 2.70 | 125 | S-Grand Am SE; O-other Grand Am |
| V-6, 231.0 | 3.80 × 3.40 | 110 | S-Bonn, Grand Prix |
| V-6, 262.0 | 4.00 × 3.48 | 130 | S-Parisienne |
| V-8, 305.0 | 3.74 × 3.48 | 150/165 | S-Trans Am, Paris wgn; O-Fbd, Bonn, GP, Parisienne |
| V-8, 305.0 | 3.74 × 3.48 | 190/205 | O-Firebird Trans Am |

## 1987

### Fiero (wb 93.4)

| | | Wght | Price | Prod |
|---|---|---|---|---|
| E37 | cpe I-4 | 2,542 | 8,299 | 23,603 |
| M37 | Sport Coupe I-4 | 2,546 | 9,989 | 3,135 |
| F37 | SE cpe I-4/V-6 | 2,567 | 11,239 | 3,875 |
| G97 | GT fstbk cpe V-6 | 2,708 | 13,489 | 15,968 |

### 1000 (wb 94.3; 4d-97.3)

| L08 | htchbk sdn 2d | 2,114 | 5,959 | 3,246 |
|---|---|---|---|---|
| L68 | htchbk sdn 4d | 2,173 | 6,099 | 2,382 |

### Sunbird (wb 101.2)

| B69 | sdn 4d | 2,366 | 7,999 | 41,248 |
|---|---|---|---|---|
| B35 | wgn 4d | 2,427 | 8,529 | 4,637 |
| D27 | SE cpe | 2,339 | 7,979 | 41,825 |
| D77 | SE htchbk cpe | 2,385 | 8,499 | 1,069 |
| D67 | SE conv cpe | 2,511 | 13,799 | 2,470 |
| U27 | GT cpe | 2,412 | 10,299 | 12,060 |
| U67 | GT conv cpe | 2,551 | 15,569 | 1,505 |
| U77 | GT htchbk cpe | 2,427 | 10,699 | 415 |
| U69 | GT sdn 4d | 2,427 | 10,349 | 1,540 |

### Firebird (wb 101.0)

| S87 | htchbk cpe V-6/V-8 | 3,186 | 10,359 | 42,558 |
|---|---|---|---|---|
| S87/W66 | Formula htchbk cpe V-8 | 3,350 | 11,829 | 13,164 |
| W87 | Trans Am htchbk cpe V-8 | 3,274 | 13,259 | 32,890 |
| W87/Y84 | T/A GTA htchbk cpe V-8 | 3,435 | 14,104 | — |

### Grand Am (wb 103.4)

| E27 | cpe | 2,525 | 9,299 | 90,146 |
|---|---|---|---|---|
| E69 | sdn 4d | 2,598 | 9,499 | 52,177 |
| V27 | LE cpe | 2,561 | 9,999 | 47,414 |
| V69 | LE sdn 4d | 2,623 | 10,199 | 21,196 |
| W27 | SE cpe | 2,641 | 12,659 | 23,142 |
| W69 | SE sdn 4d | 2,719 | 12,899 | 10,653 |

### 6000 (wb 104.9)

| F27 | cpe | 2,764 | 10,499 | 3,161 |
|---|---|---|---|---|
| F19 | sdn 4d | 2,797 | 10,499 | 72,645 |
| G19 | LE sdn 4d | 2,731 | 11,099 | 33,939 |
| E19 | S/E sdn 4d V-6 | 2,986 | 12,089 | 6,649 |
| F35 | wgn 4d | 2,943 | 10,095 | 7,740 |
| G35 | LE wgn 4d | 2,867 | 11,499 | 3,797 |
| E35 | S/E wgn 4d V-6 | 3,162 | 13,049 | 1,756 |
| H19 | STE sdn 4d V-6 | 3,101 | 18,099 | 8,802 |

### Grand Prix (wb 108.1)

| J37 | cpe | 3,286 | 11,069 | 8,599 |
|---|---|---|---|---|
| K37 | LE cpe | 3,306 | 11,799 | 6,226 |
| P37 | Brougham cpe | 3,308 | 12,519 | 1,717 |

# Pontiac

| Bonneville (wb 110.8) | | Wght | Price | Prod |
|---|---|---|---|---|
| X69 | sdn 4d | 3,316 | 13,399 | 53,912 |
| Z69 | LE sdn 4d | 3,355 | 14,866 | 69,904 |
| **Safari (wb 116.0)** | | | | |
| L35 | Brougham wgn 4d V-8 | 4,109 | 13,959 | 13,154 |

| 1987 Engines | bore × stroke | bhp | availability |
|---|---|---|---|
| I-4, 97.6 | 3.23 × 2.98 | 65 | S-1000 |
| I-4, 121.0 | 3.39 × 3.39 | 96 | S-Sunbird (ohc) |
| I-4T, 121.0 | 3.39 × 3.39 | 165 | O-Sunbird SE/GT, G Am SE (ohc) |
| I-4, 151.0 | 4.00 × 3.00 | 98 | S-Fiero exc GT, Grand Am, 6000 |
| V-6, 173.0 | 3.50 × 3.00 | 125/135 | S-Fiero GT, 6000 S/E, 6000 STE; O-Fiero SE, Fbd, other 6000 |
| V-6, 181.0 | 3.80 × 2.70 | 125 | S-Grand Am SE; O-other Grand Am |
| V-6, 231.0 | 3.80 × 3.40 | 110 | S-GP exc 2+2 |
| V-6, 231.0 | 3.80 × 3.40 | 150 | S-Bonneville |
| V-6, 262.0 | 4.00 × 3.48 | 140 | O-Grand Prix |
| V-8, 305.0 | 3.74 × 3.48 | 140 | S-Safari wgn |
| V-8, 305.0 | 3.74 × 3.48 | 150 | S-Grand Prix 2+2; O-other GP |
| V-8, 305.0 | 3.74 × 3.48 | 155 | O-Firebird |
| V-8, 305.0 | 3.74 × 3.48 | 165/205 | O-Firebird Trans Am |
| V-8, 350.0 | 4.00 × 3.48 | 210 | S-Fbd GTA; O-Fbd Formula, T/A |

## 1988

| Fiero (wb 93.4)—26,402 built | | Wght | Price | Prod |
|---|---|---|---|---|
| E37 | cpe I-4 | 2,597 | 8,999 | — |
| E37/W66 | Formula cpe V-6 | — | 10,999 | — |
| G97 | GT fstbk cpe V-6 | 2,783 | 13,999 | — |
| **Sunbird (wb 101.2)—93,694 built** | | | | |
| B69 | sdn 4d | 2,366 | 8,499 | — |
| D37 | SE cpe | 2,339 | 8,599 | — |
| D69 | SE sdn 4d | 2,427 | 8,799 | — |
| D35 | SE wgn 4d | 2,427 | 9,399 | — |
| U37 | GT cpe I-4T | 2,412 | 10,899 | — |
| U67 | GT conv cpe I-4T | 2,551 | 16,199 | — |
| **Firebird (wb 101.0)—62,467 built** | | | | |
| S87 | htchbk cpe V-6/V-8 | 3,102 | 10,999 | — |
| S87/W66 | Formula htchbk cpe V-8 | — | 11,999 | — |
| W87 | Trans Am htchbk cpe V-8 | 3,355 | 13,999 | — |
| W87/Y84 | T/A GTA htchbk cpe V-8 | — | 19,299 | — |
| **Grand Am (wb 103.4)—235,371 built** | | | | |
| E27 | cpe | 2,493 | 9,869 | — |
| E69 | sdn 4d | 2,568 | 10,069 | — |
| Y27 | LE cpe | 2,519 | 10,569 | — |
| Y69 | LE sdn 4d | 2,591 | 10,769 | — |
| W27 | SE cpe I-4T | 2,713 | 12,869 | — |
| W69 | SE sdn 4d I-4T | 2,781 | 13,099 | — |
| **6000 (wb 104.9)—61,446 built** | | | | |
| F19 | sdn 4d | 2,828 | 11,999 | — |
| G19 | LE sdn 4d | 2,846 | 11,839 | — |
| E19 | S/E sdn 4d V-6 | 2,888 | 12,739 | — |
| F35 | wgn 4d | 2,964 | 11,639 | — |
| G35 | LE wgn 4d | 2,982 | 12,299 | — |
| E35 | S/E wgn 4d V-6 | 3,041 | 13,639 | — |
| H19 | STE sdn 4d V-6 | 3,109 | 18,699 | — |
| — | STE AWD sdn 4d V-6 | 3,409 | — | — |
| **Grand Prix (wb 107.6)—86,357 built** | | | | |
| J37 | cpe | 3,038 | 12,539 | — |

| Grand Prix (wb 107.6) | | Wght | Price | Prod |
|---|---|---|---|---|
| K37 | LE cpe | 3,056 | 13,239 | — |
| P37 | SE cpe | 3,113 | 15,249 | — |
| **Bonneville (wb 110.8)—108,580 built** | | | | |
| X69 | LE sdn 4d | 3,275 | 14,099 | — |
| Z69 | SE sdn 4d | 3,341 | 16,299 | — |
| Y69 | SSE sdn 4d | 3,481 | 21,879 | — |
| **Safari (wb 116.0)—6,397 built** | | | | |
| L35 | wgn 4d V-8 | 4,109 | 14,519 | — |

| 1988 Engines | bore × stroke | bhp | availability |
|---|---|---|---|
| I-4, 121.0 | 3.39 × 3.39 | 96 | S-Sunbird (ohc) |
| I-4T, 121.0 | 3.39 × 3.39 | 165 | S-Sunbird GT, G Am SE; O-G AM LE (ohc) |
| I-4, 138.0 | 3.62 × 3.35 | 150 | O-Grand Am (dohc) |
| I-4, 151.0 | 4.00 × 3.00 | 98 | S-Fiero, GA, 6000 |
| V-6, 173.0 | 3.50 × 3.00 | 125/130 | S-6000 S/E, STE, GP; O-6000 |
| V-6, 173.0 | 3.50 × 3.00 | 135 | S-Fiero Formula/GT, Fbd base |
| V-6, 191.0 | 3.50 × 3.31 | 135 | S-6000 STE AWD |
| V-6, 231.0 | 3.80 × 3.40 | 150 | S-Bonneville LE |
| V-6, 231.0 | 3.00 × 3.40 | 165 | S-Bonn SE/SSE |
| V-8, 305.0 | 3.74 × 3.48 | 140 | S-Safari wgn |
| V-8, 305.0 | 3.74 × 3.48 | 170 | S-Fbd Trans Am/Formula; O-Fbd |
| V-8, 305.0 | 3.74 × 3.48 | 190/215 | O-Fbd Trans Am/Formula |
| V-8, 350.0 | 4.00 × 3.48 | 225/235 | S-Fbd GTA; O-Formula, T/A |

## 1989

| Sunbird (wb 101.2)—60,019 built | | Wght | Price | Prod |
|---|---|---|---|---|
| B37 | LE cpe | 2,418 | 8,849 | — |
| B69 | LE sdn 4d | 2,433 | 8,949 | — |
| D37 | SE cpe | 2,376 | 9,099 | — |
| U37 | GT cpe I-4T | 2,422 | 11,399 | — |
| U67 | GT conv cpe I-4T | 2,577 | 16,899 | — |
| **Firebird (wb 101.0)** | | | | |
| S87 | htchbk cpe V-6/V-8 | 3,083 | 11,999 | 49,048 |
| S87/W66 | Formula htchbk cpe V-8 | 3,318 | 13,949 | |
| W87 | Trans Am htchbk cpe V-8 | 3,337 | 15,999 | 15,358* |
| W87/Y84 | T/A htchbk GTA cpe V-8 | 3,486 | 20,339 | |
| **Grand Am (wb 103.4)** | | | | |
| E27 | LE cpe | 2,508 | 10,469 | 137,121 |
| E69 | LE sdn 4d | 2,592 | 10,669 | 87,385 |
| W27 | SE cpe I-4T | 2,739 | 13,599 | 13,410 |
| W69 | SE sdn 4d I-4T | 2,826 | 13,799 | 8,502 |
| **6000 (wb 104.9)** | | | | |
| F69 | LE sdn 4d | 2,760 | 11,969 | 83,014 |
| J69 | S/E sdn 4d V-6 | 2,762 | 15,399 | 7,539 |
| F35 | LE wgn 4d | 2,897 | 13,769 | 7,790 |
| J35 | S/E wgn 4d V-6 | 2,899 | 16,699 | 887 |
| H69 | STE AWD sdn 4d V-6 | 3,036 | 22,599 | 1,376 |
| **Grand Prix (wb 107.5)—136,748** built** | | | | |
| J37 | cpe | 3,167 | 13,899 | — |
| K37 | LE cpe | 3,188 | 14,849 | — |
| P37 | SE cpe | 3,217 | 15,999 | — |
| **Bonneville (wb 110.8)** | | | | |
| X69 | LE sdn 4d | 3,275 | 14,829 | 71,339 |
| Z69 | SE sdn 4d | 2,327 | 17,199 | 20,238 |
| Y69 | SSE sdn 4d | 3,481 | 22,899 | 17,076 |

# Pontiac

| Safari (wb 116.0)—5,146 built | | Wght | Price | Prod |
|---|---|---|---|---|
| L35 | wgn 4d V-8 | 4,225 | 15,659 | — |

*Includes 1,555 20th Anniversary Trans Ams
**Includes approx. 2,000 McLaren Turbo coupes

| 1989 Engines | bore × stroke | bhp | availability |
|---|---|---|---|
| I-4, 121.0 | 3.39 × 3.39 | 96 | S-Sunbird (ohc) |
| I-4T, 121.0 | 3.39 × 3.39 | 165 | S-Sbd GT, G-Am SE; O-Sbd SE (ohc) |
| I-4, 138.0 | 3.62 × 3.35 | 150 | O-Grand Am, (dohc) |
| I-4, 138.0 | 3.62 × 3.35 | 185 | O-late Grand Am (dohc) |
| I-4, 151.0 | 4.00 × 3.00 | 110 | S-Grand Am LE, 6000 |
| V-6, 173.0 | 3.50 × 3.00 | 130 | S-6000 S/E, GP; O-6000 |
| V-6, 173.0 | 3.50 × 3.00 | 135 | S-Firebird |
| V-6, 191.0 | 3.50 × 3.31 | 140 | S-6000 STE AWD, late GP |
| V-6T, 191.0 | 3.50 × 3.31 | 200 | S-McLaren Turbo GP |
| V-6, 231.0 | 3.00 × 3.40 | 165 | S-Bonneville |
| V-6T, 231.0 | 3.00 × 3.40 | 250 | S-20th An Trans Am |
| V-8, 305.0 | 3.74 × 3.48 | 140 | S-Safari wgn |
| V-8, 305.0 | 3.74 × 3.48 | 170 | S-Trans Am/Formula; O-Fbd |
| V-8, 305.0 | 3.74 × 3.48 | 215 | O-Fbd TA/Formula |
| V-8, 350.0 | 4.00 × 3.48 | 225 | S-Fbd GTA; O-Formula T/A |

## 1990

| Sunbird (wb 101.2) | | Wght | Price | Prod |
|---|---|---|---|---|
| B37 | LE cpe | 2,420 | 8,799 | 56,151 |
| B69 | LE sdn 4d | 2,487 | 8,899 | 57,911 |
| D37 | SE cpe | — | 9,204 | 12,860 |
| U37 | GT cpe I-4T | — | 11,724 | 4,813 |
| U67 | LE conv cpe | 2,662 | 13,934 | 13,197 |
| **Firebird (wb 101.0)** | | | | |
| S87 | htchbk cpe V-6 | 3,210 | 11,320 | 18,046 |
| S87/W66 | Formula htchbk cpe V-8 | — | 14,610 | |
| W87 | Trans Am htchbk cpe V-8 | — | 16,510 | 2,507 |
| W87/Y84 | T/A GTA htchbk cpe V-8 | — | 23,320 | |
| **Grand Am (wb 103.4)** | | | | |
| E27 | LE cpe | 2,508 | 10,544 | 104,950 |
| E69 | LE sdn 4d | 2,592 | 10,744 | 80,815 |
| W27 | SE cpe | 2,739 | 14,894 | 6,877 |
| W69 | SE sdn 4d | 2,826 | 15,194 | 4,378 |
| **6000 (wb 104.9)** | | | | |
| F69 | LE sdn 4d | 2,843 | 12,149 | 55,290 |
| NA | LE wgn 4d | 3,162 | 15,309 | 5,086 |
| J69 | S/E sdn 4d V-6 | — | 16,909 | 5,599 |
| J35 | S/E wgn 4d V-6 | — | 18,509 | 423 |
| **Grand Prix (wb 107.5)** | | | | |
| K37 | LE cpe | 3,186 | 14,564 | 49,492 |
| NA | LE sdn 4d | 3,250 | 14,564 | 56,410 |
| P37 | SE cpe | — | 17,684 | 16,398 |
| NA | Turbo cpe | — | 26,016 | |
| NA | STE sdn 4d | — | 18,539 | 5,773 |
| NA | STE Turbo sdn 4d | — | 23,775 | |
| **Bonneville (wb 110.8)** | | | | |
| X69 | LE sdn 4d | 3,325 | 15,744 | 55,926 |
| Z69 | SE sdn 4d | — | 19,144 | 13,064 |
| 009 | SSE sdn 4d | — | 23,994 | 16,854 |

| 1990 Engines | bore × stroke | bhp | availability |
|---|---|---|---|
| I-4, 121.0 | 3.39 × 3.39 | 96 | S-Sunbird (ohc) |
| I-4T, 121.0 | 3.39 × 3.39 | 165 | S-Sbd GT; O-Sbd conv. (ohc) |
| I-4, 138.0 | 3.62 × 3.35 | 160 | S-Grand Prix LE; O-Grand Am (dohc) |
| I-4, 138.0 | 3.62 × 3.35 | 180 | S-G Am SE (dohc) |
| I-4, 151.0 | 4.00 × 3.00 | 110 | S-GAm LE, 6000 |
| V-6, 191.0 | 3.50 × 3.31 | 140 | S-Firebird, Grand Prix SE/STE, 6000 S/E; O-6000 LE, GP LE |
| V-6T, 191.0 | 3.50 × 3.31 | 205 | S-Grand Prix Turbo |
| V-6, 231.0 | 3.00 × 3.40 | 165 | S-Bonneville |
| V-8, 305.0 | 3.74 × 3.48 | 170 | S-Fbd Fmla; O-Fbird |
| V-8, 305.0 | 3.74 × 3.48 | 225 | S-Fbd Trans Am; O-Fbd Formula |
| V-8, 350.0 | 4.00 × 3.48 | 235 | S-Fbd GTA; O-Fbd Formula, T/A |

## 1991

| Sunbird (wb 101.2)—155,429 built | | Wght | Price | Prod |
|---|---|---|---|---|
| | cpe 2d | 2,570 | 8,684 | — |
| | sdn 4d | 2,592 | 8,784 | — |
| C37 | LE cpe 2d | 2,484 | 9,444 | — |
| C69 | LE sdn 4d | 2,502 | 9,544 | — |
| B37 | SE cpe 2d | 2,484 | 10,694 | — |
| D37 | GT cpe 2d | 2,502 | 12,444 | — |
| B67 | LE conv cpe 2d | 2,775 | 14,414 | — |
| **Firebird (wb 101.0)—50,247 built** | | | | |
| S87 | htchbk cpe | 3,121 | 12,690 | — |
| S67 | conv cpe 2d | 3,280 | 19,159 | — |
| S87/W66 | Formula htchbk cpe | 3,370 | 15,530 | — |
| W87 | Trans Am htchbk cpe | 3,343 | 17,530 | — |
| W67 | Trans Am conv cpe | 3,441 | 22,980 | — |
| W87/Y84 | GTA htchbk cpe | 3,456 | 24,530 | — |
| **Grand Am (wb 103.4)—178,150 built** | | | | |
| | cpe 2d | 2,508 | 10,174 | — |
| | sdn 4d | 2,592 | 10,374 | — |
| E27 | LE cpe 2d | 2,728 | 11,124 | — |
| E69 | LE sdn 4d | 2,777 | 11,324 | — |
| W27 | SE cpe 2d | 2,804 | 16,344 | — |
| W69 | SE sdn 4d | 2,846 | 16,544 | — |
| **6000 (wb 104.9)—34,721 built** | | | | |
| F69 | LE sdn 4d | 2,843 | 12,999 | — |
| J69 | S/E sdn 4d | — | 18,399 | — |
| F35 | LE wgn 4d | 3,162 | 16,699 | — |
| **Grand Prix (wb 107.5)—101,211 built** | | | | |
| H19 | LE sdn 4d | 3,188 | 14,294 | — |
| J37 | SE cpe 2d | 3,252 | 14,894 | — |
| J19 | SE sdn 4d | 3,282 | 15,284 | — |
| P37 | GT cpe 2d | 3,390 | 19,154 | — |
| T19 | STE sdn 4d | 3,434 | 19,994 | — |
| **Bonneville (wb 110.8)—46,603 built** | | | | |
| X69 | LE sdn 4d | 3,323 | 16,834 | — |
| Z69 | SE sdn 4d | 3,362 | 20,464 | — |
| 009 | SSE sdn 4d | 3,507 | 25,264 | — |

| 1991 Engines | bore × stroke | bhp | availability |
|---|---|---|---|
| I-4, 121.0 | 3.38 × 3.38 | 96 | S-Sunbird (ohc) |
| I-4, 138.0 | 3.63 × 3.35 | 160 | S-GP; O-GAm (dohc) |
| I-4, 138.0 | 3.63 × 3.35 | 180 | O-Grand Am (dohc) |
| I-4, 151.0 | 4.00 × 3.00 | 110 | S-Grand Am, 6000 |
| V-6, 191.0 | 3.50 × 3.31 | 140 | S-Fbd, Snbd GT; O-Snbd, 6000, GP |

# Pontiac

| 1991 Engines | bore × stroke | bhp | availability |
|---|---|---|---|
| V-6, 207.0 | 3.62 × 3.31 | 200 | O-Grand Prix (dohc) |
| V-6, 207.0 | 3.62 × 3.31 | 210 | O-Grand Prix (dohc) |
| V-6, 231.0 | 3.80 × 3.40 | 165 | S-Bonneville |
| V-8, 305.0 | 3.74 × 3.48 | 170 | S-Fbd Fmla; O-Fbd |
| V-8, 305.0 | 3.74 × 3.48 | 230 | S-Firebird T/A; O-Firebird, Formula |
| V-8, 350.0 | 4.00 × 3.48 | 240 | S-Fbd GTA; O-T/A, Formula |

## 1992

| Sunbird (wb 101.2)—100,402 built | | Wght | Price | Prod |
|---|---|---|---|---|
| C37 | LE cpe | 2,484 | 9,620 | — |
| C69 | LE sdn 4d | 2,502 | 9,720 | — |
| B37 | SE cpe | 2,484 | 10,380 | — |
| B69 | SE sdn 4d | 2,502 | 10,480 | — |
| B67 | SE conv cpe | 2,694 | 15,345 | — |
| D37 | GT cpe | 2,682 | 12,820 | — |
| Firebird (wb 101.0)—52,405 built (estimated) | | | | |
| S87 | htchbk cpe | 3,121 | 12,505 | — |
| S67 | conv cpe | 3,280 | 19,375 | — |
| S87/W66 | Formula htchbk cpe | 3,370 | 16,205 | — |
| W87 | Trans Am htchbk cpe | 3,343 | 18,105 | — |
| W67 | Trans Am conv cpe 2d | 3,441 | 23,875 | — |
| W87/Y84 | GTA htchbk cpe | 3,456 | 25,880 | — |
| Grand Am (wb 103.4)—208,568 built | | | | |
| E37 | SE cpe 2d | 2,728 | 11,899 | — |
| E69 | SE sdn 4d | 2,777 | 11,999 | — |
| W37 | GT cpe 2d | 2,804 | 13,699 | — |
| W69 | GT sdn 4d | 2,846 | 13,799 | — |
| Grand Prix (wb 107.5)—119,319 built | | | | |
| H19 | LE sdn 4d | 3,243 | 14,890 | — |
| J37 | SE cpe 2d | 3,214 | 15,390 | — |
| J19 | SE sdn 4d | 3,282 | 16,190 | — |
| P37 | GT cpe 2d | 3,357 | 20,340 | — |
| T19 | STE sdn 4d | 3,434 | 21,635 | — |
| Bonneville (wb 110.8)—124,511 built | | | | |
| X69 | SE sdn 4d | 3,362 | 18,599 | — |
| Z69 | SSE sdn 4d | 3,507 | 23,999 | — |
| Y69 | SSEi sdn 4d | 3,607 | 28,045 | — |

| 1992 Engines | bore × stroke | bhp | availability |
|---|---|---|---|
| I-4, 121.0 | 3.38 × 3.38 | 111 | S-Sunbird (ohc) |
| I-4, 138.0 | 3.63 × 3.35 | 120 | S-Grand Am (ohc) |
| I-4, 138.0 | 3.63 × 3.35 | 160 | O-Grand Am (dohc) |
| I-4, 138.0 | 3.63 × 3.35 | 180 | O-Grand Am (dohc) |
| V-6, 191.0 | 3.50 × 3.31 | 140 | S-Fbd, Snbd GT; O-Sunbird SE |
| V-6, 204.0 | 3.70 × 3.16 | 160 | O-Grand Am |
| V-6, 207.0 | 3.62 × 3.31 | 210 | O-Grand Prix (dohc) |
| V-6, 231.0 | 3.80 × 3.40 | 170 | S-Bonn exc SSEi |
| V-6S, 231.0 | 3.80 × 3.40 | 205 | S-Bonneville SSEi |
| V-8, 305.0 | 3.74 × 3.48 | 170 | S-Fbd Fmla; O-Fbd |
| V-8, 305.0 | 3.74 × 3.48 | 205 | S-Fbd T/A; O-Fmla |
| V-8, 350.0 | 4.00 × 3.48 | 240 | S-Firebird GTA; O-T/A, Formula |

## 1993

| Sunbird (wb 101.2)—98,811 built | | Wght | Price | Prod |
|---|---|---|---|---|
| C37 | LE cpe | 2,484 | 9,382 | — |
| C69 | LE sdn 4d | 2,502 | 9,382 | — |
| B37 | SE cpe | 2,484 | 10,380 | — |
| B69 | SE sdn 4d | 2,502 | 10,380 | — |
| B67 | SE conv cpe | 2,694 | 15,403 | — |

| Sunbird (wb 101.2) | | Wght | Price | Prod |
|---|---|---|---|---|
| D37 | GT cpe | 2,682 | 12,820 | — |
| Firebird (wb 101.1)—14,475 built | | | | |
| S87 | htchbk cpe | 3,241 | 13,995 | — |
| V87 | Formula htchbk cpe | — | 17,995 | — |
| V87/Y82 | Trans Am htchbk cpe | — | 21,395 | — |
| Grand Am (wb 103.4)—247,498 built | | | | |
| E37 | SE cpe | 2,728 | 12,524 | — |
| E69 | SE sdn 4d | 2,777 | 12,624 | — |
| W37 | GT cpe | 2,804 | 13,924 | — |
| W69 | GT sdn 4d | 2,846 | 14,024 | — |
| Grand Prix (wb 107.5)—116,885 built | | | | |
| H19 | LE sdn 4d | 3,243 | 14,890 | — |
| J37 | SE cpe | 3,189 | 15,390 | — |
| J19 | SE sdn 4d | 3,312 | 16,190 | — |
| P37 | GT cpe | 3,357 | 20,340 | — |
| T19 | STE sdn 4d | 3,434 | 21,635 | — |
| Bonneville (wb 110.8)—104,806 built | | | | |
| X69 | SE sdn 4d | 3,362 | 19,444 | — |
| Z69 | SSE sdn 4d | 3,507 | 24,844 | — |
| Y69 | SSEi sdn 4d | 3,607 | 29,444 | — |

| 1993 Engines | bore × stroke | bhp | availability |
|---|---|---|---|
| I-4, 121.0 | 3.38 × 3.38 | 110 | S-Sunbird (ohc) |
| I-4, 138.0 | 3.63 × 3.35 | 115 | S-Grand Am (ohc) |
| I-4, 138.0 | 3.63 × 3.35 | 155 | O-Grand Am (dohc) |
| I-4, 138.0 | 3.63 × 3.35 | 175 | O-Grand Am (dohc) |
| V-6, 191.0 | 3.50 × 3.31 | 140 | S-Grand Prix, Sunbird GT; O-Sunbird SE |
| V-6, 204.0 | 3.70 × 3.16 | 160 | O-Grand Am |
| V-6, 207.0 | 3.62 × 3.31 | 160 | S-Firebird |
| V-6, 207.0 | 3.62 × 3.31 | 210 | O-Grand Prix (dohc) |
| V-6, 231.0 | 3.80 × 3.40 | 170 | S-Bonneville |
| V-6S, 231.0 | 3.80 × 3.40 | 205 | S-Bonneville SSEi; O-Bonneville SSE |
| V-8, 350.0 | 4.00 × 3.48 | 275 | S-Fbd Fmla/TA |

## 1994

| Sunbird (wb 101.2)—103,738 built | | Wght | Price | Prod |
|---|---|---|---|---|
| B37 | LE cpe | 2,484 | 9,764 | — |
| B69 | LE sdn 4d | 2,502 | 9,764 | — |
| B67 | LE conv cpe | 2,661 | 15,524 | — |
| L37 | SE cpe | 2,682 | 12,424 | — |
| Firebird (wb 101.1)—51,523 built | | | | |
| S87 | htchbk cpe | 3,232 | 14,099 | — |
| S67 | conv cpe | 3,346 | 21,179 | — |
| V87 | Formula htchbk cpe | 3,425 | 18,249 | — |
| V87 | Formula conv cpe | 3,489 | 24,279 | — |
| V87/Y82 | Trans Am htchbk cpe | 3,447 | 20,009 | — |
| V87/Y83 | Trans Am GT htchbk cpe | 3,494 | 21,509 | — |
| V87/Y83 | Trans Am GT conv cpe | 3,610 | 26,479 | — |
| Grand Am (wb 103.4)—254,919 built | | | | |
| E37 | SE cpe | 2,736 | 12,514 | — |
| E69 | SE sdn 4d | 2,793 | 12,614 | — |
| W37 | GT cpe | 2,822 | 15,014 | — |
| W69 | GT sdn 4d | 2,882 | 15,114 | — |
| Grand Prix (wb 107.5)—148,405 built | | | | |
| J37 | SE cpe | 3,275 | 16,174 | — |
| J19 | SE sdn 4d | 3,370 | 16,770 | — |
| Bonneville (wb 110.8)—87,926 built | | | | |
| X69 | SE sdn 4d | 3,446 | 20,424 | — |
| Z69 | SSE sdn 4d | 3,587 | 25,884 | — |

# Pontiac

| 1994 Engines | bore × stroke | bhp | availability |
|---|---|---|---|
| I-4, 121.0 | 3.38 × 3.38 | 110 | S-Sunbird (ohc) |
| I-4, 138.0 | 3.63 × 3.35 | 115 | S-Grand Am (ohc) |
| I-4, 138.0 | 3.63 × 3.35 | 155 | O-Grand Am (dohc) |
| I-4, 138.0 | 3.63 × 3.35 | 175 | O-Grand Am (dohc) |
| V-6, 191.0 | 3.50 × 3.31 | 140 | S-Snbd SE; O-Snbd LE |
| V-6, 191.0 | 3.50 × 3.31 | 155 | O-Grand Am |
| V-6, 191.0 | 3.50 × 3.31 | 160 | S-Grand Prix |
| V-6, 207.0 | 3.62 × 3.31 | 160 | S-Firebird |
| V-6, 207.0 | 3.62 × 3.31 | 210 | O-Grand Prix (dohc) |
| V-6, 231.0 | 3.80 × 3.40 | 170 | S-Bonneville |
| V-6S, 231.0 | 3.80 × 3.40 | 225 | O-Bonneville SSE |
| V-8, 350.0 | 4.00 × 3.48 | 275 | S-Frbd Fmla/TA |

## 1995

| Sunfire (wb 104.1) | | Wght | Price | Prod |
|---|---|---|---|---|
| B37 | SE cpe | 2,679 | 11,074 | 42,313 |
| B69 | SE sdn 4d | 2,723 | 11,224 | 32,481 |
| B67 | SE conv cpe | 2,835 | 16,764 | 990 |
| D37 | GT cpe | 2,829 | 12,834 | 5,313 |

| Firebird (wb 101.1) | | Wght | Price | Prod |
|---|---|---|---|---|
| S87 | htchbk cpe | 3,230 | 14,859 | ⎤ |
| V87 | Formula htchbk cpe | 3,372 | 19,099 | ⎬ 49,191 |
| V87/Y82 | Trans Am htchbk cpe | 3,345 | 21,069 | ⎦ |
| S67 | conv cpe | 3,346 | 21,939 | ⎤ |
| V67 | Formula conv cpe | 3,489 | 25,129 | ⎬ 7,532 |
| V67/Y82 | Trans Am conv cpe | 3,610 | 27,139 | ⎦ |

| Grand Am (wb 103.4) | | Wght | Price | Prod |
|---|---|---|---|---|
| E37 | SE cpe | 2,824 | 12,904 | 77,655 |
| E69 | SE sdn 4d | 2,881 | 13,004 | 163,991 |
| W37 | GT cpe | 2,888 | 14,854 | 28,343 |
| W69 | GT sdn 4d | 2,941 | 14,954 | 21,155 |

| Grand Prix (wb 107.5) | | Wght | Price | Prod |
|---|---|---|---|---|
| J37 | SE cpe | 3,243 | 16,634 | 60,397 |
| J19 | SE sdn 4d | 3,318 | 17,384 | 83,332 |

| Bonneville (wb 110.8) | | Wght | Price | Prod |
|---|---|---|---|---|
| X69 | SE sdn 4d | 3,446 | 20,804 | 84,362 |
| Z69 | SSE sdn 4d | 3,587 | 25,804 | 12,399 |

| 1995 Engines | bore × stroke | bhp | availability |
|---|---|---|---|
| I-4, 133.0 | 3.50 × 3.46 | 120 | S-Sunfire (ohv) |
| I-4, 138.0 | 3.63 × 3.35 | 150 | S-Grand Am, Sunfire GT; O-Snfr SE (dohc) |
| V-6, 191.0 | 3.50 × 3.31 | 155 | O-Grand Am |
| V-6, 191.0 | 3.50 × 3.31 | 160 | S-Grand Prix |
| V-6, 207.0 | 3.62 × 3.31 | 160 | S-Firebird |
| V-6, 207.0 | 3.62 × 3.31 | 210 | O-Grand Prix (dohc) |
| V-6, 231.0 | 3.80 × 3.40 | 200 | S-Firebird* |
| V-6, 231.0 | 3.80 × 3.40 | 205 | S-Bonneville |
| V-6S, 231.0 | 3.80 × 3.40 | 225 | O-Bonneville |
| V-8, 350.0 | 4.00 × 3.48 | 275 | S-Firebird Formula/Trans Am |

*Introduced in midyear. Standard only on California models.

## 1996

| Sunfire (wb 104.1)—131,759 built | | Wght | Price | Prod |
|---|---|---|---|---|
| B37 | SE cpe | 2,679 | 11,504 | — |
| B69 | SE sdn 4d | 2,723 | 11,674 | — |
| B67 | SE conv cpe | 2,835 | 17,734 | — |
| D37 | GT cpe | 2,829 | 13,214 | — |

| Firebird (wb 101.1)—32,799 built | | Wght | Price | Prod |
|---|---|---|---|---|
| S87 | htchbk cpe | 3,481 | 15,614 | — |
| S67 | conv cpe | 3,546 | 22,444 | — |
| V87 | Formula htchbk cpe | 3,512 | 19,464 | — |
| V67 | Formula conv cpe | 3,689 | 25,284 | — |
| V87/Y82 | Trans Am htchbk cpe | 3,605 | 21,414 | — |
| V67/Y82 | Trans Am conv cpe | 3,710 | 27,364 | — |

| Grand Am (wb 103.4)—229,117 built | | Wght | Price | Prod |
|---|---|---|---|---|
| E37 | SE cpe | 2,881 | 13,499 | — |
| E69 | SE sdn 4d | 2,954 | 13,499 | — |
| W37 | GT cpe | 2,932 | 15,499 | — |
| W69 | GT sdn 4d | 3,011 | 15,499 | — |

| Grand Prix (wb 107.5)—83,587 built | | Wght | Price | Prod |
|---|---|---|---|---|
| J37 | SE cpe | 3,243 | 17,089 | — |
| J19 | SE sdn 4d | 3,318 | 18,359 | — |

| Bonneville (wb 110.8)—74,191 built | | Wght | Price | Prod |
|---|---|---|---|---|
| X69 | SE sdn 4d | 3,446 | 21,589 | — |
| Z69 | SSE sdn 4d | 3,587 | 26,559 | — |

| 1996 Engines | bore × stroke | bhp | availability |
|---|---|---|---|
| I-4, 133.0 | 3.50 × 3.46 | 120 | S-Sunfire |
| I-4, 146.0 | 3.54 × 3.70 | 150 | S-Grand Am, Sunfire GT; O-Sunfire SE (dohc) |
| V-6, 191.0 | 3.51 × 3.31 | 155 | O-Grand Am |
| V-6, 191.0 | 3.51 × 3.31 | 160 | S-Grand Prix |
| V-6, 207.0 | 3.62 × 3.31 | 215 | O-Grand Prix (dohc) |
| V-6, 231.0 | 3.80 × 3.40 | 200 | S-Firebird |
| V-6, 231.0 | 3.80 × 3.40 | 205 | S-Bonneville |
| V-6S, 231.0 | 3.80 × 3.40 | 240 | O-Bonneville |
| V-8, 350.0 | 4.00 × 3.48 | 285 | S-Firebird Formula/Trans Am |
| V-8, 350.0 | 4.00 × 3.48 | 305 | O-Fbd Fmla/TA |

## 1997

| Sunfire (wb 104.1) | | Wght | Price | Prod |
|---|---|---|---|---|
| B37 | SE cpe | 2,627 | 12,059 | 80,740 |
| B69 | SE sdn 4d | 2,670 | 12,199 | 46,370 |
| B67 | SE conv cpe | 2,868 | 18,899 | 8,002 |
| D37 | GT cpe | 2,791 | 13,719 | 16,911 |

| Firebird (wb 101.1) | | Wght | Price | Prod |
|---|---|---|---|---|
| S87 | htchbk cpe | 3,311 | 17,124 | 17,463 |
| S67 | conv cpe | 3,481 | 23,034 | 1,310 |
| V87 | Formula htchbk cpe | 3,452 | 20,654 | ⎤ 12,068 |
| V87/Y82 | Trans Am htchbk cpe | 3,477 | 22,814 | ⎦ |
| V-67 | Formula conv cpe | 3,512 | 26,454 | ⎤ 1,851 |
| V-67/Y82 | Trans Am conv cpe | 3,605 | 28,374 | ⎦ |

| Grand Am (wb 103.4) | | Wght | Price | Prod |
|---|---|---|---|---|
| E37 | SE cpe | 2,835 | 14,634 | 44,592 |
| E69 | SE sdn 4d | 2,877 | 14,634 | 133,735 |
| W37 | GT cpe | 2,945 | 15874 | 33,613 |
| W69 | GT sdn 4d | 2,987 | 15,874 | 23,798 |

| Grand Prix (wb 110.5) | | Wght | Price | Prod |
|---|---|---|---|---|
| J69 | SE sdn 4d | — | 18,029 | 66,427 |
| P37 | GT cpe | 3,396 | 18,809 | 52,237 |
| P69 | GT sdn 4d | 3,414 | 19,809 | 40,369 |

| Bonneville (wb 110.8) | | Wght | Price | Prod |
|---|---|---|---|---|
| X69 | SE sdn 4d | 3,446 | 22,114 | 67,007 |
| Z69 | SSE sdn 4d | 3,587 | 27,164 | 12,385 |

| 1997 Engines | bore × stroke | bhp | availability |
|---|---|---|---|
| I-4, 133.0 | 3.50 × 3.46 | 120 | S-Sunfire |
| I-4, 146.0 | 3.54 × 3.70 | 150 | S-GA, Sunfire GT; O-Sunfire SE (dohc) |

# Pontiac

| 1997 Engines | bore × stroke | bhp | availability |
|---|---|---|---|
| V-6, 191.0 | 3.51 × 3.31 | 155 | O-Grand Am |
| V-6, 191.0 | 3.51 × 3.31 | 160 | S-Grand Prix SE |
| V-6, 231.0 | 3.80 × 3.40 | 195 | S-Grand Prix GT |
| V-6, 231.0 | 3.80 × 3.40 | 200 | S-Firebird |
| V-6, 231.0 | 3.80 × 3.40 | 205 | S-Bonneville |
| V-6S, 231.0 | 3.80 × 3.40 | 240 | O-GP, Bonn |
| V-8, 350.0 | 4.00 × 3.48 | 285 | S-Firebird Formula/Trans Am |
| V-8, 350.0 | 4.00 × 3.48 | 305 | O-Firebird Formula/Trans Am |

## 1998

| Sunfire (wb 104.1) | | Wght | Price | Prod |
|---|---|---|---|---|
| B37 | SE cpe | 2,637 | 12,495 | 65,416 |
| B69 | SE sdn 4d | 2,674 | 12,495 | 46,024 |
| B67 | SE conv cpe | 2,870 | 19,495 | 6,147 |
| D37 | GT cpe | 2,822 | 15,495 | 15,532 |
| Firebird (wb 101.1) | | | | |
| S87 | htchbk cpe | 3,340 | 17,124 | 15,909 |
| S67 | conv cpe | 3,492 | 24,305 | 911 |
| V87 | Formula htchbk cpe | 3,455 | 22,865 | ⎤ |
| V87/Y82 | Trans Am htchbk cpe | 3,477 | 25,975 | ⎦ 14,946 |
| V-67/Y82 | Trans Am conv cpe | 3,605 | 29,715 | 1,532 |
| Grand Am (wb 103.4) | | | | |
| E37 | SE cpe | 2,835 | 14,874 | 21,410 |
| E69 | SE sdn 4d | 2,877 | 15,024 | 59,785 |
| W37 | GT cpe | 2,945 | 16,324 | 16,781 |
| W69 | GT sdn 4d | 2,987 | 16,474 | 13,633 |
| Grand Prix (wb 110.5) | | | | |
| J69 | SE sdn 4d | — | 18,795 | 50,733 |
| P37 | GT cpe | 3,396 | 20,415 | 35,841 |
| P69 | GT sdn 4d | 3,414 | 20,665 | 55,772 |
| Bonneville (wb 110.8) | | | | |
| X69 | SE sdn 4d | 3,446 | 22,390 | 48,778 |
| Z69 | SSE sdn 4d | 3,587 | 29,390 | 19,551 |

| 1998 Engines | bore × stroke | bhp | availability |
|---|---|---|---|
| I-4, 133.0 | 3.50 × 3.46 | 115 | S-Sunfire |
| I-4, 146.0 | 3.54 × 3.70 | 150 | S-Grand Am, Sunfire GT; O-Sunfire SE (dohc) |
| V-6, 191.0 | 3.51 × 3.31 | 155 | O-Grand Am |
| V-6, 191.0 | 3.51 × 3.31 | 160 | S-Grand Prix SE |
| V-6, 231.0 | 3.80 × 3.40 | 195 | S-Grand Prix GT; O-Grand Prix SE |
| V-6, 231.0 | 3.80 × 3.40 | 200 | S-Firebird |
| V-6, 231.0 | 3.80 × 3.40 | 205 | S-Bonneville |
| V-6S, 231.0 | 3.80 × 3.40 | 240 | O-Grand Prix, Bonneville |
| V-8, 346.0 | 3.90 × 3.62 | 305 | S-Firebird Formula/Trans Am |
| V-8, 346.0 | 3.90 × 3.62 | 320 | O-Fbd Fmla/TA |

## 1999

| Sunfire (wb 104.1) | | Wght | Price | Prod |
|---|---|---|---|---|
| B37 | SE cpe | 2,630 | 12,745 | 52,115 |
| B69 | SE sdn 4d | 2,670 | 12,745 | 47,695 |
| B67 | GT conv cpe | 2,998 | 21,145 | 9,367 |
| D37 | GT cpe | 2,822 | 15,745 | 12,648 |
| Firebird (wb 101.1) | | | | |
| S87 | htchbk cpe | 3,340 | 18,165 | 15,088 |
| S67 | conv cpe | 3,492 | 24,785 | 1,859 |
| V87 | Formula htchbk cpe | 3,455 | 23,065 | ⎤ |
| V87/Y82 | Trans Am htchbk cpe | 3,477 | 26,175 | ⎦ 17,520 |
| V-67/Y82 | Trans Am conv cpe | 3,605 | 30,245 | 1,752 |
| Grand Am (wb 107.0) | | | | |
| E37 | SE cpe | 3,066 | 15,870 | 43,339 |
| E69 | SE sdn 4d | 3,116 | 16,470 | 195,190 |
| W37 | GT cpe | — | 19,070 | 48,803 |
| W69 | GT sdn 4d | — | 19,470 | 43,864 |
| Grand Prix (wb 110.5) | | | | |
| J69 | SE sdn 4d | — | 19,415 | 47,399 |
| P37 | GT cpe | 3,396 | 20,995 | 30,327 |
| P69 | GT sdn 4d | 3,414 | 21,145 | 44,767 |
| R37 | GTP cpe | — | 23,760 | 11,329 |
| R69 | GTP sdn 4d | — | 23,910 | 21,242 |
| Bonneville (wb 110.8) | | | | |
| X69 | SE sdn 4d | 3,446 | 22,800 | 49,064 |
| Z69 | SSE sdn 4d | 3,587 | 29,880 | 5,320 |

| 1999 Engines | bore × stroke | bhp | availability |
|---|---|---|---|
| I-4, 133.0 | 3.50 × 3.46 | 115 | S-Sunfire |
| I-4, 146.0 | 3.54 × 3.70 | 150 | S-Grand Am, Sunfire GT; O-Sunfire SE (dohc) |
| V-6, 191.0 | 3.51 × 3.31 | 160 | S-Grand Prix SE |
| V-6, 207.0 | 3.62 × 3.31 | 170 | O-Grand Am |
| V-6, 231.0 | 3.80 × 3.40 | 200 | S-Firebird, Grand Prix GT |
| V-6, 231.0 | 3.80 × 3.40 | 205 | S-Bonneville |
| V-6S, 231.0 | 3.80 × 3.40 | 240 | S-Grand Prix GTP; O-Bonneville |
| V-8, 346.0 | 3.90 × 3.62 | 305 | S-Firebird Formula/Trans Am |
| V-8, 346.0 | 3.90 × 3.62 | 320 | O-Firebird Formula/Trans Am |

## 2000

| Sunfire (wb 104.1) | | Wght | Price | Prod |
|---|---|---|---|---|
| B37 | SE cpe | 2,606 | 13,910 | 64,335 |
| B69 | SE sdn 4d | 2,644 | 14,010 | 54,670 |
| B67 | GT conv cpe | 2,906 | 21,610 | 3,958 |
| D37 | GT cpe | 2,771 | 16,210 | 11,251 |
| Firebird (wb 101.1) | | | | |
| S87 | htchbk cpe | 3,323 | 18,410 | 14,958 |
| S67 | conv cpe | 3,402 | 25,110 | 1,373 |
| V87 | Formula htchbk cpe | 3,341 | 23,520 | ⎤ |
| V87/Y82 | Trans Am htchbk cpe | 3,397 | 26,630 | ⎦ 13,685 |
| V-67/Y82 | Trans Am conv cpe | 3,514 | 30,700 | 1,910 |
| Grand Am (wb 107.0) | | | | |
| E37 | SE cpe | 3,066 | 15,920 | 33,126 |
| E69 | SE sdn 4d | 3,116 | 16,220 | 155,866 |
| W37 | GT cpe | — | 19,550 | 30,771 |
| W69 | GT sdn 4d | — | 19,850 | 36,092 |
| Grand Prix (wb 110.5) | | | | |
| J69 | SE sdn 4d | — | 19,815 | 61,993 |
| P37 | GT cpe | 3,396 | 21,395 | 23,482 |
| P69 | GT sdn 4d | 3,414 | 21,545 | 59,082 |
| R37 | GTP cpe | — | 24,160 | 10,497 |
| R69 | GTP sdn 4d | — | 24,310 | 17,718 |
| Bonneville (wb 112.2) | | | | |
| X69 | SE sdn 4d | 3,590 | 23,680 | ⎤ |
| Y69 | SLE sdn 4d | 3,650 | 27,380 | ⎦ 40,698 |
| Z69 | SSEi sdn 4d | 3,790 | 31,635 | 21,765 |

# Pontiac

| 2000 Engines | bore × stroke | bhp | availability |
|---|---|---|---|
| I-4, 133.0 | 3.50 × 3.46 | 115 | S-Sunfire |
| I-4, 146.0 | 3.54 × 3.70 | 150 | S-Grand Am, Sunfire GT; O-Sunfire SE (dohc) |
| V-6, 191.0 | 3.51 × 3.31 | 175 | S-Grand Prix SE |
| V-6, 207.0 | 3.62 × 3.31 | 170 | O-Grand Am SE |
| V-6, 207.0 | 3.62 × 3.31 | 175 | S-Grand Am GT |
| V-6, 231.0 | 3.80 × 3.40 | 200 | S-Firebird, GP GT; O-GP SE |
| V-6, 231.0 | 3.80 × 3.40 | 205 | S-Bonneville |
| V-6S, 231.0 | 3.80 × 3.40 | 240 | S-Grand Prix GTP, Bonneville SSEi |
| V-8, 346.0 | 3.90 × 3.62 | 305 | S-Firebird Formula/Trans Am |
| V-8, 346.0 | 3.90 × 3.62 | 320 | O-Firebird Formula/Trans Am |
| V-8, 346.0 | 3.90 × 3.62 | 327 | O-Fbd Fmla/TA |

## 2001

| Sunfire (wb 104.1) | | Wght | Price | Prod |
|---|---|---|---|---|
| B37 | SE cpe | 2,606 | 14,175 | 53,551 |
| B69 | SE sdn 4d | 2,644 | 14,430 | 57,933 |
| D37 | GT cpe | 2,771 | 16,295 | 7,543 |
| **Firebird (wb 101.1)** | | | | |
| S87 | htchbk cpe | 3,323 | 18,725 | 7,172 |
| S67 | conv cpe | 3,402 | 25,345 | 2,360 |
| V87 | Formula htchbk cpe | 3,341 | 23,905 | |
| V87/Y82 | Trans Am htchbk cpe | 3,397 | 27,015 | 10,716 |
| V67/Y82 | Trans Am conv cpe | 3,514 | 31,085 | 1,189 |
| **Grand Am (wb 107.0)** | | | | |
| E37 | SE cpe | 3,066 | 16,410 | 8,584 |
| F37 | SE1 cpe | — | 17,870 | 19,793 |
| E69 | SE sdn 4d | 3,116 | 16,440 | 25,471 |
| F69 | SE1 sdn 4d | — | 18,170 | 99,926 |
| W37 | GT cpe | 3,099 | 20,235 | 16,646 |
| V37 | GT1 cpe | — | 21,655 | 6,338 |
| W69 | GT sdn 4d | 3,118 | 20,535 | 25,724 |
| V-69 | GT1 sdn 4d | — | 21,805 | 7,854 |
| **Grand Prix (wb 110.5)** | | | | |
| K69 | SE sdn 4d | 3,384 | 20,300 | 46,898 |
| P37 | GT cpe | 3,429 | 21,865 | 14,484 |
| P69 | GT sdn 4d | 3,496 | 22,015 | 55,180 |
| R37 | GTP cpe | — | 25,335 | 4,816 |
| R69 | GTP sdn 4d | 3,559 | 25,535 | 9,149 |
| **Bonneville (wb 112.2)** | | | | |
| X69 | SE sdn 4d | 3,590 | 25,075 | 29,329 |
| Y69 | SLE sdn 4d | 3,650 | 28,045 | 9,322 |
| Z69 | SSEi sdn 4d | 3,790 | 32,415 | 6,787 |

| 2001 Engines | bore × stroke | bhp | availability |
|---|---|---|---|
| I-4, 133.0 | 3.50 × 3.46 | 115 | S-Sunfire |
| I-4, 146.0 | 3.54 × 3.70 | 150 | S-Grand Am, Sunfire GT; O-Sunfire SE (dohc) |
| V-6, 191.0 | 3.51 × 3.31 | 175 | S-Grand Prix SE |
| V-6, 207.0 | 3.62 × 3.31 | 170 | O-Grand Am SE1 |
| V-6, 207.0 | 3.62 × 3.31 | 175 | S-Grand Am GT/GT1 |
| V-6, 231.0 | 3.80 × 3.40 | 200 | S-Firebird, Grand Prix GT |
| V-6, 231.0 | 3.80 × 3.40 | 205 | S-Bonneville |
| V-6S, 231.0 | 3.80 × 3.40 | 240 | S-Grand Prix GTP, Bonneville SSEi |
| V-8, 346.0 | 3.90 × 3.62 | 310 | S-Firebird Formula/Trans Am |
| V-8, 346.0 | 3.90 × 3.62 | 325 | O-Firebird Trans Am |
| V-8, 346.0 | 3.90 × 3.62 | 330 | O-Firebird Formula/Trans Am |

## 2002

| Sunfire (wb 104.1) | | Wght | Price | Prod* |
|---|---|---|---|---|
| B37 | SE cpe | 2,606 | 14,540 | |
| B69 | SE sdn 4d | 2,644 | 15,040 | |
| D37 | GT cpe | 2,771 | 16,855 | |
| **Firebird (wb 101.1)** | | | | |
| S87 | htchbk cpe | 3,319 | 19,715 | |
| S67 | conv cpe | 3,484 | 26,630 | |
| V87 | Formula htchbk cpe | 3,541 | 25,660 | |
| V87/Y82 | Trans Am htchbk cpe | 3,495 | 27,690 | |
| V-67/Y82 | Trans Am conv cpe | 3,605 | 31,760 | |
| **Grand Am (wb 107.0)** | | | | |
| E37 | SE cpe | 3,066 | 16,800 | |
| F37 | SE1 cpe | — | 18,240 | |
| E69 | SE sdn 4d | 3,116 | 16,950 | |
| F69 | SE1 sdn 4d | — | 18,390 | |
| W37 | GT cpe | 3,099 | 20,690 | |
| V37 | GT1 cpe | — | 21,960 | |
| W69 | GT sdn 4d | 3,118 | 20,840 | |
| V69 | GT1 sdn 4d | — | 22,110 | |
| **Grand Prix (wb 110.5)** | | | | |
| K69 | SE sdn 4d | 3,384 | 20,965 | |
| P37 | GT cpe | 3,429 | 22,935 | |
| P69 | GT sdn 4d | 3,496 | 23,085 | |
| R37 | GTP cpe | 3,495 | 25,625 | |
| R69 | GTP sdn 4d | 3,559 | 25,805 | |
| **Bonneville (wb 112.2)** | | | | |
| X69 | SE sdn 4d | 3,590 | 25,530 | |
| Y69 | SLE sdn 4d | 3,650 | 28,720 | |
| Z69 | SSEi sdn 4d | 3,790 | 32,950 | |

| 2002 Engines | bore × stroke | bhp | availability |
|---|---|---|---|
| I-4, 133.0 | 3.50 × 3.46 | 115 | S-Sunfire |
| I-4, 146.0 | 3.54 × 3.70 | 150 | S-Grand Am, Sunfire GT; O-Sunfire SE (dohc)** |
| I-4, 134.0 | 3.39 × 3.72 | 140 | S-Grand Am, Sunfire GT; O-Sunfire SE (dohc)*** |
| V-6, 191.0 | 3.51 × 3.31 | 175 | S-Grand Prix SE |
| V-6, 207.0 | 3.62 × 3.31 | 170 | O-Grand Am SE1 |
| V-6, 207.0 | 3.62 × 3.31 | 175 | S-Grand Am GT/GT1 |
| V-6, 231.0 | 3.80 × 3.40 | 200 | S-Firebird, Grand Prix GT |
| V-6, 231.0 | 3.80 × 3.40 | 205 | S-Bonneville |
| V-6S, 231.0 | 3.80 × 3.40 | 240 | S-Grand Prix GTP, Bonneville SSEi |
| V-8, 346.0 | 3.90 × 3.62 | 310 | S-Firebird Formula/Trans Am |
| V-8, 346.0 | 3.90 × 3.62 | 325 | O-Firebird Trans Am |
| V-8, 346.0 | 3.90 × 3.62 | 345 | O-Firebird Trans Am |

*Figures not available at time of publication. **Early production. ***Late production.

# Rambler

Rambler, the successful compact begun by Nash in 1950, became a separate make after introducing larger four-door models for '55 and new styling for '56. These and subsequent events reflected the changing fortunes of American Motors Corporation, founded in April 1954 with the Nash-Hudson merger instigated by Nash president George Mason.

Mason had long dreamed of combining Nash with Hudson, then bringing in Studebaker and Packard to form a new company with the same economies of scale as the Big Three. Without this, he warned, none of these four independents could survive over the long term. As a halfway measure, he persuaded Packard president James Nance to take over ailing Studebaker, which was also accomplished in 1954 (at Packard's ultimate peril). But when Mason died suddenly that October, so did his dream of a "Big Four." His assistant, George Romney, became AMC president, completely forgot about linking with S-P, and bet the farm on Rambler to lift AMC from the financial hole dug by its parents.

It was really all Romney could do, but events worked in his favor. Rambler bounded from strength to strength, helped like no other make by the flash economic recession of 1958. By decade's end, AMC was making serious money and Rambler was firmly established as Detroit's best-selling compact.

The 1957 Ramblers were continuations of the reskinned '56 models sold with Nash and Hudson badges. Besides new "R" hood medallions, cosmetic changes were limited to reshuffled trim and a T-shaped grille ornament to fill the void above the eggcrate section. The big news was V-8 power: AMC's 250-cid, 190-bhp engine, introduced in '56 (a derivative was bored out for 1957's new AMC 327). V-8 Ramblers were available in four body styles, each of these unit-construction four-doors on the 108-inch wheelbase introduced for '55. Variations involved sedans and Cross Country station wagons with and without B-pillars—making Rambler the first in Detroit with hardtop wagons. As before, all offered a choice of Super or Custom trim. So did a parallel six-cylinder line retaining the 195.6-cid engine familiar from Nash days. However, that engine was tweaked quite a bit, going from 120 bhp to 125/135. Sixes also included a price-leader DeLuxe sedan at $1961. Other '57 Ramblers sold in the low-to-mid $2000s.

These were solid, reliable, smaller cars that could be quite stylish with optional two-toning. As in the Nash era, exterior "continental" spare tires were available for sedans. Wagons boasted a roll-down tailgate window instead of a clumsy liftgate, something Ford and GM wagons didn't have. Future AMC chairman Roy D. Chapin, Jr., later recalled: "We just rolled with those cars. We couldn't get enough." Indeed, of the roughly 119,000 cars AMC built in calendar '57, all but 7816 were Ramblers. The rest, of course, were Nashes and Hudsons, which would not return for '58—at least not as they had been.

Romney liked to assail Detroit's "gas-guzzling dinosaurs" while preaching the smaller-is-better virtues of Rambler. All the more surprising, then, that AMC had a performance Rambler for '57, a special Custom Country Club four-door hardtop aptly branded Rebel. Arriving at midyear with flashes of anodized aluminum on its flanks, Rebel carried the same 255-bhp 327-cid V-8 as the final Nashes and Hudsons, but was much quicker because it weighed significantly less than those cars. The extra power made Rebel more of a handler than other Ramblers, so AMC included stiff Gabriel shocks, a front antiroll bar, heavy-duty springs, power steering, and power brakes. Performance was impressive by most any standard, let alone for a Rambler. In one test at Daytona Beach, a Rebel covered 0-60 mph—and 50-80—in scarcely more than seven seconds. It might have been quicker still with Bendix mechanical fuel injection, but that promised option never materialized.

No matter. With 9.75:1 compression, the Rebel drank premium fuel and a fair bit of it, which hardly fit Rambler's economy image. And at $2786 it was the costliest '57 Rambler, which was another likely factor that kept production to just 1500 units.

During this period, economy imports were quickly climbing the sales charts, led by Volkswagen's already antiquated Beetle. AMC noted the trend and replied with an unprecedented move for 1958, a revival of the 100-inch-wheelbase 1955 Rambler two-door sedan. Renamed Rambler American and wearing a new mesh-type grille and full wheel openings, it offered DeLuxe, Super, and stripped "business" models at a low prices ranging from $1775 to $1874. With those prices in a recession year, the American couldn't help but sell, and over 30,000 were registered for the model year.

Regular Ramblers weren't ignored for '58, receiving a complete reskin that made the '56 bodies look a bit bulkier on unchanged wheelbases. Little canted tailfins and dual headlamps (moved from within the grille back to the fenders) were new styling touches. Hardtop wagons were omitted. AMC also adopted then-trendy pushbuttons for its optional Borg-Warner "Flash-O-Matic" self-shift transmission. Though V-8 cars were now called Rebel, they retained the 250 engine, which was boosted to 215 bhp. Sixes, now with 127 or 138 bhp, remained nameless, and were again far more popular—no real surprise.

What *did* surprise observers was a new 117-inch-wheelbase line called Rambler Ambassador. AMC brochures implied you should think of it as a distinct make ("Ambassador by Rambler"), but this was simply the 108-inch-wheelbase platform with nine extra inches ahead of the cowl, plus a standard four-barrel 327 V-8 with 270 bhp. Offerings comprised the usual four-door sedans, Country Club hardtop sedans, and pillared and pillarless wagons in Super and Custom trim. Visually, these Ambassadors were nothing like their Nash forebears and everything like regular '58 Ramblers. The only differences, other than the added length, were nameplates, a fine-checked grille, broad swathes of anodized aluminum on Customs, plusher interiors, and arguably better proportions. This is what the '58 Nash and Hudson would have been had those brands not been dropped at the last minute. In fact, the vee'd front bumper guard of the '58 Ambassador was taken directly from the stillborn Hudson, which had been all but locked up by late 1956 along with a nearly identical Nash.

Interestingly, the '58 Ambassador virtually doubled full-size '57 Nash/Hudson volume, model-year production totaling 14,570. Rarest of the breed—just 294 total—was the Custom Cross Country hardtop wagon, the only such model in AMC's '58 line. Despite Ambassador's modest sales, Rambler's '58 total of 162,182 was up 77 percent from '57—a fine showing in a generally disastrous industry year. The success ended four straight years of losses for AMC, which scored a $26 million profit on sales of $470 million.

This winning formula netted another $60 million profit on 1959 Rambler volume of nearly 375,000—a new record for the fledgling firm. Ramblers and Ambassadors received more-complicated body trim, plus a beltline that curved up gently at the rear doors to blend more smoothly with the finned fenders.

1958 American Super two-door sedan

1958 Rebel V-8 Custom Cross Country station wagon

1959 Ambassador Custom Country Club hardtop sedan

1959 American Super two-door station wagon

1960 Ambassador Custom Country Club hardtop sedan

Ambassadors got a more-ornate grille with a big "floating" horizontal bar. Powertrains were unchanged. Unlike most competitors, AMC had evidently decided the horsepower race was over.

Indisputably, the rush to compacts was on, and both Americans and the standard Ramblers had new competition in Studebaker's pert '59 Lark. Perhaps anticipating this, AMC expanded that year's American line by reviving the old two-door 100-inch-wheelbase wagon. Also offered in DeLuxe and Super trim, the compact hauler helped the smallest Rambler rack up 91,000 model-year sales. The bigger Ramblers also did very well in 1959's modest industrywide recovery. Ambassador took a satisfying leap to 23,769; standards attracted over a quarter-million sales. The latter were again mostly sixes, as Rebel V-8s found just 16,399 customers.

In all, AMC's 1957-59 sales performance was a remarkable comeback from nail-biting 1954-56. And the good times kept on rolling. For 1960, Rambler recorded about 450,000 sales—the highest annual output ever tallied by an independent manufacturer. Rambler ranked third in the 1961 production race despite volume that was 17 percent lower. Though production for 1962 increased substantially, Rambler ran fifth that year as Pontiac and Olds swept by. The following year found Rambler dropping to eighth place. Output continued to be healthy, yet Rambler/AMC kept slipping: down to ninth for '65 and tenth by 1968.

Two management changes greatly affected Rambler in this period. First, the hard-driving George Romney left in 1962 to make his successful run for the Michigan statehouse. His successor, the ebullient Roy Abernethy, was far less loyal to sensible economy cars, and began an ambitious model expansion that ultimately proved misguided. Abernethy stepped aside in 1966 for Roy D. Chapin, Jr., who became board chairman the following year, with William V. Luneberg as president. This team ordered further diversification, including new "make models" like the 1968 Javelin "ponycar." They also killed the Rambler name after the final Americans of 1969. That was probably wise because by that time, Rambler's sensible image had become more of a liability than an asset.

The compact American returned for 1960 with no fundamental change, but new Super and Custom four-door sedans helped lift model-year volume to 120,600. Though prices were slightly higher at $1781-$2235, the American remained one of the country's most-affordable cars. It also remained an anachronism with its '50s "Farina" styling and elderly L-head six. But sales were more than healthy enough to justify a full restyle for 1961.

Larger Ramblers were attractively restyled for 1960, gaining smoother lines, simple full-width grilles (fine-checked on Ambassador, eggcrate on Six/Rebel), less-intrusive sloped-back A-pillars (replacing vertical), shapelier fins (still mercifully modest), and new taillights. Ambassadors also sported a "Scena-Ramic" windshield curved at the top as well as the sides. A three-seat wagon with a novel left-hinged swing-out tailgate was added to all three series. These changes were evidently well-considered, for AMC passed the billion-dollar mark in net sales for the first time and earned a $48-million profit.

The rebodied 1961 American was a rather odd bit of work by AMC chief designer Edmund A. Anderson (a veteran of Nash days). Boxy and truncated, it was three inches narrower and 5.2 inches shorter than the old '55-vintage design. Happily, the ancient six was modernized with an overhead-valve cylinder head (actually a mid-1960 change), which boosted optional bhp to 127. Existing body styles plus a new convertible and four-door wagons were sprinkled among the usual trims. Posh "400" models were added for '62, and Custom moved down to displace Super. Series were retitled for '63—low-end 220, mid-priced 330, and top-end 440—and hardtop coupes arrived, the last a bench-seat 440 and bucket-seat 440H. Styling changed

# Rambler

only in detail each year. Though true economy cars with fair interior space, the 1961-63 Americans were hardly beautiful.

The Six/Rebel became Rambler's Classic for '61, announced by headlights moved into a checkerboard grille beneath a lower hood. V-8s departed for '62, but two-door sedans debuted, and all models wore a more-involved grille and finless rear fenders. An interesting '62 Classic option (shared with American) was "E-Stick," a manual transmission with "automatic" clutch. Though it cost just $60, it was too complex to sell really well.

Ambassador, meantime, underwent a big change. The '61s carried a dubious facelift with pointy front-fender bottoms, heavily hooded headlamps, and a raked inverted-trapezoid grille. Hardtop sedans and wagons were axed. Returning from 1960 as base power was a two-barrel 250-bhp "economy" version of the 327 V-8; the 270-bhp engine was now optional. The '62 models effectively replaced Classic V-8s, and were demoted to the same 108-inch platform and given near-identical styling. All this reflected sluggish Ambassador sales, which were little-changed for 1960 at 23,798 but only 18,842 for '61. The '62s fared much better at 36,171. Like Classic, the '62 Ambassador offered new two-door sedans, four-doors, and wagons seating six or eight in DeLuxe, Custom, and top-shelf "400" trim; the last came with an automatic transmission. Prices were $2300-$3000.

Richard A. Teague had joined the AMC styling staff by this time and would soon succeed Ed Anderson. But it was Anderson who shaped the Classic that was named *Motor Trend* magazine's 1963 "Car of the Year." Featured was a wholly new 112-inch-wheelbase unibody platform—the first since '56—with a lower silhouette, smoothly rounded flanks, and curved door glass. One-piece "Uniside" door-frame structures were a Detroit first that saved weight, increased rigidity, and reduced squeaks and rattles. Though styling remained a bit chunky, these Ramblers had never looked better.

They also went better thanks to a new 287-cid version of the familiar 327-cid V-8. Rated at 198 bhp, the 287 would remain through 1966. V-8 Classics combined good go with good mileage; even with "Flash-O-Matic" they could run 0-60 mph in about 10 seconds and return 16-20 mpg. Of course, the V-8s weighed more than six-cylinder Ramblers, so understeer was pronounced.

Teague refined the '63 Classic once Anderson left, giving '64 models stainless steel rocker moldings and a flat grille that replaced the concave design. Hardtops returned, but were now two-doors. Two- and four-door sedans and pillared four-door wagons returned in 550, 660, and 770 trim (replacing Deluxe, Custom, and 400). Hardtops comprised the bench-seat 770 and bucket-seat Typhoon. The latter introduced a new short-stroke 232-cid "Typhoon" six (later "Torque Command") that began replacing the old 195.6-cid unit throughout the AMC line. Arriving with 145 bhp, the 232 spawned a destroked 128-bhp

1962 American 400 convertible coupe

1964 Classic 770 Typhoon hardtop coupe

1962 Classic Custom two-door sedan

1965 Ambassador 990-H hardtop coupe

1963 Ambassador 990 four-door station wagon

1965 Marlin fastback hardtop coupe

199-cid version for '65-model 550s. The Typhoon itself was a year-only limited edition (2520 built) offering a black vinyl roof, Solar Yellow paint, and a sporty all-vinyl interior for $2509.

A new Classic implied a new Ambassador, but the '63 again shared Classic's wheelbase and styling (save the usual extra chrome bits). Series were retitled 800, 880, and 990, each with the previous three body styles. 800s were a tough sell and vanished for '64. So did 880s, leaving just 990s in four-door sedan and wagon body styles, plus a new hardtop coupe with altered styling *a la* Classic. Also listed was a sporty bucket-seat 990H hardtop with a standard 270-bhp 327 V-8.

Teague succeeded Anderson as AMC design chief on the strength of his pretty 1964 American. Ironically, this was a clever adaptation of Anderson's Classic, with Unisides shortened ahead of the cowl to give a 106-inch wheelbase. But that was still half a foot longer than American's previous span, and Teague used it to produce a well-proportioned compact with only modest brightwork. This styling was good enough to continue with only minor yearly changes through 1969 and the end of the Rambler marque.

The '64 American line repeated 1963's, then thinned for '66, when the bucket-seat 440H became a Rogue. A convertible Rogue was added for '67, only to vanish for '68, when the roster showed just a Rogue, two base-trim sedans, and the 440 as a four-door sedan and a wagon. Sixes continued to dominate American sales, with new-generation 199- and 232-cid engines delivering 128/145 bhp for 1967. But that same year brought American's first V-8 options: a new 290-cid small-block, derived from the 287, in 200- and 225-bhp tune. V-8s continued through Rambler's last stand, when American prices still began just shy of the magic $2000 mark.

All 1965 Ramblers were advertised as "The Sensible Spectaculars," but that fuzzy logic applied mainly to a much-revised Classic and Ambassador. The former wore a new convex "dumbbell" grille, recontoured hood, and a longer, squared-up rear deck. A convertible appeared in the 770 series, where Typhoon returned, this time as the 770H. Engine choices widened with an optional 155-bhp, 232-cid six and Ambassador's two 327 V-8s. The 770H became a Rebel for '66, when a light facelift featured new grilles and minor trim, a "crisp line" hardtop roof, and a reworked rear end for wagons.

Because the '64 Ambassador sold no better than the '63, the premium Rambler reverted to its own longer 116-inch wheelbase for 1965. Also back was an 880/990 lineup that included a pillarless 990H. Standard power was now the 155-bhp 232 six. The base V-8 was that year's new 287, with optional 327s, as before. An outer-sheetmetal redo bestowed rectilinear lines reminiscent of the Classic, plus a vee'd bilevel grille and vertically stacked quad headlights. Ambassador also followed Classic in '65 by offering its first convertible, a 990. Trunk space improved on all nonwagon models, but passenger room didn't because the extra wheelbase length was again ahead of the cowl. There were no huge changes for '66, when Ambassador became a separate AMC "make" (*see* AMC).

Also new for '65 was the Classic-based Marlin, a fastback to battle Ford Mustang and Plymouth Barracuda in the burgeoning sporty compact wars. A sweeping pillarless roof tapered down and inward at the back, and elliptical rear side windows helped keep it light-looking. This treatment had been previewed on a 1964 show car called Tarpon, based on Teague's new American, which carried it much better. Teague suggested a showroom version. Abernethy agreed, but insisted on besting rival 2+2s with a "3+3." Thus was Marlin molded on the Classic instead—and suffered ungainly overall proportions from that car's fairly stubby hood. This likely explains why the new image-maker sold none too well despite decent performance and a reasonable $3100 base price. Only 10,327 were produced for '65, after which Marlin sold with diminishing success as its own "make" for two more years (*see* AMC).

Rebel replaced Classic for an all-new group of midsize '67 Ramblers. A roomier new body/chassis rode a two-inch longer wheelbase (114 inches), and Teague contributed handsome contemporary styling marked by a floating rectangular grille, squarish front fenders flowing into "hippy" rear flanks, and a shapely deck with large, canted taillights. Besides the expected sixes, Rebels offered a new "thinwall" 290-cid V-8 option with 200 bhp; a bigger bore made for two new 343-cid engines packing 235 and 280 bhp. Other new features included extra-cost front-disc power brakes, available floorshift transmissions, and weight-saving Hotchkiss drive in place of Rambler's old torque-tube. Model choices diminished to two sedans and one wagon in 550 trim; midrange 770 sedan, wagon, and hardtop; and the sporty SST convertible and hardtop. Rebel then joined Marlin and Ambassador as a separate AMC "make" (*see* AMC).

Bidding an outrageous farewell to the Rambler name was the limited-edition 1969 SC/Rambler. This was basically a Rogue hardtop carrying a big new 315-bhp, 390-cid V-8, a working hood scoop, a four-speed manual transmission with Hurst shifter, heavy-duty suspension, and a cartoonish red-white-and-blue paint job. Priced at $2998, the "Scrambler," as it was inevitably nicknamed, was hardly sensible in the Rambler tradition, but it was a pretty spectacular junior muscle car. Published road tests confirmed AMC's claim of standing quarter-miles in the low 14s at around 100 mph. From rest, 60 mph came up in a reported 6.3 seconds. Production was only 1512, though that was triple the planned run.

Not many Rambler convertibles were built, no surprise given AMC's much smaller volume versus the Big Three. Though the ragtop American ran a full seven years (1961-67), the open Classic/Rebel lasted only four (1965-68), and the counterpart Ambassador just three (1965-67). AMC's most-productive soft-top year was 1965, when 3882 Americans, 4953 Classics, and 3499 Ambassadors were produced. All stand to grow in collector esteem and dollar value as the years roll by, as do interesting closed models like the '57 Rebel, the '64 Typhoon, and, of course, the "Scrambler."

## Specifications

### 1957*

| Six (wb 108.0) | | Wght | Price | Prod |
|---|---|---|---|---|
| 5715 | DeLuxe sdn 4d | 2,911 | 1,961 | 9,402 |
| 5715-1 | Super sdn 4d | 2,914 | 2,123 | 16,320 |
| 5715-2 | Custom sdn 4d | 2,938 | 2,213 | 10,520 |
| 5718-1 | Super Crss Cntry wgn 4d | 3,042 | 2,410 | 14,083 |
| 5718-2 | Custom Crss Cntry wgn 4d | 3,076 | 2,500 | 17,745 |
| 5719-1 | Super htp sdn | 2,936 | 2,208 | 612 |
| **V-8 (wb 108.0)** | | | | |
| 5723-2 | Custom Crss Cntry htp wgn 4d | 3,409 | 2,715 | 182 |
| 5725-1 | Super sdn 4d | 3,223 | 2,253 | 3,555 |
| 5725-2 | Custom sdn 4d | 3,259 | 2,343 | 3,199 |
| 5728-1 | Super Crss Cntry wgn 4d | 3,359 | 2,540 | 2,461 |

# Rambler

| V-8 (wb 108.0) | | Wght | Price | Prod |
|---|---|---|---|---|
| 5728-2 | Custom Crss Cntry wgn 4d | 3,392 | 2,630 | 4,560 |
| 5729-2 | Custom htp sdn | 3,269 | 2,428 | 485 |
| 5739-2 | Custom Rebel htp sdn | 3,353 | 2,786 | 1,500 |

| 1957 Engines | bore × stroke | bhp | availability |
|---|---|---|---|
| I-6, 195.6 | 3.13 × 4.25 | 125/135 | S-Six |
| V-8, 250.0 | 3.50 × 3.25 | 190 | S-V-8 exc Rebel |
| V-8, 327.0 | 4.00 × 3.25 | 255 | S-Rebel |

## 1958

| American (wb 100.0) | | Wght | Price | Prod |
|---|---|---|---|---|
| 5802 | bus sdn 3P | 2,439 | 1,775 | 184 |
| 5806 | DeLuxe sdn 2d | 2,463 | 1,789 | 15,765 |
| 5806-1 | Super sdn 2d | 2,475 | 1,874 | 14,691 |

| Six (wb 108.0) | | | | |
|---|---|---|---|---|
| 5815 | DeLuxe sdn 4d | 2,947 | 2,047 | 12,723 |
| 5815-1 | Super sdn 4d | 2,960 | 2,212 | 29,699 |
| 5815-2 | Custom sdn 4d | 2,968 | 2,327 | 16,850 |
| 5818 | DeLuxe wgn 4d | 3,050 | 2,370 | 78 |
| 5818-1 | Super Crss Cntry wgn 4d | 3,069 | 2,506 | 26,452 |
| 5818-2 | Custom Crss Cntry wgn 4d | 3,079 | 2,621 | 20,131 |
| 5819-1 | Super Cntry Club htp sdn | 2,983 | 2,287 | 983 |

| Rebel V-8 (wb 108.0) | | | | |
|---|---|---|---|---|
| 5825 | DeLuxe sdn 4d | 3,287 | 2,177 | 22 |
| 5825-1 | Super sdn 4d | 3,300 | 2,342 | 2,146 |
| 5825-2 | Custom sdn 4d | 3,313 | 2,457 | 2,595 |
| 5826-1 | Super Crss Cntry wgn 4d | 3,410 | 2,636 | 1,782 |
| 5826-2 | Custom Crss Cntry wgn 4d | 3,418 | 2,751 | 3,101 |
| 5829-2 | Custom Cntry Club htp sdn | 3,328 | 2,532 | 410 |

| Ambassador (wb 117.0) | | | | |
|---|---|---|---|---|
| 5883-2 | Custom Crss Cntry htp wgn 4d | 3,586 | 3,116 | 294 |
| 5885-1 | Super sdn 4d | 3,456 | 2,587 | 2,772 |
| 5885-2 | Custom sdn 4d | 3,462 | 2,732 | 6,369 |
| 5888-1 | Super Crss Cntry wgn 4d | 3,544 | 2,881 | 1,051 |
| 5888-2 | Custom Crss Cntry wgn 4d | 3,568 | 3,026 | 2,742 |
| 5883-2 | Custom htp wgn 4d | 3,586 | 3,116 | 294 |
| 5889-2 | Custom Cntry Club htp sdn | 3,475 | 2,822 | 1,340 |

| 1958 Engines | bore × stroke | bhp | availability |
|---|---|---|---|
| I-6, 195.6 | 3.13 × 4.25 | 90 | S-American |
| I-6, 195.6 | 3.13 × 4.25 | 127 | S-Six |
| I-6, 195.6 | 3.13 × 4.25 | 138 | O-Six |
| V-8, 250.0 | 3.50 × 3.25 | 215 | S-Rebel |
| V-8, 327.0 | 4.00 × 3.25 | 270 | S-Ambassador |

## 1959

| American (wb 100.0) | | Wght | Price | Prod |
|---|---|---|---|---|
| 5902 | bus sdn 3P | 2,435 | 1,821 | 443 |
| 5904 | DeLuxe wgn 2d | 2,554 | 2,060 | 15,256 |
| 5904-1 | Super wgn 2d | 2,554 | 2,145 | 17,383 |
| 5904-7 | Glass panel deliv 2d | — | — | 3 |
| 5904-8 | Steel panel deliv 2d | — | — | 3 |
| 5906 | DeLuxe sdn 2d | 2,476 | 1,835 | 29,954 |
| 5906-1 | Super sdn 2d | 2,492 | 1,920 | 28,449 |

| Six (wb 108.0) | | | | |
|---|---|---|---|---|
| 5915 | DeLuxe sdn 4d | 2,934 | 2,098 | 26,157 |
| 5915-1 | Super sdn 4d | 2,951 | 2,268 | 72,577 |
| 5915-2 | Custom sdn 4d | 2,956 | 2,383 | 15,242 |
| 5918 | DeLuxe Crss Cntry wgn 4d | 3,047 | 2,427 | 422 |
| 5918-1 | Super Crss Cntry wgn 4d | 3,082 | 2,562 | 66,739 |
| 5918-2 | Custom Crss Cntry wgn 4d | 3,097 | 2,677 | 38,731 |
| 5919-1 | Super Cntry Club htp sdn | 2,961 | 2,343 | 2,683 |

| Rebel V-8 (wb 108.0) | | Wght | Price | Prod |
|---|---|---|---|---|
| 5925 | DeLuxe sdn 4d | 3,283 | 2,228 | 113 |
| 5925-1 | Super sdn 4d | 3,287 | 2,398 | 3,488 |
| 5925-2 | Custom sdn 4d | 3,295 | 2,513 | 4,046 |
| 5928-1 | Super Crss Cntry wgn 4d | 3,398 | 2,692 | 3,634 |
| 5928-2 | Custom Crss Cntry wgn 4d | 3,407 | 2,807 | 4,427 |
| 5929-2 | Custom Cntry Club htp sdn | 3,338 | 2,588 | 691 |

| Ambassador (wb 117.0) | | | | |
|---|---|---|---|---|
| 5983-2 | Custom Crss Cntry htp wgn 4d | 3,591 | 3,116 | 578 |
| 5985 | DeLuxe sdn 4d | — | — | 155 |
| 5985-1 | Super sdn 4d | 3,428 | 2,587 | 4,675 |
| 5985-2 | Custom sdn 4d | 3,437 | 2,732 | 10,791 |
| 5988-1 | Super Crss Cntry wgn 4d | 3,546 | 2,881 | 1,782 |
| 5988-2 | Custom Crss Cntry wgn 4d | 3,562 | 3,026 | 4,341 |
| 5989-2 | Custom Cntry Club htp sdn | 3,483 | 2,822 | 1,447 |

| 1959 Engines | bore × stroke | bhp | availability |
|---|---|---|---|
| I-6, 195.6 | 3.13 × 4.25 | 90 | S-American |
| I-6, 195.6 | 3.13 × 4.25 | 127 | S-Six |
| I-6, 195.6 | 3.13 × 4.25 | 138 | O-Six |
| V-8, 250.0 | 3.50 × 3.25 | 215 | S-Rebel |
| V-8, 327.0 | 4.00 × 3.25 | 270 | S-Ambassador |

## 1960

| American (wb 100.0) | | Wght | Price | Prod |
|---|---|---|---|---|
| 6002 | DeLuxe bus sdn 3P | 2,428 | 1,781 | 630 |
| 6004 | DeLuxe wgn 2d | 2,527 | 2,020 | 12,290 |
| 6004-1 | Super wgn 2d | 2,549 | 2,185 | 15,093 |
| 6004-2 | Custom wgn 2d | 2,606 | 2,235 | 1,430 |
| 6005 | DeLuxe sdn 4d | 2,474 | 1,844 | 22,593 |
| 6005-1 | Super sdn 4d | 2,490 | 1,929 | 21,108 |
| 6005-2 | Custom sdn 4d | 2,551 | 2,059 | 3,272 |
| 6006 | DeLuxe sdn 2d | 2,451 | 1,795 | 23,960 |
| 6006-1 | Super sdn 2d | 2,462 | 1,880 | 17,233 |
| 6006-2 | Custom sdn 2d | 2,523 | 2,010 | 2,994 |

| Six (wb 108.0) | | | | |
|---|---|---|---|---|
| 6015 | DeLuxe sdn 4d | 2,912 | 2,098 | 37,666 |
| 6015-1 | Super sdn 4d | 2,930 | 2,268 | 88,004 |
| 6015-2 | Custom sdn 4d | 2,929 | 2,383 | 38,003 |
| 6018 | DeLuxe Crss Cntry wgn 4d | 3,051 | 2,427 | 24,011 |
| 6018-1 | Super Crss Cntry wgn 4d, 6P | 3,054 | 2,562 | 59,491 |
| 6018-2 | Custom Crss Cntry wgn 4d, 6P | 3,057 | 2,677 | 32,092 |
| 6018-3 | Super Crss Cntry wgn 4d, 8P | 3,117 | 2,687 | 8,456 |
| 6018-4 | Custom Crss Cntry wgn 4d, 8P | 3,137 | 2,802 | 5,718 |
| 6019-2 | Custom Cntry Club htp sdn | 2,981 | 2,458 | 3,937 |

| Rebel V-8 (wb 108.0) | | | | |
|---|---|---|---|---|
| 6025 | DeLuxe sdn 4d | 3,252 | 2,217 | 143 |
| 6025-1 | Super sdn 4d | 3,270 | 2,387 | 3,826 |
| 6025-2 | Custom sdn 4d | 3,278 | 2,502 | 3,969 |
| 6028-1 | Super Crss Cntry wgn 4d, 6P | 3,391 | 2,681 | 3,328 |
| 6028-2 | Custom Crss Cntry wgn 4d, 6P | 3,395 | 2,796 | 3,613 |
| 6028-3 | Super Crss Cntry wgn 4d, 8P | 3,446 | 2,806 | 718 |
| 6028-4 | Custom Crss Cntry wgn 4d, 8P | 3,447 | 2,921 | 886 |
| 6029-2 | Custom Cntry Club htp sdn | 3,319 | 2,577 | 579 |

| Ambassador (wb 117.0) | | | | |
|---|---|---|---|---|
| 6083-2 | Custom Crss Cntry htp wgn 4d | 3,583 | 3,116 | 435 |
| 6085 | DeLuxe sdn 4d | 3,384 | 2,395 | 302 |
| 6085-1 | Super sdn 4d | 3,395 | 2,587 | 3,990 |
| 6085-2 | Custom sdn 4d | 3,408 | 2,732 | 10,949 |
| 6088-1 | Super Crss Cntry wgn 4d, 6P | 3,521 | 2,881 | 1,342 |
| 6088-2 | Custom Crss Cntry wgn 4d, 6P | 3,538 | 3,026 | 3,849 |
| 6088-3 | Super Crss Cntry wgn 4d, 8P | 3,581 | 3,006 | 637 |
| 6088-4 | Custom Crss Cntry wgn 4d, 8P | 3,592 | 3,151 | 1,153 |
| 6089-2 | Custom Cntry Club htp sdn | 3,465 | 2,822 | 1,141 |

# Rambler

| 1960 Engines | bore × stroke | bhp | availability |
|---|---|---|---|
| I-6, 195.6 | 3.13×4.25 | 90 | S-American |
| I-6, 195.6 | 3.13×4.25 | 127 | S-Six; O-American |
| I-6, 195.6 | 3.13×4.25 | 138 | O-Six |
| V-8, 250.0 | 3.50×3.25 | 200 | S-Rebel |
| V-8, 250.0 | 3.50×3.25 | 215 | O-Rebel |
| V-8, 327.0 | 4.00×3.25 | 250 | S-Ambassador |
| V-8, 327.0 | 4.00×3.25 | 270 | O-Ambassador |

## 1961

| American (wb 100.0) | | Wght | Price | Prod |
|---|---|---|---|---|
| 6102 | DeLuxe bus sdn 2d | 2,454 | 1,831 | 355 |
| 6104 | DeLuxe wgn 2d | 2,549 | 2,080 | 5,666 |
| 6104-1 | Super wgn 2d | 2,556 | 2,165 | 5,749 |
| 6104-2 | Custom wgn 2d | 2,617 | 2,295 | 1,417 |
| 6105 | DeLuxe sdn 4d | 2,523 | 1,894 | 17,811 |
| 6105-1 | Super sdn 4d | 2,530 | 1,979 | 15,741 |
| 6105-2 | Custom sdn 4d | 2,557 | 2,060 | 7,549 |
| 6106 | DeLuxe sdn 2d | 2,490 | 1,845 | 28,555 |
| 6106-1 | Super sdn 2d | 2,499 | 1,930 | 14,349 |
| 6106-2 | Custom sdn 2d | 2,557 | 2,060 | 4,883 |
| 6107-2 | Custom conv cpe | 2,712 | 2,369 | 12,918 |
| 6108 | DeLuxe wgn 4d | 2,595 | 2,129 | 7,260 |
| 6108-1 | Super wgn 4d | 2,602 | 2,214 | 10,071 |
| 6108-2 | Custom wgn 4d | 2,660 | 2,344 | 3,679 |
| **Classic Six (wb 108.0)** | | | | |
| 6115 | DeLuxe sdn 4d | 2,905 | 2,098 | 40,398 |
| 6115-1 | Super sdn 4d | 2,923 | 2,268 | 62,563 |
| 6115-2 | Custom sdn 4d | 2,863 | 2,413 | 26,497 |
| 6118 | DeLuxe wgn 4d | 3,037 | 2,437 | 19,848 |
| 6118-1 | Super wgn 4d, 6P | 3,046 | 2,572 | 38,370 |
| 6118-2 | Custom wgn 4d, 6P | 2,984 | 2,717 | 16,394 |
| 6118-3 | Super wgn 4d, 8P | 3,087 | 2,697 | 4,465 |
| 6118-4 | Custom wgn 4d, 8P | 3,023 | 2,842 | 2,741 |
| **Classic V-8 (wb 108.0)** | | | | |
| 6125 | DeLuxe sdn 4d | 3,237 | 2,227 | 121 |
| 6125-1 | Super sdn 4d | 3,255 | 2,397 | 2,156 |
| 6125-2 | Custom sdn 4d | 3,262 | 2,512 | 2180 |
| 6128-1 | Super wgn 4d, 6P | 3,372 | 2,701 | 1,964 |
| 6128-2 | Custom wgn 4d, 6P | 3,378 | 2,816 | 1,777 |
| 6128-3 | Super wgn 4d, 8P | 3,408 | 2,826 | 300 |
| 6128-4 | Custom wgn 4d, 8P | 3,420 | 2,941 | 382 |
| **Ambassador (wb 117.0)** | | | | |
| 6185 | DeLuxe sdn 4d | 3,343 | 2,395 | 273 |
| 6185-1 | Super sdn 4d | 3,361 | 2,537 | 3,299 |
| 6185-2 | Custom sdn 4d | 3,380 | 2,682 | 10,100 |
| 6188-1 | Super wgn 4d, 6P | 3,493 | 2,841 | 1,099 |
| 6188-2 | Custom wgn 4d, 6P | 3,495 | 2,986 | 3010 |
| 6188-3 | Super wgn 4d, 8P | 3,560 | 2,966 | 277 |
| 6188-4 | Custom wgn 4d, 8P | 3,566 | 3,111 | 784 |

| 1961 Engines | bore × stroke | bhp | availability |
|---|---|---|---|
| I-6, 195.6 | 3.13×4.25 | 90 | S-American exc Custom |
| I-6, 195.6 | 3.13×4.25 | 125 | S-American Custom |
| I-6, 195.6 | 3.13×4.25 | 127 | S-Classic Six |
| I-6, 195.6 | 3.13×4.25 | 138 | O-Classic Six |
| V-8, 250.0 | 3.50×3.25 | 200 | S-Classic V-8 |
| V-8, 250.0 | 3.50×3.25 | 215 | O-Classic V-8 |
| V-8, 327.0 | 4.00×3.25 | 250 | S-Ambassador |
| V-8, 327.0 | 4.00×3.25 | 270 | O-Ambassador |

## 1962

| American (wb 100.0) | | Wght | Price | Prod |
|---|---|---|---|---|
| 6202 | DeLuxe bus sdn 2d | 2,454 | 1,832 | 283 |
| 6204 | DeLuxe wgn 2d | 2,555 | 2,081 | 4,434 |
| 6204-2 | Custom wgn 2d | 2,565 | 2,141 | 4,398 |
| 6205 | DeLuxe sdn 4d | 2,500 | 1,895 | 17,758 |
| 6205-2 | Custom sdn 4d | 2,512 | 1,958 | 13,884 |
| 6205-5 | 400 sdn 4d | 2,585 | 2,089 | 5,773 |
| 6206 | DeLuxe sdn 2d | 2,480 | 1,846 | 29,665 |
| 6206-2 | Custom sdn 2d | 2,492 | 1,909 | 12,710 |
| 6206-5 | 400 sdn 2d | 2,558 | 2,040 | 4,840 |
| 6207-5 | 400 conv cpe | 2,735 | 2,344 | 13,497 |
| 6208 | DeLuxe wgn 4d | 2,573 | 2,130 | 6,304 |
| 6208-2 | Custom wgn 4d | 2,600 | 2,190 | 8,998 |
| 6208-5 | 400 wgn 4d | 2,692 | 2,320 | 3,134 |
| **Classic (wb 108.0)** | | | | |
| 6215 | DeLuxe sdn 4d | 2,888 | 2,050 | 38,082 |
| 6215-2 | Custom sdn 4d | 2,898 | 2,200 | 68,699 |
| 6215-5 | 400 sdn 4d | 2,853 | 2,349 | 31,255 |
| 6216 | DeLuxe sdn 4d | 2,866 | 2,000 | 14,811 |
| 6216-2 | Custom sdn 2d | 2,876 | 2,150 | 12,652 |
| 6216-5 | 400 sdn 2d | 2,841 | 2,299 | 5,521 |
| 6218 | DeLuxe wgn 4d, 6P | 3,041 | 2,380 | 28,203 |
| 6218-2 | Custom wgn 4d, 6P | 3,024 | 2,492 | 53,671 |
| 6218-4 | Custom wgn 4d, 8P | 3,094 | 2,614 | 6,322 |
| 6218-5 | 400 wgn 4d | 2,985 | 2,640 | 2,1281 |
| **Ambassador (wb 108.0)** | | | | |
| 6285 | DeLuxe sdn 4d | 3,249 | 2,336 | 421 |
| 6285-2 | Custom sdn 4d | 3,259 | 2,464 | 7,398 |
| 6285-5 | 400 sdn 4d | 3,283 | 2,605 | 15,120 |
| 6286 | DeLuxe sdn 2d | 3,227 | 2,282 | 45 |
| 6286-2 | Custom sdn 2d | 3,237 | 2,410 | 659 |
| 6286-5 | 400 sdn 2d | 3,261 | 2,551 | 459 |
| 6288 | DeLuxe wgn 4d | 3,375 | 2,648 | 77 |
| 6288-2 | Custom wgn 4d | 3,385 | 2,760 | 4,302 |
| 6288-5 | 400 wgn 4d, 6P | 3,408 | 2,901 | 6,401 |
| 6288-6 | 400 wgn 4d, 8P | 3,471 | 3,023 | 1,289 |

| 1962 Engines | bore × stroke | bhp | availability |
|---|---|---|---|
| I-6, 195.6 | 3.13×4.25 | 90 | S-American |
| I-6, 195.6 | 3.13×4.25 | 125 | O-American |
| I-6, 195.6 | 3.13×4.25 | 127 | S-Classic |
| I-6, 195.6 | 3.13×4.25 | 138 | O-Classic |
| V-8, 327.0 | 4.00×3.25 | 250 | S-Ambassador |
| V-8, 327.0 | 4.00×3.25 | 270 | O-Ambassador |

## 1963

| American (wb 100.0) | | Wght | Price | Prod |
|---|---|---|---|---|
| 6302 | 220 bus sdn 2d | 2,446 | 1,832 | 162 |
| 6304 | 220 wgn 2d | 2,528 | 2,081 | 3,312 |
| 6304-2 | 330 wgn 2d | 2,539 | 2,141 | 3,204 |
| 6305 | 220 sdn 4d | 2,485 | 1,895 | 14,419 |
| 6305-2 | 330 sdn 4d | 2,500 | 1,958 | 9,666 |
| 6305-5 | 440 sdn 4d | 2,575 | 2,089 | 2,937 |
| 6306 | 220 sdn 4d | 2,472 | 1,846 | 27,780 |
| 6306-2 | 330 sdn 2d | 2,484 | 1,909 | 9,572 |
| 6306-5 | 440 sdn 2d | 2,556 | 2,040 | 1,486 |
| 6307-5 | 440 conv cpe | 2,743 | 2,344 | 4,750 |
| 6308 | 220 wgn 4d | 2,549 | 2,130 | 4,436 |
| 6308-2 | 330 wgn 4d | 2,561 | 2,190 | 6,848 |
| 6308-5 | 440 wgn 4d | 2,638 | 2,320 | 1,874 |
| 6309-5 | 440 htp cpe | 2,550 | 2,136 | 5,101 |
| 6309-7 | 440H htp cpe | 2,567 | 2,281 | 9,749 |

# Rambler

| Classic (wb 112.0) | | Wght | Price | Prod |
|---|---|---|---|---|
| 6315 | 550 sdn 4d | 2,729 | 2,105 | 43,315 |
| 6315-2 | 660 sdn 4d | 2,740 | 2,245 | 71,646 |
| 6315-5 | 770 sdn 4d | 2,686 | 2,349 | 35,281 |
| 6316 | 550 sdn 2d | 2,720 | 2,055 | 14,417 |
| 6316-2 | 660 sdn 2d | 2,725 | 2,195 | 11,064 |
| 6316-5 | 770 sdn 2d | 2,663 | 2,299 | 5,496 |
| 6318 | 550 wgn 4d | 2,893 | 2,435 | 27,261 |
| 6318-2 | 660 wgn 4d, 6P | 2,890 | 2,537 | 46,282 |
| 6318-4 | 660 wgn 4d, 9P | 2,885 | 2,609 | 5,752 |
| 6318-5 | 770 wgn 4d | 2,828 | 2,640 | 19,319 |
| **Ambassador (wb 112.0)** | | | | |
| 6385 | 800 sdn 4d | 3,140 | 2,391 | 437 |
| 6385-2 | 880 sdn 4d | 3,145 | 2,519 | 7,667 |
| 6385-5 | 990 sdn 4d | 3,158 | 2,660 | 14,019 |
| 6386 | 800 sdn 2d | 3,110 | 2,337 | 41 |
| 6386-2 | 880 sdn 2d | 3,116 | 2,465 | 1,042 |
| 6386-5 | 990 sdn 2d | 3,132 | 2,606 | 1,764 |
| 6388 | 800 wgn 4d | 3,270 | 2,703 | 113 |
| 6388-2 | 880 wgn 4d | 3,275 | 2,815 | 4,929 |
| 6388-5 | 990 wgn 4d, 6P | 3,298 | 2,956 | 6,112 |
| 6388-6 | 990 wgn 4d, 9P | 3,305 | 3,018 | 1,687 |

| 1963 Engines | bore × stroke | bhp | availability |
|---|---|---|---|
| I-6, 195.6 | 3.13 × 4.25 | 90 | S-American 220/330; O-440 |
| I-6, 195.6 | 3.13 × 4.25 | 125 | S-American 440; O-220/330 |
| I-6, 195.6 | 3.13 × 4.25 | 127 | S-Classic |
| I-6, 195.6 | 3.13 × 4.25 | 138 | S-American 440H; O-Classic |
| V-8, 287.0 | 3.75 × 3.25 | 198 | O-Classic |
| V-8, 327.0 | 4.00 × 3.25 | 250 | S-Ambassador |
| V-8, 327.0 | 4.00 × 3.25 | 270 | O-Ambassador |

## 1964

| American (wb 106.0)—160,321 built | | Wght | Price | Prod |
|---|---|---|---|---|
| 6405 | 220 sdn 4d | 2,527 | 1,964 | — |
| 6405-2 | 330 sdn 4d | 2,526 | 2,057 | — |
| 6405-5 | 440 sdn 4d | 2,572 | 2,150 | — |
| 6406 | 220 sdn 2d | 2,506 | 1,907 | — |
| 6406-2 | 330 sdn 2d | 2,504 | 2,000 | — |
| 6407-5 | 440 conv cpe | 2,752 | 2,346 | 8,907 |
| 6408 | 220 wgn 4d | 2,661 | 2,240 | — |
| 6408-2 | 330 wgn 4d | 2,675 | 2,324 | — |
| 6409-5 | 440 htp cpe | 2,596 | 2,133 | 19,495 |
| 6409-7 | 440H htp cpe 5P | 2,617 | 2,292 | 14,527 |
| **Classic (wb 112.0)** | | | | |
| 6415 | 550 sdn 4d | 2,755 | 2,116 | 21,310 |
| 6415-2 | 660 sdn 4d | 2,758 | 2,256 | 37,584 |
| 6415-5 | 770 sdn 4d | 2,763 | 2,360 | 14,337 |
| 6416 | 550 sdn 2d | 2,732 | 2,066 | 6,454 |
| 6416-2 | 660 sdn 2d | 2,736 | 2,206 | 3,976 |
| 6416-5 | 770 sdn 2d | 2,740 | 2,310 | 1,278 |
| 6418 | 550 wgn 4d | 2,915 | 2,446 | 13,164 |
| 6418-2 | 660 wgn 4d | 2,915 | 2,548 | 26,671 |
| 6418-5 | 770 wgn 4d | 2,921 | 2,651 | 10,523 |
| 6419-5 | 770 htp cpe | 2,789 | 2,397 | 8,996 |
| 6419-7 | Typhoon htp cpe | 2,818 | 2,509 | 2,520 |
| **Ambassador 990 (wb 112.0)—18,519 built** | | | | |
| 6485-5 | sdn 4d | 3,204 | 2,671 | — |
| 6488-5 | wgn 4d | 3,350 | 2,985 | — |
| 6489-5 | htp cpe | 3,213 | 2,736 | — |
| 6489 | 990H htp cpe | 3,255 | 2,917 | — |

| 1964 Engines | bore × stroke | bhp | availability |
|---|---|---|---|
| I-6, 195.6 | 3.13 × 4.25 | 90 | S-American 220/330; O-440 |
| I-6, 195.6 | 3.13 × 4.25 | 125 | S-American 440; O-220/330 |
| I-6, 195.6 | 3.13 × 4.25 | 127 | S-Classic |
| I-6, 195.6 | 3.13 × 4.25 | 138 | S-American 440H; O-Clsc exc Typhoon |
| I-6, 232.0 | 3.75 × 3.50 | 145 | S-Typhoon; O-other Classic |
| V-8, 287.0 | 3.75 × 3.25 | 198 | O-Classic |
| V-8, 327.0 | 4.00 × 3.25 | 250 | S-Ambassador exc 990H |
| V-8, 327.0 | 4.00 × 3.25 | 270 | S-Amb 990H; O-other Amb |

## 1965

| American (wb 106.0) | | Wght | Price | Prod |
|---|---|---|---|---|
| 6505 | 220 sdn 4d | 2,518 | 2,036 | 13,700 |
| 6505-2 | 330 sdn 4d | 2,522 | 2,129 | 15,433 |
| 6505-5 | 440 sdn 4d | 2,580 | 2,222 | 5,194 |
| 6506 | 220 sdn 2d | 2,492 | 1,979 | 26,409 |
| 6506-2 | 330 sdn 2d | 2,490 | 2,072 | 9,065 |
| 6507-5 | 440 conv cpe | 2,747 | 2,418 | 3,882 |
| 6508 | 220 wgn 4d | 2,684 | 2,312 | 5,224 |
| 6508-2 | 330 wgn 4d | 2,682 | 2,396 | 12,313 |
| 6509-5 | 440 htp cpe | 2,596 | 2,205 | 13,784 |
| 6509-7 | 440H htp cpe | 2,622 | 2,327 | 8,164 |
| **Classic 550 (wb 112.0)** | | | | |
| 6515 | sdn 4d | 2,987 | 2,192 | 30,869 |
| 6516 | sdn 2d | 2,963 | 2,142 | 7,082 |
| 6518 | wgn 4d | 3,134 | 2,522 | 13,759 |
| **Classic 660 (wb 112.0)** | | | | |
| 6515-2 | sdn 4d | 3,016 | 2,332 | 50,638 |
| 6516-2 | sdn 2d | 2,991 | 2,282 | 4,561 |
| 6518-2 | wgn 4d | 3,155 | 2,624 | 32,444 |
| **Classic 770 (wb 112.0)** | | | | |
| 6515-5 | sdn 4d | 3,029 | 2,436 | 23,603 |
| 6517-5 | conv cpe | 3,169 | 2,696 | 4,953 |
| 6518-5 | wgn 4d | 3,180 | 2,727 | 15,623 |
| 6519-5 | htp cpe | 3,063 | 2,436 | 14,778 |
| 6519-7 | 770H htp cpe | 3,089 | 2,548 | 5,706 |
| **Marlin (wb 112.0)** | | | | |
| 6559-7 | fastbk htp cpe | 3,234 | 3,100 | 10,327 |
| **Ambassador (wb 116.0)** | | | | |
| 6585-2 | 880 sdn 4d | 3,120 | 2,565 | 10,564 |
| 6585-5 | 990 sdn 4d | 3,151 | 2,656 | 24,852 |
| 6586-2 | 880 sdn 2d | 3,087 | 2,512 | 1,301 |
| 6587-5 | 990 conv cpe | 3,265 | 2,955 | 3,499 |
| 6588-2 | 880 wgn 4d | 3,247 | 2,879 | 3,812 |
| 6588-5 | 990 wgn 4d | 3,268 | 2,970 | 8,701 |
| 6589-5 | 990 htp cpe | 3,168 | 2,669 | 5,034 |
| 6589-7 | 990H htp cpe | 3,198 | 2,837 | 6,382 |

| 1965 Engines | bore × stroke | bhp | availability |
|---|---|---|---|
| I-6, 195.6 | 3.13 × 4.25 | 90 | S-American 220/330 |
| I-6, 195.6 | 3.13 × 4.25 | 125 | S-American 440/440H |
| I-6, 199.0 | 3.75 × 3.00 | 128 | S-Classic 550 |
| I-6, 232.0 | 3.75 × 3.25 | 145 | S-Classic 660/770/770H, Marlin; O-Amb, American |

# Rambler

| 1965 Engines | bore × stroke | bhp | availability |
|---|---|---|---|
| I-6, 232.0 | 3.75 × 3.25 | 155 | S-Amb; O-Classic |
| V-8, 287.0 | 3.75 × 3.25 | 198 | O-Classic, Marlin, Amb |
| V-8, 327.0 | 4.00 × 3.25 | 270 | O-Classic, Marlin, Amb |

## 1966

| American 220 (wb 106) | | Wght | Price | Prod |
|---|---|---|---|---|
| 6605 | sdn 4d | 2,574 | 2,086 | 15,940 |
| 6606 | sdn 2d | 2,554 | 2,017 | 24,440 |
| 6608 | wgn 4d | 2,740 | 2,369 | 5,809 |
| **American 440 (wb 106.0)** | | | | |
| 6605-5 | sdn 4d | 2,582 | 2,203 | 14,543 |
| 6606-5 | sdn 2d | 2,562 | 2,134 | 5,252 |
| 6607-5 | conv cpe | 2,782 | 2,486 | 2,092 |
| 6608-5 | wgn 4d | 2,745 | 2,477 | 6,603 |
| 6609-5 | htp cpe | 2,610 | 2,227 | 10,255 |
| **Rogue (wb 106.0)** | | | | |
| 6609-7 | htp cpe | 2,630 | 2,370 | 8,718 |
| **Classic 550 (wb 112.0)** | | | | |
| 6615 | sdn 4d | 2,885 | 2,238 | 22,485 |
| 6616 | sdn 2d | 2,860 | 2,189 | 5,505 |
| 6618 | wgn 4d | 3,070 | 2,542 | 9,390 |
| **Classic 770 (wb 112.0)** | | | | |
| 6615-5 | sdn 4d | 2,905 | 2,337 | 46,044 |
| 6617-5 | conv cpe | 3,070 | 2,616 | 1,806 |
| 6618-5 | wgn 4d | 3,071 | 2,629 | 24,528 |
| 6619-5 | htp cpe | 2,935 | 2,363 | 8,736 |
| **Rebel (wb 112.0)** | | | | |
| 6618-7 | htp cpe | 2,950 | 2,523 | 7,512 |

| 1966 Engines | bore × stroke | bhp | availability |
|---|---|---|---|
| I-6, 199.0 | 3.75 × 3.00 | 128 | S-American, Rogue |
| I-6, 232.0 | 3.75 × 3.50 | 145 | S-Classic, Rebel |
| I-6, 232.0 | 3.75 × 3.50 | 155 | O-all |
| V-8, 287.0 | 3.75 × 3.25 | 198 | O-Classic, Rebel |
| V-8, 290.0 | 3.75 × 3.28 | 200 | O-American |
| V-8, 290.0 | 3.75 × 3.28 | 225 | O-American |
| V-8, 327.0 | 4.00 × 3.25 | 250 | O-Classic, Rebel |
| V-8, 327.0 | 4.00 × 3.25 | 270 | O-Classic, Rebel |

## 1967

| American 220 (wb 106.0) | | Wght | Price | Prod |
|---|---|---|---|---|
| 6705 | sdn 4d | 2,621 | 2,142 | 12,078 |
| 6706 | sdn 2d | 2,591 | 2,073 | 26,196 |
| 6708 | wgn 4d | 2,767 | 2,425 | 3,667 |
| **American 440 (wb 106.0)** | | | | |
| 6705-5 | sdn 4d | 2,613 | 2,259 | 10,083 |
| 6706-5 | sdn 2d | 2,586 | 2,191 | 3,317 |
| 6708-5 | wgn 4d | 2,769 | 2,533 | 4,407 |
| 6709-5 | htp cpe | 2,643 | 2,283 | 4,994 |
| **Rogue (wb 106.0)** | | | | |
| 6707-7 | conv cpe | 2,821 | 2,611 | 921 |
| 6709-7 | htp cpe | 2,663 | 2,426 | 4,249 |
| **Rebel 550 (wb 114.0)** | | | | |
| 6715 | sdn 4d | 3,055 | 2,319 | 10,582 |
| 6716 | sdn 2d | 3,089 | 2,294 | 9,121 |
| 6718 | wgn 4d | 3,287 | 2,623 | 6,845 |
| **Rebel 770 (wb 114.0)** | | | | |
| 6715-5 | sdn 4d | 3,053 | 2,418 | 27,457 |
| 6718-5 | wgn 4d | 3,288 | 2,710 | 18,552 |
| 6719-5 | htp cpe | 3,092 | 2,443 | 9,721 |
| **Rebel SST (wb 114.0)** | | | | |
| 6717-7 | conv cpe | 3,180 | 2,872 | 1,686 |
| 6719-7 | htp cpe | 3,109 | 2,604 | 16,663 |

| 1967 Engines | bore × stroke | bhp | availability |
|---|---|---|---|
| I-6, 199.0 | 3.75 × 3.00 | 128 | S-American |
| I-6, 232.0 | 3.75 × 3.25 | 145 | S-Rebel; O-American |
| I-6, 232.0 | 3.75 × 3.25 | 155 | O-American, Rebel |
| V-8, 290.0 | 3.75 × 3.28 | 200 | O-American, Rebel |
| V-8, 290.0 | 3.75 × 3.28 | 225 | O-American |
| V-8, 343.0 | 4.08 × 3.28 | 235 | O-Rebel |
| V-8, 343.0 | 4.08 × 3.28 | 280 | O-Rebel |

## 1968

| American (wb 106.0) | | Wght | Price | Prod |
|---|---|---|---|---|
| 6805 | sdn 4d | 2,638 | 2,024 | 15,144 |
| 6806 | sdn 2d | 2,604 | 1,946 | 39,480 |
| **American 440 (wb 106.0)** | | | | |
| 6805-5 | sdn 4d | 2,643 | 2,166 | 11,179 |
| 6808-5 | wgn 4d | 2,800 | 2,426 | 10,414 |
| **Rogue (wb 106.0)** | | | | |
| 6809-7 | htp cpe | 2,678 | 2,244 | 4,765 |

| 1968 Engines | bore × stroke | bhp | availability |
|---|---|---|---|
| I-6, 199.0 | 3.75 × 3.00 | 128 | S-American |
| I-6, 232.0 | 3.75 × 3.50 | 145 | S-Rogue; O-American |
| V-8, 290.0 | 3.75 × 3.28 | 200 | O-American |
| V-8, 290.0 | 3.75 × 3.28 | 225 | O-American, Rogue |

## 1969

| American (wb 106.0) | | Wght | Price | Prod |
|---|---|---|---|---|
| 6905 | sdn 4d | 2,638 | 2,076 | 16,234 |
| 6906 | sdn 2d | 2,604 | 1,998 | 51,062 |
| **American 440 (wb 106.0)** | | | | |
| 6905-5 | sdn 4d | 2,643 | 2,218 | 11,957 |
| 6908-5 | wgn 4d | 2,800 | 2,478 | 13,233 |
| **Rogue (wb 106.0)** | | | | |
| 6909-7 | htp cpe | 2,678 | 2,296 | 3,543 |
| **SC/Rambler-Hurst (wb 106.0)** | | | | |
| 6909-7 | htp cpe | 3,160 | 2,998 | 1,512 |

| 1969 Engines | bore × stroke | bhp | availability |
|---|---|---|---|
| I-6, 199.0 | 3.75 × 3.00 | 128 | S-American |
| I-6, 232.0 | 3.75 × 3.50 | 145 | S-Rogue; O-American |
| V-8, 290.0 | 3.75 × 3.28 | 200 | O-Rogue, American 440 |
| V-8, 290.0 | 3.75 × 3.28 | 225 | O-Rogue |
| V-8, 390.0 | 4.17 × 3.57 | 315 | S-SC/Rambler-Hurst |

Note: See Nash listing for Rambler models prior to 1957. See AMC listing for related 1966-69 models, and those built after 1969.

# Reo

Reo resulted from a 1904 argument at Olds Motor Works, the first car company founded by the tenacious Ransom Eli Olds. When colleagues began pressuring him to build four- and six-cylinder models that were more substantial than his little Curved-Dash Oldsmobile, Ransom ventured down the street to set up a rival concern. By year's end, this new R.E. Olds Company was called Reo Motor Car Company, after his initials. Ransom got his "revenge": through 1917, Reo outproduced Olds Motor Works.

From the company's beginning to 1919, Reo fielded one-, two-, four-, and six-cylinder cars. The firm's all-time production record, 29,000, came in 1928, by which time Reo was selling sixes only. After seeing car sales fall almost 30 percent in calendar-year 1929, Reo posted a $2 million loss on 1930 volume of about 12,500 cars and a like number of trucks. The Depression had hit, and Reo was mortally wounded. But even though the company never sold more than 5000 cars a year after 1932, some of those it did sell were memorable, and among the handsomest automobiles ever created.

The Flying Cloud Sixes of 1930 were little changed from 1929. That year's junior Reo was the 115-inch-wheelbase Model 15, basically the previous year's low-priced Flying Cloud Mate with the same 60-bhp, 214.7-cubic-inch Continental engine. Senior models, now called Flying Cloud Master, comprised the 120-inch Model 20 and 124-inch "25" powered by a 268.3-cid Reo engine with 80 bhp. Prices were in the upper-middle bracket at $1175-$1870 (after Depression-prompted cuts). Styling, by the talented and once unappreciated Amos Northup, was classic, formal, and finely proportioned. Workmanship was solid, furnishings top-quality.

January 1931 brought an expanded line that ultimately offered two new straight-eights. Model nomenclature denoted cylinders and wheelbase. The larger eight, delivering 125 bhp from 358 cid, was reserved for magnificent new 8-35 Royales on a strong double-drop frame with 135-inch wheelbase. It also powered companion 8-30 Flying Clouds. Anchoring the line was the new 6-25 with 85-bhp 268 six, selling at around $1800.

The Royale premiered at $2495 with three closed Murray-built bodies. All were smooth and truly beautiful, Northup pointing the way for everyone else with skirted fenders, rounded corners, and raked-back radiators. The 8-30 and 6-25 wore a more-conservative version of this look. Reo also announced an immense new 152-inch Royale chassis for custom coachwork by Dietrich, comprising an imposing seven-passenger limousine and three convertibles. But apart from show models, few of those opulent Reos were ever built. Though all Royales had effortless performance with their big nine-main-bearing engine, they were hardly appropriate for hard economic times.

Reo spent $6 million on these initial 1931 models, hoping to spark sales. When sales failed to ignite, the firm threw additional variations at the market: a Royale 8-31; the Flying Cloud 8-25, with a new 90-bhp eight not much bigger than Reo's six; and the 6-21, really a 6-25 downpriced to the $995-$1100 region. But none of these caught on either, and Reo lost nearly $3 million on sales of just 6762 cars.

Still trying hard, Reo unveiled a smaller Flying Cloud in January 1932, the 117-inch-wheelbase 6-S. Carrying a debored 230-cid six with 80 bhp, this new entry-level line listed nine open and closed models in Standard and DeLuxe trim for $995-$1205. Eight-cylinder Clouds returned virtually without change. So did Royales, but the 8-31 and 8-35 were now nameless, and 8-52s were retagged Royale Custom. Of course, everything hinged on the 6-S, but it failed to make the needed impression, and Reo car sales fell to 3900 for the calendar year. Desperately seeking cash, the firm agreed to sell 6-S bodies and chassis to equally beleaguered Franklin for that company's 1933 Olympic, which was nearly identical except for grille, hood, and air-cooled Franklin power.

**1931/32 Royale four-door sedan**

With all this, Reo had no choice but to drastically cut its 1933 line. Thus, Flying Cloud Eights vanished in January. So did the 6-25, though its engine returned in a new low-end S-2 Flying Cloud that replaced the 6-S on an inch-longer wheelbase. The longest chassis was also dropped, leaving N-2 standard and Elite Royales on the 131-inch platform and N-1 Customs on the 135-inch chassis. Prices were cut too, but the cuts weren't enough to matter. Despite smoother styling and sturdier new X-member frames, Reo's calendar-year registrations fell to 3623, the lowest on record.

Most 1934 Reos appeared in July and September of 1933, essentially carryovers save more deeply skirted fenders and an eye-catching array of six vents per hoodside. Headlining the "real" "34s, unveiled in April, was the new S-4 Flying Cloud with nice streamlining and an optional built-in trunk for four-door sedans, though most everything else was continued from the S-2 and interim S-3 models.

Arriving in May 1933 was the "Self-Shifter," a new freebie for Royales and an $85 extra for S-4s. This was a semiautomatic transmission developed at a cost of about $2 million amidst mounting corporate finacial losses. Innovative and dependable, the Self-Shifter replaced the conventional gearlever with an under-dash T-handle. Pushing the handle to "Forward" brought access to a pair of driving gears that changed automatically according to road speed. You pulled the handle halfway out for Neutral, all the way out for "emergency low," which also had two automatic ratios. For Reverse, turn the handle right, then pull out. The clutch pedal was used only for starting off. Nice though this was, the Self-Shifter attracted few buyers. But surprisingly, Reo's calendar-1934 car output was slightly higher at 4460, and truck sales jumped a startling 70 percent.

Some experts cite the Self-Shifter's development cost as a key factor in Reo's demise, but management turmoil since the Great Crash also contributed. When Ransom Olds moved up to board chairman in 1923, new president Richard Scott greatly expanded production, which left Reo with money-losing excess capacity when the Depression severely shrunk the medium-price market. At Old's insistence, Scott was replaced in 1930 by William Wilson, an executive of the Murray Body Company. But when Wilson couldn't halt the sales slide, Scott got another chance. That angered Olds, yet Scott's supporters were entrenched, prompting the founder to resign in December 1933. That shook up embattled Reo stockholders, who persuaded Olds to return the following April and elected Donald E. Bates as president. Hopes were high that things would turn around.

Meanwhile, the S-4 continued into 1935 as the little-changed S-5, and Eights gave way to a lowly S-7 Royale Six coupe and sedan, essentially S-5s with a 95-bhp engine selling for $985. Both were gone by early 1936, a sorry end for the once-mighty Royale.

But somehow, Reo managed yet another new Flying Cloud for 1935. Designated A-6, this offered two- and four-door Hayes-built fastback sedans with 115-inch wheelbase and a superior new 90-bhp 228-cid six with seven main bearings, aluminum head, automatic choke, and external vibration damper. Front styling vaguely recalled Auburn, with flared fenders and vee'd bumper. For all that, Ransom Olds disliked the A-6, calling its $450,000 tooling cost a waste of money. But as at Olds Motor Works long before, his colleagues disagreed, and they pushed ahead for '36. They were doubtless encouraged by Reo's first profit in years, a slim $42,156 for the first half of 1935 on meager sales of cars and trucks. Still seeking to bolster income, the firm shared its body dies with erstwhile rival, Graham-Paige.

Reo announced "America's Finest Six" in November 1935, but it was just an A-6 with fuller fenders, rubber-tipped bumper guards, optional "Zeppelin-style" fender lamps, and a reworked hood and radiator wearing bright trim *a la* Pontiac's "Silver Streaks." The Self-Shifter was canned for conventional overdrive as a $50 extra for standard and DeLuxe models priced at $795-$895. But public confidence in Reo had nearly evaporated, so the firm built a mere 3206 cars that year, versus 4692 for calendar-year 1935.

With trucks now far more profitable than cars (the G-P deal had produced little revenue), the Reo board voted on May 18, 1936, to move truck assembly into the main Lansing plant; on September 3rd, Reo officially left the auto business. Though the company lost nearly $1.4 million on its 1936 cars, it was able to write off $604,000 for terminating its auto operations. Reo then turned exclusively to the truck field. Ironically, it would thrive there far longer than it had with cars, producing for the next 40 or so years under the Reo and Diamond-Reo nameplates.

## Specifications

### 1930

| Model C Flying Cloud Master (wb 120) | Wght | Price | Prod |
|---|---|---|---|
| rdstr 2-4P | 3,380 | 1,685 | — |
| cpe 2P | 3,465 | 1,625 | — |
| spt cpe 2-4P | 3,615 | 1,750 | — |
| victoria 4P | 3,550 | 1,695 | — |
| spt victoria 4P | 3,715 | 1,820 | — |
| brougham 2d | 3,540 | 1,595 | — |
| spt brougham 2d | 3,675 | 1,720 | — |
| sdn 4d | 3,665 | 1,745 | — |
| DeLuxe sdn 4d | 3,800 | 1,870 | — |
| spt rdstr 2-4P | 3,570 | 1,810 | — |
| **Model B-2 Flying Cloud (wb 115.0)** | | | |
| phtn 5P | — | 1,395 | — |
| spt phtn 5P 6W | — | 1,595 | — |
| Standard cpe 2P | 3,170 | 1,375 | — |
| Standard cpe 2P 5W | 3,180 | 1,435 | — |
| Standard cpe 2-4P | 3,220 | 1,395 | — |
| Standard cpe 2-4P 6W | 3,230 | 1,455 | — |

| Model B-2 Flying Cloud | Wght | Price | Prod |
|---|---|---|---|
| spt cpe 2-4P | 3,325 | 1,495 | — |
| Standard sdn 4d 5W | 3,280 | 1,395 | — |
| Standard sdn 4d 6W | 3,300 | 1,455 | — |
| spt sdn 4d | 3,390 | 1,495 | — |
| **Model 20 Flying Cloud (wb 120.0)—2,189 built** | | | |
| Standard cpe 2-4P | 3,635 | 1,595 | — |
| spt cpe 2-4P | 3,720 | 1,705 | — |
| Standard sdn 4d | 3,700 | 1,595 | — |
| spt sdn 4d | 3,785 | 1,705 | — |
| **Model 25 Flying Cloud Master (wb 124.0)—2,128 built** | | | |
| Standard sdn 4d | 3,795 | 1,795 | — |
| spt sdn 4d | 3,945 | 1,905 | — |
| **Model 15 Flying Cloud (wb 115.0)—1,789 built** | | | |
| Standard phtn 5P | 3,050 | 1,195 | — |
| spt phtn 5P | 3,140 | 1,238 | — |
| Standard cpe 2P | 3,110 | 1,175 | — |
| spt cpe 2P | 3,200 | 1,218 | — |
| Standard cpe 2-4P | 3,170 | 1,195 | — |
| spt cpe 2-4P | 3,260 | 1,238 | — |

# Reo

| Model 15 Flying Cloud | Wght | Price | Prod |
|---|---|---|---|
| Standard sdn 4d | 3,300 | 1,295 | — |
| spt sdn 4d | 3,370 | 1,338 | — |

| 1930 Engines | bore×stroke | bhp | availability |
|---|---|---|---|
| I-6, 214.7 | 3.38×4.00 | 60 | S-B-2, 15 |
| I-6, 268.3 | 3.38×5.00 | 80 | S-C, 20, 25 |

## 1931

| Model 15 Flying Cloud (wb 115) | Wght | Price | Prod |
|---|---|---|---|
| Standard phtn 5P | 3,050 | 1,195 | — |
| spt phtn 5P | 3,140 | 1,238 | — |
| Standard cpe 2P | 3,110 | 1,175 | — |
| spt cpe 2P | 3,200 | 1,218 | — |
| Standard cpe 2-4P | 3,170 | 1,195 | — |
| spt cpe 2-4P | 3,260 | 1,238 | — |
| Standard sdn 4d | 3,300 | 1,295 | — |
| spt sdn 4d | 3,370 | 1,338 | — |
| **Model 20 Flying Cloud (wb 120.0)** | | | |
| Standard cpe 2-4P | 3,635 | 1,595 | — |
| spt cpe 2-4P | 3,720 | 1,705 | — |
| Standard sdn 4d | 3,700 | 1,595 | — |
| spt sdn 4d | 3,785 | 1,705 | — |
| **Model 25 Flying Cloud (wb 124.0)** | | | |
| Standard sdn 4d | 3,795 | 1,795 | — |
| spt sdn 4d | 3,945 | 1,905 | — |
| **Model 21 Flying Cloud Six (wb 121.0)** | | | |
| cpe 2P | 3,645 | 1,295 | — |
| Custom spt cpe 2-4P | 3,800 | 1,410 | — |
| sdn 4d | 3,495 | 1,295 | — |
| Custom spt sdn 4d | 3,630 | 1,410 | — |
| **Model 21 Flying Cloud Eight (wb 121.0)** | | | |
| cpe 2P | 3,740 | 1,395 | — |
| Custom spt cpe 2-4P | 3,845 | 1,510 | — |
| sdn 4d | 3,685 | 1,395 | — |
| Custom spt sdn 4d | 3,725 | 1,510 | — |
| **Model 25 Flying Cloud Six (wb 124.0/125.0)** | | | |
| cpe 2-4P | 3,895 | 1,695 | — |
| victoria 4P | 3,880 | 1,695 | — |
| sdn 4d | 3,950 | 1,695 | — |
| **Model 25 Flying Cloud Eight (wb 125.0)** | | | |
| cpe 2-4P | 3,841 | 1,745 | — |
| victoria 5P | 3,904 | 1,745 | — |
| sdn 4d | 4,050 | 1,745 | — |
| **Model 830 Flying Cloud Eight (wb 130.0)** | | | |
| cpe 2-4P | 4,380 | 1,995 | — |
| victoria 4P | 4,400 | 1,995 | — |
| sdn 4d | 4,500 | 1,995 | — |
| **Model 831 Royale (wb 131.0)** | | | |
| cpe 2-4P | 4,310 | 2,145 | — |
| victoria 4P | 4,320 | 2,145 | — |
| sdn 4d | 4,375 | 2,145 | — |
| **Model 835 Royale (wb 135.0)** | | | |
| cpe 2-4P | 4,500 | 2,745 | — |
| victoria 4P | 4,475 | 2,745 | — |
| sdn 4d | 4,650 | 2,745 | — |

| 1931 Engines | bore×stroke | bhp | availability |
|---|---|---|---|
| I-6, 214.7 | 3.38×4.00 | 60 | S-15 |
| I-6, 268.3 | 3.38×5.00 | 80 | S-20, 25 |
| I-6, 268.3 | 3.38×5.00 | 85 | S-21 |
| I-8, 268.6 | 3.00×4.75 | 90 | S-21, 25 |
| I-8, 358.0 | 3.38×5.00 | 125 | S-830, 831, 835 |

## 1932

| Model 6-21 Flying Cloud (wb 121) | Wght | Price | Prod |
|---|---|---|---|
| cpe 2-4P | 3,495 | 995 | — |
| spt cpe 2-4P | 3,630 | 1,110 | — |
| sdn 4d | 3,645 | 995 | — |
| spt sdn 4d | 3,800 | 1,110 | — |
| **Model 6-25 Flying Cloud (wb 125.0)** | | | |
| victoria 5P | 3,880 | 1,565 | — |
| sdn 4d | 3,950 | 1,565 | — |
| cpe 2-4P | 3,895 | 1,565 | — |
| **Model 6-S Flying Cloud (wb 117.0)(from 4/32)** | | | |
| Standard cpe 2-4P | 3,300 | 995 | — |
| Standard conv cpe 2-4P | 3,220 | 1,045 | — |
| Standard sdn 4d | 3,405 | 995 | — |
| spt cpe 2-4P | 3,445 | 1,070 | — |
| spt conv cpe 2-4P | 3,360 | 1,120 | — |
| spt sdn 4d | 3,510 | 1,070 | — |
| DeLuxe spt cpe 2-4P | — | 1,155 | — |
| DeLuxe spt conv cpe 2-4P | — | 1,205 | — |
| DeLuxe spt sdn 4d | — | 1,155 | — |
| **Model 8-21 Flying Cloud (wb 121.0)** | | | |
| cpe 2-4P | 3,685 | 1,195 | — |
| spt cpe 2-4P | 3,725 | 1,310 | — |
| sdn 4d | 3,740 | 1,195 | — |
| spt sdn 4d | 3,845 | 1,310 | — |
| **Model 8-25 Flying Cloud (wb 125.0)** | | | |
| cpe 2-4P | 3,841 | 1,565 | — |
| victoria 5P | 3,904 | 1,565 | — |
| sdn 4d | 4,050 | 1,565 | — |
| **Model 8-31 Royale (wb 131.0)** | | | |
| cpe 2-4P | 4,310 | 1,985 | — |
| victoria 4P | 4,320 | 1,985 | — |
| sdn 4d | 4,375 | 1,985 | — |
| **Model 8-35-52 Royale (wb 135.0; lwb-152.0)** | | | |
| cpe 2-4P | 4,500 | 2,445 | — |
| victoria 5P | 4,475 | 2,445 | — |
| sdn 4d | 4,650 | 2,445 | — |
| lwb sdn 7P | 5,010 | 3,695 | — |
| lwb sdn 7P partition | 5,075 | 3,895 | — |
| **Model RYL Royale (131.0) (from 4/32)** | | | |
| cpe 2-4P | 4,310 | 1,785 | — |
| victoria 4P | 4,320 | 1,785 | — |
| sdn 4d | 4,375 | 1,785 | — |
| **Royale Custom (wb 135.0; lwb-152.0) (from 4/32)** | | | |
| cpe 2-4P | 4,500 | 2,445 | — |
| victoria 5P | 4,475 | 2,445 | — |
| conv cpe 2-4P | 4,440 | 2,995 | — |
| sdn 4d | 4,650 | 2,445 | — |
| lwb sdn 7P | 5,010 | 3,695 | — |
| lwb berline 7P | 5,075 | 3,895 | — |

| 1932 Engines | bore×stroke | bhp | availability |
|---|---|---|---|
| I-6, 230.0 | 3.13×5.00 | 80 | S-6-S |
| I-6, 268.3 | 3.38×5.00 | 80 | S-6-25 |
| I-6, 268.3 | 3.38×5.00 | 85 | S-6-21 |
| I-8, 268.6 | 3.00×4.75 | 90 | S-8-21, 8-25 |
| I-8, 358.0 | 3.38×5.00 | 125 | S-all Royale |

## 1933

| Model 6-S Flying Cloud (wb 117)—615 blt | Wght | Price | Prod |
|---|---|---|---|
| cpe 2-4P | 3,300 | 995 | — |
| conv cpe 2-4P | 3,220 | 1,045 | — |
| sdn 4d | 3,405 | 995 | — |
| spt cpe 2-4P | 3,445 | 1,070 | — |
| spt conv cpe 2-4P | — | 1,120 | — |
| spt sdn 4d | 3,510 | 1,070 | — |
| DeLuxe spt cpe 2-4P | — | 1,155 | — |
| DeLuxe spt conv cpe 2-4P | — | 1,205 | — |
| DeLuxe spt sdn 4d | — | 1,155 | — |
| cabriolet 2-4P | 3,710 | 1,250 | — |

| Model S-2 Flying Cloud Six (wb 118.0) | Wght | Price | Prod |
|---|---|---|---|
| cpe 2-4P | 3,450 | 995 | |
| Elite cpe 2-4P | 3,515 | 1,090 | |
| conv cpe 2-4P | 3,390 | 1,045 | 2,099* |
| Elite conv cpe 2-4P | 3,490 | 1,140 | |
| sdn 4d | 3,540 | 995 | |
| Elite sdn 4d | 3,645 | 1,090 | |

*Includes 1934 S-2.

| Royale (wb 131.0)—121 built | | | |
|---|---|---|---|
| cpe 2-4P | 4,310 | 1,785 | — |
| victoria 5P | 4,320 | 1,785 | — |
| sdn 4d | 4,375 | 1,785 | — |

| Royale Eight (wb 131.0; lwb-135.0) | | | |
|---|---|---|---|
| N-2 Standard cpe 2-4P | — | 1,745 | |
| N-2 Standard victoria 5P | 4,500 | 1,745 | |
| N-2 Standard sdn 4d | 4,725 | 1,745 | 1,150 |
| N-2 Elite cpe 2-4P | — | 1,845 | |
| N-2 Elite victoria 5P | 4,625 | 1,845 | |
| N-2 Elite sdn 4d | 4,850 | 1,845 | |
| N-1 Custom lwb cpe 2-4P | 4,540 | 2,445 | — |
| N-1 Custom lwb victoria 5P | 4,515 | 2,445 | — |
| N-1 Custom lwb sdn 4d | 4,690 | 2,445 | — |

| Royale Custom Eight (wb 135.0; lwb-152.0)—127 built | | | |
|---|---|---|---|
| cpe 2-4P | 4,500 | 2,445 | — |
| conv cpe 2-4P | 4,440 | 2,995 | — |
| victoria 5P | 4,475 | 2,445 | — |
| sdn 4d | 4,650 | 2,445 | — |
| lwb sdn 7P | 5,010 | 3,695 | — |
| lwb sdn brougham 7P | 5,075 | 3,895 | — |

| 1933 Engines | bore×stroke | bhp | availability |
|---|---|---|---|
| I-6, 268.3 | 3.38×5.00 | 85 | S-sixes |
| I-8, 358.0 | 3.38×5.00 | 125 | S-eights |

## 1934

| S-2 Flying Cloud Six (wb 118.0) | Wght | Price | Prod |
|---|---|---|---|
| cpe 2-4P | 3,500 | 845 | |
| Elite cpe 2-4P | 3,563 | 920 | |
| conv cpe 2-4P | 3,440 | 1,045 | 2,099** |
| Elite conv cpe 2-4P | 3,540 | 1,140 | |
| sdn 4d | 3,590 | 845 | |
| Elite sdn 4d | 3,695 | 920 | |

**Includes 1933 S-2.

| S-3 Flying Cloud Six (wb 118.0) | | | |
|---|---|---|---|
| cpe 2-4P | 3,500 | 795 | — |
| sdn 4d | 3,590 | 795 | — |

| S-4 Flying Cloud Six (wb 118.0) (from April 1934) | | | |
|---|---|---|---|
| bus cpe 2P | — | 795 | — |
| cpe 2-4P | 3,510 | 895 | — |
| conv cpe 2-4P | — | 925 | — |
| sdn 4d | 3,630 | 895 | — |

| S-4 Flying Cloud Six | Wght | Price | Prod |
|---|---|---|---|
| DeL cpe 2-4P | 3,530 | 945 | — |
| DeL conv cpe 2-4P | — | 975 | — |
| DeL sdn 4d | 3,650 | 945 | — |
| DeL cpe 2-4P 6W | 3,605 | 995 | — |
| DeL sdn 4d 6W | 3,725 | 995 | — |

| N-2 Royale Eight (wb 131.0) | | | |
|---|---|---|---|
| cpe 2-4P | 4,640 | 1,500 | — |
| Elite cpe 2-4P | 4,790 | 1,600 | — |
| victoria 5P | 4,730 | 1,500 | — |
| Elite victoria 5P | 4,815 | 1,600 | — |
| sdn 4d | 4,765 | 1,500 | — |
| Elite sdn 4d | 4,955 | 1,600 | — |

| N-1 Royale Custom Eight (wb 135.0) | | | |
|---|---|---|---|
| Elite cpe 2-4P | 4,825 | 1,700 | — |
| Elite victoria 5P | 4,915 | 1,700 | — |
| Elite sdn 4d | 5,015 | 1,700 | — |

| 1934 Engines | bore×stroke | bhp | availability |
|---|---|---|---|
| I-6, 268.3 | 3.38×5.00 | 85 | S-sixes |
| I-8, 358.0 | 3.38×5.00 | 125 | S-eights |

## 1935

| S-5 Flying Cloud Six (wb 118.0) | Wght | Price | Prod |
|---|---|---|---|
| bus cpe 2P | 3,445 | 795 | — |
| Standard cpe 2-4P | 3,510 | 895 | — |
| DeLuxe cpe 2-4P 5W | 3,530 | 945 | — |
| DeLuxe cpe 2-4P 6W | 3,605 | 995 | — |
| Standard conv cpe 2-4P | 3,495 | 895 | — |
| DeLuxe conv cpe 2-4P 5W | 3,515 | 975 | — |
| DeLuxe conv cpe 2-4P 6W | 3,590 | 1,025 | — |
| Standard sdn 4d | 3,630 | 895 | — |
| DeLuxe sdn 4d 5W | 3,650 | 945 | — |
| DeLuxe sdn 4d 6W | 3,725 | 995 | — |

| A-6 Flying Cloud Six (wb 115.0)—(from Jan. 1935) | | | |
|---|---|---|---|
| 6AB sdn 2d | 3,190 | 795 | — |
| 6AS sdn 4d | 3,220 | 845 | — |

| S-7 Royale Six (wb 118.0) | | | |
|---|---|---|---|
| 7SC cpe 3-5P | 3,550 | 985 | — |
| 7SS sdn 4d | 3,595 | 985 | — |

* Production not available

| 1935 Engines | bore×stroke | bhp | availability |
|---|---|---|---|
| I-6, 228.0 | 3.38×4.25 | 90 | S-A-6 |
| I-6, 268.3 | 3.38×5.00 | 85 | S-S-5 |
| I-6, 268.3 | 3.38×5.00 | 95 | S-S-7 |

## 1936

| Flying Cloud Six (wb 115.0) | Wght | Price | Prod |
|---|---|---|---|
| sdn 2d | 3,270 | 795 | — |
| sdn 4d | 3,300 | 845 | — |

| 6-75 Flying Cloud DeLuxe (wb 118.0) | | | |
|---|---|---|---|
| brougham 2d | 3,560 | 845 | — |
| sdn 4d | 3,595 | 895 | — |
| touring sdn 4d T/B | 3,625 | 895 | — |

| 1936 Engines | bore×stroke | bhp | availability |
|---|---|---|---|
| I-6, 228.0 | 3.38×4.25 | 90 | S-Six |
| I-6, 268.3 | 3.38×5.00 | 95 | S-6-75 |

**Reo Calendar Year Production 1930-1936**

1930.....11,450  1933.....3,623  1935.....4,692
1931.....6,762   1934.....4,460  1936.....3,206
1932.....3,870

# Saturn

General Motors' first new nameplate in over 60 years was born in 1982 as Project Saturn. Conceived in part by then-chairman Roger Smith, it was an all-out effort to stem the growing Japanese dominance of the U.S. small-car market that had begun in the early '70s. Smith realized that although GM was highly successful with traditional American cars, it badly lagged behind Japanese makers for small-car quality, design, and cost. As a result, younger buyers were deserting GM's smaller U.S. products for Hondas, Toyotas, and other Japanese models—and they weren't coming back.

More than eight years passed before the first Saturns were sold. For some, that long gestation reinforced doubts that GM could field a competitive, profitable, all-American small car—especially given recent efforts like the problem-plagued X-body front-drive compacts. Heady pronouncements along the way didn't help. For example, at the November 1983 unveiling of a full-scale sedan prototype (later dubbed "the little red car"), Smith promised Saturn would be a "a quantum leap ahead of the Japanese, including what they have coming in the future. In Saturn we have GM's answer—the American answer—to the Japanese challenge. It's the clean-sheet approach to producing small cars that in time will prove to have historic implications."

Initially, Project Saturn vehicles were to be sold by Chevrolet, starting with a front-drive four-door sedan somewhat smaller than a contemporary Chevy Cavalier. Projected price was $5000-$7000. Introduction was vaguely described as sometime in "the late '80s." A two-door coupe and a sport-utility vehicle (SUV) were to follow later. By the time Saturn opened for business, however, it was Saturn Corporation, a wholly owned subsidiary charged with pioneering new ideas in everything from styling to service. Presumably, the most-successful innovations would then spread throughout GM itself. Saturn was supposed to make money, of course, preferably by stealing sales from the competition, not other GM makes. The Saturn saga is therefore not so much about automobiles as about the automobile business.

In presenting the prototype, GM served notice that Saturns would be different: Body panels would be made of either metal or plastic and attached to a steel "spaceframe" as on Pontiac's then-new Fiero. The engine would be a brand-new, fuel-injected four-cylinder with an aluminum block and heads formed by a precision "lost foam" technique, in which oil passages were designed-in instead of drilled-in after casting, saving both time and material. Astonishing EPA fuel economy was predicted: 45 mpg city, 60 mpg highway. Other components need not come from corporate bins, and Saturn was free to devise its own engineering and manufacturing methods. A major goal for this experiment was finding ways to close the cost gap with the Japanese, then estimated at more than $2000 per car. The resultant savings, Smith said, would make GM a small-car power at last. In fact, he declared Saturn nothing less than "the key to GM's long-term competitiveness, survival, and success."

As announced in January 1985, Saturn Corporation would have its own plant, its own employees, its own contract with the United Auto Workers union, and a separate dealer network. Initial funding was $150 million, with up to $5 billion earmarked for future expenditures, including some $3.5 billion for building a "greenfield" factory in Spring Hill, Tennessee. Smith hoped production would start by fall 1987, and vowed to drive the first car off the line. Oldsmobile general manager Joseph Sanchez was tapped as Saturn president, but died of a heart attack less than three weeks later. Pontiac general manager Bill Hoglund was named to replace him.

A prime reason for locating in Tennessee was to distance Saturn from other GM plants, thus allowing a unique "corporate culture" to flower more easily. Just as important, tiny Spring Hill (population 1400 at the time) was about 35 miles south of Nashville and 30 miles from Smyrna, Tennessee, home of Nissan's North American factory, so vital railroad lines, interstate highways, and suppliers were all conveniently close. Groundbreaking took place in April 1986, by which time fledgling Saturn, barely a year old, had its third president: Richard G. "Skip" LeFauve, transferred from GM's Buick-Olds-Cadillac Group after Hoglund was named to head B-O-C.

Saturn's self-proclaimed mission was to "market vehicles developed and manufactured in the United States that are world leaders in quality, cost, and customer enthusiasm through the integration of people, technology, and business systems and to exchange knowledge, technology, and experience throughout General Motors." That was a tall order for an established car company, but Saturn was starting from scratch. The job was monumental, and ensuing months witnessed delays, cost overruns, and difficulties in signing up dealers that forced pushing back the production start date to summer 1990, shortly before Smith's scheduled retirement. Yearly volume was first set at a half-million units, then reduced to a more-manageable 240,000, and GM's total investment was trimmed to about $3.5 billion.

Smith envisioned the Saturn plant as the last word in automated manufacturing, with computer guided vehicles delivering parts to robots that did most assembly chores. But like so many GM leaders before him, Smith was a financial manager, not an engineer, and he did not really understand "high tech" or its limits. Spring Hill would use robots for welding, applying adhesives, and painting the cars, but the plant wasn't nearly as futuristic as Smith thought. The real innovation came in labor management relations. As LeFauve noted: "People are going to make the difference for Saturn."

The first employees were recruited from other GM operations.

**1991 SL2 four-door sedan**

**1991 SC coupe**

There were just 3800 jobs but more than 16,000 applicants, all evidently intrigued by the Saturn experiment and wanting to be part of it. Candidates were invited to Spring Hill for a two-day screening session, and 90 percent of those who came were hired. The eventual employee roster showed migrants from 46 states with average 13 years of GM experience. Being so accustomed to GM's old ways, "associates" were required to undergo comprehensive training in the new Saturn way of thinking and working.

UAW members received 350 hours of training on average, though some high-skill positions got twice as much. Base pay for all workers was 80 percent of GM's national average, but there were bonuses for meeting productivity targets and a profit-sharing plan—if Saturn turned a profit.

Saturn's labor agreement had few "shop rules" and gave employees more say in how they did their jobs. Workers were organized into teams responsible for monitoring the quality of parts and their own work, and any worker could stop the assembly line to fix safety or quality problems on the spot, a common practice in Japan but unknown in U.S. auto plants. That, in turn, allowed doing away with separate quality-control areas. In addition, workers sat alongside managers in meetings, helping to make decisions as "team members," and everyone ate in the same dining room. LeFauve even shared the executive office suite with the UAW's Saturn coordinator.

The team approach also figured in Saturn product development. Designers, factory workers, engineers, and outside suppliers were brought together for what was called "simultaneous engineering." This was in sharp contrast to the old way of having designers, once finished with their part of the car, "throw it over the wall" to engineers, who do their jobs before tossing the project to manufacturing, and so on down the line. Just as important, Saturn planners, some of whom already drove imports, put aside personal preferences to focus on what buyers wanted. Said engineering vice-president Jay Wetzel: "Most great cars in history reflect the personality of one person. In our case, that person just happens to be the consumer."

Despite myriad obstacles and much outside naysaying, Saturn production finally kicked off in time for model-year '91. Job One, a metallic-red sedan, rolled out the door at 10:57 A.M. on July 30, 1990, with Smith at the wheel in one of his last public appearances as GM chairman. With that, attention turned to the car itself.

Saturn greeted the world with four-door sedans and two-door coupes sharing a basic front-drive platform and major components. Each body style had its own styling, but neither drew rave reviews on that score. The sedan was criticized as looking like a scaled-down Oldsmobile Cutlass Supreme. (Some designers apparently worked on both, with the Saturn finished before the Olds but introduced after it.) The coupe, a swoopy 2+2 with hidden headlamps, was more favorably received, though some said it resembled the Geo Storm, an Isuzu-built hatchback coupe then sold by Chevrolet. Despite the shared platform, the sedan rode a 102.4-inch wheelbase, the coupe a 99.2-inch span. Respective overall lengths were 176.3 and 175.8 inches, making Saturns a little shorter than Chevy Cavaliers but seven inches longer than a Honda Civic, a key design benchmark. As promised, body panels bolted to a steel inner skeleton, with fenders, doors, and other vertical panels made of dent- and rust-resistant thermoplastic polymer materials. Hoods, trunklids, and roofs were steel. Galvanized underbody panels and a standard stainless-steel exhaust system reduced corrosion worries.

Also as promised, the engine was a new inline-four created expressly for Saturn, with an aluminum block and heads cast by the lost-foam technique. There were two versions of this 1.9-liter (116-cubic inch) design, both fuel-injected and mounted transversely per established front-drive small-car practice. The base 85-horsepower unit had a single overhead camshaft (sohc) and throttle-body injection with a central squirter at the intake manifold. A dual-cam (dohc) derivative with multipoint injection (a squirter for each cylinder) delivered 123 bhp. Each was available with five-speed manual transmission or optional electronically controlled four-speed automatic. As on some Japanese cars, the automatic had a switch for selecting "normal" or "performance" shift modes; the latter delayed full-throttle upshifts to higher rpm for best acceleration. Alas, no Saturn powertrain delivered anywhere near the economy touted seven years earlier. The best was 27 mpg city and 37 mpg highway for the single-cam/five-speed combination.

Initially, the sedan was offered in price-leader SL and better-equipped SL1 models with the sohc engine and as a dohc-powered SL2 with "Twin Cam" writ large on the rear bumper. The coupe, dubbed SC, was dohc only. Bumpers were black on single-cam cars, body-color on the sportier dual-cam models.

Interior design and features mimicked those of targeted competitors. Climate controls and the steering-column stalk switches for lights and wipers might have been lifted from a Civic or Toyota Corolla, and all models came with reclining cloth front bucket seats, tachometer, tilt steering column, trip odometer, split folding rear seatback, and a rear defogger—items found on most all Japanese rivals. Wheel designs emulated Honda's, including the use of four lug nuts instead of GM's usual five. With all this, some people thought Saturns were Japanese cars, but content was actually 95-percent domestic.

Early road-test verdicts were generally positive. Despite automatic transmission, Consumer Guide®'s test SL2 ran 0-60 mph in 8.8 seconds, surprisingly brisk for an affordable subcompact. A single-cam car took up to two seconds longer, but Saturn's slick-shifting manual transmission was a match for Japan's best and a welcome change from previous GM efforts. All models offered agile handling, a comfortably absorbent ride, good people and cargo space for the exterior size and, of course, convenient Japanese-style ergonomics. Fuel economy was another asset, but most reviewers judged the engines too loud and rough, especially for a modern four-cylinder under 2.0 liters. Which led to the most-telling judgment of all: Despite all-new engineering and the long gestation, Saturn was not the big breakthrough Roger Smith had promised—competitive with the Japanese, but not clearly superior.

Where Saturn did have an edge was price. At $7995 to start, the Scrooge-special SL was a whopping $1495 less than the base Civic sedan and $1000 less the cheapest Corolla (though the SL didn't offer an automatic transmission or power steering). Saturn's $275 destination charge was in line with those of Japanese makers and $180 less than Cavalier's. The SL1, starting $600 above the SL, swiftly became the volume seller. The SL2 listed at an attractive $10,295, but could be optioned up to around $14,600—a bit steep for the class, though that included antilock brakes (ABS) with rear discs (an $895 option) and CD player, features Civic and Corolla didn't yet offer. The SC2 topped the line at $11,775 and, like most other small coupes, was a tougher sell than the sedans.

Saturn sales officially began on October 25, 1990. Advertising never mentioned a GM connection—arguably wise, considering GM's reputation among the targeted buyers, though also appropriate for Saturn's free-wheeling status. Spring Hill was still moving slowly on a single shift to assure the highest possible assembly quality, now a must for even entry-level cars. The first Saturns were sold by some 30 dealers in Tennessee and neighboring states as well as on the West Coast, long an import stronghold. Dealers opened in other areas as production ramped up. By the following spring, Saturn counted 130 "retailers" in 33 states, most of them in 70 major urban markets.

It was in the retail area that Project Saturn had its greatest impact. Saturn carefully selected dealers who agreed to build separate showrooms and service facilities and to operate under strict guidelines for customer treatment. Sales personnel were trained in

# Saturn

**1991 SL1 four-door sedan**

**1991 SC coupe**

**1991 SL1 four-door sedan**

"consultative selling" to replace hard-sell tactics. A "retail associate" would sit down with customers, discuss their needs, explain their options, and arrange a test drive.

Pricing would be just as buyer-friendly. Federal laws on price-fixing prohibit car companies from forcing dealers to sell at a set price. That's why window stickers carry the legend "manufacturer's suggested retail price." But Saturn strongly urged its dealers to avoid the usual haggling, saying no customer should ever wonder about paying too much. Dealers agreed, and Saturns sold at full retail price—no more, no less. With production slowed to solve nagging quality problems, demand quickly exceeded supply during the 1991 model year. A good thing, then, that dealers obeyed another Saturn commandment: Thou shall not gouge. Buyers used to seeing "added dealer profit" signs on popular Japanese cars were pleasantly surprised by Saturn's "no ups, no extras" policy.

The red-carpet treatment didn't end there. Buyers were given a tour of their dealer's service area and met the mechanics who would work on their cars. Before driving off, new owners were photographed in their Saturns amid rousing cheers from dealership employees. Most all dealers invited owners in for weekend service clinics and even a free lunch. They also followed up with customers on a regular basis after the sale. If for any reason an owner was unhappy with a Saturn, the car could be returned within the first 30 days or 1500 miles for a free refund, no questions asked. When Saturn announced its first recall in February 1991, dealer technicians drove to where the cars were (about 1200 were involved) just to replace a seatback bracket. A few months later, Saturn learned a supplier had provided a batch of improperly formulated antifreeze that might cause engine damage. Instead of replacing the antifreeze, Saturn replaced more than 1100 cars.

This extraordinary approach to customer care drew some derisive comments from competing dealers, but it worked. With Spring Hill managing only 48,629 cars the first model year, dealers sold every one they could get. Most customers were ecstatic. Some even volunteered to help sell Saturns on their days off.

Another key part of Saturns sales strategy was giving dealers broad "market areas" so they would compete with other brands instead of each other. Thus, a metropolitan region like Chicago might have more than 60 Chevrolet stores but only nine or 10 Saturn dealers. Limiting the number of retail outlets helped Saturn become the industry leader in sales per dealer, and Saturn franchises quickly became very profitable.

This new way of doing business got an immediate endorsement with J.D. Power and Associates' 1991 surveys of new-car owners, where Saturn ranked third in both customer satisfaction and sales satisfaction. In its very first year, the "different kind of car company" leapfrogged Honda, Toyota, Nissan, and other rivals in two key measurements: how well customers liked their cars and how well they were treated by dealers. Only Lexus and Infiniti, the new Japanese luxury brands whose cars sold for three and four times as much, rated higher.

And this was no first-year fluke. Saturn again ranked No. 3 in both Power surveys for the '92 and '93 model years, and was No. 1 in sales satisfaction and third in customer satisfaction for '94 and '95. More impressive still, Saturn would remain tops in sales satisfaction each model year through 2001 except for 1999, when it tied for sixth with Lexus and Germany's BMW at a mere four points behind first-place Cadillac and Jaguar. These and many other accolades buoyed values of used Saturns, which retained a higher percentage of their original price than other cars in their class. Saturn's own research showed that fully 50 percent of its customers bought primarily of the positive shopping experience, versus 25 percent because of the product itself. This led one Saturn executive to remark, "We're not trying to sell people a car. We're helping them buy a car."

Other car companies scrambled to "Saturnize" themselves for improved customer satisfaction in hopes of better sales. Struggling Oldsmobile, in fact, soon implemented many of Saturn's policies in the "Oldsmobile Edge" program. Some other dealers switched to "one-price" and "no-haggle" appeals, but many of those also selling other brands eventually returned to high-pressure tactics. As LeFauve observed, Saturn's success stemmed from many factors, including being true to the company's mission statement. "You can't just tell your retailers to be nice to people," he said.

Saturn's first big product change occurred late in the 1992 model year: an optional driver-side airbag. The cars had debuted with motorized shoulder belts to meet the federal requirement for dual front-seat "passive restraints," but Japanese rivals were rapidly adding air bags and Saturn needed to match them. The motorized belts continued through model-year '94.

The driver-side cushion became an across-the-board standard for 1993, when four-door wagons and optional traction control arrived. The wagon, striding the same wheelbase as the sedan and otherwise identical to it from the rear doors forward, came in sohc SW1 and dohc SW2 versions. Also new was a lower-cost coupe, titled SC1, with the single-cam engine and exposed headlamps. The dual-cam coupe retained its hidden-headlamp face as the SC2. A new traction control was available for just $50 on models ordered with ABS and automatic. There was hardly any hardware involved.

1992 SL four-door sedan

1992 SL1 four-door sedan

1992 SC coupe

Saturn simply wrote new software allowing the ABS computer to counteract wheel slip in three stages: retard spark timing to reduce engine power, shift the transmission to a higher gear, and interrupt fuel flow. Traction was a Saturn class exclusive and thus a big coup for the brand; even many luxury cars didn't have it yet.

Saturn finally achieved full production during model-year '93, when Spring Hill ran two shifts to crank out 244,000 cars, nearly 75,000 more than the previous year. But dealers were still short of stock and asking for more, so a third shift was added and all shifts rescheduled to four days a week, 10 hours a day. That had the plant going six days a week to squeeze out nearly 60,000 additional cars each year.

The cars themselves were little changed for '94, but there was big news on the financial front. In January 1994, Saturn announced its first operating profit, achieved in 1993, though the amount was reported only to GM and not made public. The workforce had grown to 8500 by then, and each employee received a profit-sharing check of about $5100.

Though Saturn was still a long way from paying back GM's investment, officials hastened to point out other benefits from the new company. On the technology side were the lost-foam engine casting technique, a new water-borne paint process, and team-oriented assembly systems being adopted by other GM operations. In addition, Saturn's four-cylinder cars were earning valuable corporate average fuel economy (CAFE) credits for GM to offset the debits of gas-guzzling V-8 models. Most important, perhaps, 75 percent of Saturn sales represented "plus business," meaning they came at the expense of a non-GM brand. More than half of Saturn owners said they would have bought a Japanese car instead, thus realizing one of Roger Smith's goals—stealing customers from the likes of Honda, Toyota, and Nissan.

To say thanks, Saturn invited its customers—all 700,000 of them—to Spring Hill for a "Homecoming" weekend in late June 1994. It was another extraordinary thing for a car company to do, but even Saturn was surprised when over 44,000 people showed up. All came at their own expense, some driving in from as far away as Alaska and Hawaii. Drenching rains and muddy fields didn't dampen the family oriented festivities, which included plant tours, picnics, a concert, and sharing the gospel with fellow owners and Spring Hill workers. Two employees from Pennsylvania Saturn retailers got married during the event; Skip LeFauve gave the bride away, plus a 1995 Saturn as wedding present. Beyond great PR, the Homecoming testified to how well Saturn was making friends and fostering customer loyalty. It was judged a success, despite the soggy weather and other problems, and would be repeated in 1999.

But dark clouds were gathering. Saturn bowed amid huge losses for GM as a whole: $2 billion in 1990, $4.5 billion in 1991, then a U.S. business record. New top-level executives came in during 1992, and though they had GM back in the black by middecade, the company's total market share continued to shrink and profits were down. With funding tight, sibling rivalry broke out within the GM family. As *AutoWeek* observed in its report on the first Homecoming: "General Motors has already poured $5 billion into Saturn, and there are people at places like Chevrolet, Buick and Oldsmobile...who would frown upon more of their corporation's dollars heading south. They'd like to see their younger sister pull some of her own weight; that's how families work." Trouble was, Saturn had only small cars to sell, and the small-car market was withering.

In short, Saturn needed more funding and new models, yet other divisions were needy too, and there wasn't enough money to go around. Some observers recommended that GM cut overhead by merging Saturn with Olds Division, as both were growing ever closer in products and sales practices. By summer 1995, however, GM decided to delay additional Saturn models and shift development resources to other divisions, Olds included. This thinking probably made sense at the time, as Saturn was doing great business. Though calendar-year sales eased fractionally to 286,000, production rose 18 percent for model-year '95 to a record 303,000. Saturn's lineup would expand, but the fast-changing economics of the auto business meant future models would share more with other GM cars. Tellingly, Skip LeFauve was promoted in 1995 to head all GM small-car programs and "small-car convergence" efforts. GM veteran Don Hudler took over as president and CEO at Saturn Corporation after serving as its vice president for sales, marketing, and service since 1987.

Buyers found several changes in the 1995 Saturns. There was redesigned dashboard incorporating a passenger-side air bag, allowing manual three-point seatbelts to replace the never-liked shoulder "mousebelts." Adoption of multipoint fuel injection added a welcome 15 bhp to the single-cam engine, coupes wore mildly changed faces, and the SC2 sported a new rear panel and spoiler. A prime rationale for spaceframe construction and bolt-on body panels was to make styling updates relatively easy and cheap, but Saturn said it couldn't afford to redesign the whole car at once, so it focused on the interior first.

Exterior styling was updated for '96. Sedans and wagons retained familiar cues but were slightly longer and more rounded; a newly arched roofline increased sedan head room fore and aft. But the biggest change was reserved for coupes. After a brief run of '96 carryovers, the '97 models bowed in early 1996 on the sedan/wagon wheelbase to gain a whopping 4.5 inches of rear leg

# Saturn

1994 SL1 four-door sedan

1995 SW1 station wagon

room. All models got additional side-impact protection in advance of 1997 federal standards, plus daytime running lights (inboard of the headlamps), a safety feature spreading throughout the GM fleet. Traction control was now available with either transmission as part of the ABS option. Prices had been creeping up, ranging now from $9995 for the basic SL sedan to $12,695 for the top-line SW2 wagon. Despite the restyle, calendar-year sales slipped 2.5 percent to around 278,600—not a good sign.

A sign of the future arrived at select Saturn retailers in December 1996. The EV1 wasn't GM's first battery-powered car, but it built on decades of company experiments with electric vehicles. And it wasn't just for fun. California and other states had enacted laws requiring automakers to sell a percentage of zero-emissions vehicles (ZEVs) as a condition for doing business in those states. Though lawmakers kept fiddling with deadlines and sales counts, clean-air mandates were a fact of life demanding alternatives to the internal-combustion engine. Most automakers started with electric cars.

EV1 was built to gain real-world experience with advanced technology and, just as important, to assess consumer interest in electric vehicles. Saturn owners liked new ideas, and the small lozenge-shaped electric coupe had plastic body panels over a steel skeleton, so the EV1 was right at home in Saturn showrooms. It was not a Saturn, though, wearing the GM logo as a new one-model "make."

Evolved from the 1989 Impact prototype, the EV1 had a front-mounted AC induction motor driving the front wheels through a "1-speed" transaxle with reduction gear. The juice came from 26 lead-acid batteries arranged in a central T-structure and weighing some 1175 pounds, nearly half the car's curb weight. For maximum driving range, a "regenerative" feature reversed the main motor on braking to replace some of the power used; a transaxle "coast-down" feature gave a similar effect when coasting or descending hills. Recharging was by a 220-volt stand-alone unit or a 110V onboard charger. Recharging took 12-14 hours with the onboard unit, about three hours with the 220V equipment.

Costing a cool $350 million to develop, the EV1 would have had to sell for at least $35,000 on a retail basis, according to GM. That was deemed too much for a relatively impractical car with technology not yet fully proven. Instead, GM offered three-month leases that included all normal servicing, though not the required home charger. Fittingly, the first EV1s were delivered in smoggy Los Angeles and San Diego, CA, and Phoenix and Tucson, AZ. Sacramento, CA, was added in 1997, San Francisco the following year. "Owners" loved the car, happily passing gas stations in eerie silence and zipping through traffic or along winding roads with verve. Acceleration was strong—about 8 seconds 0-60—but you couldn't do that too often. Even feather-foot drivers were hard-pressed to get over 60 miles on a full charge. With that and the advent of more-practical and affordable gasoline/electric "hybrids," interest in the EV1 tailed off. GM ended production in late 2000 after fewer than 1000 units, though the lease program continued for a time.

Saturn No. 1,500,000, a blue SC2, rolled out of Spring Hill on January 17, 1997. There was little product news, though: just a standard low-fuel warning light for all '97 models and, with the optional keyless entry system, an antitheft feature that sounded the horn in the event of a break-in. But in another highly symbolic event, GM's import-fighting brand began selling cars in Japan, something even Roger Smith hadn't planned. Critics had long maintained that American cars weren't good enough for demanding Japanese buyers. But Saturns were selling well against many Japanese cars in the U.S., so why not Japan itself? The export models were reengineered to incorporate right-hand drive and equipped to satisfy both local regulations and, it was hoped, the local market. Unfortunately, sales commenced in April 1997 just as the Japanese economy was slipping into recession, and there were only eight dealers for the entire country. But the main problem, said one Japanese industry analyst quoted by U.S. trade weekly *Automotive News*, was that "Saturn didn't have any brand appeal. American brands are hard to sell in Japan because some people still have a low-quality image of them." After four tough years and only 4324 sales, Saturn gave up.

It was just as a well, for troubles were mounting at home. Calendar-year sales dropped nearly 10 percent for 1997 and another 7.7 percent in '98. The problem, many observers felt, was that Saturn's cars had become stale next to a steady stream of fresh competition—and not just from imports. Meantime, the '98 Saturns appeared with only retuned suspensions, for a smoother ride, and more powertrain refinements—an almost yearly ritual—aimed at reducing noise, vibration, and harshness. Soon, retailers had more cars than buyers for the first time, yet the one-price policy precluded rebates and other incentives to help reduce the backlog. The only thing left was to trim production, and Spring Hill scaled back by about 17 percent—to some 275,000 cars a year—starting in September 1997. There were no layoffs, prohibited by the UAW contract, but workers were worried.

Sales were basically flat in calendar 1999, which was relatively good news. And Saturn finally had some real product news that year: three-door coupes. A number of extended-cab pickups had lately sprouted auxiliary rear doors to improve back-seat access, and the idea made even more sense for Saturn's trim SCs. New Jersey retailer Stuart Lasser reportedly suggested it after noticing the trouble his son Hal had getting in and out of the regular two-door. Engineers worked fast, and the "back door" coupes were in dealerships by November 1998.

The extra door was on the driver's side, rear-hinged, about 19-inches wide, and could open to near 90 degrees. You had to open the driver's door first, because the rear-door latch was mounted flush in the jamb for safety's sake. Opening both created a spacious pillarless opening of 62 inches in width. The third door changed roof styling slightly—but only on the left—and added a mere 50 pounds despite required structural reinforcing. Unfortunately, it also cut rear hip room by three inches and rear shoulder room by 5.5 inches. Young Hal Lasser might have had an easier scramble in and out, but less space to move around in once ensconced.

After several years of dithering, GM had finally decided to fund the new products Saturn so badly needed. First up was the all-new midsize L-Series, launched in early 1999 for model-year 2000. A $1.2-billion effort, it was loosely based on GM's European Opel/Vauxhall Vectra, and Saturn took pains to make sure reporters understood how loose the relationship was. Though the L-Series used the Vectra's basic architecture and front-drive powertrains, only about 130 parts, mostly fasteners, were interchangeable—as one engineer demonstrated by pouring them out of a small laundry basket at the press preview. "That is literally everything this car has in common with the Vectra," he declared. Saturn took over an older GM plant in Wilmington, Delaware, and retooled it for the new models, which were built under a more-traditional labor agreement than existed in Spring Hill.

Despite similar "global GM" styling, the L-Series strode a 2.5-inch longer wheelbase than its Euro cousin and looked recognizably Saturn. It even had plastic fenders and door skins, though they attached to a conventional unibody rather than a true spaceframe. Two engines covered five models in two body styles with familiar Saturn nomenclature. Powering the LS and LS1 sedans and LW1 wagon was a dohc 2.2-liter four-cylinder, part of GM's new "L850" engine family and marketed under the "Ecotec" name. The LS2 sedan and LW2 wagon carried a twincam 3.0-liter V-6, also designed by GM Europe and shared with Saab (now part of the GM empire). The V-6 teamed only with four-speed automatic transmission, available for four-cylinder models in lieu of five-speed manual. Options included ABS with traction control across the board, leather upholstery except on the base LS sedan, and a rear spoiler for LS1/LS2. V-6 models had standard rear disc brakes.

Hopes were very high for the L-Series, though it competed in one of the most crowded and competitive market sectors, where two contenders, the Honda Accord and Toyota Camry, were perennial rivals for title as America's favorite car line. But with total sales of some 3.5 million units a year, the midsize class offered huge growth potential for Saturn and GM—an irresistible opportunity. What's more, critics found the L-Series had most everything necessary to satisfy midsize buyers. Said *Car and Driver:* "We're not about to bet against the top dogs...but the LS1 covers all the sedan bases very well and could make the others sweat a little if Saturn can persuade Americans to take notice of its new model."

Unfortunately, Saturn fumbled the ball. Unexpected production glitches kept supplies tight in the critical early weeks, and initial advertising touted "the next big thing from Saturn" without giving a clear idea of what the L-Series was. As a result, calendar-2000 deliveries were just over 94,000. Saturn had projected 192,000 the first year and up to 300,000 a year thereafter. Cars started piling up once the factory got cranking, forcing Saturn to trim production twice in quick succession. To jump-start sales, Saturn granted a $1000 per car "advertising allowance" that retailers could use any way they liked. Many simply passed it on to customers as a hidden rebate, but even that didn't help. Zero-down leases were being offered by July, when *Business Week* reported that average incentives for all Saturn models were at a record $1116 per vehicle.

With the L-Series around, the lineup of smaller Saturns was named S-Series. The SW1 wagon was dropped. Remaining models sported a new gauge cluster and switchgear, redesigned center

**1995 SL2 four-door sedan**

**1996 SL1 four-door sedan**

**1996 SW2 station wagon**

# Saturn

console, revised front seats with more rearward travel, plus new lower-body panels that increased length by 1.2 inches but were hardly noticeable. Coupes had a short model year, with slightly restyled '01s arriving in early 2000. Powertrains were fiddled with yet again, getting a new induction system and other changes in the continuing quest for smoothness and quietness. Consumer Guide® thought a decade of effort had "finally paid off—at least in the '2' models. Their twincam engine now feels coarse and buzzy only at maximum rpm. The changes don't affect [output], so acceleration with either transmission remains slightly better than the class norm." But at age 10, the original Saturn design looked old against most rivals, and sales took a beating in calendar 2000, dropping 23.7 percent to a little over 177,000. With that, Spring Hill was put on furlough to give dealers time to clear stocks—including some leftover '99s. However, total Saturn sales for the period rose 16.9 percent to 271,800. The L-Series, disappointment though it was, more than made up for the S-Series' decline.

Sounding a hopeful note in 2000 was the April 25 announcement of a new $1.5-billion cash infusion for Saturn. Two-thirds would go toward capital improvements at Spring Hill for building a new Saturn sport-utility vehicle (SUV) starting in late 2001. Remaining funds were earmarked for equipment needed to build the 2.2-liter four-cylinder engine, which Saturn would supply for all North American GM vehicles using it, as well as a new continuously variable automatic transmission (CVT). Intriguingly, the announcement hinted at a "yet undisclosed future Saturn" with a Honda V-6, to be supplied under a recently concluded agreement with GM. "Our challenge now," said Saturn president Trudell, is to keep up with customer demand for a wider variety of vehicles...and [to] position Saturn as more than just a small-car company."

Actually, it was do-or-die time. In 2000 alone, Saturn lost nearly $840 million, over $3000 on each sale. The brand created to stop buyers from deserting GM was itself being deserted. As a result, nearly half of Saturn's total factory capacity was idled that year, according to an internal report. By April 2001, GM was nearly out of patience. Saturn was told to double productivity at Spring Hill, boost production there by two-thirds while cutting employment by 18 percent, and to at least break even on operations—or else.

Suddenly, everything was riding on the new SUV. If it bombed like the L-Series, reported *Automotive News*, GM would cancel the redesigned S-Series set for model-year 2003.

Trudell expected to meet all goals, yet admitted that "If we are not successful with one product [the SUV], no one would put in more products."

But calendar 2001 was another discouraging year. Aggravated by a steady decline in the national economy, sales for the 12 months slid 4.2 percent to a little over 260,000. The L-Series was up (to just over 98,000) but the S-Series was down (by 8.6 percent to 162,110). Product news was again scant. Both lines added optional head-protecting curtain side airbags that dropped down from above the doors in a side impact, but neither yet offered torso side airbags. Midsize model names changed—four-cylinder L100 and L200 sedans, V-6 L300 sedan, LW200 and LW300 wagons. And that was about it. For 2002, the S Series lost its remaining wagon. For the L-Series, ABS, curtain side airbags, and traction control became standard across the board. L-Series options also expanded with an in-dash six-disc CD changer, minivan-style rear-seat video entertainment system, GM OnStar communications/assistance system, and 16-inch chome wheels.

The tense national mood after 9/11/01 was the unforeseen backdrop for the rollout of Saturn's vital new SUV, the Vue. Americans were flocking to car-based "crossover" wagons like the Honda CR-V and Ford Escape. Vue was designed to match or beat them in size, versatility, performance, and other respects. Significantly, Vue introduced a new "Theta" platform destined for similar models under other GM brands, but it maintained Saturn tradition with thermoplastic vertical body panels.

Vue engines were borrowed from the L-Series. The V-6 came only with a new five-speed automatic transmission and all-wheel drive (AWD) with no transfer case or low-range gearing. The four-cylinder teamed with front drive and five-speed manual transmission or with front drive or AWD operating through Saturn's new CVT, dubbed VTi (for "Variable Transmission, intelligent"). Like CVTs offered by Honda and Audi, this one (developed by GM's Hydramatic division) used a special drive belt running between two laterally expandable pulleys providing an infinite number of

**1997 Saturn SL1 four-door sedan**

**1998 SC1 coupe**

**2000 LW2 station wagon**

**2001 Saturn SC2 three-door coupe**

ratios. Electronic control assured the transmission was always in the right "gear" for efficient engine operation. Interestingly, Saturn claimed 0-60 acceleration of 10.2 seconds for the front-drive model with CVT versus 11.1 with manual. The AWD V-6 was pegged at 8.4 seconds, which *Car and Driver* verified in its first full Vue test.

The CVT was another class-exclusive for Vue. So, too, its electric power steering, with motors replacing power-sapping hydraulics. These apart, Saturn's SUV was much like its rivals for dimensions, fuel economy, and dynamic behavior. Consumer Guide® found that it "leans more in corners than Escape or CR-V and tends to nose-plow where most compact SUVs feel nimble." Steering was "vague on-center and doesn't impart much road feel." But ride was judged a "strong point. Tires and suspension [four-wheel independent] do a good job of absorbing the worst bumps...." CG's overall assessment: "What Vue lacks in handling it more than makes up for in versatility, ride quality, and interior comfort. Even more attractive are its competitive pricing [about $16,300-$22,600] and the high customer-satisfaction ratings for Saturn's dealership experience and no-haggle price strategy."

Vue was just starting out when this book was compiled, so history's verdict on this and other-new century Saturn initiatives must await a future edition. We note, however, that Saturn somehow managed to restyle the L-Series for 2003, giving it a new front end and some discreet chrome trim in hopes of achieving significant sales at last. And despite GM's threats, the long-awaited S-Series replacement, called Ion, debuted as planned for '03, sharing a new GM "Delta" front-drive platform with Chevy's next-generation Cavalier.

A pity we must close with the future of this make hanging in the balance. Had GM not waited so long to fund new, more-competitive models, Saturn's place in the automotive universe might now be far more secure. As it is, the Saturn saga stands as a cautionary tale about the perils of complacency that any car company would do well to heed.

## Specifications

### 1991—48,629 built

| Coupe (wb 99.2) | Wght | Price | Prod |
|---|---|---|---|
| G27/H27 SC | 2,375 | 11,775 | — |

| Sedan (wb 102.4) | | | |
|---|---|---|---|
| F69    SL | 2,312 | 7,995 | — |
| G69/H69 SL1 | 2,344 | 8,595 | — |
| J69/K35 SL2 | 2,408 | 10,295 | — |

| 1991 Engines | bore × stroke | bhp | availability |
|---|---|---|---|
| I-4, 116.0 | 3.22 × 3.54 | 85 | S-SL, SL1 (ohc) |
| I-4, 116.0 | 3.22 × 3.54 | 123 | S-SC, SL2 (dohc) |

### 1992—169,959 built

| Coupe (wb 99.2) | Wght | Price | Prod |
|---|---|---|---|
| G27/H27 SC | 2,375 | 11,875 | — |

| Sedan (wb 102.4) | | | |
|---|---|---|---|
| F69    SL | 2,313 | 8,195 | — |
| G69/H69 SL1 | 2,343 | 8,995 | — |
| J69/K35 SL2 | 2,407 | 10,395 | — |

| 1992 Engines | bore × stroke | bhp | availability |
|---|---|---|---|
| I-4, 116.0 | 3.22 × 3.54 | 85 | S-SL, SL1 (ohc) |
| I-4, 116.0 | 3.22 × 3.54 | 124 | S-SC, SL2 (dohc) |

### 1993—244,621 built

| Coupe (wb 99.2) | Wght | Price | Prod |
|---|---|---|---|
| E27/F27 SC1 | 2,304 | 10,995 | — |
| G27/H27 SC2 | 2,387 | 12,795 | — |

| Sedan (wb 102.4) | | | |
|---|---|---|---|
| F69    SL | 2,323 | 9,195 | — |
| G69/H69 SL1 | 2,353 | 9,995 | — |
| J69/K69 SL2 | 2,425 | 11,495 | — |

| Wagon (wb 102.4) | | | |
|---|---|---|---|
| G35/H35 SW1 | 2,368 | 10,895 | — |
| J35/K35 SW2 | 2,475 | 12,195 | — |

| 1993 Engines | bore × stroke | bhp | availability |
|---|---|---|---|
| I-4, 116.0 | 3.22 × 3.54 | 85 | S-SC1, SL, SL1, SW1 (ohc) |
| I-4, 116.0 | 3.22 × 3.54 | 124 | O-SC2, SL2, SW2 (dohc) |

### 1994—267,518 built

| Coupe (wb 99.2) | Wght | Price | Prod |
|---|---|---|---|
| E27/F27 SC1 | 2,280 | 11,695 | — |
| G27/H27 SC2 | 2,376 | 12,895 | — |

| Sedan (wb 102.4) | | | |
|---|---|---|---|
| F69    SL | 2,314 | 9,995 | — |
| G69/H69 SL1 | 2,349 | 10,795 | — |
| J69/K69 SL2 | 2,405 | 11,795 | — |

| Wagon (wb 102.4) | | | |
|---|---|---|---|
| G35/H35 SW1 | 2,362 | 11,695 | — |
| J35/K35 SW2 | 2,448 | 12,595 | — |

| 1994 Engines | bore × stroke | bhp | availability |
|---|---|---|---|
| I-4, 116.0 | 3.22 × 3.54 | 85 | S-SC1, SL, SL1, SW1 (ohc) |
| I-4, 116.0 | 3.22 × 3.54 | 124 | O-SC2, SL2, SW2 (dohc) |

### 1995

| (wb 102.4; cpe wb 99.2) | Wght | Price | Prod |
|---|---|---|---|
| E27/F27 SC1 cpe | 2,284 | 11,895 | ⎤ 62,434 |
| G27/H27 SC2 cpe | 2,360 | 12,995 | ⎦ |
| F69    SL sdn 4d | 2,345 | 9,995 | ⎤ |
| G69/H69 SL1 sdn 4d | 2,353 | 10,995 | ⎬ 221,102 |
| J69/K69 SL2 sdn 4d | 2,405 | 11,995 | ⎦ |
| G35/H35 SW1 wgn 4d | 2,380 | 11,695 | ⎤ 19,452 |
| J35/K35 SW2 wgn 4d | 2,448 | 12,695 | ⎦ |

| 1995 Engines | bore × stroke | bhp | availability |
|---|---|---|---|
| I-4, 116.0 | 3.22 × 3.54 | 100 | S-SC1, SL, SL1, SW1 (ohc) |
| I-4, 116.0 | 3.22 × 3.54 | 124 | O-SC2, SL2, SW2 (dohc) |

### 1996—294,198 built

| (wb 102.4; cpe wb 99.2) | Wght | Price | Prod |
|---|---|---|---|
| E27/F27 SC1 cpe | 2,282 | 12,195 | — |
| G27/H27 SC2 cpe | 2,363 | 13,295 | — |

## Saturn

| (wb 102.4; cpe wb 99.2) | | Wght | Price | Prod* |
|---|---|---|---|---|
| F69 | SL sdn 4d | 2,348 | 10,495 | — |
| G69/H69 | SL1 sdn 4d | 2,378 | 11,395 | — |
| J69/K69 | SL2 sdn 4d | 2,421 | 12,295 | — |
| G35/H35 | SW1 wgn 4d | 2,437 | 11,995 | — |
| J35/K35 | SW2 wgn 4d | 2,507 | 12,895 | — |

| 1996 Engines | bore × stroke | bhp | availability |
|---|---|---|---|
| I-4, 116.0 | 3.22 × 3.54 | 100 | S-SC1, SL, SL1, SW1 (ohc) |
| I-4, 116.0 | 3.22 × 3.54 | 124 | O-SC2, SL2, SW2 (dohc) |

### 1997

| (wb 102.4) | | Wght | Price | Prod |
|---|---|---|---|---|
| B27 | SC1 cpe | 2,309 | 12,495 | 70,711 |
| C27 | SC2 cpe | 2,386 | 13,695 | |
| B69 | SL sdn 4d | 2,321 | 10,595 | 213,182 |
| B69 | SL1 sdn 4d | 2,321 | 11,595 | |
| D69 | SL2 sdn 4d | 2,390 | 12,495 | |
| B35 | SW1 wgn 4d | 2,390 | 12,195 | 31,099 |
| D35 | SW2 wgn 4d | 2,454 | 13,095 | |

| 1997 Engines | bore × stroke | bhp | availability |
|---|---|---|---|
| I-4, 116.0 | 3.22 × 3.54 | 100 | S-SC1, SL, SL1, SW1 (ohc) |
| I-4, 116.0 | 3.22 × 3.54 | 124 | O-SC2, SL2, SW2 (dohc) |

### 1998

| (wb 102.4) | | Wght | Price | Prod |
|---|---|---|---|---|
| B27 | SC1 cpe | 2,309 | 12,595 | 38,591 |
| C27 | SC2 cpe | 2,380 | 13,895 | |
| B69 | SL sdn 4d | 2,326 | 10,595 | 160,759 |
| B69 | SL1 sdn 4d | 2,326 | 11,595 | |
| D69 | SL2 sdn 4d | 2,392 | 12,495 | |
| B35 | SW1 wgn 4d | — | 12,295 | 20,415 |
| D35 | SW2 wgn 4d | 2,454 | 13,295 | |

| 1998 Engines | bore × stroke | bhp | availability |
|---|---|---|---|
| I-4, 116.0 | 3.22 × 3.54 | 100 | S-SC1, SL, SL1, SW1 (ohc) |
| I-4, 116.0 | 3.22 × 3.54 | 124 | O-SC2, SL2, SW2 (dohc) |

### 1999

| (wb 102.4) | | Wght | Price | Prod |
|---|---|---|---|---|
| B27 | SC1 cpe 3d* | 2,320 | 12,445 | 52,965 |
| C27 | SC2 cpe 3d* | 2,390 | 15,505 | |
| B69 | SL sdn 4d | 2,327 | 10,595 | 203,578 |
| B69 | SL1 sdn 4d | 2,327 | 11,295 | |
| D69 | SL2 sdn 4d | 2,389 | 12,755 | |
| B35 | SW1 wgn 4d | 2,391 | 12,295 | 19,090 |
| D35 | SW2 wgn 4d | 2,449 | 14,225 | |

| 1999 Engines | bore × stroke | bhp | availability |
|---|---|---|---|
| I-4, 116.0 | 3.22 × 3.54 | 100 | S-SC1, SL, SL1, SW1 (ohc) |
| I-4, 116.0 | 3.22 × 3.54 | 124 | O-SC2, SL2, SW2 (dohc) |

*Midyear introduction of left-side rear door.

### 2000

| S-Series (wb 102.4) | | Wght | Price | Prod |
|---|---|---|---|---|
| N27/P27 | SC1 cpe 3d | 2,368 | 12,535 | 8,517 |
| R27/Y27 | SC2 cpe 3d | 2,436 | 15,145 | 8,724 |
| F69 | SL sdn 4d | 2,332 | 10,685 | 74,085 |
| G69/H69 | SL1 sdn 4d | 2,332 | 11,485 | |
| J69/K69 | SL2 sdn 4d | 2,399 | 12,895 | 68,907 |
| J35/N35 | SW2 wgn 4d | 2,452 | 14,290 | 9,633 |

| L-Series (wb 106.5) | | | | |
|---|---|---|---|---|
| R19/S19 | LS sdn 4d | 2,910 | 15,010 | 7,140 |
| T19/U19 | LS1 sdn 4d | 2,943 | 16,750 | 45,953 |
| W19 | LS2 sdn 4d | 3,152 | 20,135 | 35,099 |
| U35 | LW1 wgn 4d | 3,075 | 18,835 | 6,041 |
| W35 | LW2 wgn 4d | 3,229 | 21,360 | 9,573 |

| 2000 Engines | bore × stroke | bhp | availability |
|---|---|---|---|
| I-4, 116.0 | 3.22 × 3.54 | 100 | S-SC1, SL, SL1, SW1 (ohc) |
| | | 124 | (dohc) |
| I-4, 134.0 | 3.39 × 3.72 | 137 | S-LS, LS1, LW1 |
| V-6, 183.0 | 3.39 × 3.35 | 182 | S-LS2, LW2 |

### 2001

| S-Series (wb 102.4) | | Wght | Price | Prod |
|---|---|---|---|---|
| N27/P27 | SC1 cpe 3d | 2,368 | 12,535 | 23,584 |
| R27/Y27 | SC2 cpe 3d | 2,436 | 15,645 | 17,414 |
| F69 | SL sdn 4d | 2,332 | 10,570 | 73,428 |
| G69/H69 | SL1 sdn 4d | 2,332 | 11,485 | |
| J69/K69 | SL2 sdn 4d | — | 12,895 | |
| J35/N35 | SW2 wgn 4d | 2,452 | 14,290 | 3,416 |

| L-Series (wb 106.5) | | | | |
|---|---|---|---|---|
| R19/S19 | L100 sdn 4d | 2,944 | 14,495 | 4,023 |
| T19/U19 | L200 sdn 4d | 2,964 | 16,750 | 54,968 |
| W19 | L300 sdn 4d | 3,182 | 19,495 | 23,339 |
| U35 | LW200 wgn 4d | 3,375 | 18,835 | 4,673 |
| W35 | LW300 wgn 4d | 3,257 | 21,360 | 5,283 |

| 2001 Engines | bore × stroke | bhp | availability |
|---|---|---|---|
| I-4, 116.0 | 3.22 × 3.54 | 100 | S-SC1, SL, SL1, SW1 (ohc) |
| I-4, 116.0 | 3.22 × 3.54 | 124 | O-SC2, SL2, SW2 (dohc) |
| I-4, 134.0 | 3.39 × 3.72 | 135 | S-L100, L200, LW200 |
| V-6, 183.0 | 3.39 × 3.35 | 182 | S-L300, LW300 |

### 2002

| S-Series (wb 102.4) | | Wght | Price | Prod* |
|---|---|---|---|---|
| N27/P27 | SC1 cpe 3d | 2,367 | 12,900 | — |
| R27/Y27 | SC2 cpe 3d | 2,429 | 16,080 | — |
| F69 | SL sdn 4d | 2,341 | 10,570 | — |
| G69/H69 | SL1 sdn 4d | 2,341 | 11,850 | — |
| J69/K69 | SL2 sdn 4d | 2,393 | 13,335 | — |

| L-Series (wb 106.5) | | | | |
|---|---|---|---|---|
| R19/S19 | L100 sdn 4d | 2,948 | 14,495 | — |
| T19/U19 | L200 sdn 4d | 2,989 | 16,750 | — |
| W19 | L300 sdn 4d | 3,197 | 19,495 | — |
| U35 | LW200 wgn 4d | 3,070 | 18,835 | — |
| W35 | LW300 wgn 4d | 3,272 | 21,360 | — |

| 2002 Engines | bore × stroke | bhp | availability |
|---|---|---|---|
| I-4, 116.0 | 3.22 × 3.54 | 100 | S-SC1, SL, SL1 (ohc) |
| I-4, 116.0 | 3.22 × 3.54 | 124 | O-SC2, SL2, (dohc) |
| I-4, 134.0 | 3.39 × 3.72 | 135 | S-L100, L200, LW200 |
| V-6, 183.0 | 3.39 × 3.35 | 182 | S-L300, LW300 |

*Figures not available at time of publication.

# Shelby

When heart trouble forced Carroll Shelby to retire from driving race cars in 1960, the one-time Texas chicken rancher and oil-field roughneck decided to build stark, incredibly fast road cars to suit himself and other like-minded enthusiasts. The first were the long-since legendary Shelby-Cobras. Starting with lithe, lightweight Ace roadsters from A.C. Cars in England, Carroll replaced a plodding small six with potent Ford V-8s: initially 260- and 289-cubic-inchers with up to 306 horsepower, then mammoth 427s making up to 425 bhp. The result was a hairy thrill on the road and nearly unbeatable in major-league sports-car racing. Even the "little" 289 could do 0-60 mph in 5.5 seconds and exceed 135 mph. The otherworldly 427s needed just 4.2 seconds to go 0-60, on the way to 165 mph.

Shelby built 654 small-block Cobras and 350-odd big-block versions in 1962-68. All have since become prized collector's items fetching six-figure prices, thanks to a fabled competition background and a raw, elemental nature unmatched by other sports cars. Those same factors explain the numerous Cobra "replicars" that appeared after them and which Shelby fiercely fought against. Shelby also contributed to the midengine GT40 and Mark IV prototypes that took Ford to the racing pinnacle by winning the 24 Hours of LeMans in 1966-67.

Equally famous, but more-popular and practical, was the series of limited-edition Shelby Mustang GTs built in 1965-69. The first, named GT 350 for no particular reason, was a race-inspired conversion of Ford's new 1965-66 "ponycar" carried out by the small Shelby American shop next door to Los Angeles International Airport. Early Shelby-Mustangs were uncompromising grand tourers equally at home on the track. Post-1967 models were planned and built by Ford and were thus "softer," though still plenty exciting.

Ford Division chief Lee Iacocca had asked Shelby to modify the Mustang so it could win the Sports Car Club of America's national B-production championship. The GT 350 did just that in 1965-67, virtually running away from the field to give showroom Mustangs a "competition-proven" aura.

The 1965-66 GT 350 began as a white, blue-striped Mustang fastback supplied with the excellent small-block 289 in 271-bhp "Hi-Performance" guise. "Hi-rise" manifold, bigger four-barrel carburetor, free-flow exhaust, and other Shelby changes lifted output to 306 bhp at 6000 rpm. Carroll also specified the Mustang's optional Borg-Warner T-10 four-speed gearbox, plus a stronger rear axle from the full-size Ford Galaxie to replace the stock Mustang's Falcon unit. Other component swaps included Koni adjustable shocks, Shelby-cast 15-inch alloy wheels wearing high-performance Goodyear tires, metallic friction surfaces for both rear-drum and front-disc brakes, and fast-ratio steering (with relocated front suspension mounting points). A hefty steel tube linked the tops of the front shock towers to reduce body flex in hard cornering. The result of all this was near-neutral handling instead of the stock Mustang's strong understeer, plus 0-60 acceleration of just 6.8 seconds—impressive even today—and over 120 mph all-out. An optional Paxton supercharger, offered during 1966, allegedly boosted horsepower beyond 400 and trimmed the 0-60 time to just five seconds, though very few cars were so equipped.

As planned, Carroll also developed a race-ready GT 350R with the same engine as competition Cobra 289s. That meant a nominal 350 bhp—an outstanding 1.21 bhp per cubic inch. To minimize weight, the gearbox got an aluminum case and the interior was stripped down to a single racing seat, roll bar, and safety harness. Competition tires and super-duty suspension were specified, too. The front bumper was replaced by a rudimentary fiberglass air dam with a large central slot for feeding in extra air. A few GT 350Rs were built with all-disc brakes, 400-bhp 289s, and wide tires under flared fenders.

Hertz Rent-A-Car got into the act during 1966 by ordering 936 special GT 350H models. All carried Ford's three-speed Select-Shift Cruise-O-Matic and black paint set off by gold stripes. Hertz rented them for $17 a day and 17 cents a mile. Weekend racers eagerly lined up, and their unauthorized track outings quickly made the venture a mite unprofitable, leading Hertz to abandon it after just one year.

In all, Shelby built 562 GT 350s for '65 and another 2378 to '66 specs, including R-model racers and Hertz cars, plus six prototype '66 convertibles. That was good production for such a specialized machine, but profit-minded Ford wanted far more. As a result, the original Shelby concept began to be watered down.

Ford bowed a heavier, restyled ponycar for 1967 with a first-time 390 big-block option. Typical of the man, Carroll went one better by tossing in the division's new 428 V-8 for a companion Shelby Mustang, the GT 500. Horsepower was advertised at 335, mainly so insurance companies wouldn't worry, but was closer to 400 actual. The GT 350 returned with its previous power rating, but the true figure was now under 300 because the original steel-tube headers were eliminated to satisfy noise regulations. Both Shelbys sported a longer, more-aggressive new fiberglass nose, crisply clipped "Kamm" tail with prominent spoiler, and other appearance departures from regular Mustangs, plus small chassis refinements. Interiors gained a large black-finish roll bar with built-in inertia-reel seatbelts. Shelby built 3225 of his '67 GTs, which sold for around $4000, down some $500 from the 1965-66 cars that were themselves incredible high-performance buys.

The 350 and 500 returned for '68 in convertible and fastback form, but all were somewhat less-special than the '67s. Interiors, for instance, were stock Mustang save a console-mounted ammeter and oil-pressure gauge, and there were cushy new options like air conditioning, power steering, and automatic

**1965 GT 350 fastback coupe**

**1967 GT 350 fastback coupe**

transmission. Styling was modified via a wider hood scoop and wide Mercury Cougar taillights with sequential turn signals. Convertibles listed about $100 above comparable fastbacks. At midseason, the GT 500 became the GT 500KR—"King of the Road"—denoting Ford's latest 428 "Cobra Jet" engine with jumbo ports and a new intake manifold fed by a huge four-barrel Holley carb. Fastbacks rose to $4117 for the 350, $4317 for the 500, and $4473 for the KR. The costliest '68 Shelby was the KR ragtop, at $4594.

With Ford now calling all the shots, the '69 Shelbys became even more like that year's fully redesigned stock Mustangs. Styling remained distinctive but was busier, with a big loop bumper/grille, scoops and ducts most everywhere, and reflective tape stripes midway up the flanks. GT 350s were demoted to Ford's new 351 "Cleveland" V-8 with 290 bhp; GT 500s, no longer KRs, stayed with the Cobra Jet, still at a nominal 335 bhp. But after just 3150 of the '69s, plus 636 leftovers reserialized as '70s, Shelby and Iacocca agreed to end the Mustang GT program in the face of blossoming government regulations, spiraling insurance rates (the cars' accident record was staggering), and sales interference from hot new production Mustangs like the Mach I and Boss 302. Like the Cobras, however, these Shelbys quickly became high-priced, highly sought after collector cars.

The Mustang experience had soured Shelby on being a small-scale auto manufacturer, and he turned to other interests.

Iacocca, meantime, was promoted to Ford Motor Company president in 1970. He continued as such until the summer of '78, when he was abruptly fired by chairman Henry Ford II in a celebrated row that was as personal as it was public. (HFII was reportedly jealous, if not fearful of Iacocca's growing prominence and power.) Later that year, Iacocca made his equally celebrated move to the presidency of then-moribund Chrysler Corporation, where he was named board chairman in 1979.

After helping pull Chrysler from the financial brink, Iacocca called on old friend Shelby to add some needed pizzazz to the corporate lineup—timely, as performance was starting to make a comeback throughout Detroit. Carroll agreed, and Chrysler duly announced his arrival in 1982 as a "performance consultant" who promised to "bring excitement back to the auto industry."

The first fruit of the renewed Shelby/Iacocca partnership was the Chrysler Shelby California Development Center. Set up in Santa Fe Springs, near Los Angeles, CSCDC was assigned to work with Chrysler engineers in exploring new technology for future models and to devise specific performance packages for Chrysler's "excitement" division, Dodge. Two immediate results were the 1983-86 Shelby Charger coupe and Omni GLH ("Goes Like Hell") sedan, essentially "Shelbyized" versions of those workaday front-drive subcompacts. Both offered extra power, tight suspension, distinctive styling touches, and attractively low prices (see Dodge for additional information). Things went a step further in February 1986, when Shelby and Chrysler Motors chairman Gerald Greenwald announced formation of Shelby Automobiles, Inc. (SAI) in nearby Whittier, California, to build high-performance Dodge-based limited editions.

With that, March 1, 1986, introduced the first Shelby-marque car since the final Mustang GTs: a quicker, more-powerful GLH called GLH-S ("Goes Like Hell—Some more"). This carried a 2.2-liter (135 cid) turbocharged Chrysler four-cylinder engine that Shelby tweaked to 175 bhp via an air-to-air intercooler, equal-length intake runners, and other alterations. Helped by a mandatory five-speed manual transmission, the GLH-S offered brisk eight-second 0-60 performance—and truly horrendous front-drive torque-steer.

In February 1987, SAI began building a new Shelby Lancer spun from Dodge's recently launched "H-body" four-door hatchback sedan. Base-priced at $16,995, this also came with

1968 GT 500 convertible coupe

1968 GT 500 fastback coupe

1969 GT 500 convertible coupe

the five-speed and the 175-bhp turbo-four, but offered a tamer 146-bhp turbo 2.2 with TorqueFlite automatic for $1000 extra. The Shelby Lancer took Carroll into a new realm: the high-style European-type sports sedan. Equipment was suitably lavish, with power everything, all-disc brakes (instead of rear drums), and a special Shelby Touring Suspension (good for 0.80g on the skidpad). Handling was sharp and manual-shift acceleration lively—7.7 seconds 0-60 in most published road tests—but shift action was clunky, the ride jarring, turbo "lag" annoying, and quietness conspicuously absent.

As ever, though, Shelby wasn't building cars for the masses. After completing 800 Shelby Lancers by July of '87, SAI turned to a similarly modified Dodge Shadow compact called the Shelby CSX. Offered only as a two-door hatchback sedan, it weighed 200 pounds less than the midsize Shelby Lancer and was thus a bit quicker. The factory claimed 0-60 in 7.1 seconds and a standing quarter-mile of 15.1 seconds at 90 mph. Most road tests agreed.

Meanwhile, Carroll wrote two postscripts to his Ford experience. The first involved a dozen GT 350 convertibles built from restored Mustangs, essentially brand-new '66 models identical to Shelby's original six prototypes. All sold quickly despite stiff $40,000 price tags. Shelby sprang a similar surprise in early 1993 by announcing that four dozen "continuation" Cobra 427SCs would be assembled from never-used stock parts he had in storage for years.

A heart transplant forced Shelby to slow down for a while, yet he somehow found the time and energy to be the "spiritual

**1987 Charger GLH-S hatchback coupe**

**1987 Shelby Lancer hatchback sedan**

**1999 Series I convertible coupe**

conscience" behind the Cobra-like 1992 Dodge Viper RT/10. In late 1997, he lent his name to something rather unusual for him: a hot-rodded Dodge Durango sport-utility vehicle. Premiered as a concept at the SEMA aftermarket-industry show, the Shelby SP360 was a limited edition created by several independent tuners with hopes of getting Carroll's endorsement. The concept packed a supercharged 5.9-liter (360-cid) Dodge V-8 making 360 bhp, plus a fortified suspension and other Shelby-style features, including the trademark Cobra Blue paint and broad white dorsal stripes. Dodge said only 3000 SP360s would be built, all in 1999, but actual production was probably less.

But Shelby had long since drifted away from Chrysler (his pal Iacocca had left in 1992), and was pursuing new ventures of his own. After moving some of his enterprises to facilities near the recently opened Las Vegas Motor Speedway, he began advertising another "new-old" Cobra, the CSX4000. This looked much like an original 289, but was sold without an engine as a "component car," again to sidestep pesky "gummint" rules.

Shelby was now in his 70s, but as restless as ever. "I'm tired of imitations," he had told the press. "Folks have put the Cobra name on all sorts of stuff . . . but none of them were Shelby Cobras. Before they throw the last shovel of dirt on me, I want to take one last shot at an honest-to-goodness Cobra."

Though not exactly a Cobra, the prosaically named Series I would prove the most-vexing car of Shelby's storied career. It entered production—with great difficulty—in 1999 after some five years of second thoughts and false starts. The original plan, revealed in April 1994, was for a twin-turbo V-8 roadster with 500 bhp, a chassis made of high-tech carbon fiber, and a staggering $200,000 price tag. Only 500 would be built. The engine would come from none other than flagging Oldsmobile. General manager John Rock, a cowboy type worthy of Shelby himself, suggested the new 4.0-liter twincam Aurora V-8, hoping an Olds-powered "Cobra for the '90s" would do for his brand what the Viper had done for Dodge. Market realities soon forced downshifting to a less-ambitious $50,000 machine.

The Series I bowed as a "pushmobile" at the Greater Los Angeles Auto Show in January 1997. A running prototype was tested the following October, by which time the chassis was a steel-tube structure supporting a carbon-fiber body. Initial deliveries were planned for 1998. But, uncharacteristically, Shelby American underestimated production costs by a whopping $60,000 a car. That, plus unforeseen development glitches and construction delays with the new Las Vegas plant, pushed production back to mid-1999. By that point the price had soared to near $100,000 and soon went to nearly $114-grand. Despite sizable deposits from 300 would-be owners and a handful of Olds dealers who would sell the car, the project was almost bankrupt by year's end, when only 20 Series Is had been built.

Just when all seemed lost, Venture Industries, which supplied the carbon-fiber bodies, rode to the rescue, offering some $10 million for a 60-percent stake in Shelby American. By late April, Shelby American was honoring original contracts with dealers, depositers, and suppliers; lingering engineering bugs were fast being squashed; and production was up to 1.2 cars a day, thanks to more-efficient methods. But about 250 Series Is were still unsold, and price had to be hiked again—first to $160,000, then to near $175,000—close, ironically, to the original 1994 figure.

For the few who got to drive it, the Series I was a genuine Shelby with all the thrills that name implied. Riding a tight 96.2-wheelbase, the Series I was three inches wider than a C5 Corvette yet scaled a feathery 2650 pounds. The carbon-fiber body weighed only 130 pounds, yet was stronger than steel. So, too, the chassis, made up from extruded-aluminum members and boasting a resonance frequency of 52 hertz, more than double the best then attained in production cars. Suspension was also mostly aluminum, with four-wheel independent geometry by upper and lower control arms, an adjustable shock, and a coil spring attached to Formula 1-style pushrod-operated inboard rocker arms. This layout not only reduced undesirable unsprung weight but could be easily custom-tuned. An antiroll bar lived at each end. Brakes were contemporary Corvette discs of 13-inch diameter fore, 12 inches aft. As with the Viper, though, Shelby felt no need for antilock brake control. Steering was the expected power rack-and-pinion. Rolling stock comprised five-spoke 18-inch alloys wearing Z-rated Goodyear Eagle F1 Supercar tires sized at P265/40 front, P315/40 rear. A Corvette six-speed manual gearbox was sited in the tail, helping achieve the ideal 50/50 weight distribution. The Aurora V-8 got new camshafts, intake manifold, exhaust system, and control chip; modest changes that nevertheless yielded 320 bhp, up 70 from stock, and 30 extra pound-feet of torque, 290 in all.

With a stump-pulling 4.22:1 rear axle and carrying just 8.3 pounds per horsepower, the Series I was claimed to do 0-60 in 4.4 seconds, 0-100 in 11 flat, and a 12.8-second standing quarter-mile at 109.9 mph. *AutoWeek* found these numbers credible, though it couldn't confirm them in testing two prototypes. But the magazine did find the Series I "a blast to drive. It handles like a world-class sports car." Yet this Shelby was no raw-edged Cobra, equipped with standard air conditioning, power windows, leather-trimmed cockpit, and a booming stereo. Some GM bits were obvious inside, but the manual folding top was

# Shelby

snug and easy to operate, and workmanship improved to first-class once Venture came aboard. By February 2002, Shelby American had delivered 240 Series Is, with orders for 25 more.

Shelby's later accomplishments only enhanced his stature in the world of high-performance automobiles. Ever the complex but plain-spoken and colorful iconoclast, his dedication, passion, and the sheer driving force of his will are reflected in most every car he ever touched.

## Specifications

### 1965

| GT 350 (wb 108.0) | | Wght | Price | Prod |
|---|---|---|---|---|
| fstbk cpe | | 2,800 | 4,457 | 562 |
| **1965 Engine** | **bore × stroke** | **bhp** | **availability** | |
| V-8, 289.0 | 4.00 × 2.87 | 306 | S-all | |

### 1966

| GT 350 (wb 108.0) | | Wght | Price | Prod |
|---|---|---|---|---|
| fstbk cpe | | 2,800 | 4,600 | 2,378 |
| **1966 Engines** | **bore × stroke** | **bhp** | **availability** | |
| V-8, 289.0 | 4.00 × 2.87 | 306 | S-all | |
| V-8S, 289.0 | 4.00 × 2.87 | 400 | O-all (limited) | |

### 1967

| GT 350 (wb 108.0) | | Wght | Price | Prod |
|---|---|---|---|---|
| fstbk cpe | | 2,800 | 3,995 | 1,175 |
| GT 500 (wb 108.0) | | | | |
| fstbk cpe | | 3,000 | 4,195 | 2,050 |
| **1967 Engines** | **bore × stroke** | **bhp** | **availability** | |
| V-8, 289.0 | 4.00 × 2.87 | 290 | S-GT350 | |
| V-8, 428.0 | 4.13 × 3.98 | 400* | S-GT500 | |

* Estimated; advertised bhp 335.

### 1968

| GT 350 (wb 108.0) | | Wght | Price | Prod |
|---|---|---|---|---|
| fstbk cpe | | 3,000 | 4,117 | 1,253 |
| conv cpe | | 3,100 | 4,238 | 404 |
| GT 500 (wb 108.0) | | | | |
| fstbk cpe | | 3,100 | 4,317 | 1,140 |
| conv cpe | | 3,200 | 4,439 | 402 |
| GT 500KR (wb 108.0) | | | | |
| fstbk cpe | | 3,200 | 4,473 | 933 |
| conv cpe | | 3,300 | 4,594 | 318 |
| **1968 Engines** | **bore × stroke** | **bhp** | **availability** | |
| V-8, 302.0 | 4.00 × 3.00 | 250 | S-GT350 | |
| V-8, 390.0 | 4.05 × 3.78 | 335 | S-GT500 | |
| V-8, 428.0 | 4.13 × 3.98 | 360 | S-GT500 | |
| V-8, 428.0 | 4.13 × 3.98 | 400* | S-GT500KR | |

* Estimated; advertised bhp 335.

### 1969

| GT 350 (wb 108.0) | | Wght | Price | Prod |
|---|---|---|---|---|
| fstbk cpe | | 3,000 | 4,434 | 1,085 |
| conv cpe | | 3,100 | 4,753 | 194 |
| GT 500 (wb 108.0) | | | | |
| fstbk cpe | | 3,100 | 4,709 | 1,536 |
| conv cpe | | 3,200 | 5,027 | 335 |
| **1969 Engines** | **bore × stroke** | **bhp** | **availability** | |
| V-8, 351.0 | 4.00 × 3.50 | 290 | S-GT350 | |
| V-8, 428.0 | 4.13 × 3.98 | 400* | S-GT500 | |

* Estimated; advertised bhp 335.

### 1970

| GT 350 (wb 108.0)—350 built | | Wght | Price | Prod |
|---|---|---|---|---|
| fstbk cpe | | 3,000 | 4,500* | — |
| conv cpe | | 3,100 | 4,800* | — |
| GT 500 (wb 108.0)—286 built | | | | |
| fstbk cpe | | 3,100 | 4,800* | — |
| conv cpe | | 3,200 | 5,100* | — |

* Estimated.

| **1970 Engines** | **bore × stroke** | **bhp** | **availability** |
|---|---|---|---|
| V-8, 351.0 | 4.00 × 3.50 | 290 | S-GT350 |
| V-8, 428.0 | 4.13 × 3.98 | 375* | S-GT500 |

* Estimated; advertised bhp 335.

### 1986

| Shelby GLH-S (wb 99.1) | | Wght | Price | Prod |
|---|---|---|---|---|
| htchbk sdn 4d | | 2,300 | 10,995 | 500 |
| **1986 Engine** | **bore × stroke** | **bhp** | **availability** | |
| I-4T, 135.0 | 3.44 × 3.62 | 175 | S | |

### 1987

| Shelby Charger GLH-S (wb 96.5) | | Wght | Price | Prod |
|---|---|---|---|---|
| htchbk cpe | | 2,483 | 12,995 | 1,000 |
| Shelby CSX (wb 97.0) | | | | |
| htchbk cpe | | 2,690 | 13,495 | 750 |
| Shelby Lancer (wb 103.1) | | | | |
| htchbk sdn 4d | | 2,895 | 16,995* | 800 |
| **1987 Engines** | **bore × stroke** | **bhp** | **availability** | |
| I-4T, 135.0 | 3.44 × 3.62 | 175 | S-All | |
| I-4T, 135.0 | 3.44 × 3.62 | 146 | O-Shelby Lancer (automatic) | |

* 5-speed manual transmission, cloth upholstery; $17,995, automatic transmission, leather upholstery.

### 1988

| Shelby CSX-T (wb 97.0) | | Wght | Price | Prod |
|---|---|---|---|---|
| htchbk cpe | | 2,675 | * | 1,000 |
| **1988 Engine** | **bore × stroke** | **bhp** | **availability** | |
| I-4T, 135.0 | 3.44 × 3.62 | 146 | S | |

* All were sold to Thrifty Car Rental at fleet prices.

### 1989

| Shelby CSX (wb 97.0) | | Wght | Price | Prod |
|---|---|---|---|---|
| htchbk cpe | | 2,790 | 15,000 | 500 |
| **1989 Engine** | **bore × stroke** | **bhp** | **availability** | |
| I-4T, 135.0 | 3.22 × 3.62 | 175 | S | |

### 1999-2002

| Series 1 (wb 96.2) | | Wght | Price | Prod |
|---|---|---|---|---|
| conv 2d | | 2,650 | 175,000 | * |
| **1999-'02 Engines** | **bore × stroke** | **bhp** | **availability** | |
| V-8, 244.0 | 3.42 × 3.31 | 320 | S | |
| V-8S, 244.0 | 3.42 × 3.31 | 450-500 | O | |

* 500 maximum planned, all certified as 1999 models.

# Studebaker

Studebaker was born in 1852 when brothers Henry and Clem built three covered wagons in South Bend, Indiana. Actually there were five Studebaker brothers, all of whom participated in company affairs over the years.

J. M. "Wheelbarrow Johnny" was president in 1902, when Studebaker began building automobiles. He relinquished the president's chair in 1919 to Albert Russell Erskine, a one-time company accountant who would take the firm into the '30s. Erskine made a series of serious mistakes, starting with the ill-timed acquisition of Pierce-Arrow in 1928. His next blunder was a 1930 car named for himself. Although a pretty little six-cylinder job offered in nine models, the 70-horsepower Erskine was a weak performer and thus a slow seller. Production came to just 22,371.

Having failed with his namesake car, A. R. Erskine put the same small Studebaker six into another low-priced "companion," the Rockne, named for then-famous Notre Dame football coach Knute Rockne. This car lasted little longer than the Erskine, with just over 36,000 built in 1932-33. At $585-$735, the Rockne should have sold well in those deep Depression years, but lack of power was again a handicap, compounded by iffy workmanship. Yet another Erskine error was selling a Studebaker called Dictator. The name seemed downright unpatriotic as real-life dictators Hitler and Mussolini consolidated their power, yet it persisted through 1937.

Excluding the Erskine, Studebaker's 1930 line encompassed no fewer than six engines and seven series. A six and eight, both 221-cubic-inch inline units of similar power, featured in that year's 115-inch-wheelbase Dictator and 120-inch Commander series. Low-priced 114-inch-wheelbase Standard Sixes anchored the line. At the top were magnificent President Eights, offered on both a 125-inch-wheelbase chassis and a special 135-inch platform. These were the finest automobiles South Bend built in this decade—perhaps the best ever.

For 1931, Studebaker dropped the Dictator Six with its 221 engine while lengthening wheelbases to 124 inches on Commanders and to 130/136 on Presidents. At midyear, the 221 Dictator eight was booted from 70 to 81 bhp, and the long-stroke 250.4-cid Commander unit was pushed to 101. Prices were adjusted to cover a slightly broader range of $795-$2550, versus 1930's $895-$2595.

This same lineup returned for 1932-33, when the small 205-cid six powered the Rockne. The senior-line six, a stroked 230 with 80 bhp, went into a new 117-inch-wheelbase Standard chassis that also served Dictator Eights. The Commander's wheelbase increased an inch, and all Presidents sat atop a new 135-inch platform. Arriving for '33 was a Commander eight stroked to 235 cid and 100 bhp; the 250-cid engine gained nine bhp.

The 205 six returned with 88 bhp for a 113-inch-wheelbase 1934 Dictator line comprising Standard, Special, and Deluxe models. That year's Commanders rode a 119-inch wheelbase and carried a revived 221 eight, albeit with 103 bhp. Presidents were downgraded to the 110-bhp, 250-cid eight and now rode a 123-inch chassis.

Sales dwindled from over 123,000 for 1930 to under 26,000 for '32, dropping the make from fourth to 11th. Studebaker finished 14th for 1933, when it went into receivership after a hoped-for merger with White Motors fell through. With that, Erskine resigned, then committed suicide soon afterward.

Stepping into this managerial breach were production vice-president Harold S. Vance and sales VP Paul G. Hoffman, who would jointly guide Studebaker through 1949. They quickly got rid of Pierce-Arrow, then took steps to get idle production lines moving again. As a result, Studebaker made a small profit in 1934, enough to secure a line of credit and get out of receivership. Production promptly moved up to near 60,000 from 1933's paltry 12,500, lifting the make to eighth in the industry. Output slipped below 44,000 for '35, but recovered to near 56,000 and some 98,000 for 1936-37, respectively, when Studebaker finished 11th and tenth. Part of this success reflected a reversal of Erskine's "full-line" market approach. Studebaker's 1934-35 line comprised just three series: Dictator Six, Commander Eight, and President Eight. Commanders then took a two-year vacation.

For 1934, Studebaker introduced streamlined "Year Ahead" models with pontoon fenders and rounded grilles. Rumble-seat body types departed the following year. "Potato" shapes were evident for 1936-37, as most everywhere else, yet Studebaker managed a handsome, individual appearance. Offerings in both those years comprised 116-inch-wheelbase Dictators and Presidents that rode 125-inch chassis.

For 1938 styling, Hoffmann hired Raymond Loewy, the brilliant industrial designer who'd created the 1932-34 "Aero-dynamic" Hupmobiles. This first of many Loewy projects at South Bend produced a prominent prow-type radiator with pod headlights snugged in between it and the fenders, plus GM-style "catwalk" trim on some models. Those offerings involved a revived Commander Six with five body styles, a replacement for the departed Dictator on a slightly longer 116.5-inch chassis. The same platform supported four State Commander Eights, while a newly abbreviated 122-inch chassis appeared under four State Presidents. The 1939 models had headlamps moved out into the fenders and more horizontal grillework to match.

Though Studebaker earned a respectable $2 million for 1936, profits slimmed to just $812,000 for '37, followed by a deficit of $1.76-million in recession-plagued 1938. But things improved markedly in '39, when model-year car production jumped nearly 50 percent to almost 86,000. From there, it went nowhere but up until the war.

The big reason for this roaring success was the cleanly styled Champion, available as a new economy coupe, club sedan, and four-door Cruising Sedan on a 110-inch wheelbase. Pitched in the $660-$800 range, it cost only $25-$40 more than the "Low-Priced Three."

Though carefully weight-engineered by engineering VP Roy Cole and project chief Eugene Hardig, the Champ was no less substantial than a Commander or President. Its new 164.3-cid L-head six was smaller than rival engines and made less power—78 bhp initially—but the Champ delivered comparable performance because it weighed an average 500-600 pounds less. Though no match for a V-8/85 Ford, it would run up to 78 mph—equal to or better than Chevy, Plymouth, and the Ford V-8/60. Mileage and durability were fantastic.

With all this, the Champ scored nearly 34,000 model-year sales despite its midseason debut, lofting Studebaker back up to seventh in the industry with total 1939 car production just short of 86,000. Coupled with the much-reduced break-even point of 75,000 cars wrought by Hoffman and Vance, South Bend earned $2.9 million.

You don't mess with a savior, so Champ changes for 1940 were limited to finer grille bars, sealed-beam headlamps per industry practice, new Custom DeLuxe trim, and a second coupe with rear "opera seat." Series production nearly doubled for the model year, hitting 66,264. Commanders and Presidents returned with wheelbases and engines unchanged in 1938-39,

# Studebaker

1932 President Eight four-door sedan

1934 Commander 2/4-passenger convertible roadster

1938 Commander five-passenger coupe

1947 Commander four-door sedan

1948 Commander Regal DeLuxe convertible coupe

but lost their convertible sedans, leaving each with a coupe, Cruising Sedan, and two-door club sedan; Commander still listed a business coupe as well. Front ends were more Lincoln-like than Champion's, with sharper prows and a split, roughly heart-shaped vertical-bar grille. Presidents sold for about $125 more than comparable Commanders, which ranged upward of $200 above the Champs.

Loewy reworked the entire line for 1941, giving the cars slightly sharper noses and lower, wider vertical-bar grilles. The engines were reworked, too. Champ's was stroked to 169.6 cid and 80 bhp, while more-subtle changes lifted Commander's six to 94 bhp and the President's silky nine-main straight-eight to 117.

1941 was another excellent Studebaker sales year, though the make slipped from eighth to ninth in the model-year production race. Still, Champ attracted nearly 85,000 buyers to become the single best-selling line in Studebaker history, and Commander rose from just under 35,000 to nearly 42,000. President maintained its low-volume tradition with just under 7000 model-year sales, up only 500 from 1940.

A wider, heavier-looking, and rather Chevy-like "face" arrived for war-shortened '42, when DeLux-tone models were renamed "Deluxstyle." Studebaker touted a "new, perfected Turbo-matic Drive" as a Commander/President option. This was much like Chrysler's semiautomatic Fluid Drive, a manual transmission with a fluid coupling allowing clutchless changes within two gear ranges. Studebaker returned to eighth for the model year by building some 50,000 cars before February 1942, when the government ended consumer production for the duration of World War II.

Studebaker's military output was numerous and varied, chiefly trucks (where the firm had an equally long and successful record) but also airplane engines and "Weasel" personnel carriers. Thanks largely to the success of the '39 Champion, Studebaker had turned over its styling chores to Loewy Associates, an outside firm not entirely occupied with defense contracts. As a result, Studebaker was able to introduce all-new postwar cars in the spring of 1946—well ahead of everyone else except industry newcomer Kaiser-Frazer.

Earlier that year, Studebaker returned to civilian car sales with Skyway Champions, slightly altered versions of the 1942 Champ three- and five-passenger coupe and two- and four-door sedan. Changes were few and modest: an upper-grille molding that extended beneath the headlamps, optional lamps atop the fenders, and the elimination of hoodside moldings. Only 19,275 were built before South Bend changed over to the all-new '47s.

Costing some $11 million to develop, these appealing new Studebakers had evolved from sketches done as early as 1940 by young Robert E. Bourke. It was that work that prompted Bourke's hiring at Loewy Associates by Virgil M. Exner, the group's chief stylist. Exner had joined Loewy before the war after a career at Pontiac. Though Exner began the '47 Studebaker program, he left Loewy before the design was finalized, so the end product was a blend of Exner and Bourke ideas.

Postwar Presidents were still some years off in 1947, but Commanders returned along with Champions. The latter, no longer called Skyway, were little changed mechanically, but rode a two-inch-longer wheelbase. A special 123-inch chassis was reserved for a lush new Commander Land Cruiser priced at $2043. Other Commanders retained the prewar 119-inch wheelbase. Both series listed two- and four-door sedans (the latter now with "suicide" back doors), long-deck three-seater coupe, and a new five-passenger "Starlight" coupe with radical three-element wraparound rear window. All were available with base DeLuxe trim or, for about $120 more, in new Regal DeLuxe form. Also new were a pair of Regal convertibles, a $1902 Champ and $2236 Commander. Studebaker returned to

# Studebaker

1950 Champion Regal DeLuxe coupe

1952 Champion Starlight coupe

1953 Champion Regal Starliner hardtop coupe

1956 Sky Hawk hardtop coupe

profitability in 1947, earning more than $9 million on 58.5-percent higher calendar-year car/truck sales.

The upward trend continued in 1948, with $19 million in earnings on calendar-year output of over a quarter-million cars and trucks—both Studebaker records. Predictably, South Bend's cars changed little for '48, though a winged hood medallion provided instant identification. Another, more-significant linewide change was a price hike averaging $200, bringing stickers to $1535-$2430 in reflection of strong postwar inflation. South Bend moved up a notch on the industry roster, finishing seventh for the model year with nearly 185,000 cars.

Though brand-new styling was planned for 1949 to one-up the competition again, lack of time precluded it, so Studebaker settled for refinements. Champs sported a new grille composed of horizontal and vertical louvers forming three rows of rectangular openings, and the Commander six was stroked to 245.6 cid, good for an even 100 bhp. Despite the lack of change, profits soared to $27.5 million.

Studebaker was 98 years young in 1950, which would be its best-ever car year. Model-year production totaled 343,166. Grand preparations were underway for the firm's "second century," about which there were many equally grand predictions. But, of course, that second 100 years would be cut far short—to exactly 14.

Seeking to look fresh against newer-design rivals for 1950, Studebaker gave its basic '47 bodies a dramatic cowl-forward facelift that was controversial at the time. According to designer Bob Bourke, the new "bullet nose" front was ordered by the French-accented Loewy with the words, "Now Bob, eet has to look like zee aeroplane." It did, and had the most-bizarre face of any American car since Graham's abortive 1939-40 "Sharknose."

The new front increased wheelbase a nominal one inch for all 1950 Studebakers, bringing Champs up to 113 inches and Commanders to 120. Engines were unchanged. So was the lineup, except for a quartet of price-leading Champ Customs in the low $1400s. That year's Land Cruiser was tagged at $2187. The year's big technical news was "Automatic Drive" as an across-the-board option. Studebaker had designed this excellent new fully self-shifting transmission in cooperation with the Detroit Gear Division of Borg-Warner—the only postwar automatic developed by an independent other than Packard's Ultramatic.

Wheelbases were rearranged again for 1951, thanks to an improved chassis with better brakes, easier "center-point" steering, and a 115-inch wheelbase for all models (up two on Champions, down five on Commanders) except the Land Cruiser, which got a 119-inch spread. Champ power was unchanged, but there was big news in Studebaker's first V-8, a new standard for Commanders. Sized at 232.6 cid, it pumped out 120 bhp by conventional means, although overhead cams and hemispherical combustion chambers had been considered.

Rising production costs forced Studebaker to raise prices a bit for 1951, the range running $1560-$2380. But buyers seemed happy to pay for South Bend's lively new V-8, which boosted Commander sales no less than 70 percent. Appearance changes for '51 were slight. The bullet nose was toned down by painting its chrome outer ring, the prominent air vents above the sub-grilles were erased, and model names were spelled out on hood leading edges. However you think it looks now, the 1950-51 bullet nose was quite salable. Though Korean War restrictions held 1951 car production to 268,566, Studebaker actually increased its market share from 4.02 to 4.17 percent.

An all-new Studebaker was planned for centennial 1952, with unit construction and evolutionary bullet-nose styling. But though this "N-Series" progressed to a running prototype, it was abandoned due to continuing government restraints on civilian goods and a big upturn in Studebaker's military business.

Accordingly, the '47 platform was facelifted one last time for '52, gaining a low and toothy full-width grille dubbed "the clam digger" by Loewy stylists. Offerings stood pat with the exception of the belated addition of new Starliner hardtop coupes. As in '51, trim levels comprised Custom, DeLuxe, and Regal for Champion; Regal and State for Commander. Starliners were top-liners. To no one's surprise, Studebaker paced the 1952 Indy 500, and a Champ and Commander scored class wins in that year's Mobilgas Economy Run. But Studey's centennial saw production of just 186,239 units.

Studebaker updated its look in literal high style for the first model year of its second century. Headlining the all-new '53 line were the now-legendary "Loewy coupes." These were sleek, low, and clean—triumphs of good taste. There were six in all:

# Studebaker

1956 Golden Hawk hardtop coupe

1956 President Classic four-door sedan

1957 Commander two-door sedan

1957 Golden Hawk hardtop coupe

1957 Silver Hawk two-door coupe

1958 Commander four-door sedan

pillarless Regal Starliner and pillared Deluxe and Regal Starlights, Commander, and Champion. Despite the "Loewy" nickname, the basic design was actually the work of Bob Bourke. It was first intended only for a show car, but Loewy himself convinced Studebaker management that it should be put into production.

Perfect from every angle, the Loewy coupe mounted a new 120.5-inch Land Cruiser chassis rather than the 116.5-inch platform used for other models. Advertised as the "new European look," it's still widely regarded as America's best automotive design of the decade. Studebaker's 1953 two- and four-door sedans were almost as pretty, bearing coupe lines but necessarily stubbier and more-upright on the shorter wheelbase.

Ominously, tooling the '53 line delayed its production, which ended at a disappointing 169,899. Worse, when things finally did get rolling, demand for coupes was four times that for sedans. Management had expected just the reverse, and both time and sales were lost in switching around. For all that, Studebaker managed a slim $2.69 million profit for the fiscal year.

Eggcrate grille inserts identified the predictably little-changed '54 models, which again included the "Loewys," a pair of cheap Champ Custom sedans, and Deluxe and Regal sedans in each line. A belated newcomer was the two-door all-steel Conestoga, Studebaker's first station wagon. Named for the famous "prairie schooners" of the firm's infancy, it came as Deluxe and Regal Champs and Commanders. Also new for '54 were seven extra horses for Commanders and larger brakes across the board.

But Studebaker's weaknesses were now painfully apparent. On "pricing out" a Commander Starliner using the General Motors cost structure, Bourke found that Chevrolet could have sold it for $1900; Studebaker charged $2500. Meanwhile, the "Ford Blitz" was on, as Dearborn waged a no-holds-barred price war with GM. Though neither giant damaged the other, they wreaked havoc on independents like Studebaker, whose model-year volume plunged to 81,930.

But just as things looked blackest, Nash president George Mason persuaded Packard president James J. Nance to purchase Studebaker as a prelude to combining with Nash and Hudson to form Mason's hoped-for American Motors. The Packard takeover was duly accomplished in October 1954, ushering in the able Nance to preside over a new Studebaker-Packard Corporation. But when Mason died suddenly that same month, so did his dream of a "Big Four."

Meantime, Studebaker hitched hopes for higher sales to a group of facelifted '55s laden with chrome. Among them were the first postwar Presidents: top-line Deluxe and State four-door sedans (replacing Land Cruiser) and pillared and pillarless State coupes. More power was the order of the day. The Champ six was stroked to 185.6 cid and 101 bhp. Commander's V-8 was pumped up to 140 bhp despite a downsizing to 224.3 cid. Presidents arrived with a 232 bored out to 259 cid, good for 175 bhp. Seeking to hold production costs, Studebaker discarded Automatic Drive for Borg-Warner's cheaper "Flight-O-Matic."

But sales still lagged, so a raft of changes were made in

January '55. Commander was promoted to a 162-bhp "Bearcat" 259 (an optional "High Power Kit" added 20 bhp more), and Presidents graduated to a 185-bhp "Passmaster" version. At the same time, noncoupe Presidents and Commanders gained trendy "Ultra Vista" wrapped windshields, and a jazzy President Speedster hardtop bowed with "quilted" leather interior, full instrumentation in a tooled-metal dash, and wild two-tone paint schemes like pink and black and "lemon and lime." But because it listed at a pricey $3253, the Speedster was not a big seller (just 2215 built). Neither were its linemates. In a year when most makes set new sales records, Studebaker managed only 133,826 cars. At this point, South Bend needed about 250,000 annual car sales just to break even.

A game reskin for '56 achieved a squarer look announced by large mesh-filled grilles. Commander and Champion gained inexpensive two-door "sedanets" priced under $2000, a spiffy long-chassis Classic sedan joined the President range at $2489, and wagons got new names: Pelham (Champion), Parkview (Commander), and Pinehurst (President).

Coupes were dubbed the Hawk line of "family sports cars." The last '50s Studebakers styled by the Loewy team, they featured an admirably restrained facelift of the original 1953 coupe, with modest tailfins and a large square grille riding high on an elevated hood. Deluxe interiors featured tooled-metal dash trim, as on the '55 Speedster. There were four versions, pillared Flight Hawk and Power Hawk, and hardtop Sky Hawk and Golden Hawk. All were good-looking, competent through curves, and impressive on straights.

Topping Studebaker's '56 engine chart was a 275-bhp 352 V-8 from new partner Packard as exclusive power for the Golden Hawk. Champs, Flight Hawk, and the Pelham wagon carried an unchanged six, while 259 V-8s now delivered 170/185 bhp in Commander/Power Hawk/Parkview. A new long-stroke 289 version offered 195/210/225 bhp in Presidents/Sky Hawk/Pinehurst.

The Flight Hawk listed below $2000 and the Golden Hawk at $3061, so Studebaker's "family sports cars" were good buys in 1956. Trouble was, they were peripheral sellers appealing mainly to enthusiasts, while the bread-and-butter models appealed to few mainstream buyers. Studebaker thus managed just 85,462 of its '56 cars, including 19,165 Hawks. But the worst was yet to come: In 1957-58, Studebaker and Packard combined couldn't sell more than 80,000 cars a year.

In May 1956, Nance arranged with Curtiss-Wright Corporation, through its president, Roy Hurley, for "advisory management services"—in other words, a cash bailout. With that, plans for an expansive new 1957 S-P line were abruptly canceled and Nance resigned along with Studebaker chairman Paul Hoffman and president Harold Vance. This left Hurley to preside over a group of 1957-58 Studebakers restyled in the only possible way—on the cheap.

Duncan McRae did the deed, giving standard '57s a full-width grille and grossly distended rear fenders suggesting fins. Hawks gained prominent fins that didn't seriously detract from overall appearance. Models were cut to Deluxe and Custom Champ and Commander sedans, Pelham and Parkview wagons, three President sedans, Golden Hawk, and a new pillared Silver Hawk available with six or 289 V-8. Somehow, Studebaker also managed four-door wagons, offered as Commander Provincial and President Broadmoor. Higher compression lifted the 259-cid V-8 to 180/195 bhp, and the Golden Hawk exchanged its Packard engine for a Paxton-supercharged Studebaker 289 delivering the same 275 bhp. Another attempt to spark sales produced the midyear Scotsman, a miserly wagon and two sedans offering six-cylinder power—and very little else—for well under $2000. Some 9300 were sold, but overall '57 sales did not spark, and model-year car production ended at only 74,738.

The '58s were uglier still, with hastily contrived four-headlamp fronts and even-more-garish trim. Commander and President introduced new Starlight hardtop coupes on the 116.5-inch chassis, but the overall lineup was thinner. The Scotsmans did well in that recession year with nearly 21,000 sales. A good thing, too, for total volume dropped again, this time to 62,114.

Studebaker might have died right there had it not been for the sudden success of the compact Lark. Replacing all the old standard models for 1959, this retained the basic sedan/wagon inner structure used since '53, but shorn of all the extra sheet-metal hung on it in the intervening years, good for a loss of up to 200 pounds in curb weight. In its place, McRae applied simple, clean, well-formed styling announced by a Hawk-like grille and a return to dual headlamps. The 169.6-cid six also returned, making 90 bhp in "Lark VI" Deluxe and Regal two- and four-door sedans, two-door wagons, and Regal hardtop coupe. A Regal four-door, hardtop, and wagon comprised the "Lark VIII" series with standard two-barrel 180-bhp 259 V-8; optional "Power Pack" four-barrel carb and dual exhaust added 15 horses. Wagons rode the familiar 113-inch wheelbase, but other Larks sat on a trim new 108.5-inch span.

With all this, the Lark was lively (0-60 in under 10 seconds with 180-bhp V-8) yet economical (over 22 mpg easy) and surprisingly roomy. Aided by starting prices below $2000, it was a smash hit, garnering 131,078 sales.

Studebaker didn't give up on "family sports cars" for '59, but the only one it offered was a pillared Silver Hawk. Available with six or either Lark V-8, it added only 7788 units to total model-year production. Still, Studebaker found its way out of the financial woods, earning its first profit in six years on a startling sales gain of over 250 percent from abysmal 1958.

Lark was predictably little changed for 1960. Minor trim was shuffled, and the grille went from horizontal bars to mesh. Four-door wagons returned for the first time since 1958, and that year's Lark VIII line offered Studebaker's first convertible in eight years, a $2756 Regal. Prices were bumped up slightly across the line, and this together with new Big Three competition cost some sales. Meantime, South Bend's lone "family sports car" carried on as simply the Hawk. Its main 1960 change involved engines: V-8s were now exclusively 289s with 210 standard bhp or 225 with optional "Power Pack." Though dated, the V-8 Hawk remained a fine value at $2650, and was still a good performer. But model-year sales dropped by almost half from '59, to 3939, owing to a dearth of dealers, continued advertising emphasis on Lark, and steadily diminishing demand.

Ominously, Lark volume also fell by more than half for 1961 despite revised outer sheetmetal imparting a slightly squarer look, quad headlamps on V-8 models, a new overhead-valve head that turned the old six into a new 112-bhp "Skybolt Six," and the addition of a V-8 Lark Cruiser. The last, reviving Studebaker's luxury-sedan idea, rode the wagon chassis and boasted a richly upholstered interior with extra rear legroom. Hawk returned with a narrow contrast-color panel beneath its fins and newly optional four-speed gearbox, but sales slipped to 3340.

Studebaker got a new president in early '61 when the dynamic Sherwood H. Egbert replaced the embattled Harold Churchill, who'd held the job since August 1958. Shortly after he arrived, Egbert asked Milwaukee-based industrial designer Brooks Stevens to rework both the Lark and Hawk for 1962 on a six-month "crash" basis. Company styling chief Randall Faurot stepped aside, and Stevens whipped up cheap but remarkably effective makeovers. All Larks now wore quad headlamps, plus elongated rear quarters, large round taillights, a Mercedes-like grille (Studebaker had been the North American Mercedes-Benz distributor since 1958 via Curtiss-

# Studebaker

1960 Lark VIII convertible coupe

1961 Hawk two-door coupe

1962 Gran Turismo Hawk hardtop coupe

1963 Lark Daytona hardtop coupe

1963 Lark Daytona Wagonaire station wagon

Wright), and crisper nonwagon rooflines. Two-door wagons vanished, but there were four new Daytona models: a six and V-8 convertible and hardtop coupe with bucket seats, deluxe trim, and an available European-type sliding cloth sunroof for the hardtop.

For the '62 Hawk, Stevens resurrected the pillarless "Loewy" body and applied square, Thunderbird-style rear roof quarters, a matching tail bereft of fins, and a thrust-forward grille. He also penned a new dash with a full set of round gauges in a large rectangle with outboard ends canted in toward the driver. Retitled Gran Turismo Hawk and offered only with the previous pair of 289 V-8s, it was a deft piece of work. Quick, too, with the optional 225-bhp engine good for 120 mph all out and under 10 seconds 0-60 mph. Though heavy, the 289 was strong, with far greater power potential than its modest size implied—as we'd soon see.

Helped by an attractive $3095 base price, the GT Hawk attracted nearly 8400 buyers. Total Studebaker car sales jumped by over 30,000 to some 101,400. Regrettably, that would be the firm's only gain of the decade.

Stevens made further refinements for '63. Larks got raked A-pillars and new windshields, thinner door-window frames, a finely checked grille, and a new Hawk-style dash with round gauges, rocker switches, and a "vanity" glovebox with pop-up mirror. Also new, and quite novel, was Steven's "Wagonaire." Offered in Standard, Regal, and Daytona form, this boasted a unique rear roof panel that could be slid forward for unlimited "head room"—perfect for hauling tall loads. But Wagonaires leaked badly even when buttoned up, which likely explains why cheaper fixed-roof Stude wagons were reinstated during the year. Further expanding the '63 line were six and V-8 sedans in Standard and nicer new Custom trim, the latter priced between Regal and Daytona.

The '63 GT Hawk displayed a revised grille similar to Lark's, round parking lights (amber, per new federal law), woodgrain dash trim, and pleated-vinyl seats. By midseason, both Lark and Hawk could be ordered with new "Avanti" 289 V-8s: a 240-bhp R1 and a 290-bhp supercharged R2 respectively priced at $372 and $210. An R2-equipped "Super Hawk" exceeded 140 mph at Bonneville that year; an R2 "Super Lark" did over 132 mph.

Those engines were named for the totally unexpected grand-touring Studebaker that broke cover in early 1962. Easily the most-stunning South Bend product in a decade, the Avanti lived up to its name—"forward" in Italian—brilliantly conceived by Raymond Loewy and his stellar team of John Ebstein, Robert Andrews, and Tom Kellogg. Because Stevens was occupied with updating higher-volume models, Egbert had turned to Loewy Associates for the exotic sporty car he felt would rejuvenate Studebaker's sagging image—a swoopy four-seat coupe of the sort Loewy had been designing for years.

As with Chevrolet's first Corvette of a decade before, fiberglass was chosen for the Avanti bodyshell to minimize both time and tooling costs. Those same factors nixed an all-new chassis, but chief engineer Gene Hardig beefed up a Lark ragtop frame with front/rear antiroll bars, rear radius rods, and the Bendix front-disc power brakes newly optional for the '63 Lark and Hawk (the first caliper discs in U.S. production, by the way). The 289 V-8 was heavily revised to become a "Jet Thrust." The basic R1 employed ¾-race high-lift cam, dual-breaker distributor, four-barrel carb, and dual exhaust. Andy Granatelli's Paxton Products, then part of Studebaker, added a Paxton supercharger to create the R2. They also devised a trio of bored-out, 304.5-cid extensions: blown R3 with 9.6:1 compression and 335 bhp; naturally aspirated R4 with twin four-barrels, 12:1 compression, and 280 bhp; and the experimental R5 with twin blowers (one per cylinder bank), magneto ignition, Bendix fuel injection, and no less than 575 bhp.

Immediately generating high excitement, the Avanti promised to pack Studebaker showrooms like nothing else in years. Calamitously, production was delayed a critical six months by botched bodies from the supplier, Molded Fiber Glass Company (which also built Corvette shells), forcing Studebaker to set up its own fiberglass production. By the time these and other bugs were squashed, most buyers with advance orders had canceled and bought Corvettes. Thus, just 3834 Avantis (including 500 exports) were built for '63.

Overall, Studebaker's 1963 volume was well down from '62, skidding to 81,660. Only Lincoln and Imperial ranked lower among major U.S. makes. Egbert, who'd been repeatedly hospitalized of late, left in November, never to return. (Sadly, he would die of cancer in 1969.) A month later, new president Byers Burlingame announced the closure of Studebaker's historic South Bend plant after failed last-ditch efforts to obtain financing for future models. Operations were consolidated at the Hamilton, Ontario, assembly plant, where management hoped to return to profitability on 20,000 cars a year, all family compacts. With that, the Avanti and GT Hawk were unceremoniously dumped after a token run of little-changed '64 models: just 809 and 1767, respectively (including exports).

Also among the last South Bend Studebakers were the first '64 Larks, with crisply square new outer body panels, again courtesy of Brooks Stevens. Overall length grew six inches; the grille became more horizontal, with an eggcrate center and integral headlights; and a pointy new rear end carried high-set tail/backup lamps. The stripped Standard was retagged Lark Challenger and priced from as low as $1943. The hallowed Commander name returned to oust Custom/Regal, a four-door Daytona sedan arrived, and newly optional Avanti R3 power reduced a Super Lark's 0-60 to 7.3 seconds (though very few such cars were built). The R3 was also listed (and as rarely ordered) for the GT Hawk, which bowed out with "landau" roof styling and optional vinyl half-top, plus a smoother rear deck and matte-black dash appliqué. But Studebaker sales kept sliding, to fewer than 20,000 for calendar '64, and to about 44,400 for the model year.

For 1965, the Lark name was dropped as a liability and the line pared to just ten "Common-Sense" models: six and V-8 Cruisers, two- and four-door Commander sedans, and solid-top Commander wagon, plus V-8 Daytona Wagonaire (with and without sliding roof) and a new pillared Daytona sport coupe. Styling was virtually unchanged. Because the closure of South Bend ended production of Studebaker engines, management settled for Chevy substitutes: the 120-bhp 194 six from the compact Chevy II and the legendary 283 small-block V-8 in 195-bhp tune.

Hamilton almost managed 20,000 cars for '65, but without facilities for developing replacement models, Studebaker had no real future as an automaker. Besides, financing was all but gone. The 1966 models thus ended the marque. These were basically '65s warmed over with dual-beam headlamps (replacing quads), a new four-slot grille, and air-extractor vents in place of the upper taillight units. Studebaker built only 8947 of these cars before calling it quits.

In retrospect, Studebaker's death was a classic case of the deadly downward spiral that claimed so many makes in the Depression: insufficient sales to cover development costs for new models to replace increasingly unpopular old ones, thus further depressing sales and spurring talk of a possible demise that becomes a self-fulfilling prophecy. So although losing Studebaker was a greater shame, it was, perhaps, inevitable.

1964 Daytona R1 "Avanti-Powered" convertible coupe

1965 Daytona Sport Sedan two-door

1966 Cruiser four-door sedan

# Specifications

### 1930*

| 53 Six (wb 114.0)—22,371 built Nov/29-Nov/30 | | | |
|---|---|---|---|
| | Wght | Price | Prod |
| touring 5P | 2,840 | 965 | — |
| Regal touring 5P | 2,900 | 1,065 | — |
| bus cpe 2P | 2,835 | 895 | — |
| cpe 2-4P | 2,890 | 985 | — |
| club sdn 5P | 2,875 | 935 | — |
| sdn 4d | 2,950 | 985 | — |
| Regal sdn 4d | 3,100 | 1,085 | — |
| landau sdn 4d | 3,110 | 1,125 | — |
| **GJ Commander Six (wb 120.0)—16,019 built Dec/28-Apr/30** | | | |
| Regal rdstr 2-4P | 3,000 | 1,495 | — |
| touring 5P | 3,070 | 1,395 | — |
| touring 7P | 3,095 | 1,360 | — |
| Regal touring 5P | 3,200 | 1,495 | — |
| Regal touring 7P | 3,225 | 1,460 | — |
| cpe 2P | 3,105 | 1,345 | — |
| cpe 2-4P | 3,160 | 1,425 | — |
| victoria 4P | 3,130 | 1,425 | — |
| conv cab 4P | 3,215 | 1,545 | — |
| sdn 4d | 3,235 | 1,425 | — |

# Studebaker

| GJ Commander Six (wb 120.0) | Wght | Price | Prod |
|---|---|---|---|
| Regal sdn 4d | 3,335 | 1,545 | — |
| brougham (mohair uph.) 5P | 3,415 | 1,575 | — |
| brougham (broadcloth) 5P | 3,390 | 1,575 | — |
| **GL Dictator Six (wb 115.0)—17,561 built Jun/29-May/30** | | | |
| touring 5P | 2,955 | 1,145 | — |
| Regal touring 5P | 3,075 | 1,265 | — |
| cpe 2P | 2,915 | 1,135 | — |
| cpe 2-4P | 2,980 | 1,195 | — |
| brougham 5P | 3,250 | 1,295 | — |
| club sdn 5P | 2,970 | 1,095 | — |
| sdn 4d | 3,080 | 1,195 | — |
| Regal sdn 4d | 3,200 | 1,295 | — |
| **FC Dictator Eight (wb 115.0)—16,359 built May/29-Aug/30** | | | |
| touring 5P | 2,980 | 1,285 | — |
| Regal touring 5P | 3,100 | 1,385 | — |
| cpe 2P | 2,950 | 1,255 | — |
| cpe 2-4P | 3,010 | 1,315 | — |
| brougham 5P | 3,275 | 1,415 | — |
| club sdn 5P | 2,990 | 1,195 | — |
| sdn 4d | 3,095 | 1,295 | — |
| Regal sdn 4d | 3,230 | 1,415 | — |
| **FD Commander Eight (wb 120.0)—24,639 built Dec/28-Jun/30** | | | |
| Regal rdstr 2-4P | 3,040 | 1,595 | — |
| touring 5P | 3,100 | 1,495 | — |
| Regal touring 5P | 3,250 | 1,595 | — |
| cpe 2P | 3,150 | 1,495 | — |
| cpe 2-4P | 3,235 | 1,545 | — |
| victoria 4P | 3,200 | 1,515 | — |
| conv cab 4P | 3,345 | 1,695 | — |
| sdn 4d | 3,310 | 1,515 | — |
| Regal sdn 4d | 3,435 | 1,695 | — |
| sdn 7P | 3,355 | 1,695 | — |
| Regal sdn 7P | 3,480 | 1,845 | — |
| brougham (mohair uph.) 5P | 3,540 | 1,695 | — |
| brougham (broadcloth) 5P | 3,520 | 1,695 | — |
| **FH President Eight (wb 125.0)—17,527 built Dec/28-Jun/30** | | | |
| rdstr 2-4P | 3,810 | 1,795 | — |
| conv cab 4P | 4,000 | 1,995 | — |
| State victoria 4P | 4,050 | 1,995 | — |
| sdn 4d | 4,110 | 1,795 | — |
| State sdn 4d (mohair uph.) | 4,235 | 1,995 | — |
| State sdn 4d (broadcloth) | 4,225 | 1,995 | — |
| **FE President Eight (wb 135.0)—8,740 built Dec/28-Jun/30** | | | |
| touring 7P | 4,020 | 1,845 | — |
| State touring 7P | 4,175 | 2,145 | — |
| brougham (mohair uph.) 5P | 4,440 | 2,395 | — |
| brougham (broadcloth) 5P | 4,425 | 2,345 | — |
| sdn 7P | 4,035 | 2,095 | — |
| State sdn (mohair uph.) 7P | 4,435 | 2,295 | — |
| State sdn (broadcloth) 7P | 4,435 | 2,295 | — |
| limo 7P | 4,205 | 2,295 | — |
| State limo 7P | 4,445 | 2,595 | — |
| State victoria 5P | 4,230 | 2,295 | — |

* Includes 1929 production; FC also includes 1931.

| 1930 Engines | bore × stroke | bhp | availability |
|---|---|---|---|
| I-6, 205.3 | 3.25 × 4.13 | 70 | S-53 |
| I-6, 221.0 | 3.38 × 4.13 | 68 | S-GL |
| I-6, 248.3 | 3.38 × 4.63 | 75 | S-GJ |
| I-8, 221.0 | 3.06 × 3.75 | 70 | S-FC |
| I-8, 250.4 | 3.06 × 4.25 | 80 | S-FD |
| I-8, 337.0 | 3.50 × 4.38 | 115 | S-FH, FE |

## 1931*

| 53 Six (wb 114.0)—22,371 built Nov/29-Nov/30 | Wght | Price | Prod |
|---|---|---|---|
| rdstr 2P | 2,720 | 795 | — |
| touring 5P | 2,840 | 895 | — |
| Regal touring 5P | 2,990 | 995 | — |
| bus cpe 2P | 2,785 | 845 | — |
| cpe 2-4P | 2,840 | 895 | — |
| club sdn 5P | 2,830 | 845 | — |
| sdn 4d | 2,900 | 895 | — |
| Regal sdn 4d | 3,030 | 995 | — |
| landau sdn 4d | 3,110 | 995 | — |
| **54 Six (wb 114.0)—23,917 built Dec/30-Sep/31** | | | |
| rdstr 2P | 2,700 | 895 | — |
| bus cpe 2P | 2,790 | 845 | — |
| cpe 2-4P | 2,840 | 895 | — |
| sdn 4d | 2,930 | 895 | — |
| Regal sdn 4d | 3,075 | 970 | — |
| touring 5P | 2,805 | 895 | — |
| Regal touring 5P | 2,960 | 970 | — |
| **FC Dictator Eight (wb 115.0)—16,359 built May/29-Aug/30** | | | |
| touring 5P | 2,980 | 1,285 | — |
| Regal touring 5P | 3,100 | 1,385 | — |
| cpe 2P | 2,950 | 1,255 | — |
| cpe 2-4P | 3,010 | 1,315 | — |
| brougham 5P | 3,275 | 1,415 | — |
| club sdn 5P | 2,990 | 1,195 | — |
| sdn 4d | 3,095 | 1,295 | — |
| Regal sdn 4d | 3,230 | 1,415 | — |
| **61 Dictator Eight (wb 114.0)—14,141 built Aug/30-Sept/31** | | | |
| cpe 2P | 2,905 | 1,095 | — |
| cpe 2-4P | 2,955 | 1,150 | — |
| sdn 4d | 3,055 | 1,150 | — |
| Regal sdn 4d | 3,195 | 1,225 | — |
| **70 Commander Eight (wb 124.0)—10,823 built Jun/30-Sept/31** | | | |
| victoria 4P | 3,390 | 1,585 | — |
| cpe 4P | 3,400 | 1,585 | — |
| Regal b'ham (mohair uph.) 5P | 3,660 | 1,685 | — |
| Regal b'ham (broadcloth) 5P | 3,655 | 1,685 | — |
| sdn 4d | 3,520 | 1,585 | — |
| Regal sdn 4d | 3,660 | 1,685 | — |
| **80 President Eight (wb 130.0)—6,340 built Jun/30-Sep/31** | | | |
| rdstr 4P | 4,130 | 1,900 | — |
| cpe 2P | 3,995 | 1,850 | — |
| State cpe 4P | 4,200 | 1,950 | — |
| sdn 4d | 4,230 | 1,850 | — |
| State sdn (mohair uph.) 4d | 4,385 | 1,950 | — |
| State sdn (broadcloth) 4d | 4,380 | 1,950 | — |
| **90 President Eight (wb 136.0)—2,762 built Jun/30-Sep/31** | | | |
| State victoria 5P | 4,275 | 2,250 | — |
| State b'ham (mohair uph.) 5P | 4,460 | 2,250 | — |
| State b'ham (broadcloth) 5P | 4,450 | 2,250 | — |
| sdn 7P | 4,360 | 2,150 | — |
| State sdn 7P | 4,520 | 2,250 | — |
| touring 7P | 4,125 | 1,850 | — |
| State touring 7P | 4,265 | 2,050 | — |
| State limo 7P | 4,580 | 2,550 | — |

* Includes 1930; FC includes 1929-30.

| 1931 Engines | bore × stroke | bhp | availability |
|---|---|---|---|
| I-6, 205.3 | 3.25 × 4.13 | 70 | S-53, 54 |
| I-8, 221.0 | 3.06 × 3.75 | 70 | S-FC |
| I-8, 221.0 | 3.06 × 3.75 | 81 | S-61 |

## Studebaker

| 1931 Engines | bore × stroke | bhp | availability |
|---|---|---|---|
| I-8, 250.4 | 3.06 × 4.25 | 101 | S-70 |
| I-8, 337.0 | 3.50 × 4.38 | 122 | S-80, 90 |

### 1932

| 55 Six (wb 117.0)—13,647 built | Wght | Price | Prod |
|---|---|---|---|
| conv rdstr 2-4P | 3,035 | 915 | — |
| Regal conv rdstr 2-4P | 3,135 | 1,020 | — |
| cpe 2P | 3,025 | 840 | — |
| Regal cpe 2P | 3,125 | 945 | — |
| cpe 2-4P | 3,080 | 890 | — |
| Regal cpe 2-4P | 3,165 | 995 | — |
| St. Regis brougham 2d 5P | 3,130 | 915 | — |
| St. Regis Regal b'ham 2d 5P | 3,215 | 1,020 | — |
| sdn 4d | 3,170 | 915 | — |
| Regal sdn 4d | 3,260 | 1,020 | — |
| conv sdn 5P | NA | 985 | — |
| Regal conv sdn 5P | NA | 1,090 | — |

| 62 Dictator Eight (wb 117.0)—6,021 built | Wght | Price | Prod |
|---|---|---|---|
| conv rdstr 2-4P | 3,115 | 1,060 | — |
| Regal conv rdstr 2-4P | 3,190 | 1,155 | — |
| cpe 2P | 3,085 | 980 | — |
| Regal cpe 2P | 3,170 | 1,085 | — |
| cpe 2-4P | 3,160 | 1,030 | — |
| Regal cpe 2-4P | 3,225 | 1,135 | — |
| St. Regis brougham 2d 5P | 3,225 | 1,050 | — |
| St. Regis Regal b'ham 2d 5P | 3,280 | 1,155 | — |
| sdn 4d | 3,240 | 1,050 | — |
| Regal sdn 4d | 3,330 | 1,155 | — |
| conv sdn 5P | 3,285 | 1,125 | — |
| Regal conv sdn 5P | 3,370 | 1,230 | — |

| 71 Commander Eight (wb 125.0)—3,551 built | Wght | Price | Prod |
|---|---|---|---|
| conv rdstr 2-4P | 3,380 | 1,445 | — |
| Regal conv rdstr 2-4P | 3,480 | 1,550 | — |
| cpe 2P | 3,400 | 1,295 | — |
| Regal cpe 2P | 3,475 | 1,400 | — |
| cpe 2-4P | 3,465 | 1,350 | — |
| Regal cpe 2-4P | 3,530 | 1,455 | — |
| St. Regis brougham 2d 5P | 3,530 | 1,445 | — |
| St. Regis Regal b'ham 2d 5P | 3,585 | 1,550 | — |
| sdn 4d | 3,545 | 1,445 | — |
| Regal sdn 4d | 3,645 | 1,550 | — |
| conv sdn 5P | 3,690 | 1,560 | — |
| Regal conv sdn 5P | 3,775 | 1,665 | — |

| 91 President Eight (wb 135.0)—2,399 built | Wght | Price | Prod |
|---|---|---|---|
| conv rdstr 2-4P | 4,100 | 1,750 | — |
| State conv rdstr | 4,200 | 1,855 | — |
| cpe 2P | 4,120 | 1,595 | — |
| State cpe 2P | 4,220 | 1,700 | — |
| cpe 2-4P | 4,265 | 1,690 | — |
| State cpe 2-4P | 4,365 | 1,795 | — |
| St. Regis brougham 2d 5P | 4,200 | 1,750 | — |
| St. Regis State b'ham 2d 5P | 4,300 | 1,855 | — |
| sdn 4d | 4,260 | 1,750 | — |
| State sdn 4d | 4,390 | 1,855 | — |
| conv sdn 5P | 4,335 | 1,880 | — |
| State conv sdn 5P | 4,445 | 1,985 | — |
| sdn 7P | 4,365 | 1,890 | — |
| State sdn 7P | 4,475 | 1,995 | — |
| limo 7P | 4,415 | 1,990 | — |
| State limo 7P | 4,525 | 2,095 | — |

| 1932 Engines | bore × stroke | bhp | availability |
|---|---|---|---|
| I-6, 230.0 | 3.25 × 4.63 | 80 | S-55 |
| I-8, 221.0 | 3.06 × 3.75 | 85 | S-62 |

| 1932 Engines | bore × stroke | bhp | availability |
|---|---|---|---|
| I-8, 250.4 | 3.06 × 4.25 | 101 | S-71 |
| I-8, 337.0 | 3.50 × 4.38 | 122 | S-91 |

### 1933

| 56 Six (wb 117.0)—6,861 built | Wght | Price | Prod |
|---|---|---|---|
| rdstr 2-4P | 3,165 | 915 | — |
| Regal rdstr 2-4P | 3,260 | 1,020 | — |
| cpe 2P | 3,160 | 840 | — |
| Regal cpe 2P | 3,245 | 945 | — |
| cpe 2-4P | 3,210 | 890 | — |
| Regal cpe 2-4P | 3,300 | 995 | — |
| St. Regis brougham 2d 5P | 3,300 | 915 | — |
| St. Regis Regal b'ham 2d 5P | 3,375 | 1,020 | — |
| sdn 4d | 3,310 | 915 | — |
| Regal sdn 4d | 3,435 | 1,020 | — |
| conv sdn 5P | 3,380 | 1,015 | — |
| Regal conv sdn 5P | 3,460 | 1,120 | — |

| 73 Commander Eight (wb 117.0)—3,841 built | Wght | Price | Prod |
|---|---|---|---|
| conv rdstr 2-4P | 3,245 | 1,095 | — |
| Regal conv rdstr 2-4P | 3,335 | 1,200 | — |
| cpe 2P | 3,220 | 1,000 | — |
| Regal cpe 2P | 3,345 | 1,105 | — |
| cpe 2-4P | 3,275 | 1,050 | — |
| Regal cpe 2-4P | 3,405 | 1,155 | — |
| St. Regis brougham 2d 5P | 3,375 | 1,075 | — |
| St. Regis Regal b'ham 2d 5P | 3,475 | 1,180 | — |
| sdn 4d | 3,385 | 1,075 | — |
| Regal sdn 4d | 3,500 | 1,180 | — |
| conv sdn 5P | 3,475 | 1,195 | — |
| Regal conv sdn 5P | 3,545 | 1,300 | — |

| 82 President Eight (wb 125.0)—1,194 built | Wght | Price | Prod |
|---|---|---|---|
| conv rdstr 2-4P | 3,480 | 1,385 | — |
| State conv rdstr 2-4P | 3,560 | 1,490 | — |
| cpe 2-4P | 3,520 | 1,325 | — |
| State cpe 2-4P | 3,600 | 1,430 | — |
| St. Regis brougham 2d 5P | 3,605 | 1,385 | — |
| St. Regis State b'ham 2d 5P | 3,670 | 1,490 | — |
| sdn 4d | 3,640 | 1,385 | — |
| State sdn 4d | 3,720 | 1,490 | — |
| State conv sdn 5P | 3,745 | 1,650 | — |

| 92 President Eight (wb 135.0)—635 built | Wght | Price | Prod |
|---|---|---|---|
| conv rdstr 2-4P | 4,205 | 1,685 | — |
| State conv rdstr 2-4P | 4,285 | 1,790 | — |
| cpe 2-4P | 4,255 | 1,625 | — |
| State cpe 2-4P | 4,335 | 1,730 | — |
| St. Regis State b'ham 2d 5P | 4,400 | 1,790 | — |
| sdn 4d | 4,380 | 1,685 | — |
| State sdn 4d | 4,465 | 1,790 | — |
| State conv sdn 5P | 4,470 | 1,960 | — |
| sdn 7P | 4,470 | 1,835 | — |
| State sdn 7P | 4,565 | 1,940 | — |
| State limo 7P | 4,605 | 2,040 | — |

| 1933 Engines | bore × stroke | bhp | availability |
|---|---|---|---|
| I-6, 230.0 | 3.25 × 4.63 | 85 | S-56 |
| I-8, 235.0 | 3.06 × 4.00 | 100 | S-73 |
| I-8, 250.0 | 3.06 × 4.25 | 110 | S-82 |
| I-8, 337.0 | 3.50 × 4.38 | 132 | S-92 |

### 1934

| A Dictator Six (wb 113.0)—45,851 blt | Wght | Price | Prod |
|---|---|---|---|
| conv rdstr 2-4P | 2,860 | 790 | — |
| Regal conv rdstr 2-4P | 2,935 | 820 | — |

## Studebaker

| A Dictator Six (wb 113.0) | Wght | Price | Prod |
|---|---|---|---|
| cpe 2P | 2,795 | 740 | — |
| Regal cpe 2P | 2,860 | 770 | — |
| cpe 2-4P | 2,865 | 790 | — |
| Regal cpe 2-4P | 2,950 | 820 | — |
| St. Regis brougham 2d 5P | 2,840 | 760 | — |
| St. Regis Regal b'ham 2d 5P | 2,935 | 810 | — |
| St. Regis Custom b'ham 2d 5P | 2,890 | 810 | — |
| sdn 4d | 2,910 | 790 | — |
| Regal sdn 4d | 3,005 | 840 | — |
| Custom sdn 4d | 2,950 | 840 | — |
| *Special series:* | | | |
| cpe 2P | 2,780 | 685 | — |
| Regal cpe 2P | 2,845 | 720 | — |
| cpe 2-4P | 2,850 | 740 | — |
| Regal cpe 2-4P | 2,935 | 770 | — |
| St. Regis brougham 2d 5P | 2,825 | 710 | — |
| St. Regis Regal b'ham 2d 5P | 2,920 | 760 | — |
| St. Regis Custom b'ham 2d 5P | 2,875 | 760 | — |
| sdn 4d | 2,895 | 740 | — |
| Regal sdn 4d | 2,990 | 790 | — |
| Custom sdn 4d | 2,935 | 790 | — |
| *"Year Ahead" series (from Jul/34):* | | | |
| cpe 3P | 2,800 | 695 | — |
| Regal cpe 3P | 2,885 | 730 | — |
| cpe 5P | 2,880 | 750 | — |
| Regal cpe 5P | 2,980 | 780 | — |
| St. Regis sdn 4d | 2,850 | 720 | — |
| St. Regis Custom sdn 2d | 2,910 | 755 | — |
| St. Regis Regal sdn 2d | 2,970 | 770 | — |
| sdn 4d | 2,915 | 750 | — |
| Custom sdn 4d | 2,960 | 785 | — |
| Regal sdn 4d | 3,020 | 800 | — |
| *Deluxe subseries:* | | | |
| rdstr 3-5P | 2,900 | 800 | — |
| Regal rdstr 3-5P | 2,970 | 800 | — |
| cpe 3P | 2,830 | 750 | — |
| Regal cpe 3P | 2,920 | 780 | — |
| cpe 3-5P | 2,900 | 800 | — |
| Regal cpe 3-5P | 3,020 | 830 | — |
| St. Regis sdn 2d | 2,895 | 770 | — |
| St. Regis Regal sdn 2d | 2,985 | 820 | — |
| St. Regis Custom sdn 2d | 2,945 | 805 | — |
| sdn 4d | 2,945 | 800 | — |
| Regal sdn 4d | 3,055 | 850 | — |
| Custom sdn 4d | 2,990 | 835 | — |
| Land Cruiser sdn 4d | 3,015 | 995 | — |
| Regal Land Cruiser sdn 4d | 3,110 | 995 | — |

| B Commander Eight (wb 119.0)—10,315 built | Wght | Price | Prod |
|---|---|---|---|
| conv rdstr 2-4P | 3,255 | 970 | — |
| Regal conv rdstr 2-4P | 3,335 | 1,000 | — |
| cpe 2P | 3,205 | 920 | — |
| Regal cpe 2P | 3,290 | 950 | — |
| cpe 2-4P | 3,280 | 970 | — |
| Regal cpe 2-4P | 3,350 | 1,000 | — |
| St. Regis brougham 2d 5P | 3,235 | 940 | — |
| St. Regis Regal b'ham 2d 5P | 3,355 | 990 | — |
| St. Regis Custom b'ham 2d 5P | 3,295 | 990 | — |
| sdn 4d | 3,310 | 970 | — |
| Regal sdn 4d | 3,435 | 1,020 | — |
| Custom sdn 4d | 3,360 | 1,020 | — |
| Land Cruiser sdn 4d | 3,385 | 1,165 | — |
| Regal Land Cruiser sdn 4d | 3,480 | 1,165 | — |
| *"Year Ahead" series (began Jul/34):* | | | |
| rdstr 3-5P | 3,290 | 915 | — |

| B Commander Eight (wb 119.0) | Wght | Price | Prod |
|---|---|---|---|
| Regal rdstr 3-5P | 3,355 | 945 | — |
| cpe 3P | 3,215 | 865 | — |
| Regal cpe 3P | 3,300 | 895 | — |
| cpe 3-5P | 3,295 | 915 | — |
| Regal cpe 3-5P | 3,375 | 945 | — |
| St. Regis Regal sdn 2d | 3,385 | 935 | — |
| St. Regis Custom sdn 2d | 3,340 | 920 | — |
| Regal sdn 4d | 3,435 | 965 | — |
| Custom sdn 4d | 3,395 | 950 | — |
| Land Cruiser sdn 4d | 3,410 | 1,135 | — |
| Regal Land Cruiser sdn 4d | 3,500 | 1,135 | — |

| C President Eight (wb 123.0)—3,698 built | Wght | Price | Prod |
|---|---|---|---|
| conv rdstr 2-4P | 3,435 | 1,220 | — |
| Regal conv rdstr 2-4P | 3,510 | 1,250 | — |
| cpe 2P | 3,370 | 1,170 | — |
| Regal cpe 2P | 3,470 | 1,200 | — |
| cpe 2-4P | 3,410 | 1,220 | — |
| Regal cpe 2-4P | 3,510 | 1,250 | — |
| sdn 4d | 3,490 | 1,220 | — |
| Regal sdn 4d | 3,620 | 1,270 | — |
| Custom sdn 4d | 3,550 | 1,270 | — |
| Land Cruiser sdn 4d | 3,565 | 1,445 | — |
| Regal Land Cruiser sdn 4d | 3,655 | 1,445 | — |
| Custom berline 5P | — | 1,420 | — |
| Regal berline 5P | — | 1,420 | — |
| *"Year Ahead" series (began Jul/34)* | | | |
| rdstr 3-5P | 3,460 | 1,220 | — |
| Regal rdstr 3-5P | 3,520 | 1,250 | — |
| cpe 3P | 3,395 | 1,170 | — |
| Regal cpe 3P | 3,495 | 1,200 | — |
| cpe 3-5P | 3,465 | 1,220 | — |
| Regal cpe 3-5P | 3,535 | 1,250 | — |
| Regal sdn 4d | 3,630 | 1,270 | — |
| Custom sdn 4d | 3,560 | 1,255 | — |
| Regal berline 6P | 3,720 | 1,420 | — |
| Custom berline 6P | 3,660 | 1,405 | — |
| Land Cruiser sdn 4d | 3,595 | 1,445 | — |
| Regal Land Cruiser sdn 4d | 3,710 | 1,445 | — |

| 1934 Engines | bore × stroke | bhp | availability |
|---|---|---|---|
| I-6, 205.3 | 3.25 × 4.13 | 88 | S-Dictator |
| I-8, 221.0 | 3.06 × 3.75 | 103 | S-Commander |
| I-8, 250.0 | 3.06 × 4.25 | 110 | S-President |

### 1935

| 1A Dictator Six* (wb 114)—11,742 blt | Wght | Price | Prod |
|---|---|---|---|
| rdstr 3-5P | 2,985 | 745 | — |
| Regal rdstr 3-5P | 3,070 | 775 | — |
| cpe 3P | 2,895 | 695 | — |
| Regal cpe 3P | 3,005 | 725 | — |
| cpe 3-5P | 2,995 | 745 | — |
| Regal cpe 3-5P | 3,070 | 775 | — |
| St. Regis sdn 4d | 2,965 | 715 | — |
| St. Regis Regal sdn 2d | 3,085 | 755 | — |
| St. Regis Custom sdn 2d | 3,035 | 740 | — |
| sdn 4d | 3,030 | 745 | — |
| Regal sdn 4d | 3,160 | 785 | — |
| Custom sdn 4d | 3,085 | 770 | — |
| Land Cruiser sdn 4d | 3,100 | 880 | — |
| Regal Land Cruiser sdn 4d | 3,220 | 895 | — |

| 2A Dictator Six** (wb 114.0)—23,550 built | Wght | Price | Prod |
|---|---|---|---|
| rdstr 3-5P | 3,040 | 780 | — |
| Regal rdstr 3-5P | 3,140 | 810 | — |
| cpe 3P | 2,975 | 720 | — |

# Studebaker

| 2A Dictator Six** (wb 114.0) | Wght | Price | Prod |
|---|---|---|---|
| Regal cpe 3P | 3,075 | 760 | — |
| cpe 3-5P | 3,065 | 780 | — |
| Regal cpe 3-5P | 3,135 | 810 | — |
| St. Regis sdn 4d | 3,035 | 750 | — |
| St. Regis Regal sdn 2d | 3,170 | 790 | — |
| St. Regis Custom sdn 2d | 3,105 | 775 | — |
| sdn 4d | 3,095 | 780 | — |
| Regal sdn 4d | 3,230 | 820 | — |
| Custom sdn 4d | 3,155 | 805 | — |
| Land Cruiser sdn 4d | 3,170 | 915 | — |
| Regal Land Cruiser sdn 4d | 3,285 | 930 | — |
| **1B Commander Eight (wb 120.0)—6,085 built** | | | |
| rdstr 3-5P | 3,510 | 980 | — |
| Regal rdstr 3-5P | 3,570 | 1,010 | — |
| cpe 3P | 3,420 | 925 | — |
| Regal cpe 3P | 3,510 | 960 | — |
| cpe 3-5P | 3,520 | 980 | — |
| Regal cpe 3-5P | 3,570 | 1,010 | — |
| St. Regis Regal sdn 2d | 3,620 | 1,000 | — |
| St. Regis Custom sdn 2d | 3,550 | 985 | — |
| Regal sdn 4d | 3,685 | 1,030 | — |
| Custom sdn 4d | 3,600 | 1,015 | — |
| Land Cruiser sdn 4d | 3,692 | 1,115 | — |
| Regal Land Cruiser sdn 4d | 3,720 | 1,130 | — |
| **1C President Eight (wb 124.0)—2,305 built** | | | |
| rdstr 3-5P | 3,645 | 1,295 | — |
| Regal rdstr 3-5P | 3,740 | 1,325 | — |
| cpe 3P | 3,600 | 1,245 | — |
| Regal cpe 3P | 3,685 | 1,275 | — |
| cpe 3-5P | 3,660 | 1,295 | — |
| Regal cpe 3-5P | 3,740 | 1,325 | — |
| Regal sdn 4d | 3,900 | 1,345 | — |
| Custom sdn 4d | 3,790 | 1,330 | — |
| Land Cruiser sdn 4d | 3,820 | 1,430 | — |
| Regal Land Cruiser sdn 4d | 3,900 | 1,445 | — |
| Custom berline 5P | 3,900 | 1,430 | — |
| Regal berline 5P | 3,970 | 1,445 | — |

* conventional front suspension ** planar front suspension

Note: DeLuxe version of all Sixes also offered at $40 higher, 15 pounds more weight, and included free-wheeling, Startix, dual windshield wipers, sunvisor, taillamp, robe rail, and ash receivers. All Regal models equipped with trunks and six wire wheels all series.

| 1935 Engines | bore × stroke | bhp | availability |
|---|---|---|---|
| I-6, 205.3 | 3.25 × 4.13 | 88 | S-1A, 2A |
| I-8, 250.0 | 3.06 × 4.25 | 107 | S-1B |
| I-8, 250.0 | 3.06 × 4.25 | 110 | S-1C |

## 1936

| 3A Dictator Six* (wb 116)—26,634 blt | Wght | Price | Prod |
|---|---|---|---|
| bus cpe 3P | 2,910 | 665 | — |
| Custom cpe 3P | 2,965 | 695 | — |
| Custom cpe 5P | 3,020 | 720 | — |
| St. Regis Custom sdn 2d | 3,075 | 725 | — |
| St. Regis Cruising Sdn 2d T/B | 3,080 | 745 | — |
| Custom sdn 4d | 3,110 | 755 | — |
| Cruising Sdn 4d T/B | 3,120 | 775 | — |
| **4A Dictator Six** (wb 116.0)—22,029 built** | | | |
| bus cpe 3P | 2,980 | 685 | — |
| Custom cpe 3P | 3,035 | 705 | — |
| Custom cpe 5P | 3,090 | 740 | — |
| St. Regis Custom sdn 2d | 3,145 | 745 | — |
| St. Regis Cruising Sdn 2d T/B | 3,150 | 765 | — |

| 4A Dictator Six** (wb 116.0) | Wght | Price | Prod |
|---|---|---|---|
| Custom sdn 4d | 3,180 | 775 | — |
| Cruising Sdn 4d T/B | 3,190 | 795 | — |
| **2C President Eight (wb 125)—7,297 built** | | | |
| Custom cpe 3P | 3,460 | 965 | — |
| Custom cpe 5P | 3,515 | 995 | — |
| St. Regis Custom sdn 2d | 3,560 | 1,015 | — |
| St. Regis Cruising Sdn 2d T/B | 3,570 | 1,035 | — |
| Custom sdn 4d | 3,600 | 1,045 | — |
| Cruising Sdn 4d T/B | 3,615 | 1,065 | — |

* conventional front suspension ** planar front suspension

| 1936 Engines | bore × stroke | bhp | availability |
|---|---|---|---|
| I-6, 218.0 | 3.25 × 4.38 | 90 | S-Dictator |
| I-8, 250.0 | 3.06 × 4.25 | 115 | S-President |

## 1937

**5A Dictator Six* (wb 116)—50,000 built***

| | Wght | Price | Prod |
|---|---|---|---|
| bus cpe 3P | 2,695 | 765 | — |
| Custom cpe 3P | 3,005 | 820 | — |
| Custom cpe 5P | 3,045 | 845 | — |
| St. Regis Custom sdn 2d | 3,100 | 850 | — |
| St. Regis Cruising Sdn 2d T/B | 3,100 | 850 | — |
| Custom sdn 4d | 3,130 | 880 | — |
| Cruising Sdn 4d T/B | 3,140 | 900 | — |
| **6A Dictator Six** (wb 116.0)—39,000 built**** | | | |
| bus cpe 3P | 2,765 | 785 | — |
| Custom cpe 3P | 3,075 | 840 | — |
| Custom cpe 5P | 3,115 | 865 | — |
| St. Regis Custom sdn 2d | 3,170 | 870 | — |
| St. Regis Cruising Sdn 2d T/B | 3,170 | 890 | — |
| Custom sdn 4d | 3,200 | 900 | — |
| Cruising Sdn 4d T/B | 3,210 | 920 | — |
| **3C President Eight (wb 125.0)—9,000 built*** | | | |
| Custom cpe 3P | 3,510 | 1,087 | — |
| Custom cpe 5P | 3,540 | 1,115 | — |
| St. Regis Custom sdn 2d | 3,600 | 1,135 | — |
| St. Regis Cruising Sdn 2d T/B | 3,610 | 1,155 | — |
| Custom sdn 4d | 3,620 | 1,165 | — |
| Cruising Sdn 4d T/B | 3,635 | 1,185 | — |

* conventional front suspension ** planar front suspension *** Estimated.
Note: President State trim option $30 higher

| 1937 Engines | bore × stroke | bhp | availability |
|---|---|---|---|
| I-6, 218.0 | 3.25 × 4.38 | 90 | S-Dictator |
| I-8, 250.0 | 3.06 × 4.25 | 115 | S-President |

## 1938

**7A Commander Six (wb 116.5)—19,260 built**

| | Wght | Price | Prod |
|---|---|---|---|
| bus cpe 3P | 3,045 | 875 | — |
| Custom cpe 3P | 3,060 | 900 | — |
| Club sdn 2d 6P | 3,140 | 955 | — |
| Cruising Sdn 4d | 3,140 | 960 | — |
| conv sdn 6P | 3,390 | 1,315 | — |
| **8A State Commander (wb 116.5)—22,053 built** | | | |
| Custom cpe 3P | 3,095 | 965 | — |
| Club sdn 2d 6P | 3,160 | 1,030 | — |
| Cruising Sdn 4d 6P | 3,215 | 1,040 | — |
| conv sdn 6P | 3,400 | 1,365 | — |
| **4C State President (wb 122.0)—5,474 built** | | | |
| cpe 3P | 3,315 | 1,130 | — |

# Studebaker

| 4C State President (wb 122.0) | Wght | Price | Prod |
|---|---|---|---|
| club sdn 2d 6P | 3,400 | 1,195 | — |
| Cruising Sdn 4d 6P | 3,455 | 1,205 | — |
| conv sdn 6P | 3,640 | 1,555 | — |

| 1938 Engines | bore × stroke | bhp | availability |
|---|---|---|---|
| I-6, 226.2 | 3.31 × 4.38 | 90 | S-Commander |
| I-8, 250.0 | 3.06 × 4.25 | 110 | S-President |

## 1939

| G Champion (wb 110)—33,905 built | Wght | Price | Prod |
|---|---|---|---|
| Custom cpe 3P | 2,260 | 660 | — |
| Custom club sdn 2d 5P | 2,330 | 700 | — |
| Custom Cruising Sdn 4d | 2,360 | 740 | — |
| DeLuxe cpe 3P | 2,275 | 720 | — |
| DeLuxe club sdn 2d 5P | 2,345 | 760 | — |
| DeLuxe Cruising Sdn 4d | 2,375 | 800 | — |

| 9A Commander (wb 116.5)—43,724 built | | | |
|---|---|---|---|
| bus cpe 3P | 3,045 | 875 | — |
| Custom cpe 3P | 3,080 | 900 | — |
| club sdn 2d 6P | 3,160 | 955 | — |
| Cruising Sdn 4d | 3,200 | 965 | — |
| conv sdn 6P | 3,400 | 1,290 | — |

| 5C President (wb 122.0)—8,205 built | | | |
|---|---|---|---|
| Custom cpe 3P | 3,300 | 1,035 | — |
| club sdn 2d 6P | 3,390 | 1,100 | — |
| Cruising Sdn 4d | 3,440 | 1,110 | — |
| conv sdn 6P | 3,640 | 1,460 | — |

| 1939 Engines | bore × stroke | bhp | availability |
|---|---|---|---|
| I-6, 164.3 | 3.00 × 3.88 | 78 | S-Champion |
| I-6, 226.2 | 3.31 × 4.38 | 90 | S-Commander |
| I-8, 250.0 | 3.06 × 4.25 | 110 | S-President |

Note: Some station wagons were built on Commander chassis by Hercules Body Company in 1939. Production figures include chassis.

## 1940

| 2G Champion (wb 110)—66,264 built | Wght | Price | Prod |
|---|---|---|---|
| cpe 3P | 2,290 | 660 | — |
| cpe 5P | 2,335 | 696 | — |
| club sdn | 2,360 | 700 | — |
| Cruising Sedan 4d | 2,390 | 740 | — |
| DeLuxe cpe 3P | 2,315 | 705 | — |
| DeLuxe cpe 5P | 2,360 | 740 | — |
| DeLuxe club sdn | 2,385 | 745 | — |
| DeLuxe Cruising Sedan 4d | 2,415 | 785 | — |

| LOA Commander (wb 116.5)—34,477 built | | | |
|---|---|---|---|
| Custom cpe 3P | 3,055 | 895 | — |
| club sdn | 3,135 | 925 | — |
| Cruising Sedan 4d | 3,180 | 965 | — |

| 6C President (wb 122.0)—6,444 built | | | |
|---|---|---|---|
| cpe 3P | 3,280 | 1,025 | — |
| club sdn | 3,370 | 1,055 | — |
| Cruising Sedan 4d | 3,420 | 1,095 | — |

| 1940 Engines | bore × stroke | bhp | availability |
|---|---|---|---|
| I-6, 164.3 | 3.00 × 3.88 | 78 | S-Champion |
| I-6, 226.2 | 3.31 × 4.38 | 90 | S-Commander |
| I-8, 250.0 | 3.06 × 4.25 | 110 | S-President |

## 1941

| 3G Champion (wb 110)—84,910 built | Wght | Price | Prod |
|---|---|---|---|
| Custom cpe 3P | 2,370 | 710 | — |
| Custom Opera cpe | 2,410 | 750 | — |
| Custom club sdn | 2,450 | 755 | — |

| 3G Champion (wb 110) | Wght | Price | Prod |
|---|---|---|---|
| Custom Cruising Sedan 4d | 2,480 | 795 | — |
| Custom DeLuxe cpe 3P | 2,395 | 745 | — |
| Custom DeLuxe Opera cpe | 2,425 | 780 | — |
| Custom DeLuxe club sdn | 2,470 | 785 | — |
| Custom DeLuxe Cruis Sdn 4d | 2,500 | 825 | — |
| DeLux-Tone cpe 3P | 2,400 | 780 | — |
| DeLux-Tone Opera cpe | 2,430 | 815 | — |
| DeLux-Tone club sdn | 2,470 | 820 | — |
| DeLux-Tone Cruising Sdn 4d | 2,500 | 860 | — |

| 11A Commander (wb 119.0)—41,996 built | | | |
|---|---|---|---|
| Custom sdn cpe | 3,160 | 990 | — |
| Custom Cruising Sedan 4d | 3,210 | 1,010 | — |
| Custom Land Cruiser sdn 4d | 3,230 | 1,055 | — |
| DeLux-Tone Cruis sedan 4d | 3,225 | 1,075 | — |
| DeLux-Tone Land Cruis sdn 4d | 3,245 | 1,120 | — |
| Skyway sdn cpe | 3,200 | 1,080 | — |
| Skyway Cruising Sedan 4d | 3,240 | 1,100 | — |
| Skyway Land Cruiser sdn 4d | 3,260 | 1,130 | — |

| 7C President (wb 124.5)—6,994 built | | | |
|---|---|---|---|
| Custom Cruising Sedan 4d | 3,450 | 1,140 | — |
| Custom Land Cruiser sdn 4d | 3,475 | 1,185 | — |
| DeLux-Tone Cruis Sedan 4d | 3,475 | 1,205 | — |
| DeLux-Tone Land Cruis sdn 4d | 3,500 | 1,250 | — |
| Skyway sdn cpe | 3,440 | 1,210 | — |
| Skyway Cruising Sedan 4d | 3,500 | 1,230 | — |
| Skyway Land Cruiser sdn 4d | 3,520 | 1,260 | — |

| 1941 Engines | bore × stroke | bhp | availability |
|---|---|---|---|
| I-6, 169.6 | 3.00 × 4.00 | 80 | S-Champion |
| I-6, 226.2 | 3.31 × 4.38 | 94 | S-Commander |
| I-8, 250.0 | 3.06 × 4.25 | 117 | S-President |

## 1942

| 4G Champion (wb 110)—29,678 blt | Wght | Price | Prod |
|---|---|---|---|
| Custom cpe 3P | 2,415 | 744 | — |
| Custom Double Dater cpe 5P | 2,455 | 769 | — |
| Custom club sdn | 2,495 | 774 | — |
| Custom Cruising Sedan 4d | 2,520 | 804 | — |
| DeLuxstyle cpe 3P | 2,435 | 779 | — |
| DeLuxstyle Dble Dater cpe 5P | 2,470 | 804 | — |
| DeLuxstyle club sdn | 2,520 | 809 | — |
| DeLuxstyle Cruising Sedan 4d | 2,545 | 839 | — |

| 12A Commander (wb 119.0)—17,500 built | | | |
|---|---|---|---|
| Custom sdn cpe | 3,195 | 1,025 | — |
| Custom Cruising Sedan 4d | 3,265 | 1,045 | — |
| Custom Land Cruiser sdn 4d | 3,290 | 1,080 | — |
| DeLuxstyle sdn cpe | 3,210 | 1,070 | — |
| DeLuxstyle Cruising Sedan 4d | 3,280 | 1,090 | — |
| DeLuxstyle Land Cruis sdn 4d | 3,305 | 1,125 | — |
| Skyway sdn cpe | 3,240 | 1,105 | — |
| Skyway Cruising Sedan 4d | 3,300 | 1,125 | — |
| Skyway Land Cruiser sdn 4d | 3,315 | 1,160 | — |

| 8C President (wb 124.5)—3,500 built | | | |
|---|---|---|---|
| Custom sdn cpe | 3,440 | 1,141 | — |
| Custom Cruising Sedan 4d | 3,485 | 1,161 | — |
| Custom Land Cruiser sdn 4d | 3,510 | 1,196 | — |
| DeLuxstyle sdn cpe | 3,455 | 1,186 | — |
| DeLuxstyle Cruising Sedan 4d | 3,500 | 1,206 | — |
| DeLuxstyle Land Cruis sdn 4d | 3,515 | 1,241 | — |
| Skyway sdn cpe | 3,470 | 1,221 | — |
| Skyway Cruising Sedan 4d | 3,540 | 1,241 | — |
| Skyway Land Cruiser sdn 4d | 3,540 | 1,276 | — |

# Studebaker

| 1942 Engines | bore × stroke | bhp | availability |
|---|---|---|---|
| I-6, 169.6 | 3.00 × 4.00 | 80 | S-Champion |
| I-6, 226.2 | 3.31 × 4.38 | 94 | S-Commander |
| I-8, 250.0 | 3.06 × 4.25 | 117 | S-President |

### 1946
| 5G Skyway Champion (wb 110.0) | Wght | Price | Prod |
|---|---|---|---|
| cpe 3P | 2,456 | 1,002 | 2,465 |
| cpe 5P | 2,491 | 1,044 | 1,285 |
| club sdn | 2,541 | 1,046 | 5,000 |
| Cruising Sedan 4d | 2,566 | 1,097 | 10,525 |

| 1946 Engine | bore × stroke | bhp | availability |
|---|---|---|---|
| I-6, 169.6 | 3.00 × 4.00 | 80 | S-all |

### 1947
| 6G Champion (wb 112)—105,097 blt | Wght | Price | Prod |
|---|---|---|---|
| DeLuxe sdn 4d | 2,735 | 1,478 | — |
| DeLuxe sdn 2d | 2,685 | 1,446 | — |
| DeLuxe cpe 5P | 2,670 | 1,472 | — |
| DeLuxe cpe 3P | 2,600 | 1,378 | — |
| Regal DeLuxe sdn 4d | 2,760 | 1,551 | — |
| Regal DeLuxe sdn 2d | 2,710 | 1,520 | — |
| Regal DeLuxe cpe 5P | 2,690 | 1,546 | — |
| Regal DeLuxe cpe 3P | 2,620 | 1,451 | — |
| Regal DeLuxe conv cpe | 2,875 | 1,902 | — |

| 15A Commander (wb 119.0; LC-123.0)—56,399 built | Wght | Price | Prod |
|---|---|---|---|
| DeLuxe sdn 4d | 3,265 | 1,761 | — |
| DeLuxe sdn 2d | 3,230 | 1,729 | — |
| DeLuxe cpe 5P | 3,210 | 1,755 | — |
| DeLuxe cpe 3P | 3,140 | 1,661 | — |
| Regal DeLuxe sdn 4d | 3,280 | 1,882 | — |
| Regal DeLuxe sdn 2d | 3,245 | 1,850 | — |
| Regal DeLuxe cpe 5P | 3,225 | 1,877 | — |
| Regal DeLuxe cpe 3P | 3,155 | 1,782 | — |
| Regal DeLuxe conv cpe | 3,420 | 2,236 | — |
| Land Cruiser sdn 4d | 3,340 | 2,043 | — |

| 1947 Engines | bore × stroke | bhp | availability |
|---|---|---|---|
| I-6, 169.6 | 3.00 × 4.00 | 80 | S-Champion |
| I-6, 226.0 | 3.31 × 4.38 | 94 | S-Commander |

### 1948
| 7G Champion (wb 112)—99,282 blt | Wght | Price | Prod |
|---|---|---|---|
| DeLuxe sdn 4d | 2,720 | 1,636 | — |
| DeLuxe sdn 2d | 2,675 | 1,604 | — |
| DeLuxe cpe 5P | 2,670 | 1,630 | — |
| DeLuxe cpe 3P | 2,590 | 1,535 | — |
| Regal DeLuxe sdn 4d | 2,725 | 1,709 | — |
| Regal DeLuxe sdn 2d | 2,685 | 1,678 | — |
| Regal DeLuxe cpe 5P | 2,690 | 1,704 | — |
| Regal DeLuxe cpe 3P | 2,615 | 1,609 | — |
| Regal DeLuxe conv cpe | 2,865 | 2,060 | — |

| 15A Commander (wb 119.0; LC-123.0)—85,711 built | Wght | Price | Prod |
|---|---|---|---|
| DeLuxe sdn 4d | 3,195 | 1,956 | — |
| DeLuxe sdn 2d | 3,165 | 1,925 | — |
| DeLuxe cpe 5P | 3,150 | 1,951 | — |
| DeLuxe cpe 3P | 3,080 | 1,856 | — |
| Regal DeLuxe sdn 4d | 3,215 | 2,078 | — |
| Regal DeLuxe sdn 2d | 3,175 | 2,046 | — |
| Regal DeLuxe cpe 5P | 3,165 | 2,072 | — |
| Regal DeLuxe cpe 3P | 3,095 | 1,978 | — |
| Regal DeLuxe conv cpe | 3,385 | 2,431 | — |
| Land Cruiser sdn 4d | 3,280 | 2,265 | — |

| 1948 Engines | bore × stroke | bhp | availability |
|---|---|---|---|
| I-6, 169.6 | 3.00 × 4.00 | 80 | S-Champion |
| I-6, 226.2 | 3.31 × 4.38 | 94 | S-Commander |

### 1949
| 8G Champion (wb 112)—85,604 blt | Wght | Price | Prod |
|---|---|---|---|
| DeLuxe sdn 4d | 2,745 | 1,689 | — |
| DeLuxe sdn 2d | 2,720 | 1,657 | — |
| DeLuxe cpe 5P | 2,705 | 1,683 | — |
| DeLuxe cpe 3P | 2,645 | 1,588 | — |
| Regal DeLuxe sdn 4d | 2,750 | 1,762 | — |
| Regal DeLuxe sdn 2d | 2,725 | 1,731 | — |
| Regal DeLuxe cpe 5P | 2,725 | 1,757 | — |
| Regal DeLuxe cpe 3P | 2,650 | 1,652 | — |
| Regal DeLuxe conv cpe | 2,895 | 2,086 | — |

| 16A Commander (wb 119.0; LC-123.0)—43,694 built | Wght | Price | Prod |
|---|---|---|---|
| DeLuxe sdn 4d | 3,240 | 2,019 | — |
| DeLuxe sdn 2d | 3,215 | 1,988 | — |
| DeLuxe cpe 5P | 3,200 | 2,014 | — |
| DeLuxe cpe 3P | 3,130 | 1,919 | — |
| Regal DeLuxe sdn 4d | 3,245 | 2,141 | — |
| Regal DeLuxe sdn 2d | 3,220 | 2,109 | — |
| Regal DeLuxe cpe 5P | 3,205 | 2,135 | — |
| Regal DeLuxe cpe 3P | 3,135 | 2,041 | — |
| Regal DeLuxe conv cpe | 3,415 | 2,468 | — |
| Land Cruiser sdn 4d | 3,325 | 2,328 | — |

| 1949 Engines | bore × stroke | bhp | availability |
|---|---|---|---|
| I-6, 169.6 | 3.00 × 4.00 | 80 | S-Champion |
| I-6, 245.6 | 3.31 × 4.75 | 100 | S-Commander |

### 1950
| 9G Champion (wb 113)—270,604 blt | Wght | Price | Prod |
|---|---|---|---|
| Custom sdn 4d | 2,730 | 1,519 | — |
| Custom sdn 2d | 2,695 | 1,487 | — |
| Custom cpe 5P | 2,690 | 1,514 | — |
| Custom cpe 3P | 2,620 | 1,419 | — |
| DeLuxe sdn 4d | 2,750 | 1,597 | — |
| DeLuxe sdn 2d | 2,720 | 1,565 | — |
| DeLuxe cpe 5P | 2,705 | 1,592 | — |
| DeLuxe cpe 3P | 2,635 | 1,497 | — |
| Regal DeLuxe sdn 4d | 2,755 | 1,676 | — |
| Regal DeLuxe sdn 2d | 2,725 | 1,644 | — |
| Regal DeLuxe cpe 5P | 2,715 | 1,671 | — |
| Regal DeLuxe cpe 3P | 2,640 | 1,576 | — |
| Regal DeLuxe conv cpe | 2,900 | 1,981 | — |

| 17A Commander (wb 120.0; LC-124.0)—72,562 built | Wght | Price | Prod |
|---|---|---|---|
| DeLuxe sdn 4d | 3,255 | 1,902 | — |
| DeLuxe sdn 2d | 3,215 | 1,871 | — |
| DeLuxe cpe 5P | 3,215 | 1,897 | — |
| Regal DeLuxe sdn 4d | 3,265 | 2,024 | — |
| Regal DeLuxe sdn 2d | 3,220 | 1,992 | — |
| Regal DeLuxe cpe 5P | 3,220 | 2,018 | — |
| Regal DeLuxe conv cpe | 3,375 | 2,328 | — |
| Land Cruiser sdn 4d | 3,355 | 2,187 | — |

| 1950 Engines | bore × stroke | bhp | availability |
|---|---|---|---|
| I-6, 169.6 | 3.00 × 4.00 | 85 | S-Champion |
| I-6, 245.6 | 3.31 × 4.75 | 102 | S-Commander |

### 1951
| 10G Champion (wb 115)—144,286 blt | Wght | Price | Prod |
|---|---|---|---|
| Custom sdn 4d | 2,690 | 1,667 | — |
| Custom sdn 2d | 2,670 | 1,634 | — |
| Custom cpe 5P | 2,650 | 1,662 | — |

# Studebaker

| 10G Champion (wb 115) | Wght | Price | Prod |
|---|---|---|---|
| Custom cpe 3P | 2,585 | 1,561 | — |
| DeLuxe sdn 4d | 2,715 | 1,759 | — |
| DeLuxe sdn 2d | 2,690 | 1,716 | — |
| DeLuxe cpe 5P | 2,675 | 1,744 | — |
| DeLuxe cpe 3P | 2,610 | 1,643 | — |
| Regal sdn 4d | 2,720 | 1,833 | — |
| Regal sdn 2d | 2,690 | 1,800 | — |
| Regal cpe 5P | 2,675 | 1,828 | — |
| Regal cpe 3P | 2,615 | 1,727 | — |
| Regal conv cpe | 2,890 | 2,157 | — |

| H Commander (wb 115.0; LC-119.0)—124,280 built | | | |
|---|---|---|---|
| Regal sdn 4d | 3,065 | 2,032 | — |
| Regal sdn 2d | 3,045 | 1,997 | — |
| Regal cpe 5P | 3,030 | 2,026 | — |
| State sdn 4d | 3,070 | 2,143 | — |
| State sdn 2d | 3,045 | 2,108 | — |
| State cpe 5P | 3,030 | 2,137 | — |
| State conv cpe | 3,240 | 2,381 | — |
| Land Cruiser sdn 4d | 3,165 | 2,289 | — |

| 1951 Engines | bore × stroke | bhp | availability |
|---|---|---|---|
| I-6, 169.6 | 3.00 × 4.00 | 85 | S-Champion |
| V-8, 232.6 | 3.38 × 3.25 | 120 | S-Commander |

## 1952

| 12G Champion (wb 115)—101,390 blt | Wght | Price | Prod |
|---|---|---|---|
| Custom sdn 4d | 2,695 | 1,769 | — |
| Custom sdn 2d | 2,655 | 1,735 | — |
| Custom cpe 5P | 2,660 | 1,763 | — |
| DeLuxe sdn 4d | 2,720 | 1,862 | — |
| DeLuxe sdn 2d | 2,685 | 1,828 | — |
| DeLuxe cpe 5P | 2,675 | 1,856 | — |
| Regal sdn 4d | 2,725 | 1,946 | — |
| Regal sdn 2d | 2,690 | 1,913 | — |
| Regal cpe 5P | 2,695 | 1,941 | — |
| Regal Starliner htp cpe | 2,860 | 2,220 | — |
| Regal conv cpe | 2,870 | 2,273 | — |

| 3H Commander (wb 115.0; LC-119.0)—84,849 built | | | |
|---|---|---|---|
| Regal sdn 4d | 3,085 | 2,121 | — |
| Regal sdn 2d | 3,040 | 2,086 | — |
| Regal cpe 5P | 3,030 | 2,115 | — |
| State sdn 4d | 3,075 | 2,208 | — |
| State sdn 2d | 3,055 | 2,172 | — |
| State cpe 5P | 3,025 | 2,202 | — |
| State Starliner htp cpe | 3,220 | 2,488 | — |
| State conv cpe | 3,230 | 2,548 | — |
| Land Cruiser sdn 4d | 3,155 | 2,365 | — |

| 1952 Engines | bore × stroke | bhp | availability |
|---|---|---|---|
| I-6, 169.6 | 3.00 × 4.00 | 85 | S-Champion |
| V-8, 232.6 | 3.38 × 3.25 | 120 | S-Commander |

## 1953

| 14G Champion (wb 116.5; cpes-120.5)—93,807 built | | | |
|---|---|---|---|
| | Wght | Price | Prod |
| Custom sdn 4d | 2,710 | 1,767 | — |
| Custom sdn 2d | 2,690 | 1,735 | — |
| DeLuxe sdn 4d | 2,735 | 1,863 | — |
| DeLuxe sdn 2d | 2,700 | 1,831 | — |
| DeLuxe Starlight cpe | 2,695 | 1,868 | — |
| Regal sdn 4d | 2,745 | 1,949 | — |
| Regal sdn 2d | 2,715 | 1,917 | — |
| Regal Starlight cpe | 2,700 | 1,955 | — |
| Regal Starliner htp cpe | 2,760 | 2,116 | — |

| 4H Commander (wb 116.5; LC/cpes-120.5)—76,092 built | | | |
|---|---|---|---|
| DeLuxe sdn 4d | 3,075 | 2,121 | — |
| DeLuxe sdn 2d | 3,055 | 2,089 | — |
| DeLuxe Starlight cpe | 3,040 | 2,127 | — |
| Regal sdn 4d | 3,095 | 2,208 | — |
| Regal Starlight cpe | 3,040 | 2,213 | — |
| Regal Starliner htp cpe | 3,120 | 2,374 | — |
| Land Cruiser sdn 4d | 3,180 | 2,316 | — |

| 1953 Engines | bore × stroke | bhp | availability |
|---|---|---|---|
| I-6, 169.6 | 3.00 × 4.00 | 85 | S-Champion |
| V-8, 232.6 | 3.38 × 3.25 | 120 | S-Commander |

## 1954

| 15G Champion Six (wb 116.5; cpes-120.5)—51,431 built | | | |
|---|---|---|---|
| | Wght | Price | Prod |
| Custom sdn 4d | 2,735 | 1,801 | — |
| Custom sdn 2d | 2,705 | 1,758 | — |
| DeLuxe sdn 4d | 2,765 | 1,918 | — |
| DeLuxe sdn 2d | 2,730 | 1,875 | — |
| DeLuxe Starlight cpe | 2,740 | 1,972 | — |
| DeLuxe Conestoga wgn 2d | 2,930 | 2,187 | — |
| Regal sdn 4d | 2,780 | 2,026 | — |
| Regal sdn 2d | 2,745 | 1,983 | — |
| Regal Starlight cpe | 2,750 | 2,080 | — |
| Regal Starliner htp cpe | 2,825 | 2,241 | — |
| Regal Conestoga wgn 2d | 2,950 | 2,295 | — |

| 5H Commander (wb 116.5; LC/cpes-120.5)—30,499 built | | | |
|---|---|---|---|
| DeLuxe sdn 4d | 3,105 | 2,179 | — |
| DeLuxe sdn 2d | 3,075 | 2,136 | — |
| DeLuxe Starlight cpe | 3,085 | 2,233 | — |
| DeLuxe Conestoga wgn 2d | 3,265 | 2,448 | — |
| Regal sdn 4d | 3,120 | 2,287 | — |
| Regal Starlight cpe | 3,095 | 2,341 | — |
| Regal Starliner htp cpe | 3,175 | 2,502 | — |
| Regal Conestoga wgn 2d | 3,265 | 2,556 | — |
| Land Cruiser sdn 4d | 3,180 | 2,438 | — |

| 1954 Engines | bore × stroke | bhp | availability |
|---|---|---|---|
| I-6, 169.6 | 3.00 × 4.00 | 85 | S-Champion |
| V-8, 232.6 | 3.38 × 3.25 | 127 | S-Commander |

## 1955

| 16G Champion (wb 116.5; cpes-120.5)—50,368 built | | | |
|---|---|---|---|
| | Wght | Price | Prod |
| Custom sdn 4d | 2,790 | 1,783 | — |
| Custom sdn 2d | 2,740 | 1,741 | — |
| DeLuxe sdn 4d | 2,805 | 1,885 | — |
| DeLuxe sdn 2d | 2,780 | 1,841 | — |
| DeLuxe cpe | 2,790 | 1,875 | — |
| DeLuxe Conestoga wgn 2d | 2,980 | 2,141 | — |
| Regal sdn 4d | 2,815 | 1,993 | — |
| Regal cpe | 2,795 | 1,975 | — |
| Regal htp cpe | 2,865 | 2,125 | — |
| Regal Conestoga wgn 2d | 2,985 | 2,312 | — |

| 6G Commander (wb 116.5; cpes-120.5)—58,792 built | | | |
|---|---|---|---|
| Custom sdn 4d | 3,065 | 1,919 | — |
| Custom sdn 2d | 3,105 | 1,873 | — |
| DeLuxe sdn 4d | 3,075 | 2,014 | — |
| DeLuxe sdn 2d | 3,045 | 1,969 | — |
| DeLuxe cpe | 3,065 | 1,989 | — |
| DeLuxe Conestoga wgn 2d | 3,265 | 2,274 | — |
| Regal sdn 4d | 3,080 | 2,127 | — |
| Regal cpe | 3,065 | 2,094 | — |
| Regal htp cpe | 3,150 | 2,282 | — |

# Studebaker

| 6G Commander (wb 116.5; cpes-120.5) | Wght | Price | Prod |
|---|---|---|---|
| Regal Conestoga wgn 2d | 3,274 | 2,445 | — |
| **6H President (wb 120.5)** | | | |
| DeLuxe sdn 4d | 3,165 | 2,311 | ⎤ |
| State sdn 4d | 3,220 | 2,381 | ⎥ 22,451 |
| State cpe | 3,210 | 2,270 | ⎥ |
| State htp cpe | 3,175 | 2,456 | ⎦ |
| Speedster htp cpe | 3,301 | 3,253 | 2,215 |

| 1955 Engines | bore × stroke | bhp | availability |
|---|---|---|---|
| I-6, 185.6 | 3.00 × 4.38 | 101 | S-Champion |
| V-8, 224.3 | 3.56 × 2.81 | 140 | S-early Commander |
| V-8, 259.2 | 3.56 × 3.25 | 162 | S-late Commander |
| V-8, 259.2 | 3.56 × 3.25 | 175 | S-early President |
| V-8, 259.2 | 3.56 × 3.25 | 185 | S-early Spdstr; O-late Pres |

## 1956

### 56G Six (wb 116.5; Hawk-120.5)—28,918* built

| | Wght | Price | Prod |
|---|---|---|---|
| Champion sdn 4d | 2,835 | 1,996 | — |
| Champion sdn 2d | 2,800 | 1,946 | — |
| Champion sedanet | 2,780 | 1,844 | — |
| Pelham wgn 2d | 3,000 | 2,232 | — |
| Flight Hawk cpe | 2,780 | 1,986 | — |

### 56B V-8, 259 (wb 116.5; Hawk-120.5)—30,654* built

| | Wght | Price | Prod |
|---|---|---|---|
| Commander sdn 4d | 3,140 | 2,125 | — |
| Commander sdn 2d | 3,110 | 2,076 | — |
| Commander sedanet | 3,085 | 1,974 | — |
| Parkview wgn 2d | 3,300 | 2,354 | — |
| Power Hawk cpe | 3,095 | 2,101 | — |

### 56H V-8, 289 (wb 116.5; Classic/Hawk-120.5)

| | Wght | Price | Prod |
|---|---|---|---|
| President sdn 4d | 3,210 | 2,235 | ⎤ |
| President sdn 2d | 3,180 | 2,188 | ⎥ 18,209 |
| President Classic sdn 4d | 3,295 | 2,489 | ⎥ |
| Pinehurst wgn 2d | 3,395 | 2,529 | ⎦ |
| Sky Hawk htp cpe | 3,215 | 2,477 | 3,610 |

### 56J V-8, 352 (wb 120.5)

| | Wght | Price | Prod |
|---|---|---|---|
| Golden Hawk htp cpe | 3,360 | 3,061 | 4,071 |

* Includes 11,484 Flight Hawks and Power Hawks.

| 1956 Engines | bore × stroke | bhp | availability |
|---|---|---|---|
| I-6, 185.6 | 3.00 × 4.38 | 101 | S-Chmp, Flht Hwk, Plhm |
| V-8, 259.2 | 3.56 × 3.25 | 170 | S-Cmdr, Pwr Hwk Prkvw |
| V-8, 259.2 | 3.56 × 3.25 | 185 | O-Champ, Comm, Pwr/Flht Hwk, wgns |
| V-8, 289.0 | 3.56 × 3.63 | 195 | S-Pres, Pnhrst |
| V-8, 289.0 | 3.56 × 3.63 | 210 | S-Pres, Clsic, Sky Hwk |
| V-8, 289.0 | 3.56 × 3.63 | 225 | O-Pres, Pnhrst, Sky Hwk |
| V-8, 352.0 | 4.00 × 3.50 | 275 | S-Golden Hawk |

## 1957*

### 57G Six (wb 116.5; Hawk-120.5)

| | Wght | Price | Prod |
|---|---|---|---|
| Scotsman sdn 4d | 2,725 | 1,826 | — |
| Scotsman club sdn | 2,680 | 1,776 | — |
| Scotsman wgn 2d | 2,875 | 1,995 | — |
| Champion Custom sdn 4d | 2,785 | 2,049 | — |
| Champion Custom club sdn | 2,755 | 2,001 | — |
| Champion DeLuxe sdn 4d | 2,810 | 2,171 | — |
| Champion DeLuxe club sdn | 2,780 | 2,123 | — |
| Pelham wgn 2d | 3,015 | 2,382 | — |
| Silver Hawk cpe | 2,790 | 2,142 | — |

### 57B V-8, 259 (wb 116.5)

| | Wght | Price | Prod |
|---|---|---|---|
| Commander Custom sdn 4d | 3,105 | 2,173 | — |
| Commander Custom club sdn | 3,075 | 2,124 | — |
| Commander DeLuxe sdn 4d | 3,140 | 2,295 | — |
| Commander DeLuxe club sdn | 3,100 | 2,246 | — |
| Provincial wgn 4d | 3,355 | 2,561 | — |
| Parkview wgn 2d | 3,310 | 2,505 | — |

### 57H V-8, 289 (wb 116.5; Classic/Hawks-120.5)

| | Wght | Price | Prod |
|---|---|---|---|
| President Classic sdn 4d | 3,270 | 2,539 | — |
| President sdn 4d | 3,205 | 2,407 | — |
| President club sdn | 3,170 | 2,358 | — |
| Broadmoor wgn 4d | 3,415 | 2,666 | — |
| Silver Hawk cpe | 3,185 | 2,263 | — |
| Golden Hawk htp cpe | 3,185 | 3,182 | 4,356 |

* Total 1957 production: 74,738; includes 15,318 Silver Hawks.

| 1957 Engines | bore × stroke | bhp | availability |
|---|---|---|---|
| I-6, 185.6 | 3.00 × 4.38 | 101 | S-Scotsman, Champ, Silver Hawk, Pelham |
| V-8, 259.2 | 3.56 × 3.25 | 180 | S-Commander & 57B wagons, O-Silver Hawk |
| V-8, 259.2 | 3.56 × 3.25 | 195 | O-Commander & 57B wagons, Silver Hawk |
| V-8, 289.0 | 3.56 × 3.63 | 210 | S-President, Silver Hawk, 57H wagons |
| V-8, 289.0 | 3.56 × 3.63 | 225 | S-President Classic; O-Silver Hawk, 57H wgn |
| V-8S, 289.0 | 3.56 × 3.63 | 275 | S-Golden Hawk |

## 1958

### 58G Six (wb 116.5; Hawk-120.5)

| | Wght | Price | Prod |
|---|---|---|---|
| Silver Hawk cpe | 2,810 | 2,291 | * |
| Scotsman sdn 4d | 2,740 | 1,874 | ⎤ |
| Scotsman sdn 2d | 2,695 | 1,795 | ⎥ 20,870 |
| Scotsman wgn 2d | 2,870 | 2,055 | ⎦ |
| Champion sdn 4d | 2,835 | 2,253 | ⎤ 10,325 |
| Champion sdn 2d | 2,795 | 2,189 | ⎦ |

### 58B V-8, 259 (wb 116.5)—12,249 built

| | Wght | Price | Prod |
|---|---|---|---|
| Commander sdn 4d | 3,185 | 2,378 | — |
| Commander Starlight htp cpe | 3,270 | 2,493 | — |
| Provincial wgn 4d | 3,420 | 2,664 | — |

### 58H V-8, 289 (wb 120.5; Starlight htp-116.5)

| | Wght | Price | Prod |
|---|---|---|---|
| President sdn 4d | 3,365 | 2,639 | ⎤ 10,442 |
| President Starlight htp cpe | 3,355 | 2,695 | ⎦ |
| Silver Hawk cpe | 3,210 | 2,352 | * |
| Golden Hawk htp cpe | 3,470 | 3,282 | 878 |

* Total Silver Hawk; 7,350

| 1958 Engines | bore × stroke | bhp | availability |
|---|---|---|---|
| I-6, 185.6 | 3.00 × 4.38 | 101 | S-Scotsman, Champion, Silver Hawk |
| V-8, 259.2 | 3.56 × 3.25 | 180 | S-Commander, Provincial; O-Silver Hawk |
| V-8, 259.2 | 3.56 × 3.25 | 195 | O-Commander, Provincial, Silver Hawk |
| V-8, 289.0 | 3.56 × 3.63 | 210 | O-Silver Hawk |
| V-8, 289.0 | 3.56 × 3.63 | 225 | S-President; O-Silver Hawk |
| V-8S, 289.0 | 3.56 × 3.63 | 275 | S-Golden Hawk |

# Studebaker

## 1959

### 59S Lark VI (wb 108.5; wgns-113.0)—98,744 built

|  | Wght | Price | Prod |
|---|---|---|---|
| DeLuxe sdn 4d | 2,605 | 1,995 | — |
| DeLuxe sdn 2d | 2,577 | 1,925 | — |
| DeLuxe wgn 2d | 2,805 | 2,295 | — |
| Regal sdn 4d | 2,600 | 2,175 | — |
| Regal htp cpe | 2,710 | 2,275 | — |
| Regal wgn 2d | 2,815 | 2,455 | — |

### 59V Lark VIII (wb 108.5; wgn-113.0)—32,334 built

| | Wght | Price | Prod |
|---|---|---|---|
| Regal sdn 4d | 2,924 | 2,310 | — |
| Regal htp cpe | 3,034 | 2,411 | — |
| Regal wgn 2d | 3,148 | 2,590 | — |

### 59S/59V Silver Hawk (wb 120.5)

| | Wght | Price | Prod |
|---|---|---|---|
| cpe, I-6 | 2,795 | 2,360 | 2,417 |
| cpe, V-8 | 3,140 | 2,495 | 5,371 |

### 1959 Engines

| | bore × stroke | bhp | availability |
|---|---|---|---|
| I-6, 169.6 | 3.00 × 4.00 | 90 | S-Lrk VI, Slvr Hwk I-6 |
| V-8, 259.2 | 3.56 × 3.25 | 180 | S-Lrk VIII, Slvr Hwk V-8 |
| V-8, 259.2 | 3.56 × 3.25 | 195 | O-Lrk VIII, Slvr Hwk V-8 |

## 1960

### 60S Lark VI (wb 108.5; wgns-113.0)—70,153 built

| | Wght | Price | Prod |
|---|---|---|---|
| DeLuxe sdn 4d | 2,592 | 2,046 | — |
| DeLuxe sdn 2d | 2,588 | 1,976 | — |
| DeLuxe wgn 4d | 2,792 | 2,441 | — |
| DeLuxe wgn 2d | 2,763 | 2,366 | — |
| Regal sdn 4d | 2,619 | 2,196 | — |
| Regal htp cpe | 2,697 | 2,296 | — |
| Regal conv cpe | 2,961 | 2,621 | — |
| Regal wgn 4d | 2,836 | 2,591 | — |

### 60V Lark VIII (wb 108.5; wgns-113.0)—57,562 built

| | Wght | Price | Prod |
|---|---|---|---|
| DeLuxe sdn 4d | 2,941 | 2,181 | — |
| DeLuxe sdn 2d | 2,921 | 2,111 | — |
| DeLuxe wgn 4d | 3,161 | 2,576 | — |
| DeLuxe wgn 2d | 3,138 | 2,501 | — |
| Regal sdn 4d | 2,966 | 2,331 | — |
| Regal htp cpe | 3,033 | 2,431 | — |
| Regal conv cpe | 3,315 | 2,756 | — |
| Regal wgn 4d | 3,183 | 2,726 | — |

### 60S/60V Hawk (wb 120.5)—3,939 built

| | Wght | Price | Prod |
|---|---|---|---|
| cpe, V-8 | 3,207 | 2,650 | — |

### 1960 Engines

| | bore × stroke | bhp | availability |
|---|---|---|---|
| I-6, 169.6 | 3.00 × 4.00 | 90 | S-Lark VI |
| V-8, 259.2 | 3.56 × 3.25 | 180 | S-Lark VIII |
| V-8, 259.2 | 3.56 × 3.25 | 195 | O-Lark VIII |
| V-8, 289.0 | 3.56 × 3.63 | 210 | S-Hawk |
| V-8, 289.0 | 3.56 × 3.63 | 225 | O-Hawk |

## 1961

### 61S Lark VI (wb 108.5; wgns-113.0)—41,035 built

| | Wght | Price | Prod |
|---|---|---|---|
| DeLuxe sdn 4d | 2,665 | 1,935 | — |
| DeLuxe sdn 2d | 2,661 | 2,005 | — |
| DeLuxe wgn 4d | 2,865 | 2,370 | — |
| DeLuxe wgn 2d | 2,836 | 2,290 | — |
| Regal sdn 4d | 2,692 | 2,155 | — |
| Regal htp cpe | 2,770 | 2,243 | — |
| Regal conv cpe | 3,034 | 2,554 | — |
| Regal wgn 4d | 2,836 | 2,520 | — |

### 61V Lark VIII (wb 108.5; Crsr/wgns-113.0)—25,934 built

| | Wght | Price | Prod |
|---|---|---|---|
| DeLuxe sdn 4d | 2,941 | 2,140 | — |
| DeLuxe sdn 2d | 2,921 | 2,070 | — |
| DeLuxe wgn 4d | 3,183 | 2,505 | — |
| DeLuxe wgn 2d | 3,112 | 2,425 | — |
| Regal sdn 4d | 2,956 | 2,290 | — |
| Regal htp cpe | 3,074 | 2,378 | — |
| Regal conv cpe | 3,315 | 2,689 | — |
| Regal wgn 4d | 3,183 | 2,655 | — |
| Cruiser sdn 4d | 3,001 | 2,458 | — |

### 61V Hawk (wb 120.5)

| | Wght | Price | Prod |
|---|---|---|---|
| cpe | 3,205 | 2,650 | 3,340 |

### 1961 Engines

| | bore × stroke | bhp | availability |
|---|---|---|---|
| I-6, 169.6 | 3.00 × 4.00 | 112 | S-Lark VI |
| V-8, 259.2 | 3.56 × 3.25 | 180 | S-Lark VIII |
| V-8, 259.2 | 3.56 × 3.25 | 195 | O-Lark VIII |
| V-8, 289.0 | 3.56 × 3.63 | 210 | S-Hawk |
| V-8, 289.0 | 3.56 × 3.63 | 225 | O-Hawk |

## 1962

### 62S Lark Six (wb 113.0; 2d-109.0)—54,397 built

| | Wght | Price | Prod |
|---|---|---|---|
| DeLuxe sdn 4d | 2,760 | 2,040 | — |
| DeLuxe sdn 2d | 2,655 | 1,935 | — |
| DeLuxe wgn 4d | 2,845 | 2,405 | — |
| Regal sdn 4d | 2,770 | 2,190 | — |
| Regal wgn 4d | 2,875 | 2,555 | — |
| Regal htp cpe | 2,765 | 2,218 | — |
| Regal conv cpe | 3,075 | 2,589 | — |
| Daytona htp cpe | 2,765 | 2,308 | — |
| Daytona conv cpe | 3,075 | 2,679 | — |

### 62V Lark Eight (wb 113.0; 2d-109.0)—38,607 built

| | Wght | Price | Prod |
|---|---|---|---|
| DeLuxe sdn 4d | 3,015 | 2,175 | — |
| DeLuxe sdn 2d | 2,925 | 2,070 | — |
| DeLuxe wgn 4d | 3,115 | 2,540 | — |
| Regal sdn 4d | 3,025 | 2,325 | — |
| Regal wgn 4d | 3,145 | 2,690 | — |
| Regal htp cpe | 3,015 | 2,353 | — |
| Regal conv cpe | 3,305 | 2,724 | — |
| Daytona htp cpe | 3,015 | 2,443 | — |
| Daytona conv cpe | 3,305 | 2,814 | — |
| Cruiser sdn 4d | 3,030 | 2,493 | — |

### 62V Gran Turismo Hawk (wb 120.5)

| | Wght | Price | Prod |
|---|---|---|---|
| htp cpe | 3,230 | 3,095 | 8,388 |

### 1962 Engines

| | bore × stroke | bhp | availability |
|---|---|---|---|
| I-6, 169.6 | 3.00 × 4.00 | 112 | S-Lark Six |
| V-8, 259.2 | 3.56 × 3.25 | 180 | S-Lark Eight |
| V-8, 259.2 | 3.56 × 3.25 | 195 | O-Lark Eight |
| V-8, 289.0 | 3.56 × 3.63 | 210 | S-GT Hawk; O-Lark Cruiser |
| V-8, 289.0 | 3.56 × 3.63 | 225 | O-GT Hawk, Lark Cruiser |

## 1963

### 63S Lark Six (wb 113.0; 2d-109.0)—73,192 built (includes 63V)

| | Wght | Price | Prod |
|---|---|---|---|
| Standard sdn 4d | 2,775 | 2,040 | — |
| Standard sdn 2d | 2,650 | 1,935 | — |
| Standard wgn 4d | 3,285 | 2,430 | — |
| Regal sdn 4d | 2,790 | 2,160 | — |
| Regal sdn 2d | 2,665 | 2,055 | — |
| Regal wgn 4d | 3,200 | 2,550 | — |

## Studebaker

| 63S Lark Six (wb 113.0; 2d-109.0) | Wght | Price | Prod |
|---|---|---|---|
| Custom sdn 4d | 2,800 | 2,285 | — |
| Custom sdn 2d | 2,680 | 2,180 | — |
| Daytona wgn 4d | 3,245 | 2,700 | — |
| Daytona htp cpe | 2,795 | 2,308 | — |
| Daytona conv cpe | 3,045 | 2,679 | — |
| **63V Lark Eight (wb 113.0; 2d-109.0)** | | | |
| Standard sdn 4d | 2,985 | 2,175 | — |
| Standard sdn 2d | 2,910 | 2,070 | — |
| Standard wgn 4d | 3,435 | 2,565 | — |
| Regal sdn 4d | 3,000 | 2,295 | — |
| Regal sdn 2d | 2,925 | 2,190 | — |
| Regal wgn 4d | 3,450 | 2,685 | — |
| Custom sdn 4d | 3,010 | 2,420 | — |
| Custom sdn 2d | 2,940 | 2,315 | — |
| Daytona wgn 4d | 3,490 | 2,835 | — |
| Daytona htp cpe | 3,035 | 2,443 | — |
| Daytona conv cpe | 3,265 | 2,814 | — |
| Cruiser sdn 4d | 3,065 | 2,595 | — |
| **63V Grand Turismo Hawk (wb 120.5)** | | | |
| htp cpe | 3,280 | 3,095 | 4,634 |
| **63R Avanti (wb 109.0)** | | | |
| spt cpe | 3,140 | 4,445 | 3,834 |

* Note: Lark wagon data for sliding-roof Wagonaire models. Solid-roof versions offered from midmodel year for $100 less than comparable Wagonaires.

| 1963 Engines | bore × stroke | bhp | availability |
|---|---|---|---|
| I-6, 169.6 | 3.00 × 4.00 | 112 | S-Lark Six |
| V-8, 259.2 | 3.56 × 3.25 | 180 | S-Lark Eight |
| V-8, 259.2 | 3.56 × 3.25 | 195 | O-Lark Eight |
| V-8, 289.0 | 3.56 × 3.63 | 210 | S-Hawk, Cruiser; O-Lark Eight |
| V-8, 289.0 | 3.56 × 3.63 | 225 | O-Hawk, Lark Eight, Cruiser |
| V-8, 289.0 | 3.56 × 3.63 | 240 | S-Avanti; O-Hawk, Lark Eight (R1) |
| V-8S, 289.0 | 3.56 × 3.63 | 290 | O-Avanti, Hawk, Lark Eight (R2) |

### 1964

| 64S Six (wb 113.0; 2d-109.0)—43,884 built (includes 64V) | | | |
|---|---|---|---|
| | Wght | Price | Prod |
| Challenger sdn 4d | 2,780 | 2,048 | — |
| Challenger sdn 2d | 2,660 | 1,943 | — |
| Challenger wgn 4d | 3,230 | 2,438 | — |
| Commander sdn 4d | 2,815 | 2,168 | — |
| Commander sdn 2d | 2,695 | 2,063 | — |
| Commander Special sdn 2d | 2,725 | 2,193 | — |
| Commander wgn 4d | 3,265 | 2,558 | — |
| Daytona sdn 4d | 2,790 | 2,318 | — |
| Daytona conv cpe | 3,040 | 2,670 | — |
| Daytona wgn 4d | 3,240 | 2,708 | — |
| **64V Eight (wb 113.0; 2d-109.0)** | | | |
| Challenger sdn 4d | 3,010 | 2,183 | — |
| Challenger sdn 2d | 2,910 | 2,078 | — |
| Challenger wgn 4d | 3,480 | 2,573 | — |
| Commander sdn 4d | 3,045 | 2,303 | — |
| Commander sdn 2d | 2,945 | 2,198 | — |
| Commander Special sdn 2d | 2,975 | 2,328 | — |
| Daytona sdn 4d | 3,055 | 2,453 | — |
| Daytona htp cpe | 3,060 | 2,451 | — |
| Daytona conv cpe | 3,320 | 2,805 | — |

| 64V Eight (wb 113.0; 2d-109.0) | Wght | Price | Prod |
|---|---|---|---|
| Daytona wgn 4d | 3,555 | 2,843 | — |
| Cruiser sdn 4d | 3,120 | 2,603 | — |
| **64V Gran Turismo Hawk (wb 120.5)** | | | |
| htp cpe | 3,120 | 2,966 | 1,767 |
| **64R Avanti (wb 109.0)** | | | |
| spt cpe | 3,195 | 4,445 | 809 |

* Note: All wagons are sliding-roof Wagonaire models.

| 1964 Engines | bore × stroke | bhp | availability |
|---|---|---|---|
| I-6, 169.6 | 3.00 × 4.00 | 112 | S-Six |
| V-8, 259.2 | 3.56 × 3.25 | 180 | S-Eight exc. Cruiser |
| V-8, 259.2 | 3.56 × 3.25 | 195 | O-Eight exc. Cruiser |
| V-8, 289.0 | 3.56 × 3.63 | 210 | S-Hawk, Cruiser; O-other Eight |
| V-8, 289.0 | 3.56 × 3.63 | 225 | O-all Eight exc. Avanti |
| V-8, 289.0 | 3.56 × 3.63 | 240 | S-Avanti; O-other Eight (R1) |
| V-8S, 289.0 | 3.56 × 3.63 | 290 | O-all (R2) |
| V-8S, 304.5 | 3.65 × 3.63 | 335 | O-all exc. Challenger (R3) |
| V-8, 304.5 | 3.65 × 3.63 | 280 | O-all exc. Challenger (R4) |

### 1965—19,435 built

| C-1 Six (wb 113.0; 2d-109.0) | Wght | Price | Prod |
|---|---|---|---|
| Commander sdn 4d | 2,815 | 2,230 | — |
| Commander sdn 2d | 2,695 | 2,125 | — |
| Commander wgn 4d | 3,265 | 2,620 | — |
| Cruiser sdn 4d | 2,820 | 2,470 | — |
| **C-5 Eight (wb 113.0; 2d-109.0)** | | | |
| Commander sdn 4d | 2,995 | 2,370 | — |
| Commander sdn 2d | 2,895 | 2,265 | — |
| Commander wgn 4d | 3,465 | 2,760 | — |
| Daytona Sport Sdn 2d | 2,970 | 2,565 | — |
| Daytona wgn 4d | 3,505 | 2,890 | — |
| Cruiser sdn 4d | 3,070 | 2,610 | — |

* Note: All wagons are sliding-roof Wagonaire models.

| 1965 Engines | bore × stroke | bhp | availability |
|---|---|---|---|
| I-6, 194.0 | 3.56 × 3.25 | 120 | S-Six |
| V-8, 283.0 | 3.88 × 3.00 | 195 | S-Eight |

### 1966—8,947 built

| Six (wb 113.0; 2d-109.0) | Wght | Price | Prod |
|---|---|---|---|
| Commander sdn 4d | 2,815 | 2,165 | — |
| Commander sdn 2d | 2,695 | 2,060 | — |
| Wagonaire wgn 4d | 3,246 | 2,555 | — |
| Daytona sdn 2d | 2,755 | 2,405 | — |
| Cruiser sdn 4d | 2,815 | 2,405 | — |
| **Eight (wb 113.0; 2d-109.0)** | | | |
| Commander sdn 4d | 2,991 | 2,305 | — |
| Commander sdn 2d | 2,891 | 2,200 | — |
| Wagonaire wgn 4d | 3,501 | 2,695 | — |
| Daytona sdn 2d | 3,006 | 2,500 | — |
| Cruiser sdn 4d | 3,066 | 2,545 | — |

| 1966 Engines | bore × stroke | bhp | availability |
|---|---|---|---|
| I-6, 194.0 | 3.56 × 3.25 | 120 | S-Six |
| I-6, 230.0 | 3.88 × 3.25 | 140 | O-Six |
| V-8, 283.0 | 3.88 × 3.00 | 195 | S-Eight |

Postwar Studebaker production includes cars manufactured in South Bend, Indiana, and Hamilton, Ontario, for U.S., Canadian, and export sale. All 1965-66 Studebakers were built in Canada.

# Stutz

**1930 Model M Weymann Monte Carlo four-door sedan**

Stutz was never a high-volume producer, rising from 759 cars its first year, 1913, to just 2207 in 1917. But the firm was making its own engines by the early '20s: a big 361-cubic-inch side-valve four with 88 brake horsepower and an overhead-valve 75-bhp six. The latter was bumped up to 80 bhp and 268 cid for 1924's Speedway Six. Fours were discontinued the following year.

European-born, Frederick E. Moskovics arrived in 1925 to take over the presidency of Stutz. Moskovics introduced beautiful new open and closed "Safety Stutz" models the following year. These carried Stutz's first eight, a European-inspired inline engine with single overhead camshaft and dual ignition with two plugs per cylinder. Stutz called it the "Vertical Eight." Bowing at 289 cid and 92 bhp, it would be the heart of all Stutzes through the final 1936 models. The sole exception was the 1929-30 Blackhawk, a companion line powered by an L-head Continental eight or overhead-cam Stutz six. Though "cheap" for Stutz at a base price of $2395, the Blackhawk managed just under 1600 units. After 1930, its chassis was used for the least-costly Stutzes.

The Vertical Eight was quickly uprated, going to 298.6 cid for 1927, then to 322 cid and 113 bhp two years later. Advertised horsepower would go no further, although actual horsepower might have reached 140 by the end of the '20s. Stutz added to its racing image by dominating AAA stock car racing in '27 and giving Bentley a run for its money at the 1928 LeMans. Stutz chassis engineering changed remarkably little after 1929. For example, the same three wheelbases persisted to the end: 134.5 inches, 145, and, after Blackhawk's demise, 127.5 inches.

Though Stutz couldn't afford a 12- or 16-cylinder engine, it did experiment with a supercharger that lifted the Vertical Eight to 143 bhp. The blower was a huge affair mounted low, ahead of the radiator. Like most superchargers, it was driven directly from the crankshaft. It did the job, but it was noisy and carburetion was a problem. Accordingly, Stutz followed Duesenberg's approach for 1931 by offering a new 32-valve twincam cylinder head. This had no room for the dual ignition of what was now called the "SV16" (single-valve) engine, but improved breathing gave the new "DV32" (dual-valve) 161 bhp at 3900 rpm.

At the same time, Stutz tried to stem sliding sales in the deepening Depression with revived six-cylinder models, designated LA for '31 and LAA for 1932-33. Offering a standard coupe and sedan as well as five semicustom body styles, the LA sold for as little as $1995, the LAA for just $1620. Power came from what amounted to a Vertical Eight with two fewer cylinders—or the same 241.5-cid single-cam engine as the departed Blackhawk. But with just 85 bhp to propel better than 4300 pounds, these cars were hardly swift on the road or the sales chart, and Stutz gave up on them after 1933.

That left nothing but high-priced cars, which reflected Moskovics's no-compromise approach to sporty performance but also made Stutz an odd, slow-selling fish in luxury-car waters. Even standard-body models sold for upward of $3000-$4000—a lot for "hard times"—and some 30 custom styles were available on both SV16 and DV32 chassis from high-buck crafters like LeBaron, Fleetwood, Rollston, Weymann, Brunn, Waterhouse, and Derham. Stutz had offered Weymann's unusu-

1932 DV32 Super Bearcat convertible coupe

1932 DV32 Continental coupe by Waterhouse

1933 DV32 convertible coupe by LeBaron

al fabric bodies (actually padded leatherette) since 1928; these were light, strong, elastic, and quiet. Compared to steel shells, they soaked up more noise and road shock, and were easier to repair. Weymann bodies didn't last as long as steel or offer much protection in a crash. Also, many people disliked their dull, pebbled finish and dowdy looks. Stutz offered another Weymann novelty in 1932, the Monte Carlo, an aluminum-bodied five-passenger four-door "sport" sedan on the DV32 platform, priced at $4895 complete.

The DV32 itself debuted in chassis form at the New York Auto Show in the winter of 1930-31. Prices were announced at the end of March 1931, and production was underway by July. At about the same time, Stutz reported net earnings of just $20,000 on gross sales of only $100,000—pitifully meager, but still preferable to the red ink that had flowed since 1929.

Further changes were announced for 1932 SVs and DVs. The four-speed gearbox gave way to a very rugged "Muncie" three-speed synchronized unit, and freewheeling was a new option. The hot-air manifold was replaced with a hot-water heating system, and an oil cooler was provided. A new trunk rack and dust valance were installed at the rear, bodies were dropped down in a curving line to cover the frame, and single-bar bumpers replaced the previous double-bar design.

Stutz lost $315,000 in 1932, but continued to stumble on with the same basic lineup of SV16s and DV32s, all little changed. It's hardly surprising then that the company dropped a half-million dollars in 1933 and another quarter-million in '34. Though these were not particularly huge sums even in those days, the losses greatly accelerated the drain on Stutz's already meager resources.

Management sought refuge by contracting to build a line of small delivery trucks called Pak-Age-Cars. George H. Freers was appointed chief engineer for this effort, and the first 28 vehicles in a total order of 340 were completed by the summer of 1936. But this wasn't nearly enough to keep things going, so Stutz was forced to declare bankruptcy in April 1937. By that time, assets totaled $1.2 million and liabilities only $733,000, yet Stutz still couldn't meet its debts. When creditors couldn't agree on a reorganization plan, a federal judge ordered liquidation of all assets in April 1938. That was completed by summer, and the Pak-Age-Car program was taken over by Diamond T Truck Company.

## Specifications

### 1930

| Model M (wb 134.5; lwb 145)—649 blt* | Wght | Price | Prod |
|---|---|---|---|
| Torpedo speedster 2P | 4,595 | 3,450 | — |
| cpe 2P | 4,850 | 3,295 | — |
| sdn 4d | 4,918 | 3,695 | — |
| Weymann Versailles sdn 4d | — | 3,945 | — |
| phaeton 5P | — | 3,945 | — |
| lwb sdn 7P | 5,210 | 3,895 | — |
| lwb Weymann MC spt sdn 5P | — | 4,495 | — |
| chassis (both wbs) | — | — | — |

* Includes some 1929 production.

| 1930 Engine | bore × stroke | bhp | availability |
|---|---|---|---|
| I-8, 322.0 | 3.38 × 4.50 | 113 | S-all |

### 1931

| Model LA (wb 127.5) | | Wght | Price | Prod* |
|---|---|---|---|---|
| | sdn 4d | 4,320 | 2,245 | — |
| | cpe 2P | 4,275 | 1,995 | — |
| | five other body styles | — | — | — |
| **Model MA/MB (wb 134.5; MB-145.0)** | | | | |
| 21 | MA sdn 4d | 4,918 | 3,195 | — |
| 23 | MA cpe 2P | 4,850 | 2,995 | — |
| 24 | MA speedster 2P | 4,595 | 3,495 | — |
| 40 | MB sdn 7P | 5,210 | 3,895 | — |
| | MB dual-cowl phaeton | — | 4,495 | — |
| | MB Fltwd trans town car 7P | — | 7,495 | — |
| | chassis (both wbs) | — | — | — |
| **Model DV32 (wb 134.5; lwb-145.0)** | | | | |
| 21 | sdn 4d | 5,035 | 4,995 | — |
| 23 | cpe 2P | 4,909 | 4,995 | — |
| 24 | Bearcat speedster 2P | 4,678 | 4,995 | — |
| 40 | lwb sdn 7P | 5,270 | 5,395 | — |
| | chassis (both wbs) | — | — | — |

* Production not available.

# Stutz

| 1931 Engines | bore × stroke | bhp | availability |
|---|---|---|---|
| I-6, 241.5 | 3.38 × 4.50 | 85 | S-LA |
| I-8, 322.0 | 3.38 × 4.50 | 113 | S-MA, MB |
| I-8, 322.0 | 3.38 × 4.50 | 161 | S-DV32 |

## 1932*

| Model LAA (wb 127.5)** | | Wght | Price | Prod |
|---|---|---|---|---|
| | sdn 4d | 4,385 | 1,620 | — |
| | cpe 2P | 4,315 | 1,620 | — |
| | five other body styles | — | — | — |
| **Model SV16 (wb 134.5; lwb-145.0)** | | | | |
| 21 | sdn 4d | 4,985 | 2,995 | — |
| 23 | cpe 2P | 4,859 | 2,995 | — |
| 24 | Bearcat speedster 2P | 4,628 | 3,495 | — |
| 40 | lwb sdn 7P | 5,220 | 3,895 | — |
| | chassis (both wbs) | — | — | — |
| **Model DV32 (wb 134.5; lwb-145.0)** | | | | |
| 21 | sdn 4d | 5,185 | 3,995 | — |
| 23 | cpe 2P | 5,059 | 3,995 | — |
| 24 | Bearcat speedster 2P | 4,828 | 4,495 | — |
| 40 | lwb sdn 7P | 5,420 | 4,895 | — |
| | Super Bearcat 2P (wb 116.0) | — | 5,895 | — |
| | chassis (both wbs) | — | — | — |

\* Production not available.  ** Less than 50 built 1932-33.

| 1932 Engines | bore × stroke | bhp | availability |
|---|---|---|---|
| I-6, 241.5 | 3.38 × 4.50 | 85 | S-LAA |
| I-8, 322.0 | 3.38 × 4.50 | 113 | S-SV16 |
| I-8, 322.0 | 3.38 × 4.50 | 161 | S-DV32 |

## 1933*

| Model LAA** (wb 127.5) | | Wght | Price | Prod |
|---|---|---|---|---|
| | sdn 4d | 4,243 | 1,895 | — |
| | cabriolet cpe 5P | — | 2,185 | — |
| | three other body styles ($1900-2200) | — | — | — |
| **Model SV16 (wb 134.5; lwb-145.0)** | | | | |
| 21 | sdn 4d | 4,845 | 3,095 | — |
| 23 | cpe 2P | 4,719 | 3,095 | — |
| 24 | Bearcat speedster 2P | 4,488 | 3,195 | — |
| 40 | lwb sdn 7P | 5,080 | 3,560 | — |
| | Super Bearcat 2P (wb 116.0) | — | 5,095 | — |
| | chassis (both wbs) | — | — | — |
| **Model DV32 (wb 134.5; lwb-145.0)** | | | | |
| 21 | sdn 4d | 5,045 | 3,795 | — |
| 23 | cpe 2P | 4,919 | 3,795 | — |
| 24 | Bearcat speedster 2P | 4,688 | 3,895 | — |
| 40 | lwb sdn 7P | 5,280 | 4,260 | — |
| | Super Bearcat 2P (wb 116.0) | — | 5,795 | — |
| | Weymann MC spt sdn 5P (lwb) | 5,120 | 4,895 | — |
| 64 | LeBaron lwb sdn 4d 6P | 5,346 | 3,410 | — |
| | chassis (both wbs) | — | — | — |

\* Production not available.  ** Less than 50 built 1932-33.

| 1933 Engines | bore × stroke | bhp | availability |
|---|---|---|---|
| I-6, 241.5 | 3.38 × 4.50 | 85 | S-LAA |
| I-8, 322.0 | 3.38 × 4.50 | 113 | S-SV16 |
| I-8, 322.0 | 3.38 × 4.50 | 161 | S-DV32 |

## 1934

| SV16 (wb 134.5; lwb 145.0) | | Wght | Price | Prod* |
|---|---|---|---|---|
| 21 | sdn 4d | 4,845 | 3,095 | — |
| 23 | cpe 2P | 4,719 | 3,095 | — |
| 24 | Bearcat speedster 2P | 4,488 | 3,195 | — |
| 40 | lwb sdn 7P | 5,080 | 3,560 | — |
| | chassis (both wbs) | — | — | — |
| **DV32 (wb 134.5; lwb-145.0)** | | | | |
| 21 | sdn 4d | 5,045 | 3,795 | — |
| 23 | cpe 2P | 4,919 | 3,795 | — |
| 24 | Bearcat speedster 2P | 4,688 | 3,895 | — |
| 40 | lwb sdn 7P | 5,280 | 4,260 | — |
| | chassis (both wbs) | — | — | — |

\* Production not available.

| 1934 Engines | bore × stroke | bhp | availability |
|---|---|---|---|
| I-8, 322.0 | 3.38 × 4.50 | 113 | S-SV16 |
| I-8, 322.0 | 3.38 × 4.50 | 156 | S-DV32 |

## 1935

| SV16 (wb 134.5; lwb-145.0) | | Wght | Price | Prod* |
|---|---|---|---|---|
| 21 | sdn 4d | 4,745 | 3,095 | — |
| 23 | cpe 2-4P | 4,619 | 3,095 | — |
| 24 | Bearcat speedster 2-4P | 4,488 | 3,195 | — |
| 40 | lwb sdn 7P | 4,980 | 3,560 | — |
| | chassis (both wbs) | — | — | — |
| **DV32 (wb 134.5; lwb-145.0)** | | | | |
| 21 | sdn 4d | 4,895 | 3,795 | — |
| 23 | cpe 2-4P | 4,769 | 3,795 | — |
| 24 | Bearcat speedster 2-4P | 4,538 | 3,895 | — |
| 40 | lwb sdn 7P | 5,130 | 4,260 | — |
| | chassis (both wbs) | — | — | — |

\* Production not available.

| 1935 Engines | bore × stroke | bhp | availability |
|---|---|---|---|
| I-8, 322.0 | 3.38 × 4.50 | 113 | S-SV16 |
| I-8, 322.0 | 3.38 × 4.50 | 156 | S-DV32 |

## 1936

| SV16 (wb 134.5; lwb-145.0) | | Wght | Price | Prod* |
|---|---|---|---|---|
| 21 | sdn 4d | 4,745 | 3,095 | — |
| 23 | cpe 2-4P | 4,619 | 3,095 | — |
| 24 | Bearcat speedster 2-4P | 4,488 | 3,195 | — |
| 40 | lwb sdn 7P | 4,980 | 3,560 | — |
| | chassis (both wbs) | — | — | — |
| **DV32 (wb 134.5; lwb-145.0)** | | | | |
| 21 | sdn 4d | 4,895 | 3,795 | — |
| 23 | cpe 2-4P | 4,769 | 3,795 | — |
| 24 | Bearcat speedster 2-4P | 4,538 | 3,895 | — |
| 40 | lwb sdn 7P | 5,130 | 4,260 | — |
| | chassis (both wbs) | — | — | — |

\* Production not available.

| 1936 Engines | bore × stroke | bhp | availability |
|---|---|---|---|
| I-8, 322.0 | 3.38 × 4.50 | 113 | S-SV16 |
| I-8, 322.0 | 3.38 × 4.50 | 156 | S-DV32 |

# Terraplane

The abundant success of the 1932-33 Essex Terraplane (see Essex) prompted Hudson president Roy D. Chapin to use just Terraplane for the firm's 1934 junior models. At the same time, the existing 193-cubic-inch six and 244-cid eight gave way to a new long-stroke six with 212 cid and 80-85 horsepower, upped to 88 bhp for 1935-36. Power rose to 96/102 for 1937. Terraplane then became a Hudson, but as a separate make it literally saved the company.

Though Essex Terraplanes sold for as little as $425, their successors were pitched somewhat upmarket in the $565-$880 range. The 1934 Terraplane also offered more variety, with Special and midline Challenger on a 112-inch wheelbase and Major models on a 116-inch chassis. Majors were mustered out for '35, when Challenger was renamed DeLuxe. The 1936 line offered DeLuxes and uplevel Customs on a new 115-inch platform that was stretched two inches for the 1937 DeLuxe and Super models.

Unlike many companion makes, the separate-make Terraplanes followed period design trends but avoided excesses, though the 1936-37 "fencer's mask" grille was debatable. Body styles were the usual sort. Roadsters and phaetons were never listed, but brougham and coach sedans in regular and trunkback "touring" form were always available, as were fixed-roof and convertible coupes. A smart victoria was offered for 1934 only. A DeLuxe wood-bodied station wagon was exclusive to '36, while in '37, a small number of Terraplane chassis were built for commercial applications.

All these cars had fine performance. A British road test of a 1936 sedan showed 0-60 mph in 26.6 seconds and a top speed of 82 mph, both highly creditable for a period car weighing some 2800 pounds. Moreover, as the report observed, "The six-cylinder engine... has that suppleness and quietness in it's running that are characteristic of American design... Even at 70 there is no special fuss... [The Terraplane] can thus be a decidedly swift car for journeying over long distances, and is an easy one to handle, too... [It] gives, and does, much for its price."

**1934 K Special Six convertible coupe**

**1935 DeLuxe Six coupe**

**1936 DeLuxe Six coupe**

# Terraplane

1937 Series 70 Custom panel delivery (¾-ton)

Terraplane accounted for the lion's share of Hudson volume in each of its four years as a separate make, garnering nearly 280,000 total sales. Model-year output was around 51,000 for 1934 and '35, rose to almost 87,000 for '36, then reached 90,253 for the 1937 campaign.

With that, plus the demise of most other junior editions, the 1938 Terraplanes received Hudson badges and expanded to include standard, DeLuxe, and Super models with eight extra horsepower. But with that year's new "112" line, Terraplanes were no longer Hudson's smallest or most-affordable cars. Sales proved disappointing, so the name was dropped, though Terraplane continued to live on in spirit as the 1939 Series 91 Pacemaker and Series 92 Six.

## Specifications

Note: Production figures based on serial number spans and other calculations; may exceed actual production.

### 1934

| K Special Six (wb 112)—23,726 built | Wght | Price | Prod |
|---|---|---|---|
| cpe 2P | 2,600 | 600 | — |
| cpe 2-4P | 2,605 | 645 | — |
| conv cpe 2-4P | 2,625 | 695 | — |
| victoria 5P T/B | 2,655 | 655 | — |
| coach 5P | 2,630 | 615 | — |
| sdn 4d | 2,710 | 675 | — |
| sdn 4d T/B | 2,735 | 715 | — |
| **KS Challenger Six (wb 112.0)—20,265 built** | | | |
| cpe 2P | 2,540 | 565 | — |
| cpe 2-4P | 2,590 | 610 | — |
| coach 5P | 2,600 | 575 | — |
| sdn 4d | 2,670 | 635 | — |
| **KU Major Six (wb 116.0)—7,093 built** | | | |
| cpe 2P | 2,650 | 665 | — |
| cpe 2-4P | 2,700 | 710 | — |
| conv cpe 2-4P | 2,695 | 750 | — |
| victoria 5P T/B | 2,755 | 720 | — |
| coach 5P | 2,730 | 680 | — |
| sdn 4d | 2,780 | 740 | — |
| sdn 4d T/B | 2,805 | 780 | — |

| 1934 Engines | bore × stroke | bhp | availability |
|---|---|---|---|
| I-6, 212.0 | 3.00 × 5.00 | 80 | S-KS, K |
| I-6, 212.0 | 3.00 × 5.00 | 85 | S-KU |

### 1935

| G Special Six (wb 112)—37,772 built | Wght | Price | Prod |
|---|---|---|---|
| cpe 2P | 2,505 | 585 | — |
| cpe 2-4P | 2,555 | 625 | — |
| touring brougham 5P T/B | 2,610 | 625 | — |
| coach 5P | 2,595 | 595 | — |
| sdn 4d | 2,655 | 655 | — |
| Suburban sdn 4d T/B | 2,670 | 685 | — |
| **GU DeLuxe Six (wb 112.0)—13,362 built** | | | |
| cpe 2P | 2,565 | 635 | — |
| cpe 2-4P | 2,635 | 675 | — |
| conv cpe 2-4P | 2,590 | 725 | — |
| touring brougham 5P T/B | 2,680 | 675 | — |
| coach 5P | 2,665 | 645 | — |
| sdn 4d | 2,710 | 705 | — |
| Suburban sdn 4d T/B | 2,725 | 735 | — |

| 1935 Engine | bore × stroke | bhp | availability |
|---|---|---|---|
| I-6, 212.0 | 3.00 × 5.00 | 88 | S-all |

### 1936

| 61 DeLuxe Six (wb 115)—69,750 built | Wght | Price | Prod |
|---|---|---|---|
| cpe 2P | 2,620 | 595 | — |
| cpe 2-4P | 2,690 | 640 | — |
| conv sdn 2-4P | — | — | — |
| brougham 5P | 2,745 | 615 | — |
| touring brougham 5P T/B | 2,760 | 635 | — |
| sdn 4d | 2,805 | 670 | — |
| touring sdn 4d T/B | 2,820 | 690 | — |
| wgn 4d | — | 700 | — |
| **62 Custom Six (wb 115.0)—17,041 built** | | | |
| cpe 2P | 2,675 | 650 | — |
| cpe 2-4P | 2,745 | 690 | — |
| conv cpe 2-4P | — | — | — |
| brougham 5P | 2,800 | 665 | — |
| touring brougham 5P T/B | 2,815 | 685 | — |
| sdn 4d | 2,860 | 720 | — |
| touring sdn 4d T/B | 2,875 | 740 | — |

| 1936 Engine | bore × stroke | bhp | availability |
|---|---|---|---|
| I-6, 212.0 | 3.00 × 5.00 | 88 | S-all |

### 1937

| 71 DeLuxe (wb 117)—70,346 built | Wght | Price | Prod |
|---|---|---|---|
| bus cpe 3P | 2,370 | 595 | — |
| cpe 3P | 2,715 | 605 | — |
| victoria 4P | 2,765 | 850 | — |
| conv cpe 3P | 2,765 | 725 | — |
| brougham 6P | 2,830 | 625 | — |
| conv brougham 6P | 2,780 | 800 | — |
| sdn 4d | 2,865 | 675 | — |
| touring sdn 4d T/B | 2,865 | 695 | — |
| chassis | — | — | — |
| **72 Super (wb 117.0)—19,907 built** | | | |
| cpe 3P | 2,755 | 880 | — |
| touring sdn 4d T/B | 2,905 | 745 | — |
| victoria 4P | 2,795 | 700 | — |
| conv cpe 3P | 2,825 | 770 | — |
| conv brougham 6P | 2,915 | 845 | — |
| brougham 6P | 2,875 | 680 | — |
| touring brougham 6P | 2,875 | 700 | — |
| sdn 4d | 2,905 | 725 | — |
| chassis | — | — | — |

| 1937 Engine | bore × stroke | bhp | availability |
|---|---|---|---|
| I-6, 212.0 | 3.00 × 5.00 | 96 | S-71 |
| I-6, 212.0 | 3.00 × 5.00 | 102 | S-72 |

# Tucker

Preston Thomas Tucker was an ebullient, 200-pound, six-footer who dreamed big and could raise big money—fast. He was an industry veteran with sales experience at Studebaker, Dodge, and elsewhere, and an inveterate entrepreneur who secured financing from Henry Ford to build Indy racers in 1935. He also built a high-speed military scout car in 1937. In 1948, Tucker surprised everyone with "The Most Completely New Car in Fifty Years."

New it was. A torpedo-shaped fastback four-door sedan, the Tucker "48" looked just like the "car of the future" long expected by war-weary Americans. Styled by the forward-thinking Alex Tremulis on a 128-inch wheelbase, it was 219 inches long but only 60 inches high—low for the day. Engineering broke just as sharply from Detroit convention, with all-independent suspension and a rear-mounted flat-six. The latter derived from a wartime air-cooled helicopter unit, but boasted a fully sealed water-cooling system—an industry first. Horsepower was 166 and torque a thumping 372 pound-feet from 335 cubic inches, yet the all-alloy powerplant weighed just 320 pounds. The chassis was a sturdy box-section perimeter type with a subframe at each end.

Lack of time, money, and even technology precluded a curved windshield, disc brakes, "Torsilastic" rubber springs, and other innovations proposed by Preston. But the car still had novelties aplenty: central "cyclops-eye" headlight that turned with the front wheels, doors cut into the roof to ease entry/exit, a roomy six-passenger cabin with "step-down" floor, and interchangeable front/rear seats (to even out upholstery wear). Safety features abounded, too, and included massive bumpers; recessed or protected knobs, buttons, and levers; windshield glass that popped out harmlessly on impact; and a "Safety Chamber" where front passengers could dive "in case of impending collision."

Despite its size and 4200 pounds of heft, the Tucker could manage the 0-60 mph sprint in about 10 seconds. Top speed was at least 120 mph, thanks to the aerodynamic styling with an estimated drag factor of 0.30—good even today. Factory tests showed a creditable 20 mpg at a steady 50-55 mph. Just as nice, the rear-engine layout, all-independent suspension, and center-point steering combined for surprisingly easy handling and secure roadholding.

The Tucker would probably have sold well despite a Cadillac-like projected price of some $4000. But production ended at only 50 cars, plus the famous "Tin Goose" prototype. All were built before August 1948, the last 37 on a short assembly line in a refurbished wartime Dodge plant on Chicago's South Side.

Preston always claimed the Tucker was too good to live, and evidence suggests that the Detroit establishment felt threatened by it. But Tucker himself doomed the venture by moving with suspicious haste in issuing $15 million worth of stock to finance it. This led to charges of "fast-sell" tactics and a probe by the Securities and Exchange Commission that was attended by a mountain of adverse publicity. With that, Tucker and seven associates went to trial in October 1949 on 31 counts of conspiracy and securities and mail fraud. All were acquitted in January 1950 after what the jury termed a farce proceeding. Ironically, Tucker Corporation still had funds to produce its car, but public confidence was long gone. Receivers briefly considered going ahead before auctioning everything off at 18 cents on the dollar. Tucker's dream was dead.

Tremulis later sketched a stunning fastback coupe called Talisman as a proposed new '50s Tucker, and even Preston apparently still had hopes of building a car after his ordeal in Chicago. Though broken by the experience, Tucker moved to Brazil and was planning a two-seat kit sports car, the Carioca, when he died on December 26, 1956. He was only 53.

The Tucker saga has since been committed to film in *Tucker: The Man and His Dream*, released in 1988. Though the movie is good drama, director/producer Francis Ford Coppola plays fast and loose with some facts—just as Preston occasionally did. For example, the closing "parade" sequence shows most every Tucker built, including two owned by Coppola himself, but those precious few cars never made a triumphant procession right after the Tucker verdict was announced, let alone in unpredictable springtime Chicago weather. At least you shouldn't fret over the Tuckers that get smashed in an earlier scene; they're replicas.

**1948 Torpedo "48" four-door sedan**

# Willys

Willys built passenger cars for nearly 35 years before it ever built a Jeep—and for some years afterward, too. It started when John North Willys, an Elmira, New York, car dealer, bought ailing Overland of Indianapolis in 1907. A year later he renamed the firm Willys-Overland, moved into the old Pope plant in Toledo, Ohio, and began rebuilding the firm's fortunes. He did that in spectacular fashion. For most of the Teens, the four-cylinder Overland was second in sales only to the Model T Ford. By 1918, J. N. Willys owned the world's second-largest auto company.

Willys-Overland entered the Twenties offering four-, six-, and eight-cylinder models spanning the low- and medium-price ranges. Sixes and Eights were temporarily dropped after 1921, the company concentrating on four-cylinder models. Sixes returned in 1925, and fours were dropped the following year to appear under a new Whippet nameplate. Whippet flourished at first, but died after 1931 when Willys elected to concentrate all its dwindling resources on its own four-cylinder model. Meanwhile, an Eight joined the Willys line in mid-1930 carrying a 245.4-cid 75-bhp Continental engine.

An association with visionary engineer Charles Yale Knight led to the Willys-Knight. Early-'30s Willys-Knights were sixes offered in two series. Smaller models had 178 cid, 53-60 bhp, and wheelbases of 113 or 115 inches; the larger ones used a 255-cid engine with 72-87 bhp in 120- and 121-inch chassis. Prices were rather stiff—$1075 to around $1300—so demand tailed off quickly as the Depression took hold.

Willy's production withered to only some 27,000 for '32. With that, J. N. Willys, who had held the largely honorary post of board chairman since 1929, resigned his recent appointment as U.S. ambassador to Poland and returned to rescue his company, something he'd done twice before. But not this time, despite chipping in $2 million of his own money and personally assuring dealers and creditors that all would be well. After being forced to declare bankruptcy, Willys-Overland was reorganized and resumed production, but managed only about 13,000 units in 1934. It would not fully emerge from receivership until 1937, two years after John North Willys succumbed to heart troubles.

Meantime, Willys-Overland decided to bet its dwindling bank on a new low-priced small car, which it managed to develop for next to nothing. Called the Willys 77, it was unveiled in June 1932 with a 100-inch wheelbase and an ultrathrifty four-cylinder engine making 48 bhp from 134.2 cid. It was the only car Willys would sell from early 1933 through 1936.

The 1933 reorganization ushered in a new chairman, the bespectacled Ward Canaday. A pillar of the Toledo business community with a strong sense of loyalty to his employees, Canaday ached to get things moving again. His first real chance came with the 1937 line, for which he ordered a full restyle. The result was less than ideal, with lumpy looking rounded bodies carrying pontoon fenders and a bizarre bulging front not unlike that of Graham's forthcoming "sharknose." The new sheetmetal increased overall length by over a foot to 175.5 inches. Again, only a coupe and sedan were tried, albeit in standard and DeLuxe variations. Priced from $500 to near $600, these new Model 37s met with some success despite their odd looks, and model-year volume shot up to 63,467. But 1937 was a recovery year for most of the industry, so despite building twice the number of cars it had in '36, Willys only improved from 15th to 14th in the overall standings.

The 1938 recession resulted in dramatically lower sales, pushing Willys back to 16th. Changes for that year's Model 38 were few, but offerings expanded with a pair of two-door sedans called Clipper.

A sharper prow announced "Slip-Stream" styling for 1939, and the lineup again included Overlands: standard, DeLuxe, and Speedway Special sedans and coupes with two extra inches of wheelbase ahead of the cowl. Designated Model 39, they differed from that year's Model 38/48 in having 62 bhp (via higher compression, improved carburetor, and new camshaft), standard hydraulic brakes, larger tires, and headlamps carried in fender-top pods rather than within the fenders. Overlands cost an average of $100 more than other Willys models, but the extra money bought markedly better performance. And at $596-$689, the Overlands were still some $32 below the cheapest Chevys. As a result, Overland's model-year production was fairly respectable. But total Willys output was only 17,839—a worrisome decline in a year when most automakers did better than the year before.

It was in 1939 that Joseph W. Frazer, the dynamic sales manager of Chrysler Corporation, went to Toledo and W-O as president and general manager; Canaday remained board chairman. Frazer knew how to cut losses, and decreed more-orthodox styling for 1940. Still, it's doubtful even he could have saved Willys' passenger cars.

Designated Series 440—for four cylinders, 1940—Frazer's

**1931 Series 97 Six two-door Coach**

**1939 Series 39 Overland two-door sedan**

1941 Americar DeLuxe four-door station wagon

1946-48 Station Wagon two-door

1948 Jeepster phaeton-convertible

1953 Aero-Eagle hardtop coupe

1955 Custom four-door sedan

revised models were essentially '39 Overlands with sealed-beam headlamps and a vertical prow (instead of undercut). Model-year production improved to nearly 27,000.

Frazer and company made further improvements for the following year's Series 441. All models were dubbed "Americar," providing patriotic appeal, and gained two more horsepower and two more inches in wheelbase. Models expanded to seven with the addition of a new Plainsman coupe and sedan. Frontal styling was now quite Ford-like, with an even shapelier nose above a small vertical-bar grille. Prices were hiked nearly $100, now ranging from $634 to $916.

Willys had started building military Jeeps by now, so its 1942 model year was even shorter than for most other U.S. automakers. That year's Series 442 Americars were the same as the '41s save a prominent vertical grille bar (carrying a line down from the hood trim) and slightly higher prices. Just under 29,000 of the '41 and '42 models combined were built before W-O shifted entirely to war production. Frazer would leave Toledo in 1943, ultimately to take over Graham-Paige. Taking over as W-O president was Charles E. Sorensen, the famed former production boss at Ford. "Cast-Iron Charlie" then stepped aside in 1946 for James D. Mooney.

Willys postponed returning to passenger cars, resuming peacetime production with Jeep-based vehicles instead. These included the inevitable civilian version of the military Jeep, plus two hybrids. The first was a station wagon introduced in 1946 and destined to live on for 20 years. Though usually considered a truck and not a car, it arguably qualifies as the first modern all-steel wagon. In any case, it was W-O's main civilian product through 1947.

More directly automotive was the Jeepster, a jaunty open tourer designed during the war by Brooks Stevens, who also did the wagon. Announced in 1948, the Jeepster offered seating for four on the 104-inch wagon wheelbase, plus a manual soft top and clip-in side curtains. Initial power was provided by the prewar Americar four, but a six with 148.5 cid and 72 bhp was added for 1949. Former Studebaker engineer Barney Roos converted both engines from L-head to overhead-valve F-head configuration by 1950. That year's Jeepsters sported an eggcrate grille (replacing vertical slats), somewhat less-deluxe appointments, and a six enlarged to 161 cid and 75 bhp.

Priced in the $1400-$1500 range, the Jeepster was relatively popular for such a specialized product. First-year sales were strong at 10,326. But this evidently satisfied demand, for 1949 production was just 2960. The 1950 figure was a healthier 5844, but some were unsold at year's end and registered as '51 models. Today, all Jeepsters are avidly sought collectibles.

Willys could likely have lived just fine on Jeeps, Jeep wagons, trucks, and military vehicles. But the high optimism and booming seller's market of the early postwar years made returning to the passenger-car business seem like a no-lose proposition. Ward Canaday, who had taken over as president in 1950, entertained numerous ideas. His final choice was a trim 108-inch-wheelbase unitized proposal engineered by the distinguished Clyde Paton and inventively styled by Phil Wright. It was ready for the road by 1952, when it was trumpeted as "The Revolutionary New Aero-Willys."

It was a fine effort. Fashionably square and slab-sided, the Aero was relatively light (2500-2600 pounds), roomy, and blessed with good handling. There were four models at first: Aero-Eagle hardtop coupe and three two-door sedans. The Aero-Lark used the 75-bhp, 161-cid six from late Jeepsters; Eagle and the Aero-Wing and Aero-Ace sedans ran the overhead-valve version with 90 bhp. Though small, the 161 six delivered good performance, plus fuel economy on the order of 25 miles per gallon.

# Willys

Despite high pricing ($2155 for the Eagle), 1952-model production of 31,363 was good, if not great; the midrange Aero-Wing accounted for well over a third.

Offerings expanded for 1953, when appearance changed only in detail—notably red hubcap emblems and a gold-plated "W" in the grille, honoring Willys' 50th anniversary. About 500 Aero-Larks were built for export with the old F-head fours, but engines were otherwise unchanged. Aero-Wing was retitled Aero-Falcon, and a new four-door sedan arrived in Lark, Falcon, and Ace versions. The hardtop Eagle was again rather pricey, though up only $2 from '52. Helped by the end of government curbs on consumer production instituted because of the Korean War, Willys had another modestly good year, selling about 42,000 cars.

The situation changed in 1954, when Willys-Overland was purchased by Henry Kaiser, who combined it with ailing Kaiser-Frazer to form Kaiser-Willys Sales Corporation. K-F sold its sprawling Willow Run, Michigan, plant to General Motors (which would use it into the 1990s), and Kaiser production was transferred to Toledo.

The Kaiser takeover didn't immediately affect the '54 Aero-Willys, which was little more than a '53 with larger taillights and revised interior. But March 1954 brought a raft of changes. Chief among them was Kaiser's 226-cid L-head six, which was shoehorned in as optional power for all models. There were also new Ace and Eagle Customs, basically the standard articles with a "continental" spare tire.

Though heavier than the Willys 161, the Kaiser 226 engine produced a useful 25 extra horsepower that made the Aero relatively fast. Top speed was little higher at 85 mph, but the big six dropped typical 0-60 mph times to around 14 seconds. As an experiment, a few Aeros were fitted with 140-bhp supercharged Kaiser Manhattan engines, which made the lighter Willys a performance match for many contemporary V-8 cars—or so company engineers claimed.

All '54s handled much better than earlier Aeros, thanks to a revised front suspension. In all, the best Aeros yet failed to convince many customers, and production dropped to 11,717.

By early 1955, Kaiser-Willys decided to abandon the U.S. car market. No longer called Aero, the '55s comprised Custom two- and four-door sedans and a Bermuda hardtop (formerly called Eagle); Willys also built 659 Ace four-doors, again for export. Engine choices did not change save for deletion of the Lark's 134-cid four, but prices were drastically cut in a last-ditch effort to attract sales. The Bermuda, for instance, was slashed to $1895, and was thus honestly advertised as America's lowest-priced hardtop.

Sales considerations also prompted an ambitious '55 facelift by Kaiser stylists Buzz Grisinger and Herb Weissinger. The restyles' main elements were a busy two-tier grille (replacing the simple horizontal-bar motif of prior years) and Z-line side moldings that made for an odd two-toned appearance. In the meantime, a neat hardtop wagon was in the works for 1955-56, and designers "Dutch" Darrin and Duncan McRae were conjuring more-ambitious restyles for the years beyond. But Willys wouldn't live to see them, at least not with passenger cars. So after a final 5986 units, most carrying the 226 engine, Willys returned to making nothing but Jeeps.

Happily, the Aero would live a good while longer in South America, where Kaiser's Willys do Brasil subsidiary took over the Aero dies and offered a cleaned-up '55 with F-head Willys power during 1960-62. Designer Brooks Stevens then applied handsome new square-rigged outer panels, and the car continued all the way through 1972, first as the Aero-Willys 2600, then Willys Itamaraty, and finally Ford Itamaraty (Dearborn acquired Willys do Brasil via American Motors in 1967). That's eloquent testimony to the sound basic design of the original Aero-Willys. A pity it wasn't more appreciated in its native land.

## Specifications

Note: production figures based on serial number spans; may exceed actual production.

### 1930

| 98B Six (wb 110.0)—27,870 built* | Wght | Price | Prod |
|---|---|---|---|
| rdstr 2-4P | 2,497 | 725 | — |
| sdn 4d | 2,641 | 795 | — |
| rdstr 2P | — | 695 | — |
| DeLuxe sdn 4d | 2,650 | 850 | — |
| cpe 2P | — | 745 | — |
| DeLuxe cpe 5P | — | 800 | — |
| DeLuxe rdstr 2P | — | 750 | — |
| DeLuxe rdstr 2-4P | — | 780 | — |
| **8-80 Eight (wb 120.0)—1,901 built (from Jan/30)** | | | |
| cpe 2P | — | 875 | — |
| rdstr 2-4P | — | 855 | — |
| sdn 4d | — | 895 | — |
| rdstr 2P | — | 825 | — |
| DeLuxe cpe 5P | — | 900 | — |
| DeLuxe rdstr 2-4P | — | 910 | — |
| DeLuxe sdn 4d | — | 950 | — |
| DeLuxe rdstr 2P | — | 910 | — |
| **87-Knight (wb 112.5; sdn-115.0)—3,627 built (from Jun/30)** | | | |
| rdstr 2-4P | 2,718 | 975 | — |
| cpe 2-4P | 2,922 | 1,075 | — |

| 87-Knight (wb 112.5; sdn-115.0) | Wght | Price | Prod |
|---|---|---|---|
| sdn 4d | 2,989 | 1,075 | — |
| **70B-Knight (wb 112.5; sdn 115.0)—10,723 built** | | | |
| rdstr 2-4P | 2,748 | 1,045 | — |
| DeLuxe cpe 2-4P | 2,916 | 1,145 | — |
| sdn 4d | 3,015 | 1,145 | — |
| **66B-Knight (wb 120.0)—5,820 built** | | | |
| rdstr 2-4P | 3,592 | 1,895 | — |
| cpe 2-4P | 3,815 | 1,895 | — |
| sdn 4d | 3,934 | 1,895 | — |

* Includes 1931 Model 97.

| 1930 Engines | bore × stroke | bhp | availability |
|---|---|---|---|
| I-6, 177.9 | 2.94 × 4.38 | 53 | S-70B |
| I-6, 177.9 | 2.94 × 4.38 | 55 | S-87 |
| I-6, 193.0 | 3.25 × 3.88 | 65 | S-98B |
| I-6, 255.0 | 3.38 × 4.75 | 72 | S-66B |
| I-8, 245.4 | 3.13 × 4.00 | 75 | S-Eight |

### 1931

| 97 Six (wb 110.0)—37,678 built* | Wght | Price | Prod |
|---|---|---|---|
| rdstr 2P | 2,407 | 495 | — |
| cpe 2P | 2,528 | 565 | — |
| sdn 4d | 2,670 | 675 | — |

# Willys

| 98B Six (wb 110.0)—27,870 built* | Wght | Price | Prod |
|---|---|---|---|
| rdstr 2-4P | 2,430 | 725 | — |
| sdn 4d | 2,623 | 795 | — |
| **98D Six (wb 113.0)—3,653 built** | | | |
| victoria cpe 5P | 2,656 | 795 | — |
| sdn 4d | 2,706 | 795 | — |
| **8-80D Eight (wb 120.0; lwb-121.0)—1,686 built** | | | |
| 80 cpe 2-4P | 3,061 | 1,245 | — |
| 80 sdn 4d | 3,076 | 1,295 | — |
| 80D lwb vict cpe 5P (from Jan/31) | 3,063 | 995 | — |
| 80D lwb sdn 4d (from Jan/31) | 3,131 | 995 | — |
| **66B-Knight (wb 120.0)—2,189 built** | | | |
| rdstr 2-4P | 3,515 | 1,795 | — |
| cpe 2-4P | 3,745 | 1,795 | — |
| sdn 4d | 3,868 | 1,795 | — |
| **66D-Knight (wb 121.0)—4,982 built (from Jan/31)** | | | |
| victoria cpe 5P | 3,336 | 1,095 | — |
| sdn 4d | 3,400 | 1,095 | — |
| **87-Knight (wb 112.5; sdn-115.0)—2,541 built** | | | |
| rdstr 2-4P | 2,739 | 975 | — |
| cpe 2-4P | 2,882 | 1,075 | — |
| sdn 4d | 3,001 | 1,075 | — |

*Includes 1930 Model 98B.

| 1931 Engines | bore × stroke | bhp | availability |
|---|---|---|---|
| I-6, 177.9 | 2.94 × 4.38 | 55 | S-87 |
| I-6, 193.0 | 3.25 × 3.88 | 65 | S-97, 98B, 98D |
| I-6, 255.0 | 3.38 × 4.75 | 87 | S-66B, 66D |
| I-8, 245.4 | 3.13 × 4.00 | 80 | S-Eight |

## 1932

| 6-90-Overland Six (wb 113)—13,148 blt | Wght | Price | Prod |
|---|---|---|---|
| rdstr 2P | 2,570 | 415 | — |
| cpe 2P | 2,749 | 530 | — |
| sdn 4d | 2,814 | 610 | — |
| **97 Six (wb 110.0)—9,754 built** | | | |
| rdstr 2P | 2,407 | 495 | — |
| cpe 5P 2W | 2,648 | 595 | — |
| sdn 4d | 2,670 | 675 | — |
| **98D Six (wb 113.0)—245 built** | | | |
| victoria cpe 4P | 2,656 | 795 | — |
| sdn 4d | 2,706 | 795 | — |
| **8-80D Eight (wb 121.0)—452 built** | | | |
| victoria cpe 4P | 3,100 | 995 | — |
| sdn 4d | 3,131 | 995 | — |
| **8-88-Overland Eight (wb 121.0)—1,296 built** | | | |
| rdstr 2P | 2,981 | 730 | — |
| cpe 2P | 3,148 | 780 | — |
| Custom victoria 4P | 3,337 | 1,030 | — |
| sdn 4d | 3,250 | 830 | — |
| **95-Knight (wb 113.0)—1,300 built (est.)** | | | |
| Silver Ann. cpe 2P | 2,915 | 745 | — |
| Silver Ann. cpe 2-4P | 2,994 | 775 | — |
| Silver Ann. coach 5P | 2,982 | 745 | — |
| Silver Ann. sdn 4d | 3,031 | 795 | — |
| **66D-Knight (wb 121.0)** | | | |
| victoria cpe 5P | 3,360 | 1,095 | ⎤ 718 |
| sdn 4d | 3,400 | 1,095 | ⎦ |
| **66D-Knight (wb 121.0)** | Wght | Price | Prod |
| Silver Ann. Cust victoria 5P | 3,664 | 1,145 | ⎤ 900 |
| Silver Ann. Custom sdn 4d | 3,775 | 1,295 | ⎦ |

| 1932 Engines | bore × stroke | bhp | availability |
|---|---|---|---|
| I-6, 177.9 | 2.94 × 4.38 | 60 | S-95 |
| I-6, 193.0 | 3.25 × 3.88 | 65 | S-97, 98D, 6-90 |
| I-6, 255.0 | 3.38 × 4.75 | 87 | S-66D |
| I-8, 245.4 | 3.13 × 4.00 | 80 | S-8-80D, 8-88 |

## 1933

| 6-90A-Overland Streamlined Six (wb 113.0)—6,775 built | Wght | Price | Prod |
|---|---|---|---|
| rdstr 2P | 2,569 | 535 | — |
| cpe 2P | 2,781 | 650 | — |
| sdn 4d | 2,913 | 740 | — |
| **8-88A-Overland Streamlined Eight (wb 121.0)—1,022 built** | | | |
| cpe 2P | 3,217 | 955 | — |
| sdn 4d | 3,368 | 995 | — |
| **77 (wb 100.0)—12,820 built** | | | |
| cpe 2P | 2,058 | 395 | — |
| Custom cpe 2P | 2,072 | 415 | — |
| cpe 2-4P | 2,072 | 425 | — |
| Custom cpe 2-4P | 2,105 | 445 | — |
| sdn 4d | 2,136 | 445 | — |
| Custom sdn 4d | 2,156 | 475 | — |
| **66E-Knight Streamlined Six (wb 121.0)** | | | |
| Custom sdn 4d | 3,830 | 1,420 | 574 |

| 1933 Engines | bore × stroke | bhp | availability |
|---|---|---|---|
| I-4, 134.2 | 3.13 × 4.38 | 48 | S-77 |
| I-6, 193.0 | 3.25 × 3.88 | 65 | S-6-90A |
| I-6, 255.0 | 3.38 × 4.75 | 87 | S-66E |
| I-8, 245.4 | 3.13 × 4.00 | 80 | S-8-88A |

## 1934

| 77 (wb 100.0)—13,235 built | Wght | Price | Prod |
|---|---|---|---|
| cpe 2P | 2,058 | 395 | — |
| Custom cpe 2P | 2,072 | 415 | — |
| cpe 2-4P | 2,072 | 425 | — |
| Custom cpe 2-4P | 2,105 | 445 | — |
| sdn 4d | 2,131 | 445 | — |
| Custom sdn 4d | 2,156 | 475 | — |
| *Second Series (from Jan/34):* | | | |
| cpe 2P | 2,058 | 430 | — |
| sdn 4d | 2,131 | 450 | — |

| 1934 Engine | bore × stroke | bhp | availability |
|---|---|---|---|
| I4, 134.2 | 3.13 × 4.38 | 48 | S-all |

## 1935

| 77 (wb 100.0)—10,715 built | Wght | Price | Prod |
|---|---|---|---|
| cpe 3P | 2,034 | 475 | — |
| sdn 4d | 2,111 | 495 | — |

| 1935 Engine | bore × stroke | bhp | availability |
|---|---|---|---|
| I-4, 134.2 | 3.13 × 4.38 | 48 | S-all |

# Willys

## 1936

| 77 (wb 100.0)—30,826 built | Wght | Price | Prod |
|---|---|---|---|
| cpe 2P | 2,034 | 395 | — |
| sdn 4d | 2,131 | 415 | — |

| 1936 Engine | bore × stroke | bhp | availability |
|---|---|---|---|
| I-4, 134.2 | 3.13 × 4.38 | 48 | S-all |

## 1937

| 37 (wb 100.0)—63,467 built | Wght | Price | Prod |
|---|---|---|---|
| cpe 2P | 2,146 | 499 | — |
| DeLuxe cpe 2P | 2,146 | 579 | — |
| sdn 4d | 2,200 | 538 | — |
| DeLuxe sdn 4d | 2,306 | 589 | — |

| 1937 Engine | bore × stroke | bhp | availability |
|---|---|---|---|
| I-4, 134.2 | 3.13 × 4.38 | 48 | S-all |

## 1938

| 38 (wb 100.0)—26,691 built* | Wght | Price | Prod |
|---|---|---|---|
| Standard cpe 2P | 2,145 | 499 | — |
| Deluxe cpe 2P | 2,155 | 574 | — |
| Clipper sdn 2d | 2,258 | 539 | — |
| Standard sdn 4d | 2,247 | 563 | — |
| Deluxe Clipper sdn 2d | 2,258 | 575 | — |
| Deluxe sdn 4d | 2,263 | 614 | — |
| Custom sdn 4d | 2,336 | 700 | — |

* Includes 1939 Model 38 production.

| 1938 Engine | bore × stroke | bhp | availability |
|---|---|---|---|
| I-4, 134.2 | 3.13 × 4.38 | 48 | S-all |

## 1939

| 38 (wb 100.0)* | Wght | Price | Prod |
|---|---|---|---|
| Standard cpe 2P | 2,181 | 499 | — |
| Standard sdn 2d | 2,258 | 539 | — |
| Standard sdn 4d | 2,300 | 563 | — |
| Deluxe cpe 2P | 2,181 | 574 | — |
| Deluxe sdn 2d | 2,258 | 575 | — |
| Deluxe sdn 4d | 2,306 | 614 | — |

| 39 Overland (wb 102.0)—15,214 built | Wght | Price | Prod |
|---|---|---|---|
| Standard Speedway cpe 2P | 2,137 | 596 | — |
| Standard Speedway sdn 2d | 2,217 | 616 | — |
| Standard Speedway sdn 4d | 2,249 | 631 | — |
| Deluxe cpe 2P | 2,193 | 646 | — |
| Deluxe sdn 2d | 2,262 | 667 | — |
| Deluxe sdn 4d | 2,306 | 689 | — |
| Speedway Special cpe 2P | 2,193 | 610 | — |
| Speedway Special sdn 2d | 2,262 | 631 | — |
| Speedway Special sdn 4d | 2,306 | 646 | — |

| 48 (wb 100.0)—2,625 built | Wght | Price | Prod |
|---|---|---|---|
| cpe 2P | 2,181 | 524 | — |
| sdn 2d | 2,258 | 565 | — |
| sdn 4d | 2,300 | 586 | — |

* Included in 1938 Model 38 production.

| 1939 Engines | bore × stroke | bhp | availability |
|---|---|---|---|
| I-4, 134.2 | 3.13 × 4.38 | 48 | S-38, 48 |
| I-4, 134.2 | 3.13 × 4.38 | 62 | S-39 |

## 1940

| 440 (wb 102.0)—26,698 built | Wght | Price | Prod |
|---|---|---|---|
| Speedway cpe | 2,146 | 529 | — |
| Speedway sdn 4d | 2,238 | 596 | — |
| DeLuxe cpe | 2,190 | 641 | — |
| DeLuxe sdn 4d | 2,255 | 672 | — |
| DeLuxe wgn 4d | 2,124 | 830 | — |

| 1940 Engine | bore × stroke | bhp | availability |
|---|---|---|---|
| I-4, 134.2 | 3.13 × 4.38 | 61 | S-all |

## 1941

| 441 Americar (wb 104.0)* | Wght | Price | Prod |
|---|---|---|---|
| Speedway cpe | 2,116 | 634 | — |
| Speedway sdn 4d | 2,230 | 674 | — |
| DeLuxe cpe | 2,135 | 685 | — |
| DeLuxe sdn 4d | 2,265 | 720 | — |
| DeLuxe wgn 4d | 2,483 | 916 | — |
| Plainsman cpe | 2,175 | 740 | — |
| Plainsman sdn 4d | 2,305 | 771 | — |

| 1941 Engine | bore × stroke | bhp | availability |
|---|---|---|---|
| I-4, 134.2 | 3.13 × 4.38 | 63 | S-all |

## 1942

| 442 Americar (wb 104.0)* | Wght | Price | Prod |
|---|---|---|---|
| Speedway cpe | 2,142 | 695 | — |
| Speedway sdn 4d | 2,261 | 745 | — |
| DeLuxe cpe | 2,184 | 769 | — |
| DeLuxe sdn 4d | 2,295 | 795 | — |
| DeLuxe wgn 4d | 2,512 | 978 | — |
| Plainsman cpe | 2,242 | 819 | — |
| Plainsman sdn 4d | 2,353 | 845 | — |

| 1942 Engine | bore × stroke | bhp | availability |
|---|---|---|---|
| I-4, 134.2 | 3.13 × 4.38 | 63 | S-all |

* Total 1941-42 Americar production: 28,935.

## 1948

| 463 Four (wb 104.0) | Wght | Price | Prod |
|---|---|---|---|
| Jeepster phtn conv 2d | 2,468 | 1,765 | 10,326 |

| 1948 Engine | bore × stroke | bhp | availability |
|---|---|---|---|
| I-4, 134.3 | 3.13 × 4.38 | 63 | S-all |

## 1949

| 463 Four/VJ-3 Four (wb 104.0)—2,307 built | Wght | Price | Prod |
|---|---|---|---|
| Jeepster phtn conv 2d | 2,468 | 1,495 | — |

| VJ-3 Six (wb 104.0) | Wght | Price | Prod |
|---|---|---|---|
| Jeepster phtn conv 2d | 2,392 | 1,530 | 653 |

# Willys

| 1949 Engines | bore × stroke | bhp | availability |
|---|---|---|---|
| I-4, 134.2 | 3.13 × 4.38 | 63 | S-463 Four |
| I-4, 134.2 | 3.13 × 4.38 | 72 | S-VJ3 Four (F-head) |
| I-6, 148.5 | 3.00 × 3.50 | 72 | S-Six |

## 1950

### 443 Four/VJ-3 Four (wb 104.0)—4,066 built

|  | Wght | Price | Prod |
|---|---|---|---|
| Jeepster phtn conv 2d | 2,459 | 1,390 | — |

### VJ-3 Four (wb 104.0)

|  | Wght | Price | Prod |
|---|---|---|---|
| Jeepster phtn conv 2d | 2,468 | 1,495 | — |

### 673VJ Six (wb 104.0)

|  | Wght | Price | Prod |
|---|---|---|---|
| Jeepster phtn conv 2d | 2,485 | 1,490 | 1,778 |

| 1950 Engines | bore × stroke | bhp | availability |
|---|---|---|---|
| I-4, 134.2 | 3.13 × 4.38 | 63 | S-Four, 1st series, L-head |
| I-4, 134.2 | 3.13 × 4.38 | 72 | S-Four, 2nd series, F-head |
| I-6, 148.5 | 3.00 × 3.50 | 72 | S-Six, 1st series, L-head |
| I-6, 161.0 | 3.13 × 3.50 | 75 | S-Six, 2nd series, F-head |

## 1951

### 473-VJ Four (wb 104.0)

|  | Wght | Price | Prod |
|---|---|---|---|
| Jeepster phtn conv 2d | 2,459 | 1,426 | * |

### 673-VJ Six (wb 104.0)

|  | Wght | Price | Prod |
|---|---|---|---|
| Jeepster phtn conv 2d | 2,485 | 1,529 | * |

* Combined with 1950 totals; includes 1950 leftovers sold as '51s.

| 1951 Engines | bore × stroke | bhp | availability |
|---|---|---|---|
| I-4, 134.2 | 3.13 × 4.38 | 72 | S-Four |
| I-6, 161.0 | 3.13 × 3.50 | 75 | S-Six |

## 1952

### 652-K Aero-Lark (wb 108.0)

|  | Wght | Price | Prod |
|---|---|---|---|
| KA2-675 sdn 2d | 2,487 | 1,731 | 7,474 |

### 652-L Aero-Wing (wb 108.0)

|  | Wght | Price | Prod |
|---|---|---|---|
| LA1-685 sdn 2d | 2,570 | 1,989 | 12,819 |

### 652-M Aero (wb 108.0)

|  | Wght | Price | Prod |
|---|---|---|---|
| MA1-685 Ace sdn 2d | 2,584 | 2,074 | 8,706 |
| MC1-685 Eagle htp cpe | 2,575 | 2,155 | 2,364 |

| 1952 Engines | bore × stroke | bhp | availability |
|---|---|---|---|
| I-6, 161.0 | 3.13 × 4.38 | 75 | S-Lark |
| I-6, 161.0 | 3.13 × 4.38 | 90 | S-Wing, Ace, Eagle |

## 1953

### 653-K Aero-Lark (wb 108.0)

|  | Wght | Price | Prod |
|---|---|---|---|
| KA1-675 sdn 2d | 2,487 | 1,646 | 8,205 |
| KB1-675 sdn 4d | 2,509 | 1,732 | 7,692 |

### 653-M Aero (wb 108.0)

|  | Wght | Price | Prod |
|---|---|---|---|
| MA1-685 Ace sdn 2d | 2,584 | 1,963 | 4,988 |
| MB1-685 Ace sdn 4d | 2,735 | 2,038 | 7,475 |
| MC1-685 Eagle htp cpe | 2,575 | 2,157 | 7,018 |

### 653-P Aero-Falcon (wb 108.0)

|  | Wght | Price | Prod |
|---|---|---|---|
| PA1-675 sdn 2d | 2,507 | 1,760 | 3,054 |
| PB1-675 sdn 4d | 2,529 | 1,861 | 3,117 |

| 1953 Engines | bore × stroke | bhp | availability |
|---|---|---|---|
| I-4, 134.2 | 3.13 × 4.38 | 72 | S-Lark 4 |
| I-6, 161.0 | 3.13 × 4.38 | 75 | S-Lark 6, Falcon |
| I-6, 161.0 | 3.13 × 4.38 | 90 | S-Ace, Eagle |

## 1954

### 654-K Aero-Lark (wb 108.0)

|  |  | Wght | Price | Prod |
|---|---|---|---|---|
| KA2 | sdn 2d, (226) | 2,740 | — | 59 |
| KB2 | sdn 4d, (226) | 2,730 | — | 282 |
| KA3-685 | sdn 2d | 2,623 | 1,737 | 1,370 |
| KA3-685 | Custom sdn 2d | 2,678 | 1,798 | 1,132 |
| KB3-685 | sdn 4d | 2,661 | 1,823 | 1,482 |
| KB3-685 | Custom sdn 4d | 2,722 | 1,878 | 548 |

### 654-M Aero (wb 108.0)

|  |  | Wght | Price | Prod |
|---|---|---|---|---|
| MA1 | Ace DeLuxe sdn 2d (226) | 2,751 | — | 1,195 |
| MA1 | Ace DeL Cust sdn 2d (226) | 2,806 | — | 7 |
| MB1 | Ace DeLuxe sdn 4d (226) | 2,778 | — | 1,498 |
| MB1 | Ace DeL Cust sdn 4d (226) | 2,833 | — | 9 |
| MA2-685 | Ace sdn 2d | 2,682 | 1,892 | 2 |
| MA2-685 | Ace Custom sdn 2d | 2,737 | 1,947 | 586 |
| MB2-685 | Ace sdn 4d | 2,709 | 1,968 | 1,380 |
| MB2-685 | Ace Custom sdn 4d | 2,764 | 2,023 | 611 |
| MC1 | Eagle htp cpe (226) | 2,847 | — | 660 |
| MC1 | Eagle Custom htp cpe (226) | 2,904 | — | 11 |
| MC2 | Eagle Special htp cpe (226) | — | — | 302 |
| MC3-685 | Eagle DeLuxe htp cpe | — | 2,222 | 84 |
| MC3-685 | Eagle DeL Cust htp cpe | — | 2,411 | 499 |

| 1954 Engines | bore × stroke | bhp | availability |
|---|---|---|---|
| I-4, 134.2 | 3.13 × 4.38 | 72 | S-Lark 4 |
| I-6, 161.0 | 3.13 × 4.38 | 90 | S-Lark 6, Ace, Eagle |
| I-6, 226.2 | 3.31 × 4.38 | 115 | O-Lark 6, Ace, Eagle |

## 1955

### 522/6 Ace (wb 108.0)

|  | Wght | Price | Prod |
|---|---|---|---|
| 52367 sdn 4d (226) | — | — | 659 |

### 523/4 Custom (wb 108.0)

|  | Wght | Price | Prod |
|---|---|---|---|
| 52367 sdn 4d (226) | 2,778 | 1,795 | 2,822 |
| 52462 sdn 2d (161) | — | — | 2 |
| 52467 sdn 2d (226) | 2,751 | 1,725 | 288 |

### 525 Bermuda (wb 108.0)

|  | Wght | Price | Prod |
|---|---|---|---|
| 52527 htp cpe (161) | — | 1,895 | 59 |
| 52567 htp cpe (226) | 2,831 | 1,997 | 2,156 |

| 1955 Engines | bore × stroke | bhp | availability |
|---|---|---|---|
| I-6, 161.0 | 3.13 × 3.50 | 90 | S-Custom, Bermuda |
| I-6, 226.2 | 3.31 × 4.38 | 115 | S-Ace; O-Custom, Bermuda |

Willys production does not include steel-bodied station wagons manufactured from 1946 through 1961, or Wagoneers (wagons) manufactured from 1960 onward. Aero production does not include export or taxi models. Aero production continued in Brazil through 1962.

# Minor Makes

The following compilation lists American-built automobiles, 1930 onward, not dealt with in the main body of this book. The vast majority of these saw very limited production; some never progressed beyond the prototype stage; a rare few were sold for several years. Facts about some are unavoidably elusive.

We have omitted all unsubstantiated, experimental, racing, and Canadian cars; likewise products designed for children. Only those prototypes that show evidence of serious intent to manufacture vehicles in complete form have been included. Kit cars are included only where fully assembled models were also available from the manufacturer or dealer.

Dates and factory locations are as accurate as possible. A question mark, as in "1965-?," indicates that the editors have not been able to determine when production ceased. When "c." (circa) is shown, it is not possible to determine the precise date company activity began and/or was terminated. "NA" indicates that precise production-figure information is not available.

### Aerocar 1948-c.70
Aerocar Inc.; Longview, WA
Production: 7
Developed by Moulton P. Taylor, the Aerocar was a car/plane powered by a 100-bhp Franklin engine. It was first sold in late 1954 for $7500, and had a top speed of 50 mph on the ground, 110 mph in the air. Wings and propeller assembly were towed in a 14-foot trailer when in road use; conversion from car to plane took five minutes for one person with a wrench.

### Aircar 1970-c.73
Advanced Vehicle Engineers; Van Nuys, CA
Production: NA
This car/plane conversion had Cessna Skymaster control surfaces placed on a Pontiac Firebird chassis. A later Ford Pinto-based model flew in 1973 as the Mizar.

### Airphibian 1946-52
Continental, Inc. (Robert E. Fulton, Jr.); Danbury, CT
Production: NA
Another car/plane conversion, this one with an aluminum passenger compartment with detachable wings, propeller, and fuselage. The conversion from plane to car took five minutes. It was powered by a 6-cylinder, 150-bhp engine that produced a top speed of 45 mph on the ground, 120 in the air.

### Airscoot 1947
Aircraft Products Company; Wichita, KS
Production: NA
The Airscoot was intended to be carried in an airplane for ground transportation upon landing. It was foldable and made of lightweight tubing; it weighed 72 pounds and was 37 inches long. Power came from a single-cylinder 2.6-bhp engine that produced a top speed of 25 mph while promising 60 mpg. It apparently never reached production.

### Airway 1948-50
Airway Motors, Inc.; San Diego, CA
Production: 2
A two-door fastback sedan was produced in 1948-49; a notchback coupe followed in 1950. Both were powered by a 10-bhp air-cooled aluminum engine with fluid drive. Total weight was 600-775 pounds, with a top speed of 45-50 mph.

### American Buckboard 1955
American Buckboard Corp.; Los Angeles, CA
Production: NA
This tiny roadster was powered by a rear-mounted two-cylinder air-cooled motorcycle engine that drove a fifth wheel. It sat on a 70-inch wheelbase and measured 10 feet overall. Projected price was $750, but production is doubtful, though a version called the Bearcat was built in 1956.

### American Steam Car 1929-c.1931
American Steam Automobile Co.; West Newton, MA
Production: NA
Made-to-order steamers that used Hudson components, bodies, and chassis were the product of engineer Thomas Derr, who founded the company in 1924 to provide replacements and improvements for Stanley Steamers still on the road.

### Amitron 1967-?
Gulton Industries; Metuchen, NJ
Production: NA
Wedge-shaped three-passenger electric vehicle powered by lithium-nickel batteries was a co-operative venture with American Motors Corp. It was claimed to do 0-50 mph in about 20 seconds with a range of about 150 miles.

### Apache 1966-?
Interco Development Corp.; New York, NY
Production: NA
Similar to European economy cars in size, engine displacement, and seating, but the Apache had an unusual collapsible roof that transformed it from a fastback coupe to an open roadster.

### Apollo 1962-65
International Motor Cars, Inc. (Newt Davis & Milt Brown); Oakland, CA
Production: 88
A high-performance sports car with coachwork by

Carrozzeria Intermeccanica of Turin built to a Ron Plescia design modified by Scaglione. It was powered by a 215-cid Buick aluminum V-8. Added in 1964 was the 5000 GT with a 300-cid Buick V-8 that could do 0-60 mph in 7.5 seconds and had a top speed of 150+ mph. They were never advertised nationally and had a spotty dealer network. Some bodies were later sold to a Dallas, Texas, firm that assembled them as the Vetta Ventura (*see entry*).

**Argonaut 1959-63**
Argonaut Motor Machine Co.; Cleveland, OH
Production: NA, but doubtful
Aluminum-bodied luxury cars thaat were built in the Duesenberg/Pierce Arrow mold. Seven models were announced, ranging from the two-seat Steed sports coupe (126.5-inch wheelbase) to a huge limousine (154-inch wheelbase). Overall lengths varied from 218-258 inches. The proposed air-cooled, overhead-cam aluminum V-12 was to produce a whopping 1020 horsepower, enough to provide an equally whopping 240-mph top speed. Factory-direct prices ranged from $25,150-$36,000.

**Arnolt 1952-c.58**
S. H. Arnolt, Inc, (S. H. "Wacky" Arnolt); Chicago, IL
Production: 65 MG; 142 Bristol
These two sports cars carried specially designed bodywork by Bertone of Italy. The Arnolt-MG was a pleasant, square-cut two-seater hampered by an anemic 4-cylinder engine and lofty $3195 price. The follow-up Arnolt-Bristol had a 2.0-liter, 130-bhp six built by Bristol in England, and was offered as a closed coupe and a roadster with or without top. Prices varied from $4000-$6000. The Bristol weighed but 2100 pounds and was quick: 0-60 mph took about 8.7 seconds, the standing quarter-mile passed in 17 seconds at 82 mph. Top speed was 110 mph. Production reportedly continued after Arnolt's death in 1963, but few were likely completed after '58.

**Arrowbile/Aerobile c.1937-c.58**
Waldo D. Waterman; Santa Monica, CA
Production: 8 (est.)
An early serious attempt to produce a flying car for commercial sale in U.S. The first examples used a Studebaker Commander six-cylinder engine; final Aerobile used a horizontally opposed, water-cooled Franklin six. Studebaker intended to sell Arrowbile through selected dealers, but backed out because of a downturn in the economy.

**Asardo 1959**
American Special Automotive Research and Design Organization; North Bergen, NJ
Production: NA
This fiberglass sport coupe with an 88-inch wheelbase, 150-inch overall length, and total weight of 1350 pounds was powered by a 91.3-cid Alfa Romeo four with 135 bhp. It could do 0-60 mph in just 6.4 seconds; top speed was 135. Price: $5875.

**Ascot 1955**
Glasspar Co.; Santa Ana, CA
Production: NA
Ascot was a 1700-pound fiberglass roadster with a 94-inch wheelbase and a height of 48 inches. It featured butterfly-type fenders, freestanding headlights, square grille, and external deck-mounted spare. Engines included a 172-cid Ford industrial unit, Studebaker six, and others.

**Auburn 1967-81**
Glenn Pray Co.; Auburn, IN
Production: NA
From the maker of the mid-'60s Cord 8/10 replicar came the "866," a fiberglass, 3100-pound replica of the 1935-36 Auburn 851/852 Speedster. It was built on a modified Ford Galaxie frame with a 127-inch wheelbase and standard 365-bhp 428-cid Thunderbird V-8. Top speed was 130 mph. Priced at $8450, options were limited to a choice of exterior color and upholstery materials. It was later joined by the Model 874, a dual-cowl phaeton with no 1930s counterpart.

**Aurora 1954**
Father Alfred A. Juliano; Branford, CT
Production: 1
This one-off safety prototype was built at a cost of $30,000. Mounted on a 1954 Buick Roadmaster chassis, it featured a fiberglass body, transparent plastic roof, and forward-raked bubble windshield.

**Auto Cub 1956**
Randall Products; Hampton, NH
Production: NA
Auto Cub was a single-passenger, tiller-steered runabout with an overall length of just 51 inches. It weighed 115 pounds, and its rear-mounted 1.6-bhp Briggs & Stratton or Clinton engine could push it along at up to 15 mph while getting 75 mpg. It was priced at $169.50, and was a companion to the Daytona (*see entry*).

**Autoette 1952-57**
Autoette Electric Car Co.; Long Beach, CA
Production: NA
This small, steel-bodied, two-passenger three-wheeler (single wheel at front) was available in three versions. All carried a 24-volt DC electric motor powered by four heavy-duty six-volt batteries. Prices ranged from $775-$950.

**Bassons Star 1956**
Bassons Industries Corp.; Bronx, NY
Production: NA
An open, three-wheeled (single wheel at front), two-passenger delivery-service car, the Star had a fiberglass body and single-cylinder German J.L.O. two-cycle engine producing 10 bhp. It was 33 inches high, 49 inches wide, 124 inches long, and weighed 400 pounds. Maximum cruising speed was 40 mph; top speed 70. It was advertised at $1000. Bassons also showed the Stationette, an enclosed fiberglass-bodied delivery van based on an ear-

# Minor Makes

1948 Beechcraft Plainsman sedan

lier wood-body model designed by James V. Martin (*see* Martinette).

### Baymont 1955
Baymont Co.; Redwood City, CA
Production: NA
Baymont's Suburban Model 240 was basically a two-passenger electric golf cart modified for local running on city streets. It boasted a top speed of 20 mph, and a range of 60 miles.

### Bearcat 1956
American Buckboard Corp.; Los Angeles, CA
Production: NA
Not at all like its Stutz namesake, this unusual five-wheeled vehicle had a rear-mounted fifth wheel that was chain-driven by a two-cylinder engine. With a wheelbase of 70 inches and an overall length of 120 inches, it was claimed to get 50 mpg. Cost: $1000

### Beechcraft Plainsman 1948
Beech Aircraft Co.; Wichita, KS
Production: 1
This one-off prototype had a four-cylinder Franklin air-cooled engine that drove an electric generator, which in turn powered four electric motors—one at each wheel. It had a large six-passenger body and all-independent air suspension with air-filled shocks at each wheel. Though its price was projected at $5000, production models would likely have cost more.

### Bergermobile 1948
Berger Air-Turbine Car Co.; Mount Vernon, NY
Production: 1
The Bergermobile started life as a Chevrolet. The engine was replaced by a 30-gallon air tank and Ingersoll-Rand compressed-air turbine engine. A 24-volt storage battery supplied electrical power to drive the turbine and run the car's electrical equipment.

### Blackhawk 1929-30
Stutz Motor Car Co.; Indianapolis, IN
Production: 1929: 1310; 1930: 280
Stutz's companion make was derived from the parent company's 1928 Model BB. It was built on a 127½-inch wheelbase and offered with open and closed body styles. The four-door sedan sold for $2395. An 85-bhp overhead-cam six was initially available, followed by a 90-bhp Continental L-head eight. Curb weight was nearly two tons, so performance was leisurely.

### B.M.C. 1952
British Motor Car Co.; San Francisco, CA
Production: NA
This B.M.C. had no connection with British Motor Corporation. Its fiberglass-bodied two-seater was designed around the engine and chassis of a Singer 1500, built by the Rootes Group in England. Plans were to produce 400 units a year, but the venture folded after a few months.

### Bobbi-Kar 1945-47
Bobbi Motor Car Corp.; San Diego, CA
Production: NA
A two-passenger roadster with a four-cylinder, 25-horsepower engine, the Bobbi-Kar had a wheelbase of 80 inches and an overall length of 132 inches. Projected price was $500. (*Also see* Keller)

### Bocar 1958-60
Bocar Racing Cars, Inc.; Denver, CO
Production: Less than 100
Though occasionally seen on the street, these were sports cars built primarily for racing. The XP-4 had a 90-inch wheelbase, tubular frame, and a Pontiac 370 or Chevrolet 283 V-8; the latter engine was coaxed to an alleged 350 horsepower in 1959. The later XP-5, an evolution of the XP-4, had sleek, aerodynamic lines and a price of $11,000. It was followed by the XP-6, with a

**1974 Bricklin SV-1 coupe**

Supercharged Chevy 283 with GMC blower claimed to produce 400 horsepower. It was priced at $11,700, weighed 2300 pounds, had a wheelbase of 104 inches, and a top speed of 135+ mph.

### Bolide 1969-70
Bolide Motor Car Corp.; Huntington, NY
Production: NA
Bolide's Can-Am 2 was a midengined, fiberglass-bodied car that rode a 105-inch wheelbase and used 351-cid Ford power. It was based on the Can-Am 1 prototype shown at the 1969 New York Auto Show and was expected to enter production for $3500. Also offered was an XJ002 two-passenger sports car with four-wheel-drive and a Jeep V-6 engine. Both were the work of Andrew J. Griffith, Jr., who was involved with the Griffith (*see entry*).

### Brewster 1934-36
Springfield Manufacturing Co.; Springfield, MA
Production: approx. 300
An attempt to salvage the Brewster coachbuilding company resulted in open and closed bodies on contemporary Ford, Buick, and other chassis. However, the venture was killed by steep prices that started at $3000.

### Bricklin 1974-75
Bricklin Vehicle Corp. (Malcolm Bricklin);
St. John, New Brunswick, Canada
Production: 2897
The "Safety sports car," designated SV-1, was a two-seat, fiberglass-bodied coupe with gullwing doors, large impact-resistant front bumper, and ungainly high-waisted styling. A grainy paint finish resulted from the color being impregnated into the outer acrylic shell. It was first powered by a 175-bhp (SAE net) AMC 360 V-8; later a 162-bhp Ford 351. Suspension was basically that of the AMC Javelin. Prices ranged from $7490-$9775, though each car may have cost at least $15,000 to build.

### Brogan 1946-c.52
B & B Specialty Co.; Rossmoyne, OH
Production: NA
The first model was a two-seat three-wheeler (single wheel in front) with a 10-bhp rear-mounted air-cooled twin. With a total weight of 450 pounds, the top speed was 45 mph with claimed 65-mpg economy. Later Broganette model was smaller than the first, delivering 85 mpg but a top speed of barely 40 mph. The Brogan name was phased out in 1951, when a revised Broganette was built that moved its single wheel to the rear. This car was 10 feet long and 52 inches wide, delivering a top speed of 50 mph while getting 55-60 mpg. Price was $550. Some 1947 models were sold under the name B & B Three Wheel.

### Buckaroo 1957
Manufacturer unknown; Cleveland, OH
Production: NA
Little is known about the Buckaroo, but it was a very small car with a top speed of only 18 mph that sold for about $400.

### Buckboard 1956
Don Bruce; Bronx, NY
Production: 1 show car; additional examples unlikely
With a name like Buckboard, it had to be good—if, that is, any were actually sold. This wood-bodied cycle car was powered by an Ariel "Square-4" motorcycle engine, mounted amidship on a Renault 4CV frame. It had a 94-inch wheelbase and an overall length of 143 inches. Curb weight was 738 pounds, top speed 90+ mph. While production is doubtful, construction plans were available for do-it-yourselfers.

### Bugetta c.1968-?
Bugetta, Inc.; Costa Mesa, CA
Production: NA
Bugetta was a fiberglass-bodied two/four-passenger open

# Minor Makes

design with midengine Ford 302-cid V-8. Its $3695 starting price included fiberglass and fabric tops. The same firm also made off-road vehicles.

1946 Californian convertible

**Californian 1945-46**
California Motor Car Co.; Los Angeles, CA
Production: NA
Three-wheel convertible with 58-bhp engine boasted a top speed of 100 mph with 40-mpg economy. The prototype was built by former race driver Frank Curtis, and was a predecessor of the Davis (*see entry*).

**Clenet 1976-?**
Clenet Coachworks; Santa Barbara, CA (to 1982) and Carpinteria, CA (from 1985)
Production: NA, but limited
French-born AMC stylist and industry consultant Alain Clenet's entry into the "neoclassic" market appeared as a prototype first shown at the '76 Los Angeles Auto Expo. Several orders were taken for the $24,500 two-seat, steel-bodied convertible. Series I blended basic MG Midget cabin with a 351-cid V-8 on a Lincoln Continental Mark IV chassis. Longer four-passenger Series II convertible—built around a Volkswagen Super Beetle cowl and 302-cid Ford V-8—debuted in mid-'79. The firm closed during 1982, but was revived in '85 by former Clenet employee Alfred DiMora. Renewed Series II ($98,000) was accompanied by the two-seat Series III "Asha" with fixed ($78,500) or folding ($82,500) top. The 118-inch wheelbase Series IV Sportster announced for 1988 was an effort to revive the original Clenet concept but with more amenities.

**Chadwick 1960**
Chadwick Engineering Works; Pottstown, PA
Production: NA
Chadwick was an open car only 87 inches long on a 58-inch wheelbase, which contributed to its overall weight of just 680 pounds. It was powered by a single-cylinder 13-bhp air-cooled BMW motorcycle engine connected to a four-speed BMW transmission with enclosed chain drive. Features included a tubular chassis, independent front suspension, quarter-elliptic rear leaf springs, and four-wheel hydraulic brakes.

**Charles Town-About 1958-59**
Stinson Aircraft Tool & Engineering Corp.; San Diego, CA
Production: NA
Electric conversion of a VW Karmann-Ghia with DeSoto fins and taillights. A 3.2-bhp motor was used at each rear wheel; top speed was 58 mph, range 77 miles. A utility model with protruding cargo box was called Van-About.

**Chicagoan 1952-54**
Triplex Industries, Ltd.; Blue Island, IL
Production: 15 (est.)
Two-passenger fiberglass sports car with six-cylinder Willys engine seemingly got a name change to Triplex around 1954.

**CitiCar 1974-76**
Sebring Vanguard, Corp.; Sebring, FL
Production: 2225
Small, two-seat runabout with triangular-shaped body made of Cycolac ABS plastic had a wheelbase of 65½ inches and an overall length of 94 inches. Eight General electric 6-volt batteries wired in sequence provided 6 net horsepower. Initial factory price was $2988. It was succeeded by the Comute-Car.

**Colt 1958**
Colt Manufacturing Co.; Milwaukee, WI, or Colt Motors Corp.; Boston, MA
Production: NA
Fiberglass-bodied, two-passenger car weighed 700 pounds. It was powered by an air-cooled 23-cid Wisconsin single-cylinder engine that provided a top speed of 50 mph. It was claimed to get 60 mpg with its standard automatic transmission. Price: $995

**Comet (i) c.1946-48**
General Developing Co.; Ridgewood, NY
Production: NA
Comet was a 114-inch-long three-wheeler (single wheel mounted at front) with tubular frame, plastic body, and a 4.5-bhp rear-mounted engine. It was claimed to get 100 mpg.

**Comet (ii) 1951-55**
Comet Manufacturing Co.; Sacramento, CA
Production: NA
The Comet name later appeared on a two-seat roadster, available as a kit or fully assembled. It was offered with a 6-horsepower engine, automatic transmission, heavy-duty brakes, and oversized balloon tires. It was said to reach 40 mph and get 60 mpg. The manufacturer (whose bread and butter was micro-midget race cars) claimed running costs of 50 cents a week.

**Continental 1933-34**
Continental Automobile Co.; Detroit, MI

Production: NA
Four- and six-cylinder cars were produced by the famed engine company. They were based on DeVaux body styles. Fours rode a 101.5-inch wheelbase, with prices starting at $335; Beacon Six and Ace Big Six had 65- and 85-bhp engines; 107- and 114-inch wheelbases.

**Convaircar 1941-48**
Consolidated-Vultee Aircraft Corp.; San Diego, CA
Production: NA
Car/plane powered for the road by a 26.5-horsepower Crosley engine; for flight by 190-bhp Lycoming. It had a four-seat fiberglass body and a 34½-foot wingspan; the wings were attached to the roof at three points. It was known as the Hall Flying Auto by 1950.

**Cord 1964-66; 1968-70**
Cord Automobile Co.; Tulsa, OK
Sports Automobile Manufacturing Co.; Mannford, OK
Production: approx. 100
Front-wheel-drive (with Corvair drivetrain) replicar revival of the 1936-37 Cord 810/812, was just 80 percent of the original's size, and thus named Cord 8/10. It was styled by Gordon Buehrig, who had worked on the original. The car was redesigned in rear-drive form by a new manufacturer in 1968; it got a Ford 302-cid V-8 as standard, with a Chrysler 440-cid Magnum V-8 optional.

**Cortez c.1947-c.50**
North American Motors; Dallas, TX
Production: NA
Full-size car intended for volume sale at $1000 was designed by Lincoln-Zephyr designer John Tjaarda.

**1960 Crofton**

**Crofton 1959-61**
Crofton Marine Engine Co.; San Diego, CA
Production: approx. 200
Jeep-style vehicle with Crosley engine had a wheelbase of 63 inches and overall length of 106 inches. The base price was $1350, but a "Brawny Kit" for an additional $450 brought a six-speed transmission, limited-slip differential, crash pan, deluxe seats, and upsize tires.

**1949 Cubster roadster**

**Cubster 1949**
Osborn Wheel Co.; Doylestown, PA
Production: NA
The "racing" chassis and a 6.6-horsepower engine sold for $299.50, but there was a Cubster body available at extra cost. The two-passenger, fenderless roadster had a top speed of 35 mph.

**Cunningham (i) 1907-33**
James Cunningham and Sons Co.; Rochester, NY
Production: NA, but limited
Open- and closed-model luxury cars were powered by a 355-cid V-8 rated at 110-140 bhp. Unfortunately, prices that reached $9000 discouraged Depression-era buyers, and the firm returned to coachbuilding after 1933.

**1953 Cunningham C-3 coupe**

**Cunningham (ii) 1953-55**
B. S. Cunningham Co.; West Palm Beach, FL
Production: 27 (C-3 model)
Grand-touring production cars evolved from sportsman Briggs Cunningham's fleet C-1 and C2-R. They were designed by Giovanni Michelotti, built by Vignale of Italy on a Cunningham chassis. Power came from a Chrysler 331-cid V-8 rated at 220-235 bhp. Prices ranged from $9000-$11,422.

**Curtis-Wright Air-Car 1959-60**
Curtis-Wright Corporation; South Bend, IN
Production: NA
Wheelless, four-passenger vehicle traveled 6-12 inches above land or water on a cushion of low-pressure air, and had a claimed top speed of 60 mph. Planned versions included Air-Bus and Air-Car pickups and trucks.

## Minor Makes

**1960 Cushman**

**Cushman 1945-**
Cushman Motor Works; Lincoln, NE
Production: NA
Shopper car from the manufacturer of motor scooters and golf carts had a one-cylinder, air-cooled engine; electric models were occasionally available as well. Town & Fairway model, c. 1969, could be converted from a four-passenger minicar to a golf cart or carryall.

**Custer 1959-60**
Custer Specialty Co.; Dayton, OH
Production: NA
Two-passenger "buckboard" vehicle was offered with a Custer Special electric motor or a 6-horsepower gas engine. Top speed was 18 mph in electric versions, 40 mph in gas models. Custer had offered cars in 1898 or '99 and 1920-46; company abandoned cars for good after 1960.

**Darrin 1946-47**
Howard A. "Dutch" Darrin/Lehman Brothers; New York, NY
Production: 1
Fiberglass-bodied, five-seat convertible from noted prewar designer of custom coachwork rode a 115-inch wheelbase. It was powered by a 100-bhp 226-cid Kaiser six. An elaborate hydraulic system powered the top, front seat, and jacking and hood-raising mechanisms. Sadly, the sole prototype was destroyed by flood some years later.

**1948 Davis coupe**

**Davis 1947-49**
Davis Motor Co.; Van Nuys, CA
Production: 17
This wide three-wheeler had a single four-passenger bench seat. Early examples had Continental engines, but later models got a 113-cid 60-bhp Hercules four. When the enterprise collapsed, owner Glen Gordon "Gary" Davis was convicted of fraud.

**Daytona 1956**
Randall Products; Hampton, NH
Production: NA
Rich man's version of the Auto Cub (*see entry*) was a two-passenger runabout that was 72 inches long and weighed 235 pounds. It had a steel chassis with Formica body panels. Power came from a rear-mounted 2-horsepower Briggs & Stratton engine providing a top speed of 18 mph and up to 75 mpg.

**Debonnaire 1955**
Replac Corp.; Euclid, OH
Production: NA
It's unclear whether this was a complete car or just a kit; contemporary accounts price it (with top) at about $1800. The fiberglass body was designed to fit the 1941-48 Ford platform.

**1947-49 Delcar truck**

**Delcar 1947-49**
American Motors, Inc.; Troy, NY
Production: NA
Delcar specialized in small delivery trucks, but at least one boxy Delcar station wagon was built. Its four-cylinder engine was mounted beneath the front floor. It claimed room for six, despite a short 60-inch wheelbase and 102-inch overall length.

**Del Mar 1949**
Del Mar Motors, Inc.; San Diego, CA
Production: less than 10 (est.)
Only prototypes exist of this 100-104-inch-wheelbase

**1949 Del Mar convertible**

subcompact. The Hillman-like bodies were made of aluminum, plastic, and steel, and the drivetrain consisted of a 160-cid 63-bhp Continental four and Warner three-speed transmission. It had a claimed 80 mph top speed and 30 mpg. Most had transverse leaf springs front and rear; a few had semielliptic rear springs. Planned price: $1200.

**Detroiter 1953**
Detroit Accessories Co.; St. Clair Shores, MI
Production: NA, but likely minuscule
Fiberglass-bodied convertible conceived by Raymond Russell (*see* Gadabout) was built on a 115-inch Ford or shortened Cadillac chassis. It was powered by a Ford drivetrain, with 110-bhp 239.4-cid flathead V-8.

**Detroit Electric 1907-38**
Detroit Electric Car Co.; Detroit, MI
Production: Several hundred (approx.)
Perhaps the best-known and most-successful American electric car was noted for its tall, glassy "china cabinet" bodies, but '30s cars could be had with false fronts that gave Detroits a contemporary look. Cars built on 100- and 112-inch-wheelbases were offered between 1930 and 1935. Innovations included safety glass, balloon tires, and four-wheel brakes, all of which were featured on '30s versions.

**DeVaux 1931-33**
DeVaux-Hall Motor Corp.; Grand Rapids, MI
Production: 1931: 4315; 1932-33: 1239
1931 Model 6-75 had a 113-inch wheelbase and 70-bhp 214.7-cid Continental L-head six, and carried prices of $645-$885. The 1932 Model 6-80 was slightly more expensive, and was marketed as the Continental DeVaux.

**Devin 1954-64**
Devin Motors, Inc. (Bill Devin & Malcolm MacGregor); El Monte, CA
Production: 15 (SS model)
These high-performance, fiberglass-bodied sports cars were sold fully assembled (few actually built) and as kits (hundreds sold). The original body mold was pulled from an aluminum Scaglietti design mounted on an Ermini 1100 chassis; the body was later modified to fit MacGregor's state-of-the-art steel-tube frame, with de Dion rear suspension and all-disc brakes. Drivetrain was

**1957 Devin SS roadster**

a stock Corvette 283 V-8 and Borg-Warner T-10 four-speed manual transmission. Thanks to low weight, they were quick: 0-60 mph in 4.8 seconds; 0-100 in 12 seconds. 1958 Devin D had the same body but with VW Beetle powertrain, and the later Devin C was similar but with a Chevy Corvair powertrain; these were not so quick.

**Diehlmobile 1962-64**
H.L. Diehl, Co.; South Willington, CT
Production: NA
The tiny three-wheeler weighed 225 pounds, and could be folded up and carried in the trunk of a normal car. Powered by a 3-bhp Briggs & Stratton engine, it was priced at $299.50.

**1952 Die Valkyrie convertible**

**Die Valkyrie 1952**
Brooks Stevens Design Assoc.; Milwaukee, WI, and Spohn Carosserie, Ravensburg, West Germany
Production: 1
Special-order car on contemporary Cadillac chassis was commissioned by a Cleveland syndicate. One model was manufactured; it was shown at the 1952 Paris Salon.

**Doble 1924-31**
Doble Steam Motors, Corp. (Abner Doble); Emeryville, CA
Production: NA
Luxurious, technically sophisticated steam cars wearing a variety of body styles, most supplied by Murphy. Power came from a 125-bhp 213-cid four-cylinder engine, with

# Minor Makes

automatic-boiler ignition system. They had a 75 mph cruising speed, 100 mph top speed, and cost up to $12,000—a huge sum in late-'20s dollars.

**Doray 1950**
Doray, Inc.; Miami Springs, FL
Production: NA, production beyond prototype stage unlikely
Steel-bodied three-seat roadster was based on the contemporary Willys Jeepster chassis, with styling similar to the Cord 810/812. Front fenders were hinged to allow wheel turning clearance. Power came from F- and L-head Willys engines that gave mediocre performance at best, and rock-hard Jeepster suspension made for a rugged ride.

**Dow Electric 1960**
Dow Testing Laboratory, Inc. (Douglas Dow); Detroit, MI
Production: none
Two-passenger electric minicar weighed 447 pounds and was 74 inches long. It was powered by two 0.3-horsepower motors driven by three 12-volt and four 24-volt batteries providing a top speed of 15-20 mph and a range of 30 miles. Projected price was $500-$800, but no backers could be found.

1957 Dual Ghia convertible

**Dual-Ghia 1956-63**
Dual Motors Corp. (Eugene Casaroll); Detroit, MI
Production: 1956-58: 117; 1961-63: 26
Italo-American GT was inspired by the 1952 Dodge Firearrow show car styled by Virgil Exner and built by Ghia. A stock Dodge chassis was modified by Ghia's Giovanni Savonuzzi; wheelbase was 115 inches with a Hudson-like step-down floor. It was powered by a 315-cid Dodge Red Ram V-8 rated at 230, 260, and 285 bhp, teamed with floorshift PowerFlite automatic. Initial price was $7650. The design was revised for 1960 as a sleek, glassy semifastback coupe called L6.4. That version had a purpose-designed chassis and fewer stock Chrysler parts, and was powered by a Chrysler 325-bhp wedgehead 383. By this time, the price had risen to $15,000. Casaroll's death in the late 1960s scuttled a planned third generation.

**Duesenberg (ii) 1966**
Duesenberg Corp. ("Fritz" Duesenberg); Indianapolis, IN
Production: 1
Duesie revival with Virgil Exner-inspired neoclassic styling was a 5700-pound prototype built by Ghia on 137.5-inch wheelbase. It was 245 inches overall and powered by a Chrysler 440 V-8. Announced price: $19,500. Stillborn were a massive brougham sedan with center-opening doors, plus a limousine and convertible sedan.

**Duesenberg (iii) 1970-75**
Duesenberg Co.; Gardena and Inglewood, CA
Production: NA
Another Duesie revival attempt, this one a $24,500 replica of the two-seat SSJ roadster on a 128-inch wheelbase, with an overall length of 116.5 inches. It tipped the scales at 3600 pounds. Automatic transmission was standard, with a four-speed manual optional; both were coupled to a Chrysler 383 V-8 with a claimed 500 bhp. The firm moved from Gardena to Inglewood in 1974, and the already-steep price was hiked to $41,500 while the engine became a detoxed 440 V-8 rated at 215 net bhp.

**Duesenberg (iv) 1979**
Duesenberg Brothers Co. (Harlan & Kenneth Duesenberg and Robert Peterson); Mundelein and Evanston, IL
Production: 1
Yet another Duesie revival, this one based on a thinly disguised Cadillac Fleetwood Brougham with the same 133-inch wheelbase and 195-bhp (net) fuel-injected 425 V-8. It carried a projected price of $100,000, which may explain why only one was produced.

**duPont 1920-32**
duPont Motors, Inc. (E. Paul duPont); Moore, PA
Production: less than 100
The Model G had a 144-inch wheelbase, 140-bhp Continental side-valve straight eight, and bodywork by Merrimac; a few were also bodied by Waterhouse and Derham. The Model E (only three built) had a smaller supercharged engine and 146-inch wheelbase.

**Durant 1921-32**
Durant Motors of America (William Crapo Durant); Detroit, MI
Production: 1930: 21,440; 1931: 7229; 1932: 1135
By 1930, a half-dozen models were built with a 112-inch wheelbase and 58-70-bhp Continental six. In 1931, the remaining four models were priced between $695-$775. That was cut to just a pair of models for 1932 (621 and 622) with 71-bhp Continental engine; starting price $700. The company closed its doors that year, but continued to sell cars in Canada under the Frontenac name through 1933.

**Edwards 1953-55**
Edwards Engineering Co. (Sterling H. Edwards);

**1954 Edwards America hardtop coupe**

San Francisco, CA
Production: 6
Edwards America was a slab-sided convertible built on a Mercury station wagon chassis. One car had a 303.7-cid Olds V-8; two had 205-bhp Lincoln engines; the three remaining cars carried 210-bhp Cadillac V-8s. High prices ($7800 by 1955) and factory setup costs prevented volume production.

### Elcar 1915-31
Elcar Motor Company; Elkhart, IN
Production: NA
Thirty-two models in four series were offered in 1930. The Model 75 had a 117-inch wheelbase and was powered by a 61-bhp Lycoming six. The Model 95/96 rode a 123-inch wheelbase and had a 90-bhp Lycoming eight. The Model 130 sat on a 130-inch wheelbase and was fitted with a 140-bhp Lycoming straight eight. The 1931 Model 140 had a 135-inch wheelbase.

### Electra 1974-76
Die Mech Corp.; Pelham, NY
Production: NA
Basically a Fiat 850 Sport Spyder converted to electric operation, with 10 horsepower from triple motors. Heavy batteries increased weight from Fiat's 1620 to more than 3000 pounds, resulting in a range of about 40 miles.

### Electra King 1961-c.81
B & Z Electric Car Co.; Long Beach, CA
Production: NA
Tall, two-passenger, fiberglass-bodied electric car was available in three- or four-wheeled models that were usually powered by five 6-volt batteries in series, though sometimes by 24-, 30-, and 36-volt systems. The 1970s brought a choice of four motors producing from 1 to 3.5 bhp, resulting in top speeds of 16-29 mph and ranges from 18-36 miles. For electric cars they were light, tipping the scales at just 675 pounds.

### Electricar 1950-c.66
Boulevard Machine Works; North Hollywood, CA
Production: NA
Small electric runabouts were offered in three versions. Two-seat Boulevard was 106 inches long, with four ⅙-bhp electric motors, one driving each wheel. The single-seat Cutie had two such motors, one in front and one in back; top speed 25 mph. The Cutie Junior had but one motor giving a top speed of 10 mph.

**1960 Electric Shopper**

### Electric Shopper 1956-?
Electric Car Co.; Long Beach, CA
Production: NA
Three-wheeled, battery-powered shopping car had a fiberglass body; it was 86 inches long with a 61-inch wheelbase. It was powered by a 1.5-bhp 24-volt DC series-wound motor providing a top speed of 18 mph and a range of 30-35 miles. It was priced at $945, though metal-bodied models were available at about $750.

### Electrobile 1951
Manufacturer unknown; probable Chicago location
Production: NA, but doubtful
Three-wheel runabout had a fiberglass body molded over an aluminum framework. A high-speed DC motor and built-in charger gave a range of 25-35 miles. The proposed price was $350, but only sketches of the car were shown; prototype may not have been built.

### Electro Master 1962-64(?)
Nepa Manufacturing Co.; Pasadena, CA
Production: NA
Fiberglass-bodied shopping car was powered by a 2-bhp motor connected to six 6-volt batteries, which gave a top speed of 20 mph and a range of 40 miles. It weighed 680 pounds. Production may have continued past 1964.

### Electronic 1955
Electronic Motor Car Corp.; Salt Lake City, UT
Production: 1
An innovative hybrid-power car with gasoline or diesel engine charging an 80-cell battery pack connected to "Dual-Torque" electric motor within the rear axle housing that was far ahead of its time. "Electro-Magnetic Differential" aimed to provide limited-slip effect. Proposed were sedan, station wagon, panel truck, and sports car body styles, all on a 110-inch wheelbase; though, sadly, none materialized.

# Minor Makes

**1956 El Morocco convertible**

### El Morocco 1956-57
Rueben Allenden; Detroit, MI
Production: approx. 30
A styling conversion that brought Cadillac cues to contemporary Chevrolet convertible and two- and four-door hardtops carried altered bumpers, side trim, and fins.

### Erskine 1927-30
Studebaker Corp.; South Bend, IN
Production: 22,371
Six-cylinder companion make for Studebaker was named for company president Albert R. Erskine. The final 1930 Model 53 was offered in nine variations, all powered by a 205.3-cid L-head six with 70 bhp.

### Fergus 1949
Fergus Motors, Inc.; New York, NY
Production: Prototype stage only
Followup to this firm's 1915-22 attempt to become an automaker was based on a restyled Austin A40 patterned after the relatively uncommon Austin A40 Sports.

### Ferrer 1966
Ferrer Motors Corp.; Miami, FL
Production: NA
A steel-reinforced fiberglass body on a VW Beetle chassis carried styling that mimicked contemporary Ford GT endurance racers. It had an overall length of 158 inches, a width of 60 inches, and a height of 42 inches. The basic kit sold for $990; a deluxe kit cost $1750; and a fully assembled version was $2950 with a 50-bhp engine, or $3800 with a reworked 70-bhp VW flat four. The standard model claimed a 90-mph top speed, 0-60 mph in 12.5 seconds, and 29 mpg at a steady 68 mph.

### Fibersport 1953-54
Fibersport, Inc.; Bloomington, IN
Production: NA
Unusually well-engineered fiberglass sports roadster based on the Crosley Hot Shot platform was sold as a kit for $650-$750, or fully assembled for $2850. It weighed 1150 pounds and claimed a top speed of 100 mph. Following the demise of Crosley, Fibersport designed its own new tubular frame and adopted Morris Minor gearboxes.

### Fina 1953-c.55
Fina, Inc. (Perry Fina); New York, NY
Production: NA
Fina's Sport was available as a convertible or hardtop on a 115-inch-wheelbase Ford chassis. Its 188-inch-long body was made by Vignale of Italy. The standard powerplant was a 210-bhp Cadillac unit (300-bhp engine available at extra cost), though most any Detroit V-8 could be ordered. GM's Dual-Range Hydra-Matic was the sole transmission. It was priced at about $10,000.

### Fitch (i) 1949
Sports and Utility Motors, Inc. (John Fitch); White Plains, NY
Production: NA; single prototype built
Race-and-ride sports-car prototype was a proposed Type A model. Proposed Type B model would have used Fiat 1100 chassis with 96-inch wheelbase, modified Crosley Hot Shot body, and tweaked flathead Ford V-8/60 with 105 bhp.

### Fitch (ii) 1961-69
John Fitch and Co., Inc.; Falls Village, CT
Production: NA
A modified Chevrolet Corvair, called the Fitch GT, was also offered in separate packages, including an engine kit and an appearance package for '65 Corvairs. The Fitch Phoenix, offered for 1966, was a 2150-pound targa-top two-seater with modified 170-bhp Corvair engine good for 0-60 mph in 7.5 seconds and a top speed of 130 mph. The Phoenix body was built by Intermeccanica in Italy. But the planned Phoenix run of 500 units was scuttled because of the expense in meeting federal safety standards. As a result, only a prototype was built.

### Fletcher 1954
Fletcher Aviation Corp.; Rosemead, CA
Production: NA
The Fletcher Flair was a four-wheel-drive Jeep-like vehicle powered by a 1500cc Porsche flat four. It had a wheelbase of 78 inches, an overall length of 115-126 inches.

### Flintridge-Darrin 1957
Flintridge Motor Manufacturing Corp.; Los Angeles, CA
Production: 15 (est.)
A contemporary German DKW sedan with two-stroke engine and low-slung fiberglass roadster body (from Woodill; *see entry*) styled by Howard "Dutch" Darrin, was priced at $3195, contrasted with $2275 for the DKW. It was also known as the Flintridge, Darrin-DKW, or Flintridge-DKW.

### Ford 1901 Replica 1968
Horseless Carriage Corp.; Ft. Lauderdale, FL
Production: NA, but limited
It was sold as a three-quarter replica "of the 1901 Ford," though Henry's first production car, the Model A, was not built until 1903. Specs have been lost, though production lasted only a few months.

### France Jet 1961
France Jet Motors, Ltd.; New York, NY
Production: NA, but limited
Fiberglass-bodied two-seater was priced at $1595 with a 17-cid four-cycle one-cylinder engine. An optional 66-cid 40-bhp twin was available for an additional $250.

### Frazen 1951-62
Ray Green, Co.; Toledo, OH
Production: NA, but limited
Powered by 161-cid Henry J flathead six, this fiberglass sports roadster was available fully assembled ($2795 in 1952) and as a kit.

### Frick 1955
Bill Frick Motors; Rockville Centre, NY
Production: NA; beyond single prototype unlikely
Ferrari-like coupe, bodied by Vignale of Italy, was based on Cadillac running gear. It sat on a 110-inch-wheelbase box-channel chassis of Bill Frick's own design, with conventional independent front suspension and live-axle/leaf-spring rear suspension. Total weight was 3000 pounds. (*See also* Studillac)

### Gadabout 1945
Ray Russell; Grosse Pointe, MI
Production: none
Three-seat roadster on an 80-inch wheelbase was a home workshop project from industrial designer Russell. It had a flush-fender duraluminum body over an MG chassis and running gear; top speed was 50 mph. Crash protection was provided by an unobtrusive bumper-height steel perimeter tube. An 1100-pound curb weight contributed to a claimed 50 mpg. Front- and rear-engine models were planned, but no backer could be found.

### Gardner 1916-31
Gardner Motor Car Co.; St. Louis, MO
Production: NA
1930 Models 136 and 140 used Lycoming 70-bhp six and 90-bhp eight, respectively; Model 150 had a Lycoming 126-bhp eight. The 1930 Gardner Front-Drive rode a 133-inch wheelbase and was powered by an 80-bhp Lycoming six. The firm turned to hearses and ambulances in 1931 and folded a year later.

### Gaslight 1960-61
Gaslight Motors Corp.; Detroit, MI
Production: NA
A 640-pound replica of a 1902 Rambler, the Gaslight was built on a 77-inch wheelbase and powered by a 4-bhp air-cooled single-cylinder engine. Price: $1495. (*See also* Rambler 1902 Replica)

### Gaylord 1955-57
Gaylord Cars, Ltd. (Edward & Jim Gaylord); Chicago, IL
Production: 3
Luxury two-seater in retractable hardtop convertible form was styled by Brooks Stevens and executed by Spohn coachworks in Ravensburg, West Germany. It had

**1955-57 Gaylord coupe**

a purpose-built chassis with conventional suspension, and was powered by a Chrysler hemi-head V-8. Despite weighing nearly two tons, the Hemi provided decent performance: 120 mph top speed, 0-60 in 8 seconds. The target price was $17,500, but the project fell apart following a quality dispute with the body contractor.

### Glassic 1966-72; 1972-75
Glassic Industries, Inc. (Jack & Joel Faircloth); West Palm Beach, FL
Glassic Motor Car Co. (Fred Pro); West Palm Beach, FL
Production: NA
Model A-style fiberglass bodywork was mounted on an International Scout chassis with its 94-bhp four; cars built after 1972 used a 210-bhp Ford 302 V-8. Initial price of $3800 grew to $10,000 by 1972. The firm did business as Replicar after 1976-77.

### Glasspar 1950-54
Glasspar, Inc. (Bill Tritt); Santa Ana, CA
Production: 200 (est.; number may include kits)
Sleek, two-seat fiberglass-body roadsters usually rode a 100-inch wheelbase. They were typically sold as kits, though a few were sold fully assembled for $3000 and up through 1954; kits only afterward. The G-2 model was fitted with Ford or Mercury flathead or ohv V-8s.

### Goff 1956
Charles Goff; Texarkana, TX
Production: NA; a handful, at most
Five-passenger, fiberglass-bodied sports model was conceived around a '39 Ford chassis and running gear; other engines and matching top were available at extra charge. It was priced at $600 for a kit, or $1500 for a fully assembled car.

### Gordon c.1947-48
H. Gordon Hansen; San Lorenzo, CA
Production: 1
This 3750-pound one-off was dubbed the "Diamond" because of its unusual, diamond-pattern wheel placement: one in front, one in back, and one on either side. The end wheels were 156 inches apart, with side wheels halfway between. Power was supplied by a 100-bhp Ford truck engine, providing a 95-mph top speed.

# Minor Makes

**1966 Griffith coupe**

### Griffith 1964-66
Griffith Motors (Jack Griffith); Syoset, NY
Griffith Motor Car Co. (Jack Griffith); Plainview, NY
Production: 285
These 138-inch-long sports cars, dubbed Series 200, consisted of a modified fiberglass body from the British TVR on a purpose-built tubular chassis. Power came from a Ford 289 V-8 that produced 0-60-mph times of less than four seconds. Price was $3995-$4800. The cut-off of TVR body supplies caused a switch to Vetta Ventura (*see entry, and* Apollo *entry*); new $6095 GT model had a body by Intermeccanica of Italy and power from a 235-bhp Plymouth 273 V-8 with standard Torque-Flite automatic or optional four-speed manual. This car was continued after 1966 as the Omega (*see entry*) and Intermeccanica.

### Henney Kilowatt 1960-c.64
Henney Motor Co. (C. Russell Feldman); Canastota, NY
Production: 100 (max.)
Electric conversion of a Renault Dauphine was powered by a dozen 6-volt batteries and a 7-bhp motor. At 2250 pounds, it was 750 pounds heavier than a Dauphine. Top speed was 40 mph; range 40 miles.

### Hoppenstand 1948-49
Hoppenstand Motors, Inc.; Greenville, PA
Production: NA
Two-passenger, aluminum-body open economy car was powered by an 8.5-bhp 21.4-cid air-cooled flat twin mounted at the rear of its 90-inch-wheelbase chassis. It had all-independent suspension and standard automatic torque converter. Top speed was 50 mph with claimed 35-mpg economy. Overall length was 162 inches; weight 684 pounds. Base price was $1000.

### Hydramotive c.1960
Hydramotive Corp.; Charlotte, NC
Production: 1
Small, diesel-engine car, designed by Durward Willis, had no transmission, universal joints, driveshaft, differential, axles, or brakes. Though it was intended to be sold for $1200, the plan failed when the company was the focus of a 1961 SEC stock-fraud investigation.

**1949-51 Imp**

### Imp 1949-51
International Motor Products; Glendale, CA
Production: NA
The 1949 Imp prototype featured a rear-mounted 7.5-horsepower Gladden 75 engine and doorless, fiberglass-laminate body on a 63-inch wheelbase. It was 120 inches long, weighed 475 pounds, had a top speed of 35 mph, and was claimed to run 180-240 miles on a 3-gallon tank of gas. 1951 models were 108 inches long and priced at $500.

### Jetmobile 1952
Richard Harp; Frederick, MD
Production: NA
Missile-shaped single-seat three-wheeler (single wheel at front) was made from an aircraft fuel tank. Its rear-mounted 75-bhp Lycoming was later swapped for a 60-bhp Ford flathead V-8.

### Jomar c.1954-60
Saidell Sports Racing Cars (Ray Saidell); Manchester, NH
Production: NA
British TVR chassis mated to a specially designed aluminum body was powered by a 71.5-cid British Ford Anglia four; optional alternatives included a supercharged version and at least three Coventry-Climax units. Price: $2995-$4595.

### Jordan 1916-31
Jordan Motor Car Co., Inc.; Cleveland, OH
Production: 2851
Great Line 80 (120-inch wheelbase) and Great Line 90 (125-inch-wheelbase) were powered by 80-85-bhp straight eights in a variety of body styles priced from $1495-$2295. Series 90 roadsters and touring cars rode a 131-inch wheelbase, which was shared with a seven-seat limousine and sedan. Model Z Speedway rode a 145-inch wheelbase mounting a 125-bhp 318-cid Continental straight eight. Sportsman sedan and Ace roadster with custom Coburn aluminum bodywork were capable of an easy 100 mph. Price: $5500.

1968 Keen Streamliner convertible

### Keen Streamliner c.1955-67; c.1968
Charles F. Keen; Madison, WI
Thermal Kinetics Corp.; Rochester, NY
Production: NA

Original version was a shortened 1946-48 Plymouth converted to steam power; follow-up car was a fiberglass-bodied convertible based on the Victress shell also used for the Williams steamer (*see entry*). Cars carried a V-4 engine of unknown origin. Top-speed claims vary from 60 mph to 100 mph.

### Keller 1948-40
Keller Motors Corp. (George D. Keller); Huntsville, AL
Production: 18 (est.)

Outgrowth of Bobbi Motor Car Co. (*see* Bobbi-Kar) was slightly longer and more-powerful than the Bobbi-Kar. It was first offered as a wagon (two-door; 2100 pounds) and convertible (three-seats, with front- or rear-mounted engine; 2400 pounds), in two series: Chief models were powered by a 47-bhp 133-cid Hercules engine; Super Chiefs had a 58-bhp 162-cid Continental unit. The company claimed to have a network of 1150 dealers in 1948, but the hoped-for annual production of 150,000 never came close to being achieved, and the firm went bankrupt in 1950.

1953 King Midget Deluxe roadster

### King Midget 1946-c.69
Midget Motors Supply Co. and Midget Motors Corp.

1946 King Midget racer

(Claud Dry & Dale Orcutt); Athens, OH
Production: approx. 5000

Tiny, buckboard-type vehicle, first available as a kit only, was sold fully assembled from about 1949. A more car-like replacement was offered from 1951-57. A third generation arrived in 1957. Two different engines were used; 1946-66 models had 7.3-8.5-bhp single-cylinder Wisconsin units, while those built from 1967 onward had 9.3-12-bhp Kohlers. Overall length ranged from 96 to 117 inches; all models rode a 76.5-inch wheelbase. Weight ranged from 400-700 pounds; prices from $350-$1000+. Overall fuel economny was claimed to be 60 mpg.

### Kissel 1906-31
Kissel Motor Company; Hartford, WI
Production: 1930:77; 1931: 16

The last production year of these finely crafted cars included the Model 6-73 (117-inch wheelbase powered by a 70-bhp six), Model 95 (125-inch wheelbase with a 246 cid and 95 bhp) and Model 8-126 White Eagle (wheelbases up to 139 inches with a 126-bhp 298-cid eight.) Prices extended to well above $3000. The company was reorganized in 1931 and went on to produce outboard motors.

### Krim-Ghia 1966
Krim Car Import Co.; Detroit, MI
Carrozzerria Ghia; Turin, Italy
Production: NA, but limited

The 1500 GT was a sports coupe powered by an 86-bhp Fiat four. Also offered was a roadster on a Plymouth Barracuda chassis, powered by that car's 245-bhp V-8.

### Kurtis 1948-49
Kurtis-Craft (Frank Curtis); Glendale, CA
Production: fewer than 50

The initial version of this 169-inch sports car was built using stock production pieces and a supercharged L-head Studebaker Champion engine. Later models were powered by Ford flathead V-8s or 160-bhp Cadillac V-8s. The firm was purchased by Earl "Madman" Muntz in 1949 (*see* Muntz).

# Minor Makes

### LaFayette 1934-36
Nash Motors; Kenosha, WI
Production: 1934: 5000; 1935: 9400; 1936: 27,860
Nash's lower-priced "junior" make was priced from $585-$715. They rode a 113-inch wheelbase and were powered by a 217.8-cid 75-83-bhp Nash six.

### Honey Bee 1959
Swift Manufacturing Co.; El Cajon, CA
Production: NA
Tiny, fiberglass-bodied open three-wheeler (single wheel in front) had a teardrop shape and low, rounded nose. It was powered by a rear-mounted, four-cycle Briggs & Stratton 1.5-bhp engine. The same firm also made replicars under the Swift name (*see entry*).

### La Saetta 1955
Testaguzza Brothers; Detroit, MI
Production: approx. 15
Fiberglass-bodied two-passenger roadster was powered by a variety of Hudson and Oldsmobile engines, and no two cars were alike. Wheelbases were about 110 inches, with overall length ranging from 200-210 inches. A late-1955 partnership with Electronic Motor Corporation of Salt Lake City resulted in a turbo-electric called Electronic.

### Lawler Steamobile 1948-50
James H. Lawler; Huntington Park, CA
Production: NA
Originally a steam-powered conversion of a 1938 Terraplane; conversions of other cars may have been carried out at nearby South Gate.

### MK III 1968
Auto Craft Northwest; Portland, OR
Production: NA
This sports car was built to owner specifications, and was available with midengine 327- or 427-cid Chevy V-8 or rear-engine 164-cid Corvair flat six. It was also available in kit form.

### Marketour 1964
Marketour Electric Cars; Long Beach, CA
Production: NA
In addition to a boxy, two-passenger, three-wheel electric (single wheel in front), a quarter-ton pickup model was also built. They were fitted with six heavy-duty batteries that powered a 36-volt motor. Range was 35-40 miles. The steel body had a removable leatherette-covered top.

### Markette 1967-68
Westinghouse Electric Corp.; Pittsburgh, PA
Production: 1
Boxy electric car was 116 inches long and powered by twelve 6-volt batteries that comprised about half the car's 1730-pound weight. Projected price was $2000.

**1967 Markette coupe**

### Marquis 1954
Plasticar; Doylestown, PA
Production: NA
While the prototype of this two-door fastback sports coupe on a 4CV Renault chassis had an aluminum body, the production cars were to be bodied in "plastic," perhaps fiberglass, and priced at $3100.

### Marquette 1929-30
Buick Motor Division, General Motors Corp.; Flint, MI
Production: 35,007
The 1930 lineup of Buick's "junior" edition offered six body styles on a 114-inch wheelbase, all powered by a 67.5-bhp 213-cid enlargement of the contemporary Olds L-head six. Price: about $1000.

### Mars II 1966-c.70
Electric Fuel Propulsion, Inc.; Ferndale, MI
Production: NA
Electric car based on the Renault 10 body was powered by four 3-volt battery packs, each consisting of five lead-cobalt batteries. These battery packs accounted for 1900 of the car's 4160 pounds. Five-year or 50,000-mile battery life was claimed. Top speed was 68 mph, and 0-40 mph was claimed to take 12 seconds.

### Martinette 1954
Martin Development Laboratories (James Vernon Martin); Rochelle Park, NY
Production: NA
Two- and three-passenger, teardrop-shaped three wheelers (single wheel at the rear) were based on the firm's 1948 prototype; one panel delivery was produced in 1955. Power came from a rear-mounted 24-bhp Hercules engine. Price: $1000. Firm was sold to Bassons Industries Corp. in 1955 or 1956 (*see* Bassons Star).

### Maverick 1953-55
Maverick Motors; Mountain View, CA
Production: approx. 7
Three-passenger car mounted on a Cadillac chassis had a 122-128-inch wheelbase with an overall length of 16 feet. A sleek fiberglass body was available with one, two, or three doors. The drivetrain consisted of a Cadillac engine with Borg-Warner overdrive transmission.

**1955 Maverick roadster**

### Mighty Mite 1953
Mid-America Research Corp.; Wheatland, PA
Production: NA
Full-time 4WD car offered in a wide range of body styles was designed by Ben F. Gregory. The prototype was fitted with an air-cooled Porsche engine; production models were to have modified Lycoming 65-bhp aircraft engines.

### Minicar 1969
Minicars, Inc.; Goleta, CA
Production: 1
Three-passenger car that was 108 inches overall in length, powered by a Corvair six. Anticipated price: $2500.

### Mohs 1967-78
Bruce Baldwin Mohs; Madison, WI
Production: 3 or 4 cars a year
The company dates to 1948 but did not build its first car until 1967. Huge Ostentatienne Opera coupe weighed 5740 pounds and measured 246 inches overall on a 119-inch wheelbase—meaning there was substantial overhang on each end. International Harvester built the chassis to Mohs' specs, and also supplied its 304-cid 193-bhp V-8; a 549-cid V-8 was optional. Instead of regular doors, entry was gained though a large rear "hatch" that extended from roof to bumper. Features included a water-cooled automatic transmission, butane furnace-heater, ¾-inch Ming Dynasty-style carpet, velvet upholstery, and a walnut-covered instrument panel inlaid with 24-karat gold. By the late 1960s, the base price was $19,600, or $25,600 with the 549 V-8. A second model, the Safarikar, was added in 1971. It was a metal-topped dual-cowl phaeton with side-mounted doors that extended outward on rails, and the body was covered in padded Nau-gahyde. Its initial base price was $14,500.

### Mota 1953
Banning Electric Products Corp.; New York, NY
Production: NA
Little is known about the Mota save for that it was a fiberglass-bodied gas/electric hybrid.

**1952 Multiplex roadster**

### Multiplex 1952-54
Multiplex Manufacturing Co.; Berwick, PA
Production: 3
This two-passenger sports car was built on a tubular truss frame and powered by a modified Willys F-head four- (87 hp) or six-cylinder (124 hp) engine.

### Mustang (ii) 1948
Mustang Engineering Corp.; Seattle, WA
Production: NA
Six-passenger car (two in front, four in back) was designed by Lincoln-Mercury service alumnus Roy C. McCarty. Its aluminum body was mounted on a tubular-steel frame. Power was supplied by a rear-mounted 59-bhp Hercules four, which was accessible by a door on car's left side. Projected price: $1235.

### Navajo c.1954
Navajo Motor Car Co.; New York, NY
Production: NA
Three-passenger sports car, visually similar to a Jaguar XK-120, was powered by a tweaked Mercury flathead V-8 rated at 130 hp that was good for a claimed 7.8-second run from 0-60 mph.

### Nu-Klea 1959-60
Nu-Klea Automobile Corp.; Lansing, MI
Production: NA
Small, two-passenger electric car with steel chassis and fiberglass body had leaf springs at the rear, coil springs in front. It was powered by a separate motor at each rear wheel. Range was claimed to be 75-85 miles.

### Oakland 1907-31
Oakland-Pontiac Division, General Motors Corp.; Pontiac, MI
Production: 1930: 21,943; 1931: 13,408
Companion make to Pontiac, which eventually overshadowed it. 1930-31 Oaklands rode a 117-inch wheelbase and were offered in a variety of open and closed body types priced from $895-$1055. All were powered by an 85-bhp 250-cid V-8; oversquare cylinder dimensions and 180-degree crankshaft made for rough running.

# Minor Makes

## Olds 1901 Replica 1968
Horseless Carriage Corp.; Fort Lauderdale, FL
Production: NA
Three-quarter-scale replicar of the famed curved-dash Olds.

## Omega 1967-68
Suspensions International Corp.; Manhasett, NY
Production: NA
Stillborn '66 Griffith GT (*see* Griffith) was continued in 1967 as the steel-bodied (by Intermeccanica of Turin, Italy) Omega. It was constructed by Holman and Moody of Charlotte, North Carolina. The Griffith's Plymouth V-8 was replaced by a Ford 289 engine and driveline. Base price was $8950. The car continued after 1968 as the Torino, Italia, and IMX, all presumably assembled by Intermeccanica.

## Panda 1955-56
Small Cars, Inc.; Kansas City, KS
Production: NA
Two-passenger fiberglass-body roadster was styled like a child's pedal car, but built on a 70-inch wheelbase. Two engines were offered: a 44-cid Aerojet four and a 67-cid Kohler flat twin ('55 prototype had a Crosley engine).

1962 Panther roadster

## Panther 1962-c.63
Panther Automobile Co.; Bedford Hills, NY
Production: NA
This two-passenger fiberglass sports car was built on a 94-inch wheelbase and powered by a Daimler V-8.

## Paxton Phoenix 1951-54
Paxton Engineering Co.; Los Angeles, CA
Production: NA
Five-passenger, fiberglass-body car was styled by Brooks Stevens. Steam engines were considered (with key development work done by steam-engine pioneer Abner Doble) but the ultimate powerplant was a rear-mounted Porsche 1500.

1932 Peerless V-16 sedan

## Peerless 1900-32
Peerless Motor Car Corp.; Cleveland, OH
Production: NA
A respected luxury make rivaling the best in America closed out its history with the beautiful, aluminum-bodied (by Murphy) V-16 of 1932, of which only one was completed. Peerless' car-making activities were killed by the Depression, and the company moved into brewing.

## Pioneer 1959-c.60
Nic-L-Silver Battery Co.; Santa Ana, CA
Production: NA
Fiberglass-bodied electric car was powered by twin motors that drove the rear wheels. It was 157 inches long, had a curb weight of 1800 pounds, and a range of 40-100 miles. It was also known as the Lippencott Pioneer and the Nic-L-Silver.

1948 Playboy retractable convertible

## Playboy 1947-51
Playboy Motor Car Corp.; Buffalo, NY
Production: approx. 90
This three-passenger convertible minicar with folding steel top was powered by a 40-bhp Hercules four (some cars had a Continental engine of similar power) driving through a three-speed Warner Gear automatic transmission. Built on a 90-inch wheelbase, it measured 155 inches overall and weighed 2035 pounds.

1955 Powell Sport Wagon pickup

**Powell 1954-56**
Powell Manufacturing Co.; Compton, CA
Production: approx. 2400
Steel-bodied Powell Sport Wagon (the nose panel was fiberglass) rode on a remanufactured Plymouth chassis with 90-bhp engine. Initial price was $998. A pickup truck was styled along similar lines.

**Publix 1947-48**
Publix Motor Car Co.; Buffalo, NY
Production: NA
Two-passenger three-wheeler (single wheel at the front) was offered with a choice of fabric or Plexiglas top. It had an aluminum tube frame, body, and engine that combined for a total weight of just 150-200 pounds. It was claimed to get 70-80 mpg at speeds up to 60 mph.

1948-49 Pup coupe

**Pup 1948-49**
Pup Motor Car Co.; Spencer, WI
Production: NA
Two wood-bodied versions were offered: an open two-seat roadster with separate fenders and no doors or top, and an enclosed, slab-sided coupe. Engine choices included a 7.5-bhp single-cylinder Briggs & Stratton or a 10-bhp two-cylinder unit. Top speed was claimed to be 35-40 mph while getting 50-60 mpg. Price: $500-$600.

**Quantum 1962-63**
Quantum Corp.; Rockland, MA
Production: NA
Rebodied Saab weighed just 900 pounds, and was distributed in the U.S. through individual Saab dealers.

**Rambler 1902 Replica c.1959-60**
American Air Products; Fort Lauderdale, FL
Production: NA
Replica of the 1902 Rambler continued as the Gaslight (*see entry*).

**Roadable 1946**
Portable Products Corp.; Garland, TX
Production: 1
Three-wheel car/plane with single wheel at the front. When airborne, ailerons and elevators were controlled by the steering wheel. A 130-bhp Franklin engine provided a top ground speed of 60 mph. Aloft it had a cruising airspeed of 110 mph and a range of 600 miles. Five minutes were needed to convert the vehicle to road use.

**Rockefeller Yankee 1953**
Rockefeller Sports Car Corp.; Rockville Centre, NY
Production: NA
Four-passenger, fiberglass- and Vibrin-bodied sports car was fitted with a Ford engine and driveline. It had a 100-inch wheelbase, overall length of 14 feet, and a claimed top speed of 100 mph.

**Rocket 1948**
Hewson Pacific Corp.; Los Angeles, CA
Production: NA
Aluminum-bodied three-passenger car sat on a 106-inch wheelbase with an overall length of 161 inches. Two engines were available: a 65-bhp four or a 95-bhp six; a torque-convertor automatic transmission was standard with either engine. It was priced at about $1500.

**Rockne 1932-33**
Studebaker Corp.; South Bend, IN
Production: 1932: 22,715; 1933: 13,326
Less-expensive companion make for Studebaker was named after Notre Dame's lengendary football coach Knute Rockne. Rockne died in a plane crash shortly before the car was introduced. The car was offered in two series priced from $585-$735. The base Model 65 had a 66-bhp 190-cid flathead six and rode a 110-inch wheelbase; it was redesignated the Model 10 for 1933 when horsepower was increased to 70. The Model 75 was designed by Studebaker's Barney Roos and had a 72-bhp 205-cid six and rode a 114-inch wheelbase. The Model 75 was dropped after 1932. Financial conditions forced Studebaker to reduce its model range and drop the Rockne make altogether after the 1933 model year.

**Rollsmobile 1958-c.61**
Starts Manufacturing Co.; Fort Lauderdale, FL
Production: NA
Replicars of the 1901 Olds and "1901" Ford (the first Ford was a 1903 model) were powered by an air-cooled 3-bhp Continental engine, claimed to provide a top speed of 30 mph and economy of over 100 mpg.

# Minor Makes

1967 Rowan coupe

### Rowan 1967-69
Rowan Controller Co.; Westminster, MD and/or Oceanport, NY
Production: NA
Closed electric runabout with Ghia body borrowed some mechanical parts from DeTomaso. Dynamic-braking method regenerated power during coasting and deceleration to help provide a range of 200 miles.

### Ruger 1968-c.72
Sturm Ruger & Co., Inc.; Southport, CT
Production: NA
Built by the famous gun maker and inspired by the 4.5-liter Bentley tourer, the Ruger had fiberglass body panels covered with Naugahyde. Powered by a 427-cid Ford V-8, it could do 0-60 mph in 7.7 seconds despite a 3500-pound curb weight. Price: $13,000.

1930 Ruxton sedan

### Ruxton 1930
New Era Motors, Inc. (Archie Andrews); New York, NY
Production: approx. 500
A one-year-only marvel, yet one of the most-interesting and beautiful cars of the 1930s. It featured a ground-hugging front-wheel-drive chassis, ultralow hood and fenders, no running boards, and a Continental 85-bhp straight eight. New York stage designer Joseph Urban created a paint scheme featuring eight horizontal bands of complementary colors. Only a handful of show cars sported the rainbow treatment.

### Saviano Scat 1960
Saviano Vehicles, Inc.; Warren, MI
Production: 4
Two-door, four-passenger Jeep-type car weighed 1700 pounds and was built on an 80-inch wheelbase. It was powered by an air-cooled 25-bhp Kohler engine teamed with Borg-Warner transmission. A steel body covered a rectangular-tube frame. Price: $1395.

### Scooter Car 1947
Manufacturer unknown
Production: NA
Two-passenger vehicle available in several forms, including a 5-bhp model with no body and angular mud guards.

1960 Seagrave coupe

### Seagrave 1960
Seagrave Fire Apparatus Co.; Columbus, OH
Production: 3
Compact car sat on a 93-inch wheelbase and was powered by a four-cylinder Continental engine. Of the three built, two had fiberglass bodies, the third was bodied in aluminum. Projected price was $3000.

### Scootmobile c.1946-52
Norman Anderson, Vernon Servoss, Lester Sworthwood; Corunna, MI
Production: NA, but unlikely
Three-wheeler (using airplane wheels; single wheel at the rear) was built from a modified auxiliary aircraft fuel tank and was equipped with an automatic transmission. Though claimed to be capable of 70 mph, top speed was probably closer to 40. Price: $350.

1952 Skorpion roadster

## Skorpion 1952-54
Wilro Co.; Pasadena, CA
Production: NA
Fiberglass sports car was available as a kit ($445) or fully assembled ($1200). It was designed to accept several different chassis and engines; the best combination was a Crosley Hot Shot chassis and Ford flathead V-8.

1953 Skyline convertible

## Skyline c.1953
Skyline, Inc.; Jamaica, NY
Production: NA
Safety-minded two-passenger hardtop-convertible that shared its L-head six, chassis, and most lower body panels with the Henry J. Projected price was less than $3000.

1968 Spook Electric coupe

## Spook Electric 1968
Dynamic Development; Pasadena, CA
Production: NA
This 99-inch-long electric was powered by six 6-volt batteries and a 36-volt DC ball-bearing motor connected to the rear wheels by chain drive. A steel and fiberglass body on a steel-channel frame combined for a total weight of 750 pounds.

## Star Dust 1953
Grantham Motor Car Co.; Los Angeles, CA
Production: NA
Built on an altered Ford chassis with 110-inch wheelbase, this 2650-pound car was powered by a Ford engine located five inches lower and 19 inches farther back in the chassis than normal. Estimated price: $3750.

## Starlite c.1959-?
Kish Industries, Inc.; Lansing, MI
Production: NA
Electric "sports" model with 82-inch wheelbase measured 148 inches overall. It was a soft-top convertible, though a clear-plastic hardtop was planned. Approximate price: $3000.

## Stearns-Knight 1899-1930
F. B. Stearns Co.; Cleveland, OH
Production: NA
The final (1930) model of this luxury car was powered by a 385-cid 127-bhp S-K engine. Eight body styles were offered, included sedans and a cabriolet roadster. Wheelbases ranged from 126-145 inches; base price was $5000.

## Storm 1954
Sports Car Development Corp.; Detroit, MI
Production: NA
Little is known about the Storm aside from the fact it had a two-passenger Bertone body and a 250-bhp Dodge V-8.

## Stout Project Y 1946
Kaiser-Frazer, Corp.; Detroit, MI
Production: 1
The brainchild of inventor/engineer William B. Stout, who developed the Scarab in 1936, the Project Y had a sleek fiberglass body, Mercury V-8, and 74-inch-wide rear seat. Production expense and a probable $10,000 selling price quickly killed the project.

1962 Stuart coupe

## Stuart 1962
Stuart Motors; Kalamazoo, MI
Production: 1
Two-passenger, fiberglass-bodied electric car was powered by eight 6-volt batteries and a 4-bhp motor, which provided a 40-mile range at 35 mph. The car was 115 inches long, 64 inches wide, and 56 inches high, and offered in two forms: a passenger model for $1600, and a commercial version for $1500.

## Studillac 1953-55
Bill Frick Motors; Rockville Centre, NY
Production: NA

## Minor Makes

Studebaker hardtops fitted with Cadillac V-8s and three-speed manual ($3695) or Dual-Range Hydra-Matic ($4195) were good for 0-60 mph in 8.5 seconds and a top speed of 125 mph. (*See also* Frick.)

### Stutz 1969-85
Stutz Motor Car of America, Inc.; New York, NY
Production: NA
A Stutz in name only, this revival, styled by Virgil Exner, was similar in appearance to the '66 Duesenberg (*see* Duesenberg ii *entry*). Based on a Pontiac Grand Prix chassis with 116-inch wheelbase, it was offered as a two-door hardtop, convertible, limo, and ceremonial parade car. Prices ranged from $22,500-$110,000+.

### Super Station Wagon 1954
Henney Motor Co.; Freeport, IL
Production: NA
This 12-passenger wagon, based on the contemporary '54 Packard Cavalier sedan, included an observation-lounge arrangement with curved rear seat and a table. Projected price was $7500.

### Surrey c.1960
E. W. Bliss Co.; Canton, OH
Production: NA
Curved-dash Olds replicar offered a 4.8-bhp standard engine or an 8-bhp air-cooled Cushman unit. It was available fully assembled and as a kit. Top speed was 35 mph, with claimed 65-mpg economy. The base model cost $1045, the DeLuxe $1145.

### Swift 1959
Swift Manufacturing Co.; El Cajon, CA
W. M. Manufacturing Co.; San Diego, CA
Production: NA
This trio of ⅝-scale replicars included the Swift-T (styled after a 1910 Model T Ford), Swift Cat (Stutz Bearcat), and Swifter (1903 Cadillac). All were powered by a single-cylinder air-cooled Clinton engine and belt drive. None were actually swift; top speed was 27 mph. Approximate price was $795.

### Tasco (The American Sports Car Co.) 1948
Derham Body Co.; Rosemont, PA
Production: NA
Produced by a firm organized by members of the SCCA, the Tasco was designed by Gordon Buehrig, with removable plastic roof panels and front fenders that turned with the wheels. It was powered by a modified Mercury V-8, and the projected price was $7500.

### Taylor-Dunn 1948-68
Taylor-Dunn Manufacturing Co.; Anaheim, CA
Production: NA
Two-to-four passenger electric vehicles were built in car and truck form with three or four wheels. Wheelbase ranged from 98 to 101 inches. They had a top speed of 12 mph and a range of 30 miles.

### Thrif-T 1947-55
Tri-Wheel Motor Corp.; Oxford, NC
Production: 50 per month, maximum
These three-wheelers were offered in pickup, closed delivery, and open utility body types on a wheelbase of 85 inches; overall length was 126 inches. They were powered by a 62.6-cid Onan flat-twin mounted on a detachable cradle. Curb weight was 900 pounds, payload about 500 pounds, and top speed about 35-40 mph. Price: $800.

**1948 Town Shopper**

### Towne Shopper 1948
International Motor Car Co.; San Diego, CA
Production: NA
Predominantly made of aluminum, this open two-seater was built on a 63-inch wheelbase. A 10.5-bhp Onan twin provided a top speed of 50 mph with 50 mpg economy. A late-1948 variant, the "Town Shopper" from the Carter Motor Corp., had a steel body and frame and 79-inch wheelbase; it's not known if this was a new venture or a revised design from International Motor Car.

### Tri-Car 1955
Lycoming Division, Avco Corp.; Williamsport, PA
Tri-Car Co.; Wheatland, PA
Production: NA
Sources disagree on which company built this 117-inch-long, rear-engine three-wheeler (single wheel at the rear), but it had a closed, three-passenger fiberglass body and a Goodrich rubber suspension system. The rear wheel was driven via torque converter by a Lycoming vertical twin. Top speed was 65 mph, and up to 41.5 mpg was claimed.

### Triplex c. 1954-55
Kethem's Automotive Corp.; Chicago, IL
Production: NA
Two-place sports car with one-piece fiberglass body was derived from the earlier Chicagoan (*see entry*). Its box-section chassis could accommodate a variety of engines, but was intended to accept a contemporary Ford V-8.

### U.S. Mark II 1956
U.S. Fiberglass Co.; Norwood, NJ
Production: NA

Fiberglass-bodied convertible was built on wheelbases of 110-118 inches; sold fully assembled and in kit form.

**Valkyrie 1967-69**
Fiberfab, Inc.; Los Angeles, CA
Production: NA
Kit-car manufacturer put its Valkyrie body on a ladder-type frame and stuffed in a 450-bhp Chevy 427 V-8 and five-speed ZF transaxle. Not surprisingly, it was very quick: The company claimed 3.9 seconds 0-60 mph and a top speed of 180+. A drag chute was provided for high-speed braking. Price: $12,500.

**Vetta Ventura 1964-66**
Vanguard Motors Corp.; Dallas, TX
Production: NA
Identical to the Apollo (*see entry*), the name changed to Vetta Ventura after the Apollo was phased out during 1965. It was offered as both a coupe ($6897) and convertible ($7237).

**Viking 1929-30**
Oldsmobile Motor Division, General Motors Corp.; Lansing, MI
Production: 1390
Introduced as an upmarket extension of Olds, the Viking had styling similar to the "baby Cadillac" LaSalle. Three body styles were offered for 1930, all powered by an 81-bhp 260-cid V-8.

**Voltra c.1962**
Voltra, Inc.; New York, NY
Production: NA
Compact electric car rode a 106-inch wheelbase, was 170 inches overall, and weighed 1600 pounds. It was powered by a General Electric DC motor, which provided a top speed of 45 mph.

**Warrior 1964**
Vanguard Products, Inc.; Dallas, TX
Production: NA
Two-seat targa-roof sports car sat on a 94-inch-wheelbase rectangular steel-tube chassis. Offered by an air conditioner manufacturer, it was powered by a rear-mounted Ford of Germany V-4.

**Westcoaster 1960**
Manufacturer unknown
Production: NA
Tiny, three-wheel electric car, suited for golf-cart duty or light shopping, was powered by a 36-volt GE system with built-in battery charger and automatic voltage relay. Doorless, rudimentary fiberglass body offered an optional snap-on fiberglass hardtop.

**Whippet 1926-31**
Willys-Overland Motors; Toledo, OH
Production: 43,422
Whippet was introduced as Willys' "price leader" at $505-$685. The Model 96A had a 103.3-inch wheelbase and a 40-bhp 136-cid four; the Model 98A rode a 112.5-inch wheelbase and had a 50-bhp 179-cid six. Coupes, sedans, and roadsters were offered in both series.

**Williams 1957-68**
Williams Engine Co. (Calvin Williams & sons); Ambler, PA
Production: NA
Williams built a variety of steam-operated cars with converted gasoline engines. The company's 1963 model used a fiberglass S-4 kit-car body from Victress; a later effort was a converted '66 Chevelle priced at $10,250.

**1953 Woodill Wildfire roadster**

**Woodill Wildfire 1952-56**
Woodill Motor Co. (B. R. "Woody" Woodill); Downey, CA
Production: 15
America's first fiberglass-bodied production sports car had bodywork by Glasspar (*see entry*). It was conceived as a kit, but was also sold fully assembled for $2900-$4500. The 101-inch-wheelbase frame was designed by ex-hot rodder Shorty Post and carried a Willys 90-bhp F-head six with three-speed overdrive manual transmission.

**Yank 1950**
Custom Auto Works; San Diego, CA
Production: NA
Two-seat aluminum-bodied sports car was built on a 100-inch wheelbase and was powered by a Willys four-cylinder engine that provided a top speed of 78 mph. Price: $1000.

**Yankee Clipper 1953-54**
Strassberger Motor Co.; Menlo Park, CA
Production: NA
Purpose-designed car rode a 101-inch wheelbase chassis, weighed 1900 pounds, and stood but 37 inches high. It used many '54 Ford components, including a 130-bhp V-8.

**Yenko Stinger 1965-71?**
Yenko Sportscars, Inc. (Don Yenko); Cannonsburg, PA
Production: NA
Five modified versions of the Corvair Corsa coupe were available, all intended mainly for competition. Engines included the 164-cid Corvair flat six or an overbored 176-cid version with ratings of from 160-240 bhp. Two Camaro-based cars were offered for 1969 with engines rated at 435 and 450 bhp. The Turbo Stinger, a blown version of Chevy's Vega, was announced in 1971.